2022 世界交通运输大会(WTC2022)论文集

(交通工程与航空运输篇)

世界交通运输大会执委会 编

人民交通出版社股份有限公司

北京

内 容 提 要

本书为2022世界交通运输大会(WTC2022)论文集　交通工程与航空运输篇,是由中国公路学会、世界交通运输大会执委会精选的136篇论文汇编而成。此论文集重点收录了交通工程与航空运输领域的前沿研究及创新成果,可供从事交通运输工程等领域的人员参考,也可供院校相关师生学习。

图书在版编目(CIP)数据

2022世界交通运输大会(WTC2022)论文集 : 交通工程与航空运输篇 / 世界交通运输大会执委会编. — 北京: 人民交通出版社股份有限公司, 2022.8

ISBN 978-7-114-18286-0

Ⅰ.①2… Ⅱ.①世… Ⅲ.①交通工程—文集②航空运输—文集 Ⅳ.①U-53

中国版本图书馆CIP数据核字(2022)第194352号

2022 Shijie Jiaotong Yunshu Dahui(WTC2022) Lunwenji　Jiaotong Gongcheng yu Hangkong Yunshu Pian

书　　名:**2022世界交通运输大会(WTC2022)论文集　交通工程与航空运输篇**

著 作 者:世界交通运输大会执委会

责任编辑:韩亚楠　郭晓旭

责任校对:席少楠　赵媛媛

责任印制:刘高彤

出版发行:人民交通出版社股份有限公司

地　　址:(100011)北京市朝阳区安定门外外馆斜街3号

网　　址:http://www.ccpcl.com.cn

销售电话:(010)59757973

总 经 销:人民交通出版社股份有限公司发行部

经　　销:各地新华书店

印　　刷:北京建宏印刷有限公司

开　　本:889×1194　1/16

印　　张:59.25

字　　数:1794千

版　　次:2022年8月　第1版

印　　次:2022年12月　第2次印刷

书　　号:ISBN 978-7-114-18286-0

定　　价:280.00元

编 委 会

目　录

交通工程篇

航空运输篇

交通工程篇

考虑旅客运输服务的轨道交通系统总体运能计算方法研究*

李文新[1,2,3] 刘 静[1,3] 马 超*[1,3]
(1. 湖北文理学院汽车与交通工程学院;2. 西南交通大学交通运输与物流学院;
3. 湖北文理学院纯电动汽车动力系统设计与测试湖北省重点实验室)

摘 要 轨道交通系统总体运能作为衡量系统内旅客协同运输组织效率和运输服务水平的重要指标,其计算方法应体现出旅客运输服务质量对系统总体运能的影响。考虑到现有的系统总体运能计算方法存在模型简单、形式单一的缺点,本文提出的轨道交通系统总体运能新型计算方法能够将旅客运输服务质量对系统总体运能的影响转化为定量计算。接着结合实际调研数据,利用数据拟合函数模型对该计算模型的主要影响参数进行测定。最后通过案例研究对该计算模型的准确性进行了验证以及对该计算模型的主要影响因素进行了灵敏度分析。结果表明:该计算模型能够较好地体现出旅客运输服务质量对系统总体运能的影响。

关键词 铁路运输 总体运能 旅客运输服务 数据拟合 灵敏度分析

0 引言

近年来,随着区域轨道交通线网的不断扩张和发展,旅客出行环境和出行类型也在不断发生变化[1-3]。轨道交通系统作为市域内单制式旅客和城市间跨制式旅客输送的主要方式之一,其系统总体运能计算方法的研究也一直受到专家学者的广泛关注和青睐。系统总体运能作为衡量区域内各制式轨道交通旅客协同运输组织效率和运输服务水平的重要指标,其计算方法应体现出旅客运输服务质量对系统总体运能的影响,而现有的系统总体运能计算方法存在模型简单、形式单一的缺点[4-5],难以反映出旅客运输服务质量对系统总体运能产生的动态影响。综上所述,考虑旅客运输服务质量影响的轨道交通系统总体运能计算方法研究已经迫在眉睫。

崔艳萍等从铁路车站、区段和路网能力的研究现状入手,分析现有方法在测算方法和参数设置上的不足,提出了铁路运输能力未来需要深入研究和改进的方向[6]。梁栋等分析了国内外铁路运输能力在计算方法上的优缺点,对我国铁路运输能力计算方法存在的问题进行了改进,并以实际案例验证了改进计算方法的合理性[7]。陆晓军等针对南宁铁路局现有运输能力不足的现状,分析了造成这种现象的深层次原因,从均衡运输、施工优化、增重增载等方面实现了铁路局运输能力的大幅度提升[8]。帖立彬等对影响铁路通道能力提升的影响因素进行了识别,并构建数学模型从理论层面上提出了一定消解办法,最后采用实际案例证明了消解方法的可行性[9]。何世伟等提出并研究了铁路运输路网系统总体运能、有效运能和潜在运能力,构建了基于短路的铁路运输路网系统总体有效运能数学模型[10]。徐瑞华采用概率论的方法对城市轨道交通线网共线运营情况下的通过能力进行了研究,并利用计算机对城市轨道交通线网进行仿真研究[11]。雷中林等提出了铁路路网运输能力概念体系以及对铁路路网系统有效使用运输能力进行剖析,构建了铁路路网运能的数学模型[12]。

综上可知,目前国内外学者对轨道交通系统运输能力的研究主要集中在单一轨道交通制式总体运输能力研究和单一评价指标或评估方法,缺少系统的研究理论和方法。此外,对于多制式路网运输能力的评估多是从运营效益的角度来考虑,

1. 基金项目:湖北文理学院高层次引进人才科研基金(2059164)。

缺少从运输效率和旅客运输服务质量方面考虑的研究。本文提出的考虑旅客运输服务质量影响的轨道交通系统总体运能计算方法,从线(旅客站间出行OD,车站→车站)的研究入手,克服了传统系统总体运能计算模型中车站旅客发送量和中转量为"点"数据的缺陷,将旅客运输服务质量对系统总体运能的影响转化为定量计算。此外,本文构建的考虑旅客运输服务质量影响的轨道交通系统总体运能计算方法不仅能够根据系统旅客运输服务质量计算当前轨道交通系统的总体运能,还能对该系统总体运能弹性进行测算。

1　问题描述与假设

1.1　问题描述

现有文献对轨道交通系统总体运能的研究主要集中在线网通过能力、系统有效承载力等网络通过能力的计算,而有关多制式系统总体运能计算方法的研究少之甚少,仅有的关于区域轨道交通系统总体运能计算方法研究也依托于车站的发送量和中转站的换乘站,停留在以点(车站)为核心构建的系统总体运输能力计算模型,无法体现系统总体运能在旅客运输服务质量影响下的动态变化过程,如式(1)和式(2)所示。其中,式(1)是现有轨道交通系统的路网通过能力计算方法,表示的是单位时间内系统能够通过的列车对数。式(2)为现有轨道交通系统的路网运能计算方法,表示的是单位时间内系统能够运输的旅客人次。

$$N_{\text{network}} = \sum_{i \in L} N_{\text{line}}(l) \tag{1}$$

$$C_{\text{network}} = \sum_{i \in V} q(i) + \sum_{k \in K} q(k) \tag{2}$$

式中:N_{network}——单位时间内路网所能通过的最大列车数;

$N_{\text{line}}(l)$——线路 l 单位时间内线路所能通过的最大列车数;

l——路网所包含的线路数;

C_{network}——路网单位时间内输送的旅客量,人次;

V——路网所有的车站的集合;

i——路网的车站编号;

$q(i)$——车站 i 的旅客发送量,人次;

$q(k)$——路网内跨制式换乘车站 k 的旅客中转换乘量,人次;

K——路网内跨制式换乘车站的集合;

k——路网换乘车站的编号。

本文研究旅客运输服务质量对系统总体运能计算方法的定量影响,提出旅客运输服务质量作用下的系统总体运能计算模型,结合实际调研数据,利用数据拟合函数模型对该计算模型的主要影响参数进行测定,从而得到考虑旅客运输服务质量影响下的系统总体运能新型计算模型。

1.2　假设条件

为了后续研究的顺利展开,本文对模型构建提出以下假设条件:

假设1:考虑跨制式旅客输送具有双向性,为了研究与建模方便,本文研究区域轨道交通系统内旅客单向跨制式出行为例。

假设2:地铁和铁路作为轨道交通系统中最重要和常见的两种轨道交通制式,为了描述方便,本文以研究地铁与铁路两种轨道交通制式构成的轨道交通系统。

2　考虑旅客运输服务质量影响的系统总体运能计算模型

为便于后续系统总体运能计算模型的建立和描述,首先对该模型中出现的主要符号和变量做如下定义,见表1。

符号与变量　　表1

符号和变量	描　述
m, r	地铁、铁路制式
$(t_o, t_d), (t_o^m, t_d^m), (t'_o, t'_d), (t_o^{\text{transfer}}, t_d^{\text{transfer}})$	计划时段范围
$\mathbf{K}_m, \mathbf{K}_r$	地铁、铁路列车的集合
$\mathbf{I}_m, \mathbf{I}_r, \mathbf{I}_{m,r}$	地铁、铁路车站和跨制式换乘车站的集合
i_m, j_m, i_r, j_r	车站编号
$i_{m,r}$	跨制式换乘车站编号
$q(i_m, j_m)$	地铁车站 i_m 到 j_m 的单制式客流输送量(人次)

续上表

符号和变量	描　述
$q(i_r,j_r)$	铁路车站 i_r 到 j_r 的单制式客流输送量(人次)
$q(i_m,i_r)$	地铁车站 i_m 到铁路车站 i_r 的跨制式换乘客流输送量(人次)
$q(i_{m,r})$	跨制式换乘车站 $i_{m,r}$ 的换乘旅客中转量(人次)
$Q_{total}^{dynamic}(t_o,t_d)$	考虑旅客运输服务质量下的轨道交通系统单方向跨制式出行下的总体运能(人次)
Q_{totol}^{static}	轨道交通系统单方向跨制式出行下的总体运能(人次)
wt_m^{cur}	当前旅客运输服务质量下地铁旅客的平均等待时间(s)
wt_m^{opt}	旅客运输服务质量提升下地铁旅客的平均等待时间(s)
$\alpha(wt_m^{opt})$	旅客运输服务质量提升下地铁旅客将再次选择地铁出行的出行率
$\alpha(wt_m^{cur})$	当前旅客运输服务质量下地铁旅客将再次选择地铁出行的出行率
$Q_{m,totol}^{cur}$	当前旅客运输服务质量下地铁的总体运能(人次)
$wt_{m,r}^{cur}$	当前旅客运输服务质量下由地铁换乘到铁路的跨制式换乘旅客平均换乘等待时间(s)
$wt_{m,r}^{opt}$	旅客运输服务质量提升下由地铁换乘到铁路的跨制式换乘旅客平均换乘等待时间(s)
$\alpha(wt_{m,r}^{opt})$	旅客运输服务质量提升下跨制式换乘旅客将再次选择轨道交通出行的出行率
$\alpha(wt_{m,r}^{cur})$	当前旅客运输服务质量下跨制式换乘旅客将再次选择轨道交通出行的出行率
$Q_{(m,r),totol}^{cur}$	当前旅客运输服务质量下由地铁换乘铁路的跨制式换乘旅客中转量(人次)

2.1　旅客运输服务质量影响因素

站台拥挤、候车等待时间过长作为影响轨道交通运输服务质量的重要因素，一直备受旅客的关注。本文对旅客运输服务质量调研结果表明，超70%的调研对象认为乘坐轨道交通出行的过程中最令其无法忍受的就是站台拥挤造成的候车时间过长，站台拥挤、旅客候车时间过长将造成旅客服务质量大打折扣，降低旅客选择轨道交通出行的概率，从而减少轨道交通旅客运输量。因此，优化旅客候车等待时间可有效降低旅客全出行链旅行时间，提高单位时间内轨道交通系统设施设备服务频率，从而达到提升系统总体运能的目的。

综上，本文将轨道交通系统内的出行旅客分为单制式旅客和跨制式换乘旅客，将单制式旅客站台候车平均等待时间和跨制式旅客中转换乘平均等待时间作为旅客运输服务质量的主要影响因素，以研究旅客运输服务质量对系统总体运输能力的定量影响。

2.2　模型构建

本文首先基于旅客站间出行OD，构建单方向跨制式出行下的轨道交通系统总体运能计算模型(OTC)如式(3)所示。其中，式(3)中括号部分表示单方向跨制式出行下的各制式轨道交通旅客输送量，公式后部分表示单方向跨制式出行下的轨道交通系统旅客中转量。然后考虑单制式旅客站台候车平均等待时间(ATWTP)和跨制式旅客中转换乘车站平均等待时间(ATWTTP)对系统总体运能的定量影响，构建考虑运输服务质量影响下的系统总体运能计算模型(OTCSQ)，如式(4)所示。

$$Q_{OTC}=\left[\sum_{i_m\in \mathbf{I}_m}\sum_{j_m\in \mathbf{I}_m}q(i_m,j_m)+\sum_{i_m\in \mathbf{I}_m}\sum_{i_r\in \mathbf{I}_r}q(i_m,i_r)+\sum_{i_r\in \mathbf{I}_r}\sum_{j_r\in \mathbf{I}_r}q(i_r,j_r)\right]+\sum_{i_{m,r}\in \mathbf{I}_{m,r}}q(i_{m,r}) \tag{3}$$

$$Q_{OTCSQ}(t_o,t_d)=Q_{OTC}(t_o,t_d)+\left(\frac{\alpha(wt_m^{opt})-\alpha(wt_m^{cur})}{\alpha(wt_m^{cur})}\right)Q_{m,total}^{cur}+\left(\frac{\alpha(wt_{m,r}^{opt})-\alpha(wt_{m,r}^{cur})}{\alpha(wt_{m,r}^{cur})}\right)Q_{(m,r),total}^{cur} \tag{4}$$

其中，$\alpha(wt_m^{opt})$、$\alpha(wt_m^{cur})$和$\alpha(wt_{m,r}^{opt})$、$\alpha(wt_{m,r}^{cur})$可通过问卷调查收集的相关数据，利用数据拟合方法，选择合适的数学拟合函数对各类型旅客平均等待时间和旅客再次出行选择进行拟合，比较不同拟合函数的拟合度的大小，选择拟合度最高的拟合函数作为两者之间的数学拟合函数。然后，根据拟合出来的函数模型计算出不同类型旅客平均等待时间下的旅客再次出行率。

2.3　模型主要参数测定

为得到ATWTP、ATWTTP分别与旅客再次乘坐轨道交通出行率间的数学函数关系式。本文在成都地铁二号线车站候车站台和犀浦同站台换乘车站换乘平台分别对单制式地铁出行旅客和跨制式出行旅客进行调研和数据收集,得到 500 份旅客出行行为选择的有效调查问卷,包括对不同运营时段下的 ATWTP、ATWTTP 以及旅客再次选择轨道交通出行的概率等相关数据进行调研。

随后,本文运用线性拟合函数、二次拟合、指数拟合、对数拟合和幂指数拟合回归方程分别对调查问卷所得的 ATWTP 与再次出行率的数据和 ATWTTP 与再次出行率的数据进行拟合。然后,分析比较各拟合函数的拟合度 R^2 的值,选择拟合度最高的数学拟合函数作为 ATWTP、ATWTTP 分别与旅客再次乘坐轨道交通出行率间的数学函数关系式,见表 2。

不同拟合回归方程的拟合度比较　　表 2

场景	ATWTP 与再次出行率拟合回归方程的拟合度 R^2					ATWTTP 与再次出行率拟合回归方程的拟合度 R^2				
	线性拟合	二次拟合	指数拟合	对数拟合	幂指数拟合	线性拟合	二次拟合	指数拟合	对数拟合	幂指数拟合
平峰	0.9622	0.9698	0.9659	0.9645	0.9618	0.9736	0.9964	0.9627	0.9084	0.89
高峰	0.9925	0.9962	0.9944	0.9960	0.9954	0.9948	0.9958	0.9854	0.9666	0.9423

因此,平峰时段下选择了指数拟合回归方程和二次拟合回归方程分别对 ATWTP 与再次出行率的数据和 ATWTTP 与再次出行率的数据进行拟合,其拟合函数模型、拟合度 R^2 分别如式(5)和式(6)所示。其中,图 1 和图 2 分别给出了平峰运营下 ATWTP 与再次出行率拟合函数和 ATWTTP 与再次出行率拟合函数示意图。高峰时段下均选择了二次拟合回归方程对 ATWTP 与再次出行率的数据和 ATWTTP 与再次出行率的数据进行拟合,其拟合函数模型分别如式(7)和式(8)所示。其中,图 3 和图 4 分别给出了高峰运营下 ATWTP 与再次出行率拟合函数和 ATWTTP 与再次出行率拟合函数示意图。

$$y_{A,1} = 1 \times 10^{-6} x_{A,1}^2 - 0.0016 x_{A,1} + 1.13361 \times R^2 = 0.9698 \tag{5}$$

$$y_{A,2} = -2.9 \times 10^{-7} x_{A,2}^2 + 3.29 \times 10^{-5} x_{A,2} + 0.9647 R^2 = 0.9964 \tag{6}$$

$$y_{B,1} = 2.64 \times 10^{-6} x_{B,1}^2 - 0.00211 x_{B,1} + 1.08487 R^2 = 0.9962 \tag{7}$$

$$y_{B,2} = -1.44 \times 10^{-7} x_{B,2}^2 - 3.7 \times 10^{-4} x_{B,2} + 1.08834 R^2 = 0.9958 \tag{8}$$

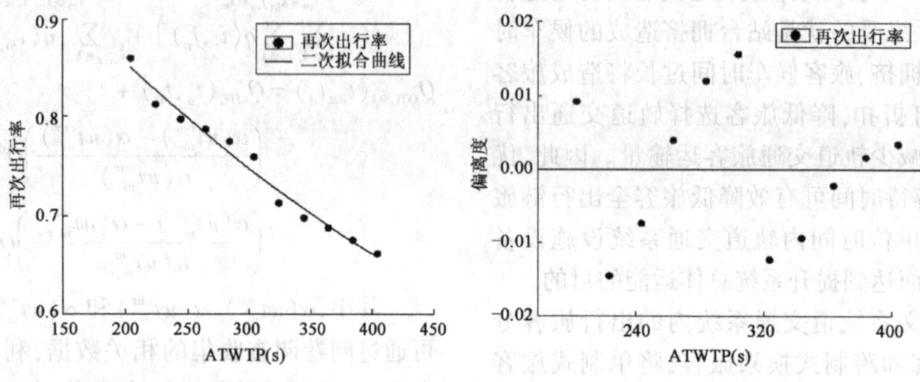

图 1　平峰运营时段下 ATWTP 与再次出行率拟合函数关系示意图

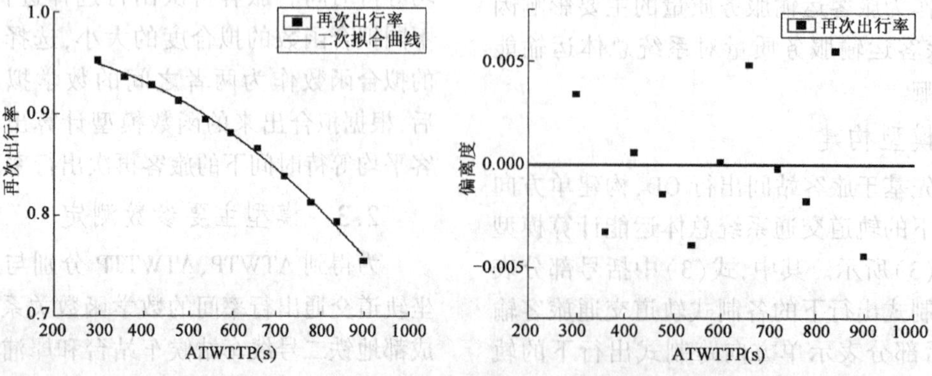

图 2　平峰运营时段下 ATWTTP 与再次出行率拟合函数关系示意图

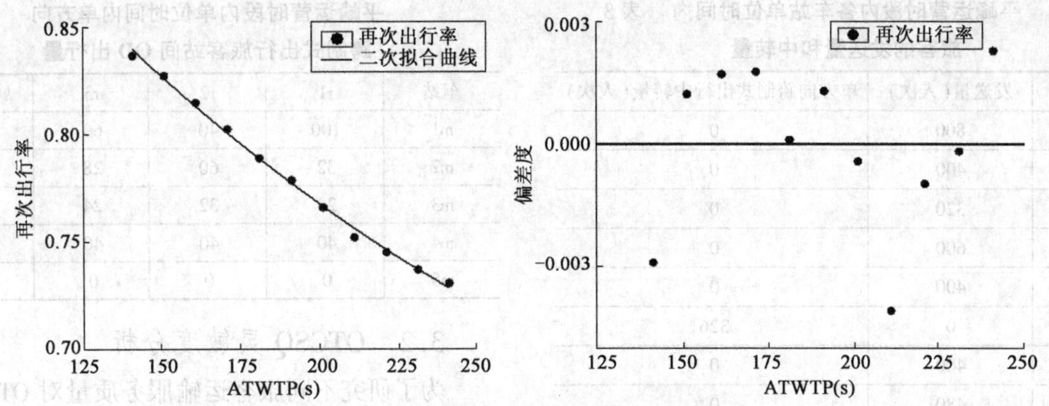

图 3　高峰运营时段下 ATWTP 与再次出行率拟合函数关系示意图

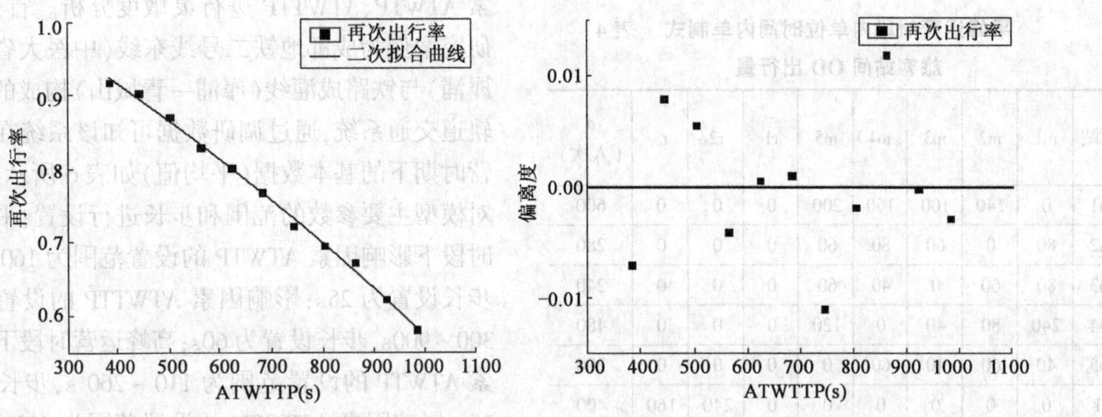

图 4　高峰运营时段下 ATWTTP 与再次出行率拟合函数关系示意图

综上，在得到 ATWTP、ATWTTP 分别和再次乘车率之间的数学拟合函数后，可以计算出不同类型旅客平均等待时间下的旅客再次出行率，结合不同当前旅客运输服务质量下的系统总体运能，可以计算出优化后的旅客运输服务质量下的系统总体运能。

3　案例分析

3.1　OTCSQ 准确性验证

从式(3)可以看出，OTCSQ 模型是基于 OTC 模型构建的一种能够体现运输服务质量影响的系统总体运能计算模型。因此，要证明本文构建的 OTCSQ 模型准确性，只需证明 OTC 模型是正确的即可。因此，本文利用不同系统总体运能模型分别计算由一条地铁线与铁路线构成的区域轨道交通系统在平峰运营时段下的总体运能，以此作为案例验证提出的 OTC 模型的准确性。

案例分析：地铁线由 5 座车站构成，命名为 m1 ~ m5，铁路线由 3 座车站构成，命名为 r1 ~ r3。两线路衔接的跨制式中转换乘车站为 m5 和 r1 构成的同站台换乘车站，命名为 m5-r1。系统在平峰运营时段内各车站单位时间内旅客的发送量和中转量如表 3 所示，系统在平峰运营时段内单位时间内单制式旅客站间 OD 出行量(用 d 表示)如表 4 所示，系统在平峰运营时段内单位时间内单方向跨制式出行旅客站间 OD 出行量(用 k 表示)如表 5 所示。利用传统区域轨道交通系统总体运能计算模型[式(2)]和本文构建的 OTC 模型[式(3)]分别计算该系统平峰运营时段下单位时间内的旅客总体运输能力，发现两者计算结果完全相同，如式(9)和式(10)所示。证明了本文构建的 OTC 模型和基于 OTC 模型构建的 OTCSQ 模型的准确性。

$$C_{\text{network}} = \sum_{i \in V} q(i) + \sum_{k \in K} q(k) = 800 + 400 + 320 + 600 + 400 + 400 + 480 + 320 + 326 = 4046 \tag{9}$$

$$Q_{\text{total}}^{\text{static}} = \Big[\sum_{i_m \in \mathbf{I}_m} \sum_{j_m \in \mathbf{I}_m} q(i_m, j_m) + \sum_{i_m \in \mathbf{I}_m} \sum_{i_r \in \mathbf{I}_r} q(i_m, i_r) + \sum_{i_r \in \mathbf{I}_r} \sum_{j_r \in \mathbf{I}_r} q(i_r, j_r) \Big] + \sum_{i_{m,r} \in \mathbf{I}_{m,r}} q(i_{m,r}) \tag{10}$$

$$= (600 + 280 + 240 + 480 + 200) + (200 + 120 + 80 + 120 + 0) + (400 + 480 + 320) + 326 = 4046$$

平峰运营时段内各车站单位时间内旅客的发送量和中转量　　表3

车　站	发送量(人次)	单方向跨制式出行中转量(人次)
m1	800	0
m2	400	0
m3	320	0
m4	600	0
m5	400	0
m5 - r1	0	326
r1	400	0
r2	480	0
r3	320	0

平峰运营时段内单位时间内单制式旅客站间 OD 出行量　　表4

车站	m1	m2	m3	m4	m5	r1	r2	r3	d(人次)
m1	0	140	100	160	200	0	0	0	600
m2	80	0	60	80	60	0	0	0	280
m3	80	60	0	40	60	0	0	0	240
m4	240	80	40	0	120	0	0	0	480
m5	40	60	40	60	0	0	0	0	200
r1	0	0	0	0	0	0	240	160	400
r2	0	0	0	0	0	360	0	120	480
r3	0	0	0	0	0	120	200	0	320

平峰运营时段内单位时间内单方向跨制式出行旅客站间 OD 出行量　　表5

车站	r1	r2	r3	k(人次)
m1	100	40	60	200
m2	32	60	28	120
m3	24	32	24	80
m4	40	40	40	120
m5	0	0	0	0

3.2　OTCSQ 灵敏度分析

为了研究不同旅客运输服务质量对 OTCSQ 的影响程度,需要对影响旅客运输服务质量的影响因素 ATWTP、ATWTTP 进行灵敏度分析。首先,确定研究案例为成都地铁二号线东线(中医大省医院—犀浦)与铁路成灌线(犀浦—青城山)构成的多制式轨道交通系统,通过调研数据可知该系统在不同运营时期下的基本数据(平均值)如表6所示。其次,对模型主要参数的范围和步长进行设置:平峰运营时段下影响因素 ATWTP 的设置范围为160～410s,步长设置为25s;影响因素 ATWTTP 的设置范围为300～900s,步长设置为60s;高峰运营时段下影响因素 ATWTP 的设置范围为110～260 s,步长设置为15s;影响因素 ATWTTP 的设置范围为400～1000s,步长设置为60s。图5、图6给出了不同运营时段下 ATWTP、ATWTTP 分别对 OTCSQ 的灵敏度分析。

基本运营数据　　表6

运营时段	OTC(人次)		ATWTP (s)	ATWTTP (s)
	$Q^{cur}_{m,total}$(人次)	$Q^{cur}_{(m,r),total}$(人次)		
平峰	3195	851	198.17	280.65
高峰	4191	1388	140.13	391.05

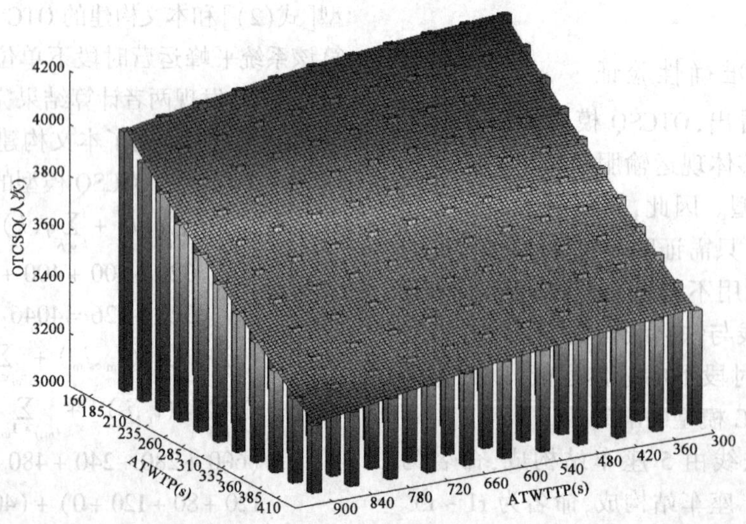

图5　平峰运营时段下 ATWTP、ATWTTP 对 OTCSQ 的灵敏度分析

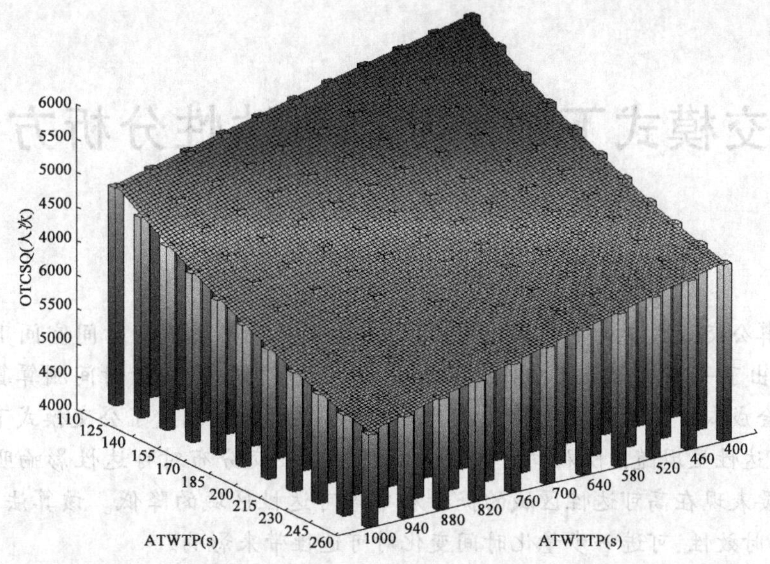

图 6 高峰运营时段下 ATWTP、ATWTTP 对 OTCSQ 的灵敏度分析

从图 5、图 6 可以看出影响因素 ATWTP、ATWTTP 的变化与 OTCSQ 演变趋势间的关系。假设以引起 OTCSQ 单位变化所需的 ATWTP、ATWTTP 的变化量作为 OTCSQ 的灵敏度，可以看出灵敏度由高到低的排序为：ATWTP 大于 ATWTTP。意味着 ATWTP 对 OTCSQ 的影响度较大，ATWTTP 对 OTCSQ 的影响度较小。

4 结语

为弥补现有研究的不足，论文构建了考虑旅客运输服务质量影响的轨道交通系统总体运能计算方法，主要得出以下结论：

(1)分析本文调研结果可知，就旅客服务质量对系统总体运能的影响而言，减少单制式旅客等待时间和跨制式出行旅客换乘等待时间可有效提升旅客运输服务质量，从而吸引更多旅客选择轨道交通方式出行。

(2)本文提出的 OTC 模型是一种优于传统系统总体运能计算方法的系统总体运能计算模型。其中，依托 OTC 模型构建的 OTCSQ 模型能够有效地将旅客运输服务质量对系统总体运能的动态影响转化为定量计算。

(3)当优化目标为系统总体运能最大化时，就优化效果而言，提升城市轨道交通(地铁、轻轨等)单制式旅客的运输服务质量比提升跨制式换乘客流的运输服务质量更加有效。

参考文献

[1] 陈敏，缪磊磊，张奕. 德国轨道交通发展的借鉴与启示[J]. 浙江经济，2014(3)：38-39.

[2] 南敬林. 京津冀区域轨道交通功能层次分析[J]. 铁路工程造价管理，2016，31 (2)：5-8.

[3] 孙霁. 上海市轨道交通网络规划建设思考与建议[J]. 中国市政工程，2018(01)：73-75.

[4] Helbing D, Farkas I, Vicsek T. Simulating dynamical features of escape panic. Nature[J]. 2000，407(603)：487-490.

[5] Hoogendoorn S. Daamen W. Microscopic pedesteian traffic data collection and analysis [J]. 2003，3(2)：89-100.

[6] 崔艳萍，肖睿. 铁路运输能力研究综述[J]. 铁道运输与经济，2015，37(06)：20-26.

[7] 梁栋，肖睿，赵颖. 铁路运输能力计算理论方法改进研究[J]. 铁道经济研究，2011(06)：1-4 +8.

[8] 陆晓军，黎国敏. 提高铁路运输能力和运输总量的实践[J]. 铁道运输与经济，2012，34 (08)：17-19.

[9] 帖立彬，王志美，陈昂扬. 铁路通道能力瓶颈识别与消解技术研究[J]. 铁道运输与经济，2020，42(S1)：118-124.

[10] 何世伟，宋瑞等. 路网运输能力及计算方法的研究[J]. 铁道学报，2003，25 (02)：5-9.

[11] 徐瑞华. 城市交通列车共线运营的通过能力和延误[J]. 同济大学学报，2005，33 (03)：301-305.

[12] 雷中林，何世伟. 铁路路网系统运输能力灵活性研究[J]. 铁道学报，2009，31(01)：26-30.

公交模式下个体动态可达性分析方法

程　静*
(长安大学运输工程学院)

摘　要　为计算公交模式支持下的个体可达性,更加直观地描述不同时间空间下个体可达性差异,利用 Python 语言提出了一种基于公交拓扑网络模型的“基于门到门”出行时间测算算法,并结合最邻近设施时间和累积机会成本方法度量可达性。以南昌市四个区县为例测度了公交模式下个体就医可达性。结果表明,区域内可达性呈现随医院群向外递远递减特性且公交分布对可达性影响明显,不同出发时间下的可达性变化主要表现在高可达性区域的提升和中等可达性区域的降低。该算法省去了传统拓扑建模的烦琐过程,更具时效性,可进一步量化时间变化对可达性带来影响。

关键词　交通工程　个体动态可达性　门到门出行时间成本　公共交通　换乘网络特性

0　引言

可达性作为公交服务质量的主要指标,在出行者出行模式选择中扮演着重要的角色。现有城市公共交通可达性分析大体可分为供给和需求两个角度,分别测度了公共交通的服务能力和公交模式下出行个体城市不同空间位置所能获取的最邻近服务设施的便利程度[1]。公交可达性作为公共交通出行者的活动—出行决策的一种重要影响因素发挥着调控居民出行行为的作用[2]。为吸引更多居民选择公共交通方式出行,公交可达性研究应更多关注需求角度,探寻公交模式支持下个体可达性。

为实现公交运营效率更优,公交管理部门常根据历史客流数据动态调控不同时段发车班次、线路,这导致了公交设施服务能力的波动,人们也逐渐意识到可达性是动态变化的。早期的可达性研究多集中于求解静态线路、站点间的时间距离[3],实际上线路运营状态不可能如传统假设中恒定[4]。部分研究将特定时间的可达性[5]作为研究重点,这过于乐观地估计了公交设施的供给能力,因为一天当中最佳的公交服务质量只在特定时段出现。研究可达性的挑战之一是合理引入时间维度,准确评估实际出行时间[6],特别是量化分析可达性在一天当中的动态变化,传统数据源的限制增加了这一问题的难度[7]。

地理空间数据和 GTFS 等数据集的可获得性为研究可达性的动态变化提供了可能。例如,Borja 等使用路段平均出行时间和推特数据分析了一天当中旅行时间和目的地吸引力动态变化下的可达性[8];Fayyaz 等基于 GTFS 数据集计算了 4 点至 22 点时段内不同出发时间下公交站点的可达性[8,9]。公交网络节点、线路交织复杂,基于换乘网络拓扑模型的可达性测度为研究提供了有益思路[10],但探寻如何将动态数据集成到公交网络模型中以建立公共交通模式动态可达性仍是一个挑战。

基于此,本文基于公交到站时间数据、站点地理信息数据及高德爬取的 POI 数据集,设计了一种基于复杂网络的公交模式下个体动态可达性算法,可有效计算出行个体在一天中多个出发时间下到达最邻近设施的公交旅行时间,从而实现公交模式下个体动态可达性分析。

1　研究方法

1.1　基于公交拓扑网络模型的“门到门”出行时间测度

提出的算法自出行起点出发,基于公交站点间的拓扑关系寻找到达行程终点的所有可行路径,进一步基于公交运营时刻表数据更新不同出发时间下起讫点间完整出行链的最短行程时间。假定公共交通使用者都愿意最多采取两个换乘和步行 700m 的步行时间到达目的地,基于这一假设,算法描述如下:

(1)网络节点间行程时间获取。为便于更新不同出发时间下的最短出行时间,将出行起讫点、公交站点均抽象为网络节点，基于公交数据集生成两两节点间的行程时间表。其中，公交站点间行程时间矩阵由公交运营时刻表数据生成，记录了同一线路两两站点间的行程时间数据（仅保留上车站序小于下车站序数据），包含公交线路、车牌号、方向、上下车时间、上下车站序信息；其余节点间的行程时间矩阵则根据公交线路地理信息数据记录的地理位置信息，结合 ArcGIS 近邻分析模块获取起讫点间最邻近公交站点的距离，设定步行速度为 5km/h，得到包含起讫点和行程时间信息的数据，如图 1 所示。

图 1　公交出行行程示意图

（2）基于复杂网络的公交换乘网络模型。基于 Space-P 网络模型，将公交站点抽象为节点，公交站点间的拓扑关系为边。当且仅当同一公交线路的两个不同公交站点认定为有边连接，其拓扑关系为 1，其余连接方式的拓扑关系均为 0，即上一步骤所得的公交站点间行程时间数据中的起点与终点为有边连接，以站点名称为索引值生成公交换乘网络邻接矩阵表。

（3）基于深度优先搜索的可行路径搜索：针对该有向拓扑网络结构图，设定起讫点最邻近的公交站点为起点、终点，分别记为 u、v；由 u 出发，访问其某一邻接顶点 w_1；再从 w_1 出发，访问与 w_1 相邻且还没有访问过的顶点 w_2；以此类推，遍历所有邻接顶点，直至沿着该搜索路径的拓扑距离满足换乘次数约束条件或到达终点。由此可求得满足换乘假设的所有可行路径解。

（4）动态最短路径：遍历给定起终点的可行路径，并根据出发时间更新给定出发时间下两两节点间的最短行程时间，最后拼接所有路径的时间得到起讫点间的最短出行时间。

假定出行起讫点分别为 o、d，其最邻近公交站点分别为 i、j，第 1、2 次中转换乘站点为 c_1、c_2。

$$\begin{cases} t_{\text{odt0}} = \min\{T_{\text{aco}} + T_{\text{vi}} + T_{\text{egrj}}\} \\ t_{\text{odt1}} = \min\{T_{\text{aco}} + T_{\text{vi}} + T_{\text{trc1}} + T_{\text{vc1}} + T_{\text{egrj}}\} \\ t_{\text{odt2}} = \min\{T_{\text{aco}} + T_{\text{vi}} + T_{\text{trc1}} + T_{\text{vc1}} + T_{\text{trc2}} + \\ \quad T_{\text{vc2}} + T_{\text{egrj}}\} \end{cases} \tag{1}$$

式中：t_{odt0}、t_{odt1}、t_{odt2}——t 时刻出发 0、1、2 次换乘情形下 od 间的最短行程时间，s；

T_{aco}——t 时刻从 o 点出发到 i 站的步行时间及最短等待时间之和，s；

T_{vi}、T_{vc1}、T_{vc2}——从 i 站、c_1 站、c_2 站点出发到达下一站点间的行程时间，s；

T_{trc1}、T_{trc2}——c_1 站点、c_2 站点的换乘等待时间，s；

T_{egrj}——到达 j 站后，从 j 站到终点的步行接入时间，s。

1.2　公交动态可达性计算

本文采用最邻近设施时间方法来分别计算不同出发时间下城市公共服务设施的可达性，步骤如下：

（1）出行起讫点坐标拾取。

（2）t 时刻出发情形下的各起讫点最短行程时间成本测算。

$$t_{\text{odt}} = \min\{t_{\text{odti}}\},\ i = 0、1、2 \tag{2}$$

式中：t_{odt}——t 时刻出发 od 间的最短行程时间，s。

（3）依据最短出行时间成本，运用最邻近设施方法分别计算 o 点的可达性，其公式可表达为：

$$A_{ot} = \min\{t_{\text{odt}}\} \tag{3}$$

式中：A_{ot}——t 时刻 o 点到所有同类设施目的地 j 的最短行程时间，即可达性，s。

（4）运用累计机会成本指标计算一定时间阈值范围下接入目的地的面积和人口。

$$A = \sum O_i \cdot \beta \tag{4}$$

式中：A——区域整体可达性；

O_i——出行点 i 的机会数，如人口/面积等；

β——二进制值变量，当 i 点在时间阈值内时取 1，否则为 0。

2　应用分析

2.1　研究区域与数据来源

研究选取南昌市四个主要城区(东湖区、西湖区、青山湖区、青云谱区)为研究对象,基于上述研究方法分析各居住单元的就医可达性。所需的公交数据集(包括公交运营时刻表数据、公交线路及站点信息)均来自南昌市公交运营管理部门。医疗服务设施相关数据来源于高德地图 API 服务提供的兴趣点 POI,并通过相关医疗行业网站进行数据核查,最终仅保留二级及以上公立综合医院数据。研究区域内大部分医院分布于东南侧,“医院群”格局明显。

2.2　可达性空间测算结果及特征分析

在一个典型的工作日 2020 年 6 月 10 日(周三),计算了 7:00 出发研究区域内各居住单元的最邻近医疗设施时间,对各出行起点的可达性测算结果进行一维密度分布估计,估计结果如图 2 所示。研究区域内前往二级以上综合医院的可达性均值为 15.8min,多集中于 5 ~ 20min 且 15min 后可达性递减趋势明显,整体可达性水平较高,但仍存在部分区域的可达时间高于 30min。

为进一步分析研究区域内可达性的空间分布特征,利用 ArcGIS 克里金插值功能填充空白区域可达性值。研究范围内高可达性区域主要分布在东湖区、西湖区及青云谱区北侧。青山湖区(北)与东湖区的个体就医可达性呈现出类似的圈层分布结构,即医院群周边可达性优良,越往外延伸,可达性水平越低。此外,可达性空间分布格局与公交站点核密度格局相似,可推断公交分布对可达性高低存在明显影响。

尽管区域整体可达性较高,但青山湖区大部分区域可达性差,如蛟桥镇、冠山管理处等地,这与南昌市就医资源格局有关系,医疗资源过于集中,这为其他区域居民就医带来极大不便。

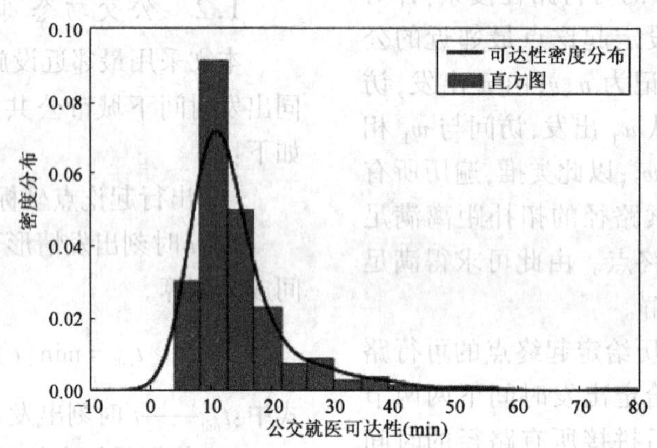

图 2　就医可达性密度分布图

此外,基于门到门出行时间成本测度结果表明近 1/3 的居住单元在前往医院的途中,自公交站点下车后步行前往医院的时间超过总行程时间的 20%,建议医疗设施周边的公交站点应配置尽可能多的共享单车以支持就医人群换乘。

2.3　时间差异

为度量时间变化给公交可达性带来的变化,计算了早高峰时段 7:00 到 8:00 每 15min 间隔的可达性。本文还使用了不同可达性等时圈的累积面积和累积人口比例(表 1),用于量化时间变化对公交模式下就医活动所带来的影响。

7:00 ~ 8:00 间区域整体可达性水平显著提升,主要表现在高可达性范围的增大和中等可达性范围的降低,其中,8:00 与 7:15 出发时间下的差异尤为明显,前者 10 分钟阈值下的累积面积和累积人口分别是后者的 1.84 倍和 1.47 倍,15 ~ 20min 内出行的累积人口和面积分别降低了 73% 和 80%。这表明不同时间下的可达性测度有较大差异,集中于最高服务水平的可达性测度有局限性。

不同出发时间下的个体就医可达性统计 表1

可达性(min)	7:15		7:30		7:45		8:00	
	A	P	A	P	A	P	A	P
<10	26.42	47.27	38.23	61.55	48.52	64.96	48.67	69.83
10~15	49.49	39.88	55.79	35.58	37.75	29.74	45.52	27.82
15~20	21.72	11.63	5.77	2.77	12.20	4.49	5.81	2.35
20~25	2.15	1.11	0.21	0.11	1.35	0.70	—	—
25~30	—	—	—	—	0.19	0.11	—	—

注:A代表累积面积率(%),P代表累积人口率(%)。

3 结语

本文基于公交运营时刻表数据、公交线网地理信息数据与高德开发者平台爬取的POI数据,利用Python语言设计了一种算法将公交运营时刻表数据集成到公交拓扑模型中,以有效计算一天中多个出发时间下公交模式支持下的个体可达性分析。基于此,研究对南昌市四个区的个体就医可达性进行了测度。结果表明,南昌市就医可达性格局随医院群圈层式分布且可达性与公交设施分布联系紧密,值得注意的是,公共交通作为就医的重要交通方式,应做好和周边公交设施的换乘衔接以减少就医人群步行时长。本文还发现,不同时间下的可达性存在较大差异,高可达区域的累积面积和人口覆盖率可相差1.5倍,未来基于时间成本的可达性测度应更加注重不同时段带来的影响。

本研究围绕常规公交展开,未考虑地铁出行,与实际的交通出行方式存在出入,此外本文在出行时段选择上应进一步增加不同情景比较研究,如平峰期、高峰期对比及工作日与非工作日的对比,上述情景将在未来研究中进行更为深入的分析。

参考文献

[1] 艾廷华,雷英哲,谢鹏,等.等时线模型支持下的深圳市综合医院空间可达性测度分析[J].地球信息科学学报,2020,22(01):113-121.

[2] 陈丽昌.社区公交可达性对居民活动—出行决策的影响研究[D].昆明理工大学,2014.

[3] 张亦汉,乔纪纲,李建程,等.广州地铁网络的可达性分析[J].测绘与空间地理信息,2014,37(02):9-11.

[4] 于文涛,张可,李静,等.基于出行数据的城市公交网络可达性研究[J].交通运输系统工程与信息,2020,20(04):106-112.DOI:10.16097/j.cnki.1009-6744.2020.04.016.

[5] Djurhuus Sune, Sten Hansen Henning, Aadahl Mette, Glümer Charlotte. Building a multimodal network and determining individual accessibility by public transportation:[J]. Environment and Planning B:Planning and Design,2016,43(1).

[6] 陈杰,李昂,符峥,等.公交模式对公共服务设施可达性的影响[J].地球信息科学学报,2019,21(07):983-993.

[7] Borja Moya-Gómez, María Henar Salas-Olmedo, Juan Carlos García-Palomares, Javier Gutiérrez. Dynamic Accessibility using Big Data:The Role of the Changing Conditions of Network Congestion and Destination Attractiveness[J]. Networks and Spatial Economics,2018,18(2).

[8] S. Kiavash Fayyaz, Xiaoyue Cathy Liu, Richard J. Porter. Dynamic transit accessibility and transit gap causality analysis[J]. Journal of Transport Geography,2017,59.

[9] S Kiavash Fayyaz S, Xiaoyue Cathy Liu, Guohui Zhang. An efficient General Transit Feed Specification (GTFS) enabled algorithm for dynamic transit accessibility analysis.[J]. PLoS ONE,2017,12(10)

[10] 王宇环,靳诚,杜家禛.基于Space-P复杂网络的南京市轨道交通换乘可达性研究[J].地理与地理信息科学,2020,36(01):87-92.

基于多元数据融合的ETC系统全生命周期管理研究及应用

王长华　于涵诚　朱熙豪*　郑于海　陶　杰
(浙江省机电设计研究院有限公司)

摘　要　随着ETC系统的不断建设完善,ETC设备日常巡检及故障检修已经成为保障ETC系统稳定运行的一项重要工作。为了进一步提高ETC系统的服务水平,本文通过构建高速公路ETC运行状态评估系统拟提高ETC设备巡检维护工作的水平和效果。通过对接获取ETC门架系统设备运行物理数据及门架业务交易数据等,基于自组织映射网络(SOM)和最小量化误差(MQE)相结合的模型,利用数据偏离正常特征空间的量化误差进行模式识别。并将其应用于ETC门架系统的全生命周期数据,对设备故障预警有效性进行评估。通过测试集数据对SOM、SOM-MQE和BP分别测试性能,验证了SOM-MQE模型通过追踪MQE值来定量描述设备的健康状态,有效降低了评估时耗,在一定程度上也减少了误检率。为了验证算法在实际中的准确性,本文依托高速公路工程,构建以不同车流量为环境参数变量的试验场景验证本系统在实际环境下的实用性。总体状态评估准确率接近94%,具备提升ETC门架综合保障能力。

关键词　ETC系统　状态评估　SOM神经网络　最小量化误差　故障预警

0　引言

目前,全国各省新建电子不停车收费(ETC)系统已基本实现高速公路全面联网。ETC系统作为高速公路收费系统的关键组成部分,不仅是道路业主方良好生产效益的重要载体,更是驾乘人员便捷通行、准确计费的可靠保障。ETC系统的稳定运行是全网收费业务顺利开展的基础和保障,因此需要定期开展相关系统的运行检测工作,及时发现系统隐患,确保全网收费系统的稳定运行。当前ETC系统检测工作主要依靠运维人员定期巡查,普遍需要封闭部分道路的方式进行,不仅效率低下,而且不能及时排除安全隐患。并且ETC系统运行状态数据采集的周期较长,不能对其进行有效监测和故障预测分析,传统的人工运维模式已无法满足ETC门架系统的运维管理要求。为指导ETC系统的监测管理,2019年交通运输部发布了《高速公路ETC门架系统及关键设备检测规程》(以下简称《规程》)。《规程》明确提出ETC门架系统及关键设备运行检测由管理单位或运营单位定期或不定期组织实施,运行检测间隔宜不大于6个月。同时运行检测应在ETC门架系统正常工作状态下进行,且不影响高速公路正常通行能力。

目前国内外对于ETC系统状态评估的研究已经展开。由于ETC系统是实现车辆的不停车收费,因此要求路侧单元(RSU)和车载单元(OBU)能够在很短的时间内完成整个交易,并对交易的过程和结果进行校验,才能保证车辆在不停车的情况下通过ETC车道。由此可见,ETC系统状态评估中很重要的一点就是RSU与OBU的微波通信和交易流程的稳定性和准确性。以往技术人员一般都是以测试设备来判断这两个专用短程通信技术(DSRC)设备出现问题,从而依靠经验评估ETC系统状态,但DSRC设备检测仪仅采集了部分关键的数据,缺乏数据实时分析等功能,难以对ETC设备进行实时的状态评估。国外应用DSRC设备比我国要早,测试设备的研究也比我国要早。TOSHIBA公司的ETC通信监视装置及ETC通信监视方法,可用于对RSU和OBU间微波信号的监听。ROHDE&SCHJWARZ公司的模块化仪器经过模块的组装,可以对ETC系统数据进行采集和波形分析,但是接收到的数据却不能够进行DSRC协议的解析。我国也有专家研究和设计DSRC设备检测仪运用于ETC系统的检测。许泽斌研究了一种DSRC设备监测仪,体积小、成本低、功耗低、易携带,可以很方便地与 RSU 和 OBU 完成通信,设备检测仪能有效对 ETC 关键设备提供方便快捷的检测,但是该仪器只能获取数据不能直接评估状态,还需要进一步完善。罗佳研究和开发了专用于电子不停车收费系统中 DSRC 设备综合性能测试仪,主要实现三大功能:应用于 ETC 系统中的 DSRC 设备模拟、链路通信测试和 DSRC 设备间交易协议分析,在不停车收费系统中,具备广泛的应用性,对提升 DSRC 产品的品质和产品升级改进起着重要的作用,但是系统在调试过程中较为复杂,功能难以完全实现。

由上述可知,目前基于 RSU 和 OBU 的检测技术已经成熟,针对 ETC 系统的评估模型还处于起步阶段,但是对于 ETC 系统的设备状态评估已经有了较为丰富的数据来源。本文通过分析 ETC 检测的技术现状和存在的问题,结合未来智慧高速发展的方向,ETC 运行状态评估系统将具备较大的应用场景。

1 ETC 评估系统的设计

本系统拟从 ETC 系统天线检测设备研发、运行状态的在线监测研究、多源数据融合评估等重点内容展开对 ETC 评估系统的研究。ETC 评估系统框架如图 1 所示。

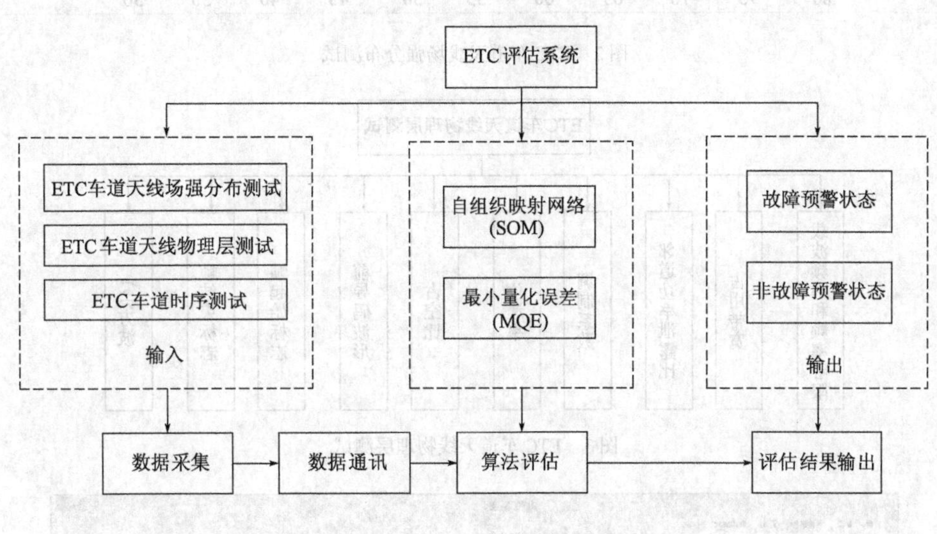

图 1 ETC 评估系统框架

通过研发一套 ETC 系统天线检测设备安装于测试车辆,模仿车辆的正常行驶过程,进行交易过程和物理数据进行采集,实现对 ETC 系统不封路、快速有效地检测;通过检测采集的 ETC 天线设备状态数据和收费数据实现统计分析、动态监测,并融合多源数据基于 SOM-MQE 算法进行运行状态评估、寿命预测,实现 ETC 系统有针对的预防性维护,提升营运单位的运维管理水平。

1 ETC 系统天线检测设备研发

1.1 ETC 系统天线检测内容

根据《规程》中 ETC 系统定检要求及 ETC 设备实际运行情况,本文对 ETC 系统的检测内容进行了分类整理,主要的检测内容包括 ETC 车道天线场强分布测试、ETC 车道天线物理层测试和 ETC 车道时序测试。

(1) ETC 车道天线场强分布测试

检测车辆驶入 ETC 车道,通过自动化采集系统,测量出该车道 ETC 天线的场强分布信息图,直观的得出 ETC 车道天线的信号覆盖范围,可对 ETC 车道天线运行状态、是否存在邻道干扰的潜在性等进行评价(图 2)。

(2) ETC 车道天线物理层测试

采取全自动化集成测试的方式,抓取 ETC 车道天线发射的射频信号并进行物理层测试与分析,测试指标如图 3 所示。

(3) ETC 车道时序测试

测试车辆通过 ETC 车道,自动采集交易数据并进行解析并整合数据时序分析,例如交易时间统计、交易状态等,如图 4 所示。

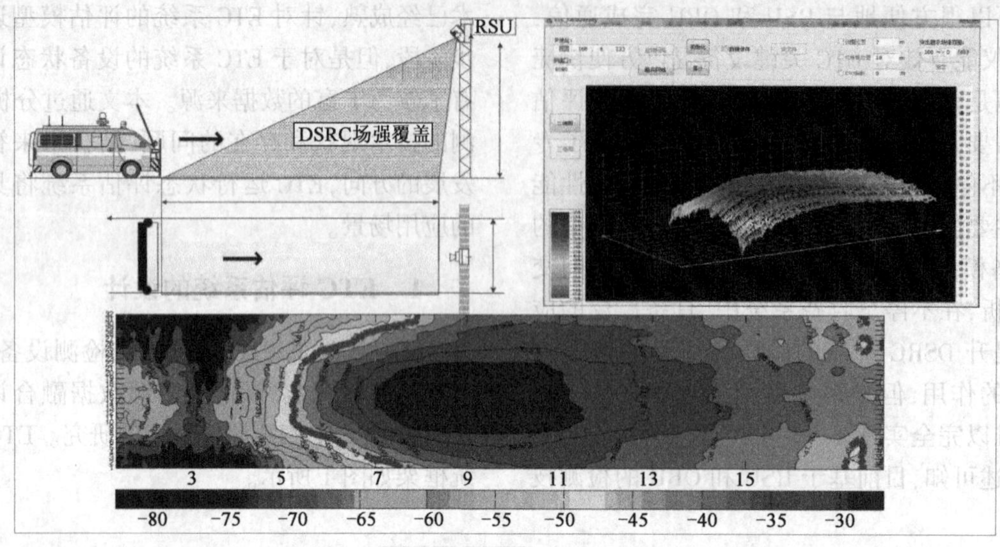

图 2　ETC 车道天线场强分布测试

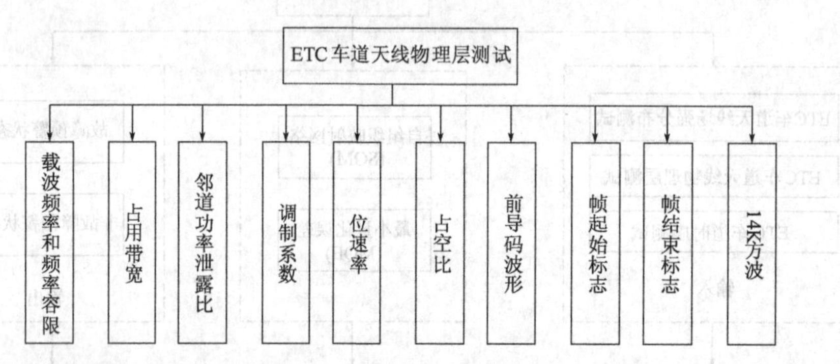

图 3　ETC 车道天线物理层测试

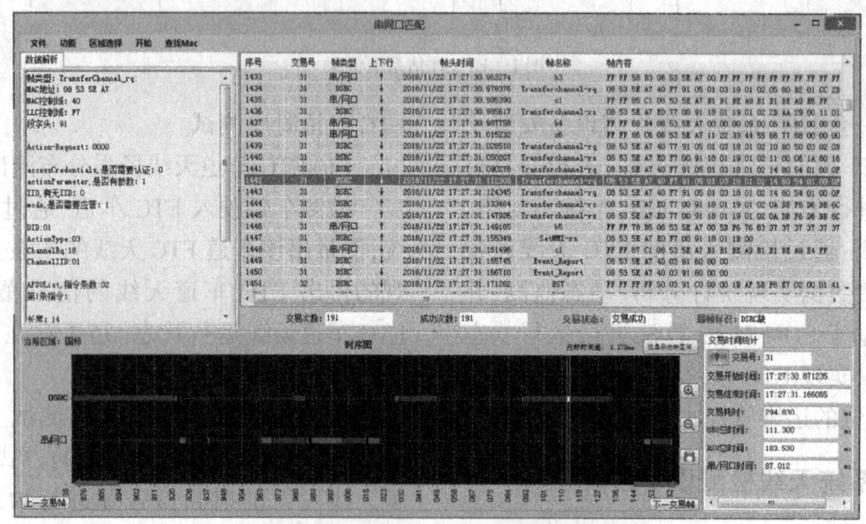

图 4　ETC 车道时序测试

1.2　DSRC 综合测试仪的研发原理和功能

DSRC 综合测试仪安装在测试车辆上。在测试过程中,通过综测仪上的射频前端和混频器与 ETC 车道天线实现射频信号的传输和转换,高速采样 ADC 完成对 ETC 车道天线的物理数据采集。结合省部中心的后台车辆交易数据,实现 ETC 系统天线设备的动态监测。其构成原理如图 5 所示。

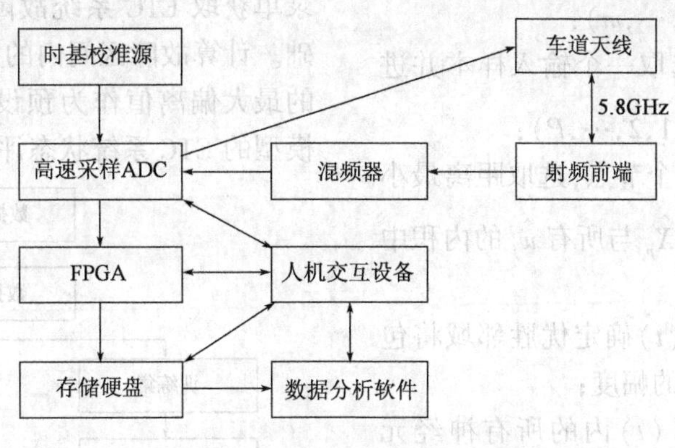

图5 DSRC综合测试仪的构成原理

(1)射频前端:主要对ETC系统中5.8G射频信号预处理,降噪,放大活衰减,功率分配,信道分配等功能。

(2)混频器:主要将射频信号变频为基带信号,用于后端ADC采样。

(3)高速采样ADC:进行物理数据采样,采样率越高,对数据物理指标分析越精准。

(4)FPGA:采样后的数据送入大容量FPGA,进行实时解码,并分析物理层指标。

(5)硬盘:用于数据存储,原始采样数据会实时存入大容量硬盘。

(6)人机交互设备:主要包括设备的配置管理,实时运算结果信息的显示,或者后期数据再查看,分析等显示。

(7)时基校准源:采样数据的时间戳是从GPS或北斗中获取。

2 基于SOM-MQE模型的ETC设备运行状态评估

本文基础数据来源包括ETC设备物理数据以及省部中心提供的后台车辆交易数据。物理数据是检测车辆驶入ETC车道,通过车道天线场强分布测试、车道天线物理层测试和车道时序测试得到的包括场强信号数据、天线射频信号、时序分析数据等,而后台车辆交易数据为收费站ETC设备心跳数据和运行监测数据,包括ETC门架断面交易成功率等。

由于物理数据通过检测车采集获取,采集频率周期较长,而且检测通常按照检测标准以是否合格为结果,对设备状态的反映较为单一,不能准确反映设备状态。因此针对这一问题,本项目接入省部中心提供的后台车辆交易数据,该数据来源于车辆通过ETC门架所采集的交易数据,具有实时性和真实性。通过该交易数据可及时反映设备的使用状态,但是设备交易状态并不能完全反映其运行状态,因为交易成功率还与车辆通过速度、车流量等因素有关。

根据以上情况,借助机器学习算法进行设备状态评估是保证设备安全可靠运行的有效手段,但故障数据样本难以获取,成为相关设备推广应用的一大挑战。多数情况下,故障数据非常难以准确采集,而正常状态数据往往可以方便且准确地获取,所以故障预警可以基于偏离正常特征空间的量化误差来进行。因此本文构建一种结合自组织映射网络(SOM)和最小量化误差(MQE)的SOM-MQE模型,提出基于SOM-MQE模型的ETC系统运行状态监测方法,利用数据偏离正常特征空间的量化误差进行模式识别。SOM-MQE模型易于构建,检测速度快,适用于大多数实际工业场景。

2.1 SOM算法

SOM算法的基本思想接近于竞争神经网络,差别在于竞争神经网络中只有唯一获胜神经元才能调整权向量,其他神经元无权调整权向量;而在SOM中,获胜神经元对其邻近神经元的影响是由近及远,由兴奋逐渐变为抑制。不仅获胜神经元要训练调整权值,其周围的神经元也受到影响,要不同程度地调整权向量。具体调整过程是:以获胜神经元为中心设定一个邻域半径R,该邻域半径圈定的范围称为优胜邻域,优胜邻域初始状态较大;随着训练次数的增加,优胜邻域将不断收缩,直至半径为0。具体学习步骤如下:

(1)学习率η初始化,建立初始优胜邻域$N_{j*}(0)$,使用小随机数对输出层各神经元权重赋初

值、归一化,得到 $\hat{w}_j(j=1,2,\cdots,m)$;

(2)从训练集中随机选取一个输入样本并进行归一化处理,得到 $\hat{X}_p(p=1,2,\cdots,P)$;

(3)遍历输出层中每一个节点,选取距离最小的节点作为优胜节点,即从 $\hat{X}_p$ 与所有 $\hat{w}_j$ 的内积中找到最大的 j^*;

(4)根据优胜邻域 $N_{j^*}(t)$ 确定优胜邻域将包含的节点,并计算各自更新的幅度;

(5)更新优胜邻域 $N_{j^*}(t)$ 内的所有神经元权重:

$$w_{ij}(t+1)=w_{ij}(t)+\eta(t,N)[x_i^p-w_{ij}(t)]$$
$$(i=1,2,\cdots,n,j\in N_{j^*}(t)) \quad (1)$$

式中:i——一个神经元所有输入边的序标;

$\eta(t,N)$——训练时间 t 和邻域内第 j 个神经元与获胜神经元 j^* 之间的拓扑距离 N 的函数。

(6)完成一次迭代,返回步骤(2),直至满足设定的迭代次数。

2.2 MQE 算法

大多数情况下,故障数据非常难以采集,而正常状态数据往往可以方便且准确地采集,所以故障预警可以基于偏离正常特征空间的量化误差来进行。首先,用正常状态数据训练 SOM 模型;然后,将特征矢量与所有图元中的权值矢量作比较,若 MQE 超过了预设临界点,则表示可能已需要预警。借助于当前状态偏离正常运行基准模型的距离,可以设计新的故障预警指标,其做法是通过将新获取的状态监测数据输入到正常状态数据训练过的 SOM 网络,计算其 MQE,并将该误差作为一种新的故障预警评估指标。MQE 定义为:

$$M_{\mathrm{MQE}}=\|D-m_{\mathrm{BMU}}\| \quad (2)$$

式中:M_{MQE}——最小量化误差;

D——输入矢量;

m_{BMU}——最佳匹配单元的权值矢量。

通过追踪 MQE 值,可以定量描述设备的健康状态。

2.3 基于 SOM-MQE 模型的 ETC 系统状态评估

在本系统中,为了取得并分析 ETC 系统异常数据样本,需要对 ETC 系统的物理数据与交易数据等进行长期监测,并结合 ETC 系统历史巡检记录单获取 ETC 系统故障数据作为构建模型的基础。计算故障区间内的所有监测指标与正常指标的最大偏离值作为预设临界点。基于 SOM-MQE 模型的 ETC 系统状态评估流程如图6所示。

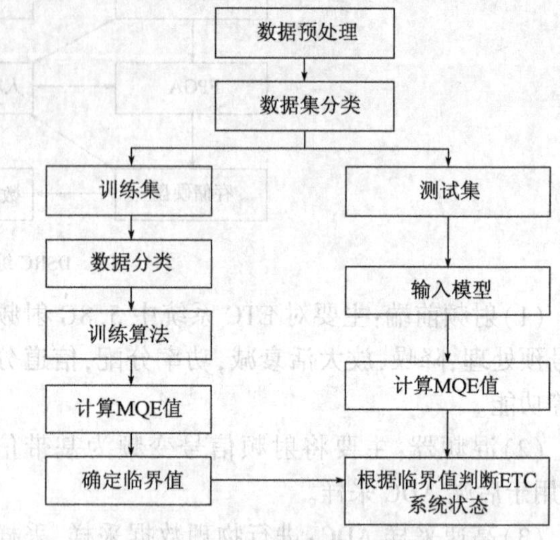

图6 ETC 系统状态评估流程

(1)划分训练集和测试集,将训练集和测试集中的每组数据划分为正常数据和故障数据,分别做标签设置;

(2)利用训练集的正常数据训练 SOM 模型;

(3)计算训练集数据中故障数据的 MQE 值;

(4)将特征矢量与所有图元中的权值矢量作比较,若 MQE 超过了预设临界点,则表示可能已需要预警;

(5)计算判断准确率,评估模型的性能。

该方法的优势在于,即使缺少明确的故障标签,也能够充分利用历史数据中的海量健康数据和使用经验构建基准模型,并基于观测数据与正常状态数据的偏差实时判定设备的健康状态,快速有效地对设备进行故障预警,降低意外故障导致的设备维修次数。

2.4 故障分类识别

由于目前 ETC 故障数据缺乏,难以构建具有故障分类的状态评估。目前本系统只能实现对正常状态和异常状态两种模式的识别,如果能后期获取足够的故障数据就能实现对异常状态原因的自动判别,因此本文拟通过依托项目进行对 ETC 系统进行全生命周期的数据监测,为后期对本系统的优化提升奠定数据基础。

3 实验分析与评估

评估算法的性能则是本系统的核心,将2045

组测试集数据通过 SOM 算法、SOM-MQE 算法和主流的 BP 算法分别测试评估的性能,并多次验证统计其平均值。将 3 种算法的识别能力进行对比,见表 1。

评估算法性能对比 表 1

测试类型	SOM	BP	SOM-MQE
评估耗时(ms)	57	46	36
漏检率	0.52%	1.70%	0.35%
误检率	2.35%	1.50%	0.6%
准确率	97.13%	96.80%	99.05%

其中 BP 的识别速度是快于 SOM,但在识别上的漏检率较为严重,误检率略低于 SOM。而 SOM-MQE 通过追踪 MQE 值来定量描述设备的健康状态,有效降低了评估时耗,在一定程度上也减少了误检率。通过测试集数据证实了 SOM-MQE 在 ETC 系统状态评估中的可靠性。

为了验证算法在实际中的准确性,本文依托高速公路工程,通过选取 3 组 ETC 门架系统作为实验数据集。A 组为使用寿命前中期正常状态,B 组为使用寿命中后期衰退状态,C 组为使用寿命末期故障状态。因为 ETC 门架系统的工作负荷与车流量因素有密切相关,因此需要以不同车流量为环境参数变量以验证本系统在实际环境下的实用性。由于测试时难以保证每次车流量的完全一致,则通过按范围来划分并分别进行多次实地测试。最后采用人工验证的办法统计各车流量区间下的平均准确度,见表 2。

状态评估准确度统计 表 2

车流量 [veh(h · ln)]	A 组正常运行时间占比	A 组识别率	B 组正常运行时间占比	B 组识别率	C 组正常运行时间占比	C 组识别率
250 ±20	99.23%	98.35%	97.58%	97.33%	83.58%	94.50%
80 ±20	99.68%	98.70%	98.35%	97.76%	89.15%	96.66%
20 ±20	100%	99.10%	99.6%	98.86%	92.22%	96.80%

表 2 中的车流量单位表示辆/(每小时 × 每条车道),分别对应日高峰值、日均值和日低谷值,可以发现随着车流量的增大,A 组 ETC 系统仍然能保持正常运行;B 组 ETC 系统仍能较好保持正常运行;而 C 组 ETC 系统出现较多异常情况。SOM-MQE 模型的识别率在 A 和 B 组能保持较高的水平,在 C 组由于异常数据的大量增加使得识别率略有下降,总体仍然保持了一定的水平,具备实用性。

4 结语

取消省界收费站后,ETC 门架系统作为收费系统的重要组成部分,如何对其实施智能化管控和监测显得尤为重要,本文介绍了一种基于 SOM-MQE 模型的 ETC 状态评估方法。由于 ETC 故障数据较少,该方法在即使缺少明确的故障标签的情况下,也能够充分利用历史数据中的海量健康数据和使用经验构建基准模型,并基于观测数据与正常状态数据的偏差实时判定设备的健康状态,快速有效地对 ETC 系统进行故障预警。并通过大量试验仿真验证了 SOM-MQE 模型算法的有效性,其评估效果优于传统 SOM、BP 网络。但是该算法仍有局限性,只能有限提高原有 SOM 神经网络的检测精度,其检测精度的核心仍然基于 BP 神经网络的性能。尤其对一些少量的负样本的学习问题,优化后的网络识别检测能力不能得到明显提高。后期将继续对识别检测能力进行研究优化。

参考文献

[1] Abdulla R, Abdillahi A, Abbas M K. Electronic toll collection system based on radio frequency identification system[J]. International Journal of Electrical and Computer Engineering, 2018, 8 (3):1602.

[2] Abboud K, Omar H A, Zhuang W. Interworking of DSRC and cellular network technologies for V2X communications: A survey [J]. IEEE transactions on vehicular technology, 2016, 65

(12):9457-9470.

[3] Ghafoor K Z, Guizani M, Kong L, et al. Enabling efficient coexistence of DSRC and C-V2X in vehicular networks [J]. IEEE Wireless Communications, 2019, 27(2):134-140.

[4] Xu Zebin. Research and design of DSRC equipment tester [D]. Wuhan University of technology, 2012.

[5] Luo Jia. Implementation of DSRC comprehensive tester in non-stop toll collection system [D]. Central China Normal University, 2011.

[6] Tao C C, Fan C C. A modified decomposed theory of planned behaviour model to analyze user intention towards distance-based electronic toll collection services [J]. Promet-Traffic&Transportation, 2017, 29(1):85-97.

[7] Qian C, Yang M, Li P, et al. Application of customer segmentation for electronic toll collection: a case study [J]. Journal of Advanced Transportation, 2018.

[8] Qu N, Chen J, Zuo J, et al. PSO-SOM neural network algorithm for series arc fault detection [J]. Advances in Mathematical Physics, 2020.

[9] Zhang Q, Gu J Y, Liu J M, et al. Pick wear condition identification based on wavelet packet and SOM neural network [J]. Journal of China Coal Society, 2018, 43(7):2077-2083.

[10] Zair M, Rahmoune C, Benazzouz D. Multi-fault diagnosis of rolling bearing using fuzzy entropy of empirical mode decomposition, principal component analysis, and SOM neural network [J]. Proceedings of the Institution of Mechanical Engineers, Part C: Journal of Mechanical Engineering Science, 2019, 233 (9):3317-3328.

[11] Nan F, Li Y, Jia X Y, et al. Application of improved som network in gene data cluster analysis[J]. Measurement, 2019, 145:370-378.

[12] Xu J, Miao J, Gao Z, et al. Analysis and modeling of quantization error in spike-frequency-based image sensor [J]. Microelectronics Reliability, 2020, 111:113705.

[13] Lv Wenyuan, Hua Bin. Economic production batch model considering equipment fault repair time [J]. Computer integrated manufacturing system, 2015, 21 (05):1309-1314.

[14] Ge Z, Haiyan W. Linear precoding design for massive MIMO based on the minimum mean square error algorithm [J]. EURASIP Journal on Embedded Systems, 2017, 2017(1):1-6.

[15] Dresp-Langley B, Wandeto J M, Nyongesa H O. Using the quantization error from Self-Organizing Map (SOM) output for fast detection of critical variations in image time series[J]. 2018.

Analysis of Spatiotemporal Characteristics of Online Car Hailing Based on k-means Clustering

Yan Li　Lin Cheng*　Chenhao Zhang　Hanqing Zhao

(School of transportation, Southeast University)

Abstract　With the continuous growth of the shared transportation market and the rapid increase of the number of private cars, the urban network car Hailing market has rapidly entered a prosperous period. Taking Didi behaviours with high utilization rate in China as an example, this paper studies the Spatiotemporal joint characteristics of online car Hailing based on the big data information of transportation platform. Through the k-means clustering method, comprehensively considering the three factors of demand hot spot area, Manhattan distance and OD speed, this paper analyzes the speed spatiotemporal characteristics of Didi travel, and classifies the online car Hailing operation status based on this. Summarize the operation status of Didi travel to characterize the travel status of urban network car Hailing traffic, provide a basis for the research of traffic managers, promote urban traffic design, planning and construction, and strengthen the management of traffic system.

Keywords Traffic planning and management Spatiotemporal characteristics K-means Clustering Online car hailing Passenger carrying intensity division Manhattan distance

0 Introduction

With the increasing progress of social economy and the continuous improvement of living standards, the online car hailing mode relies on the use of mobile big data technology and Internet technology to offset many shortcomings of other means of transportation, significantly improve passengers' comfort and improve passengers' travel experience. Didi travel in China has about 2 million registered drivers and provides more than 1.1 billion taxi services across the country.

In recent years, online car Hailing has brought a noticeable impact on traffic order, and the practical research on its spatiotemporal data should be gradually put on the agenda. Yu H. et al. (2020) proposed an online carpool matching scheme to protect the privacy of passengers and drivers in the process of carpooling. Aravinda D. et al. (2020) the impact of sociodemographic characteristics, location characteristics and IPT mode on the availability of taxi Hailing service. McAfee A. et al. (2012) believe that comprehensive processing and analysis of big data can generate a new business structure pattern in a domain. Daniel S. et al. (2019) proposed a two-tier growth model to identify potential factors affecting the demand for online car Hailing services, and estimated the relative market share of online car Hailing express to reveal possible relevant spatial and temporal factors. Yu H. et al. (2019) analyzed the close relationship between ride demand and building environment variables by capturing the spatial heterogeneity of online car Hailing travel data. Raymond G. et al. (2018) used the public Uber travel data to study the time trend of weekly demand for Uber in Manhattan, and considered heteroscedasticity and autocorrelation effects based on the panel random effect model. Edouard D. et al. (2019) transformed the dynamic spatiotemporal model into a recurrent neural network for modeling the time series of spatial processes. Ke J. et al. (2017) proposed the fusion convolution long-term and short-term memory network (FCL net), which solves the three dependencies of spatial dependence, time dependence and exogenous dependence in the data of on-demand ride service platform in an end-to-end learning architecture.

This paper takes Didi travel online car Hailing as the research object. Aiming at the traffic problems of travelers when using Didi online car hailing, starting from the analysis of Didi's space-time data, this paper analyzes the relationship between online car Hailing demand and urban building environment, characterizes and grasps the current situation of urban Didi travel, so as to better guide urban traffic operation. The rest of the paper is organized as follows: Section 2 introduces the data processing methods used in this paper, such as k-means clustering, spatio-temporal velocity calculation and so on. Section 3 analyzes according to the visualization results and regional conditions. Section 4 is the summary and prospect.

1 Processing Analysis Method

1.1 Data Source and Preconditioning

The data source of this paper is the public data in Gaia open data Didi platform. A total of 1689126 Didi travel order data in Chengdu from Monday, November 21, 2016 to Sunday, November 27, 2016 is selected. Chengdu, China is the capital of Sichuan Province and a megacity. With the increase of urban population, it has strengthened its dependence on private cars and newly developed online car Hailing. Therefore, its Didi travel accounts for a large proportion in residents' daily transportation life.

After eliminating the abnormal data such as repetition, travel time greater than 1h, longitude and latitude exceeding the geographical coordinate range of Chengdu, according to the projection calculation, 105E of 3-degree zoning of CGCS2000 projection coordinate system is adopted. This paper captures Chengdu from "bbbike" website GIS electronic road network map in SHP format.

1.2 Spatiotemporal Joint Analysis

The travel demand on weekdays and non-weekdays is divided into three characteristic time periods: morning peak (6:00-10:00), afternoon peak (12:00-15:00) and evening peak (17:00-22:00). Use tools such as "spatial analyst" in ArcGIS to count the boarding demand in three time periods. Using the natural break point method, the boarding places in different periods are divided into 15 levels according to the travel frequency of Didi. The 2D thermal map covers the distribution of 20 types of land such as subway, residence and commerce, so as to analyze the relationship between the demand for online car hailing and the urban building environment.

1.3 Estimation of Characterization Speed Based on OD Points

Because the data in this paper only have the starting and ending time and position, the trajectory velocity cannot be obtained accurately. In order to accurately characterize the speed characteristics of Didi travel, the concept of Manhattan distance based on the starting and ending points of Didi travel is introduced.

1.3.1 Manhattan Distance

Manhattan distance is also known as taxi geometry or taxi distance. It represents the sum of the projection distance of the line segment formed by two points on a fixed rectangular coordinate system to the coordinate axis in Euclidean space. For example, on a plane, the Manhattan distance between the point M with coordinates (x_M, y_M) and the point N with coordinates (x_N, y_N) is Eqs. (1) expressed as $d(M, N)$. Manhattan distance is also known as "taxi distance". Didi travel studied in this paper has similar driving track and mode to taxi. When only the longitude and latitude of the starting point and the longitude and latitude of the ending point are known, the Manhattan distance is closer to the real travel situation of residents reflected by Didi travel than the Euclidean distance as shown by Xie W. et al. (2011).

$$d(M,N) = |X_M - X_M| + |Y_N - Y_N| \quad (1)$$

1.3.2 Longitude Latitude Conversion

The earth's longitude and latitude coordinates use spherical coordinates (x, y) in the terrestrial coordinate system, where x is the earth's longitude and y is the earth's latitude. In order to calculate and analyze the earth data, the first thing is to convert the spherical coordinates into rectangular coordinates (x, y, z). If the earth radius is r, there are conversion formulas: $x = r \cdot \cos(y) \cdot \cos(x)$, $y = r \cdot \cos(y) \cdot \sin(x)$, $z = r \cdot \sin(y)$. It is obtained that the starting point (x_1, y_1) and the ending point (x_2, y_2) are expressed as (X_1, Y_1, Z_1) and (X_2, Y_2, Z_2) in the rectangular coordinate system.

1.3.3 Calculate Manhattan Arc Length Distance

In order to obtain the Manhattan arc length distance between AB, point A (X_1, Y_1, Z_1), point B (X_2, Y_2, Z_2), point C (X_1, Y_1, Z_2) and point D (X_1, Y_2, Z_2) are introduced as shown in Fig. 1. The Manhattan arc length distance between point A and point B can be expressed as $\overset{\frown}{AB} = \overset{\frown}{AC} + \overset{\frown}{CD} + \overset{\frown}{DB}$. From the chord length formula $L = 2r\sin\left(\frac{\theta}{2}\right)$, the spherical central angle θ corresponding to the three arc lengths can be calculated, the arc length of each section also can be obtained, and the sum of the three arc lengths is the Manhattan distance of each Didi travel order.

1.3.4 Passenger Carrying Intensity Division based on K-means Clustering

The core idea of K-means clustering in this paper is to assign each sample to the nearest center (mean) class, so as to find K classes in a given data set as shown by Cai X. et al. (2020) and G Venkatesh. et al. (2018). The Euclidean distance is used as the similarity index, and the center of each class is obtained according to the average Euclidean distance of all values in the class. According to the Lagrange principle, the cluster center is the average value of each object data point in the corresponding category. At the same time, combined with the least square method, the location or value of the cluster center can be calculated as shown by Deng Y. et al. (2016).

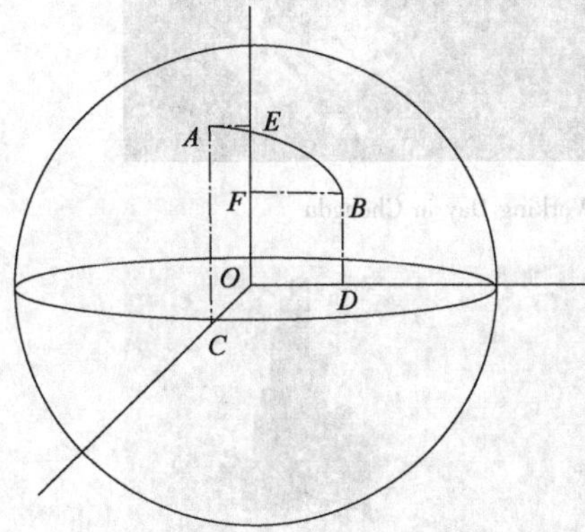

Fig. 1 Spherical Diagram of Manhattan Distance Calculation

The passenger carrying intensity area is determined by three factors: demand hot spot area, Manhattan distance coverage and OD speed distribution. Now perform K-means cluster analysis on the three data respectively. The specific steps are as follows.

(1) Determination of K value: according to the analysis of temporal and spatial distribution, Didi's travel demand is mainly concentrated in the center of Jinjiang District, the south of Jinniu District and the west of Chenghua District, that is, the classified K value of demand intensity is determined to be 3. The travel is divided into long-distance, midway and short-distance travel, and the K value of Manhattan distance is determined to be 3. According to the basic statistical analysis of OD speed, the speed range is divided by its mode, average and 85% quantile, and the K value of speed is determined to be 4.

(2) Eliminate abnormal values: in addition to the normal distribution principle for data elimination processing, in order to analyze the OD speed in the following paper, the speed limit rules and traffic flow characteristics of urban roads in Chengdu are also used here to eliminate the outliers of speed greater than 100km/h and speed lower than 10km/h.

(3) Through clustering, different clustering centers of three factors are obtained.

(4) Determine the radiation range of each factor: take the Manhattan distance at the cluster center as the reference value, according to the number of data contained in each category after clustering. The radiation range of each cluster in the three factors is determined according to the quantitative proportion.

(5) Draw buffer: according to the radiation influence range of each cluster, use ArcGIS to draw the influence buffer for each cluster of the three factors.

(6) Passenger carrying strength extraction: the buffer areas of three factors are "intersected" and "cut", the strength areas with different influence degrees of each factor are obtained, and they are classified and displayed in color.

2 Results Discussion and Analysis

2.1 Spatiotemporal Joint Distribution Characteristics

The visual 3D thermal diagram of travel demand characteristics on working days and non-working days is shown in Fig. 2 and Fig. 3, and there are three intervals consists of morning peak, afternoon peak and evening peak respectively from right to left. The specific time period is the same as the above. According to the hot spot map, the distribution characteristics of working days and non-working days are similar as a whole. The hot spots of morning peak travel are mainly distributed in the core business circle in the second ring road and the core residential area in the north. In the residential areas and tourist attractions near the North Third Ring Road, due to the rigid demand for going to work and school, the travel hot spots are also obvious. There is less demand for industrial bases and sports parks outside the Fourth Ring Road. The hot spots of afternoon peak travel are mainly distributed at the intersection of the three golden business districts in the first ring road, with a peak of 884 person times per hour. The demand is also large in the area from the northwest of the city center to the North Second Ring Road near residential land. The evening peak is the peak of work, school and night activities. The travel hot spots are mainly distributed in the core office area, sports center and other entertainment and leisure places and commercial shopping blocks. The overall travel demand level in each time period of non-working days is lower than that in working days, but its hot spots are more widely distributed.

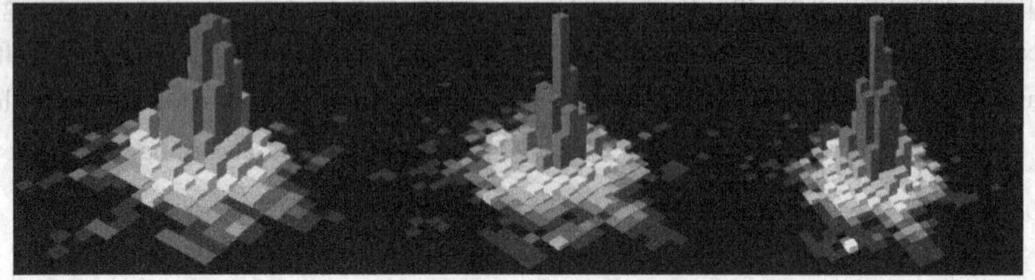

Fig. 2 The 3D Heat Map at Different Time of the Working Day in Chengdu

Fig. 3 The 3D Heat Map at Different Time of the Non-Working Day in Chengdu

2.2 Analysis of Spatiotemporal Characteristics of Speed Based on Carrying Intensity

2.2.1 Strength Classification of Passenger Carrying Area

The passenger carrying strength extraction is shown in Fig. 4 and Fig. 5. It can be found that Didi has the greatest travel demand in the center of Jinjiang District, the south of Jinniu District and the west of Chenghua District. Jinniu District and Chenghua District are residential areas, and Jinjiang District is a commercial area. Due to the needs of commuting, leisure and entertainment, Didi's travel orders are also exchanged in these three regions.

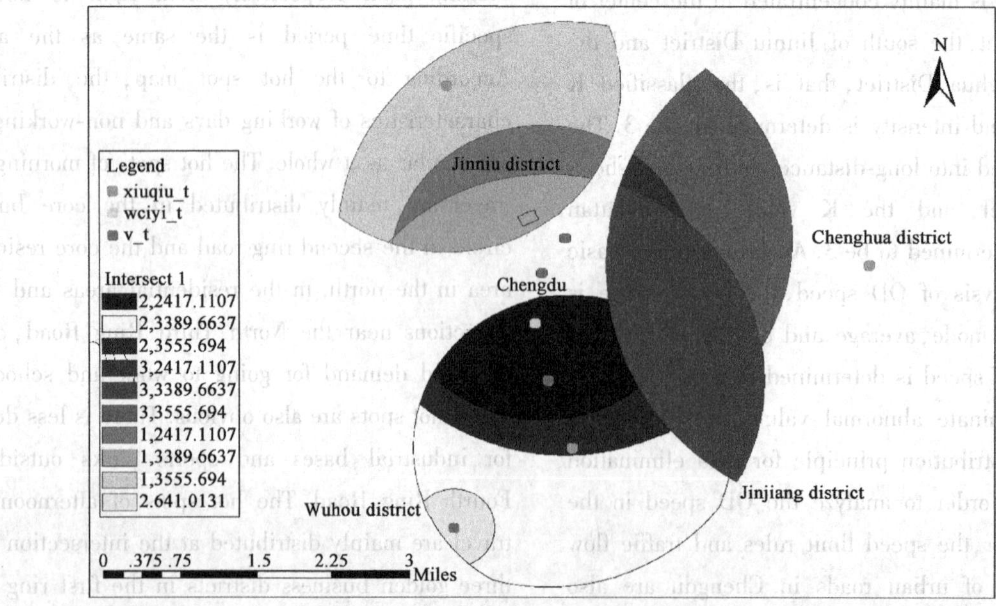

Fig. 4 The Map of Passenger Hotspots

Fig. 5 The 3D Map of Passenger Hotspots

2.2.2 Velocity Characteristics in Different Directions at Same Time

Select two representative time periods in the morning, afternoon and evening peak, respectively (6:00 ~ 7:30), (7:30 ~ 9:00), (11:30 ~ 13:00), (13:30 ~ 15:00), (17:00 ~ 18:30), (20:00 ~ 21:30). The average travel speeds of Didi in the four directions of "Jinniu District get on-get off in the city center", "Chenghua District get on-get off in the city center", "downtown get on-get off in Jinniu District" and "downtown get on-get off in Chenghua District" are counted respectively. As shown in Fig. 6, the automatic variable is the time period and the dependent variable is the average travel speed of Didi in different time periods.

The operating speed conditions in different operating directions in the same time period are shown in Fig. 7 to Fig. 12. The darker the color or the thicker the line, the faster. It can be found that in the same time period, Didi's travel speed is different with different running directions. This also reflects the situation of Didi travel roads in different operation directions in Chengdu.

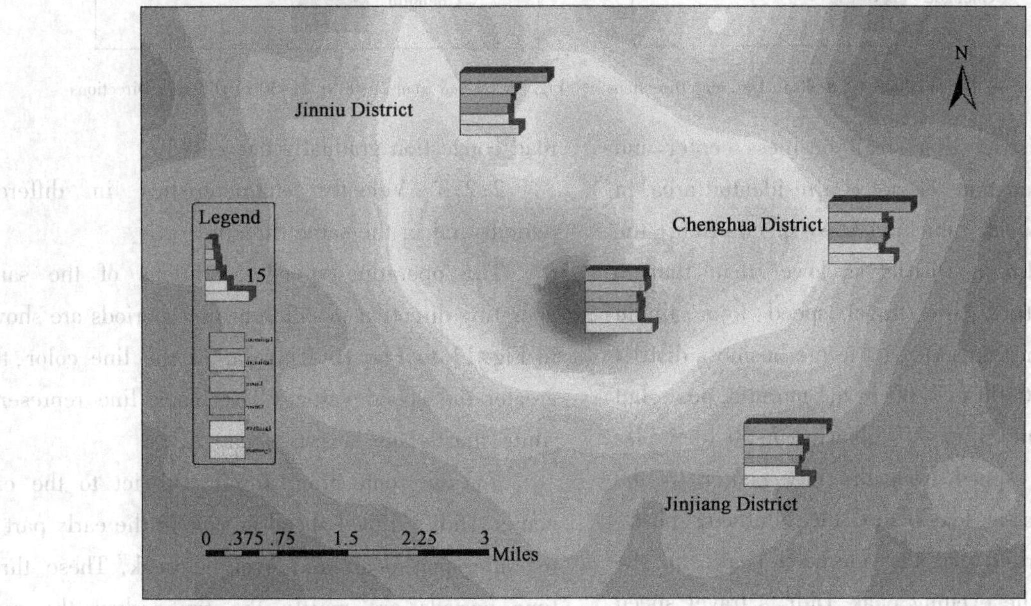

Fig. 6 Overall Bar Chart of Average Speed at Different Time Periods and in Different Directions

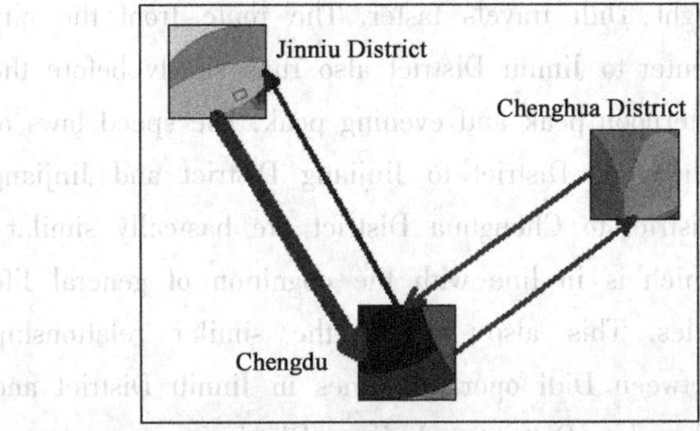

Fig. 7 Speed from 6:00 to 7:30 in Different Directions

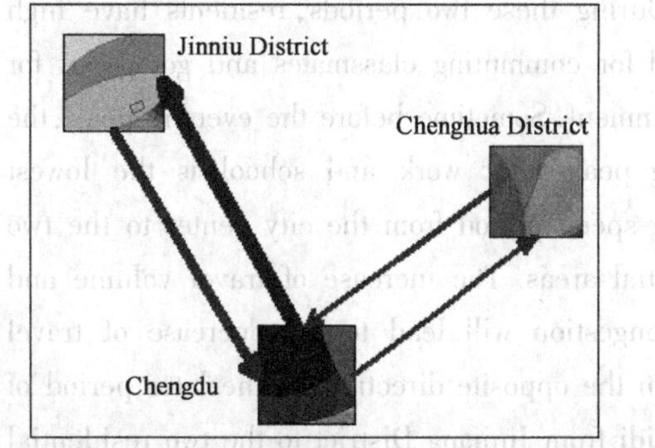

Fig. 8 Speed from 7:30 to 9:00 in Different Directions

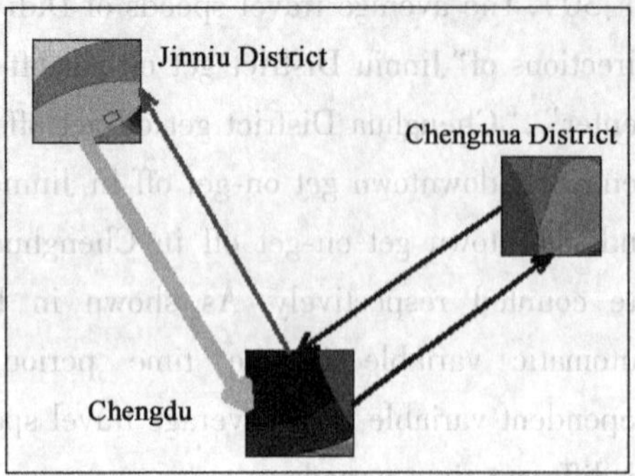

Fig. 9 Speed from 11:30 to 13:00 in Different Directions

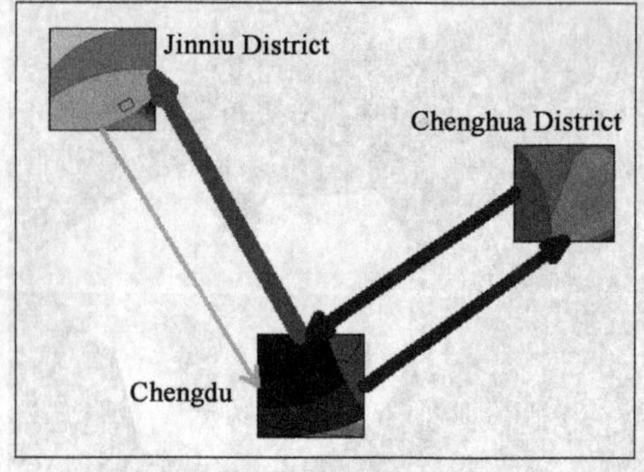

Fig. 10 Speed from 13:30 to 15:00 in Different Directions

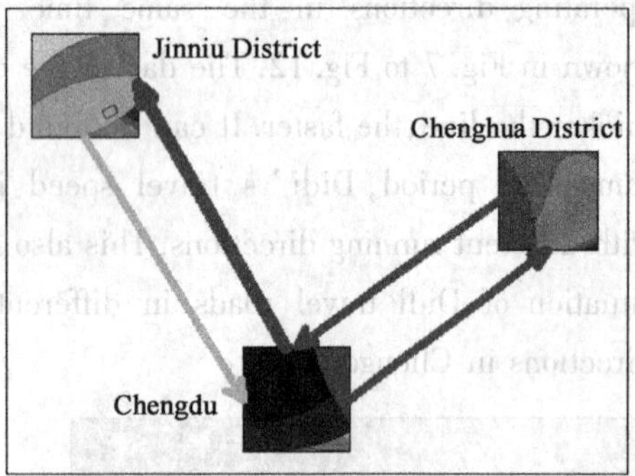

Fig. 11 Speed from 17:00 to 18:30 in Different Directions

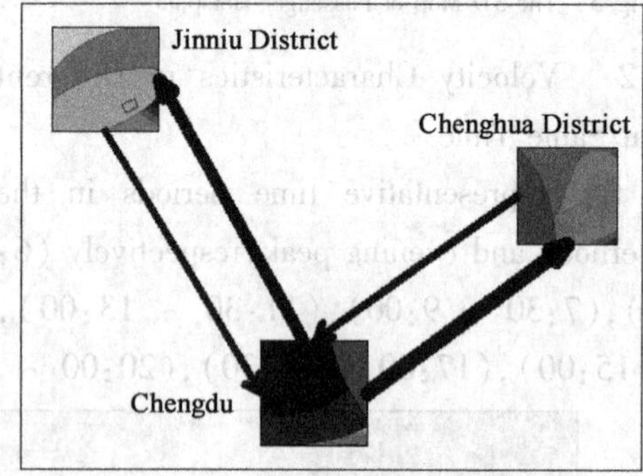

Fig. 12 Speed from 20:00 to 21:30 in Different Directions

Jinniu District is a small business center and school, and Chenghua District is a residential area. In the morning peak, the average speed from the downtown to Jinniu District is lower than that to Chenghua District. The travel speed from Jinniu District and Chenghua District to the business district is higher from 6:00 to 7:00 in the morning peak, but it decreases quickly in the following 7:30 to 9:00. Didi's travel speed from the city center to the residential area is low before the afternoon peak. During the period after the afternoon peak and the period before the evening peak, Didi's travel speed from the two residential areas is maintained at a low level. During these two periods, residents have high demand for commuting classmates and going out for entertainment. Sometime before the evening peak, the evening peak after work and school is the lowest running speed period from the city center to the two residential areas. The increase of travel volume and road congestion will lead to the decrease of travel speed in the opposite direction. In the later period of time, Didi from Jinjiang District to the two residential areas increased its running speed, and the degree of road congestion gradually decreased.

2.2.3 Velocity characteristics in different periods and in the same direction

The operating speed conditions of the same operating direction in different time periods are shown in Fig. 13 to Fig. 16. The darker the line color, the greater the speed value (The black line represents white, that is, the lowest speed).

For the route from Jinniu District to the city center, Didi's travel speed is slow in the early part of the afternoon peak and evening peak. These three time periods are mostly the time when the road congestion is serious. In the early morning and late at night, Didi travels faster. The route from the city center to Jinniu District also runs slowly before the afternoon peak and evening peak. The speed laws of Chenghua District to Jinjiang District and Jinjiang District to Chenghua District are basically similar, which is in line with the cognition of general life rules. This also reflects the similar relationship between Didi operation lines in Jinniu District and Chenghua District to Jinjiang District.

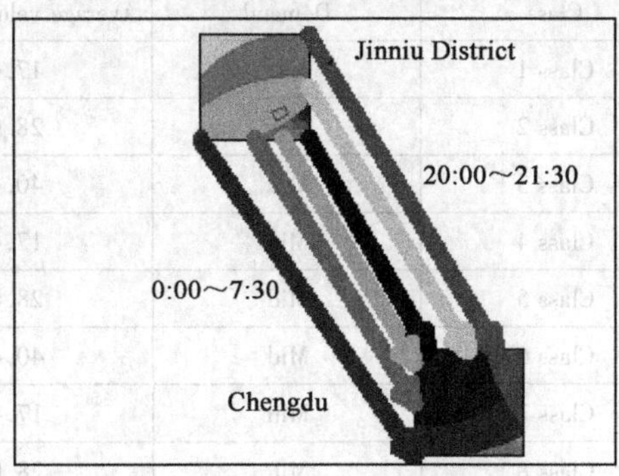

Fig. 13 The Speed of Jinniu District to Jinjiang District in 6 Time Slots

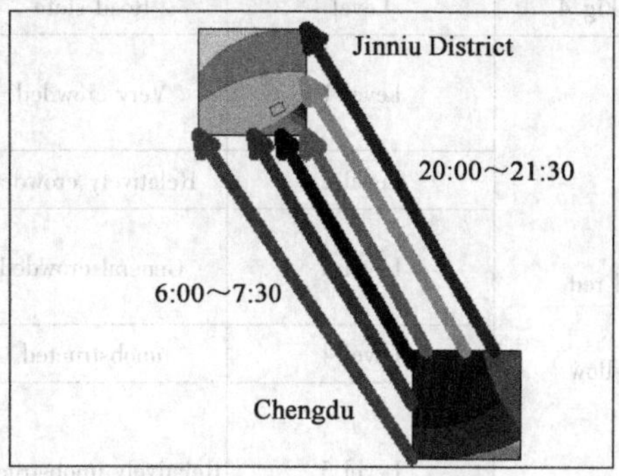

Fig. 14 The Speed of Jinjiang District to Jinniu District in 6 Time Slots

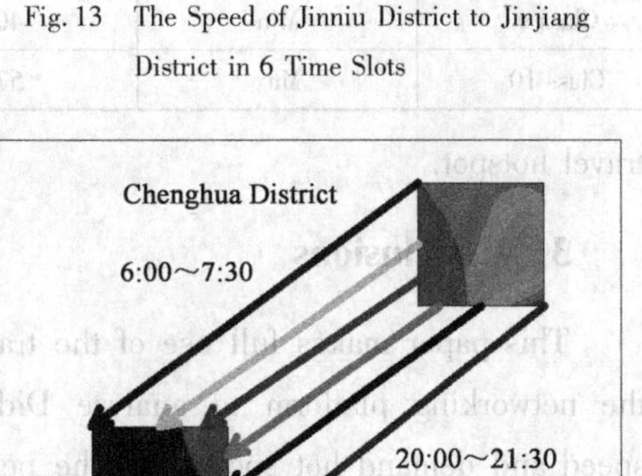

Fig. 15 The speed of Chenghua District to Jinjiang District in 6 Time Slots

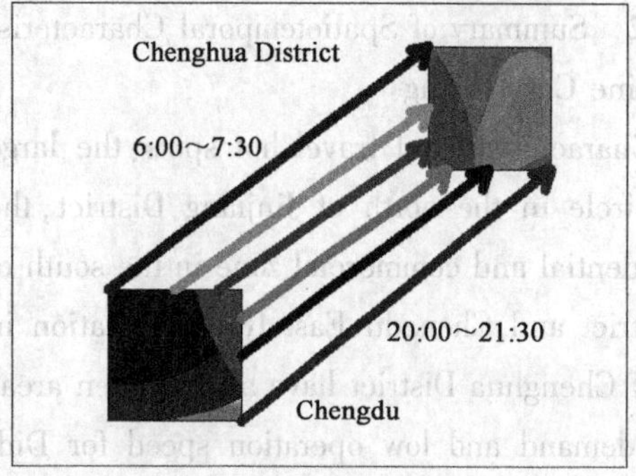

Fig. 16 The Speed of Jinjiang District to Chenghua District in 6 Time Slots

2.3 Evaluation on the Running State of Online Car Hailing Traffic in Urban Road Network

This section classifies and evaluates the operation status of Didi's travel roads according to the degree of congestion, locates each hot spot area in Chengdu, evaluates the degree of congestion, and summarizes the temporal and spatial characteristics of Didi's travel.

2.3.1 Classification of Traffic Operation Status

Based on k-means clustering, urban traffic congestion is divided into 1-6 levels. The discrimination criteria are shown in Tab. 1. The larger the level number, the smoother the traffic of Didi travel. Among them, most of the travel distances in Manhattan fall within the cluster of 5000 meters, and they are no longer distinguished. The demand degree is described by "Max", "Mid" and "Min" when the demand is 88389, 78434 and 62647 respectively. The column "status" describes the traffic congestion characteristics of Didi travel at this level.

According to the 3D diagram of passenger hot spot extraction shown in Fig. 5, most of the travel displacement of Didi in Chengdu is within the 5000m buffer zone. In the hot area in the center of Jinjiang District, Didi's travel traffic status evaluation can be divided into class 1 and class 2 "very crowded" in the core business district and class 10 "very unobstructed" with good road design. Hot spots in the south of Jinniu District can be divided into 7 and 8 "relatively unobstructed" in industrial parks and 9 "very unobstructed" in university campuses. The hot spots in the west of Chenghua District can be divided into 4 and 5 "general congestion" of the company group and 6 "unobstructed" of a small number of residential areas.

Didi Traffic Status Evaluation Level Division Discrimination Standard Table Tab. 1

Color in Fig. 4	Level	Road state	Class	Demand	Average velocity(km/h)
Oxblood red ↓ Light yellow	Level 1	Very crowded	Class 1	Max	17.464
			Class 2	Max	28.086
	Level 2	Relatively crowded	Class 3	Max	40.409
	Level 3	General crowded	Class 4	Mid	17.464
			Class 5	Mid	28.086
	Level 4	unobstructed	Class 6	Mid	40.409
	Level 5	Relatively unobstructed	Class 7	Min	17.464
			Class 8	Min	28.086
			Class 9	Min	40.409
	Level 6	Very unobstructed	Class 10	Max	57.961

2.3.2 Summary of Spatiotemporal Characteristics of Online Car Hailing

(1) Characteristics of travel hot spots: the large business circle in the north of Jinjiang District, the mixed residential and commercial zone in the south of Jinniu District and Chengdu East Railway Station in the west of Chenghua District have always been areas with high demand and low operation speed for Didi travel on weekdays and non-weekdays. This shows that the business circle and comprehensive transportation hub have a strong attraction to residents.

(2) Time characteristics of travel hotspots: Didi travel hotspots in many regions are temporal. For example, during weekdays, morning and evening peaks form obvious Didi travel hotspots in the education and scientific research base where the entertainment shopping center and university campus are located. The residents gathering areas in Jinniu District and Chenghua District formed obvious hot spots in these two periods. During non-working days, travel hot spots will be formed in scenic spots, hospitals, markets and other places.

(3) Accidental characteristics of travel hotspots: it is accidental that some areas become travel hotspots. For example, the shopping mall in the middle of Jinniu District is located in the northern suburb, which has no geographical advantage like the commercial shopping center in the center of the city. Therefore, there are accidental factors that make it a travel hotspot.

3 Conclusions

This paper makes full use of the traffic data in the networking platform to analyze Didi's travel speed and demand hot spots from the perspective of time, space and space-time combination, from qualitative analysis to mining quantitative analysis data indicators. Based on the division of Didi travel hot spots based on demand, OD operation speed and travel displacement, the urban road traffic operation state is distinguished in detail, and the congestion level is divided, so as to grasp the road traffic network rules of online car hailing in Chengdu from a macro perspective, and put forward a theoretical basis for the formulation of urban traffic strategy and the improvement methods of road operation state.

Due to the limited length of the paper and limited data, this paper still has deficiencies in the following two aspects, which need to be further explored and expanded in the future work:

(1) The research data based on this paper is the spatiotemporal data of Didi travel start and end, and there is no trajectory data in the process of operation. In the future, the processing and analysis of trajectory data can be added on the basis of more detailed data sources to more deeply and accurately reflect the current situation of road traffic operation.

(2) This paper does not do cluster analysis on the variables themselves, and the determination of

cluster K value of samples is qualitative analysis, and the specific quantitative basis remains to be discussed. Therefore, in the future, we can try to use other clustering methods to cluster not only the samples, but also the variables themselves.

4 Acknowledgements

This work is supported by the National Natural Science Foundation of China (General Program 52172318 and General Program 52131203).

References

[1] Cai, X. , Lei, C. , Peng, B. , Tang, X. , Gao, Z. (2020). Road traffic safety risk estimation method based on vehicle onboard diagnostic data. Journal of Advanced Transportation, 2020 (10), 1-13.

[2] Daniel, S. , Ding, X. (2019). Spatiotemporal evolution of ridesourcing markets under the new restriction policy: A case study in Shanghai. Transportation Research Part A, (130): 227-239.

[3] Delasalles, E. , Ziat, A. , Denoyer, L. , Gallinari, P. (2019). Spatio-temporal neural networks for space-time data modeling and relation discovery. Knowledge and Information Systems, 61(3), 1241-1267.

[4] Deng, Y. , Zou, F. , Xiang, X. , Rong, H. An Algorithm for Identifying the Change of Road Restriction Based on K-means Clustering.

[5] Devaraj, A. , Ramakrishnan, G. A. , Nair, G. S. , Srinivasan, K. K. , Pendyala, R. M. (2020). Joint model of application-based ride hailing adoption, intensity of use, and intermediate public transport consideration among workers in Chennai city. Transportation Research Record Journal of the Transportation Research Board (3), 036119812091223.

[6] Ke, J. , Zheng, H. , Yang, H. , Chen, X. (2017). Short-term forecasting of passenger demand under on-demand ride services: a spatio-temporal deep learning approach. Transportation Research, 85c(dec.), 591-608.

[7] Mcafee, A. , Brynjolfsson, E. (2012). Big data: the management revolution. Harvard business review, 90(10), 60-6, 68, 128.

[8] Raymond, G. , Konduri, K. , Naveen, E. (2018). Is there a limit to adoption of dynamic ridesharing systems? evidence from analysis of uber demand data from new york city. Transportation Research Record Journal of the Transportation Research Board, 2672, 036119811878846.

[9] Venkatesh, G. , Arunesh, K. (2018). Map reduce for big data processing based on traffic aware partition and aggregation. Cluster Computing.

[10] Xie, W. , Wang, H. , Gu, X. , Guo, Y. (2011). Research on outlier mining algorithm oriented to traffic information. Advanced Materials Research, 299-300, 1312-1315.

[11] Yu, H. , Peng, Z. (2019). Exploring the spatial variation of ridesourcing demand and its relationship to built environment and socioeconomic factors with the geographically weighted poisson regression. Journal of Transport Geography, 75(FEB.), 147-163.

[12] Yu, H. , Zhang, H. , X Yu. (2020). Hail the closest driver on roads: privacy-preserving ride matching in online ride hailing services. Security and Communication Networks, 2020 (2), 1-13.

Research on the Prediction of Intercity Passenger Waiting Time Based on Random Forest of Survival Analysis

Haofei Guo*[1] Jiaxin Du[2]

(1. College of Ocean Science and Engineering, Shanghai Maritime University;

2. College of Transport, Shanghai Maritime University)

Abstract The waiting time of intercity passengers is a decisive factor affecting the station's crowd density, which is also the key to the station's epidemic prevention control and daily management. In this study, a stochastic survival forest model is used to carry out passenger waiting time research, which overcomes the disadvantages of traditional decision tree models that are prone to transitional fitting and traditional survival analysis that requires restrictive assumptions. The study is based on Zheng-jiao intercity passenger waiting time data, combined with personal and social attributes, etc. The final model results show that cost source, age, income, and education level have significant effects on intercity passenger waiting time, and the model has a prediction accuracy of over 90% for the dataset. The study can be used by station decision makers and scholars in related fields to develop corresponding strategies for the characteristics of different groups of intercity passengers, reducing operating costs and improving station management level and turnover.

Keywords passenger waiting time survival analysis random survival forest railway station

0 Introduction

Since October 27, 2021, Zheng-Kai (Zhengzhou East Station to Songcheng Road Station), Zheng-Airport (Zhengzhou East Station to Xinzheng Airport Station) and Zheng-Jiao (Jiaozuo Station to Nanyangzhai Station) intercity railroads have started high-density bus operation mode, marking the further development of the "half-hour" traffic circle in the Central Plains city cluster. China's intercity railroads have begun to undertake the passenger flow between cities and major central towns along the route, and take into account the passenger flow between urban clusters and sub-central towns (Wang, 2017).

The station, as a grassroots unit for waiting passengers, is a significant place in intercity passenger transportation. Therefore, the management of passenger crowd density in railroad stations has been the focus of station management (Li et al., 2016). Controlling the density of passengers in the station is of great importance both to the improvement of the service level in the station and the control under the current epidemic (Li et al., 2021). Keking Liu realized multi-target detection and tracking positioning through machine vision methods, thus realizing intelligent monitoring of station passenger flow and constructing a passenger flow safety warning index system (Liu, 2018). Jinmei Xiao derived the optimal layout of station facilities under different passenger flow conditions by simulating experiments with Anylogic simulation software (Xiao, 2012); while Rui Li et al. introduced an attention mechanism processing module in the density estimation model of deep neural network to achieve crowd density estimation under different scenarios for the special characteristics such as uneven crowd distribution in railroad stations (Li et al., 2021).

The waiting time of intercity passengers is the fundamental reason affecting the density of passengers at stations (Jia and Wang, 2018), and some stations implement a 2-4 hour advance entry rule to control the density of stations, and it is not known whether this rule will be effective in today ' s Novel Coronavirus Pneumonia. Therefore, studying the waiting time of intercity passengers and the influencing factors affecting their waiting time can provide some implications for intercity railroads similar to Zheng-jiao in terms of the frequency of intercity bus service and station management schemes.

It has been shown that the timing of intercity passenger travel has a considerable relationship with passengers' own attributes(Wei,2015). In addition, the choice behavior of intercity passengers causes dynamic changes in the distribution of passenger flow at stations and it may easily lead to the propagation of congestion, which is one of the key factors in the creation of carrying capacity bottlenecks (Huang et al., 2018). Therefore, it is particularly important to fully understand the characteristics of different passengers' own demands and grasp the determinants of intercity passengers' detention time(Da Hensher and Aj Reyes, 2000). In addition, Chen Tuan-sheng et al. argued that with the continuous improvement of the railroad line network, the alternatives for rail travel passengers have gradually increased, and as decision makers in the travel process, passengers have their own subjectivity, preference and other various unpredictable influencing factors on waiting time. Thus the economic and time factors of passengers have a certain influence on their detention time (Chen et al., 2007).

This study is based on the data of passenger arrival time at Jiaozuo waiting station of Zheng-Jiao intercity in April 2021 and the original data consisting of personal attributes and social attributes of passengers obtained by distributing questionnaires. The 80% of the data are used as the training data set and the 20% are used as the test data set. The modeling of significant influencing factors and weights for the intercity passenger detention time is analyzed by establishing a random survival forest method. Finally, the model accuracy is tested based on the 20% test data set, and the model prediction accuracy is tested with three typical evaluation indexes of standardized mean absolute variance, mean square error and mean absolute error, and the results obtained in this study are summarized to conclude the whole study.

1 Data Description

The Zheng-Jiao line undertakes daily activities such as commuting and tourism in Zhengzhou and Jiaozuo, and the survey results can better reflect the personal characteristics of intercity passengers. While the waiting room on the second floor of Jiaozuo North Station is full of intercity passengers of the Zheng-Jiao line, which improves the efficiency of the sample to a certain extent. In this study, the information of passengers boarding the train at Jiaozuo station of Zheng (Zhou)-Jiao (Zuo) line is studied(Fig. 1).

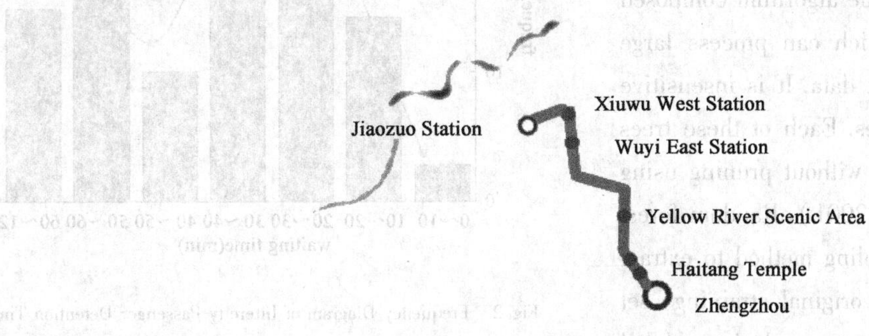

Fig. 1 Schematic Diagram of the Zheng-jiao Line

This study is based on the data of the arrival time of the Zheng-Jiao intercity passenger flow at Jiaozuo Station in April 2021 and the personal and social attribute data of passengers obtained by issuing questionnaires as a complete data set. In the end, 150 questionnaires were issued and 141 questionnaires were returned (recovery rate of 94%), which met the requirements, see Tab. 1.

Summary of Intercity Passenger Arrival Time Survey Tab. 1

	Content
Time	April 2021
Location	Second floor of Jiaozuo Railway Station-Zheng-jiao Intercity Waiting Hall
Study Subjects	Zheng-jiao intercity (Zhengzhou direction) passengers
Recycling samples	141
Survey Content	Personal attributes (e. g. , gender, age, etc.) Objective attributes (e. g. , interchange, distance, etc.)

It is not difficult to see from Fig. 2 that passengers with a waiting time of 20-30 minutes and 30-40 minutes have a higher frequency, accounting for 42% of the total. While passengers with the waiting time of one hour account for 85% of the total, which basically represents the entire waiting time of the passenger group, and the distribution of the waiting time of the whole passenger is represented by a typical bimodal graph. Through the random sampling method, 80% of the data set is used to train the intercity passenger waiting time prediction model, and the 20% is used as the test set to test the prediction accuracy of the model. The data characteristics of the two sets of data are basically the same.

2 Intercity Passenger Waiting Time Prediction Model Based on Survival Random Forest

Random forest is a machine algorithm composed of multiple tree classifiers, which can process large and multi-dimensional complex data. It is insensitive to collinearity between variables. Each of these trees is composed of a decision tree without pruning using the CART algorithm (Breiman, 2001). Random forest is the use of Bootstrap re-sampling method to extract multiple samples from the original training set samples. Secondly, each Bootstrap sample is modeled by a decision tree, then the predictions of multiple decision trees are combined, and finally the final prediction result is obtained through voting. Among them, the probability of each sample being drawn in the Bootstrap re-sampling method is:

$$P = \left(1 - \frac{1}{N}\right) \tag{1}$$

When $N \to \infty$,

$$\lim_{N\to\infty} P = \lim_{N\to\infty}\left(1 - \frac{1}{N}\right)^N = e^{-1} \approx 0.368 \tag{2}$$

In the formula, P represents the probability that the sample is not drawn; N is the number of samples in the original training set. Among them, about 37% of the samples in the original training set will not appear in the Bootstrap samples. These data are taken out as out-of-bag OOB.

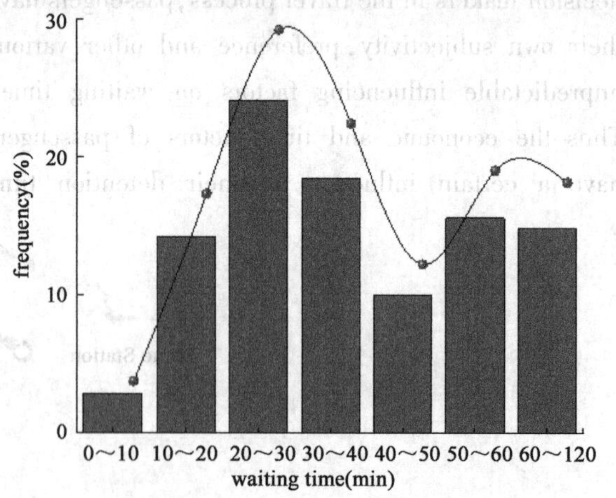

Fig. 2 Frequency Diagram of Intercity Passenger Detention Time

Each tree in the random survival forest is estimated by the end point KM risk when the survival function is used. For any end point h, the definition

$d_{i,h}$ and $Y_{i,h}$ respectively represent the number of individuals and the expected number that end at time $t_{i,h}$. Cumulative survival function for endpoint h:

$$\hat{H}_h(t) = \sum_{t_{i,h}} \leqslant t \frac{d_{i,h}}{Y_{i,h}} \tag{3}$$

If the survival tree has multiple nodes, then the tree has multiple KM risk estimates. If the endpoint h is under the action of the covariate x_i, the survival function of the corresponding single tree is:

$$\hat{H}(t|x_i) = \hat{H}_h(t), \text{if } x_i \in h \tag{4}$$

So as to get the survival function of the random survival forest $H_e^*(t|x_i) = \frac{1}{N_{\text{tree}}} \sum_{b=1}^{N_{\text{tree}}} \hat{H}_b(t|x_i)$

$\hat{H}_b(t|x_i)$ is the survival function of survival tree b; N_{tree} is the number of survival trees in the random survival forest.

In order to determine the reasonable forest scale, thisstudy studies the model error corresponding to the random survival forest scale in the interval of [1,1000]. As shown in Fig. 3, when the number of trees in the survival forest is less than 200, the error fluctuates markedly. When the survival forest scale is after 300, the error is small and the fluctuation is stable. The model error is the smallest when the optimal survival forest scale is finally determined to be 325.

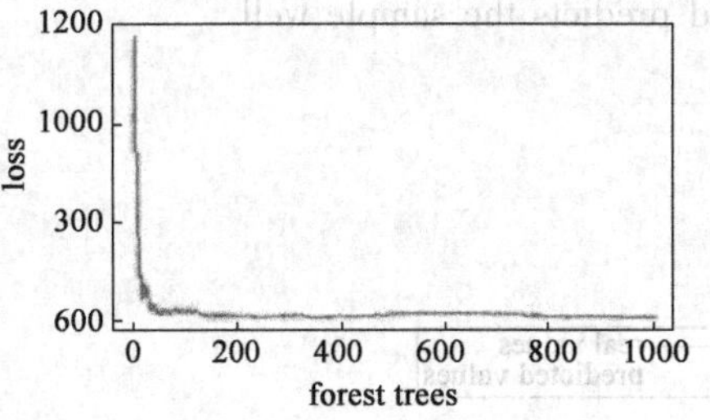

Fig. 3 The Relationship Between the Number of Decision Trees and Model Error in Random Survival

In this study, there are 10 independent variables involved in the establishment of a random survival model. In order to determine the specific number of nodes, the number of variables should be randomly selected and the corresponding model errors at 1-10 need to be calculated. As shown in Fig. 4, through calculation and information of the figure, it can be obtained that when the characteristic variable of the decision tree split node in the random survival forest is 4, the error change of the model reaches the minimum.

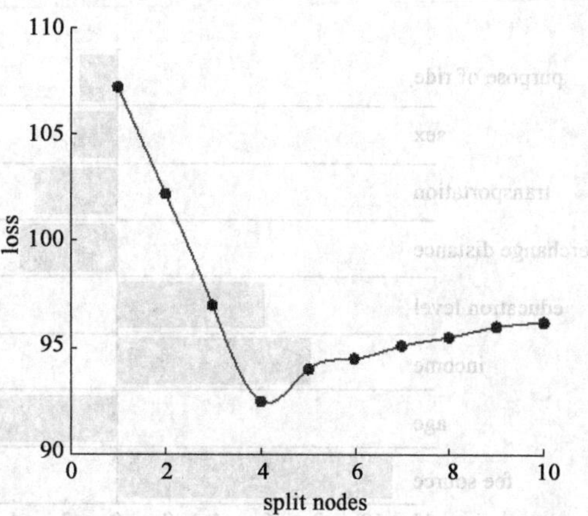

Fig. 4 The number of Preselected Variables and the Change of Model Error

There is no fixed function model expression in the random survival forest model. This article uses the random forest model established by the "randomforest" package in the R software to analyze the importance of the independent variables. Among them, Random Survival Forest provides two methods for screening variables, namely screening the importance of variables (VIMP) by machine-selected OOB error rate. The greater the value of VIMP, the greater the degree of its impact on the event, and the stronger the predictive ability. This article chooses the method of VIMP to filter the variables, and the results obtained are shown in Fig. 5. The source of expenses, age, income and education level have a significant impact on the prediction results of the model.

The random survival forest variable screening method VIMP sorts the importance of variables according to the absolute value of the OOB error rate. The sorting result is shown in Fig. 5. From the data obtained in Fig. 5, it can be seen that thefee source, age, income, and education level are the main factors that affecting the waiting time of intercity passengers. When the source of expenses is public expense, income level, and higher education level, this type of passenger group pays more attention to time cost, and their waiting time is shorter, while groups over 50 years old have no higher requirements for time. Arrive at the station a long time in advance and wait for the train to run.

The residual error of the model training setdata is shown in Fig. 6. It can be seen that the deviation between most of the model predictions and the actual passenger waiting time data is 0, indicating that the model fits the test set data quite well.

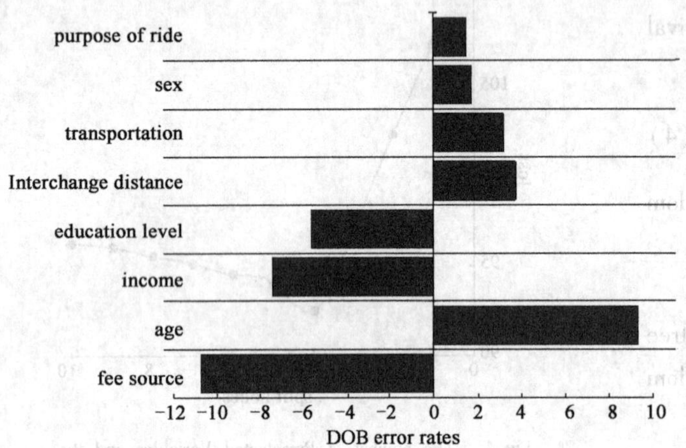

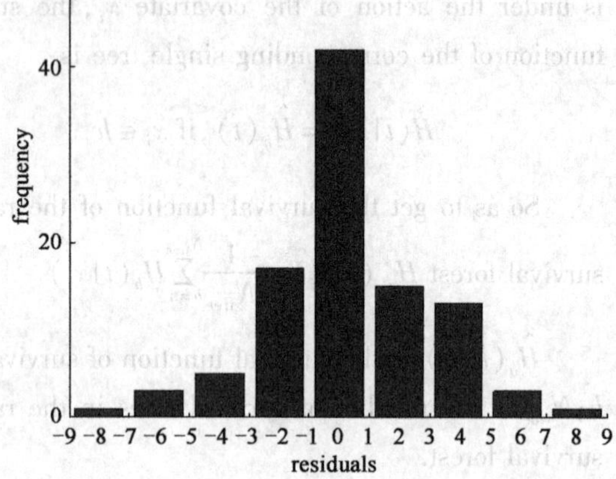

Fig. 5 The Importance of Random Survival Forest Feature Variables

Fig. 6 Fitting Residual Distribution of the Training Data

Although the out-of-bag data is used for prediction in the process of establishing the random survival model, in order to further understand and verify the predictive ability of the model, this study uses the remaining 20% of the data set to verify the predictive ability of the model. The prediction results are shown in Fig. 7.

The model prediction results use mean absolute error (MAE), mean square error (MSE), and standardized mean absolute error (NMSE) as the main evaluation indicators. Tab. 2 shows the calculation accuracy of the random survival forest model on the training data set and the test set. What can be seen from the table is that the average absolute error of the model for all samples is within 5 minutes, the standardized average absolute error is less than 0.3, and the errors of each predictions are lower than those during training. This manifests that the model fits and predicts the sample well.

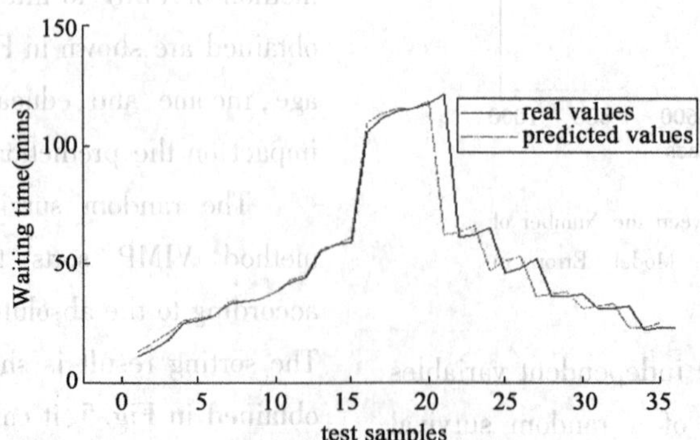

Fig. 7 Model Prediction Results

Computational Accuracy Metrics of the Stochastic Survival Forest Model Tab. 2

Evaluation Metrics	Training dataset	Test dataset
Average absolute error(MAE)	4.05	5.42
Mean Square Error(MSE)	20.03	26.21
Standardized mean absolute variance(NMSE)	0.28	0.30

3 Conclusions

Through the intercity passenger waiting time and related data of Zheng-jiao, this study uses the random survival forest model to construct an intercity passenger waiting time prediction model. The random survival forest model combines the advantages of random forest and survival analysis, which has a strong generalization ability. Through the research on the waiting time of intercity passengers, the significant variables that affect the waiting time of passengers are mainly: source of expenses, age, income, and education level. Among them, the source of expenses refers to the most significant factor for the waiting time of intercity passengers. Generally, the waiting time of intercity passengers traveling at public expense is relatively short, which is basically consistent with the previous research conclusions. In addition, the higher the level of income and education, the higher the awareness of time costs, and the relatively shorter waiting time. What's more, the increase in age is positively correlated with the waiting time, especially for passengers over 50 years old, and this type of passengers is more inclined to advance. After arrival, there is no major requirement for time.

According to the distribution of various variables and the relationship between the variables, a random survival forest prediction model for predicting the waiting time of intercity passengers is established. The model validity test and prediction results show that:

(1) The random survival forest model can better fit the data of intercity passenger detention time;

(2) The random survival forest model has high prediction accuracy for intercity passenger detention time. When the allowable error is within 5 minutes, the prediction accuracy of the model exceeds 90%.

The prediction results can be used to estimate the behavior information of individual passengers and even inter-city passenger groups. Not only can the average and median of the waiting time of inter-city passengers be obtained, but also the probability that the waiting time of passengers at the station exceeds a certain point in time can be estimated. Station decision-makers and scholars in related fields can use the research results to formulate corresponding strategies for different groups of people, thereby reducing operating costs and increasing turnover. In subsequent studies, the flow of intercity passengers at stations and the optimal departure interval of intercity trains can be optimized based on the results of this research, so as to meet the needs of passenger transportation while meeting the lowest operating costs.

References

[1] Breiman, L. Random forests [J]. Machine Learning 45, 2001: 5-32.

[2] DA Hensher, AJ Reyes. Trip chaining as a barrier to the propensity to use public transport [J]. Transportation, 2000.

[3] Jia, N., Wang, Y. A Model of High-Density Passenger Boarding and Alighting in Urban Rail Transit Station, in: Jia, L., Qin, Y., Suo, J., Feng, J., Diao, L., An, M. (Eds.), Proceedings of the 3rd International Conference on Electrical and Information Technologies for Rail

Transportation (EITRT) 2017, Lecture Notes in Electrical Engineering. Springer Singapore, Singapore, pp. 779-789.

[4] Liu Kejing. Research on intelligent monitoring of passenger flow safety in stations based on machine vision [D]. Southwest Jiaotong University, 2018.

[5] Li, R., Wu, H., Yang, W. T.. Design of an early warning system for monitoring passenger flow in railroad passenger stations based on ticketing data [J]. Railway Transportation and Economy, 2016, 38, 54-58 + 73.

[6] Li R, Li P, Wang W Q, et al. Study on adaptive scenario estimation and application of passenger density in railroad stations [J]. Railway Transportation and Economy, 2021, 43, 19-26.

[7] Wang Wanying. Study on functional positioning and characteristics of intercity railroads [J]. Journal of Railway Engineering, 2017, 34, 74-77.

[8] Xiao Jinmei. Study on the scale and layout of passenger service facilities in intercity railroad stations [D]. Southwest Jiaotong University, 2012.

[9] Chen Tuan-Sheng, Mao Bao-Hua, Gao Li-Ping, et al. Analysis of passenger travel choice behavior on special lines [J]. Journal of Railways, 2007.

[10] Wei Wei. Passenger flow sensitivity analysis based on intercity passenger travel behavior [D]. Chang'an University, 2015.

[11] Huang Jiajun, Xu Ruihua, Deng Ying, et al. A bottleneck identification method for subway station carrying capacity considering passenger choice behavior [J]. Journal of Tongji University, 2018, 46, 1080-1088.

增加考虑出行者非理性特征对决策结果的影响分析

曹 悦*[1] 程引南[2]

(1. 长安大学运输工程学院;2. 贵州宏信创达工程检测咨询有限公司)

摘 要 为分析增加考虑出行者非理性特性时路径决策行为的变化,分别用期望效用理论(Expected Utility Theory, EUT)和前景理论(Prospect Theory, PT)对出行者的决策过程进行建模。通过算例检验模型的可行性,计算对出行者做不同假设时的出行路径决策结果,并讨论不同迟到风险下,考虑出行者的非理性特性是否会对决策结果的影响。结果显示:基于期望效用理论的假设,出行者选择路径2出行,基于前景理论时,出行者选择路径1出行。这表明面对风险,作为非理性人的出行者的决策结果将发生改变。分析讨论的结果可以佐证前景理论中对出行者非理性人假设的合理性,同时可为面对出行准时性需求不同的出行者的诱导提供分析思路。

关键词 交通工程 出行者路径决策 前景理论 非理性决策行为

0 引言

出行者的出行决策影响着道路交通流的分布、各交通方式的协同运转。随着 MaaS(出行及服务)等理念的提出,研究出行者的路径决策行为进而预测出行者的决策结果是研究居民出行方式比例以及道路交通流的分配的基础,对提升城市道路交通流运行效率以及优化多模式交通间的换乘衔接具有重要意义。

进行决策过程建模时,对出行者这一决策主

体特征的假设经历了从"理性"到"非完全理性"的变化。早期常采用的期望效用理论(Expected Utility Theory,EUT)认为人是完全理性的个体,当面对选择时,其一定会作出最优的决策结果[1]。后来,Ellsberg 悖论、Allais 悖论引起了人们对期望效用理论的适用性及可行性的质疑。从心理学和行为科学的研究成果角度,认为人们在具有不确定因素的环境下做出的决策应是有限理性的。Kahneman 和 Tversky 基于心理学实验的研究结果提出前景理论(Prospect Theory,PT),用来描述人们面对风险时的决策行为[2]。后续的相关研究证明了其在出行者决策建模方向的合理性[3-5]。实际上路径决策通常结合交通分配问题进行研究。前景理论应用于路径决策问题时,利用前景理论优化交通分配中的阻抗函数[6],综合考虑多策略下(交通出行者角度的 UE 策略,交通管理者角度的 SO 策略,大型客货运输企业的 CN 策略等)的交通分配目标,改进 UE 模型[7],能更好地模拟交通量在道路网络上的分布。或改进 SUE 模型,得到含交通系统不确定性、出行者感知误差及建模者观测误差的交通分配结果[8]。由于前景理论内存在参照点等根据不同出行情景、不同出行者个体可能会变化的参数,因此探讨了参数变化对前景理论计算结果的影响[9]。作为路径决策及分配研究的拓展,有研究将前景理论应用于获取大型建筑如轨道交通车站[10-11]、道路交通[12]的应急疏散路径方案,并通过与仿真结果的对比证明了此应用方向的可行性。

通过综述上述研究可以发现,PT 更适用于解决出行者的路径决策问题,为对比基于 EUT 和基于 PT 的路径决策模型的建模过程及计算结果的差异,本文首先建立基于两个理论的出行者路径决策过程模型,然后利用一小路网进行数值检验,计算出行者的决策结果。最后对比分析不同风险概率对"理性"人、"非理性"人决策的影响。

1 路径决策模型

1.1 基于期望效用理论的路径决策模型

EUT 通过计算效用函数来表现决策者对选择的"偏好"。在决策问题中建立效用值(Utility Value)来描述对可能出现的选择的偏好程度。而每种选择的结果是不确定的,可将其看作一个概率分布。

当建立以时间为决策变量的出行者路径决策模型时,基于 EUT 的有关概念,假设出行起讫点间有多条合理路径备选。同时由于道路出行过程中,路段、交叉口节点运行情况的不确定性,每条路径理论上均有迟到、准时、早到可能。由此,第 k 条路径的期望效用值可用式(1)表示。由于出行时间越短,出行者收到的效用越大,因此在理性人假设下,出行者将比较起讫点间 k 条路径的期望时间值,选择该值最小但相应的使出行者效用最大的路径出行。

$$\mathrm{EU}_k = \sum_i (u_i P_i) \tag{1}$$

式中:EU_k——第 k 条路径的期望时间值;

u_i——第 k 条路径第 i 种可能出行时间;

P_i——第 k 条路径第 i 种可能出行时间结果的概率。

1.2 基于前景理论的路径决策模型

PT 指出人们的决策过程分为编辑、评价两个阶段。第一个阶段是编辑阶段,考虑决策影响因素对决策者的影响,建立决策者进行比较时的"参照点",服务于已有的决策过程。第二个阶段是评价阶段,计算已编辑过的各个选择的前景,对前景值进行排序,决策者将选择前景值最大的选择,从而完成决策过程。当 PT 用于研究出行者的路径决策时,可做如下假设:每次出行的起讫点之间会有多条备选路径,出行者需要选择其中一条路径出行。基于 PT 的原理,出行者将按照图 1 所示的步骤完成决策过程。

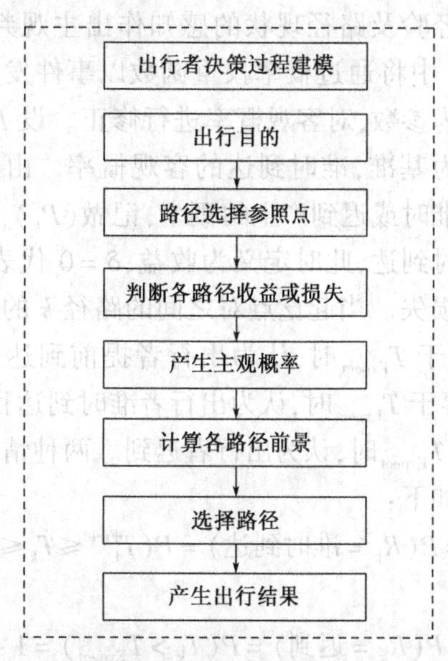

图 1 出行者决策流程图

首先,出行者通过自身出行经验、对路网的了解程度、当时路网状态、诱导信息等对此次出行的时间产生主观判断,得到预计出行时间 T_{Expect},并将此预计出行时间作为参照点。然后出行者将对备选路径的价值进行评估。假定价值函数以实际出行时间与参照点的差值 $T_{\text{Expect}}-T_{\text{pk}}$ 作为自变量,$T_{\text{Expect}}-T_{\text{pk}}$ 越大,对应的价值越大。假定路径 k 的价值函数形式为 $V(T_{\text{Expect}}-T_{\text{pk}})$,将其做如下定义:

$$V(T_{\text{Expect}}-T_{\text{pk}})=\begin{cases}(T_{\text{Expect}}-T_{\text{pk}})^{\alpha}, & T_{\text{Expect}}-T_{\text{pk}}\geqslant 0\\ -\lambda\left[-(T_{\text{Expect}}-T_{\text{pk}})\right]^{\alpha}, & T_{\text{Expect}}-T_{\text{pk}}\leqslant 0\end{cases}\tag{2}$$

式中:$V(T_{\text{Expect}}-T_{\text{pk}})$——路径 k 的价值;

α——风险态度系数,其取值范围为(0,1),α 的值越小,出行者越倾向于回避风险;

λ——损失规避系数,λ 一般大于1,其取值越大,出行者对损失的态度更加敏感。

在过往的研究中,学者对参数 α,λ 进行了标定,其中较为常用的取值为:$\alpha=0.88$,$\lambda=2.25$[2]。

当采用备选路径完成出行时,均可能出现准时到达、迟到、早到三种情况。基于既往的出行结果,可统计其对应概率。前景理论认为出行者在进行路径决策时,一般是根据自己对路径的了解及过往经验及路径现状的感知作出主观判断,因此在PT中将通过概率权重函数以事件发生的客观概率为参数,对客观概率进行修正。设 P_{k} 为以参照点为基准,准时到达的客观概率。由此产生了路径准时或迟到产生的概率,记做 $(P_{\text{k}})_{\delta}$。$\delta=1$ 代表准时到达,此时定义为收益;$\delta=0$ 代表迟到,定义为损失。当起讫点对之间的路径 k 的出行时间 T_{k} 小于 T_{Expect} 时,认为出行者提前到达了目的地;T_{k} 等于 T_{Expect} 时,认为出行者准时到达目的地;T_{k} 大于 T_{Expect} 时,认为出行者迟到。两种情况的计算公式如下:

$$(P_{\text{k}})_1=P(R_{\text{k}}=\text{准时到达})=P(T_{\text{k}}^{\text{Free}}\leqslant T_{\text{k}}\leqslant T_{\text{Expect}})\tag{3}$$

$$(P_{\text{k}})_0=P(R_{\text{k}}=\text{迟到})=P(T_{\text{k}}>T_{\text{Expect}})=1-(P_{\text{k}})_1\tag{4}$$

式中:$T_{\text{k}}^{\text{Free}}$——路径 k 自由流行驶时间;

$(P_{\text{k}})_1$——准时到达的概率;

$(P_{\text{k}})_0$——迟到的概率。

再根据 $(P_{\text{k}})_{\delta}$ 计算准时到达或迟到情况下的概率权重。取得收益即准时到达时的概率权重为:

$$W(P_{\text{k}})=\frac{(P_{\text{k}})^{\gamma}}{\left[(P_{\text{k}})^{\gamma}+(1-P_{\text{k}})^{\gamma}\right]^{\frac{1}{\gamma}}}\tag{5}$$

受到损失即迟到时的概率权重为:

$$W(P_{\text{k}})=\frac{(P_{\text{k}})^{\chi}}{\left[(P_{\text{k}})^{\chi}+(1-P_{\text{k}})^{\chi}\right]^{\frac{1}{\chi}}}\tag{6}$$

式中:$W(P_{\text{k}})$——表示路径 k 的概率权重;

γ——由Kahneman经试验标定,结果为收益时,取0.61[2];

χ——由Kahneman经试验标定,结果为损失时,取0.69[2]。

在这一阶段利用路径 k 的价值及概率权重计算得出路径 k 的前景值,通过比较各路径的前景完成评价阶段,见式(7)。

$$(PS)_{\text{k}}=\sum W(P_{\text{k}})V(d_{\text{k}})=\frac{(d_{\text{k}})^{\alpha}(P_{\text{k}})^{\gamma}}{\left[(P_{\text{k}})^{\gamma}+(1-P_{\text{k}})^{\gamma}\right]^{\frac{1}{\gamma}}}-\frac{\lambda(-d_{\text{k}})^{\alpha}(P_{\text{k}})^{\chi}}{\left[(P_{\text{k}})^{\chi}+(1-P_{\text{k}})^{\chi}\right]^{\frac{1}{\chi}}}\tag{7}$$

式中:$(PS)_{\text{k}}$——路径 k 的前景值。

出行者在进行路径选择时遵循如下原则:比较各路径的前景,选择前景最大的路径出行,即最终选定路径的前景值应符合如下条件:

$$(PS)_{\text{k}}=\max\left[(PS)_1,(PS)_2,\cdots,(PS)_{\text{k}}\right]\tag{8}$$

2　数值检验

2.1　路网信息

采用如图2所示的路网对上述两个模型的可行性及合理性进行数值检验,路网内共含13个节点,18个路段。以起点为1终点为13的一次出行为例讨论路径决策结果。

为获取模型内决策变量:合理路径集、路径出行时间,经交通分配得路段交通量及路段行驶时间后,采用 K 条最短路径算法(KSP,k-shortest paths)得前三条时间最短路作为合理路径集。统计各路径的出行时间、出行距离信息如表1。同时由于各路径途经交叉口数目不同,结合实际道路内出行情况,对出行时间的迟到、早到、准时概率做如表1所示假设。

路网基础信息 表1

路径	路径长度(km)	出行时间(min)/对应概率		
路径1:1-3-10-12-17	8.7	17/0.15	22.8/0.7	26/0.15
路径2:2-4-6-8-10-12-17	8.8	14/0.3	24.5/0.5	28/0.2
路径3:2-4-6-9-13-18	8.2	17/0.15	24.6/0.65	28/0.2

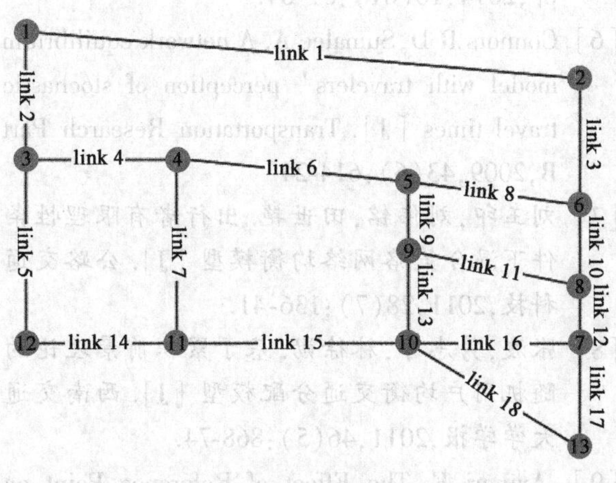

图2 算例路网

2.2 前景理论参数标定

为了标定模型内的期望出行时间这一变量,应用问卷调查法对出行者决策的特性进行调查。本次调查内容主要包括出行者个体特征、不同自由流行驶时间下出行者能接受的最大出行时间预期等变量。调查的对象为居住于各市的市民。调查采用互联网络数据调查方式,总发放500份,回收487份。为了消除调查中由于问卷填写者的随意性等因素对数据造成的影响,需对数据进行筛选处理及校核,剔除控制性强的数据以及不符合逻辑的数据,最终获取有效样本465份,有效率为93%。

将不同年龄段、不同性别的出行者针对不同自由流行驶时间的出行所能接受的最大出行时间统计见表2,可以看出,在不同的自由流行时间下,出行者能接受的出行时间延误也不同。因此根据调查结果,当自由流行驶时间为10min即路径长度为10km左右时,出行者的期望出行时间为20min。

出行者能接受的最大出行时间统计表 表2

自由流行驶时间(min)	能接受的最大出行时间(min)	占比
10	20	47.5%
20	30	40.0%
30	40	42.5%
40	60	32.5%
50	60	27.5%
60	90	25.0%

2.3 路径决策结果

分别将各条路径的出行时间及各出行时间对应概率代入两个模型内求解,可得到各路径的期望值和前景值,结果见表3。从表3中可见,基于EUT,出行者将选择期望时间值最小、效用最大的路径2出行;而基于PT出行者将选择前景值最大的路径1出行。

路径决策结果 表3

路径	期望值计算结果	选择路径	前景值计算结果	选择路径
路径1:1-3-10-12-17	22.41	路径2	-5.036	路径1
路径2:2-4-6-8-10-12-17	22.05		-5.902	
路径3:2-4-6-9-13-18	24.14		-7.765	

分析路径的基本信息,可佐证EUT与PT的差异。出行路径1途经4个交叉口,路径2途经6个交叉口。由于途经交叉口数目的增加,出行者在道路出行的不确定性增加,早到、迟到风险均发生变化。在EUT的建模过程中,认为出行者是完全理性的,通过综合路径的可能出行时间及对应概率计算得到路径出行时间期望值。虽然选择的路径2将为完全理性出行者带来最大效用,但未能体现交叉口数目增加等路况信息对出行者决策过程的影响。而PT认为出行者是非完全理性的,会对比期望出行时间与可能的出行时间结果得到自己评判的路径价值,而且还会结合自身经验及获

取的出行信息对客观概率进行修正。最后结合价值和概率权重得到前景值。在 PT 描述的决策过程中体现了出行者面临损失时的风险喜好与面临收益时的风险规避。以上建模思想应用于路径决策过程中的差异导致了出行者在两种模型内做出不同的路径决策结果。

3　结语

本文从对比不同路径决策模型的决策结果的角度出发,建立基于 EUT 和基于 PT 的路径决策模型。采用发放调查问卷的方式获取出行者的出行时间期望,并通过小路网进行数值检验,计算两种模型下的路径决策结果。结果显示在算例路网的情况下,路径决策结果不同。从模型的假设和建模过程对比分析,决策结果的差异机理。通过以上的研究,可以看出:出行者更适合于非完全理性人的假设。在未来的研究中,可基于 PT,针对出行者个体的决策特性,在结合交通分配建模的基础上考虑如何进行出行诱导。

参考文献

[1] 钱晨,祖永昶,顾金刚,等.基于前景理论的路径选择方法研究[J].中国公共安全(学术版),2018(04):71-74

[2] Kahneman D, Tversky A. Prospect theory: An analysis of decision under risk [M]. Handbook of the fundamentals of financial decision making: Part I. World Scientific. 2013:99-127.

[3] Amit Kothiyal, Vitalie Spinu, Peter P. Wakker. An experimental test of prospect theory for predicting choice under ambiguity [J]. Journal of Risk and Uncertainty ,2014,48(1):1-17.

[4] Yang J F, Jiang G Y. Development of an enhanced route choice model based on cumulative prospect theory. Transportation Research Part C,2014,47(2):168-178.

[5] 陆雯雯,姜康,黄志鹏.基于前景理论诱导信息的出行者路径选择模型[J].交通科技与经济,2014,16(01):61-64.

[6] Connors R D, Sumalee A. A network equilibrium model with travelers' perception of stochastic travel times [J]. Transportation Research Part B,2009,43(6):614-24.

[7] 刘玉印,刘伟铭,田世艳.出行者有限理性条件下混合策略网络均衡模型 [J].公路交通科技,2011,28(7):136-41.

[8] 张波,隽志才,林徐勋.基于累积前景理论的随机用户均衡交通分配模型 [J].西南交通大学学报,2011,46(5):868-74.

[9] Avineri E. The Effect of Reference Point on Stochastic Network Equilibrium [J]. Transportation Science,2006,40(4):409-20.

[10] 毛亚兰,张锦.考虑乘客不完全理性行为的轨道交通车站应急疏散方法研究[J].工业工程,2020,23(03):138-144+153.

[11] 卢勇利,朱昌锋,侯耀文.城市轨道交通车站应急疏散方案决策研究[J].中国安全生产科学技术,2019,15(03):128-134.

[12] 龙雪琴,王建军,关宏志.交通事故下出行者非理性出行行为研究[J].交通运输系统工程与信息,2015,15(02):156-162.

居民出行方式选择模型的估计与分析

南彦洲*　曾明哲　陶　锋

(长安大学运输工程学院)

摘　要　为建立居民出行方式选择模型,本文基于实际案例的调查数据,通过对出行方式选择影响因素相关性分析,以出行方式的出行时间、出行费用和步行时间等作为自变量,出行者年龄、性别和出行目的为虚拟变量,并考虑构建新的变量,建立了多项、嵌套和混合三种不同类型的离散选择模型,分别用于出行方式选择研究。对比三种类型方式选择模型似然比检验结果,并据最优拟合模型评估出行方式分担率。结果表明,汽车出行平均高于地铁和公交出行总和,占出行总数的55%;依据灵活性进行嵌套方式划分模型最优;基于嵌套模型的汽车、地铁和公交三种出行方式分担率分别为56.70%、29.05%和14.25%,误差均小于1.5%,平均误差0.93%。本文建立最适合本案例的NL模型,对依据居民出行选择评估的城市交通方式分担率预测有较高的应用价值。

关键词 出行方式选择 离散选择模型 Logit模型 参数估计 相似性检验

0 引言

居民出行交通方式选择趋于多元化,研究表明出行对交通方式的选择受到众多因素影响。汽车、地铁和公交出行涉及因素包括出行时间、出行成本和步行时间等。除此之外,出行者本身的年龄、性别、出行目的和转车次数属性也会影响其对出行方式的选择。基于出行方式选择的交通方式分担率对城市总体交通运行及管理有重要意义。因此,如何有效估计居民出行方式选择是首要任务。

多元Logit模型广泛使用于多因素影响下的离散选择。温慧英研究车辆属性、驾驶员特征、道路状况和环境等因素与路口自行车事故严重程度的关系,建立了一种离散选择模型,采用最大似然法估计模型参数,通过拟合度检验和独立性检验。李军利用浮动车出行数据研究城市路网多OD和Logit随机路径选择模型参数估计,将离散多叉Logit模型转化为相对阻抗的连续概率模型,准确反映实际路径选择行为。滕靖等考虑在途时间、非在途时间和费用等出行者异质性和偏好性,建立出行方式离散选择模型。张文会建立拥挤度实测数据与乘客主观感知对应关系,对行程时间、拥挤度和出行费用分级,建立常规公交和地铁出行方式选择离散Logit模型。综上可知,出行方式选择从出行者属性和出行方式特征两个维度以新变量和虚拟变量形式进行的研究较少。

本研究针对影响出行者方式选择的多种因素,从出行者和出行方式两个角度出发,分别考虑MNL、NL和ML模型建立出行方式选择的多元Logit模型,建立模型并评估分析,以期对出行方式分担率进行评估。

1 数据收集分析

1.1 数据描述

本案例使用荷兰梅亨市实际调查收集获得的235个调查对象出行特征数据,为居民提供了三种可供选择的出行方式,即汽车、地铁和公交车。影响每个调查对象出行方式选择的因素主要包括年龄、性别、换乘次数、出行目的、出行成本、出行时间和不同出行方式的额外时间等,见表1。

出行不同属性对应表 表1

变量值	0	1	2	3	4
年龄	—	≤25	26~40	41~59	≥60
换乘地铁	0次	1次	2次	3次	—
换乘公交	0次	1次	2次	—	—
出行目的	—	商业	购物或再生产	其他	—
性别	男性	女性	—	—	—

1.2 数据统计分析

根据调查数据,经过数据统计,图中横坐标对应表1中年龄、出行目的和性别各自属性值区分,并从三个维度对出行方式进行分析,如图1所示。

图1显示三种出行选择在年龄、出行目的、性别下的分布。汽车出行方式占三种出行方式的55%,图1a)中26~40岁年龄段人群选择汽车出行的比例占53%,且各出行方式在各个年龄段出行者中的比例相似;相比之下,图1b)中出行目的为商业而选择汽车出行的比例反而更小,以商业为出行目的人更加偏向地铁方式。图1c)中男性选择汽车出行比女性高10%,女性选择地铁出行方式比男性高8%,而选择公交的比例接近,且公交方式与出行者年龄、出行目的和性别之间的关系更加不明显,与出行者特殊属性关联性最弱,因此建模中不优先考虑。

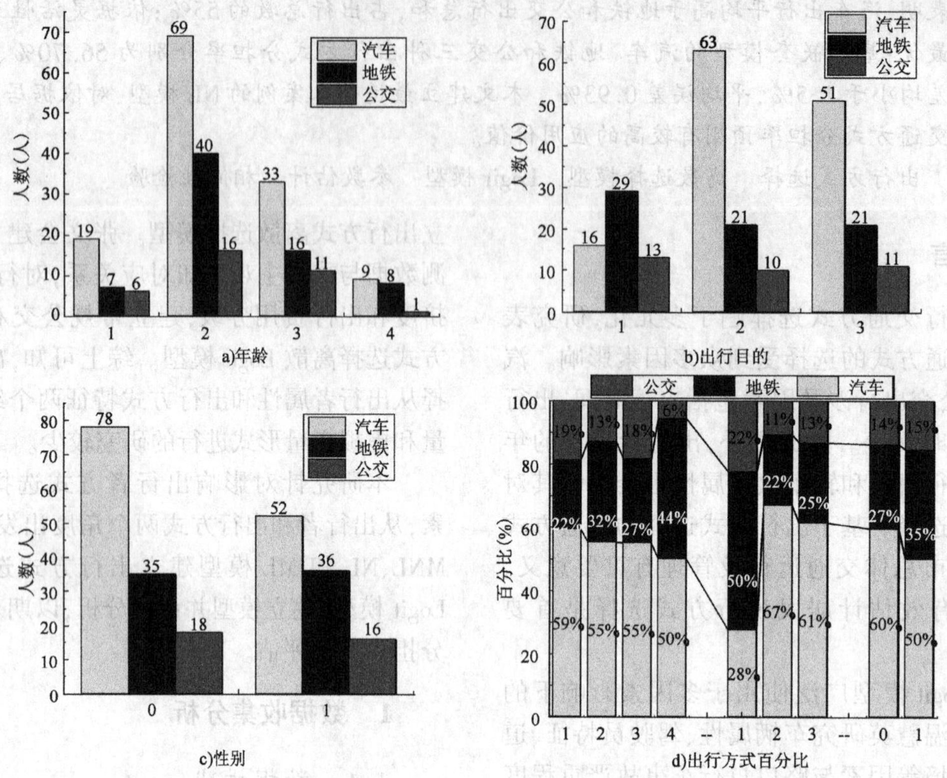

图 1　年龄—出行目的—性别与出行方式选择

2　模型分析

2.1　变量

出行方式有汽车、地铁和公交,出行方式的属性主要有时间、票价和换乘次数,通常 Logit 会考虑方式选择常量 ASC 和出行者属性的离散变量,见表 2。

方式选择和出行者属性变量　　表 2

分　类	名　称	符　号	数据类型
汽车	常量	ASC1	固定值
	出行费用	TCCAR	连续变量
	出行时间	TTCAR	
	步行时间	VOTCAR	
公交	常量	ASC2	固定值
	出行费用	TCBUS	连续变量
	出行时间	TTBUS	
	步行时间	VOTBUS	
	换乘次数	CHANGEB	
地铁	常量	ASC3	固定值
	出行费用	TCRAIL	连续变量
	出行时间	TTRAIL	
	步行时间	VOTRAIL	
	换乘次数	CHANGESR	
其他	虚拟变量	dum	0 ~ 1 变量
	参数	B	

变量的选择主要有加入新变量和增加虚拟变量，新变量 TCCAR_new = $TCCAR^{1/2}$，虚拟变量 dum_1 =（PURPOSE = 2），表示当出行者的出行目的是为了再生产或购物时，虚拟变量 dum_1 的值为 1，否则 dum_1 = 0。虚拟变量取法见表 1。根据不同因素对出行方式选择的影响，在最简单离散选择模型的基础上，选择、估计和修改变量。在此情况下，离散选择模型如下。

car：ASC1 · one + B_1 · TCCAR + B_2 · TTCAR

rail：ASC2 · one + B_3 · TCRAIL + B_4 · TTRAIL

bus：ASC3 · one + B_5 · TCBUS + B_6 · TTBUS

2.2 多项式(MNL)模型估计

首先，当出行选择模型中没有新的变量或虚拟变量时，基本模型运行检验结果见表 3 、表 4。

效 用 参 数 表3

参 数	值	调整标准差	调整 t 检验	P 值
ASC1	0.00			
ASC2	−4.42	1.05	−4.21	0.00
ASC3	6.32	1.81	3.48	0.00
B_1	−0.000275	7.85e−005	−3.50	0.00
B_2	−0.0347	0.00804	−4.32	0.00
B_3	−0.000398	0.000167	−2.38	0.02
B_4	0.00846	0.00800	1.06	0.29
B_5	−0.00233	0.000437	−5.34	0.00
B_6	−0.0507	0.0108	−4.70	0.00

相似性及模型 t 检验 表4

似然比检验	调整 R^2
183.217	0.324

其中，拟合优度 $R^2 > 0.2$ 即可初步接受模型效果，但是 B_4 的 t 检验为 1.05 < 1.96，未通过 t 检验，说明其对模型未产生显著影响，模型需要进一步调整。

(1)考虑出行方式步行时间及对应其他变量重建，对模型进行调整并检验。经检验汽车和公交的额外步行时间变量对应参数未通过 t 检验，因此步行时间对其出行方式选择的影响并不显著，新建变量如下。

TCCAR_new = $TCCAR^{1/2}$

TCBUS_new = $TCBUS^{1/2}$

TCRAIL_new = $TCRAIL^{1/2}$

OVTRAIL_new = $OVTRAIL^2$

TTCAR_new = $TTCAR^{1/2}$

TTRAIL_new = $TTRAIL^{1/2}$

TTBUS_new = $TTBUS^{1/2}$

模型运行结果中未通过 t 检验的参数见表 5。

未通过 t 检验的效用参数 表5

参 数	值	调整标准差	调整 t 检验	P 值
B_4	0.104	0.168	0.62	0.53
B_7	−2.02e−005	1.35e−005	−1.50	0.13
B_9	−0.000330	0.000265	−1.25	0.21

从结果来看，$R^2 > 0.2$ 模型效果可接受，但新添加变量的参数 B_7 和 B_9 的 t 检验均小于 1.96，未通过 t 检验，且通过修改变量调整模型，运行模型的参数仍未通过 t 检验，说明对居民出行方式选择模型并没有显著影响，因此这些参数对应的变量被舍弃。

(2)根据数据分析考虑虚拟变量。当出行选择为汽车时，即“购物或再生产”的目的对汽车出行方式的选择有显著影响，因此可以考虑设置为虚拟变量 dum_1。当性别为男性时，对汽车出行方式的选择有显著影响，可考虑设为虚拟变量 dum_2。当年龄代码为 4 时，对公交车出行方式的选择影响比较大，可以考虑设为虚拟变量 dum_3。当性别代码为 1 时，即女性对公交出行方式的选择有显著影响，可以设置为虚拟变量 dum4。虚拟变量如下：

dum_1 =（PURPOSE = 2） dum_1 =（GENDER = 0） dum_1 =（AGE = 4） dum_1 =（GENDER = 1）

出行选择模型如下：

car：ASC1 · one + B_1 · TCCAR_new + B_2 · TTCAR_new + B_7 · OVTCAR_new + B_{10} · dum_1 + B_{11} · dum_2rail：ASC2 · one + B_3 · TCRAIL_new + B_4 · TTRAIL_new + B_8 · OVTRAIL_new

bus：ASC3 · one + B_5 · TCBUS_new + B_6 · TTBUS_new + B_9 · OVTBUS_new + B_{12} · dum_3 + B_{13} · dum_4 模型运行结果中未通过 t 检验变量的效用函数如表 6。

未通过 t 检验的效用参数 表6

参数	值	调整标准差	调整 t 检验	P 值
B_{13}	−0.842	0.612	−1.38	0.17
B_3	−0.0294	0.0177	−1.66	0.10
B_4	0.399	0.869	0.46	0.65
B_7	-1.67×10^{-6}	1.59e−006	−1.06	0.29

无论如何修改变量,变量TTRAIL对应的参数t检验都未通过。由于B_3、B_{13}、B_4和B_7未能通过t检验,最终舍弃这些参数对应变量,调整得到如下选择模型:

car:ASC1·one + B_1·TCCAR_new + B_2·TTCAR_new + B_6·dum_1 + B_7·dum_2

rail:ASC2·one + B_3·TCRAIL + B_8·OVTRAIL

bus:ASC3·one + B_4·TCBUS_new + B_5·TTBUS_new + B_9·dum_3

模型运行结果见表7,相似性检验见表8。

效用参数　　表7

参数	值	调整标准差	调整t检验	P值
ASC1	0.00			
ASC2	−8.06	1.99	−4.04	0.00
ASC3	16.3	5.01	3.25	0.00
B_1	−0.0425	0.0101	−4.19	0.00
B_2	−0.859	0.173	−4.96	0.00
B_3	−0.000270	0.000154	−1.76	0.00
B_4	−0.243	0.0465	−5.23	0.00
B_5	−1.41	0.316	−4.46	0.00
B_6	1.13	0.321	3.51	0.00
B_7	0.762	0.307	2.48	0.00
B_8	−0.0511	0.0154	−3.31	0.00
B_9	−2.36	1.20	−1.97	0.00

相似性及模型t检验　　表8

似然比检验	调整R^2
228.896	0.443

表7表明在置信水平95%条件下,所有变量参数都通过了t检验1.96,且表8中模型似然比检验为$228.896 > \chi_{0.05}(11)$,$R^2 = 0.443$说明该出行方式选择模型拟合良好,表明所建立的出行方式选择模型中的变量对该地区居民出行有显著性影响。从模型的似然比检验、特设方程和t检验的综合比较得到该模型是最优出行方式选择模型。

2.3　基于灵活性的嵌套(NL)模型估计

由于居民出行选择依赖出行方式灵活性,依灵活性的出行方式划分结果如图2所示。对NL嵌套模型进行修改,使汽车和公交车在同一选择支,地铁在另一选择支。

模型结果见表9,相似性检验见表10。

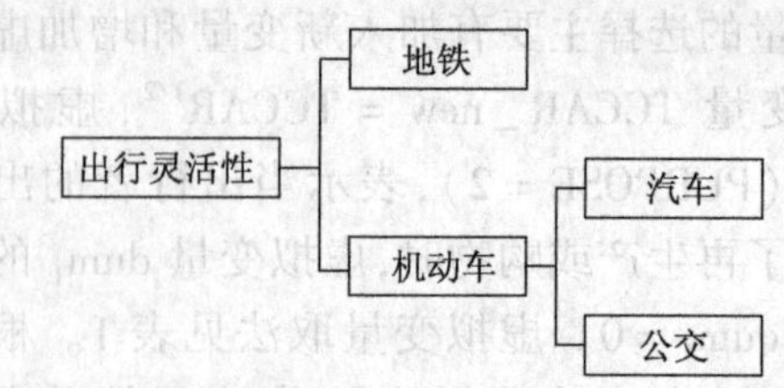

图2　嵌套模式图

效用参数　　表9

参数	值	调整标准差	调整t检验	P值
ASC1	0.00			
ASC2	−7.20	1.81	−3.98	0.00
ASC3	11.0	3.87	2.85	0.00
B_1	−0.0353	0.00990	−3.56	0.00
B_2	−0.778	0.157	−4.95	0.00
B_3	−0.000269	0.000147	−1.83	0.02
B_4	−0.186	0.0415	−4.48	0.00
B_5	−1.06	0.268	−3.95	0.00
B_6	0.905	0.280	3.23	0.00
B_7	0.546	0.289	2.31	0.00
B_8	−0.0483	0.0147	−3.28	0.00
B_9	−1.82	1.02	−1.79	0.01

相似性及模型t检验　　表10

似然比检验	调整R^2
233.065	0.451

表9说明在置信水平95%条件下,所有变量参数都通过了t检验1.96,且表10中模型似然比检验为$233.065 > \chi_{0.05}(11)$,$R^2 = 0.451$说明该出行方式选择模型拟合良好,表明所建立的出行方式选择模型中的变量对该地区居民出行有显著性影响。从模型的似然比检验、特设方程和t检验的综合比较中可以发现,所得模型即为最优出行方式选择模型。

2.4　混合(ML)模型估计

选择TTCAR_new、dum_1和dum_3等其他变量分别作为被混合的变量,混合模型会出现两种情况,一种是似然比降低,另一种是参数没有通过95%置信水平下的t检验,而且调整后仍然没有通过,所以对应的出行方式选择混合模型判定为无效。选择变量dum_2作为被混合的变量,那么可以得到以下混合表达式。

car:exp(B7[SIGMA1])·dum_2

选择混合出行模式选择模型如下:

car: ASC1 · one + B_1 · TCCAR_new + B_2 · TTCAR_new + B_6 · dum_1 + exp(B_7[SIGMA1]) · dum_2

rail: ASC2 · one + B_3 · TCRAIL + B_8 · OVTRAIL

bus: ASC3 · one + B_4 · TCBUS_new + B_5 · TTBUS_new + B9 · dum_3

该模型的运行结果见表 11，相似性检验见表 12。

混合模型效用参数 表 11

参数	值	调整标准差	调整 t 检验	P 值
ASC1	0.00			
ASC2	−9.01	2.30	−3.92	0.00
ASC3	17.7	5.53	3.20	0.00
B_1	−0.0513	0.0139	−3.70	0.00
B_2	−0.948	0.202	−4.69	0.00
B_3	−0.000381	0.000173	−2.20	0.03
B_4	−0.268	0.0477	−5.62	0.00
B_5	−1.55	0.358	−4.35	0.00
B_6	1.21	0.352	3.43	0.00
B_7	−1.93	2.88	−2.01	0.04
B_8	−0.0524	0.0157	−3.34	0.00
B_9	−2.43	1.14	−2.13	0.03
SIGMA1	−3.07	2.40	−2.33	0.30

相似性及模型 t-检验 表 12

似然比检验	调整 R^2
231.009	0.447

表 11 表明除了随机参数 B7_SIGMA1 通过 80% 置信水平下的 t 检验，其他所有变量参数都通过了置信水平 95% 条件下的 t 检验 1.96，且表 12 中模型似然比检验为 231.947 $>\chi_{0.05}(11)$，R^2 = 0.447说明该出行方式选择模型拟合良好，表明所建立的出行方式选择模型中的变量对该地区居民出行有显著性影响。从模型的似然比检验、特设方程和 t 检验的综合比较中可以发现，得到的模型是最优出行方式选择模型。

3 模型对比及方式分担

MNL 模型、NL 模型和 MA 模型比较见表 13。通过比较，NL 模型似然比和调整 R^2 均大于 MNL 模型和 ML 模型，因此 NL 模型能够更好地拟合本案例的居民出行方式选择。

MNL/NL/ML 模型相似性检验对比 表 13

模 型	MNL	NL	ML
似然比检验	228.896	233.065	231.009
调整 R^2	0.443	0.451	0.447

三种出行方式分担率的计算公式如下（以 P(Car)为例）。

$$P(\mathrm{Car}) = P(\mathrm{Car}|\mathrm{NM}) \cdot P(\mathrm{NM})$$

$$= \frac{e^{\mu_{NM}V_{Car}}}{e^{\mu_{NM}V_{Car}} + e^{\mu_{NM}V_{Bus}}} \cdot \frac{e^{\frac{\mu}{\mu_{NM}}\ln(e^{\mu_{NM}V_{Car}} + e^{\mu_{NM}V_{Bus}})}}{e^{\frac{\mu}{\mu_M}\ln(e^{\mu_M V_{Rail}})} + e^{\frac{\mu}{\mu_{NM}}\ln(e^{\mu_{NM}V_{Car}} + e^{\mu_{NM}V_{Bus}})}}$$

式中：V_{Car}、V_{Rail} 和 V_{Bus}——分别代表汽车、地铁和公交出行方式的效用价值；

μ_M——NESTA；

μ_{NM}——NESTB，$\mu = 1$。

那么两种方案下三种出行方式的分担率结果见表 14。

模型预测出行方式分担率检验 表 14

项目	汽车	地铁	公交
原始分担率	55.54%	30.45%	14.01%
模型预测分担率	56.70%	29.05%	14.25%
误差	1.16%	1.40%	0.24%

与原始调查样本进行比较，基于 NL 选择模型对出行方式分担率预测平均误差为 0.93%，即汽车、地铁和公交三种出行方式分担率估计误差均小于 1.5%，这对该地区交通组织运行及管理具有重要的参考意义，通过合理组织出行方式，保证交通畅通，便利居民出行。

4 结语

（1）本文基于出行者属性和出行方式属性建立了出行方式的 Logit 离散选择模型，并对 MNL 模型、NL 模型和 ML 模型进行对比分析，表明依据出行灵活性进行划分出行方式的 NL 嵌套模型更加适合本案例研究，能更好地表述出行方式的选择行为。

（2）基于 NL 嵌套模型的出行方式选择模型评估的汽车、地铁和公交的分担率分别为 56.70%、29.05% 和 14.25%，与调查的方式分担率相比，其估计误差分别为 1.16%、1.40% 和 0.24%，平均误差 0.93%，表明该出行方式选择模型对本案例适用性强。

(3)变量的选择以与出行方式划分最相关为原则,通时构造新变量和添加虚拟变量也是提高模型拟合性能的有效方式。

(4)案例研究样本数量受调查方式和问卷设置影响因素数量的限制,因此对出行方式选择的估计精度和拟合优度有待进一步提升。因此下一步研究将优化模型影响因素设置和丰富调查手段,对出行方式选择模型进行优化调整。

参考文献

[1] 刘建荣,郝小妮. 基于随机系数 Logit 模型的市内出行方式选择行为研究[J]. 交通运输系统工程与信息,2019,19(05):108-113.

[2] 王灿,王德,朱玮,等. 离散选择模型研究进展[J]. 地理科学进展,2015,34(10):1275-1287.

[3] 温惠英,汤左淦. 道路交叉口单车事故严重程度影响因素分析[J]. 公路工程,2019,44(02):55-61+102.

[4] 李军,赵长相,唐晓宇,等. 基于浮动车数据的随机路径选择模型参数估计[J]. 交通运输系统工程与信息,2014,14(05):37-42.

[5] 滕靖,薛晖. 考虑出行者异质性的城际出行选择行为研究[J]. 铁道运输与经济,2020,42(S1):60-66+80.

[6] 张文会,秦佳琪,李洪涛,等. 考虑拥挤度的常规公交与地铁出行方式选择模型[J]. 吉林大学学报(工学版),2021,51(01):200-205.

[7] 朱善伟. 三元 Logit 模型的贝叶斯推断与应用[J]. 安阳师范学院学报,2016(5):75-78.

[8] 陈瑞,姜海. 基于 Logit 离散选择模型的品类优化问题综述[J]. 运筹学学报,2017,21(04):118-134.

[9] N Sopitpongstor n, Silvapulle P, Gao J, et al. Local logit regression for loan recovery rate[J]. Journal of Banking & Finance,2021,126.

[10] Shanmugam L, Ramasamy M. Study on mode choice using nested logit models in trel towards Chennai metropolitan city[J]. Journal of Ambient Intelligence and Humanized Computing,2021.

Spatiotemporal Travel Characteristics of Urban Residents and Their Travel Choice in an Aging City, China

Hui Zhang*　Xu Li

(Shandong Jianzhu University)

Abstract With the development of ageing in cities, the travel structure and mode of urban residents are undergoing obvious changes. Understanding the difference of travel characteristics between the elderly and non-elderly people is helpful to provide targeted policies to ensure high-quality services. In this paper, we use 2019 travel interview survey data to analyze the travel characteristics and travel choice of residents in an ageing city. The residents are divided into two groups: elderly people (≥60 years old) and non-elderly people (<60 years old). A structural equation model is proposed to explore the relationships among travel characteristics, personal attributes, family attributes and travel mode. The results show that elderly people prefer to travel in non-peak time, while non-elderly people tend to travel in morning and evening peaks. Moreover, there are 72.98% of elderly people and 61.66% of non-elderly people travel within the same district. In addition, the results implies that gender, age, personal income, family monthly transportation expenditure have significant impacts on travel behaviour. The female and the elderly with lower personal monthly income are more likely to choose buses as their travel mode. When the travel time is longer, the non-elderly people are more likely to choose private cars.

Keywords Urban traffic Travel behavior Structural equation Aging Travel characteristics

0 Introduction

Population ageing has become a serious challenge in most countries. The population aging leads to many social problems such as healthcare and travel issues (Szeto et al., 2017; Zhang et al., 2019; Du et al., 2020). The travel behaviours between elderly and young adults are different, which brings a great challenge for transport managers (Ahmad et al., 2019; Cheng et al., 2019b). Understanding the travel behaviour and provide a better travel service are two critical challenges.

Travel mobility plays a key role in urban planning, transport planning and operations. However, it is hard to measure people's travel mobility. (Wang and Zhou, 2017; Ding et al., 2017; De Vos, 2018; Rahimi et al., 2020). Elderly people prefer to use private car in most developed countries, while elderly people usually use public transport. In China, elderly people who use private car account for 1% and most of them (>80%) travel on foot or use public transport (Hu et al., 2013). The paper contributions on two aspects. Firstly, the residents are divided into elderly group and non-elderly group, and comparison analysis is given to find the differences. Secondly, structural equation model has been introduced to study the relationships between variables incorporating travel characteristics, personal attributes, family attributes and travel mode. The paper is organized as follows. Section 2 gives the literature review. Section 3 introduces the study area and data description. Travel characteristic analysis is given in section 4. Model and results are exhibited in section 5. Section 6 concludes the paper.

1 Litrrature Review

Travel mobility is an important part of travel characteristics of residents. During the last two decades, there have been many studies focusing on it. Model-based and data-driven methods are two main approaches to study the travel mobility. Shen et al. constructed a SEM model for urban rail transit (Shen et al., 2016). Ding et al. found thattravelers in a household with more children are more likely to choose transit, walking or cycling (Ding et al., 2017). Weng et al. proposed a binary logit model to examine public transport commuters' travel choice (Weng et al., 2018). Molin et al. found low-income young people prefer using cars when they can afford it (Molin et al., 2016). In recent years, data-driven methods have applied successfully to detect travel behaviour. Faroqi et al. used transit smart card data to measure passengers' activity similarity (Faroqi et al., 2018). Zhang et al. constructed dynamic networks with taxi trajectory data to reveal travel behaviour and found taxi trip length follows a lognormal distribution (Zhang et al., 2020). The new emerging machine learning methods combining with traditional methods provide a powerful tool to analyze travel behaviours (Wang and Ross, 2018; Cheng et al., 2019a; Zhou et al., 2019; Zhao et al., 2020).

Elderly people tend to have fewer trips and shorter distance compared with young adults in the UK and US (Giuliano and Narayan, 2003). Income is recognized as an important factor that affect mode choice and trip length for elder people (Moniruzzaman et al., 2013; Hahn et al., 2016). Truong and Somenahalli pointed out that elderly people who avoid driving at peak hours are more likely to utilize public transport (Truong and Somenahalli, 2015). Habib and Hui suggested that increasing accessibility would increase the out-of-home activity for elderly people (Habib and Hui, 2017). Elderly people preferred traveling during noon off-peaks to avoid crowd (Szeto et al., 2017). They preferred traveling in old town with high elderly people's density (Shao et al., 2019). In a transit-oriented city, older people prefer traveling to service-rich zones and those older people with more family members are less likely to go out (Yang, 2018). Ahmad et al. pointed out that older women in Pakistan were particularly influenced by poor access to public transport and had to walk long distance by foot (Ahmad et al.,2019). Sundling et al. found that more personal assistance, better driving behaviour and swift maintenance were key facilitators that would improve the predictability in traveling (Sundling et al.,2016). Mohd et al. found that elderly people had less than five trips a day and the trip distances are within five kilometers (Mohd,2019).

Travel mode choice plays a key role in urban and transportation planning. Nowadays, there are many travel modes for urban inhabitants such as private cars, public transport, taxi, sharing bike, walking, etc. Cars are the most crucial travel mode to elderly people in West countries. In Australia, cars are dominant travel mode, public transport accounts for only 7% (Truong and Somenahalli, 2015). Age was found to play a negative role in public transport usage for elderly people in most Western countries (Pettersson and Schmöcker, 2010), while elderly people tend to use tram more because of cheaper fares (Szeto et al.,2017). Van den Berg et al. found that highly educated elderly conducted more trips by public transport (Van den Berg et al., 2011). Hanson and Hildebrand revealed that older people living in the suburbs rely more on cars than those who live in highly dense neighborhoods (Hanson and Hildebrand, 2011). It seems that free bus policy for elderly people has positive role to enhance their mobility (Zhang et al.,2019). Moreover, study shows bus and walking are main modes for elderly to seek medical treatment (Du et al., 2020). Yuan et al. found that time schedule and reliability are less important for the elderly, while other dimensions such as service, security and convenience needs to be improved (Yuan et al.,2019).

2 Study Area and Data Description

2.1 Study Area

This data survey is carried out in Jinan. As of 2019, the city has 10 districts and 2 counties, with a total area of 10244 square kilometers and permanent population of 8.987 million.

2.2 Data Description

The data contains 19551 households and 38133 members. The households mainly concentrate in six districts. The household interview comprises four levels: (1) household information; (2) household members' information; (3) trip information made with the past 24 hours for every household member; (4) transit-related information for each member.

In this paper, we divided household members into two groups: elderly people whose age is larger or equal to 60 years old, and other people (non-elderly) whose age is smaller than 60. Totally, we achieve 13088 trips for elderly people and 67015 trips for non-elderly people, which account for 16.3% and 83.7% respectively. Tab. 1 shows the basic socio-demographic attributes information. From the perspective of gender, the proportion of men and women is almost balanced. The Pearson's Chi-Square test show that there are obvious differences between elderly people and other people in terms of occupation, personal monthly income, monthly transportation cost of family and whether owning a private car.

Basic Socio-demographic Characteristics of Data Tab. 1

Project description		Elderly	Non-elderly	P-value
Age	Male	49.8%	47.4%	0.000
	Female	50.2%	52.6%	
Occupation	Ordinary employees	6.5%	85.5%	0.000
	Retired person	87.3%	6.1%	
	Student	0.0%	1.9%	
	Unemployed person	6.2%	6.5%	
Personal monthly income (yuan)	<3000	41.7%	23.6%	
	3000~5000	41.6%	39.9%	

continued

Project description		Elderly	Non-elderly	P-value
Personal monthly income (yuan)	5000 ~ 7000	12.5%	24.7%	0.000
	>7000	4.2%	11.8%	
Monthly transportation cost of family(yuan)	<100	44.8%	15.4%	0.000
	100 ~ 499	32.5%	38.3%	
	500 ~ 899	12.7%	25.2%	
	900 ~ 1399	7.2%	15.2%	
	>1400	2.8%	5.9%	
Own a private car?	Yes	37.7%	69.8%	0.000
	No	62.3%	30.2%	

3 Travel Characteristics Analysis

This section provides the statistical analysis of trip distribution, travel distance, travel mode, travel purpose, etc. The analysis result could reflect the differences between elderly people and non-elderly people. The spatiotemporal characteristics of travelers will be analyzed to better understand the travelers' behaviour.

3.1 Temporal Distributions of Trips

Fig. 1 shows the travel trip distributions of elderly people and non-elderly people in a day. For elderly people, the trips are concentrated on two periods. One is 8:00-12:00 that after morning peak hours and the other one is 16:00-18:00 that before evening peak hours. For other non-elderly people, we can see there are two sharp peaks. One peak is around 8:00 and the other peak is around 18:00. The reason is that non-elderly people are mainly comprised of commuters and students whose travel time is almost fixed. Elderly people prefer to travel in the forenoon to avoid morning travel congestion.

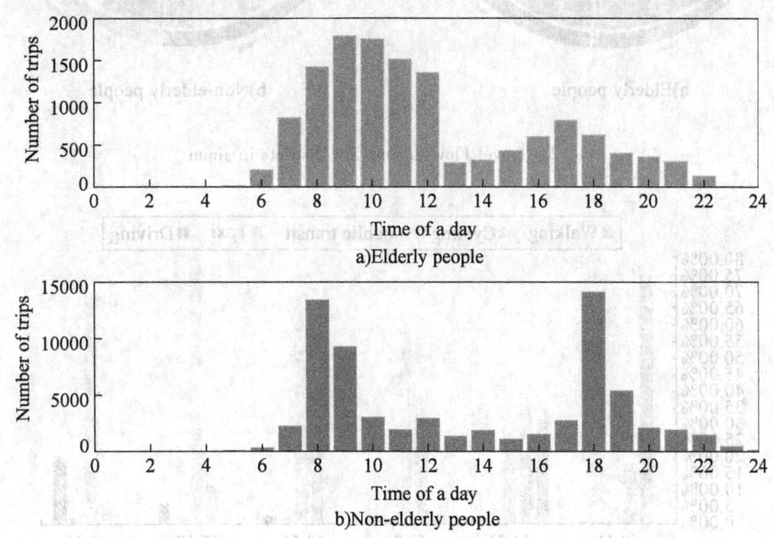

Fig. 1 Travel Trips Distributions

3.2 Spatial Distributions of Trips

Fig. 2 shows the travel flows among the six districts in Jinan. As shown in the figure, 72.98% of elderly people and 61.66% of non-elderly people travel within the same district. Compared with elderly people, more non-elderly people have to travel longer to work. It can be seen that there is no trip between Licheng and Changqing for elderly people. Moreover, there is a very smaller proportion of non-elderly travel between them. Because the distance between the two districts is large.

3.3 Travel Mode

According to travel modes involved in the survey data, they are divided into the following five categories: public travel, walking travel, cycling travel, taxi travel, and private driving travel. The cycling mode accounts for 35.9%, which is the largest in the survey. Due to the development of bike-sharing and electric bicycle, there are more commuters choose cycling devices because they are more convenient and feasible to ride on crowded roads. Urban manger should make efforts to enhance the proportion of public transit to alleviate the increasingly serious traffic congestions.

3.4 Travel Modes with Different Distances

Fig. 3 and Fig. 4 exhibit the proportions of travel modes with different distances for elderly people and non-elderly people respectively. When the distance is smaller than 1 km, they prefer walking. When the distance is getting longer, elderly people choose public transit as their main travel mode. For non-elderly people, they use various modes to travel when the distance is between 1 km and 10 km. Cycling is the main travel mode when the distance is between 1 km and 5 km. When the distance is larger than 10 km, private car become the main travel mode for non-elderly people.

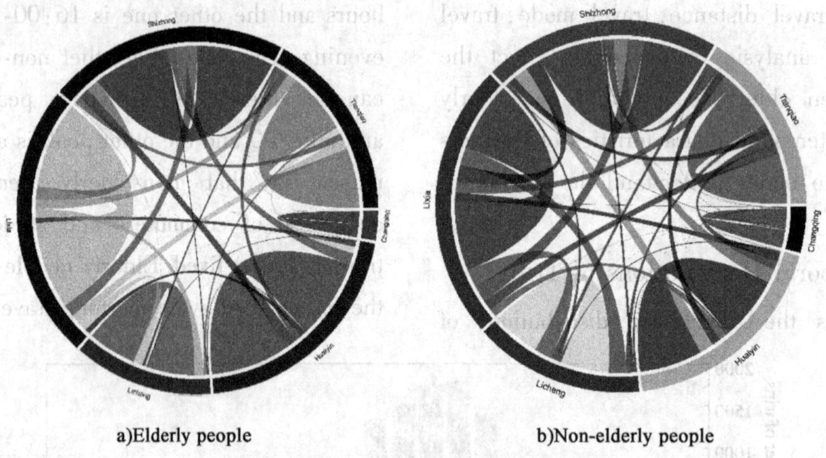

Fig. 2 Travel Flows among Six Districts in Jinan

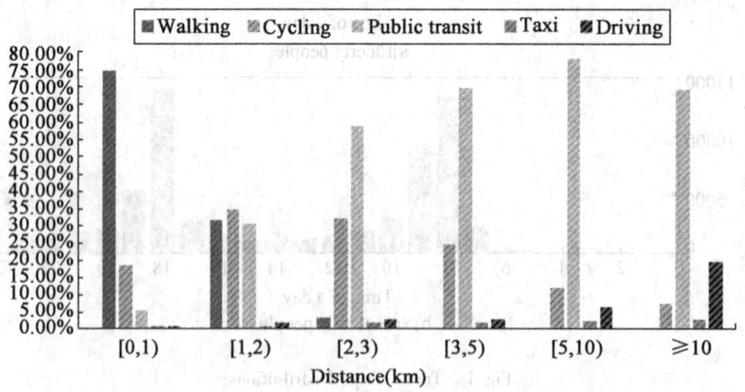

Fig. 3 Travel Mode Proportion of Elderly Group under Different Distances

3.5 Relationship between Travel Mode and Age

In this part, multiple logistic regression analysis is applied to show the relationship between travel mode and age. Age and travel distance are taken as the main covariates for analysis. Tab. 2 shows the results of multiple logistic regression. The significance of the final model is less than 0. 05. Cox and Snell were 0. 547 and 0. 473 (greater than 0. 300), Nagelkerke were 0. 601 and 0. 505 (greater than 0. 300), and McFadden were 0. 328 and 0. 233 (greater than 0. 200), respectively, which were all within the acceptable range. In elderly group, ageing people prefer to choose taxi and public transit.

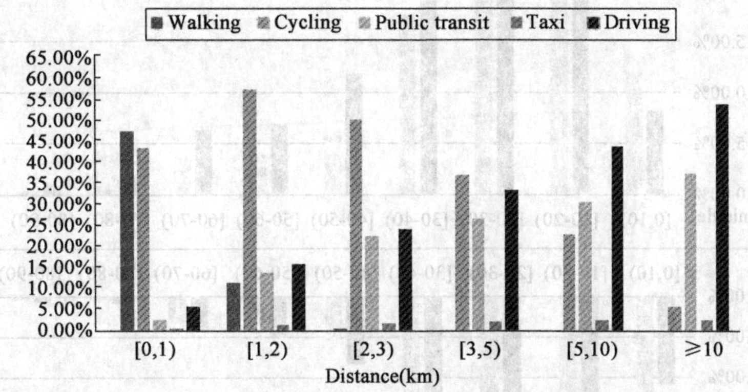

Fig. 4 Travel Mode Proportion of Non-elderly Group under Different Distances

Multiple Logistic Regression Analysis Results Tab. 2

Age	Travel mode	Age coefficient	Distance coefficient
≥60 years old	Taxi travel	0. 082	2. 553
	Public travel	0. 018	2. 533
	Drive travel	-0. 096	2. 616
	Cycling travel	-0. 097	2. 054
<60 years old	Taxi travel	-0. 073	2. 672
	Public travel	-0. 029	2. 688
	Drive travel	-0. 038	2. 679
	Cycling travel	-0. 032	2. 328
≥60 years old: Cox and Snell = 0. 547, Nagelkerke = 0. 601, McFadden = 0. 328			
<60 years old: Cox and Snell = 0. 473, Nagelkerke = 0. 505, McFadden = 0. 233			

3. 6 Travel Time Distributions

Fig. 5 shows the travel proportion of residents of different age groups and genders according to travel time. The travel time is classified by 10 minutes as a group interval. In all the time periods, the travel time is within 30 minutes and reaches the peak within 10-20 minutes. Especially in the elderly group, the proportion of men reaches 32. 77% and the highest proportion of women reaches 35. 64%. When the travel time is more than 60 minutes, the highest proportion is about 6. 41% of the male in non-elderly group and the lowest is about 0. 50% of the elderly group. In terms of gender and age groups, 18. 06% of non-elderly respondents spent more than 60 minutes traveling, slightly more than 12. 22% of elderly respondents. It is also worth mentioning that the length of travel time is not exactly the same as the actual travel distance, which depends on the mode of travel used and the corresponding average travel speed.

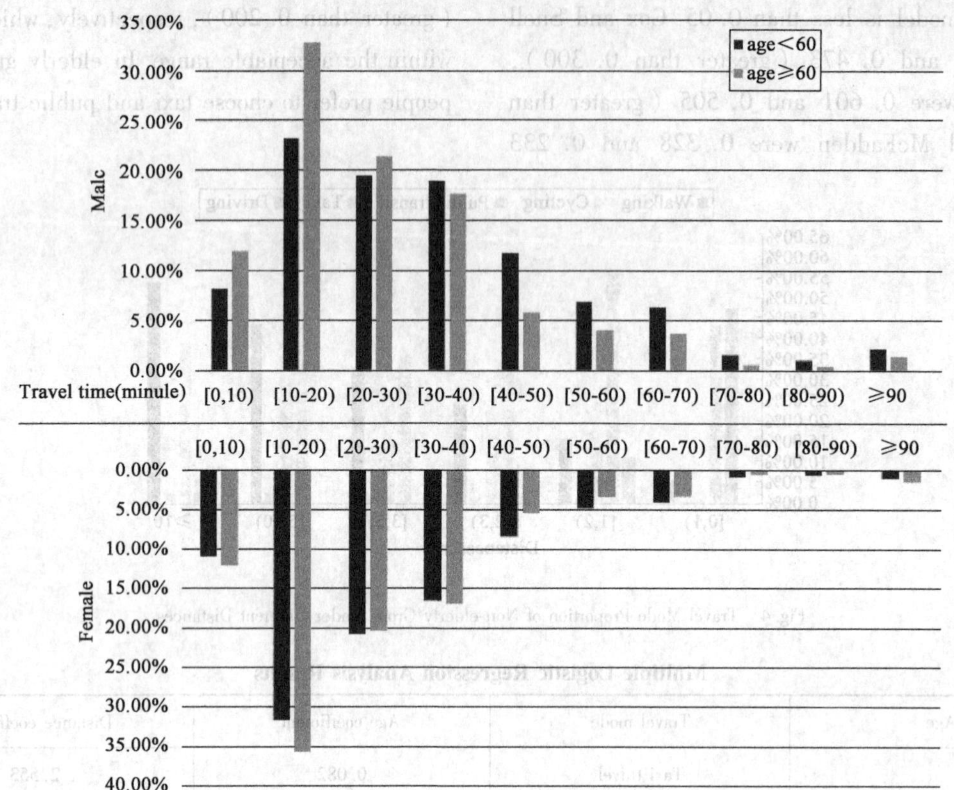

Fig. 5　Travel Time Distributions of Different Age and Gender Groups

4　Model and Results

Residents are affected by a variety of factors when they choose their travel mode. There are certain relationships between these factors and the travel mode that they choose. In order to describe the influenced relationships between various factors more clearly, structural equation model is introduced in this part.

4.1　Structural Equation Model

Structural EquationModeling (SEM) is a statistical method to analyse the relationship between variables based on the covariance matrix of variables. It is a method to establish, estimate and test causality model. The model contains not only significant variables that can be observed, but also potential variables that cannot be directly observed.

4.1.1　Model Form

Structural equation model includes measurement model and structural model. Measurement model describes the relationship between indicators and latent variables, while structural model describes the relationship between latent variables. The specific matrix equation can be expressed as follows:

$$X = \Lambda_X \xi + \delta \tag{1}$$

$$Y = \Lambda_Y \eta + \varepsilon \tag{2}$$

$$\eta = B_\eta + \Gamma \xi + \zeta \tag{3}$$

where X and Y are variables composed of exogenous and endogenous explicit variables respectively; Λ_X and Λ_Y are the index variables, ξ is the exogenous potential variable, η is the endogenous potential variable; δ is the error term of the exogenous explicit variable, ε is the error term of the endogenous explicit variable; B is the coefficient matrix describing the interaction between endogenous latent variables; Γ is the coefficient matrix describing the influence of exogenous variables on endogenous variables; ζ is the residual term of the model, which means the part that cannot be explained by the model.

4.1.2　Model Evaluation

In order to better test the goodness of fit of the model, we use the following four evaluation indexes: the goodness-of-fit index (GFI), adjusted goodness-of-fit index (AGFI), standardized root mean square residual (SRMR) androot mean square error of approximation (RMSEA).

(1) GFI and AGFI

GFI value is between 0 and 1. The closer the value is to 1, the better the fitness of the model is. The general criterion is GFI > 0.900, which means that the path map of the model is better than the actual data. It is defined as follows:

$$\mathrm{GFI} = 1 - \frac{F(S;\hat{\Sigma})}{F(S;\hat{\Sigma}(0))} \quad (4)$$

AGFI value is between 0 and 1. It is similar with GFI. Large value indicates better the fitness of the model. The formula is as follows:

$$\mathrm{AGFI} = 1 - (1 - \mathrm{GFI})\left[\frac{k(k+1)}{2df}\right] \quad (5)$$

where k is the number of variables in the model and df is the degree of freedom of the model.

(2) The SRMR value is the sum of the standardized root mean square residual, with the range of 0 ~ 1. Its acceptable range is below 0.050.

(3) RMSEA is root mean square error of approximation. The value is usually regarded as the most important fitness index information. The smaller the RMSEA value is, the better the fitness of the model is. The value between 0.080 ~ 0.100 indicates that the model has ordinary fitness. The value between 0.050 ~ 0.080 indicates that the model has reasonable fitness and the value less than 0.050 indicates that the model has a very good fitness. The formula is as follows:

$$\mathrm{RMSEA} = \sqrt{\frac{F_0}{df}} = \sqrt{\max\left(\frac{F_{ML}}{df} - \frac{1}{N-1}, 0\right)} \quad (6)$$

4.1.3 Model Variable Selection

Combined with the actual factors affecting travel choice, this paper comprehensively selects personal attributes, family attributes, travel characteristics and travel modes as four types of variables. Tab. 3 shows the calibration and notes.

Explanation Table of Structural Equation Variable Assignment Tab. 3

Variables	Definitions and notes
Travel attributes	
Travel distance(km)	0 ~ 5→1; 5 ~ 10→2; 10 ~ 15→3; 15 ~ 20→4; 20 ~ 30→5; >30→6
Travel mode	Bus→1; Walking→2; School Bus→3; Unit bus →4; Bike sharing →5; Electric bicycle →6; Motorcycle →7; Online booking / Special / Express →8; Taxi→9; Rail transit →10; Carpooling→11; Private car→12
Purpose of travel	Go to work→1; Go home→2; Sports and entertainment →3; Shopping and catering →4; Pick up family and children →5; Visiting relatives and friends→6; Park and scenic spot tour→7; Official business →8; Seeing a doctor→9; Go to school→10; Other→11
Travel time(min)	0 ~ 10→1; 10 ~ 20→2; 20 ~ 30→3; 30 ~ 45→4; 45 ~ 60→5; >60→6
Walking time to bus stop	Within 5 minutes→1; 5-10 minutes→2; 10-15 minutes→3; 15-20 minutes→4; More than 20 minutes→5
Personal attributes	
Gender	Male→1; Female→2
Age	0 ~ 18→1; 18 ~ 24→2; 24 ~ 40→3; 40 ~ 60→4; 60 ~ 70→5; >70 →6
Personal monthly income(yuan/month)	<3000→1; 3000 ~ 5000→2; 5000 ~ 7000→3; 7000 ~ 10000→4; 10000 ~ 15000→5; >15000→6
Occupation	Clerk→1; Service industry employees→2; Science, education, culture and health workers→3; Personnel of government organs, enterprises and institutions→4; Workers→5; Retired person→6; Self-employed→7; Student→8; Unemployed person→9; Military and police personnel→10; Production personnel in agriculture, forestry, animal husbandry, fishery and water conservancy→11; Other→12
Family attributes	
Monthly transportation expenditure of family(yuan/month)	<100→1; 100 ~ 499→2; 500 ~ 899→3; 900 ~ 1399→4; 1400 ~ 1799→5; 1800-2199→6; 2200-2599→7; >2600→8
Total number of households	Actual value
Administrative region	Lixia District →1; Huaiyin District→2; Licheng District→3; Shizhong District→4; Tianqiao District→5; Changqing District→6

continue

Variables	Definitions and notes
Number of cars	Actual value
Number of bicycles	Actual value
Number of electric vehicles	Actual value
Number of motorcycles	Actual value
Number of fixed parking spaces	Actual value

4.2 Results

According to the above model assumptions, the SEM model of residents' travel mode selection is constructed. The path of the structural equation model is shown in Fig. 6 e1 to e17 are used to represent the residual term.

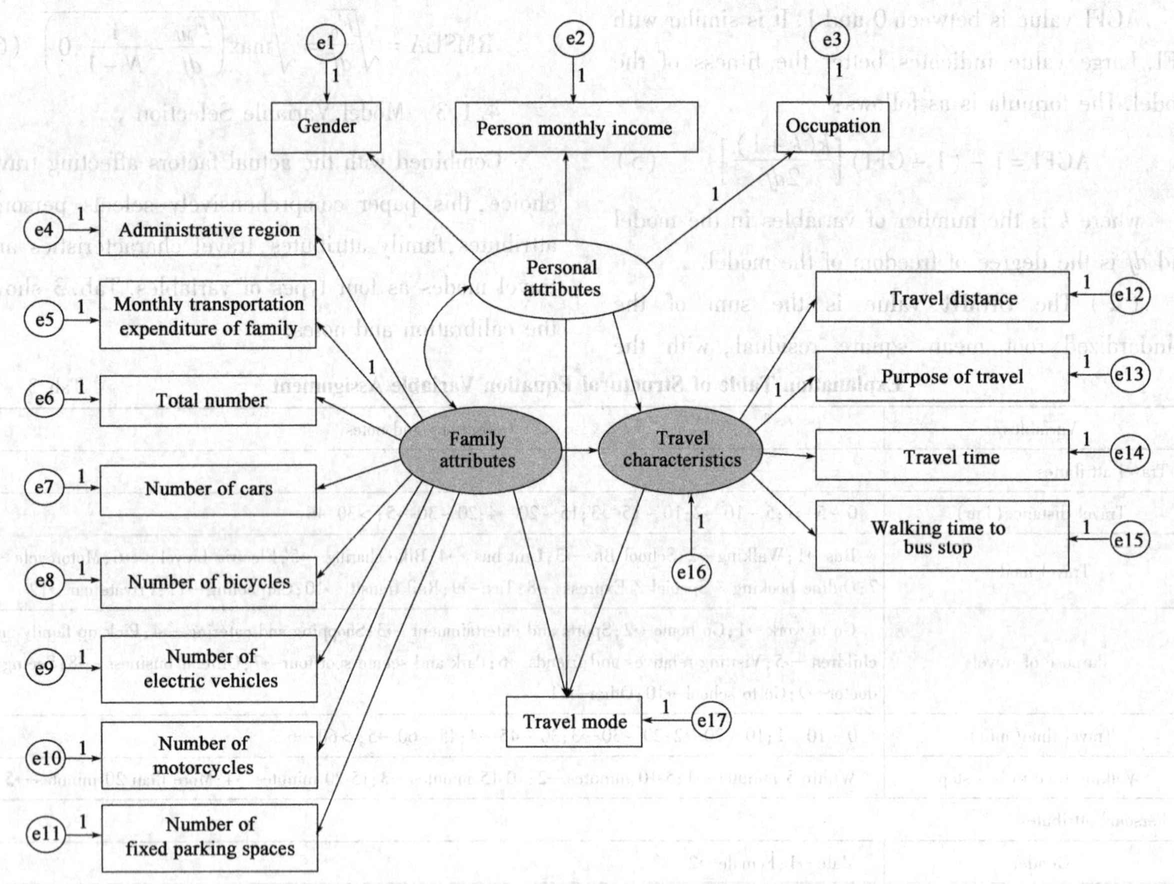

Fig. 6 Model Path Map

We applied the model to elderly people and non-elderly people respectively. Tab. 4 shows the goodness of fit, which indicates the performance of the model is acceptable. Tab. 5 exhibits the regression weight between indicators and variables. Fig. 7 shows the parameter estimation results of the elderly people standardized model. The results implies that the female and the elderly with lower personal monthly income are more likely to choose buses. Moreover, those people who own more cars and fixed parking spaces tend to use more private car as their main travel mode. Fig. 8 shows the parameter estimation results of the non-elderly people standardized model. We can see that women of non-elderly people with lower monthly income are more likely to choose private cars as their travel mode, with the shorter travel distance and travel time. Moreover, the shorter travel time or the shorter travel distance, the more likely they are to choose bus as the travel mode. The longer travel time or the longer travel distance, the more likely they are to choose private cars as the travel method.

Results of Goodness of Fit Test of Standardized Model Tab. 4

Evaluating indicator	Test results		Good range of fitness
	≥60	<60	
GFI	0.965	0.974	>0.900
AGFI	0.951	0.963	>0.900
SRMR	0.0413	0.0396	<0.050
RMSEA	0.053	0.047	<0.080

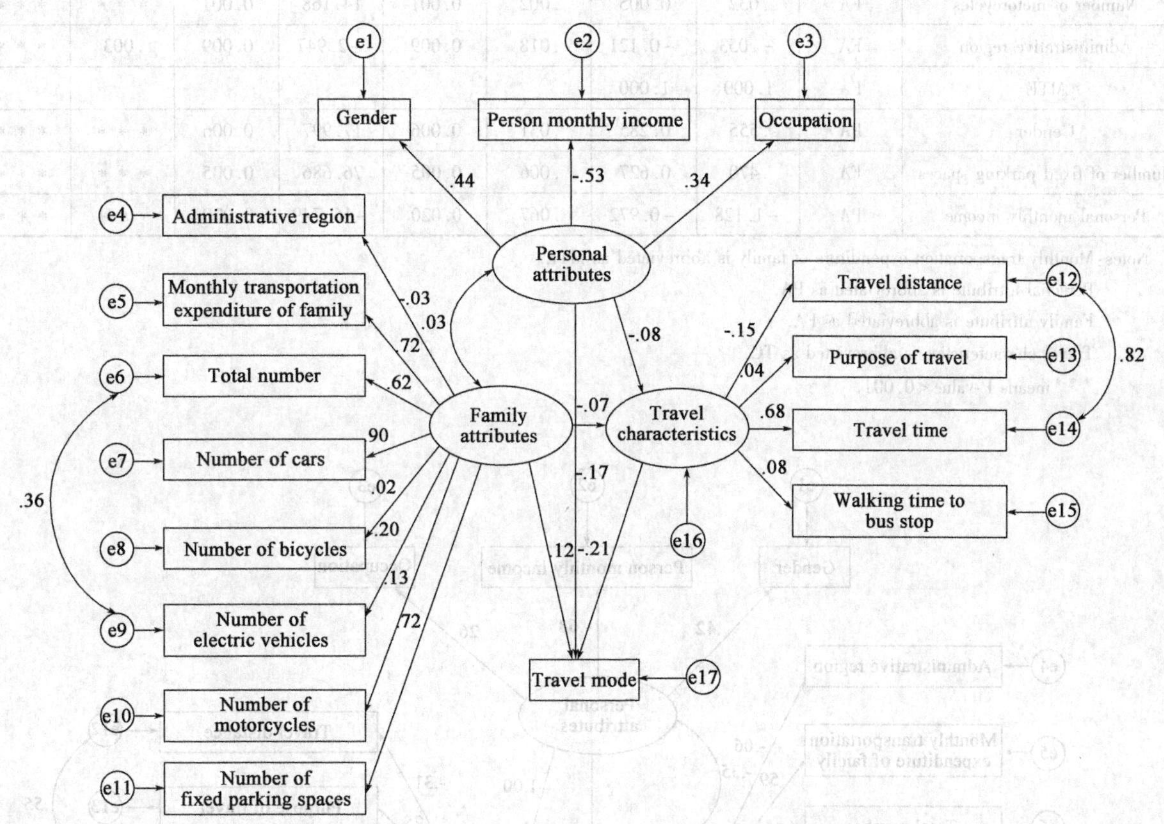

Fig. 7 Parameter estimation results of the elderly people standardized model

Regression Weight Table between Indicators and Variables Tab. 5

Hypothetical path		Standardized regression coefficient		Standard error		C. R.		P-value	
		≥60	<60	≥60	<60	≥60	<60	≥60	<60
Travel characteristics	PA	-.018	0.584	.009	0.017	-1.965	34.713	.049	* * *
Travel characteristics	FA	-.008	0.029	.004	0.007	-2.034	3.851	.042	* * *
Occupation	PA	1.000	1.000						
Travel time	TC	9.716	-1.071	4.587	0.027	2.118	-40.255	.034	* * *
Travel distance	TC	-.909	-0.600	.484	0.015	-1.878	-39.684	.060	* * *
Purpose of travel	TC	1.000	1.000						
Walking time to bus stop	TC	.743	-0.103	.198	0.010	3.748	0.010	* * *	* * *
Total number of households	FA	.915	0.360	.014	0.006	65.538	0.006	* * *	* * *

continue

Hypothetical path	Standardized regression coefficient			Standard error		C. R.		P-value	
Number of cars	FA	.644	0.727	.007	0.005	86.078	0.005	* * *	* * *
Number of bicycles	FA	.015	−0.005	.008	0.003	2.008	0.003	.045	0.117
Number of electric vehicles	FA	.189	−0.225	.009	0.005	20.953	0.005	* * *	* * *
Travel mode	TC	−5.644	−4.564	1.370	7.147	−4.121	7.147	* * *	0.523
Travel mode	FA	.366	1.391	.035	0.213	10.517	0.213	* * *	* * *
Travel mode	PA	−1.039	0.324	.102	4.182	−10.211	4.182	* * *	0.938
Number of motorcycles	FA	.032	0.005	.002	0.001	14.168	0.001	* * *	* * *
Administrative region	FA	−.053	−0.121	.018	0.009	−2.947	0.009	.003	* * *
MTE	FA	1.000	1.000						
Gender	PA	.555	0.285	.031	0.006	17.997	0.006	* * *	* * *
Number of fixed parking spaces	FA	.470	0.627	.006	0.005	76.686	0.005	* * *	* * *
Personal monthly income	PA	−1.128	−0.972	.067	0.020	−16.749	0.020	* * *	* * *

Notes: Monthly transportation expenditure of family is abbreviated as MTE.
Personal attribute is abbreviated as PA.
Family attribute is abbreviated as FA.
Travel characteristics is abbreviated as TC.
* * * means P-value < 0.001.

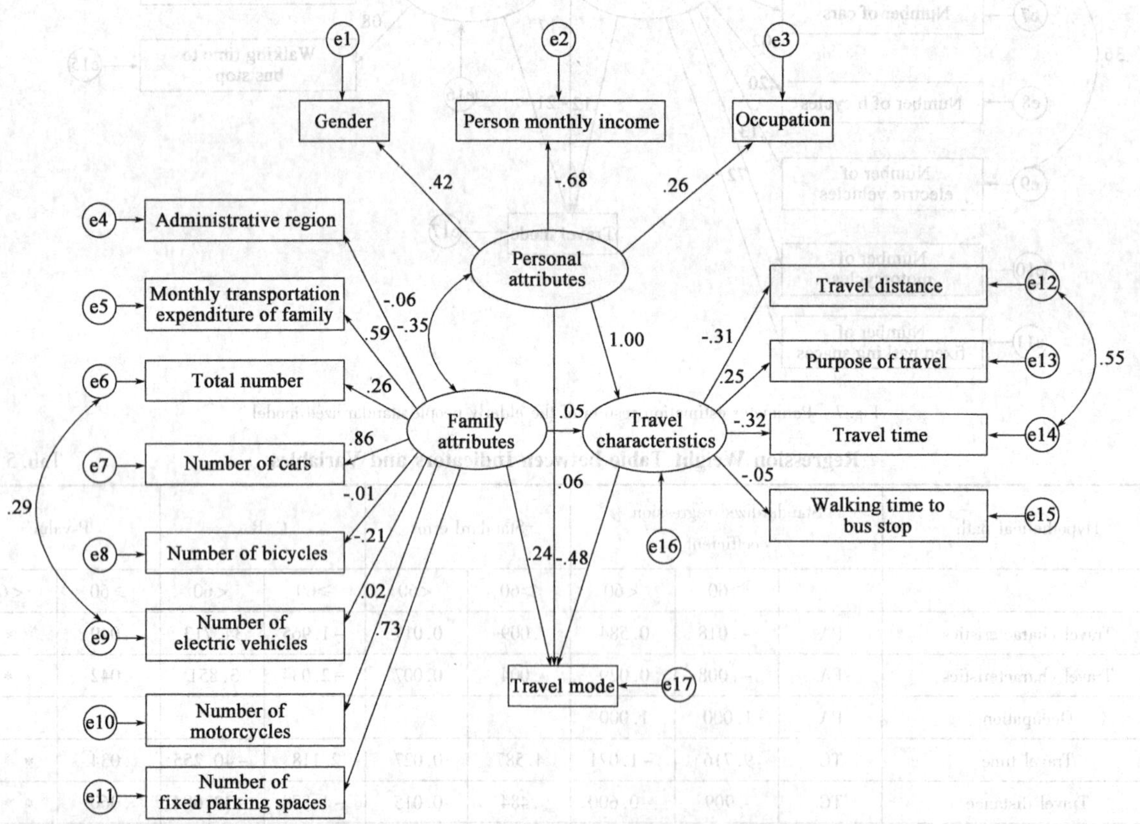

Fig. 8 Parameter Estimation Results of Non-elderly People Standardized Model

5 Conclusions

Travel characteristics and mode choice of residents play key roles in urban transportation planning. Due to continuous low fertility rate and higher life expectancy, the proportion of elderly people become an increasingly larger. The travel behaviours of elderly people and non-elderly people are different. Understanding the travel features and mode choice is conducive to providing better transport service.

Based on a massive number of travel interview survey data, this paper divided residents into elderly group and non-elderly group. A spatiotemporal analysis framework has been proposed. The results show that elderly people prefer to travel avoiding peak hours when most non-elderly people commute. People tend to travel within the same district. Compared with non-elderly people, elderly people like using public transport as their main travel mode. Most trips cost less than 30 minutes and concentrated between 10 and 20 minutes. Structural equation model is introduced to analyse the relationships between variables. The results implies that the female and the elderly with lower personal monthly income are more likely to choose buses as their travel mode. Moreover, those people who own more cars and fixed parking spaces tend to use more private cars as their main travel mode.

In light of the findings, this study suggests that city managers should improve the transport facilities to enhance the accessibility for elderly people. Establishing more subway lines to solve long-distance travel problem because many elderly people choose bus as their main travel mode for long distance trips in Jinan at present.

6 Acknowledgements

This work is supported by National Natural Science Foundation of China (Grant No. 42001396), and Graduate Education Quality Improvement Plan program of Shandong Jianzhu University (YZKC202115).

References

[1] Ahmad Z, Batool Z and Starkey P. (2019). Understanding mobility characteristics and needs of older persons in urban Pakistan with respect to use of public transport and self-driving. Journal of Transport Geography, 74, 181-190.

[2] Cheng L, Chen XW, De Vos J, Lai XJ and Witlox F. (2019a). Applying a random forest method approach to model travel mode choice behavior. Travel Behavior and Society, 14, 1-10.

[3] Cheng L, De Vos J, Shi KB, Yang M, Chen XW and Witlox F. (2019b). Do residential location effects on travel behavior differ between the elderly and younger adults? Transportation Research Part D, 73, 367-380.

[4] De Vos J. (2018). Do people travel with their preferred travel mode? Analysing the extent of travel mode dissonance and its effect on travel satisfaction. Transportation Research Part A, 117, 261-274.

[5] Ding C, Wang DG, Liu C, Zhang Y and Yang JW. (2017). Exploring the influence of built environment on travel mode choice considering the mediating effects of car ownership and travel distance. Transportation Research Part A, 100, 65-80.

[6] Du MY, Cheng L, Li XF and Yang JZ. (2020). Factors affecting the travel mode choice of the urban elderly in healthcare activity: comparison between core area and suburban area. Sustainable Cities and Society, 52, 101868

[7] Faroqi H, Mesbah M, Kim J and Tavassoli A. (2018). A model for measuring activity similarity between public transit passengers using smart card data. Travel Behaviour and Society, 13, 11-25.

[8] Giuliano G and Narayan D. (2003). Another look at travel patterns and urban form: the US and Great Britain. Urban studies, 40 (11), 2295-2312.

[9] Habib KMN and Hui V. (2017). An activity-

based approach of investigating travel behaviour of older people. Transportation, 44 (3), 555-573.

[10] Hahn JS, Kim HC, Kim JK and Ulfarsson GF. (2016). Trip making of older adults in Seoul: Differences in effects of personal and household characteristics by age group and trip purpose. Journal of Transport Geography, 57, 55-62.

[11] Hanson TR and Hildebrand ED. (2011). Can rural older drivers meet their needs without a car? Stated adaptation responses from a GPS travel diary survey. Transportation, 38 (6), 975-992.

[12] Hu XW, Wang J and Wang L. (2013). Understanding the travel behavior of elderly people in the developing countries: a case study of Changchun, China. Procedia Social and Behavioral Sciences, 96, 873-880.

[13] Mohd S, Latiff ARA and Senadjki A. (2019). Travel behavior of elderly in George Town and Malacca, Malaysia. Sustainability, 11 (19), 5251.

[14] Molin E, Mokhtarian P and Kroesen M. (2016). Multimodal travel groups and attitudes: A latent class cluster analysis of Dutch travelers. Transportation Research Part A, 83, 14-29.

[15] Moniruzzaman M, Paez A, Habib KMN and Morency C. (2013). Mode use and trip length of seniors in Montreal. Journal of Transport Geography, 30, 89-99.

[16] Pettersson P and Schmöcker JD. (2010). Active ageing in developing countries? -trip generation and tour complexity of older people in Metro Manila. Journal of Transport Geograph, 18(5), 613-623.

[17] Rahimi A, Azimi G and Jin X. (2020). Examining human attitudes toward shared mobility options and autonomous vehicles. Transportation Research Part F, 72, 133-154.

[18] Shao FJ, Sui Y, Yu X and Sun RC. (2019). Spatio-temporal travel patterns of elderly people-A comparative study based on buses usage in Qingdao, China. Journal of Transport Geography, 76, 178-190.

[19] Shen WW, Xiao WZ and Wang X. (2016). Passenger satisfaction evaluation model for urban rail transit: A structural equation modeling based on partial least squares. Transport Policy, 46, 20-31.

[20] Sundling C, Nilsson M, Hellqvist S, Pendrill L, Emardson R and Berglund B. (2016). Travel behaviour change in old age: the role of critical incidents in public transport. European Journal of Ageing, 13(1), 75-83.

[21] Szeto WY, Yang LC, Wong RCP, Li YC and Wong SC. (2017). Spatio-temporal travel characteristics of the elderly in an ageing society. Travel Behaviour and Society, 9, 10-20.

[22] Truong LT and Somenahalli SVC. (2015). Exploring frequency of public transport use among older adults: A study in Adelaide, Australia. Travel Behaviour and Society, 2 (3), 148-155.

[23] Van den Berg P, Arentze T and Timmermans H. (2011). Estimating social travel demand of senior citizens in the Netherlands. Journal of Transport Geography, 19(2), 323-331.

[24] Wang DG and Zhou M. (2017). The built environment and travel behavior in urban China: A literature review. Transportation Research Part D, 52, 574-585.

[25] Wang F and Ross CL. (2018). Machine learning travel mode choices: Comparing the performance of an extreme gradient boosting model with a multinomial logit model. Transportation Research Record, 2672(47), 35-45.

[26] Weng JC, Tu Q, Yuan RL, Lin PF and Chen ZH. (2018). Modeling mode choice behaviors for public transport commuters in Beijing. Journal of Urban Planning and Development, 144(3), 05018013.

[27] Yang LC. (2018). Modeling the mobility choices of older people in a transit-oriented city: Policy insights. Habitat International, 76, 10-18.

[28] Yuan YL, Yang M, Wu JX, Rasouli S and Lei D. (2019). Assessing bus transit service from the perspective of elderly passengers in Harbin, China. International Journal of Sustainable Transportation, 13(10), 761-776.

[29] Zhang H, Zhang LL, Che F, Jia JM and Shi BY. (2020). Revealing urban traffic demand by constructing dynamic networks with taxi trajectory data. IEEE Access, 8, 147673-147681.

[30] Zhang YS, Yao EJ, Zhang R and Xu H. (2019). Analysis of elderly people's travel behaviours during the morning peak hours in the context of the free bus programme in Beijing, China. Journal of Transport Geography, 76, 191-199.

[31] Zhao XL, Yan X, Yu A and Van Hentenryck P. (2020). Prediction and behavioral analysis of travel mode choice: A comparison of machine learning and logit models. Travel Behaviour and Society, 20, 22-35.

[32] Zhou XL, Wang MS, Li DY (2019) Bike-sharing or taxi? Modeling the choice of travel mode in Chicago using machine learning. Journal of Transport Geography, 79, 102479.

考虑低碳心理变量的出行方式选择行为模型

——基于 TPB-VBN 复合框架

林 涛[1] 邵海鹏[*1,2] 方瑞韬[1]

(1. 长安大学运输工程学院;2. 长安大学生态安全屏障区交通网设施管控及循环修复技术交通运输行业重点实验室)

摘 要 通勤者使用低碳出行方式对减少二氧化碳排放和缓解城市交通拥堵问题有着至关重要的作用。为更好地探究通勤者的低碳出行行为机理,提出了将低碳知识和低碳行为习惯引入离散选择模型的研究方法。基于计划行为理论(TPB)和价值—信念—规范理论(VBN)复合框架分别对公共交通和私家车构建了两个多指标多因果(MIMIC)模型。把模型预测后的潜变量加入离散选择模型中,构建带有低碳心理变量的 TPB-VBN 复合框架混合选择模型。结果表明:通勤者个人社会经济属性对部分潜变量有显著影响;出行习惯、个人规范和责任归属是影响通勤方式选择的三个最重要的影响因素。与传统模型相比,所建的混合选择模型分类正确率整体提高了 3.08%。该成果为制定促进公共交通使用的低碳政策提供支持。

关键词 出行行为 计划行为理论 价值—信念—规范理论 混合选择模型 MIMIC 模型

0 引言

碳排放是全球变暖现象的最大原因之一[1]。进入 21 世纪,交通运输行业产生了近 1/4 的全球二氧化碳排放量。此外,具国际能源署(IEA)统计推测,预计 2030 年交通运输行业的碳排量将占全球碳排量的 41%[2]。此外,我国于 2020 年在应对气候变化《巴黎协定》中郑重承诺:中国将提高国家自主贡献力度,采取更加有力的政策和措施,二氧化碳排放力争于 2030 年前达到峰值,努力争取 2060 年前实现碳中和的“双碳”目标。

在此背景下,如何减少交通运输行业的碳排量成为各研究学者所关注的焦点。随着人均收入快速增长和生活水平的提高,中国等发展中国家的交通模式正快速地向城市交通模式进行转变。在过去几十年中,私家车保有量和使用频率也出现了极大的增长[3]。虽然,机动化水平的提高给社会经济和旅游出行带来了有利作用,但从长远

1. 基金项目:国家重点研发计划(2019YFB1600300);中央高校基本科研业务费专项资金(300102219210,300102210201)。

来看,这将对城市居民生活质量产生严重的不利影响[4]。

由于通勤在城市交通需求中是主导因素之一,鼓励通勤者使用公共交通系统出行而不是私人交通系统便是减少二氧化碳排放和缓解城市交通拥堵的一个较为理想的措施。这是因为公共交通系统的容量远高于私人交通系统,增加公共交通系统的使用量不仅有助于减少人均碳排放还能减缓城市交通拥堵的难题。因此,各国的政策制定者试图实施旨在减少私人交通系统使用的政策,并鼓励通勤者使用更低碳清洁、更可持续发展的公共交通[5]。在经济学方面,普遍认为增加碳排放收费和拥堵收费是减少私人交通系统使用的有效方法[6],但在国外的实践中发现,通勤者普遍对使用公共交通的意愿不大且不易被大众所接受[7-8]。在国内,地方政府尝试车牌号出行限制和增加道路收费等措施,虽然这些方法在短期内是有效的[9],许多发展中国家政策制定者常采纳的政策,但有研究表明,交通条件的变化会导致一部分通勤者又转回使用私家车[10]。

因此,仅靠决策者出台或改变政策并不能从宏观角度很好地保证减少碳排放和缓解城市交通拥堵这两个方面取得长期的成效,为此有必要研究决定通勤者低碳出行方式选择意向的影响因素。目前,关于低碳出行行为意向影响因素的研究主要有两种方式。第一种方式基于计划行为理论(the Theory of Planned Behavior,TPB),该理论通过态度、主观规范和知觉行为控制来概括通勤者个体所受外在因素的影响,从而解释其低碳行为意向与实际行为[11];第二种方式基于价值—信念—规范理论(Value-belief-norm Theory,VBN),此理论是由Stern将价值理论、新环境范式和规范—行为理论进行结合,通过价值观、后果意识、责任归属和个人规范来解释低碳行为的形成[12]。单独使用计划行为理论或价值—信念—规范理论,以及后来发展的扩展TPB或扩展VBN理论,均在低碳环保行为研究领域都得到了验证[13-17]。

然而,无论是单独使用计划行为理论还是价值—信念—规范理论,均无法较为满意地解释低碳环境行为意图[18]。在TPB理论中,缺乏对重复行为的预测,在对低碳价值观的影响上也缺乏考虑;而在VBN理论中,忽略了行为态度等影响个体行为的重要因素[19]。为此,有学者尝试对模型进行改良,Jia等[20]将TPB理论与物质占有理论(Material Possession Theory,MPT)相结合来考察低碳方式选择的行为影响因素,但并没有明确改良后的模型解释力有无提升。因此,Lane和Potter[21]提出考虑将TPB和VBN两个理论结合,并通过实证分析发现模型的解释力有所提高,而且还可以探索二者理论中变量之间的相互作用。Liu等[22]通过天津市的调查数据也验证了该复合TPB-VBN理论的合理性。可是,迄今为止很少有研究者在改良后的复合TPB-VBN理论的研究中明确考虑通勤者的心理因素[23]。在此,有必要从通勤者的微观心理角度,在考虑低碳心理因素的情况下,更加深入地研究决定其低碳出行方式选择意向的主要影响因素。

此外,在以往研究出行方式选择时,通常以通勤者个人经济特征和出行方式属性作为选择行为的解释变量,这使得个体异质性(如心理特征)和一些无法被直接观测的因素无法得到解释,并被学者批评该选择过程为"黑箱"[24-25]。为此离散选择建模领域对其进行多次改进,从而整合发展出了混合选择模型(Hybrid Choice Model,HCM),该模型将关于个体异质性的"软信息"和"硬信息"(例如社会经济特征)相结合,从而为实际行为所受到的潜在影响因素提供结构和意义[24,26]。在过去有关低碳出行方式选择的研究中,往往假设出行方式选择意向与实际行为是一致的[20],缺乏对各低碳变量对通勤者低碳出行实际行为的影响研究,为此本文提出了带有低碳心理变量的TPB-VBN复合框架混合选择模型。

基于以上理念,本文基于计划行为理论(TPB)和价值—信念—规范理论(VBN)的复合框架,通过预调查,确定公共交通和私家车是通勤者最常用的两种出行模式,以此为基础,分别对公共交通和私家车构建两种多指标多因果(MIMIC)模型,研究低碳心理因素对低碳出行方式选择意向的影响。在此过程中,把模型预测后的潜变量加入离散选择模型中,构建带有低碳心理变量的TPB-VBN复合框架混合选择模型,以深入了解各低碳变量对通勤者低碳出行实际行为的影响。该研究不同于以往从宏观调控角度出发,以通勤者的微观心理角度为切入点,研究成果为制定促进公共交通使用的低碳政策提供启示。

1 模型理论框架与假设

1.1 计划行为理论

计划行为理论(Theory of Planned Behavior, TPB)通过态度(Attitude, AT)、主观规范(Subjective Norms,SN)和知觉行为控制(Perceived Behavioral Control,PBC)来概括个体所受到的外在因素的影响,从而解释其行为意向与实际行为。首先,对于行为的态度(AT),要么积极,要么悲观;其次,对于主观规范(SN),它代表了一种来自社会的压力,要求从事或不从事一种行为;第三个是感知行为控制(PBC),指的是一个人对自己执行给定行为的能力的感知。行为意向会受到上述三个变量的复合影响[11]。该模型的基本假设为:主观规范、态度、知觉行为控制都对出行意向产生正向影响;主观规范、知觉行为控制正向影响态度。

1.2 价值—信念—规范理论

价值—信念—规范理论(Value-belief-norm Theory,VBN)最早是由Stern等[27]提出的,该理论结合了价值理论、新生态范式(New Ecological Paradigm)和规范活动理论(Norm-Activity Theory)。在本文中,个人规范(Personal Norms,PN)指的是个人认为采取环保行为的义务。内在心理感知被视为个人规范的本质,当一个人感到后悔、内疚,甚至是一系列负面情绪时,行为意向就会受到影响。后果意识(Consequence Awareness,AC)是指当个体意识到对自己或对外部环境的负面后果时,个体决策受到影响;责任归属(Responsibility Awareness,AR)是指个体在采取行动之前考虑其决策的更广泛后果而做出的行为决策。环境行为主要受个人规范的刺激。该模型的基本假设为:个人的责任归属和后果意识正向影响个人规范,后果意识正向影响责任归属。

1.3 低碳心理变量

由于上述两个理论都还在不断的发展中,可能存在其他潜变量对低碳行为意向有着重要影响,此外,计划行为理论和价值—信念—规范理论均不是完全独立的模型框架,增加新的潜变量能提高模型解释能力。为此,本文从通勤者的微观心理角度,将低碳认知和低碳习惯作为低碳心理潜变量引入模型中。

低碳认知(Understanding of Low-carbon,U):低碳认知是指关于低碳知识的了解程度。在低碳方面了解程度更高的人,可能会更了解个人行为对有关碳排放效果的影响。这样的人也可能会对全球变暖和温室效应等全球性低碳环保问题有更多的了解。低碳认知已被证实对低碳行为有积极影响,如低碳旅行[28]。Frick等[29]研究表明,低碳环保的认知有可能影响个人的亲环境行为,以上研究表明,低碳认知可在影响个体知觉行为控制和塑造个人规范中起到不可或缺的作用。基于此,我们假设H1~H3:

假设H1:低碳认知正向影响知觉行为控制。

假设H2:低碳认知正向影响个人规范。

假设H3:低碳认知正向影响行为意向。

低碳习惯(Low-carbon Habit,HAB):低碳习惯是旨在减少个人总体碳排放的习惯。Stern等人[27]指出,低碳习惯的概念是环保行为的一个子集,它可以显著提高对未来低碳行为的预测[30]。以往研究发现,习惯几乎和初始的大部分变量有显著正向影响关系[31-33]。因此,低碳习惯是我们不可忽略的重要因素。基于此,我们假设H4~H7:

假设H4:低碳习惯正向影响态度。

假设H5:低碳习惯正向影响知觉行为控制。

假设H6:低碳习惯正向影响个人规范。

假设H7:低碳习惯正向影响行为意向。

1.4 多指标多因果模型

为检验计划行为理论和价值—信念—规范理论的复合框架中各潜变量间的内在作用机理以及各潜变量与通勤者个人属性之间的关系,建立多指标多因果模型(Multiple Indicators and Multiple Causes,MIMIC)。该模型的主要优点是可以通过结构方程清晰地表达出潜变量的外生原因与内生指标之间的关系,并得到各解释变量与潜变量之间的影响系数,其本质上是结构方程模型(Structural Equation Mode,SEM)的一种形式,结构方程模型的基本表达式为:

$$\begin{aligned}\eta &= \Gamma x + \xi \\ y &= \Lambda\eta + \varepsilon\end{aligned} \tag{1}$$

式中:η——潜变量向量;

x——和潜变量η有因果关系的外生可观测变量的向量;

y——η的可观测的指标变量向量;

Γ、Λ——待估计的参数矩阵;

ξ、ε——测量误差。

MIMIC模型可分解为两部分：第一部分是计划行为理论和价值—信念—规范理论的复合框架的各潜变量进行验证性因子分析的过程[33]。由潜变量和指标以及相应的测量误差 组成；第二部分是通勤者个人特征属性的外生变量与计划行为理论和价值—信念—规范理论的复合框架中的内生潜变量及潜变量的指标变量之间的结构方程模型，类似回归分析[33]。每部分的模型表达式分别为：

$$\begin{cases} y_{\text{lv1}} = \lambda_{\text{lv1}}\ \eta_{\text{lv1}} + \varepsilon_{\text{lv1}} \\ y_{\text{lv2}} = \lambda_{\text{lv2}}\ \eta_{\text{lv2}} + \varepsilon_{\text{lv2}} \\ \cdots \\ y_{\text{lvn}} = \lambda_{\text{lvn}}\ \eta_{\text{lvn}} + \varepsilon_{\text{lvn}} \end{cases} \tag{2}$$

$$\eta_{\text{lvi}} = \gamma_{\text{lv1}} x_i + \gamma_{\text{lv2}} x_i + \gamma_{\text{lv3}} x_i + \cdots + \gamma_{\text{lvn}} x_i + \xi_i \tag{3}$$

式中：λ——因子载荷；

lv——计划行为理论和价值—信念—规范理论的复合框架中的潜变量；

n——观测变量数量；

γ——待估参数；

x——个人经济属性；

i——被观测的个体。

1.5　混合选择模型

通过MIMIC模型估计计算后得出潜变量拟合值，将其作为解释自变量加入传统离散选择模型形成混合选择模型[32]。根据式(3)表明，通勤者对于低碳出行方式的潜在偏好，受到通勤者个体的性别、受教育程度、月收入、年龄等因素的影响，因此建立潜变量与离散选择模型结合的混合选择模型。设通勤者采用第 j 种出行方式的效用函数 u_j 为：

$$u_j = a_j \cdot I + b \cdot T_j + c_j \cdot \eta + \varepsilon_j, j = 0,1 \tag{4}$$

式中：I——可观测的通勤者个人社会经济属性向量；

T_j——可观测的出行特征属性向量；

η——潜变量向量；

a_j、b、c_j——待估计参数向量；

ε_j——随机项。

效用最大化的函数 $U_{\max}$ 为：

$$U_{\max} = \begin{cases} 1, u = \max\limits_j(u_j) \\ 0, \text{其他} \end{cases} \tag{5}$$

采用最大似然估计法在AMOS 24.0软件中对MIMIC模型进行求解，然后将求得的潜变量值代入离散选择模型，并使用STATA 16.0软件求解。本文建立的混合选择模型是考虑了潜变量的离散选择BL模型(Binary Logit Model)。模型可表示为：

$$P(y=j|x) = F(x,\beta) = \Lambda(x'\beta) \equiv \frac{e^{x'\beta}}{1+e^{x'\beta}}, j = 0,1 \tag{6}$$

式中：$x'\beta$——通勤者选择其中一种出行方式的影响因素，具体变量有出行距离、出行费用、出行时间、月收入、驾驶证、拥有公交卡和车辆拥有；

β——影响因素对于某种出行方式相对于另一种出行方式选择概率的影响。

混合选择模型的框架如图1所示。

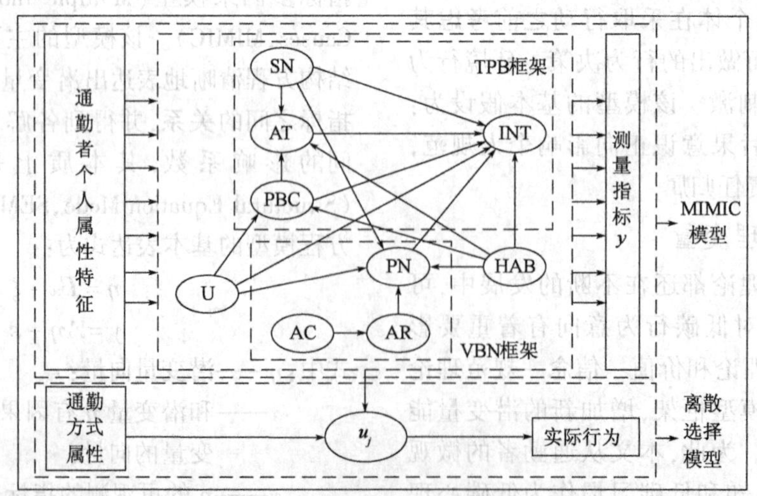

图1　混合选择模型的全路径框架

2 研究方法

2.1 预调查

通勤者可能使用几种不同类型出行方式,包括公共汽车、地铁、出租车、私家车、摩托车、自行车、步行等。其中步行、骑自行车和其他非机动车不在本研究范围内,因此被归类为“其他模式”。预调查以国内的一线及部分新一线城市为对象,分别是北京、上海、广州、深圳、天津、杭州、武汉、长沙、重庆、成都、西安,在这些城市中,交通网络较为发达,交通出行模式丰富,且在国内的总碳排量占比中较高。采用问卷调查的方式收集预调查数据。预调查数据收集自2021年4月至5月,通过问卷星问卷平台进行的在线随机抽样。

本研究在预调查中所收集的数据显示,一共回收有效样本1034份问卷,在所有可供的选择中,公共汽车、轨道交通和私家车这三种出行方式共845份,占总样本量的81.7%。考虑到后续建模的简便性和二者的共同性,本文将公共汽车、轨道交通这两种出行模式合并为公共交通方式。因此,本文后续研究只考虑私家车和公共交通两种主要的出行方式。

2.2 问卷调查设计

问卷由三部分组成:

(1)通勤者个人社会经济属性特征;

(2)潜变量的可观测变量题;

(3)RP调查实际通勤的出行方式选择。

个人社会经济属性特征部分包括被调查者的性别、年龄、收入、汽车拥有、驾驶证和是否拥有(实体、电子)公交卡的信息。第二部分的所有问题采用李克特五分制来衡量的,范围从“非常不同意(=1)”到“非常同意(=5)”。与低碳心理相关的方面分为两个潜变量:低碳认知和低碳习惯,均采用了三个可观测变量问题来衡量,见表1。调查数据收集自2021年6月至7月,被调查的城市对象分别是北京、上海、广州、深圳、天津、杭州、武汉、长沙、重庆、成都、西安,通过问卷星问卷平台进行的在线随机抽样。第三部分是RP调查实际通勤的出行方式选择,包括:出发地(当地)、目的地(当地)、出行距离(km)、出行时间(min)、出行费用(元)、换乘次数(次)。

各潜变量的具体描述 表1

潜变量	编号	可观测变量	假设来源及参考文献
态度(AT)	AT1	低碳出行让我快乐	Liobikien G[16],Liu[22]
	AT2	低碳出行让我很舒服	
	AT3	低碳出行比较方便	
主观规范(SN)	SN1	家人鼓励我选择低碳出行方式	Mancha[13],Liu[22]
	SN2	身边的同事朋友鼓励我选择低碳出行方式	
	SN3	新闻媒体鼓励我选择低碳出行方式	
知觉行为控制(PBC)	PBC1	低碳出行方式完全可以满足我日常出行的需要	Mancha[13],Liobikien éG[16]
	PBC2	我有信息未来一段时间内我会选择低碳出行方式	
	PBC3	我认为很容易采取低碳出行方式	
个人规范(PN)	PN1	低碳出行符合我的环保价值观	Lane and Potter[21],Liu[22]
	PN2	不管别人怎么做,我都会选择低碳出行模式	
	PN3	基于我个人的价值观,我认为选择低碳出行方式是我的职责	
责任归属(AR)	AR1	我认为减少空气污染是政府和企业的责任	Lane and Potter[21],Liu[22]
	AR2	我认为大家都有责任走低碳出行模式	
	AR3	我认为我有负责使用低碳出行模式	
后果意识(AC)	AC1	我认为低碳出行可以减少城市拥堵	Lane and Potter[21],Liu[22]
	AC2	我认为低碳旅行可以减少空气污染	
	AC3	我认为低碳出行可以降低能耗	

续上表

潜 变 量	编号	可观测变量	假设来源及参考文献
低碳认知(U)	U1	我相信我知道哪些行为会导致碳排放增加	Jia[20]
	U2	突然加速、低速高速行驶等行为会增加油耗	
	U3	推广使用新能源汽车可以节约资源,减少碳排放	
低碳习惯(HAB)	HAB1	低碳出行方式是我的固有习惯	Jia[20],Chen C F[34],许冰[33]
	HAB2	平时,我使用低碳方式出行的频率很高	
	HAB3	平时购买当地季节性物品,因为运输和包装需要消耗能源	
出行意向(INT)	INT1	我强烈希望进行低碳旅行	Liobikien éG[16],Liu[22],许冰[33]
	INT2	未来一年我会尽可能选择低碳出行	
	INT3	我会鼓励身边的家人和朋友选择低碳出行方式	

2.3　问卷调查设计

正式调查收回有效样本 811 份。从有效样本的个人属性特征上看,被调查者男性占 57.5%;年龄以中青年为主,其中 26～35 岁占比接近一半;月收入以中等收入为主,2001～4000 元占30.7%,4001～6000 元占 29.5%;受教育程度以大专和本科为主,占总体的 49.8%;大部分样本均拥有汽车,占总体的 69.9%;有 66.3% 的调查者有驾驶证,稍低于汽车拥有比例,说明少数调查者拥有至少一辆汽车;高达 85.2% 的调查者拥有公交卡,见表 2。

个人属性特征　　表 2

变量名称		定 义	频 数	占 比
性别	Gender	男性(1)	466	57.5
		女性(0)	345	42.5
年龄(岁)	Age	18～25	165	20.3
		26～35	395	48.7
		36～45	178	21.9
		46～60	69	8.5
		60 以上	4	0.5
月收入(元)	Income	低于 2000	60	7.4
		2001～4000	249	30.7
		4001～6000	239	29.5
		6001～8000	121	14.5
		8001 及以上	142	17.5
教育程度	Education	初中及以下	88	10.9
		高中/中专	157	19.4
		大专/本科	404	49.8
		硕士及以上	162	20.0
拥有汽车	Car ownership	有(1)	567	69.9
		无(0)	244	30.1
驾驶证	Driving license	是(1)	538	66.3
		否(0)	273	33.7
拥有公交卡	Owning bus card	是(1)	691	85.2
		否(0)	120	14.8

3 数据与模型估计

3.1 信度效度分析

信度系数通过 Crobrach's α 系数来检验,收敛效度通过平均方差提取值(Average Variance Extracted,AVE)来表征,通过 KMO 检验与 Bartlett 球形检验对问卷的因子分析适宜性进行初步判断。分别以公共交通和私家车的数据进行信效度分析,见表3。信度方面,公共交通和私家车的各变量 Crobrach's α 大于等于0.7,说明具有较强的一致性。效度方面,KMO 值均高于0.5,其他变量的 AVE 值都接近或高于0.7,说明具有很好的收敛效度。

潜变量的信度效度分析 表3

出行方式	潜变量	AVE	KMO	Bartlett	Crobrach's α
公共交通	AT	0.71	0.73	613.2***	0.93
	SN	0.75	0.75	760.9***	0.90
	PBC	0.72	0.78	821.5***	0.92
	PN	0.78	0.73	705.2***	0.89
	AR	0.76	0.77	794.7***	0.91
	AC	0.72	0.76	722.4***	0.90
	U	0.80	0.74	528.7***	0.87
	HAB	0.72	0.71	591.4***	0.85
	INT	0.82	0.78	785.7***	0.91
私家车	AT	0.70	0.75	701.9***	0.91
	SN	0.73	0.74	656.2***	0.89
	PBC	0.70	0.76	780.5***	0.90
	PN	0.76	0.71	599.7***	0.86
	AR	0.78	0.77	682.3***	0.88
	AC	0.75	0.76	722.4***	0.91
	U	0.78	0.72	593.7***	0.84
	HAB	0.75	0.75	653.9***	0.89
	INT	0.79	0.73	604.8***	0.88

注:"***"表示 $p<0.001$。

3.2 模型拟合评价

本文选取采用卡方自由度比(χ^2/df)、近似均方跟误差(Root Mean Squared Error of Approximation,RMSEA)、适配度指数(Goodness of Fit Index,GFI)、比较拟合指数(Comparative Fit Index,CFI)、塔克-刘易斯指数(Tucker-Lewis Index,TLI)作为 MIMIC 模型的拟合度评价指标。一般认为,小于3.0的模型拟合度较好。RMSEA 的值越小表示模型的拟合度越好,当小于0.05时其拟合度良好。GFI 值越高表示模型的契合度越好,CFI 和 TLI 两个指标是把独立模型与定义模型的绝对拟合进行比较,三者越接近1越好。考虑到采用公共交通与私家车两种出行方式的差异性,对其分别建立 MIMIC 模型,模型的拟合指标见表4。

MIMIC 模型拟合指标统计与推荐值 表4

项目	公共交通	私家车	推荐值
CMIN/df	1.716	1.612	<3.0
RMSEA	0.043	0.039	<0.050
GFI	0.910	0.921	>0.90
CFI	0.948	0.953	>0.90
TLI	0.934	0.941	>0.90

3.3 MIMIC 模型估计

两种不同出行方式 MIMIC 模型中潜变量之间的路径关系如图2和图3所示,潜变量之间的路径适配系数为标准化后的系数。其中"*"表示 $p<0.1$;"**"表示 $p<0.01$,"***"表示 $p<0.001$。

总体上看,MIMIC 模型对公共交通和私家车这两种出行方式的选择行为均得到良好的解释效果,行为意向的解释程度分别为 73% 和 77%。根据标准化路径适配系数和显著性检验结果得出以下结论。

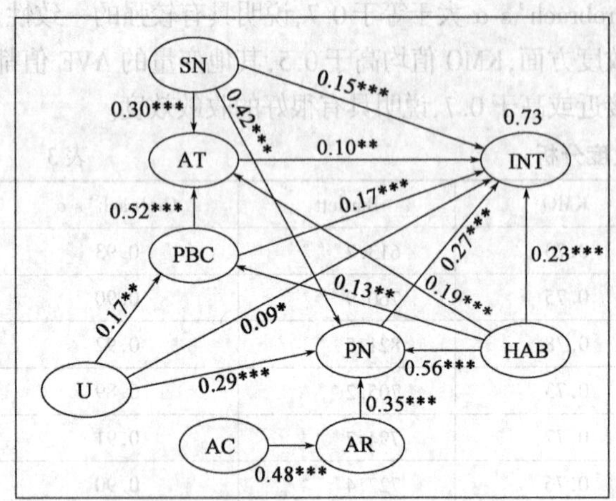

图 2　公共交通 MIMIC 模型中潜变量之间的标准化系数

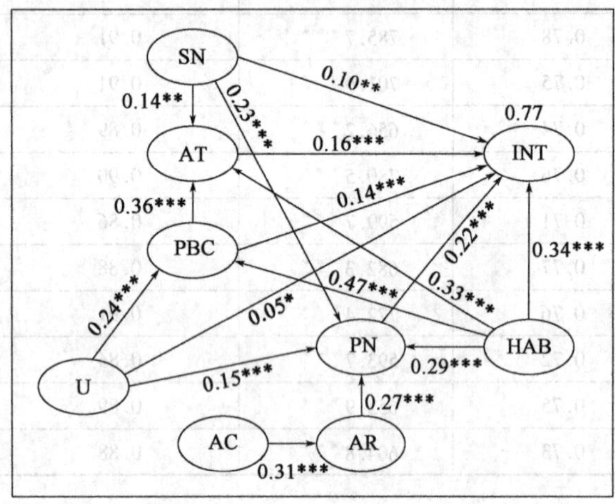

图 3　私家车 MIMIC 模型中潜变量之间的标准化系数

(1)公共交通和私家车这两种出行方式中,主观规范对态度有显著正向影响,说明在低碳出行行为中,通勤者选择这出行方式的倾向程度受到周边社会期望与认同的影响,并且它的影响程度在公共交通中更大。知觉行为控制也对态度有显著正向影响,说明通勤者同样受到掌控出行信念的影响,该因素对公共交通的影响更大,意味着通勤者在低碳出行中所预期的阻碍相对较少。两种出行方式中的态度、主观规范和知觉行为控制都对行为意向有显著正向影响,说明通勤者的个人行为评价判断、社会认同和出行掌控对低碳方式选择的行为意愿有显著的推动作用。

(2)两种出行方式中,后果意识正向影响责任意识,责任意识显著的正向影响个人规范,个人规范可以解释低碳出行选择意向分别达到 27% 和 22%,这意味着在公共交通方式中,价值—信念—规范理论起到了较好的解释效果。对于有较好低碳环保价值观的通勤者,当意识到非环保、高碳行为发生时,预期到的不良后果就会唤起责任意识,从而激活个人规范,阻止这一行为发生。因此,意识到使用机动车会对环境造成污染的后果,环保责任感会使其倾向于选择低碳方式出行。

(3)行为习惯对大部分潜变量均有显著正向影响,这意味着通勤者在选择这两种出行方式时,均受到不同程度的习惯影响。值得注意的是,在公共交通中,行为习惯对低碳出行选择意向的直接解释程度只有 23%,但是在通过个人规范这一个中介变量后,其解释程度有所提升,说明公共交通中,通勤者的行为习惯受个人规范的间接影响;而私家车则相反,其行为习惯可以更好地直接地解释选择意向。

(4)通勤者的低碳认知对知觉行为控制和个人规范均有较为显著的正向影响,但其影响程度弱于行为习惯,同样地,低碳认知对行为选择意向的影响显著性不佳,尤其对私家车的选择意向中,其影响程度极其微弱,说明低碳认知对私家车的选择意向并没有显著的驱动力。

3.4　混合选择模型估计结果分析

在对 MIMIC 模型估计之后,对公共交通与私家车这两种出行方式模型中的潜变量分别进行了预测,然后代入离散选择模型中与通勤者的社会经济特征属性一起进行估计。为了便于比较,本文分别用不带潜变量的离散选择 BL 模型和带潜变量的混合选择模型进行参数估计;同时为了较为全面地研究各种因素对低碳出行方式的影响,分别以公共交通与私家车出行方式作为效用基础项进行回归分析,并列出概率比(Odds Ratio,OR)。由于篇幅所限,仅列出以公共交通为效用基础项的回归结果,见表 5。

参与分析的样本共有 811 个。一般认为优度比系数达到 0.2 以上即可认为模型具有较高的精度。由表 5 可知:不带潜变量的离散选择模型和带潜变量混合选择模型的优度比系数 R2 分别为 0.3826 和 0.4350,这说明这两个模型的精度是可以接受的,且带潜变量混合选择模型的优度比系数 R2 提高了 0.0524。从拟合指标上可以看出,带潜变量混合选择模型要明显优于不带潜变量的离散选择模型,模型的分类正确率提高了 3.08%。

以公共交通为基础效用项的模型估计结果　表5

变　量	不含潜变量离散选择模型			含潜变量混合选择模型		
	参数	z 值	OR 值	参数	z 值	OR 值
Distance	−0.85***	−6.03	0.43	−0.79***	−5.60	0.45
Time	−0.62***	−4.38	0.54	−0.60***	−3.99	0.55
Cost	−0.78***	−5.76	0.46	−0.72***	−4.86	0.49
Driving license	−0.39***	−2.89	0.68	−0.31***	−2.31	0.73
Own bus card	0.41***	3.12	1.51	0.39**	−2.56	1.48
Car ownership	−0.37***	−2.87	0.69	−0.29**	−2.28	0.75
Income	−0.24*	−1.95	0.79	−0.35***	−2.78	0.70
Change	−0.19*	−1.82	0.83	−0.11	−1.58	0.89
Education	−0.12	−0.96	0.89	—	—	—
Age	−0.16	−1.27	0.85	—	—	—
Gender	0.25	1.07	1.28	—	—	—
_cons	0.93**	2.56	2.53	1.39***	3.32	4.01
AT	—	—	—	0.32***	2.54	1.38
SN	—	—	—	0.21***	2.28	1.23
PBC	—	—	—	0.19*	1.89	1.21
PN	—	—	—	0.48***	3.92	1.62
AR	—	—	—	0.37**	2.52	1.45
AC	—	—	—	0.25**	2.05	1.28
U	—	—	—	0.15*	1.68	1.16
HAB	—	—	—	0.53***	3.92	1.70
样本数	811			811		
对数似然估计值	−405.88			−367.87		
优度比系数 R2	0.3826			0.4350		
分类正确率	77.07%			80.15%		

注："*"表示 $p<0.1$；"**"表示 $p<0.05$，"***"表示 $p<0.01$。

从表5还可以看出，不是所有的因素对低碳出行方式都有显著性影响。在不带潜变量的离散选择模型中，传统出行时间、出行距离和出行费用均对公共交通的出行选择为负向影响。驾驶证、汽车拥有、拥有公交卡、月收入和换乘次数这五个变量显著影响低碳出行选择。其中，驾驶证(−0.39)、汽车拥有(−0.37)、月收入(−0.24)和换乘次数(−0.19)四个变量的公共交通的出行选择为负向影响，同时可以看出，拥有驾驶证与汽车对低碳出行行为影响程度相近，且比月收入和换乘次数的影响程度大。随着月收入的增加、换乘次数的增加，选择公共交通的可能性比选择私家车的可能性将降低，意味着高收入的通勤者往往更倾向使用私家车出行，而换乘次数意味着通勤者会同时考虑交通工具的便利性。

在带潜变量混合选择模型中，所有的潜变量都对低碳出行方式的选择有显著性影响。所有的潜变量均对低碳方式选择有正向的显著性影响。在定义潜变量时考虑了不同出行方式之间的差异，所以即使对于同一个通勤者，不同的出行方式也会产生不同的潜变量影响因素。对于选择公共交通方式的低碳心理潜变量而言，每提高1个指标值，在保持其他影响因素不变的前提下，通勤者选择公共交通出行的概率对数分别是私家车出行方式的1.16和1.70倍,可以看出,低碳出行习惯的可能性提升幅度明显比低碳认知大,这说明低碳出行习惯比低碳认知更具有影响力;对于TPB框架中的主观规范、态度和知觉行为控制三个潜变量,每提高1个指标值,除了潜变量态度,选择公共交通出行的可能性提升幅度较小,均低于1.25倍,而VBN框架中的个人规范、责任归属这两个潜变量的增长比例更加明显,分别高达1.62和1.45倍,这意味着在TPB-VBN复合框架中,态度、个人规范和责任归属成为更为重要的影响因素。在引入低碳心理因素的TPB-VBN复合框架中,模型中出行习惯、个人规范和责任归属的影响最大。以私家车为效用基础项的分析类似。

4 结语

(1)在低碳出行行为中,通勤者的低碳心理因素(低碳认知和出行习惯)对出行意向起到重要的作用。围绕选择公共交通和私家车出行方式的潜变量来制定相应的低碳出行需求引导模式和策略,应该是基于微观心理影响因素进一步研究低碳出行选择行为的重要方向之一。

(2)混合选择模型比传统不带潜变量的离散选择模型具有更高的拟合度和分类准确率。通过对混合选择模型显著自变量参数估计值的分析,能够从通勤者的社会经济属性特征和低碳心理因素两个方面着手去考虑对通勤者出行方式选择行为的干扰,为实现城市的主要出行方式系统结构优化提供支撑和参考。

(3)尽管本文将计划行为理论和价值—信念—规范理论相结合成复合框架,并适当考虑了微观心理潜变量,但模型仍有很大的改进空间,这也是今后需要进一步研究的问题。此外,本研究的样本量还不足够大,样本不同年龄比例与实际有一定偏差,今后可考虑与大数据结合,使研究结果更具说服力。

参考文献

[1] Hu X, Moura S J, Murgovski N, et al. Integrated Optimization of Battery Sizing, Charging, and Power Management in Plug-In Hybrid Electric Vehicles[J]. IEEE Transactions on Control Systems Technology, 2016, 24(03): 1036-1043.

[2] International Energy Agency, 2010. World Energy Outlook 2010: Fact Sheet.

[3] Huo H, Zhang Q, He K, et al. Vehicle-use intensity in China: Current status and future trend [J]. Energy Policy, 2012, 43: 6-16.

[4] Steg L, Vlek C. Encouraging pro-environmental behaviour: An integrative review and research agenda [J]. Journal of Environmental Psychology, 2009, 29(03): 309-317.

[5] Du H, Liu D, Southworth F, et al. Pathways for energy conservation and emissions mitigation in road transport up to 2030: A case study of the Jing-Jin-Ji area, China [J]. Journal of Cleaner Production, 2017, 162: 882-893.

[6] Small K A, Gomez-ibañez J A. Road pricing for congestion management: the transition from theory to policy [M]. UK, K. J. Button, E. T. Verhoef (Eds.), Road pricing, Traffic Congestion and the Environment, 1998, 213-246.

[7] Rouwendal J, Verhoef E T. Basic economic principles of road pricing: from theory to applications [J]. Transport Policy, 2006, 13(02): 106-114.

[8] Schade J, Schlag B. Acceptability of urban transport pricing strategies [J]. Transportation Research Part F: Traffic Psychology and Behaviour, 2003, 6(01): 45-61.

[9] Wang L, Xu J, Qin P. Will a driving restriction policy reduce car trips? — The case study of Beijing, China [J]. Transportation Research Part A: Policy and Practice. 2014, 67: 279-290.

[10] Jia N, Zhang Y, He Z, et al. Commuters' acceptance of and behavior reactions to license plate restriction policy: A case study of Tianjin, China [J]. Transportation Research Part D: Transport and Environment, 2017, 52 (Part B): 428-440.

[11] Ajzen I. The theory of planned behavior [J]. Organizational Behavior and Human Decision Processes, 1991, 190(2): 179-211.

[12] Stern P C, Dietz T, Abel T, et al. A value-belief-norm theory of support for social movements: The case of environmentalism [J]. Hu-

man Ecology Review,1999,6(2):81-97.

LI Gen. Merging model in freeway weaving section based on gradient boosting decision tree[J]. Journal of Southeast University (Natural Science Edition), 2018, 48 (03): 563-567.

[13] Mancha R M,Yoder C Y. Cultural antecedents of green behavioral intent: An environmental theory of planned behavior[J]. Journal of Environmental Psychology,2015,43:145-154.

[14] 陈月霞,陈龙,查奇芬,等.基于低碳心理潜变量Logit模型的出行方式预测模型[J].公路交通科技,2017,34(09):100-108+137.

[15] 陈坚,张弛,庹永恒,等.考虑环保意识和出行习惯的公交出行选择行为模型[J].交通运输系统工程与信息,2020,20(04):128-135.

[16] LiobikienE G,MandravickaitE J,BernationienE J. Theory of planned behavior approach to understand the green purchasing behavior in the EU:A cross-cultural study[J]. Ecological Economics,2016,125:38-46.

[17] Gärling T,Fujii S,Gärling A,et al. Moderating effects of social value orientation on determinants of proenvironmental behavior intention [J]. Journal of Environmental Psychology, 2003,23(01):1-9.

[18] Abrahamse W, Steg L. Factors related to household energy use and intention to reduce it:the role of psychological and socio-demographic variables[J]. Human Ecology Review, 2011,18(01):30-40.

[19] Bamberg S,Hunecke M,BLÖBAUM A. Social context,personal norms and the use of public transportation:Two field studies[J]. Journal of Environmental Psychology, 2007, 27 (03): 190-203.

[20] Jia N,Li L,Ling S,et al. Influence of attitudinal and low-carbon factors on behavioral intention of commuting mode choice-A cross-city study in China [J]. Transportation Research Part A: Policy and Practice, 2018, 111: 108-118.

[21] Lane B,Potter S. The adoption of cleaner vehicles in the UK: exploring the consumer attitude-action gap [J]. Journal of Cleaner Production,2007,15(11-12):1085-1092.

[22] Liu D, Du H, Southworth F, et al. The influence of social-psychological factors on the intention to choose low-carbon travel modes in Tianjin, China [J]. Transportation Research Part A:Policy and Practice,2017,105:42-53.

[23] Hafner R J, Walker I, Verplanken B. Image, not environmentalism:A qualitative exploration of factors influencing vehicle purchasing decisions[J]. Transportation Research Part A:Policy and Practice,2017,97:89-105.

[24] Ben-akiva M,Walker J,Bernardino A T,et al. Integration of Choice and Latent Variable Models[J]. NLD, Mahmassani H S(Eds.), Perpetual Motion:Travel Behaviour Research Opportunities and Application Challenges,2002, 431-470.

[25] Kamargianni M,Dubey S,Polydoropoulou A,et al. Investigating the subjective and objective factors influencing teenagers' school travel mode choice-An integrated choice and latent variable model [J]. Transportation Research Part A: Policy and Practice, 2015, 78: 473-488.

[26] Ramezani S, Laatikainen T, Hasanzadeh K, et al. Shopping trip mode choice of older adults: an application of activity space and hybrid choice models in understanding the effects of built environment and personal goals [J]. Transportation,2021,48:505-536.

[27] Stern P C,Dietz T,Troy A,et al. A Value-Belief-Norm Theory of Support for Social Movements:The Case of Environmentalism[J]. Human Ecology Review,1999,6(2):81-97.

[28] Kaplowitz M D,Thorp L,Coleman K. et al. Energy conservation attitudes,knowledge,and behaviors in science laboratories[J]. Energy Policy,2012,50(11):581-591.

[29] Frick J, Kaiser F G, Wilson M. Environmental knowledge and conservation behavior: exploring prevalence and structure in a representative sample [J]. Personality and Individual Differences, 2004, 37(8): 1597-1613.

[30] Stern P C. New Environmental Theories: Toward a Coherent Theory of Environmentally Significant Behavior [J]. Social Issues, 2002, 56(3): 407-424.

[31] Gardner B. Modelling motivation and habit in stable travel mode contexts[J]. Transportation Research Part F: Traffic Psychology and Behaviour, 2009, 12(1): 68-76.

[32] 景鹏,隽志才,查奇芬. 考虑心理潜变量的出行方式选择行为模型[J]. 中国公路学报, 2014, 27(11): 84-92 + 108.

[33] 许冰,邵春福,钱剑培,等. 扩展计划行为理论框架下城际出行方式选择建模[J]. 交通工程, 2018, 18(03): 28-35.

[34] Chen C F, Chao W H. Habitual or reasoned? Using the theory of planned behavior, technology acceptance model, and habit to examine switching intentions toward public transit[J]. Transportation Research Part F: Traffic Psychology andBehaviour, 2011, 14(2): 128-137.

基于共享单车骑行数据的通勤识别研究

王建伟[1,2]　崔梦妍*[1,2]　付　鑫[1,2]　刘旭旭[1,2]

(1. 长安大学运输工程学院大数据管理与应用系;2. 长安大学道路基础设施数字化教育部工程中心)

摘　要　通勤群体作为城市交通出行最具规律性的群体,对其分析可以为城市交通规划与管理提供许多思路。因此,本文基于共享单车骑行的订单数据,对共享单车通勤的订单与用户进行识别。首先根据早晚高峰时段,一周出行天数指标初步筛选可能为通勤出行的订单数据;然后通过空间聚类筛选空间上具有规律性的订单数据;最终,根据类内到达时间差来确保时间上的规律性。经参数验证,发现共享单车空间聚类最优的簇内最小距离为 100m,即人们骑车前往同一个地点时,不同行程间的停车距离不会超过 100m。最终识别到的通勤订单占一周总订单的 22%,占早晚高峰时段订单的 40%。本文提出的基于共享单车订单数据的通勤识别研究,通过参数验证,提出了一个适合共享单车数据的空间聚类距离阈值。在以往通勤识别研究的基础上,考虑了将用户分为一周骑行不同天数的群体后再进行识别,研究结果更加符合实际通勤特征,可以为城市交通规划与管理者提供思路。

关键词　共享单车　通勤识别　空间聚类　通勤用户　指标筛选

0　引言

通勤出行占据着城市交通出行的一大部分,通过对通勤出行的分析,可以为城市交通规划与管理提供很多有效的信息。目前,已有很多学者对公共交通的通勤人群识别做了研究,这些研究也为公共交通的运营提供了很多思路。从研究思路来看,常常通过对时空规律性两个方面的分析,来进行通勤出行的识别。衡量时间规律性的常见指标有出行频次[4,12,14]、出发时间差或到达时间差[1,2,11,12]等。衡量空间规律性的方法分为指标筛选法和空间聚类法。常见的指标有 OD 点的到访频率、首次出行站点、停留时间最长的站点[4,11,12]等。空间聚类[1-8]则是通过 K-means 或 DBSCAN 聚类等,来确定空间上的规律性。从研究方法来看,可以分为聚类[1-8]、指标筛选[9-14]、神经网络[15]等方法。从研究结果来看,龙瀛[11]识别通勤用户以后,对通勤用户的职住地分布进行了分析,周亚楠[13]利用识别结果进行了通勤定制公交的探讨,李娜等[5]对通勤人群的出行时间分布,出行频率分布等进行了分析。

现有研究较多对公交和地铁的通勤人群进行

识别,在进行空间筛选时通常以刷卡站点为判断指标,阈值设点主观性较强。而共享单车作为近几年新型的公共交通,有着机动灵活,使用不受站点限制,接驳其他公共交通的特点。当对共享单车的通勤出行进行判断时,适用于公交地铁的一些参数设定不再适用,且大多数研究的参数设定为主观设定,并无理论依据。因此,本文基于西安市哈啰共享单车的骑行订单数据,提出一种集空间聚类与指标筛选的通勤识别方法,根据数据情况,适当的选取距离阈值,时间差阈值等参数,能够为后续相关研究提供一定的参考,为共享单车管理优化提供一定依据。

1 研究数据

1.1 数据描述及预处理

本研究以西安为研究对象。自2016年起,共享单车开始流行于中国的各个城市。截至2021年10月,西安目前在运营的共享单车包括哈啰,美团,青桔。2020年9月,哈啰在西安的日均使用人数达到了60万人。我们使用了西安2020年9月14日至9月20日期间的共享单车出行订单数据,数据来源于哈啰单车,运营主体为上海钧正网络科技有限公司。数据涵盖了约67万名用户,285万份订单。每条订单包含的字段有:车辆编号,用户ID,行程开始和结束时间,行程开始和结束经纬度,骑行时间,骑行距离。数据预处理包括以下步骤:

(1)缺失数据删除。由于数据丢失等原因,会有数据缺乏某个字段的情况出现,因此,将缺乏字段的行数进行删除。

(2)无效数据删除。由于车辆故障、车辆调度等原因,会出现一些骑行时间,骑行距离严重不符合常识的数据。故将骑行时间小于1min,骑行距离小于50m的数据进行剔除。

1.2 骑行数据分类

相关研究表明,早晚高峰时段出行和周骑行天数较多用户的出行,为通勤出行的可能性比较高[10],所以通过以下两个步骤来对骑行数据进行筛选和分类。第一步是通过计算一天24h的分时骑行订单分布,对早晚高峰的数据分别进行提取;第二步计算用户一周骑行天数,将用户分为14类,早晚高峰分别骑行了7d、6d、5d、4d、3d、2d、1d的用户。孙世超[10]的研究还表明,通勤人群与非通勤人群的一周刷卡天数差别较大,因此本文将数据按一周骑行天数分类后,再进行分析。

共享单车的分时出行量分布如图1所示,因此认为西安市共享单车通勤的高峰时段为6:00~10:00以及17:00~20:00。以此早晚高峰通勤时段为基础,统计每个用户ID在这一周中在早晚高峰时段分别骑行过的天数,将数据分为早晚高峰分别骑行了7d、6d、5d、4d、3d、2d、1d的用户数据。最终分类后的数据分布如图2所示。从图2可以看出,一周骑行1d的用户数量最多,应是骑行1d的用户中包含了很多不规律的偶然出行。然后随着天数的增加,骑行的用户数开始依次递减,但在5d时出现了一个很小的峰值,这与人们双休的工作规律是相符的。而一周骑行7d的用户数量则最少,如图1、图2所示。

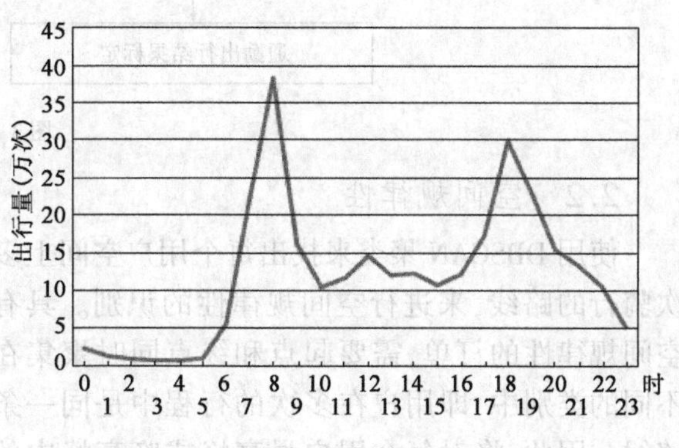

图1 分时出行量

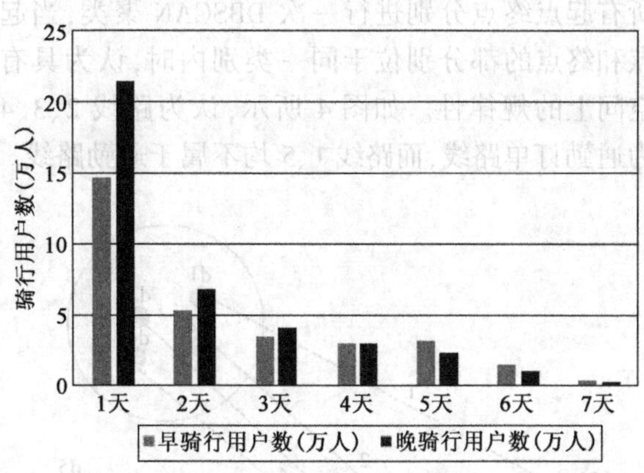

图2 骑行用户分类

2 骑行数据的通勤出行识别方法

2.1 研究思路

本文通过识别用户在时间和空间上都具有规律性的骑行订单来识别通勤出行。首先根据早晚高峰时段,一周出行天数指标初步筛选可能为通勤出行的订单数据;然后通过对乘客一周内早高峰或晚高峰的所有骑行订单起终点进行聚类,来识别起终点空间上聚集在一起的起点或终点;最后对同一类别内的订单再进行时间上的筛选,剔除出发时间点相差较大的订单,如图3所示。

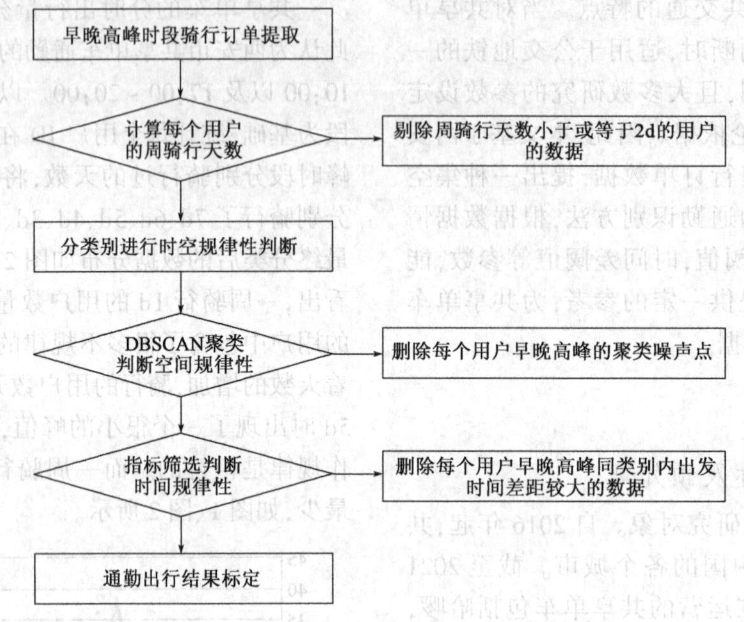

图3　技术路线图

2.2　空间规律性

使用DBSCAN聚类来找出每个用户空间上多次骑行的路线,来进行空间规律性的识别。具有空间规律性的订单,需要起点和终点同时聚集在不同的类别中,即用户在多次的行程中是同一条路线。因此,将对每个用户早高峰或晚高峰内的所有起点终点分别进行一次DBSCAN聚类,当起点和终点的都分别位于同一类别内时,认为具有空间上的规律性。如图4所示,认为路线2、3、4为通勤订单路线,而路线1、5均不属于通勤路线。

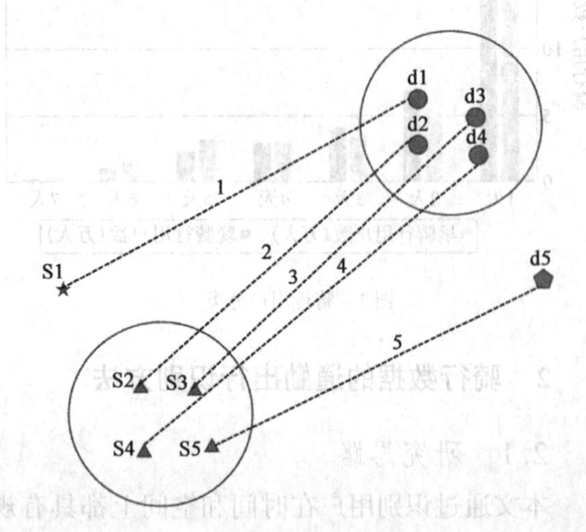

图4　起终点空间聚类示意图

DBSCAN聚类

在DBSCAN聚类方法应用的过程中,需要确定两个参数,簇内最大距离和簇内最小点数。簇内最大距离即该类别内点与点之间的最大距离,可以看作距离阈值;簇内最小点数即该类别内至少要包含的点的数量,可以看作出行频次。

出行频次指同一出行者在一周或一个月中出行的次数,距离阈值指同一出行者在一周或一个月中每天出行的起终点之间的距离。现有的有关通勤识别的研究大部分是使用公交刷卡数据,因此出行频次与距离阈值的设定也都是有关公交出行的。在出行频次的设定上,大多数研究者一般设置为2~4次/周[12-14];在距离阈值的设定上,李娜[11]的研究使用1000m作为距离阈值,龙瀛[5]使用500m作为距离阈值。

由于公交与共享单车公共交通的共性,其出行频次没有太大的区别,因此设置了早高峰或晚高峰到达3次以上;但考虑到公交和共享单车有出行距离的区别,所以本研究通过设置不同的簇内最大距离来寻找共享单车出行的最优距离阈值。由于共享单车起到的是最后一公里和接驳的作用,因此,将距离阈值设置为了500m以内,分别为500m、400m、300m、200m、100m、75m、50m这些值。

2.3 时间规律性

本研究将通过出发时间差来衡量时间上的规律性。但由于经过空间聚类以后,已经筛选出来了一批空间上具有规律性的行程,因此,时间差基于空间聚类的结果进行计算。本研究定义一个指标为类内到达时间极差,其具体的计算方式见表1。通过这样的计算可以确保聚类后的行程中不同天之间骑行的时间是相近的。

类内出发时间极差 表1

出发时间		类内到达时间极差
2020-9-14 6:49:31		
2020-9-15 6:50:27		
2020-9-16 6:49:32		
2020-9-17 6:52:53		57 - 40 = 17min
2020-9-18 6:53:06		
2020-9-19 6:40:35	最早出发的一天	
2020-9-20 6:57:50	最晚出发的一天	

3 参数验证

由于过去的研究关于识别共享单车通勤的较少,因此,在沿用既往方法时,参数的选取需要进行新的验证。因此本章节对 DBSCAN 的参数和类内到达时间极差的阈值进行验证,其中 DBSCAN 的参数指的是簇内最大距离。

3.1 DBSCAN 参数验证

首先是对 DBSCAN 的参数,簇内最大距离的验证。由于共享单车的作用是最后一公里和接驳,因此,将距离阈值在 500m 之内进行验证。每隔 100m,设置一个值,100m 之内,又每隔 25m 设置一个值。不同簇内最大距离下的识别结果如图5所示。其中横坐标表示的是不同的簇内最大距离,纵坐标表示的是在该簇内最大距离下,最终识别到的具有空间规律性的出行占该类别出行的比例。每一条折线代表一个类别的用户,分别是在早高峰骑行 7d、6d、5d、4d、3d 的用户,由于这里设置了簇内最少点数为 3,因此,对骑行 2d 和 1d 的用户类别不再进行聚类。

从图 5 可以看出,在同一个聚类距离下,随着骑行天数的减少,识别的通勤出行比例逐渐下降;在同一个骑行天数下,随着聚类距离的减小,识别的通勤比例也逐渐下降。并且骑行天数越多,距离减小对识别到的通勤比例的影响越小,即识别到的通勤比例下降的幅度越小。一周骑行 5d、6d、7d 的用户出行中,无论聚类距离是多少,识别到的通勤出行的比例基本都可以达到 80%,且聚类距离对其识别结果的影响并不大;而骑行 4d 和骑行 3d 的出行识别通勤比例则大大下降,且聚类距离对其识别结果的影响较大。

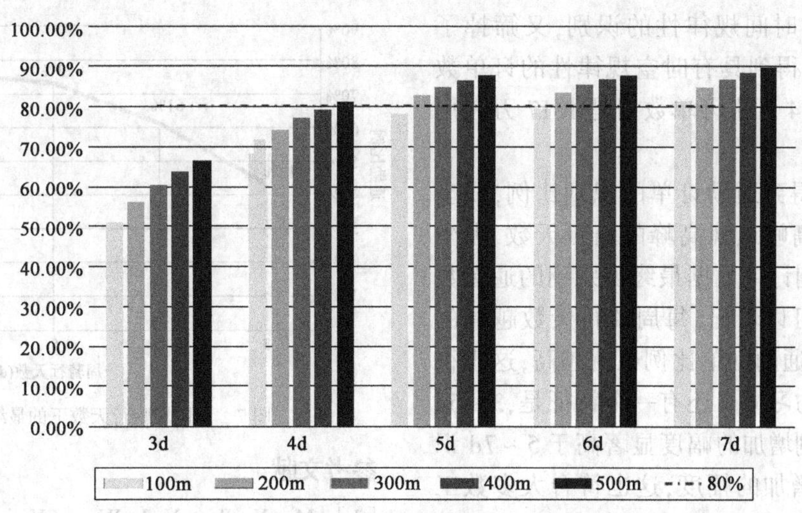

图5 早高峰不同聚类距离下识别比例的变化

借鉴判断轮廓系数的肘部法则对不同聚类距离下的识别比例结果进行分析,可以看出当距离由 100m 再减小过程中,识别比例下降幅度大于由 500m 变为 100m 的过程。因此本研究选取 100m 的 DBSCAN 聚类后的通勤标定结果作为最终的通勤标定结果。即认为大多数通勤者去往同一个地点的话,其不同行程停下共享单车的距离不会超过 100m。

3.2　类内到达时间极差

接下来是对类内到达时间极差的阈值的分析。通过计算可以发现80%的类内到达时间极差小于60min,具体类内到达时间极差的分布如图6左边箱线图所示。因此本研究将类内到达时间极差的阈值设为60min,剔除之后的类内到达时间极差的分布如图6右边箱线图所示。在将异常值剔除之后,可以保证所有极差位于1h以内,且75%的极差位于20min以内。

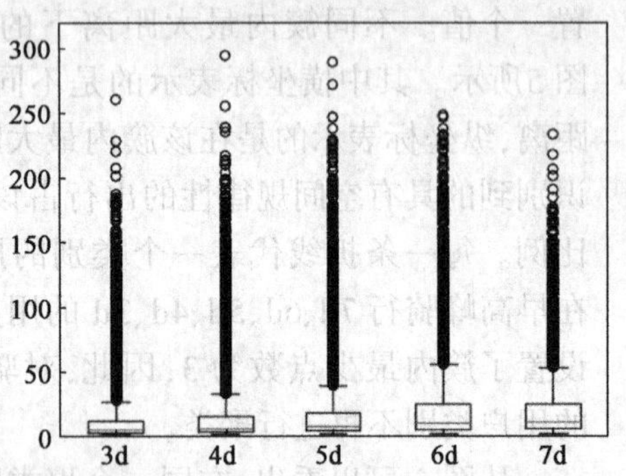

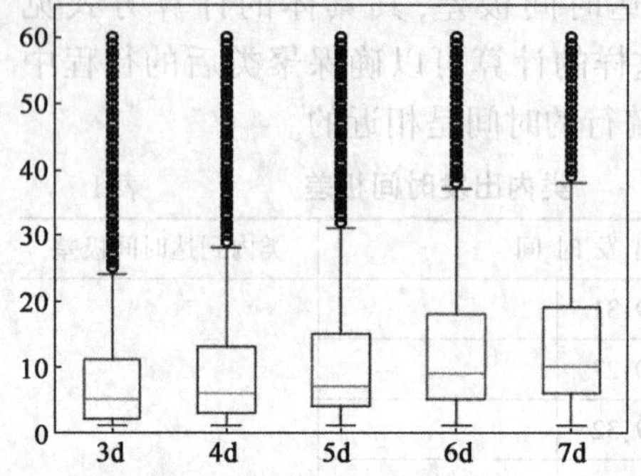

图6　剔除前后数据的类内到达时间极差

4　结果分析

本研究对2020年9月14日到20日这一时间段的67万名用户的285万份订单数据进行分析。首先对早晚高峰时段的订单进行了提取,提取出了161万份订单数据;然后对早晚高峰时段订单中每个用户的骑行天数进行了计算,去除了一周中只骑行1d和2d的用户,筛选得到了115万份订单数据;接下来对空间规律性进行识别,通过起终点的聚类得到空间上具有规律性的订单共81万份;最后通过对时间规律性的识别,又筛掉了20%的数据,最终得到具有时空规律性的订单数据共64万份,这64万份订单数据是由17万名用户产生的。

图7是最终得到通勤订单的识别比例,横坐标表示的是在早高峰或晚高峰的骑行天数,纵坐标表示的是该类别订单数据最终识别到的通勤数据所占的比例。可以看出,每周骑行天数越高的类别,其识别到的通勤订单比例也就越高,这也符合城市人口通勤的习惯。还有一个特征是,3~5d识别到的通勤比例增加的幅度显著高于5~7d识别到的通勤比例增加的幅度,这也符合大多数工作人员双休的工作习惯,同时也反映出目前的很多工作类型还不能为人们提供双休的福利。

5　结语

本文通过早晚高峰时段、一周骑行天数、时间规律性、空间规律性4个步骤对通勤订单进行筛选和识别,综合运用空间聚类和指标筛选的思路,以DBSCAN算法为基础算法,类内出发时间极差进行指标二次筛选。基于西安市的哈啰共享单车9月某一周的数据,最终识别到了22%的具有时空规律性的订单。从一周骑行天数进行细分的话,一周骑行5~7d的用户订单中,识别到规律性的比例更高。本文识别过程与结果的分析都较为细致,考虑了对一周骑行天数不同的用户群体进行分类分析,能识别出对共享单车通勤依赖度不同的用户,更符合人们的出行习惯。

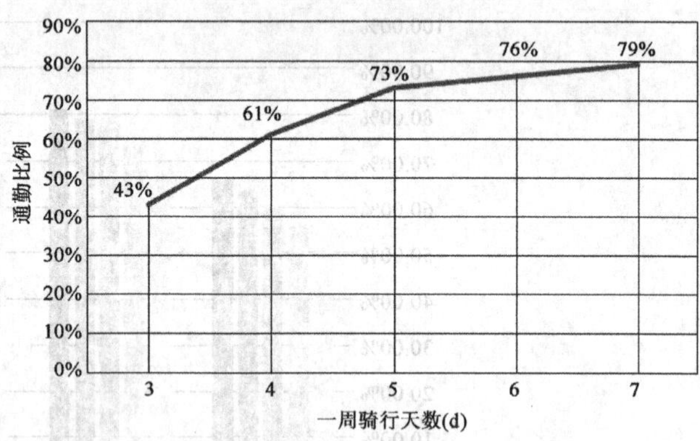

图7　不同周骑行天数下的最终识别比例

参考文献

[1] Ma X, Wu Y J, Wang Y, et al. Mining smart card data for transit riders' travel patterns[J]. Transportation Research, 2013, 36C(nov.): 1-12.

[2] Ma X, Liu C, Wen H, et al. Understanding commuting patterns using transit smart card

data[J]. Journal of Transport Geography, 2017, 58(JAN.): 135-145.

[3] 孙世超,杨东援. 基于朴素贝叶斯分类器的公交通勤人群辨识方法[J]. 交通运输系统工程与信息,2015,15(6):46-53.

[4] 周航,陈学武. 集时空聚类和指标筛选的公共交通通勤者识别[J/OL]. 交通运输工程与信息学报,2021,1(11):115-126.

[5] 李娜,严海,曹佳,等. 基于公交IC卡数据的跨区通勤出行者识别研究[J]. 交通世界,2021(1):4.

[6] Jya D, Lza C, Xm B, et al. Mining metro commuting mobility patterns using massive smart card data [J]. Physica A: Statistical Mechanics and its Applications, 2021, 584: 116-132.

[7] Kieu L M, Bhaskar A, Chung E . A modified Density-Based Scanning Algorithm with Noise for spatial travel pattern analysis from Smart Card AFC data [J]. Transportation Research Part C: Emerging Technologies, 2015, 58: 193-207.

[8] Langlois G G, Koutsopoulos H N, Zhao J. Inferring patterns in the multi-week activity sequences of public transport users [J]. Transportation Research Part C, 2016, 64 (Mar.): 1-16.

[9] Hadachi A, Pourmoradnasseri M, Khoshkhah K. Unveiling large-scale commuting patterns based on mobile phone cellular network data [J]. Journal of Transport Geography, 2020, 89: 102-118.

[10] 孙世超,杨东援. 基于朴素贝叶斯分类器的公交通勤人群辨识方法[J]. 交通运输系统工程与信息,2015,15(6):46-53.

[11] 龙瀛,张宇,崔承印. 利用公交刷卡数据分析北京职住关系和通勤出行[J]. 地理学报,2012,67(10):1339-1352.

[12] 李军,邓红平. 基于公交IC卡数据的乘客出行分类研究[J]. 重庆交通大学学报(自然科学版),2016,35(6):109-114.

[13] 周亚楠. 基于一卡通数据分析的通勤性定制公交线路规划[D]. 吉林:吉林大学,2003.

[14] 陈君,杨东援. 基于APTS数据的公交卡乘客通勤OD分布估计方法[J]. 交通运输系统工程与信息,2013,013(004):47-53.

[15] 梁泉,翁剑成,林鹏飞,等. 基于个体出行图谱的公共交通通勤行为辨别方法研究[J]. 交通运输系统工程与信息,2018,18(2).

基于地铁导向标识系统的乘客信息需求分析
——以西安地铁小寨站为例 *

陈　龙[1*]　彭　辉[1]　田　凯[1]　王曲顺[1]　韩紫鹃[1]

(长安大学)

摘　要　随着经济的发展,越来越多的中国城市修建了地铁,而地铁站是我们乘坐地铁的重要场所,地铁站的导向标识系统提供给我们重要的地铁站内信息,是地铁站的重要组成部分。本文以西安地铁小寨站为例,通过对地铁站内的乘客及导向标识系统进行调查,分析了地铁站乘客的信息需求及导向标识系统现状。结果表示导向标识系统的设计需要考虑到不同行为方式的乘客,同时小寨地铁站导向标识系统存在设置多且乱、连贯性不够和内容表达不准确的问题。

关键词　西安地铁　地铁小寨站　导向标识　信息需求

1. 基金项目:国家自然科学基金面上项目(52072044)。

0　引言

随着经济的发展,地铁或者轨道交通系统被越来越多的城市所选择,地铁也慢慢成了这些城市新的“名片”。而在这张“名片”中,地铁站的导向标识系统已经成为这张“名片”中不可或缺的组成部分。一个地铁站的导向标识系统在给予乘客地铁站信息的同时,可节省乘客在站厅和站台的时间,提高车站通行效率和人们生活的便利性[1,2]。

西安小寨地铁站是西安地铁 2 号线和 3 号线的换乘站,同时小寨站 500m 内有着赛格购物中心、金沙国际和华旗国际等商业广场,这都使小寨地铁站成为西安地铁线网客流量最大的车站[3]。随着客流的增加,小寨地铁站拥堵现象愈加明显,这时小寨站地铁导向标识系统所提供的乘客需求信息直接影响站内乘客的出行效率[4,5]。

由此,本文通过对小寨站导向标识系统进行调研,并对小寨地铁站空间及导向标识系统进行分析,来研究地铁站乘客的信息需求。为优化地铁站内部空间导向流线设计、缓解地铁站行人拥挤和提高地下空间的通行效率等提供支撑。

1　小寨地铁站导向标识调查

1.1　调查目的

通过实地与网络调查了解小寨车站内外的空间环境;对地铁小寨站导向标识现状调研结果进行数据统计分析,将实地调研与问卷调查相结合,从心理认知角度对小寨站地铁导向标志设计可行性进行评价,并分析小寨站乘客信息需求。

1.2　调查对象及时间安排

在 2021 年 9 月 12 日至 13 日期间,通过网络及实地勘察对小寨站外部环境、内部结构和导向标识等进行实地调;在 2021 年 9 月 14 日至 18 日期间,通过线上和线下问卷形式对小寨站导向标识认知情况进行调查。

1.3　调查样本容量的确定

由于小寨地铁站进出站客流较大,所以本次采用简单随机抽样的方法抽取样本,由相关数理统计和误差理论得到样本容量公式和抽样率公式如下:

$$n=\frac{(u_{a}S/d)^{2}}{1+(u_{a}S/d)^{2}/N} \tag{1}$$

$$f=\frac{n}{N}=\frac{(u_{a}S)^{2}}{d^{2}N+(u_{a}S)^{2}} \tag{2}$$

式中:n——样本容量;

f——抽样率;

S——标准差,一般取 1.1;

d——随机变量在 $1-\alpha$ 的置信水平下的绝对误差限;

N——地铁站日均进出站客流量。

根据西安地铁公司统计数据,小寨地铁站日均进出站客流在 17 万人次左右,所以 N 为 17 万人次/每日,在绝对误差 3% 和 85% 的置信水平时 $u_{a}=1.04$, $n=246.84$, $f=0.1452\%$。所以至少收取 247 份有效问卷,才能满足抽样误差在 3% 以下,置信水平为 85% 的要求。同时考虑 n 过小时样本对总体的代表性降低和会产生无效问卷,所以发放的问卷应适当增加。最终决定发放问卷 300 份左右。

1.4　调查方案

1.4.1　空间布局调查

在预定调查日期内,通过线上和线下对小寨站内外环境进行了调查实地测量。包括了小寨地铁站站厅层、站台层、扶楼梯、基础设施设备的容量等。

1.4.2　乘客问卷调查

选取西安地铁小寨站,对乘客情况、小寨站导向标识数量与位置、连续性、内容设计以及总体评价 5 个方面进行问卷设计,由乘客做出评测。拟在小寨站口及车站内部附近发放问卷 200 份,如图1 所示,另利用 Credamo 平台制作网络调查问卷 100 份,如图 2 所示。

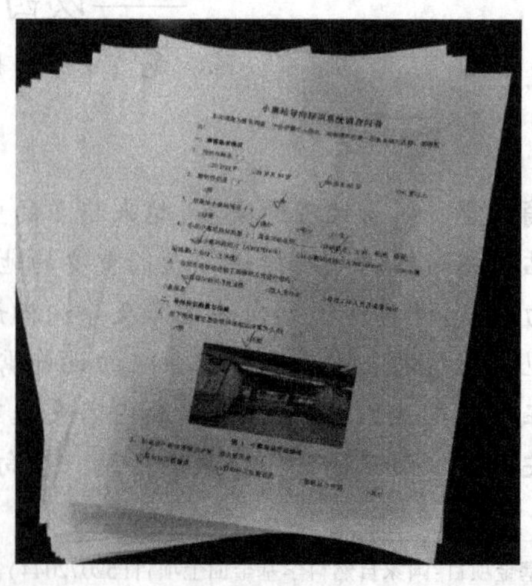

图1　调查问卷图片

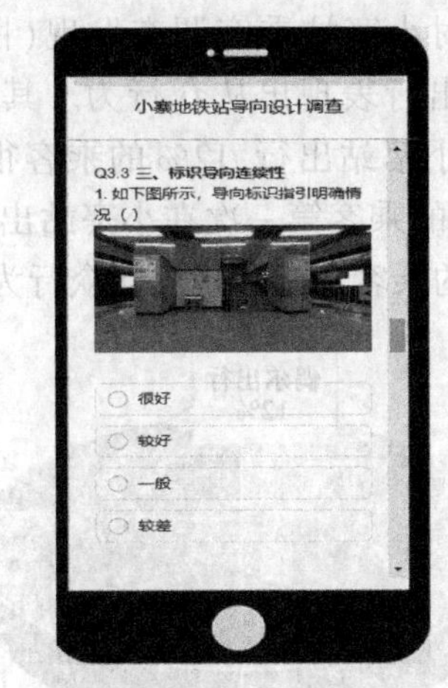

图 2 网络调查问卷图片

1.5 问卷的发放与回收

本次调查预计发放问卷 300 份，共回收问卷 289 份，其中有效问卷 260 份。

2 乘客信息需求分析

2.1 小寨站乘客特征

本次调查发放问卷 300 份，共回收有效问卷 260 份，有效的样本分布情况见表 1。

2.1.1 乘客基本属性

乘客年龄、性别和携带行李情况见表 1，参与者群体的主要是 20～40 岁，性别以女性乘客居多，同时大多数旅客都携带了行李。对于儿童、老年人和携带行李箱的旅客，他们步行速度相对较慢，在车站乘车及换乘难度较大，导向标识的导向性需求较高。

小寨站乘客性别与年龄情况　　表 1

项目	选　项	选择人数(人)	占比(%)
年龄	20 岁以下	39	15
	20～40 岁	169	65
	40～60	52	20
	60 岁以上	13	5
性别	男	112	43
	女	148	57
携带行李	无行李	89	34
	携带背包(手提包)	117	45
	携带行李箱	54	21

2.1.2 出行目的

小寨站乘客的调问卷查数据显示(图 3)，小寨地铁站是以购物、娱乐、换乘、上班客流为主。出行的目的比较多样性，反映出目前小寨站是一个比较综合性的换乘站，不同类型的人流对换乘的要求也不同，行走速度和路径的选择也不同，不同目的的乘客也会提出不同的需求。

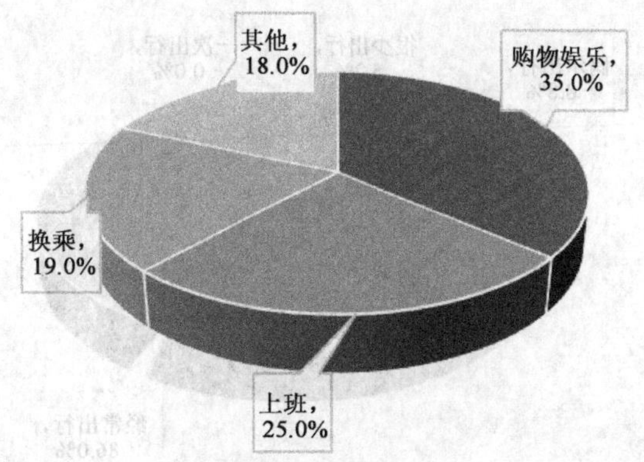

图 3 小寨站出行目的比例

2.2 乘客活动方式分析

小寨站乘客乘坐情况见表 2，在乘坐小寨站情况总体构成上，调查到许多乘客都是本地乘客，频率为"经常"的乘客最多占比 49%，但同时"第一次到小寨站"的乘客也很多占 23%，然后是"偶尔出行"占比 16%，"很少出行"占比 13%。

小寨站乘客乘坐情况　　表 2

项目	选　项	选择人数(人)	占比(%)
乘坐小寨站情况	经常	127	49
	偶尔	42	16
	很少	34	13
	第一次	60	23
在小寨站出行一般借助	利用标志引导寻找道路	141	54
	跟随人流行走	31	12
	询问工作人员或乘客	25	10
	直接走	63	24

2.2.1 自主行为

自主行为是乘客在地铁站内时，因为对车站比较熟悉而直接知道要走行的路径的行为方式[3]。对小寨站乘客调查发现，有 24% 的乘客站内出行表现出自主行为。其中，86% 的乘客经常在小寨站出行。5.2% 的乘客很少在小寨站出行，8.8% 的乘客偶尔在小寨站出行，第一次在小寨站出行的乘客均未表现出自主行为。

调查结果说明(图 4)，表现出自主行为的乘客通常是经常在该站出行的乘客，他们非常了解车站的空间布局与功能分区，站内出行时通常依靠累积的出行经验和思维模式。在出行过程中,这类乘客目的明确、方向准确、行动快捷,对标识的需求性不高,仅关注动态标识信息或根据标识确认自己行为是否准确。

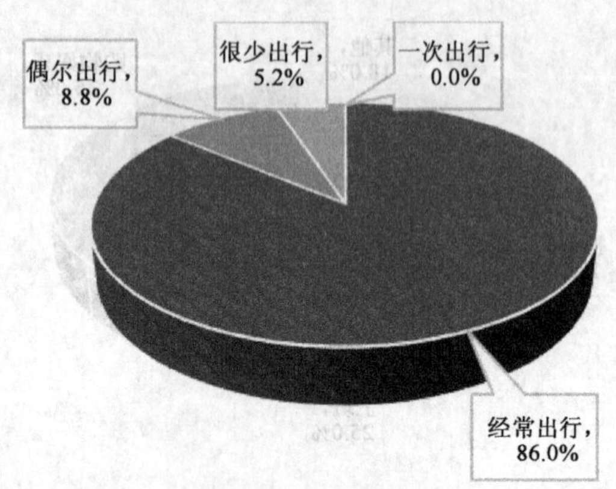

图 4　自主行为乘客组成

2.2.2　依赖行为

依赖行为是乘客在车站出行时由于对于地铁站不太熟悉,需要借助导向标识行进的行为方式[3]。对小寨站乘客调查发现(图 5),有 54% 的乘客站内出行表现出依赖行为。其中,18% 的乘客偶尔在小寨站出行,42% 的乘客经常在小寨站出行,15% 的乘客很少在小寨站出行,23% 的乘客第一次在小寨站出行。

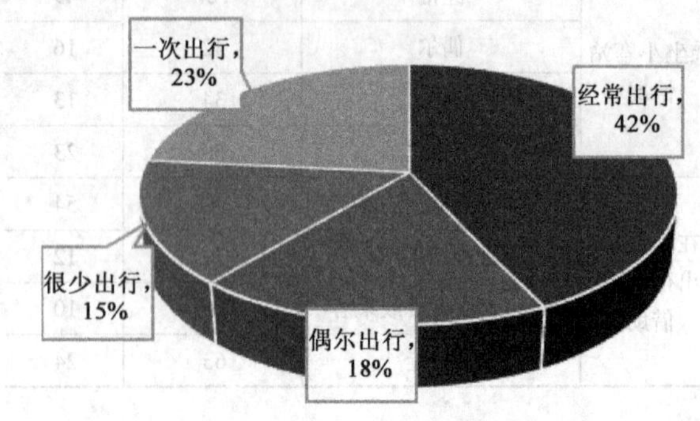

图 5　依赖行为乘客组成

根据对小寨站乘客调查,无论经常出行、偶尔出行、很少出行,还是第一次到小寨站的乘客,这些乘客都有相当大一部分表现出依赖行为。这类行为的乘客往往对车站环境不够熟悉,在车站中活动需要通过标识获取自己所需的出行信息,甚至需要结合询问确认获取信息及自己行为的准确性,方可完成出行。

2.2.3　从众行为

从众行为是乘客在地铁车站出行时,由于对车站很不熟悉,直接随人流行进或咨询别人的行为方式[3]。对小寨站乘客调查发现(图 6),22% 的乘客站内出行表现出从众行为。其中,12% 的乘客偶尔在小寨站出行,12% 的乘客很少在小寨站出行,26% 的乘客第一次在小寨站出行,经常在小寨站出行的乘客均为表现出从众行为。

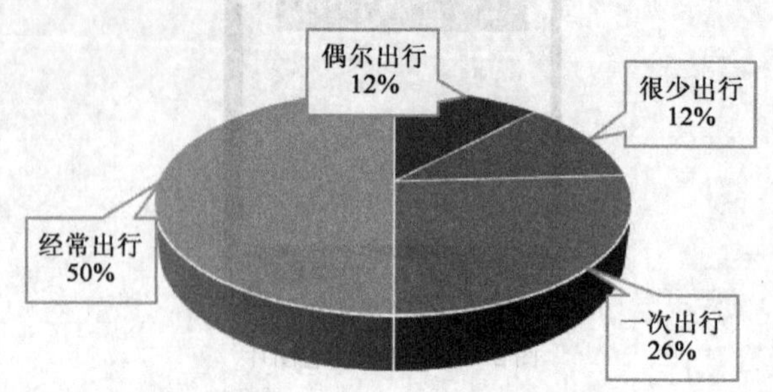

图 6　从众行为乘客组成

根据对小寨站乘客调查,到小寨站频率越低的乘客表现出从众行为的乘客越多。这类乘客通常也是对车站环境不了解的乘客。他们不通过标识获取信息判断行走方向,而是直接随人流行走,在出站客流中该行为表现最明显。当车站人流量较低时,这类乘客只能被迫依靠标识或通过询问帮助自己完成出行。

2.3　导向标识认知分析

乘客对于小寨站导向标识总体上比较满意,平均满意度达 90 分以上(满分 100 分),但针对问卷调查结果分析,乘客对于小寨站导向标识的认知总体上有以下的问题。

2.3.1　导向标识设置多且乱

小寨站使用了大量标识,其中临时标识又占很大的一部分,这使小寨站站内的导向标识系统与小寨站内空间环境明显不协调。站厅层通向 2 号线站台层的楼梯入口处如图 7 所示,是小寨站重要的乘车通道之一。

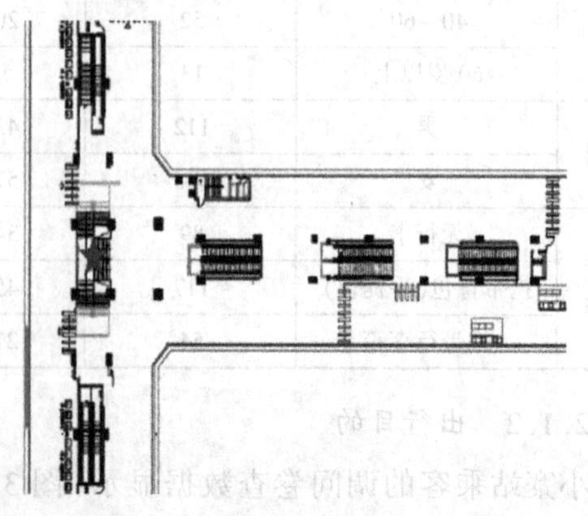

图 7　小寨站站厅层楼梯位置平面图

调查结果显示(图8),小寨站大部分乘客进站后看到导向标识后不能快速做出决策,这时候会乘客会驻足停下来观看每一块不同的导向标识信息并思考接下来的行动路径,这就导致了行进速度变慢,乘车或换乘的效率变低。

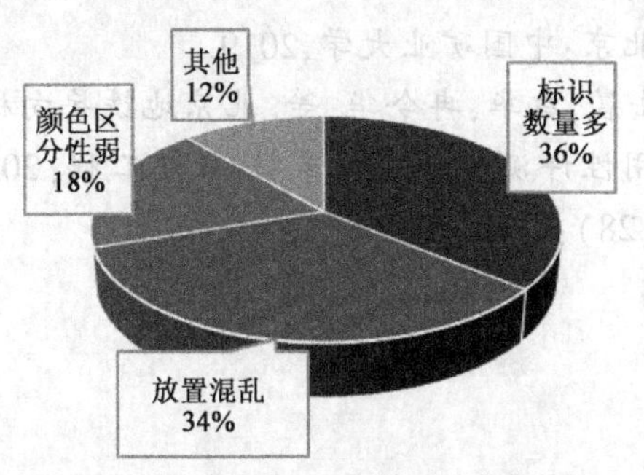

图8 不能快速做出决策的原因数据饼状图

2.3.2 标识连贯性不够

在导向标识连续性调查中,2号线站台层连接楼梯的出口处如图9所示。在问卷调查中有89.2%的人选择增加贴地式导向标识更好,7%的人认为此方案一般,其余人则认可现在的导向标识,如图10所示。

图9 小寨站2号线站台层楼梯出口处位置平面图

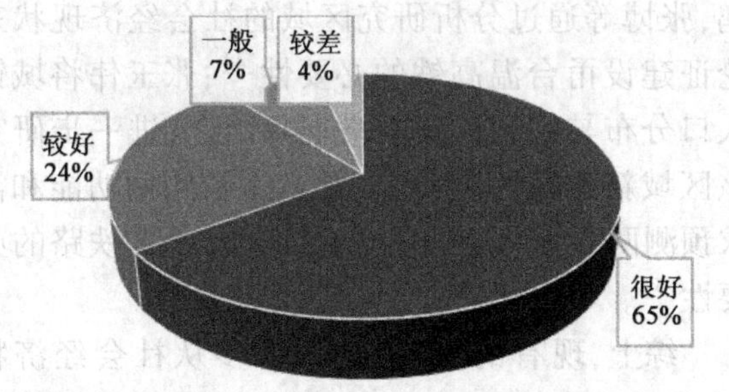

图10 小寨站2号线楼梯口处优化调查数据饼状图

调查结果显示在小寨站导向标识系统中部分导向标识并不连续,当对小寨站不熟悉的乘客经过这些地方时,需要花费一些时间来寻找路径,但是在早晚高峰或者客流量较大的时间段中,一部分人需要时间作决策,而另一部分人不需要,就会加剧客流拥挤。

2.3.3 标识内容设计需改进

导向标识的内容设计应与现实活动相匹配,针对导向标识内容设计问卷调查。例如,问卷调查所在位置是站厅层如图11所示,由于正前方有立柱障碍物,因此要乘坐2号线的乘客需拐弯才能到达进入2号线的楼梯口。

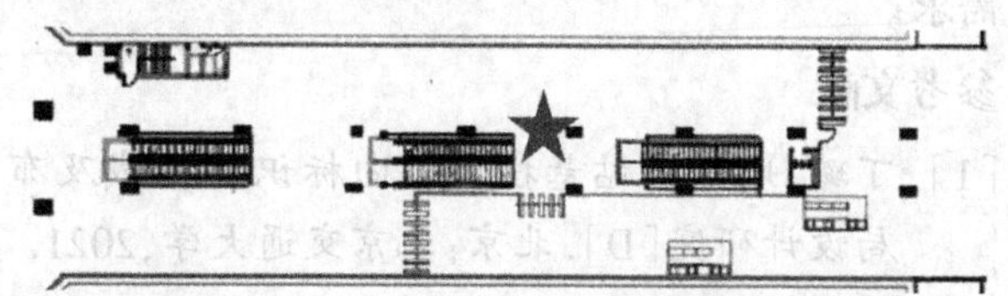

图11 小寨站站厅层“乘坐2号线”导向标识位置平面图

调查数据显示(图12),大部分乘客在此地方虽然不用花费过多时间来思考寻找径路,但是仍有很多人认为折叠状箭头能更好地发挥导向作用。

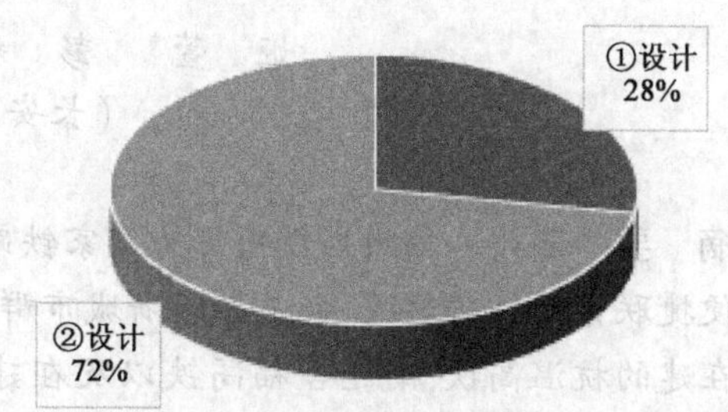

图12 “乘坐2号线”导向标识优化前后对比调查数据饼状图

3 结语

本研究通过对西安地铁小寨站导向标识系统进行线上和线下调查,从小寨地铁站乘客特征、乘客活动方式和地铁站导向标识认知三方面对乘客信息需求进行了分析。研究结果表明:

(1)对于目的性明确、行动迅速、熟悉路径的旅客,引导标志的信息内容应具有较高的针对性,其布局应相对容易识别,以便有效识别引导标志,使旅客快速获取信息;对于不了解车站环境,表现出依赖和从众行的旅客,引导标志需要高度系统性、完备性和连续性,以减少旅客出行过程中的决策和停留时间。

(2)小寨地铁站现有的导向标识系统仍有不能满足乘客需求信息的地方,比如导向标识设置多且乱、标识连贯性不够和一些标识内容设计需改进。

研究结果可为优化地铁站内部空间导向流线设计提供支持,从而提高地下空间的通行效率和缓解地铁站行人拥挤。本文主要通过问卷调查法对地铁站导向标识系统和乘客信息需求进行分析,存在一定局限性,未来可引入轨道交通AFC数据或者应用眼动仪等更先进设备进行数据调查,形成地铁站行人大数据集,提高研究结论可靠性,深入研究乘客对于地铁导向标识系统的信息需求。

参考文献

[1] 丁璐.地铁车站悬挂式导向标识可视域及布局设计研究[D].北京:北京交通大学,2021.

[2] 高瑜甜.地铁文化标识系统对城市文化传播的作用[J].新闻研究导刊,2021,12(14):51-53.

[3] 韩玉琦.基于乘客行为和信息需求的地铁导向标识系统优化[D].西安:长安大学,2019.

[4] 周颖川.地铁站地下空间导向设计研究[D].北京:中国矿业大学,2019.

[5] 岳晨,秦华,冉令华,等.北京地铁导向标志可用性评测[J].科学技术与工程,2020,20(28):11761-11766.

沿海高铁(温州—福州段)建设必要性研究

——基于旅客特征与出行意愿分析*

姬 萱* 彭 辉 韩紫鹏 田 凯 陈 龙

(长安大学运输工程学院)

摘 要 温州—福州高铁项目为国家铁路网规划“八纵八横”中沿海高铁主通道组成部分,是浙闽两省便捷联系的铁路通道,也是粤闽浙城市群连接珠三角城市群、长三角城市群的重要纽带。温福高铁北接在建的杭温高铁,南连合福高铁以及在建的福厦高铁。本文通过分析沿线旅客出行特征及出行意愿,具体为分析沿线旅客出行基本特征、社会经济特性、出行方式选择意愿和疫情出行等特征,来进行新建温州—福州高铁的必要性分析。

关键词 温州—福州高铁 建设必要性 出行特征 选择意愿

0 引言

本路线起于温州枢纽,基本沿既有温福铁路通道,经浙江省瑞安、平阳、苍南,福建省福鼎、宁德至福州枢纽,整条高铁辐射粤闽浙城市群城市,覆盖浙江和福建的11个县市区,线路全长约313.8km。

目前的研究和文献中鲜有论述沿海高铁温州—福州段的建设必要性,廖怡从宏观角度、通道运输需求和其他交通方式的可替代性等方面分析了沿江铁路建设的必要性[1];任峥峥通过研究沿江铁路通道的发展现状、现存问题、运输需求,以及拟建项目的功能定位,分析沿江铁路规划建设的必要性[2];江佳璐通过论述该通道对国家战略的支撑作用,并结合运输需求预测分析了兰州—汉中—十堰高铁建设的必要性[3];李志鹏,张博等通过分析研究区域的社会经济现状来论证建设甬台温高铁的必要性[4];张玉伟将城镇人口分布与区域铁路网络现状结合,进一步研究该区域新建高铁走向[5];常占奎从路网功能和需求预测两方面入手,论述了新建温武吉铁路的必要性[6]。

综上,现有的研究中,学者多从社会经济特征、运输网络结构、路网的功能定位、通道运输需求预测等方面来分析铁路建设必要性,而本文通过对线路沿线区域旅客出行特性及出行选择意愿进行分析,来研究温福客专的必要性。

1.基金项目:基于空间活动理论的城市群城际轨道交通客流预测模型及方法,国家自然科学基金(项目资助号:52072044)。

1 区域旅客出行特征调查

1.1 调查时间

调查工作自2021年3月10日自温州市,途径瑞安县、宁德市等16县市于3月25日结束,历时15天。

1.2 调查内容

1.2.1 样本容量的确定

由于温州—福州影响区域内交通流动性及流量较大,所以在进行样本抽样时采用简单随机抽样的方法,由有关数理统计和误差理论可知:

$$n=\frac{(u_aS/d)^2}{1+(u_aS/d)^2/N} \quad (1)$$

式中:n——样本容量;

S——标准差,一般取1.10;

d——随机变量在$1-\alpha$的置信水平下的绝对误差限;

N——运输通道的总客流量。

由此可确定抽样率为:

$$f=\frac{n}{N}=\frac{(u_aS)^2}{d^2N+(u_aS)^2} \quad (2)$$

由历年统计资料,温州—福州交通走廊的旅客对外出行流量日均为120万人次左右,因此在绝对误差3%和85%的置信水平时$U_\alpha=1.04$,抽样率为:

$$f=0.12103\%$$

相应地,$n=1453$,即至少取1453份,才能满足抽样误差不超过3%,置信水平为85%的要求。

考虑到n过大,会使调查费用显著增加;n过小,又会使样本对总体的代表性降低,增大抽样误差。另外,又由于此条城际线路较长,影响范围较广,涉及区域较大,因此,根据经验和调查经费预算,最终确定$n=1150$。

1.2.2 具体内容

本次调查主要包括旅客基本信息和旅行基本情况两部分:

(1)旅客基本信息:旅客职业、旅行目的、旅费来源、月均收入等。

(2)旅行基本情况:旅客起讫点、乘降车站、乘坐等级、车次号、车类型及型号、旅程票价、乘降区间运行时间、进出乘车点的时间及费用、时间、疫情出行情况等。

1.3 调查地点

本次交通调查选择沿线较为重要的汽车站、火车站和机场进行,对13个铁路客运站点、20个汽车客运站点、2个机场进行旅客出行意愿调查。客运站旅客出行意愿调查点(问卷)一览表见表1。

客运站旅客出行意愿调查点(问卷)一览表

表1

编号	节点名称	调查地点(公路客运站)	问卷数/份	调查地点(铁路客运站、机场)	问卷数/份
1	温州市辖区	温州牛山客运站	20	温州南站	70
		温州汽车南站	20	温州站	60
		—	—	温州龙湾机场	100
2	瑞安	瑞安市客运中心站	20	瑞安站	40
3	文成	文成车站	20	—	—
4	平阳	平阳鳌江客运中心	20	平阳站	40
5	龙港	龙港车站	20	—	—
6	苍南	苍南汽车站	20	苍南站	40
7	泰顺	泰顺客运北站	20	—	—
8	寿宁	寿宁汽车站	20	—	—
9	福鼎	福鼎汽车北站	20	福鼎站	40
		福鼎汽车南站	20		
10	柘荣	柘荣汽车站	20	—	—
11	福安	福安汽车站	20	福安站	40
12	霞浦	福宁长途汽车站	20	霞浦站	30
13	宁德市辖区	宁德客运枢纽站	20	宁德站	40
		宁德汽车南站	20		

续上表

编号	节点名称	调查地点(公路客运站)	问卷数/份	调查地点(铁路客运站、机场)	问卷数/份
14	罗源	罗源汽车站	20	罗源站	40
15	连江	连江汽车站	20	连江站	40
16	福州	福州汽车南站	20	福州南站	70
		福州汽车北站	20	福州站	50
		—	—	福州长乐机场	100

1.4　调查方式

具体的调查,采取电子问卷(图1)快速录入结合纸质问卷填写后录入的方式。

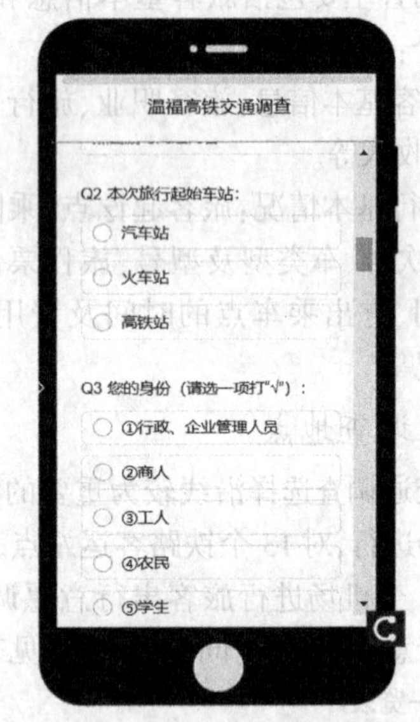

图1　电子问卷

(1)在调查地点(公路客运站、铁路客运站)向旅客分发出行意愿调查问卷(电子及纸质),由旅客本人填写完毕后收回,发放700份。

(2)通过调查员询问出行者,由调查员填写问卷相关内容,发放450份。

1.5　问卷的发放、回收与处理

1.5.1　问卷的发放与回收

本次调查共发放问卷1150份,回收有效问卷约1110份(收回率约为97.3%),见表2。

旅客出行意愿调查问卷统计　　表2

类　别	实地调查			合计
	汽车站	火车站	机场	
计划调查旅客	400	550	200	1150
实际调查旅客	392	532	195	1119

1.5.2　数据处理、扩样与校核

数据分为调查原始数据、直接扩样数据、校核扩样数据三个层面。

(1)数据处理。在编码和录入后,修正异常的编码,并将无法统计的数据剔除,得到原始数据。

(2)直接扩样。以调查区域内铁路、公路客运站为调查基点,按照确定的的抽样率,使被调查样本能够与总体一致,保证调查数据的准确性和真实性。

(3)校核扩样。根据实际调查结果和交通运营数据,对旅客出行调查相关指标进行修正,从而客观、真实的反映项目影响区交通需求状况和发展趋势。

2　调查数据分析

2.1　出行者的社会经济特性

2.1.1　旅客职业分布

旅客职业反映了旅客的经济水平,而经济水平很大程度上影响了旅客的出行方式选择。

此次调研根据统计资料和劳动人事部门对职业的分类规范,根据道路沿线区域的实际情况,将出行者的职业分类为七类,扩样后受访者的职业结构如图2所示,不同交通方式出行者职业调查统计图如图3所示。

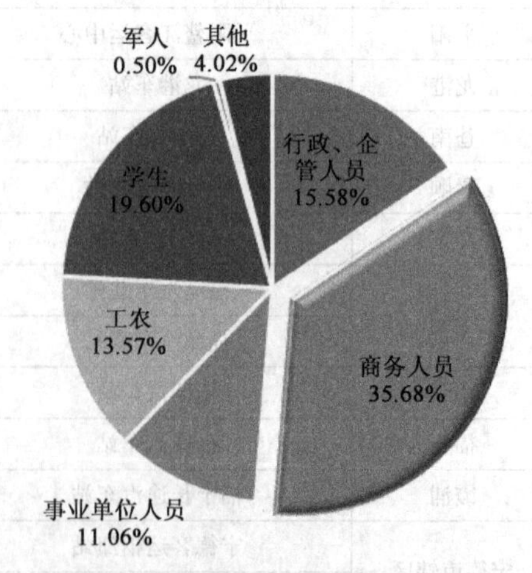

图2　旅客职业结构

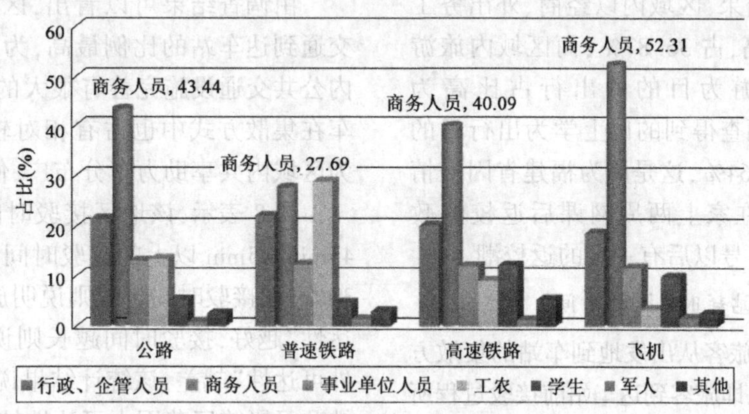

图3　不同交通方式出行者职业调查统计图

旅客职业构成商务人员所占比例最多，为35.68%。而经商者，个体户等占比多，区域经济发展将变得活跃且迅速，符合项目区域内的整体发展趋势。

区域内出行的交通方式主要为公路及高速铁路。从商务人员的视角分析，出行中公路交通中占比43.44%，而高速铁路占比则为40.09%，一定程度上可以映射出区域内旅客出行选择高铁和公路的意愿较强，这与区域内交通路网发达及设施完善程度高有关，也说明了经商者的出行更注重方便、快捷、速度等因素。

2.1.2　旅客收入情况

出行者的收入水平是影响出行者选择交通方式的重要因素。在问卷调查之前，首先对收入范围进行划分定义：5000以下为低收入，5000以上为较高收入。以此为基础对旅客收入水平进行统计分析，如图4、图5所示。

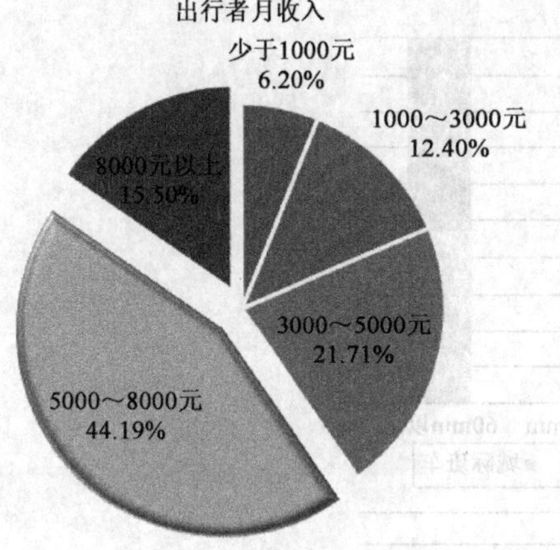

图4　出行者月收入

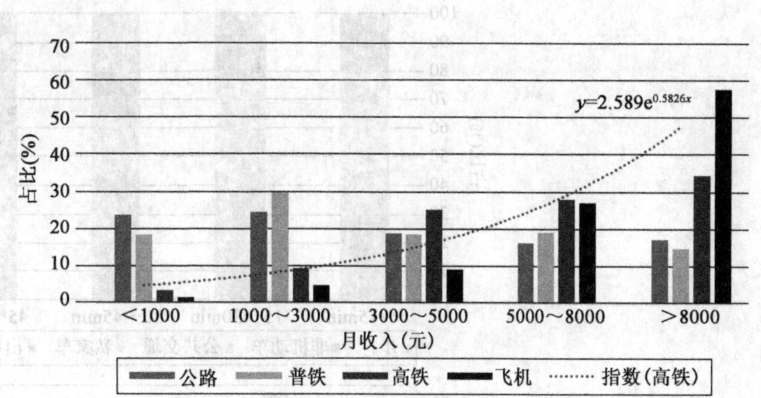

图5　不同交通方式出行者月收入统计图

通过调查结果可以看出，随着月收入的提高，出行者开始追求更舒适、高效的出行方式。各阶层乘坐高铁比例均较高，这与域内有完善的高铁设施且票价适中有关。

2.2　出行者出行特性

2.2.1　旅客出行目的

出行目的多种多样，本次调研将出行者的目的分为公差、经商、外出务工、上学、旅游、探亲访友、就医疗养及其他8种类型，如图6所示。

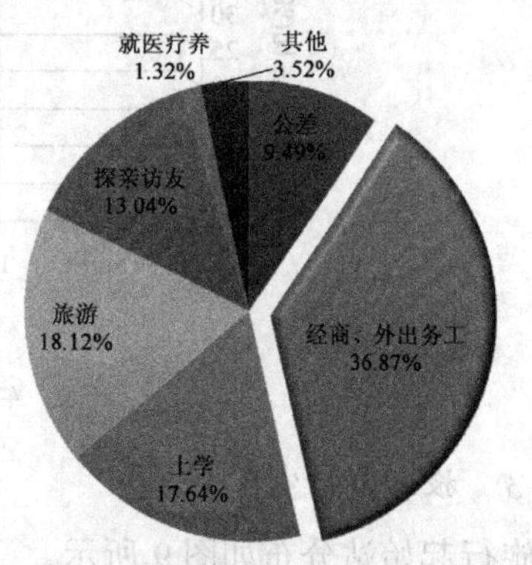

图6　出行目的统计图

通过分析调查结果,区域内以经商、外出务工为出行目的比例最高,占36.87%;而区域内旅游景点较多,故以旅游为目的的出行占比高为18.12%;此外本次调查得到的以上学为出行目的的比例也较高为17.64%,这是因为福建省因疫情防控所采取的学生在家上两周网课后返校的政策,致使域内3月10号以后有一定的返校潮。

2.2.2　出行到站耗时(接驳时间)

本次调查统计了旅客从出发地到车站的集散方式及其所耗费的时间,即旅客到达车站前接驳过程所使用的交通方式及其所需要的时间,如图7所示。

由调查结果可以看出,区域内旅客选择公共交通到达车站的比例最高,为36.90%,这与区域内公共交通设施完善有很大的关系;此外,非机动车在集散方式中也占有相对较高的比例,这是因为区域内共享助力车分布广,使用人群多。

图8表示,该地区接驳时间大多分布在15~45min,45min以上的接驳时间所占比例在20%~30%,而接驳时间越短则说明旅客出行的"途外可达性"越好,接驳时间越长则说明旅客出行的"途外可达性"越差,该统计结果说明了温州—福州高铁项目影响区范围内可达性较低。

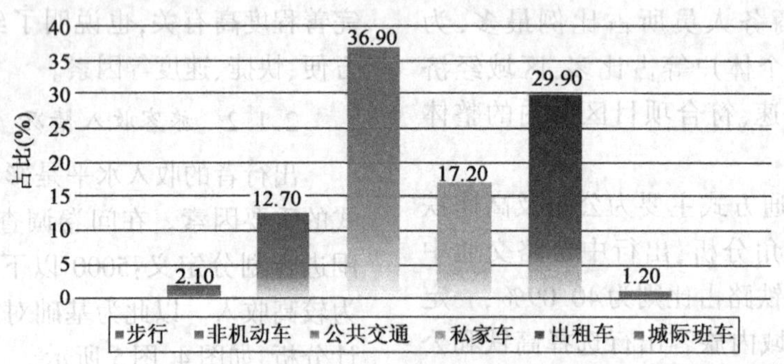

图7　到达车站集散方式统计图

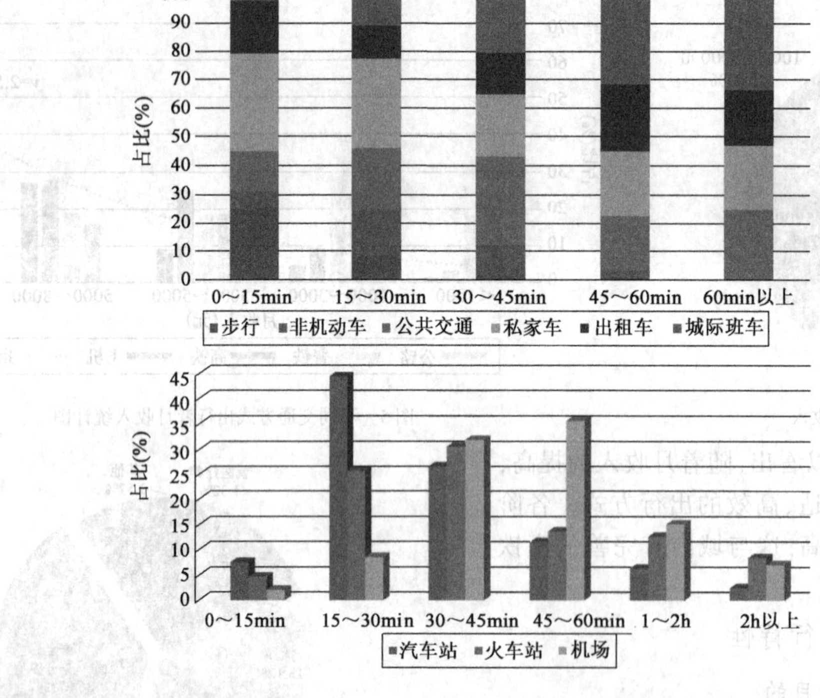

图8　车站集散交通方式及接驳时间分布统计图

2.2.3　旅客出行空间分布

(1)旅行起始站分布如图9所示。

(2)出行换乘

经统计分析,旅客旅行的换乘情况如图10所示。

经过调查得知,域内规划有专门的客运专线,即原有时速为250km/h的温福沿海通道高铁，承担了项目沿海区域的密集客流。对于域外出行的打工、经商等需乘坐普速铁路的出行者需前往温州站、宁德站及福州站换乘。而区域内陆地区如文成、泰顺、寿宁、柘荣等地只运营客运班车，故出行方式以公路为主，去往就近的县市换乘铁路或民航。

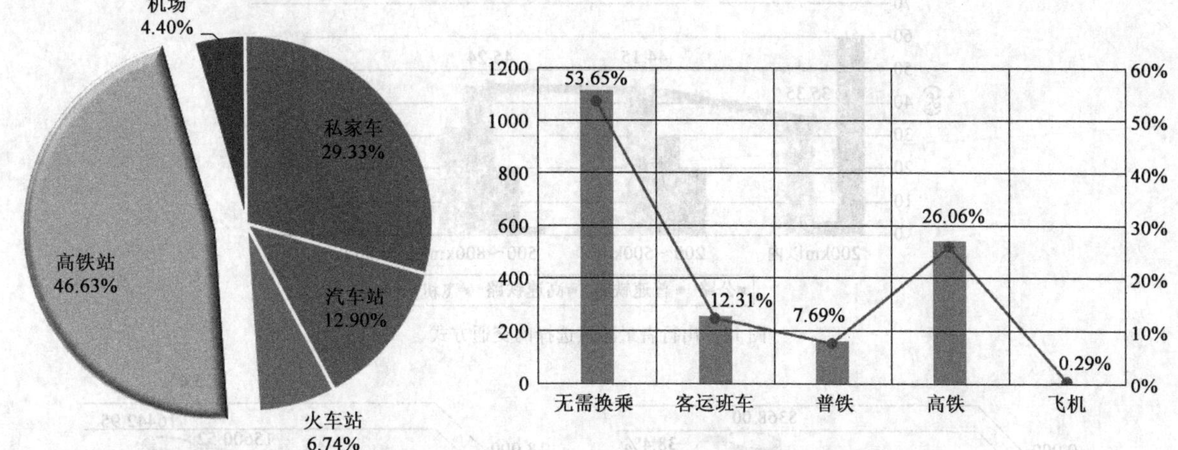

图9 旅行起始站分布统计图

图10 旅客出行换乘情况

2.3 出行者对交通方式的选择意愿

针对沿线居民每次出行(出行距离50km以上或出行时间2h以上)，询问其在本客运专线开通后是否愿意转变乘坐。经调查，约有74.59%的居民愿意改变原有出行方式，改乘本客专。约有25.41%的出行居民不愿意改乘，其原因主要为沿线站点设置离家较远，不在本市，需进行换乘，如图11所示。

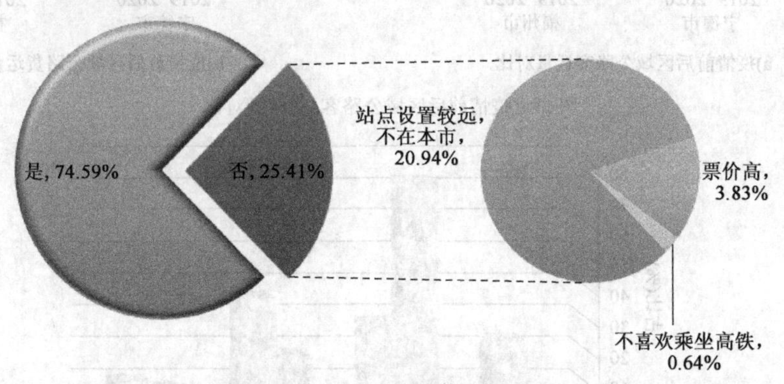

图11 出行者对交通方式的选择意愿

由表3及图12可知，短距离内县市之间客运班车联系频繁，故公路承担着大多数旅客的短距离出行，但选择高速铁路的比例较高，这是由于高铁具有速度快、环境舒适等优势，以及居民的经济和生活水平在逐渐提高。

出行者最愿意选择的交通方式(单位:%) 表3

交通方式	200km以内	200~500km	500~800km	800km以上
公路	60.42	19.67	2.55	1.34
普速铁路	4.23	30.29	19.48	14.17
高速铁路	35.35	44.15	45.24	22.61
飞机	—	5.89	32.73	61.88
合计	100	100	100	100

中长距离出行主要由火车和飞机承担。随着距离的增加，旅客选择高速公路和出行的比例逐渐减少，选择铁路的比例先增后减，选择飞机出行的比例逐渐增大。

2.4 疫情影响下的出行分析

受疫情影响，区域内客运量总体下降约40%，而货运量有小幅增加，增幅在0~10%，如图13所示。

在疫情期间内，城际客运班车停运，铁路等人流密集的出行方式比例下降，出行结构以私家车为主，如图14所示。

结合调查期间客运站发送人数及 2019 ~ 2021 年春运情况对比,在疫情好转的情况下,城际班车运营线路、班次等已恢复正常,但发送旅客较疫情前减少约 20%,这与班车可达性较差,旅途时间较长有关;而区域内铁路运营基本已恢复正常,载客率在 70% ~85% 波动,如图 15 所示。

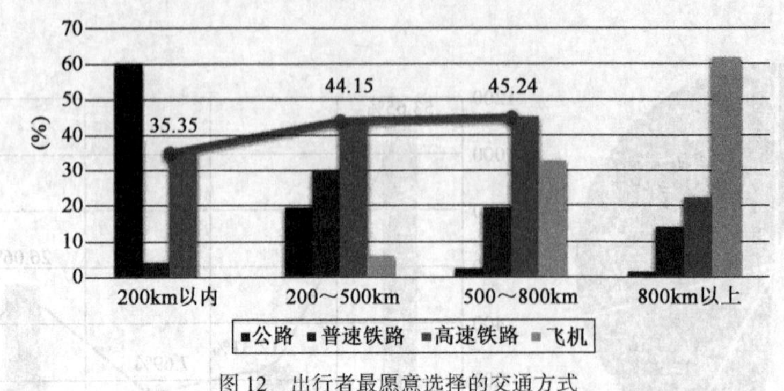

图 12　出行者最愿意选择的交通方式

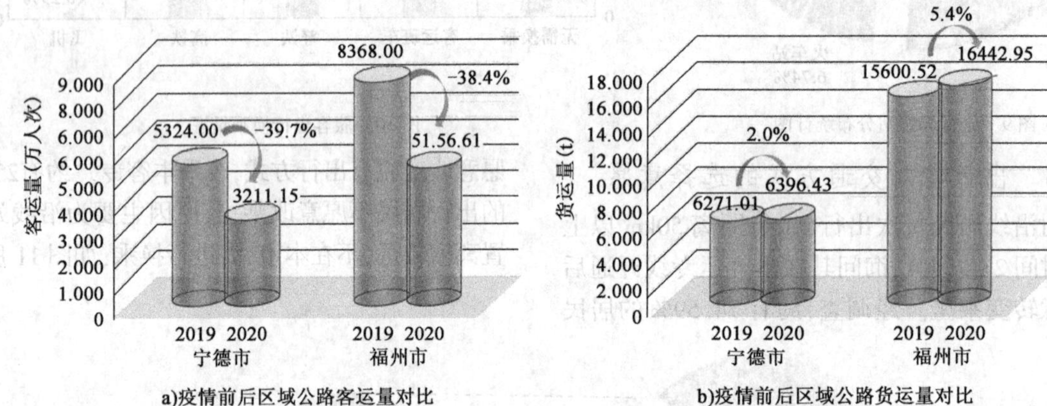

图 13　疫情前后区域公路客、货运量对比

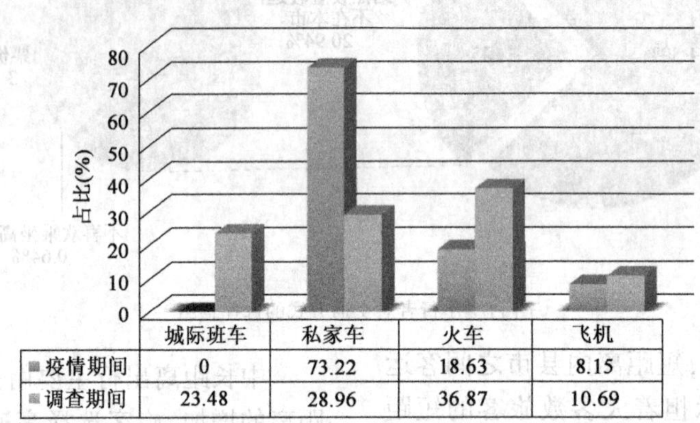

图 14　跨区域出行方式对比

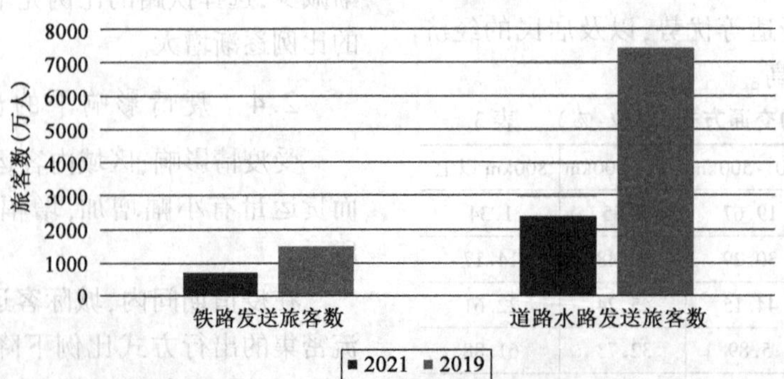

图 15　2019、2021 年福州市春运期间发送旅客数(万人)

可见,受疫情影响域内旅客出行方式更加倾向于高运力,速度快,可达性高的出行方式。

3 结语

研究区域内经济活力高,人口流动大,客运需求旺盛,形成了以经商、外出务工为主的出行。

从旅客收入分析,各阶层乘坐高铁比例均较高,且随着收入的提高,旅客高铁出行的比例越来越高,月收入大于5000的旅客选择高铁出行的比例达44.19%。可见,随着人民经济水平的提高,高铁客运需求数量将持续增长。

从出行特性分析,目前域内并未规划建设为域内出行服务的高铁客运专线,交通运输网络可达性较低,大多需要通过换乘至较高等级的车站出行,且接驳时间较长,增大了出行时间。

从出行意愿分析,受访者中约有74.59%的旅客愿意改乘温福客专。而出行距离调查显示,区域内旅客在短距离出行时愿意乘坐高铁的比例高达35.35%,而在200~500km的远距离出行时,旅客选择高铁的比例为44.15%。

从疫情影响下的出行分析,铁路运营较公路受影响较小,列车开行及运营恢复较快。

综上所述,铁路尤其是高铁是域内居民出行选择的重要交通方式。而当地客运需求日益增加,居民的经济和生活水平也日益提高,该区域迫切需要一条具有高运力的高速铁路线路。建设沿海通道高铁温州—福州段,有利于促进沿线城市人文交流、产业融合,加快区域经济协调发展,形成高铁沿线全面繁荣的格局。

参考文献

[1] 廖怡. 关于沿江铁路通道建设模式的分析[J]. 价值工程,2016,35(11):88-89.

[2] 任峥峥. 长江经济带沿江铁路通道规划建设必要性分析[J]. 铁道标准设计,2017,61(06):49-52.

[3] 江佳璐. 兰州—汉中—十堰高速铁路建设必要性研究[J]. 山西建筑,2021,47(21):125-128.

[4] 李志鹏,张博. 建设甬台温高铁的必要性研究[J]. 铁道建筑技术,2020(08):60-63.

[5] 张玉伟. 新建杭州至温州铁路走向方案研究[J]. 铁道建筑技术,2016,(01):5-8.

[6] 常占奎. 新建温武吉铁路建设必要性研究[J]. 高速铁路技术,2020,11(04):13-16.

基于场论的城市居民地铁出行时空特征探索

——以西安市为例

付 鑫[1,2] 熊国芳*[1] 王建伟[1,2] 姚禹璠[1]

(1. 长安大学运输工程学院;2. 长安大学道路基础设施数字化教育部工程研究中心)

摘 要 城市居民出行对社会城市经济、城市公共交通、商品贸易、疾病传播等都有着重要的影响。本文基于城市地铁刷卡数据,以西安市为例对居民地铁客流进行时空特征分析。首先从分时段及分周内周末对城市地铁出行客流进行时间特征分析,其次通过借鉴物理学场论理论,对城市地铁客流出行网络进行矢量化表征对居民地铁出行进行空间特征分析。研究结果表明,西安市居民地铁出行有明显的高峰时段,尤其是表现在工作日时段,并且工作日与休息日的地铁出行客流存在差异;在空间上西安市地铁客流出行场是一个有源无旋场,此外地铁矢量站点场势超过7000的有一个,超过6000的有两个站点,因此西安是一个“一主一副”的双中心发展结构城市,并且城市居民地铁客流呈现分级递减的态势。

关键词 居民出行 时空分析 场理论 地铁刷卡数据

0　引言

城市居民出行作为城市交通的重要组成部分,与城市经济、交通[1]、土地利用[2,3]、疾病传播[4]等密切相关。从出行行为的简单研究[5]到对居民出行目的、出行方式选择[6,7]、居民出行网络研究(如网络效率、出行链)[8,11]等方面,城市居民出行行为特征的研究越来越细致。随着大数据的兴起发展,相关学者通过将出租车轨迹数据[12]、手机信令数据[13]等多种数据与居民出行行为相结合对居民出行特征进行研究,还有学者通过结合其他学科(如物理学)来研究城市居民出行特征[14,16]。城市轨道交通作为承担大量客流的主要交通方式,在城市公共交通系统中起着至关重要的作用;地铁 IC 卡中丰富的乘客出行记录可以有效支持居民出行特征的分析。通过对城市居民出行行为特征进行分析研究,能更好地了解城市功能结构,对城市的管理与规划发展具有重要意义[17]。

总体而言,目前对城市居民出行行为的研究比较丰富,场论在交通领域也有相关研究,但是用场论来探索出行网络属性特征,揭示由居民出行行为带来的流动性所具有的空间特征,是具有进一步探索价值的。本文主要利用地铁刷卡数据,对居民出行行为的时空特征进行分析,研究城市居民在时间与空间维度上所呈现出来的分布规律。

1　研究区域及数据准备

西安是中国内地第 14 座开通城市轨道交通的城市、西北地区第 1 个开通地铁的城市,第一条线路于 2011 年 9 月 16 日开通试运营。本文利用西安地铁 2019 年 4 月 1～4 号线 88 个站点共计 55392201 人次的刷卡数据作为主要数据源。通过地铁刷卡记录来获取相应数据信息。相关数据信息的形式见表 1。

地铁刷卡数据示例　　表 1

名　称	含　义	格　式	示　例
ENTRYSTATIONID	进站车站编号	x_x	2_3
INTIME	进站时间	yyyy/mm/dd hh:mm	2019/4/17 2:09
STATIONID	出站车站编号	x_x	3_6
OUTTIME	出站时间	yyyy/mm/dd hh:mm	2019/4/17 2:11
CARDID	用户 ID	xxxxxxxxxxx	0200＊＊＊＊fc5fb1a

本文所选取的研究区域为西安市,相应研究范围内的地铁线路和站点分布如图 1 所示。

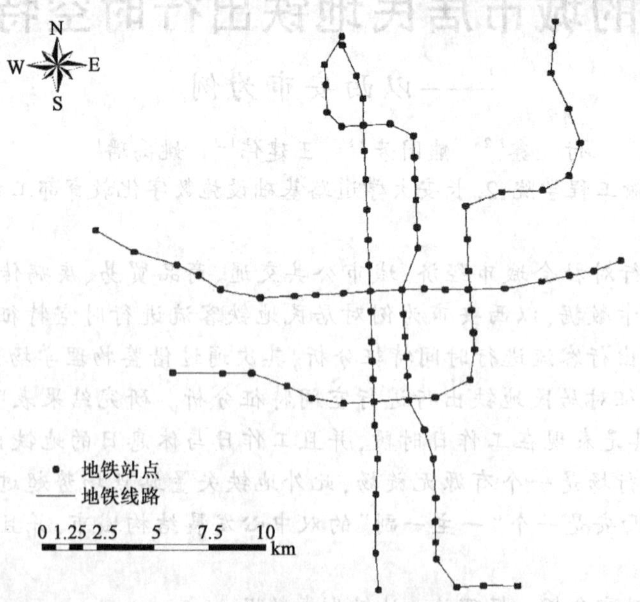

图 1　研究区域示意图

本研究选取西安地铁出行客流进行实证分析,收集 POI 数据描述地铁站的属性特征。本文用到的 POI 数据有 22 个类别,共计 554925 条。对 POI 数据进行清洗及重分类[18],最后分为 8 个类别,即日常服务、教科文旅、机构团体、医疗卫生、住宅服务、风景名胜、休闲娱乐、公司企业。通过对所研究区域进行网格划分,并计算每个网格内重分类后的 POI 密度。本文规定网格内单种类 POI 密度超过 50% 即为单一功能区,位于单一功能去内的地铁站点为单功能站点,反之由网格内混合度前二的 POI 类别共同决定,为混合功能区[19],位于混合功能区内的地铁站点为混合功能站点。

2 研究方法

本研究基于矢量场理论[9]并以场势作为表征量对城市居民出行进行矢量化表征,进而对城市居民出行进行时空特征的分析研究。

2.1 场模型

本研究中将各地铁站视为客流发生点,各地铁站在产生出行客流时有一个结合大小与方向的客流矢量。将城市地铁客流的完整出行过程在城市内呈现出的规模强度大小、关联关系等定义为如下客流出行场。

$$\overrightarrow{W}_i = \overrightarrow{R}_i = \sum_j R_{ij}\overrightarrow{u}_{ij} \tag{1}$$

式中:R_{ij}——i 站到 j 站的总客流量;

$\overrightarrow{u}_{ij}$——i 站到 j 站的单位矢量;

$\overrightarrow{R}_i$——i 站产生的终客流矢量。

2.2 场势

客流出行场与静电场不同,地铁客流所形成的矢量分布并不均匀。本研究中客流出行场场势代表各矢量点在其所属区域发展等因素影响下产生客流能力的大小。场势大小规定如下:

$$\overline{\omega} = m\frac{R}{l} \tag{2}$$

式中:m——地铁场势的影响因素;

R——地铁站产生的起始客流,万人;

l——各地铁站与所规定零势点之间的实际地理距离,km。

本研究规定将研究区域的几何中心视为客流出行场的零势点。

3 实证研究

本文以西安市地铁站客流数据作为验证数据,对城市居民地铁客流的出行进行一般性时空特征的探索研究。结合物理场理论对城市居民地铁出行客流进行矢量化表征,利用场势这一特征量来分析研究由城市地铁客流出行网络反映出的城市发展中心特征。

3.1 居民出行时间特征分析

对城市居民地铁出行从时间角度做特征分析在一定程度上能反映出城市地铁运营的热点时间段以及各条地铁线路的运营时况,在这一定程度上有助于缓解城市的交通问题。本节分别从日出行总量、分工作日与周末不同时间下的居民地铁出行时间特征、各地铁线路的居民出行时间特征这三个方面研究城市居民地铁出行的时间特征。

3.1.1 一周日出行总量

选择 4 月 15—21 日一周的数据对居民地铁出行进行客流总计,如图 2 所示。从图中可知,周一至周四居民地铁出行总量波动不大,在周五出行量呈现大幅增长,占一周出行客流总量的 16.18%。周末两天的客流出行总量均小于工作日的客流出行总量,并呈现出递增的态势。由此可看出地铁是通勤者出行的一种重要交通方式。在工作日居民出行会选择时间准确性更高的交通方式,周五是一周内客流出行量最高的一天,在这一天除了正常工作日出行外,还会伴随一些休闲式出行;在周末对于可能产生的休闲式出行,人们会更考虑出行舒适度。

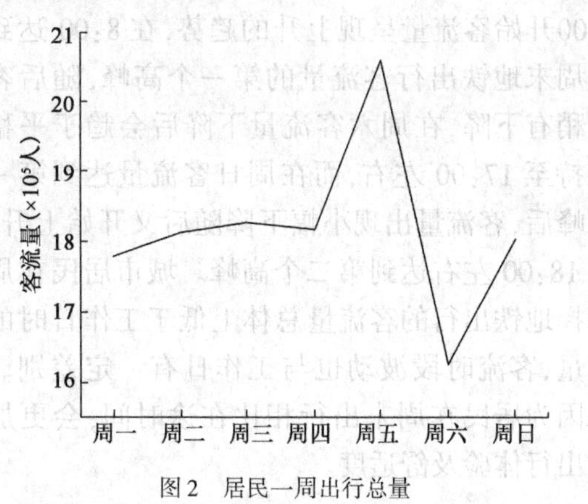

图 2 居民一周出行总量

3.1.2 工作日与周末居民出行对比分析

本研究以一周内五天工作日的地铁刷卡数据对城市居民地铁工作日出行进行时间特征分析研究。如图 3 所示,周内工作日各时段居民地铁出行客流量呈现出相似的分布态势。从 6:00 开始客流量开始增长,在 7:00,客流量呈现出显著的跳跃式增长,在 8:00 ~9:00,到达第一个出行客流高峰,这与城市居民在工作日的上班早高峰比较贴合。9:00 后客流急速下降并趋于平缓,12:00 ~16:00,客流量处于一个相对稳定的状态,16:00 ~17:00,出行量开始逐渐上升,并在 17:00 ~18:00,到达第二个出行客流高峰,这与城市居民在工作日的下班晚高峰比较贴合。19:00 开始,客流量逐渐下降直至最低。

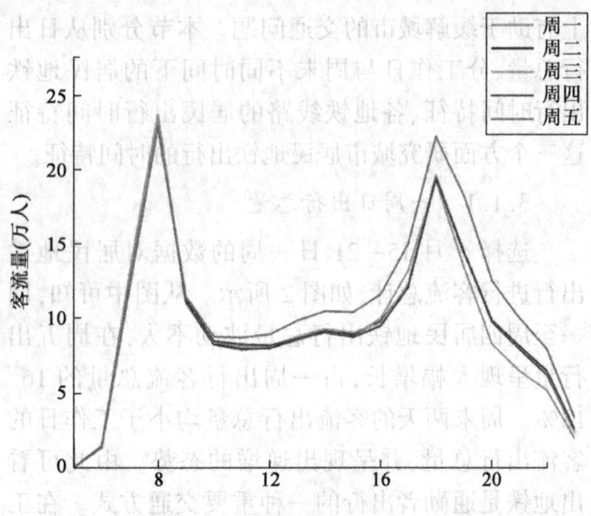

图3　居民工作日地铁出行客流量

本研究以一周内两天周末时间的地铁刷卡数据对城市居民地铁休息日出行进行时间特征分析研究。如图 4 所示,在周末居民选择地铁出行时的客流分布差异较小,总体态势基本一致。从 6:00开始客流量呈现上升的趋势,在 8:00 达到居民周末地铁出行客流量的第一个高峰,随后客流量稍有下降,在周六客流量下降后会趋于平稳并保持至 17:00 左右,而在周日客流量达到第一个高峰后,客流量出现小幅下降随后又开始上升,并在 18:00 左右达到第二个高峰。城市居民在周末选择地铁出行的客流量总体上低于工作日时的客流量,客流时段波动也与工作日有一定差别。这是因为居民在周末出行相比在途时间,会更加注重出行体验及舒适度。

3.1.3　不同地铁线路居民出行时间特征分析

本文所选择的西安市 1 ~4 号线地铁在地域上覆盖了主城区的相关区域,地铁线路有着重要的客流运输作用,在不同时段具有不同的交通职能。如图 5、图 6 所示,四条地铁线在工作日早晚高峰的客流分布特征十分显著,2 号线承担工作日居民地铁出行的主要客流量,1、3 号线次之,4 号线最少;在休息日,同样也是 2 号线承担了主要的出行客流量,其次是 1、3 号线,4 号线最少,1 ~3 号线分别在 8:00 与 18:00 左右都有较为明显的客流高峰,4 号线总体较为平缓,没有明显波动。与工作日相比,周末地铁出行客流分布虽然也有高峰客流时段,但没有工作日的高峰客流明显,客流量的波动程度较小,数量上也相对较少。

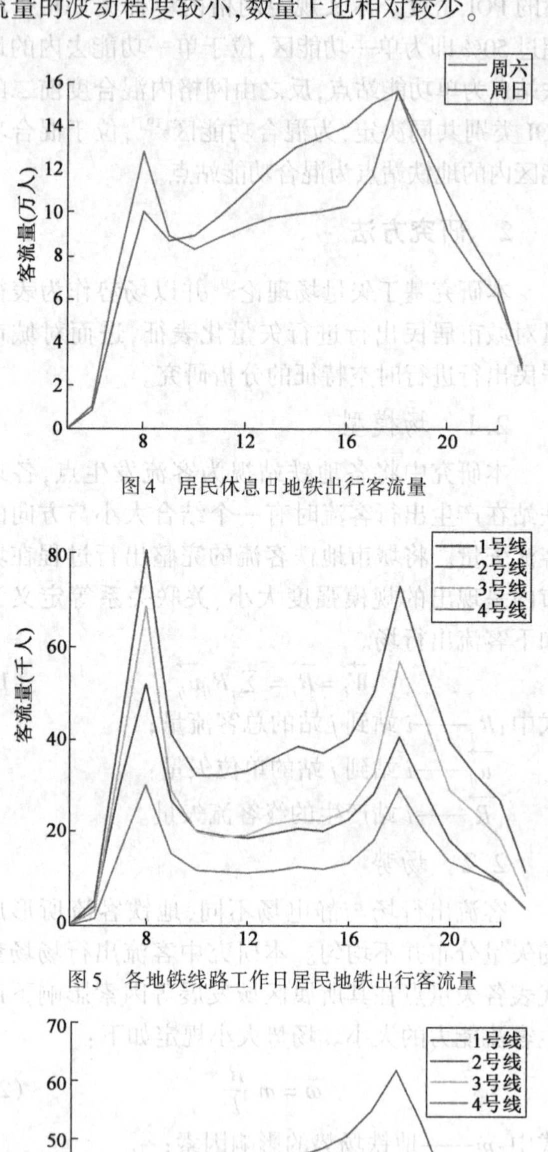

图4　居民休息日地铁出行客流量

图5　各地铁线路工作日居民地铁出行客流量

图6　各地铁线路休息日居民地铁出行客流量

3.2 居民出行空间特征分析

对城市居民地铁出行进行空间特征分析有助于加深了解居民日常地铁出行行为，进而对居民出行热点区域、城市集聚客流中心等进行清楚的认知，在一定程度上对城市资源规划建设、交通管理决策等可以提供有效的数据支撑。

3.2.1 矢量化表征

本文选择的西安市 1 ~ 4 号地铁线具有西安市地铁网络的基本形状。结合矢量场模型对西安市居民地铁出行客流网络进行矢量化表征，构建西安市地铁客流出行场，如图 7 所示（小图为矢量合成示意图；以各地铁站点为客流出发点，以该站产生的前往其余各站的客流形成分矢量，对这些分矢量进行矢量加和，最终形成构成地铁客流出行场中每一地铁站的子矢量）。

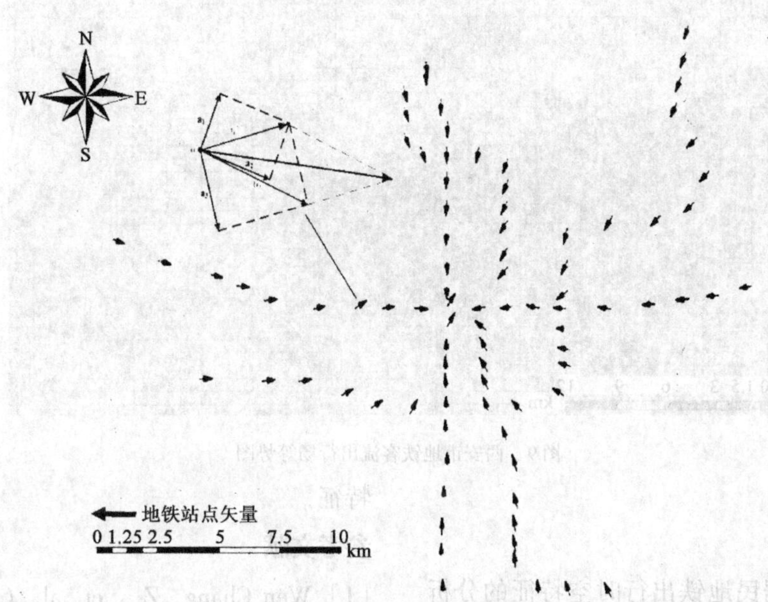

图 7 西安市地铁客流出行场

不同于风场、静电场，构成地铁客流出行场的子矢量没有呈现出规律大小的角度，无法构成旋转分布式场。这也说明了地铁客流出行场可以进行场标量势的计算；场中存在源点式吸引中心；最终构成的地铁客流出行场是一个有源无旋场。

3.2.2 场势特征

通过对西安市 POI 数据进行重分类预处理，并与各地铁站相结合呈现出各地铁站的功能属性，在此基础上，对地铁客流出行场进行场势特征量的研究分析。如图 8 所示，为西安市排名前十的地铁客流出行场场势情况。西安市地铁客流出行场场势在数值上呈现缓慢下降的态势，并且在排名前 10 的地铁站中，混合功能的地铁站点占比 90%，单一功能的地铁站点仅有一个。

通过对场势前十地铁站的功能特征进行研究，发现场势排名前十的地铁站主要由教科文旅、日常服务、机构团体和公司企业四种特色用地组成。进一步对场势的等值情况进行分析，如图 9 所示，可以看出西安市地铁客流出行场存在显著的分级现象，势值较高的地区多为混合功能性质的地铁站。从整体数量上来看，西安市地铁客流出行场的场势集中度不高，势值大小呈现出逐层递减的分布特征；场势峰值（场势数值超过 7000）有且仅有一个，此外还有另外两个势值较高的点（场势数值超过 6000），这反映出西安市是一个“一主一副”的双发展中心城市。

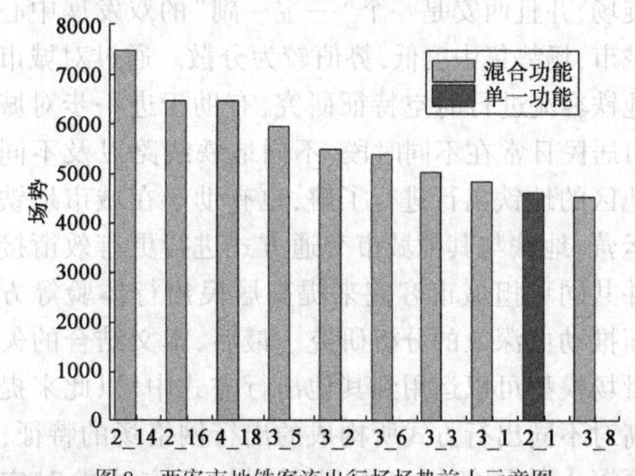

图 8 西安市地铁客流出行场场势前十示意图

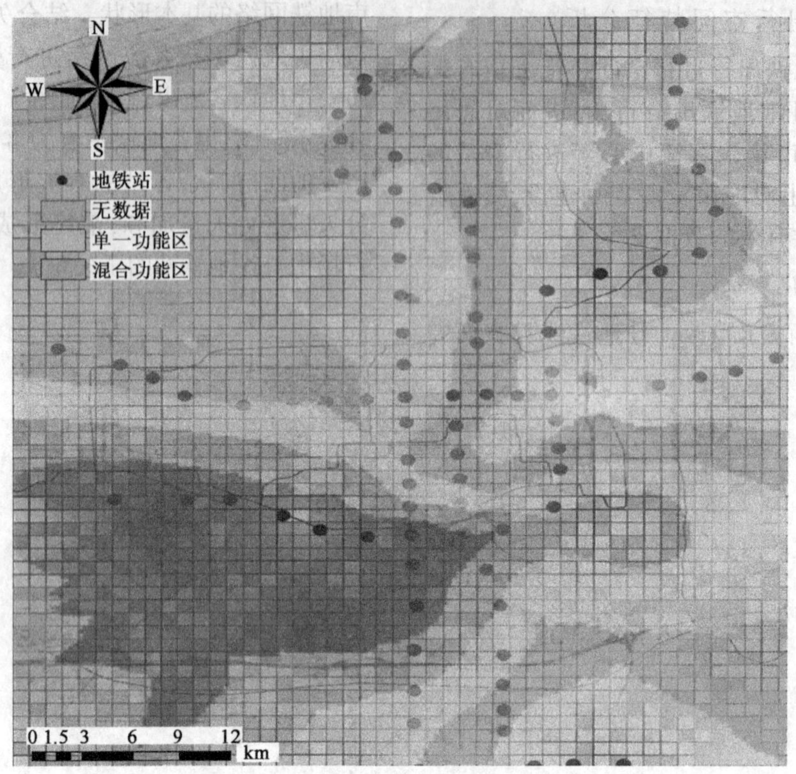

图 9　西安市地铁客流出行场等势图

4　结语

为了进行城市居民地铁出行时空特征的分析研究,本文以西安市为例,对居民地铁出行进行一般性时空特征分析,结合物理场论理论对居民地铁出行进行矢量化表征,从矢量场的角度对城市地铁客流出行网络进行特征分析。研究表明,在时间维度上,工作日有两个明显的高峰时间点,分别为 8:00、18:00;休息日的高峰时段没有工作日的显著,并且客流总量低于工作日的客流总量。在空间维度上,通过对西安市地铁客流进行分析研究,发现西安市地铁客流出行场是一个有源无旋场,并且西安是一个"一主一副"的双发展中心城市,场势集中度低,势值较为分散。通过对城市地铁客流进行时空特征研究,有助于进一步对城市居民日常在不同时段、不同地铁线路以及不同地区的地铁出行进行了解,也有助于在城市地铁运营、地铁与其他城市交通方式进行更有效衔接并共同承担城市客流来提高居民出行体验等方面推动更深入的分析研究。最后,本文结合的矢量场模型可以运用到其他出行方式中,以此来提高对不同出行方式所构成的出行网络场的特征,更深入的了解城市居民不同出行方式的时空特征。

参考文献

[1] Wen Chang, Z., et al. (2007). "Spatial-Temporal Characteristics of Urban Resident Trips and Influence Factors in China." Scientia Geographica Sinica 27(6):737-742.

[2] Chai, Y., et al. (2012). "Low-carbon optimization strategies based on CO_2 emission mechanism of household daily travels: A case study of Beijing." Geographical Research 31(2):334-344.

[3] Xu, X., et al. (2014). "Characteristics And Impact Mechanism of Carbon Emission for Urban Residents' Transport in The Yangtze River Delta, China." Resources and Environment in the Yangtze Basin 23(8):1064-1071.

[4] Ma Jing, Chai Yanwei, Fu Tingting. Progress of research on the health impact of people's space-time behavior and environmental pollution exposure[J]. Progress in Geography, 2017, 36(10):1260-1269.

[5] Karel, J. K. Travel Patterns of Urban Residents[J]. Transportation Science, 1967, 1:261-285.

[6] Forinash C V, Koppelman F S. Application and interpretation of nested logit models of intercity mode choice[M]. 1993.

[7] Cao Rui, Tu Wei, Chao Baichong, Luo Nianxue, Zhou Meng, LI Qingquan. Identification and Analysis of Home and Work Regions in the Vicinity of Metro Stations Using Smart Card Data [J]. Journal of Geomatics, 2016, 41(03): 74-78.

[8] Hu Bei-bei, Lin Ke-xin, Dong Xian-lei, MA Xu-jun. Research on Spatial Differentiation Characteristics of Urban Taxi Trip Trajectory Network [J]. Journal of Statistics and Information, 2021, 36(01): 119-128.

[9] Yuan Yun, Xu Ge, Jia Jianmin. Spatiotemporal Characteristics and Network Analysis of Car-Hailing Mobility Behavior [J]. Journal of Systems & Management, 2021, 30(01): 28-39.

[10] Sun Qiuxia, Sun Lu, Liu Xinmin. Study of the Traffic Network Efficiency Based on Individual Traveler's Behavior[J]. Journal of Chongqing Jiaotong University(Natural Science), 2016, 35(02): 110-113 + 168.

[11] Xue Yuxuan. Spatial and Temporal Travel Characteristics Analysis of Urban Residents Based on APTS Data [D]. Shandong University of Science and Technology, 2020.

[12] Li, J., et al. (2020). "Trajectory data extract of O/D temporal and spatial distribution of urban residents." Science of Surveying and Mapping 45(2): 150-158.

[13] Su Yue-jiang, Wen Hui-ying, Wei Qing-bo, Wu De-xin. Resident Travel Characteristics Analysis Method Based on Multi-source Data Fusion[J]. Journal of Transportation Systems Engineering and Information Technology, 2020, 20(05): 56-63.

[14] Mazzoli, M., Molas, A., Bassolas, A. et al. Field theory for recurrent mobility. Nat Commun 10, 3895 (2019).

[15] Li Xue. Study on the influence scope of mountain city track station based on the Field theory [D]. Chongqing Jiaotong University, 2019.

[16] Schläpfer Markus, Dong Lei, O Keeffe Kevin, Santi Paolo, Szell Michael, Salat Hadrien, Anklesaria Samuel, Vazifeh Mohammad, Ratti Carlo, West Geoffrey B.. The universal visitation law of human mobility[J]. Nature, 2021, 593(7860):

[17] Zhou Yingdi, Zhang Xingguo, Pan Xiaofang, Wu Chaohong. Spatio-temporal analysis of residential travel based on taxi trajectories [J]. Urban Geotechnical Investigation & Surveying, 2020(03): 17-23.

[18] Zhang Ling. Research on POI Classification Standard [J]. Bulletin of Surveying and Mapping, 2012(10): 82-84.

[19] Zhang Ting, Wang Hongyuan. Research on Identification and Visualization of Nanning City Functional Area Based on POI Data[J]. Chinese & Overseas Architecture, 2021(03): 102-107.

实时公交信息对乘客出行行为影响研究*

张生瑞　杨小红*
（长安大学运输工程学院）

摘　要　随着社会生活质量提高，人们对公交出行要求也增高，在出行中公交到站时间、车辆运行状

1. 基金项目：国家自然科学基金资助(52102404,71871029)；长安大学中央高校基本科研业务费专项资金资助(300102210301)。

况及车内拥挤程度等出行需求日益突出。本文通过问卷调查实时公交信息下乘客出行意愿,建立Logit模型,利用SPSS进行模型参数估计,并分析影响出行方式选择关键因素,经统计实时公交信息能降低乘客候车不确定性、缓解焦虑、候车更有耐心。影响公交线路选择的主要因素为所需候车时长、车内拥挤度、是否换乘等。本文研究对于社会经济具有非常可观效益和重要现实意义。

关键词 实时公交信息 出行行为 出行时间 Logit模型

0 引言

公交运行会受到诸多因素影响,使公交发生串车及车内拥挤分布不均等会降低车辆到站、乘客候车时间规律性。因此,提供车辆到站时刻、车内拥挤度等实时公交信息,可降低乘客候车时间焦虑和线路选择盲目性。目前,国内外学者在交通信息对乘客出行行为影响方面,涉及众多。

钱依楠等[1]分析实时信息对出行行为意向影响,结果显示乘客候车时间、是否使用公交到站服务、是否有道路拥挤等而有出行延误经历、信息准确性是否有必要提示同公交线路连续班次的到站时间等因素对乘客出行方式转移作用显著。

史远[2]对多种公交到站信息发布形式下乘客出行行为进行研究,其以乘客出行行为为研究对象,以公交信息发布为出发点,将二者结合,公交资源得到利用,乘客出行成本得到有效控制。

孟嘉铭等[3]对公交实时信息对乘客出行影响进行研究,结果表明使用实时公交App和不使用的乘客在步行速度、乘车时间及候车情绪等方面差异显著。

张蒙迪[4]分析了实时公交信息对乘客出行行为影响及效用,结果表明实时公交信息对缩短乘客感知等待时间有着非常重要作用。

侯现耀等[5]研究公交出行信息条件下出行者通勤出发时间选择影响因素,研究表明出行距离、道路拥挤、公交换乘等会影响出发时间。

以上研究在研究方法与思路上有一定创新,但仍有不足,大多数研究都针对小汽车驾驶员,对出行者个人属性及其公交车之间的相互作用欠考虑。另外大部分学者都是基于理论建模和数值仿真来研究实时公交信息提供下出行者的出行行为,还应该结合乘客的乘车选择行为作进一步的探讨。

1 实时公交信息概述

1.1 出行决策分析

生活中,出行者会根据出行目的、经验对出行时间、方式、路径等选择,这种选择过程称为出行决策,如图1所示。

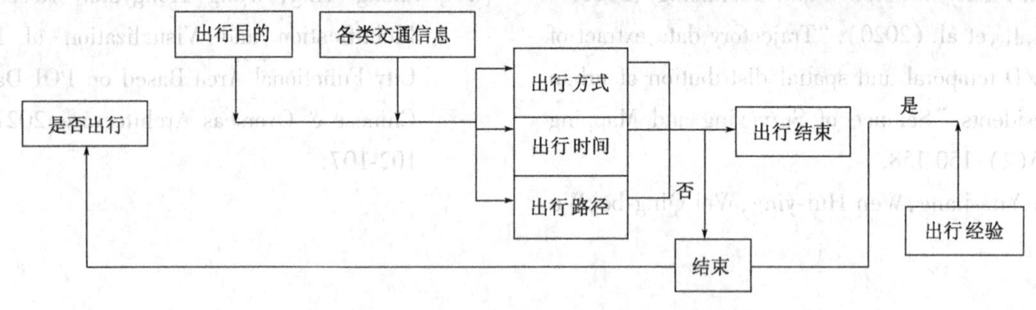

图1 出行决策示意图

1.2 原理及影响

公交公司通过安装在公交车上全球定位系统(GPS系统),将公交车实时位置传到交通监管平台,实现对公交合理调配,同时将公交数据处理后发送至公交电子站牌、实时公交应用程序App、高德地图等,出行者按需求来选择查询方式,提前规划出行时间,减少出行不确定性,使个人出行效用最大化。此外,对于交通系统,信息诱导出行者做出高效出行决策,使路网上出行均匀分布,防止交通拥堵发生。

2 问卷设计与研究方法概述

本文通过对比交通行为两种调查方法及结合本章研究,采用RP调查法设计问卷。下面对实时公交信息对各个方面影响方法进行说明。

2.1 对出行方式影响研究方法

对于出行方式选择分为乘坐公交车和选择其他方式，因此采用二元 Logit 模型。对于参数估计，通过问卷调查，用 SPSS 进行估计与结果分析。

2.1.1 二元 Logit 模型

Logit 模型是基于随机效用论的离散模型。由效用理论，出行者会选择对自身效用最大的出行方案，随机效益由函数 $U(k)$ 表示，包括固定效益 $V(k)$ 和随机项 $e(k)$，假设随机项 $e(k)$ 相互独立，且服从同一干贝尔分布。具体如下：

$$U(k)=V(k)+e(k) \tag{1}$$

式中：$V(k)$——方案 k 的固定效益；

$e(k)$——随机项。

当方案 k 的随机效益 $U(k)$ 比其他方案大时，则方案 k 被选择，选择概率为：

$$P(k)=[U(k)>U(j),\forall j(\neq k)\in K] \tag{2}$$

式中：K——方案集。

由式(1)、式(2)得：

$$P(k)=P[e(j)<V(k)-V(j)+e(k),\forall j(\neq k)\in K] = \int_{e(k)} F[V(k)-V(j)+e(k),\forall j(\neq k)\in K]\, f_k(x)\mathrm{d}x \tag{3}$$

式中：$F(x)$——概率分布函数；

$f_k(x)$——概率变量 $x=e(k)$ 的概率密度函数。

用概率变量 x 表示 $e(k)$，θ 作为参数，随机项分布函数为：

$$F_e(x)=\exp\{-\theta\exp(-x)\}(\theta>0,-\infty<x<\infty) \tag{4}$$

由式(4)、式(3)推导得：

$$P(k)=\frac{e^{V(k)}}{\sum_j e^{V(j)}} \tag{5}$$

式(5)即为 Logit 模型，由此得二元 Logit 模型：

$$P(k)=\frac{e^{V(k)}}{\sum_j e^{V(j)}}=\frac{1}{1+e^{-[V(k)-V(j)]}} \tag{6}$$

两方案效益函数固定效益之差为：

$$V=V(k)-V(j)=c+\sum_i b_i x_i \tag{7}$$

式中：c——与方案 k 有关的常数项；

x_i——影响改变出行方式解释变量；

b_i——x_i 对应参数，由 SPSS 求解。

2.1.2 SPSS 软件参数估计

利用 SPSS 对解释变量参数进行估计，先将解释变量数值化，见表 1。

解释变量选项数值化设置 表 1

变量名称	变量定义	变量赋值
性别	X_1	男 =1　女 =2
年龄	X_2	18 岁以下 =1　18 ~30 岁 =2　30 ~45 岁 =3　45 岁以上 =4
受教育程度	X_3	高中或中专及以下 =1　大专或大学本科 =2　研究生及以上 =3
每天乘坐次数	X_4	0 ~2 次 =1　3 ~5 次 =2　5 次以上 =3
每周乘坐天数	X_5	从不 =1　1 ~2d =2　3 ~5d =3　6 ~7d =4
信息获取情况	X_6	不获取 =1　偶尔获取 =2　经常获取 =3
等待容忍度	X_7	0 ~5min =1　6 ~10min =2　11 ~15min =3　15min 以上 =4
信息准确度	X_8	不准确 =1　一般 =2　准确 =3
信息有用性	X_9	无用 =1　一般 =2　有用 =3

表中变量名称为因变量，对自变量进行筛选，筛选方法选择"向后：有条件"，利用 SPSS 得最优解。

2.2 对乘客候车心理、出行时间、公交线路选择影响研究方法

实时公交信息对乘客候车心理、出行时间、公

交线路选择影响通过问卷调查来研究,即相比无实时公交信息,在实时公交信息下乘客候车心理情绪的变化,通过对感知时间研究来分析其是否能够影响出发时间;通过调查乘客在改变公交线路时考虑因素,了解主要因素。然后,对其如何影响乘客线路选择进行分析。

3　数据分析

3.1　问卷整体分析

本次共得到有效问卷 159 份,分析如下。

3.1.1　个人属性

被调查者中女性占 55.97%;年龄中占比最大 18~30 岁,为 88.68%;受教育程度中大专或本科占比为 76.73%;另外,多数人等待容忍度在 6~10min 内,如图 2 所示。

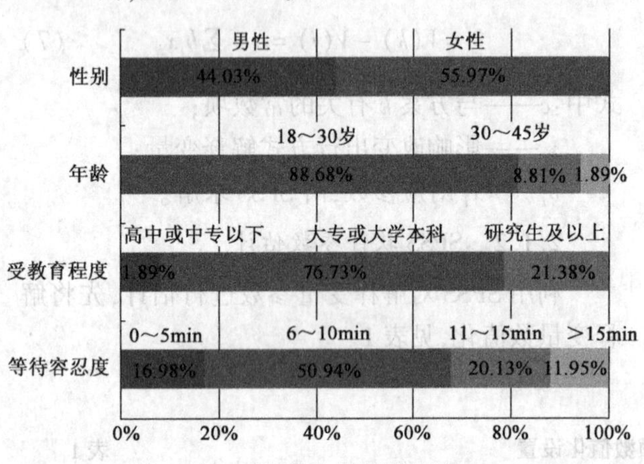

图 2　出行者个人属性统计图

3.1.2　出行属性

此次问卷中,对以下出行属性进行分析,如图 3~图 6 所示。

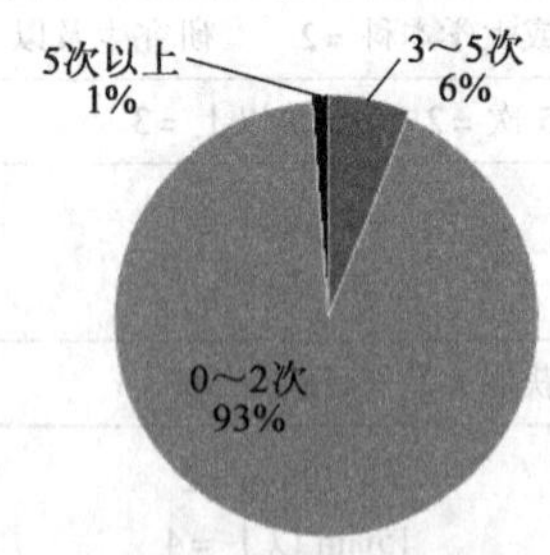

图 3　每天乘坐公交车次数

由图 3、图 4 知,乘客每天乘坐公交频率不高,由于正是疫情期间,此类问题会受到限制出行影响。由图 5、图 6 知,83.65% 主要以电子站牌和手机 APP 获取实时公交信息,可见实时公交信息广受欢迎。

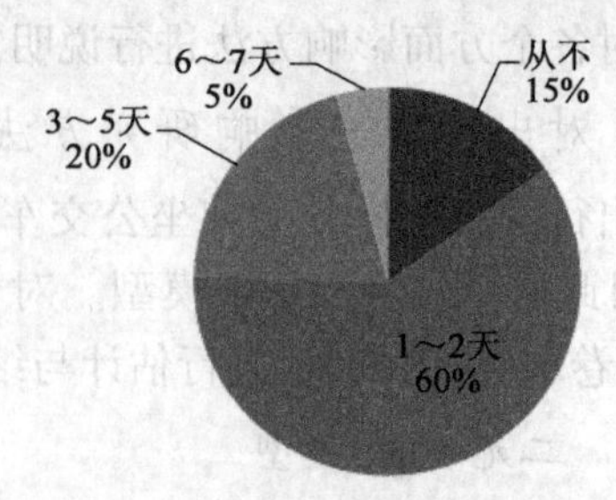

图 4　每周乘公交车天数

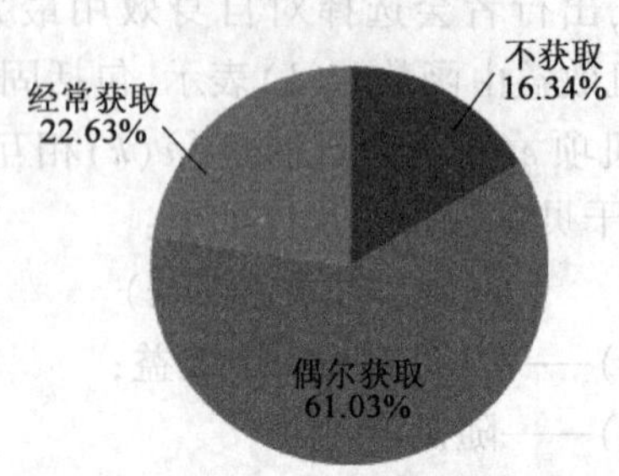

图 5　实时公交信息获取情况

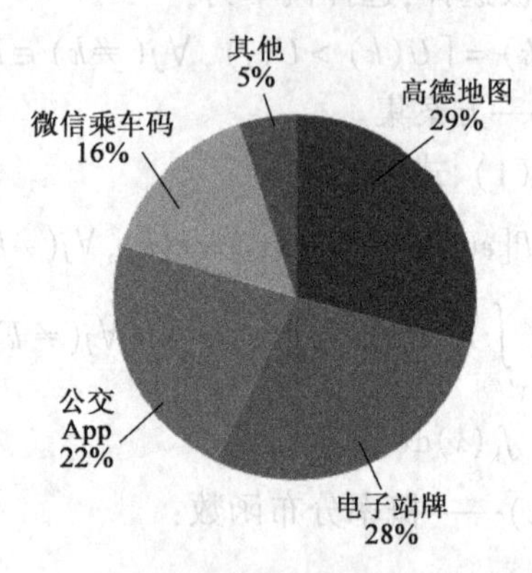

图 6　获取信息途径

3.1.3　乘客对信息评价

由图 7、图 8 知,认为实时公交信息不准确、作用不大的占比极少,可见,实时公交信息给予出行者有利条件,但其准确性有待提高。

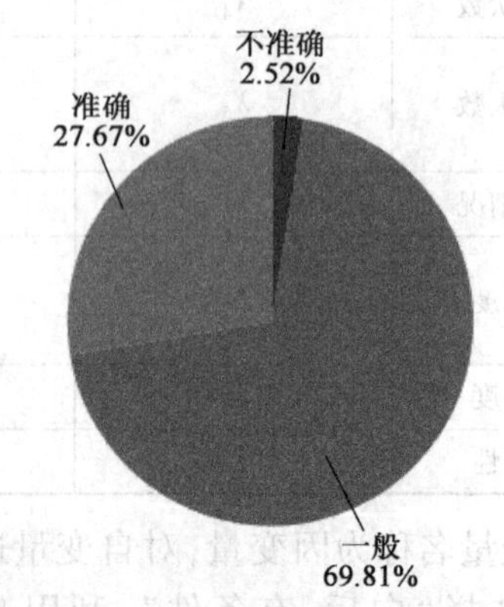

图 7　实时公交信息准确性

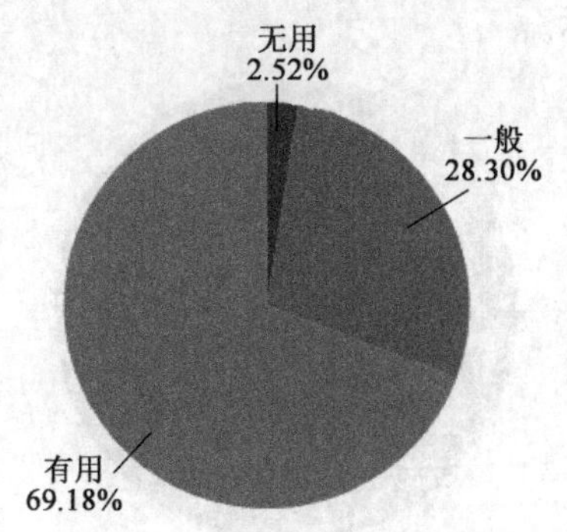

图8　实时公交信息是否有用

3.2　实时公交信息对乘客出行方式影响

3.2.1　改变出行方式影响因素

通过调查乘客改变出行方式时的考虑因素，分析如图9所示。

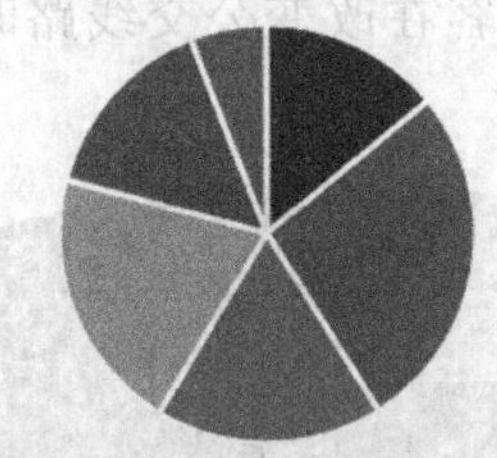

图9　乘客在改变出行方式时考虑因素

由图9知，乘客在改变出行方式时考虑最多是候车时长，其次为是否出现拥堵，这一因素与候车时长密切相关，出行者考虑费用可能性最小。

3.2.2　模型参数估计与结果分析

(1)参数估计。

根据二元Logit模型，由2.1节所提方法筛选自变量，利用SPSS得最优解。通过剔除显著性水平在95%以下解释变量，得迭代结果见表2。

Logit回归分析最终迭代结果　表2

项　目	b	P	exp(b)
受教育程度		0.090	
受教育程度(1)	4.086	0.030	59.479
受教育程度(2)	3.325	0.112	27.796
实时公交信息获取情况		0.024	
实时公交信息获取情况(1)	2.586	0.007	13.276
实时公交信息获取情况(2)	2.040	0.068	7.691
等待容忍度		0.092	
等待容忍度(1)	-3.929	0.028	0.020
等待容忍度(2)	-4.671	0.013	0.009
等待容忍度(3)	-1.631	0.590	0.196
实时公交信息准确性		0.057	
实时公交信息准确性(1)	2.056	0.032	7.815
实时公交信息准确性(2)	2.476	0.025	11.888
实时公交信息有用性		0.003	
实时公交信息有用性(1)	2.624	0.007	13.793
实时公交信息有用性(2)	3.407	0.001	30.182
常量	-4.130	0.037	0.016

当$P<0.05$时，说明该影响因素显著。由表2知，最终自变量为受教育程度、等待容忍度、实时公交信息：获取情况、信息准确性、有用性。将估计得到参数代入式(7)得出行方式选择模型：

$$P(k)=\frac{1}{1+\mathrm{e}^{-V}}$$

$$P(j)=1-P(k) \tag{8}$$

式中：$V=V(k)-V(j)=c+\sum_i b_i x_i=-4.130+4.086x_3(2)+2.586x_6(2)-3.929x_7(2)-4.671x_7(3)+2.056x_8(2)+2.476x_8(3)+2.624x_9(2)+3.407x_9(3)$；

$P(k)$——选择k方案的概率；

$P(j)$——选择j方案的概率；

$x_3(2)$——大专或大学本科；

$x_6(2)$——偶尔获取实时公交信息；

$x_7(2)$——能接受最长等待时间为6～10min；

$x_7(3)$——能接受最长等待时间为11～15min；

$x_8(2)$——实时公交信息一般准确；

$x_8(3)$——实时公交信息准确；

$x_9(2)$——实时公交信息一般有用；

$x_9(3)$——实时公交信息有用。

模型拟合优度检验见表3。

霍斯默—莱梅肖检验　表3

步　骤	卡　方	自由度	显著性
1	6.215	8	0.623
4	5.215	8	0.734

由显著性$0.734>0.05$，故拟合度高，模型拟合质量好。

(2)结果分析。

由结果知各变量对出行方式产生显著影响,分析如下:

①受教育程度:系数为正,且其参考类别为中专或高中及以下,说明受教育程度越高,改变出行方式概率越大。

②实时公交信息获取情况:系数为正,以从不获取信息为参考类别,实时公交信息获取越频繁,改变出行方式可能性越大,且获取信息乘客改变出行方式可能性是不获取信息的13.3倍,可见实时公交信息对出行方式选择影响显著。

③等待容忍度:系数为负,以等待容忍度为0~5min为参考类别,说明等待容忍度越小,乘客改变出行方式可能性越大。

④实时公交信息准确性:系数为正,说明其对改变出行方式有正向作用,出行者越认为实时公交信息准确,易改变出行方式。

⑤实时公交信息有用性:系数为正,以信息无用为参考类别,说明出行者若认为实时公交信息对出行决策有用,则易受其影响而改变出行方式。

3.3 实时公交信息对乘客候车心理、出行时间、公交线路选择影响

3.3.1 对乘客候车心理情绪影响

通过了解实时公交信息对乘客候车心理影响,分析如下。

由图10知,多数乘客认为实时公交信息能减小乘客候车不确定性,缓解焦虑,由于对时间有把握,使候车更有耐心。

图10 实时公交信息对乘客心理情绪的影响

3.3.2 对乘客出行时间影响

实时公交信息对乘客感知等待时间影响如图11所示。

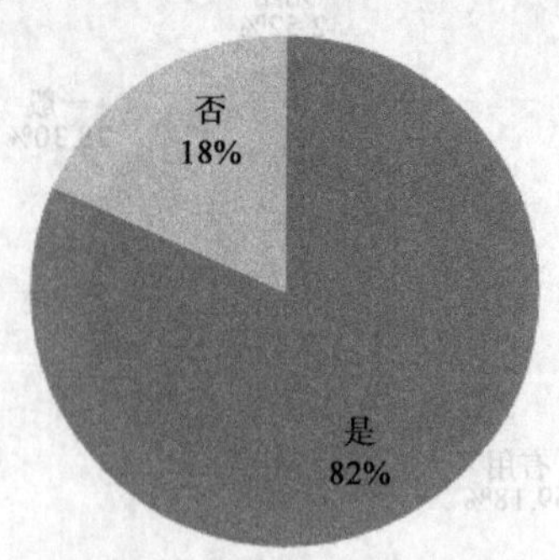

图11 无实时公交信息下等待时间是否更加漫长

由图11知,82%乘客认为无实时公交信息时等车时间更长。说明实时公交信息能减少乘客感知候车时间,从而提前改变出发时间。

3.3.3 对乘客公交线路选择影响

通过调查乘客在改变公交线路时的考虑因素,如图12所示。

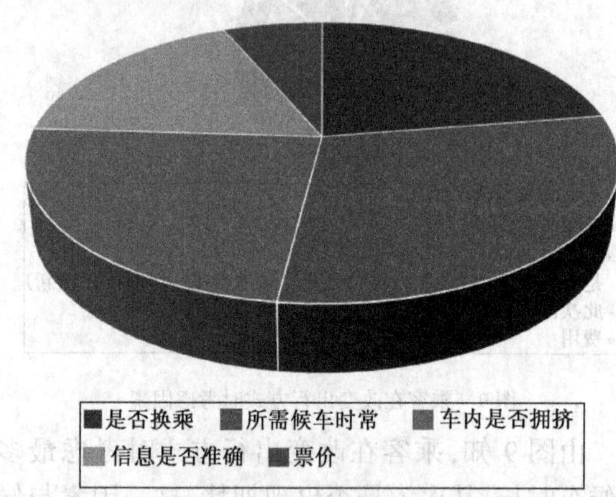

图12 实时公交信息下改变公交线路的影响因素

由图12知,在实时公交信息提供下,乘客改变线路时最多考虑候车时长,其次为车内是否拥挤、乘坐此车是否需换乘以及实时公交信息是否准确等。

主要因素统计分析如下:

(1)等待容忍度对改变公交线路影响如图13所示。

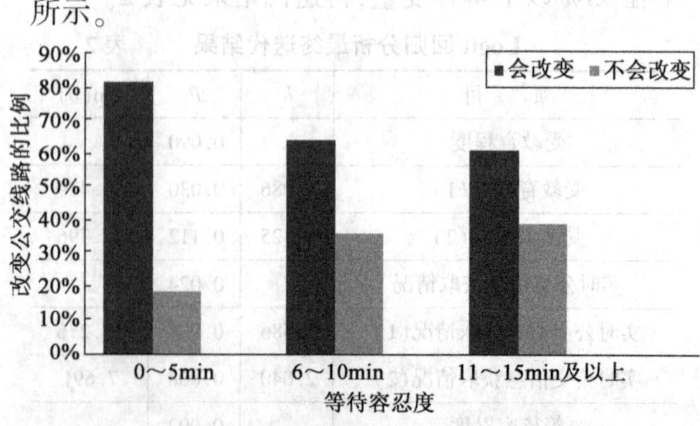

图13 等待容忍度与改变公交线路关系

由图13知乘客可接受最长候车时间越短，其改变线路比例越高，随容忍时间增大，其改变公交线路可能性降低，说明等待容忍度与改变公交线路呈负相关。

(2)信息准确度对改变公交线路影响。

由图14可知，随实时公交信息准确性提高，乘客改变公交线路比例提高，即实时公交信息准确性与改变公交线路的趋势正相关。

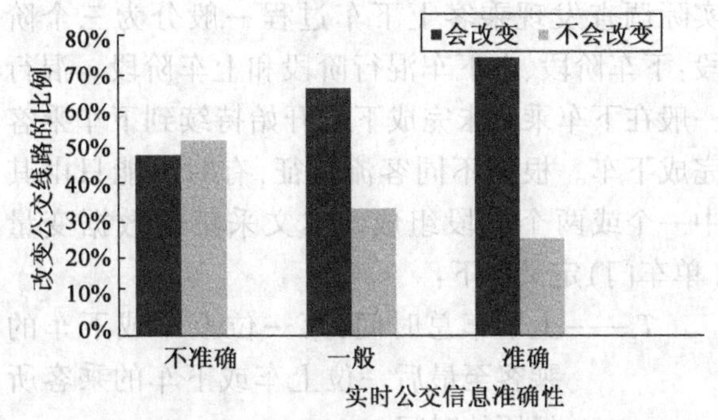

图14 实时公交信息准确性与改变公交线路关系

4 结语

(1)影响乘客改变出行方式因素有：受教育程度、乘客等待容忍度、实时公交信息：获取情况、准确性、有用性，其中等待容忍度与改变出行方式呈负相关，其他因素对方式改变有正向作用。

(2)实时公交信息能减少乘客出行不确定性，缓解焦虑，更好把握候车时间，降低感知候车时间。

(3)在实时公交信息提供下，乘客改变公交线路考虑最多因素是等车时长，其次是车厢拥挤度、是否需换乘及实时公交信息是否准确。此外，乘客最大容忍时间越短或实时公交信息越准确，其改变线路可能性越大。

此外，本文仍有不足，调查问卷样本不足、变量水平值需增加；实时公交信息对乘客出行行为影响分时段、分目的不同，今后研究仍需改进。

参考文献

[1] 钱依楠，申华鹏，吴静娴.公交实时信息化服务对乘客出行行为意向影响[J].物流技术，2022，41(02).

[2] 史远.多种公交到站信息发布形式下的乘客出行行为研究[D].西安：长安大学，2020.

[3] 孟嘉铭，林南南，史宏飞.公交实时信息对乘客出行的影响[J].公路交通科技(应用技术版)，2018，14(11).

[4] 张蒙迪.实时公交信息对乘客出行行为的影响及其效用研究[D].西安：长安大学，2018.

[5] 侯现耀，陈学武，曾隽.公交出行信息条件下出行者通勤出发时间选择影响因素[J].东南大学学报(自然科学版)，2016，46(04)：893-898.

混行行为对地铁乘客上下车时间影响分析及时间预测*

彭丽如[1] 刘伟铭*[1] 郭雨鑫[2]

(1.华南理工大学土木与交通学院；2.湖北省交通规划设计院股份有限公司)

摘 要 地铁站台上下车时间是列车停站时间的重要组成部分。乘客上下车过程中普遍存在的混行行为(车门处同时存在无序上车和下车乘客)是影响列车停站时间的重要因素。本文利用机器视觉和深度学习结合的方法所采集的站台门与地铁间乘客上下车实时数据，分析研究不同客流规模下混行行为对乘客上下车时间的影响，并进一步提出了基于混行因素的高斯过程回归时间预测模型。实验结果表明，在混行发生的情况下，上、下车时间分别增加了33.78%、24.84%。不同客流规模的混行行为对上下车总时间影响不同。与传统线性回归模型相比，高斯过程回归模型有效实现了上下车总时间概率意义上的预测，拟合优度提高了9.21%，均方根误差减少15.6%。对上下客时间进行分析及预测可以优化列车停站时间，缩短列车最小发车间隔，提高列车运行效率。

关键词 城市轨道交通 时间预测 高斯过程回归 上下车时间 混行行为

1.基金项目：国家重点研发计划(2016YFB1200402)。

0　引言

地铁在站时间包括开关门时间、上下车时间、确认和等待信号时间。上下车时间是地铁在站时间的主要组成部分，影响着列车最小发车间隔。上下车时间的确定是列车运行仿真的基础，有助于优化列车运行效率。目前大多数地铁站都建议乘客先下后上，但在实际上下客过程中混行行为十分常见。因此探讨混行行为对乘客上下车时间的影响并据此建立上下车时间模型具有重要的意义。

为了能够准确预测地铁在站时间，Puong[1]和Kim等[2]以不同地铁站台为例建立了关于乘客数量和车厢拥挤度的上下车时间模型。曹守华等[3]分析乘客上车时间特性以建立分段式数学模型。学者建立的上下车时间模型均为参数回归方法且样本较少，为确定性模型，无法对预测值的不确定性进行定量分析。高斯过程回归[4]是使用高斯过程先验对数据进行回归分析的非参数模型，输出预测的同时还能得到预测值的95%置信区间，可以实现预测值概率意义上的预测。

为了研究影响上下客效率因素，Daamen等[5]研究人数和方向组成、站台与车辆之间的宽度与高度等10个因素对车门通过能力的影响。Yang等[6]改变期望速度和身体半径等参数，研究人群异质性对乘客下车效率的影响；Zhang等[7]研究上下车客流规模与时间的关系，发现同一下车客流规模平均下车时间随着上、下车人数的比例增大而增加。上述学者对影响上下车效率因素的研究大都局限于上、下车乘客数量、上下车乘客比例和基础设施等，乘客上下车行为特性如混行行为等通常被忽略。

研究混行行为对上下客效率的影响的学者有，Li等[8]通过仿真研究不同车厢拥挤度混行下车人数对总人均时间的影响，结果表明总人均时间在中等拥挤时随着混行下车人数的增加先减少后增加，临界阈值为5人。陈伽申[9]对不同客流规模，只考虑上(下)人数并将其拆分为混行人数和非混行人数进行多元线性回归分析。上述研究证明混行行为对乘客上下车时间具有直接影响。

综上，本文基于站台屏蔽门与地铁间乘客上下车获取的498组实时数据，分析不同客流规模下混行行为对乘客上下车时间的影响，并进一步建立基于混行因素的高斯过程回归上下车时间预测模型。

1　基本参数定义及数据来源

早高峰时段居民出行较为集中，本文数据采集于2020年9月两个工作日早高峰时段(7:30～9:00)广州某地铁站台同一行驶方向列车的各个车门，候车区域地面标识为中间下车，两边上车。实际调查发现乘客上下车过程一般分为三个阶段：下车阶段、上下车混行阶段和上车阶段。混行一般在下车乘客未完成下车开始持续到下车乘客完成下车。根据不同客流特征，有时可能只由其中一个或两个阶段组成。本文采集的数据变量(单车门)定义如下：

T_t——上下车总时间，第一位上车或下车的乘客至最后一位上车或下车的乘客所经历的时间；

T_r——混行时间，混行行为持续的时间；

T_a、T_b——下车时间即乘客下车持续时间、上车时间即乘客上车持续时间；

N_{ra}、N_{rb}——混行时间内下车人数、混行时间内上车人数；

N_{a-r}、N_{b-r}——非混行时间内下车人数、非混行时间内上车人数；

N_a、N_b——下车人数，等于N_{a-r}与N_{ra}之和、上车人数，等于N_{a-r}与N_{ra}之和；

通过机器视觉和深度学习结合的方法对每个乘客的运动轨迹方向进行统计，再计算得到客流相关数据。检测精度在每万次上下客流检测中达到97.10%[10]，获取手段较人工计算更为智能且数据比仿真数据更贴近实际。剔除时间间隔大于4s的数据[11]，共采集498组有效数据，其中有78.50%的数据存在混行行为，并且混行时间占总时间的最大比重达到88.67%，因此分析混行行为在不同客流规模下对乘客上下车时间的影响十分必要。

2　混行行为对上下车时间影响分析

为分析混行行为对人均上下车时间影响，对客流规模为1～10人，11～20人和21～30人时存在混行行为和不存在混行行为的人均上、下车时间和总人均时间进行统计，结果如图1中A、B、C所示。三类客流规模样本数量分别为124组，166

组和 123 组，存在混行行为的组别的比例分别为 41.13%，22.89%，13.00%。数据标注表示存在混行行为相较于不存在混行行为的人均时间变化百分比。混行行为对人均上下车时间影响具体分析如下：

(1)由图 1 中 A、B 部分可以看出在同一客流规模存在混行行为时人均上、下车时间均大于不存在混行行为时，总体上、下车时间分别增加了 33.78%，24.84%。

(2)尽管混行行为造成人均上、下车时间的增加，但对总人均时间影响不同，由图 1 中 C 部分可知，当客流规模为 0～10 人，11～20 人时，存在混行行为时总人均时间比不存在混行行为时分别少 23.65%和 11.36%，客流规模大于 20 人时，存在混行行为时总人均时间比不存在混行行为时多 15.2%。

上述分析表明混行行为会增加人均、下车时间，但是对总人均时间的影响则与客流规模相关，在 0～10 人和 11～20 人组别总人均时间减少，但是在 0～10 人组减少更多，21～30 人组别总人均时间增加。

为找出混行行为发生对总人均时间的影响发生变化的阈值，对不同分类条件总人均时间进行统计，如图 2 所示。图 2a)为采用移动平均法以上下车总人数 5 人为一组，移动步长为 1 时总人均时间统计图，平滑后可以直观看出在总人数大于 20 人的组别时，存在混行行为时总人均时间大于不存在混行行为时的总人均时间。图 2b)为不同总人数时总人均时间统计，总人数不大于 20 人时，存在混行行为时总人均时间均小于不存在混行时，大于 20 人时除了 26 人时，存在混行行为时总人均时间均大于不存在混行时。因为人数为 26 人时不存在混行行为的样本量只有一个，所以可能存在偶然性。

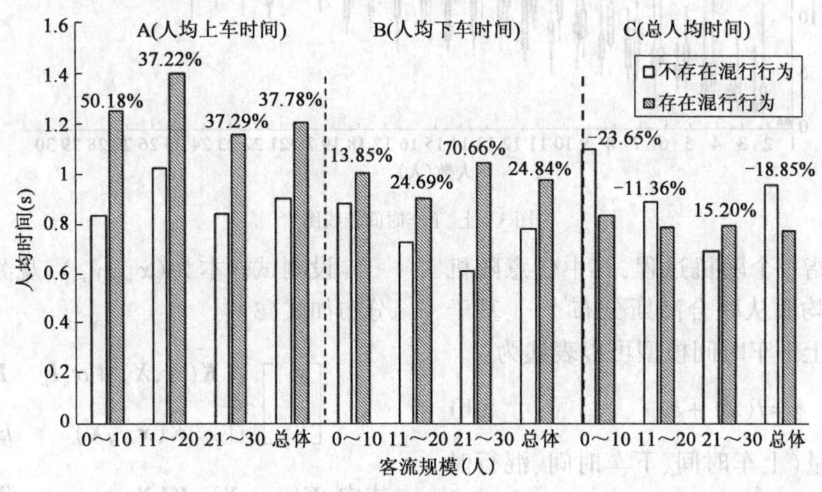

图 1 不同客流规模人均上下车时间

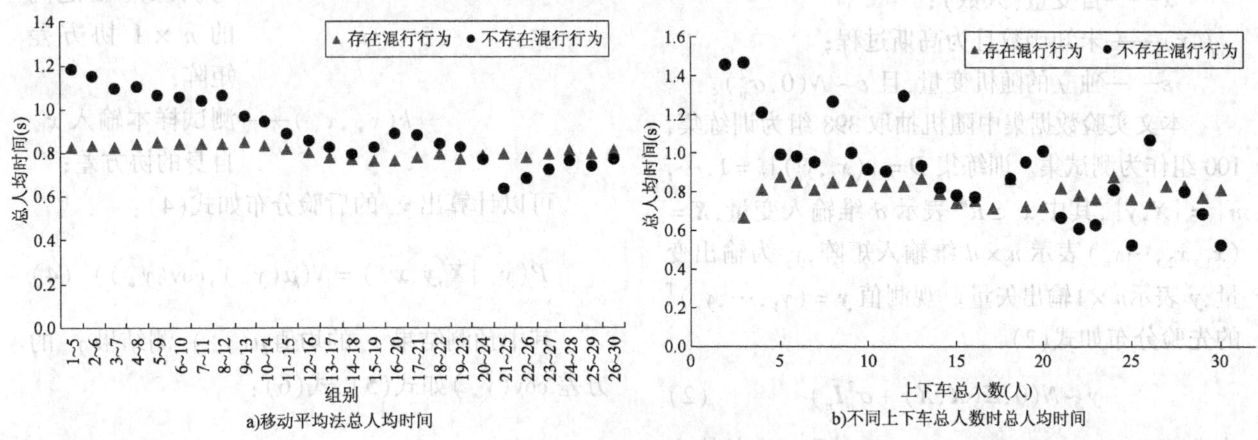

图 2 混行行为对总人均时间影响

综合上述分析，在乘客上下车过程中混行行为发生并不是一定降低上下车效率，尽管混行行为在任何客流规模都会增加人均上车时间和人均下车时间,但是只有在大于 20 人时才会增加总人均时间,在小于 20 人时反而会减少总人均时间。

3　基于混行因素的高斯过程回归时间预测模型

大部分学者建立的上下车时间模型使用传统参数回归方法,然而该方法只对平滑曲线的预测效果较好,并且一般使用最小二乘法求解方程从而得出唯一确定的预测值,无法对预测值的不确定性做出定量分析。

对乘客上下车时间与人数关系进行分析,如图 3 所示。可以看出,时间具有一定波动性,因此传统参数回归模型不适用于该波动曲线预测。高斯过程回归模型是使用高斯过程先验对数据进行回归分析的非参数模型,对高维数、小样本和非线性等问题具有良好的适应性和泛化能力,并且能够输出预测值及其 95% 置信区间[12],可以实现上下车时间概率意义上的预测。因此本文使用高斯过程回归模型对乘客上下车时间进行预测。

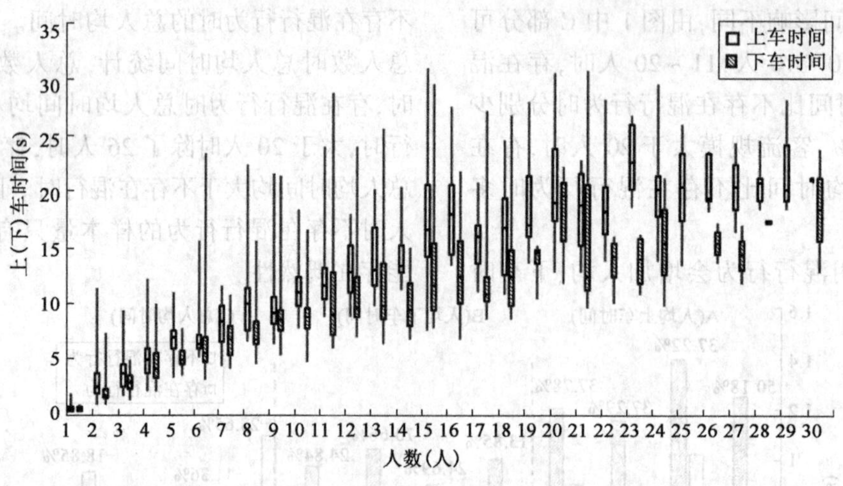

图 3　上、下车时间箱线图

高斯过程是指一个随机过程,其中任意随机变量的有限子集均服从联合高斯分布[13]。基于高斯过程回归的上下车时间模型可以表述为:

$$y = f(\boldsymbol{x}) + \varepsilon \tag{1}$$

式中:y——自变量(上车时间、下车时间、混行时间、上下车时间);

$\boldsymbol{x}$——自变量(人数);

$f(\boldsymbol{x})$——未知函数且为高斯过程;

ε——独立的随机变量,且 $\varepsilon \sim N(0,\sigma_n^2)$。

本文实验数据集中随机抽取 398 组为训练集,100 组作为测试集。训练集 $D=\{(\boldsymbol{x}_i,y_i)\mid i=1,\cdots,n\}=\{\boldsymbol{X},y\}$,其中 $\boldsymbol{x}_i \in R^d$ 表示 d 维输入变量,$\boldsymbol{X}=(x_1,x_2,\cdots x_n)$ 表示 $n\times d$ 维输入矩阵,y_i 为输出变量,$\boldsymbol{y}$ 表示 $n\times 1$ 输出矢量。观测值 $\boldsymbol{y}=(y_1,\cdots,y_n)^{\mathrm{T}}$ 的先验分布如式(2):

$$\boldsymbol{y} \sim N(0,\boldsymbol{K}(\boldsymbol{X},\boldsymbol{X})+\sigma_n^2\boldsymbol{I}_n) \tag{2}$$

式中:$\boldsymbol{K}(\boldsymbol{X},\boldsymbol{X})=\boldsymbol{k}(\boldsymbol{x}_i,\boldsymbol{x}_j)_{n\times n}$——对称正定的协方差矩阵;

$\boldsymbol{I}_n$——n 维单位矩阵。

设测试样本为$(\boldsymbol{x}_*,y_*)$,观测值和预测值 y_* 分布如式(3):

$$\begin{bmatrix} \boldsymbol{y} \\ y_* \end{bmatrix} \sim \begin{bmatrix} \boldsymbol{K}(\boldsymbol{X},\boldsymbol{X})+\sigma_n^2\boldsymbol{I}_n & \boldsymbol{K}(\boldsymbol{X},\boldsymbol{x}_*) \\ \boldsymbol{K}(\boldsymbol{x}_*,\boldsymbol{X}) & k(\boldsymbol{x}_*,\boldsymbol{x}_*) \end{bmatrix} \tag{3}$$

式中:$\boldsymbol{K}(\boldsymbol{x}_*,\boldsymbol{X}),\boldsymbol{K}(\boldsymbol{X},\boldsymbol{x}_*)$——测试样本输入 $\boldsymbol{x}_*$ 与训练集 $\boldsymbol{X}$ 之间的 $n\times 1$ 协方差矩阵;

$k(x_*,x_*)$——测试样本输入 $\boldsymbol{x}_*$ 自身的协方差;

可以计算出 y_* 的后验分布如式(4):

$$P(y_*\mid \boldsymbol{X},\boldsymbol{y},\boldsymbol{x}_*)=N(\mu(y_*),\mathrm{cov}(y_*)) \tag{4}$$

其中预测结果 y_* 的均值 $\mu(y_*)$、测结果 y_* 的方差 $\mathrm{cov}(y_*)$ 如式(5)、式(6):

$$\mu(y_*)=\boldsymbol{K}(x_*,\boldsymbol{X})[\boldsymbol{K}(\boldsymbol{X},\boldsymbol{X})+\sigma_n^2\boldsymbol{I}_n]^{-1}y \tag{5}$$

$$\mathrm{cov}(y_*)=\boldsymbol{k}(\boldsymbol{x}_*,\boldsymbol{x}_*)-\boldsymbol{K}(\boldsymbol{x}_*,\boldsymbol{X})$$

$$[\boldsymbol{K}(\boldsymbol{X},\boldsymbol{X})+\sigma_n^2\boldsymbol{I}_n]^{-1}\boldsymbol{K}(\boldsymbol{y},\boldsymbol{x}_*) \tag{6}$$

高斯过程回归模型预测结果的好坏取决于是否选择了合适的核函数作为协方差函数。本数据集采用核函数为平方指数协方差函数,表达式见式(7):

$$\boldsymbol{k}(\boldsymbol{x},\boldsymbol{x}')=\sigma_f^2\exp\left[-\frac{1}{2}(\boldsymbol{x},\boldsymbol{x}')^{\mathrm{T}}\Lambda^{-1}(\boldsymbol{x},\boldsymbol{x}')\right] \tag{7}$$

式中: σ_f^2——核函数的信号方差;

$\Lambda=\mathrm{diag}(l_1^2,l_2^2,\cdots,l_d^2)$——每个输入属性的长度尺度参数 l 的集合。

称参数集合 $\theta=[\Lambda,\sigma_f^2,\sigma_n^2]$ 为超参数,超参数优化依据贝叶斯原理,通过极大似然法求得参数的最大后验估计。

为了评价预测效果,采用拟合优度 R^2 和均方根误差 RMSE 来分析预测结果和实际值的精确值。其计算公式分别为:

$$R^2=1-\frac{\sum_{i=1}^{m}(y_i-y_{i*})^2}{\sum_{i=1}^{m}(y_i-\bar{y})^2} \tag{8}$$

$$\mathrm{RMSE}=\sqrt{\frac{1}{m}\sum_{i=1}^{m}(y_i-y_{i*})^2} \tag{9}$$

式中:m——观测变量数;

y_{i*}——预测变量;

$\bar{y}$——观测值的平均值。

基于混行因素的高斯过程回归时间预测模型从三个方面进行实验。首先,对混行时间进行实验,分析混行时间与人数关系;其次,对上、下车时间进行实验,分析混行因素对上、下车时间预测效果影响;最后,在相同条件下对线性回归模型和高斯过程回归模型进行实验并对比。实验数据集为前述所采集的 498 组数据,在其中随机抽取 100 组作为测试集,剩余 398 组作为训练集。实验性能指标及高斯过程回归模型参数如表 1 所示,结果分析如下:

(1)混行时间与混行上车和混行下车人数具有显著线性关系。第 1 组中线性回归模型中 R^2 大于 0.9,因此混行人数决定混行程度。

(2)第 2~5 组实验证明混行行为对下车乘客影响大于上车乘客。第 2、3 组为是否虑混行因素的上车时间回归模型,两组 R^2 和 RMSE 变化较小。第 4、5 组为是否虑混行因素的下车时间回归模型,第 5 组 R^2 比第 4 组高 42.37%,RMSE 比第 4 组低 36.97%。

(3)基于高斯过程回归时间模型预测效果均优于线性回归模型,第 2~6 组实验中高斯过程回归模型 R^2 均高于线性回归模型,RMSE 则均低于线性回归模型。其中基于混行因素的上车、下车高斯过程回归时间预测模型均方根误差分别为 1.33s 和 2.04s。高斯过程回归上下车总时间预测模型均方根误差 2.16s。第 3、5、6 组高斯过程回归时间预测模型预测结果如图 4 所示,该模型给出预测值及 95% 置信区间,测试集中只有少部分实际值在预测值 95% 置信区间外。证明本文提出的高斯过程回归时间预测模型有效实现了时间概率意义上的预测。

上下车时间高斯过程回归模型性能指标 表 1

组别	因变量	自变量	线性回归模型				高斯过程回归模型						
			训练集		测试集		训练集		测试集		$l_1,l_2,\cdots l_d$	σ_f	σ_n
			RMSE	R^2	RMSE	R^2	RMSE	R^2	RMSE	R^2			
1	T_r	N_{ra},N_{rb}	1.27	0.92	0.78	0.92	0.49	0.99	1.13	0.84	[1.50,1.69]	8.54	0.54
2	T_b	N_b	3.60	0.77	2.53	0.77	3.23	0.82	2.15	0.83	[3.12]	7.99	3.29
3		N_{r-b},N_{rb},N_{ra}	3.26	0.82	2.21	0.81	2.48	0.89	2.04	0.85	[2.69,3.30,3.21]	7.68	2.82
4	T_a	N_a	3.98	0.48	2.30	0.51	3.73	0.54	2.11	0.59	[3.52]	8.12	3.78
5		N_{r-a},N_{rb},N_{ra}	2.58	0.78	1.45	0.80	2.12	0.85	1.33	0.84	[3.51,6.83,4.46]	8.32	2.54
6	T_t	N_a,N_b	3.35	0.82	2.56	0.76	2.94	0.86	2.23	0.82	[13.35,9.86]	4.54	3.38

4 结语

本文根据实际数据分析混行行为对乘客上下车时间的影响并提出了基于混行因素的高斯过程回归时间预测模型,通过研究得到以下结论:

(1)通过对实验数据进行分析得出混行行为在任何客流规模均会增加人均上、下车时间,总体样本人均上、下车时间增加分别增加了 33.78%,

24.84%，但总人均时间在大于20人时才会增加，而不大于20人时总人均时间则会减少。

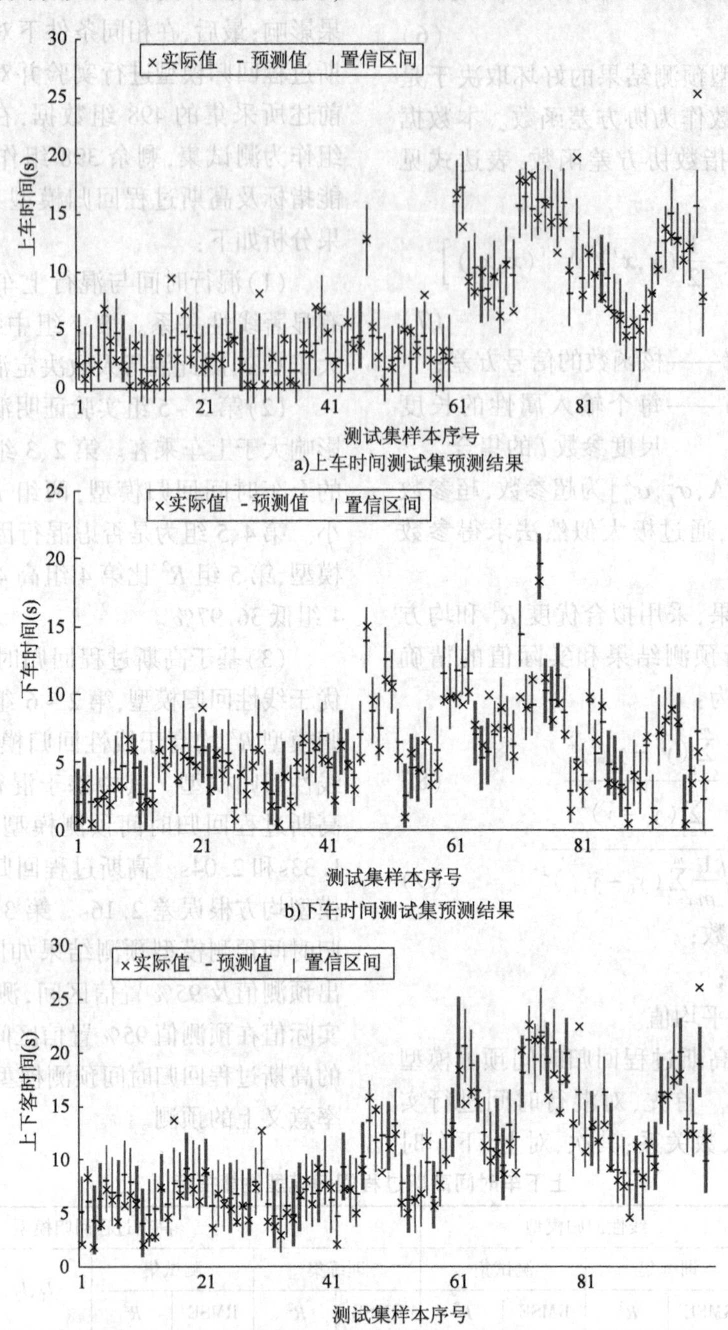

图4　测试集时间预测结果

(2)基于混行因素的高斯过程回归时间预测模型进行三部分实验。首先，对混行时间进行实验，发现混行时间与混行人数存在显著线性关系；其次，进行考虑混行因素的上、下车时间实验，比较是否考虑对向混行人数的拟合结果，结果表明混行行为对下车乘客影响大于上车乘客；最后，在相同条件下对线性回归模型和高斯过程回归模型进行实验进行对比，实验表明高斯过程回归时间预测模型均优于传统线性回归模型。本文提出的高斯过程回归时间模型给出了预测值及其置信区间，且实际值与预测值十分接近，只有少部分实际值在预测值的置信区间外，能够有效实现概率意义上的上下车时间预测。

本文以广州某站台为例，研究混行行为对上下车时间的影响和提出的上下车时间模型，可以为站台上下车引导提供依据并且有效预测上下车时间。下一步工作可以获取不同线路、站台的数据,针对混行行为特性提出有效管理措施来提高上下车效率,并对大规模的应用进行深入的验证。

参考文献

[1] Puong A. Dwell Time Model and Analysis for the MBTA Red Line [J]. Massachusetts Institute of Technology Research Memo, 2020: 1-8.

[2] Kim J, Kim M S, Hong J S, et al. Development of a Boarding and Alighting Time Model for the Urban Rail Transit in a Megacity [J]. Urban Transport XXI, 2015: 675-685.

[3] 曹守华,袁振洲,赵丹. 城市轨道交通乘客上车时间特性分析及建模[J]. 铁道学报, 2009, 31(03): 89-93.

[4] Rasmussen C E, Williams C K I. Gaussian Processes for Machine Learning [M]. Cambridge: MIT Press, 2006.

[5] Daamen W, Lee Y C, Wiggenraad P. Boarding and Alighting Experiments [J]. Transportation Research Record: Journal of the Transportation Research Board, 2008, 2042(1): 71-81.

[6] Yang X X, Yang X L, Pan F Q, et al. The Effect of Passenger Attributes on Alighting and Boarding Efficiency Based on Social Force Model[J]. Physica A: Statistical Mechanics and its Applications, 2021: 565.

[7] Zhang Q, Han B, Li D. Modeling and Simulation of Passenger Alighting and Boarding Movement in Beijing Metro Stations [J]. Transportation Research Part C: Emerging Technologies, 2008, 16(5): 635-649.

[8] Li Z T, Lo S M, Ma J, et al. A Study on Passengers' Alighting and Boarding Process at Metro Platform by Computer Simulation [J]. Transportation Research Part A: Policy and Practice, 2020, 132: 840-854.

[9] 陈伽申,蒲琪,涂颖菲. 城市轨道交通乘客上下车行为与停站时间研究[J]. 城市轨道交通研究, 2017, 20(01): 61-64 + 78.

[10] Zheng Z X, Liu W M, Wang H, et al. Real-time Enumeration of Metro Passenger Volume Using Anchor-free Object Detection Network on Edge Devices [J]. IEEE Access, 2021: 21593-21603.

[11] Qu Y C, Xiao Y, Liu H, et al. Analyzing Crowd Dynamic Characteristics of Boarding and Alighting Process in Urban Metro Stations-Science Direct [J]. Physica A: Statistical Mechanics and its Applications, 2019, 526: 121075.

[12] 康军,段宗涛,唐蕾,等. 高斯过程回归短时交通流预测方法[J]. 交通运输系统工程与信息, 2015, 15(04): 51-56.

[13] 汪晓臣,郭长青,黄志威,等. 基于视频图像和轴重分析的地铁客流密度显示系统[J]. 现代城市轨道交通, 2019(12): 66-70.

基于离散选择模型的居民出行方式研究

张 敏*[1] 白 杰[1] 王亚楠[2] 黄春富[2] 刘 斌[2]

(1. 长安大学运输工程学院; 2. 长安大学公路学院)

摘 要 为了缓解我国大、中、小城镇的交通拥挤,必须大力发展公交和提高公交运输系统的分载量,所以通过研究出行方式选择行为从而诱导居民尽可能乘坐公共交通出行是非常有意义的。以往对居民出行方式选择的研究存在以下两方面不足:一是过分注重交通方式本身的特点,没有考虑到人、路、环境因素的潜在影响;二是以往研究常常把群体的平均偏好值直接作为每个个体的偏好值,未能重视每个个体的自身特点。所以本文从个体角度出发,围绕出行者的特点进行变量的选取,即受访者性别、年龄、出行目的、三种不同出行方式对应的出行中时间和出行成本,并基于三种不同的logit模型研究了城市居民对不同出行方式选择的机理。基于此本文把用户最终选择的各种不同的出行方式作为因变量,选择其他9个潜在变量作为自变量进行回归分析。对例如性别等单个因素是否影响出行方式选择的结果进行假设检验,并通过可视化构建虚拟变量。使用bigeme软件对数据集进行建模,使用MNL模型建立两个了模型,并进行横向对比。在此基础上,利用bigeme软件对程序代码进行修改,分别使用NL模型和混合logit模型对实例进行研究。通过比较三种模型,得出了三种模型在解释居民出行方式选择行为时的优先级:嵌套logit模型>MNL模型>混合logit模型。结果表明利用该模型的效用函数值,可以得到外部因素变化时各出行方式模式变化的比例,能够从计量统计意义上表述外部条件变化时,公共交通出行分担率的变化情况。

关键词　出行选择行为　嵌套logit模型　MNL模型　混合logit模型　潜在变量　出行分担率

0　引言

众所周知,在道路资源有限的城市空间内,我国交通基础设施的发展速度一直追不上交通需求的速度,造成了城市的交通拥挤,使得居民出行的幸福指数直线下降。在此情况下仅仅依增大规道路建设的规模对减轻城市交通压力来说是不能从根本上解决问题的,只有从居民出行的选择行为入手,研究出行者出行时进行交通方式选择的心理因素和外部因素,才能掌握出行者选择出行方式的规律,诱导居民在出行方式选取上更偏向于公共交通,增大公共交通出行在城市总客流上的分担率,只有这样才能从根本上解决城市的交通拥堵问题。可见对居民的出行选择行为展开研究为城市道路交通诱导治理提供了一定的理论依据。

在运输网络中,出行者的出行行为仅仅是个体在一系列的思维过程中所作出的决策,但在决策之前可经历了很多阶段。首先居民在日常生活中由于“衣食住行”等各种目的产生了需要出行的想法;然后进行出行前的准备,如思考乘坐什么出行方式出行、什么时间段出行、经过哪条道路出行等问题,通常的人们会考虑不同交通方式的便利度、经济性、当然,有些时候,人们在选择出行的时候,还会受到其他因素影响,比如人的心理状态和天气的好坏等。在获得了一定数量的出行规划信息后,人们往往会采用主观或特定的评估方法来比较出各种出行方案的优劣,制定最适合自己的出行计划;其次经过前期多个方案的对比,居民可以依据自身的需要和喜好来确定最佳的出行方式;最后一个阶段,也是尤为重要的一个阶段,即在彻底完成此次出行活动后,出行者将会对自身的体验做出相应的真实评价。若是此次出行结果满意,说明自己各个步骤获取的信息比较充分且正确,以后出行可继续采取该模式进行出行方式的选取。要是对出行结果不是很满意,可能是由于搜集到的资料与现实不符,或是由于未预见到的状况影响了自己规划行程的幸福度。这样的反馈不但会作用以后自己的出行选择,相关经验也会被其他乘客所接受,从而为他们的出行提供一定的参考。

国外学者很早就开始对居民的出行方式选择行为进行研究,并发现相比于集计模型,出行者在选取出行方式时的心理状况更适合用基于效用值的非集计模型来研究。自从Ben[1]在1985年第一次给出了Logit模型的定义后,后世许多学者在此基础上丰富了很多有关非集计模型的研究内容,Logit模型作为非集计模型的代表之一也经常被拿来进行出行方式选择行为的研究。但Logit模型都有一个固有缺陷就是它对目标选择支的选择会受到其他无关选择支的影响,但实际上不同选择支之前应该是互不影响的,业界把这种缺陷称之为IIA缺陷。之后Koppelman等学者在前人研究的基础上[2,3]提出的嵌套Logit(NL)模型,NL模型具有不同分项选择支相互独立和同一分项的选择支之间存在一定相关性的特点,所以它虽然相比于Logit模型在研究出行行为选择机理时多多考虑了分类的情形,但模型本身仍然具有IIA缺陷的弊端。为了彻底解决此问题McFadden D等[4]于1989年提出了一种随机参数Logit模型,克服了IIA的缺陷,形成了一个相对科学的非聚集性出行方式选择行为研究模型。

国内对出行方式选择行为的研究大多是在借鉴国外相关研究之后,根据我国的具体情况,对模式进行了相应的修改与完善。在我国学者们最开始围绕着多元Logit模型进行了一系列的研究:例如,戴晓明[5],魏金丽[6]使用多元 Logit 模型对影响居民出行选择行为的因素进行分析。张磊等[7]从微观的角度上研究了停车费这一经济因素对出行者出行行为的影响,并总结出停车收费的变化对出行方式的选择变化的规律。秦焕美等[8]基于北京市市中心城区的停车调研资料,采用非集计模型的方法,构建了基于多因子的综合评价模式,并对停车费波动带来的出行行为变化的灵敏度进行了研究。符韦苇[9]使用多重 Logit 模型分析了停车费用不同引起的私家车车主的出行意愿变化状况,精确的求解了私家车转乘公共交通的停车费用价格区间。如上文提到随着学者们对 Logit 模型的不断研究,发现该模型固有的 IIA 缺陷始终会给分析结果的准确性带来很大的误差。所以国内学者也普遍的开始研究了其他非集计模型来研究居民出行行为。如杨励雅[10]等基于最大随机效用理论的研究结果表明,在研究经济因素对出行者的选择行为时,嵌套 Logit 模型在模型拟合程度优劣上和传统的多项 Logit 模型相比效果更好,指出了高峰时段提前向车主收费,并未显著降低用车频率这一现实规律。岳利[11]基于嵌套 Logit 模型研究了居民在假期、工作日和周末三个不同时间段内的租车行为差异的因素。

过去的研究都是建立在对出行方式选择结果的基础上,强调从整体出发未能重视个人偏好,这与实际情况并不相符。随机参数 Logit 模型的效用函数系数不是固定的,可以有效地考虑个体偏好。目前,基于随机变量的 Logit 模型已经得到了越来越多的应用,但是涉及出行方式的选择问题的研究还很少见。主要应用在一些其他领域:如罗彦发运用随机参数 Logit 模型研究由于产品差异引起的中国家用汽车市场的变化[12];谭家美等[13]研究了因个人特征引起出行者选择行为差异化的原因。程谦[14]等综合考虑影响铁路出行中的各个因素,分别采用多项式 Logit 模型构建混合 Logit 模型对获得的客流资料拟合,表明混合 Logit 模型的拟合优度更能精细化的反映铁路出行方式选择的特点。盛冬冬[15]利用 NLOGIT 软件分别对传统 Logit 模型、横截面混合 Logit 模型和面板混合 Logit 模型等方法进行了参数估算,验证了面板混合 Logit 模型在行为的解释和预测中更具有准确性的结论。

本文在综合比较多种因素相关性基础上,用 bigeme 软件对数据集进行建模,分别建立了 MNL 模型,NL 模型和混合参数 Logit 模型。结合同一份实际数据分别研究三种模型在解释居民出行方式选择行为时优劣情况,最终利用该模型的效用函数值,量化外部条件变化时,公共交通出行分担率的变化情况。

1 出行方式选择行为机理研究

居民选择交通方式时一般来说会首先考虑目的地距离的远近,但随着研究的不断深入,出行者的自身原因和外部原因在影响出行者出行方式选择时的重要性越来越大。如何精确分析这些自身因素和外部因素对出行方式选择行为的机理有必要进行更深一步的研究。非集计模型(又称离散模型)起源于经济学基础理论,贴近人们在出行方式选择过程中的心理决策,所以也适合应用于人们在出行方式选择中的心理行为研究。在非集计模型中居民出行时对出行方式的选择时是基于个体视角出发的,因此本文认为选用非集计模型来研究居民出行方式的选择行为在理论上和方法上均是可取的。

非集计模式以顾客进行多种选择时"效用"最大化假设为理论依据。该定义最早是经济专业的观点,也就是顾客在购物或购物后的满意程度。决策人员在进行抉择时,其思维的进程看似是相当复杂的,但是事实上却是有理可据的。在离散选择模型中出行者基于各种不同选择支的效用进行选择。由于出行者接收到的资讯难免会有误差,而且特定交通方式的效用也很难被全面地观测,因此一般将效用分成两种:能直接观察到且能被定量研究的称为固定效用,不能定量描述但可被虚拟化处理的称为随机效用。效用最大的学说是决策人员在决策过程中,从最优的角度进行决策。在选择集合中,每一项选择分支都必须满足有限性、互斥性和完整性的需求,但同时选择集中的选择应当涵盖全部可能的情况确保模型的严谨。

2 出行方式影响因素分析

2.1 影响因素的筛选

假设出行者出行选择选择受到许多因素的影响,如出行者的年龄、目的和性别,各种不同出行方式对应的成本,时间等。使用以下回归模型对初步出行调查所获得的数据分析每个因素对出行

者最终选择结果的显著性:

在数据分析中,把出行方式的选择结果设为因变量,其他九个因素是线性拟合的自变量。九个自变量包括出行者年龄、性别、出行目的、三种出行方式对应的出行中时间、出行成本和等待时间。假设回归估计表达式:

$$y = b_0 + b_1 \cdot x_1 + b_2 \cdot x_2 + b_3 \cdot x_3 + b_4 \cdot x_4 + b_5 \cdot x_5 + b_6 \cdot x_6 + b_7 \cdot x_7 + b_8 \cdot x_8 + b_9 \cdot x_9 \tag{1}$$

选择235个调查数据进行研究,对小汽车、地铁、公交三种交通方式中的出行者选择行为的研究中,得到初步结果如图1所示。

SUMMARY OUTPUT

回归统计	
Multiple R	0.57916
R Square	0.335426
Adjusted R	0.308843
标准误差	0.607097
观测值	235

方差分析

	df	SS	MS	F	gnificance F
回归分析	9	41.85548	4.650609	12.6181	3.52E-16
残差	225	82.9275	0.368567		
总计	234	124.783			

	Coefficient	标准误差	t Stat	P-value	Lower 95%	Up
Intercept	1.838499	0.39587	4.644199	5.81E-06	1.058412	2.[illegible]
TCCAR	6.29E-05	1.83E-05	3.442154	0.000688	2.69E-05	9.[illegible]
TCRAIL	-5.1E-05	3.45E-05	-1.49058	0.137472	-0.00012	1.[illegible]
TCBUS	-0.0003	4.41E-05	-6.69517	1.7E-10	-0.00038	-[illegible]
TTCAR	0.008484	0.002008	4.225364	3.47E-05	0.004527	0.[illegible]
TTRAIL	0.001241	0.002037	0.609408	0.542869	-0.00277	0.[illegible]
TTBUS	-0.00757	0.001412	-5.35928	2.06E-07	-0.01035	-[illegible]
AGE	-0.06745	0.054509	-1.23737	0.217238	-0.17486	0.[illegible]
PURPOSE	-0.12327	0.055576	-2.218	0.027555	-0.23278	-[illegible]
GENDER	0.102201	0.081864	1.248427	0.213172	-0.05912	0.[illegible]

图1　影响因素的回归统计分析

F检验用于所有自变量x对y的总体线性显著性。显著性$F<0.05$,F检验通过。

T检验用于独立变量X_i到Y的线性意义。如果变量不显著,则意味着该变量可以从模型中移除,使模型更加简洁。从图1中的p值可以看出,tcrail(轨道交通出行成本)、ttrail(轨道交通出行中时间)、年龄、性别、t统计的p值均大于0.05,说明上述这些自变量和因变量不适合用于构造回归函数。可以再次假设回归估计表达式:

$$y = b_0 + b_1 \cdot \mathrm{TCCAR} + b_2 \cdot \mathrm{TCBUS} + b_3 \cdot \mathrm{TTCAR} + b_4 \cdot \mathrm{TTBUS} + b_5 \cdot \mathrm{PUPPOSE} \tag{2}$$

2.2　单因素假设检验和虚拟变量的构建

经统计在235位受访者人中,三种出行方式及性别统计见表1。

性别和出行方式统计表　　　　表1

男性			女性		
小汽车	火车	公交汽车	小汽车	火车	公交汽车
78	35	15	52	36	16

在研究居民出行方式的选择是否与性别有关时假设:H0:$P(x_i = I) = P_i$ $I = 1,2,3,4,5,6$H1:$P_i = 1/6$。检验统计时取卡方 = 11.07(置信系数取0.05)。因为实际计算统计的卡方为96.38 > 11.07。因此拒绝了原来的假设,认为出行方式的选择与性别无关。

从图2中还可以看出,性别并不影响人们对旅行方式的选择。无论男性还是女性,各种交通方式的比例大致相同。例如,与其他出行方式相比,人们开车更为普遍。但稍有不同的是,男性开车比女性多。

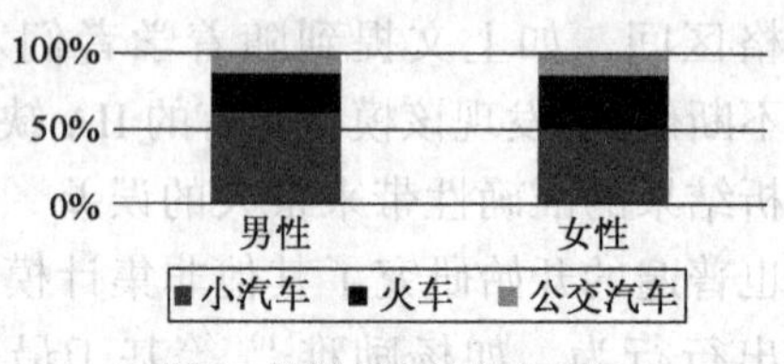

图2　性别与出行方式对比

3　离散选择模型在预测出行方式中的应用

Biogeme是一款开源免费软件,专为参数模型的最大似然估计而设计,特别强调离散选择模型。本章在Biogeme源码的基础上,分别运用了MNL模型(多项Logit模型)、NL模型(巢式Logit模型)、混合Logit模型来预测外部因素变化时出行方式比例的变化。

3.1　两种MNL模型的比较

在样本模型的基础上,此处为不同出行模式的属性提供了一个新的参数BETA6,其中BETA7表示虚拟变量的系数。将虚拟变量dum_1(出行选择方式)添加到模型中(代码见图3)。在样本模型的基础上,定义新的变量(如TCCAR_new是TCCAR的平方),并将性别列为虚拟变量(代码见图4)。

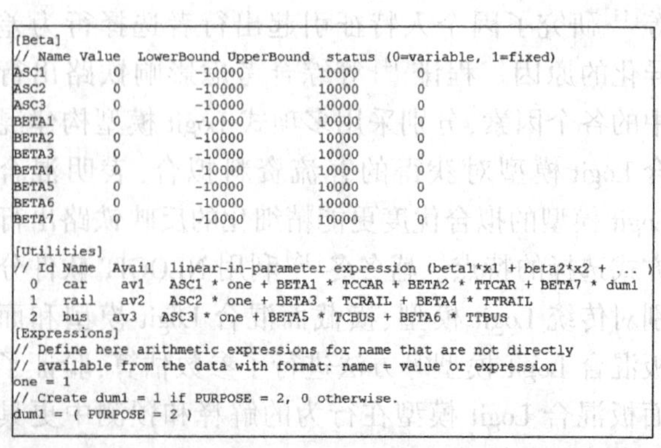

```
[Beta]
// Name Value  LowerBound UpperBound  status (0=variable, 1=fixed)
ASC1      0      -10000      10000      0
ASC2      0      -10000      10000      0
ASC3      0      -10000      10000      0
BETA1     0      -10000      10000      0
BETA2     0      -10000      10000      0
BETA3     0      -10000      10000      0
BETA4     0      -10000      10000      0
BETA5     0      -10000      10000      0
BETA6     0      -10000      10000      0
BETA7     0      -10000      10000      0

[Utilities]
// Id Name  Avail  linear-in-parameter expression (beta1*x1 + beta2*x2 + ... )
  0   car    av1   ASC1 * one + BETA1 * TCCAR + BETA2 * TTCAR + BETA7 * dum1
  1   rail   av2   ASC2 * one + BETA3 * TCRAIL + BETA4 * TTRAIL
  2   bus   av3   ASC3 * one + BETA5 * TCBUS + BETA6 * TTBUS
[Expressions]
// Define here arithmetic expressions for name that are not directly
// available from the data with format: name = value or expression
one = 1
// Create dum1 = 1 if PURPOSE = 2, 0 otherwise.
dum1 = ( PURPOSE = 2 )
```

图3　MNL模型(1)代码

```
ASC2        0     -10000     10000     0
ASC3        0     -10000     10000     0
BETA1       0     -10000     10000     0
BETA2       0     -10000     10000     0
BETA3       0     -10000     10000     0
BETA4       0     -10000     10000     0
BETA5       0     -10000     10000     0
BETA6       0     -10000     10000     0
BETA7       0     -10000     10000     0
BETA8       0     -10000     10000     0
BETA9       0     -10000     10000     0
BETA10      0     -10000     10000     0
BETA11      0     -10000     10000     0
BETA12      0     -10000     10000     0
[Utilities]
// Id Name  Avail  linear-in-parameter expression (beta1*x1 + beta2*x2 + ... )
  0   car    av1   ASC1 * one + BETA1 * TCCAR_new + BETA2 * TTCAR + BETA3 * dum1 + BETA4 * dum2
  1   rail   av2   ASC2 * one + BETA5 * TCRAIL_new + BETA6 * TTRAIL + BETA7 * dum1 + BETA8 * dum2
  2   bus    av3   ASC3 * one + BETA9 * TCBUS_new + BETA10 * TTBUS + BETA11 * dum1 + BETA12 * dum2
[Expressions]
// Define here arithmetic expressions for name that are not directly
// available from the data with format: name = value or expression
one = 1
// Create dum1 = 1 if PURPOSE = 1, 0 otherwise.
dum1 = ( PURPOSE = 1 )
// Create dum2 = 1 if female = 1, 0 otherwise.
dum2 = ( GENDER = 1 )
// This is equivalent to define the following expressions
TCCAR_new  =  TCCAR   ^  2
TCBUS_new  =  TCBUS   ^  2
TCRAIL_new =  TCRAIL  ^  2
```

图4 MNL模型(2)代码

两个模型的输出结果如下所示。图5显示了模型1的结果,图6显示了模型2的结果。

```
                          Model: Multinomial Logit
er of estimated parameters: 14
    Number of observations: 235
     Number of individuals: 235
       Null log-likelihood: -258.174
        Cte log-likelihood: -227.677
       Init log-likelihood: -258.174
      Final log-likelihood: -197.170
     Likelihood ratio test: 122.008
               Rho-square: 0.236
      Adjusted rho-square: 0.182
      Final gradient norm: +3.915e+001
               Diagnostic: Radius of the trust region is too smal
               Iterations: 44
                 Run time: 00:01
      Variance-covariance: from analytical hessian
              Sample file: mnl-sample.dat
```

图5 MNL模型(1)结果

```
                          Model: Multinomial Logit
Number of estimated parameters: 10
        Number of observations: 235
         Number of individuals: 235
           Null log-likelihood: -258.174
            Cte log-likelihood: -227.677
           Init log-likelihood: -258.174
          Final log-likelihood: -163.570
         Likelihood ratio test: 189.208
                   Rho-square: 0.366
          Adjusted rho-square: 0.328
          Final gradient norm: +6.984e-004
                   Diagnostic: Convergence reached...
                   Iterations: 20
                     Run time: 00:00
          Variance-covariance: from analytical hessian
                  Sample file: mnl-sample.dat
```

图6 MNL模型(2)结果

从各个方面可以看出,模型2的效果优于模型1。0.182 <0.328。最终得到两个MNL模型的效用函数如下:

模型1效用函数:

公交汽车:5.70 + −0.00234 · TCBUS + −0.0503 · TTBUS

小汽车:0.841 + −0.000260 · TCCAR −0.0553 · TTCAR +0.770 · dum_1

火车:−4.86 −0.000413 · TCRAIL −0.0205 · TTRAIL

模型2效用函数:

公交汽车:$0.00518-3.01\cdot10^{-7}\cdot TCBUS^2-0.0148\cdot TTBUS-0.000701\cdot dum_1+0.000302\cdot dum_2$

小汽车:$1.77\cdot10^{-8}\cdot TCCAR^2-0.0210\cdot TTCAR-0.0094\cdot dum_1-0.000724\cdot dum_2$

火车:$-0.00105-6.81\cdot10^{-8}\cdot TCRAIL^2-0.0205\cdot TTRAIL+0.00123\cdot dum_1-0.000422\cdot dum_2$

3.2 MNL模型和NL模型的比较

基于给定的数据,使用bigeme软件继续修改代码,建立NL模型和混合Logit模型,NL模型中dum_1为出行目的的虚拟变量,dum_2为性别的虚拟变量。并讨论哪个Logit模型更适合于解释本数据中居民的出行方式选择行为。在biogeme软件中更改NL模型代码(图7)并输出结果表(图8)。

```
ASC1        0     -10000     10000     1
ASC2        0     -10000     10000     0
ASC3        0     -10000     10000     0
BETA1       0     -10000     10000     0
BETA2       0     -10000     10000     0
BETA3       0     -10000     10000     0
BETA4       0     -10000     10000     0
BETA5       0      10000     10000     0
BETA6       0     -10000     10000     0
BETA7       0     -10000     10000     0
BETA8       0     -10000     10000     0
BETA9       0     -10000     10000     0
BETA10      0     -10000     10000     0
BETA11      0     -10000     10000     0
BETA12      0     -10000     10000     0

[Utilities]
// Id Name  Avail  linear in parameter expression (beta1*x1 + beta2*x2 + ... )
  0   car    av1   ASC1 * one + BETA1 * TCCAR_new + BETA2 * TTCAR + BETA3 * dum1 + BETA4 * dum2
  1   rail   av2   ASC2 * one + BETA5 * TCRAIL_new + BETA6 * TTRAIL + BETA7 * dum1 + BETA8 * dum2
  2   bus    av3   ASC3 * one + BETA9 * TCBUS_new + BETA10 * TTBUS + BETA11 * dum1 + BETA12 * dum2
[Expressions]
// Define here arithmetic expressions for name that are not directly
// available from the data with format: name = value or expression
one = 1
// Create dum1 = 1 if PURPOSE = 1, 0 otherwise.
dum1 = ( PURPOSE = 1 )
// Create dum2 = 1 if female = 1, 0 otherwise.
dum2 = ( GENDER = 1 )
// This is equivalent to define the following expressions
TCCAR_new  =  TCCAR   ^  2
TCBUS_new  =  TCBUS   ^  2
TCRAIL_new =  TCRAIL  ^  2
```

图7 NL模型代码

```
                          Model: Nested Logit
Number of estimated parameters: 15
        Number of observations: 235
         Number of individuals: 235
           Null log-likelihood: -258.174
            Cte log-likelihood: -227.677
           Init log-likelihood: -257.821
          Final log-likelihood: -195.289
         Likelihood ratio test: 125.769
                   Rho-square: 0.244
          Adjusted rho-square: 0.185
          Final gradient norm: +7.958e+001
                   Diagnostic: Radius of the trust region is too small
                   Iterations: 105
                     Run time: 00:02
          Variance-covariance: from finite difference hessian
                  Sample file: mnl-sample.dat
```

图8 NL模型结果

3.1节中MNL模型2的参数化输出结果如图9所示。图10为NL模型参数化输出结果。很明显,NL模型的t参数小于MNL模型。对于本案例研究,我们认为NL模型比MNL模型更合适。

Name	Value	Std err	t-test	p-value
ASC1	0.00	fixed		
ASC2	-0.00105	1.80e+308	-0.00	1.00
ASC3	0.000518	1.80e+308	0.00	1.00
BETA1	-1.77e-008	5.97e-009	-2.96	0.00
BETA10	-0.0148	0.00689	-2.15	0.03
BETA11	0.000701	0.323	0.00	1.00
BETA12	0.000302	0.252	0.00	1.00
BETA2	-0.0210	1.80e+308	-0.00	1.00
BETA3	-0.00194	0.254	-0.01	0.99
BETA4	-0.000724	0.163	-0.00	1.00
BETA5	-6.81e-008	2.44e-008	-2.79	0.01
BETA6	-0.0205	0.0108	-1.90	0.06
BETA7	0.00123	0.241	0.01	1.00
BETA8	0.000422	0.279	0.00	1.00
BETA9	-3.01e-007	7.52e-008	-4.00	0.00

图 9　MNL 模型(2)参数输出

Utility parameters

Name	Value	Std err	t-test	p-value	
ASC1	0.00	fixed			
ASC2	-0.0470	1.98	-0.02	0.98	*
ASC3	0.0235	3.50	0.01	0.99	*
BETA1	-1.72e-008	8.66e-009	-1.98	0.05	
BETA10	-0.0150	0.0108	-1.38	0.17	*
BETA11	0.0299	1.80e+308	0.00	1.00	*
BETA12	0.0138	1.80e+308	0.00	1.00	*
BETA2	-0.0207	0.0152	-1.36	0.17	*
BETA3	-0.0823	1.80e+308	-0.00	1.00	*
BETA4	-0.0335	1.80e+308	-0.00	1.00	*
BETA5	-6.80e-008	2.42e-008	-2.81	0.00	
BETA6	-0.0202	0.00398	-5.09	0.00	
BETA7	0.0524	1.80e+308	0.00	1.00	*
BETA8	0.0198	1.80e+308	0.00	1.00	*
BETA9	-3.01e-007	8.38e-008	-3.59	0.00	

Model parameters

Name	Value	Std err	t-test 0	p-value	t-test 1	p-val
NESTA	1.00	fixed				
NESTB	1.00	0.00436	229.10	0.00	0.00	1.00

图 10　NL 模型参数输出

3.3　MNL 模型和混合 Logit 模型比较

在 Biogeme 软件中修、改代码(图 11)和输出结果表(图 12)。来讨论混合 Logit 模型(又称为随机参数 Logit 模型)是否比 MNL 更适合本案例研究。

```
BETA7     0     -10000     10000     0
BETA8     0     -10000     10000     0
BETA9     0     -10000     10000     0
BETA10    0     -10000     10000     0
BETA11    0     -10000     10000     0
BETA12    0     -10000     10000     0

[LaTeX]
ASC1  "Constant for alt. 1"
ASC2  "Constant for alt. 2"
ASC3  "Constant for alt. 3"
BETA1  "$\beta_1$"
BETA2  "$\beta_2$"
SIGMA1  "$\sigma_1$"

[Utilities]
// Id Name  Avail  linear-in-parameter expression (beta1*x1 + beta2*x2 + ... )
 0   car    av1   ASC1 * one + BETA1 * TCCAR_new + BETA2 * TTCAR + BETA3 * dum1 + BETA4 * dum2
 1   rail   av2   ASC2 * one + BETA5 * TCRAIL_new + BETA6 * TTRAIL + BETA7 * dum1 + BETA8 * dum2
 2   bus    av3   ASC3 * one + BETA9 * TCBUS_new + BETA10 * TTBUS + BETA11 * dum1 + BETA12 * dum2

[GeneralizedUtilities]
1 exp( BETA1 [ SIGMA1 ] ) * TTCAR
2 exp( BETA1 [ SIGMA1 ] ) * TTRAIL
3 exp( BETA1 [ SIGMA1 ] ) * TTBUS

[Draws]
5

[Expressions]
// Define here arithmetic expressions for name that are not directly
// available from the data
one = 1
// Create dum1 = 1 if PURPOSE = 1, 0 otherwise.
```

图 11　ML 模型代码

```
                         Model: Mixed Multinomial Logit
               Number of draws: 5
Number of estimated parameters: 15
        Number of observations: 235
         Number of individuals: 235
           Null log-likelihood: -258.174
            Cte log-likelihood: -227.677
           Init log-likelihood: -14437.920
          Final log-likelihood: -5512.944
         Likelihood ratio test: -10509.540
                   Rho-square: -20.354
          Adjusted rho-square: -20.412
          Final gradient norm: +9.462e+005
                   Diagnostic: Maximum number of iterations reached
                   Iterations: 1000
                     Run time: 00:54
          Variance-covariance: from finite difference hessian
                  Sample file: mnl-sample.dat
```

图 12　ML 模型结果

MNL 模型参数化结果如图 13 所示,ML 模型(混合 Logit 模型)如图 14 所示。由于与 MNL 模型相比,ML 模型的 t 检验次数没有显著变化,因此认为混合 Logit 模型不适合本研究。通过比较,得出对于此案例模型适用的优先级:NL 模型 > MNL 模型 > ML 模型。

Name	Value	Std err	t-test	p-value
ASC1	0.00	fixed		
ASC2	-0.00105	1.80e+308	-0.00	1.00
ASC3	0.000518	1.80e+308	0.00	1.00
BETA1	-1.77e-008	5.97e-009	-2.96	0.00
BETA10	-0.0148	0.00689	-2.15	0.03
BETA11	0.000701	0.323	0.00	1.00
BETA12	0.000302	0.252	0.00	1.00
BETA2	-0.0210	1.80e+308	-0.00	1.00
BETA3	-0.00194	0.254	-0.01	0.99
BETA4	-0.000724	0.163	-0.00	1.00
BETA5	-6.81e-008	2.44e-008	-2.79	0.01
BETA6	-0.0205	0.0108	-1.90	0.06
BETA7	0.00123	0.241	0.01	1.00
BETA8	0.000422	0.279	0.00	1.00
BETA9	-3.01e-007	7.52e-008	-4.00	0.00

图 13　MNL 模型参数输出

Name	Value	Std err	t-test	p-val
ASC1	0.00	fixed		
ASC2	-3.46e-011	9.85	-0.00	1.00
ASC3	-2.31e-011	10.8	-0.00	1.00
BETA1	-2.21e-007	6.91e-008	-3.20	0.00
BETA10	-3.93e-009	0.0640	-0.00	1.00
BETA11	2.02e-012	4.90	0.00	1.00
BETA12	-1.42e-011	2.49	-0.00	1.00
BETA2	5.45e-009	0.0505	0.00	1.00
BETA3	1.78e-013	4.25	0.00	1.00
BETA4	2.48e-011	2.03	0.00	1.00
BETA5	-8.10e-006	6.28e-007	-12.90	0.00
BETA6	-2.65e-009	0.122	-0.00	1.00
BETA7	-2.19e-012	2.97	-0.00	1.00
BETA8	-1.05e-011	2.66	-0.00	1.00
BETA9	-2.46e-005	1.46e-006	-16.84	0.00
SIGMA1	-1.50e-008	1.80e+308	-0.00	1.00

图 14　ML 模型参数输出

公交汽车:$0.0235 - 3.01 \cdot 10^{-7} \cdot TCBUS^2 - 0.0150 \cdot TTBUS + 0.0299 \cdot dum_1 + 0.0138 \cdot dum_2$

小汽车:$-1.72 \cdot 10^{-8} \cdot TCAR^2 - 0.0207 \cdot TTCAR - 0.0823 \cdot dum_1 - 0.0335 \cdot dum_2$

火车：$-0.0470-6.8\cdot10^{-8}$ TCRAIL$^2-0.0202\cdot$ TTRAIL $+0.0524\cdot$ dum$_1$ $+0.0198\cdot$ dum$_2$

4 结语

已有235条数据中，71个人选择公交，34人选择小汽车，130人选择轨道出行。实地政策表明：若地铁提速使的出行中时间减少10%，根据NL模型效用函数知，公交车和小汽车受影响较小，地铁选择比例将会提高0.002，其他两种出行方式分担比例基本保持不变。如果燃料价格下降20%，地铁出行分担比例不变，公交车出行增加量占比系数为$3.01\cdot10^{-7}\cdot0.04$，小汽车出行增加量占比系数为$1.72\cdot10^{-8}\cdot0.04$，即1:500的比例，相当于油价若降低20%，每500个人仅有1个人还愿意乘坐公交车出行，这反映了价格对需求影响的客观经济规律，说明模型预测相对准确。

参考文献

[1] Ben Akiva M. Steven R. I. Diserete Choice Analysis: The Theory and Application to Travel Demand [M]. The MIT Press, Cambridge Massachusetts, 1985: 348-349.

[2] Koppelman F. S. Non-Linear Utility Function in Models of Travel Choice Behavior [J]. Transportation 1981, 10: 1224-1233.

[3] Hensher D. A., Reyes A. J. Trip chaining as a barrier to the Porpensity to use Public transport [J]. Transportation, 1990, 27(4): 314-361.

[4] McFadden D. A method of simulated moments for estimation of discrete response models without numerical integration [J]. Econometrica, 1989, 57(5): 995-1026.

[5] 戴晓明. 基于MNL模型的城市交通方式选择研究[J]. 交通技术与经济, 2016, 18(1): 33-37.

[6] 魏金丽，周建伟. 基于多项Logit模型下胶州居民出行行为选择研究[J]. 现代电子技术, 2021, 44(19): 169-172.

[7] 张磊. 基于logit模型的停车费率变化对居民出行方式的影响分析[J]. 交通与运输(学术版), 2015(01): 211-214.

[8] 秦焕美，关宏志，殷焕焕. 停车收费价格对居民出行方式选择行为的影响研究——以北京市居民小汽车、公交、出租车选择行为为例[J]. 土木工程学报, 2008(08): 93-98.

[9] 符韦苇. 广州市停车收费对居民出行方式选择的影响研究[D]. 广州：华南理工大学, 2011.

[10] 杨励雅，邵春福，HAGHANI A. 出行方式与出发时间联合选择的分层Logit模型[J]. 交通运输工程学报, 2012, 12(02): 76-83.

[11] 岳利，吴丽霞. 基于NL模型的居民租车选择行为研究[J]. 现代商贸工业, 2018, 39(35): 76-77.

[12] 罗延发. 产品差异化视角下的中国家庭轿车市场—基于随机系数logit模型的实证研究[D]. 杭州：浙江大学, 2007.

[13] 谭家美，徐瑞华. 影响交通信息支付意愿的关键因素实证研究[J]. 系统管理学报, 2009, 18(05): 572-576+600.

[14] 程谦，杨光，胡启洲. 基于混合Logit模型的旅客对短途高速铁路列车选择行为[J]. 中国铁道科学, 2021, 42(02): 183-192.

[15] 盛冬冬，孙明姝. 基于面板混合Logit模型的中长途高速客运方式分担率预测[J]. 山东科学, 2021, 34(01): 62-71.

基于NL模型的城市轨道交通接驳方式选择研究

杨逍遥[1] 梁国华[*1] 李国栋[2]

(1. 长安大学运输工程学院；2. 深圳市城市交通规划设计研究中心股份有限公司)

摘 要 为深入探索城市轨道交通不同站点接驳方式选择的差异性规律，本文采用K-Means聚类算法对城市轨道交通站点进行聚类分析,并以嵌套Logit模型为基础构建以出发时刻为上层选择枝,以步行、共享单车、常规公交接驳方式为下层选择枝的接驳方式选择模型。结果表明,本文构建的NL模型在预测轨道交通接驳方式选择方面优于MNL模型。接驳距离与接驳时间是影响轨道接驳方式选择的重要因素,而出行目的与年龄在很大程度上决定着出行时刻的选择。通过对比不同类别站点发现,"商业型"车站的步行接驳受路网密度的影响最为显著;公交接驳线路数对常规公交的接驳选择行为在"商业型""枢纽型"轨道车站表现出明显的促进作用。本文研究了轨道接驳行为在时间与空间上的差异性规律,可为不同类型轨道站点周边的接驳设施、接驳环境配置提供指导意见。

关键词 出行行为分析 方式选择 NL模型 城市轨道接驳

0 引言

由于城市轨道交通的定线路、高造价等特性决定了其较低的线网覆盖率与可达性,难以较好地满足乘客的出行需求,构建与之匹配的接驳设施就愈显重要。深入了解各类轨道站点的接驳出行特性,可为城市轨道交通与其他出行方式间的顺畅衔接提供解决思路。为此,国内外相关学者对居民出行方式选择行为进行了大量研究。

目前,国内、外学者主要从出行者特性、出行环境特性、接驳设施条件以及模型探索等方面对出行方式选择行为进行了大量研究。Zachary通过构建NL模型与MNL模型,发现男性选择公共交通出行的概率大于女性,女性对于时间的敏感度大于男性[1]。部分学者通过建模分析发现建筑功能混合度、步行道路环境能够促进非通勤步行方式出行[2],但对学生的出行行为影响较小[3]。孙斌栋发现居住地的人口密度、用地混合度与交叉口占比与小汽车通勤出行量成反比[4]。在轨道交通接驳行为的研究中,部分学者发现步行、自行车与公共交通是最常见的轨道接驳方式,其中步行为主要轨道接驳方式;接驳距离、接驳时间与道路的连通性是影响乘客接驳方式选择的重要因素,其中接驳时间占据了总出行时间的19% ~ 64%[5,6]。Rahul发现地铁站位置、出行距离、地铁站周边人口密度与车辆拥有情况与轨道接驳方式选择显著相关[7]。此外,国内学者对于轨道交通接驳行为的模型开发与适用性探索研究较为成熟。韩晓玉、岳芳、秦观明等运用Logit模型对城市轨道交通接驳方式的分担率进行预测,验证了该模型在预测轨道交通接驳分担率方面具有较强的适用性[8,9,10]。裴玉龙发现模型对于预测不同轨道接驳方式分担率的适用性不同[11]。部分学者对轨道交通出行两端的接驳特性进行对比研究,发现到站客流相比于离站客流对接驳便捷程度的敏感性更高[10,12,13]。

现有研究较少考虑出行时刻、轨道站点类型差异对轨道接驳方式选择行为的影响。为更好地剖析城市轨道接驳方式选择行为的差异,本文考虑了不同出行时刻接驳行为的差异性,构建了以嵌套Logit模型为基础的城市轨道接驳方式选择模型,并对轨道站点接驳行为选择差异的影响因素进行分析。

1 数据来源与影响因素

1.1 数据来源

本文选择2020年11月期间的周末,对西安地铁1号、2号、3号线各站点的接驳方式选择特性进行问卷发放,共发放调查问卷350份,收回有效问卷334份。

1.2 轨道接驳影响因素分析

基于调查数据统计分析并结合已有文献,从轨道交通出行者个人特性、出行特性以及出行环境特性对轨道接驳出行方式的影响因素进行分析。

1.1.1 轨道交通出行者特性

性别、年龄、收入与受教育程度是影响出行者出行方式选择的主要个人因素。男性更倾向于选择私家车出行;不同年龄段对选择轨道的接驳交通方式有较大的差别;低收入人群在进行出行方式选择时会更多地考虑接驳成本与出行总费用;教育程度越高的人更倾向于选择绿色出行方式。

1.1.2 出行特性

出行者在进行方式选择时,主要考虑的因素有出行时间、出行距离、出行费用,这些变量的取值一旦超过出行者的心理忍受阈值,则会考虑选择其他方式出行。在不同的出发时段与出行目的下,出行者对出行的时耗、舒适度、准点率、便捷性要求不同,从而导致出行接驳方式的选择上也相继呈现出差异性。

1.1.3 出行环境特性

轨道接驳方式选择不仅受轨道线网规模的影响[14]，同时也受轨道车站接驳环境的影响。轨道站点周边较强的土地利用混合度、路网密度、出行环境与基础服务设施都对轨道乘客接驳方式的选择有着很大的影响；车站所处位置、车站性质也是导致不同种类站点接驳方式选择结构差异的主要原因。

采用SPSS软件对轨道接驳影响变量进行相关性分析，得到影响轨道站点接驳方式的显著因素，见表1。

轨道交通接驳显著因素 表1

变量属性	变量	变量定义	变量名
出行者特性	年龄(x_1) （岁）	当年龄为≤18,19～28,29～39,40～60,>60，变量分别取0,1,2,3,4	Age
出行特征	出行目的(x_2)	非通勤=0,通勤=1	Goal
接驳环境特征	接驳距离(x_3) （m）	距离≤500,501～1000,1001～1500,1501～2000,2001～2500,2501～3000,>3000，变量分别取0,1,2,3,4,5,6	Distance
	接驳时间(x_4) （min）	实际值	Time
	路网密度(x_5) （km/km²）	实际值	Density
	公交线路数(x_6) （条）	实际值	Busroute
	公交站点数(x_7) （个）	实际值	Busstop

2 城市轨道站点接驳方式选择模型

本文章考虑到在不同时刻居民出行特性的差异会引起轨道接驳决策行为的差异，构建了以NL(Nested Logit)模型为基础的城市轨道接驳方式选择模型。NL(Nested Logit)模型是在基于多个MNL模型嵌套而成，该模型根据备选方案间的相似属性进行分类，再将各大类细分为若干小类，逐层以此类推从而形成多层树状结构[6]，其中每一层均可以看作一个MNL模型[15]。

2.1 MNL离散选择模型

非集计模型遵循随机效用理论(Random Utility Theory)，追求"效用"最大化假说。某个选择枝(方案、交通方式、路径等)的效用由固定效用与随机效用两部分加和构成[16]。选择枝被选中的概率如式(1)所示：

$$U_{in}=V_{in}+\varepsilon_{in}=\beta X+\varepsilon_{in}$$
$$U_{in}>U_{jn},(i\neq j;\ \forall j\in An) \tag{1}$$

式中：U_{jn}——出行者n选择方案j的效用；

V_{in}——固定效用；

ε_{in}——随机效用。

轨道乘客选择方案i的概率P_{in}可通过式(2)计算：

$$\begin{aligned}P_{in}&=\mathrm{Prob}(U_{in}>U_{jn};i\neq j;\ \forall j\in An)\\&=\mathrm{Prob}(V_{in}-V_{jn}>\varepsilon_{jn}-\varepsilon_{in};i\neq j)\end{aligned} \tag{2}$$

假定效用随机项ε_j是相互独立的，且服从(0,1)的最大极值Gumble随机分布[17]。多元Logit模型的分布形式使得任意两个选择枝之间的协方差为0。根据效用最大化的原则可以推导出乘客选择i的概率为：

$$P_{in}=\frac{\exp(V_{in})}{\sum\limits_{k\in An}\exp(V_{kn})} \tag{3}$$

2.2 NL离散选择模型

本文依据城市轨道乘客接驳出行选择行为建立NL模型，分为出发时刻选择枝(Level 2)和出行方式选择枝(Level 1)。L_1中的选择枝为高峰时段与平峰时段[18]。乘客接驳轨道交通的方式选择集中包括步行、共享单车、常规公交三种方式。据NL模型的树状结构如图1所示。

出行者n在水平1上选择任意出行方案tm的概率等于n在选择出发时间t的条件下选择出行方式m的条件概率与选择出发时间t的概率的乘积[6]，即：

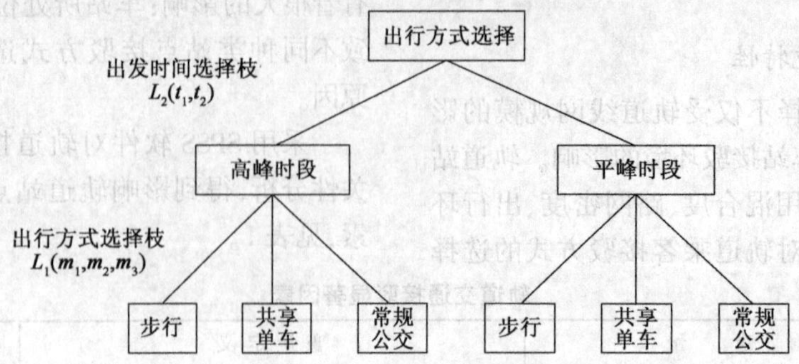

图1　轨道站点乘客出行换乘方式选择结构图

$$P_n(tm)=P_n(m|t)P_n(t),$$

$$(t_1,t_2\in t;m_1,m_2,m_3\in m) \tag{4}$$

$$P_n(m|t)=\frac{\exp(\lambda_1 V_{(m|t)_n})}{\sum_{m'=m_1}^{m_3}\exp(\lambda_1 V_{(m'|t)_n})} \tag{5}$$

$$P_n(t)=\frac{\exp[\lambda_2(V_{tn}+V_{tn}^*)]}{\sum_{t'=t_1}^{t_2}\exp[\lambda_2(V_{t'n}+V_{t'n}^*)]} \tag{6}$$

$$V_{tn}^*=\frac{1}{\lambda_1}\ln\sum_{m=m_1}^{m_3}\exp(\lambda_1 V_{(m|t)n}) \tag{7}$$

式中：$P_n(tm)$——出行者 n 在 L_1 上选择接驳备选方案 tm 的概率；

$P_n(m|t)$——第 n 个出行者在选择 t 的前提下选择 m 的条件概率；

$P_n(t)$——n 选择 t 的概率；$V_{(m|t)_n}$ 为 n 在选择 t 的前提下选择 m 的固定效用；

V_{tn}——n 选择 t 时的固定效用；

V_{tn}^*——合成效用。

λ_1 是只与方式选择层(L_1)相关的效用概率项的方差参数，λ_2 是与 L_1、L_2 均有关的概率项的方差参数[18]。其中，λ_1 与 λ_2 应满足 $0<\frac{\lambda_2}{\lambda_1}\leq 1$。

3　结果与分析

本文选用工作日小时平均进出站客流、周六、周日小时进出站客流量为指标，采用 K-means 算法将轨道站点分为五类，并根据进出站客流时空分布特征将各类车站定义为“居住型”“对外枢纽型”“枢纽型”“商住混合型”“商业型”轨道交通站点。图2～图6所示为各类轨道站点工作日与非工作日6:00～24:00(共18×2个小时)平均日小时客流进、出站人数分布特征。

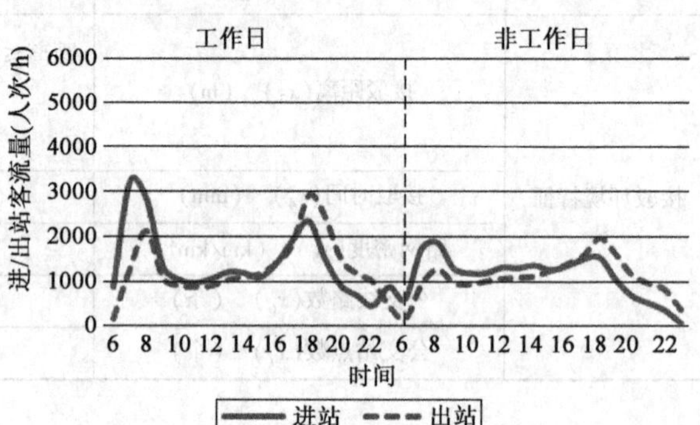

图2　“居住型”车站客流时间分布

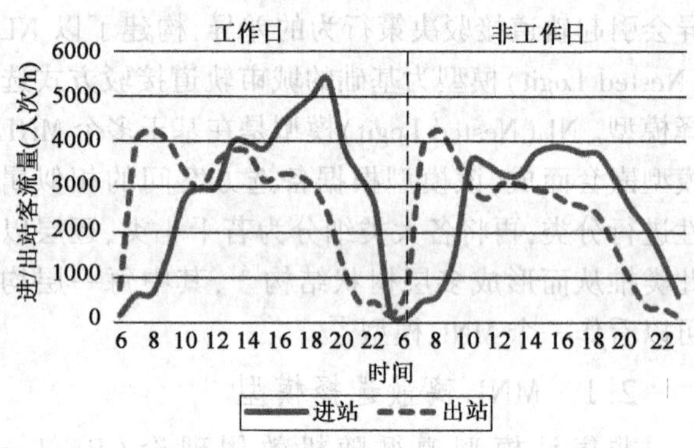

图3　“对外枢纽型”车站客流时间分布

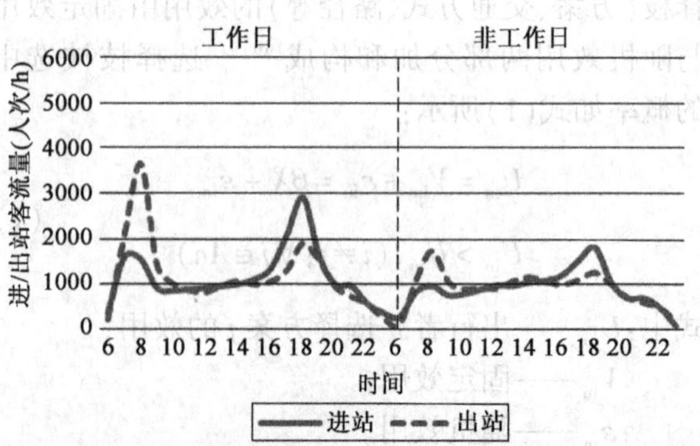

图4　“枢纽型”车站客流时间分布

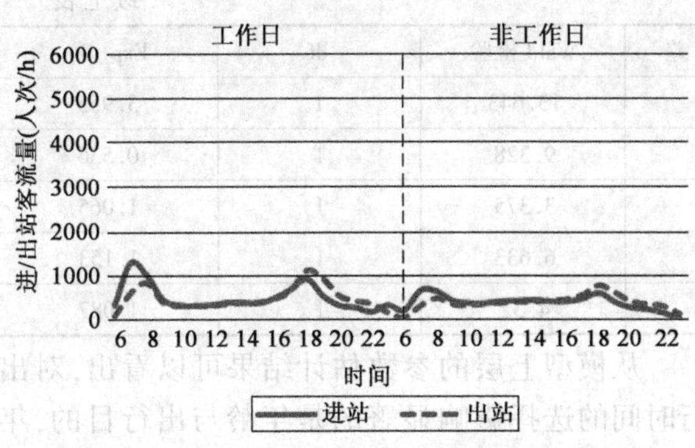

图5 "商住混合型"车站客流时间分布

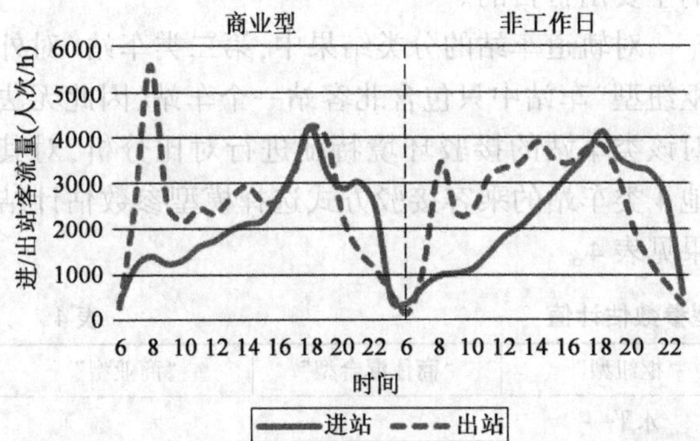

图6 "商业型"车站客流时间分布

3.1 模型结果

本文以类别1"居住型"车站为例,采用最大似然参数估计法,利用SPSS软件分别对各类别轨道车站的接驳方式选择模型进行参数估计,NL模型方式选择层(L_1)的参数估计结果见表2。

在自由度为1,置信度$\alpha = 0.05$的条件下,Wald值大于3.841,说明自变量和因变量显著相关;Wald略小于3.841,认为自变量对因变量的影响较小;Wald远小于3.841,则认为自变量和因变量显著无关[19]。

从参数的估计结果可以看出,接驳距离与接驳时间是影响轨道接驳方式选择的重要因素,随着接驳距离的增加,乘客更倾向于选择常规公交接驳;年龄越大的乘客,更倾向于选择步行、公交等较为安全、舒适的接驳方式;有着通勤目的的乘客更愿意选择共享单车进行接驳;公交接驳线路数与乘客选择常规公交的概率呈正相关;路网密度对步行相比于其他两种接驳方式有更强的相关性,路网密度越高的站点,道路可达性越高,乘客步行活动越密集。

模型下层参数估计表　表2

变量		B	标准误差	Wald检验	df	Exp(B)
步行	Constant	1.865	0.935	3.641	1	
	Age	1.104	0.044	4.051	1	1.110
	Goal	-0.036	0.017	1.027	1	0.965
	Distance	-1.305	0.178	10.743	1	0.271
	Time	-0.632	0.214	9.540	1	0.532
	Density	0.602	0.110	8.027	1	1.826
	Busroute	-0.017	0.009	0.832	1	0.983
	Busstop	-0.012	0.007	0.801	1	0.988
共享单车	Constant	-11.463	1.500	53.649	1	
	Age	-0.179	0.100	5.506	1	0.836
	Goal	0.121	0.047	4.572	1	1.129
	Distance	-0.546	0.110	5.659	1	0.579
	Time	-1.146	0.165	10.736	1	0.318
	Density	0.115	0.043	4.204	1	1.122
	Busroute	-0.045	0.018	4.380	1	0.956
	Busstop	-0.012	0.007	0.638	1	0.988
常规公交	Constant	-4.035	2.387	5.781	1	
	Age	0.174	0.102	4.393	1	1.190
	Goal	-0.136	0.076	3.801	1	0.873

续上表

变量		B	标准误差	Wald 检验	df	Exp(B)
常规公交	Distance	1.375	0.198	13.643	1	3.955
	Time	-0.623	0.125	9.328	1	0.536
	Density	0.063	0.034	3.375	1	1.065
	Busroute	0.142	0.034	6.633	1	1.153
	Busstop	0.083	0.029	4.32	1	1.087

在模型的水平2上,以非高峰时段为参照类别,得到模型该层的参数进行估计结果见表3。

模型上层参数估计表 表3

变量	B	标准误差	Wald 检验	df	Exp(B)
Constant	-4.16	1.056	5.644	1	
Age	-0.375	0.04	3.813	1	0.687
Goal	0.882	0.12	5.192	1	2.416
λ_2	0.326	0.035	7.222	1	1.385

从模型上层的参数估计结果可以看出,对出行时间的选择影响显著的是年龄与出行目的,年轻人在高峰时刻出行的概率高,通勤是高峰期间的主要出行目的。

对轨道车站的分类结果中,第二类车站"对外枢纽型"车站中只包含北客站一个车站,因此无法对该类车站的接驳环境特征进行对比分析,对其他4类车站的乘客接驳方式选择模型参数估计结果见表4。

各类别车站 NL 模型参数估计值 表4

车站类型 / 接驳方式	变量	"居住型"	"枢纽型"	"商住混合型"	"商业型"
			水平一		
步行	Constant	1.865	1.376	2.403	1.934
	Age	1.104	0.132	0.115	0.113
	Goal	-0.036	-0.04	-0.032	-0.032
	Distance	-1.305	-1.503	-1.101	-0.607
	Time	-0.632	-0.872	-0.65	-0.353
	Density	0.602	0.901	0.581	1.152
	Busroute	-0.017	0.031	0.015	-0.034
	Busstop	-0.012	-0.023	-0.017	-0.023
共享单车	Constant	-11.463	-11.299	-10.783	-13.342
	Age	-0.179	-0.180	-0.164	-0.176
	Goal	0.121	0.232	0.274	0.211
	Distance	-0.546	-0.755	-0.511	-0.521
	Time	-1.146	-0.856	-1.057	-0.324
	Density	0.115	0.443	0.118	0.577
	Busroute	-0.045	-0.543	-0.042	-0.878
	Busstop	-0.012	-0.051	-0.022	-0.054
常规公交	Constant	-4.035	-3.584	-3.837	-6.038
	Age	0.174	0.175	0.171	0.171
	Goal	-0.136	-0.067	-0.121	-0.244
	Distance	1.375	1.787	1.264	1.205
	Time	-0.623	-0.566	-0.759	-0.320
	Density	0.063	0.069	0.063	0.089
	Busroute	0.142	1.012	0.169	1.175
	Busstop	0.083	0.110	0.097	0.124

续上表

车站类型	变　量	"居住型"	"枢纽型"	"商住混合型"	"商业型"
	水平二				
	Constant	-4.16	-5.458	-1.394	-7.743
	Age	-0.375	-0.361	-0.331	-0.432
	Goal	0.882	0.753	0.824	0.975
	λ_2	0.326	0.184	0.214	0.202

从各类轨道车站的方式选择模型标定结果可以看出，年龄、出行目的、接驳距离、接驳时间对以上4类城市轨道站点周边的接驳行为的影响无显著性差异。

路网密度、公交接驳数与公交站台数对不同类型轨道站点的接驳行为呈现出明显的差异性影响。研究结果显示，"商业型"车站接驳行为受路网密度的影响较大，其中对选择步行接驳的影响最为显著。该类站点周边用地具有较高的客流吸引量，当路网密度越高，道路通达性越强时，将产生较高的轨道接驳需求，乘客则更倾向于选择步行或共享单车进行接驳。轨道站点周边公交接驳线路数相比于公交站台分布数对常规公交的接驳选择行为表现出更强的促进作用，并在"商业型""枢纽型"轨道车站处更为明显。这是由于公交接驳数越多，公交通达性越高，乘客选择常规公交进行轨道接驳的概率越大，尤其是在"商业型""枢纽型"乘车需求较高的轨道站点，便捷的公交接驳设施可大大提高公交接驳的分担率。

3.2　模型精度检验

为验证构建模型的有效性与准确性，本文主要通过T检验、命中率对NL模型进行精度检验，并与传统的MNL模型进行对比。

T检验用来说明参数的显著程度及有效性。当置信水平$\alpha=0.1$时，$|t|\geqslant1.65$，说明有90%的概率认为该因素对出行选择行为影响显著[20]，由检验结果可知各变量标定的参数结果均为有效值，且显著程度均较高。

命中率是通过将模型预测结果与实际的居民出行行为选择数据进行对比，以检验模型精度的指标[20]。将观测值代入模型，命中率大于50%的接驳方案可作为备选方案；如果命中率能大于80%，说明该模型的精度相当高。两种模型的命中率见表5～表7，得到NL模型的上、下层的命中率分别为80.54%、87.13%，MNL模型的命中率为76.35%，可见NL模型在本案例中预测精度较高。

NL模型下层命中率表　　表5

观　察　值	预　测　值			
	步行	共享单车	常规公交	百分比校正(%)
步行	155	10	3	92.26
共享单车	9	55	2	83.33
常规公交	8	11	81	81.00
总百分比(%)	51.50	22.75	25.75	87.13

NL模型上层命中率表　　表6

观　察　值	预　测　值		
	高峰时段	平峰时段	百分比矫正(%)
高峰时段	145	11	92.95
平峰时段	54	124	69.66
总百分比(%)	59.58	40.42	80.54

MNL模型命中率表　　表7

观　察　值	预　测　值			
	步行	共享单车	常规公交	百分比校正(%)
步行	142	17	9	84.52
共享单车	13	41	12	62.12
常规公交	15	13	72	72.00
总百分比(%)	50.90	21.26	27.84	76.35

4　结语

(1)本文在对轨道车站分类的基础上，考虑不同出发时间与不同类型的轨道站点在接驳行为上可能存在差异性，以"居住型"轨道站点为例，构建上层为出发时刻选择枝、下层为三种出行方式选择枝的NL模型。研究发现，出行距离与出行时间是出行者在轨道接驳方式选择时考虑的主要因素，出行目的与出行者年龄分布在不同时刻呈现出较大差异。决策者可依据轨道站点周边的各类POI点的数量与距离合理配置各类轨道接驳设施比例,并在高峰时段加强对轨道接驳交通的管控力度。

(2)通过对多类站点构建NL模型,结果显示对于“商业型”轨道站点,路网密度对步行接驳选择的影响最为显著;对于“商业型”“枢纽型”轨道车站,公交接驳线路数对选择常规公交接驳具有明显的促进作用。可为不同类型的轨道车站设置差异化接驳环境提供指导依据。

(3)在后续的研究中,可进一步丰富接驳方式选择的影响因素变量,以增强模型的解释力度,为决策者提供更加科学的理论支持,为城市轨道站点周边的接驳设施规划提供更加全面的理论支持。

参考文献

[1] Zachary Patterson, Gordon Ewing, Murtaza Haider. Gender-Based Analysis of Work Trip Mode Choice of Commuters in Suburban Montreal, Canada, with Stated Preference Data [J]. Transportation Research Record, 2005, 1924(1).

[2] Jayanthi Rajamani, Chandra R. Bhat, Susan Handy, et al. Assessing Impact of Urban Form Measures on Nonwork Trip Mode Choice After Controlling for Demographic and Level-of-Service Effects [J]. Transportation Research Record, 2003, 1831(1).

[3] Reid Ewing, William Schroeer, William Greene. School Location and Student Travel Analysis of Factors Affecting Mode Choice [J]. Transportation Research Record, 2004, 1895(1).

[4] 孙斌栋,但波.上海城市建成环境对居民通勤方式选择的影响[J].地理学报,2015,70(10):1664-1674.

[5] Moshe, Givoni, et al. The access journey to the railway station and its role in passengers' satisfaction with rail travel [J]. Transport Policy, 2007.

[6] 王文红,关宏志,王山川.Nested-Logit模型在轨道交通衔接方式选择中的应用[J].城市轨道交通研究,2008(07):25-30.

[7] Rahul, Goel, Geetam, et al. Access-egress and other travel characteristics of metro users in Delhi and its satellite cities[J]. Iatss Research, 2016.

[8] 韩晓玉,朱从坤,何承韡.Logit模型在轨道交通接驳方式预测中的应用[J].交通科技与经济,2016,18(01):25-29.

[9] 岳芳,毛保华,陈团生.城市轨道交通接驳方式的选择[J].都市快轨交通,2007(04):36-39.

[10] 秦观明.城市轨道交通接驳方式选择及客流吸引范围研究[D].哈尔滨:哈尔滨工业大学,2010.

[11] 裴玉龙,潘跃.城市轨道交通站点接驳设施规模预测方法[J].交通信息与安全,2018,36(04):106-112.

[12] 黄杉,关宏志,严海.轨道交通衔接方式选择行为研究——以北京市轨道交通为例[J].土木工程学报,2009,42(07):126-130.

[13] 周家中.出行链视角下城市轨道交通接驳方式联合选择模型[J].铁道标准设计,2016,60(04):4-7.

[14] 李妍锦.慢行交通环境对轨道交通接驳方式选择的影响与优化研究[D].西安:长安大学,2017.

[15] 关宏志.非集计模型－交通行为分析的工具[M].北京:人民交通出版社,2004.

[16] 鲜于建川.出行方式选择:神经网络与多项Logit模型的比较研究[J].上海电机学院学报,2009,12(004):323-327.

[17] 毛伟.基于旅客出行行为分析的通道客运分担率预测研究.[J].交通运输工程与信息学校,2009(1):75-79.

[18] 向红艳,何素贞,徐韬.基于NL模型的轨道停车换乘行为建模分析[J].武汉理工大学学报(交通科学与工程版),2016,40(003):413-417.

[19] 陈俊励,马云龙,朱楠.基于巢式Logit模型的公交出行方式选择行为研究[J].交通运输系统工程与信息,2011,11(1):120-125.

[20] 徐佳欢.基于SP/RP数据融合的新建地铁对居民出行方式选择的影响[D].大连:大连理工大学,2018.

新冠肺炎疫情防控常态化时期大学生出行行为特征分析

孙 皓* 吴 瑜
(西北大学城市与环境学院)

摘 要 随着各地区政府的不断努力,我国已进入了新冠肺炎疫情防控常态化时期。通过分析特定人群的出行行为特征可为城市交通系统的优化升级、防疫工作的精准化提供依据。因此,本文以线上、线下结合发放调查问卷的方式得到了疫情防控常态化时期西安市长安区大学生出行行为的相关数据。通过对调查数据进行描述性统计分析,得出大学生群体的出行特征。根据统计数据可发现在疫情防控常态化时期,大学生群体的出行频率下降,出行方式主要依赖慢行交通,大部分大学生在离校出行时都有陪同者同行等出行行为特征。同时,根据大学生的出行特征并结合现有城市交通体系中存在的不足,提出针对性的改善方法与优化策略。

关键词 出行行为 统计分析 大学生 新冠肺炎疫情 优化策略

0 引言

2019 年年底,发生的新冠肺炎疫情(COVID-19)作为一场严重的公共卫生安全突发事件,对人类命运共同体的健康发展敲响了警钟。其历时之久,涉及范围之广,在人类传染疾病学、社会学、公共管理学等诸多领域引起了各界学者的高度重视。新冠肺炎疫情发展趋势的深远性对于城市建设工作而言无疑也是一次严峻的挑战。而城市交通系统作为城市巨系统中的重要子系统,它的稳定性、环境适应性对于城市系统的可持续发展至关重要,在防疫工作中发挥着不可替代的作用。

研究表明,交通运输系统加大了流感和冠状病毒在全球范围内的扩散和传播,尤其是高密度的出行人群、封闭的交通环境增加了污染物间接传播的概率[1,2]。自新冠肺炎疫情产生以来,学者们针对新冠肺炎疫情的外部因素影响下对城市居民交通出行行为的影响进行了不少有价值的研究。李之明[3]等通过对比 2019 年与 2020 年 1—6 月广东省的公共交通一卡通交易数据,发现新冠肺炎疫情对公共交通出行的影响强度大、时间久,截至 2020 年 6 月 30 日(复工 4 个月)的公共交通出行量仅恢复到 2019 年同期出行量的 70% 左右。Bucsky[4]发现布达佩斯所有交通方式的出行量都有大幅度的下降,而公共交通的下降幅度最大。周江平[5]将公共交通出行者分为了六类,并讨论了新冠肺炎疫情冲击下和新冠肺炎疫情后时代公共交通出行稳定性、变化性、柔韧性和恢复力的认知框架和量化指标。赵彦勇[6]等通过抓取 10 个城市的微博评论数据,探讨了关于新冠肺炎疫情的网络舆情、民众情感与城市轨道交通客流量之间的关系。姜楠[7]等通过对在线调查问卷进行数据分析发现,新冠肺炎疫情极大地改变了我国人群出行频次及交通方式,其中,私家车、公共交通的出行比例变化明显。刘建荣[8]等通过对后疫情时期针对老年人的调查,发现新冠肺炎疫情、老年人对新冠肺炎疫情严重程度的感知对老年人使用公共交通的可能性、出行频率影响明显。李洁[9]基于美国公布的疫情数据、居民出行数据发现,新冠肺炎疫情的发生提高了居民使用共享自行车、小汽车的出行比例,同时,应用因子分析法分析了新冠肺炎疫情对纽约市居民出行行为的影响。通过文献梳理可发现,现有研究主要关注了新冠肺炎疫情暴发期及后疫情时代的居民出行行为,较少涉及疫情防控常态化时期的居民出行行为。同时,现有研究将调查研究对象进行特征分类时,针

1. 基金项目:陕西省教育厅自然科学一般专项(21JK0932)。

对不同特征人群的出行行为分析存在理论空缺。

随着我国各地区政府的不断努力,新冠肺炎疫情逐渐得到了控制。2020年6月7日,《抗击新冠肺炎疫情的中国行动》白皮书发布,将我国抗击新冠肺炎疫情的历程分为5个阶段。其中,明确自2020年4月29日以后我国居民的生产、生活已逐步恢复,我国的疫情防控进入常态化[6]。2020年夏季,随着各地“复工复学”相关工作的稳步推进,全国各高等学校学生群体陆续返校。综上所述,为深入探索城市交通系统存在的不足,助力防疫工作的完善与优化,应当充分把握新冠肺炎疫情防疫不同阶段、不同特征人群的出行特征,促进城市交通的韧性建设。本文就大学生群体在疫情防疫常态化下的交通出行行为展开分析,以期在得到大学生出行行为特征分析结果的基础上,为城市交通管理和高等教育部门制定管理政策提供理论依据。

1 大学生个体属性分析

西安市自2020年8月后,全市各高校安排各年级学生分地区、分时段、分批次返校报道,教学工作逐步正常展开,高校的疫情防控工作也进入常态化。本研究的调研时间为2021年4月30日至2021年6月1日,调研对象为西安市长安区大学城的在读本科大学生群体,调研方式为随机的线上、线下相结合的问卷调查。调研获得共计260组原始样本数据,通过筛除数据缺失严重的样本,获得有效样本257组进行后续的数据分析工作。问卷调查内容包括大学生个人基本特征、出行特征、出行方式选择三个内容,包括大学生性别、经济水平、出行距离、出行时间、出行方式选择等共计11项调查项。调查问卷中涉及的学生个体属性的描述性统计结果见表1。

学生个体属性调查项描述性统计 表1

调查变量	测度	频数	比例(%)
性别	男	132	51
	女	125	49
学生年级	2016级	29	11.28
	2017级	33	12.84
	2018级	47	18.29
	2019级	109	42.41
	2020级	39	15.18
月生活费	1000元以下	56	21.79
	1000~2000元	85	33.07
	2000~2500元	69	26.85
	2500元以上	47	18.29

根据统计结果可知,被调查者中男性男生132人,占调查总人数的51%;女性学生125人,占调查总人数的49%,被调查者的性别结构基本为1:1。被调查者中2020级学生39人,2019级学生109人,2018级学生47人,2015级学生33人,2016级学生29人;分别占总人数的15.18%、42.41%、18.29%、12.84%和11.28%,可知本次被调查者多集中于较低年级。

通过对大学生月生活费水平的调查结果,约45%的学生月生活费在2000元以上。通过和2010年的大学生月生活费进行对比可知[10],西安市大学生的月生活费水平增长明显。

2 大学生出行行为分析

2.1 出行频率

考虑到大学生群体的生活、学生规律,在进行调查问卷设计时,分别对大学生的周内(周一至周五)出行频率和周末出行(周六及周日)频率进行了调查,这里的出行均指离校出行。根据统计结果可知,大学生的周内出行频率和周末出行频率呈现出统一的分布规律,如图1所示。根据统计,大学生群体在周内的日均出行次数约0.55次/(人·日),周末的日均出行次数约1.16次/(人·日),初步可得结论:大学生离校外出频率在周末明显高于周内。

通过对比疫情前西安市居民的日均出行次数[11]，可发现大学生在疫情防控常态化时期的出行频率降低。同时，对比同时期其他人群[7]（企业员工、事业员工等）的出行频率，大学生的校外出行频率偏低，可以侧面说明大学生的社会出行需求较低。

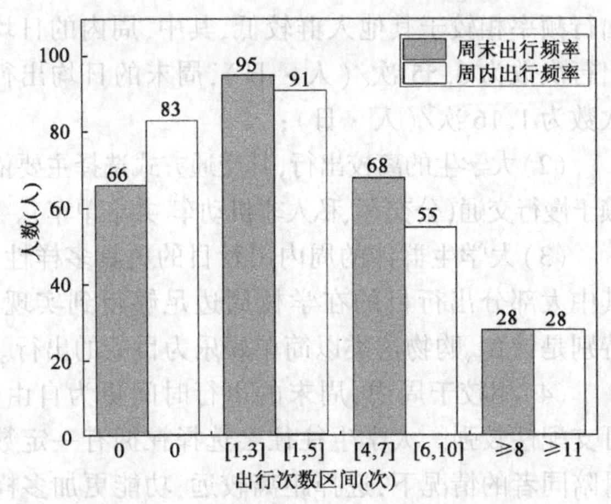

图1 大学生周内、周末出行频率统计图

2.2 出行目的

大学生离校外出的目的可大致概括为：娱乐、学习与休憩三方面。通过调查大学生在周内、周末的最近一次出行行为，获得统计数据。不管是在周末还是在周内，出行目的的分布由高到低依次为：娱乐目的、学习目的与休憩目的。区别在于：相较于周末的出行目的，周内出行目的为回家会友等休憩目的的外出行为下降，出行目的为娱乐与学习的出行增多。此外，新增2%的其余外出目的。可见，大学生群体于周内的离校外出行为相较于周末更加多元化，如图2所示。

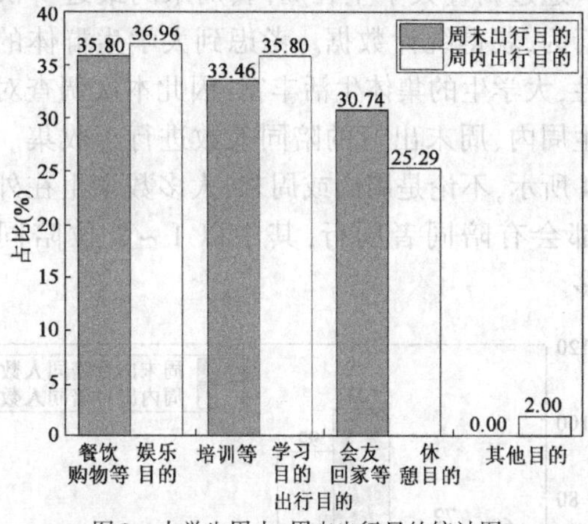

图2 大学生周内、周末出行目的的统计图

2.3 出行方式

通过调查大学生在周内、周末的最近一次出行行为，获得统计数据。在调查问卷选项中，将出行方式分为步行、公交地铁、自用自行车等私人非机动车、共享单车等共享非机动车、出租车、滴滴等机动车以及其他方式六个选项，以多选题的形式进行数据收集。由收集到的结果分析，大多数样本数据为两种及以上多种出行方式结合构成。通过统计各出行方式选择的单项计次统计结果由多到少依次为公交地铁、私人非机动车、共享非机动车、步行、出租车、滴滴等机动车和其他方式。由初步统计结果可知，大学生离校的出行选择方式主要依赖于公共交通和非机动交通，如图3所示。

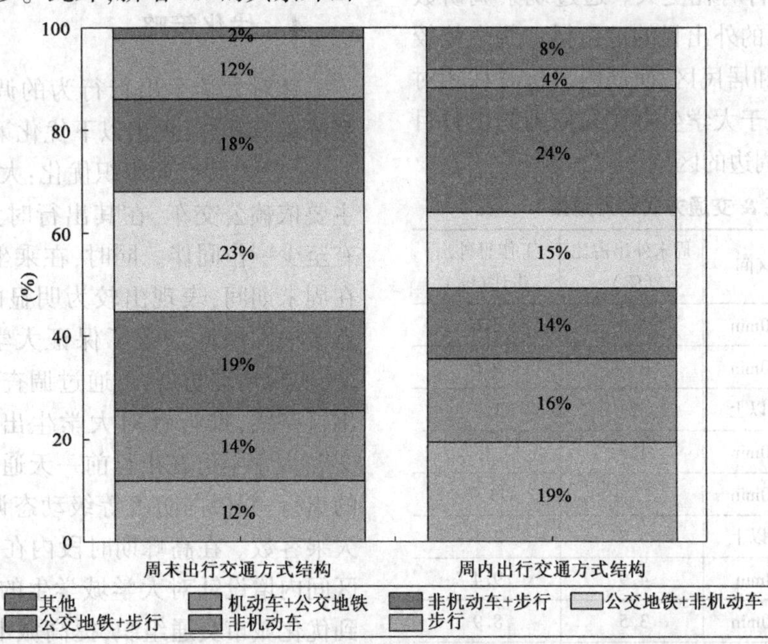

图3 大学生周内、周末出行交通方式结构统计图

2.4　出行陪同

通过调查大学生在周内、周末的最近一次出行行为,获得统计数据。考虑到大学生群体的特殊性,大学生的集体生活丰富,因此本次调查对大学生周内、周末出行的陪同人数进行了收集。如图4所示,不论是周内或周末,大多数学生在外出时都会有陪同者同行,其中以1～3位陪同者居多。

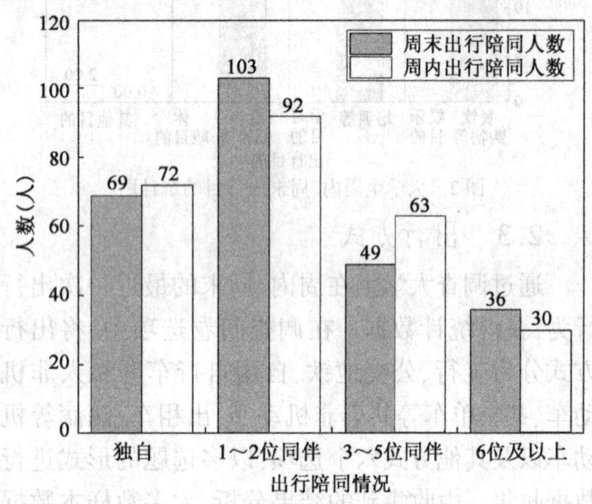

图4　大学生周内、周末出行陪同情况

2.5　出行时耗

依旧对大学生的周内、周末上一次出行进行统计,表2为出行方式与时耗结合的部分统计结果。由数据分析可知,大学生群体在周末时间段内相较于工作日周期内出行时耗更久。通过观察调研数据发现,大学生周末的外出目的地包括一些离校较远的重要商业区域和居民区,而周内出行时耗相对较短,其原因主要在于大学生群体在周内的出行目的地多集中在学校周边的区域。

出行时耗 & 交通方式调查数据　　表2

出行方式	时耗区间	周末外出占比(%)	工作日外出占比(%)
公交	10～30min	6.8	2.6
	30～60min	10.4	9.6
	60min 以上	2	1.4
公交+非机动车	10～30min	1.3	1
	30～60min	17.4	11.7
	60min 以上	4.7	2.1
步行	0～10min	4.9	9.4
	10～20min	3.5	8.9
	20～30min	0.8	1.1

3　数据分析结论

结合本次调查数据的描述性统计结果,防疫常态化下大学生外出行为方式分析结论如下:

(1)防疫常态化下的大学生群体出行,其离校出行频率相较于其他人群较低,其中,周内的日均出行次数为0.55次/(人·日),周末的日均出行次数为1.16次/(人·日);

(2)大学生的离校出行,其交通方式选择主要依赖于慢行交通(公交车、私人非机动车、共享单车)。

(3)大学生群体的周内出行目的更具多样性,其中大部分出行目的在学校周边足够得到实现,特别是饮食、购物这类以简单娱乐为目的的出行。

(4)相较于周内,周末的出行时间更为自由,可支配性较强。大学生往往会选择在拥有一定数量陪同者的情况下,选择距离较远、功能更加多样的商业空间完成娱乐目的的实现。观察调查数据可发现,在周末出行距离增加、外出陪同人员数量相对增多的情况下,大学生群体的交通方式选择有两方面变化:一方面为多种交通方式的组合出行比例增加,非机动交通方式更多地成为衔接公共交通工具(特别是地铁)与最终目的地之间的过渡性工具;另一方面,在陪同者数量相较增多的情况下,学生群体选择出租车、滴滴等机动车交通工具时可通过拼单等途径降低经济成本,于是选择该类交通工具的比例产生一定增加。

4　优化策略

针对大学生出行行为的调查结果,结合城市系统现有状况,提出以下优化策略:

(1)公共交通组织优化:大学生群体校外出行主要依赖公交车,在其出行时大部分的大学生都有至少一位同伴。同时,在乘坐公共交通时,尤其在周末期间,表现出较为明显的时段集中性与地点集中性因此。为了保证大学生出行的防疫安全,实现精准防疫,可通过调查大学城学生的热门出行路线,推行针对大学生出行的可预约“微公交”,大学生可在出行前一天通过手机预约第二天的出行,并根据防疫等级动态调整“微公交”的最大乘客数。在高峰期时段内在客流量集中的线路区间内增设针对大学城学生的“微公交”,可以达到优化城市交通组织,提高城市交通效率的目的。同时,还可以使出行者在公共交通工具内的人均面积得到一定的提升,特别是在常态化防疫的特殊社会氛围下,公共交通工具内更加宽敞的空间尺度对于出行者的心理安全感知有一定的积极作用。

(2)非机动交通系统优化:新冠肺炎疫情过后,乘客换乘时需要付出额外的时间以配合防疫需求,导致了出行的时间成本增加。非机动车属于健康绿色的个体交通工具,随着共享非机动车的普及,并且非机动车属于无直接接接触式交通方式,其新冠病毒的传播概率小,非机动车成了大学生实现交通出行、交通换乘的重要交通方式。而对于大学而言,学生数量多,学生的出行时间也相对随机,对非机动车的需求量巨大,且需求高峰期持续时间久。目前在很多校园暴露出共享非机动车供给量不足、非机动交通道路的缺乏与停放空间缺乏等不合理之处。因此,可考虑在高校附近打造非机动车专用道,根据大学城区域的共享非机动车需求量动态跟进市场投放量,同时科学布局高校附近的共享非机动车停放点及停放点数量,以进一步提高非机动车的使用率并保证高校的交通秩序。

(3)机动车接驳场地优化:由调查问卷收集到的数据分析可知,一部分选择网约车、出租车等机动车作为出行工具的大学生同时选择了公交地铁这一选项,可见,对于学生群体而言,机动车在离校外出的整个行为过程中,主要承担着接驳公共交通的角色。而现实情况是,在很多客流量较大的公共交通枢纽位置,存在着出租车服务站点缺乏,网约车停车困难的问题。因此,通过规划增设相关接驳服务场地,可以有效优化出租车及网约车的服务质量。

5 结语

本文通过对2021年4月30日至2021年6月1日获取的新冠肺炎疫情防控常态化时期西安市长安区本科大学生的离校出行调查问卷进行描述性统计及分析,分别对大学生的个人基本属性、出行行为特征进行了分析。本文能够为合理引导大学生出行提供一定的参考,但仍有需要深入研究之处,后续可以加大调查数量,增加数理模型的分析,进一步探究大学生出行的行为机理,并基于可持续理论提出城市交通系统优化策略。

新冠肺炎疫情自爆发至今已两年多,我国的防疫工作也已经进入了新冠肺炎疫情防护的常态化时期。城市交通系统在面临突发的重大安全卫生事件、重大自然灾害时能否经得住检验,是城市建设者们应该思考的重大议题。通过对疫情防控常态化时期各类出行群体的出行特征、出行差异性进行分析,有针对性地提出城市交通系统的优化策略,这是提升城市交通系统韧性及防疫性能的有效途径。随着人们对防疫工作的日益成熟,如何能够在保证经济发展的前提下,满足城市居民的各类出行需求、精准防疫、实现城市的可持续发展是亟待解决的问题。

参考文献

[1] 新型冠状病毒感染的肺炎诊疗方案(试行第三版)[EB/OL].中华人民共和国人民政府官方网站,2020-1-22. http://www.gov.cn/zhengce/zhengceku/2020-1/23/content_5471832.htm.

[2] World Health Organization. Global alert and response: severe acute respiratory syndrome (SARS): multi-country outbreak [EB/OL]. Geneva: World Health Organization, 2003-04-30 [2020-03-29]. http://www.who.int/csr/don/2003_04_30/en.

[3] 李之明,王宁,吴金成,等.新冠肺炎疫情对公共交通出行影响分析及因素探究[J].综合运输,2021,43(07):22-26.

[4] Bucsky P. Modal. Share Changes Due to Covid-19: The Case of Budapest[J]. Transportation Research Interdisciplinary Perspectives. 2020. https://doi.org/10.1016/j.trip.2020.100141.

[5] 周江评.以变应变——外部大冲击背景下公共交通出行及其量化指标[J/OL].城市规划:1-8[2022-01-20]. http://kns.cnki.net/kcms/detail/11.2378.TU.20211012.1706.002.html.

[6] 赵彦勇,周家静,厉海,等.新冠舆情、民众情感与城市公共交通[J].统计学报,2021,2(01):71-82.

[7] 姜楠,李赛,曹素珍,等.新冠肺炎疫情期间我国人群交通出行行为分析[J].环境科学研究,2020,33(07):1675-1682.

[8] 刘建荣,郝小妮,石文瀚.新冠肺炎疫情对老年人公交出行行为的影响[J].交通运输系统工程与信息,2020,20(06):71-76+98.

[9] 李洁.新型冠状病毒肺炎疫情对纽约市交通出行的影响[J].公路工程,2020,45(06):91-98.

[10] 黄当玲.西安市大学生消费现状的调查与分析[J].西安邮电学院学报,2010,15(04):63-65+74.

[11] 牛凯,田甜,余丽洁.西安城市发展与居民出行特征变迁分析[C]//2019世界交通运输大会论文集(下),2019:901-912.

基于图卷积网络的交通流预测方法综述

龙佰超　肖建力*

(上海理工大学光电信息与计算机工程学院)

摘　要　实时、准确的交通流预测是交通管理系统的基础。随着深度学习快速发展,图卷积网络(Graph Convolutional Networks,GCNs)在交通流预测任务中受到更多关注。本文回顾了交通流预测任务的经典模型,以基于图卷积网络的混合模型为主,分别介绍了引入时序模型、图注意力机制和考虑外部因素的混合模型的结构和特点。近年来,图卷积网络的混合模型考虑多重因素的影响,使模型性能进一步提高。本文还介绍了基于图卷积网络的常用交通数据集以及获取方法。

关键词　交通流预测　综述　图卷积网络　深度学习　智能交通

0　引言

随着智能交通系统的快速发展,交通流预测任务受到越来越多人的重视。实时、准确的交通流预测,有助于缓解交通拥堵、减少交通事故和降低能源消耗等问题。交通流预测任务包括:交通流量预测、交通流速度预测和交通流密度预测等。交通流量为交通流速度和交通流密度的乘积。但是由于交通流复杂的时间依赖性和空间依赖性,交通流预测任务一直都是智能交通领域的热点研究话题。

交通流预测方法可以大致分为三种:参数模型、非参数模型和混合模型[1]。参数模型算法简单,计算方便。但其依赖于系统模型的静态假设,不能反映交通数据的非线性和不确定性。对于非参数模型,只需要足够的历史数据,就可以很好地解决这些问题。自回归综合移动平均模型[2]、灰色预测模型[3]和卡尔曼滤波模型[4]是较为常见的参数模型。支持向量机回归模型[5]、K最近邻模型[6]、贝叶斯模型[7]、模糊逻辑模型[8]和人工神经网络模型[9]是常见的非参数模型。但是,这些方法只考虑了时间依赖性而忽略了空间依赖性,使得交通流的变化不受路网的约束,无法准确地预测实际交通。近年来,随着深度学习的快速发展,基于深度学习的混合模型可以很好地解决这一类问题。基于深度学习下的时序模型有深度置信网络[10]和回归模型组成的网络结构、递归神经网络[11]、长短期记忆[12]和门控递归单元[13]等。有学者将卷积神经网络[14]引入空间依赖模型中,在交通流预测任务中取得了很好的进展,但是卷积神经网络本质上适用于欧几里得空间,对于拓扑结构复杂的交通路网有局限性。无法从本质上描述空间依赖性。近年来,随着图卷积网络[15]的发展,其可以用来捕获图数据的结构特征。许多学者将空间模型与时序模型相结合组成混合模型[16],混合模型同时考虑了时间依赖性和空间依赖性。

交通流预测发展到现在,许多学者利用当前热门的图卷积网络和时序模型组合成混合模型,对交通大数据进行时间尺度和空间尺度的特征提取并预测,并且取得了显著效果。本文首先回顾图卷积网络与递归神经网络及其变种组合的混合模型,然后介绍将图卷积扩展到时空域的模型,接着说明考虑外部因素对模型的影响,最后介绍引入注意力机制的混合模型。

1.基金项目:国家自然科学基金资助项目(61603257,61906121)。

1 基于图卷积网络的交通流预测方法

随着深度学习的发展，卷积神经网络在处理规则的网格数据上面效果是很显著，但在处理具有拓扑结构的图数据即非欧式结构的数据上面，图卷积网络更具有优势。图卷积网络作为经典卷积神经网络的延伸，由于所面对的数据结构的差异，其在交通流预测任务方面取得了良好的效果。现有的预测方法主要是通过图卷积网络和递归神经网络的结合来实现的。本章将介绍近年来基于图卷积网络的交通流预测方法。

1.1 基于图卷积网络的混合模型

由于图卷积网络只能解决交通数据的空间依赖性，而交通数据是标准的时间序列数据，因此许多学者基于图卷积网络提出了既能满足时间尺度，还能满足空间尺度的混合模型。

(1)在基于图卷积网络的混合模型中，无论采取哪一种时序模型，研究人员都取得了很好的效果。Azzedine 等[17]利用图卷积网络和门控循环单元的深度聚合结构(即序列到序列结构)，将图卷积网络与基于注意的序列结合到具有双向门控递归单元核的序列模型中。中南大学的赵玲等人[1]也将图卷积网络与门控循环单元结合，提出时间图卷积网络。其中，图卷积网络用于学习复杂拓扑结构，获取空间相关性；门控循环单元用于学习交通数据的动态变化，获取时间相关性。北京航空航天大学的彭浩[18]等人提出了基于动态图的长期交通流预测方法。通过动态交通流概率图对交通网络进行建模，对动态图进行图卷积，学习空间特征，再结合长短期记忆单元学习时间特征。彭浩等还进一步提出利用基于强化学习的图卷积策略网络来生成由于数据稀疏而导致的不完整的动态图。Zhang 等[19]提出了时间图卷积网络的演变模型，用基于相似度的注意力方法来融合多个图邻接矩阵。然后，将门控循环单元与图卷积网络结合，同时捕获时空相关性及其变化状态。张帅等[20]提出了基于动态特征编码的时空模糊图卷积网络模型，以实现准确的交通流预测。该模型结合了图卷积网络和长短期记忆网络，提取交通数据复杂的时空依赖特征。此外，设计了一种新的基于模糊 C 均值聚类的图生成方法，以增强交通网络站点间空间相关性的表达能力。

(2)在时序问题处理上，除了典型时序模型外，北京大学的 Yu 等[21]提出时空图卷积网络，该模型将问题建立在图上，并建立具有完整卷积结构的模型，使训练速度更快，参数更少。相比于时空图卷积网络，北京交通大学的 Song 等[22]提出了时空同步图卷积网络模型，该模型通过精心设计的时空同步建模机制，能够有效地捕捉复杂的局部性时空关联。同时，在模型中设计了针对不同时间段的多个模块，有效地捕捉局域时空图中的异质性。

(3)考虑到外部因素对模型的影响同样十分重要，Yu 等[23]模拟了基于可变邻接矩阵的真实交通传播。对相邻链路的连通性强度进行参数化，并根据大量的观测数据进行估计。此外，通过图卷积模型，还考虑了路段的通行能力和长度等特性。Ye 等[24]提出了基于注意的考虑外部因素的时空图卷积网络，用于多步交通流预测。该模型将交通流建模为有向图上的扩散，并通过图卷积网络提取交通流的空间特征。在编码器-解码器中添加有意义的时隙注意，以形成一个注意编码器网络来处理时间相关性。同时考虑了三个外部因素(白天、工作日和交通事故标记)对交通流预测任务的影响。

1.2 基于图注意力机制的混合模型

图注意力机制与图卷积网络分别在空域上和频域上对图进行卷积。图注意力机制与时序模型组成的混合模型也取得了很好的交通预测效果。

(1)Wu 等[25]提出的基于图注意力机制的混合模型，建立端到端可训练的编码器预测模型，解决多链路流量预测问题。Zhang 等[26]提出了基于图的深度学习框架用于交通速度预测。该模型集成了图注意网络和递归神经网络，共同学习交通网络的时空依赖性，将注意图卷积用于空间特征学习，并将学习到的注意系数作为空间依赖关系。通过集成长短期记忆网络来捕获时间动态，提高相对长期预测的性能。该框架继承了图注意力机制和长短期记忆的优点。

(2)单独的图卷积网络不太容易作用于动态图，因此许多学者在交通流预测上面引入图注意力机制。近年来，在时空图卷积网络的基础上加入注意力机制以更好的捕获路网的时空特征。Guo 等[27]提出了基于注意力的时空图卷积网络模型来解决交通流预测问题。该模型结合了时空注意力机制和时空卷积，包括空间维度上的图卷积和时间维度上的标准卷积,同时捕获交通数据的动态时空特征。基于注意力的时空图卷积网络主要由三个独立的分量组成,分别模拟交通流的三种时间特性,即近期依赖性、日周期性依赖性和周周期性依赖性。具体来说,每个分量包含两个主要部分:①有效捕获交通数据动态时空相关性的时空注意力机制;②时空卷积,使用图卷积来捕获空间模式,同时使用通用标准卷积来描述时间特征。将三个分量的输出进行加权融合,生成最终的预测结果。

(3)无论混合模型的构成如何,图卷积网络与递归神经网络等结合以及是否引入图注意力机制等,模型必须考虑时间尺度与空间尺度。南方科技大学的余剑峤[28]通过图卷积和注意力机制捕获几何交通数据相关性,并使用生成式对抗学习框架内的编码器—解码器体系结构提取和扩展时间数据相关性。目前的注意力机制对动态依赖关系具有很好的捕捉能力。湖南大学的安吉尧等[29]提出了用于城市道路交通流预测的时空图卷积网络模型,其利用信息几何方法确定不同传感器之间的动态数据分布差异。注意力机制采用信息几何方法,通过分析传感器数据的分布得到矩阵,交通流数据特征中的时空动态连接更能捕捉城市道路网络中不同传感器之间的交通空间依赖关系。该模型充分考虑了信息几何方法和基于注意力机制并且首次利用信息几何技术来增强注意力机制。

2　基于图卷积网络的交通流预测方法常用数据集

数据集的真实性对于训练模型是至关重要的。本文描述了基于图卷积网络的交通流预测方法常用公开数据集,这些数据集包含由道路环形探测器、收费站和其他道路设备检测记录的交通数据。

(1)PeMS:PeMS为加利福尼亚州交通流数据库,其收集了加利福尼亚州高速公路上39000多个独立探测器的实时数据。数据包括,车道的流量、占有率和速度等,数据的最小时间间隔为5min,非常适合短期预测。其启用历史平均值方法自动填充丢失的数据。在交通流预测任务中,常使用子数据集PeMS-D4/D8/BAY/LA等。该数据集获取地址:http://pems.dot.ca.gov/。

(2)CityPulse Smart City Datasets:该数据集采自丹麦第二大城市和主要港口奥胡斯,数据集为有记录的每5分钟平均速度和车流量。数据集包括每个探测器的地理信息,并且提供了污染状况,天气和特殊事件信息。这些信息可以作为外部因素来训练模型。该数据集获取地址:http://iot.ee.surrey.ac.uk:8080/datasets.html。

(3)其他数据集:该数据资源收集了多个国家和地区的交通数据集和获取方式,不同数据集包含多种真实交通信息,例如,交通流量、道路是否封闭、交通事故和天气情况等。该数据资源获取地址:https://github.com/graphhopper/open-traffic-collection/。

3　结语

本文深入回顾了基于图卷积网络的交通流预测方法,基于图卷积网络的混合模型成了当下主流的交通流预测方法,其引入时序模型、注意力机制和外部因素等使模型的性能获得了不错的效果。在未来的研究中,为了使模型预测准确度提高,其必须考虑多种外部因素。对交通中的多参与者(如行人等)进行研究和分析,考虑节假日、交通事故、温度湿度和降水等多因素的影响。

参考文献

[1] Zhao Ling, Song Yu-jiao, Zhang Chao, et al. T-GCN: A Temporal Graph Convolutional Network for Traffic Prediction[J]. IEEE Transactions on Intelligent Transportation Systems, 2020, 21(9):3848-3858.

[2] 刘星委.基于ARIMA与长短时记忆神经网络的高速公路交通流预测及比较的研究[D].成都:西南交通大学,2018.

[3] Duan Hui-ming, Xiao Xin-ping. A Multimode Dynamic Short-Term Traffic Flow Grey Prediction Model of High-Dimension Tensors[J]. Complexity, 2019, 2019:1-18.

[4] 申雷霄,陆宇航,郭建华.卡尔曼滤波短时交通流预测普通国省道适应性研究[J].交通信息与安全,2021,39(05):117-127.

[5] 郑义彬,赖伟伟.基于支持向量机的高速短时交通流量预测[J].工程与建设,2020,34(02):201-204.

[6] 陈娇娜,张翔,张生瑞.高速公路行程时间

Bootstrap-KNN 区间预测分析与实证[J]. 控制与决策,2018,33(11):2080-2086.

[7] 林培群,夏雨,周楚昊. 引入时空特征的高速公路行程时间预测方法[J]. 华南理工大学学报(自然科学版),2021,49(08):1-11.

[8] 程山英. 基于模糊神经网络的短时交通流预测方法研究[J]. 计算机测量与控制,2017,25(08):155-158.

[9] 杨凤满. 基于人工神经网络的交通流预测方法综述[J]. 公路交通科技,2020,37(S1):130-135.

[10] 孔繁辉,李健. 深度信念网络优化 BP 神经网络的交通流预测模型[J]. 管理评论,2020,32(03):300-306.

[11] 王体迎,时鹏超,刘蒋琼,等. 基于门限递归单元循环神经网络的交通流预测方法研究[J]. 重庆交通大学学报(自然科学版),2018,37(11):76-82.

[12] Wang Sheng-you, Zhao Jin, Shao Chun-fu, et al. Truck Traffic Flow Prediction Based on LSTM and GRU Methods With Sampled GPS Data [J]. IEEE Access, 2020, 8: 208158-208169.

[13] Seng De-wen, Lu Fan-shun, Liang Zi-yi, et al. Forecasting Traffic Flows in Irregular Regions with Multi-Graph Convolutional Network and Gated Recurrent Unit [J]. Frontiers of Information Technology & Electronic Engineering, 2021, 22(9):1179-1193.

[14] 马永杰,程时升,马芸婷,等. 卷积神经网络及其在智能交通系统中的应用综述[J]. 交通运输工程学报,2021,21(04):48-71.

[15] Defferrard M, Bresson X, Vanderg Heynst P. Convolutional neural networks on graphs with fast localized spectral filtering [C] // Proceedings of the 30th International Conference on Neural Information Processing Systems. New York: Curran Associates, 2016: 3844-3852.

[16] Du Sheng-dong, Li Tian-rui, Xun Gong, et al. A Hybrid Method for Traffic Flow Forecasting Using Multimodal Deep Learning [J]. International Journal of Computational Intelligence Systems, 2018, 13(1).

[17] Boukerche Azzedine, WANG Jia-hao. A Performance Modeling and Analysis of a Novel Vehicular Traffic Flow Prediction System Using a Hybrid Machine Learning-Based Model[J]. Ad Hoc Networks, 2020, 106: 102224.

[18] Peng Hao, Du Bo-wen, Liu Ming-sheng, et al. Dynamic Graph Convolutional Network for Long-Term Traffic Flow Prediction with Reinforcement Learning [J]. Information Sciences, 2021, 578: 401-416.

[19] Zhang Zi-kai, Li Yi-dong, Song Hai-feng, et al. Multiple Dynamic Graph Based Traffic Speed Prediction Method [J]. Neurocomputing, 2021, 461: 109-117.

[20] Zhang Shuai, Chen Yong, Zhang Wen-yu. Spatiotemporal fuzzy-graph convolutional network model with dynamic feature encoding for traffic forecasting. [J]. Knowledge-Based Systems, 2021, 231: 107403.

[21] Yu Bing, Yin HaoTeng, Zhu Shengnan. Spatio-Temporal Graph Convolutional Networks: A Deep Learning Framework for Traffic Forecasting [C] // Proceedings of the Twenty-Seventh International Joint Conference on Artificial Intelligence. 2017(3634-3640).

[22] Song Chao, Lin You-fang, Guo Sheng-nan, et al. Spatial-Temporal Synchronous Graph Convolutional Networks: A New Framework for Spatial-Temporal Network Data Forecasting [J]. Proceedings of the AAAI Conference on Artificial Intelligence, 2020, 34(1): 914-921.

[23] Yu Byeonghyeop, Lee Yong-jin, Sohn Keemin. Forecasting road traffic speeds by considering area-wide spatio-temporal dependencies based on a graph convolutional neural network (GCN)-Science Direct[J]. Transportation Research Part C: Emerging Technologies, 2020, 114: 189-204.

[24] Ye Ji-hua, Xue Sheng-jun, Jiang Ai-wen. Attention-based spatio-temporal graph convolutional network considering external factors for multistep traffic flow prediction[J]. Digital Communications and Networks, 2021.

[25] Wu Tianlong, Chen Feng. Graph Attention LSTM Network: A New Model for Traffic Flow Forecasting [C] // 2018 5th International Conference on Information Science and Control Engineering (ICISCE). 2018:241-245.

[26] Zhang Chen-han, James J. Q. Yu, Liu Yi. Spatial-Temporal Graph Attention Networks: A Deep Learning Approach for Traffic Forecasting [J]. IEEE Access, 2019, 7: 166246-166256.

[27] Guo Sheng-nan, Lin You-fang, Feng Ning, et al. Attention Based Spatial-Temporal Graph Convolutional Networks for Traffic Flow Forecasting [J]. Proceedings of the AAAI Conference on Artificial Intelligence. 2019: 922-929.

[28] James J. Q. Yu. Citywide traffic speed prediction: A geometric deep learning approach-ScienceDirect [J]. Knowledge-Based Systems, 2020, 212:106592.

[29] An Ji-yao, Guo Liang, Liu Wei, et al. IGAGCN: Information geometry and attention-based spatiotemporal graph convolutional networks for traffic flow prediction [J]. Neural Networks, 2021, 143:355-367.

基于时空特征的路内泊位停车需求短时预测

刘俚宁[1] 叶晓飞[*1,2] 王金芬[1] 胡怡洁[1] 朱 羿[1] 陈 峻[3]

(1. 宁波大学海运学院;2. 宁波市港口贸易合作与发展协同创新中心;3. 东南大学交通学院)

摘 要 城市停车问题日益严重,停车资源精细化管理迫在眉睫。停车需求短时预测作为停车资源精细化管理的基础,其预测普适性和精准度尚未得以有效解决。为了充分挖掘停车需求的空间特征和时间特征,本文提出了基于卷积神经网络(CNN)和长短期记忆神经网络(LSTM)的路内停车短时需求预测模型。以宁波东方一品区域的路内泊位为研究对象,对其停车需求数据进行预测,并对预测模型进行对比分析。结果表明:CNN-LSTM模型的在"宁波_东方一品_15min"数据集下预测误差MAE仅为0.2935,拟合优度R^2已达99.62%;同时CNN-LSTM模型在增加一定的训练时间条件下大幅提高了预测精度以及模型稳定性,能有效应用于实际停车需求的短时预测当中。

关键词 交通数据挖掘 停车需求短时预测 CNN-LSTM模型 路内泊位 停车资源精细化管理

0 引言

城市机动化水平快速增长,汽车保有量和使用量逐年增加,城市有限的停车资源难以匹配持续上涨的停车需求,停车难问题日益严重[1]。随着城市数字化水平的提高,各种检测硬件设施的完善,停车资源精细化管理这一理念逐渐被大众所关注[2]。停车需求短时预测作为停车资源精细化管理的基础,是停车管理策略设计的关键技术之一,其预测普适性和精准度尚未得以有效解决[3]。

现有对停车需求预测的方法主要有两种,即基于统计学理论的预测方法以及基于机器学习的预测方法[4]。基于统计学理论的停车需求预测方法主要包括:多元回归模型[5]、马尔可夫模型[6]、卡尔曼滤波[7]、自回归滑动平均(ARIMA)[8]以及时间序列模型等。这些模型较为简单,且求解速度较快,但由于基于统计学的预测模型对于历史需求数据没有很好的自适应和自学习能力,导致其不能很好地反映停车需求数据中的不确定性和非线性特征,在短时预测精度方面不能满足实际需要。得益于计算机设备的高速发展,计算机性能大幅提升,使得机器学习方法在停车需求预测

1. 项目基金:国家重点研发计划项目(2017YFE9134700);国家自然科学基金资助项目(71701108);浙江省自然科学基金项目(LY20E080011);宁波市交通科技计划项目(201920)。

领域得以广泛应用,主要包括:支持向量机[9]、随机森林模型[10]、梯度提升决策树(GBDT)[11]、模糊神经网络[12]、基于小波神经网络的预测方法[13]、基于卷积神经网络(CNN)的预测方法[14]以及基于长短期记忆神经网络(LSTM)的预测方法[15]等。这些模型通过训练大量样本数据,不需任何经验公式,便可建立良好的输入、输出映射模型,具有较强的自适应、自学习能力。基于机器学习的预测方法虽然能获取较优的预测精度,但现有研究通常将单一的基于时间序列的数据作为模型输入,忽视了停车需求的空间相关性特征,减弱了模型对停车需求变化规律的挖掘与学习。

基于上述研究的不足,本文将考虑停车需求的时间相关性以及空间相关性特征,设计模型输入结构。同时,将设计一种基于卷积神经网络(CNN)和长短期记忆神经网络(LSTM)的组合预测模型,充分挖掘停车需求间的时空关系,对停车需求进行短时预测。

1 数据收集及特征分析

1.1 数据说明及采集

选取2019年4月1日至2019年4月30日宁波东部新城东方一品区域(数据量约4.85万条,路内停车泊位317个)停车设施自动采集数据进行分析。原始数据主要内容包含:车牌识别信息、停车区域信息、停车驶入时间、停车驶出时间以及停车费用,见表1。

原始数据形式 表1

号牌号码	停车区域信息	驶入时间	驶出时间	停车费用
浙 BX＊＊＊8S	区划:鄞州区 片区:东方一品 停车点:定宁街交警中队北侧 泊位:H1030009	2019-4-12 18:14	2019-4-12 22:51	免费离开
浙 B1＊＊＊XV	区划:鄞州区 片区:东方一品 停车点:安顺路东方一品西侧 泊位:E1030026	2019-4-12 18:14	2019-4-12 18:29	免费离开
浙 B7＊＊＊V5	区划:鄞州区 片区:东方一品 停车点:安顺路东方一品西侧 泊位:Z1030032	2019-4-12 18:15	2019-4-12 21:38	免费离开
浙 B8＊＊＊S1	区划:鄞州区 片区:东方一品 停车点:瑞庆路恒元悦庭西侧 泊位:A1031042	2019-4-12 18:15	2019-4-12 17:46	免费离开

1.2 停车需求特征分析

对原始数据按照15min的时间间隔进行聚类统计,东方一品区域四月整体停车需求量时间变化规律如图1、图2所示。每日停车需求量出现周期性变化且具有相似的波动性,能观察到明显的高峰和平峰。非工作日的时间变化规律与工作日相似。

停车区域的空间相似性表现为路内停车需求受到相邻路段停车需求的影响,因此,分别对东方一品区域内各路段的路内停车需求进行相关性分析,以实际区域的路段分布为依据,将东方一品区域划分为一个"5×3"的矩阵,以区块1、2、3做可视化,结果如图3所示。可见,东方一品区域内,相邻区块之间的路内停车需求往往具有更高的相关性。

上述分析可得,路内停车需求具有明显的时间相关性的同时也受到空间特征的影响。因此,为了更加精确的挖掘停车数据的变化规律,应设计一种能综合考虑停车需求的时间特征和空间特征的短时预测模型,实现停车需求的短时预测。

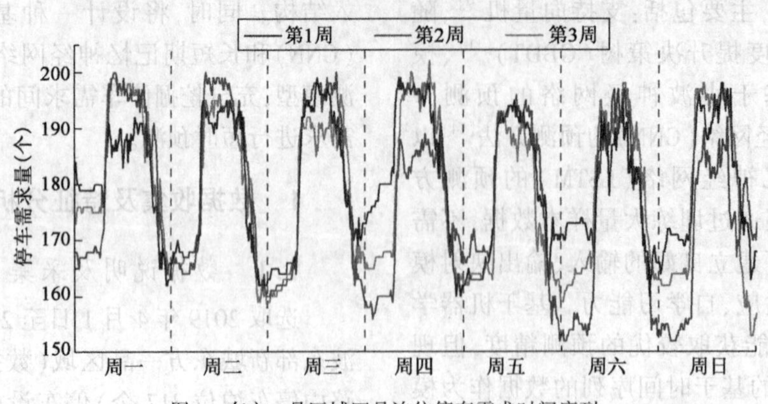

图1　东方一品区域四月泊位停车需求时间序列

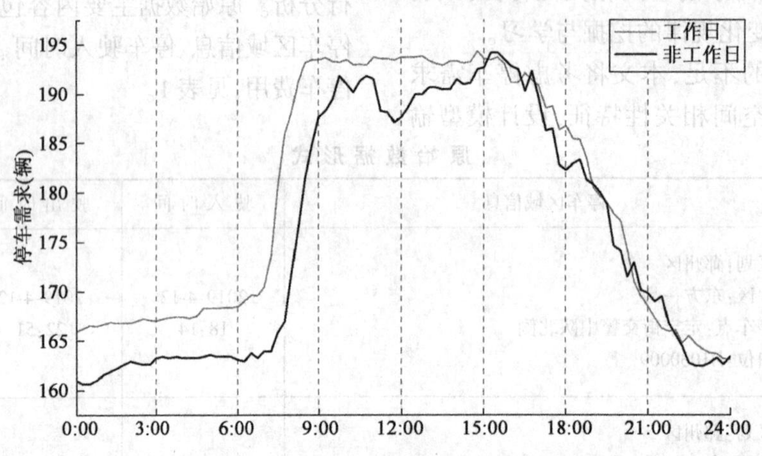

图2　东方一品区域单日泊位停车需求时间序列

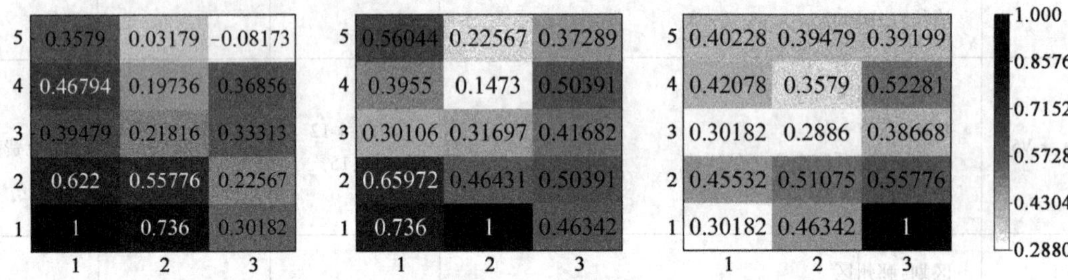

图3　东方一品区域停车需求空间相关性(以区块1、2、3为例)

2　基于 CNN-LSTM 的停车需求短时预测方法

2.1　卷积神经网络

卷积神经网络(CNN)能够挖掘历史数据中的空间相关性,结合局部感知区域、共享权、空间或时间的向下采样,减少网络训练参数,提高模型运算效率[16]。其结构与普通的多隐含层神经网络有所不同。CNN 的输入通常为多组二维矩阵,隐含层由功能不同的卷积层和池化层组合而成,如图 4 所示。具体来看,卷积层通过设置卷积核,对输入样本进行离散卷积运算,进行特征提取;池化层则通过对卷积层的输出数据进行最大值提前,或平均值提取等操作,去除数据噪声,映射关键特征。

卷积层的原理如下:

$$y_{ij}^{k} = \sigma(W_{k} \otimes x_{ij}^{k-1} + b_{k}) \tag{1}$$

$$W_{k} \otimes x_{ij}^{k-1} = \sum_{m=0}^{a-1}\sum_{n=0}^{a-1} w_{mn}^{k} * x_{(i+m)(j+n)}^{k-1} \tag{2}$$

式中:x_{ij}^{k-1}——代表该卷积层输入数据;

y_{ij}^{k}——代表输出数据;

$\otimes$——卷积运输;

W_k——代表卷积层对应卷积核的权重;

b_k——代表卷积核的偏置参数;

σ——卷积层的激活函数。

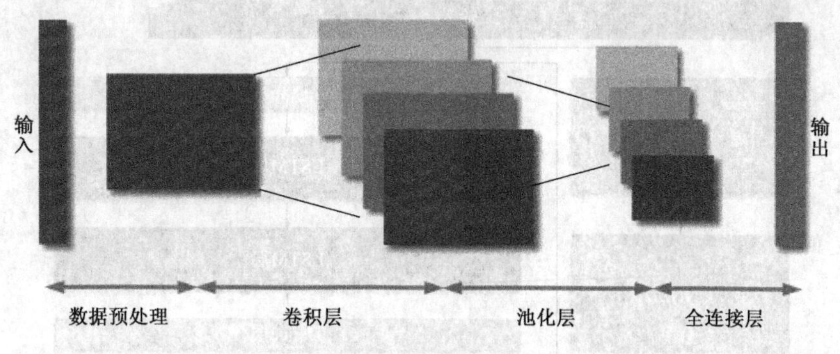

图4 简单卷积神经网络示意图

卷积层的神经元与上一层对应分量中的接收域内的神经元相连接，将连接权值与接收域内神经元的输出做点乘，并通过激活函数进行输出。

2.2 长短期记忆神经网络

长短期记忆神经网络（LSTM）是循环神经网络（RNN）的一种变体，其在解决RNN的梯度消失以及梯度爆炸问题的同时，大幅提高了在时序数据预测问题上的预测精度[17]。LSTM单元是由三个不同的通过门限控制信息通信的网络层组成，三个门限组织过滤了原始数据中影响较小的数据，记忆重要信息，提高网络的记忆能力，同时提高了训练效率。工作机制如图5所示，原理如下：

$$f_t = \sigma[W_f \cdot (h_{t-1}, x_t) + b_f] \quad (3)$$

$$i_t = \sigma[W_i \cdot (h_{t-1}, x_t) + b_i] \quad (4)$$

$$\widetilde{C}_t = \mathrm{Relu}[W_C \cdot (h_{t-1}, x_t) + b_C] \quad (5)$$

$$C_t = f_t \cdot C_{t-1} + i_t \cdot \widetilde{C}_t \quad (6)$$

$$o_t = \sigma[W_o \cdot (h_{t-1}, x_t) + b_o] \quad (7)$$

$$h_t = o_t \cdot \mathrm{Relu}(C_t) \quad (8)$$

式中：f_t——遗忘门；

i_t——输入门；

o_t——输出门；

$\widetilde{C}_t$、C_t——分别表示即时状态和长期状态；

h_{t-1}——上一时刻隐藏状态；

x_t——当前时刻输入特征；

σ、Relu——两种不同的激活函数；

W_f、W_i、W_C、W_o——模型需要训练的参数；

b_f、b_i、b_C、b_o——模型需要训练的偏置。

2.3 CNN-LSTM模型

单一的CNN虽然可以有效地对空间特征进行抽象化处理，但在长期的预测过程中容易陷入过拟合状态，LSTM无法处理空间特征，但通过记忆机制筛选高影响特征，能有效解决梯度消失问题以及模型过拟合问题。可见，单一模型在停车需求短时预测领域具有局限性。因此，本文提出CNN-LSTM混合模型，发挥CNN在空间特征挖掘的优势以及LSTM在时序特征挖掘方面的优势，既解决单一模型存在的过拟合问题和梯度问题，又提升模型深度，提升模型学习能力。模型结构如图6所示。

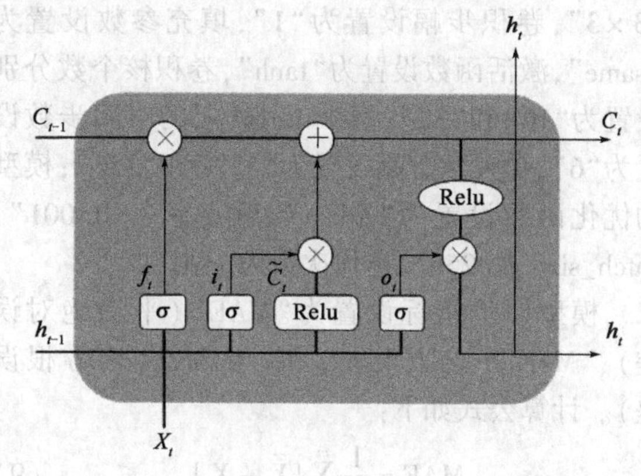

图5 LSTM单元工作机制

具体建模流程如下：

(1)利用CNN单元挖掘停车需求的空间相关性。采用两层CNN模型，提取空间特征。

(2)重塑CNN单元的输出结果。将CNN输出的二维数据转化成LSTM可以训练的一维数据。

(3)利用LSTM单元挖掘停车需求的时间相关性。采用两层LSTM模型，提取时间特征。

(4)利用全连接层输出预测结果。采用一层全连接层解码被CNN-LSTM模型编译后的数据，输出预测结果。

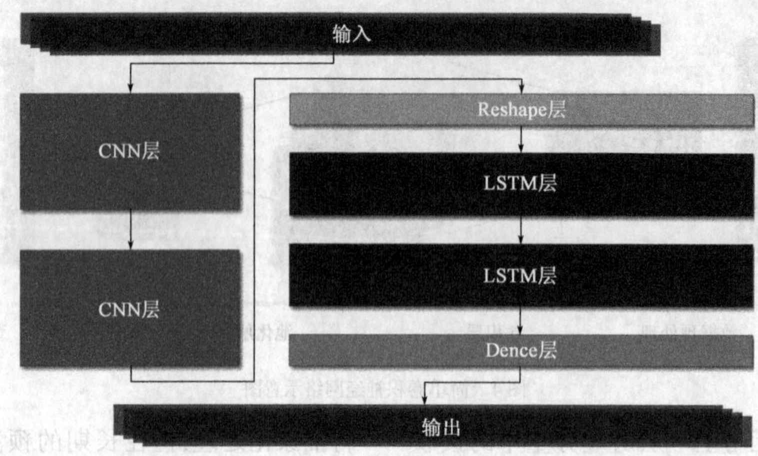

图6　CNN-LSTM模型流程结构图

3　模型验证

3.1　模型参数设置

本文选择使用Keras框架搭建并训练CNN-LSTM停车需求短时预测模型。依据东方一品区域停车位的分布情况，将东方一品区域划分为15个停车区块，并将模型输入设计为5×3的矩阵形式。模型中，两个卷积层的卷积核尺寸设置为"3×3"，卷积步幅设置为"1"，填充参数设置为"same"，激活函数设置为"tanh"，卷积核个数分别设置为"16"和"32"；两个LSTM层的时间步数设置为"6"，单元数分别设置为"128"和"256"；模型的优化函数设置为"Adam"，学习率为"0.001"，batch_size为"256"，迭代次数为"300"。

模型评价指标设置为"MAE"（平均绝对误差）、"MSE"（均方误差）和"RMSE"（均方根误差）。计算公式如下：

$$MAE = \frac{1}{m}\sum_{i=1}^{m}|\overline{X}_i - X_i| \tag{9}$$

$$MSE = \frac{1}{m}\sum_{i=1}^{m}(\overline{X}_i - X_i)^2 \tag{10}$$

$$RMSE = \sqrt{\frac{1}{m}\sum_{i=1}^{m}(X_i - X_i)^2} \tag{11}$$

3.2　预测结果分析

通过对东方一品区域的停车数据分别进行15min和30min的聚类，得到"宁波_东方一品_15min"和"宁波_东方一品_30min"两个数据集，并以7∶3的比例划分训练集和测试集验证模型效用。

CNN-LSTM模型的训练误差收敛情况如图7，模型对各训练集的预测误差见表2。相较于30min数据集，15min数据集的预测精度提高了不少。一方面，时间间隔越短，停车需求的变化越能被更好的观察；另一方面，更短的统计间隔将带来更多的数据样本，同一时间长度内，15min数据集的样本数是30min数据集的两倍，样本数的增加也带来这更好的预测精度。CNN-LSTM停车需求短时预测模型在"宁波_东方一品_15min"数据集下拟合优度已达99.62%，说明该模型已深度挖掘了数据间的空间特征和时间特征，极大减小了预测误差，对真实值的拟合程度极高。选取了4月29日和30日停车需求数据的真实值和预测值进行对比，拟合情况如图8所示。

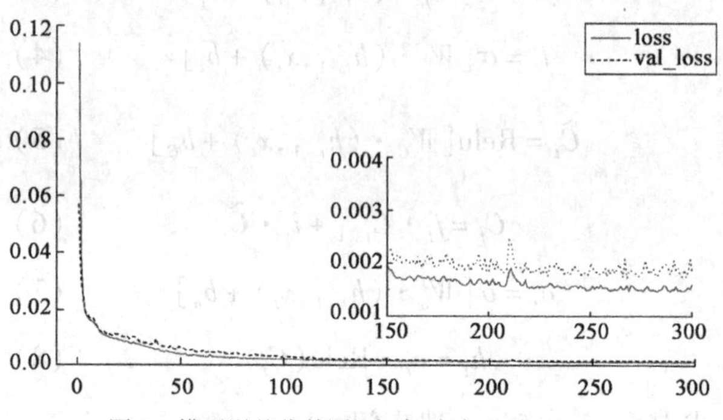

图7　模型误差收敛图(宁波_东方一品_15min)

预测误差　　表2

数据集	宁波_东方一品_15min	宁波_东方一品_30min
MAE	0.2935	0.3845
MSE	0.4028	0.6750
RMSE	0.6346	0.8216
R^2(拟合优度)	99.62%	90.33%

3.3　模型效用对比分析

本文将选用以下4种现有的停车需求短时预测方法与CNN-LSTM模型进行对比。

(1)WNN[13]：基于小波神经网络的停车需求预测模型；

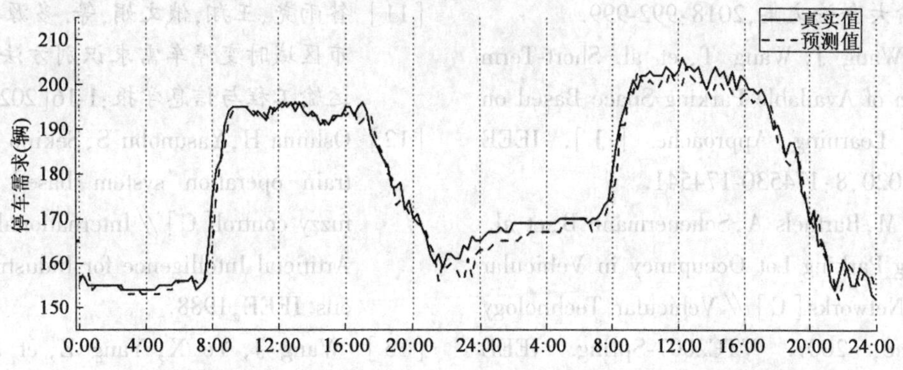

图8　“宁波_东方一品_15min”数据集中停车需求数据的真实值和预测值对比

(2) CNN[14]：基于卷积神经网络的停车需求预测模型；

(3) LSTM[15]：基于长短期记忆神经网络的停车需求预测模型；

(4) ConvLSTM[18]：基于卷积长短期记忆神经网络的停车需求预测模型。

模型的稳定性通过训练五次模型的均方误差的标准差来衡量：

$$S_{\mathrm{MSE}} = \sqrt{\frac{1}{5}\sum_{i=1}^{5}(\mathrm{MSE}_i - \mathrm{MSE})^2} \tag{12}$$

通过训练“宁波_东方一品_15min”数据集可得模型效用情况对比如表3和图9所示。

模型性能对比　表3

模　型	CNN-LSTM	CNN	LSTM	WNN	ConvLSTM
MAE	**0.2935**	0.5338	0.4254	0.7978	0.6928
RMSE	**0.6346**	0.9496	0.8306	1.2695	1.1342
R^2_score	**0.9962**	0.9914	0.9934	0.9846	0.9877
ACC	**0.9596**	0.9393	0.9469	0.9189	0.9278
模型稳定性 S_{MSE}	**0.0201**	0.0451	0.0345	0.0806	0.0643
训练时长(s)	1200	**150**	750	600	1350

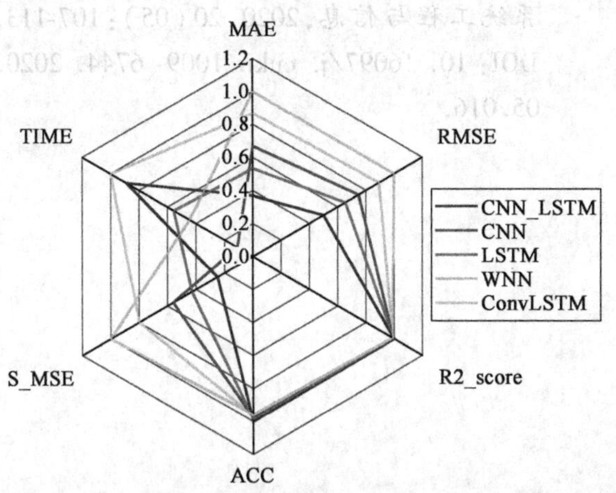

图9　模型预测性能比较

通过对现有停车需求短时预测模型对比，可以明显发现CNN-LSTM模型在各个预测性能指标上表现优异。从预测误差上看，CNN-LSTM模型无论是在MAE、RMSE、R2_score还是ACC指标方面都具备一定优势；从模型稳定性来看，CNN-LSTM模型更是具有压倒性优势，这在实际运用中无疑更具普适性；从训练时长来看，CNN-LSTM模型的训练速度低于单一的CNN和LSTM模型，但是整体训练时长也未超过短时预测的要求。总的来看，CNN-LSTM模型以延长一定的训练时间为代价，换取了更优的预测精度和更稳定的训练效果，在停车需求短时预测领域具有明显优势。

4　结语

本文提出了一种基于时空特征的路内泊位停车需求短时预测模型，该模型通过两层卷积神经网络对停车需求的空间相关性建模，同时运用长短期记忆神经网络对停车需求的时间相关性进行挖掘，并将两者融合，形成的CNN-LSTM预测模型能更好地学习复杂场景的停车特征，为停车需求的短时预测提供更准确的预测方法。在真实的停车数据集上实验表明，本文提出的停车需求预测模型的预测效果优于当前已有的停车需求预测方法，同时在预测稳定性方面，本文模型也得到大幅提高。因此，本文提出的基于CNN-LSTM的停车需求短时预测模型能有效运用于实际停车需求短时预测当中，并支撑停车管理策略的设计。

参考文献

[1] 叶晓飞，陈峻，冯树民，等. 路内停车影响下非机动车流速度模型[J]. 哈尔滨工业大学学报，2016，48(03)：115-119.

[2] 朱安康，宋丹丹，欧阳松寿，等. 北京市机动车停车设施资源管理机制研究[C]//2018世界

交通运输大会论文集,2018:992-999.

[3] Ye X, Wang J, Wang T, et al. Short-Term Prediction of Available Parking Space Based on Machine Learning Approaches [J]. IEEE Access,2020,8:174530-174541.

[4] Caliskan M, Barthels A, Scheuermann B, et al. Predicting Parking Lot Occupancy in Vehicular Ad Hoc Networks[C]//Vehicular Technology Conference, 2007. VTC2007-Spring. IEEE 65th. IEEE,2007.

[5] 汪磊,左忠义.基于MLR的公交车行程时间预测模型[J].大连交通大学学报,2015,36(02):1-5. DOI:10.13291/j.cnki.djdxac.2015.02.001.

[6] 刘东辉,肖雪,张珏.基于粒子群和LSTM模型的变区间短时停车需求预测方法[J].交通信息与安全,2021,39(04):77-83.

[7] 唐克双,郝兆康,衣谢博闻等.停车场泊位占有率预测方法评价[J].同济大学学报(自然科学版),2017,45(04):533-543.

[8] Aslanargun A, Mammadov M, Yazici B, et al. Comparison of ARIMA, neural networks and hybrid models in time series: tourist arrival forecasting [J]. Journal of Statistical Computation and Simulation,77:1,29-53, DOI:10.1080/10629360600564874

[9] 梁迪,郭启航,姜廷霖.布谷鸟搜索算法优化支持向量机的停车位预测[J].沈阳大学学报(自然科学版),2021,33(03):234-239+266. DOI:10.16103/j.cnki.21-1583/n.2021.03.007.

[10] 叶骐铭,叶晓飞,李敏等.巡游出租车运力规模动态调整回归树模型[J].宁波大学学报(理工版),2020,33(04):89-96.

[11] 昝雨尧,王翔,俄文娟,等.多源数据融合的城市区域时变停车需求识别方法[J/OL].交通运输工程与信息学报:1-16[2021-12-21].

[12] Oshima H, Yasunobu S, Sekino S I. Automatic train operation system based on predictive fuzzy control[C]//International Workshop on Artificial Intelligence for Industrial Applications. IEEE,1988.

[13] Wang J, Ye X, Yang Z, et al. Short-Term Prediction of Available Parking Space Based on Improved Wavelet Neural Network[C]//20th COTA International Conference of Transportation Professionals,2020.

[14] Yu D, Yang L, Yu X. A Data Grouping CNN Algorithm for Short-Term Traffic Flow Forecasting[C]//Asia-Pacific Web Conference. Springer International Publishing,2016.

[15] Wang Xiangxue, Xu Lunhui, Chen Kaixun. Data-Driven Short-Term Forecasting for Urban Road Network Traffic Based on Data Processing and LSTM-RNN [J]. Arabian Journal for Science and Engineering,2019,44(4):3043-3060.

[16] 陈先昌.基于卷积神经网络的深度学习算法与应用研究[D].杭州:浙江工商大学,2014.

[17] 山世光,阚美娜,刘昕,等.深度学习:多层神经网络的复兴与变革[J].科技导报,2016,34(14):60-70.

[18] 赵聪,朱逸凡,李兴华等.动态管理模式下路侧停车泊位占有率预测方法[J].交通运输系统工程与信息,2020,20(05):107-113. DOI:10.16097/j.cnki.1009-6744.2020.05.016.

肇事逃逸车辆危险驾驶行为对事故伤害严重程度影响分析

柏 伟*[1,2] 蒋乙豪[1]

(1.四川警察学院道路交通管理系;2.四川警事科学研究院)

摘 要 为探究肇事逃逸车辆危险驾驶行为与事故伤害严重程度的关系,本文在充分考虑逃逸事故特征及各统计分析模型特性的基础上,采用有序 Logit 模型、随机参数 Logit 模型和有序广义线性模型鉴别各危险驾驶行为对事故伤害严重程度的关联,并论述各类危险驾驶行为对不同伤害程度事故的影响规律特征。研究结果表明:有序广义线性模型的拟合程度最优;且肇事逃逸车辆的闯红灯、制动失败、鲁莽驾驶、速度过快和停车不当行为会显著加剧事故伤害严重程度。根据数据分析结果,应加强安全驾驶及交通法规的宣教工作,同时倡导车辆主动安全提醒技术应用配置,并结合道路交通监测等技术手段,提升逃逸事故的应对效率。

关键词 数据挖掘 影响因素 逃逸事故 有序广义线性模型 危险驾驶行为 伤害程度

0 引言

逃逸事故是一类颇受社会各界及学界内部关注的道路交通事故,且被广泛定性为一种严重的违法行为;危险驾驶行为则是导致道路交通事故发生和损害产生的关键因素之一。研究肇事逃逸车辆危险驾驶行为与事故伤害严重程度之间的关系,不仅有助于加深对逃逸事故特征规律的理解和掌握,更利于完善防治逃逸事故的策略措施,并借此降低逃逸事故所引起的人身伤害和财产损失。

现阶段关于逃逸事故的研究多集中在通过逻辑回归模型(Logistic Regression Model)等方法探讨逃逸事故发生的影响特征因素等方面[1,2]。逃逸行为抉择影响因素[3]、分心驾驶与逃逸行为之间的关联[4]、城市下穿隧道处逃逸事故典型特征[5]、机动车与自行车碰撞逃逸事故[6]和逃逸事故伤害严重程度[7]等方向均引起学者的关注。此外,有序/广义有序 Logit 模型等方法多被用在从定量研究角度阐述事故伤害严重程度与各特征因素变量之间的关联[8~10]。因此,现阶段关于逃逸事故的相关研究未能有效阐述肇事逃逸车辆危险驾驶行为与事故伤害严重程度之间的关系。本文通过数据筛选,并与非逃逸事故的对比,从定量分析角度探究肇事车辆各类危险驾驶行为对逃逸事故和非逃逸事故的伤害严重程度影响差异性,以及影响逃逸事故伤害严重程度的规律特征,最后借此给出防治逃逸事故在驾驶行为方面的措施重点,为有效降低逃逸事故的发生和减轻事故伤害严重程度提供依据和参考。

1 数据描述与筛选

1.1 数据来源

本文基于 2014 年道路交通事故数据进行研究,其中不论危险驾驶行为是否导致事故发生,凡调查人员在进行事故调查时发现其存在危险驾驶,均进行标定。共筛选出逃逸事故 13463 起(双车事故,其中肇事方存在危险驾驶和逃逸行为,受害方无任何违法驾驶行为)[11]。同时,采取同样的数据甄选方法,随机选择 13612 起非逃逸双车事故(占该类型样本总量的 9.5%)作为对比分析组。

1.2 变量定义

考虑到研究事故样本中的死亡与重伤事故占极少数,在建模过程中将二者一并考虑,作为因变量的事故伤害严重程度依次为:未受伤(=1),轻伤(=2),中伤(=3)及重伤或死亡(=4),作为自变量的各危险驾驶行为详细定义见表1。

1. 基金项目:四川警察学院 2020 度平台团队科研专项(CJKY202007);四川警察学院博士科研启动经费项目(2018YJBSQD29)。

变量定义及统计结果　表 1

变　量	描　述	逃逸事故		非逃逸事故	
		期望	标准差	期望	标准差
事故严重程度	未受伤 = 1,轻伤 = 2,中伤 = 3,重伤或死亡 = 4	—	—	—	—
速度过快	速度过快 = 1,否则 = 0	0.06	0.23	0.06	0.25
制动失败	制动失败 = 1,否则 = 0	0.15	0.36	0.27	0.44
闯红灯	闯红灯 = 1,否则 = 0	0.06	0.25	0.05	0.22
偏离道路中心	偏离道路中心 = 1,否则 = 0	0.02	0.16	0.01	0.10
不当超车	不当超车 = 1,否则 = 0	0.03	0.17	0.01	0.11
车道使用错误	车道使用错误 = 1,否则 = 0	0.10	0.30	0.05	0.22
不当转向	不当转向 = 1,否则 = 0	0.02	0.15	0.03	0.16
倒车不当	倒车不当 = 1,否则 = 0	0.06	0.24	0.05	0.21
停车不当	停车不当 = 1,否则 = 0	0.25	0.43	0.37	0.48
鲁莽驾驶	鲁莽驾驶 = 1,否则 = 0	0.04	0.20	0.00	0.06
分心驾驶	粗心驾驶 = 1,否则 = 0	0.11	0.31	0.03	0.17
其他	其他违法行为 = 1,否则 = 0	0.09	0.29	0.07	0.25

2　事故伤害程度分析模型

现代统计理论与方法的发展为交通安全定量研究提供便捷,适用不少于 3 个无序因变量的多元 Logit 模型以及适用于若干有序(3 个及以上)因变量的有序 Logit 模型被广泛应用于道路交通安全的鉴定、分析和影响作用研究上。鉴于本文研究因变量的定义为 4 类有序等级,选择有序 Logit 模型探究危险驾驶行为对逃逸事故伤害程度的影响。其模型表达式为:

$$P(Y_i > j) = g(X\beta) = \frac{\exp(\alpha_j + X_i\beta)}{1 + \exp(\alpha_j + X_i\beta)} \tag{1}$$

式中:j——表示事故伤害严重等级,且 $j = 1,2,3\cdots$;

i——表示第 i 起事故,且 $i = 1,2,3\cdots$;

Y_i——表示第 i 起事故的伤害程度;

X——表示各类危险驾驶行为集合(自变量);

β——表示自变量 X 的系数;

α_j——表示第 j 等级伤害程度方程的常数项。

由于有序 Logit 模型中的常数项 α_j 随事故伤害等级的变化而变化,而自变量系数 β 则保持不变,制约了模型中各自变量对事故不同伤害等级程度的影响作用效果,存在着明显的缺陷[10]。

区别于有序 Logit 模型,随机参数 Logit 模型通过允许与每个自变量相关联的参数(如系数)根据预先指定的分布进行随机变化来体现样本数据的异质性。依据随机效应最大化的假设,可有:

$$U_{ij} = \beta_j X^{\mathrm{T}} + \varepsilon_{ij} \tag{2}$$

式中:U_{ij}——表示第 i 起事故的伤害程度为 j 时的效应;

X^{T}——自变量集合;

β_j——X^{T} 的对应系数;

ε_{ij}——扰动项。

假设 ε_{ij} 服从广义极值分布,则对于第 i 起事故,伤害严重程度为 j 的概率,即标准 Multinomial logit 模型可表示为:

$$P_i(j) = \frac{\exp(X_i^{\mathrm{T}}\beta_j)}{\sum_{j\in L}\exp(X_i^{\mathrm{T}}\beta_j)} \tag{3}$$

对式(3)在其密度函数上进行积分,可有随机参数 logit 模型:

$$P_i(j) = \int \frac{\exp(X_i^{\mathrm{T}}\beta_j)}{\sum_{j\in L}\exp(X_i^{\mathrm{T}}\beta_j)} f(\beta_j \mid \varphi_s)\, d\beta_j \tag{4}$$

式中:L——事故伤害严重程度的所有类别集合;

$f(\beta_j \mid \varphi_s)$——表示符合某类概率分布的密度函数(如正态分布等),其密度函数可由参数集合 φ_s 进行定义。

有序广义线性模型的特殊之处在于其允许通过模拟异方差性的形式来避免由同方差性假设所带来估计偏差,避免了由对异方差性的忽视所导致的边际效应实质偏差估计[12]。假设 y 表示各伤害严重程度等级,且满足 $y \in \{0,1,2,\cdots,J-1\}$;存在潜变量 y^* 满足式(5):

$$y^* = X\beta + \sigma\varepsilon \quad (5)$$

式中：ε——平均零随机误差项；

σ——允许误差项的方差向上或向下移动的参数。

确定 $\alpha_1 < \alpha_2 < \alpha_3 < \cdots < \alpha_{J-1}$ 为观察结果的阈值，在给定误差项 ε，参数向量 β 和阈值参数集的分布函数条件下，可有：

$$\begin{cases} P(y=0) = P(y^* \leqslant \alpha_1) = P\left(\varepsilon \leqslant \dfrac{\alpha_1 - X\beta}{\sigma}\right) \\ P(y=1) = P(y^* \leqslant \alpha_2) - P(y^* \leqslant \alpha_1) = P\left(\varepsilon \leqslant \dfrac{\alpha_2 - X\beta}{\sigma}\right) - P\left(\varepsilon \leqslant \dfrac{\alpha_1 - X\beta}{\sigma}\right) \\ P(y=J-1) = P(y^* \geqslant \alpha_{J-1}) = P\left(\varepsilon > \dfrac{\alpha_{J-1} - X\beta}{\sigma}\right) \end{cases} \quad (6)$$

在 $\alpha_0 \to -\infty$ 及 $\alpha_J \to +\infty$ 时，则存在：

$$P(y=j) = P\left(\varepsilon \leqslant \frac{\alpha_{j+1} - X\beta}{\sigma}\right) - P\left(\varepsilon \leqslant \frac{\alpha_j - X\beta}{\sigma}\right) = F\left(\frac{\alpha_{j+1} - X\beta}{\sigma}\right) - F\left(\frac{\alpha_j - X\beta}{\sigma}\right) \quad (7)$$

3 分析与讨论

3.1 结果分析

针对 1.1 节筛选数据样本，采用 R 软件中的 MASS 包、Rchoice 包和 oglmx 包对逃逸事故和非逃逸事故样本分别进行有序 Logit、随机参数 Logit 和有序广义线性模型回归计算，取显著性水平 $p = 0.05$，各模型回归结果见表 2 ~ 表 4。

有序 Logit 模型参数估计结果 表2

变量	行为	逃逸事故			非逃逸事故		
		参数估计	标准差	p 值	参数估计	标准差	p 值
截距 1		1.972	0.120	<0.001*	1.331	0.110	<0.001*
截距 2		3.527	0.126	<0.001*	2.728	0.114	<0.001*
截距 3		5.073	0.152	<0.001*	4.173	0.129	<0.001*
X1	速度过快	0.339	0.154	0.028*	−0.080	0.139	0.568
X2	制动失败	0.617	0.132	<0.001*	0.253	0.117	0.030*
X3	闯红灯	0.864	0.143	<0.001*	0.905	0.133	<0.001*
X5	不当超车	−0.677	0.239	0.005*	−0.752	0.279	0.007*
X6	车道使用错误	−0.862	0.168	<0.001*	−1.346	0.192	<0.001*
X8	倒车不当	−1.698	0.256	<0.001*	−2.918	0.353	<0.001*
X9	停车不当	0.330	0.129	0.010*	−0.260	0.116	0.025*
X10	鲁莽驾驶	0.490	0.163	0.003*	0.767	0.335	0.022*
X12	其他	0.207	0.144	0.151	−0.141	0.140	0.314

*表示显著因素。后同。

随机参数 Logit 模型参数估计结果 表3

变量	行为	逃逸事故			非逃逸事故		
		参数估计	标准差	p 值	参数估计	标准差	p 值
kappa1		1.665	0.049	<0.001*	1.453	0.034	<0.001*
kappa2		3.303	0.108	<0.001*	2.964	0.075	<0.001*
截距		−1.969	0.120	<0.001*	−1.328	0.110	<0.001*
X1	速度过快	0.340	0.154	0.028*	−0.079	0.139	0.571
X2	制动失败	0.620	0.132	<0.001*	0.255	0.117	0.029*
X3	闯红灯	0.869	0.143	<0.001*	0.913	0.133	<0.001*
X5	不当超车	−0.679	0.239	0.005*	−0.756	0.280	0.007*
X6	车道使用错误	−0.864	0.168	<0.001*	−1.350	0.192	<0.001*
X8	倒车不当	−1.701	0.256	<0.001*	−2.923	0.354	<0.001*
X9	停车不当	0.332	0.129	0.010*	−0.261	0.116	0.025*
X10	鲁莽驾驶	0.492	0.163	0.003*	0.773	0.336	0.022*
X12	其他	−1.210	0.365	<0.001*	−0.964	0.298	0.001*

有序广义线性模型参数估计结果　　表 4

变量	行为	逃逸事故			非逃逸事故		
		参数估计	标准差	p 值	参数估计	标准差	p 值
阈值 1		1.140	0.062	0.001*	0.746	0.060	0.001*
阈值 2		1.970	0.064	0.001*	1.515	0.061	0.001*
阈值 3		2.659	0.073	0.001*	2.191	0.066	0.001*
X1	速度过快	0.177	0.081	0.028*	−0.078	0.076	0.302
X2	制动失败	0.325	0.069	<0.001*	0.096	0.063	0.132
X3	闯红灯	0.459	0.076	<0.001*	0.458	0.074	<0.001*
X5	不当超车	−0.340	0.115	0.003*	−0.464	0.144	0.001*
X6	车道使用错误	−0.447	0.082	<0.001*	−0.775	0.096	<0.001*
X8	倒车不当	−0.811	0.112	<0.001*	−1.449	0.143	<0.001*
X9	停车不当	0.137	0.067	0.040*	−0.228	0.063	<0.001*
X10	鲁莽驾驶	0.280	0.086	0.001*	0.445	0.191	0.020*
X12	其他	−0.432	0.160	0.007*	−0.505	0.145	<0.001*

综上,汇总有序 Logit 模型、随机参数 Logit 模型及有序广义线性模型的参数估计结果,危险驾驶行为与逃逸事故伤害严重程度之间影响关系如下:

(1)制动失败、闯红灯、车道使用错误、倒车不当、鲁莽驾驶、不当超车、速度过快、停车不当 8 类危险驾驶行为对逃逸事故伤害严重程度有显著影响;闯红灯、车道使用错误、倒车不当、停车不当、不当超车、鲁莽驾驶 6 类危险驾驶行为对非逃逸事故伤害严重程度影响显著;制动失败与速度过快对逃逸事故伤害严重程度的影响较非逃逸事故凸出。

(2)加剧逃逸事故伤害严重程度的危险驾驶行为,按其影响程度大小排序依次为闯红灯、制动失败、鲁莽驾驶、速度过快、停车不当;相较于非逃逸事故,仅有闯红灯、鲁莽驾驶两类危险驾驶行为可显著增加其发生严重伤害程度事故的可能性。

(3)闯红灯与鲁莽驾驶两类危险驾驶行为常伴随有忽视通行环境、放松警惕、缺乏对驾驶环境的正确预判及车辆速度过快等特征,进而造成所引起的道路交通事故伤害严重程度增大的可能性递增;制动失败常由驾驶人分心驾驶或未及时制动导致,速度过快则不利于车辆紧急制动,进而导致发生严重伤害的逃逸事故可能性较大;停车不当则由于肇事车辆选择的停车位置或方式不当,给正常通行的车辆秩序带来干扰,从而导致产生严重伤害程度的逃逸事故概率增大。

(4)可促使逃逸事故伤害严重程度增大的可能性显著降低的危险驾驶行为,依其影响程度大小依次为倒车不当、车道使用错误、不当超车;而除上述三类危险驾驶行为外,停车不当行为也可显著降低非逃逸事故伤害严重程度增大的可能性。

(5)鉴别显著影响逃逸事故伤害严重程度的逃逸车辆危险驾驶行为,有助于从规范驾驶行为角度提升防治逃逸事故的效率与水平,借此加强安全驾驶及交通法规的宣教工作,促使驾驶人养成懂法守法的驾驶习惯,杜绝主观逃逸的可能性;同时,倡导车辆主动安全提醒技术应用配置,并结合道路交通监测等技术手段,提升交通事故的发现和应对效率,以达到有效提升逃逸事故防治效率的目的。

3.2　模型拟合优度对比

以所选用分析模型的 AIC、BIC 值来分析模型拟合效果,计算公式如下:

$$\mathrm{AIC} = 2k - 2\ln(L) \tag{8}$$

$$\mathrm{BIC} = k\ln(n) - 2\ln(L) \tag{9}$$

式中:k——表示各模型中纳入参数个数;

L——表示似然函数;

n——表示样本数量。

从表 5 计算结果可知,相较于有序 Logit 模型,随机参数 Logit 模型和有序广义线性模型的拟合优度较优,有序广义线性模型的拟合优度最好。

模型 AIC 与 BIC 准则值计算结果　表 5

模　型	AIC		BIC	
	逃逸事故	非逃逸事故	逃逸事故	非逃逸事故
有序 Logit 模型	13693.44	17277.45	13791.04	17375.20
随机参数 Logit 模型	13665.93	17249.61	13778.55	17362.39
有序广义线性模型	13658.29	17219.48	13770.90	17332.26

4　结语

本文通过有序 Logit 模型、随机参数 Logit 模型和有序广义线性模型探究各类危险驾驶行为对逃逸事故伤害严重程度的影响特征，阐述危险驾驶行为对逃逸事故和非逃逸事故的伤害严重程度影响差异性。通过数据分析发现：有序广义线性模型对危险驾驶行为与逃逸事故伤害严重程度的拟合优度最好；闯红灯、制动失败、鲁莽驾驶、速度过快、停车不当 5 类危险驾驶行为可显著加剧发生严重伤害逃逸事故的概率；相较于非逃逸事故，仅有闯红灯、鲁莽驾驶两类危险驾驶行为可显著增加其发生严重伤害程度事故的可能性。并在此基础上给出倡导车辆主动安全提醒技术应用配置，加强道路交通监测技术手段应用等措施来完善逃逸事故的防治。

参考文献

[1] Richard Tay, Upal Barua, Lina Kattan. Facts contributing to hit-and-run in fatal crashes [J]. Accident Analysis and Prevention, 2009 (41):227-233.

[2] Kara E. Macleod, Julia B. Griswold, Lindsay S. Arnold, et al. Factors associated with hit-and-run pedestrian fatalities and driver identification [J]. Accident Analysis and Prevention, 2012(45):366-372.

[3] Goro Fujita, Kazuko Okamura, Makoto Kihira, et al. Facts contributing to driver choice after hitting a pedestrian in Japan [J]. Accident Analysis and Prevention, 2014(72):277-286.

[4] Arash M. Roshandeh, Bei Zhou, Ali Behnood. Comparison of contributing factors in hit-and-run crashes with distracted and non-distracted drivers [J]. Transportation Research Part F, 2016(38):22-28.

[5] Chenming Jiang, Linjun Lu, Shengdi Chen, Jian John Lu. Hit-and-run crashes in urban river-crossing road tunnels [J]. Accident Analysis and Prevention, 2016(95):373-380.

[6] Dahianna Lopez, Mark E. Glickman, Stephen B. Soumerai, et al. Identifying factors related to a hit-and-run after a vehicle-bicycle collision [J]. Journal of Transport & Health, 2018(8): 299-306.

[7] Meiquan Xie, Wen Cheng, Gurdiljit Singh Gill, et al. Investigation of hit-and-run crash occurrence and severity using real-time loop detector data and hierarchical Bayesian Binary Logit model with random effects [J]. Traffic Injury Prevention, 2018, 19(2):207-213.

[8] Haqverdi M Q, Seyedabrishami S, Groeger J A. Identifying psychological and socio-economic factors affecting motorcycle helmet use [J]. Accident Analysis & Prevention, 2015 (85): 102-110.

[9] 赵跃峰，张生瑞，马壮林. 基于部分优势比的公路隧道交通事故严重程度分析模型[J]. 中国公路学报，2018，31(9)：159-166.

[10] 江欣国，章国鹏，石小林，等. 交互危险行为对双责事故严重程度的影响分析[J]. 西南交通大学学报，2018，53(2)：378-384.

[11] Michigan Department of Transportation. Michigan Crash Data (2014) [DB/DK]. [S. L.]: Michigan Department of Transportation, 2015.

[12] Fred L. Mananering, Chandra R. Bhat. Analytic methods in accident research: Methodological frontier and future directions [J]. Analytic Methods in Accident Research, 2014 (1): 1-22.

城市公交车速等级特征提取及影响因素分析

明秀玲　肖　梅*　黄洪滔　刘　倩　王竟涛
(长安大学运输工程学院)

摘　要　为了探究显著影响公交车速的主要因素,本文基于西安市公交 GPS 数据,依据平均车速将公交车速划分为三个等级,从道路条件、周围土地利用性质、公交运行条件、时间和天气五个方面,选取了 12 个因素。首先,利用了轻量级梯度提升机(LightGBM)特征选择算法计算各因素的重要性,对因素进行降维。然后,构建了广义有序 Logit 模型,对重要因素进行验证分析,并结合弹性分析确定了显著因素对公交车速各等级影响程度的大小。研究表明:对公交车速等级最为重要的 8 个因素依次为:进入驶出公交站、交叉口、弯道、时段、站码间距、人流通行辅助设施、假日、公交专用道,并且均影响显著。研究结果对城市公交网络的优化提供了理论依据。

关键词　交通工程　影响因素分析　广义有序 Logit 模型　城市公交车　LightGBM　弹性分析

0　引言

目前,我国公交运营线路总里程已超百万千米,公交网络的蓬勃发展缓解了交通拥堵问题。但公交车在运营中的问题也日益突出,如因速度受外部因素影响造成的准点率低、线路重叠等问题,严重影响了公交车的服务质量。

车速是评价车辆运行安全性的重要指标之一,刘莹莹等[1]建立了多元线性回归确定了快速路车速离散的主要影响因素。朱建全等[2]运用统计学方法对城市快速路的车速分布特征进行了分析,并在此基础上进行了车速影响因素的研究。杨俊儒等[3]在建立车辆转向行驶动力学模型研究弯道安全车速的基础上,利用正交试验对各弯道车速影响因素进行敏感性分析,确定了因素的主次。陈铭等[4]选取了 6 类道路和运行环境特征,运用多元线性回归方法分析主干路车速影响因素。Fitzpatrick[5]分别针对 4 车道郊区公路的平曲线段和直线段采集自由流车速,研究发现路段限速对运行车速影响最为显著。Figueroa[6]等采集 2 车道和 4 车道的郊区公路路段的道路几何、切线、平曲线和交叉口等特征,研究平均车速和车速偏差的显著因素。Liu[7]观测在市/郊区交叉口进口道的驾驶行为,探究交叉口接近速度的影响因素。Cruzado[8]等在 Pennsylvania 采集道路与环境特征,并建立了 20 个转移区的速度影响因素模型。Ma[9]等结合公交车和出租车数据集,将公交线路自动分为居住段和公交段,在考虑多个影响因素的情况下,分别建立了独立的模型预测。王丰元等[10]建立了公交车停靠过程影响因素层次结构模型,通过层次分析法,结合实车验证发现对公交车停靠过程影响最大的因素。

当前,车速影响因素的研究主要聚焦于其他机动车,公交车方面仍处于匮乏状态,其研究方法主要为统计分析模型,如线性回归、Logit 模型等。本文将公交车速分级,简化了研究问题,同时,广义有序 Logit 模型在保证车速等级有序性的同时放宽了比例假设,具有更好的适用性。再将 LightGBM 特征提取算法和广义有序 Logit 模型结合,减少了计算量,并通过弹性分析,探究了各显著因素对每个等级车速的影响程度。研究结果为提高城市公交系统的运行效率提供了理论支持。

1　变量选取

1.1　因变量的选择与定义

本文因变量为公交车速度等级,利用西安市 2017 年某线路公交车 GPS 数据,选用 8 月 12、14、16 和 17 日共 5 天的数据,计算得公交车的平均车速为 18.89km/h,据此将公交车速划分为:低速 0～15km/h,中速 15～25km/h 和高速大于 25km/h

1. 基金项目:浙江省科技厅软科学重点项目(2021C25005)。

三个等级,对应着因变量 Y 设置为:低速 $Y=1$,中速 $Y=2$,高速 $Y=3$。

1.2 自变量的选择与定义

自变量为从道路条件、周围土地利用性质、公交运行条件、时间和天气5个方面选取的12个特征。数据集个案数为422,各变量的具体定义见表1。

自变量的定义 表1

变量名称	变量符号	描述
弯道	X_1	1:直行* 2:左转 3:右转
交叉口	X_2	0:非交叉口* 1:交叉口
公交专用道	X_3	0:非公交专用道* 1:公交专用道
学校	X_4	0:非学校区域* 1:半径为200m的学校区域
商业区	X_5	0:非商业区* 1:商业区中心前后100m范围
近交通枢纽	X_6	0:非交通枢纽区* 1:地铁站/车站为中心,半径100m范围的交通枢纽区
进入驶出公交站	X_7	0:未处于公交站半径50m范围内* 1:处于公交站半径50m范围内的进入驶出公交站状态
人流通行辅助设施	X_8	1:无* 2:人行横道 3:人行天桥/地下通道
站码间距	X_9	1:公交车当前站与始发站间的站数≤6* 2:7≤公交车当前站与始发站间的站数≤12 3:公交车当前站与始发站间的站数>12
时段	X_{10}	0:平峰* 1:高峰(7:00~9:00、17:00~19:00)
假日	X_{11}	0:周末* 1:周内
天气	X_{12}	0:非雨天* 1:雨天

注:"*"表示参照类别。

由表1可知,自变量是分类变量,当分类数 $m \geqslant 3$ 时,需设置 $m-1$ 个虚拟变量。以弯道(X_2)为例,虚拟变量设置结果见表2。

弯道的虚拟变量设置 表2

弯道	虚拟变量		
	X_{1_1}	X_{1_2}	X_{1_3}
直行	1	0	0
左转	0	1	0
右转	0	0	1

2 研究方法

2.1 基于LightGBM的特征选取

LightGBM是对GBDT(Gradient Boosting Decision Tree)算法的一种改进算法,该算法采用的是每次只对分裂增益最大的叶子进行分裂的叶子生长(Leaf-wise)策略,保证在相同的分裂次数下模型的偏差更低,适用于本研究中分类特征的选取。由于各特征间并不是完全不相关的,且对因变量分类的贡献度存在优劣,当特征数量增加时,重复的冗余量、噪声和误差也会增大,影响分析结果。LightGBM 算法根据特征划分时产生的信息增益对特征重要性排序,删除重要性较小的特征,达到降低特征冗余量的目的。本文遵循分类准确率最大原则,对特征进行降维。

2.2　广义有序 Logit 模型

本文中速度是有序的分类变量,适用于广义有序 Logit 模型。广义有序 Logit 模型在保证公交车速等级有序性的同时放宽了比例优势假设,其回归系数对公交车速各等级可以不同。假设有序因变量有 M 个类别,其广义有序 Logit 模型的表达式为:

$$P(Y_i > j) = g(X\beta_j) = \frac{\exp(\alpha_j + X_i\beta_j)}{1 + \exp(\alpha_j + X_i\beta_j)}$$

$$j = 1,2,3,\cdots,M-1 \tag{1}$$

式中:$P(*)$——公交车速某一等级发生的概率;

α_j——第 j 个等级的截距;

β_j——第 j 个等级的回归系数向量。

因此,广义有序 Logit 模型的概率模型为:

$$P(Y_i = 1 | X) = 1 - g(X_i\beta_1) \tag{2}$$

$$P(Y_i = j | X) = g(X_i\beta_{j-1}) - g(X_i\beta_j)$$

$$j = 2,3,\cdots,M-1 \tag{3}$$

$$P(Y_i = M | X) = g(X_i\beta_{M-1}) \tag{4}$$

本文中因变量是 3 分类,通过将 3 个速度等级分成 2 组来进行比较分析,当 $j=1$ 时,表示速度等级 1、2 与速度等级 3 对比;当 $j=2$ 时,表示速度等级 1、2 与速度等级 3 对比。

2.3　弹性分析

广义有序 Logit 模型的参数估计只能定性反映各个自变量对某个类别的影响趋势,为弥补不足,本文结合弹性系数来评估显著性自变量对公交车速等级的影响程度,计算式为:

$$E_{X_{jk}}^{P(Y_i=j)} = \frac{\partial P(Y_i = j)}{\partial X_{jk}} \cdot \frac{X_{jk}}{P(Y_i = j)} \tag{5}$$

式中:X_{jk}——与第 j 个公交车速等级相关的第 k 个显著性自变量。

本文中变量是离散型的,故 X_{jk} 的弹性系数可用式(6)进行计算:

$$E_{X_{jk}} = \frac{\exp(\beta_k) - 1}{\exp(\beta_k)} \tag{6}$$

弹性系数的绝对值越大,则自变量对因变量的影响程度就越大。

3　结果与讨论

3.1　特征选择

LightGBM 算法的操作环境为 python3.8.5,得到的特征重要性排序如图 1 所示。

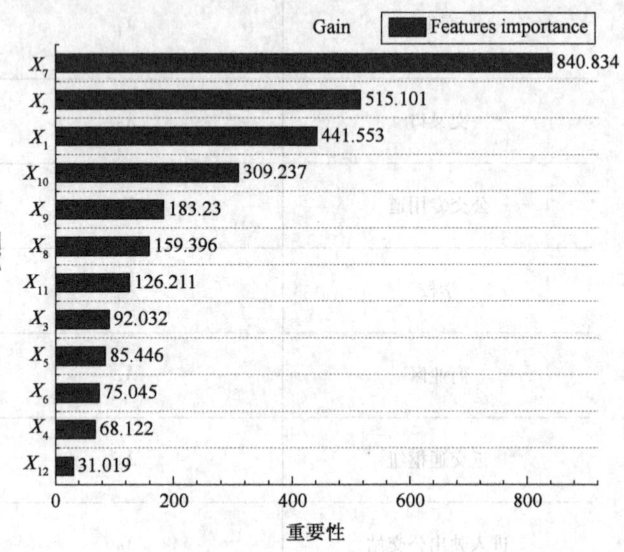

图 1　重要性排序

图 1 为各特征的重要性,并根据重要性程度对特征进行了降序排列。为降低特征的冗余量,得到最优特征子集,使用 LightGBM 算法进行进一步的评估,对当前特征子集的准确率进行计算。然后,逐步删除重要度最小的特征,分别计算准确率,得到图 2 所示的分类准确率曲线图。

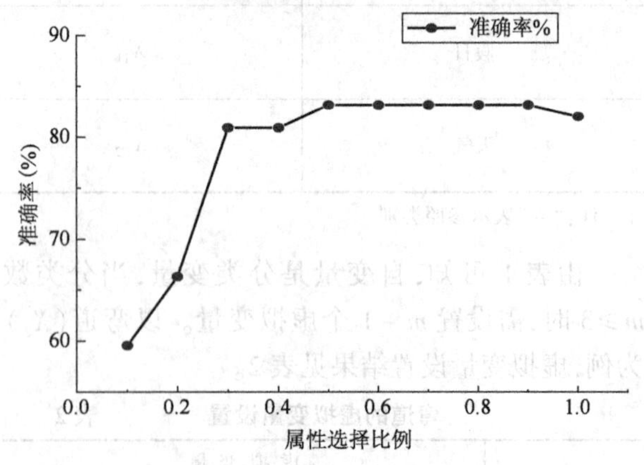

图 2　LightGBM 分类结果

由图 2 可知,当特征选择比例为 0.7 时,准确率达到稳定且最大。因此,本文依据图 1 提取了重要度前 70% 的 8 个特征:进入驶出公交站(X_7)、交叉口(X_2)、弯道(X_1)、时段(X_{10})、站码间距

(X_9)、人流通行辅助设施(X_8)、假日(X_{11})和公交专用道(X_3),即对城市公交车速等级分类最重要的前八个因素,进入后续的模型分析。

3.2 公交车速等级影响因素分析

本文利用STATA16.0中的gologit2程序进行广义有序logit模型分析,对最优特征组合验证分析。本文取0.05的显著性水平,即显著性小于0.05时表现显著。模型分析结果见表3。显著变量的弹性分析结果见表4。

广义有序Logit模型的参数估计 表3

变量	$j=1$(1vs2,3)		$j=2$(1,2vs3)	
	参数估计	显著性	参数估计	显著性
弯道(左转)	-3.8684	0.0000	-6.0325	0.0000
弯道(右转)	-4.3463	0.0000		
交叉口	-1.1264	0.005	-3.2251	0.0000
公交专用道	0.8833	0.031		
进入驶出公交站	-5.0184	0.0000	-6.5915	0.000
人流通行辅助设施设置(人行道)			-1.8560	0.003
站码间距([7,12])			-1.4636	0.015
时段(高峰)	-2.3282	0.0000	-1.6607	0.001
假日(周内)	-0.9603	0.01		
Model goodness-of fit statistics				
Number of observations		442		
Likelihood ratio(LR) chi-square		510.94		
Prob > chi-square		0.0000		
Log likelihood		-186.09957		
Pseudo R^2		0.5786		

广义有序Logit模型中显著影响因素的弹性分析 表4

变量	低速	中速	高速
弯道(左转)	0.321	0.004	-0.326
弯道(右转)	0.364	-0.016	-0.348
交叉口	0.089	0.081	-0.17
公交专用道	-0.07	0.034	0.036
进入驶出公交站	0.396	-0.048	-0.348
人流通行辅助设施设置(人行道)	0.043	0.061	-0.104
站码间距([7,12])	-0.032	0.114	-0.082
时段(高峰)	0.184	-0.096	-0.088
假日(周内)	0.076	-0.041	-0.035

3.2.1 道路特性分析

(1)弯道 左、右转弯在第一级中均显著,回归系数均为负值,表明与直行相比,公交车在左转和右转时趋向于低速行驶,对应的概率分别增加了32.1%和36.4%。左转在第二级中也显著,表明左转使公交车高速行驶的概率降低,且会降低32.6%。

(2)交叉口 在第一级和第二级中均显著,回归系数为负,表明与非交叉口处相比,公交车在交叉口时处于高速状态的概率会降低,对应的概率降低17%。

(3)公交专用道 在第一级中显著,回归系数为正,表明与在非公交专用道上相比,公交专用道利于速度提升,中速和高速的概率分别增加

3.4%、3.6%。

3.2.2 公交运行特性分析

(1)进入驶出公交站 在第一级和第二级中均显著,回归系数均为正,说明公交车在进入和驶出公交站时的速度大概率是处于一个低速的正常状态的,处于高速的概率会降低 34.8%。

(2)人流通行辅助设施设置 与道路上没有任何行人通行设施相比,公交车经过人行道时,速度显著偏低,高速行驶的概率会降低 10.4%;而人行天桥或者地下通道对速度的影响并不显著,表明该路段下此设施对公交车速度的提升效果不显著。

(3)站码间距 当站码间距在[7,12]范围内时,在第二等级中显著,回归系数为负。说明与站码间距小于 7 相比,该情况下公交车速为高速的概率降低,对应降低 8.2%。站码间距大于 12 时,对公交车速的影响相对不显著,说明公交车的运行速度会受站码间距的影响,不同的站码间距对公交车速的影响程度是不同的。

3.2.3 时间特性分析

(1)时段 高峰时段在第一、二级中均显著,回归系数均为负,说明高峰对公交车速影响更大。此时,公交车中速和高速行驶的概率分别降低 9.6% 和 8.8%。由于研究路段周围学校、大型商业区聚集,并存在车站等,人流量较大,使路段整体在高峰时段速度降低的幅度较小。

(2)假日 与周末相比,由于路段环境的特殊性,公交车在周内的速度趋于低速,在第一等级中表现显著,公交车在周内行驶时中速和高速降低的概率分别为 4.1% 和 3.5%,降低的幅度并不大。

4 结语

(1)本文从道路条件、周围土地利用性质、公交运行条件、时间和天气五个方面,通过 LightGBM 算法对特征降维,再利用广义有序 Logit 模型分析得到弯道、交叉口、公交专用道、进入驶出公交站、人流通行辅助设施设置、站码间距、时段和假日对公交车速等级贡献最大,并影响显著。结合弹性分析可知,弯道和进入驶出公交站对车速影响程度最大,公交专用道和时间特性影响反而较小。

(2)本文提出以下改进措施:有关部门应加强管理,提高公交专用道的利用率;优化公交车的运营调度,提高公交站点的效率;改善交通基础设施,如设置公交专用道隔离带、非机动车道等。

(3)本文存在的不足:由于数据缺失,商业区等可能对车速产生影响的因素未在文中分析,且个别因素如时段和假日,可能因未考虑到存在的异质性,导致分析结果中影响程度较小,需在未来的研究中进一步完善研究内容和方法。

参考文献

[1] 刘莹莹,李健,陈小鸿. 城市快速路车速离散特征及其影响因素研究[J]. 交通运输系统工程与信息,2018,18(5):112-120.

[2] 朱建全,石琴. 城市快速路路段车速分布特征及影响因素研究[J]. 合肥工业大学学报(自然科学版),2018,41(1):96-101.

[3] 杨俊儒,褚端峰,王维峰,等. 弯道安全车速建模及影响因素分析[J]. 交通信息与安全,2018,36(6):1-8.

[4] 陈铭,王雪松. 城市主干路车速影响因素研究[J]. 交通与运输(学术版),2011,12:20-24.

[5] Kay Fitzpatrick, Paul Carlson, Marcus Brewer et al. Design Factors That Affect Driver Speed on Suburban Streets[C]. Transportation Research Record 1751, Washington D. C. 2001:18-25.

[6] Alberto M. Figueroa, Andrew P. Tarko. Speed Factors on two-lane rural highways in free-flow conditions[C]. The 84th Annual Meeting of the Transportation Research Board, Washington D. C. 2005.

[7] Bor-Shong Liu. Association of intersection approach speed with driver characteristics vehicle type and traffic conditions comparing urban and suburban areas [J]. Accident Analysis and Prevention, 2007, 39:216-223.

[8] Ivette Cruzado, Eric T. Donnell, P. E. Factors Affecting Driver Speed Choice along Two-Lane Rural Highway Transition Zones[J]. Journal of Transportation Engineering, 2010, 135: 755-764.

[9] Jiaman Ma, Jeffrey Chan, Goce Ristanoski et al. Bus Travel time prediction with real-time traffic information[J]. Transportation research part C, 2019(105):536-539.

[10] 王丰元,梁星,何施,等.公交车停靠过程影响因素分析及试验研究[J].青岛理工大学学报,2017,38(3):100-107.

基于手机信令数据的轨道站点核心影响域时空变化研究

——以深圳市为例

李泳霖[1] 彭文楷[1] 李效光[1] 吕竞晴[1] 辜智慧*[1,2]
(1.深圳大学建筑与城市规划学院;2.深圳市建筑环境优化设计研究重点实验室)

摘 要 轨道站点核心影响域的合理划定是预测居民出行行为、优化站点配套接驳设施、规划轨道线网的基础。本文基于手机信令数据获取轨道站点出行的用户来源,划定轨道站点核心影响域,以深圳市为例,分析2018—2021年轨道站点核心影响域的空间形态特征及出行特征变化。并通过K-Means聚类对站点进行分类,分析站点的年际类型变化特征及核心影响域变化趋势。研究表明:①2018—2021年深圳市站点的核心影响域整体呈先增大后缩小趋势,不同区位的站点核心影响域面积差异较大;②根据站点在站域的相对位置,可以将站点核心影响域形态分为中心型、偏态型、边缘型,主要受站域周边建成环境影响;③根据圈层轨道出行占比特征,可将站点分为6类,部分站点随时间变化类别也发生了变化,结合站点核心影响域变化可以进一步分析站点类型变化趋势以及具体变化区域。

关键词 站点核心影响域 时空变化 轨道交通 手机信令数据 深圳市

0 引言

以地铁为代表的城市轨道交通是高速且客运量大的运输工具,发展城市轨道交通是特大城市及超大城市缓解交通拥堵、带动城市发展、减少环境污染的重要措施。城市轨道交通系统与城市其他空间的相互作用发生在城市轨道交通站点周边的一定范围内。对这一范围的合理划定是分析预测居民出行行为特征、改善站点周边建成环境、站点配套接驳设施优化及轨道线网规划的基础。

国内外学者从不同的角度探讨了对站点周边一定范围城市空间进行定义,提出了合理吸引范围[1]、潜在吸引范围[2]、步行接驳范围[3]、合理步行可达范围[4]、站点辐射区[5]、站点影响域等概念[6]。界定站点影响域的方法也大致可以分为四类:第一类方法通常基于步行可接受的距离,以轨道站点为核心划定圆形缓冲区作为站点影响域,如基于居民出行调查数据,统计居民步行到地铁站点的距离,从而确定地铁站点吸引范围[7]。第二类通常结合问卷调查,以划定在一定的时间阈值内不同接驳方式下的覆盖范围,该类研究较好地考虑了各种接驳方式的差异,但问卷调查样本数据量有限,且地理位置标记误差较大。如有研究基于武汉市轨道交通接驳出行调查,分析轨道接驳出行结构和接驳距离,运用成本加权距离分析方法划分轨道站点的多级影响区(即步行接驳区域、自行车接驳区域、公交接驳区域)距离依次为800m、2400m、4200m[8]。第三类研究结合理论模型估算法,考虑主观因素及客观建成环境影响下的站点影响域。相比于前两类方法,该方式更好地考虑了居民出行的主观选择特性及轨道站点周边实际建成环境对站点影响域的影响,但缺乏与实际数据的比较与验证,实际效果不太理想。如采用沿城市路网步行750m范围作为站点影响域直接研究武汉市不同站域建成环境与轨道交通站点客流特征间的关系[9]。

随着手机信令数据、AFC数据等数据的广泛应用,追踪客流来源以真实划定地铁站点影响域的第四类方法应运而生。这类方法可以有效解决传统问卷调查样本有限、模型推断缺乏实证数据验证的问题。如使用手机信令数据基于乘客实际站外全程轨迹对比杭州2号线西段站点建成前后实际服务范围与理论服务范围的差异,建立城市轨道交通线网建设时序的评估预测模型[10]。

总体而言,在划定站点影响域及挖掘站点影响域的特征及其影响因素上的研究成果已较为丰富,并为站点客流预测、周边用地布局优化、接驳设施完善等提供了较多有用建议,但缺少对某一城市所有站点影响域特征的整体认识。而且很少采用跨年度连续跟踪数据对站点影响域的变化过程进行分析,难以比较站点影响域面积、空间形态及其客流特征的变化。

综上,本文引用“站点影响域”这一名词,并提出“站点核心影响域”的概念。本文定义的站点影响域是指使用轨道站点出行的所有乘客的来源地的网格集合,而站点核心影响域是指在轨道站点影响域内的轨道出行集聚的网格集合。在该区域内的居民出行特征会受到轨道站点的影响,同时居民的出行行为也会反映在站点核心影响域的面积大小及形态特征。不同于同心圆划定影响范围的方法,站点核心影响域更加强调居民的出行行为与轨道站点周边城市空间形态,更加直观地反映居民轨道出行特征,是一个相对准确的空间载体。本研究拟在多源及多时间序列数据的基础上,从时间、空间两个维度对深圳市2018—2021年地铁站点的站点核心影响域进行划定,探讨站点核心影响域的形态类型及年际变化,分析站点客流在轨道快速建设过程中的变化特征,挖掘影响已有站点核心影响域变化的原因,以期为深圳的轨道交通站点规划建设提供参考和建议。

1　研究区域及数据

1.1　研究区域

本文研究区域为深圳市。深圳市总面积为1997.47km^2。深圳市自2004年正式开通1号线一期工程并投入运营始,至2020年底已建成11条线路,运营里程共410.7km,其建设时序如表1所示。据统计,2020年,深圳日均客运量已超过400万人次,城市轨道交通客运量约占深圳市公共交通客运量的60%,城市轨道交通线网密度及日均客运强度居全国第一[11]。由此可见城市轨道交通已经成为深圳公共交通的骨干,为优化深圳市居民的出行体验、提升出行效率做出了重大贡献。

深圳市轨道站线建设时序表　　表1

线路名称		站点数量	线路长度	开通时间
1号线	罗湖—世界之窗	15座	40.98km	2004年12月
	世界之窗—深大	3座		2009年9月
	深大—机场东	12座		2011年6月
2号线	赤湾—世界之窗	12座	约38km	2010年12月
	世界之窗—新秀	17座		2011年6月
	新秀—莲塘	3座		2020年10月
3号线	双龙—草埔	16座	41.94km	2010年12月
	草埔—益田	14座		2011年6月
	益田—福保	1座		2020年10月
4号线	福田口岸—福民	1座	31.30km	2007年8月
	福民—少年宫	4座		2004年12月
	少年宫—清湖	10座		2011年6月
	清湖—牛湖	8座		2020年10月
5号线	前海湾-黄贝岭	27座	47.65km	2011年6月
	前海湾—赤湾	7座		2019年9月
6号线(松岗—科学馆)		27座	49.35km	2020年8月
7号线(西丽湖—太安)		28座	30.17km	2016年10月
8号线(梧桐山南—盐田路)		6座	12.36km	2020年10月

续上表

<table>
<tr><th colspan="2">线路名称</th><th>站点数量</th><th>线路长度</th><th>开通时间</th></tr>
<tr><td rowspan="2">9号线</td><td>文锦—红树湾南</td><td>22座</td><td rowspan="2">36.18km</td><td>2016年10月</td></tr>
<tr><td>红树湾南—前湾</td><td>10座</td><td>2019年12月</td></tr>
<tr><td colspan="2">10号线(双拥街—福田口岸)</td><td>24座</td><td>29.30km</td><td>2020年8月</td></tr>
<tr><td colspan="2">11号线(碧头—福田)</td><td>18座</td><td>51.94km</td><td>2016年6月</td></tr>
</table>

1.2 研究数据

本文采用的是联通公司2018—2021年10月深圳市手机信令数据,由智慧足迹DaaS(Data as a Service)能力开放平台提供,其预置了以城市边界范围绘制的标准250m网格。据统计,深圳市联通用户约600万户,市场占有率约为20%[12]。该平台基于联通全量手机用户信令数据,通过DaaS大数据平台处理后生成用户驻留位置网格、出行日期、出行时长、出行距离以及出行方式等数据,得到涵盖所有出行方式的全出行链。根据乘客进入城市轨道交通地下站点手机会强制进行位置区码切换的原理,可以准确识别城市地下轨道交通乘客选择的出行站点,并根据地上行动轨迹来判断乘客的来源及去向,实现用户轨道出行链的提取。在提取过程中,首先将地上轨道站点及受影响的站点相关数据剔除,将其他站点作为可用站点保留其数据。然后将轨道出行居民数量大于30(正态分布的最小样本数)的网格作为轨道出行影响网格,以提取基于格网的轨道出行链统计数据。最终得到的轨道出行链数据包括使用轨道出行用户的起始位置网格、终止位置网格、起始轨道站点、终止轨道站点、出行日期、出行次数等。全出行链及轨道出行链提取流程如图1所示。

基于上述处理流程,最终提取了129个站点相关的全出行链及轨道出行链数据量如表2所示,可用站点的空间分布如图2所示。

数据提取结果　表2

年份	全出行链数据条数	轨道出行链数据条数	比例
2018	8156216	4909067	60.19%
2019	10578256	9987850	94.42%
2020	10175016	8954923	88.01%
2021	76864854	10212939	13.29%

注:比例=轨道出行链数据条数/全出行链数据条数。

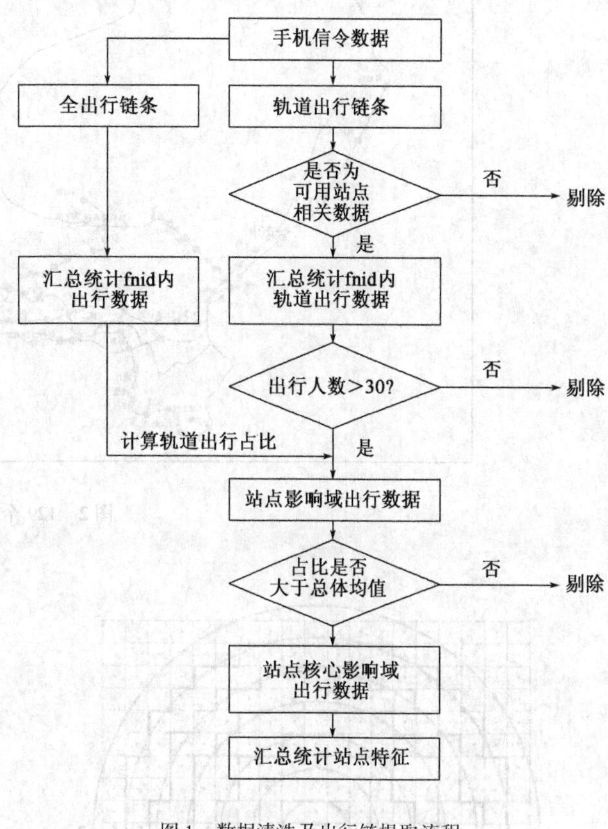

图1　数据清洗及出行链提取流程

2 研究内容与方法

2.1 站点核心影响域划定

基于轨道出行链数据库,将与出行起始站点相关的用户出行起始网格视为站点影响域,并计算影响域内各格网内的轨道出行占比,即各格网内轨道出行总量占所有交通方式出行总量的比值。将轨道出行占比大于总体平均值的起始网格划入该站点核心影响域,最后使用Python及Arcgis Pro对站点核心影响域进行可视化。

2.2 圈层聚类统计

将站点核心影响域依照相同半径增量进行圈层划分,圈层的多少可以反映站点对周边空间辐射能力的强弱;不同圈层的轨道出行占比差异,可以体现站点在不同距离区间内的影响力大小。取所有核心影响域的最大半径为划分依据,结合网格大小,定义圈层范围如图 3 所示。

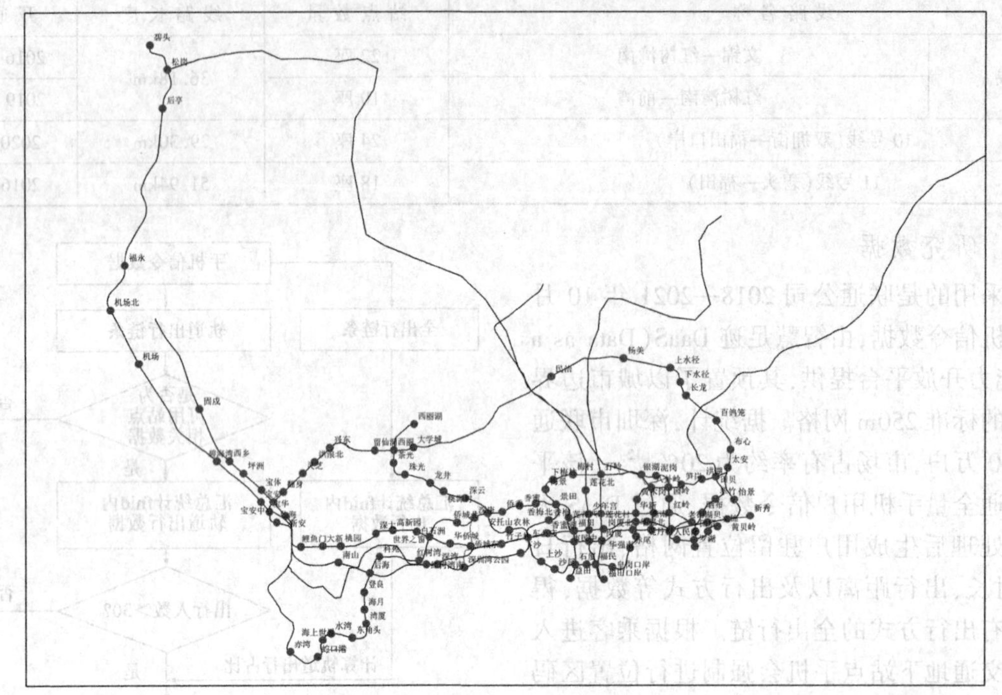

图 2　129 个站点空间分布

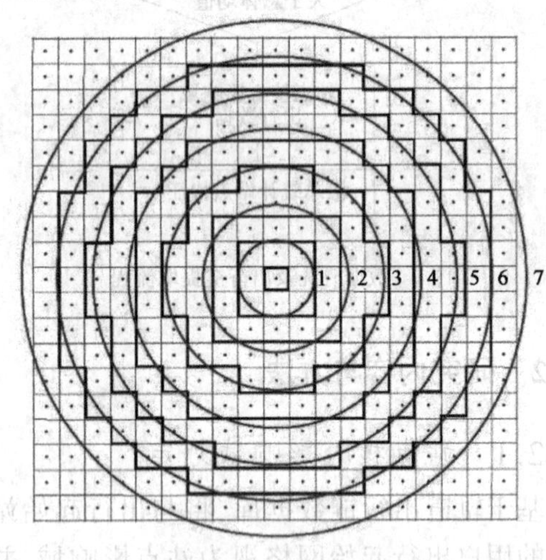

图 3　圈层图

2.3　k-means 聚类分析

k 均值聚类算法(k-means clustering algorithm)是一种迭代求解的聚类分析算法,其步骤是,预将数据分为 k 组,则随机选取 k 个对象作为初始的聚类中心,然后计算每个对象与各个种子聚类中心之间的距离,把每个对象分配给距离它最近的聚类中心,每分配一个样本,聚类的聚类中心会根据聚类中现有的对象被重新计算。这个过程将不断重复直到满没有(或最小数目)聚类中心再发生变化,误差平方和局部最小。利用不同站点核心影响域的统计变量进行聚类分析,将圈层特征具有相似性的站点进行分类,不同类别的站点反映了站点影响范围的大小和对周边空间影响力的强弱。并在站点的类型发生年际变化时,对影响变化的原因进行探究。

3　研究结果

3.1　站点核心影响域

对 129 个站点的核心影响域范围逐年提取,提取数据结果如表 3 所示,面积统计结果如表 4 及图 4 所示。可以发现核心影响域的范围整体呈先增大后缩小的趋势,与深圳市整体轨道出行占比变化趋势相符。此外,从空间上来看,中心区轨道站点越密集,站点核心影响域范围越小,如 2 号线燕南站,位于福田区中心部分,其核心影响域面积仅为 0.31km^2,而 11 号线机场站,位于宝安机场航站楼,核心影响域面积 7.70km^2。尤其是靠近城市边缘以及端点的轨道站点,核心影响域范围随时间增加明显,说明随着深圳市轨道交通网络的不断完善,其影响范围在不断扩大。

核心影响域数据筛选结果　表3

年份	核心影响域轨道出行次数	核心影响域起止一致性全出行次数	起止一致性轨道出行占比
2018	3481031	22153572	15.71%
2019	8976637	42310311	21.21%
2020	10239433	45629593	22.44%
2021	9412803	49423173	19.05%

注：起止一致性轨道出行占比＝核心影响域轨道出行次数/核心影响域起止一致性全出行次数。

站点影响域特征统计　表4

年份	站点影响域平均面积（km^2）	站点影响域面积变异系数	站点核心影响域平均面积（km^2）	站点核心影响域面积变异系数
2018	6.90	(−1.17,4.82)	1.79	(−1.11,5.28)
2019	11.85	(−1.14,4.07)	1.92	(−1.13,5.16)
2020	10.83	(−1.07,3.80)	1.99	(−1.18,4.52)
2021	8.74	(−1.15,4.16)	2.11	(−1.39,3.81)

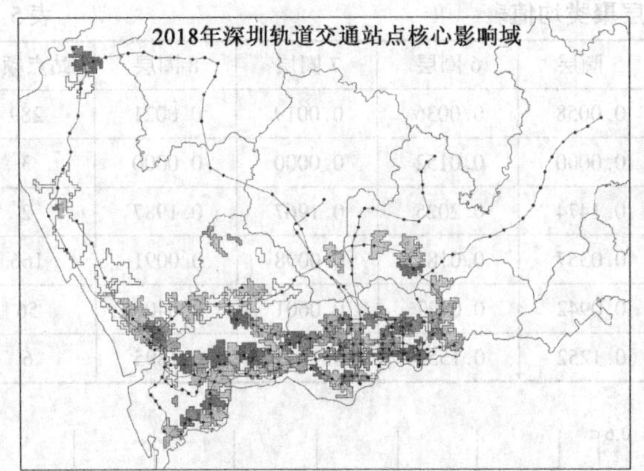

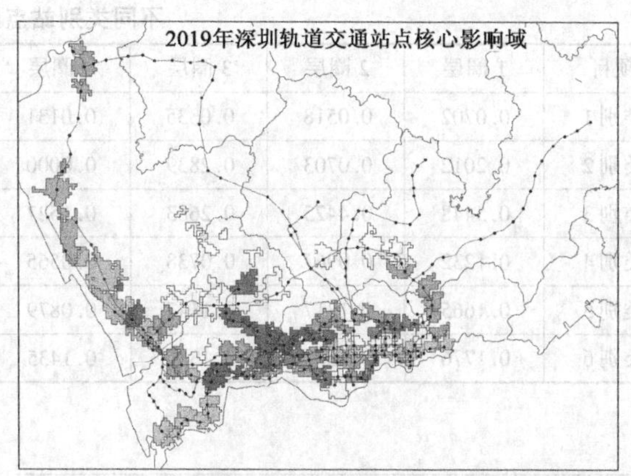

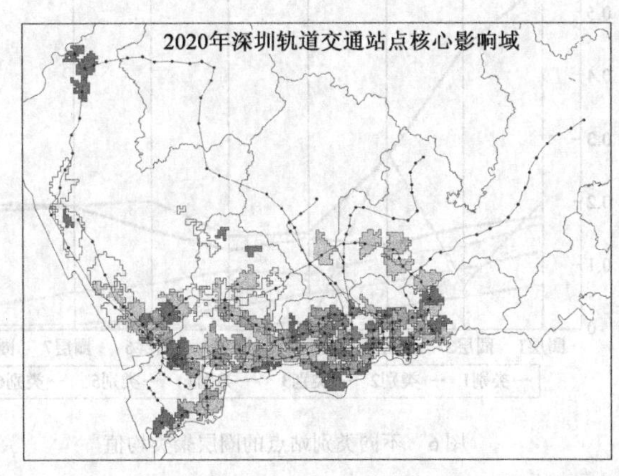

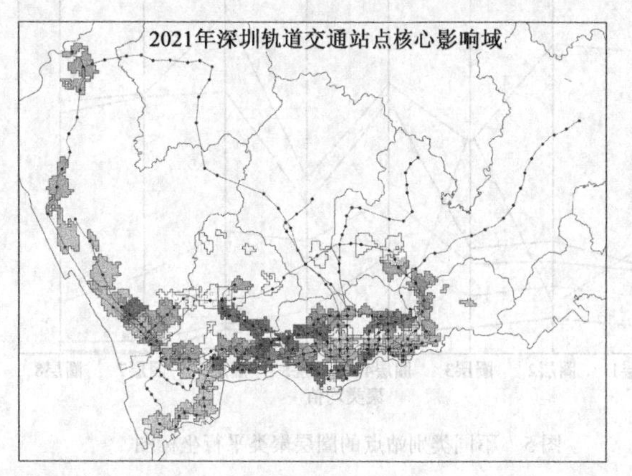

图4　2018—2021年深圳市轨道交通站点核心影响域分布

此外，根据站点在核心影响域的相对位置还可将站域形态分为中心型、偏态型、边缘型。中心型站域的站点位于站域几何中心，该类站点主要分布于深圳南山福田心区及站点密集区，大多站点站域面积较小，客流来源集中于800m以内。偏态型站域的站点的相对位置偏置于站域一侧，站域面积普遍较大。该类站点受到周边用地性质、道路及周边站点分布的影响，其站域呈现偏态分布。边缘型站域的站点一般位于城市建设用地边缘、轨道线路外圈或末端。在本次研究的站点中，中心型站点约占32.82%，偏态型站点约占47.18%，边缘型站点约占20%。根据站域的不同形态和站点周边的路网、用地性质等因素分析，影响站域形态的因素可能有以下几种：

（1）站点周围存在自然地形地貌，如山体、河流等，会对站点的影响范围起到阻断作用。

（2）站点周围的通过性主干道由于其空间上的割裂效果，造成通往站点的可达性较差，使得站域影响力突然减小。

（3）站点周围其他站点的分布状态，会对该站点的核心影响域形态造成影响，越靠近其他站点的区域影响力越弱。

3.2　分类站点年际变化特征

采用8个圈层的平均轨道出行占比作为站点

的特征指标,通过 JMP 数据分析软件对 129 个站点 4 年数据分别进行 K-Means 聚类分析,本次研究根据手肘法确定选聚类 K 值为 6,在该 K 值下能够较合理地区分不同性质的站点。不同类别的变量均值如表 5、图 5 及图 6 所示。其中,类别 1 站点轨道出行占比低,且逐圈衰减趋势不明显,代表站点的吸引力较差且随距离增加变化不明显;类别 2 站点轨道出行占比中等但波动较大,且在第四个圈层上锐减,代表站点的吸引力中等且随距离增加变化差异较大;类别 3 站点轨道出行占比高但逐圈衰减趋势较明显,代表站点的吸引力较好但随距离增加急剧减弱;类别 4 站点轨道出行占比低且逐圈衰减趋势缓慢,代表站点的吸引力较差且随距离增加不断减弱;类别 5 站点轨道出行占比中等且逐圈衰减趋缓慢,代表站点的吸引力中等且随距离增加不断减弱;类别 6 站点轨道出行占比中等且无衰减趋势,代表站点的吸引力中等且随距离增加变化不明显。

不同类别站点圈层聚类均值表　　表 5

项目	1 圈层	2 圈层	3 圈层	4 圈层	5 圈层	6 圈层	7 圈层	8 圈层	站点频数
类别 1	0.0702	0.0518	0.0335	0.0131	0.0058	0.0036	0.0019	0.0021	289
类别 2	0.2012	0.0703	0.2839	0.0000	0.0000	0.0152	0.0000	0.0000	3
类别 3	0.5448	0.4425	0.2683	0.1527	0.1474	0.2025	0.1967	0.1987	2
类别 4	0.1232	0.0967	0.0738	0.0565	0.0357	0.0181	0.0098	0.0091	166
类别 5	0.1665	0.1317	0.1147	0.0879	0.0942	0.0727	0.0601	0.0408	56
类别 6	0.1776	0.1608	0.1339	0.1435	0.1252	0.1557	0.1943	0.1895	6

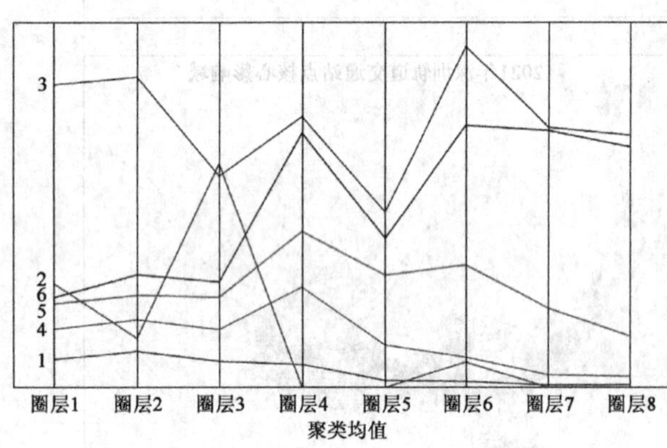

图 5　不同类别站点的圈层聚类平行坐标图

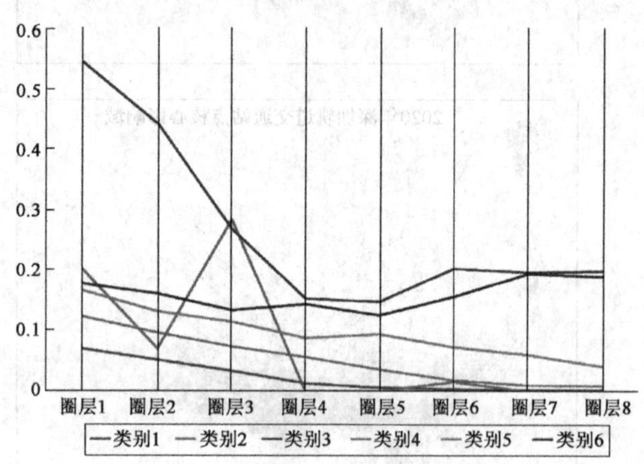

图 6　不同类别站点的圈层聚类均值

在对站点进行四个年份的比较后统计出有 35 个站点类型基本保持一致,其中宝安中心及车公庙站四年均为类别 4;岗厦北、石厦、华强南等 33 个站点四年均为类别 1。但部分站点的核心影响域的出行占比特征发生了变化,其中,变化频次最多的是从类别 4 变化成类别 1,共计 67 次(表 6),此类变化代表着站点的吸引力变差但其随距离的衰减趋势有所减缓,发生此类变化的站点有深大站(2020—2021 年)、下沙站(2019—2020 年)、深湾站(2018—2019 年)等,结合深大站核心影响域变化可以看出其吸引力减弱的主要区域位于科苑路及其周边产业园区(500m 以内);变化频次第二多的是从类别 1 转变为类别 4,共计 44 次,此类变化代表着站点的吸引力增强但其随距离的衰减趋势有所加剧,也意味着站点对较近距离(1 ~ 5 圈层:1700m)人群的吸引力显著提高,发生此类变化的站点有大新站(2018—2019 年)、购物公园站(2019—2020 年)等,结合大新站核心影响域变化猜测其吸引力增强及衰减趋势的减弱与新站线(五号线)的开通有关;变化频次第三多的是从类别 5 转变为类别 1,共计 20 次,此类变化代表着站点的吸引力有明显减弱但其随距离的衰减趋势变缓,也意味着站点对较近距离(1 ~ 5 圈层:1700m)人群的吸引力显著降低,发生此类变化的站点有后海站(2020—2021 年)、西丽站(2020—2021 年)等,结合后海站核心影响域变化可以看出其吸引力减弱的主要区域位于海岸城及万象城。此外可以统计出与类别 3 相关的类别转化较少且仅有两例,分别为类别 6 转变为类别 3(机场站 2018—2019 年)、类别 3 转变为类别 4(机场站 2020—2021 年),结合机场站核心影响域变化,可以看出其吸引力急剧增强和减弱的主要区域位于机场北侧 1700m 左右(1~5 个圈层)的范围内。

类型变化频数 表 6

终止类别	起始类别					
	1	2	3	4	5	6
1	112	1	0	67	20	2
2	1	1	0	0	0	0
3	0	0	1	0	0	1
4	44	1	1	69	14	0
5	10	0	0	18	21	1
6	0	0	0	2	1	2

4 结语

本文使用了 2018—2021 年手机信令数据对深圳市轨道站点核心影响域进行划定,发现深圳市不同区位的站点核心影响域型态及面积差异较大。2018—2021 年深圳市站点的核心影响域整体呈现先增大后缩小的趋势,与深圳市整体轨道出行占比变化趋势相符。根据站点在站域的相对位置,可以将站点核心影响域形态分为中心型、偏态型、边缘型,中心型站域的站点位于站域几何中心,主要分布于深圳南山福田区及站点密集区,大多站点站域面积较小,客流来源集中于 800m 以内;偏态型站域的站点的相对位置偏置于站域一侧,其站域面积普遍较大,且受到周边用地性质、道路及周边站点分布的影响,呈现偏态分布;边缘型站域的站点一般位于城市建设用地边缘、轨道线网外圈或末端。通过 K-Means 聚类对每一年的站点进行分类,比较分析不同类别的站点及其变化,总结出站点类型的主要变化方式,对应着不同的站点吸引力变化和圈层衰减趋势,结合站点核心影响域能够更好地了解站点的年际变化趋势及变化区域。

参考文献

[1] 叶益芳.城市轨道交通车站不同接驳方式合理吸引范围研究[J].铁道运输与经济,2014,36(6):77-81.

[2] 王淑伟,孙立山,荣建.北京市轨道站点吸引范围研究[J].交通运输系统工程与信息,2013,13(3):183-188.

[3] 张宁,戴洁,张晓军.基于多项 Logit 模型的轨道交通站点步行接驳范围[J].城市轨道交通研究,2012,15(5):46-49.

[4] 申犁帆,王烨,张纯,等.轨道站点合理步行可达范围建成环境与轨道通勤的关系研究——以北京市 44 个轨道站点为例[J].地理学报,2018,73(12):2423-2439.

[5] 赵金宝,邓卫,王晓原,等.考虑居民出行 OD 或居住地的出行方式选择巢式 Logit 模型[J].东南大学学报(自然科学版),2016,46(4):899-904.

[6] 魏书祥.城市轨道交通站点影响域界定的若干关键问题[J].西部人居环境学刊,2015(6):75-79.

[7] Schlossberg M, et al. How far, by which route, and why? A spatial analysis of pedestrian preference[R]. MTI Report 06-06, 2007.

[8] 刘思涵,林诗佳,张竹君,等.基于手机信令数据的城市轨道交通线网建设时序决策支持模型[J].西部人居环境学刊,2021,36(05):113-120.

[9] 李清嘉,彭建东,杨红.武汉市不同站域建成环境与轨道交通站点客流特征关系分析[J].地球信息科学学报,2021,23(7):1246-1258.

[10] 郭瑞利,黄正东.基于成本加权距离分析的轨道站点多级影响区划分研究[J].现代城市研究,2021(08):73-82.

[11] http://jtys.sz.gov.cn/.

[12] http://www.sz.gov.cn/cn/zjsz/nj/content/post_7148528.html#.

高速公路出口匝道分流车辆的驶出特征

马强强[1]　邵海鹏*[1,2]　方瑞韬[1]　林　涛[1]
(1. 长安大学运输工程学院;2. 长安大学生态安全屏障区交通网设施管控
及循环修复技术交通运输行业重点实验室)

摘　要　为探究高速公路出口匝道区域车辆分流特性,本文基于无人机采集出口匝道区域车辆视频,利用 Tracker 软件以渐变段分隔线为 X 轴,垂直该方向为 Y 轴建立空间直角坐标系提取分流车辆的纵向和横向的位置、速度、加速度等指标,使用聚类分析法,横向以 5m 为一个区间,纵向以 0.2m 为一个区间,对提取出的参数进行分析。研究结果表明:横向速度在(-5~30m)的范围呈逐渐增大的趋势,纵向速度在(-2.4~2m)的范围内呈 U 型曲线;横向加速度在(30~115m)的范围内有逐渐减小的趋势;分流点的位置主要集中在(30~50m)的区段内,占其总数的 57.28%,分流车辆更倾向于以较低速度进行分流。本研究对高速公路出口匝道管理以及未来无人驾驶、车路协同等场景下为分流车辆位置及速度提供理论依据。

关键词　交通工程　车辆分流特征　聚类分析法　出口匝道　无人机视频

0　引言

高速公路出口匝道是高速公路网中的典型瓶颈区域,由于该区域频繁的分流换道、速度波动、复杂的几何线性以及各种各样的驾驶行为等因素,不仅会导致主线车流的紊乱和通行能力的降低,还会导致主线车辆的冲突和碰撞。因此有必要对出口匝道区域车辆的驶出特性进行深入研究。

目前,对出口匝道的研究主要集中在匝道的类型、事故安全和通行能力等宏观方面。Chen H 等[1]利用佛罗里达州 343 个高速公路路段的事故数据,比较不同类型高速公路出口匝道的事故频率、事故发生率和事故严重程度,并基于事故预测模型发现,将平衡型出口匝道替换为不平衡型出口匝道时,高速公路分流区事故数量将增加 68.33%。M. Pilar Martínez a 等[2]通过 VISSIM 仿真方法,对平行式出口匝道和直接式出口匝道的通行能力进行比较,发现平行式出口匝道的通行能力最低。Xie J 等[3]同样对比了平行式出口匝道和直接式出口匝道的速度标准差和通行能力,得出平行式出口匝道的通行能力高于直接式,且速度的波动性小于直接式出口匝道,这与 M. Pilar Martínez a 得出的结论相反。

除了宏观层面的研究,在微观交通层面,张驰等[4]利用西安、广州和佛山三市 12 条高速公路出口匝道为研究对象,建立小汽车在分流点和小鼻点处速度预测模型,得出分流点和小鼻点的运行速度随渐变段起点速度的增大而增大,随渐变段长度增大而减小。白浩晨和柳银芳[5]建立满足不同需求下的运行速度过渡段长度模型,得出当匝道设计速度为 30~40km/h 时,车辆变速行驶需求是运行速度过渡段长度的主要控制因素,匝道设计速度为 50~80km/h 时,超高过渡、3s 行程时间是主要控制因素。乔建刚等[6]基于驾驶模拟实验,利用速度、横向加速度、纵向加速度等参数分析下匝道运行特性发现,以 85% 车速作为匝道运行车速,发现当与相邻路段的运行速度差的绝对值小于 10m/s 时,匝道具有良好的安全性。张智勇等[7]按照车辆在匝道上的运行速度特性将匝道分为减速段、匀速段和加速段,在匝道减速段,超高与车辆运行速度呈正相关关系,曲率变化率与车辆运行速度呈负相关关系;在匝道减速段。Gong J 等[8]分析出口匝道分流区不同车道下的运行特征,得出减速车道的车头时距服从负指数分布。

1. 基金项目:国家重点研发计划(2019YFB1600300);中央高校基本科研业务费专项资金(300102219210,300102210201)。

由于之前技术条件的限制，匝道区域车辆数据的获取主要是通过链式开普勒雷达测速仪[4,5]、人工采集法[3]、GPS 轨迹数据[7]或模拟驾驶[6]。白浩晨和柳银芳[5]、张驰等[4]利用链式开普勒雷达测速仪获取匝道区域车辆的速度特性，从而进行相应的分析建模，这些数据采集方法由于视野条件、数据获取连续性等的限制，难以准确刻画车辆驶出匝道的全过程运行。随着无人机技术的发展，无人机因其可以以高空视角获得对象全息运行状态而逐渐应用于交通数据的采集[9-13]。Wan Q 等[14]基于无人机航拍视频，探究车辆在入口匝道的合流换道机理，结果表明当换道车辆的目标间隙在 15 ~ 30m 之间时，换道车辆会导致目标车道的车辆进行强制减速。但目前对于出口匝道渐变段处全过程的分流特性研究较少。

因此本研究将基于无人机航拍视频获取出口匝道分流车辆驶出减速车道的全过程，提取车辆在匝道区域全过程的横向、纵向速度加速度和位置特性，探究车辆在出口匝道处全过程速度、加速度运行特性以及分流点的位置分布，为高速公路管理部门以及未来车路协同、车车通信下分流车辆驶出匝道的位置及速度提供理论依据。

1 数据采集与参数提取

1.1 数据采集

本研究采用 DJ Phantom 4Pro 2.0 无人机在 100m 高空对出口匝道进行航拍数据采集，视频帧率为 24 帧/s，拍摄地点为西安市绕城高速西高新立交，由西向东方向的出口匝道，主线设计速度为 120km/h，匝道设计速度为 40km/h，该匝道的渐变段长度为 120m。拍摄的位置如图 1 所示。

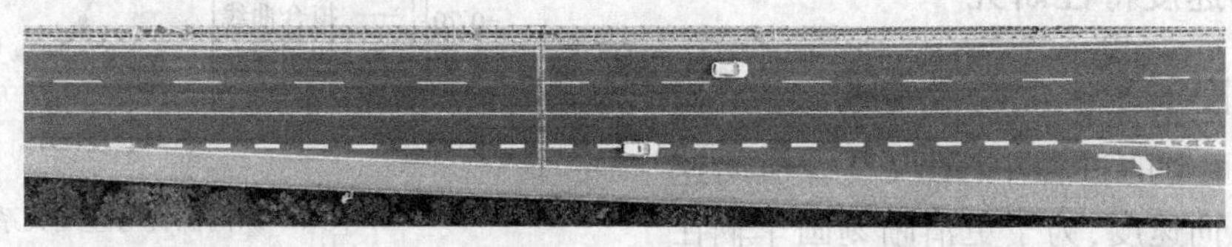

图 1 拍摄实景图

1.2 参数提取

本研究采用物理软件 Tracker 提取分流驶入匝道的车辆轨迹数据特征，Tracker 软件是一款物理影像分析和建模工具，能够实现包括提取目标追踪、位置、速度和加速度等功能。将航拍视频导入 Tracker 软件，以渐变段分隔线为 X 轴，垂直该方向为 Y 轴建立空间直角坐标系，具体如图 2 所示。对分流换道的车辆以车辆中点为标记点，每 3 帧为一个采集点进行数据提取，最终提取的参数包括车辆轨迹的采集点，横向、纵向坐标；横向、纵向、总的速度和加速度这 9 个指标的数据。表 1 为提取的部分数据样式。

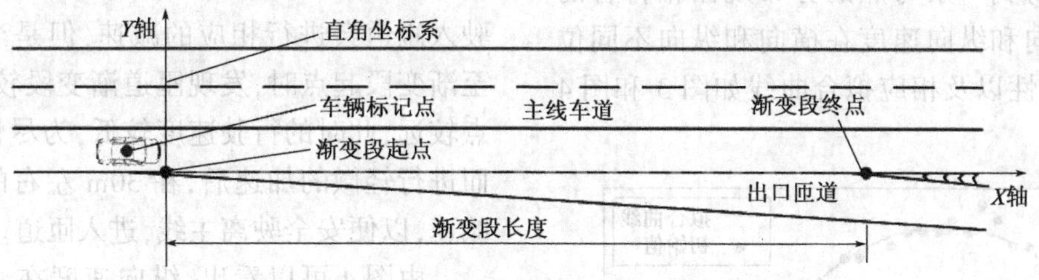

图 2 直角坐标系示意图

数据样式 表 1

采集点	横向坐标 (m)	纵向坐标 (m)	横向速度 (m/s)	纵向速度 (m/s)	总速度 (m/s)	横向加速度 (m/s²)	纵向加速度 (m/s²)	总加速度 (m/s²)
0	−7.83	2.29						
1	−5.55	2.27	18.01	−0.18	18.01			
2	−3.32	2.24	17.98	−0.35	17.99	0.52	−0.52	0.73
3	−1.05	2.18	18.21	−0.36	18.21	0.80	0.41	0.90

续上表

采集点	横向坐标(m)	纵向坐标(m)	横向速度(m/s)	纵向速度(m/s)	总速度(m/s)	横向加速度(m/s^2)	纵向加速度(m/s^2)	总加速度(m/s^2)
…	…	…	…	…	…	…	…	…
56	124.62	-1.50	20.30	-0.52	20.31	0.23	0.55	0.59
57	127.14	-1.59	20.24	-0.48	20.24	0.75	-0.43	0.86
58	129.68	-1.62	20.49	-0.49	20.49			
59	132.26	-1.71						

初步提取驶出匝道车辆数据 342 组，剔除以下两种场景下的数据：

(1)剔除大货车、大客车等特殊车辆的数据，因为本研究的对象是小汽车；

(2)对于直接换两车道的车辆不予考虑。最终得到小汽车驶出匝道渐变段的数据 302 组。

2　速度、加速度特性研究

2.1　出口匝道处速度特性分析

车辆在驶出匝道的过程中，不仅具有横向速度，而且还具有纵向速度，为了更清晰刻画车辆在出口匝道渐变段的速度分布特性，本研究分别对出口匝道的横向速度和纵向速度进行聚类分析，因为横向速度与总速度的差异较小，因此只使用横向速度。首先对所有轨迹上的采集点横向以 5m 为一个区间段，纵向以 0.2m 为一个区间段进行聚类，该区间段内所有轨迹点速度求平均值，利用 python 编程环境中的 matplotlib 绘制出各个区间段的点，并得到一条与点的分布规律相符合的拟合曲线，横向和纵向速度在横向和纵向不同位置处的分布特性以及相应拟合曲线如图 3 和图 4 所示。

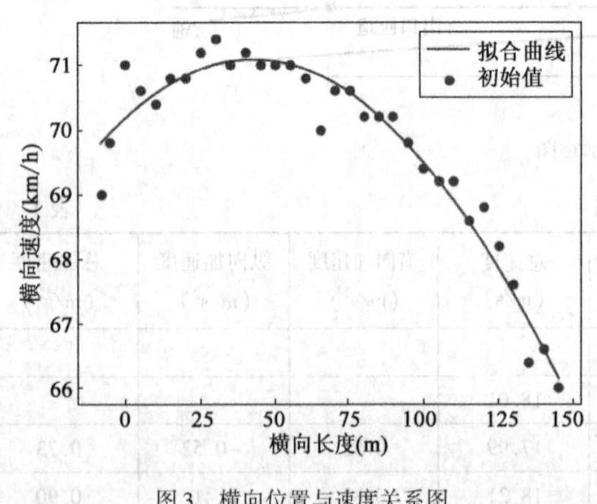

图 3　横向位置与速度关系图

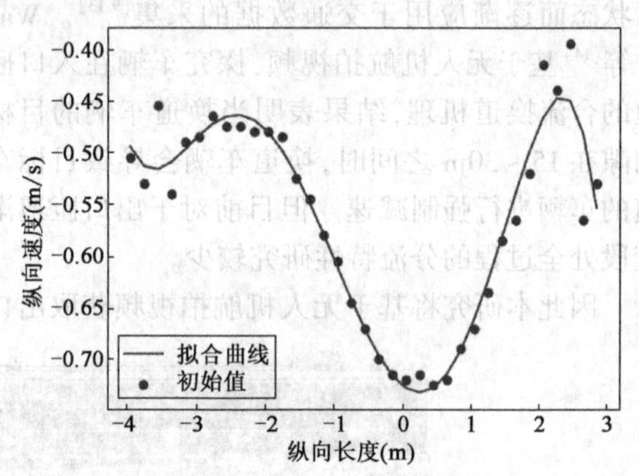

图 4　纵向位置与速度关系图

图 3 表明，横向速度在(-5~30m)的范围内呈逐渐增大的趋势；在 30~145m 之间呈逐渐下降的趋势，速度在 30m 的位置处达到最大，为 71.4km/h。速度在 30~145m 之间下降是因为车辆需要在匝道渐变段逐渐减速到匝道的限制速度，但是本研究发现在 -5~30m 的范围内，速度从 69.0km/h 逐渐增加到 71.4km/h，分析其原因为驾驶员在出口匝道上游首先看到出口匝道的标志牌，为安全驶入匝道会进行相应的减速，但是当驾驶员行驶至渐变段起点时，发现匝道渐变段较长，距离分流点较远，此时的行驶速度较低，为尽快到达分流点而进行轻微的加速后，在 30m 左右的位置再进行减速，以便安全驶离主线，进入匝道。

由图 4 可以看出，纵向速度在 -2.4~2m 的范围内呈 U 形曲线，在 0m 的位置达到最低。纵向速度在 -2.4~0m 之间逐渐减小，此区间为车辆由主线至变道点的位置，表明车辆在该区域逐渐转向，进行变道操作，且速度越来越大。当到达分流点位置时，纵向速度达到最大。纵向速度在 0~2m 之间逐渐增大。此区间为车辆由分流点点至匝道车道的位置，反映出车辆分流驶入渐变段减速车道后，速度纵向波动越来越平稳。

2.2 出口匝道处加速度特性分析

加速度的大小可以反映出匝道区域分流车辆的波动程度。同样,加速度也分为横向加速度和纵向加速度,采集点也是横向以5m为一个区间段,纵向以0.2m为一个区间段,对落入该区间段的所有轨迹点的加速度求平均值。与速度类型不同的是加速度还包含车辆在行驶过程中的总加速度。与分析速度特性类似,绘制出各个区间段加速度的点,并得到一条与点的分布规律相符合的拟合曲线,横向、纵向和总的加速度在不同位置点的分布特性以及相应的拟合曲线如图5~图7所示。

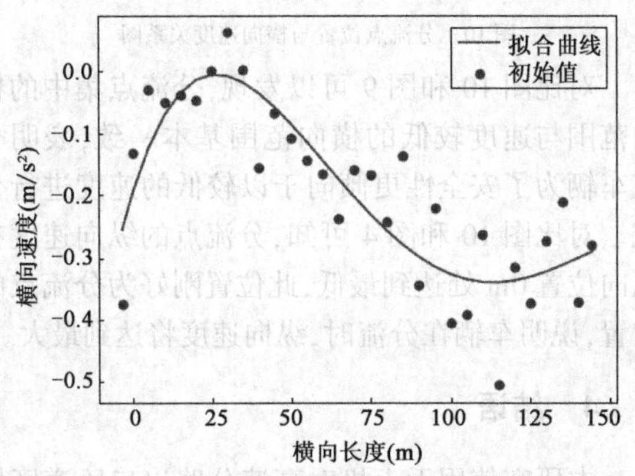

图5 横向位置与加速度的关系图

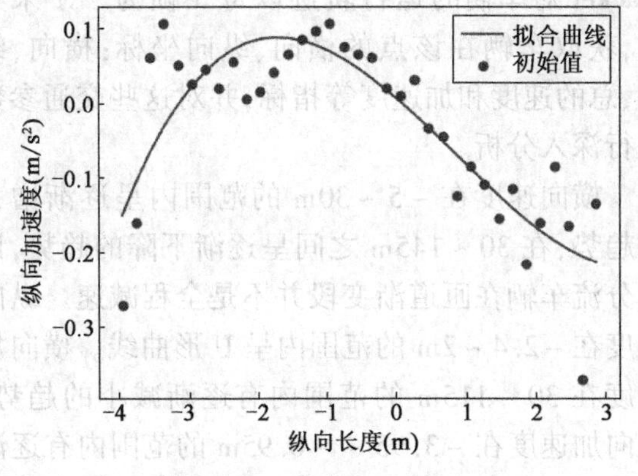

图6 纵向位置与加速的关系图

根据图5可得,横向加速度在-3.5~30m的范围内有逐渐增大的趋势,最大加速度为$0.062m/s^2$,其中最大加速度大于0,证明速度在该段范围内是增加的,与速度特性得出的结论一致;在30~115m的范围内有逐渐减小的趋势,最小加速度为$-0.506m/s^2$;在115~145m的范围内又有逐渐增大的趋势,但仍然小于0,为减速阶段。

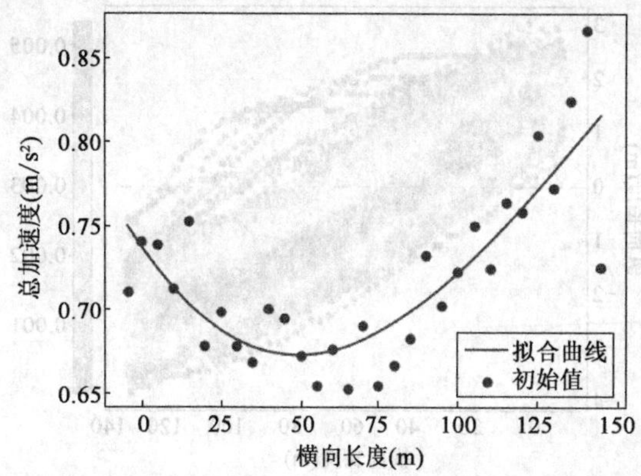

图7 横向位置与总加速度的关系图

由图6知,纵向加速度在-3.95~-0.95m的范围内有逐渐增加的趋势;在-0.95~2.85m的范围内有逐渐减小的趋势。纵向加速度在-3.95~0.05m的范围内为正值,表明在该区域进行加速,在0.05m之后为负值,表明在该区域进行减速,该结论与图4纵向长度与纵向速度反应出来的结论基本一致。总加速度是根据横向加速度与纵向加速度求均方根得到的,因此总加速度均为正值,但代表的应为减速度。根据横向位置与总加速的关系图7可知,总加速度在-3.5~60m的范围内有逐渐减小的趋势,最小值为$0.652m/s^2$;在60~145m的范围内有逐渐增加的趋势,最大加速度为$0.866m/s^2$,在该范围内加速度逐渐增加,其原因为在该范围内,车辆在换道后要迅速减速至匝道限制速度,以便安全进入匝道。

3 分流点特性研究

3.1 分流点位置特性分析

本文分流点定义为车辆中心通过渐变段分隔线的位置,即车辆轨迹线与X轴的交点,提取每条轨迹在该点处的横、纵坐标位置和速度特性。对于轨迹标记点刚好为分流点的位置,则直接提取相应的参数;对于标记点不在分流点的情况,则分别取距离X轴上下最近的两个标记点相应指标的平均值作为该分流点的参数。首先利用Python编程环境中的matplotlib绘制所有轨迹点的核密度图,具体如图8所示。其次在横向以5m为一个区间段,统计落入该区间段的分流点的数量,并求其概率密度,分流点位置的概率密度如图9所示。

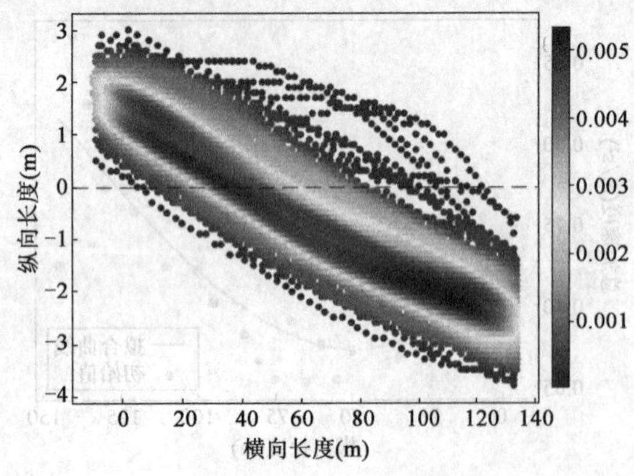

图8　轨迹核密度图

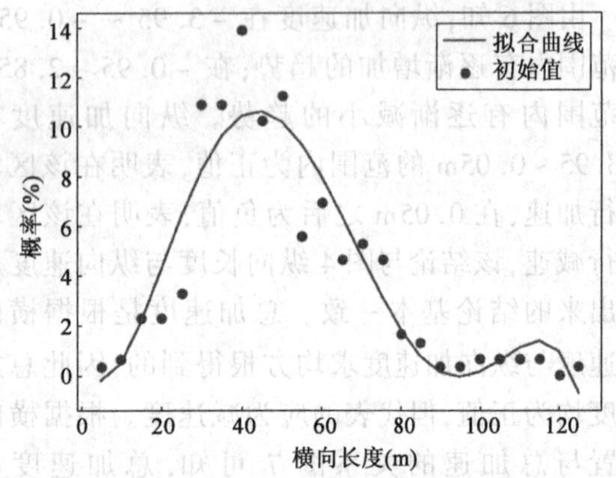

图9　分流点位置与概率密度关系图

由图8可以看出,分流车辆的轨迹具有一定的集聚效应。图9显示分流点的位置以10~75m的范围为主,主要集中在30~50m的区间内,该区段占分流点总数的57.28%,分流点在50m以后的区段占总数的30.13%,分流点在30m以前的区段占总数的12.59%。

3.2　分流点速度特性分析

由于分流点的位置主要集中在10~75m的范围内,因此探究该区域分流点位置与速度之间的关系。在横向以5m为一个区间段,统计落入该区间段的分流点所对应的横向速度平均值,分流点的位置与速度之间的关系如图10所示。

由图10可知,分流点的速度在69~76km/h的区间波动,其中速度在区间10~35m的范围内,一直呈下降趋势;在35~60m的范围内呈上升趋势;在60~75m的范围内呈下降趋势,在35~55m的范围内,驶出匝道的车辆以71km/h左右的速度到达分流点。这种变化趋势表明车辆在以较高的速度到达渐变段起点附近,速度较高的可能会首先进行分流,对于渐变段中部区域,低速行驶的车辆更倾向于在该区域进行分流;在渐变段后半部分车速有回升的原因可能是该部分车辆未进行及时分流,因此只能以较高速度进行强制分流。

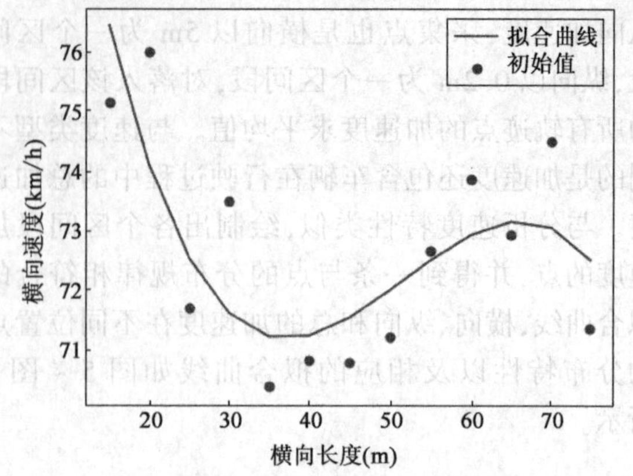

图10　分流点位置与横向速度关系图

对比图10和图9可以发现,分流点集中的横向范围与速度较低的横向范围基本一致,表明分流车辆为了安全性更倾向于以较低的速度进行分流。对比图10和图4可知,分流点的纵向速度在纵向位置0m处达到最低,此位置刚好为分流点的位置,说明车辆在分流时,纵向速度将达到最大。

4　结语

本研究使用无人机对高速公路出口匝道区域分流车辆运行状态进行视频拍摄,基于物理软件Tracker对车辆的运行轨迹以每3帧为一个采集点,获取车辆在该点的横向、纵向坐标;横向、纵向、总的速度和加速度等指标,并对这些交通参数进行深入分析。

横向速度在-5~30m的范围内呈逐渐增大的趋势,在30~145m之间呈逐渐下降的趋势,说明分流车辆在匝道渐变段并不是全程减速。纵向速度在-2.4~2m的范围内呈U形曲线。横向加速度在30~115m的范围内有逐渐减小的趋势。纵向加速度在-3.95~-0.95m的范围内有逐渐增加的趋势;在-0.95~2.85m的范围内有逐渐减小的趋势。

分流点的速度在69~76km/h的区间波动,位置主要集中在30~50m的区段内,占其总数的57.28%。其中分流点的速度在35~60m的范围内呈上升趋势;在60~75m的范围内呈下降趋势,在35~55m的范围内,驶出匝道的车辆以71km/h左右的速度到达分流点,分流车辆更倾向于以较低速度进行分流。

本文对出口匝道分流车辆速度、加速度、分流点的位置特性研究对高速公路车辆分流安全管理具有一定参考意义,也可以为未来无人驾驶、车路协同等场景下车辆的分流位置及速度提供理论依据。本文只研究了直接式出口匝道的车辆运行特性,不同类型的出口匝道可能存在不同的运行特性,因此未来可以对比不同类型出口匝道的车辆运行特性。

参考文献

[1] Chen H, Zhou H, Zhao J, et al. Safety performance evaluation of left-side off-ramps at freeway diverge areas[J]. Accident Analysis & Prevention,2011,43(3):605-612.

[2] M. Pilar Martínez a, B A G, C A T M. Traffic Microsimulation Study to Evaluate Freeway Exit Ramps Capacity-ScienceDirect [J]. Procedia-Social and Behavioral Sciences, 2011, 16 (1): 139-150.

[3] Xie J, Ma Y, Yuan L, et al. Safety and Capacity Performances of Single-lane Right Exit Ramp on Freeway: A Case Study in Jiangsu Province, China[J]. Procedia Engineering, 2016, 137: 563-570.

[4] 张驰,闫晓敏,李小伟,等.互通式立交单车道出口小客车运行速度模型[J].中国公路学报,2017,30(6):8.

[5] 白浩晨,柳银芳.互通式立交出口匝道运行速度过渡段长度研究[J].中外公路,2020,40(1):6.

[6] 乔建刚,刘轲,李瑞.基于小客车运行特性的立交桥出口匝道安全性分析[J].科学技术与工程,2018,018(033):244-248.

[7] 张智勇,郝晓云,吴文斌,等.互通立交匝道运行速度预测模型[J].交通运输系统工程与信息,2015,15(1):7.

[8] Gong J, Guo X, Dai S, et al. Research on the Operational Characteristics of Diverging Area on Expressway Off-Ramp Based on Different Restricted Strategy of Lane[J]. Procedia-Social and Behavioral Sciences,2013,96:1156-1164.

[9] 马小龙,余强,刘建蓓,等.基于无人机视频拍摄的高速公路小型车换道行为特性[J].中国公路学报,2020,33(6):11.

[10] 严亚丹,李杨,王东炜,等.公交车辆进出停靠站对城市主干路路段的交通影响[J].交通运输系统工程与信息,2019,19(3):8.

[11] 周雨阳,龚艺,姚琳,等.无人机广域视频的机动车交通参数计算及分析[J].交通运输系统工程与信息,2015,15(6):7.

[12] Outay F, Mengash H A, Adnan M. Applications of unmanned aerial vehicle (UAV) in road safety, traffic and highway infrastructure management: Recent advances and challenges [J]. Transportation Research Part A Policy and Practice,2020,141:116-129.

[13] Khan M A, Ectors W, Bellemans T, et al. Unmanned Aerial Vehicle-based Traffic Analysis: A Case Study to Analyze Traffic Streams at Urban Roundabouts[J]. Procedia Computer Science,2018,130:636-643.

[14] Wan Q, Peng G, Li Z, et al. Spatiotemporal trajectory characteristic analysis for traffic state transition prediction near expressway merge bottleneck[J]. Transportation Research Part C Emerging Technologies,2020,117(4-6):102682.

基于函数型数据的交通流量特征分析

王得圣*

(长安大学运输工程学院)

摘 要 交通流量特征分析可以更好地描述和反应波动的交通状态,但目前多数的交通流量特征分析都没有考虑交通流量的函数特征。本文将历史交通流量作为函数型数据,提出了一种利用函数型数据来识别交通流量特征的方法。根据粗糙度惩罚和广义交叉验证选取基函数个数及惩罚系数,对离散数据进行函数拟合,分析交通流量均值函数以及一阶导函数和二阶导函数的变化来获取交通流量特征。本研究使用的函数型数据分析方法产生足够详细的交通流量剖面,同时增强了交通流量特征的解释性。

关键词 交通工程 交通流量特征 函数型数据分析 交通流量拟合曲线

0 引言

交通流量特征分析是分析交通系统性能的一种重要手段,通过对交通流量特征的分析可以获取未来交通变化的趋势,为道路工作者给出相应的参考依据,因此,交通流量特征的准确分析在交通系统占有十分重要的地位。大部分学者研究了交通流量随时间变化的交通特征,以开发有效的交通预测模型、控制和监测方法[1]。其中,有大量的文献分析和模拟交通流量在一天内系统地变化的程度来获取相应的交通流量特征[2],还有部分学者分析几天之间交通流量的变化模式[3]。本文的研究重点同时包含日内和日间的交通流量特征。

目前,交通流量数据已被广泛用于网络实时监控系统的开发和短时交通流量预测。但由于数据类型的不同,模型的建立也各不相同,最常见的交通流量预测模型有时间序列分析[4]、动态网络模型[5]、随机模型[6]、神经网络[7]、非参数回归[8]等。上述研究是在离散时间段上对交通流量的分析,但是,将时间离散化偏离了实际的简化假设前提,忽略了相邻时间段之间的相关性。因此,对于交通流量特征识别的研究,最适合用连续变量表示一天的时间,但天数应被视为离散变量。加拿大学者 Ramsay[9] 提出的函数型数据分析(Functional Data Analysis,FDA)方法考虑了时间相关性和连续性,可以有效获取交通流量中的关键特征。

FDA 在交通领域中的应用相对较少,少数国外研究采用函数型数据来监测交通流量的变化趋势[10],检测交通流量异常值和计算日常的缺失部分[11],分析交通流量的波动状态[12]。结果表明 FDA 方法能有效获取交通流量的时变特征,目前国内相关研究中均未涉及 FDA 方法。然而,国外学者对 FDA 方法的应用仅限于某一方面的交通识别和波动性的描述,并没有给出具体的交通流量特征。本文结合 FDA 分析日内交通流量变化和日间交通流量变化,获取交通流量的时变特征,为交通流量研究提供一种新的思路。

1 数据来源

本论文采用的交通数据集 PeMSD3 来自加利福尼亚州交通委员会。PeMS 是由美国加州交通局性能测量系统(Caltrans Performance Measurement System)部署在加州超过3.9万个传感器站实时收集的数据。每个传感器每隔30s采集一次数据,并以5min为间隔,将间隔内的数据进行集合并返回给系统。本次实验选取加州第三街区 Yolo 县 I80-E 路段318092号环行线圈采集的交通流量断面数据。时间范围为2020年7月1日—2020年12月31日,其中7月22日数据丢失,故将其剔除,所以有183天的交通流量断面数据可用于实验。

本次收集的数据以每5min为间隔,一天从00:00:00—24:00:00共288段间隔,本次研究将每段时间间隔以自然数表示,则一天24h可以表示为1,2,3,……,288。

2 模型算法

与传统的数据分析方法相比,FDA 是一种将时间序列数据平滑为连续曲线并作为输入的分析方法,同时 FDA 只需要较少的先验假设条件。将每日交通流量曲线作为观测结果,输入模型可以充分考虑时间特征之间的相关性,同时利用平滑技术对原始数据进行匀修,在一定程度上可以消除误差。FDA 存在一阶和高阶的导数估计,通过分析不同时间点的一阶导数和高阶导数,可以更详细地研究交通流量之间的变化差异和其他相关特征。此外,FDA 可以避免交通流量时间序列在不同时间点之间的滞后性,提高交通流量特征的解释性。

在对交通流量数据进行分析之前,对获得的原始离散数据进行预处理,拟合成函数型数据,将离散的单日交通流量观测数据点转化为曲线形式。基函数拟合指运用一组已知且相互独立的基函数估计原始数据,基函数最常用的是B样条基函数[12]。将待拟合交通流量数据的整体区间通过断点 $T_i(i=1,2\cdots)$ 切分成 L 个子区间，这与采集的每 5min 交通流量数据在时间轴上十分契合。这里对 B 样条做简要介绍：对于给定的递增交通流量节点序列 $\{t_1,\cdots,t_i,\cdots,t_{i+k},\cdots,t_n\}$，定义 K 阶多项式 $B_{i,k}$ 为第 i 个子区间的 B 样条基函数。要求 $t_i<t_{i+k}$，K 阶多项式定义如下：

$$B_{i,0}(t)=\begin{cases}1, t_k<t<t_{k+1}\\0, \text{其他}\end{cases} \tag{1}$$

$$B_{i,k}(t)=\frac{(t-t_k)}{t_{k+i-1}-t_k}B_{i,k-1}(t)+\left(1-\frac{t_{k+i}-t}{t_{k+i}-t_{i+1}}\right)B_{i+1,k-1}(t) \tag{2}$$

在实际应用中发现运用三阶 B 样条对数据的拟合效果较好[11]，如图 1 所示，重叠产生的拟合交通流量轨迹比单个考虑时间区间的方法能够更好地表示交通流量数据中的局部特征。高阶 B 样条拟合数据时会产生过拟合现象，增加计算成本，因此，本文在拟合交通流量数据时运用三阶 B 样条。

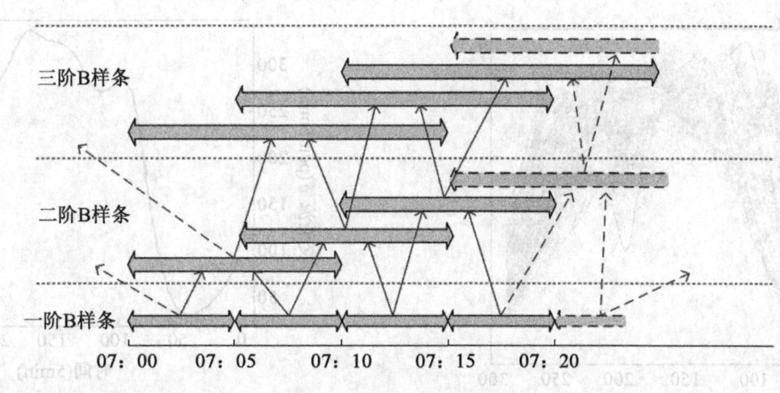

图 1 B 样条覆盖范围示例图

假定使用 K 个已知的基函数 $\{\phi_k(t)\}$，$k=1,2,\cdots,K$ 来拟合交通流量轨迹曲线，则所拟合的交通流量轨迹函数可以表示为：

$$\hat{x}(t)=\sum_{k=1}^{K}c_k\phi_k(t) \tag{3}$$

拟合后交通流量轨迹函数的导数可以表示为：

$$D^m[\hat{x}(t)]=\sum_{k=1}^{K}c_kD^m[\phi_k(t)] \tag{4}$$

其中，$D^m(\cdot)$ 表示函数的 m 阶导数。

在基函数确定之后，需要求解各基函数所对应的系数 $\{c_k\}$，$k=1,2,\cdots,K$。一般采用的方法是最小二乘法：

$$\min\sum_{i}^{n}\left[x(t)-\sum_{k=1}^{K}c_k\phi_k(t)\right]^2 \tag{5}$$

其中，$x(t)$ 表示真实的交通流量轨迹曲线。

为选择合适的基函数个数近似交通流量轨迹曲线，必须要在拟合度和光滑度之间进行权衡，在实际问题的研究中，基函数个数通过粗糙度惩罚法[13]来选取。一般而言，描述函数波动性采用函数二阶导平方的积分，其表达如下：

$$PENSSE=\sum_{i=1}^{n}\left[x(t_j)-\hat{x}(t_j)\right]^2+\lambda\int\left[D^2\hat{x}(t_j)\right]^2\mathrm{d}t \tag{6}$$

式(6)中，平滑参数 λ 通常用广义交叉验证法[13]选取。图 2 展示了 9 月 15 日一天的交通流量时间序列和 B 样条拟合后的交通流量轨迹曲线，通过图 2 的对比，不难发现，拟合后的交通流量轨迹随时间的推移更加流畅，更加方便获取一天之内交通流量随时间变化的特征。

3 案例分析

交通流量数据由每 5min 记录一次收集的，一天的交通流量由 288 条记录组成。交通流量轨迹曲线通过拟合每 5min 离散的交通流量数据获得，如图 3 所示，本文一共拟合 183 条交通流量曲线。三阶 B 样条基函数个数通过粗糙度惩罚和广义交叉验证方法计算比较误差后选择 $K=50$ 较合适，曲线呈现光滑趋势，同时对原始数据的拟合度也较高。惩罚系数 $\lambda=0.01$[13]，λ 的选取不是本文的重点，故不做详细讨论。

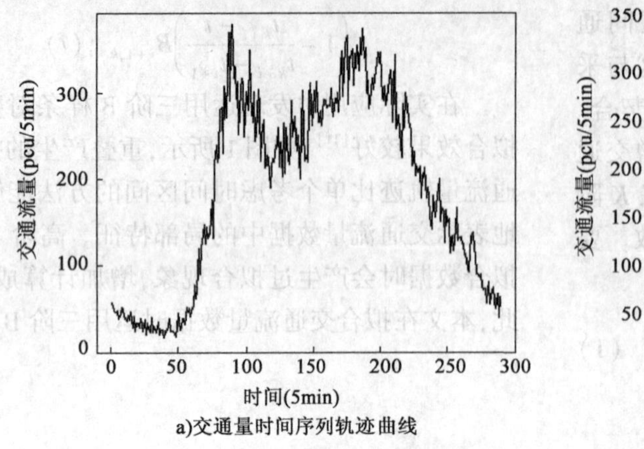

a)交通量时间序列轨迹曲线

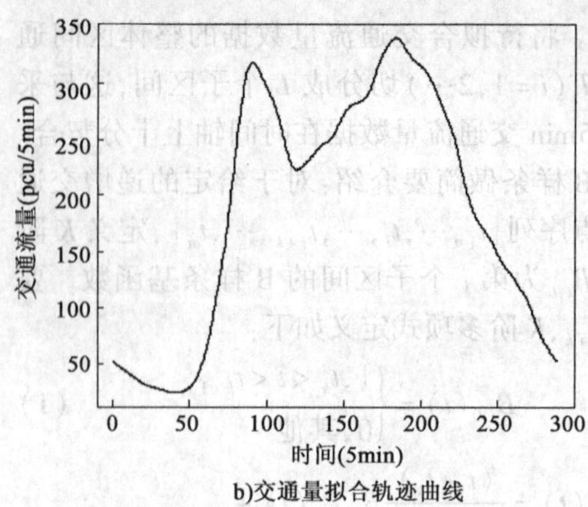

b)交通量拟合轨迹曲线

图 2　交通流量的时间序列与 B 样条平滑交通流量对比

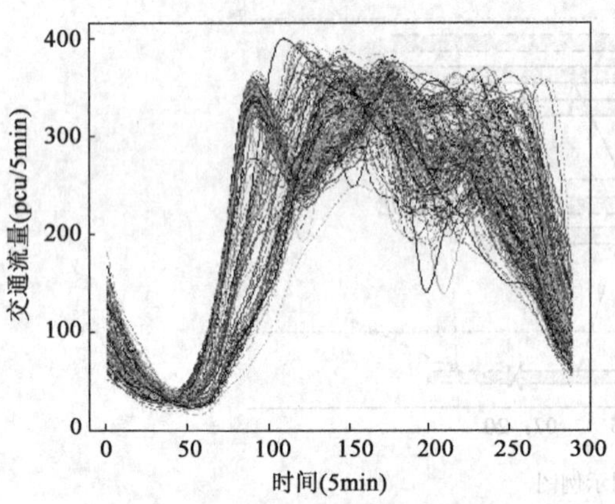

图 3　183d 的交通流量曲线

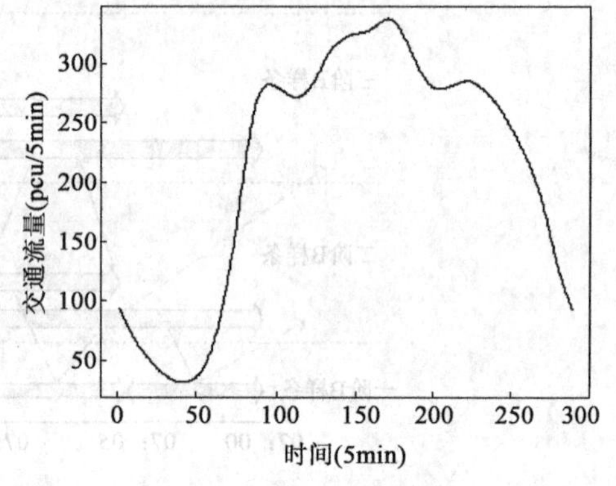

图 4　交通流量均值曲线

183d 交通流量拟合函数型曲线的均值如图 4 所示。均值曲线体现了 183d 交通流量的总体平均走势,总体来说,夜间交通流量较小,白天交通流量偏大。在 3:30(T_{42})交通流量均值曲线达到波谷状态,13:30(T_{162})达到波峰状态。在 3:30—6:30($T_{42}-T_{78}$)时间段交通流量迅速上升,18:00(T_{216})后又迅速下降至波谷,显然这是由夜间与白天出行需求的差异造成的;6:30—18:00(T_{78}—T_{216})时间段内交通流量在一天之中最高,同时交通流量轨迹曲线表现为波动形态。

交通流量均值函数曲线的一阶导函数和二阶导函数如图 5 所示。如图 5a)所示一阶导函数表明交通流量均值函数变化的速度,说明交通流量一直处于不断变化趋势,整体大致表现出 3:30—6:30(T_{42}—T_{78})上升速度快,18:00—3:30(T_{216}—T_{288+42})下降速度快,6:30—18:00(T_{78}—T_{216})起伏波动缓慢。如图 5b)所示的二阶导函数表明交通流量变化的加速度;当二阶导函数为负时,说明在相应时间段内交通流量变化的加速度减小;当二阶导函数为正时,表示在相应时间段内交通流量变化的加速度增大。

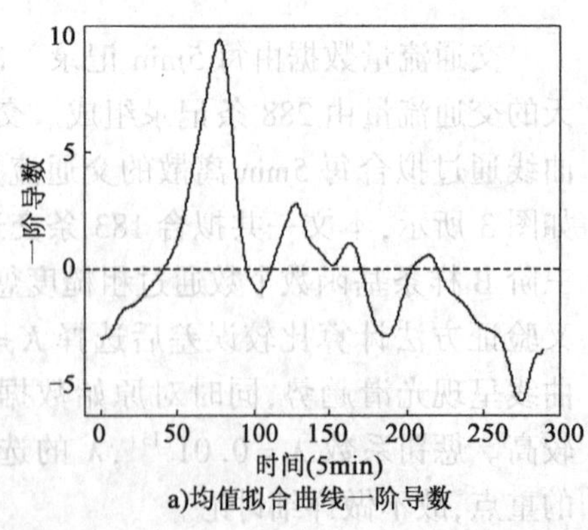

a)均值拟合曲线一阶导数

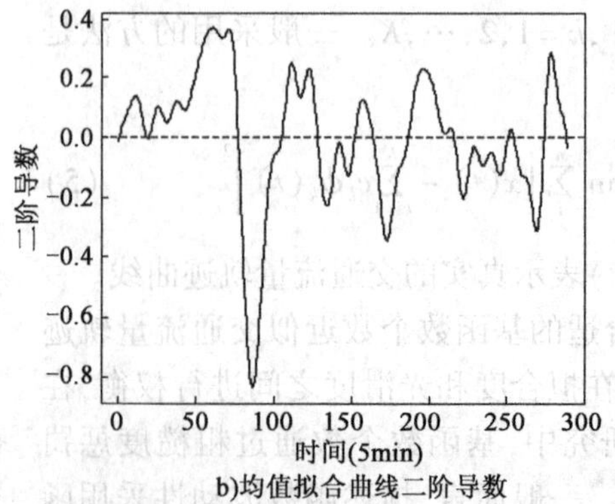

b)均值拟合曲线二阶导数

图 5　交通流量均值曲线一阶导函数和二阶导函数

4 结语

本文提出了一种获取交通流量特征的函数型方法,与时间息息相关。该方法使用函数型数据分析方法,利用历史数据,对183d的交通流量进行数据拟合,分析了交通流量均值曲线及一阶和二阶导数曲线,强调了函数型数据分析在获取交通流量变化特征方面的优势,为交通建模和解释交通现象提供了一种新的视角。然而,本文只考虑了单一位置的单个交通变量,后续的研究还应考虑占有率、速度等相关变量,结合道路网整体的交通状况,获取更多的交通特征。

参考文献

[1] Tan M C, Wong S C, Xu J M, et al. An aggregation approach to short-term traffic flow prediction [J]. IEEE Transactions on Intelligent Transportation Systems,2009,10(1):60-69.

[2] Ke H, Terry L, Friesz W Y, et al. Elastic demand dynamic network user equilibrium: Formulation, existence and computation [J]. Transportation Research Part B,2015,81(81): 183-209.

[3] Hazelton M L, Parry K. Statistical methods for comparison of day-to-day traffic models [J]. Transportation Research Part B,2016,92(92): 22-34.

[4] Xiao F, Yang H, Ye H. Physics of day-to-day network flow dynamics [J]. Transportation Research Part B,2016,86(86):86-103.

[5] Du L, Peeta S, Kim Y H. An adaptive information fusion model to predict the short-term link travel time distribution in dynamic traffic networks [J]. Transportation Research Part B,2011,46(1):235-252.

[6] Saif E J, Henry X. A stochastic model of traffic flow: Gaussian approximation and estimation [J]. Transportation Research Part B,2013,47 (47):15-41.

[7] Kit Y C, Dillon T S, Singh J, et al. Neural-Network-based models for short-term traffic flow forecasting using a hybrid exponential smoothing and Levenberg-Marquardt algorithm [J]. IEEE Transactions on Intelligent Transportation Systems,2012,13(2):644-654.

[8] Wei C H, Yucheng D, Feifeng Z, et al. Hybrid evolutionary algorithms in a SVR traffic flow forecasting model. Applied Mathematics and Computation[J]. 2011,217(15):6733-6747.

[9] Ramsay J O. When the data are functions[J]. Psychometrika,1982,47(4):379-396.

[10] I. G. Guardiola, T. Leon, F. Mallor. A functional approach to monitor and recognize patterns of daily traffic profiles [J]. Transportation Research Part B, 2014, 65 (65):119-136.

[11] Chiou J, Zhang Y, Chen W, et al. A functional data approach to missing value imputation and outlier detection for traffic flow data [J]. Transportmetrica B: Transport Dynamics, 2014,2(2):106-129.

[12] Crawford F, Watling D P, Connors R D. A statistical method for estimating predictable differences between daily traffic flow profiles [J]. Transportation Research Part B,2017,95 (95):196-213.

[13] 王国华. 中国股票市场日内波动率研究——基于函数型数据分析[D]. 武汉:中南财经政法大学,2017.

基于出租汽车轨迹数据的城市居民出行时空特征分析

曹　悦[*1]　刘玖樽[2]

(1.长安大学运输工程学院;2.西安电子科技大学网络与信息安全学院)

摘　要　为挖掘城市居民出行的时空特性,利用西安市工作日及周末的出租汽车GPS轨迹数据,计算每30min每单位距离的平均出行时间为指标的拥挤系数,分析出行状态随时间的变化特征;并制作西安市雁塔区晚高峰期间某区域内的出租汽车轨迹热力图、出租汽车上下客热力图,捕捉居民高峰时段的出行起终点的空间分布特性。分析结果表明:与周末相比,工作日具有较明显的早晚高峰;工作日晚高峰时段大致为17:30—19:30,在该时段研究区域内的出行起点热点为工作地、商圈、高校,终点热点为居住区、商圈、景点。上述研究成果可为管理部门针对西安出行现状制定出租汽车调度及交通管控措施提供依据。

关键词　交通大数据　轨迹数据时空分析　拥堵系数　热点区域

0　引言

居民的出行规律是制定管控措施以缓解城市交通拥堵问题及辅助城市规划研究的重要依据。在现代信息技术环境下,随着各类检测器及车辆运行数据获取途经的发展,出现应用手机信令数据、蓝牙数据、Wi-Fi数据、车载全球定位系统(GPS)轨迹数据等来分析其包含的交通信息的方法。出租汽车是居民出行的一种重要公共交通方式。不同于公交、轨道交通等其他具有固定的线路和站点的公共交通方式,出租汽车具有的随叫随停的运行特点,可以为居民出行提供更便捷的出行服务。并且其运行数据是通过GPS得到的轨迹数据,具有覆盖范围广、位置精度高、采样间隔小等优点,数据内包括是否有乘客、行驶速度、车辆位置等信息,利用轨迹数据进行交通研究已经成为新趋势[1-3]。

居民出行同时具有时间和空间两个维度的分布特征。时间分布特征的分析一般通过计算评价指标得到其随时间的变化趋势,再判断出行者在不同时段内的行为特征。道路运行情况的评价指标一般以速度、时间、流量数据为基础,再进行处理获得。如通过衡量道路交通密度,描述拥堵强度和持续情况的道路拥堵指数(RCI);或计算通勤人员的年均延误时间、总延误等综合得到出行时间指数(TTI),用来描述交通拥堵的程度[4];而拥堵度(DC)指标以某路段实际交通量与24h或白天12h的评价基准量之比来描述道路的拥堵状况[5]等。国内的道路拥堵值的评价方法主要包括拥堵里程比例、出行时间和综合评价,如以车辆平均速度、拥堵指数、停车时间比例、加速度噪声和平均速度梯度标线交通拥堵的程度[6]。

居民出行的空间分布特征主要利用数据挖掘中的K-MEANS算法、DBSCAN算法、BIRCH算法等对空间位置数据进行聚类获得。如基于DBSCAN算法和改进的DTW距离的时间序列聚类算法,通过提取具有相似性出行特征的时空模式,进而研究城市人群出行行为的时空差异[7];或采用基于网格密度的GScan聚类算法,合并可达热点网格单元得到城市的热点区域[8];还可基于出租汽车载客的起终点数据,利用DBSCAN方法和Web组件技术实现热点区域的在线可视化交互[9]等。虽然通过以上的聚类算法可以直观得到空间位置的分布热点,但其大多为数据驱动。但处理大规模的空间数据需要较大的计算内存、耗费较长的计算时间。

从空间纬度向时间纬度的扩展形成了空间聚类方法,是一种综合时空特点进行时空聚类提取热点区域来分析居民出行规律[10-12]的方法。时空聚类方法需解决时序相似性度量和模式聚类两大核心问题。其中现有的时序相似性度量方法主要是基于距离的相似性度量,最常用的有欧式距离和DTW距离;关于模式聚类,在噪声处理、参数选择、密度分布等方面的研究已经很成熟[13-14]。

为获知西安市城市居民出行的时间与空间特征,本文利用出租汽车 GPS 轨迹数据计算全天各时段拥挤系数,从时间角度分析居民工作日及周末的出行规律以及出租汽车的运行状况,并针对高峰时段出租汽车轨迹热点区域及居民出行起讫热点(OD)区域分析其空间特性。

1 实验数据

1.1 数据来源

选取 2019 年 11 月 8 日(周五)11 月 9 日(周六)的西安市出租汽车轨迹数据作为数据来源。数据具有如下基础特征:①数据量方面,每天包含 5000 辆出租汽车营运时间内的轨迹数据;②数据内容方面,每个文件为一辆出租汽车的轨迹数据,每条数据包含车牌号、时间、空重、纬度、经度、速度、订单编号等属性信息。

1.2 数据清洗

主要采用 Python 处理数据。首先对数据进行清洗和筛选,按如下规则进行数据的预处理:①划定研究范围为大致西安市三环以内区域,剔除三环外轨迹数据;②对于每个滑行轨迹,移除具有相同的坐标和时间戳的重复顶点;③剔除数据行内无用数据,保留车牌号、时间、速度、经度、纬度、空重信息。

2 居民出行时间特征分析

2.1 拥挤系数计算

道路拥堵指标大多基于行程时间、行驶速度、道路交通量。本文将表征交通状况的拥挤系数定义为单位距离的平均行驶时间,具体为以 30min 为时间间隔,计算出租汽车每行驶 1km 所用时间。具体的计算流程为:完成原始轨迹数据清洗后,将全天 24h 划分为 48 个时段,对出租汽车数据进行划分,计算每时段内车辆的平均行驶速度 $\bar{v}$,然后通过以下公式得到每辆车以 min 为单位的单位距离的行驶时间 t。由拥挤系数的定义可知:拥挤系数越大,道路的运行状态越差。

$$t = \frac{1 \times 60}{\bar{v}} \tag{1}$$

2.2 分析方法

通过上述计算得到每辆出租汽车在全天 48 个时段内的拥挤系数,由于每条拥挤系数具有车辆、时段、值大小多个属性,因此可以分别从拥挤系数各时段的分布比例,以及拥挤系数每一取值区间的时间分布特征两个角度对居民出行的时间特征进行分析。

2.2.1 道路拥挤系数占比分析

根据拥挤系数的定义,当其值大于 9 时,出租汽车的行驶速度已小于 7km/h,因此在分析过程中主要采用 0~9 的拥挤系数值进行统计。为分析各时段车辆的运行状态,将每个时段内拥挤系数以 1 为间隔划分,统计每个区间内车辆频数并计算其在时段内占比,得到工作日及周末各时段各拥挤系数值的分布折线,如图 1 和图 2 所示。

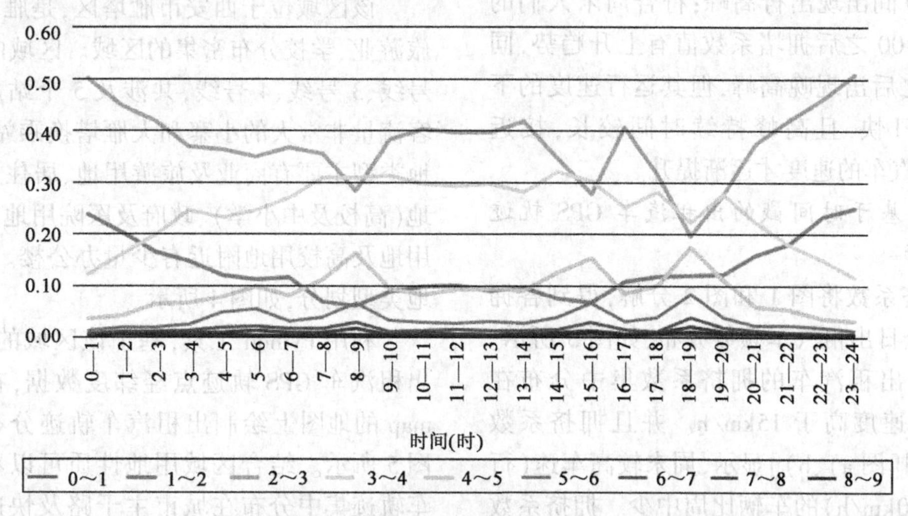

图 1 工作日出租汽车 GPS 轨迹拥挤系数占比

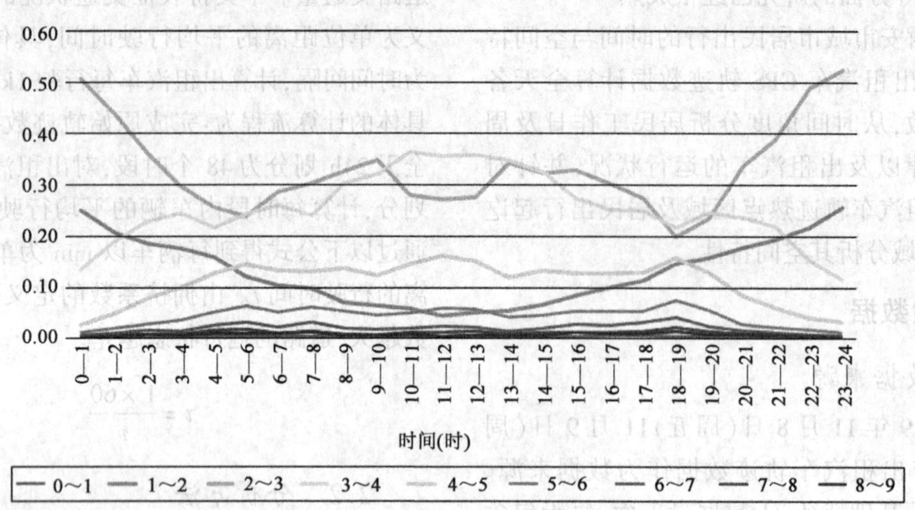

图 2　周末出租汽车 GPS 轨迹拥挤系数占比

从图 1 和图 2 中可以看出,与周末相比,工作日的早晚双峰特性更加明显。工作日在 6:00 之后车辆行驶速度开始减慢,在 7:00—9:00 间呈现早高峰状态,早高峰后行驶速度得到恢复;下午 15:00—16:00 附近车辆行驶速度再次有所减低,其原因可能有两方面,一方面西安市出租汽车在每天 15:00—15:30、15:30—16:00、16:00—16:30 时段实行错时交接班,另一方面可能受到部分学校放学影响;晚高峰大概开始于 17:00,18:00—19:00 行驶拥挤系数均值最高,对应的行驶速度最慢,20:00 之后开始逐渐缓解。

从整体分布趋势看,周末出租汽车的 3 以上拥挤系数占比要高于工作日,且双峰不明显,尤其是早高峰。6:00 之后出租汽车速度逐渐减慢,10:30—13:00 间出现出行高峰;符合周末人们的出行习惯;15:00 之后拥堵系数值有上升趋势,同样在 17:00 之后出现晚高峰,但其运行速度的下降没有工作日快,且高峰持续时间较长,接近 21:00时出租汽车的速度才逐渐提升。

2.2.2　基于时间戳的出租汽车 GPS 轨迹频数分布分析

按照拥挤系数将图 1 和图 2 分解,得到各拥挤系数下的全日出租汽车频数分布,如图 3 所示。从整体上看,出租汽车的拥挤系数集中分布在 0 ~4,即行驶速度高于 15km/h。并且拥挤系数 0 ~2区间的图[图 a)、b)]显示,周末较高车速(行驶速度高于 30km/h)的车辆比周中少。拥挤系数 2 ~4 区间内,周末与周中都具有较明显的早晚高峰。拥挤系数 4 ~6 区间内,出租汽车频数大致呈梭形。拥挤系数 4 ~9 区间内,出租汽车的行驶速度低于 15km/h,此时在周中的早晚高峰时段内,出租汽车分布频数有显著增加,说明了工作日早晚高峰的拥堵程度要强于周末。

3　居民出行空间特征分析

3.1　晚高峰小时出租汽车轨迹分布

以工作日晚高峰时段内 18:30—19:30 这 1h 的轨迹数据为基础,分析居民出行的空间分布特征。对数据按时间进行筛选处理,得时段内出租汽车的 GPS 轨迹点,将其结合西安市路网导入 ArcMap 软件内,可以看出,出租汽车的轨迹在主干路及快速路上分布较多。

该区域位于西安市雁塔区,是雁塔区内商业、旅游业、学校分布密集的区域。区域内经过地铁 2 号线、3 号线、4 号线,共涉及 5 个站点,内含两个客流量非常大的小寨和大雁塔换乘站。区域内用地类型主要有商业及旅游用地、居住用地、教育用地(高校及中小学)、政府及医院用地,另外由商业用地及高校用地附近有少量办公楼。将区域按用地类型划分,如图 4 所示。

利用 Python 工具,基于该区域的高峰小时内出租汽车 GPS 轨迹点经纬度数据,在 open street map 的地图上绘制出租汽车轨迹分布热力图,如图 5 所示。结合区域用地性质可以看出:出租汽车轨迹集中分布在城市主干路及快速路上,集中在商业区、景区、学校附近。

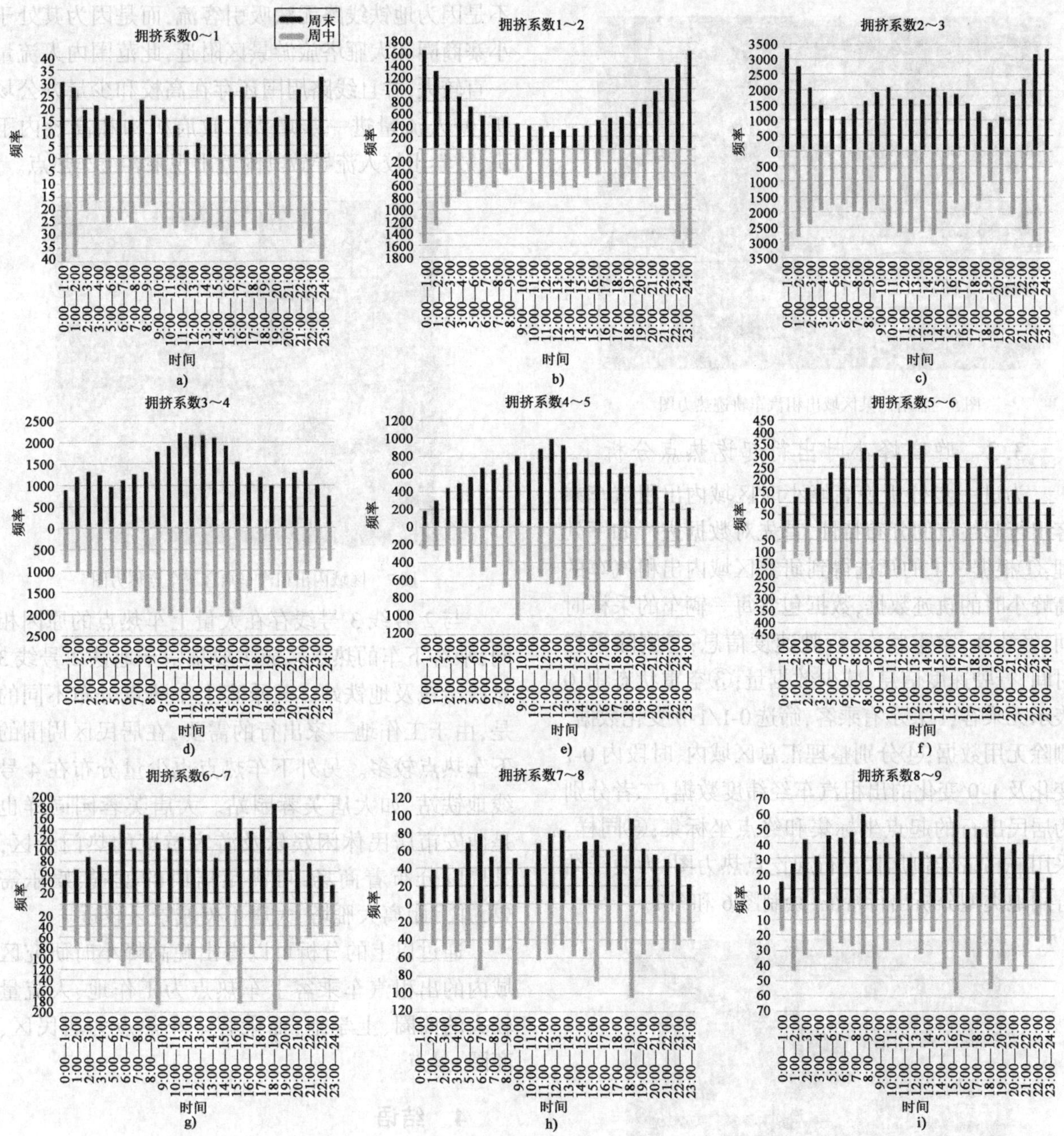

图3 基于拥挤系数的出租汽车GPS轨迹频率分布

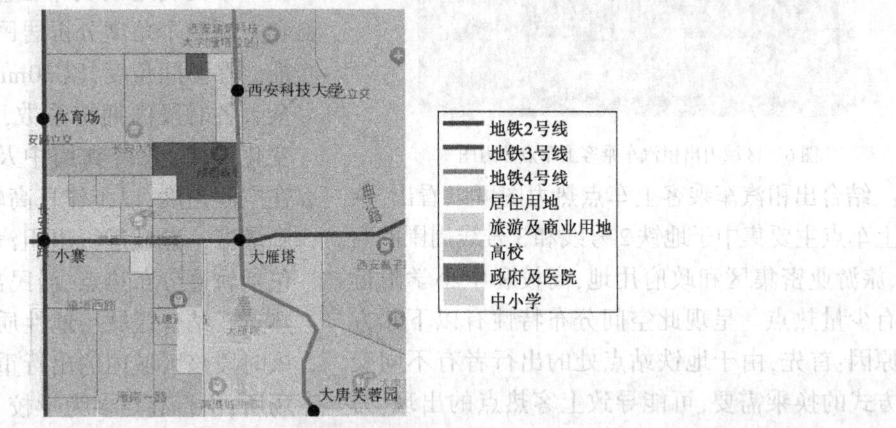

图4 区域内用地类型划分

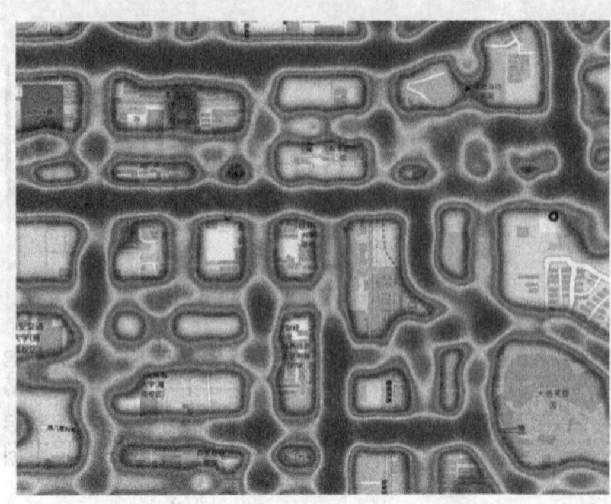

图 5　雁塔区某区域出租汽车轨迹热力图

3.2　晚高峰小时出行起讫热点分析

为进一步分析晚高峰小时区域内出租汽车乘客出行起终点的分布特性,首先对数据进行如下处理:①根据 3.1 的筛选得到研究区域内出租汽车的高峰小时的轨迹数据,数据包含每一辆车的采样时间、经纬度、空重状态、行驶速度信息;②删除采样时间、行驶速度信息,减少数据量;③空重状态中,0 表示无乘客,1 表示有乘客,筛选 0-1/1-0 变化数据,删除无用数据;④分别整理汇总区域内、时段内 0-1 变化及 1-0 变化的出租汽车经纬度数据,二者分别为居民出行的起点坐标集和终点坐标集;⑤同样,采用 python 绘制居民出行起讫点热力图,为便于结合用地类型分析出行特征,绘制图 6 和图 7。

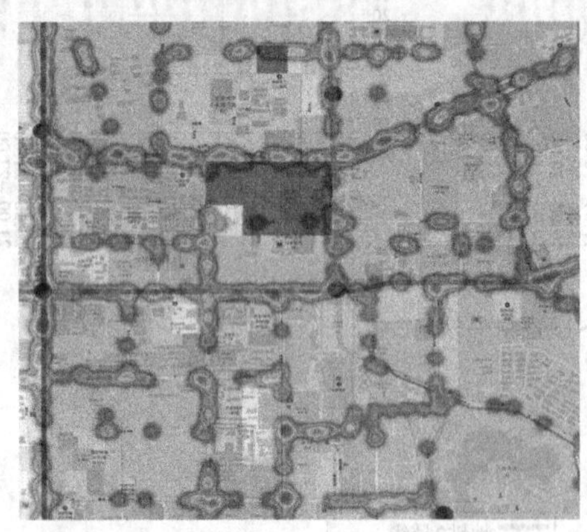

图 6　区域内出租汽车乘客上车点热力图

结合出租汽车乘客上车点热力图可以看出,乘客上车点主要集中于地铁 2 号线和 3 号线周围的商业、旅游业密集区和政府用地,高校和中小学附近也有少量热点。呈现此空间分布特性有以下几方面原因:首先,由于地铁站点处的出行者有不同交通方式的换乘需要,可能导致上客热点的出现,另外,此区域内的地铁沿线出现大量的乘车热点,并不是因为地铁线路无法吸引客流,而是因为其处于小寨商圈和大雁塔旅游景区附近,此范围内人流量一直较大,并且线路周围还存在高校和少量办公场所,使人流量进一步增大。政府机构和高校内下班、放学出校人流导致其附近出现乘客上车热点。

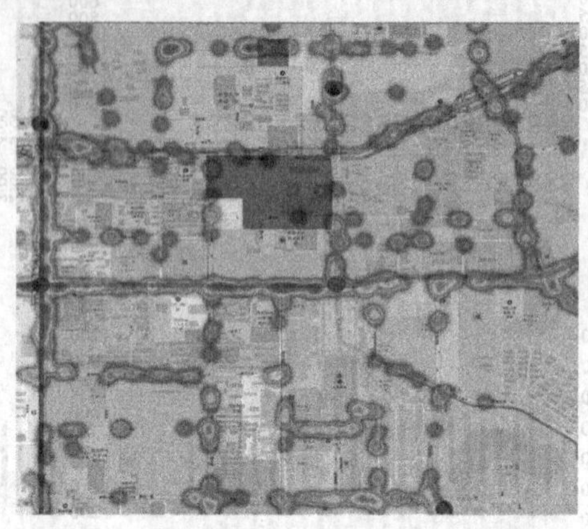

图 7　区域内出租汽车乘客下车点热力图

与 2 号线 3 号线存在大量上车热点的原因相同,乘客下车的热点区域主要集中于地铁 2 号线 3 号线沿线及地铁站。与乘客上车热点分布不同的是,由于工作地—家出行的需要,在居民区周围的下车热点较多。另外下车热点也少量分布在 4 号线地铁站,如大唐芙蓉园站。大唐芙蓉园同样也是西安市居民休闲娱乐及游客游览的热门景区,其周围分布着商场,可满足居民的就餐、娱乐需要,并且距离大雁塔、大唐不夜城景区较近。

通过以上的分析可以得出晚高峰小时研究区域内的出租汽车乘客上车热点为工作地、人流量较大的商圈、上学地;而乘客下车热点为居民区、商圈、景点。

4　结语

本文利用西安市出租汽车轨迹数据,从时间和空间两个角度分析居民在周中和周末的出行特征。在时间角度,以 30min 为间隔切分数据,计算全天各时段内拥挤系数,分析拥挤系数随时间的变化规律,并得到周中及周末的早晚高峰时段。在空间角度,以工作日高峰时段为例,选取西安市雁塔区一区域进行出租汽车分布热点分析。热点包括轨迹分布热点、居民出行起点热点、出行终点热点。结合区域用地性质,经分析发现:出行者在该时段该区域内的出行重点大多为家或休闲娱乐场所,出行起点多为学校、商业区和工作地。在后续的研究中,为缓解高峰路网拥堵和打车难问题,可以结合出租汽车 OD 热点优化出租汽车在热点区域的调度诱导,还可划定拥挤禁停区域,引导区域内出行者采用轨道交通、公交、自行车出行,在区域外进行与出租汽车的换乘衔接。

参考文献

[1] 郑宇. 城市计算概述[J]. 武汉大学学报(信息科学版),2015,40(01):1-13.

[2] 邱端昇,邬群勇,刘萌,等. 一种基于出租车轨迹数据的优质客源评价模型及实证研究[J]. 福州大学学报(自然科学版),2018,46(02):199-203.

[3] 刘萌,邬群勇. 基于出租车 OD 数据的居民活动强度时空特征研究[J]. 福州大学学报(自然科学版),2018,46(02):204-209.

[4] Eisele B, Lomax T, Schrank D. Tti's 2011 urban mobility report [R]. Texas: Texas Transportation Institute,2011.

[5] 饭田恭敬. 交通工程学[M]. 邵春福,等译. 北京:人民交通出版社,1994.

[6] 王力,张海,范耀祖. 移动式道路交通状态模糊评价方法研究[J]. 系统仿真学报,2008(01):178-181.

[7] 邸少宁,朱杰,郑加柱,等. 出租车轨迹数据的南京人群出行模式挖掘[J]. 测绘科学,2021,46(01):203-212.

[8] 郑林江,赵欣,蒋朝辉,等. 基于出租车轨迹数据的城市热点出行区域挖掘[J]. 计算机应用与软件,2018,35(01):1-8.

[9] Jahnke M, Ding L, Karja K, et al. 2017. Identifying Origin/Destination Hotspots in Floating Car Data for Visual Analysis of Traveling Behavior[C]. // Progress in Location-Based Services 2016. Berlin: Springer International Publishing,253-269.

[10] 腾巧爽,孙尚宇,秘金钟. 众源地理空间数据的城市热点区域探测[J]. 测绘科学,2018,43(5):74-80.

[11] 陈婷. 基于移动时空轨迹的路网热点区域挖掘系统设计与实现[D]. 成都:电子科技大学,2019.

[12] Shen, Liu, Chen. Discovering Spatial and Temporal Patterns from Taxi-based floating Car Data: a Case Study from Nanjing [J]. GIScience: Remote Sensing,2017,54(5):617-638.

[13] 伏家云,靖常峰,杜明义. 空间密度聚类模式挖掘方法 DBSCAN 研究回顾与进展[J]. 测绘科学,2018,43(12):50-57.

[14] Liu X, Gong L, Gong Y, et al. Revealing Travel Patterns and City structure with Taxi Trip Data [J]. Journal of Transport Geography, 2015, 43:78-90.

2021 年春运综合客流规律研究

龚露阳* 陈 硕 闫 超

(交通运输部科学研究院)

摘 要 为支撑交通运输部门和企业制定春运的运营组织管理措施,基于人口迁徙、各种运输方式运营数据,本文应用大数据分析方法对 2021 年春运期间的铁路、公路、水运、民航等客流数据进行分析。结果表明,2021 年春运期间,营业性客运量显著下降,“翘尾”现象明显;公路客流下降幅度最大;铁路客流中短距离出行增长明显;东北、京津冀地区迁徙规模指数下降幅度明显;中心城市迁徙潮汐特征明显;公路旅客出行半径缩短,更多为省内中短途出行,且出行计划性降低,提前购票比例下降;城市内出行需求旺盛,出行强度明显增长;疫情防控形势和防控措施对 2021 年春运客流特征规律产生了显著影响。

关键词 综合运输 春运 大数据 客流出行 疫情防控

0　引言

春节是中国人的传统节日,代表辞旧迎新时刻的到来,也是个团圆、喜庆、吉祥的日子。为了欢庆这个重要而又特殊的节日,每年的这个时候,全国各地的游子们从四面八方奔回老家。这种特殊“迁徙”带来的超乎平日的客流,对担任主要运输工作的交通运输部门来说,无疑是巨大的压力和考验。在这样的大背景下,春节前后客流出现数倍于平日的特殊现象后来被称为“春运”。关于“春运”的时间界定是以春节为界,节前15天,节后25天,共40天,由国家发改委统一发布,铁道部、交通部、民航局按此进行专门运输安排。铁道部实行特殊运行图,加开大量临时客车。据调查,从1954年起,铁道部就存在“春运”记录,但客流量与现在相差很远:当时日均客流量73万人次,高峰客流量90万人次,时间为春节前后15天。20世纪80年代以后,大量农民外出打工,“春运”成为社会热点。1989年“民工潮”引起媒体注意,从那时起媒体开始使用“春运”一词。据统计,自20世纪90年代以来,春节旅客人数年平均增长5.6%,前几年接近10%,年净增长量达到2亿人次。春运综合客流规律研究具有重要意义,有利于提高未来春运客流特点及趋势判断的准确性,有利于提升春运期间交通运输管理部门的决策水平和运输企业的服务水平,有利于推动综合运输业的发展。

1　疫情形势和防控措施

在疫情防控常态化的背景下,疫情形势和防控措施将对春运客流产生重大影响。2021年春运开始前和春运期间呈现了局部疫情集中爆发、防控措施趋严的特点。

1.1　疫情形势

2021年1月1日至1月27日(春运开始前一天),全国累计新增新冠肺炎确诊病例2255例,其中,新增本土病例1871例,日均新增约69例;新增境外输入病例384例,日均新增约14例。春运开始前,北京、河北、山西、辽宁、吉林、黑龙江、上海、陕西等10个省(市)爆发本土疫情,其中,河北、吉林、黑龙江等省份疫情集中爆发,新增本土确诊病例分别为934例、303例、540例。春运开始前各省(市)新增本土确诊病例数见表1。

春运开始前各省(市)新增本土确诊病例数　表1

省(市)	新增本土病例(例)	省(市)	新增本土病例(例)
北京市	43	辽宁省	27
广西壮族自治区	1	山东省	1
河北省	934	山西省	4
黑龙江省	540	陕西省	2
吉林省	303	上海市	16

注:其他省份无新增本土病例

春运开始后,疫情迅速得到有效控制,新增确诊病例数快速下降。春运期间,全国共新增确诊病例676例,其中,本土病例仅为234例,日均新增约6例;境外输入病例442例,日均新增约11例。2021年2月7日起至春运结束(共计30天),全国无新增本土确诊病例。2021年春运开始前和春运期间全国新增确诊病例数如图1所示。

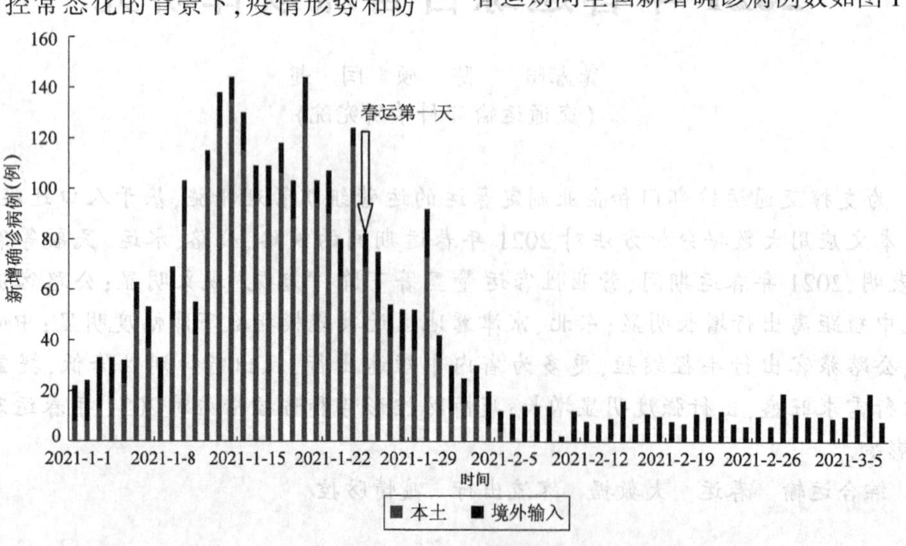

图1　2021年春运开始前和春运期间全国新增确诊病例数

1.2 防控措施

2021年春运开始前,国家高度重视疫情防控工作,在国务院联防联控机制下成立了春运工作专班,印发了《2021年综合运输春运疫情防控总体工作方案》,指导各地切实做好春运期间疫情防控和错峰控流相关工作;引导公众避峰错峰出行,减少不必要出行,特别是非必要不前往中高风险地区;严格控制交通运输工具载客率。

截至春运开始前,全国31个省(市)均发出了非必要不出行或不返乡的倡议,其中北京、河北、贵州3个省(市)提出了机关干部带头就地过节,天津、河北、黑龙江、江西、河南、湖北、湖南、海南、重庆等9个省(市)发出了前往中高风险地区的提示,河北、山西、上海、江苏、湖南、重庆、陕西、甘肃、宁夏等9个省(市)发出了错峰返乡返岗的倡议,浙江、福建、广东采取发送"春节礼包"等形式鼓励人们留在本地过年,河北、福建、广东、重庆等4个省(市)提出鼓励灵活弹性休假。

全国31个直辖市或省会城市,除河北石家庄实行严格管控措施外,针对高风险地区人员,北京、天津、太原、呼和浩特、沈阳、长春、哈尔滨、上海、南京、杭州、合肥、福州、济南、郑州、武汉、长沙、广州、南宁、海口、成都、贵阳、昆明、西安、兰州、西宁、乌鲁木齐、银川等27个城市明确要求集中或居家隔离,南昌、重庆、拉萨3个城市需要做核酸检测。针对中风险地区人员,北京、上海、天津、太原、沈阳、长春、哈尔滨、南京、合肥、福州、济南、郑州、武汉、广州、南宁、成都、贵阳、西安、兰州、西宁、乌鲁木齐、银川等22个城市要求居家或集中隔离,呼和浩特、杭州、南昌、长沙、海口、重庆、昆明、拉萨等8个城市不要求隔离,但需要核酸检测证明。针对低风险地区人员,各市均不需要隔离,合肥、武汉、西安、兰州、拉萨等5个城市要求核酸检测证明;沈阳要求从重点区域外的地区来沈的人员携带7日内核酸检测阴性报告,贵阳要求所在城市有确诊病例的人员进行1次核酸检测,未出结果前不得自由流动。

2 总体客流情况

2.1 营业性客运量显著下降,"翘尾"现象明显

受疫情形势、防控政策以及就地过年政策的影响,春运40天,全国铁路、公路、水路、民航共发送旅客8.7亿人次,比2019年同期下降70.9%,比2020年同期下降40.8%。与往年客流运行趋势不同,今年春运客流运行"翘尾"现象明显,节后客流持续增加,节前节后客流量之比为31∶69,与2019年的37∶63相比,节后客流比重明显提高,客流高峰出现在2月28日(正月十七),达到3152.4万人次。2019、2020年和2021年春运客流走势如图2所示。

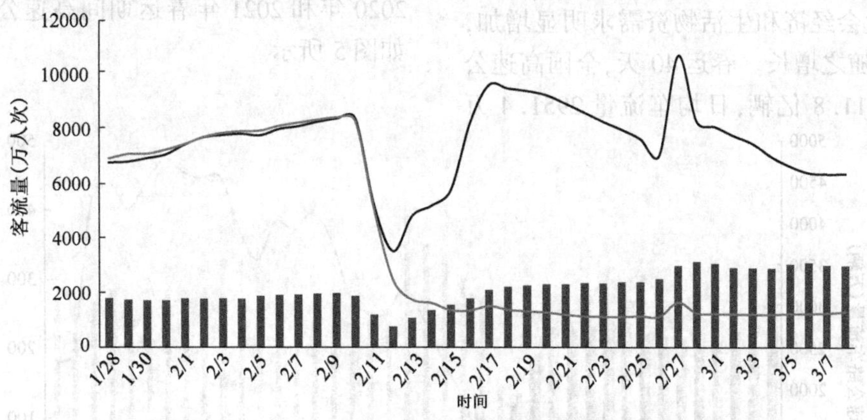

图2 2019—2021年春运客流走势图

2.2 公路客流下降幅度最大,铁路客流中短距离出行增长明显

近几年,受高铁成网运行、民航航班加密影响,公路中长距离客运量明显下降。疫情暴发以来,群众对出行安全性、私密性、便捷性要求更高,私家车出行需求较往年明显增加。同时,铁路不断提升运力供给能力,提高客运服务能力,推广应用电子客票、候补购票、互联网订餐等服务,试点浮动定价机制,以及外延旅游、购物、住宿、租车等相关服务,在保持中长距离出行竞争优势的基础上,也逐步成为旅客短途出行的重要选择。2021

年春运期间铁路旅客发送量占春运客流总量的25.0%，公路旅客发送量占比自2013年统计口径调整算起首次下降到70%以下(2014年占比最高，为90.3%)，水路、民航旅客发送量占比分别由2014年的1.2%和1.2%提升至1.8%和4.2%。其中，铁路客运量较2020年增长3.5%，各铁路局集团公司管内旅客发送量较去年增长13.4%，中短距离出行旅客比例明显增加；公路发送旅客量较2019年下降75.5%，较2020年下降50.2%，降幅明显；铁路、民航旅客发送量降幅相对较小，同比2019年分别下降46.5%和51.5%，同比2020年分别增长3.5%和下降8.4%。2021年春运期间各运输方式客运量及其占比如图3、图4所示。

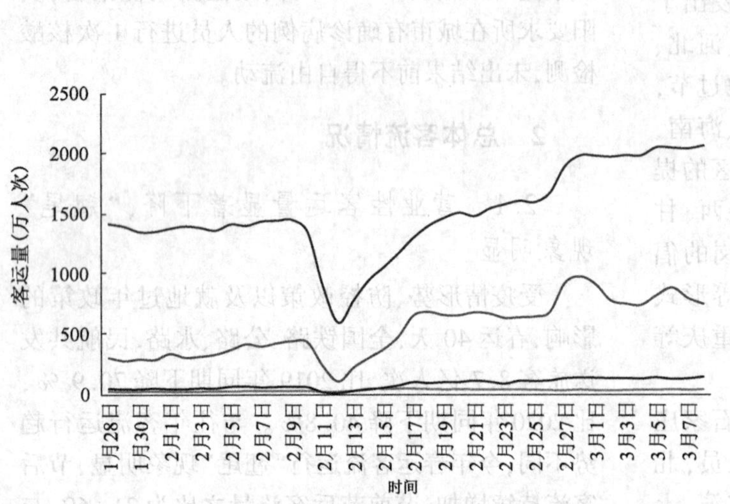

图3　2021年春运期间各运输方式客运量

图4　2021年春运期间各运输方式客运量占比

2.3　高速公路车流量快速增长，货运车辆增加明显

在就地过年政策的引导下，更多群众选择在工作地过年，社会经济和生活物资需求明显增加，货物运输需求随之增长。春运40天，全国高速公路累计车流量11.8亿辆，日均车流量2951.4万辆，较2019年上升0.5%，较2020年上升77.6%，其中节后高速公路日均车流量较2020年增长2倍。春运期间，全国高速公路货车流量1.9亿辆，较2019年上升28.1%，较2020年上升87.7%。2020年和2021年春运期间高速公路车流量变化如图5所示。

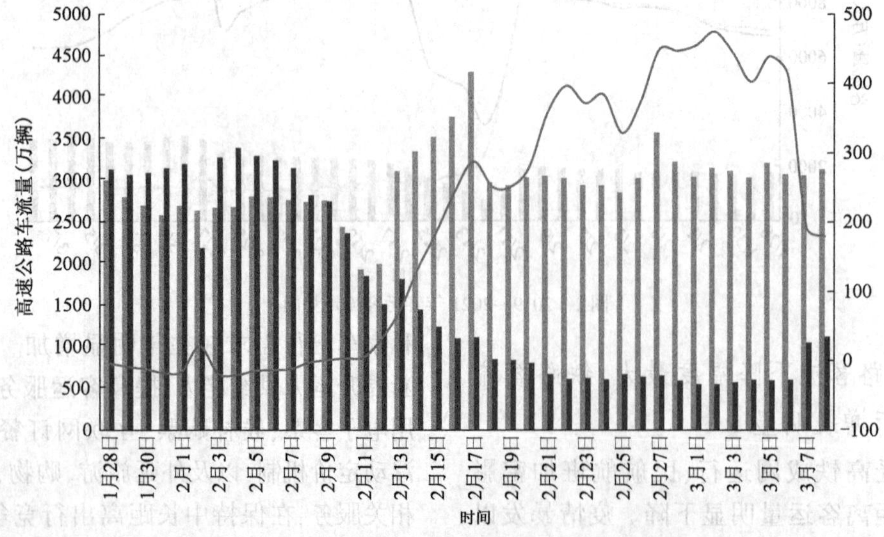

图5　2020年和2021年春运期间高速公路车流量变化图

3 人口迁徙情况

3.1 总体情况

百度迁徙数据显示,2021 年春运期间,全国日均迁徙规模指数为 621(含迁入迁出),同比 2019 年、2020 年分别下降 35.9%、上升 14.2%。迁徙高峰为 2 月 18 日(正月初七),迁徙规模指数为 931;迁徙低谷为 2 月 12 日(正月初一),迁徙规模指数为 351。2019—2021 年春运全国迁徙规模指数如图 6 所示。

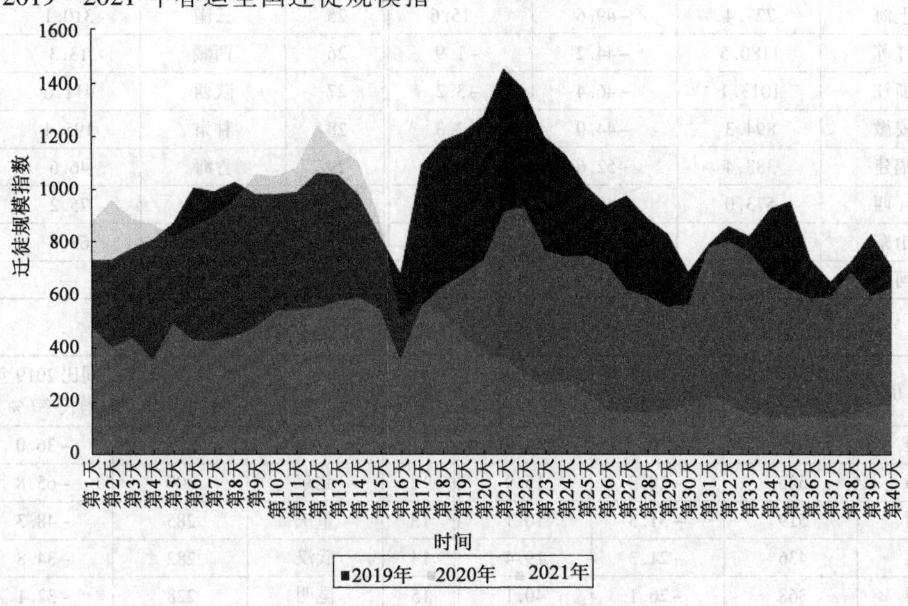

图 6 2019—2021 年春运全国迁徙规模指数

从春运 40 天全国迁徙规模指数的波动情况来看,2021 年春运总体走势比较平稳,与 2019 年及之前春运的走势基本一致,回归常态。节前、节后和春节期间的迁徙强度占比分别为 30.3%、69.7%、19.9%,2019 年同期比例分别为 36.6%、63.4%、19.9%。尤其是春运后期,客流迁徙呈回升态势,“翘尾”现象较为明显。春节假期后 18 天,迁徙强度占比为 49.9%,比 2019 年和 2020 年分别提高了 8.4%、34.3%。

3.2 省份迁徙情况

全国 31 个省(市)中,迁徙规模指数排名前 10 的是广东、江苏、浙江、河南、安徽、四川、河北、湖南、上海、山东,迁徙指数排名后 10 的是西藏、青海、新疆、宁夏、黑龙江、海南、吉林、甘肃、辽宁、内蒙古。

受疫情影响,各省(市)迁徙规模也呈现差异化态势,2021 年东北、京津冀地区客流下降幅度最为明显,黑龙江、北京、吉林、辽宁、河北的迁徙强度下降幅度排名前 5,天津排在第 8 位,同比 2019 年分别下降 70.2%、65.8%、63.4%、56.4%、52.9%、49.4%。这主要是因为年黑龙江、吉林、河北等地春运期间疫情形势较为紧张,执行了严格的疫情防控政策,导致客流出行大幅减少。西藏、青海、宁夏、甘肃等西部省份受疫情影响较小,本身出行基数较低,迁徙规模指数下降幅度最小,同比 2019 年分别下降 22.8%、37.8%、39.5%、40.3%。贵州、河南、云南、广西、湖南、海南、江西、山东、安徽、江苏等 10 个省份迁徙强度相对较小,下降幅度不超过 45%。各省(市)春运迁徙规模指数见表 2。

从节前迁入迁出情况来看,节前迁入大于迁出的输出型省(市)有广东、浙江、西藏、上海、北京、新疆、天津、江苏、青海、福建、海南、内蒙古、宁夏。其中,迁入迁出比最低的是广东和浙江,仅为 17.4%、32.1%;最高的是湖南、江西、广西,达到 327.1%、321.5%、304.1%。从迁入迁出量来看,广东、浙江、上海、北京、江苏净输出排名前 5。

3.3 城市迁徙情况

春运期间,全国城市平均迁徙规模指数为 66,迁徙规模指数排名前 20 的城市是广州、成都、深圳、东莞、郑州、上海、佛山、西安、长沙、苏州、杭州、北京、重庆、武汉、昆明、合肥、南京、惠州、南宁、贵阳,详见表 3、图 7。

2021 年各省(市)春运迁徙规模指数　　表 2

序号	省(市)	2019 年迁徙规模指数	同比 2019 年增长率(%)	同比 2020 年增长率(%)	序号	省(市)	2019 年迁徙规模指数	同比 2019 年增长率(%)
1	北京	877.1	-65.8	-40.4	17	湖北	617.1	-48.6
2	天津	313.0	-49.4	-11.2	18	湖南	721.7	-42.2
3	河北	885.2	-52.9	-16.6	19	广东	1584.6	-45.1
4	山西	300.6	-45.5	-3.6	20	广西	548.1	-42.2
5	内蒙古	253.5	-49.2	-8.5	21	海南	113.2	-43.5
6	辽宁	280.3	-56.4	-28.8	22	重庆	551.5	-48.3
7	吉林	182.4	-63.4	-39.5	23	四川	761.0	-45.1
8	黑龙江	195.1	-70.2	-50.1	24	贵州	437.6	-40.5
9	上海	727.4	-49.6	-15.6	25	云南	310.1	-42.1
10	江苏	1180.5	-44.2	-1.9	26	西藏	13.3	-22.8
11	浙江	1013.1	-46.4	-3.2	27	陕西	411.6	-46.6
12	安徽	894.3	-44.0	-2.3	28	甘肃	195.4	-40.3
13	福建	383.4	-52.6	-17.7	29	青海	46.6	-37.8
14	江西	573.0	-43.6	-3.0	30	宁夏	75.2	-39.5
15	山东	631.8	-43.8	-2.7	31	新疆	63.6	-45.0
16	河南	900.7	-41.4	7.3	—	—	—	—

2021 年春运迁徙规模指数排名前 20 的城市　　表 3

排名	城市	2021 年迁徙规模指数	同比 2019 年增长率(%)	同比 2020 年增长率(%)	排名	城市	2021 年迁徙规模指数	同比 2019 年增长率(%)	同比 2020 年增长率(%)
1	广州	602	-30.1	19.3	11	杭州	301	-36.0	21.8
2	成都	525	-28.3	15.9	12	北京	300	-65.8	-40.4
3	深圳	519	-31.3	10.1	13	重庆	285	-48.3	-4.9
4	东莞	436	-21.3	19.4	14	武汉	282	-34.8	50.9
5	郑州	368	-26.1	40.1	15	昆明	228	-32.1	17.6
6	上海	366	-49.6	-15.6	16	合肥	226	-29.3	23.9
7	佛山	355	-23.7	31.9	17	南京	218	-38.9	5.4
8	西安	351	-31.5	32.6	18	惠州	217	-20.8	31.6
9	长沙	325	-19.5	28.2	19	南宁	198	-27.9	21.7
10	苏州	306	-39.9	1.7	20	贵阳	196	-24.6	30.4

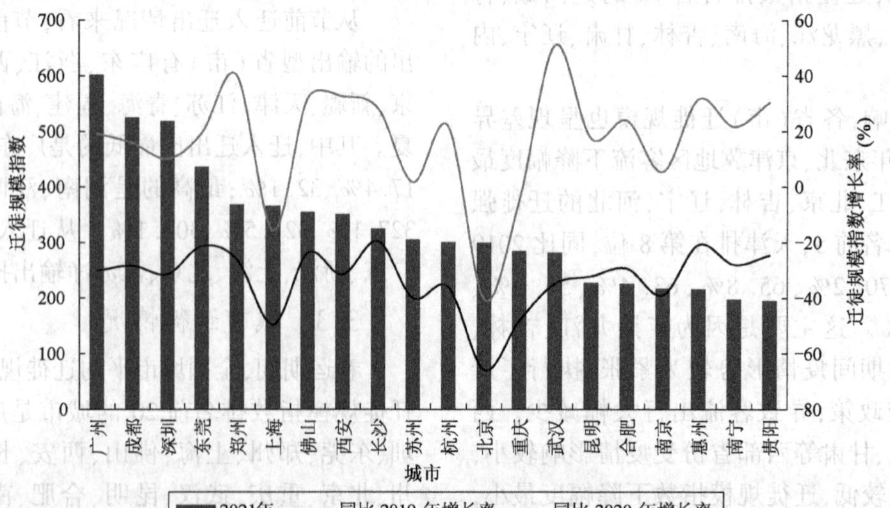

图 7　2021 年春运迁徙规模指数排名前 20 的城市

2021年春运迁徙规模指数同比2019年下降幅度最大的20个城市(地区)是伊春、绥化、大兴安岭地区、哈尔滨、黑河、鹤岗、牡丹江、齐齐哈尔、鸡西、大庆、通化、延边朝鲜族自治州、七台河、北京、佳木斯、克孜勒苏柯尔克孜自治州、呼伦贝尔、双鸭山、白山、石家庄,详见表4、图8。其中,排名前10的城市均为黑龙江省城市。

2021年春运迁徙规模指数同比2019年降幅前20的城市地区 表4

排名	城市(地区)	2021年迁徙规模指数	同比2019年增长率(%)	同比2020年增长率(%)	排名	城市(地区)	2021年迁徙规模指数	同比2019年增长率(%)	同比2020年增长率(%)
1	伊春	4	-74.4	-49.9	11	通化	11	-67.2	-43.6
2	绥化	26	-73.4	-48.6	12	延边朝鲜族自治州	8	-66.6	-42.7
3	大兴安岭地区	2	-71.3	-46.0	13	七台河	4	-66.2	-33.6
4	哈尔滨	61	-71.3	-46.6	14	北京	300	-65.8	-40.4
5	黑河	6	-70.0	-42.2	15	佳木斯	14	-65.3	-33.3
6	鹤岗	4	-68.9	-41.8	16	克孜勒苏柯尔克孜自治州	2	-65.3	-45.0
7	牡丹江	9	-68.8	-45.9	17	呼伦贝尔	10	-65.1	-33.0
8	齐齐哈尔	21	-68.8	-43.0	18	双鸭山	7	-64.8	-32.2
9	鸡西	6	-68.4	-41.6	19	白山	6	-64.0	-37.1
10	大庆	21	-67.3	-41.5	20	石家庄	82	-62.9	-33.6

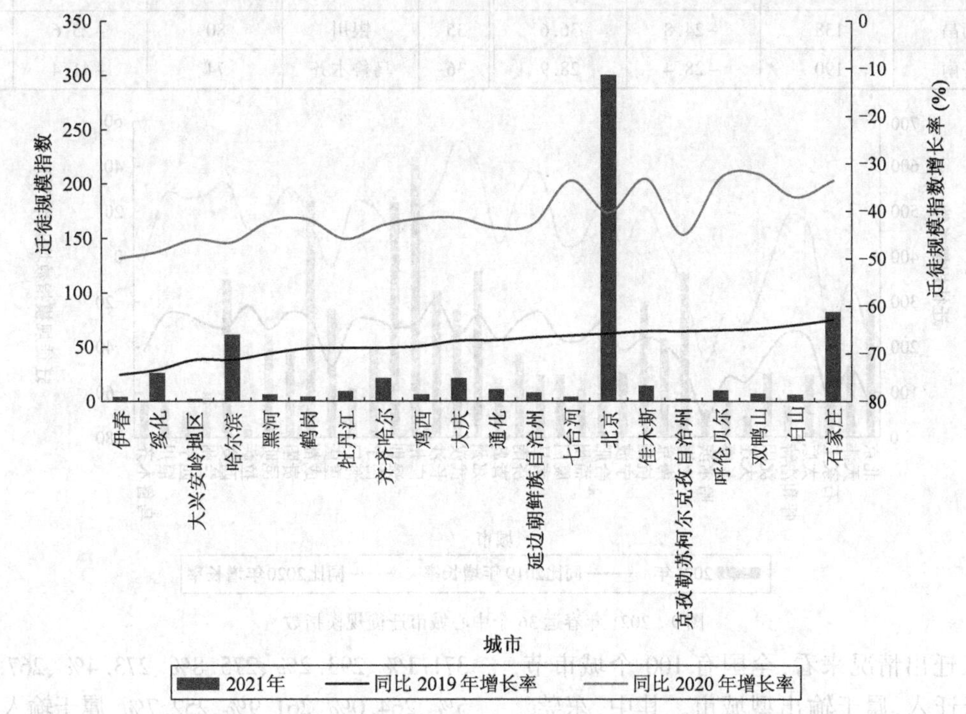

图8 2021年春运迁徙规模指数同比2019年降幅前20的城市

全国36个中心城市平均迁徙强度为204,比全国其他城市平均高出209%。广州、成都、深圳、郑州、上海、西安、长沙、杭州、北京、重庆迁徙规模指数排名前10。与2019年同期相比,长沙、拉萨、贵阳、南昌、西宁、银川、郑州、南宁、成都、济南等10个城市迁徙规模指数降幅相对较小。与2020年同期相比,武汉、郑州、南昌、西安、贵阳、济南、长沙、兰州、银川、西宁、合肥、海口、杭州、南宁、广州、呼和浩特、昆明、成都、太原、拉萨、深圳、福州、厦门、青岛、南京、宁波等26个城市实现了迁徙规模指数正增长,哈尔滨、北京、石家庄、大连、长春、上海、天津、沈阳、重庆、乌鲁木齐等 10 个城市迁徙规模指数下降。2021 年春运 36 个中心城市迁徙规模指数见表 5、图 9。

2021 年春运 36 个中心城市迁徙规模指数　　表 5

序号	城　市	2021 年迁徙规模指数	同比 2019 年增长率(%)	同比 2020 年增长率(%)	序号	城　市	2021 年迁徙规模指数	同比 2019 年增长率(%)	同比 2020 年增长率(%)
1	北京	300	-65.8	-40.4	19	青岛	132	-36.9	6.0
2	天津	158	-49.4	-11.2	20	郑州	368	-26.1	40.1
3	石家庄	82	-62.9	-33.6	21	武汉	282	-34.8	50.9
4	太原	138	-36.5	13.0	22	长沙	325	-19.5	28.2
5	呼和浩特	69	-33.5	18.3	23	广州	602	-30.1	19.3
6	沈阳	141	-43.0	-6.6	24	深圳	519	-31.3	10.1
7	大连	48	-55.2	-29.5	25	南宁	198	-27.9	21.7
8	长春	86	-53.6	-24.2	26	海口	108	-29.0	23.3
9	哈尔滨	61	-71.3	-46.6	27	重庆	285	-48.3	-4.9
10	上海	366	-49.6	-15.6	28	成都	525	-28.3	15.9
11	南京	218	-38.9	5.4	29	贵阳	196	-24.6	30.4
12	杭州	301	-36.0	21.8	30	昆明	228	-32.1	17.6
13	宁波	143	-41.5	4.8	31	拉萨	19	-21.6	12.3
14	合肥	226	-29.3	23.9	32	西安	351	-31.5	32.6
15	福州	108	-37.0	6.6	33	兰州	100	-29.9	27.4
16	厦门	139	-36.6	6.4	34	西宁	59	-25.5	25.9
17	南昌	138	-24.8	36.6	35	银川	80	-25.6	27.3
18	济南	190	-28.4	28.9	36	乌鲁木齐	74	-41.4	-1.1

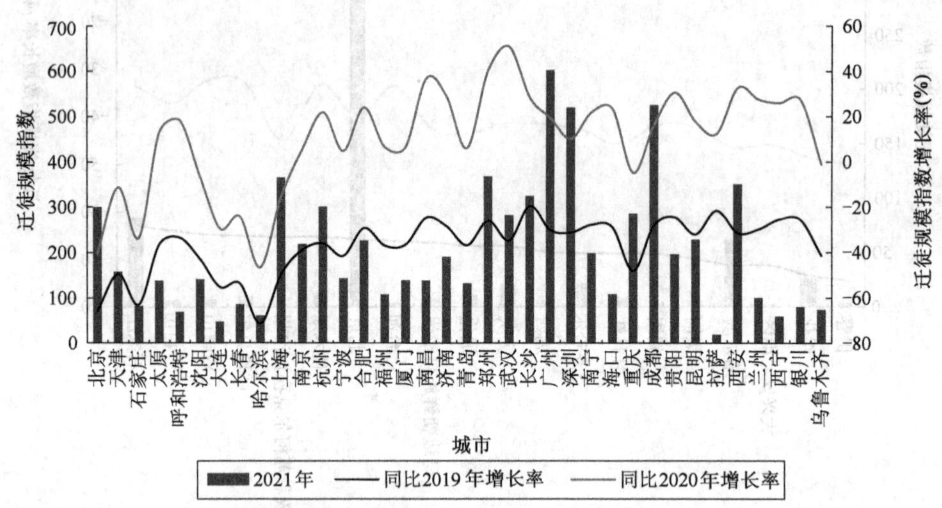

图 9　2021 年春运 36 个中心城市迁徙规模指数

从迁入迁出情况来看,全国有 100 个城市节前迁出大于迁入,属于输出型城市。其中,东莞、深圳、宁波、厦门、上海、北京、广州、中山、佛山、成都迁出比例最高,迁入迁出比分别为 35.0%、36.3%、40.7%、41.4%、41.4%、43.5%、45.6%、47.4%、47.4%、48.9%,属于输出型城市;梅州、茂名、湛江、贵港、玉林、邵阳、龙岩、云浮、汕尾、吉安迁入比例最高,迁入迁出比分别为 407.8%、371.1%、293.2%、275.8%、273.4%、267.7%、264.5%、264.0%、261.9%、252.7%,属于输入型城市。

4　铁路客流情况

4.1　时间波动

从时间上看,2021 年春运节前铁路发送旅客量整体明显小于节后,呈现出不同于往年的显著特征,节前、春节假期和节后铁路旅客发送量比例为22.9∶11.0∶66.0,这与2021年春节前我国在全国范围内鼓励和实施“就地过年”的疫情防控措施有关。2021年春运期间铁路旅客发送量时间分布如图10所示。

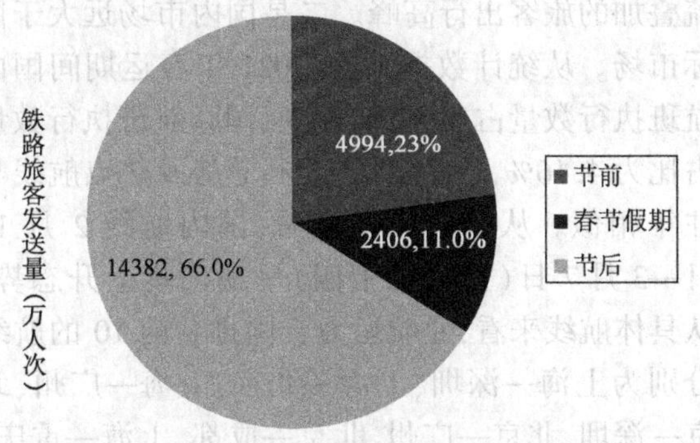

图10 2021年春运期间铁路旅客发送量时间分布

4.2 空间分布

从空间上看,全国铁路到达旅客量排名前3的区域为华东、华南和华中,说明这三个区域仍然是我国劳动人口输入量较大、经济活动较为活跃的区域。华北地区受河北疫情、北京“两会”召开等因素的影响,2021年春运期间到达旅客量较少。2021年春运期间全国铁路各区域到达旅客量如图11所示。

2021年春运期间全国发送和到达旅客量最大的10个车站为广州南、深圳北、成都东、上海虹桥、杭州东、长沙南、重庆北、郑州东、西安北、南京南。其中,广州南站发送和到达旅客量均为全国第一,且明显高于其他铁路车站。各大铁路车站节后旅客到达量整体大于节前,这与其所在城市是务工就业集中地的现实相吻合。除广州南和深圳北外,其他铁路车站节前旅客发送量整体小于节后,与全国铁路总体规律相一致。2021年春运期间十大铁路车站日均客流量如图12所示。

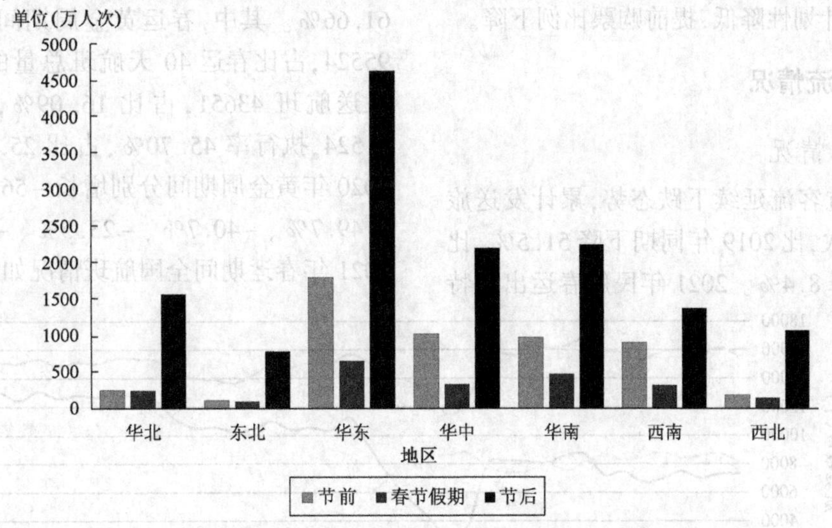

图11 2021年春运期间全国铁路各区域到达旅客量

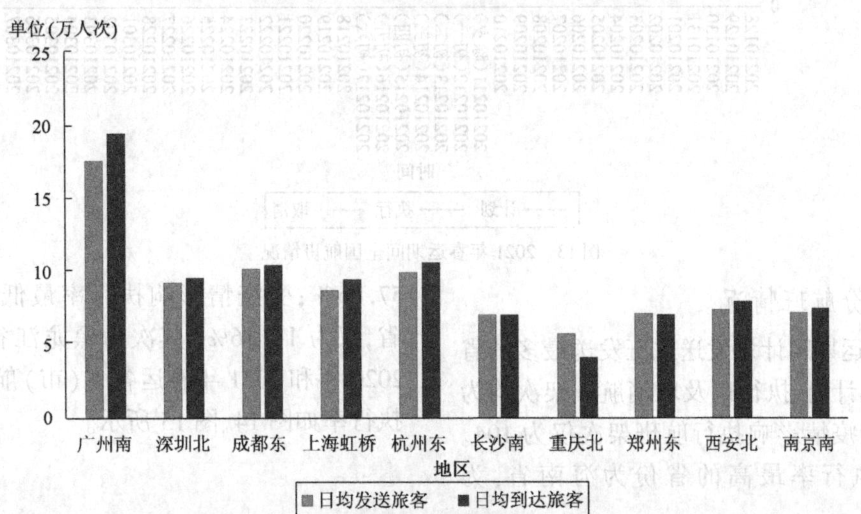

图12 2021年春运期间十大铁路车站日均客流量

5　公路客流情况

从全国 11 个省份 223 个道路客运站客流情况来看,受多地春运期间实行查验核酸检测证明等防控措施的影响,部分旅客选择在春运开始之前返程,1 月 27 日道路旅客发送量达到小高峰,春运开始后迅速回落。

2021 年春运期间公路旅客发送量较 2019 年下降 47.6%,较 2020 年增长 32.3%;网上购票比例较低,但占比逐步提高,分别较 2019 年和 2020 年提高了 5% 和 3%;当天购票比例明显高于往年,达到 81.6%。从出行起讫点来看,2021 年春运跨省出行客流比例仅占总出行客流的 12%,较 2019 年降低 8%,较 2020 年提高 3%。公路旅客与铁路旅客表现出类似出行习惯,即受疫情形势和防控政策影响,出行半径缩短,更多为省内中短途出行,且出行计划性降低,提前购票比例下降。

6　民航客流情况

6.1　总体情况

2021 年民航客流延续下跌态势,累计发送旅客 3539.8 万人次,比 2019 年同期下降 51.5%,比 2020 年同期下降 8.4%。2021 年民航春运出行特征大致表现在以下几点:一是节前各类旅客未出现出行叠加,节前客流相对平稳,客流高峰在节后较为突出。与 2020 年春运相比,2021 年春运较去年错后 32 天,春运后期迎来务工流、学生流、探亲流叠加的旅客出行高峰。二是国内市场远大于国际市场。从统计数据来看,2021 年春运期间国内航班执行数量占比为 95.84%,国际航班执行数量占比为 4.16%。三是国内出行趋势及热点航线与往年相似。从预定数据来看,国内航线 2 月 12 日—3 月 7 日(正月二十四)呈现稳步上升态势;从具体航线来看,通航运力全国排名前 10 的航线分别为上海—深圳、上海—北京、上海—广州、北京—深圳、北京—广州、北京—成都、上海—重庆、上海—成都、广州—杭州、广州—成都。

2021 年春运期间航班计划 585051 班次[1],执行 360751 班次,取消 221234 班次,执行率 61.66%。其中,春运黄金周期间,计划发送航班 95524,占比春运 40 天航班总量的 19.94%;执行发送航班 43651,占比 16.09%,取消发送航班 51524,执行率 45.70%,占比 25.06%,执行率较 2020 年黄金周期间分别增长 -56.2%、-58.2%、-49.7%、-40.7%、-23.5%、-5.0%、12.0%。2021 年春运期间全国航班情况如图 13 所示。

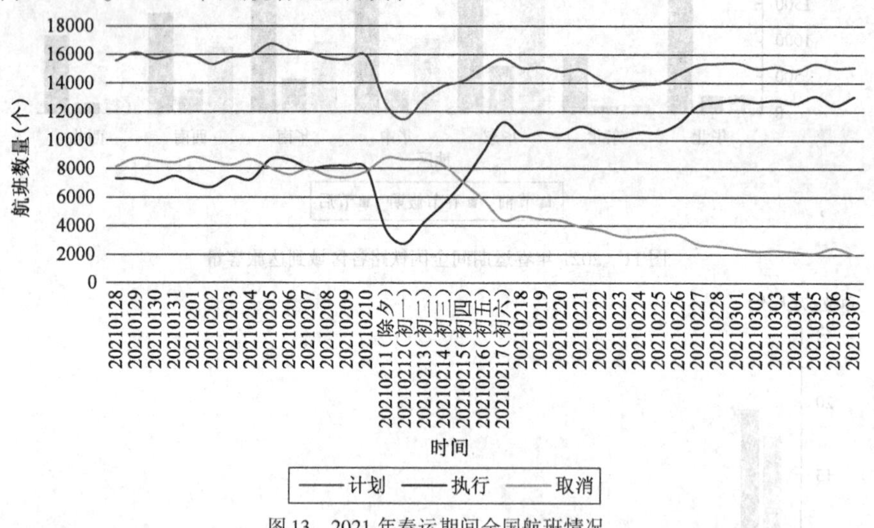

图 13　2021 年春运期间全国航班情况

6.2　省份航班情况

2021 年春运期间计划发送航班发送最多的省份为广东省,其计划、执行以及取消航班架次均为最高,河北省受疫情影响执行航班架次仅为 104。2021 年航班执行率最高的省份为海南省,为 57.66%;受疫情影响执行率最低的省份为河北省,仅为 11.16%,其次为黑龙江省,为 31.13%。2020 年和 2021 年春运各省(市)航班运营情况及执行率如图 14、图 15 所示。

[1] 截至 2021 年 3 月 7 日,春运第 39 天,下同。

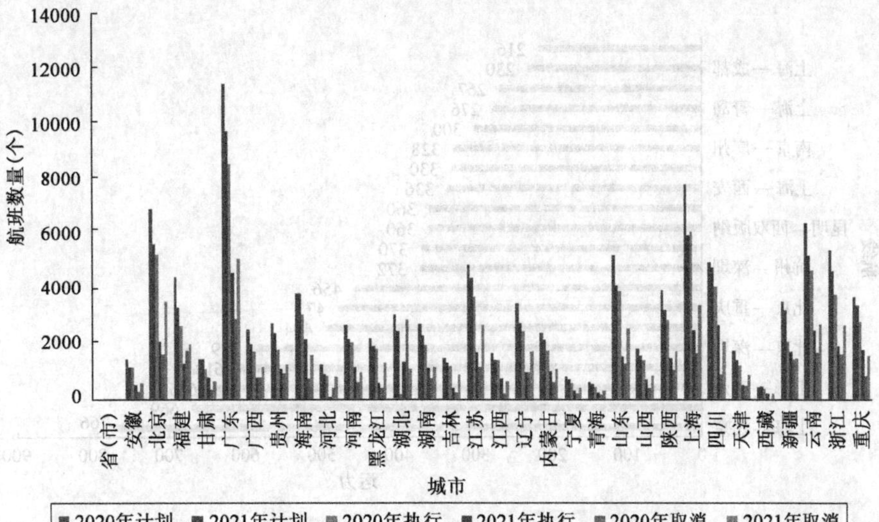

图 14　2020 年和 2021 年春运各省(市)航班运营情况

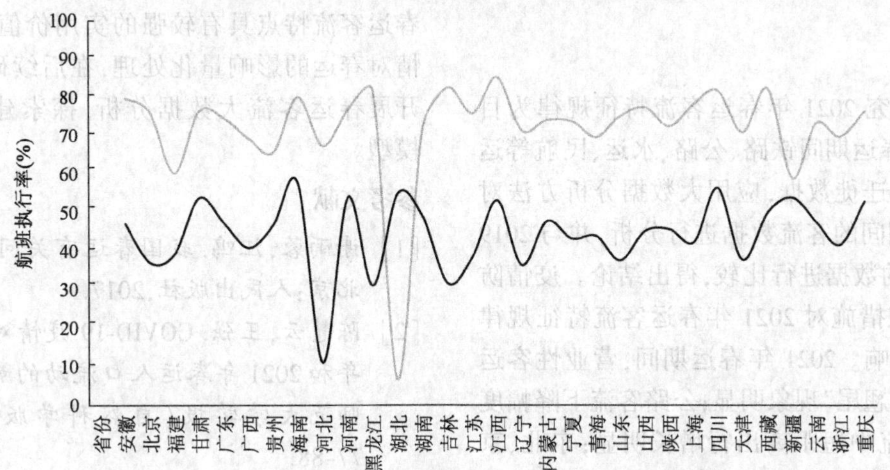

图 15　2020 年和 2021 年春运各省(市)航班执行率

6.3　航线情况

春节假期期间,全国通航运力最为活跃的 10 条航线以北上广深为主,分别为上海—北京、上海—深圳、上海—广州、北京—广州、北京—深圳、北京—杭州、北京—重庆、广州—杭州、杭州—深圳、北京—西安运力情况如图 16、图 17 所示。

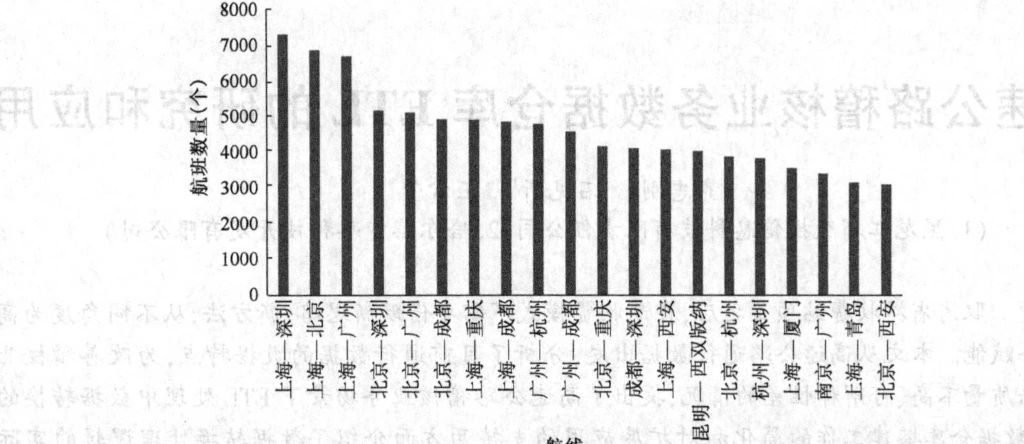

图 16　2021 年春运期间全国主要航线通航运力情况

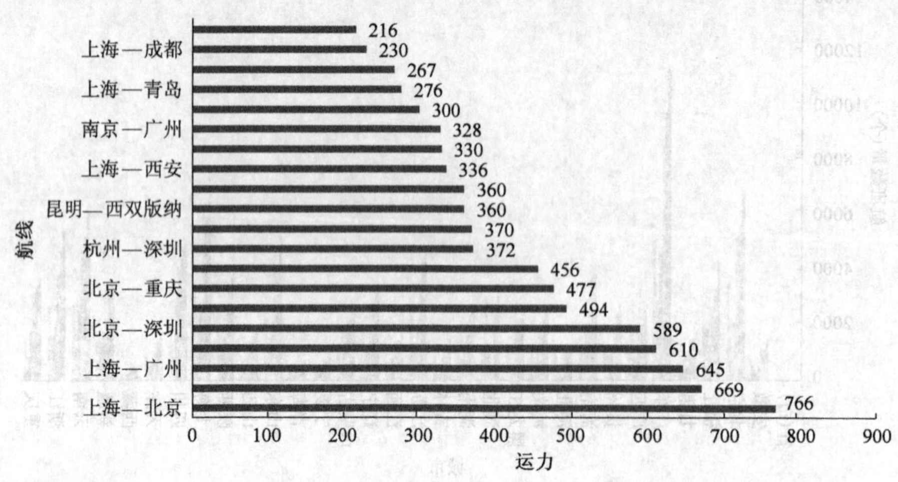

图17　2021年春节假期全国主要航线通航运力情况

7　结语

本文以研究2021年春运客流特征规律为目的,通过收集春运期间铁路、公路、水运、民航等运营数据和人口迁徙数据,应用大数据分析方法对2021年春运期间的客流数据进行分析,并与2019年和2020年的数据进行比较,得出结论。疫情防控形势和防控措施对2021年春运客流特征规律产生了显著影响。2021年春运期间,营业性客运量显著下降,"翘尾"现象明显;公路客流下降幅度最大;铁路客流中短距离出行增长明显;东北、京津冀地区迁徙规模指数下降幅度明显;中心城市迁徙潮汐特征明显;公路旅客出行半径缩短,更多为省内中短途出行,且出行计划性降低,提前购票比例下降;城市内出行需求旺盛,出行强度明显增长。本文对于交通运输管理部门和企业科学研判春运客流特点具有较强的实用价值,但未能将疫情对春运的影响量化处理,在后续研究中将继续开展春运客流大数据分析,探索建立疫情影响模型。

参考文献

[1] 谢雨蓉,汪鸣.我国春运有关问题研究[M].北京:人民出版社,2017.

[2] 陈慧云,王强.COVID-19疫情对福建省2020年和2021年春运人口流动的影响[J].福建师范大学学报(自然科学版),2021(5):77-88.

[3] 刘海洋,王录仓.腾讯迁徙数据下的春运中国人口流动时空格局分析[A].活力城乡 美好人居——2019中国城市规划年会论文集(16区域规划与城市经济)[C].2019.

高速公路稽核业务数据仓库ETL的研究和应用

齐志刚[1]　石见昕[1]　王雪莹*[2]

(1.黑龙江省交投信息科技有限责任公司;2.哈尔滨智路科技开发有限公司)

摘　要　取消省界收费站项目之后,在新收费模式下需要借助新思路、新方法,从不同角度为高速公路稽核业务赋能。本文从高速公路通行数据出发,分析了目前通行数据的数据特点,为改善稽核业务数据模型数据质量不高、可解释性差的情况,提出了高速公路稽核业务场景下ETL处理中数据转换的处理逻辑,从对数据仓库搭建工作的简化和对扩展应用的支持两方面介绍了数据转换处理逻辑的实际应用价值。

关键词 高速公路 稽核 数据仓库 ETL 数据转换

0 引言

撤站项目之后,收费模式的变化在提高车辆通行效率的同时,也加大了车辆逃费的可能性和对逃费车辆的打击难度,传统人工稽核已无法承载挽回通行费流失和威慑逃费行为的职责,稽核业务更加依赖对通行数据的分析和应用,更需要通过信息化手段提高从业人员的数据分析和应用技能,提高稽核业务工作开展的质量和效率,从而减少通行费收益的流失[1-2]。

新形势下的稽核业务引入了 AI(人工智能)、数据挖掘、数据仓库等多种前沿技术手段[3-4],但在实际工作过程中,稽核系统的模型结果往往存在着数据质量不高、可解释性差的情况,造成稽核系统与业务人员的实际工作脱节、模型逻辑对业务人员不友好等现实问题,其根本原因是忽视了高速公路收费系统的数据特点和数据质量。

本文基于黑龙江省稽核管理系统中分析模块的数据仓库架构,提出适用于稽核业务场景的数据转换逻辑,对数据进行降噪降维,提高数据仓库数据质量,从而提高模型结果的准确性、可信性和可解释性。

1 高速公路稽核业务数据仓库

1.1 高速公路通行数据特点

在目前的收费模式下,高速公路的通行业务数据根据采集设备的不同,可以分为由天线产生的交易数据、由车牌识别设备产生的牌识数据、由车型识别设备产生的车型识别数据,采集设备种类多样、产生场景丰富,对其数据特点总结如下:

(1)单对象、高实时。通行业务数据所描述的是单台通行车辆的单次通行行为,但由于高速公路业务侧重于保障通行,车辆的单次通行并不会只产生一条记录,存在一对多的关系,车辆的通行记录会实时传输至上级节点进行处理和存储。

(2)多场景、高维度。入口数据、途径门架数据和出口数据分别产生于收费站入口、途径门架、收费站出口,在数据库中存储在不同的数据表中,代表了车辆在不同场景下的通行行为。通行数据中包含车辆信息、通行节点信息、通行介质信息、操作人员信息和交易状态信息等上百个字段,从多个维度来描述单次通行行为。

(3)弱关联、低质量。ETC 门架的牌识数据和交易数据由两套独立的数据采集设备产生,数据本身没有可以关联的直接条件,只能依靠后期根据车辆信息、通行节点信息和通行时间进行关联。对于收费站入出口场景下产生的数据,包含闯关、倒车等地感线圈识别到的特殊通行行为和车队、车辆引出等人工判断的特殊通行行为数据,对于稽核业务而言,数据质量低、噪声大,需要进行严格且口径一致的数据清洗。

1.2 高速公路稽核业务数据仓库

数据仓库的最初定位是为企业提供分析性报告和决策支持,在架构上可以概括为源数据经过 ETL 处理集中到数据仓库,如图 1 所示。其中 ETL [抽取(Extract)、转换(Transform)、装载(Load)]的工作量约占 70% ~80%,是数据仓库的基石[5]。ETL 处理是从数据源抽取所需数据,经过清洗和转换,按照预先定义好的模型将数据加载到数据仓库中,例如对数据进行名称、数据类型、编码、位数的统一,消除重复数据、处理空值以及有限性检查等,以保证装载到数据仓库中的数据质量[6]。

在 ETL 处理中,主要由数据转换过程进行数据处理,传统 ETL 处理的数据转换过程在处理高速公路通行数据特点时难以达到数据仓库的质量要求,例如在数据间没有建立关联、在业务而非数据层面仍存在重复等。通过将数据转换过程拆分为数据清洗、数据关联、特征判断三个子过程,对高速公路稽核业务的数据仓库架构进行完善,如图 2 所示,从根源改善稽核系统数据质量不高、可解释性差的现状。

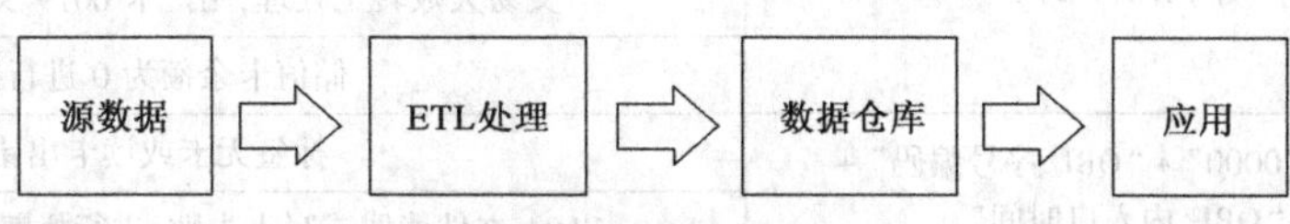

图 1 数据仓库架构

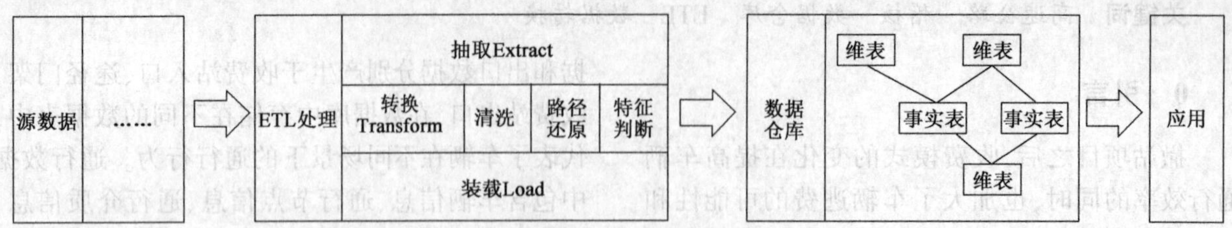

图2　稽核业务场景下的数据仓库架构

2　ETL 处理中的数据转换逻辑

本章根据高速公路通行数据特点，对高速公路稽核业务下 ETL 处理中数据转换过程的处理逻辑进行举例介绍。

2.1　数据清洗

2.1.1　入出口数据清洗

(1)倒车数据清洗。

车辆在经过车道时，先后压过第一、第二个线圈产生一条交易数据，先后压过第二、第一个线圈产生一条倒车数据，当同一台车在同一车道先后产生交易数据和倒车数据时，在业务场景上判断为该辆车没有经过收费站，在入口上表现为未驶入高速公路，在出口上表现为未驶离高速公路，需要清洗掉此类数据。

(2)重复数据清洗。

为防止车辆在车道停留时间长、导致产生重复交易数据，车道软件一般会设置若干分钟之内相同车道内的相同车辆不允许重复交易，但是仍会有不同车道间的临道干扰，在同一场景下的重复数据通常表现为产生收费站相同、车牌号及颜色相同、业务时间间隔较近，需要将此类数据清洗掉，避免无效的“有入无出”或“有出无入”的模型结果产生。

(3)交易数据清洗。

高速公路的外部稽核业务关注车辆是否合法驶入高速公路，及驶离高速公路时是否收取相应通行费，对车辆在收费站场景产生的非交易类数据不做关注，因此需要将入出口数据区分为交易类数据和非交易类数据，非交易类数据主要包含特殊通行行为数据。

2.1.2　门架数据清洗

(1)门架交易数据清洗。

根据门架流水中的特情字段(SPECIALTYPE)，将字段值包含 154、186(反向干扰)、193(前排已经处理，查询共享后拒绝处理)的流水剔除，避免影响数据关联的准确度。

(2)门架牌识数据清洗。

对于“2 +1”车道类型的高速公路，黑龙江的 ETC 门架配备 8 套车牌识别设备，包括车头抓拍设备 5 套和车尾抓拍设备 3 套，车辆通行门架时会产生车头 + 车尾两条牌识流水和两张抓拍图片，在稽核业务中，需要将车辆通过同一门架节点产生的两条牌识流水整合成一条，作为该辆车通行过当前节点门架的依据。

(3)整合门架交易数据和牌识数据。

为了门架交易数据和车牌识别数据可以进行便捷的关联分析，程序需要为符合匹配条件的牌识数据赋值上对应的 PASSID 值，作为其和交易数据的绑定关系记录。

2.2　通行数据关联

2.2.1　根据 PASSID 关联通行数据

PASSID 在车辆通行过车道及门架时由程序生成，生成规则见表 1，通过 PASSID 可以将车辆通行高速公路的一趟完整通行路径的收费数据进行关联。

PASSID 生成规则　　表 1

<table>
<tr><td rowspan="6">ETC</td><td rowspan="4">1</td><td rowspan="4">“01” + “卡网络编号” + “用户卡编号” + “卡内入口时间”</td><td>正常交易的 ETC 车辆</td></tr>
<tr><td>标签无卡或读卡出错后又重新交易成功</td></tr>
<tr><td>交易失败转工处理，用户卡 0019 文件中已写入本站</td></tr>
<tr><td>储值卡余额为 0 进行拦截</td></tr>
<tr><td rowspan="2">2</td><td rowspan="2">“00” + “0000” + “OBU 序号编码” + “OBU 内入口时间”</td><td>标签无卡或读卡出错的</td></tr>
<tr><td>EF04 文件读取或写入失败，进行拦截转人工发放 CPC 卡</td></tr>
<tr><td>CPC</td><td>3</td><td>“02” + “0000” + “CPC 卡编码” + “入口时间”</td><td>CPC 卡交易</td></tr>
</table>

2.2.2 通过车牌号关联通行数据

对于无法用PASSID进行关联的情况,应用车牌号、入口时间、入口站HEX码等信息进行数据关联,该情况下主要包含出口计费方式为在线计费和最小费额两种情况,如图3所示。

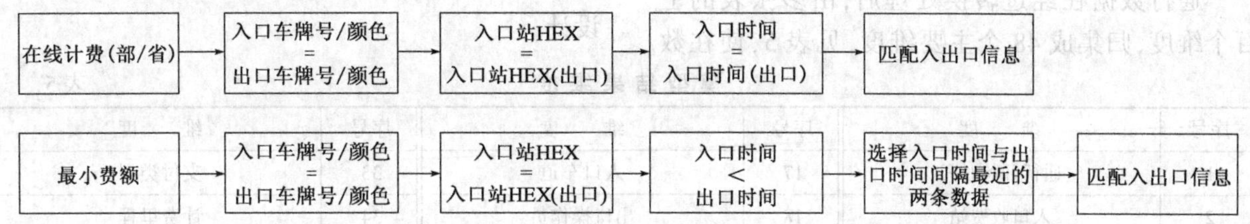

图3 通过车牌号进行路径还原

2.2.3 其他情况

对于出省车辆但是省界门架没有采集到交易数据的情况,通过入口数据与出省牌识数据进行数据关联,关联依据为无法通过上述方式关联的入口数据,且该车辆存在入口时间后24h内的出省门架牌识数据。

2.3 判断通行特征

2.3.1 特情特征

特情特征包括收费业务中门架节点和入出口收费站节点数据中由程序判断生成的特情维度,代表了数据所属的特情类别,见表2。特情是对车辆经过节点时,对于本次交易情况的记录。特情数据有上百种,需要对于不同节点的特情数据提取出关键信息形成通行路径的特情特征,见表3。

门架特情类型 表2

特情类型	特情取值
标签拆卸	101
标签无卡	102
标签锁定	103
标签未到启用日期	104
……	……

特情特征举例 表3

特情类型	数据源
出口坏卡	出口流水
出口无卡	出口流水
出口按照最短路径收费	出口流水
……	……

2.3.2 业务特征

业务特征从真实业务场景出发,通过构建符合稽核需求的业务特征标签对数据进行分类和降维,业务特征的判断逻辑通常包含多个维度,是对一趟通行路径的客观描述,可以实现对通行数据的快速定位,增强单趟通行路径的可解释性,见表4。

业务特征举例 表4

特情类型	数据源
入口11min内有相同车辆的重复数据	入口流水
入口交易车牌号 入口牌识车牌号(剔除未识别成功的车牌号)	入口流水
出口交易车牌号 出口牌识车牌号(剔除未识别成功的车牌号)	出口流水
出口识别车牌号 入口识别车牌号(剔除未识别成功的车牌号)	入/出口流水
完整的通行路径中包含省界门架通行记录	入/出口/门架流水
出口/省车型<入口/省轴数对应车型	入/出口/门架流水
超时低速	入/出口流水
无对应出口,但是该车牌号入口时间一天内有出省门架牌识	入/出口/门架流水
根据PASSID对应的出口数据为非有效交易数据	入/出口流水
……	……

3　ETL 处理结果的应用

3.1　稽核业务数据仓库

通行数据在经过转换处理后,由多张表的上百个维度,归集成 48 个主要维度,见表 5,使在数据装载进数据仓库前已经具备业务层面的准确性和一致性,将数据处理逻辑前置到 ETL 过程中,在此基础上建设数据仓库只需要进行简单的映射,可以简化逃费模型的判断逻辑和数据仓库的维度设计。

模型结果维度　　表 5

序号	维　度	序号	维　度	序号	维　度
1	通行开始时间	17	入口车道	33	支付类型
2	入口收费站	18	出口操作员	34	计费里程
3	入口车道	19	出口车牌	35	通行时长
4	入口操作员	20	出口识别车牌	36	是否跨省
5	入口车牌	21	出口通行介质	37	通过交易门架数量
6	入口识别车牌	22	出口卡类型	38	首个交易门架
7	入口通行介质	23	出口车型	39	首个通过门架时间
8	入口卡类型	24	出口车种	40	末个交易门架
9	入口车型	25	出口的入口轴数	41	末个通过门架时间
10	入口车种	26	出口 CPC_ID	42	通过牌识门架数量
11	入口轴数	27	出口 OBU_ID	43	首个牌识门架
12	入口 CPC_ID	28	出口 ETC_ID	44	首个通过牌识门架时间
13	入口 OBU_ID	29	计费方式	45	末个牌识门架
14	入口 ETC_ID	30	应收金额	46	末个通过牌识门架时间
15	通行结束时间	31	优惠金额	47	特征类型
16	出口收费站	32	实付金额	48	匹配类型

以倒换通行介质嫌疑车辆为例,此类逃费方式可以通过多种判断逻辑实现,例如入口交易短时间内多次交易、以图搜车、出口超时车辆分析等,均可得到倒换通行介质的嫌疑车辆[7-8],但每类判断逻辑之间无关联,且对嫌疑数据需要进行进一步的信息补充,本文应用 ETL 的结果作为数据仓库中的预设维度,来明确逃费模型的边界。对于模型结果可以清晰地看出嫌疑车辆在完整通行路径语境下的所有信息,以及各种判断逻辑之间是否存在交叉,如图 4 所示。

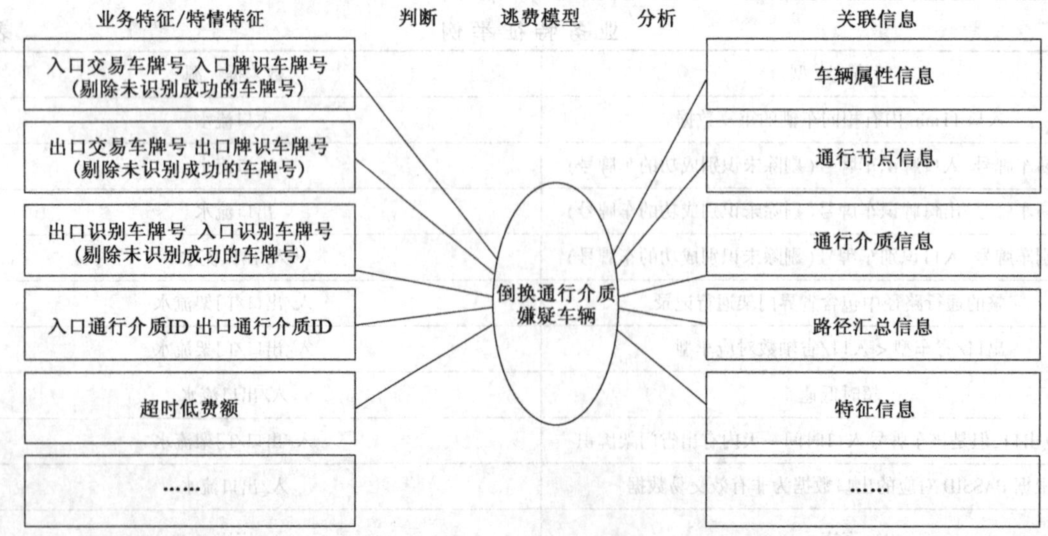

图 4　倒换通行介质嫌疑车辆模型逻辑

3.2 稽核业务数据仓库的展示

应用BI工具作为数据仓库的展示层嵌入到稽核系统中,让业务人员可以全程使用拖、拉、拽操作,无须编写SQL语句,来实现数据的分析和探索,同时业务人员可以借助BI工具内置的多种报表、图表样式制作报表,实现对数据更大程度的利用[9]。另外,通过对已定义特征的提前汇总,减小结果数量,避免直接从海量的原始数据中执行计算,可以在不用增加硬件资源的前提下,给业务人员提供大数据量分析的体验。

3.3 ETL处理结果的扩展应用

3.3.1 对接以图搜图模块

以图搜图功能在高速公路业务上的应用是独立在结构化数据之外的功能模块,而且很多情况下需要配合车型识别设备的车侧图片来完成图像特征结构化和搜索。将经过关联的路径各节点数据所对应的图片进行融合后,图片作为通行路径的新增通行特征,以图搜图的结果不仅是零散的节点图像信息,更加可以关联出其对应的路径信息。

3.3.2 对接数据挖掘工具

对接数据挖掘工具,例如Oracle的ODM,可以更充分地利用稽核模型结果包含的丰富维度,对于长时间跨度下的模型结果,应用聚类、逻辑回归、关联规则挖掘等数据挖掘算法,来实现对逃费行为规律判断的进一步探索。

4 结语

本次研究通过对高速公路稽核业务场景下ETL处理中数据转换的处理逻辑进行改进,提高了模型结果的准确性、可信性和可解释性。通过改进后的ETL处理逻辑,实现了对通行数据的清洗和降维,并定义可扩展的特征类型和匹配类型等信息,用贴合实际业务的48个维度来描述一次通行行为,在简化后期数据仓库的构建工作的同时,本次研究结果在应用场景上具备可扩展性,可作为对稽核业务信息化手段的进一步探索的数据基础。

参考文献

[1] 欧毕华,廖勇.基于新形势下高速公路收费业务管理创新研究[J].管理,2021,S1,015:72-76.

[2] 刘睿健.消界去站论"自由"——高速公路取消省界收费站背景下自由流收费探讨[J].中国交通信息化,2019,04,002:29-35.

[3] 刘春成,吴博,倪悝,等.基于AI的收费稽核研究与实践[J].中国交通信息化,2021,S1,034:135-138.

[4] 张西亚.大数据时代的"云上稽核"——江苏高速公路云稽核探索与实践[J].中国公路,2020,(18):30-32.

[5] Ralph K.数据仓库生命周期工具箱[M].清华大学出版社,2003.

[6] 张宁,贾自艳,史忠植.数据仓库中ETL技术的研究[J].计算机工程与应用.2002,24,071.

[7] 邱伟明.数据挖掘技术在打击倒卖OBU逃费中的应用浅析[J].中国交通信息化,2020,01,007:40-41+46.

[8] 李嘉.基于数据的高速公路智慧型稽核系统的研究与实现[D].合肥:电子科技大学,2015.

[9] 项丽燕.基于高速公路收费数据的交通状态分类与可视化分析方法[D].南京:南京师范大学,2019.

基于LSTM的短时交通速度预测

彭 昆 肖代全* 徐学才

(华中科技大学土木与水利工程学院)

摘 要 交通预测是智能交通中的重要研究方向,特别是在智能网联环境下,在误差允许范围内实时对交通速度进行预测,通过交通速度来实时评价交通状况,能起到疏导交通拥堵、减少环境污染、减少驾乘人员等待时间、提高交通参与者的安全、为驾驶人提供出行信息服务的作用。本文采用长短期记忆网络来进行速度预测,首先对数据进行归一化处理,再搭建多层LSTM网络,最后选取合适的参数,让模型完美拟合,泛化能力强。基于此模型进行的交通速度预测的均方误差为89.54km^2/h^2,均方根误差为9.46km/h,平均绝对误差为4.30km/h,决定系数为0.83,均在可接受范围内。此模型在训练数据量足够大的情况下,预测速度的精度和可信度较高,需要的训练时间短,可应用性较强。

关键词 智能交通 短时交通速度预测 LSTM 深度学习

0 引言

短时交通速度预测是近年来智能交通的研究热点方向,在误差允许范围内实时对交通速度进行预测,通过交通速度来实时评价交通状况,能起到疏导交通拥堵、减少环境污染、减少驾乘人员等待时间、提高交通参与者的安全、为驾驶人提供出行信息服务的作用,同时给交通工具的调度和城市管理者实行的交通管制提供可靠的依据,可以有效保护人民生命财产安全,提升城市居民对于交通的满意程度。

预测短时交通速度的方法大致可以分为4类:传统的统计理论方法、人工神经网络的方法、机器学习的方法和深度学习的方法。

(1)传统的统计理论方法:基于传统的统计理论来进行交通速度预测的前提是假设预测的速度与历史上的速度存在相似的特征,具有相关性,再通过曲线拟合和参数估计来进行预测。预测精度较高的方法有:卡尔曼滤波器、马尔可夫预测模型和时间序列模型。其中预测效果比较好的是时间序列的分析模型,有代表性的是根据自动回归积分滑动平均模型(Autoregressive Integrated Moving Average,ARIMA)模型改进的季节性整合移动平均自回归模型(Seasonal Autoregressive Integrated Moving Average,SARIMA),该模型考虑到季节性变化对交通速度的影响,预测误差相比传统ARIMA模型更小。但是简单的时间序列模型通常依赖平稳假设,这与城市交通的动态性不符。

(2)人工神经网络的方法:包括BAM神经网络、Hopfield神经网络、RBF神经网络和BP神经网络等。人工神经网络进行速度预测的优点是记忆能力和学习能力很强,但缺点是依赖大量的数据,数据量不够时预测结果难以让人满意,同时要人工调节网络参数与节点,如果操作不当,会让预测结果误差较大。

(3)机器学习的方法:包括支持向量机模型、贝叶斯网络、K近邻算法[1-2],还有高斯模型和卡尔曼滤波方法。机器学习方法需要自己来选择与速度相关的交通特征,根据这些特征来训练模型,但是这些特征不一定准确,往往由模型建立者的主观意愿来决定,所以速度预测的场合一旦变化,选取特征的方法也要随之变化,在较为复杂的情况下预测速度不能让人满意。

(4)深度学习的方法:由于城市越来越智能化,越来越多的交通数据可以被采集,这些数据可以建立相关的深度学习模型进行交通速度的预测。深度学习模型提取交通速度的相关特征并不依靠人工选,而是机器自动提取。深度学习的优点是学习能力强、可覆盖性广,并且数据越大,效果越好。比较常用的深度学习模型有循环神经网络(Recurrent Neural Network,RNN)[3-4]。本文使用的长短记忆网络(Long Short Term Memory Networks,LSTM)是循环神经网络的一种变体。还有一些文献利用卷积神经网络(Convolutional Neural Network,CNN)来进行空间相关性的建模,来解决交通速度预测问题[5]。

本文以深度学习为框架,利用Python语言和TensorFlow平台来实现交通速度预测。LSTM网络LSTM是RNN的一个优秀的变种模型,继承了大部分RNN模型的特性,在序列建模问题上有一定优势,具有长时记忆功能,实现起来简单的优点,同时解决了梯度反传过程由于逐步缩减而产生的梯度消失和梯度爆炸问题。具体到语言处理任务中,LSTM非常适合用于处理与时间序列高度相关的问题,例如交通速度预测。

1 长短期记忆网络

长短期记忆网络的设计灵感来自于计算机的逻辑门。长短期记忆网络引入了记忆(Memory Cell),或简称为单元(Cell)。一些文献认为记忆元是隐状态的一种特殊类型,它们与隐状态具有相同的形状,其设计目的是用于记录附加的信息。

LSTM 有很多门来控制这些记忆单元。其中一个门用来从单元中输出条目,称为输出门(Output Gate)。另外一个门用来决定何时将数据读入单元,称为输入门(Input Gate)。此外还需要一种机制来重置单元的内容,由遗忘门(Forget Gate)来管理。就如在门控循环单元中一样,当前时间步的输入和前一个时间步的隐状态作为数据送入 LSTM 的门中,如图 1 所示。它们由三个具有 Sigmoid 激活函数的全连接层处理,以计算输入门、遗忘门和输出门的值。因此,这三个门的值都在(0,1)的范围内。

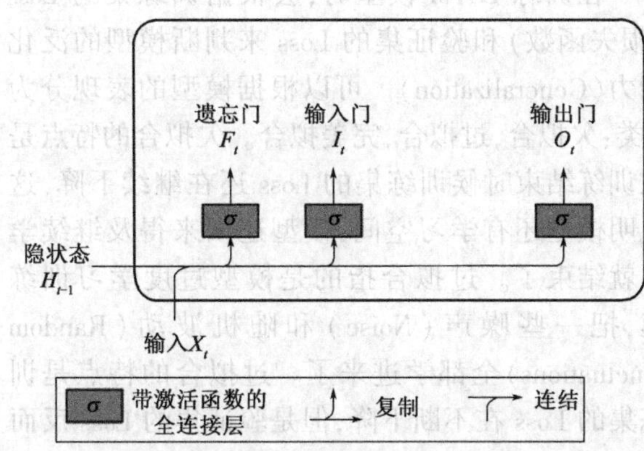

图 1　长短期记忆模型中的输入门、遗忘门和输出门

长短期记忆网络的数学表达式:假设有 h 个隐藏单元,批量大小为 n,输入数为 d,由此得到输入$X_t \in R^{n\times d}$,前一时间步的隐状态为$H_{t-1} \in R^{n\times h}$。时间步 t 的门被定义为输入门$I_t \in R^{n\times h}$,遗忘门$F_t \in R^{n\times h}$,输出门$O_t \in R^{n\times h}$,它们的计算方法如式(1)所示:

$$\begin{aligned} I_t &= \sigma(X_t W_{xi} + H_{t-1} W_{hi} + b_i), \\ F_t &= \sigma(X_t W_{xf} + H_{t-1} W_{hf} + b_f) \\ O_t &= \sigma(X_t W_{xo} + H_{t-1} W_{ho} + b_o), \end{aligned} \tag{1}$$

其中,W_{xi}、W_{xf}、$W_{xo} \in R^{n\times d}$和W_{hi}、W_{hf}、$W_{ho} \in R^{h\times h}$是权重参数,b_i、b_f、$b_o \in R^{1\times h}$是偏置参数。

在门控循环单元中,有一种机制来控制输入和遗忘(或跳过)。类似地,在长短期记忆网络中,也有两个门用于这样的目的:I_t输入门控制采用多少来自$\widetilde{C}_t$的新数据,而遗忘门F_t控制保留多少过去的记忆元$C_{t-1} \in R^{n\times h}$的内容。使用按元素乘法,得出式(2):

$$C_t = F_t \odot C_{t-1} + I_t \odot \widetilde{C}_t \tag{2}$$

最后定义隐状态$H_t \in R^{n\times h}$,如图 2 所示,H_t的值如式(3)所示,需要确保H_t的值始终保持在(-1,1)内:

$$H_t = O_t \odot \tanh(C_t) \tag{3}$$

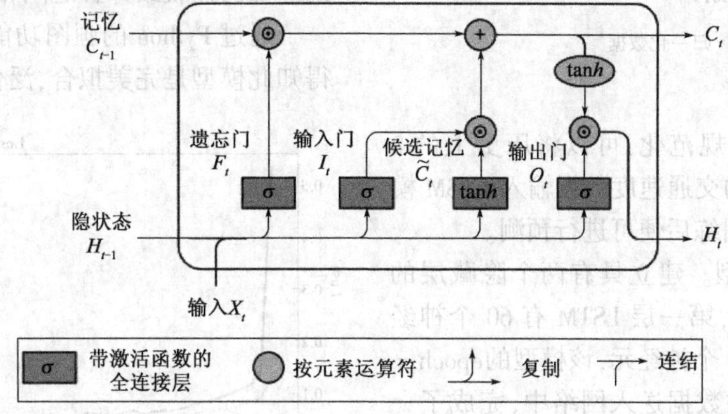

图 2　长短期记忆模型中计算隐状态

在实际预测交通速度时,基于已经训练好的 LSTM 模型输入历史上的交通速度数据,就可以得到预测速度。

2　LSTM 模型预测及结果分析

2.1　规范数据

本次模型所训练的数据来源于英国的高速数据网站,包含了英国大部分 M、A 级高速公路,数据非常全面,数据类型包括时间、流量、速度、占有率等。这里只选择时间、速度两个变量来预测交通速度。所选择预测的站点位于位置在 M25 高速希思罗机场附近,随着机场客流的变化,此站点速度也会发生较大变化,大部分时间位于 110km/h 附近,拥堵时间段会降至 20km/h 附近。

首先需要对已有的交通数据进行规范处理,使之适合用 LSTM 来进行预测。

第一步,选取用于模型训练的数据。数据的起始时间为 2019 年 8 月 1 日 0:00:00,截止时间为 2019 年 10 月 1 日 0:00:00,数据时间间隔为 15min,累计时间为两个月。将数据保存为 csv 类型,分别记录时间,点位速度便于模型进行训练。

第二步,选取用于和预测速度进行对比的实际速度,用于确定模型预测效果。

第三步,在 Python 中使用 Numpy 函数库。它可以储存和运算各种大型矩阵,解决数学问题。

第四步,对数据进行归一化处理[6],使用的方法是 MIN - MAX 标准化(线性函数归一化),也称为离差标准化,是对原始数据的线性变换,使得结果映射到 0 和 1 之间。转换函数:$(X - \text{MIN})/(\text{MAX} - \text{MIN})$。结果如图 3 所示。

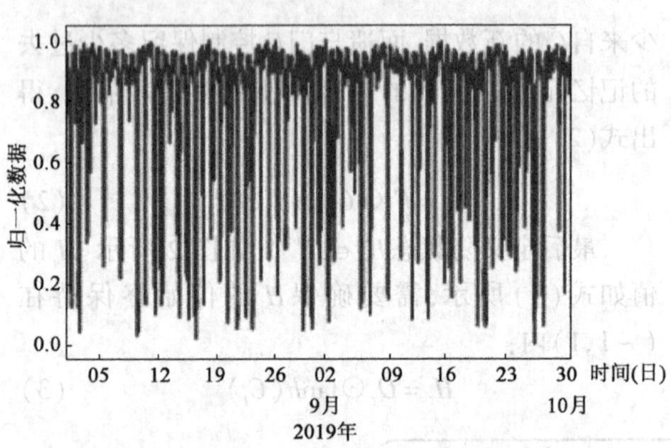

图 3 归一化数据

2.2 训练数据

经过之前的数据规范化,可以将历史上的 8 月 1 日至 9 月 30 日的交通速度数据输入 LTSM 模型,模型经过数据的训练后便可进行预测。

第一步,建立模型。建立具有两个隐藏层的 LSTM 模型,该模型中,第一层 LSTM 有 60 个神经元,第二层 LSTM 有 60 个神经元,该模型的epoch = 50(epoch 表示所有的数据送入网络中,完成了一次前向计算 + 反向传播的过程)。LSTM 模型可以利用有效的随机梯度下降 Adam 模型进行拟合,并利用均方误差损失函数进行优化。速度预测中使用的是一个单变量序列,因此特征数(Features)为 1。这里设定序列长度为 20,也就是一个样本中包含观测值的数量。具体的代码如下:

```
model = Sequential()
model.add(LSTM(60,activation = 'relu',return_sequences = True,input_shape = (SEQ_LEN,1)))
model.add(LSTM(60,activation = 'relu',))
model.add(Dense(1))
model.compile(optimizer = 'adam',loss = 'mse')
```

第二步,建立数据的训练集和测试集。训练集是用来学习的样本,测试集是用来评估模型的预测性能和准确率的样本。这里将数据的 80% 作为训练集来供模型学习。为了更直观地表现出预测值与实际值的区别,下文将直接用图表来说明模型的准确率。

2.3 预测结果及分析

2.3.1 Loss 曲线

在训练 LSTM 模型时,会根据训练集的 Loss(损失函数)和验证集的 Loss 来判断模型的泛化能力(Generalization)。可以根据模型的表现分为 3 类:欠拟合,过拟合,完美拟合。欠拟合的特点是在训练结束时候训练集的 Loss 还在继续下降,这说明模型还有学习空间,模型还没来得及继续学习就结束了。过拟合指的是模型过度学习训练集,把一些噪声(Noise)和随机波动(Random Fluctuations)全都学进来了。过拟合的特点是训练集的 Loss 在不断下降,但是验证集的 Loss 反而不断上升。完美拟合是我们模型的目标,它在 Loss 曲线上的特点是训练集的 Loss 和验证集的 Loss 都已经收敛并且之间相差很小很小。

通过 Python 的画图功能可以得到图 4。可以得知此模型是完美拟合,泛化能力强。

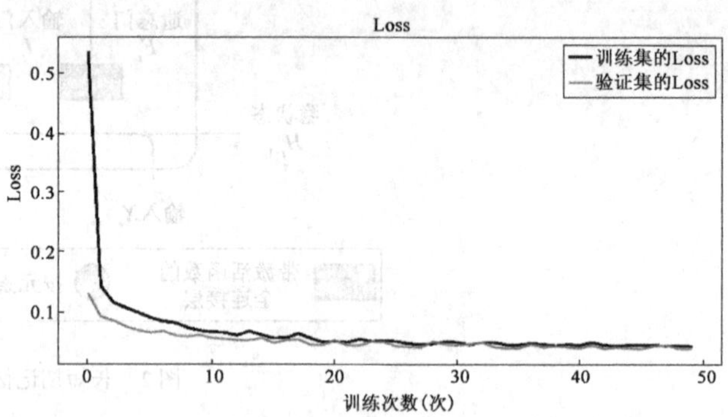

图 4 训练集与验证集的 Loss 图

2.3.2 预测结果

根据已经训练好的 LSTM 模型,对数据点位的速度进行实时预测。当训练样本占样本总量(5856)的 80% 时,图 5 和图 6 分别为路段的速度预测(15min)结果和误差分布图(横坐标为时间,每一点的跨度为 15min,纵坐标为速度,单位为

km/h)。可以很明显地看出,LSTM 模型可以实现完全实时跟踪交通流的变化趋势,且预测的速度较为准确。但是有一个明显的问题,当交通流出现拥堵时,预测误差可能会出现较大幅度的波动,如图 6 后半段所示,当出现交通拥堵时,预测的误差比较大。但是当交通流平稳时,如图 6 前段所示,时间序列的预测误差在 5km/h 以内,基本上实现了准确预测交通速度。

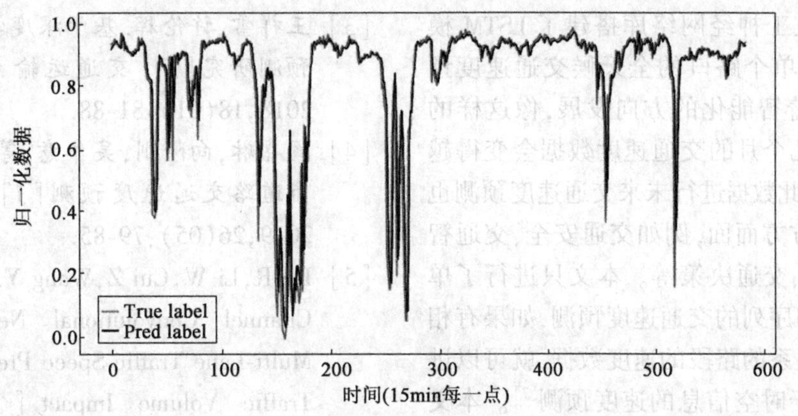

图 5　预测速度与真实速度对比图

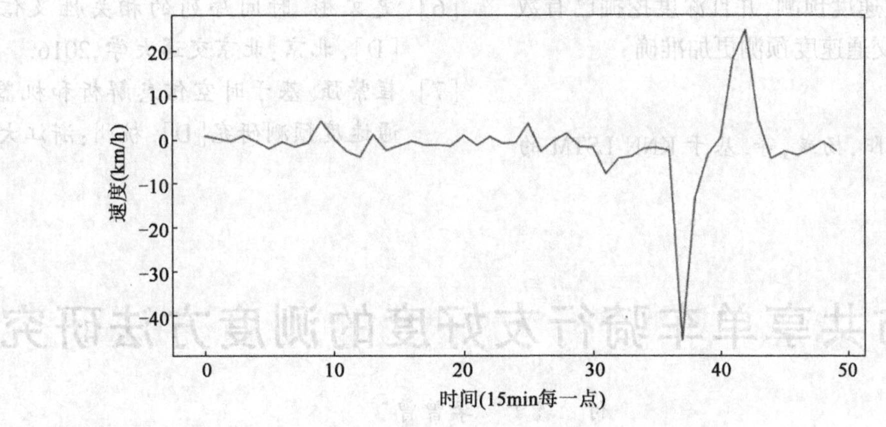

图 6　误差分布图

2.3.3　误差分析

首先提出一些衡量预测速度与实际速度的误差衡量指标:MSE(均方误差)、RMSE(均方根误差)、平均绝对误差(MAE)、R2(决定系数)。根据 R2 的取值,可以判断模型的好坏,越接近 1 说明模型拟合效果越好。式(4)表达如下:

$$\mathrm{MSE}=\frac{1}{n}\sum_{i=1}^{n}(y_{ti}-y_{pi})^2$$

$$\mathrm{RMSE}=\sqrt{\mathrm{MSE}}$$

$$\mathrm{MAE}=\frac{1}{n}\sum_{i=1}^{n}|y_{ti}-y_{pi}| \tag{4}$$

$$R_2=1-\frac{\sum_{i=1}^{n}(y_{ti}-y_{pi})^2}{\sum_{i=1}^{n}(\overline{y_{ti}}-y_{ti})^2}$$

其中,y_{ti} 为实际速度,y_{pi} 为预测速度,n 为测试集样本量,$\overline{y_{ti}}$ 为实际速度的平均值。由于此路段位于机场附近的高速公路,不拥堵的情况下速度很快,接近 110km/h,但是拥堵时的速度会降至 10km/h,对速度预测造成了一定影响。最后通过数据分析得出 MSE = 89.54km^2/h^2, RMSE = 9.46km/h, MAE = 4.30km/h。这些误差说明本模型的预测值与真实值之间的差距不大,在可以接受的范围内。R_2 = 0.83(保留两位小数),说明本模型的拟合效果较好。

传统的 ARIMA(3,1,3)模型对速度进行预测的 RMSE = 9.15km/h, MAE = 4.38km/h。相较而言 LSTM 模型的提升并不是很大,原因是高速公路的速度变化较为符合平稳性要求,受影响因素较少,这种条件下传统的 ARIMA 模型精度较高,但在普通城市的信号控制道路上,LSTM 模型的表现会更加优异,且不用人为提取交通相关特征。

3 结语

本文基于深度学习中的长短期记忆网络,对数据进行归一化处理,利用TensorFlow机器学习库和Keras开源人工神经网络库搭建了LSTM模型,最后实现了对单个路口的全天候交通速度预测。随着交通朝着智能化的方向发展,像这样的单路口时间累计几个月的交通速度数据会变得越来越易获得,基于此数据进行未来交通速度预测也将运用到生活的方方面面,例如交通安全、交通智能管理、拥堵治理、交通决策等。本文只进行了单一路口的基于时间序列的交通速度预测,如果有相邻几个存在空间关系的路段的速度数据,就可以进行一个区域的基于时空信息的速度预测[7]。本文的后续工作是随着深度学习的快速发展,找到更好的模型来进行交通速度预测,并且深度挖掘已有数据的特征,从而让交通速度预测更加准确。

参考文献

[1] 罗向龙,李丹阳,杨彧,等.基于KNN-LSTM的短时交通流预测[J].北京工业大学学报,2018,44(12):1521-1527.

[2] 陈佳良,胡钊政,李飞.基于时空特征序列匹配的交通流状态估计方法[J].交通信息与安全,2021,39(03):68-76+120.

[3] 王祥雪,许伦辉.基于深度学习的短时交通流预测研究[J].交通运输系统工程与信息,2018,18(01):81-88.

[4] 阎嘉琳,向隆刚,吴华意,等.基于LSTM的城市道路交通速度预测[J].地理信息世界,2019,26(05):79-85.

[5] Ke R, Li W, Cui Z, Wang Y. Two-Stream Multi-Channel Convolutional Neural Network for Multi-Lane Traffic Speed Prediction Considering Traffic Volume Impact [J]. Transportation Research Record, 2020, 2674(4):

[6] 史文彬.时间序列的相关性及信息熵分析[D].北京:北京交通大学,2016.

[7] 崔紫强.基于时空信息解析和机器学习的交通速度预测研究[D].杭州:浙江大学,2020.

城市共享单车骑行友好度的测度方法研究

付 鑫[1,2] 李曾曾*[3]

(1.长安大学运输工程学院大数据管理与应用系;

2.交通基础设施数字化教育部工程中心;

3.长安大学经济与管理学院管理科学与工程系)

摘 要 城市交通体系建设、综合治理以及社会发展等环境因素是影响城市慢行交通,尤其是骑行交通方式发展的重要因素。为了探索城市综合环境对于骑行的影响,找出关键因素并为改善提供量化支撑,进而提高居民骑行出行意愿,本文构建了包括舒适性、安全性、连通性和交通可达性四个方面在内的共享单车骑行友好度测度体系,采用多元线性回归结合零膨胀负二项回归分别对骑行速度和骑行频次进行建模,结果表明,安全性是提高骑行速度首要考虑的因素,舒适度是影响道路骑行频次的主要因素,人们偏好在具有较多的公交站、距离地铁站的距离较近并且路网密度高和信号交叉口少的道路上骑行。对西安市的实证分析表明,对骑行影响最大的是舒适度和安全度方面的指标,城市中南部的骑行友好度大于城市北部,并且自行车道的友好度要高于其他类型的道路。

关键词 慢行交通 骑行优化 回归分析 共享单车

0 引言

伴随大数据、移动互联网等前沿技术在交通系统中不断的应用,共享单车已经成为城市综合交通系统中的重要出行方式。共享单车由于其使用自由、服务灵活、支付便利的特点,被广泛地用来解决"最后一公里"的出行问题,用于接驳公交或者地铁出行,有效地促进了公共交通出行,减少了小汽车出行的比例,提高了人们出行方式的选择,有助于城市交通出行结构的改善,缓解交通拥堵[1],降低交通污染[2]。然而,随着共享单车骑行与建成环境的不断碰撞,越来越多的城市问题不断暴露,如骑行道路质量差、乱停乱放、骑行不通畅等,这种现象反映出,城市的慢行系统与居民的骑行需求存在失衡,即街道的骑行环境未提供给单车出行充足的空间和吸引力。因此如何找出影响骑行的关键道路因素,在最需要的地方提供舒适的骑行环境以满足城市居民的骑行需求是目前亟需解决的问题。

建成环境特征、自行车基础设施、公共交通设施和共享自行车使用之间的联系已被广泛地探讨研究[3-7]。Meng 等[7]利用多元回归分析探讨了街道形态对于共享单车使用率的影响,选取了中间性、分流比和最大凸包半径这三个指标,从出行距离和出行量两个方面考察了街道形态对于共享单车出行的影响。Gao 等[8]通过多元线性回归分析了无桩式共享单车系统使用距离衰减与建筑环境因素的关系。结果表明,人口密度、土地利用熵、支路密度、地铁站密度等因素与无桩式共享单车使用距离衰减显著相关,而商业用地比例、工业用地比例、高速公路密度等因素与上海使用距离衰减显著相关。但他们的研究都是基于对出行距离的考量,而出行距离大多时候并非由街道环境决定,可能取决于其他因素。在使用的数据上,以往研究多采用问卷调查或实地调查数据[9-12]。相比传统数据,大数据源以其数量、速度和多样性为特征,为以前所未有的细节水平理解非机动交通的详细时空出行模式提供了巨大的潜力[13-14]。在研究方法上,大多数研究采用线性回归来探讨各变量对于自行车出行行为的影响[15-18]。考虑到计数数据容易存在零膨胀现象,有的研究采取了零膨胀负二项模型[19-20]。

综上所述,已有对于探索共享单车出行行为影响因素的研究,大多从建筑环境的角度出发,探索建筑环境因素对于出行需求或者出行距离的影响,而对能反映骑行偏好和骑行适宜性的骑行频次和骑行速度研究较少。因此本文研究道路环境因素对这两个反映骑行行为的指标的影响。传统的数据多为基于问卷调查或者实地调查获得,数据获取难度大,耗费人力物力,近年来,随着大数据与物联网技术的广泛应用,开放的大数据源为探究共享单车出行行为提供了更多的细节数据。大多数研究在探究共享单车出行影响因素时采用线性回归的方法,多元线性回归可用于探索不同因素对于因变量的影响。因此,本文从几个典型角度,如骑行的舒适度、安全度、连通性、交通可达性选取了 9 个指标来构建道路骑行友好度评价指标体系,利用多元回归分析和零膨胀负二项回归,来分析道路环境对于共享单车的友好度。

1 研究数据

本研究使用来自哈啰出行提供的中国西安的共享单车订单数据,利用 2020 年 9 月 14 日—2020 年 9 月 20 日共一周早高峰期间的数据,如表 1 所示,每条记录包括交易日期,车辆 ID,用户 ID,行程开始时间,行程结束时间,起点经度、纬度,终点经度、纬度,行驶距离等。为了删除错误的行程信息,本文设定了三个标准来过滤异常值:①行程时间小于 1h 和大于 2min;②骑行距离小于 10km 和大于 50m;③经纬度在西安市界内。不符合上述标准的记录数据将被排除在数据集之外,数据清理后,得到 763021 条记录。

共享单车订单数据结构及样例

表 1

日期	车辆 ID	用户 ID	起始时间	结束时间
20200917	9150570400	b58650783f5843bf81b0a9204b237225	2020-09-17 09:20:25.001	2020-09-17 09:24:09.0
20200918	9150112678	5860aab732aa4f508c6e781b1d7215ff	2020-09-18 08:33:40.955	2020-09-18 08:48:42.0
20200919	5110029854	7b9afb1be0184a79b068dabe65ca714d	2020-09-19 07:27:16.523	2020-09-19 08:36:20.0
起始经度	起始纬度	终点经度	终点纬度	骑行距离
121.640884	29.907184	121.640174	29.904114	440
121.529373	29.872441	121.537492	29.873377	799
121.638914	29.906124	121.637180	29.907930	294

在此基础上,根据订单的起止点信息利用高德API获取轨迹点数据,从中提取出距离、时长和轨迹点字段。为了使爬取的路径规划轨迹数据尽量与实际行驶轨迹一致,将路径规划的距离与交易记录里的实际距离相差200m以上的数据记录剔除,总共得到124950条轨迹数据,如表2所示数据字段包括起点经纬度,终点经纬度,行驶距离,规划距离,轨迹点。

轨迹数据结构及样例　　表2

起始经纬度	终点经纬度	骑行时长(s)	规划时长(s)	骑行距离(m)	规划距离(m)	轨迹点
108.945138,34.248382	108.949364,34.252034	331	183	833	762	108.945135,34.248294;108.945438,34.248294;108.945477,34.248294;108.945586,34.24832;…
108.979649,34.290470	108.985821,34.290874	236	136	448	565	108.97964,34.290937;108.980152,34.290942;108.980152,34.290942;108.982053,34.290942;…
108.9632563,34.2504042	108.988270,34.257213	1316	840	3623	3498	108.96332,34.250404;108.963312,34.250755;108.963312,34.250755;108.963303,34.250894;…

为了了解不同道路的信息特征,本文使用从openstreetmap.org(OSM)上提取的2020年的基本道路网络矢量数据,经过道路数据筛选后获得11974条道路,然后将获得的数据进行拓扑处理后得到路段31098条这些道路覆盖了市中心的城市地区,由于数据可用性低,其他道路没有包括在内。

截至2021年6月,西安市开通运营地铁线路共有8条,共设车站154座,其中换乘车站14座(图1)。西安公交拥有数百条公交线路,随着西安城市建设的不断发展,市政府提出"公交先行"的发展思路。西安公交在城市的建设当中起到了重要的推动作用,截至2019年11月西安公交线路达到409条。本文中研究的地铁数据包含7条线路的156个站点,公交数据包含西安市内11544个公交站点。

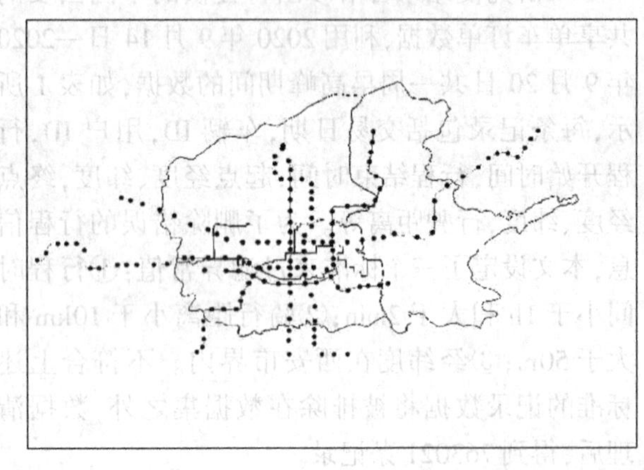

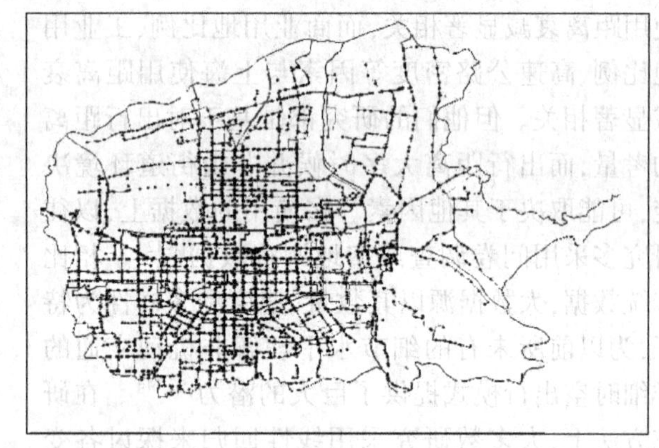

图1　地铁和公交站点数据

2　研究方法

2.1　指标体系

为了研究无桩式共享单车(DBSS)使用与路网环境之间的关系,在现有研究的基础上,结合《中国城市步行与自行车交通系统规划设计技术指南》中提出的安全、连续性、便利性三大原则,我们扩展了现有自行车骑行环境评价的框架,构建了包括舒适性、安全性、连通性和交通可达性四个方面在内的共享单车骑行友好度的测度体系,通过骑行速度和骑行频次的双回归模型,测算了不同道路环境因素对于骑行行为的影响。其中,舒适度包括道路类型,道路长度和该街道红绿灯等待时长;安全度指标包括转弯频次和是否是单行道;连通性指标选取路网密度和交叉口密度两个指标;交通可达性[22]指标选取道路中心点到地铁站的距离和道路周边公交站的密度两个指标;因变量选择骑行速度和骑行频次。变量的描述性统计见表3。

变量的描述性统计 表3

维度	变量	描述	均值	最小值	最大值	标准差
因变量	速度	骑行速度	5.381054	0	17.11579	4.000678
	骑行频次	经过该路段的骑行数量	110.534021	0	1610	199.537636
舒适度	道路类型	道路类型(共6种)	—	—	—	—
	道路长度	路段的长度	0.160473	0.000004	3.426499	0.211606
	红绿灯延误时长	骑行过程中等待红黄绿等的时长	219.012502	0	1619	203.379316
安全度	转弯频次	骑行中转弯的数量	2.091285	0	14	1.711434
	单行道	1(是)or 0(否)	—	—	—	—
连通性	路网密度	道路周边20m的路网密度	11.746469	0.51375	44.241727	4.712467
	交叉口密度	道路周边20m的交叉口密度	197.211276	0	954	160.470042
交通可达性	公交站密度	道路周边20m内的公交站的密度	1.241226	0	71.356955	4.613715
	距地铁站距离	道路中心点到地铁口的距离	658.767636	4.192877	999.904914	261.428627

(1)因变量概述

因变量选取骑行速度和骑行频次。骑行速度是所有经过该路段的轨迹的骑行速度的均值,骑行速度反映该街道骑行的适宜性,速度越快表明该街道越适合骑行。骑行频次是骑行经过该路段的次数,频次越高表明该街道利用率越高,骑行偏好越高。通过对街道骑行速度和频次分析,可以挖掘街道的利用率,对整体道路网络的使用情况进行分析,探索影响道路使用的道路环境因素,进而构建各道路的友好度评价指标体系。

(2)舒适度指标

舒适度指标包括道路类型,道路长度和该街道信号灯等待时长。道路类型包括城市主干道、城市次干道、城市支路、内部道路、人行横道、自行车道六种类型,分别用1、2、3、4、5、6来表示。道路长度是指某路段的长度,路网中的各条道路纵横交错,不尽相同。信号灯等待时长由实际订单时长与路径规划时长相减得出,因为路径规划得出的骑行时长假设道路畅通无阻,并不考虑路况。信号灯等待时长会降低骑行的舒适性,某路段信号灯等待时长越长,该路段骑行舒适性越低。

(3)安全度指标

安全度指标包括转弯频次和是否是单行道。直行发生交通事故的可能性远远小于转弯,转弯时难以判断各方来车,容易发生碰撞等交通事故。每条轨迹的转弯频次由爬取的每条轨迹数据中"左转"和"右转"的总数得出,即骑行过程中的转弯总次数。转弯频次越高,安全性越低。而单行道的安全性可能会高于双行道或者多行道,因为单行道只有单方向的车流,车流较少,而多行道车流较多,且车流方向不一,会降低骑行的安全性。

(4)连通性指标

连通性指标选取路网密度和交叉口密度两个指标。路网密度越高连通性越高,交叉口密度同理。路网密度是利用路网数据和西安市市区做统一投影,然后将西安市区划分为1000m×1000m的交通分析区域TAZ(Transportation Analysis Zone),对TAZ里的路网长度统计分析,计算出每个TAZ的面积,然后利用路网长度/TAZ面积计算出每个TAZ的路网密度,单位:km/km^2,然后用道路数据与路网密度数据做相交处理,计算每条道路周边(20m)的路网密度。

交叉口密度是利用路网数据和西安市市区数据,先将路网数据做拓扑处理在每个交叉点将路网打断,再将端点处的点数据去除得到路网和交叉点数据,然后对数据做统一投影,然后将西安市区划分为1000m×1000m的交通分析区域TAZ,对TAZ里的交叉点统计分析,计算出每个TAZ的面积,然后利用交叉点个数/TAZ面积计算出每个

TAZ的交叉口密度,单位:个/km²,然后用道路数据与交叉口密度数据做相交处理,计算每条道路周边(20m)的交叉口密度。

(5)交通可达性指标

交通可达性指标选取道路中心点到地铁站的距离和道路周边公交站的密度两个指标。计算道路中心点到地铁站的距离需要用到的数据有道路数据和地铁站点数据,利用道路数据计算出各条道路的道路中心点,然后计算各条道路的中心点到1000m范围内的地铁站的距离。

计算道路周边公交站的密度需要对道路做20m的缓冲区,统计路网缓冲区内的公交车站个数,利用公交站点数量除以道路长度计算出该路段公交车站密度,单位:个/km²。道路中心点到地铁站的距离越长说明该道路距离地铁站越远,交通可达性较低。道路周边公交站的密度越大,说明该道路周边公交站较多,交通可达性较高[22]。

2.2　模型构建

根据选取的指标构建道路骑行友好度的评价模型,首先对数据预处理后进行指标的计算,然后根据骑行速度和骑行频次的不同特点分别构建多元线性回归模型和零膨胀负二项回归模型,然后利用熵权法确定骑行速度和骑行频次的权重,最后根据两者的权重将骑行速度和骑行频次合称为友好度,然后利用构建的评价模型对各条街道进行骑行友好度的测算及评价(图2)。

利用提出的指标体系,对影响骑行友好度的道路环境因素构建多元线性回归模型(Multivariable Linear Regression Model,MLR)。多元线性回归模型通常用来描述变量y和x之间的随机线性关系,即:

$$y_i = \beta_0 + \beta_1 x_1 + \beta_2 x_2 + \cdots + \beta_k x_k + \delta \tag{1}$$

$$y_i\,(i=1,2)$$

$$x_k\,(k=1,2,\cdots 9)$$

$$\beta_k\,(k=1,2,\cdots 9)$$

式中:y_i——每条街道的骑行速度和骑行频次;

x_k——9个解释变量;

β_k——每个自变量x_k的回归系数,表示当其他解释变量不变时,该解释变量变化一个单位时因变量的变化值;

β_0——常数项;

δ——随机误差项。

零膨胀现象:在计数数据中,若0的个数明显多于泊松、负二项等标准离散分布随机产生的个数,称此现象为零过多现象(Zero-Inflated,ZI)。骑行频次是典型的计数数据,并且骑行频次的方差远大于均值,属于过离散数据,由骑行频次取值分布直方图可知,数据中含有大量(11206/31098,36.03%)为0的数据,该数据为典型的零膨胀数据。

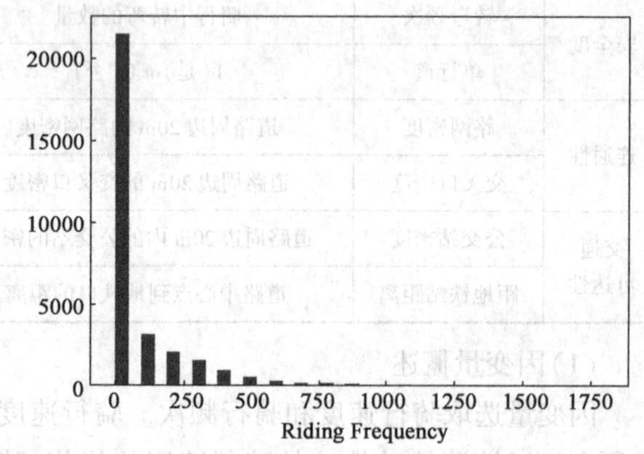

图2　共享单车骑行频次分布

骑行频次的这些特征决定了数据比较适合做零膨胀负二项回归(Zero-Inflated Negative Binomial,ZINB)。ZINB模型是二项分布和负二项分布两种形式的复合体,该模型把原始数据集视为由一个全零数据集和一个服从负二项分布的数据集混合而成,ZINB模型分为两部分,概率密度函数为:

$$P(Y=y_i|x_1,x_2,\cdots\cdots x_n)$$

$$=\begin{cases} p_i+(1-p_i)\left(\dfrac{1}{1+\alpha\lambda_i}\right)^{\frac{1}{\alpha}} & y_i=0(\text{logit 部分}) \\ (1-p_i)\dfrac{\Gamma\left(y_i+\dfrac{1}{\alpha}\right)}{\Gamma(y_i+1)\Gamma\left(\dfrac{1}{\alpha}\right)}\left(\dfrac{\alpha\lambda_i}{1+\alpha\lambda_i}\right)^{y_i}\left(\dfrac{1}{1+\alpha\lambda_i}\right)^{\frac{1}{\alpha}} & y_i\geq 1(\text{负二项部分}) \end{cases} \tag{2}$$

$$\lambda_i = \exp\left(\beta_i x_i + \varepsilon_i\right) \tag{3}$$

式中:y_i——分析单元i的行程到达次数;

p_i——回归过程可能产生多余零的概率;

α——散度参数。

对骑行速度和骑行频次分别建模后需要将两

个指标合成为友好度,这里采用熵权法分别确定骑行速度和骑行频次的权重,然后将两个指标合成。熵值(Entropy)是一种物理计量单位;熵越大说明数据越混乱,携带的信息越少,效用值越小,因而权重也越小。熵权法则是结合熵值提供的信息值来确定权重的一种研究方法。熵权法计算步骤:

(1)数据标准化

将各个指标的数据进行标准化处理。假设给定了 k 个指标,其中 $X_1, X_2, \cdots, X_k$,其中 $X_i = \{x_1, x_2, \cdots, x_n\}$。假设对各指标数据标准化后的值为 $Y_1, Y_2, \cdots, Y_k$,那么,

$$Y_{ij} = \frac{X_{ij} - \min(X_{ij})}{\max(X_i) - \min(X_i)} \tag{4}$$

(2)求各指标的熵值

$$E_j = -\frac{1}{\ln n}\sum_{i=1}^{n} p_{ij} \ln p_{ij} \tag{5}$$

其中,$p_{ij} = Y_{ij} / \sum_{i=1}^{n} Y_{ij}$,如果 $p_{ij} = 0$,则定义 $\lim_{p_{ij} \to 0} p_{ij} \ln p_{ij} = 0$。

(3)求各指标权重

$$W_i = \frac{1 - E_i}{\sum(1 - E_i)} (i = 1, 2, \cdots, k) \tag{6}$$

3 结果与讨论

3.1 结果

3.1.1 多重共线性

方差膨胀系数是衡量多元线性回归模型中多重共线性严重程度的一种度量。它表示回归系数估计量的方差与假设自变量间不线性相关时方差相比的比值。可利用方差膨胀系数(VIF)检验。表4展示了VIF检验的结果,由VIF检验的结果可知,所有的解释变量的VIF值均小于10,因此所有解释变量都通过了多重共线性检验,可用于模型拟合。

解释变量的VIF值 表4

维度	变量	VIF 值
舒适度	道路长度	1.12
	等待时长	2.36
	城市次干道	1.26
	城市支路	1.47
	内部道路	1.40
	人行道	1.33
	自行车道	1.02
安全度	转弯频次	2.45
	单行道	1.01
连通性	路网密度	5.95
	交叉口密度	5.81
交通可达性	距地铁站距离	1.18
	公交站密度	1.06

3.1.2 骑行速度影响因素回归结果

对道路的骑行速度的回归分析结果表明,模型的 R^2 值为0.824,调整后的 R^2 值为0.824,说明有82.4%的解释变量变化能够被模型解释。模型的回归结果如表5所示。从速度的回归结果来看,除了单行道之外的所有因素都在0.05的显著性水平下是显著的。

骑行速度回归结果 表5

维度	模型1(因变量速度) $R^2=0.824$	未标准化系数 B	未标准化系数 标准错误	标准化系数	t	显著性	VIF
	(常量)	0.977	0.046		21.284	0.000	
舒适度	道路长度	-0.174	0.048	-0.009	-3.667	0.000	1.118
	信号灯延误时长	0.004	0.000	0.193	52.846	0.000	2.355
	城市次干道	-0.353	0.032	-0.030	-11.068	0.000	1.261
	城市支路	-0.426	0.025	-0.049	-17.082	0.000	1.470
	内部道路	-0.736	0.032	-0.064	-22.682	0.000	1.396
	人行道	-0.988	0.037	-0.072	-26.412	0.000	1.330
	自行车道	-0.294	0.123	-0.006	-2.377	0.017	1.017
安全度	转弯频次	1.627	0.009	0.696	186.855	0.000	2.452
	单行道	-0.243	0.208	-0.003	-1.169	0.242	1.008

续上表

维度	模型1(因变量速度) $R^2=0.824$	未标准化系数		标准化系数	t	显著性	VIF
		B	标准错误				
	(常量)	0.977	0.046		21.284	0.000	
连通性	路网密度	0.103	0.005	0.121	20.820	0.000	5.949
	交叉口密度	-0.002	0.000	-0.085	-14.904	0.000	5.814
交通可达性	距地铁站距离	-0.00005283	0.000	-0.061	-23.761	0.000	1.176
	公交站密度	0.038	0.002	0.043	17.711	0.000	1.063

从表5可以看出,模型公式为:

骑行速度=0.977-0.174×道路长度+0.004×红绿灯延误时长-0.353×城市次干道-0.426×城市支路-0.736×内部道路-0.988×人行道-0.294×自行车道+1.627×转弯频次-0.243×单行道+0.103×路网密度-0.002×交叉口密度-0.00005283×距地铁站距离+0.038×公交站密度 (7)

3.1.3 骑行频次影响因素回归结果

在进行骑行频次的回归时,考虑到本文统计的据地铁站的距离为1km以内的,最先本文对据地铁站距离1km以外的道路赋值10000,表示这条道路周围并没有地铁站,得到的模型拟合结果较差,于是剔除了据地铁站距离大于1km的道路数据,对剩下的17180条道路数据进行模型拟合。

表6展示了ZINB模型的结果,包括了负二项部分(Count Model)和Logit(Zero-inflation model)部分两部分结果,Logit部分对数据中的零频数建立模型,负二项部分是针对数据中骑行频次大于0的计数建立负二项回归模型。

非零部分骑行频次建模为:

骑行频次=7.039+0.276×道路长度-0.003×红绿灯延误时长-0.437×城市支路-1.018×内部道路-0.696×人行道-0.297×自行车道-0.324×转弯频次+0.077×路网密度-0.002×交叉口密度-0.0004795×距地铁站距离+0.027×公交站密度 (8)

ZINB模型的结果 表6

变量	Count model coefficients (negbin with log link)				Zero-inflation model coefficients (binomial with logit link)			
	β	Std. Error	z	$Pr(>\|z\|)$	β	Std. Error	z	$Pr(>\|z\|)$
(常量)	7.039	0.085	83.197	<0.000***	21.391	3.850	5.557	0.000***
路网密度	0.077	0.007	11.496	<0.000***	-0.718	0.206	-3.483	0.000***
交叉口密度	-0.002	0.000	-12.319	<0.000***	0.019	0.006	3.116	0.002**
距地铁站距离	-0.0004795	0.000	-13.496	<0.000***	-0.009	0.002	-4.625	0.000***
公交站密度	0.027	0.002	13.403	<0.000***	-0.116	0.162	-0.715	0.475
转弯频次	-0.324	0.022	-14.719	<0.000***	-4.552	0.693	-6.571	0.000***
信号灯延误时长	-0.003	0.000	-16.495	<0.000***	-0.099	0.014	-7.098	0.000***
道路长度	0.276	0.072	3.806	0.000***	-0.483	2.153	-0.225	0.822
单行道	-0.214	0.258	-0.829	0.407	32.293	4.897	6.595	0.000***
城市次干道	-0.030	0.034	-0.872	0.383	-0.334	3.208	-0.104	0.917
城市支路	-0.437	0.026	-16.715	<0.000***	5.811	1.947	2.985	0.003**
内部道路	-1.018	0.034	-29.538	<0.000***	-0.856	1.921	-0.446	0.656
人行道	-0.696	0.043	-16.041	<0.000***	2.533	4.592	0.552	0.581
自行车道	-0.297	0.119	-2.493	0.013*	1.824	18.769	0.097	0.923
Log(theta)	-0.327	0.011	-30.039	<0.000***				

Signif. codes: 0 '***' 0.001 '**' 0.01 '*' 0.05 '.' 0.1 ' ' 1
Theta = 0.7208
Number of iterations in BFGS optimization: 60
Log-likelihood: -8.354e+04 on 29 Df

3.1.4　骑行速度和骑行频次权重

骑行频次和骑行速度的权重值分别是0.683、0.317。由此可得出友好度 = 0.3167 × 骑行速度 + 0.6833 × 骑行频次(表7)。

熵权法计算权重结果汇总　　表7

项	信息熵值	信息效用值	权重系数
骑行频次	0.9208	0.0792	68.33%
骑行速度	0.9633	0.0367	31.67%

3.2　讨论

3.2.1　各影响因素分析讨论

就道路环境因素对骑行速度的影响来看，路网密度会对骑行速度产生显著的正向影响，这是因为密集的路网能够提高出行的连通性，骑行的连续性较好。道路周围公交车站的密度和转弯频次对骑行速度有正向影响。模型结果显示信号灯等待时长越长骑行速度越快，这是由于在工作日早高峰骑共享单车用于通勤的人数较多，如果路上用于等信号灯的时间超出预期，人们就会加快速度，以免上班迟到。而城市次干道、城市支路、内部道路、人行横道、自行车道对骑行速度的建模结果为负，说明城市主干道的骑行速度要快于其他类型的道路，城市主干道一般道路质量较好，路面宽敞，有利于骑行。交叉口密度则不利于骑行速度的加快，这是因为交叉口一般有信号灯，并且车流复杂，不利于骑行。

从道路环境对骑行频次的建模结果来说，模型的负二项部分表示对骑行频次大于0的道路进行建模，结果表明，路网密度和道路长度对骑行频次的增加有正向影响，这不难理解，如前所述，路网密度越高，道路连通性越高，就会提供到达更多目的地的途径，这无疑会增加通过该路段的骑行。公交车站的密度增加也会使骑行频次增加，这是由于公交站越多该道路就会有越多用于接驳公交的骑行行为发生。距离地铁站的距离对骑行频次呈现负面影响，这是由于据地铁站距离越远，越不利于通过该道路进行接驳地铁。交叉口密度、信号灯等待时长和转弯频次对骑行频次具有负面影响，可能的原因是交叉口密度、信号灯等待时长和转弯频次的增加会使骑行变得困难。相较于城市主干道来说，城市次干道、城市支路、内部道路、人行横道、自行车道的骑行频次较少，因为主干道遍布整个城市，连接着各条城市次干道和支路，是去往目的地的必经之路，因此骑行经过城市主干道的人会多于其他类型的城市道路(图3)。

在对各因素对骑行速度和骑行频次的影响进行排序后发现，对骑行速度影响最大的三个因素为转弯频次、信号灯等待时长、路网密度，对骑行频次影响最大的三个因素为交叉口密度、据地铁站距离、路网密度。由此可见，要想改善骑行的友好度，需要考虑多方面的因素，其中道路的安全性和连通性是重要考虑因素，政府可根据实际情况合理规划建设骑行的路线，使城市道路骑行尽可能连续，并且考虑到用于接驳地铁的骑行，距离地铁站的距离不宜过远。

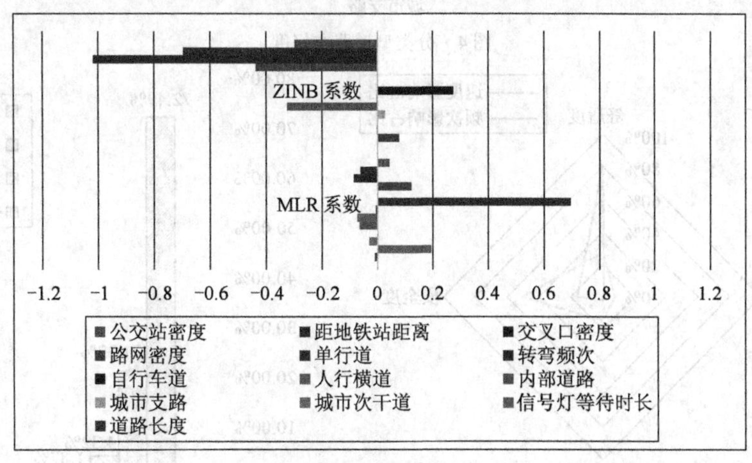

图3　回归系数相对大小

3.2.2　道路友好度评估

表8给出了预测值的描述性统计,骑行速度的预测均值为5.457km/h,骑行频次的均值为3.626,意味着平均每条道路一周内在工作日早高峰期间经过的次数为3.626次,平均每条道路的友好度值为4.206。

预测值的描述性统计　　表8

预测变量	计数	均值	最大值	最小值	标准差
骑行速度	31098	5.457	25.462	−0.609	3.672
骑行频次	31098	3.626	7.975	−3.576	2.240
友好度	31098	4.206	13.513	−2.636	2.694

西安市路网的友好度值分级显示,城市中南部的骑行友好度大于城市北部,这是因为西安的市中心位于中南部的雁塔区、碑林区和莲湖区,这些区域内的用地类型丰富,有多种类型的目的地分布,并且道路连通性高,骑行行为也多发生于这些区域,因此这些区域的骑行频次较高,进行道路骑行环境的改善时应首先考虑这些区域。

另外对道路分类型的骑行友好度做了分类汇总,从图4中可以看出,自行车道的友好度要高于其他类型的道路,自行车道由于与机动车道隔离,提供了较好的骑行环境。其次是人行道路,内部道路,在OSM的道路分类中内部道路是指公园居住区等的车行道路,这些道路由于与城市道路分离,机动车流较少,骑行较为适宜。而城市主干道、城市次干道和城市支路由于车流较多,骑行适宜性较差,因此骑行的友好度较差。

对舒适度、安全度、连通性和交通可达性四个维度的指标对骑行的影响大小进行分析,将各维度的评价指标按标准化系数进行影响度大小的排序,由图5可知,对骑行速度的影响里,安全度的指标影响占比最大,可采用一些措施,例如增设自行车专用道来提高骑行的安全性,而舒适度指标对骑行频次的影响最大,政府可采用诸如改善路面质量、合理调控红绿灯等待时长等措施来提高骑行的舒适性。总的来说,对骑行影响最大的是舒适度和安全度方面的指标,可采用适当措施提高这两个方面的道路环境,以便于人们更多地采用骑行出行。

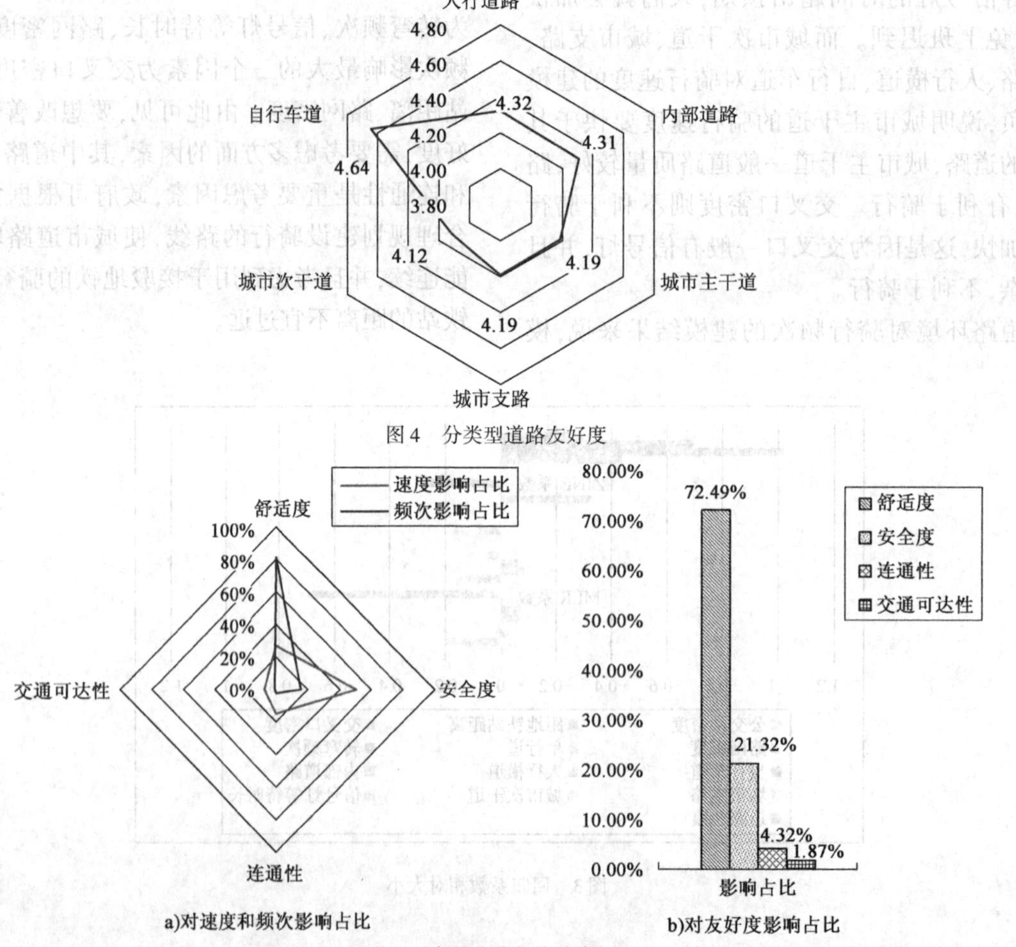

图4　分类型道路友好度

a)对速度和频次影响占比　　b)对友好度影响占比

图5　各维度指标影响占比

4 结语

本文通过构建骑行速度和骑行频次的双回归模型，测算了不同道路环境因素对于骑行行为的影响，结果发现，安全性是提高骑行速度首要考虑的因素，而对骑行速度影响最大三个因素为转弯频次、信号灯等待时长、路网密度。舒适度是影响道路骑行频次的主要因素，对骑行频次影响最大的三个因素为交叉口密度、据地铁站距离、路网密度。值得注意的是，人们偏好在具有较多的公交站、距离地铁站的距离较近并且路网密度高和信号交叉口少的道路上骑行。

然后通过熵权法合成道路友好度，评估的结果显示，城市中南部的骑行友好度大于城市北部，并且自行车道的友好度要高于其他类型的道路，建议政府尽可能修建骑行专用自行车道，以提高道路骑行友好度。分析不同维度的指标对骑行友好度的影响，发现对骑行影响最大的是舒适度和安全度方面的指标，可采用适当措施提高这两个方面的道路环境，以提高人们的骑行出行意愿。

道路环境错综复杂，是一个庞大的交通体系，影响骑行的道路环境因素更是不胜枚举，本研究由于数据获取和技术的限制，仅考虑了道路环境中的9个指标，未来应该从更完整的角度考虑更多的影响因素进一步进行骑行友好度评价研究。此外，本研究只针对了一个城市的道路友好度的对比，后续研究可考虑使用更多的具有代表性的城市进行研究对比。本文另一个局限性在于，本文由于数据获取的缺乏，只考虑了早高峰期间的道路环境因素，未能从各个时间段上进行对比分析。

参考文献

[1] Barbour N., Zhang Y., Mannering F. A statistical analysis of bike sharing usage and its potential as an auto-trip substitute[J]. Journal of Transport & Health,2019,12:253-262.

[2] Zhang Y.,Mi Z. Environmental benefits of bike sharing:A big data-based analysis[J]. Applied Energy,2018,220:296-301.

[3] Eca B., Zya B. Identifying the nonlinear relationship between free-floating bike sharing usage and built environment[J]. Journal of Cleaner Production,2020,280.

[4] Shen Y.,Zhang X.,Zhao J. Understanding the usage of dockless bike sharing in Singapore [J]. International Journal of Sustainable Transportation,2018,12(9):686-700.

[5] El-Assi W., Mahmoud M. S., Habib K. N. Effects of built environment and weather on bike sharing demand: a station level analysis of commercial bike sharing in Toronto [J]. Transportation,2017,44(3):589-613.

[6] Zhao P. J. The Impact of the Built Environment on Bicycle Commuting: Evidence from Beijing [J]. Urban Studies,2014,51(5).

[7] Meng S., Zacharias J. Street morphology and travel by dockless shared bicycles in Beijing, China[J]. International Journal of Sustainable Transportation,2020(1).

[8] Gao, K., Yang, Y., Li, A., et al. Spatial heterogeneity in distance decay of using bike sharing: An empirical large-scale analysis in Shanghai[J]. Transportation Research Part D-Transport and Environment,2020,94,102814.

[9] Zhu S.,Zhu F. Cycling comfort evaluation with instrumented probe bicycle[J]. Transportation Research Part A:Policy and Practice,2019,129.

[10] Grabow M. L., Bernardinello M., Bersch A. J., et al. What moves us: Subjective and objective predictors of active transportation [J]. Journal of Transport & Health, 2019, 15:100625.

[11] Li H., Chen Z., Li X., et al. Friendliness Analysis for Bike Trips on Urban Roads Using Logistic Regression Model[M]. 2019.

[12] Schmid-Querg J.,Keler A.,Grigoropoulos G. The Munich Bikeability Index: A Practical Approach for Measuring Urban Bikeability [J]. Sustainability,2021,13.

[13] 付学梅，隽志才. 时间维度下上海市共享单车骑行模式研究[J]. 交通运输系统工程与信息,2020,20(3):8.

[14] Munira S., Sener I. N. A geographically weighted regression model to examine the spatial variation of the socioeconomic and land-use factors associated with Strava bike

activity in Austin, Texas-ScienceDirect [J]. Journal of Transport Geography,88.

[15] Zhang Y., Thomas T., Brussel M, et al. Exploring the impact of built environment factors on the use of public bikes at bike stations:Case study in Zhongshan, China[J]. Journal of Transport Geography, 2017, 58 (JAN.):59-70.

[16] 曹小曙,罗依.中国大陆城市建成环境与共享单车配置的关系[J].中山大学学报(自然科学版),2020,267(01):83-91.

[17] Strauss J., Miranda-Moreno L. F. Speed, travel time and delay for intersections and road segments in the Montreal network using cyclist Smartphone GPS data [J]. Transportation Research Part D Transport & Environment, 2017,57(dec.):155-171.

[18] Wang K., Chen Y. J. Joint analysis of the impacts of built environment on bikeshare station capacity and trip attractions [J]. Journal of Transport Geography,2020,82.

[19] Zhao D., Ong G. P., Wang W., et al. Effect of built environment on shared bicycle reallocation:A case study on Nanjing, China [J]. Transportation Research Part A: Policy and Practice,2019,128.

[20] Wang K., Akar G., Chen Y. J. Bike sharing differences among millennials, Gen Xers, and baby boomers: Lessons learnt from New York City's bike share[J]. Transportation research part A:policy and practice,2018,116:1-14.

[21] Ministry of Housing and Urban-Rural Development. China's Urban Pedestrian and Bicycle Transportation System Planning and Design Technical Guideline. Ministry of Housing and Urban-Rural Development,2013.

[22] 龙瀛,周垠.街道活力的量化评价及影响因素分析——以成都为例[J].新建筑,2016, No.164(01):54-59.

基于POI数据的电动汽车充电站选址规划

吴 鹏*

(重庆交通大学交通运输学院)

摘 要 针对不断恶化的气候环境,电动汽车成为新的交通出行。但是我国电动汽车发展历程较短,相关配套设施还不完善,尤其是电动车充电设施规划以及规模还存在不合理之处。在POI数据的基础上,本文提出了一种基于加权K-Means聚类算法的电动汽车充电桩选址规划模型。该模型根据POI数据的一级分类对充电需求的吸引和聚类半径分别确定POI数据权值、聚类中心簇个数,然后进行选址规划。以重庆市POI数据为例,提出了两种拟建充电站选址方案。

关键词 城市POI K-Means聚类算法 充电站选址规划

0 引言

气候变化是当今世界面临的最大挑战,引起气候变化的主要原因就是化石燃料的使用,煤炭、石油、汽油等使用率远高于新能源,因此发展和使用新能源成为新的趋势和环境治理的有效手段。国内碳排放行业中,交通行业位于第二位,占比达到28%。在可持续发展的背景下,发展电动汽车成为减少污染排放、应对能源危机的重要举措。

我国电动车的发展历史比较短,目前还存在着续驶里程较短、配套设施不完善等问题,仅从充电设施来看,还存在着设施利用率、覆盖率低的问题。充电桩可以分为分散式充电桩、专用充电桩以及公共充电桩。在城市中由于在建设规划阶段缺少大数据的科学引导,在规划公共充电桩时会产生电桩布局不合理的问题[1]。有些地方需求量大但是充电桩数量少,而有些地方闲置数目较多,而且充电桩的规模不一,且不同于传统加油站,单次充电耗时较长,常常存在排长队等充电的情况。通过科学有效的手段对充电桩的选址进行合理规划具有重要意义。

兴趣点数据(Point of Interest,POI)包含名称、坐标、类别、分类四方面信息,源于基础测绘成果数字线划地图(Digital Line Graphic,DLG)产品中点类地图要素矢量数据集;在地理信息系统(Geographic Information System,GIS)中指可以抽象成点进行管理、分析和计算的对象。随着互联网电子地图服务与LBS应用的普及,POI无论从概念范畴,还是从信息纵深都有了长足发展,在O2O、电商、社交、互联网金融、共享经济等领域都得到了广泛应用。一方面各行各业把越来越多的内容包装成POI供其用户消费,如互联网电子地图提供的周边搜索服务中的各类商家门店,网约车平台提供的上车点,O2O行业提供的推荐收货地址等等。另一方面POI所包含的属性也越来越多,如商家信息、服务介绍、点评信息、排行榜、推荐、状态、社交互动信息、消费金融信息等等。以高德地图为例,其POI数据中对外开放的基础字段就有45个之多。因此POI也具备了跨行业、跨部门整合数据,基于空间位置进行大数据挖掘的天然优势。

在电动汽车充电站选址问题上,有学者以社会总成本为目标建立选址优化模型以得到充电站的最优选址和充电订单[2-5]。Bian C[6]等针对电动汽车充电站投资收益问题,提出一种基于利润最大化的混合整数线性规划(MILP)模型来确定城市充电站的最优选址。Mak HY[7]等建立了考虑建设成本最小和收益目标概率最大的选址优化模型。从充电用户的角度来看,用户不仅希望充电的成本越低越好,还希望整个充电过程所付出的时间代价尽可能最小。Zhang S[8]等基于K-Means方法建立电动出租车(ET)的动态分布聚类模型并利用重心法建立电动出租车充电站(ETCS)的位置模型,得到各集群区块的充电需求和经纬度位置。钱斌[9]等利用"油—电"热值折算的方法确定公交车的换电电量需求,并使用近邻传播聚类(AP)算法对换电需求的空间分布进行聚合分析,完成充电站的选址。从电网配电供给的角度来看,电动车充电站的选址对配电网造成的负面影响越小越好。Jamian J J[10]等从减少配电网电能损失的角度研究电动汽车换电站的选址布设问题。此外,换电站选址决策评价在选址最优决策的过程中扮演着重要角色。有研究者基于层次分析法[11-12]建立选址综合评价体系,采用相似度排序法(TOP-SIS)确定最优EVCS[12-15]选址。

1 研究背景及意义

在POI数据的视角下,可以对城市交通的总体规划进行评价和规划。结合GIS数据和POI数据,可以对城市交通供需以及公共交通供需匹配进行评价[16]以及对景点游客最优游客接待中心、城区养老设施进行选址规划[17-18]。帅春燕[19]等人基于K-Means算法对POI数据聚类进行电动自行车的换电柜选址规划。相对于传统的交通需求预测的数据,POI数据具有可挖掘性强、数据易得的特点,在交通行业中,POI数据常常用于解决网约车上车位置推荐,以及快递收货地址选择等问题,并且取得了良好的效果。

充电设备作为发展绿色交通,低碳出行的必要保障,其规模化建设是电动汽车的推广和发展的前提下,有必要超前于电动汽车的发展。尽管电动汽车和充电基础设施的发展趋势良好,但是仍存在供小于求的问题,电动车使用者充电难、充电设施资源配置不均衡的问题亟需解决。那么以交通需求为引领,使用数据融合的方式进行充电需求预测与相关设施建设就成为解决这一问题的重要手段之一。

综上所述,POI数据在指导城市公共设施选址规划中具有一定的指导意义,但是专门针对电动车公共充电设备的选址规划的研究还比较少,大部分是基于电动车续航里程以及充电需求的充电桩选址规划,在城市道路中,这些模型不能实时反映充电需求的发生。本文提出了一种基于K-Means算法和POI数据的充电桩选址规划方法,从需求侧引导交通发生,将地理信息技术融合交通规划,按照POI对应权重确定电动车充电桩规模、位置,以及对现有充电桩规模进行优化配置。

2 数据采集与初步分析

2.1 城市POI数据

本文使用Python脚本对高德地图的API接口的POI数据进行爬取,爬取时间为2021.12.25。

按照一级分类、二级分类,可以将POI数据分为基础设施服务设施类、商业服务设施类、行政办公设施类以及医疗养老设施类。POI数据的分类见表1。

POI主要数据分类　　表1

一级分类	二级分类	具体设施名称
基础服务设施	交通设施	飞机场、火车站、长途汽车站、地铁站、公交车站等
	科教文化	图书馆、科技馆、高等院校、中小学等
	体育休闲	体育场馆、健身中心、农家院、电影院等
	旅游景点	公园、动物园、植物园等
	生活服务	邮局、照相馆、公共厕所等
商业服务设施	金融	银行、ATM、信用社等
	酒店	星级酒店、快捷酒店、公寓式酒店等
	购物	购物中心、百货商场、超市、便利店、家居建材等
	餐饮美食	中餐厅、小吃快餐店、蛋糕甜品店、咖啡厅等
行政办公设施	政府机构	各级政府、行政单位、福利机构
	公司企业	公司、园区、农林园艺等
	房地产	写字楼、住宅区、宿舍
医疗养老设施	医疗服务	综合医院、专科医院、诊所、药店、疗养院、急救中心、疾控中心等
	养老设施	养老院、老年养护中心、敬老院、老年大学、老年公寓、照料中心、社会福利中心等

所选取的POI类型应该对交通出行具有较大的吸引,如住宅、商场等,对于出行需求较大,对于充电设备的需求较大,而对于图书馆、银行等弱交通出行吸引场所,对于充电桩的需求较低。所以本文主要选取商务住宅、交通设施服务、餐饮服务、医疗保健服务、体育休闲服务为爬取关键词,得到的数据如表2所示。

POI数据示例　　表2

Name	ID	Location	Type	CityName	AdName	Address
钢哥土鲫鱼(南滨路店)	B0FFGMND4E	106.550472,29.537853	餐饮服务;中餐厅;中餐厅	重庆市	南岸区	铜元局城投天邻水岸附34号(菜园坝大桥下)
铜元酒馆	B0FFHHS4L0	106.550265,29.537723	餐饮服务;中餐厅;中餐厅	重庆市	南岸区	铜建村509号20号商铺
驿米速食(菜园坝汽车站店)	B0FFI7SC6Q	106.549991,29.548189	餐饮服务;中餐厅;中餐厅	重庆市	渝中区	菜袁路3号长途汽车站
老麻抄手(菜园坝店)	B0FFGFW2IB	106.550536,29.548344	餐饮服务;中餐厅;中餐厅	重庆市	渝中区	菜袁路德克士对面
车站便民餐厅	B0FFGXZFWP	106.548381,29.548053	餐饮服务;中餐厅;中餐厅	重庆市	渝中区	菜袁路12号附11号

本文主要以重庆市的POI数据为研究对象,重庆市属于山地城市,道路坡度大,路网密度大,车辆对能源需求也强。重庆市呈现出“多中心、组团式”的发展格局,多中心、组团式形态是集中与分散的有机统一,让重庆的每个区域可以形成一个较为独立的空间,相对完整的区域配套和生产、生活功能,让大部分人的日常活动都能在一个空间里完成。一个组团内,住宅区、办公场所和商贸用地等交错布局,有效减少了城市空置率,又有助于缩短交通里程,减少交通拥挤、环境污染,节省社会生活成本。

2.2 城市 POI 数据分析

基于高德地图 API 接口,得到以 106.550985,29.542659 为初始点坐标,半径为 5km 的重庆市 POI 数据共计 5000 余条,按照分类,其分布如图 1 所示。

从图中可以看出 POI 点的分布规律:

(1)交通设施分布比较分散,呈环绕式分布在餐饮服务、医疗保健服务以及商务住宅附近,单个交通设施分布之间距离在 100m 以上;

(2)商务住宅分布呈现组团式特点,且多个组团之间距离较远,周围分布着医疗保健服务设施、小部分餐饮服务设施以及体育休闲设施;

(3)医疗保健服务设施、餐饮设施分布集中,结合地图数据可知,主要集中在组团式商业中心地带。

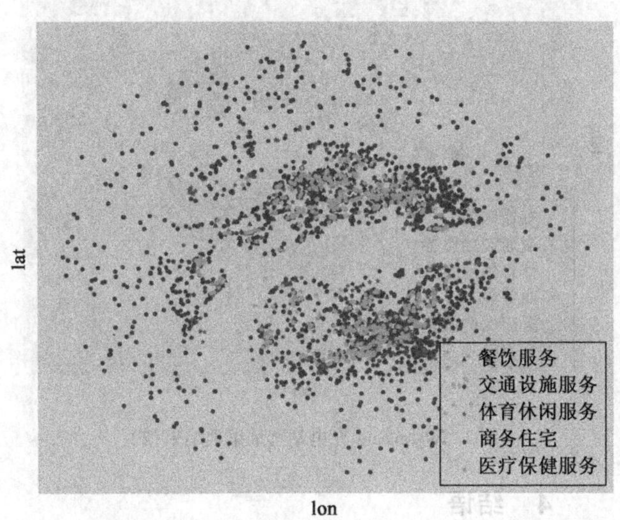

图 1 重庆市 POI 分布

3 基于加权 K-Means 聚类的充电桩选址规划

3.1 加权 K-Means 算法

K-Means 算法是最常用的聚类算法,主要思想是:在给定 K 值和 K 个初始类簇中心点的情况下,把每个点(亦即数据记录)分到离其最近的类簇中心点所代表的类簇中,所有点分配完毕之后,根据一个类簇内的所有点重新计算该类簇的中心点(取平均值),然后再迭代的进行分配点和更新类簇中心点的步骤,直至类簇中心点的变化很小,或者达到指定的迭代次数。

假定给定数据样本 X,包含了 n 个对象 $X=\{X_1,X_2,\cdots,X_n\}$,其中每个对象都具有 m 个维度的属性。K-Means 算法的目标是将 n 个对象依据对象间的相似性聚集到指定的 k 个类簇中,每个对象属于且仅属于一个其到类簇中心距离最小的类簇中。对于 K-Means,首先需要初始化 k 个聚类中心 $\{C_1,C_2,\cdots,C_k\}$,$1<k\leqslant n$,然后通过计算每一个对象到每一个聚类中心的欧式距离,如式(1)所示:

$$\mathrm{dis}(X_i,C_j)=\sqrt{\sum_{t=1}^{m}(X_{it}-C_{jt})^2} \tag{1}$$

式中:X_i——第 i 个对象,$1\leqslant i\leqslant n$;

C_j——第 j 个聚类中心的 $1\leqslant j\leqslant k$;

X_{it}——第 i 个对象的第 t 个属性,$1\leqslant t\leqslant m$;

C_{jt}——第 j 个聚类中心的第 t 个属性。

依次比较每一个对象到每一个聚类中心的距离,将对象分配到距离最近的聚类中心的类簇中,得到 k 个类簇 $\{S_1,S_2,S_3,\cdots,S_k\}$。K-Means 算法用中心定义了类簇的原型,类簇中心就是类簇内所有对象在各个维度的均值,其计算公式如式(2)所示:

$$C_t=\frac{\sum_{x_i\in Sl}X_i}{|S_l|} \tag{2}$$

式中:C_l——第 l 个聚类的中心,$1\leqslant l\leqslant k$;

S_l——第 l 个类簇中对象的个数;

X_i——第 l 个类簇中第 i 个对象,$1\leqslant i\leqslant |S_l|$。

加权 K-means 算法简称为 Wkmeans 算法,是基于传统 K-Means 算法的改进。其核心思想就是给每个特征维度初始化一个权重值,等到目标函数收敛时,噪声维度所对应的权重就会趋于 0,从而使得在计算样本间的距离时能够尽可能地忽略噪声维度的影响。

WKmeans 聚类算法的目标函数如式(3)所示:

$$P(U,Z,W)=\sum_{p=1}^{k}\sum_{i=1}^{n}u_{ip}\sum_{j=1}^{m}\omega_j^{\beta}(x_{ij}-z_{pj})^2 \tag{3}$$

式中:ω_j^{β}——权重参数,其意义在于在计算簇内距离时计算的是每个维度的加权平均和,即通过不同的权重值来调节每个维度对于聚类结果的影响。对于权重 ω_j^{β},满足 $\sum_{j=1}^{m}\omega_j^{\beta}=1$ 的约束条件。

3.2　基于 POI 数据的充电桩选址规划

为了方便车主在停留点处充电,聚类半径不宜过大。最小样本数需结合充电站的充电预期为参考,假定每个充电站的最佳充电设备台数为 10,每台设备的小时利用率最低为 20%,此时平均聚类半径为 150m。将地图划分为 150×150 的网格,即每个网格内至少应有 1 个充电站。初步确定聚类个数为 100 个,即拟建设 100 个充电站。

根据各种 POI 点的一级分类,认为其对交通吸引的大小和充电需求成正比,即交通需求大的 POI 点其电动车充电需求也大。按照其对交通吸引的大小,可以得到各个一级分类 POI 点的对于 W-Kmeans 聚类权重。原始 POI 数据分类繁杂,且多个类型的 POI 数据之间存在重复交叉现象,根据 POI 占地面积并参考公共认知度排序[20-21],认为占地面积大且公共认知度高的 POI 对于交通具有较大的影响力,权重也就更高,对于各类 POI 数据赋予的权重值结果见表 3。

不同类别 POI 点的权重值　　表 3

设施类别	餐饮类	购物类	科教类	金融类	交通类	生活类	商务类	政府类
权重	0.2	0.2	0.15	0.1	0.1	0.1	0.1	0.05

根据爬取的 POI 数据和聚类权值,使用 W-Kmeans 算法进行聚类选址规划,当聚类簇中心为 150 个点时,得到的结果如图 2 所示。

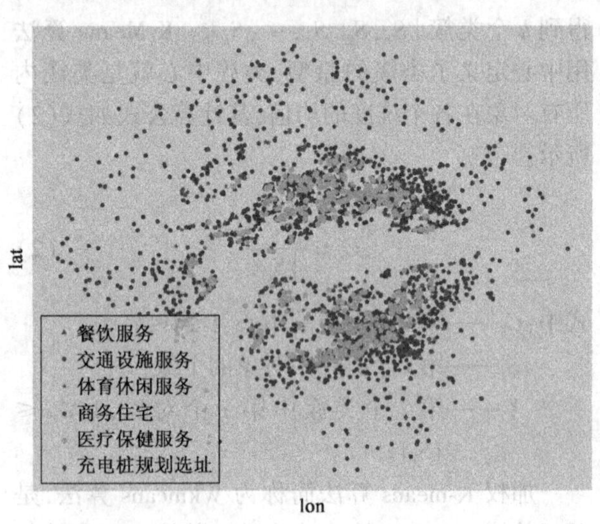

图 2　W-Kmeans 充电站选址聚类结果(1)

从图 2 中可以看出,在充电站应该布局的位置,在餐饮服务、商务住宅密集的地方,充电需求较大,所以充电桩分布比较密集,而对于 POI 点分布较少的地方,充电站聚类簇点较少。对于拟建 150 个充电站的方案,应该在 POI 较少的地点建设大型充电站,以满足充电需要,以及形成新的充电需求引导。

当聚类簇中心为 300 个点时,得到的结果如图 3 所示。

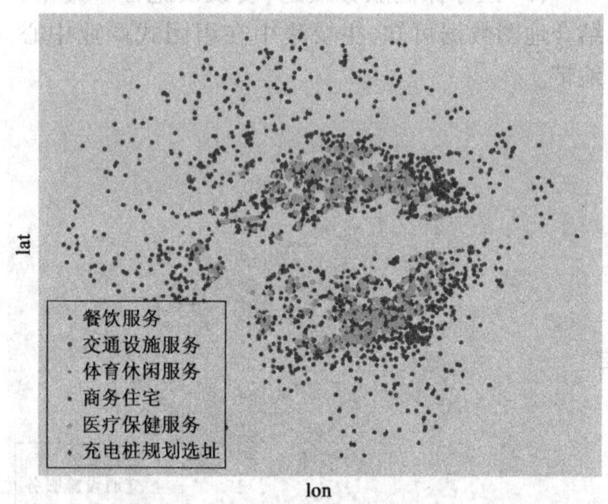

图 3　W-Kmeans 充电站选址聚类结果(2)

对于拟建 300 个充电站的方案,充电站之间距离不超过 200m,但是建设成本较大,在实际建设时,尤其是重庆这样的山地城市,更应该考虑城市道路的可达性。

4　结语

4.1　结论

本文提出了一种基于 POI 数据的充电站选址模型,该方法基于加权 K-means 模型,基于 POI 对于充电需求的吸引,确定电动车充电站的选址。根据充电站的充电站的最佳充电设备台数、每台设备的小时利用率等指标,确定聚类半径,从而确定拟建充电站的个数,根据权值,提出了两种建设方案。

4.2　展望与不足

在当今时代,数据的应用与分析,能够促进科学技术与社会的共同进步。POI 数据也不例外,POI 数据的分析与应用,促进了数据挖掘技术与城市地理学相互发展。基于本文的数据挖掘技术与城市服交通研究的基础上,在后续的研究中仍然有值得探讨的问题,主要可以从以下几个方面进行改进：

(1)提出的模型仅基于POI数据的一级分类，没有考虑到更加细致的二级分类对于充电吸引的不足，如交通设施中，认为公交车站和高速铁路车站对于充电需求是一致的；

(2)近似认为交通需求和充电需求一致，需要对两者的相关性进行进一步研究；

(3)在算法选择上，单一使用K-Means算法，该算法需要手动设置聚类点个数，应该探究其他聚类算法与本文使用算法的优劣。

参考文献

[1] 陈德忠.基于充电行为的电动出租车充电站选址优化及推荐算法研究[D].北京：北京交通大学，2021.

[2] 张勇，顾腾飞.电池交换式电动汽车换电站优化模型研究[J].华南理工大学学报(自然科学版)，2018，46(12)：128-138.

[3] 刘志鹏，文福拴，薛禹胜，等.电动汽车充电站的最优选址和定容[J].电力系统自动化，2012，36(03)：54-59.

[4] 赵明宇，吴峻，张卫国，等.基于时空约束的城市交流充电桩优化布局[J].电力系统自动化，2016，40(04)：66-70+104.

[5] Nie Y M, Ghamami M. A corridor-centric approach to planning electric vehicle charging infrastructure[J]. Transportation Research Part B: Methodological, 2013, 57: 172-190.

[6] Bian C, Li H, Wallin F, et al. Finding the optimal location for public charging stations-a GIS-based MILP approach [J]. Energy Procedia, 2019, 158: 6582-6588.

[7] Mak H Y, Rong Y, Shen Z J M. Infrastructure planning for electric vehicles with battery swapping [J]. Management Science, 2013, 59(7): 1557-1575.

[8] Zhang S, Wang H, Zhang Y, et al. A novel two-stage location model of charging station considering dynamic distribution of electrictaxis [J]. Sustainable Cities and Society, 2019, 51: 101752.

[9] 钱斌，石东源，谢平平，等.电动公交车换电站—电池充电站优化规划[J].电力系统自动化，2014，38(02)：64-69+84.

[10] Jamian J J, Mustafa M W, Mokhlis H, et al. Simulation study on optimal placement and sizing of Battery Switching Station units using Artificial Bee Colony algorithm [J]. International Journal of Electrical Power & Energy Systems, 2014, 55: 592-601.

[11] 冯超，周步祥，林楠，等.Delphi和GAHP集成的综合评价方法在电动汽车充电站选址最优决策中的应用[J].电力自动化设备，2012，32(09)：25-29.

[12] Erbaş M, Kabak M, Özceylan E, et al. Optimal siting of electric vehicle charging stations: A GIS-based fuzzy Multi-Criteria Decision Analysis[J]. Energy, 2018, 163: 1017-1031.

[13] Guo S, Zhao H. Optimal site selection of electric vehicle charging station by using fuzzy TOPSIS based on sustainability perspective [J]. Applied Energy, 2015, 158: 390-402.

[14] Ju Y, Ju D, Gonzalez E D R S, et al. Study of site selection of electric vehicle charging station based on extended GRP method under picture fuzzy environment [J]. Computers & Industrial Engineering, 2019, 135: 1271-1285.

[15] Xu J, Zhong L, Yao L, et al. An interval type-2 fuzzy analysis towards electric vehicle charging station allocation from a sustainable perspective[J]. Sustainable cities and society, 2018, 40: 335-351.

[16] 吴玲玲，彭念.城市空间结构与公共交通通达性匹配研究——以重庆市核心城区为例[J].重庆理工大学学报(自然科学)，2021，35(11)：173-181.

[17] 汪晓春，熊峰，王振伟，等.基于POI大数据与机器学习的养老设施规划布局——以武汉市为例[J].经济地理，2021，41(06)：49-56.

[18] 杜兰，葛军莲，王宏志，等.基于POI网络信息的景区最优游客接待中心选址研究——以南京钟山景区智慧旅游为例[J].华中师范大学学报(自然科学版)，2014，48(04)：613-619.

[19] 帅春燕，许庚，何民，等.基于城市POI聚类的需求不确定情况下电动自行车换电柜选址[J].重庆理工大学学报(自然科学)，

2021,35(07):169-175.

[20] 张玲. POI的分类标准研究[J]. 测绘通报, 2012(10):82-84.

[21] 赵卫锋,李清泉,李必军. 利用城市POI数据提取分层地标[J]. 遥感学报, 2011, 15(05):973-988.

基于大样本GPS数据的公交线路行驶工况构建

刘　斌*[1]　白　杰[2]　王亚楠[1]　魏东东[1]　宋潮安[2]

(1.长安大学公路学院;2.长安大学运输学院)

摘　要　为了构建符合青岛市交通特征的公交车行驶工况,对青岛市公交车GPS数据进行采集,获得428644条有效数据,从中划分得到7151个短行程,采用主成分分析法和碎石法相互验证,将数据维数降为4维,应用K均值聚类与最佳增量选择法选取代表性片段,最终构建了青岛市公交车行驶工况。结果表明:拟合工况与样本的特征参数对比平均相对误差为4.97%,构建的工况可以反映青岛市公交车辆行驶特点;与美国FTP75和欧洲NEDC工况相比,青岛市公交车行驶工况加速和减速比例存在一定差异,与欧洲NEDC工况对比匀速比例甚至低30%以上,国外工况标准不能完全反映青岛市实际交通状况。

关键词　城市交通　行驶工况构建　短行程划分　GPS数据　大样本

0　引言

汽车行驶工况,又称为汽车行驶循环,是衡量车辆在给定的行驶环境下行驶状况的重要指标[1]。目前世界各国都开发并构建了各自的汽车行驶工况标准,以反映真实的驾驶情况,为控制车辆能耗与排放量的评估、性能试验等提供重要参考[2-3]。

目前世界广泛使用的行驶工况主要有美国、欧洲和日本三大体系[4]。许多国家与地区也针对自身交通特征对驾驶工况进行进一步的研究[5-6]。Fotouhi等[7]利用安装在私家车上的高级车辆定位数据,应用K均值聚类法建立了包含1533s的速度时间序列的行驶工况,Mohd Azman Abas等[8]利用在马来西亚众多城市道路上的实际发动机参数及其特性构建了马来西亚乘用车行驶工况,John Brady等[9]利用爱尔兰全国电动汽车示范项目为期6个月的试验数据构建了符合爱尔兰电动汽车真实状况的行驶工况。我国各城市也对驾驶工况展开了研究,并建立了部分城市的行驶工况。孙强等[10]以环卫车为研究对象通过两阶段聚类法构建了西安市环卫车行驶工况,张宏等[11]通过专用设备收集了74台车辆的样本构建了呼和浩特轻型车辆的驾驶工况。国内还有部分学者对驾驶工况研究方法进行改进,徐婷等[12]利用改进的短行程法将传统的工况构建方法适用于高原山区的复杂路段,苏小会等[13]对行驶工况聚类算法引入了加权欧式距离与最大最小距离进行改进,建立了汽车行驶工况分析瞬时油耗。

目前我国对于行驶工况的构建与构建方法上有一定的研究,但是,现有研究一方面对于城市公交车的行驶工况构建研究较少,公交车的运行规律不同于普通车辆,具有日行驶距离远、路线规律性强等特点,因此构建其行驶工况具有重要意义。另一方面,不同的城市具有不同的交通特征与道路条件,国内对于青岛市的行驶工况研究较少,本文基于大样本GPS数据,利用主成分分析和碎石法互相验证,对数据维度进行降维,通过K均值聚类提取代表性短行程片段,构建出青岛市公交车的行驶工况。

1　数据采集与预处理

1.1　道路试验规划及数据采集

一般行驶工况构建常用数据采集方法为车辆追踪法、自主行驶法和平均车流统计法等[14]。本文所用到的数据源为青岛市公交公司一条固定线路上41个不同编号公交车车载设备采集的GPS数据,青岛市公交车日行驶里程长、行驶范围广,适合采用自主行驶法进行采集,该法不影响驾驶员驾驶车辆,采集数据前只要与公交公司商量好,提前安装好设备,于汽车运营过程中即可采集数据。

公交车在运行路线上行驶时,车载设备会自动记录车辆的相关运行信息并储存。通过试验车辆可以获得的运行信息主要包括车辆编号、运行时间、实时速度、经纬度、方向等。为了最大限度降低采样频率对研究结果的负面影响,本文 GPS 的采样频率为 1s,最终采集的数据样本大小为 428703 行 8 列,参照同类研究,符合大样本的特点[15-16]。

1.2 数据预处理

GPS 车载设备记录的数据会因为种种原因引起数据的漂移和失真[17],这些原始数据须经进一步的筛选处理才能用于工况的构建。

需要删除的数据包括数据毛刺和数据尖点。数据毛刺指的是在较长怠速时间内,速度却不为零的样本点,这些数据会影响怠速时长的计算;数据尖点指的是加速度绝对值大于 $3m/s^2$ 的数据,在正常的公交运营过程中加速度限值为 $3m/s^2$[18]。

异常值主要针对速度突变,一般来说城市公交车的运行速度不能大于 70km/h,将速度大于 70km/h 的片段视为异常片段,并删除含异常片段的整个短行程。

重复值采用均值法,取相同时间内车速的均值,对重复值进行删除。处理结果见表 1。

数据处理结果 表1

原有数据数量(条)	删除数据数量(条)	异常数据数量(条)	重复数据数量(条)
428703	16	25	18
经处理后保留数据	428687	428662	428644
数据保存率	0.9999	0.9999	0.9998

2 数据分析

定步长截取法在划分短行程时只考虑了持续时间这一个因素,并未考虑其他因素对划分短行程的影响。结合青岛市交通特征,本文采用短行程法构建工况。

2.1 短行程划分

短行程指的是车辆行驶工况图中的一个片段,如图 1 所示,基本上每个短行程均可由一个行驶片段和一个怠速片段构成,故速度为 0 可视为一个短行程的起点或终点,以此为依据进行短行程划分,将 428703 条数据划分为 7151 个短行程。

统计性特征值分类见表 2,分别求出每个短行程的各个特征参数,特征参数见表 3。

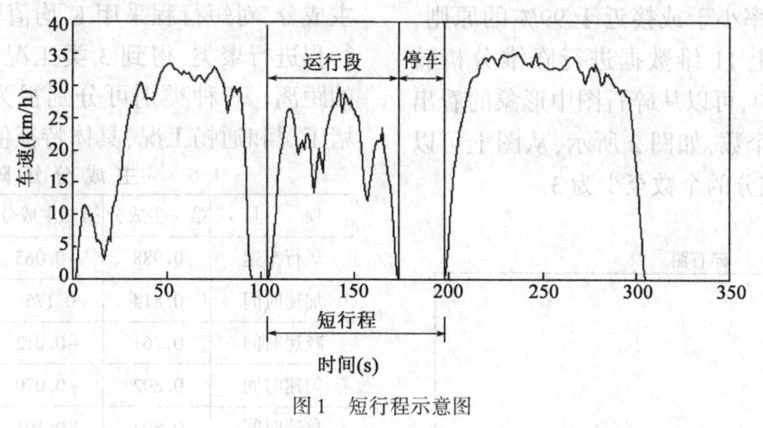

图 1 短行程示意图

特征值的分类 表2

描述性特征值		统计性特征值	
运行时间(s)	平均运行车速(km/h)	加速时间比例	0~10km/h 速度段的比例
加速时间(s)	速度标准差(km/h)		10~20km/h 速度段的比例
减速时间(s)	平均加速度(m/s^2)	减速时间比例	20~30km/h 速度段的比例
匀速时间(s)		匀速时间比例	……
怠速时间(s)	平均减速度(m/s^2)	怠速时间比例	60~70km/h 速度段的比例
平均车速(km/h)	加速度标准差(m/s^2)		

短行程的特征参数 表3

序号	运行时间	加速时间	减速时间	匀速时间	……	加速度标准差
1	96	29	47	5	……	0.07
2	151	22	65	9	……	0.07
3	334	53	114	30	……	0.07
4	339	111	68	27	……	0.12
……	……	……	……	……	……	……
7151	77	11	24	5	……	0.06

2.2 主成分分析和聚类分析

短行程片段的特征值有11个维度,采用所有的特征值计算数据量巨大,也会导致信息冗余重叠,而采用几个特征值作为分类指标会导致信息丢失,为了降低数据维度,需要进行主成分分析,提取出主要的成分进行研究。本文采用Python的Scikit-Learn库中的主成分分析实现,分析结果见表4。

主成分分析结果表 表4

向量	成分1	成分2	成分3	成分4	……	成分11
向量维度1	0.8786	-0.0022	0.0001	0.1661	……	-0.4472
向量维度2	0.2868	0.3817	-0.7123	-0.2542	……	0.4472
向量维度3	0.2854	0.3974	-0.7018	-0.2601	……	0.4472
……	……	……	……	……	……	……
向量维度11	……	……	……	……	……	……
方差百分比	0.8953	0.0749	0.0244	0.0003	……	0.0000
累计贡献率	0.8953	0.9702	0.9946	0.9949	……	1.0000

若按照累计贡献率小于或接近于80%原则来确定主成分的话[19],只有一个主成分,不符常规,本文采取累计贡献率小于或接近于99%的原则,并采用SPSS对以上11维数据进行降维分析验证,SPSS因子分析中,可以从碎石图中形象的看出来提取出的主成分个数,如图2所示,从图上可以直观地看出来,主成分的个数至少为3。

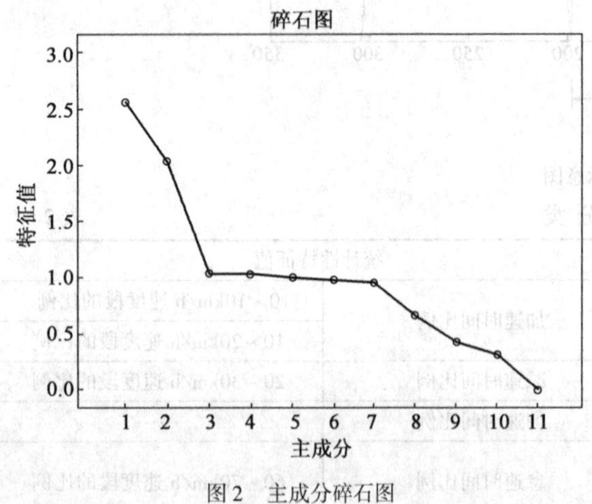

图2 主成分碎石图

在SPSS中生成主成分矩阵表见表5。

由表5可知,SPSS把11维数据降维成了4个主成分,对短行程采用K均值聚类法对7151个短行程进行聚类,得到3类工况的聚类中心及之间的距离。三种类别可分别视为拥堵工况、比较拥堵工况和通畅工况,具体特征值见表6。

主成分矩阵 表5

项目	第一主成分	第二主成分	第三主成分	第四主成分
运行车速	0.988	-0.065	-0.001	0.004
加速时间	0.814	0.175	-0.004	0.009
减速时间	0.761	-0.012	-0.017	0.000
匀速时间	0.802	-0.070	0.020	-0.013
怠速时间	0.803	-0.191	0.008	0.005
平均车速	0.070	0.993	0.015	-0.004
平均运行车速	-0.006	0.004	-0.049	0.737
车速标准差	0.009	-0.007	0.678	0.007
平均加速度	0.009	0.004	0.131	0.521
平均减速度	-0.013	-0.027	0.671	-0.245
加速度标准差	-0.019	-0.014	0.324	0.394

各类平均特征值汇总 表6

特征值	第一类	第二类	第三类
最大速度(km/h)	58.9	26.2	35.7
平均速度(km/h)	40.5	21.4	31.0
平均运行速度(km/h)	38.5	20.3	28.2
平均加速度(m/s^2)	0.65	0.58	0.55
平均减速度(m/s^2)	0.39	0.56	0.48
加速时间比例	0.25	0.26	0.24
减速时间比例	0.38	0.29	0.33
匀速时间比例	0.07	0.08	0.07
怠速时间比例	0.30	0.37	0.36
0~10km/h速度段的比例	0.00	0.02	0.04
10~20km/h速度段的比例	0.00	0.04	0.18
20~30km/h速度段的比例	0.00	0.18	0.11
30~40km/h速度段的比例	0.56	0.43	0.31
40~50km/h速度段的比例	0.43	0.32	0.20
50~60km/h速度段的比例	0.02	0.00	0.00
60~70km/h速度段的比例	0.00	0.00	0.00

3 行驶工况构建

由聚类结果可知,第一类工况有1994个片段,第二类工况有1951个片段,第三类工况有3206个片段,三类短行程片段比例约为1:1:2。本文预计构建600s(10min)的工况,为了保证所构建的工况能够较为全面的反应各种运动状态,所以应该根据三类工况中所包含短行程片段的数量比,来确定构建工况时每类工况中应该抽取的短行程数目。

应用最佳增量选择法,在1994个通畅工况中选出与该类总体特征值最相近的短行程片段,比较两者特征值的相似度,通过比较选出各个特征值都与通畅类总体特征值最为相似的短行程片段。经过对比,选取序号为1056的短行程片段作为通畅时的候选工况。同理,选出序号为2987的短行程片段作为比较拥堵时的候选工况,选出序号为5432、6928的两个短行程片段作为拥堵时的候选工况。最终,由4个短行程构成青岛市线路一城市公交车综合行驶工况如图3所示。

由图3可以看出,公交车运行速度总体偏低且加减速比较频繁,可能是因为青岛城区车辆较多,驾驶员驾驶车辆总体速度较慢,但由于市民节奏较快,车辆起动或制止车辆频数都较多。速度为0的时间段比较多,可认为遭遇红灯或拥堵地段,该工况参数总体上符合城市公交车的运行状况。

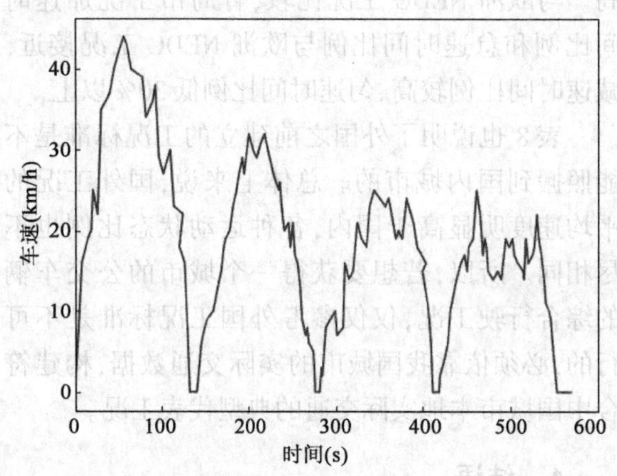

图3 青岛市城市公交车综合行驶工况

对本文工况进行验证,将本文工况的特征参数与样本数据特征参数进行对比,结果见表7。

由表7可知,样本数据各项特征参数与本文构建的工况特征参数误差最大值为7.7%,平均相对误差仅为4.97%,说明本文构建的能够较真实的反映青岛市公交的实际运行状态。将本文工况与国际上常用的标准测试工况进行对比,结果见表8。

样本数据和工况的特征参数对比 表7

特征参数	样本数据特征参数	工况特征参数	误差(%)	平均相对误差(%)
平均速度(km/h)	32.1	31.0	3.4	—
平均加速度(m/s^2)	0.65	0.66	1.5	—
平均减速度(m/s^2)	-0.43	-0.40	7.0	—
加速比例	0.25	0.26	4.0	4.97
减速比例	0.22	0.21	3.8	—
匀速比例	0.26	0.24	7.7	—
怠速比例	0.27	0.29	7.4	—

三类工况特征参数对比　表 8

工　况	平均速度 (km/h)	平均加速度 (m/s^2)	平均减速度 (m/s^2)	加速时间比例 (%)	减速时间比例 (%)	匀速时间比例 (%)	怠速时间比例 (%)
FTP75	34.1	0.66	-0.75	19.1	28.8	25.6	26.5
NEDC	33.2	0.48	-0.67	23.2	17.3	36.8	23.7
本文工况	31.0	0.66	-0.40	26.2	23.6	24.5	25.7

由表 8 可知,本文所构建的青岛市工况与美国 FTP75 和欧洲 NEDC 的典型工况有很明显的差异。美国 FTP75 和欧洲 NEDC 的平均速度要比青岛市平均速度略高。与美国 FTP75 工况比较,青岛市匀速时间比例和怠速时间比例与美国 FTP75 工况接近,减速时间比例较低,加速时间比例较高。与欧洲 NEDC 工况比较,青岛市工况加速时间比例和怠速时间比例与欧洲 NEDC 工况接近,减速时间比例较高,匀速时间比例低 30% 以上。

表 8 也说明了外国之前建立的工况标准是不能照搬到国内城市的。总体上来说,国外工况的平均速度明显高于国内,各种运动状态比例也不尽相同。所以,若想要获得一个城市的公交车辆的综合行驶工况,仅仅参考外国工况标准是不可行的,必须依靠我国城市的实际交通数据,构建符合中国城市本地实际交通的典型代表工况。

4　结语

(1)采集了 428703 条数据进行数据清洗,得到 428644 条有效数据,划分为 7151 个短行程,计算短行程片段的特征值参数,并应用主成分分析法和碎石法互相验证进行降维分析,应用 K 均值聚类和最佳增量选择法,按各类工况的比例来组成基于大样本并符合青岛市公交车交通特征的综合行驶工况。

(2)构建的青岛市公交车综合行驶工况通过多个特征值参数的对比,与整体数据特征值的平均相对误差为 4.97%,误差最大值为 7.7%,表明构建的驾驶工况能够代表青岛市的实际行驶状况。

(3)青岛市公交车行驶工况在加速时间比例和减速时间比例等与美国 FTP75 和欧洲 NEDC 工况存在一定差异,采用外国工况标准不能完全反映青岛市实际的交通状况,应针对我国城市实际情况建立能够反映当地交通特点的行驶工况。

(4)样本数据实际采集的主要是青岛城区的某一公交线路,线路覆盖率较低,不具有整体代表性,不能代表整个城市的行驶工况。在今后的研究中应考虑采集多条线路数据来构建青岛市的公交车行驶工况。

参考文献

[1] 张璇. 西安市公交工况构建方法研究[D]. 西安:长安大学,2017.

[2] Shen P, Zhao, et al. Development of a typical driving cycle for an intra-city hybrid electric bus with a fixed route[J]. Transportation Research Part D: Transport & Environment, 2018.

[3] 罗玉涛,胡红斐,沈继军. 混合动力电动汽车行驶工况分析与识别[J]. 华南理工大学学报:自然科学版,2007,35(6):7.

[4] Chauhan B P, Joshi G J, Purnima P. Driving cycle analysis to identify intersection influence zone for urban intersections under heterogeneous traffic condition [J]. Sustainable Cities & Society, 2018, 41:180-185.

[5] Zhao X, Ma J, Wang S, et al. Developing an electric vehicle urban driving cycle to study differences in energy consumption [J]. Environmental Science and Pollution Research, 2019.

[6] Kim W, Kyum C, et al. Characteristics of nanoparticle emission from a light-duty diesel vehicle during test cycles simulating urban rush-hour driving patterns[J]. Journal of Nanoparticle ResearchAn Interdisciplinary Forum for Nanoscale Science & Technology, 2018.

[7] Fotouhi A, Montazeri-Gh M. Tehran driving cycle development using the k k -means clustering method[J]. Scientia Iranica, 2013, 20(2):286-293.

[8] Abas M A, Rajoo S, Abidin S. Development of Malaysian urban drive cycle using vehicle and

engine parameters [J]. Transportation Research,2018,63(AUG.):388-403.

[9] Brady J, O'Mahony M. Development of a driving cycle to evaluate the energy economy of electric vehicles in urban areas [J]. Applied Energy,2016,177(sep.1):165-178.

[10] 孙强,白书战,韩尔樑,等.基于试验测量的瞬时行驶工况构建[J].吉林大学学报:工学版,2015(2):7.

[11] 张宏,姚延钢,杨晓勤.城市道路轻型汽车行驶工况构建[J].西南交通大学学报,2019,54(6):9.

[12] 徐婷,崔世超,刘明,等.高原山区乘用车行驶工况构建方法研究[J].公路交通科技,2021,38(2):8.

[13] 苏小会,张玉西,徐淑萍,等.改进K-means聚类算法行驶工况及油耗研究[J].计算机工程与科学,2021,43(11):7.

[14] 李宁.城市道路车辆行驶工况的构建与研究[D].保定:河北农业大学,2013.

[15] Andre M, Hickman A J, Hassel D, et al. Driving cycles for emission measurements under European conditions [J]. SAE transactions,1995:562-574.

[16] Haan P D, Keller M. Real-world driving cycles for emission measurements: ARTEMIS and Swiss cycles[J]. 2001.

[17] 李耀华,苟琦智,任田园,等.城市公交线路模态行驶工况构建研究——以西安市公交线路为例[J].交通信息与安全,2018,36(3):7.

[18] 张翠平.城市道路公交车行驶工况特征研究——以南京市为例[D].南京:东南大学,2017.

[19] 石琴,马洪龙,丁建勋,等.改进的FCM聚类法及其在行驶工况构建中的应用[J].中国机械工程,2014,25(10):7.

新发展格局下交通强国昆明方案研究

孙莉芬*[1]　李　军[2]　彭　伟[2]　张旭东[1]　张建明[3]

(1.昆明市城市交通研究所;2.昆明市交通运输局;3.昆明市建设服务中心)

摘　要　昆明市进入新的发展时期,交通强国建设为破解城市交通问题提供了新的机遇与发展方向。为认真贯彻落实《交通强国建设纲要》精神,深入推进交通强市建设,对标学习国际国内先进城市经验,突出昆明特色和引领全省发展,通过发展形势和需求分析,科学谋划制定建设交通强国的昆明方案,建立三阶段的发展目标,实现三张交通网、三个交通圈的构建,推动十大体系的交通运输高质量可持续发展,切实体现昆明担当。

关键词　交通强国　国际性综合交通枢纽　公交都市　交通治理

0　引言

在新的发展时期,《交通强国建设纲要》作为交通运输的顶层设计正式印发,自此"交通强国"作为国家战略自上而下在全国各地开展实施,各地陆续在重点领域推出了一系列的交通强国建设的试点工作。云南省作为交通强国的第二批试点省份,为积极落实云南省对昆明市的定位要求,发挥昆明区域辐射和省会引领作用,先行开展交通强国方案在昆明的落地,推出昆明机场枢纽一体化、昆明市交通运行智能化协调指挥系统、昆明市智慧停车信息平台等一批试点任务,并列入云南省交通强国试点工作,在全省先行开展、推广经验。

1　现实基础

随着昆明市国际性综合交通枢纽的建设,昆明市交通运输行业进入了全面提速的发展阶段,疫情前昆明长水国际机场完成运输起降架次35.71万架次、旅客吞吐量4807.61万人次、货邮吞吐量41.58万t;铁路旅客发送量6508.3万人,高速铁路动车发送旅客3968.0万人,占旅客发送比例的61.0%;货物运输量14224.1万t,增长8.8%;全市公路总里程突破20367km,高速公路通车里程突破1160km的大关;公路、铁路、民航客运总量比为14.5:48.4:37.1,相较上一年,航空客流比重相对稳定,公路客运比重大幅降低,向铁路方式转移。昆明中心城道路长度2243.1km,较上一年增长3.2%,公交专用道达194km,轨道交通通车总里程达139.4km,串联机场、高速铁路车站、公路客运枢纽及各大商圈,昆明轨道交通进入"五线齐发、三线共建"的崭新阶段,昆明市公共交通日均服务261.11万人次,公共交通机动化出行分担率达58%;昆明全市机动车保有量达282.4万辆,年度增长6.6%,主城区早高峰主要道路平均车速为22.84km/h,较上一年下降1.96km/h,在机动车快速增长、城市空间扩张和城市功能集聚所引发的交通需求增长迅猛,昆明依然面临各种复杂的交通问题和挑战。

2　规划构思

为进一步发挥优势、弥补短板,立足目标导向和问题导向,聚焦当前存在的问题和主要矛盾,凸显新时代昆明的国家战略地位和区域引领作用,准确把握未来昆明交通运输发展趋势和结构优化、发展短板和提升空间,落实推进创新驱动、转型发展、供给侧结构性改革,综合谋划好昆明未来的交通发展战略定位、空间格局和要素配置,推动交通强国建设试点在昆明落地,以"通达全球、面向全国、辐射区域、建设枢纽上的中心城市、轨道上的滇中核心"为战略目标,坚持从全局谋划一域、以一域服务全局,展现交通强国的省会担当,按照一条主线、三个阶段来实现三张交通网、三个交通圈的构建,推动十大体系的交通运输高质量可持续发展,如图1所示。

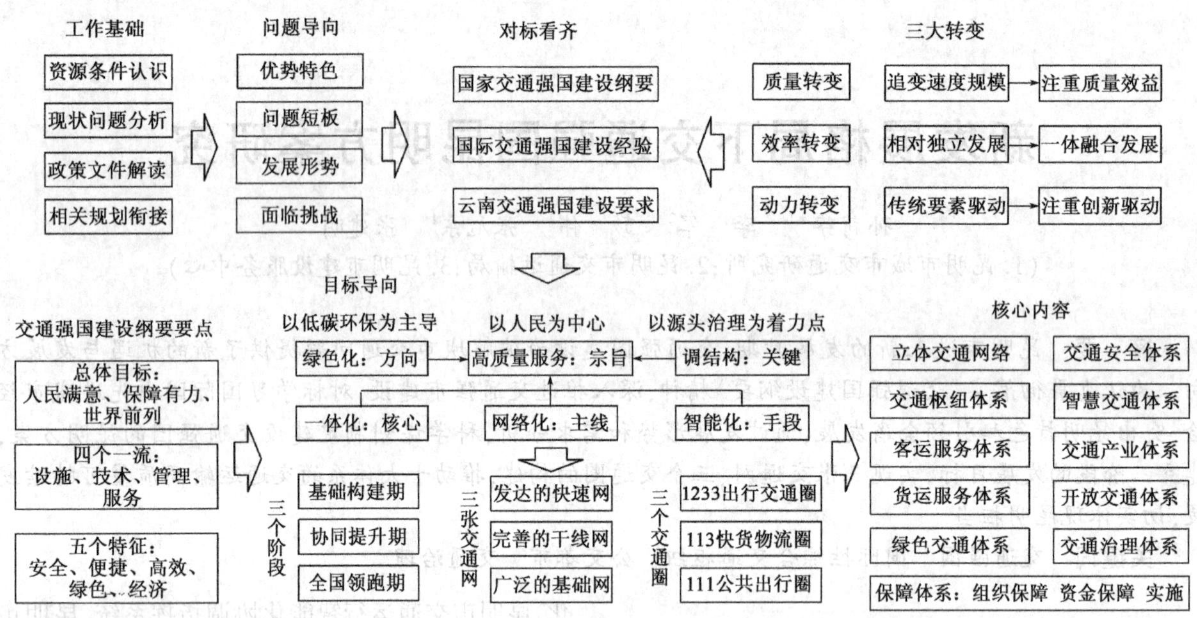

图1　技术路线图

3　趋势分析

3.1　交通需求结构不断提升,跨区域、跨方式、网络化的出行日益增多

随着滇中城市群和区域性国际中心城市战略的推进,昆明市的发展不能仅局限在滇池流域范围,需全域全要素地统筹市域国土空间格局,在昆明全域范围内谋求城市的新的发展走廊,加快推进南部都市区城镇空间向城市发展核心、四大协作发展片区集聚,逐步引导北部山区城镇空间向各县(市、区)域中心城镇、重点镇集聚。以网络化城镇空间布局结构为发展目标,跨越以往以环湖为核心的"一湖四片""一主四辅"的发展形态,构建"两核两翼、多片多点、山水相间、网络发展"的昆明都市区发展格局,城际铁路、高速公路、轨道交通等形成的立体交通网络将构筑城镇

空间的发展骨架,改变单核心、放射状的出行向多中心、网络化出行的转变。都市圈内人流与物流的空间大范围、高密度位移,要求交通方式的多样化,越来越多的出行需求采取多种方式组合在一起来完成,进而促进都市区不同圈层的一体化发展。

3.2 轨道交通引领空间重构,高频化、日常化、同城化的区际联系加强

随着高速铁路、城际铁路、市域(郊)铁路、高速公路等立体交通网络的逐渐完善,居民人均出行率将逐步提高,未来客运出行量年均增速将保持在4.5%左右。云南省内高速铁路营运里程1105km,云南高铁已基本形成了1h覆盖滇中城市群,2~3h覆盖滇西、滇南、滇东南地区,2~5h通达周边省会城市,高速铁路引发城市和区域时空距离变形,拉近了城市与城市之间的距离,使得城市之间的同城效应得到体现,催生了一个个不同层次、大大小小的跨区域"城市圈"和"经济圈"。昆明城内6条地铁线路投入运营,拓展了城市的出行空间,将昆明市的交通出行半径增加至25km以上,地铁促进了中心城区与外围组团的联系的同时带动了城市空间形态和结构升级,地铁的大容量、准时、快捷的服务特征吸引了大量的人流量。区域中心城市带动城镇群发展的交通需求快速增长,以中心城区向心交通和以边界跨城交通需求旺盛。

3.3 客运需求保持增长态势,多样化、个性化、高品质的出行特征显著

经济的增长将带来人均出行次数的上升,2035年昆明都市核心区人均全方式出行强度将由现状的2.3次/日增长到2.6~2.7次/日。随着生活水平从生存型、温饱型向发展型、美好型的转变,人民对美好生活的向往表现在出行消费倾向于选择更快速、更舒适、更自由的交通方式,从"走得了"向"走得快、走得好"转变,多元化、个性化的交通出行要求逐步增加,交通消费结构进一步升级,对出行的安全性、舒适性提出更高的质量要求,客运需求由基本出行向品质出行转变,未来休闲、旅游、度假等娱乐性出行需求增加显著,将带动民航、高铁、自驾游市场的快速增长,另外,信息化、"互联网+"将改变人的出行行为,即时性、体验性和个性化出行成为一种新趋势。

3.4 产业结构升级优化调整,敏捷性、时效强、高价值的物流快速攀升

随着昆明市产业高质量发展进程加快,内陆开放高地建设稳步推进,全市货运需求稳步增长,外贸货物运输保持长期较快增长态势,昆明市作为国际班列枢纽节点城市,未来货运量年均增速将保持在3.5%左右,邮政快递业务量年均增速将保持在6.5%左右。产业结构的升级要求提升物流货运系统的敏捷性,进而满足对货物运输的高时效性要求;随着产业结构的优化,第二产业比重的下降导致货运需求和强度下降,敏捷性、时效强、高价值的物流快速攀升,运输结构进一步优化,中长距离货物运输以铁路、航空为主导,高速公路货运重点辐射滇中城市群周边毗邻地区。

4 昆明交通强国建设发展目标

以"通达全球、面向全国、辐射区域、建设枢纽上的中心城市、轨道上的滇中核心"为战略目标,按照一条主线、三个阶段落实交通强国战略,从2020年到21世纪中叶,分阶段推进交通强国建设。第一阶段从2020—2025年为基础构建期,聚焦补短板,聚力提效能,推进综合交通枢纽建设,加快交通基础设施"能通全通""互联互通"建设,进一步提升"公交都市"建设,绿色交通出行方式达75%以上,物流成本降低至15%(占地区生产总值)以下,初步构建现代化的综合交通运输体系;第二阶段从2026—2035年为协同提升期,推进各方式一体化发展、注重全面融合,建成国际性综合交通枢纽,强力支撑云南省出行交通圈和快货物流圈的构建,实现滇中城市群1h城际圈、都市区1h通勤圈、综合客运枢纽平均5min换乘、慢行或公交15min内可达公共服务设施点;重点镇30min上高速公路、县市核心区30min进机场或高铁站,中心城1h通达市域各县市。绿色交通出行方式达80%以上,物流成本降低至9%(占地区生产总值)以下,基本建成现代化综合交通运输体系。第三阶段从2036年到21世纪中叶为全面领跑期,注重现代化治理、彰显卓越品质。建成"一带一路"战略支点城市、面向南亚东南亚和环印度洋地区的桥头堡和区域性国际中心城市,绿色交通出行方式达90%以上,物流成本降低至7%以下(占地区生产总值),全面实现现代化综合交通运输体系。

5　推进昆明交通强国战略的发展路径

5.1　立体互联,打造高质量的综合交通网络

构建区域一体的立体交通快速网络,通过拓展航线、直通高速铁路、加密高速公路、提升航道等,着力增强"五向九廊"战略性复合运输通道对外辐射能力,实现与重要城市的直连直通;构筑外联内通的干线交通网络,新建城际铁路"一环四射"的铁路网昆明境内段及两市域线,如图6所示;对接城乡空间发展,加快国省干线公路线网优化和提质升级改造,在全域范围内实现国省道等级达到二级以上;打通从东川港到水富港的金沙江流域航道,连通长江航道。打造全域畅达的交通基础网络,推行小街区密路网布局,高水平织密"四好农村路",高标准打造"美丽公路",实现农村公路成环成网。

5.2　多网融合,打造国际性综合交通枢纽体系

加快长水国际机场设施改扩建工程,以机场为中心打造超级交通枢纽联合体,推进昆明第二机场建设,与长水国际机场形成联动效益,与省内多类型机场协调发展,形成面向全球的航空枢纽机场群;建设高速铁路引领的国际铁路枢纽,改扩建昆明站、升级昆明南、新建昆明西和长水机场高速铁路车站,提升公路客运枢纽体系,强化与轨道网的零距离换乘,形成一港两核四纽多星的客运枢纽布局。推进中心城区公路货运站搬迁和物流资源整合,建成"一圈两轴"货运枢纽格局。

5.3　多元便捷,打造高水准的客运运行体系

构建民航和地面交通一体化协同运行体系,依托高速铁路、城际铁路、城市轨道、机场巴士等交通方式延伸航空运输服务链,以提高整网效率、扩大中转旅客规模为中心,打造层次分明、高效衔接的优质航班波。建立在集约化和高效率之上高质量发展由高速铁路、城际轨道交通、市域轨道交通、城市轨道交通为主导的城际出行,推动城际铁路、市域(郊)轨道交通线的统一规划建设和跨界运营,建成以环滇铁路为核心形成一环多射的市郊铁路布局,实现滇中城市群城镇间30min至1h到达。保障公交核心竞争力,强化大运量轨道网,1~9号线全网建成,加密补强轨道网,新增10、11、12井字形轨道网;保障公交路权、提速地面公交,在向外放射道路、城市发展轴、轨道交通覆盖盲区,新建、改建的城市快速路、主次干道,优先配置公交专用道;创新多元化公共交通服务,实施"全域公交",全面推进城市公交、城乡班线和镇村公交三级客运网络融合。

5.4　降本增效,打造集约化的货运服务体系

基于以腾俊国际陆港、安宁南亚陆港、空港物流集聚区、东川港等整合物流资源,构建三级城市物流配送网络,建立网格化管理体系。以昆明集装箱中心站为核心,打造大宗商品集散中心与国际班列集结中心,发展面向南亚东南亚的跨境物流,提升中越国际货运班列、中老国际货运班列、中缅"海公铁"联运货运组织能力,推动与中欧班列、西部陆海新通道等国际集装箱多式联运项目深度融合。依托商区、居住区等社区配送集散点,建立三级物流配送节点,大力发展"互联网+"物流新业态、新模式,构建一大批特色平台,完善城市末端服务网络。

5.5　绿色环保,打造高品质的低碳交通体系

促进交通运输结构性减排,加快构建以高速铁路和城际铁路为主体的大容量快速客运系统,形成与铁路、民航、水运相衔接的道路客运集疏网络,稳步提高铁路客运比重,促进各种运输方式的有效衔接和深度融合;按照"宜陆则陆、宜空则空、宜水则水"的原则,促进不同运输方式各展其长,发展多式联运提高综合运输的组合效率。继续深入推进公交优先战略,进一步提高公交出行分担率,鼓励发展城市慢行交通系统,建设绿色出行友好环境,增加绿色出行方式吸引力,让人民群众更多更好分享绿色交通的成果。

5.6　安全可靠,打造高标准的平安交通体系

加大交通基础设施安全防护投入,深入推进交通安全工程建设,继续加大公路、轨道交通、站场、枢纽、航道等交通运输安全设施建设投入;加强重点领域安全管控和全程数字化监管。推进交通安全体系建设,强化企业安全生产、隐患排查与交通安全风险管控;提升安全应急保障能

力，完善交通行业突发事件应急预案，建立上下联动、水陆空协同、军民融合的综合交通应急管理体制机制，建立全天候通行保障和应急通道，加强物资配备、应急保障车辆，提升应对突发公共卫生事件、极端天气、国际会议和赛事等的应急响应能力。

5.7 产城融合，打造高层级的交通产业体系

围绕机场、高速铁路车站、地铁站、物流园区等枢纽载体，进行圈层拓展、产城融合的产业空间布局，形成站城一体、产城融合的综合枢纽，建成各枢纽联动互补、多种交通方式交汇融合的枢纽经济区，大力发展枢纽经济，加速交通枢纽偏好型产业集聚。深度融合旅游+交通，将城际铁路、米轨线路、环滇轨道与沿线旅游资源有效统筹，打造“快旅”骨干体系，实现旅客出发地与目的地城市的快速到达及云南城市之间的快速移动，同步发展城郊环带式旅游线路；围绕公园、绿地、林荫道路和旅游景点，开发郊野环山绿道、环湖绿道、滨河绿道等，建设339km绿道串联旅游景点、市民公园，形成“建团成环”的绿道布局；基于生态修复要求，有节制开发金沙江、滇池、盘龙江为核心的“一江一湖一轴”，其他库湖区为补充的生态航道；深度开发公路自驾游、房车营地、游艇旅游、低空飞行旅游等发展。

5.8 创新驱动，打造高水平的智慧交通体系

推进大数据、5G技术、云计算、区块链、人工智能等新技术在交通运输领域的深度应用，积极发展自动驾驶、无人递送，推动工程云建设，完善综合交通智慧云平台，开发大数据集成应用，打造交通大脑。推动交通基础设施和载运工具数字化，制定多式信息共享和数据传输、交换标准，加强信息共享融合。实现建管养数据互联互通，构建智能化建管养体系；加强安全运行管控系统建设，实现全生命周期健康性能监测，实现路网智慧管控；推动公共服务智慧化，以“互联网+交通”的思维，聚焦公众出行需求，推动铁路、机场、公路等设施智能化升级，整合交通出行服务信息。

5.9 互利互赢，打造高潜力的开放交通体系

强化昆明与周边国家在国际航空航线、铁路联运、道路运输、水陆联运等方面的衔接，打通对外开放通道，积极支持海外仓建设，加快王家营片区铁路枢纽申报国家级口岸，鼓励开展面向南亚东南亚的国际多式联运试点；积极争取第五航权在内的国际航权，支持昆明长水国际机场开展航班时刻改革试点。打造通往南亚东南亚快速冷链通道。创新发展航空口岸物流，打造临空经济增长点。发展面向南亚东南亚的跨境物流，推进中老、中越、中缅跨境直达运输试点工作。建设数字口岸交通，建设智能化口岸交通查验设施，构建国际道路运输市场信用体系。

5.10 协同高效，打造规范化的交通治理体系

构建多方参与、共建、共治、共享的交通治理体系，从经济杠杆、交通环境等角度出发研究降低小汽车使用强度，制定科学合理的私人汽车使用政策，实施工作日高峰时段区域限行措施，主动建立长效的交通需求管理机制；从城市规划设计、创新开发模式、优化公共政策、增强智能化管理等视角，不断探索多方式、多手段、多维度的交通综合治理工作模式，推动交通治理从侧重治理小汽车拥堵向提供高品质的交通服务转变。建设和谐礼让、共建共享的文明交通，将交通违法行为纳入信用体系，构建人、车、路和谐共处的良好交通氛围，实现人车互让的高度文明出行。

6 结语

随着中老铁路的开通，以昆明为中心的出境大通道、集结中心雏形已现，昆明与南亚东南亚国家、环印度洋国家的交通更加便捷，联系更加紧密，为以昆明为中心打造面向南亚东南亚和环印度洋周边经济圈的国际新通道提供了新的历史机遇。通过深入推进交通强市的建设，主动服务和融入国家发展战略，市、区各级在交通强国昆明方案的指引下推行试点任务、实施细则，认真贯彻落实交通强国部署，发挥昆明省会引领作用，为辐射南亚东南亚、促进云南跨越式发展发挥更大的作用。

参考文献

[1] 汪光焘. 贯彻交通强国建设纲要 推进城市交通高质量发展[J]. 城市规划，2020，44(3)：31-35.

[2] 昆明机场总体规划修编[R].云南:云南省人民政府,中国民用航空局,2020.
[3] 孙莉芬,等.昆明市贯彻落实《交通强国建设纲要》实施意见课题研究[R].昆明:昆明市城市交通研究所,2021.

大城市高速铁路枢纽公共交通可达性提升研究

郑姝婕[1] 陈学武*[2,3,4] 齐 超[2,3,4]
(1.上海市城市建设设计研究总院(集团)有限公司;2.东南大学江苏省城市智能交通重点实验室;3.东南大学现代城市交通技术江苏高校协同创新中心;4.东南大学交通学院)

摘 要 为提升高速铁路枢纽与城市交通的衔接性,提升乘客出行体验,论文提出了一种枢纽公共交通可达性提升方法。首先定义枢纽公共交通可达性评价标准,构建枢纽公共交通衔接网络,利用地图开放应用程序接口(API)批量爬取枢纽到公交网络各个节点的出行时间,然后通过划分交通小区将站点可达性转换为小区可达性,之后依据枢纽公共交通可达性标准和交通小区客流规模筛选待改善区,通过轨道交通接驳公交线路生成和枢纽直达公交线路优化两种策略的合理选用,实现待改善区的公共交通服务优化。南京南高铁枢纽案例展示了方法的可行性,共筛选了待改善区36个,案例经改善后均满足可达性标准要求。

关键词 城市公共交通设施规划 可达性提升 地图API爬取 高速铁路枢纽 公交线路优化

0 引言

近年来,我国高速铁路飞速发展,截止到2020年底,我国高铁营业里程达到3.8万km。随着高速铁路里程的增长,高速铁路枢纽的建设也愈发受到关注。但当前高速铁路枢纽与城市交通的衔接不尽如人意,存在换乘不便、乘坐公共交通出行时间过长等突出问题。

高速铁路枢纽与城市交通的衔接通常通过各类衔接方式实现。常见的衔接方式可以分为公共交通(主要指轨道交通及地面公交)、个体机动化交通、慢行交通三大类。大城市高速铁路枢纽由于客流集散总量较大,一般采取以公共交通为主体的衔接模式,因此大城市高速铁路枢纽的公共交通可达性提升尤为重要。

关于高速铁路枢纽公共交通可达性,目前已有一些研究。一部分文献以枢纽与传统城市市中心的公共交通出行时间为枢纽可达性评估标准,然后分析影响枢纽可达性的因素。还有一部分文献[3]利用开放数据平台API接口批量获取城市内部点位到达枢纽站的公共交通出行时间,从而评估整个城市范围内不同区域的可达性。但目前对枢纽可达性的研究主要停留在评估方面,对于如何提升枢纽可达性,此类文献并未给出可行方法。

而关于枢纽公共交通衔接网络的定量优化方法,已有研究主要集中在枢纽接运公交的优化设计。Prabhat Shrivastava等人设计了一种混合算法来优化设计接驳公交线网和发车频率。Guo等人设计了一种多目标编程的方法,在最大限度满足可服务的乘客数量的同时,尽可能缩短接运公交的线路长度。张英群[6]以高铁快巴服务网络TOD效用最大和广义成本最小为目标建立了快巴网络优化模型。但目前大城市高速铁路枢纽的公共交通接驳,不单依赖接运公交,而是依靠以轨道交通为主体的整体公共交通网络,而现有研究缺乏对整体公共交通衔接网络的评价与优化。

因此,本文以大城市高速铁路枢纽为研究对象,提出枢纽公共交通可达性提升方法。论文构建了高速铁路枢纽公共交通衔接网络,通过对整个城市进行交通小区划分,梳理枢纽公共交通衔接网络的可达性评价和优化的整体思路。针对轨道交通接驳公交和枢纽直达公交,进行线路优化,以提升部分区域的可达性。最后对南京南高速铁路枢纽进行案例研究。

1 枢纽公共交通可达性评价及提升方法

1.1 可达性评价标准

根据美国 TCQSM 手册,公共交通—小汽车出行时耗比是衡量一个公共交通系统服务水平的重要依据。该指标指完成同一出行起讫点间位移时,使用公共交通与小汽车耗费时间的比值,体现了公共交通方式的出行效率。TCQSM 对不同公共交通—小汽车出行时耗情况下的乘客感受总结如表 1 所示。

公共交通—小汽车出行时耗比　　表 1

公共交通-小汽车出行时耗比	乘客感受
≤1	公交出行比小汽车出行快
>1~1.25	车内出行时间相当(对于 40min 的通勤出行,公交比小汽车多花 10min)
>1.25~1.5	对于乘客来说公交出行时间还可以容忍(对于 40min 的通勤出行,公交比小汽车多花 20min)
>1.5~1.75	对于 40min 的单程出行,公交耗时 1h 以上
>1.75~2	公交出行时间为小汽车的近 2 倍
>2	对于所有乘客都不具有吸引力

当比值大于 2 时,公共交通对乘客基本不再有吸引力。因此,本研究中将高铁枢纽的公共交通衔接网络的可达性评价标准定义为城市内部某点到达高铁枢纽的公共交通时耗 T_{transit} 与小汽车时耗 T_{car} 的之比 R 是否小于或等于 2,如式(1)所示。

$$R=\frac{T_{\text{transit}}}{T_{\text{car}}}\leqslant 2 \tag{1}$$

若 R 小于或等于 2,认为枢纽的公共交通衔接服务可达性可接受,否则应该对该地区的公共交通接驳服务进行改善。

1.2 枢纽公共交通衔接优化思路

本文采用的优化枢纽公共交通衔接网络的思路如图 1 所示。

具体流程如下:

(1)公共交通网络构建。首先,通过地图 API 爬取城市的公共交通站点(包括地铁站点及常规公交站点),构建公共交通网络。本研究认为,城市的整个公共交通网络都有承担枢纽客流集疏运的功能,因此对整体的公共交通网络进行分析,而不局限于枢纽接运公交。

(2)各站点的公共交通出行时耗爬取。通过地图 API 路径规划功能计算枢纽站到达所有站点的公共交通出行时耗。基于地图 API 爬取出行时间的方法在一些研究中已经有应用,具有数据准确且获取速度快的优势。利用此方法可大批量获取城市间任意两个点之间的出行时间。

(3)交通小区划分。对所研究枢纽所在的城市进行交通小区划分,划分交通小区的目的是从区域的角度研究哪些区域到枢纽的可达性不足,以进行针对性改善。仅从单个公交站点评价枢纽可达性,覆盖率较低,也不便于进行整体公交线路的优化。

(4)交通小区客流统计。基于枢纽客流在城市内的空间分布结果,统计每个交通小区内的客流总量及客流密度。

(5)小区质心公共交通出行时耗及驾车时耗爬取。利用地图 API 路径规划功能计算所有小区质心到达枢纽站的公共交通出行时耗及驾车出行时耗。

(6)小区公共交通出行时耗确定。由于小区的质心可能远离公交站点,无法采用公共交通方式从枢纽站到达小区质心或者爬取到的公共交通出行时耗的值可能过大,这时直接利用质心的公共交通出行时耗与驾车时耗对比显然是不合理的。因此本研究中计算小区内所有公交站点的公共交通平均出行时耗,与小区质心到达枢纽站的公共交通出行时耗作比较,取较小值,作为小区到枢纽站的公共交通出行时耗。

(7)小区公共交通—驾车出行时耗比计算。计算小区到枢纽站的公共交通出行时耗与驾车出行时耗的比值,作为判定该区域是否需要改善的重要依据。

(8)待改善区域判定。将小区公共交通—驾车出行时耗比大于 2,客流量大于客流量筛选阈值,客流密度大于密度筛选阈值的小区,判定为待改善区域。阈值的大小根据实际客流情况确定,本研究取客流量和客流密度的均值分别作为筛选阈值,以保障待改善区域客流达到一定规模,利用有限客流资源服务更多客流。

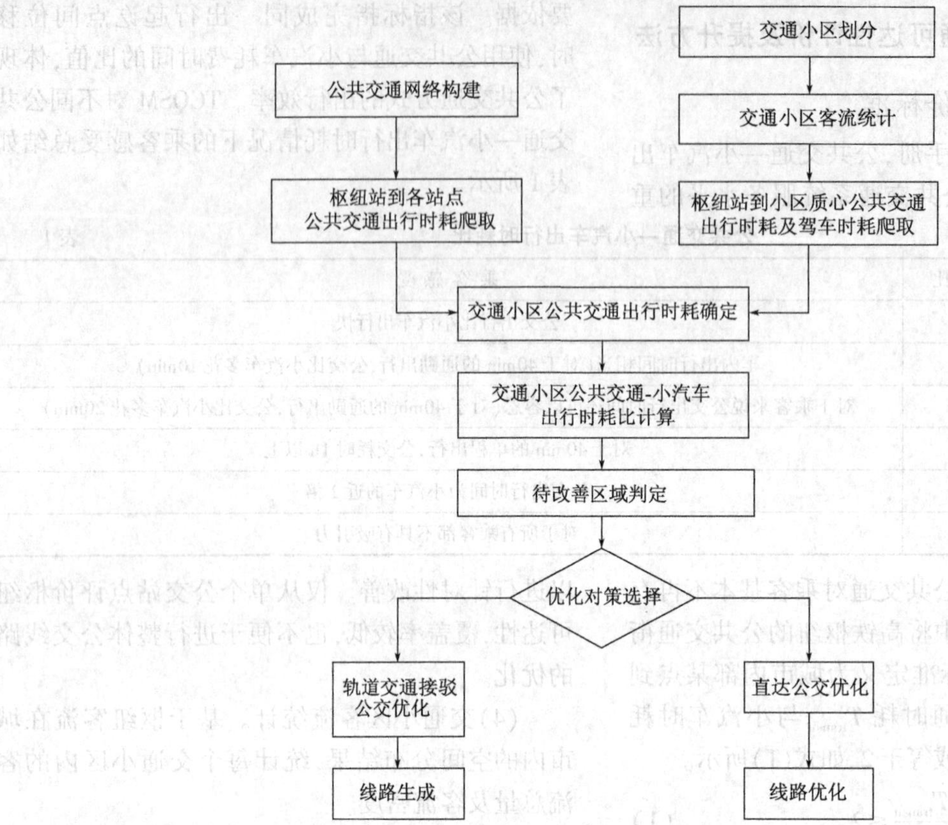

图1　枢纽公共交通衔接网络优化流程

(9)优化对策选择。大城市高速铁路枢纽的公共交通衔接网络一般以轨道交通为主体。因此本研究中主要采用两种优化策略,以减少公共交通出行时耗。一是提供轨道交通接驳公交,指起终点或者中间站必须经过轨道接驳站点,主要目的是为轨道交通集散客流的线路;二是对现有直达枢纽站的公交进行优化,指的是与枢纽站直接衔接的公交线路,也即前文所述的枢纽接运公交。计算小区质心与不需换乘可直达枢纽站的地铁站的距离 d_1 和质心与直达枢纽站的公交线路的站点的距离 d_2,若 $d_1 \leqslant 2d_2$(由于地铁站覆盖范围大于公交车站,因此采用 $2d_2$),说明客流点距离地铁站较近,采用轨道交通接驳公交较为合适,否则,通过优化直达枢纽的公交线路增加该区域的可达性。

(10)线路生成及优化。

①对于轨道交通接驳公交,依据待改善区域内的客流,设计合理公交线路。该问题为公交线路生成问题。本论文首先对客流源点进行聚类生成备选公交站点,然后以运营商收入最大为目标函数,将接驳公交线路布设问题转换为一个双层规划模型,上层模型解决选择哪些站点以构建站点集的问题,下层为特定站点集下的经典TSP问题,然后采用枚举法和贪婪算法进行求解。

②对于直达公交,依据待改善区域内的客流和已开通的直达公交历史客流,优化线路走向,该问题为公交线路优化问题。对该问题论文的主要思路是根据待改善区客流分布聚类生成站点,与直达线路在待改善区内的站点共同构成备选站点集,然后以所有乘客总出行时间最小为目标函数,是否采取某些站点构成的某一路径作为决策变量,采用 k-最短路算法对模型进行求解,对原线路在待改善区附近的部分进行优化。

由于篇幅限制本文仅简单介绍两类线路模型的构建思路与相应求解算法,不展开具体论述。

2　案例研究

2.1　可达性评价及优化对策判断

以南京南高铁枢纽为实例,进行公共交通衔接网络可达性评价。

1)公共交通网络构建

利用百度地图API爬取南京市的地铁网络和公交网络(不包括溧水区和高淳区)。经整理,南京市地铁网络由10条地铁线、159个站点构成,公交网络由631条线路,5619个站点构成。地铁网络和公交网络共同构成公共交通网络,为枢纽乘客的集疏运提供服务。在整个公共交通网络中,直接衔接南京南站的地铁线路共有4条,直接接入南京南站的公交线路共有12条。

2)各站点公共交通出行时耗爬取

通过百度地图API路径规划功能计算南京南站到达所有地铁站点及公交站点的换乘次数及公共交通出行时耗。

3)交通小区划分

参考南京市城市与交通规划设计研究院股份有限公司在南京年度居民出行调查中所划设的交通小区,将研究区域划分为770个小区,从区域的角度观察客流和服务供给是否匹配。

4)交通小区客流统计

在前期研究中基于手机信令数据获取了枢纽客流在城市内的空间分布,以此为基础统计每个交通小区内的客流量及客流密度。计算客流量筛选阈值和客流密度筛选阈值,分别为360人次和340人次/km^2。

5)小区质心公共交通出行时耗及驾车时耗爬取

利用地图API路径规划功能计算所有小区质心到达枢纽站的公共交通出行时耗及驾车出行时耗,并进行批量爬取,信息整理后如表2所示。

公共交通-小汽车出行时耗比 表2

小区ID	质心 X	质心 Y	公共交通出行距离(km)	公共交通出行时间(min)	公共交通换乘次数	驾车距离(km)	驾车时间(min)
756	118.858	31.7347	37.62	145.67	1	33.8	31.33
755	118.809	31.7493	31.61	79.33	1	31.14	36.58
754	118.825	31.7587	27.15	41.53	0	31.03	28.85
753	118.841	31.7638	30.79	70.05	1	28.81	25.98
740	118.79	31.7626	29.26	95.65	1	28.55	31.4

6)小区公共交通出行时耗确定

利用ArcGIS中的空间连接功能,将各个站点分配到所属的小区内,计算小区内所有站点的公共交通平均出行时耗,将其与小区质心到达枢纽站的公共交通出行时耗对比,取较小值,作为小区到枢纽站的公共交通出行时耗。

7)小区公共交通—驾车出行时耗比计算

计算各个小区到枢纽站的公共交通出行时耗与驾车出行时耗的比值,得到各小区的公共交通-小汽车出行时耗比。

8)待改善区域判定

将公共交通—驾车出行时耗比大于2,客流量大于360人次,客流密度大于340人次/km^{2}的小区,作为待改善区域,共计36个。

9)优化对策选择

计算小区质心与直达枢纽站的地铁线路站点的直线距离 d_1 和直达枢纽站的公交站点的距离 d_2,若 $d_1 \leqslant 2d_2$,则采用轨道交通接驳公交优化策略,否则,采用直达枢纽的公交线路优化策略。

2.2 公交线路生成及优化

2.2.1 轨道交通接驳线路生成案例

选取南京市建邺区的两个相邻待改善区(编号11和编号14)进行轨道交通接驳公交线路生成的案例展示。

建议设置地铁接驳公交线路,线路长度约9.7km,站点300m覆盖范围内共能服务2312个乘客,占总客流(2922人次)的79.1%,能满足大部分乘客的需求。且经估算,从该线路采用地铁+接驳公交这一方式的公共交通出行时间约41min,而对应的驾车时间为23min,满足公共交通-小汽车出行时耗比小于或等于2的可达性要求。

2.2.2 直达公交线路优化案例

选择编号为17、18、21、22的交通小区构成的一片区域(下文简称"秦淮待改善区")进行直达公交优化的案例展示。

优化后,除了过于偏远的客流源点,流量较大的客流源点基本能被覆盖。经估算,该待改善区内的84路公交服务范围内的,最远的大客流源点到达枢纽站的公共交通出行时间约为40min,而驾车时间为25min,满足公共交通-小汽车出行时耗比小于或等于2的可达性要求。

3 结语

论文提出了一种枢纽公共交通可达性提升方

法。首先定义了可达性评价标准,判定公共交通-小汽车出行时耗比大于2的区域为可达性不足区域,结合可达性和枢纽客流分布进行待改善区筛选,并根据待改善区质心与公交站点和轨道站点的距离,采用轨道交通接驳公交和枢纽直达公交两种不同策略进行优化。对于提出的公共交通网络优化方法,以南京南站为案例进行实例研究,验证了方法的可行性。

论文利用地图API爬取手段快速构建了枢纽公共交通网络,并创新性地以交通小区的公共交通-小汽车出行时耗比为可达性评价标准,实现了全市范围内的枢纽可达性评价。此外,还从整体网络的角度,为提升枢纽公共交通可达性提供了可行的定量优化方法。但由于知识水平和精力有限,论文还有一定不足,后续还需在公交线路时刻表编制等方面进行深入研究,以进一步提升方法的实践价值。

参考文献

[1] 国家铁路局. 2020年铁道统计公报[J]. 铁道技术监督,2021,49(05):34.

[2] 王祥. 我国高铁车站的可达性研究[C]//中国城市规划学会城市交通规划学术委员会. 创新驱动与智慧发展——2018年中国城市交通规划年会论文集. 北京:中国建筑工业出版社,2018:2450-2461.

[3] 周雨阳,李芮智,潘利肖,等. 北京南站公共交通可达性计算与评价[J]. 北京工业大学学报,2020,46(12):1365-1376.

[4] O'Mahony M. Use of a Hybrid Algorithm for Modeling Coordinated Feeder Bus Route Network at Suburban Railway Station[J]. Journal of Transportation Engineering. 2009, 135(1):1-8.

[5] Guo Xiao-le, Song Rui, HE Shi - wei, et al. A multi-objective programming approach to design feeder bus route for high-speed rail stations[J]. Symmetry. 2019,11(4):514.

[6] 张英群,宋瑞,何世伟,等. TOD理念下高铁快巴服务网络设计研究[J]. 铁道学报. 2019,41(09):12-19.

[7] Kittelson Associates, Parsons Brinckerhoff, Group K. Transit capacity and quality of service manual (TCQSM)[M]. 3rd edition ed. Washington, DC: Transportation Research Board,2013.

[8] 郑姝婕,程剑珂,张锦阳,等. 高铁枢纽客流特征与城市交通衔接性分析[C]//中国城市规划学会城市交通规划学术委员会. 交通治理与空间重塑——2020年中国城市交通规划年会论文集. 北京:中国建筑工业出版社,2020:1357-1370.

基于车路协同的智能网联小巴运营评价指标体系研究

张霁扬[1,2]　刁含楼*[1,2]　华禹凯[1,2]　王立超[3,4]

(1. 华设设计集团股份有限公司;2. 江苏省综合交通智能感知与管控重点实验室;
3. 东南大学交通学院;4. 东南大学江苏省城市智能交通重点实验室)

摘　要　新技术驱动下,基于车路协同的智能网联公交引领传统公交发展方向。微循环智能网联小巴作为主干公交接驳,能够充分发挥灵活度高、可达性强、需求响应及时等优势,已经成为智能网联公交的重要业态。本文基于智能网联小巴的车辆特征和通用应用,首次从安全性、舒适性、效率性和环保性四个方面提出了面向智能网联小巴运营期的评价指标并开展专家调查,运用层次分析法计算各指标类型和

1. 基金项目:国家自然科学基金项目(52072066)、江苏省交通运输科技项目(2020Y01)、江苏省杰出青年基金项目(BK20200014)。

各具体指标项的权重，形成了智能网联小巴运营评价指标体系，为进一步提升优化智能网联小巴运营水平提供依据。

关键词 智能网联汽车 自动驾驶小巴 运营评价 层次分析法

0 引言

基于车路协同的智能网联汽车在单车智能自动驾驶的基础上，依据数据和信息交互约定协议，能够实现车与车、车与路侧设备、车与交通参与者之间不同程度的信息动态交互共享，助力自动驾驶车辆在环境感知、计算决策和控制执行等方面能力升级，进而通过一系列车辆和交通管控手段，提供更安全、更高效、更优质的出行服务[1]。国家高度重视基于车路协同的智能网联汽车发展。《国家综合立体交通网规划纲要》中明确推进包括智能汽车、自动驾驶和车路协同的智能网联汽车应用。国家发改委发布的《第十四个五年规划和2035年远景目标纲要》中提出加快研发智能(网联)汽车基础技术平台，扩大发展自动驾驶和车路协同出行服务等数字化应用场景，推广交通信号联动和公交优先通行控制。住建部、科技部、工信部等七部委发布的《关于加快推进新型城市基础设施建设的指导意见》中要求推动智能网联汽车在城市公交、景区游览、特种作业、物流运输等多场景应用。由于智能网联公交具有更安全、更高效、更绿色、更便捷的特点，现已被广泛视为传统公交的发展方向。

近年来，基于车路协同的智能网联公交在全国多地试点运营，呈现出两种模式：一类是主干公交智慧化升级，如图1所示，通过为已经投入运营的公交车加装辅助自动驾驶设备，为公交行驶线路加装智能路侧设施，实现高通行效率保障、强驾驶行为规范等功能[2]；另一类是建设基于车路协同的微循环智能网联小巴(简称“智能网联小巴”)，如图2所示，通过L4级别小巴短距离固定线路巡游或者预约乘坐，解决“最后一公里”的公交干线接驳问题[3]。目前国内两类智能网联公交的典型试点示范建设情况如表1所示。

图1 主干公交智慧化升级

图2 微循环智能网联小巴

国内智能网联公交典型试点示范建设情况 表1

类型	城市	主要建设情况
主干公交智慧化升级	长沙	现已完成超过2000辆公交车的智慧化升级，开通两条智慧通勤线路，实现驾驶行为监测、速度动态控制、绿波通行、事故预警等应用
	郑州	已完成郑东新区全长17.4km道路智能化改造以及相关线路公交车智慧化升级，实现信号优先、盲区监测、车速诱导、精准进站等功能
	重庆	已完成永川区双向近10km道路的智能化改造以及5辆公交车的智慧化升级，实现盲区预警、绿波通行、APP预约出行等功能
智能网联小巴	郑州	在龙子湖智慧岛开放运营，采用L4级自动驾驶微循环小巴，实现智慧岛内环多站点间的全流程自动驾驶接驳
	苏州	覆盖高铁新城周边10km^{2}范围，采用L4级自动驾驶微循环小巴，实现4条线路、14个路口间的全流程自动驾驶接驳
	深圳	覆盖坪山站和坪山区政府之间范围，采用L4级自动驾驶微循环小巴，实现总长约5km、沿途10个站点间的全流程自动驾驶接驳

两种智能网联公交模式中,智能网联小巴由于灵活度高、可达性强、需求响应及时等优势,现已逐步应用于地铁接驳专线、微循环公交、园区摆渡车等固定线路低速运行场景,作为地铁、主干公交等传统公交的重要补充[4]。综合比较郑州、苏州和深圳等地的试运营情况以及沈峰[5]、汲安志[6]、吴士一等人[7]的相关研究,可归纳出智能网联小巴普遍建设了包括前向碰撞预警、行人过街预警、转弯盲区预警、车辆轨迹跟踪等安全保障类应用,信号优先、车速引导等效率提升类应用以及平稳驾控、平台叫车等服务优化类应用,而具有上述场景应用的智能网联小巴相比一般同类型车辆效能提升的效果,现有研究中仅有针对车辆测试期的探索[8],而并无聚焦运营期的体系化评价指标。为弥补该研究空白,本文基于智能网联小巴的特点,分别从安全性、舒适性、效率性和环保性等角度提出一系列区别于智能网联汽车测试的智能网联小巴运营评价指标,通过基于层次分析法的专家调查标定各指标类型和各具体指标项的权重,形成智能网联小巴运营评价指标体系。

1　智能网联小巴运营期评价指标

现阶段业内针对智能网联汽车测试评价指标已进行了初步探索。中国智能网联汽车产业创新联盟发布的《智能网联汽车测试评价白皮书》从安全、体验和配置三个方面提出了一系列评价指标,中国汽车研究中心则从安全、舒适、能效和智能四个方面提出了智能网联自动驾驶车辆测试的评价指标。考虑到进入运营期的智能网联车辆已通过相关测试,运营期评价无需再关注包括设计运行域、配置计算能力等面向测试的评价指标,而应更聚焦测试质量达标后的长期运营特征。基于智能网联小巴建设的一系列安全保障、效率提升和服务优化应用,运营后相比传统公交驾驶行为更平稳、需求响应更及时、通行过程更顺畅,故针对智能网联小巴运营期的评价指标需充分体现上述特点。

本文基于智能网联小巴运营应用特征调研,从安全、舒适、高效和环保四个方面构建树状结构,提出智能网联小巴运营期评价指标,如图3所示。

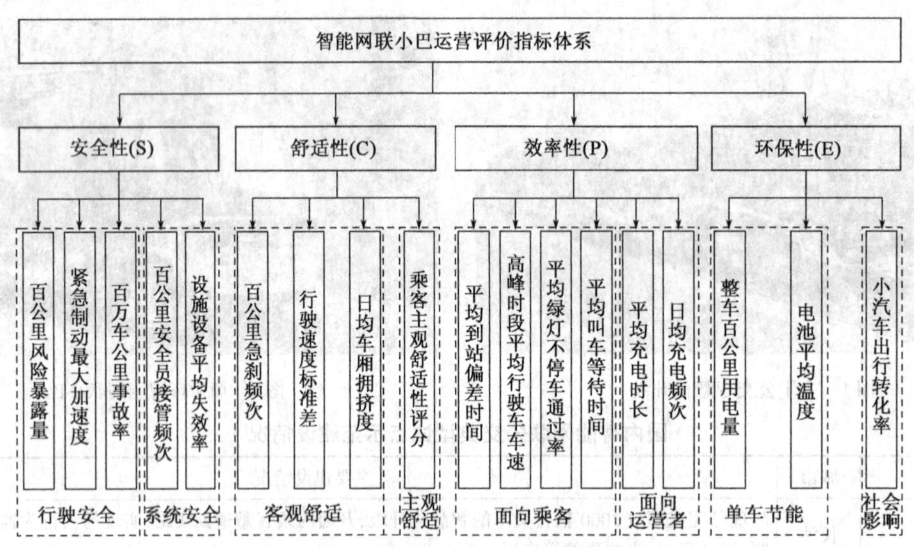

图3　智能网联小巴运营评价指标体系

1.1　安全性指标(S)

智能网联小巴通过前向碰撞预警、行人过街预警、转弯盲区预警、车辆轨迹跟踪等安全类场景建设,能够全方位强化行驶过程中的安全风险预判能力,从源头上减少交通事故。通过设施设备接入网联管理平台以及紧急状态下随车安全员接管控制的机制,能够有效监控小巴的运营安全状态,降低设施设备突发脱离带来的安全危害。故本文从行驶安全、系统安全的角度提出智能网联小巴运营安全性评价指标,主要包括百公里风险暴露量、紧急制动最大加速度、百万车公里事故率、百公里安全员接管频次和设施设备平均失效率,具体如下:

(1)百公里风险暴露量 S_1(s/km)

风险暴露量被定义为碰撞预估时间(TTC)小于关键碰撞预估时间值的持续时长,是衡量行驶碰撞风险的重要指标。风险暴露量越小，发生碰撞的可能性越低，车辆行驶安全性越高。为使评价结果标准化，本文引入百公里风险暴露量作为智能网联小巴运营的行驶安全性评价指标，可以充分评估前向碰撞预警、行人过街预警、转弯盲区预警等防碰撞场景的建设效果。

$$S_1 = \frac{\sum_{m=0}^{m=R_{\text{total}}} \sum_{r=0}^{r=F_{\text{mtotal}}} \text{Time}\{\text{TTC}_{m,r} < \text{TTC}_{\text{critical}}\} \times 100}{l_{\text{total}}} \tag{1}$$

式中：R_{total}——小巴运营总车次；

l_{total}——小巴运营总里程(km)；

F_{mtotal}——第 m 次运营中遇到碰撞风险的总频次；

$\text{TTC}_{m,r}$——第 m 次运营中遇到第 r 次碰撞风险时的碰撞预估时间(s)；

$\text{TTC}_{\text{critical}}$——关键碰撞预估时间(s)($0 < m \leqslant R_{\text{total}}, 0 \leqslant r \leqslant F_{\text{mtotal}}$)。

(2)紧急制动最大加速度 S_2(m/s^2)

紧急制动最大加速度被定义为碰撞风险发生时车辆发生紧急制动的最大加速度，是评价智能网联小巴风险最小化策略的重要指标。紧急制动最大加速度值越大，车辆的风险最小化策略越保守，避免碰撞的可能性越高，但会增加后车碰撞风险，也会对车内乘客产生一定的安全风险，故智能网联小巴的紧急制动最大加速度应综合考虑碰撞风险发生时车内、车外的安全性。本文引入紧急制动最大加速度作为智能网联小巴运营的行驶安全性评价指标，可以充分评估小巴风险最小化策略和行驶控制系统的建设效果。

$$S_2 = \max\{a_{\text{break}}\} \tag{2}$$

式中：a_{break}——运营期内每次碰撞风险发生时车辆的制动加速度。

(3)百万车公里事故率 S_3(/km)

百万车公里事故率被定义为运营期间发生的事故数乘100万再与实际运营里程的比值，是常用衡量运营期事故发生数量的直接指标[9]。百万车公里事故率越低，智能网联小巴运营期内的行驶安全性越高。

$$S_3 = \frac{N_{\text{accidents}} \times 1000000}{l_{\text{total}}} \tag{3}$$

式中：$N_{\text{accidents}}$——运营期内发生事故的总数；

l_{total}——运营总里程(km)。

(4)百公里安全员接管频次 S_4(/km)

现阶段营运智能网联小巴均随车配备安全员，当发生智能车辆无法处理的紧急事件时，车载系统会警示安全员接管控制。运营期安全员的接管频次是衡量车辆紧急控制能力和系统安全的重要指标。平均接管频次越少，车辆的紧急控制能力和系统安全性越强。为使结果标准化，本文引入每百公里的安全员接管频次作为小巴行驶安全性评价指标。

$$S_4 = \frac{C_{\text{total}} \times 100}{l_{\text{total}}} \tag{4}$$

式中：C_{total}——运营期安全员接管总频次；

l_{total}——小巴运营总里程(km)。

(5)设施设备平均失效率 S_5(%)

智能路侧设施和智能网联小巴各类设备均接入网联管理平台中，实现统一管理。设施设备失效率被定义为管理平台监测到的设施设备离线总时长与运营总时长的比值，是衡量各类设施设备运行状态稳定性和通信网络安全等系统安全性的重要指标。平均失效率越低，小巴的系统安全性越强。本文引入设施设备平均失效率作为智能网联小巴运营的系统安全性评价指标，可以充分评估路侧设施和小巴设备的稳定性以及通信网络安全建设情况。

$$S_5 = \frac{O_{\text{time}}}{R_{\text{time}}} \tag{5}$$

式中：O_{time}——设施设备离线总时长(s)；

R_{time}——小巴运营总时长(s)。

1.2 舒适性指标(C)

智能网联小巴普遍采用线控底盘技术进行整车控制，通过线控转向、线控制动、线控换挡、线控油门及线控悬挂五大关键系统，保障车辆行驶平稳，提高出行者的乘车舒适性。此外，智能网联小巴的乘车空间、内饰和车内明亮度相比传统公交也都有显著提升。

故本文从客观舒适和主观舒适的角度[2]提出智能网联小巴运营舒适性指标，主要包括百公里刹率、行驶速度标准差、车厢平均拥挤度和乘客主观舒适性评分，具体如下：

(1)百公里紧急制动频次 C_1(/km)

图4中的红圈显示了智能网联小巴在开放道路试运营时实测的紧急制动事件，可见遇到安全预警时，智能网联小巴通常采用制动方式规避碰

撞风险。而如果车辆行驶过程中出现频繁紧急制动行为,势必会对乘客舒适性造成负面影响。故从客观舒适性的角度,要求智能网联小巴能够更提前预判危险性事件,尽可能延长碰撞预估时间(TTC),减少行驶过程中的紧急制动事件。为使评价结果标准化,本文引入百公里紧急制动频次作为智能网联小巴运营的舒适性评价指标,充分评估小巴预警和控制系统的舒适性考量。百公里紧急制动频次越低,舒适性越高。

$$C_1 = \frac{\sum_{m=0}^{m=R_{\text{total}}} B_m \times 100}{l_{\text{total}}} \tag{6}$$

式中:R_{total}——小巴运营总车次;

l_{total}——小巴运营总里程(km);

B_m——第 m 次运营时的紧急制动总频次($0<m\leqslant R_{\text{total}}$)。

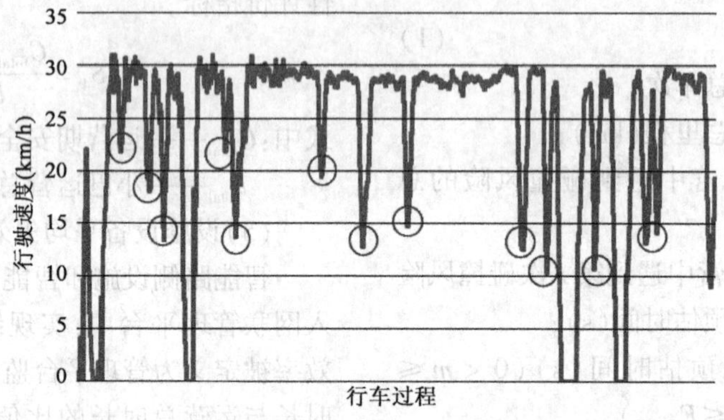

图4　智能网联小巴开放道路试运营实测速度变化情况

(2)行驶速度标准差 C_2(km/h)

行驶速度标准差表征车辆行驶的平稳性,是衡量乘客舒适性的重要指标。智能网联小巴通过先进的驾驶控制策略,相比传统的人驾公共交通行驶更平稳。如图4所示,所选开放道路环境下智能网联小巴的自由流速度设定在30km/h左右,而遇到安全预警、红灯等事件时,智能网联小巴会制动减速,随后加速恢复自由流速度,影响行驶平稳。本文引入行驶速度标准差作为智能网联小巴运营的客观舒适性评价指标,可以衡量车辆的驾驶控制策略对于舒适性的影响。行驶速度标准差越小,表明行驶过程中加减速行为越少,舒适性越高。

$$C_2 = \sigma_{(\text{speed})} \tag{7}$$

式中:$\sigma_{(\text{speed})}$——运营期小巴行驶速度的标准差(km/h)。

(3)车厢平均拥挤度 C_3(%)

智能网联小巴作为需求响应式接驳公交,支持乘客在线预约出行,具有灵活性强、运力实时性高等特点,相比传统公交更能满足旅客的弹性出行需求,乘车空间也更宽敞。定义车厢平均拥挤度为运营期内智能网联小巴载客总数与总运力的比值,衡量乘客所能占有的车内空间大小,是评价智能网联小巴运营客观舒适性的重要指标。

$$C_3 = \frac{N_{\text{passenger}}}{V_{\text{capacity}} \times R_{\text{total}}} \tag{8}$$

式中:$N_{\text{passenger}}$——运营期智能网联小巴载客总数;

V_{capacity}——智能网联小巴的额定座位数;

R_{total}——智能网联小巴运营总车次。

(4)乘客主观舒适性评分 C_4

平均紧急制动频次、行驶速度标准差和车厢拥挤度之外,乘客的舒适性评价还包括一些非客观指标,例如对车厢内饰、车内明亮度、座椅柔软度等项目的满意度感知。本文引入主观舒适性评分归纳乘客对于上述项目的体验感,作为客观舒适性指标的有效补充。该指标一般通过满意度调查获得。

1.3　效率性指标(P)

智能网联小巴通过信号优先、车速引导、平台叫车等场景建设,能够有效改善车辆交叉口和路段通行效率,降低乘客的出行总时间,进而提升运营效率。另外,智能网联小巴作为一种新能源汽车,其充电频次和充电时长也是影响运营效率的重要因素。

故本文从乘客和运营管理者的角度提出智能网联小巴运营效率性指标,主要包括车辆平均到站偏差时间、高峰时段平均行驶车速、平均红灯停车率、平均叫车等待时间、日均充电频次和平均充电时长[10-11]。

(1)平均到站偏差时间 P_1(s)

准点到站是公交出行效率的重要保障。智能网联小巴通过信号优先、车速引导等场景建设,相比传统公交行驶时间更加可控,到站时间应更加精准。本文引入运营期平均到站偏差时间作为智能网联小巴到站准点性的评价指标,平均偏差时间越小,智能网联小巴运营准点性越强,面向乘客的运营效率越高。

$$P_1 = \frac{\sum_{m=0}^{m=R_{\text{total}}} \sum_{r=0}^{r=N_{\text{station}}-1} |t_{m,r} - t_{\text{rplan}}|}{N_{\text{station}}} \tag{9}$$

式中:N_{station}——运营期累积停站数;

R_{total}——智能网联小巴运营总车次;

$t_{m,r}$——第 m 次运营中智能网联小巴在第 r 个车站和第 $r+1$ 个车站区间之内行驶时间(s);

t_{rplan}——为保证准时到站智能网联小巴在第 r 站和 $r+1$ 站区间内的设计行驶时间(s)$(0<m\leqslant R_{\text{total}}, 0\leqslant r\leqslant N_{\text{station}}-1)$。

(2)高峰时段平均行驶车速 P_2(km/h)

高峰时段平均行驶车速是对于高峰时段智能网联小巴通行效率的直观评价指标。智能网联小巴通过信号优先、车速引导等场景建设,相比传统公交通行效率应更高,高峰时段的平均行驶车速也应更高。

$$P_2 = \frac{\sum_{m=0}^{m=R_{\text{ptotal}}} \frac{l_m}{t_m}}{R_{\text{ptotal}}} \tag{10}$$

式中:R_{ptotal}——高峰时段智能网联小巴运营总车次;

l_m——第 m 次高峰时段运行的行驶里程(km);

t_m——第 m 次高峰时段运行的行驶时间(h)$(0<m\leqslant R_{\text{ptotal}})$。

(3)平均绿灯不停车通过率 P_3(%)

智能网联小巴通过与信号灯信息交互不断调整驾驶行为和行驶车速,最大可能实现全绿灯通行。本文引入平均绿灯不停车通过率作为面向乘客运营效率性的评价指标,平均绿灯不停车通过率越高,智能网联小巴的运营效率越高。

$$P_3 = \sum_{m=0}^{m=R_{\text{total}}} \frac{n_{m,s}}{n_{m,i}} \tag{11}$$

式中:R_{total}——智能网联小巴运营总车次;

$n_{m,s}$——第 m 次运行中不停车通过的绿灯数;

$n_{m,i}$——第 m 次运行路线经过的全部信控交叉口数量$(0<m\leqslant R_{\text{total}})$。

(4)平均叫车等待时间 P_4(s)

智能网联小巴通过线上预约、定制出行实现需求响应,发起预约后的平均等待时间(s)是衡量其需求响应能力的重要指标,也是评价智能网联小巴面向乘客运营效率性的重要依据。平均叫车等待时间越低,小巴运营效率高。

$$P_4 = \frac{\sum_{m=0}^{m=d_{\text{total}}} t_{m,c}}{d_{\text{total}}} \tag{12}$$

式中:d_{total}——运营期叫车总人数;

$t_{m,c}$——第 m 个叫车者预约后等待车辆的时长(s)$(0<m\leqslant d_{\text{total}})$。

(5)平均充电时长 P_5(s)与日均充电频次 P_6

智能网联小巴由电力驱动,其充电平均时长和频次是影响运营时长的重要因素,也是运营者进行排班设计必须考虑的指标。本文引入智能网联小巴的平均充电时长(s)和日均充电频次(次)作为面向运营者的智能网联小巴运营效率评价指标。

1.4 环保性指标(E)

智能网联小巴采用新能源驱动,通过高效的电控策略尽可能降低整车电能浪费和电池损耗,实现节能减耗和碳减排的目标[12-13]。本文从单车节能和社会影响的角度提出智能网联小巴环保性评价指标,主要包括整车百公里用电量、电池平均温度和小汽车出行转化率。

(1)整车百公里用电量 E_1(kW·h)

智能网联小巴电驱动系统、自动线控系统、车载感知设备、计算单元、空调、电子显示器等设备的使用情况都会对车辆能耗产生影响。相比一般的新能源公交,智能网联小巴通过更高效的线控动力传动、更精准的设备耗电调控和更平稳的驾驶行为控制,预期达到“精准用电”的效果。为标准化评价结果,本文引入整车百公里用电量作为评价智能网联小巴的单车环保性指标,可充分评估智能网联小巴整车电控策略的效果。

(2)电池平均温度 E_2(℃)

智能网联小巴电池寿命受到电池温度的显著影响。通常情况下,电池工作适宜温度在15~40℃,当温度高于或者低于适宜温度时,电池都会出现充放电限流乃至失效。相比一般的新能源公交,智能网联小巴通过网联化设备和更精准的电池热管理系统,能够更有效地维持电池组温度在安全、合理的工作区间内,降低电池的损耗,从而减少电池废弃对环境的影响。本文引入运营期电池平均温度作为评价智能网联小巴的单车环保性指标,可充分评估智能网联小巴电池热管理系统的使用效果。

(3)小汽车出行转化率 E_3(%)

智能网联小巴通过建设定制化、预约化的出行应用,能够充分发挥微循环接驳效能,在常态化运营后可显著提升公共交通出行吸引力,减少小汽车使用和相应的道路交通碳排量。定义小汽车出行转化率为选择智能网联小巴而放弃小汽车出行的人员比率,可以衡量智能网联小巴对出人们出行方式的影响,从社会影响的角度间接评价智能网联小巴的环保效果。

2　智能网联小巴评价指标权重

智能网联小巴评价指标权重见表2。

智能网联小巴评价指标权重　表2

指标类型	指标类型权重值	指标项	指标项权重值
安全性	0.50	百公里风险暴露量	0.17
		紧急制动最大加速度	0.19
		百万车公里事故率	0.18
		百公里安全员接管频次	0.25
		设施设备平均失效率	0.21
舒适性	0.18	百公里紧急制动率	0.50
		行驶速度标准差	0.24
		日均车厢拥挤度	0.14
		乘客主观舒适性评分	0.12
效率性	0.20	平均到站偏差时间	0.22
		高峰时段平均行驶车速	0.21
		平均绿灯不停车通过率	0.18
		平均叫车等待时间	0.27
		平均充电时长	0.06
		日均充电频次	0.06
环保性	0.12	整车百公里用电量	0.15
		电池平均温度	0.17
		小汽车出行转化率	0.68

本文运用层次分析法(AHP)标定各评价指标类型和每个评价指标项的权重[9,14]。

基于本文提出的一系列智能网联小巴评价指标,建立以智能网联小巴运营评价为目标层,安全性、舒适性、效率性和环保性四个评价角度为准则层,各具体指标为指标层的递阶层次结构。进一步开展调查,得到智能网联公交领域专家对评价指标体系中各准则层以及同一准则层中各指标项两两重要性比较的结果,根据1~9位标度法对比较结果进行量化,构建判断矩阵,再运用熵权法进行权重分配[15],得到各类评价指标和各具体指标项的权重值,形成智能网联小巴运营评价指标体系。

本文回收的专家问卷通过问卷一致性检验,经过AHP方法标定的各项权重如表2所示。

权重标定结果从指标类别上看,安全性指标的类别权重最大,占比达到50%。舒适性指标和效率性指标的类别权重相近,而环保性指标的类别权重相对最低,占比仅11%,充分说明安全、效率和体验感在智能网联小巴运营中的重要性。

从具体指标项看,安全性指标中"百公里安全员接管频次"和"设施设备平均失效率"两个系统安全相关指标的权重较高,三个行驶安全相关指标权重略低且接近,表明智能网联小巴运营期系统级的设备和网络安全更受到重视。舒适性指标中"百公里紧急制动率"和"行驶速度标准差"两个行驶平稳性相关的指标权重分别达到50%和24%,剩余两个指标权重相对较低,表明行驶平稳性被认为更能影响旅客的舒适体验。效率性指标中"平均叫车等待时间"、"平均到站偏差时间"和"高峰时段平均行驶车速"三个从"出行前"延伸到"出行中"的乘客出行过程性指标权重相对较高,而"平均充电时长"和"日均充电频次"两个面向运营者的指标权重较低,仅为6%,表明乘客的出行效率更受到重视。环保性指标中,"小汽车出行转化率"这一社会影响指标显著高于两个权重相近的单车节能指标,达到68%,表明专家对智能网联小巴改变人们出行方式以实现环保的预期远高于通过车辆自身节能实现环保的预期,这与智能网联小巴的实际运营特点相一致。

3 总结

本文从现有智能网联小巴的通用应用场景和建设特点出发,结合智能网联小巴试点运营现状调研和智能网联汽车测试评价指标分析,提出了包含安全性、舒适性、效率性和环保性的18项评价指标,首次建立了面向智能网联小巴运营期的评价指标体系,是对现有该空白领域的创新探索。基于智能网联公交领域的专家调查,本研究运用AHP法计算了各指标类型和各具体指标项的权重,得出了安全性指标具有最高权重而环保性指标权重相对最低等结论,形成了智能网联小巴运营评价指标体系。

由于智能网联汽车测试评价的标准和依据在业内仍未成熟[16],智能网联小巴运营也尚处初级阶段,故本研究暂未提出每项指标的具体评价方法。未来应在本文提出的运营评价指标体系基础上,为每项评价指标制定评分分级区间,将指标的实际取值标准化为无量纲的评价分数,建立智能网联小巴运营评价模型,最终计算运营情况的整体评分,为进一步提升智能网联小巴运营水平提供定量依据。

参考文献

[1] 清华大学智能产业研究院,百度 Apollo. 面向自动驾驶的车路协同关键技术与展望白皮书[R],2021.

[2] Pigenon C, Alauzet A, Paire-Ficout L. Factors of acceptability, acceptance and usage for non-rail autonomous public transport vehicles: A systematic literature review[J]. Transportation Research Part F: Traffic Psychology and Behaviour, 2021, 81: 251-270.

[3] Weschke J, Bahamonde-Birke F J, Gade K, et al. Asking the Wizard-of-Oz: How experiencing autonomous buses affects preferences towards their use for feeder trips in public transport[J]. Transportation Research Part C: Emerging Technologies, 2021, 133: 103454.

[4] Bernhard C, Oberfeld D, Hoffmann C, et al. User acceptance of automated public transport[J]. Transportation Research Part F: Traffic Psychology and Behaviour, 2020, 70: 109-123.

[5] 沈峰. 车路云一体智能网联公交系统研究[J]. 科学与信息化, 2020, (8): 64-67.

[6] 汲安志. 无人公交:引领交通新变革[J]. 智能网联汽车, 2021(5): 45-47.

[7] 吴士一,杨辰兮,王春香,等. 无人小巴关键技术与商业化应用进展[J]. 智能驾驶, 2021(2): 19-28.

[8] 申静峰. 自动驾驶汽车车辆在环测试方法研究[D]. 长春:吉林大学, 2021.

[9] 秦佳琪. 城市常规公交服务水平综合评价研究[D]. 哈尔滨:东北林业大学, 2021.

[10] Nagy V, Horvath B. The effects of autonomous buses to vehicle scheduling system[J]. Procedia Computer Science, 2020, 170: 235-240.

[11] Bartuska L, Labudzki R. Research of basic issues of autonomous mobility[J]. Transportation Research Procedia, 2020, 44: 356-360.

[12] 王虹霞. 车路协同环境下纯电动公交车节能驾驶策略研究[D]. 西安:长安大学, 2020.

[13] Pan S, Fulton L M, Roy A, et al. Shared use of electric autonomous vehicles: Air quality and health impacts of future mobility in the United States[J]. Renewable and Sustainable Energy Reviews, 2021, 149: 111380.

[14] 潘隽. 快速公交线路运行效率分析与评价[D]. 济南:山东大学,2020.

[15] 王羽. 中国智能汽车评价体系研究[J]. 智能驾驶,2021(1):27-33.

[16] 燕迪. 自动驾驶车辆道路测试行政法规制问题研究[D]. 南京:东南大学,2019.

基于区块链的城市交通大数据平台构建与算法设计

范嘉婕[1]　方　轲[1]　于　滨*[1,2]

(1. 北京航空航天大学交通科学与工程学院;

2. 北京市大数据科学与脑机智能高精尖创新中心(北京航空航天大学))

摘　要　为解决城市交通中信息共享滞后和日益突显的用户隐私保护问题,考虑到区块链去中心化、不可篡改和可追溯的技术特征和联盟链的权限管理特征,采用联盟链搭建了多方参与的城市交通大数据共享平台,实现数据的去中心化管理和平台化共享。针对数据共享问题,提出了基于数字货币和积金激励的城市交通数据共享算法,阐述了智能合约执行的流程,并通过设置数据共享资质门槛保证数据的有效性和可信性。同时,在数据加密、数据上链、数据访问等环节使用基于属性的加密算法 CP-ABE 进行用户隐私安全保障算法的设计,保障用户隐私安全。

关键词　城市交通　算法设计　区块链　激励算法　隐私安全　大数据平台

0　引言

随着城市交通信息化进程不断加快,作为人-车-路交互的城市交通数据平台面临的信息孤岛和隐私安全问题愈发突出。大数据时代,海量的城市交通数据依靠更多的交通参与者自发提供和共享,激励用户共享有效数据和保障用户隐私安全尤为重要。

区块链是分布式数据库系统,具有去中心化、数据不可篡改和可追溯特征[1]。近些年,区块链在交通领域应用场景日益增多,特别是在车联网和自动驾驶领域。Rathee[2]和 Jiang 等[3]分别研究了基于区块链的车辆安全连接和传输应用框架。之后,Duong 等[4]、Cebe 等[5]提出了去中心化的自动驾驶驾驶应用机制与概念模型;龚奕等[6]在多方交通公司及机构参与的场景下,搭建了城市交通大数据平台概念模型;在概念模型和框架搭建的基础上,学者们将关注点集中在交通信息共享的激励机制研究。现有的共享激励机制可大致分为数字货币激励和信誉值激励;Fujihara 等[7]普通市民参与的道路状态异常监测,并通过数字货币激励和协调收集到的数据;Devi 等[8]鼓励用户在不泄露身份的情况下生成和认可事故区域的事故警报消息,并向消息生成者和背书者支付货币奖励;Zhang 等[9]通过后验和先验鉴定收集到的数据,并给与车辆广播的货币奖励;Chen 等[10]提出将平台作为拍卖人购买数据,保障链上和链下数据的可信度;在信誉值激励方面,Chen 等[11]通过信誉评估设计保障消息真实性,但是计算较为复杂;Chai 等[12]则在共识机制部分补充了信誉证明机制,适用于范围不大的系统;Kang 等[13]利用三权重主观逻辑实现了车辆的高质量信誉管理;李志展等[14]提出了车联网信誉共识机制,使得记账权集中在信誉高的车辆,保障车联网消息的可信度;类似的,翟宝琴等[15]采用自上而下的双层共识结构,赋予每辆车信任值并提出组领导节点算法。货币激励和信誉值激励的研究丰富,但是二者结合的激励研究有待完善。因此,本文在搭建城市交通大数据平台的基础上,结合数字货币激励和信誉积金激励进行算法设计。

1. 基金项目:国家自然科学基金项目(U1811463)。

在隐私泄露问题频发的技术过渡期,针对数据共享过程中的用户隐私保护也是国内外专家关注的热点。信誉值属性一定程度上能筛选不良用户,禁止其访问和共享数据;李永强等[16]、龚丽娜等[17]、翟宝琴[18]引入了双重过滤的信誉机制来排除网络恶意信息,并基于用户隐私需求提出了随机加密和生成毫不相干的伪身份;在算法研究层面,基于属性的加密方案 CP-ABE 可以使用属性刻画用户资格,并由数据加密方来制定密文访问策略[19],相较于传统的嵌入式策略更加灵活,特别是在一对多的数据文件分享中,只需制定一条仅限 N 位用户才能满足的访问策略即可实现共享操作。

Bethencourt[20]首次引入属性授权的 CP-ABE 算法,设计了一个可信的安全隐私保护方案以访问数据;近几年,相继有学者对区块链与 CP-ABE 结合进行探索,保障分布式系统上的数据共享隐私安全。Lin 等[21]、Wang 等[22]基于 CP-ABE 实现了可以进行细粒度访问控制的云数据加密存储与共享访问系统;之后,王静宇等[23-24]、刘帆等[25]、谭跃生等[26]许多学者针对系统的密文策略属性基加密方案进行研究,验证了 CP-ABE 算法较传统加密算法单笔交易处理时间减少,效率提高;李峰等[27]提出了一种基于信任机制的访问控制策略,利用智能合约技术将原始数据文件的元数据信息以及经 CP-ABE 加密,并通过实验验证 CP-ABE 算法可达到更短的整体消耗时间和更高的安全级别。现有成果表明 CP-ABE 与区块链融合设计具有高效性与极大发展空间,对城市交通应用场景中的隐私安全算法设计具有重要实践意义。因此,本文基于 CP-ABE 加密方案对用户隐私安全保护进行算法层设计。

综上,国内外专家依托区块链的技术特征,围绕交通领域的隐私保护和激励数据共享问题进行概念模型的搭建和框架研究,合约层激励算法和用户隐私安全的算法设计仍有待完善。因此,本文采用区块链架构,搭建了城市交通大数据共享平台,设置了数据共享和访问的最小门槛,进行了基于数字货币和积金激励结合的数据共享和隐私保护算法研究。

1 城市交通大数据平台构建

传统城市交通数据平台下,各种交通基础设施的信息、气象信息、车辆信息由不同机构进行分散采集和内部处理,效率低下且难以验证。而基于区块链架构下的城市交通大数据平台,各数据源直接通过区块链节点链接入网,处理分析由网络本身完成,保证数据完全“共享”,避免了各层级间数据传输损失等问题。搭建联盟链进行节点部署,保证用户深度隔离,并通过准入机制和多组织联合的方式,实现网络拓展和自适应管理,使各节点间高可靠通信。

城市交通数据共享平台设计如图 1 所示。驾驶者账户在达到共享数据门槛后,可通过车载设备上传有效高质量的交通数据,同时获得一定的奖励计入账户;公交车、出租车等车辆和交通检测设备的监控作为单独的区块链节点,可直接上传车辆及路况信息,避免多次信息采集上传造成的信息延时和失真;各交通运营企业基础数据库、政府交管部门基层数据库、其他气象部门基层数据库存档共享信息,为公众提供系统实时准确的出行信息,实现出行决策的优化;同时方便营运企业及时掌握交通系统的实时动态,调整规划方案。

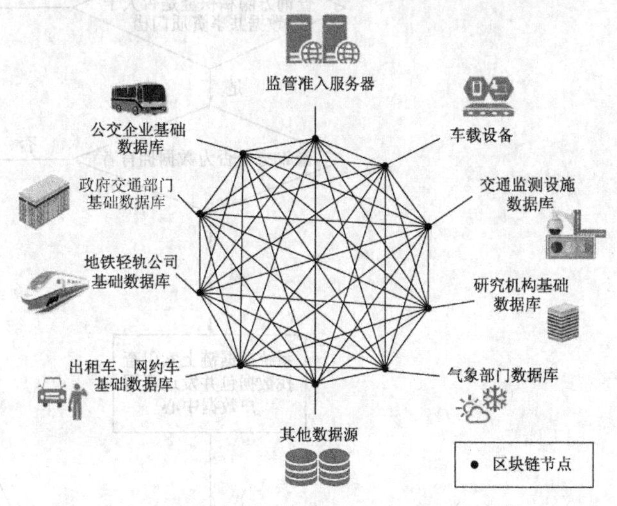

图 1 平台区块运营关系图

2 激励算法设计

考虑到驾驶人、行人等道路参与者往往能够提供更具实际应用价值和参考价值的信息,在智能合约层设计激励机制,设置隐私“钱包”,激励利益相关者或第三方共享数据尤为重要。隐私“钱包”主要用于交易或访问数据资产,当“钱包”内信誉积金低于最小门槛时,用户不具备分享数据和访问数据资质。收到共享数据请求后,检验请求人是否为联盟链内成员;若是,数据所有者启动数据共享发送,否则直接结束。一旦提交数据共享

SA,数据所有者就会获得奖励,分享后清算账户金额与信誉积金并结束。在这种情况下,如果利益相关者的账户中没有足够支付奖励,发送将失败。智能合约流程图如图 2 所示。

符号及含义表　　表1

符　号	含　义	符　号	含　义
Dat	共享数据	SminS	支付所需最低币数
SA	安全执行方式	j	账户金额计数
Registry	数据集注册表	AccessSH	共享数据的利益相关者集
ReMin	共享资质最小积金门槛	SHId	利益相关者唯一标识
ReCoins	信誉积金数	Owner	拥有者
StakeHolder	利益相关者	Coins	账户金额
operatorId	操作者唯一标识		

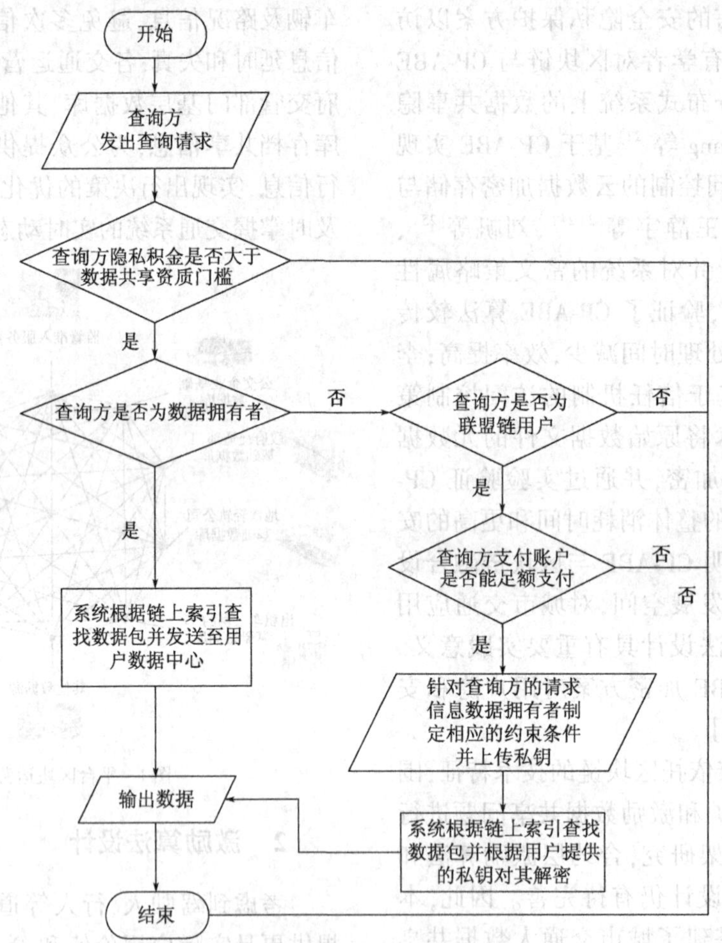

图 2　智能合约激励算法流程图

算法 1 为基于数字货币与信誉积金奖励的数据共享传输伪代码。符号及含义表如表 1 所示。算法分为四个步骤。首先,采用安全的执行方式获得共享的数据资产,数据上链与访问参见算法 2 和算法 3。其次,检查共享数据的结构与内容是否正确完整,并对共享数据请求方进行核验。然后,算法检查资产是否已经与利益相关者共享。之后,利益相关者向数据所有者支付数字货币。最后,更新资产状态,并通知利益相关者。

算法 1:基于数字货币与信誉积金奖励的数据共享传输算法。

输入:联盟链成员共享数据

输出:共享数据成功交易记录

①if ReCoins of Dat. Owner >= ReMin then

②Dat ← DatRegistry. get(SA. Dat Reference)/ * Step1:核验分享资质,获取共享数据 */

③End if

④for all StakeHolder In SA. StakeHolders do /* Step2:检查是否已与利益相关方共享数据(数据上链与解密过程见隐私保护算法)*/

⑤if Dat. AccessSH is not Empty then

⑥ if j >= SminS do /*账户金额是否足以支付*/

⑦ SHId ← StakeHolder. operatorId /*共享操作完成,获取此操作共享的利益相关者唯一标识*/

⑧ if SHId exists in Dat. AccessSH then

⑨ return Data has been shared successfully/*核验成功,返回共享成功消息*/

⑩ continue to the next StakeHolder/*继续操作*/

⑪ else

⑫ push SHId into Dat. AccessSH/*将已分享者的唯一标识压入共享成员集*/

⑬ end if

⑭ else

⑮ return coin is not enough

⑯ end if

⑰ else

⑱ Dat. AccessSH ← SHId

⑲ end if /* Step2 结束*/

⑳Coins ← Coins belonging to StakeHolder/* Step3:分享者获取奖励,存入账户*/

㉑ for j >= SminS do /*钱包金额不小于支付所需*/

㉒ Coins[j]. Owner ← Dat. Owner

㉓Update coin status and ReCoins/* 更新账户钱包金额*/

㉔ end for

㉕ Broadcast sharing event

㉖end for

㉗Update Dat status/* Step4:共享记录完成*/

㉘return Sharing Successfully

3 隐私保护算法设计

城市交通数据平台涉及用户多、功能复杂,用户隐私保护不容忽视。个人数据的收集、处理或使用应遵守用户和第三方之间协议和标准,只有在数据所有者同意的情况下,才能对个人数据及信息进行处理。而用户有权知晓哪些第三方有权获得哪些数据以及如何使用这些数据。一旦不再需要这些数据,数据所有者有权立即删除。

任何依赖用户数据的技术都必须通过设计来保护用户隐私。因此,引入联盟链,通过对数据的上链和加密、解密环节设计智能合约机制,对用户数据进行保护。基于联盟链的性质和 CP-ABE 算法(Ciphertext Policy Attribute Based Encryption,基于密文策略的属性加密)的优异表现,本文使用 CP-ABE 加密算法进行设计,分为初始化、数据加密、数据上链和数据访问四部分。表 2 为算法中应用的相关符号及含义。

算法符号及其含义表 表2

符 号	含 义
MESS	数据拥有者制定的访问控制策略
DataFiles	数据文件
Dat. Owner	数据拥有者
Dat. User	数据消费者
UID	用户标识码
SPK	系统主密钥
PK	系统公钥
SK	用户私钥
ASF	加密后的数据文件
ASK	加密后的对称密钥
FID	文件标识码
Encry_K	AES 加密算法,K 为对称密钥
Deci_K	AES 解密算法,K 为对称密钥
Addr. Ipfs	文件在 IPFS 上的索引地址
β	安全参数

初始化主要输出为系统随机生成的公钥和主密钥。数据拥有者将待共享数据文件上传到数据平台并生成原始数据文件;再使用具备高速度、高安全级别特性的 AES 对称加密算法,随机生成密钥对原始数据文件进行加密得到密文 ASF。最后将密文上传到 IPFS 私有集群,得到密文存储的地址 Addr. Ipfs,并使用系统公钥和制定的访问策略

MESS 对对称密钥进行加密。

区块链的不可篡改、可溯源特性能保障安全有效的访问控制管理。数据上链是将共享数据的原始数据文件描述信息、文件存储地址和加密密钥存储在链上,并全网同步以供各区块链节点检索和访问。整个共享数据文件的数据加密和数据上传伪代码如算法 2 所示。

算法 2:数据上链隐私保护算法

输入:DataFiles、安全参数 β、UID、FID

输出:区块成功交易信息

①(PK, SPK) ← Set (1^{β})／* Part1:初始化*／

②DataFile←Data. registry／*生成原始数据文件*／

③Module executes:／* Part 2:数据加密及上链*／

④K← generate a symmetric key／*生成系统密钥*／

⑤EncryDataFile ←AESEncry (DataFiles, K) ／*文件加密*／

⑥Addr. Ipfs← store EncryDataFile to IPFS／*获取文件存储地址*／

⑦DAT. Owner develop control strategy MESS

⑧PK, SPK←CP-ABEset (1^{β})　／* CP-ABE 对称加密算法初始化*／

⑨ASK←CP-ABEEncry (PK, K, MESS)／*得到 MESS 隐私保护策略下加密后密钥*／

数据访问主要是进行密钥解密和文件解密。数据访问者发出访问请求后,检索到链上的加密对称密钥并获取私钥 SK,再通过私钥 SK 解密获取明文。为减少数据篡改等潜在破坏性风险,在密钥生成阶段,可将访问机制获取到的用户信誉积金添加到用户属性。在解密阶段,若用户符合密文的访问控制策略 MESS,并且用户的信誉积金达到控制策略中的可信任范围时,则可对密文正常解密从而获得对称加密密钥。

通过链上的索引地址 Addr. Ipfs 得到原始密文数据文件,和解密密钥阶段获得的文件对称加密密钥一起使用即可完成加密文件的解密,获取共享数据。数据访问阶段的算法伪代码如算法 3 所示。

算法 3:数据访问隐私保护算法

输入:UID、FID

输出:DataFiles

①DAT. USER send request　／*访问请求发送*／

②if registry ContractAuthCheck (UID) = true／*核验注册表用户标识*／

③ Addr. Ipfs, ASK←Trace ContractGetInfo (FID)

④end if

⑤S←UserAttributes&Requested_Trust　／*获取请求方的隐私属性*／

⑥if user's attribute S satisfy access tree MESS Then／*请求方的隐私属性满足要求*／

⑦K←CP-ABEDeci (ASK, SK)

⑧ Get IPFSEncryDataFiles ← get DataFiles according to Addr. Ipfs／*获得加密文件*／

⑨ DataFiles←AESdeci (IPFSEncryDataFiles get, K)／*解密得到明文*／

⑩else

⑪return Access failed because of low credits

⑫end if

⑬return DataFiles

4　案例研究

4.1　案例研究

针对数据共享中的激励机制和信誉积金门槛进行模拟操作,各用户初始账户信息及隐私属性如表 3 所示。操作中,用户 Wang 为数据共享者,用户 Li、Liu 与 Zeng 为数据请求方;设定本次文件分享者为用户 Wang,需在满足最低隐私门槛的状态下支付 5 个数字货币,数据共享过程如表 4 所示;表 4 中用户 Li 虽然满足 5 个数字货币的支付要求,但由于隐私属性不佳,低于数据分享和访问的最低门槛导致共享数据失败,最终返回了算法中的"Access failed because of low credits"语句。用户 Zeng 信誉积金高于分享门槛,但由于不能完成共享的支付需要,最终返回"coin is not enough"语句;用户 Liu 的信誉积金超过最低门槛要求,同时具备支付共享数据所需数字货币的能力,返回"Sharing Successfully",得到用户 Wang 分享的数据文件,数据共享操作成功。

共享操作结束后的更新状态信息如表 5 所示。通过表中框出的数字,可以发现由于用户 Li 和用户 Zeng 未能得到 Wang 共享的数据,故其账户数字货币数额并未变化；而用户 Liu 在支付数字货币后金额减少，减少金额转移至数据分享者 Wang 账户中。

初始用户账户信息及信誉积金属性表 表 3

属性	用户			
	Wang	Li	Zeng	Liu
账户金额(数字货币)	10	5	3	10
信誉积金	12	3	8	8

注：模拟操作中设定最小信誉积金门槛 SminS 为 5。

数据共享操作说明表 表 4

属性	Li		Zeng		Liu	
	账户金额	信誉积金	账户金额	信誉积金	账户金额	信誉积金
数量	5	3	3	8	10	8
是否满足访问共享的隐私门槛需要	—	NO	—	YES	—	YES
是否满足共享操作支付需要	YES	—	NO		YES	
是否共享成功	Access failed because of low credits		coin is not enough		Sharing Successfully	

共享操作后用户账户信息及信誉积金属性表 表 5

属性	用户			
	Wang	Li	Zeng	Liu
账户金额(数字货币)	15	5	3	5
信誉积金	13	3	8	8

4.2 算法对比分析

通过设计数据共享激励算法和设置最小信誉积金门槛，能有效筛选信用度佳的用户共享可信度高、安全性好的高质量的数据，进一步规避了数据篡改和隐私泄露的风险；通过积金奖励的方式激励共享行为，也能一定程度上起到惩戒危险分享行为的用户的作用。此外，信誉积金属性可与新型社会信用体系衔接，将个人的社会信用嵌入隐私属性中，成为隐私门槛的设置的基础和规范标准，助力智慧城市交通平台的构建。

同时，算法采用的 CP-ABE 属性加密适用于云上数据的加密存储和细粒度共享；相较于传统的公钥加密算法而言，CP-ABE 属性加密更加高效安全。CP-ABE 能在一对多的数据文件分享中，只需制定一条仅限 N 位用户才能满足的访问策略，加密一次即可形成唯一密文，再分别发送给 N 位用户即可；传统公钥加密则需利用 N 个不同公钥，将共享明文加密 N 次，形成 N 份不同密文分别发送给 N 个用户；另外，CP-ABE 可以使用属性刻画用户资格，并由数据加密方来制定密文访问策略，相较于传统的嵌入式策略更加灵活。因此，采用 CP-ABE 属性加密算法能有效为城市交通大数据平台的构建提供技术支撑。

5 结论

在分析城市交通智能化进程中面临的信息共享滞后和用户隐私安全难题的基础上，采用联盟链搭建了多方共同参与的城市交通大数据共享平台，提出了参与者共享数据的门槛限制和积金激励的算法；同时在智能合约层设计了基于奖励的数据共享算法与数据加密上链、数据访问等隐私保护算法。未来在海量数据的基础上，可以通过搭建城市交通数据共享区块链平台，仿真实验算法水平及平台的运营效果。

参考文献

[1] Li X, Jiang P, Chen T, et al. A survey on the security of blockchain systems [J]. Future Generation Computer Systems, 2020, 107: 841-853.

[2] Rathee G, Sharma A, Iqbal R, et al. A Blockchain Framework for Securing Connected and Autonomous Vehicles[J]. Sensors (Basel,

Switzerland),2019,19(14).

[3] Jiang X, Yu F R, Song T, et al. Blockchain-enabled cross-domain object detection for autonomous driving: A model sharing approach [J]. IEEE Internet of Things Journal, 2020, 7 (5):3681-3692.

[4] Duong T, Todi K K, Chaudhary U, et al. Decentralizing Air traffic Flow management with blockchain-based reinforcement learning[C]// 2019 IEEE 17th International Conference on Industrial Informatics (INDIN). IEEE, 2019, 1: 1795-1800.

[5] Cebe M, Erdin E, Akkaya K, et al. Block4forensic: An integrated lightweight blockchain framework for forensics applications of connected vehicles[J]. IEEE Communications Magazine, 2018, 56(10):50-57.

[6] 龚奕,廖金花.区块链技术的城市智能交通大数据平台及仿真案例分析[J].公路交通科技,2019,36(12):117-126.

[7] Fujihara A. Proposing a system for collaborative traffic information gathering and sharing incentivized by blockchain technology [C] // International Conference on Intelligent Networking and Collaborative Systems. Springer, Cham, 2018: 170-182.

[8] Devi G S P, Pamila J C M J. Accident alert system application using a privacy-preserving blockchain-based incentive mechanism [C] // 2019 5th International Conference on Advanced Computing & Communication Systems (ICACCS). IEEE, 2019: 390-394.

[9] Zhang L, Luo M, Li J, et al. Blockchain based secure data sharing system for Internet of vehicles: A position paper [J]. Vehicular Communications, 2019, 16: 85-93.

[10] Chen W, Chen Y, Chen X, et al. Toward secure data sharing for the IoV: a quality-driven incentive mechanism with on-chain and off-chain guarantees[J]. IEEE Internet of Things Journal, 2019, 7(3): 1625-1640.

[11] Chen C, Wang C, Qiu T, et al. A secure content sharing scheme based on blockchain in vehicular named data networks [J]. IEEE Transactions on Industrial Informatics, 2019, 16(5): 3278-3289.

[12] Chai H, Leng S, Zhang K, et al. Proof-of-reputation based-consortium blockchain for trust resource sharing in internet of vehicles [J]. IEEE Access, 2019, 7: 175744-175757.

[13] Kang J, Yu R, Huang X, et al. Blockchain for secure and efficient data sharing in vehicular edge computing and networks [J]. IEEE Internet of Things Journal, 2018, 6 (3): 4660-4670.

[14] 李志展,王永利,宫小泽.基于DAG分布式账本的车联网信誉值模型[J].信息安全研究,2022,8(01):55-61.

[15] 翟宝琴,王健,韩磊,等.基于信任值的车联网分层共识优化协议[J].网络与信息安全学报,2022.

[16] 李永强,刘兆伟.基于区块链的车联网安全信息共享机制设计[J].郑州大学学报(工学版),2022,43(01):103-110.

[17] 龚丽娜.基于区块链的众包式无人机配送系统框架及隐私保护方案研究[D].合肥:安徽大学,2021.

[18] 翟宝琴.基于区块链的车联网数据共享安全技术研究[D].北京:北京交通大学,2021.

[19] Wan Z, Deng R H. Hasbe: A hierarchical attribute-based solution for flexible and scalable access control in cloud computing [J]. IEEE transactions on information forensics and security, 2011, 7(2): 743-754.

[20] Bethencourt J, Sahai A, Waters B. Ciphertext-policy attribute-based encryption security and privacy [C] // Proceedings of Security and Privacy, CA, USA, 2007: 321-334.

[21] Lin C, He D, Huang X, et. al BSe In: A blockchainbased secure mutual authentication with fine-grained access control system for industry 4.0 [J]. Journal of Network and Computer Applications, 2018, 116: 42.

[22] Wang S, Wang X, Zhang Y. A secure cloud

storage framwork with access control based on blockchain [J]. IEEE Access, 2019, 7:112713.

[23] 王静宇,董昊.基于DAG区块链的密文策略属性加密模型[J].内蒙古科技大学学报,2021,40(04):355-363.

[24] 王静宇,周雪娟.一种支持属性撤销的密文策略属性基加密方案[J].计算机工程,2021,47(07):95-100.

[25] 刘帆,杨明.一种用于云存储的密文策略属性基加密方案[J].计算机应用研究,2012,29(04):1452-1456.

[26] 谭跃生,章世杨,王静宇.基于多授权中心的CP-ABE属性撤销方案[J].计算机工程与应用,2019,55(13):78-84.

[27] 李峰,梁任纲,李雪聪,等.结合区块链和属性基的可信数据分发[J].小型微型计算机系统,2021,42(07):1524-1531.

新时期杭州公交专用道发展现状及策略研究

赵晨阳[1] 冯 伟*[2] 傅佳楠 李家斌 姚 遥

(1.杭州市规划设计研究院;2.杭州市规划设计研究院)

摘 要 公交专用道是推动公交优先发展,缓解城市交通拥堵的重要措施。在城市空间格局不断优化、轨道交通快速网络化、私人机动化快速发展背景下,本文分析了杭州公交专用道的现状问题与发展瓶颈,通过相关城市经验借鉴,认为公共交通是城市客运的基础,依然有必要发展与优化公交专用道网络,使之与轨道交通共织公共交通骨架网络,满足人民群众对高品质出行的需求。基于此,本文建议研究确定杭州公交专用道设置条件,并提出了针对核心城区、放射廊道、星城差异化的公交专用道的布局策略以及运行保障策略。

关键词 杭州 常规公交 公交优先 公交专用道

0 引言

公交专用道在国内外城市公共交通优先发展过程中,得到普遍应用和推广[1]。杭州公交专用道已经过多年的发展,近年来伴随着轨道交通的快速网络化,以及城市道路的提升改造,公交专用道发展进入了瓶颈期。

在此背景下,本文对当前杭州公交专用道发展困境进行分析,结合发展环境分析与国内城市经验借鉴,并考虑杭州城市空间与公共交通实际发展情况,提出公交专用道发展的布局策略与运行保障策略。

1 杭州公交专用道发展现状分析

1.1 结合"公交都市"创建及治堵工作,公交专用道快速发展后趋于平缓

2006年,杭州在城市核心城区设置了第一条公交专用道。2013年,杭州成功申报创建国家"公交都市"示范城市,同时启动五年交通治堵工作,在《杭州市公交专用道专项规划》的指导下,公交专用道进入快速发展期[2];2014年杭州全年新增公交专用道道路长度达45.5km,同比增长47.3%。2015—2019年期间,杭州公交专用道受轨道交通快速网络化以及道路改扩建工程等多重因素影响,增速逐渐放缓,四年仅增长17.7km,如图1所示[3]。

1.2 公交专用道发展水平低,远落后于国内同等水平城市

杭州市现状人均轨道交通和公交专用道长度较低,2019年底,杭州市轨道线网和公交专用道总长度为约295km,人均拥有率仅为0.25km/万人,远低于国内主要城市均值(0.46km/万人)。2019年主要城市人均轨道交通与公交专用道长度如图2所示。

如图3所示,国内主要城市2015—2019年的轨道交通和公交专用道均在有序增加;而杭州市

2015年的轨道交通和专用道建设基础也比较薄弱,而截至2019年底,公交专用道基本没有增加,总长度和年增量远低于其他主要城市;轨道交通直到2019年以后才大幅度增加。

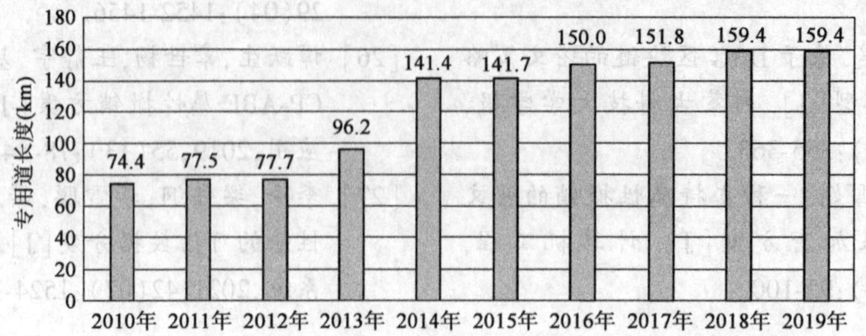

图1　历年杭州市区公交专用道规模发展情况示意图

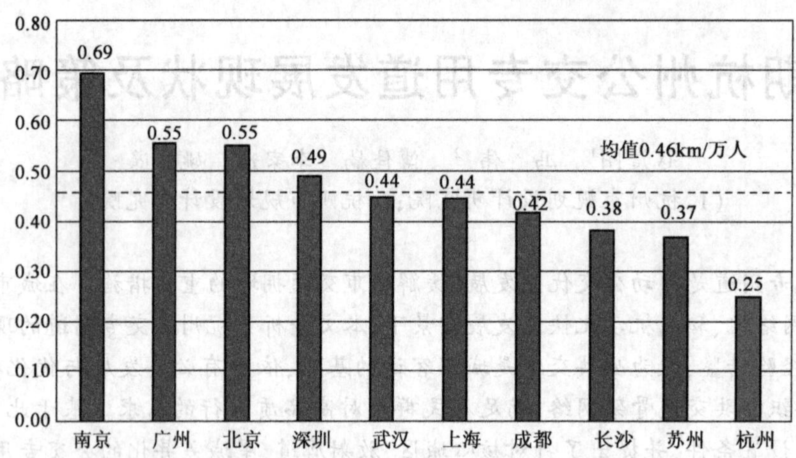

图2　2019年主要城市人均轨道交通与公交专用道长度

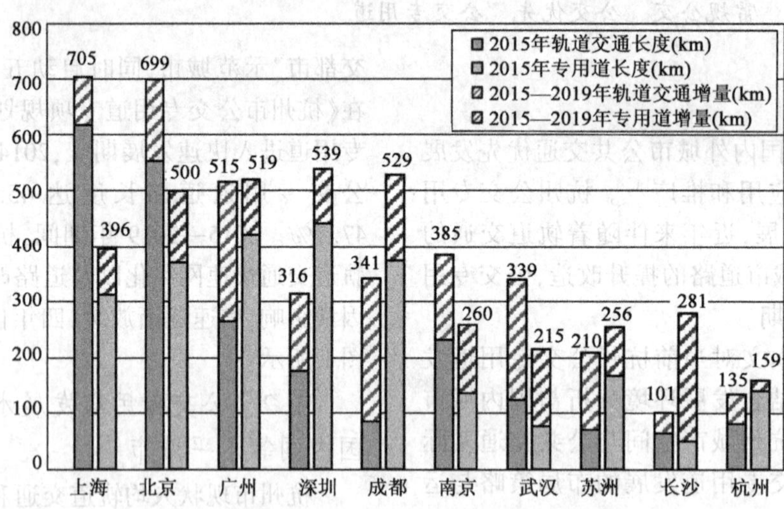

图3　主要城市轨道交通与公交专用道发展增量图

1.3　公交专用道主要布局于核心城区10km范围内,星城及放射走廊专用道尚未成型

现状杭州公交专用道主要集中在核心城区10km范围以内,基本实现网络化发展,且匹配重要的常规公交客流走廊;周边星城整体上缺乏公交专用道布设,仅钱塘和萧山城区各施划了1条公交专用道。从放射廊道上来看,仅核心城区至钱塘方向施划了1条公交专用道。

1.4 受制于道路通行压力，公交专用道使用时段不断调整

为了缓解部分道路的拥堵问题，杭州先后四次调整公交专用道使用时间，道路路权分配逐渐向社会车辆倾斜，由全天型为主转变为工作日高峰时段为主。在 2016 年，杭州市交通警察局第四次调整公交专用道使用时间后，杭州市多数公交专用道除工作日 7—9 时、16 时 30 分—18 时 30 分之外的其他时段准许社会车辆借道通行，意味着绝大部分时间，公交专用道上公交车需要与社会车辆共享路权。

1.5 公交专用道对于运营提速效果不明显，相对于社会车辆难以形成竞争优势

根据杭州市“公交云”平台数据，在同一条道路上，高峰时期常规公交车辆在有专用道路段的运营速度比无专用道路段的运营速度仅提升 7.7%；公交车辆相对于社会车辆的优势并不明显。导致公交专用道平均运行速度不高的主要原因有以下几点：

（1）现状杭州公交专用道存在局部路段施划不连续特征。如图 4 所示，部分路段如天目山路、环城北路、文一路等因受既有道路红线限制或道路提升改造工程影响，公交专用道在局部路段施划中断或被擦除。

（2）杭州取消了多条道路路口公交专用进口道，导致高峰时段进一步加剧了公交车辆在交叉口的拥堵情况（图 5）。

（3）杭州市现状公交车专用道多为路侧式，两侧地块车辆进出、借道区较短等造成社会车辆与公交车辆互相干扰，存在潜在冲突点（图 6）。

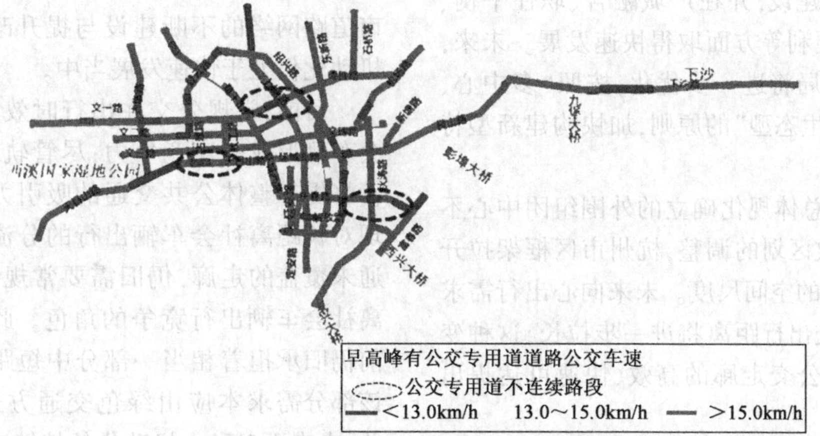

图 4 现状杭州公交专用道局部路段不连续及早高峰运行速度示意图

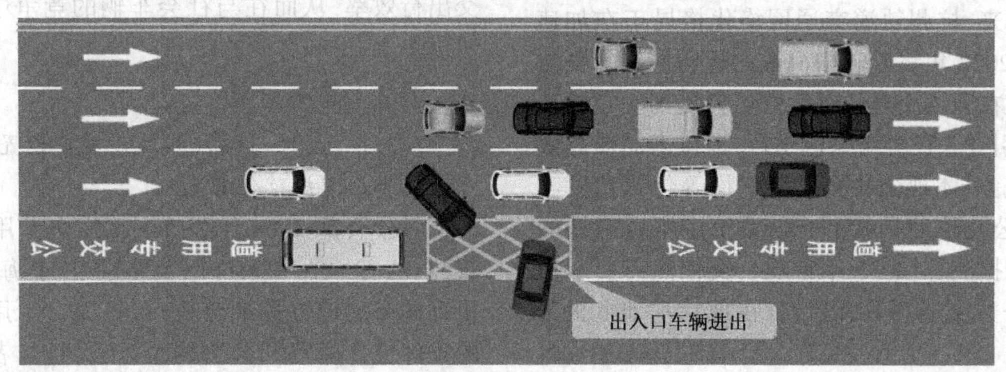

图 5 两侧地块车辆进出示意图

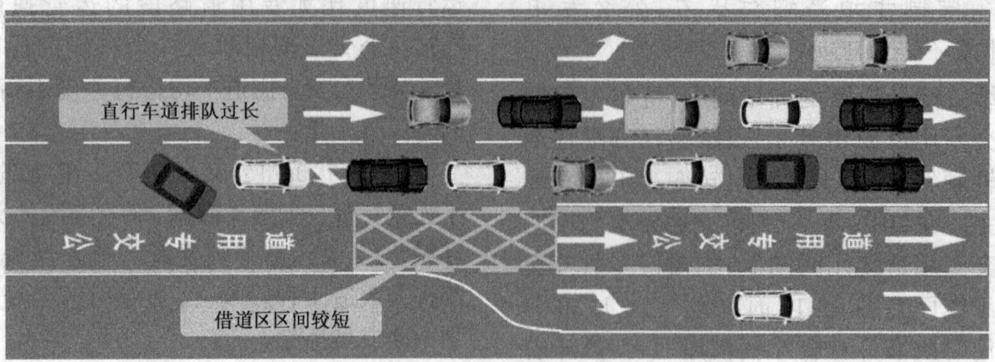

图6　进口道直行车道排队过长及借道区区间过短示意图

2　公交专用道发展相关城市经验启示

2.1　发展环境分析

2.1.1　城市空间格局不断优化，要求放射公交走廊提质提速

现状杭州城市总体上遵循“主城-副城-组团”的空间结构展开建设，并在产城融合、职住平衡、生态宜居、交通便利等方面取得快速发展。未来，杭州城市空间布局将进一步优化，按照“多中心、网络化、组团式、生态型”的原则，加快构建新型特大城市空间格局。

随着上一轮总体规化确立的外围组团中心不断发展，以及行政区划的调整，杭州市区框架拉开到东西向100km的空间尺度。未来向心出行需求将持续增长，公交出行距离将进一步拉长，这种变化趋势将对放射公交走廊的高效、快速可达提出了更高的要求。

2.1.2　轨道交通网络化背景下，常规公交将依旧承担重要职能

近年来，杭州轨道交通网络化格局正在加速形成，至2022年将形成516km的运营网络。虽然常规公交在轨道交通开通运营后会受到一定的冲击，但从引导人民群众绿色出行、提供高品质高效率出行服务、体现公共交通服务均等化等角度考虑，常规公交依旧是城市交通系统中不可或缺的一部分。据测算，2035年常规公交依然需要承担40%的公共交通客流，出行量在现状基础上提升近80%。

轨道交通网络化成熟后，高、大公共交通客流走廊基本都有轨道交通覆盖，常规公交客流分布也将会发生较大变化，存在及时调整和优化公交线路的必要，以及优化公交专用道网络布局的需要。因此，需结合城市与空间发展进程以及轨道交通建成后的常规公交运行情况对公交专用道系统进行相应的优化调整。

2.1.3　私人机动化仍处于快速发展当中，常规公交需提升吸引力

在小客车总量调控政策的影响下，杭州市区机动车保有量增长率已降低至5%左右，但随着城市道路网络的不断建设与提升改造，整体上私人机动化仍处于快速发展当中。

目前，常规公交在出行时效方面仍难以对社会车辆形成一定竞争力；尽管轨道交通的逐步运营将提升整体公共交通的吸引力，一定程度上实现对长距离社会车辆出行的分流，但对于轨道交通未覆盖的走廊，仍旧需要常规公交扮演与长距离社会车辆出行竞争的角色。此外，社会车辆目前仍旧承担着相当一部分中短距离出行需求，而该部分需求本应由绿色交通方式主要承担。因此，未来面对私人机动化的持续冲击，必须加快引导公交优先发展，保障专用路权供给，提升常规公交出行效率，从而在与社会车辆的竞争中取得相对优势。

2.2　经验启示

2.2.1　刚性与弹性相结合确定设置门槛，引导公交专用道规范化布局

对公安部2004年发布的《公交专用车道设置》(GA/T 507—2004)以及北京市、上海市、深圳市等颁布的地方标准分析，可见公交专用道设置的条件包含道路和公交两个方面，且二者缺一不可[4-7]。设置条件中，利用“应、宜、可”关系，体现刚性要求和灵活设置的需要，利用“或、且”关系，强化公交专用道设置的门槛条件。国家及部分国内城市公交专用道设置标准见表1。

国家及部分国内城市公交专用道设置标准一览表　　表1

项目		道路条件		公交条件			逻辑关系
		单向车道数（条）	单向交通流量（pcu/h）	单向断面客流量（人次/h）	单向断面车流量（车/h）	车辆运行速度（km/h）	
国标	应设置	≥3	≥500	≥6000	≥150	—	或
		≥4	—	—	≥90	—	—
	宜设置	3	—	≥4000	≥100	—	且
		2	—	≥6000	≥150	—	且
北京	应设置	≥2	—	≥1500	≥60	≤20	或
	宜设置	≥2	—	1200～1500	45～60	20～25	或
上海	应设置	≥3	—	≥4000	≥90	—	或
		≥2	—	≥3000	≥70	—	或
	宜设置	≥3	—	≥4000（预测3年内）	≥90（预测3年内）	—	或
		≥3	—	≥3000	≥70	—	或
		≥2	—	≥2500	≥60	—	或
	可设置	—	—	≥1500	≥40	—	且
		—	—	—	≥60%通道客流量	<15	且
深圳	应设置	≥3	—	≥4000	≥90	—	且
	宜设置	≥3	—	—	≥60	—	且
		≥2	—	≥4000	≥120	—	且

道路条件主要考虑单向车道数以及单向交通流量，是公交专用道设置的基本要求。公交条件可分为单向断面客流量、车流量及运行速度等[8]。

目前，杭州尚未出台公交专用道的设置标准。面向未来，建议一方面充分结合相关标准要求以及国内城市经验，另一方面需结合城市空间结构以及走廊道路条件、客流条件，制定适合杭州的公交专用道设置标准，使得公交专用道设置有据可循。

2.2.2　推进放射形公交专用道布局，提升外围片区向心出行时效

在社会车辆全面进入家庭之前，杭州在核心城区至下沙副城方向的放射廊道上开通了快速公交1号线。在设计之初，面对当时较为畅通的道路运行环境，杭州仍然在艮山路—下沙路上施划放射形公交专用道，并坚持到现在。良好的公交车辆通行环境保障了公交车辆运行速度（现状艮山路-下沙路早高峰时段公交车平均运行速度可达到30km/h）；也吸引了较为稳定的客流，产生了较高的公交出行分担率（现状下沙方向走廊的公交机动化出行分担率为72%，显著高于临平方向的48%、良渚方向的60%、未来科技城方向的48%）。

未来随着城市空间外拓及星城向心需求的不断增加，杭州需继续推进放射公交专用道建设，培育居民公共交通出行习惯，提升公交出行体验。

2.2.3　轨道交通网络化背景下，仍继续加强公交专用道建设

北京、上海、广州、深圳等城市轨道交通网络化速度快于杭州，但其仍注重保障常规公交的基础地位，持续秉持公交优先的发展理念，通过不断推进公交专用道的施划工作，提升常规公交的出行效率。国内相关城市轨道及公交专用道建设情况如表2所示。

表2 国内相关城市轨道与公交专用道建设情况一览表

城市	轨道现状里程(km)	专用道现状里程(km)	专用道规划里程(km)
北京	799.4	500	1020
广州	531.9	519	840
深圳	423.4	539	1015
南京	394.7	260	670
杭州	306.3	159	—

由上述城市的轨道与公交专用道的建设情况可知,面向未来,杭州轨道交通网络化后,仍应继续推动公交优先发展战略,结合道路条件以及客流条件,注重公交专用道网络与轨道交通网络的协同关系,继续重视公交专用道建设。

2.2.4 积极探索在重要走廊的快速路上设置公交专用道,提高常规公交客流运输能力

国内北京、深圳、成都、武汉等城市均开始尝试在快速路主线上设置公交专用道,通过路权的重新分配来提升道路瓶颈段的客流输送能力,进而转变走廊上的交通出行模式。以北京京通快速路为例,2011年京通快速路路中式公交专用道开始启用,早晚高峰期由公交车辆专用。京通快速路公交专用道使用后,早高峰公交车辆运行速度提升100%;公交客流量明显增加,早高峰进城公交客流量增加8000人次,而社会车辆与地铁客流均有不同程度的下降,高峰客流拥挤情况得到缓解[9-10]。京通快速路公交专用道开通前后道路运行对比如图7所示。

a)开通前

b)开通后

图7 京通快速路公交专用道开通前后道路运行对比图

京通快速路公交专用道的实践,体现了其提升公交出行效率,转变走廊交通出行模式,破解道路拥堵瓶颈的作用。杭州可探索在合适的快速路主线上(重要走廊、跨江桥梁)设置公交专用道,强化公交服务水平,提高道路通行效率,减轻高、大客流走廊轨道压力,建立起相对社会车辆更具竞争力的常规公交体系。

3 杭州公交专用道发展策略

3.1 公交专用道布局策略

3.1.1 策略一:结合客流、车流、道路等条件明确公交专用道布局条件标准

根据《城市综合交通体系规划标准》(GB/T 51328—2018):规划高峰小时单向断面公交客流量达到3000人次/h的公共交通走廊,应设置公交专用道[11]。当走廊上布置大运量城市轨道交通时,应根据交通衔接和客运需求特征,设置公交专用道。结合标准要求以及国内其他城市经验,同时结合未来杭州的城市空间结构构想,杭州公交专用道设置条件建议如表3所示,考虑到绕城高速内外地区在城市发展及客流强度的差异,为了在绕城高速外地区提前预留公交专用道,培养公共交通出行习惯,对于绕城高速外地区适当降低专用道施划条件。此外,为了避免绕城外地区道路资源的浪费,对于宜设置公交专用道的道路,必须同时满足单向客流量及车流量的门槛。

杭州公交专用道设置条件建议表　　表3

项目		道路条件	公交条件		
		单向车道数(条)	单向断面客流量(人次/h)	单向断面车流量(标准车/h)	逻辑关系
绕城高速内	应设置	≥3	≥3000	≥75	或
		2	≥4000	≥100	或
	宜设置	≥3	≥2500	≥60	或
		2	≥3000	≥75	或
绕城高速外	应设置	≥3	≥2500	≥60	或
		2	≥3000	≥75	或
	宜设置	≥3	≥1500	≥40	且
		2	≥2000	≥50	且

3.1.2　策略二:核心城区——打通既有运行公交专用道瓶颈,优化完善公交专用道网络

杭州现状核心城区的公交专用道总体上已形成一定规模,其中核心城区双向六车道以上的主干路施划公交专用道比例已经超过80%,但由于受道路及交通组织条件限制,难以形成相对完善的公交专用道网络,其系统效益收到较大影响。

核心城区从路网角度应减少专用道施划中断的情况、打通施划瓶颈,对公交专用道系统进行优化、完善。此外,核心城区应在保留现有专用道的基础上,结合道路资源优化组织交通,例如在西湖景区、历史文化街区等一些道路资源紧张、环保要求较高,同时公共交通需求较大的特殊区域考虑设置公交专用路。

3.1.3　策略三:放射廊道——持续推进放射状公交专用道建设,与轨道交通共同支撑客流走廊

杭州公交专用道现状基本布局于留石快速路、秋石快速路、钱塘江、绕城高速西线围合的区域内,强化了对于公交出行集中区域的服务。但随着城市空间的进一步拓展,面对居住人口以及就业岗位的逐步外溢,单一的轨道交通通道将难以承担日益增长的出行需求,需要常规公交与之形成合力,共同服务于客流走廊。

放射廊道需契合"东整、西优、南启、北建、中塑"的城市发展方向,结合轨道交通线网规划以及重要放射客流走廊布局,在下沙方向基础上重点谋划至临平、大城北、良渚、大城西、萧山等方向的核心城区放射状公交专用道,与轨道交通共织公共交通骨架网络,如图8所示。

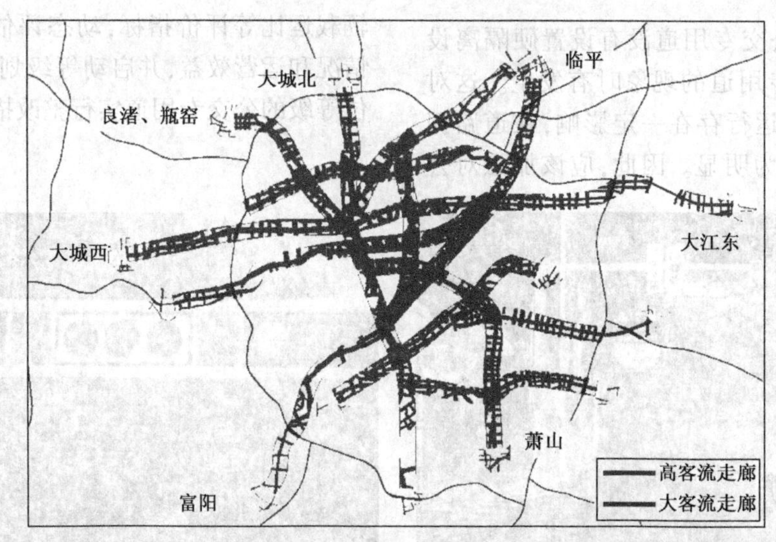

图8　杭州核心城区重要放射客流走廊情况示意图

3.1.4　策略四:星城——适度超前设置公交专用道,引领公交优先发展

星城是未来新增居住人口与就业岗位集聚的主要地区,也是现状私人机动化交通发展最为迅猛的区域。星城应抓住基础设施大建设的时机,依托轨道交通站点规划设置公交专用道,构建公交系统主骨架,培养居民公交出行习惯。因此,可围绕轨道交通站点与网络,结合杭州公交专用道设置条件建议,积极增加公交专用道(图9)。

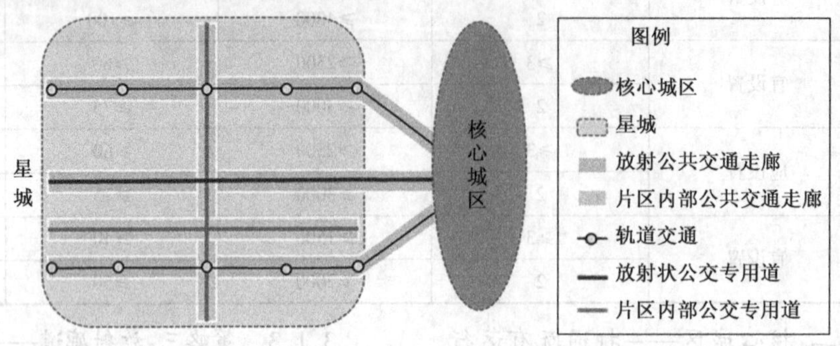

图9　杭州星城公交专用道布局模式示意图

3.2　公交专用道运行保障策略

3.2.1　策略一:因地制宜,细化设计提升公交专用道运行效率

目前,核心城区公交专用道走廊内仍有较多的路口未设置公交专用进口道,易形成堵点。此外,现状公交专用道基本设置在道路路侧,易受到地块出入口、社会车辆临时停车及借道、交叉口处右转车辆等影响,交通运行效率受到较大制约。因此,有必要结合道路条件及交通运行状况,建议骨架公交专用道尽可能采用路中式布置,加强公交专用进口车道的设置,并辅助以公交信号优先,保障公交专用道运行效率,如图10所示。

3.2.2　策略二:加强公交专用道运行监管力度,保障专用路权

目前,大部分公交专用道没有设置硬隔离设施,违章使用公交专用道的现象时有发生。这对公交车辆在专用道运行存在一定影响,在道路拥挤情况下的影响更为明显。因此,应该加强对公交专用道违章使用的管理力度,保障公交车辆正常使用公交专用道,保持道路通行秩序。通过新增公交车辆车载式违章拍照摄像头,可以增大违章监管覆盖范围。此外,注重标志标线设施,加强宣传引导工作,避免社会车辆误入公交专用道,影响公交车辆的正常运行(图11)。

3.2.3　策略三:建立公交专用道长效动态评估机制

基于杭州市道路交通和公共交通发展环境,建立一套完善的公交专用道评价体系,通过筛选道路断面形式、车道数、交叉口间距、路段出入口数量、公交车站设置形式、公交车站据交叉口距离、早晚高峰单向断面小汽车流量、单向断面公交客流量、单向断面公交车辆数、社会车辆与公交车辆载运比等评价指标,动态评估公交专用道运行情况和运营效益,并启动等级划分机制,对处于末位等级的公交专用道实行整改措施(图12)。

图10　公交信号优先示意图

图 11　公交专用道运行监管示意图

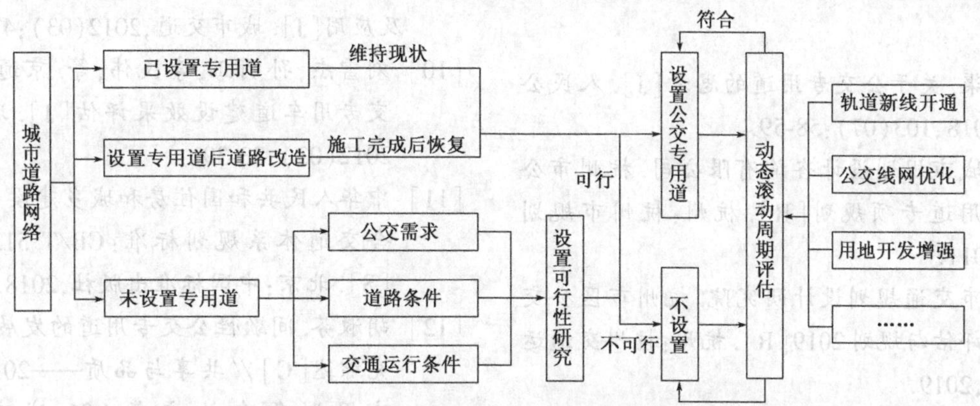

图 12　公交专用道监管评估体系示意图

3.2.4　策略四：适时探索多形式公交专用道，为路权分配破局

国内许多城市广泛推广建设的多为完全性公交专用道，会存在道路通行空间减少、通行能力降低的现象[12]。因此，结合杭州城市空间格局和道路交通特点，开展多形式的公交专用道研究与实施工作势在必行。

(1)间歇式公交专用道(Intermittent Bus Lane，IBL)。通过可变情报板、路面下感应设备等装置主动动态控制公交专用道对社会车辆的开放时间，类似于可变车道，其可以在保证公交优先的前提下，有效地提高公交专用道的利用率(图 13)[13]。

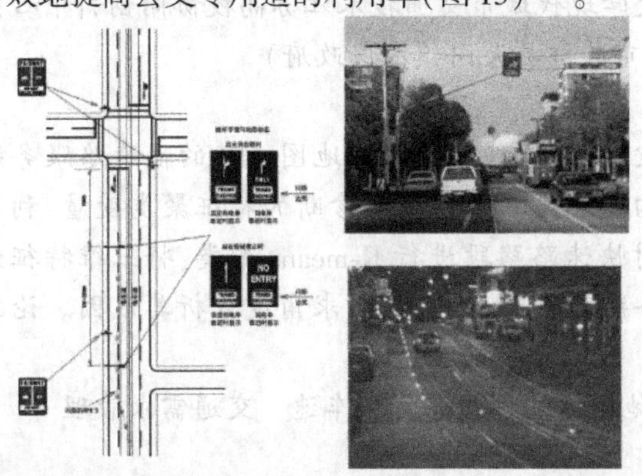

图 13　墨尔本间歇式公共交通专用公路工程

(2)逆向公交专用道(Contraflow Bus Lane，CBL)。多设置在单向或单循环组织的道路街区上，结合次支路灵活管理，并配备公交专用信号灯，用以解决公交车辆绕行等问题，目前杭州市浣纱路、文二路、文三路等道路设有逆向公交专用道(图 14)。

图 14　杭州市文二路逆向公交专用道

4　结语

本文认为杭州公交专用道发展取得了一定的成绩，但也正面临着困境，在布局和运行上存在进一步提升的空间。本文借鉴相关城市经验，认为

新时期杭州继续加强公交专用道的布局与优化是必要的,建议应建立本地化的公交专用布局条件与标准;对于不同区域,公交专用道布局应体现差异化。

受制于研究水平与精力,本文仅侧重宏观层面对于杭州公交专用道网络发展策略的分析,对于量化指标方面考量较少。在未来的研究中,可叠加杭州公交线网、站点、客流、车流等多源数据,使得分析与策略更有针对性,有利于更加精准地直接指导公交专用道的布设。

参考文献

[1] 蔡少渠.关于公交专用道的思考[J].人民公交,2018,103(07):58-59.

[2] 杭州城市规划设计咨询有限公司.杭州市公交专用道专项规划[R].杭州:杭州市规划局,2011.

[3] 杭州市交通规划设计研究院.杭州市区公交线网评估与规划2019[R].杭州:杭州交通运输局,2019.

[4] 中华人民共和国公安部.公交专用车道设置:GA/T 507—2004[S].北京:中国标准出版社,2004.

[5] 北京市质量技术监督局.公交专用车道设置规范:DB11/T 1163—2015[S],2015.

[6] 上海市城乡建设和管理委员会.公交专用道系统设计规范:DG/TJ 08-2172—2015[S],2015.

[7] 深圳市交通运输委员会.深圳市公交专用道设置标准及建设指引(征求意见稿)[R].深圳:深圳交通运输委员会,2014.

[8] 赵紫琴.佛山市公交专用道设置条件及网络化方案研究——以佛山市中心城区为例[J].黑龙江交通科技,2017,40(011):179-180.

[9] 王晓峰,邹平.北京市道路交通仿真平台建设及应用[J].城市交通,2012(03):47-53.

[10] 刘雪杰,孙明正,李民伟,等.京通快速路公交专用车道建设效果评估[J].城市交通,2012(03):33-39.

[11] 中华人民共和国住房和城乡建设部.城市综合交通体系规划标准:GB/T 51328—2018[S].北京:中国标准出版社,2018.

[12] 胡淑芬.间歇性公交专用道的发展历程及研究综述[C]//共享与品质——2018中国城市规划年会论文集(06城市交通规划),2018.

[13] Hongzhao D, Chenxin Z, Fengjie F. Sharing Bus Lanes: A New Lanes Multiplexing-based Method using a Dynamic Time Slice Policy[J]. Transport,2018:1-38.

快速路服务瓶颈诊断及成因分析

矫仟慧*[1,2,3] 罗荣根[4] 陈文栋[1,2,3] 陈学武[1,2,3]

(1.东南大学江苏省城市智能交通重点实验室;2.东南大学现代城市交通技术江苏高校协同创新中心;3.东南大学交通学院;4.福建省龙岩市长汀县大同镇人民政府)

摘 要 为了解析交通拥堵特征,辅助交通需求调控,提出一种基于高德地图API的快速路服务瓶颈诊断方法。首先,从拥堵性、原发性、周期性三个维度构造快速路服务瓶颈诊断的特征聚类变量,利用高德地图API获得聚类变量数据源并进行计算。然后,对快速路路段进行K-means聚类,将三维特征最显著的一类路段定义为快速路服务瓶颈。最后,结合服务瓶颈特征,从交通需求角度分析其成因。论文以南京市快速路网为例,验证了方法的有效性。

关键词 城市公共交通设施规划 服务瓶颈诊断 地图API调用 行程车速 交通需求管理

0 引言

近年来,机动车保有量逐年攀升,交通拥堵问题随行相伴,城市功能的正常运转受到了严重威胁。据相关研究显示,交通拥堵往往首先形成于道路网络中的瓶颈区段(如快速路),随后蔓延至其他路段[1]。快速路是大城市交通主骨架,作为最高等级的城市道路,其以少量的道路资源承担了大量的交通出行,是分析交通拥堵、诊断服务瓶颈的重点研究对象。

当前,众多学者都对交通服务瓶颈的识别进行了研究。Chen 等[2]在对圣地亚哥 7 条高速公路瓶颈识别的研究中,发现前 10 个最严重瓶颈产生的延误占所有瓶颈产生总延误的 61%,这证明了服务瓶颈在交通拥堵延误中所起的主导作用。现有对服务瓶颈识别的数据主要来源于历史检测线圈数据[3-8],识别方法主要分为累计曲线法[3,4]、自动识别算法[5-7]、交通仿真算法[8]三类,对高速路服务瓶颈点位置与瓶颈激活时间进行识别。刘立[9]通过道路实验证明了道路实际通行能力的参数与行程车速是相关联的,进而证明可以用行程车速表征道路交通运行状态。冯星宇[10]与郑凌瀚[11]以快速路为研究对象进行服务瓶颈诊断,进一步证明了可以依据快速路路段的速度变化与交通运行状态对快速路的服务瓶颈进行状态划分与成因分析。

根据交通拥堵发生地点的固定性,交通拥堵可划分为常发性拥堵和偶发性拥堵两大类别。相应的,可将导致交通拥堵的服务瓶颈划分为常发性服务瓶颈与偶发性服务瓶颈。相较于偶发性服务瓶颈的不可预测与影响短期性,具有周期性的常发性服务瓶颈对城市交通正常运转有长期影响。因此,常发性服务瓶颈的诊断与成因分析一直备受关注,也是本文重点研究的对象。

通过服务瓶颈诊断方面的文献研读,发现既有研究多对服务瓶颈现象进行静态识别与解释,重点研究服务瓶颈所属路段,缺少对服务瓶颈的动态时空分布特性进行分析,且多停留在服务瓶颈本身的位置和特性识别,而缺少从需求侧对服务瓶颈成因进行深入分析。

针对上述问题,本文从拥堵性、原发性、周期性三个维度构造快速路服务瓶颈诊断的特征聚类变量,利用高德地图 API 获取快速路各路段全天的交通状态以及行程车速等开放数据,将 API 获取数据转换为三维特征变量值,采用聚类分析的方法从快速路网中识别出最具瓶颈特征的路段,将其定义为快速路服务瓶颈,深入分析服务瓶颈的时空特征,并结合南京案例,从需求侧探讨其产生的原因。

1 服务瓶颈诊断方法

1.1 构造聚类变量

为解决拥堵特征评价分散化、平均化的问题,相关学者[12]引入了常发性拥堵路段的三维特征,即拥堵性、原发性、周期性,对常发性交通拥堵状态进行评价。导致常发性拥堵的常发性服务瓶颈可采用同样的三维特征指标进行评价。

1)拥堵性指标

行程车速通常用来表征道路交通运行状态,图 1 所示为南京市某天路段行程车速分布特征。本文利用行程车速构造如下聚类变量表征拥堵性:

(1)路段自由流速度 v_f:自由流速度是指不受上下游条件影响的交通流运行速度。一般情况下,道路等级越高、路况条件越好,自由流速度便越高。选取该聚类指标,可反映服务瓶颈与道路等级和条件的关系。本研究取最大行程车速作为自由流速度。

(2)路段平均速度 v_{avg}:平均速度是路段在一天中所有时刻的行程车速的平均值,能够反映快速路路段的平均运行水平。

(3)路段最低速度 v_{lowest}:最低速度是路段一天中的最低行程车速,能够反映路段受交通拥堵影响的程度。

(4)路段速度方差 $var^2(v)$:速度方差反映了一天当中路段行程车速的波动,也即行程车速变化的剧烈程度,为各时刻路段行程车速与路段平均速度的差的平方和。

2)原发性指标

高德地图将每一时刻路段所处的状态划分为“畅通”“缓行”“拥堵”“严重拥堵”四类。北京市地方标准《城市道路交通运行评价指标体系》将工作日早高峰定义为 7:00 至 9:00,晚高峰为 17:00 至 19:00[13]。南京市某路段在不同时刻所处的交通状态如图 2 所示,图中,1、2、3、4 分别代表畅通、缓行、拥堵、严重拥堵。

图1　南京市某路段全天行程车速

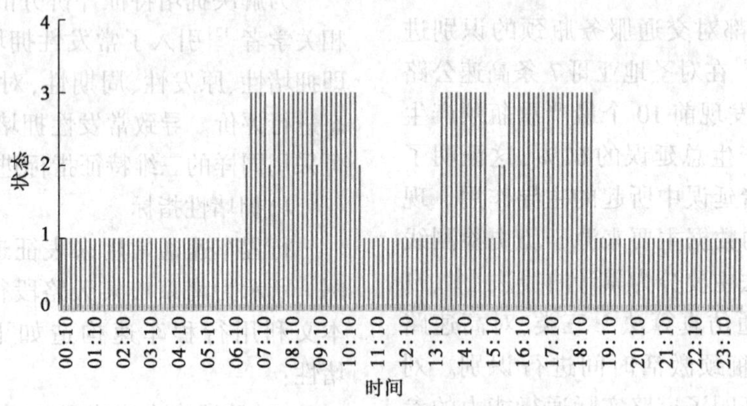

图2　南京市某路段全天交通状态

以不同状态在早晚高峰出现的时刻与高峰开始时刻的时间差作为聚类变量表征原发性:

(1)早高峰第一次"缓行"出现时刻与早高峰开始时刻的时间差 $t_{缓行.am}$。

(2)早高峰第一次"拥堵"出现时刻与早高峰开始时刻的时间差 $t_{拥堵.am}$。

(3)早高峰第一次"严重拥堵"出现时刻与早高峰开始时刻的时间差 $t_{严重拥堵.am}$。

(4)晚高峰第一次"缓行"出现时刻与晚高峰开始时刻的时间差 $t_{缓行.pm}$。

(5)晚高峰第一次"拥堵"出现时刻与晚高峰开始时刻的时间差 $t_{拥堵.pm}$。

(6)晚高峰第一次"严重拥堵"出现时刻与晚高峰开始时刻的时间差 $t_{严重拥堵.pm}$。

3)周期性指标

以不同交通状态在一天中出现的频率来表征周期性,具体包括:

(1)"缓行"频率 $frequency_{缓行}$。

(2)"拥堵"频率 $frequency_{拥堵}$。

(3)"严重拥堵"频率 $frequency_{严重拥堵}$。

各聚类变量的数量级存在差异。为了保证聚类结果的可靠性和有效性,需要对原始聚类变量数据进行归一化处理。本文选取最大最小归一化[14]对各指标变量进行归一化处理,归一化在 SPSS 软件中完成。

$$Z_{ij}=\frac{X_{ij}-\min(X_j)}{\max(X_j)-\min(X_j)} \tag{1}$$

式中:X_{ij}——第 j 个变量在第 i 个路段尚未归一化的值;

$\min(X_j)$——第 j 个变量的最小值;

$\max(X_j)$——第 j 个变量的最大值。

1.2　获取变量数据

本文使用高德开放的 Web 服务应用程序接口(Application Programming Interface,API)的驾车路径规划服务获取变量数据。本文以快速路卡口行程数据作为 URL 构造参数向高德地图 API 发送请求,采集南京市快速路网 2021 年 4 月 6—15 日共 10 天的全天 24 小时行程车速数据,采集频率为每 10min 一次,行程数据格式如表 1 所示。

高德地图 API 返回的数据是默认的 JS 对象简谱(JavaScript Object Notation,JSON)格式,JSON 格式数据的一个花括号"{}"代表一个对象,同时里面是一种键值对的存储形式。返回的导航路段信息 step 如表 2 所示。

为获得三维聚类变量值,利用高德地图 API 可以获取路段行程车速与交通状态,数据格式如表 3 所示。其中,路段运行状态是高德地图根据用户回传以及与各地交警合作获得的大量实时数据,反映了道路交通的运行状态以及交通参与在该路段行驶的真实感受。将表 3 按照路段编号和记录插入时间进行排序,得到各路段一天中的行程车速序列和交通状态序列。某快速路路段全天的行程车速如图 3 所示。

快速路卡口行程数据示例 表 1

字段名称	字段说明	示例
SEQ	行程序号	42
START_POINT	起点卡口点位经纬度	118.820909,31.887252
END_POINT	终点卡口点位经纬度	118.795212,32.054169
MEDIUM_POINT	中间经过卡口点位经纬度	118.803289,32.035304;118.76168,32.071477; 118.756499,32.06627;118.755834,32.057776

导航路段信息 step 列表 表 2

名称		含义	规则说明
tmcs		驾车导航详细信息列表	其中包含 tmc 对象
	distance	此路段的长度	单位:m
	status	此路段的交通情况	未知、畅通、缓行、拥堵、严重拥堵
	polyline	此路段的轨迹	—

计算聚类变量所用数据格式 表 3

行程序号	记录插入时间	道路名称	速度	状态	路段编号
30708	2021-03-29 11:58:17	南庄枢纽	14	畅通	899
30709	2021-03-29 11:58:17	G42 沪蓉高速	33	畅通	900
30710	2021-03-29 11:58:17	扬子江大道	66	畅通	901
30711	2021-03-29 11:58:17	草场门隧道	64	畅通	902

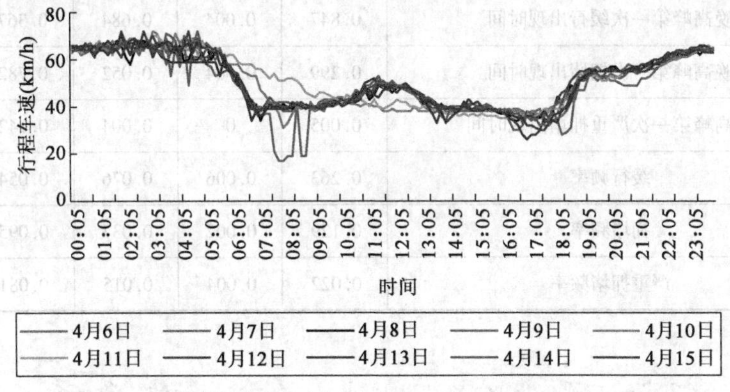

图 3 南京市某快速路路段全天行程车速

1.3 基于 K-means 聚类的服务瓶颈诊断

本文选取 K-means 聚类算法对快速路路段进行聚类分析,识别快速路服务瓶颈,聚类分析通过将研究对象划分为相对同质的若干群组(Clusters),以期达到簇(类)内的相似度尽可能高,簇(类)间的相似度尽可能低的目标。

K-means 均值聚类算法原理为:首先,随机地选择 k 个聚类中心,每个中心初始地代表了一个簇的平均值或中心;对剩余的每个样本,根据其与各簇中心的距离,将它赋给最近的簇;然后重新计算每个簇的平均值。随后反复迭代这一过程,直到其结果不再发生变化。K-means 聚类的优势在于只需要给定聚类个数 k,无需调整其他参数,即可完成分析。聚类个数的确定本文采用轮廓系数法 SC(Silhouette Coefficient)。SC 描述聚类结果中每个簇内外差异的指标,其取值范围为(-1,

1),SC越接近于1,则聚类效果越好。

以南京快速路网为例进行K-means聚类,结果如图4所示,当聚类簇数为6时,对应的轮廓系数SC值最大,聚类效果最好,因此确定最佳聚类簇数为6。

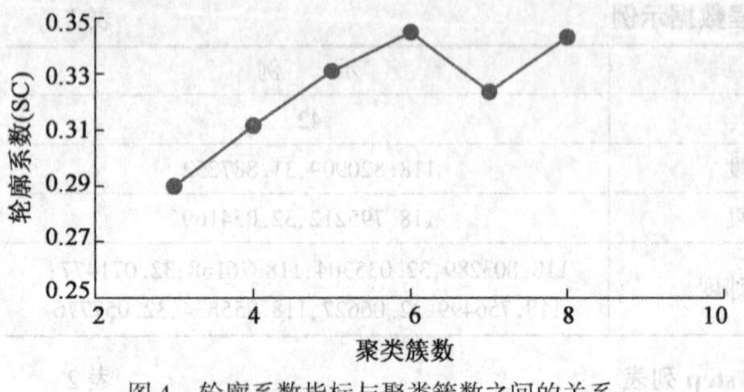

图4　轮廓系数指标与聚类簇数之间的关系

使用SPSS软件应用K-means算法将南京市快速路路段聚为6类,表4为各类的聚类中心,图5为各类别快速路路段的空间分布,综合考虑各类路段的聚类中心及空间分布,对各类路段的三维特征进行分析确定快速路服务瓶颈所属类别。由于类别2的路段占了所有快速路路段的70%(3209/4563),且其各类指标均不符合服务瓶颈的特性,排除类别2;同时,因为类别3~5的路段周期性指标过低,不符合常发拥堵的实际发生频率,排除类别3~5;类别6路段的平均车速和最低车速均小于类别1,并且类别6的原发性指标明显要比类别1的高,故选定三维聚类特征更明显的类别6为快速路服务瓶颈路段。

聚类中心　　表4

类别	变量	1	2	3	4	5	6
拥堵性指标	路段自由流速度	0.548	0.524	0.499	0.474	0.49	0.556
	路段平均速度	0.412	0.468	0.418	0.382	0.411	0.375
	路段最低速度	0.115	0.255	0.147	0.106	0.111	0.083
	路段速度方差	0.121	0.03	0.062	0.064	0.062	0.174
原发性指标	早高峰第一次缓行出现时间	0.856	0.011	0.093	0.125	0.454	0.191
	早高峰第一次拥堵出现时间	0.479	0.006	0.072	0.148	0.471	0.932
	早高峰第一次严重拥堵出现时间	0.054	0.002	0.005	0.01	0.065	0.341
	晚高峰第一次缓行出现时间	0.847	0.004	0.684	0.367	0.023	0.299
	晚高峰第一次拥堵出现时间	0.299	0.004	0.052	0.782	0.01	0.922
	晚高峰第一次严重拥堵出现时间	0.005	0	0.004	0.142	0.007	0.074
周期性指标	缓行频率	0.263	0.006	0.076	0.054	0.039	0.109
	拥堵频率	0.129	0.007	0.037	0.095	0.05	0.451
	严重拥堵频率	0.022	0.004	0.015	0.081	0.018	0.122

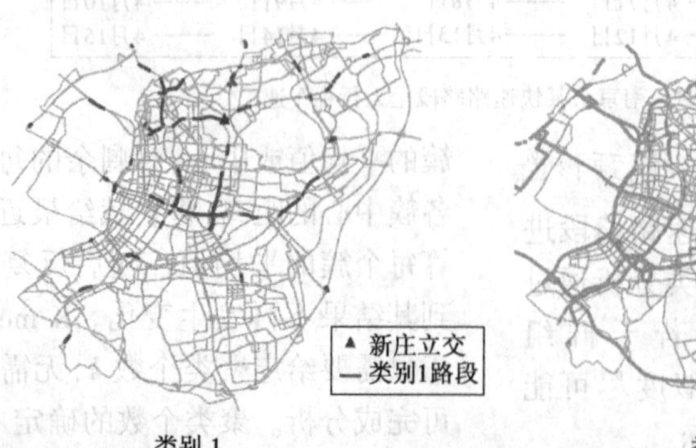

类别1

类别2

图　5

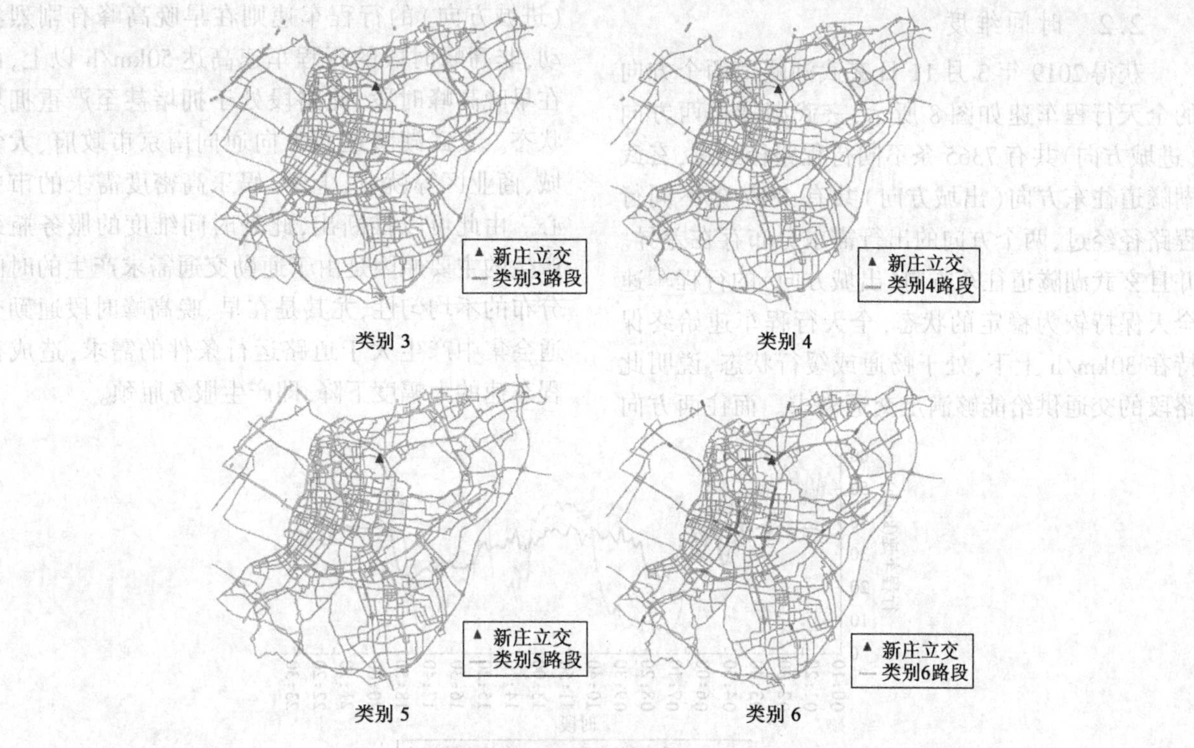

图5 各类别快速路路段的空间分布

图5中的类别6橙色路段即为本文研究识别出的南京市快速路网服务瓶颈。成片出现服务瓶颈的地区有卡子门地区、新庄立交、赛虹桥立交等;独立出现的有大桥北路、浦滨路隧道进城方向,油坊桥立交合流处,双龙大道牛首山河桥梁段等,这与实际情况非常符合。

2 服务瓶颈需求侧成因分析

2.1 空间维度

本文以新庄立交的服务瓶颈——玄武湖隧道(西方向)为例,综合快速路行程车速数据与卡口行程数据分析服务瓶颈产生的需求侧原因。如图6所示,新庄立交往玄武湖隧道方向行驶的三股车流,分别来自①玄武大道、②新庄立交普通地面道路和③九华山隧道左转,值得注意的是货车被禁止进入新庄立交。可以得知,不同方向客流需求在瓶颈路段交织、合流造成此路段交通需求集中。同时,比对高德地图可以发现玄武湖隧道是过玄武湖的重要通道,直接连接内环,连通区域就业人口与出行需求密集。由图7可知,玄武湖西侧的主要行程终点,对照高德地图可以发现玄武湖隧道西侧是南京市居住人口高密度地区,经济发达、就业岗位众多,吸引大量就业、上学、娱乐人口涌入,交通需求大。

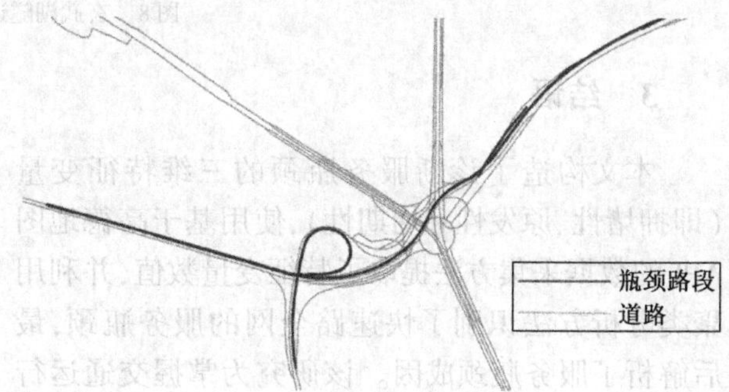

图6 新庄立交处服务瓶颈

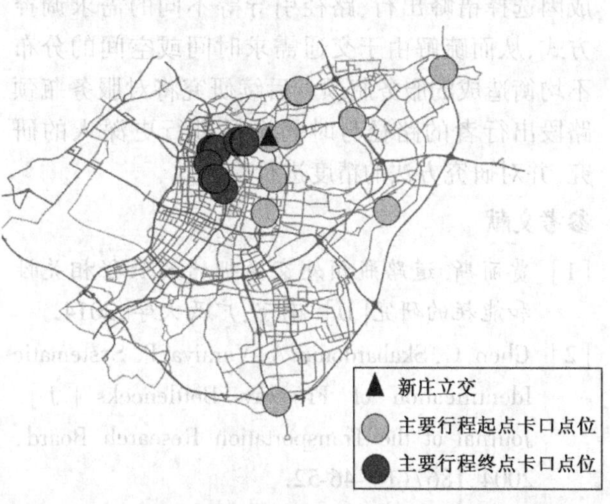

图7 玄武湖隧道西方向(进城方向)主要行程起终点

2.2　时间维度

获得2019年3月11日玄武湖隧道两个方向的全天行程车速如图8所示,玄武湖隧道西方向(进城方向)共有7365条不同行程路径经过,玄武湖隧道往东方向(出城方向)共有4807条不同行程路径经过,两个方向的出行需求分布存在差异。并且玄武湖隧道往东方向(出城方向)的行程车速全天保持较为稳定的状态,全天行程车速始终保持在30km/h上下,处于畅通或缓行状态,说明此路段的交通供给能够满足交通需求。而往西方向(进城方向)的行程车速则在早晚高峰有剧烈波动,非高峰时段的行程车速高达50km/h以上,而在早晚高峰时段,此路段处于拥堵甚至严重拥堵状态。玄武湖隧道西方向通向南京市政府、大学城、商业区等就业、上学、娱乐高密度需求的市中心。由此可以推断出,此处时间维度的服务瓶颈产生的主要原因是由于通勤交通需求产生的时间分布的不均匀性,尤其是在早、晚高峰时段通勤交通会集中产生大于道路运行条件的需求,造成行程车速的大幅度下降,即产生服务瓶颈。

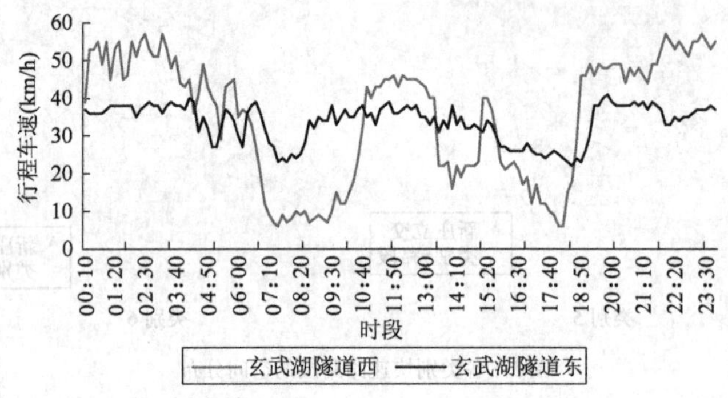

图8　玄武湖隧道双向行程车速对比

3　结语

本文构造了诊断服务瓶颈的三维特征变量(即拥堵性、原发性和周期性),使用基于高德地图API的数据采集方法提取了特征变量数值,并利用聚类分析方法识别了快速路全网的服务瓶颈,最后解析了服务瓶颈成因。该研究为掌握交通运行规律、剖析交通拥堵原因、辅助交通管理决策提供了理论指导与方法支撑,如根据差异化服务瓶颈成因选择错峰出行、路径引导等不同的需求调控方式,从而疏解由于交通需求时间或空间的分布不均衡造成的服务瓶颈。后续研究将对服务瓶颈路段出行者的路径与时间选择进行更深入的研究,并对研究方法的精度进行检验。

参考文献

[1] 贾丽斯.道路瓶颈处交通拥堵的长程相关性和能耗的研究[D].南宁:广西大学,2014.

[2] Chen C, Skabardonis A, Varaiya P. Systematic Identification of Freeway Bottlenecks [J]. Journal of the Transportation Research Board, 2004,1867(1):46-52.

[3] Wang C, Li W, Tong X, et al. An automatic identification algorithm for freeway bottleneck based on loop detector data [J]. Journal of Southeast University (English Edition), 2014, 30(4):495-499.

[4] Zhang L, Levinson D. Ramp metering and freeway bottleneck capacity [J]. Transportation Research Part A, 2010, 44(4):218-235.

[5] Zuduo Zheng, Soyoung, Ahn, et al. Applications of wavelet transform for analysis of freeway traffic: Bottlenecks, transient traffic, and traffic oscillations [J]. Transportation Research Part B. 2011, 45:372-384.

[6] 张建波,宋国华,于雷,等.基于浮动车数据的城市快速路瓶颈识别与特征分析[J].中南大学学报:英文版,2018,25(8):11.

[7] Chu, Benouar. Bottleneck Identification and Calibration for Corridor Management Planning [J]. Journal of the Transportation Research Board, 2007, 1999(1999):40-53.

[8] Song T J, Williams B M, Rouphail N M. Data-driven approach for identifying spatiotemporally recurrent bottlenecks [J]. IET Intelligent Transport Systems, 2018, 12(8).

[9] 郑凌瀚.基于高德地图数据的上海市快速路

路网拥堵成因分析. 中国城市规划学会城市交通规划学术委员会. 创新驱动与智慧发展——2018年中国城市交通规划年会论文集[C]. 中国城市规划学会城市交通规划学术委员会:中国城市规划设计研究院城市交通专业研究院,2018:9.

[10] 闫小倩. 基于微波数据的城市快速路常发性拥堵评价方法研究[D]. 北京:北京交通大学,2015.

[11] 北京交通发展中心. 城市道路交通运行评价指标体系:DB11/T 785—2011[S]. 北京市质量监督局,2011.

[12] 苏为华. 多指标综合评价理论与方法问题研究[D]. 厦门:厦门大学,2000.

[13] 周爱武,于亚飞. K-Means聚类算法的研究[J]. 计算机技术与发展,2011,21(2):4.

附录

(1)行程车速与交通状态获取代码,详见https://github.com/xuxinkun0591/gaode2

(2)高德地图API调用返回的数据及各参数意义说明。

返回结果参数说明 附表

名　称	含　义	规则说明
status	结果状态值,值为0或1	0:请求失败;1:请求成功
info	返回状态说明	status为0时,info返回错误原因,否则返回“OK”
count	驾车路径规划方案数目	—
route	驾车路径规划信息列表	—
origin	起点坐标	规则:lon,lat(经度,纬度),“,”分割,如117.500244,40.417801经纬度小数点不超过6位
destination	终点坐标	规则:lon,lat(经度,纬度),“,”分割,如117.500244,40.417801经纬度小数点不超过6位
paths	驾车换乘方案列表	—
path	驾车换乘方案	—
distance	行驶距离	单位:m
duration	预计行驶时间	单位:s
strategy	导航策略	—
steps	导航路段列表	—
step	导航路段	—
tmcs	驾车导航详细信息列表	其中包含tmc对象
distance	此路段的长度	单位:m
status	此路段的交通情况	未知、畅通、缓行、拥堵、严重拥堵
polyline	此路段的轨迹	

"status":"1",——本次向高德地图 API 发送的请求是成功的
"info":"OK",
"infocode":"10000",
"count":"3",——共返回 3 条躲避拥堵的驾车路径规划方案
"route":{——route 对象存储了本次请求返回的规划方案
"origin":"118.820909,31.887252",——起点经纬度，东南大学九龙湖校区
"destination":"118.795212,32.054169",——终点经纬度，东南大学四牌楼校区
"taxi_cost":"62",——打车预计花费 62 元
"paths":[——paths 对象存储了本次请求的 3 条规划路径的详细方案
{——第一条规划路径的详细信息
"distance":"24335",——本条路径预计行驶距离为 24335 米
"duration":"2868",——本条路径预计花费 2868 秒
"strategy":"速度最快",——本条路径所属出行策略
"tolls":"0",——收费站收费为 0 元
"toll_distance":"0",——收费里程为 0 米
"steps":[——steps 存储了本条规划路径的途经路段详细信息
{
"instruction":"沿南工路向西行驶 913 米右转",——行驶指示
"orientation":"西",——向西行驶
"road":"南工路",——本路段属于"南工路"
"distance":"913",——在该路段的行驶距离为 913 米
"tolls":"0",——收费站收费为 0 元
"toll_distance":"0",——收费里程为 0 米
"toll_road":[],——不存在收费道路
"duration":"189",——预计花费时间为 189 秒
"polyline":"118.820946,31.886714;118.818364,31.88658;118.816762,31.88648;118.816502,31.88648;118.815972,31.886476;118.815217,31.886424;118.813863,31.886345;118.813832,31.886345;118.812318,31.88625;118.812218,31.886215;118.811884,31.886168;118.811306,31.886094",——在该路段行驶的轨迹坐标点串
"action":"右转",——在该路段终点的主要驾驶动作
"assistant_action":[],——在该路段终点的辅助驾驶动作
"tmcs":[——分段统计途径路段的详细信息
{
"lcode":[],
"distance":"244",
"status":"未知",——由于是校园内部道路，状态未知
"polyline":"118.820946,31.886714;118.818364,31.88658"
},——该子路段的坐标点串

附图 请求返回的路段导航信息示例

路外公共停车设施的时空适用性探讨

皮 文[1] 王树盛[2] 邓惠章[*3]

(1.滨海县公安局交通警察大队;2、3.江苏省规划设计集团有限公司交通规划与工程设计院)

摘 要 路外公共停车设施是城市停车设施的重要组成部分,停车设施规范里明确了"以配建停车为主、公共停车为辅、路内停车为补充"的停车供应结构,并给出了路外公共停车设施的具体供应比

例[1]。在现实中,城市路外公共停车设施建设往往达不到规范比例,甚至严重缺乏。从城市管理者的角度来讲,路外公共停车设施占地面积多、经济效益小,其建设确实得不偿失。本文尝试从车辆使用者出行目的、停车供需的根本角度出发,探讨路外公共停车设施建设的时空适用性。文章结合理论和现实,提出应从近期和远期两个阶段、老城和新城两个范围来分析路外停车设施建设的适用性,对于老城区的近期规划建设,路外公共停车场建设适用性高,而对于其他时空组合情况,路外公共停车场建设适用性较低。

关键词　路外公共停车设施　停车供需　时空适用性

0　引言

路外公共停车设施作为一种服务于小汽车弹性出行的停车设施,到底服务于哪种出行目的?其建设适用性如何?在苏南(泛指江苏省在长江以南部分地区)城区设置1处独立占地3000m² 的公共停车场,考虑机会成本,如作为居住用地性质,考虑楼面单价、容积率、建筑密度等因素,成本不菲。根据已有项目资料,苏南一个普通县级市动辄规划20ha² 以上的路外公共停车设施用地(独立占地),按照当地土地出让价值计算,其土地机会成本可达70亿元,而普通县级市的一年财政收入也就100亿元左右。因此,在进行用地规划时,应慎重考虑路外公共停车场是否确实需要这么多,换言之,其建设是否具有适用性。

事实上,结合大量停车规划现状调查数据发现,没有哪个城市实打实地按照规划来建设路外公共停车场,因此,规划人员在停车设施现状分析时,往往会给出“停车设施供给结构不合理”“路外公共停车设施用地控制不足”“路外公共停车设施建设滞后”等结论。那么,到底是哪里出问题了,是规划的问题,还是地方执行的问题。这个问题的明晰不仅关系到地区交通的畅达,而且与用地的布局、经济的发展有着密切的联系,因此具有重要意义。本文尝试从停车需求的根本角度出发,剖析路外公共停车设施建设的时空适用性。

1　停车供需分析

根据停车需求的不同,停车设施可分为基本车位和出行车位。基本车位是满足车辆拥有者在无出行时车辆长时间停放需求的相对固定停车位,是刚性需求;出行车位是满足车辆使用者在有出行时车辆临时停放需求的停车位,是弹性需求。基本车位的供给形式主要为居住建筑物配建停车位(以下简称居住配建),出行车位的供给形式主要为公共建筑物配建停车位(以下简称公共配建),根据车辆使用者的不同出行目的,公共配建可分为办公配建(对应通勤出行)、商业配建(对应购物出行)或其他配建(对应旅游出行、健身出行、就医出行等等)。

基于以上的车位供需内涵,基本车位作为刚需,理应足额配建供给,以免造成历史欠账;对于弹性需求的出行车位,基于每种用地、建筑类型(对应各种车辆出行的目的),城市停车配建标准也应适当设置一定的车位指标满足其需求。表1是南京市2019年的机动车标准车位配建指标表。可以看出,对应于各类用地(包括居住、商办等各种用地类型),均明确了基本车位或出行车位的配建指标。

南京市机动车标准车位配建指标表(部分)　表1

<table>
<tr><th colspan="3" rowspan="3">建筑物类型</th><th rowspan="3">计算单位</th><th colspan="4">机动车指标</th></tr>
<tr><th colspan="2">一类区</th><th>二类区</th><th>三类区</th></tr>
<tr><th>下限</th><th>上限</th><th>下限</th><th>下限</th></tr>
<tr><td rowspan="6">住宅</td><td rowspan="5">商品房、共有产权房</td><td>$S_{建}>200m^2$</td><td>车位/户</td><td>1.4</td><td>1.6</td><td>2</td><td>2</td></tr>
<tr><td>$144\ m^2<S_{建}\leqslant 200\ m^2$</td><td>车位/户</td><td>1.2</td><td>1.4</td><td>1.5</td><td>1.5</td></tr>
<tr><td>$90\ m^2<S_{建}\leqslant 144m^2$</td><td>车位/户</td><td>1</td><td>1.2</td><td>1.2</td><td>1.2</td></tr>
<tr><td>$S_{建}\leqslant 90m^2$</td><td>车位/户</td><td>0.8</td><td>1</td><td>1</td><td>1</td></tr>
<tr><td>未分户</td><td>车位/100m²建筑面积</td><td>0.9</td><td>1.1</td><td>1.1</td><td>1.1</td></tr>
<tr><td colspan="2">租赁住房</td><td colspan="5">按照商品房指标值执行;其中,公共租赁住房按照商品房指标值的70%执行</td></tr>
</table>

续上表

建筑物类型			计算单位	机动车指标			
				一类区		二类区	三类区
				下限	上限	下限	下限
酒店式公寓			车位/100m^{2}建筑面积	0.9	1.1	1.1	1.1
集体宿舍			车位/100m^{2}建筑面积	0.3	0.4	0.4	0.4
饭店、宾馆、培训中心			车位/客房	0.4	0.5	0.5	0.5
办公	行政办公	拥有执法、服务窗口的单位	车位/100m^{2}建筑面积	1.2	1.5	1.8	1.8
		其他		0.8	1	1	1.2
	商务办公		车位/100m^{2}建筑面积	0.8	1	1	1.2
	生产研发、科研设计、物流办公		车位/100m^{2}建筑面积	0.8	1	1	1.2
	配套办公管理用房		车位/100 m^{2}建筑面积	0.6	0.8	0.8	1
餐饮娱乐	独立餐饮娱乐		车位/100m^{2}建筑面积	2	2.5	2.5	3
	附属配套餐饮娱乐		按独立餐饮、娱乐指标的80%执行				
商业	中小型商业设施(50000m^{2}及以下)		车位/100m^{2}建筑面积	0.5	0.7	0.8	0.7
	大型商业设施(50000m^{2}以上)、大型超市		车位/100m^{2}建筑面积	0.8	1	1.1	1.3
	配套商业设施(小型超市、便利店、专卖店)		车位/100m^{2}建筑面积	0.25	0.35	0.4	0.6
	专业、批发市场		车位/100m^{2}建筑面积	0.5	0.7	0.9	1

2　路外公共停车设施建设的适用性分析

综上,停车需求来源于车辆拥有或者车辆出行,车辆的拥有或出行与各种建筑类型相对应,而配建标准已考虑所有建筑种类的停车需求。因此,从理论上来讲,无论是路外还是路内公共停车设施,均无“立足之地”。然而,从城市建设的现实来看,由于历史的局限性,城市老城区里的老旧小区往往配建不足,造成基本车位不足;老城区里的商业、办公等建筑同样配建不足,特别是零散的沿街商业,由于用地的局限,配建严重不足。

因此,结合理论和现实,公共停车设施,特别是路外公共停车设施的设置,应从近期和远期两个阶段、老城和新城两个范围来分析其适用性。

从近期来看,对于老城区小区的基本车位不足问题,除了小区周边的路内或路侧(建筑退让空间内停车)公共停车设施,还需要通过路外公共停车设施的挖潜来满足,如在边角空地、绿地广场、人防设施、学校操场等空间建设地上或地下立体停车库;对于老城区的商业、办公等公共建筑配建不足问题,这种配建停车主要满足小汽车弹性出行需求,而在老城区应着重控制小汽车出行、鼓励公交(轨道)慢行,因此这种配建不足问题可通过适当设置路内或路侧停车泊位来解决,而非必须建设路外公共停车场。对于新城区,由于各类配建车位标准执行到位,基本车位和出行车位需求基本能满足,路外公共停车没有建设的必要性;由于用地条件限制,新城区里的沿街商铺的配建车位较为缺乏,可通过适当设置路内或路侧停车设施来解决。

从远期来看,老城区内的老旧小区、商办等用地均进行了有效更新(合理假设),其配建车位标准也同步执行到位,基本车位和出行车位需求基本能满足,路外公共停车设施的建设并不适用;同样,如上所述,由于用地的局限,零散沿街商业的配建车位也可通过路内或路侧停车设施来解决。对于新城区,由于各类配建车位标准执行到位,基本车位和出行车位需求基本能满足,路外公共停车同样没有建设的必要;由于用地的局限,零散沿街商业的配建车位可通过路内或路侧停车设施来解决。

上述分析的结果见表 2。

城市停车设施供需对应一览表　　表2

规划范围	停车需求	近期停车供给	远期停车供给
老城区	基本车位	居住配建、路外公共、路内或路侧公共	居住配建
	出行车位	公共配建、路内或路侧公共	公共配建、路内或路侧公共
新城区	基本车位	居住配建	居住配建
	出行车位	公共配建、路内或路侧公共	公共配建、路内或路侧公共

3　结论

基于上述分析,可以得出以下结论:

(1)对于近期来说,老城区的停车设施规划建设,路外公共停车设施适用性高;新城区的路外公共停车设施适用性较低。

(2)对于远期来说,无论是老城区还是新城区,路外公共停车设施适用性均较低。

(3)在进行城市停车规划时,近期方案应重点计算老旧小区的基本车位缺口,进而有针对性的在老旧小区附近进行路外公共停车设施的挖潜布局;远期方案应重点合理调整城市建筑物配建停车指标,并提出相应的标准执行保障措施。

参考文献

[1] 中华人民共和国住房和城乡建设部. 城市停车规划规范:GB/T 51149—2016[S]. 北京:中国标准出版社,2016.

[2] 江苏省城市规划设计研究院. 张家港市综合交通规划(2012年版)[M].

[3] 南京市建筑物配建停车设施设置标准与准则(2019年修订)[S].

基于K-Means聚类的共享单车停放区域选址与规模测算方法

成　骋[1,2,3]　华明壮[1,2,3]　齐　超[1,2,3]　陈学武*[1,2,3]

(1. 东南大学江苏省城市智能交通重点实验室;2. 东南大学现代城市交通技术江苏高校协同创新中心;3. 东南大学交通学院)

摘　要　随着传统的停放管理方式已经不足以应对当下尖锐的供需矛盾,以北斗定位系统为基础的"电子围栏"式的停放管理手段,为共享单车停放秩序的维护提供了新的可能。本文结合各家共享单车企业在南京的出行订单数据,采用K-means聚类的方法确定了共享单车停放的"虚拟站点"及其空间分布。以虚拟站点为共享单车集中运行的单元,结合订单数据估计了各站点的共享单车停放需求。研究结果为北斗系统的应用提供了停放区域选址与规模测算方面的指导,有利于共享单车运营过程中的秩序改善及效率提升。

关键词　城市公共交通设施规划　虚拟站点　聚类分析　共享单车　需求测算

0　引言

近年来,无桩式共享单车在国内各大城市迅速推广,吸引了众多的用户,成为居民通勤的重要方式之一。然而,过度的车辆投放与粗放的供给模式导致了停放秩序的混乱,进一步加剧了城市内部非机动车停车空间的供需矛盾。针对停放秩序问题,管理者通常采取划定停车区域的方式进行应对。

1. 基金项目:国家自然科学基金面上项目(52172316)。

然而停放区域的选址与规模的确定,多依赖于管理人员的经验判断,缺乏科学性与效率性。且该手段对乘客仍以指导性原则为主,其效果取决于乘客的素质,无法从本质上提高停放管理的效果。

在传统的停放管理方式已不足以保证良好的停放秩序的情况下,北斗卫星系统的逐步完善,使得利用卫星系统划定高精度的“电子围栏”来对共享单车进行实时的停放监督与管理成为可能。目前,深圳已经尝试利用北斗系统对共享单车实施停放区域的约束,用户只能在卫星划定的区域内才能够完成还车,从而实现车辆的定点取还与规范停放。

然而,上述系统的使用,对停放区域的规划提出了更高的要求。停放区域的选址及规模,必须精准地反映和满足用户的停放需求,才能真正提高共享单车的停放管理效率。因此,科学地制定停放区域的地址与规模,为北斗系统的使用提供良好的指导,是目前亟待解决的问题。

关于共享单车停放区域的选址与规模,学术界已有大量的研究。李林凤等[1]利用 ArcGIS 的空间分析与统计功能,对影响共享单车停放适宜性的因素进行分级和综合叠加,得出选址适宜性的分级,对现有站点位置进行调整;Kumar 等[2]根据人口统计、个人信息等社会经济基础资料来选择合适的站点位置。郭彦茹等[3]考虑了微观层面的因素,将行人、单车与汽车之间的影响纳入到社会力模型中进行仿真,分析共享单车使用者的最优停放区选择;赖建智[4]借助 ArcGIS 软件,提出了一种共享单车停放区的自动编码方法,为共享单车停放的精准化、规范化提供了技术上的支持;Martinez 等[5]提出以建设成本最小为决策目标,利用混合整数线性规划模型来优化站点的选址。李婷婷[6]从自行车用户的出行行为角度出发,结合用户的出行选择,构建双层规划模型进行自行车租赁点的地址选择。总体来说,现有的研究多是基于停放点的步行距离或周边环境因素,结合出行订单数据及客流需求本身的研究较少。

本文利用 K-Means 聚类的方法,根据南京主城区的共享单车出行数据,分析得出其主要集中的虚拟站点,以虚拟站点为单位进行停放区域的指导,并结合出行数据,对各站点所需的停放需求进行估计,为北斗系统“电子围栏”的划定提供一定的借鉴与指导。

1　研究范围与数据处理

1.1　研究范围

本文的研究区域为南京城区(不包括浦口、六合、高淳、溧水、江北新区)。

1.2　数据来源

本文使用的数据来源于南京市共享单车监管平台提供的 2021 年 10 月、11 月共享单车订单数据,包括美团、哈啰、青桔三家企业。数据结构及字段如表 1 所示。其中,经纬度数据坐标系为 WGS84 坐标系。

订单数据字段及示例数据　　表 1

字　段	示　例
订单编号	hellobike16352637966711487090739
车辆编号	7960856399
开始时间	2021-10-26 23:56:41
起点经纬度	{“lon”:118.75933112726896, “lat”:32.03001045879231}
结束时间	2021/10/27　0:18:08
终点经纬度	{“lon”:118.7482863215334, “lat”:32.035150529552105}
开始时间戳	1635263989
结束时间戳	1635265088

1.3　数据预处理

(1)无效数据剔除

利用 Python 编程读取数据,剔除数据集中的异常值、缺失值与重复值,剔除后的数据集共包含 589072 条数据。

(2)字段分离与提取

由于原数据集中的经纬度处于同一列字段下,为了聚类分析的方便,将经纬度字段拆分为经度与纬度两列。

(3)坐标系转换

对经纬度的坐标系进行转换。本文研究中采用了基于欧式距离的 K-means 聚类方法,为了获得精确的欧式距离聚类结果,需要进行坐标系转换,将 WGS84 地理坐标系转换为 WGS84 EASE-1 Grid Global 投影坐标系,以保证欧式距离计算的精确性。

2 研究方法

2.1 技术路线

由于共享单车无车桩的特性,其车辆的流动性较大,在各区域的数量处于常态的变化中,很难利用某一时刻的数量和位置分布来估计各区域的停车需求。因此,为了简化共享单车的停车问题,需要找到能够代表不同区域出行的基本单元。本文首先采取聚类的方法,通过挖掘订单数据,将每一区域的共享单车出行起点的集合转化为一个虚拟站点,以虚拟站点作为研究的基本单元,每一虚拟站点即代表该区域内的所有车辆出行或停放需求,可以作为停放区域选址的参考依据。

在生成虚拟站点后,需要确定每个站点的服务范围,作为分析停放需求的依据。由于传统的划定缓冲区作为服务范围的方法会使得服务范围产生重叠,不利于后续停放需求的分析。因此,本文采取缓冲区与泰森多边形相交的方式,来避免各站点服务范围的冲突。

在服务范围确定的基础上,利用 ArcGIS 软件,统计各站点一天内服务的车辆数,并探究其服务车辆数在一天中随时间变化的规律,其中的峰值即为该站点一天内需要停放的最大车辆数,即可作为该站点停放区域规模的最终取值。

技术路线如图1所示。

2.2 K-Means 聚类方法

聚类分析的方法是机器学习中常用的一种无监督的分类方法。聚类分析的特点在于,能够在缺少先验信息的情况下,通过挖掘数据本身的特性对其进行分类。该分析方法与共享单车的特点不谋而合,因此,可以利用聚类分析的方法,将共享单车的出行划分为不同的集合,每个集合即可抽象为一个虚拟站点,集合的质心作为虚拟站点的位置。经过聚类分析,即可用各个虚拟站点来代表南京全市的共享单车出行,并获得其分布的具体位置。由于共享单车的出行与停放具有一致性,一次出行的出发地即为上一次出行的停放地,因此,其出行的聚类结果即可代表其停放需求。

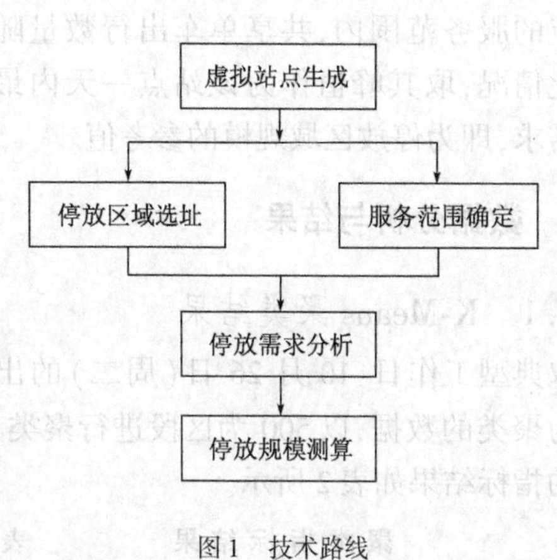

图1 技术路线

本文选取聚类分析中的 K-means 方法,其算法原理为:首先,随机地选择 k 个聚类中心,每个中心初始地代表了一个簇的平均值或中心。对剩余的每个样本,根据其与各簇中心的距离,将它赋给最近的簇。然后重新计算每个簇的平均值。随后反复迭代这一过程,直到其结果不再发生变化。K-means 聚类的优势在于只需要给定聚类个数 k,无需调整其他参数,即可完成分析。

利用 Python 编程来实现 K-means 聚类,在聚类过程中,给出每次聚类的评价指标轮廓系数 SC 及 Calinski-Harabasz 指数(CH 指数)。其中,轮廓系数 SC 是用以描述聚类结果中每个簇内外差异的指标,其取值范围为$(-1,1)$,SC 越接近于 1,则聚类效果越好。CH 指数表示每个簇内的相似度及簇与簇之间的非相似性。CH 指数评价的目的在于,用尽量少的类别聚类尽量多的样本,同时获得较好的聚类效果。其数值越大,则簇内相似度越高,簇与簇之间的界限越清晰,聚类效果越好。根据 SC 与 CH 指数,可以确定合适的分类个数。

2.3 停放需求计算方法

根据聚类分析得到的结果,确定每一虚拟站点的服务范围。将站点数据导入 ArcGIS 中,求解各站点在研究范围内的泰森多边形,并与 500m 的缓冲区相交,以最终的交集为各虚拟站点的服务范围。

由于停车区域的规模需要满足该区域一天内最大的停放需求,因此,需要计算各站点的服务范围在一天内停放的最大共享单车数量。将服务范围与一天内的共享单车订单总数相交,得到各站点服务范围一天内发生的出行数量。统计每个虚拟站点的服务范围内,共享单车出行数量随时间的变化情况,取其峰值作为该站点一天内最高的停放需求,即为停放区域规模的参考值。

3 数据分析与结果

3.1 K-Means 聚类结果

取典型工作日:10 月 26 日(周二)的出行数据作为聚类的数据,以 500 为区段进行聚类,聚类分析的指标结果如表 2 所示。

聚类指标结果　　表 2

聚类簇数量	轮廓系数 SC	CH 指数
500	0.4475	958307
1000	0.4641	1140812
1500	0.4766	1289045
2000	0.4884	1420924
2500	0.4944	1550273
3000	0.4972	1678319
3500	0.4982	1799110
4000	0.4992	1817520
4500	0.4944	1833957
5000	0.4963	1858661
5500	0.4965	1881064
6000	0.4929	1901486
6500	0.4909	1919892
7000	0.4905	1939649
7500	0.4897	1964866
8000	0.4895	1981569
8500	0.4884	2002328
9000	0.4895	2100900

由表 2 可知,聚类簇数量在(3500,4000)区间时,聚类效果最好。为了进一步细化聚类效果,对该分段以 100 为区段,再次进行聚类,指标结果如表 3 所示。

二次聚类指标结果　　表 3

聚类簇数量	轮廓系数 SC	CH 指数
3500	0.4982	1799110
3600	0.4957	1817520
3700	0.4986	1833957
3800	0.5008	1858661
3900	0.4972	1881064
4000	0.4992	1901486

由表 3 可知,聚类簇数量为 3800 时,聚类效果最好。因此,选择 3800 作为最终的聚类簇数量。该聚类结果代表了研究区域内共享单车用户的停放需求,可以作为共享单车停放区域选址的参考依据。

3.2 停放需求估计与站点规模测算

对每个虚拟站点,利用 ArcGIS 软件,求得其 500m 范围缓冲区与研究范围内泰森多边形的交集,作为其覆盖的服务范围。统计各站点服务范围在一天内存放的最高共享单车数量,可以得出每个虚拟站点的停车位需求。统计结果如表 4 所示。

各行政区虚拟站点停放需求　　表 4

行政区	虚拟站点数量(个)	停放需求 >250 的虚拟站点数量(个)	站点停车位需求(万辆)
秦淮区	535	178	12.8
玄武区	410	104	9.1
鼓楼区	557	144	13.3
建邺区	554	131	12.8
栖霞区	540	55	7.8
江宁区	871	48	8.7
雨花台区	333	46	6.1
总计	3800	706	70.6

分析结果显示,南京市各区共享单车的出行比例存在一定的差异,秦淮、鼓楼、玄武、建邺的高需求站点数量较多,表明当地用户的使用意愿更高。其中,有 707 个虚拟站点需求的停车位超过了 250,可以作为共享单车停放规划的重点,根据现实条件规划大规模非机动车停车场、共享单车调度站点等。根据统计结果,全市虚拟站点的总停放需求为 70.6 万个停车位。依据中华人民共

和国住房与城乡建设部于2013年发布的《城市步行和自行车交通系统规划设计导则》,单个自行车停车位的面积至少为1.5m²,因此,南京市虚拟站点的总停车面积需求为105.9万m²。此结果可以作为南京市共享单车停放区域地址选择与规模测算的参考,根据聚类分析的站点分布结果以及计算得出的各站点停放需求,结合相关政策与用地条件,即可确定停放区域的规划方案,为北斗系统的使用提供科学依据。

4 结语

本文通过挖掘南京地区的共享单车订单数据,利用K-means聚类分析的方法,获得了研究区域内共享单车主要聚集的"虚拟站点",并确定了站点的服务范围,为南京市共享单车停放区域的规划提供了基本的研究单元。在此基础上,结合数据挖掘了南京市共享单车出行的时空分布特性,估算了各站点所需的停放车位数。相比于以往多以建成环境因素或出行距离为核心的研究,本文从用户的车辆使用行为本身出发,能够更为真实地反映出用户在车辆使用过程中的实际停放需求。

本文的研究结果,为南京市共享单车停放区域的选址与容量提供了科学的测算方法,为北斗系统应用中"电子围栏"的布设提供了理论依据,有助于北斗系统的合理使用及城市共享单车停放管理效率的提高。本文的研究仍有许多不足。首先,本文对停放区域容量的测算仅考虑了停放需求,除此之外,可以考虑利用各虚拟站点的周转率对停放容量的测算方法进行优化。其次,还需考虑站点周边的用地状况的约束,停放容量进行调整。最后,可以结合共享单车企业的日常调度方案,对各站点容量进行进一步的细化,从而提高共享单车的运转效率,真正体现"共享经济"的本质。

参考文献

[1] 李林凤,李进强,耿莲.基于GIS的城市共享单车虚拟站点选址规划——以闽江学院校区为例[J].智能城市,2019,5(20):4-8.

[2] Kumar V P, Bierlaire M. Optimizing Locations for a Vehicle Sharing System[J]. 2012.

[3] 郭彦茹,罗志雄,王家川,等.数据驱动的共享单车停放区规划方法研究[J].交通运输系统工程与信息,2021,21(06):9-16.

[4] 赖建智.一种城市共享单车停放区自动编码方法研究[J].测绘地理信息,2020:1-5.

[5] Martinez L M, Caetano L, Eiró T, et al. An Optimisation Algorithm to Establish the Location of Stations of a Mixed Fleet Biking System: An Application to the City of Lisbon[J]. Procedia, social and behavioral sciences, 2012, 54: 513-524.

[6] 李婷婷.城市公共自行车租赁点选址规划研究[D].北京:北京交通大学,2010.

基于用地性质的共享单车"时空"分布特征

李书新[1] 李 辉[1] 张 旭*[1] 郭亚辉[1] 林秋雨[2]

(1.河南工业大学 土木工程学院;2.中国农业发展银行富顺县支行)

摘 要 针对部分地区存在共享单车冗余不足的情况,提出了一种基于用地性质的共享单车分配优化方案。分别对不同时间段内住宅区、办公区和商业区进行相应的单车数据调查,并通过调查问卷的形式对共享单车使用和分布情况进行统计;以不同用地的面积和兴趣点(Point of Interest,POI)数量之比得出相应共享单车密度,比较不同时间段内各地区共享单车密度,提出分配方案;运用SPSS进行多元线性回归模拟验证该方案有效性。结果表明,以郑州市高新区为例,空间上对共享单车的吸引程度从大到小分别是商业区、办公区、住宅区;商业区、办公区高峰时段共享单车分布密度比非高峰时段略高;住宅区非

1.基金项目:河南工业大学高层次人才科研启动基金项目(2018BS029)。

高峰时段共享单车分布密度比高峰时段略高。用该方法分析并预测共享单车“时空”分布特征与用地性质的关系,为解决目前共享单车分配问题,提出相关意见。

关键词　交通工程　时空特征　多元线性回归　共享单车　用地性质　分布密度;POI

0　引言

为了最大限度地减少对环境的影响,同时保证交通设施的可持续性发展,共享单车系统应运而生,慢慢融入了我们的生活[1]。当公共交通运行能力降低时,共享单车系统在一定程度上也能作为传统交通的替代者[2]。作为解决出行“出行最后一公里”的共享单车设施,由于是采用无桩式设计,所以单车本身享有的自由度是极高的,企业对于单车的投放以及用户出行起点和终点都不会受到太大的限制[3]。但随着市场投放量过大,且共享单车的自由度极高,就很容易造成共享单车运转效率低下、乘客无车可用的情况。而有些区域则单车泛滥,造成堵塞车道、停放过多等问题。分析用地性质对共享单车分布特征的影响,合理调控单车数量的分配,可提高共享单车的利用率和共享单车系统运行效率,满足乘客高峰需求。

从个人属性、用户骑行行为、用地功能、交通布局、时间等多个方面的研究,包含在时间和空间这两大因素之中。在空间上,邓力凡等[4]基于单车用户数据,通过单车的分布特征对共享单车调度提出意见。周川[5]通过共享单车分布密度,提出优化算法和方案,提高共享单车的区域利用率。为了更加合理的观察到单车的分布特征,在空间特征的基础上还应考虑时间特征的影响,SUN等[6]在研究中还加入了“时间”变量,实现了时空同时测量。目前共享单车系统中“时空因素”对于单车分布的影响较为普遍且具有逻辑关联性。以往研究中也有通过时空聚类[7]和共享单车订单与轨迹数据[8]对共享单车的时空特征进行分析,对共享单车的调度和站点规划提出意见。已有研究的研究对象单一,获取用户骑行信息为同一共享单车公司,研究较为局限,且以不同用地性质的共享单车密度为目标的研究较少。

本文细化空间因素和时间因素,以不同用地性质的共享单车密度为研究目标,根据实际统计的数据采用相应的数据分析模式,综合比较得出结论。通过调研数据预测导致共享单车分布特征变化的原因,并针对用地性质的不同,提出一种解决共享单车供需不等问题的优化方案。

1　共享单车“时空”分布特征机理

1.1　空间特征影响机理

因为各区域的用地功能不同以及区域内各种基础设施的完善程度不等,共享单车的分布密集程度在不同区域有所差异。两个建筑面积完全相同住宅区和商业区,住宅区只对住房拥有者具有吸引力,而商业区这种集成餐饮、娱乐、休闲为一体的综合化区域则对全部人群均产生吸引力,因此导致的人流量就会有所差异。从某种概率上来讲,较多人流量的商业区则会产生更多的骑行需求,导致共享单车聚集程度就会显著提高,从而影响到共享单车的分布。其次,区域内的基础设施建设,交通网路的布局也是重要的原因之一。不同地区的共享单车分布受到POI数量的影响,POI包含名称、地址、坐标、类别四个属性,用于导航定位、地理编码、周边搜索、热度分析、密度分析、选址决策分析等。

多家共享单车品牌企业并存,共享单车数量基数巨大,如此多的单车是如何分配到不同区域的,这就要依据共享单车的调度方式了,正面来说,共享单车企业会根据市场需求和政府规定来分别对不同区域投放不等量的共享单车,这也是形成共享单车最初分布特征的原因之一。共享单车的调度方式需要依据用地性质等多方面因素来实现,有研究表明,共享单车的运营调度主要发生在相对固定的区域范围之内。另外一方面,由于企业对于共享单车资源的争抢,导致的供需不等的现象,都会影响到对共享单车的运营。疏于管理的地区可能产生共享单车堆积泛滥的现象,而某些地方又无车可用,所以说,企业在不同地区对于单车的调度方式也是空间特征影响的机理之一。

1.2　时间特征影响机理

时间因素的影响机理其表现出的波动性,很大程度上表现为用户的骑行特征,对于共享单车系统的用户来说,在一天24小时之内,不同时间段的使用频率以及出行目的都有所差异。以高峰期为例,单车的使用频率会在这一时段显著增加,这是由于在这个时段内,用户群体产生了大面积的集体出行需求。总的来说,在受到例如社会因素的制约,或者是环境因素的影响下,都会导致公众的出行时间段有所差异。所以,时间特征对于共享单车分布特征的影响原因表现为用户的主观意愿。

2 实例分析

2.1 数据获取与分析

2.1.1 调查区域

以郑州市高新区及其附近为例,该地区不同功能的建筑设施分界相对较为明显,且呈现出完整的、区域性的块状分布,易于划分和调查。调查区域在研究范围内定义并选取30个住宅型区域,30个办公型区域,30个商业型区域,为保证研究的准确性,在选定区域时保证除主要研究属性以外的其他客观因素保持一致。

2.1.2 调查内容和方法

调查获取上述区域中出行非高峰时段和高峰时段的共享单车的实际数量、区域的面积以及区域内POI数量等基础信息,并了解用户的相关骑行特征与个人意愿。

调查分两个时间段进行:①非高峰时段(21:00—7:30)②高峰时段(9:00—18:00),总计90个区域180组数据,所有车辆和POI数据均为现场人工计数,区域面积则是通过谷歌地图实景图直接测量网格面积得到。

为避免一定程度上调查结论的误差,在方法中加入问卷调查的模式,总计200份问卷,22来源于实地统计的纸质版数据,178份来源于APP问卷星的网络收集,作补充说明,加强论证的效用。问卷调查针对于不同类型的人群,保证了被调查群体的综合性,结合线上和线下两种方式同时进行。

2.1.3 调查数据统计

(1)住宅区数据收集

为保证研究数据的准确性,调查采用实地人工计数的办法。郑州住宅区的调查主要于河南省郑州市高新区范围内进行,区域内建筑设施布局合理,居住人口适宜,个人属性综合多样且调查区域尽可能避免了特殊情况的存在。例如万丰慧城住宅区容积率3.11,绿化率38.75%。以高层和小高层为主。小区右邻莲花公园和主干道莲花街,环绕多个工业园区,交通状况良好,整体基础情况均满足共享单车出行条件,极具调查意义。具体数据收集情况见表1。

住宅区信息统计 表1

编号	地　点	出行非高峰时段车辆数(辆)	出行高峰时段车辆数(辆)	区域面积(m^2)	POI(个)
R1	谦祥万和城	351	186	379312.83	195
R2	大谢新区	68	28	24641.42	31
R3	莲花苑	41	25	22408.79	22
R4	裕华满园	92	40	68557.13	42
R5	翰林国际城西区	107	45	173889.63	57
R6	翰林国际城东区	181	69	223077.44	108
R7	高新锦华苑	221	94	156094.9	136
R8	东史马小区南区	73	30	62679.58	45
R9	荣邦城南区	147	49	137620.32	78
R10	东史马小区中区	51	27	25678.8	30
R11	荣邦城中区	49	25	38302.06	45
R12	学府嘉园	100	65	121991.8	92
R13	中鸿花园	72	67	32,349.68	48
R14	高新·锦绣苑	79	37	51,846.32	40
R15	万丰慧城	207	199	80,587.93	130
R16	金盾花园	24	9	14144.94	15

续上表

编号	地　点	出行非高峰时段车辆数(辆)	出行高峰时段车辆数(辆)	区域面积(m^2)	POI(个)
R17	朗悦公园道 1 号南苑	73	27	55942.96	39
R18	翡翠华庭	124	67	115,010.50	69
R19	万科城紫兰苑(东)	44	25	48260.91	31
R20	万科城紫兰苑(西)	153	54	70,630.88	90
R21	万科城锦枫苑(西)	15	6	17,656.59	9
R22	万科城锦枫苑(东)	78	43	57,108.66	60
R23	祥瑞苑	98	43	127,748.83	68
R24	万科城采薇苑	78	25	86,604.41	49
R25	祥晖苑	21	9	32,871.82	12
R26	玉兰雅庭	9	4	7,904.32	6
R27	紫薇小区	44	23	39,600.43	30
R28	美景菩提	35	29	51,136.05	26
R29	菁翠园(西北)	17	11	14,432.12	16
R30	宏莲花园	23	13	15,462.06	17

(2)办公区数据收集

办公区调查以分布于高新区的工业园区或写字楼大厦片区为主,此类办公区具有明显的功能性分界,区域内凝聚了密集的工作岗位,建筑功能主要以办公为核心。办公区的调查以工业园区为例,整个区域划分为一个或者多个企业并存,大面积的整体性规划导致区域具有一定的封闭性,所有出入口仅有少数几个,单车的分布具有了一定的集中性。调查结果见表 2。

办公区信息统计　　表 2

编号	地　点	出行非高峰时段车辆数(辆)	出行高峰时段车辆数(辆)	区域面积(m^2)	POI(个)
O1	国家 863 中部软件园	218	563	86906.65	50
O2	郑州国家信息安全产业基地孵化中心	29	71	14133.22	8
O3	教育科技产业园	101	272	59285.26	27
O4	汉威国际传感器科技园	53	151	45512.32	20
O5	总部企业基地 3 期	86	185	35270.72	19
O6	总部企业基地 2 期	194	368	72437.16	46
O7	河南省煤炭科学研究院	13	25	40903.25	3
O8	郑州机械研究所	35	73	111027.25	11
O9	中国电建十一局	67	118	28730.32	25
O10	高新区检察院	15	37	20390.90	4
O11	郑州拓普轧制技术有限公司	14	41	22346.04	4
O12	舜华文创园	17	38	12602.66	5
O13	河南省智能计量仪表工程技术研究中心	10	26	8345.07	3
O14	郑州永和制药	5	18	6971.17	2
O15	中钢集团郑州金属制品研究院	10	37	19850.06	4
O16	高新数码港	17	39	37917.19	6
O17	郑州新材料产业园	28	53	34253.09	6

续上表

编号	地　点	出行非高峰时段车辆数(辆)	出行高峰时段车辆数(辆)	区域面积(m^2)	POI(个)
O18	银发工业园	11	36	32078.20	4
O19	郑州高新区创业中心五号园	9	33	11548.51	4
O20	郑州高新企业加速器产业园(西北区)	48	174	103243.77	21
O21	郑州燃气发电有限公司(梧桐街)	14	41	122372.50	5
O22	河南省电子商务产业园	68	139	90409.30	32
O23	地质科技大厦	14	23	13081.24	6
O24	河南省大学科技园西区(北)	89	253	86017.20	29
O25	总部基地	201	430	67137.67	47
O26	纽科科技园(北)	39	72	27582.39	9
O27	中国烟草总公司郑州烟草研究院	69	186	93501.58	17
O28	郑州高新技术产业开发区创业中心	89	194	57912.67	18
O29	高新区管委会	37	92	60816.45	11
O30	河南宏伟电气	14	37	20731.67	4

(3)商业区调查

调查选取以朗悦公园茂、潮流茂、丹尼斯等商业广场为代表的30个商业区,朗悦公园茂,拥有包括郑州大学、河南工业大学等高校在内超过10万名大学生的消费人群,朗悦公园道一号、万科、恒大、升龙等住宅不断交付带来的新入住人口。形成了庞大的人流量同时也产生了相应的共享单车使用需求,调查结果如表3所示。

商业区信息统计　表3

编号	地　点	出行非高峰时段车辆数(辆)	出行高峰时段车辆数(辆)	区域面积(m^2)	POI(个)
B1	朗悦公园茂	202	456	22341.03	28
B2	朗悦家庭茂	197	399	22150.41	25
B3	朗悦潮流茂	106	223	7608.96	11
B4	丹尼斯全日鲜(石楠路段)	6	21	7703.60	2
B5	蜀香门第(雪松路段)	14	32	7452.52	4
B6	博大五交化	19	34	7272.37	3
B7	阿彬美食	11	19	6148.04	2
B8	师新庄美食路	43	91	7256.85	8
B9	乐辉商贸卖场	24	33	6742.39	4
B10	东方金博(银杏路)	35	48	11071.87	9
B11	亿丰商贸	135	264	7248.16	17
B12	丹尼斯	91	232	40302.15	15
B13	鑫瑞祥卖场	88	143	7804.26	12
B14	正道思达超市	11	23	13999.28	4
B15	高兴区酒业中心	7	26	1872.15	3
B16	紫荆街	13	28	14017.39	10
B17	湘乡心语	19	31	5482.87	3
B18	蔷薇街	84	187	65429.58	21
B19	一家人擀面酒楼	14	22	2409.34	3

续上表

编号	地　点	出行非高峰时段车辆数(辆)	出行高峰时段车辆数(辆)	区域面积(m^2)	POI(个)
B20	世纪华联	10	15	16407.45	2
B21	裕丰商贸	39	85	9834.21	7
B22	凯旋酒行	74	153	6620.19	10
B23	升龙商业广场	53	76	27098.96	15
B24	爱位半永久美妆中心	10	35	17315.85	4
B25	新艺艺术中心	8	13	7303.46	1
B26	东方风度	6	22	11825.69	3
B27	VANKE LIVING CENTER	10	8	30192.32	1
B28	文利书店	11	25	10662.84	4
B29	万科星光广场	32	38	29,261.48	4
B30	丹尼斯全日鲜(枫杨街段)	9	7	2,058.06	1

(4)问卷反馈

问卷数据总计200份,22份为纸质版,于现场分发,178份为问卷星的网络调查结果,被调查人群里个人属性综合多样,保证了问卷的有效性。在选择共享单车出行的人群中,32人有私人自行车,168人无私人自行车;80人有电动自行车,120人没有电动自行车。用户骑行选择和车辆分配统计如图1所示。

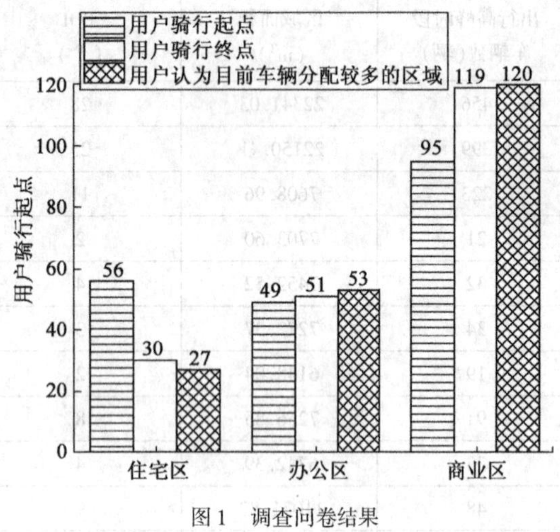

图1　调查问卷结果

2.1.4　数据分析

观察图2中不同时段下区域内单车数量,调查结果显示在不同时间段,多数区域共享单车数量均产生了较大的变化,由此可初步预测大量用户在不同时段下的不同出行需求导致车辆在区域间发生了交互转移的情况。在不同时间段,多数区域共享单车数量均产生了较大的变化,由此可初步预测大量用户在不同时段下的不同出行需求导致车辆在区域间发生了交互转移的情况。

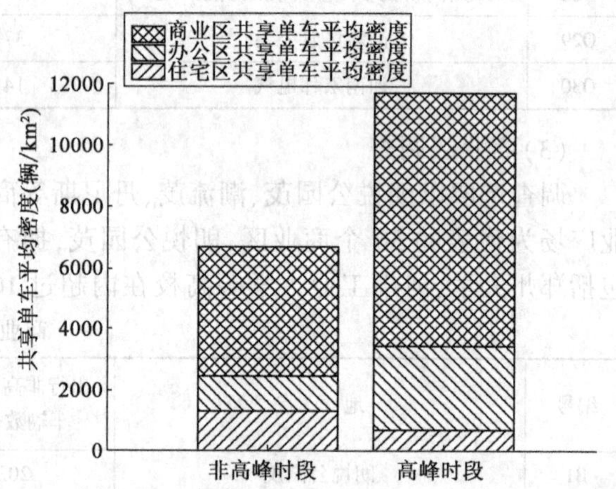

图2　不同时空共享单车平均密度统计图

由调查问卷反馈,基于目前私有出行工具并不是大面积普及的社会背景下,在短距离的出行中,共享单车系统仍能有效地满足我们的骑行愿望,体现出本次调查研究是具有意义的。由图1可知,在200份问卷总计400组数据中,共有214组骑行位置位于商业区,86组骑行位置位于住宅区,100组骑行位置位于办公区。这种差异说明了商业区对于共享单车的吸引程度远远高于住宅区和办公区,用户在人流量巨大的商业区有着更明显的出行需求。

时间因素上以出行高峰期为例,200组数据,164人在高峰期出行目的为上下班,36人出行目的为其他。200组数据,30人在非高峰期出行目的为上下班,170人出行目的为其他。经对比总结,这些数据能反映出用户在高峰期时段出行目的以通勤为主,非高峰时期出行目的为了通勤的人数较少,而具体的单车转移情况则需要对所有数据进一步处理以后才能进行说明。关于共享单车运营管理与社会环境之间的矛盾,148 人认为共享单车的运营情况尚可接受。换句话说,统计结果表明:共享单车系统的运营问题确实存在,但极大程度上存在优化的可能性,总的来说目前共享单车系统的整体情况还算良好。基于上述统计数据,共享单车的分布特征确实和"时空"因素有着密不可分的直接联系。

2.2 多元线性回归模型

为进一步探究空间因素和时间因素对共享单车分布特征的影响权重并更加深入地了解分布特征产生变化的具体情况,本次研究将对数据纳入到多元线性回归模型之中进行回归分析。本次模型中自变量的选取仅以研究内容为主,即分别以住宅区密度、办公区密度、商业区密度为自变量,车辆密度为因变量,具体公式如下:

$$Y = b_1X_1 + b_2X_2 + b_3X_3 + a \tag{1}$$

式中:Y——车辆密度,即调查所得共享单车总数量(辆)与调查区域总面积之比(km^2);

X_1——住宅区密度,即调查区域内 POI 数量(个)与调查区域面积(km^2)之比;

X_2——办公区密度;

X_3——商业区密度;

a——随机误差;

b_1、b_2、b_3——回归系数。

本文利用 SPSS 软件进行多元回归分析,检验结果显示在不同时段,住宅区密度与住宅区车辆密度,办公区密度与办公区区域密度,商业区密度与商业区车辆密度的皮尔森相关系数均在 0.7 ~ 0.9 之间,表现为较强或者是强相关性。这里表明每个区域自身而言,随着密度的增加,共享单车的数量也会得到即时的提高,基本符合线性关系。非高峰时段车辆密度的模型调整后的 R^2 为0.814,模型拟合优度较好。同理高峰时段车辆密度模型调整后 R^2 为 0.833,模型拟合优度较好。方程通过显著性检验,说明因变量 Y 车辆密度随至少一个因变量的变化而变化。

为了在同等数量级的影响下继续探究住宅区和办公区对于共享单车分布特征的影响,将再对数据进行两次拟合,如表 4 所示,自变量取 X_1(住宅区密度)和 X_2(办公区密度),因变量 Y 为两区域总车辆数与总面积之比,拟合中,非高峰时段车辆密度模型中方程回归系数的显著性检验均通过($P<0.05$),表明高峰时段内两个因子在同等数量级下对于共享单车的影响都具有意义,此时比较系数的大小,办公区密度标准化系数 0.779 大于住宅区密度标准化系数 0.395,说明办公区密度对于车辆密度的影响权重高于住宅区密度。高峰期的回归系数检验仅办公区表现为显著影响,住宅区由高峰期前的显著影响变为不显著影响是因为高峰期后,住宅区密度和办公区密度影响力的差距进一步加大,导致了住宅区密度与车辆密度的正相关性急剧减弱,从而形成了在方程中体现为不显著的现象。接着我们可以观察到从非高峰时段到出行高峰时段,办公区密度的回归参数由 4.008 上升到 7.818,而住宅区密度的由显著影响变为不显著影响,由此我们可以判断共享单车发生了区域间的转移,即出行高峰期时从住宅区向办公区转移。

不同时段二元拟合回归系数 表 4

区域密度	非高峰时段			高峰时段		
	非标准化系数	标准化系数	显著性	非标准化系数	标准化系数	显著性
住宅区密度	1.222	0.395	0	0.353	0.067	0.43
办公区密度	4.008	0.779	0	7.818	0.892	0

3 结论

(1)商业区在不同时间段对共享单车的分布特征的影响都表现得最为明显,该区域内更是在每日出行平稳期之间达到共享单车数量的最大值。研究建议,加派人员及时对区域内的单车进行管理调度,防止共享单车产生堆积现象,同时又要保证留有足够多的共享单车来满足庞大的人流量。

(2)住宅区对于共享单车的吸引力为三种区域中最小,其共享单车的分布特征的变化主要以高峰期为界限。经早高峰后大量共享单车主要由住宅区向办公区转移,导致住宅区和办公区对于共享单车的吸引力发生了倒置的现象。研究建议,对将周边溢出需求的共享单车在高峰期前向住宅区调度转移,既满足居民高峰时出行的需求,又提高了共享单车系统的运转效率。

(3)办公区对于共享单车的吸引力次于商业区高于住宅区。由上述结论可知,晚高峰时,由于用户下班回家,会导致大量单车由办公区向住宅区转移。研究建议,在该时段地区的相关工作人员做好单车的整理维护工作即可,尽可能地避免单车损坏的情况发生。

(4)本文只考虑了工作日的共享单车数据,未考虑工作日和节假日不同时期的数据,在之后研究中会将其完善。并将多角度分析共享单车分配问题,向共享单车平衡配流方向探索。

参考文献

[1] Abolhassani L, Afghari A P, Borzadaran H M. Public Preferences Towards Bicycle Sharing System in Developing Countries: the Case of Mashhad, Iran[J]. Sustainable Cities and Society, 2019(44):763-773.

[2] Fuller D, Luan Hui, Buote R, Auchincloss A H. Impact of a Public Transit Strike on Public Bicycle Share Use: an Interrupted Time Series Natural Experiment Study [J]. Journal of Transport & Health, 2019, (13):137-142.

[3] 高楹,宋辞,舒华,等.北京市摩拜共享单车源汇时空特征分析及空间调度[J].地球信息科学学报,2018,20(8):1123-1138.

[4] 邓力凡,谢永红,黄鼎曦.基于骑行时空数据的共享单车设施规划研究[J].规划师,2017,33(10):82-88.

[5] 周川.基于改进樽海鞘算法的共享单车分布密度优化[J].计算机科学,2021,48(S2):106-110.

[6] Sun Ye-ran, Mobasheri A, Hu Xu-ke, et al. Investigating Impacts of Environmental Factors on the Cycling Behavior of Bicycle-Sharing Users[J]. Sustainability, 2017, 9(6):1-12.

[7] 陈植元,林泽慧,金嘉栋,等.基于时空聚类预测的共享单车调度优化研究[J].管理工程学报,2022,36(01):1-13.

[8] 徐春玲,赵祥,张溪,等.共享单车骑行时空特征分析——以北京市为例[C]//2020中国城市规划年会论文集.中国城市规划学会:中国建筑工业出版社,2021:686-692.

智能网联车专用车道对人工驾驶车的影响分析

靳雅寓[1]　何赏璐*[2]　苏　宁[3]　刘英舜[4]

(南京理工大学自动化学院)

摘　要　具有较高自动化水平的高等级智能网联车投入市场应用指日可待。为了适应并加快智能网联车的落地应用,智能网联车专用车道技术受到了越来越多的关注。本研究通过了解驾驶员应对不同智能网联车专用车道设置策略的行为变化,为完善智能网联车专用车道技术提供一定的支撑。具体来说,本研究采用意向调查法(Stated Preference, SP),从个人信息、设置策略、行为影响等方面设计了包含16个问题的问卷,并通过网络发放和收集了613份有效反馈;运用频数分析和卡方分析探讨了驾驶员性别、年龄、驾龄等基本属性与智能网联车专用车道不同设置策略之间的影响关系,分析出对人工驾驶车行为具有显著性影响的因素。研究发现,女性更支持设置CAV专用车道,认为严格的隔离方式和动态调控的智能道钉的指示十分安全;驾驶习惯偏保守的驾驶员更倾向配合CAV专用车道使用策略;青年人和习惯固定限速值驾驶人都属于虽然不完全接受对限速值的动态调控,但依旧愿意配合协助。

关键词　智能网联车　专用车道策略　SP调查　统计分析　动态调控　出入口　限速值

1.基金项目:国家重点研发计划政府间国际科技创新合作项目(2019YFE0123800);国家自然科学基金青年项目(52102380);中国博士后科学基金(2021T140325);中央高校基本科研业务费专项资金资助(30920021140)。

0　引言

近年来,智能网联车(Connected and Autonomous Vehicle,CAV)因其在促进交通安全和提升效率等方面的潜在优势而获得了政府、行业和学术界的强烈关注。与传统的人工驾驶汽车(Human-driven Vehicle,HV)相比,CAV有很多潜在的优势,如减少交通事故、增加道路通行能力、降低车辆能耗等。许多研究指出,CAV在未来将落地实施,且早于预期。目前,学术界主要聚焦于CAV环境下的交通安全、出行行为等领域,但尚未全面、细致的研究与CAV配套的基础设施。

鉴于路权规则,专用车道是道路基础设施中特殊的一部分,而CAV专用车道的设置是否对HV的驾驶行为产生了影响,目前仍是研究的关注点。例如He S[1]指出,应更新交通基础设施(即专用车道)和相关法律法规,以适配CAV的使用;席海南[2]得到用户的教育程度与对CAV了解程度会影响其对自动驾驶公交的接受度;范鹤亭[3]指出设置CAV专用车道有助于大家选择购买CAV。CAV可以借助自身的通信设施和路侧设施实现智能网联化驾驶,而专用车道的引入在提高道路通行能力的同时,避免CAV和HV之间的相互影响。既有研究表明CAV专用车道被认为是提升CAV效益和提高CAV市场渗透率的有效途径[4-6];然而,专用车道的建设会占用原有的道路资源,而不合理的规划会带来负面效益。在此基础上,本研究进一步探索CAV专用车道的使用权限、路权分配、出入方式等不同策略对驾驶员的影响,为专用车道策略的完善和后续应用提供一定支撑。

1　调查及统计结果

1.1　调查问卷设计

本研究采用SP调查方法设计问卷。本研究拟探讨不同智能网联专用车道设置方案对驾驶员驾驶行为的影响。具体来说,问卷由16个问题组成,设计框架如图1所示,其中,专用车道及出入方式的图在调查问卷中有相应的图文解释,智能道钉是本文新提出的隔离方式,其含义见本文1.3.2节。

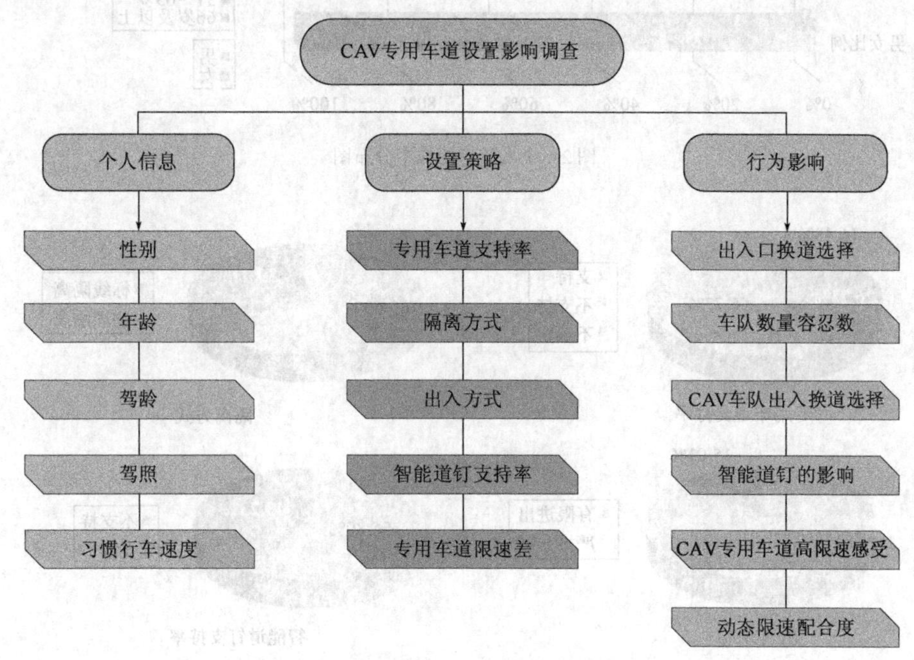

图1　拟建问卷的设计框架图

1.2　问卷的发放和收集

本研究利用了在中国比较常用的网络调查工具“问卷星”,发放时间为2022年1月3日至15日。最后,共收集得到613份有效问卷。在置信度为95%,相对抽样误差小于或等于4%时,要求的最小样本量为600,本次回收的有效问卷数量满足了最小样本量需求。

1.3　统计结果

1.3.1　个人信息调查结果

性别、年龄、驾龄、驾照分布和安全驾驶程度的分布状况如图2所示,样本数据表明被调查者中男女受访者数量接近,男女比例是1.2:1,这基本等同于2022年发布的全国男女比例(1.04:1);调查对象在18~40岁年龄区间内的数量近七成,总体趋于年轻化,原因在于问卷的传播途径是朋友圈,面对CAV专用车道的信息处理,他们有着更开放、更与众不同的思想;按驾龄来说,在1年内和3~7年的占比约为四分之一。鉴于驾驶员有一定驾驶经验,因此道路环境中的潜在风险更容易被经验丰富的驾驶人感知,其行车反应对安全合理的道路设计具有参考。从驾驶行为习惯来看,近四分之三的人偏向保守驾驶。

1.3.2 智能网联车专用车道设置策略调查结果

在设置CAV专用车道条件下,接受的态度、车道间隔离方式和出入方式等因素分布状况如图3所示。本调查创新性提出了智能道钉的隔离方式,智能道钉是专用车道在有限出入口的前提下,安装在出入口的隔离带上,动态显示前方专用车道出入口开放的范围。例如,绿色代表没有CAV进出,黄色代表有CAV进出,红色代表有CAV车队或多辆CAV车进出。

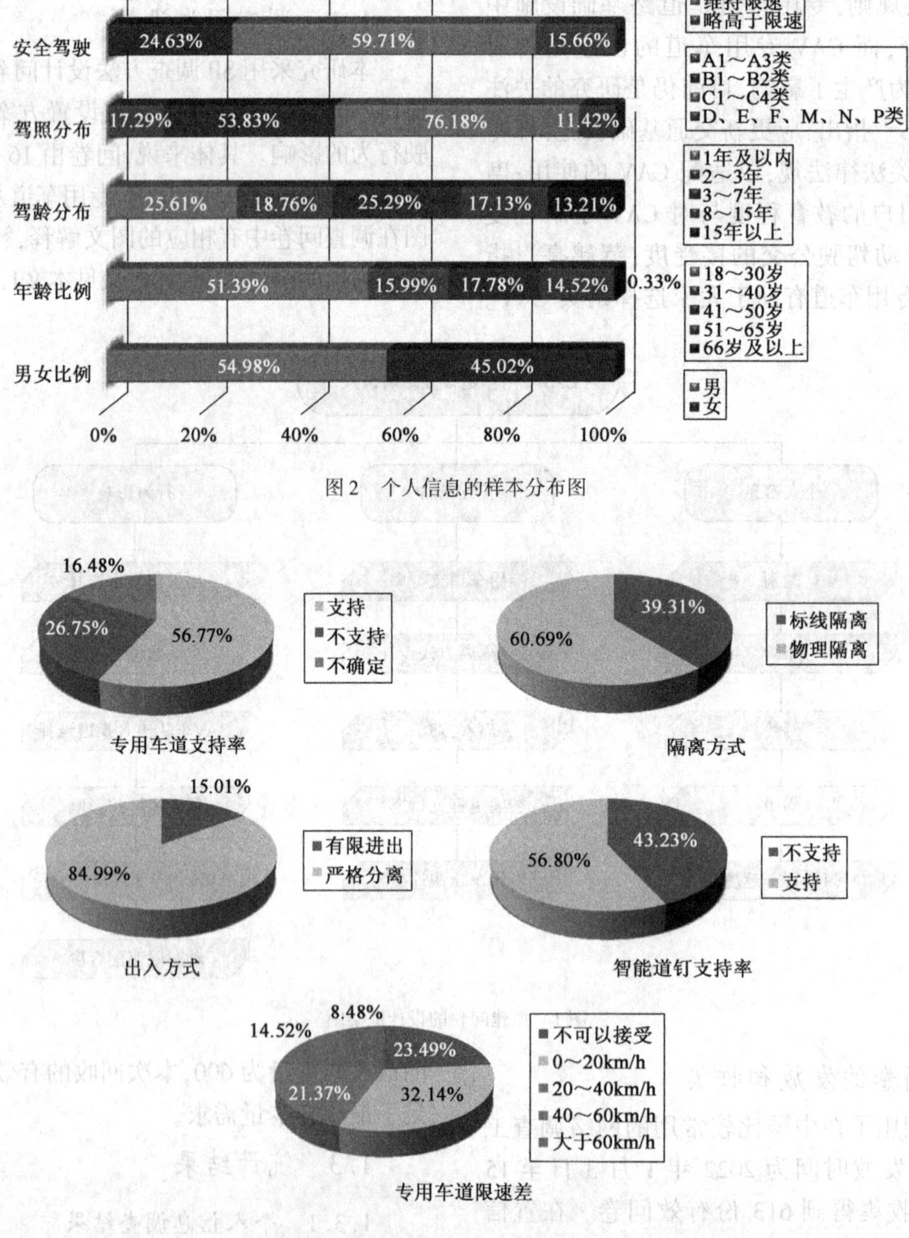

图2 个人信息的样本分布图

图3 智能网联车专用车道设置策略样本分布图

不难看出,超过半数的人支持 CAV 专用车道,这个结果和 He S[1] 在 2020 年的调查结果相一致,说明驾驶员愿意接受专用车道这一未来道路基础设施,且大多数人认为物理隔离更为安全;近九成的驾驶员支持出入方式的严格隔离;超过半数的人支持设置动态智能道钉,有利于后期对于此方法的宣传;在高速专用车道接受度上,仅四分之一的人完全不能接受高速行驶的 CAV 车辆,应针对此类人群进行针对性分析。

1.3.3 不同场景下行为影响调查结果

不同场景下,对出入口换道选择、容忍 CAV 车队数、CAV 车队出入的换道选择以及智能道钉等因素进行频数分析,结果如图 4 所示。

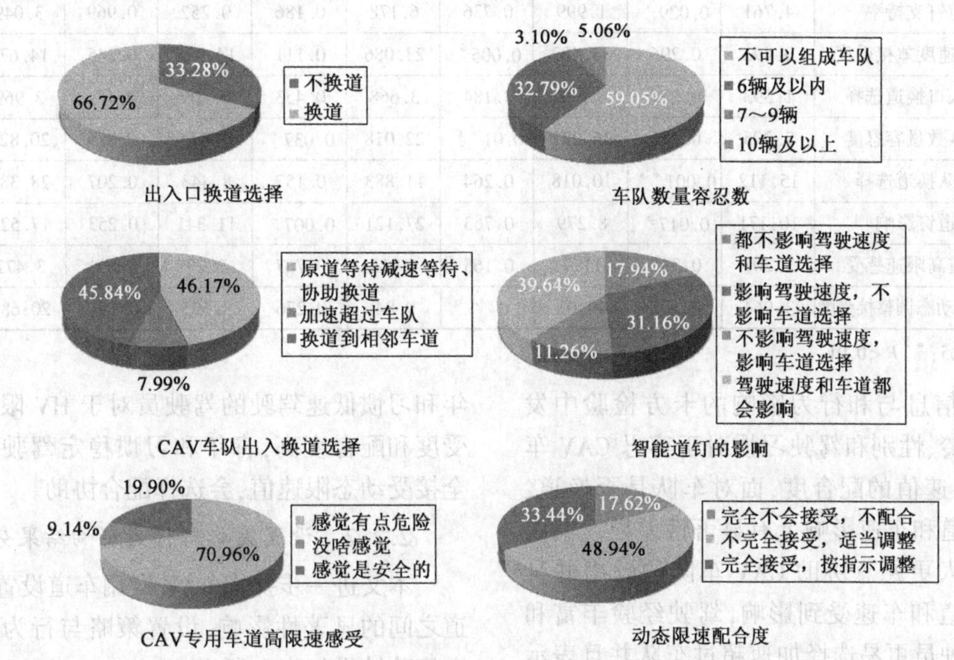

图 4 不同场景下行为影响样本分布图

结果表明,约五分之三的人会在 CAV 驶出专用车道时选择换道,尽量避免与智能网联车在同一车道内混行;CAV 车队规模方面,五分之三的驾驶员表示不接受其组成车队;面对 CAV 车队驶离专用车道时,愿意配合的保守驾驶员占九成以上;也有五分之二的人认为使用智能道钉动态控制对驾驶员影响较大,比较担心设置的安全性。

2 卡方分析

2.1 各因素对设置策略与驾驶行为的相关性分析

本文采用了 SPSS 软件进行卡方分析,本次选用皮尔逊和费希尔精确检验输出的 P(显著性值)值:当 n(总样本量)≥40 且所有的单元格的 T(理论频数)≥5,选用皮尔逊检验;当总样本量 $n<40$ 或最小理论频数 $T<1$,选用费希尔精确检验。理论上,如果 P 值小于 0.05,则认为该自变量对因变量具有显著影响。

2.2 分析结果

2.2.1 个人信息与设置策略和行为影响结果分析

表 1 所示为个人信息与设置策略和行为影响的卡方检验表,其中,驾龄对设置策略无影响,驾照类型对设置策略和行为影响均无显著性差异。表 1 中,* 代表 $P<0.05$,有显著影响;** 代表 $P<0.01$,显著性更强。

从个人信息与设置策略的卡方检验中发现,年龄、性别及驾驶习惯在 CAV 专用车道支持率、智能道钉支持率和隔离方式、高限速专用车道的感受上有显著性差异。设置 CAV 专用车道在男性和偏向保守驾驶的人群支持率最低,设置动态智能道钉和物理隔离对于保守驾驶的女性接受度更高;青年人最能接受提速的速度差在较低。

个人信息与设置策略和行为影响的卡方检验表　　表1

χ^2 和 P		个人信息									
		性别		年龄		驾龄		驾照		习惯车速	
		χ^2	P	χ^2	P	χ^2	P	χ^2	P	χ^2	P
设置策略	专用车道支持率	10.718	0.005**	7.413	0.512	15.227	0.055	3.901	0.69	13.35	0.01**
	隔离方式	5.815	0.016*	6.557	0.161	8.042	0.09	5.382	0.164	1.263	0.532
	出入方式	0.017	0.896	3.826	0.43	3.468	0.483	3.015	0.389	5.649	0.058
	道钉支持率	4.761	0.029*	1.999	0.736	6.178	0.186	0.252	0.969	3.049	0.218
	提速速度差接受度	0.492	0.296	34.402	0.005*	23.086	0.111	14.928	0.245	14.671	0.066
行为影响	出入口换道选择	1.393	0.238	6.208	0.184	3.668	0.453	2.809	0.422	2.969	0.227
	车队数量容忍度	7.205	0.066	26.272	0.01**	22.018	0.037*	4.374	0.885	20.826	0.002*
	车队换道选择	15.112	0.001**	10.018	0.264	11.883	0.157	8.443	0.207	28.384	0**
	道钉影响	10.171	0.017*	8.279	0.763	27.121	0.007*	11.341	0.253	17.528	0.008
	车道高限速感受	2.207	0.332	11.7	0.165	4.912	0.767	2.29	0.891	3.472	0.482
	限速值动态调整接受度	3.964	0.138	40.01	0**	9.84	0.276	8.695	0.191	20.689	0**

注：* $P<0.05$；** $P<0.01$。

从个人信息与和行为影响的卡方检验中发现,年龄、驾龄、性别和驾驶习惯对于容忍CAV车队数、动态限速值的配合度、面对车队是否换道、换道时对车道和车速影响上有显著性差异。偏向保守驾驶的人更愿意协助CAV车队的驶出并且表示会对车道和车速受到影响,驾驶经验丰富和激进性的驾驶员更易选择加速超过车队并且表示对车道和车速都不受影响;青年、驾龄长和习惯更保守驾驶的人对CAV车队数量容忍程度较低,中年和习惯低速驾驶的驾驶员对于HV限速值的接受度和配合度高,青年和习惯稳定驾驶的人不完全接受动态限速值,会选择配合协助。

2.2.2　设置策略与行为影响结果分析

本文进一步探究CAV专用车道设置与HV车道之间的显著性影响,设置策略与行为影响的卡方检验结果如表2所示。

设置策略与行为影响的卡方检验表　　表2

χ^2 和 P		个人信息									
		专用车道支持率		隔离方式		出入方式		道钉支持率		提速速度差接受度	
		χ^2	P	χ^2	P	χ^2	P	χ^2	P	χ^2	P
设置策略行为影响	出入口换道选择	1.367	0.505	5.862	0.015*	2.522	0.112	5.71	0.017*	11.69	0.02*
	车队数量容忍度	18.569	0.005**	2.141	0.544	4.291	0.232	35.383	0**	40.305	0**
	车队换道选择	17.139	0.002**	0.719	0.698	1.096	0.578	3.429	0.18	6.318	0.612
	道钉影响	13.523	0.035*	4.727	0.195	7.438	0.059	7.02	0.071	28.287	0.005**
	车道高限速感受	12.791	0.012*	4.059	0.131	6.812	0.033*	17.952	0**	58.74	0**
	限速值动态调整接受度	23.182	0**	1.334	0.513	0.908	0.635	42.511	0**	80.732	0**

注：* $P<0.05$；** $P<0.01$。

对于接受提速车速差越小、不支持设置专用车道和道钉的驾驶员来说,也无法接受有CAV车队驶出,表示会影响其行驶速度和车道选择;但会配合协助人工车道的动态限速值。选择物理隔离的人在出入口更注重安全,会选择换道避让。信任智能化的设备支持新提出的动态智能道钉的人也更信任CAV专用车道,认为对其毫无影响。接受提速车速差越小的人更愿意配合协助CAV车队,且接受提速车速差越大的人动态限速值的配合度高。

3 结语

本研究采用SP调查面向驾驶员开展了其应对不同CAV专用车道设置策略的态度和选择行为的调查,利用皮尔逊检验和费希尔精确检验,分析了不同CAV专用车道设置策略对于被调查驾驶员驾驶行为的影响关系。从调查结果的分析中,可以看出现阶段驾驶员对于CAV专用车道的接受度仍不高,仅略超半数。若未来要推广应用专用车道及相关策略,需提高驾驶员对其接受度。其中,男性驾驶员相对于女性驾驶员的接受度更低,驾驶习惯偏激进的驾驶员更不配合使用CAV专用车道,因此是未来CAV专用车道动态调控的智能道钉和限速等普及宣传重点受众群体。此外,调查结果也反映出驾驶员对于未来路权分配带来的公平性问题和提高专用车道限速带来的安全隐患等方面的担忧,因此,在规划设计CAV专用车道的车道分布、出入、限速等方案时,需要保障HV的路权并充分论证专用车道方案。

研究结果可以为专用车道未来的应用提供一定支持。本文一定程度上解释了个人信息、专用车道设置策略和行为影响三种因素间的相互影响,为交通工作者、政策制定者、企业和广大驾驶员等利益相关者提供一些新的研究方向和观点,为设置专用车道提供理论依据。未来仍需持续的研究工作,如扩大样本量、细化专用车道设置策略、分析影响驾驶员对CAV专用车道策略接受度的原因并提出提升方法。

参考文献

[1] He S, Qiao R, Qi Y. Multinomial Logit-Based Analysis on Users' Perceptions and Expectations to the High-Level Connected and Autonomous Vehicles[C]//3rd International Forum on Connected Automated Vehicle Highway System through the China Highway & Transportation Society. US: SAE Technical Paper, 2020:1-7.

[2] 席海角. 自动驾驶公交接受度及选择意愿研究[D]. 大连:大连理工大学,2020.

[3] 范鹤亭. 基于混合Logit模型的自动驾驶汽车购买意愿实证研究[D]. 大连:大连理工大学,2019.

[4] Chen Z, He F, Yin Y, et al. Optimal design of autonomous vehicle zones in transportation networks[J]. Transportation Research Part B: Methodological, 2017, 99:44-61.

[5] Liu Z, Song Z. Strategic planning of dedicated autonomous vehicle lanes and autonomous vehicle/toll lanes in transportation networks [J]. Transportation Research Part C: Emerging Technologies, 2019, 106:381-403.

[6] Chen S, Wang H, Meng Q. Designing autonomous vehicle incentive program with uncertain vehicle purchase price [J]. Transportation Research Part C: Emerging Technologies, 2019, 103:226-245.

附录

调查问卷原网址:https://www.wjx.cn/vm/OSSa9Sr.aspx.

参数解释表　　附表

参　数	解　释
P	显著性值
n	总样本量
T	理论频数
χ^2	卡方值

高速公路改扩建的圆曲线半径可靠性分析方法

梁家明* 张 航

(武汉理工大学交通与物流工程学院)

摘 要 为探究高速公路改扩建工程中圆曲线半径的定量安全设计方法,引入可靠度理论,对高速公路改扩建工程的圆曲线半径进行可靠性分析和设计。以车辆在圆曲线路段行驶时不发生滑移为约束条件,建立功能函数,对莞深高速公路从100km/h提升至120km/h设计速度的第一期改扩建工程进行了可靠度分析,并按失效概率不大于0.1%的要求,对不满足可靠度设计要求的圆曲线路段进行了可靠性设计。研究结果表明,从100km/h提升至120km/h设计速度的改扩建工程中,超高为4%、5%的圆曲线路段对应的可靠性安全半径分别为1200m和1100m。

关键词　交通工程　失效概率　可靠性理论　圆曲线半径　路线设计　交通安全

0　引言

随着我国人民生活水平的不断提高,机动车数量逐年上升,据公安部统计,截至2021年,全国机动车保有量已达到3.72亿辆。为了满足交通量增长的需要,同时做到缩短建设周期、少占建设用地,对已有高速公路的改扩建就显得十分必要。在对已有高速公路的改扩建工程中,曲线路段由于线形特殊,驾驶人在曲线路段的驾驶行为也较为复杂,已经成为交通事故的高发区域,而圆曲线半径的大小又是决定曲线路段行车安全的重要因素。因此,对高速公路改扩建工程中的圆曲线半径值进行研究势在必行。

高速公路改扩建一直是我国公路建设中的热门话题。程国柱等[1]提出一种高速公路改扩建作业区昼夜渐变限速标志间距的计算方法;李刚[2]分析了高速公路改扩建新旧路基差异沉降的影响因素;王保群等[3]对高速公路改扩建项目中的既有桥梁承载力进行评定分析;YANG等[4]对改扩建项目中绿色道路的评价指标体系进行了研究。上述学者对高速公路改扩建项目进行了各个方面的研究,但对高速公路改扩建工程中圆曲线半径值的探究较少。

在现行的高速公路改扩建工程中,对圆曲线路段均采用确定性的设计方法,即按照《公路路线设计规范》(JTG D20—2017)判断旧路段的圆曲线半径值是否满足改扩建后的公路等级在规范中对应的圆曲线半径值。运用这种方法,设计人员只能判断旧路段的设计值是否满足规范,而无法了解设计值对应的具体安全水平,导致改扩建后的设计目标和预期安全效果不明确。运用可靠性理论对圆曲线半径值进行分析,能够避免确定性设计方法的缺点。对于可靠度理论在道路路线设计中讨论设计指标安全程度的运用,Navin等[5-6]最先做出了尝试;张航[7]运用可靠度理论对高速公路的停车视距进行研究;王路[8]基于可靠度计算高速公路临界坡长等。因此,考虑利用可靠度理论,在高速公路改扩建工程中,以车辆在曲线路段行驶时不发生侧滑为约束条件,推导功能函数,提出一种能定量表示改扩建工程安全程度的圆曲线半径可靠性分析方法,并通过实例予以说明。

1　可靠性功能函数建立

1.1　可靠性理论

可靠度为工程结构在确定的条件下,达到预期成果的概率。将可靠度理论应用于圆曲线设计,车辆在圆曲线路段行驶时,要保证车辆不会发生横向倾覆和横向滑移的现象,而车辆只要不发生横向滑移就能保证车辆不发生横向倾覆,因此,考虑以车辆在圆曲线路段行驶时不发生横向滑移作为约束条件进行研究。

将车辆在弯道行驶时保持稳定的概率称为可靠概率P_S,发生滑移的概率称为失效概率P_f,两者关系为$P_S+P_f=1$。在实际应用时,失效概率比可靠概率更具有明确的物理意义,同时为了表达和计算方便,所以通常以失效概率P_f描述结构的可靠程度,失效概率P_f越小,系统的可靠性越高,失效概率的计算公式为:

$$P_f = P(Z<0) = \int_{-\infty}^{0} f(Z)\mathrm{d}Z \tag{1}$$

李国强等学者在《工程结构荷载与可靠度设计原理》一书中指出,根据公众心理对危险程度的感知从危险至可以接受再到安全的顺序,将失效概率分为0.1%、0.01%以及0.001%三个层次,心理承受能力较强的人可以接受0.1%的失效概率,谨慎的人可以接纳的失效概率为0.01%,而当失效概率低于或等于0.001%时,一般都不再考虑其危险性。考虑以失效概率不大于0.1%作为圆曲线半径的可靠性设计标准。

将车辆在高速公路上平稳行驶所需要的圆曲线安全最小半径值,记为R_D;将设计道路所提供的圆曲线设计半径值,记为R_S,当设计半径值小于安全最小半径值,可以认为设计值失效。因此,可靠性功能函数设为:

$$Z = g(X_1, X_2, \cdots, X_n) = R_S - R_D \quad (2)$$

1.2 功能函数建立

对在圆曲线路段行驶的车辆进行受力分析，如图1所示。

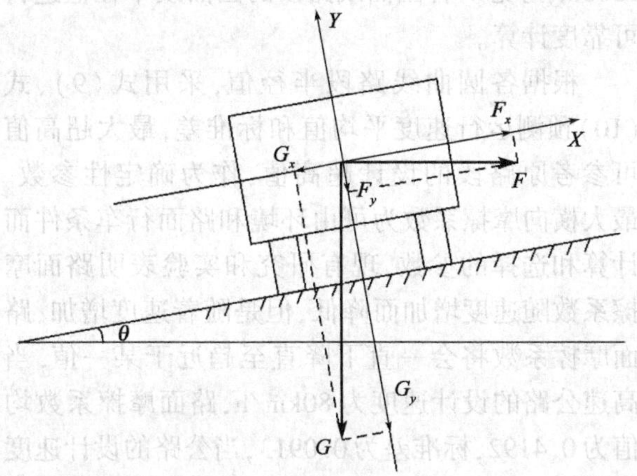

图1 车辆在曲线路段上行驶受力分析图

车辆在曲线路段上行驶时会产生离心力，方向为背向圆心，作用点在车辆重心处，计算公式为：

$$F = \frac{GV^2}{127R} \quad (3)$$

其中，F 为离心力，N；G 为汽车重力，N；V 为车辆行驶速度，km/h；R 为圆曲线半径值，m。

图1中 $F_x = F\cos\theta$、$F_y = F\sin\theta$、$G_x = G\sin\theta$、$G_y = G\cos\theta$，θ 为超高横坡度，设路面超高为 i_h，则有：

$$i_h = \tan\theta \quad (4)$$

根据力学平衡条件得，汽车不发生横向滑移的稳定性条件为：

$$F\cos\theta - G\sin\theta \leqslant f(F\sin\theta - G\cos\theta) \quad (5)$$

其中，f 为横向摩擦系数。又因为 θ 取值一般很小，所以 $\sin\theta \approx \tan\theta = i_h$，$\cos\theta = 1$。将式(5)化简为：

$$F - Gi_h \leqslant Gf \quad (6)$$

由式(3)、式(6)可得，此状态下在拟改扩建高速公路上不产生横向滑移的最小圆曲线半径 R 大小表达式为

$$R = \frac{V^2}{127(f + i_h)} \quad (7)$$

将式(7)代入式(2)，得到式(8)作为可靠度功能函数，计算改扩建高速公路圆曲线半径的可靠度模型较简单，参数互相独立。

$$Z = g(X_1, X_2, \cdots, X_n) = R_S - R_D = R_S - \frac{V^2}{127(f + i_h)} \quad (8)$$

2 可靠性分析

2.1 基本变量分析

2.1.1 运行车速

公路的运行速度一般采用测定速度的第85百分位的速度表示。车辆在圆曲线路段行驶时的运行车速与圆曲线半径有着一定程度的关联，陈富坚[9]在文章中指出运行车速与圆曲线半径具有正态相关性，并给出回归模型，模型为

$$V_{均值} = 16.015\ln R - 5.7882 \quad (9)$$

$$S = 0.14V_{均值} \quad (10)$$

其中，S 为运行车速标准差。

2.1.2 最大横向摩擦系数

汽车与路面的摩擦系数与路面材料类型、路面等级、天气、车速、轮胎材料性能等因素有关。FAMBRO[10]的研究表明，路面摩擦系数可以被看作是服从正态分布的随机量。路面在潮湿和干燥条件下的摩擦系数的均值和标准差见表1。

不同状态路面在不同速度下的路面摩擦系数

表1

路面状况	速度(km/h)	摩擦系数均值	摩擦系数标准差
潮湿	80	0.4192	0.0913
潮湿	85	0.4013	0.0913
潮湿	90	0.3826	0.0913
潮湿	95	0.3571	0.0913
潮湿	99.8	0.3498	0.0913
干燥	任意速度	0.8852	0.0949

2.1.3 超高值

道路设计时设置超高是为了让车辆能克服离心力，保证车辆在弯道时的稳定和安全，在道路设计时将弯道的道路做成向内侧的单向横向坡度形式。超高的选取不能过小也不能过大，过小时，车辆可能因为离心力较大，向道路外侧滑移甚至侧

翻;超高过大时,在弯道行驶的车辆可能因为自身重力,发生向内侧滑移的危险,因此,道路的超高值有一个最大限值,即最大超高值。我国现有公路的最大超高值见表2。

公路最大超高值(%)　表2

公路等级	高速公路	一级公路	二级公路	三级公路	四级公路
一般地区	8或10	8或10	8	8	8
冰雪影响较大地区	6	6	6	6	6

2.2　改扩建工程圆曲线半径可靠性分析

在道路设计过程中,设计人员对圆曲线半径的取值都会有一定程度的富余,只在个别特殊地形或极端环境的条件下采用规范中的一般或极限最小半径值。因此,在改扩建工程中,当旧路的圆曲线半径值满足新路对应规范中的一般最小半径值要求时,设计人员便认为这部分旧路可以沿用,这样的做法有很大的安全隐患,无法定量地评价改扩建后高速公路的安全程度。《公路路线设计规范》(JTG D20—2017)中规定的高速公路各设计速度条件下的圆曲线一般最小半径值和极限最小半径值见表3。

最小半径值　表3

设计速度(km/h)	最大超高(%)	一般最小半径值(m)	极限最小半径值(m)
80	8	400	250
100	8	700	400
120	8	1000	650

下面以位于广东省的莞深高速公路第一期改扩建工程的设计施工为背景,阐述改扩建工程中圆曲线半径可靠性分析方法。

2.2.1　工程项目简介

莞深高速公路第一期改扩建工程,起点为莞深高速公路与梅观高速公路交界处,终点设在大有园互通立交桥,路线全长20.675km,途经塘厦镇、黄江镇等镇区。遵照使用功能要求,原设计全线按100km/h设计车速双向6车道标准设计,现进行由100km/h提高到120km/h设计速度的方案可靠性研究。

2.2.2　工程可靠性分析

全线共设16个圆曲线路段,JD3、JD5、JD12的圆曲线半径值未达到规范中规定的120km/h的一般最小半径值1000m,其他交点半径值均大于1000m,考虑对各圆曲线路段的圆曲线半径值进行可靠度计算。

根据各圆曲线路段半径值,采用式(9)、式(10)预测运行速度平均值和标准差,最大超高值可参考原路段的设计超高值,作为确定性参数。最大横向摩擦系数为可由环境和路面行车条件而计算和选择的参数,现有研究和实验表明路面摩擦系数随速度增加而降低,但是随着速度增加,路面摩擦系数将会一直下降直至趋近于某一值,当高速公路的设计速度为80km/h,路面摩擦系数均值为0.4192,标准差为0.0913,当公路的设计速度增加至100 km/h及以上时,路面摩擦系数可以参照表1中速度为99.8km/h的路面摩擦系数均值和标准差,得到计算结果见表4。

最大横向摩擦系数　表4

道路运行速度(km/h)	路面养护较好	路面磨光
80	0.2934	0.16
100	0.2449	0.1399
120	0.2449	0.1399

根据以上分析,针对出现的环境不利情况,可以在MATLAB软件中运用蒙特卡洛法计算莞深高速公路第一期改扩建工程各圆曲线路段半径值的失效概率,计算步骤如图2所示。

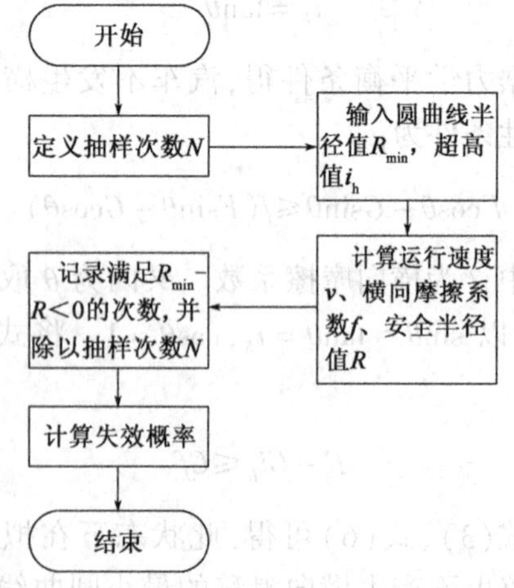

图2　可靠度计算步骤

按照上述计算步骤得到莞深高速公路第一期改扩建工程中各路段圆曲线半径的失效概率见表5。

圆曲线失效概率 表5

交 点 号	交点桩号	半径(m)	超高(%)	可靠指标β	失效概率(%)
JD2	K0 + 294.82	1000	4	2.9677	0.15
JD3	K1 + 082.46	800	5	2.9291	0.17
JD4	K4 + 784.59	1500	3	3.1559	0.08
JD5	K6 + 822.35	727.46	5	2.8943	0.19
JD6	K7 + 955.30	1043.95	4	2.9889	0.14
JD7	K8 + 669.91	2061.04	2	3.2389	0.06
JD8	K10 + 291.34	4520	—	3.7190	0.01
JD9	K12 + 210.29	1178.33	4	3.0618	0.11
JD10	K13 + 147.98	1500	3	3.1559	0.08
JD11	K14 + 323.36	1091.81	4	3.0115	0.13
JD12	K14 + 927.95	873.34	5	2.9478	0.16
JD13	K16 + 328.28	1500	3	3.1559	0.08
JD14	K17 + 463.95	1400	3	3.1213	0.09
JD15	K18 + 555.76	1200	4	3.0902	0.10
JD16	K19 + 892.36	2000	2	3.1947	0.07

从表5中可以看出,JD4、JD7、JD8、JD10、JD13、JD14、JD15、JD16 的圆曲线半径值失效概率小于0.1%,满足可靠度设计的标准;JD2、JD3、JD5、JD6、JD9、JD11、JD12 的圆曲线半径值失效概率大于0.1%,不满足失效概率小于0.1%的可靠度设计标准。且JD2、JD9、JD11 的圆曲线半径值大于规范中设计速度为120km/h的一般最小半径值1000m。

因此,在改扩建工程中,当旧路的圆曲线半径值满足新路在规范中的一般值就认为可以沿用旧路的设计参数,这种做法存在安全隐患。

2.2.3 工程项目可靠性设计

可靠性设计是上文中可靠性分析的逆过程,是以确定的可靠程度反算出达到要求的圆曲线半径值的设计方法。对于莞深高速公路第一期改扩建工程中,JD4、JD7、JD8、JD10、JD13、JD14、JD15、JD16 的圆曲线半径值满足设计速度达到120km/h后的可靠性设计要求,可保留原路继续使用;JD2、JD3、JD5、JD6、JD9、JD11、JD12 的圆曲线半径值不满足可靠性设计要求,需要对其进行重新设计,以失效概率0.1%作为设计标准进行可靠性设计,保持原路线中各曲线路段的超高值不变,得到JD2、JD3、JD5、JD6、JD9、JD11、JD12 的圆曲线半径可靠性设计推荐值见表6。

圆曲线半径推荐值 表6

交 点 号	交点桩号	超高(%)	失效概率(%)	可靠指标β	推荐半径值(m)
JD2	K0 + 294.82	4	0.10	3.0902	1200
JD3	K1 + 082.46	5	0.10	3.0902	1100
JD5	K6 + 822.35	5	0.10	3.0902	1100
JD6	K7 + 955.30	4	0.10	3.0902	1200
JD9	K12 + 210.29	4	0.10	3.0902	1200
JD11	K14 + 323.36	4	0.10	3.0902	1200
JD12	K14 + 927.95	5	0.10	3.0902	1100

由表6可知,在道路圆曲线半径设计中运用可靠性理论,可以预先设置目标失效概率,计算道路的圆曲线半径值。该方法既满足规范中设计速度为120km/h的圆曲线一般最小半径值为1000m的要求,还可以考虑车辆、路面等多种因素,减少人为主观因素影响,有更好的安全性,更有利于交

通安全。

3　结语

(1)现行改扩建圆曲线段的确定性设计方法存在安全隐患。

(2)在高速公路改扩建工程中使用可靠性设计方法可以解决现行方法无法定量表现改扩建后道路安全程度的问题,可以定量表示改扩建后的预期成效。

(3)以失效概率0.1%作为圆曲线半径可靠度设计标准,对于由100km/h提高到120km/h设计速度的高速公路,当圆曲线路段的超高值为4%、5%时,圆曲线可靠性推荐半径值分别为1200m、1100m。

(4)本研究对于汽车在高速公路上曲线路段行驶时,道路的最大摩擦系数、超高值等参数都是基于其他学者的研究成果,建议今后进一步对各个参数的取值进行研究,以提高高速公路可靠性设计的准确性。

参考文献

[1] 程国柱,程瑞,薛长龙,等.高速公路改扩建的渐变安全限速设置方法[J].哈尔滨工业大学学报,2020,52(09):185-192.

[2] 李刚,郭艳玲.高速公路改扩建新旧路基差异沉降影响因素分析[J].公路交通科技,2021,38(07):22-28.

[3] 王保群,邢德进,陈成勇,等.高速公路改扩建既有桥梁承载力评定[J].公路,2021,66(08):216-220.

[4] Yang Y G, Xia J P, Zhao R, et al. Research on Evaluation Index System of Green Highway in Reconstruction and Expansion Projects[J]. E3S Web of Conferences, 2021, 233:01136.

[5] Navin F P D. Safetyfactors for road design: Can they be estimated[J]. Transportation Research Record, 1990, 1280:181-189.

[6] Navin F P D. Reliabilityindices for road geometric design[J]. Canadian Journal of Civil Engineering. 1992, 19(5):760-766.

[7] 张航,张肖磊,吕能超.高速公路停车视距可靠性设计[J].公路交通科技,2019,36(04):44-49+87.

[8] 王路,程建川.基于可靠度的高速公路准临界坡长[J].东南大学学报(自然科学版),2018,48(01):181-187.

[9] 陈富坚,郭忠印,陈富强.公路平曲线半径的可靠性设计[J].哈尔滨工业大学学报,2012,44(04):100-104.

[10] Fambro D B, Koppa R J, Picha D L, et al. Driver braking performance in stopping sight distance situations [J]. Transportation Research Record, 2000(1701):9-16.

城市快速路 HOV 车道设置位置研究

李丙烨　陈嘉乐　赵一静　高佳鑫　张　敏*

(长安大学运输工程学院)

摘　要　随着HOV车道在我国城市道路中的不断发展,HOV车道设置条件的研究逐渐成为研究的重点。本文在分析国内外对于HOV车道研究的基础上,指出了HOV车道设置条件理论的缺乏,分析了城市快速路内外侧设置HOV车道的交通运行特性,考虑了车道位置不同而造成的交通效率不同,以此为依据构建了交通效率模型,并以西安市南三环早高峰实际情况为基础,对交通效率模型进行计算分析;实验结果表明:西安市南三环某段在总交通流量为2342pcu/h,合乘车辆流量占比28%,转向车辆占比10%时,内侧设置HOV车道合乘车辆的运行时间为743s,外侧设置HOV车道合乘车辆的运行时间为766s,在此种交通条件下适宜在内侧HOV车道,本文介绍的交通效率模型可以在对比分析HOV车道设置方案优劣方面提供理论参考。

关键词 城市交通 城市快速路 HOV 车道 交通效率模型 设置条件

0 引言

交通管理策略的主要目标通常集中于改善安全、缓解拥挤和节省成本[1-3]。其中,HOV(High Occupancy Vehicle,多乘员车)车道是一种交通管理措施,可最大化平均车辆占有率[4]。对于 HOV 车道的研究大多基于美国的研究案例,在设置 HOV 车道后,规定合乘人员达两人或以上的汽车可在车道上正常行驶,过往国外对 HOV 车道的研究主要集中在新增 HOV 车道方法、HOV 车道配置、HOV 车道的交通安全问题等[5-7]。国内对 HOV 车道研究较少,陈玮等[8]介绍了 HOV 车道的起源和 HOV 车道的应用实例,并阐述了 HOV 车道在我国的发展前景;范文博等[9]基于交通行为构建了双层规划模型,分析了 HOT 车道的拥挤管理效果;邓社军等[10]以南京市两条城市快速路路段为例,研究了 HOV 车道设置方案,并利用仿真手段,确定了运营效率最大化的车道管理方案;韩得利[11]和刘晨阳[12]分别对深圳市和大连市的 HOV 车道进行了现状调查,并评估了 HOV 车道的实施效果,近期王瑜等[13]利用模糊评价方法对成都市 HOV 车道的云霄效果进行了评估,并对 HOV 车道的管理方面提出了优化建议;田丽君等[14]基于累积前景理论,考虑了通勤者的出行时间,研究了出行者的出行方式会受到风险偏好的影响;况雪[15]调查了人们的出行意愿,并进行了出行方式选择建模,为研究 HOV 车道的出行行为提供了思路;邵春福等[16]分析了公交专用道的使用现状,并结合 HOV 车道的使用意愿,提出了将 HOV 车道与公交专用道合并的思路,拓展了 HOV 车道的设置方案。

以上对 HOV 车道研究大多集中在运行效果的评估以及 HOV 车道的设置方案中,HOV 车道的有效设置,可在保障交通安全的基础上,提升交通运行效率。HOV 车道的设置位置研究是 HOV 车道的首要问题,然而,对于 HOV 车道的设置位置研究较少。对于一般 HOV 车道路段采用的道路断面形式一般分为两种,一种是道路内侧车道设置为 HOV 车道,另一种是道路外侧车道设置为 HOV 车道。我国在设置 HOV 车道时,考虑到国内相关标准规范涉及 HOV 车道设置条件的内容较少,故大多借鉴国外的设置经验。国外设置 HOV 车道大多设置在道路内侧,故目前多在道路内侧设置 HOV 车道,但国外实施 HOV 车道的大多是高速公路,导致了国内在城市快速路中设置内侧车道为 HOV 车道时,HOV 会受到左转车辆的影响,故需要进一步对国内城市快速路 HOV 车道的设置位置展开研究。

综上所示,本文在分析 HOV 车道运行特征的基础上,对内外侧设置 HOV 车道的交通效率问题进行建模研究,并通过数值仿真方法,分析了内外侧设置 HOV 车道在交通效率方面的优劣。

1 HOV 车道设置位置运行特征

HOV 车道允许合乘车辆(即车辆内部人数达到规定人数的车辆)行驶,禁止非合乘车辆行驶,与此同时,HOV 车辆也可以在通用车道上行驶。在 HOV 车道的运行特征基础上分析 HOV 车道设置位置不同时的不同交通运行特征。

1.1 内侧 HOV 车道

内侧设置 HOV 车道,即为将原有道路内侧的普通车道改造为 HOV 车道,此时非合乘车辆禁止在此车道上行驶,但考虑到部分设置 HOV 车道的路段存在与主干路交叉情况,参考大连 HOV 车道在交叉口处的解决办法,将内侧车道临近交叉口部分,更换为通用车道,左转车辆可驶入内侧车道,完成左转交通需求,内侧设置 HOV 车道的示意图如图 1a)所示。

1.2 外侧 HOV 车道

外侧设置 HOV 车道,即为将原有道路外侧的普通车道改造为 HOV 车道,为了满足交叉口交通流中右转车辆交通需求,将外侧车道临近交叉口部分改善为通用车道,外侧设置 HOV 车道的示意图如图 1b)所示。

综上所述,在我国城市快速路中 HOV 车道的设置位置,影响着合乘车辆的交通效率。下文研究了量化两种 HOV 车道的交通效率方法,可以用此来比较两种方案在交通效率上的优劣。

2 运行时间计算模型

在研究 HOV 车道因设置位置不同而导致的交通运行特征不同的基础上,各自分析方案的交通效率。考虑到交通效率与交通运行时间息息相关,故在交通效率建模时,以交通运行时间为主。为了便于计算交通运行时间,将道路分段划分,假设在路段存在 n 个交叉口,则将路段划分为 $2n+1$ 个路段,路段编号规则如图2所示。

a)内侧设置HOV车道

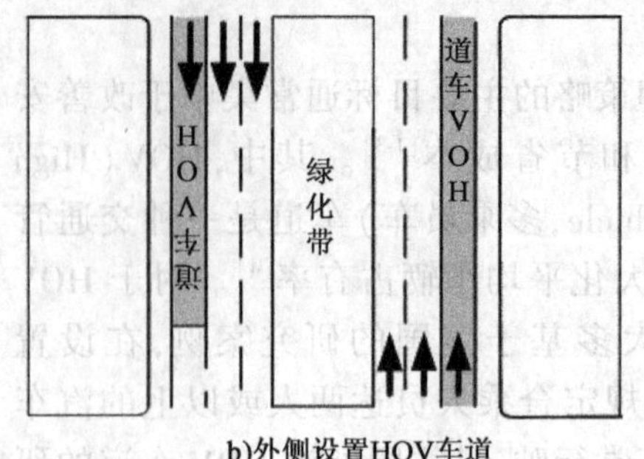

b)外侧设置HOV车道

图1　HOV车道设置位置图

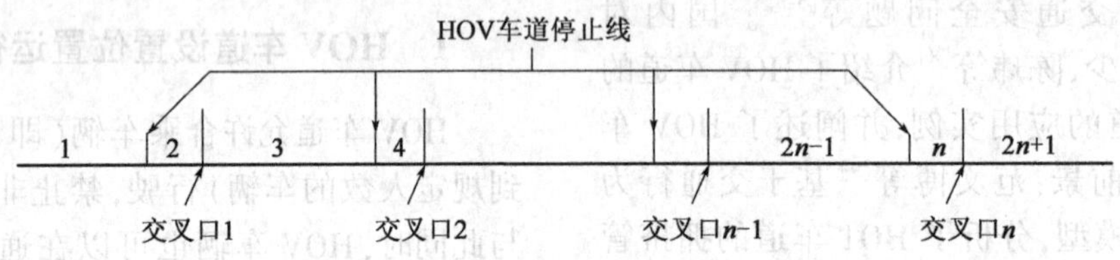

图2　HOV路段编号规则

2.1　内侧HOV车道

如若内侧设置HOV车道,在临近交叉口附近,左转车辆会驶入内侧通用车道,并受信号灯控制,此时内侧车道为直行和左转车道,车辆组成为合乘车辆和左转车辆,在中间车道的交通组成为直行非合乘车辆和部分由HOV车道分流的合乘车辆。本文采用BPR函数用于计算运行时间,BPR基本函数表达式如式1所示:

$$t = t_0\left[1 + \alpha\left(\frac{Q}{C}\right)^{\beta}\right] \tag{1}$$

其中,t 为当前交通流量下车辆通过路段的行程时间;t_0 为车辆自由流通过路段的时间;C 为路段通行能力;Q 为路段车流量;α、β 为待定系数。

在道路内侧设置HOV车道时,合乘车辆的运行时间为所有路段的运行时间之和,与此同时,路段是由一段HOV车道和一段直行左转车道组成,故将两车道的运行时间表示如下:

$$t_n = \frac{L_n}{V_n}\left[1 + \alpha\left(\frac{Q_i}{C_i}\right)^{\beta}\right], i = \begin{cases}\text{HOV} \\ n - \text{HOV}\end{cases} \tag{2}$$

其中,t_n 为合乘车辆通过第 n 个路段的行程时间;L_n 为第 n 个路段的长度;V_n 为第 n 个路段的自由流速度;Q_i 为车道 i 的交通流量;C_i 为车道 i 的道路通行能力;α、β 为待定系数。

由上述计算可知,精准计算车道 i 的道路通行能力是一项重要工作。文献[17]等计算直行左转通行能力的计算方法得出:

$$C_{sl} = \frac{3600}{t_c}\left(\frac{t_g - t_1}{t_{is}} + 1\right) \times \varphi \times \left(1 - \frac{\beta_1}{2}\right) \tag{3}$$

其中,C_{sl} 为直行左转车道的通行能力;t_c 为信号灯周期时间;t_g 为信号灯周期内绿灯时间;t_1 为绿灯开始时直行车辆通过停车线的反应时间,通常取2.3s;t_{is} 为车辆通过停车线的车头时距;φ 为折减系数,通常取0.9;β_1 为直行左转车道中左转车辆比例。

合乘车辆的运行时间是所有路段运行时间之和,表达式如下:

$$t_{\text{HOV}} = \sum_{i=1}^{2n+1} t_i \tag{4}$$

其中,t_{HOV} 为合乘车辆通过路段的行程时间;t_i 为合乘车辆通过第 i 个路段的时间。

2.2　外侧HOV车道

如若外侧设置HOV车道,在临近交叉口,右转车辆会驶入外侧通用车道,但不受到信号灯控制,可即时通行,但直行的合乘车辆受到信号灯控制,在停车线前停车等待。在交叉口附近外侧设置成为HOV车道的运行效率明显优于内侧设置为HOV车道,但受我国机非混行的影响,如若在道路外侧设置HOV车道,在路段上合乘车辆的运行会受到非机动车违规行驶影响,运行速度降低,通行能力下降,与此同时,外侧设置HOV车道的路段运行时间增长。外侧设置HOV车道的运行时间主要由路段运行时间、交叉口运行时间、交叉口等待时间组成。

路段外侧设置 HOV 车道,合乘车辆的路段运行时间和交叉口运行时间可表示为:

$$t_n = \frac{L_n}{V_n}\left[1 + \alpha\left(\frac{Q_i}{C_i}\right)^{\beta}\right], i = \begin{cases} \text{HOV} \\ n - \text{HOV} \end{cases} \quad (5)$$

其中,t_n 为合乘车辆通过第 n 个路段的行程时间;L_n 为第 n 个路段的长度;V_n 为第 n 个路段的自由流速度;Q_i 为车道 i 的交通流量;C_i 为车道 i 的道路通行能力;α、β 为待定系数。

在交叉口处的直行右转车道中因右转车辆可直接转入交叉口,对直行车辆影响较小,故直行右转车道的通行能力与直行车道的通行能力一致。在路段中 HOV 车道的道路通行能力可表示为:

$$C_{\text{HOV}} = N_0 \times \gamma \times \eta \times C \times n' \quad (6)$$

其中,C_{HOV} 为 HOV 车道的道路通行能力;N_0 为道路理论通行能力;γ 为自行车影响修正系数;η 为车道宽度影响修正系数;C 为交叉口影响修正系数;n' 为车道数修正系数;

合乘车辆的运行时间是所有路段运行时间之和,表达式如下:

$$t_{\text{HOV}} = \sum_{i=1}^{2n+1} t_i \quad (7)$$

其中,t_{HOV} 为合乘车辆通过路段的行程时间;t_i 为合乘车辆通过第 i 个路段的时间。

3 实例分析

以西安市南三环某段为例,全长共计 11km,设计速度为60km/h,存在 5 个交叉口共组成了 11 个路段,车道宽度 3.5m,并按上述编号方法编号 1-11,据《城市道路交叉口规划规范》(GB 50647—2011),HOV 车道的停止线距离交叉口 100m,以供转弯车辆完成换道行为,据早高峰 7:00—9:00,实际调查,合乘车辆占比 28%,总流量为 2342pcu/h,交叉口左、右转流量占比均为 10%。

3.1 内侧设置 HOV 车道

通过计算得出,路段中 HOV 车道的道路通行能力为 1080pcu/h,交叉口直左车道的通行能力为 940pcu/h,则合乘车辆在路段行驶的时间:

$$t'_{\text{HOV}} = t_1 + t_3 + t_5 + t_7 + t_9 + t_{11} = 643\text{s}$$

合乘车辆在交叉口附近通用车道的行驶时间:

$$t^*_{\text{HOV}} = t_2 + t_4 + t_6 + t_8 + t_{10} = 100\text{s}$$

则如在内侧设置 HOV 车道,合乘车辆通过此路段需要消耗:

$$t_{\text{HOV}} = \sum_{i=1}^{2n+1} t_i = 743\text{s}$$

3.2 外侧设置 HOV 车道

如若外侧设置 HOV 车道,在运行过程中会受到非机动车影响,则通过计算得出路段中 HOV 车道的道路通行能力为 864pcu/h,则合乘车辆在路段行驶的时间:

$$t'_{\text{HOV}} = t_1 + t_3 + t_5 + t_7 + t_9 + t_{11} = 661\text{s}$$

合乘车辆在交叉口附近通用车道的行驶时间:

$$t^*_{\text{HOV}} = t_2 + t_4 + t_6 + t_8 + t_{10} = 105\text{s}$$

则如在内侧设置 HOV 车道,合乘车辆通过此路段需要消耗:

$$t_{\text{HOV}} = \sum_{i=1}^{2n+1} t_i = 766\text{s}$$

综上所述,在此种交通条件下,内侧设置 HOV 车道的交通效率比右外设置 HOV 车道的交通效率高,如若在内侧设置 HOV 车道,每辆车的平均运行时间减少 23s,在交通系统中,HOV 车道的交通运行效率会大大提高。

4 结语

(1)本文以首先分析了内外侧设置 HOV 车道交通运行特性,根据交通运行特性研究,发现内外侧设置 HOV 车道的交通效率方面有些不同,故对内外侧设置 HOV 车道的交通效率展开研究。

(2)分别建立内外侧 HOV 车道的交通效率模型,并提供了交通效率的研究方法,为未来交通效率研究提供参考方法。并以西安市南三环的实际道路为对象展开研究,得出结论:在此种交通条件下,适宜在道路左侧设置 HOV 车道,为城市快速路内外侧设置 HOV 车道的条件提供参考。

(3)在设置 HOV 车道时,需要考虑的因素众多,目前仅从交通效率的角度出发研究了设置 HOV 车道的位置条件,后续可综合考虑交通安全、交通效率、土地利用等方面进行综合研究。

参考文献

[1] Barth M, Boriboonsomsin K. Energy and emissions impacts of a freeway-based dynamic eco-driving system[J]. Transportation Research Part D: Transport and Environment, 2009, 14

(6):400-410.

[2] Gkritza K, Karlaftis M G. Intelligent transportation systems applications for the environment and energy conservation (part 2)[J]. Journal of Intelligent Transportation Systems, 2013, 17(3):177-178.

[3] Shladover S E. Challenges to evaluation of CO_2 impacts of intelligent transportation systems[C]//2011 IEEE Forum on Integrated and Sustainable Transportation Systems. IEEE, 2011:189-194.

[4] Zhong L, Zhang K, Nie Y M, et al. Dynamic carpool in morning commute: Role of high-occupancy-vehicle (HOV) and high-occupancy-toll (HOT) lanes[J]. Transportation Research Part B: Methodological, 2020, 135:98-119.

[5] Boriboonsomsin K, Barth M. Impacts of freeway high-occupancy vehicle lane configuration on vehicle emissions[J]. Transportation Research Part D: Transport and Environment, 2008, 13(2):112-125.

[6] Johnston R A, Ceerla R. The effects of new high-occupancy vehicle lanes on travel and emissions[J]. Transportation Research Part A: Policy and Practice, 1996, 30(1):35-50.

[7] Kitali A E, Kidando E, Kutela B, et al. Safety Evaluation of High-Occupancy Toll Facilities Using Bayesian Networks [J]. Journal of Transportation Engineering, Part A: Systems, 2021, 147(5):04021018.

[8] 陈玮,陈白磊.将HOV优先引入我国城市交通规划的管理[J].城市规划,2003(06):93-96.

[9] 范文博.美国高承载率车道拥挤收费方案建模[J].交通运输系统工程与信息,2015,15(3):204-213.

[10] 邓社军,陈峻,李春燕,等.我国城市快速路基本路段HOV车道设置方案研究[J].交通运输工程与信息学报,2013,11(2):11-18.

[11] 韩得利.深圳市HOV车道设置条件及实施效果评估研究[D].北京:中国人民公安大学,2018.

[12] 刘晨阳.公交专用3+合乘共用车道规划设置与优化研究——以大连市软件园路为例[D].大连:大连理工大学,2020.

[13] 王瑜,李勇.基于模糊综合评价的HOV车道综合效益分析[J].公路交通科技,2020,37(9):148-158.

[14] 田丽君,吕成锐,黄文彬.基于累积前景理论的合乘行为建模与研究[J].系统工程理论与实践,2016,36(6):1576-1584.

[15] 况雪.HOV车道选择模型及应用条件研究[D].成都:西南交通大学.2020.

[16] 邵春福,郭润航,董春娇,等.基于HOV理念的公交专用道交通组织优化[J/OL].北京交通大学学报:1-10[2021-12-10].http://kns.cnki.net/kcms/detail/11.5258.U.20210611.0837.002.html.

[17] 王炜.交通工程学[M].南京:东南大学出版社,2000.

Study on Vehicle Lane Changing Trajectory Model in Expressway Diverging area

Junjie Cai[*a] Binghong Pan[b] Lin Zong[a] Zhenjiang Xie[a]

([a]School of Highway, Chang'an University;

[b]Key Laboratory for Special Area Highway Engineering of Ministry of Education)

Abstract Due to its complex process, the lane changing behavior is affected by the driver's behavior characteristics and the interaction behavior with the front and rear vehicles in the lane changing process, and restricted by the data acquisition technology, it is difficult to obtain a large number of micro trajectory data describing the vehicle lane changing behavior. At present, it has not been widely and deeply studied. In order to establish a more accurate vehicle lane changing trajectory model in the expressway diverging area, based on the measured data, this paper uses the quintic polynomial trajectory model, cosine curve lane changing trajectory model, uniform transverse cosine curve model and hyperbolic tangent trajectory model to fit the lane changing vehicle trajectory in the diverging area, and improves the hyperbolic tangent trajectory model. A hyperbolic tangent trajectory width correction model is creatively proposed.

Keywords Expressway Diverging area Lane change behavior Lane change trajectory model

1 Introduction

Lane changing behavior is one of the core driving behaviors in the micro traffic flow model, which controls the lateral movement of vehicles during driving. Vehicle lane change behavior refers to the behavior of vehicles changing from one lane to another. Lane change modeling is the abstraction of this behavior, which is used to simulate and analyze the logical level and influence of lane change behavior. Under certain traffic flow density conditions, frequent and unreasonable lane changing behavior may interfere with the normal driving of surrounding vehicles and cause traffic shock. If the traffic shock spreads upstream under certain conditions, it may produce traffic congestion and threaten the safety of expressway. In addition, the lane change trajectory model is also the basis for establishing the minimum clear distance of expressway interchange. Therefore, vehicle lane changing trajectory is of great significance to study the traffic characteristics and linear indicators of expressway.

Scholars in china and abroad have done some research on vehicle lane changing trajectory. In 1986, Gipps first put forward in the vehicle lane changing model; Based on the Gipps model, Yang and Koutsopoulos divided the lane change behavior into mandatory lane change behavior and arbitrary lane change behavior, and divided the lane change process into four stages: lane change intention, lane selection, finding plausible gap and lane change execution, and established the expressway lane change model; Bin Zhou et al. used the tachograph installed on the taxi to record the vehicle lane change data, extracted the lane lines and angles between the vehicle and both sides in the video, and proposed a vehicle lane change trajectory model based on hyperbolic tangent function to describe the vehicle lane change trajectory. With the continuous progress of data acquisition technology, and researchers gradually realize the importance of real vehicle lane changing trajectory data to the study of lane changing trajectory model, some researchers began to collect detailed vehicle lane changing trajectory data, including speed, acceleration position, steering wheel angle, etc. Zhang Yingda and others selected the data to construct a semi logarithmic model and quintic polynomial model on the basis of smoothing to analyze the micro characteristics of lane changing behavior; Wang Xuesong and others obtained natural driving data through a data acquisition system composed of a radar system, GPS positioning system, three-axis accelerometer and camera to analyze driver lane changing characteristics. However, only a few scholars have studied the detailed lane changing trajectory of vehicles; Pei Yulong et al. use β spline curve reverse algorithm, and simulate the expected trajectory of lane change; Yang Zhigang et al. Proposed a new lane changing model combining the constant velocity migration trajectory model and the sine function lane changing trajectory. Although the above lane change trajectory model can match the data with the modeling results, most of them fit the trajectory data through simple mathematical equations. The model has little correlation with the driver's driving behavior, and the model parameters do not have practical physical significance. In addition, the above research is mainly based on the simulation data, which are difficult to match the actual driving situation, and there are some potential errors.

The vehicle lane changing behavior in the expressway diverging area is the most frequent, and the expressway diverging area is also the accident prone area of the expressway. Research on the vehicle lane changing trajectory model in the expressway diverging area is of great significance for reasonably setting the clear distance of the expressway interchange and ensuring the driving safety of the expressway. Based on the measured data, this paper will study the lane changing trajectory of vehicles in the diverging area of expressway. Firstly, the lane change data in the diverging area are collected by UAV, then the lane change data are extracted by tracker software, and then the lane change data are processed by Kalman filter. Finally, the lane change vehicle trajectory in the diverging area is fitted by quintic polynomial trajectory model, cosine curve type lane change trajectory model, uniform transverse cosine curve model and hyperbolic tangent trajectory model, In order to establish a reasonable vehicle lane changing trajectory model in highway diverging area.

2 Data Acquisition and Processing

In this paper, the diverging area is defined as the section between the exit warning sign and the starting point of the deceleration lane. In order to study the characteristics of vehicle lane changing trajectory in the diverging area of multi lane expressway, this paper uses DJI air 2S UAV to collect the lane changing video data in the diverging area of Baotou Maoming Expressway and Xi' an Ring Expressway (Qujiang interchange and Baqiao Interchange) from 11:00 to 16:00. The collected data sections have adopted interval speed measurement for traffic control, and the traffic signs and markings in the sections are complete, as shown in Fig. 1.

Fig. 1　UAV Shooting Lane Change Video

2.1 Lane changes trajectory data extraction

For the lane change video collected by UAV, the track of vehicle lane change is extracted by tracker software. The processing steps are as follows:

(1) Import captured video data (Fig. 2).

The captured video is divided into several small videos. Each small video contains a complete lane changing process, and the video is imported into tracker software.

(2) Establish coordinate system.

Establish a coordinate system at a reasonable position, which shall be parallel to the lane line.

(3) Setting benchmark.

In order to determine the actual length of the vehicle in the video, the benchmark needs to be determined first. In this paper, a lane width is used as the benchmark.

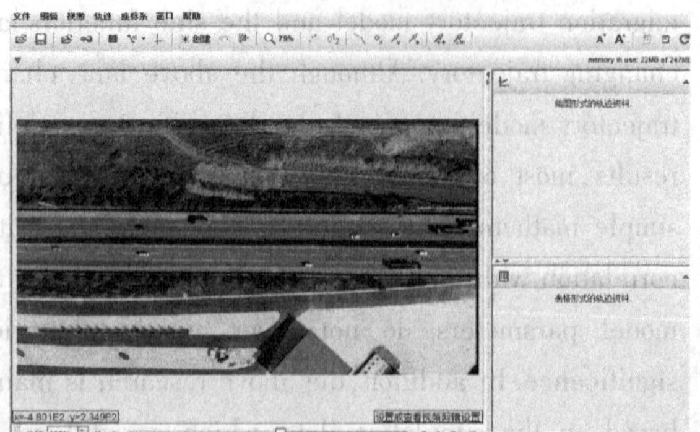

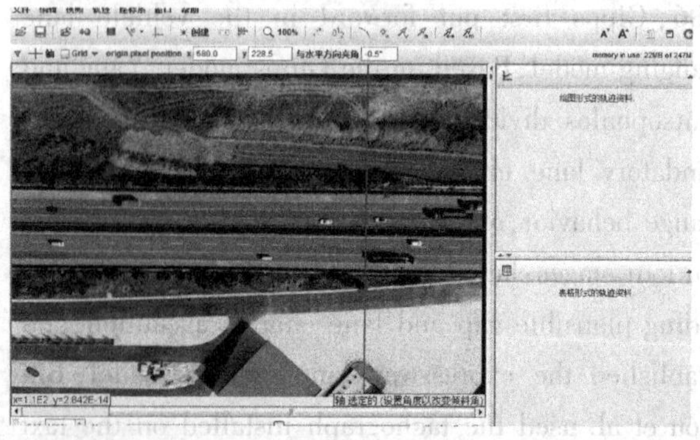

Fig. 2　Import the Captured Video Data and Establish the Coordinate System

(4) Determining particles and tracking objects.

Determine the tracking objects. At present, tracker software provides two tracking methods: automatic tracking and manual tracking. In this paper, two methods are combined for data processing (Fig. 3).

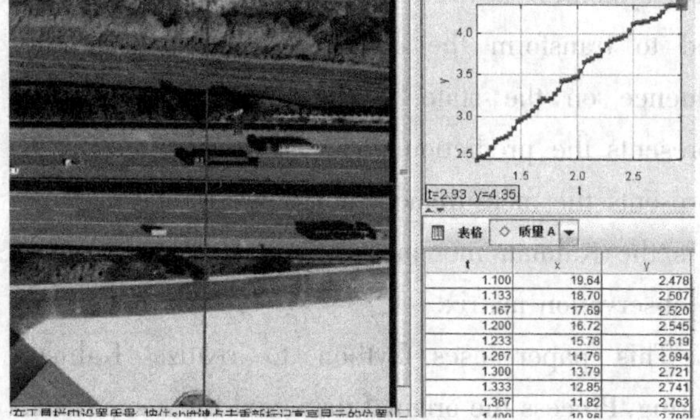

Fig. 3 Trajectory Data

2.2 Data Processing of Lane Changing Trajectory Based on Kalman Filter

The lane change trajectory data extracted by tracker software are an uneven curve, which is determined by the recognition error of the software itself. Therefore, it is particularly important to filter and smooth the trajectory data extracted by tracker software. Filtering is a very important concept in signal processing. The so-called filtering refers to the operation of filtering the specific band frequency in the signal. It is an important measure to prevent interference.

At present, commonly used filters include IIR digital filter, Kalman filter, Wiener filter, Gaussian filter and amplitude limiting filter. IIR digital filter is often used to determine the signal bandwidth, but its computation is large and the result output is unstable; Kalman filtering has a wide range of applications. At present, it has been popularized in many forms, such as "adaptive filtering", relaxing the restriction on noise uncorrelation and approximating nonlinear systems with linear systems; The wiener filter is derived from the spectral decomposition of stationary processes, so it is difficult to be extended to non-stationary processes and multi-dimensional cases, so its application range is narrow; the gaussian filter is suitable for eliminating Gaussian noise and is widely used in the noise reduction process of image processing. It is a kind of linear smoothing filter; Amplitude limiting filtering can effectively overcome the pulse interference caused by accidental factors, but it can not suppress the periodic interference and the smoothness is poor. Considering the advantages and disadvantages of various filters, Kalman filter is selected for lane change trajectory data processing.

Kalman filtering is a linear filtering and prediction method, which was proposed by R. E. Kalman in the 1960s in order to adapt to the development of high-speed electronic computer and solve the technical problems of satellite orbit determination and navigation. The basic assumption is that the estimated process X is the output of a finite order multidimensional linear dynamic system under the influence of random noise, and the observed value Z_k at time k is a partial component of the state X_k at time k or the superposition of its linear function and the measurement noise.

Kalman filtering is divided into two processes: the prediction process and prediction process. The prediction process estimates the current time state based on the previous time state, and the correction process estimates the optimal state by combining the current time state and the observed state.

Kalman filter prediction process:

$$X_k = AX_{k-1} + BX_{k-1} \tag{1}$$

$$E_k = AE_{k-1}A^{\mathrm{T}} + Q \tag{2}$$

Kalman filter correction process:

$$G_k = E_k H^{\mathrm{T}}\ (HE_k H^{\mathrm{T}} + R) - 1 \tag{3}$$

$$X_k = X_k + G_k (Z_k - HX_{k-1}) \tag{4}$$

$$E_k = (1 - G_k H) E_k \tag{5}$$

Where: X_k is the state at time k. A is the state transition matrix, which is related to the specific linear system. B is the input control matrix, which is used to transform the external influence into the influence on the state. E_k is the error matrix. Q represents the prediction noise covariance matrix. R represents the measurement noise covariance matrix. G_k is the Kalman increment at time k. H represents the observation matrix.

This paper uses Python to realize Kalman filtering. Process the original data, and the comparison before and after processing is shown in the Fig. below (Fig. 4).

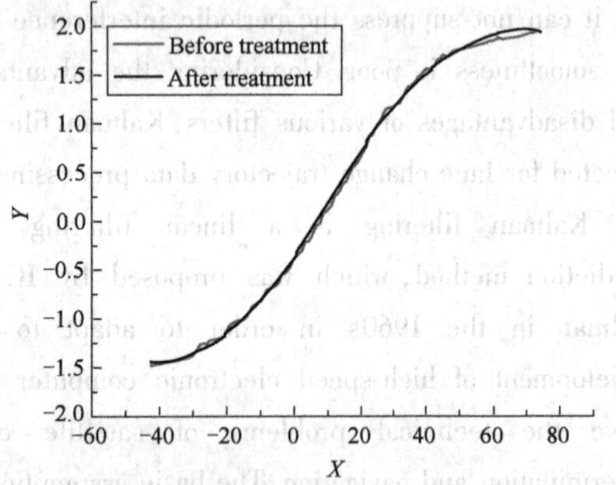

Fig. 4 Data Diagram Before and After Kalman Filtering

2.3 Statistical analysis of sample data of vehicle lane change indiverging area

A total of 143 groups of lane changing samples in the diverging area were collected, including 103 groups of right lane changing vehicles and 40 groups of left lane changing samples. The proportion of right lane changing accounted for 72.03%. It is found that drivers with diversion intention are guided by signs and will choose to change to the outer lane in advance before shunting ramps; in order to pursue higher driving speed and avoid the interference of shunting vehicles, drivers without shunting intention often choose to change lanes to the inner lane. In addition, it is observed that a small number of drivers with diversion intention miss the signboard or cannot complete the lane change in advance due to the large traffic flow on the inner side, so there are certain potential safety hazards at the exit of the interchange.

(1) Sample size.

The sample size depends on the accuracy requirements. In order to ensure the accuracy of the survey, it is necessary to ensure a certain number of samples. In this paper, the formula is used to determine the minimum observation sample size.

$$n = \frac{\sigma^2 \cdot t^2}{E^2}\left(1 + \frac{U^2}{2}\right) \tag{6}$$

Where: n is the minimum observed sample size. σ^2 is the variance of the population. This paper uses point estimation to estimate the parameters and according to the point estimation, $s^2 = \sigma^2$. t is a t-distribution statistic that depends on the confidence level and the degree of freedom. In this paper, the confidence level $\alpha = 0.05$. When the sample size is greater than 120, $t = 1.96$. E represents the required accuracy value of observation parameters, which can range from ± 8.0km/h ~ ± 1.6 or less. U is a constant determined by the required statistical type, and its value is selected according to the Tab. 1.

Value Tab. of γ Tab. 1

Percentile speed	Average velocity	15% Speed/85% Speed	5% Speed/95% Speed
γ	0.00	1.04	1.64

In this paper, the variance DX of vehicle speed is estimated by using the measured data and the point estimator s^2, and $s^2 = 140.63$ is obtained. The accuracy of vehicle speed is taken as $E = 2$ km/h. The minimum observation sample size of vehicle average speed is 136, and the sample number meets the minimum sample size requirements.

(2) Shapiro Wilk sample normality test based on Python.

Testing whether the observation data obey the normal distribution is called the normality test. The commonly used normality tests include Shapiro wilktest method, skewness kurtosis test method and Kolmogorov test method. This paper uses Python programming and Shapiro Wilk method to test the normality of samples. Shapiro wilktest test, also known as W test, mainly tests whether the research object conforms to the normal distribution. The inspection steps are as follows:

① Put forward a hypothesis and establish a hypothesis test. The sample data accord with normal distribution.

②The observed values of n samples are arranged from small to large:

$$x_{(1)} \leqslant x_{(2)} \leqslant \cdots \leqslant x_{(i)} \leqslant \cdots \leqslant x_{(n)} \tag{7}$$

③Construct the test statistics and calculate the statistical indexes of Shapiro wilktest normality test:

$$W = \left(\sum_{i=1}^{n} a_i x_{(i)} \right)^2 \Big/ \sum_{i=1}^{n} (x_{(i)} - \bar{x})^2 \tag{8}$$

$$a = (a_1, \cdots, a_i, \cdots, a_n) = \frac{m^{\mathrm{T}} K^{-1}}{C} \tag{9}$$

$$C = \| K^{-1} m \| = (m^{\mathrm{T}} K^{-1} K^{-1} m) \tag{10}$$

Where: W is the statistical indicator. $\bar{x}$ is the sample mean. $\left(\sum_{i=1}^{n} a_i x_{(i)} \right)^2$ is the best linear unbiased estimate of $(n-1)\sigma^2$; And σ is the standard deviation of the sample from the normal distribution; K is the covariance matrix, which belongs to the order statistics of random variables with standard normal distribution. m is the vector of expectations of these variables. C is the vector norm.

④ Considering the alternative hypothesis, the small probability event is constructed and the rejection domain is obtained. Set a certain significance level α, and then obtain its quantile or critical value W_{α}. If $W < W_{\alpha}$, reject H_0, otherwise accept H_0.

This paper implements Shapiro wilktest normality test based on python programming. Take the confidence level $\alpha = 0.05$. If P-value is greater than 0.05, the original hypothesis cannot be rejected, that is, the data conforms to the normal distribution. In this paper, it is calculated that p-value = 0.096, which is greater than 0.05, so the average velocity data conforms to the normal distribution. The Shapiro Wilk method is used to test the normality of lane change duration, lane change length and lane change width. The results show that the lane change duration, lane change length and lane change width accordance with the normal distribution (Fig. 5).

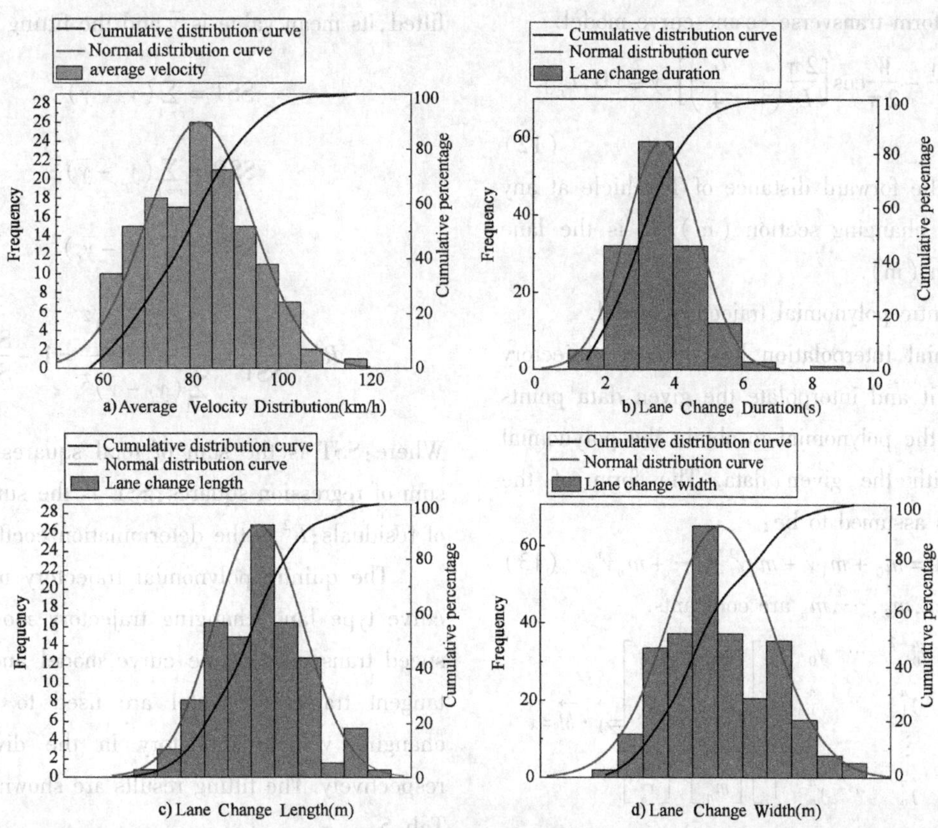

Fig. 5 Sample Normality Test

3 Lane Changing Trajectory Fitting of the Left Lane Changing Vehicles in Diverging Area

3.1 Introduction to Common Lane Change Trajectory Models

(1) Cosine curve lane changing trajectory model.

The trajectory curvature and lateral acceleration of cosine curve lane changing trajectory model change continuously, and the trajectory is smooth without abrupt points. In addition, its calculation method is simple and easy to operate. Therefore, cosine model is widely used in many lane changing models. The expression is as follows:

$$x(t)=\frac{W}{2}\left[1-\cos\left(\frac{t}{T}\pi\right)\right]-\frac{W}{2},0\leqslant t\leqslant T \quad (11)$$

Where: $x(t)$ represents the transverse position of the vehicle relative to the lane line at any time (m). T represents the time required for a vehicle lane change, i. e. lane change time (s). W is the width of vehicle lane change (m).

(2) Uniform transverse cosine curve model.

$$x(t)=\frac{Wy}{L_c}-\frac{W}{2\pi}\cos\left[\frac{2\pi}{L_c}\left(y-\frac{L_c}{4}\right)\right],y\in[0,L_c] \quad (12)$$

Where: y is the forward distance of T vehicle at any time in lane changing section (m). L_c is the lane change length (m).

(3) Quintic polynomial trajectory model.

Polynomial interpolation lane change trajectory model is to fit and interpolate the given data points according to the polynomial to obtain the polynomial consistent with the given data. The form of the polynomial is assumed to be:

$$p(y)=m_0+m_1y+m_2y^2+\cdots+m_ny^n \quad (13)$$

Where $m_0,m_1,m_2,\cdots,m_n$ are constants.

$$\begin{bmatrix} y_0^n & y_0^{n-1} & y_0^{n-2} & \cdots & y_0 & 1 \\ y_1^n & y_1^n & y_1^n & \cdots & y_1^n & 1 \\ \vdots & \vdots & \vdots & & \vdots & \vdots \\ y_n^n & y_n^n & y_n^n & \cdots & y_n^n & 1 \end{bmatrix}\begin{bmatrix} m_0 \\ m_1 \\ \vdots \\ m_n \end{bmatrix}=\begin{bmatrix} x_0 \\ x_1 \\ \vdots \\ x_n \end{bmatrix}\Rightarrow \vec{y}\cdot\vec{M}=\vec{x} \quad (14)$$

(4) Hyperbolic tangent trajectory model.

The hyperbolic tangent model uses the hyperbolic tangent function to describe the lateral position of the lane change, and its lane change trajectory model is:

$$x(t)=\frac{W}{2}\tanh\left[\frac{\tau}{T}\cdot\left(t-\frac{T}{2}\right)\right]+\frac{x_0+x_{-1}}{2},0\leqslant t\leqslant T \quad (15)$$

Where: x_0 and x_{-1} respectively represent the transverse position of the vehicle relative to the lane line at the beginning and end of the vehicle lane change track (m); τ is the emergency coefficient, indicating the emergency degree of lane change. The greater its value, the more urgent the lane change.

3.2 Lane Changing Trajectory Fitting of the Left Lane Changing Vehicles in Diverging Area

Goodness of fit refers to the fitting degree of the regression line to the observed value, and the statistic to measure the goodness of fit is the determination coefficient R^2. Assuming that x is the value to be fitted, its mean value is $\bar{y}$ and the fitting value is y:

$$\text{SST}=\sum_{i=1}^{n}(y_i-\bar{y})^2 \quad (16)$$

$$\text{SSR}=\sum_{i=1}^{n}(y_i-\bar{y})^2 \quad (17)$$

$$\text{SSE}=\sum_{i=1}^{n}(y_i-\bar{y}_i)^2 \quad (18)$$

$$R^2=\frac{\text{SSR}}{\text{SST}}=\frac{\sum_{i=1}^{n}(\bar{y}_i-\bar{y})^2}{\sum_{i=1}^{n}(y_i-\bar{y})^2}=1-\frac{\text{SSE}}{\text{SST}} \quad (19)$$

Where: SST is the sum of total squares; SSR is the sum of regression squares; SSE is the sum of squares of residuals; R^2 is the determination coefficient

The quintic polynomial trajectory model, cosine curve type lane changing trajectory model, constant speed transverse cosine curve model and hyperbolic tangent trajectory model are used to fit the lane changing vehicle trajectory in the diverging area respectively. The fitting results are shown in Tab. 2 ~ Tab. 5.

Fitting Results of Uniform Transverse Cosine Curve Model Tab. 2

Lane change direction	Sample number	SSE	SST	R^2	$E(R^2)$
Right lane change	1	2.7362	30.3697	0.9099	0.8236
	2	5.5002	69.5231	0.9209	
	3	2.7361	30.3697	0.8985	
	⋮	⋮	⋮	⋮	
	102	1.0932	9.1082	0.8800	
	103	4.7439	39.5898	0.8802	
	104	9.0259	30.5188	0.7042	
Left lane change	1	0.9371	7.2766	0.8712	0.8413
	2	4.3484	35.7263	0.8783	
	3	1.2755	13.0671	0.9024	
	⋮	⋮	⋮	⋮	
	39	0.4964	33.6030	0.9852	
	40	3.0073	12.7128	0.7634	
	41	19.4850	87.6994	0.7778	

Fitting Results of Uniform Transverse Cosine Curve Model Tab. 3

Lane change direction	Sample number	SSE	SST	R^2	$E(R^2)$
Right lane change	1	0.1068	2.4576	0.9565	0.9980
	2	0.0139	17.2401	0.9992	
	3	0.0536	30.3697	0.9982	
	⋮	⋮	⋮	⋮	
	102	0.0820	8.8695	0.9908	
	103	0.0354	67.8106	0.9994	
	104	0.1424	88.6832	0.9984	
Left lane change	1	0.1839	5.3771	0.9658	0.9879
	2	3.4442	73.2423	0.9530	
	3	0.0128	15.7072	0.9992	
	⋮	⋮	⋮	⋮	
	39	0.0035	7.2766	0.9995	
	40	0.2448	13.0671	0.9813	
	41	0.0009	11.9123	0.9999	

Fitting Results of Cosine Curve Type Lane Change Trajectory Model Tab. 4

Lane change direction	Sample number	SSE	SST	R^2	$E(R^2)$
Right lane change	1	0.2899	17.2401	0.9832	0.8796
	2	1.2005	30.3697	0.9605	
	3	3.9091	30.3048	0.8710	
	⋮	⋮	⋮	⋮	
	102	6.0475	39.9575	0.8487	
	103	1.0265	5.0303	0.7959	
	104	4.3389	67.8107	0.9360	

continue

Lane change direction	Sample number	SSE	SST	R^2	E(R^2)
Left lane change	1	9.4535	73.2423	0.8709	0.8832
	2	13.3732	87.6994	0.8475	
	3	1.7272	35.7263	0.9517	
	⋮	⋮	⋮	⋮	
	39	0.4119	7.2766	0.9434	
	40	1.1404	14.1858	0.9196	
	41	2.3133	15.3006	0.8488	

Fitting Results of Hyperbolic Tangent Trajectory Model Tab. 5

Lane change direction	Sample number	R^2	τ	E(R^2)
Right lane change	1	0.9935	2.98	0.9140
	2	0.9824	2.75	
	3	0.9719	3.07	
	⋮	⋮	⋮	
	102	0.9862	2.5	
	103	0.8313	2.72	
	104	0.9538	2.70	
Left lane change	1	0.9882	2.45	0.9106
	2	0.8934	2.87	
	3	0.8755	2.74	
	⋮	⋮	⋮	
	39	0.9895	2.53	
	40	0.9370	3	
	41	0.9879	2.48	

3.3 Establishment of Hyperbolic Tangent Trajectory Width Correction Model

Through the fitting of vehicle lane changing trajectory, it is concluded that the determination coefficient R^2 of each model fitting is as follows: Quintic polynomial trajectory model fitting model > hyperbolic tangent trajectory model > cosine curve lane changing trajectory model > uniform transverse cosine curve model. Compared with the fitting model of quintic polynomial trajectory model, the parameters of the hyperbolic tangent trajectory model have clear physical significance, so the hyperbolic tangent trajectory model has high applicability for the fitting of vehicle lane changing trajectory in the confluence area.

However, in the process of fitting the lane change trajectory in the confluence area through the hyperbolic tangent trajectory model, we find that the lane change width of the fitted trajectory is not equal to the measured data due to the existence of the emergency coefficient τ.

In order to make the lane changing width fitted by the fitting model equal to the lane changing width of the measured data, the width correction coefficient is introduced to modify the hyperbolic tangent trajectory model. Finally, the hyperbolic tangent trajectory width correction model is obtained:

$$x(t) = \frac{W}{2\alpha}\tanh\left[\frac{\tau}{T}\left(t - \frac{T}{2}\right)\right] + \frac{x_0 + x_{-1}}{2}, 0 \leqslant t \leqslant T \tag{20}$$

Bring $t = 0$ and $t = T$ into the above formula to obtain the transverse position of the vehicle relative to the lane line at the beginning and end of the fitting lane change track:

$$x(0)=\frac{W}{2\alpha}\tanh\left(-\frac{\tau}{2}\right)+\frac{x_0+x_{-1}}{2} \quad (21)$$

$$x(T)=\frac{W}{2\alpha}\tanh\left(\frac{\tau}{2}\right)+\frac{x_0+x_{-1}}{2} \quad (22)$$

Subtract the above two formulas to obtain the model fitting lane change width W_1, and use the model fitting lane change width equal to the actual lane change width to solve the width correction coefficient α:

$$W_1=x(T)-x(0)=\frac{W\tanh\left(\frac{\tau}{2}\right)}{\alpha}=W \quad (23)$$

$$\alpha=\tanh\left(\frac{\tau}{2}\right) \quad (24)$$

Where: α is the width correction coefficient, which modifies the measured data to ensure that the lane change width conforms to the reality.

The hyperbolic tangent trajectory width correction model is used to fit the lane change trajectory data in the confluence area. The results are shown in Tab. 6.

Through fitting, it can be found that the hyperbolic tangent trajectory width correction model not only corrects the lane changing width problem in the hyperbolic tangent trajectory model, but also has higher goodness of fit than the hyperbolic tangent trajectory model. Therefore, this paper uses the hyperbolic tangent trajectory width correction model as the lane changing model of vehicles in the confluence area (Fig. 6).

Fitting Results of Hyperbolic Tangent Trajectory Width Correction Model Tab. 6

Lane change direction	Sample number	R^2	α	τ	E(R^2)
Right lane change	1	0.9967	0.7595	1.99	0.9230
	2	0.9897	0.6169	1.44	
	3	0.9745	0.7969	2.18	
	⋮	⋮	⋮	⋮	
	102	0.9856	0.6230	1.46	
	103	0.9969	0.4621	1	
	104	0.8366	0.5979	1.38	
Left lane change	1	0.9977	0.4621	1	0.8259
	2	0.8886	0.7397	1.9	
	3	0.9792	0.8617	2.6	
	⋮	⋮	⋮	⋮	
	39	0.9751	0.4621	1	
	40	0.9415	0.7615	2	
	41	0.9971	0.4621	1	

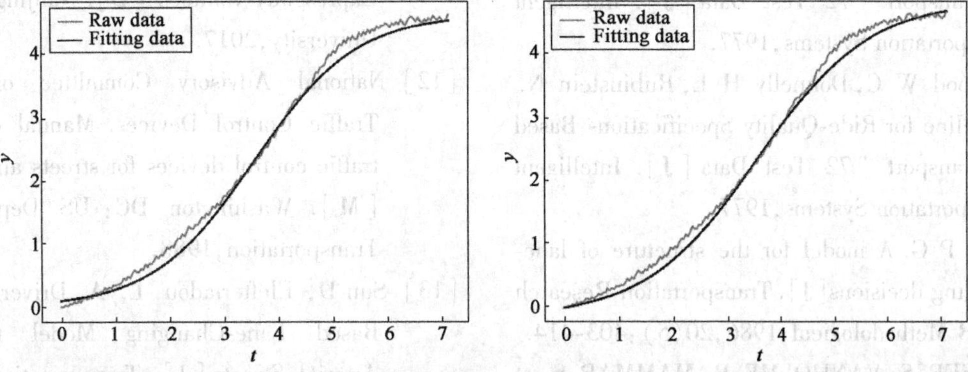

Fig. 6 Fitting Results of Hyperbolic Tangent Trajectory Model and Hyperbolic Tangent Trajectory Correction Model

4 Conclusions

Based on the measured data, this paper establishes the vehicle lane changing trajectory model in the diverging area.

(1) The video of lane change trajectory in expressway diverging area is taken by UAV, the lane change data is extracted by tracker software, and the normality of the samples is tested by Shapiro Wilk method.

(2) Through the quintic polynomial trajectory model, cosine curve type lane changing trajectory model, uniform transverse cosine curve model and hyperbolic tangent trajectory model, the lane changing vehicle trajectory in the diversion flow area is fitted. In the fitting process, the shortcomings of the hyperbolic tangent trajectory model are creatively found, the hyperbolic tangent trajectory model is modified, and the hyperbolic tangent trajectory width correction model is established . The results show that the hyperbolic tangent trajectory width correction model can better fit the vehicle lane change model in the diverging area of expressway.

(3) Only two expressways are collected for lane change trajectory sample data, the data sample size is small, and the universality of research scope and conclusion is limited. In future research, it is necessary to increase the data collection scope and sample size.

References

[1] Caywood W C, Donnelly H L, Rubinstein N. Guideline for Ride-Quality Specifications Based on Transport '72 Test Data [J]. Intelligent Transportation Systems, 1977.

[2] Caywood W C, Donnelly H L, Rubinstein N. Guideline for Ride-Quality Specifications Based on Transport '72 Test Data [J]. Intelligent Transportation Systems, 1977.

[3] Gipps P G. A model for the structure of lane-changing decisions[J]. Transportation Research Part B Methodological, 1986, 20(5): 403-414.

[4] GLASER S, VANHOLME B, MAMMAR S, et al. Maneuver-based trajectory planning for highly autonomous vehicles on real road with traffic and driver interaction [J]. IEEE Transactions on Intelligent Transportation Systems, 2010, 11(3): 589-606.

[5] GLASER S, VANHOLME B, MAMMAR S, et al. Maneuver-based trajectory planning for highly autonomous vehicles on real road with traffic and driver interaction [J]. IEEE Transactions on Intelligent Transportation Systems, 2010, 11(3): 589-606.

[6] Hou H. Research on recognition method of Expressway driver's lane changing intention [D]. Changchun: Jilin University, 2013.

[7] Keyvan-Ekbatani M, Knoop V, Daamen, W. Categorization of the lane change decision process on freeways [J]. Transportation Research Part C: Emerging Technologies, 2016, 69.

[8] Khattak A J, Khattak A J, Council F M. Effects of work zone presence on injury and non-injury crashes. [J]. Accid Anal Prev, 2002, 34(1): 19-29.

[9] Lin Z. West German specification for highway facilities (RAL), Part II, Chapter I, linear elements (ral-l-1) [J]. Sino foreign highway, 1978 (2).

[10] Lu J, Li Y. Review and Prospect of vehicle lane changing behavior modeling [J]. Transportation system engineering and information, 2017, 17 (04): 48-55.

[11] Nie Jianqiang Research on Modeling of autonomous lane changing behavior of Expressway vehicles [D]. Nanjing: Southeast University, 2017.

[12] National Advisory Committee on Uniform Traffic Control Devices. Manual on uniform traffic control devices for streets and highways [M]. Washington DC: US Department of Transportation, 1988.

[13] Sun D, Elefteriadou L. A Driver Behavior-Based Lane-Changing Model for Urban Arterial Streets [J]. Transportation Science, 2014, 48(2): 184-205.

[14] Salvucci D, Liu A. The time course of a lane change: Driver control and eye-movement behavior[J]. Transportation Research Part F Traffic Psychology & Behavior, 2002, 5(2): 123-132.

[15] Salvucci D, Liu A. The time course of a lane change: Driver control and eye-movement behavior[J]. Transportation Research Part F Traffic Psychology & Behavior, 2002, 5(2): 123-132.

[16] Tang J, Yu S, Liu F, Chen X, Huang H. A hierarchical prediction model for lane-changes based on combination of fuzzy C-means and adaptive neural network[J]. Expert Systems with Applications, 2019, 130.

[17] Wang Zh, Sun B, Sui W. Research on the current situation of road design in Japan [M]. Hefei: Hefei University of Technology Press, 2016.

[18] Yuan W, Fu R, Guo Y, et al Driver's lane changing intention recognition based on visual characteristics [J]. Chinese Journal of highway, 2013, 26(04): 132-138.

[19] Yang Q I, Koutsopoulos H N. A Microscopic Traffic Simulator for evaluation of dynamic traffic management systems[J]. Transportation Research Part C Emerging Technologies, 1996, 4(3): 113-129.

自动驾驶条件下城市道路横断面优化设计探讨

宋 欣[1] 梁昌征[2] 张 震[3] 张志清*[1]

(1. 北京工业大学城市交通学院;2. 中国城市规划设计研究院)

摘 要 自动驾驶将会在一定条件下改善道路的通行效率,从而影响道路横断面的设计。文章运用交通流仿真技术,在自动驾驶车辆不同比例条件下,对单车道交通流通行能力和运行速度进行预测分析。从车道宽度和通行能力的角度,分析自动驾驶对城市道路横断面设计的影响。研究表明:自动驾驶对城市主干路横断面设计影响较大,在相同的交通条件下,当自动驾驶比例为50%时,可使双向八车道优化为双向六车道;当自动驾驶比例达到70%时,可使双向六车道优化为双向四车道。可见,随着自动驾驶技术的实现,将会提高城市主干路通行效率,缓解主干路横断面空间不足的矛盾。研究成果可对未来城市道路规划提供参考。

关键词 公路工程 自动驾驶 交通流仿真 通行能力 横断面

0 引言

随着自动驾驶技术发展,未来城市交通流将变为由自动驾驶车辆和传统车辆组成的混合行驶交通流。自动驾驶车辆先进的感知、控制等技术使得其与传统车辆相比具有更小的反应时间和车头间距,这将导致城市交通流特性发生较大变化[1]。横断面作为承担城市交通流的空间载体,其布置形式应与城市交通流特性的发展相适应[2]。因此,有必要对自动驾驶条件下城市道路横断面的优化设计进行研究。

合理预测自动驾驶条件下的交通流特性是横断面设计的基础。国内外关于自动驾驶混合交通特性的研究主要以构建仿真模型,进行交通流仿真实验为主,大多数研究表明自动驾将会明显改变道路的运行速度和通行能力[3-7],从而影响道路横断面的布置。Friedrich、Steven 等的研究表明通过自动驾驶通过实现车距精确控制与车队化运行,可将单车道通行能力最高提升100%,机动车道数的需求将缩减一半,且自动驾驶带来的平稳空间将缩减单车道宽[8]。Alessandrini 的研究认为自动驾驶车辆对道路宽度和停车空间的需求较小,

1. 基金支持:国家自然科学基金项目(52178403)。

在横断面设计时可以缩减机动车行道宽度,取消路侧停车带,用于慢行交通空间的建设[9]。洛杉矶 Wilshire 街区完成了全球首例基于无人驾驶汽车的街道空间概念设计,在研究了无人驾驶私家车和公交车的运输能力的基础上,对横断面宽度进行了充分分配。周明妮从行为学的角度分析了目前和未来城市多模式出行的行为特征,提出了与城市多模式交通出行需求相适应的主干路横断面布置形式[10]。刘凯在总结目前街道设计和自动驾驶相关研究的基础上,就未街道设计中安全设计、车道设置等多个关键问题展开研究[11]。王维礼基于人机混合驾驶环境下交通流变化特征,提出了适宜人机混合驾驶环境的城市主干路横断面空间设计方案[12]。

目前,国内外关于自动驾驶对交通流特性影响的研究呈现出不同观点,而考虑自动驾驶横断面设计的相关研究仅对自动驾驶混合交通特性进行了定性分析,研究成果较为主观。因此,本文将以单车道混合交通流元胞仿真模型为基础进行仿真实验,从速度和通行能力角度定量分析自动驾驶对横断面设计的影响,并基于分析结果对典型横断面进行优化设计。结果表明:自动驾驶将会改变道路断面通行效率,优化城市道路空间,可为未来城市道路规划提供参考。

1　混合交通流运行特性

1.1　单车道混合流仿真模型

自动驾驶车辆与手动驾驶车辆相比具有更小的反应时间和车头间距,本文选择可以同时描述反应时间和车头间距的 GIPPS 安全距离模型,结合经典的 Nagle-Schreckenberg 交通流元胞模型,以设计速度为 60km/h 的城市交通性主干路为研究对象,建立单车道混合交通流元胞自动机模型,依托 MATLAB 进行仿真实验。

GIPPS 安全距离模型认为,在车流运行过程中,后车为了避免在前车紧急制动时与其发生碰撞必须保持的一个安全车距,并选择一个安全车速来保证车辆间距不能小于安全车距。该模型对安全距离的严格约束与自动驾驶车辆对交通安全的高要求相契合,因此采用 GIPPS 安全距离模型对 N-S 模型进行改进[13],并以此制定车辆的速度、纵向位置演化规则。

$$\begin{aligned}\mathrm{Gap}_s &= x_{n+1}(t) - x_n(t) - s \\ &= v_n(t)\tau + \frac{v_n(t)^2}{2b_m} - \frac{v_{n+1}(t)^2}{2b_m}\end{aligned} \tag{1}$$

$$v_s(t) = -b_m\tau + \sqrt{b_m\tau^2 + b_m\left\{2[x_{n+1}(t) - x_n(t) - s] - \tau v_n(t) + \frac{v_{n+1}^2(t)}{b_m}\right\}} \tag{2}$$

1.2　仿真模型验证

为验证交通流仿真模型的准确性,对自动驾驶车辆比例为0%时的交通流仿真结果与理论计算结果进行对比分析。如图1所示,在流量密度图中,交通流量最大值代表在理想的道路和交通条件下,单车道所能通过的最大车辆数,即单车道基准通行能力。

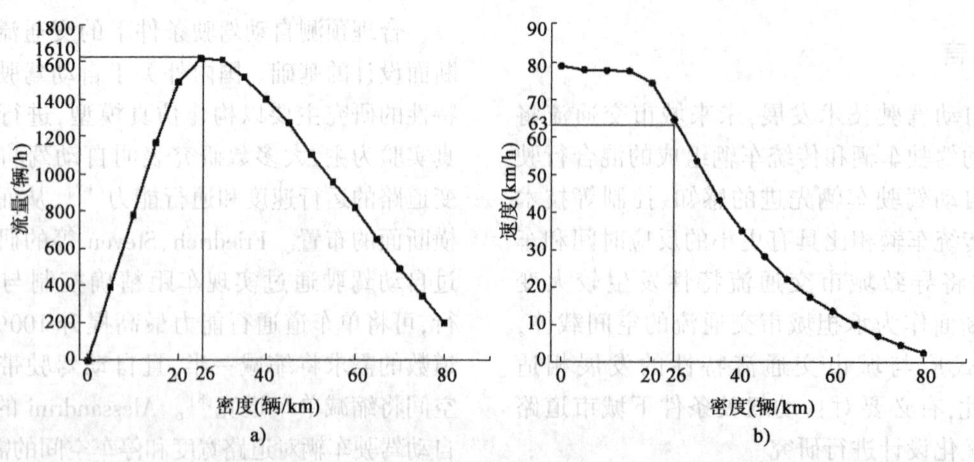

图1　流量-密度-速度图(0%)

如图 1a)中交通流仿真结果所示,交通密度在 26 辆/km 时单车道达到其理论通行能力,即 1610pcu/h,通过计算得出当前条件下车头间距和跟车距离为 39.76m 和 33.76m。通过对比图 1a)与图 1b),仿真交通流速度为 63km/h。

根据《交通工程学》中有关城市道路路段通行能力的分析和计算,当交通流运行速度为 60km/h 时,车道的理论通行能力为 1552pcu/h,此时交通流中平均车头间距为 38.67m,平均跟车距离为 34.67m,并计算得到对应的交通密度为 26.7 辆/km。通过表 1 中理论计算结果与仿真结果的对比分析,发现本文所建立的交通流仿真模型与理论计算模型之间各项指标的误差均在 5.0% 之内,可以较好地反映出实际交通流现象,可以用于后续的研究。

交通流仿真模型与理论计算结果对比 表 1

项目	速度(km/h)	通行能力(pcu/h)	密度(辆/km)	车长(m)	车头间距(m)	跟车距离(m)
理论结果	60	1552	26.7	5	38.67	33.67
仿真结果	63	1610	26	5	39.76	34.76
误差	5.0%	3.7%	2.7%	—	2.8%	3.2%

1.3 混合交通流特性分析

1.3.1 通行能力

混合交通流通行能力特性通过流量—密度基本图进行分析,如图 2 所示,交通流量变化曲线的最大值代表车道的基准通行能力。

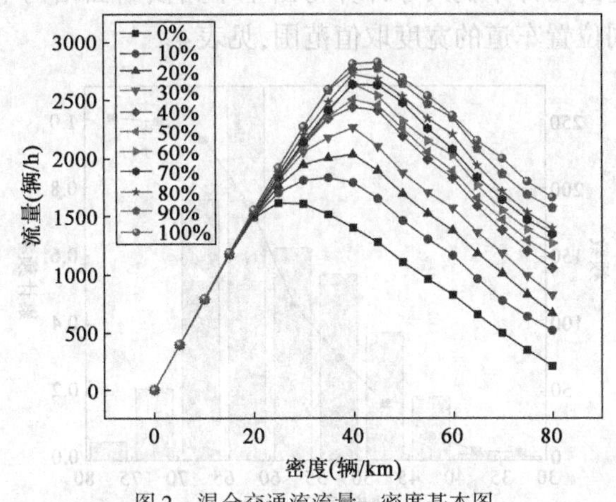

图 2 混合交通流流量—密度基本图

由仿真结果可以得出,自动驾驶比例达到 50% 前,通行能力提升速度较快,而后开始减缓。根据 GIPPS 安全距离模型,自动驾驶车辆行驶所需的车头间距小于手动驾驶车辆,随着自动驾驶比例的增加,交通流中车辆平均车头间距减小,导致车道通行能力提升。当自动驾驶比例超过 50% 后,混合交通流中自动驾驶车辆开始占据主要部分,因此单车道通行能力提升速度开始减缓。

自动驾驶车辆的加入使单车道通行能力得到不同程度的提升,在纯自动驾驶环境下单车道通行能力将提高 1.84 倍。在相同的交通出行需求条件下,机动车道需求数将减少,机动车行车空间降低。根据自动驾驶比例对通行能力的影响,得到城市道路常见单向车道数以及后自动驾驶影响后的车道数缩减情况,见表 2。从表中可以得出,自动驾驶对通行能力的提升可使双向八车道和六车道结构对应改造为双向六车道和四车道结构,同时也说明城市道路中主干路的横断面结构受自动驾驶的影响最大。

受自动驾驶影响的机动车道数量缩减情况 表 2

车道缩减情况	2→1	3→2	4→3	4→2
通行能力提升倍数	2	1.5	1.33	2
自动驾驶比例	—	60% ~70%	40% ~50%	—

1.3.2 运行速度

通过速度-密度基本图分析混合交通流运行速度特性,如图 3 所示。

由仿真结果可以得出,自动驾驶比例达到 50% 前,交通流运行速度提升较快,而后开始减缓。由于自动驾驶车辆行驶所需的车头间距较小,自动驾驶车辆能够更加充分地交通流空间,车辆加速行为增加,导致整体运行速度提高。当自动驾驶比例超过 50% 后,混合交通流中自动驾驶车辆开始占据主要部分,车辆间行驶差异性减弱,运行速度的提升逐渐减缓。

同时,对交通密度为 40 辆/km 时的交通流仿真速度进行分析后,发现当自动驾驶比例由 0% 增长到 50% 时,交通流速度提升了 69.3%,而自动驾驶比例由 50% 增长到 100% 时,交通流速度仅提升了 13.9%。速度是车道宽度计算的关键依据,该变化说明自动驾驶比例 50% 是影响横断设计中机动车道宽度确定的关键参数,在城市交通流中自动驾驶比例达到 50% 前,与交通流运行速度相适应的车道宽度变化频繁,而达到 50% 后机动车道宽度变化趋于稳定(表 3)。

不同自动驾驶比例下的交通流仿真速度　　表 3

自动驾驶反应时间	交通流仿真速度(km/h)				
	0%	30%	50%	80%	100%
0.1s	35.0	56.7	61.1	68.1	70.4

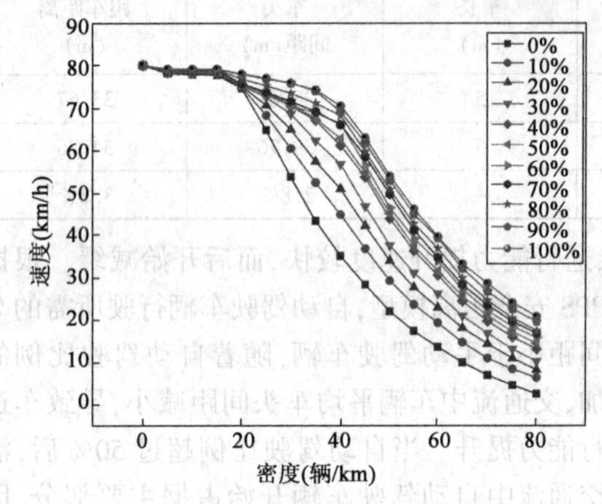

图 3　混合交通流速度-密度基本图

2　横断面优化设计

2.1　车道宽度分析

车道宽度由车辆宽度与侧向安全距离共同构成。随着汽车技术迅猛发展,车辆行驶稳定性大幅度提升,安全行驶需要的侧向安全距离减少,传统的车道宽度计算模型已不适用。本文将按照车道宽度模型修正公式[14]进行计算:

$$c = 0.3 + 0.0053V \tag{3}$$

$$d = 0.58 + 0.0589V^{0.51} \tag{4}$$

$$x = 0.9 + 0.0589\ (V_1 + V_2)^{0.51} \tag{5}$$

其中,c 为车身边缘到路缘石的安全间距;d 为同向行驶车辆间的安全间距;x 为反向行驶车辆间的安全间距;V 为车辆行驶速度;V_1、V_2 为对向车辆行驶速度。

在交通流仿真过程中随机抽取 1000 个瞬时速度样本进行速度累计频率分布分析,结果如图 4 所示。根据速度频率分布结果,当自动驾驶比例为 50% 时,第 85% 分位行驶速度位于 62.5 ~ 67.5km/h范围内,代入上述公式计算得到车辆行驶所需的侧向安全距离范围,并根据不同位置车道的设计车辆尺寸计算得出主干路横断面结构不同位置车道的宽度取值范围,见表 4。

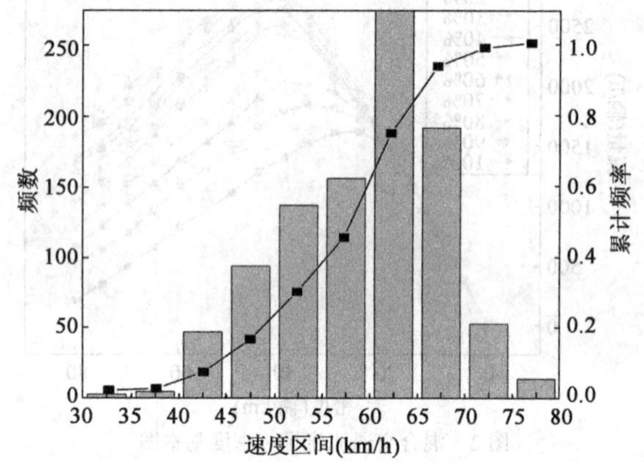

图 4　运行速度频率分布图

车道宽度组成计算结果　　表 4

结　构	车道位置		B	c	d	x	合　计
四块板	外侧车道		2.5	0.63 ~ 0.66	1.07 ~ 1.08	—	3.67 ~ 3.70
	中间车道		1.8	—	1.07 ~ 1.08	—	2.87 ~ 2.88
			2.5	—	1.07 ~ 1.08	—	3.57 ~ 3.58
	内侧车道		1.8	0.63 ~ 0.66	1.07 ~ 1.08	—	2.97 ~ 3.00
三块板	外侧车道		2.5	0.63 ~ 0.66	1.07 ~ 1.08	—	3.67 ~ 3.70
	中间车道		1.8	—	1.07 ~ 1.08	—	2.87 ~ 2.88
			2.5	—	1.07 ~ 1.08	—	3.57 ~ 3.58
	内侧车道	中分带	1.8	0.63 ~ 0.66	1.07 ~ 1.08	—	2.97 ~ 3.00
		无	1.8	—	1.07 ~ 1.08	1.59 ~ 1.62	3.13 ~ 3.15

速度是决定车道宽度的重要参数，自动比例对交通流速度特性的影响将会导致车道宽度发生变化。当自动驾驶比例达到50%后，随着自动驾驶比例的增加，自动驾驶对交通运行速度的影响逐渐减弱，仅10km/h范围内变化，说明在这个阶段车道宽度只会存在小幅度的变化。同时，外侧车道和混合行驶车道的交通运行速度会受到公交车等大型车的影响而降低，车辆对车道宽度的需求减少。综合考虑以上因素，对车道宽度计算结果进行适度的调整，确定自动驾驶比例达到50%及以后车道宽度推荐值，见表5。

城市主干路车道宽度建议值　　表5

车道位置		设计车辆宽度(m)	车道宽度计算值(m)	车道宽度建议值(m)
外侧车道		2.5	3.67~3.70	3.50
中间车道		2.5	3.57~3.58	3.50
内侧车道	有中分带	1.8	2.97~3.00	3.00
	无中分带		3.13~3.15	3.20

2.2 通行能力分析

设计通行能力是横断面设计中确定车道数规模的重要依据，其含义是根据一个车道的基准通行能力进行修正后得到的道路实用通行能力。设计通行能力受多种影响因素，综合考虑城市道路实际道路交通条件，城市道路单车道设计通行能力为：

$$C_d = C_0 \cdot \alpha_w \cdot \alpha_n \cdot \alpha_b \cdot \alpha_i \quad (6)$$

设计通行能力影响修正系数取值与横断面结构有较大关系，在通行能力分析时应考虑到横断面结构之间的差异性。通过对北京市五环内160余条城市主干路路段处的横断面结构进行调研，发现城市主干路横断面以三块板和四块板结构下的双向八车道和双向六车道为主。因此本文主要对三块板和四块板结构下的横断面单向通行能力进行计算。

通过对单车道混合交通流基准通行能力与自动驾驶比例间的关系进行线性拟合，如图5所示，得到：当自动驾驶比例为50%时，单车道基准通行能力提升至2300pcu/h左右；当自动驾驶比例为70%时，单车道基准通行能力提升至2530pcu/h左右，从而计算得到自动驾驶混合交通特性下城市主干路常见横断面结构优化后对应的单向设计通行能力，见表6。

$$C_{0m} = 1718.32 + 1165.96 P_{cav} \ (R^2 = 0.9135) \quad (7)$$

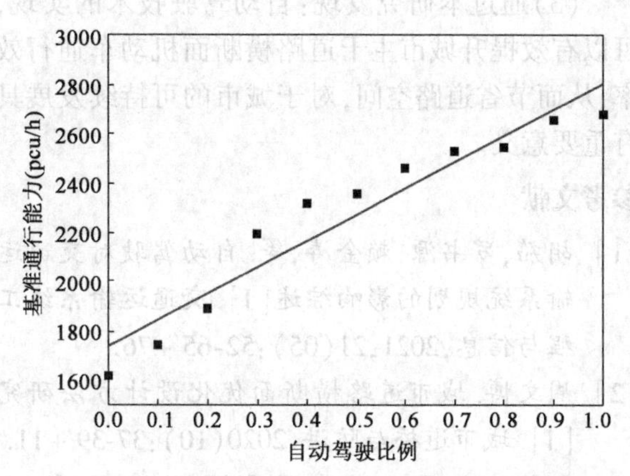

图5　自动驾驶比例与通行能力拟合结果

主干路不同横断面结构优化后单向通行能力　　表6

结构	无自动驾驶			存在自动驾驶		
	车道数	C_0	C_d	车道数	C_0	C_d
四块板	4	1800	4331.52	3	2300	4385.33
	3		3594.24	2	2530	3784.88
三块板	4		4331.52	3	2300	4544.80
	3		3594.24	2	2530	3784.88

通过对比单向通行能力计算结果，当自动驾驶比例为50%时，城市主干路双向六车道横断面机动车单向通行能力大于双向八车道；当自动驾驶比例达到70%时，城市主干路双向四车道横断面机动车单向通行能力大于双向六车道。自动驾驶对通行能力提升作用使城市主干路机动车道需

求数减少,在红线宽度确定的情况下,可将横断面宽度用于慢行交通空间,推动城市道路空间由机动车尺度向行人尺度转变。

3　结语

本文基于交通流元胞仿真模型,从交通流通行能力和运行速度角度,分析了自动驾驶技术对城市主干道路横断面设计的影响,提出城市主干路典型横断面结构优化设计方案,结论如下:

(1)自动驾驶车辆的混入可以明显提升交通流运行速度。随着自动驾驶车辆占比的提高,交通流运行速度呈现出先快后慢的变化趋势。当自动驾驶比例达到50%后,交通流运行速度受车道宽度的变化趋于稳定。

(2)自动驾驶车辆可明显缩减车头间距,提升单车道通行能力。当自动驾驶比例为50%时,单车道基准通行能力提升至2300pcu/h;当自动驾驶比例为70%时,单车道基准通行能力可达2530pcu/h,双向八车道和六车道断面可对应优化为双向六车道和四车道断面。

(3)通过本研究发现:自动驾驶技术的实现,可以有效提升城市主干道路横断面机动车通行效率,从而节省道路空间,对于城市的可持续发展具有重要意义。

参考文献

[1] 胡茹,罗书源,赖金涛,等.自动驾驶对交通运输系统规划的影响综述[J].交通运输系统工程与信息,2021,21(05):52-65+76.

[2] 周文博.城市道路横断面优化设计方法研究[J].城市道桥与防洪,2020(10):37-39+11.

[3] Csikóss A, Tettamanti T, VARGA I. Nonlinear gating control for urban road traffic network using the network fundamental diagram [J]. Journal of Advanced Transportation, 2015, 49(5):597-615.

[4] Zhu H B, Zhou Y J, Wu W J. Modeling traffic flow mixed with automated vehicles considering drivers' character difference [J]. Physica A: Statistical Mechanics and its Applications, 549.

[5] Varotto H, Van A. Empirical Longitudinal Driving Behavior in Authority Transitions Between Adaptive Cruise Control and Manual Driving [J]. Transportation Research Record: Journal of the Transportation Research Board, 2015 (2489):105-114.

[6] 胡明伟,施小龙,翟素云,等.自动驾驶混合交通流的交通和环境效益评估[J].重庆交通大学学报(自然科学版),2021,40(08):7-14.

[7] 常鑫,李海舰,荣建,等.混有智能网联车队的交通流基本图模型分析[J].东南大学学报(自然科学版),2020,50(04):782-788.

[8] S E Shladover, Su D Y. Transportation Research Record: Journal of the Transportation Research Board[J]. 2012(2324):63-70.

[9] Alessandrini A, Campagna A, Site P D. Automated vehicles and the rethinking of mobility and cities [J]. Transportation Research Procedia, 2015, 5:145-160.

[10] 刘凯,常四铁.面向自动驾驶的城市街道设计研究[C].2019中国城市交通规划年会.

[11] 周明妮,黄宝涛,马荣国,等.适合多模式交通需求的城市主干路横断面[J].公路,2018,63(07):249-255.

[12] 王维礼,郑苹莫,朱杰.无人驾驶环境下城市交通空间优化设计探讨[J].天津建设科技2020,30(5):75-80.

[13] Yang D, Qiu X P, Ma L N, et al. Modeling and simulation of the traffic flow mixed by the manual and automated vehicles based on Cellular Automata [J]. Transportation Research Record: Journal of Transportation Research Board, 2017.

[14] 侯宗霖.武汉市机动车道宽度与横渡面组合形式研究[D].武汉:华中科技大学,2006.

基于心理旋转的行人二次过街安全岛交通改善研究

杨 柳 杜志刚* 许富强 王首硕 韩 磊
(武汉理工大学交通学院)

摘 要 城市交叉口行人二次过街安全岛需要满足多个方向、多种交通流的视认需求,以保障驾驶人与行人的通行安全。本文从颜色恒常性与形状恒常性两方面针对安全岛交通设施进行设计分析,通过采用球形、圆柱形、圆形、弧形视线诱导设施组合设置,实现交叉口行人二次过街安全岛的多级线形诱导、多级轮廓诱导功能,以提升各个方向交通流的视认距离,缓解心理旋转效应。利用3ds Max软件构建城市道路交叉口安全岛模型进而开展室内仿真实验,以驾驶人视认距离作为评价指标。实验结果表明:不同安全岛改善方案对驾驶人视认距离影响显著,前进方向上视认距离普遍大于对向方向视认距离,且随着方案等级的提高,视认距离呈单调递增趋势,采用改善后的设计方案能够有效缓解驾驶人心理旋转现象,提高安全岛的安全性。

关键词 交通安全 心理旋转 仿真实验 行人二次过街安全岛 视认距离 反应时间

0 引言

随着国民经济的发展,我国汽车保有量呈爆发式增长,城市道路交叉口安全岛交通事故不断增加,仅2019年深圳市就发生15起安全岛交通事故[1],造成8人死亡、16人受伤,其中,安全岛视认性不佳、缺乏警示诱导防撞功能以及车辆超速行驶为交通事故的主要诱因。而合理的安全岛视线诱导设施能够显著提升驾驶人视距视区,进一步降低其在驾驶任务中的安全操纵时间,从而获得基于人因的安全保障,减少或避免因视距不足、视认不清、方向不明而诱发的道路交通事故。

关于行人二次过街岛的设置必要性、具体设置方法以及对行人的影响等相关议题备受社会关注,国内外学者在相关方面研究成果颇多。在安全岛设置的必要性方面,Dixon等[2-3]通过分析设置安全岛前后的交通事故数据,发现安全岛可以有效降低交通事故;赖元文等[4]则指出在交叉口设置安全岛能够使交叉口通行能力得到有效提升。至于安全岛的设置方法,我国相关规范[5]提出了具体的设计标准和推荐参数;李淑庆[6]以行人过街量为判断依据,提出了不同过街方式的适用条件和范围。在二次过街安全岛对行人的影响方面,Kim等[7-8]认为在人行横道上增设安全岛后,行人的过街行为更加规范,违反交通规则的概率大大降低;余昕宇[9]则结合驾驶人在停车视距和决策视距位置的视觉需求对城市过街路段进行安全改善设计。

通过上述国内外研究发现,目前的研究大多针对不同条件下安全岛的选用形式,对于详细的设施设置比较模糊;另外安全岛存在缺乏行人防撞设施、视线不佳等问题,亟须新的设计方法提高其安全性;同时现有安全岛改善方法缺乏相关理论支撑,导致无法评价其设置方法的优劣。因此,本文在相关研究基础之上,结合心理旋转诱导理念,提出一种安全有效、生命周期成本低的安全岛改善方法,并通过室内仿真实验对改善前后效果进行评价。

1 改善原理与方法

1.1 心理旋转效应

心理旋转[10]是指人在头脑中运用表象对物体进行二维或三维旋转的过程,是衡量一个人空间认知能力的标准。在具体的交通应用中,当驾驶人驾驶车辆行进时,不断被动接受来自导航或道路两端交通标识等信息的客体旋转,需要持续转换、对比这类信息在大脑中的呈现与现实中的方位,由此使得驾驶人产生心理旋转效应。而知觉的恒常性则有助于降低心理旋转效应造成的影响,其中颜色恒常性和形状恒常性在道路交通环境中广泛应用。

颜色恒常性是指当照射物体表面的颜色光发生变化时,人们对该物体表面颜色的知觉仍然保持不变的知觉特性;形状恒常性即保持对物体形状的感知完整性,当人在观察熟悉物体时,物体原本的形状知觉仍具有保持相对不变的特征。

由于交叉口车流动线复杂,行人二次过街安全岛所处地理位置与交叉口四个方向车流轨迹存在一定范围的交织;同时不同类型车辆混合通行,由此导致不同注视点高度下的视距视区需求不一致,不同等级道路其所对应的安全岛警示诱导及防撞等级亦应有所不同。因此,本文基于心理旋转效应,在平面交叉口安全岛设计一套完整连续、安全有效的警示诱导信息系统,主要将突起路标、交通柱、防撞桶、贝里莎球等不同高度设施相结合,这些圆柱形、球形、圆形及弧形设施能够满足360°全方向驾驶人视觉需求,同时不同颜色的高低组合设计能够有效降低驾驶人驾驶负荷,缓解心理旋转所产生的影响,提高交叉口安全性。

1.2　行人二次过街安全岛设施设计方法

交叉口安全岛改善设计方法分为四个等级,等级越高其对于缓解驾驶人心理旋转效果越好,方案主要是在中分带安全岛岛头、行人驻足区设置不同颜色、不同尺寸的警示诱导信息,同时利用逆反射及自发光技术,使得各种设施在不同照度不同天气条件下仍保持颜色的恒常性,多采用圆柱形、球形设施保持安全岛的形状恒常性,由此降低交叉口安全岛心理旋转效应,具体设计方案如图1、表1所示。

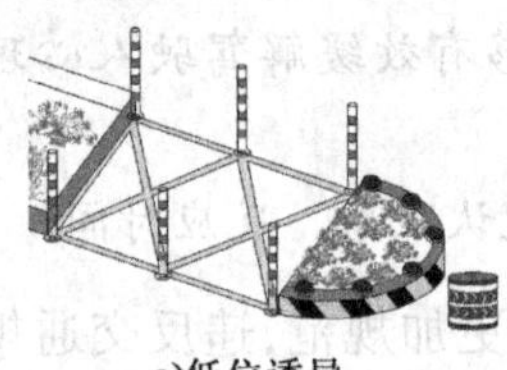
a)低位诱导

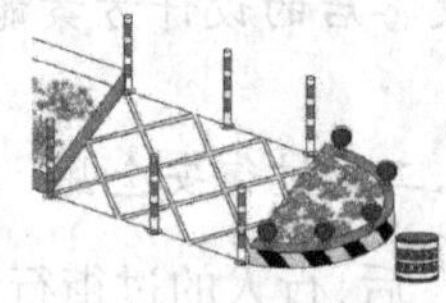
b)中位诱导

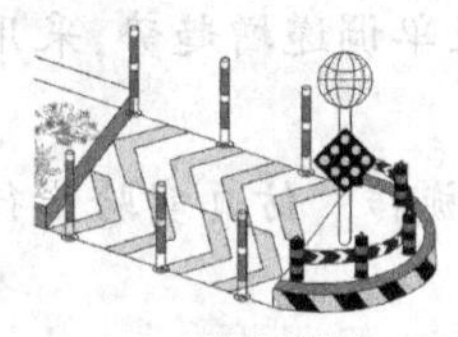
c)高位诱导

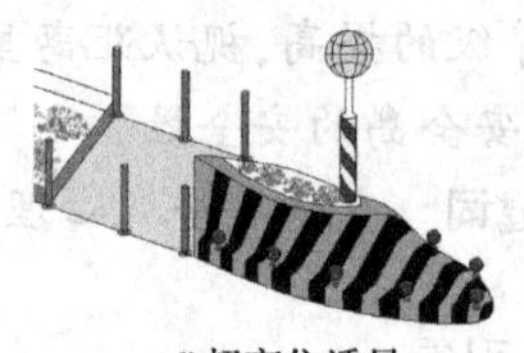
d)超高位诱导

图1　设计方案

交叉口行人二次过街安全岛改善方案　　表1

设施类型	低位心理旋转 一级	中位心理旋转 二级	高位心理旋转 三级	超高位心理旋转 四级	设施功能	视认适用方向	适用距离
低位圆弧形反光膜	√	√	√		低位轮廓诱导,不易造成二次伤害	三个方向	大于停车视距
低位球形突起路标	√	√	√		低位线形诱导,360°反光	四个方向	小于停车视距
低位圆形坐式轮廓标		√		√	低位轮廓诱导为主,低位线形诱导为辅	对向	大于停车视距
中位圆柱形刚性交通柱			√		中位轮廓诱导为主、线形诱导为辅	四个方向	大于简单识别视距
中位圆柱形防撞桶	√	√			防撞为主,警示为辅,降低车辆伤害	三个方向	大于简单识别视距
中位圆柱形柔性柱	√短条	√中短条	√中长条	√长条	不同柔性柱随着等级的提高,警示效果依次增加	四个方向	大于简单识别视距
中位联株式半圆弧护栏			√		防撞为主、警示为辅,保护驻留区行人	三个方向	大于简单识别视距
高位轮廓标			√	√	增强警示作用,使驾驶人进一步控制车辆速度	四个方向	大于复杂识别视距
高位贝里沙球			√	√	高位警示,显著提升驾驶人视距,分解驾驶任务	四个方向	大于复杂识别视距
一体式圆弧形防撞岛头				√	防撞为主,警示为辅,将车辆动能转化为重力势能	三个方向	大于复杂识别视距

注:表中三个方向为对向、左侧向、右侧向,四个方向为当前方向、对向、左侧向、右侧;设施高度 $0<h<0.3$m 为低位,$0.3\text{m}<h<0.6$m 为中位,$0.6\text{m}<h<2.5$m 为高位,$h>2.5$m 为超高位。

2 实验设计及数据分析

2.1 实验方案

受城市道路交叉口管理等因素限制，本文采用3ds Max软件构建仿真模型，并基于E-prime2.0平台进行仿真实验。选取28人（男性21名，女性7名）作为被试，被试者身体健康，视力矫正后达到1.0，设计仿真场景为运行车速40km/h的双向六车道，以驾驶人的视认距离作为实验指标，视认距离指驾驶人看清安全岛轮廓时与其之间的距离。实验共涉及10个场景，驾驶人前进方向上的安全岛对应于现状方案以及四种不同等级方案的场景1、场景2、场景3、场景4与场景5；对向车道方向则依次对应场景6、场景7、场景8、场景9与场景10。

2.2 实验流程

仿真实验步骤如下：①实验开始前，告知被试者需要熟悉的操作流程，并随机播放1min的预实验视频；②实验正式开始，车辆从距离对向行人二次过街安全岛前300m开始以40km/h的速度匀速行驶，电脑自动记录实验起始时刻为t_1，当驾驶人视认出安全岛时记录此时刻为t_2，则驾驶人的视认距离为$S=300-\left(\frac{40}{3.6}\right)\times(t_2-t_1)$；③当每个场景完成后，驾驶人休息5min，继续进行下一组实验；④导出实验数据，并对数据进行整理分析。实验场景如图2所示。

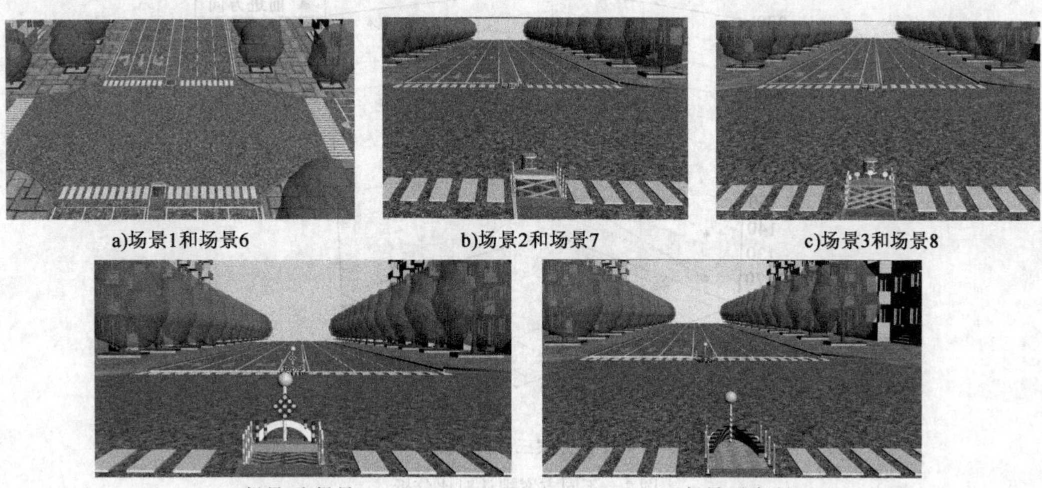
a)场景1和场景6 b)场景2和场景7 c)场景3和场景8 d)场景4和场景9 e)场景5和场景10

图2 设计方案

2.3 数据分析

根据实验得到前进方向车道及对向方向车道安全岛的视认距离数据，实验结果见表2、表3，采用单因素重复测量方差分析数据，利用Origin软件得出前进方向与对向方向安全岛视认距离箱线图以及三维折线图，如图3所示。

视认距离表 表2

不同场景	场景1	场景2	场景3	场景4	场景5
评价指标	视认距离(m)	视认距离(m)	视认距离(m)	视认距离(m)	视认距离(m)
前进方向	137.678	182.258	189.54	201.801	216.790
不同场景	场景6	场景7	场景8	场景9	场景10
评价指标	视认距离(m)	视认距离(m)	视认距离(m)	视认距离(m)	视认距离(m)
对向方向	119.7631	157.03	163.01	172.96	186.689

视认距离提升程度 表3

比较项目	场景2较场景1提升程度	场景3较场景1提升程度	场景4较场景1提升程度	场景5较场景1提升程度
前进方向车道	32.38%	37.67%	46.57%	57.46%
比较项目	场景7较场景6提升程度	场景8较场景6提升程度	场景9较场景6提升程度	场景10较场景6提升程度
对向方向车道	31.12%	36.11%	44.42%	55.88%

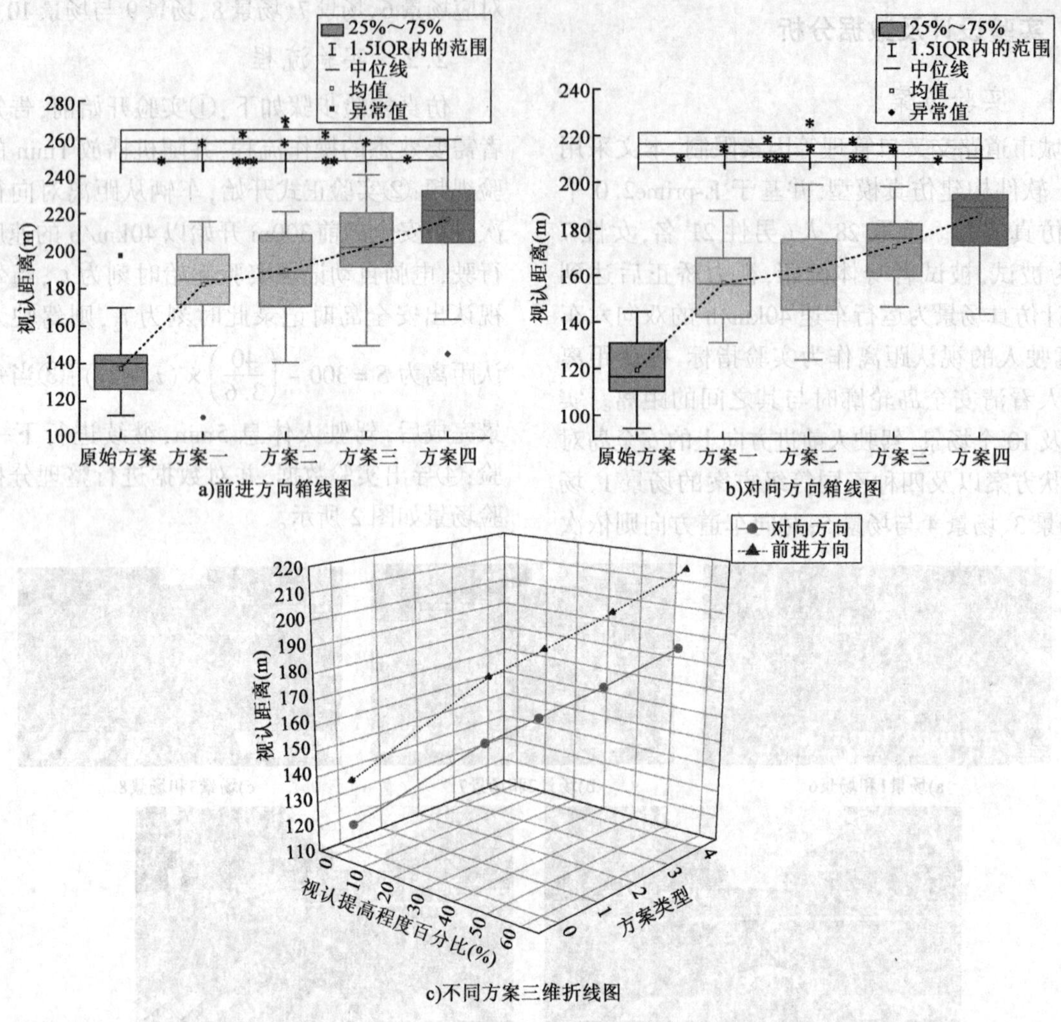

图3　不同方案视认对比分析

(1)对比表2、3及图3发现,驾驶人在前进方向和对向方向上对行人二次过街安全岛视认距离相较于现有方案都有所提升,前进方向安全岛视认距离均大于对向方向安全岛视认距离。就同一方向而言,方案等级与视认距离呈现单调递增趋势,即圆柱形、球形设施越多,对优化驾驶人视距效果越佳,同时对向方向上对安全岛视认距离的提升程度均略低于前进方向,表明改善后的方案对同向视认效果的提升更为有效。

(2)采用单因素重复测量方差分析同一方向上不同方案对驾驶人视认距离的影响,不同方案视认距离平均值见表4,由表可知视认距离在不同方案下存在总体显著性差异(前进方向 $F = 47.23$, $P = 0.000$,对向方向 $F = 99.38$, $P = 0.000$),由图3可知(＊表示 $P < 0.02$,＊＊表示 $0.05 < P < 0.05$,＊＊＊表示 $P > 0.05$),除方案一与方案二无显著性差异外,其余改善后的方案均对视认距离影响显著,且方案二与方案三之间的差异性小于其他方案。

同一方向上不同方案视认距离平均值　　表4

方案类型	前进方向		对向方向	
	视认距离平均值(m)	标准差(m)	视认距离平均值(m)	标准差(m)
原始方案	137.68	17.44	119.76	13.51
方案一	182.26	22.53	157.04	17.17
方案二	189.54	25.88	163.01	20.15
方案三	201.80	21.86	172.96	13.95

续上表

方案类型	前进方向		对向方向	
	视认距离平均值(m)	标准差(m)	视认距离平均值(m)	标准差(m)
方案四	216.79	27.79	186.17	17.33
F	47.23		99.38	
P	0.000		0.000	

3 结论

(1)由于现有安全岛设计无法满足不同方向不同交通流的视认需求,当驾驶人行车至交叉口时,容易产生心理旋转效应,而本文提出的针对安全岛改善设计能有效缓解驾驶人的心理紧张,驾驶人无论从何种方向驶入交叉口,均能获得安全岛上恒定不变的交通信息,提高设施对驾驶人的警示诱导作用,同时保护岛上行人安全。

(2)与现状安全岛设计方案相比,改善后的方案能够有效提高驾驶人的视认距离,扩大视距视区。不同等级的改善方案使得驾驶人视距得到不同程度的提升,方案等级越高,驾驶人视认距离提升程度越大,同时同方向的视认距离与提升程度均要显著大于对向。

(3)在实际工程实例中,可根据经济状况、道路等级、车辆运行速度等选择合适的行人二次过街安全岛安全改善方案,道路等级越高,车辆运行速度越大,则选择的安全岛等级应越高。

参考文献

[1] 毛应萍,刘轼介,洪泽佳,等.深圳市道路交通岛安全性分析及改善研究[J].交通与运输,2020,33(S2):100-105.

[2] Dixon K K, Hibbard J L, Nyman H. Right-turn treatment for signalized intersections[C]// Urban Street Symposium, Transportation Research Circular E-C019. 1999,3(5556):036.

[3] Zegeer C V, Esse C T, Stewart J R, et al. Safety analysis of marked versus unmarked crosswalks in 30 cities[J]. ITE journal, 2004, 74(1): 34-41.

[4] 赖元文.设置导流岛的信号交叉口运行效果评价[J].道路交通与安全,2016,16(03):13-16.

[5] 中华人民共和国住房和城乡建设部.城市道路交叉口规划规范:GB 50674—2011[S].北京:中国计划出版社,2011.

[6] 李淑庆.灯控交叉口行人过街设施设置依据研究之一——人行横道行人通行能力分析与计算[J].重庆交通大学学报(自然科学版),1991(1):59-70.

[7] Kim T H, Won J M, Bae G M, et al. The development of pedestrian signal timing models considering pedestrian behavior and location [J]. KSCE Journal of Civil Engineering, 2006, 10(2):131-136.

[8] Bungum T J, Day C, Henry L J. The association of distraction and caution displayed by pedestrians at a lighted crosswalk[J]. Journal of community health, 2005, 30(4):269-279.

[9] 余昕宇,杜志刚,倪玉丹.基于视距视区优化的夜间过街安全改善研究[J].武汉理工大学学报(交通科学与工程版),2020,44(02):358-362.

[10] 王鹏,黄艳华.心理旋转概述[J].宁波大学学报,2006,28(5):1457-1464.

掉头位置设置对道路运行效率影响研究

郭亚辉[1]　李　辉[1]　张　旭*[1]　李书新[1]　杨　锦[2]
(1.河南工业大学土木工程学院;2.锦屏县交通运输局)

摘　要　为提升常规十字路口左转掉头混合车道的车辆通行效率,以左转掉头混合车道道路通行能力最大为评价指标提出了最佳掉头位置的计算方法。该方法将车流量、交叉口尺寸,信号时间等作为影响因素分析同一车道上左转车辆与掉头车辆相互影响造成的延误时间和各种延误情况的发生概率,建立了掉头车辆阻挡左转车辆时产生的损失总时间模型和左转车辆阻挡掉头车辆时的有效通行总时间模型,并将这两种模型计算结果作为参数,构建起了左转掉头混合车道的通行能力计算模型。结果表明,掉头位置优化后,左转掉头车道通行能力提升了21.93%。该掉头位置模型能有效降低该车道车辆平均延误,提高车道通行能力,可为左转掉头车道设计提供参考。

关键词　交通工程　掉头位置　仿真模拟　掉头车道　通行能力　延误

0　引言

左转交通是最易发生交通事故的地方,由于它与多个交通流存在冲突点,所以是交叉口是否能正常通行的关键。在常规情况下,掉头交通与左转交通共道,所以掉头位置的正确设置,能减少掉头车辆与左转车辆的冲突,提高左转掉头混合车道的通行能力。

目前,国内外关于掉头位置设计的研究主要集中在左转车流远引掉头位置设计或者左转+直行车流远引掉头位置设计这两种情况,如:张卫华等以延误最小为指标,构建了次路左转+直行远引的掉头位置模型;成卫等通过实地调查平均饱和车头时距的方法计算饱和流率并引入掉头调整系数,得出的结论表明当掉头流量百分比小于21%时,支路左转远引掉头的运行效率高于直接左转;潘兵宏等提出一种新型U形转弯方式,当道路上大型车比例增加时能够有效改善路网的运行效率。

上述研究对于减少交叉口冲突点,提升通行效率很有帮助,但都把重心放在了远引掉头。目前对于常规左转+掉头车道的设计研究相对很少,设计者往往是将掉头位置设置在交叉口处或者凭借感性经验设置掉头位置。Al-OMARI M M A等通过研究73个中间带掉头道路探究不同掉头位置对交通通行及安全的影响,结果表明在掉头车辆在中间带适当位置掉头比常规交叉口掉头更加高效和安全,邵海鹏等在仿真车辆掉头行为的基础上,分析车辆运行轨迹特性,建立了掉头空间计算判别模型,同时基于车辆排队理论与车辆换道理论,建立了适用于交叉口进口道导向车道上游位置设置掉头开口的位置计算模型。但都缺乏对掉头车辆与左转车辆之间相互影响的研究。因此,需要在现有的关于掉头位置的研究理论上,结合我国的交通情况以及左转交通与掉头交通的关系,推导适用于掉头交通流方法,确定相关模型以此对左转掉头混合车道掉头位置设置对道路运行效率进行研究。

综上,本文主要通过研究左转掉头混合车道掉头位置的设置,在已有的掉头位置设计的基础上,考虑交通量、掉头车辆、左转车辆等因素,建立不同掉头位置对道路通行能力的影响模型,结合交通仿真软件分析不同掉头位置对道路通行能力的影响,得出掉头位置设置的方法,提出合理的掉头位置,结果可为道路设计提供参考。

1　掉头车道交通特性

1.1　掉头位置设置条件

掉头位置如果设置在交叉口,掉头车辆会受到信号灯的管控,增加掉头等待时间,且掉头车辆

1.基金项目:河南工业大学高层次人才科研启动基金项目(2018BS029)。

会与慢行交通之间产生冲突，造成延误且可能会引起安全问题；如果距离交叉口过短，则左转车辆堵住掉头口的概率会很高，且有可能会导致掉头车辆无法及时换道至掉头口；如果掉头位置距离交叉口过长则会增加车辆延误，因此确定掉头位置对交叉口的运行起着关键作用(图 1)。

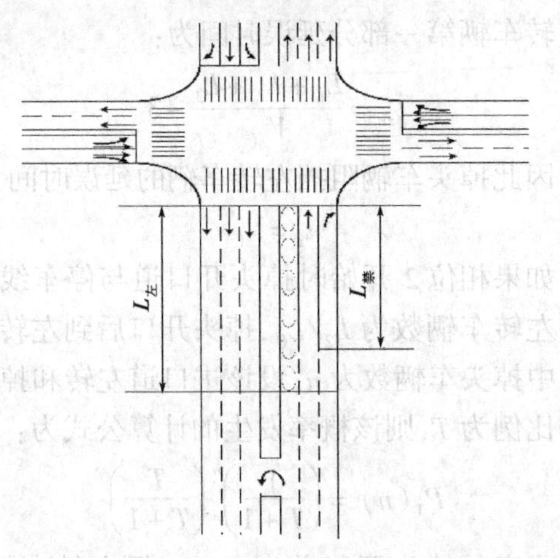

图1 交叉口示意图

综上所述，掉头位置应设置于左转排队长度 $L_{左}$，禁止变道线长度 $L_{禁}$ 之后，同时掉头位置前还应留出一辆车的换道所需长度 $L_{换}$ 以保证掉头车辆有足够的换道距离。

左转排队车辆长度计算模型为

$$L_{左}=q_{左}\ r_{左}\ l_{Q} \tag{1}$$

式中：$L_{左}$——左转车道车辆排队长度；

$q_{左}$——左转车辆高峰小时交通量；

$r_{左}$——一个信号周期内的左转红灯时间；

l_{Q}——平均停车车头时距。

通过对交通高峰期间城市道路车辆强制换道情况进行调查，以 60s 为间隔统计目标车道流率并转换成小时交通量，得到车辆强制换道时目标车道车流量数据与对应的车辆换道行驶距离数据，并利用 Jupyter 生成线性回归模型如图 2 所示。

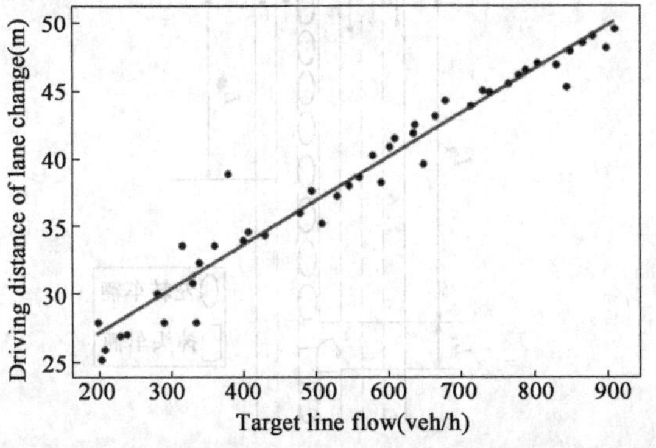

图2 流量与车辆强制变道行驶距离的关系

$$L_{换}=0.0324x+20.5167(x\geqslant 200) \tag{2}$$

则掉头位置 L 的模型为

$$L=(L_{左},L_{禁})_{\max}+L_{换} \tag{3}$$

1.2 掉头车辆运行特性

根据现有交通掉头位置，由掉头交通的运行特性，可将交叉口进口道的左转掉头混合车道掉头位置设为三种：交叉口内部掉头、停止线前掉头，距离停车线适当距离掉头。由于交叉口内部掉头会增加掉头车辆与慢行交通的冲突点，且掉头车辆也需受到红绿灯的管控，势必会增加交叉口的车辆延误时间；停止线前掉头会导致左转车辆在前车掉头时无法通过变道的方式越过前车，也会增加车辆延误时间，两种掉头方式都有明显的弊端。因此，本文会重点分析距离停车线适当距离掉头设置方式。

图 1 为常规十字交叉口示意图，该交叉口为三相位十字交叉路口，第一相位为南北直行，第二相位为南北左转，第三相位为东西直行左转。掉头车辆在南北路段的中央分隔带开口处掉头可以分为以下四个过程：

过程一：看见行驶的路段前方有可掉头的交通标志，车辆调整车速驶入可掉头的车道并注意与前后车保持车距然后驾驶进中央分隔带开口处。

过程二：对向车道如果没有来车或对向车辆出现可插入间隙，即可直接掉头驶入对向车道。

过程三：发现对向车辆没有可插入的间隙，那么就在中央分隔带开口处等待，注意观察对向车流的情况，一旦发现可插入的间隙，注意与前后车保持车距后，进行掉头转向，驶入目标车道。

过程四：完成掉头，驶入目标车道后，变速到与此路段车辆平均行驶速度，再进行变道以便直行或右转。

掉头位置设置在距停车线适当距离的位置，如遇到掉头车辆正在掉头，左转车辆可以通过变道的方式越过掉头口，左转车辆就不用在掉头车辆后排队等待。掉头车辆也可以不受交叉口信号灯的管控。此掉头位置适用于两交叉口间距较大时，因为交叉口间距短的路段中间掉头，会因掉头车辆排队长度而影响后续其后的直行和左转车辆通行。当掉头开口过大时，行人与非机动车可能会为求便利。利用其开口横穿街道，这种行为会与各交通流发生交通冲突，容易发生交通事故。

1.3　通行能力

1.3.1　通行能力

单位时间内的信号周期个数乘以一个信号周期内车道能够通过的最多的车辆数即是该车道的实际通行能力，由此可得左转掉头混合车道通行能力的计算模型为：

$$N_{通行} = \frac{3600}{T_{周}} \times \left(\frac{g_2 - Z_1}{t_h} + \frac{Z_2}{t_d}\right) \tag{4}$$

式中：$T_{周}$——一个信号周期时长；

g_2——第二相位绿灯时间；

Z_1——掉头车阻挡左转车产生的总损失时间；

Z_2——左转车受到掉头车阻挡后的有效通行总时间；

t_h——左转掉头混合车流的饱和车头时距；

t_d——掉头车流饱和车头时距。

1.3.2　掉头阻挡左转车损失时间

考虑左转掉头混合车道的通行能力会与左转流量与掉头流量有关。如图 3 所示，所研究的进口道停车线到对向进口道停车线之间的距离为 L_1，该进口道停车线到掉头开口处的距离为 L_2，掉头开口处宽度为 L_3，进口道禁止变道线长为 $L_{禁}$，进口道直行车道行驶速度为 $V_{直}$，进口道左行车道行驶速度为 $V_{左}$。

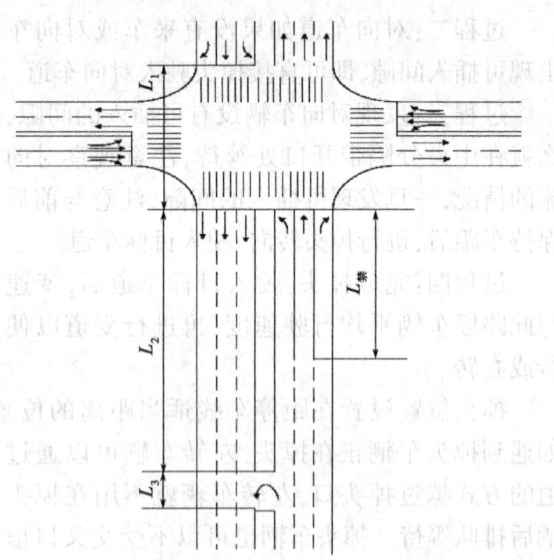

图 3　距离停车线适当距离掉头示意图

如图 3 所示，此时将掉头开口设置于进口道实线外。如遇掉头车辆在掉头开口掉头，此时左转车辆可以通过在直行车道变道到左转车道的方式，绕开掉头开口处。当掉头开口前的左转排队车辆达到最大时，后续到达的车将不能变道，只能紧跟掉头车辆排队通过。此时会出现掉头车辆阻挡左转车辆而造成延误。

当相位一时，对向直行车辆最后一辆从对向停车线通过当前研究掉头口时，掉头车辆才能进行掉头，减掉 3s 的黄灯时间，所以此时等待时间为左转车辆第一部分延误时间为：

$$t_{z1} = \frac{L_1 + L_2 + L_3}{V_{直}} - 3 \tag{5}$$

因此掉头车辆阻挡左转车辆的延误时间为：

$$t_z = t_{z1} \tag{6}$$

如果相位 2 开始时掉头开口道与停车线的距离中左转车辆数为 L_2/L_Q，掉头开口后到左转车辆距离中掉头车辆数为 n，设该进口道左转和掉头车辆的比例为 T，则该概率发生的计算公式为：

$$P_1(n) = \left(\frac{1}{T+1}\right)^n \left(\frac{T}{T+1}\right) \tag{7}$$

此公式表示掉头开口前有 L_2/L_Q 辆左转车辆，其后到第一辆左转车辆间有 n 辆掉头车辆。当 n 辆掉头车辆其后跟着首辆左转车辆的概率。

掉头车辆对左转车辆延误模型为：

$$Z_1 = \frac{\sum_{n=0}[t_z P_1(n)]}{\sum_{n=0} P_1(n)} \tag{8}$$

1.3.3　左转车辆阻挡掉头车辆时的有效通行总时间

如图 4 所示，当左转处于红灯时，左转车辆先于掉头车辆到达并堵住掉头口，就会给掉头车辆造成延误。

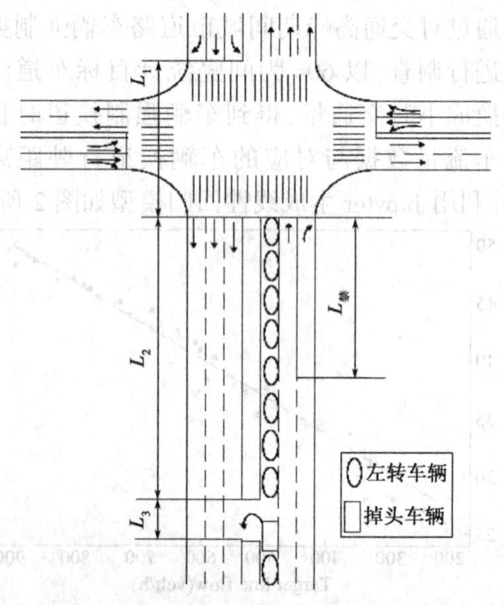

图 4　掉头车辆阻挡左转车辆通行示意图

假设左转车道车辆到达率符合泊松分布，那么通过泊松分布求出到达左转排队车辆堵住掉头口的概率为：

$$P_k = \frac{(\lambda t)^k}{k!} e^{-\lambda t} \tag{9}$$

式中：P_K——在左转红灯时间内到达 K 辆左转车的概率；

λ——左转车辆到达率。

$$P\left(\leqslant \frac{L_2}{l_Q}\right) = \sum_{i=0}^{\frac{L_2}{l_Q}} P_i \tag{10}$$

则左转红灯时间内左转排队车辆数在 L_2/L_Q 以上的概率为：

$$P\left(> \frac{L_2}{l_Q}\right) = 1 - \sum_{i=0}^{\frac{L_2}{l_Q}} P_i \tag{11}$$

左转红灯时车辆损失总时间：

$$K = T_E \times P\left(> \frac{L_2}{l_Q}\right) \tag{12}$$

式中：T_E——左转车道的红灯黄灯时间。

左转车辆在左转车道遇到红灯排队时，左转车辆排队长度大于或等于掉头口位置且其后跟着第一辆掉头车辆时就是左转车辆对掉头车辆造成的延误，此时有效通行总时间为：

$$Z_2 = \frac{T_E - K}{(T+1)} \tag{13}$$

2 实例分析

2.1 交通调查数据

按照上文左转车道掉头位置距停车线适当距离的应用环境。本次选取了郑州市长椿路与冬青街交叉口路段，该路段为常规十字交叉口，东西路段双向四车道，南北路段双向六车道，南北进口道均为一个左转掉头混合车道，一个直行车道，一个右转车道；东西进口道均为一个左转直行车道和一个右转直行车道。南北左转车道掉头位置距离停车线 8m，本次调查选择了星期三，避开节假日交通量偶然增加的情况。

表 1 ~ 表 4 为在郑州市长椿路与冬青街早高峰时期现场采集的实际交通数据。

长椿路与冬青街交叉口高峰小时交通量 表1

进口道	流向	早高峰交通量1	合计 1	早高峰交通量2	合计 2
东进口道	左转	126	683	158	671
	直行	471		445	
	右转	86		68	
西进口道	左转	117	624	128	603
	直行	405		388	
	右转	102		87	
北进口道	左转	275	1256	227	1087
	掉头	44		49	
	直行	722		657	
	右转	215		154	
南进口道	左转	227	1083	255	117
	掉头	57		39	
	直行	692		752	
	右转	10		125	

长椿路与冬青街交叉口信号配时方案 表2

相位	车流方向	绿灯时间(s)	黄灯时间(s)	红灯时间(s)	周期(s)
第一相位	南北直行	57	3	68	128
第二相位	南北左转	24	3	101	
第三相位	东西直行左转	38	3	8	

交通流数据　　表3

数据类型	数据名称	数据
交通流数据	l_Q	8m
	T	5
	t_h	2.32s
	t_d	3.28s
	λ	241vec/h

交叉口数据　　表4

数据类型	数据名称	数据
交叉口数据	L_1	33m
	L_3	6m
	L_4	48m
	$V_{直}$	10.8m/s
	$V_{左}$	10.8m/s

南进口道左转高峰小时交通量取平均值241veh/h,左转红灯时长101s,禁止变道线长48m,由式(1)~式(3)可得掉头位置应为84.4m,取85m。

2.2　仿真模拟

采用前文中所算掉头位置的结果将北进口左转道掉头位置设置在距离停车线85m处,利用前述通行能力计算模型计算左转掉头混合车道通行能力。并利用VISSIM对现状交叉口及优化掉头后的交叉口分别进行仿真。

由图5可知,利用前述模型计算出的左转掉头车道通行能力最大时所对应的掉头位置区间在80~88m之间,这与计算所得出的最佳掉头位置相符合。

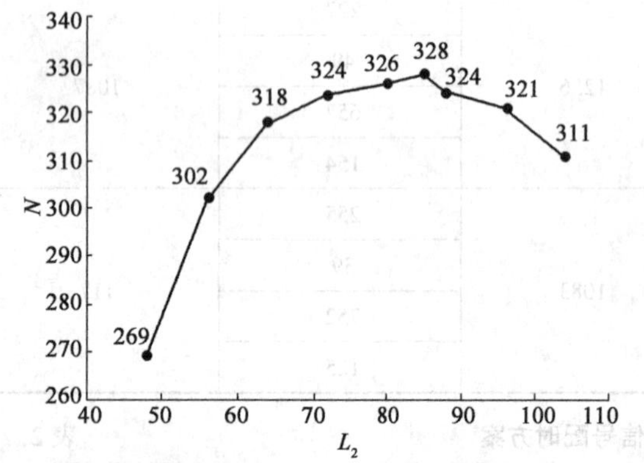

图5　掉头位置与左转掉头车道通行能力的关系

将现状交叉路口和优化掉头位置后的交叉路口分别进行VISSIM仿真,将仿真结果和模型计算结果进行对比分析,使用相对误差值进行评价分析,验证模型的有效性。

由表5计算结果可得,掉头位置优化后,左转掉头车道通行能力提升了21.93%。计算值与仿真值的相对误差值均在20以内,其结果验证了前述通行能力计算模型的准确性,也表明了提出的掉头位置优化方案适用于该交叉口。

不同掉头位置下通行能力的仿真值与模型计算值

表5

左转掉头车道通行能力	现状(掉头位置距停车线8m)	优化(掉头位置据停车线85m)
计算值	269	328
仿真值	278	342
相对误差值	9	14

3　结论

(1)针对常规十字交叉口的掉头位置展开研究,建立了左转掉头混合车道掉头位置的计算方法,与以往研究不同的是,该方法着重考虑了左转车辆与掉头车辆之间相互影响下的延误时间和有效通行时间。

(2)利用VISSIM仿真软件对所选取的交叉口进行路网建模,结果表明左转掉头车道通行能力提升了21.93%。验证了左转掉头位置的合理设置会在很大程度上提升左转掉头车道的通行能力,并将仿真结果与计算结果进行对比,相对误差在可接受范围。此方法可以结合左转车辆,掉头车辆,在交叉口提出合理的掉头位置,提高道路的运行效率。

(3)本文未考虑到慢行交通对左转车辆产生的影响,可能会导致交通环境过于理想,对通行能力的计算结果也会产生一定的影响;且仅考虑了常见的十字交叉口的掉头位置对道路运行效率影响,并不适用于其他类型交叉路口,因此其他类型交叉口的掉头位置对道路运行效率影响有待进一步研究。

参考文献

[1] 潘兵宏,单慧敏,任卉,等.新型非常规U型转弯交叉口的运行效率研究[J].深圳大学学报理工版,2020,37(3):305-313.

[2] 张卫华,陈靖生,董瑞娟.道路平面交叉口次路远引几何参数设置及通行效率研究[J].土木工程学报,2017,50(10):121-128.

[3] 成卫,李冰,雷建明,等.远引调头对下游交叉口通行能力的影响[J].公路交通科技,2015,32(11):107-112+119.
[4] AL-OMARI M M A, ABDEL-ATY M, LEE J, et al. Safety Evaluation of Median U-turn Crossover-based Intersections[J]. Transportation Research Record,2020,2674(7):1-13.
[5] 王晨,夏井新,陆振波,等.基于微观仿真与极值理论的城市交叉口安全评价方法[J].中国公路学报,2018,31(4):288-295+303.
[6] 林栋.信号交叉口左转车流通行能力研究[D].北京:北京工业大学,2014.
[7] 孙峰,孙立,李庆印,等.基于通行效率最优的交叉口掉头选位[J].西南交通大学学报,2017,52(02):334-339.
[8] 邵海鹏,王宇轩,陈兴影,等.信号交叉口进口道掉头设置条件研究(英文)[J].系统仿真学,2018,30(11):4429-4436.

城市地下互通立交交通特性研究

宋潮安　赵一静　潘夏卓　张　敏*
(长安大学运输工程学院)

摘　要　随着城市地下道路的不断建设,地下互通逐渐成为城市地下道路发展的关键节点,而由于其复杂的交通运行环境,对其开展交通特性研究显得尤为必要。本文在对地下互通立交进行路段划分的基础上,以厦门万石山隧道与钟鼓山隧道交叉所设地下互通作为研究对象,采集监控视频数据,利用人工计数法以及Kinovea视频分析软件获取交通流数据,结合已有地上互通立交交通特性研究成果,从交通量分布特性、换道特性以及速度特性三个方面,对地上、地下互通分合流区的交通运行特征进行对比分析。结果表明:相较于地上互通路段,在地下互通分合流区,驾驶人更倾向在最内侧车道行驶;在分流区容易提前变道,在合流区需要更长的时间来观察主线车辆情况;外侧与中间车道速度差值较高。研究结果可为城市地下互通的规划、设计与运营管理提供一定的理论依据。

关键词　交通工程　交通特性分析　视频识别　城市地下互通　分合流区

0　引言

随着城市化进程的不断推进,交通建设用地紧缺已经成为制约我国经济快速发展的重要因素,为了实现经济和交通的可持续发展,一些城市地下互通式立交工程应运而生。目前,在国内或者是国外,小规模的地下快速通道建设已经有了很多的先例,在欧美的一些国际化大都市里,大规模地下互通立交也已经有了实质进展。

目前,国内外对于地下互通的研究主要集中在地下立交道路设计和路网规划方面,有关交通特性方面的研究较少。国外相关研究调查显示,道路环境越复杂,交通事故率越高[1-2]。Jane 等[3]认为,道路环境,如交通标志标线、照明及其他附属设施设置的方式或位置会对驾驶人的驾驶特性产生显著的影响。

国内也有学者对城市地下道路开展了大量研究。陈雨人等[4]从视觉信息负荷角度解析地下快速路车辆运行特征差异机理,为完善和提高地下快速路视觉环境交通安全性的技术研究奠定理论基础。刘硕等[5]采用驾驶模拟技术研究地下快速路车道宽度、侧向净宽等横断面因素对车辆运行速度和轨迹的影响。李素艳等[6]依据变速特点,将地下道路变速车道分成不同的段落,并根据速度变化规律得到不同段落长度的计算式,并通过计算得到不同工况下变速车道长度的建议值。周灿[7]采用实车实验,采集厦门市万石山隧道与钟鼓山隧道的互通立交实车数据,发现加速车道成功合

1. 基金项目:四川省交通运输科技项目(2019-ZL-12)。

流车辆数受主线交通量和匝道交通量影响以及主线车速和加速车道剩余长度对合流点分布的影响关系。袁胜强等[8]根据城市地下互通立交特点,计算出城市地下互通立交主线路段、匝道路段以及分合流区的通行能力。

从以上研究可以看出,城市地下道路交通是当下研究热点,但关于地下互通立交的研究还较少,而地下互通立交作为未来城市交通建设的重要组成部分,对其进行交通特性分析有着重要意义。因此,本文在分别获取地上互通立交和地下互通立交视频数据的基础上,利用视频识别技术,采集交通流数据,进而对两者进行差异性分析,以获得地下互通分、合流区的交通特性。

1　地下互通式立交路段划分

1.1　路段划分目的

城市地下互通式立交路段交通环境复杂,在不同路段具有不同的交通特性,因此需要对道路进行路段划分。本研究路段划分的主要目的是根据路段划分结果,针对不同路段,采取相应的交通安全管控措施,并为城市地下互通立交的规划、设计与运营管理提供相应的理论依据。

1.2　路段划分方法及依据

在速度管控、事故分析、道路养护等方面研究中,聚类法被广泛应用于道路路段划分,包括系统聚类法、动态聚类法、有序聚类法等[9-10]。在地下互通立交工程交通安全管控措施研究中,也可采用聚类思想进行路段划分。根据路段划分后的结果,对现有交通特性研究较为成熟的路段,可参考已有研究;而其他路段,则作为本次研究重点。

路段划分的主要依据是交通特性,包括道路交通环境特性、交通流特性、驾驶人行为特性等。

1.3　路段划分结果

对于本研究而言,采用聚类法根据车辆通行限界以及行车环境特性,从宏观上将道路划分为地上道路和地下道路。地上道路指车辆通行限界位于地表以上的道路,而地下道路指车辆通行限界位于地表以下的道路。对于地上道路,交通安全管控措施已有较多研究,并形成了系列规范,本研究可参考已有交通安全管控措施执行,故不再进一步细分。

对于地下道路,则可根据整个地下道路内是否存在交通分、合流,将地下道路进一步划分为一般地下道路和地下互通。一般地下道路指的是整个地下道路范围内不存在交通分、合流的道路,因此其交通特性与公路隧道类似,交通安全管控措施也可参考隧道执行,故也不再进一步细分。

众多研究表明,互通分、合流区交通特性差别较大,同时与一般路段交通特性差别也较大。因此对于地下互通路段,则可根据分、合流交通特性的不同,将其进一步划分为地下分流路段、地下合流路段和地下基本路段(图1)。

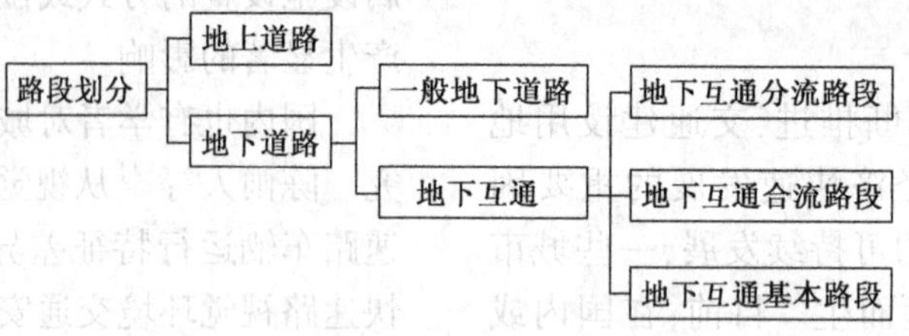

图1　城市地下互通式立交路段划分

根据上文分析以及路段划分结果可知:对于地上道路而言,交通特性、交通管控措施相关研究较多,也较为成熟。对于一般地下道路,以及地下互通基本路段而言,因其不存在隧道内的分合流,因此其与一般公路隧道路段交通特性类似,相关研究及交通管控措施也较为成熟。而对于地下互通分流路段及合流路段而言,国内外相关研究还较少,交通管控措施也还有待完善。因此,本文主要对地下互通分流路段和合流路段交通特性进行详细分析。

2　交通数据采集及处理

2.1　交通数据采集

本研究对地下互通分流路段和合流路段进行交通特性分析时,主要将其与地上互通分流路段和合流路段进行对比分析。

地下互通路段交通数据采集地点位于厦门万石山隧道与钟鼓山隧道交叉所设地下互通处,万石山隧道段设计速度 60km/h。本研究采集了 2020 年 8 月的分、合流区域各特征点监控视频，各个关键特征点的监控位置示意图如图 2 所示，共 5 个测点。各观测点中，测点 1 和测点 2 位于 C 匝道与万石山隧道分流路段处，测点 3、测点 4 和测点 5 位于 B 匝道与万石山隧道合流路段处。其中，C 匝道减速车道及其渐变段长度约 120m，B 匝道加速车道及其渐变段长度约 200m。

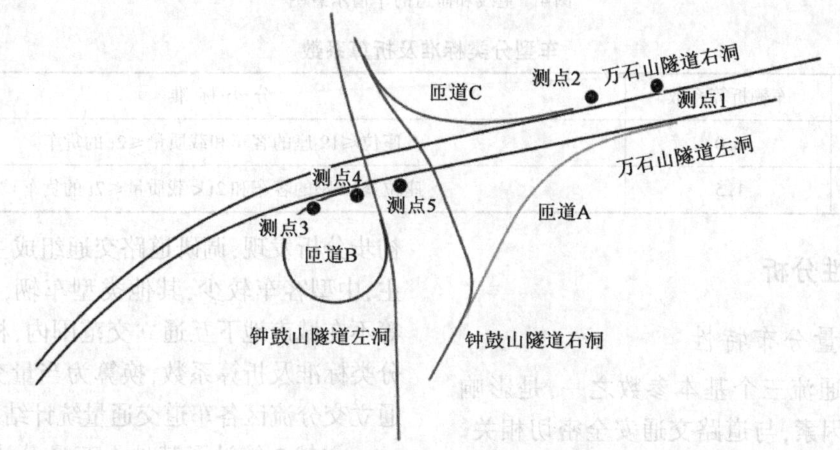

图 2 城市地下互通式立交路段划分

地上互通路段交通数据来源于现有研究中相关数据及结论。本研究中地上互通交通数据主要来源于东南大学侯佳博士学位论文《多车道高速公路分流影响区交通特性及通行能力分析》[11]（记为文献 1），合肥工业大学陈乾坤硕士学位论文《快速路互通立交分合流区交通冲突机理研究》[12]（记为文献 2），以及陈而越所发表的期刊论文《基于行驶轨迹的合流区车辆换道特性研究》[13]（记为文献 3）

2.2 交通数据处理

地下互通立交交通量及交通组成数据基于采集的视频数据由人工计数方法进行统计，方法较为简单，不做详述；速度数据则基于采集的视频数据，利用 Kinovea 视频分析软件进行获取。

用 Kinovea 软件的逐帧播放功能对目标车辆的行车轨迹进行分析。首先观察车辆的运动方向与拍摄角度的空间关系，在图像中找到清晰的固定标尺。再采用固定标尺法，即选取各个特征点附近的虚线标线或立面标记等作为标尺，并在标尺附近布设网格，并以汽车的后轮与地面的交点作为跟踪点，通过坐标数据输出后对行车轨迹进行分析，从而计算出车辆的运行速度。以万石山地下互通式立交减速车道上游路段某车辆为例，其监控录像视频处理如图 3 所示。

为便于后文表述，主线各车道名称从外侧至内侧分别记为 L1、L2 和 L3 等（若还有其他车道，则进一步记为 L4、L5 等），匝道各车道名称从内侧至外侧分别记为 ZD1、ZD2（同理，若还有其他车道，则进一步记为 ZD3、ZD4 等），入口匝道各车道名同出口匝道。对于本研究中实地调研道路而言，主线单向均为 3 车道，且均采用单车道出口、入口，因此加、减速车道均只有 1 条车道，即调研道路主线车道从外至内分别为 L1、L2、L3，共 3 条车道，出、入口仅有 ZD1。具体车道划分如图 4 所示。

图 3 地下互通行车轨迹分析示意图

根据车辆长度与载客人数，对观察到的车辆进行分类，根据分类结果将不同类型的车辆换算为标准车当量数。本研究对象为城市地下互通立交，因此仅涉及小客车与中型车两类车型。车型分类标准与折算系数见表 1。

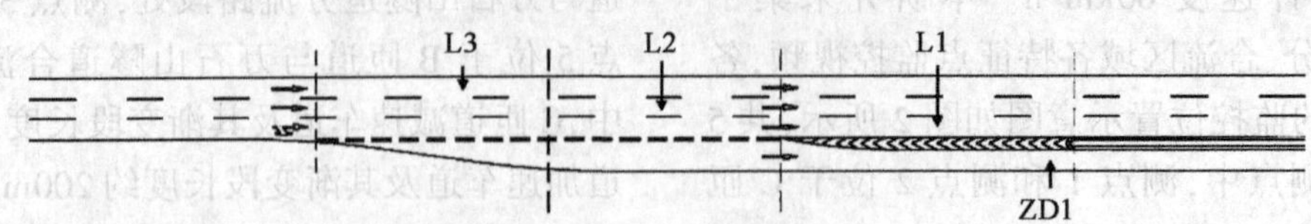

图4　主线和匝道的车道示意图

车型分类标准及折算系数　　表1

车辆代表车型	车辆折算系数	分类标准
小客车	1.0	座位≤19 座的客车和载质量≤2t 的货车
中型车	1.5	座位≥19 座的客车和 2t < 载质量≤7t 的货车

3　交通特性分析

3.1　交通量分布特性

交通量是交通流三个基本参数之一，是影响车辆运行的直接因素，与道路交通安全密切相关。与道路一般路段相比，因互通车辆的分流、合流影响，主线交通量会在各车道进行重新分布。本文主要分析分、合流区交通量在不同车道上的分布情况，分析中将分流区、合流区分别进行分析，同时与地上互通进行对比分析。

3.1.1　分流区交通量分布特性

对地下互通立交分流区渐变段附近交通量平峰时段在各个车道的分布比例进行了统计分析。初步分析发现，调研道路交通组成主要以小客车为主，中型客车较少，其他类型车辆，如大客车、货车等不在城市地下互通立交范围内，根据表1中车型分类标准及折算系数，换算为当量交通量。地下互通立交分流区各车道交通量统计结果见表2。

文献2统计了某地上互通分流区各车道交通占比情况，并将其分为平峰时段、早高峰、晚高峰时段3种时段，每种时段各3个视频数据。鉴于本研究中统计地下互通交通量分布的时间为平峰时段，因此对文献2中平峰时段3个视频数据进行了整理，得到地上互通分流区各车道平均交通量分布情况见表3。

地下互通分流区各车道交通量分布　　表2

车道位置	L3	L2	L1
交通量(pcu/h)	460	650	53
交通量占比(%)	39.55	55.89	4.56

地上互通分流区各车道交通量分布　　表3

车道位置	L3	L2	L1
交通量(pcu/h)	260	427	87
交通量占比(%)	33.59	55.17	11.24

注：表中外侧车道 L1 交通量仅为直行交通量，不包括分流交通量。

由表2和表3可知：

(1)地下互通外侧车道 L1 交通量占比约4.56%，中间车道 L2 和内侧车道 L3 交通量占比分别为55.89%和39.55%；地上互通外侧车道 L1 交通量占比约11.21%，中间车道 L2 和内侧车道 L3 交通量占比分别为55.17%和33.62%。这表明，无论是地上互通还是地下互通，直行车辆中，外侧车道 L1 的交通量均明显低于中间车道 L2 和内侧车道 L3。这是因为分流车辆对外侧车道车辆影响相对较大，因此绝大部分直行车辆倾向于在内侧两条车道行驶。

(2)地下互通外侧车道 L1 交通量占比约4.56%，地上互通外侧车道交通量占比约11.21%，与地上互通相比，地下互通直行车辆中外侧车道交通量占比相对更低。这表明，与地上互通分流区相比，地下互通分流区车辆在内侧两条车道行驶的意愿更为强烈。这是因为对于地下互通而言,绝大部分分流车辆在距出口较远位置就驶入了外侧车道,外侧车道车流密度较大,舒适性相对较差,因此地下互通分流区直行车辆在内侧两条车道行驶的意愿更为强烈。

3.1.2 合流区交通量分布特性

探讨合流区交通量分布特性时,交通量观测位置选在加速车道合流鼻附近。同前文所述,调研道路交通组成主要以小客车为主,因此统计分析时未对车型进行细分,以断面自然车数量进行统计分析。平峰时段地下互通立交分流区各车道交通量统计结果见表4。

同前文,将文献2中平峰时段3个视频数据进行处理,得到地上互通合流区各车道平均交通量分布情况见表5。

地下互通合流区各车道交通量分布 表4

车道位置	L3	L2	L1
交通量(pcu/h)	341	466	40
交通量占比(%)	40.26	55.02	4.72

地上互通合流区各车道交通量分布 表5

车道位置	L3	L2	L1
交通量(pcu/h)	273	420	53
交通量占比(%)	36.60	56.30	7.10

注:表中外侧车道L1交通量仅为直行交通量,不包括汇入交通量。

由表4和表5可知:

(1)地下互通外侧车道L1交通量占比约4.32%,中间车道L2和内侧车道L3交通量占比分别为55.08%和42.60%;地上互通外侧车道L1交通量占比约7.14%,中间车道L2和内侧车道L3交通量占比分别为56.25%和36.61%。合流区交通量分布特性与分流区类似,无论是地上互通还是地下互通,直行车辆中,外侧车道L1均明显低于中间车道L2和内侧车道L3。这是因为匝道车辆的汇入会对主线车辆产生一定的干扰,而对于L1、L2、L3三条车道而言,汇入车辆对L1干扰最大,因此驾驶人更倾向于走内侧两条车道。

(2)地下互通外侧车道L1交通量占比4.32%,该值明显低于地上互通外侧车道L1交通占比7.14%,这表明地下互通合流区驾驶人倾向于走内侧两条车道的意愿较地上互通驾驶人更为强烈。这可能与地下互通、地上互通标线施划方式有关,地上互通、地下互通标线施划方式如图5所示。由图5可知,因为地下互通外侧车道L1与中间车道L2之间为实线,所以可认为匝道驶入车辆几乎不会干扰中间车道L2及内侧车道L3,而地上互通外侧车道L1与中间车道L2之间为虚线,因此匝道驶入车辆对中间车道L2及内侧车道L3仍有一定影响;此外,因地下互通外侧车道L1与中间车道L2之间为实线,若匝道驶入交通量较大,在不考虑由外车车道L1压实线强行变道至中间车道L2的情况下,匝道驶入车辆对外侧车道干扰更大,严重时甚至会产生拥堵。综上,地下互通驾驶人倾向于走内侧两车道的意愿较地上互通驾驶人更为强烈。

3.2 换道特性

车辆的换道会导致所在区域甚至相邻车道和上下游的交通流紊乱,影响其他车辆的正常行驶,与道路交通安全密切相关。本研究将对车辆在地下互通和地上互通分、合流区的换道位置分别进行对比分析。本研究将车辆从某一车道跨越标线变道至另一车道过程中跨越标线的位置视作换道点,如图6所示。为便于表述车辆具体换道位置,现做如下规定:

对于分流区而言,换道点特指由中间车道L2变道至外侧车道L1过程中车辆跨越标线的位置,换道位置指该换道点与减速车道渐变段起点之间的距离;对于合流区而言,换道点特指由加速车道ZD1变道至外侧车道L1过程中车辆跨越标线的位置,换道位置指该换道点与加速车道起点之间的距离。

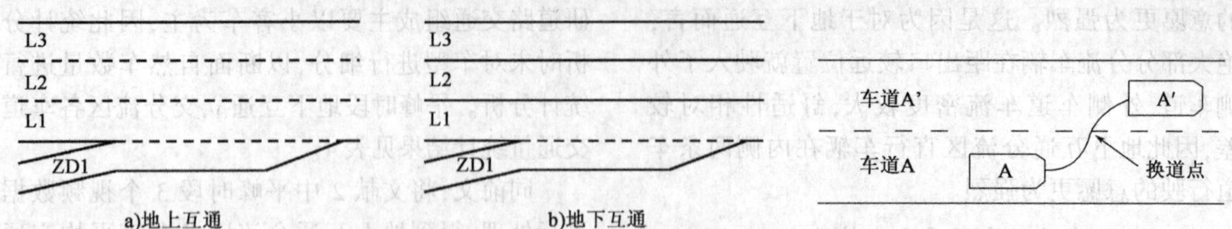

图5　合流区标线对比

图6　车辆换道点示意图

3.2.1　分流区换道特性

探讨地下互通分流区换道特性时,限于视频数据录制范围,观测位置位于地下互通分流区减速车道渐变段起点上游约200m处。以100m为间隔,将其划分为两段,其中减速车道渐变段起点上游200~100m记为路段1,减速车道渐变段上游100~0m记为路段2。该范围内车辆换道情况统计结果见表6。

地下互通分流区车辆换道位置　　表6

换道方式及位置	L2变L1(路段1)	L2变L1(路段2)	L1变L2(路段1)	L1变L2(路段2)
交通量(pcu/h)	35	7	15	2
交通量占比(%)	6.89	1.38	2.95	0.39

注:1.观测时间内分流交通量为508pcu/h,直行交通量957pcu/h;

2.观测时间内未见车辆从内侧车道L3变道至中间车道L2,或由L2变道至L3。

文献1统计了地上互通分流区在不同车道数、不同交通量情况下减速车道渐变段起点上游车辆换道位置。其中与地下互通较为接近的条件是车道数采用双向六车道,交通量 $q < 1700$pcu/h时,该条件下地上互通分流区减速车道渐变段起点上游200m内车辆换道情况见表7。

地上互通分流区车辆换道位置　　表7

换道位置	路段1	路段2	路段1上游
交通量占比(%)	9.8	0	90.2

由表6和表7可知:

(1)地下互通分流车辆中,于路段1从中间车道L2变至外侧车道L1的交通量占比约为6.89%,该值低于地上互通的9.8%。这说明对于地下互通而言,更多分流车辆于更上游位置就已经变道至外侧车道,需要分流的驾驶人提前变道至外侧车道的意识更明显。

(2)地下互通分流车道中,于路段2从中间车道L2变道至外侧车道L1的交通量占比为1.38%,而地上互通该值为0。这说明对与地上互通相比,地下互通分流路段处有相对更多的驾驶人未能准确识别到出口,临近出口渐变段时才强行变道至外侧车道,地下互通路段出口识别更加困难。这是因为,地下互通采用人工照明,与地上互通相比,驾驶人视觉条件相对较差;地下互通行车环境封闭,汽车尾气浓度增加,会影响驾驶人能见度,进一步恶化驾驶人视觉条件;此外,因隧道侧墙为实体,严重影响通视条件,三者均会影响驾驶人对出口标志及出口的识别。

3.2.2　合流区换道特性

将合流区以20m为间隔进行分组,调研道路加速车道及其渐变段长度约为200m,因此共被划分为10组,从加速车道起点至渐变段终点处分别为路段1、路段2……路段10。共统计了合流区100辆车从加速车道(包括其渐变段)ZD1换道至外侧车道L1的换道位置,结果见表8。

地下互通合流区车辆换道位置　　表8

换道位置	路段1	路段2	路段3	路段4	路段5	路段6	路段7	路段8	路段9	路段10
	0~20m	20~40m	40~60m	60~80m	80~100m	100~120m	120~140m	140~160m	160~180m	180~200m
频率(%)	0	2	3	7	20	33	24	10	1	0

文献[3]对将地上互通全长250m的合流区断面坐标以10m为间隔分组,共分为25组,统计每个网格内的换道频数。为使结果便于与地上互通对比,将文献[3]中地上互通合流区重新划分为

10组,每组25m,再统计每组的换道频数,结果见表9。

地上互通合流区车辆换道位置　表9

换道位置	路段1	路段2	路段3	路段4	路段5	路段6	路段7	路段8	路段9	路段10
	0~20m	20~40m	40~60m	60~80m	80~100m	100~120m	120~140m	140~160m	160~180m	180~200m
频率(%)	0	9	32	14	8	17	14.5	3.5	2	0

地下互通换道位置主要集中于路段5~路段8,而地上互通换道位置主要集中于路段3~路段7,地下互通车辆换道处距加速车道起点距离较地上互通大。这说明与地上互通相比,地下互通匝道汇入主线车辆需要更长的时间来观察主线车辆情况。这是因为对于地上互通而言,合流三角区一般能满足通视要求,因此匝道车辆可提前观察到主线车辆情况;而对于地下互通而言,因受隧道侧墙等影响,三角区通视情况很难满足要求,匝道车辆无法提前观察到主线车辆情况,因此地下互通匝道汇入主线车辆需要更长的时间来观察主线车辆情况,进而导致地下互通车辆换道处距加速车道起点距离比地上互通大。

3.3　速度特性

本研究关于速度特性的分析从速度横向分布特性及速度纵向分布特性两个方面展开。速度横向分布特性是以某断面为例,分析该断面处不同车道速度差异性;速度纵向分布特性是分车道分析速度沿道路纵向的变化情况。

3.3.1　分流区速度特性

1)速度横向分布特性

在探讨地下互通分流区速度横向分布特性时,将观测断面选于分流区减速车道(包括其渐变段)中间位置。

根据《道路交通标志与标线》(GB 5768—2017),当道路设计速度60km/h,最低断面测速样本量为85辆,本研究中各车道均采集100辆车的速度进行统计分析,地下互通分流区各车道速度区间频率分布规律如图7所示,各车道速度特征值见表10。

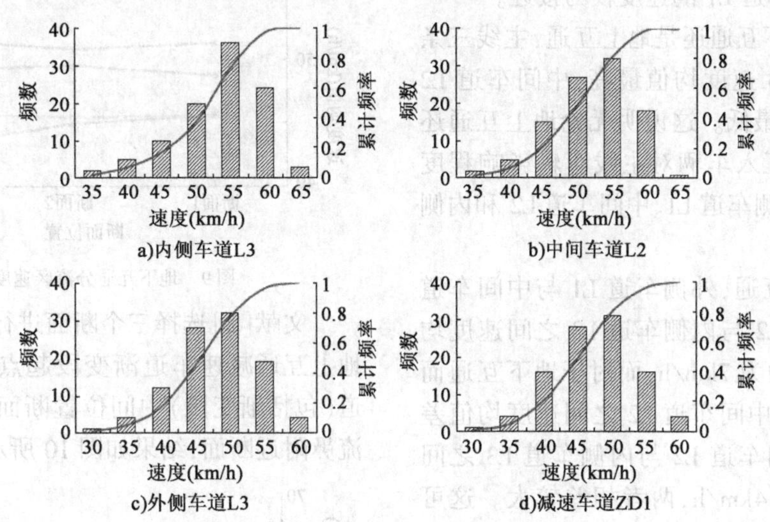

图7　地下互通分流区各车道速度的区间频率分布

地下互通分流区速度特征值　表10

车道位置	L1	L2	L3	ZD1
速度均值(标准差)(km/h)	45.48(5.47)	49.48(5.76)	50.78(6.03)	44.93(5.56)

文献[2]统计了某地上互通分流区主线3条车道L1、L2、L3及2条减速车道ZD1、ZD2的车辆速度特征值,以及各车道速度区间及频率分布。该分流区主线3条车道及内侧匝道车辆速度的区间频率分布如图8所示,各车道速度特征值见表11。

地上互通分流区速度特征值　表11

车道位置	L1	L2	L3	ZD1
速度均值(标准差)(km/h)	48.10 (8.54)	55.50 (10.80)	62.30 (9.89)	47.30 (8.07)

由以上图表可知:

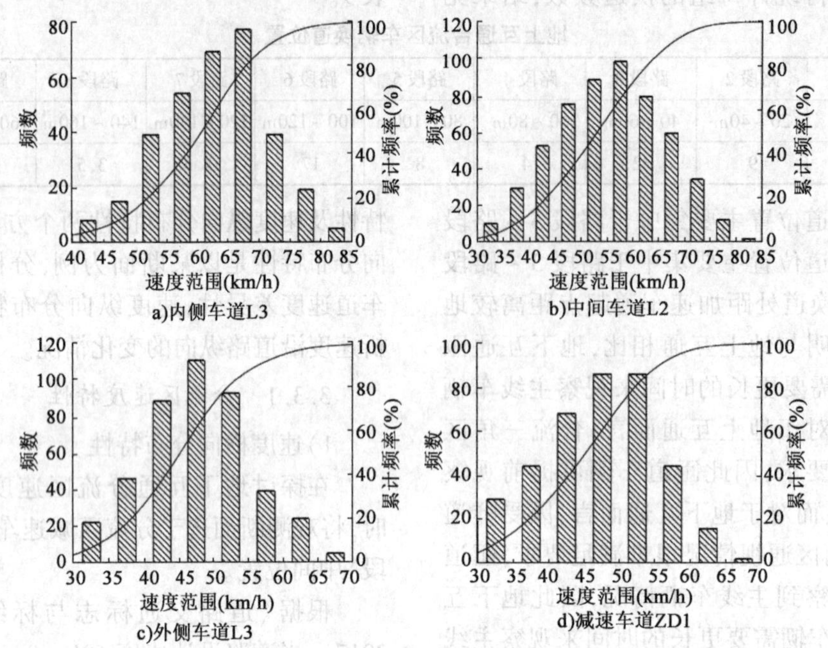

图8　地上互通分流区各车道速度的区间频率分布

(1)无论是地下互通还是地上互通,匝道ZD1速度均明显低于主线内侧两条车道L2、L3的速度,而与主线外侧车道L1的速度较为接近。

(2)无论是地下互通还是地上互通,主线三条车道中内侧车道L3速度均值最高,中间车道L2次之,外侧车道L1最低。这说明无论地上互通还是地下互通,匝道汇入车辆对主线车辆影响程度从高到低分别为外侧车道L1、中间车道L2和内侧车道L3。

(3)对于地上互通,外侧车道L1与中间车道L2,以及中间车道L2与内侧车道L3之间速度均值差值相差无几,约为7km/h;而对于地下互通而言,外侧车道L1与中间车道L2之间速度均值差值约为1km/h,中间车道L2与内侧车道L3之间速度均值差值约为4km/h,两者相差较大。这可能也是由地上互通、地下互通合流区标线施划方式不同所致,具体分析同前文。

2)速度纵向分布特性

为获取分流区交通流速度纵向分布特性,本文在互通立交分流区减速车道渐变段起点附近、减速车道(包括渐变段)中部位置以及减速车道分流鼻附近各选定了1个测速断面。在各断面处,每条车道各采集100辆车的速度进行统计分析,结果如图9所示。图中断面1表示减速车道渐变段起点附近断面,断面2表示减速车道(包括渐变段)中部位置断面,断面3表示减速车道分流鼻附近断面。

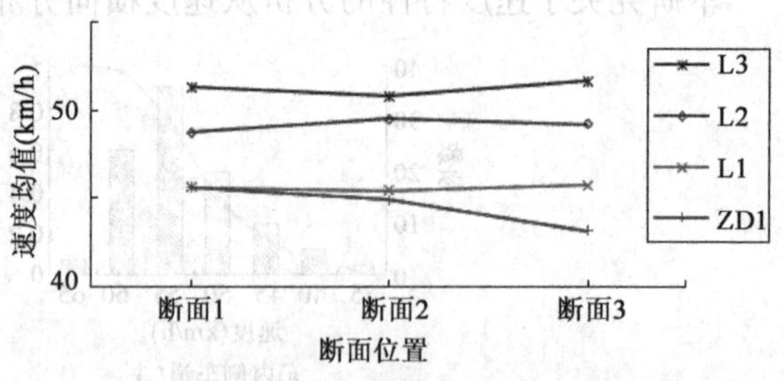

图9　地下互通分流区速度纵向分布

文献[2]选择三个断面进行作图分析,分别为地上互通减速车道渐变段起点附近断面,减速车道(包括渐变段)中间位置断面,以及减速车道分流鼻附近断面,结果如图10所示。

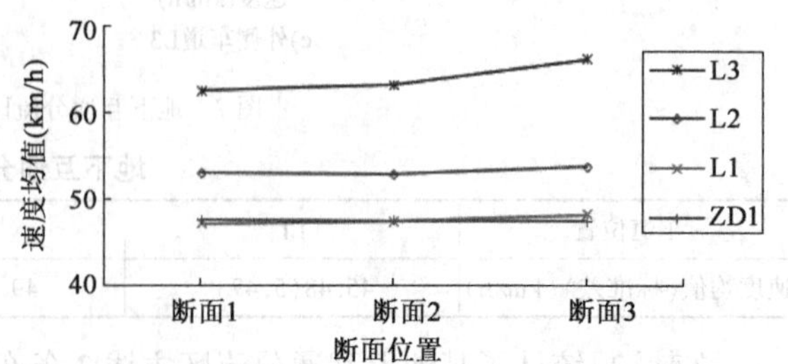

图10　地上互通分流区速度纵向分布

由图9和图10可知:

(1)地上互通内侧车道L3速度均值呈上升趋势,可能是因为地上互通驾驶人为避免分流车辆对其影响,有希望快速驶离分流区的意愿;而地下互通内侧车道 L3 速度均值呈波动趋势,基本维持恒定,这可能是因为地下互通分流区内侧车道 L3 与中间车道 L2 之间行车道分隔线为实线,分流车辆对内侧车道 L3 影响很小,因此地下互通分流区驾驶人该种意愿不明显。

(2)地上互通中间车道 L2 速度均值呈先下降后上升的变化趋势,这可能是因为地上互通外侧车道 L1 与中间车道 L2 之间行车道分割线为虚线,因此仍有部分车辆在断面 1 至断面 2 范围内进行变道,受其影响,速度有所降低;而从断面 2 至断面 3,因分流车辆基本已经完成分流,因此速度有所上升。与之相比,地下互通中间车道 L2 呈波动趋势,基本维持恒定,这可能也是因为地下互通分流区中间车道 L2 与外侧车道 L1 之间行车道分隔线为实线,因此分流车辆对中间车道 L2 影响很小,其呈现出波动趋势。

(3)断面 1 至断面 2 范围内,无论是地上互通还是地下互通,外侧车道 L3 速度变化趋势与减速车道基本一致,且速度均值大小基本相同。这主要是因为分流车辆主要在该范围由外侧车道 L3 驶入减速车道 ZD1,因此外侧车道 L3 受分流车辆影响较为严重,其速度均值降至与减速车道 ZD1 相当水平。

(4)断面 2 至断面 3 范围内,无论是地上互通还是地下互通,外侧车道 L1 均呈上升趋势,这是因为在断面 1 至断面 2 范围内分流车辆基本已经完成分流,因此断面 2 后速度有所上升;而减速车道 ZD1 均呈下降趋势,这与驾驶人在减速车道上的减速过程相对应。

(5)断面 2 至断面 3,与地上互通相比,地下互通 ZD1 速度降低更为明显,这可能与所接匝道线形有关。

3.3.2 合流区速度特性

1)速度横向分布特性

根据车道换道位置分析结果可知,地下互通合流区由匝道汇入外车车道车辆的换道位置主要集中于路段 5—路段 8,而其他路段相对较少。因此,在探讨合流区速度特性时,将观测断面选于路段 5—路段 8 中间位置。

合流区各车道也均采集 100 辆车的速度进行统计分析,合流区各车道速度区间频率分布规律如图 11 所示,各车道速度特征值见表 12。

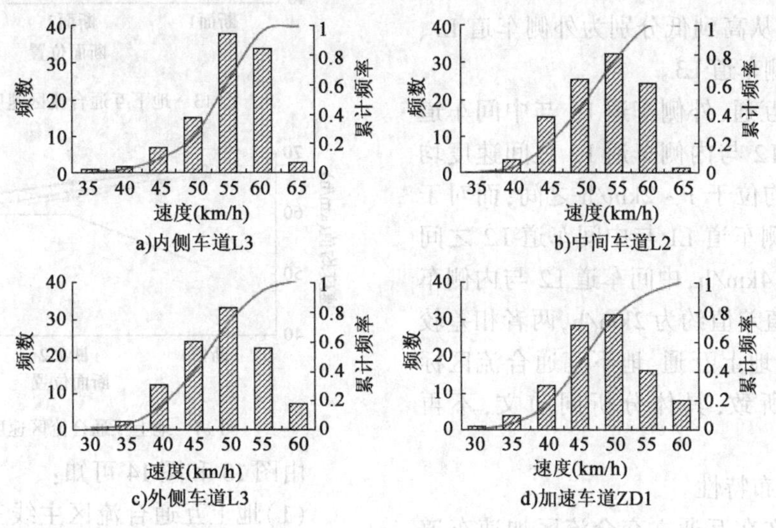

图 11 地下互通合流区各车道速度区间频率分布

地下互通合流区速度特征值 表 12

车道位置	L1	L2	L3	ZD1
速度均值(标准差)(km/h)	46.60 (5.9)	50.58 (5.48)	52.48 (5.27)	45.73 (5.58)

文献[2]中地上互通合流区主线 3 条车道及内侧匝道车辆速度的区间频率分布如图 12 所示,各车道速度特征值见表 13。

地上互通合流区速度特征值 表 13

车道位置	L1	L2	L3	ZD1
速度均值(标准差)(km/h)	63.0 (7.69)	64.6 (7.52)	65.8 (6.79)	57.3 (6.52)

由以上图表可知:

(1)无论是地下互通还是地上互通,匝道 ZD1 速度均明显低于主线三条车道 L1、L2、L3 的速度。

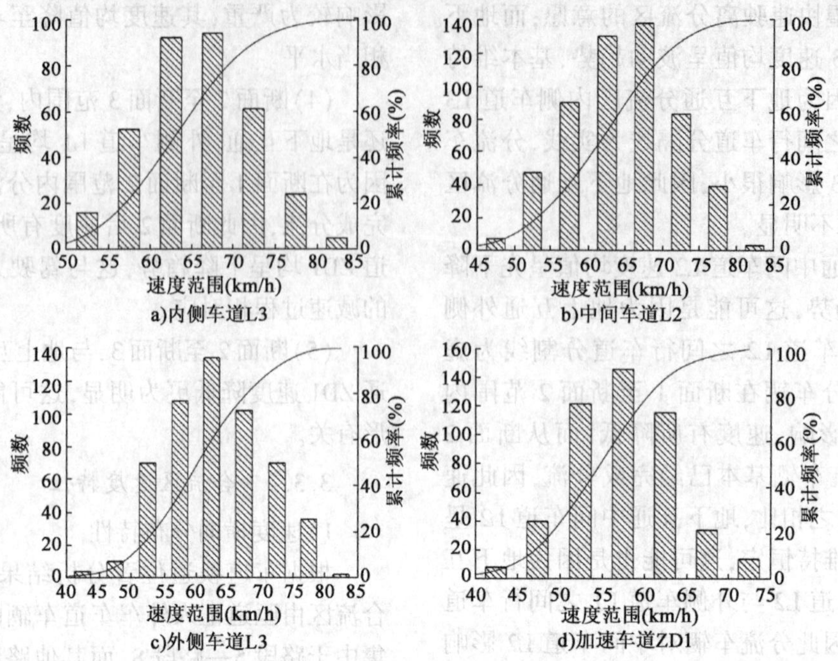

图12　地上互通合流区各车道速度区间频率分布

(2)无论是地下互通还是地上互通,主线三条车道中内侧车道L3速度均值最高,中间车道L2次之,外侧车道L1最低;内侧车道L3速度标准差最低,中间车道L2次之,外侧车道L1最高。这说明无论地上互通还是地下互通,匝道汇入车辆对主线车辆影响程度从高到低分别为外侧车道L1、中间车道L2和内侧车道L3。

(3)对于地上互通,外侧车道L1与中间车道L2,以及中间车道L2与内侧车道L3之间速度均值差值相差无几,均位于1~2km/h之间;而对于地下互通而言,外侧车道L1与中间车道L2之间速度均值差值约为4km/h,中间车道L2与内侧车道L3之间速度均值差值约为2km/h,两者相差较大。这可能也是因地上互通、地下互通合流区标线施划方式不同所致,具体分析同前文,不再详述。

2)速度纵向分布特性

同分流区,本文在互通立交合流区加速车道起点附近,断面2表示路段5—路段8中间位置以及加速车道渐变段终点附近各选定了1个测速断面。各断面处,每条车道各采集100辆车的速度进行统计分析,结果如图13所示。

文献2也选择三个断面作图进行分析,三个断面分别为地上互通加速车道起点附近断面,路段5—路段8范围内断面,以及渐变段终点附近断面,统计结果如图14所示。

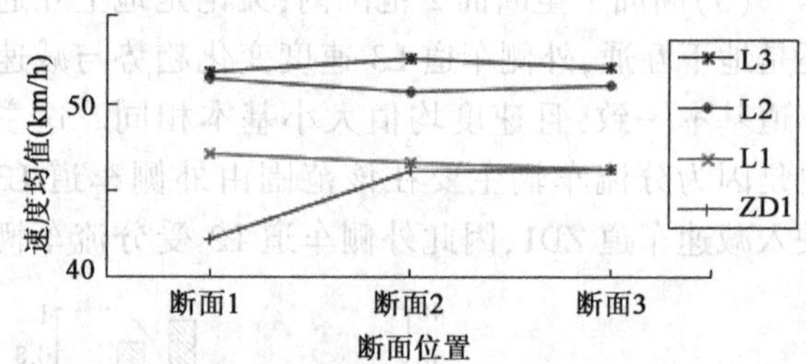

图13　地下互通合流区速度纵向分布

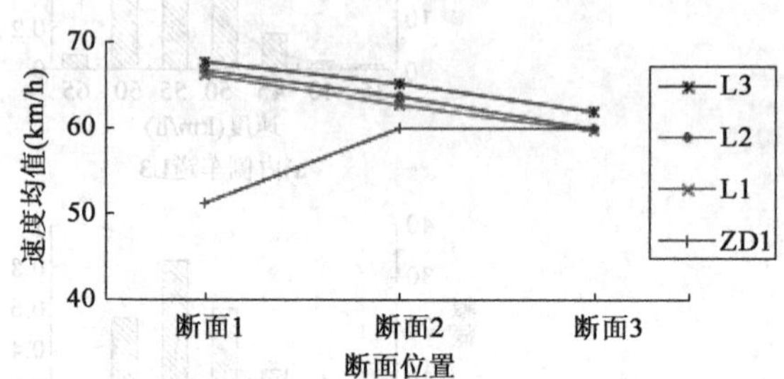

图14　地上互通合流区速度纵向分布

由图13和图14可知:

(1)地上互通合流区主线三条车道速度均值均呈下降趋势,这是因为地上互通合流区行车道分割线均为虚线,因此匝道合流车辆可变道至主线三条车道,因此合流车道对主线三条车道均有影响,使其速度均值有所下降。

(2)对于地下互通而言,合流区内侧车道L3和中间车道L2速度均值呈波动趋势,外侧车道L1速度均值呈下降趋势,这是因为地下互通合流区仅加速车道与外侧车道之间行车道分隔线为虚线，而主线三条车道之间行车道分割线均为实线，因此合流车道仅对外侧车道L1有明显影响。

(3)无论地上互通还是地下互通加速车道ZD1速度均值均呈先上升，再基本保持恒定的变化趋势。这分别反映了合流车辆的加速以及伺机汇入主线的过程。

4 结语

本文在对比分析了地上和地下互通分合流路段的交通量分布、换道位置、速度分布特征后，得出了以下具体结论：

(1)地上和地下互通分合流路段的最内侧车道交通量占比大于88%，表明直行驾驶人在互通分合流路段倾向于走内侧两条车道，而且驾驶人的该倾向在地下互通分合流路段更为明显。

(2)驾驶人在地下互通分流路段容易提前变道，但也有驾驶人在出口处强行变道。驾驶人在地下互通合流路段的换道集中于变速车道及渐变段的中间区域，而且汇入主线车辆需要更长的时间来观察主线车辆情况。

(3)地上和地下互通分合流路段外侧车道速度最低，其次是中间车道、内侧车道。相较于地上互通分合流路段，地下互通外侧与中间车道速度差值较高。

参考文献

[1] Wood J M, Chaparro A, Lacherez P, et al. Useful Field of View Predicts Driving in the Presence of Distracters [J]. Optometry and vision science: official publication of the American Academy of Optometry, 2012, 89(4): 373-381.

[2] Barkley R A, D Cox. A review of driving risks and impairments associated with attention-deficit/hyperactivity disorder and the effects of stimulant medication on driving performance. [J]. Journal of Safety Research, 2007, 38(1): 113-128.

[3] Stutts J, Feaganes J, Reinfurt D, et al. Driver's exposure to distractions in their natural driving environment [J]. Accident Analysis & Prevention, 2005, 37(6): 1093-1101.

[4] 陈雨人，郑仕文. 地下道路视觉环境影响车辆运行特征机理分析[J]. 同济大学学报(自然科学版)，2013，41(07)：1031-1039.

[5] 刘硕，王俊骅，张兰芳，等. 城市地下道路车速特征及运行车速模型[J]. 同济大学学报(自然科学版)，2015，43(11)：1677-1683.

[6] 李素艳，杨东援，俞明健. 城市地下道路出、入口变速车道长度设计研究[J]. 交通标准化，2006(12)：22-25.

[7] 周灿，王红，陈勇. 基于路上实验的地下互通立交合流区交通流特性研究[J]. 工程与建设，2020，34(03)：404-406.

[8] 袁胜强，景啸，史程祥. 城市地下互通立交通行能力计算[J]. 同济大学学报(自然科学版)，2021，49(02)：236-242.

[9] 崔玉姣，李波，王静，等. 基于主成分-聚类法的高速公路沥青路面养护路段划分[J]. 公路，2019，64(03)：290-296.

[10] 张鑫，张卫华. 考虑安全的快速路合流区主线车道宽度研究[J]. 华中科技大学学报(自然科学版)，2021，49(06)：26-30.

[11] 侯佳. 多车道高速公路分流影响区交通特性及通行能力分析[D]. 南京：东南大学，2018.

[12] 陈乾. 快速路互通立交分合流区交通冲突机理研究[D]. 合肥：合肥工业大学，2019.

[13] 陈而越，陈金山，郭建钢，等. 基于行驶轨迹的合流区车辆换道特性研究[J]. 哈尔滨商业大学学报(自然科学版)，2020，36(02)：231-237.

Evaluation of Urban Road Network Resilience Based on Three-dimensional Space Vector Model

Jianjun Wang* Shiyu Zheng
(School of Transportation Engineering, Chang' an University)

Abstract The ability of urban road network to resistdisturbances is a problem which attract high attention in the field of transportation.

Based on previous studies on the reliability and vulnerability of road network, in this paper we propose the concept of urban road network resilience. At first, the urban road resilience assessment model is constructed from three latitudes of absorption capacity, adaptive capacity and recovery capacity. Secondly, the road speed difference and meteorological environment index are adopted to construct the road section importance model to quantify the absorptive capacity. And then the adaptive and recovery ability are quantified by the proportion of sections in different speed ranges. Finally, the resilience value is calculated through the three-dimensional space vector model. Major holiday and severe weather are compared with regular period. We take Hefei Demonstration Area as an example.

The results show that the range of resilience value is 0.54 and the variance is 0.025 during the regular period. The range and variance of resilience value have increased by 38% and 80% during major holiday. In terms of severe weather, they are increase by 31% and 4%. The resilience of the two disturbances scenes fluctuates greatly. However, the absorption capacity of roads during major holiday is stronger.

This research can provide a theoretical basis for the performance evaluation of urban road network and provide relevant suggestions for taking recovery measures.

Keywords Urban Roads Resilience Disturbance Scenes Three-dimensional space Vector Model

0 Introduction

In order to research the potential impact of disturbance events on the urban network, the previous approach is to use reliability or vulnerability indicators to measure the possible adverse effects of the system. With the increasing complexity of the urban network, how to scientifically evaluate the operation status of the road network and improve its resilience in the face of disturbance has attracted great attention.

In the previous research, road network reliability and vulnerability are the main concerns. The research on reliability mainly includes the use of the relative size of the largest connected subgraph to measure the degree of road network connectivity (Feng et al., 2019), and the use of Bayesian network to calculate the reliability of the overall road network connection (Jia et al., 2019). Cui et al. (2019) evaluated the reliability of road network connectivity based on the goal of the lowest cost of reinforcement and optimization.

The research on vulnerability mainly includes the use of vulnerability indicators to describe the road network performance under normal and abnormal events (Lu et al., 2019), and the use of strong connection value of the road section (Yang et al., 2019). Shen (2014) evaluated the vulnerability of the urban road network at the topological structure level. Du et al. (2020) proposed road network vulnerability analysis method based on weighted flow betweenness centrality. Cloud model and spectral analysis also be used to measure road network traffic vulnerability (Deng 2019; Li et al., 2020). Some scholars proposed to evaluate the vulnerability of the road network from the perspective of time.

such as using the average travel time of the road network, the total travel time of the road segment, and the total service time at the intersection (Rong 2018; Li et al., 2016). An et al. (2018) constructed comprehensive indicators to evaluate the vulnerability of urban roads based on changes in the total travel time of traffic flow sections and the total service time at intersections. With the development of complex network, some researchers use complex network methods to identify faulty road network (Nourzad 2016). Qian et al. (2015) constructed a complex network model of the road traffic system, and studied the situation of road cascading failures under the influence of different delays, time dissipation factors and load capacity. Dynamic research is also gradually emerging, such as the use of taxi trajectory data, mathematical model methods for dynamic routes (Ausk 2014).

However, the existing research fails to start from the evolutionary nature of the network itself to deal with disturbance, and rarely considers the adaptive capacity and recovery capacity of the system after disturbance. These are the focus of traffic participants and managers, and they are also an important basis for systematic evaluation of the state of the road network.

With the integration of the concept of resilience and system science, researchers began to use resilience to evaluate the performance of road network under disturbances. Regarding the definition of resilience, scholars have conducted extensive research. Lin (2017) believed that urban network resilience is the ability of affected regions to respond to shocks and restore, maintain or improve the original system features and key functions. Ip et al. (2011) defineded the resilience of the road traffic system as the weighted sum of the resilience of all nodes, and the resilience of the nodes is determined by the weighted average reliability value of the channel. Lv and Gao (2020) believed that resilience is the ability of a system to absorb disturbances and recover from disturbances. Sai (2020) thought that resilience is the ability of the road system to resist, absorb, adapt and recover from its impact in a timely and effective manner in the face of emergencies. Wan, Yang, et al. (2018) believed that resilience reflects the inherent ability of the network to respond to disasters and the ability to return to a normal state or service level within a specific time.

Based on previous research, this paper defines the resilience of urban roads: the ability of urban road sections to recover to their normal service level and maintain normal operation after partial loss of functions when they are invaded by disasters, accidents.

At present, some scholars have carried out research on network resilience. Lv et al. (2020) aimed at problems such as incomplete evaluation of system performance by existing resilience indicators and failure to consider the impact of traffic flow. They also proposed an urban network resilience assessment model based on day-to-day traffic assignment (DTA) (CALVERTSC 2018). Simeon et al. (2019) considered the resilience of the network and proposed the resilience of the link performance index to evaluate the resilience level of a single road section.

Previous researches have studied the actual network based on the theory of resilience, but the resilience assessment method is relatively simplified. Thus, it's difficult to deeply analyze the specific state tendency of the urban network. In order to solve the problem that the assessment index is relatively single and lacks systemicity, based on the systematic analysis of the resilience theory, the resilience evaluation method of urban roads is proposed. The resilience model is calculated from the three dimensions of absorptive capacity, adaptive capacity and recovery capacity. Then, considering major holiday and severe weather, the three-dimensional space vector is used to calculate the resilience modulus.

1　Materials and Methods

1.1　Study Area and Data Source

OpenITS Hefei Demonstration Zone (https://www.openits.cn/) is located along Huangshan Road in Hefei Economic and Technological Development Zone, Anhui Province. The distribution of road sections and microwave detectors in the demonstration area is shown (Fig. 1). It mainly includes the seven sections: Yulan Road, Xiangzhang Road, Tianzhu Road, Tianhu Road, Science Road, Huangshan Road and Tianzhi Road. The obtained microwave detection data are shown in Tab.1.

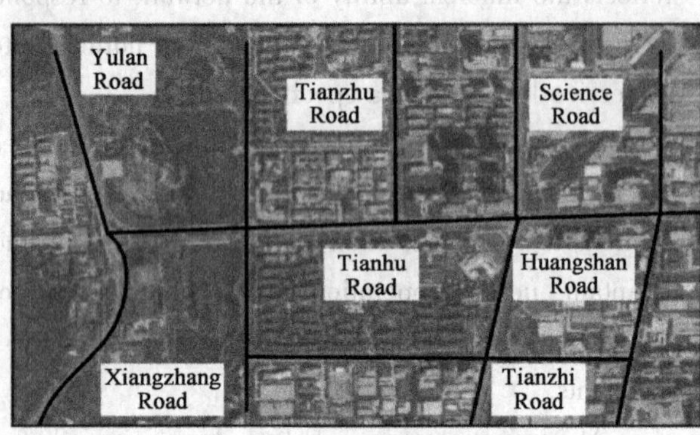

a)Regional Road Sections

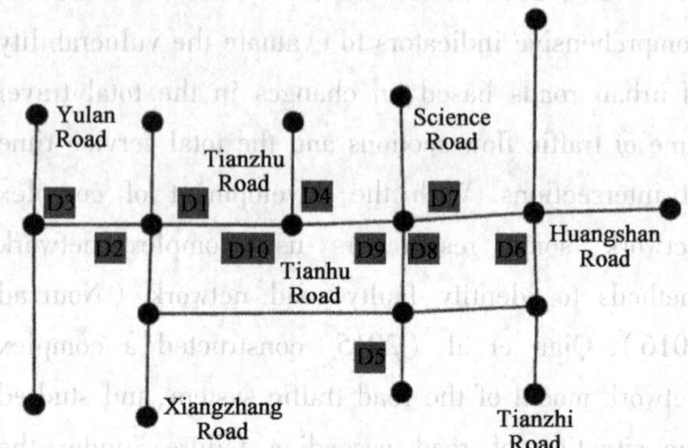

b)Distribution of Microwave Detectors

Fig. 1　Study Area

Microwave Detection Data　　Tab. 1

Field Name	Data Type	Remark
ID	NUMBER	ID Number
DETECT_CLASS	VARCHAR	Equipment Type C: Microwave Detector
DETECT_ID	VARCHAR	Device ID
ROAD_ID	NUMBER	Section Number
COLLECT_TIME	VARCHAR	Acquisition Time
ROOM_OCCUPANCY	VARCHAR	Time Occupation Rate (%)
SPEED	NUMBER	Average Lane Speed(km/h)
LANE	VARCHAR	Lane Number 0: 1st lane from left to right 1: 2nd lane from left to right 2: 3rd lane from left to right 3: 4th lane from left to right
VEHICLE_CLASS	VARCHAR	Vehicle Type 0: pedestrian 1: pedestrian 2: bike 3: passenger car 4: truck
VOLUME	NUMBER	Traffic flow in a Statistical Period (vehicles)

The time range of the data is from September 9, 2016 to September 18, 2016. We use PYTHON to process the raw data. For missing data, the method of filling in the average value of adjacent periods before and after is used.

Considering the design speed and the actual operation status of the actual road section, operating speed is divided into three sections: low(<20km/h), normal (20-40 km/h) and high (40-60 km/h). The value after calculating the variance is normalized, so that the result is between [0, 1]. The historical weather conditions are obtained by querying the network weather software, and the meteorological environment index is calculated by combining relevant documents and meteorological industry standards.

1.2 Selection of Urban Road Operation Scenes

The main disturbance factors of Hefei's urban roads are severe weather and major holiday. The resilience of urban network under three scenes: regular period, major holiday, and severe weather are evaluated (Tab. 2).

Related Characteristics of the Research Scenes Tab. 2

Scenes	Regular Period	Major Holiday	Severe Weather
Time	September 10, 2016	September 17, 2016	September 14, 2016
Scene Description	Good weather and good road conditions	On the last day of the Dragon Boat Festival, the service capacity of the network was impacted.	Heavy rains have severely influenced the service capacity of the network.
Operating Conditions	General traffic conditions	Withstand greater traffic	Suffering from severe weather

1.3 Methods

Definition of Resilience

Resilience evaluation takes the entire process from disturbance occurs to recovery as the research object, and divides the system operating state into five stages: initial state, degradation process, steady state, recovery process, and state after recovery.

The horizontal axis is time t, and the vertical axis is system performance F. The curve is called the system performance curve. The period between t_e and t_d is the stage where the disturbance occurs. The degradation curve of system performance represents a time-related event, which is not necessarily linear. The recovery system performance may be consistent with the initial state, or may be reduced or improved (Fig. 2).

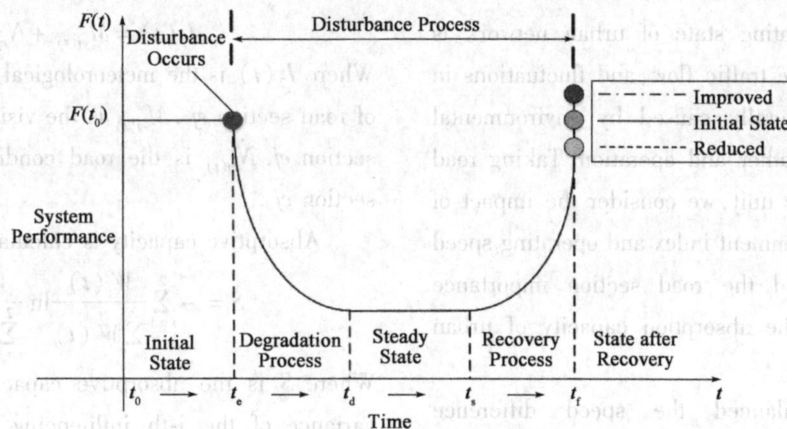

Fig. 2 Changes in System Performance from the Perspective of Resilience

Resilience is the ability of a system to absorb disturbance and recover from disturbance. Its connotation includes three steages. The first is the ability to absorb disturbance, which is reflected by the degradation of system performance under disturbance. The second is the ability to adapt after disturbance, which is a steady state after disturbance. The third is the ability to recover from disturbance, which is reflected by the speed and degree of system recovery. Therefore, the resilience evaluation index should comprehensively consider the different stages of system performance changes.

Urban Network Resilience Assessment Method

The absorptive capacity is expressed by the speed difference of the road section and the meteorological environment index. The adaptive capacity and recovery capacity are expressed by the ratio of the average speed of the road section. The following table is the urban network resilience assessment framework (Fig. 3).

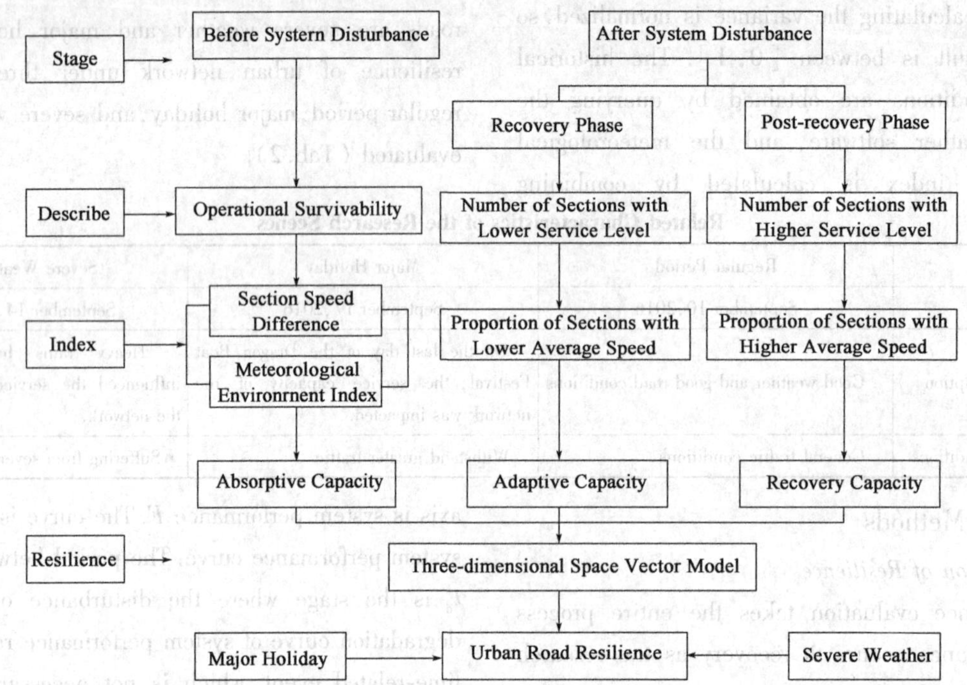

Fig. 3 Urban Network Resilience Assessment Framework

- Absorptive capacity

Absorptive capacity is the ability of the network to resist disturbance and be able to resume normal operation. The operating state of urban network is easily affected by the traffic flow, and fluctuations in traffic flow are generally caused by environmental changes such as weather and operation. Taking road sections as the basic unit, we consider the impact of meteorological environment index and operating speed difference, and build the road section importance model to quantify the absorption capacity of urban road resilience.

The more balanced the speed difference distribution is, the stronger the network's ability to resist disturbance. Road section ej's speed difference $I_1(t)$ is calculated with Eq. 1:

$$I_1(t) = V_{ej} - V_{dej} \tag{1}$$

Where $I_1(t)$ is the speed difference of section e_j at time t. V_{ej} is the average driving speed of section ej. V_{dej} is the design speed of section ej. Road section e_j's meteorological environment index $I_2(t)$ is calculated with Eq. 2:

$$I_2(t) = M_{ej(t)} + N_{ej(t)} \tag{2}$$

Where $I_2(t)$ is the meteorological environment index of road section ej. $M_{ej(t)}$ is the visibility index of road section ej. $N_{ej(t)}$ is the road condition index of road section ej.

Absorptive capacity is calculated with Eq. 3:

$$S = -\sum_{i=1}^{2} \frac{W_i(t)}{\sum_{i=1}^{2} W_i(t)} \ln \frac{W_i(t)}{\sum_{i=1}^{2} W_i(t)} \tag{3}$$

Where S is the absorptive capacity. $W_i(t)$ is the variance of the i-th influencing factor. $W_i(t)$ is calculated with Eq. 4:

$$W_i(t) = \frac{1}{n} \sum_{i=1}^{n} [I_i(t) - \overline{I_i(t)}]^2 \tag{4}$$

- Adaptive capacity

Adaptive capacity refers to the ability of the network to reorganize itself to adapt to the environment and to accelerate the system's recovery to a stable state when the network faces disturbance,

When urban roads are disturbed, the vehicle speed usually decreases, which in turn leads to a decrease in the flow of sections per unit time. Therefore, the change of average vehicle speed on the road section can be used to describe the adaptive capacity. In order to ensure the practicability of the model, it is necessary to divide the speed range. Adaptive capacity is calculated with Eq. 5:

$$A = \frac{\sum_{j=1}^{n} T_{nej}(t)}{T_{ej}(t)} \quad (5)$$

Where A is the adaptive capacity. $T_{nej}(t)$ is the time in the lower average speed range of the road section ej. n is the number of road section in the lower average speed range, and $T_{ej}(t)$ is the total number of road section at time t.

- Recovery capacity

Recovery capacity is the ability to recover from a lower service level to normal operation after disturbance. The time taken to change the operating state is used as an indicator to reflect the restoration process.

We use the ratio of the number of road segments with a higher service level to the total number of road segments to indicate the recovery capacity of urban roads. Recovery capacity is calculated with Eq. 6:

$$C = \frac{\sum_{j=1}^{k} P_{kej}(t)}{P_{ej}(t)} \quad (6)$$

Where C is the recovery capacity. $P_{kej}(t)$ is the time in the section ej in the higher average speed range at time t. k is the number of road sections in the higher average speed range, and $P_{ej}(t)$ is the total number of road sections at time t.

Urban RoadResilience Value Measurement Based on Space Vector Model

The absorption capacity, adaptive capacity and recovery capacity are included in the same coordinate system, and the resilience of urban roads is measured by calculating the modulus.

Absorptive capacity and adaptive capacity are the negative indicators, and need to be positively processed. They can beformulated with Eq. 7:

$$y_a = \frac{l_{\min}}{l_g} \quad (7)$$

Where l_g is the g-th value in a certain index. $l_{\min}$ is the smallest value at a certain time in the index.

A three-dimensional coordinate system with O as the origin is established, and the three ability indicators are quantified and projected on the x, y, and z axes. The projection points are respectively $S'(x', 0, 0)$, $A'(0, y', 0)$, $C'(0, 0, z')$, and the corresponding vectors are $\overrightarrow{OS'}$, $\overrightarrow{OA'}$, $\overrightarrow{OC'}$. The spatial vector of urban road resilience is $\overrightarrow{OR'} = (x', y', z')$ (Fig. 4). Taking the modulus length of the vector r as the resilience value of urban roads, is calculated with Eq. 8:

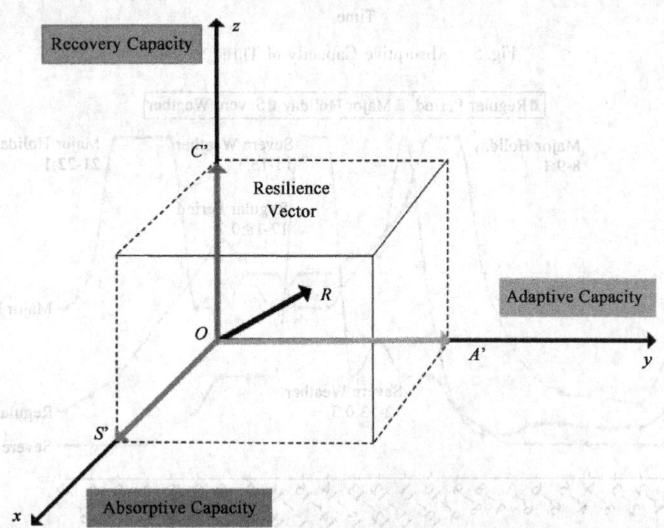

Fig. 4 Three-dimensional Space Vector Model

$$|r| = |\overrightarrow{OR'}| = \sqrt{\overrightarrow{OR'} \cdot \overrightarrow{OR'}} = \sqrt{x^2 + y^2 + z^2} \quad (8)$$

Where $|r|$ is the resilience value. $\overrightarrow{OR'}$ is the resilience vector. $|\overrightarrow{OR'}|$ is the vector modulus length.

The resilience of the study area is determined by absorptive capacity, adaptive capacity andrecovery capacity. Generally speaking, the resilience value can reflect the ability of the network to recover its operating state after being disturbed.

2　Result and Discussion

2.1　Analysis of Urban Road Resilience in Three Dimensions

• The absorptive capacity during major holiday and regular period is significantly higher than that in severe weather

During the daytime on major holiday, the absorptive capacity is generally weak and fluctuating, and the network is less invulnerable. In the regular period from 0 to 6, the absorptive capacity is relatively weak. During the period from 7 to 20, the absorptive capacity is generally higher than that of major holiday, indicating that the high traffic during the daytime on major holiday has caused the performance of urban roads to decline (Fig. 5).

• The adaptive capacity of the three scenes at night time is lower than that in the daytime.

In severe weather, the adaptive capacity during the whole period is low. Compared with the regular period, the adaptive capacity of major holiday is slightly stronger at night and weaker during the daytime.

In contrast, the traffic flow of major holiday has reduced the entire adaptive capacity of the network, and severe weather has caused it at a lower level (Fig. 6).

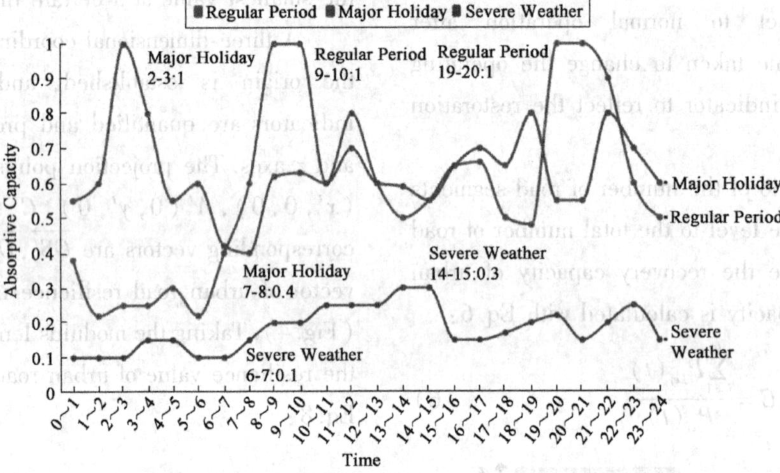

Fig. 5　Absorptive Capacity of Three Scenes

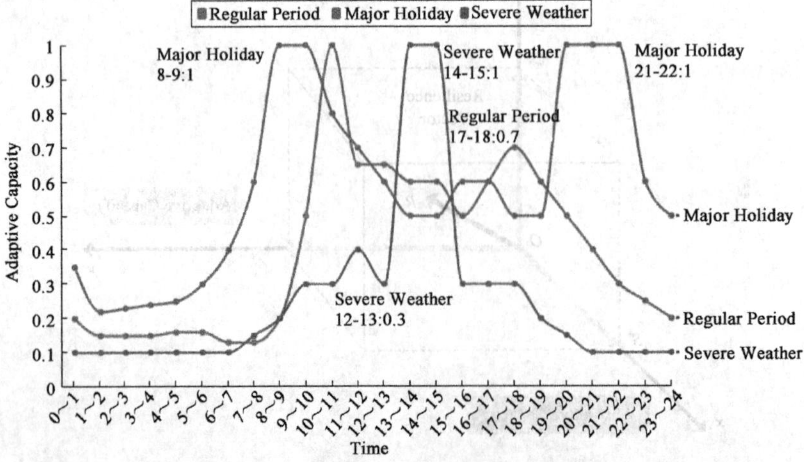

Fig. 6　Adaptive Capacity of Three Scenes

• The recovery capacity in severe weather and major holiday is greater than that of regular period.

During the regular period, the recovery capacity fluctuates slightly. Compared with severe weather, the average value of major holiday is 0. 14, which is higher than 0. 12 for severe weather. The range is 0. 29, which is higher than 0. 20 for severe weather. In contrast, the stability of the recovery ability of major holiday is poor. The recovery ability of bad weather is greatly affected by the outside world, and has obvious characteristics of time (Fig. 7).

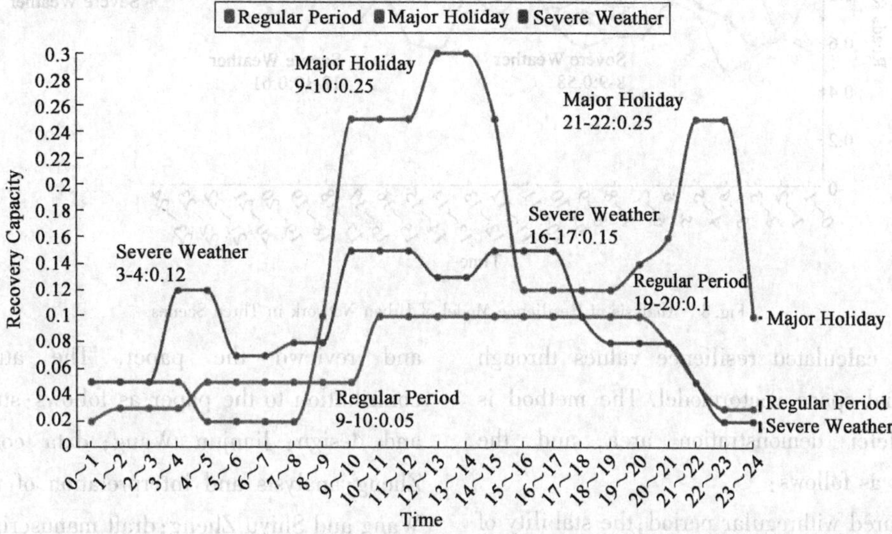

Fig. 7 Recovery Capacity of Three Scenes

2. 2 Evaluation Results of Urban Road Resilience in Different Scenes

According to the three-dimensional space vector model, the resilience value of urban roads is measured (Fig. 8). Compared with regular period, severe weather and major holiday have a significant impact on the resilience of urban roads. During the regular period, the network has the best resilience in the 19-20 period, and the 4-7 period also has better resilience. It can be found that the network has better resilience before the morning and evening peak hours. There is a small fluctuation trend, while the network resilience under major holiday and severe weather is distributed in a fluctuating manner. The range of resilience values during the regular period is 0. 54, and the variance is 0. 025. The range of resilience values during major holiday is 0. 75, which is an increase of 38% compared to the regular period. The variance of the regular values during the study period is 0. 045, which is an increase of 80% compared with the regular period. The range in severe weather is 0. 71, which is an increase of 31% compared to the regular period. The variance of the resilience value is 0. 026, which is an increase of 4% compared to the regular period. In contrast, the resilience value of the network under severe weather and major holiday scenes fluctuates greatly. That is, the stability of the major holiday network is worse, and the resilience of the bad weather is generally low.

3 Conclusions

We have presented the concept of resilience and constructed an urban road resilience assessment model which combines absorptive capacity, adaptive capacity, and recovery capacity.

Based on the meteorological environment index and the operating speed difference of the road section, a road section importance model is constructed to quantify the absorption capacity. Once the urban roads are disturbed, the vehicle speed usually decreases. Therefore, the change of average vehicle speed on the road section can be used to describe the adaptability of urban roads. The recovery capacity of urban roads is reflected in the time it takes to change the operating state.

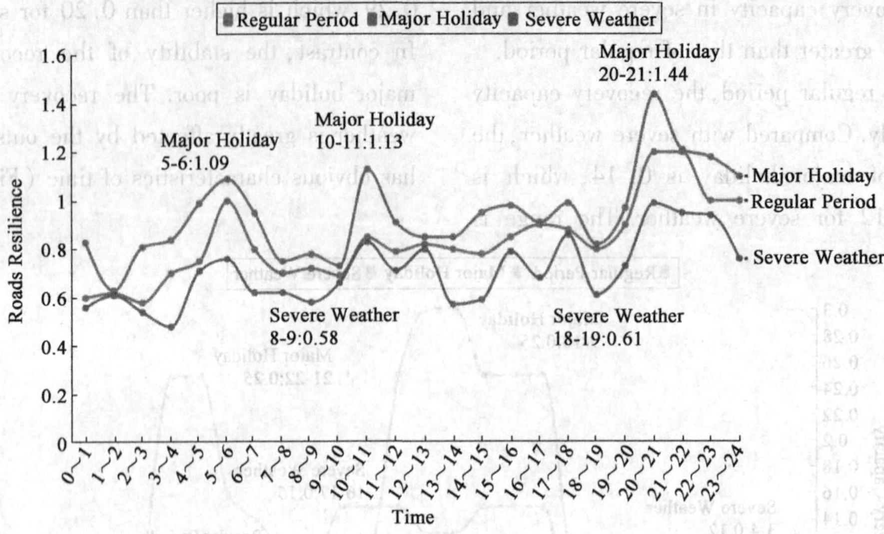

Fig. 8　Analysis of Resilience Model of Urban Network in Three Scenes

Next, we calculated resilience values through three-dimensional space vectormodel. The method is applied to Hefei demonstration area, and the conclusions are as follows:

(1) Compared withregular period, the stability of urban roads is poorer during major holiday, reflecting poorer overall resistance. The overall level of urban road resilience in severe weather is lower, reflecting poorer levels of the three capabilities of the network.

(2) In the three scenes, the absorptive capacity and adaptive capacity of bad weather are low, while the recovery capacity presents a fluctuating trend with the changes of the weather. During the daytime in the regular period, the absorptive capacity and adaptive capacity are both stronger than the major holiday.

(3) The shortcoming of this article is that it does not include the number of lanes and the speed limit in the section. Therefore, further research can consider more influencing factors of the road network, expand the scope of research, and explore changes in the resilience of a large-scale road network.

4　Acknowledgments

This research was supported by theXi ' an Special Funds for Urban Construction Program (Grant Nos. SZJJ2019-22).

5　Author Contributions

All authors contributed to the general concept and reviewd the paper. The authors confirm contribution to the paper as follows: study conception and design: Jianjun Wang; data collection: Shiyu Zheng; analysis and interpretation of results: Jianjun Wang and Shiyu Zheng; draft manuscript preparation: Shiyu Zheng. All authors reviewed the results and approved the final version of the manuscript.

References

[1] Aksu D T, Ozdamar L A. Mathematical Model for Post-disaster Road Restoration: Enabling accessibility and evacuation[J]. Transportation Research Part E Logistics & Transportation Review, 2014, 61(1):56-67.

[2] An S., Yue J. Q., Hu X. W. Evaluation of urban network vulnerability based on OD inversion. Journal of Dalian Jiaotong University, 2018, 39 (01):11-16.

[3] Calvertse, Anelderm. A Methodology for Road Traffic Resilience Analysis and Review of Related Concepts. Transportmetrica A-Transport Science, 2018, 14, (1):130-154.

[4] Cui H. J., You T. T., Li X., et al. Seismic Optimization and Reinforcement of Regional Network Based on Connectivity Reliability[J]. Science Technology and Engineering, 2019, 19 (14):346-350.

[5] Deng Z. P. Research on the Vulnerability of Network Traffic system considering the

characteristics of congestion propagation[D]. Chongqing Jiaotong University,2019.

[6] Du J. X. ,Zhang F. ,Du Z. H. ,et al. Network Vulnerability Analysis Based on Weighted Flow Betweenness Centrality——Taking Wuxi City as an example [J]. Journal of Zhejiang University (Science Edition),2020,47(02):223-230+243.

[7] Feng J. ,Huang Y. ,Wan D. Research on Fault Simulation and Reliability Evaluation of Pedestrian Network in Commercial District[J]. Journal of Chongqing University, 2019, 42(09):93-105.

[8] IP W H,Wang D. Resilience and Friability of Transportation Network: Evaluation, Analysis and Optimization[J]. IEEE Systems Journal, 2011,5(2):189-198.

[9] Jia D. W. ,Wu Z. Y. ,Wang Q. A. Network Seismic Reliability Evaluation Based on Bayesian Network [J]. Journal of Natural Disasters,2019,28(04):151-158.

[10] Jun X. F,Xie J,Wu J. Q. Highway resilience assessment Method Considering Different Disturbance Scenarios[J]. China Work Safety Science and Technology, 2019, 15 (01): 12-19.

[11] Li X. ,Dai J. F. ,Lin J. X. ,et al. Summary of Research on Vulnerability Assessment Indicators of Urban Network [J]. Highway Transportation Science and Technology (Applied Technology Edition), 2016, 12 (01):155-157.

[12] Li Y. C. ,Liu S. M. ,Yu Y. ,et al. Network vulnerability identification mechanism taking into account road sections and intersections [J]. Journal of Beijing University of Posts and Telecommunications,2020,43(01):14-20.

[13] Lin Y. Z. Urban Network Structure Resilience Assessment and Optimization Strategy Research[D]. Huazhong University of Science and Technology,2017.

[14] Lu B. ,Gao Z. Q. ,Guan X. Y. ,et al. Urban Network Resilience Assessment Based on Daily Varying Traffic Distribution. Journal of Southwest Jiaotong University,2020,55(06):1181-1190.

[15] Lu B. ,Gao Z. Q. ,Liu Y. L. et al. Road Traffic System Resilience and Road Section Importance Evaluation [J]. Transportation System Engineering and Information, 2020, (02):114-121.

[16] Lu B. ,Liu Y. L. ,Liu H. X. Urban Network Design Considering Vulnerability and Reliability Together[J]. Journal of Southwest Jiaotong University, 2019, 54 (05): 1093-1103.

[17] Nourzad S H H,Pradhan A. Vulnerability of Infrastructure Systems: Macroscopic Analysis of Critical Disruptions on Network[J]. Journal of Infrastructure Systems, 2016, 22 (1):04015014.

[18] Qian Y,Wang B,Xue Y,et al. A Simulation of the Cascading Failure of a Complex Network Model by Considering the Characteristics of Road Traffic Conditions. Nonlinear Dynamics, 2015,80(1-2):413 -420.

[19] Rong X. Research on the design of dynamic network based on vulnerability[D]. Southwest Jiaotong University,2018.

[20] Sai W. Y. Resilient Road Construction[J]. Urban Roads, Bridges and Flood Control, 2020,(09):1-4+8.

[21] Shen L. B. Research on the Safety Assessment Method of Urban Network Traffic Reliability Based on Vulnerability and Resilience[D]. Chongqing Jiaotong University,2014.

[22] Wan C. ,Yang Z. ,Zhang D. Resilience in Transportation Systems: A Systematic Review and Future Directions[J]. Transport Reviews, 2018,38(4):479-498.

[23] Yang Y. X. Based on Actual Network Connectivity Reliability and Critical Road Section Identification and Analysis [D]. Southwest Jiaotong University,2009.

高速公路服务区交通安全设施设计方案探讨

陶盼盼* 李 元 刘保卫 马东旭
(北京国道通公路设计研究院股份有限公司)

摘 要 在充分调研的基础上,梳理与分析了服务区交通安全设施的现状问题,并对现状问题进行总结分类。针对服务区交通安全设施"如何做更好"的问题,结合现存标准规范与驾乘人员需求,在充分借鉴以往工程经验与先进设计理念的基础上,提出服务区部分区域交通安全设施的优化设计方案。为了解驾乘人员对服务区交通安全设施优化设计方案的接受度与满意度,确保设计方案实施的可行性,进一步开展了设施现状及优化设计方案的网络问卷调查。结合问卷调查与设施应用现况,提出高速公路服务区交通安全设施的设置建议。

关键词 高速公路服务区 交通安全设施 优化设计方案 设置建议

0 引言

近年来,我国高速公路建设总里程持续增长,高速公路服务区需求量也在逐年递增。按照《高速公路交通工程及沿线设施设计通用规范》中"高速公路服务区平均间距不宜大于50km"的要求,截至2020年年底,我国高速公路总里程为16.10万km,高速公路服务区需求量大致在3220对左右[1-3]。高速公路服务区数量的不断增加,给服务区各项工作提出了更高的要求。在各项政策的推动下,高速公路服务区功能设施的服务水平有了较大改善,但由于交通安全设施在服务区总功能设施中占比较小,因此在设施服务提升过程中常常被忽视,从而导致一些服务区交通组织混乱、综合体验感差的现象难以彻底根除。

在政策文件层面,为推进服务区设施提质升级,交通运输部发布了多项文件要求,其中也多次提及有关服务区交通安全设施的完善内容与要求。2014年,《交通运输部关于进一步提升高速公路服务区服务质量的意见》在"加强服务区运行秩序维护"一条中提出,结合场地条件及车型构成情况,优化停车区域设置,确保交通标识齐全清晰[4];2016年,交通运输部印发《2016年全国公路服务区工作要点》,在"继续加强公共场区秩序管理"一条中要求,进一步规范服务区交通标识,保持公共场区停车秩序规范,科学规划设置不同车型的专用停车位[5];交通运输部在《2018年全国公路服务区工作要点》中指出,要合理设计服务区交通流向,规范交通标志标线,引导不同车型分区按序停放,适当增加人行横道线,引导顾客安全通行[6];交通运输部印发的《2020年全国公路服务区工作要点》为服务区各项工作指明了方向,提出聚焦打造"四个一流",并在"一流管理"方面提出要完善服务区标准规范体系[7]。在标准规范层面,日本的《高速公路设计要领》一书中详细介绍了服务区内各种设施的设计要素、要求及原因,具有较高的参考价值;而交通运输部及部分省市的标准规范对高速公路服务区交通安全设施的设置要求有所提及,但论述不多,在具体技术要求方面仍基本空白。在理论研究层面,戴国仲、林广明、陈兴文及王建伟等人均指出我国高速公路服务区交通标志标线存在设计混乱、不规范、不清晰的现象[8-11];于瑾根据服务区内各功能区的位置和需求,将服务区场区划分为6个区域,并提出相应区域标志标线的设计原则和内容[12];欧志霖在对高速公路服务区交通标志需求分析的基础上设计了服务区内各等级交通标志的版面[13];Wang Jiaxian等人指出国内许多服务区的交通线路标识模糊,布局混乱,且大部分服务区域没有施划人行道和人行横道[14]。

综上所述,管理单位对服务区设施的重视程度不断加强,但由于目前尚未形成专门且明确的

1. 基金项目:北京建工集团有限责任公司支撑发展项目(RZCA501020200001);北京市政路桥集团(股份)有限公司技术创新项目(2020-07)。

服务区交通安全设施设置方法与标准体系指导工程应用,导致在实际设计、实施过程中,仍存在服务区交通安全设施设置主观随意性强、不规范的现象,在一定程度上制约了服务区整体服务水平的提升。因此必要且亟须明确服务区交通安全设施的设置要求,提升服务区交通安全设施的保障能力与服务水平,改善驾乘人员的出行体验。

1 服务区交通安全设施现状问题分析

通过实地调查,发现目前高速公路服务区交通安全设施除管理与养护问题外,以下几类问题较明显。

1.1 设置标准不统一

同一区域的高速公路服务区内存在交通标志规格形式不统一、停车位标线施划形式不统一、地面指示箭头规格不统一等设置标准不统一的现象,如图1~图3所示。

图1 交通标志规格形式不统一

图2 停车位标线施划形式不统一

图3 地面指示箭头规格不统一

1.2 停车位标线施划不规范

部分服务区停车场区存在停车位标线施划不规范的现象,例如,小型车停车位尺寸过于富裕,大型车停车位尺寸不足等,如图4、图5所示。

1.3 服务区入口匝道减速设施效果差

部分高速公路服务区入口匝道未设置减速设

施,导致匝道处车辆行驶速度较快,存在一定的安全隐患。此外,服务区入口匝道减速设施存在一道减速丘、多道减速丘、横向减速标线、纵向减速标线及几种减速设施组合等多种设置形式,且部分减速设施破损,减速效果受到较大影响,如图6所示。

图4 停车位尺寸过长

图5 停车位尺寸不足

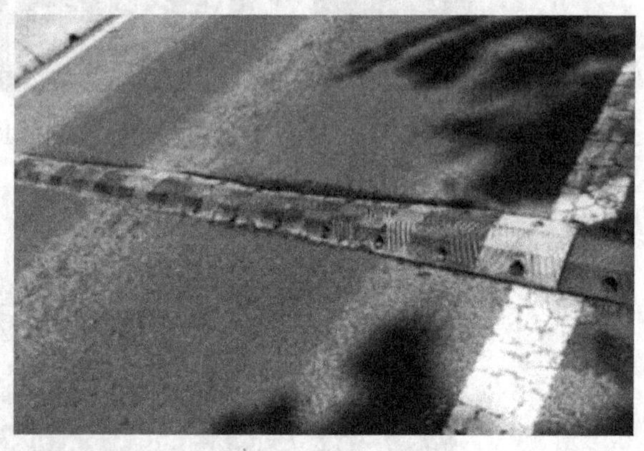

图6 服务区入口匝道减速设施现状

1.4 服务区入口分流处指引设施不完善

部分高速公路服务区入口分流处存在导向指引标志缺乏、标志标线未配合使用、分流指引形式不统一等现象,如图7所示。

图7 导向指引标志缺乏

1.5 服务区场区人行步道缺乏

经调查,大部分高速公路服务区内未设置人行步道,交通基本处于人车混行状态,存在较大安全隐患,如图8所示。

图8 人行步道缺乏

经分析,目前服务区交通安全设施存在的问题主要分为两大类:一类是通过开展标准化工作即可完善的问题,如设施设置标准不统一、停车位标线施划不规范等;另一类则是需要探讨“如何做更好”的问题,该类问题应结合现状情况与驾乘人员需求分析研究确定,如服务区入口匝道减速设施设置形式、入口处地面分流方式、是否设置场区人行步道等。

2 服务区交通安全设施方案设计

针对高速公路服务区交通安全设施存在的第二类问题,即需要探讨“如何做更好”的问题,结合现存标准规范与驾乘人员需求,在充分借鉴以往工程经验与先进设计理念的基础上,开展对应交通安全设施的优化方案设计。

2.1 入口匝道减速设施方案设计

2.1.1 横向减速标线方案设计

服务区入口匝道最少设置5道横向减速标线,第一道减速标线距服务区入口20~50m,其余标线可按表1的要求设置。横向减速标线设计方案如图9所示。

横向减速标线设置参数　　表1

车道	第二道	第三道	第四道	第五道	第六道	第七道	……
间隔(m)	$L_1=5$	$L_2=9$	$L_3=13$	$L_4=17$	$L_5=20$	$L_6=23$	……
标线条数(条)	1	1	2	2	2	2	……

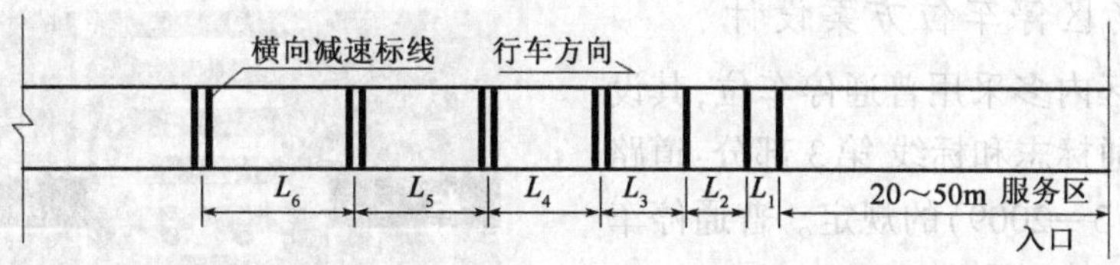

图9 服务区入口匝道横向减速标线设计方案

2.1.2 纵向减速标线方案设计

纵向减速标线起点为服务区入口匝道处,终点为服务区入口处,在纵向减速标线起点处设置30m的渐变段。纵向减速标线的设计参数参考国标《道路交通标志和标线 第3部分:道路交通标线》(GB 5768.3—2009)的规定[15]。纵向减速标线设计方案如图10所示。

2.1.3 减速丘方案设计

目前,对于减速丘的设置暂无明确规范规定。通过数据可知,驼峰式减速带对于车辆速度的影响大概在减速带前30m到通过后20m左右的范围[16]。因此,本文的设计方案将减速丘设置在服务区入口前20m处。减速丘设计方案如图11所示。

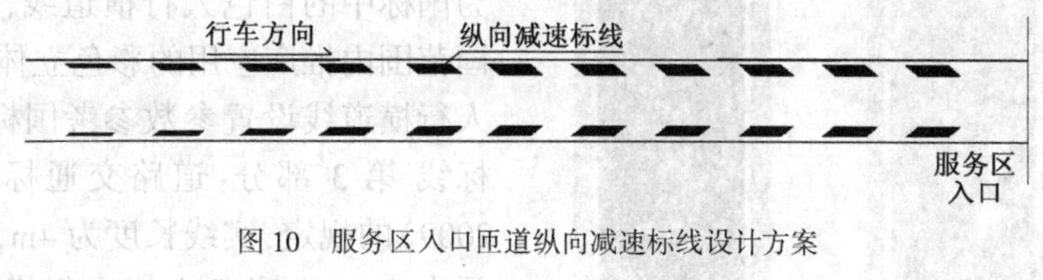

图10 服务区入口匝道纵向减速标线设计方案

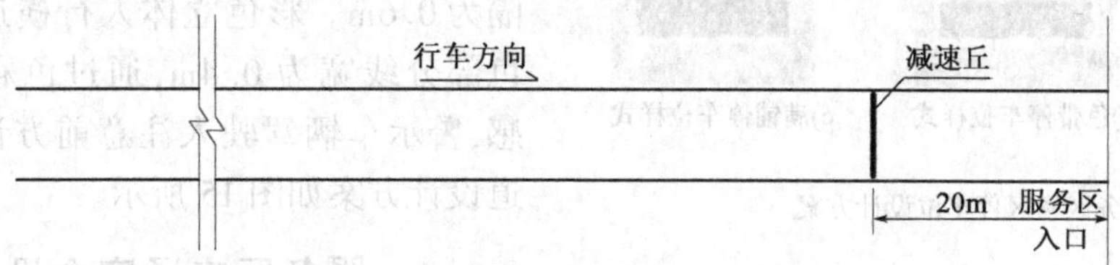

图11 服务区入口匝道减速丘设计方案

2.2 服务区入口地面分流设施方案设计

2.2.1 “注字+箭头”分流方案设计

调查发现,现状服务区入口处地面多采用“注字+箭头”的形式进行车辆分流,“注字+箭头”地面分流设施设计方案如图12a)所示。

2.2.2 “注字+箭头+彩铺”分流方案设计

为提高服务区入口处地面分流设施的醒目程度及驾驶人的视认性,可在地面“注字+箭头”分流的基础上增加彩铺,小型车方向可采用蓝色铺装,大型车方向可采用绿色铺装,彩铺应填满整个车道并凸显出大小型车的行驶轨迹,彩铺长度可视服务区入口情况而定。“注字 + 箭头 + 彩铺”地面分流设施设计方案如图 12b)所示。

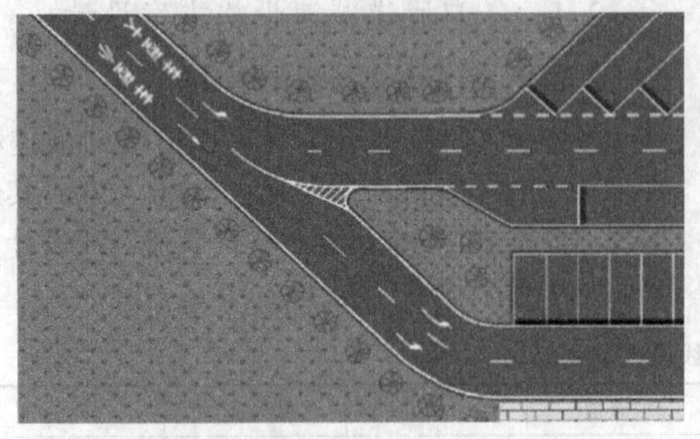

a)服务区入口地面“注字+箭头”分流设计方案

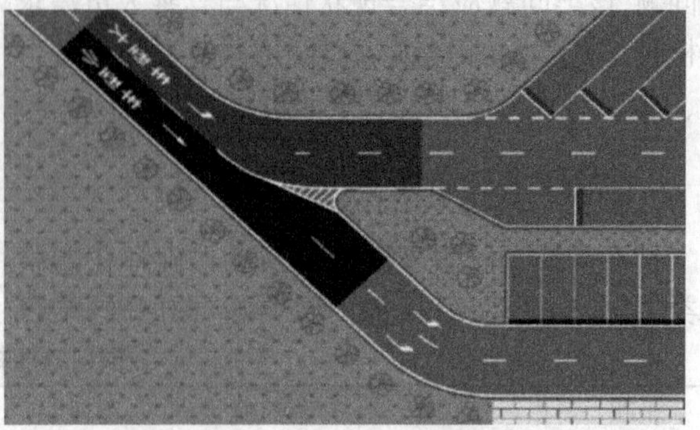

b)服务区入口地面“注字+箭头+彩铺”分流设计方案

图 12　服务区入口地面分流设施设计方案

2.3　服务区场区停车位方案设计

目前,服务区场区内多采用普通停车位,其设置参数参照《道路交通标志和标线 第 3 部分:道路交通标线》(GB 5768.3—2009)的规定。普通停车位标线设计方案如图 13a)所示。

为提高场区停车位的视认性,优化不同车型分区停放的功能,停车位标线可与地面彩铺配合使用,彩铺分为“色带”与“全铺”两种样式,“色带”式彩铺设置在供车辆进出停车位的一侧,在停车位内的彩铺长度为 60cm。彩铺式停车位设计方案如图 13b)与图 13c)所示。

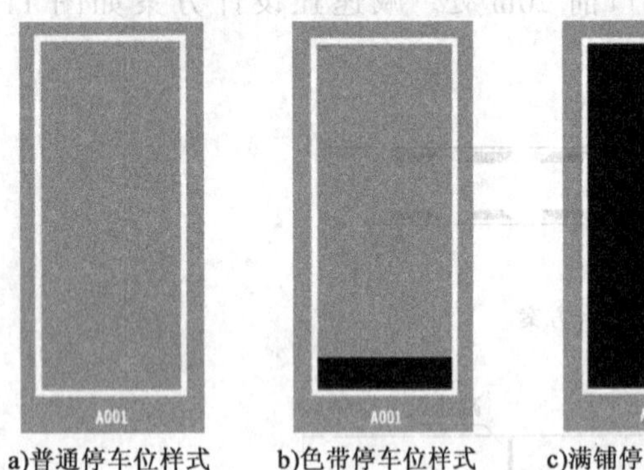

a)普通停车位样式　b)色带停车位样式　c)满铺停车位样式

图 13　服务区场区停车位设计方案

2.4　服务区场区人行设施方案设计

2.4.1　场区人行步道方案设计

在场区车行道旁设置人行步道,步道采用红色铺装,宽为 1 ~ 1.5m。场区人行步道设计方案如图 14 所示。

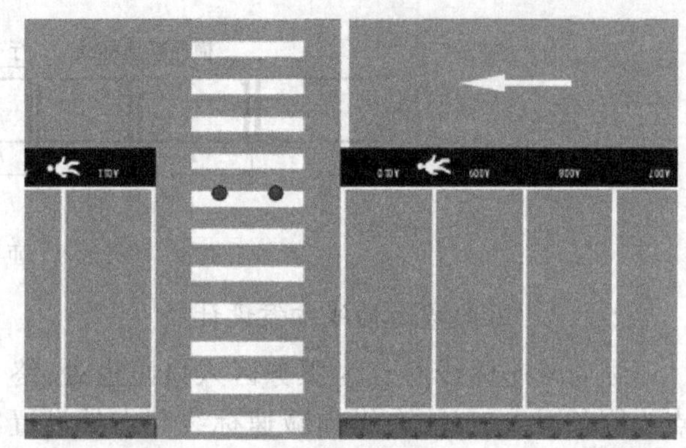

图 14　服务区场区人行步道设计方案

2.4.2　场区人行横道方案设计

目前,服务区人行横道主要有两种形式,一种为国标中的白色人行横道线,另一种为逐渐在全国范围内推广应用的彩色立体人行横道线。白色人行横道线设置参数参考国标《道路交通标志和标线 第 3 部分:道路交通标线》(GB 5768.3—2009)的规定,实线长度为 4m,线宽为 0.4m,线间隔为 0.6m。彩色立体人行横道线长度为 4m,白色部分线宽为 0.4m,通过色彩搭配增强其立体感,警示车辆驾驶人注意前方让行。场区人行横道设计方案如图 15 所示。

3　服务区交通安全设施设计方案问卷调查分析

为了解驾乘人员对高速公路服务区交通安全设施优化设计方案的接受度与满意度,确保设计方案实施的可行性,针对服务区交安设施现状及拟定优化方案进行网络问卷调查。本次共收集网络问卷1053份,高速公路服务区入口匝道减速设施、入口地面分流设施、场区停车位形式及场区人行设施设置方案的分析结果如图16~图20所示。

a)白色人行横道线

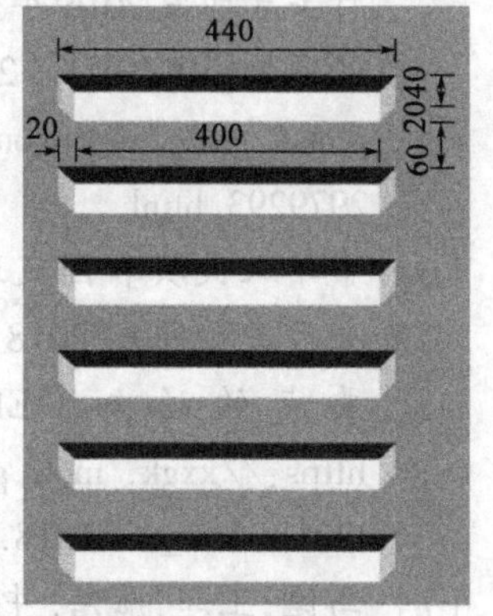

b)彩色立体人行横道线

图15 服务区场区人行横道设计方案(单位:cm)

由图16可知,驾乘人员对服务区入口匝道设置横向减速标线或纵向减速标线两种方案的支持率较高,分别为41.98%与35.8%;19.75%的驾乘人员支持在服务区入口匝道设置减速丘,仅有2.47%的驾驶人不支持在服务区入口匝道设置减速设施。该统计结果表明,几乎全部驾驶人都支持在服务区入口匝道设置减速设施。

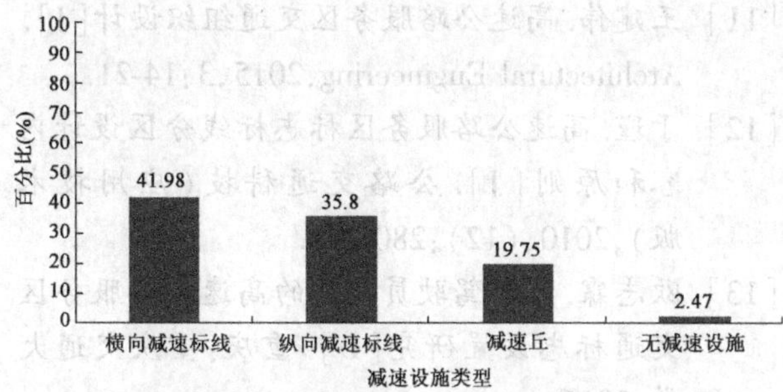

图16 服务区入口匝道减速设施方案比选统计结果

由图17可知,在服务区入口处,有85.19%的驾乘人员支持“注字+箭头+彩铺”的地面分流形式,14.81%的驾乘人员支持“注字+箭头”的地面分流形式。该结果表明,驾乘人员更倾向于在服务区入口分流处设置地面彩铺来辅助分流。

由图18可知,在服务区场区内,有70.37%的驾乘人员支持设置彩色立体人行横道线,29.63%的驾乘人员支持设置普通人行横道线。该结果表明,大部分人更倾向于在服务区内设置彩色立体人行横道线。

由图19可知,83.48%的驾乘人员认为有必要在服务区内设置人行步道进行人车分离,16.52%的驾乘人员认为没有必要在服务区内设置人行步道。该结果表明,大部分驾乘人员支持在服务区内设置人行步道,认为人车分离可提升服务区内行人的安全水平。

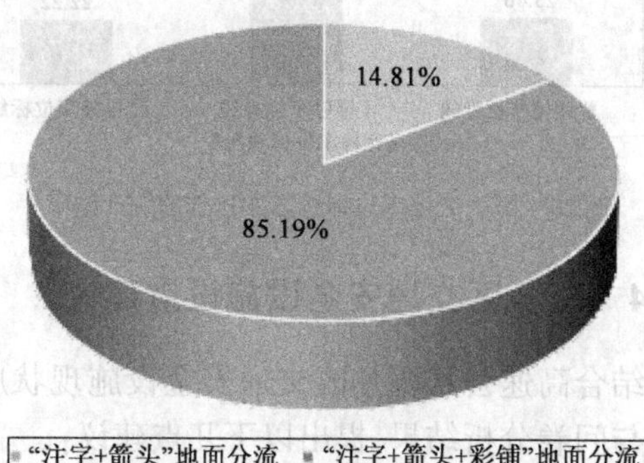

图17 服务区入口地面分流设施方案比选的统计结果

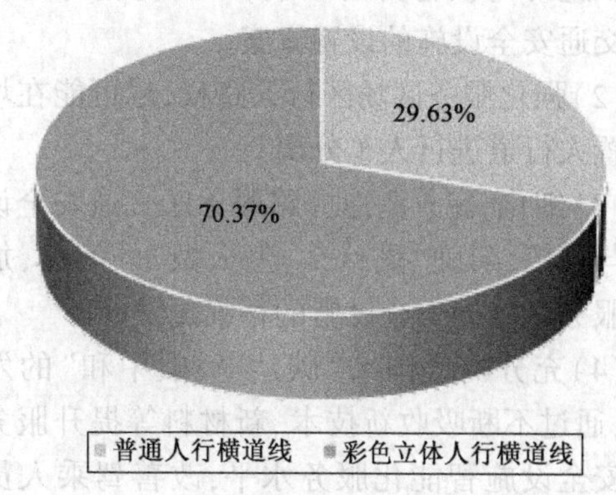

图18 服务区人行横道方案比选的统计结果

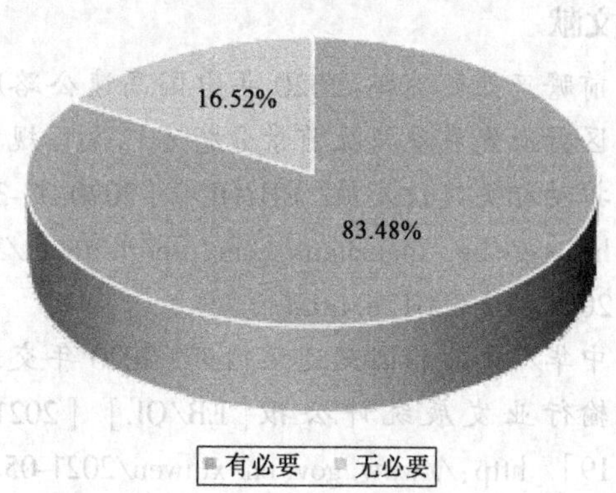

图19 服务区人行步道方案比选的统计结果

由图20可知,54.32%的驾乘人员支持服务区内采用“色带”式的彩铺停车位形式,驾乘人员对普通停车位与“全铺”式彩铺停车位的支持率相差不大,分别为23.46%与22.22%。该统计结果表明,仅有一半左右的驾乘人员支持在服务区内采用“色带”式的彩铺停车位形式,对“全铺”式彩铺停车位支持率不高。

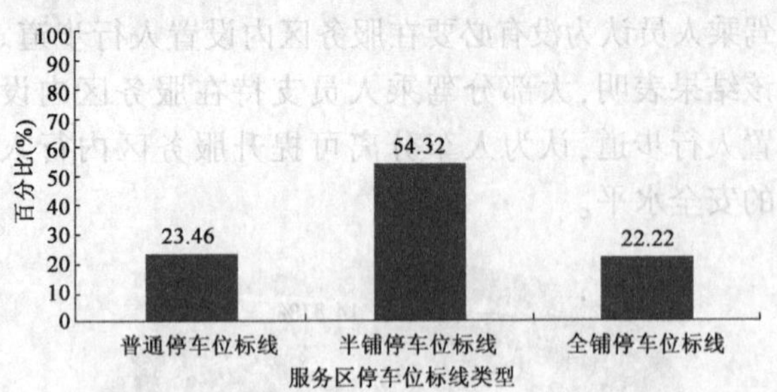

图 20　服务区停车位标线方案比选的统计结果

4　服务区交通安全设施设置建议

结合高速公路服务区交通安全设施现状应用实际与问卷分析结果,提出以下几点建议:

(1)在问卷调查与实践经验总结的基础上,建议利用驾驶模拟等技术,进一步论证服务区交通安全设施对驾驶行为的影响,不断优化与完善服务区交通安全设施的设置方案。

(2)强化服务区场区行人路权,尽可能在场区内设置人行道进行人车分离。

(3)细化、完善高速公路服务区交通安全设施标准与规范,明确"做什么、怎么做"的问题,加快推进服务区交通安全设施的精细化设计。

(4)充分响应国家"碳达峰、碳中和"的发展战略,通过不断吸收新技术、新材料等提升服务区交通安全设施智能化服务水平,改善驾乘人员出行体验。

参考文献

[1] 前瞻产业研究院. 2020 年中国高速公路服务区行业发展现状及前景分析万亿投资规模将推动相关建设发展[EB/OL]. [2020-07-30]. https://bg. qianzhan. com/report/detail/300/200730-29f8612e. html.

[2] 中华人民共和国交通运输部. 2020 年交通运输行业发展统计公报[EB/OL]. [2021-05-19]. http://www. gov. cn/xinwen/2021-05/19/content_5608523. htm.

[3] 中华人民共和国交通部. 高速公路交通工程及沿线设施设计通用规范: JTG D80—2006[S]. 北京:人民交通出版社,2006.

[4] 中华人民共和国交通运输部. 交通运输部关于进一步提升高速公路服务区服务质量的意见[EB/OL]. [2014-10-14]. https://xxgk. mot. gov. cn/jigou/glj/201410/t20141014_2978998. html.

[5] 中华人民共和国交通运输部. 交通运输部办公厅关于印发 2016 年全国公路服务区工作要点的通知[EB/OL]. [2016-05-10]. https://xxgk. mot. gov. cn/jigou/glj/201605/t20160510_2979293. html.

[6] 中华人民共和国交通运输部. 交通运输部办公厅关于印发 2018 年全国公路服务区工作要点的通知[EB/OL]. [2018-05-03]. https://xxgk. mot. gov. cn/jigou/glj/201805/t20180517_3021818. html.

[7] 马健,王超,臧浩. 中国服务区的 2020[J]. 中国公路,2021,(04):58-65.

[8] 戴国仲. 服务区交通组织设计问题探讨[J]. 运输经理世界,2009,(08):74.

[9] 林广明. 高速公路服务区交通标志标线设计问题探讨[J]. 交通工程,2014,(3/4):234-236.

[10] 陈兴文,庹永丽,袁帅,等. 高速公路既有服务区优化提升研究[J]. 公路,2021,(2):219-223.

[11] 王建伟. 高速公路服务区交通组织设计[J]. Architectural Engineering,2015,3:14-21.

[12] 于瑾. 高速公路服务区标志标线分区设计内容和原则[J]. 公路交通科技(应用技术版),2010,(12):280-281.

[13] 欧志霖. 基于驾驶员视觉的高速公路服务区交通标志设置研究[D]. 重庆:重庆交通大学,2016.

[14] Wang J, Zhao B, Jia W, et al. Research on the traffic organization optimization countermeasures in highway service area under the abnormal condition[C]. International Conference on Civil and Hydraulic Engineering,2019.

[15] 中国国家标准化管理委员会. GB 5768.3—2009 道路交通标志和标线 第 3 部分:道路交通标线[S]. 北京:中国标准出版社,2009.

[16] 关于减速带的设置(依据国家标准 GB 5768—2009)[EB/OL]. http://www. jsgdlines. com/news. asp? id = 15.

考虑行程时间波动的电动公交充电排班协同优化

贾作宁　马万经　安　琨*

(同济大学 道路与交通工程教育部重点实验室)

摘　要　为了应对城市交通迅速发展带来的交通拥堵、环境污染等问题,结合公共交通和电动汽车两者优点的纯电动公交在城市公交企业中得到广泛应用。纯电动公交由于受到续航里程和充电时间的限制,其行车计划编制问题较为复杂,大多缺乏科学合理的模型求解,纯电动公交充电计划和排班计划之间协同性较差,致使公交企业运营成本难以进一步降低。本研究采用时空网络模型对纯电动公交充电与排班方案进行协同优化,突破了传统相关研究中对充电条件和充电时间的限制,提出了一种去除车辆角标的排班变量建模方法,使得模型求解速度进一步提高,并在不改变网络规模的前提下将任务行程时间的波动性纳入模型中,使得模型更符合公交实际运营情况;最后选取嘉定公交的多条线路班次进行测试,得出多线路纯电动公交充电排班的协同方案,验证了本研究提出模型的有效性。

关键词　电动公交　充电排班　时空网络　时间波动　协同优化

0　引言

随着经济的快速发展,城市交通问题日益突出,交通拥堵和空气污染等问题已成为制约城市出行绿色可持续发展的瓶颈。

城市常规公交作为一种常见的公共交通方式,在载客量、人均具用面积和价格等方面具有极大优势,在我国城市公共交通结构中占有重要地位,能够有效地缓解交通拥堵问题。电动汽车作为一种新型的交通方式,具有节能环保等优势,越来越受到出行者的青睐,能够有效缓解交通出行给城市环境带来的空气污染问题。纯电动公交兼具常规公交和电动汽车的优势,已经成为市民日常出行中不可或缺的交通工具。截至2020年,上海市新能源公交占比已经超过60%,北京市电驱动公交车超过公交车保有量的50%,深圳市在2017年年底就已基本实现公交车全部电动化。由此可以看出,在国家和地方的大力支持和不断推进下,纯电动公交在城市出行中占据极为重要的地位。

公交行车计划编制问题一直是公交企业运营调度的核心,由于我国城市公交路网规模较大、发车班次较多、频率较高,该问题求解规模十分庞大,大多缺乏科学合理的模型求解,依靠经验编制行车计划的现象较为普遍,各线路之间的车辆缺乏统一的调度指挥。纯电动公交行车计划编制较传统燃油公交而言更为复杂,由于电池容量的限制,纯电动公交日均运营里程远低于传统燃油公交,同时在运营时间内纯电动公交需要返回充电场站进行补电,这都对行车计划编制造成影响。现有纯电动公交充电计划和运营排班计划之间协同性较差,考虑续航里程和充电时间的纯电动公交车充电排班计划的研究,是实现大规模低成本运营纯电动公交的重要支撑。

城市公交充电排班问题通常可以通过连接网络和时空网络进行描述,并将该问题转化为网络流问题进行求解。Janovec[1]、Bie Y[2]、Niekerk[3]和姚恩建[4]分别基于连接网络和时空网络建立了电动公交充电排班模型。

由于续航里程的约束,模型中对充电条件和充电时间的约束尤为关键。Jingquan Li[5]在模型中假定纯电动公交采用换电模式。姚恩建[4]将充电时间以常量表示;程春阳[6]规定当车辆剩余电量不能满足下一班次运营时必须进行充电,充电时间与充电深度、当前车辆剩余工作时长及运营里程有关;高佳宁[7]则采用有序充电的策略根据前后序车次任务的时间限制确定充电时长。

网络模型中的变量表示与求解速度直接相关,变量往往包含车辆角标,这使得模型结果存在

1. 基金项目:国家自然科学基金项目(72101186);上海市科学技术委员会科技创新行动计划(21692110900);中央高校基本科研业务费专项资金资助(16002150068)。

对称性,如何对角标进行简化也是研究热点之一。Cattaruzza D[8]在对车辆调度问题的综述中,分别总结了不含车辆角标、不含任务角标以及不含车辆和任务角标的建模思路并给出了具体模型表示。Cheng[9]在对无人机路径规划的研究中,基于载重限制和任务里程建立了不包含无人机角标的模型。但现有去除车辆角标的模型均采用连接网络进行描述,鲜有在时空网络中去除车辆角标的模型方法。

在现实运行情况中,公交行程时间会因实际路网状况产生波动。Yiming Bie[2]和 Yindong Shen[10]均通过定义行程时间的概率分布曲线将其波动性纳入连接网络模型中。但这种通过增加节点数考虑波动性的方法实际上增大了原有网络的规模,且在时空网络中鲜有不改变网络规模而考虑波动性的建模方法。

本研究采用时空网络进行建模,实现了考虑行程时间波动性的纯电动公交充电计划和排班计划的协同优化;突破了以往对纯电动公交的里程约束和充电约束,允许纯电动公交在满足后序任务所需的续航里程前提下,任何时间驶入车场进行充电且充电时间任意,不必须充满才能离开车场;提出了一种在时空网络模型中去除车辆角标的方法,并且在不增加网络节点的情况下将行程时间波动性纳入模型当中。这对于提高纯电动公交行车计划的编制水平具有一定的实践指导意义。

1　时空网络的搭建和波动性表示

1.1　时空网络的搭建

1.1.1　基本概念和改进思路

公交车辆在运营时间内存在四种状态,分别是任务状态、连接状态、等待状态和充电状态,利用时空网络可以较好地表示出公交车辆在运营时间内的状态变化过程。时空网络的节点表示车辆在某时刻位于某站点,各节点之间由任务弧、连接弧、等待弧和充电弧进行连接。通过时空网络对模型进行描述可以理解为:通过连接弧、等待弧和充电弧的某种组合,实现任务弧之间的连接,保证所有任务弧被且仅被经过一次,找出若干条串联起任务弧和其他弧的路径,所有路径就构成了能满足时刻表安排的一种可行的充电排班方案。

在利用网络进行描述的传统研究思路中,模型中决策变量角标中往往包含车辆信息,模型输出结果为优化后公交车队各车辆的排班计划,这就导致模型结果的对称性。本文提出了一种去除对称性的时空网络模型,决策变量角标设置中不包含车辆信息,模型结果仅输出不同车辆可供选择的单车充电排班计划,根据单车充电排班计划数量确定公交车队调用规模。

在去除对称性的过程中,难点是区分同时流经某节点的弧,使其在流经该节点后仍归属于原单车充电排班计划。在时空网络的车场节点中,由于存在多车辆同时充电或等待,流经车场节点的弧数量会大于1,导致无法区分离开车场节点的车辆的前序站点,车辆电量状态无法追踪,如图1所示。因此,本研究去除对称性的时空网络模型主要解决的是车场中的节点分离问题,详细思路在弧生成过程中阐述。

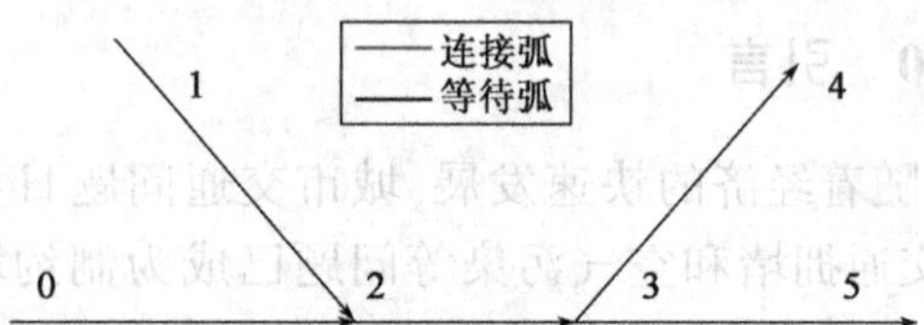

图1　两股流分别为1-2-3-4、0-2-3-5,但在经过(2,3)弧后,会出现1-2-3-5、0-2-3-4的情况

1.1.2　时空网络搭建步骤

Step Ⅰ:获取空驶时间矩阵。根据公交时刻表得到各线路的始末站,获得非运营情况下各线路始末站与车场之间的空驶时间并构成空驶时间矩阵。

Step Ⅱ:创建任务弧。根据公交时刻表中各班次的始末站点和到发时间,创建表示车辆任务状态的任务弧。

Step Ⅲ:创建连接弧。连接弧根据空驶时间矩阵和任务弧创建,表示不同站点之间非任务过程的衔接,包含车辆的空驶过程和在站点的等待过程。生成连接弧需满足一定规则:①两任务弧间隔时间大于等于两站点的空驶时间;②各任务弧首节点向前引出长度为空驶时间的连接弧至车场,并称该弧为流出弧;③各任务弧末节点向后引出长度为空驶时间的连接弧至车场,并称该弧为流入弧。连接弧创建过程如图2所示。

Step Ⅳ:创建等待弧。等待弧由流入弧和流出弧生成,且需满足一定规则:①由流入弧生成:

将流入弧末节点确定为等待弧节点,并从该节点开始以15分钟为间隔生成节点直至运营结束;将时间晚于该节点的流出弧首节点确定为等待弧节点。将同一流入弧生成的节点首尾依次相连创建等待弧。②由流出弧生成:将运营初节点与流出弧首节点相连创建等待弧。

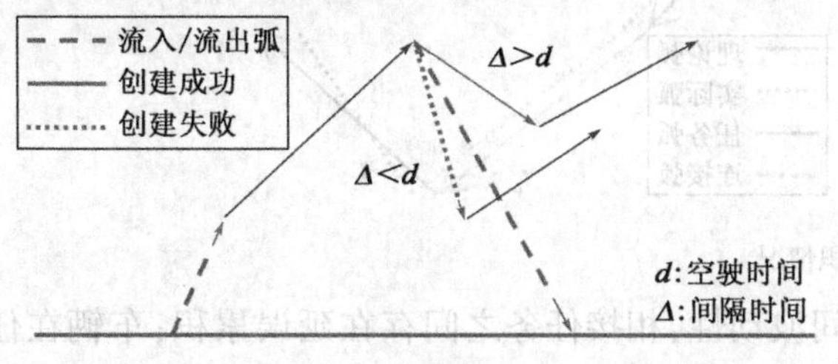

图2 连接弧创建过程

Step V:创建充电弧。充电弧即车场站点上的等待弧,表示车辆在车场的等待状态,其生成方式与等待弧相同。在实际充电过程中,本研究假定车辆充满电自动停止。

在创建等待弧和充电弧时,在不同生成过程中会存在节点重复的问题,进而难以实现去对称性。针对此问题,设定以下规则用于分离节点。假设t时刻存在k次重复现象,创建该时刻的时间集合$T=\{t,t+\varepsilon,t+2\varepsilon\cdots,t+k\varepsilon\}$,其中$\varepsilon$为大于0的极小常数,在每次节点生成过程中,取$T$内时间作为该节点的时刻。由此,实现了节点时间的分离,保证了每个节点最多被经过一次,即每个节点仅属于一个单车充电排班计划。

1.2 网络的行程时间波动性表示

本研究提出了不改变网络结构情况下考虑行程时间波动性的新思路。任务行程时间在一定范围内随机分布并设置最长发车等待时间,即允许车辆推迟从任务首节点出发,允许车辆提前或推迟到达任务末节点。本研究将考虑波动性的实际弧均表示为原始网络中的理论弧,不会增大原有网络中节点和弧的规模,如图3所示。

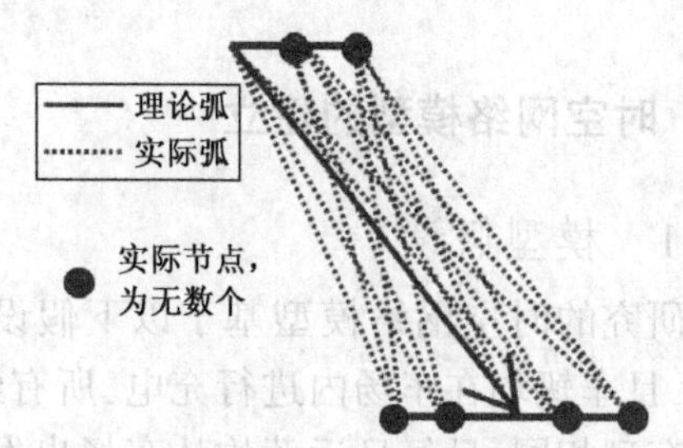

图3 理论弧和实际弧

设定如下规则判断波动情况下连接弧能否被占用:若前一任务结束节点的车辆通过空驶过程到达下一任务开始节点的时间,超过考虑最大发车延误时间的下一任务开始时间,则该连接弧被判定为不会被占用。详细情况如图4所示。

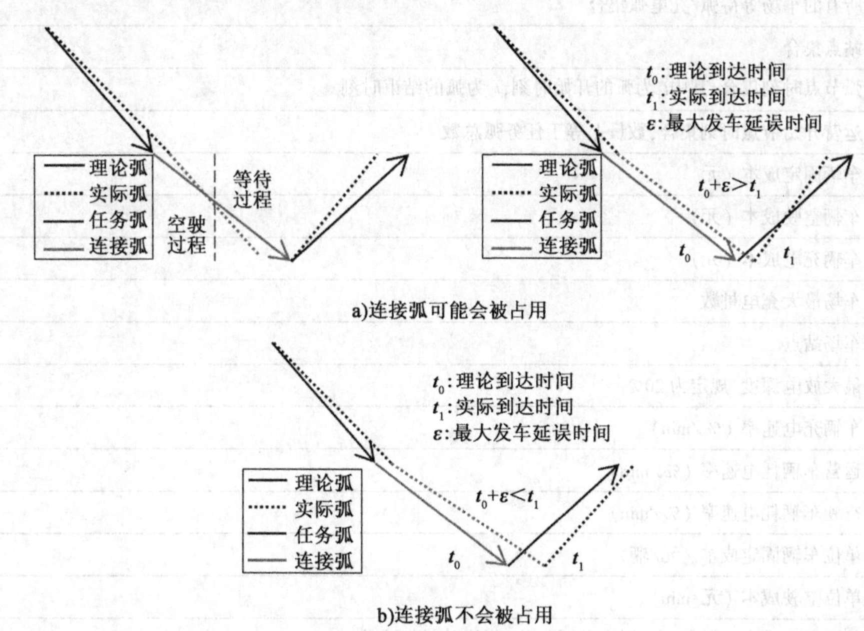

图4 连接弧状态

同时考虑相接任务的延误累积情况,设上一任务的延误传递值为Δ,计算前一任务结束节点的车辆通过空驶过程到达下一任务开始节点的时间与下一任务开始时间的差值,Δ为该差值与0之间的较大值。如图 5 所示。

在涉及车场充电过程时,需要考虑流入弧的时间波动情况以精确判断车辆的充电时间,因此设定流入弧的时间波动与其所连接任务弧的时间波动一致。

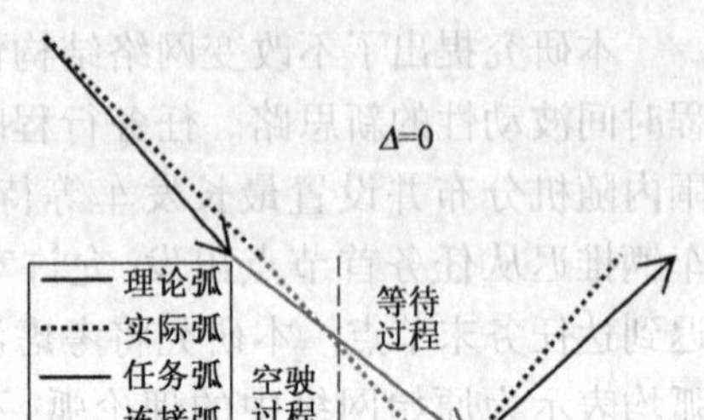

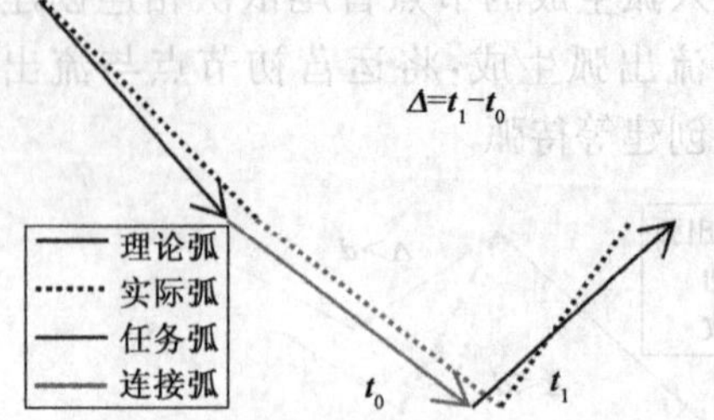

图 5　延误累积情况

2　时空网络模型的建立

2.1　模型假设

本研究的时空网络模型基于以下假设:考虑单车场,且车辆均在车场内进行充电,所有纯电动公交的车型相同,且每日运营均从车场出发,运营结束后均返回车场;车辆在各站点之间的任务时间、空驶时间已知,在车辆执行任务过程中考虑时间波动性,相接任务之间存在延误累积;车辆在任务始站点可接受等待发车的延误时间存在上限,但不会存在提前发车的情况;车场内可供同时充电的充电桩有数目限制。

2.2　模型建立

2.2.1　参数变量设置

基于时空网络建立纯电动公交充电排班模型,参数变量设置如表 1 所示。

时空网络参数变量设置　　表 1

参数变量	含　义
$\{A^T\}$	所有任务弧集合
$\{A^B\}$	所有连接弧集合
$\{A^D\}$	所有的车场等待弧/充电弧集合
$I:\{i,j\cdots\}$	站点集合
$T:\{t,t_s,t_e\cdots\}$	弧节点时刻集合,其中t_s为弧的开始时刻,t_e为弧的结束时刻
$T_s:\{t_1,t_2,t_3\cdots\}$	运营开始节点时刻集合,数量上等于任务弧总数
C_f	车辆固定成本 (元)
C_b	车辆空驶成本 (元)
C_d	车辆充电成本 (元)
N	车场最大充电桩数
d	车场站点
$S_{\min}$	最大放电深度,规定为 20%
V_c	车辆充电速率 (%/min)
V_f	运营车辆耗电速率 (%/min)
V_e	空驶车辆耗电速率 (%/min)
e_f	单位车辆固定成本 (元/辆)
e_b	单位空驶成本 (元/min)
e_d	单位充电成本 (元/min),引入分时电价,取值随时间波动
$d_{i,j}$	i,j 站点间空驶时间(min)
$\varepsilon_{\max}$	车辆执行任务的时间初始最大波动值(min)
$delay_{\max}$	车辆在任务始站点可接受等待发车的延误时间上限(min)

续上表

参数变量	含　义
$S_{i,t}$	连续变量,表示车辆在 i 站点在 t 时刻的电量
T_{i,t_s,j,t_e}	任务弧,0-1 变量,表示车辆执行任务,t_s 时刻从 i 站点出发,t_e 时刻到达 j 站点,其中 $(i,t_s,j,t_e)\in A^T$
B_{i,t_s,j,t_e}	连接弧,0-1 变量,表示车辆连接两任务,t_s 时刻从 i 站点出发,t_e 时刻到达 j 站点,其中 $(i,t_s,j,t_e)\in A^B$
W_{i,t_s,i,t_e}	等待弧,0-1 变量,表示车辆在车场等待,i 站点从 t_s 时刻等待到 t_e 时刻,其中 $(i,t_s,i,t_e)\in A^D$,$i=d$
C_{i,t_s,i,t_e}	充电弧,0-1 变量,表示车辆在车场充电,i 站点从 t_s 时刻充电到 t_e 时刻,其中 $(i,t_s,i,t_e)\in A^D$,$i=d$
$\varepsilon^0_{i,t_s,j,t_e}$	任务弧时间初始波动情况,连续变量,表示车辆在执行任务前确定的时间波动情况,其中 $-\varepsilon_{max}\leqslant\varepsilon^0_{i,t_s,j,t_e}\leqslant\varepsilon_{\max}$,$(i,t_s,j,t_e)\in A^T$
$\varepsilon^1_{i,t_s,j,t_e}$	任务弧时间累积波动情况,连续变量,表示车辆在执行任务时的时间波动情况,即时间波动累积情况,其中 $(i,t_s,j,t_e)\in A^T$
$\varepsilon_{i,t_s,j,t_e}$	流入车场的连接弧时间波动情况,连续变量,表示该连接弧受上一任务影响而产生的时间波动,其中 $(i,t_s,j,t_e)\in A^B$,$j=d$
M	临时变量,用于约束的线性化过程,为极大数
δ	临时变量,用于约束的线性化过程,取值为 0 或 1
$\in$	临时变量,用于约束的线性化过程,为大于 0 的极小数

2.2.2　目标函数的确定

模型以最小化运营成本为目标,其中运营成本包括固定成本、空驶成本和充电成本。

目标函数:

$$\min Z=C_f+C_b+C_d$$

其中:

$$C_f=e_f\cdot\sum_{(i,t_s,i,t_e)}W_{i,t_s,j,t_e}t_s\in T_s \tag{1}$$

$$C_b=e_b\cdot\sum_{(i,t_s,j,t_e)}B_{i,t_s,j,t_e}\cdot d_{i,j} \tag{2}$$

$$C_d=e_d\cdot\sum_{(i,t_s,j,t_e)}C_{i,t_s,j,t_e}\cdot(t_e-t_s) \tag{3}$$

式(1)为车辆固定成本,与被调用车辆总数有关,统计运营开始前等待弧占用情况;式(2)为车辆空驶成本,统计连接弧占用情况,并根据连接弧中的车辆空驶过程确定车辆空驶成本;式(3)为车辆充电成本,统计充电弧占用情况,并基于分时电价机制确定车辆充电成本。

2.2.3　约束条件的确定

$$T_{i,t_s,j,t_e}=1\ \forall(i,t_s,j,t_e)\in A^T \tag{4}$$

$$\sum_j\sum_{t_s}T_{j,t_s,i,t}+\sum_j\sum_{t_s}B_{j,t_s,i,t}+\sum_{t_s}W_{i,t_si,t}+\sum_{t_s}C_{i,t_si,t}$$
$$=\sum_j\sum_{t_e}T_{i,t,j,t_e}+\sum_j\sum_{t_e}B_{i,t,j,t_e}+\sum_{t_e}W_{i,t,i,t_e}+$$
$$\sum_{t_e}C_{i,t,i,t_e}\ \forall i,t \tag{5}$$

$$S_{i,t}\geqslant S_{\min}\cdot\Big(\sum_j\sum_{t_s}T_{j,t_s,i,t}+\sum_j\sum_{t_s}B_{j,t_s,i,t}+\sum_{t_s}W_{i,t_si,t}+\sum_{t_s}C_{i,t_si,t}\Big)\forall i,t \tag{6}$$

$$S_{i,t}=100\cdot W_{i,t,i,t_e}i=d;\ \forall t\in T_s \tag{7}$$

$$S_{i,t}\geqslant\sum_j\sum_{t_e}T_{i,t,j,t_e}\cdot V_f\cdot(t_e-t+\varepsilon_{\max})+$$
$$\sum_j\sum_{t_e}B_{i,t,j,t_e}\cdot V_e\cdot d_{i,j}\ \forall i,t \tag{8}$$

$$S_{i,t}=\sum_j\sum_{t_s}T_{j,t_s,i,t}\cdot(S_{j,t_s}-V_f\cdot(t-t_s+$$
$$\varepsilon^1_{j,t_s,i,t}))+\sum_j\sum_{t_s}B_{j,t_s,i,t}\cdot(S_{j,t_s}-V_e\cdot$$
$$d_{j,i})+\sum_{t_s}W_{i,t_si,t}\cdot S_{i,t_s}+\sum_{t_s}C_{i,t_s,i,t}\cdot(S_{i,t_s}+$$
$$V_c\cdot(t-t_s-\varepsilon_{*,*,i,t_s}))\ \forall i,t$$

$$S_{i,t}=\min\{S_{i,t},100\%\}\ \forall i,t \tag{9}$$

$$W_{i,t_s,i,t_e}+C_{i,t_si,t_e}\leqslant 1\ \forall(i,t_s,i,t_e)\in A^D \tag{10}$$

$$\sum_{t_s\leqslant t\leqslant t_e}C_{i,t_s,j,t_e}\leqslant N\ \forall t\ in\ operationtime \tag{11}$$

$$t_e{}^1+\varepsilon^1{}_{i^1,t_s{}^1,j^1,t_e{}^1}+d_{j^1,i^2}-(t_s^2+delay_{\max})\geqslant$$
$$(\delta-1)\cdot M$$
$$t_e{}^1+\varepsilon^1{}_{i^1,t_s{}^1,j^1,t_e{}^1}+d_{j^1,i^2}-(t_s{}^2+delay_{\max})\leqslant$$
$$\delta\cdot M-\in$$
$$B_{j^1,t_e{}^1,i^2,t_s{}^2}\leqslant(1-\delta)\cdot M$$
$$B_{j^1,t_e{}^1,i^2,t_s{}^2}\geqslant(\delta-1)\cdot M$$
$$\forall(i^1,t_s{}^1,j^1,t_e{}^1),(i^2,t_s{}^2,*,*)\in A^T;$$
$$\forall(j^1,t_e{}^1,i^2,t_s{}^2)\in A^B \tag{12}$$

$$\varepsilon^1{}_{i^2,t_s{}^2,j^2,t_e{}^2}=\varepsilon^0_{i^2,t_s{}^2,j^2,t_e{}^2}j^1=d$$
$$t_s{}^2-(t_e{}^1+\varepsilon^1{}_{i^1,t_s{}^1,j^1,t_e{}^1})-d_{j^1,i^2}\geqslant(\delta-1)\cdot M$$
$$t_s{}^2-(t_e{}^1+\varepsilon^1{}_{i^1,t_s{}^1,j^1,t_e{}^1})-d_{j^1,i^2}\leqslant\delta\cdot M-\in$$
$$\varepsilon^1{}_{i^2,t_s{}^2,j^2,t_e{}^2}-\varepsilon^0{}_{i^2,t_s{}^2,j^2,t_e{}^2}\leqslant(1-\delta)\cdot M$$
$$\varepsilon^1{}_{i^2,t_s{}^2,j^2,t_e{}^2}-\varepsilon^0{}_{i^2,t_s{}^2,j^2,t_e{}^2}\geqslant(\delta-1)\cdot M$$
$$\varepsilon^1{}_{i^2,t_s{}^2,j^2,t_e{}^2}-\varepsilon^0{}_{i^2,t_s{}^2,j^2,t_e{}^2}+(t_s{}^2-$$
$$(t_e{}^1+\varepsilon^1{}_{i^1,t_s{}^1,j^1,t_e{}^1})-d_{j^1,i^2})\cdot B_{j^1,t_e{}^1,i^2,t_s{}^2}\leqslant\delta\cdot M$$
$$\varepsilon^1{}_{i^2,t_s{}^2,j^2,t_e{}^2}-\varepsilon^0{}_{i^2,t_s{}^2,j^2,t_e{}^2}+(t_s{}^2-(t_e{}^1+$$

$\varepsilon^{1}_{i^1,t_s^1,j^1,t_e^1}) - d_{j^1,i^2}) \cdot B_{j^1,t_e^1,i^2,t_s^2} \geq -\delta \cdot M$

$\forall (i^1,t_s^1,j^1,t_e^1),(i^2,t_s^2,j^2,t_e^2) \in A^T;$

$$\forall (j^1,t_e^1,i^2,t_s^2) \in A^B \tag{13}$$

$\varepsilon_{i,t_s j,t_e} = \varepsilon^{1}_{*,*,i,t_s} \forall (i,t_s,j,t_e) \in AB, j = d;$

$$\forall (*,*,i,t_s) \in A^T \tag{14}$$

约束(1)为任务执行约束；约束(2)为流平衡约束，即保证任意时空节点的流入弧和流出弧平衡；约束(3) ~ (6)为时空节点电量约束，其中约束(3)为节点剩余电量约束，保证在车辆能够到达的节点上剩余电量不小于最大放电深度，约束(4)则规定节点初始电量，约束(5)为节点电量满足后续行程约束，应满足后续任务存在最大时间波动的情况，约束(6)为时空节点电量变化过程约束，其中任务弧要考虑时间累积波动，连接弧仅需考虑车辆空驶过程，充电弧需考虑流入弧的时间波动，节点电量不大于100%；约束(7)则规定了车辆不能同时充电和等待；约束(8)规定了最大可同时充电的车辆数；约束(9)为连接弧判断约束，通过前一任务弧的时间波动情况来判断两任务弧间的连接弧能否被占用；约束(10)为任务弧波动时间更新约束，表示任务弧的波动时间累积过程；约束(11)为流入弧时间波动约束，与其所连接任务弧的时间波动一致。

3　实例验证

为了验证模型在实际公交网络中的效果和适用性，本研究选取嘉定公交线路作为算例进行验证。本研究所涉及模型代码均使用 Python 语言编写，并使用 Gurobi 9.1 进行模型求解。算例在配置 Apple M1 处理器和 16GB 内存的计算机上运行。

3.1　算例选取和参数设定

本研究选取上海市嘉定区公交枢纽站中的嘉定北站为中心向外辐射的三条线路，公交嘉定北站既作为公交线路的始末站，又作为供车辆停放和充电的车场，选取的三条线路为嘉定 3 路、嘉定 10 路和嘉定 61 路。

该算例下的各站点空驶时间如表 2 所示。

选择时间跨度为 6 小时左右的 20 个任务进行小样本建模求解。具体任务如表 3 所示。

模型中的各参数设定如表 4 所示。由于选取算例为小样本，为表征充电情况，耗电速率和充电速率的设定与实际情况存在偏差。

各站点空驶时间　表2

分钟	嘉定北站	塔新东路徐南路	塔新路倪家浜路	牛头泾	车场/充电站
嘉定北站	0	18	15	30	0
塔新东路徐南路	18	0	7	35	18
塔新路倪家浜路	15	7	0	45	15
牛头泾	30	35	45	0	30
车场/充电站	0	18	15	30	0

任务样本　表3

线　路	出发时刻			
嘉定 3 路上行	05:30	07:15	09:24	10:15
嘉定 3 路下行	05:20	06:50	07:25	09:58
嘉定 10 路上行	05:55	07:35	09:55	10:25
嘉定 10 路下行	05:20	06:45	08:35	10:20
嘉定 61 路上行	05:20	06:55	08:30	09:50

参数设定　表4

耗电速率	0.5%/min	车辆固定成本	232 元/天	谷时电价	0.27 元/min
充电速率	0.56%/min	车辆空驶成本	0.3 元/min	平时电价	0.621 元/min
最小荷电状态	20%	最大生成波动时间	10min	峰时电价	0.964 元/min
充电桩数量	10	最大可接受延误时间	50min		

3.2　算例结果

将上述算例进行建模求解,得出收敛小于5%的近似最优解为1543.71元/天。该可行解调用车队规模为6辆,同时在该可行解下:总空驶时间237min/天、总空驶费用71.08元/天、总充电时间125min/天、总充电费用80.63元/天。车辆在结束当天运营任务返回车场后,集中在夜间进行充电,故调整后的充电费用为209.39元/天,调整后的总成本为1672.47元/天。各车辆执行任务班次情况如表5所示。

在得到模型结果后,会发现存在车辆充电时段离散情况,经过充电时间连续化处理并再次验证满足充电桩数目约束后,得到车队状态随时间变化情况,如图6所示。

模型结果　表5

车辆编号	线路/发车时刻			
1	嘉定3路上行/05:30	嘉定3路下行/06:50	嘉定61路上行/08:30	嘉定10路下行/10:20
2	嘉定3路下行/05:20	嘉定10路上行/07:35	嘉定10路下行/08:35	嘉定3路上行/10:15
3	嘉定3路下行/07:25	嘉定61路上行/09:50	—	—
4	嘉定10路上行/05:55	嘉定10路下行/06:45	嘉定3路上行/09:24	嘉定10路上行/10:25
5	嘉定10路下行/05:20	嘉定61路上行/06:55	嘉定10路上行/09:55	—
6	嘉定61路上行/05:20	嘉定3路上行/07:15	嘉定3路下行/09:58	—

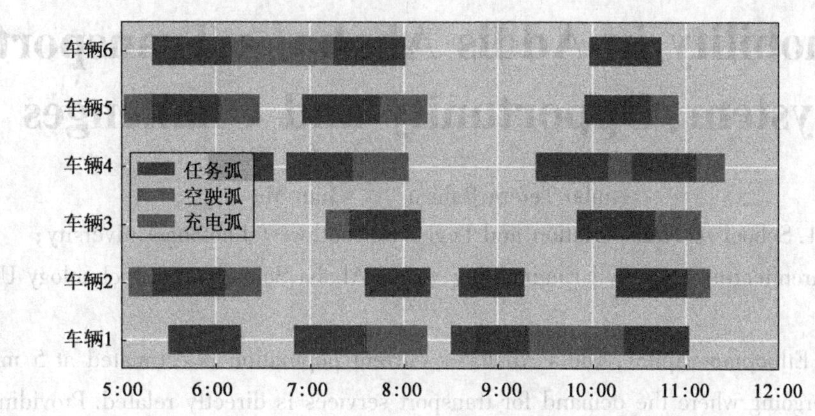

图6　模型结果

4　结语

针对纯电动公交行车计划编制缺乏科学性的问题,本文打破了传统研究中对续航里程和充电时间的限制,提出了一种纯电动公交充电计划和排班计划协同优化的方法。在网络结构中,选取了计算复杂度更小且表达更为清晰明了的时空网络模型,提高了模型运算速度。在模型表达中,提出了去除车辆角标的方法,模型结果给出多个单车的充电与排班计划而不明确特定车辆,模型求解速度进一步提高。在充电设定中,允许车辆不必电量耗尽再充电或单次必须充满电,使得纯电动公交的充电安排更加灵活妥当。同时,为更贴近实际情况,提出了一种不会改变原有网络规模的考虑行程时间波动性的方法,在不牺牲模型求解速度的情况下将班次到达提前或延误纳入模型。最后选取嘉定公交多条线路进行算例验证,从结果中可以看出本模型的可行性。本研究对提高纯电动公交行车计划的编制水平具有一定的实践指导意义。

参考文献

[1] Maroš Janovec, Michal Koháni. Exact approach to the electric bus fleet scheduling [J]. Transportation Research Procedia, 2019, 40: 1380-1387.

[2] Bie Y, Ji J, Wang X, et al. Optimization of electric bus scheduling considering stochastic volatilities in trip travel time and energy consumption [J]. Computer-Aided Civil and Infrastructure Engineering, 2021, 36 (12): 1530-1548.

[3] Van Kooten Niekerk M E, Van den Akker J M,

Hoogeveen J A. Scheduling electric vehicles [J]. Public Transport, 2017, 9(1): 155-176.

[4] 姚恩建,卢沐阳,刘宇环,等.考虑充电约束的电动公交区域行车计划编制[J].华南理工大学学报(自然科学版),2019,47(9):68-73.

[5] Jingquan Li. Transit bus scheduling with limited energy [J]. Transportation Science, 2014, 48 (4): 521-539.

[6] 程春阳.公交电动车辆的智能排班方法研究[D].北京:北京邮电大学,2019.

[7] 高佳宁.考虑分时电价的纯电动公交行车计划编制方法研究[D].北京:北京交通大学,2018.

[8] Cattaruzza D, Absi N, Feillet D. Vehicle routing problems with multiple trips [J]. Annals of Operations Research, 2016, 14(3): 223-259.

[9] Cheng C, Adulyasak Y, Rousseau L M. Drone routing with energy function: Formulation and exact algorithm [J]. Transportation Research Part B: Methodological, 2020, 139 (C): 364-387.

[10] Shen Y, Xu J, Li J. A probabilistic model for vehicle scheduling based on stochastic trip times [J]. Transportation Research Part B: Methodological, 2016, 85: 19-31.

Micromobility in Addis Ababa's Transportation System: Opportunity and Challenges

Ambo Tefera Bahiru *[1,2] Jian Ma[1]

(1. School of Transportation and Logistics, Southwest Jiaotong University;

2. College of Architecture and Civil Engineering, Addis Ababa Science and Technology University)

Abstract The Ethiopian capital, Addis Ababa's current population is estimated at 5 million, and rapid urban spread is undergoing where the demand for transport services is directly related. Providing a safe, green, reliable, and sustainable response to the ever-increasing demand for the city's mobility is a rapidly growing concern. The emerging micromobility transportation plays a significant role as a cost-effective contemporary mobility alternative in many parts of the world. Micromobility reduces dependence on private cars, congestion, greenhouse gas emissions, and better existing space use.

The paper summarizes key points fromthe literature on the opportunities and challenges of micromobility transportation alternatives, focusing on developing countries. The main aim is to explore and disclose insights on micromobility transportation and investigate the challenges and opportunities it will bring in a city like Addis Ababa if widely applied. The paper may help as valuable information for the city governments, transport planners, policymakers, micromobility providers, and researchers to understand the key elements of such an active transportation alternative.

Keywords Addis Ababa Opportunity Challenge Ethiopia Micromobility Mobility Shared bikes

0 Introduction

The population of Africa is increasing rapidly; currently, the continent has estimated over 1 billion people with about 40% of whom living in urban areas, and more than 60% of the population are young people with age below 25 years. These are active, energetic, and highly mobile groups of people who need sustainable transportation and power for the continent's future development. Providing a reliable response to the demand for mobility of many urban dwellers is an urgent growing concern in the continent. Compared to the mobility demand of the people, efforts made towards transportation developments are inadequate. In many cases, most individuals use walking as an effective means of their daily trip in the continent. For example, about 75% of daily commuters in sub-Sahara Africa's main trip is walking, where the region is often regarded as the world's fastest urbanizing region.

Addis Ababa is the capital of Ethiopia and seat for many international diplomats, including the African Union and Economic Commission for Africa. The city's estimated current population is about 5 million. According to UN-Habitat forecasts, 10 million people will live in Addis Ababa by 2025. Addis Ababa is considered one of the fastest-growing economies in Africa. The city's development, driven by the country's vibrant economic health, is moving forward and attracting several foreign investors in most investment sectors. However, motorization and per capita car ownership is low in Ethiopia, like many African cities. The international organization of motor vehicle manufacturers reports revealed that Ethiopia had an estimated 2 vehicles per 1000 inhabitants. Despite its relatively low rate of motorization, vehicle registration in Ethiopia continues to rise, where the capital Addis Ababa hosts about 70% of all registered vehicles in the country. Most of these vehicles are aged and entered the country as second-hand vehicles and cause serious air pollution and multidimensional negative impacts to the environment.

A survey conducted by the Africa transport program on mobility in Addis Ababa revealed that 35% of daily trips are performed by public transport, 10% by private vehicles, and the remaining 55% is by walking. The World bank estimated this daily walking trip as 54%.

Therefore, with this massive urbanization on the rise and consequently enormous demand for short-distance trips/walking, trips people take in Addis Ababa, and most cities of Africa can generally fall within the category of micromobility. Thus, it is essential to practice the micromobility transport alternatives by understanding its opportunities and carefully considering the related challenges. However, micromobility transportation is not well known in Addis Ababa, even in most African cities; generally, it's understood as motorcycle transportation for low and middle-class commuters.

The main objective of this review is to disclose the significant opportunities Addis Ababa will gain by integrating micromobility transportation alternatives in its transport system and pointing out the main challenges of such mobility options through a thorough review of research articles, blogs, reports, policies, and news. This can help to reveal important information that can be used by the city governments, transport planners, policymakers, micromobility providers, and researchers to understand and play their role in bringing sustainable green transportation in the city.

1 Method

The review summarizes studies conducted on opportunities and challenges of micromobility transportation, emphasizing shared bikes. Three focused review procedures are followed. The first focus is on the benefits of micromobility for sustainable transportation. Detail review of scientific research, reports, articles, blogs, news, etc., were applied to achieve the first focus point. The second focus is on the challenges of micromobility, which was again done through an in-depth exploration of the literature on the area. The final focus explores the failure and lesson learned on micromobility, particularly in developing countries.

Furthermore, for additional analysis, six-year traffic crash data were also collected from the traffic police department of the Addis Ababa police commission. Finally, concluding remarks were forwarded, which summarizes the commitment to bring this emerging mobility option into the transportation systems of Addis Ababa. Micromobility transportation alternatives play a significant role and have the power to create affordable and sustainable transportation services for most populations, particularly in developing countries.

2 Results

2.1 Mobility in Addis Ababa and its challenges

Transportation contributes to achieving much of society's development. Well-planned and managed transportation systems play a significant role in long-term and sustainable economic growth. It facilitates access to opportunities, education, medical services and improves the overall quality of life. However, if all the relevant considerations are not considered, constructing new roads and transport infrastructure yields the opposite result.

A typical transportationsystem in Addis Ababa comprises public transportation, including buses, twelve to twenty-four seat minibus taxis, light rail transit (LRT), taxis, and private car. In addition, auto-rickshaws locally called Baja (Fig. 1) are also another common means of transportation in most parts of Ethiopia, including the capital Addis Ababa for short to medium-distance trips. Moreover, the majority of the population utilizes the oldest form of transit, walking, in their daily lives, and it's assumed that more than 55% of the transport trips per day in Addis Ababa is walking which is an important means of transportation in the city. Recently, several bike users have been seen in most parts of Addis Ababa.

Fig. 1　Three-wheeled auto rickshaw/Baja in Addis Ababa(Source: Photo by the author)

A light rail transit(Fig. 2) constructed by China Railway Group and partly financed by the Export-Import Bank of China, is among the public transport alternatives in Addis Ababa. The LRT's total length is about 34.24km which has two lines running from north-south and east-west of Addis Ababa and was inaugurated in September 2015. In its planning stage, the LRT system was aimed to transport up to 60000 passengers per hour. However, after nearly one year of operation, it commutes 15000 passengers per hour in each direction. It's the first LRT in Sub-Saharan Africa and plays a significant role in reducing travel time delay congestion and providing cost-effective alternative transportation services. The LRT system also brought enormous advantages in emission reduction, estimated to reduce 170000t of CO_2 per year by 2030. As an efficient mode of transportation, it stimulates the local economy and attracts new investments. While the LRT system helps to improve residents' mobility, the lack of frequency, trains, and integration into the existing transport network is a major challenge.

Fig. 2　Light rail transit in Addis Ababa (Source: SUSTAINIA, 2018)

Despite various initiatives taken by the agencies responsible forproviding and managing the public mass transportation system in the city, numerous factors challenge the transportation system in Addis Ababa. For example, a queue of people with long waiting time at stations, inconvenient and unsatisfactory connectivity along with the transfer stations, traffic congestion, travel delays, uncomfortable public transports, costly tariff systems, and onboard cash-based fare payment and absence of prepaid tickets/electronic payment and travel information are a few to list. Fig. 3 shows the common feature of Addis Ababa's daily long queue of people waiting for public transportation, mainly taxis.

Fig. 3 Queue of people waiting for taxis in Addis Ababa (Source: ABDU,2015)

2.2 Traffic safety problem

Road traffic safety problem is the other main challenge in Addis Ababa's daily transportation system. About 85% of the total fatalities in the country are concentrated on roads in the central part of the country, including the Addis Ababa City Administration, Oromia regional state, Amhara regional state, and South nations nationality people region. Furthermore, road traffic fatality in Addis Ababa has become a daily life-threatening concern, particularly on vulnerable road users/pedestrians. Although efforts are made towards combating the problem, it is insufficient by any standard relative to the worsening situation, hundreds of citizens' precious lives are lost year to year. The ten-year crash record trend (Fig. 4) in the city proves that traffic safety is among the city's top challenges. The figure is constructedbased on the crash data record obtained from the Addis Ababa police commission traffic police department (AAPCTPD). A total of 186182 road traffic crashes have been registered in Addis Ababa in the last ten years. As shown in the Fig., there is a sharp year-to-year increment in total vehicle crash records from 2010 to 2019. According to the police justification, most of the crashes in the city were caused by human behavior-related factors. With well-designed infrastructure effectively managed micromobility, transportation traffic crashes may reduce by minimizing the number of car users on the streets. Some city authorities in high micromobility transportation users' countries believed that fewer car trips and more micromobility are good for safety.

Furthermore, fatal crashes are compared between the victims (pedestrians, vehicle occupants, and drivers). From the comparison result shown in Fig. 5, one can easily understand that the fatal crash rate also sharply increased from year to year, indicating the seriousness of the problem in the city. Among those fatal crash victims, the vulnerable road users, particularly the pedestrians, take the massive share, which is an important sign of how dangerous for people to walk on the city's streets.

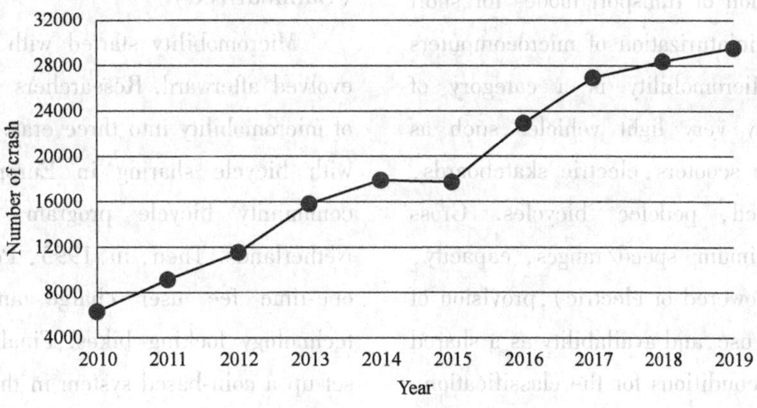

Fig. 4 Ten-year crash trend

In addition, the crash injury risk is highest in the active age groups, aged between 18 ~ 30, and males take the highest proportion of injury risk. Tab. 1 summarizes the ten-year crash victims' demographic characteristics.

In general, traffic crash in Addis Ababa is a silent killer that needs great attention with possible mitigation measures. It seems Addis Ababa somewhat understood this issue and is cooperating with international partners working on the city's road safety, like Bloomberg initiatives for Global Road Safety Facility (GRSF). Providing multiple transportation alternatives is among the intervention strategy for road safety challenges. Micromobility transportation can reduce pedestrian deaths and bring safe mobility to the city. A recent study revealed that micromobility transportation has the potential to improve traffic safety by reducing the number of car trips, increasing the waiting area of public transport, and allowing more access to stations.

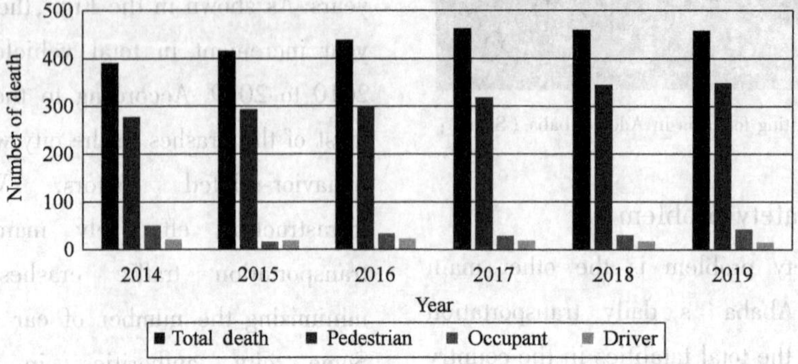

Fig. 5　Addis Ababa' s fatal traffic crash comparison among victims

Crash by demographic characteristics of victims(2010—2019 年)　　Tab. 1

	Variable	Frequency (n)	Percent (%)
Gender	Male	166837	88.33
	Female	17589	9.31
	Unknown	4464	2.36
Age Group	Below 18	1793	0.95
	18 ~ 30	81737	43.27
	31 ~ 50	74234	39.30
	Above 50	26671	14.12
	Unknown	4455	2.36

2.3　Micromobility

The miniaturization of transport modes for short journeys peers the miniaturization of microcomputers for personal use. Micromobility is a category of transport provided by very light vehicles such as shared bikes, electric scooters, electric skateboards, electric pedal-assisted, pedelec bicycles. Gross vehicle weight, maximum speed/ranges, capacity, powertrain (human-powered or electric), provision of motor, primary utility use, and availability as a shared service are the main conditions for the classification. In another way, micromobility can be defined as a form of transport that can share space with bicycles. Although, in general, multiple criteria can be applied to define what micromobility is, availabilities as a shared service are the focus of this review. Shared micromobility refers to any of these vehicles used as a shared resource between multiple users.

2.4　Evolution of micromobility (Summarized)

Micromobility started with bicycle sharing and evolved afterward. Researchers groupe the evolution of micromobility into three eras. The first was started with bicycle sharing in Europe in 1975 with a community bicycle program in Amsterdam, the Netherlands. Then, in 1995, Portsmouth brought a one-time fee user charge and smart card/rack technology locking bikes. Finally, Copenhagen also set up a coin-based system in this era.

The second era initiated dockless bikes with the advancement of smartphone and GPS communication technologies in 2000. Ofo and Mobike in China took this idea to an extreme extent by deploying 20 times more bikes in one year than all the station-based systems put together.

The third micromobility era took root and

flourished in the US with shared electric stand-up scooters designed for consumer throttle-operated products in late 2017 with Bird in Santa Monica. The availability of relatively inexpensive batteries, displays, and GPS receivers enabled by the smartphone supply chains provided easily accessible components for dockless services in many cities worldwide.

2.5 Multidimensional benefits of micromobility

Shared bikes and scooters reduce the physical walking required to move people over relatively short distances in developed countries. The wide-spreading of these transportation options motivates users worldwide within a short period. Micromobility has the potential to connect people with public transit in a better way, reduce dependence on private cars, reduce greenhouse gas emissions, and make better use of existing space. Micromobility addresses some of the most common transportation challenges in urban areas of developing countries, such as congestion, parking problems, excessive auto Emissions, air quality, poor coordination, and uneven access to public transport. The main benefits are summarized in the following section.

2.6 Reduce congestion

It's known by city planners and researchers that it can't always be simple to add more routes as a remedy for congestion problems because it would cost too much or result in other undesirable outcomes. And most of the time, a recommended traffic management technique to tackle congestion is encouraging public transport, which is not practical. The first mile/last mile problem is one potential issue that can discourage cities with an excellent public transportation system. In addition, people may not live/work within short walking distance of a transit station or bus stop. Therefore, cities can't escape suffering from traffic congestion. Micromobility integrated transportation systems, including public transportation and shared bikes, can help overcome this gap. Though using micromobility on a large scale and its new challenge still needs additional investigation, the micromobility vehicle provides, and the public needs to work out the best and safest implementation methods.

2.7 Environmental benefits

Micromobility has significant potential in reducing carbon dioxide and nitrogen emissions in the environment and energy consumption. For example, a study by Yongping et al. indicated that bike-sharing in Shanghai saved 8358 tons of petrol and decreased CO_2 and NO_X emissions by 25240 and 64 tones, respectively, and they also added the amount is much higher in more developed districts with higher population density. Furthermore, Ethiopia is committed to reducing emissions and mitigating climate change. In 2011 the country developed a document called "Climate-Resilient Green Economic strategy" to hold 145 metric tons of CO_2 equivalent per year, implemented across all society levels. Therefore, adopting micromobility programs and promoting green transportation in Addis Ababa plays a significant role in achieving this goal and creating a healthy environment for the citizen.

2.8 Health benefits

An increased level of bicycle riding brings more physical activity, positively impacting people's health. Promoting bicycling and bicycle commuting has shown the potential to increase the levels of physical activity among the population. When all factors were considered, including the risks associated with cycling, the improvement in physical activity among bike-sharing users resulted in significant health gains at the population level, decrease in heart disease, reduction in depression are few to list. In addition, researchers estimated a reduction in the death rate of 3.3 ~ 10.9 per million users per year. Riding a bicycle to work can also reduce physical inactivity and overweight/obesity (Raustorp and Koglin, 2019), the world's fourth and fifth leading risk factors for non-communicable diseases as concluded by the World Health Organization. With a poor habit of city-dwellers exercise in Addis Ababa, micromobility can play a significant role in keeping people's health besides its mobility benefit.

3 Main challenges of micromobility

With itsenormous potentials/opportunities, micromobility comes with challenges, especially for cities like Addis Ababa. Therefore, it's important to understand the primary challenges of micromobility transportation order to be put into practice in cities like Addis Ababa. The following major challenges should be considered when adopting micromobility transportation services in Addis Ababa.

3.1 Infrastructure

One big challenge that Addis Ababa will face to bring into practicethe micromobility program is the infrastructure. It is a common challenge for many developing cities in Africa, even in cities where the micromobility program has been applied widely. Addis Ababa's total road network is about 6000km. Most of the road elements lack bicycle lanes which are crucial for micromobility programs. Therefore, building more micromobility vehicle-friendly infrastructure is vitally crucial as adopting a micromobility program. However, the commitment by the city Administration to construct more than 100km of non-motorized infrastructure in the coming ten years is a great promising startup initiation to overcome this challenge. Research revealed that constructing a bike lane is highly cost-effective if observed from the point of reducing injury risks and more use of active modes of transportation. The other significant opportunity here is that some micromobility service providers are committed to supporting governments to build bike lanes. For example, Bird, one of the known micromobility service providers, offers one dollar per vehicle per day to the city government to build bike lanes, promote safe riding, and maintain shared infrastructure. Currently, there is some controversy on this fact. Another bright future is that the World Bank allocated funding to the consultancy service to prepare a road transport design guide that emphasizes the transport service program's bicycling and public transport guide.

3.2 Technology

Technology advancements are changing our world from time to time. The same is true in micromobility. It's unreasonable to think of providing micromobility services without satisfying access to telecommunication services and the internet. For example, Dockless shared e-bikes services use GPS and cellular connectivity/smartphone applications to track the locations of their vehicles and charge the users, which needs good internet services and continuous electricity supply. It will be another challenge that Addis Ababa will face to apply micromobility transport services. So, planning and adjusting to this fundamental condition is vital for making micromobility feasible in Addis Ababa.

3.3 Theft and vandalism

For micromobility providers, particularly for small micromobility companies, theft and vandalism of bikes is a major discouraging barrier in some countries, which leads them out of business. For example, one of the bike companies in Paris, Gobee bike, is out of business in France due to mass destruction/damage of their bikes in February 2018. Micromobility providers must deal with the expenses associated with replacing stolen hardware and hire enough workforce to repair damaged ones. Some micromobility vehicle provider companies redesigned their shared bike hardware to make more durable, solid-core bike tires.

3.4 Cultural stigma

Cultural stigma is anotherissue that should not be ignored while planning to bring micromobility options in Addis Ababa. Gender and cultural barriers hold bicycling back from being a viable alternative transportation option in many parts of Africa. For example, in South Africa, using a bicycle is seen as either for the illiterate or the poor. Such understanding is currently changing due to many bike riders in the city. People's perspective of cyclists as lower-classes challenges Egypt and Kenya. Such challenges can be solved by providing good infrastructure, attractive micromobility vehicles, and creating awareness among citizens of the immeasurable benefits of micromobility transportation alternatives.

3.5 Promising initiatives towards micromobility program in Addis Ababa

3.5.1 Car Free Day

Addis Ababa monthly celebrates "Car Free Day" to promote a healthy living style and reduce pollution on roads usually congested with traffic, primarily initiated by the government and started in Ethiopia in December 2018. The government's commitment demonstrates the cheerful willingness to practice the micromobility transportation option because micromobility can play a significant role in a healthy lifestyle and reduce congestion by minimizing individual car usage.

3.5.2 Bicycle lane and non-motorized transport strategy

Addis Ababa also publicized the first protected bicycle lane witha length of around 2.7km on one of the city's busiest road strips. Furthermore, the city administrations have a plan to build 100km non-motorized transport infrastructure in the coming ten years, which proves the commitment/good initiative of the government to further widen for more advanced mobility options like that of micromobility transportation services. Moreover, the non-motorized transport strategy of Ethiopia highly encourages such mobility options to come into practice.

The 2019 demographic and health survey (DHS) program data also revealed among the sample of 23007 households, around three percent have bicycle owners (Tab. 2). As one category of micromobility vehicles, Bicycles can play an important role as a cost-effective micromobility alternative, especially for the younger age group. The implication of such data may prove the people's interest in using micromobility transportation alternatives like shared bikes.

Households with Bicycle Tab. 2

	Frequency	Percent(%)
No	22153	96.3
Yes	676	2.9
Not adejure resident	178	0.8
Total	23007	100

Source: The DHS Program, 2022.

In addition, a survey study conducted by Tulu, Hadgu and Tarekegn to assess the awareness and experience of bicycling on 291 samples of Addis Ababa dwellers aged above 15 years also revealed that about 25% of them have experience on a bicycle as their transportation alternative within the last six months, and most of them have not experienced bicycle in the last six month which is related with various factors.

4 Concluding Remarks

Mobility demand in Addis Ababa is growing at an unprecedented rate with the growth of the population. To balance such a rapid increment in population and the demand for sustainable transportation, the provision of multiple alternatives of transport service is indispensable. Micromobility transport alternatives, particularly shared bikes, are increasingly used in cities worldwide and are simplifying people's lives with their multidimensional benefits. Micromobility transportation can give door-to-door transport services with the technological advancement of smartphones and other connected devices on a scale of individual users. They can be used to transport people for small and medium-distance coverage. Therefore, Addis Ababa, as a good city for micromobility transportation alternatives, can benefit a lot if it considers the wide application of such alternatives in its transportation system by careful examinations of the factors that should be considered. The major promising initiation to bring into practice micromobility transportation in Addis Ababa includes:

(1) Addis Ababa's transport policy adopted in 2011 and the Ethiopia non-motorized transport strategy 2020—2029 promote the expansion of non-motorized and mass transport systems to achieve a more socially inclusive, economically affordable, environmentally friendly, and technologically advanced transport system in the city.

(2) The city master plan released in 2017 (renewed every ten years) calls for development focused on a transportation plan with more pedestrian and bicycle infrastructure. The rationale behind this great idea was to bring sustainable and lasting socio-

economic development to the citizen.

(3) More than 55% of daily trips in Addis Ababa were short-distance trips done through walking, which is a promising input for the city's success of a micromobility transportation alternative.

(4) Accessibility is the most crucial feature of a modern transportation system in which properly designed micromobility infrastructure and services can satisfy this fundamental urban transportation element.

Therefore, as proved by research and experience of many cities, the provision of micromobility transportation options (e. g., shared bikes) can bring reliable, accessible, and environmentally friendly transport services and also helps to achieve the country's green transportation strategy.

Reference

[1] Addis TV, 2020. Lebu-Jemo Interim Cycling Corridor.

[2] Agence France-Presse. Gobee. bike pulls out of France due to "mass destruction" of its dockless bike fleet [WWW Document]. Guard. URL https://www.theguardian.com/world/2018/feb/25/gobeebike-france-mass-destruction-dockless-bikes (accessed 8.12.20).

[3] Akloweg Y, Hayshi Y, Kato H. The effect of used cars on African road traffic accidents: A case study of Addis Ababa, Ethiopia[J]. Int. J. Urban Sci, 2011(1): 61-69.

[4] American Library Association. "Micro-Mobility" [WWW Document]. ala. org. URL http://www.ala.org/tools/future/trends/micromobility (accessed 8.25.20).

[5] B. David Zarley. The future of micromobility in Africa [WWW Document]. freethink. com. URL https://www.freethink.com/articles/the-future-of-micromobility-in-africa (accessed 8.12.20).

[6] BBC News. Thousands walk on Ethiopia Car Free Day-BBC News [WWW Document]. bbc. com. URL https://www.bbc.com/news/world-africa-46499036 (accessed 3.2.20).

[7] BeltonPadraig, Padraig Belton. How cheap dockless hire bikes are flooding the world [WWW Document]. BBC News. URL https://www.bbc.com/news/business-44066083 (accessed 8.12.20).

[8] Breathelife, 2018. Ethiopia launches first car-free day [WWW Document]. breathelife2030. org. URL https://breathelife2030.org/news/ethiopia-launches-first-car-free-day/ (accessed 8.11.20).

[9] Brookshire K, Sandt L, Sundstrom C, et al. Advancing pedestrian and bicyclist safety: A primer for highway safety professionals. Washington, DC: National Highway Traffic Safety Administration.

[10] Cbinsights. The micromobility revolution: how bikes and scooters are shaking up urban transport worldwide [WWW Document]. cbinsights. com. URL https://www.cbinsights.com/research/report/micromobility-revolution/ (accessed 8.6.20).

[11] Celis-Morales C. A, Lyall D. M, Welsh P, et al. Association between active commuting and incident cardiovascular disease, cancer, and mortality: prospective cohort study. BMJ 357, j1456. https://doi.org/10.1136/bmj.j1456

[12] Charlie Campbell. China's bike-sharing fever has reached saturation point [WWW Document]. Time. URL https://time.com/5218323/china-bicycles-sharing-economy/ (accessed 8.12.20).

[13] Cusick D. Ethiopia aims for a bright, green climate future [WWW Document]. Sci. Am. URL https://www.scientificamerican.com/article/ethiopia-aims-for-a-bright-green-climate-future/ (accessed 8.19.20).

[14] Cynthia Nanjekho Sitati K. O. O. Electric mobility in Addis Ababa [WWW Document]. Next Gener. City Action. URL http://nextgenerationcityaction.com/16-electric-mobility-in-addis-ababa/ (accessed 8.18.20).

[15] Damilola Soladoye S. O. Getting around in Africa: The tale of micro mobility [WWW Document]. movmi. net. URL https://movmi.net/

micro-mobility-in-africa/ (accessed 2. 29. 20).

[16] Dediu Horace. The Micromobility Definition [WWW Document]. micromobility. io. URL https: // micromobility. io/blog/2019/2/23/the-micromobility-definition (accessed 8.6.20).

[17] Dediu Horace. The Three Eras of Micromobility [WWW Document]. micromobility. io. URL https: // micromobility. io/blog/2019/4/29/the-three-eras-of-micromobility (accessed 8. 6.20).

[18] Dews F. Charts of the Week: Africa's changing demographics [WWW Document]. brookings. edu. URL https: // www. brookings. edu/blog/brookings-now/2019/01/18/charts-of-the-week-africas-changing-demographics/ (accessed 2.27.20).

[19] Downs A. Traffic: Why It's getting worse, what government can do. J. Policy Pract. Intellect. Disabil. 1, 186-186. https: // doi. org/10. 1111/j. 1741-1130. 2004. 04033.

[20] Ethiopia Construction, 2016. Addis Ababa City Spends Big on Roads [WWW Document]. ethiopiaconstruction. com. URL https: // ethiopiaconstruction. com/news/addis-ababa-city-spends-big-on-roads/ (accessed 8.15.20).

[21] FHWA, n. d. Traffic congestion and reliability: Linking solutions to problems [WWW Document]. ops. fhwa. dot. gov. URL https: // ops. fhwa. dot. gov/congestion_report_04/chapter4. htm (accessed 8.26.20).

[22] GRSF, 2018. Global Road Safety Facility Annual Report Annual Report, rtda. gov. rw.

[23] Jamal Saghir, J. S., 2018. Urbanization in Sub-Saharan Africa [WWW Document]. csis. org. URL https: // www. csis. org/analysis/urbanization-sub-saharan-africa (accessed 2.19.20).

[24] Jarrett Walker, 2016. Can public transport investment really fix traffic congestion? | CityMetric [WWW Document]. citymetric. com. URL https: // www. citymetric. com/transport/can-public-transport-investment-really-fix-traffic-congestion-1870 (accessed 8.26.20).

[25] Jill Barker, 2014. Bike-sharing has health benefits [WWW Document]. montrealgazette. com. URL http: // www. montrealgazette. com/health/bike + sharing + health + benefits + study + finds/9572544/story. html (accessed 8.12.20).

[26] Ministry of Transport, 2020. Ethiopia non-motorised transport strategy 2020-2029, unhabitat. org.

[27] Ministry of Transport, 2011. The Federal Democratic Republic of Ethiopia Ministry of Transport Transport Policy of Addis Ababa.

[28] Nieuwenhuijsen, M., Khreis, H., 2019. Urban and Transport planning, environment and health, in: Integrating Human Health into Urban and Transport Planning. Springer, pp. 3-16.

[29] OICA, 2015. World Vehicles in Use [WWW Document]. oica. net. URL http: // www. oica. net/wp-content/uploads/Total_in-use-All-Vehicles. pdf (accessed 2.29.20).

[30] Oja, P., Titze, S., Bauman, A., de Geus, B., Krenn, P., Reger-Nash, B., Kohlberger, T., 2011. Health benefits of cycling: a systematic review. Scand. J. Med. Sci. Sports 21, 496-509. https: // doi. org/10. 1111/j. 1600-0838. 2011. 01299. x

[31] Population Stat, 2020. Addis Ababa, Ethiopia Population (2020) [WWW Document]. populationstat. com. URL https: // populationstat. com/ethiopia/addis-ababa (accessed 8. 15. 20).

[32] Raustorp, J., Koglin, T., 2019. The potential for active commuting by bicycle and its possible effects on public health. J. Transp. Heal. 13, 72-77. https: // doi. org/10. 1016/j. jth. 2019.03.012.

[33] Sam Mehmet, 2020. ITF report examines traffic safety of micromobility vehicles [WWW Document]. Int. Transp. Forum. URL https: // www. intelligenttransport. com/transport-news/97163/itf-report-examines-traffic-safety-of-mi-

cromobility-vehicles/ (accessed 8.24.20).

[34] Schmitt, A., Angie Schmitt, 2019. Bird Quietly Ends a Much-Hyped Bike Lane Subsidy [WWW Document]. Streetsblog USA. URL https://usa.streetsblog.org/2019/01/10/bird-quietly-ends-a-much-hyped-bike-lane-subsidy/ (accessed 8.6.20).

[35] Sebastian Ibold, D. C. N., 2018. The Evolution of Free-Floating Bike-Sharing in China [WWW Document]. Sustain. Transp. China. URL https://www.sustainabletransport.org/archives/6278 (accessed 8.18.20).

[36] SSAP, 2018. Addressing Africa's Urban Transport and Mobility Challenge [WWW Document]. ssatp.org. URL https://www.ssatp.org/en/page/urban-transport-mobility (accessed 2.19.20).

[37] Stucki, M., 2015. Policies for Sustainable Accessibility and Mobility in Urban Areas of Africa. https://doi.org/10.1038/nchem.1002.

[38] The World Bank Implementation Status & Results Report, 2019. The World Bank Ethiopia: Transport Systems Improvement Project (TRANSIP) (P151819) Implementation Status and Key Decisions.

[39] Wikipedia, 2020a. Micromobility [WWW Document]. en.wikipedia.org. URL https://en.wikipedia.org/wiki/Micromobility (accessed 8.12.20).

[40] Wikipedia, 2020b. Luud Schimmelpennink [WWW Document]. en.wikipedia.org. URL https://en.wikipedia.org/wiki/Luud_Schimmelpennink (accessed 8.12.20).

[41] Witze, S., Sandra Witzel, 2018. How micro mobility solves multiple problems in congested cities [WWW Document]. skedgo.com. URL https://skedgo.com/how-micro-mobility-solves-multiple-problems-in-congested-cities/ (accessed 8.6.20).

[42] World Bank, 2016. PROJECT APPRAISAL DOCUMENT ON A PROPOSED CREDIT IN THE AMOUNT OF SDR213 MILLION (US $300 MILLION EQUIVALENT) TO THE THE THE FEDERAL DEMOCRATIC REPUBLIC OF ETHIOPIA FOR A TRANSPORT SYSTEMS IMPROVEMENT PROJECT, Annals of Tropical Medicine and Parasitology. https://doi.org/10.1179/136485908X337463

[43] World Health Organization, 2009. Global Health Risks.

[44] Zarif Rasheq, Derek Pankratz, B. K., 2019. Making micromobility work for citizens, cities, and service providers [WWW Document]. www2.deloitte.com. URL https://www2.deloitte.com/us/en/insights/focus/future-of-mobility/micro-mobility-is-the-future-of-urban-transportation.html#endnote-sup-1 (accessed 8.6.20).

[45] Zhang, Y., Mi, Z., 2018. Environmental benefits of bike sharing: A big data-based analysis. Appl. Energy 220, 296-301. https://doi.org/10.1016/j.apenergy.2018.03.101.

[46] ABDU, B. (2015). Mass Transportation Mess: The Poor Traffic Management in Addis Abeba. Addisfortune. Retrieved from https://addisfortune.net/columns/mass-transportation-mess-the-poor-traffic-management-in-addis-abeba/.

[47] B. David Zarley. (2019). The future of micromobility in Africa. Retrieved from https://www.freethink.com/social-change/the-future-of-micromobility-in-africa.

[48] Clelie Nallet. (2018). The Challenge of Urban Mobility: A Case Study of Addis Ababa Light Rail, EThiopia. Retrieved from https://www.ifri.org/sites/default/files/atoms/files/nallet_urban_mobility_addis_ababa_2018.pdf.

[49] SUSTAINIA. (2018). Addis Ababa: Sub-Saharan Africa's First Light-Rail Train. Retrieved from. https://goexplorer.org/addis-ababa-sub-saharan-africas-first-light-rail-train/.

[50] The DHS Program. (2022). Ethiopia: Interim DHS, 2019 Dataset. Retrieved from https://dhsprogram.com/data/dataset/Ethiopia_

Interim-DHS_2019. cfm? flag = 1.

[51] Tulu, G. S., Hadgu, M., & Tarekegn, A. G. (2019). Bicycling in Addis Ababa, Ethiopia: Opportunities and challenges. Journal of Sustainable Development of Transport and Logistics, 4(2), 50-59. doi: 10.14254/jsdtl.2019.4-2.5.

[52] VOI. (2021). Safer streets with shared micromobility. Retrieved from https://www.voiscooters.com/wp-content/uploads/2021/08/Voi-Safety-Report_2021-august-update-2.pdf.

共享电动汽车网点布局及运营综述

艾合太木·艾斯凯尔 孙小慧*
(新疆大学建筑工程学院)

摘 要 作为一种基于共享经济的新型出行模式,共享电动汽车既有私家车的舒适性和灵活性,又具有低碳环保等优点,在我国一线城市得到了快速发展。然而,共享电动汽车在发展过程中存在用户借车还车难、用户实际步行距离远、用户和工作人员充电难以及运营商调度成本高等问题,合理布局网点和充电基础设施,并建立高效的后期运营模式可有效解决共享电动汽车发展中面临的问题。目前,共享电动汽车网点布局和运营管理得到了众多国内外专家学者的广泛研究,主要集中在用户需求预测、网点选址和车辆调度方面,少数学者研究了共享电动汽车充电站选址与定容问题。本文从共享电动汽车用户出行特征、网点选址布局、充电站选址布局和网点运营等方面对共享电动汽车网点布局和运营管理的既有研究成果进行梳理和总结,以期为共享电动汽车未来研究方向提供有益的借鉴。

关键词 共享电动汽车 网点布局 充电站布局 运营管理 文献综述

0 引言

目前,交通运输系统消耗的化石燃料是温室气体排放的主要来源。公安交通局统计数据显示,截至2021年5月,全国机动车保有量达3.8亿辆,交通领域化石燃料的消耗和温室气体的排放形势愈加严峻。汽车电气化是实现绿色交通的有效途径之一。相关研究表明,与传统燃油车相比,一辆电动汽车每千米可节省约6美分燃油费,并减少50%的温室气体排放[1]。然而,目前私人电动汽车拥有量仍然很低,电动汽车的市场认可度和公众接受度不高,主要原因除了续航里程短及其带来的里程焦虑问题外,还有前期购车成本高、维修和保养费用高、技术更新迭代周期快带来的潜在折旧率高等问题[2]。因此,对于电动汽车的推广,除了进一步完善电动汽车技术、合理建设充电设施以缓解电动汽车消费者的里程焦虑外,还需要降低车辆的购买和使用成本。共享电动汽车作为一种新兴的出行方式,用户在使用时无须支付购置车辆费用、购买保险费用和维修费用等,只需要按计费模式支付使用费用,在用户购车养车难、汽车限牌和限行的政策环境下,可以为居民提供一种新的出行选择,满足用户多样化和个性化的出行需求。

目前有关共享电动汽车网点布局和运营管理研究较多,同时还有少量关于共享电动汽车充电站选址定容的研究。然而,全面阐述共享电动车网点布局及运营问题的综述性文献相对较少。本文旨在系统地整理共享电动汽车网点布局及运营管理相关研究,从用户出行特征、网点选址布局、充电站选址布局和网点运营管理四个方面进行归纳总结,并提出未来研究趋势和方向,以期为共享电动汽车研究提供有价值的参考。

1 用户出行特征

共享电动汽车投入市场时间较短,其相比于传统燃油车在续航里程、能耗和驾驶体验等方面存在着明显的差异,为了更好地吸引潜在用户并进行有效的后期运营管理,需要充分了解用户的出行特征。下文分别从影响用户出行行为的因素、用户宏观出行特性和用户微观出行特性三个方面来进行综述。

1.1 影响用户出行的因素

Prieto 对伦敦、马德里和巴黎城市居民发起问卷调查,用最小二乘法(OLS)回归分析数据,研究结果显示,知识、环保、自主性及参与度是影响汽车共享市场消费者行为的重要因素[3]。Yoon 基于北京的调查数据对比分析了基于站点的单程式共享汽车和往返式共享汽车用户的使用偏好差异,分析结果表明,年龄、可用车辆数、预定价格和寒冷天气对选择使用单程式共享汽车有显著影响,而对于往返式共享汽车而言,影响其使用的重要因素是拥有车辆、收入、性别、环保意识[4]。Kim 发现低收入社区的出行者在共享汽车使用行为偏好方面与常规地区的出行者没有明显差异[5]。Efthymiou 发现中低收入人群、经常采用公共交通的人倾向于使用共享汽车,26~35 岁、博士学历人群不倾向使用共享汽车[6]。Sioui、Luca、Efthymiou 等对来自线上或线下的用户出行行为调查问卷数据进行了分析,结果表明用户的出行行为受年龄、性别和收入等多种因素的影响[7-9]。

1.2 用户宏观出行特性

Hui 发现共享汽车与私家车的出行链特征存在差异,以长时间停车为目的的出行中,用户倾向使用私人汽车,然而在一些短程出行或停车时间短暂的出行中,用户倾向使用共享汽车[10]。Müller 应用负二项分布来分析柏林自由浮动式共享汽车用户订单数据,研究发现自由浮动式共享汽车在城市中心区域的可持续发展性更好[11]。Stefan 对自由浮动式共享汽车系统的大规模订单数据进行分析、评估,通过共享汽车的时空分布特征得到工作日订单频率明显更高[12]。为了探究需求的时空分布特性,Martínez 开发了一种基于 Agent 的模型来模拟共享电动汽车系统,将该模型应用于里斯本城市,发现需求在全天的分布不均衡,客流峰值发生在早上 8 点左右,其次是中午,再次是晚上 5 点左右[13]。

1.3 用户微观出行特性

鞠鹏基于南京市的实证调查数据,运用混合选择模型对出行者的汽车共享选择行为进行研究,结果表明共享汽车的选择行为不仅受到社会人口统计属性和出行方式属性的影响,还会受到感知有用性、感知易用性、行为态度等态度潜变量的影响[14]。Kim 等考虑了驾驶乐趣、环保态度、小汽车个人价值、隐私保护四个潜在变量,探究态度与共享汽车使用的关系,研究发现环保态度的影响最显著[15]。余静财构建包含潜变量的混合选择模型,研究发现对共享电动汽车的了解程度、行为态度、车辆障碍和个人障碍等因素,对选择共享电动汽车出行存在显著影响[16]。朱振涛研究发现,使用共享电动汽车的关键影响因素依次为环保意识、社会影响、价格价值、绩效期望和政府政策[17]。

2 网点选址布局

共享电动汽车网点选址布局的研究方法可分为两大类:一类是数据驱动的优化选址方法,另一类是基于数学规划的选址方法。

2.1 数据驱动的优化选址方法

数据驱动的优化选址方法主要依据手机订单数据、GPS 轨迹数据和手机信令数据结合启发式算法分析来确定网点的位置。Li 将地理信息系统与大数据相结合,通过对兴趣点(POI)数据、共享电动汽车运营数据、手机订单数据与 GPS 轨迹数据等多源数据的挖掘和预处理,预测共享汽车需求并确定网点位置[18]。Willing 采用核密度估计(KDE)方法合并兴趣点(POI)数据和运营商租赁数据,开发了一种空间决策支持系统,可以预测共享汽车需求,以便合理布局网点位置[19]。Liu 提出一种 AP 聚类算法,对出租车起讫点(OD)进行聚类分析来确定网点选址的优化方法,根据分析 AP 聚类算法的特点,基于服务区对出租车 OD 进行划分,考虑出租车 OD 点稀疏相似矩阵和自适应 AP 聚类的特点输入参数,进行层次优化,最终确定网点的数量和位置[20]。

2.2 基于数学规划的优化选址方法

基于数学规划的优化选址方法主要以利润最大化、建设成本最小化、调度成本最小化和用户最便利为优化目标建立优化模型。Çalık 以运营商利润最大化为目标,提出一个混合整数线性规划模型,解决了共享电动汽车网点的最优位置和容量确定问题[21]。Huang 提出一种混合整数非线性规划模型,用于确定网点位置和容量,优化目标中考虑了调度流程和调度成本,解决了用户出行需求和车辆可用性之间的不平衡问题[22]。Biesinger以总利润最大化为目标,将网点的选址、网点充电桩的数量和网点容量作为一个组合优化问题,并建立双层规划模型,第一层使用变领域搜索算法确定网点的位置、网点充电桩的数量和每个网点的车辆数,第二层使用贪婪算法迭代对第一层生成的候选解进行评估[23]。徐文结合选址因素分析、网点分类,建立以建设成本最小、用户最便利为目标的多目标优化模型,以 Yalmip 优化工具对模型进行求解[24]。

3 充电站选址布局

共享电动汽车的高效运营离不开完善的充电设施。然而,目前充电桩的布局和容量与共享电动汽车需求不相匹配,严重制约了共享电动汽车的运营效率。如何合理规划充电设施的位置和容量,成为亟待研究的问题。

多数学者研究共享电动汽车充电站选址布局时,以充电设施建设总成本最小、利润最大化、充电等待时间最小和提高用户满意度为目标建立优化模型。Miao 提出两阶段多目标优化模型,第一阶段优化地理服务区域,第二阶段解决充电基础设施配置问题;建立需求点到充电设施距离最小和充电设施建设总成本最小的多目标模型,保证用户和运营商同时受益[25]。Roni 研究了车队车辆闲置时间与充电站数量之间的关系,以最小化充电等待时间为目标,建立一个整数规划模型,从充电站的数量和位置以及共享电动汽车在充电站间的分配等方面进行联合优化;研究表明,通过增加 5 ~ 20 个新的充电站,运营期间的车辆闲置时间减少了 2% ~ 4%[26]。Brandstätter 为了确定共享电动汽车充电站位置,构建以利润最大化为目标的一个时变整数线性规划,并提出了一种求解优化问题的启发式算法,通过使用基于维也纳市的运营数据对模型进行了验证[27]。Brandstätter 为寻求共享电动汽车充电站最佳位置和规模,把用户可接受里程数作为首要目标,提出了两个整数线性规划公式,跟踪每辆共享电动汽车的电池剩余量,还设计了迭代寻找最短路径和迭代寻找最小成本两种启发式算法对问题进行求解[28]。Calık 假设车辆网点的充电桩数量与停车位数量相同,构建了最大化利润的混合整数线性规划模型,确定充电站位置及数量,并用纽约市曼哈顿区的出租车出行数据对模型进行了验证[29]。Cocca 针对自由流动式的共享电动汽车系统,提出了基于用户停车行为和不同充电策略的精确轨迹驱动的仿真方法,以最小化充电站数量和降低乘客不满意度为目标,优化充电站布设位置[30]。

4 网点运营研究

由于用户出行需求的潮汐特性,随着运营时间的增加,会出现网点间车辆需求和供给失衡的问题,某些时段无法有效满足用户的出行需求,导致用户体验较差,极大地制约了共享电动汽车的发展,采用合理的调度策略可使车辆供需失衡问题得以解决。按照调度主体可分为员工调度和用户调度两类。

4.1 基于员工的调度

基于员工的调度方式,就是雇佣员工,更加有目的性地对车辆进行调度,虽然调度成本较高,但是可以显著的平衡网点间的车辆供需关系。Xu 通过建立一个混合整数非线性规划模型,确定了车队规模和车辆调度策略,并以新加坡的汽车共享公司 move 为例,验证了模型的有效性[31]。王宁基于完全满足用户用车需求的前提,建立成本最低的调度需求模型,采用遗传算法求解得出调度需求;构建了电动汽车共享站点间车辆员工调度策略,以运营公司收益最大为目标函数规划模型,并采用分支定界法求解模型[32]。Huo 为了兼顾用户出行需求,将利润表示为具有不确定用户需求的离散随机变量的数学期望,构建线形规划模型,用于平衡需求和供给以及实现企业利润最大化,并使用了北京市某企业 30 个网点的真实数据对模型进行验证[33]。Wang 提出两阶段调度策略,第一阶段根据网点内车辆数预测调度需求,第二阶段提出混合整数线性规划模型,对车辆需要从哪些网点进行调度进行了优化计算[34]。

4.2 基于用户的调度

用户调度所使用的方法主要是调节用户的车辆租赁价格,通过价格激励用户自发改变原计划的取、还车点,以此完成用户调度。王宁提出基于用户激励的共享电动汽车自适应调度成本最优模型,引入共享单车调度与价格激励手段,并提出将多时段可变的上下阈值作为调度决策的关键变量,引入价格优惠激励机制,引导用户实现自适应调度,并通过遗传算法求解获得最优价格优惠、初始站点车辆数、多时段可变最优阈值[35]。Stokkin引入了一种基于用户需求预测的调度策略,该策略根据系统当前网络中的车辆分布和预计未来用户需求来确定最优激励,通过预测未来用户的需求,避免未知需求的损失[36]。姚恩建提出面向自组织平衡的车辆调度优化方法,在员工调度的基础上,为实现自组织平衡,基于用户的共享电动汽车站点选择行为偏好,制定动态折扣策略,以引导用户改变默认的最近取还车网点,在满足用户出行需求的同时,由用户完成部分调度任务,从而提高各站点车辆的供需平衡,降低员工调度任务数量与调度成本[37]。

5　总结与展望

本文从共享电动汽车用户出行特征、网点选址布局、充电站选址布局和网点运营管理等方面对共享电动汽车网点布局和运营管理的既有研究成果进行了梳理和总结。基于上述总结分析,未来共享电动汽车网点布局和运营管理可从以下几个方面开展。

(1)无论是国内还是国外,目前都没有提出关于共享电动汽车充电设施参与碳交易的发展方案,对其运营机制的研究也属空白。我国节能减排的需求以及电动汽车绿色节能特性决定了共享电动汽车具有巨大的发展潜力,伴随着未来更多政策的实施,共享电动汽车充电基础设施参与碳交易市场有望成为我国实行节能减排的重要举措,未来可考虑开展共享电动汽车充电站参与碳交易增加收益的情形下网点布局和运营管理方面的研究。

(2)随着自动驾驶的发展,车辆调度也有望实现无人驾驶。未来的研究中,可以开发车辆调度的控制逻辑,用户无须到网点取车,而是预订车辆后,就近的共享电动汽车自动驾驶到用户的所在地,用户也无须到网点还车,而是付完钱后,车辆检测自身电量及安全状态,根据情况自动驾驶到共享站点或者继续提供服务,提高共享车辆的利用率。

(3)大多数车辆调度的研究中,未考虑交通中断对调度车辆的影响,而实际情况中,交通中断是不可忽略的因素,因此在未来研究中,可以在车辆调度研究中加入交通中断的影响,将不确定性纳入共享电动汽车网点规划,以提高整个交通网络的韧性。

(4)为了提高共享电动汽车的利用率,把车辆调度到高需求区,从运营商的角度来看可以直接转化为更高的利润,然而从社会的角度来看,让车辆远离低需求区可能不太可取,因为它剥夺了居民在低需求区出行的机会,未来可考虑社会公平性的因素,从更全面的城市流动性角度来研究。

参考文献

[1] He L, Mak H, Rong Y, et al. Service Region Design for Urban Electric Vehicle Sharing Systems [J]. Manufacturing & Service Operations Management, 2017, 19(2): 309-327.

[2] Latinopoulos C, Sivakumar A, Polak J. Modeling electric vehicle charging behaviour: What is the relationship between charging location, driving distance and range anxiety[C]. Meeting of the Transportation Research Board, 2017.

[3] Prieto M, Stan V, Baltas G, et al. Shifting consumers into gear: car sharing services in urban areas[J]. International Journal of Retail & Distribution Management, 2019, 47(5): 552-570.

[4] Yoon T, Cherry C R, Jones L R. One-way and round-trip carsharing: A stated preference experiment in Beijing [J]. Transportation Research Part D: Transport and Environment, 2017, 53: 102-114.

[5] Kim, Kyeongsu. Can carsharing meet the mobility needs for the low-income neighborhoods? Lessons from carsharing usage patterns in New York City[J]. Transportation Research Part A Policy and Practice, 2015, 77: 249-260.

[6] Efthymiou D, Antoniou C. Modeling the propensity to join carsharing using hybrid choice models and mixed survey data[J]. Transport Policy, 2016, 51: 143-149.

[7] Efthymiou D, Antoniou C, Waddell P. Factors affecting the adoption of vehicle sharing systems by young drivers[J]. Transport Policy,2013,29(SEP.):64-73.

[8] Luca S D, Pace R D. Modelling users' behaviour in inter-urban carsharing program: A stated preference approach [J]. Transportation Research Part A,2015,71(jan.):59-76.

[9] Sioui L, Morency C, Trépanier M. How Carsharing Affects the Travel Behavior of Households: A Case Study of Montréal, Canada[J]. International Journal of Sustainable Transportation, 2013,7(1):52-69.

[10] Hui Y, Ding M, Zheng K, et al. Observing Trip Chain Characteristics of Round-Trip Carsharing Users in China: A Case Study Based on GPS Data in Hangzhou City[J]. Sustainability,2017,9(6):949.

[11] Müller J, Correia G, Bogenberger K. An Explanatory Model Approach for the Spatial Distribution of Free-Floating Carsharing Bookings: A Case-Study of German Cities[J]. Sustainability,2017,9(7):1290.

[12] Schmoeller S, Weikl S, Mueller J, et al. Empirical analysis of free-floating carsharing usage: The Munich and Berlin case[J]. Transportation Research Part C,2015,56(jul.):34-51.

[13] Martínez L M, Correia G H D A, Moura F, et al. Insights into carsharing demand dynamics: Outputs of an agent-based model application to Lisbon, Portugal[J]. International journal of sustainable transportation,2017,11(2):148-159.

[14] 鞠鹏,周晶,徐红利,等.基于混合选择模型的汽车共享选择行为研究[J].交通运输系统工程与信息,2017,17(02):7-13.

[15] Kim J, Rasouli S, Timmermans H J P. The effects of activity-travel context and individual attitudes on car-sharing decisions under travel time uncertainty: A hybrid choice modeling approach[J]. Transportation Research Part D: Transport and Environment, 2017, 56: 189-202.

[16] 余静财,李文权,王顺超,等.共享电动汽车选择行为分析[J].东南大学学报(自然科学版),2021,51(01):153-160.

[17] 朱振涛,杜明阳,刘颖.共享电动汽车使用意愿的关键影响因素研究[J].江汉大学学报(社会科学版),2020,37(06):91-102.

[18] Li W, Li Y, Fan J, et al. Siting of Carsharing Stations Based on Spatial Multi-Criteria Evaluation: A Case Study of Shanghai EVCARD [J]. Sustainability,2017,9(1):152.

[19] Willing C, Klemmer K, Brandt T, et al. Moving in time and space-Location intelligence for carsharing decision support[J]. Decision Support Systems,2017[C],99:75-85.

[20] Liu Z, Jia Y, Zhu X. Deployment Strategy for Car-Sharing Depots by Clustering Urban Traffic Big Data Based on Affinity Propagation [J]. Scientific Programming,2018,2018:1-9.

[21] Calik H, Fortz B. Location of stations in a one-way electric car sharing system, 2017 [C]. IEEE,2017.

[22] Huang K, Correia G H D A, An K. Solving the station-based one-way carsharing network planning problem with relocations and non-linear demand[J]. Transportation Research Part C: Emerging Technologies,2018,90:1-17.

[23] Biesinger B, Hu B, Stubenschrott M, et al. Optimizing Charging Station Locations for Electric Car-Sharing Systems [C]. European Conference on Evolutionary Computation in Combinatorial Optimization,2017.

[24] 徐文.共享汽车网点选址与调度方法研究[D].南京:东南大学,2019:87.

[25] Miao H, Jia H, Li J, et al. Autonomous connected electric vehicle (ACEV)-based carsharing system modeling and optimal planning: A unified two-stage multi-objective optimization methodology [J]. Energy, 2019, 169: 797-818.

[26] Roni M S, Yi Z, Smart J G. Optimal charging

management and infrastructure planning for free-floating shared electric vehicles [J]. Transportation Research Part D:Transport and Environment,2019,76:155-175.

[27] Brandstätter G, Kahr M, Leitner M. Determining optimal locations for charging stations of electric car-sharing systems under stochastic demand[J]. Transportation Research Part B: Methodological,2017,104:17-35.

[28] Brandstätter G,Leitner M,Ljubic I. Location of Charging Stations in Electric Car Sharing Systems [J]. Transportation science, 2020, 54 (5):1408-1438.

[29] Calik H,Fortz B. Location of Stations in a One-Way Electric Car Sharing System [C]. 2017 IEEE Symposium on Computers and Communications (ISCC),2017.

[30] Cocca M, Giordano D, Mellia M, et al. Data Driven Optimization of Charging Station Placement for EV Free Floating Car Sharing [C]. 2018 IEEE International Conference on Intelligent Transportation Systems (ITSC), 2018.

[31] Xu M, Meng Q, Liu Z. Electric vehicle fleet size and trip pricing for one-way carsharing services considering vehicle relocation and personnel assignment[J]. Transportation Research Part B:Methodological,2018,111:60-82.

[32] 王宁,张文剑,刘向,等.电动汽车共享站点间车辆人工调度策略[J].同济大学学报(自然科学版),2018,46(08):1064-1071.

[33] Xiang H A,Xwa B,Ming L A,et al. The allocation problem of electric car-sharing system: A data-driven approach [J]. Transportation Research Part D:Transport and Environment, 78.

[34] Wang L,Liu Q,Ma W. Optimization of dynamic relocation operations for one-way electric carsharing systems [J]. Transportation Research Part C:Emerging Technologies,2019, 101:55-69.

[35] 王宁,郑文晖,刘向,等.基于用户激励的共享电动汽车调度成本优化[J].同济大学学报(自然科学版),2018,46(12):1668-1675.

[36] Stokkink P, Geroliminis N. Predictive user-based relocation through incentives in one-way car-sharing systems [J]. Transportation Research Part B Methodological,2021,149(3): 230-249.

[37] 姚恩建,何媛媛,金方磊,等.面向自组织平衡的共享电动汽车调度优化方法[J].交通运输系统工程与信息,2020,20(5): 135-141.

共享汽车需求及时空分布研究综述

王飞燕 孙小慧*

(新疆大学建筑工程学院)

摘 要 共享汽车对交通领域的碳减排起着不可替代的作用,准确预测其需求及时空分布可为站点布局和车辆调度提供依据。基于此,本文对国内外研究进行梳理,首先,从个人属性、出行属性、共享汽车系统属性以及建成环境属性总结影响需求的因素;其次,明确基于运营订单数据探究的共享汽车需求的时空分布特性;最后,概述需求预测的常用方法。在此基础上,从影响因素、多源数据融合等方面提出未来研究方向,并进一步考虑个人碳交易、MaaS理念等对共享汽车选择影响机理研究的可能性。

关键词 共享汽车 需求预测 时空特性 出行行为 综述

0　引言

随着全球能源短缺和环境污染问题日趋严重,各国都在加速推进节能减排,我国提出“2030年碳达峰,2060年碳中和”的双碳目标。据国际能源署预测,截至2040年,交通领域将有可能是唯一不能实现中国碳达峰、目标的领域[1],交通领域碳中和面临严峻挑战。随着理论与实践的推进,交通领域电气化、共享化进程成为助力碳达峰、碳中和的重要途径。

共享汽车多采用电动汽车,其发展可有效减少私家车的保有量和行驶里程[2],从而降低碳排放量,有效缓解交通拥堵、停车难等问题。然而,现有共享汽车的网点布局以及车辆调度不尽合理,导致出现“无车可取、无位可停”等现象。准确预测共享汽车的需求及其分布,可为运营商高效布设共享站点及车辆调度提供理论依据。现有研究大多从个人属性、出行属性、共享汽车系统属性以及建成环境属性四个方面来探讨共享汽车需求的影响因素,并常采用建模或仿真方法预测需求总量,鲜有学者探究需求时空分布特性及其形成机理。

本文从影响需求的因素、需求分布特性及需求预测方法三个方面梳理已有研究成果,总结研究不足并提出未来展望,以期为未来进一步研究共享汽车需求提供思路。

1　共享汽车需求影响因素

共享汽车需求影响因素主要包括个人属性、出行属性、共享汽车系统属性以及建成环境属性四个方面的因素。

1.1　个人属性

个人属性是居民自身特征的表征,主要分为可直接观测的社会经济属性和不可观测的心理属性。已有研究表明,影响共享汽车需求的可观测变量主要有性别、年龄、学历、职业等,大多研究指出,年轻人、中低收入人群、无车人群、受教育程度较高的人群、机关/事业单位人员更有意愿使用共享汽车[3-5]。此外,部分研究探讨了移民和本地人口的出行行为差异,发现相较于本地人口,移民更有可能使用共享汽车出行[6]。

随着研究的深入,不可观测的心理属性成为共享汽车使用意愿影响因素探讨的重点。部分国内外学者以计划行为理论为基础,探究主观规范、知觉行为控制及态度对使用意向的影响。研究发现,知觉行为控制是影响共享汽车使用选择行为最重要的因素;主观规范对其有积极影响;而接受态度的影响并不显著[7-10]。另有部分学者考虑了其他心理变量对共享汽车使用选择的影响,如习惯、环保意识、里程焦虑等。习惯会使人拒绝改变,成为共享汽车发展的障碍之一[8],Ramos 等发现,高频率驾驶私家车的群体会将共享汽车作为第二或第三选择[11],但少有学者深入探讨习惯对共享汽车选择行为的影响机理。目前,关于环保意识如何影响共享汽车使用选择行为还没有统一的定论。朱振涛等将环保意识、政府政策、感知风险引入 UTAUT2 改进模型,运用 Lasso 回归和随机森林算法,得出环保意识的重要性最高的结论[12];而陈月霞等通过构建混合选择模型,发现低碳出行态度对共享汽车使用选择没有显著影响[13]。由于共享汽车多以电动汽车为主,学者通过描述性分析发现,公众对富余里程和电量补充存在很大的焦虑[14-15],但未进一步深入研究“里程焦虑”对共享汽车选择行为的影响。

1.2　出行属性

出行属性指出行时间、出行距离、出行目的及用车费用。研究发现,步行时间、候车时间、车内时间及出行费用是影响共享汽车出行的关键因素,其中步行时间的影响最为显著[4,16-17]。王佳雨等对共享汽车的用车费用、共享汽车系统属性及个人社会经济属性进行弹性分析,发现用车费用是影响最大的因素[18]。张圆等发现共享汽车的出行距离多为10～15km[5],中长途出行将是共享汽车服务的潜在领域。出行目的因其极强的不确定性对共享汽车出行选择具有很大的影响,张圆等发现以购物为出行为目的个体更愿意使用共享汽车;张晚笛等以共享汽车用户为研究对象,发现近郊出游是共享汽车使用频率最高的场景,其次是通勤或业务外出,最后是休闲娱乐出行[19]。

1.3　共享汽车系统属性

共享汽车系统属性不仅包括系统中的车辆属性,如车辆类型、续航里程等,还包括共享系统的服务水平,如配套停车服务、车队规模、站点位置、运营模式等。已有研究表明,车辆属性如燃料类型、印花外观、品牌等并不影响共享汽车的使用选择行为[20],而用户选择共享汽车的概率会随着车辆续航里程的增加而增大[18,21]。王佳雨指出,提供相关配套停车服务如专有车位,会增强人们对共享汽车的使用意愿[18]。Li 等以租赁价格和车队规模对共享汽车需求的影响进行敏感性分析,表明价格一定的情况下,车队规模越大共享汽车的需求越大[22]。刘向等通过敏感度分析得到取还车的站点距离较远是选择共享汽车出行的最大障碍[21],应将站点设置于交通枢纽、住宅区、工作区等区域。Scott 等通过分析伦敦共享汽车的需求发现,自由浮点式比基于站点往返式的运营模式对公众更具吸引力,被认为是公共交通的替代,而基于站点往返式则是一种补充模式[23]。

1.4 建成环境属性

建成环境指为居民生活提供所需空间的人为环境[24],如土地类型、交通系统及城市设计,交通系统包括交通基础设施及其服务水平。

建成环境属性比社会经济属性更易影响公众出行选择[25-26],近年来学者才开始考虑建成环境属性对共享汽车需求的影响,发现交通发达区、人口密度、目的地可达性及各类兴趣点(Point of Interest,POI)数量对共享汽车的需求有积极影响,就业密度和到工作地的距离对共享汽车使用选择影响不显著[6,27-29]。Chen 等考虑共享汽车站点属性、建成环境属性(密度、多样性、城市设计和目的地可达性)等对共享汽车需求的影响,通过自适应弹性网络回归分析发现道路交叉密度越高使用共享汽车出行的强度越大;街道小巷和单向道路的长度对需求有负向影响,而双向道路的长度对需求有正向影响[27]。孙立山等通过构建多元回归模型发现,站点周边建筑总面积、各站点间用地类型多样性均对共享汽车需求有正向影响[30]。

交通基础设施及其服务水平对共享汽车使用意向的影响主要表现在交通方式自身特性、距市中心的距离等方面。不同交通方式对共享汽车的需求有不同作用,轻轨、公交及火车为积极的促进作用,地铁在高峰期具有抑制作用而在非工作日具有促进作用[29,31-32]。此外,Müller 等发现,到市中心的距离和周边是否可以停车显著影响共享汽车需求,中心地区比郊区需求量更大[33]。而 Dong 等发现,在公共交通不发达的地区,人们使用共享汽车的频率更高[34]。

2 需求的时空分布特性

共享汽车需求影响因素的确定可为其出行分担率的预测提供基础,但难以描述需求的时空分布特性。为了对运营商优化站点布局和车辆调度提供依据,既有研究通过运营订单数据挖掘共享汽车需求的时空分布规律。

陈小鸿等通过多元线性回归和二项 Logistic 回归分析共享汽车高频用户和通勤用户的特征,发现用车需求、高峰出行主要发生在城市外围区域,市中心无通勤特征[35];苑尊根据订单数据挖掘不同时空尺度下的共享汽车需求分布特性,结果表明用车量主要集中于早 8 时到晚 8 时,且在工作日存在早高峰现象,而非工作日无明显高峰期[36]。Klemmer 等通过核密度估计处理 POI 数据和车辆数据,并建立具有 Gamma 分布值的广义线性模型,探究时空因素对共享汽车需求量的影响,发现零售服务和交通站点附近的共享汽车需求在任何时段均较大;休闲娱乐如健身房、电影院等,在工作日晚上和周末需求量大,而在工作时间需求量小;政府机构,社会宗教如学校、图书馆、教堂等仅在工作日需求量大[37]。Willing 等发现多数共享汽车需求发生在中午 12 点之后,且工作日出行量比非工作日多;对于同一 POI 类型在不同时段也有不同影响,如“餐厅”,12—16 时用车需求较大而在 16—18 时、0—4 时需求较弱;需求的空间分布较为分散,仅夜间需求会集中在运营站点的中心区[38]。

3 需求预测的方法

基于上述对共享汽车需求的影响因素及时空特性的梳理,可为预测需求提供基础。学者多以建模和仿真的方法进行预测,建模主要用于数据可获取的情况,而仿真主要是在数据获取较难时模拟不同场景下居民的出行选择。

3.1 建模

建模所用数据通常有 SP 数据和 RP 数据两类,SP 数据多被用以离散选择模型预测共享汽车的分担率,RP 数据多被用以机器学习挖掘出行规律并制定相同学习规则预测需求。

通过离散选择模型分析 SP 数据时,多项 Logit (Multinominal Logit,MNL)模型是最基本的模型,假设效用函数的随机项服从相互独立同 Gumbel

分布。陈金升等通过 MNL 模型探究公众对共享电动汽车、共享单车、网约车及出租车的选择行为,确定共享电动汽车的效用函数,进而预测其在不同小区间的分担率[39]。但 MNL 模型具有 IIA 特性(Independence from Irrelevant Alternatives),即非相关选项相互独立特性,为减轻此限制,学者们使用巢式 Logit(Nested Logit,NL)模型,将相似方案聚集为一个巢,同时考虑同一巢中选项之间的相关性,不同巢仍为相互独立。Catalano 等建立 NL 模型预测共享汽车分担率,研究结果表明,随着出行费用从 0.4 欧元/km 下降到 0.08 欧元/km,共享汽车分担率从 0.02% 增长到 10%[31]。刘向通过建立 NL 模型,预测共享汽车的分担率为 3.3%,较为接近实际分担率 2.36%[21]。由于 MNL 和 NL 模型未考虑出行者的异质性,为适应偏好差异,Yin 等建立混合 Logit(Mixed Logit,ML)模型,假设参数随机分布,研究公共交通、私家车及共享汽车的使用选择,以区域日均出行量和共享汽车分担率为基础估计其需求量[40]。此外,也有学者用 Probit 模型研究出行行为,假设效用函数的随机项服从多元正态分布。Henrik 等对比单变量和多变量 Probit 模型预测共享汽车的分担率,发现多变量 Probit 模型解释力更好[41]。但是 Probit 模型的随机项两两相关,模型较为复杂,难以求解。随着心理潜变量的引入,混合选择模型被应用于共享汽车的需求预测,Kim 等在出行时间不确定的情况下,建立混合选择模型分析环保意识、个人隐私意识等心理变量对共享汽车使用选择的影响,进而预测共享汽车的市场潜力[42]。

通过机器学习分析以共享汽车历史订单数据为主的 RP 数据,其常用算法包括神经网络、决策树、回归算法等。学者多采用神经网络建立需求预测模型,并以实际数据验证模型,如长短期记忆神经网络、径向基函数神经网络、多层感知机神经网络及进化神经网络等[43-46],Henrik 等对比回归分析、时间序列法和神经网络预测一年中不同时间段的出行需求,结果表明神经网络的预测精度最高[41]。此外,学者以决策树为基础,建立梯度提升树、随机森林等模型预测需求[47]。苑尊通过基于统计学的时间序列模型和基于机器学习的梯度提升树模型预测区域各站点的短时需求,发现梯度提升树模型的预测精度更高,因为该模型不仅考虑了历史时间序列的影响,还考虑站点属性、天气等多因素的影响[36]。

3.2 仿真

由于车辆的可用性本质上取决于出行次数,其不确定性导致共享汽车需求建模困难[48]。此外,建模难以表示供需之间复杂的演变过程,而仿真可以模拟不同场景下共享汽车的系统设置和用户行为选择。

Ciari 等第一次在 MATSim 平台建立基于代理的模型,通过设置共享汽车的不同使用场景,发现基于站点式的共享汽车系统有较大发展潜力,自由浮点式系统可作为前者的补充模式,不会降低其吸引力[31]。Martinez 等在单向共享汽车系统下建立基于代理的仿真模型,并结合离散选择模型估算共享汽车的潜在用户,结果发现共享汽车的潜在需求为总出行次数的 3%,其中 40% 的共享汽车潜在用户来自步行,26% 来自私家车,22% 和 10% 分别来自公交车和地铁[49]。Li 等考虑共享汽车的动态流量、出行者的异质性及不同的定价方案,提出基于公差的活动-出行调度动态用户均衡模型,并预测个人日常的多模式多活动出行链中对自由浮动式共享汽车的选择[22]。

4 结语

本文综述共享汽车需求及时空分布的研究,首先从个人属性、出行属性、共享汽车系统属性以及建成环境属性四个方面梳理显著影响需求的因素;其次,总结既往研究中共享汽车的时空分布特征;最后,归纳需求预测所用到的方法包括建模和仿真。针对已有研究成果,对于未来研究提出如下展望:

(1)既有研究针对共享汽车使用选择行为的影响因素仍考虑不全,需要进一步探究是否为外来人口、里程风险、习惯、环保意识等因素对其的影响;此外,建成环境对共享汽车需求的影响显著,但表征建成环境的变量多为人口或道路密度、土地利用多样性、目的地可达性、距交通设施的距离等,还需要不断完善表征变量并形成完整体系。

(2)交通领域的碳减排是实现双碳目标的重要环节,随着碳交易市场的逐步扩大,部分学者提出个人碳交易,即允许自由买卖个人固定碳量,以进一步激励公众低碳出行,未来研究可考虑探究实行该措施对共享汽车使用选择行为的影响机理,进而为相关部门制定政策提供依据。

(3)不同数据类型各有其优缺点,SP数据不仅考虑到居民选择过程中各因素的影响,还可以分析非用户的使用意向和潜在需求,但选择结果可能会与实际选择不一致;RP数据是居民的真实出行行为,但只体现行为的结果,不能描述选择过程,即仅可描述共享汽车需求的时空分布,而无法探寻其分布机理。各类大数据可以挖掘居民的出行行为规律,如:手机信令数据可获得出行轨迹和出行时间;POI数据可描述某个位置的用地特性及周边建筑环境,进一步结合公众的社会经济属性和心理潜变量等个人因素,融合多源数据提高共享汽车需求的预测精度,为优化站点布局及车辆调度提供基础。

(4)针对数据较难获取的情况,通过仿真预测居民的出行选择方式、出行时间等。其最大的不足是模型的校准和验证,长期的影响效应并不能直接在模拟范围内显示出来,且很难解释输入参数与输出服务需求之间的因果关系,解决此类问题还需要未来更深入的研究。

(5)通过需求预测可以使运营商在高需求区域投放更多车辆,并减少低需求区域的投放量,但这剥夺了公众获取平等交通的机会,未来可以深入探究运营商利润与社会公平之间的平衡关系。

(6)紧扣“出行即服务”(MaaS)理念,涵盖从出行计划、路线规划到预定购票和支付的一系列过程,不仅融合公共交通、小汽车、步行等传统出行方式,还可以考虑共享汽车、网约车等新型出行方式,形成一种新型的出行服务体系。融合多种交通方式,进而减少私家车的使用,为社会带来多重效益。未来可探究在MaaS理念下,多种交通方式的融合对共享汽车需求的影响。

参考文献

[1] 中国交通低碳转型发展战略与路径研究课题组.碳达峰碳中和目标下中国交通低碳转型发展战略与路径研究[M].北京:人民交通出版社股份有限公司,2021.

[2] Khan M, Machemehl R. The Impact of Land-Use Variables on Free-Floating Carsharing Vehicle Rental Choice and Parking Duration [M]. Seeing Cities Through Big Data, 2017.

[3] 贺珊,李锦莹,王伟嘉.基于Logit模型衡阳市居民关于共享汽车加入意愿的影响因素分析[J].商场现代化,2020(16):173-175.

[4] 周彪,周溪召,李彬.基于上海市消费者的汽车共享选择分析[J].上海理工大学学报,2014,36(1):6.

[5] 张圆,邓院昌.基于Logit模型的共享汽车出行影响因素分析[J].科学技术与工程,2019,19(04):254-258.

[6] Lee S, Smart M J, Golub A. Difference in travel behavior between immigrants in the u. s. and us born residents: The immigrant effect for car-sharing, ride-sharing, and bike-sharing services [J]. Transportation Research Interdisciplinary Perspectives, 2021, 9(4): 100296.

[7] Mattia G, Mugion R G, Principato L. Shared mobility as a driver for sustainable consumptions: The intention to re-use free-floating car sharing [J]. Journal of Cleaner Production, 2019, 237(Nov. 10): 117401-117404.

[8] Ramos R M S, Bergstad C J. The Psychology of Sharing: Multigroup Analysis among Users and Non-Users of Carsharing [J]. Sustainability, 2021, 13(12): 6842.

[9] 金方磊.共享电动汽车使用选择行为建模及潜在转移需求估计[D].北京:北京交通大学,2020.

[10] 赵敏,王善勇.电动汽车共享的使用意向研究[J].大连理工大学学报:社会科学版,2018,39(3):7.

[11] Ramos É M S, Bergstad C J, Chicco A, et al. Mobility styles and car sharing use in Europe: attitudes, behaviours, motives and sustainability [J]. European Transport Research Review, 2020, 12(1).

[12] 朱振涛,杜明阳,刘颖.共享电动汽车使用意愿的关键影响因素研究[J].江汉大学学报(社会科学版),2020,37(06):91-102.

[13] 陈月霞,陈龙,查奇芬,等.基于低碳心理潜变量Logit模型的出行方式预测模型[J].公路交通科技,2017,34(9):10.

[14] Wang Y Y, Chi Y Y, Xu J H, et al. Consumer Preferences for Electric Vehicle Charging Infrastructure Based on the Text Mining Method[J]. Energies, 2021, 14(15): 4598.

[15] 尹治.共享汽车用户的满意度分析[D].昆

明:云南大学,2019.

[16] 吴娇蓉,王宇沁,林子旸,等.综合体分时租赁小汽车对出行方式转移行为影响[J].同济大学学报(自然科学版),2020,48(01):60-67.

[17] 杨飞,侯宗廷,王亮,等.考虑个体异质性的汽车分时租赁选择行为[J].西南交通大学学报,2021:1-8.

[18] 王佳雨.二线城市居民汽车共享加入意愿分析[D].大连:大连理工大学,2017.

[19] 张晚笛,尹志芳,李超,等.基于RP/SP调查的汽车分时租赁用户出行特征分析——以成都市为例[J].交通运输研究,2021,7(02):66-73.

[20] Yoon T,Cherry C R,Jones L R. One-way and round-trip carsharing: A stated preference experiment in Beijing [J]. Transportation Research Part D Transport & Environment, 2017,53:102-114.

[21] 刘向,董德存,王宁,等.基于Nested Logit的电动汽车分时租赁选择行为分析[J].同济大学学报(自然科学版),2019,47(01):47-55.

[22] B L Q A,B F L,B H J P T,et al. Incorporating free-floating car-sharing into an activity-based dynamic user equilibrium model: A demand-side model[J]. Transportation Research Part B:Methodological,2018,107:102-123.

[23] Aruna,Sivakumar,Scott,et al. A new approach to predict the market and impacts of round-trip and point-to-point carsharing systems: Case study of London[J]. Transportation Research Part D Transport & Environment,2014.

[24] Ewing R, Cervero R. "Does Compact Development Make People Drive Less?" The Answer Is Yes[J]. Journal of the American Planning Association,2017,83(1):19-25.

[25] 王建军,王赛,宋明洋,等.大数据背景下城市建成环境对出行行为影响研究综述[J].长安大学学报(自然科学版),2021:1-18.

[26] Mokhtarian P L,Cao X. Examining the impacts of residential self-selection on travel behavior: A focus on methodologies [J]. Transport Reviews,2008,42(3):204-228.

[27] Chen X,Cheng J,Ye J,et al. Locating Station of One-Way Carsharing Based on Spatial Demand Characteristics [J]. Journal of advanced transportation,2018,2018(PT. 3):1-16.

[28] 惠英,唐磊,解英堃,等.区域建成环境对共享单车日变特征的影响——以厦门市为例[J].城市交通,2021:1-14.

[29] Tai,Stillwater,Patricia,et al. Carsharing and the Built Environment:Geographic Information System-Based Study of One U. S. Operator [J]. Transportation Research Record,2018, 2110(1):27-34.

[30] 孙立山,王顺超,罗薇,等.基于用地分布特征的共享汽车需求估计模型[J].重庆交通大学学报(自然科学版),2020,39(05):1-6.

[31] Catalano M,Casto B L,Migliore M. Car sharing demand estimation and urban transport demand modelling using stated preference techniques [J]. European Transport Trasporti Europei, 2008(40):33-50.

[32] Wagner S, Brandt T, Neumann D. Data Analytics in Free-Floating Carsharing: Evidence from the City of Berlin: Hawaii International Conference on System Sciences, 2015[C].

[33] Müller, Johannes, Correia, et al. An Explanatory Model Approach for the Spatial Distribution of Free-Floating Carsharing Bookings:A Case-Study of German Cities[J]. Sustainability,2017(9):1290.

[34] Dong H,Yang X,Wang W. Influencing factor analysis of car-sharing demand based on point of interest data [J]. Journal of Physics: Conference Series,2021,1972(1).

[35] 陈小鸿,成嘉琪,叶建红,等.共享汽车用户及出行时空特征分析[J].同济大学学报:自然科学版,2018,46(6):9.

[36] 苑尊.基于数据驱动的共享汽车需求预测及动态定价研究[D].北京:北京交通大学,2020.

[37] Klemmer K, Willing C, Wagner S, et al. Explaining Spatio-Temporal Dynamics in Carsharing:A Case Study of Amsterdam[C]. 22nd Americas Confrence on Information Systems (AMCIS 2016),2016.
[38] Willing C, Klemmer K, Brandt T, et al. Moving in time and space -Location intelligence for carsharing decision support [J]. Decision Support Systems,2017.
[39] 陈金升.新能源汽车分时租赁需求预测及调度方法研究[D].武汉:武汉理工大学,2018.
[40] Yin Y, Wang H, Xiong J, et al. Estimation of optimum supply of shared cars based on personal travel behaviors in condition of minimum energy consumption [J]. Environment, Development and Sustainability: A Multidisciplinary Approach to the Theory and Practice of Sustainable Development, 2021,23.
[41] Becker H, Loder A, Schmid B, et al. Modeling car-sharing membership as a mobility tool: A multivariate Probit approach with latent variables[J]. Travel Behaviour and Society, 2017,8:26-36.
[42] Kim J, Rasouli S, Timmermans H J P. The effects of activity-travel context and individual attitudes on car-sharing decisions under travel time uncertainty: A hybrid choice modeling approach[J]. Transportation Research Part D Transport and Environment, 2017, 56 (oct.): 189-202.
[43] 崔晓敏.基于需求预测的单向共享电动汽车车辆调度方法研究[D].大连:大连理工大学,2019.
[44] 赛秋玥.基于共享汽车数据驱动的用户用车特征分析与预测建模[D].北京:北京交通大学,2019.
[45] Xu J X, Lim J S. A new Evolutionary Neural Network for forecasting net flow of a car sharing system [C]. Evolutionary Computation,2007. CEC 2007. IEEE Congress on,2007.
[46] Yu D, Li Z, Zhong Q, et al. Demand Management of Station-Based Car Sharing System Based on Deep Learning Forecasting [J]. Journal of Advanced Transportation, 2020,2020:8935857.
[47] Abstreiter A S. Characterization and Prediction of Car Sharing usage exploiting Points of Interest information[D]. Torino: Politecnico di Torino,2018.
[48] Golalikhani M, Oliveira B B, Carravilla M A, et al. Carsharing: A review of academic literature and business practices toward an integrated decision-support framework[J]. Transportation Research Part E Logistics and Transportation Review, 2021, 149(2):102280.
[49] Martínez L M, de Almeida Correia G H, Moura F, et al. Insights into carsharing demand dynamics: Outputs of an agent-based model application to Lisbon, Portugal[J]. International Journal of Sustainable Transportation,2016.

用户使用体验对共享电动汽车站点布局的影响综述

王远峰　孙小慧*
(新疆大学建筑工程学院)

摘　要　随着电动汽车以及共享经济的发展,共享电动汽车迎来了广阔的发展空间。但是,目前共享电动汽车的发展还面临着盈利困难、用户满意度低、站点等基础设施不完善等问题。合理地进行网点以及充电设施的布局,并且充分考虑用户使用体验,是共享电动汽车长远发展的重要保障。本文对考虑用户使用体验的共享电动汽车需求、网点以及充电设施布局的相关研究进行综述,旨在对目前研究的现状以及存在的问题进行总结梳理,并据此提出未来可开展基于满足用户差异化需求配置共享电动汽车网点及车辆的研究,以及通过相关激励手段鼓励用户参与充电的方式开展网点布局和运营管理的相关研究。

关键词 共享电动汽车 用户使用体验 网点布局 充电设施布局 综述

0 引言

2021 年全国两会上,“碳达峰、碳中和”首次被写入政府工作报告,随着交通运输领域电动化、共享化趋势的发展,共享电动汽车开始被企业及公众所认知并逐渐接受。共享电动汽车相比燃油汽车,在缓解能源紧张、环境污染、交通拥堵、资源大量闲置等方面具有明显的优势。在市场、资本以及政策的推动下,共享电动汽车的发展前景广阔,但是目前共享汽车的发展仍面临着盈利困难的困境,一方面前期购车成本高、后期运维人力成本高,另一方面公众接受度不高、车辆使用率不高。并且通过金方磊学者对共享电动汽车潜在转移需求研究表明,当共享电动汽车具有较好的站点覆盖和车辆分布条件下(平均取还车距离为 0.5km 时),共享电动汽车的方式分担率约为 4%,具体地,这些潜在转移需求有 99.44% 来自公共交通,总计转移 7.66% 的原公共交通出行需求,因此,共享电动汽车的大规模站点布局与车辆投放会在一定程度上加重道路交通的拥堵[1]。为了促进共享电动汽车行业的可持续发展,提高公众接受度以及站点的合理布局是其关键环节。

Ikezoe 等对日本私家车车主进行调查研究发现,有 74% 的车主表示,无论共享电动汽车服务有多么便宜,即使没有车辆不可用的风险,他们也不会停止拥有私家车;如果共享电动汽车旨在减少私家车的拥有量,服务必须具有情感激励,包括更高水平的便利性等[2]。Acheampong 等利用结构方程对汽车共享使用意向进行建模发现,62% 的潜在用户将在推出汽车共享服务的第一年内加入该服务,并且用户对于目前公共交通的不满是其加入共享汽车的基础,要想更好地推广汽车共享需要配套更好的服务[3]。因此,为了提高共享电动汽车的公众接受度,需要注重对潜在用户的情感激励,通过提高服务质量、完善配套基础设施,提升用户出行便利性、满意度等出行体验。

站点及相关基础设施的布设直接影响运营商的服务水平,从而影响用户的需求满意度、车辆的利用率,站点及相关基础设施的合理布设对提升用户使用体验有重要影响。本文主要对现有研究中从用户角度考虑共享电动汽车站点布局的相关问题进行综述,包括考虑用户使用体验的共享电动汽车需求、网点和充电设施布局等方面,以期为运营商、进行相关研究的学者提供有价值的参考。

1 共享电动汽车需求

根据公安部交通管理局统计,2020 年我国机动车保有量达 3.72 亿辆,而全国有 4.18 亿名汽车驾驶人,共享电动汽车的市场十分广阔。准确地分析潜在用户的用车需求影响因素并对需求进行预测,从而有针对性地提供相关设施及服务,能够提升服务质量,增强用户使用体验。下文从共享电动汽车需求影响因素及需求预测两方面进行综述。

1.1 共享电动汽车需求影响因素

尹治的研究表明,消费者对于共享电动汽车的使用体验主要有个人信息保密满意、临时解决用车需求满意、相关制度法规满意[4]。目前,用户在使用共享电动汽车时,需要向服务商提供驾驶证信息等个人信息,Huang 等为了解决隐私保密的问题,提出了一个分散的、负责的、保护隐私的汽车共享服务架构,采用多个动态验证服务器替代单个可信第三方授权,帮助客户建立分布式信任[5]。用车是否方便也对共享电动汽车需求有很大影响,Liao 等通过对荷兰持有驾照、拥有汽车或打算在未来 3 年内购买汽车的人群进行陈述选择实验,并通过潜类别模型对数据进行分析,结果显示,有 20% 的人表示如果附近有汽车共享,他们可能会放弃购买车辆或放弃使用现有车辆[6]。朱振涛等运用因子分析和 Lasso 回归以及机器学习中特征提取的方法,对 527 份调查问卷进行了分析,发现共享电动汽车的关键影响因素依次为环保意识、社会影响、价格价值、绩效期望和政府政策[7]。余静财等通过分析研究发现,用户对共享电动汽车的了解程度、是否拥有机动车、舒适性、快捷性、行为态度、使用偏好、行为意向、使用障碍、站点障碍、车辆障碍、个人障碍等因素对共享电动汽车的使用需求存在显著影响[8]。

1.2 共享电动汽车需求预测

Wang等为了满足实时监控、管理和车辆分配的需要,以提升服务灵活性提高服务质量增进用户使用体验,提出了一种全球定位系统数据驱动的方法,通过历史车辆GPS数据匹配用户当前轨迹并推断其可能的目的地,对共享系统动态目的地进行预测,以满足共享系统实时监控、管理和车辆分配的需要[9]。Li等考虑了用户的有限理性,从用户使用体验出发,考虑异质性,将用户分为不同类别和不同定价方案,建立了自由浮动式共享汽车动态用户需求侧均衡模型,在不同场景下模拟表明,自由浮动式共享汽车的车队规模、车辆分布和用车价格显著影响用户对共享汽车出行的选择[10]。Wang等为满足不同用户出行需求,考虑了“取车间隔”“出行时间”“工作日与否”“每日天气状况”和“每分钟费用”对需求的影响,建立了单向电动汽车共享系统的微观需求预测模型,通过分析发现,在不同的时空条件下,各需求影响指标所产生的需求量不同,“取车间隔”与“每分钟费用”对需求影响较大,而“工作日与否”与“每日天气状况”对需求的影响几乎可以忽略不计[11]。

2 考虑用户使用体验的共享电动汽车网点布局

共享电动汽车的网点布局与运营商的收益密切相关,然而,还应以人为本,在考虑成本与收益的同时考虑用户使用体验,以实现共享电动汽车行业的长远可持续发展。下文将从共享电动汽车网点布局的影响因素及布局方法两个方面进行综述。

2.1 共享电动汽车网点布局影响因素

在网点布局问题上,影响用户使用体验的因素主要包括网点的易达性与便利性等,因此,网点的地理位置是否优越、是否临近生活区工作区、交通是否便利以及是否方便换乘等就显得尤为重要。

由孙依哲的研究总结可知,共享电动汽车网点布局的影响因素包括地理因素、交通因素、企业因素以及社会因素[12]。地理因素是共享电动汽车网点布局的一个重要因素,好的地形地势以及地理位置能够使用户更方便地到达工作区生活区等,极大程度地影响用户的使用体验,同时方便基础设施布设。Hui等对杭州“车纷享”一年的共享汽车项目数据进行了分析,以确定站点土地利用特征、位置、规模等属性对站点的影响,结果表明车辆使用频率和周围的土地特征与车站使用频率有一定的相关性[13]。交通是否便利、是否临近换乘站点、企业能否提供便捷舒适的服务、政策是否优惠等社会因素,都对共享电动汽车用户的使用体验产生影响。

2.2 共享电动汽车网点布局方法

Xiao等通过选取汽车共享选址的相关影响指标,其中包含了公共场所、生活区、是否便利等影响用户使用体验的指标,采用模糊层次分析法对共享汽车备选停放位置进行评价,以供运营商参考,发现共享汽车选址的协调性和社会经济效益对共享汽车选址有相当大的影响[14]。孙依哲以共享电动汽车的需求点和备选停放区域之间的加权出行总成本最小,以及用户的综合满意度加权最大为优化目标,建立了共享电动汽车停放区域选址的双目标整数规划模型[12],该研究综合评价用户对不同站点的满意度,能够在实现运营商盈利的同时兼顾用户的使用体验。田静静通过潜在需求确定需求满足程度,并考虑了车辆利用程度,建立了一个基于数据驱动的共享汽车站点选址的混合整数规划模型,结果显示需求满足率对于站点选址具有重要影响,且车辆利用率很大程度上决定了站点的车辆容量[15],学者考虑了站点需求满足率,而站点车辆能否解决用户临时用车需求对用户的使用体验有直接的影响,也影响了共享电动汽车从“可用、易用”向用户“爱用”进行转变。

3 考虑用户使用体验的共享电动汽车充电设施布局

目前学者对于共享电动汽车充电设施布局的研究较少,但对于电动汽车充电站布局的研究相对更加丰富,可为共享电动汽车充电设施布局提供参考。充电站的合理选址能够促进电动汽车产业的发展,基于用户的心理及使用行为建立充电设施是电动汽车得以大规模推广的关键因素。同样,合理的共享电动汽车充电设施布局也是共享电动汽车系统健康运行的保障。虽然共享电动汽车系统中用户一般不参与充电过程,但由于充电问题导致的车辆利用率、需求满足率以及续航里程等问题将很大程度的影响用户的使用体验。下文将从共享电动汽车充电设施布局以及电动汽车充电站的选址定容两个方面进行综述。

3.1 共享电动汽车充电设施布局

国内外对于共享电动汽车充电设施的布局问题研究处于起步阶段。在现有的研究中,学者们多考虑充电站的位置与数量、建设运营成本以及站点流量平衡等问题对充电设施进行布局,较少学者考虑用户的使用体验等问题。

Michele 等考虑了充电站位置、数量以及还车模式,建立了共享电动汽车充电站的位置及数量的优化模型,并采用基于爬山法的局部搜索算法以及改进的遗传算法对模型进行求解[16]。Michele 等考虑了租车时间、行驶距离以及停车时间开发了一个离散事件跟踪驱动的模拟器,模拟表明,将充电站设置在共享汽车停放时间短的区域,就可以仅在城市 8% 的区域规划充电站,而共享汽车用户的行程不会因为电池耗尽结束[17]。Georg 等考虑了同一点取还车的情况,但不考虑车辆调度等操作活动,建立了充电设施选址整数线性规划模型,并利用启发式算法对模型进行求解[18]。Miao 等考虑车辆调度、车辆行驶范围和充电时间等,提出了一个两阶段多目标优化模型,先对地理服务区域进行优化,再对充电基础设施进行分配,并在每个阶段同时使用户和运营商受益[19]。Antoine 考虑了车辆调度以及站点流量平衡,建立了混合整数线性规划模型,对每个充电站的车辆和停车位需求进行匹配,以限制网络中的供应不平衡[20]。Georg 等考虑可接受的预期续航里程,建立了整数线性规划优化模型,利用启发式算法对模型求解,其间考虑并跟踪每辆车的电池电量[21]。Mohammad 等考虑了充电站数量、位置以及共享电动汽车到充电站的位置,建立了整数规划模型,对充电站的分配进行联合优化[22]。Mustafa 等考虑了现有充电基础设施、充电站的车辆排队以及新建充电站和扩大现有充电站之间的权衡,提出了一个优化充电基础设施开发的框架,以提高自动驾驶汽车在共享系统中的使用率[23]。田静静考虑详细的充电过程,默认到达站点的车辆均有充电桩可用,建立了一个考虑需求满足率及充电时间的充电站选址规划模型[15]。Wang 考虑到共享电动汽车用户在行驶过程中充电的便利性,提出了一种结合充电站和分散充电桩的两阶段规划方法,在第一阶段中,根据区域划分和出行特点,预测每个网点的充电需求;然后,以年总成本最小为目标,采用均值聚类算法和排队论方法确定充电站的位置和容量;在第二阶段,引入用户中途充电满意度,建立基于均值漂移算法的离散充电桩规划模型,以平衡共享电动汽车运营商的经济性和用户的便利性[24]。

3.2 电动汽车充电站的选址定容

梁梦梦对用户满意度进行定义,以用户对充电过程的满意程度作为评价指标,建立了一个考虑社会综合成本最小的电动汽车充电站规划模型,并采用混合布谷鸟算法对模型进行求解[25]。Yang 等提出了一个考虑与“范围焦虑”和“损失焦虑”相关的基于客户满意度的电动汽车充换电站选址的线性整数规划模型,并利用禁忌搜索启发式算法对模型进行了求解[26]。贾永基等提出了一种基于满意优化理论的用户满意度评价函数,通过引入充电站等级概念,建立了以平均电动汽车用户满意度最大为目标函数的多等级电动汽车充电站选址的混合整数规划模型,并基于免疫算法对模型进行求解[27]。Kong 等通过考虑运营商的经济问题、用户充电的满意度、车辆的功率损耗、交通系统的拥堵以及电网的安全性等,建立了多目标线性规划模型,并利用迭代算法对模型进行求解[28]。Yi 等考虑用户充电便利性、充电成本和充电时间,建立电动汽车充电站选址定容模型,采用基于人工免疫算法的模型进行优化求解[29]。

也有学者将用户成本、运营商利润以及电网负荷进行综合考虑,建立社会综合成本最小化的目标函数,对电动汽车充电站进行优化规划[30-34]。其中,部分学者使用 Voronoi 图的方法对规划模型进行求解[33,35],较多的学者基于遗传算法对规划模型进行求解[32,34,36-38]。

4 结语

目前对于共享电动汽车充电设施布局的研究较少,大多数学者采用整数线性规划模型对充电站进行建模,并采用启发式算法等对模型求解。

学者在考虑用户使用体验时考虑的因素较为单一,或仅在共享电动汽车停放区域的规划上考虑了用户的满意度。共享电动汽车的用户使用体验对共享电动汽车的发展具有重要意义,不仅极大程度上影响着共享电动汽车的使用需求,而且对共享电动汽车后期的运营管理具有决定性作用。

本文通过对现有文献进行总结,从用户使用体验的角度出发,对共享电动汽车的需求、网点布局以及充电设施的布局进行了综述。基于对既有研究的总结,对未来研究提出以下几点展望。

(1)在今后的研究中,可以考虑用户用车前的电量或续航里程心理预期的满足率,对共享电动汽车充电设施进行布局,通过合理的布局,提升车辆闲时的充电效率,进而提高车辆的利用率。

(2)运营商应使用相关激励政策,通过返还消费红包、优惠券、减免部分用车费用等方法鼓励用户对车辆进行充电,以此来降低运营期间的车辆调度工作量,同时能够提升用户的消费体验。

(3)挖掘不同用户的出行习惯、载人载物情况等对车辆配置进行优化,进而对网点进行布局。比如在不同的网点配备不同数量的2座车、5座车、7座车等,为用户提供多样化的选择,在节省资源的同时满足差异化需求,提高用户使用体验。

(4)随着科技的发展,无人驾驶技术将在未来成为主流,用户可在运营区域内任意位置产生用车需求并等待用车,车辆自动计算剩余电量及与充电站位置,用户用车结束后或运行过程中车辆主动前往充电位置进行充电续航等。学者可以超前规划,将无人驾驶的因素考虑在内,对共享电动汽车网点及充电设施的布局进行研究。

参考文献

[1] 金方磊. 共享电动汽车使用选择行为建模及潜在转移需求估计[D]. 北京:北京交通大学,2020.

[2] Ikezoe K, Kiriyama E, Fujimura S. Car-sharing intention analysis in Japan by comparing the utility of car ownership for car-owners and non-car owners[J]. Transport Policy,2020,96:1-14.

[3] Acheampong R A, Siiba A. Modelling the determinants of car-sharing adoption intentions among young adults: the role of attitude, perceived benefits, travel expectations and socio-demographic factors[J]. Transportation, 2020,47(5):2557-2580.

[4] 尹治. 共享汽车用户的满意度分析[D]. 昆明:云南大学,2019.

[5] Huang C, Lu R, Ni J, et al. DAPA: A Decentralized, Accountable, and Privacy-Preserving Architecture for Car Sharing Services [J]. IEEE Transactions on Vehicular Technology,2020,69(5):4869-4882.

[6] Liao F, Molin E, Timmermans H, et al. Carsharing: the impact of system characteristics on its potential to replace private car trips and reduce car ownership[J]. Transportation,2020, 47(2):935-970.

[7] 朱振涛,杜明阳,刘颖. 共享电动汽车使用意愿的关键影响因素研究[J]. 江汉大学学报(社会科学版),2020,37(06):91-102.

[8] 余静财,李文权,王顺超,等. 共享电动汽车选择行为分析[J]. 东南大学学报(自然科学版),2021,51(01):153-160.

[9] Wang L, Zhong Y, Ma W. GPS-data-driven dynamic destination prediction for on-demand one-way carsharing system[J]. IET Intelligent Transport Systems,2018,12(10):1291-1299.

[10] Li Q, Liao F, Timmermans H J P, et al. Incorporating free-floating car-sharing into an activity-based dynamic user equilibrium model: A demand-side model [J]. Transportation research. Part B: methodological, 2018, 107: 102-123.

[11] Ning W A, Jg A, Xiang L B, et al. A service demand forecasting model for one-way electric car-sharing systems combining long short-term memory networks with Granger causality test-Science Direct [J]. Journal of Cleaner Production,244.

[12] 孙依哲. 新能源共享汽车停放区域的选址研究[D]. 上海:上海大学,2020.

[13] Hui Y, Ding M, Qian C, et al. Research on the operational characteristics of car sharing service stations: A case study of a car sharing program in Hangzhou [J]. Transportation Research Procedia,2017,25:4140-4156.

[14] Xiong X, Xia J, Ni B. The Construction of Car-

Sharing Location Index System[J]. 2017.

[15] 田静静. 共享汽车站点选址优化模型与算法[D]. 北京:北京交通大学,2020.

[16] Cocca M, Giordano D, Mellia M, et al. Free floating electric car sharing design: Data driven optimisation [J]. Pervasive and Mobile Computing, 2019, 55: 59-75.

[17] Cocca M, Giordano D, Mellia M, et al. Free Floating Electric Car Sharing: A Data Driven Approach for System Design [J]. IEEE Transactions on Intelligent Transportation Systems, 2019, 20(12): 4691-4703.

[18] Brandstätter G, Kahr M, Leitner M. Determining optimal locations for charging stations of electric car-sharing systems under stochastic demand[J]. Transportation Research Part B: Methodological, 2017, 104: 17-35.

[19] Miao H, Jia H, Li J, et al. Autonomous connected electric vehicle (ACEV)-based car-sharing system modeling and optimal planning: A unified two-stage multi-objective optimization methodology[J]. Energy, 2019, 169: 797-818.

[20] Deza A, Huang K, Metel M R. Charging station optimization for balanced electric car sharing [J]. Discrete Applied Mathematics, 2020.

[21] Brandstätter G, Leitner M, Ljubic I. Location of charging stations in electric car sharing systems[J]. 2017.

[22] Roni M S, Yi Z, Smart J G. Optimal charging management and infrastructure planning for free-floating shared electric vehicles [J]. Transportation Research Part D: Transport and Environment, 2019, 76: 155-175.

[23] Lokhandwala M, Cai H. Siting charging stations for electric vehicle adoption in shared autonomous fleets[J]. Transportation Research Part D: Transport and Environment, 2020, 80: 102231.

[24] Wang N, Wang C, Niu Y, et al. A Two-Stage Charging Facilities Planning Method for Electric Vehicle Sharing Systems [J]. IEEE Transactions on Industry Applications, 2021, 57(1): 149-157.

[25] 梁梦梦. 基于用户满意度的电动汽车充电站规划研究[D]. 成都:西南交通大学,2020.

[26] Yang J, Guo F, Zhang M. Optimal planning of swapping/charging station network with customer satisfaction [J]. Transportation Research Part E: Logistics and Transportation Review, 2017, 103: 174-197.

[27] 贾永基,邢芳芳. 基于满意优化的电动汽车充电站选址[J]. 东华大学学报(自然科学版),2017,43(05):739-745.

[28] Kong W, Luo Y, Feng G, et al. Optimal location planning method of fast charging station for electric vehicles considering operators, drivers, vehicles, traffic flow and power grid[J]. Energy, 2019, 186(C).

[29] Yi T, Cheng X, Zheng H, et al. Research on Location and Capacity Optimization Method for Electric Vehicle Charging Stations Considering User's Comprehensive Satisfaction [J]. Energies, 2019, 12(10).

[30] 贾龙,胡泽春,宋永华. 考虑不同类型充电需求的城市内电动汽车充电设施综合规划[J]. 电网技术,2016,40(09):2579-2587.

[31] 罗清玉,田万利,贾洪飞. 考虑通勤需求的电动汽车充电站选址与定容模型[J]. 吉林大学学报(工学版),2019,49(05):1471-1477.

[32] 李涛,罗旭,温力力,等. 考虑充电站需求特性的电动汽车充电站与配电网联合规划方法[J]. 现代电力,2020,37(05):491-500.

[33] 谢远德,张邻,邓沙丽,等. 电动汽车充电设施优化网络布局研究[J]. 数学的实践与认识,2020,50(10):168-176.

[34] Ren X, Zhang H, Hu R, et al. Location of electric vehicle charging stations: A perspective using the grey decision-making model[J]. Energy, 2019, 173: 548-553.

[35] 徐青山,蔡婷婷,刘瑜俊,等. 考虑驾驶人行为习惯及出行链的电动汽车充电站站址规划[J]. 电力系统自动化,2016,40(04):59-65.

[36] 舒隽,唐刚,韩冰. 电动汽车充电站最优规划的两阶段方法[J]. 电工技术学报,2017,32(03):10-17.

[37] 付凤杰,方雅秀,董红召,等. 基于历史行驶

路线的电动汽车充电站布局优化[J]. 电力系统自动化,2018,42(12):72-80.
[38] 田梦瑶,汤波,杨秀,等. 综合考虑充电需求和配电网接纳能力的电动汽车充电站规划[J]. 电网技术,2021,45(02):498-509.

车道级调控策略对通行效率性能差异比较研究

付　鑫[1,2]　吕夏合*[1]　王建伟[1,2]　岳雨晴[1]　崔睿颖[1]
(1. 长安大学 运输工程学院大数据管理与应用系;2. 交通基础设施数字化教育部工程中心)

摘　要　高速公路正逐渐向高精度科学化方向发展,车道协调管控策略受到越来越多学者的广泛关注。因此,本文基于高速公路事故拥堵区车辆运行状态,结合拥堵区域特征,在车辆跟驰模型基础上引入换道压力,模拟车辆在高速公路行驶时遇到事故区域后的换道行为。分析混合流车辆在多车道交通事故情况下,不同换道点所引起的交通状况的变化,提出合理的车道管控策略。仿真结果表明,对车道进行不同距离的换道提示,提前约 150~200m 左右进行换道提示效果较好,能有效缓解交通拥堵,更好地利用道路资源,提高交通效率,达到更高精度的交通流车道级管控。

关键词　道路交通流理论与出行能力　变道提示距离　跟驰模型　交通流

0　引言

各类交通事故发生率的频繁增加,给社会带来了一定的负面影响,高速公路智慧交通面临着基础信息化建设数据不全面、不充分、不协同的难题。然而发生交通事故时,因存在多方联动,事件的处置效率、协同水平极大地影响路网恢复通行时间和道路性能通行效率。因此,对车辆进行有效引导以及车道级协调管控,以数字化手段提升道路性能通行能力就显得尤为重要。

针对高速公路事故发生点产生拥堵问题,研究者们从宏观[1-4]与微观层面[5-6]提出各种方法来解决交通拥堵的实际问题。然而,交通运输部门仍将重点放在交通设计、秩序管控、事故处理以及信息服务等交通管控上,单点的统一控制已经不能满足道路的快速发展,分车道协调管控策略的提出能够有效预防交通事故的二次发生,对交通事故引发的拥堵的快速消散带来积极的作用。

所以,本文对不同交通条件多事故车道影响下的交通流进行分析,构建了在交通事故影响下的车辆跟驰模型,在事故区上游适当距离增设诱导标志牌,给予驾驶人信息提示,使驾驶人有充分时间进行提前预判,降低前方车辆的变道频次,更好地缓解交通拥堵,提高道路利用率以及道路安全性,有效地实现车路协同。同时,减少极端交通状况对国民经济发展带来的损失以及造成的人员伤亡问题,对于建立更加科学有效的交通轻微事故快速处理机制、缓解交通事故带来的拥堵有重要的意义。

本文的组织结构如下:第一节研究背景、目的及意义;第二节对交通流仿真模型以及预警位置最佳点仿真方法进行系统综述,明确本文章的研究切入点和研究方向;第三节介绍了考虑换道压力的车辆跟驰换道模型;其次在第四节进行了数值实验;最后,在第五节给出了结论。

1　综述

交通事故后拥堵占道势必会影响车辆的正常运行,导致道路通行能力降低、车辆延误等,给人们的出行造成诸多不便。随着数据不断精细化,发生交通事故的高速道路上的交通行为研究备受学者们关注,以期得到更高精度的交通流车道集管控的理论方法和应用。早在 1935 年,Greenshields 首次对交通流进行系统的研究[7]。此后,众多研究学者开始了新的探索与进步,涌现了大量的对交通流进行系统管理的建模和方法。这些模型主要包括:微观跟驰模型[8]、宏观流体力学模型[9]以及介观气体动理论模型[10]。2019 年,Liu 等提出了一种用于车道变换的高精度元胞自动机交通流模型[11]。随着科技的逐渐进步,道路上的车辆类型不止有一种,此后众多研究学者将重点放在了混合交通流的情况。2017 年,Qian 等基于原来的交通流场景,对车辆类型进行细分,建立新的交通流模型,并对交通流特征进行了一系列分析[12]。2019 年,Liu 等在自动驾驶车辆混合流的情况下,建立了一套优于基本换道规则的车辆换道模型[13]。2020 年,Jiang 等建立了考虑驾驶人意图的双车道混合交通流模型的换道规则,该模型更加接近实际的交通流情况[14]。在混合交通流模型逐渐取得进一步发展时,越来越多的研究者期望得到更高精度的车道级管控策略研究。2021 年,Chen、Lingjuan 等在元胞自动机模型的基础上,对普通车辆混行状态下的车流跟驰模型即换道模型进行分析,对不同车辆建立了不同的换道规则,利用 Matlab 进行仿真,得出不同换道点与混合车辆车流之间的关系[15]。

本文在混合交通流的情况下,建立了考虑换道压力的车辆换道模型,对不同交通情况下的多车道事故进行建模仿真,找到最佳换道点,提出了一种交通流车道级管控策略,进一步探索和发现更为细致的交通流系统随机行为的车道集管控策略所对应的机制与规律性。

2 方法

在实际情况中,驾驶人在高速公路上行驶时,受到不同距离的警示标志诱导所做出的决策对交通流的影响也不同。本节对原有的车辆跟驰模型进行改进,引入换道压力的概念,更好地描述了当驾驶人行驶至事故拥堵区时,能够及时根据警示牌预警更好地做出随机决策的过程,该模型在有利于保持较高交通密度的同时,也使道路能够容纳较高的交通流量。

考虑换道压力的车辆跟驰换道模型:基于元胞自动机的交通流模型上,进一步考虑在不同距离设置警示点对交通驾驶行为引导的影响因素,引入换道压力(λ)的概念。换道压力是车辆距离车道失效区域不同距离的加权函数值的大小,即车辆变换车道受外界因素的影响程度。随着驾驶人越来越接近车道失效区,换道位置的压力也越来越大,它与换道距离有关(图 1)。根据动力学经验可知[16],负梯度的线性函数可以更贴近实际情况去描述随距离越远值越小的特征,使得对车辆行驶和换道行为建模过程更符合实际交通中越靠近车辆警示的影响越大的事实。

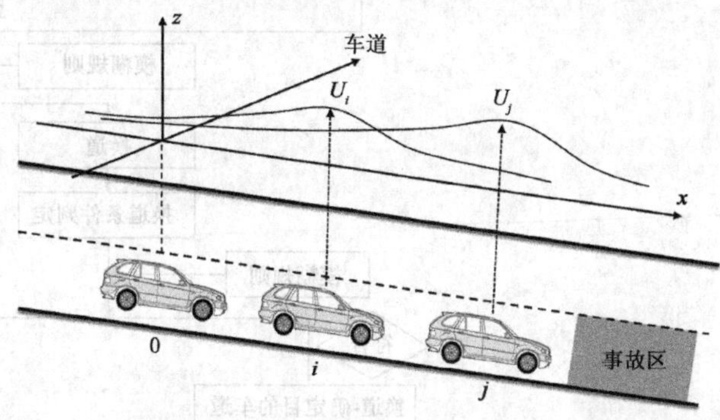

图 1 换道压力车辆示意图,其中U_i和U_j分别表示车辆的换道压力

换道压力 λ 表达式如下:

$$\lambda = \frac{1}{d_{\min} + T v_n}\sqrt{1-\left(\frac{v_n}{v_0}\right)^{\delta}} \tag{1}$$

在实际的交通流中,当第一辆车接近车道事故区时,驾驶人接受预警换道指示,为了通过该车道失效区域路段,会择机换道绕行,本文模型是在交通流中发生车道发生事故的场景下,将车辆绕行与车辆变道结合起来,考虑车辆速度的影响,对整体交通流进行分析。实际情况下,多车道的换道情况更为复杂,要考虑相邻左右车道车辆的情况。当前方发生车道失效时,在预警位置进行提示,驾驶人发生换道行为。驾驶人首先应该判断周围两车道的驾驶情况,比较两边车道的相邻前后车速度与距离,判断总体是否可以换道,最终做出换道决定。为了使得交通流的仿真更加符合实际驾驶人的操作情况,得到更好的驾驶环境,获取更高的驾驶速度,使用模糊逻辑的换道模型规则,对换道车辆相邻车道前后车距离进行模糊化处理,当产生换道需求后,根据换道规则进行换道绕行。图 2 为多车道换道判定过程示意图。

具体规则如下:记 L 为距离车道失效区的预警距离,该车在收到提醒后会进行减速并择机变道。δ 是一个参数,无论之前的车速是多少,在面临换到提醒时,车辆会减速降至一个较低水平绕过事故发生点,控制车辆加速度a_s的减小。x_n和v_n分别代表第 n 辆车的位置和速度,$v_{\max}$代表车辆所能达到的最大速度,v_0是车辆初始速度。d_{n+1}为 n 车车头距离相邻车道上前方车辆第 $n+1$ 辆车的车尾的最小值,d_n为该车车尾距离相邻车道后方车辆第 $n-1$ 辆车的车头的最小值,$d_{\min}$是车辆变换车道所需要的最小长度(这里取 5m)(图 3)。

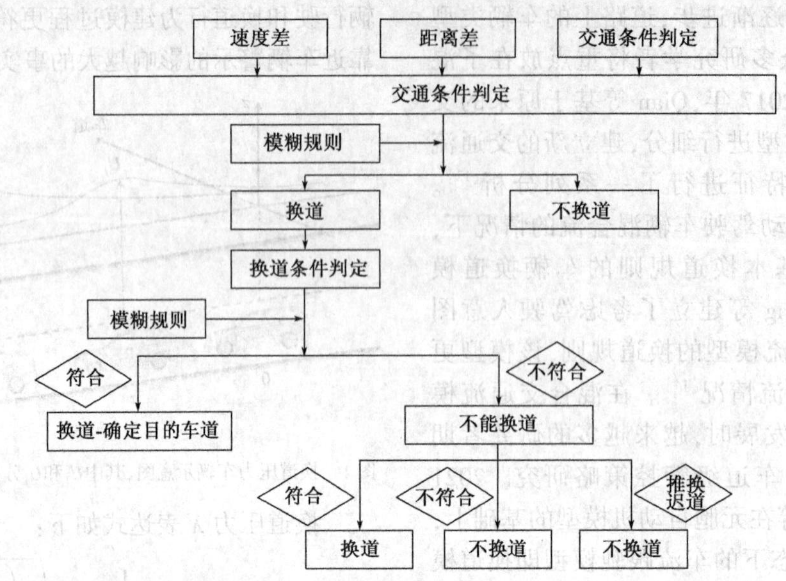

图2　多车道换道判定过程示意图

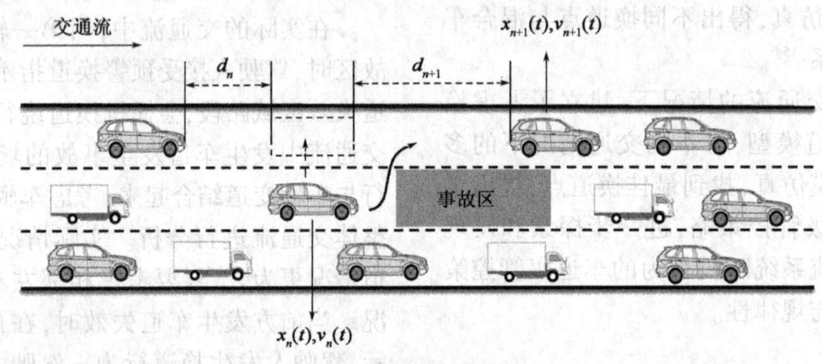

图3　参数标定示意图

由此可通过P_{pass}计算得到车辆在行驶过程中的慢化概率公式,随着距离警示区越近,换道压力越大,其慢化概率逐渐减小,其中 T 表示车辆时间间隔,$T=1.2s$:

$$P_{slow}=1-P_{pass}^{[L\lambda]}=1-\left(1-e^{-\lambda(d_n+l_c)}\right)^{[L\lambda]}$$

$$=1-\left(1-e^{-\frac{1}{d_{\min}+Tv_n}\sqrt{1-\left(\frac{v_n}{v_0}\right)^{\delta}}(d_n+l_c)}\right)^{\left[L\frac{1}{d_{\min}+Tv_n}\sqrt{1-\left(\frac{v_n}{v_0}\right)^{\delta}}\right]} \tag{2}$$

考虑交通事故的车辆换道规则具体描述如下;

换道条件:$d_{k+1}>d_{safe}$,$d_k>d_{safe}$,且 $rand()<p_{change}$。

第一步;换道。当车辆换道当前时刻的通过概率小于目标车道位置虚拟车辆的通过概率时,车辆 n 所在的位置对元胞赋值为0,即有 $\delta(x)=0$。

第二步:加速。当 $v_n<v_{max}$ 时,则第 n 车的速度加1,即$v_n\to\min\{v_n+1,v_{max}\}$,当$v_n$保持不变时,如当$v_n=v_{max}$时,$v_n=\min\{v_n+1,v_{max}\}$。

第三步:(因为其他车)减速。当$d_n<v_n$时,则第 n 车的速度减至d_n。即$v_n\to\min\{v_n,d_n\}$。

第四步:考虑换道压力的慢化。如果$v_n>0$,且$p_{rand}<p_{slow}$,则当前车辆会减速即$v_n\to\min\{v_n-1,0\}$。但是,当$v_n=0$时,v_n并不发生改变。

第五步:车辆位置更新车辆,即 $x_n\to x_n+v_n$。

3　仿真实验

本节考虑不同交通条件的多事故车道道路上预警点的最佳位置,通过分析可选择路径的车辆平均速度与交通流时间之间的关系,得到整体交通事故带来拥堵的恢复时间,通过对车道进行有效管控,能够加快恢复车道的正常行驶。

3.1　模型的基本假设

本文模型采用的是周期型边界条件的车道模型。仿真道路 $L=600$(元胞)$=3000$m,事故发生时长为30min,覆盖道路长度为50个元胞,约150m。模型设定场景如下:(1)事故仅发生在一条车道上,对相邻的同向车道没有影响;(2)在多车道的情况下，事故在多个车道同时发生；(3)假设短时间内事故的影响程度不变；(4)道路上的车辆由泊松分布随机生成。

3.2 事故发生在一个车道上

本次实验实在混合车流车辆密度条件不变的情况下，对多车道仅一个车道发生交通事故进行仿真，基于不同的预警位置，得到平均速度与时间的关系，判断其最佳预警位置。因双车道事故位于1车道和2车道效果相似，这里仅举发生在1车道的情况进行说明(图4~图8)。

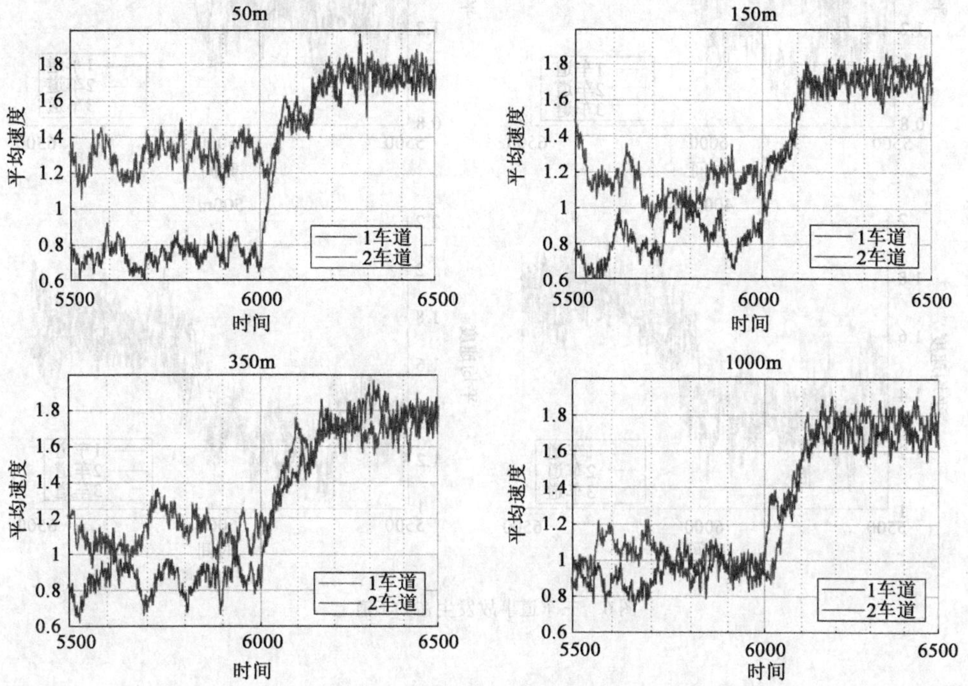

图4 双车道事故发生在1车道上

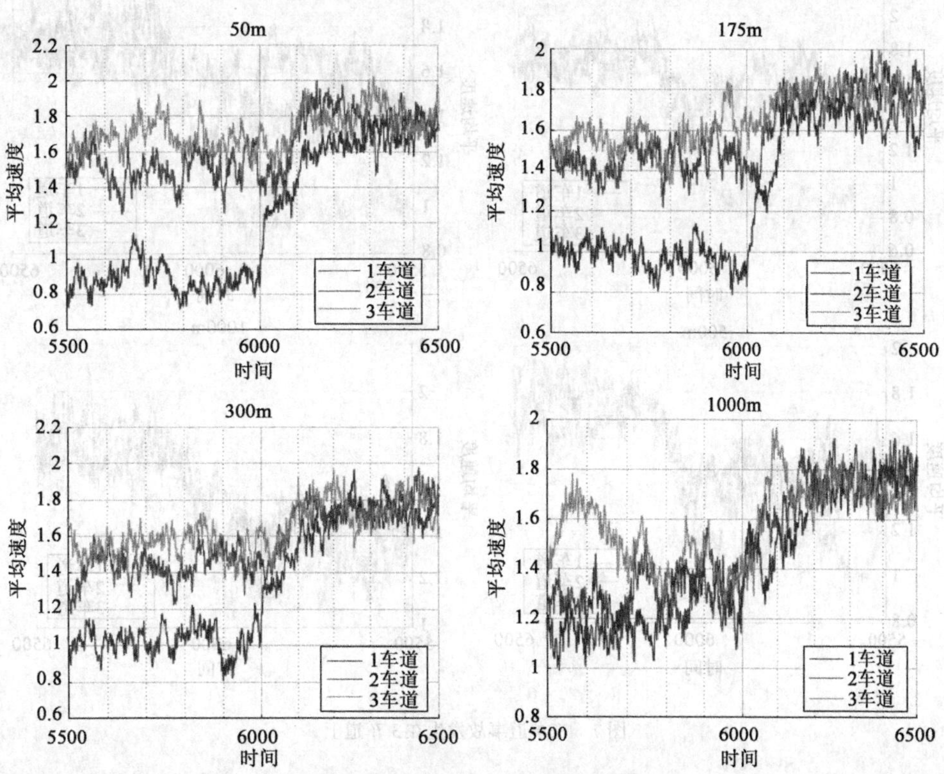

图5 三车道事故发生在1车道上

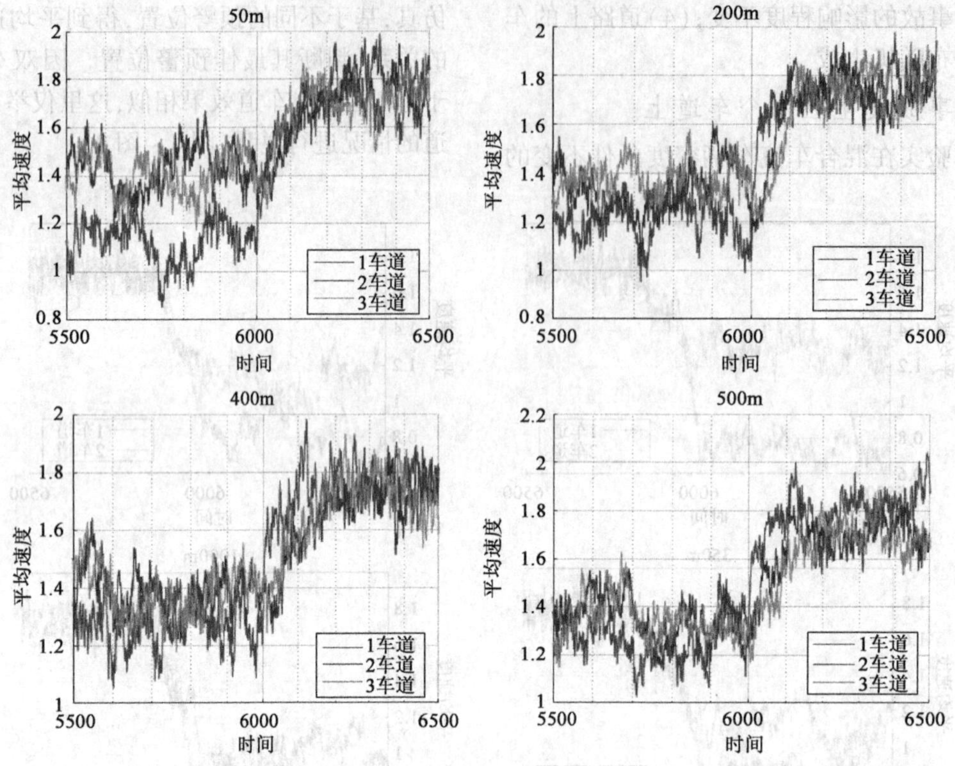

图 6　三车道事故发生在 2 车道上

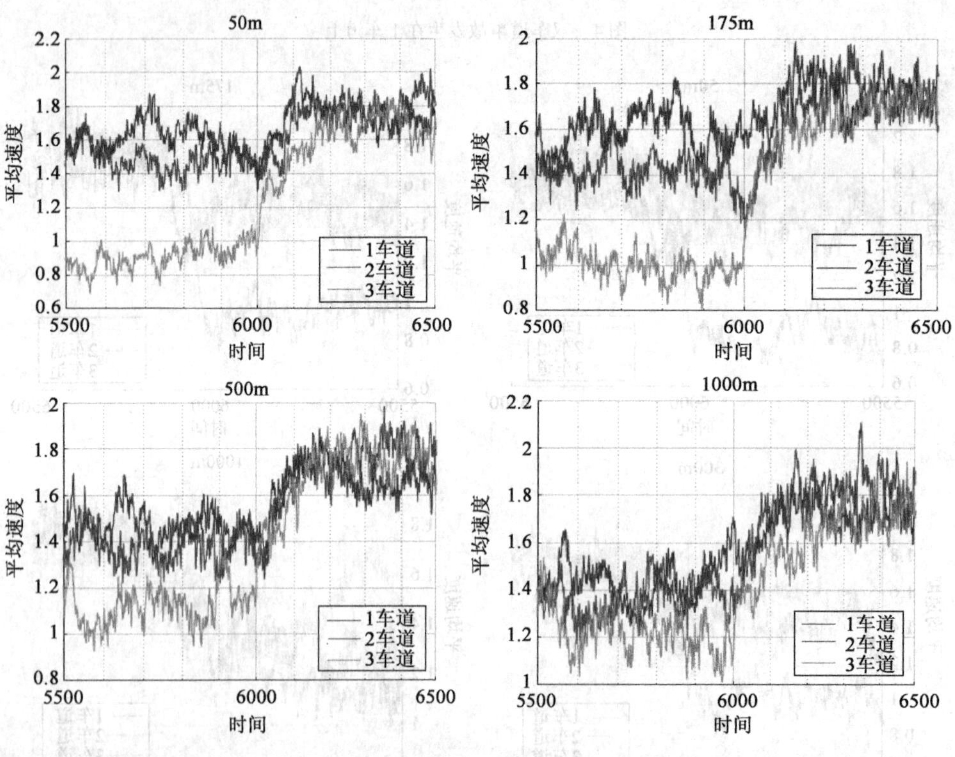

图 7　三车道事故发生在 3 车道上

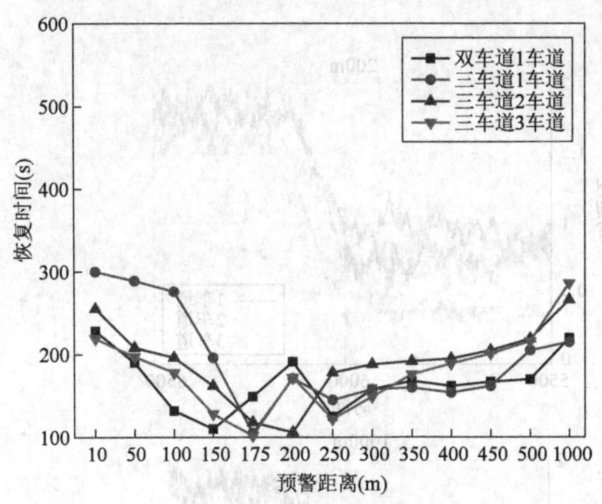

图8 事故恢复时间

对以上四种场景进行分析,得到如下结论:

(1)从整体上来看,事故车道拥堵瘫痪导致其余正常车道车辆平均速度降低,经过一段时间又逐渐上升,拥堵逐渐消散。正常车道的车速随着事故车道车辆的换道而产生波动,随着警示距离的逐渐变大,对正常车道的车辆行驶干扰也越大,进行提示时距离越远,平均速度越低,越容易导致正常车道交通瘫痪;且预警距离不应离事故发生点过近。

(2)从图8来看,双车道应在150m处进行预警提示效果最佳,三车道在150~200m进行提示能较大限度改善交通事故所造成的拥堵现象。若事故发生在中间二车道,对其余两车道的交通干扰较大,事故拥堵消散的时间略有增加。所以对中间车道发生交通事故时,预警位置应稍有提前,在200m处进行预警效果最佳

3.3 事故发生在多个车道上

本次实验实在混合车流车辆密度条件不变的情况下,对多车道多个车道发生交通事故进行仿真,基于不同的预警位置,得到平均速度与时间的关系,判断其最佳预警位置(图9~图12)。

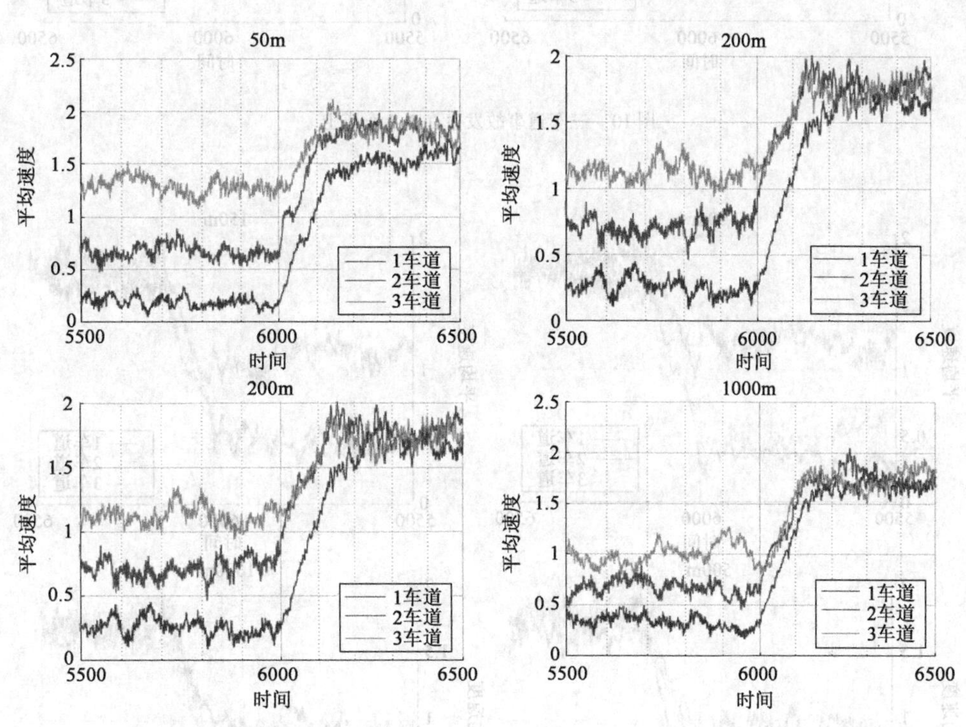

图9 三车道事故发生在1、2车道上

对以上三种场景进行分析,得到如下结论:

(1)从整体上来看,正常车道受事故车道的影响,平均速度下降后又逐渐上升。从图5~图7与图9~图11的对比来看,当多车道发生交通事故时,尽管在最佳位置进行预警提示,其道路拥堵消散时间会略有增加。

(2)从图12可以看出,若有事故发生在中间车道时,因最左1车道向安全车道换道判断条件较为复杂,所以受事故干扰影响最大,平均车速最低,预警位置应稍提前,在200m处左右进行预警效果最佳;当交通事故发生在1、3车道时,在150m处进行预警,能最大限度地利用道路资源,带来最有优效果。

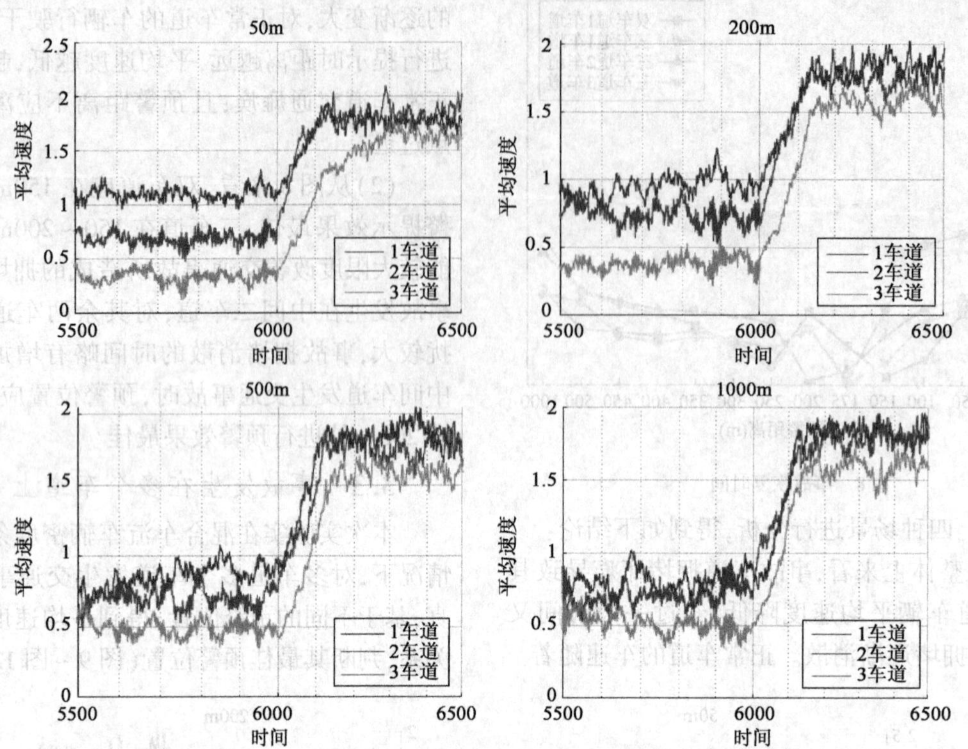

图10　三车道事故发生在2、3车道上

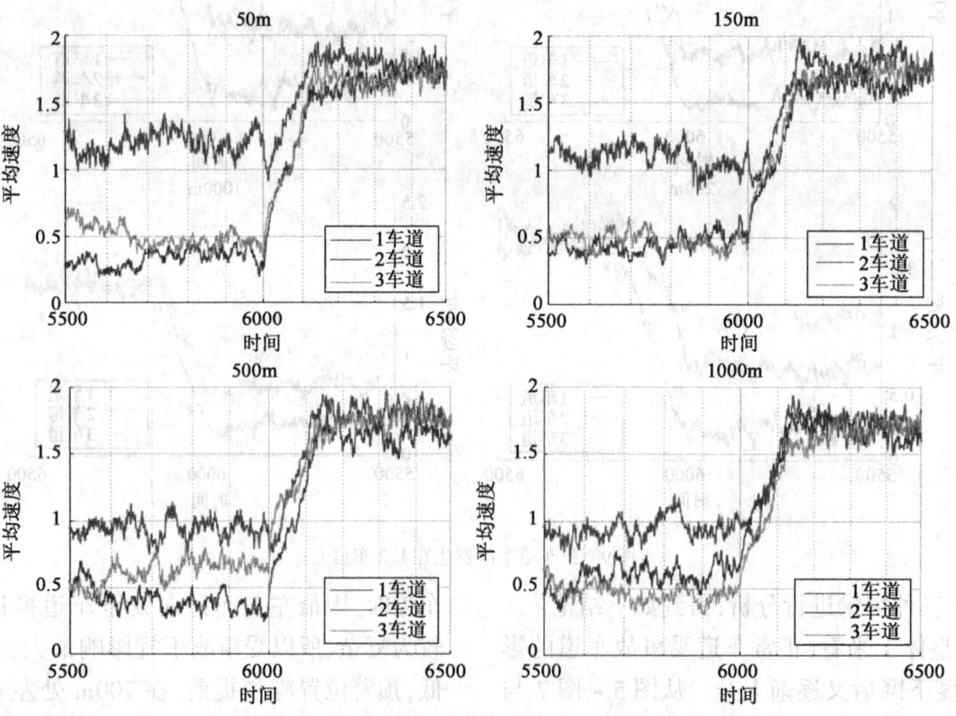

图11　三车道事故发生在1、3车道上

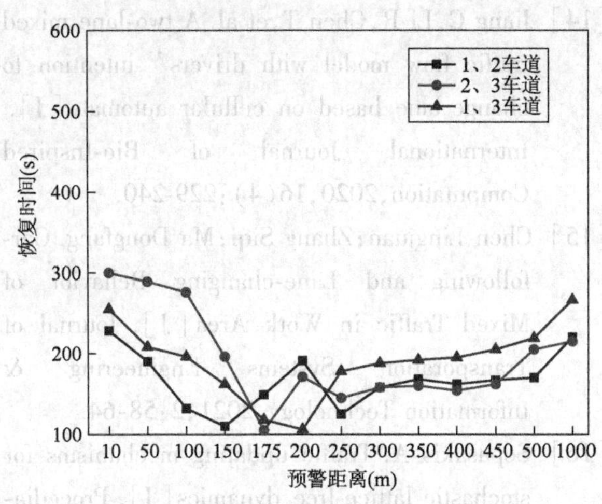

图 12 事故恢复时间

4 结论

为解决实际道路交通中因为严重的交通事故带来的各种问题,本文通过构造一个接近实际交通流分析的连续状态集元胞自动机模型。以多车道发生交通事故,车辆需要强制换道为背景,对车辆在事故区道路上不同场景下的行驶状况进行仿真,得到了在多车道下的交通流换道提示基本规律。实验结果表明,在混合交通流车流不变的情况下,驾驶人在收到预警信息后,降低速度发生换道行为,在合适的距离进行换道,有利于充分利用事故区前的道路资源。若事故仅发生在一个车道,在 150 ~ 200m 处左右进行提示效果最好。当事故发生在多个车道时,道路整体交通情况有所下降,拥堵消散时间均有所增加。根据实际情况在适当位置进行预警,以期得到更高精度的车道集管控策略。

不足与展望:

(1)本实验结果数据未经经验数据验证。

(2)该模型仅在交通条件较好的情况下准确率较高。

因实际情况下每条道路的交通流输入不同,且随着道路数字化的进一步发展,车道级的精度也越来越高,未来应进一步考虑不同车道交通流输入,以及对不同车道进行不同距离换道提示的车道级管控策略。

参考文献

[1] Payne H J. FREFLO: A macroscopic simulation model of freeway traffic [J]. Transportation Research Record, 1979 (722).

[2] Tang T Q, Caccetta L, Wu Y H, et al. A macro model for traffic flow on road networks with varying road conditions [J]. Journal of Advanced Transportation, 2014, 48 (4): 304-317.

[3] Amirgholy M, Shahabi M, Gao H O. Optimal design of sustainable transit systems in congested urban networks: A macroscopic approach [J]. Transportation Research Part E: Logistics and Transportation Review, 2017, 103: 261-285.

[4] Adacher L, Tiriolo M. A macroscopic model with the advantages of microscopic model: A review of Cell Transmission Model's extensions for urban traffic networks [J]. Simulation Modelling Practice and Theory, 2018, 86: 102-119.

[5] Maroto J, Delso E, Felez J, et al. Real-time traffic simulation with a microscopic model [J]. IEEE Transactions on Intelligent Transportation Systems, 2006, 7(4): 513-527.

[6] Mardiati R, Ismail N, Faroqi A. Review of microscopic model for traffic flow [J]. ARPN Journal of Engineering and Applied sciences, 2014, 9(10): 1794-1800.

[7] Greenshields B D, Bibbins J R, Channing W S, et al. A study of traffic capacity [C]. Highway research board proceedings. National Research Council (USA), Highway Research Board, 1935.

[8] Li X G, Jia B, Gao Z Y, et al. A realistic two-lane cellular automata traffic model considering aggressive lane-changing behavior of fast vehicle [J]. Physica A: Statistical Mechanics and its Applications, 2006, 367: 479-486.

[9] Ngoduy D, Hoogendoorn S P, Van Zuylen H J. Comparison of numerical schemes for macroscopic traffic flow models [J]. Transportation Research Record, 2004, 1876 (1): 52-61.

[10] Hoogendoorn S P, Bovy P H L. Generic gas-kinetic traffic systems modeling with applications to vehicular traffic flow [J]. Transportation Research Part B:

Methodological,2001,35(4):317-336.
[11] Liu M, Shi J. A cellular automata traffic flow model combined with a BP neural network based microscopic lane changing decision model[J]. Journal of Intelligent Transportation Systems,2019,23(4):309-318.
[12] Qian Y S, Feng X, Zeng J W. A cellular automata traffic flow model for three-phase theory[J]. Physica A: Statistical Mechanics and its Applications,2017,479:509-526.
[13] Liu Y, Wang X, Li L, et al. A novel lane change decision-making model of autonomous vehicle based on support vector machine[J]. IEEE Access,2019,7:26543-26550.
[14] Jiang C, Li R, Chen T, et al. A two-lane mixed traffic flow model with drivers' intention to change lane based on cellular automata[J]. International Journal of Bio-Inspired Computation,2020,16(4):229-240.
[15] Chen Lingjuan; Zhang Siqi; Ma Dongfang. Car-following and Lane-changing Behavior of Mixed Traffic in Work Area[J]. Journal of Transporation Systems Engineering & Information Technology,2021,2:58-64.
[16] Sopasakis A. Traffic updating mechanisms for stochastic lattice-free dynamics[J]. Procedia-Social and Behavioral Sciences,2013,80:837-845.

网联环境下考虑驾驶人异质性的基本图模型

张柯娜 王来军* 洪中荣
(长安大学运输工程学院)

摘 要 随着车联网技术的发展与应用,由网联车辆和人工车辆组成的异质交通流是当前研究重点,为研究驾驶人异质性对异质交通流特性的影响。基于全速度与加速度差模型作为人工车辆模型,协同自适应巡航控制模型(Cooperative Adaptive Cruise Control,CACC)作为网联车辆模型,推导考虑驾驶人异质性的异质交通流宏观基本图模型,并分析不同驾驶人类型对道路通行能力的影响。最后,在Matlab中对驾驶人异质性的混合交通流受到扰动后的演化过程进行仿真。仿真结果表明:激进型驾驶人比标准型驾驶人平均最大通行量增加18.6veh/h,而保守型比标准型驾驶人则减少16.46veh/h。当异质交通流网联车比例低于33%时,激进型驾驶人比标准型驾驶人的交通流稳定性增强了90%左右,而保守型驾驶人的交通流稳定性大约降低15%;当网联车比例为66%时,激进型驾驶人比标准型驾驶人对交通流稳定性降低约3%,保守型驾驶人对交通流稳定性没有影响;网联车比例为100%时,驾驶人异质性对交通流稳定性没有影响。

关键词 交通工程 异质交通流 CACC 驾驶人异质性 智能网联车辆

0 引言

随着中国新一代通信技术的发展,车与车、车与路、车与人之间通过云平台实现了实时信息共享,达到了全方位的网络连接。基于车联网技术的发展,未来交通流将由人工驾驶车辆和网联车辆混合组成,即异质交通流,这是当前国内外的研究热点。

基于网联环境下异质交通流的研究,国内外学者主要从提高交通流稳定性[1-3]与通行能力[4-5]和基本图推导[6-8]等方面展开。例如Xie等[1]基于智能驾驶人模型提出了混合常规车辆的通用跟车模型,并得出网联车辆可以明显增强交通流稳定性的结论。李霞等[2]解析不同通信技术下网联车辆与普通车辆构成的异质交通流稳定性理论。Cao等[4]采用智能驾驶人模型和CACC模型作为

1. 基金项目:交通运输部科技司项目"车路协同标准体系构建研究"(211434210059)。

普通车辆和网联车辆的跟驰模型，计算不同 CACC 车辆占比下车辆通过拥堵路段的排队时间和长度。秦严严等[7-8]求解了混有人工车辆与 CACC 车辆和 ACC 车辆的异质交通流基本图模型，并进行参数敏感性分析；推导考虑不同平衡态速度和不同 CACC 车辆比例时的异质流基本图模型。

基于驾驶人异质性对交通流影响的研究，如曾友志等[9]基于驾驶人差异，提出驾驶人扰动风险偏好的优化速度类模型。华雪东等[10]构建了考虑驾驶人心理的元胞自动机模型，并分析了驾驶人的不同心理对城市道路交通流特性的影响。但他们都未考虑驾驶人异质性在网联环境下对异质交通流的影响。

鉴于此，为充分研究现实中驾驶人差异性对交通流特性的影响。提出考虑驾驶人异质性和网联车混行的交通流基本图模型，进而求解驾驶人异质性对网联环境下交通流通行能力的影响。最后，利用 Matlab 对不同网联车混行和驾驶人异质的交通流进行数值扰动仿真，探究驾驶人异质性对混合交通流稳定性影响。为未来网联车在复杂交通流环境中的应用提供相关理论依据。

1 跟驰模型

1.1 交通流异质性模型的建立

1.1.1 人工车辆跟驰模型

优化速度（Optimal Velocity，OV）模型由 Bando 等[11]于 1995 年提出，其微分方程为：

$$a_n(t) = a_1[V(\Delta x_n) - v_n(t)] \tag{1}$$

其中，$v_n(t)$第 n 辆车的在第 t 时刻的速度；同理 $\Delta x_n(t) = x_{n+1}(t) - x_n(t)$ 表示第 n 辆车与前车在 t 时刻的车间距；$V(\Delta x_n)$ 表示期望速度函数。1998 年，Helbing 和 Tilch[12]根据实测数据将 $V(\Delta x_n)$ 函数定义为：

$$V(\Delta x_n) = V_1 + V_2\tanh[C_1(\Delta x_n - l_c) - C_2] \tag{2}$$

其中，$V_1 = 6.75\text{m/s}$；$V_2 = 7.91\text{m/s}$；$C_1 = 0.13\text{m}^{-1}$；$l_c = 5\text{m}$；$C_2 = 1.57$。

结合 JIANG R 等提出的全速度差（Full Velocity Difference，FVD）[13]模型。使用全速度差与加速度差（Full Velocity Acceleration Difference，FVAD）模型作为人工车辆跟驰模型：

$$a_n(t) = a[V(\Delta x_n(t)) - v_n(t)] + b\Delta v_{n-1}(t) + c\Delta a_{n-1}(t-1) \tag{3}$$

其中，a、b、c 分别表示人工车辆的期望函数敏感系数、速度差敏感系数与加速度差敏感系数，这里 $a = 0.9$、$b = 0.15$、$c = 0.05$；$a_n(t)$表示车辆 n 在 t 时刻的速度；Δv_n 表示第 n 辆与前车的速度差；$\Delta a_n(t)$表示第 n 辆车与前车的加速度差。

1.1.2 CACC 车辆跟驰模型

2001 年，美国加州伯克利大学 PATH 实验室经过实车验证总结提出 CACC 模型。其表达式如下[14]：

$$a_{n+1}(t+T) = a_n(t) + \rho[\Delta x_n - t_g v_n(t) - L - S_0] + \lambda[v_n(t) - v_{n+1}(t)] \tag{4}$$

其中，$a_{n+1}(t+T)$为车辆 $n+1$ 在 $t+T$ 时刻的速度；t_g 为期望车头时距；$L = 5\text{m}$ 为车头间距，$S_0 = 5\text{m}$ 为安全停车间距，$\rho = 0.2$、$\lambda = 3.0$ 为 CACC 车辆的期望函数敏感系数。

1.2 驾驶人异质性场景设计

考虑到现实中驾驶人的年龄，驾驶时长和出行目的等因素存在差异性，所以本文将驾驶人分为 3 类：标准型驾驶人、保守型驾驶人、激进型驾驶人。

1.2.1 标准型驾驶人

在车辆直行工况下，车辆前向加速度 $<0.9\text{m/s}^2$ 或制动减速度 $<1.1\text{m/s}^2$ 的概率为 95%[15]。设驾驶人有 20% 的认知差异，标准驾驶人加速度变化量为 $a_n(t)$，驾驶人异质行为参数 $e = 0.2\text{m/s}^2$。

1.2.2 保守型驾驶人

当车辆处于加速状态时，保守型驾驶人的加速度会低于 $a_n(t)$，称之消极型加速；而减速状态时则会高于 $a_n(t)$，称之积极型减速。

消极型加速和积极型减速的加速度变化见式（5）和式（6）：

$$\text{如果}(a_n(t) > 0),\ a_n(t) = a_n(t) - e \tag{5}$$

$$\text{如果}(a_n(t) < 0),\ a_n(t) = a_n(t) - e \tag{6}$$

1.2.3 激进型驾驶人

当车辆处于加速状态时，激进型驾驶人的加速度会高于 $a_n(t)$，称之积极型加速；而减速状态时则会低于 $a_n(t)$，称之消极型减速。

积极型加速和消极型减速的加速度变化见式（7）和式（8）：

$$\text{如果}(a_n(t) > 0),\ a_n(t) = a_n(t) + e \tag{7}$$

$$\text{如果}(a_n(t) < 0),\ a_n(t) = a_n(t) + e \tag{8}$$

2　基本图模型

基本图模型是体现流量、密度和速度之间的函数关系模型。基本图模型的计算是基于车队的平衡态。当车队行驶至平衡态时,车辆加速度 $a_n(t)$ 为 0,相邻车辆的速度差 $\Delta v_n(t)$ 为 0,所有速度达到平衡态速度 v。

2.1　同质交通流基本图模型

同质交通流分为人工车辆同质交通流和网联车辆同质交通流。

2.1.1　人工车辆基本图计算

将平衡态条件代入式(3)得到人工车辆的车头间距 h_f,见式(9)。

$$h_f=\frac{\operatorname{arctanh}\left(\frac{1.25v-V_1}{V_2}\right)+C_2}{C_1}+l_c \tag{9}$$

根据交通流理论可知,交通流密度与车头间距之间互为倒数关系,流量等于密度和速度的乘积。则人工车辆同质交通流密度 k_f 和流量 q_f 的表达式见式(10)。

$$\begin{cases}k_f=\frac{1}{h_f}=\frac{C_1}{\operatorname{arctanh}\left(\frac{1.25v-V_1}{V_2}\right)+C_2+C_1l_c}\\q_f=k_fv\end{cases} \tag{10}$$

2.1.2　CACC 车辆基本图计算

将平衡态条件代入式(4),可得 CACC 车辆同质交通流车头间距 $h_c=t_gv+L+S_0$,对应的交通流密度 k_c 流量 q_c 见式(11)。

$$\begin{cases}k_c=\frac{1}{h_c}=\frac{1}{t_gv+L+S_0}\\q_c=k_cv\end{cases} \tag{11}$$

2.1.3　同质交通流基本图

设平衡态速度 v 的取值范围为 0 ~ 33.3m/s,根据式(9) ~ 式(11),求得同质交通流流量与密度之间的函数关系。如图 1 所示,在相同的交通流密度下,不同类型驾驶人的基本通行能力比较:激进型 > 标准型 > 保守型,相同类型驾驶人的基本通行能力比较:CACC 车辆 > 人工车辆。人工车辆同质交通流基本通行能力,激进型比标准型的 414pcu/h 提高了 2.26%,保守型则降低了 2.25%。CACC 车辆同质交通流基本通行能力,激进型比标准型的 1234pcu/h 提高了 3.84%,保守型则降低了 3.57%。CACC 车辆比人工车辆平均基本通行能力增加 821.5pcu/h。

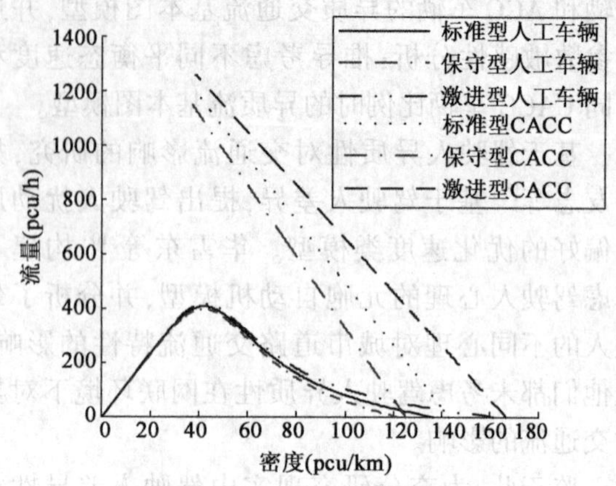

图 1　同质交通流通行能力基本图

2.2　异质交通流基本图模型

异质交通流是指人工车辆和 CACC 车辆一起组成的交通流。计算不同比例 CACC 车辆下的基本图模型,并分析驾驶人异质性模型的变化趋势和规律。

2.2.1　异质交通流基本图计算

设异质交通流中人工车辆的比例为 S_f,CACC 车辆的比例为 S_c,且 $S_f+S_c=1$。异质交通流的跟驰模式类型和比例见表 1。

跟驰模式比例　　表 1

跟驰模式	比例
人工车辆跟驰人工车辆	S_fS_f
人工车辆跟驰 CACC 车辆	S_fS_c
CACC 车辆跟驰人工车辆	S_cS_f
CACC 车辆跟驰 CACC 车辆	S_cS_c

因 CACC 车辆跟驰人工车辆时,人工车辆无法通信,故 CACC 车辆转变成人工车辆。计算可得异质交通流中人工车辆跟驰模式的比例 P_f 和 CACC 车辆跟驰模式的比例 P_c,见式(12)。

$$\begin{cases}P_f=S_fS_f+S_fS_c+S_cS_c=1-S_c^2\\P_c=S_cS_c=S_c^2\end{cases} \tag{12}$$

异质交通流中稳态车头间距 h、密度 k、流量 q,见式(13)、式(14)。

$$h=P_fh_f+P_ch_c \tag{13}$$

$$\begin{cases}k=\frac{1}{h}=\frac{1}{P_fh_f+P_ch_c}\\q=kv\end{cases} \tag{14}$$

2.2.2　异质交通流基本图

根据式(12)~式(14),可得异质交通流流量和密度的关系曲线,以及驾驶人异质性对道路通行量的影响。如图2所示,在同一密度下,交通流量随着网联车比例的增加而增大。当网联车占比为20%时,基本通行能力增强3.42%,交通量变化不明显。当网联车占比为40%时,基本通行能力增强13.43%。当网联车占比为60%时,基本通行能力增强28.23%,当网联车占比为80%时,基本通行能力增强45.28%。不同网联车比例下激进型驾驶人的平均基本通行能力比标准型增加18.60pcu/h,保守型则减少16.46pcu/h。

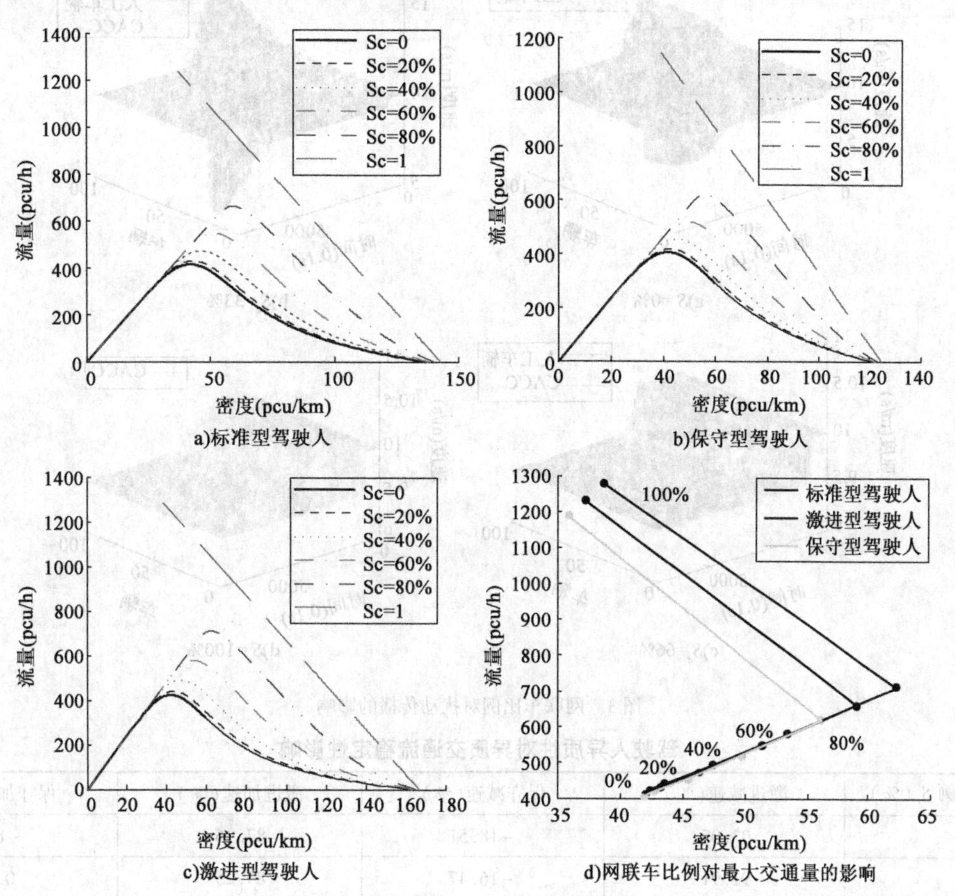

图2　异质交通流通行能力基本图

3　数值仿真

应用本文的跟驰模型在MATLAB中进行数值仿真,研究网联车辆占比对交通流稳定性影响。仿真车队长度为100辆车,车辆1为头车,依次类推为跟驰车辆。其中CACC车辆与人工车辆的位置随机确定,二者的数量由CACC车辆的占比确定。头车的初始速度为10m/s,车头间距为20m,跟驰车辆按照各自的驾驶模式跟驰。当车队达到稳定的跟驰速度和车头间距,头车以-0.01m/s^2的减速度运行3s,接着以减小后的速度运行至仿真结束。仿真步长为0.1s,总运行时间为700s。仿真结果如图3所示。

由仿真结果可知,扰动在车队中的传播具有延时性,随着CACC车辆渗透率的增大,传播速度变快,交通流对干扰的抑制越强,交通流越平稳。当车队全部为CACC车辆时,车队中扰动的传播时间为0s,当网联车占比低于33%时,稳定性提升的比例较小,当网联车比例大于66%时,交通流稳定性提升93%左右,稳定性增强效果十分显著。交通流宏观特征随网联车比例变化见表2。

异质交通流宏观特征　　表2

网联车辆比例 S_c(%)	速度波峰平均值(m/s)	速度波谷平均值(m/s)	稳定性上升比例(%)	延迟时间(s)
0	12.01	4.95	0.00	112.2
33	11.65	5.64	14.98	102.2
66	10.00	9.54	93.42	62.1
1	10.02	9.54	93.20	0

异质驾驶人与标准驾驶人的交通流稳定性仿真结果的对比见表3。激进型驾驶人对交通流稳定性的影响程度大于保守型驾驶人。当网联车占比低于33%时,激进型驾驶人可以显著改善交通流稳定性,而保守型驾驶人对扰动的抑制效果低于标准型驾驶人,其交通流稳定性有所降低。当网联车比例为66%,驾驶员异质性不能改善交通流稳定性。当网联车辆占比为1时,驾驶人异质性对交通流稳定性没有影响。

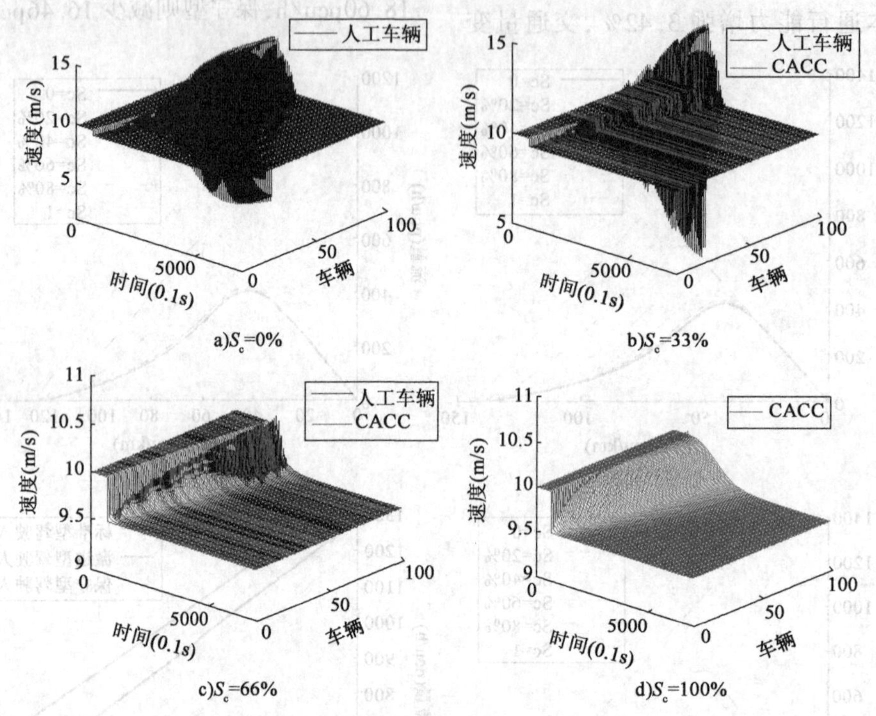

图3　网联车比例对扰动传播的影响

驾驶人异质性对异质交通流稳定性影响　　表3

网联车辆比例 S_c(%)	激进减速(%)	保守减速(%)	激进加速(%)	保守加速(%)
0	93.05	-18.51	87.96	-8.41
33	91.91	-16.47	89.25	0.00
66	-4.14	0.00	-2.77	0.00
1	0.00	0.00	0.00	0.00

4　结论

应用FVAD模型和CACC模型分别作为人工和网联车辆跟驰模型。通过引入驾驶人异质性参数,提出考虑驾驶员异质性的异质交通流基本图模型,并得出如下结论:

(1)驾驶人异质性对异质交通流稳定性的影响随着网联车占比不同而改变。当网联车占比较低时,激进型驾驶人对交通流稳定性有改善作用,而保守型驾驶人对交通流扰动有放大作用。当车队中车辆全部为网联车辆时,驾驶人异质性对交通流稳定性没有影响。

(2)考虑驾驶人异质性的异质交通流,随网联车占比的增大,其交通流最大通行能力和车队整体稳定性提升作用越明显,车队中扰动的传播速度就越快。

(3)未来可在单车道基本图模型的基础上加入换道和超车模型,计算和推导多车道基本图模型,研究驾驶人异质性对多车道混合交通流的影响。

参考文献

[1] Xie D F, Zhao X M, He Z. Heterogeneous Traffic Mixing Regular and Connected Vehicles: Modeling and Stabilization [J]. IEEE Transactions on Intelligent Transportation

Systems,2019,20(6).
[2] 李霞,汪一戈,崔洪军,等.智能网联环境下复杂异质交通流稳定性解析[J].交通运输系统工程与信息,2020,20(6):114-120.
[3] Yao Z,Hu R,Wang Y,et al. Stability analysis and the fundamental diagram for mixed connected automated and human-driven vehicles [J]. Physica A: Statistical Mechanics and its Applications,2019:533(c).
[4] Cao Z, Lu L, Chen C, et al. Modeling and Simulating Urban Traffic Flow Mixed With Regular and Connected Vehicles [J]. IEEE Access,2021,9.
[5] 马庆禄,傅宝宇,曾皓威.智能网联环境下异质交通流基本图和稳定性分析[J].交通信息与安全,2021,39(05):76-84.
[6] 徐桃让,姚志洪,蒋阳升,等.智能网联车环境下考虑反应时间影响的基本图模型[J].公路交通科技,2020,37(08):108-117.
[7] 秦严严,王昊,王炜,等.混有CACC车辆和ACC车辆的异质交通流基本图模型[J].中国公路学报,2017,30(10):127-136.
[8] 秦严严,王昊,王炜,等.混有协同自适应巡航控制车辆的异质交通流稳定性解析与基本图模型[J].物理学报,2017,66(09):257-265.
[9] 曾友志,张宁,刘利娟.考虑司机扰动风险偏好异质的跟驰模型[J].物理学报,2014,63(06):378-384.
[10] 华雪东,王炜,王昊.考虑驾驶心理的城市双车道交通流元胞自动机模型[J].物理学报,2011,60(08):404-411.
[11] Bando M, Hasebe K, Nakayama A, et al, Dynamical model of traffic congestion and numerical simulation[J]. Physical Review E, 1995,51(2):1035-1042.
[12] Helbing D,Tilch B. Generalized force model of traffic dynamics[J]. Physical Review E,1998,58(1):133-138
[13] JIANG R,WU Q,ZHU Z,Full velocity difference model for a car-following theory [J]. Physical Review E,2001,64(1):017101.
[14] Milanes V,Shladover S E. Modeling cooperative and autonomous adaptive cruise control dynamic responses using experimental data[J]. Transportation Research Part C: Emerging Technologies,2014,48:285-300.
[15] 刘瑞,马志雄,武彪,等.驾驶员驾驶行为的统计学特性[J].同济大学学报(自然科学版),2019,47(06):832-841.

基于元胞自动机的三车道超车变道行为影响分析

李喻萍* 马超群
(长安大学运输工程学院)

摘 要 本文基于元胞自动机模型,建立高速公路单向三车道连续超车变道模型,利用MATLAB仿真平台研究分析高速公路单向三车道变道过程中车道长度,平均速度与车流密度参数之间的关系。通过分析输出参数数据判断道路上是否发生交通拥堵或其他交通事故,进而优化改善道路交通条件。结果表明,车道长度越短,车流密度变化幅度越大,越容易出现交通拥堵情况或者其他交通问题。

关键词 高速公路 超车变道 元胞自动机 单向三车道

0 引言

随着社会科学技术的迅猛发展和经济水平的持续增长,居民私家车保有量逐年递增,各类道路安全问题频发。在驾驶人行驶的过程中,由于驾驶操作失误引发的交通事故占据94%以上[1]。高速公路驾驶过程中,驾驶人的超车变道行为均会对整条道路的车辆密度,车流量以及安全性产生影响。若在超车变道驾驶过程中,安全距离不够或者驾驶人完成超车行为立刻折返原车道,都极易引发交通安全事故。

目前,许多学者对车辆在道路行驶过程中的超车变道行为都展开了大量的研究,其中元胞自动机模型能够较好地模拟超车换道的交通状况。交通流元胞自动机模型是 Wolfram 最早提出的一维元胞自动机模型,又称 184 号模型。即道路被划分为等格的格子,每一个格点表示一个元胞。在每一个时间步长内,若第 N 辆车前方元胞为 0,该车辆前进一格。若第 N 辆车前的元胞被第 $N+1$ 个元胞所占据,第 N 辆车无法前进[2]。随着计算机技术的不断发展,李庆元等基于改进元胞自动机原理构建最小纵向双车道超车变道模型,实验表明该模型能够有效地模拟高速公路车辆行驶交通状况[3]。王婷等对初始元胞自动机模型进行改进,提出双车道混合车辆超车变道模型,得出不同情景下的时空斑图[4]。孔德文构建基于车型差异性的元胞自动机换道模型,对多车道高速公路进行仿真,实验表明,与传统元胞自动机模型相比,该模型能够有效模拟车辆换道行为[5]。卫妮娜等提出基于安全参数的双车道元胞自动机超车变道模型,实验表明,在超车变道规则下,当安全系数增大时,道路流量增大[6]。杨巧丽构建基于智能网联汽车背景下的三车道换道元胞自动机跟车变道模型,对人工驾驶下的交通流模型和智能网联汽车下的交通流模型展开仿真分析[7]。郝思淳等通过元胞自动机交通流模型,对自动驾驶汽车和人工驾驶车辆混行情景下的超车变道行为展开仿真,实验得出当自动驾驶车辆比例为 0.6 时,道路交通行驶环境最佳[8]。唐汐茹等将驾驶人特性和车辆动力性能引入元胞自动机模型,建立了改进型双向双车道元胞自动机模型,分别对流量对称型双车道和流量不对称型双车道展开超车变道行为模拟仿真[9]。

元胞自动机交通流模型能够有效地模拟车辆超车、换道、跟驰行为下的真实交通流,从而精准分析是否产生交通事故。目前大多数学者将高速公路双车道超车变道行为作为研究重点展开深入研究,对三车道连续超车行为研究较少。基于此研究背景,本文基于元胞自动机模型,对单向三车道超车变道中连续变道行为进行仿真,研究分析高速公路下不同车道长度,车流密度和车辆平均速度三者之间的影响情况。

1　模型基本假设

第一,本文研究高速公路上三车道超车行为,即由右车道连续变道超车两次至最左车道返回中间车道的超车行为进行仿真分析。第二,利用元胞自动机模型模拟的交通流具有连续性,不考虑实际道路状态下的交通停止信号并且假设道路为直行道路,无十字路口和左右转弯。第三,每一个元胞模拟一辆车,设置快速车道和慢速车道,考虑车道的最高时速和是最低时速的限制。第四,模拟车道上的所有车辆的行驶状态均为匀速行驶,车辆进行超车换道行为时,仍旧保持匀速状态,不考虑实际超车变道过程中车辆加速情况。第五,需要考虑驾驶人的随机性和不确定性,即车道入口处车辆概率具有随机性。需要对车道入口处车辆进入的概率进行随机赋值,保证其数据具有随机性和有效性。最后,利用元胞自动机交通流模型进行的仿真路段车辆密度为常数,即模拟仿真过程中,车辆密度变化为 0,可以对不同区段内不同的车辆密度进行分析研究。

2　超车变道模型围观规则设计

2.1　超车变道模型

假设三车道高速公路上不分主要行驶车道和超车车道,道路上的车辆采用自由对称换道超车。同一车道在第 t 时刻前后依次行驶的车辆的间距为 $S_{n+1}(t)$。其中 $X_n(t)$ 为在第 t 时刻第 n 辆车的位置,$X_{n+1}(t)$ 为在第 t 时刻第 $n+1$ 辆车的位置。

$$S_{n+1}(t)=X_n(t)-X_{n+1}(t) \tag{1}$$

车道上第 $n+1$ 辆车在第 t 时刻时与相邻车道前方紧邻车辆之间的距离为 $S_{n+1,\text{other}}(t)$,其中 $X_{n,\text{other}}(t)$ 为第 t 时刻第 $n+1$ 辆车相邻车道的前方紧邻车辆的位置。

$$S_{n+1,\text{other}}(t)=X_{n,\text{other}}(t)-X_{n+1}(t) \tag{2}$$

车道上第 $n+1$ 辆车在第 t 时刻与相邻车道后方紧邻车辆之间的距离为 $S_{n+1,\text{back}}(t)$,其中 $X_{n+2,\text{other}}(t)$ 为在第 t 时刻时第 $n+1$ 辆车与相邻车道后方紧邻车辆的位置。

$$S_{n+1,\text{back}}(t)=X_{n+1}(t)-X_{n+2,\text{other}}(t) \tag{3}$$

高速公路单向三车道超车变道规则应遵循两点基本规则:①车辆超车变道后避免与变道后方

行驶的车辆发生碰撞；②拟换道的车道行驶条件比本车道好，即车辆的换道动机，如式(4)和式(5)所示。

$$S_{n+1,\mathrm{other}}(t)+X_{n+1}(t)>X_{n+2}(t) \tag{4}$$

$$S_{n+1}(t)+\alpha X_{n+1}(t)<X_n(t)<S_{n+1,\mathrm{other}}(t)+\alpha X_{n+2,\mathrm{other}}(t) \tag{5}$$

其中，α 为车辆换道概率，$\alpha\in[0.1]$。

本文主要针对单向三车道车辆由右车道超车变道至左车道返回到中间车道的情况进行研究。该模拟状态下，车辆均为匀速行驶状态，通过根据车道空位数来判断是否可以进行超车行为。车辆在右车道进行行驶，当中间车道车辆空位数大于或等于3个时，车辆即可向左变道完成超车后返回原车道。当中间车道车辆空位数等于2个且左车道空位数大于等于3个时，车辆由右车道向左连续变道至左车道，完成超车后返回中间车道。当中间车道车辆空位数小于2个时，车辆无法完成超车。

2.2 元胞交通流模型

(1)车流密度(P)：一个车道单位长度内某一瞬间存在的车辆数，单位为辆/km，即

$$p=\frac{N_{\mathrm{total}}}{N_C\cdot N_L} \tag{6}$$

其中，N_C表示测试路段的长度；N_L代表车道数目，N_{total}表示位于路段内所有车辆数。

(2)平均车速(V)：在固定路段内不同车道上所有车辆的平均时速的平均值，其定义如下：

$$v=\frac{1}{N_{\mathrm{total}}\cdot T}\sum_{t=1}^{T}\sum_{j=1}^{N_{\mathrm{total}}}E \tag{7}$$

其中，E 代表第 j 辆车在 t 时刻的速度；T 表示计测周期。

(3)交通流量(Q)：单位时间内通过某一固定点的车辆数，根据交通流的理论，交通流量可定义为车流密度与平均车速的乘积，即

$$Q=v\cdot p \tag{8}$$

本文主要对右行左超车规则高速公路单方向三车道超车行为利用元胞自动机进行仿真模拟。假设每一条车道划分为1000个元胞，则三条车道分为3×1000元胞矩阵。设定仿真步长d_t为0.01s。考虑不同车道长度对超车变道模型的影响，车道长度分别为设置为10、100、1000。在模拟状态中，分别用第 t 时刻车辆行驶速度(av)，车辆变道频率(ad)和车流密度(ap)三个参数来描述元胞状态。

3 单向三车道元胞自动机仿真

3.1 仿真步骤

步骤一：输入初始参数。输入模拟车道数目、车道长度、仿真步长时间、仿真步长数目和车道入口处车辆进入概率。车道数目初始值为3，为测试不同车道长度下的车流密度与车流速度的变量关系，车道长度初始值分别为10、100、1000，仿真步长时间初始值为0.1s，仿真步长数目初始值设定为1000，本文确定车道入口处车辆概率从2.5以0.25的速度减少至0.5。同时，本文将模拟仿真状态下，车流密度，车辆速度和车辆换道次数初始参数值设置为0。

步骤二：构建元胞矩阵并且对元胞车辆初始化。设置 cc 表示车道上的车辆数。当 $cc=0$ 时，车道上的车辆数为0，当 $cc=1$ 时，车道上的车辆数大于或等于1。初始化每个元胞模型，将每个元胞即每个车辆的行驶速度，换道频率以及车流密度的初始值均设置为0。

步骤三：获取所有元胞数据。模拟道路上，确定前 $n-2$ 个元胞车辆的行驶状态分别为加速行驶状态，匀速行驶状态，减速行驶状态中的哪一种。随后，确定后2个元胞车辆的行驶状态。从而确定整条模拟车道上所有的元胞车辆数据。

步骤四：超车换道且确定元胞车辆位置变化。元胞车辆通过判断中间车道和左车道的车辆空位数来确定是否满足超车条件。当中间车道车辆空位数为2个，且左车道车辆空位数大于等于3个时，元胞车辆即可完成超车行为。超车变道后，重新设置道路上的元胞车辆，获取所有元胞车辆数据。当元胞车辆匀速前进，元胞车辆位置前进1格。同时，记录模拟车道的车辆数目，车流密度及车辆行驶速度。

步骤五：引入道口车辆。在车道入口处随机引入新车辆，重新构建元胞矩阵，绘制交通流量与仿真步长的关系曲线图，重新获取所有元胞数据，并且返回步骤三进行循环仿真。

步骤六：输出第 t 时刻的车辆行车速度(av)，车辆变道频率(ad)，车流密度(ap)。得出车辆平均行驶车速与车辆密度关系图和车流密度与仿真车道长度关系图。

3.2 仿真结果分析

本文针对单向三车道右行左超车进行模拟分

析,设置仿真参车道数目 $N_c = 3$,仿真时长 $d_t = 0.01$s,仿真步长数目 $N_L = 1000$,车道长度分别设定为 10、100、1000。

3.2.1　车道长度与平均速度-车流密度关系

由图 1 可知横坐标表示车流平均速度,纵坐标表示车流密度。当车道长度取 10、100、1000 时,平均车速与车流密度曲线走势大致一致,且三种车道长度的车流密度均随平均速度的增大而降低。同时,当车道长度越长,车流速度较高时,车流密度波动较大且降幅更快。这说明当车道越长时车道车辆平均速度升高,车道的车辆数降低,从而车流密度降低。

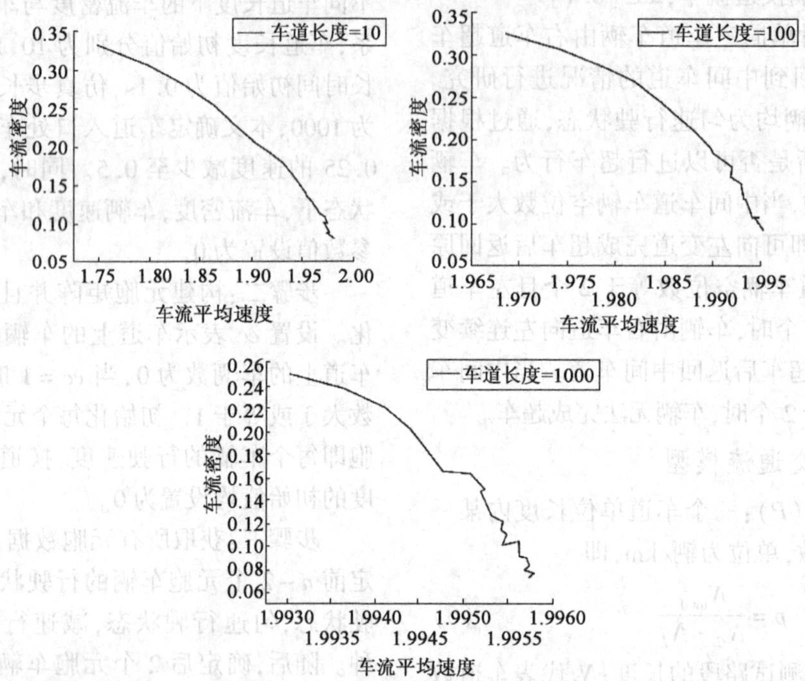

图 1　不同车道长度下车流密度和车流平均速度关系图

3.2.2　车道长度与车流密度关系

由图 2 分析得出,当车道长度分别取 10、100、1000 时,车流密度曲线越连续。这说明,对于高速公路单向三车道模型,车道长度越长,车流密度变化越平滑,道路交通情况越平稳;车道长度越短,车流密度变化幅度越大,交通拥堵情况或者其他交通问题越容易发生。

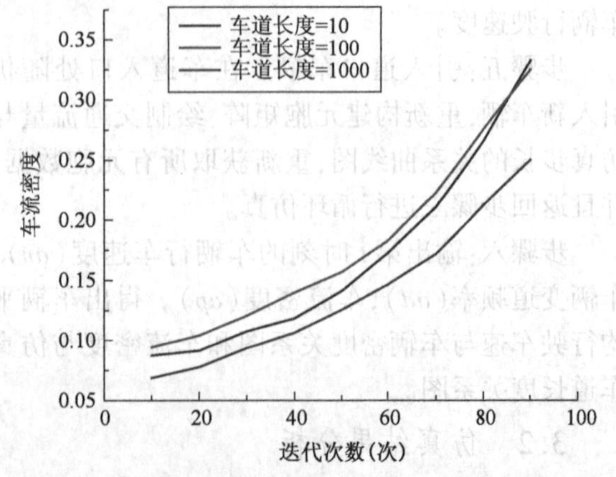

图 2　不同车道长度下车流密度变化图

4　结论

本文基于元胞自动机模型,对高速公路三车道超车变道行为展开仿真,研究分析不同车道长度、车流密度和车辆平均速度三者之间的影响情况。实验表明,当车道长度越长,车流密度变化越平滑,道路交通情况越平稳。当车道长度越短,车流密度变化幅度越大,交通拥堵情况或者其他交通问题越容易发生。本文构建的三车道超车变道模型可以为交通安全、交通管制提供相应的理论依据。

实际交通环境复杂多变,在后续的研究中可以增加不同车型的车辆数目和增加车道数,对多车道的同种类似连续超车变道情况进行仿真模拟,增加超车模型的实用性。

参考文献

[1] Dingus T A, Guo F, Lee S, et al. Driver crash risk factors and prevalence evaluation using

naturalistic driving data [J]. Proceedings of the National Academy of Sciences, 2016, 113(10): 2636-2641.

[2] 黄志鹏,石琴.交通流元胞自动机模型综述[EB/OL].(2017-1-22)[2018-12-26].

[3] 李庆宇,陈凌珊.基于元胞自动机的智能车辆超车规则研究[J].农业装备与车辆工程,2020,58(06):64-69.

[4] 王婷,周石鹏.基于元胞自动机双车道混合车辆变道规则的交通流模型研究[J].物流科技,2017,40(10):90-93+110.

[5] 孔德文.大型车辆对多车道高速公路交通运行影响研究[D].南京:东南大学,2018.

[6] 卫妮娜,俞礼军,李少龙.基于安全参数的双车道元胞自动机交通流模型及两种交通规则下的模拟分析[J].公路与汽运,2017(01):40-43+56.

[7] 杨巧丽.智能网联驾驶环境下的三车道交通流模型研究[D].长沙:湖南大学,2019.

[8] 郝思淳,霍梦真,姚皓楠.自动与非自动驾驶车辆在高速路上的互动策略[J].现代电信科技,2017,47(06):30-36.

[9] 唐夕茹,徐丽萍.基于改进型元胞自动机模型的双车道公路交通冲突分析[J].公路交通科技,2016,33(03):109-115.

附录

参数解释表

参数	解释
$S_{n+1}(t)$	同一车道在第 t 时刻前后依次行驶车辆的间距
$X_n(t)$	第 t 时刻第 n 辆车的位置
$X_{n+1}(t)$	第 t 时刻第 $n+1$ 辆车的位置
$S_{n+1,\text{other}}(t)$	车道上第 $n+1$ 辆车在第 t 时刻时与相邻车道前方紧邻车辆之间的距离
$X_{n,\text{other}}(t)$	第 t 时刻第 $n+1$ 辆车相邻车道的前方紧邻车辆的位置
$S_{n+1,\text{back}}(t)$	车道上第 $n+1$ 辆车在第 t 时刻与相邻车道后方紧邻车辆之间的距离
$X_{n+2,\text{other}}(t)$	在第 t 时刻时第 $n+1$ 辆车与相邻车道后方紧邻车辆的位置
α	车辆换道概率
P	车流密度
V	车流平均速度
N_C	测试路段长度
N_L	车道数目
N_{total}	路段内所有车辆数
Q	交通流量
E	第 j 辆车在 t 时刻的速度
t	计测时刻
T	计测周期
d_t	仿真步长
av	第 t 时刻车辆行车速度
ad	第 t 时刻车辆变道频率
ap	第 t 时刻车流密度
B_i	车辆行驶的车道位置
cc	车道上的车辆数

Variable Speed Limit Control Method in Work Zone of Multi-lane Freeway Based on METANET Model

Yiheng Lu[1] Chunjie Li[*1,2] Chengcheng Xu[1] Qikang Zheng[1] Ling Deng[1]
(1. School of Transportation, Southeast University;
2. Hebei Provincial Communications Planning, Design and Research Institute)

Abstract In order to alleviate the traffic congestion caused by the traffic bottleneck in thefreeway work zone, such as the decline of traffic capacity, the extension of travel time and the increase of travel delay, the variable speed limit control method in the multi-lane freeway work zone is studied, and an improved METANET model suitable for the traffic characteristics of different lanes and the variable speed limit method is proposed. A variable speed limit control model in the work zone is constructed to improve the traffic volume and shorten the travel time. The paper uses a work zone of Jingde freeway as an example to display the implementation effect of the control method model. The results reveal that the method can reduce the sudden reduction of traffic capacity, maintain a certain traffic capacity in the work zone, save 25% of the travel time, increase the average speed of vehicles passing through the work zone by 23%, and effectively improve the traffic efficiency in the work zone.

Keywords Freeway work zone Variable speed limi METANET model Control method Traffic bottleneck

0 Introduction

The freeway work zone as the bottleneck area of freeway traffic operation, has closed some lanes due to pavement construction, resulting in frequent speed change and lane change of vehicles, increasing traffic conflicts, easily inducing accidents and sudden drop of traffic capacity, resulting in road congestion. In order to find a reasonable and effective highway control method to alleviate or eliminate the congestion in the bottleneck area, scholars have carried out research from different perspectives and put forward many control schemes[1-7].

As an emerging freeway control method, variable speed limit control has been widely used in freeway traffic control and achieved satisfying effects. Variable speed limit control is to limit the driving speed upstream of the bottleneck area to form a section of high-density and low-flow area upstream to reduce the traffic flow flowing into the bottleneck, keep the traffic flow below the critical value of traffic capacity and prevent the queue from spreading upstream. The core of variable speed limit control method is to determine the reasonable speed limit value. The determination methods of speed limit value include traffic flow model and artificial intelligence model. The artificial intelligence algorithm model relies on massive measured data for training and parameter calibration. The model itself has weak correlation with traffic flow, which is unpredictable, and the solution is complex, so it is difficult to obtain a reasonable speed limit value in practical application[8]. The traffic flow model can truly reflect the traffic situation. By analysing the operation characteristics of traffic flow, a model is established for the traffic flow data according to the reasonable traffic relationship to solve the speed limit value of the road section, and its parameter setting is closely related to the operation of traffic flow. Based on the traffic flow METANET model, this paper constructs a variable speed limit control model suitable for the work zone of multi -lane freeway based on analysing the operation characteristics of traffic flow in the work zone of multi-lane freeway, considering the impact of variable speed limit control on traffic state, and combined with the congestion characteristics of freeway work zone. The prediction model can predict the traffic operation status of each lane in the work zone in advance, avoid congestion and ensure the initiative of variable speed limit control.

1 Principle and Application of Metanet Model

METANET model is a macro traffic flow model. The continuous conservation equation of traffic flow is discretized in time and space by selecting Taylor formula and difference equation, to realize the description of the operation situation change of traffic flow in space-time domain. Its remarkable feature is that it can realize the traffic flow operation modelling of basic sections, diversion areas, work zones and other sections of the freeway, and effectively describe the free flow state, congestion state, steep decline state of traffic capacity. The METANET model takes the prediction of average speed as the core and considers the relationship between the average speeds of upstream and downstream units. The speed parameters at the next period are affected by the traffic conditions such as upstream and downstream speed, density, and driver's expected speed at the current time, which is more convenient to analyse the impact of variable speed limit control[9]; The model can be used for real-time feedback correction, and the expression effect is more accurate.

METANET model divides the freeway main line into m basic sections with consistent road attributes, and describes the operation status of traffic flow in the basic sections. Take section m as an example, take length Δx_m as a unit, road section m is divided into N_m basic units, and each unit $i$contains traffic flow parameters: Traffic volume of inflow (outflow) unit i ($q_{m,i-1}(k)$), traffic flow density ($\rho_{m,i}(k)$), average speed ($v_{m,i}(k)$). Where $T$is the discrete time interval, k is the number of time interval steps, t is the sampling time, $t = KT$.

The METANET model consists of the following basic equations:

The outflow flow of section m in the sampling period k is equal to the product of traffic flow density, speed, and the number of lanes in the unit, i.e.,

$$q_{m,i}(k) = \rho_{m,i}(k) v_{m,i}(k) \lambda_m \tag{1}$$

The unit i density in the sampling period is equal to the sum of the unit density and the change of unit density in the previous time interval,

$$\rho_{m,i}(k+1) = \rho_{m,i}(k) + \frac{T}{\Delta x_m \lambda_m}[q_{m,i-1}(k) - q_{m,i}(k)] \tag{2}$$

The speed of vehicles onfreeway is related to driver characteristics, traffic characteristics and environment, and its change is more complex. The driver mainly depends on the distance from the front traffic flow (traffic flow density) to adjust the speed, and the driver's response characteristics are delayed, so drivers can't respond to the real-time state change of traffic in time. Moreover, the driver acts after reaction, and the vehicle also needs a certain speed adjustment time. Therefore, it is assumed that the change of vehicle speed lags the change of traffic density at the front Δx as τ, constructing a description model of the relationship between the average speed of unit road section, density parameters and expected speed.

$$v_{m,i}(k+1) = v_{m,i}(k) + \frac{T}{\tau}\{V[\rho_{m,i}(k)] - v_{m,i}(k)\} + \frac{T}{\Delta x_m}[v_{m,i-1}(k) - v_{m,i}(k)]v_{m,i}(k) - \frac{\nu T}{\Delta x_m \tau}\frac{\rho_{m,i-1}(k) - \rho_{m,i}(k)}{\rho_{m,i}(k) + \kappa} \tag{3}$$

In the METANET model, the dynamic speed value in the K + 1 sampling interval is equal to the sum of the difference between the average vehicle speed and the driver's expected speed in the K sampling interval, the speed change caused by traffic volume change and the impact of traffic flow density on the driver's speech speed:

$$V[\rho_{m,i}(k)] = v_{f,m} \exp\left[-\frac{1}{\alpha_m}\left(\frac{\rho_{m,i}(k)}{\rho_{c,m}}\right)^{\alpha_m}\right] \tag{4}$$

Where, $v_{f,m}$ is the expected speed value at $t = kT$ time. Expected speed refers to the speed when the traffic flow is in a stable state, which reflects the driver's expectation of traffic stability during driving, and can be expressed by the statistical relationship equation between speed and density

2 Multi-lane Metanet Model Under Variable Speed Limit Control

METANET is a macro traffic flow model, concentrating on the division of unit sections and the above traffic parameter relationship equations. Under variable speed limit control, due to the lane management measures taken by multi-lane freeway, the speed limit values of each lane are different, so it is necessary to improve the model based on lane, and further consider the improvement of variable speed limit on flow equation and steady-state speed density equation. There are differences in vehicle types and legal speed limit values of each lane of multi-lane freeway, and the traffic operation state and traffic flow parameters of each lane are also different in practical operation. However, the traditional METANET model describes the traffic operation state of the whole section, which can't reflect the characteristics of each lane under multi-lane conditions, it is necessary to refine the model, introducing lane indicator variables j ($j \in (1,2,3\cdots)$).

According to the traditional METANET model, the traffic, density, and speed models are extended based on lane, if vehicles only change lanes on adjacent lanes, there is no lane change, the amount of lane change $q_{i,j,\text{change}}(k)$ is introduced, the average speed equation is extended to lane-based speed change,

$$\rho_{m,i,j}(k+1) = \rho_{m,i,j}(k) + \frac{T}{\Delta x_m}[q_{m,i-1,j}(k) - q_{m,i,j}(k) + q_{i,j,\text{change}}(k)] \quad (5)$$

$$v_{m,i,j}(k+1) = v_{m,i,j}(k) + \frac{T}{\tau}\{V[\rho_{m,i,j}(k)] - v_{m,i,j}(k)\} + \frac{T}{\Delta x_m}[v_{m,i-1,j}(k) - v_{m,i,j}(k)]v_{m,i,j}(k) - \frac{\nu T}{\Delta x_m \tau}\frac{\rho_{m,i+1,j}(k) - \rho_{m,i,j}(k)}{\rho_{m,i,j}(k) + \kappa} \quad (6)$$

For multi-lane freeway, the traffic volume and vehicle type distribution of each lane and the composition of traffic flow of the lane are different, resulting in the differences of traffic operation characteristics of each lane under the same state. Therefore, there are some differences in the steady-state value of speed, the steady-state speed of lane is stable can be described as,

$$V[\rho_{m,i,j}(k)] = v_{f,m,i,j}\exp\left[-\frac{1}{\alpha_{m,j}}\left(\frac{\rho_{m,i,j}(k)}{\rho_{c,m,i,j}}\right)^{\alpha_{m,j}}\right] \quad (7)$$

Because the variable speed limit control urges the driver to change the speed artificially, the existing steady-state speed equation can't better describe the expected speed change under the changing speed limit value, so it needs to be improved. When the road traffic is in the free flow state, the driver expects the speed to be higher than the speed limit, but due to the limit of the speed limit, the driver can only drive the vehicle at the limited speed; When the road density is greater than the critical density, the mutual interference between vehicles is serious, and the driver's expected speed is lower than the speed limit. Therefore, the empirical expected speed of the driver and the minimum expected speed under speed limit conditions can be taken as the speed density relationship under speed limit conditions, and the obedience rate of driver correlation coefficient β is introduced.

$$V[\rho_{m,i}(k)] = \min\left(v_{f,m}\exp\left[-\frac{1}{\alpha_m}\left(\frac{\rho_{m,i}(k)}{\rho_{c,m}}\right)^{\alpha_m}\right],(1+\beta)V_{VSL,i}(k)\right) \quad (8)$$

In addition, under variable speed limit control, the speed limit value is a spatiotemporal variable, which changes with time and space. The speed limit value will affect the free flow speed, density, and model parameters of the lane. Carlson[10] better described the impact of variable speed limit control on other traffic flow parameters in their research. The paper introduces the coefficient of variable speed limit proportion to indicates the application of variable speed limit.

$$R_i(k)=\frac{V_{VSL,i}(k)}{V_{VSL,i,max}} \tag{9}$$

$$v'_{f,m}(k)=R_i(k)v_{f,m}(k) \tag{10}$$

$$\rho'_{c,m}(k)=\rho_{c,m}[1+C_i(1-R_i(k))] \tag{11}$$

The above equations are used to describe the operation state of traffic flow under variable speed limit control. At the same time, the three traffic parameters of any period and section can be obtained, and the offline or online parameter acquisition can becollected.

3 Optimal Control Model of Variable Speed Limit in Work Zone of Multi-lane Freeway

When the upstream flow of the bottleneck section is greater than Q_m, the maximum traffic volume of the bottleneck section, the bottleneck section is activated. At this time, queuing will occur in the upstream of the bottleneck section, and the traffic state in the bottleneck area will deteriorate. In order to reduce the vehicle arrival rate and alleviate the congestion in the bottleneck area, speed limit sections should be set in the upstream of the bottleneck.

Freeway has the characteristics of high service level, high traffic volume and high speed. Generally, the total travel time or total capacity of vehicles in the bottleneck area of freeway is used as the variable speed limit control target. For example, taking the shortest total travel time as the optimization control target, the bottleneck area maintains low density and high speed. When the flow is low, the control effect is obvious; When the flow increases greatly, there will be a serious queuing phenomenon in the upstream of the control area. If the control goal is to increase the total traffic volume, the road traffic flow operates at low speed and high density, and the road traffic volume is close to its capacity to the greatest extent, which can reduce queuing, but will reduce the stability of road traffic flow.

Previous studies haverevealed that static speed limit control can't effectively alleviate the traffic problems in the bottleneck area. Based on the analysis of the traffic operation characteristics in the bottleneck area of the freeway work zone, the traffic flow state prediction model under the condition of multi-lane is determined. In order to prevent and alleviate the congestion in the work zone, this paper mainly aims to improve the traffic efficiency in the work zone of multi-lane freeway. In order to balance the low-speed driving caused by less restrictions caused by the total traffic time and the total traffic volume, the total travel time and the total traffic volume are comprehensively selected as the control indexes, and a variable speed limit control model in the bottleneck section with the maximum traffic volume and the minimum travel time as the comprehensive control objectives is proposed with the speed limit of each lane.

Total Travel Time (TTT):

$$TTT=\sum_i\sum_j\sum_k \Delta x_m\rho_{i,j}(k)T \tag{12}$$

The total traffic capacity TTC is the sum of the traffic volume in each time period of each lane of each unit:

$$TTC=\sum_i\sum_j\sum_k \Delta x_m\rho_{i,j}(k)v_{i,j}(k) \tag{13}$$

Therefore, the control objective of variable speed limitmethod shall be the minimum total travel time and the maximum total traffic volume as the objective function:

$$\min \quad TOTAL=C_{TTT}TTT-C_{TTC}TTC \tag{14}$$

In order to ensure the rationality and effectiveness of variable speed limitmethod, it is necessary to set up constraints based on variable speed limit control

(1) Maximum speed constraint

The speed limit value under the variable speed limit control in the freeway work zone shall not exceed the upper limit of the fixed speed limit value of the lane to ensure driving safety

$$V_{VSL,i,j}(k)\leqslant V_{\max,j}$$

For multi-lane highways, according to the lane management method, the maximum speed limit value of the inner lane should be greater than that of the outer lane

$$V_{VSL,1},V_{VSL,2}\leqslant 120\text{km/h},V_{VSL,3},V_{VSL,4}\leqslant 100\text{km/h}$$

(2) Minimum speed constraint

In order to ensure the efficient and fast traffic of the freeway, the speed limit value in the freeway work zone shall be greater than the minimum value of the fixed speed limit value of the lane. Generally, the minimum speed limit value of the freeway is 60km/h,

$$V_{VSL,i,j}(k) \geqslant V_{\min,j}$$

(3) Lane speed limit difference constraint

As the multi-lane Freeway adopts the vehicle management method of separated lanes, the speed limit values of each lane are different, so the speed limit value of the outer lane shall not be greater than the speed limit value of the inner lane and shall be less than the threshold value. For example, there are two-way six lane Freeway

$$V_{VSL,1} \geqslant V_{VSL,2} \geqslant V_{VSL,3}$$

$$|V_{VSL,i,j} - V_{VSL,i,j+1}| \leqslant 20\text{km/h}$$

(4) Difference of speed limit value between adjacent time and adjacent units

Considering the driver's adaptability to the change of speed limit and improving the implementation effect and safety of dynamic speed limitmethod, the difference of speed limit value between adjacent time intervals and adjacent units shall be controlled below the threshold. According to the existing research results, the difference of speed limit value is usually 10km / h, and the maximum difference threshold is usually 20km / h.

$$|V_{VSL,i,j} - V_{VSL,i+1,j}| \leqslant 20\text{km/h}$$

The variable speed limit optimization controlmethod in the work zone of multi-lane freeway based on METANET traffic flow prediction model proposed in this paper is shown in Fig. 1.

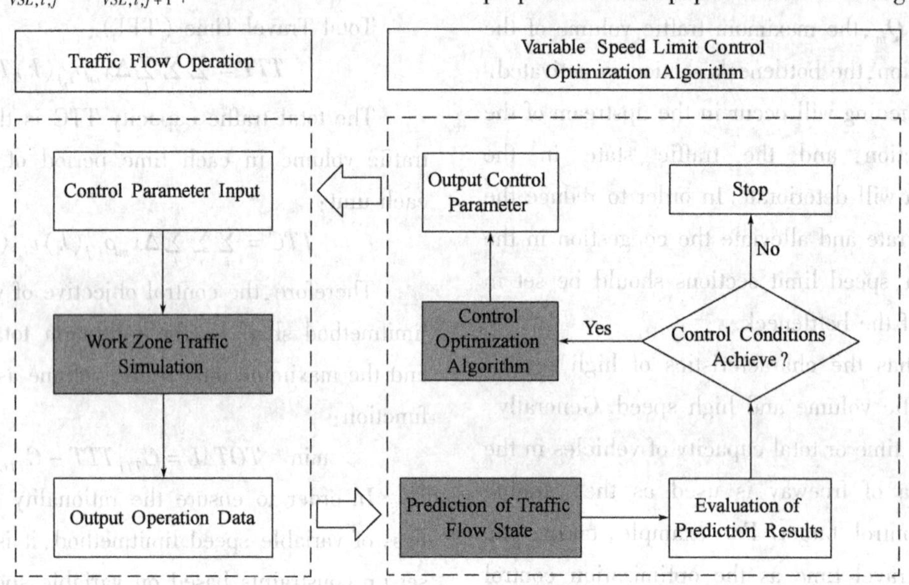

Fig. 1　Variable Speed Limit Control Method Flow Chart

4　Example Analysis of Variable Speed Limit Control in Construction Area of Multi-lane Freeway

4.1　Simulation scheme design

A section ofJingde Freeway in Hebei Province is selected as the simulation instance. This section is a two-way six lane section. According to the layout specification of freeway work zone and the requirements of variable speed limit control, the length of the work zone is 200m. The study area is 2000m downstream of the bottleneck of the work zone, which is divided into four units in 500 meters. The overview of the simulation section in the work zone is shown in Fig. 2.

The VISSIM simulation software is calibrated according to the actual data collected from thefreeway. The proportion of passenger vehicles and trucks is set at 75% and 25%, the bottleneck capacity in the work zone is 3300veh / h, the fixed speed limit in the work zone is 60km / h, and the parameter settings of each lane are shown in Tab. 1.

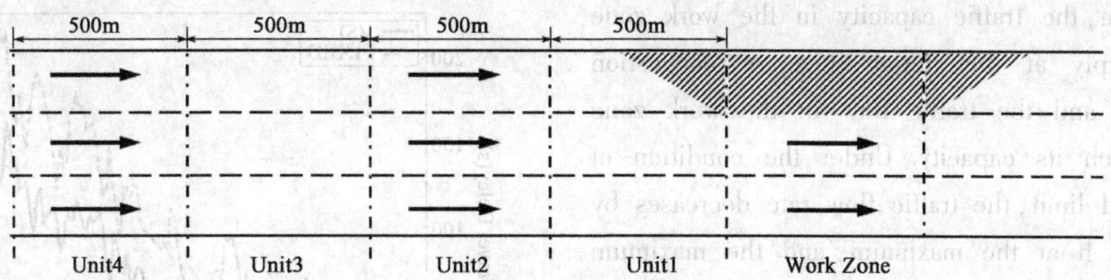

Fig. 2 Schematic Diagram of Simulation Section in Work Zone

Section Foundation Parameters Tab. 1

	Free flow speed(km/h)	Critical density(veh/km)	Fixed speed limit(km/h)
Lane1	125	30	100 ~ 120
Lane2	120	25	90 ~ 120
Lane3	100	22	60 ~ 100

Referring to the existing research results, the parameters of multi-lane METANET prediction model is calibrated. The macro parameters α, τ and κ in METANET model are related to the characteristics of road sections and belong to static parameters. α is the fitting coefficient of the expectation equation, τ is the driver's response time constant to speed, κ is the model compensation coefficient set to avoid too small density value, δ is the characterization of sensitivity between steady-state speed and road section density, the parameters of each lane are shown in Tab. 2.

Calibration of Model Parameter Tab. 2

	α	τ	κ	δ
Lane1	2.22	24.80	60.00	40.00
Lane2	2.95	20.10	60.00	40.00
Lane3	4.00	13.84	60.00	40.00

The simulation time is set as 6000s, of which the first 1200s is the preparation time to stabilize the traffic flow. The sampling time interval is set as 30s and the control cycle is 60s. In order to balance the influence of sub objective functions of different dimensions on the objective function, the coefficients of TTT model and TTC model are set as $C_{TTT} = 2.5$, $C_{TTV} = 1.0$.

4.2 Analysis of Simulation Results

Through simulation, the traffic flow parameter data of the simulated section in the freeway work zone under static speed limit conditions and variable speed limit conditions are compared. The traffic conditions and queuing conditions of the bottleneck section in the work zone under the two speed limit conditions are shown in Fig. 3 ~ Fig. 7.

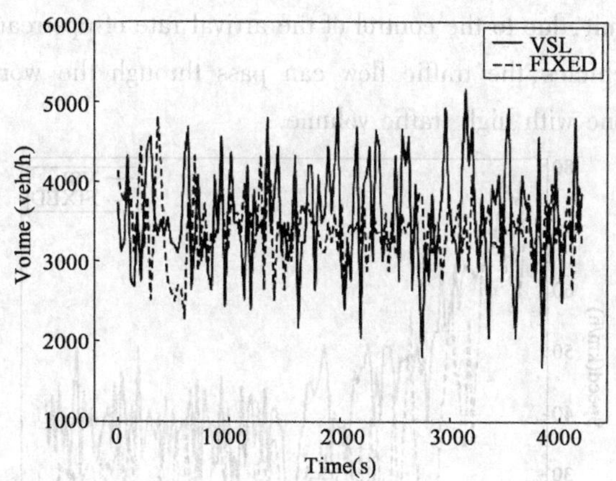

Fig. 3 Comparison of Traffic Volume in Work Zone

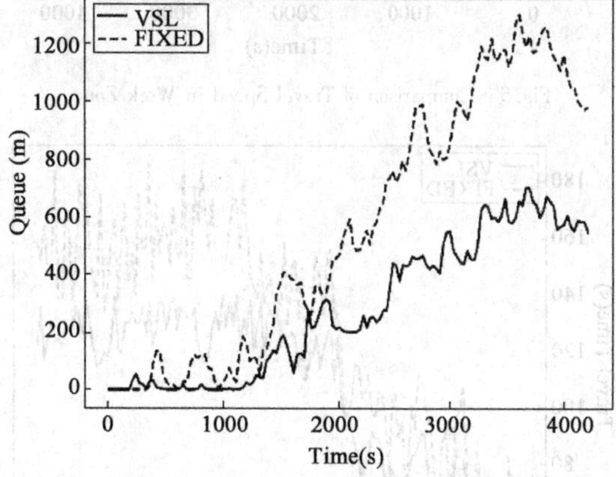

Fig. 4 Comparison of Vehicle Queue Length in Work Zone

As can be seen from Fig. 3, with the increase of input flow, the bottleneck in thework zone begins to generate congestion around 300 seconds. Due to the interference of lane change caused by vehicle deceleration, the traffic capacity in the work zone drops sharply at the initial stage of congestion generation, and the traffic flow in the work zone cannot reach its capacity. Under the condition of static speed limit, the traffic flow rate decreases by 1800veh / h at the maximum, and the maximum decline reaches 35%; Under the condition of variable speed limit, the maximum reduction of traffic flow rate is 1200veh / h, and the maximum reduction is 26%. Compared with the static speed limit scheme, the use of variable speed limit can still maintain a certain traffic capacity and prevent excessive sudden reduction. After the congestion is formed, the traffic flow through the work zone under the static speed limit is maintained at about the capacity of the work zone, about 3300veh / h. under the dynamic speed limit, due to the control of the arrival rate of upstream vehicles, the traffic flow can pass through the work zone with high traffic volume.

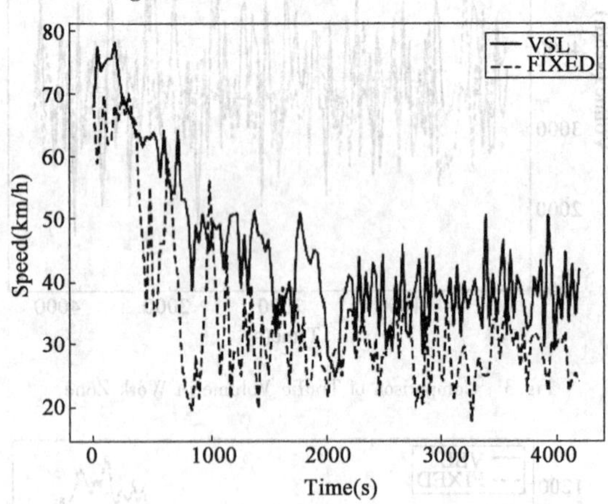

Fig. 5 Comparison of Travel Speed in Work Zone

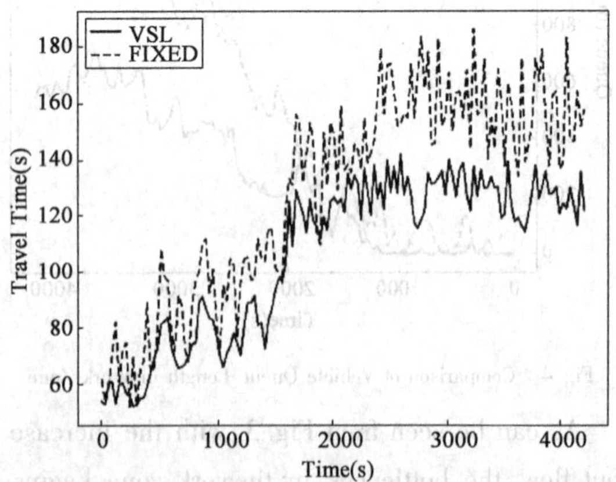

Fig. 6 Comparison of Travel Time in Work Zone

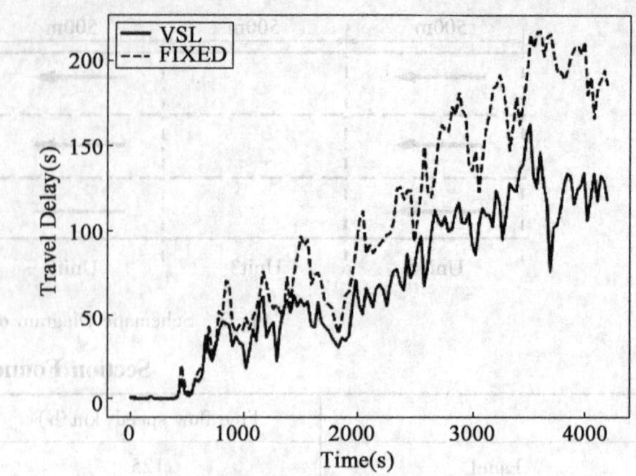

Fig. 7 Comparison of Travel Delay in Work Zone

From Fig. 4 ~ Fig. 7, under the static speed limit condition, due to the failure to control the arrival traffic flow, the congestion in the upstream lane of the work zone tends to be serious, and the traffic flow queue spreads upstream at a faster speed. The maximum queue length during the experiment can reach 1200 meters. Under the condition of dynamic speed limit control, the queuing in the work zone is relatively late, and the propagation speed slows down. The maximum queuing length is about 500m. Under the condition of static speed limit, the queue behind the work zone is serious, the vehicle speed decreases, the travel time is significantly increased compared with the dynamic speed limit method, and the vehicle delay increases. Under the condition of static speed limit, the average travel time through the work zone reaches 160S, the average speed is only 27km/h, and the vehicle traffic delay reaches 200 seconds. If the dynamic speed limit method is adopted, the average travel time is about 120s, which can save 25% of the traffic time. The average speed of vehicles passing through the work zone is increased to 35km/h, an increase of 23%, and the average traffic delay of vehicles is reduced to 140s, a decrease of 30%.

5 Conclusions

This paper studies the traffic bottleneck variable speed limitmethod and implementation effect in the work zone of multi-lane freeway. Aiming at the congestion problem in the work zone of multi-lane freeway at high traffic flow, the improved METANET model under multi-lane conditions is applied to the lane-level traffic flow prediction and management under the lane management method. Through the variable speed limit control model of freeway, the input flow into the work zone is adjusted to prevent the steep drop of traffic capacity, and a satisfying control effect is obtained. Through the simulation experiment, compared with the static speed limit condition, under the condition of applying the variable speed limit control method, the maximum traffic volume decreases less in peak hours, which can save 25% of the traffic time. The average speed of vehicles passing through the work zone increases by 23% and the decrease in traffic delay reaches 30%.

The variable speed limit management method proposed in this paper is applicable to the bottleneck management of freeway work zone under multi-lane conditions, but this paper only studies the implementation effect of the method for the construction of inner lane. In the future, it will study the cooperative control effect of work zone arranged in various forms and other strategies.

6 Acknowledgements

Thi sstudy was sponsored by the National Natural Science Foundation of China (51925801), National key R&D Program (2020yfb1600500), National Natural Science Foundation of China (52172343). The authors would like to thank the editor and the reviewers for their constructive comments and valuable suggestions to improve the quality of the article.

References

[1] Raddaoui O, Ahmed M M, Gaweesh S M. Assessment of the effectiveness of connected vehicle weather and work zone warnings in improving truck driver safety [J]. IATSS research, 2020, 44(3), 230-237.

[2] Van Leeuwen B. The impact of connected and automated vehicles on highway work zone traffic efficiency and safety: A simulation study [D]. Delft University of Technology, 2020.

[3] Abdulsattar H, Mostafizi A, Wang H. Surrogate safety assessment of work zone rear-end collisions agent-based modeling framework [J]. Journal of Transportation Engineering, Part A: Systems, 2018, 144(8): 04018038.

[4] Li Z, Jin M, Liu P, et al. Evaluation of impact variable speed limits on improving traffic efficiency on freeways [J]. Journal of Jilin University, 2013, 43, 1204-1209.

[5] Jiao Y, Yanyong G, Lei W. A Study of vehicle speed limit in freeway work zone [J]. China Safety Science Journal, 2014, 4(06): 74-79.

[6] Rista E, Barrette T, Hamzeie R, et al. Work zone safety performance: Comparison of alternative traffic control strategies [J]. Transportation Research Record, 2017, 2617(1), 87-93.

[7] Ge H, Xia R, Sun H, et al. Construction and simulation of rear-end conflicts recognition model based on improved TTC algorithm [J]. IEEE Access, 2019, 134763-134771.

[8] Zhu S, Zou H, et al. Traffic conflict model for confluence section in highway work zone [J]. Journal of Harbin Institute of Technology, 2020, 52(09): 70-76.

[9] Ma M, Yang Q, et al. A method of variable speed limit control for traffic flow on freeway mainline [J]. Journal of Harbin Institute of Technology, 2015, 47(09): 107-111.

[10] Carlson R C, Papamichail I, Papageorgiou M. Local Feedback-Based Mainstream Traffic Flow Control on Motorways Using Variable Speed Limits [J]. IEEE Transactions on Intelligent Transportation Systems, 12 (4): 1261-1276.

高速公路立交分流区的主线速度研究

张兴林*
(长安大学公路学院)

摘　要　高速公路立交分流区是立交区通行能力的瓶颈和立交区安全的薄弱点,立交路段的交通流状态影响着整个高速公路的交通安全与通行效率。本文为研究高速公路立交分流区的主线速度,对西安绕城高速曲江立交分流区进行调研,通过实地实验获得了大量的调研数据。对比国内外规范和研究,使用交通量、分流比、重车混入率作为反映交通流状态的基本指标,用主线平均速度来表征主线速度特性,使用Origin软件对数据进行处理和分析。结果表明:在低交通量下,分流比、重车混入率对主线速度影响不大,随着交通量的增加,分流比、重车混入率对主线速度的影响加剧。相关研究结论对于缓解分流区的瓶颈、提高交通安全性、保证互通立体交叉路口的通行能力和服务水平有着十分重要的意义。

关键词　高速公路分流区　通行效率　数理统计　主线速度　重车混入率

0　引言

高速公路立交分流区是立交区通行能力的瓶颈和立交区安全的薄弱点,立交路段的交通流状态影响着整个高速公路的交通安全与通行效率。近年来,高速公路立交分流区的拥堵现象越来越常见,拥堵问题给人们的出行带来极大的负担,不仅浪费了出行者的时间,也影响人们的生活质量。同时,在拥堵过程中,由于燃油时间的持续性,将带来更高的油耗、排烟,这不仅浪费了资源,还污染了空气,不利于生态的可持续发展。此外,交通拥堵还可能会引发一系列的交通事故,给人们的生命和财产也带来损失。因此,高速公路的立交区分流区拥堵已经成为我国社会发展中亟须解决的问题。

目前,高速公路立交分流区拥堵问题已经引起相关学者、交通从业者和道路管理部门甚至整个社会层面的广泛关注,许多学者对此都已经开展了一系列的研究,取得了不错的成果。大量学者运用交通流的理论与方法进行拥堵的研究分析[1],这些理论大部分将交通流划分为拥挤和非拥挤两种状态,并设置了一个临界密度值,认为交通流中密度超过该临界值时,便会形成拥堵。Guo等[2]针对高速公路出口匝道拥堵现象,通过宏观和微观模拟验证了分析结果,并研究了高速公路系统总需求、总流入、总出口和车辆数量之间的一般关系。高学辉等[3]学者研究发现,当交通量较大时,货车比例的增加会导致车流平均速度快速降低、道路通行能力的下降,进而产生拥堵;张喆康[4]从分流区的运行特性入手,结合实际调查数据,分析了分流区交通流运行特性,基于移动瓶颈理论解释了货车对分流区交通流的影响。综上所述,立交分流区的不同交通流状态(交通量、分流比、重车混入率)会影响着立交分流区通行效率,导致立交分流区主线速度等交通流参数发生变化。因此,若能得出不同交通状态对立交分流区的主线速度影响程度,对于解决分流影响区的交通实际问题,并缓解分流区的瓶颈,提高交通安全性,保证互通立体交叉的通行能力和服务水平有着十分重要的意义。

本文以西安绕城高速曲江立交实地收集的交通数据为基础,对立交分流区分流比和重车混入率进行区段划分,选取主线平均速度作为交通流参数,分析交通量、分流比、重车混入率这三个指标对高速公路分流区主线速度的影响,为高速公路分流区交通管理与控制提供理论依据和技术支持。

1　数据采集与处理

1.1　数据采集地点及方式

正确选择观测点的主要目的在于能够得到正确反映互通立交交通流特性的数据。观测点的选择必须以数据后期分析要求为依据,选点应具有代表性。

调查点的选择主要有以下几个原则:

(1)一般情况下,应选择常见立交形式,视野良好,没有遮挡物,并适合雷达测速枪测速;

(2)观测地点应有较少的外界干扰,即保证在实验时不受意外事件影响,保证实验数据的确定性;

(3)交通量及分流交通量波动范围应足够大,尽可能观测分流区的多种情况下交通流状态及通行效率。

高速公路的分流区主要分为两种,分别是主线交通分流的上游分流区、主线与出口匝道相连接的匝道分流区,相对而言,匝道分流区在高速公路上较为多见,交通运行状态更为复杂,更容易发生交通事故,当高速公路出口匝道下游段与地面段连接部分发生交通拥堵时,车辆队列可能由出口匝道路段向上游蔓延,让分流区成为高速公路交通运行的瓶颈路段,故本文所分析的高速公路立交分流区是指高速公路立交匝道出口与公路主线相交附近的一部分区域,不讨论主线分流的情况不讨论。

根据美国《公路通行能力手册》对高速公路各组成部分的划分,高速公路分流影响区被定义为:匝道从主线分流,出口匝道与主线连接处上游450m内、包含减速车道以及主线上第1、第2车道在内的区域。这里所定义的分流区影响范围在对高速公路各级服务水平等级下大部分车辆运行都受到分流行为的影响,即这里定义的影响区范围和高速公路的服务水平无关。而分流区的定义在本质上是不同于分流影响区的,分流区是指从出口匝道和主线连接处到主线上游450m内、含所有车道的区域。本文主要研究的是中高交通量下分流区的主线速度,在中高交通量情况下,分流区交通流会处于稳定流或拥挤流,存在小部分车辆从最内侧车道换道至最外侧的现象,由于交通量较大,车与车之间的相互影响会变大,这种情况会对主线交通流产生一定的影响,故需要同时考虑三个车道的车速情况。基于以上原则和定义,对西安绕城高速上的立交桥不断实地勘测,最后选取曲江立交桥主线东行方向分流区为实验地点,于人行天桥上进行数据采集。

2021年9月至10月,在西安绕城高速曲江立交分流区进行多次实地实验。在现场数据采集时,实验人员使用计数器来获取主线交通量、分流交通量等数据,用雷达测速枪获取受影响的主线车辆速度。采用秒表计时,国内外学者在研究交通流的时候,通常以15min作为统计间隔[5]。荣建[6]研究发现,采用15min和5min的统计间隔,在相同的流量下,不论是速度、密度的均值,还是出现频率最高的速度、密度值都没有明显的差异,故将统计间隔控制在5~15min是较为合适的。所以,在统计开始后,实验过程中如观察到交通流状态发生较大的变化(特别是前后速度相差较大),即结束此段测量,否则在15min时终止统计。统计间隔时间最少是5min,否则排除这一样本,这样才能保证测得数据的准确性、完整性。实验观测地点如图1所示。

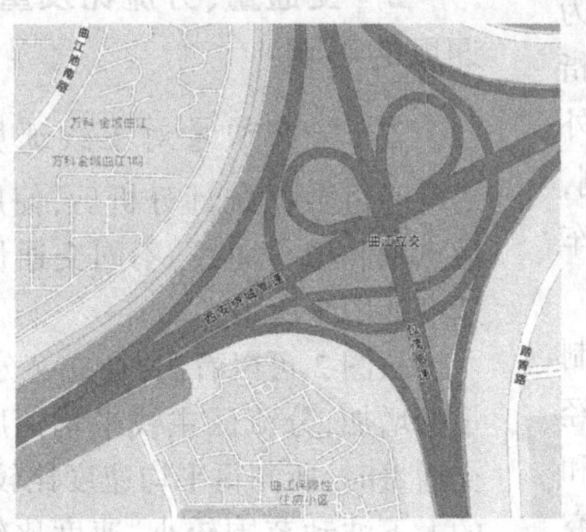

图1 现场调查

1.2 指标选取及数据的预处理

为了更加明确立交分流区交通流状态对主线速度的影响,本研究选择交通量、分流比和重车混入率等作为交通流状态指标。在实验过程中,可能存在统计间隔不同的数据,为了便于后期进行数据分析,需要对所测得的数据进行统一。在交通流分析过程中通常以流率作为自变量,即当量小时交通量,故需要将所测到每条数据中的交通量换算成当量小时流率[7]，对应的其他数据也应该进行等量换算。同时对收集到的自然交通量数据，需要对不同的车型进行当量折算，根据《公路工程技术标准》将车辆分型分为四类，分别是小客车、中型车、大型车、汽车列车。具体折算系数见表1。

各汽车代表车型及车辆折算系数　　表1

汽车代表车型	车辆折算系数	说　明
小客车	1.0	座位≤19 座的客车和载质量≤2t 的货车
中型车	1.5	座位 >19 座的客车和 2t < 载质量≤7t 的货车
大型车	2.5	7t < 载质量≤20t 的货车
汽车列车	4.0	载质量 >20t 的货车

由于分流车辆的存在，相较于高速公路基本路段，立交分流区的交通状态更为复杂。在一定交通量情况下，随着分流的车辆增多，分流车辆与正常行驶的车辆产生的冲突情况会越多，立交分流区的交通流状态会越发的不稳定，可能会对整个立交分流区的行驶速度产生影响，影响整个通行效率。所以，本研究选择分流比作为立交分流区交通状态的一个指标，同时将分流比定义为从主线分流、进入出口匝道的交通量与分流区主线交通量的比例。

在立交分流区，有分流任务的驾驶人为了能够顺利进入出口匝道，一般都会提前换道至最外侧车道。一般来说，载重汽车都是在高速公路的最外侧车道行驶，但是载重汽车的行驶速度慢，小客车的速度快，当重车较多的时候，沿着主线正常行驶的载重汽车会压低最外侧车道这股车流的速度，可能会对后面已经提前换道至最外侧车道的分流车辆的速度产生影响，严重的时候会在最外侧车道形成排队。故本研究选择重车混入率作为立交分流区交通状态的另一个指标。本研究所指的重车混入率是除客车和载质量小于 2t 的货车外其他货车在立交分流区车辆总数中所占的比例，即两轴及以上平车、自卸车、牵引车、箱车、半挂车等货车在分流区车辆总数中所占的比例[8]。

行车速度既是公路规划车中的一项重要控制指标，又是车辆运营效率的一项重要评价指标，经常作为交通管制的依据，反映了道路通行能力和车辆运行状况。在对交通流速度参数的相关研究中，一般有 V85、V50、V15、平均速度等等特征速度指标。V85 一般可以反映交通流高速运行车辆特别是小客车的速度特征；V15 可了解交通流低速运行车辆特别是重型车的速度特征，高速管理部门通常以 V15 作为最低限制速度的设置依据；在车流速度符合正态分布的情况下，V50 可以视为交通流平均速度，它和平均速度都反映驾驶人最关注的运行效率问题；本文主要研究立交分流区的效率问题，故选择平均速度作为研究指标。一般用时间平均速度和空间平均速度来表征交通流平均速度。其中，时间平均速度指的是交通流经过特定断面时的平均速度，而空间平均速度指的是某一时刻路段上所有车辆的平均速度。在进行交通流和通行能力的相关研究中，通常采用空间平均速度作为研究指标，实验中雷达测速仪获取的速度是地点车速，地点速度的算术平均值就是时间平均速度，由时间平均速度推算空间平均速度的公式如下[9]：

$$\bar{v}_s = \bar{v}_t - \frac{\sigma_t^2}{\bar{v}_t} \tag{1}$$

式中：$\bar{v}_s$——空间平均速度；

$\bar{v}_t$——时间平均速度；

σ_t——时间平均速度的标准差。

2　交通量、分流比及重车混入率对主线速度的影响

2.1　交通量对主线速度的影响

经过数据统计分析后，使用 Origin 软件绘制散点图和拟合曲线，不同交通量情况下空间平均速度如图 2 所示。

从图 2 可以看出，在立交分流区内，随着交通量的增加，分流区主线平均速度逐渐下降。在低交通量时，所测得平均速度比较贴近拟合线，速度的上下波动范围较小，速度比较集中。当交通量超过 4000pcu/h 之后，平均速度波动呈现出更加离散与混乱的状态，尤其是交通量在 5000pcu/h 左右时，最大的速度差距可以达到 23km/h，而在低交通量时，平均速度差只是个位数。结合线性拟合可以看出，速度与交通量具有显著的相关性，

这说明交通量对主线速度的影响比较大,同时随着交通量的增加,可能存在一些除了交通量之外的因素对主线平均速度产生了不能忽视的影响。

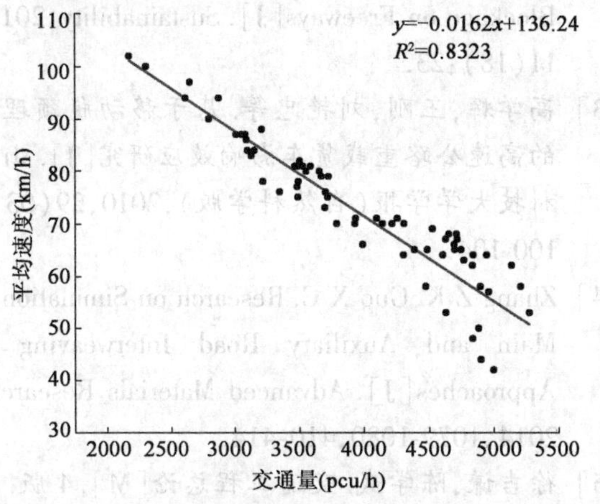

图2 主线平均速度与交通量关系图

2.2 分流比对主线速度的影响

考虑到重车的混入可能会对主线速度造成影响,故选取重车混入率10%以下的速度数据进行研究。由于实验条件的限制和实验数据的有限,将分流比划分为3部分,分别是20%~30%、30%~40%、40%~60%。对数据统计分析后,使用Origin软件绘制散点图和拟合曲线,不同分流比情况下的主线速度与交通量之间关系如图3所示。

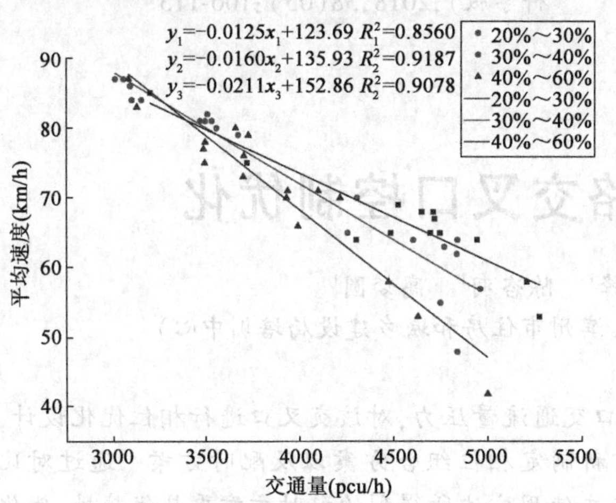

图3 不同分流比情况下的主线平均速度与交通量关系图

从图3可以看出,在同一分流比范围内,随着交通量的增加,分流区主线平均速度逐渐下降。这三条拟合直线的斜率分别是-0.0125、-0.0160、-0.0211,可以看出,在高分流比的情况下,拟合直线斜率的绝对值最大,说明此时交通量对速度的影响较大,而在低分流比情况下,速度随交通量下降的慢一些。此外,在交通量较低的情况下,三种不同分流比条件下速度差异较小,说明此时分流比对速度的影响不大,主要受交通量的影响。原因可能是分流区交通量较少,各车道的车与车间隙较大,能给分流车辆提供足够的换道间隙,此时车与车之间的干扰较小,对交通流运行状况影响不大。而在高交通量时,各车道的车辆间隙较小,驾驶人较难找到合适的换道间隙,此时分流车辆的增多导致车辆之间的干扰变大,对交通流运行状况产生较大影响,导致不同分流比间的速度差异较大。总之,在低交通量下,分流比对速度影响不大,随着交通量的增加,分流比对主线速度的影响加剧。

2.3 重车混入率对主线速度的影响

对数据统计分析后,使用Origin软件绘制散点图和拟合曲线,不同重车混入率情况下的主线速度与交通量之间关系如图4所示。

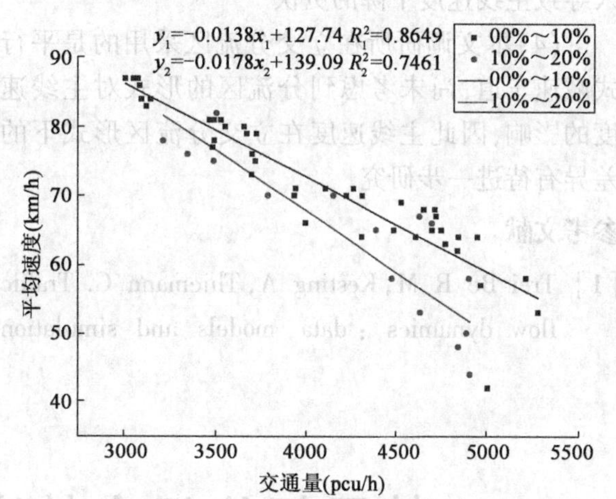

图4 不同重车混入率情况下的主线速度与交通量关系图

从图4可以看出,在同一重车混入率范围内,随着交通量的增加,分流区主线平均速度逐渐下降。这两条拟合直线的斜率分别是-0.0138、-0.0178,可以看出,在重车混入率为10%~20%情况下,拟合直线斜率的绝对值最大,说明此时交通量对速度的影响较大,而在低重车混入率情况下,速度随交通量下降的慢一些。同时可以看出,重车比例对整体运行效率的影响还是比较大的。不论交通量大小,重车混入率的增加都会使分流区平均速度下降。在交通量较低的情况下,不同重车混入率之间的速度差异较小,小客车可以通过超车来弥补货车造成的影响,一定程度上能够减少主线速度的降低。随着交通量增加,超车发生的可能越来越低,导致随着重车混入率的增加,速度下降得更快。

3 结论

本文通过对实地测量的西安绕城高速曲江立交分流区交通流数据的处理与分析,选取主线平均速度作为表征指标,研究了以交通量、分流比、重车混入率作为反映交通流状态的基本指标对高速公路分流区主线速度的影响,结果表明:

(1)交通量对主线速度的影响较大,随着交通量的增加,可能存在一些除了交通量之外的因素对主线平均速度产生了不能忽视的影响。

(2)在低交通量下,分流比对速度影响不大,随着交通量的增加,分流比对主线速度的影响加剧。

(3)无论交通量大小,重车的混入都会导致分流区平均速度的下降。在低交通量下,重车混入率对速度影响不大,随着交通量的增加,重车的混入导致主线速度下降的更快。

(4)本文调研所在立交分流区采用的是平行式减速车道,尚未考虑到分流区的形式对主线速度的影响,因此主线速度在立交分流区形式下的差异有待进一步研究。

参考文献

[1] Trei Be R M, Kesting A, Thiemann C. Traffic flow dynamics : data, models and simulation [M]. Springer,2013.

[2] Guo J Q, Chen X Y, Pang Y Q, et al. Bottlenecks, Shockwave, and Off-Ramp Blockage on Freeways[J]. Sustainability,2019, 11(18):23.

[3] 高学辉,王刚,刘艳忠等.基于移动瓶颈理论的高速公路重载货车影响效应研究[J].山东科技大学学报(自然科学版),2010,29(03):100-104.

[4] Zhang Z K, Guo X C. Research on Simulation of Main and Auxiliary Road Interweaving at Approaches[J]. Advanced Materials Research, 2014,1079-1080,410-414.

[5] 徐吉谦,陈学武.交通工程总论[M].4版.北京:人民交通出版社股份有限公司,2015.

[6] 荣建,常成利,刘小明,等.标定交通流模型时最小统计间隔的选择[J].北京工业大学学报,1999,04):49-55.

[7] 周荣贵.公路通行能力手册[M].北京:人民交通出版社,2017.

[8] 景立竹,李群善,许金良,等.基于v/C比和载重汽车混入率的高速公路基本路段车辆平均行程时间预测模型[J].长安大学学报(自然科学版),2018,38(05):106-113.

基于相位组合的道路交叉口控制优化

王瑞聪[1] 范宜卿[*2] 陈秀锋[1] 陈咨羽[1] 高梦圆[1]

(1.青岛理工大学机械与汽车工程学院;2.滨州市住房和城乡建设局培训中心)

摘 要 为缓解青岛市海尔路—海口路T形交叉口交通流量压力,对该交叉口进行相位优化设计,采用聚类思想的相位组合优化模型,结合渠化设计重新制定相位组合方案以及配时方案。通过对比Webster配时法,改善绿信比的方案。仿真分析表明,本文使用方法所得到的配时方案更具优越性,优化后整体车辆延误改善20%左右,服务水平由D变为C。

关键词 交通工程 控制优化 相位组合 交叉口

0 引言

单点交叉口是城市主要交叉口,当下我国主要采用单路口固定信号控制,平峰时交通流量较少,易造成一定的绿灯时间浪费;高峰时期交通流量增加,绿灯时间分配不均,导致车辆延误增加。

1.基金项目:基金项目:国家自然科学基金(51678320);山东省自然科学基金(ZR2019MG012,ZR2020MG021);山东省重点研发计划(2019GGX101038)。

Webster[1]提出了最早的单点信号交叉口固定配时的优化方法,即 Webster 法。该方法是以车辆平均延误最小为优化目标,受到业内学者的普遍认可。张鹏和常玉林[2]提出了延误-通行能力联合优化配时模型,取得较好仿真结果。Chin 和 Yong 等[3]通过最小延误和通行能力等信号控制参数,以此实现信号配时优化,仿真分析表明该方法能适应交通流的实时变化。张小雨等[4]提出以延误、通行能力、停车次数、车辆尾气排放等因素的多目标模型,实现了良好控制。Gao 等[5]确定了信号配时、排队长度和行驶速度之间的关系,结果显示关系模型的多维优化控制可以显著提高道路的服务水平。Terraza 等[6]通过对每个周期的车辆延迟以及加权车辆和行人延迟,提出了一种信号配时优化方法,适应变化的交通量,最大限度地减少与交叉口相关的进入交叉路口的延迟。

综上所述,诸多学者对单点交叉口信号控制进行了研究,主要是优化周期、绿信比、饱和度等配时参数,而较少涉及相位设计与信号配时的组合优化。海尔路—海口路交叉口由于景区吸引力容易产生较大的交通负荷,且有着特殊的交通流特性。本文针对海尔路—海口路交叉口通行能力较差的现状,采用相位组合优化模型设计配时方案,并且通过 Vissim 仿真,对不同方式的优化方案进行评价。

1 相位组合优化模型

1.1 相位组合原则

相位原则设计一般遵循车流均衡原则和相位放行安全性原则[7],从而实现相位组合内各车流的相对均衡相位并且避免在某个相位内部相互冲突。

同一相位的各进口道交通流量不是固定不变的,可能由于某一进口道流量比较大,另一进口道流量较小,该相位的绿灯时间就得不到充分利用,从而产生绿灯损失[8]。车流到达产生的相位绿灯损失如图 1 所示。

图中 $Q_1(t)$、$Q_2(t)$ 为同一相位两股交通流的单位时间内车辆到达率函数,红灯时间为 R,消散时刻分别为 t_1,t_2,d_k,为车辆延误时间,线段 RA 的斜率为进口道饱和流率 S_j。如果该相位的两股车流都以相同饱和流率通过,都为 S,则经过计算可以得到相位的损失绿灯时间为

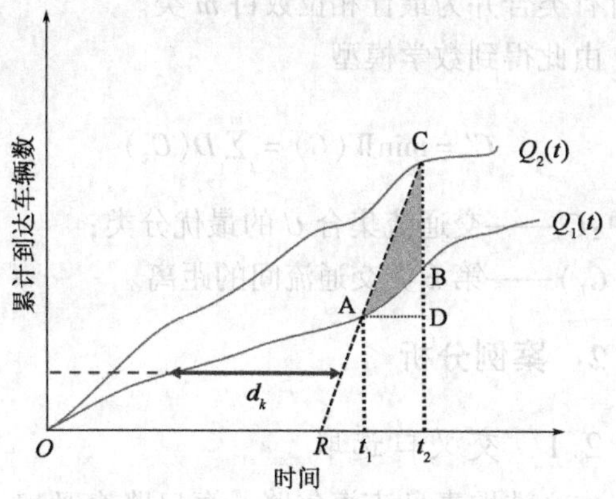

图 1 车流到达产生的相位绿灯时间损失

$$D_i = \frac{R^2 \cdot S_j^2 (Q_1 - Q_2)^2}{2(S_j - Q_2)^2 (S_j - Q_2)^2} \tag{1}$$

当 $Q_1 \approx Q_2$ 时,可知 $D_i = 0$,即

$$\lim_{Q_1 = Q_2} D_i = 0 \tag{2}$$

则周期绿灯损失 L

$$L = \sum_{i=1}^{4} D_i \tag{3}$$

这说明,要使周期内绿灯损失时间最小,交通流量相近的流向应该放在同一相位。

1.2 聚类思想

聚类是根据数据对象自身的属性,用数学方法按照某种相似性或差异性的指标,定量确定不同对象之间的亲疏关系,并按这种亲疏关系程度对样本进行聚类[9]。

当用样本获得数据矩阵后,通过计量相似度的方法来进行样本分类。一般的相似度计量方法有两种:距离度量和相似性度量[10]。为合理描述各交通流对象间差异的大小,本文采用距离度量的方法。对象间距离定义的方法有很多种,采用的度量公式也就各不相同,为真实客观地反应对象间的绝对差异,采用欧氏距离来定义各股交通流之间的距离。

1.3 模型建立

聚类分析的过程可以概括为:特征值确定、计算相似度、分类和检验四个步骤。

若交叉口存在 n 股交通流,最佳的相位数目为 m,将 n 股交通流流向流量比作为特征值;当两股交通流之间的距离小于给定的最大距离值时,将这两个交通流聚为一类,然后计算类与类之间的距离,即通过欧氏距离矩阵来显示两股交通流的流量相似性差异。按照规定组合所有流向,直

至所有类合并为最佳相位数目 m 类。

由此得到数学模型

$$C' = \min W(C) = \sum_{k=1}^{m} D(C_k) \tag{4}$$

式中：C'——交通流集合 U 的最优分类；

$D(C_k)$——第 k 类交通流间的距离。

2　案例分析

2.1　交叉口选取

本文选取青岛市海尔路—海口路交叉口。海口路为东西方向双向四车道，东与东海东路交汇，西与云岭路交汇，北与海尔路交汇，研究区域的交通负荷主要来自于过境交通以及景区和商业用地对吸引的周边居民与游客。风景区现状如图2所示。

2.2　海口路—海尔路交通特性

海口路—海尔路交叉口由信号控制，根据电子卡口数据随机提取旅游旺季(7—8月)某个非工作日时段和工作日时段，绘制车辆数与时间的关系图。由图3a)可知，旅游旺季非工作日车流量与工作日车流量从整体趋势上来看，交叉口总流量与各个方向的流量趋势基本一致。非工作日早上7:00开始各个方向车流量开始急速上升，11:00左右到达第一个峰值，此后各进口流量逐渐达到一个相对波动不大的状态，但总流量仍多次呈现高峰，这与一般城市交叉口早高峰达到最高峰值不同，这是由于景区的吸引力造成车流量不同时段进出交叉口。晚上7点左右车流量开始呈现逐渐下降趋势，由于景区返程时间相对不固定，虽然车流量并未达到新的峰值，但仍保持一定的数量，这与一般城市交叉口晚高峰较为相似。由图3b)可知，工作日车流量从早上7:00开始几乎呈现直线上升，到达第一个峰值，和城市早高峰交通特性较为相似，随后车流量短暂下降14:00左右又开始极速上升，18:00左右到达全天最高峰值，这与城市晚高峰现状有些差异，可能由于景区车流量返程高峰所致。数据证明开放式风景区对于附近交叉口产生了一定的交通影响，造成了差异性。

图2　风景区现状

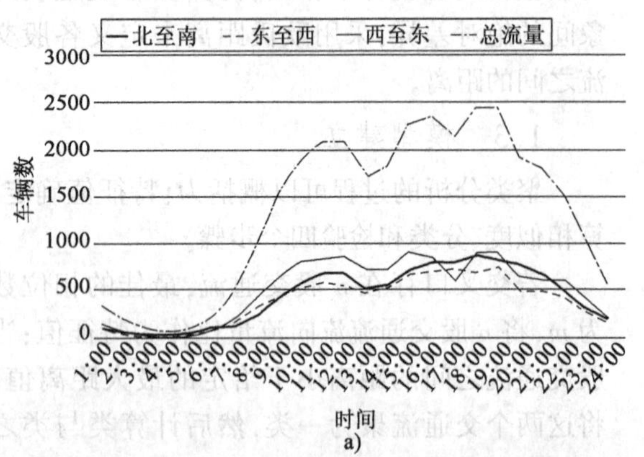

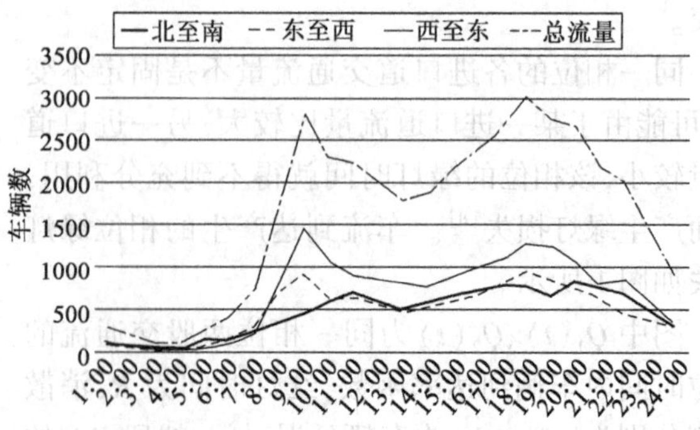

图3　非工作日与工作日交叉口全天流量变化

2.3 信号配时

本文研究的海口路—海尔路T形交叉口，控制方式为两相位定时信号控制，控制方案如图4所示，相位配时方案如图5所示。该交叉口全天采用同样的相位组合进行信号控制，周期时长90s，其中东西向交通流量最长，分配的绿灯时长最大，为56s。北进口道左转车辆放行时间为19s。每一相位黄灯时间为3s，为避免浪费绿灯时间设置第一相位全红时间为6s，第二相位全红时间为3s。不难看出，西进口左转车辆和东进口道直行车辆有冲突，并且左转车辆量较多也加剧了这一冲突。

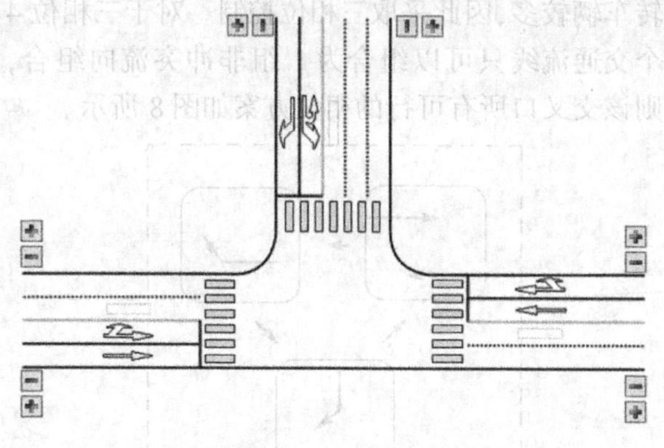

图4 交叉口现状

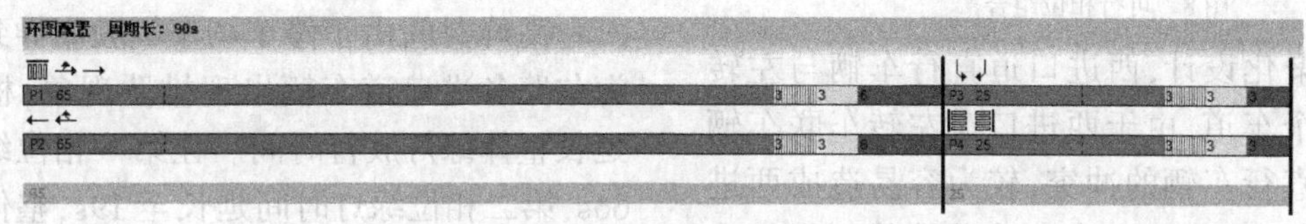

图5 交叉口相位配时图

2.4 交叉口配时优化

根据人工现场计数采集车流量，绘制流量流向图如图6所示。

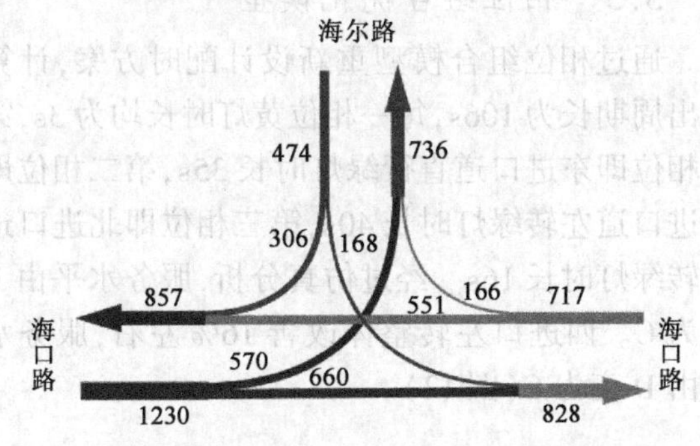

图6 某工作日高峰小时流量流向图

从实际的车流量不难看出，东西进口道流量占主要比例，且西进口道左转与东进口直行存在冲突，北进口道左转车流量相对较少，因此北进口道绿灯可能存在绿灯时长冗余现象。

因为右转车辆不受控制，故只考虑东西北方向的直行和左转，根据二维交通流线以东直、北左、西直、西左为顺序(图7)，采用实际测量交通量构建欧氏距离矩阵，D_{ij}为第i个交通流和第j个交通流之间距离，矩阵如下：

$$D=\begin{bmatrix}0 & 0.4141 & 0.3051 & 0.2319\\0.4141 & 0 & 0.1090 & 0.1822\\0.3051 & 0.1090 & 0 & 0.0732\\0.2319 & 0.1822 & 0.0732 & 0\end{bmatrix}$$

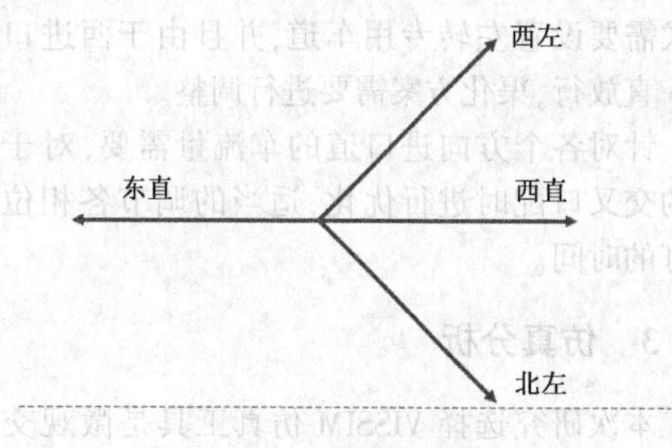

图7 二维交通流线图

定义P_{ij}作为冲突系数，若两股交通流之间不存在冲突则取0，否则取1，根据交通实际流向绘制二维交通流线图构建冲突距离矩阵如下：

$$d=\begin{bmatrix}0 & 1 & 1 & 0\\1 & 0 & 1 & 0\\1 & 1 & 0 & 0\\0 & 0 & 0 & 0\end{bmatrix}$$

为了合理度量交叉口各个流向之间的距离，采用欧氏距离与冲突距离的代数和来表示，根据矩阵运算法则，交通流之间距离为：

$$D'=\begin{bmatrix}0 & 1.4141 & 1.3051 & 1.2319\\0.4141 & 0 & 0.1090 & 1.1822\\1.3051 & 1.1090 & 0 & 1.0732\\0.2319 & 0.1822 & 0.0732 & 0\end{bmatrix}$$

由上述距离矩阵可知，对于两相位的信号控制，无论怎样相位组合都不可能解决冲突，并且左转车辆较多,因此采取三相位控制。对于三相位4个交通流线只可以组合为1组非冲突流向组合,则该交叉口所有可行的相位方案如图8所示。

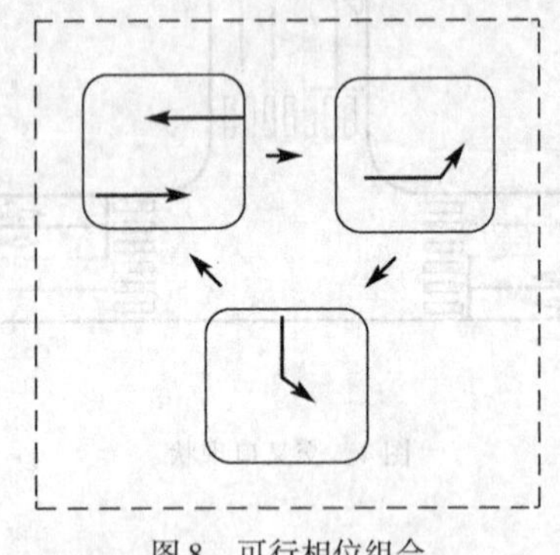

图8 可行相位组合

现有的渠化设计,西进口道直行车辆与左转车辆共用一个车道,由于西进口道左转车联车辆与东进口道直行车辆的冲突,较为容易造成西进口道排队长度过长。由相位组合优化模型根据聚类的思想得到一组相位组合,三相位的信号控制方式需要设置左转专用车道,并且由于西进口直行一直放行,渠化方案需要进行调整。

针对各个方向进口道的车流量需要,对于现有的交叉口配时进行优化,适当的调节各相位信号灯的时间。

3 仿真分析

本次研究选择VISSIM仿真工具是微观交通流仿真系统。随机选取某一天交通量进行仿真分析,以平均停车延误、平均停车次数、平均排队长度作为评价指标。

3.1 Webster配时法

T形交叉口信号配时同样是Webster配时法以延误最小所得,求得周期长为135s,第一相位有效绿灯时间98s,第二相位有效绿灯时间25s。根据仿真结果,从整体上来看如图9a)所示。优化后服务水平由D变为C,但是具体到每个进口道,虽然每个进口道均得到一定的改善但是相对而言幅度很小,尤其是西进口道左转车辆和东进口道直行车辆依旧有冲突,优化结果显示西进口左转整体改善8%左右如图9b)所示,服务水平依然是D。

3.2 改善绿信比

高峰时间由于停车场车辆驶离导致海口路—海尔路各进口道车辆出现排队现象,根据流量比延长整体绿灯放行时间。让第一相位绿灯延长至66s,第二相位绿灯时间延长至19s,整体周期增加至100s(图10)。

经过仿真分析,总体上和Webster法优化程度相似,服务水平由D变为C。西进口左转整体改善16%左右,服务水平依旧是D(图11)。

3.3 相位组合优化模型

通过相位组合模型重新设计配时方案,计算得出周期长为106s,每一相位黄灯时长均为3s,第一相位即东进口道直行绿灯时长35s,第二相位即西进口道左转绿灯时长40s,第三相位即北进口道左转绿灯时长16s。经过仿真分析,服务水平由D变为C。西进口左转整体改善16%左右,服务水平由D变为C(图12)。

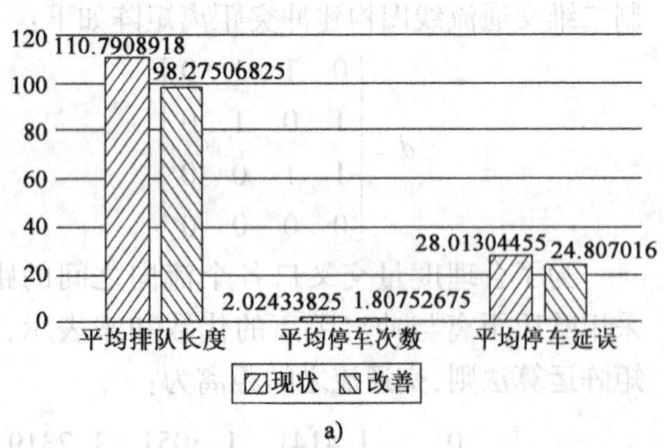

a)

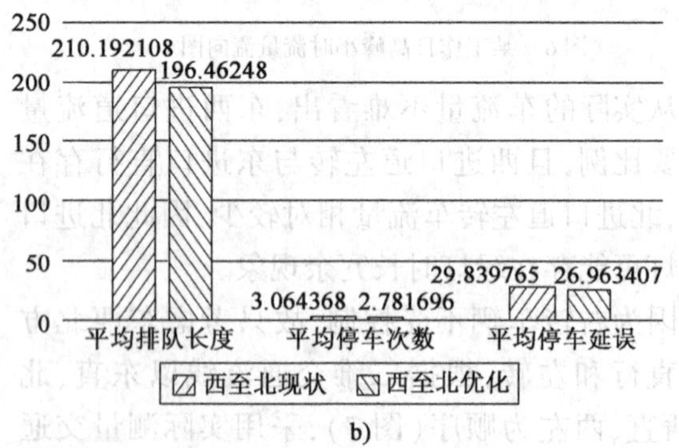

b)

图9 Webster仿真结果

图10 优化信号配时图

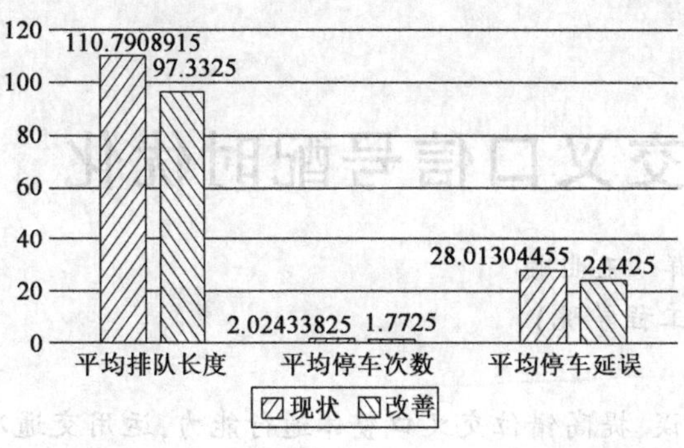

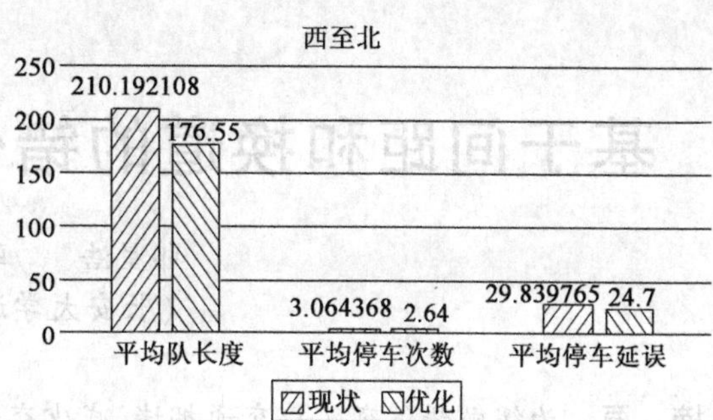

图 11 改善绿信比优化结果

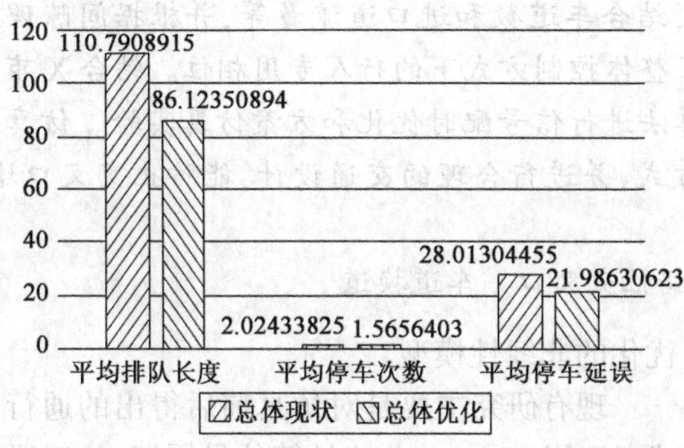

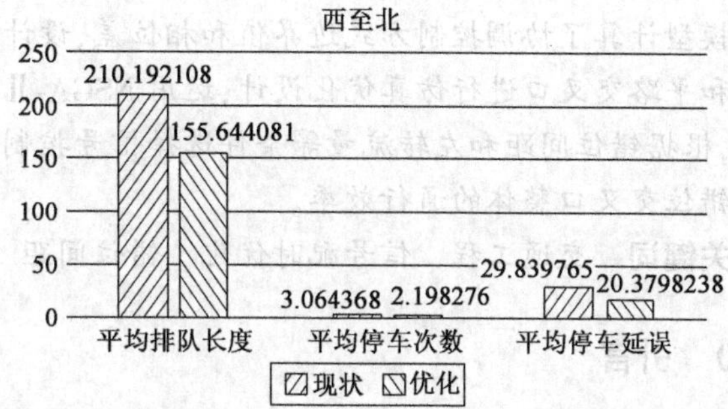

图 12 相位优化组合优化结果

4 结语

针对海尔路—海口路交叉口实际拥堵情况，通过相位组合优化模型对相位重新设计，仿真结果表明，新的配时方案对比 Webster 配时法和改善绿信比的方案，极大地改善了西进口左转流量大而导致的排队问题。交叉口的流量随着时间而变化，会导致聚类结果发生变化，本文只是选取了比较具有代表性的高峰小时流量，并且单个交叉口的信号配时往往具有一定局限性，没有考虑相邻交叉口，仅为局部最优的结果，未来应进一步研究相邻交叉口协调控制，达到区域最优结果。

参考文献

[1] Webster F V. Traffic signal settings[J]. Road Research Technical Paper, 1958, 39.

[2] 张鹏，常玉林. 信号交叉口延误—通行能力联合优化配时方法研究[J]. 交通运输系 统工程与信息，2008, 8(1): 118-122.

[3] Chin Y K, Yong K C, Bolong N, et al. Multiple Intersections Traffic Signal Timing Optimization with Genetic Algorithm [C] // IEEE International Conference on Control System, Computing and Engineering. IEEE, 2011: 454-459.

[4] 张小雨，邵春福. 城乡结合部道路交叉口多目标信号配时优化模型[J]. 系统仿真学报，2020, 32(04): 709-717. DOI: 10. 16182/j. issn1004731x. joss. 18-0392.

[5] Gao Y, Qu Z, Song X, et al. A Novel Relationship Model between Signal timing, Queue Length and Travel Speed [J]. Physica A: Statistical Mechanics and Its Applications, 2021.

[6] Terraza M, Zhang J, Li Z. Intersection Signal Timing Optimisation for an Urban Street Network to Minimise Traffic Delays. Promet-Traffic&Transportation. 2021; 33(4): 579-92. DOI: 10. 7307/ptt. v33i4. 3694.

[7] Florida U O, Gainesville. Florida Intersection Desing Guide for New Construction and Major Reconstruction of At-Grade Intersections on the State Highway System[J]. 2002.

[8] 刘娅欣. 基于 RFID 技术的交叉口信号配时优化研究[D]. 重庆：重庆交通大学，2018.

[9] 陈文斌. 单点信号控制交叉口相位相序优化模型研究[D]. 成都：西南交通大学，2015.

[10] 唐东明. 聚类分析及其应用研究[D]. 成都：电子科技大学，2010.

基于间距和换道的错位交叉口信号配时优化

邱星浩* 马超群 王曲顺
(长安大学运输工程学院)

摘 要 为缓解错位交叉口交通拥堵,减少交通延误,提高错位交叉口整体通行能力,运用交通冲突理论分析了城市错位交叉口的交通流运行特性,从错位交叉口间距和中间段的车道变换两个方面探讨了错位信号交叉口交通设计和信号控制方式的约束条件,结合车道数和进口道流量等,并根据间隙理论和换道模型计算了协调控制方式边界值和相位差,设计了整体控制方式下的行人专用相位。结合X市西五路与和平路交叉口进行仿真优化设计,运用NSGA-Ⅱ算法进行信号配时优化和方案仿真实验。仿真结果表明,根据错位间距和左转流量等条件选择信号控制方式,并进行合理的交通设计,能防止交叉口堵塞,提高错位交叉口整体的通行效率。

关键词 交通工程 信号配时优化 错位间距 错位交叉口 车道换道

0 引言

平面错位交叉口是畸形交叉口的一种特殊形式,主要是由两个T形交叉口和相距几十米到几百米的中间连接路段L组成。错位交叉口与一般交叉口相比具有交通流运行特性更加复杂的特性,主要体现在车辆在错位距离内多次实现分流—合流—分流增加了车辆冲突。

针对错位交叉口的研究大多集中在交通流特性分析和交通管理控制方面。Jack Haddad[1]对错位交叉口进行分析,当错位交叉口之间的距离较短时会出现车辆排队现象,通过对信号周期进行调整来保证错位交叉口通行能力最大化。Cai Zhengyi[2]基于排序策略和预信号,利用连接段作为存车区域对错位交叉口进行渠化和相位设计,研究表明,该方法能减少交叉口内各流向的平均延误和最大排队长度。Liu Xiaoming[3]等应用元胞自动机规则分析了无灯控错位交叉口主路进口道交通流密度变化对不同路段交通流平均速度的影响,结果表明,错位交叉口主路上较小的车流密度也能导致主路进口道及两T形交叉口中间路段发生交通堵塞。陈林圻[4]建立不同设计速度下的错位平面交叉口节点间距计算模型,得出将错位交叉口间距增加至模型计算值后,能够减少错位交叉口各进口道的平均延误与停车次数的结论。李硕[5]提出了左转车辆损失时间的计算方法,以信号周期、绿灯时长为约束条件,建立了信号配时优化的非线性模型。

现有研究主要是对仿真前后得出的通行能力或者运用Webster公式计算信号周期,然后通过合理的信号协调控制来改善错位交叉口的通行能力。本文主要从间隙理论和换道模型研究入手,分析错位交叉口几何形式以及交通特性,从错位交叉口的错位间距和交通流量等方面分析研究影响错位交叉口信号控制方式和信号配时的因素,确定在不同错位间距和交通流量条件下的合理控制方式。

1 错位交叉口信号控制约束分析

图1为错位交叉口类型,本文以右转错位交叉口为例,分析错位交叉口交通设计方法和信号控制方式选择的两个约束条件:连接段约束和换道约束。

1.1 连接段长度约束

以图2为例,次路交叉口进口在有效绿灯时间内到达的左转车辆在中间段的排队长度L为:

$$L = q \times p \times g \times l \tag{1}$$

式中:L——车辆排队长度,m;

q——有效绿灯时间内车辆到达率,pcu/s;

p——主路左转车到达比例;

g——主路左转相位红灯时间,s;

l——车辆排队的平均车头间距,m/veh。错位间距阈值为车辆最大排队长度L_{max}小于两个T形交叉口的距离L_0,即$L_{max} \leq L_0$。

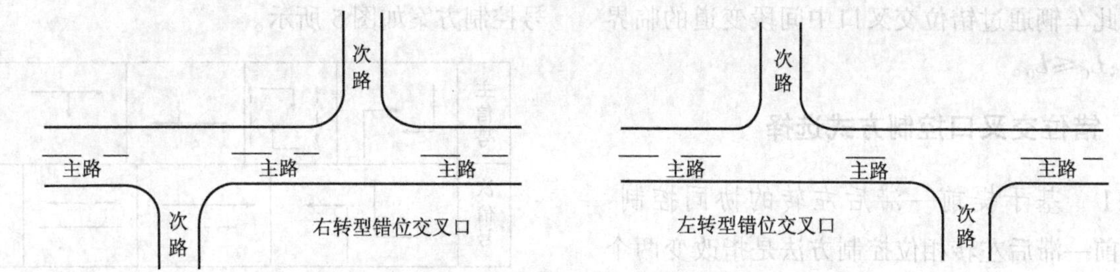

图1 城市错位交叉口类型

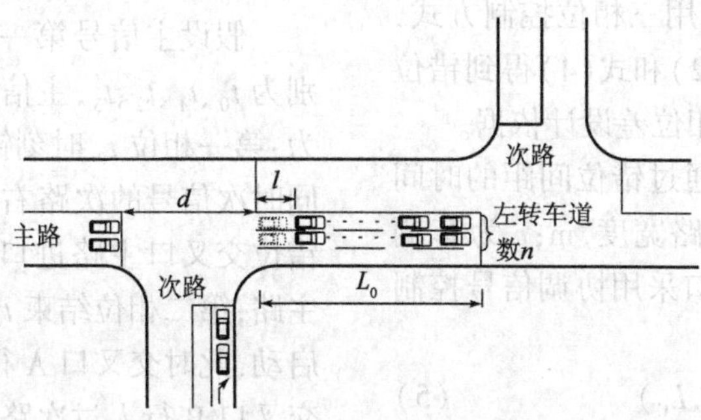

图2 错位交叉口临界距离分析图

为防止次路车辆与前一相位下游交叉口处排队的左转车辆相遇，上游T形交叉口的右转相位需要在下游T形交叉口最后一辆排队车辆起动时放行，这一阶段排队车辆消散时间 t_d 为：

$$t_d = \frac{L}{v_w} = -L \times \frac{k_j - k_m}{q_m} + \tau \quad (2)$$

式中：t_d——排队车辆消散时间，s；

v_w——消散波速度，m/s；

k_j——车辆排队时的交通流密度，pcu/m；

k_m——下游T型口饱和流密度，pcu/m；

q_m——下游T形交叉口饱和流率，pcu/s；

τ——消散时间的修正系数，s。

$$\tau = \frac{\sum_{i=1}^{k}(h_i - h_{ip})}{k} \quad (3)$$

式中：h_i——第 $i(i<k)$ 辆车的车头时距，s/veh；

h_{ip}——平均车头时距，s/veh；

k——车辆数，veh，默认值为4。

1.2 连接段车道变换约束

本文主要探讨连接段车道数 $n=3$ 时，车道分布为直左、直行和右转的情形。中间车道混行的右转车辆要在较短的时间内完成变道，车辆变道场景如图3所示。

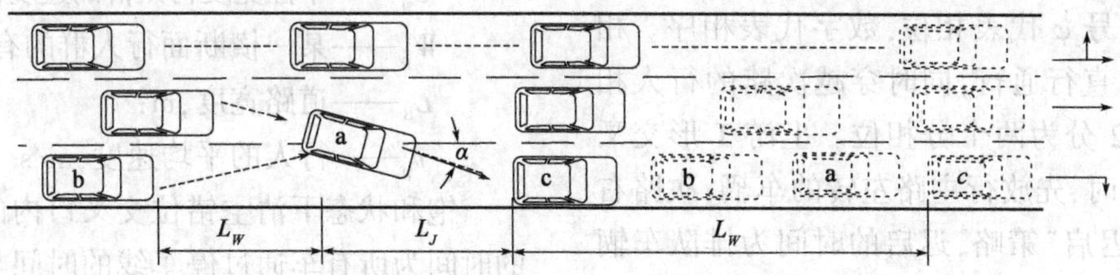

图3 错位交叉口中间段变道示意图

在换道过程中，车辆完成变道过程行驶的距离包括：车辆变道前在等待可接受间隙时间内行驶的距离 L_W(m)，驾驶员变道时在判断-反应时间内行驶的距离 L_J(m)，车辆完成变道所需要的距离安全 L_S(m)，因此整个变道过程的行驶距离 L_C 为：

$$L_C = L_W + L_J + L_S = \frac{v}{3.6}(t_w - t_j) + vt_a\cos\alpha + \frac{1}{2}at_a^2 + \Delta d \quad (4)$$

式中：L_C——车道变道所需总距离，m；

t_w——等待变道的时间，s；

t_j——驾驶员判断-反应时间，s；

a——变道时的加速度，m/s²；

α——车辆变道时与车道线夹角，°；

t_a——变道时的加速时间，s。

Δd——正态随机变量，默认值为服从 $\Delta d \sim N(-10,10)$ 的随机数，s。

因此车辆通过错位交叉口中间段变道的临界条件为:$L_C \leqslant L_0$。

2　错位交叉口控制方式选择

2.1　基于提前—滞后左转的协同控制

提前—滞后左转相位控制方法是指改变两个相邻协调控制交叉口的直行和左转相序,按照相邻交叉口协调控制的原理,采用三相位控制方式,相位差的取值为 φ。结合式(2)和式(4)得到错位交叉口采用协调信号控制的相位差设计依据。

①主路上游 T 形交叉口通过错位间距的时间 $t_0=(L_0+d)/v$,其中:d 为支路宽度,m;v 为车辆的平均速度,m/s。错位交叉口采用协调信号控制方式的临界条件为:

$$L_0 > \max(L_{\max}, L_C) \tag{5}$$

②第一相位产生的左转车排队从第一辆车启动到最后一辆车启动交通波的传播时间,相位差 φ 的取值为:

$$\varphi = \max(t_0, t_d) \tag{6}$$

对主要道路的交通流采用协调控制,相位设计原理和配时方案如图 4 所示。

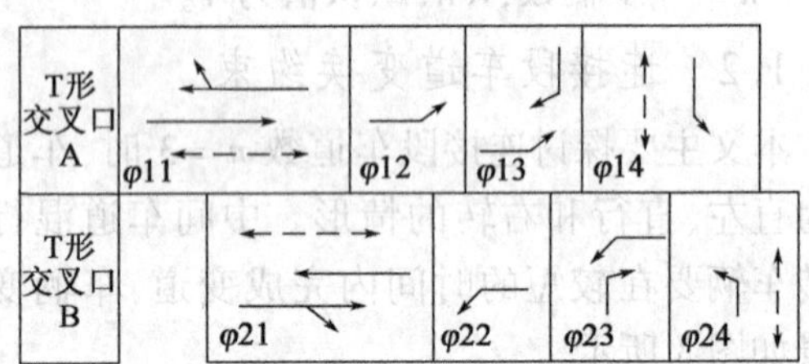

图 4　协调信号相位设计图

图 4 中符号 φ 代表相位,数字代表相序。相位 1 表示主路直行通行,同时穿越次路的行人相位启动;相位 2 分为两个分相位。上游 T 形交叉口的绿灯结束时,先放行主路左转的车辆,次路右转采用信号"迟启"策略,迟启的时间为排队车辆启动波传播的时间 t_d;相位 3 表示次路左转交通放行,同时穿越主路的行人相位启动。

2.2　基于待行区次信号的整体控制设计

根据相序优化模型,将上游和下游 T 形交叉口流向相同的交通同时放行。这种方案的优点是在时间上分离了各个方向的交通量,将次路的右转作为搭接相位,既节省了周期时间,也避免了错位间距内车辆的换道行为,信号相位方案交通信号控制方案如图 5 所示。

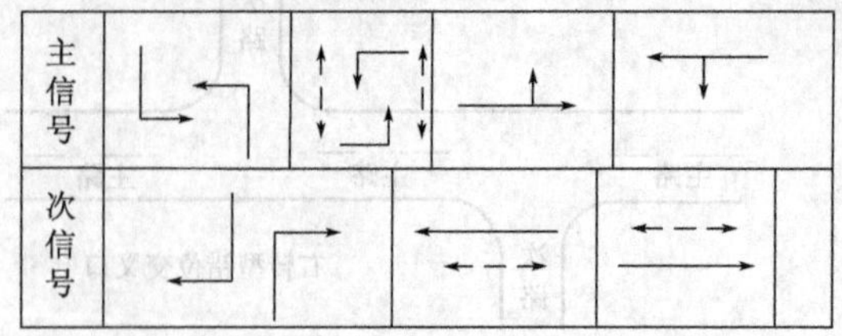

图 5　整体控制信号相位

假设主信号第一、二、三、四相位起始时刻分别为 t_0、t_1、t_2、t_3,主信号与次信号的协同控制机理为:第一相位 t_0 时刻错位交叉口次路的左转放行,同时次信号的次路右转绿灯亮;第二相位 t_1 时刻错位交叉口主路进口道左转放行,此时行人通过主路;第二相位结束 t_d 时间段后,t_2 时刻第三相位启动,此时交叉口 A 行人过次路;第四相位 t_3 时刻交叉口 B 行人过次路。图 6 为不同时刻的交通运行流线。

在第二、第三相位结束后,增设行人和非机动车专用相位,当上游交叉口的机动车绿灯时间结束时,行人专用相位和下一相位的绿灯同时启亮,此时上一相位放行进入错位交叉口中间段的直行车辆继续通行,行人和非机动车穿越次路。行人专用相位时间为行人绿灯时间和行人绿闪时间之和,即

$$g_p = \frac{Q_P}{S_p \times W_p} + \frac{L_R}{v_p} \tag{7}$$

式中:g_p——行人相位绿灯时间,s;

Q_p——行人绿灯时间开始时集结的人数,人;

S_p——单位宽度行人群的速度,人/(m·s);

W_p——某一横断面行人群的有效宽度,m;

L_R——道路宽度,m;

v_p——行人的平均速度,m/s。

饱和状态下清空错位交叉口内的车辆所需要的时间为所有车通过停车线的时间与第一辆车和剩余车辆的车头时距之和,可表示为下式:

$$t_c = k \times t_0 + h_{ip} \times \frac{k \times (k-1)}{2} \tag{8}$$

式中:t_c——相位绿灯时间错位交叉口内车辆清空时间,s;

t_0——车辆通过停车线所需要的时间,s。

为保证行人过街不与主信号左转冲突,行人最佳相位绿灯时间 g_{ps} 应小于相位转换时间,即:

$$g_{ps} = \min[g_p, t_c] \tag{9}$$

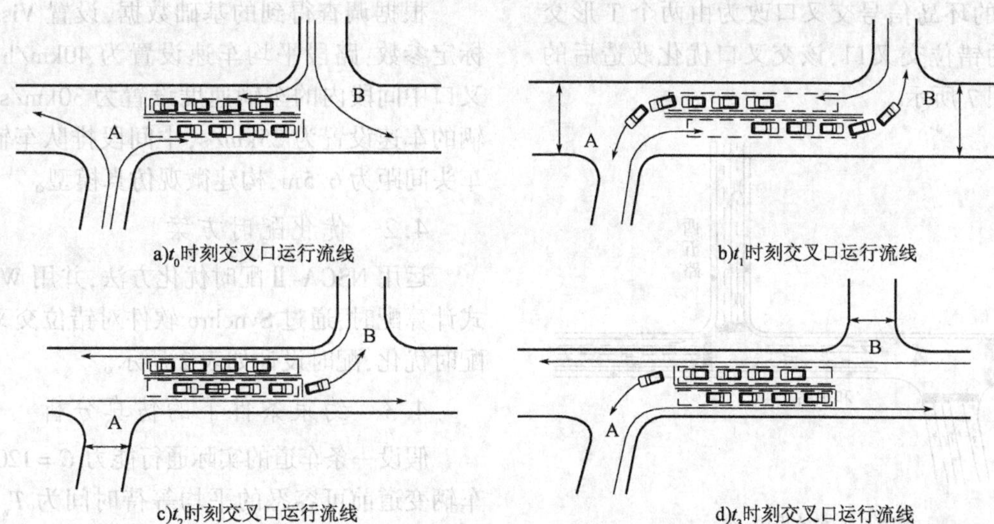

a) t_0时刻交叉口运行流线　b) t_1时刻交叉口运行流线

c) t_2时刻交叉口运行流线　d) t_3时刻交叉口运行流线

图6　错位交叉口整体信号控制策略

3　信号配时优化

3.1　算法思想

通过算法直接对交叉口信号配时进行优化，然后和 Synchro 等软件配时进行比较，校检信号配时的可靠性。

3.2　算法的目标优化函数

制约错位交叉口通行能力 Z 最主要的因素是主路的左转交通流 N_{ZZ} 和次路穿越主路的直行交通 N_{CZ}，这两种交通流最终汇集为下一个 T 形交叉口的左转交通量，因此建立以通过下游 T 形交叉口左转交通量最大为目标的模型[6]，即：

$$Z = \max[N_{ZZ} + N_{CZ}] \tag{10}$$

除了考虑左转交通量，还要考虑连接段车辆通过能力最大和车辆排队最小两个目标函数。其中通过能力最大主要是由交叉口处的关键路径决定，即：

$$Q_c = \max \sum_{i=1} c_i w_i \tag{11}$$

式中：Q_c——错位交叉口连接段通过能力，pcu/h；

c_i——连接段第 i 个进口道的通行能力，pcu/h；

w_i——第 i 个进口道的权重系数。

车辆排队最小是由等待的车辆数决定，即：

$$Q_l = \min \sum_{i=1} \frac{l_i}{L_i} \tag{12}$$

式中：Q_l——评价连接段排队情况指标；

l_i——交叉口第 i 个相位的车辆排队长度，m；

L_i——交叉口第 i 个相位可容纳的车辆排队长度，m。

3.3　约束条件

协调信号控制和整体信号控制的约束条件分别为式(12)和式(13)。

$$\begin{cases} L_C < L_0 \\ t_d = \dfrac{L}{v_w} = -L \times \dfrac{k_j - k_m}{q_m} + \tau \\ L_{\max} \leqslant L_0 \\ \varphi = \max(t_0, t_d) \end{cases} \tag{13}$$

$$\begin{cases} L_C < L_0 \\ t_d = \dfrac{L}{v_w} = L \times \dfrac{k_j - k_m}{q_m} + \tau \\ L_{\max} \leqslant L_0 \\ g_{ps} = \min(g_p, t_c) \end{cases} \tag{14}$$

除此之外，还要考虑绿灯显示时间的约束，绿灯显示时间不能小于最小绿灯显示时间 g_{pmin}，不能大于最大绿灯显示时间 g_{pmax}，即：

$$g_{pmin} \leqslant g \leqslant g_{pmax} \tag{15}$$

$$g_{pmax} = g_{pmin} + g_{po} \tag{16}$$

式中：g_{po}——单位绿灯延长时间，延长时间一般为 30～60s。

4　案例分析

以 X 市西五路与和平路的错位交叉口为案

例,将原来的环岛信号交叉口改为由两个T形交叉口组成的错位交叉口,该交叉口优化改造后的渠化图如图7所示。

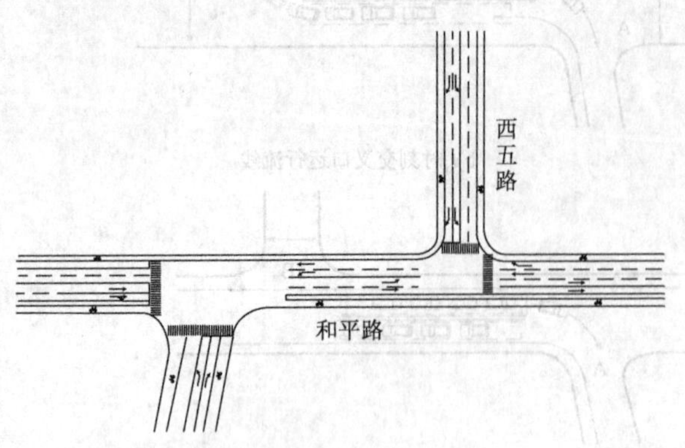

图7　方案效果图

4.1　交通数据调查与仿真分析

调查时段为一周工作日晚高峰,调查了该错位交叉口的四个进口道,调查结果如表1所示。

根据调查得到的基础数据,设置Vissim仿真标定参数:路段平均车速设置为40km/h,错位交叉口中间段内的车辆速度设置为30km/s,右转车辆的车速设置为25km/s,中间段排队车辆的平均车头间距为6.5m,构建微观仿真模型。

4.2　优化配时方案

运用NSGA-Ⅱ配时优化方法,并用Webster公式计算配时,通过Synchro软件对错位交叉口进行配时优化,配时设计如表2所示。

4.3　约束条件下的仿真分析

假设一条车道的实际通行能力$C=1200$pcu/h,车辆变道前可容忍的平均等待时间为$T_w=3.5$s,驾驶人反应时间为$t_f=2.5$s,变换车道的时间$t_a=2.5$s,车辆加速度$a=2.25\text{m/s}^2$,摩阻系数$f=0.015$,目标车辆的平均速度$v_1=30$km/h,车辆变道前的速度$v_0=25$km/s。

各路口各流向流量表(pcu/h)　　表1

流　量	南进口		西进口		北进口		东进口	
	右转	直行	右转	直行	右转	直行	右转	直行
小时交通量	198	792	235	940	598	153	449	837
比例	0.2	0.8	0.2	0.8	0.66	0.34	0.34	0.48

西五路-和平路交叉口信号配时　　表2

情　形	相位1(s)	相位2(s)	相位3(s)	相位4(s)	周期(s)
现状	23	23	63	—	109
协调控制	46	34	20	—	100
整体控制	25	17	34	22	98

从表3可以看出,现状交叉口最大排队长度达到35.4m,优化后排队长度明显缩短。在3种优化后的控制方案中,整体信号控制错位交叉口的平均延误最小,比现状减少了15.9s,而采用协调信号控制时错位交叉口内最大排队长度最小,比现状减少了17.8m。由此可见,两种信号控制方式对错位交叉口内各流向的延误时间和排队长度有着不同程度的改善,显示了各自的优点。

西五路与和平路交叉口仿真评价指标　　表3

情　形	平均延误时间(s)	最大排队长度(m)
现状	41.9	35.4
协调信号控制	34.6	17.6
整体信号控制	26	29.4

5　结语

本文针对影响错位信号交叉口通行能力的两个因素——交叉口间距和车辆换道,建立了错位交叉口几何条件、交通条件与信号控制方案之间的联系。结果发现:错位交叉口的信号配设和相位相序设计不是固定的,需要根据两个T形交叉口之间的距离以及每个进口道流量选择协调控制或整体控制,而协调控制中相位差是控制错位交叉口内部排队溢出的重要因素;当错位交叉口间距大于上游车辆产生的排队长度或连接段车辆变道长度的最大值时,宜采用协调信号控制方式;当采用整体信号控制时,平均延误时间显著下降。

参考文献

[1] Haddad J, Mahalel D. Offset Effects on the Capacity of Paired Signalised Intersections during Oversaturated Conditions[J]. Transport metrica A: Transport Science, 2014, 10(8): 740-758.

[2] Cai Z, Xiong M. Traffic Design and Signal Timing of Staggered Intersection Based on a Sorting Strategy[J]. Advance in Mechanical Engineering, 2016, 8(4): 1-9.

[3] Liu X, Zheng S. Traffic Flow Model for Staggered Intersection without Signal Lamp[J]. Journal of Transportation Systems Engineering and Information Technology, 2012, 12(5): 82-89.

[4] 陈林圻,周磊,潘兵宏. 城市双车道错位交叉口合理间距分析[J]. 中国科技论文,2020,15(08):906-914.

[5] 李硕,付珊,贺文,等. 基于遗传算法的左转待行区交叉口信号配时优化研究[J]. 公路工程,2018,43(5):131-137.

[6] 吴伟,马万经,杨晓光. 信号控制交叉口左转相位协调设计方法[J]. 同济大学学报(自然科学版),2013,41(1):66-71.

城市道路平面交叉口信号优化设计

李 梅[1] 孙战丽[*2] 何美玲[3] 赵建有[1]

(1. 长安大学汽车学院;2. 河南省交通运输发展集团有限公司航空港分公司;3. 江苏大学 汽车与交通工程学院)

摘 要 本文的主要内容是总结国内外研究现状和城市道路平面交叉口信号相关理论基础,学习城市交叉口交通信号控制的各项参数指标,进行实例计算分析,通过调查纬三路与楚桥路交叉口的相位配时、渠化方案和实际交通量,对现行交叉口进行 VISSIM 仿真并评价其平均延误等相关参数;然后应用经典配时方法——Webster 法,结合所调查的楚桥路与纬三路交叉口的交通量,重新计算该交叉口的各项信号配时参数;接下来根据计算结果对楚桥路与纬三路交叉口信号配时进行优化,进而提高楚桥路与纬三路交叉口的通行能力,减少该交叉口的交通延误,缓解城市道路交通拥堵现象,降低交通事故的发生率;优化完成后,应用 VISSIM 仿真软件对楚桥路与纬三路交叉口进行仿真并与优化前的仿真评价进行比较。

关键词 道路交叉口 信号优化 Webster 法 VISSIM 仿真

0 引言

1960 年加拿大多伦多建成了世界上第一个中心式交通信号控制系统,是道路交通控制技术发展的里程碑[1-2]。

1998 年,陈森发等提出了两个概念,分别是"关键车流"和"非关键车流",并且对 Pappis[3] 提出的城市单向单路口模糊控制方法进行了优化。在城市交叉路口左转车流较小时可用此优化方法,因此该方法建立在理想化模型路口的基础上,但在实际应用中运用较为困难[4]。

2006 年,王秋平、谭学龙、张生瑞以单点信号控制交叉口为例,建立了一个以平均延误时间最小、平均停车次数最小为目标的函数,以有效绿灯时间、饱和度及周期长度为约束条件的单个交叉口非线性函数模型,并采用遗传算法和遗传模拟退火算法相结合的全局搜索算法对其进行求解[5]。

对于一般常规的道路交叉口,已有很多研究考虑了交通需求,并提出了信号鲁棒优化[6]、感应式控制[7]和自适应控制[8]等应对措施。其中,鲁棒优化方法目前大多用于常规交叉口优化中。

此外,还有在重大活动事件发生的背景下建立的双层优化模型[9]、结合 PFI 车流运行特征提高

1. 基金项目:基于交通行为安全性的河南省高速公路运行控制技术研究(2019G-2-11)。

十字路口运行效率的优化模型[10]、提高车辆通行效率的一种平面交叉口交通拥堵多方向交通灯运行时间自适应算法[11]等。

本文应用经典配时方法——Webster法,结合所调查的镇江市楚桥路与纬三路交叉口的交通量,重新计算该交叉口的各项信号配时参数,然后根据计算结果对楚桥路与纬三路交叉口信号配时进行优化,进而提高楚桥路与纬三路交叉口的通行能力。

1　数据采集

1.1　交通量调查

本文以镇江市楚桥路与纬三路交叉路口为例,进行交通量的调查。楚桥路与纬三路交叉口位于镇江市东边,在图1中用红点标出。

图1　楚桥路与纬三路交叉口位置

1.1.1　目前渠化方案

镇江市楚桥路与纬三路交叉路口形式如图2所示、目前渠化方案如图3所示。

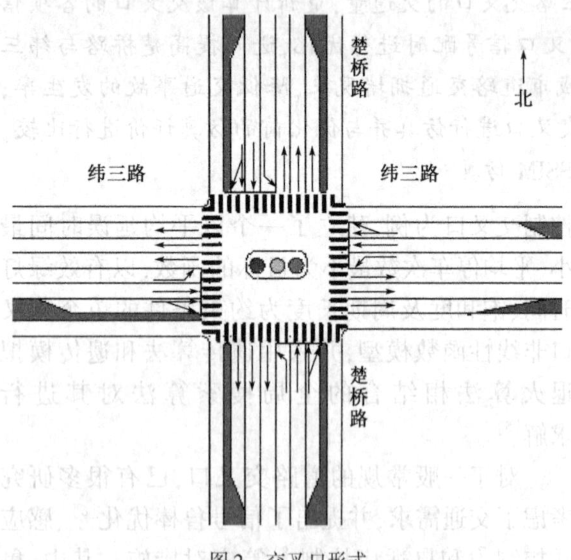

图2　交叉口形式

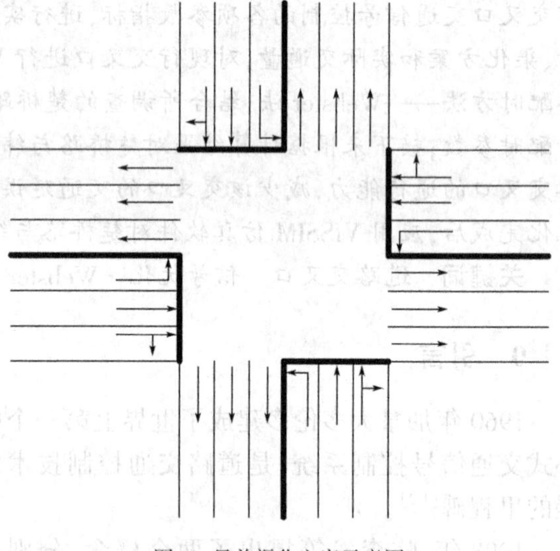

图3　目前渠化方案示意图

1.1.2　目前信号相位及配时图

楚桥路与纬三路交叉口采用了三相位的信号控制,信号周期为103s,一天内周期不随时间的变化而改变。具体相位如图4～图6所示。

目前配时方案如图7所示。

1.1.3　调查数据

根据交通运输部办公厅印发的《关于调整公路交通情况调查车型分类及车辆折算系数的通知》,本文将各类车型的数量通过表1的机动车车型分类标准和表2的折算系数转换为标准车数。

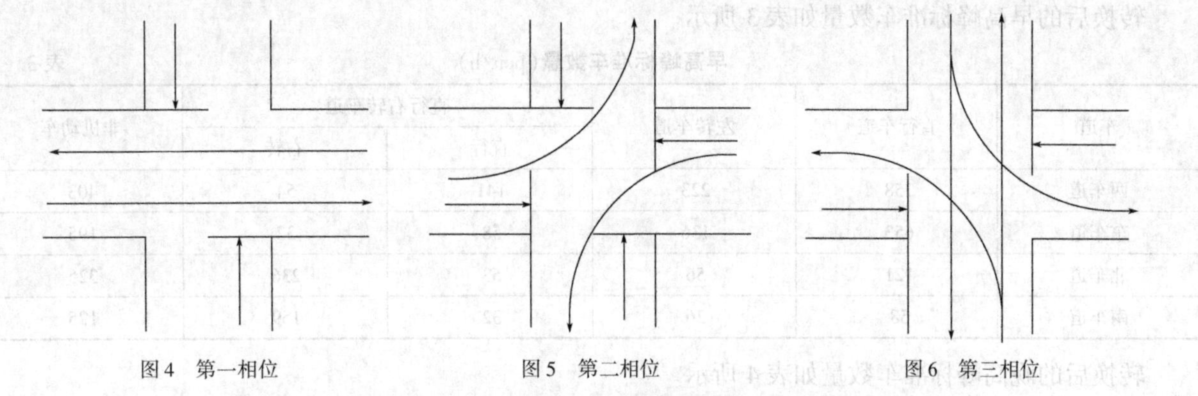

图4　第一相位　　　　图5　第二相位　　　　图6　第三相位

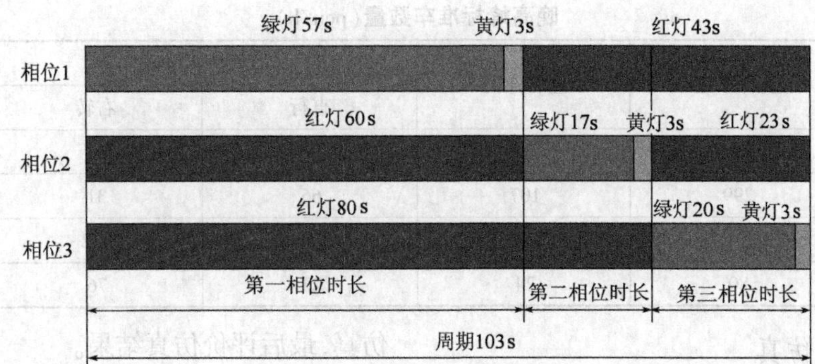

图7　目前信号配时图

公路交通情况调查机动车车型分类　　　　表1

车型	一级分类	二级分类	额定荷载参数	轮廓及轴数特征参数	备注
汽车	小型车	中小客车	额定座位≤19座	车长<6m,2轴	—
		小型货车	载质量≤2t		包括三轮载货汽车
	中型车	大客车	额定座位>19座	6m≤车长≤12m,2轴	—
		中型货车	2t<载质量≤7t		包括专用汽车
	大型车	大型货车	7t<载质量≤20t	6m≤车长≤12m,3轴或4轴	—
	特大型车	特大型货车	载质量>20t	车长>12m或4轴以上,且车高<3.8m或车高>4.2m	—
		集装箱车		车长>12m或4轴以上,且3.8m≤车高≤4.2m	—
摩托车	摩托车		发动机驱动	—	包括轻便、普通摩托车
拖拉机	拖拉机		—	—	包括大、小拖拉机

注:各车型的额定荷载、轮廓及轴数的特征参数均可作为判别车型的依据。

公路交通情况调查机动车车型折算系数参考值　　　　表2

车型	汽车							摩托车	拖拉机
一级分类	小型车		中型车		大型车	特大型车		摩托车	拖拉机
二级分类	中小客车	小型货车	大客车	中型货车	大型货车	特大型货车	集装箱车		
参考折算系数	1	1	1.5	3	4	4	4	1	4

注:交通量折算采用小客车为标准车型。

转换后的早高峰标准车数量如表3所示。

早高峰标准车数量(pcu/h) 表3

车道	直行车道	左转车道	直行右转车道		非机动车
			直行	右转	
西车道	758	223	141	54	403
东车道	653	136	58	32	195
北车道	121	56	53	236	325
南车道	58	26	32	159	125

转换后的晚高峰标准车数量如表4所示。

晚高峰标准车数量(pcu/h) 表4

车道	直行车道	左转车道	直行右转车道		非机动车
			直行	右转	
西车道	747	325	155	83	480
东车道	299	107	66	31	199
北车道	54	30	19	232	140
南车道	80	24	23	76	376

1.2 交叉口仿真

1.2.1 仿真过程简述

本文使用VISSIM软件进行交叉口路段绘制，并结合调查统计的交通量和正确的信号控制进行仿真，最后评价仿真结果。

1.2.2 仿真评估

早高峰的仿真评估如表5所示。

晚高峰的仿真评估如表6所示。

早高峰的仿真评估 表5

仿真运行	时间间隔	转向	排队长度(s)	排队长度(最大)(m)	车辆延误(平均值)(所有)(s)	静态停车延误(平均值)(所有)(s)	停车次数(所有)
平均值	0~3600	南直行—北入道口	3.01	12.73	59.39	51.81	1.00
平均值	0~3600	南左转—西入道口	1.18	12.17	30.57	20.72	1.42
平均值	0~3600	南直行右转—北入道口	1.48	20.24	50.60	43.33	1.00
平均值	0~3600	南直行右转—东入道口	0.02	6.70	3.99	2.21	0.21
平均值	0~3600	西直行—东入道口	10.19	38.46	7.98	6.22	0.22
平均值	0~3600	西左转—北入道口	8.66	32.61	35.44	28.96	0.77
平均值	0~3600	西直行右转—南入道口	0.00	0.00	1.84	0.00	0.00
平均值	0~3600	西直行右转—东入道口	2.47	12.83	16.07	12.54	0.45
平均值	0~3600	东直行—西入道口	6.47	45.20	8.44	5.83	0.34
平均值	0~3600	东左转—南入道口	3.84	21.62	26.44	20.34	0.79
平均值	0~3600	东直行右转—西入道口	0.56	4.45	11.80	8.56	0.44
平均值	0~3600	东直行右转—北入道口	0.00	0.00	0.00	0.00	0.00
平均值	0~3600	北直行—南入道口	1.66	16.26	16.35	11.49	0.53
平均值	0~3600	北左转—东入道口	0.85	4.43	58.07	46.95	1.33
平均值	0~3600	北直行右转—南入道口	5.30	35.94	42.92	37.34	0.76
平均值	0~3600	北直行右转—西入道口	0.10	13.06	5.63	4.83	0.10

晚高峰的仿真评估 表6

仿真运行	时间间隔	转　向	排队长度(m)	排队长度(最大)(m)	车辆延误(平均值)(所有)(s)	静态停车延误(平均值)(所有)(s)	停车次数(所有)
平均值	0~3600	南直行—北入道口	0.75	9.80	19.12	14.11	0.53
平均值	0~3600	南左转—西入道口	1.11	7.15	43.15	30.56	1.83
平均值	0~3600	南直行右转—东入道口	0.00	0.00	0.12	0.00	0.00
平均值	0~3600	南直行右转—北入道口	0.32	3.23	18.66	14.21	0.67
平均值	0~3600	西直行—东入道口	6.34	28.81	4.31	3.23	0.13
平均值	0~3600	西左转—北入道口	12.61	31.75	36.65	31.51	0.63
平均值	0~3600	西直行右转—南入道口	0.00	0.00	1.34	0.08	0.15
平均值	0~3600	西直行右转—东入道口	1.06	16.55	9.23	5.49	0.46
平均值	0~3600	东直行—西入道口	0.94	8.57	3.11	2.12	0.11
平均值	0~3600	东左转—南入道口	3.00	11.83	35.34	29.55	0.78
平均值	0~3600	东直行右转—西入道口	0.10	3.33	2.10	1.07	0.08
平均值	0~3600	东直行右转—北入道口	0.00	0.00	0.00	0.00	0.00
平均值	0~3600	北直行—南入道口	1.56	9.13	37.91	30.66	0.92
平均值	0~3600	北左转—东入道口	1.19	8.12	39.01	29.49	0.80
平均值	0~3600	北直行右转—南入道口	11.64	34.78	37.59	32.09	0.73
平均值	0~3600	北直行右转—西入道口	0.16	9.00	12.99	9.78	0.33

2　信号配时模型

2.1　现行交叉口各参数的计算

2.1.1　现行交叉口信号配时参数

通过公式(1)、(2)、(4)计算,结果如表7所示。

2.1.2　每条车道的设计交通量

设计交通量如公式(1)所示:

$$q_{mn} = 4 \times Q_{15mn} \tag{1}$$

式中:q_{mn}——配时时段中车道 m 与流向 n 的设计交通量,pcu/h;

Q_{15mn}——配时时段中车道 m 与流向 n 的高峰小时中最高15min的流率,pcu/15min。

每个车道在各个流向的最高15min的流率如表8所示。

由公式(1)可得各个车道的设计交通量,如表9所示。

现行信号配时各参数 表7

配 时 参 数	相位划分		
	第一相位	第二相位	第三相位
显示绿灯时间/s	57	17	20
黄灯时间/s	3	3	3
有效绿灯时间/s	52	12	15
绿信比/s	0.5	0.12	0.15
周期/s	103	103	103
绿灯间隔/s	3	3	3

各个车道在各个流向的最高15min的流率(pcu/15min) 表8

车　道	直行车流量	左转车流量	直行右转车流量	
			直行车流量	右转车流量
西车道	212	72	43	21
东车道	202	49	25	15
北车道	41	20	20	73
南车道	19	12	10	50

设计交通量(pcu/h) 表9

车道	直行车流量	左转车流量	直行右转车流量	
			直行车流量	右转车流量
西车道	848	288	172	84
东车道	808	196	100	60
北车道	164	80	80	292
南车道	76	48	40	200

2.1.3 各车道大车数比率

各车道大车占该车道总车辆的比率如表10所示。

各车道大车比率(%) 表10

车道	直行大车率	左转大车率	直行右转大车率	
			直行大车率	右转大车率
西车道	5.8	1.6	1.7	0.9
东车道	6.6	1.7	1	0.6
北车道	0.7	0.4	0	5.1
南车道	0.7	0.4	0	4.1

2.2 交叉口饱和流量计算

饱和流量的估算如公式(2)所示:

$$S_f = S_{bi} \times f(F_i) \quad (2)$$

式中:S_f——各车道的估算饱和流量,pcu/h;

S_{bi}——第 i 条车道基本饱和流量,i 取直行、左转和右转;

$f(F_i)$——各车道各项校正系数。

2.2.1 基本饱和流量

各车道的基本饱和流量如表11所示。

各车道的基本饱和流量(pcu/h) 表11

车道	基本饱和流量S_{bi}(pcu/h)
直行车道	1550~1750(平均1650)
左转车道	1350~1550(平均1450)
右转车道	1450~1650(平均1550)

2.2.2 各类车道通用校正系数

(1)车道宽度校正。

车道宽度校正系数如公式(3)所示:

$$f_w = \begin{cases} 0.4(W-0.5) & 2.7 \leqslant W < 3.0 \\ 1 & 3.0 \leqslant W \leqslant 3.5 \\ 0.05(W+16.5) & W > 3.5 \end{cases} \quad (3)$$

式中:f_w——车道宽度校正系数;

W——车道宽度,m。

本文中的交叉口车道宽度是3m,故在计算过程中 $f_w = 1$。

(2)坡度及大车校正。

坡度及大车校正系数如公式(4)所示:

$$f_g = 1-(G+HV) \quad (4)$$

式中:f_g——坡度及大车校正系数;

G——道路纵坡,下坡时取0;

HV——大车率,这里 HV 不大于0.50。

根据公式(4),各车道的坡度及大车校正系数如表12所示。

各车道坡度及大车校正系数 表12

车道	西车道		东车道		北车道		南车道	
	直行车道	左转车道	直行车道	左转车道	直行车道	左转车道	直行车道	左转车道
f_g	0.942	0.984	0.934	0.983	0.993	0.996	0.993	0.996

2.2.3 直行车道饱和流量

直行车道饱和流量如公式(5)所示:

$$S_T = S_{bT} \times f_w \times f_g \times f_b \quad (5)$$

式中:S_T——直行车道的饱和流量,pcu/h;

S_{bT}——直行车道的基本饱和流量,pcu/h,根据表11取1650(pcu/h);

f_b——自行车校正系数,取1。

根据公式(5),各车道的直行车道的饱和流量如表13所示。

各车道的直行车道的饱和流量(pcu/h)

表13

车道	西车道	东车道	北车道	南车道
S_T	1554	1541	1638	1638

2.2.4 左转专用车道有左转专用相位时的饱和流量

本文中的交叉口东西方向有左转专用车道且有左转专用相位,其饱和流量计算如公式(6)所示:

$$S_L = S_{bL} \times f_w \times f_g \quad (6)$$

式中:S_L——左转专用车道有专用相位时的饱和流量,辆/h;

S_{bL}——左转专用车道有专用相位时的基本饱和流量,辆/h,根据表10取1450(pcu/h)。

根据公式(6),东西车道的左转专用车道的饱和流量如表14所示。

东西车道的左转专用车道的饱和流量(pcu/h)

表14

车道	西车道	东车道
S_L	1427	1425

2.2.5 左转专用车道无左转专用相位时的饱和流量

本文中的交叉口南北方向有左转专用车道但无左转专用相位,其饱和流量计算如公式(7)所示:

$$S'_L = S_{bL} \times f_w \times f_g \times f_L \quad (7)$$

式中:S'_L——左转专用车道无专用相位时的饱和流量,pcu/h;

S_{bL}——左转专用车道有专用相位时的基本饱和流量,pcu/h,根据表10取1450(pcu/h);

f_L——左转校正系数。

左转校正系数可按公式(8)进行估算:

$$f_L = \exp\left(-0.001\varepsilon \frac{q_{T_0}}{\lambda}\right) - 0.1 \quad (8)$$

式中:ε——对向直行车道数影响系数;

q_{T_0}——对向直行车流量,pcu/h;

λ——绿信比。

对向直行车道数影响系数如表15所示。

对向直行车道数影响系数 ε 表15

对向车道数	1	2	3	4
ε	1.0	0.625	0.51	0.44

本文中 ε 取1.0。

根据公式(8),南北车道的左转校正系数如表16所示。

南北车道的左转校正系数 表16

车道	北车道	南车道
f_L	0.84	0.71

根据公式(7),南北车道的左转专用车道的饱和流量如表17所示。

南北车道的左转专用车道的饱和流量(pcu/h)

表17

车道	北车道	南车道
S'_L	1213	1025

2.2.6 直行右转合用车道饱和流量

本文中的交叉口四个方向均有直行右转合用车道,其饱和流量计算如公式(9)所示:

$$S_{TR} = S_T \times f_{TR} \quad (9)$$

式中:S_{TR}——直行右转合用车道的饱和流量,pcu/h;

S_T——直行车道的饱和流量,pcu/h;

f_{TR}——直右合流校正系数。

f_{TR}的计算如公式(10)所示:

$$f_{TR} = \frac{q_R + q_T}{q'_T} \quad (10)$$

$$q'_T = K_R q_R + q_T \quad (11)$$

$$K_R = \frac{S_T}{S'_R} \quad (12)$$

式中:q_T——合用车道中直行车交通量,pcu/h;

q_R——合用车道中右转车交通量,pcu/h;

q'_T——合用车道直行车当量,pcu/h;

K_R——合用车道中的右转系数;

S'_R——无专用相位时右转专用车道饱和流量。

由于本文中的交叉口无右转专用车道,故S'_R采用建议值,取1550pcu/h,故根据公式(12),各车道的合用车道中的右转系数K_R的数值如表18所示。

各车道的合用车道中的右转系数　表 18

车道	西车道	东车道	北车道	南车道
K_R	1.00	0.99	1.06	1.06

则根据公式(11),各车道的合用车道直行车当量 q'_T 的数值如表 19 所示。

合用车道直行车当量(pcu/h)　表 19

车道	西车道	东车道	北车道	南车道
q'_T	195	88	313	200

根据公式(10),各车道的直右合流校正系数 f_{TR} 的数值如表 20 所示。

直右合流校正系数　表 20

车道	西车道	东车道	北车道	南车道
f_{TR}	1.00	1.01	0.92	0.95

根据公式(9),各车道的直行右转合用车道饱和流量如表 21 所示。

各车道直行右转合用车道饱和流量(pcu/h)　表 21

车道	西车道	东车道	北车道	南车道
S_{TR}	1553	1561	1513	1564

综上所述,各相位饱和流量如表 22 所示。

各相位饱和流量(pcu/h)　表 22

相位	第一相位		第二相位		第三相位	
车道	西车道	东车道	西车道	东车道	北车道	南车道
饱和流量	3107	3102	1427	1425	4364	4227

3　交叉口信号优化与评价

3.1　信号配时的优化

3.1.1　用 Webster 法计算交叉口信号配时参数

3.1.1.1　第 i 相位的最大流量比

第 i 相位的最大流量比如公式(13)所示:

$$Y_i = \frac{q_i}{s_i} \tag{13}$$

式中:q_i——第 i 相位实际到达流量;

s_i——第 i 相位流向的饱和流量。

一般流量比不应大于 0.9。

各相位实际到达流量如表 23 所示。

根据公式(13),各相位的最大流量比如表 24 所示。

3.1.1.2　最大流量比之和

所在周期内全部相位的最大流量比之和的计算如公式(14)所示:

$$Y = \sum_{i=1}^{n} \max(Y_i) \tag{14}$$

式中:Y_i——第 i 个相位的最大流量比。

各相位实际到达流量(pcu/h)　表 23

相位	第一相位		第二相位		第三相位	
车道	西车道	东车道	西车道	东车道	北车道	南车道
实际到达流量	953	743	223	136	466	275

各相位的最大流量比　表 24

相位	第一相位		第二相位		第三相位	
车道	西车道	东车道	西车道	东车道	北车道	南车道
Y_i	0.31	0.24	0.16	0.10	0.11	0.07

则最大流量比之和为 $Y = 0.31 + 0.16 + 0.11 = 0.58$。

3.1.1.3　信号总亏损时间

信号总亏损时间的计算如公式(15)所示:

$$L = \sum_k (L_s + I - A)_k \tag{15}$$

式中:k——一个周期内的绿灯间隔数;

I——绿灯间隔时间(s);

L_s——起动损失时间,可定为 3s;

A——黄灯时长,可定为 3s。

则信号总亏损时间为 $L = 9$s。

3.1.1.4　信号最佳周期

信号最佳周期的计算如公式(16)所示:

$$C_0 = \frac{1.5L + 5}{1 - Y} \tag{16}$$

则信号最佳周期为 $C_0 = \frac{1.5 \times 9 + 5}{1 - 0.58} = 45$s

3.1.1.5 总有效绿灯时间

总有效绿灯时间的计算如公式(17)所示：

$$G_e = C_0 - L \tag{17}$$

则总有效绿灯时间为$G_e = 36s$

3.1.1.6 各相位有效绿灯时间

各相位有效绿灯时间的计算如公式(18)所示：

$$g_i = G_e \frac{\max\ (Y_i)}{Y} \tag{18}$$

则各相位有效绿灯时间如表25所示。

各相位的有效绿灯时间(s) 表25

相位	第一相位	第二相位	第三相位
g_i	19	10	7

3.1.1.7 各相位绿信比

各相位绿信比的计算如公式(19)所示：

$$\lambda_j = \frac{g_i}{C_0} \tag{19}$$

则各相位绿信比如表26所示。

各相位绿信比 表26

相位	第一相位	第二相位	第三相位
λ_j	0.53	0.28	0.19

3.1.1.8 各相位绿灯显示时间

各相位绿灯显示时间的计算如公式(20)所示：

$$g_j = g_i - Y + L_s \tag{20}$$

式中：Y——黄灯时间。

则各相位绿灯显示时间如表27所示。

各相位绿灯显示时间(s) 表27

相位	第一相位	第二相位	第三相位
g_j	19	10	7

3.1.2 优化后的配时方案

通过Webster法优化后的各相位配时参数如表28所示。

优化后各相配时位参数 表28

配时参数	相位划分		
	第一相位	第二相位	第三相位
显示绿灯时间/s	19	10	7
黄灯时间/s	3	3	3
有效绿灯时间/s	19	10	7
绿信比/s	0.53	0.28	0.19
周期/s	45	45	45
绿灯间隔/s	3	3	3

优化后交叉口配时图如图8所示。

3.2 评价分析

优化后的仿真评估如表29所示。

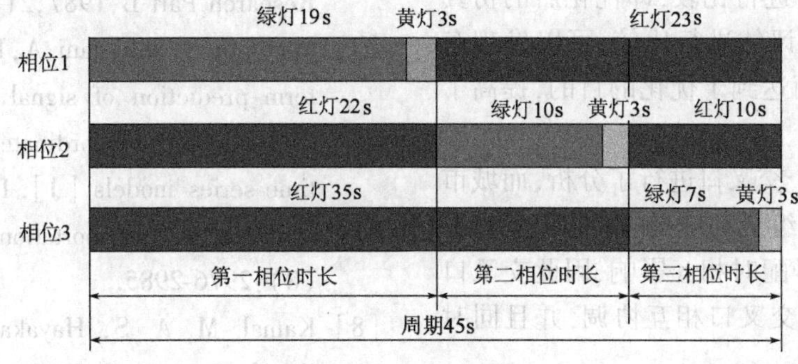

图8 优化后交叉口配时图

优化后的仿真评估 表29

仿真运行	时间间隔	转向	排队长度(m)	排队长度(最大)(m)	车辆延误(平均值)(所有)(s)	静态停车延误(平均值)(所有)(s)	停车次数(所有)
平均值	0~3600	南直行—北入道口	0.47	5.02	18.07	11.33	0.90
平均值	0~3600	南左转—西入道口	0.86	6.47	30.30	19.49	1.57
平均值	0~3600	南直行右转—东入道口	0.00	0.00	5.97	3.19	0.30
平均值	0~3600	南直行右转—北入道口	2.40	20.92	30.36	24.05	0.93
平均值	0~3600	西直行—东入道口	12.37	46.35	7.31	4.48	0.35

续上表

仿真运行	时间间隔	转　向	排队长度(m)	排队长度(最大)(m)	车辆延误(平均值)(所有)(s)	静态停车延误(平均值)(所有)(s)	停车次数(所有)
平均值	0~3600	西左转—北入道口	2.48	25.71	9.55	4.73	0.39
平均值	0~3600	西直行右转—南入道口	0.00	0.00	0.39	0.00	0.00
平均值	0~3600	西直行右转—东入道口	1.40	10.93	9.82	5.26	0.49
平均值	0~3600	东直行—西入道口	5.15	42.04	5.74	2.85	0.35
平均值	0~3600	东左转—南入道口	1.54	9.62	10.79	6.33	0.55
平均值	0~3600	东直行右转—西入道口	0.10	2.98	5.34	2.90	0.24
平均值	0~3600	东直行右转—北入道口	0.00	0.00	0.00	0.00	0.00
平均值	0~3600	北直行—南入道口	2.27	12.70	16.22	8.83	0.73
平均值	0~3600	北左转—东入道口	0.54	7.91	16.36	8.48	0.74
平均值	0~3600	北直行右转—南入道口	6.49	34.17	27.40	20.38	0.86
平均值	0~3600	北直行右转—西入道口	0.55	7.63	11.04	6.99	0.48

4　结语

(1)未优化前该交叉口的车流量主要由东西方向负担,但西侧车流量更多,南北车流量相对较小,则东西方向更易造成车辆拥堵。由表5和表6可以看出,早高峰的车辆延误大于晚高峰的车辆延误,则优化设计的过程中选用早高峰的交通流量。

(2)表6与表28进行比较,即优化后的仿真评估与早高峰的仿真评估进行比较,可以发现车辆延误大大降低,从而达到了优化的目的,提高了道路的通行能力。

(3)本文仅对单个交叉口进行了分析,而城市道路是由多条交叉口组合而成的,并且各个交叉口之间联系紧密,信号配时相互影响,因此交叉口信号配时需要与其他交叉口相互协调,并且同时进行。

参考文献

[1] 栗红强.城市交通控制信号配时参数优化方法研究[D].长春:吉林大学,2004.

[2] 常宏顺.城市单交叉口实时控制方法研究[D].大连:大连理工大学,2008.

[3] Pappis C P, Mamdani E H. A Fuzzy logic controller for a traffic junction [J]. IEEE Transacions on systems, man and cybernetics, 1977,7(10):707-711.

[4] 陈森发,陈洪,徐吉谦.城市单路口交通的两级模糊控制及其仿真[J].系统仿真学报,1992,10(2):35-38.

[5] Gartner N H, Tarnoff P J, Andrews C M. Valuation of the optimized policies for adaptive control (OPAC) strategy [J]. Transportation Research Board,1991,1324:105-114.

[6] Heydecker B. Uncertainty and variability in traffic signal calculations [J]. Transportation Research Part B,1987,21 (1):79-85.

[7] Moghimi B, Safikhani A, Kamga C, etal. Short-term prediction of signal cycle on an arterial with actuated-uncoordinated control using sparse time series models [J]. IEEE Transactions on Inter-ligent Transportation Systems, 2018, 20 (8):2976-2985.

[8] Kamal M A S, Hayakawa T, Imura J I. Development and Evaluation of an Adaptive Traffic Signal Control Scheme Under a Mixed-automated Traffic Scenario [J]. IEEE Transactions on Intelligent Transportation Systems,2019,21 (2):590-602.

[9] 徐泽洲,刘祥泽,贾彦峰,等.重大事件下的路网交通疏散双层优化模型[J].山东科技大学学报(自然科学版),2021,40(5):117-119.

[10] 薛禹胜,郁琛,赵俊华,等.关于短期及超短期风电功率预测的评述[J].电力系统自动化,2015,39(6):141-151.

[11] 闫鹤鸣,李相俊,麻秀范,等.基于超短期风电预测功率的储能系统跟踪风电计划出力控制方法[J].电网技术,2015,39(2):432-439.

考虑车辆排放的交叉口信号控制优化模型

冀浙明　邵海鹏*　陈帅铭
(长安大学运输工程学院)

摘　要　在城市交通系统中,车辆运行过程中产生的污染气体给城市的生态环境带来了显著的恶劣影响,本文通过考虑车辆通过交叉口过程中产生的排放,构建了一种单点交叉口信号配时优化模型。基于Webster车均延误模型和VT-micro微观排放模型,建立了能够综合优化交叉口总延误和总排放的信号配时优化模型,运用遗传算法对其进行优化求解。选取珠海市柠溪路—兴业路交叉口作为实验交叉口,利用SUMO仿真平台对提出的优化模型进行对比检验,结果表明本文所提出的优化模型能够在不增加车均延误的同时,有效降低交叉口的车辆总排放,尤其在平峰时段,优化模型下实验交叉口的CO_2和NO_x排放量分别降低了59.55%和56.06%,证明了本文所提出的信号配时优化模型能够实现交叉口延误和排放的综合优化。

关键词　交通工程　信号控制优化　VT-micro模型　车辆排放

0　引言

交叉口作为城市交通系统中的重要节点,承担着复杂的交通任务,车辆在此反复地分流、合流,交织出各个流向的冲突点,因此交通系统的运行效率和安全性与交叉口运行状况息息相关。信号控制系统的快速发展在很大程度上缓解了城市路网关键节点的无序冲突,在保证交叉口通行安全性的同时提高了交叉口的运行质量。然而,随着机动车出行需求的快速增长,当前的城市交叉口信号控制系统暴露出了一些不可忽视的问题。比如,城市交叉口信号控制系统配时方案大多侧重于对交通运行指标的优化,比如延误、排队长度、通行时间等,而忽略了信号配时方案对环境产生的影响,因此,在优化信号配时方案时,与生态环境相关的指标也应该被着重考虑。在"双碳"目标下,全社会再次深刻认识到了碳排放给生态环境带来的恶劣影响,减少交通碳排放也成为了交通领域的重要话题。通过优化信号配时方案来减少交叉口车辆碳排放作为一种聪明的调控方法,已经被国内外学者广泛关注。如何实现信号配时策略中交通运行效率和排放的多维优化,是值得研究的重要问题。

目前国内外的交通尾气排放模型按照适用范围和功能用途可以分为宏观、中观、微观三个层面。其中,宏观模型基于平均速度的排放因子,运用统计方法得到区域的车辆排放状况[1],最具代表性的为美国环保局研发的MOBILE(Vehicle Emission Factor Model)模型;中观排放模型一般基于驾驶工况计算机动车排放,能够估计某条道路或某一路段上的交通尾气排放状况,比如美国环保局开发的MEASURE模型[2];微观排放模型则把单一汽车作为研究对象,输入瞬时速度、加速度等瞬时行驶参数逐秒估算单车排放,典型的微观排放模型有VT-micro模型[3]等。

随着车辆排放逐渐得到国内外学者更深的思考,一些学者[4]发现交通控制策略会影响车辆排放,因此,通过交通控制手段来辅助减少车辆运行过程中的排放成为了一些学者的研究重点。P. Fernandes等[5]针对一个包含有环形交叉口、信号控制交叉口和停车控制交叉口的交通廊道进行了控制方案的多目标优化,利用VISSIM模型和VSP(Vehicle Specific Power)模型对该交通廊道进行评价,对比不同控制方案的延误和排放,采用快速非支配排序遗传算法(NSGA-Ⅱ)对延误和排放进行优化来寻找最佳交叉口间距。结果表明,与信号控制相比,环岛可以实现更小的排队长度和排放量,而交叉口间距保持在200m会在交通运营和排放方面具有优势。Chen等[6]将宏观交通分析模型与宏观排放估算模型相结合来考虑车辆排放,采用遗传算法来优化各相位绿灯时间,以减少路网内的平均出行时间和排放为优化目标。利用AIMSUN软件对西安市的一个拥堵区域进行仿真,对比当前的信号策略和优化后的信号策略,结果表明,提出的优化策略减少了研究区域的车辆通行时间和四种污染物的排放量。Yukimasa Matsumoto等[7]选取两个交叉口,其中一个交叉口有行人信号灯,另一个交叉口没有行人信号灯,除此之外,两个交叉口的特征几乎一样,而行人信号灯被认为可以为驾驶员提供减速信息。运用微观仿真软件模拟观察到的车辆运动,并估算CO_2排放量。通过对比未提供减速信息、较晚提供减速信息、较早提供减速信息、多次提供减速信息多种情景,得出为车辆提供减速信息可以有效减少CO_2排放,其中较早提供减速信息对CO_2排放的减少最为明显。然而,提供减速信息这一策略在交通量小的时候可以明显降低CO_2排放,在交通量大的时候会造成拥堵和CO_2排放的显著增加。Chen等[8]基于有限容量排队模型提出了一种基于左转车道的交叉口宏观交通模型,同时结合宏观排放模型,构建了信号控制优化框架。该优化框架能够确切地得到预信号和主信号的绿灯时间占比,模型求解采用非支配排序遗传算法Ⅱ(NSGA-Ⅱ)。利用AIMSUN对实际交叉口数据进行仿真,对比提出的优化策略与传统交通控制方法下的延误和排放,结果表明该优化策略能有效降低借道左转交叉口的行驶延误和车辆排放。

从目前的研究现状可以看出,虽然国内外学者对于以排放为优化目标的信号控制策略有较深的研究,但是大多基于较为宏观的排放模型,针对单个车辆运行过程中瞬时排放的优化研究相对较少。本文则在相关研究的基础上,立足于微观排放模型,通过估算单车排放,集计得到交叉口总排放,以交叉口总排放和总延误为优化目标,构建低延误、低排放的交叉口信号控制优化模型。

1　模型构建

1.1　车均延误模型

在车均延误模型中,最为经典的是1958年Webster[9]提出的延误模型,他假设车辆到达服从泊松分布,通过修正得到了延误计算模型,如式(1)所示。

$$d_i = 0.9\left[\frac{C(1-\lambda_i)^2}{2(1-\lambda_i x_i)} + \frac{x_i^2}{2q_i(1-x_i)}\right] \quad (1)$$

式中:d_i——车道组i的平均延误,s/pcu;

C——信号周期时长,单位为s;

λ_i——绿信比;

x_i——车道组i的饱和度;

q_i——车道组i的通行能力(pcu/h)。

1.2　VT-micro微观排放模型

Kyoungho Ahn等[3]于2002年提出了VT-micro(Virginia Tech Microscopic Energy and Emission Model)模型,该模型由线性回归方法得出,以单一汽车为研究对象,通过输入瞬时速度、加速度等瞬时行驶参数,逐秒估算机动车的排放。其具体表达式如式(2)所示。

$$\ln(\mathrm{MOE}_e) = \begin{cases} \sum_{i=0}^{3}\sum_{j=0}^{3}(L_{i,j}^{e} \times s^i \times a^j), a \geqslant 0 \\ \sum_{i=0}^{3}\sum_{j=0}^{3}(M_{i,j}^{e} \times s^i \times a^j), a < 0 \end{cases} \quad (2)$$

式中:MOE_e——某车辆在t时刻的能耗或排放值,单位为liters/s或mg/s;

s——该车辆在t时刻的速度,单位为km/h;

a——该车辆在t时刻的加速度,单位为km/h/s;

i——速度幂指数;

j——加速度幂指数;

$L_{i,j}^{e}$——$a \geqslant 0$,速度幂指数为i,加速度幂指数为j时的回归系数;

$M e_{i,j}$——$a < 0$,速度幂指数为i,加速度幂指数为j时的回归系数。

在计算机动车排放时,不同的排放物对应不同的回归系数,如表1(CO_2)、表2(NO_x)所示。

1.3　考虑排放的信号配时模型

本研究以交叉口的总延误和总排放为优化目标,将两个目标融合为单目标优化函数,并对两个目标赋予不同的权重,权重的选取依照表3中的规则,选取α为0.7,β为0.3,在此基础上来优化各相位的有效绿灯时间,目标函数如式(3)所示。

CO_2 回归系数　　表 1

a	i	$j=0$	$j=1$	$j=2$	$j=3$
$a \geqslant 0$	$i=0$	6.916	0.217	2.354×10^{-4}	-3.639×10^{-4}
	$i=1$	0.02754	0.968×10^{-2}	-0.175×10^{-2}	8.35×10^{-5}
	$i=2$	-2.070×10^{-4}	-1.0138×10^{-4}	1.966×10^{-5}	-1.02×10^{-6}
	$i=3$	9.80×10^{-7}	3.66×10^{-7}	-1.08×10^{-7}	8.50×10^{-9}
$a<0$	$i=0$	6.915	-0.032	-9.17×10^{-3}	-2.886×10^{-4}
	$i=1$	0.0284	8.53×10^{-3}	1.15×10^{-3}	-3.06×10^{-6}
	$i=2$	-2.266×10^{-4}	-6.594×10^{-5}	-1.289×10^{-5}	-2.68×10^{-7}
	$i=3$	1.11×10^{-6}	3.20×10^{-7}	7.56×10^{-8}	2.95×10^{-9}

NO_x 回归系数　　表 2

a	i	$j=0$	$j=1$	$j=2$	$j=3$
$a \geqslant 0$	$i=0$	-1.08	0.2369	1.47×10^{-3}	-7.82×10^{-5}
	$i=1$	1.79×10^{-2}	4.05×10^{-2}	-3.75×10^{-3}	1.05×10^{-4}
	$i=2$	2.41×10^{-4}	-4.08×10^{-4}	-1.28×10^{-5}	1.52×10^{-6}
	$i=3$	-1.06×10^{-6}	9.42×10^{-7}	1.86×10^{-7}	4.42×10^{-9}
$a<0$	$i=0$	-1.08	0.2085	2.19×10^{-2}	8.82×10^{-4}
	$i=1$	2.11×10^{-2}	1.07×10^{-2}	6.55×10^{-3}	6.27×10^{-4}
	$i=2$	1.63×10^{-4}	-3.23×10^{-5}	-9.43×10^{-5}	-1.01×10^{-5}
	$i=3$	-5.83×10^{-7}	1.83×10^{-7}	4.47×10^{-7}	4.57×10^{-8}

$$F = \min \alpha \frac{E}{E_0} + \beta \frac{D}{D_0} \tag{3}$$

式中：α 和 β——权重系数；

E——优化后配时方案下的交叉口车辆总排放；

E_0——原始配时方案下的交叉口总排放；

D——优化后配时方案下的交叉口车辆总延误；

D_0——原始配时方案下的交叉口总延误。

约束条件如式(4)所示。

$$\text{s.t.} \begin{cases} \sum_{i=1}^{3} g_i + l = C \\ 0 < g_i < C, i \in \{1,2,3\} \\ \alpha + \beta = 1 \end{cases} \tag{4}$$

式中：g_i——i 相位的有效绿灯时间；

l——绿灯损失时间。

权重系数取值　　表 3

环境污染程度(PM2.5)	α	β
重度污染(PM2.5 >150)	0.3	0.7
轻度污染(75 < PM2.5 <150)	0.5	0.5
良(75 < PM2.5 <150)	0.7	0.3

2　基于遗传算法的模型求解

20 世纪 70 年代 John holland 提出了遗传算法，该算法是一种模拟自然界生物进化机制的随机全局搜索和优化方法，借鉴了达尔文的进化论和孟德尔的遗传学理论，通过模拟自然进化过程寻求最优解。在遗传算法求解中，优化问题的求解被转化成类似生物进化中染色体基因的交叉、变异等过程，产生更适应环境的个体种群，通过不断繁衍进化，最终收敛得到最适应环境的个体，以此作为最优解。本文基于遗传算法的求解步骤如图 1 所示。

在遗传算法模块中，以研究交叉口的原配时方案作为初始种群；根据本文所建立的目标函数，选取适应度函数为 $f=1/F$。除此之外还需设置交叉概率和变异概率，其中交叉运算是将群体内个体随机配对，个体间以一定的概率交换部分染色体，从而得到新一代个体，本文的交叉概率设置为 0.8；变异运算则是随机选择的个体以特定概率改变某一个或某一些基因座上的基因值，即可变异成为新的个体，本文的变异概率设为 0.1。

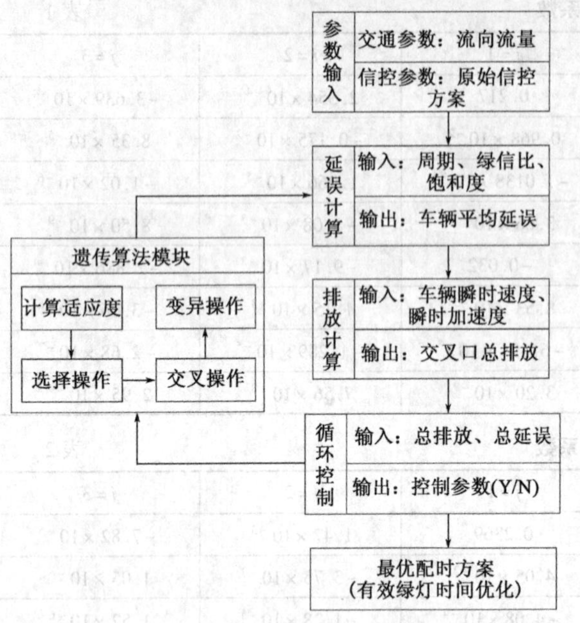

图 1　模型求解

3　实例分析

3.1　实验交叉口

本文选取珠海市柠溪路—兴业路交叉口为案例交叉口，数据来源为交通运输部开放数据(https://www.mot.gov.cn/sjkf/)[10]。该交叉口是由柠溪路与兴业路交叉形成的十字路口，路口周边分布众多居民楼，幼儿园、医院以及大型的购物广场，是重要的人员、车流集散地，是重要的交通节点。该交叉口某工作日早高峰(7:00—9:00)和平峰(14:00—15:00)的分向流量如图 2、图 3 所示。

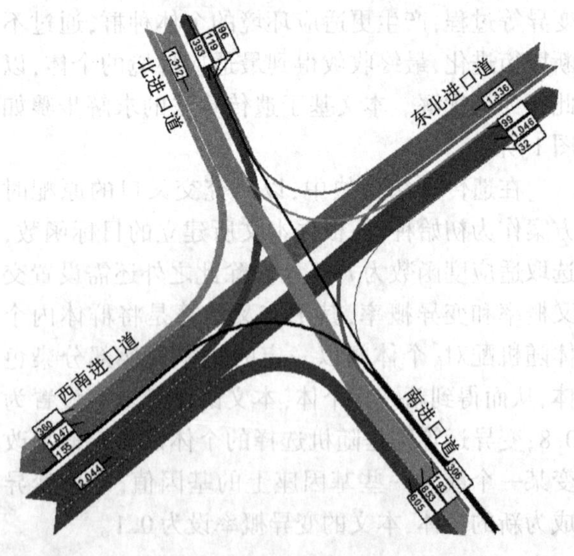

图 2　早高峰分向流量图

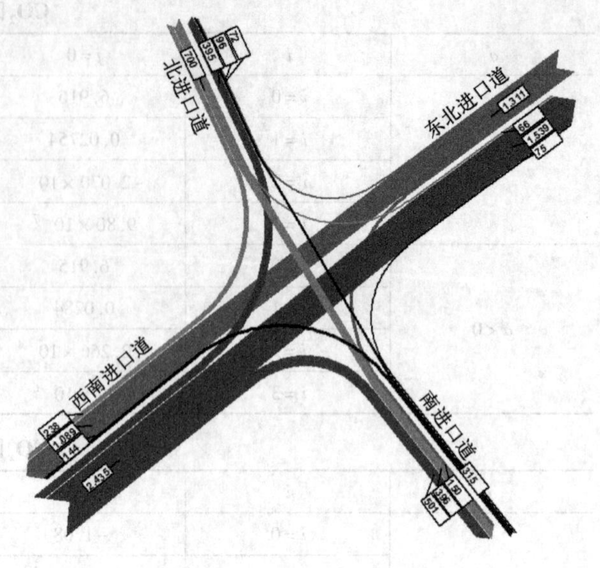

图 3　平峰分向流量图

该交叉口的实际信控方案是根据不同日期与不同时段的道路数据计算得来的，日期主要分为工作日(周一到周四)、周五、休息日(周六、周日)，每天分为 14 个时段，共 17 套定时信号配时方案，根据不同日期不同时段的交通运行状况选择特定的配时方案。本文选取工作日的高峰和平峰两个时段，对其相应配时方案的有效绿灯时间进行优化，该时段的原信控方案如图 4 所示，两个信控方案的相位和相序一致，信号周期和绿灯时间不同，图中黄灯时间均为 3s。

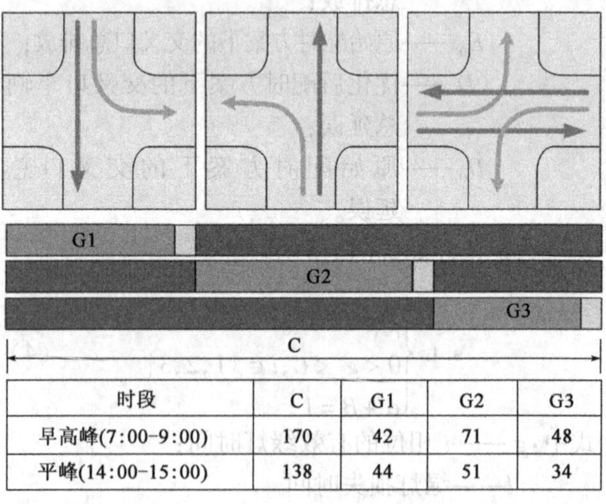

时段	C	G1	G2	G3
早高峰(7:00-9:00)	170	42	71	48
平峰(14:00-15:00)	138	44	51	34

图 4　实验交叉口原配时方案

3.2　仿真结果

本文首先通过 SUMO 微观仿真平台还原出实验交叉口在原配时方案下的运行状况，获取单车瞬时速度和瞬时加速度来计算单一车辆通过交叉口过程中产生的排放,进而集计出交叉口的总排放;然后借助 PyCharm 2021.3.1 与 SUMO 1.11.0,在 Python 3.9 环境下完成基于优化模型的仿真实验,计算出优化后的信号配时参数以及该配时方案下实验交叉口的总延误和总排放,其中车辆排放考虑了 CO_2 和 NO_x 两类排放物。两个时段优化后的配时方案如表 4 所示,优化前后的排放指标和延误指标如图 5、图 6 所示。

优化后信号配时方案 表 4

时段	C	G1	G2	G3
早高峰(7:00—9:00)	170	25	64	72
平峰(14:00—15:00)	138	57	26	46

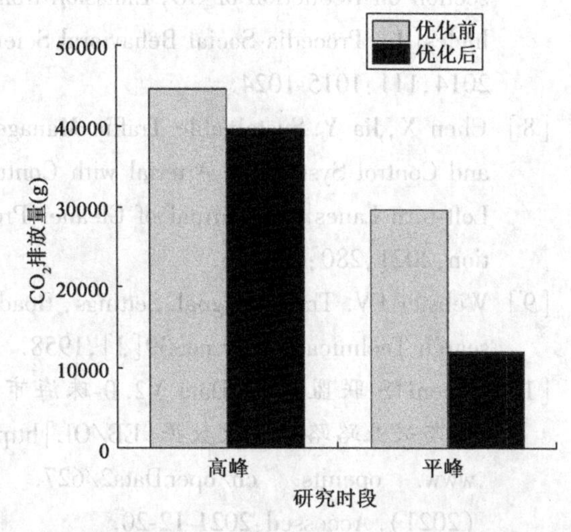

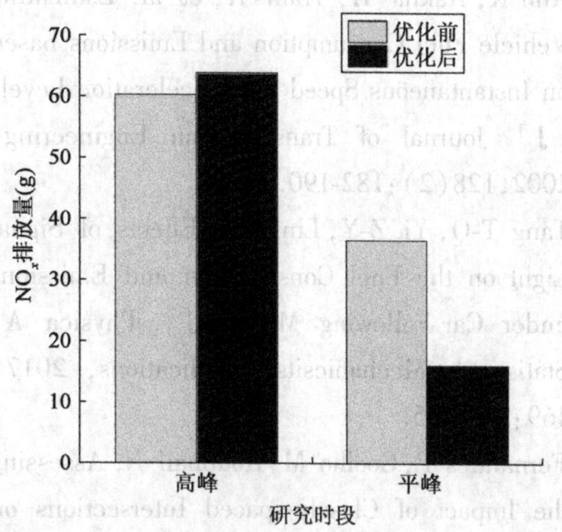

图 5 优化前后排放指标对比

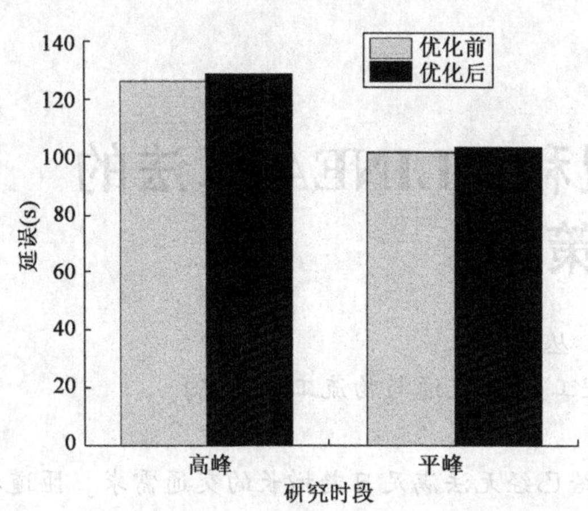

图 6 优化前后总延误指标对比

从图 5 和图 6 可以看出,在优化后的配时方案下,实验交叉口的 CO_2 总排放量在高峰时段降低了 11.22%,在平峰时段降低了 59.55%;NO_x 总排放量在高峰时段增加了 5.84%,在平峰时段降低了 56.06%;而一个信号周期内交叉口各流向的总延误,在高峰时段增加了 2.34s,在平峰时段仅增加了 1.34s。仿真结果表明,本文提出的考虑排放的信号优化模型,能够在几乎不改变交叉口单车延误的基础上,较为显著地降低交叉口的 CO_2 和 NO_x 的总排放量,尤其在平峰时段,优化后的 CO_2 和 NO_x 总排放量分别降低了 59.55% 和 56.06%,证明了提出的信号优化模型能在很大程度上减少交叉口机动车运行带给生态环境的负面影响。

4 结语

本文基于 Webster 车均延误模型与 VT-micro 微观排放模型,构建了综合考虑交叉口延误和排放的配时参数优化模型,并利用遗传算法对其进行求解。研究结果表明,本文所提出的信号配时优化模型在几乎不增加车均延误的基础上,可以显著减少交叉口车辆尾气排放量,尤其是在平峰时段,实验交叉口的 CO_2 和 NO_x 排放量分别降低了 59.55% 和 56.06%,验证了本文所提出的信号配时参数优化模型能够在保证交叉口不增加车均延误的同时,有效降低交叉口的车辆总排放。然而,本研究依然存在许多不足,在未来,还将考虑电动车辆与燃油车辆混合流状态下考虑车辆排放的信号配时优化模型以及考虑排放的自适应信号控制策略。

参考文献

[1] 赵佳,闫学东,王江锋.机动车尾气排放和扩散研究综述[J].公路交通科技,2011,28(S1):147-153.

[2] Fomunung I, Washington S, Guensler R, et al. Validation of the MEASURE Automobile Emissions Model: A Statistical Analysis [J]. Journal of TransportationStatistics,2001:65-84.

[3] Ahn K, Rakha H, Trani A, et al. Estimating Vehicle Fuel Consumption and Emissions based on Instantaneous Speed and Acceleration Levels [J]. Journal of Transportation Engineering, 2002,128(2):182-190.

[4] Tang T-Q, Yi Z-Y, Lin Q-F. Effects of Signal Light on the Fuel Consumption and Emissions under Car-Following Model [J]. Physica A: Statistical Mechanicsits Applications, 2017, 469:200-205.

[5] Fernandes P, Coelho M, Rouphail N. Assessing the Impact of Closely-spaced Intersections on Traffic Operations and Pollutant Emissions on a Corridor Level[J]. Transportation Research Part D:Transport Environment,2017,54:304-320.

[6] Chen X, Yuan Z. Environmentally Friendly Traffic Control Strategy-A Case Study in Xi'an City[J]. Journal of Cleaner Production,2020, 249:119397.

[7] Matsumoto Y, Oshima T, Iwamoto R. Effect of Information Provision around Signalized Intersection on Reduction of CO_2 Emission from Vehicles[J]. Procedia-Social Behavioral Sciences, 2014,111:1015-1024.

[8] Chen X, Jia Y. Sustainable Traffic Management and Control System for Arterial with Contraflow Left-turn Lanes[J]. Journal of Cleaner Production,2021,280:124256.

[9] Webster FV. Traffic Signal Settings, Road Research Technical Paper no. 39[J],1958.

[10] OpenITS 联盟. OpenData V2. 0-珠海市柠溪路与兴业路路口开放数据[EB/OL] https://www.openits.cn/openData2/627.jhtml (2021). Accessed:2021-12-20.

一种基于宏观交通流模型和 ALINEA 算法的匝道控制策略

刘海燕[1]　李载宁[*1]　丛　喆[2]

(1.中南大学 交通运输工程学院;2.武汉理工大学 交通与物流工程学院)

摘　要　随着汽车保有量的增加,高速公路的交通供给已经无法满足日趋增长的交通需求。匝道控制是缓解高速公路主线行车压力的有效手段,对其控制算法和控制效果的研究是十分必要的。本文设计了一个具体的高速公路局部路网以及相对应的交通需求场景,并针对该场景建立了宏观交通流模型METANET,设定无控制的空白对照组,通过 MATLAB 仿真实验的方式验证和比较 ALINEA(Asservissement Linéaire d'Entrée Autoroutière)控制算法对总旅行时间(TTS)、交通流速度等相关评价指标的优化效果,结果表明经典 ALINEA 控制方法在局部匝道控制领域具备显著效用,缓解了合流冲突和交通拥堵、提升了行车效率。

关键词　匝道控制　ALINEA　高速公路　负反馈控制　METANET

0　引言

在国民经济大发展的时代背景下,交通需求的急速增长造成高速公路拥堵,增加了高速公路行车的安全隐患。匝道控制(ramp metering)作为高速公路控制最主要、应用最广泛的方式,已被理论和实践证实为改善高速公路安全性,提高通行效率最有效可行的方法之一[1]。该方法的原理是通过灯光控制进入高速公路主线的交通量,减少交织区合流冲突,提高主线运行效率。

国际上交通学者对匝道控制的研究开始于20世纪60年代,从实时性角度来看,入口匝道控制方法可分为静态定时控制(Pre-timed Metering)和自适应控制(Responsive Metering)。由Wattleworth提出的单点匝道定时控制方法是最早得到应用的方法[2],但是,该方法容易出现过饱和,导致拥堵或交通能力利用不充分的现象。随着检测技术的发展和互联网技术的引入,现有的匝道控制大都采用自适应控制方法,其中最具代表性的有Msher提出的Demand-Capacity方法、Papageorgiou提出的ALINEA(Asservissement Linéaire d'Entrée Autoroutière)闭环控制方法。美国广泛使用的Demand-Capacity方法是基于对主线上游交通量的测量并将其与饱和流进行比较。然而,由于仅凭交通量的值不足以确定高速公路是拥堵还是畅通[3],该方法存在平稳交通流能力不足的缺陷;ALINEA控制方法可以保持交通流的稳定高效,并且操作容易,因此在单点匝道控制中具有广泛应用[3]。陆克丽霞等人[4]通过分析上海内环武夷路上匝道,考虑匝道排队长度限制,将ALINEA算法运用于实际的工程实践,可使主线速度提高、匝道流量的激波现象平滑。从控制点的选择来看,匝道控制方法还可以分为单点匝道控制方法和多点匝道协调控制方法,其中,后者中的典型方法有多匝道协调控制方法METALINE。Papageorgiou在巴黎Boulevard环城大道的实地实验中,发现ALINEA和METALINE两种反馈控制策略在正常情况下得到的结果大致相同,但METALINE方法在突发事件发生时的控制效果较好[5]。

但是,当前研究缺乏对匝道控制对交织区不同细分路段的交通流运行状态影响的进一步分析。因此,本文拟通过METANET模型对研究路段进行拓扑结构化,探究ALINEA控制方法对匝道入口处不同路段交通流的影响以及对总旅行时间、排队长度等宏观关键指标的影响,论证ALINEA算法对高速公路交织区运行效率的改善效果。

1 研究方法

1.1 高速公路系统交通运行状态分析

高速公路作为一个相对封闭和独立的系统,其交通流存在明显的特征。如图1a)所示,用q_{out}表示匝道下游的主线车流量,o_{out}表示占有率,其与交通流密度的关系为:

$$o = \frac{1}{1000}\bar{L} \times \rho$$

式中:$\bar{L}$——车辆平均长度,单位为m;

ρ——交通流密度,单位为veh/km。

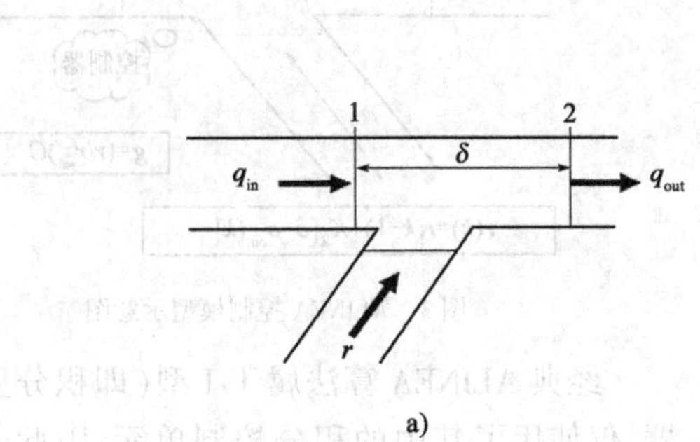

a)

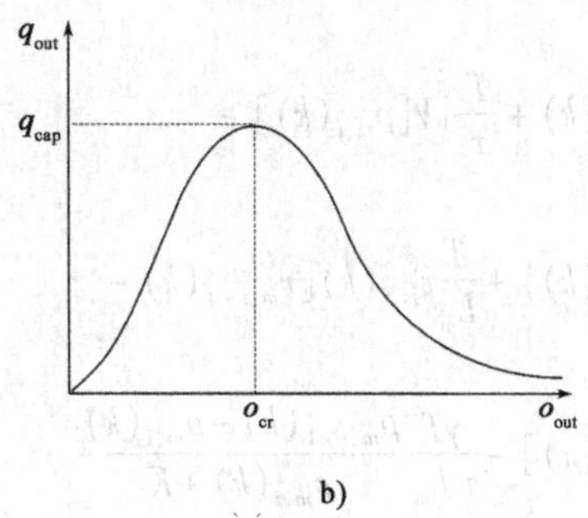

b)

图1 流量与占有率基本原理图

根据Greenshields速度-密度线性模型,速度和密度之间呈线性关系:

$$v = a\rho + b$$

$$q = \rho v = \rho(a\rho + b) = a\rho^2 + b\rho$$

式中:a、b——待确定的模型参数,其中a通常情况下是负数。

将占有率的密度计算公式中的密度ρ分离出来,代入上式中可得:

$$q = \frac{1000^2 a}{L^2} \cdot o^2 + \frac{1000b}{L} \cdot o$$

根据以上分析可知,交通流量和占有率之间的关系属于二元一次函数,符合著名的基本原理

图 $q=Q(o)$。如图1b)所示[5],其中 $o=o_{cr}$ 是对应最大流量 $q_{cap}=Q(o_{cr})$ 的临界占有率。当高速公路的占有率处于临界值 o_{cr} 附近时,车流量最大,系统运行状态最优。对流量 q 求微分即可得到临界占有率。

$$o_{cr}=-\frac{bL}{2000a}$$

1.2　宏观交通流模型 METANET

基于对宏观交通流集总行为分析的模型有很多种,其中,交通流的流体力学模型将流体力学的重要理论运用于交通流之中,即将交通流视作由大量车辆组成的可压缩连续流体介质,并以密度、速度和流量这三个宏观要素对其进行特征描述。模型的研究对象仅仅是这一特殊流体,而非系统中的每一个微观的车辆。Papageorgiou 针对高速公路交通流特点建立了宏观交通流稳态数值模型 META。在此基础上,Papageorgiou 与 Messmer 建立了二阶交通流模型 METANET,该模型将高速公路网络以有向图的形式进行拓扑结构化,对于路段之间较小的线形差异,模型予以忽略;而对于较大的线性变化则设置节点。入口匝道和出口匝道处也设置节点。高速公路的路段 m 被划分为 N_m 个长度为 L_m 的区间,如图2所示[6]。

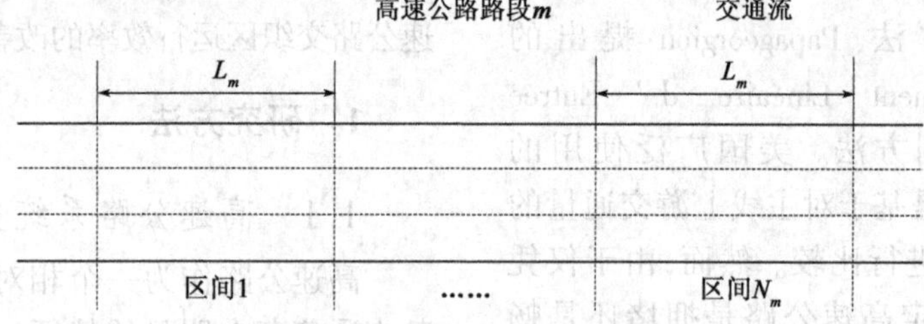

图2　METANET 模型示意图

模型的公式表述如下:

$$\rho_{m,i}(k+1)=\rho_{m,i}(k)+\frac{T}{L_m\lambda_m}[q_{m,i-1}(k)-q_i(k)]$$

$$q_{m,i}(k)=\rho_{m,i}(k)\cdot v_{m,i}(k)\cdot\lambda_m$$

$$v_{m,i}(k+1)=v_{m,i}(k)+\frac{T}{\tau}\{V[\rho_{m,i}(k)]-v_{m,i}(k)\}+\frac{T}{L_m}v_{m,i}(k)[v_{m,i-1}(k)-v_{m,i}(k)]-\frac{\gamma T}{\tau L_m}\frac{\rho_{m,i+1}(k)-\rho_{m,i}(k)}{\rho_{m,i}(k)+K}$$

$$V[\rho_{m,i}(k)]=v_{f,m}\exp\left\{-\frac{1}{a_m}\left[\frac{\rho_{m,i}(k)}{\rho_{cr,m}}\right]a_m\right\}$$

Papageorgiou 从定性和定量两个方面,在荷兰阿姆斯特丹 A10 等组成的高速公路网对其进行了实地的验证分析,得出结论,即 METANET 模型对高速公路交通流的描述精确,具备工程适用性,还可以精确再现交通拥堵。

1.3　经典 ALINEA 匝道控制理论

ALINEA 控制方法基于 PID 技术,模型原理示意图如图3所示。

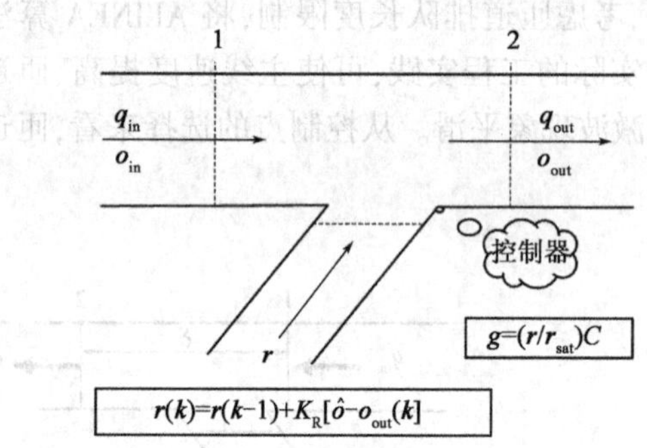

图3　ALINEA 控制模型示意图

经典 ALINEA 算法属于 I 型(即积分型)控制器,仅使用了其中的积分控制单元,因此,其控制原理可表达为:

$$r(t)=K_R\int e(t)\,dt$$

式中:$e(t)$——误差函数,$e(t)=\hat{o}=o_{out}(t)$;

对以上控制表达式求导,并进行离散化处理,得到 ALINEA 算法表达式[5]:

$$r(k)=r(k-1)+K_R[\hat{o}-o_{out}(k)]$$

式中:r——入口匝道交通量(veh/h);

式中出现的 $r(k-1)$ 的值应设为与上一时段实测的实际匝道交通量相等。

模型的基本原理是：以入口匝道下游占有率作为被控量，以一个略低于主线饱和流所对应的入口匝道下游设定占有率作为系统的输入量，在实时监测被控量的基础上，对进入主线的匝道入口交通量进行调节。具体说来，当下游占有率超过设定值时，就降低入口匝道调节率；反之，则增加入口匝道调节率[7]。这样不断修正，将入口匝道下游占有率维持在设定值附近，从而将主线交通流维持在饱和流附近，达到通过能力最大化。

由于 METANET 模型较好地平衡了仿真的速度和精度，具有确定性、离散性、离散空间性和宏观性等特点，适用于交通控制的需求。此外，该模型可以再现在交通激波的影响下造成的入口匝道交通量阈值下降的现象，因此，可以将该模型与 ALINEA 控制算法进行结合，进行仿真实验，从而对该控制算法的有效性进行评价。

2 仿真实验与结果讨论[1]

2.1 高速公路交织区场景搭建

高速公路主线设定为全长 6km 的双车道公路，以匝道入口为节点分为两个路段，其中路段 L_1 长 4km，L_2 路段长 2km。每隔 1km 将路段划分为一个区间，其中路段 L_1 被划分为区间 1-4，路段 L_2 被划分为区间 5 和 6，如图 4 所示。

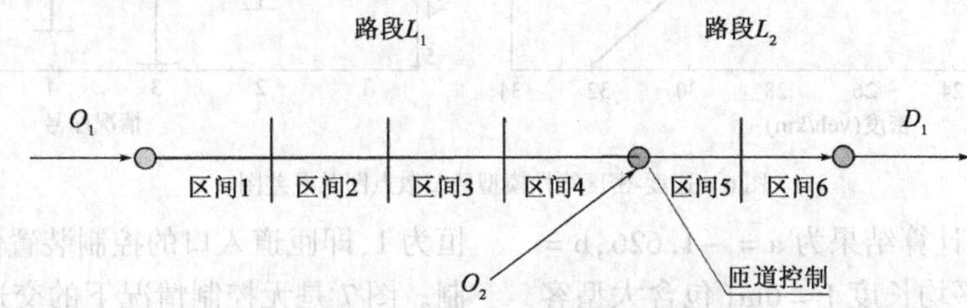

图 4 高速公路交织区场景 METANET 模型示意图

系统有两个交通流输入，其中主线上游交通流输入 O_1 是主要的交通流生成，饱和交通流量为每条车道 2000veh/h，合计 4000veh/h；入口匝道 O_2 是一条单车道公路，饱和交通流量为 2000veh/h。

2.2 仿真实验的初始化设置

2.2.1 仿真时间步长以及实验需求情况的设置

仿真时间取 $T=2.5$h，仿真时间步长 $k=10$s，对各指标进行离散化处理。然后确定控制器的进行控制和采样间隔时间 $Tc=1$min。需求场景如下：主线交通需求在前 2h 维持在 3500veh/h，2h 后下降至 1000veh/h；匝道交通需求在前 0.5h 出现 1500veh/h 的峰值，随后减少至 500veh/h 并维持不变（图 5）。

2.2.2 ALINEA 控制算法的模型参数标定

（1）临界占有率 o_{cr} 的确定

根据 ALINEA 控制方法的原理，需要首先确定回归系数，从而计算高速公路主线的临界占有率取值。根据 Greenshields 速度-密度线性模型进行一元线性回归，本设计的需求场景得到的密度和速度数据如表 1 所示。

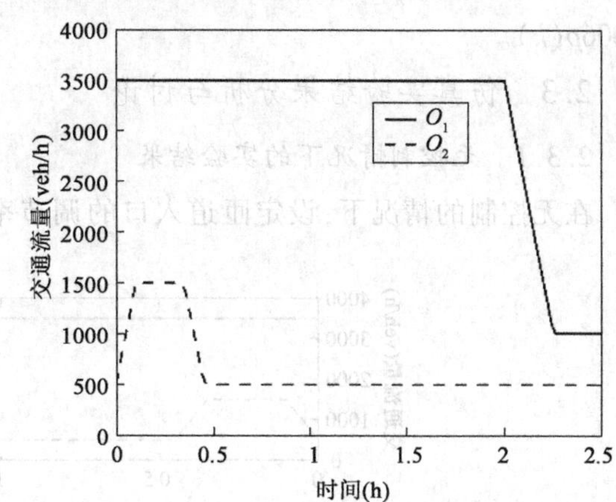

图 5 仿真实验采取的交通需求折线图

O_1-主线；O_2-匝道

1. 本论文所基于的仿真实验思路和 MATLAB 代码参考自 András Hegyi 的论文（参考文献[6]），本文的原创性在于对实验的部分重要参数进行了标定，特此声明。

实验需求场景的交通流密度和速度　　表1

数据组数	1	2	3	4	5	6
密度(veh/km)	21.870	21.963	22.387	24.121	30.323	32.184
速度(km/h)	80.017	79.679	78.171	72.552	65.957	62.143

一元线性回归结果如图 6 所示。

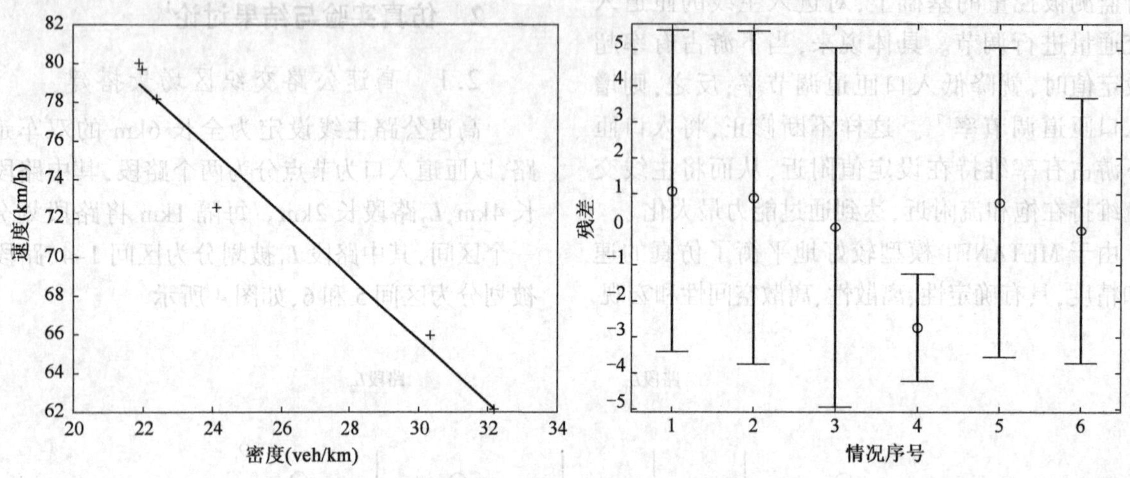

图 6　速度-密度线性模型回归散点图及残差图

模型的回归系数计算结果为 a = −1.626，b = 114.514。取车辆的平均长度 L = 6m(包含大型客车)，根据临界占有率公式计算可得 o_{cr} = 21.13%，仿真实验中取略低于它的 20%。

(2)实时占有率 $o(k)$ 的确定

由占有率的密度计算公式可知，占有率 o 与交通流密度之间呈线性正相关，相关系数为 $L/1000 = 0.006$，因此可确定实时占有率 $o(k) = 0.006\rho(k)$。

2.3　仿真实验结果分析与讨论

2.3.1　无控制情况下的实验结果

在无控制的情况下，设定匝道入口的调节率恒为 1，即匝道入口的控制装置保持绿灯不加以限制。图 7 是无控制情况下的交通流需求和调节率变化折线图。

(1)交通流三要素变化曲线

两个交通流来源 O_1 和 O_2 在高峰时段进行合流之后的交通流量为 5000veh/h，超出饱和交通流量，导致交通拥堵。仿真得到 6 个区间的交通流三要素的变化曲线如图 8 所示。

分析图 8a)可以得出以下结论：

①在入口匝道的交通流输入高峰时段，也即 0.5h 之前，由于入口匝道的交通需求大，出现了合流冲突，导致路段 L_1 的交通流量下降；

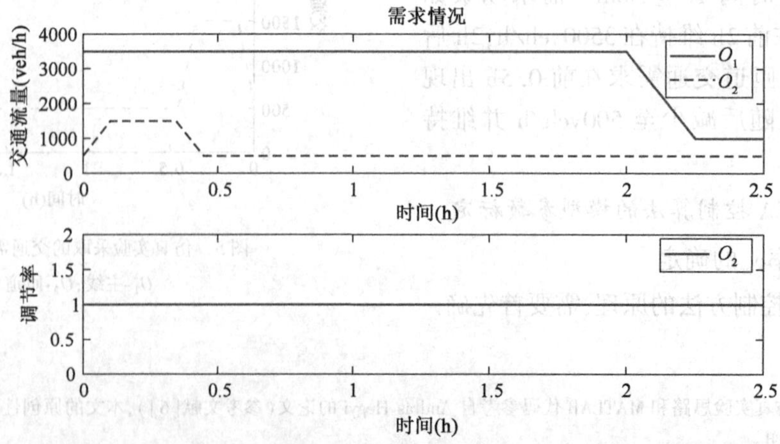

图 7　无控制情况下的交通需求和调节率设定值

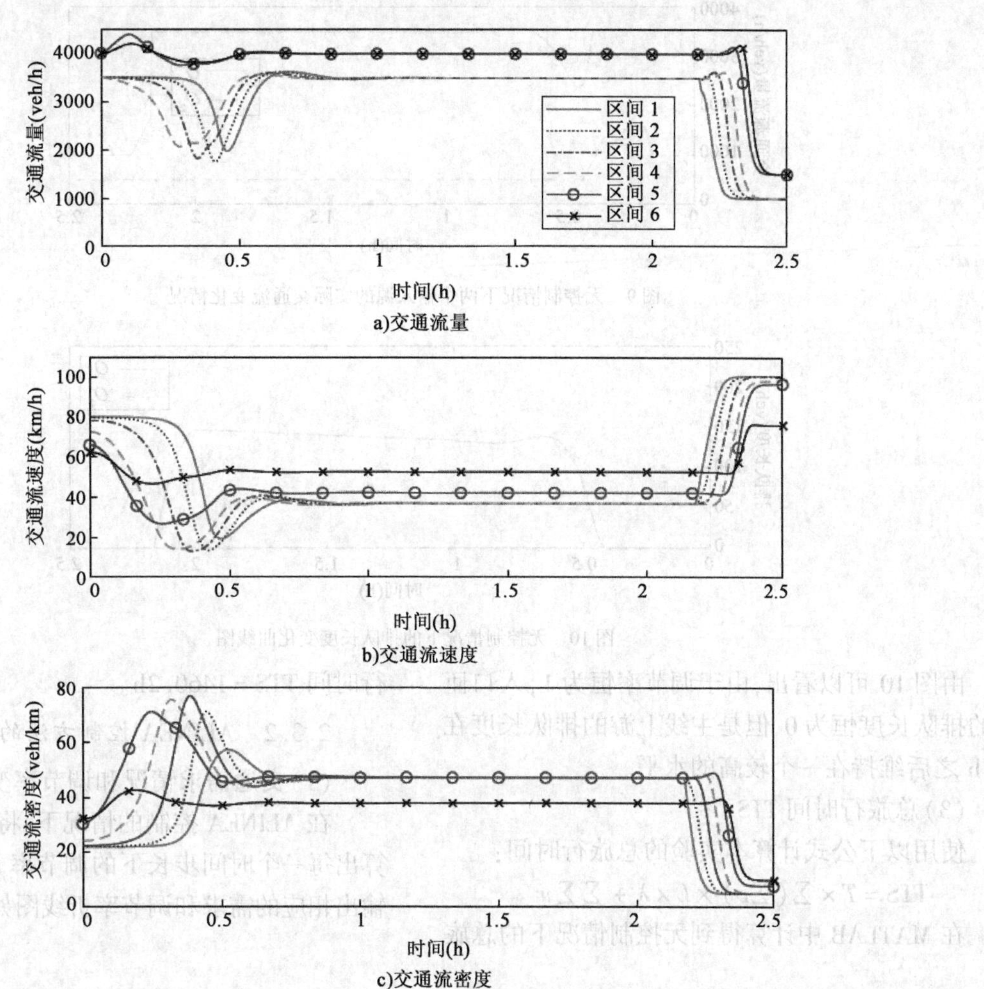

图 8 无控制情况下 6 个区间交通流三要素变化曲线图

②在 2h 之后，当高速公路主线的交通需求降低至小于主线的饱和交通流量时，拥堵消失，路段 L_1 的交通流量逐渐稳定至 1000veh/h，路段 L_2 的交通流量逐渐稳定至 1500veh/h。

分析图 8b) 可以得出以下结论：

①在 0.5h 之前，各个路段和区间的交通流速度均出现了一个低谷，且越靠近上游的区间，速度最小值出现的时间越滞后，可见入口匝道不加以控制时带来的合流冲突首先影响了路段 L_2 的交通畅通，随后拥堵范围不断扩大至主线上游；

②在 2h 之后，高速公路主线的交通需求降低至 1000veh/h，速度出现显著提升。

分析图 8c) 可以得出以下结论：

①在 0.5h 之前，各个区间的交通流密度均出现峰值，同样的，越靠近高速公路主线上游的区间，峰值出现的时间越滞后。此外，区间 6 的交通流密度峰值和稳定值较之其他区间都更低，可以看出合流冲突对距离入口匝道节点较远的下游路段影响较小；

②在 2h 之后，交通压力减小，各个区间的交通流密度均大幅降低。

(2) 实际交通流以及排队长度变化统计

在无控制的情况下，两个交通流输入源 O_1 和 O_2 实际进入目标路段的交通流随时间变化的曲线如图 9 所示。

无控制情况下，匝道入口的交通流全部进入主线，但是这阻碍了主线上游交通流 O_1 的输入，使其出现了急速的下降。当 O_2 的交通需求降至 500veh/h 时，O_1 的交通流量逐渐增加，并维持在 3500veh/h 的水平。

图 10 是主线和入口匝道排队长度变化曲线图。

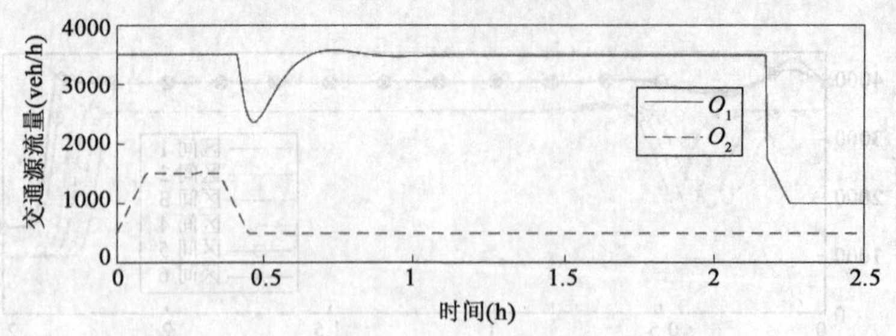

图9 无控制情况下两个输入源的实际交通流变化情况

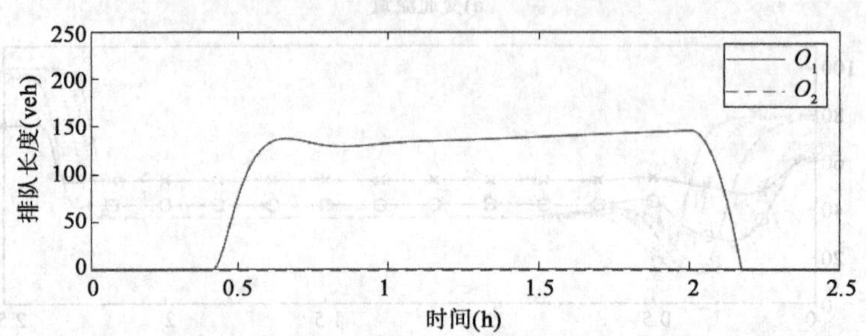

图10 无控制情况下的排队长度变化曲线图

由图10可以看出,由于调节率恒为1,入口匝道的排队长度恒为0,但是主线上游的排队长度在0.5h之后维持在一个较高的水平。

(3)总旅行时间TTS

使用以下公式计算本实验的总旅行时间:

$$TTS = T \times \sum(\sum\rho) \times L \times \lambda + \sum\sum w$$

在MATLAB中计算得到无控制情况下的总旅行时间TTS=1460.2h。

2.3.2 ALINEA控制方法的实验结果

(1)交通需求情况和调节率变化曲线图

在ALINEA控制的情况下,将参数代入模型计算出每一个时间步长下的调节率r。使用MATLAB输出相应的需求和调节率折线图如图11所示。

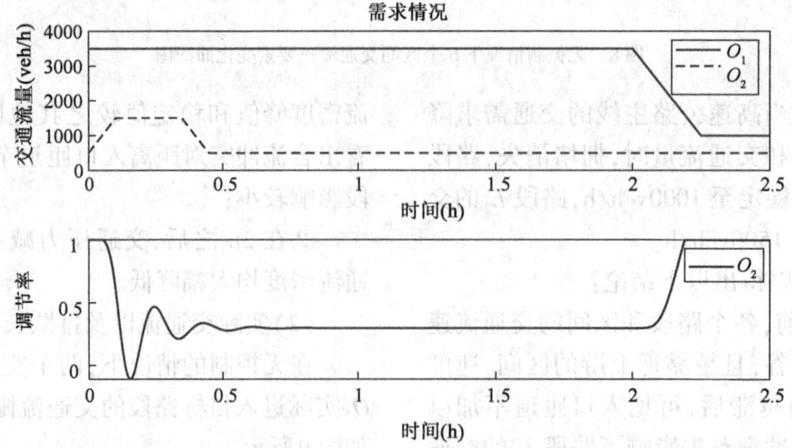

图11 ALINEA控制情况下的交通需求和调节率设定值

由上图可以看出,调节率r在交通需求高峰时期(前半个小时)减幅震荡,当交通需求稳定后,很快收敛于$r=0.3$;最后,当O_1的交通需求减少至小于主线饱和交通量,调节率就上升到$r=1$,并保持不变。

(2)交通流三要素变化曲线图

通过数值仿真得到6个区间的交通流三要素的具体数值变化曲线图,如图12所示。

分析图12a)可以得出以下结论:

①在0.5h之前,原本区间1-4会出现合流冲突并导致路段L_1的交通流量下降,但是在ALINEA控制情况下,主线上游交通流仅仅有区间4出现了一个微弱波动,交通流整体趋势平稳;区间5、6的交通流也同样在短时间的震荡之后被平滑;

②在 2h 之后,需求降低,各个区间的交通流量和密度均降低,速度提升。

分析图 12b)可以得出以下结论:

①在 0.5h 之前,4、5、6 三个区间的交通流速度在出现小低谷并短暂波动后稳定,区间 1 的速度最快,靠近合流点的三个区间速度稍慢,但在控制系统的作用下都较为稳定;

②在 2h 之后,交通需求降低,路段 L_1 和 L_2 的交通流速度提升分别至 100km/h 和 75km/h 左右。

分析图 12c)可以得出以下结论:

①在 0.5h 之前,4、5、6 三个区间的交通流密度在出现小高峰并短暂波动后稳定,同样的,区间 1 的密度最大,靠近合流点的区间密度稍小;

②在 2h 之后,交通需求降低,交通压力减小,各个区间的交通流密度均降低。

(3)实际交通流以及排队长度变化统计图

在 ALINEA 控制的情况下,两个交通源 O_1 和 O_2 实际进入高速公路主线的交通流随时间变化的曲线如图 13 所示。

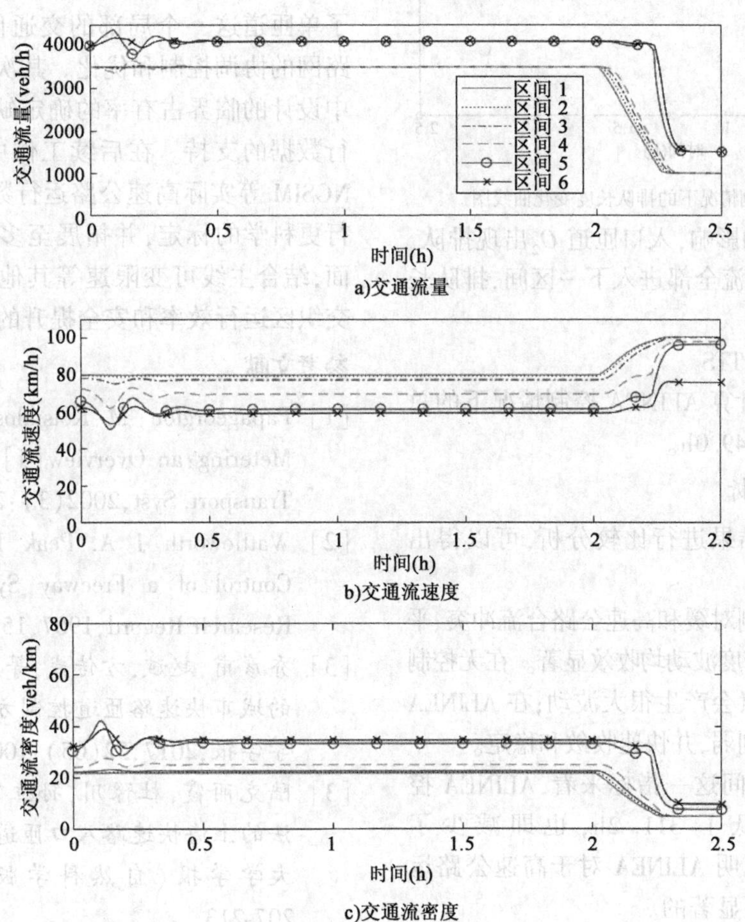

图 12 ALINEA 控制情况下 6 个区间交通流三要素变化曲线图

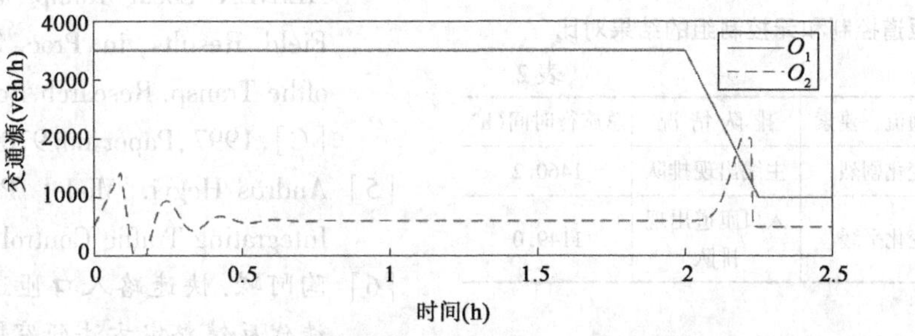

图 13 ALINEA 控制情况下两个交通源的实际交通流变化情况

在 ALINEA 控制下,O_2的实际交通流呈减幅震荡后稳定至500veh/h;当O_1需求减少之后,r逐渐增加至1,O_2的实际交通流也迅速上升,直至O_2的交通需求降低。

图14是主线和入口匝道排队长度变化曲线图。

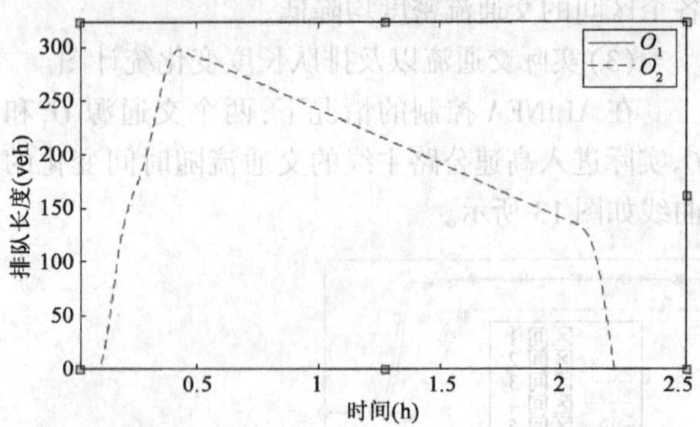

图14　ALINEA控制情况下的排队长度变化曲线图

受到匝道控制的影响,入口匝道O_2出现排队,相反,主线O_1的交通流全部进入下一区间,排队长度始终为0。

(4)总旅行时间TTS

在MATLAB中计算ALINEA控制情况下的总旅行时间为TTS = 1149.0h。

2.3.3　比较分析

根据仿真实验结果进行比较分析,可以得出以下结论:

(1)ALINEA控制对缓和高速公路合流冲突、平滑交通流量、速度和密度波动均收效显著。在无控制情况下,交通流三要素会产生很大波动;在ALINEA控制下,这一波动被削弱,并快速收敛和稳定。

(2)从总旅行时间这一指标来看,ALINEA控制将TTS整体降低了311.2h,也即减少了21.31%,这一数据说明ALINEA对于高速公路运行效率的提升效果是显著的。

ALINEA控制方法和无控制组的结果对比总结如表2所示。

ALINEA匝道控制和无控制组的结果对比

表2

控制方法	交通流三要素	排队情况	总旅行时间(h)
无控制	变化剧烈	主线出现排队	1460.2
ALINEA	变化平缓	入口匝道出现排队	1149.0

3　结语

为探究ALINEA匝道控制策略对高速公路主线运行效率的提高作用,本文通过仿真实验的方式设定了一个常见的高峰期需求场景,使用METANET模型对交通流进行模拟,并分别设定无控制情况和ALINEA控制情况进行对比实验,结果发现ALINEA方法在稳定交通流、提高运行效率、减少主线排队等方面具有显著的优势。此外,由于METANET模型的特点,本文还对入口匝道附近的不同主线路段交通流特点进行了细分讨论,进一步完善了对ALINEA控制效果的研究。

本研究尚存在一些不足。首先,本文仅考虑了单匝道这一个局部的交通优化,没有考虑整个路网的协调控制和优化。其次,ALINEA控制算法中设计的临界占有率的确定缺乏实际高速公路运行数据的支持。在后续工作中,将考虑通过使用NGSIM等实际高速公路运行数据集对模型参数进行更科学的标定,并拓展至多匝道甚至路网的层面,结合主线可变限速等其他策略进行高速公路交织区运行效率和安全提升的研究。

参考文献

[1] Papageorgiou, M Kotsialos A. Freeway Ramp Metering: an Overview[J]. IEEE Trans. Intell. Transport. Syst, 2002(3):271-281.

[2] Wattleworth J A. Peak Period Analysis and Control of a Freeway System[J]. Highway Research Record, 1967, 157:1-21.

[3] 乔彦甫,赵斌,方传武,等.基于ALINEA算法的城市快速路匝道控制方法[J].西南交通大学学报,2017,52(05):1001-1007.

[3] 陆克丽霞,杜豫川,孙立军.基于ALINEA算法的上海快速路入口匝道控制方法[J].同济大学学报(自然科学版),2009,37(02):207-213.

[4] M Papageorgiou, H Hadj-Salem, F Middelham. ALINEA Local Ramp Metering: Summary of Field Results, in Proc. 76th Annual Meeting ofthe Transp. Research Board, Wash ington D C[C]. 1997, Paper no. 970032.

[5] András Hegyi. Model Predictive Control for Integrating Traffic Control Measures, 2004.

[6] 陶阿嵘.快速路入口匝道ALINEA控制器的迭代反馈整定方法研究[D].青岛:青岛科技大学,2010.

针对公交优先协调控制的混行车流延误计算方法

邹 亮* 李智凡
(深圳大学土木与交通工程学院)

摘 要 延误是公交优先协调控制的关键指标,对于公交车和小汽车的混行车流,现有单一折算标准的延误计算方法,将公交车折算成小汽车,同时计算两种车辆的延误;但公交车和小汽车的特性差异较大,导致计算结果存在较大的误差。为获得更加精确的车辆延误计算结果,优化公交优先协调控制配时方案,本文在现有的干道协调控制车辆延误研究的基础上,针对混行公交车和小汽车的加速度、速度和停站差异大,不同公交线路的停站时间和载客量不同的问题,提出了多折算标准的延误计算方法,分别计算小汽车和各公交线路车辆的延误;然后生成178组干道协调控制算例,计算车辆延误,并通过仿真验证该方法的准确度。结果表明:较单一折算标准的延误计算方法,该方法的小汽车、公交车车均延误计算误差分别降低了22.27%、82.07%。

关键词 公交车速 公交停站时间 车型折算系数 Vissim仿真

0 引言

近年来,为改善城市交通拥堵问题,我国大力发展公共交通。公交优先是公共交通发展的趋势,2017年交通运输部发布的《城市公共交通"十三五"发展纲要》明确提出深入贯彻落实公交优先发展战略。目前,主要的公交优先策略包括路权优先和信号优先两方面,其中路权优先发展迅速[1],2020年全国共设置公交专用车道16551.6km,自2017年增加了51.65%。相比之下,我国公交信号优先控制技术较为滞后,需要深入研究。

我国干道协调控制技术日趋成熟,已广泛应用于很多城市,且效果较好。截至2021年,北京市区内已对50条道路路段实施双向绿波协调控制,包括信号灯交叉路口289处,优化后道路整体通行效率提升了40%以上;深圳市设置了574条绿波路段,涉及1742个信号灯路口,累积绿波道路总长为520km,优化后干道车辆通行状况得到了较大的改善,以和平路为例,其双向行程时间分别降低了31%和46%。

干道协调控制方法主要包括最大绿波带法和最小延误法[2],其中最小延误法考虑了车辆的运行状况,与实际情况更加吻合,能更大程度地提升车辆通行效率。针对干道协调控制的公交车和小汽车混行车流,现有单一折算标准的延误计算方法,将公交车折算成小汽车,先计算出所有车辆的延误,然后得到公交车和小汽车的延误,未考虑不同车型运行特性的差异。由于公交车速度、停站与小汽车差异较大[3],不同公交线路的停站时间和载客量也不同,所以得到的车均延误和人均延误都存在较大误差。此外,在车辆延误的研究基础上,有学者提出了干线总延误最小优化方法[4-5];部分学者在社会车辆干线协调的基础上,通过车速引导[6]、主动优先、车速引导和信号调整相结合等措施优化公交车辆的路口特性[7-8];也有学者提出公交信号优先对车辆延误影响的分析方法[9]和公交优先效果的评价方法[10],这些研究都与车辆延误计算密切相关,延误计算结果存在较大误差将会影响研究结论的准确性。

干道协调控制的车辆延误计算结果精度,直接影响交叉口信号配时方案与交通需求的匹配程度,进而影响车辆在交叉口的通行效率。本文以干道协调控制为研究对象,为得到更加精确的公交车和小汽车延误,为优化公交优先协调控制提供基础,首先在现有的干道协调控制延误研究的基础上,针对混行公交车和小汽车加速度、速度和停站差异大,不同公交线路的停站时间和载客量不同的问题,提出了多折算标准的延误计算方法,分别计算不同车型和公交线路的延误;然后生成算例,计算车辆延误;最后通过仿真验证该方法的准确度。

1　单一折算标准延误计算方法

本文参考了卢凯的《干道协调控制相位差模型及其优化方法》[11]中的车辆总延误计算方法。该方法针对干道协调控制的相邻交叉口,考虑了车队从上游交叉口到下游交叉口的离散现象,分析一个行车方向上的车队在下游交叉口的到达和驶离情况,将车队产生延误的情形分为6类,分别计算车队总延误。

而针对混行的公交车和小汽车车流,两种车辆相互影响,不能直接计算出两种车辆的总延误。现有单一折算标准的延误计算方法,将公交车折算成小汽车,先计算出所有车辆的延误,进而求出两种车辆的延误,但公交车和小汽车的特性差异较大,导致计算结果存在较大的误差。因此,考虑到公交车与小汽车的加速度、速度和停站等特性不同,本文提出了多折算标准的延误计算方法,分别计算小汽车和公交车的延误,计算公交车延误时将小汽车进行折算,且不同公交线路的停站时间存在差异,因此分线路计算公交车延误。

下面介绍延误计算的输入参数和单一折算标准延误计算方法,并对公交车与小汽车的特性差异进行分析。

1.1　参数定义

针对干道协调控制的相邻交叉口,计算一个行车方向上的混行公交车和小汽车延误时,输入参数及定义如表1所示。

参数定义　　表1

参数	定义
l	相邻交叉口间距(m)
C	交叉口公共信号周期(s)
λ	下游交叉口干道方向(协调控制相位)绿信比
o	下游交叉口对于上游交叉口的相对相位差(s)
N_c	下游交叉口干道方向的小汽车数(辆)
N_b	下游交叉口干道方向的公交车数(辆)
N_i	下游交叉口干道方向公交线路 i 的车辆数(辆)
v_c	小汽车速度(m/s)
v_i	公交线路 i 的速度(m/s)
v_b	公交车速度(m/s)
s	交叉口干道方向的饱和流率(pcu/h)
q	下游交叉口的车辆到达率(pcu/h)
E_b	公交车辆折算系数

1.2　单一折算标准

对于公交车与小汽车的混行车流,计算两种车辆延误时,通常以小汽车为折算标准,将公交车进行折算,先计算出所有车辆的总延误,然后根据小汽车数与公交车折算后的数量比,同时计算出两种车辆的延误。具体计算过程如下:

(1)以小汽车为折算标准,将公交车进行折算,确定车辆总延误计算的输入参数,然后计算出所有车辆的总延误。车辆总延误计算的输入参数取值如下:

车辆数

$$N = N_c + E_b \times N_b \tag{1}$$

速度

$$v = \frac{v_c \times N_c + E_b \times v_b \times N_b}{N_c + E_b \times N_b} \tag{2}$$

车辆到达率依据交通流三参数的关系进行推算,由于干道协调控制不适用于车流量大的交叉口,且一般干道上的车辆不会特别少,可采用车辆密度与速度的单段式直线关系模型,推导出车辆到达率与速度的关系表达式[12],具体公式如下:

$$q = k \times v \tag{3}$$

$$k = k_{jc} \times \left(1 - \frac{v}{v_f}\right) \tag{4}$$

$$q = k_{jc} \times v \times \left(1 - \frac{v}{v_f}\right) \tag{5}$$

式中:k——车辆密度(辆/km);

k_{jc}——小汽车阻塞密度(辆/km);

v_f——自由流速度(m/s)。

确定输入参数的取值后,据参考文献[1]中的总延误计算方法,计算出所有车辆的总延误 D。

(2)根据小汽车数与公交车折算后的数量比,同时计算出两种车辆的总延误,进而得到车均延误。

小汽车车均延误

$$d_c = \frac{D}{N_c + E_b \times N_b} \tag{6}$$

公交车车均延误

$$d_b = \frac{2 \times D}{N_c + E_b \times N_b} \tag{7}$$

1.3　车辆特性差异分析

公交车与小汽车的加速度、速度和停站特性存在差异,对车辆延误有影响,下面将具体分析两种车辆的加速度、深圳市 2011—2019 年高峰时段小汽车、公交车速度和深圳部分干道的公交停站情况。

1.3.1 加速度差异

根据现有研究可知,公交车进站的减速度区间通常为(0.15,2.5)、出站加速度区间为(0,2.5)[13];小汽车的制动减速度区间通常为(1.2,3.2)、最大加速度区间为(2,4)[14];两种车辆的加速度差异较大。

1.3.2 速度差异

由图 1 可知,小汽车的速度明显高于公交车,小汽车平均速度为 27.53km/h,公交车平均速度为 19.77km/h,速度差异较大。

1.3.3 公交停站

由图 2 可知,每公里干道平均包含 1.43 个公交站台,车站较密集,停站次数较多,对于公交车速度影响较大。

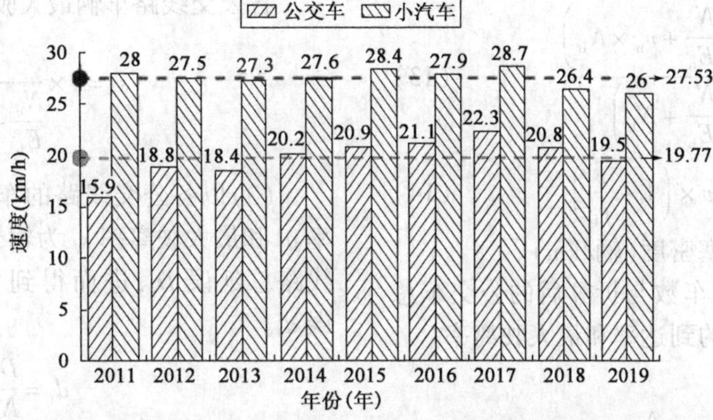

图 1 2011—2019 年深圳市高峰时段小汽车和公交车平均速度

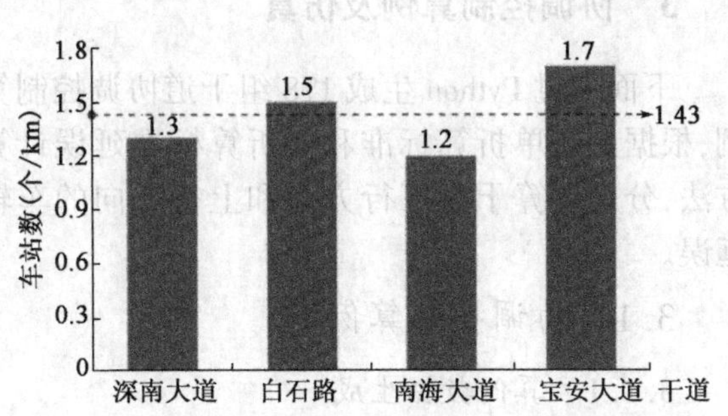

图 2 干道每公里包含的公交车站数量

2 多折算标准延误计算方法

以小汽车为单一折算标准的延误计算方法,未考虑到公交车和小汽车的特性差异,导致两种车辆的延误计算结果存在较大误差。为得到更加精确的车辆延误结果,本文提出了多折算标准延误计算方法,分别计算小汽车和各线路公交车的延误,下面将介绍多折算标准延误计算方法的具体计算步骤。

2.1 分车型

公交车的加速度、速度和停站与小汽车相比存在一定差异,以至于两种车辆在下游交叉口的到达和驶离情况不同,延误产生情况也不相同。因此,本文将公交车和小汽车看成两股车队,提出多折算标准的延误计算方法,分别计算两种车辆延误,同时考虑了混行车辆之间的影响。以公交车延误计算为例,为考虑小汽车的影响,将其折算成公交车,首先计算出下游交叉口的车辆到达率;由于两交叉口间的公交车与小汽车总体分布较均匀,然后依据输入的公交车数与折算后的公交车总数的比例,计算出下游交叉口的公交车到达率和最大驶离率;最后计算出公交车延误。两种车辆延误计算的具体过程如下。

(1)计算小汽车车均延误

①以小汽车为折算标准,将公交车进行折算,计算车辆到达率 q。

$$v = \frac{v_c \times N_c + E_b \times v_b \times N_b}{N_c + E_b \times N_b} \tag{8}$$

$$q = k_{jc} \times v \times \left(1 - \frac{v}{v_f}\right) \tag{9}$$

②依据输入的小汽车数与折算后的小汽车总数的比例,计算小汽车的到达率和最大驶离率。

小汽车到达率

$$q_c = q \times \frac{N_c}{N_c + E_b \times N_b} \tag{10}$$

小汽车最大驶离率

$$s_c = s \times \frac{N_c}{N_c + E_b \times N_b} \tag{11}$$

③以小汽车的车辆数 N_c、速度 v_c、到达率 q_c 和最大驶离率 s_c 为输入参数,计算出小汽车总延误 D_c,进而得到小汽车车均延误 d_c。

$$d_c = \frac{D_c}{N_c} \tag{12}$$

(2)计算公交车车均延误

①以公交车为折算标准,将小汽车进行折算,计算车辆到达率 q。

$$v = \frac{\left(v_c \times \frac{N_c}{E_b} + v_b \times N_b\right)}{\left(\frac{N_c}{E_b} + N_b\right)} \tag{13}$$

$$q = k_{jb} \times v \times \left(1 - \frac{v}{v_f}\right) \tag{14}$$

式中:k_{jb}——公交车阻塞密度(辆/km)。

②依据输入的公交车数与折算后的公交车总数的比例,计算公交车的到达率和最大驶离率。

公交车到达率

$$q_b = q \times \frac{N_b}{\frac{N_c}{E_b} + N_b} \tag{15}$$

公交车最大驶离率

$$s_b = s \times \frac{N_b}{\frac{N_c}{E_b} + N_b} \tag{16}$$

③以公交车的车辆数 N_b、速度 v_b、到达率 q_b 和最大驶离率 s_b 为输入参数,计算出公交车总延误 D_b,进而得到公交车车均延误 d_b。

$$d_b = \frac{D_b}{N_b} \tag{17}$$

2.2　分线路

除了公交车与小汽车特性存在差异之外,各公交线路的停站时间和载客量也不同,对公交车车均延误和人均延误计算结果也有较大影响。因此,可将每条线路的公交车视为一股车队,分别计算每条公交线路的车均延误。具体计算过程如下:

(1)以公交车辆为折算标准,将小汽车进行折算,计算下游交叉口的车辆到达率 q。

$$v = \frac{v_c \times \frac{N_c}{E_b} + \sum_{i=1}^{m} v_i \times N_i}{\frac{N_c}{E_b} + \sum_{i=1}^{m} N_i} \tag{18}$$

$$q = k_{jb} \times v \times \left(1 - \frac{v}{v_f}\right) \tag{19}$$

(2)依据输入的各公交线路车辆数与折算后的公交车总数的比例,计算各公交线路车辆的到达率和最大驶离率。

各公交线路车辆到达率

$$q_i = q \times \frac{N_i}{\frac{N_c}{E_b} + \sum_{i=1}^{m} N_i} \tag{20}$$

各公交线路车辆最大驶离率

$$s_i = s \times \frac{N_i}{\frac{N_c}{E_b} + \sum_{i=1}^{m} N_i} \tag{21}$$

(3)以各公交线路的车辆数 N_i、速度 v_i、到达率 q_i 和最大驶离率 s_i 为输入参数,计算出各公交线路总延误 D_i,进而得到各线路公交的车均延误 d_i。

$$d_i = \frac{D_i}{N_i} \tag{22}$$

3　协调控制算例及仿真

下面通过 Python 生成 178 组干道协调控制算例,根据上述单折算标准和多折算标准延误计算方法,分别计算干道下行方向和上行方向的车辆延误。

3.1　协调控制算例

3.1.1　算例数据生成

算例数据生成分为 3 部分:首先确定交叉口属性参数,然后生成车流量相关参数,最后确定信号配时参数,下面将分别介绍每部分的参数生成依据及取值。

(1)交叉口属性参数

研究表明,干道协调控制的交叉口间距宜为 300~800m,本文基于实际的两相邻交叉口,确定交叉口间距 l 为 495m[15],该值在适宜的范围之内;然后参考文献《信号交叉口饱和流率和启动延误的影响分析》[16],确定交叉口直行方向的饱和流率 s 为 1800pcu/h。

(2)车流量相关参数

首先生成各方向输入的小汽车流量和各流向的车辆比例,根据上游交叉口的小汽车输入量及流向比,计算出下游交叉口干道方向的小汽车流

量 N_c；然后设置公交车与小汽车的数量比为 10% ~20%，随机生成每个方向的公交车总数 N_b，且设置公交车线路取值范围为 2 ~6 条，随机生成干道双向的公交线路数量，并确定每条公交线路的车辆数 N_i；最后，参考信号交叉口服务水平评估标准，控制交叉口的饱和度在 0.75 以下[17]，对输入的小汽车和公交车流量进行调整。

本文设定小汽车和公交车的行驶速度分别为 45 ~55km/h 和 40 ~50km/h，计算车辆延误时取小汽车的平均速度 v_c，同时利用广州市实际公交运营数据，以其中部分公交线路的停站时间作为算例数据，并确定每条公交线路的行程速度 v_i，进而可得到公交车的速度 v_b，v_i 计算公式如下。

$$v_i = \frac{l}{l/v_{行驶} + t_i} = \frac{l \times v_{行驶}}{l + t_i \times v_{行驶}} \tag{23}$$

式中：t_i——公交线路 i 的停站时间；

$v_{行驶}$——公交车的行驶速度。

参考现有研究，确定公交车折算成小汽车的系数 E_b 为 2[18]，然后计算小汽车阻塞密度 k_{jc} 和公交车阻塞密度 k_{jb}，并根据交通流三参数的关系推算出下游交叉口的车辆到达率 q，k_{jc} 和 k_{jb} 的取值如下[19]：

根据小汽车的长度为 5m 左右，最小车头间距约为 2m，确定 $k_{jc} = \frac{1000}{7} \approx 143$ 辆/km；

根据公交车的长度为 12m 左右，最小车头间距约为 2m，确定 $k_{jb} = \frac{1000}{14} \approx 71$ 辆/km。

（3）信号配时参数

首先确定两交叉口的信号相位；然后根据 Webster 配时法确定信号配时参数，包括公共周期长度 C、协调控制相位的绿信比 λ；最后设定干道下行方向的相对相位差 o 为 30s，由于两个行车方向的相对相位差的和为信号周期，上行方向的相对相位差等于公共周期减去 30s。

基于上述数据生成原则，生成 178 组算例。

3.1.2 算例数据分布

下游交叉口干道方向的车辆数是根据上游交叉口各进口道生成的车辆数及流向比计算得到的，具有随机性。因此，需进一步分析 178 组算例中数为小汽车车辆数、公交车车辆数和两种车辆数量比的分布情况。

（1）小汽车数量分布

下游交叉口干道方向的小汽车数量分布情况如图 3 所示，车辆数为 550 ~950 辆，以 50 辆为间隔进行分析，小汽车数量整体分布较为均匀，其中车辆数为 550 ~600 辆和 900 ~950 辆的算例略少，所占比例分别为 6.75% 和 8.58%；其他数量区间的比例均为 13% ~15%。

（2）公交车数量分布

下游交叉口干道方向的公交车数量分布情况如图 4 所示，车辆数为 90 ~120 辆，以 5 辆为间隔进行分析，公交车数量整体分布均匀，各数量区间的比例均为 15% ~19%。

（3）两种车辆数量比分布

下游交叉口干道方向的公交车与小汽车的数量比分布情况如图 5 所示，比例为 9% ~21%，以 2% 为间隔进行分析，整体分布不均匀，大部分为 11% ~17%。

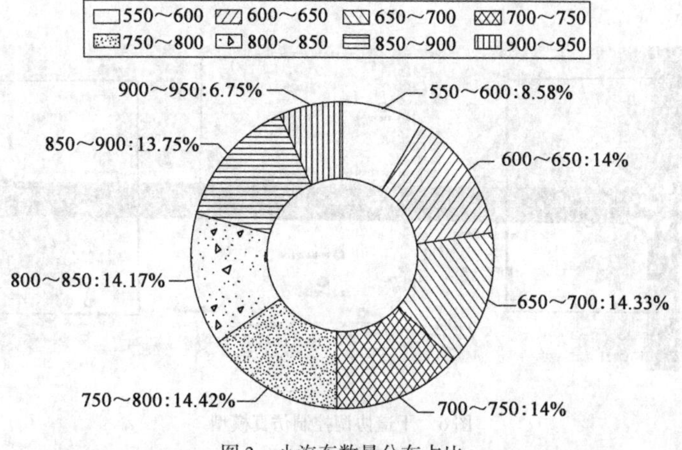

图 3 小汽车数量分布占比

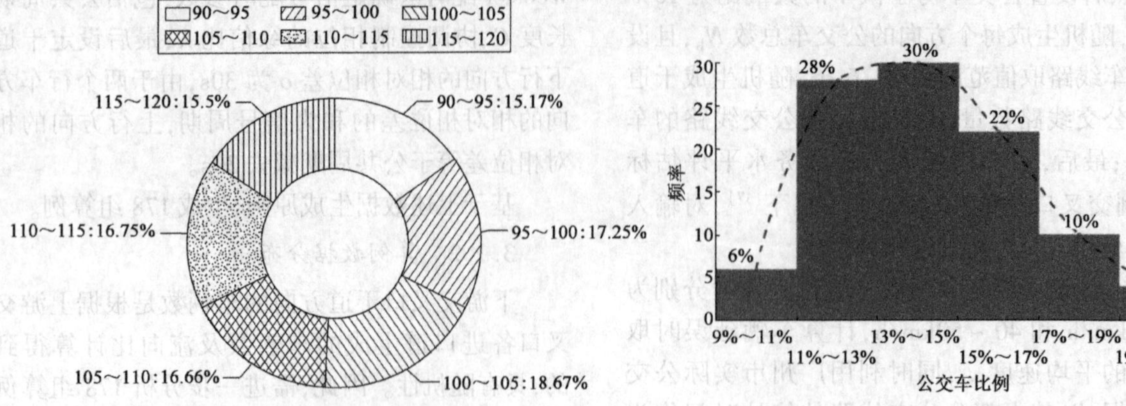

图4　公交车数量分布占比

图5　公交车与小汽车的数量比例分布

3.1.3　延误计算

生成178组算例后,用上述单一折算标准延误计算方法和多折算标准延误计算方法分别计算干道双向的车辆延误,单一折算标准计算得到公交车和小汽车车均延误;多折算标准包括分车型、分线路两种,其中分车型计算得到公交车和小汽车车均延误,在分车型的基础之上,分线路计算得到各线路公交的延误。

3.2　仿真

基于实际干道上两相邻交叉口,首先建立干道协调控制 Vissim 仿真模型,然后对仿真参数进行标定;最后通过 Vissim 二次开发对生成的178组算例进行仿真,并获取车均延误仿真结果。

3.2.1　仿真模型的构建

以深圳市某干道上两个间距为495m的相邻交叉口为例,通过 Vissim 软件建立干道协调控制仿真模型,干道双向均设有公交线路与公交站台,并且设置了行程时间检测器用于采集车辆延误数据。仿真模型如图6所示。

3.2.2　仿真参数的标定

Vissim 仿真软件中的跟驰模型和换道模型对于车辆行驶状态有较大的影响,为了获得更加真实的仿真效果,对这两个模型中的以下6个参数进行标定:平均停车间距、安全距离的附加部分、安全距离的倍数部分、最小车头空距、超车最大减速度和超车最大减速度[20]。

参数标定的过程为:

(1)统计实际交叉口数据,以车辆的平均延误和停车次数作为评价指标。

(2)确定6个参数的合理取值范围及取值步长,然后向仿真模型中输入实际交叉口的数据,改变参数取值进行多次仿真,并提取各进口道的车均延误和停车次数结果。

(3)将仿真的车均延误和停车次数结果与统计的实际值进行对比,计算出每次仿真的误差,确定最合适的参数组合。参数标定前后的误差分别为25.5%和20%,降低了5.5%,更加符合车辆的实际运行状况,标定结果如表2所示。

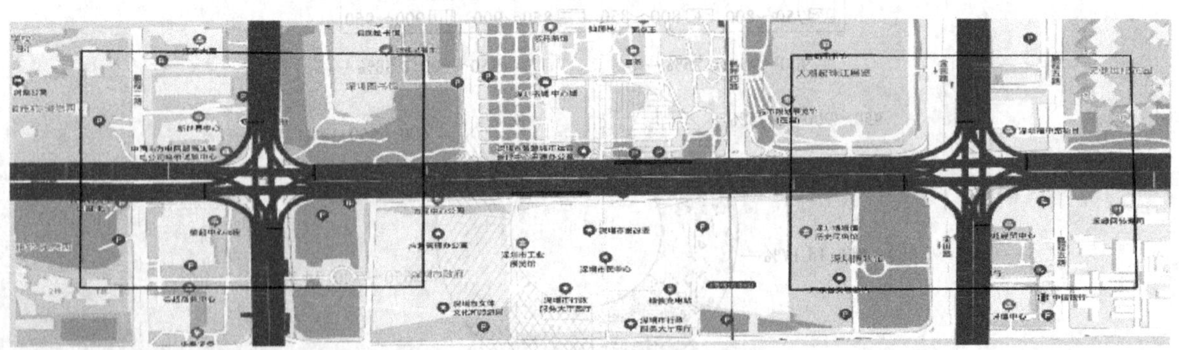

图6　干道协调控制仿真模型

驾驶行为参数标定结果 表2

参　　数	平均停车间距	安全距离的附加部分	安全距离的倍数部分	最小车头空距	超越车最大减速度	被超车最大减速度
默认值	2	2	3	0.5	-4	-3
标定结果	2.2	2	3	0.5	-4	-3.5

3.2.3　仿真结果

标定仿真参数后,通过Vissim二次开发对178组算例分别进行仿真,并获取干道双向的小汽车、公交车和各线路公交的车均延误结果。

4　延误计算误差分析

下面将以178组算例的仿真结果为基准,首先对单一折算标准和多折算标准中分车型的延误计算结果进行分析,对比两种方法计算小汽车车均延误和公交车车均延误的误差值,验证多折算标准延误计算方法准确度更高;然后对比多折算标准中分车型和分线路的延误计算误差,进而确定公交优先协调控制的延误计算方法。

4.1　单一折算标准与多折算标准中分车型的误差

基于178组算例的车均延误仿真结果,计算出单一折算标准和多折算标准中分车型的延误计算误差。由图7、图8可知,两种方法计算小汽车车均延误的平均误差分别为7.32s、5.69s,公交车车均延误的平均误差分别为21.75s、3.52s;多折算标准延误计算方法的准确度更高,小汽车车均延误和公交车车均延误的误差分别降低了1.63s、18.23s,降低率分别为22.54%、83.82%。

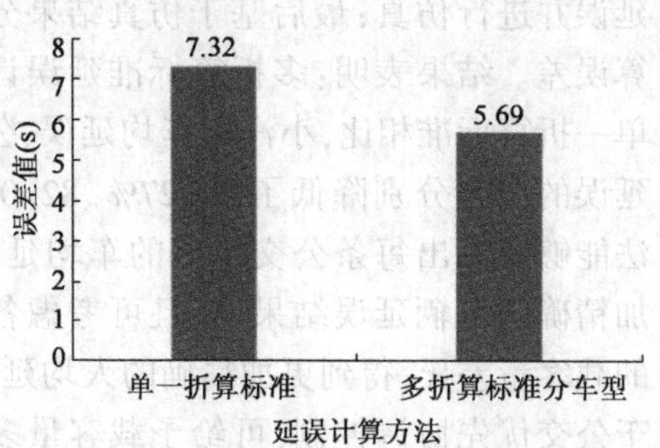

图7　小汽车车均延误平均误差

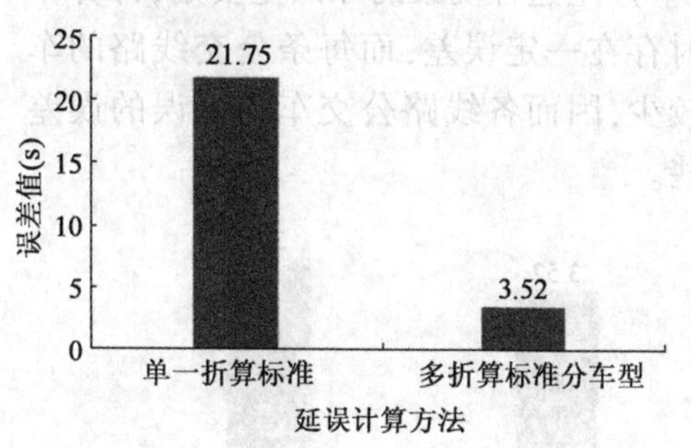

图8　公交车车均延误平均误差

下面为178组算例的小汽车车均延误和公交车车均延误,其中包括仿真结果、单一折算标准和多折算标准中分车型的延误计算结果。

(1)小汽车延误结果

由图9可知,多折算标准与单一折算标准相比,99%的延误计算结果都更加靠近仿真结果,误差更小。

(2)公交车延误结果

由图10可知,多折算标准与单一折算标准相比,98%的延误计算结果都更加靠近仿真结果,且误差降低幅度较大。

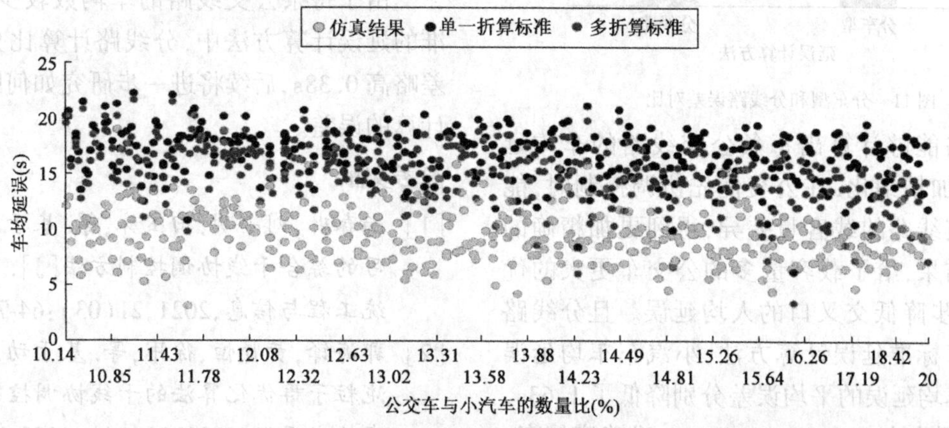

图9　小汽车车均延误

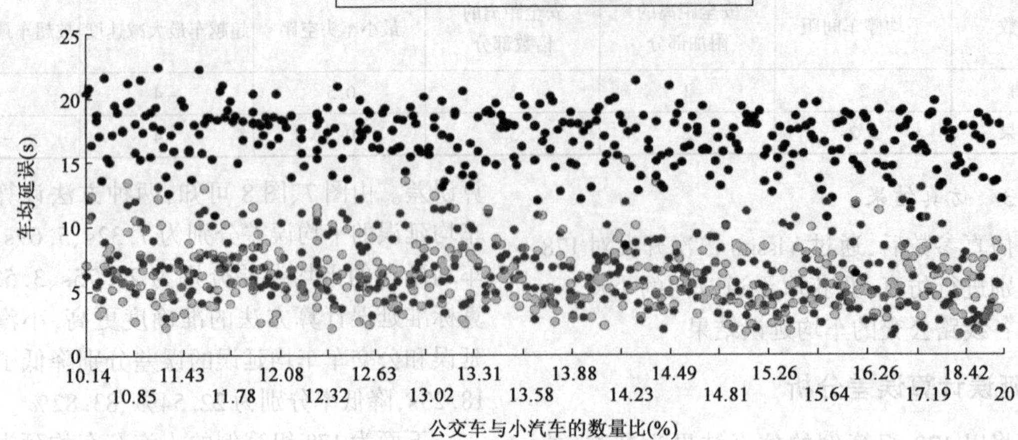

图10　公交车车均延误

4.2　多折算标准中分车型和分线路的误差

基于178组算例的车均延误仿真结果,对比分析多折算标准中分车型和分线路的延误计算结果,得到的小汽车车均延误的平均误差均为5.69s。公交车车均延误的平均误差如图11所示,其中分车型的平均误差为3.52s。分线路的平均误差为3.9s。两种结果相差不大,分线路的误差略高0.38s。产生这种现象的原因主要是,计算车队总延误时存在一定误差,而每条公交线路的车辆数相对较少,因而各线路公交车均延误的误差会更大一些。

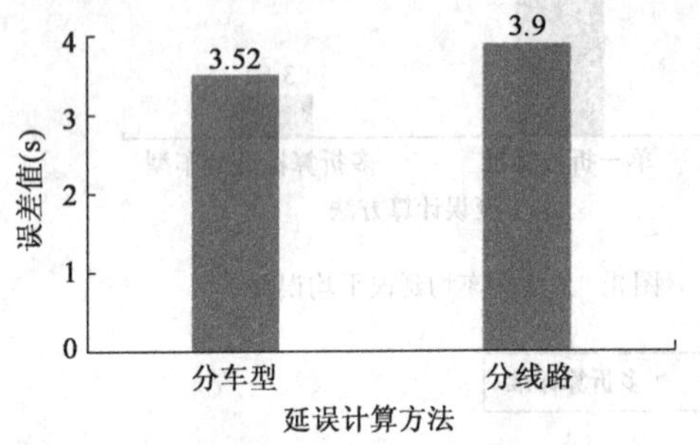

图11　分车型和分线路误差对比

分线路能够计算出每条公交线路的车均延误,结果更加精细化,在公交优先协调控制时,能考虑各公交线路的载客量差异,得到更加精确的人均延误结果,给予载客量多的公交车更大的优先权,进一步降低交叉口的人均延误。且分线路较单一折算标准延误计算方法,小汽车车均延误和公交车车均延误的平均误差分别降低了1.63s、17.85s,降低率为22.27%、82.07%,准确度较高。因此,对于公交优先协调控制,宜采用多折算标准中分线路延误计算方法。

5　结语

本文在现有的干道协调控制车辆延误研究的基础上,针对公交车与小汽车的混行车流,分析两种车辆加速度、速度和停站特性差异,提出多折算标准延误计算方法,分别计算小汽车和各线路公交的延误;然后生成干道协调控制算例,计算车辆延误并进行仿真;最后基于仿真结果分析延误计算误差。结果表明:多折算标准延误计算方法与单一折算标准相比,小汽车车均延误、公交车车均延误的误差分别降低了22.27%、82.07%。该方法能够计算出每条公交线路的车均延误,得到更加精确的车辆延误结果,并且可考虑各公交线路的载客量差异,得到更加精确的人均延误结果,对于公交优先协调控制,可给予载客量多的公交车更大的优先权,降低交叉口的人均延误。

由于每条公交线路的车辆数较少,多折算标准的延误计算方法中,分线路计算比分车型的误差略高0.38s,后续将进一步研究如何降低分线路计算的误差。

参考文献

[1]　尚春琳,刘小明,田玉林,等.基于深度强化学习的综合干线协调控制方法[J].交通运输系统工程与信息,2021,21(03):64-70.

[2]　郭海锋,黄贤恒,徐甲,等.基于动态自适应混沌粒子群优化算法的干线协调控制方法[J].高技术通讯,2021,31(11):1189-1201.

[3] 强添纲,刘涛,裴玉龙,等.考虑绿灯延长的干线公交绿波优化控制模型[J].交通信息与安全,2021,39(2):87-94.

[4] Liu Y, Chang G. An arterial signal optimization model for intersections experiencing queue spillback and lane blockage [J]. Transportation Research Part C,2010,19(1):130-144.

[5] Li Z. Modeling Arterial Signal Optimization with Enhanced Cell Transmission Formulations[J]. Journal of Transportation Engineering,2011,137(7):445-454.

[6] Truong L T, Currie G, Wallace M, et al. Coordinated transit signal priority model considering stochastic bus arrival time [J]. IEEE Transactions on Intelligent Transportation Systems,2019,20(4):1269-1277.

[7] Colombaroni C, Fusco G, Isaenko N. A simulation-optimization method for signal synchronization with bus priority and driver speed advisory to connected vehicles [J]. Transportation research procedia, 2020, 45:890-897.

[8] Zhang W H, Li J, Ding H. Arterial traffic signal coordination model considering buses and social vehicles [J]. Journal of Southeast University (English Edition),2020,36(2):206-212.

[9] Zeeshan R. Abdy, Bruce R. Hellinga. Analytical Method for Estimating the Impact of Transit Signal Priority on Vehicle Delay[J]. Journal of Transportation Engineering,2011,137(8).

[10] Bagherian M, Mesbah M, FERREIRA L. Using delay functions to evaluate transit priority at signals[J]. Public Transport,2015,7(1).

[11] 卢凯,徐建闽.干道协调控制相位差模型及其优化方法[J].中国公路学报,2008(01):83-88.

[12] 庄焰,吕慎.城市道路交通流三参数关系研究[J].深圳大学学报(理工版),2005,22(4):373-376.

[13] 张雅丽,袁伟,付锐,等.纯电动公交车进出站节能驾驶策略的设计与仿真[J].交通运输系统工程与信息,2021,21(04):106-117.

[14] 陆涛,刘箴,刘婷婷,等.基于跟驰模型的车辆虚拟仿真方法[J].计算机工程,2016,42(06):305-309.

[15] 施群.城市干道信号控制交叉口间距研究[D].福州:福州大学,2014.

[16] 杨晓光,庄斌,李克平.信号交叉口饱和流率和启动延误的影响分析[J].同济大学学报(自然科学版),2006,34(6):738-743.

[17] 中华人民共和国行业标准.建设项目交通影响评价技术标准:CJJ/T 141—2010[S].北京:中国建筑工业出版社,2010.

[18] 徐建闽,鄢小文,马莹莹,等.MFD 对车型构成的敏感性分析及车辆换算系数计算方法[J].中国公路学报,2018,31(8):145-154.

[19] 刘萍.基于 wiedemann 跟驰行为的中观交通流模型[D].长沙:长沙理工大学,2016.

[20] 张鹍鹏,刘鼎,谢秉磊.基于 VISSIM 的微观交通仿真模型参数标定研究[J].价值工程,2020,39(28):189-193.

基于元胞自动机的高速公路施工区上游过渡段长度仿真研究

唐志耀[*1]　雷仕轩[2]

(1.长安大学运输工程学院;2.西安工业大学经济管理学院)

摘　要　高速公路施工区上游过渡段由于车道数缩减,造成车辆强制换道的流线冲突问题,影响车流正常运行。利用 Python 语言,建立三车道缩减二车道元胞自动机模型,模拟高速公路施工区上游段场景并进行数值仿真,研究施工区上游过渡段长度对混入货车交通流的运行影响。结果表明:针对高速公路施工区三车道缩减二车道场景,施工区上游过渡段长度在110~130m范围内时,缩减段具有最优的道路通行能力,且车流运行的平均速度、换道率保持在较好水平。本研究可以为高速公路施工区设置提供理论依据,具有一定的实践与应用价值。

关键词 交通仿真 元胞自动机 高速公路施工区 混行交通流

0 引言

随着我国高速公路网络的不断建成与完善,高速公路交通负荷呈现逐年增长趋势,部分在役高速公路已出现通行能力不足、服务水平降低及基础设施老化损坏等现象,对高速公路进行施工养护与改扩建成为解决此类问题的重要解决措施。高速公路施工期间需要进行围挡施工导致部分车道封闭,行驶在即将被封闭车道的车辆需要在进入施工段前,换道进入相邻的未封闭车道,此时车流换道率增大从而影响整体运行速度,加快形成车流延误排队。

国内外对高速公路施工区的研究主要集中与通行能力、交通流特性、服务水平评价等方面。Kou等对高速公路车道缩减区交通流的合流行为进行了研究[1];Jin等对高速公路合流区交通流与车辆驾驶员行为特点进行了分析[2];Yeom等基于美国的已有成果数据,提出了新的描述高速公路施工区通行能力模型[3];多项研究分析了施工区上游过渡段物理隔离、限速标志设置等指标对通行能力的影响[4-7];薛飞等通过建立局部车道缩减双车道元胞自动机模型,分析了封闭车道的交通运行状况[8];李永义等构建了高速公路施工区服务水平评价指标体系,基于VISSIM仿真得出指标值并进行了评价[9]。然而,目前的研究针对高速公路施工区上游过渡段长度变化对交通流影响的研究较少。元胞自动机模型简单灵活、易于模拟,被广泛应用于交通流仿真研究中[10-13];鲁翠娥等通过建立货车渗入的双车道元胞自动机模型,研究了货车比例对高速公路交通流的影响[14];杨柳等利用实际数据标定验证了双车道元胞自动机模型,并对货车动力性能对高速公路交通流的影响进行了研究[15];黄青霞等通过建立高速公路施工区仿真模型,研究了多个施工区独立与合并设置情况对交通流的影响[16];龙科军等建立了城市道路缩减区元胞自动机模型,分析了两车道缩减区、三车道缩减区车辆的驾驶行为特点[17];杭佳宇等建立了车道缩减区模型,分析车道缩减区长度对道路通行能力的影响[18]。

由此,本研究基于元胞自动机模型,利用Python语言编写仿真程序,以目前我国常见的三车道高速公路为场景,研究不同货车比例下高速公路施工区上游过渡段长度对运行车流的影响规律,从而为高速公路施工区设计、交通管理与控制方案提供理论依据。

1 模型搭建

1.1 仿真场景

仿真场景选用目前我国常见的三车道高速公路,施工区位于行驶方向的最外侧车道,车道由外向内分别编号为L_1、L_2、L_3;道路分为三个部分:A_1为正常的三车道路段,A_2为进入施工区前的上游过渡段,A_3为封闭车道的施工路段,如图1所示。

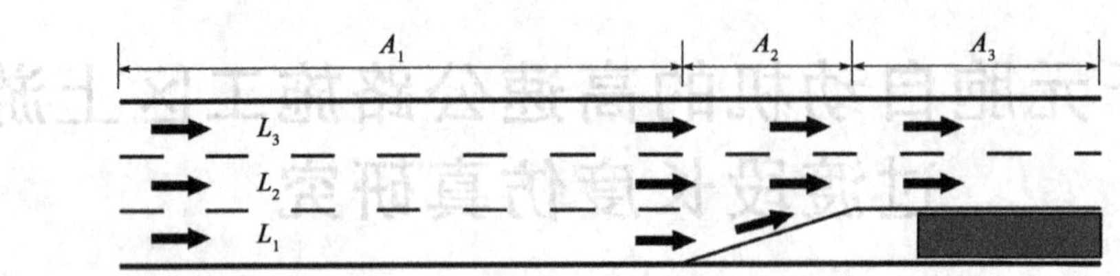

图1 仿真场景示意图

车辆在A_1段可以正常行驶;在进入A_2段后,由于施工区上游过渡段的车道缩减,使得位于L_1车道行驶的车辆需强制换道以合流的方式进入L_2车道,涉及车辆减速、相互干扰等过程,对正常运行于L_2、L_3车道的车辆造成影响;A_3段车辆可正常行驶于L_2、L_3车道。因此,本文针对高速公路施工区上游过渡段(即 A_2 段)的合流效应造成的车流流线冲突现象,研究上游过渡段长度对交通流运行的影响。

1.2 基本假设

正在运行的车辆总希望与前车保持一个合适的间距紧随前车运行,当与前车的间距受限时车辆将会产生换道动机,这一合适间距成为车辆运行中的期望跟车间距。车辆在运行过程中的跟驰与换道过程符合一下假设条件:

(1)与传统元胞自动机 NaSch 模型不同的是,本模型中的车辆在跟车中的加减速行为仅取决于其与前车的间距,车辆运行不会随机加减速;

(2)当车辆与前车的间距为 0 或 1 时车辆将处于静止状态,并通过事先设定值的方式划分处于低速与高速运行的车辆;

(3)为保证车辆同步行进更新,假定每车辆为"人-车共同体",即驾驶员反应时间小于仿真时间间隔;

(4)车辆仅在低速或静止状态下才能进行换道,高速行驶车辆在换道前需要先减速;

(5)车辆在 A_1 与 A_3 段可实施自由换道,车辆总是优先考虑向远离被施工封闭车道的方向进行换道;车辆在 A_2 段时静止的车辆可实现自由换道,在 L_2 车道上低速或高速运行的车辆仅能向 L_3 车道换道,在 L_3 车道上静止的车辆只要 L_2 车道空位数大于 1 个仿真步长内车辆最大行驶距离即可换道。

1.3 运行规则

模型在文献[17]基础上进行改进。为更好地表达模型运行规则,对涉及的参数意义进行说明:$X_{i,k}(t)$为第 i 车道上第 k 辆车在 t 时刻的位置;dt 为仿真时间间隔;V_α 为在 dt 时间内车辆的平均运行速度;V_β 为在 dt 时间内车辆的最大运行速度;$V_{i,k}$ 为第 i 车道上第 k 辆车的速度;$Dist_{i,k}$ 为第 i 车道上第 k 辆车与前车之间的距离;$Dist^j_{i,k}$ 为第 i 车道上第 k 辆车与其相邻的第 j 条车道上相应位置与前车间的距离;$Disth^j_{i,k}$ 为第 i 车道上第 k 辆车与其相邻的第 j 条车道上相应位置与后车间的距离;$Dist_{hp}$ 为高速车辆跟驰行驶的期望跟车间距;$Sta_{i,k}$ 为第 i 车道上第 k 辆车在 t 时刻的运行状态:$Sta_{i,k}=1$ 代表车辆以平均速度行驶,$Sta_{i,k}=2$ 代表车辆以高速行驶,$Sta_{i,k}=1$,代表车辆静止。

1.3.1 跟驰规则

与 NaSch 规则相比,本模型的跟驰规则引入"车辆状态"指标,对于不同状态的车辆设定固定运行速度,且车辆在跟车中的加减速行为仅取决于其与前车的间距,车辆运行不会随机加减速,具体规则如下:

(1)静止车辆。对于一辆车,若其与前车间隔的空元胞数小于或等于 1,则在下一仿真时刻里该车为静止车辆,即:

$$Dist_{i,k} \leqslant 1 \quad \rightarrow \quad Sta_{i,k}=3, V_{i,k}=0$$

(2)低速车辆。对于一辆车,若其与前车间隔的空元胞数大于 1 且小于高速车辆的期望跟车间距,则在下一仿真时刻里该车为低速车辆,车辆以平均速度行驶,即:

$$1 < Dist_{i,k} < Dist_{hp} \quad \rightarrow \quad Sta_{i,k}=1, V_{i,k}=V_\alpha$$

(3)高速车辆。对于一辆车,若其与前车的间距大于等于高速车辆的期望跟车间距,则在下一仿真时刻里该车为高速车辆,车辆以最大速度行驶,即:

$$Dist_{i,k} \geqslant Dist_{hp} \quad \rightarrow \quad Sta_{i,k}=2, V_{i,k}=V_\beta$$

1.3.2 换道规则

根据 1.2 中设定的车辆运行基本假设条件,车辆换道的具体规则如下:

(1)在 A_1 段:

对于行驶在 L_2 车道上需进行换道的车辆应优先向 L_3 车道换道,条件不满足时再考虑向 L_1 车道换道,即:

$$\begin{cases} Sta_{2,k}=2; Dist^3_{2,k} \geqslant Dist_{hp}, Disth^3_{2,k} \geqslant V_\beta \\ Sta_{2,k}=3; Dist^3_{2,k} \geqslant V_\alpha, Disth^3_{2,k} \geqslant V_\beta \end{cases} \rightarrow \text{车辆向 } L_3 \text{ 换道}$$

上式不满足时:

$$\begin{cases} Sta_{2,k}=2; Dist^1_{2,k} \geqslant Dist_{hp}, Disth^1_{2,k} \geqslant V_\beta \\ Sta_{2,k}=3; Dist^1_{2,k} \geqslant V_\alpha, Disth^1_{2,k} \geqslant V_\beta \end{cases} \rightarrow \text{车辆向 } L_1 \text{ 换道}$$

对于行驶在 L_1 车道上需进行换道的车辆应在满足如下条件时向 L_2 车道换道,否则不进行换道:

$$\begin{cases} Sta_{1,k}=2; Dist^2_{1,k} \geqslant Dist_{hp}, Disth^2_{1,k} \geqslant V_\beta \\ Sta_{1,k}=3; Dist1^2_{1,k} \geqslant V_\alpha, Disth^2_{1,k} \geqslant V_\beta \end{cases} \rightarrow \text{车辆向 } L_2 \text{ 换道}$$

对于行驶在 L_3 车道上需进行换道的车辆应在满足如下条件时向 L_2 车道换道,否则不进行换道:

$$\begin{cases} Sta_{3,k}=2: Dist_{3,k}^{2} \geqslant Dist_{hp}, Disth_{3,k}^{2} \geqslant V_{\beta} \\ Sta_{3,k}=3: Dist1_{3,k}^{2} \geqslant V_{\alpha}, Disth_{3,k}^{2} \geqslant V_{\beta} \end{cases} \rightarrow \text{车辆向 } L_2 \text{ 换道}$$

(2)在 A_2 段:

对于行驶在 L_3 车道上需进行换道的车辆,在满足 A_1 段该两条车道上换道条件的情况下可执行换道;对于行驶在 L_2 车道上的车辆,在车辆静止时才可向 L_1 车道换道,否则仅能向 L_3 车道换道,即:

$$Sta_{2,k}=3: Dist_{2,k}^{1} \geqslant V_{\alpha}, Disth_{2,k}^{1} \geqslant V_{\beta} \rightarrow \text{车辆向 } L_2 \text{ 换道}$$

对于行驶在 L_1 车道上的车辆强制向 L_2 车道换道,但换道仍需满足在 A_1 段该两条车道上车辆换道的条件;若车辆到达最后一个元胞点仍未换道成功,需静止在该位置处等候至满足换道条件在进行换道。

(3)在 A_3 段:L_2 与 L_3 车道上的车辆与在 A_1 段行驶规则一致。

1.3.3　位置更新

车辆完成换道后,各车道上的车辆执行位置更新。

(1)对于低速行驶的车辆,按平均运行速度向前移动格点,即:

$$Sta_{i,k}=1 \quad \rightarrow X_{i,k}(t+\mathrm{d}t)=X_{i,k}(t)+V_{\alpha}$$

(2)对于高速行驶的车辆,按最大运行速度向前移动格点,即:

$$Sta_{i,k}=2 \quad \rightarrow X_{i,k}(t+\mathrm{d}t)=X_{i,k}(t)+V_{\beta}$$

1.4　参数说明

以双向六车道高速公路的单向三车道道路为仿真场景,将其模拟为采用开放性边界条件的三条相邻离散元胞链,每个元胞格代表 3.75m × 3.75m的道路空间。每条道路初始状态下为 400 个元胞格,即初始状态下仿真道路总长度为 1650m;其中,A_1 段为 300 个元胞格、A_2 段为 40 个元胞格、A_3 段为 100 个元胞格。当某段道路被车辆占据时,元胞赋值为 1,否则为 0;车型分为小汽车与货车,其中小汽车占据 2 个元胞格、货车占据 4 个元胞格。车辆在车道起点处以泊松分布随机生成输入车辆,货车占比分别为 0、0.1、0.25、0.5,其中小汽车 $V_{\alpha}=2$、$V_{\beta}=4$、$Dist_{hp}=11$,货车 $V_{\alpha}=2$、$V_{\beta}=3$、$Dist_{hp}=12$。

2　仿真分析

2.1　仿真设置

利用 Python 语言对搭建的模型进行数值仿真,研究高速公路施工区上游三车道缩减二车道过渡段长度对交通流的影响。将 A_2 段初始长度设定为 150m,以 7.5m(即 2 个元胞)为单位逐渐缩短长度直至 60m,A_1 与 A_3 长度保持不变。模型由初始状态开始运行,仿真时长为 5000s,为保障数据的稳定性,仅记录最后 1000s 的仿真结果进行分析。

2.2　指标分析

图 2a)为各货车比例下 A_2 段长度与通行能力的关系图。可以看出,随着货车比例增大,A_2 段通行能力整体下降,且通行能力随 A_2 段长度缩减有一定变化;这是由于货车比例的增大会造成车流中的移动瓶颈增多,道路时空资源利用率下降,车辆间的相互影响加重。单独分析每一货车比例下的通行能力变化情况,见图 2b) ~ 图 2e),A_2 段通行能力随 A_2 段长度的缩减均呈现一定的先上升后下降趋势,通行能力峰值约在 110 ~ 130m 处取得。因此可以得出,当 A_2 段长度在 110 ~ 130m 范围内时,具有最优的通行能力。

图 3 为各货车比例下 A_2 段长度与平均速度的关系图。可以看出,随着货车比例增大,A_2 段平均速度整体下降;这是由于货车的动力性能压制了整体运行速度,货车增多使小汽车换道安全空档减少,导致其被迫跟随前方货车行驶,造成一定车流排队低速运行,降低整体速度。在各货车比例下,平均速度随 A_2 段长度缩减具有减小的趋势;当 A_2 段长度大于 110m 时,平均速度随 A_2 段长度缩减保持较低程度的降低;当 A_2 段长度处于 90 ~ 110m 时,平均速度随 A_2 段长度缩减有明显程度降低;当 A_2 段长度小于 90m 时,平均速度随 A_2 段长度缩减保持相对稳定。因此可以得出,当 A_2 段长度在大于 110m 时,具有较快的运行速度。

图 4 为各货车比例下 A_2 段长度与换道率的关系图。可以看出,随着货车比例增大,A_2 段换道率整体上升;这是由于货车比例较大时,车道内小汽车运行速度较低导致换道动机大量产生,小汽车实施换道的频数增加。在各货车比例下,换道率随 A_2 段长度缩减具有增加的趋势;当 A_2 段长度大于 100m 时,平均速度随 A_2 段长度缩减保持较低程度的增加;当 A_2 段长度小于 100m 时,换道随 A_2 段长度缩减明显增大。因此可以得出,当 A_2 段长度在大于 100m 时,具有较为稳定的交通流运行状态。

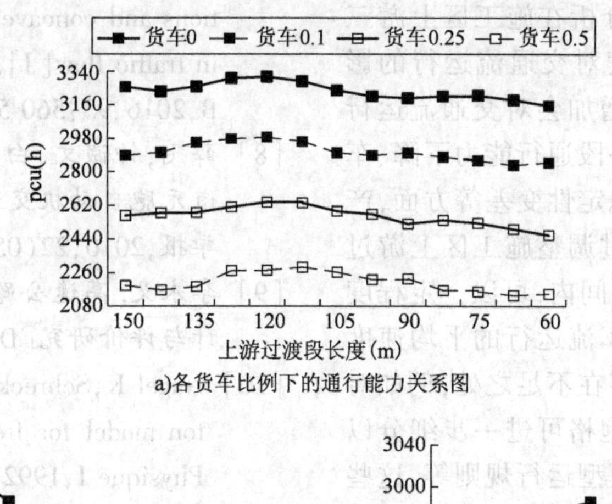

a)各货车比例下的通行能力关系图

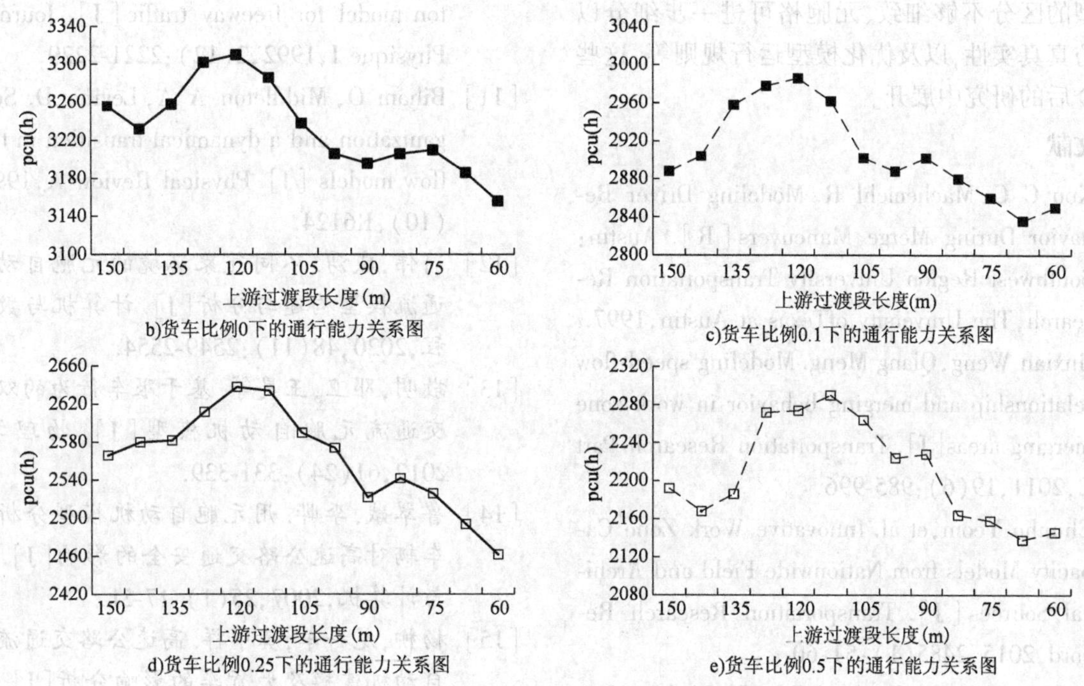

b)货车比例0下的通行能力关系图

c)货车比例0.1下的通行能力关系图

d)货车比例0.25下的通行能力关系图

e)货车比例0.5下的通行能力关系图

图2 上游过渡段长度与通行能力关系图

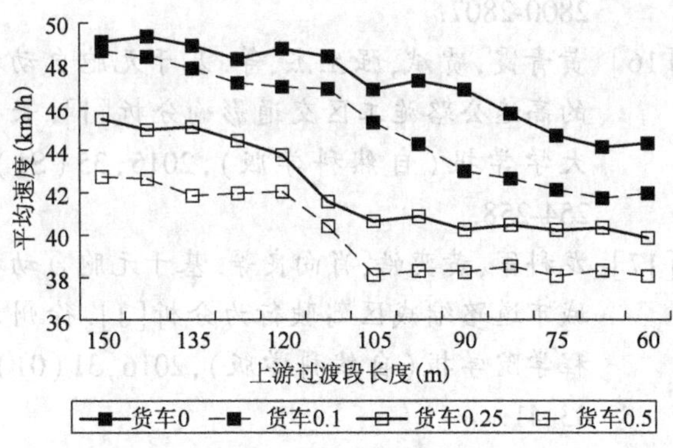

图3 上游过渡段长度与平均速度关系图

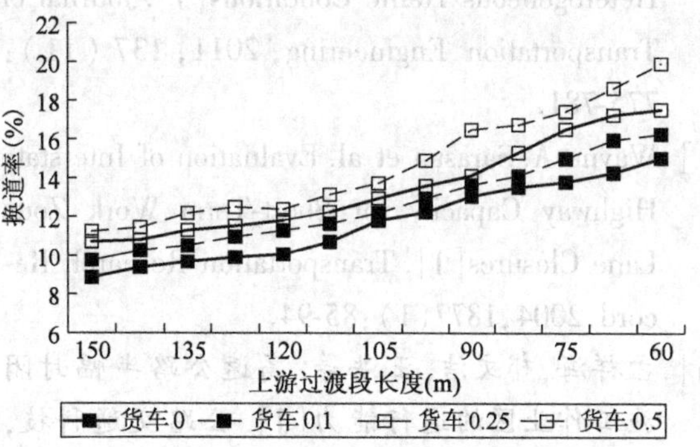

图4 上游过渡段长度与换道率关系图

通过对交通流通行能力、平均速度与换道率指标的分析的可知，当 A_2 段(即施工区上有过渡段)长度处于 110～130m 时，车流具有效率较高、运行较快、安全稳定的运行状态。同时，应对货车比例较高的车流进行合理监管，保障车流运行的安全性。

3 结语

本文基于元胞自动机模型理论建立了双向六车道高速公路施工区上游的仿真场景，并利用

Python语言进行数值模拟,分析在施工区上游三车道缩减二车道过渡段长度对交通流运行的影响。分析可知,货车比例的增加会对交通流运行造成不利影响,具体表现在路段通行能力下降、车流运行速度降低、车流运行稳定性变差等方面,产生移动瓶颈效应。同时,通过调整施工区上游过渡段长度在110~130m的区间内,可以一定程度提高该段的通行能力,以及车流运行的平均速度与换道率。最后,本研究仍存在不足之处,例如对于车型的区分不够细致、元胞格可进一步细分以提高仿真真实性,以及优化模型运行规则等,这些会在今后的研究中展开。

参考文献

[1] Kou C C, Machemehl R. Modeling Driver Behavior During Merge Maneuvers[R]. Austin: Southwest Region University Transportation Research, The University ofTexas at Austin, 1997.

[2] Jinxian Weng, Qiang Meng. Modeling speed-flow relationship and merging behavior in work zone merging areas[J]. Transportation Research Part C, 2011, 19(6): 985-996.

[3] Chunho Yeom, et al. Innovative Work Zone Capacity Models from Nationwide Field and Archival Sources[J]. Transportation Research Record, 2015, 2485(1): 51-60.

[4] K. V. R. Ravishankar and Tom V. Mathew. Vehicle-Type Dependent Car-Following Model for Heterogeneous Traffic Conditions[J]. Journal of Transportation Engineering, 2011, 137(11): 775-781.

[5] Wayne A. Sarasua et al. Evaluation of Interstate Highway Capacity for Short-Term Work Zone Lane Closures[J]. Transportation Research Record, 2004, 1877(1): 85-94.

[6] 孟祥海,祁文洁,王浩等. 高速公路半幅封闭施工作业区的通行能力[J]. 公路交通科技, 2012, 29(05): 109-113.

[7] Junfang Tian et al. Cellular automaton model simulating spatiotemporal patterns, phase transitions and concave growth pattern of oscillations in traffic flow[J]. Transportation Research Part B, 2016, 93: 560-575.

[8] 薛飞,钟诚文,白存儒. 局部车道缩减的双车道元胞自动机交通流模型研究[J]. 系统仿真学报, 2010, 22(05): 1114-1116.

[9] 李永义. 高速公路施工路段交通组织方案设计与评价研究[D]. 东南大学, 2006.

[10] Nagel K, Schreckenberg M. A cellular automaton model for freeway traffic[J]. Journal De Physique I, 1992, 2(12): 2221-2229.

[11] Biham O, Middleton A A, Levine D. Self-organization and a dynamical transition in traffic-flow models[J]. Physical Review A, 1992, 46(10): R6124.

[12] 芮伟,戚湧. 不同气象环境的元胞自动机交通流模型构建与分析[J]. 计算机与数字工程, 2020, 48(11): 2549-2554.

[13] 敬明,邓卫,王昊等. 基于跟车行为的双车道交通流元胞自动机模型[J]. 物理学报, 2012, 61(24): 331-339.

[14] 鲁翠娥,李晔. 用元胞自动机模型分析货运车辆对高速公路交通安全的影响[J]. 交通与计算机, 2007, 25(1): 17-21.

[15] 杨柳,龙科军,黄中祥. 高速公路交通流元胞自动机建模及大货车的影响分析[J]. 中南大学学报(自然科学版), 2017, 48(10): 2800-2807.

[16] 黄青霞,贾斌,强生杰,等. 基于元胞自动机的高速公路施工区交通影响分析[J]. 长安大学学报(自然科学版), 2015, 35(S1): 254-258.

[17] 龙科军,黄奕皓,肖向良等. 基于元胞自动机城市道路缩减区驾驶行为分析[J]. 徐州工程学院学报(自然科学版), 2016, 31(01): 33-41.

[18] 杭佳宇,王嘉文,周溪召. 基于元胞自动机的城市道路车道缩减区渐变段长度研究[J]. 系统工程, 2018, 36(09): 139-145.

面向驾驶人行为演化机制的交通流仿真研究

魏 雯 秦 丹 谢 培 杜雨萌 董傲然 朱 彤*
（长安大学 运输工程学院）

摘 要 为重现驾驶人行为演化过程并分析其对交通流状态和交通安全的影响，以 NetLogo 平台中 Traffic 2 Lanes 模型为基础，构建了基于多智能体系统的三车道交通仿真环境，并建立考虑驾驶人异质性及驾驶行为演化、车辆碰撞等因素的交通模型。通过合理的模型标定得到仿真数据，进而研究异质驾驶人的行为演化和车辆时空分布。仿真结果表明：加入驾驶人行为演化机制后的交通仿真结果更能反映现实状况；平均车速提高近 20%，事故率明显降低；综合各方面指标，普通型驾驶人驾驶过程中收益最高；基于驾驶人收益的行为演化机制对驾驶人属性产生短暂影响；少量事故造成道路拥堵，但交通流整体处于动态平衡。

关键词 交通工程 行为演化模型 交通仿真 异质驾驶人

0 引言

驾驶人作为有思维的复杂个体，善于在环境中总结经验，不断提高驾驶能力，对驾驶人因素的研究一直是交通仿真建模的关键。以往文献将驾驶人因素和车辆交互现象纳入仿真模型，实现了对异质驾驶行为和车辆交互的研究。卢守峰等认为，驾驶人的期望速度差异是影响车流平均速度的主要因素之一[1]。Taheri 等研究表明，驾驶人特性和周边道路环境都会对驾驶行为产生影响[2]。Lee 说明高速公路合并间隙接受模型受干线平均车速、与前车和后车的相互作用、合并的紧急程度等交通条件的影响[3]。Matjaz 引入了博弈理论，对车辆间的交互行为所造成的宏观交通流特性进行了剖析[4]。Yan 等考虑到周边环境影响，通过博弈模型来更准确地描述车辆间的交互行为[5]。

驾驶人试图通过驾驶行为调整获得更好的驾驶体验，如高速、平稳、安全等。杨晓芳等基于现实数据，体现了驾驶人在驾驶过程中的博弈行为和相应的驾驶行为意图演化现象[6]。王梦莎初步揭示了环境嬗变下驾驶人驾驶倾向性的转移机制并建立了相应的转移模型[7]。Wang 等认为车辆集群和转化现象与驾驶人认知能力相互影响，体现了行为因环境而改变的机制，但并未明确行为的稳态特质[8]。

现有的交通流仿真模型大多反映车辆运行的交互特性和不同驾驶人的个人偏好，驾驶人不能实现综合考虑周边交通状况和自身行为收益的行为调整，使驾驶人行为仿真研究存在一定局限。论文建立一种具有演化功能的交通仿真平台，进一步研究各类驾驶人的行为特性及演化现象，进行更贴近实际的考虑驾驶人行为倾向演化的交通仿真，对重现路网交通流动态特性、优化管理有现实意义。

1 模型与仿真

1.1 路段—车辆智能体与多智能体系统

路段智能体是道路交通环境的主体，论文结合参考文献将驾驶人分为激进型、普通型和保守型[9-10]，将不同类型的驾驶人特性赋予车辆智能体，形成不同类型的车辆智能体。路段—车辆智能体系统结构如图 1 所示。

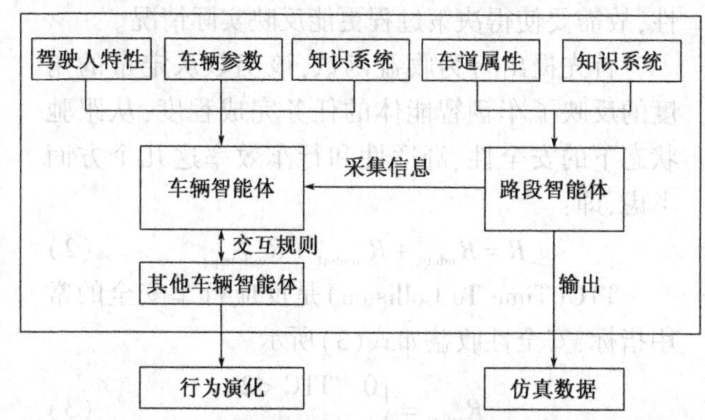

图 1 路段—车辆智能体系统结构图

1. 基金项目：国家重点研发计划（2019YFE0108000）。

1.2　车速调整模型

车速改变通过设置合理的加速度($m \cdot s^{-2}$)得以实现,提出一种加速度调整规则,如式(1)所示。

$$(v_i \times a_i) < (v_m \times a_m) \tag{1}$$

式中:v_i——目标车辆速度(m/s);

a_i——目标车辆加速度(m/s^2);

v_m——目标车辆一定感知内的车辆平均速度(m/s);

a_m——目标车辆一定感知内的车辆平均加速度(m/s^2)。

车速调整过程如图2所示。

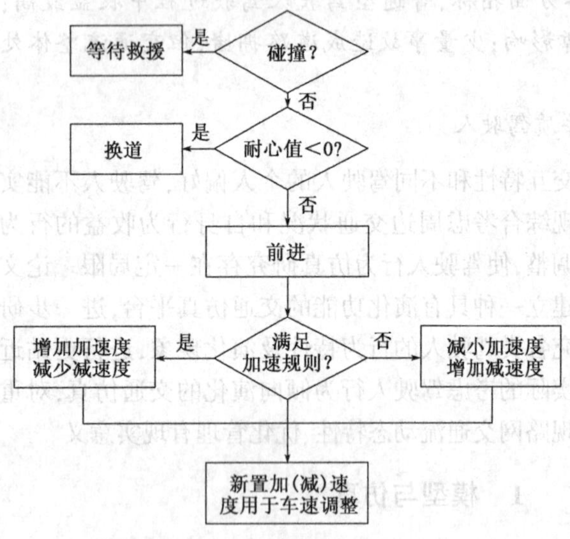

图2　车速调整过程

1.3　驾驶行为倾向演化模型

论文建立了一个基于驾驶人收益的属性转换机制来研究驾驶行为倾向的演化过程。需要说明的是,这种基于驾驶人历史经验和主观感知的决策不一定是最佳策略,这反映了人类认知的局限性,故需要使得决策过程更能反映实际情况。

首先提出行为收益函数,该函数从定量的角度的反映了车辆智能体的任务完成程度,从跟驰状态下的安全性、舒适性和行车效率这几个方面考虑,即:

$$R = R_{safety} + R_{comfort} + R_{efficiency} \tag{2}$$

TTC(Time To Collision)是反应行车安全的常用指标,安全性收益如式(3)所示。

$$R_{safety} = \begin{cases} 0 & TTC < 2 \\ 1 & TTC \leqslant 2 \end{cases} \tag{3}$$

乘坐舒适性也是驾驶人需要考虑的因素,应避免驾驶动作的频繁切换,同时尽量避免急刹车,安全性收益如式(4)所示。需要说明的是,由于驾驶行为受交通状况影响,故舒适与否由固定的减速度来界定是不合理的,故采取本车减速度在周边车辆减速度中的百分位数来定义,如式(4)所示。

$$R_{comfort} = \begin{cases} 0 & dec_i > dec_{65\%} \\ 1 & dec_i \leqslant dec_{65\%} \end{cases} \tag{4}$$

式中:dec_i——目标车辆减速度(m/s^{-2});

$dec_{65\%}$——感知范围内由小到大位于65%的车辆减速度(m/s^{-2})。

驾驶人期望在遵守交通规则的前提下尽量提高行车效率,主要指车速。与减速度相同,车速也是动态变化的,因此,针对行车效率的收益值定义如下:

$$R_{efficiency} = \begin{cases} 0 & (v_i > 0) \wedge (v_i \leqslant v_{35\%}) \\ 1 & v_i > v_{35\%} \end{cases} \tag{5}$$

式中:v_i——目标车辆车速(m/s^{-1});

$v_{35\%}$——感知范围内由小到大位于35%的车速(m/s^{-1})。

收益函数确定后,驾驶人会根据本车的收益值调整当前驾驶行为,使本车的行驶状态向高收益者靠近,具体过程可用如下算法表示:

```
if R^sub < 2
then find R^ref = 3
    adt←0
    repeat S^sub(v,acc,dec)←S^ref(v,acc,dec)
        adt←adt + 1
    until adt > 30
    find Breed^ref = breeds-with-R_max
    Breed^sub←Breed^ref
else remain breed
```

其中,R^{sub}、R^{ref}分别为目标车辆、参照车辆收益值;S为车辆行驶状态;adt为驾驶行为调整次数;$Breef^{sub}$、$Breef^{ref}$分别为目标车辆、参照车辆属性。

这种根据环境信息与自身状态确定收益值,然后进行行为调整与属性转换,这个过程即为驾驶行为倾向演化过程。

1.4　平台搭建与模型标定

基于NetLogo软件中的Traffic 2 Lanes模型,建立异质驾驶人交通流仿真平台,将多车道换道、碰撞、驾驶人异质性、行为演化规则等因素部署其中,展现驾驶人行为演化过程并分析其规律。

参照现实交通环境对仿真环境进行设置。以西安市主干路为实例,车辆限速应按照Ⅰ级道路设置,取16.67m·s^{-1}(60km·h^{-1}),车道宽度为3.75m,单向车道数不少于3条。道路总长设置为100个瓦片,每个瓦片长度为4m。车辆智能体参照小型汽车的一般型号设置为长4m,宽1.8m。仿真初始时刻,每个车辆智能体随机占据一个瓦片。当两车辆智能体中心间距小于二者长度的一半时,车辆发生碰撞。车辆参数设置如表1所示。

有关驾驶人异质性的参数标定,如表2所示。

利用不同车辆的颜色形状区分不同类型驾驶人,仿真界面如图3所示。图中有白色@标签的车辆表示其发生了碰撞,正处于恢复中,图中箭头形状的车辆代表此车辆的驾驶人之前发生了属性转换。

车辆智能体参数标定 表1

参数	说明	实验标定
车辆位置	—	仿真获得
车辆速度(m/s)	—	—
路网限速(m/s)	参考城市主干路最高限速:16.67m/s	0.2 patches · tick-1
转换阈值	车辆智能体直到转换属性的调整次数	多次仿真获得优化值
收益值	动作收益函数的计算值	仿真计算获得
安全距离	跟驰与换道中感知障碍以调速的距离	(1 + Speed) patches/45°
感知范围	调整加减速计算收益值等可感知的周边环境	5 patches /180°
目标车道	换道过程中车辆判断的目标车道	车辆自主判断
恢复时间	车辆间距离不足发生碰撞后等待恢复时间	360ticks

驾驶人异质性参数的标定 表2

驾驶人种类	初始人数	最高限速(m/s)	初始速度(m/s)	初始加速度(m/s^2)	初始减速度(m/s^2)①	初始耐心值	事故易发率②
激进型驾驶人	20	16.67	12.5	0.4	2.4	13	1/800
普通型驾驶人	50	13.89	10.56	0.36	2	25	1/1000
保守型驾驶人	30	11.11	8.33	0.32	1.6	50	1/1200

注:①减速度主要用于车辆防撞,其标定参考现实生活中百公里起步时间,进行换算得到。加速度则用于小幅调速,故数值上远小于减速度。

②参考以往研究,赋予激进型驾驶人最大的事故易发率,普通型驾驶人次之,保守型驾驶人最小[11]。

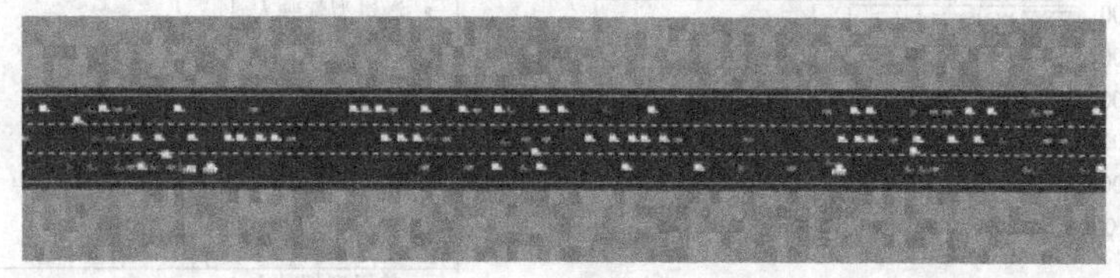

图3 仿真道路与车辆

2 仿真结果

以下分析基于1000ticks内的仿真结果。图4为转换阈值对事故数量与平均车速的影响。随着转换阈值增大,事故数量先减少后增多,平均车速总体上先增大后减小;转换阈值为30时,平均每个时间步发生交通事故最少,为0.54起,平均车速为12.35m/s,也处于较高水平,因此我们认为基于转换阈值设置为30可以保证相对良好的交通状况,充分发挥驾驶行为倾向演化机制的作用。

图5为驾驶人行为演化机制在一定时间内道路事故率和车辆平均速度的影响。随着车辆密度增大,平均车速降低,事故率增加。与未加入演化机制相比,加入演化机制后车辆平均车速明显提高,在密度为83.33veh/(km·lane)时车速提高近20%,这表明加入驾驶行为倾向演化机制能有效提高行车效率;加入演化机制后事故率明显降低,说明该机制可提高行驶安全性。该图也证明对于车辆密度的初始标定[83.33veh/(km·lane)]的合理性。

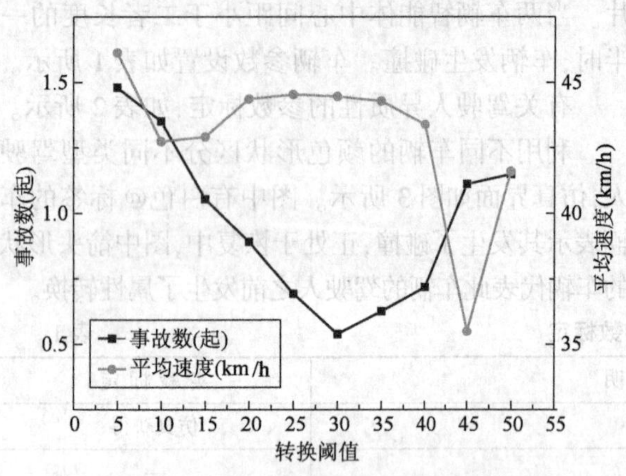

图 4　转换阈值对事故数量与平均车速的影响

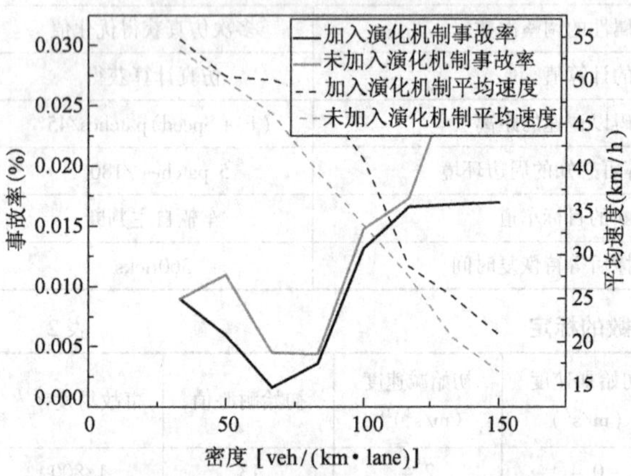

图 5　是否加入演化机制交通状况对比曲线

图 6 对各类驾驶人收益相关参数平均值进行了统计。TTC 的统计结果显示，行驶过程中保守驾驶行为最安全，激进驾驶行为危险系数最高；三类驾驶人的舒适性指标减速度相差不多；激进型驾驶人行车效率高，保守型驾驶人行车效率低。以下基于这三类指标分析驾驶人的收益值及驾驶行为倾向演化过程。

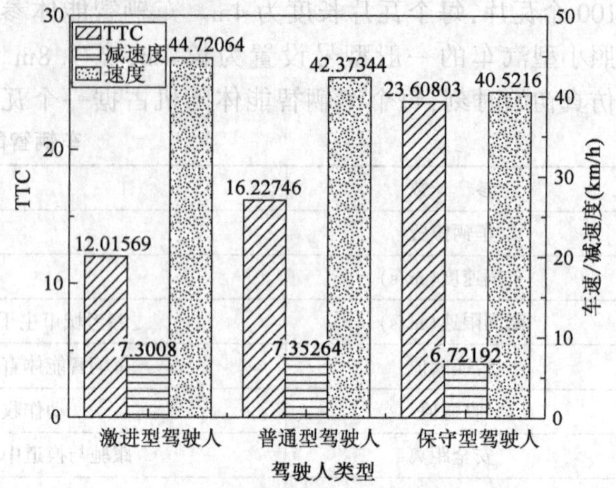

图 6　驾驶人关于收益的参数统计

图 7 为驾驶人收益值分布和人数变化情况。图 7a) 显示普通驾驶人收益值处于较高水平且较为集中，激进型驾驶人收益值整体偏低且较为分散；驾驶行为倾向的演化表现为各类驾驶人数的变化，图 7b) 显示各类型驾驶人数稳定在初始值，只在个别时刻出现浮动，统计得知 1000ticks 内激进型、普通型、保守型驾驶人属性转换概率分别为 4.2%、5.4%、5.8%。可见驾驶人对自身属性的调整有限且暂时，很难通过一次行驶经历有效改变驾驶倾向。以往研究也得出了相似结果[7]。

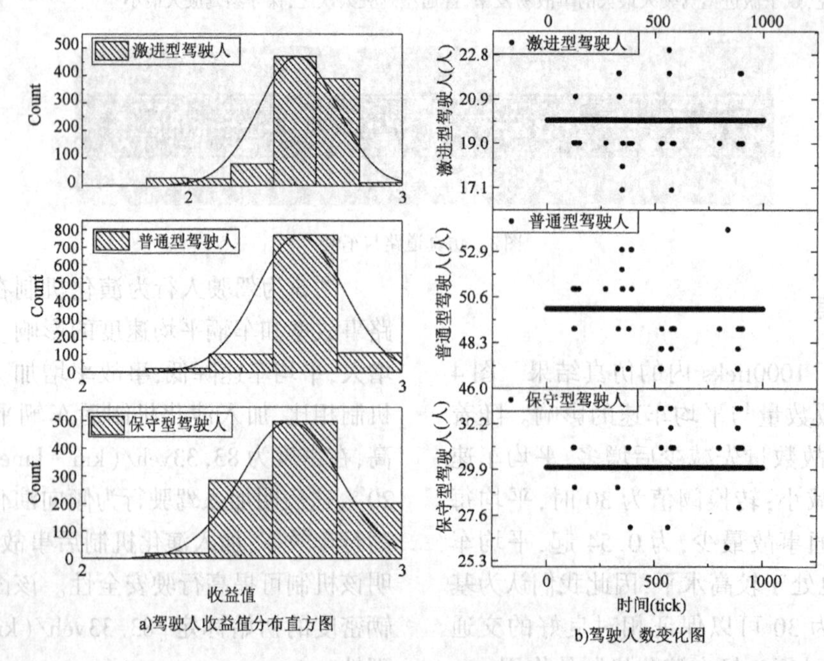

图 7　驾驶人收益值与人数变化对比

图8为不同类型驾驶人的车辆在1000ticks内的时空分布图，折线斜率可直观展现车辆速度，不同颜色折线代表不同车辆个体，操作界面的拓扑结构造成了图中的折线分割。可以看出，激进型驾驶人车速高，保守型驾驶人则相反。仿真途中部分折线在纵向位置未达到100时便已经中断，这表明驾驶人属性发生了转换，原始的数据记录中断。与X轴平行的折线表示此时车辆由于事故或拥堵处于停滞状态。

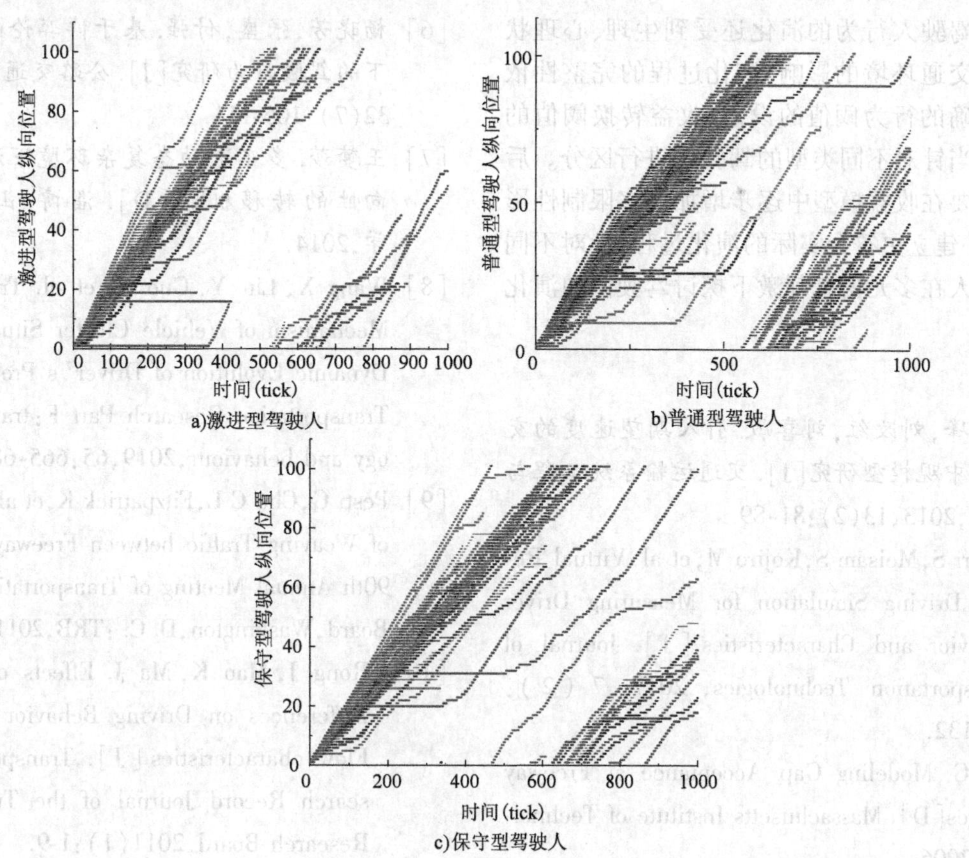

图8 各类型驾驶人时空分布

图9为3车道车辆分布图。由图得知，在86ticks处开始的碰撞大概率发生在3车道，其造成的拥堵使后续车辆大量换道至邻近的2车道；525ticks开始的碰撞发生在车道2，后续车辆向两侧车道换道。从仿真全程来看，尽管碰撞事故造成局部车辆分布不均，但整体处于动态平衡。

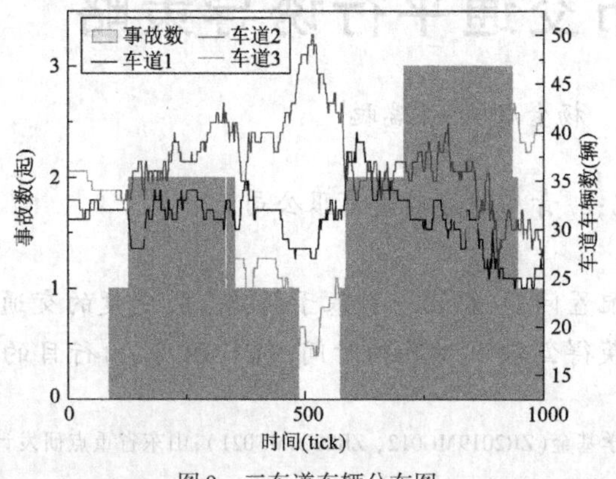

图9 三车道车辆分布图

3 结语

(1)与未考虑驾驶人行为演化相比，在驾驶人属性转换阈值为30、车辆密度为83.33veh/(km·lane)时加入行为倾向演化机制，平均车速提高近20%，事故率明显减小，体现了考虑驾驶人行为演化的必要性。

(2)激进型驾驶行为行车效率高，安全性差，保守型驾驶人行为行车效率低，但安全性高，普通型驾驶行为由于既不急减速也不频繁减速保持较大安全距离所以舒适性好，综合来看，普通型驾驶人收益较好。以上结论验证并完善了以往研究中对于驾驶人异质性的论述。

(3)驾驶人行为演化机制下，不同类型驾驶人数基本稳定在原始值，仿真全程属性转换比例为4%～6%，可见驾驶人行为的改变是少量且暂时的,驾驶习惯很难通过一次驾驶经历得到改变;交通事故造成道路拥堵,使后续来车向邻近车道换道,但整体车辆分布处于动态平衡。

论文基于驾驶人收益模型初步实现了驾驶人行为调整和属性转换这一过程,但模型设置仍存在不足。驾驶人行为的演化还受到生理、心理状态及周围交通环境的影响,演化过程的完整性依赖于更准确的行为阈值的设定,收益转换阈值的设定也应当针对不同类型的驾驶人进行区分。后续研究需要在收益模型中逐步增加更多限制性影响因素,并建立更符合实际的演化过程,针对不同类型驾驶人在多元信息刺激下探讨驾驶倾向演化规律。

参考文献

[1] 卢守峰,刘改红,刘喜敏.引入期望速度的交通流中观模型研究[J].交通运输系统工程与信息,2013,13(2):81-89.

[2] Taheri S,Meisam S,Kojiro M,et al. Virtual Reality Driving Simulation for Measuring Driver Behavior and Characteristics[J]. Journal of Transportation Technologies, 2017, 7(2): 123-132.

[3] Lee G. Modeling Gap Acceptance at Freeway Merges[D]. Massachusetts Institute of Technology,2006.

[4] Perc M. Premature Seizure of Traffic Flow Due to the Introduction of Evolutionary Games[J]. New Journal of Physics,2007,9(1):3-17.

[5] Yan Z, Wang J, Zhang Y. A Game-theoretical Approach to Driving Decision Making in Highway Scenarios[C]//2018 IEEE Intelligent Vehicles Symposium (IV). IEEE, 2018: 1221-1226.

[6] 杨晓芳,张盛,付强.基于博弈论的完全信息下的驾驶行为研究[J].公路交通科技,2015,32(7):105-111.

[7] 王梦莎.多车道动态复杂环境下汽车驾驶倾向性的转移机制[D].淄博:山东理工大学,2014.

[8] Wang X, Liu Y, Guo Y, et al. Transformation Mechanism of Vehicle Cluster Situations under Dynamic Evolution of Driver's Propensity[J]. Transportation Research Part F: traffic psychology and behaviour,2019,65:665-684.

[9] Pesti G,Chu C L,Fitzpatrick K,et al. Simulation of Weaving Traffic between Freewayramps[C]. 90th Annual Meeting of Transportation Research Board,Washington,D. C.:TRB,2011.

[10] Rong J, Mao K, Ma J. Effects of Individual Differences on Driving Behavior and Traffic Flow characteristics[J]. Transportation Research Record Journal of the Transportation Research Board,2011(1):1-9.

[11] 许志鹏.基于驾驶行为特性的交通流动力学建模与稳定性分析研究[D].桂林:广西师范大学,2017.

基于驾驶人接受度的城市交通平行诱导策略

陈咨羽[1]　韩业利[*2]　陈秀锋[1]　杨金顺[1]　王瑞聪[1]

(1.青岛理工大学机械与汽车工程学院;2.青岛城建集团有限公司)

摘　要　为解决城市路网中平行路段空间资源优化配置问题,提出一种基于驾驶人接受度的交通平行诱导策略。问卷调查在年龄、性别和驾龄个性特征下,获得驾驶人对节约时间、绕行距离、出行目的接

1.基金项目:基金项目:国家自然科学基金(51678320);山东省自然科学基金(ZR2019MG012, ZR2020MG021);山东省重点研发计划(2019GGX101038)。

受度;多种因素进行显著性分析选取最大等待时间作为效用函数变量,建立Logit路径选择模型,并结合绕行成本指标对路径选择概率进行调整;以车辆实际通行时间为诱导约束条件,提出了车流诱导策略。实例仿真分析表明,区域交通拥堵情况下实施本文诱导策略后,主干道行程时间减少31.7%,平行道路次干道行程时间增加19.7%,区域整体路网通行效率增加17.2%,说明诱导策略能够有效缓解区域交通拥堵现象。

关键词 交通工程 驾驶人接受度 Logit选择模型 平行诱导 VISSIM仿真

0 引言

城市汽车保有量的激增导致路网交通压力剧增,交通拥堵呈现常态化的显著特征。特别是,部分道路交叉口因进口道某转向比例车辆过多,积压排队过长,造成路段拥堵,交叉口通行效率低下[1]。现有的交通控制研究成果多是应用于非饱和状态,对于饱和状态和过饱和状态的信号控制效果并不理想[2]。交通诱导综合考虑人、车、路等因素,诱导出行者选择最优路径来改善路面交通系统,尤其是定时控制和诱导协同以实现信号控制优化,可实现区域路网流量的时空均衡分布,已成为解决城市道路拥堵的重要手段之一[3]。

龙琼[4]等基于驾驶人个性化需求特性,采用不确定型多属性决策方法得到驾驶人最优选择路径。但实际拥堵路段的出行目的往往较单一,文中路径优化方法在仿真实验中得到的结果与真实情况相差较大。Pang[5]等提出引用模糊控制方法应用到路网自动路径选择中,此方法路径选择效率较高,但对于路网的不确定性以及突发事件的随机性处理效率较为低下。龚奕等[6]在根据不同驾驶人需求提供路径后,对于诱导效果的驾驶人满意度进行调查,作为判断诱导策略的指标。李炼恒[7]等针对高速公路突发事故引起的拥堵进行驾驶人意愿调查,并根据调查结果提出诱导路径选择模型。目前主要的分流诱导策略为三种。(1)交通诱导与交通预测相结合。通过交通预测模型预测道路运行状态,实时调整诱导控制方法。该方法效率较高,但当面临相邻道路饱和度差异较大以及导航车辆达到一定规模时,有时无法获得最优解并且此类预测模型鲁棒性有待考究[8-9]。(2)考虑路径选择行为和整体交通设施投资的诱导策略。在保证用户平衡与系统最优的前提下,进行车流动态分配。该方法考虑了驾驶人自身因素接受性高,但对于单点交叉口发生异常交通事件,交通流波动较大的路段处理效果不好[10]。(3)基于大数据的深度学习诱导策略,将机器学习思想推广于交通量短时预测等问题中,该方法适用性广,对数据处理较准确。但学习架构的建立需要大量的数据和数据库的支撑,面对交通中突发事件导致的交通流波动,处理效率较慢[11]。

以上学者的研究成果对本文有很好的借鉴意义,但涉及城市道路的文献较少,研究手段多为区域协调诱导与信号周期相结合,其诱导策略需要大量的数据基础,对信息采集设备铺设在密度上有较高要求[12]。在城市道路智能化程度初级阶段,相关数据信息不够完善,诱导策略的工程应用价值不高。本文针对城市道路空间资源利用不均衡,以区域内平行道路交通运行为研究对象,提出了一种基于驾驶人接受度的平行诱导策略。问卷调查获得不同因素对于驾驶人诱导接受度的影响,采用最长等待时间为变量的效用函数建立Logit路径选择模型,并结合驾驶人对绕行路径时间、距离成本的接受度对路径选择概率进行调整。

1 驾驶人接受度调查与分析

1.1 问卷设计与统计

1.1.1 问卷设计

针对城市道路单路段或交叉口拥堵,本文开展了驾驶人对交通诱导的接受度调查。选取年龄、性别、驾龄3个驾驶人代表性属性,对绕行节约时间、出行目的、绕行距离等因素下的驾驶人诱导接受度进行调查。

1.1.2 调查结果统计

本次调查采取网上调查问卷形式,共采集551份问卷,其中未完成问卷45份,信息明显错误问卷20份,共计有效问卷486份。

(1)驾驶人个人特性

问卷样本中,男性驾驶人占比57%;驾驶人年龄多分布在18~25岁这一区间,占整体40%;其次为31~40岁,占比22%;其余岁数均匀分布在26~30岁、41~50岁、51~60岁这三个区间。参与调查的驾驶人中,半数驾龄在5年以内;驾龄在

5～10年的驾驶人占比28%；驾龄超过10年以上占比19%。

(2)诱导接受度统计

假设在城市道路出行中遇到前方路段或交叉口拥堵的情况。由于驾驶人出行目的不同、绕行距离和节约时间等因素接受程度的不同，分别对各因素不同情况下的驾驶人对交通诱导接受度进行统计，其累计频率结果见表1。

调查结果统计　　表1

因素		小计	比例(%)
节约时间	≤10min	213	44
	10～20min	156	32
	20～30min	63	13
	>30min	54	11
目的地距离	≤1km	102	21
	1～5km	165	34
	5～10km	117	24
	>10km	102	21
绕行距离	≤2km	258	53
	2～5km	192	40
	>5km	36	7
出行目的(多选)	上班	210	43
	回家	177	36
	上学	165	34
	出差	204	42
	外出游玩	303	62

1.2　基于驾驶人认知效用函数的logit模型

1.2.1　哑变量转换

使用Logit选择模型，首先对因变量(诱导接受率)进行哑变量转换，在保证行时间、距离成本皆为最优即理想状态，即节约时间大于30min，绕行距离小于2km情况，得到驾驶人对诱导系统的接受情况如图1所示。

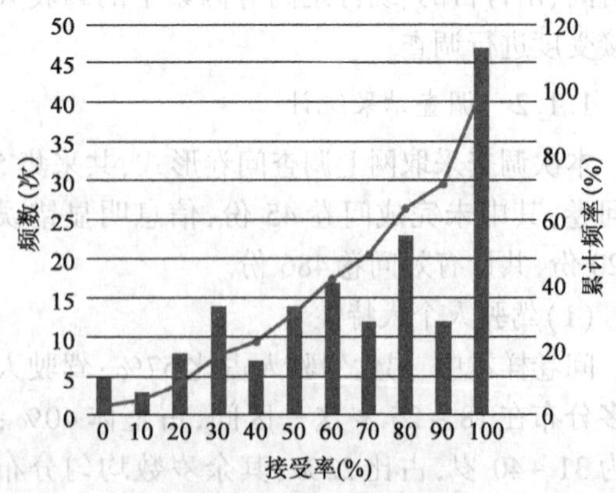

图1　接受度频率累计图

接受度频率调查结果中，50%累计频率对应的驾驶人接受度为72%，将72%接受度作为划分驾驶人是否接受交通诱导的阈值，对接受度进行哑变量转换，接受度大于72%则为服从诱导"$Y=1$"，接受度小于72%则为不服从诱导"$Y=0$"。

1.2.2　因素分析

分析驾驶人不同因素对交通诱导接受度的影响，将问卷中所有因素进行显著性分析，得到结果见表2。

因考虑到在实际的交通运行过程中无法确定驾驶人的性别、年龄、驾龄等特性，则不将出行者个人属性作为自变量。在城市道路网中，因为不同驾驶人目的地不同，因此拥堵发生地点距目的地距离无法定量化处理，不作为变量考虑。

1.2.3　模型建立

传统道路分流Logit模型所采用的效用函数多为路阻函数(BPR)，表达式如下：

$$t_i = t_{i0} \times \left[1 + \alpha\left(\frac{Q}{C}\right)^{\beta}\right] \tag{1}$$

影响因素显著性分析结果表　　表2

	B	标准误差	Wald	自由度	显著性	Exp(B)
平均行驶距离	0.032	0.153	0.044	1	0.834	1.033
平均出行时间	0.116	0.220	0.280	1	0.597	1.123
最大等待时间	0.540	0.207	6.799	1	0.009	1.716
节约时间	-0.008	0.197	0.001	1	0.969	0.992
目的地距离	-0.159	0.186	0.730	1	0.393	0.853
绕行距离	-0.018	0.304	0.003	1	0.953	0.982
年龄	0.195	0.178	1.200	1	0.273	1.215
驾龄	0.026	0.300	0.007	1	0.932	1.026
性别	0.345	0.349	0.973	1	0.324	1.411
常量	-1.922	0.889	4.673	1	0.031	0.146

路阻函数常用指标为交通量、通行能力。传统路阻函数所得分流结果是基于系统最优角度，驾驶人在实际行驶过程中，因个人对路径的偏好不同，驾驶人实际路径选择结果与模型预测结果相差较大。

在对影响交通诱导的因素主次调查分析中得到，在出行路径选择中，时间成本对驾驶人的决定起主导地位。调查中所涉及3个时间因素分别为最大等待时间、平均出行时间和绕行节约时间，其中平均出行时间为出行前因素，不能作为行程中诱导考虑因素，对其余两个指标进行赋值分析见表3。

变量转化　　表3

变　量	系数	赋　值
最大等待时间(x)	α	1:0~5min;2:5~10min; 3:10~15min;4:>15min
绕行节约时间(y)	β	1:0~10min;2:10~20min; 3:20~30min;4:>30min

使用SPSS 26.0分别对所研究的两个变量进行二元logit分析，得到只有最大等待时间，该因素满足显著性要求，因此将采用道路拥堵时间承受度(最大等待时间)与交通诱导接受度的关系作为效用函数，建立更符合驾驶人心理认知的路径选择logit模型，效用函数如下：

$$V = C + \alpha x \tag{2}$$

SPSS分析结果见表4。

表4中，B表示各变量参数，即C，α分别为-0.988、0.559，显著性(Sig)均小于0.05表示所研究自变量对因变量影响较大，拟合所得函数能大概率反映实际情况。

效用函数为：

$$V = -0.988 + 0.559x \tag{3}$$

选择路径的逻辑概率为P_1，则logit离散选择模型为：

$$P_1 = \frac{\exp(-0.988 + 0.559x)}{1 + \exp(-0.988 + 0.559x)} \tag{4}$$

根据驾驶人对绕行路径信息对P_1进行修正，实际选择路径i的概率P_i计算公式为：

$$P_i = P_1 \varepsilon \mu \tag{5}$$

式中：ε——绕行距离影响系数；

μ——节约时间影响系数。

影响系数根据问卷调查结果中累计频率转化得到，如表5所示。

方程中的变量　　表4

项　目	B	标准误差	$Wald$	自由度	显著性	Exp(B)
最大等待时间	0.559	0.195	8.190	1	0.004	1.748
常量	-0.988	0.376	6.900	1	0.009	0.372

影响系数取值　　表5

项目	绕行距离			节约时间			
范围	<2km	2~5km	>5km	<10min	10~20min	20~30min	>30min
ε取值	1	0.47	0.07	—	—	—	—
μ取值	—	—	—	0.44	0.76	0.89	1

2　平行诱导策略

2.1　平行诱导定义

平行诱导策略,是一种对于城市网状道路结构的交通诱导策略。在日常出行中,由于OD点的分布和驾驶人个性倾向,导致承载过境交通的主干道往往交通压力过大而产生拥堵现象,但与主干道平行的次干路、支路路段交通量小,交通运行流畅。针对交叉口交通流量不均衡和相邻平行道路空间资源利用不充分的现象,提出通过上游交通诱导车辆绕行的方式使各流向通行能力最大化,以提高交叉口通行效率、减少交叉口区域延误的优化思想。由于固有道路资源的限制,需要考虑道路交叉口区域的车流状况是否适合采用绕行方式。首先,在运行状态较差的主干道驾驶人可接受绕行区域内有相邻平行路段可供绕行选择。利用相对饱和度较低的次干道为原驶入主要交叉口车辆提供绕行路径选择(图2),使得道路资源均衡分配,提高区域各交叉口通行效率。

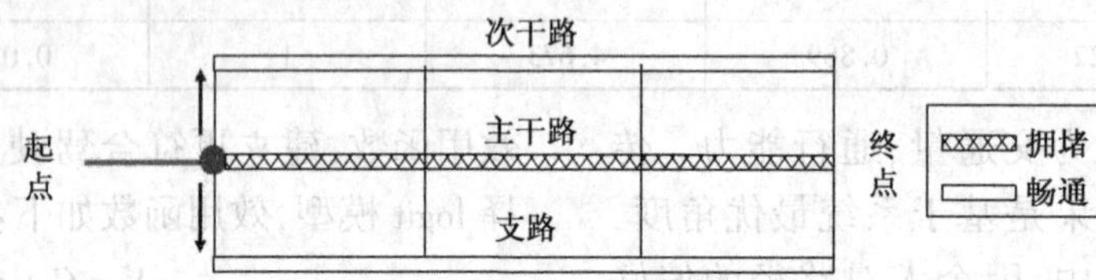

图2 绕行示意图

2.2　关键参数选取

2.2.1　行程时间

路段及交叉口的信息采集手段主要有车辆导航、多目标雷达和视频监控。GPS定位会受到信号干扰,又因为多基于手机信令,对实时路况描绘准确性有待考证;多目标雷达对交通运行指标的采集较全面,但造价过高、铺设密度低,城市道路网信息协同使用难度大。目前国内信号交叉口大多设置视频采集设备。本文基于违章车辆抓拍思想,提取目标车辆驶入和驶出路段的时间差,作为路段实际行程时间。对比原路径行程时间与绕行路径行程时间得出绕行节省时间作为路径选择指标。

简化复杂路网为子区路网见图3,路段分别标号a、b、c、d、e。

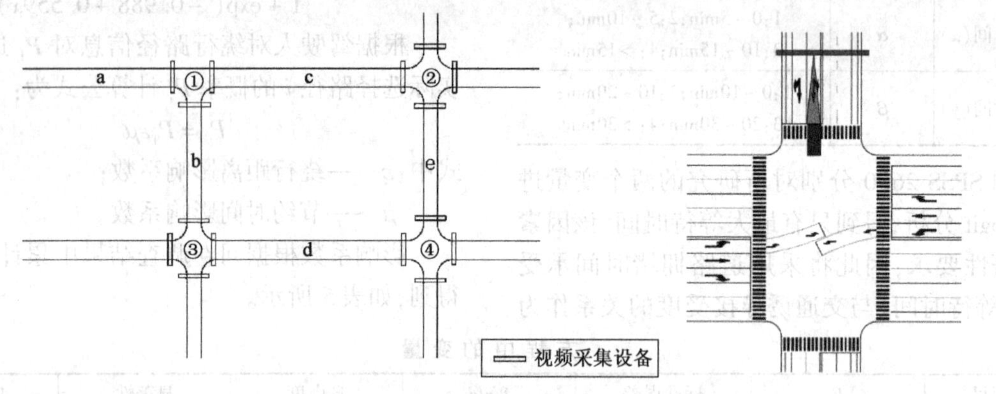

图3　简化子区路网示意图

记录目标车辆行驶离开a路段车道停车线时刻为t_a^i,车辆驶入路段a经过人行横道线的时刻记录为t_a^o。根据车牌特征识别目标车辆,检测其驶入和驶出道路时间做差即为路段实际行程时间,所测得实际通行时间能直观反映道路拥堵条件。车辆在路段a上的实际行程时间见式(6):

$$t_a^{\mathrm{T}} = \left| t_a^i - t_a^o \right| \tag{6}$$

式中:t_a^i——驶离路段a的时刻;

t_a^o——驶入路段a的时刻;

t_a^{T}——路段a实际行驶时间。

绕行路径节约时间即为所行驶路径上路段行驶时间差,即绕行总时间与原路径时间之差。设

图2中交叉口①、②为OD点,原行驶路径为路段c,绕行路段为b→d→e,则节约时间为

$$t^S_{1,2}=t^D_{b,d,e}-t^T_c \tag{7}$$

$$t^D_{b,d,e}=t^T_b+t^T_d+t^T_e \tag{8}$$

式中:$t^S_{1,2}$——起始点为①,②点诱导绕行节约时间;

$t^D_{b,d,e}$——绕行路径b→d→e的行程时间。

2.2.2 行程时间比(TTI)

实际行程时间与自由流行程时时间比值称为行程时间比(TTI)[13],TTI值越大表示交通运行状况越差。计算方法见式(9)。

$$\mathrm{TTI}_{kj}=\frac{\bar{t}_{kj}}{t^f_j} \tag{9}$$

式中:TTI_{kj}——路段j在某一时间间隔k内的行程时间比,时间间隔不应大于15min(0.25h);

$\bar{t}_{kj}$——时间间隔k内车辆行驶过路段j所使用的平均时间(h),$\bar{t}_{kj}=\frac{\sum_{i=1}^{n}t_{kji}}{n}$或者$\bar{t}_{kj}=\frac{L_j}{V_{kj}}$,$n$为车辆数;

t_{kji}——使用视频监控捕捉第i辆目标车辆实际行程时间(h);

t^f_j——路段j在自由流状态下的行程时间(h)。

当路段行程时间小于自由流时间时,设定TTI等于1。

根据我国现有标准行程时间比与运行状态转化如表6所示。

道路行程时间比与运行状态转换关系 表6

行程时间比(TTI)	[1,1.3)	[1.3,1.6)	[1.6,1.9)	[1.9,2.2)	≥2.2
运行状态等级	畅通	基本畅通	轻度拥堵	中度拥堵	严重拥堵

2.3 平行诱导策略设计

交通空间资源分配不均现象产生的主要原因有:①驾驶人偏好导致大部分车辆驶入以距离成本最优的最短路径;②驾驶人对交通诱导信息服从率较低。

针对以上原因并根据前文研究所得驾驶人个性偏好以及道路运行效率指标,建立以下选择策略:根据交叉口视频数据计算下游路段TTI指标,判断主干道运行状态是否拥堵,同时判断平行路段交通运行状态是否满足绕行要求,并在信息发布端为驾驶人提供拥堵时间以及绕行节约时间信息作为路径选择参考指标,驾驶人根据自身特性选择路径完成诱导。具体流程图如图4所示。

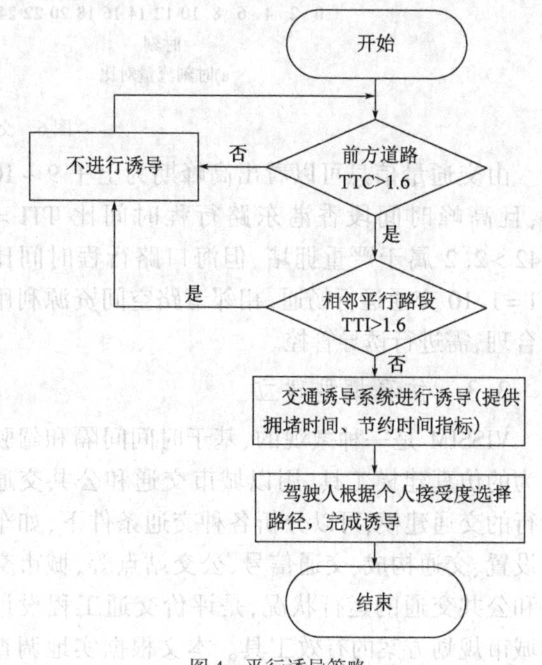

图4 平行诱导策略

3 案例分析

3.1 路网现状

本文路网主干道选择青岛市崂山区香港东路。香港东路北部毗邻大量商业用地,南部以居住用地为主,主要承载东西向的过境交通以及景区和商业用地周边居民与游客。同时区域内有与香港东路相邻平行路段的路段海口路,并在关键交叉口处均有道路联通,可供驾驶人绕行选择。具体区域路网如图5所示。

3.2 交通特性现状

以香港东路与海尔路交叉口为例,东西向排队长度较长,导致交叉口服务水平较低。但与之相邻的海口路由于驾驶人选择意愿以及路况信息未知,交通量较小,导致道路资源分配不合理的情况。选取历史数据,对比同一时刻香港东路、海口路各时刻流量以及行程时间(图6)。

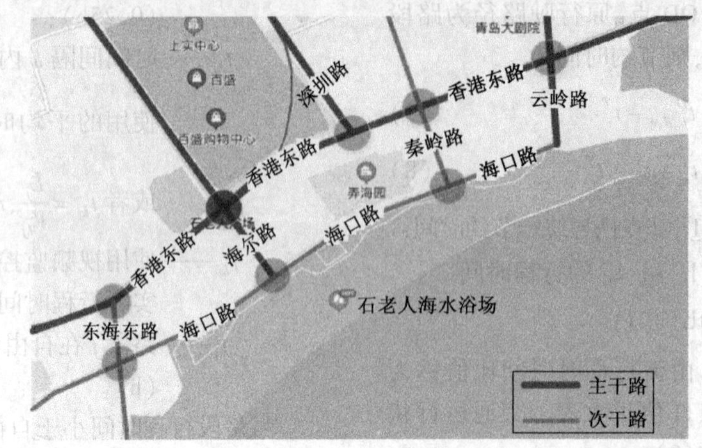

图5 区域路网示意图

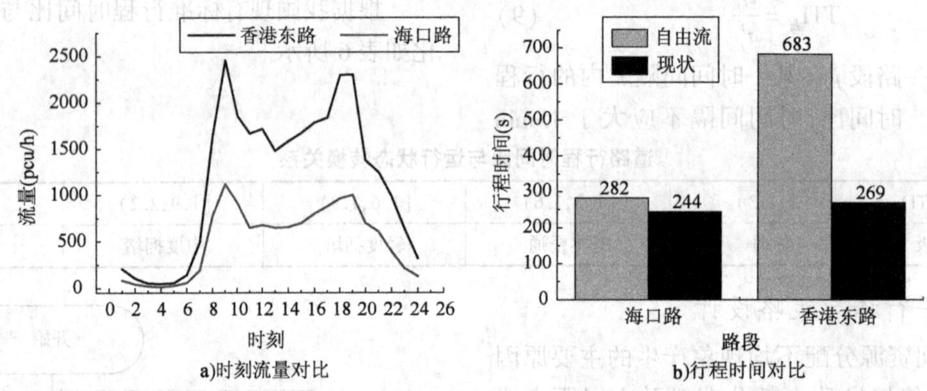

图6 交通运行状态对比

由交通量信息可以看出高峰期为上午9~10时,且高峰时间段香港东路行程时间比TTI=2.42>2.2属于严重拥堵,但海口路行程时间比TTI=1.10交通运行畅通,相邻道路空间资源利用不合理,需进行诱导管控。

3.3 仿真模型建立

VISSIM是一种微观的、基于时间间隔和驾驶行为的仿真建模工具,用以城市交通和公共交通运行的交通建模,可以分析各种交通条件下,如车道设置、交通构成、交通信号、公交站点等,城市交通和公共交通的运行状况,是评价交通工程设计和城市规划方案的有效工具。本文根据实地调查道路基本数据,相位配时方案以及交通量,选取仿真软件VISSIM构建路网模型(图7)。

为验证仿真模型的可信度,选用路网中香港东路—海尔路交叉口各进口道排队长度作为量化评价指标。使用平均绝对误差(MAE)、平均绝对相对误差(MARE)对模型结果进行评价,对比仿真值与实际观测值差距,各评价指标表达式分别为:

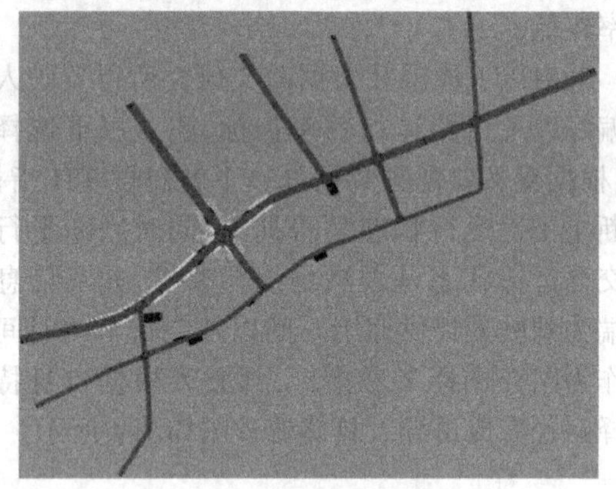

图7 仿真路网示意图

$$\mathrm{MAE}=\frac{1}{M}\sum_{k=1}^{M}\left|z_{\mathrm{r}}-z_{\mathrm{s},k}\right| \tag{10}$$

$$\mathrm{MARE}=\frac{1}{M}\sum_{k=1}^{M}\left(\frac{z_{\mathrm{r}}-z_{\mathrm{s},k}}{z_{\mathrm{r}}}\right) \tag{11}$$

式中:z_{r}——实测数据;

$z_{\mathrm{s},k}$——第k次仿真数据;

M——仿真总次数,取$M=5$。

通过实测数据与仿真结果的对比完成了4个进口道排队长度的误差分析,由于误差值是5次仿真结果的平均值,所以对仿真结果保留两位小数,实际观测值取整,结果见表7。

模型可信度评价　表7

评价指标	L_e	L_w	L_s	L_n
MAE	10.65	12.2	1.19	4.35
MARE	0.08	0.05	0.09	0.05

表中 L_e、L_w、L_s、L_n 分别为交叉口东进口道、西进口道、南进口道、北进口道排队长度。

仿真模型测定交通运行指标与实际观测 MARE 均小于 10%,证明该仿真模型可信度高,能够真实反映区域道路交通流运行情况。

根据历史数据,在早高峰时间香港东路西起东海东路,东至云岭路沿线交通流运行速度较慢,出现拥堵情况,故将诱导点设置在香港东路—东海东路交叉口上游,将原驶向香港东路的车流诱导至海口路,示意图如图8所示。

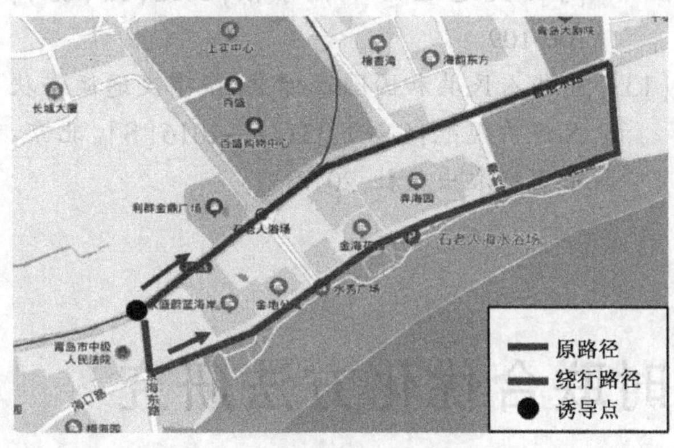

图8　诱导绕行示意图

3.4　仿真结果分析

所选案例原路径由香港东路—海口路交叉口沿香港东路行驶至云岭路,由东海东路行至海口路完成绕行,根据原路径调查得到拥堵等待时间为5~10min这一区间,即 $x=2$ 代入式(4)。

$$P_1=\frac{\exp(-0.988+0.559)}{1+\exp(-0.988+0.559)}=0.53 \quad (12)$$

该绕行路径绕行距离300m,节约时间约为300s,即 $\varepsilon=1$,$\mu=0.44$ 代入式(4),对路径选择概率进行修正,得到最终选择绕行概率:

$$P_i=P_1\times1\times0.44=0.23 \quad (13)$$

计算得出驾驶人接受交通诱导比例占23%,调整仿真场景下路径选择比例以达到诱导效果;对仿真模型进行实验,以路段自由流行程时间作为参照组,得到车流在有无诱导策略下的通行时间对比如图9所示。表8为行程时间结果对比。

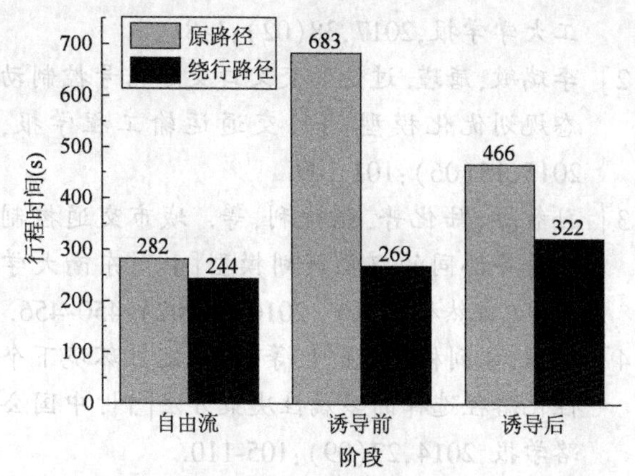

图9　行程时间对比

行程时间结果对比　表8

情况	原路径	绕行路径
自由流(s)	282	244
诱导前(s)	683	269
诱导后(s)	466	322
改善(%)	-31.70	19.70

从上述结果可见在交通诱导策略下,主干道香港东路行程时间减少31.7%,平行道路次干道海口路行程时间增加19.7%,区域整体路网通行效率增加17.2%。基于以上结果本文提出的一种考虑驾驶人接受度的平行诱导策略相比传统解决区域拥堵的方法更为优越,能够实现对空间资源的合理使用,改善交通运行状况。

4　结语

(1)本文针对城市道路空间资源利用不均衡问题,提出了一种基于驾驶人接受度的平行诱导策略。相较于传统交通诱导系统,此方法采集交通运行效率指标简单,无需额外布设其他设备且能实时反映路段运行情况。同时,在信息发布端,通过SP问卷调查的方法分析出影响诱导接受率最为显著的因素作为关键信息进行发布。根据调查结果,改进得出以驾驶人接受度为效用函数的Logit,选择模型运用到仿真验证中,并取得良好效果。

(2)本文诱导策略只考虑空间上进行绕行诱导,可以将绕行路线上的信号一起考虑,进行协同配合,进一步提升通行效率。

(3)实际调查数据有限,后续可在复杂度更高的路网验证该诱导策略的有效性。

参考文献

[1] 曲大义,杨建,王进展,等.基于雷达多目标检测技术的交通信号智能控制系统[J].青岛理

工大学学报,2017,38(02):1-8.

[2] 李瑞敏,唐瑾.过饱和交叉口交通信号控制动态规划优化模型[J].交通运输工程学报,2015,15(06):101-109.

[3] 孙智源,陆化普,张晓利,等. 城市交通控制与诱导协同的双层规划模型[J]. 东南大学学报(自然科学版),2016,46(02):450-456.

[4] 龙琼,胡列格,张谨帆,等.不确定性环境下个性化路径选择的多属性决策方法[J].中国公路学报,2014,27(09):105-110.

[5] Pang G,Takahashi K,Yokota T,et al. Adaptive Route Selection for Dynamic Route Guidance System Based on Fuzzy-neural Approaches[C]// Vehicle Navigation and Information Systems Conference, 1995. Proceedings. In conjunction with the Pacific Rim TransTech Conference. 6th International VNIS. A Ride into the Future'. IEEE', 1999.

[6] 龚奕,李苏剑,刘启生.驾驶员分类的路径诱导系统及评价指标[J].武汉理工大学学报,2013,35(01):75-81.

[7] 李炼恒,曹光斌.基于驾驶员意愿的交通诱导路径选择模型[J].公路,2016,61(02):137-141.

[8] 周永华.交通诱导预测控制仿真研究[J].控制与决策,2009,24(12):1869-1872.

[9] 徐天东,孙立军,郝媛.基于模型预测的快速交通网络路由诱导方法[J].同济大学学报(自然科学版),2010,38(06):827-831+838.

[10] 陈芳,张卫华,丁恒,等.基于出行者路径选择行为的 VMS 诱导策略研究[J].系统工程理论与实践,2018,38(05):1263-1276.

[11] HE G, MA S. AI-based Dynamic Route Guidance Strategy and Its Simulation[C]// IEEE Inteligent Transportation System Conference. Oakland:IEEE,2001:28-32.

[12] 史忠科,乔羽.城市道路排队车辆检测方法[J].交通运输工程学报,2012,12(05):100-109.

[13] 中华人民共和国国家标准.城市交通运行状况评价规范:GB/T 33171—2016[S].北京:中国标准出版社,2016.

交通拥挤费与信号灯配时联合优化方法研究

王　笛*　陈　笑
(长安大学运输工程学院)

摘　要　为了缓解城市交通拥堵,提高系统运行效率,本文研究针对拥挤收费与信号控制联合优化的交通管理与控制措施,建立目标为系统出行者广义出行成本最小化的非线性优化模型,并运用 interior-point 算法求解,同时得出最优拥挤收费费率与信号灯配时方案,最后通过一个小型路网对该组合优化模型进行验证。结果表明:相较于实施单一的信号控制措施而言,实施组合措施的系统广义出行成本降低 8.94%,出行效率得到了提高。

关键词　联合优化　拥挤收费　信号灯配时　路网建模

0　引言

随着汽车保有量的持续增长,全球几乎所有的城市都面临着交通能否可持续发展的问题,由于无节制使用私家车造成的交通拥堵已使得一些地区现有的交通系统不堪重负。因此,实施高效可行的交通管理措施迫在眉睫。针对具体的管控方法,国内外学者进行了大量的研究,包括拥挤收费政策、交通诱导、信号控制、流量限制等[1]。其中,拥挤收费作为一种基于经济调节手段的交通需求管理方法,已被证实在改善城市交通拥挤方面效果显著[2]。

考虑到决策部门与出行者之间的相互关系,研究者们常用可以实现上下联动的双层规划模型来探究实施拥挤收费政策的影响;针对双层优化模型,上层目标函数根据内容大致可以分为出行成本[3]、系统运行效率[4]、环境影响[5]和公平性[6]四类,而模型下层通常是该收费政策影响下的出行行为选择。双层模型的求解方法有解析法和基于方向迭代的启发式算法等。此外,考虑到双层模型求解较为困难,通常是不可求导的最优化问题[7],也有不少学者选择单层优化模型,程铁信等[8]建立考虑车辆碳排放在内的社会成本最小化的单层模型,模型通过VISSIM仿真求解得出最优定价方案;任涛等[9]研究系统总收费最小时的单层收费模型,在满足用户平衡条件下获取最优收费策略。

纵观针对拥挤收费政策的研究,不难发现,大部分研究的对象是单一的,仅限于动态收费或静态收费,而有关拥挤收费与其他管理措施相结合的研究内容较为缺乏。理论上而言,将多种管理方式组合起来联合实施,充分利用每种方式的优势,取长补短,相较于仅实施单一的管理措施而言能更有效地缓解交通问题[10]。为了减少交通堵塞的发生,提高出行效率,当目标为出行者在系统中的广义出行成本[11]最小时,本文提出一种将拥挤收费与信号灯配时联合优化的管理措施,通过构建单层非线性优化模型,同时得出满足目标和约束条件下最优的收费费率和信号控制方案。

1 构建组合优化模型

1.1 目标函数

本文构建同时优化进入中心商贸区路段的拥挤收费与交叉口信号控制的组合模型,模型目标为系统中出行者的广义出行成本最小化,此时广义出行成本 Z 既包含总出行时间 T 又包含总出行花费 N。当针对目标中出行者总出行时间 T 的计算时,模型考虑运用混合交通运行公式[12],该公式分别基于BPR(Bureau of Public Roads)路段阻抗函数[13]计算路段耗时以及简化的韦伯斯特(Webster)延误公式[14]计算交叉口延误。其中,在计算交叉口延误时,将所有受信号控制的路段根据行驶方向划分为队列,研究不同队列上出行者在受不同信号灯配时影响下的延误情况;当针对目标中出行者总出行花费 N 的计算时,考虑拥挤收费费率,引入时间价值系数 ν,将出行者在路网中花费的金额与出行时间计算单位进行统一。具体计算系统中出行者广义出行成本最小化的目标函数如下所示:

$$\min Z = \min[T + \nu^{-1}N] \tag{1}$$

$$T = \sum_{a \in A} t_a^0 \left[1 + 0.15\left(\frac{f_a}{S_a}\right)^4\right] f_a + \sum_{l \in L} \frac{C_d(1-g_p)^2}{2(1-f_l/M_d)} f_l \tag{2}$$

$$N = \sum_{a \in A} \tau_a f_a \tag{3}$$

式中:Z——路网中出行者的广义出行成本(s);

T——出行者的总出行时间(s);

N——出行者的总出行花费(元);

ν——时间价值系数;

A——路网中所有路段集合,$\forall a \in A$;

l——将受信号控制的路段按照左转,直行,右转行驶方向划分为同向队列 $\forall l \in L, L \in A$;

t_a^0——路段 a 上自由流的行驶时间(s);

f_a——路段 a 上的交通流量($\mathrm{pcu \cdot h^{-1}}$);

f_l——信号控制队列 l 上的交通流量($\mathrm{pcu \cdot h^{-1}}$);

τ_a——路段 a 的收费费率(元);

S_a——路段 a 的饱和流量($\mathrm{pcu \cdot h^{-1}}$);

C_d——交叉口 d 的周期时长(s),D 表示路网中所有交叉口集合,$\forall d \in D$;

g_p——信号交叉口相位 p 的绿信比,$\forall p \in P$;

M_d——交叉口 d 的饱和流量(pcu/h)。

1.2 约束条件

(1)收费费率约束。路段实施拥挤收费的费率约束:

$$\tau_a^{\min} \leqslant \tau_a \leqslant \tau_a^{\max} \tag{4}$$

式中:$\tau_a^{\min}$——路段a的收费费率最小值(元);

$\tau_a^{\max}$——路段a的收费费率最大值(元)。

(2)交通分配约束。考虑到路段实施拥挤收费对于出行者出行决策的影响,运用Logit模型计算出行者对于OD对间各路径的选择概率,其中,选择概率依据路径的效用函数计算得出:

$$D_{od} = \sum_{r \in R_{od}} f_{odr} \tag{5}$$

$$f_a = \sum_{od \in OD} \sum_{r \in R_{od}} f_{odr} \delta_{ar}^{od} \tag{6}$$

$$f_l = \sum_{od \in OD} \sum_{r \in R_{od}} f_{odr} \delta_{lr}^{od} \tag{7}$$

$$f_{odr} = D_{od} P_{odr} \tag{8}$$

$$P_{odr} = \frac{e^{(-\theta V_{odr})}}{\sum_{r \in R_{od}} e^{(-\theta V_{odr})}} \tag{9}$$

$$V_{odr}=\sum_{a\in A}t_a^0\left[1+0.15\left(\frac{f_a}{S_a}\right)^4\right]\delta_{ar}^{od}+$$

$$\sum_{l\in L}\frac{C_d\ (1-gp)^2}{2(1-f_l/M_d)}\delta_{lr}^{od}+\sum_{a\in A}\frac{\tau_a}{v}\delta_{ar}^{od} \tag{10}$$

式中:OD——路网中 OD 对集合,$\forall od\in OD$;

f_{odr}——从出发点 o 到目的地 d 之间经过路径 r 的交通流量($\mathrm{pcu\cdot h^{-1}}$);

D_{od}——每小时从出发点 o 到目的地 d 之间的交通需求量(pcu);

R_{od}——od 对之间的所有路径集合,$\forall r\in Rod$;

V_{odr}——od 对之间选择路径 r 的效用函数;

P_{odr}——od 对之间选择路径 r 的概率;

θ——路径选择模型中的常量;

δ_{ar}^{od}——如果从 o 出发的车辆经由路段 a 通过路径 r 到达目的地 d,则 δ_{ar}^{od} 为1,否则为0;

δ_{lr}^{od}——如果从 o 出发的车辆经由信号控制队列 l 通过路径 r 到达目的地 d,则 δ_{lr}^{od} 为1,否则为0。

(3)信号控制绿信比约束。一般交叉口信号控制设计满足如下约束:

$$b_d=\sum_{p\in P_d}g_p \tag{11}$$

$$\mu_l-\sum_{p\in P_l}g_pM_d=0 \tag{12}$$

$$g_p\geqslant g_{\min} \tag{13}$$

式中:b_d——交叉口 d 的有效周期比;

μ_l——信号控制队列 l 的服务率;

$g_{\min}$——绿信比的最小值,每个相位所对应的最小绿灯时间为4s;

P_l——信号控制队列 l 上的所有相位集合;

P_d——交叉口 d 上的所有相位集合。

2 算例分析

2.1 路网概况

图1给出了一个包含7个节点的小型路网模型,路网中所有的路段均由3条车道组成,路段设计车速为30km/h,各节点之间的距离和路段通行能力如表1所示。此外,路网中共有4个OD对,分别为1-2,2-1,3-4,4-3,各OD对之间的交通需求量分别为 $D_{12}=5200$pcu/h,$D_{21}=5400$pcu/h,$D_{34}=5500$pcu/h,$D_{43}=5300$pcu/h。路网中节点7为中心商贸区,拟对进入该中心商贸区的所有路段(已加粗标记)实施拥挤收费(设置收费费率的上下限分别为0元和10元[13],且时间价值系数 v 为56.2元/h[14],约0.0156元/s)。节点5,6表示为两个信号控制交叉口,两个交叉口均为4相位控制交叉口(4个相位分别控制东西向直行,东西向左转,南北向直行和南北向左转),交叉口信号灯的周期时长均设置为100s,黄灯时长为3s。

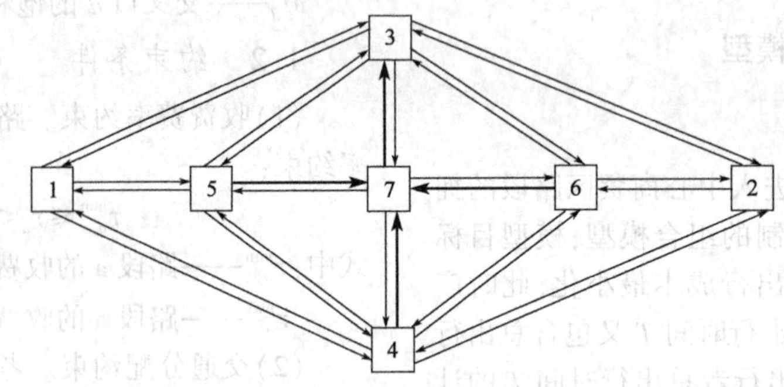

图1 路网模型

路网参数说明 表1

路段	距离(m)	通行能力(pcu/h)	路段	距离(m)	通行能力(pcu/h)
1-3,3-1	3000	4500	3-6,6-3	2500	4500
1-4,4-1	3000	4500	3-7,7-3	600	4500
1-5,5-1	500	4500	4-5,5-4	2500	4500
2-3,3-2	3000	4500	4-6,6-4	2500	4500
2-4,4-2	3000	4500	4-7,7-4	600	4500
2-6,6-2	3000	4500	5-7,7-5	500	4500
3-5,5-3	2500	4500	6-7,7-6	500	4500

2.2 模型求解

基于所构建的拥挤收费和信号控制组合优化模型,本文在 MATLAB 软件中输入有关小型路网的外部参数(路段长度,道路容量,路段设计时速,交叉口周期时长等),并借助 trust-region-reflective 算法求得满足所有约束条件的可行初值。对优化模型进行求解时调用非线性多变量优化函数 fmincon,运用其中 interior-point 算法对包含收费费率和绿信比两个决策变量在内的所有初值进行迭代,最后得到广义出行成本最小化时的拥挤收费费率和信号灯配时方案。

为验证组合优化模型的效果,在上述小型路网中考虑联合实施拥挤收费与信号控制措施以及单独实施信号控制措施对于计算系统广义出行成本的影响,对路网中 4 条拟收费路段(3-7,4-7,5-7,6-7)实施收费前后的模型求解结果进行对比(表 2,表 3)。

模型输出费率及目标函数结果 表 2

输出参数	路段收费费率(元)				系统广义出行成本(min)
	3 ~ 7	4 ~ 7	5 ~ 7	6 ~ 7	
单一信号控制措施	0	0	0	0	43699.95
拥挤收费与信号控制组合措施	4.25	4.19	4.13	4.21	39793.1

模型输出信号灯配时方案 表 3

输出参数	相位绿信比									
	交叉口 5					交叉口 6				
	东西直行	东西左转	南北直行	南北左转	有效周期比	东西直行	东西左转	南北直行	南北左转	有效周期比
单一措施	0.23	0.23	0.12	0.30	0.88	0.16	0.11	0.17	0.44	0.88
组合措施	0.33	0.20	0.11	0.24	0.88	0.30	0.12	0.34	0.12	0.88

由上述对比结果可知,在路网中实施拥挤收费与信号控制组合措施相较于实施单一的信号控制措施而言,系统广义出行成本由原来的 43699.95min减少为 39793.1min,降低 8.94%;交通总延误减小,出行效率整体得到改善。同时,在满足信号控制约束条件下,拥挤收费政策的加入没有对信号灯配时的优化方案产生明显负面影响。

3 结语

本文选取拥挤收费和信号控制进行联合管理措施的研究,在考虑信号控制约束以及实施拥挤收费对于出行决策的影响下,构建以系统广义出行成本最小化为目标的优化模型,整个模型使用非线性函数 fmincon 中 interior-point 算法求解,并通过一个小型路网完成数值计算。计算结果表明将拥挤收费与信号控制两者组合起来的研究是有效的,有助于充分发挥实施拥挤收费对于交通流量引导以及优化信号控制对于减缓交通压力的积极作用。

但该模型也存在一定不足,目前仅适用于交通需求固定且交通拥堵时有发生的路网中;对于堵塞程度严重、交通需求动态变化、交通过饱和状态路网中的组合优化计算,模型误差较大;缺乏对路网中各个交叉口之间协调性和相互影响的考虑,不具有普遍适用性。因此,未来工作还将考虑该组合模型在实际中的应用,进一步完善和改进模型中的目标函数及约束条件,期望研究出从出行成本和环境两个维度实现交通系统可持续发展的多目标组合优化模型,使社会资源得到充分利用。

参考文献

[1] Othman, B, De Nunzio, G, Di Domenico, et al. Ecological traffic management: A review of the modeling and control strategies for improving environmental sustainability of road transportation[J]. Annual Reviews in Control, 2019, 48: 292-311.

[2] Lehe, L. Downtown congestion pricing in practice. Transportation Research Part C: Emerging Technologies, 2019, 100: 200-223.

[3] Aboudina A, B Abdulhai. A bi-level distributed

approach for optimizing time-dependent congestion pricing in large networks: A simulation-based case study in the Greater Toronto Area[J]. Transportation Research Part C:Emerging Technologies 85:684-710.

[4] Cheng Q,et al. A cell-based dynamic congestion pricing scheme considering travel distance and time delay [J]. Transportmetrica B-Transport Dynamics 7(1):1286-1304.

[5] Lv Y,et al. A sustainable road pricing oriented bilevel optimization approach under multiple environmental uncertainties [J]. International Journal of Sustainable Transportation.

[6] Paleti C,et al. Design of income-equitable toll prices for high occupancy toll lanes in a single toll facility [J]. Transportation Planning and Technology 39(4):389-406.

[7] 张小宁.双层优化交通模型及其算法[J].同济大学学报(自然科学版),2005(02):169-173.

[8] 程铁信,李奇,赵颖.考虑碳排放的城市交通拥堵定价模型及其仿真分析[J].中国管理科学,2016,24(S1):932-937.

[9] 任涛,黄海军,刘天亮.区分车辆起讫信息的拥挤道路使用收费模型[J].系统工程理论与实践,2019,39(05):1189-1197.

[10] Ye Y, Wang H. Optimal design of transportation networks with automated vehicle links and congestion pricing [J]. Journal of Advanced Transportation,2018.

[11] Chen R, L Nozick. Integrating congestion pricing and transit investment planning [J]. Transportation Research Part A: Policy and Practice 89:124-139.

[12] Qu Z, Xing Y, Song X, et al. A study on the coordination of urban traffic control and traffic assignment[J]. Discrete Dynamics in Nature and Society,2012.

[13] Bureau of Public Roads. Traffic assignment manual [M]. US Department of Commerce,1964.

[14] Webster F V. Traffic Signal Settings[R]. Road Research Technical Paper No. 39, Road Research Laboratory.

自动化集装箱码头双场桥调度的接力区选址研究

王彦琳　王晓蕾*

(同济大学经济与管理学院)

摘　要　针对自动化码头中的不可穿越式双场桥调度问题,研究适应任务特征的可变接力区选址方案。提出了5种不同的根据任务特征的可变接力区选址规则,利用模拟退火算法优化了给定接力区选址下的场桥调度,在不同场景下,对不同的接力区选址规则的优劣进行了对比。研究结果表明:混合接力模式能够有效减少集卡等待时间;海陆两侧任务量不均衡以及存箱任务的比例越高时,混合接力模式对比不接力模式的优势更加明显;考虑海陆两侧的任务量以及主任务起止点分布的接力规则更适用于确定最优的接力区位置。

关键词　自动化集装箱码头　场桥调度　接力区选址　不可穿越式双场桥　模拟退火

1.基金项目:国家自然科学基金国际合作研究项目"突发及特殊事件下的多模式公共交通系统应急管理研究"(72061127003)。

0 引言

随着世界集装箱海运量不断增长,集装箱码头的堆场也越来越大。堆场作业效率的高低,越来越成为码头提高作业效率的关键和核心。堆场作业的主要内容是以码头的堆存计划为依据,调动堆场内的场桥设备来完成来自海侧船舶的集装箱进场和离场作业以及来自陆侧集卡的集装箱入港和提箱作业。

轨道式龙门起重机(轨道吊)是目前大型集装箱码头堆场中常用的场桥类型。由于有固定的轨道,通常在每个箱区内布置两个轨道吊负责固定箱区内的集装箱进场和离场任务。具体而言,在轨道吊双场桥模式下,根据两个轨道吊是否大小不同可以相互穿越,又可分为双轨可穿越以及同轨不可穿越两种。本文研究的同轨不可穿越双场桥是指由大小相同、不可互相穿越的两个场桥来完成单个箱区海陆两侧集装箱进场和离场任务的模式。我国最大的集装箱自动化码头——上海洋山港四期采用的即为同轨不可穿越式双场桥模式。

科学合理的场桥调度可以有效提升海侧进出口箱的装卸船效率,减少集卡等待时间,增加港口的吞吐量,提高港口的竞争力;而低效的场桥操作会成为港口装卸作业中的瓶颈[1]。对于同轨不可穿越式双场桥,由于两个场桥在作业的过程中很可能发生作业区间冲突,需要彼此避让,其调度的关键是如何在避免两个场桥的作业区间冲突的条件下平衡两个场桥的作业任务,确定各场桥的任务分配以及任务完成顺序,优化任务的总完成时间、AGV/集卡的平均等待时间或任务延迟数等目标。为了减少两个场桥间的避让带来的额外成本,目前文献中的方法主要有两种:一种是通过优化任务顺序尽可能减少干扰的发生;另一种是通过设置接力区划分两侧场桥各自的作业贝位区间,让两侧场桥接力完成跨区间任务来减少干扰。

在没有固定接力区的情形下,早期对双场桥调度问题的研究一般不考虑任务可由两个场桥接力完成的情况,所有任务都由对应场桥独立完成。例如,在考虑场桥不可穿越且保持安全距离的约束下,乐美龙等[2]建立了混合整数规划模型,并设计两阶段求解算法进行求解,但该研究仅考虑了出口集装箱。Gharehgozli 等[3]进一步考虑堆场内同时存在进出口集装箱的情形,给出了场桥在堆场内操作以及移动时间的计算,将双场桥调度问题转化为具有优先约束的多重非对称广义旅行商问题,并通过自适应大邻域搜索启发式算法进行求解。Hu 等[4]分析了避免双场桥干扰的任意两个任务作业中间时间的最小时间间隔,并通过精确算法和遗传算法求解,但假设场桥在完成每个任务后都需要返回相应的交接点,对场桥的作业过程进行了简化。对于双场桥调度中存在的场桥干扰问题,Carlo 等[5]提出了在产生干扰时的 14 种优先级规则。由于接力作业可以更好地平衡两个场桥的任务分配,近年来也出现了一些在没有固定接力区情形下考虑任务接力完成的场桥调度研究。例如,Dominik 等[6]在海侧任务可中断、而后由陆侧场桥接力完成的假设下,构建了动态规划模型,并设计了定向搜索启发式算法。由于没有固定接力区,在这些研究中接力任务中箱子的中间停放一般作为决策变量生成。Park 等[7]考虑了每个任务都可由两个场桥配合完成的情形,将问题转化为求解有向图中最短路径的问题,提出了基于启发式和局部搜索的实时调度方法。邱亚等[8]提出考虑作业顺序的动态接力点模式,将每次任务的接力点设置在距离下次任务目标位置一个贝位的地方,通过与固定中间贝位的接力模式对比证明了规则的有效性。

在有固定接力区情形下,Han 等[9]分析了接力区双场桥产生干扰的 4 种情况,在给定接力区位置的情形下提出了基于遗传算法的场桥任务分配和作业顺序优化。Gharehgozli 等[10]通过仿真比较了接力区的位置和大小对任务完成时间的影响,考虑了不同的任务处理顺序规则,优先级分配规则等多种因素的影响。

已有的研究表明,接力区的选址对于堆场任务的完成时间、集卡的等待时间等有显著的影响。但是,在这些研究中,普遍假定接力区设置在堆场箱区的固定贝位[11-12],没有考虑如何根据任务特征来优化接力区选址。本文提出根据作业任务特征和起止点分布确定接力区位置的方案,以期为采用不可穿越双场桥模式的自动化码头优化场桥调度决策、提升堆场作业效率提供算法支持。

1 问题描述

我们考虑一个由两台不可穿越式双场桥 RMG1 和 RMG2 服务的自动化码头箱区,其最大

贝位、最大列数和最大层高分别为 T_X、T_Y 和 T_Z。箱区中的任意位置用 $m=(X,Y,Z)$ 来表示(图1),其中 $X\in\{1,2,\cdots,T_X\}$、$Y\in\{1,2,\cdots,T_Y\}$、$Z\in\{1,2,\cdots,T_Z\}$。在箱区两端,分别有 T_Y 个海侧交接点和 T_Y 个陆侧交接点,我们用 $(0,Y,1)$ 表示位于第 Y 列的陆侧交接点,$(T_X+1,Y,1)$ 表示位于第 Y 列的海侧交接点。两个场桥沿 X,Y,Z 三个方向的移动速度分别为 v_x,v_y 和 v_z,则场桥从任意位置 $m_1=(X_1,Y_1,Z_1)$ 到位置 $m_2=(X_2,Y_2,Z_2)$ 的移动时间可以表示为 $t(m_1,m_2)=\max\{|X_1-X_2|/v_x,|Y_1-Y_2|/v_y\}+(|T_Z-Z_1|+|T_Z-Z_2|)/v_z$[3,13]。提箱与进箱操作的作业时间相同且为固定值,用 t_0 表示;两个场桥的安全距离为 1 个贝位。

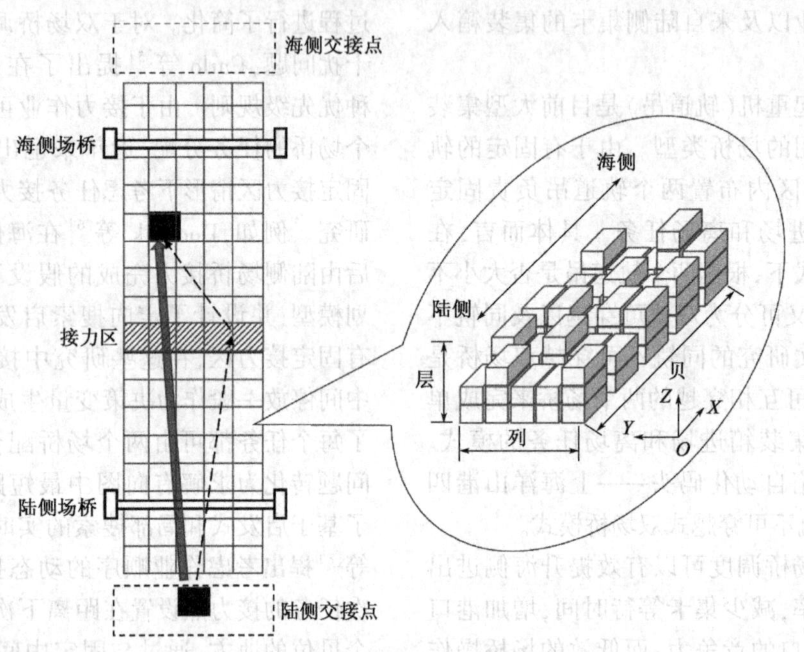

图 1　堆场箱区布置

令 I 为该箱区在一次调度优化中考虑的所有作业任务的集合。对于任意作业任务 $i\in I$,命 $O_i=(x_i^o,y_i^o,z_i^o)$ 表示其作业开始位置,$D_i=(x_i^d,y_i^d,z_i^d)$ 表示其作业结束位置。场桥的作业任务主要可以分为进箱任务以及提箱任务两类。进箱任务是指需要场桥将目标集装箱从陆侧/海侧交接点转移到堆场内进行储存的任务,我们用 I_{in} 表示所有进箱任务的集合;提箱任务是指需要场桥将目标集装箱从堆场内移动至陆侧/海侧交接点的任务,我们用 I_{out} 表示所有提箱任务的集合。所有海侧的存提箱任务由内集卡(或 AGV)完成,所有陆侧的存提箱任务由外集卡完成。令 d_i 表示任务 $i\in I$ 对应的集卡到达时间。进箱任务需要等到相应的集卡到达才能进行提箱操作开始任务,提箱任务需要等待相应的集卡到达才能进行进箱操作结束任务。在本文中,我们假设码头对每个任务 $i\in I$ 有准确的集卡/AGV 到达时间预估。由于集卡的等待时间,特别是内集卡,直接影响码头装船等其他任务的作业效率,本文设定堆场作业的目标是最小化内外集卡的加权总等待时间,其中外集卡的等待时间权重为 1,内集卡的等待时间权重为 θ $(\theta\geqslant 1)$。

对于同轨不可穿越式双场桥,单个提箱任务或进箱任务可以由两个场桥接力完成。当存在固定接力区时,起止点没有跨越接力区的任务由对应场桥独立完成,而对于起止点跨越接力区的任务,我们假设它可以由一侧场桥运送至接力区再由另一侧场桥完成余下任务,也可以由单侧场桥跨接力区单独完成,由场桥调度优化来决定采用哪一种模式。为了减少两个场桥在接力区的冲突,接力区大小通常设置为 1 个贝位。令 k 为接力区所在贝位,$1\leqslant k\leqslant T_x$。在本文余下的章节中,我们将提出 5 种不同的接力区选择规则,并通过仿真检验他们在实际堆场运作中的效果。

2　接力区选址规则

在给出接力区选址规则之前,我们首先讨论任意给定的接力选址给两个场桥任务分配带来的影响。假设第 k 贝位被选为接力区，那么所有跨接力区的进箱或提箱任务将被拆分为两个任务。令 $I^c(k)$ 为选定接力区 k 后所有需要接力完成的任务的集合，即：

$$I^c(k)=\{i\in I\mid (x_i^o-k)(x_i^d-k)<0\}$$

对于任意 $i\in I^c(k)$，我们假设其拆分后在接力区的放箱位置已知，用 $M_i(k)=(k,y_i^m,z_i^m)$ 表示。命 $i_1(k)$ 表示任务 $i\in I^c(k)$ 在接力区为 k 时从 O_i 到 $M_i(k)$ 的第一阶段任务，$i_2(k)$ 表示其从 $M_i(k)$ 到 D_i 的第二阶段任务。则当接力区为 k 时，我们可得到所有第一阶段任务集合 $I_1^c(k)$，所有第二阶段任务的集合 $I_2^c(k)$ 以及所有任务的集合为 $I(k)=[I/I^c(k)]\cup I_1^c(k)\cup I_2^c(k)$。对于任意 $i\in I(k)$，其起止点必然位于接力区的同一侧。根据其起止点位于 $[0,k]$ 还是 $[k,T_X+1]$，我们定义 $I_S(k)$ 为起止点贝位都位于海侧 $[k,T_X+1]$ 的任务集合，即 $I_S(k)=\{i\in I(k)\mid x_i^d\geqslant k,x_i^o\geqslant k\}$；$I_L(k)$ 为起止点贝位都位于陆侧 $[0,k]$ 的任务集合，即 $I_L(k)=\{i\in I(k)\mid x_i^d\leqslant k,x_i^o\leqslant k\}$。令 $TD_S(k)$ 和 $TD_L(k)$ 分别表示当接力区选址为 k 时任务集合 $I_S(k)$ 对应的总提箱移动距离和任务集合 $I_L(k)$ 对应的总提箱移动距离，其计算公式如下：

$$TD_S(k)=\sum_{i\in I_S(k)}|x_i^o-x_i^d| \tag{1}$$

$$TD_L(k)=\sum_{i\in I_L(k)}|x_i^o-x_i^d| \tag{2}$$

在本文中，我们讨论 5 种接力区选址规则。

R1：选择箱区的中间贝位作为接力区，即 $k=[T_X/2]$，其中 $[a]$ 表示向下取整。

R2：命 x_i^w 表示任务 $i\in I(k)$ 在堆场内的作业位置，即对于进箱任务，$x_i^w=x_i^d$；对提箱任务，$x_i^w=x_i^o$。接力区设置在所有任务堆场内作业位置的中位数处。

R3：选择拆分后两个场桥任务量相同的贝位作为接力区，即 $k=[x_i^w+x_j^w/2]$，$i,j\in I$，使得 $|I_S(k)|=|I_L(k)|$。

R4：命 x_i^m 表示任务 $i\in I$ 开始和结束位置的中间贝位，即 $x_i^m=(x_i^o+x_i^d)/2$。接力区设置在所有任务起止点中间贝位的均值处。

R5：选择能够最小化两个场桥提箱距离最大值的 k 作为接力区，即 $k\in\arg\min\limits_{k\in\{1,2,\cdots T_X\}}\max\{TD_S(k),TD_L(k)\}$。

3 给定接力区选址下的场桥作业仿真

为了评估不同接力区选址规则对于减小集卡等待时间的作用，我们建立了如下场桥作业仿真平台。该仿真平台的作用是在给定的接力区选址 k 下，通过模拟退火算法给出场桥作业顺序优化后的任务开始时间、任务完成时间和集卡等待时间。

3.1 基于模拟退火的场桥调度优化

从前面的分析可知，在接力区贝位 k 选定后，箱区内的任务集合为 $I(k)$，其中海侧任务集合为 $I_S(k)$，陆侧任务集合为 $I_L(k)$。其中，一些提箱任务对应的目标集装箱并不都在顶层（图 2）。此时就需要进行翻箱操作，将位于目标集装箱上面的集装箱都移到附近的空位，然后才搬运目标集装箱。对于需要翻箱的作业任务 $i\in I(k)$，我们在初始化时为其生成若干个翻箱任务。命 $I_r(k)\subseteq I(k)$ 表示需要翻箱的作业任务集合，对每一个需要翻箱的任务，我们为其生成一系列翻箱任务。每一个翻箱任务将位于目标箱顶层的箱子移至一个附近的进箱位置，假设该位置不跨接力区，且不位于任何当前其他主任务对应的目标集装箱之上[14]。对于任意任务 $i\in I_r(k)$，命 R_i 表示其翻箱任务的集合。当产生翻箱任务后，所有任务的集合变为 $\hat{I}(k)=I(k)\cup(\cup_{i\in I_r(k)}R_i)$。

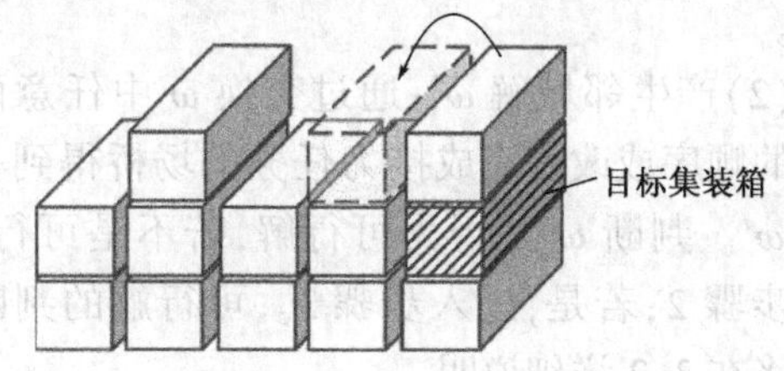

图 2 集装箱翻箱示意图

命 $\omega=[(i_j,RMG_j),j=1,2,\cdots,|\hat{I}(k)|]$ 表示任意的一组场桥调度解（图 3），其中 $i_j\in\hat{I}(k)$ 表示这个任务序列中的第 j 个任务，$RMG_j\in\{RMG1,RMG2\}$ 表示第 j 个任务所分配的 RMG。

任务序列	i_1	i_2	…	$i_{\|\hat{I}(k)\|}$
分配场桥	RMG_1	RMG_2	…	$RMG_{\|\hat{I}(k)\|}$

图 3 场桥调度解示意图

对任意的解 ω，命 t_j^s 和 t_j^e 分别表示其第 $j=1,\cdots,|\hat{I}(k)|$ 个任务的开始时间和完成时间，$T(\omega)$ 表示 ω 对应的总的集卡等待时间，则

$$T(\omega)=\sum_{i\in I_{in}\cap I_s(k)}\theta\left(\sum_{j=1}^{\hat{I}(k)}t_j^s\delta_{ij}-d_i\right)+\sum_{i\in I_{out}\cap I_S(k)}\theta\left(\sum_{j=1}^{\hat{I}(k)}t_j^e\delta_{ij}-d_i\right)+\sum_{i\in I_{in}\cap I_L(k)}\left(\sum_{j=1}^{\hat{I}(k)}t_j^s\delta_{ij}-d_i\right)+\sum_{i_j\in I_{out}\cap I_L(k)}\left(\sum_{j=1}^{\hat{I}(k)}t_j^s\delta_{ij}-d_i\right) \tag{3}$$

式中：$I_{\text{in}}\cap I_{\text{s}}(k)$、$I_{\text{out}}\cap I_{\text{s}}(k)$——海侧进箱和海侧提箱任务的集合；

$I_{\text{in}}\cap I_{\text{L}}(k)$、$I_{\text{out}}\cap I_{\text{L}}(k)$——陆侧进箱和陆侧提箱任务的集合。

$\delta_{ij}, i\in\hat{I}(k), j=1,2,\cdots,|\hat{I}(k)|$是指示每个任务排序的参数，若任务$i\in\hat{I}(k)$在$\omega$中被排在第$j$位，则$\delta_{ij}=1$，否则$\delta_{ij}=0$；$\theta$是大于1的参数，给予海侧作业任务更高的权重。对于进箱任务$i\in I_{\text{in}}$来说，集卡等待时间是任务开始时间$\sum_{j=1}^{\hat{I}(k)}t_j^s\delta_{ij}$与集卡到达时间$d_i$的差；对于提箱任务来说，集卡等待时间是任务结束时间与集卡到达时间d_i的差。

对于给定接力区选址k、作业任务集合$\hat{I}(k)$以及每个任务对应的集卡到达时间($d_i, i\in I$)，我们采用如下的模拟退火算法来优化任务作业顺序和场桥分配，最小化集卡等待时间$T(\omega)$。

模拟退火算法：

(1)初始化：设置初始温度T_0，终止温度T_f，退火速率a，迭代次数N，随机产生一个初始解ω，$n=0$。

(2)产生邻域解ω'：通过交换ω中任意两个任务的顺序或改变完成接力任务的场桥得到一个新解ω'。判断ω'是否为可行解，若不是可行解，重复步骤2；若是，进入步骤3。可行解的判断规则在将在3.2详细说明。

(3)计算$\Delta\Pi=\Pi(\omega')-\Pi(\omega)$。若$\Delta\Pi\leqslant 0$，则接受$\omega'$为新的当前解；若$\Delta\Pi>0$，则以概率$\exp(-\Delta\Pi/T_k)$接受$\omega'$为新的当前解。

(4)若$n<N, T_k=a\times T_k$，转第2步；否则，输出当前解为最优解，程序结束。

3.2　可行解的判断

模拟退火中新解是通过交换当前解中任意两个任务的顺序或改变完成接力任务和翻箱任务的场桥来产生的，但由于任务序列中存在具有优先约束的接力任务和翻箱任务，则会出现新解不满足任务完成的前后顺序约束的情况，因此模拟退火中产生的新解并不一定都是可行解，所以需要对新解的可行性进行判断。

我们将存在优先约束的两个任务称为关联任务，需要先完成的任务称为优先任务，优先任务完成后才能进行的任务为随后任务。令L_i表示任务$i\in\hat{I}(k)$在ω中的位置，则有$L_i=\sum_{j=1}^{\hat{I}(k)}j\delta_{ij}$。

(1)当关联任务由同一个场桥完成时，优先任务与随后任务的任务顺序不满足先后约束则该解不可行。

即对于任务$i\in\hat{I}(k)$，若$i\in I_r(k)$，存在$i'\in\hat{I}(k)\cap R_i$，$x_{i'}^o=x_i^o$，$y_{i'}^o=y_i^o$，$z_{i'}^o=z_i^o+1$且$\text{RMG}_{Li}=\text{RMG}_{Li'}$，当$L_i<L_{i'}$时，该解不可行；若$i\in I_2^c(k)$，存在$i'\in I_1^c(k)$，$D_{i'}=O_i$且$\text{RMG}_{Li}=\text{RMG}_{Li'}$，当$L_i<L_{i'}$时，该解不可行。

(2)当关联任务由不同的场桥完成时，如果存在多对关联任务，可能会出现两个场桥都需要等待对方完成优先任务然后才能进行各自当前的随后任务而无法作业的情况，此时的解是不可行的。

即对于任务$i\in\hat{I}(k)$，若$i\in I_r(k)$，存在$i'\in\hat{I}(k)\cap Ri$，$x_{i'}^o=x_i^o$，$y_{i'}^o=y_i^o$，$z_{i'}^o=z_i^o+1$且$\text{RMG}_{Li}\neq\text{RMG}_{Li'}$，如果存在任务$p\in\hat{I}(k)(p\neq i)$，若$p\in I_r(k)$并存在$p'\in\hat{I}(k)\cap R_p$，$x_{p'}^o=x_p^o$，$y_{p'}^o=y_p^o$，$z_{p'}^o=z_p^o+1$，$\text{RMG}_{Lp'}\neq\text{RMG}_{Lp}$且$\text{RMG}_{Lp'}=\text{RMG}_{Li}$，则当$L_i<L_{p'}$且$L_p<L_{i'}$时，该解不可行；若$p\in I_2^c(k)$并存在$p'\in I_1^c(k)$，$D_{p'}=O_p$，$\text{RMG}_{Lp'}\neq\text{RMG}_{Lp}$且$\text{RMG}_{Lp'}=\text{RMG}_{Li}$，则当$L_i<L_{p'}$且$L_p<L_{i'}$时，该解不可行。

若$i\in I_2^c(k)$，存在$i'\in I_1^c(k)$，$D_i'=O_i$且$\text{RMG}_{Li}\neq\text{RMG}_{Li'}$，如果存在任务$p\in\hat{I}(k)(p\neq i)$，若$p\in I_r(k)$并存在$p'\in\hat{I}(k)\cap R_p$，$x_{p'}^o=x_p^o$，$y_{p'}^o=y_p^o$，$z_{p'}^o=z_p^o+1$，$\text{RMG}_{Lp'}\neq\text{RMG}_{Lp}$且$\text{RMG}_{Lp'}=\text{RMG}_{Li}$，则当$L_i<L_{p'}$且$L_p<L_{i'}$时，该解不可行；若$p\in I_2^c(k)$并存在$p'\in I_1^c(k)$，$D_{p'}=O_p$，$\text{RMG}_{Lp'}\neq\text{RMG}_{Lp}$且$\text{RMG}_{Lp'}=\text{RMG}_{Li}$，则当$L_i<L_{p'}$且$L_p<L_{i'}$时，该解不可行。

3.3　给定任务序列的任务开始和完成时间确定

对于给定的任务序列和场桥分配方案，任务开始和完成时间的确定是各种调度方案评估和调度方案优化的基础，一般需要通过场桥的作业轨迹绘制来完成。下面我们将对场桥作业轨迹的产生以及任务开始和完成时间确定进行详细说明。

3.3.1 场桥作业轨迹图

场桥执行任意任务的过程都可以分为4个步骤:

(1)场桥从当前位置移动到任务的起始位置;

(2)提取目标集装箱;

(3)场桥将目标集装箱移动到任务的目的地;

(4)释放目标集装箱。

其中,步骤(1)和步骤(3)时场桥处于移动状态,步骤(2)和步骤(4)时场桥处于装卸操作状态,此时场桥的操作是不可中断的。由此根据场桥完成任务的4个步骤及其对应位置贝位的变化,我们可以得到场桥完成任意任务时的移动轨迹图,如图4中实线所示。

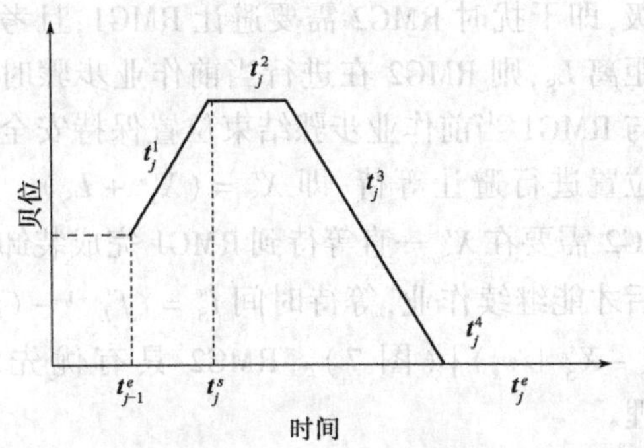

图4 场桥完成单个任务的作业轨迹图

t_j^p 表示场桥执行第 j 个任务的第 p 个步骤所需要的时间,f_j^{sp} 和 f_j^{ep} 分别表示场桥执行第 j 个任务的第 p 个步骤的开始和完成时间,其中 $p=1,2,3,4$,有 $t_j^2=t_j^4=t_0$,$t_j^1=t_{D_{ij-1}O_{ij}}$,$t_j^3=t_{O_{ij}D_{ij}}$,$f_j^{s1}=f_{j-1}^{e4}$,完成第 j 个任务需要的固定时间 $t_j=\sum_{p=1}^{4}t_j^p$。第 j 个任务的开始时间 t_j^s 为场桥提取目标集装箱的开始时间,任务结束时间 t_j^e 为释放目标集装箱的完成时间。对于场桥执行的任意任务,都有 $(f_j^{s2}-t_j^1)\geqslant f_{j-1}^{e4}$,即场桥结束上一个任务并从结束位置移动到当前任务的开始位置时才能开始执行当前任务。翻箱任务和取箱任务的一阶段任务都可以在集卡到达前提前完成,此时 $f_j^{s2}=f_{j-1}^{e4}+t_j^1$,而存箱任务需要集卡到达后才能开始提箱操作,取箱任务需要集卡到达后才能开始放箱操作,则当 i_j 为存箱任务以及存箱任务一阶段任务时,$f_j^{s2}=\max\{f_{j-1}^{e4}+t_j^1,d_{i_j}\}$,$i_j$ 为取箱任务以及取箱任务的二阶段任务时,$f_j^{s2}=\max\{f_{j-1}^{e4}+t_j^1,d_{i_j}-t_j^2-t_j^3\}$,且由于接力任务的二阶段任务需要在一阶段任务完成后进行,故当 i_j 为接力任务的二阶段任务时,$f_j^{s2}=\max\{f_{j-1}^{e4}+t_j^1,f_{j'}^{e4}\}$,其中任务 $i_{j'}$ 为任务 i_j 对应的一阶段任务即 $i_j\in I_2^c(k)$,$i_{j'}\in I_1^c(k)$,$D_{i_j}=O_{i_{j'}}$。在确定场桥作业顺序且不中断任务的情况下,$f_j^{ep+1}=f_j^{sp}(p\neq1)$,$f_j^{ep}=f_j^{sp}+t_j^p$,对所有任务 i_j 都有 $t_j^e=f_j^{s2}$,$t_j^s=f_j^{e4}$。由此我们可以得到任意给定可行的任务序列下,不考虑场桥干扰时的作业步骤开始结束时间以及任务的开始完成时间,进而得到场桥的作业轨迹图,如图5中实线所示。

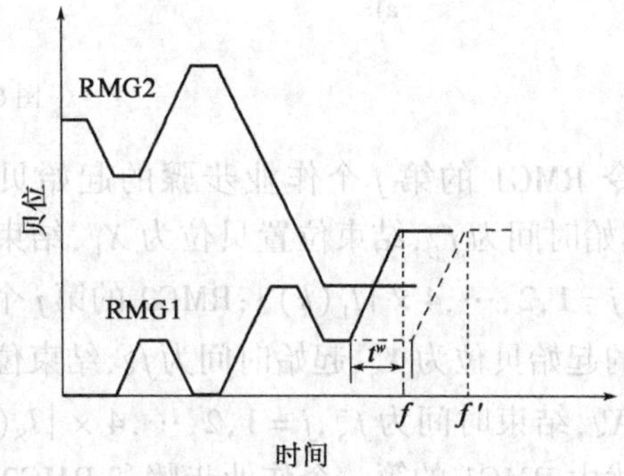

图5 双场桥作业轨迹图

由图5可以看出此时RMG1与RMG2的作业区间发生冲突,RMG1需要越过RMG2执行任务,图中表现为RMG1与RMG2的作业轨迹发生了交叉。但实际作业时由于共用轨道两台场桥不能互相穿越,因此发生如图5所示的干扰时,需要场桥避让到安全位置等待直到可以顺利进行作业。图5中虚线所示的即为干扰时将优先级赋予RMG2,由RMG1避让等待RMG2再进行作业的轨迹图。由图5可知,不考虑干扰时RMG1当前作业步骤的结束时间 $f_j^{ep}=f$,考虑干扰时RMG1避让RMG2后等待时间为 t^w,RMG1当前作业步骤的结束时间 $f_j^{ep}=f'$,其中 $f'=f+t^w$,并且RMG1的当前步骤结束时间变化也将影响后续步骤作业的开始与结束时间。由此我们可以确定避免场桥干扰的任意作业步骤的开始与结束时间,进而确定任意任务的开始和完成时间。

3.3.2 场桥避让等待时间的确定[15]

通过上述分析可知,给定调度方案下任务的开始和完成时间主要取决于干扰产生下场桥的避让等待时间,因此我们需要确定场桥在不同避让规则下的等待时间。

根据干扰时场桥所处的状态——移动或装卸,可将干扰分为三种形式:(1)两个场桥均在移动(图6a));(2)陆侧移动海侧装卸(图6b));(3)海侧移动陆侧装卸(图6c))。两个场桥均在装卸可以看作是以上3种形式的特殊情况。

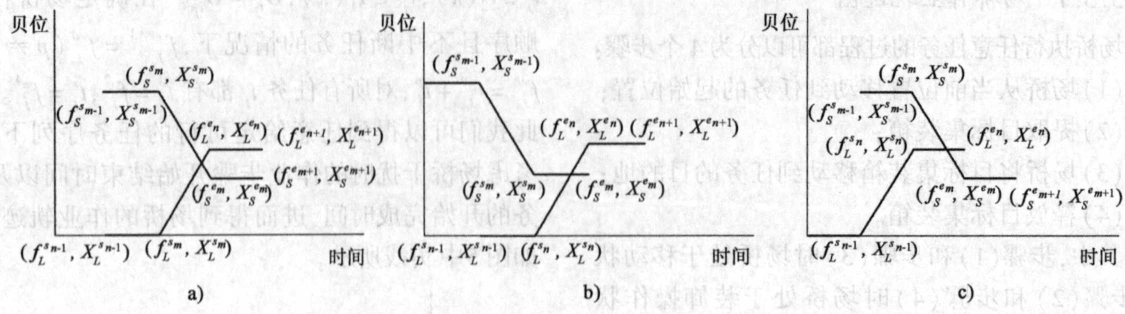

图6　场桥干扰类型示意图

令 RMG1 的第 j 个作业步骤的起始贝位为 $X_{\mathrm{L}}^{s_j}$,起始时间为 $f_{\mathrm{L}}^{s_j}$,结束位置贝位为 $X_{\mathrm{L}}^{e_j}$,结束时间为 $f_{\mathrm{L}}^{e_j}$,$j = 1,2,\cdots,4 \times |I_{\mathrm{L}}(k)|$;RMG2 的第$j$个作业步骤的起始贝位为 $X_{\mathrm{S}}^{s_j}$,起始时间为 $f_{\mathrm{S}}^{s_j}$,结束位置贝位为 $X_{\mathrm{S}}^{e_j}$,结束时间为 $f_{\mathrm{S}}^{e_j}$,$j = 1,2,\cdots,4 \times |I_{\mathrm{S}}(k)|$。设干扰由 RMG1 的第 n 个作业步骤和 RMG2 的第 m 个作业步骤产生,X_{L}^{r},X_{S}^{r} 分别表示 RMG1,RMG2 发生干扰时的避让等待位置贝位,t_{L}^{w},t_{S}^{w} 分别表示 RMG1,RMG2 产生干扰时的避让等待时间。

(1)两个场桥均处于移动状态

如图6a)所示,干扰发生时RMG1 和RMG2 均处于移动状态,则在当前作业步骤结束后 RMG1 和 RMG2 都将进行装卸操作。假设 RMG1 具有优先级,即干扰时 RMG2 需要避让 RMG1,且考虑安全距离 L_{S},则 RMG2 在进行当前作业步骤时需要在与 RMG1 当前作业步骤结束位置保持安全距离的位置进行避让等待,即 $X_{\mathrm{S}}^{r} = (X_{\mathrm{L}}^{e_n} + L_{\mathrm{S}})$。并且 RMG2 需要在 X_{S}^{r} 一直等待到 RMG1 完成装卸并离开后才能继续作业,等待时间 $t_{\mathrm{S}}^{w} = [f_{L}^{e_{n+1}} - (f_{\mathrm{S}}^{s_m} + |X_{\mathrm{S}}^{r} - X_{\mathrm{S}}^{s_m}|/v_x)]$(图 7)。RMG2 具有优先级时同理。

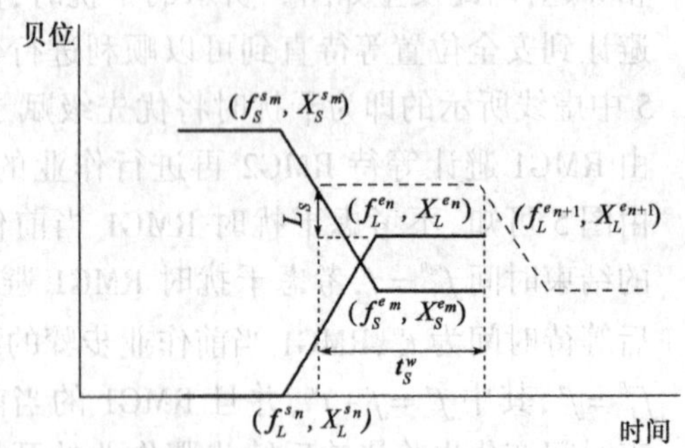

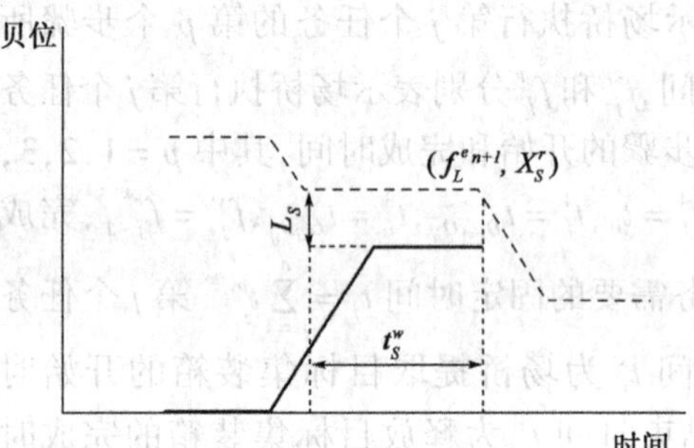

图7　RMG1 拥有优先权的避让轨迹图

(2)一个场桥处于移动状态,一个场桥处于装卸状态

如图6b)所示,产生干扰时RMG1 处于移动状态,RMG2 处于装卸状态。假设 RMG1 拥有优先级,则 RMG2 在当前作业步骤时的避让等待位置应为$(X_{\mathrm{L}}^{e_n} + L_{\mathrm{S}})$,并且 RMG2 应该在$(X_{\mathrm{L}}^{e_n} + L_{\mathrm{S}})$一直等待 RMG1 完成装卸并离开。但是由于 RMG2 处于装卸状态,此时 RMG2 的作业步骤不能中断,且该作业步骤的起始地点和目的地相同,所以 RMG2 在前一个作业步骤时就应当避让到与 RMG1 的目的地保持安全距离的位置,即 $X_{\mathrm{S}} = (X_{\mathrm{L}}^{e_n} + L_{\mathrm{S}})$,且 RMG2 在 X_{S}^{r} 一直等待 RMG1 完成装卸并离开后再继续作业,等待时间为 $t_{\mathrm{S}}^{w} = [f_{\mathrm{L}}^{e_{n+1}} - (f_{\mathrm{S}}^{s_{m-1}} + |X_{\mathrm{S}}^{r} - X_{\mathrm{S}}^{s_{m-1}}|/v_x)]$(图8)。

假设 RMG2 拥有优先级,由于 RMG1 处于移动状态,则 RMG1 在当前作业步骤的避让等待位置为$(X_{\mathrm{S}}^{e_m} - L_{\mathrm{S}})$,即 $X_{\mathrm{L}}^{r} = (X_{\mathrm{S}}^{e_m} - L_{\mathrm{S}})$。并且 RMG1 应在 X_{L}^{r} 一直等待 RMG2 完成装卸并离开后再继续作业,等待时间 $t_{\mathrm{L}}^{w} = [f_{\mathrm{S}}^{e_m} - (f_{\mathrm{L}}^{s_n} + |X_{\mathrm{L}}^{r} - X_{\mathrm{L}}^{s_n}|/v_x)]$(图9)。RMG1 处于装卸状态 RMG2 处于移动状态时同理。

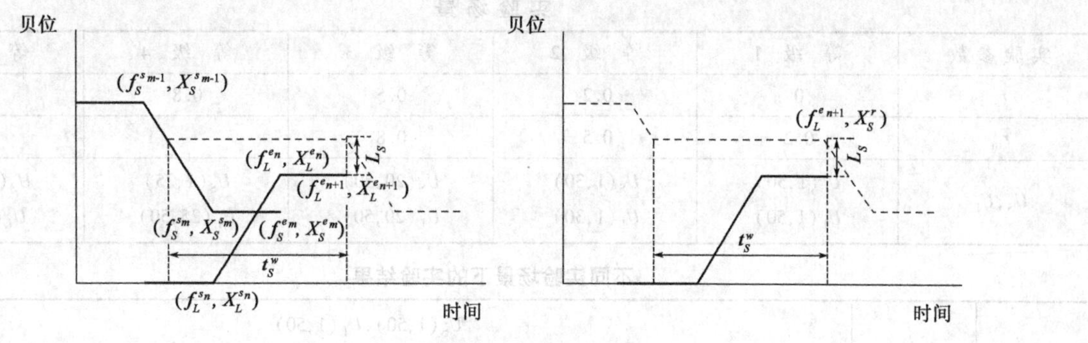

图 8 RMG1 拥有优先级的场桥避让轨迹图

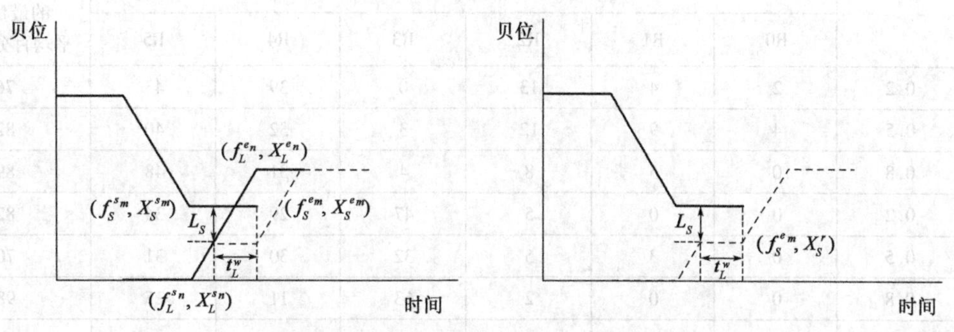

图 9 RMG2 拥有优先级的场桥避让轨迹图

通过上述对不同干扰情况下场桥避让轨迹的分析可以知道，对于产生干扰时的非优先权场桥而言，如果当前作业步骤场桥状态为移动，则非优先权场桥在进行当前作业步骤时的避让等待位置为优先权场桥当前作业目的地 ± 安全距离，且非优先级场桥的避让等待时间为非优先级场桥在当前作业步骤到达与优先级场桥保持安全距离的位置直到优先级场桥完成当前作业步骤以及装卸操作的时间；如果当前作业步骤场桥状态为装卸，则非优先权场桥在前一个作业步骤的避让等待位置为优先权场桥当前作业目的地 ± 安全距离，此时非优先级场桥的避让等待时间为非优先级场桥在前一个作业步骤到达与优先级场桥保持安全距离的位置直到优先级场桥完成当前作业步骤以及装卸操作的时间。由此可以在给定优先权规则下，确定任意给定的任务排序和场桥分配方案所导致的任务开始和完成时间。

4 算例分析

4.1 参数设置

每个箱区设置 50 个贝位，跨距为 10 列，最高堆垛为 5 层，箱区的初始集装箱数量为容量的 70%，陆侧交接点为 0 贝位，海侧交接点为 51 贝位。两侧场桥不可穿越，始终保持匀速运动，速度为 0.05min/bay；提箱和进箱的操作时间相同，为 1.2min，场桥间的安全距离为一个贝位。接力区规则 R0 为不设置接力区。

影响作业时间以及集卡等待时间的因素主要是任务数、两侧场桥的任务比例以及存提箱任务的比例，而作业的起止点分布将会影响接力区的位置选择。考虑到堆场的存储能力以及实验的复杂度，本文将主任务数设置为 20，每个实验重复 100 次，为了分析不同接力区规则的适用情况，设置了不同的实验场景，将海侧任务比例 r_s、进箱任务比例 r_{in} 以及海陆侧作业起止点分布 U_S, U_L 划分了不同的实验等级，如表 1 所示。

4.2 结果分析

从表 2 的实验结果可以看出，当海陆两侧的主任务起止点在 1 ~ 50 均匀分布时，对比不设置接力区的独立作业模式，5 种接力规则所代表的混合接力模式下场桥的效率更高，在 90% 以上的实验中都能够得到更好的解。而随着进箱任务比例的增加和海陆两侧任务量变得不均衡，不接力模式与接力模式的最优等待时间平均百分比差异越来越大，说明海陆两侧任务量越不均衡，进箱任务比例越高，混合接力模式比不接力模式的优势更明显，接力模式越有利。

实验场景　　表1

实验参数	等级1	等级2	等级3	等级4	等级5
r_s	0	0.2	0.5	0.8	1
r_{in}	0.2	0.5	0.8	—	—
U_S,U_L	$U_S(1,50)$ $U_L(1,50)$	$U_S(1,30)$ $U_L(1,30)$	$U_S(20,50)$ $U_L(20,50)$	$U_S(1,25)$ $U_L(25,50)$	$U_S(25,50)$ $U_L(1,25)$

不同实验场景下的实验结果　　表2

r_s	r_{in}	$U_S(1,50),U_L(1,50)$						
		在重复试验中找到最优解的次数(%)						不接力模式与接力模式的最优等待时间平均百分比差异(%)
		R0	R1	R2	R3	R4	R5	
0	0.2	2	4	13	0	39	43	76.4102
0	0.5	4	9	12	3	32	40	82.6978
0	0.8	0	5	8	4	31	48	89.6486
0.2	0.2	0	0	5	47	29	34	82.5154
0.2	0.5	0	3	5	32	30	31	70.5462
0.2	0.8	0	0	2	63	11	25	98.2045
0.5	0.2	0	9	28	28	31	41	47.0628
0.5	0.5	1	11	35	35	39	36	43.0969
0.5	0.8	6	20	35	35	20	34	36.9745
0.8	0.2	0	0	3	46	22	32	112.2295
0.8	0.5	0	2	2	64	41	52	122.5193
0.8	0.8	0	0	0	84	7	10	187.2982
1	0.2	0	3	18	2	36	40	86.2992
1	0.5	1	6	7	0	40	46	87.9935
1	0.8	2	5	15	3	30	45	90.0534

对比直接将接力区设置在箱区中间的规则R1,考虑任务特征和起止点分布的规则R2、R3、R4和R5优势更为明显,无论海陆两侧任务量以及存取任务量是否均衡,在不同实验场景下的结果都优于R1,说明R2、R3、R4和R5能够有效地找到适合当前作业任务序列的接力区位置。

当海陆两侧任务量相同时,R2和R3确定的接力区位置相同,从R3、R4和R5得到的结果可以看出,3种规则在海陆两侧任务量均衡时的表现差异不大。而海陆侧任务量不均衡时即$r_{in}=0.2$或者$r_{in}=0.8$时,R3的表现优于R4和R5,且随着进箱任务的比例增加R3更有利。$r_s=0$和$r_s=1$时,即只存在陆侧任务和只存在海侧任务的情况下,R3虽然可以平衡工作量但对任务特征的考虑失效,此时R4和R5更优。

由于R2和R3在海陆两侧任务量相同时确定的接力区位置相同因此无法对R2和R3进行对比。因此对海陆两侧任务量不均衡时不同主任务起止点分布的情况进行实验,结果如表3所示,海侧任务比例分别设置为0.2和0.8,而由于进箱任务比例较高时接力模式的优势更明显,所以将实验的进箱任务比例设置为0.8。由表3可知,R2由于仅考虑了的起始点分布,没有考虑海陆两侧任务的比例,因此在海陆两侧任务数差异较大时可能无法找到最优的交接区位置,与表2中海陆两侧任务量均衡时R2的相比,R2受海陆侧任务比例以及主任务起止点分布的影响较大,不能在各种实验等级下取得较为稳定的结果。而在不同的主任务起止点分布以及海陆任务比例下,可以认为R3在大部分实验中都能得到更好的结果。值得注意的是任务起止点都在1~30均匀分布时即任务起止点分布在靠近陆侧的位置时,陆侧任务比例越高,R3 越有利,海侧任务的比例越高,R5 越有利;而任务起止点都在 20 ~50 均匀分布时即任务起止点分布在靠近海侧的位置时,陆侧任务比例越高,R5 越有利,海侧任务的比例越高,R3 越有利。

不同主任务起止点分布的实验结果 表3

U_S	U_L	在重复试验中找到最优解的次数(%)									
		$r_S=0.2, r_{in}=0.8$					$r_S=0.8, r_{in}=0.8$				
		R1	R2	R3	R4	R5	R1	R2	R3	R4	R5
$U_S(1,25)$	$U_L(25,50)$	1	1	33	47	45	2	0	26	40	54
$U_S(25,50)$	$U_L(1,25)$	14	0	48	11	26	7	2	44	15	32
$U_S(1,30)$	$U_L(1,30)$	2	4	66	14	11	0	2	10	19	69
$U_S(20,50)$	$U_L(20,50)$	0	0	4	24	72	4	0	68	21	7

5 结语

本文围绕自动化集装箱堆场的同轨不可穿越式双场桥机械调度问题,针对双场桥作业接力区设置,以最小化集卡等待时间为目标,通过仿真实验比较分析了 5 种接力区设置规则,结果表明:

(1)对比双场桥的独立作业模式,混合接力模式下双场桥的作业效率更高。

(2)两侧场桥的任务量不平衡时,接力模式更有利。接力模式下一侧场桥可以协助另一侧场桥完成部分的任务,减少了该侧场桥的作业时间。

(3)优化目标为集卡等待时间时,进箱任务比例越高,接力模式越有利。进箱任务的集卡等待时间为集卡到达直到任务开始场桥提取目标集装箱的时间。混合接力模式下,进箱任务被分成两个阶段,一阶段任务的相应场桥可以更快结束当前任务并进入下一个任务,由此减少其他任务的集卡等待时间。

(4)在主任务的起止点分布不均时,对比将接力区设置在中间贝位的接力规则 R1,考虑作业任务的特征和起止点分布的接力规则更具有优势。R2 只适用于海陆侧任务量均衡的情况,且受任务的起止点分布影响较大;如果只存在海侧任务或只存在陆侧任务,R4 和 R5 更优;同时存在海陆侧任务时,海陆侧任务量不均衡时 R3 更具有优势。

参考文献

[1] Chung Y G, Randhawa S U, Mcdowell R. A simulation analysis for a transtainer-based container handling facility[J]. Computers & Industrial Engineering,1988.

[2] 乐美龙,林艳艳,范志强.基于两阶段启发式算法的多场桥作业调度研究[J].武汉理工大学学报,2012,34(01):60-65.

[3] Gharehgozli A H, Laporte G, Yu Y G, et al. Scheduling Twin Yard Cranes in a Container Block[J]. Transportation Science, 2015, 49(3):686-705.

[4] Hu Z H, Sheu J B, Luo J X. Sequencing twin automated stacking cranes in a block at automated container terminal[J]. Transportation Research Part C Emerging Technologies,2016, 69(aug.):208-227.

[5] Carlo H J, Martínezacevedo F L. Priority rules for twin automated stacking cranes that collaborate [J]. Computers & Industrial Engineering [J]. Computers & Industrial Engineering,201,6(1):5-20.

[6] Dominik K, Jan D, Florian J. An exact solution approach for scheduling cooperative gantry cranes[J]. European Journal of Operational Research,2018,273.

[7] Park T, Choe R, Ok R M, et al. Real-time scheduling for twin RMGs in an automated container yard[J]. OR Spectrum,2010,32(3):593-615.

[8] 邱亚,梁承姬,张悦.动态接力点模式下双自动化轨道吊协调调度[J].上海海事大学学报,2020,41(3):7.

[9] Han X L, Wang Q, Huang J. Scheduling cooperative twin automated stacking cranes in automated container terminals[J]. Computers & Industrial Engineering, 2019, 128(FEB.):

553-558.

[10] Gharehgozli A H, Vernooij F G, Zaerpour N. A simulation study of the performance of twin automated stacking cranes at a seaport container terminal[J]. European Journal of Operational Research, 2017, 261(1): 108-128.

[11] 魏亚茹,朱瑾.自动化码头双场桥调度与集装箱存储选位建模[J].计算机应用,2018,38(04):1189-1194+1206.

[12] Guo P, Wang L, Xue C, et al. Dispatching Rules for Scheduling Twin Automated Gantry Cranes in an Automated Railroad Container Terminal[J]. Arabian Journal for Science and Engineering, 2020, 45(3): 2205-2217.

[13] 丁一,陈杭钦,林国龙.成对自动堆垛起重机在集装箱码头中的实时调度研究[J].重庆师范大学学报(自然科学版),2017(02):16-24.

[14] 郑红星,刘保利,匡海波,等.考虑实时预倒箱的出口箱堆场多场桥调度优化[J].中国管理科学,2018,26(09):85-96.

[15] Vis I F A, Carlo H J, Diaz P, et al. Control policies for a dynamic storage system with multiple lifts and shuttles[C]//In K. P. Ellis, K. R. Gue, R. B. M. de Koster, R. D. Meller, B. Montreuil, & M. K. Ogle (Eds.). Progress in Material Handling Research: 2010. Charlotte, North Carolina: Material Handling Institute, 2010: 494-509.

Study on Night Bus Scheduling Based on Passenger Flow Time Sensitivity

Xiangjun Tan Xiaolei Li*

(Transportation Engineering, College of traffic&transportation, Chongqing Jiaotong University)

Abstract Bus timetable and departure frequency are the key bridge between bus companies and passengers. The unreasonable bus scheduling will lead to fewer shifts and congestion in the vehicle at night. By applying the calculation model of departure frequency in transportation organization, the scheduling is optimized for night bus routes. By investigating and analyzing the operation of domestic night bus, including the operation time period of night bus, the operation mode of bus and the departure frequency of the line. Aiming at the operation mode of night bus, this paper puts forward the time-division scheduling (TDS) method of night bus scheduling, so as to solve the problem of high time sensitivity of night bus passenger flow. Through the field follow-up survey of a typical night bus line, the passenger flow of the bus line in different periods is obtained. The optimal departure frequency of the line is calculated by using the calculation model of departure frequency of transportation organization. The results show that compared with the traditional fixed-point routing, scheduling method, the TDS method can better adapt to the passenger flow of night bus. This method can provide reference for night bus scheduling in China.

Keywords departing frequency bus timetable night bus passenger flow

0 Introduction

Public transportation plays a vital role in satisfying residents' travel. In the wake of the development of the Chinese social economy, residents' public transportation travel is gradually increasing. According to the data of the Ministry of Transport of the Peoples' Republic of China, the passenger volume of urban buses and trolleybuses in China has been up to 1,526,132 as of August 2021, with a year-on-year growth rate of 28%. However, there are still some shortcomings in the aspect of night transportation. Taking Chongqing as an example, according to the data of"8684 Bus Platform" in 2018, there are 1, 128 bus routes in Chongqing ' s main urban area. 31% of bus routes are in operation after 21:00 while only 14% are in operation after 22:00. Since the advent of the " three shifts" system, traffic congestion occurs during the early hours of the night bus operation while empty car operation during the late operating hours, which indicates the problem of inappropriate bus departure frequency and timetable at night currently, resulting in the inability to coordinate the relationship between the cost of the bus company and the travel demand of passengers.

Yao et al. (2021) studied on re-examines the interactions among bus service quality, car ownership, car use and bus use. The research showed that think high quality bus service can effectively reduce the increase of car usage. Developing public transport and reducing car ownership can effectively reduce traffic congestion. Therefore, optimizing bus schedule can reduce urban traffic congestion to some extent. Gkiotsalitis et al. (2017) combined the travel time of passengers with their needs when considering the generation of timetables. The prediction of traffic demand is of great significance for traffic planning. Zhou et al. (2019) selected the geographically and temporally weighted regression model (GTWR) for prediction and verified it with the license plate data of Hangzhou in 2016. Compared with least squares regression model (OLS) and geographically weighted regression model (GWR), GTWR can better capture the temporal and spatial characteristics of traffic demand and the relationship between traffic demand and built environment. The traffic demand for public transport is mainly reflected by factors such as waiting time and capacity utilization. The basic idea of a planning departure schedule is to determine bus scheduling by traffic demand forecasting. Zhang et al. (2021) considered the traffic jam in formulating the bus departure timetable and thought that the problem was a nonlinear problem in mathematics. Therefore, they used the compass search algorithm without derivative constraint for optimization calculation and conducted a simulation experiment on the departure timetable of a typical bus line in Beijing, It is proven that the optimization method can effectively improve passenger comfort and bus service level. Zhang, et al. (2021) established the bus timetable model of balanced operation and service by calculating the operating cost and service value after the bus departure, so that the experimental results were closer to the objective reality. Dou et al. (2016) optimized the timetable of cooperative dispatch in order to take the weighted average minimum value of transfer waiting time and average deviation as the optimization target. By utilizing robust model and genetic algorithm, the randomness in the operation of public transportation vehicles was taken into account, and the approximate optimal solution was obtained, which effectively reduced the negative utility of the total transfer. Yao et al. (2020) put forward the quota system optimization method for the departure interval of conventional bus routes under the mixed vehicle operation mode. With comprehensive consideration about the interests of both passengers and public transportation companies, a multi-objective optimization model for synchronou optimizing the departure interval and vehicle configuration was established, whose effectiveness was verified by combining enumeration method and genetic algorithm for example solution. Ci et al. (2021) proposed a bi-level optimization method for regional dispatching of urban public transportation, and established a bi-level planning model integrating fleet size and timetable optimization, which can effectively eliminate the negative impact of timetable optimization on fleet size adjustment, as well as provide alternative scheme boundaries for public transportation companies. In the study carried out by Jiang et al. (2016), genetic algorithm was adopted to solve the model by considering the layout and timetable of the bus route network, taking the transfer station at the route connection as the entry point, and from the perspective of maximizing the interests of public transportation companies and passengers, and the connection efficiency of public transport vehicles at the transfer station was thus improved. Gu et al. (2016) explained in layer the relationship between bus services and routes with connection at transfer stations, coordinated the time of arrival at the transfer stations according to the hierarchical service relationship among routes, and solved it by genetic algorithm In this process, the connection efficiency of transfer stations in the multi-level conventional bus network was fully brought into play, and the balance of interests between public transportation companies and passengers was effectively weighed. With the development of rail transit, many scholars study the transfer between conventional bus and rail transit. At the beginning of operation, more night buses will involve the transfer with rail transit. Therefore, when planning night bus lines, we should consider the transfer between rail and conventional bus. Lv et al. (2019) took Suzhou urban area as an example, took the four modernizations of public transport as the core, identified the problem lines by establishing the problem line screening model. Finally, the evaluation mechanism of route network optimization with the four modernizations of public transport as the core is established. Li et al. (2019) took Kunming as an example, analysed the impact of the addition of rail transit on conventional public transport and optimized the public transport lines. It provides ideas for optimizing and adjusting the city's transportation mode structure. Hu et al. (2021) constructed a bi-level planning model that takes into account the demand of random passenger flow and the operation efficiency of the timetable, through which the relationship between the demand of random passenger flow and the timetable was analysed based on the service quality of passenger travel. Dial-msa and genetic algorithm were used to solve the model, which could effectively optimize the benefit contradiction between passengers and public transportation companies. Chu et al. (2019) proposed a Mixed-integer linear programming models and a heuristic algorithm for the transfer synchronization planning of bus timetables. The model optimizes the bus schedule and passengers' choice of travel path. It can improve the accuracy of bus schedule planning. However, this model is a nonlinear model, and whether the optimal solution can be obtained in the actual bus schedule planning remains to be further studied. At present, the application of big data in traffic planning is more and more widely. Ma et al. (2020) Developed a data-driven bus schedule. Timetable optimization model of passenger demand and inter station travel time are based on bus GPS data and IC card data. Compared with the traditional timetable planning method, this method can achieve a more satisfactory result with the increase of traffic. Shang et al. (2019) proposed a bustimetabling method which is practical and applicable in China. An optimization method of bus schedule and headway based on passenger satisfaction is established. However, this paper only takes into account the one-way travel demand during the afternoon peak, and the effectiveness of this method remains to be further studied. He et al. (2019) By adjusting the speed of the bus in the bus lane to reduce traffic congestion and uneven distribution of bus lines. The experimental results show that the more dedicated bus lanes in a bus line, the more effective the strategy becomes. This method can be applied to night bus scheduling. Yu et al. (2019) proposed a method for identifying urban rail passenger flow paths based on mobile signaling data. Under the condition that only the base station ID corresponding to each rail station is obtained, the trajectory similarity matching method is used to identify the urban rail passenger flow path through the mobile phone signaling data. As more and more public transport passengers use bus cards and mobile phone APPs to pay for public transport costs, this method can also be applied to the passenger flow survey of public transport.

To put it in a nutshell, numerous factors should be considered in optimizing the optimal departure frequency and timetable of bus routes, including travel time, ride satisfaction, passenger flow, actual traffic conditions of bus routes, operating costs of public transportation companies, etc. The ultimate goal is to minimize the total cost of passengers and public transportation companies (Zhang et al., 2021). In view of the long waiting time of night buses and the congestion of passengers on the bus caused by the unreasonable time intervals of night bus, in this paper, the night bus operation period is divided into high peak period (HPP) and flat peak period (FPP) by analyzing the sensitivity of passenger flow to time. The optimal departure frequency in different periods is calculated and analyzed by using the calculation model of transportation histology, and the TDS according to different time periods is worked out.

1 Night bus Operation

1.1 Development status of urban night bus

Large cities usually boast of a perfect night bus system and daytime buses that lasts until the night. There are still bus running after 21:00, and even many large cities have opened night buses from 23:00 p.m. and the early morning hours to meet the needs of passengers travelling at night. The operational status of night buses in some large cities is shown in Tab. 1.

Night Bus Operation in Large Cities. Tab. 1

City	Operation mode	Number of lines	Operation time	Departure frequency (min)
Beijing	Fixed point positioning	47	22:50 ~ 04:50	20 ~ 30
Shanghai		41	22:30 ~ 06:30	30 ~ 40
Chengdu		30	21:20 ~ 06:30	25 ~ 40
Chongqing		11	21:40 ~ 06:30	30 ~ 40
Guangzhou		45	21:00 ~ 05:30	10 ~ 30

Only a small minority of small and medium-scale cities own the planning of night bus routes. The daytime bus routes in most ordinary prefecture-level cities are sufficient to meet the bus demand of most residents. The number of bus routes that are still operating after 21:00 in some small and medium-scale cities is shown in Fig. 1.

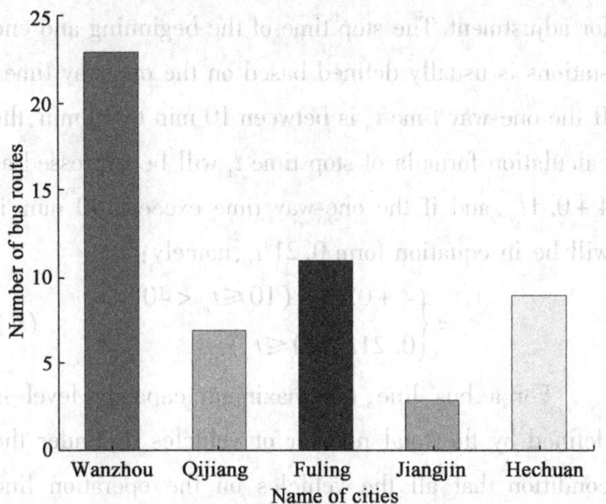

Fig. 1 Number of Bus Lines in Small and Medium-sized Cities after 21:00

It is concluded that the operation scale of night buses varies with the size of the city. In large cities, the entire night bus service is opened so that residents can enjoy the public transportation service at night; By contrast, in medium-sized cities, only part of the daytime bus routes will be served from 21:00 to 23:00 to provide travel services for residents and certain cities will select a time period to operate night bus after this time period. However, these night bus routes are relatively simple and few in number, mainly covering areas with a high concentration of urban population. For small cities, the bus network is inherently underdeveloped with a shortage of bus routes. Most bus routes will be stopped before 19:30 while few bus routes will be running after 19:30 in very few cities, and they basically only go through the main urban roads. We can analyze the status of the night bus based on these characteristics. It can be seen from the number of night buses that there is little room for improvement in small and medium-sized cities due to residents' less strong demand for night bus ride. While in the night bus routes of large cities, the scheduling method of fixed-point routing can be optimized due to the high sensitivity of passenger flow to time.

1.2　Bus passenger flow

Bus passenger flow, in the process of bus operation, mainly refers to passenger volume on the bus route per unit time, with the following three characteristics:

1.2.1　Time distribution characteristics

Bus passenger flow shows fluctuation, periodicity and tendency to time, as shown in Tab. 2.

Time Distribution Characteristics　Tab. 2

Nature	Specific performance
Fluctuation	Passenger flow shows changes in fluctuation
Periodicity	Passenger flow renders periodic law
Tendency	Passenger flow changes with a certain law

1.2.2　Spatial distribution characteristics

In terms of spatial distribution, the passenger flow at different stations on the same line remains unbalanced, as well as in the upstream and downstream directions, as shown in Tab. 3.

Spatial Distribution Characteristics　Tab. 3

Imbalance	Specific performance
At stations	The distribution of passenger flow in different stations keeps unbalanced
In direction	The passenger flow in the upward and downward directions shows tidal changes

1.2.3　Short-term distribution characteristics

Except for some emergencies, short-term bus operation is highly affected by the time changes, illustrating its high sensitivity of time.

As the main body of travel, passengers will choose different travel modes due to their own influencing factors, including age, transportation preference, occupation, income and so on. Night bus refers to the bus that operates between 21:30 and 6:00. With the advancement of society, the emergence of"three shifts"system in many enterprises brings the late peak of bus passenger flow between 20:00 and 23:00, while the number of residents who take night bus after 23:00 will decrease, making night bus passenger flow highly sensitive to time.

2　Calculation Model of Departure Frequency

The departure interval I and the departure frequency g_i are reciprocal, and the available interval time t of the departure interval I is divided by the total number of vehicles on the line A, namely:

$$I = \frac{A}{t} \tag{1}$$

The optimal departure interval can be calculated according to the passenger flow.

Let the turnaround time equal t_0 including the one-way time t_n of the complete bus operation in its line and the stop time t_t at the beginning and end stations, namely:

$$t_0 = 2(t_n + t_t) \tag{2}$$

One-way time equals to t_n, which refers to the time consumed by the bus to complete a one-way transportation. It includes the sum of one-way driving time t_{nT} and stop time t_{ns} at the intermediate station, namely:

$$t_n = t_{nT} + t_{ns} \tag{3}$$

The stop time at the beginning and end of the station is t_t, including the necessary time for shunting the vehicle, handling driving formalities, cleaning the vehicle, rest and succession of drivers, getting passengers on and off the bus and station dwell time for adjustment. The stop time of the beginning and end stations is usually defined based on the one-way time. If the one-way time t_n is between 10 min to 40 min, the calculation formula of stop time t_t will be expressed as $4 + 0.1t_n$, and if the one-way time exceeds 40 min, it will be in equation form $0.21\,t_t$, namely:

$$t_t = \begin{cases} 4 + 0.21t_n (10 \leq t_n < 40) \\ 0.21t_n (40 \leq t_n) \end{cases} \tag{4}$$

For a bus line, the maximum capacity level is defined by the total number of vehicles A. Under the condition that all the vehicles on the operation line operate in the whole journey mode, the calculation method of the total number of vehicles A is shown as formula (5).

$$A = \frac{Q''_s t_0}{60 q_0 \gamma_s^0} \tag{5}$$

Where, Q''_s stands for road passenger flow (person/time), q_0 for the rated passenger capacity (person/time) of the vehicle, and γ_s^0 for the planned full rate quota.

Assuming that each section of the road between bus stops in the whole journey is independent of each other. According to the arrival schedule of each stop on the line, we can calculate the time for the bus to arrive at each stop on the route through the departure time of the first and last stops. T_i is used to denote the time when the bus arrives at the i station:

$$T_i = T_{i-1} + t_{i-1} \tag{6}$$

In the above formula, T_i means the time when the vehicle arrives at i station and t_{i-1} means the time required from $i-1$, station to i station. Assuming the known departure time is t_1, the running time t_i of operated bus in the first section can be obtained through field investigation, so that the time when the bus of this route arrives at each station can be deduced following formula (6).

When calculating the expected running time t_i, a corrected value t_1 of the confidence interval can be set, so that the corrected value T_i can be expressed as:

$$T'_i = T_i \pm t_1 \tag{7}$$

The value of confidence interval equals the punctuality rate of the bus, which is one of the evaluation indexes of bus service level, as shown in Tab. 4 (Xia et al., 2020).

Reference Range of Bus Punctuality Rate under Different Bus Service Levels Tab. 4

Service level	Reference range(%)
A	95.0—100
B	90.0—94.9
C	85.0—89.9
D	80.0—84.9
E	75.0—79.9

3 Model Validation

Take Chongqing 0301 night bus line as an example to optimize the departure frequency and time table. A total of 18 buses are in operation on Chongqing No. 0301 bus route. The model used in this line is CKZ3416N4 car of Hengtong Company, with a rated passenger capacity of 82 people.

No. 301 night bus runs from Ciqi Street Station to Lijiatuo South Station, with differences between the stations in the ascending direction and descending direction, as shown in Fig. 2.

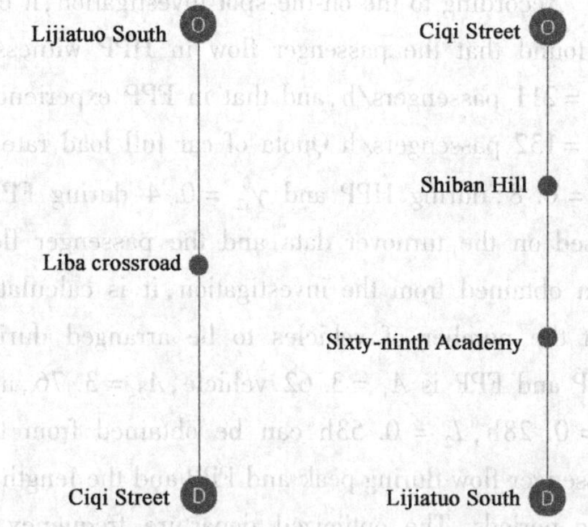

Fig. 2 0301 Road Night Bus Direction Difference Site

Despite of these differences, the total length l of the route is the same, which is 14.6km. By 22:00—1:00 a. m. as the operation time and 0.45h as the average vehicle running time t, the average vehicle running speed $V = l/t = 32\text{km/h}$ can be calculated. The departure frequency is 0.33h per shift in accordance with the fixed-point routing operation mode. The departure schedule is shown in Tab. 5.

Departure Timetable Tab. 5

Down direction	Departure time	Up direction	Departure time
Ciqi Street	00:00	Lijiatuo South	00:10
	00:20		21:40
	00:40		22:00
	1:00		22:20
	22:00		22:40
	22:20		23:00
	22:40		23:20
	23:00		23:40
	23:20	—	
	23:40		

According to the above-mentioned method of bus

dispatching by time period, the operation period of Chongqing No. 0301 bus is divided into 22:00—23:00 as HPP and 23:00—1:00 as FPP. Calculated time data: the one-way time of HPP and FPP is t_{n1} = 0.52h and t_{n2} = 0.37h, respectively, the stop times of the first and second stations are t_{t1} = 0.12h and t_{t2} = 0.1h; respectively, and the turnover time is t_{01} = 1.27 h and t_{02} = 0.93h, respectively.

According to the on-the-spot investigation, it can be found that the passenger flow in HPP witnesses Q''_{s1} = 211 passengers/h, and that in FPP experiences Q''_{s2} = 132 passengers/h Quota of car full load rate is γ^0_{s1} = 0.8, during HPP and γ^0_{s2} = 0.4 during FPP. Based on the turnover data and the passenger flow data obtained from the investigation, it is calculated that the number of vehicles to be arranged during HPP and FPP is A_1 = 3.62 vehicle, A_2 = 3.76, and I_1 = 0.28h, I_2 = 0.53h can be obtained from the passenger flow during peak and FPP and the length of time periods. The optimized departure frequency is that: the departure frequency remains about 0.25h during the HPP (22:00—23:00), and remains about 0.5h during FPP (23:00—1:00). The optimized departure schedule is shown in Tab. 6.

Departure Schedule of Chongqing 0301 Bus Line

Tab. 6

Down direction	Departure time	Up direction	Departure time
	00:00		00:00
	00:30		00:30
	1:00		01:00
	22:00		22:00
Ciqi Street	22:15	Lijiatuo South	22:15
	22:30		22:30
	22:45		22:45
	23:00		23:00
	23:30		23:30

It is calculated that the average travel speed duringHPP and FPP is v_1 = 19.08km/h and v_2 = 39.96km/h respectively. Following the average travel time, it can be obtained that the upstream and downstream stations on the No. 0301 road are in HPP and FPP. Assuming that the service level is Class A, the travel time between adjacent site and the 95% confidence zone are shown in Fig. 3 and Fig. 4 The site name is shown in Tab. 7.

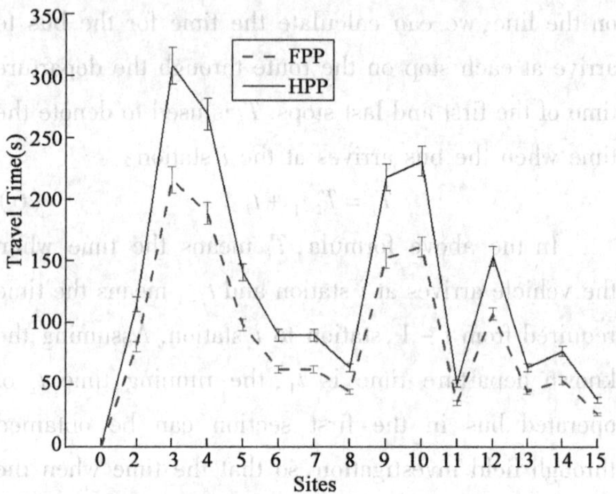

Fig. 3 Travel Time of Downlink Adjacent Sites and 95% Confidence Interval Table

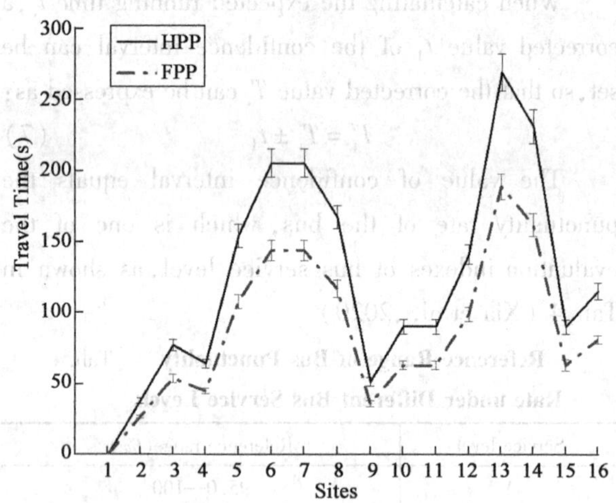

Fig. 4 Travel Time of Uplink Adjacent Sites and 95% Confidence Interval Table

Name of Uplink and Downlink Sites

Tab. 7

Downlink site	Name	Uplink site	Name
1	Ciqi Street	1	Lijiatuo South
2	Zhongxing Street	2	Lijiatuo East
3	Exhibition Center	3	Mid of Banan Avenue

continued

Downlink site	Name	Uplink site	Name
4	Nanping South Road	4	Banan Avenue
5	Four Kilmetres	5	Jiangnan Vechile Management
6	Five Kilometres	6	Eight Kilometres
7	Six Kilometres of Rail	7	Sixty-ninth Academy
8	Six Kilometres	8	Six Kilometres
9	Eight Kilometres	9	Six Kilometres of Rail
10	Liba crossroad	10	Five Kilometres
11	Jiangnan Vechile Management	11	Four Kilometres
12	Banan Avenue	12	Nanping South Road
13	Mid of Banan Avenue	13	Exhibition Center
14	Lijiatuo East	14	Shiban Hill Street
15	Lijiatuo South	15	Zhongxing Street
—	—	16	Ciqi Street

4 Conclusions

(1) In this paper, a scheduling method for the use of night bus by different time periods is proposed. On the basis of the passenger flow gap betweenHPP and FPP of night bus and by utilizing the time sensitivity of passenger flow, it shows that the use of bus scheduling in different time periods can meet both the cost requirements of public transportation companies and the travel needs of passengers by optimizing the departure frequency and schedule of a typical night line.

(2) Compared with other methods, TDS pays more attention to the matching degree with passenger flow, which can intuitively improve the bus ride experience of passengers. Under the passenger flow during different time periods, increasing departure frequency during HPP can reduce the waiting time of bus passengers, and to some extent unclog crowded buses and enhance the passenger experience. During FPP, the departure frequency and the bus scheduling cost will be reduced. Generally speaking, the bus scheduling shifts before and after optimization are close, which will have little significant impact on the total operating cost of public transportation companies.

(3) TDS is proposed based on the sensitivity of passenger flow to time, which is featured by many night bus passenger flows, demonstrating that the method can be applied to most night bus scheduling, as well as daytime buses that feature passenger flow characteristics, which provides a new idea for bus route scheduling.

(4) In this paper, the effectiveness of TDS operation for night bus dispatching is verified for single-route buses, but the specific bus dispatching needs to be investigated in the entire bus operation mode. It will be the further research direction to adjust the timetable of each time interval on the basis of consideration of the entire traffic environment.

References

[1] Yao D, Xu L, Zhang C, et al. Revisiting the interactions between bus service quality, car ownership and mode use: A case study in Changzhou China[J]. Transportation Research Part A: Policy and Practice, 2021, 154: 329-344.

[2] Gkiotsalitis K, F Alesiani. Robust timetable optimization for bus line subject to resource and regulatory constraints [J]. Transportation Research Part E Logistics and Transportation Review, 2019, 128(8): 30-51.

[3] Zhou Y, Shen X, Jin S. Geographically and Temporally Weighted Regression Model for Traffic Demand Forecasting and Its Application

[C] // in 2019 World Transport Convention (WTC2019), Beijing, China, June 13-16, 2019:1411-1420.

[4] Zhang W, Xia D, Liu T. Optimization of single-line bus time tables considering time-depeng-dent travel times: A case study of Beijing, China[J]. Computers & Industrial Engineering, 2021, 158(4):870-885.

[5] Zhang H, Zheng C. Research on Bus Timetable Optimization Considering Operation and Service Balance [J]. Journal of Guizhou University (Natural Sciences), 2021, 38(5):119-124.

[6] Dou X, Guo X, Gong X. Robust timetable optimization model for coordinated scheduling in a bus network [J]. Journal of Southeast University (Natural Science Edition), 2016, 46 (5):1110-1114.

[7] Yao E., Liu T., Huan N. and Liu W. (2020) Study on optimization of departure interval and vehicle type configuration of regular bus lines [J]. Journal of Beijing Jiaotong University, 44 (4):86-93.

[8] Ci Y, Han Z, Wu L. Bi-level Optimization Method for Urban Public Transport Regional Dispatching[J]. China Journal of Highway and Transport, 2021, 34(6):196-204.

[9] Jiang Z, Gu J. Compilation of Regional Timetable Based on Transit Network Layout [J]. Journal of Highway and Transportation Research and Development, 2016, 33 (12), 113-117.

[10] Gu J, Yang Y, Zhang J. Timetable of Multi-level Transit Considering Arrivaal Time Difference [J]. Journal of Highway and Transportation Research and Development, 2016, 33(6):128-133.

[11] Lv B, Yao C, Xiu Y, et al. Research on Bus Line Network Optimization Based on Problem Line Screening Model-Taking Suzhou City as an Example [C] // World Transport Convention (WTC2019), Beijing, China, June 13-16, 2019:91-97.

[12] Li X, Wang H, Yang Y. Bus Route Network Connection Planning after Rail Transit Preliminary as a Network: Take Kunming as an Example [C] // World Transport Convention (WTC2019), Beijing, China, June 13-16, 2019:47-57.

[13] Hu J. Optimization of Bus Regional Timetable Considering Operating Efficiency[J]. Journal of Transportation Systems Engineering and Information Technology, 2021, 21 (2): 139-144.

[14] Chu J, Korsesthakarn K, Hsu Y, et al. Models and a solution algorithm for planning transfer synchronization of bus timetables [J]. Transportation Research Part E: Logistics and Transportation Review, 2019, 131:247-266.

[15] Hm A, Xiang L, Hy B. Single bus line timetable optimization with big data: A case study in Beijing [J]. Information Sciences, 2020, 536:53-66.

[16] Shang H, Huang H, Wu W. Bus timetabling considering passenger satisfaction: An empirical study in Beijing[J]. Computers & Industrial Engineering, 2019, 135 (9): 1155-1166.

[17] He S, Dong J, Liang S, et al. An approach to improve the operational stability of a bus line by adjusting bus speeds on the dedicated bus lanes. Transportation research, 2019, 107 (10):54-69.

[18] Yu Y, Cheng X. Path Recognition Method of Urban Rail Passenger Flow Based on Mobile Signaling Data: A Case Study of Nanjing Metro [C] // World Transport Convention (WTC2019), Beijing, China, June 13-16, 2019:1681-1688.

[19] Xia X. Research on Bus Punctuality Rate Control Method Based on Signal Timing and Schedule Optimization[D]. Guangdong: South China University of Technology, 2020.

基于车路协同的寒区网联自动驾驶关键技术研究

崔星灿[1] 刘嘉庆*[1] 屈桢深[2] 张英涛[2] 刘 研[2]
(1.黑龙江省交投智能网联汽车产业创新有限公司;2.哈尔滨工业大学)

摘 要 交通建设是现代化经济体系建设的先行领域,车联网技术为现代化智慧交通提供了重要的支持。由于我国北方地区冬季漫长、气候寒冷,路况复杂等特点,研究和开发适合于寒区的基于车路协同的智能网联自动驾驶系统对于提升北方地区交通安全和效率具有重要意义。本文以黑河市自动驾驶测试场为背景,采用多元传感器对车辆和道路进行信息全方位协同采集。然后采用基于边缘计算平台,开发深度学习、机器学习和模式识别等相关智能算法,实现路况感知、识别危险和提供预警等功能,有效提升车端驾驶的安全性及事故危害的预警能力。

关键词 车路协同 车联网 自动驾驶 高寒地区

0 引言

交通在当前国际经济发展战略环境和地位中起到了十分重要的作用,一个便捷、安全、绿色和畅通的交通环境是国家经济可持续发展的有效保障[1]。随着公路工程实施技术以及智慧城市的发展和提高,世界各国都将发展基于现代化的智能交通体系作为未来交通事业发展的主要方向,从而为稳定经济增长、区域城乡协同发展、国土经济开发、生产力布局完善、产业结构优化等提供战略支持[2]。

在社会经济高速发展的环境下,中国道路交通建设也实现了大幅度的提升。由于北方环境及人文的特殊性,冬季时间长,路况复杂,因此车辆在进行高速行驶过程中,环境路面条件及前方车辆状态是导致交通事故的两种重大安全隐患。受车辆行驶道路和极寒天气的影响,导致驾驶员对突发事件的反应降低,不能地对驾驶过程中所遇到的突发事件进行及时地反应,进而产生交通事故;驾驶员不能在极短时间内,在极端环境下的道路上对因汽车本身状况出现的问题(如因失控或故障等因素的影响)而导致交通事故的发生。此外,由于驾驶员自身的驾驶素质和不良驾驶习惯,如超速行驶、闯红灯、驾驶过程中接打电话等违规行为使得在突发情况面前不能进行对车辆进行及时控制而酿成危险。在影响驾驶安全的诸多因素中,道路因素可以通过提高公路基础设施建设增加安全系数;环境因素因受天气尤其是极寒地区的极端天气变化影响难以对其进行针对性的实时防范。相对于上述外界因素,由车辆故障和驾驶员违规驾驶行为等内部因素产生的安全隐患则更加难以进行有效预防。因此,需要开发一种适应北方高寒气候地区的车辆安全预警和控制系统,使得汽车在环境感知、智能决策、协同控制等方面得到有效提升,从而为驾驶员在危险天气中行驶的安全性提供保障。

随着计算机通信技术及传感技术的飞速发展,基于车路协同技术的危险智能感知和预警技术逐渐被应用到安全驾驶领域中[3]。车路协同通过采用先进的无线通信和互联网技术,全方位实现车与车之间、车与路之间的联通与数据共享,并根据各项数据实现交通行为的分析和共同决策[4]。车路协同融合了通信、汽车、交通几大产业领域,是多重拉动经济途径的汇聚点。通过布设路侧传感器,路侧通信单元以及边缘计算设备,融合数字信号机、数字化交通标识标牌等全系列感知设备,最终形成车路协同的一体化应用。当前,车联网已经成为全球核心战略。早在20世纪90年代,欧美及日本就开始陆续地在车路协同领域进行研究和探索。我国关于该领域的研究相对欧美等国家起步较晚,我国智能交通系统(ITS)中心于2000年开始研究车路协同领域的相关技术。在之后的十年里,智慧公路系统的发展以道路基础设施智能化为核心,以智能道路与智能车载的协同工作为基础,重视人的因素应用研究,促进人车路三维一体协调发展。随着我国机动车辆保有量的高速增长,研究开发一套符合我国综合驾驶环境的智能车路协同技术是一个重大的社会热点和难点。当前我国已在车联网、网联汽车、基于路由和MAC层的协议、基于车路协动的数据采集及安全应用等关键领域开展进行了大量和广泛的研究。实际应用和理论研究证明,基于车路协同技术的安全预警技术可有效提升驾驶员在危险天气中行驶的安全性[5]。

此外,由于北方一些区域地广人稀,传统的集中式车载网络因受地域和通信距离的制约,不能充分、良好地利用网络资源条件。综上所述,本文以黑河市自动驾驶测试场为背景,采用基于V2X技术,融合视觉、毫米波雷达、气象等传感器对当前道路的运行状况和周边环境进行感知,采集车辆和车辆的位置、距离和速度等信息。基于边缘计算平台,开发深度学习、机器学习和模式识别等相关智能算法,实现路况感知、识别危险和提供预警等功能,进而通过V2X网络,将路面状况、前方道路及车辆状况及预警信息转至车端(驾驶员)及指挥中心(云端)。针对集中式车载网络受远距离的约束而不能满足移动状态下的实时通信需求的问题,本文将移动边缘计算(Mobile edge computing,MEC)技术引入车载网络以增强车辆的计算能力,从而有效地解决任务传输过程的丢包、时延问题,缩短任务执行时间,提升处理效率。本文的研究可为在高寒地区的复杂交通环境下,全方位实现车与车、车与路之间动态信息实时交互和反馈。在基于全时空多元动态交通信息采集、识别与融合的基础上充分有效地实现车路协同控制与管理,优化交通环境,保证交通安全,减少交通事故,提高通行效率,从而形成的安全、高效、畅通和绿色的道路交通系统,解放驾驶员,提升社会幸福感,以对高速公路驾驶安全提供关键支撑。

1 基于车路协同的组网架构设计

本文以黑龙江省黑河市自动驾驶测试场为实验场景以开展系统部署和验证。黑河自动驾驶测试场在提供自动驾驶汽车寒区测试验证环境的同时,还搭建了寒区车路协同新技术规模化落地的应用场景。其在东北地区率先积累了智能网联汽车的测试数据、丰富了车路协同自动驾驶车辆的场景库、完善了车路协同自动驾驶的测试流程。黑河自动驾驶测试场力争成为国内首家将高寒地区汽车传统测试、自动驾驶汽车测试与智能网联应用示范相结合的第三方测试、认证、示范平台;力争成为首个拿到国家级寒地检测牌照的官方检测机构,为取得未来寒区智能网联汽车标准制定的行业话语权而努力,也为打造国内一流、世界领先的寒区智能网联汽车示范区奠定基础。背景测试场地如图1所示。

图1 背景实验场地演示

本文系统可以概括为"感知-计算-决策"三个部分。首先,利用括固定相机视觉、云台相机视觉、雷达、结冰路面检测相机及气象站等感知设备获取车、路以及气象等信息。其中固定相机视觉采用固定位置及角度安装的监控相机,实时采集监控路段视频并进行处理,对车辆进行识别与跟踪,获取车型、车辆位置及行驶轨迹等信息。云台相机雷达利用安装与立杆的半球监控单元实现对路面的视频监控,并在必要时,通过手动或自动控制进行云台转动及变焦操作,实现对特定监控细节的近景监控识别。毫米波雷达传感器可实时感知多台车辆的位置及运动,且不受光照及天气影响,因此可与视觉传感数据进行互补,以准确提取路面车辆信息。气象站可返回多项气象监测信息,包括温湿度、气压、降水、风量等,为交通气象情况报道及路面状况处理分析提供信息源。结冰相机采用红外观测相机结合结冰检测算法,通过实时采集的红外图像实现对路面结冰及湿滑状况的分析判断。信息融合模块将上述传感信息进行融合判断,同时综合指挥中心下行的道路参考数据和道路车辆车载平台 OBU 信息,给出最终车、路信息处理结果及警告信息。

在此基础上,使用边缘计算节点和总控节点对获取的数据进行算法处理和二次融合,得到更加直观的信息。最后,基于基本的交通规则和人的思维逻辑,将必要的预测或危险信息进行可视化处理,呈现给交通管理者和驾驶员,从而保证交通安全,或进一步地,实现一定路段的自动驾驶。系统工作流程如图 2 所示。

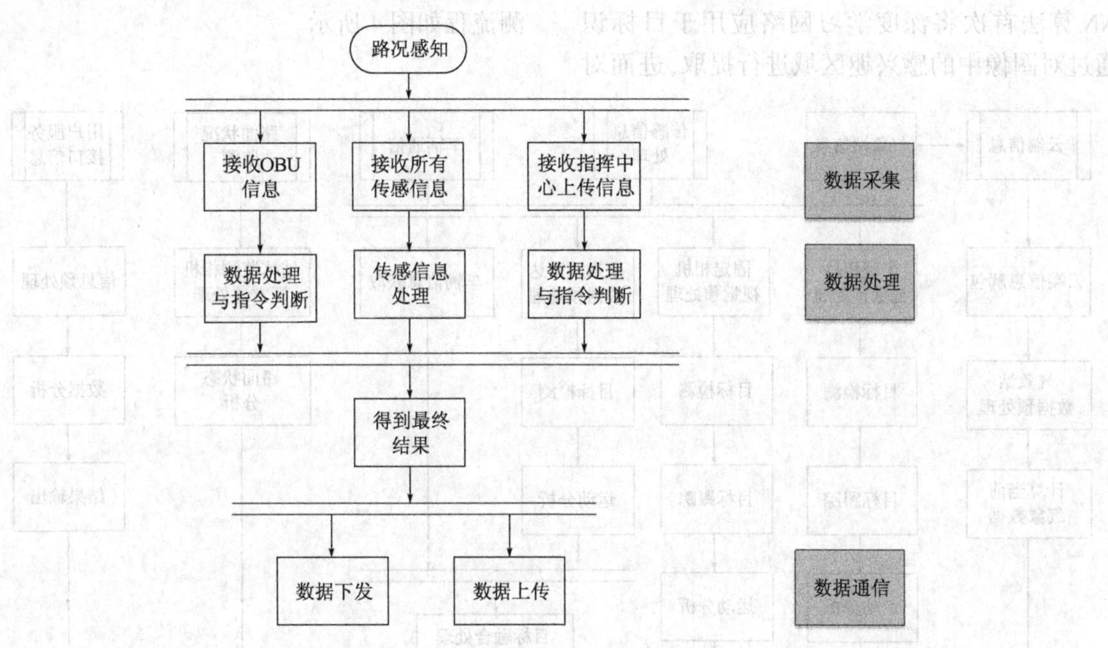

图 2　系统工作流程

从图 2 可以看出,本文系统是由数据采集、处理和通信三部分组成。首先通过数据采集系统,分别对车辆位置、运动速度、车流量等交通信息以及积水、结冰、积雪等路面状态信息进行采集和识别,为车辆提供实时路段信息。其中,数据处理是系统功能的核心,主要完成对各种传感器采集的数据信息进行加工处理,获取有助于决策信息生成的各种有用数据。数据来源包括传感信息,车辆通信信息,用户服务接口信息以及云端信息,其中各传感器信息采用并行处理。对于视觉传感器,主要在于计算道路车辆运行信息,因此需要重点在于车辆目标的检测、跟踪及运动轨迹分析,取得车辆的运动位置及车型等信息。对于雷达传感器,同样需要计算车辆位置及速度信息。与视觉相比,其速度信息计算更为准确,但无法感知车辆准确外观信息。通过气象站可获取当前温湿度等气象信息,同时结合视觉处理计算,推断当前路面结冰状况。然后分别对传感器信息和上层指令信息进行处理,结合云端信息和由扩展用户接口提供的其他信息,进行融合和判断处理,得到最终有用的决策结果。最后,由数据通信模块,将处理结果一方面通过 RSU 实时发送到道路行驶车辆,给出必要信息;另一方面通过路侧光纤发送至指挥中心,基于多传感器协同的工作流程如图 3 所示。

2　基于视觉的场景目标检测技术

由于高速公路场景中的相机的工作环境较为恶劣,尤其是在阴天、刮风、下雨、下雪及其他复杂天气等环境下,这些条件的干扰给基于视觉场景目标识别算法的鲁棒性和实时性的带来了重大挑战。传统机器视觉检测方法首先提取视觉场景的局部灰度和彩色对目标所处的感兴趣区域(Regions Of Interest, ROI)进行定位;然后基于全局的特征对 ROI 进行验证。该策略对在无复杂背景变化和周围运动物体干扰的特定场景较为使用。但由于其训练样本规模和泛化能力的限制,在有着复杂背景变化的场景则难以达到预期效果,如在漂浮物遮挡、雨雪天气等环境中易发生漏检和误检的现象,对基于复杂背景的场景目标识别的有效性提出了挑战。本文采用基于回归思想的深度学习目标检测算法用作相机的目标检测算法,首先采用基于 R-CNN 的卷积神经网络抽取图像中特征。在众多基于深度学习网络的算法中,R-CNN 算法首次将深度学习网络应用于目标识别,通过对图像中的感兴趣区域进行提取,进而对场景中的模板进行定位及类别的划分[6]。其具体方法是首先通过对图像不同局部区域的扫描获得次级目标区域,然后采用缩放等方式对候选区域进行处理之后将其输入到 CNN 中,并将的 CNN 对应输出作为输入上传到支持向量机中,获得对物体的最终分类结果。对于初步分类结果,当由于其对应的识别框处于的位置可能不是最佳区域,则要采用基于非极大值抑制算法对识别结果在场景中的位置进行优化,基于 R-CNN 的场景目标检测流程如图 4 所示。

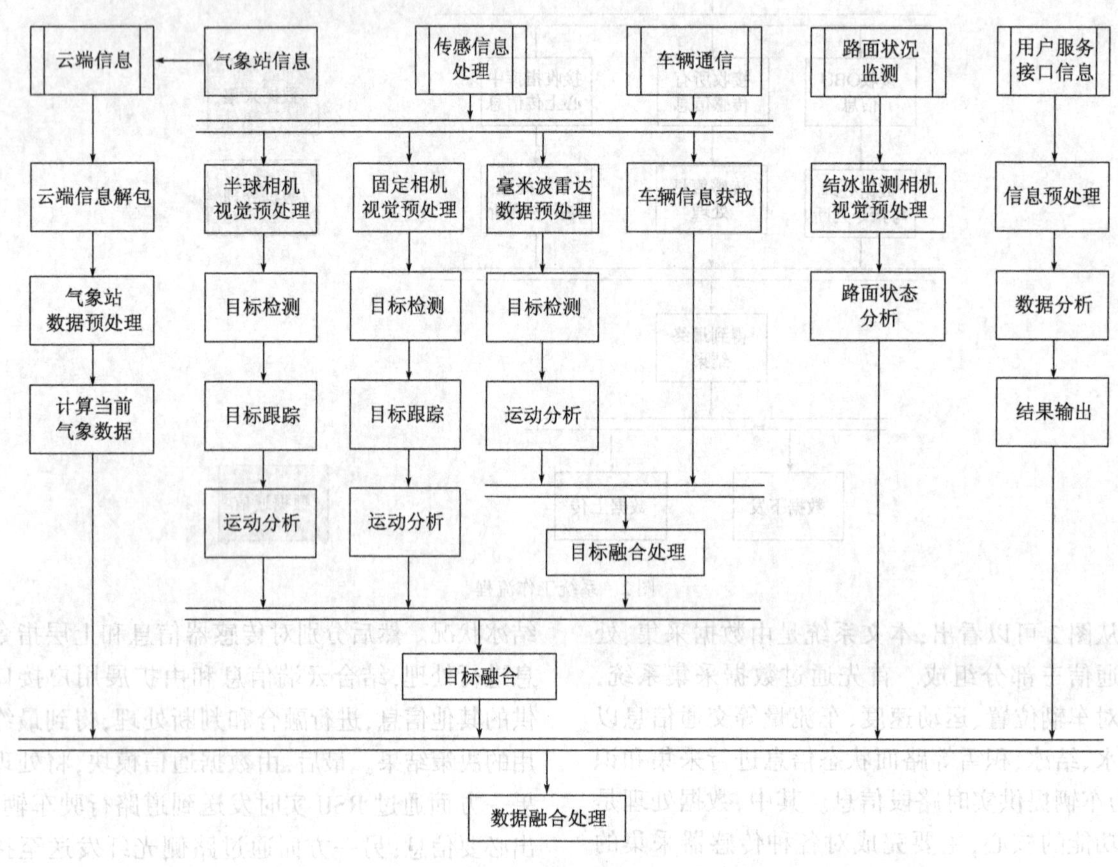

图 3　传感信息处理流程

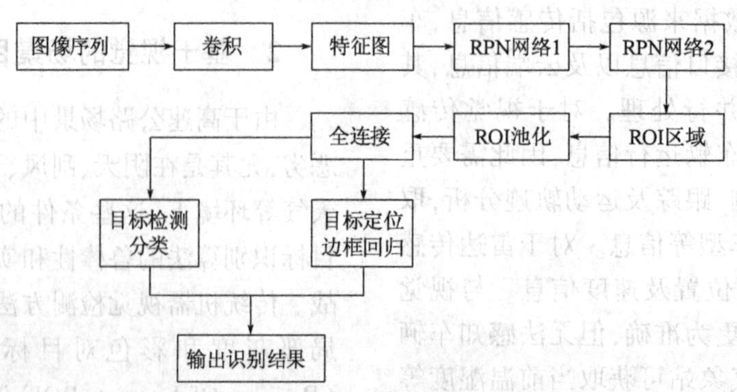

图 4　基于 R-CNN 算法的场景目标检测流程

在对图像的特征进行骨干网络提取的基础上，将提取的特征输入 SPPNet，通过固定输入最终的分类网络的特征图的通道数以及尺寸来扩大感受野，进而提升模型的泛化能力，其主要步骤为：首先输入任意大小的特征图并将其分割为不同的尺度的块，然后在每个块上计算最大池化，再将所有尺度下对应的池化特征通过 Concate 进行拼接并输出一个固定维度的结果，从而满足分类和边界框回归所需的条件。本文采用的 SPP 网络结构如图 5 所示。

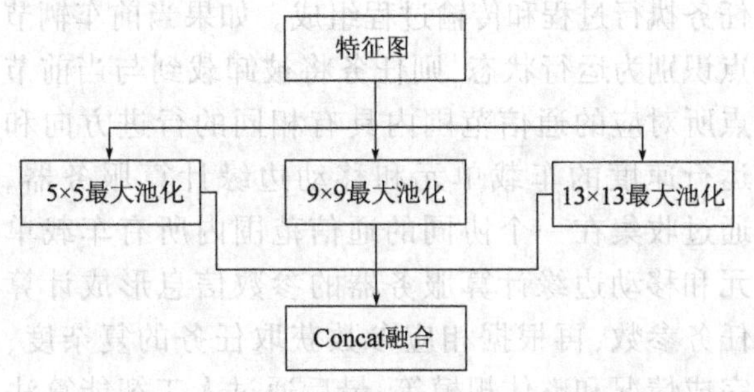

图 5 SPP 模块网络结构

在此基础上，本文采用基于 PANet 的多尺度目标特征融合方法，利用特征金字塔的上下级联对深层和浅层特征进行融合。该模型首先采用 FPN 网络作为融合的主体框架，然后在 FPN 做完处理后加入了一个下采样操作，将 SPP 结构的输出作为 FPN 的最底层进行上采样做特征融合。在基于 FPN 的特征融合基础上，本文将融合结果的最顶端输出进行两次下采样操作，再与之前上采样步骤中的 SPP 和 Resblock3 模块的输出结果进行特征融合以形成基于多尺度融合的特征信息，最后将基于多尺度融合的特征图输入 YOLO HEAD 完成对目标所处 ROI 边界的识别和回归分类。

3 基于视觉的场景目标跟踪技术

本文首先采用 Alexnet 构建跟踪模型骨干网络，其理由在于 Alexnet 的特征提取层的参数设置规模远小于其他学习网络，且因本文方法的应用背景为车辆目标跟踪，对网络模型结构的深度的要求不是很高。由于对于 Alexnet 对网络深度需求较低的特点，在特征融合方面的相对于其他神经网络需求资源较小，对于整体的目标跟踪网络而言，随着特征融合要求的降低，其网络的参数量也随之减少，即意味着网络整体计算规模的进一步缩减[7]。在此基础上，采用 LeakyReLU 函数对原始 Alexnet 网络模型中的 ReLU 函数进行改进，提高神经元的学习效能。在将目标模板与实时传输的图像进行卷积后，分别将 Alexnet 网络中的第三和第五个卷积所对应的输出输送到 SiameseRPN-block 中进行特征识别，然后将通道与待识别目标场景所对应特征图在相应的通道上进行卷积，然后将卷积结果传至 YOLO HEAD 中进行 ROI 分类和回归。最后，在将全部 SiamRPN-block 计算结果进行线性加权融合的基础上，获得场景中的目标的跟踪位置和其所对应的分类评分。

为了提高系统在复杂寒地天气和场景中对于目标跟踪的鲁棒性，本文采用基于孪生网络的 ReID 技术对目标丢失后进行重新定位和跟踪。孪生数字技术的所采用的原理是将现实空间中的事物、关系、过程等对象全时空一致地复现为信息空间中的数字模型（称为数字孪生体），并通过观测、分析、推演和操作数字孪生体来实现对现实中事物的研究和控制[8-9]。通过孪生网络进行相似度的计算、生成计算结果响应图并采用分类的方法来区分背景和具有最高响应的特征。在场景目标跟踪丢失时，目标标记框仍会停留在目标丢失时所处的位置。此时网络将持续图像的特征提取和匹配。如目标重新出现，网络会根据之前目标的特征再次进行特征匹配和分类，将目标以正样本的形式进行输出、定位和反馈，从而完成对丢失目标的再识别与追踪。

4 基于多传感器的融合技术

本文所设计的多信息融合模型通过将路侧感知信息和视觉信息进行融合，获得对路面情况分析及车辆运动速度分析，为系统提供路面结冰、路面积雪、路面积水和路面破损等情况的识别功能。为了发挥不同传感器的优势，本文采用基于决策层的融合策略来定制最符合不同传感器使用特性的识别方法，利用毫米波雷达和视觉摄像头进行数据采集来获取场景中不同的目标类别及位置的信息描述，然后采用多信息融合策略，将不同传感器获取的信息计算其交并比，根据计算结果合适的目标。为了实现不同种类设备所采集的多源信息全方位的融合，本文通过对不同设备的坐标系进行统一，使得多源数据能够在统一的坐标系下相融合,实现多源信息在空间上同步。本文采用决策级融合策略,将多源信息映射至至统一的坐标系中,并利用毫米波雷达获取的场景目标信息标定为潜在的感兴趣区域,然后对这些标记区域采用基于深度学习的快速检测算法划分类别。最后采用基于交并比的方法从而确定其最终的属性。

多信息融合流程如图6所示。

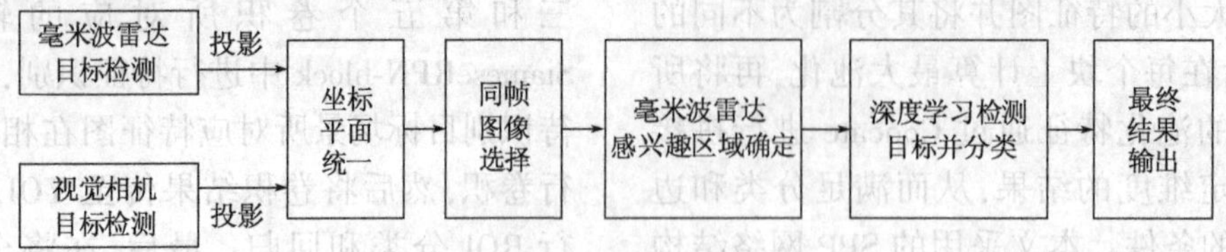

图6　多信息融合流程

5　基于移动边缘计算的车载网络任务优化技术

本文采用的车载网络任务优化技术是根据簇头单元的行驶状态对该群组内其他单元的行驶状态(速度及方向等信息)进行估计,从而建立运行车辆的参考点群组移动模型。依照任务资源分配方案,将计算任务分派到移动边缘计算平台和本地设备,从而将优化过程分派为移动边缘平台计算、车辆单元任务计算以及任务传输等过程。其中,移动边缘计算平台的任务计算由任务执行、等待和传输等部分组成,车辆单元任务计算由车辆任务执行过程和传输过程组成。如果当前车辆节点识别为运行状态,则任务将被卸载到与当前节点所对应的通信范围内具有相同的行进方向和运行速度的车载单元和移动边缘计算服务器。通过收集在一个协同的通信范围内所有车载单元和移动边缘计算服务器的参数信息形成计算任务参数,再根据相应参数获取任务的复杂度、完成情况和整体规模等,最后通过人工智能算法如马尔可夫算法、遗传算法等选择最优的联合决策方案。

基于移动边缘计算的车载网络任务优化流程如图7所示。

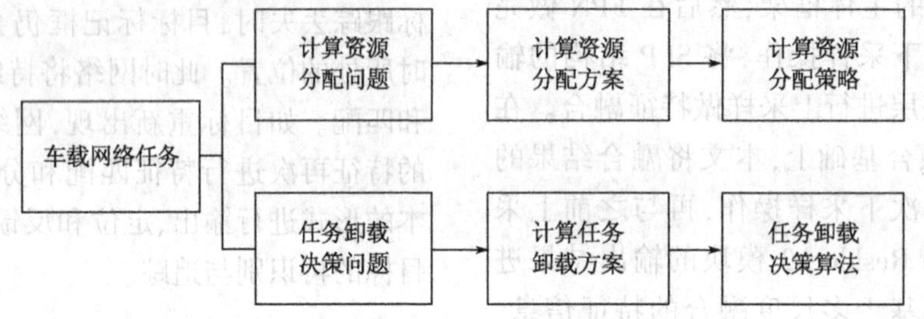

图7　基于移动边缘计算的车载网络任务优化流程

6　结语

本文基于寒地特殊环境下的车联网需求和挑战出发,针对车路协同V2X的关键技术和标准给出了全方位的设计和解决方案,为推动我国智慧交通的发展提供有效的支持。

参考文献

[1] 李大成.车路协同在智慧高速领域的应用探索[J].互联网经济,2020(11):64-70.

[2] Sukuvaara T, Nurmi P. Wireless Traffic Service Platform for Combined Vehicle-to-Vehicle and Vehicle-to-Infrastructure Communications[J]. IEEE Wireless Communications, 2009, (6): 54-61.

[3] 蔡赫.基于车联网技术的车路协同系统设计研究[J].时代汽车,2019(3):198-199.

[4] 熊小敏,杨鑫,刘兆璘,等.车路协同的云管边端架构及服务研究[J].电子技术应用,2019,45(8):14-18,31.

[5] C. Guo, L. Liang, G. Y. Li. Resource Allocation for Low-Latency Vehicular Communications: An Effective Capacity Perspective[J]. IEEE Journal on Selected Areas in Communications, 2019,37(4):905-917.

[6] Girshick R, Donahue J, Darrell T, et al. Rich Feature Hierarchies for Accurate Object Detec-

tion and Semantic Segmentation[C]//. Proceedings of the IEEE Conference on Computer Vision and Pattern Recognition. Columbus: IEEE, 2014: 580-587.

[7] Simonyan K, Zisserman A. Very Deep Convolutional Networks for Large-scale Image Recognition[J]. arXiv preprint arXiv: 1409. 1556, 2014.

[8] W. Ji, R. Guo, Z. Zhao, et al. Bridging the Physical, the Digital, and the Social[J]. IEEE Internet of Things Magazine, 2019, 2(3): 4-6.

[9] A. Fuller, Z. Fan, C. Day, et al. Digital Twin: Enabling Technologies, Challenges and Open Research[J]. IEEE Access, 2020, (8): 108952-10897.

动态多目标优化及其在若干交通优化问题中的应用综述

孙 晨 段续庭*

(大数据科学与脑机智能高精尖创新中心,车路协同与安全控制北京市重点实验室,
北京航空航天大学交通科学与工程学院)

摘 要 本文以动态多目标优化问题为研究对象,基于比较研究法、文献调查法等研究方法,首先对动态多目标优化问题进行了理论概述,接着总结了求解动态多目标优化问题的典型算法,然后重点梳理了动态多目标优化理论在军事交通领域、应急交通领域以及城市交通领域的诸多应用点。交通领域的部分实际问题属于动态多目标优化问题的研究范畴,其在具体交通应用场景中通常采用模型驱动的方式解决实际问题,即综合分析该实际问题的关键影响因素后,构建由决策变量、目标函数和约束条件组成的动态多目标优化模型,再运用适用的算法求解帕累托最优方案,最后总结了目前动态多目标优化理论发展存在的问题,并展望了动态多目标优化问题的未来应用前景。

关键词 动态多目标优化 交通优化 Pareto 最优

0 引言

动态多目标优化问题(Dynamic Multi-objective Optimization Problems, DMOPs)是包含多个目标,且其目标、约束或参数可能随时间变化的问题[1]。由于 DMOPs[2-3]具有多个矛盾的目标函数,其解一般无法最优化所有目标,涉及通过同时优化冲突目标来找到一组折中的解决方案。现实世界中的优化问题常在动态或不确定的环境中解决[4],因此优化的目标不仅仅是进化出一个接近最优的帕累托前沿面,而且要实现当环境变化时对帕累托最优解或者帕累托最优前沿面的有效追踪和定位。近年来,针对动态多目标优化(Dynamic Multi-objective Optimization, DMO)的理论研究越来越普遍,应用进化算法求解多目标优化问题引起研究者广泛关注,已有文献[5]中有一些对动态多目标优化算法研究的综述。而 DMOPs 是具有挑战性的工程问题,在交通工程领域有着典型应用场景,应用 DMO 可为解决交通系统中实际优化问题提供一种理论指导,辅助进行合理决策。故本文总结和归纳了动态多目标优化问题的相关理论、典型算法及其在交通领域中的实际应用场景,较已有的算法综述而言,涵盖范围更为全面,且结合了实际。

本文在第 1 节对动态多目标优化问题的定义和分类进行总结;在第 2 节从求跟踪环境动态变化后的最优解和求动态鲁棒的最优解两个角度对动态多目标优化典型算法和特点进行归纳;在第 3

1. 项目资助:国家重点研发计划项目(No. 2018YFB1601300)。

节对动态多目标理论分别在军事交通领域、应急交通领域、城市交通领域中具体实际问题的应用进行总结;在第 4 节对动态多目标优化问题研究中存在的问题和未来发展趋势进行分析,最后在第 5 节进行了总结。

1 动态多目标优化概述

1.1 动态多目标问题定义

本文参考国内外文献总结其最小化形式定义[6-8]如下:

$$\begin{cases} \min F(x,t) = \{f_1(x,t), f_2(x,t), \cdots, f_m(x,t)\} \\ \text{s.t. } k_i(x,t) \geqslant 0, \\ r_j(x,t) = 0, \\ i = 1,2,\cdots,p, j = 1,2,\cdots,q \end{cases}$$

式中: t——时间(环境)变量向量;

x——决策空间向量;

$F(x,t)$——t 时刻的 m 维目标函数向量;

$k_i(x,t)$、$r_j(x,t)$——不等式和等式约束。

针对该动态多目标优化问题给出如下定义:

(1)t 时刻的决策向量支配。t 时刻,假设决策变量空间中的两个向量为 x_1 和 x_2,则有 $f_e(x_1,t)$ 和 $f_e(x_2,t)$。如果有 $f_e(x_1,t) \leqslant f_e(x_2,t)$, $\forall e \in \{1, 2, \cdots, m\}$,且存在 m_1 时,$f_{m_1}(x_1,t) < f_{m_1}(x_2,t)$,则认为 x_1 支配 x_2,记作 $x_1 < x_2$。

(2)非支配解。t 时刻,若解 $x_1 \in x$ 是该问题的非支配解,在解空间内不存在解 x_2,使 $x_2 < x_1$。

(3)Pareto 最优解。t 时刻,不存在任何一个个体 $x' \in x$ 支配个体 x,那么称个体 x 为 t 时刻下该动态多目标优化问题的一个 Pareto 最优解。

(4)Pareto 最优解集。t 时刻,帕累托最优解的集合称为帕累托最优解集(Pareto Set, PS)。

(5)Pareto 最优前沿面。t 时刻,帕累托最优解集在目标空间的映射称帕累托最优前沿面(Pareto Front, PF)。

1.2 动态多目标问题类型

多个时变冲突和不可通约的目标可能导致变化的帕累托最优前沿。Farina 等[6]根据 Pareto 最优解集 PS 和 Pareto 最优前沿面 PF 的动态变化组合,将该问题分为 4 类(表 1)。

动态多目标优化问题的类型 表 1

类 型	PS 不变	PS 变化
PF 不变	Type Ⅳ	Type Ⅰ
PF 变化	Type Ⅲ	Type Ⅱ

Type Ⅰ:当前环境状态 t 下,Pareto 最优解集为 PS_t,Pareto 最优前沿面 PF_t,当环境变化后,PS_t 随环境变化而改变,PF_t 不随环境变化而改变。

Type Ⅱ:当前环境状态 t 下,Pareto 最优解集为 PS_t,Pareto 最优前沿面 PF_t,当环境变化后,PS_t 随环境变化而改变,PF_t 也随环境变化而改变。

Type Ⅲ:当前环境状态 t 下,Pareto 最优解集为 PS_t,Pareto 最优前沿面 PF_t,当环境变化后,PS_t 不随环境变化而改变,PF_t 随环境变化而改变。

Type Ⅳ:当前环境状态 t 下,Pareto 最优解集为 PS_t,Pareto 最优前沿面 PF_t,当环境变化后,PS_t 不随环境变化而改变,PF_t 不随环境变化而改变。

本文研究的动态多目标优化问题属于前 3 类。其中,可对现有的 Type Ⅳ类型可应用静态多目标优化问题的算法。而现有的动态多目标优化算法一般用于求解前 3 种类型。

2 动态多目标优化算法

动态多目标优化问题在工程和日常中普遍存在,该问题具有多个制约的目标,且目标函数、约束函数、决策变量等都可能随环境变化,因此该问题的算法应快速有效跟踪随环境动态移动的 Pareto 最优前沿或 Pareto 最优解集。目前,国内外许多专家学者针对其高效求解算法的研究已取得相关研究成果,总结其求解思路大致分为两类:一是求跟踪环境动态变化后的最优解,二是求动态鲁棒的最优解。

2.1 第一类求解算法研究现状

针对第一类求解方法的关键,在于优化时兼顾种群多样性和收敛性。准确找到此刻的帕累托最优解。环境变化时,再次初始化种群并重新寻优。即该类算法应当灵敏感知和检测环境变化并快速有效响应环境变化,因此环境变化检测机制和环境应答机制是此类算法的重要组成部分。

2.1.1 环境变化检测

对于环境变化检测机制的研究,Farina 等[6]采用重评估的方法,从每一代种群中随机选取 10% 的个体重新评价,若相邻两次迭代的个体适应度值不同,则说明环境发生了变化。Wei[9]兼顾了对环境变化敏感的点,提出了均匀设计的方法来产生均匀分布的向量,利用所产生的向量将Pareto前沿划分区域,从所划分的区域中取点进行评估检测,从而判定环境是否发生变化。杨圣祥等[10]提出一种稳态检验方法,首先对所有个体进行随机排列,再逐一进行重评估,若某个个体的评估存在差异则说明环境发生了变化。Janson等[11]通过观察种群树的层次结构变化来判断含有噪声的多目标优化问题的环境是否发生了变化。Richter等[12]通过比较连续两代,即当前代和下一代的目标解集的分布是否具有显著差异来判定问题是否变化。张世文等[13]定义了自检算子,选取种群中一定比例的个体生成候选集,重新评估个体适应度值,采用所定义的公式检测环境是否变化。Cobb[14]提出了通过比较一定迭代次数内的最优解的平均值,若其值减小则说明环境发生了变化。

2.1.2 环境应答机制

对于环境应答机制的研究,主要分为种群多样性保持策略、记忆机制、预测机制以及多种群策略。

(1)种群多样性保持策略。

在求解动态多目标优化问题时,若种群多样性缺乏则很难在环境发生变化后跟踪并找到新环境下的最优解,Deb等[15]对种群部分个体采用随机初始化的方式来提高其多样性。Zheng等[16]在保持最优个体的同时用随机产生的解替代其他解,并提出超级突变机制。Cobb[14]提出了超级变异法,环境发生变化后为重新发散种群而大幅增加变异率,但这存在变异率不可控问题,而且当环境变化较小时没必要采用较高的变异率;对此,Vavak等[17]提出采用可变局部搜索变异算子逐步增大变异率的方法。Grefenstette[18]提出了利用生成的随机个体替换每代部分原个体的随机移民法,从而确定每一代均有新的基因被引入种群以保持多样性。Azevedo等[19]提出了一种基于优秀个体的移民和随机移民相结合的混合移民策略以保持种群多样性。Yang等[20]提出了自组织随机移民算法。Du和Li[21]提出了利用差分变异更新微粒速度的方式保持种群多样性。

(2)记忆机制。

由于外界环境变化可能具有周期性,即当前的环境可能以前出现过,故在后续进化中针对历史最优解信息的有效利用的研究十分必要,引入记忆技术可以通过利用不同环境下的最优解提高新环境的寻优效率。记忆机制通常分为两类,即显性记忆模式和隐性记忆模式。其中显性记忆主要利用了引入额外存储空间的记忆集来储存较好的解。YANG[22]提出联想记忆模式,环境变化后根据等位基因分布向量采样生成新随机个体。Branke[23]在变化后从记忆体中取最优解替换等量的原个体。隐性记忆主要利用染色体冗余表达来降低种群收敛速度。Goldberg等[24]针对动态背包问题提出基于二倍体和基因显性机制的遗传算法,而Hadad等[25]对频繁环境变化采用多倍体的算法。RYAN[26]所提出的采用当满足某特定条件时基因为1否则为0的额外二倍体隐式记忆方法可以更优地适用于周期性的环境变化。Wang和Li[27]针对克服显性记忆和局部搜索记忆策略的不足提出了混合记忆策略。Koo等[28]提出了利用历史记忆的方法来改善种群的分布并优化种群的收敛。Bendtsen和Krink[29]提出了一种能够使得记忆体自身可以跟踪检测动态环境的不断变化,并且可以随之进行可自我调整的动态记忆模型。记忆机制可以有效应对环境呈周期性变化的动态多目标问题。

(3)预测机制。

由于外界环境变化可能遵循某些规律,为了使算法可以提前为环境变化做准备,估计未来动态环境下的最优解,故引入预测技术。通过预测模型对历史最优解信息进行处理,期望在新环境中生成甚至覆盖真实Pareto解集的初始种群,从而提高快速响应环境的能力。Hatzakis和Wallace[30]通过记录最优前沿的边界点的历史信息,采用自回归模型预测新环境中个体位置,由此提出一种前馈预测策略。Bosman[31]提出了通过结合机器学习和统计学习方法预测未来,构建进化计算和机器、统计学习融合的算法框架。Rossi[32]采用了基于卡尔曼滤波并引入偏差修改变异算子的预测方法,以在预测位置产生引导个体的方式引导后续搜索。Zhou等[33]采用加入白噪声的时间序列预测模型产生新环境的初始种群。又提出了基于中心形和流形的种群预测方法[34],即采用中心点和流形信息预测下一时刻的初始种群。Koo[35]对最优解历史信息通过加权平均预测下次环境变化的预测方向和大小,基于此提出了动态预测梯度策略。Peng 等[36]提出了采用线性时间模型预测种群的进化方向,将环境变化后的记忆池的非支配个体和预测产生的个体共同组成新的初始种群。预测机制可有效改善算法跟踪 Pareto 解集变化的性能。Li 等[37]提出了一种基于特殊点(SPPS)的预测策略,该策略由利用前馈中心直接预测的非支配集、在预测总体中引入一个诸如边界点和膝点的特殊点集、基于边界点和中心点的自适应多样性维持这三种机制组成,实验表明该算法能较好实现动态多目标优化。Li 等[38]设计了一种特殊的基于点的混合预测策略(SHPS),并将其与基于分解的差分进化多目标优化算法相结合。该预测策略下新环境的初始种群由预测的特殊点和种群预测策略(PPS)预测的种群(特殊点除外)这两部分个体组成,实验表明该算法对处理 DMOPS 问题具有良好前景。

(4)多种群策略。

通过利用对多个种群的独立区域进行搜索来提高算法跟踪 Pareto 最优解的能力。Rong 等[39]通过基于所提出的分类方法将种群聚类为若干具有代表性的群体,由此提出了一种多种群预测算法。Xu 等[40]将决策变量按照与时间相关性划分两类从而构建两个子种群,各种群的进化机制不同,由此提出了一种多种群协同进化优化方法。胡成玉等[41]首先采用多种群竞争模式进行勘探式搜索解集空间,当竞争失败后自适应切换到协作模式进行开采式搜索解集空间。Oppacher[42]将种群划分为一个追踪最优解的大种群和若干用于探索的小种群,由此设计了一种漂移平衡算法。Mendes 和 Mohais[43]提出了基于差分进化策略的多种群进化算法以保持整个种群的多样性。多种群策略利于搜索未开发的区域,对于多峰优化问题的求解适用性较优。

随着对于动态多目标优化问题求解算法的不断深入研究,国内外学者针对不同实际问题提出了相应的高效求解算法。Orouskhani 等[44]提出了一种由变更检测、变更相应和优化过程三部分组成的新型动态多目标优化算法。第一步采用 Sentry 解决方案检测环境变化,再采用 Borda 技术方法选出最坏的解,然后利用新的解重新初始化种群,来增加解的多样性。应用多目标猫群算法(CSO)从上一步改进的解中求取最优解,能够有效收敛到最优帕累托前沿。De Carvalho Bento 等[45]研究了具有约束条件的凸函数差分的帕累托临界点的多目标优化问题,基于行为科学中著名的群体动态问题,考虑采用每次迭代利用凸逼近最小化的方式来保证向量的改进过程,每一步的这种上升过程都保证了群体的稳定。李志勇[46]基于历史信息采用自回归模型来获得新环境下的预测种群。徐标[47]针对不同类型的动态多目标问题分别提出检测和响应策略,如针对区间参数变化,提出基于区间相似度的动态区间多目标协同进化优化方法。刘淳安等[48]将时间变量等区间离散化,提出一种自动检测环境变化的应答算子的动态多目标进化算法。Zhang 等[49]针对目标空间维数随时间变化时,提出了新型动态多目标优化免疫算法。许多国内外专家学者通过在对克隆免疫算法、遗传算法、粒子群算法以及蚁群算法等进行相应的改进和扩展后进行问题求解。

总结第一类求解算法的相关研究现状如表 2 所示。

第一类求解算法的相关研究现状　　表 2

第一类求解算法的重要组成部分		现状主要研究方法
环境变化检测机制		重评估法; 均匀设计法; 稳态检验法; 种群树法; 定义环境自检算子法; 最优解平均值法
环境应答机制	记忆机制	基于部分个体随机初始化法; 基于超级突变机制法; 基于超级变异法; 基于局部搜算算子法; 随机移民法; 自组织随机移民法; 差分变异法

续上表

第一类求解算法的重要组成部分		现状主要研究方法	
环境应答机制	记忆机制	显性记忆模式	借鉴等位基因的联想记忆法
			基于某种替换策略法
		隐形记忆模式	基于二倍体和基因显性机制法
			基于额外二倍体法
		混合记忆策略	利用历史记忆改善种群分布优化法
			基于自我调整式的动态记忆模型
	预测机制	前馈预测策略法； 结合机器学习和统计学习法； 基于卡尔曼滤波引入偏差修改变异算子法； 基于流形的种群预测法； 动态预测梯度策略； 基于线性时间模型预测进化方向法； 一种基于特殊点(SPPS)的预测策略； 一种特殊的基于点的混合预测策略(SHPS)； 一种基于参考点的预测策略	
	多种群策略	基于种群聚类的多种群预测法； 多种群协同进化优化方法； 多种群竞争模式和协作模式法； 基于大小种群的漂移平衡法； 基于差分进化策略的多种群进化算法	

2.2 第二类求解算法研究现状

针对第二类求解方法，目前相关研究尚不多见。鲁棒解以较好的合适满意度适合多个连续环境。Chen 等[50]描述了 Pareto 解环境适应性的新型鲁棒帕累托最优解(Robust Pareto Optima Over Time，RPOOT)定义及其时间和性能鲁棒性，时间鲁棒性为任意鲁棒帕累托最优解的生存时间，即可适用于多个连续动态环境。性能鲁棒性是鲁棒帕累托最优解逼近其所适用的多个连续动态环境下多目标优化问题的真实 Pareto 前沿的能力。

陈美蓉等[51]构建了两种求解动态鲁棒 Pareto 最优解的模型，即基于固定时间窗的模型和基于约束的模型。其中定义 L_u 来反映鲁棒最优解集 *RPS* 种任意鲁棒 Pareto 最优解 RPS_u 的时间鲁棒性。第 1 种采用了传统基于分解的多目标进化算法，分解方法是基于罚值的边界交集法。第 2 种采用无参数惩罚约束处理法。根据历史信息和动态环境变化趋势，估计当前解在未来连续环境下的适应度值，通过移动平均预测模型(Moving average，MA)实现每代种群中所有解在多个目标上的未来适应度值的多维时间序列预测。

Guo 等[52]提出了一种能够随时间变化寻找到鲁棒帕累托最优解集的基于网格的混合变异操作的多目标头脑风暴算法，提出了一种综合高斯、柯西、混沌的变异算子的混合变异策略，实验表明该算法能在可接受的适应度阈值下在更多的后续环境中找到能够逼近 Pareto 前沿的鲁棒 Pareto 最优解。

该方法相关公式及解释说明如表 3 所示。

其中，表 3 中涉及的变量及变量含义见附录。

综上所述，目前针对动态多目标优化算法的研究成果集中体现第一类求解算法上，主要注重对于 PF/PS 的有效定位和追踪，通过对保持种群多样性策略以及对记忆机制和预测机制的设计和改进来保证算法的收敛性。降低算法的复杂度，而在进化算法中的预测策略能够充分利用历史信息对未来环境下的最优解，在处理 DMOPS 问题上表现优良，一度成为该领域的研究热点问题。此外，目前对于经典的具有鲁棒性的动态多目标优化算法的研究相对缺乏，但是近年来该领域研究热度逐步攀升，求取鲁棒帕累托最优解也成为动态多目标优化算法的重点研究领域。

第二类求解算法相关公式及解释说明　表3

<table>
<tr><th colspan="2">第二类求解算法</th><th>相关公式</th></tr>
<tr><td rowspan="5">评价指标</td><td rowspan="3">时间鲁棒性</td><td>$$L_u = \min_{x_u^v \in RPS_u} \bar{l}(x_u^v)$$</td></tr>
<tr><td>$$\bar{l}(x_u^v) = \max\{l(x_u^v) \mid \Delta[l(x_u^v)] \leqslant \eta, l(x_u^v) = 0,1,\cdots K-k\}$$</td></tr>
<tr><td>$$\Delta[l(x_u^v)] = \frac{\| A[x_u^v,\alpha(k)] - \hat{A}\{x_u^v,\alpha[k+l(x_u^v)]\} \|}{\| A(x_u^v,\alpha(k)) \|}$$</td></tr>
<tr><td rowspan="2">性能鲁棒性</td><td>$$A^{\mathrm{ave}}[x_u^v,\alpha(k)] = \{a_1^{\mathrm{ave}}[x_u^v,\alpha(k)],\cdots,a_M^{\mathrm{ave}}[x_u^v,\alpha(k)]\}$$</td></tr>
<tr><td>$$a_s^{\mathrm{ave}}[x_u^v,\alpha(k)] = \frac{1}{T}\{a_s[x_u^v,\alpha(k)] + \sum_{l=1}^{T-1}\hat{a}_2[x_u^v,\alpha(k+l)]\}$$</td></tr>
<tr><td rowspan="2">转化模型</td><td>基于固定时间窗</td><td>基于固定时间窗的转化模型以最小化固定时间窗 T 内的平均适应度值为目标函数:
$$\min A^{\mathrm{ave}}[X,\alpha(k)] = \{a_1^{\mathrm{ave}}[X,\alpha(k)],\cdots,a_M^{\mathrm{ave}}[X,\alpha(k)]\}$$</td></tr>
<tr><td>基于约束</td><td>基于约束的转化模型将解对未来环境的适应程度转化成固定时间窗内的 T 个鲁棒约束:
$$\min A^{\mathrm{ave}}[X,\alpha(k)] = \{a_1^{\mathrm{ave}}[X,\alpha(k)],\cdots,a_M^{\mathrm{ave}}[X,\alpha(k)]\}$$
$$\text{s.t.} \frac{\| A^{\mathrm{ave}}[X,\alpha(k)] - \hat{A}[X,\alpha(k+g)] \|}{\| A^{\mathrm{ave}}[X,\alpha(k)] \|} \leqslant \eta, g = 0,1,\cdots,T-1$$
当 $g=0$ 时 $\hat{A}[X,\alpha(k+g)]$ 指当前时刻 k 的真实适应度值</td></tr>
</table>

2.3　两类研究算法优缺点

2.3.1　第一类求解算法优缺点

第一类算法本质上是检测到环境状态改变后重新初始化种群并触发寻优过程,在有限时间内找到当前环境下的最优解。

该算法的优点在于考虑了环境变化的检测、种群多样性的保持以及历史信息的有效利用,在优化的过程中使得决策空间的探索得以有效的平衡和开发,保证算法快速收敛。该方法虽然为动态多目标优化问题提供了有效的求解思路,但也存在一些缺点。当决策空间维数较高或者目标函数复杂时,该方法难以在有限时间内搜索到每一环境下的最优解。此外,对于实际工程问题,当环境变化较快时,每次变化都跟踪新环境下的最优解通常耗费较高计算代价,甚至无法在有限时间内执行该最优解,导致算法不可行。

2.3.2　第二类求解算法优缺点

第二类算法本质上是寻求一组鲁棒帕累托最优解集,其中每一个鲁棒帕累托最优解以一定的满意度可以适应多个连续的动态环境。

该类算法的优点是无须在每次环境变化时都频繁重新触发寻优过程求解执行每个环境下的最优解,从而避免了导致较高计算代价和资源。通过鲁棒帕累托最优解对连续环境的适应度,为环境变化快但不剧烈以及每次寻优代价较大的动态多目标优化问题提供了有效解决思路。但是该算法所求的鲁棒帕累托最优解是以一定适应度值适应变化的动态环境,并不是环境变化后的真实的帕累托最优解,对于需要获得当前环境下精确的帕累托最优解的问题不适用。

3　动态多目标优化问题应用点

针对动态多目标优化问题在交通系统优化与决策方面的应用点,本文归纳总结了动态多目标优化问题在军事交通领域、应急交通领域和城市交通领域内的主要实际应用。

3.1　交通领域

随着人工智能、大数据等信息技术的革新,现代战争趋向于发展战争智能化。数据信息对于军事交通领域相关问题的优化决策具有重要指导意义。一方面,军用物资随着作战过程不断消耗,需要军事后勤补给持续供应以维持前方作战能力。科学合理地对不确定的动态战时条件下军事交通领域中的后勤车辆调度及路径优化问题进行深入研究,是军队后勤部门正确决策的前提,是军用物资快速安全送往前方部队的保障。另一方面,战场环境复杂时变,无人机在战前目标跟踪侦察及战时作战任务分配中具有重要应用价值,对于动态环境变化下的无人机的作战路径优化及航迹规划问题的研究是保证取得可靠敌情,占据战争主动性,保证作战胜利的重要手段,在军事交通领域中具有重要研究意义。将动态多目标优化理论应用于军事交通领域的物资运输线路优化以及无人机航迹路径优化的实际问题,具有较强合理性和可行性。动态多目标优化问题在军事交通领域中的应用点如图1所示。

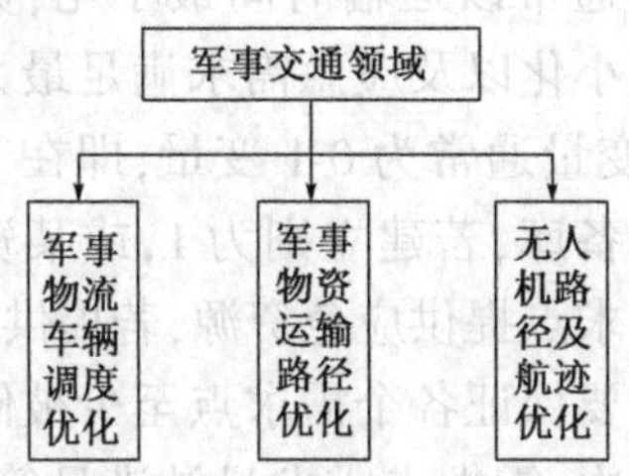

图1 动态多目标优化问题在军事交通领域中的应用点

3.1.1 军事物流车辆调度优化

针对军事物流车辆调度优化问题的研究,该类动态多目标优化问题通常以总运输距离和运输时间最小化以及通行安全性最大化为目标函数进行研究。决策变量通常为0-1变量,如车辆是否经过任务节点,若经过则为1。约束条件通常考虑为任务节点的时间限制,车辆载重量和运输量的关系以及任务节点被服务的次数等。通过对相关影响因素的具体分析建立军事物流车辆调度模型,解决军事物流车辆的优化调度问题。

针对不确定作战环境下的军事物流车辆的合理安排与优化调度问题,杨凯[53]针对面向军事物流的集群智能优化车辆调度问题,设置参数条件,以现有车辆数、物流中心数、载重量、节点需求量、节点间距离、车辆行驶速度、路况信息,道路的安全威胁等信息为基础数据,构建了以最小化节点总等待时间和最小化车辆总行驶路程为双目标函数的多目标优化模型,同时加入了时效性、优先级以及安全性考虑,采用结合混合粒子群算法和A*算法求解。张建光[54]针对战时车辆调度问题,综合考虑了时间、经济和安全等影响因素,以总安全通过概率最大化以及总运输距离最小化为目标函数构建考虑时间窗的动态多目标优化模型。基于需求地的时间要求、需求量以及军用车辆的类型、容量、平均车速数据,采用退火遗传算法求解带有硬时间窗的多车型战时非满载车辆调度的多目标决策问题。陈军[55]等针对军事物流配送车辆调度优化问题建立了蚁群算法的多目标优化模型并设计了其求解的流程。以配送中心和需求点数量,需求点的需求量,交通工具类型、数量、载重量以及单位运输成本为基础数据,应用模型算法求解最优车辆调度方案。

3.1.2 军事物资运输路径优化

针对军事物资运输路径的优化问题,该类动态多目标优化问题的优化目标通常考虑时间和安全两个因素,以最小化车队运输总时间和最大化运输总风险为目标函数。决策变量通常为0-1变量,如路段是否包含在规划的运输路径中,若包含则为1。约束条件通常考虑合法的可行路径的界定,保证需求点的需求可满足等,通过对关键影响因素分析建立动态多目标优化模型来解决军事物资路径优化的问题。

针对不确定作战环境下的军事物资的运输路径及调度策略优化问题,海军[56]基于路段实时通行能力及通行时间,以配送运输网络两点间的运行时间最短和通行能力最大为目标函数建立了军事动态配送网络的最小时间最大能力路径问题的优化模型,为解决动态军事网络配送问题提供了新的解决途径。在弹药运输调度的运输路径优化中,部队只有在正确的时间和地点接受充足的弹药才能保证部队的持续战斗力,侯德飞等[57]针对运输路径优化研究弹药的调配问题,由于在作战过程中弹药调配需满足不同的部队的弹药需求,因此存在互相矛盾和冲突的目标,故基于不同部队间的利益冲突,充分考虑弹药调度过程中时间和安全因素两个目标,以作战部队的弹药需求量、作战部队作战程度级别、弹药储备点到作战部队的距离、弹药运输通过路段的速度、路段的道路容量以及路段交通流量大小等数据为基础进行弹药运输策略的优化,以期用尽可能短的时间和尽可能安全的方式将所需的药从弹药储存点配送至所需作战部队,构建博弈模型,以遗传算法求解。在战时备件供应配送问题优化中,Wang Y D 等人[58]考虑了作战场景和参数的不确定性及多样性。在供应过程中,备件从后方仓库供应到前线部队,野战仓库作为配送中心接受后方仓库备件并实现给作战单位的配送分发,由此建立了有限离散的任务场景集,以交货时间最小化和缺货成本最小化为优化目标,以填充率和风险条件为约束,建立起战时备件供应的鲁棒优化模型。采用了自适应罚函数法进行无约束处理,利用改进进化策略的多目标差分进化算法求解模型。该鲁棒优化模型的最优解可为最坏情况下提供可行优化方案。

3.1.3　无人机路径及航迹优化

针对无人机路径及航迹优化问题,该动态多目标优化问题的优化通常考虑以无人机燃油消耗、任务完成时间以及执行任务的威胁程度等因素为目标。决策变量通常为 0-1 变量,如无人机是否经过任务节点,若经过则为 1。通常以任务完成后的无人机有足够的油量返回无人机基地等为约束条件,由此通过建立动态多目标优化模型为无人机路径及航迹的优化问题提供解决方案。

在集群作战中,无人机集群技术的应用前景广阔,随着大数据等智能技术的兴起,基于数据驱动下无人机执行作战任务的航迹路径规划的研究具有重要意义。Zhu 等[59]针对不确定复杂动态环境下的无人机作战的任务规划问题,基于不确定理论和多目标规划方法建立了考虑无人机飞行时间最小化、燃料消耗最小化、敌方威胁最小化的动态多目标优化模型并求解。冯慧等[60]以雷达威胁代价最小化和燃油消耗代价最小化为目标,提出基于多目标模糊优化的方法建立航迹规划性能指标;基于雷达自身的性能,利用启发式 A^* 搜索算法,选取对应的不同燃油权值和启发函数组合,从而优化无人机执行飞行任务时的航迹规划问题。

3.2　应急交通领域

在自然灾害、重大卫生事件等现象发生后,执行救援任务的时间有限,救援资源储备有限,而灾区的救援需求具有动态性,救援过程具有不确定性,救援目标具有多重性。基于所获取的有关灾情及路况等数据信息,在应急交通领域中,可驱动在应急交通领域中关于应急资源储备点选址和资源配置以及驱动救援物资调运配送的路径优化问题的研究,有利于辅助应急交通进行科学高效优化并做出合理的应急救援决策,因此动态多目标优化问题在应急交通领域中有较高应用价值,可为科学合理的应急交通决策提供一系列帕累托最优的备选方案,保障救援任务顺利实施。动态多目标优化问题在应急交通领域中的应用点如图 2 所示。

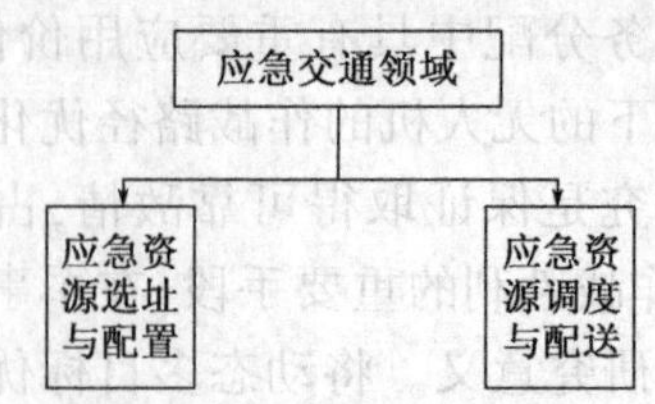

图 2　动态多目标优化问题在应急交通领域中的应用点

3.2.1　应急资源选址与配置

针对应急资源选址与配置问题,该动态多目标优化问题通常以运输时间最小化、资源调度运输等成本最小化以及应急需求满足最大化为目标函数,决策变量通常为 0-1 变量,即在节点处是否建立资源储备库,若建立则为 1,或某资源储备地是否向某需求点提供应急资源,若提供则为 1。约束条件通常要保证各个需求点至少被储备地服务范围覆盖一次,需求点需求量被满足等。由此,通过建立动态多目标优化模型为应急资源选址配置的优化问题提供解决方案。

由于灾害或紧急事件的发生具有不确定性,基于现有的数据对应急资源的储备点选址以及资源的配置问题的研究是保证救援顺利进行的基础,资源配送中心的选址优化问题也是应急交通领域的重要组成部分。高升等[61]针对非常规突发事件的资源布局问题,基于资源储备库的固定、运行及单位资源成本,需求点经济重要性、人口数、最晚应急时间数以及资源储备库到应急需求点之间的交通条件信息、平均距离、通行时间等信息,以成本和时间最小化为目标。运输成本是灾害发生后产生的,故将其设置为资源储备库的权重,采用改进的蚁群算法求解储备库地址点以及覆盖范围,通过合理的资源布局以便为非常规突发事件做好充分准备。许建国等[62]考虑将时间因素划分成时间周期,在一个时间周期内确定资源储备点的位置并在选址点配置资源,再根据随时间周期性变化的需求量调整相应储备资源地址点的配置资源量。基于各周期内需求点的需求量,候选点与需求点个数及位置信息、候选点与需求点之间的距离及交通因素等,建立了以整个周期内被满足的需求量最大以及因调整资源量产生的总成本最小为双目标函数,并纳入了时间因素的动态双目标非线性整数规划模型,有效刻画了应急设施选址和资源配置问题,为其优化决策提供指导基础。在突发事件或自然灾害发生后,高效的应急交通是保障伤员得到及时有效救治的前提,依据现有数据信息在不确定环境中科学合理的对医疗应急救援设施选址问题的研究是伤员得以快速转运保证。在综合考虑来对应急医疗设施选址和伤员转运计划集成问题上,孙华丽等[63]针对震后应急医疗设施选址—伤员转运问题,考虑临时医院和后方医院的选址以及轻、重伤员的转运,基于临时医院及后方医院的数量、位置及容量限制、受灾点数量及位置信息,临时医院、后方医院、受灾点之间的路况信息及运输时间、伤员受伤类型、救援工具可用容量等数据,建立了以伤员生存数量最大和心理成本最小为目标函数的医疗设施选址—伤员转运的动态双目标规划模型,驱动医疗设施位置的选址优化,有利于在应急交通关于伤员转运的优化问题方面提供最佳医疗救援决策方案。

3.2.2 应急资源调度与配送

针对应急资源调度与配送的问题,该动态多目标优化问题通常以应急救援运输时间最小化,物资延迟损失最小化,运输物流成本最小化,运输路径的可靠度最大化,需求点未满足的需求量最小化等为目标函数。决策变量通常为资源储备点向需求点提供的某种应急资源的数量。约束条件通常为每个需求点的需求量必须满足,资源储备点向需求点提供的资源量不能超过其相应资源拥有量等。由此,通过建立动态多目标优化模型为应急资源调度配送的优化问题提供解决方案。

灾害发生后,资源储备点或救援物资配送中心根据各灾区实际受灾情况和救助需求等数据信息,进行救援物资的分配调度和运输配送,是应急救援领域的研究重点。文仁强等[64]针对在资源有限条件下,从多个资源供应地向多个受灾地进行对多种类型资源调度优化的问题,考虑了自然灾害的不确定性以及因道路受损导致的安全性问题,基于应急资源的种类及数量、应急资源需求点位置、需求量及未满足量、应急资源供应点位置及储备量、应急资源中转站的位置及资源中转延迟时间、不同站点间路径可靠程度及通行时间等数据,构建了以所有调度路线可靠度最大、调度任务所消耗时间和最短、需求点未被满足的资源量最小等为目标函数的协同配备资源的动态多目标优化调度模型,采用了引入精英策略的多蚁群优化算法求解,可为灾后应急资源调度提供可靠的调运方案。王永奇[65]考虑了在灾害发生初期,资源储备点有限,物资发放点的需求量不固定,路网节点的通行时间动态变化等不确定因素,基于应急资源存储量、需求点需求量、应急响应时间要求、路网结构信息及相应路段通行时间等数据,构建了以当前阶段各物资分配接近水平的平均值最大化,以累计到当前阶段各物资分配接近水平的平均值之间的差异最小化,以总运输时间最小化为目标函数的多阶段应急物资动态调度模型并设计动态调度算法求解,为决策时提供该阶段下的合理救援方案。康斌等[66]针对突发事件发生后应急救援物资配送路径的优化问题,假设配送中心唯一,引入道路阻断修复及可靠性影响的约束条件,以应急道路网络情况、路网中链路距离及安全通过概率、应急资源可用量、需求点需求量、车辆在需求点的处服务时间、车辆载重量、车辆运行平均速度等数据为基础,构建了以未满足需求和最晚服务结束时间最小为目标的模型,利用引入优先邻点交叉算子的非支配排序遗传算法进行应急资源配送的路径的优化与决策,为应急交通领域中物资配送的路径优化提供了有效方案。王悦宸等[67]针对应急交通领域中救援情况不同且对于救援时间有着非常严苛的时间限制的应急资源调度配送问题,基于救援任务个数、截止时间、救援资源个数、救援资源单独执行救援任务的时间及效果等数据,构建了以完成救援任务的效果、个数最大化以及救援任务执行时间最小化为目标函数的资源调度优化模型,采用了动态规划的多阶段资源分配方式进行模型求解。巩青歌等[68]针对应急保障资源的实时动态调度问题,以应急资源种类、资源保障供应点和受灾点数量、各供应点资源存储量、受灾点动态资源需求量、受灾严重程度以及对各种资源需求紧急程度、资源成本及运输成本等参数信息为基础数据,构建了最大化包括时间效用和使用效用在内的资源效用值,最小化包括运输成本、物资本身成本以及应急响应延时损失在内的物资调度成本,最大化各个任务点的最小满意度的动态多目标后勤应急保障资源调度模型,从而保证各个任务点资源调度任务的均衡性。采用遗传算法求解,生成应急资源合理高效调配的优化方案。

云服务技术可以对物联网中各类物资进行实时动态管理,有利于实时数据的更新和获取,从而确保驱动模型的输入数据具有时效性和可靠性。将云服务应用至城市应急事件响应中,可对应急交通领域中的动态环境下物资配送问题提供科学合理的优化决策方案,实现快速响应和高效部署。刘宏志等[69]针对当前突发情况的基于云服务的应急物流动态部署问题中的物资生产与配送问题,基于物资供应地和应急集散地数量、供应地和集散地距离、需求地的需求量、物资单位运输成本以及单位生产成本等,构建了以在最短的时间内最大限度满足资源需求为目标函数的模型,并利用多目标遗传算法求解,通过获取实时地理信息和物流信息,及时依据实时数据进行动态地决策方案调整。

在应急交通领域中关于配送物资储备点的选址和物资配送线路优化相结合的实际应用中,沈晓冰[70]针对基于灾情特征的震后应急物资选址—联运问题,以物资供给点和受灾点数量、受灾点需求资源量、供给点容纳物资量,各运输方式工具的数量、运力限制及运输时间等基本数据信息为基础,构建了未满足物资需求所造成的相对损失最小化和应急救援时间最小化的双目标函数,并考虑多种运输方式以及配送时间等约束条件,建立多周期混合联运的动态选址-路径模型,以数据为驱动进行应急交通领域中救援物资集散点定位以及路线安排问题的优化和联合方案的制定。

3.3　城市交通领域

随着社会经济水平持续发展及城市化进程的不断推进,居民收入大幅增长,汽车保有量攀升,也带来了一系列交通问题。而随着大数据、5G 等信息技术的发展,革新了交通信息采集与集成的技术手段。此外,通过城市居民智能手机的使用可提供动态海量的众包数据,实现了多源异构的城市交通信息的实时动态获取及城市交通运行状态的实时动态监控。动态多目标优化问题在城市交通系统的优化中有诸多应用点,通过挖掘和分析数据中潜在的知识和应用价值,进行动态多目标优化问题的研究,保障了输入数据的时效性和精确性,使得交通系统优化结果更具说服力,交通系统优化决策更加科学合理。故应用动态多目标优化问题于城市交通系统的优化与决策,有利于提高城市交通系统的整体运行效率。动态多目标优化问题在城市交通领域中的应用点如图 3 所示。

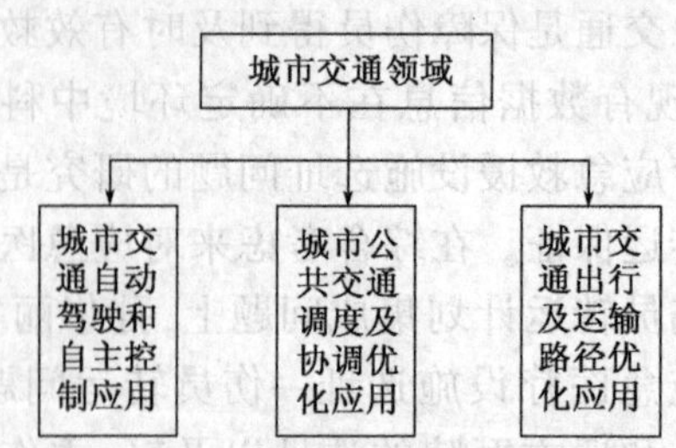

图 3　动态多目标优化问题在城市交通领域中的应用点

3.3.1　城市交通自动驾驶和自主控制应用

随着城市智慧交通的发展,自动驾驶及自主控制在城市交通系统中得以应用发展。在城市轨道交通智能化发展过程中,列车自主运行(Autonomous Train Operation,ATO)技术应用广泛,轨道交通的列车自主运行装置可使得列车在无人驾驶或者有人监控状态下,收到信号系统指示后,通过该装置实现自动控制开关车门、列车自动驾驶、自动开停车、自动折返、自动控制列车速度等功能,为轨道列车司机提供了手动驾驶和自动驾驶两种方式,有利于减少司机的人为失误,有利于减少列车加速或减速的时间,从而达到增加列车班次的目的。

轨道列车的 ATO 系统运行模式曲线优化是根据列车运行时刻表进行运行区间的时间计算,结合列车的基本参数信息和线路各种信息,以安全准时和能耗最小为目标,通过多目标优化算法计算出列车在此区间内的最大运行能力曲线。ATO 运行曲线如图 4 所示。

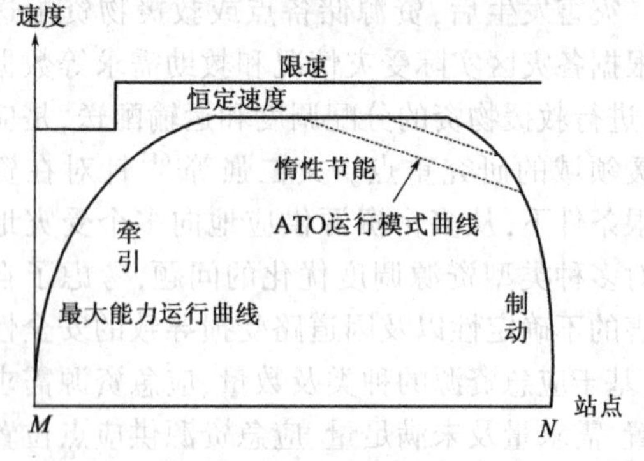

图 4　ATO 运行曲线图

针对 ATO 运行模式曲线优化问题,该动态多目标优化问题通常以列车的准时准点、安全舒适为目标,以最小化列车能耗和最小化列车运行时间为目标函数,约束条件通常考虑列车时刻表、速度及加速度等,决策变量通常为 ATO 系统在各个阶段的节点速度,通过建立动态多目标优化模型为轨道列车

ATO 运行模式曲线优化问题提供解决方案。

ATO 运行模式曲线优化是具有高实时性的动态多目标优化问题。丁文君[71]针对轨道交通的 ATO 运行模式曲线优化问题,基于地铁线路站点坡道、坡度以及限速信息等数据,在列车运行站之间进行多阶段区间划分,将问题转化成明确各阶段节点状态构成的最优曲线序列问题,以每个阶段节点间状态转移的 ATO 运行时间最小化、运行耗能最小化为目标函数构建运行曲线优化模型,在收到列车运行计划和运行时刻表的数据信息后结合当前列车的位置、线路及限速信息、速度等数据,进行满足准时、安全、舒适等多目标的决策,采用动态规划方法得到 ATO 系统运行目标速度-距离曲线,即确定列车最优运行曲线。熊仲夏[72]针对列车自动驾驶系统的优化问题上,基于数据预处理后的列车线路数据及列车参数,以牵引能耗和运行时间最小为目标,采用动态规划得到满足要求的优化曲线。选取北京地铁亦庄线小红口—旧宫段的列车运行线路数据进行了实例验证。孟建军等[73]针对列车自动驾驶系统各个性能指标的优化问题,构建了以准时性、能耗最小、精准停车、舒适性为目标函数,以列车动力学方程为约束条件的多目标优化模型,基于列车自身参数,如车辆最高限速、平均运行加速度数据等,结合线路基本属性参数,如站内限速、站间限速、坡度等数据驱动来计算列车的运行目标曲线。设计提出了一种改进灰色预测模糊 PID 控制算法,获取了使速度和加速度跟随效果较好的列车跟踪目标曲线,有利于实现 PID 控制的实时在线调整。城市公交实际运营过程中存在着受人为因素干扰导致的调度方式单一、调度方案不合理等的现象,故研究自动驾驶环境下的公交运营方式对于提高公交系统运行效率十分必要。马晓磊等[74]针对自动驾驶环境下的公交调度优化问题,考虑了乘客需求的动态性,构建了以公交利用程度最大化和乘客总等待时间最小化为目标的自动驾驶公交运营调度优化模型,基于公交实际运营数据,即从智能卡交易数据和 GPS 数据中挖掘实时更新的参数作为模型的数据输入,采用拉格朗日松弛算法求解。将基于实时数据的公交运营状态与实际公交数据对比分析,表明了在公交运营中投入自动驾驶车辆可使得公交在合理承载乘客需求的基础上避免超载,实现载客量分布均衡。

3.3.2 城市公共交通调度及协调优化应用

针对城市公共交通,包括轨道交通运行车辆和常规公交运行车辆的车辆调度以及其协调衔接程度的优化研究,有利于充分发挥“公交优先”政策的优势。

针对城市公交的优化调度问题,该动态多目标优化问题通常考虑出行者和公交公司两个主体利益,以乘客候车等待时间最小化以及公交运营收益最大化为目标函数,以公交车辆的发车间隔和满载率为约束条件,将车辆在站点的发车时刻作为决策变量。由此,通过建立动态多目标优化模型为城市公交调度优化问题提供解决方案。

针对城市公交车的优化调度问题,王莹莹[75]应用全球卫星定位系统和通信装置,并结合自动乘客计数装置采集获取的客流实时数据,分析客流时空变化的周期性及时空分布不均衡性,构建乘客损失成本最小和公交运营企业收益最大的动态双目标优化模型,采用改进的遗传-退火模拟算法进行求解,对公交车的调度时刻表进行了以站点实时客流数据为基础的优化,更好地满足了乘客公交出行需求。秦政[76]充分利用公交 IC 卡数据和 GPS 数据信息。选取公交 IC 卡数据中的 IC 卡号、线路号等作为基础数据,选取 GPS 数据中站点号、经纬度等作为基础数据,分析获取公交客流的动态分布特征,由此构建以乘客等车时间最小化、出行拥挤时间最小化、公交企业成本最小化为目标的优化模型,以各时段的最优发车间隔方案编制优化的发车时间表。赵倩阳[77]针对城际公交系统的动态调度的优化问题,基于公交车辆速度、公交车辆位置、道路实时交通条件等动态信息进行公交车辆和班次的灵活运营调整。通过兼顾乘客和公交运营公司两方面的利益,构建了乘客等候时间最小化和公交公司利润最大化的双目标公交调度优化模型,同时考虑公交车辆满载约束、舒适性约束和拼车条件约束等,基于公交 IC 卡数据提取的班次时间及车内人数进行优化求解。崔诚[78]针对运营过程中公交车队越站调度优化问题,以某条公交运行线路为例,构建了最小化乘客总站点等候时间、最小化乘客车内时间以及最小化公交总运行时间的多目标优化模型,将公交车辆在各站点的进出站时间、不同站点间运行时间、各个站点的停靠时间等为优化模型的基础数据,采用了元胞遗传算法进行求解优化。邹智杰[79]

针对双向公交调度问题,考虑了乘客候车时间最小、乘车舒适度最大、公交运营成本最低等因素为优化目标,建立了以包括上行和下行候车成本的总乘客成本最小化,以及包括上行和下行运营成本的总公交运营成本最小化为目标的双向公交调度优化模型,同时兼顾了运力方向不均衡系数、发车间隔的最大和最小约束、车辆可用性和满载率约束,以真实的客流数据、研究路段的通行状况数据、公交运营时长等数据为基础,采用了遗传算法求解双向公交调度合理方案。赵萌迪[80]针对城市公交线路调度问题,以乘客等待时间最小化和公交运营效益最大化为目标函数,以线路上的各个公交站点的客流量数据为基础,分析得到线路上客流时空分布规律,利用Matlab遗传工具箱进行模型求解得到公交发车时刻表。姜少毅等[81]考虑乘车效用,以高峰和非高峰时段的乘客等候公交车的满意度最大化和乘坐公交车拥挤度最大化为多目标函数,基于各个站点每个时刻点乘客上车和下车的历史数据和随机特征数据,此动态优化模型可利用Cplex软件进行求解。穆礼彬[82]基于公交线路上客流量数据,构建了出行者和公交公司利益最大的双目标线路发车间隔模型,模型参数可由常规公交调查或智能公共交通系统记录获取,基于此得到满足出行需求的公交发车时刻表。而实际公交运营中会受到诸多不确定性因素的影响,需要根据这些异常事件进行动态调度,通过IC卡数据信息及乘客自动计数系统获取的信息实时检测,进而判断客流量异常;通过GPS数据信息实时检测,进而判断线路运行和车辆运行的异常,针对发生的异常事件重新对行车计划进行实时调度优化。针对城市轨道列车的优化调度问题,汪林等[83]基于自动售检票系统采集的历史交易信息数据进行深入挖掘,基于实时客流信息建立以全体乘客平均候车和平均乘车满意度最高、列车公司运营满意度最高为目标函数的模型。基于站台实时客流及客流概率转移矩阵,使用伪并行遗传算法求解得到南京地铁二号线优化后的发车方案,并与当日实际发车方案进行对比分析,验证了以实时数据为驱动的优化决策方案的有效性。针对轨道交通和公共交通的衔接协调度优化问题,郭淑霞[84]考虑了轨道交通和常规公交之间换乘客流的影响,针对IC卡数据和GPS数据,构建以换乘平均候车时间最小、营运商成本最小、拥挤里程比例最小为目标函数的模型。前两个目标基于客流量,后一个目标基于公交车辆行程时间预测结果。刘华胜[85]针对轨道交通和常规公交营运协调模型的构建,设计双层规划模型。系统总成本随路径流量和换乘流量动态变化。上层规划中以居民出行成本、常规公交和轨道交通线路营运成本最小为目标函数。上层模型的决策变量结果作为下层规划模型的输入数据。基于换乘网络分配客流量,而客流量动态分配的结果又是上层规划模型的输入数据,上层模型是一个动态多目标优化模型,双层模型形成动态反馈。

3.3.3 城市交通出行及运输路径优化应用

针对城市出行路径选择和运输路径优化问题,该类动态多目标优化问题通常以出行者出行或运输时间最小化、出行或运输成本最小化、出行或运输距离最小化等为目标函数,决策变量通常为0-1变量,即是否选择路网中某路段,若是则为1。通常以保证路径无环路、道路通行能力和路段阻抗等因素为约束。由此,通过建立动态多目标优化模型为城市出行及运输优化问题提供解决方案。

城市化进程推进带来严峻城市交通问题,也推动着智能交通发展。而随着车载GPS的发展,基于浮动车技术等先进交通信息采集与集成方法为解决动态多目标的交通路径优化提供了海量的大数据支撑,有利于对现有道路交通资源进行整合利用,为人们出行提供最优路径选择,从而有效解决交通问题。于泉等[86]以路网状况数据、路段限制数据、车辆平均速度数据为模型的输入数据,构建了以出行时间最小化,出行距离最小化和道路拥挤度最小化为目标函数的实时环境下的多目标路径选择模型,运用逆向A^*算法优化全局路径,将变化后的数据反馈至系统,驱动增量更新算法,动态更新路径,实现实时的车辆动态路径规划问题。陈海鹏等[87]在考虑出行者出行需求多样性的基础上,在获取实时车流量、车辆交叉口等待时间、车辆行驶时间和行驶速度等数据的基础上,构建了以时间最短和费用最小为双目标的实时路径选择模型,采用广义自适应A^*算法求解。

随着电子商务快速发展,物流配送运输影响城市交通,对物流配送运输的车辆路径进行科学合理的动态优化,有利于确保物流配送服务的准时性,提高城市交通系统的整体运行效率。马春连等[88]针对动态车辆路径的优化应用,将配送中心车辆数、顾客数、顾客需求量、不同顾客间距离、车辆载重量、车辆在顾客间行驶时间以及在每个顾客处的服务时间等信息作为输入数据，由此构建了以运输总路程最小化、运输总成本最小化、使用车辆数最小化为目标函数的多目标优化模型，设计了基于聚集密度的人工免疫多目标进化算法。胡明伟等[89]针对快递服务相关的带时间窗口的动态车辆路径优化问题的实际应用场景，基于客户信息，构造了基于词典式的排序方法的动态多目标优化模型，通过基于事件驱动的算法根据新增客户请求实时更新路径方案。通过在不同基准问题数据集上进行仿真实验证明了模型优化的有效性。周慧等[90]以车辆数、车辆运行成本、车辆行驶距离、行驶速度、行驶时间以及路网结构情况作为输入数据，构建了以成本最低和客户满意度最高为目标函数的动态多目标物流配送模型。采用多目标混合粒子群优化算法并结合贪婪插入和变邻域搜索方法实时调整。

此外，随着民用无人机技术的发展进步，利用无人机技术进行城市交通信息采集和城市交通状况实时监测，对交通管控方面具有重要应用价值。关于这类民用无人机的动态路径优化问题，Liu等[91]基于对有足够数量的无人机监视所有目标和只有一定数量的无人机监视部分目标两种场景，针对场景1建立了以无人机总巡航距离最小化和无人机使用数量最小化为目标函数的多目标优化模型，针对场景2建立了无人机总巡航距离最小化和未被检测的目标数量最小化为目标函数的多目标优化模型，并基于强度帕累托进化算法(Strength Pareto Evolutionary Algorithm，SPEA)和帕累托归档进化策略(Pareto Archived Evolutionary Strategy，PAES)提出了一种无人机巡航路线的进化算法。王亮等[92]针对由于侦察目标的不确定性而产生的无人机在交通监控过程中的动态路径规划问题，引入了时间轴概念。将其路径规划分成两个阶段，一是在动态目标未出现时通过静态优化使无人机按预定路径巡航，二是当动态目标出现时及时响应变化，重新规划巡航路线。基于无人机在初始时刻、有新侦查任务时刻、执行新巡航路径时刻的信息，构造以最小化无人机使用数量和最小化广义巡航距离为目标函数的动态多目标优化模型，用基于Pareto最优改进的非支配排序遗传算法进行求解得到规划路径，为满足无人机的交通监控需求提供一种有效解决思路。

3.3.4 城市枢纽群选址与布局优化应用

针对城市间枢纽群的选址与布局优化问题，学者提出了一种基于遥感卫星图像数据驱动的城市群综合客运枢纽集散点客流密度识别技术，在此基础上，以客运需求量以及综合客运枢纽点和需求点之间的距离数据为模型基础输入数据，进行其选址布局的优化，针对优化确定的枢纽点，以集散点智能识别技术预测的客运量数据为基础进行综合客运枢纽点的优化决策方案的确定。此方法可为京津冀城市群交通系统中综合客运枢纽选址布局优化提供一种优化决策方法。关键技术路线如图5所示，研究思路如图6所示。

利用综合客运枢纽的遥感卫星图像构建数据集，通过YOLOv3方法识别综合客运枢纽周边土地利用类型，通过ArcGIS影像分类平台计算不同土地利用类型面积，利用已有数据构建综合客运枢纽客流预测模型来进行客流密度识别。基于此，可由卫星图像和其他输入信息(如手机信令数据)获取个体联程出行链信息，进行联程集散点客流密度识别，从而获取广域互联出行链信息。基于智能识别的客流量大小数据，进行城市群综合客运枢纽选址布局与优化决策。在综合客运枢纽布局优化时，首先定量分析综合客运枢纽选址布局的影响因素，构建基于枢纽魅力度的备选点筛选模型确定枢纽的备选集合。在枢纽备选点集确定的基础上利用P-中位选址模型，即以备选点与需求点之间距离与各需求点的客运量乘积之和最小化为目标函数，以每个需求点只有一个综合客运枢纽站点为其服务以及只有当备选枢纽点被确定枢纽场站时才能够对需求点进行服务为约束条件，输入相应的数据进行综合客运枢纽的布局优化。该方法可为京津冀地区的枢纽群布局优化实践提供一定的参考。

综上所述，目前动态多目标优化理论在诸多交通领域均有广泛应用，在军事交通、应急交通和城市交通领域中普遍存在应用与不同场景下的资源调度与分配的优化问题、运输路径与线路规划的优化问题等，同时也存在某交通领域内专有的动态多目标优化问题，如城市交通下轨道运行的自主控制优化问题。目前，在实际应用中通常基于综合考虑解决该实际问题的主要影响因素进行数学建模，构造适用于优化该问题的有效目标函数和合理的约束条件,再通过设计求解动态多目标优化问题的高效算法,利用模型所需的基础数据对所构造的数学模型进行求解,从而获取解决相关动态多目标优化问题的科学合理的优化方案,为该问题在对应的实际场景应用中提供一定的优化决策思路。

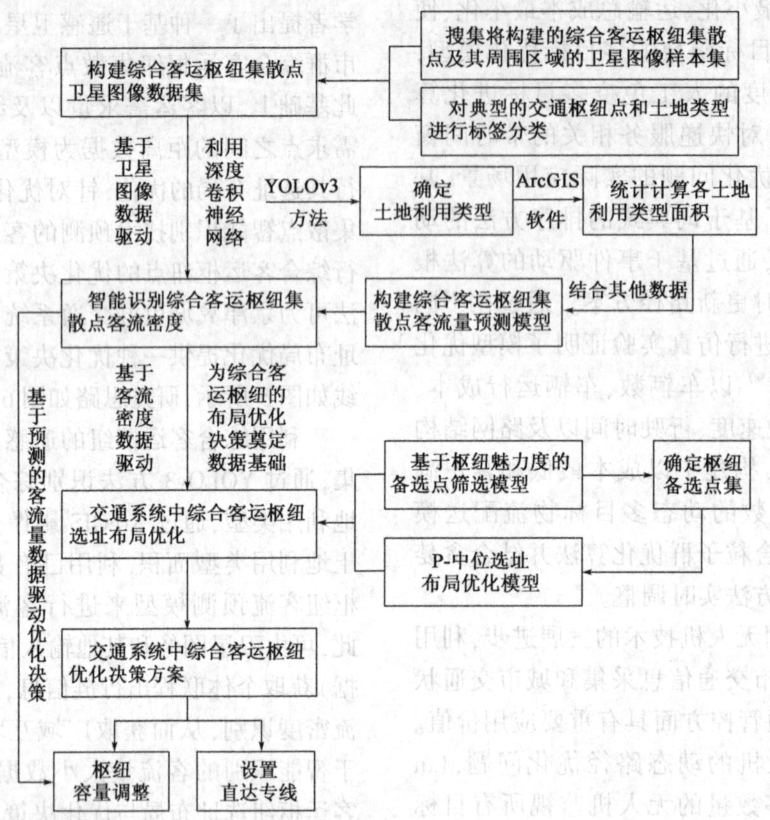

图5　关键技术路线图

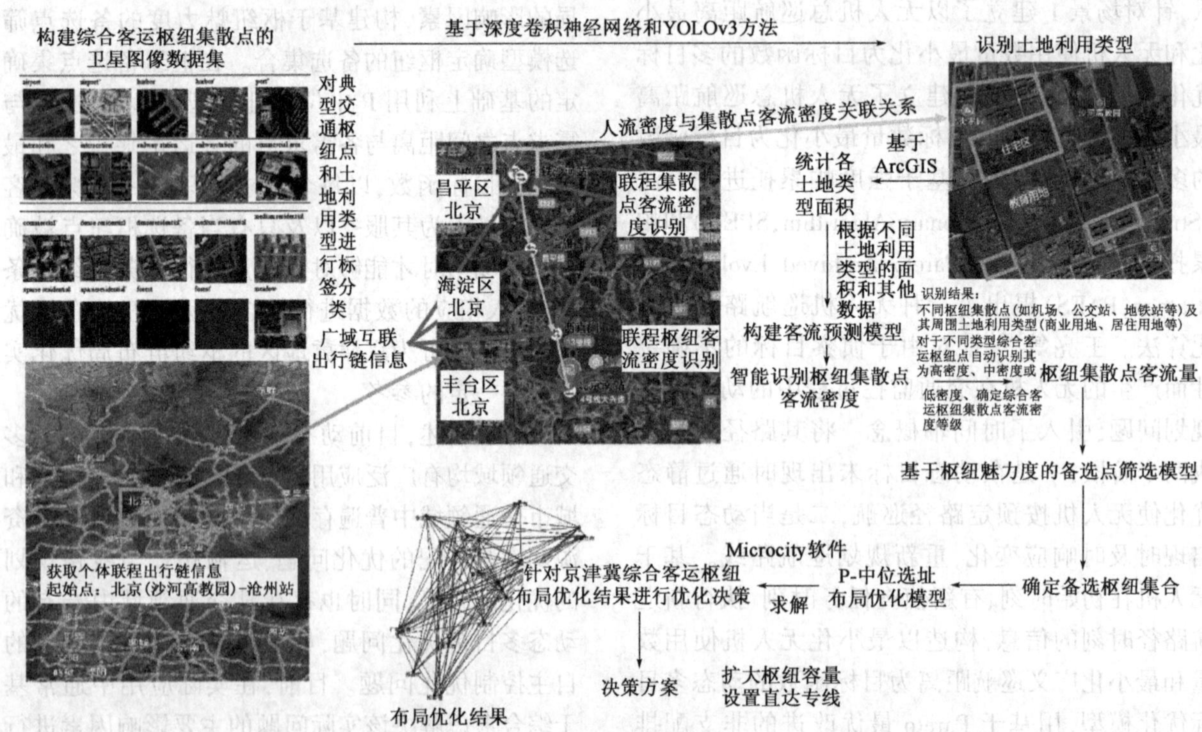

图6　研究思路

4 动态多目标优化问题的挑战和发展

4.1 需要进一步的开展的研究工作

虽然国内外学者针对动态多目标优化问题的应用以及动态多目标优化算法进行了大量的研究,但是由于动态多目标问题具有随着环境变动而变化的高度不确定性和复杂性,难以设计出适用于各种各样的动态多目标优化问题的通用算法,在最优解求取和实际应用上仍具有很大挑战,需要进行进一步研究和探索。

(1)在环境检测机制上,目前通常使用的诸如基于重评估的方法只能判断是否发生环境变化,无法确定环境变化的强度、频率和类型。同时现有处理方法多针对已知的环境变化,对于环境变化未知和环境不可检测的情况研究较少,造成了现有环境检测方法不能全面适应各种类型环境改变。此外,目前大多数动态多目标优化算法的研究相对集中在最大化满足问题条件的基础上求取问题的最优解,但普遍存在缺少多样性和收敛速度慢的问题,对于算法的有效性、收敛性、计算量和计算成本的考虑相对较少。如在动态多目标求解方面,基于预测机制的研究是热点,而在预测时如果预测所有的解,那么计算量过大,导致算法时间复杂度过高等;预测模型的选取和建立影响预测误差,从而影响求取 Pareto 最优解。故有效利用历史信息进行关键特征点的选取以及设计合适的方法增强预测结果的准确度方面,是提高算法性能的研究重点。根据实际的求解问题,要结合各种策略和方法设计具有较高性能的算法。

(2)目前很多动态多目标优化问题仅限于理论层面的研究,在实际的交通问题应用上仍需要进一步衔接。实际交通问题,如军事领域、应急交通领域和城市交通领域中的车辆调度和运输路径规划等动态多目标问题的不确定性和变化性会更加复杂多样,其目标函数以及约束条件等均可能会随着时间变化而实时变动,这种实时性和复杂性会导致在应用动态多目标优化方法求解实际交通问题时计算代价过大,计算资源耗费太高,使该方法不具实际可操作性,这也引发诸多学者对动态多目标优化方法解决实际交通问题可行性和实用性产生质疑。

4.2 未来研究发展趋势

一方面,在不同领域的交通系统优化与决策问题上,应用动态多目标优化方法建立动态多目标优化模型后,通常采用第一类求解算法进行求解。而现实中交通问题的应用场景中环境变化更加频繁和复杂,不确定性和随机性更加显著。对于环境每次改变都重新触发寻优过程的求解方式将导致对实际交通问题的求解所需的计算资源代价过大,甚至无法在有限时间内执行最优解。故在未来的研究中,对于动态多目标问题在交通系统优化与决策的应用求解上,可以重点研究本文所述的第二种求鲁棒 Pareto 最优解的方式,由于求得的鲁棒 Pareto 最优解能够以一定的满意度来适应连续多个动态过程,使算法无须在每次环境变化时都频繁重新触发寻优过程求解,一定程度上避免了较高的计算代价和资源消耗,是未来实际交通领域应用动态多目标优化求解算法的重要发展趋势。

另一方面,随着大数据、5G 智能技术、群智决策的不断创新突破以及相关理论和学科的进一步发展完善,传统的模型驱动的动态多目标优化方法应用于实际交通系统优化决策时存在一定的局限性,如求解该问题的计算资源过大而导致实用性不强。未来,在深入研究动态多目标优化理论时应结合先进科学技术获取的实时可靠的数据信息为优化和决策驱动,推动将模型驱动模式向数据驱动模式发展转变,以数据为驱动的动态多目标优化将成为解决交通领域中相关优化与决策问题强有力的支撑,这将对解决随着环境动态变化的多目标实际交通系统优化决策问题具有重大贡献。

5 结语

本文首先描述了有关动态多目标优化问题的相关概念,总结了动态多目标优化问题的类型。其次,将动态多目标求解算法划分两种求解思路并分别总结归纳了相关典型算法的研究现状。接着,重点归纳梳理了动态多目标问题在描述刻画军事交通领域、应急交通领域和城市交通领域中相关实际优化决策问题的应用点,最后总结了动态多目标优化问题面临的未来挑战和未来发展趋势。

DMOPs 在现实生活中有着广泛应用前景,在未来的研究中可着重从环境变化检测机制和环境应答机制两方面改进快速有效追踪环境变化后的最优解的策略以及重点研究求取鲁棒 Pareto 最优解的算法设计。随着大数据和 5G 技术的不断突破,在解决交通领域实际问题时,可考虑转变基于模型驱动的动态多目标优化问题应用向基于数据的动态多目标优化问题应用。

参考文献

[1] Yang C E, Ding J L. Constrained dynamic multi-objective evolutionary optimization for operational indices of beneficiation process[J]. Journal of Intelligent Manufacturing, 2019, 30(07): 2701-2713.

[2] Hu Z Y, Yang J M, Cui H H, et al. MOEA3D: a MOEA based on dominance and decomposition with probability distribution model[J]. Soft Computing, 2019, 23(04): 1219-1237.

[3] Fan R, Wei L X, Sun H, et al. An enhanced reference vectors-based multi-objective evolutionary algorithm with neighborhood-based adaptive adjustment[J]. Neural Computing & Applications, 2020, 32(15): 11767-11789.

[4] Wei L X, Guo Z Y, Fan R, et al. A prediction strategy based on special points and multiregion knee points for evolutionary dynamic multiobjective optimization[J]. Applied Intelligence, 2020, 50(12): 4357-4377.

[5] Rong M, Gong D W, Pedrycz W, et al. A Multimodel Prediction Method for Dynamic Multiobjective Evolutionary Optimization[J]. IEEE Transactions on Evolutionary Computation, 2020, 24(02): 290-304.

[6] Farina M, Deb K, Amato P. Dynamic multiobjective optimization problems: test case, approximations and applications[J]. IEEE Transactions on Evolutionary Computation, 2004, 8(05): 425-442.

[7] Farina M, Deb K, Amato P. Dynamic Multiobjective Optimization Problems: Test Cases, Approximation, and Applications[C]//IEEE. Proceedings of Genetic and Evolutionary Computation Conference. New York: IEEE, 2003: 71-71.

[8] Blackwell T, Branke J. Multi-swarm Optimization in Dynamic Environments[C]//Springer. Lecture Notes in Computer Science. Berlin: Springer, 2004: 489-500.

[9] Wei J X, Jia L P. A novel particle swarm optimization algorithm with local search for dynamic constrained multi-objective optimization problems[C]//IEEE. Proceedings of the 2013 IEEE Congress on Evolutionary Computation. New York: IEEE, 2013: 2436-2443.

[10] Jiang S Y, Yang S X. A Steady-State and Generational Evolutionary Algorithm for Dynamic Multiobjective Optimization[J]. IEEE Transaction on Evolutionary Computation, 2017, 21(01): 65-82.

[11] Janson S, Middendorf M. A hierarchical particle swarm optimizer for noisy and dynamic environments[J]. Genetic Programming and Evolvable Machines, 2006, 7(04): 329-354.

[12] Richter H. Detecting change in dynamic fitness landscapes[C]//IEEE. Proceedings of the 2009 IEEE Congress on Evolutionary Computation. New York: IEEE, 2009: 1613-1620.

[13] 张世文,李智勇,陈少淼,等. 基于生态策略的动态多目标优化算法[J]. 计算机研究与发展, 2014, 51(06): 1313-1330.

[14] Cobb H G. An investigation into the use of hypermutation as an adaptive operator in genetic algorithms having continuous, time-dependent nonstationary environments (Technical Report AIC-90-001)[R]. Washington: Naval Research Laboratory, 1990.

[15] Deb K, Rao N U B, Karthik S. Dynamic Multi-objective Optimization and Decision-Making Using Modified NSGA-II: A Case Study on Hydro-thermal Power Scheduling[C]//Springer. Lecture Notes in Computer Science. Berlin: Springer, 2007: 803-817.

[16] Zhang B J. A New Dynamic Multi-objective Optimization Evolutionary Algorithm[C]//IEEE. Proceedings of the third International Conference on Natural Computation. New York: IEEE, 2007: 565-570.

[17] Vavak F, Fogarty T C, Jukes K. A Genetic Al-

gorithm with Variable Range of Local Search for Tracking Changing Environments [C] // Springer. Parallel Problem Solving from Nature. Berlin: Springer, 1996: 376-385.

[18] Grefenstette J J. Genetic algorithms for changing environments [C] // Springer. Parallel Problem Solving from Nature. Berlin: Springer, 1992: 137-144.

[19] Azevedo C R B, Araujo A F R. Generalized immigration schemes for dynamic evolutionary multiobjective optimization [C] // IEEE. Proceedings of the 2011 IEEE Congress on Evolutionary Computation. New York: IEEE, 2011: 2033-2040.

[20] Tinós R, Yang S. A self-organizing random immigrants genetic algorithm for dynamic optimization problems [J]. Genetic Programming and Evolvable Machines, 2007, 8(03): 255-286.

[21] Du W L, Li B. Multi-strategy ensemble particle swarm optimization for dynamic optimization [J]. Information Sciences, 2008, 178(15): 3096-3109.

[22] Yang S X. Associative memory scheme for genetic algorithms in dynamic environments [C] // Springer. Applications of Evolutionary Computing. Berlin: Springer, 2006: 788-799.

[23] Branke J. Memory Enhanced Evolutionary Algorithms for Changing Optimization Problems [C] // IEEE. Proceedings of the 1999 IEEE Congress on Evolutionary Computation. New York: IEEE, 1999: 1875-1882.

[24] Goldberg D E, Smith R E. Nonstationary Function Optimization Using Genetic Algorithms with Dominance and Diploidy [C] // Lawrence Erlbaum Associates. Proceedings of the Second International Conference on Genetic Algorithms on Genetic Algorithms and Their Application, Hillsdale: Lawrence Erlbaum Associates, 1987: 59-68.

[25] Hadad B S, Eick C F. Supporting Polyploidy in Genetic Algorithms Using Dominance Vectors [C] // Springer. Proceedings of the Sixth International Conference on Evolutionary Programming. Berlin: Springer, 1997: 223-234.

[26] Ryan C. Diploid without dominance [C] // IEEE. Proceeding of the third Nordic Workshop on Genetic Algorithms. New York: IEEE, 1997.

[27] Wang Y, Li B. Investigation of memory-based multi-objective optimization evolutionary algorithm in dynamic environment [C] // IEEE. Proceedings of the 2009 IEEE Congress on Evolutionary Computation. New York: IEEE, 2009: 630-637.

[28] Koo W T, Goh C K, Tan K C. A predictive gradient strategy for multiobjective evolutionary algorithms in a fast changing environment [J]. Memetic Computing, 2010, 2(02): 87-110.

[29] Bendtsen C N, Krink T. Dynamic memory model for non-stationary optimization [C] // IEEE. Proceeding of the 2002 Congress on Evolutionary Computation. New York: IEEE, 2002: 145-150.

[30] Hatzakis I, Wallace D. Dynamic multi-objective optimization with evolutionary algorithms: a forward-looking approach [C] // ACM. Proceedings of the 8th Annual Conference on Genetic and Evolutionary Computation. Kuwait: ACM, 2006: 1201-1208.

[31] Bosman P. Learning and Anticipation in Online Dynamic Optimization [C] // Springer. Evolutionary Computation in Dynamic and Uncertain Environments. Berlin: Springer, 2007: 129-152.

[32] Rossi C, Abderrahim M, D' laz J C. Tracking Moving Optima Using Kalman-Based Predictions [J]. Evolutionary Computation, 2008, 16(01): 1-30.

[33] Zhou A M, Jin Y C, Zhang Q F, et al. Prediction-Based Population Re-initialization for Evolutionary Dynamic Multi-objective Optimization [C] // Springer. Proceeding of the 4th International Conference on Evolutionary Multi-Criterion Optimization. Berlin: Springer, 2007: 832-846.

[34] Zhou A M, Jin Y C, Zhang Q F. A Population Prediction Strategy for Evolutionary Dynamic Multiobjective Optimization[J]. IEEE Transactions on Cybernetics, 2014, 44(01): 40-53.

[35] Koo W T, Goh C K, Tan K C. A predictive gradient strategy for multi-objective evolutionary algorithms in a fast changing environment[J]. Memetic Computing. 2010, 2(02): 87-110.

[36] Peng Z, Zheng J, Zou J, et al. Novel prediction and memory strategies for dynamic multiobjective optimization[J]. Soft Computing, 2015, 19(9): 2633-2653.

[37] Li Q Y, Zou J, Yang S X, et al. A predictive strategy based on special points for evolutionary dynamic multi-objective optimization[J]. Soft Computing, 2019, 23(11): 3723-3739.

[38] Li J X, Liu R C. Wang R N, et al. A Special Points-Based Hybrid Prediction Strategy for Dynamic Multi-Objective Optimization[J]. IEEE Access, 2019, 07: 62496-62510.

[39] Rong M, Gong D W, Zhang Y, et al. Multidirectional Prediction Approach for Dynamic Multiobjective Optimization Problems[J]. IEEE Transactions on Cybernetics, 2019, 49(09): 3362-3364.

[40] Xu B, Zhang Y, Gong D W, et al. Environment Sensitivity-Based Cooperative Coevolutionary Algorithms for Dynamic Multiobjective Optimization[J]. IEEE/ACM Transactions on Computational Biology and Bioinformatics, 2018, 15(06): 1877-1890.

[41] 胡成玉,姚宏,颜雪松.基于多粒子群协同的动态多目标优化算法及应用[J].计算机研究与发展,2013,50(06):1313-1323.

[42] Oppacher F, Wineberg M. The shifting balance genetic algorithm: improving the GA in a dynamic environment[C]//ACM. Proceedings of the Genetic and Evolutionary Computation Conference. Kuwait: ACM, 1999: 504-510.

[43] Mendes R, Mohais A S. DynDE: a differential evolution for dynamic optimization problems[C]//IEEE. Proceeding of the 2005 IEEE Congress on Evolutionary Computation. New York: IEEE, 2005: 2808-2815.

[44] Orouskhani M, Teshnehlab M, Nekoui M A. Evolutionary dynamic multi-objective optimization algorithm based on Borda count method[J]. International Journal of Machine Learning and Cybernetics, 2019, 10(08): 1931-1959.

[45] de Carvalho Bento G, Bitar S D B, da Cruz Neto J X. Soubeyran A, de Oliveira Souza J. A proximal point method for difference of convex functions in multi-objective optimization with application to group dynamic problems[J]. Computational Optimization and Applications. 2020, 75(01): 263-290.

[46] 李智勇,李峥,陈恒勇,等.基于正交设计的动态多目标优化算法[J].计算机工程与应用,2016,52(14):42-49.

[47] 徐标.动态多目标协同进化优化理论与方法[D].徐州:中国矿业大学,2019.

[48] 刘淳安,王宇平.动态多目标优化的进化算法及其收敛性分析[J].电子学报,2007(06):1118-1121.

[49] Zhang Z H. Multiobjective optimization immune algorithm in dynamic environments and its application to greenhouse control[J]. Applied Soft Computing, 2007, 8(02): 959-971.

[50] Chen M R, Guo Y N, Liu H Y, et al. The Evolutionary Algorithm to Find Robust Pareto-Optimal Solutions over time[J]. Mathematical Problems in Engineering, 2015, 2015: 1-18.

[51] 陈美蓉,郭一楠,巩敦卫,等.一类新型动态多目标鲁棒进化优化方法[J].自动化学报,2017,43(11):2014-2032.

[52] Guo Y N, Yang H, Chen M R, et al. Grid-based dynamic robust multi-objective brain storm optimization algorithm[J]. Soft Computing, 2020, 24(10): 7395-7415.

[53] 杨凯.面向军事物流的群集智能优化车辆调度研究[D].长沙:国防科学技术大学,2010.

[54] 张建光.基于退火遗传算法的战时非满载车辆调度问题研究[D].长沙:国防科学技术

大学,2009.

[55] 陈军,智军,王毓龙. 基于蚁群算法的军事物流配送车辆调度优化问题研究[J]. 物流工程与管理,2015,37(05):131-132+74.

[56] 海军. 战区联勤配送运输路径优化问题研究[D]. 北京:清华大学,2009.

[57] 侯德飞,田德红,林聪仁,等. 基于博弈的多目标弹药调度策略优化研究[J]. 南京航空航天大学学报,2019,51(06):841-847.

[58] Wang Y D,Shi Q. Multi-objective Robust Optimization Model for Spare Parts Supply in Wartime[J]. Engineering Letters,2019,27(04):17-24.

[59] Zhu J Y,He Q F,Wang T Z,et al. Multiobjective Mission Planning for UAV under Uncertain Environment. Applied Mechanics and Materials,2014,556-562:4435-4438.

[60] 冯慧,屈香菊. 基于多目标模糊优化方法的无人机航迹规划[J]. 飞行力学,2007,25(02):25-29.

[61] 高升,庄亚明. 基于多目标的非常规突发事件资源布局模型[J]. 西安电子科技大学学报(社会科学版),2011,21(01):8-13.

[62] 许建国,池宏,祁明亮,等. 应急资源需求周期性变化的选址与资源配置模型[J]. 运筹与管理,2008(01):11-17.

[63] 孙华丽,柴丽萍,张玲,等. 震后多目标动态应急医疗设施选址-伤员转运问题研究[J]. 中国管理科学,2020,28(03):103-112.

[64] 文仁强,钟少波,袁宏永,等. 应急资源多目标优化调度模型与多蚁群优化算法研究[J]. 计算机研究与发展,2013,50(07):1464-1472.

[65] 王永奇. 面向自然灾害的应急物资多目标调度问题研究[D]. 合肥:合肥工业大学,2016.

[66] 康斌,刘权,黄健,等. 突发事件下多目标应急救援物资配送路径规划[J]. 科学技术与工程,2020,20(04):1521-1527.

[67] 王悦宸,苏醒,贾熹滨,等. 应急救援中基于线性规划的多目标多资源分配模型[J]. 中国科学技术大学学报,2018,48(06):458-466.

[68] 巩青歌,谭海佩,赵鹏皓,等. 后勤应急保障资源调度模型动态多目标算法研究[J]. 计算机测量与控制,2017,25(09):273-277.

[69] 刘宏志,刘钊,魏小兵. 基于云服务的应急物流动态部署模型的研究[J]. 计算机安全,2013,(05):43-47.

[70] 沈晓冰. 震后应急物资配送中选址—联运的优化问题研究[D]. 徐州:江苏师范大学,2017.

[71] 丁文君. 基于多目标决策的轨道交通 ATO 运行模式曲线优化研究[J]. 电子测量技术,2020,43(12):65-69.

[72] 熊仲夏. 基于自适应动态规划的 ATO 优化研究[D]. 北京:北京交通大学,2017.

[73] 孟建军,张宏强. 基于改进灰色预测模糊 PID 控制的列车多目标优化研究[J]. 铁道标准设计,2020,64(05):173-181.

[74] 马晓磊,沈宣良,张钊,等. 基于拉格朗日松弛算法的自动驾驶公交调度优化研究[J]. 中国公路学报,2019,32(12):10-24.

[75] 王莹莹. 基于实时客流数据的公交车辆调度优化研究[D]. 北京:北京交通大学,2015.

[76] 秦政. 基于数据挖掘的客流特征提取及公交调度优化研究[D]. 成都:西南交通大学,2017.

[77] 赵倩阳. 城际公交运输效率分析与优化[D]. 北京:北京工业大学,2018.

[78] 崔诚. 基于多目标优化的城市公交越站调度研究[D]. 南京:东南大学,2017.

[79] 邹智杰. 数据驱动的公交调度分析与优化研究[D]. 福州:福州大学,2018.

[80] 赵萌迪. 城市公交调度策略与方案优化研究[D]. 兰州:兰州交通大学,2017.

[81] 姜少毅,王博,闫哲. 基于候车与乘车满意度的公交车调度优化模型[J]. 工程数学学报,2017,34(04):375-382.

[82] 穆礼彬. 智能公交系统背景下的公交调度优化研究[D]. 成都:西南交通大学,2013.

[83] 汪林,张宁,邵家玉,等. 基于历史交易信息的城市轨道交通运营调度优化研究[J]. 铁路通信信号工程技术,2018,15(10):58-63.

[84] 郭淑霞.基于时变二源数据的城市公交调度协调模型与算法[D].北京:北京交通大学,2010.
[85] 刘华胜.城市轨道交通与常规公交协调优化关键方法研究[D].长春:吉林大学,2015.
[86] 于泉,姚宗含.动态重规划的多目标路径产生方法研究[J].交通运输工程与信息学报,2019,17(04):105-112.
[87] 陈海鹏,刘陪,申铉京,等.实时环境下多目标的路径选择模型[J].哈尔滨工程大学学报,2017,38(08):1285-1292.
[88] 马春连,许峰.人工免疫多目标进化算法在动态车辆路径优化中的应用[J].软件导刊,2014,13(04):25-27.
[89] 胡明伟,唐浩.动态车辆路径问题的多目标优化模型与算法[J].深圳大学学报理工版,2010,27(02):230-235.
[90] 周慧,周良,丁秋林.多目标动态车辆路径问题建模及优化[J].计算机科学,2015,42(006):204-209.
[91] Liu X F, GAO L M, GUAN Z W, et al. A Multi-Objective Optimization Model for Planning Unmanned Aerial Vehicle Cruise Route[J]. International Journal of Advanced Robotic Systems,2016,13(3):116-124.
[92] 王亮,刘晓锋,刘少堂,等.面向交通监控的动态无人飞机路径多目标优化[J].数学的实践与认识,2017,47(22):173-182.

附录1

涉及的符号名称及含义说明

符　号	符号意义	上标与下标意义
t	在动态多目标最小化形式定义中表示时间(环境)变量	—
x	在动态多目标最小化形式定义中表示决策空间向量	—
m	在动态多目标最小化形式定义中表示目标函数的维度	—
p	在动态多目标最小化形式定义中表示不等式约束的个数	—
q	在动态多目标最小化形式定义中表示等式约束的个数	—
$F(x,t)$	在动态多目标最小化形式定义中表示目标函数向量	—
$k_i(x,t)$	在动态多目标最小化形式定义中表示第 i 个不等式约束	i 是变量,表示第 i 个不等式约束,$i=1,2,\cdots,p$
$r_j(x,t)$	在动态多目标最小化形式定义中表示第 j 个等式约束	j 是变量,表示第 j 个等式约束,$j=1,2,\cdots,q$
$f_e(x_1,t)$	在动态多目标最小化形式定义中表示第 e 个目标函数	e 是变量,表示第 e 个目标函数,$i=1,2,\cdots,m$
PS_t	表示在环境状态 t 下的 Pareto 最优解集向量	t 是环境变量
PF_t	表示在环境状态 t 下的 Pareto 最优前沿面向量	t 是环境变量
RPS_u	表示第 u 个鲁棒 Pareto 最优解向量	u 是变量,表示第 u 个鲁棒 Pareto 最优解
L_u	表示鲁棒 Pareto 最优解集中任意鲁棒 Pareto 解 RPS_u 的生存时间	u 是变量,表示第 u 个鲁棒 Pareto 最优解
x_u^v	表示鲁棒 Pareto 解 RPS_u 中的某个个体	u 是变量,表示第 u 个鲁棒 Pareto 最优解;v 是变量,表示鲁棒 Pareto 最优解中的第 v 个个体
$\Delta(l(x_u^v))$	表示鲁棒 Pareto 解 RPS_u 中的某个个体 x_u^v 在相邻动态环境中的相对适应度差值	—
η	稳定性阈值,表示对个体 x_u^v 在相邻动态环境中的相对适应度差值 $\Delta[l(x_u^v)]$ 的容忍程度,取值由决策者偏好决定	—
$A(x_u^v,\alpha(k))$	表示个体 x_u^v 在当前环境 $\alpha(k)$ 下的适应度值向量	—

续上表

符　号	符号意义	上标与下标意义
$A\{x_u^v,\alpha[k+l(x_u^v)]\}$	表示个体 x_u^v 在未来动态环境 $\alpha[k+l(x_u^v)]$ 下的适应度的预测值向量	—
T	表示固定时间窗,指鲁棒 Pareto 解的环境适应能力的期望	—
$A^{ave}[x_u^v,\alpha(k)]$	表示鲁棒 Pareto 解 RPS_u 中的某个个体 x_u^v 当前环境 $\alpha(k)$ 的时间窗 T 内的平均适应度值向量	ave,表示平均的意思
M	表示适应度函数的个数	—
$a_s^{ave}[x_u^v,\alpha(k)]$	表示鲁棒 Pareto 解 RPS_u 中的某个个体 x_u^v 当前环境 $\alpha(k)$ 的时间窗 T 内的第 s 个适应度函数的平均适应度值	ave,表示平均的意思 s 是变量,表示第 s 个适应度函数,$s=1,2\cdots,M$
g	表示第 g 个时间窗	—
X	表示鲁棒 Pareto 解 RPS_u 中的个体向量集合	—

基于 YOLOv3 和 DeepSORT 的车流量检测方法

邓韩聪　徐学才*　肖代全

(华中科技大学土木与水利工程学院)

摘　要　在智能交通领域中,特别是智能网联环境下对车流量进行自动检测具有非常重要的作用。传统的车流量检测算法存在复杂网络模型计算速度慢,简单网络模型检测精度低两大问题。针对这两大问题,本文提出了基于 YOLOv3 和 DeepSORT 算法的车流量检测方法。采用 YOLOv3 算法对视频中车辆进行识别,兼顾了计算速度和检测精度。采用 DeepSORT 算法对 YOLOv3 算法检测得到的车辆进行追踪和计数,提高检测精度。研究结果表明,该方法准确度较高,可行性好,适用于视频车流量检测。

关键词　智能网联　车流量检测　YOLOv3 算法　DeepSORT 算法

0　引言

近年来,随着交通领域的发展进入新的阶段,智能化成为了交通领域发展的新方向和大趋势。而高效且及时的车流量检测是实现智能交通最基础的保障。常规的车流量检测方法耗时长,工作量大,耗费大量人力物力,并且对于大范围的交通网难以做到及时检测。基于视频的车流量检测是解决这些问题的有效方法。随着机器学习和图像处理技术的快速发展,越来越多研究者实现了基于视频的车流量检测。

视频车流量检测通常分为两个步骤:视频车辆识别和车辆追踪计数。目前广泛应用的是基于深度学习的目标检测算法和基于滤波的目标追踪算法。

基于深度学习的目标检测算法分为基于候选区域的两阶段算法和基于回归的一阶段算法。两阶段算法的代表算法为 R-CNN(Regions with CNN Features)[1]系列。宋焕生等(2018)[2]基于 Faster R-CNN(Faster Regions with CNN Features)算法进行不同场景的车辆目标检测,取得了较好的效果,但该算法对于远场景中的小目标的识别和检测的效果较差。一般来说,两阶段算法的识别精度和准确率较高,但检测速度较慢。一阶段算法的代表算法为 YOLO(You Only Look Once)[3]系列。袁小平等(2021)[4]针对 YOLOv3 中小目标检测效果不佳的问题,提出了改进算法 DX-YOLO(Densely ResneXt with YOLOv3),提高了算法对中小目标的检测精度。一阶段算法的检测速度快于两阶段算法,但检测精度不如两阶段算法。

基于滤波的目标追踪算法的代表算法为 SORT(Simple Online and Real-time Tracking)算法和 DeepSORT(Simple Online and Realtime Tracking with a Deep Association Metric)算法。纪筱鹏和魏志强(2011)[5]提出了一种基于车辆轮廓特征拐点的卡

尔曼滤波车辆追踪扩展方法,对于车辆重叠遮挡的情况适应性较强。SORT算法使用卡尔曼滤波和匈牙利算法处理目标追踪问题,DeepSORT算法在SORT算法上进行改进,通过级联匹配解决了SORT算法无法处理长时间遮挡目标的追踪这一问题。

考虑到实用性的要求,在基于深度学习的目标检测算法中,选择了基于回归的一阶段算法。作为一阶段算法的代表,YOLOv3算法结构简单、鲁棒性好、检测速度快、检测精度较高,是应用性较强的一种目标检测算法;而DeepSORT算法进行目标追踪的准确性高,稳定性好,在相机抖动情况下也能取得较好的跟踪结果,适应性强。将YOLOv3算法与DeepSORT算法相结合,不仅能够精准识别视频中的车辆,而且通过目标追踪对所识别的车辆进行计数,得到的车流量更加准确,可以有效完成视频车流量检测的实验。算法首先使用YOLOv3对视频中的车辆进行识别,再将YOLOv3的检测结果作为DeepSORT算法的输入,完成检测器与追踪器的关联与匹配,最后统计车流量,在传统车流量检测算法的基础上提升了检测性能和鲁棒性。

1　YOLOv3算法

YOLOv3是一种基于全卷积网络的目标检测算法,主干网络采用Dark Net-53。YOLOv3使用了Dark Net-53网络的前52层,在32倍降采样,16倍降采样,8倍降采样时分别进行检测并完成深层特征的提取,最终产生三个尺度的输出。借鉴于FPN的多尺度特征检测加强了算法对小目标的检测精确度。输出的内容包括三部分:检测框位置、置信度、类别概率值。YOLOv3对图像中检测到的对象执行多标签分类,减少了重叠现象的产生,通过回归的方法得出预测结果,兼顾了检测精度和检测速度。YOLOv3的网络结构模型如图1所示。

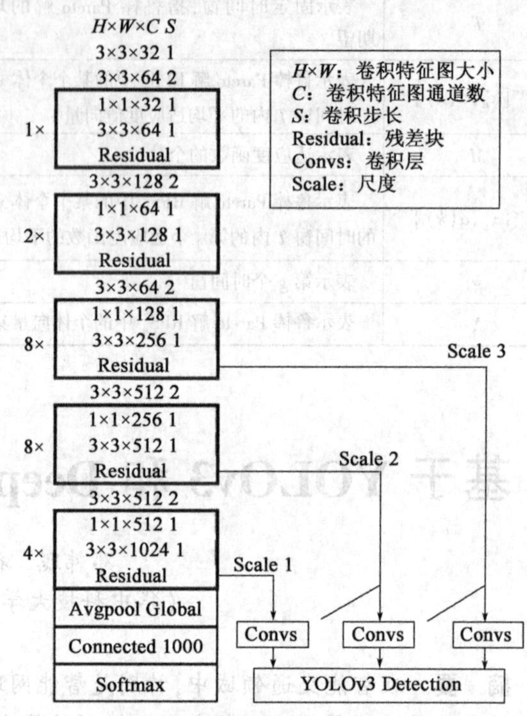

图1　YOLOv3网络结构

2　DeepSORT算法

DeepSORT算法是在Sort目标追踪算法上的改进。DeepSORT算法延续了SORT算法使用卡尔曼滤波和匈牙利算法进行目标追踪的总体思路,在此基础上增加了鉴别网络,在流程上增加级联匹配和新轨迹确认两个步骤。DeepSORT算法的流程图如图2所示。

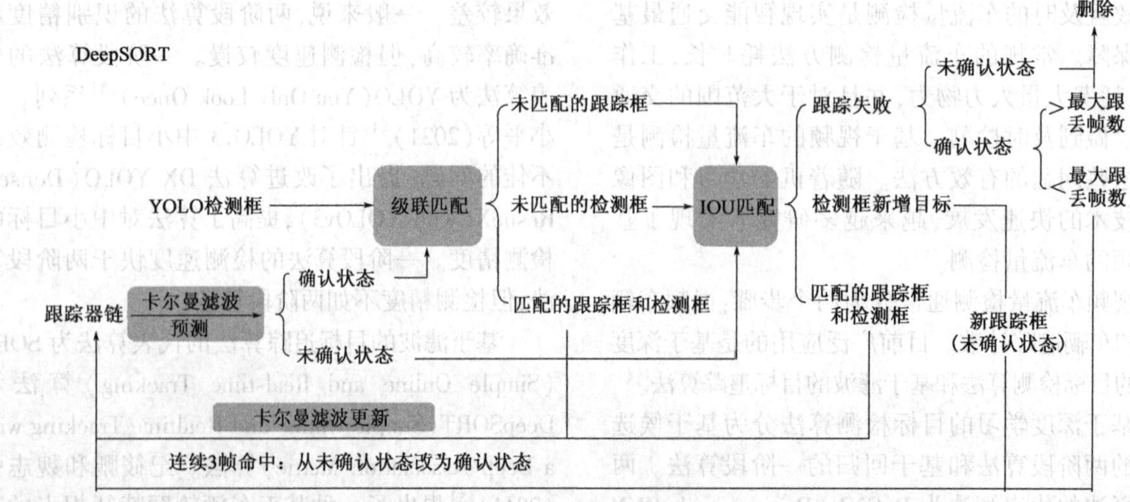

图2　DeepSORT流程图

DeepSORT算法在实时追踪检测中,提取目标的表现特征进行最近邻匹配,可以改善有遮挡情况下的目标追踪效果。同时也减少了目标ID跳变的问题。其核心思想还是一个传统的单假设追踪方法,使用了递归的卡尔曼滤波和逐帧的数据关联。

2.1 轨迹处理和状态估计

2.1.1 运动状态估计

针对多目标跟踪中可能出现的一个目标覆盖多个目标或者同一目标被多个检测器检测的情况,DeepSORT算法使用8个参数$(u,v,\gamma,h,\dot{x},\dot{y},\dot{\gamma},\dot{h})$来进行运动状态的描述,其中$(u,v)$为检测框中心位置,$\gamma$是框的长宽比,$h$表示框的高度,$(\dot{x},\dot{y},\dot{\gamma},\dot{h})$表示图像在坐标系中对应的速度信息,DeepSORT算法以一个基于匀速模型和线性观测模型的标准卡尔曼滤波器来进行目标在下一帧的运动轨迹的预测,其预测的结果为(u,v,γ,h),也就是以检测框坐标作为目标运动轨迹的预测。

2.1.2 目标的创建与移除

对每一个追踪目标k,记录其上一次检测结果与追踪结果匹配之后的帧数a_k,如果一个目标的检测结果与追踪结果相匹配,该参数设置为0。假如a_k超过了设置的最大阈值$A_{\max}$,则认为目标离开场景,对该目标的追踪结束。如果某个目标无法与已有的追踪器匹配,就假定产生了新目标,生成一个新追踪器。如果连续的3帧中新的追踪器都能够与检测结果相匹配,那么就出现了新目标;如果不能,就需要删除该目标。

2.2 信息关联

DeepSORT算法中处理检测结果与追踪预测结果的关联的方法是匈牙利方法。包括运动信息的关联和目标外观信息的关联。

DeepSORT算法使用马氏距离来衡量卡尔曼滤波器的预测结果与检测结果之间的匹配度,以此完成运动信息的关联。马氏距离指的是检测目标背离目标轨迹平均位置的偏离程度,通过计算检测位置和平均追踪位置之间的标准差将状态测量的不确定性进行了考虑。其计算公式为:

$$d^{(1)}(i,j)=(d_j-y_i)^{\mathrm{T}}S_i^{-1}(d_j-y_i) \tag{1}$$

式中:d_j——第j个检测框的位置;

y_i——第i个追踪器对目标的预测位置;

S_i——检测位置与平均追踪位置之间的协方差矩阵。

使用马氏距离对检测到的目标进行筛选,当某次关联的马氏距离小于指定的阈值$t^{(1)}$,那么设置运动状态匹配成功,其函数表达式为:

$$b_{i,j}^{(1)}=l[d^{(1)}(i,j)\leqslant t^{(1)}] \tag{2}$$

式中,$t^{(1)}$设置为9.4877。

当运动的不确定性很低的时候,马氏距离可以较好地衡量预测结果与检测结果之间的匹配度。当相机运动较为剧烈时,马氏距离匹配方法失效,此时会出现目标ID跳变的问题。此时采用卷积神经网络关联法。对每一个检测目标d_j求的特征向量,用r_j表示,且$/\!/ r_j /\!/=1$。然后对每个追踪器i构建一个存储其成功匹配的最近100帧的特征向量的集合,用$\{r_k^{(i)}\}_k^{L_k}$表示,其中$L_k=100$。新的衡量方法就是使用第i个追踪器的特征集合$\{r(i)_k\}_k^{L_k}$与当前帧第j个检测结果的特征向量间的最小余弦距离表示检测结果与追踪结果的关系,其计算公式如下:

$$d^{(2)}(i,j)=\min\{1-r_j^{\mathrm{T}}r_k^{(i)}\mid r_k^{(i)}\in R_i\} \tag{3}$$

如果上式求得的距离$d^{(2)}(i,j)$小于指定的阈值$t^{(2)}$,那么匹配成功,阈值$t^{(2)}$是从单独的训练集中得到的。

最后使用两种衡量方法的线性加权作为最终的衡量方法,计算公式如下:

$$c_{i,j}=\lambda d^{(1)}(i,j)+(1-\lambda)d^{(2)}(i,j) \tag{4}$$

只有当$c_{i,j}$位于两个指定的阈值的交集之内时,得到的匹配才是正确的。

2.3 级联匹配

当目标被长时间遮挡时,卡尔曼滤波预测的不确定性大大增加,状态空间的可观察性也大大降低。两个追踪器进行同一个检测结果的匹配时,遮挡时间较长的那条轨迹会因为位置信息的长时间不更新,追踪预测位置的不确定性更大,协方差更大,而马氏距离计算之时使用的时协方差的倒数,因此马氏距离会更小,那么检测结果就更可能和遮挡时间较长的那条轨迹相关联,这种不理想的效果往往会破坏追踪的持续性。级联匹配的核心思想是由小到大对消失时间相同的轨迹进行匹配,这样保证了对最近出现的目标赋予最大的优先权,解决了上述问题。

3　实验流程

3.1　环境配置

本实验在 Windows10 系统下的 Visual Studio Code 开发平台实现,以 Python 3.6 作为编程语言,以 Keras 2.2.4 为深度学习框架,通过 Open CV 3.4.4 实现跟踪可视化。算法最终集成于 Tensorflow 平台并结合 Pytorch 1.1.0 环境完成车流量检测。实验所用硬件 GPU 为 NIVDIA GeForce GTX1650。

3.2　YOLOv3 数据集训练

本实验的 YOLOv3 数据集训练在原作者提供的 YOLOv3 模型的基础上进行,以其预训练网络为基础网络。数据集中识别类型由原本的 80 类改为车辆这一类,以此加快目标识别的速度并提高检测精度。合适的预选框大小是影响 YOLOv3 模型训练速度的关键。本实验中所选的用于模型训练的 9 组预选框的宽和高分别为:(10,13),(16,30),(33,23),(30,61),(62,45),(59,119),(116,90),(156,198),(373,326)。训练设置的动量参数为 0.9,权重衰减因子为 0.0005,初始学习率设置为 0.001。

3.3　实验流程图

本实验使用 YOLOv3 模型对视频中的车辆进行识别,再将 YOLOv3 的检测结果作为 DeepSORT 算法的输入,完成检测器与追踪器的关联与匹配,车辆进入跟踪区域时进行计数。算法的流程图如图 3 所示。

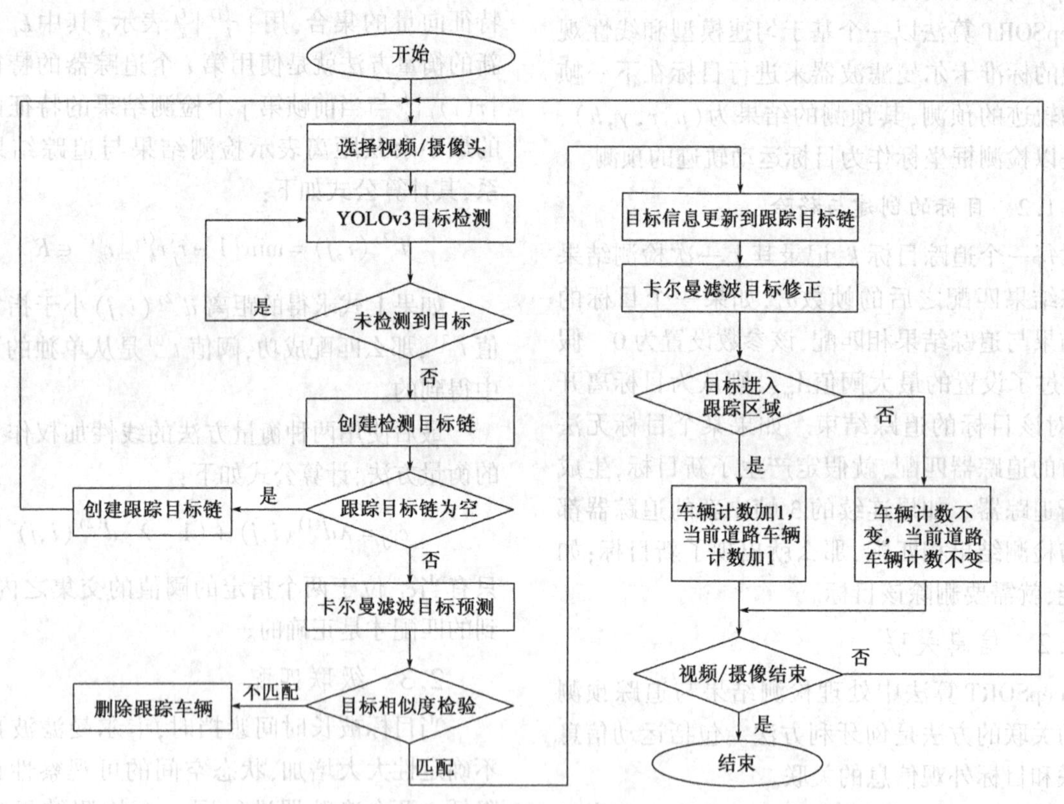

图 3　算法流程图

4　实验结果及分析

4.1　车辆目标识别

为了检验本实验中所用 YOLOv3 模型对视频中车辆的识别精确度,选取了 10 个不同的车流量视频作为检测对象。检测结果表明,模型对不同角度的车辆视频的识别效果较好,准确率高。但在实验中也同样发现了漏检现象。其一是模型对于场景中位置偏僻且尺寸小的车辆图像的检测精度较低。其二是当两辆车车头间距过近时,模型无法准确识别,会将两辆车视为一辆车。这两个问题都属于 YOLOv3 算法本身的不足,需要对 YOLOv3 算法做出改进才能够有所改善。图 4 是从检测视频中截取的画面。

图4 检测画面

4.2 车辆追踪计数

在这一步,DeepSORT算法根据上一步YOLOv3模型得到的检测结果进行检测器与追踪器的关联与匹配,当车辆进入跟踪区域时进行计数,并在检测视频中分别显示当前视频画面中的车辆数和视频累计车辆数。同时采用虚拟线圈法对相同的视频进行检测计数作为对照。表1是两种算法对10个不同车流量视频进行检测计数的实际效果。

表1 计数准确率

车流量视频	实际车辆数(辆)	DeepSORT算法检测结果(辆)	准确率(%)	虚拟线圈法检测结果(辆)	准确率(%)
视频1	49	60	81.6	41	83.7
视频2	25	27	92.6	20	80.0
视频3	70	73	95.9	61	87.1
视频4	26	29	89.6	22	84.6
视频5	28	32	87.5	25	89.3
视频6	53	58	91.3	47	88.7
视频7	40	44	90.9	35	87.5
视频8	29	32	90.1	26	89.7
视频9	31	34	91.1	27	87.0
视频10	43	47	91.5	38	88.4

从表1可以看出,基于YOLOv3和DeepSORT的车流量检测算法对10个不同的车流量视频都有较好的检测效果,平均精度达到了90.21%。高于虚拟线圈法的86.66%平均精度。这10个视频中的车流速度和密度各不相同,拍摄的角度也有差异,这表明本文提出的算法对实际情况的适应性强,在高密度或者高速的情况下也有不错的检测精度,算法的应用价值较大。

同时,在10个检测视频中,基于YOLOv3和DeepSORT的车流量检测算法检测车辆数均大于实际车辆数,经过检查发现,主要原因是当车辆被其他车辆或物体遮挡时,YOLOv3模型无法识别被遮挡的车辆,车辆不再被遮挡时,又再次被检测到,导致DeepSORT算法对被遮挡的车辆进行了两次甚至两次以上的重复计数,因此检测车辆数会大于实际车辆数。视频1的检测精度显著低于其他视频就是因为视频1中存在一个固定的遮挡物,影响了车辆识别的准确性。

而虚拟线圈法的检测结果则与之相反。10 个检测视频中,基于 YOLOv3 和虚拟线圈法的车流量检测算法检测车辆数均小于实际车辆数,出现这种情况主要原因有两个。第一个原因是虚拟线圈法需要在检测画面中绘制一条固定的检测线,当车辆检测框与检测线相交时才开始判断是否计数,而检测线覆盖范围小,在视频开始和结束时出现在视频中但还没有行驶到检测线处的车辆就不会被计数。第二个原因是当多辆车同时通过检测线时,如果车辆横向间距过近,就会有车辆被遮挡导致 YOLO 算法无法识别,检测框消失,无法计数,而 DeepSORT 算法不需要绘制检测线,在整个视频范围内进行跟踪计数,避免了上述情况的发生,因此取得了更好的检测效果。

5　结语

本文给出了一种具有可行性的能帮助人们实时获取交通流量的方法,通过 YOLOv3 模型识别车辆,结合 DeepSORT 算法跟踪计数,改善了传统的车流量检测算法准确率低和鲁棒性差的问题。实验结果表明,基于 YOLOv3 和 DeepSORT 算法的车辆跟踪和计数检测精度高,适应性强,使用简单方便,减轻了人工计数耗费大量人力和时间的问题。检测过程中所绘制的车辆轨迹也为进一步的研究诸如道路异常事件的检测等问题奠定了基础。但本文提出的算法无法分车道,分种类进行车辆计数,且检测精度会因车辆被遮挡而降低,未来还需要进一步的研究和优化。

参考文献

[1] Girshick R, Donahue J, Darrell T, et al. Rich Feature Hierarchies for Accurate Object Detection and Semantic Segmentation [C] // Advances in Neural Information Processing Systems. ICLR Press, 2014:1055-1061.

[2] 宋焕生,张向清,郑宝峰,等. 基于深度学习方法的复杂场景下车辆目标检测[J]. 计算机应用研究,2018,35(04):1270-1273.

[3] Redmon J, Farhadi A. Yolov3: An Incremental Improvement [C] // IEEE Conference on Computer Vision and Pattern Recognition, 2018:85-89.

[4] 袁小平,马绪起,刘赛. 改进 YOLOv3 的行人车辆目标检测算法[J]. 科学技术与工程, 2021,21(08):3192-3198.

[5] 纪筱鹏,魏志强. 基于轮廓特征及扩展 Kalman 滤波的车辆跟踪方法研究[J]. 中国图像图形学报,2011,16(02):267-272.

[6] 陈佳倩,金晅宏,王文远,等. 基于 YOLOv3 和 Deep Sort 的车流量检测[J]. 计量学报, 2021,42(06):718-723.

深度学习军事领域应用综述

段续庭*[1]　周宇康[1]　田大新[1]　张　龙[2]　刘　赫[3]

(1. 北京航空航天大学交通科学与工程学院;2. 军事科学院系统工程研究院;
3. 中国人民解放军军需工业学院)

摘　要　随着深度神经网络研究的突破,深度学习技术得到了快速发展,已经广泛应用于目标检测与识别、图像语义分割与决策规划问题中,并取得了巨大成功。在军事领域,美国国防高级研究计划局针对深度学习技术开展了一系列应用研究,党的十九大也提出“加快军事智能化发展”。本文对深度学习技术在军事目标检测与识别、战场大数据处理与作战决策智能支持三方面的应用进行了总结。并进一步探讨了军事领域深度学习技术应用所面临的重大挑战及未来发展方向,为深度学习在军事领域的进一步研究提供参考。

1. 基金项目:国家自然科学基金资助项目(62173012;U20A20155;61822101);北京市自然科学基金资助项目(L191001);国家自然科学基金中英牛顿高级学者计划(62061130221)。

关键词 深度学习 军事 目标识别 大数据 决策支持系统

0 引言

随着计算机算力的增强,以及深度学习神经网络训练难题的重大突破,深度学习技术取代传统方法,为目标检测与识别带来了新的发展,并在场景语义分割与理解、决策与规划领域中,取得了众多成果[1]。目前深度学习使用的主要算法包括卷积神经网络(Convolutional Neural Networks, CNN)[2]、循环神经网络(Recurrent Neural Network, RNN)[3-4]、生成对抗网络(Generative Adversarial Networks, GAN)等。在国防领域,各类电子军事产品的广泛应用与进步,为深度学习技术在电子终端的部署创造了良好条件。各国军事科研机构纷纷开始相关领域的研究,应用深度学习技术解决军事目标检测、语义识别等问题,以提升各类军事装备的智能化水平。我国国防部发布《抢占人工智能制高点》《让人工智能成为提升国防实力的助推器》,肯定人工智能技术在国防领域的应用潜力,提出"把握人工智能的发展契机",推进国防建设发展。

目前,深度学习在国防领域的应用大多处于研究、试验阶段,相关应用还需要进一步研究与论证。已有一些学者对深度学习在军事领域的应用进行了总结。魏敬和等[11]对深度学习技术的硬件与算法进行了介绍,阐述了深度学习技术在雷达与红外图像及声呐信号处理中的应用。朱丰等[12]基于深度学习在大数据处理中的应用,对深度学习技术在战场态势评估中的现有研究进展及其优势进行了综述。张晓海等[13]聚焦军事决策支持系统,对深度学习技术的发展沿革、经典模型及深度学习在决策支持系统中的应用与挑战进行了系统综述。以上工作都是对军事领域某一特定方面深度学习技术应用的介绍,缺乏对近年来整体情况的综述。

本文将深度学习在国防领域的应用划分为军事目标自动识别、军事大数据挖掘与处理、指挥决策智能辅助三个主要方面,并对每一方面的研究背景、主要成果及国内外研究进展内容进行了综述。另外,针对军事领域信息环境的特殊性及深度学习算法的技术限制,本文阐述了深度学习在军事领域应用面临的挑战与发展趋势。深度学习技术已经越来越成为军事领域研究的热点,在国防领域机械化、信息化的浪潮结束后,国防智能化革命已经在地平线处显现了其曙光。

1 深度学习在军事目标识别中的应用

识别敌方军事目标(图1)是作战的前提,快速、准确地识别各类型目标能够使己方在战斗中获得主动权,对智能决策、数据处理具有重要价值。深度学习技术通过多层卷积神经网络学习识别模式,使得计算机能够有效提取到图像、语音等抽象材料的特征,从而解决许多目标识别问题。

图1 军事目标识别示例

目前使用深度学习技术进行目标识别的方法主要有两种,一种是端到端式:直接输入图片,使用端到端网络回归出含有特定目标的概率和目标的具体位置(四个坐标);另一种是基于区域的算法,先提取出可能包含物体的区域,再进行边框(Bound Box)回归,回归出物体在图像中的具体位置。基于区域的算法一般都包含区域提名(提取候选区域)、特征提取和分类回归(分类器识别,边框回归)三个步骤,具体顺序与方法根据不同算法变化。总的来说,端到端方法计算量小,识别速度更快,而基于区域的算法应用更广,精度更高,结果更准确。图2为深度学习目标识别的一般流程。

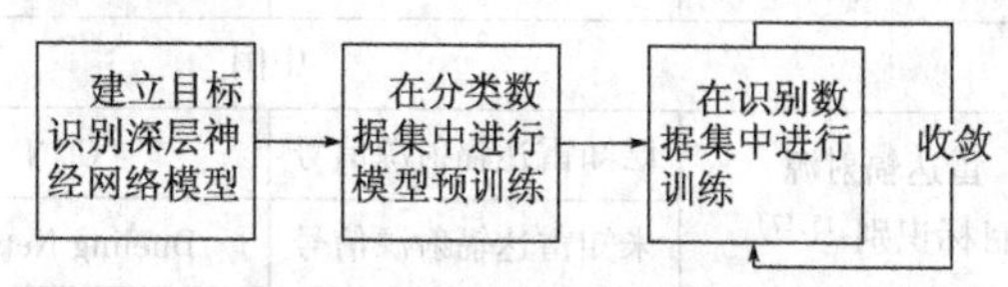

图2 深度学习目标识别一般流程

在军事领域,世界上许多国家都已经注意到深度学习技术在目标检测方面的潜力。美国国防部高级计划局(DARPA)[14]开展的TRACE项目,旨在针对基于飞机的雷达传感器,利用深度学习技术完成军事目标识别[15]。同时在满足飞行器平台算力与能量限制的情况下,实现系统的低识别功耗与低虚警率,并能利用有限的训练数据学习。该项目的目的在于使用深度学习和迁移学习等智能算法解决传统基于飞行平台识别系统的高功耗与高虚警率问题。2010 年 3 月,DAPRA 启动"思想之眼"(Mind's Eye)项目[16],旨在(通过深度学习算法)为机器建立视觉上的仿生智能,并赋予其处理视频信息的能力。

国内开展军事目标自动识别研究较晚,将深度学习技术结合其中的步伐也落后于西方国家。但近年来,国内也有一批学者和研究人员致力于将深度学习技术应用于军事目标识别领域,并取得了一定的成果。冷鹏飞等针对雷达辐射源的识别,对已知辐射源信号设计了一种基于 CNN 的识别方法,对未知辐射源使用 Dueling Network 构造深度强化学习模型进行识别,对两种信号均实现了 98% 以上的识别率[17]。然而,深度学习的良好表现很大程度上依赖于训练数据集的尺度,当能用于训练的样本很少时,其效果往往差强人意。针对以上限制,陈龙等设计了一种基于 GAN 与深度森林算法相结合的方法[18]。该算法首先使用 GAN 与传统方法进行样本扩展与优化,之后使用深度森林算法从扩展后的样本获得识别模型。测试表明,在样本数据集较少的情况下,该方法对战斗机目标的识别率仍能达到 78.4%,优于许多传统深度学习算法。

以上是针对特定目标的识别研究,在综合识别方面,中北大学的马奇锋[19]针对 YOLOv3 网络,对其中 NMS 算法置信度直接置零的缺陷进行改进,提出了一种针对军事目标的改进 YOLOv3 算法,与 YOLOv3 算法相比,该算法在测试中表现出了更好的性能(表 1)。

改进 YOLOv3 算法与原算法性能对比　表 1

类　别	算法	
	YOLOv3	改进 YOLOv3
装甲车辆	0.842	0.864
战舰	0.945	0.963
战斗机	0.960	0.988
直升机	0.954	0.976
导弹	0.911	0.932
士兵	0.919	0.942
坦克	0.821	0.843

袁秋壮等人使用深度学习技术构建了一套基于星载 SAR 数据的目标识别系统[20]。在训练完成后,使用该系统对 MSTAR 数据库包含的 11 类军事目标进行识别测试,该系统对 ZSU 型自行高炮类目标的识别准确率达到 99.64%,11 类目标识别的总体准确率 96.29%。

表 2 所示为基于深度学习的军事目标识别系统。

基于深度学习的军事目标识别系统　表 2

目标识别项目	数据来源	深度学习方法	识别目标类型	
美国			目标	
TRACE	雷达探测数据	—	多类型军事目标	低识别功耗;低虚警率;低所需样本量
Mind's Eye	可见光图像/视频数据	—	—	赋予机器处理视频信息的能力
MAVEN	视频数据	—	多目标类型识别(如人员、车辆等)	针对无人机探测视频,进行综合目标识别
中国				识别准确率(%)
雷达辐射源目标识别[15,17]	已知雷达辐射源信号	CNN	雷达辐射源	98.28
	未知雷达辐射源信号	Dueling Network		98.13
无人机多目标识别[19]	可见光图像	CNN(改进 YOLOv3)	多类型军事目标	—
SAR 星上识别系统[20]	SAR 图像	CNN	综合目标识别	96.29%(平均识别率)
俄罗斯				
空天目标智能识别系统	雷达数据	—	空天飞行器目标识别与跟踪	—

就目前成果而言,我国仍缺少成熟的军事目标识别综合系统,目前大多数研究在功能上着眼于解决某一类军事目标识别需求,在应用层次上着眼于辅助人员完成任务。已经进行的研究大多着眼于针对单类型传感器数据识别较小型号范围内的军事目标,缺少一类能够融合多传感器数据进行大范围军事目标识别的成熟系统。

2 深度学习在军事大数据中的应用

军事大数据泛指与宏大战场环境、复杂军事系统和军事安全相关的大规模数据集以及与之紧密相关的存储、处理、分析和运用等技术与军事应用的集合[21]。有效搜集、处理军事大数据,是穿透战场信息不透明困境,洞悉战场态势对比,做出最优决策的基础。Viktor Mayer Schönberger 在《大数据时代》中提出,大数据具有"4V"特性,即规模性(Volume)、多样性(Varitey)、高速性(Velocity)、价值性(Value)[22]。而相比民用大数据,军事大数据数据质量更差,价值密度更低,且无论是获取还是转存处理都涉及到网络攻防与信息安全。因此,军事大数据分析的难度远超民用大数据,需要使用新方法新理论来解决以上问题。近年来兴起的深度学习技术因其对数据内在规律与表示特征的强大学习能力,表现出解决军事大数据所面临难题的强大潜力。

图 3 为军事大数据平台架构,图 4 为军事大数据搜集流程。

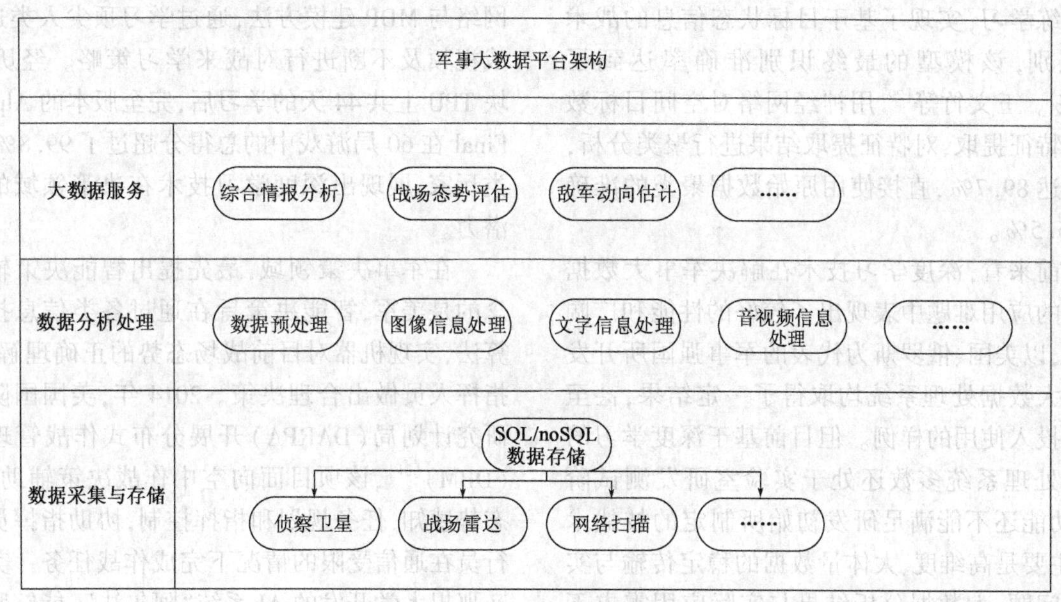

图 3 军事大数据平台架构

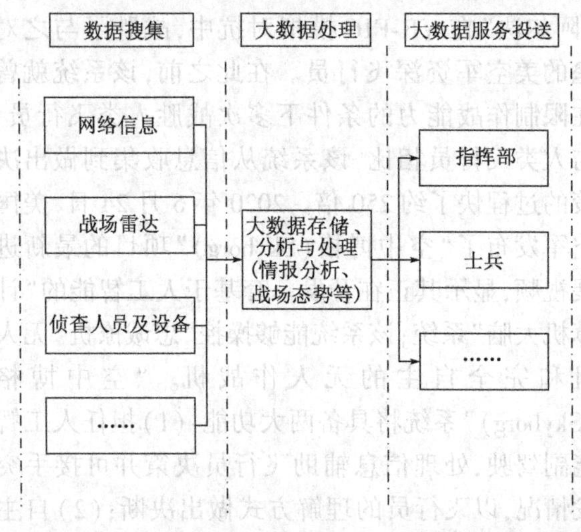

图 4 军事大数据搜集应用流程

2012 年,白宫发布《大数据研究和发展倡议》,倡议以国防部门为首,推进大数据搜集与分析技术。2019 年,美国又发布《DoD Cloud Strategy》,提出利用机器学习技术,实现数据智能。

2010 年 8 月,DARPA 启动"Insight"[23]项目,基于战场环境的多种数据来源,综合处理多种类型的数据,有效识别战场威胁目标,综合评估态势对比。2012 年,DARPA 启动的 DEFT(Deep Exploration and Filtering of Text)[24]项目针对作战过程中产生的文本材料,利用深度学习技术,对其进行识别处理。此项目将用于情报分析与作战规划。俄罗斯发布的《俄联邦科技发展战略》中,将大数据与机器学习作为优先发展方向。2016 年,俄军宣布开始研究战场大数据分析技术,并以此建立信息指挥系统,该系统已于 2019 年底向集团军等单位配发[25]。

在国内,深度学习技术在军事大数据处理中的潜力越来越得到重视。国内相关单位也逐步开展了关于这方面的研究。孙志军等人首先通过无监督预训练对已有数据进行处理,之后采用基于深度学习的算法进一步提取数据特征[26],实现了对小样本数据集的有效特征提取。张乐等使用深度学习中的自编码神经网络实现武器系统评估指标的简化[27],在不显著影响指标体系评估效能的条件下,大大简化了效能指标评价体系,明显降低后续评估工作复杂度。欧微等[28]利用基于 SAE 的自动识别模型,使用某作战仿真系统空战数据进行训练学习,实现了基于目标状态信息的战术意图识别,该模型的最终识别准确率达到了 82.65%。王文竹等[29]用神经网络对空间目标数据进行特征提取,对特征提取结果进行聚类分析,准确率达 89.7%,直接使用原始数据聚类的准确率为 45.5%。

目前来看,深度学习技术在解决军事大数据所面临的应用难题中表现出了较好的性能和广阔的潜力,以美国、俄罗斯为代表的军事强国所开发的战场大数据处理系统均取得了一定结果,甚至有已经投入使用的样例。但目前基于深度学习的大数据处理系统多数还处于实验室研发测试阶段,其功能还不能满足研发初始所制定的技战术目标,主要是高维度、大体量数据的稳定传输与实时处理问题,大数据分析结果与实际应用需求不匹配的问题以及大数据与精准作战数据无法混合运用的问题。此外,就我国而言,大数据的应用主要着眼于某一具体领域或问题,如武器系统评估[27]、战术意图识别[28]等,还没有较成熟的综合军事大数据处理系统。

3　深度学习在决策支持中的应用

战场决策是指挥领域的核心,是指对影响战场态势与敌我力量对比的关键问题做出决断。优秀的决策必须全方面考虑战场内外信息,并考虑到敌我信息不对称的情况,实现决策收益最大化。曾经,合理的战场决策是人类名将的专属,但随着信息时代的到来、深度学习技术的突破使得机器在智能决策领域也显示出巨大潜力。

基于深度学习的决策系统最先在棋牌游戏和电子竞技领域进行试验,取得了突破性进展,并且已经涌现了一批较成熟的智能决策模型。AlphaGo[30]因接连击败人类顶尖围棋高手李世石与柯洁而受到大众的广泛关注,其核心技术是将深度学习与传统的蒙特卡洛树搜索方法结合,使 AI 的蒙特卡洛树大量剪枝,只搜索较优良的下法。2020 年,由中央军委装备部主办的“谋略方寸 · 联合智胜”AI 指挥系统挑战赛开幕,赛事针对真实岛屿作战情景,以 AI 模型作为博弈双方,进行包括目标侦察、电磁对抗和火力协同打击等复杂作战行动的决策规划,模拟攻防双方进行对抗。Google 旗下的 DeepMind 公司与美国电子游戏公司暴雪娱乐共同研制的 AlphaStar 使用深层神经网络与 MDP 建模方法,通过学习顶尖人类选手对战视频及不断进行对战来学习策略。经历在 32 块 TPU 上共 44 天的学习后,完全版本的 AlphaStar Final 在 60 局游戏中的总得分超过了 99.8% 的人类玩家,展现出深度学习技术在决策领域的非凡潜力。

在军事决策领域,最先提出智能决策辅助概念的是美军,智能决策旨在通过各类信息技术与算法,实现机器对目前战场态势的正确理解,辅助指挥人员做出合理决策。2014 年,美国国防预先研究计划局(DARPA)开展分布式作战管理研究(DBM)[31],该项目面向空中作战决策辅助,进行态势感知,任务规划和指挥控制,协助指挥员与飞行员在通信受限的情况下完成作战任务。美国辛辛那提大学开发的 AI 系统“阿尔法”,能够胜任空军飞行编队僚机的智能控制任务。2016 年 6 月,“阿尔法”在 VR-F16 模拟对抗中,战胜了与之对垒的美空军资深飞行员。在此之前,该系统就曾在限制作战能力的条件下多次战胜人类飞行员。与人类飞行员相比,该系统从信息收集到做出决策的过程快了约 250 倍。2020 年 6 月 24 日,美国空军发布了“空中博格(Skyborg)”项目的最新进展视频,显示其正在开发一套基于人工智能的“计算机大脑”系统;该系统能够操控“忠诚僚机”无人机和完全自主的无人作战机。“空中博格(Skyborg)”系统将具备两大功能:(1)担任人工智能副驾驶,处理信息辅助飞行员决策并可接手突发情况,以飞行员的理解方式做出决断;(2)自主驾驶无人机。可以集成在低成本消耗性无人机中,人类飞行员只负责无人机的投送。在国内,深度学习也被广泛应用于智能决策支持系统中,并且涌现了一批比较成熟的决策辅助系统。潘耀宗等[32]使用深度Q网络(Deep Q-Network,DQN)构建角度捕获网络与距离捕获网络,使用双网络协同控制战机作战机动,并对其进行了计算机仿真,机动成功率达到83.2%。张宏鹏等[33]提出了一种基于深度神经网络(DNN)的战机机动决策模型,从给定272160种飞行样本训练决策网络,以使其能够从给定机动动作库选出一种机动动作使决策最优,仿真实验显示,相比基于统计学的决策方法,该决策方法用时缩短9ms,并在多次均等态势对抗中取得胜利。深度学习方法还可用于作战预案分析。赵晓晓等[34]使用深度学习技术进行作战任务规划合理性分析,最终建立的深度信念网络模型的均方根误差和平均绝对误差均小于0.01,具备较强的分析与泛化能力。

深度学习决策支持系统的优势在于其强大的数据分析能力、多线程工作能力与自我学习增强能力。与传统方法和其他机器学习方法相比较,深度学习算法在解决辅助决策问题中具有种种优势,包括善于解决非线性问题、能有效提取大数据特征、迁移能力强等。金欣等[35]将指控控制问题分解为多个子问题,并基于不同的学习方法,对各个子问题的适用性进行了分析。

军事智能指挥决策将具有广阔的发展空间及研究前景。但当前的智能决策系统决策正确率仍然偏低,常常不能有效处理态势理解、决策取舍等问题,在目前的技术水平下,深度学习决策支持系统主要是用于辅助人、启发人,提高决策效率,避免低级错误。表3列出了几种深度学习决策辅助系统。

几种深度学习决策辅助系统 表3

决策支持系统	基础网络	主要用途	达成成果
美国			
DBM	—	空中作战决策辅助	—
阿尔法 AI	—	战机副驾驶/僚机智能飞行员	完成虚拟仿真测试,并在VR对抗中战胜空军飞行员
SkyBorg	—	智能副驾驶+无人机自主控制	完成无人机概念模型及软件原型设计
我国			
战机机动决策模型[30]	DQN	战机向攻击区域机动决策	机动成功率83.2%
战机机动决策模型[31]	DNN	战斗机空战中机动动作决策	平均决策时间0.063s,与统计学对比方法相比快9ms
作战辅助决策模型[34]	CNN	根据战场数据寻找最优作战决策	建立了用于决策的深层CNN模型

4 深度学习应用挑战及发展方向

在军事领域深度学习技术主要应用于目标识别、大数据处理、决策支持等方面,并越来越成为领域内的研究热点。但由于军事领域问题普遍具有信息来源复杂、有价值样本稀少、规则边界不明确、信息安全性与算法鲁棒性要求高等特点,深度学习技术的应用主要处于实验室测试阶段,距离满足军事装备要求的稳定性、准确率、便捷性、低成本等还有一定距离。

4.1 军事目标识别领域

在军事目标识别领域。深度学习技术的应用面临着如下挑战:

(1)识别模型训练方面存在高价值样本的稀缺性。

深度学习方法的突出优势根基于大量的训练样本,然而,在军事实际应用中,受限于侦查手段及敌方保密处理,军事目标样本数据集往往较小,价值密度也较低[37]。这就对军事目标识别算法的学习效率和鲁棒性提出了较高的要求。

(2)识别任务执行方面存在目标识别的大小和数目问题。

在军事问题的处理中,因为战场形势复杂多变,战场环境也随之呈现出多样性和复杂性,这给目标识别任务提高了难度:一方面是由于战场的广阔性、非典型性,目标识别的背景可能出现多种情况,如丛林、雪地、山地、训练营地等等;另一方面是由于战场交战及侦查的高风险性,侦查手段及时间都受限,对于所得到的目标识别数据,所要识别的目标可能在其中所占像素点/数据空间很少。

(3)识别平台方面受到平台算力限制。

基于深度学习技术的目标识别系统大多搭载

于有人或无人作战及侦查平台上,如战斗机、无人侦察机、卫星等。但这些平台的硬件装载空间与所耗能量都受到限制,使得其计算能力不足。这一方面导致目标识别系统只能在外部训练好后部署在相应平台上,不能实现训练学习-任务执行一体化,另一方面也使得目标识别系统处理图像等数据的能力受限,智能识别并分类多种不同物体的能力不足,如美军无人机就曾在伊拉克等地多次发生误击平民事故。

面对以上挑战,基于深度学习的目标识别技术在未来的发展中,着眼的研究重点可能在于:一是解决在小样本数据集情况下深度学习网络训练的准确性及鲁棒性问题;二是研究深度神经网络优化方法,降低其所占用的计算资源,降低在算力受限情况下目标识别的时间;三是目前目标识别系统主要是基于单一数据来源对某一类型战斗目标的识别,未来将向多元传感器信息融合与识别方向发展,并且能够同时识别多种类型的军事目标。

4.2　军事大数据领域

在军事大数据分析领域,随着现代军事数据在体量和维度上的急速扩大,传统基于简单线性方式的数据分析与处理技术已经不能满足需求,深度学习技术因其在非线性问题解决上的卓越性能及对抽象特征的良好提取能力而越来越在军事大数据处理领域受到重视。但军事大数据本身及其服务具有种种限制,也为深度学习的应用带来了以下挑战:

(1)军事领域大数据往往带有多个维度,以准确描述所处领域的种种特点,但高维数据的处理要求处理单元具备极高的算力。卷积神经网络能够处理高维数据,研究人员使用卷积神经网络在256×256RGB的ImageNet数据集上得到了理想的结果[38],但卷积神经网络的问题在于其神经元连接简化指的仅仅是同一空间区域内的神经元,并且越接近网络高层,图像的分辨率也就越低。未来高维数据处理将是深度学习技术的一个重点探索方向,如何实现高维数据处理的快速性、准确性、完整性是其核心问题。

(2)军事领域大数据也包含多个种类,大数据的主要特点之一即是其多样性,目前深度学习算法在整合处理多来源数据中已经有了一定的成果,例如,Ngiam等成功地使用深度学习技术从音频与视频两类数据中进行表征学习[39]。但对于不同来源数据的冲突处理和有效融合问题,目前研究涉及较少;此外,目前的深度学习算法主要在双模式(双数据来源:音频与视频)下进行测试,但实际应用中数据来源远多于两个,在未来应用中,实现对多来源数据的有效融合与理解将是发展趋势之一。

(3)军事领域大数据相比一般大数据,具有低价值性、不确定性、不完全性,并且常常要面临信息安全问题,这些特性要求深度学习算法更加高效、稳定、精确,且能够识破虚假信息的欺骗行为。同时,军事大数据为保证信息安全,每次读取都需要经过"加密-解密"过程,这大大增加了处理时延,对算法设计与计算能力提出了很高的要求。

4.3　军事决策支持领域

在军事决策领域,一方面所获得的军事数据具有不完全性,对战双方都不能对作战态势有全面了解,一方面各类决策取舍难于用量化指标来衡量,这都成为智能决策支持系统发展的障碍。基于深度学习的独立智能决策系统如AlphaGo、AlphaStar、CASIA-先知等已经在棋类竞技、电子即时策略竞技游戏及兵棋推演等项目中取得了成果,但真实战争所面临的决策问题无论是在处理数据维度还是在决策难度上都远远超过棋类竞技和兵棋推演游戏。将深度学习技术用于军事决策支持还面临着许多挑战:

(1)深度学习模型的认知智能问题。作战指挥和棋牌竞技有着本质的区别,一场战斗或战役的得失不是简单的吃子失子,决策的最优价值衡量也不是简单的得分失分。在有限的样本下,如何让机器通过学习真正理解战场态势对比与决策价值内核,将是决策支持领域未来的一个重要发展方向。此外,深度学习目前接近于"黑匣子"状态,模型可以做出决策,但无法向用户解释决策的依据,研究人员也无法以人类思维解释其来由,这就大大降低了决策的可信度和参考性。

(2)不完全信息下的博弈问题解决。目前深度学习主要应用于信息完全、规则一致的情境,在此假设下,深度学习技术在决策问题中取得了一系列成果,但对于不完全信息条件下的博弈问题,深度学习成果较少。DeepMind公司在试验AlphaStar的过程中发现,一旦引入游戏中的"战争迷雾"设置(即每一方只能看见己方单位与建筑视野之内的区域),AI 的决策就显得呆板而僵化,后来,DeepMind 通过更新算法和延长训练时间解决了"战争迷雾"造成的决策信息差问题。同样,在现实战争中敌人的动向、资源等很可能是未知的,他们所能采取的策略也更加复杂、更难以预测[38]。因此,应用与创新深度学习算法,使其能出色解决不完全信息下的复杂博弈问题,将是未来的重要研究方向。

5 结语

近年来,计算机及通信技术快速发展,军事领域智能化浪潮方兴未艾,在十九大报告中的"全面推进国防和军队现代化"部分,出现了"加快军事智能化发展,提高基于网络信息体系的联合作战能力"这一重要论述。战争对信息技术与即时处理的依赖性前所未有,这一方面为深度学习技术的应用提供了巨大机遇。深度学习技术应用多种深层神经网络,能够对传统算法难以处理的抽象材料(如图片、语音、文字等)进行特征提取与辨识,从而降低军事信息处理所消耗的人力物力与时间成本,提高军事装备的智能化水平。另一方面,这也对其鲁棒性、快速性与学习的效率提出了更高的要求,如要求深度学习算法能够解决小样本情况下的学习性能问题、不完全信息下的决策问题等。文章以目标自动识别、军事数据处理、作战决策综合辅助等系统为代表,从问题背景、研究进展、国内外研究对比等多个方面对其进行了分析,概述了研究中面临的关键问题,并指出了其解决方向,可为国防领域深度学习技术的应用研究提供参考。

参考文献

[1] Shinde PP, Shah S. A Review of Machine Learning and Deep Learning Applications[C]. 2018 Fourth International Conference on Computing Communication Control and Automation (ICCUBEA). IEEE, 2019.

[2] LeCun, Boser, Denker, et al. Backpropagation Applied to Handwritten Zip Code Recognition [J]. Neural Computation, 1989.

[3] Hochreiter S, Schmidhuber J. Long Short-Term Memory[J]. Neural Computation, 1997, 9(8): 1735-1780.

[4] Schuster M, Paliwal K K. Bidirectional Recurrent Neural Networks[J]. IEEE Transactions on Signal Processing, 1997, 45(11): 2673-2681.

[5] Good Fellow J, Pouget-Abadie J, Mizra M, et al. Generative Adversarial Nets [C]. International Conference on Neural Information Processing Systems Montreal: MIT Press, 2014: 2672-2680.

[6] Wang X, Yang R, Lu Y, et al. Military Named Entity Recognition Method Based on Deep Learning[C]. 2018 5th IEEE International Conference on Cloud Computing and Intelligence Systems (CCIS). IEEE, 2018.

[7] Hiippala T. Recognizing Military Vehicles in Social Media Images Using Deep Learning[C]. Proceedings of the 2017 IEEE International Conference on Intelligence and Security Informatics. IEEE, 2017.

[8] Belloni C, Aouf N, Balleri A, et al. Pose-informed Deep Learning Method for SAR ATR [J]. Post-Print, 2020.

[9] 中华人民共和国国防部. 抢占人工智能技术发展制高点[EB/OL]. (2019-7-25)[2020-10-10]. http://www.mod.gov.cn/jmsd/2019-07/25/content4846531.htm.

[10] 中华人民共和国国防部. 让人工智能成为提升国防实力的助推器[EB/OL]. (2019-7-25)[2020-10-10]. http://www.mod.gov.cn/jmsd/2019-07/25/content_4846531.htm

[11] 魏敬和, 林军. 深度学习算法、硬件技术及其在未来军事上的应用[J]. 电子与封装, 2019, 19(12): 1-6+22.

[12] 朱丰, 胡晓峰. 基于深度学习的战场态势评估综述与研究展望[J]. 军事运筹与系统工程, 2016, 30(03): 22-27.

[13] 张晓海, 操新文. 基于深度学习的军事智能决策支持系统[J]. 指挥控制与仿真, 2018, 40(02): 1-7.

[14] 易比一, 黄世亮, 雷二庆. DARPA 在国防科技创新链中的定位[J]. 科研管理, 2017, 38(S1): 297-300.

[15] DARPA. Target recognition and adaption in contested environments (TRACE)[R]. DARPA-BAA-15- 09. Virginia: DARPA, 2014. 12.01.

[16] DARPA. Mind's Eye[EB/OL]. (2018-02-28)[2020-10-10]. https://web.archive.org/web/20121014043008/http://www.darpa.mil/Our_Work/I2O/Programs/Minds_Eye.aspx.

[17] 冷鹏飞. 基于深度学习的雷达辐射源识别技术[D]. 扬州:扬州船用电子仪器研究所,2018.

[18] 陈龙,张峰,蒋升. 小样本条件下基于深度森林学习模型的典型军事目标识别方法[J]. 中国电子科学研究院学报,2019,14(03):232-237.

[19] 马奇锋. 基于深度学习的军事目标检测技术研究[D]. 太原:中北大学,2020.

[20] 袁秋壮,魏松杰,罗娜. 基于深度学习神经网络的SAR星上目标识别系统研究[J]. 上海航天,2017,34(05):46-53.

[21] 战晓苏. 军事大数据现状与展望[J]. 军事文摘,2020(09):57-61.

[22] Mayer-Schonberger V, Cukier K. Big data: a revolution that will transform how we live, work, and think[M]. [S. l.]: John Murray Publishers,2013.

[23] DARPA. Insight[EB/OL]. (2017-10-13)[2020-10-10]. https://www.darpa.mil/program/insight.

[24] DARPA. Deep Exploration and Filtering of Text(DEFT)[EB/OL]. (2017-9-25)[2017-09-25]. https://www.darpa.mil/program/deep-exploration-and-filtering-of-text.

[25] 刘智慧,张泉灵. 大数据技术研究综述[J]. 浙江大学学报(工学版),2014,48(6):957-972.

[26] 孙志军,薛磊,许阳明. 基于深度学习的边际Fisher分析提取算法[J]. 电子与信息学报,201 3,35(4):805-811.

[27] 张乐,刘忠,张建强,等. 基于自编码神经网络的装备体系评估指标约简方法[J]. 中南大学学报,2013,44(10):4130-4137.

[28] 欧微,柳少军,贺筱媛. 基于时序特征编码的目标战术意图识别算法[J]. 指挥控制与仿真,2016,38(6):36-41.

[29] 王文竹,李智,来嘉哲,等. 基于卷积神经网络的空间目标特性聚类分析研究[J]. 指挥与控制学报,2020,6(02):141-146.

[30] Chen J X. The Evolution of Computing: AlphaGo[J]. Computing in Science &Engineering, 2016,18(4):4-7.

[31] DARPA. Distributed battle management program[R]. DARPA-BAA-14-17. Virginia: DARPA,2014.02.11.

[32] 潘耀宗,张健,杨海涛,等. 战机自主作战机动双网络智能决策方法[J]. 哈尔滨工业大学学报,2019,51(11):144-151.

[33] 张宏鹏,黄长强,轩永波,等. 基于深度神经网络的无人作战飞机自主空战机动决策[J]. 兵工学报,2020,41(8):1613-1622.

[34] 赵晓晓,肖玉杰,马吟龙,等. 基于深度学习的作战任务规划合理性分析[J]. 指挥与控制学报,2019,5(02):153-158.

[35] 金欣. 指挥控制智能化问题分解研究[J]. 指挥与控制学报,2018,4(01):64-68.

[36] 国海峰,侯满义,张庆杰,等. 基于统计学原理的无人作战飞机鲁棒机动决策[J]. 兵工学报,2017,38(1):160-167.

[37] 罗荣,王亮,肖玉杰,等. 深度学习技术在军事领域应用[J]. 指挥控制与仿真,2020,42(01):1-5.

[38] Hinton G E, Zemel R S. Autoencoders, Minimum Description Length and Helmholtz Free Energy[J]. Advances in neural information processing systems,1993,6.

[39] JNgiam, A Khosla, M Kim, J Nam, et al. Multimodal deep learning[C]. in Proc. 28th Int. Conf. Mach. Learn., Bellevue, WA, USA,2011.

L3 自动驾驶接管操纵行为研究

潘梦妞　张子号　曲彦菘　刘　钦　李振龙*
(北京工业大学，城市建设学部)

摘　要　为挖掘安全的接管操纵动作，需要确定 L3 自动驾驶接管过程中驾驶员操纵行为的差异性。根据非驾驶相关任务(NDRT)、接管请求时间(TORT)、接管场景设计 2×2×4 驾驶模拟实验，招募 42 名驾驶员参与。基于驾驶模拟器采集驾驶员行为数据，反应时间为系统发出接管请求至驾驶员发生动作的时间，定义反应时间的最小值作为接管第一操纵，按时间顺序排列反应时间获得接管操纵序列。通过接管第一操纵和接管操纵序列研究接管操纵行为，使用无序多元 Logit 模型分析不同属性(年龄、驾龄和性别)的驾驶员接管操纵行为的差异性以及 NDRT、TORT、接管场景对接管操纵行为的影响。结果表明，驾龄($p=0.000$)、接管请求时间($p=0.005$)及接管场景($p=0.005$)对接管第一操纵的选择有显著影响，驾龄($p=0.001$)及接管场景($p=0.000$)对接管操纵序列有显著影响。研究结果可为安全接管操纵行为模式的发现奠定基础，为驾驶员接管培训提供支持，提高接管成功率及道路安全性。

关键词　驾驶员接管行为　无序多元 Logit 模型　非驾驶相关任务　接管请求时间　接管操纵序列

0　引言

车辆自动化水平的提升，可减轻驾驶员的驾驶任务。然而由于技术和立法的限制，未来很长一段时间，车辆控制权将由驾驶员和车辆共同掌控，即 L3(有条件自动驾驶)级。在 L3 级自动驾驶中，车辆在大多数情况下可独立行驶，驾驶员无须实时关注驾驶环境，但当出现系统无法应对的情况时，系统将提前请求驾驶员接管车辆控制权，驾驶员需要及时接管车辆。如果驾驶员无法安全接管车辆，很有可能导致交通事故。为了挖掘安全的接管行为模式，须确定不同驾驶员接管操纵行为的差异性以及影响因素。

国内外学者研究发现多种因素导致驾驶员行为存在差异，而驾驶行为的差异导致不同程度的驾驶风险。Wang 等利用 11 个驾驶参数，基于 k-means 算法分类纵向驾驶行为，结果发现纵向驾驶行为可以通过驾驶风格与驾驶技能分类[1]。Jade 记录了 108 名驾驶员的自然驾驶数据，分析发现男性的制动时间比女性晚，年轻驾驶员的刹车时间比年长驾驶员晚[2]。Korber 等研究了不同条件下 L3 自动驾驶中年龄对接管行为的影响，发现年长车手制动更频繁，制动更猛[3]。Nikiforo 调查了年龄和性别对事故倾向影响的统计学意义，结果表明驾龄和性别对驾驶安全有显著影响[4]。侯海晶等分析了不同风格的驾驶员驾驶行为参数的区别，结果表明驾驶风格更激进的驾驶员更容易产生急加速、急减速行为[5]。张梦航发现在任何风险场景下，经验组都能够更早地感知到危险，从而提早采取减速措施[6]。吕能超等人在研究不同驾驶员在追尾事故中的驾驶行为特征时，发现女性驾驶人更倾向于紧急制动，熟练驾驶员制动时间更长，制动过程更加平稳[7]。房曰荣发现不同年龄段驾驶员在行驶速度与操控频次上呈现显著性差异，从制动触发次数看，青年组的操控频次更多[8]。庄明科等发现激进型人格的人更容易出现攻击性驾驶行为，而具备安全驾驶习惯的驾驶员更少出现风险驾驶行为[9]。Bryan 等发现，随着认知负荷的增加，驾驶员会默认地降低对驾驶任务的注意，并降低加速踏板压力导致减速，且年龄较大的驾驶员行车更加保守[10]。鲁光泉等使用统计学方法分析 29 名年轻驾驶员的接管反应特性，发现场景中障碍物的出现会显著增加制动比例[11]。高岩等将次任务分为不同等级，发现分心程度的增加导致制动接管比例增加[12]。国内外学者研究不同驾驶员行为时，通常通过量化制动次数或经验性的描述，且固定单一外部变量。但驾驶员的行为习惯不止由一个驾驶动作表征，本文

1. 基金项目：国家自然科学基金项目(10038002201801)。

对多个驾驶行为进行描述统计,且综合多项外界因素。

本研究的目的是分析不同驾驶员接管操纵行为的差异性以及 TORT、NDRT 和接管场景对接管操纵行为的影响。首先,利用驾驶模拟器开展实验,采集驾驶员的操纵数据。其次,使用无序多元 Logit 模型分析不同驾驶员接管操纵行为的统计学意义以及 TORT、NDRT 和接管场景对接管操纵行为的影响。研究结果可为发现安全接管行为模式奠定基础,为驾驶员接管培训提供支持,提高接管成功率。

1　自动驾驶接管实验

1.1　试验设计

1.1.1　NDRT

当处于自动驾驶状态时,驾驶员无须实时关注驾驶环境,将有选择性地从事非驾驶相关任务。本实验选择娱乐任务(看娱乐视频)和工作任务(发微信语音)作为非驾驶相关任务,均在手机上完成。

1.1.2　接管场景

实验道路按风格分为内蒙古草原高速以及北京城郊高速两种,总长为 22km;按驾驶模式分为自动驾驶路段、接管路段和人工驾驶路段。设计 4 种典型的自动驾驶接管场景:主线接管、团雾接管、事故接管以及匝道接管,为了探究交通流对驾驶员的影响,另增设稳定流的团雾接管。

1.1.3　TORT

TORT 是系统发出接管请求到系统边界的时间(Time to Collision,TTC),代表系统预留给驾驶员接管的时间[13]。

当系统向驾驶员发出接管请求时,驾驶员需要在系统预留时间内接管车辆控制权。本文为对比分析不同 TORT 对驾驶员接管操纵行为的影响,将 TORT 设定为 5s、10s。

1.1.4　接管请求方式

基于华为平板开发人机交互界面(Human-Machine Interface,HMI)提供视觉和听觉结合的接管请求方式,共设计如图 1 所示的 4 种 HMI 界面。

1.2　实验对象

本次实验共招募 42 名驾驶员,所有被试者视力、听力正常,并都持有驾照,均按照要求完成实验。驾驶员信息如表 1 所示。

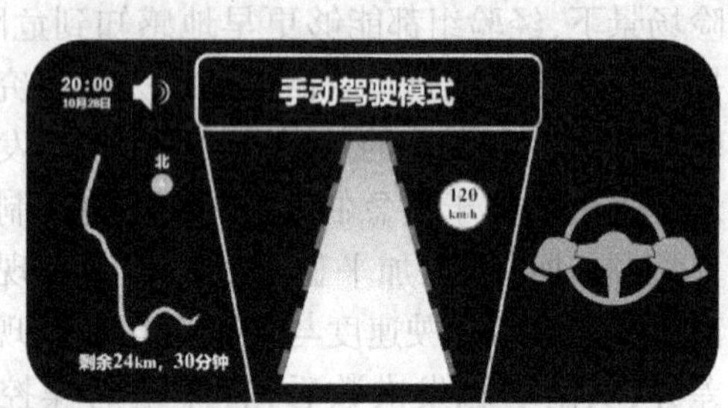

a)手动驾驶模式-自动驾驶功能不可用

b)手动驾驶模式-自动驾驶功能可用

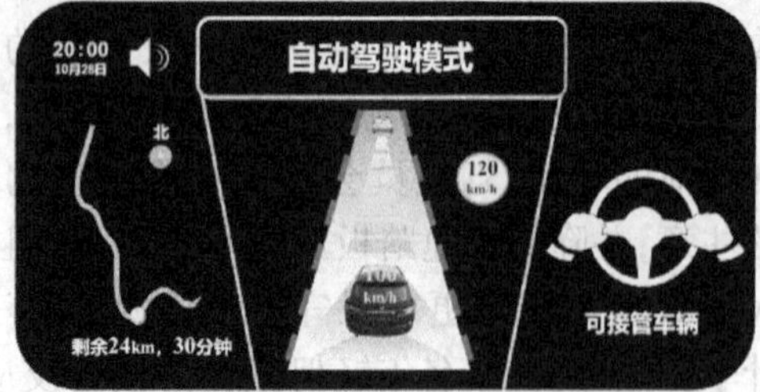

c)自动驾驶模式-自动驾驶功能已激活

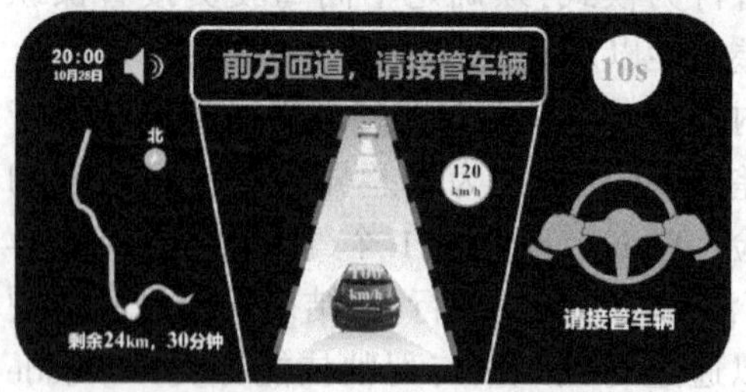

d)自动驾驶模式-请求接管预警

图 1　HMI 界面设计

驾 驶 员 信 息　　表 1

基本特征	指 标 值	数量(人)	比例(%)	平均值(岁)	标准差(岁)
性别	男	32	76.2	—	—
	女	10	23.8	—	—
年龄	青年(18~35 岁)	15	35.7	23.2	2.0

续上表

基本特征	指标值	数量(人)	比例(%)	平均值(岁)	标准差(岁)
年龄	中年(36~60岁)	14	33.3	46.5	6.6
	老年(60岁以上)	13	31.0	63.7	2.9
驾龄	低驾龄(1~12年)	18	42.9	4.1	2.7
	中驾龄(13~26年)	14	33.3	20.2	4.7
	高驾龄(26年以上)	10	23.8	32.0	4.4

1.3 实验设备

本实验采用北京工业大学 AutoSimAS 驾驶模拟系统,硬件主要包括驾驶模拟设备、华为平板、高性能计算机 6 台、Eye Tracking Core + 眼动仪等设备。软件为 SCANeR1.9,它可以 20Hz 的频率动态采集车辆运行过程中的速度、坐标、横向偏移、刹车踏板开度、油门踏板开度以及方向盘转角等运行和操纵数据。实验设备示意图见图 2。

图2 实验设备示意图

1.4 实验因变量

实验的因变量为接管第一操纵和接管操纵序列。接管第一操纵为减速反应时间、转向反应时间以及加速反应时间的最小值,接管操纵序列由三种反应时间按时间顺序排列而成。减速(加速)反应时间为系统发出接管请求至驾驶员踩踏制动(加速)踏板的时间。转向反应时间为系统发出接管请求至驾驶员转动转向盘的时间。

1.5 数据预处理

本实验共采集了 42 组(756 条)数据,剔除了发生碰撞、接管失败等导致的一些异常数据;为了避免交通流对驾驶员行为的干扰,删除增设稳定流的团雾接管数据,共获得 667 条数据。由于车辆控制权切换到驾驶员的过程中,车辆未接受外界的操纵,踏板深度及转向盘转角将逐渐归零,驾驶员接管车辆后,踏板深度及转向盘转角将增加。因此,可定义踏板深度的增加为踏板激活,方向盘角度变化为转向盘激活,基于 Matlab 编程提取[14]。

2 实验数据分析方法

本文通过接管第一操纵以及接管操纵序列研究接管操纵行为。接管第一操纵为制动、转向盘或者加速踏板,统计整个接管过程中驾驶员的操纵行为,发现接管操纵序列共 11 种。选择性别、年龄、驾龄、NDRT、TORT 以及接管场景作为解释变量,分析其对操纵行为的影响。其中,除年龄与驾龄变量为有序型分类变量外,其他变量均为无序型分类变量。因此,本文采用无序多分类 Logit 回归模型检验不同变量对驾驶员接管操纵行为的影响。

假设有 m 个自变量,n 个因变量,可随机从因变量的 n 个水平中选择一个作为参照,其余作为对照,将拟合得到 $n-1$ 个回归模型。本文选择因变量取值于第 n 个水平为参照,此时第 k 个水平的 Logit 回归模型为:

$$\ln\left(\frac{\pi_k}{\pi_n}\right)=\beta_{k0}+\beta_{k1}x_1+\cdots+\beta_{ki}x_i,\quad k\in[1,n-1],i\in[1,m] \tag{1}$$

式中:x_i——性别、年龄、驾龄、NDRT、TORT 以及接管场景的取值;

π_k——因变量取值于第 k 类的概率;

β_{ki}——第 k 个水平第 i 个自变量 x_i 的系数。

3 结果与讨论

实验数据获取过程中涉及到重复测量,考虑到自变量之间可能存在相关性,一个自变量的变化会引起另一个自变量的变化,因此有必要在使用无序多分类 Logit 模型之前检验多重共线性。本文使用方差膨胀因子统计指标(VIF)检验多重共线性,当 $0<\text{VIF}<10$,判定不存在严重的多重共线性[15]。利用软件 SPSS26.0 进行运算,结果显示,解释变量的方差膨胀因子最大是 2.973,因此

可以判定模型不存在严重的多重共线性。

定义置信水平为95%，利用软件SPSS26.0建立无序多分类Logit模型分析不同变量对接管操纵行为的影响。表2显示，驾龄、TORT及接管场景对接管第一操纵的选择有显著影响，驾龄及接管场景对接管操纵序列影响显著，对其进行统计描述。

接管操纵行为统计分析　　表2

自变量	性别	年龄	驾龄	NDRT	TORT	接管场景
接管第一操纵(显著性检验sig*)	0.485	0.950	0.000	0.431	0.005	0.005
接管操纵序列(显著性检验sig*)	0.527	0.489	0.001	0.618	0.152	0.000

注：Sig* <0.05代表有显著性差异。

3.1　不同驾龄接管操纵行为统计分析

由图3可知，随着驾龄的增加，第一操纵为加速(A)的比例越来越小，“中驾龄”中选择减速(B)作为第一操纵的驾驶员比“低驾龄”高116.086%，比“高驾龄”高70.20%，“低驾龄”和“高驾龄”驾驶员选择转动转向盘(W)的比例几乎相同。由图4可知，相比“中驾龄”驾驶员，“低驾龄”以及“高驾龄”驾驶员更倾向采用WBA作为接管操纵序列。

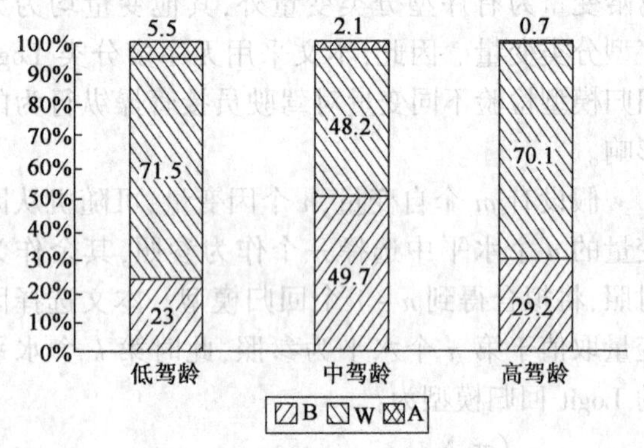

图3　驾龄对接管第一操纵的影响

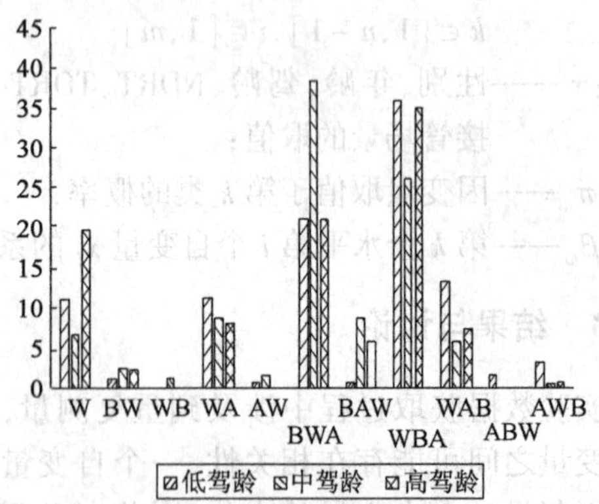

图4　驾龄对接管操纵序列的影响

回看驾驶模拟视频发现，“低驾龄”和“高驾龄”驾驶员习惯接管后首先调整车辆位置，或接管后立刻换道，随后调整车辆速度。而“中驾龄”驾驶员更倾向于先减速降低车辆速度后观察驾驶环境，做出后续选择。

3.2　不同接管场景接管操纵行为统计分析

图5显示事故场景下驾驶员选择减速作为第一操纵的比例最高，匝道场景下驾驶员选择加速的比例为所有场景中最高。由图6可知，匝道场景下，接管操纵序列为WAB的比例，远远高于其他接管场景。

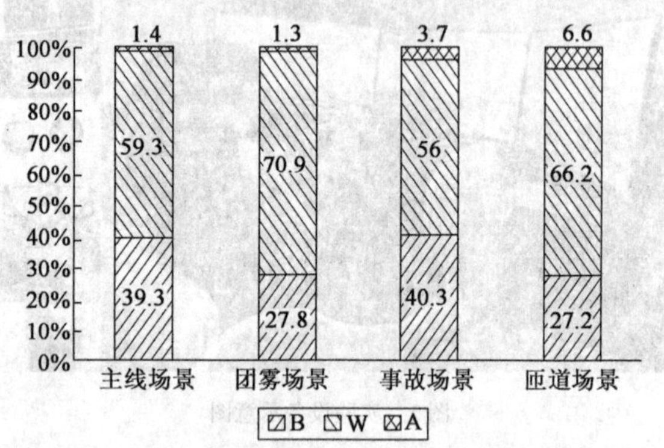

图5　接管场景对接管第一操纵的影响

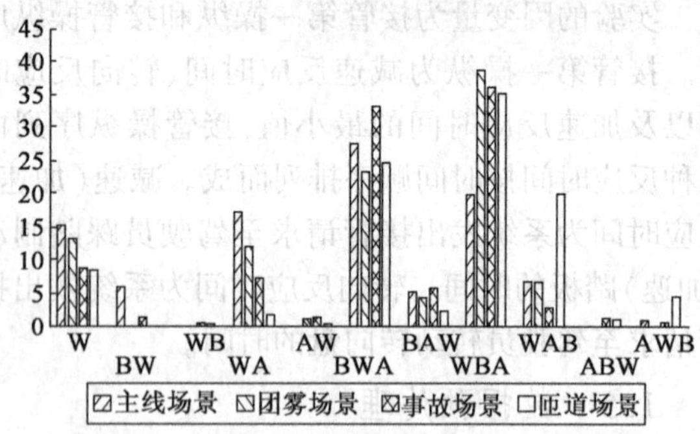

图6　接管场景对接管操纵序列的影响

事故场景设定的是前方出现事故，因此有更多驾驶员先减速避让，制动踏板的使用将使得驾驶员有更多的时间应对前方险情。而匝道场景下，系统提醒驾驶员接管时，车辆位于限速值为120km/h的普通路段，因此部分驾驶员选择调整车辆位置，并加速通过普通路段。由此可见，驾驶员行为与驾驶环境有着密不可分的关系。

3.3 不同TORT下接管操纵行为统计分析

由图7得到,TORT为10s时,第一操纵为减速的比例比TORT为5s时高37.5%,为转动方向盘的比例低22.2%。图8表明,TORT为5s时的最频繁接管操纵序列为WBA,TORT为10s时的为BWA。

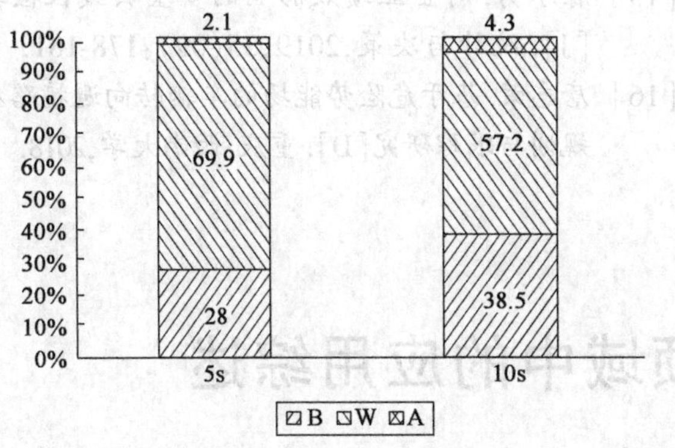

图7 TORT对接管第一操纵的影响

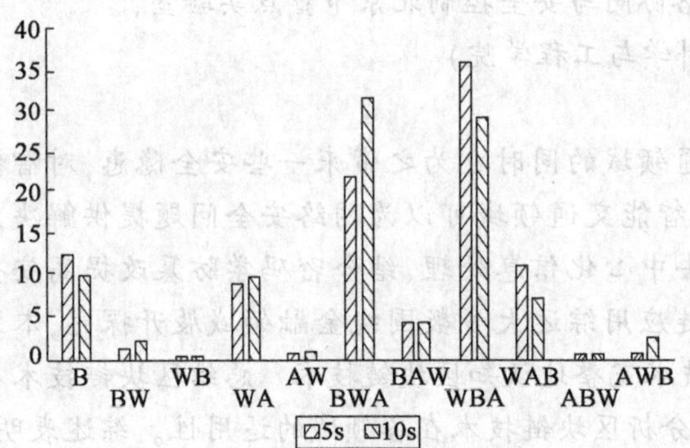

图8 TORT对接管操纵序列的影响

唐志荣指出,当情况紧急或车速较高,与障碍物之间的距离不足以驾驶员通过制动安全避让时,通过转向实现避撞的效果会更好。因此当TORT为5s时,驾驶员为了避让,更多的选择先调整方向,再减速[16]。

4 结语

本研究基于驾驶模拟实验,研究不同驾驶员接管操纵行为的差异以及TORT、NDRT、接管场景对接管操纵行为的影响,结论如下:

(1)"中驾龄"驾驶员更倾向于选择减速作为接管第一操纵,"低驾龄"和"高驾龄"的驾驶员第一操纵更相近。

(2)接管操纵行为与接管场景关联性较强,不同接管场景及TORT下,驾驶员的接管操纵行为不同。

(3)研究不同变量对驾驶员接管操纵行为的影响,有助于结合驾驶环境发现安全的接管操纵行为模式,可为驾驶员培训提供支持。此外,为提高操纵序列的完整度,以后将加入眼动行为,并将制动踏板、转向盘以及加速踏板的使用划分不同类别,挖掘安全的接管操纵行为模式。

参考文献

[1] Wang J, Lu M, Li K. Characterization of Longitudinal Driving Behavior by Measurable Parameters [J]. Transportation Research Record, 2018:15-23.

[2] Montgomery J, Kusano K D, Gabler H C. Age and Gender Differences in Time to Collision at Braking from the 100-Car Age and Gender Differences in Time to Collision at Braking from the 100-Car Naturalistic Driving Study [J]. Traffic Injury Prevention, 2014, 15: S15-S20.

[3] Körber M, Gold C, Lechner D. The Influence of Age on the Take-Over of Vehicle Control in Highly Automated Driving [J]. Transportation Research Part F Traffic Psychology and Behaviour, 2016, 39: 19-32.

[4] Stamatiadis N, Deacon J A. Trends in Highway Safety: Effects of an Aging Population on Accident Propensity [J]. Accident Analysis and Prevention 1995, 27(4): 443-459.

[5] 侯海晶,金立生,关志伟. 驾驶风格对驾驶行为的影响[J]. 中国公路学报,2018,31(4):10-10.

[6] 张梦航. 基于实车仿真的不同风险等级下新手驾驶人跟车行为研究[D]. 上海:上海交通大学,2014.

[7] 吕能超,任泽远,段至诚,等. Near-crash事件中驾驶人行为特征分析[J]. 中国安全科学学报,2017,27(6):2-7.

[8] 房曰荣. 不同类别驾驶员的驾驶行为特性差异实验研究[J]. 安全与环境工程,2020,27(5):5-5.

[9] 谢晓非,庄明科,白海峰. 驾驶人员风险驾驶行为分析及相关因素研究[J]. 北京大学学报:自然科学版,2008,44(3):8-8.

[10] Reimer B, Donmez B, LavalliÈRe M, et al. Impact of Age and Cognitive Demand on Lane

Choice and Changing under Actual Highway Conditions [J]. Accident Analysis and Prevention, 2013, 52: 125-132.

[11] 鲁光泉,赵鹏云,王兆杰. 自动驾驶中视觉次任务对年轻驾驶人接管时间的影响[J]. 中国公路学报,2018,31(4):7-7.

[12] 高岩,尤志栋,罗毅,等. 基于驾驶模拟的自动驾驶接管行为研究[J]. 中国安全生产科学技术,2021,17(2):140-146.

[13] HAPPEE R, GOLD C, RADLMAYR J, et al. Take-over Performance in Evasive Manoeuvres [J]. Accident Analysis and Prevention, 2017, 106: 211-222.

[14] Papazikou E, Thomas P, Quddus M. Developing personalised braking and steering thresholds for driver support systems from SHRP2 NDS data[J]. Accident Analysis and Prevention, Elsevier Ltd, 2021, 160(August): 106310.

[15] 滕承秀. 对企业绩效影响的多重共线性检验[J]. 统计与决策,2019,35(09):178-181.

[16] 唐志荣. 基于危险势能场的车辆转向避撞路径规划与跟踪研究[D]. 重庆:西南大学,2018.

区块链技术在交通领域中的应用综述

张　傲　段续庭*

(大数据科学与脑机智能高精尖创新中心,车路协同与安全控制北京市重点实验室,北京航空航天大学交通科学与工程学院)

摘　要　随着智能交通不断发展,新兴技术引入交通领域的同时也为之带来一些安全隐患,对智能交通系统网络安全的关注逐渐增多。将区块链技术融入智能交通领域可以为网络安全问题提供解决方案。区块链技术以计算机网络为基础、依靠智能合约对去中心化信息处理、结合密码学防篡改提高安全性、通过共识算法解决分布式一致性问题。但有关区块链应用综述大多数围绕金融领域展开探究,本文回顾区块链的发展历程,并通过介绍区块链架构与关键技术完整地认知区块链技术。总结区块链技术在交通领域、车联网领域与军事领域的应用与研究进展,并分析区块链技术在各领域的适用性。综述表明,区块链技术驱动各领域的革新,将成为支撑智能交通系统网络安全的核心技术。

关键词　网络安全　交通　区块链技术　车联网　应用

0　引言

随着科技革命的不断演进,促进交通行业的数据驱动发展,推动人工智能与大数据等前沿技术与交通运输相结合发展成为智能交通。交通运输逐渐自动化、数字化与智能化是交通发展的必然趋势。将人工智能应用在交通领域以实现网联车辆的发展目标,应用大数据使交通数字化以提高智能交通的发展水平[1]。

智能交通发展离不开大数据分析、人工智能、信息技术等先进技术的创新,但这些新兴技术的融入也给智能交通系统带来了一定程度的安全风险,引起社会对智能交通系统网络安全的关注。在发展创新技术的同时转向安全、高质的发展阶段,目前智能交通系统网络中跨区域的共享机制不完善、部门之间的协作效率低,还存在一系列的海量数据共享与存储、信息获取与篡改及用户隐私泄露等网络安全问题。为解决上述一系列问题,在智能交通系统网络中引入区块链技术,在区块链技术下的数据是真实可信不可篡改的、可以为海量数据的存储与共享提供技术支撑、实现交通数据可追溯防攻击等。

近年来区块链为交通领域的建设提供了技术支撑,如利用区块链技术共享交通拥堵情况、道路车流量等数据信息以解决交通运输中的信息闭塞与数据整合困难的问题;与边缘计算等技术相结合应用至车联网中提升系统整体安全与协同能力,为交通出行提供安全保障。由此,区块链技术将逐渐成为解决智能交通系统网络安全问题的关键技术之一。

区块链技术在各行业的应用进展迅速，得到高度关注。区块链在去中心化、溯源、信任等方面都展现了显著优势，逐渐被应用到金融、物流、医疗等方面，有关区块链技术应用的综述也仅围绕这些方面展开。目前，区块链的应用场景较多且繁杂，为加快新一代技术与交通运输融合、提升交通运输质量、交通管理逐渐智能协同、交通系统网络安全可靠，对目前区块链在交通领域的相关应用进行梳理。

本文首先回顾区块链发展历程，并介绍区块链基础架构与原理，针对区块链在交通运输、车联网与军事领域的应用与研究成果进行总结，并对未来区块链在智能交通领域的发展趋势进行展望。

1 区块链技术概述

1.1 区块链技术发展

区块链的概念由中本聪[2]首次提出，它的本质是一种由密码学与验证技术作为技术支撑、根据时间的顺序进行存储的分布式共享数字账本。通过共同管理的组网方式逐渐成为解决信任危机的革命性技术。区块链的发展阶段如图1所示。区块链技术在第一阶段中诞生，但这个阶段只体现在数字货币中；在第二阶段中解决智能合约技术难题，逐渐在金融领域崭露头角；第三阶段引领了新一代的技术革命，将广泛应用到各行各业。

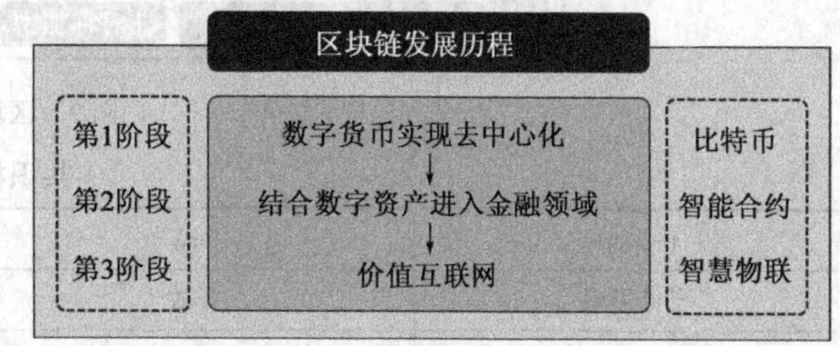

图1 区块链的发展阶段

在区块链的发展过程中，逐渐被分为以读写权限公开的公有链、只有指定节点达成共识的联盟链以及形成组织节点的私有链三类，如表1所示。

区块链分类 表1

区块链	非许可链	许可链	
	公有链	联盟链	私有链
共识	所有节点	指定节点集	指定组织
读写权限	公开	公开/限制	公开/限制
安全性	高	低	低
效率	低	高	高
信任	去信任	去信任	相互信任
去中心化	是	局部	否

公有链实现完全去中心化、不受第三方约束；私有链中心化节点的权限被不同程度限制；而联盟链事为一个或多个组织一起对区块链管理。整体来看，这三类区块链都是区块链技术在适应不同的应用需求，区块链技术及其应用仍然处于一个探索的阶段，它的概念验证目前多于实际的应用落地，商业模式也有待更加清晰。

1.2 区块链架构与关键技术

区块链可以通过多种技术得以实现，其系统由数据层、网络层、共识层、激励层、合约层和应用层组成，为了清晰理解各层执行功能，本文结合已有研究，给出如图2所示的系统架构。

数据层：数据层封装应用过程中的交易数据至数据区块，根据区块中的时间戳对各区块排序到主区块链中，从而对网络中的区块进行更新。

网络层：在网络层中制定验证机制与传播协议来满足不同的应用需求，区块链的节点都可以参与检验和记账，并且满足仅当区块数据通过全网大部分节点验证后，才能记入区块链。

共识层：使网络中的分布式节点的数据形成共识，典型的共识层中的共识机制如表2所示。这些共识机制各有优劣，可以根据实际情况具体分析与应用。

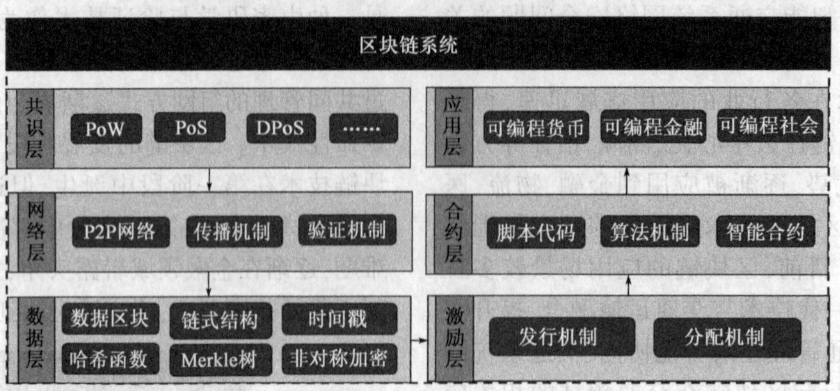

图2　区块链系统架构

共识机制特点　　表2

Property	PoW	PoS	DPoS
节点身份	开放	开放	开放
能耗节约	否	局部	局部
允许恶意节点	<51%算力	<51%股份	<51%验证
所需资源	算力	财富/股份	财富/股份
奖励	是	否	否

激励层:在激励层制定适当的奖励机制可以实现共识节点自身的收益最大化同时鼓励网络中多数节点参与共识过程进而实现稳定的分布式网络。

合约层:在完成对数据的表示、传播及验证的工作后需要形成具体的应用逻辑与算法来实现后面对数据的操作。

应用层:区块链技术可以延伸至金融、物流、物联网等较多领域。本文就是围绕区块链的实际应用,探究区块链技术对交通、车联网领域的研究成果与推进作用,如图3所示。

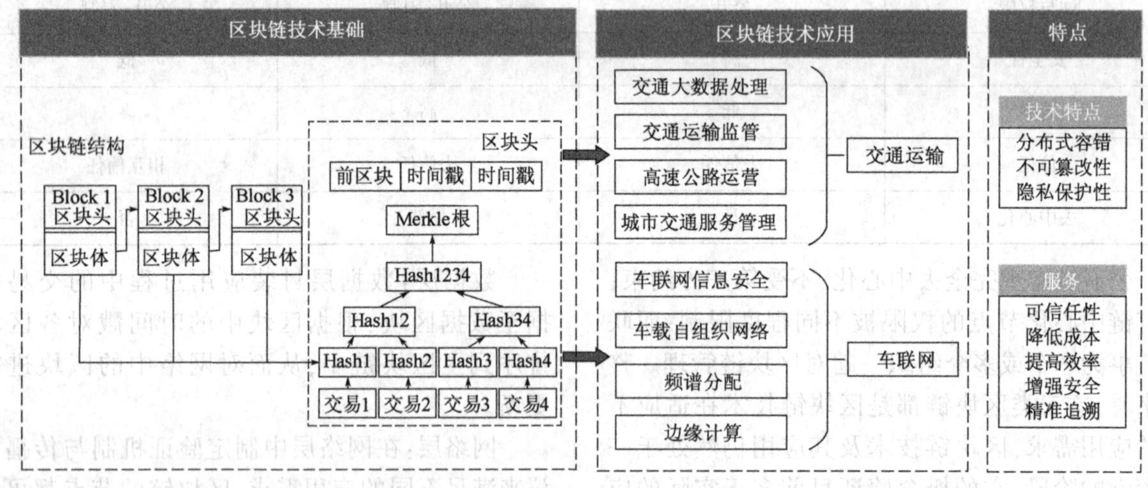

图3　区块链技术应用领域

2　区块链在交通运输领域应用

目前区块链技术正促进许多领域发展模式的创新,特别是可以为交通运输领域的建设方面提供便利并促进其进一步发展。交通运输行业是国民经济的基础性行业[3],区块链技术在交通领域有着无限的应用前景。

以交通运输的各类数据作为数据主链,应用区块链技术进一步建立数据层,数据与区块链账本间利用合约层的智能合约等技术进行数据的交互,最后构建成适用于交通运输的区块链应用平台,为交通运输的数据交互安全与共享提供便利与技术支持。本节将从交通大数据处理、交通运输监管、高速公路运营、城市交通服务管理,如图4介绍区块链技术在交通运输领域的应用。

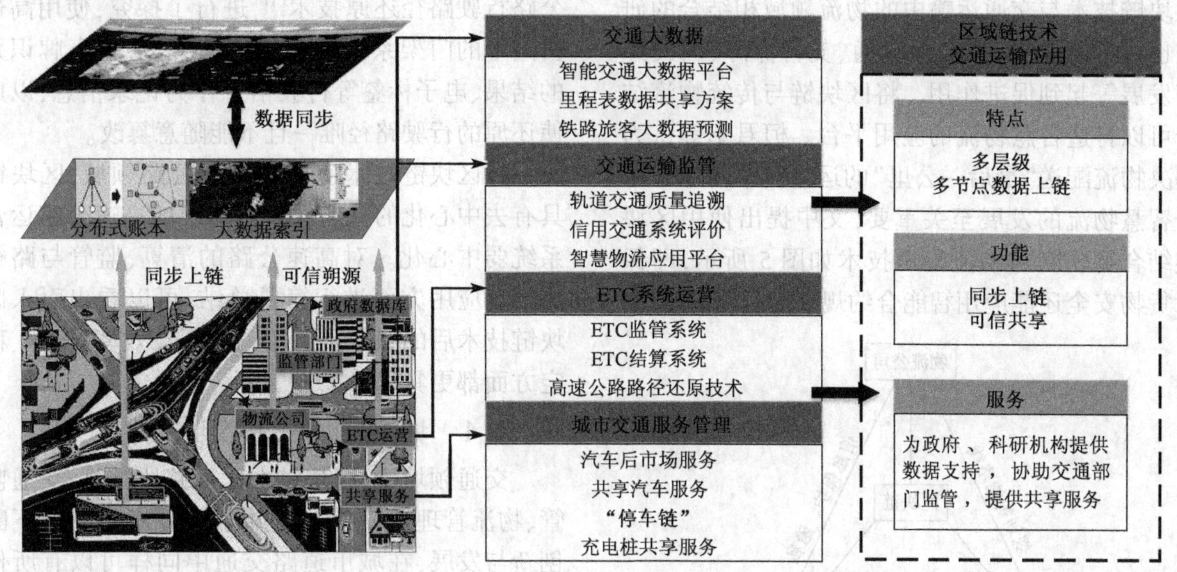

图4 区块链技术应用领域

2.1 交通大数据处理

借助区块链技术中的权限控制特性,可以将各个地区、部门或企业等交通领域参与方进行权限分配,形成交通区块链成员访问控制权限,实现交通领域的信息可控与共享,解决交通运输领域信息闭塞、数据整合困难等问题。数据的共享对于提高交通安全和增强交通服务是十分重要的。为了确保数据共享的隐私与安全,很多研究会采用区块链技术对交通领域的数据构建共享平台或应用。

交通数据的智能化一般体现在层级式的网络架构,有关交通部门会对数据进行独立的上传或处理,从而使数据共享面临巨大难题。针对这类问题,龚奕等提出基于区块链的智能交通大数据平台的方法[4]。利用区块链特性实现交通部门的去中心化管理,在数据层对不同的数据源进行数据格式与更新等要求的统一、在共识层等层面构建数据监管等处理机制,最终符合统一标准的数据通过新生成的区块链节点入网,应用此多源平台提高数据共享效率、实现分布式计算。在交通运输领域中,汽车里程数可以作为汽车估值或定价的重要指标,当前的里程表数据十分容易被修改进而导致估价造假甚至更严重的道路安全问题。Preikschat 等[5]提出了一种基于区块链的里程表数据共享分布式数据库,保障数据不可篡改,提高里程表数据的公开透明性。近几年,在交通领域中高速铁路结合共享汽车也在不断发展,喻麒睿提出将区块链技术融入铁路旅客大数据中[6],实现旅客信息跨行业流通。在这种模式中分析各利益相关群体的数据交互方式并提出数据流通机制。

区块链技术的信息上链实现可追溯、保障安全及不可篡改,这些特点都在交通领域的数据共享发挥着巨大的作用。区块链技术使信息间摩擦降低、突破了“信息孤岛”,保障并解决了交通领域中数据量庞大且整合难度高的问题,进一步促进了智慧交通、智慧城市的构建。

2.2 交通运输监管

区块链实时动态更新的分布式账本。在区块链中节点信息上链,任何节点的信息增删等都需要全网大多数节点验证。这种实时更新记录的信任机制可以被应用到监管部门中,以此提高工作效率。把对交通领域的监管与区块链结合,可以提高交通监管部门的安全性和透明化。

在交通领域中车联网日益发展,车辆会根据接收其他车辆的消息来判断当前路况进而制定行车策略,但由于系统不完善会存在恶意车辆发布干扰信息的情况。对于这类问题,Yang 等利用区块链提出车联网的信任管理系统[7],主要是利用贝叶斯模型验证接收到的信息并计算信任偏移值,将数据结合区块链以提高交通信息可靠性。区块链技术与交通运输中的物流领域相结合的研究也在不断发展,对商品流通、支付保障、国民经济发展等起到促进作用。将区块链与传统物流结合可以打造智慧物流的应用平台。柯君卓等认为解决物流配送"最后一公里"的运输效率问题[8]对于智慧物流的发展至关重要,文中提出使用区块链结合物联网与物流配送技术如图 5 所示,即保障货物安全还能应用智能合约规划配送路线。

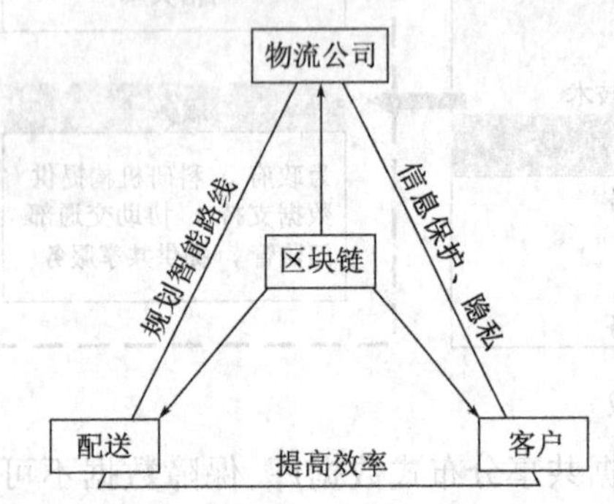

图 5　区块链结合物流配送

区块链技术结合交通领域的行业监管,使各参与监管部门的数据信息汇集到分布式账本并采用加密算法进行保存,保证了监管数据的安全与可信度,从而提升交通监管效率,对智慧交通系统有明显的优化作用。

2.3　ETC 系统运营

区块链技术在金融领域的应用技术已经逐渐成熟。2020 年,我国开始全面实施 ETC 收费,取消省界收费站。目前 ETC 收费属于中心化记账模式,收费周期较长。而且高速公路的车流量、里程及数据信息逐年增长,使 ETC 面临结算数据易丢失、数据整合安全性低、跨区域间不兼容等问题。

随着车流量、里程及用户逐年增加,ETC 面临着数据存储与管理效率低、跨地域不兼容、系统安全性低等问题。针对以上问题,杨洪路等进一步提出基于区块链技术的电子不停车收费系统[9],由于系统采用去中心化的区块链技术,可以将车辆通行与交易记录保存在区块链系统中,进而实现道路数据记录上链以此缩短清算时间,提高高速公路工作效率。罗江等考虑将区块链技术结合射频信号来对接收信号进行整合与分析,提出了基于区块链的高速公路 ETC 监管系统[10],主要内容为结合区块链对射频信号有关数据进行记录与分析,对信号或数据的异常采取预警,为交通管理与车辆通行提高效率。王棚对基于区块链的高速公路行驶路径还原技术[11]进行了探究,使用高速公路上的门架系统作区块链的节点,将车牌识别的结果、电子标签等行驶信息作为记录信息,以此使还原的行驶路径唯一且不能随意篡改。

将区块链技术应用到高速公路领域,区块链具有去中心化的特点可以对传统的高速公路运营系统弱中心化。对高速公路的清算、监管与路径还原等应用方面进行简要总结,可以看出引入区块链技术后的高速公路相关应用在效率、安全、稳定方面都更具优势。

2.4　城市交通服务管理

交通领域中,区块链在区域路段结算、交通监管、物流管理及交通数据共享等方面的应用不断创新与发展,在城市道路交通中同样可以有所作为。将区块链应用到交通公共服务中,可以提升服务质量、简化工作流程、数据公开透明并且可以提升政府或有关部门的公信力。

我国汽车保有量逐年增长使汽车后市场及商机增大,但行业景象还处在逐步发展阶段。邹亚强等构建了基于联盟链的汽车售后服务的应用模型[12],通过建立汽车售后服联盟链对用户身份、相关认证及链上服务等进行管理,其中运营平台及管理员作为联盟节点,其余普通节点只享受服务但不允许参与数据记录。由于近年来共享经济的快速普及与渗透,国家大力提倡"绿色出行",因此共享汽车行业得以快速发展。然而共享汽车行业在起步阶段就遇到了滴滴顺风车等安全性漏洞事件,陶云杰等提出了新模式的共享汽车服务[13]。

目前区块链在交通运输领域的应用大部分仍停留在理论设想与方案构想层面,缺少实际应用落地。但随着区块链技术逐渐成熟,理论研究足够支撑实际的应用需求。区块链在交通运输领域的应用主要是与数据共享、交通数据安全隐私两方面,未来区块链技术将结合物联网、通信等技术赋能交通运输。

3　区块链在车联网领域应用

根据区块链特性将区块链技术全面应用在移动通信领域,以此优化移动通信性能,保护用户隐私,提高通信安全性与稳定性。

由于车辆网络的高移动性和可变性,安全、隐私和信任管理问题仍然是促进安全、高效和智能交通的未决问题。区块链技术被认为是车联网的核心技术之一,但目前来看将区块链结合车联网的研究还处在初步探索阶段。本节将从车载自组织网络、车联网信息安全、边缘计算以及频谱分配方面介绍区块链在车联网领域的有关研究及应用,如图6所示。

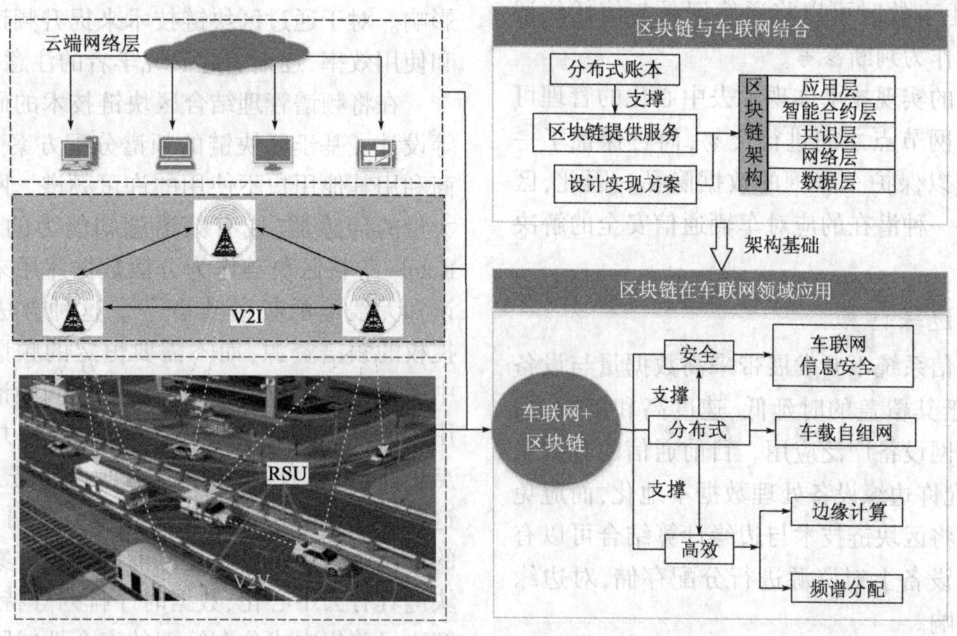

图6　车联网在区块链领域应用

3.1　车载自组织网络

智能化的城市交通依赖于车载自组织网络,车载自组网可以有效解决当前城市道路交通的问题。车载自组网中,车-车与车-基础设施通过无线通信预告道路具体情况,有利于车辆提前进行预判,从而缓解城市交通状况。

在车载自组网中,车辆对道路状况判断会耗费额外的资源,需要激励机制鼓励其参与进来,进而保证车载自组网的安全性、有效性。李春燕提出依靠区块链技术对车载自组网道路状况预警的方案[14],利用激励机制促进车辆积极参加车载自组织网络路况预警。由于区块链保证了数据的一致性和抗篡改性,Zhang 提出基于区块链的数据共享和存储系统[15],该系统具有车载自组织网络中的数字签名。路边单元(RSU)通过部署智能合约设置数据共享条件,并以分布式方式存储副本传感器的数据。由此,研究多基于密码学中数字签名、假名机制等为车辆身份提供隐私保障,同时在车载自组网中设计共识合约与奖励机制等促进车辆作为节点在网络中共享信息并解决历史信息的追溯难题。

目前,国内外对区块链在车载网应用中的研究主要集中在去中心化管理,匿名网络可信性,多方安全交易等方面,通过应用区块链技术充分利用车辆节点通信能力,并从区块链的存储方式上满足移动特性,进而满足车载自组织网络可扩展性和可靠性。

3.2　车联网信息安全

车联网依赖的相关通信技术不断发展,由此给人们的生活带来许多便利。车联网应用新一代的通信技术来实现车辆与车辆或车辆与一些基础设施等的协作通信,其中安全问题是当前研究的重点。

目前车联网中存在一些安全与信任问题,考虑将区块链技术结合到车联网中。Yuan 等提出了一个智能交通系统的区块链网络架构模型,成构建了安全可信的分布式智能交通系统[16],为后续的研究提供基础。Rowen S 提出了基于区块链的车辆通信方案[17],从理论和实验等方面对侧信道进行研究,提出新的车辆间会话密钥建立协议,利用区块链技术对车联网中信息保护,去中心化的相互作用能力提高车联网的安全性,以此实现了 V2V 通信。区块链技术源于加密货币,如比特币也可用来在对等网络中建立信任与可靠性。

Singh 中提出了使用区块链技术进行基于奖励的智能车通信[18],定义了信任比特作为车辆可信行为的象征。这种通信机制可以实现车辆与车辆间的快速可靠通信,并将车辆间通信记录与信任位存储,当发生事故时可以将通信记录与信任位记录有关数据作为判断参考。

区块链的实现技术体现了去中心化的管理可以允许在全网节点之间进行交易,而且保证了一份共识数据以保护车联网的数据隐私。因此,区块链技术是一种潜在的应对车辆通信安全的解决方案。

3.3 边缘计算

移动通信系统不断发展带来高数据量与设备的连接,由于其覆盖的时延低、速度高和范围大,可以使车联网设备广泛应用。目前通信的数据量不断增加,允许边缘设备处理数据本地化,而避免集中授权。将区块链技术与边缘计算结合可以有效地在边缘设备上对资源进行分配存储,对边缘计算产生影响。

目前对于区块链和边缘计算的有关研究多数是关于边缘计算解决区块链算力的问题。Xiong 等为解决这类问题提出方案[19],利用移动边缘计算服务器解决区块链中的计算问题,用户对边缘资源进行访问并利用其计算服务。QIU 等[20]指出传统的卸载方案不能根据环境的变化做出相应的调整策略,在考虑挖矿任务和数据处理的基础上,提出了基于深度强化学习的在线计算卸载方案。降低 PoW 的资源消耗也是需要解决的问题。为了提供有效的数据存储和共享,Kang 等中提出了一种基于安全信誉的数据共享系统[21],该系统具备车载计算能力与智能合约。所提出的基于声誉的方案主要考虑三重主观逻辑模型,提高可信度、确保高质量的数据共享。可以看出,区块链与边缘计算可以互补结合,边缘计算为区块链提供计算能力与存储空间等,区块链保证边缘节点的数据安全,所以边缘计算与区块链协同应用成为提升整体系统的重要方案。

车联网设备的有限计算与存储能力成为制约区块链相关应用的重要因素,可以通过边缘计算解决这类问题。区块链与边缘计算的结合可以提高车联网的性能。后续可以对分配与协调区块链网络下的边缘计算进一步研究。

3.4 频谱分配

无线频谱资源属于稀缺国家战略资源,并且其需求逐渐增长。无线频谱作为无线通信的载体,它的使用与配置对其应用领域会产生一定的影响。对于通过区块链技术来提升频谱资源配置和使用效率,逐渐引起研究学者的注意。

在将频谱管理结合区块链技术的研究中,Jiao 等设计了基于区块链的频谱分配方案[22],使运营商利用其他用户不使用的许可频谱。网络需要有大量的传感器,或有频谱感知能力的邻居节点。Kotobi 等将区块链作为分散数据库用来验证移动认知无线电的频谱共享[23]。这种方法可以访问授权的频谱资源,而不需要恒定的频谱感知。文中引入一种虚拟货币用来支付访问频谱的所需费用。所有交易记录都会在区块链中,并由志愿节点更新,可以使用区块链对所有事务进行验证。这种介质访问协议中度和重度衰落时,共享可用的未使用频谱可以超越以前的传统方案。由于区块链具有去中心化、数据时序排列等特点,对于就解决目前集中式分布管理的安全性威胁与资源短缺等问题具有优势。研究中节点通过区块链分布式数据库获得频谱感知信息,在频谱交易过程中发起频谱请求并与指定节点进行交易认证。区块链与频谱管理结合的新模式将有发挥频谱分配的运作能力,极大提升频谱资源的有效利用。

区块链技术应用在移动通信频谱管理中,可以改善网络安全、提高频谱的利用率、实现高效的频谱管理,为移动通信提供良好的共享环境。

区块链是信息基础设施的重要组成部分,逐渐成为车联网的关键技术之一。由于车联网中越来越多的数据交互在安全、隐私与信任等方面造成威胁。本章针对区块链技术在车联网领域的应用,主要分析区块链技术在车载自组织网络、车联网信息安全、频谱管理与边缘计算中的应用。目前许多研究还是起步阶段,但区块链在车联网领域的应用具有广阔的发展前景。

4 发展与挑战

根据区块链特性将区块链技术全面应用在移动通信领域,以此优化移动通信性能,保护用户隐私,提高通信安全性与稳定性。

在交通数字化、信息化、智能化快速发展的新阶段,区块链技术会以去中心化、防篡改可溯源、数据安全共享等特点得到广泛关注。随着区块链技术逐渐与交通领域融合,使其能够为当前智能交通系统网络中跨部门数据共享、自动驾驶信息安全、物流信息隐私加密、公众出行信任共识等提供解决方案,进一步助力交通运输行业的发展并驱动其发展模式的革新。

通过区块链技术以交通运输业数据作为数据主链从而构建数据层,以智能合约等实现区块链账本与大数据控制层的数据交互。在交通运输领域,区块链将有效解决交通数据上链、数据朔源以及数据准确性的难题,为交通基础建设与交通行业监管提供可靠信任数据与共享机制、保障信息溯源与安全、确保隐私不泄露。

随着网联车辆越来越多,车联网逐渐遭受数据信任、安全与可持续性的难题,在智能交通系统网络中信息安全逐渐成为先进技术广泛应用的隐患。利用区块链技术将前端感知传感器的所获数据进行信息上链,如将道路监控数据、车载传感器与交通信号灯等信息数据上链,海量数据接入设备后在边缘侧进行数据分析,完成身份识别、轨迹分析等上传至云端平台。网联车辆、自动驾驶车辆通过区块链技术可以共享位置信息数据、车辆轨迹数据等;路侧交通信号灯、摄像头及毫米波雷达等路侧感知设备也可以应用区块链技术对数据进行存储与共享。车联网中的区块链技术可以实现海量数据的存储,并利用边缘计算与云边协同全局监控与本地应用协作,区块链中去中心化的特点支持网络由单点向全局可控转变,可以使网联车辆由单车智能逐渐发展为群体智能,实现大范围的联网联控,形成城市级的交通协调调度。将区块链技术融入到车联网领域,通过共识机制与加密技术对数据进行可靠的存储与安全认证,并提供实时的信息上链,为车联网安全提供技术保障。

总体来看,区块链在交通领域的应用可以分为两方面,一是协同与共享:随着车路协同、自动驾驶、车联网等技术等不断发展,交通领域面临着大量的信息交互与数据共享,借助区块链技术实现异构网络的互联互通。在交通领域的应用中实现可信数据传输与同步、异构节点合作与资源共享。二是隐私与安全:区块链的不可篡改性与数据传输完整性为交通领域的应用构建相关安全信任机制,实现去中心化管理,有效防止恶意节点攻击,加解密技术保障用户隐私。以上,区块链技术将成为提升交通运输科技水平、全面综合交通调度与智能交通系统网络安全的核心技术支撑。

5 结语

智能交通系统的发展目前面临着许多安全问题,通过引入区块链技术可以将人工智能、大数据等先进技术更好的与智能交通相结合。

区块链技术在许多复杂的环境中有利于解决去中心化、不可篡改、可追溯与隐私保护、去信任等问题,由于这些特性可以赋能许多行业的应用而逐渐成为研究热点。目前区块链技术驱动着各领域应用技术的革新。本文重点讨论了区块链技术在交通领域、车联网领域与军事领域的应用与研究现状:在交通领域,区块链技术主要与大数据、人工智能等技术结合为交通建设提供便利;在车联网领域,结合边缘计算、频谱分配等将区块链引入车联网中,保障车辆用户信息隐私、降低通信成本。

区块链技术正驱动着各领域的管理,大力推广区块链技术在各个领域的应用是必然的发展趋势,同时各类领域的应用也会随着与区块链的结合而产生新的变革。区块链技术在未来将成为支撑智能交通系统网络安全的核心技术,在更多的应用中得到发展。

参考文献

[1] Zhu L, Yu F R, Wang Y, et al. Big Data Analytics in Intelligent Transportation Systems: A Survey[J]. IEEE Transactions on Intelligent Transportation Systems,2018:1-16.

[2] 韩璇,袁勇,王飞跃. 区块链安全问题:研究现状与展望[J]. 自动化学报,2019,45(01):206-225.

[3] Li Y, Liu D, Ke S . Research on Fuzhou Logistics Development Status under the Background of National Logistics Hub City Construction[J]. IOP Conference Series Earth and Environmental Science,2020,508:012093.

[4] 龚斐,廖金花. 区块链技术的城市智能交通大数据平台及仿真案例分析[J]. 公路交通科技,2019,36(12):117-126.

[5] Preikschat K, Bhmecke-Schwafert M, Buchwald J P, et al. Trusted systems of records based on

Blockchain technology-a prototype for mileage storing in the automotive industry [J]. Concurrency and Computation Practice and Experience,2020,2020(3).
[6] 喻麒睿.高铁共享汽车数据流通机制及关键技术研究[D].北京:中国铁道科学研究院,2019.
[7] Yang Z,Yang K,Lei L,etal. Blockchain-based Decentralized Trust Management in Vehicular Networks[J]. IEEE Internet of Things Journal,2018:1-1.
[8] 柯君卓,汪驰升,高青,等.区块链在最后一公里物流配送的应用分析[J].物流科技,2019,42(02):38-41.
[9] 杨洪路,张伊,邓静.基于区块链的ETC管理系统设计与实现[J].中国交通信息化,2020,(02):18-24.
[10] 罗江,高林,郑婧,等.基于区块链的高速公路ETC监测管理系统[J].中国交通信息化,2020,(05):18-22.
[11] 王棚.基于区块链的高速公路行驶路径还原技术探究[J].中国交通信息化,2020,(07):93-95,101.
[12] 邹亚强,朱小燕,蒋小健,等.联盟链技术在汽车售后服务的应用模型[J].科学技术创新,2020,(17):71-73.
[13] 陶云杰,余伟.基于区块链的共享汽车服务[J].电子商务,2019,(03):59-60.
[14] 李春燕.基于区块链技术的车载自组织网络路况预警方案研究[D].北京:北京交通大学,2019.
[15] Zhang X,Chen X. Data Security Sharing and Storage Based on a Consortium Blockchain in a Vehicular Ad-hoc Network[J]. IEEE Access,2019:58241-58254.
[16] Yuan Y,Wang F Y. Towards blockchain-based intelligent transportation systems[C]// IEEE International Conference on Intelligent Transportation Systems. IEEE,2016.
[17] Rowan S, Clear M, Gerla M, et al. Securing Vehicle to Vehicle Communications using Blockchain through Visible Light and Acoustic Side-Channels[J]. 2017.
[18] Singh M, Kim S. Trust Bit: Reward-based intelligent vehicle commination using blockchain paper[C]//2018 IEEE 4th World Forum on Internet of Things (WF-IoT). IEEE,2018.
[19] Xiong Z H, Feng S H, Wang W B, et al. Cloud/fog computing resource management and pricing for blockchain networks[J]. arXiv:1710.01567,2018.
[20] QIU X Y,LIU L B,CHEN W H,etal. Online deep reinforcement learning for computation offloading in blockchain-empowered mobile edge computing[J]. IEEE Transactions on Vehicular Technology, 2019, 68(8): 8050-8062.
[21] Kang J,Yu R,Huang X,et al. Blockchain for Secure and Efficient Data Sharing in Vehicular Edge Computing and Networks[J]. IEEE Internet of Things Journal, 2019, 6(3): 4660-4670.
[22] Jiao Y,Wang P, Niyato D, et al. Auction Mechanisms in Cloud/Fog Computing Resource Allocation for Public Blockchain Networks[J]. IEEE Transactions on Parallel and Distributed Systems,2019:1-1.
[23] Kotobi K, Bilén S G. Secure blockchains for dynamic spectrum access: a decentralized database in moving cognitive radio networks enhances security and user access[J]. IEEE Vehicular Technology Magazine,2018,13(1): 2-9.

智慧交叉口车路协同控制优化研究综述

肖七瑞　刘　伟*
(重庆交通大学交通运输学院)

摘　要　自动驾驶的车路协同控制优化研究是当前智慧交通领域的一个重要研究方向,大量学者针对该问题进行了深入研究,涵盖了道路交叉口信号优化控制、车辆自动驾驶、交通流及智慧路口等领域的相关理论和方法。本文从实践的角度出发,首先综述了传统交叉口信号控制策略,其次进行自动驾驶/混合驾驶环境下车辆行为及其交通流特征研究,最后取得自动驾驶环境下交叉口车路协同控制策略和智慧路口建设等方面的成果。综合上述研究内容,提出一种技术路线,采用 VISSIM/SUMO 工具来实现自动驾驶道路交叉口场景的动态仿真分析,探究自动驾驶场景下的道路交叉口通行能力、排队长度、绿灯使用率等主要参数指标的变化规律。

关键词　智能交通　研究综述　交叉口信号优化　自动驾驶车辆(AV)　车路协同系统(IVICS)

0　引言

随着城市空间的拓展,汽车保有量快速增长,而地形地貌等因素的限制,使道路的发展受阻,与车辆发展的不匹配,导致城市交通拥堵加剧、矛盾突出。一方面,依靠智慧道路安全、高效、绿色等优势,可在一定程度上弥补地形地貌等难以改变的因素带来的限制,从而提升道路功能,缓解拥堵;另一方面,智慧道路对车路协同的有力支撑将助力道路运输系统的协同管控,实现路网的科学管理与高效运行,提供更加优质的运输服务,从而改善道路发展与车辆发展之间的不匹配问题。

"智慧车还需智慧路",与自动驾驶相适配的智慧道路是自动驾驶车辆 V2I、V2V 乃至 V2X 等的通信基础,是车路协同的重要支撑。车路协同通过车辆信息化、道路信息化、云计算和大数据计算中心形成的体系化整体应用,成为了智慧道路的关键技术,可为复杂环境下自动驾驶提供技术支撑。

1　现状分析

1.1　传统信号控制

交叉口信号控制即通过控制交通信号灯,合理分配交叉口各进口的通行权。按照控制区域可分为单点信号控制、干线协调控制、区域协调控制等方式。

交叉口信号配时首先需要进行相位设计,确定饱和流量以及其他参数,使用韦伯斯特(Webster)配时法以及其他方法确定信号周期,再根据流量比分配绿灯时间以及其他参数。

感应式信号控制通过路口的检测设备感知道路状况,反馈给信号控制机来调整信号配时方案。感应信号控制相比固定配时可以提高绿灯使用率,减少交叉口停车延误。

单点自适应控制在感应式信号控制的基础上,内置基于逻辑规则或优化策略的优化配时算法,生成适合当前需求的配时方案。

干线协调控制是在单点信号控制的基础上,协调多个信号交叉口,使干线通行能力达到最优或次优。

1.2　智慧路口现状

智慧交叉口即结合物联网、互联网、边缘计算、人工智能等方面技术,使现代交叉口侧重于实时反应路口的本地实时态势、实时感知、实时应用联动,具有移动互联、仿真模拟、高精度地图、信息播报等功能。

1.2.1　国内现状

在国内,哈尔滨工业大学构建的交通电子智慧路口,使用增强现实(AR)技术和交通仿真技术来实现新建路口的渠化设计和评估;重庆车检院联合中国移动重庆公司,采用 5G + 北斗高精度定位技术,在重庆高新区实施了车路协同与自动驾驶示范项目;长沙智能驾驶研究院[1]研发了智能网联交叉路口管理系统,集成传感器感知技术、智能网联技术、传感器融合算法、交通优化算法,可实现交叉路口行人、非机动车辆、红绿灯与智能网联汽车之间的信息传递。

1.2.2　国外现状

在国外,美国思科公司[2]以 Wi-Fi 无线技术将路侧设备与手机端、车端互联互通,结合物联网计算平台进行数据处理,上传到云端,分析出每个车道一天的交通流变化;本田公司[3]、Miovision 公司[4]等打造的智能交叉口,包含云端平台、开放 API 以及硬件,应用案例主要有远程性能诊断、实时事件检测和自动响应、预测分析并改善多模式交通流等;欧洲 IoT-COMM 项目[5]开发了协作式智能十字路口,路口的摄像头将高质量视频实时发送至路侧单元,将监测信息通过无线网络从路侧设备传输到车载设备。

2　驾驶行为特征及交通流特征分析

2.1　驾驶行为特征

据目前的研究,车辆驾驶的行为特征方面主要集中在车辆环境感知、路径规划决策、行为决策等方面[6]。

2.1.1　车辆环境感知

车辆环境感知反映了车辆的环境感知能力特征和数据清洗能力特征,通过激光雷达、超声波雷达、摄像头等设备,感知路网结构、车辆位置、外部环境信息(如动静态障碍物位置等)用于决策处理,达到车辆对外界环境自主感知或协同感知[7]。

2.1.2　路径规划决策

路径规划决策体现了车辆宏观的驾驶轨迹特征与微观的动态运行特征,根据环境感知信息,决定车辆的驾驶路径和动态驾驶行为,包括任务规划、行为决策与运动规划等组成部分。其中,任务规划综合考虑道路的静态和动态变化因素,如线路条件、限行、限速、拥堵等,规划车辆前往目的地的最优路径,典型方法包括基于迭代搜索的最优路径规划方法[8]、图论方法[9]等。

2.1.3　行为决策

行为决策即根据车辆动态感知信息,生成加速、减速、车辆换道、车道车速保持等驾驶行为指令;典型方法包括基于有限状态机[10]、自动推理[11]等基于规则的决策方法以及基于机器学习[12]的决策方法等。运动规划根据行为决策指令,考虑车辆动力学特性、外界环境动静态障碍、前方线路特征等因素,优化生成目标运动轨迹作为车辆横纵向控制目标量。根据决策目标的不同,典型的运动规划方法可分为局部路径规划方法[13]、路线规划[14]、动作规划[15-16]和轨迹规划[17]等。车辆控制及根据规划决策的车辆横纵向控制目标量,使控制车辆沿指定轨迹行驶,典型的控制方法包括模型预测控制、自适应控制、PID 控制和滑模控制等[18]。

2.2　交通流特征模型

围绕交通流特征方面的现有研究主要集中在微观尺度、中观尺度和宏观尺度的交通流建模等方面。

2.2.1　微观尺度模型

微观尺度模型用于刻画自动驾驶车辆个体外在的跟驰特征,主要研究车辆跟驰特征对交通流效率和安全的影响,典型的微观尺度模型包括期望测量模型[19-21]、安全距离模型[22]、最优速度模型[23]、控制模型[24-25]等。此外,还有一部分微观尺度模型用于刻画车辆的安全换道过程,并量化该过程对交通流的影响,典型的模型包括基于规则的模型、机器学习模型[26]等。

2.2.2　中观尺度模型

中观尺度模型填补了微观尺度模型和宏观尺度模型之间的空白,包括气体动力学模型、连续气体动力学模型、车头时距分布模型[27-28]等,可用于描述混合车辆和自动驾驶汽车的交通流特征。

2.2.3　宏观尺度模型

宏观尺度模型刻画更大的时间和空间范围的交通流特征,可用于分析路网的通行能力[29-30]和交通流的稳定性[31-34]等。

3　自动驾驶环境下交叉口车路协同控制策略

车联网下的智能车辆交叉口信号控制策略研究主要集中在车辆通行控制策略研究、信号控制策略研究、车辆信号协同控制策略研究等方面。

3.1　控制策略研究

3.1.1　车辆通行控制策略研究

交叉口车辆通行控制主要以信号灯配时为基础,结合智能网联汽车与交叉口交互的信息,实现

速度和加速度的调整,包括有以下几个方向:

(1)假设车辆的组成为自动驾驶车辆,可以实时地被信号灯控制,对车辆的加减速进行控制,如Ahn 等[35]和 Meng 等[36-37]。

(2)假设车辆的组成为自动驾驶和人工驾驶车辆混合,可以实时地被信号灯控制,对车辆的加减速进行控制,如 Jiang 等[38]。

(3)假设车辆的组成为自动驾驶车辆,不采用传统的信号灯控制方法,而是直接根据车辆到达状态数据,规划出每辆车通过交叉口的先后顺序,进而对每辆车的轨迹控制方案进行求解,如 Park[39]和 Lee[40-41]。

3.1.2 信号控制策略研究

交叉口信号控制主要根据车联网环境下智能汽车和交叉口之间信息交互的结果,对交叉口信号灯相位进行调整,从而实现交叉口更大的通行能力,减少车辆在交叉口的等待时间。Beak 等[42]提出了一种改进多模态智能交通信号系统优先信号控制模型的方法,利用点对点交叉口通信从相邻交叉口发送优先请求,有效地减少优先合格车辆的停车次数和延误。Song 等[43]提出了一种基于行程时间预测模型的交通信号优先权优化方法,针对汽车联网环境下的双向实时信息传输,建立交通出行时间预测模型,实现了下一周期绿灯时间的补偿。

3.1.3 车辆信号协同控制策略研究

针对交叉口车联网情境下智能车辆与信号协同优化研究领域,主要有以下几个研究方向:

(1)在所有车辆都是自动驾驶且能与交叉口控制中心实时交互的理想条件下,对单车道的车辆与信号协同优化进行理论模型和求解算法的研究,如 Li 等[44]和 Feng 等[45]。

(2)在考虑不同类型车辆混合条件下,构建混合条件下的单车道的车辆与信号协同优化模型和求解算法,将智能车辆的渗透率作为一个实验控制参数,通过仿真实验探究模型算法的实际效果,如 Yang 等[46]和高书涛[47]。

(3)考虑交叉口多车道以及智能车辆在控制区域内换道的行为因素,建立了更加贴近真实情景的控制理论模型和响应的优化问题求解方法,如晏松[48]和梁晶伟[49]。

3.2 现有研究总结及其问题分析

现有研究针对自动驾驶的交叉口车路协同控制优化问题做出了积极贡献。然而,现有研究在面向自动驾驶的交叉口交通流特征变化机理、车路协同框架下的道路交叉口信息交互模型与框架、道路交叉口车路协同控制与信号优化配时等方面还存在诸多问题,具体如下。

(1)道路交叉口的交通流变化特征是实施交叉口信号优化控制的重要依据,现有方法主要根据车辆自身的驾驶行为特征和跟驰行为特征,分析了车辆跟驰行为为交通流效率和安全的影响,然而,现有方法未能站在道路交叉口控制的角度进行问题分析,缺乏对于交叉口类型、典型场景、行车特点等因素的挖掘辨识与综合考虑,造成面向自动驾驶的交叉口典型场景交通流特征变化规律研究尚处于空白。

(2)车路协同框架下的道路交叉口信息交互模型及框架有待建立。道路交叉口信息交互模型可为交叉口信号优化控制提供具体实施指导,然而,现有方法主要围绕交叉口车路协同控制的策略展开研究,并未针对交叉口车路协同控制进行过系统性探讨,使得智慧交叉口的建设目前主要停留在测速、监控、播报信息、获取信号配时等基础层面,缺乏车路协同框架下的交叉口信息交互需求系统化体系,涉及交叉口控制与安全行车的应用层关键信息交互需求及其交互机制有待完善。

(3)道路交叉口车路协同控制与信号优化配时仍有提升空间。现有研究在交叉口车路协同控制方面主要关注车联网环境下的单个交叉口信号相位调整,然而,现有研究未能充分利用 5G 通信与 V2X 体系(以下简称 5G + V2X)的优势,未能基于体系化的信息交互机制实现车路协同框架下的交叉口安全高效控制,尤其缺乏针对两难区域的车路协同控制研究以及面向自动驾驶的多交叉口网络化协同控制研究,使得交叉口的信号优化配时仍有提升空间。

3.3 技术路线

采用资料调研→特征分析→理论研究→方法提出→模型构建→问题求解的总体思路,围绕道路交叉口场景特征定义、交叉口车路协同信息交互模型与架构、交叉口车路协同控制与信号优化配时三个核心内容展开研究,具体技术路线如图 1 所示。

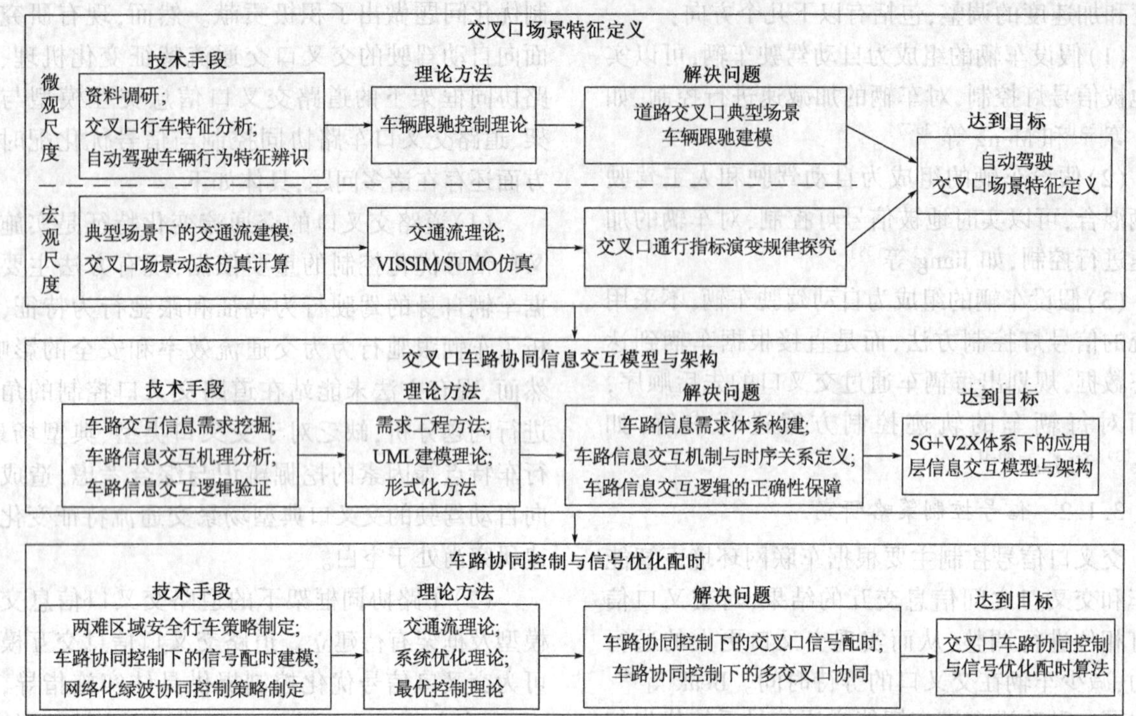

图 1　面向自动驾驶的交叉口车路协同控制优化研究技术路线图

对于道路交叉口场景特征定义,拟采用自动驾驶车辆跟驰控制理论、交通流理论和 VISSIM/SUMO 仿真等方法,围绕道路交叉口典型场景车辆跟驰建模、交叉口同行指标演变规律探究等关键问题展开研究,最终形成自动驾驶场景交叉口特征定义规格。

对于交叉口车路协同信息交互模型与架构,拟通过需求工程方法、UML 建模理论和形式化方法等,针对车路信息需求体系构建、车路信息交互机制与时序关系定义和车路信息交互逻辑的正确性保障等问题开展研究,形成 5G 和 V2X 体系下的应用层信息交互模型的架构。

对于车路协同控制与信号优化配时,拟采用交通流理论、系统优化控制理论和最优控制理论等手段,针对车路协同控制下的交叉口信号配时和多交叉口协同问题,设计交叉口车路协同安全控制策略和信号优化配时算法,实现面向自动驾驶的交叉口车路协同控制优化。

4　结语

对于自动驾驶的研究还需进一步加深,相关的规范尚未制订。面向道路自动驾驶场景,针对道路交叉口的车路协同控制问题,根据上述研究现状,可围绕面向自动驾驶的道路交叉口场景特征定义、车路协同框架下的道路交叉口信息交互模型与架构,道路交叉口车路协同控制与信号优化配时算法等方面开展研究,具体如下。

(1)面向自动驾驶道路交叉口场景的交通特征研究。

可分别从微观和宏观两个角度分析定义面向自动驾驶的道路交叉口场景的交通特征开展研究。

在微观层面,通过调研相关文献研究成果,分析自动驾驶车辆的行为特征,并根据自动驾驶跟驰控制理论,结合道路交叉口实际行车特点,构建面向自动驾驶道路交叉口场景的车辆跟驰模型和交通参数传递函数。

在宏观层面,以三路交叉口、四路交叉口和环路交叉口为研究对象,研究自动驾驶、自动驾驶与人工驾驶混合等工况,建立交叉口各入口交通量不均衡场景、路口有优先请求信号需求场景、流线强制优先场景等主要典型场景的交通参数与函数,采用 VISSIM/SUMO 工具实现对自动驾驶道路交叉口场景的动态仿真分析,探究自动驾驶场景下的道路交叉口通行能力、排队、绿灯使用率等主要参数指标的变化规律。

(2)研究车路协同框架下的道路交叉口信息交互模型与架构。

采用需求工程分析方法，以交叉口车路协同控制为目标导向，以自动驾驶车辆的安全可控、高效运行为原则和前提，挖掘和建立面向不同等级自动驾驶的车路信息交互需求体系；基于 UML (Unified Modelling Language) 建模技术，围绕车路信息交互需求，从交通信号灯状态、左转排队、车辆轨迹、车速、定位校正、危险预告、两难区域决策等关键信息交互需求入手，提出车路协同框架下的路侧-车端信息双向交互机制，定义信息交互的时序关系特征，构建基于 5G 通信与 V2X 技术体系框架的道路交叉口路侧-车端应用层信息交互模型与架构；采用 Petri 网理论、时间自动机理论等严格的形式化方法，围绕通信死锁、状态可达性、功能完备性等关键内容进行模型检测和性质验证，保障车路双向信息交互模型的逻辑正确性。

(3)研究道路交叉口车路协同控制与信号优化配时算法。

根据自动驾驶车辆车速可控的特点，基于车路协同框架下的关键信息交互机制，研究车路协同控制框架下的道路交叉口两难区域安全行车策略；基于上述研究(1)和研究(2)的结论，以三、四路交叉口和环路交叉口为驾驶环境，根据交叉口各入口交通量不均衡场景、路口有优先请求信号需求场景、流线强制优先场景等主要典型场景下的交通流特征，分阶段、分模式建立车路协同控制框架下的道路交叉口信号自适应优化配时模型，采用系统优化理论，提出适用于交叉口信号自适应优化配时的智能算法；在此基础上，进一步考虑多交叉口在不同组合类型下的网络化协同控制问题，提出车路协同环境下的网络化区域绿波协同控制策略，为车路协同环境下的自动驾驶车辆提供安全高效的路网车速引导方案。

参考文献

[1] 长沙智能研究院. 长沙智能驾驶研究院——智能网联交叉路口技术[EB/OL]. https://jingyan. baidu. com/article/4dc4084873c40fc8d946f1d6. html.

[2] Cisco. Smart Intersections-IoT insights using Wi-Fi [EB/OL]. https://www. cisco. com/c/dam/global/ en_au/products/pdfs/cisco-smart-intersection-iot-insights-using-wi-fi-v1. pdf.

[3] Honda. Honda Demonstrates New-Smart Intersection ‖ Technology [EB/OL]. https://csr. honda. com/2018/10/04/honda-demonstrates-new-smart-intersection-technology.

[4] MIOVISION. THE WORLD ' S SMARTEST INTERSECTION [EB/OL]. https://www. smartestinter section. com/innovation.

[5] European Projects. Cooperative Intersection Safety (INTERSAFE-2)[EB/OL]. https://www. up2europe. eu/ european/projects/? q = intersection.

[6] Urmson C, Anhalt J, Bagnell D, et al. Autonomous Driving in Urban Environments: Boss and the Urban Challenge[J]. Journal of Field Robotics, 2008, 25(8): 425-466.

[7] 张毅，姚丹亚. 基于车路协同的智能交通系统体系框架[M]. 北京：电子工业出版社，2015.

[8] 程向红，祁艺. 基于栅格法的室内指示路径规划算法[J]. 中国惯性技术学报，2018, 26(02): 236-240, 267.

[9] BoroujeniZ, Goehring D, Ulbrich F, et al. Flexible unit A-star trajectory planning for autonomous vehicles on structured road maps [C] // IEEE International Conference on Vehicular Electronics & Safety. IEEE, 2017.

[10] Chen Y, ZhaJ, Wang J. An Autonomous T-Intersection Driving Strategy Considering Oncoming Vehicles Based on Connected Vehicle Technology [J]. IEEE/ASME Transactions on Mechatronics, 2020, 24(6): 2779-2790.

[11] ZhaoL, Ichise R, Sasaki Y, et al. Fast Decision Making using Ontology-based Knowledge Base [C] // Intelligent Vehicles Symposium. IEEE, 2016.

[12] 王玉龙，裴锋，刘文如，等. 基于开关式深度神经网络的拟人化自动驾驶决策算法[J]. 中国机械工程，2021, 32(6): 689-696. DOI: 10.3969/j. issn. 1004-132X. 2021. 06. 008.

[13] 吴黎兵，范静，聂雷，等. 一种车联网环境下的城市车辆协同选路方法[J]. 计算机学报，2017, 040(007): 1600-1613.

[14] Ohn-BarE, Trivedi M M. Looking at Humans in the Age of Self-Driving and Highly Automated Vehicles[J]. IEEE Transactions on

Intelligent Vehicles,2016:90-104.

[15] CkA,Mq A,Whc B,et al. Real-time motion planning methods for autonomous on-road driving: State-of-the-art and future research directions-ScienceDirect [J]. Transportation Research Part C: Emerging Technologies, 2015,60:416-442.

[16] EvestedtN, Ward E, Folkesson J, et al. Interaction aware trajectory planning for merge scenarios in congested traffic situations[C]// 2016 IEEE 19th International Conference on Intelligent Transportation Systems (ITSC). IEEE,2016.

[17] ZhangS,Shen Y,Sun Z. Mobile Robot Local Path Planning Based on Improved T-S Fuzzy Neural Network[C]// International Industrial Informatics & Computer Engineering Conference. 2015.

[18] 唐志荣,冀杰,吴明阳,等.基于改进人工势场法的车辆路径规划与跟踪[J].西南大学学报(自然科学版),2018,40(6).

[19] NishinariK. Traffic Flow Dynamics: Data, Models and Simulation [J]. Physics Today, 2014,67(3):54-54.

[20] Laval J,Toth C,Yi Z. A parsimonious model for the formation of oscillations in car-following models[J]. Transportation Research Part B,2014,70(dec.):228-238.

[21] Zheng,Liang,Guan,et al. A simple nonparametric car-following model driven by field data [J]. Transportation research,Part B. Methodological,2015.

[22] ZhengL,Zhu C,He Z,et al. Safety Rule-Based Cellular Automaton Modeling and Simulation under V2V Environment[J]. Transportmetrica A:Transport Science,2018:1-37.

[23] Xie D,Gao Z,Zhao X. The effect of ACC vehicles to mixed traffic flow consisting of manual and ACC vehicles [J]. Chinese Physics B,2008,17(12):4440-4445.

[24] Naus G J L,Ploeg J,Molengraft M J G V D,et al. Design and implementation of parameterized adaptive cruise control: An explicit model predictive control approach [J]. Control Engineering Practice,2010,18(8):882-892.

[25] GeigerA,Lauer M,Moosmann F,et al. Team Annie WAY's Entry to the 2011 Grand Cooperative Driving Challenge [J]. IEEE Transactions on Intelligent Transportation Systems,2012,13(3):1008-1017.

[26] WolfP,Kurzer K,Wingert T,et al. Adaptive Behavior Generation for Autonomous Driving using Deep Reinforcement Learning with Compact Semantic States[C]// 2018 IEEE Intelligent Vehicle Symposium. IEEE,2018.

[27] Nowakowski,O'Connell J,Shladover S E,et al. Cooperative Adaptive Cruise Control:Driver Acceptance of Following Gap Settings Less than One Second [J]. Human Factors & Ergonomics Society Annual Meeting Proceedings,2010,3(24):2033-2037.

[28] Gunter G,JanssenC,Barbour W,et al. Model-Based String Stability of Adaptive Cruise Control Systems Using Field Data[J]. IEEE Transactions on Intelligent Vehicles,2020,5(1):90-99.

[29] ZhouJ, Zhu F. Modeling the fundamental diagram of mixed human-driven and connected automated vehicles [J]. Transportation Research Part C:Emerging Technologies,115.

[30] GhiasiA,Hussain O,Qian Z S,et al. A mixed traffic capacity analysis and lane management model for connected automated vehicles: A Markov chain method [J]. Transportation Research Part B Methodological, 2017, 106 (dec.):266-292.

[31] Sun, Jie, Zheng, et al. Stability analysis methods and their applicability to car-following models in conventional and connected environments [J]. Transportation Research Part B Methodological,2018.

[32] Ngoduy D, Jia D. Multi anticipative bidirectional macroscopic traffic model considering cooperative driving strategy[J]. Transportmetrica,2017,5(1-4):96-110.

[33] HuangK,Di X,Du Q,et al. Scalable traffic

stability analysis in mixed-autonomy using continuum models [J]. Transportation Research Part C Emerging Technologies, 2020,111:616-630.

[34] IoannouPA, Chien C, Autonomous intelligent cruise control [J]. IEEE Transactions on Vehicular Technology, 1993, 42(4):657-672.

[35] Ahn K, Rakha H A, Park S. Ecodrive Application: Algorithmic Development and Preliminary Testing[M]. 2013.

[36] Meng W, Da AmenW, Hoogendoorn S P, et al. Rolling horizon control framework for driver assistance systems. Part I: Mathematical formulation and non-cooperative systems[J]. Transportation Research Part C, 2014, 40 (mar.):271-289.

[37] Meng W, DaamenW, Hoogendoorn S P, et al. Rolling horizon control framework for driver assistance systems. Part II: Cooperative sensing and cooperative control [J]. Transportation Research Part C: Emerging Technologies, 2014, 40(mar.):290-311.

[38] Jiang H, HuJ, An S, et al. Eco approaching at an isolated signalized intersection under partially connected and automated vehicles environment[J]. Transportation Research Part C Emerging Technologies, 2017, 79 (JUN.): 290-307.

[39] Park B B, Malakorn K, LeeJ, et al. Sustainability Assessment of Cooperative Vehicle Intersection Control at Urban Intersections with Low Volume Condition [M]. Springer Berlin Heidelberg, 2012.

[40] Lee J, ParkB. Development and Evaluation of a Cooperative Vehicle Intersection Control Algorithm Under the Connected Vehicles Environment [J]. IEEE Transactions on Intelligent Transportation Systems, 2012, 13 (1):81-90.

[41] LeeJ, Park B B, Malakorn K, et al. Sustainability assessments of cooperative vehicle intersection control at an urban corridor[J]. Transportation Research Part C Emerging Technologies, 2013, 32(jul.):193-206.

[42] Beak B, ZamanipourM, Head K L, et al. Peer-to-Peer Priority Signal Control Strategy in a Connected Vehicle Environment [J]. Transportation Research Record Journal of the Transportation Research Board, 2018, 2672 (18):036119811877356.

[43] Song X, YuanM, Di L, et al. Optimization Method for Transit Signal Priority considering Multirequest under Connected Vehicle Environment[J]. Journal of Advanced Transportation, 2018, 2018 (PT. 3): 7498594. 1-7498594. 10.

[44] Li Z, ElefteriadouL, Ranka S. Signal control optimization for automated vehicles at isolated signalized intersections [J]. Transportation Research Part C, 2014, 49:1-18.

[45] Feng Y, YuC, Liu H X. Spatiotemporal intersection control in a connected and automated vehicle environment [J]. Transportation Research Part C Emerging Technologies, 2018, 89(APR.):364-383.

[46] Yang K, Guler SI, Menendez M. Isolated intersection control for various levels of vehicle technology: Conventional, connected, and automated vehicles [J]. Transportation Research Part C, 2016, 72(11):109-129.

[47] 高书涛.基于车路协同的交叉口车辆通行方法研究[D].长春:吉林大学,2017.

[48] 晏松.智能网联环境下复杂交叉口信号控制研究[D].北京:中国人民公安大学.2019.

[49] 梁晶伟.车路协同条件下交叉口优化控制方法[D].长春:吉林大学,2019.

公众监督下的政府与超载运输企业的演化博弈分析

洪中荣　王来军*　张柯娜
(长安大学运输工程学院)

摘　要　为了探究公众监督举报机制在运输企业超载运输问题的监管上的可行性,构建了以运输企业和监管部门为主体的演化博弈模型。在引入公众监督举报机制后,分析各种条件下的演化博弈均衡,并利用模拟仿真分析双方的博弈过程,揭示超载运输罚款、监管部门的监管效率以及公众监督举报率对运输企业和监管部门决策施加影响的过程。研究表明,建立成熟完善的超载运输举报平台能够降低监管部门的监管成本从而有效控制超载运输,但只有在监管效率与举报概率处于较高水平时监管部门进行提升惩罚力度的提升才会对抑制超载运输起到积极作用。

关键词　交通组织与运营管理　超载治理　演化博弈　公众监督

0　引言

随着我国公路总里程不断攀升,路网格局不断完善,到 2020 年末全国公路运输量达到 342.64 亿 t,同时也对政府的监管水平提出了新的更高的要求。一些运输企业为了追求超额收益,利用多种手段躲避监管进行超载运输[1]。超载的车辆还会对道路和桥梁造成损害[2],因此,如何进一步提升对运输企业监管效果,减少超载运输现象成为了相关部门的一大难题。由于无法对运输企业进行完全实时的监管,相关部门对超载运输的监管往往达不到想要的效果,此外政府监管的手段单一、监管力度不足等问题也是超载运输现象屡禁不止的重要原因[3]。

在过往对超载运输的研究中,Eric 等[4]提出了一种双层建模的方法,用于探究货运承运人超载对于道路的损害和道路规划部门的惩罚金额之间的关系,但是模型变量较少,没有考虑其他因素可能造成的影响。曹长慧[5]从静态博弈的角度出发,对运输企业的超载情况和监管部门的监管力度进行研究,但是缺少对博弈双方的决策的动态演绎;崔红建[6]从经济学角度分析超载的原因,但是缺少量化研究。超载运输的车辆的制动性能会大大下降[7],一旦事故发生,不仅会对公众的生命财产造成严重损失,而且将会降低公众对相关监管部门的信任度。因此,公众对于超载运输进行监督,是主动承担社会责任的体现,也是对于自身的安全的保护。

目前少有研究针对超载运输监管领域内的公众参与监督的研究。本研究在以往研究的基础上,以运输企业的运输行为和监管部门的监管行为作为基础,运用演化博弈理论,建立演化博弈模型,并在博弈过程中引入公众对运输企业的监督情况,探究不同参与度情况下公众监督对于博弈双发演化结果的影响,进一步得出影响最终博弈演化结果的关键因素,从而为实际的超载运输监管提供理论支持。

1　博弈模型构建

1.1　基本假设

根据演化博弈理论与实际情况作出假设。

假设 1:监管部门与运输企业各主体都为有限理性。

假设 2:对于监管部门,策略集为强监管与弱监管,令监管部门在时间 t 选择强监管的概率为 $x(t)$,则选择弱监管的概率为 $1-x(t)$。监管部门采取强监管成本为 C_{11},采取弱监管的成本为 C_{12}。在监管部门采用强监管条件下,运输企业的合规运输行为降低了道路安全风险,监管部门获得社会

1. 基金项目:长安大学重点科研平台开放基金项目(300102341505)。

效益 R_{11};假设强监管下监管部门发现超载行为的概率为 $q(0<q<1)$,称 q 为监管效率。对被发现的超载运输企业需要缴纳罚金 F,同时监管部门收获一定的社会效益 R_{12}。监管部门采取弱监管条件下,监管部门发现运输企业的超载行为的概率为 $p(0<p<q<1)$,运输企业的超载运输行为造成不良社会影响,给监管部门带来负面效益 R_{13}。

假设3:对于运输企业,策略为合规运输和超载运输,令运输企业在时间 t 选择合规运输的概率为 $y(t)$,则选择超载运输的概率为 $1-y(t)$。企业进行合规运输的收益为 R_{21},进行超载运输将获得更大的收益 R_{22}。

假设4:公众监督举报起到协助监管部门的作用,公众举报运输企业的超载行为的概率为 $\lambda(0<\lambda<1)$,并且所有举报都是有效举报,被举报的运输企业将同样被监管部门处罚金 F。

1.2 收益矩阵与动态复制方程

基于以上的假设,可以得到博弈双方的策略组合与收益矩阵,如表1所示。

博弈双方的战略组合与收益矩阵 表1

博弈主体		运输企业	
		合规运输	超载运输
监管部门	强监管	$(R_{11}-C_{11},R_{21})$	$(R_{12}-C_{11}+qF+\lambda F,R_{22}-qF-\lambda F)$
	弱监管	$(-C_{12},R_{21})$	$(-C_{12}-R_{13}+\lambda F+pF,R_{22}-\lambda F-pF)$

在表1的收益矩阵中,监管部门与运输企业都在博弈过程中不断更换自己的策略,以求获得更大的收益。根据演化博弈理论,当选择的某个策略的期望收益高于博弈系统的平均期望时,该策略就会在系统中扩散[8]。

1.2.1 监管部门的复制动态方程

设监管部门采取强监管的期望收益 E_{11}、采取弱监管的期望收益 E_{12} 与平均期望收益 $\overline{E_x}$,可得:

$$E_{11}=y(R_{11}-C_{11})+(1-y)(R_{12}-C_{11}+qF+\lambda F) \tag{1}$$

$$E_{12}=y(-C_{12})+(1-y)(-C_{12}-R_{13}+\lambda F+pF) \tag{2}$$

$$\overline{E_x}=xE_{11}+(1-x)E_{12} \tag{3}$$

进一步得到监管部门采用强监管的动态复制方程:

$$\frac{dx}{dt}=F(x)=x(E_{11}-\overline{E_x})=x(1-x)(E_{11}-E_{12}) \tag{4}$$

1.2.2 运输企业的复制动态方程

设运输企业采取合规运输的期望收益 E_{21}、超载运输的期望收益 E_{22} 与平均期望收益 $\overline{E_y}$,可得:

$$E_{21}=x(R_{21})+(1-x)(R_{21}) \tag{5}$$

$$E_{22}=x(R_{22}-qF-\lambda F)+(1-x)(R_{22}-\lambda F-pF) \tag{6}$$

$$\overline{E_y}=yE_{21}+(1-y)E_{22} \tag{7}$$

进一步得到运输企业采取合规运输的动态复制方程:

$$\frac{dy}{dt}=F(y)=y(E_{21}-\overline{E_y})=y(1-y)(E_{21}-E_{22}) \tag{8}$$

2 演化博弈模型分析

2.1 演化博弈演化稳定策略求解

在上述的博弈模型中,监管机构在 t 时刻采取强监管的概率为 $x(t)$,运输企业在 t 时刻采取合规运输的概率为 $y(t)$,两个概率都是与 t 相关的函数,并且 $x(t),y(t)\in[0,1]$。令 $F(x)=0$,$F(y)=0$,此时策略的选择率不再变化,可以得到演化过程的中的4个纯策略解(0,0),(0,1),(1,0),(1,1)与一个混合策略解(x^*,y^*)。

根据两主体的动态复制方程式(4)、式(8)可以得到对应的雅可比矩阵:

$$\boldsymbol{J}=\begin{bmatrix}\frac{\partial F(x)}{\partial x} & \frac{\partial F(x)}{\partial y}\\ \frac{\partial F(y)}{\partial x} & \frac{\partial F(y)}{\partial y}\end{bmatrix}=\begin{bmatrix}G_{11} & G_{12}\\ G_{21} & G_{22}\end{bmatrix} \tag{9}$$

式中:$\boldsymbol{J}$——演化系统的雅克比矩阵;

G_{11}、G_{12}——分别为复制动态方程 $F(x)$ 对 x 和 y 的偏导数;

G_{21}、G_{22}——复制动态方程 $F(y)$ 对 x 和 y 的偏导数。

$G_{11}, G_{12}, G_{21}, G_{22}$ 计算式如下：

$$G_{11}=(1-2x)[y(R_{11}-C_{11}+C_{12})+(1-y)(R_{12}-C_{11}+qF+C_{12}+R_{13}-pF)]$$

$$G_{12}=x(1-x)(R_{11}-R_{12}-R_{13}-qF+pF)$$

$$G_{21}=y(1-y)(qF-pF)$$

$$G_{22}=(1-2y)(R_{21}-R_{22}+xqF-xpF+\lambda F+pF)$$

2.2　均衡点演化稳定性分析

根据 Lyapunov 稳定性理论，可以用雅可比矩阵来确定演化系统中某些点的稳定性[9]。就某个具体的点来说，当对应雅可比矩阵中所有特征值都为负时，也就是说雅可比矩阵的行列式应大于 0 而迹小于 0，即 $\det\boldsymbol{J}>0$ 且 $\mathrm{tr}\boldsymbol{J}<0$ 时，可以确定该点为演化稳定策略（ESS）。5 个局部均衡点的稳定性分析如表 2 所示。

均衡点的稳定性分析　　表 2

均衡点	$\det\boldsymbol{J}$	$\mathrm{tr}\boldsymbol{J}$
(0,0)	$(R_{12}-C_{11}+qF+C_{12}+R_{13}-pF)(R_{21}-R_{22}+\lambda F+pF)$	$R_{12}-C_{11}+qF+C_{12}+R_{13}-pF+R_{21}-R_{22}+\lambda F+pF$
(1,0)	$-(R_{12}-C_{11}+qF+C_{12}+R_{13}-pF)(R_{21}-R_{22}+qF+\lambda F)$	$R_{21}-R_{22}+qF+\lambda F-(R_{12}-C_{11}+qF+C_{12}+R_{13}-pF)$
(0,1)	$-(R_{11}-C_{11}+C_{12})(R_{21}-R_{22}+\lambda F+pF)$	$R_{11}-C_{11}+C_{12}-(R_{21}-R_{22}+\lambda F+pF)$
(1,1)	$(R_{11}-C_{11}+C_{12})(R_{21}-R_{22}+qF+\lambda F)$	$-(R_{11}-C_{11}+C_{12})-(R_{21}-R_{22}+qF+\lambda F)$
(x^*,y^*)	+	0

均衡点 (x^*, y^*) 作为混合策略解，其对应行列式的迹始终为 0，因此该点为鞍点，无法成为 ESS。其余 4 点在不同情形下有成为 ESS 的可能性。

情形 1：当 $C_{11}>R_{12}+qF+C_{12}+R_{13}-pF$，$R_{22}>R_{21}+\lambda F+pF$ 时，系统在（0,0）处达到稳定，此时监管部门强监管成本高于所带来的社会效益，同时企业超载运输被公众监督举报的概率低，不足以起到有效的协助监管作用，企业最终选择超载运输策略，演化相位图如图 1 所示。

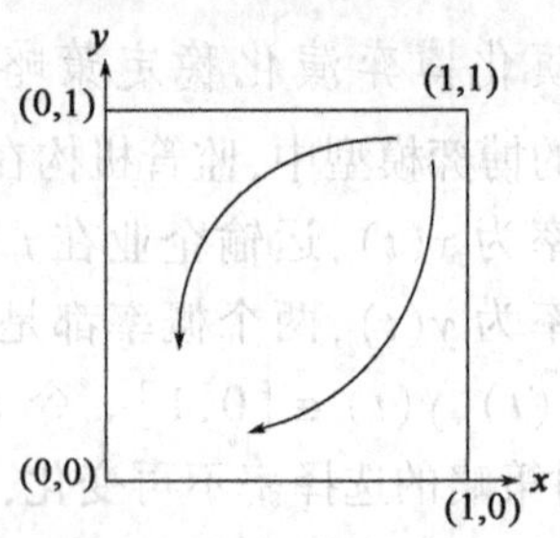

图 1　情形 1 的政企演化图

情形 2：当 $C_{11}<R_{12}+qF+C_{12}+R_{13}-pF$，$R_{22}>R_{21}+\lambda F+qF$ 时，系统在（1,0）处达到稳定，此时监管部门强监管成本低于强监管所带来的社会效益，在监管部门与公众的双重监管下，获得正向效益高于强监管成本。而运输企业合规运输的期望依旧较低，同时监管部门惩罚力度不足，对于运输企业来说，依旧选择超载运输作为稳定策略，演化相位图如图 2 所示。

情形 3：当 $C_{11}>R_{11}+C_{12}$，$R_{22}<R_{21}+\lambda F+pF$ 时，系统在（0,1）处达到稳定，此时监管部门强监管成本很高，监管部门选择弱监管；但是对于运输企业，由于超载运输被处罚罚金过高，以及公众监督举报的存在导致企业超载运输期望下降，最终选择合规运输，演化相位图如图 3 所示。

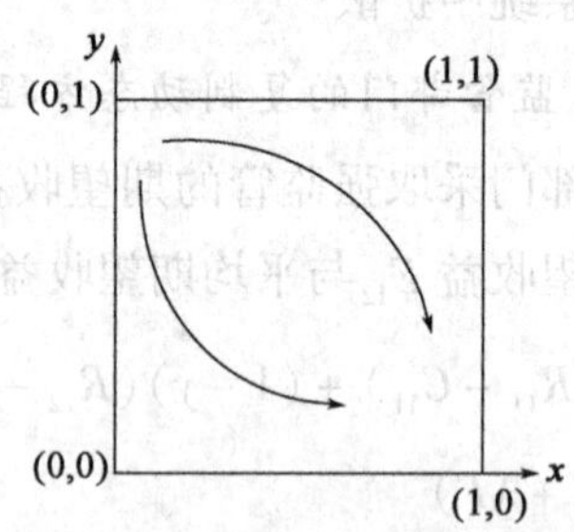

图 2　情形 2 的政企演化图

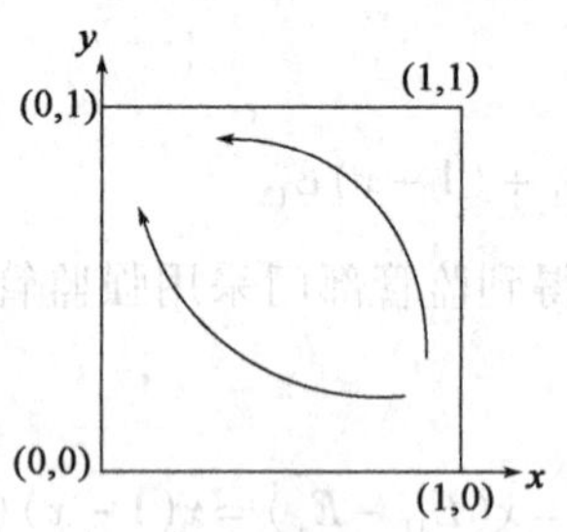

图 3　情形 3 的政企演化图

情形 4：当 $C_{11}<R_{11}+C_{12}$，$R_{22}<R_{21}+\lambda F+qF$ 时，系统在（1,1）处达到稳定，此时监管部门强监管能够带来良好的社会效益，同时由于公众监督与高额罚金的存在，运输企业最终合规运输策略。这是一种良好的状态，利用社会资源对运输企业进行约束，不仅规范了运输企业的行为，也加强了监管部门与社会群众的联系，演化相位图如图 4 所示。

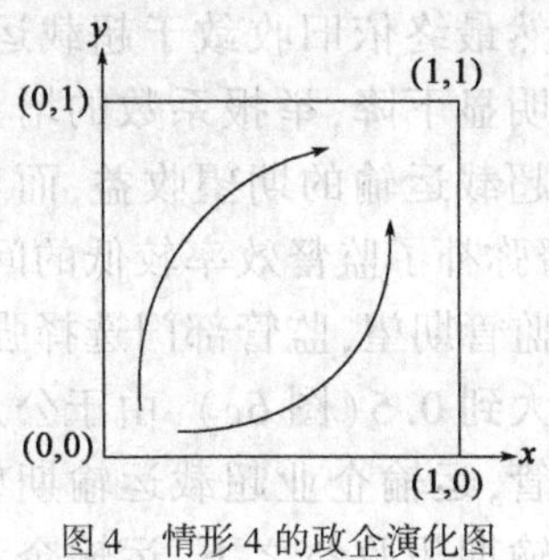

图4 情形4的政企演化图

3 演化模拟分析

基于以上讨论,成功确定了各个演化均衡点的条件。为了进一步研究在监管部门、运输企业的演化过程中,监管部门监管效率 q、监管部门对超载运输企业所处罚金 F、公众监督举报超载运输行为的概率 λ 3个参数对于演化结果的影响,利用Matlab R2017b模拟博弈双方的演化过程。为了突出这些参数波动对最终演化结果的影响,基于设计模型的结果和稳定性分析,对参数进行调整,分析其对控制超载运输的有效性。对参数进行如下初始取值:$C_{11}=15$,$C_{12}=3$,$R_{11}=17$,$R_{12}=4$,$R_{13}=2$,$p=0.1$,$F=5$,$\lambda=0.1$,$R_{21}=5$,$R_{22}=8$。

3.1 监管效率与超载运输罚金的变化对演化均衡影响的仿真结果

为了深入探究监管效率与超载所处罚金之间的联系,保持其他参数不变,取监管部门的监管效率 $q=0.5$,罚金 $F=5$ 作为参照,在监管效率不变的情况下令罚金 $F=7$,再保持罚金 $F=7$,降低监管效率到 $q=0.3$ 三种情况下的演化结果如图5所示,其中横、纵坐标分别表示演化时间进程与博弈双方做出决策的概率变化,实线与虚线分别表示监管部门与运输企业在不同初始决策概率下的决策演化过程。图5a)显示了监管效率 $q=0.5$,罚金 $F=5$ 时的演化情况,此时监管部门的强监管的期望收益较高,监管部门最终选择强监管策略,但是由于罚金设置较小,并不能够使得降低运输企业超载运输期望,运输企业依旧选择超载运输。图5b)显示,在监管效率处于合适水平,罚金 F 的提升能有效令运输企业的超载运输期望降低,同时提升了监管部门强监管期望,最终监管部门进行强监管而运输企业进行合规运输。图5c)显示,即使提高了罚金,但是由于监管部门的监管效率较低,无法及时发现超载行为,进一步来说,运输企业的超载运输收益仍然高于合规运输收益,最终运输企业选择超载运输策略。因此,从监管效率与罚金的角度来讲,要对超载运输行为进行控制,只依靠罚金的提高是不行的,从内部提高监管部门的监管效率,提高监管积极性也对于超载运输的控制有非常大的帮助。

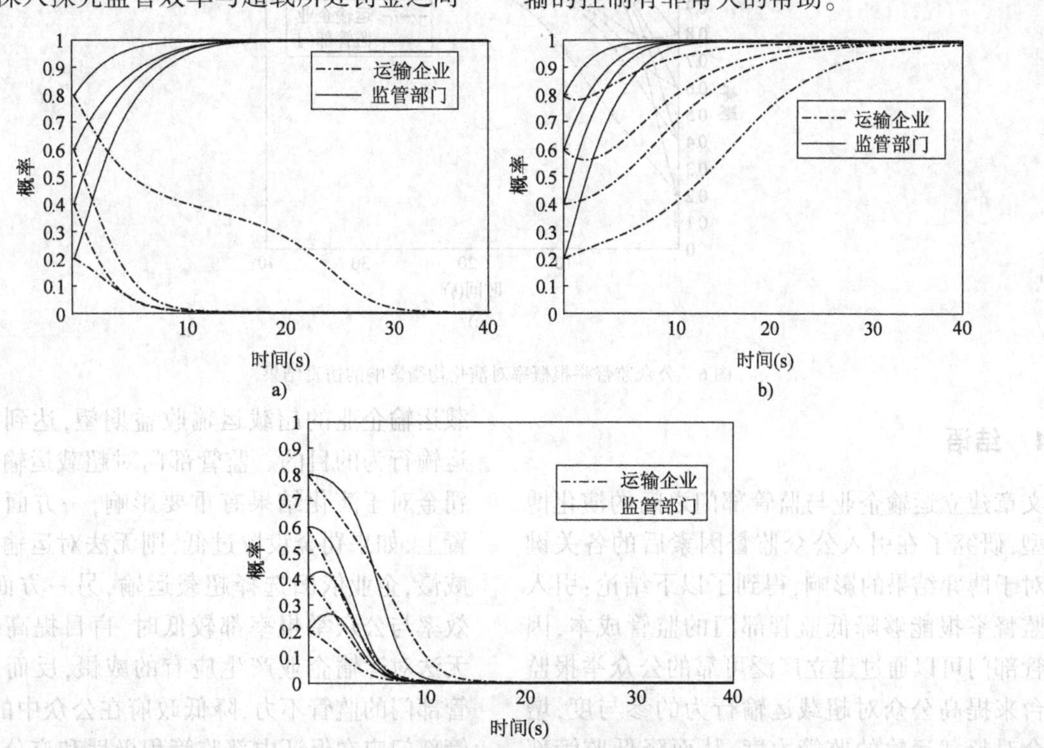

图5 超载运输罚金与监管效率对演化均衡影响的仿真结果

3.2　公众监督举报的概率对演化均衡影响的仿真结果

为了体现公众监督在协助监管部门对运输企业进行监管的作用,在适当的处罚条件下,改变监管部门的监管效率与公众举报率,在其他参数不变的条件下,令 $q=0.3$,分别取 $\lambda=0.1$、$\lambda=0.3$、$\lambda=0.5$,演化结果如图6所示。在 $q=0.3,\lambda=0.1$ 时,如图6a)所示,监管部门的监管效率与公众举报率都较低时,无法对运输企业进行有效监管,导致运输企业超载运输期望高,选择超载运输,监管部门由于监管效率低,弱监管期望收益较高最终选择弱监管。当 λ 增大到0.3时,如图6b)所示,运输企业虽然最终依旧收敛于超载运输策略,但是收敛速度明显下降,举报系数的增大有效降低了运输企业超载运输的期望收益,而对于监管部门,公众监督弥补了监督效率较低的问题,提升了监管部门强监管期望,监管部门选择强监管;举报系数继续增大到0.5(图6c),由于公众和监管部门的共同监管,运输企业超载运输期望收益已降低至合规运输期望收益之下,运输企业将自觉进行合规运输,监管部门进行强监管。因此,建立并完善一套可行的公众举报制度对于控制超载运输行为有非常重要的意义,可以有效弥补监管部门的监管漏洞,加强对超载运输行为的监管。

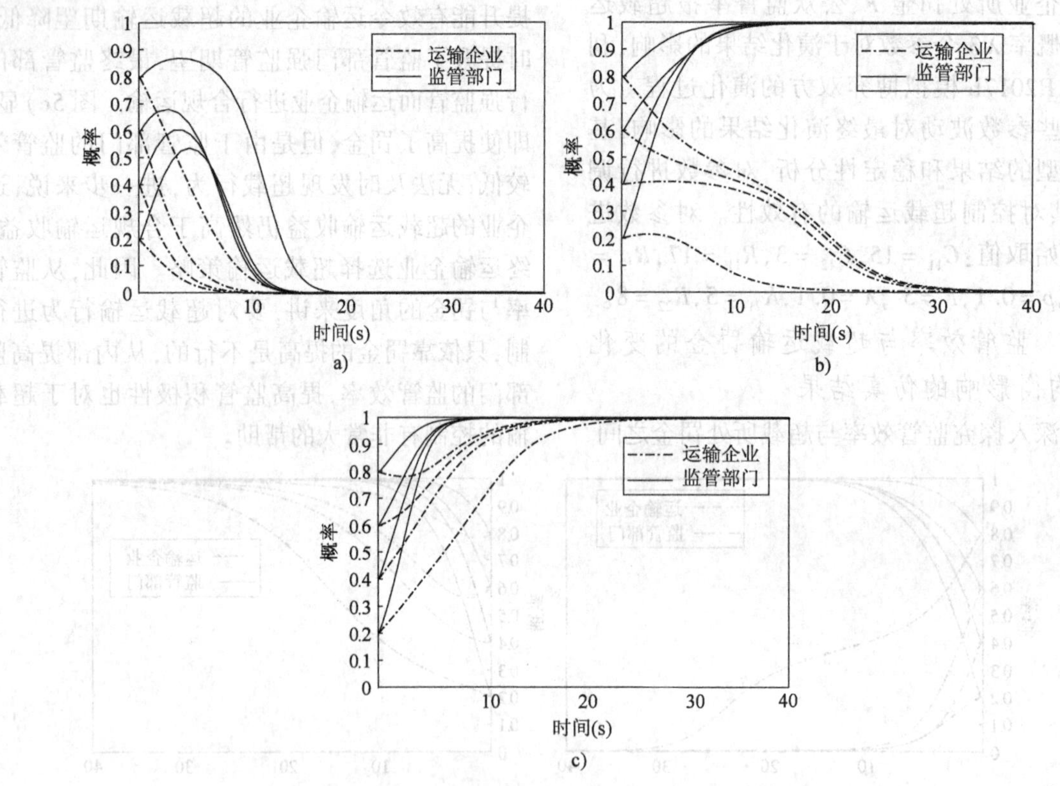

图6　公众监督举报概率对演化均衡影响的仿真结果

4　结语

文章建立运输企业与监管部门之间的演化博弈模型,研究了在引入公众监督因素后的各关键条件对于博弈结果的影响,得到了以下结论:引入公众监督举报能够降低监管部门的监管成本,因此监管部门可以通过建立广泛可靠的公众举报监管平台来提高公众对超载运输行为的参与度,增大群众对超载运输的监管力度,从而降低监管部门的监管成本,提高监管积极性同时也降低了超载运输企业的超载运输收益期望,达到控制超载运输行为的目的。监管部门对超载运输企业所处罚金对于演化结果有重要影响,一方面在罚金设置上,如果罚金设置过低,则无法对运输企业造成威慑,企业依旧选择超载运输,另一方面,在监管效率与公众举报率都较低时,盲目提高罚金不仅无法对运输企业产生应有的威慑,反而会由于监管部门的监管不力,降低政府在公众中的形象,监管部门应在保证内部监管积极性和充分发挥群众监督作用的基础上,增大超载运输的罚金,从而控制超载运输行为。

文章仅考虑了公众对于运输企业的监督,在以后的研究中可以考虑公众对于政府管理部门的监督作用。

参考文献

[1] 蒋劲羽,杨忠振.基于移动治超模式的农村公路治超站选址[J].公路交通科技,2020,37(04):125-132.

[2] 孙信文.公路货运车辆超限超载运输治理现状、困境与对策研究——以郑州为例[D].济南:济南大学,2020.

[3] 王伟,王晓楠,丁黎黎,等.考虑公众监督的政府与危险品运输企业的演化博弈分析[J].系科学学报,2022(01):92-96,136.

[4] Eric Moreno-Quintero, Tony Fowkes, David Watling. Modelling planner-carrier interactions in road freight transport Optimisation of road maintenance costs via overloading control [J]. Transportation Research PartE,50(2013)68-83.

[5] 曹长慧,李豪.超载运输与政府监管博弈分析及治理机制[J].重庆交通大学学报(社会科学版),2020,20(04):47-52.

[6] 崔红建,马天山.基于经济机理的公路超限超载运输长效治理机制研究[J].武汉理工大学学报(社会科学版),2010,23(02):194-198.

[7] 程强.公路超限超载运输问题探究-以新疆伊犁为例[D].西安:长安大学,2020.

[8] Taytor P D, Jonker L B. Evolutionarily Stable Strategies and Game Dynamics[J]. Mathematical Bioences,1978,40(1-2):145-156.

[9] Blanchini F, Giordano G. Polyhedral Lyapunov functions structurally ensure global asymptotic stability of dynamical networks iff the Jacobian is non-singular [J]. Automatica, 2017, 86: 183-191.

基于视频识别定位的室内反向寻车系统

马宇康[1] 徐良杰*[2] 殷子健[1]

(1.武汉理工大学交通与物流工程学院;2.湖北文理学院汽车与交通工程学院)

摘 要 随着一线城市的停车需求日益增加,室内停车场趋于大型化、多层化,由此产生了在大型停车场易迷路、难找车等问题,而室内停车场由于GPS信号弱,难以精确定位。为了解决大型室内停车场反向寻车难的问题,设计了基于视频识别定位的地下停车场反向寻车系统。在停车场立柱上布置车位标识作为定位标志,运用视频图像识别技术识别停车场内布置的定位标志来确定人与车的位置;手机App实时接收和处理相关信息并计算出车位和用户之间的最优路径,结合平面图线路和增强现实导航的形式引导用户寻车。导航过程一方面显示导航路径,另一方面提取并识别视频图像来更新位置和导航线路,两者相辅相成。实地测试结果表明,该室内停车场的反向寻车系统可有效辅助车主快捷、高效地找到自己的车辆,节省寻车用时约30%。

关键词 静态交通管理 室内停车场 反向寻车 视频识别 增强现实

0 引言

随着汽车保有量与日俱增,地面上的车位已远远不能满足停车需求,由此带来的是大型地下停车场数量激增[1-2]。但是地下停车场存在许多问题,如空间大、障碍物多、出入口多、结构复杂、信号差、光线差且没有明显标志物,对于不熟悉停车场的车主,无法快速找到自己的车辆[3]。同时,由于GPS和手机信号差,车主也无法利用GPS和网络技术实现室内定位和导航[4],这些问题都给车主反向寻车带来了一定的困扰。

目前针对反向寻车的研究很多,所实现的技术有刷卡定位、条码定位、有源RFID卡定位、车牌识别定位、基于BLE、Wi-Fi、ZigBee等无线信号源的室内定位、环境特征匹配定位等[6]。上述定位及反向寻车技术主要存在以下不足：

刷卡定位包括有源 RFID 卡、条形码卡片、ID 卡、IC 卡等多种形式,该方法涉及取还卡过程,影响效率,卡片容易遗失。虽然借助手机生成二维码可免去此过程[7],在停车场分布终端上扫描定位,但须到指定位置扫码,不能实时引导,硬件成本较高,用户体验差。

车牌识别定位通过在车位的前上方安装的摄像头来获取车辆的车牌号及所停泊的位置,然后在出入口的查询终端上输入车牌号码获取停车位置信息和推荐的寻车引导图,采用的设备成本较高,安装架构工程量大,不能实时引导寻车。

环境特征匹配定位利用用户获得的图像与离线数据库中的图像进行特征匹配,进而得到在线照片的位置信息[15-16]。该方案的主要优点在于无需添加附加设备,直接利用手机摄像头实现图像识别,但是效率较低,稳定性不足,图像匹配准确性不高,定位精度不高[4]。

在无线定位方面,BLE 定位方法采用蓝牙信号,缺点是穿透能力小、作用范围小、信号干扰影响大、定位精度和准确性不高[8-10];基于 Zigbee 技术,通过若干个待定位的盲节点和一个已知位置的参考节点与网关之间形成组网,每个微小的盲节点之间相互协调通信从而实现全部定位[14],该方法成本较高,延时也较高,作用的距离短且精度容易受外部因素影响;基于 Wi-Fi 定位可分为基于 RSSI 信号衰减模型和三角交汇算法和基于指纹特征库比对的方法,但 AP 节点布设成本较高,室内空间环境复杂,信号源多,容易形成信号间的干扰,定位精度具有较大的误差[11-13];后者定位特征库会随环境变化而失效,人工采集定位特征的部署成本和特征库定期更新的维护成本过高,限制了其普适化和规模化应用。室内停车场环境具有干扰动态性、结构复杂性等显著特征,其室内无线信号传播所表现出的多径效应、反射衍射、信道时变等特性与室外环境相比产生了本质差异,传统室内无线定位方法在定位精确度、可靠性、响应速度等方面面临全新挑战。

综合以上各种定位技术的问题,提出一种基于视频识别定位的 AR 室内反向寻车系统,利用手机摄像头进行识别和定位,用于大型室内停车场的寻车导航。将车位编号印刷在框架柱上作为定位标志,通过手机摄像头提取定位标志进行定位,运用了现实增强(Augmented Reality,AR)技术,将真实的环境和虚拟的导航叠加到同一个画面或视频中,给车主提供寻车路线指引,有效解决车主寻找车辆时位置不清、方向迷失等问题[3,5]。

1　反向寻车系统架构

本系统由停车场定位标志、智能手机及 App、后台服务器三部分组成,如图 1 所示。

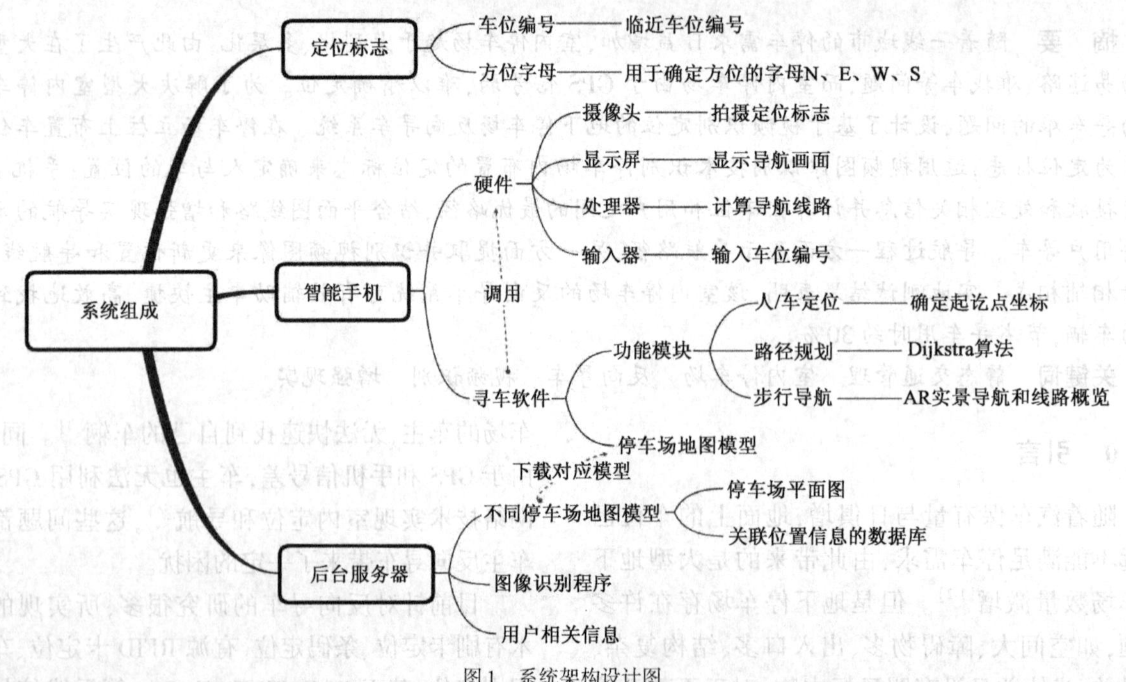

图 1　系统架构设计图

1.1　基于车位编号设置的定位标志

现有室内停车场内都设有分区和具有唯一性的车位编号,但地面上的车位编号容易被车辆遮挡或污迹掩盖不易识别。为了方便车主观察,拍摄定位标志,特将定位标志布置于停车场内行车道两侧的框架柱上,如图 2 所示。位于直线路段的定位标志布置于框架柱上与道路方向垂直的两面上;位于拐角处的定位标志则布置于框架柱四周。为简化定位标志设计,标志编号采用框架柱旁边的车位编号加方位字母的形式。定位标志既有利于手机拍摄识别具体的位置和方位,又可在实际寻车过程中方便车主确认大致方向。

图 2　定位标志设计

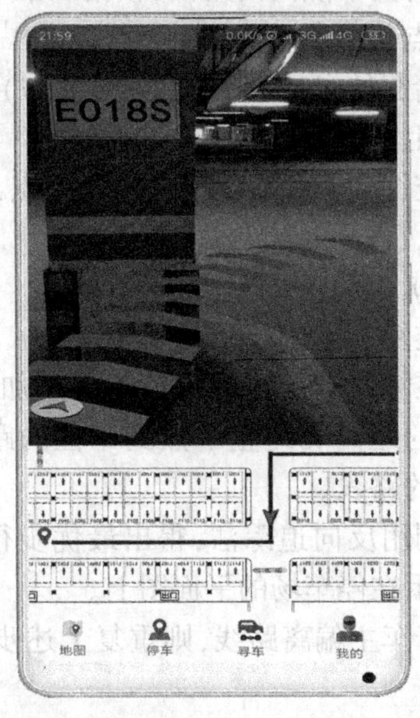

图 3　反向寻车 App 寻车界面

1.2　智能手机与反向寻车 App

现有的智能手机都配备了摄像头、显示屏、处理器、输入界面等设施。反向寻车 App 可调用智能手机的这些硬件,同时结合停车场地图模型数据,实现人车定位、路径规划、AR 步行导航等功能,如图 3 所示。摄像头用于获取视频或图像;显示屏用于交互式导航,上半部分用于显示 AR 实景导航,下半部分显示平面规划路线;处理器用于对视频画面进行预处理并进行最优路径的规划;输入界面可用于输入用户信息和停车时的车位编号。

1.3　基于边缘计算的后台服务器

后台服务器包含图像识别、停车场地图模型数据和用户信息存储三大功能,后台服务器中的图像识别程序用于识别智能手机发送图像中的定位标志,并将识别结果返回给智能手机;同时后台服务器内含有不同室内停车场的地图模型供用户下载使用,停车场地图模型包含停车场的平面矢量图和关联定位标志、车位编号和位置坐标的数据库。

在某些停车场中,由于信号不好,智能手机获取的图像无法发送至后台服务器进行识别,因而无法进行定位。为了解决该问题,可在停车场内布设若干边缘计算单元,并通过手机蓝牙进行数据通信;也可以向用户提供可下载至智能手机的图像识别工具包,用户在有信号的情况下提前下载好图像识别工具包,在进入没有信号的停车场时,不需要依靠后台服务器来实现图像识别的功能,实现自主定位。

2　反向寻车系统工作原理分析

基于视频识别定位技术,通过用户用手机拍摄定位标志或直接手动输入车位编号,得到停车时的车辆位置信息。反向寻车时,用户通过手机扫描当前所处位置视野内的定位标志。手机将图像进行预处理后,将含有定位标志图片上传至后台服务器。后台服务器对图像进行识别后,将文本信息返回给手机。寻车 App 根据定位标志匹配起讫点的位置和停车场地图模型,结合 Dijkstra 算法规划出最优的步行路线,并通过平面线路图和 AR 指示箭头显示路径方向,直至到达停车点附近,从而达到实时引导[3],系统实现流程如图 4 所示。

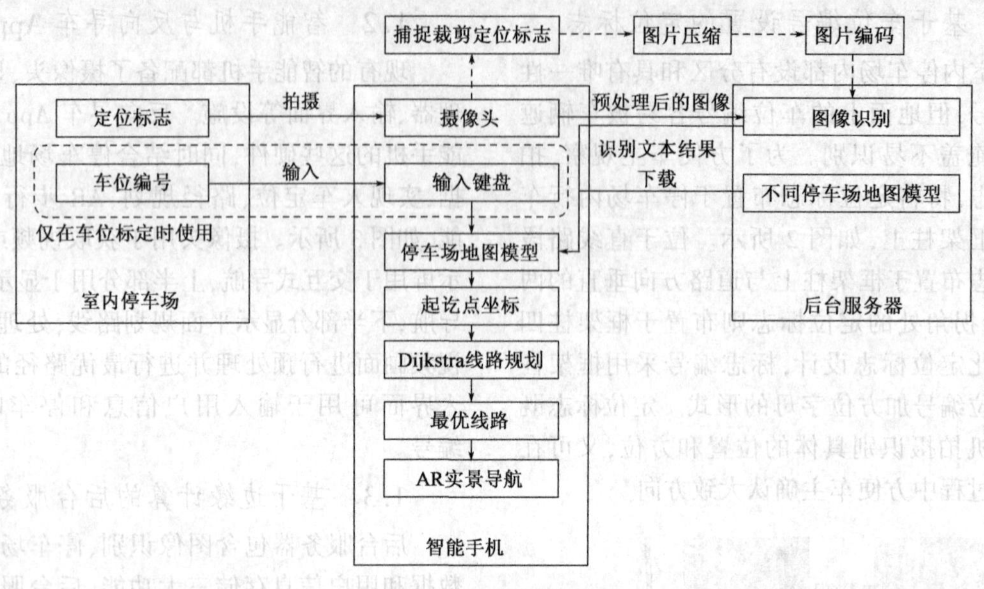

图4　系统实现流程图

2.1　用户与车辆的定位

2.1.1　停车位置标定

用户在完成停车后，可打开软件自主拍摄当前车位临近框架柱上的定位标志，或者手动输入停车位编号，完成停车位置标定。系统将得到的车位编号或定位标志与该停车场数据模型进行匹配即可获得当前车辆的位置坐标。

此外，随着物联网的普及与应用，还可以根据车载智能行车记录仪的视频进行定位。行车记录仪检测到车辆熄火后，可自动拍摄当前场景画面，并传输给手机软件识别定位标志，可以简化车位标定的过程。

2.1.2　用户定位

当用户需要寻车时，打开手机反向寻车App获取视频画面，软件可根据一定的时间间隔自行截取当前图像。通过对图像中的定位标志进行截取，压缩和编码后，上传至后台服务器。后台服务器程序识别出图像内容后，将文本数据传回给手机，软件根据返回得到的定位标志文本与停车场的数据模型进行匹配，找到该定位标志对应的位置坐标，并将该点显示在停车场平面图上。用户在软件引导下不断前行，用手机持续拍摄视频，可以实时更新用户当前的位置和引导路径。

2.2　寻车路径规划

停车场地图模型由平面矢量图和关联数据库组成。首先将平面图进行抽象化处理，将每个转折点作为一个节点，并将两节点之间分布的框架柱作为子节点，也可以根据定位精度调整子节点的密度；标出每个节点的相对位置坐标；再测出互通的两节点之间的距离作为路权，这里得到停车场步行路网的权矩阵。

反向寻车App接收服务器识别的位置信息，或自主识别当前视频中的定位信息，与手机内的停车场数据进行匹配，得到寻车的起点。用户在停车时通过拍摄定位标志或手动输入车位编号，标记为寻车的终点。结合手机内导入的停车场数字地图，构建带权值的有向图 $G=(V,E)$，其中每条边的权为两节点间的距离，根据以下Dijkstra算法计算起点与终点之间的最短路径[17-18]。

(1)给起始点标上 P 标号，令 $P(i)=0$；其余各点均标上 $T_0(j)$，并令 $T_0(j)=\infty$。

(2)查询与 i 相连且是 T 标号的点，修改其 T 标号，令 $T_1(j)=\min[T(j),P(i)+D_{ij}]$，并将其标号改为 $P(j_0)=T_1(j_0)$。

(3)重复步骤(2)直至算法结束。

(4)在算出的路径的权值中分别加上初始节点到车主的距离和终止节点到车位的距离，选择权值最小的路线。

(5)利用反向追踪法，得出最优步行路径，并将路径显示在停车场的平面图上。

(6)若车主偏离路线，则重复上述步骤(1)～(5)。

2.3　AR实时步行导航

步行导航采用AR显示和平面线路图相结合

的方式,导航界面上半部分用于显示寻车引导路径对应的实景路线和指示箭头,同时界面下面显示本停车场的平面图导航路线和定位点。AR 导航过程一方面显示导航路径,一方面提取视频图像用于更新位置和线路。AR 显示和平面线路图相辅相成,前者为后者提供图像信息,后者为前者提供导航路径信息,如图 5 所示。

图 5　实地导航测试界面

3　实地测试与结果分析

为了测试反向寻车系统的适用性,选取武汉市丽水南路某小区地下停车进行实验。首先将实验区域的室内地图数据化导入反向寻车系统,根据现场车位编号和框架柱位置编制,张贴定位标志。选取 5 名未曾到访该停车场的受试者进行模拟停车与反向寻车,每名受试者随机选择两处车位进行寻车,实验过程中测量使用该软件寻车和独立寻车各花费的时间,同步记录导航过程中定位标志识别的速度、准确率。

实验操作步骤如下:受试者在停车场内随机完成停车后,打开手机反向寻车软件,点击“停车”按钮,输入车位编号或拍摄该车位临近框架柱上的定位标志,完成车辆位置的标定。休整一段时间后,当受试者从另一入口返回停车场寻车时,打开手机反向寻车 App,点击“寻车”按钮获取当前含有定位标志的画面。反向寻车 App 显示出寻车引导路径,并且通过 AR 显示虚拟导航箭头,进行实景导航,直至引导至车辆附近。

对实验数据进行处理和计算,结果显示:反向寻车系统在 5 次导航过程中运行正常,无闪退现象出现,能明显提升寻车体验,但识别速度和准确率受画面稳定性和室内照度影响较大,缓慢步行状态下,定位标志识别准确率可达 86%,基本可实现大型地下停车场的反向寻车功能,并且寻车平均用时可节省约 30%。

4　结语

本文通过调研分析现有反向寻车技术的工作原理与优缺点,提出了一种基于视频识别定位的 AR 室内反向寻车系统。该方案因地制宜在室内停车场内行车道两侧的框架柱上布置定位标志,通过视频识别技术提取定位标志来实现室内实时定位,解决了室内无法接收 GPS 信号、无线定位不精准、固定端定位操作复杂、成本高等问题。同时,结合现实增强技术,可在识别定位的同时将虚拟导航箭头与实景相叠加,通过自主开发的反向寻车 App 实时显示导航信息实现用户交互,为解决室内停车场寻车难的问题提供了新方案[5]。

但本文提出的室内反向寻车方案需要依托专门的手机应用,导致推广困难,后续可在微信、支付宝中开发轻量化小程序,无须下载即可使用。此外,本寻车系统在图像识别速度和准确率上受环境光线和像素影响较大,有待进一步改进。

参考文献

[1] 贾雪婷,索琰琰,黄楚昌. 对反向寻车系统技术的探讨[J]. 数码世界,2018 (2):247-248.

[2] 毕昕远. 大型停车场智能反向寻车系统的设计[D]. 黑龙江:哈尔滨理工大学,2021.

[3] 蒋方艳,颜路梦,张笑语,等. 基于 AR 技术的大型地下停车场反向寻车系统设计[J]. 盐城工学院学报:自然科学版,2018,31(1):64-69.

[4] Chia W C, Salimi N. A Smart Parking and Reservation System for QR-Code-Based Car Park[M]. Innovation in the High-Tech Economy. Springer Berlin Heidelberg,2013.

[5] Tonnis M, Klein L, Klinker G. Perception thresholds for augmented reality navigation schemes in large distances[C]. 7th IEEE/ACM International Symposium on Mixed and Augmented Reality,Cambridge,UK,2008.

[6] Davidson P, RobertPiché. A Survey of Selected Indoor Positioning Methods for Smartphones[J]. IEEE Communications Surveys & Tutorials, 2017,19(2):1347-1370.

[7] 毛頔,李明兰,罗云飞. 基于人工神经网络和智能 RFID 的室内定位导航系统[J]. 传感器

与微系统,2021,40(10):98-101,105.

[8] 张立东,孙煜,万明俊.基于蓝牙技术的城市轨道交通室内定位导航及应用[J].城市轨道交通研究,2019,22(5):166-170,177.

[9] 彭金栓,舒麟棹,刘银,等.基于蓝牙识别的反向寻车系统[J].重庆交通大学学报(自然科学版),2019,38(3):110-115.

[10] Sheng-Shih, W. A BLE-Based Pedestrian Navigation System for Car Searching in Indoor Parking Garages[J]. Sensors,2018,18(5):1442-1459.

[11] 廖兴宇.基于Wifi的指纹定位系统在室内定位中的应用研究[D].南昌:江西师范大学,2015.

[12] 黎海涛,齐双.基于室内地图环境信息的多楼层WiFi定位技术研究[J].电子科技大学学报,2017,46(1):32-37.

[13] Jun L R F, Guang G. WiFi-based location services attack on dual-band hardware[C]. 2014 IEEE International Symposium on Electromagnetic Compatibility, Raleigh, NC, USA,2014.

[14] 何文华.基于ZigBee技术的超市智能定位导购系统设计与应用研究[J].重庆理工大学学报(自然科学版),2020(7).

[15] Tan H C, Zhang J, Xin-Chen Y E, et al. Intelligent car-searching system for large park[C]. International Conference on Machine Learning & Cybernetics,Baoding,China,2009.

[16] 万柯.视觉室内定位中图像特征点匹配算法研究[D].哈尔滨:哈尔滨工业大学,2016.

[17] 王艺,蔡磊,梅辉扬,等.一种反向寻车装置及方法[P].CN108447297A,中国,2018.

[18] Dijkstra E W . A note on two problems inconnexion with graphs [M]. New York: Springer-Verlag New York Inc.,1959.

十车道及以上高速公路标志布设仿真研究

许云红　刘　兵*

(武汉理工大学交通与物流工程学院)

摘　要　基于十车道及以上高速公路车道多、车辆行驶干扰因素复杂等特性,本文拟对十车道高速公路做仿真实验,设计不同场景下的交通标志布设方案,在UC-win/Road中进行模拟驾驶;考虑行驶车速和横向偏移两方面,最后分析得出适合十车道高速公路的交通标志布置方案,即交通量为1100pcu/h,大车比为30%,车道划分方式为3+2(内幅三车道+外幅两车道),交通标志设置为门架错开式。该研究为十车道及以上高速公路的交通设计、交通管理与控制提供了理论与数据支撑。

关键词　交通工程　交通标志方案设计　UC-win/Road　十车道高速公路　交通仿真

0　引言

我国高速公路修建规模以四、六车道为主,随着经济持续发展导致的机动车保有量增加,现有高速公路交通供给已经满足不了日益增长的交通需求。上海—南京等高速公路均已由原本的双向四车道改扩建为双向八车道,有些高速公路更是建成了十车道,如深圳水官高速十车道等。由此可见,多车道高速公路比例逐渐增大是我国高速公路建设的主要发展趋势。

国内外学者对多车道标志的研究多侧重标志的视认性、版面设计、支撑形式、结构设计等方面。视认性方面,MT Pietrucha等认为驾驶人视线是否被遮挡与车辆之间的相对位置和交通量等因素有关,并结合这些因素利用概率论建立了相应的遮挡模型[1];Vivek Agarwal and Partha Chakroborty研究了门架式交通标志的遮挡模型,并利用线性规划和概率论的相关知识来构建遮挡概率计算模型[2]。李苗苗对八车道高速公路上门架式标志遮挡和路侧标志遮挡进行了系统研究,并借助

VISSIM软件来分析研究交通标志遮挡问题[3]。邓亚娟等以多车道高速公路门架式交通标志遮挡模型为研究对象,借助VISSIM软件分析不同交通条件与遮挡概率的关系[4]。版面设计方面,Barbara Meta等对设置较多的提示标志对驾驶人注意力的影响进行研究,得出较多的道路标志信息对驾驶人行驶没有太多坏处[5]的结论。关伟通过认知实验分析驾驶员P300脑波,获取了驾驶员对交通标志信息转换过程的认知特性,提出了基于信息置信度的驾驶员决策模型[6]。支撑形式方面,李海南通过应用力学仿真软件,分析多车道高速公路门架式交通标志板的抗风结构强度,对门架式指路标志结构的侧面形式、立柱、横梁、交通标志板及反光膜等进行了设计[7]。

综上可以看出,目前国内外高速公路的标志研究理论已比较成熟、丰富,但研究对象大多集中于正常的四、六车道,十车道及以上的高速公路标志研究极少。因此,本文就十车道高速公路的标志布设进行仿真研究分析,探寻有效的交通标志布设方案。

1 研究目的

随着未来十车道及以上高速公路的发展,已有的高速公路建设理论已经不适用于十车道及以上高速公路的需求。这就要求以需求为导向不断探索研究合适的理论方法。因此,本文以十车道高速公路为研究对象,借助UC-win/Road搭建仿真环境,根据实验条件设置、开展一系列驾驶模拟实验,得出适合十车道及以上高速公路的交通标志布设方法。

2 仿真建模

2.1 实验目的

本实验通过采用模拟驾驶手段采集在不同交通标志设置方案下的交通流特征数据,进而分析模拟数据,得到效果最优的交通标志设置方案。本研究采用UC-win/Road软件制作模拟驾驶仿真场景,开展驾驶实验。

2.2 实验设计

本实验设置四个变量:变量1为交通量,变量2为车型比例,变量3为车道划分方式,变量4为交通标志设置。具体实验设计如下。

(1)实验路段。

实验路段为双向十车道,设计车速120km/h,车道宽度3.75m,右侧硬路肩宽度3.5m,中分带1m,左右路缘带0.5m,纵坡2%,双黄线0.5m,路段为一般平直线段。

(2)影响因素。

自变量包括交通量、车型比例、车道划分方式交通标志设置。

①交通量:一级服务水平:880pcu/h,模拟自由车流;二级服务水平:1100pcu/h,模拟延误小的稳定车流;三级服务水平:1500pcu/h,模拟接近不稳定车流时的交通状况。

②车型比例:车型构成中大型车的相对数量比例采取10%、20%、30%三个水平。

③车道划分方式:车道划分方式分为三种,即内外幅分隔2+3(内侧两车道为小汽车专用道,外侧三车道为混行车道)、内外幅分隔3+2(内侧三车道为小汽车专用道,外侧两车道为混行车道)、客货混行(五车道皆为混行车道)。

④交通标志设置:标志分幅分车道、标志分幅、标志错开。

(3)评价指标。

因变量包括速度、车距、制动情况及横向偏移距离等。

本实验根据制动减速度大小将车辆制动分为紧急制动(减速度为5.5~8.0m/s^2)、正常制动(减速度为3~4m/s^2)以及平缓制动(减速度为1.5~2.5m/s^2)。实验数据每隔0.05s采集一次,以此来记录车辆制动次数。

(4)实验设计方法。

为研究不同因素对驾驶人车速、车距和制动距离的影响,本研究分别将交通量、车型比例、车道划分方式进行组合,构建"四因素三水平"的实验,实验的全样数量为$3^4=81$。实验较为复杂,为了简化实验数量,采用正交实验设计方法进行简化实验,最终共需要$L_9(3^4)=9$次试验。见表1。

2.3 场景设计

根据实验目的及实验设计,本研究使用模拟驾驶软件UC-win/Road对场景进行建模编辑。实验场景分为不同车道划分方式和不同交通标志设置方案两种条件,其中车道组合形式包括:①内侧三条车道为客车专用道、外侧两条车道为混行车道;②内侧两条车道为客车专用道、外侧三条车道为混行车道;③五条车道都为混行车道。交通标志设置方案包括内外错开设置和并列设置两种情况。合计9种场景,如图1所示。

正交实验设计　　表1

实验号	因素			
	交通量(pcu/h)	车型比例(%)	车道划分方式	交通标志设置
1	880	10	3+2	门架标志并列
2	880	20	2+3	门架标志错开
3	880	30	混行	两侧悬臂
4	1100	10	2+3	两侧悬臂
5	1100	20	混行	门架标志并列
6	1100	30	3+2	门架标志错开
7	1500	10	混行	门架标志错开
8	1500	20	3+2	两侧悬臂
9	1500	30	2+3	门架标志并列

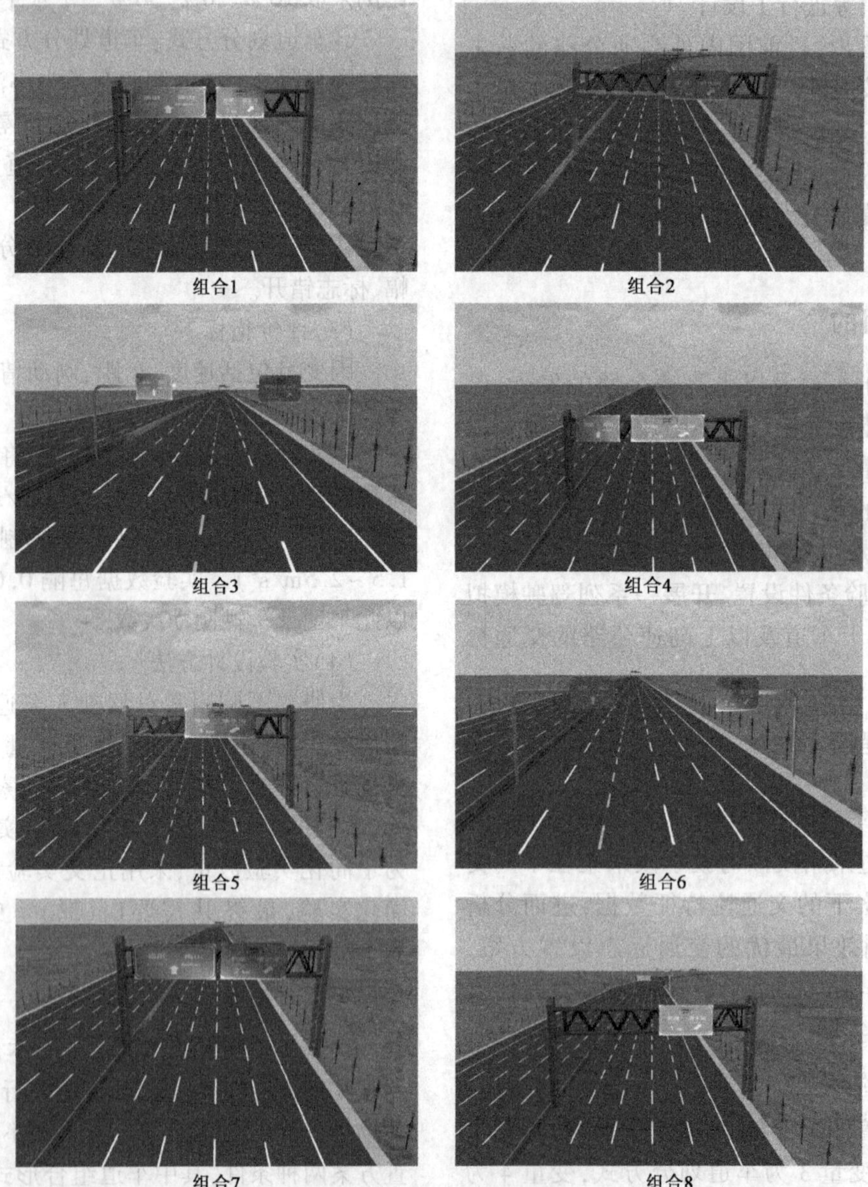

图　1

图1　场景设计

组合形式1:内外幅分隔3+2、门架标志并列;

组合形式2:内外幅分隔3+2、门架标志错开;

组合形式3:内外幅分隔3+2、两侧悬臂;

组合形式4:内外幅分隔2+3、门架标志并列;

组合形式5:内外幅分隔2+3、门架标志错开;

组合形式6:内外幅分隔2+3、两侧悬臂;

组合形式7:客货混行、门架标志并列;

组合形式8:客货混行、门架标志错开;

组合形式9:客货混行、两侧悬臂。

3　仿真实验

3.1　实验设备

(1)模拟驾驶软件UC-win/Road。

本研究使用的模拟驾驶软件是日本FORUM 8公司的UC-win/Road 13.0。

(2)基于实车开发的模拟驾驶实验平台。

基于真实汽车驾驶座舱开发的驾驶模拟器用于进行模拟驾驶实验并采集数据。为了使驾驶人获取更佳的沉浸式驾驶体验,本实验建立了180°环形视野的驾驶模拟平台。如图2所示。

图2　驾驶模拟平台

3.2　实验人员

为了确保实验过程的真实性,尽量避免驾驶人较少的驾驶经验、驾驶习惯差异等因素对实验数据产生较大的影响,本实验对驾驶人进行了筛选。

本次共招募15名驾驶人进行模拟驾驶实验。其中,5名为职业驾驶人(代驾及出租车司机),10名为非职业驾驶人。

3.3　实验流程

实验流程如图3所示。

在实验过程中,驾驶人要尽可能保持较高的速度稳定行驶于内侧车道实验场景中。道路开始会设置车道限速标志,提醒驾驶人控制车速。实验中每个场景全程约为2km,驾驶时间需要10min。如图4所示。

4　数据获取及处理

在驾驶人完成模拟驾驶实验后,通过UC-win/Road软件中自带的log数据导出功能导出驾驶人模拟驾驶过程中自身车辆的各项数据。在本次实验中,数据采集的频率为20Hz,即每隔0.05s采集一次数据。通过这些高密度的数据,可以分析出车辆在各个位置的运动状态。如图5所示。

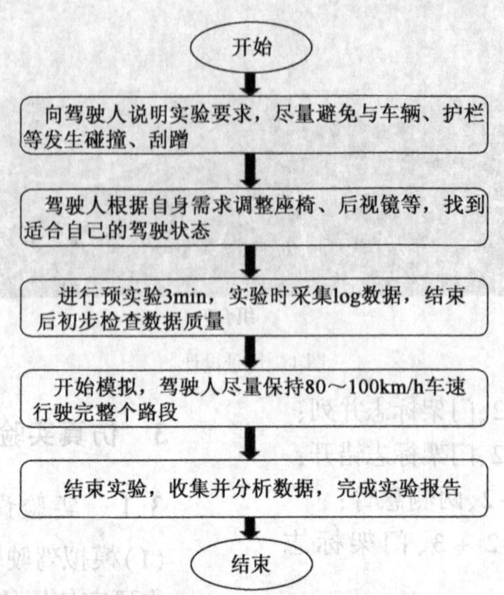

图3　实验流程

图4　实验过程

Time	Model	ID	descriptio	position X	position Y	position Z	yawAngle	pitchAngl	rollAngle	direction X	direction Y
0	expensive	38307	自身车辆	30.70599	11	4671.206	1.570795	0	0	1	0
0.059523	expensive	38307	自身车辆	31.48963	11	4671.206	1.570795	0	0	1	0
0.118784	expensive	38307	自身车辆	32.2094	11	4671.206	1.570795	0	0	1	0
0.18125	expensive	38307	自身车辆	33.00419	11	4671.206	1.570795	0	0	1	0
0.248799	expensive	38307	自身车辆	33.87378	11	4671.206	1.570795	0	0	1	0
0.308761	expensive	38307	自身车辆	34.65435	11	4671.206	1.570795	0	0	1	0
0.378172	expensive	38307	自身车辆	35.48446	11	4671.206	1.570795	0	0	1	0
0.438658	expensive	38307	自身车辆	36.23835	11	4671.206	1.570795	0	0	1	0
0.500437	expensive	38307	自身车辆	37.01663	11	4671.206	1.570795	0	0	1	0
0.567065	expensive	38307	自身车辆	37.93203	11	4671.206	1.570795	0	0	1	0
0.634716	expensive	38307	自身车辆	40.00975	11	4671.206	1.570795	0	0	1	0
0.797341	expensive	38307	自身车辆	40.73444	11	4671.206	1.570795	0	0	1	0
0.858071	expensive	38307	自身车辆	41.48346	11	4671.206	1.570795	0	0	1	0
0.919402	expensive	38307	自身车辆	42.25682	11	4671.206	1.570795	0	0	1	0
0.984481	expensive	38307	自身车辆	43.06698	11	4671.206	1.570795	0	0	1	0
1.058315	expensive	38307	自身车辆	43.98886	11	4671.206	1.570795	0	0	1	0
1.123547	expensive	38307	自身车辆	44.79925	11	4671.206	1.570795	0	0	1	0
1.193841	expensive	38307	自身车辆	45.68664	11	4671.206	1.570795	0	0	1	0
1.260919	expensive	38307	自身车辆	46.51461	11	4671.206	1.570795	0	0	1	0
1.321909	expensive	38307	自身车辆	47.28291	11	4671.206	1.570795	0	0	1	0
1.386362	expensive	38307	自身车辆	48.105	11	4671.206	1.570795	0	0	1	0
1.453851	expensive	38307	自身车辆	48.95619	11	4671.206	1.570795	0	0	1	0
1.522853	expensive	38307	自身车辆	49.83689	11	4671.206	1.570795	0	0	1	0
1.594979	expensive	38307	自身车辆	50.7733	11	4671.206	1.570795	0	0	1	0
1.660537	expensive	38307	自身车辆	51.61124	11	4671.206	1.570795	0	0	1	0
1.737525	expensive	38307	自身车辆	52.60914	11	4671.206	1.570795	0	0	1	0
1.801717	expensive	38307	自身车辆	53.44301	11	4671.206	1.570795	0	0	1	0

图5　UC-win/Road部分采集数据

在采集到的由UC-win/Road软件导出的所有数据中,仅有少部分数据是本次实验所需要的,因此首先需要去除本次实验不需要的数据,只保留需要的部分。如图6所示。

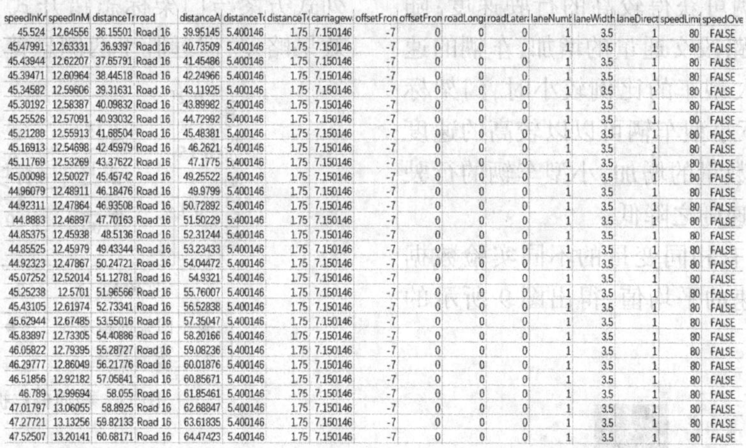

speedInKr	speedInM	distanceTr	road	distanceA	distanceT(	distanceT(	carriagew	offsetFron	offsetFron	roadLongi	roadLater	laneNumb	laneWidth	laneDirect	speedLimi	speedOve
45.524	12.64556	36.15501	Road 16	39.95145	5.400146	1.75	7.150146	-7	0	0	0	1	3.5	1	80	FALSE
45.47991	12.63331	36.9397	Road 16	40.73509	5.400146	1.75	7.150146	-7	0	0	0	1	3.5	1	80	FALSE
45.43944	12.62207	37.65791	Road 16	41.45486	5.400146	1.75	7.150146	-7	0	0	0	1	3.5	1	80	FALSE
45.39471	12.60964	38.44518	Road 16	42.24966	5.400146	1.75	7.150146	-7	0	0	0	1	3.5	1	80	FALSE
45.34582	12.59606	39.31631	Road 16	43.11925	5.400146	1.75	7.150146	-7	0	0	0	1	3.5	1	80	FALSE
45.30192	12.58387	40.09832	Road 16	43.89982	5.400146	1.75	7.150146	-7	0	0	0	1	3.5	1	80	FALSE
45.25526	12.57091	40.93032	Road 16	44.72992	5.400146	1.75	7.150146	-7	0	0	0	1	3.5	1	80	FALSE
45.21288	12.55913	41.68504	Road 16	45.48381	5.400146	1.75	7.150146	-7	0	0	0	1	3.5	1	80	FALSE
45.16913	12.54698	42.45979	Road 16	46.2621	5.400146	1.75	7.150146	-7	0	0	0	1	3.5	1	80	FALSE
45.11769	12.53269	43.37622	Road 16	47.1775	5.400146	1.75	7.150146	-7	0	0	0	1	3.5	1	80	FALSE
45.00098	12.50027	45.45742	Road 16	49.25522	5.400146	1.75	7.150146	-7	0	0	0	1	3.5	1	80	FALSE
44.96079	12.48911	46.18476	Road 16	49.9799	5.400146	1.75	7.150146	-7	0	0	0	1	3.5	1	80	FALSE
44.92311	12.47864	46.93508	Road 16	50.72892	5.400146	1.75	7.150146	-7	0	0	0	1	3.5	1	80	FALSE
44.8883	12.46897	47.70163	Road 16	51.50229	5.400146	1.75	7.150146	-7	0	0	0	1	3.5	1	80	FALSE
44.85375	12.45938	48.5136	Road 16	52.31244	5.400146	1.75	7.150146	-7	0	0	0	1	3.5	1	80	FALSE
44.85525	12.45979	49.43344	Road 16	53.23433	5.400146	1.75	7.150146	-7	0	0	0	1	3.5	1	80	FALSE
44.92323	12.47867	50.24721	Road 16	54.04472	5.400146	1.75	7.150146	-7	0	0	0	1	3.5	1	80	FALSE
45.07252	12.52014	51.12781	Road 16	54.9321	5.400146	1.75	7.150146	-7	0	0	0	1	3.5	1	80	FALSE
45.25238	12.5701	51.96566	Road 16	55.76007	5.400146	1.75	7.150146	-7	0	0	0	1	3.5	1	80	FALSE
45.43105	12.61974	52.73341	Road 16	56.52838	5.400146	1.75	7.150146	-7	0	0	0	1	3.5	1	80	FALSE
45.62944	12.67485	53.55016	Road 16	57.35047	5.400146	1.75	7.150146	-7	0	0	0	1	3.5	1	80	FALSE
45.83897	12.73305	54.40886	Road 16	58.20166	5.400146	1.75	7.150146	-7	0	0	0	1	3.5	1	80	FALSE
46.05822	12.79395	55.28727	Road 16	59.08236	5.400146	1.75	7.150146	-7	0	0	0	1	3.5	1	80	FALSE
46.29777	12.86049	56.21776	Road 16	60.01876	5.400146	1.75	7.150146	-7	0	0	0	1	3.5	1	80	FALSE
46.51856	12.92182	57.05841	Road 16	60.85671	5.400146	1.75	7.150146	-7	0	0	0	1	3.5	1	80	FALSE
46.789	12.99694	58.055	Road 16	61.85461	5.400146	1.75	7.150146	-7	0	0	0	1	3.5	1	80	FALSE
47.01797	13.06055	58.8925	Road 16	62.68847	5.400146	1.75	7.150146	-7	0	0	0	1	3.5	1	80	FALSE
47.27721	13.13256	59.82133	Road 16	63.61835	5.400146	1.75	7.150146	-7	0	0	0	1	3.5	1	80	FALSE
47.52507	13.20141	60.68171	Road 16	64.47423	5.400146	1.75	7.150146	-7	0	0	0	1	3.5	1	80	FALSE

图6 实验数据预处理结果

5 不同实验方案的驾驶行为分析

本实验从车辆的运行速度和横向偏移来分析驾驶人的驾驶行为。

5.1 变量相关性分析

本实验采用皮尔逊(Pearson)相关系数进行变量的相关性分析,结果见表2。

变量相关性分析 表2

	交通量	大车比	车道划分	行驶速度
交通量	1	—	—	—
大车比	0.554**	1	—	—
车道划分	0.305	0.539	1	—
行驶速度	-0.826**	-0.614**	0.541**	1

注:** 在0.01级别(双尾),相关性显著;* 在0.05级别(双尾),相关性显著。

由此可得:

(1)"交通量"与"大车比"有较显著的正相关性,与"行驶速度"有较显著的负相关性。交通量增大,大车比例也相应增大,行驶速度则减小。

(2)"大车比"与"行驶速度"有较显著的负相关性。随着车辆中的大车比例增加,车辆行驶干扰增大,行驶速度相应减小。

(3)"车道划分"与"行驶速度"有较显著的正相关性。车道划分方式从客货混行到内外幅分隔3+2再到内外幅分隔2+3逐渐优化,车辆行驶稳定性提高,行驶速度增大。

5.2 行驶速度分析

本实验采集模拟2km范围内的车速,驾驶人以50km/h的初始速度行驶;主要利用EXCEL软件对不同交通组合的行驶速度数据进行分析。由于驾驶过程中两侧的景物单一,驾驶人不易判断当前的驾驶位置,行驶速度呈现一定波动,因而取平均速度对比分析。

首先,分别针对服务水平、大车比对不同交通标志设置方案的影响进行单独分析。如图7、图8所示。

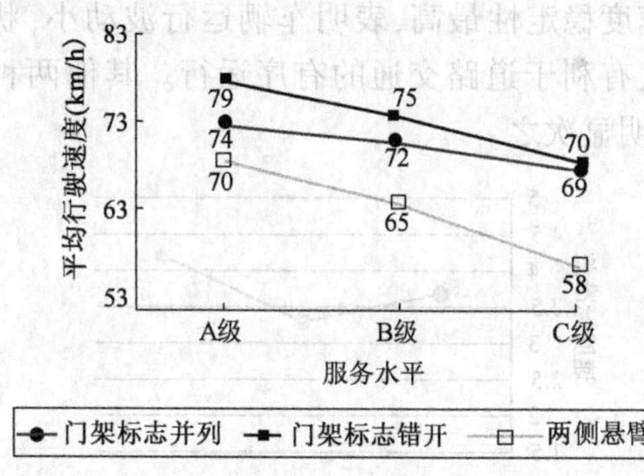

图7 服务水平—行驶速度

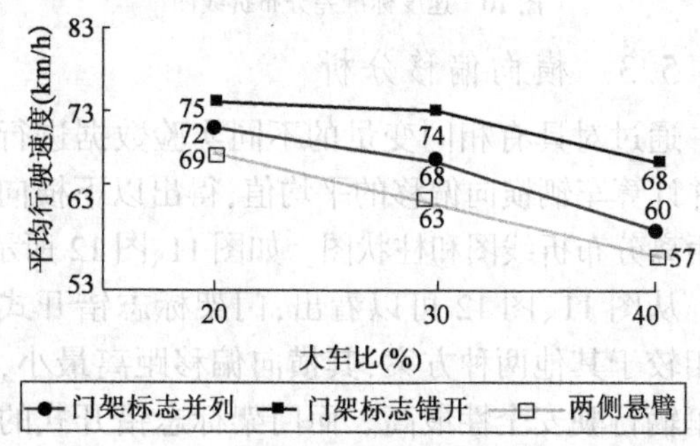

图8 大车比—行驶速度

从图7、图8可知,当服务水平较高时,门架标志错开式设置方案下车辆可获得较高的行驶速度;随着服务水平的降低,路段交通量的增加,车辆的速度也逐渐降低。当大型车的比例较小时,门架标志错开式设置方案下小型车辆可以以较高的速度行驶;但随着大型车数量的增加,小型车辆的行驶受到的影响变大,车速随之降低。

其次,通过对具有相同变量的不同实验数据进行汇总并计算车速的平均值,得出图 9 所示的车速分布柱状图。

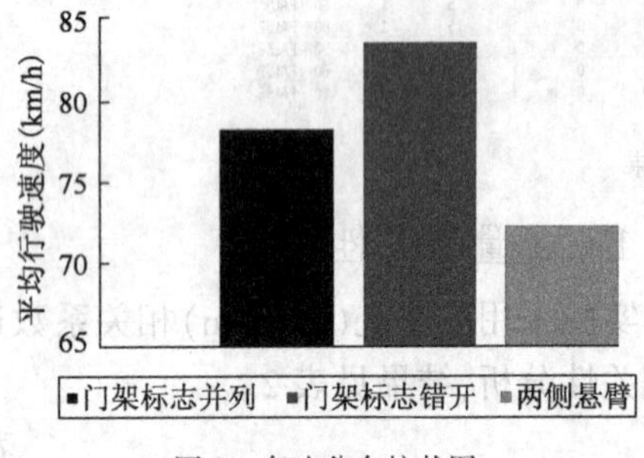

图 9　车速分布柱状图

图 9 可知,门架标志错开式的三种实验方案车辆速度比另外两个设置方案要高,说明模拟车辆行驶速度较高,道路通行效率较高,交通状态较好。另外,从速度标准差分布折线图(图 10)中可以看出,门架标志错开式方案下的速度标准差最小,速度稳定性最高,表明车辆运行波动小,状态良好,有利于道路交通的有序运行。其他两种方案都明显次之。

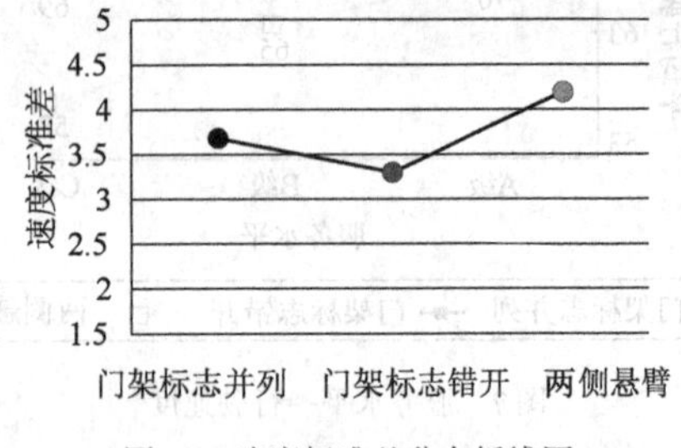

图 10　速度标准差分布折线图

5.3　横向偏移分析

通过对具有相同变量的不同实验数据进行汇总并计算车辆横向偏移的平均值,得出以下横向偏移距离分布折线图和柱状图。如图 11、图 12 所示。

从图 11、图 12 可以看出,门架标志错开式方案相较于其他两种方案,其横向偏移距离最小,说明车辆行驶安全性最高。而门架标志错开式的三个实验方案的横向偏移距离较大,车流稳定性下降。由此说明内外幅分隔 3 + 2 与内外幅分隔 2 + 3 的车道划分方式优于客货混行方式;门架标志并列式方案与门架标志错开式方案相比,车辆运行效果略差,但远胜于两侧悬臂式方案。

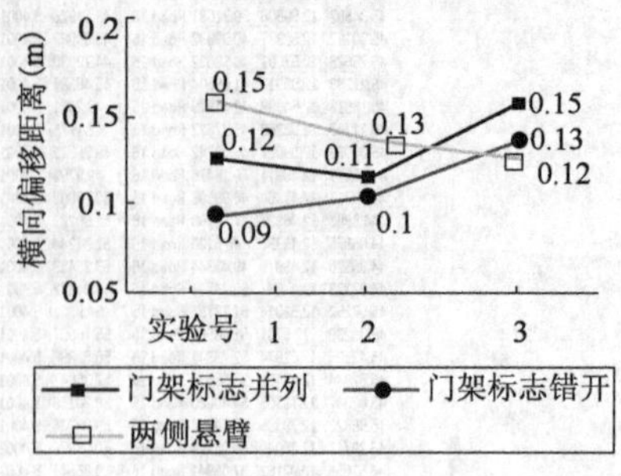

图 11　横向偏移折线图

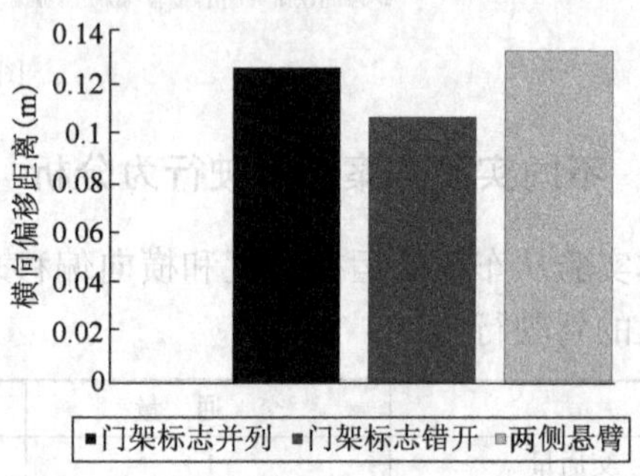

图 12　横向偏移柱状图

6　结语

本文以十车道高速公路为研究对象,对其展开 UC-win/Road 仿真实验,探索十车道及以上高速公路的交通标志方案设计。通过对实验数据的分析,最终得到实验 6 方案的模拟驾驶效果优于其他方案,即交通量为 1100pcu/h,大车比为 30%,车道划分方式为 3 + 2,交通标志设置为门架标志错开式。这方案下驾驶视认效果和车辆行驶状态更好,更有利于交通安全。

当然本次实验中也存在不足之处,如实验方案设置的合理性、模拟驾驶人的随机因素、数据分析存在不确定性偏差等问题,需要继续深入研究。

参考文献

[1] MTPietrucha, ET Donnell, P Lertworawanich, et al. Effects of Traffic Characteristics and Mounting Location on the Visibility of On-Premise Commercial Signs. Journal of Transportation Engineering, 2006, 132(11): 862-871.

[2] V Agarwal, P Chakroborty, Stochastic Analysis of the Duration of Occlusion of an Overhead Sign by a Leading Heavy Vehicle: Application

to Sign Design. Journal of Transportation Engineering,2014,140(8):04014036
[3] 李苗苗.基于大型车遮挡的多车道高速公路交通标志优化研究[D].长安大学,2017.
[4] 邓亚娟,李苗苗,胡小霞,等.多车道高速公路门架式交通标志遮挡概率研究[J].公路,2018,63(4):179-184.
[5] Barbara Metz, Hans-Peter Kruger. Do supplementary signs distract the driver [J]. Transportation Research Part F.2014,23:1-14.
[6] 关伟.驾驶员对交通标志的视觉信息认知过程实验研究[D].北京工业大学,2014.
[7] 李海南.多车道高速公路指路标志设计研究[D].河北工业大学,2015.

基于K最近邻方法的驾驶人身份辨识方法研究

黄 衍[1,2] 张 晖*[1,2]
(1.武汉理工大学智能交通系统研究中心;2.国家水运安全工程技术研究中心)

摘 要 智能网联汽车的出现和发展,为驾驶行为研究提供了精细化多维数据和网联条件,相关研究表明通过驾驶人之间行为差异可对驾驶人的身份进行辨识,但现有研究仍然存在特征提取方法优化不足等问题。

为此,本研究首先通过组织自然驾驶实验获取了20位被试,每位被试不少于6h的行车数据,包括车速、三轴加速度等4类参数;本文选择了交叉验证法对数据集进行构建,针对所构建的数据集,采用K最近邻模型(KNN)进行了身份识别;同时在模型分析过程中考虑了模型超参数、被试数据样本特征对结果的影响:如直方图区间和加速度组合参数。研究结果显示,使用KNN算法对五名驾驶人的驾驶数据进行身份识别的准确率测试结果为93.4%。

关键词 驾驶人身份识别 K最近邻

0 引言

研究表明,不同驾驶人的驾驶行为间存在显著的差距,而驾驶人驾驶车辆所产生的各种行车数据,如车速、加速度、转向盘转角、加速踏板位、制动踏板位等数据能够反映这一差距。有学者指出,即使在10000名驾驶人的行车数据当中,也能够通过行车数据,以40%以上的成功率准确分辨出驾驶人的身份[1]。

为了准确捕捉驾驶人行车数据中的差异性,首先需要对行车数据类型的进行筛选,挑出最能够反映驾驶人之间差异的行车数据类型。常用的行车数据类型包括车速、加速度、转向盘转角、加速踏板位、制动踏板位等。Miro Enev等分析了18类行车数据与驾驶人身份识别的相关性,分析结果显示制动踏板位、最大发动机转矩、转向盘转角、横向加速度、驾驶人请求转矩等五类数据最能反映驾驶人的驾驶特性[2]。Arijit Chowdhury等仅利用被试手机的GPS数据对驾驶人身份进行了识别,按照驾驶人所属地区的差异将38名驾驶人分为了9个小组,在每个小组内4~5名驾驶员组的平均身份识别准确率达到了82.3%[3]。Xun Y等人直接将CAN中的原始数据经过筛选后导入卷积神经网络,对10名驾驶人身份的识别率最高位为100%,最低识别率为92.74%[4]。Mina Remeli等人使用卷积神经网络作为特征提取器,LSTM网络作为分类器,使用组合神经网络对CAN原始数据进行分类,对33名被试进行驾驶人身份识别的精度为85%[5]。

特征工程步骤能够从原始数据当中筛选出更好的数据特征。Virojboonkiate N等通过将加速度转化为频率分布直方图,然后将频率分布直方图作为神经网络的输入[6]。高斯混合模型(Gaussian Mixture Model,GMM)通过提取原始数据中的高斯

1.基金项目:国家重点研发计划项目(编号:2019YFB1600800);国家自然科学基金(编号:52072289)。

分量进而提取出原始数据的分布特征[5,7,8]。主成分分析(Principal Component Analysis,PCA)通过正交变换,提取出不同维度原始数据中的一组线性不相关的变量,达到特征提取或数据降维的目的[8-9]。Bouhoute A 等通过区间域和图论的方法,将驾驶人的一次出行转化为一张状态转移图,通过比较不同样本的状态转移图之间的编辑距离来比较样本间的相似性[10]。还可以通过简单的统计数据来进行特征的提取,如最大最小值、均值、方差、变化率等[1,3]。

构建好的分类模型需要进行测试,早期的研究给出了多种衡量分类模型效果的指标。常用的做法有,将初始数据集按照一定的比例随机划分或按照时间顺序划分为训练集、验证集、和测试集,使用测试集的数据来测试使用训练集和验证集的数据训练得到的模型,用该结果表示模型的分类效果[11-12]。或者采用 K 折交叉验证的方法[5,7,11]。也有通过自定义一些评价指标来衡量模型效果[7]。Abdellah 等研究和分析了不同的验证方式,他们认为,不同的验证和数据集构建方式会对模型的结果产生较大的影响,有些验证方式所得到的优异结果通常在现实世界中不可重现的[13]。

本文首先将对试验场景及试验条件进行详细介绍,使用随机划分方式对数据集进行构建,分析 KNN 模型的建立步骤及超参数优化过程,然后实验不同的特征提取参数对模型的效果进行检验、测试及对比。最后根据结果进行讨论和总结。

1　实验

为了构建基于驾纹的驾驶人身份辨识模型,团队进行了一次自然驾驶试验,以收集驾驶人在不受任何数据采集设备影响、最接近日常驾驶状态下的行车数据,自然驾驶数据能够更加真实地反映驾驶人的驾驶行为和驾驶习惯。

1.1　实验对象

组织20名(男性15人,女性5人)有熟练驾驶技能的职业驾驶人(被试)进行实验。平均驾龄16年,平均年龄46岁。

1.2　实验流程

选择汉十高速公路为实验道路,大部分道路为平直路段或者大半径弯道(图1)。每次实验被试由府河收费站驶入,行驶约2h到达随州服务区,停车休息1h后行至襄阳北出口掉头,返回起点府河收费站,1次实验时长约6h,总里程约600km。实验共获得20位被试的自然驾驶行为数据。

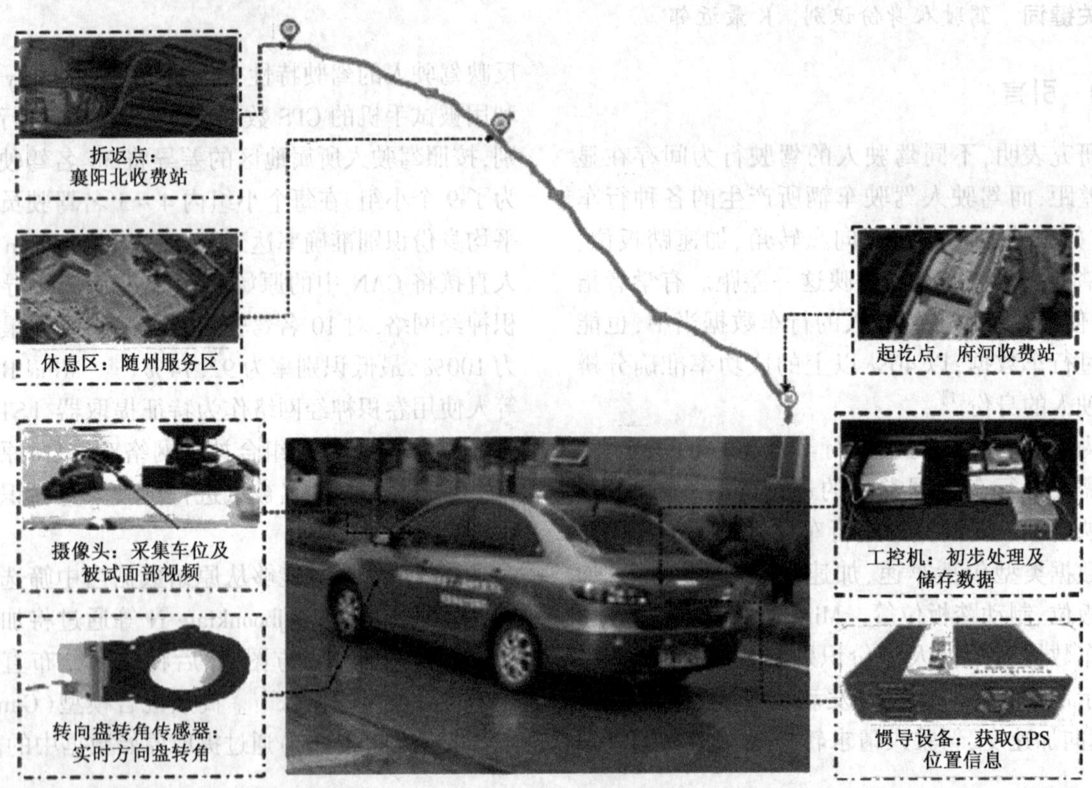

图1　实验路线

2 模型与方法

此部分将讨论对原始数据的预处理以及如何用两种不同的方式构建数据集，其次介绍了构建基于驾纹的驾驶人身份辨识模型所使用的K近邻算法。本文的技术路线如图2所示。

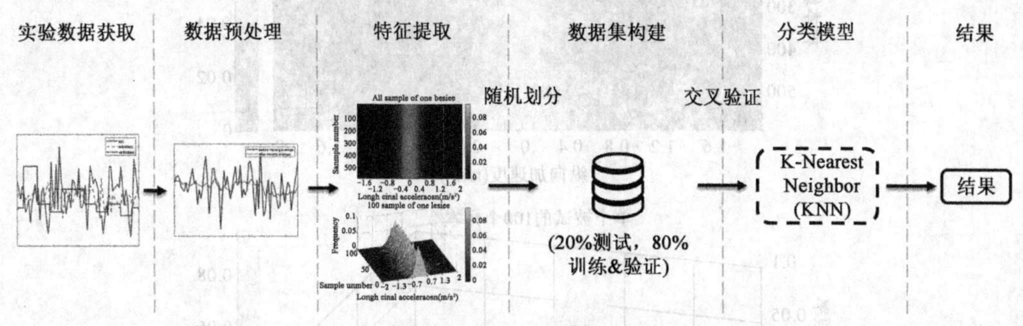

图2 技术路线图

2.1 数据预处理

在自然驾驶实验中，传感器会不断受到外部干扰，导致传感器采集数据的时间间隔是不完全相同的。同时不同的传感器之间采集得到的数据在时间上存在不同步的现象。因此需要采用插值的步骤对不同传感器的数据进行时间的同步和采样间隔的统一。本文采用修正Akima三次Hermite插值方法进行插值，经过插值步骤后的数据采样率统一为15Hz。

受车身振动及其他外部因素的影响，传感器采集的数据中存在一定的噪声，因此需要对数据进行滤波处理。本文采用滑动平均的方法对插值后的数据进行滤波处理，滑动平均的窗口为20个数据点。数据经滑动平均处理之后变得平缓，消除了许多尖峰。

2.2 数据集构建

考虑到驾驶人在高速公路及非高速公路道路上驾驶行为的差异性及驾驶人驾驶特征的稳定性，需要将非高速公路的数据进行剔除。本文以速度为筛选依据，设定80km/h为速度阈值，剔除了所有速度小于该速度阈值的数据。

本文使用滑动时间窗法对经过预处理和筛选的数据进行取样。时间窗长度为W_L，时间窗重叠度为O_V。时间窗沿着时间轴移动依次取样，取样的过程如图3所示。

经过数据的预处理以及滑窗采样后，每个被试都有约600个样本，每个样本被转化为3张频率分布直方图，其中第25号被试的纵向加速度样本直方图数据见图4。

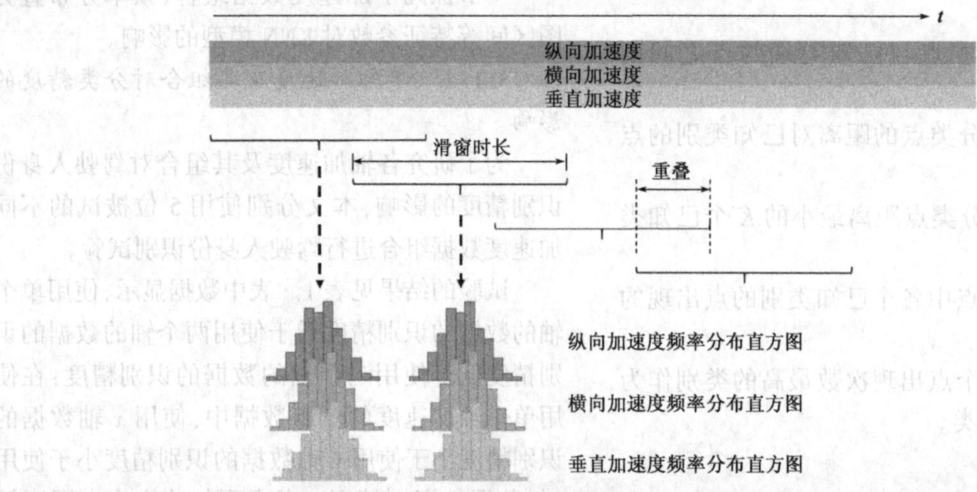

图3 数据集构建过程示意图

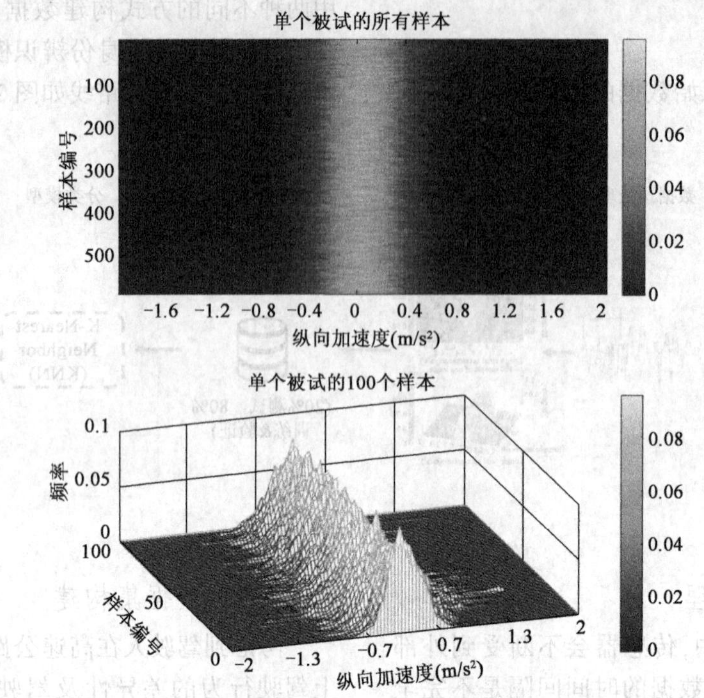

图4　单个被试的纵向加速度样本集

按照机器学习的一般模式,数据集一般被划分为三部分,分别是训练集(Training set)、验证集(Validation set)和测试集(Test set)。

本文在整个数据集中随机抽取10%作为测试集,剩余的数据作为训练集和验证集;训练集和验证集均按照10折交叉验证的方式划分。使用交叉验证的方式划分好数据集后分别进行10轮训练,得出训练好的模型,再将测试集的数据作为输入导入到训练好的模型中,得出测试结果。

2.3　K近邻

K最近邻算法是一种常用的监督学习算法,其计算步骤为:

(1)计算待分类点与已知类别的点之间的距离;

(2)按照离待分类点的距离对已知类别的点进行排序;

(3)选取与待分类点距离最小的 K 个已知类别的点;

(4)确定 K 个点中各个已知类别的点出现的次数;

(5)返回前 K 个点出现次数最高的类别作为待分类点的预测分类。

3　实验结果

本章通过一系列的实验分析了特征提取参数、模型超参数对模型效果的影响。所有的实验通过MATLAB R2020a平台进行,对5名驾驶人的行车数据进行身份辨识。模型的输入为未知驾驶人在一个时间窗内的数据样本,输出为驾驶人的编号。若模型输出的编号与真实编号相同,则认为模型分类正确,反之分类错误。模型分类准确率的计算公式为:

$$准确率 = \frac{分类正确样本数S_1}{测试集样本数S}$$

3.1　特征提取参数对模型的影响

本节探究了加速度数据组合、频率分布直方图区间等特征参数对KNN模型的影响。

3.1.1　单轴加速度及其组合对分类精度的影响

为了研究各轴加速度及其组合对驾驶人身份识别精度的影响,本文分别使用5位被试的不同加速度数据组合进行驾驶人身份识别试验。

试验的结果见表1。表中数据显示,使用单个轴的数据的识别精度低于使用两个轴的数据的识别精度低于使用三个轴的数据的识别精度;在使用单个轴加速度的三组数据中,使用 x 轴数据的识别精度小于使用 y 轴数据的识别精度小于使用 z 轴数据的识别精度。考虑到加速度直方图区间对识别精度的影响,暂时无法对各个轴数据对驾驶人身份识别精度贡献度的大小进行分析讨论，将在下文对此内容进行进一步的研究。

使用各轴加速度及其组合数据的分类结果　　表1

使用数据类型	x	y	z	xy	xz	yz	xyz
第一次训练	59.1	66.6	70.4	80.3	82.3	82.9	88.5
第二次训练	59.4	67	69.8	80.5	83.7	83.2	89.9
第三次训练	61	67.3	70.1	81.8	81.9	82	88.9
第四次训练	60.2	67.1	70	80.8	83	83.4	88.4
第五次训练	59.5	67.8	69.9	80.9	83.5	82.9	89.5
平均识别精度	59.84	67.16	70.04	80.86	82.88	82.88	89.04

3.1.2　直方图区间对分类精度的影响

由于驾驶人驾驶习惯的差异，驾驶人的行车加速度的频率分布在不同区间上也具有一定的特征。因此，除以上因素之外，本文还对加速度直方图的区间对识别精度的影响进行了分析。试验结果见图5。

图中结果显示，对于KNN模型，在一定范围内，缩小加速度频率分布直方图区间能够显著提升驾驶人身份识别精度，继续缩小加速度频率分布直方图区间会导致精度趋于平缓或者下降。在调整频率分布直方图区间后，通过单个轴的加速度数据对五名驾驶人进行身份识别的精度均可以达到90%以上。

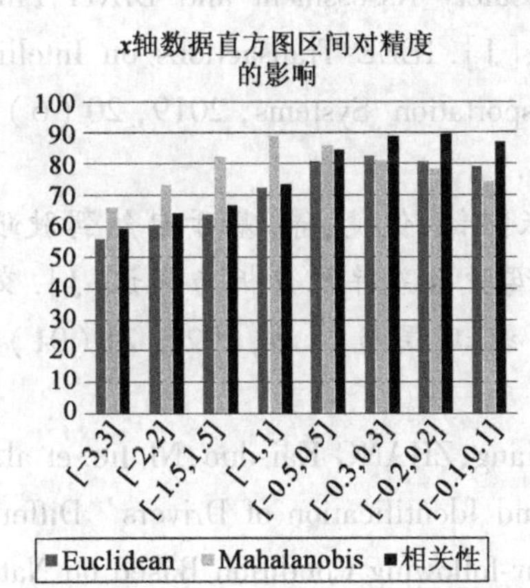

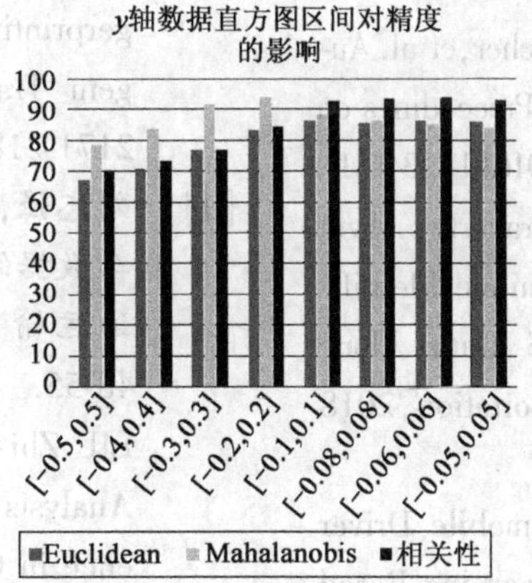

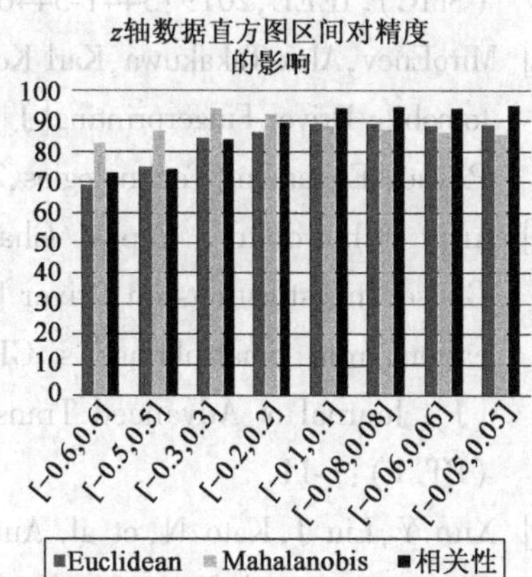

图5　各轴加速度区间对驾驶人身份识别精度的影响

3.2　超参数对模型的影响

在机器学习中，超参数是在开始学习过程之前设置值的参数，而不是通过训练得到的参数数据。通常情况下，需要对超参数进行优化，以提高学习的性能和效果。

KNN算法中的超参数包括邻近点个数、距离度量方式等，本小节将讨论不同距离度量方式对模型的影响。

MATLAB中的Classification Learner工具包提供了多种距离度量方式，包括Eulidean、相关性、Mahalanobis、City block、Chebyshev、Spearman、Hammming、Jaccard等。设空间中x,y两点的坐标为$x(x_1,x_2,\cdots,x_n)$，$y(x_1,x_2,\cdots,x_n)$，用不同方法计算其距离$d(x,y)$。各个距离度量方式对应的识别精度见表2。结果显示在此参数设定条件下，马氏距离具有最优的识别精度，其次是相关性距离和City block距离。

不同距离度量方式对识别精度的影响　　表2

距离度量方式	Eulidean	相关性	Mahalanobis	City block	Chebyshev	Spearman	Hammming	Jaccard
准确度(%)	88.80	90.60	93.20	90.00	51.50	88.40	69.50	69.50

4 小结

本文首先通过自然驾驶试验采集得到20名被试的行车数据,通过滑窗法和频率分布直方图构建驾驶行为数据集,随后使用KNN模型对驾纹特征进行身份识别测试。测试结果显示,使用x、y、z三轴数据对5名驾驶人进行身份识别的准确率最高可以达到96.6%。

此外,在未来的深入研究中,还可以使用其他算法模型对该数据集进行识别,以及使用其他类型的驾驶行为数据,例如转向盘转角、加速踏板开度、制动踏板开度等。

参考文献

[1] Tanaka D, Baba Y, H Kashima, et al. Large-scale Driver Identification Using Automobile Driving Data [C]//2019 IEEE International Conference on Systems, Man and Cybernetics (SMC). IEEE,2019:3441-3446.

[2] MiroEnev, Alex Takakuwa, Karl Koscher, et al. Automobile Driver Fingerprinting[J]. Proceedings on Privacy Enhancing Technologies,2016(1):34-51.

[3] Arijit Chowdhury, Tapas Chakravarty, Avik Ghose. Investigations on Driver Unique Identification from Smartphone's GPS Data Alone [J]. Journal of Advanced Transportation, 2018 (PT.1):1-11.

[4] Xun Y, Liu J, Kato N, et al. Automobile Driver Fingerprinting: A New Machine Learning Based Authentication Scheme [J]. IEEE Transactions on Industrial Informatics, 2020, 16 (2): 1417-1426.

[5] Remeli M, S Lestyán, Acs G, et al. Automatic Driver Identification from In-Vehicle Network Logs[J]. IEEE,2019:27-30.

[6] Virojboonkiate N, Chanakitkarnchok A, Vateekul P, et al. Public Transport Driver Identification System Using Histogram of Acceleration Data [J]. Journal of advanced transportation, 2019,2019(PT.1):1-15.

[7] Putri R, Yang C H, Chang CC, et al. Smartwatch-Based Open-Set Driver Identification by Using GMM-Based Behavior Modeling Approach [J]. IEEE Sensors Journal, 2020, PP (99):4918-4926.

[8] Zhezhang Ding, Donghao Xu, Huijing Zhao. Driver Identification through Multi-state Car Following Modeling [C] // 2019 IEEE Intelligent Transportation Systems Conference (ITSC). Auckland, New Zealand, 2019: 1580-1587.

[9] Hua Y, Jiang H, Tian H, et al. A Comparative Study of Clustering Analysis Method for Driver's Steering Intention Classification and Identification under Different Typical Conditions[J]. Appliedences,2017,7(10):1014.

[10] Bouhoute A, Oucheikh R, Boubouh K, et al. Advanced Driving Behavior Analytics for an Improved Safety Assessment and Driver Fingerprinting[J]. IEEE Transactions on Intelligent Transportation Systems, 2019, 20 (6): 2171-2184.

[11] 刘志强,张凯铎,倪捷,等.基于自然驾驶跟车数据的驾驶人差异性分析与辨识[J].交通运输系统工程与信息,2021,21(01):48-55.

LIU Zhi-qiang, ZHANG Kai-duo, NI Jie. et al. Analysis and Identification of Drivers' Difference in Car-following Condition Based on Naturalistic Driving Data[J]. Journal of Transportation Systems Engineering and Information Technology,2021,21(01):48-55.

[12] Chen Jie, Wu ZhongCheng, Zhang Jun. Driver Identification Based on Hidden Feature Extraction by Using Deep Learning[J]. Applied Soft Computing,2019,74:1-9.

[13] Abdellah El Mekki, Afaf Bouhoute, Ismail Berrada. Improving Driver Identification for the Next-Generation of In-Vehicle Software Systems [J] IEEE Transactions on Vehicular Technology,2019,68:7406-7415.

基于认知负荷的接管安全性预测模型

刘永杰[1,2] 吴超仲[1,2] 张 晖*[1,2] 肖逸影[3] 张 琦[1,2]
(1. 武汉理工大学智能交通系统研究中心;2. 国家水运安全工程技术研究中心;
3. 武汉市交通发展战略研究院)

摘 要 未来较长时间内,自动驾驶汽车仍将面对"人机共驾"的局面,为了保障驾驶人接管车辆的安全,通过分析不同驾驶环境下的驾驶人在接管请求发出前的认知负荷变化,对驾驶人接管安全性进行预测。首先选取37名被试设计并开展模拟驾驶实验,针对前方车辆事故和车道线消失两种接管场景,每位被试进行16次接管。采集不同驾驶环境下的瞳孔数据(认知负荷表征指标)和驾驶行为数据(接管安全性表征指标);提出考虑不同典型场景的基于驾驶行为指标的接管安全性评价方法,将接管情况分为安全和不安全;分别以接管请求发出前不同时间窗长度的瞳孔数据转换后的灰度图像作为输入,以接管安全或不安全作为输出,利用卷积神经网络搭建基于认知负荷的接管安全性预测模型,借助混淆矩阵的多级评价指标分析不同预测模型的优劣。结果表明,当时间窗长度大于30s后,模型准确率均能达到80%,且时间窗长度再增加,模型准确率变化不大。建议选择发出接管请求前30s内的瞳孔数据作为输入,对驾驶人接管车辆后的安全性进行预测,准确率可达到82%。

关键词 交通工程 接管预测模型 卷积神经网络 自动驾驶 接管驾驶

0 引言

随着汽车辅助驾驶技术的发展,车辆的智能化水平不断提升,自动驾驶也成为了近些年来交通领域的研究热点[1]。未来较长时间内,大部分自动驾驶车辆会以"有条件自动驾驶"(Level 3)存在[2]。近来自动驾驶车辆事故频频发生,研究驾驶人接管自动驾驶汽车对道路交通安全具有重要意义。

已有研究证明接管过程及其绩效评估是L3级车辆人机交互最为基础和重要的研究部分[3]。而接管绩效受多种因素影响,包括驾驶人是否参与非驾驶任务[4]、非驾驶任务的类型[5]、驾驶场景的复杂性[6]、驾驶场景天气状况[7]、交通密度[8]、接管请求的方式[9]和强度[10]、接管请求的紧迫度[11]、人机界面(HMI)设计[12]、驾驶人年龄、性别、情绪等。

接管时间预算(Time Budget,TB)和接管场景对人机共驾下的接管安全有显著影响。有研究指出,在观看视频时,TB设置为2s驾驶人很难安全地通过路障路段,TB设置为5s或8s时,大多数驾驶人能安全的进行接管[13]。接管时间预算越短,驾驶人可用于情境认知的时间更短,驾驶人的接管反应时间有所减少,但接管质量会下降。更长的时间预算或紧急情况的减少反而会导致更长的反应时间[14]。

研究表明,当车辆发起接管请求时,认知负荷对驾驶人接管安全性有显著影响。已有大量研究证明,眼动指标具有随认知负荷变化敏感的特性,还具有实时、客观的优点。但需要注意的是,眼动指标容易受到环境光线的影响,在实验过程中,需要对此干扰量进行控制。在眼动与认知负荷的众多研究中,专家指出瞳孔直径、瞳孔大小、注视次数及时间、眨眼频率等指标与认知负荷关联紧密。Alrefaie等[15]研究发现归一化瞳孔直径在电子邮件任务期间比不执行非驾驶相关任务(Non Driving Related Task,NDRT)平均增加了0.314,在TQT期间比不执行平均增加了0.06。刘鑫[16]发现驾驶人在有认知负荷状态下的瞳孔大于无认知负荷状态下,并且两种状态下的瞳孔大小存在显著

1. 国家重点研发计划项目:新能源汽车运行安全风险评估预警技术及系统研发;2019YFB1600803。国家自然科学基金面上项目:考虑架纹特征和时变规律的加速疲劳协同计算模型与调控方法研究;52072289。

差异。周鹏生[17]发现注视时间、注视次数、瞳孔直径这些指标可以体现驾驶人对任务的认知过程。因此通过眼动数据量化认知负荷具有一定支撑性。

在研究分析各因素对接管绩效的影响后,国内外学者进行了接管绩效评估建模工作。Michael等[18]研究视觉分心对驾驶人接管行为的影响,利用K-means聚类算法可将驾驶人按高、中、低风险分为三类,可以评估自动驾驶情况下驾驶人的道路监控行为和NDRT后的接管行为。Zeeb等[19]提出了一种贝叶斯网络统计危险估计方法,适用于两种场景下的半自动驾驶车辆(驾驶人手动驾驶和车辆自动驾驶)。

本研究针对自动驾驶过程中驾驶人认知负荷变化规律开展研究,探索不同认知负荷条件下驾驶人接管车辆能力的变化特征,对于提升自动驾驶车辆安全水平有重要意义。本研究基于驾驶人眼动数据提出考虑不同典型场景下驾驶行为指标接管安全性评价方法,最后基于认知负荷建立接管安全性预测模型,为自动驾驶车辆预警系统和城市道路安全提供依据和保障。

1 试验概况

1.1 被试

根据实验目的,驾驶人需满足以下要求:①被试年龄相近,有驾照,并且熟知交通法规;②身体健康,最近5年内无重大疾病史;③作息正常,无酗酒等不良嗜好;④无3D眩晕症,对模拟驾驶器有较好的适应性;⑤无高度闪光,眼睛未动过手术。本次实验通过校内外招募,招募了37名符合要求的驾驶人作为被试(其中,有12名女性驾驶人),年龄为24.11岁±2.23岁,驾龄为3.68年±1.36年。

1.2 试验设备

本实验利用UC-win/Road13.0软件来设计模拟实验驾驶场景,使用的模拟驾驶器由实车改造。UC-win/Road13.0软件控制7台分控电脑,其中2台电脑生成左右后视镜的模拟场景,投送至模拟驾驶器两边充当后视镜的小型液晶显示屏中;5台电脑生成模拟驾驶的道路场景,投递至模拟器正前方的5个大型显示屏,形成模拟驾驶环境,如图1所示。

图1 试验所用驾驶模拟器

本研究使用眼动仪记录人的眼动特征。本实验使用的是德国Ergoneers公司的Dikablis Glasses 3.55版本的眼动仪仪器。Dikablis Glasses眼动仪是一款非侵入式的人眼跟踪系统,包含三路采集摄像头,其中第一路和第二路为视觉特性获取摄像头,负责采集左右眼的眼动数据,第三路为场景信息获取摄像头,负责采集视线前方场景信息。可以采集驾驶人的视线、兴趣区域、眨眼率、凝视、眼跳、瞳孔等数据。眼动仪识别左右瞳孔和第三路摄像头拍摄画面如图2所示。

图2 眼动仪三路摄像头拍摄画面

1.3 自变量

本研究将接管时间预算、接管场景作为自变量。

针对接管时间预算,根据文献可知,绝大多数的驾驶人在接管时间预算为7s时能安全的进行接管[20],在接管时间预算为3s时,接管质量明显下降,影响接管安全性。本实验选择3s和7s作为接管时间预算。

针对接管场景,选择前方有故障车辆作为车辆纵向受阻场景,车道线消失作为车辆横向受阻场景,示意图如图3所示。

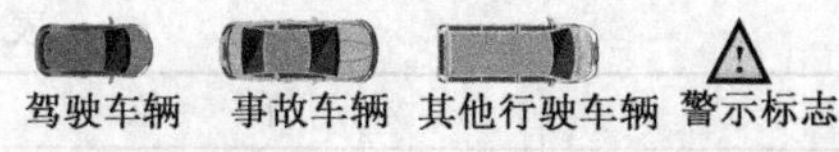

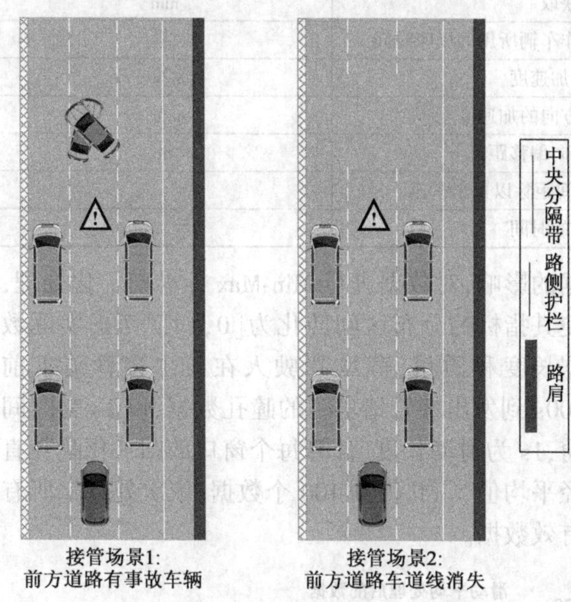

图3 接管场景示意图

1.4 试验设计

实验时间为9点至12点之间,整个实验约为90min。实验开始前,被试需要签署知情同意书、数据使用协议、个人信息登记表,在实验人员介绍实验整体流程后被试进行试驾,待被试熟悉模拟驾驶环境后给其佩戴眼动仪并进行标定。模拟驾驶实验行驶的整体路线如图4所示,接管过程会经历自动驾驶、接管车辆、手动驾驶三个阶段。实验开始后,车辆最初会以90km/h的速度匀速自动行驶,自动驾驶时长为2min,当车辆行驶到实验场景中的接管点处时,会向驾驶人发出接管请求提示音,驾驶权由车辆转移到驾驶人,驾驶人接管车辆。接管平稳后需尽可能使车辆回到中间车道,速度需保持在80~120km/h之间,手动驾驶一段时间后,会看到右前方"stop"的停车标识,待车辆超过停车标识后,将车停至紧急车道,即完成一次接管。车辆再次以自动驾驶模式抵达下一接管点,发出接管请求提示音,驾驶人接管车辆,驾驶至指定位置停车。每位被试的整个实验中共有16次接管,参考拉丁方实验设计三因素五水平的设计理念,固定16次接管场景顺序,从而抵消实验顺序的影响。

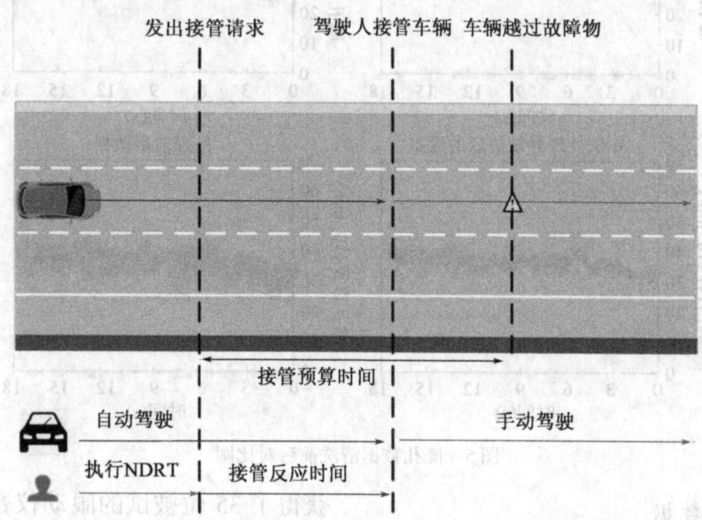

图4 接管示意图

1.5 数据预处理

模拟驾驶实验共获得37位被试的眼动仪数据、车辆操纵行为数据等多源数据。根据研究需要,针对不同的数据类型进行预处理,包括数据筛选、剔除异常数据、补充缺失值、归一化处理等,最终得到35位被试的数据集作为本次研究的样本数据集。

根据前文实验设计考虑的因素,筛选眼动指标(瞳孔直径)作为客观认知负荷依据,所获得的接管反应时间作为接管及时性表征指标,车辆横纵向行为数据(车辆横向加速度、纵向加速度、最小碰撞时间等)作为驾驶人接管绩效中接管质量的表征指标。各项数据的具体说明和单位如表1所示。

数据说明表　　表1

参　数	参数说明	单　位
瞳孔直径	通过眼动仪获取	mm
接管反应时间	驾驶人收到接管请求信号至操作车辆所用的反应时间	s
纵向加速度	车辆行驶方向的加速度	m/s^2
横向加速度	与车辆行驶方向垂直方向的加速度	m/s^2
车道偏离标准差SDLP	距离车道中心线的横向偏移距离	m
车头时距TH	距离碰上前车的时间,为车间距除以自车车速	s
碰撞时间TTC	距即将发生碰撞的时间	

1.5.1　眼动数据

首先剔除眨眼时的瞳孔直径数据;借助Matlab中的Fillmissing函数,使用窗口长度为5(包括左右5个数据点)的移动中位数替换原始数据中的0值;使用拉依达准则(3σ准则)剔除异常值。瞳孔直径数据清洗前后对比如图5所示。为了消除不同驾驶人原始瞳孔直径的差别对实验数据的影响,对数据进行Min-Max标准归一化处理,使其指标的分布区间转化为[0,1]。考虑实际数据长度和质量,截取驾驶人在发出接管请求前100s到发出接管请求时的瞳孔数据,以1s为时间窗,1s为滑动长度,计算每个窗口的归一化瞳孔直径平均值,一共得到100个数据,依次处理完所有有效数据。

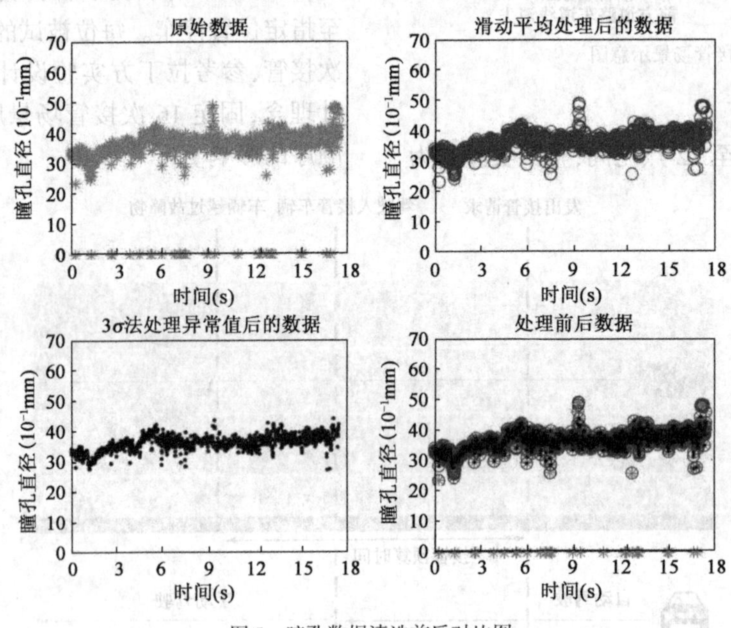

图5　瞳孔数据清洗前后对比图

1.5.2　驾驶行为数据

实验过程中,会出现因系统误差和实验误操作导致数据异常或丢失的情况,结合实验数据的实际情况需要对操作数据进行数据筛选、剔除异常值,然后采用线性插值的方法来补全缺失数据,最后计算速度、车辆横向加速度、车辆纵向加速度、车道偏移标准差的二级指标。

2　接管安全性预测模型

2.1　接管安全性评价

前文设计模拟驾驶实验收集数据并预处理后获得了35位被试的眼动仪数据、车辆操纵行为数据等多源数据。基于此,本研究提出考虑不同典型场景下驾驶行为指标接管安全性评价方法,接管安全性评价结果为安全或不安全。

根据先前研究,评估驾驶人的接管绩效从接管及时性和接管质量两个方面着手。对于不同的接管场景,使用不同的指标评估驾驶人的接管绩效[21]。针对避障场景,选择接管反应时间、TTC最小值、横向加速度最大值、车道偏移最大值作为评价指标;针对车道保持场景,选择接管反应时间、车道偏移标准差、横向加速度最大值、车道偏移最大值作为评价指标。

参考先前研究[22]的处理方法,使用 3σ 原则确定某次接管中的某个评价指标是否安全。结合 Braunagel 等研究,需要验证指标是否满足正态分布或近似正态分布,如不满足,需要先转换为正态数据,再计算阈值。在接管中若出现与护栏碰撞、与前方事故车辆碰撞、在接管时间预算内未接管车辆的极端情况都被判定为此次接管不安全。为了防止极端值对数据的影响,剔除发生碰撞事故和未在规定时间内接管车辆的极端情况数据,极端情况不参与后续的 3σ 原则数据处理。

将接管场景和 TB 组合后形成如表 2 所示的 4 种典型场景。利用 P-P 图对 4 个典型场景的评价指标进行正态性验证并对非正态分布数据进行转换。

不同典型场景说明　　表 2

典型场景	接管场景	TB(s)
1	避障	3
2	避障	7
3	车道保持	3
4	车道保持	7

在 3σ 原则中,利用均值 μ 和标准偏差 σ 计算上述指标的上限阈值和下限阈值,数值分布在 $(\mu-2\sigma,\mu+2\sigma)$ 中的概率为 0.9545。对于所有的接管事件,任一针对该接管事件的评估指标分布在阈值外即被认定为“不安全接管”,反之为“安全接管”。上述极端事件也被归类为“不安全接管”。最终得到安全接管次数为 389 次,不安全接管次数为 78 次。

2.2 模型构建

本研究利用卷积神经网络搭建基于认知负荷的接管安全性预测模型。该模型以接管请求发出前不同时间窗长度数据作为输入,以接管安全与否作为输出,使用卷积神经网络搭建接管安全性预测模型,并利用混淆矩阵多级指标评价不同预测模型的优劣,分析了输入不同时间窗长度数据对预测模型的影响及其原因,为自动驾驶车辆预警系统和城市道路安全提供依据和保障。

本研究结合 SMOTE 过采样算法和卷积神经网络进行模型搭建,用混淆矩阵的多级指标对模型进行评价。流程图如图 6 所示。

结合前文所得到的接管安全性评价结果,统计得到,原始不安全样本为 78 个,原始安全样本为 389 个。当分类样本不平衡时(类别比例超过 4:1),会导致样本量少的分类中所包含的特征过少,导致很难从中提取到规律。故本研究利用 SMOTE 算法进行过抽样处理,平衡分类样本。

在使用卷积神经网络前,需要将样本数据转换为灰度图像,并打上所属标签(安全或不安全)。以接管请求发出前不同时间窗长度数据作为输入,以接管安全与否作为输出,利用卷积神经网络搭建接管安全性预测模型。

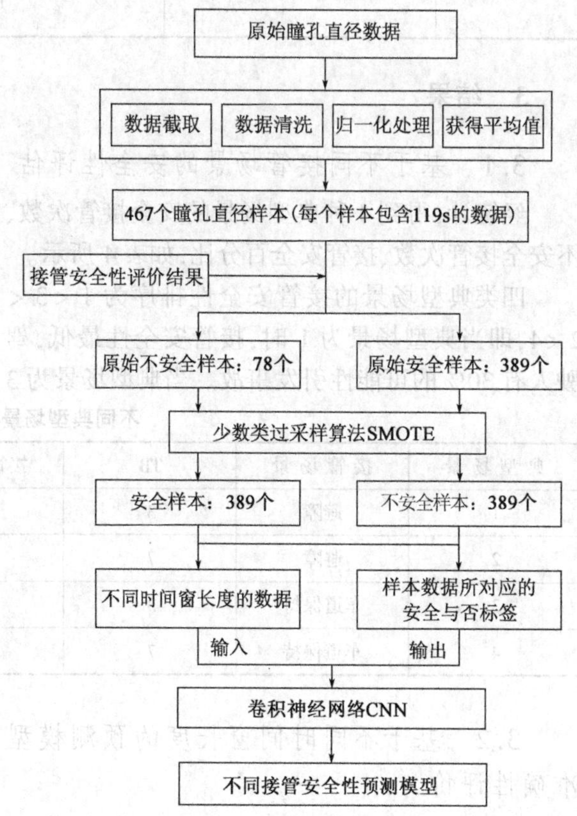

图 6　搭建不同接管安全性预测模型流程图

2.3 模型评估

混淆矩阵多用于判断分类器(Classifier)的优劣,本研究中的模型属于二分类模型,可利用混淆矩阵的一级、二级、三级指标评判接管安全性预测模型的好坏。所选指标如表 3 所示。

二分类模型评价指标　　表3

指　标		全称及公式	说　明
一级指标	TP	True Positive	实际值是 positive,预测值是 positive 的数量
	FN	False Negative	实际值是 positive,预测值是 negative 的数量
	FP	False Positive	实际值是 negative,预测值是 positive 的数量
	TN	True Negative	实际值是 negative,预测值是 negative 的数量
二级指标	ACC(准确率)	$\text{Accuracy}=\frac{TP+TN}{TP+TN+FP+FN}$	分类模型所有判断正确的结果占总观测值的比例
	PPV(精确率)	$\text{Precision}=\frac{TP}{TP+FP}$	在预测值是 Positive 的所有结果中,预测值对的比例
	TPR(灵敏度)	$\text{Sensitivity}=\text{Recall}=\frac{TP}{TP+FN}$	在实际值是 Positive 的所有结果中,预测值对的比例
	TNR(特异度)	$\text{Specificity}=\frac{TN}{TN+FP}$	在实际值是 Negative 的所有结果中,预测值对的比例
三级指标	F1 Score	$\text{F1 Score}=\frac{2PR}{P+R}$	表示模型输出能力的好坏,取值范围为[0,1],其中,1 代表模型的输出最好

3　结果

3.1　基于不同接管场景的安全性评估

经统计,得到4种典型场景的安全接管次数、不安全接管次数、接管安全百分比,如表4所示。

四类典型场景的接管安全性排序为 1 < 3 < 2 < 4,即当典型场景为1时,接管安全性最低,驾驶人有30%的可能性引发事故。当典型场景为3时,只需要驾驶人进行车道保持操纵即可,但由于所设定的TB仅为3s,驾驶人操纵车辆前的准备时间较少,故其接管安全性也不高。当典型场景为2和4时,TB为7s,驾驶人在听到接管请求发出后,有充足的时间观察行车环境,对车辆的操控力更好,安全接管的比例均在90%以上。当场景复杂度为更低的4时,超过95%的驾驶人安全接管。

不同典型场景的安全性评价结果　　表4

典型场景	接管场景	TB	接管总次数	安　全	不安全	安全性
1	避障	3	125	88	37	70.40%
2	避障	7	128	119	9	92.97%
3	车道保持	3	125	91	34	72.80%
4	车道保持	7	129	124	5	96.12%

3.2　基于不同时间窗长度的预测模型准确性评价

本模型使用带动量的随机梯度算法(Stochastic Gradient Descent with Momentum, SGDM)训练模型,该算法可以使训练速度变快。初始学习率设置为0.01,验证频率设置为30次,监控训练期间神经网络的准确性。

规定时间窗口的结束时间为发出接管请求TOR的时间,时间窗口开始的时间是TOR之前的x秒。分别取x为10、20、30、40、50、60、70、80、90、100时的数据作为输入,设定训练集与验证集的比例为7:3,对神经网络进行10次训练后取平均值作为不同模型最终结果。每迭代30次模型会计算测试集正确率和损失函数,为防止过拟合,设置"ValidationPatience"为5,即在网络训练停止之前,允许验证损失大于或等于先前的最小损失的次数为5次。对10次训练结果求平均值后,分类器的混淆矩阵多级指标如表5所示。

基于不同时间窗长度的预测模型的评价指标 表5

时间窗长度	ACC	PPV	TPR	TNR	F1 Score
10	74.37%	76.52%	70.31%	78.43%	0.7328
20	78.40%	80.51%	74.96%	81.85%	0.7763
30	81.98%	84.73%	77.95%	85.99%	0.8120
40	80.95%	85.53%	74.51%	87.39%	0.7964
50	82.28%	86.53%	76.47%	88.10%	0.8119
60	81.26%	86.05%	74.62%	87.90%	0.7993
70	81.26%	85.36%	75.46%	87.06%	0.8011
80	80.92%	86.22%	73.61%	88.24%	0.7942
90	81.41%	86.00%	75.04%	87.78%	0.8014
100	83.45%	89.33%	75.97%	90.92%	0.8211

将不同时间窗长度的数据转换为灰度图片输入神经网络训练得到不同预测模型，其 ACC 和 F1 Score 的变化趋势如图7、图8所示。可以看到当时间窗长度为10和20时，准确率分别为74.37%、78.40%。当时间窗长度大于30s时，模型平均准确率均能达到80%，且此时时间窗长度增加，模型准确率变化不大，说明选择发出接管请求时间前30s内的瞳孔数据作为输入，平均预测准确率为82%。

以任一 $x=10$ 和 $x=30$ 的模型训练过程图和混淆矩阵为例进行分析说明。图9为时间窗长度为10s的模型训练过程，为了防止过拟合，当验证损失大于或等于先前的最小损失的次数为5次时，训练停止。

从图9可以得知，在 $x=10$ 的模型停止训练时，训练集的准确率只有90%，而 $x=30$ 的模型停止训练时，训练集的准确率几乎达到100%。

由图10可知，当 $x=10$ 时，模型中实际分类为0但预测为1的有19例，将1预测为0的有41例，即将不安全接管情况误判为安全接管的有19例，错将安全接管预测为不安全接管的有41例，模型辨识安全接管情况的正确率只有65.5%。对安全接管情况的辨识度较低，导致模型整体的准确率不高。

当 $x=30$ 时，模型中实际分类为0但预测为1的有13个，对于不安全的正确识别率较 $x=10$ 时有所提升。错将1预测为0的有30例，模型辨识安全接管情况的正确率变为74.8%。模型对两个分类的辨识能力都有所上升，模型整体准确率上升，为81.9%。

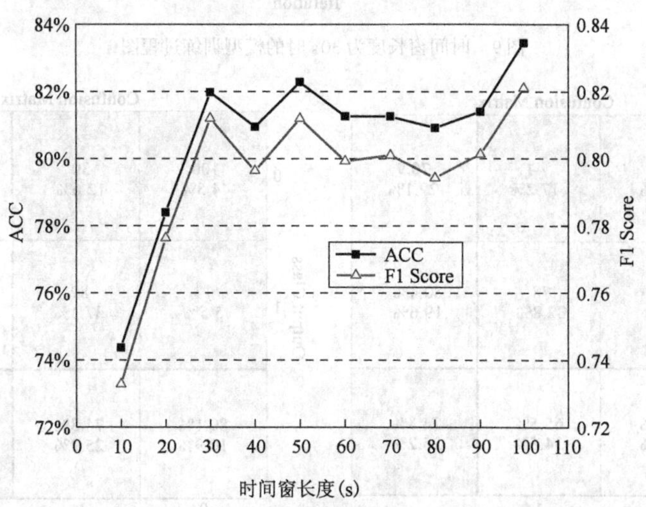

图7 输入不同时间窗长度数据的预测模型的 ACC 和 F1 Score

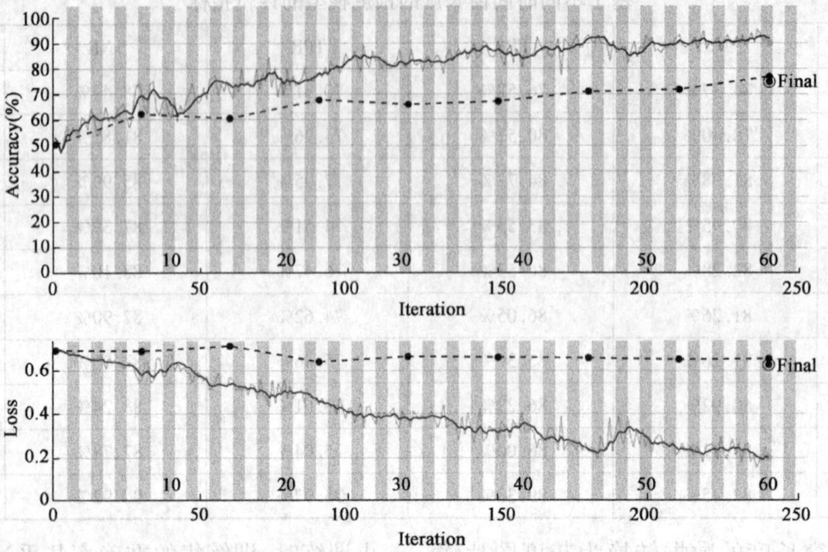

图 8　时间窗长度为 10s 时的模型训练过程图

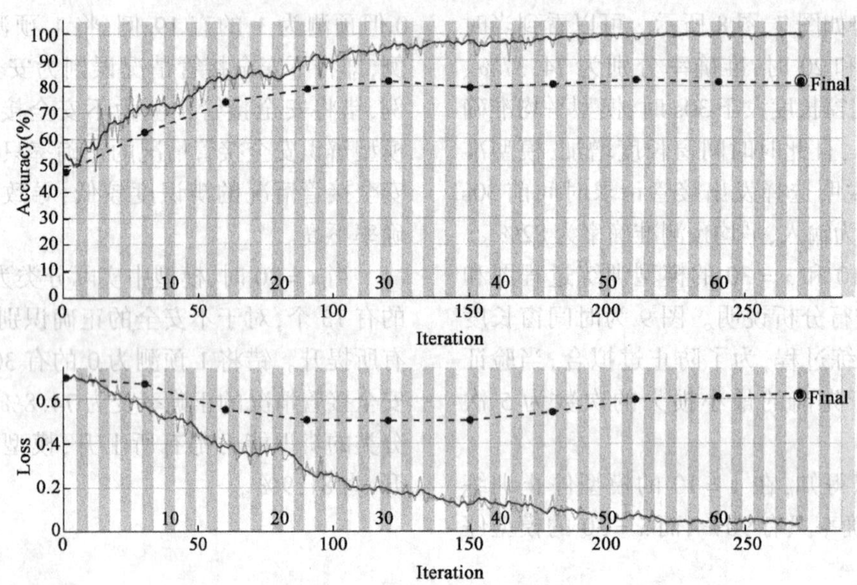

图 9　时间窗长度为 30s 时的模型训练过程图

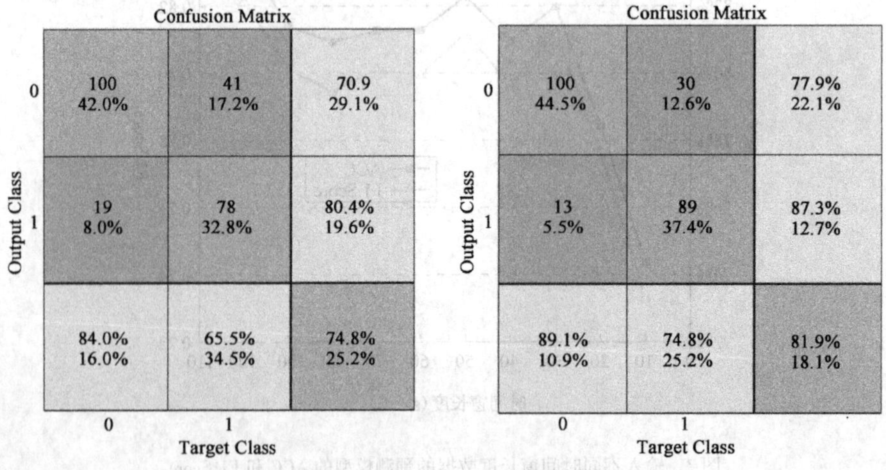

图 10　时间窗长度为 10s(左)、30s(右)时的混淆矩阵

结合以上分析,当时间窗长度大于30s后,模型平均准确率均能达到80%。可能原因是,当样本长度小于30s时,安全样本中的特征较少,模型无法提取充分的特征用以识别安全与否。

建议在对驾驶人进行实时面部监控时,实时分析最近30s内驾驶人瞳孔直径的变化,若在自动驾驶过程中,车辆发出接管请求时,预测模型得出驾驶人不适合接管车辆的结论,建议启动靠边停车服务,首先保障行车安全。

4 结语

本研究使用卷积神经网络搭建基于认知负荷的接管安全性预测模型。分别以接管请求发出前不同时间窗长度数据转换后的灰度图像作为输入,以接管安全与否作为输出,利用混淆矩阵的多级评价指标分析不同预测模型的优劣。结果表明,当时间窗长度大于30后,模型准确率均能达到80%,且时间窗长度增加,模型准确率变化不大。建议选择发出接管请求前30s内的瞳孔数据作为输入,预测驾驶人接管车辆后的安全性,准确率可达到82%。为自动驾驶车辆预警系统和城市道路安全提供依据和保障。

本研究的一个局限是本研究的数据源于模拟驾驶器,其数据分析结论和接管安全性预测模型与实车驾驶的契合程度还未可知。期望在未来的研究中,在技术条件、法律法规等都满足条件的情况下,采集实车实验数据对所得结论和预测模型进行验证。

本研究中所挑选的被试均为22~29岁的年轻人,未来可以综合考虑年龄、驾龄、性别、驾驶风格、性格特质等个体因素,结合不同复杂程度的驾驶环境,多角度、深层次探索在人机共驾环境下驾驶人的接管安全性。

本研究中评价接管安全性的方式基于车辆操纵指标,即驾驶人接管时的驾驶行为指标,现有文献中也没有统一、有效的度量方式来衡量接管安全性,未来有必要建立一套考虑多要素的普适性方法,既有主观评价法的经验指导性,又有客观评定法的客观真实性。

本研究所使用的数据集有限,因采用单个在时间序列上的数据作为输入,模型识别精度不高,未来的研究可能会使用更大的数据集,使用包含生理信号等多因素输入训练模型的方式来预测驾驶人的接管安全性。在安全性的分类上也可以进行更细致的划分,而不是局限于安全或不安全的二分类结果,以此来提高预测模型的实用性。

参考文献

[1] Hu Y F, Qu T, Liu J, et al. Human-machine Cooperative Control of Intelligent Vehicle: Recent Developments and Future Perspectives (Review)[J]. Acta Automatica Sinica, 2019, 45(7):1261-1280.

[2] SAE J3016, Taxonomy and Definitions for Terms Related to Driving Automation Systems for On-Road Motor Vehicles[R]. 2016. Detroit.

[3] Christian Gold, Riender Happee, Klaus Bengler, Modeling take-over performance in level 3 conditionally automated vehicles, Accident Analysis & Prevention, 2018, 116:3-13.

[4] 马舒,章薇,史金磊,等.基于认知机制的有条件自动驾驶接管中的人因问题[J].心理科学进展,2020,28(1):150-160.

[5] Choi D, Sato T, Ando T, et al. Effects of Cognitive and Visual Loads on Driving Performance after Take-Over Request (TOR) in Automated Driving [J]. Applied ergonomics, 2020, 85:103074.

[6] Merat N, Jamson A, Lai F, et al. Highly Automated Driving, Secondary Task Performance, and Driver State. [J]. Human Factors, 2012, Vol. 54(5):762-771.

[7] Louw T, Madigan R, Carsten O, et al. Were They in the Loop during Automated Driving? Links Between Visual Attention and Crash Potential [J]. Injury Prevention, 2017, 23(4):281-286.

[8] Radlmayr J, Gold C, Lorenz L, et al. How Traffic Situations and Non-Driving Related Tasks Affect the Take-Over Quality in Highly Automated Driving[C]. Proceedings of the Human Factors and Ergonomics Society Annual Meeting, Los Angeles, 2014, 58(1):2063-2067.

[9] Petermeijer S, Bazilinskyy P, Bengler K, et al. Take-Over Again: Investigating Multimodal and Directional TORs to Get the Driver Back into the Loop [J]. Applied Ergonomics, 2017, 62: 204-215.

[10] Gold C, Damböck D, Lorenz L, et al. "Take over!" How Long does It Take to Get the Driver Back into the Loop? [J]. Proceedings of the Human Factors and Ergonomics Society Annual Meeting, 2013, 57(1): 1938-1942.

[11] Wan J, Wu C. The Effects of Lead Time of Take-Over Request and Non Driving Tasks on Taking-Over Control of Automated Vehicles (Article) [J]. IEEE Transactions on Human-Machine Systems, 2018, 48(6): 582-591.

[12] Carsten O, Martens M H. How can Humans Understand Their Automated Cars? HMI Principles, Problems and Solutions [J]. Cognition, Technology and Work, 2019, 21(1): 3-20.

[13] Walch M, Lange K, Baumann M, et al. Autonomous Driving: Investigating the Feasibility of Car-Driver Handover Assistance [C]. the 7th International Conference on Automotive User Interfaces and Interactive Vehicular Applications, 2015.

[14] Izquierdo Reyes J, Ramirez Mendoza R A, Bustamante Bello M R, et al. Emotion Recognition for Semi-Autonomous Vehicles Framework [J]. International Journal on Interactive Design and Manufacturing, 2018, 12(4): 1447-1454.

[15] Alrefaie M T, Summerskill S, Jackon T W. In a Heart Beat: Using Driver's Physiological Changes to Determine the Quality of a Takeover in Highly Automated Vehicles [J]. Accident Analysis & Prevention, 2019, 131: 180-190.

[16] 刘鑫. 基于眼动数据测量认知负荷水平[D]. 重庆:西南大学, 2017.

[17] 周鹏生, 周爱保. THOG 推理影响因素的眼动研究[J]. 西南大学学报(自然科学版), 2021, 33(2): 167-172.

[18] Michael S, Kathrin Z, Axel B. What Determines the Take-Over Time? An Integrated Model Approach of Driver Take-Over after Automated Driving [J]. Accident Analysis and Prevention, 2015, 78: 212-221.

[19] Zeeb K, Buchner A, Schrauf M. Is Take-Over Time All that Matters? The Impact of Visual-Cognitive Load on Driver Take-Over Quality After Conditionally Automated Driving [J]. Accident Analysis & Prevention, 2016, 92: 230-239.

[20] Walch M, Lange K, Baumann M, et al. Autonomous Driving: Investigating the Feasibility of Car-Driver Handover Assistance [C]. the 7th International Conference on Automotive User Interfaces and Interactive Vehicular Applications, 2015.

[21] Braunagel C, Rosenstiel W, Kasneci E. Ready for Take-Over? A New Driver Assistance System for an Automated Classification of Driver Take-Over Readiness [J]. IEEE Intelligent Transportation Systems Magazine, 2017, 9(4): 10-22.

[22] Sevastianov P, Dymova L, Bartosiewicz P. A framework for rule-base evidential reasoning in the interval setting applied to diagnosing type 2 diabetes [J]. Expert Systems with Applications, 2012, 39(4): 4190-4200.

考虑不同驾驶工况的电动汽车热失控风险分析

丰红霞[1,2] 张 晖*[1,2] 陈 枫[1,2] 李少鹏[1,2] 黄 衍[1,2]

(1. 武汉理工大学智能交通系统研究中心;2. 国家水运安全工程技术研究中心)

摘 要 为保障电动汽车的安全运行,从更多维度对电动汽车动力电池进行分析十分关键。本研究基于国家重点研发课题中电动汽车的高频监测数据以及 K-means 聚类算法将车辆运行状态划分为三种不同的工况,即激进型、普通型、保守型,并分别计算了不同工况下的电池单体最大电压差(Voltage Difference,VD)和电池单体最大电压差的方差(Voltage Difference Variance,VDV);以电压不一致性为切入点,分析了不同工况下电压不一致性对电池热失控风险的影响。结果表明,保守型工况下的 VDV 最大值为 2.275×10^{-5},普通型工况下 VDV 最大值为 3.983×10^{-5},激进型工况下 VDV 最大值为 4.706×10^{-5}。由此说明,考虑工况进行电动汽车热失控风险分析是必要且可行的,其中激进型工况对热失控风险的影响最大,普通型工况次之,保守型工况影响最小。

关键词 交通安全 电动汽车 驾驶工况 热失控

0 引言

随着化石能源枯竭的威胁,大气污染等环境问题逐渐恶化,以电动汽车为代表的新能源汽车的发展应运而生。

作为中国战略性新兴产业之一以及我国实现"双碳"目标的有效手段,新能源汽车产业规模和技术水平发展迅速,截至 2021 年年底,国内新能源汽车保有量超过 784 万辆。动力电池作为电动汽车的核心部件,直接决定着电动汽车的整体性能和发展前景。动力电池热失控引发的车辆失火爆炸事故是新能源汽车安全性不足的主要表现,而热失控发生的原因多样、机理复杂。动力丧失、部件故障、疲劳驾驶、风险驾驶、域内他车异常等导致的碰撞可能会进一步引发动力电池热失控及车辆失火,目前电动汽车安全风险预警存在考虑因素不全面、风险评估不精准等问题。因此,考虑行车工况进行驾驶行为与热失控风险的关联规则研究,是电动汽车热失控风险预测预警技术的新思路。

历史研究中,Fu Li 等定义了四种危险驾驶行为,即异常加减速、急转向、频繁换道、在驾驶时操作手机,并采用中值滤波器和均值滤波器对手机采集的数据进行降噪处理后,基于规则的方法进行了上述危险驾驶行为的识别。Jichao Hong 等将新能源汽车国家监测与管理平台上的车辆运行状态与驾驶人状态、天气状态三方面的大数据结合起来,利用长短时记忆神经网络(LSTM)对电动汽车动力电池的电压异常进行预测,且预测精度可靠。此外,基于实际的车辆运行数据,结合报警阈值证实了预测模型的稳定性、可靠性。Li 等建立了长短时记忆神经网络(LSTM)与等效电路模型(ECM)相结合的电动汽车电池电压预测模型,并通过统计方法对电压预测值与实际值的残差进行评估以实现电池电压故障诊断及热失控的风险预警。

少量学者利用新能源汽车国家监测与管理平台的实际车辆运行数据开展研究,并考虑了行车工况、气象条件等对电池电压状态的影响,却无法深入分析电池安全特征参数与行车工况的动态映射机理,也无法真正地耦合行车工况以进一步提高电动汽车实际运行中电池故障诊断与风险预警方法的准确性和可靠性。

本文基于电动汽车热失控事故的高频监测数据,探究了不同风格工况下电动汽车热失控电池参数的特征。首先将处理过的车辆监测数据按照等时间长度划分为多个片段;然后基于 K-means 聚类算法以电动汽车的驾驶行为特征参数为切入点,对行车工况片段进行风格划分,将具有不同特征的工况片段分类为激进型、普通型、保守型三种

1. 基金项目:国家重点研发计划项目(编号:2019YFB1600800);国家自然科学基金(编号:52072289)。

风格;最后选取电池组最大电压差(VD)表征电动汽车的热失控电池参数差异,分析了不同风格工况片段下VD的变化特征,从而实现耦合行车工况的电动汽车热失控风险预测。

1　数据处理

1.1　数据简介及预处理

本研究的数据主要包括3台三元锂电池电动车辆发生热失控事故前后合计5~11个月的自然驾驶数据,采样频率为0.1Hz,采集的车辆信息包括电池信息、车速、行驶里程等。

由于采集的原始数据存在无效数据字段导致原始数据体量巨大,汽车启停时的电压波动、车载终端异常断电等情况都可能对数据采集产生一定影响,数据采集和数据传输过程受到的干扰都可能导致采集到的数据存在波动、异常或缺失等异常情况。为减少数据体量造成的计算困难,避免数据可能存在的波动、异常等情况,本研究进行了以下数据预处理:

首先剔除无效字段信号数据(采集数据为空或无效的信号字段),然后剔除充电状态、其他状态等片段数据,仅保留未充电状态数据。此外,检查采集的数据,将数值明显偏离观测值的异常数据剔除,如剔除了速度超过140km/h的数据,避免异常值给数据的计算分析带来的不利影响甚至误导性结论。

1.2　数据片段划分

为研究不同行车工况对动力电池参数影响的变化,需要将工况划分片段。本研究按照时间长度,每30min划分为一个工况片段,保证每个数据片段的时间长度一致;并使用滑动时间窗法对经过预处理和筛选的数据进行取样,其中时间窗长度为1800s,时间窗重叠度为50%,时间窗沿时间轴移动依次取样,使两相邻片段重叠50%时间长度(900s)的数据;接着剔除数据片段中数据样本不足180,即存在数据缺失情况的部分。

最终,原始的7.89×10^5组监测数据,处理得到6614个数据片段。

2　工况片段风格识别

2.1　风格识别特征指标提取

车辆速度、加速度是描述驾驶员驾驶行为最直接的参数,是驾驶员操纵制动、加速踏板的宏观表现,冲击率的大小直接反映乘坐舒适性。因此本章选择速度、加速度、冲击率作为驾驶行为特征参数,旨在研究与行车安全有关的各特征参数构成的行车工况片段的特性,并以驾驶风格的划分方式进行特性区分。

本研究将驾驶行为特征参数(车速、加速度、冲击率)的统计值构成风格识别特征参数数据集,其符号与含义见表1。

风格识别特征参数　　　　表1

符　号	含　义
Over_th_s	行车工况片段中车速超过车速阈值的次数
Over_th_a	行车工况片段中加速度超过加速度阈值的次数
Over_th_j	行车工况片段中冲击率超过冲击率阈值的次数

其中,车速、加速度、冲击率的阈值是分析3个参数的分布特性后拟定的,阈值根据参数的75%概率分布确定。由于行车工况片段的风格辨识实质上是将具有不同数据特征的片段进行整理归类,本研究将驾驶行为参数超过阈值的次数代替驾驶行为参数作为风格识别特征参数,实际上是初步将具有不同特性的工况进行代表性特征(数值大)提取的过程。

2.2　基于K-means聚类算法的工况片段风格辨识

2.2.1　K-means聚类算法

聚类算法是一种区别于分类算法的无监督学习算法,其中K-means算法因原理易懂、计算速度快的优点得到广泛应用。

本研究选取的聚类算法为K-means方法,它以距离作为相似性的评价指标,其基本思想是按照距离将样本聚成不同的簇,两个点的距离越近,其相似度就越大,以得到紧凑且独立的簇作为聚类目标。

K-means聚类算法的实现过程可大致表示如下:

(1)随机选取一个初始聚类中心。

(2)计算每个样本到各聚类中心的距离(欧氏距离),将每个样本归到其距离最近的聚类中心。

(3)以所有样本的均值作为每个簇新的聚类中心。

(4)重复第(2)~(3)步,直到聚类中心不再变化或达到设定的迭代次数。

2.2.2 工况片段分类结果分析

本文运用 Matlab 工具进行编程，通过 K-means 聚类方法对工况片段进行聚类，经对比发现划分为三类时，聚类效果最好。因此，本文参照驾驶风格分类方法，将每台车的工况片段划分为三种风格，分别定义为激进型工况、普通型工况、冷静型工况，为工况片段打上风格标签。聚类效果如图 1 所示。图中，X 轴、Y 轴、Z 轴为特征参数 Over_th_s、Over_th_a、Over_th_j，从左到右依次为第一类、第二类、第三类样本。分类结果中各类特征参数平均值如表 2 所示。

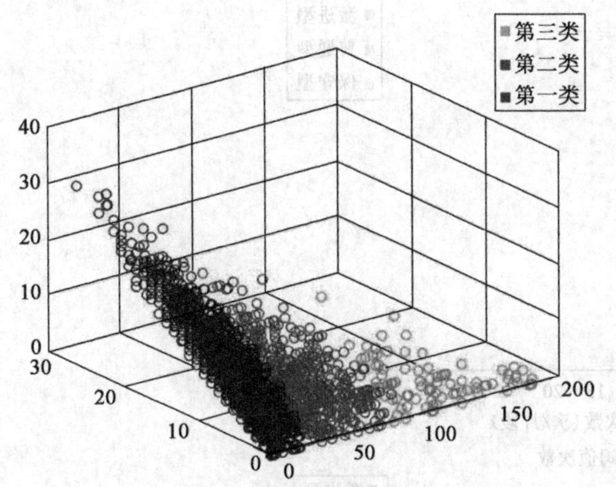

图1 工况片段风格聚类效果

各类特征参数平均值 表2

类　别	Over_th_s	Over_th_a	Over_th_j
第一类	1.7103	5.2892	9.0989
第二类	43.5395	4.4774	7.2368
第三类	124.6667	1.9896	3.2917

结合图表，通过分析各类特征参数平均值结果发现，第一类样本中，Over_th_s 这一参数虽然样本量最高，但其平均值却远低于其他两类，而速度是驾驶员驾驶行为最直接的反应参数，因此推断第一类为保守型风格工况片段；相对而言，第三类样本中 Over_th_s 的平均值为 124.6667，远高于其他两类，故推断第三类为激进型风格、第二类为普通型风格。

图 2 为不同风格工况片段的各类特征参数分布情况。

由图 2a）可知，激进型工况片段速度超过阈值的次数在高发区间的占比远远高于其他两类，且都分布在次数高于 75 的区间内，普通型工况片段速度超过阈值的次数在 0 ~ 100 区间分布，保守型工况片段速度超过阈值的次数在 0 ~ 25 区间占比 100%，这说明激进型工况片段中，驾驶员的速度高、高速行车发生频次多，而普通型、保守型工况片段中，驾驶员谨慎驾驶，车辆速度较低、行驶平稳。由图 2b）、图 2c）可知，加速度、冲击率的分布情况相似，普通型、保守型工况超过加速度阈值的次数多分布在 0 ~ 10，超过冲击率阈值的次数多分布在 0 ~ 15，且各区间占比相差不大；而激进型工况虽然加速度、冲击率超过阈值的次数分布在较小的区间，但各区间的百分比波动最剧烈，说明此类风格工况中驾驶员加速程度不稳定，容易出现急加速行为，对车速控制能力最差。

综上所述，激进型工况中车辆行驶速度高，驾驶员易发生急加速行为、车速控制能力差，对电动汽车动力电池放电要求更高，存在安全隐患。

3 热失控风险分析

3.1 电池热失控与行车工况关联性分析

电动汽车在各种道路条件和交通流状态下运行，随着驾驶行为的变化会相应地出现多种行车工况，不同的工况对应着不同的能量和功率输出，即对应着不同的电池放电特性和温度、电压、电流等多维特征值的变化规律。例如，在城市拥堵路段，车辆势必出现加速与减速工况频繁甚至急剧切换的运行状态；而在多坡道、长坡道、陡坡道的山区路段，车辆往往需要急加速，且单次加速行为持续时间长，这意味着放电电流急剧上升、大电流放电持续时间长。

从以往的研究可知，电池热失控常见诱因是，长期的滥用条件耦合自然老化效应慢慢引发电池内短路直至热失控。而在道路上行驶放电也是动力电池生命周期内充放电循环的一个重要方面，行车工况决定着放电过程特性，放电过程是电、热滥用与电池自然老化叠合作用发生的重要来源。因此，在一定程度上，行车工况影响着电池的安全状态。

新能源汽车国家监测与管理平台的数据统计表明，新能源汽车着火时的车辆状态比例是：静置状态为 35.35%，充电状态为 25.77%，行驶状态为 37.88%。各组织与单位统计的热失控失火事故中，车辆处于行驶状态的情况最多。行驶中的车辆发生电池热失控，很可能是由于车辆“带病”行驶，在行驶过程中行车工况变化触发放电，进而引发热失控。

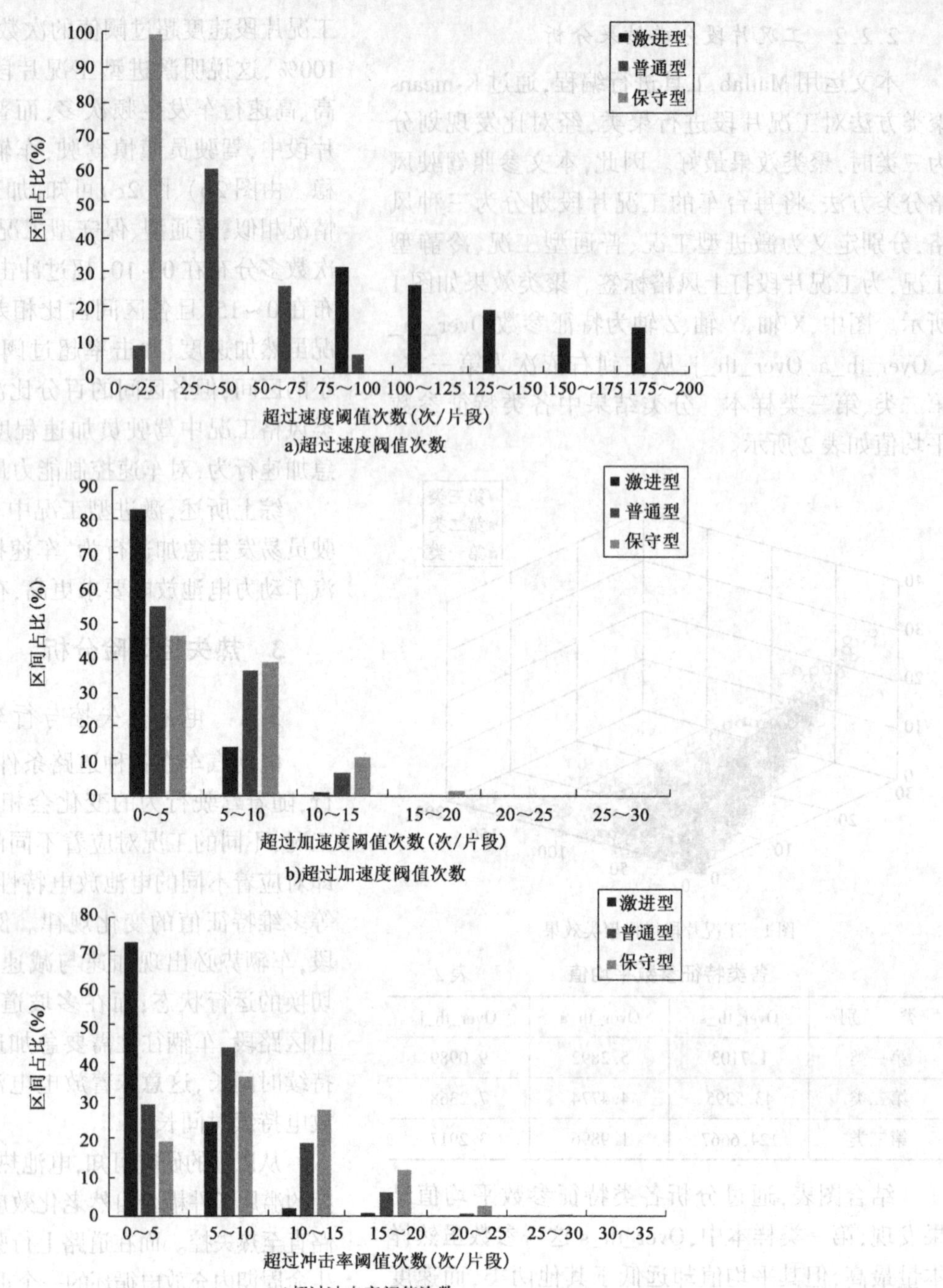

图2 各类特征参数分布情况

行车工况与电池滥用的主要联系在于:由急加速、加速行为持续时间长等行车工况引起的大功率或大电流的放电,易造成部分电池单体过放电和过热。当电池组一致性较差时,会有部分单体处于过放电的状态,而在大功率输出工况下,大电流的过放电会带来更严重的后果。

3.2 电池热失控风险分析

电动汽车锂离子电池在正常循环使用中会出现一定的性能衰退,这是锂离子电池的固有性质,属于正常现象。但当电池质量不合格或工况超出正常范围时(温度过高或过低、过充或过放电、短路或虚接等),锂离子电池有发生故障的概率更大,这些故障轻则造成电池性能加速衰退,重则导致锂离子电池出现热失控,影响车内乘员生命安全。

2016年国家制定的《电动汽车远程服务与管理系统技术规范》(GB/T 32960.1—2016)中,规范了新能源汽车远程数据传输通信格式。本研究中数据源均为实车上传数据,且符合 GB/T 32960 国标要求,数据项与国标数据项保持一致。其中,针对电动汽车装置,国标拟定了 19 项通用报警标志,包括温度差异报警、电池高温报警、单体电池过压报警、单体电池欠压报警等,故障报警频次越多,发生热失控风险的概率越大。

本文对车辆 1 中的故障报警信息进行统计发现,只有在车辆发生热失控,温度骤升时,才会发生电池高温报警,但这并不代表车辆无过压、欠压等故障。查阅国标可知,各类报警阈值均为车企自拟,阈值无法统一,存在故障报警不及时和不精准的情况,这也是对车辆热失控风险不能提前准确预警的主要原因。因此,本文基于已有文献对电压不一致性的研究,选取电池单体最大电压差(VD)来表征电压的差异,选取电池单体最大电压差的方差(VDV)来表征电压不一致性,进行不同风格工况下电动车辆热失控风险分析。

3.3 不同风格工况下热失控风险分析

基于 2.2 划分的工况片段的三种风格,激进型工况片段共 96 个,普通型工况片段共 532 个,保守型工况片段共 5986 个。计算不同风格工况下每个片段的 VD 值,如图 3 所示。从图中可以看出,保守型工况下的最大电压差分布在 0.05V 的范围内,普通型和激进型工况下的最大电压差分布在 0.07V 的范围内,说明保守型工况下电压的差异相对较小。

进一步计算不同风格下每个片段的 VDV 值,如图 4 所示。从图中可以看出,保守型工况下 VDV 值分布在 $0 \sim 1.3 \times 10^{-5}$,方差最大值为 2.275×10^{-5};普通型工况下 VDV 值略大于保守型工况,多分布在 $0.3 \times 10^{-5} \sim 2 \times 10^{-5}$,方差最大值为$3.983 \times 10^{-5}$;激进型工况下 VDV 值分布区间多位于 $0.5 \times 10^{-5} \sim 5 \times 10^{-5}$,方差最大值为 4.706×10^{-5}。

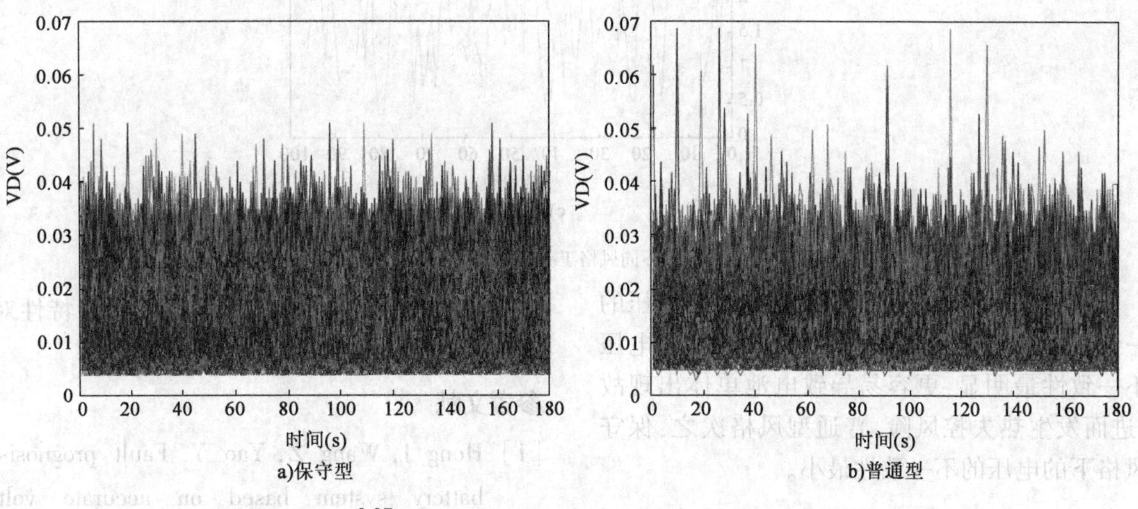

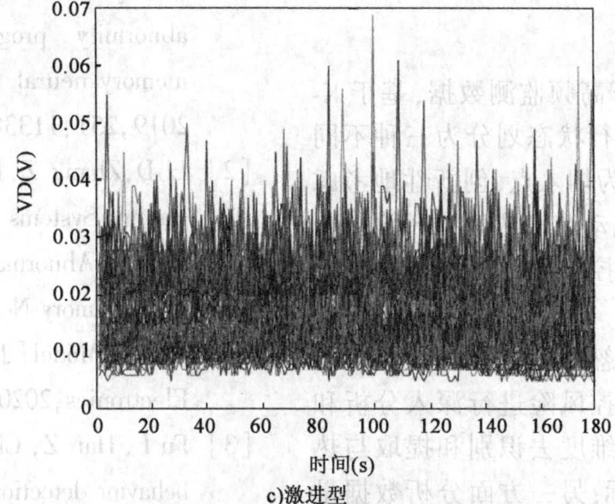

图 3 不同风格工况下的 VD 值

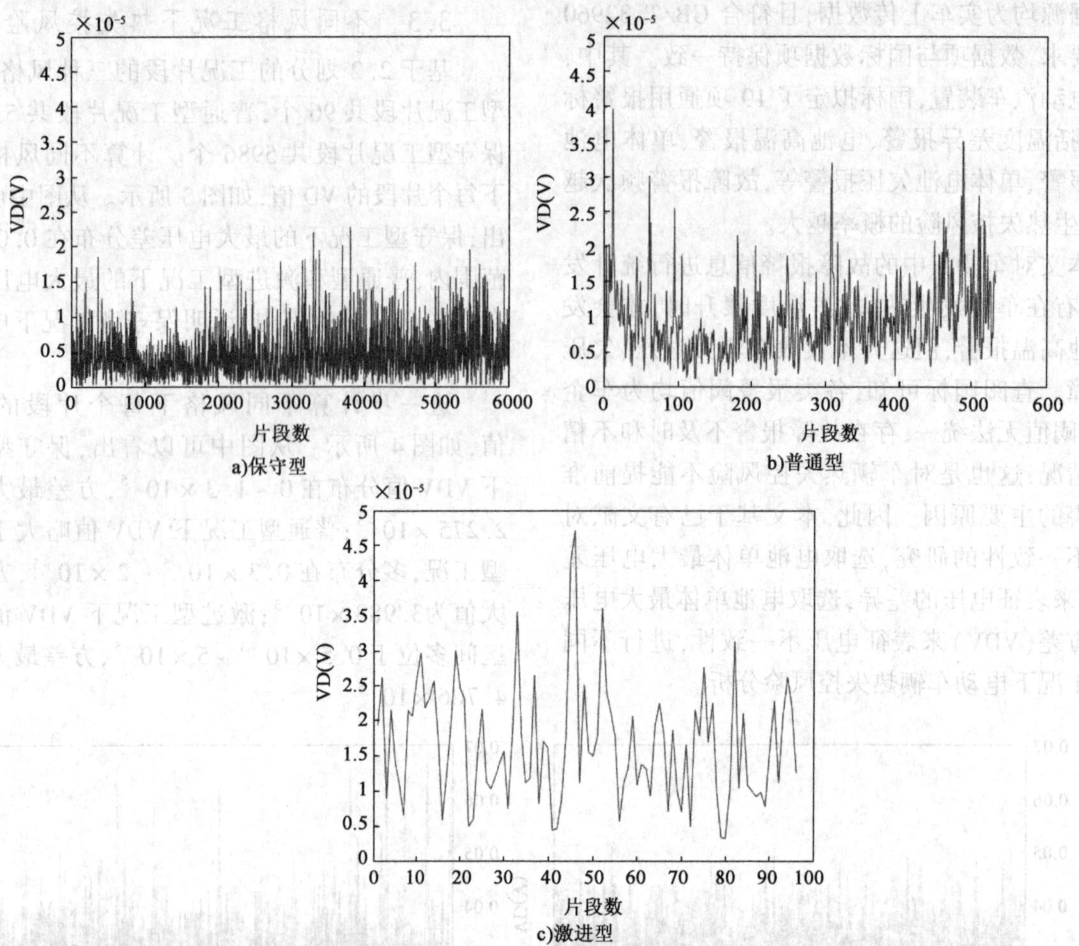

图 4　不同风格工况下的 VDV 值

方差分析反映出在不同的驾驶风格下电压的不一致性存在差异。其中,激进型风格下的电压的不一致性最明显,更容易导致电池单体出现故障,进而发生热失控风险,普通型风格次之,保守型风格下的电压的不一致性最小。

4　结语与展望

本研究通过电动汽车高频监测数据,基于 K-means 聚类算法将车辆运行状态划分为三种不同的工况,以电压不一致性为切入点,创新性地考虑了不同驾驶行为特性对电动汽车热失控风险的影响,为将来电动汽车热失控风险预测预警提供了一种可行的新思路。

但是,本研究一方面忽略了电动汽车故障报警的发生机理,来对热失控风险进行深入分析和解释,后续还需要从更多维度去识别和提取与热失控风险相关的特征指标;另一方面分析数据量较少,车辆运行状态工况风格划分未考虑转向控制等参数,根据所提取的有效数据划分的工况风格有待精进,以更精准地评估驾驶行为特性对电动汽车热失控风险的影响。

参考文献

[1] Hong J, Wang Z, Yao Y. Fault prognosis of battery system based on accurate voltage abnormity prognosis using long short-term memory neural networks[J]. Applied Energy, 2019,251:113381.

[2] Li D,Zhang Z, Liu P, et al. Fault Diagnosis of Battery Systems for Electric Vehicles Based on Voltage Abnormality Combining the Long Short-term Memory Neural Network and the Equivalent Circuit Model[J]. IEEE Transactions on Power Electronics,2020(99):1.

[3] Fu L, Hai Z, Che H, et al. Dangerous driving behavior detection using smartphone sensors[C]. 2016 IEEE 19th International Conference on Intelligent Transportation Systems (ITSC),2016.

[4] 李伦.基于纯电动汽车高频运行数据的驾驶行为研究[D].济南:山东大学,2021.

[5] 冯旭宁.车用锂离子动力电池热失控诱发与扩展机理、建模与防控[D].北京:清华大学,2016.

[6] Satyam P, Scott M, Roydon F, et al. Thermal Management of Lithium-Ion Pouch Cell with Indirect Liquid Cooling using Dual Cold Plates Approach[J]. S AE International Journal of Alternative Powertrains,2015,4(2):2011-2015.

隧道群设置遮阳棚对驾驶人视觉负荷影响研究

尚 婷[1] 黄 安*[1] 夏 瑜[2] 连 冠[3] 唐郃安[1]

(1.重庆交通大学交通运输学院;2.中国路桥工程有限责任公司;3.重庆交通大学土木工程学院)

摘 要 为研究在隧道群间距路段,遮阳棚长度对驾驶人视觉负荷的影响,本文首先以不设置遮阳棚为对照组,50m、100m和150m的遮阳棚为实验组,分别建立缩尺模型;其次,采集10名驾驶人在仿真隧道进出口的眼动数据,对不同长度隧道群连接段有无遮阳棚的驾驶人瞳孔面积变化规律进行对比分析;最后,采用瞳孔面积最大瞬态速度值和换算视觉震荡持续时间两项评价指标,并结合隧道出入口驾驶人视觉舒适度评价体系对隧道群遮阳棚路段驾驶人视觉负荷强度进行评价。结果表明:隧道入口产生的"黑洞效应"较隧道出口的"白洞效应"对驾驶人的视觉负荷产生的影响更大;在隧道群连接路段设置遮阳棚能有效缓解驾驶人的视觉负荷,50m、100m、150m遮阳棚路段驾驶人瞳孔面积最大瞬态速度值与未设置遮阳棚分别下降了28.75%、14.99%、39.84%。隧道群连接段越短,遮阳棚对于缓解驾驶人的视觉负荷效果越明显。此研究结果可为类似隧道群连接路段遮阳棚的设计方案研究提出理论依据。

关键词 隧道群连接路段 遮阳棚 缩尺模型 眼动分析 视觉负荷

0 引言

我国西部山区由于地形限制,公路隧道日益增多,隧道群作为隧道建设的衍生物,其运营安全问题一直困扰着道路管理者、执法者与研究者,其原因主要是隧道群连接路段前后光照变化剧烈,造成驾驶人员的明暗适应困难,严重影响行车安全。因此,在隧道洞口合理设置减光措施,能够有效缓解驾驶人在隧道群路段行驶时,由隧道洞口产生的频繁"黑白洞效应"带来的视觉负荷从而改善行车安全。目前,国内外主要通过设置遮阳棚、遮光棚、通透式棚洞等减光结构进行减光,除此还有利用植被、改变隧道洞口外部景观明亮程度等举措进行减光。有学者发现在隧道洞口设有减光结构是最有效可控的主动式减光保护措施,可有效缓解驾驶人视觉负荷[1]。因此,研究隧道洞口遮阳棚对于驾驶人视觉负荷影响机理,探究其改善效果,具有重要意义。

近年来,国内外学者在隧道洞口光环境及驾驶人视觉特性、隧道洞口减光设施方面开展了大量研究。在隧道洞口光环境和驾驶人视觉特性方面,大量文献集中于隧道出入口处驾驶人视觉负荷的研究,如Eran Aronson MSc[2]通过室内模拟实验研究了隧道入口段光环境过渡安全可见阈值,结果显示比CIE推荐的暗适应时间短;He S Y[3]运用实验光平台对隧道光环境进行模拟,得到被试驾驶人在不同光照强度下的反应时间和探测率,最后得出结论:在隧道过渡段设置白色目标比绿色更好,在隧道内部设置蓝色目标的敏感性高于红色目标;崔洪军等[4]采用瞳孔面积变化率和反应时间表征高速公路隧道入口段驾驶人行车舒适性及安全性,建立行车安全与亮度折减系数及车速的回归模型,确定了照明动态阈值区间;潘晓东、杜志刚等[5-6]均引用车辆桥头瞬时跳车对人员

1.基金项目:重庆市教育委员会青年科技项目(KJQN201900722);重庆市科技局基础与前沿面上项目(cstc2019jcyj－msxmX0695);国家自然科学基金项目(52172341)。

产生的振动原理,对隧道出入口段驾驶人的视觉负荷进行了研究,定量评价了驾驶人在隧道出入口的视觉负荷及行车安全;段萌萌等[7]利用“负荷重复累积效应”的概念来表达驾驶人在隧道群路段的视觉变化现象,并选取瞳孔面积最大瞬态速度值(MTPA)及换算视觉震荡持续时间(t_c)为评判指标,并根据建立的隧道出入口驾驶人视觉舒适度评价体系来对隧道进出口驾驶人视觉负荷进行评价。在隧道洞口减光设施的研究方面,国内外学者大多从安全性、经济性的角度出发进行研究,如 Dionysia Drakou[8-10]等针对隧道洞口设置减光设施的安全性和经济性进行研究,研究结果表明遮阳棚等遮光设施对于隧道安全和节约能源具有积极意义。L. M. Gil-Martina 等[11]验证了在隧道洞口设置遮阳棚,其光照环境相当于隧道的延展组成部分,并经过实验证明,该构造物还可有效减少光照线路的电灯数量,节省电力。任龙军[12]选用注视比例,注视时间占比,眨眼次数以及视觉广度收缩速率作为表征驾驶人视觉特性的指标,对比分析了在公路隧道出入口设置遮阳棚对驾驶人视觉特性的影响,结果发现,注视时间变长,眨眼次数减少,搜索广度增加;包逸帆等[13]以隧道连接段的间距长度为研究对象,提出连接式和非连接式两种形式的遮阳棚设计,运用视觉适应曲线原理对隧道群连接段的遮阳棚的透光率和长度进行了研究设计;韩凯旋[14]对封闭型、半封闭型及开放型三种毗邻隧道间遮阳(光)棚设计方案进行了定性比较,结果表明:开放型隧道群遮阳棚从遮阳效果、排烟换气及防灾救援等方面都优于其他两种类型的遮阳棚。

纵观国内外对隧道洞口段光环境、驾驶人视觉特性以及减光设施的研究可以发现,现有研究无论从研究方法还是研究内容上都为隧道洞口的交通安全改善措施提供了参考价值。然而鲜有研究从驾驶人的角度对隧道群连接路段如遮阳棚一类的减光设施设置进行量化的评价,同时缺少针对隧道群不同长度连接段设置遮阳棚对驾驶人视觉特性影响的研究。鉴于此,本文通过建立缩尺模型进行室内仿真实验,将不设置遮阳棚为作对照组,50m、100m、150m 作为试验组,分别测得隧道群连接段不同长度遮阳棚的驾驶人眼动参数,以驾驶人瞳孔面积变化为分析指标,对不同遮阳棚长度路段驾驶人视觉特性变化进行分析,以瞳孔面积最大瞬态速度值为评价指标,评价遮阳棚对于驾驶人视觉负荷的作用效果,以期为高速公路管理部门在隧道群连接路段合理设置遮阳棚一类的减光设施提供理论参考依据,提升高速公路隧道群路段的行车安全。

1　试验

1.1　试验方法

由于山区高速公路车流量大,隧道群路段危险系数高,采用实车试验的方法对不同长度的隧道群遮阳棚进行对比研究,其实验数据不易采集且受外部因素影响较大。由此本文拟建立缩尺模型进行仿真试验,缩尺模型指将物体尺寸等比例缩小后,以相似原则为理论指导研究物体的尺寸大小进行等比例缩小后,使工程中产生的现象能够在试验室中重复显示出来,同时还能够在试验中对各主要因素加以独立控制便于分析[10]。

1.2　模型搭建

由于实际搭建遮阳棚试验的特殊性以及费用等因素的限制,为此本文搭建缩尺模型(比例1:50),同时利用微型无线小型摄像头、Tobii 眼动仪(60Hz)、迷你智能感应遥控车、可调 LED 灯、不透光幕布、遮光膜等作为本次试验的试验材料。

本文以 G65 渝湘高速公路白马至黔江段作为仿真试验路段,全线 172km,该路段桥隧比高达到90%,其中隧道群小间距路段众多,据调查,该路段隧道群间距多集中在 50m、100m、150m 左右。此外,《公路隧道设计细则》(JTG/T D70—2010)中规定,高速公路隧道建筑限界横断面中车道宽度不小于 3.75m×2、检修道宽度不小于 0.75m、建筑界限高度不小于 5m。基于以上规定和试验路段设计资料,本文设计并搭建比例尺为 1:50 的缩尺模型,灯光排布基于渝湘高速照明设施设计图设计,利用遮光膜来做遮阳棚的仿真材料,课题组通过对公路上已有遮阳棚进行大量调研,选用工程中常用的蓝色,透光系数为 0.15 的遮光膜作为遮阳棚的外贴材料,根据上述试验路段 3 类具有代表性的隧道间距,分别设置 50m、100m、150m 遮阳棚长度进行隧道群遮阳棚缩尺模型的搭建,并以三种隧道群间距路段不设置遮阳棚作为对照组进行分析比较。由于隧道外部光环境的变化对驾驶人影响较大,因此本试验选择天气晴朗,上午

10:00—16:00 的某天开展试验，根据试验路段限速 80km/h 的规定，控制仿真试验遥控车速度为 5.75m/s。本次试验的基本试验布置如图 1 所示。

图 1 缩尺模型展示图

1.3 试验设计

本次试验选取持有 C1 驾驶证的被试 10 名，

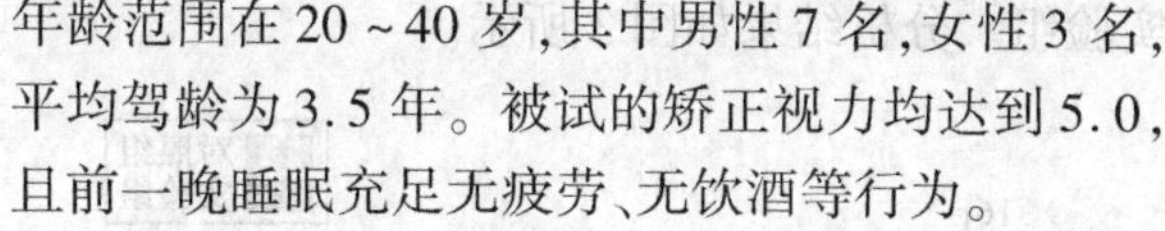

年龄范围在 20～40 岁，其中男性 7 名，女性 3 名，平均驾龄为 3.5 年。被试的矫正视力均达到 5.0，且前一晚睡眠充足无疲劳、无饮酒等行为。

为研究在隧道群路段设置遮阳棚与遮阳棚长度对驾驶人视觉特性产生的各类影响，本文在缩尺模型中间路段设置透光系数为 0.15 的蓝色遮阳棚，通过模型车以及摄像机获得行车视频（图 2）。10 名被试分别佩戴眼动仪，模拟手握转向盘，在无照明的室内环境中观看试验视频，模拟隧道环境中的“明暗效应”，为了实验数据的准确性，每位被试驾驶人进行 3 次模拟驾驶试验。再利用眼动仪获取驾驶人的相关眼动信息，根据眼动信息计算试验人员各类眼动指标，最后将仿真实验眼动指标进行对比分析，得到有无遮阳棚以及不同长度的隧道群遮阳棚对驾驶人视觉负荷的影响程度。

图 2 缩尺模型实验流程

1.4 数据收集及处理

本文利用 BeGaze3.5 数据分析软件对试验人员的眼动信息数据进行提取，驾驶人眼动的基本形式包括注视、眨眼和扫视。通过对驾驶人在仿真驾驶中注视持续时间的分析，发现约 99% 的单次注视行为持续时间在 1000ms 以下，因此仅保留小于 1000ms 的注视行为样本，扫视持续时间从 30～120ms 不等，因此剔除 100ms 以内的数据。经过验证，数据符合正态分布，因此本文选取拉依达准则法（3σ 准则）和标准化数值来进行样本数据中异常数据剔除，利用剔除后的有效数据进行后续研究。

2 不同长度遮阳棚路段驾驶人瞳孔面积变化分析

驾驶人白天进出隧道洞口会产生明显的“黑白洞”现象。现有研究表明，驾驶人在明暗适应过程中最为显著的变化为瞳孔大小的变化[6,15-16]，瞳孔大小变化剧烈，会引起驾驶人出现短暂“失明”现象，从而影响行车安全。基于此，本文选定连续位置序列下驾驶人瞳孔面积的变化为指标，以不设置遮阳棚为对照组，设置 50m、100m 及 150m 遮阳棚为实验组，分别对其驾驶人的瞳孔面积变化规律进行对比分析，研究有无遮阳棚及不同遮阳棚长度下各驾驶人瞳孔面积变化情况。瞳孔面积 S 表达式为

$$S = \frac{1}{4}\pi d^2 \tag{1}$$

2.1 遮阳棚设置对隧道群连接段驾驶人瞳孔面积的影响研究

针对隧道群连接路段的行驶过程中，分别对 3 种隧道群间距长度设置遮阳棚和不设置遮阳棚两种情况驾驶人瞳孔面积变化进行对比分析，其中未设置遮阳棚为对照组，设置不同长度遮阳棚为

实验组。分析结果如图 3 所示。

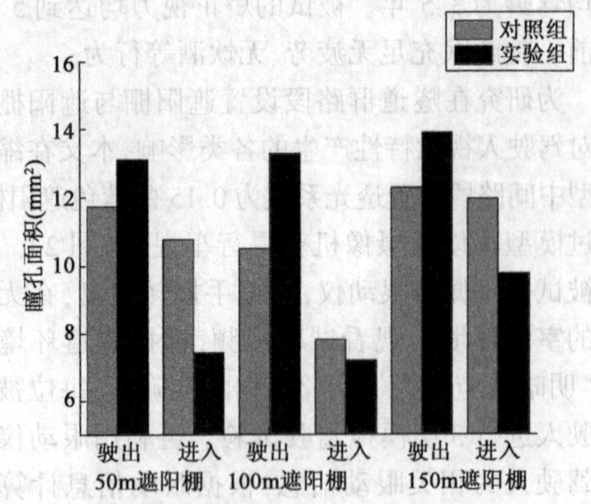

图 3　有无遮阳棚瞳孔面积变化对比分析

从图 3 可以看出,驾驶人驾驶车辆通过隧道群路段,在驶出隧道时,有遮阳棚较无遮阳棚的驾驶人瞳孔面积较大,说明设置遮阳棚后,瞳孔变化和缓,有利于驾驶人适应"白洞效应";驾驶人在进入下游隧道时,设置遮阳棚后驾驶人的瞳孔面积明显小于无遮阳棚进入隧道洞口时,说明遮阳棚可以在一定程度上缓解驾驶人暗适应过程。其次,可以看出,驾驶人驶出上游隧道时瞳孔面积均小于进入下游隧道,这是由于隧道入口产生的"黑洞效应"与隧道出口的"白洞效应"相比,给驾驶人视觉负荷造成的影响更大[5]。

2.2　不同长度遮阳棚驾驶人瞳孔面积变化规律

上述结果证明了在隧道群连接段设置遮阳棚能有效缓解驾驶人"明暗适应"的过程,为进一步研究不同长度遮阳棚对驾驶人瞳孔面积的影响,本文采集对 10 名驾驶人分别通过 50m、100m、150m 遮阳棚路段瞳孔面积 S 变化规律进行了分析,结果如图 4 ~ 图 6 所示。

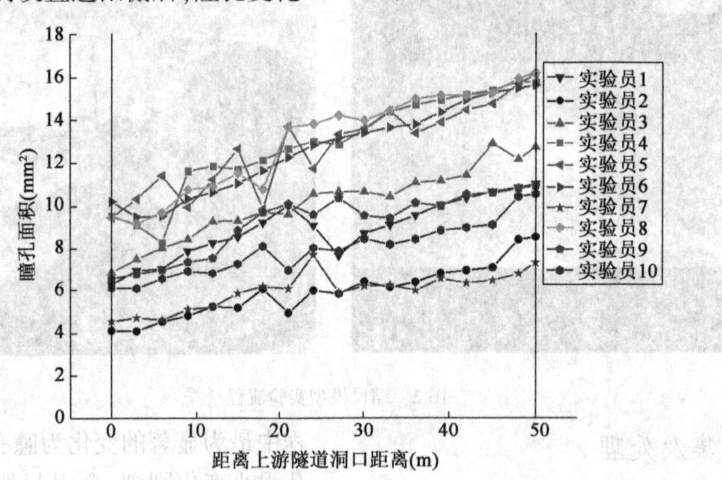

图 4　50m 遮阳棚驾驶人瞳孔面积变化规律

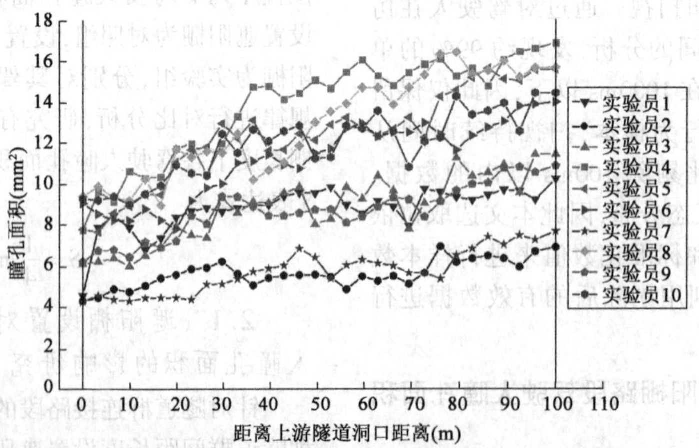

图 5　100m 遮阳棚驾驶人瞳孔面积变化规律

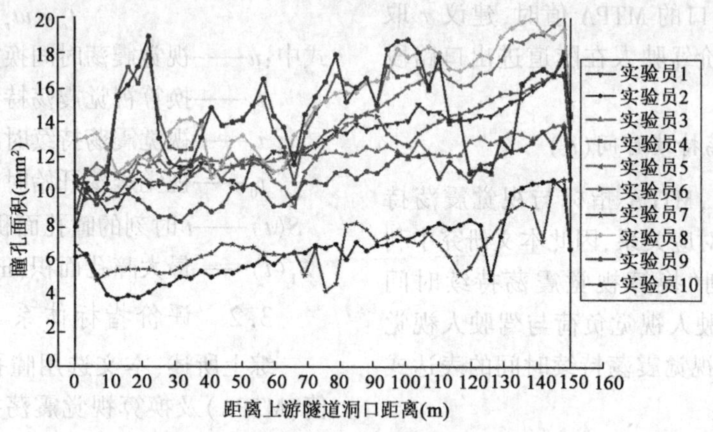

图6 150m 遮阳棚驾驶人瞳孔面积变化规律

从图4～图6可以看出，在三种长度的遮阳棚路段，驾驶人瞳孔面积变化规律具有一致性，总体上呈现缓慢上升趋势，且在接近下游隧道入口处，瞳孔面积达到最大。以50m遮阳棚为例，对三种路段驾驶人瞳孔面积变化规律进行描述，当驾驶人驶出上游隧道洞口进入遮阳棚路段时，瞳孔面积主要分布在4.13～9.51mm^2之间；随后，大部分驾驶人瞳孔面积开始减小，这是由于上游隧道内光环境照度相较于遮阳棚路段较暗，驾驶人需要将瞳孔缩小以适应这种光环境的变化，这就是明适应的过程；之后，驾驶人逐渐适应了遮阳棚路段的光照环境，瞳孔面积开始缓慢上升，行驶到遮阳棚路段15～30m时，驾驶人瞳孔面积出现下降趋势，可能是受遮阳棚透光率或光照强度的影响；最后驾驶人瞳孔面积继续增大，当驶出遮阳棚路段进入下游隧道洞口时，驾驶人瞳孔面积达到最大值，主要分布在7.28～16.14mm^2之间，这是由于隧道内光照环境相较于遮阳棚路段较低，驾驶人进入下游隧道时需要将瞳孔放大来完成暗适应的过程。

将驾驶人通过三种长度的遮阳棚路段时瞳孔面积变化规律进行对比分析发现，驾驶人通过50m、100m、150m遮阳棚路段时，其平均瞳孔面积分别为10.23mm^2、9.87mm^2、11.17mm^2，且3种长度遮阳棚路段的驾驶人瞳孔面积均呈现逐渐增加的趋势，在接近下游隧道入口即遮阳棚路段末端时，瞳孔面积达到最大，这是由于驾驶人即将进入下游隧道洞口产生的“暗适应”现象导致的，且驾驶人瞳孔面积均是逐渐增加到最大值，3种长度遮阳棚进出口处驾驶人瞳孔面积变化差值分别在3.15～6.63mm^2、2.64～7.46mm^2、0.5～1.82mm^2之间，均没有出现隧道洞口瞳孔面积剧增的现象，说明遮阳棚对驾驶人通过三种长度的隧道间距路段并进入下游隧道所产生的“黑洞效应”均有所改善，能够有效缓解由“黑洞效应”给驾驶人视觉造成的不利影响。

3 隧道群遮阳棚路段驾驶人视觉负荷评价

3.1 评价方法

相关研究表明[7]，以瞳孔面积最大瞬态速度值（MTPA）和换算视觉震荡持续时间（t_c）作为评价高隧道比路段驾驶人视觉负荷的依据是可行的。因此本文选用MTPA与t_c值来评价隧道群间距路段，不同长度遮阳棚下驾驶人的视觉负荷。

3.1.1 瞳孔面积最大瞬态速度值(MTPA)

驾驶人瞳孔面积的剧烈变化可能会使驾驶人出现瞬时的“失明”现象，对驾驶人视觉负荷产生巨大影响，从而引发交通事故。本文采用驾驶人瞳孔面积最大瞬态速度来描述驾驶人瞳孔面积变化剧烈程度的规律。

瞳孔面积瞬时速度加权值的计算公式见式(2)：

$$V_\omega(t_0)=\left[\frac{1}{\tau}\int_{t_0-\tau}^{t_0}V_\omega^2(t)\,dt\right]\frac{1}{2} \qquad (2)$$

式中：$V_\omega(t_0)$——瞬时瞳孔面积频率加权速度幅值（mm^2/s）；

τ——持续积分时间（s），一般情况下建议值取1s；

t——时间（s），积分变量；

t_0——瞬时考察时间（s）。

瞳孔面积最大瞬态速度值简称MTPA，单位是（mm^2/s），其表达式如式(3)所示：

$$MTPA=\max\{V_\omega(t_0)\} \qquad (3)$$

当测定隧道进出口的 MTPA 值时，建议 τ 取值 1s，结果可用于评价驾驶人在隧道进出口路段的视觉负荷。

3.1.2　视觉震荡持续时间(t_c)

相关研究表明[6]，MTPA 指标与视觉震荡持续时间 t_c 具有一定的对应关系，因此本文研究中利用 MTPA 值换算得到"换算视觉震荡持续时间 t_c"，将其作为评价驾驶人视觉负荷与驾驶人视觉舒适性的指标。换算视觉震荡持续时间的表达式如式(4)、式(5)所示：

$$u = \int_{t_0}^{t_0+t_v} \frac{S(t)\,\mathrm{d}t}{S_1(t)\,t_v} t_c S_1 \tag{4}$$

$$t_c = ut_v \tag{5}$$

式中：u——视觉震荡时间换算系数；

t_c——换算视觉震荡持续时间(s)；

t_v——视觉震荡持续时间(s)；

t_0——视觉震荡开始时间(s)；

$S(t)$——t 时刻的瞳孔面积(mm^2)；

$S_1(t)$——最大瞳孔面积(mm^2)。

3.2　评价指标体系

综上所述，本文选用瞳孔面积最大瞬态速度值(MTPA)及换算视觉震荡持续时间 t_c 两个指标对隧道群遮阳棚路段视觉舒适度评价指标体系进行建立，如表 1 所示[6]。

视觉舒适度评价指标体系　　表 1

MTPA(mm^2/s)		换算视觉震荡持续时间 t_c(s)	视觉负荷评价结果
隧道进口	隧道出口		
<20	<30	≤0.1	没有不舒适
[20,30)	[30,40)	(0.1,0.2]	稍不舒适
[30,70)	[40,85)	(0.2,1.0]	不舒适
[70,105)	[85,105)	(1.0,1.5]	很不舒适
≥105	≥105	≥1.5	极不舒适

3.3　试验分析

对本文试验中建立的三种不同长度的遮阳棚分别求取驾驶人通过未设遮阳棚和通过各长度遮阳棚过程中瞬时瞳孔面积加权速度 $V_\omega(t)$ 值，并对 10 名驾驶人 $V_\omega(t)$ 值取平均值进行对比分析，结果如下所示。

3.3.1　不同长度遮阳棚驾驶人 $V_\omega(t)$ 变化规律分析

从图 7 ~ 图 9 可以看出，在 3 种隧道群间距的路段，设置遮阳棚与不设遮阳棚相比，驾驶人的 $V_\omega(t)$ 值均有所下降，证明了遮阳棚对隧道群连接路段驾驶人视觉负荷有改善作用。其中驾驶人通过 50m 和 100m 的遮阳棚路段时，其瞬时瞳孔面积加权速度 $V_\omega(t)$ 值波动幅与 150m 遮阳棚相比较大，由此说明，隧道群间距越短，驾驶人所受影响越大，其视觉负荷越不稳定。3 种遮阳棚路段驾驶人的 $V_\omega(t)$ 值变化趋势大致相似，在刚出上游隧道进入遮阳棚路段时，驾驶人平均 $V_\omega(t)$ 值均较大，分别达到 21.12mm^2、25.17mm^2、9.82mm^2，这是由于隧道内与遮阳棚路段的光照强具有一定差异，导致出隧道洞口的"白洞效应"对驾驶人视觉产生影响，但与未设置遮阳棚均有所减少，其中 50m 遮阳棚驾驶人的 $V_\omega(t)$ 值减少了 6.54mm^2、100m 遮阳棚驾驶人的 $V_\omega(t)$ 值减少了 2.35mm^2、150m 遮阳棚驾驶人的 $V_\omega(t)$ 值下降了 2.47mm^2，说明遮阳棚的设置一定程度上缓解了驶入隧道洞口的"白洞效应"。随之驾驶人开始适应遮阳棚路段的光照强度，在靠近下游隧道入口即遮阳棚路段末端时，驾驶人 $V_\omega(t)$ 值迅速上升，这是由于驾驶人进入下游隧道洞口产生的"黑洞效应"，使驾驶人需要经历暗适应的过程，此时 3 种遮阳棚路段驾驶人平均 $V_\omega(t)$ 值分别达到42.50mm^2、27.78mm^2、9.82mm^2，与未设置遮阳棚相比分别下降了 12.22mm^2、4.91mm^2、9.80mm^2，说明遮阳棚对缓解驾驶人进入隧道时的"黑洞效应"也有显著效果。除此，由图 7 ~ 图 9 可知，驾驶人进入隧道洞口时的 $V_\omega(t)$ 值明显高于出隧道洞口，由此判断"黑洞效应"比"白洞效应"对驾驶人视觉负荷的影响更大。

3.3.2　结果分析

综上所述，将驾驶人通过三种长度的隧道间距路段设置遮阳棚和未设遮阳棚时的瞬时瞳孔面积加权速度 $V_\omega(t)$ 值变化规律进行对比分析发现，遮阳棚的设置均能够有效缓解驾驶人进出洞口时所产生的"黑白洞效应"。其次驾驶人刚进入遮阳

棚路段时的 $V_\omega(t)$ 值均小于驶出遮阳棚时，这是由于“黑洞效应”较“白洞效应”对驾驶人视觉舒适性的影响更大。除此，对比图7～图9可以发现，无论是否设置遮阳棚，驾驶人通过50m隧道间距段时的平均 $V_\omega(t)$ 值最大，150m时的平均 $V_\omega(t)$ 值最小，且驾驶人通过150m遮阳棚的瞬时瞳孔面积加权速度值 $V_\omega(t)$ 值波动范围最小即最为稳定，驾驶人在刚进入和驶出150m遮阳棚路段时的 $V_\omega(t)$ 值较50m和100m遮阳棚的均较小，这是由于隧道群间距越小，驾驶人会越容易经历频繁的“明暗适应”过程，从而形成视觉负荷重复累积效应，严重影响行车安全。

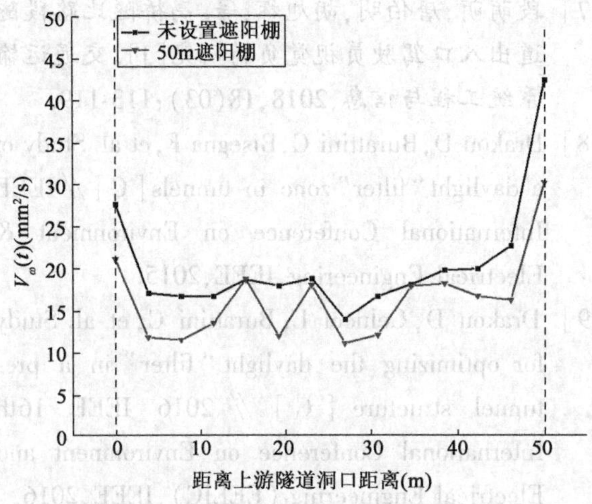

图7　50m遮阳棚驾驶人 $V_\omega(t)$ 值变化规律

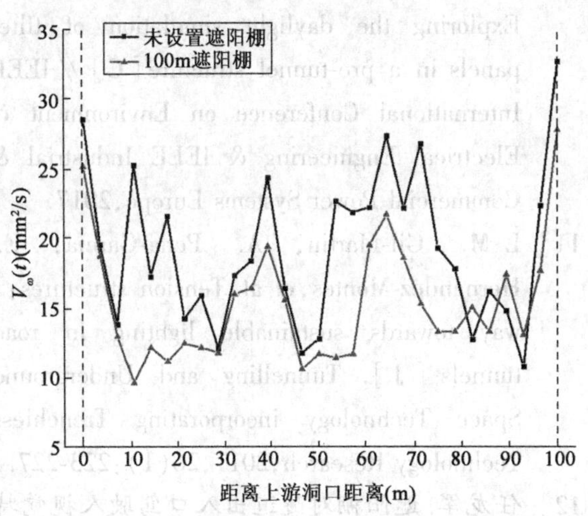

图8　100m遮阳棚驾驶人 $V_\omega(t)$ 变化规律

本文通过导出的驾驶人瞳孔数据，根据式(3)～式(5)计算得到瞬时瞳孔面积加权速度值 $V_\omega(t)$、瞳孔面积最大瞬时速度值(MTPA)、换算视觉震荡持续时间 t_c 值，并对照表3，结合上述两项指标，对不同长度隧道群连接段未设和设置遮阳棚的驾驶人视觉舒适度进行评价并对比分析，考虑到真实路段并不是单一的隧道入口段和隧道出口段，为保障驾驶人行车安全，在评价过程中选择结果最不利于行车安全的结果进行换算与分析。计算结果见表2、表3。

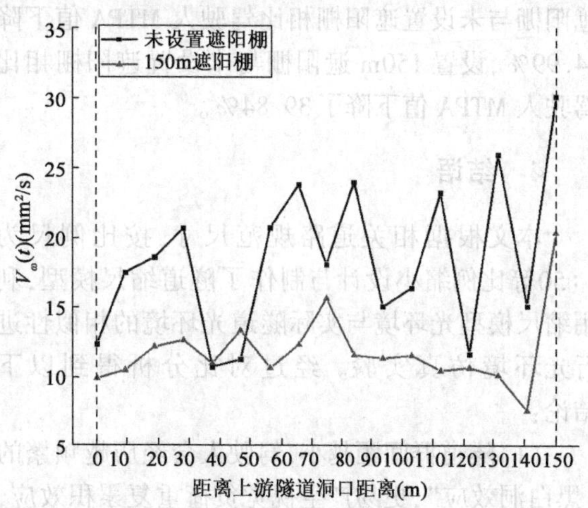

图9　150m遮阳棚驾驶人 $V_\omega(t)$ 变化规律

未设遮阳棚视觉震荡评价结果　表2

隧道群间距段长度(m)	平均 $V_\omega(t)$ (mm²/s)	MTPA (mm²/s)	t_c (s)	评价结果
50	20.56	42.51	0.26	不舒适
100	19.27	32.68	0.21	不舒适
150	17.77	25.95	0.17	稍不舒适

设置不同长度遮阳棚视觉震荡评价结果　表3

遮阳棚长度(m)	平均 $V_\omega(t)$ (mm²/s)	MTPA (mm²/s)	t_c (s)	评价结果
50	16.38	30.29	0.18	稍不舒适
100	15.34	27.78	0.15	稍不舒适
150	11.64	15.61	0.08	没有不舒适

由表2、表3可以看出，驾驶人通过3种长度的隧道群间距路段，MTPA值与换算视觉震荡持续时间 t_c 结果一致，且设置遮阳棚的MTPA值均小于未设遮阳棚时。当隧道群间距为50m和100m时，未设置遮阳棚时驾驶人视觉震荡评价结果为不舒适，设置遮阳棚后，驾驶人视觉舒适度评价结果为稍不舒适，视觉负荷有所改善，当隧道群间距为150m时，未设置遮阳棚时驾驶人视觉震荡评价结果为稍不舒适，设置遮阳棚后驾驶人视觉舒适度变为没有不舒适。上述结果均表明在隧道群间距路段设置遮阳棚能有效改善驾驶人的视觉负荷，从而保证行车安全。其次当隧道群间距为

50m时,其驾驶人MTPA值最大,表明驾驶人在该路段行驶时,视觉负荷最大,进一步证明隧道群间距越小,驾驶人视觉负荷越大的结论。从遮阳棚的改善效果来看,设置50m遮阳棚与未设置遮阳棚相比驾驶人MTPA值下降28.75%,设置100m遮阳棚与未设置遮阳棚相比驾驶人MTPA值下降14.99%,设置150m遮阳棚与未设置遮阳棚相比驾驶人MTPA值下降了39.84%。

4　结语

本文根据相关道路规范尺寸,按比例尺为1:50等比例缩小设计与制作了隧道缩尺模型,利用缩尺模型光环境与实际隧道光环境的相似性进行光环境仿真实验。经过对比分析得到以下结论:

(1)隧道群间距越小,驾驶人会经历越频繁的"黑白洞效应",更易产生视觉负荷重复累积效应,从而影响行车安全。除此隧道入口的"黑洞效应"对驾驶人视觉造成的影响较隧道出口的"白洞效应"更大,即驾驶人的"暗适应"过程较"明适应"更加困难,且在隧道入口的视觉负荷较隧道出口的更大。

(2)本文以MTPA和t_c作为遮阳棚对驾驶人视觉负荷改善效果的评价指标,研究结果表明在隧道群连接段合理设置遮阳棚能有效缓解驾驶人通过隧道群所产生的频繁"黑白洞效应",减小驾驶人视觉负荷,具有一定的理论参考价值。

(3)研究成果可以为隧道群不同间距路段减光设施、交通安全设施、交通引导设施的合理布设提供理论依据。由于试验场地和设备有限,本文仅搭建了50m、100m、150m三种长度的遮阳棚进行对比分析,结合当地隧道光环境搭建更多长度和类型的遮阳棚,探究在遮阳棚路段,照明环境变化以及道路线形特色等因素对驾驶人视觉负荷的影响将会是课题组下一步研究工作的重点。

参考文献

[1] 翁季,潘贝贝.公路隧道入口减光措施研究[J].西部人居环境学刊,2013(06):10-14.

[2] Eran Aronson MSc. Research Project: Visual adaptation for tunnel entrance[R]. TRAFIKVERKET,2013.

[3] He S Y, Tähkämö L, Maksimainen M, et al. Effects of transient adaptation on drivers' visual performance in road tunnel lighting [J]. Tunnelling & Underground Space Technology, 2017,70:42-54.

[4] 崔洪军,由婷婷,李霞.高速公路隧道入口段照明动态阈值区间研究[J].交通信息与安全,2018,36(03):48-55,78.

[5] 潘晓东,宋永朝,杨轸,等.基于视觉负荷的公路隧道进出口环境改善范围[J].同济大学学报(自然科学版),2009,37(6):777-780.

[6] 杜志刚,潘晓东,杨轸,等.高速公路隧道进出口视觉震荡与行车安全研究[J].中国公路学报,2007,20(5):101-105.

[7] 段萌萌,唐伯明,胡旭辉,等.高桥隧比路段隧道出入口驾驶员视觉负荷研究[J].交通运输系统工程与信息,2018,18(03):113-119.

[8] Drakou D, Burattini C, Bisegna F, et al. Study of a daylight "filter" zone in tunnels [C] // IEEE International Conference on Environment & Electrical Engineering, IEEE, 2015.

[9] Drakou D, Celucci L, Burattini C, et al. Study for optimizing the daylight "filter" in a pre-tunnel structure [C] // 2016 IEEE 16th International Conference on Environment and Electrical Engineering (EEEIC), IEEE, 2016.

[10] Drakou D, Burattini C, Mangione A, et al. Exploring the daylight simulation of filter panels in a pre-tunnel structure [C] // IEEE International Conference on Environment & Electrical Engineering & IEEE Industrial & Commercial Power Systems Europe, 2017.

[11] L. M. Gil-Martin, A. Pena-Garcia, E. Hernandez-Montes, et al. Tension structures: a way towards sustainable lighting in road tunnels [J]. Tunnelling and Underground Space Technology incorporating Trenchless Technology Research, 2011, 26(1):223-227.

[12] 任龙军.遮阳棚对隧道出入口驾驶人视觉特性影响研究[D].长春:吉林大学,2019.

[13] 包逸帆,王明年,秦鹏程,等.遮阳棚对隧道进出口明暗适应的影响规律研究[J].现代隧道技术,2021,10(21):1-9.

[14] 韩凯旋.基于运营安全与节能的公路隧道群遮光棚设计方案[C]//中国土木工程学会

隧道及地下工程分会.第八届全国运营安全与节能环保的隧道及地下空间学术研讨会论文集[C]//中国土木工程学会隧道及地下工程分会,2017:2.
[15] 胡江碧,李然,马勇.高速公路隧道入口段照明安全阈值评价方法[J].中国公路学报,2014,27(03):92-99.
[16] 杜志刚,潘晓东,郭雪斌.高速公路隧道进出口视觉适应实验[J].哈尔滨工业大学学报,2007(12):1998-2001.

非机动车侵入对无物理隔离路段运行安全的影响研究

杨　威[*1]　梁国华[1]　董辰昊[2]
(1.长安大学运输工程学院;2.西安市城市规划设计研究院)

摘　要　非机动车侵入无物理隔离路段行驶会严重干扰机动车通行,造成交通拥堵加剧、交通事故增加等一系列问题,影响道路交通安全。研究基于无物理隔离路段中非机动车侵入行为对机动车正常通行造成的干扰现象进行分类,针对摩擦干扰和阻滞干扰现象,制定了相关运行安全评价方法。将非机动车对机动车的侧向干扰和紧急制动次数作为安全评价指标,从横向、纵向的多维空间角度定量评价了无物理隔离路段非机动车比例及道路服务水平对道路交通通行安全的影响。研究结果表明:在摩擦干扰路段,随道路服务水平降低,干扰次数在非机动车比例为[0.5,0.6]范围内时会出现激增,机动车采取紧急制动措施次数增幅为40%~50%;在阻滞干扰路段,随道路服务水平降低,机动车受到侧向间距影响增幅为60%~125%,制动次数增幅为20%~50%,且道路服务水平越低,机动车紧急制动次数受自行车比例影响越大,道路通行安全风险越高。从我国目前的非机动车发展形势以及道路交通条件来看,研究对于改善无物理隔离路段道路通行秩序及安全具有良好的作用。

关键词　交通安全　干扰模型　安全评价　无物理隔离路段　非机动车侵入

0　引言

受前期规划影响,我国城市道路尤其是老城区道路普遍较窄,多为单幅路或双幅路,无物理隔离条件下非机动车混入机动车道行驶是导致许多城市交通拥堵加剧,交通事故数量不断增加的重要因素之一。在城市范围内,不同道路条件下非机动车混入机动车道行驶会对道路交通运行造成不同程度的影响。结合道路交通实际运行条件,定量评价无物理隔离路段非机动车比例及道路服务水平对道路交通安全的影响,有助于减少交通事故,为城市规划及管理提供有力的数据支持。

机非混行问题一直是国内外学者的研究热点,根据研究方法可以将其分为两类,一类是建立机非混行交通流模型探究机非混行路段交通运行状况[1-3],另一类是利用数据分析对机非混行路段安全风险进行评价分析[4-6]。

机非混行交通流模型评价方法主要包括:Timothy George Oketch 及 George Gould 等[7-8]建立微观混合交通流模型,定义并分析了非机动车横向运动的决策过程;M. J. Wierbosa 和 Parkin 等[9-10]构建了机非混行宏观模型,深入探究非机动车对机动车行驶时间的影响;关宏志[11]等利用交通流原理构建了基本路段机非混合交通流模型;杨佩昆[12]基于三参数模型建立了自行车交通流运动模型;龙小强[13]等运用流体力学的动力粘度概念建立的非机动车道对机动车道干扰的流体内摩擦模型等;王晓原等[14]利用冲突点法对驾驶行为进行建模仿真,从而研究机动车和非机动车之间的干扰作用。

基于数据统计的安全风险评价方法主要包括:Allen 等[15]考虑自行车与右转车辆之间的冲突,量

1.基金项目:国家自然科学基金项目(项目编号:52172338)。

化分析混行交通流对交叉口容量的影响；周旦等[16]建立了自行车三参数模型，分析了不同情况下机、非车辆的速度特征；陈永恒[17]等通过建立回归统计模型，分析机动车车速与非机动车流量、机动车与非机动车之间最小横向距离等参数的关系；罗石贵等[18]对路段冲突进行了分类和定义，建立道路冲突技术模型；高熙等[19]考虑了交通安全因素，研究了机非混行车道最小宽度；徐程等[20]机非混行路段安全风险进行评估；Liu[21]等利用回归分析方法明确了自行车对道路交通安全的影响；Kroll 等[22]发现机非混行路段，路侧非机动车驶过时，机动车车身会向机动车道内侧横移。

以上针对非物理隔离路段非机动车混入机动车道行驶的研究，尽管在模型建立与评价分析方面进行了有益探索，但仍存在不足。首先，已有研究中模型主要依据传统非机动车流建立，未考虑电动车与普通自行车的性能差异；其次，评价指标单一，无法全面的反映机非混行现象对道路交通的影响。

鉴于以往不足，研究首先通过采集视频，提取轨迹数据，探究非物理隔离路段非机动车混入机动车道行驶的交通流特征；接着将非机动车混入对机动车正常行驶的干扰行为进行细化分类，对应建立相关微观模型；最后，根据模型进行交通仿真，采用机动车交互状态数据等多重评价指标对车辆通行状况进行评价，量化评价不同道路条件下非机动车混入机动车道行驶对道路安全的影响。

1　非机动车干扰机动车类型

在无物理隔离设施的机非混行路段，存在非机动车非法闯入机动车道行驶的交通行为，干扰了机动车辆的正常运行，随着非机动车侵入机动车道的横向宽度增加，对机动车辆的影响程度不断提高。为了保证机动车和非机动车的行驶安全，两者之间需要满足最小安全侧向距离，非机动车对机动车干扰如图1所示。本文按照机动车与非机动车的侧向距离与最小安全侧向距离将干扰行为分为两类。

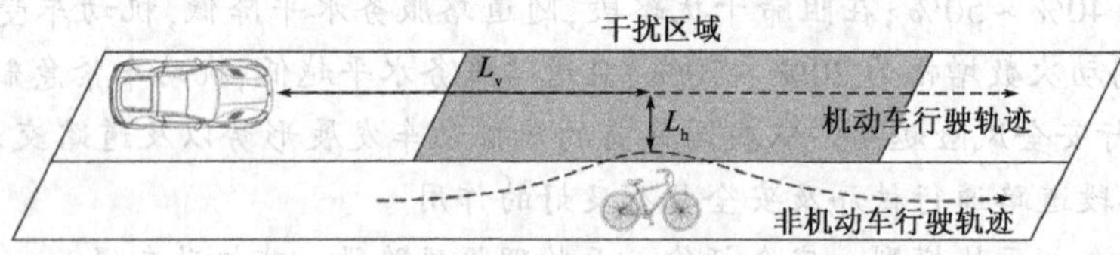

图1　非机动车对机动车行驶干扰示意图

1.1　摩擦干扰

摩擦干扰指非机动车侵入机动车道的宽度较少，对机动车影响较小，此时非机动车和机动车之间的侧向距离小于最小安全侧向距离，即 $L_h < L_{min}$，驾驶员为了保证安全行车，可在决策位置做出减速操作，等待安全超越非机动车后，再以一定的加速度加速至初始行驶速度。

1.2　阻滞干扰

阻滞干扰是指非机动车侵入机动车道的宽度较大，严重影响了机动车正常行驶，此时非机动车与机动车之间的侧向距离大于最小安全侧向距离，即 $L_h > L_{min}$，驾驶员为了保证行车安全，在决策位置被迫做出减速甚至停滞操作，等待非机动车与机动车之间的侧向距离小于最小安全侧向距离时，机动车以一定的加速度加速至初始速度，达到正常行驶的状态。

2　数据处理

2.1　视频数据采集

(1)调查地点的选取

调查地点选取机动车道与非机动车道之间无物理隔离设施，仅由白色标线隔开，非机动车可进入机动车道行驶的单幅路或双幅路路段。根据调查地点要求，选取西安市长安中路晚高峰(17:00—18:00)进行调查，路段横断面示意如图2所示。

(2)调查方法

本次视频采集方法为录像法，在较高的工作位置对目标路段进行连续摄像，得到一定时间连续的机非车辆交通流数据。

2.2　视频数据处理

对交通调查数据进行处理，获取机动车及非机动车流轨迹、速度、加速度等数据，在调查时间内,机动车与非机动车共发生冲突 111 次,交通量统计如表 1、图 3 所示。

a)路段卫星示意图

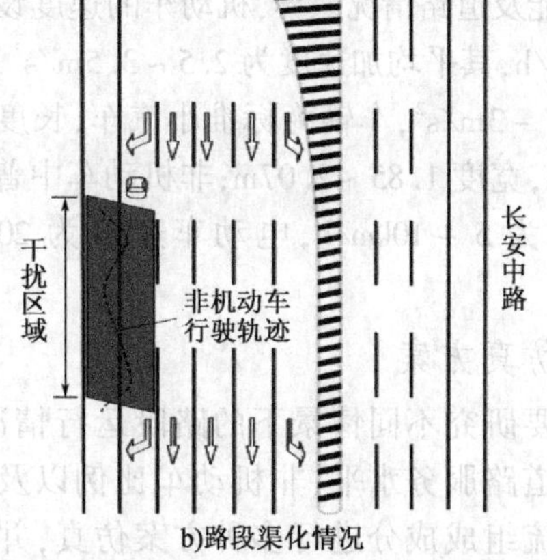

b)路段渠化情况

图 2　路段横断面示意图

调查期间交通量统计结果　表 1

项目	机动车流量		闯入机动车道		正常行驶	
小客车	小货车	大客车	电动车	自行车	电动车	自行车
307	16	37	292	37	492	320

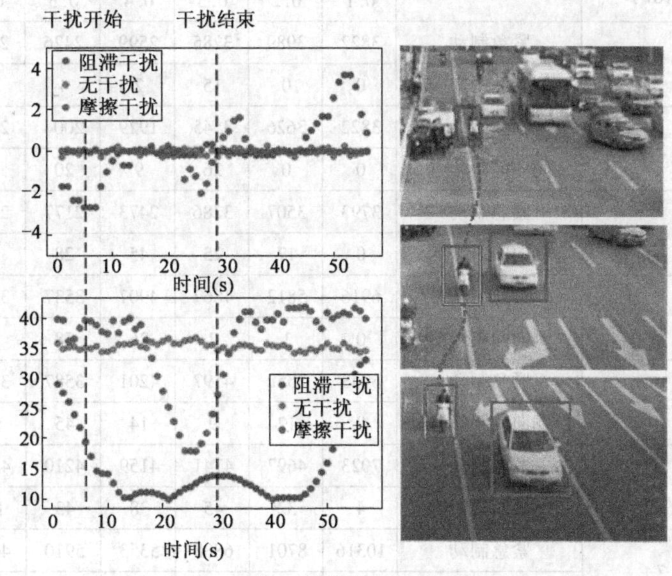

图 3　数据提取结果

3　混合非机动车流仿真模型的建立

本文利用 VISSIM 软件进行仿真,在传统机非混行交通流模型上,增加对非机动车流组成成分的考虑,同时,按照实际调查数据,对路段运行环境及各项参数进行设置,并制定相应的仿真规则,进行模型验证,使仿真模型与道路实际运行情况更加贴近。

3.1　基础参数设置

基础数据设置参考现行《道路交通标志和标线》(GB 5768)、《城市道路工程设计规范》(CJJ 37)相关规范要求,非机动车混入机动车道行驶摩擦干扰和阻滞干扰分类及大量的文献资料,最终确定各类参数数值如下:

3.1.1　车辆通行环境

根据调查路段的基本情况设置车辆通行环境。车辆通行环境主要包括路段长度,车道数及交通控制等条件;本次仿真模型设置 800m 双车道路段,道路横断面形式为单幅路,机动车道宽度为 3.5m,非机动车道宽度为 2.5m,且机动车道与非机动车道间无物理隔离设施,仅由道路标线隔开,非机动车可混入机动车道行驶。

3.1.2　车辆性能特性

由于性能及道路情况差异,机动车的速度设定为30~50km/h,其平均加速度为2.5~3.5m/s^2,减速度为-2~-3m/s^2,车辆为标准小汽车,长度为3.75~4.76m,宽度1.85~2.07m;非机动车中普通自行车速度为5~10km/h,电动车速度为20~25km/h。

3.2　仿真方案

本文主要研究不同情景下的路段运行情况,故主要改变道路服务水平、非机动车比例以及混合非机动车流组成成分进行多种方案仿真,并对方案仿真结果进行深入分析。

考虑到道路服务水平较高时,非机动车闯入机动车道的空当较少,以及服务水平较低时,非机动车对机动车影响较小,故本文选取B、C、D三种服务水平条件,设置机动车与非机动车总交通量为为600pcu/h,800pcu/h,1000pcu/h三种情况,即对应v/c分别为0.486、0.648、0.810;同时,根据调查结果仿真设置混合非机动车流,即电动车与自行车比例为7:3,为拓宽研究结果适用范围,增加电动车与自行车比例为3:7及5:5的情况,并以0.1为步长改变机动车与非机动车的比例,模拟不同交通流混行状态下的道路运行干扰情况。

3.3　车辆交互状态数据

非机动车混入机动车道行驶的安全评价指标主要为车辆交互状态类型及次数。通过仿真不同情形下的道路交通运行状况,获取机动车与非机动车辆交叉行驶的状态数据,如表2所示。

车辆交互状态数据汇总　　表2

道路服务水平	自行车与电动车比例	交互状态	非机动车比例								
			0.1	0.2	0.3	0.4	0.5	0.6	0.7	0.8	0.9
B等级	3:7	紧急制动	3822	3989	3285	2599	2426	2400	2365	2016	2762
		侧向间距影响	0	0	15	2	4	55	82	95	74
	5:5	紧急制动	3822	3626	3545	1929	2004	2623	2299	2433	3322
		侧向间距影响	0	0	26	9	20	53	46	90	136
	7:3	紧急制动	3793	3507	3286	2473	2177	2617	2849	3608	4647
		侧向间距影响	0	17	25	45	28	37	56	113	195
C等级	3:7	紧急制动	6916	5812	4867	4907	3537	3007	3224	3169	2676
		侧向间距影响	0	1	2	26	58	95	95	182	258
	5:5	紧急制动	6943	5552	4197	4201	3587	3424	4610	5702	5594
		侧向间距影响	0	12	9	14	45	90	125	196	317
	7:3	紧急制动	7023	4697	4741	4159	4210	4599	4960	6390	6307
		侧向间距影响	4	32	45	38	43	113	225	260	308
D等级	3:7	紧急制动	10316	8701	6888	5353	5910	4643	3939	3610	4963
		侧向间距影响	0	15	4	58	137	89	241	250	420
	5:5	紧急制动	9890	8469	6466	5403	5760	6325	6199	6399	8126
		侧向间距影响	0	32	20	45	102	177	283	397	630
	7:3	紧急制动	10394	8384	6639	6026	6714	6696	6989	8596	11037
		侧向间距影响	7	17	28	43	144	222	356	402	667

3.4　仿真模型验证

通过阅读文献发现对计算与实际调查数据进行检验的方法较多,但由于GEH统计检验方法既考虑两种数据的绝对值,又考虑二者之间的差异性,能较好的体现结果的相关性,因此采用GEH对模型进行检验。

$$\mathrm{GEH}=\sqrt{\frac{(N_{\mathrm{cal}}-N_{\mathrm{sur}})^2}{(N_{\mathrm{cal}}+N_{\mathrm{sur}})/2}} \tag{1}$$

式中:N_{cal}——仿真冲突数;

N_{sur}——实际调查冲突数。

根据调查结果,路段机动车与非机动车冲突次数共计111次,根据仿真得到交互状态为2447

次,涉及车辆 103 辆,计算得到 GEH 值为 0.77 < 1.00,因此模型有效。

4 非机动车混入机动车道行驶安全评价

4.1 评价指标

根据摩擦干扰与阻滞干扰的干扰行为,选取侧向间距影响与紧急制动两种干扰状态发生次数作为安全评价指标,干扰状态发生次数即干扰持续时间/仿真步长。

侧向间距影响:用以达到允许速度的加/减速度,取决于经过相同或相邻车道上其他车辆时的侧向间距;

紧急制动:刹车至所需的安全距离(到达安全距离后)。

4.2 摩擦干扰

4.2.1 侧向间距影响

如图 4 所示,非机动车比例在[0.3,0.6]范围内干扰增幅较大,约为 3 ~ 5 倍;随自行车比例的提高,干扰次数呈增加趋势,当服务水平较高时,增长较平稳,而随道路服务水平降低,干扰次数在非机动车比例为[0.5,0.6]范围内时会出现激增。

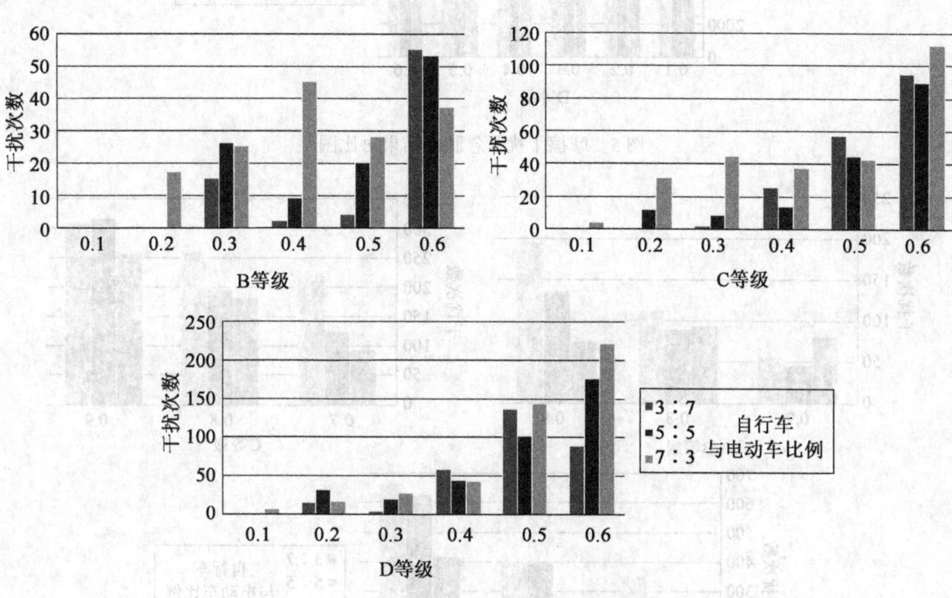

图 4 摩擦干扰侧向间距影响对比图

4.2.2 紧急制动

如图 5 所示,随非机动车比例的增加,机动车流量降低,机动车间干扰少,制动次数呈降低趋势,但由于非机动车流量增加机非之间干扰加剧;当道路服务水平降低时,机动车采取紧急制动措施次数急剧增加,增幅为 40% ~50%;在非机动车比例为[0.1,0.4]时,随电动车比例增加,机动车紧急制动次数增加;非机动车道接近饱和后,自行车比例高会造成非机动车道通行受阻,追求较高速度的非机动车借机动车道超车,对机动车通行造成较大影响。

4.3 阻滞干扰

4.3.1 侧向干扰

相比于摩擦干扰而言,阻滞干扰的侧向间距影响次数增幅约为 3.07 倍,如图 6 所示,D 服务水平的干扰程度明显高于另外两种服务水平,机动车受到侧向间距影响增幅为 60% ~125%;随道路服务水平的降低,自行车比例的增加对道路通行的影响越大,道路通行安全性越差。

4.3.2 紧急制动

如图 7 所示,在阻滞干扰路段随机动车比例增加,机动车采取紧急制动措施次数呈增加趋势;随道路服务水平降低制动次数增多,且 B 等级与 C、D 等级差距较大,增幅为 20% ~50%,随自行车比例增加,机动车紧急制动次数增加,增幅为 18% ~37.5%,且道路服务水平越低,机动车紧急制动次数受自行车比例影响越大,道路通行安全风险越高。

5 结语

研究针对无物理隔离路段机动车及非机动车的微观加、减速过程,在传统模型的基础上对干扰行为进行细化分类,定量评价行驶安全,深入探究道路服务水平及混合非机动车流组成成分对交通运行安全的影响规律。

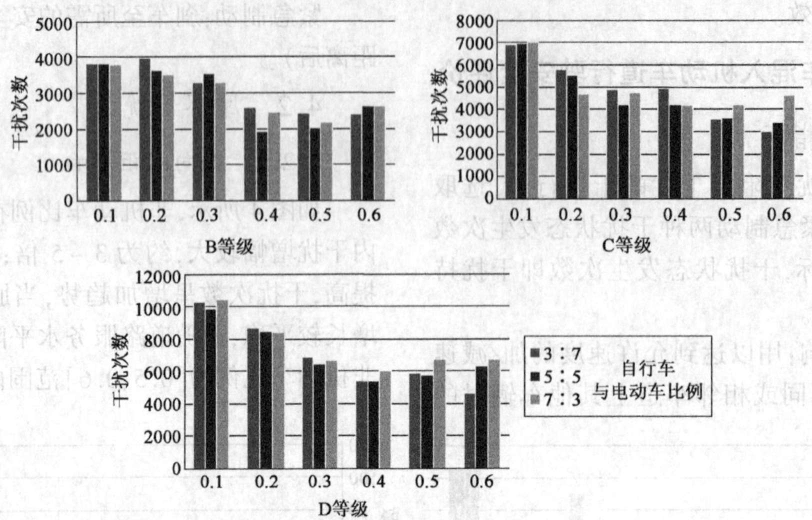

图5　摩擦干扰紧急制动结果对比图

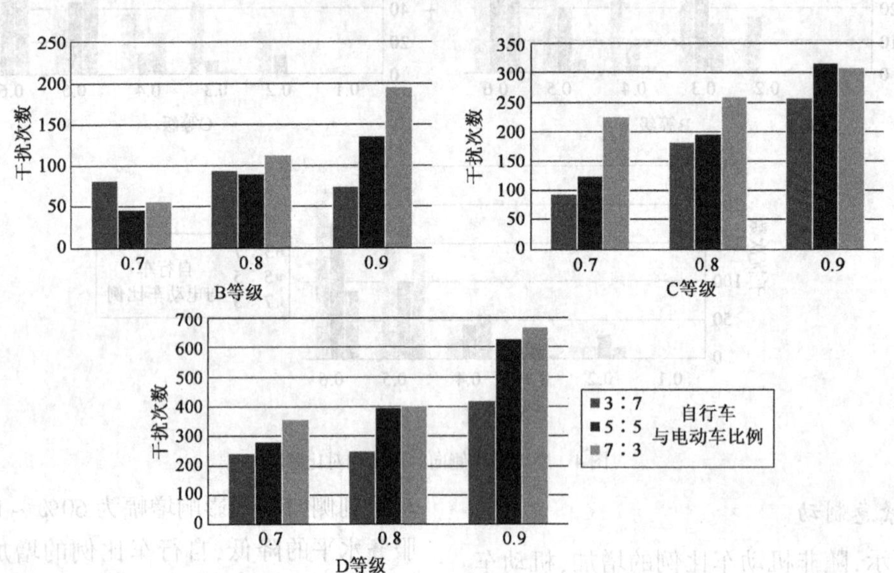

图6　阻滞干扰侧向干扰影响结果对比图

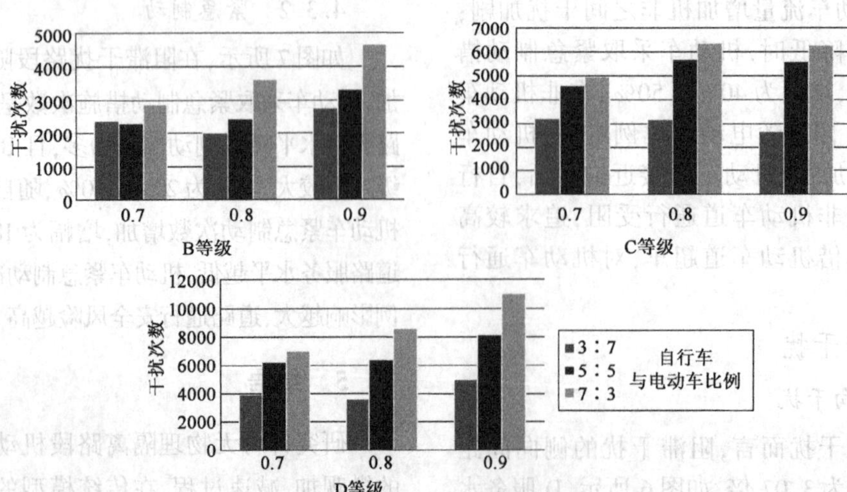

图7　阻滞干扰紧急制动次数对比图

(1)在摩擦干扰路段当道路服务水平降低、非机动车比例增加,机动车受侧向干扰及紧急制动次数持续增加;且非机动车比例在[0.1,0.2]范围内对机动车的正常通行影响较小,在[0.3,0.4]范围内时,电动车对道路安全影响较大,在[0.5,0.6]范围内时,自行车比例越高对道路通行安全影响越大。

(2)相比摩擦干扰,阻滞干扰路段对机动车的干扰次数会增加1.5~2倍;当道路服务水平及非机动车比例变化时,干扰次数大幅度增长;当阻滞干扰路段电动车比例增加时,机动车受干扰次数降低15%~25%,紧急制动次数减少21%~33%,安全性在一定程度上有所提高。

(3)在实际道路运行过程中,要加强对非机动车的监管,利用宣传教育及违规罚款等手段控制规范非机动车的行为。非机动车比例在[0.1,0.2]内可采用划线隔离的方式;非机动车比例在[0.3,0.4]范围内时,骑行行为较规范路段可不设置物理隔离设施;非机动车比例大于0.4时,建议设置硬性物理隔离设施。

(4)研究所取混合非机动车比例步长跨度较大,在后期进一步研究时可以将步长缩短,使评价更加精细化,便于精准分析非机动车比例对道路交通运行安全的影响,给出更具有针对性的路段改善意见。

参考文献

[1] Botma H, Papendrecht H. Traffic operation of bicycle traffic [J]. Transportation Research Record, 1991 (1320).

[2] Allen D P, Hummer J E, Rouphail N M, et al. Effect of bicycles on capacity of signalized intersections [J]. Transportation research record, 1998, 1646(1): 87-95.

[3] 陈永恒,王殿海,陶志兴. 无物理隔离路段机动车与非机动车速度特性研究[J]. 交通运输系统工程与信息,2009,9(5):53-57.

[4] Li X, Sun J Q. Studies of vehicle lane-changing dynamics and its effect on traffic efficiency, safety and environmental impact [J]. Physica A: Statistical Mechanics and its Applications, 2017, 467: 41-58.

[5] Afghari A P, Haque M M, Washington S. Applying fractional split model to examine the effects of roadway geometric and traffic characteristics on speeding behavior[J]. Traffic injury prevention, 2018, 19(8): 860-866.

[6] Ma C, Zhou J, Yang D, et al. Personal characteristics of e-bike riders and illegal lane occupation behavior [J]. Journal of advanced transportation, 2020.

[7] George Oketch T. New modeling approach for mixed-traffic streams with nonmotorized vehicles [J]. Transportation research record, 2000, 1705 (1): 61-69.

[8] Gould G, Karner A. Modeling bicycle facility operation: Cellular automaton approach [J]. Transportation research record, 2009, 2140(1): 157-164.

[9] Wierbos M J, Knoop V L, Hänseler F S, et al. A macroscopic flow model for mixed bicycle-car traffic [J]. Transportmetrica A: transport science, 2021, 17(3): 340-355.

[10] Parkin J, Meyers C. The effect of cycle lanes on the proximity between motor traffic and cycle traffic [J]. Accident Analysis & Prevention, 2010, 42(1): 159-165.

[11] 关宏志,陈艳艳,刘小明,等. 基本路段机非混合交通流的解析模型[J]. 北京工业大学学报,2001,27(1):12-15.

[12] 彭锐,杨佩昆. 自行车交通流基本模型[J]. 同济大学学报:自然科学版,1993,21(4):463-468.

[13] 龙小强,晏启鹏. 非机动车道对机动车道干扰的流体内摩擦模型[J]. 中国公路学报,2002,15(1):100.

[14] 王晓原,邢丽. 机非混行环境下驾驶员行为建模及仿真[J]. 中国公路学报,2009,22(2):98-104.

[15] Allen D P, Hummer J E, Rouphail N M, et al. Effect of bicycles on capacity of signalized intersections [J]. Transportation research record, 1998, 1646(1): 87-95.

[16] 周旦,马晓龙,金盛,等. 基于Logistic模型的混合自行车流量-密度关系[J]. 交通运输工程学报,2016,16(3):133-141.

[17] 陈永恒,王殿海,陶志兴. 无物理隔离路段机动车与非机动车速度特性研究[J]. 交通运输系统工程与信息,2009,9(5):53-57.

[18] 罗石贵,周伟.路段交通冲突技术研究[J].公路交通科技,2001,18(1):65-68.
[19] 高熙.机非混行车道最小宽度的研究探讨[J].科技信息,2013(16),387-388.
[20] 徐程.路段混合自行车交通运行特性与风险评估[D].长春:吉林大学,2016.
[21] Liu P, Marker S. Evaluation of contributory factors' effects on bicycle-car crash risk at signalized intersections [J]. Journal of Transportation Safety & Security, 2020, 12 (1): 82-93.
[22] Kroll B. J, Ramey M. R. Effects of bike lanes on driver and bicyclist behavior [J]. Transportation engineering journal of the American Society of Civil Engineers. 1977, 103(2):243-256.

机动车交通事故预测模型评估与特征分析

——随机森林和XGBoost的比较

林　涛[1]　邵海鹏*[1,2]　方瑞韬[1]
(1.长安大学运输工程学院;2.生态安全屏障区交通网设施管控及循环修复技术交通运输行业重点实验室)

摘　要　交通安全问题一直被人们高度关注,交通安全机构依靠预测模型进行事故预测,但是现有模型的性能评估存在不足。本文基于随机森林和XGBoost算法分别进行了模型预测,通过八个预测性能指标同时进行模型的评估比较。此外,利用SHAP解释器对XGBoost模型进行解释。结果表明,准确度、敏感度、特异度、FPR指标、精确度、NPV指标、F1分数和马修斯相关系数能够表现出模型在不同类别的预测性能,同时避免了模型过度拟合。随机森林模型和XGBoost模型在大部分测量指标的表现几乎都优于其他常用的数据挖掘模型。随机森林模型和XGBoost模型显著地提高了预测准确度,而没有提供额外的错误预测。与常用的机器学习算法相比,随机森林模型和XGBoost模型对交通事故不平衡数据的分析能力更佳。利用SHAP对模型进行特征依赖分析,为交通管理者提供合理的参考意见。

关键词　交通工程　交通安全　随机森林　XGBoost　预测准确度　SHAP解释器

0　引言

交通事故是世界各国关注的一个交通安全问题。全球道路安全状况报告(Global Status Report on Road Safety)显示,随着大多数国家高速公路和机动车辆数量的迅速增加,世界上的事故总数大幅增加。美国国家公路交通安全管理局(NHTSA)的报告显示,2021年上半年约有2万多人死于车祸,比2020年增加18.4%。中国统计年鉴显示,2020年我国道路交通事故万车死亡人数下降至1.66人,尽管近年万车死亡人数在逐年稳步下降,但是与发达国家相比依旧较高。跟据世界卫生组织报告,在世界范围内,每年有上百万人死于交通事故。如何提前预测交通事故,防止交通事故的发生以减少事故人员伤亡,一直是各国交通研究者所关注的问题。

机动车交通事故预测建模多年来一直是一个重要的安全研究课题。预测模型利用历史数据和数据统计,以此分析事故成因和预测事故发生的可能性,交通安全规划者依靠交通事故预测模型来分配未来几年的安全改进预算。因此,模型预测的准确性至关重要,尤其是在预测事故发生与事故严重程度方面。

非参数数据挖掘以及机器学习方法近年来广受欢迎,并以此建立预测模型并得到较好的预测结果。常见的方法包括:神经网络[1-2]、聚类分析[3-5]、分类和回归树分析[6-7]。大部分学者建议使用这种方法研究交通事故。但是,以往文献往往将重点注重于模型预测的准确率,较少研究者关注模型预测的综合指标,尤其是对于提高安全性至关重要的虚报率和严重程度的错误估计。因为

基金项目:国家重点研发计划(2019YFB1600300);中央高校基本科研业务费专项资金(300102219210,300102210201)。

大量的错误预测以及事故严重程度的高估或低估,不仅会浪费大量的资金和时间,还会使最需要重视最需要安全改进的地方发生误导。

随机森林(Random Forest,RF)方法是用于回归和分类树的集成方法。随机森林模型的一个已知优点是,它不仅可以限制过拟合,而且不会显著降低预测准确度。此外,随机森林是一个包含多棵决策树的分类模型,由于其结合了 Bootstrap 采样和随机属性选择的优点,在分类问题中取得了良好效果。随机森林不仅可以用于二分类,还可以用于多分类问题,其泛化能力好,一般不会出现过拟合,在有偏差的数据上,随机森林也能够获得较好的效果,随机森林算法具有更好的分类精度,且不会产生过拟合问题[8]。Dogru[9]利用随机森林进行交通事故进行分类预测,结果表明 RF 比其他监督机器学习(如 SVM、ANN 等)具有更佳的预测效果,模型评估指标为准确率、敏感度和特异度。Atumo[10]对密歇根州国际公路的交通事故热点识别和预测,同样验证了随机森林具有更好的预测性能,模型评估指标为敏感度和精确度和 F1 分数。Yassin[11]在随机森林的基础上,结合 K-means 聚类进行交通事故严重性预测,结果表明其模型预测准确度高达 99.86%,模型评估指标为准确度、敏感度、特异度、精确度和 F1 分数。

提升决策树是一种广泛而有效的集成学习方法,而 XgBoost 作为一种新型提升决策树算法,于 2016 年被提出,它能够自动利用 CPU 的多线程进行并行运算,可在缩短时间的同时提高精度。Meng[12]利用 XGBoost 方法,对多种数据源预测了事故的发生和持续时间,模型评估指标为准确率、敏感度和精确度。此外,Hamilton[13]和 Schlögl[14]表明,XGBoost 在预测事故可能性方面的表现优于其他几种机器学习技术,包括逻辑回归、贝叶斯正则化神经网络、SVM 和深度神经网络,Hamilton 的模型评估指标为准确率、灵敏度和特异度,Schlögl 的模型评估指标为准确率、灵敏度、特异度和 FPR 指标。Parsa[15]利用 XGBoost 对芝加哥高速公路交通事故进行事故预测,主要评估指标为准确率和灵敏度,结果表明 XGBoost 具有优异的预测能力,其预测准确率高达 99%。此外,XGBoost 还被用于预测交通事故的严重性,并取得了较好的效果,尤其是在使用空间数据时[16]。可以看出,随机森林模型和 XGBoost 在交通事故预测方面均能表现出良好的性能,但是以往研究对预测模型的全面评估还较少。

非参数数据挖掘及机器学习模型的可解释性较差,一般被认为是黑箱模型,无法了解样本特征值是如何影响最终的预测结果。近年来,一些研究已经开始利用 SHAP 解释器(Shapley Additive exPlanation)对模型进行进一步地分析。SHAP 最初是由 Shapley[17]提出,它基于博弈论,它提供了一个可以衡量模型中特征重要性的方法。2017 年,Lundberg 和 Lee[18]用 Python 开发了一个实用程序包,能够计算不同技术的 SHAP,包括 LightGBM、GBoost、CatBoost、XGBoost 模型。在交通安全方面,Mihaita[19]使用 SHAP 分析不同特征对事故持续时间的影响。Parsa[15]使用 SHAP 对基于 XGBoost 的交通事故检测模型特征进行分析和解释。

综上所述,本文研究的目的是评估随机森林模型和 XGBoost 模型等常用的数据挖掘方法在预测机动车交通事故中的应用,计算模型预测的准确度、敏感度、特异度、FPR 指标、精确度、NPV 指标、F1 分数和马修斯相关系数,并分析比较尤其是事故严重程度预测中容易出现虚报的指标,可为帮助相关部门进行安全优化改进从而减少不必要的资金支出。在本文中,采用了六种常用的数据挖掘方法,对决策树(DT)、随机森林(RF)、XGboost、支持向量机(SVM)、朴素贝叶斯(NB)和逻辑回归(Logistic)进行了比较,并评估各预测模型的全面性能。最后,利用 SHAP 解释器对 XGBoost 模型的预测结果进行进一步解释,在提高该模型的可解释性的同时,为交通安全管理者提供合理的意见。

1 数据

1.1 数据预处理

本研究中使用的数据为 2015—2020 年陕西省某市所发生的所有机动车交通伤亡事故。剔除含有缺失值的数据后,最后共保留 6977 条机动车事故数据作为研究对象,期间,有 4998 起伤人事故和 1979 起死亡事故。关于因变量的设置,借鉴国外对事故发生和严重程度的研究[20-21],在本文采用了二分类方法,将事故严重程度分为 2 类:伤人事故和死亡事故。

数据集分为两部分:随机选择 60% 作为训练数据集的观测值,其余 40% 的观测值作为测试数据集。训练数据集中的样本数为4186,测试数据集中的样本数为2791。数据集中共有32个变量。参考以往文献[22]并综合考虑各方面影响,最终使用26个自变量来构建随机森林模型及XGboost模型,具体如表1所示。

表中仅有年龄、驾龄、事故发生时间、涉事机动车数量是连续变量,而其他的变量均为分类变量。本研究使用分类树建立随机森林模型和XGboost模型,并运用Python3.7进行建模和后续的数据分析。

自变量分类表　表1

变量名	分　类	赋　值
事故时间	无	连续变量
事故形态	侧翻	1
	成员跌落或抛出	2
	刮撞行人	3
	滚翻	4
	碾压行人	5
	碰撞后碾压行人	6
	碰撞静止车辆	7
	碰撞运动车辆	8
	其他车辆间事故	9
	其他车辆与行人事故	10
	其他事故	11
碰撞程度	无	0
	其他	1
	同向剐蹭、护栏	2
	对向剐蹭、护栏	3
	其他角度碰撞、侧面碰撞角度不确定	4
	侧面碰撞同向	5
	侧面碰撞对向	6
	追尾碰撞	7
	侧面碰撞直角	8
	正面碰撞	9
道路类型	高速公路	1
	一级道路	2
	城市快速路	3
	二级道路	4
	一般城市道路	5
	三级道路	6
	四级道路	7
	其他	8
道路线型	平直	1
	一般坡	2
	一般弯	3
	一般弯坡	4
	陡坡	5
	连续陡坡	6
	急弯	7
	一般弯陡坡	8
	一般坡急弯	9
	急弯陡坡	10
天气	晴	1
	阴	2
	雨	3
	雾	4
	雪	5
	其他	6
能见度	200m以上	1
	100~200m	2
	50~100m	3
	50m以下	4
照明条件	白天	1
	黎明、黄昏	2
	夜间有路灯	3
	夜间无路灯	4
肇事者性别	男	0
	女	1
年龄	其他	连续变量
户口性质	非农业	0
	农业	1
交通方式	驾(驶)非机动车	1
	驾摩托车	2
	驾驶其他机动车	3
	驾驶汽车	4
驾龄	无	连续变量
血液酒精含量	无	0
	0~19	1
	20~79	2
	80以上	3
安全带、头盔使用情况	无	0
	有	1
地形	平原	1
	丘陵	2
	山区	3
涉事机动车数量	无	连续变量
事故原因	其他违法	1
	非违法过错	2
	非机动车违法	3
	机动车违法	4
事故道路横断面位置	其他	1
	人行道、人行横道	2

续上表

变量名	分　类	赋　值
路面状况	路面完好	1
	凹凸	2
	路障	3
	施工	4
	塌陷	5
	其他	6
路面结构	沥青	1
	水泥	2
	沙石	3
	土路	4
	其他	5
路表情况	干燥	1
	潮湿	2
	泥泞	3
	油污	4
	积水	5
	漫水	6
	冰雪	7
	其他	8
路侧防护设施	无	0
	波形护栏	1
	柔性护栏	2
	混凝土护栏	3
	金属护栏	4
	绿化带、行道树	5
	活动护栏	6
	护栏墩(柱)	7
	其他	8
事故道路横断面位置	非机动车道	3
	机非混合道	4
	机动车道	5
道路物理隔离	无隔离	0
	中心隔离与机非隔离	1
	机非隔离	2
	中心隔离	3
中央隔离措施	无	0
	波形护栏	1
	柔性护栏	2
	混凝土护栏	3
	金属护栏	4
	绿化带	5
	活动护栏	6
	隔离墩(柱)	7
道路安全隐患督办等级	无	0
	县级	1
	市级	2
	省级	3
道路安全属性	正常路段	1
	已经治理但仍存在隐患道路	2
	正在治理隐患路段	3
	已排查尚未治理隐患路段	4
	尚未排查隐患路段	5
交通控制方式	无控制	0
	标志标线	1
	信号灯、民警指挥	2
	其他	3

1.2　不平衡数据处理

某一类数据稀少的数据集被定义为不平衡数据[23]。交通事故数据就是典型的不平衡数据，因为在交通事故中无人伤亡的数量是远高于伤亡事故的，而伤人事故又高于死亡事故，在其他事故领域中，也表现出同样的现象。当使用传统方式预测时，往往偏向对有充足数据量的类别进行预测。这会导致对数据量较大的类别表现出良好的预测性能，但对数据量稀少的类别预测能力相对较差，甚者无法预测罕见事件，这可以在以前的研究[24-26]中得到类似的结果。处理不平衡数据有几种常用的技术，分别是数据加权、过采样和欠采样。以往文献中，过采样容易导致模型过拟合，为了解决过拟合问题，文献常使用 SMOTE 法[27]，即利用少数类的每个数据生成新的数据集，使少数类数据量与多数类数量持平，但该方法适合连续变量的数据集，与 SMOTE 相近的还有 ADASYN 法。而欠采样技术往往会大致大量数据的丢失，从而导致模型的精度大幅下降。

指定先验概率通常可为模型中的不平衡数据获得更好的预测结果，一般来说，先验概率由每个类别的频率来表示[28]。当增加不平衡数据的先验概率时，也增加后验概率，从而改变不平衡数据的分类边界，使得更多的样本被分类到该类别中。

考虑到数据集中的本身特点,因此,本文的解决办法是对不平衡数据增加权重,在模型训练时调整损失函数的惩罚系数,使模型能平等对待多数的伤人事故与少数的死亡事故这两个不平衡类别。

2　模型建立与评价

2.1　随机森林

随机森林模型是一种用于分类和回归的集成方法。由随机森林模型做出的决策是基于由许多决策树做出的决策集合。在本研究中,决策树拆分的算法选择 ID3 信息熵算法。ID3 信息熵算法测量信息增益,以确定是否应该选择属性变量作为拆分器以及节点是否应该进一步拆分。假设一个变量 S 有 c 个不同的值,S 的熵 $E(S)$ 的计算公式见式(1):

$$E(S) = \sum_{i=1}^{C} -p_i \log_2 p_i \tag{1}$$

式中:p_i——取某个确定值的概率。

如果变量在某个属性上被划分为子集 $s_1, s_2, \cdots, S_c$,期望熵(EH)可以衡量变量 S 分裂后计算结果数学期望的不确定性,计算公式见式(2):

$$\mathrm{EH} = \sum_{i=1}^{C} \frac{a_i}{a} \times (-p_i \log_2 p_i) \tag{2}$$

式中:a_i——每个子集 $s_1, s_2, \cdots, s_c$ 中的样本总数;

a——父节点 S 中的样本总数。

信息增益 IG(S,A)是将属性 A 分割成 S 个集合之前到之后熵差的度量[29]。换句话说,在属性 A 上拆分集合 S 后,S 中的不确定性减少的值。信息增益 IG(S,A)按等式(3)计算:

$$\mathrm{IG}(S,A) = E(S) - \mathrm{EH} \tag{3}$$

信息增益为零的节点被认为是不需要进一步分裂的终端节点。决策树总是对训练数据进行完美分类,随着决策树不断分裂数据,树变得越来越大,对训练数据集的准确率会有所提高,但其应用于测试数据集时,所做出的预测结果不理想。决策树倾向于过度拟合训练数据,这在应用完整数据集时可能会产生较差的结果。RF 的最大优势之一是它可以在不显著降低预测准确度的情况下限制过度拟合。

RF 模型主要基于两种方法构建:袋装法和随机子空间。袋装法是使用 Bootstrapping 随机重采样得到训练样本,然后对每个 Bootstrapping 样本进行学习的过程。Bootstrapping 是一种带替换的统计随机重采样方法,用于处理不平衡数据。随机子空间随机选择属性变量来分割 RF 模型中每个决策树的节点。而不被 Bootstrapping 采用的样本被称为袋外样本,常被用于模型选择和评估。具有较低袋外 OOB 误差率的 RF 模型是最优的结果,因为它可以提供较高的预测准确度。通常,包含更多树的 RF 模型具有较低的袋外误差率,也不会导致过度拟合,但在某些情况下,过多的决策树会存在缺点[30]。

在本研究中,使用袋装法的 RF 模型作为预测工具。此外,还进行了完整的预测准确度分析,以更好地理解所提出的 RF 方法的预测性能。对于模型训练,选取 60% 数据进行训练,40% 进行模型测试,本文使用了 Scikit-learn 库中的随机森林包。通过五折交叉验证选择最优超参数值:树的个数 n estimators:200;最大深度 max depth:9;使用袋装法 bootstrap:True;分裂算法 criterion:entropy 信息熵 ID3 算法;不平衡数据加权 class weight:balanced;叶子节点最少样例数 min samples leaf:2;分裂内部节点所需最少样例数 min samples split:2。

2.2　XGBoost

XGBoost 是一种高效的梯度提升决策树。决策树的结构类似于具有根节点(最顶端的节点)、内部节点和叶节点(末端节点)的树,决策树算法常使用简单的规则,从根节点开始分支,经过内部节点,最后在叶子中结束。相比之下,梯度增强决策树是一种集成学习技术,它使用一系列决策树,其中每个决策树从先前的树中学习,并影响下一棵树来改进模型并构建强大的学习者。详细可参考陈天奇和 Guestrin 的相关研究[31]。

给定一个具有 n 个样本的数据集,存在独立变量 x_i,并且这些变量中的每一个都具有 m 个特征,因此 $x_i \in R^m$。对于每一个变量,都有相应的因变量 y_i,$y_i \in R$。树集合模型使用自变量和 k 个函数预测因变量 $\overset{\$}{y}_i$:

$$\overset{\$}{y}_i = \sum_{k=1}^{K} f_k(x_i), f_k \in F \tag{4}$$

式中:f_k——一个具有叶分值的独立的树结构;

F——树的空间。

目标是最小化公式(5):

$$L(\phi) = \sum_i l(\overset{u}{y}_i, y_i) + \sum_k \Omega(f_k) \tag{5}$$

式中:l——损失函数;

Ω——惩罚模型复杂性的系数,并且:

$$\Omega(f)=\Upsilon T+\frac{1}{2}\lambda\ \|\omega_i\|^2 \tag{6}$$

式中：T——叶节点个数；

ω_i——第 i 个叶节点的得分。

通过解方程式(4)～式(6)，ω_j^* 的最佳值和相应值为：

$$\omega_j^*=-\frac{\sum_{i\in Ij}\partial_{\hat{y}^{t-1}}l(y_i,\hat{y}^{t-1})}{\sum_{i\in Ij}\partial^2_{\hat{y}^{t-1}}l(y_i,\hat{y}^{t-1})+\lambda} \tag{7}$$

$$\tilde{L}_{(q)}=-\frac{1}{2}\sum_{j=1}^{T}\frac{\left(\sum_{i\in Ij}\partial_{\hat{y}^{t-1}}l(y_i,\hat{y}^{t-1})\right)^2}{\sum_{i\in Ij}\partial^2_{\hat{y}^{t-1}}l(y_i,\hat{y}^{t-1})+\lambda}+\lambda T \tag{8}$$

因为在实践中，很难为所有可能的树结构计算该值，所以使用了以下公式：

$$L_{split}=\frac{1}{2}\left[\frac{\left(\sum_{i\in IL}\partial_{\hat{y}^{t-1}}l(y_i,\hat{y}^{t-1})\right)^2}{\sum_{i\in IL}\partial^2_{\hat{y}^{t-1}}l(y_i,\hat{y}^{t-1})+\lambda}+\frac{\left(\sum_{i\in IR}\partial_{\hat{y}^{t-1}}l(y_i,\hat{y}^{t-1})\right)^2}{\sum_{i\in IR}\partial^2_{\hat{y}^{t-1}}l(y_i,\hat{y}^{t-1})+\lambda}-\frac{\left(\sum_{i\in I}\partial_{\hat{y}^{t-1}}l(y_i,\hat{y}^{t-1})\right)^2}{\sum_{i\in I}\partial^2_{\hat{y}^{t-1}}l(y_i,\hat{y}^{t-1})+\lambda}\right]-\gamma \tag{9}$$

式中：$I=I_L\cup I_R$。作为决策树算法，XGBoost 不受多重共线性的影响。因此，即使两个变量在一个系统中捕捉到相同的现象，两个变量都可以保留下来。

对于模型训练，选取 60% 数据进行训练，40% 进行模型测试，本文使用了 XGBoost 包的分类器和 Scikit-learn 库。五折交叉验证后选择的最优超参数值为：迭代次数 n estimators：200；最大深度 max depth：9；随机抽取样本比例 subsample：0.9；学习率 eta：0.1；不平衡数据加权 scale pos weight：6；子采样参数 colsample bytree 和 colsample bylevel 分别取 0.8 和 0.7；节点分裂最小损失函数下降值 gamma：1.0；alpha 和 lambda 分别是 L1 和 L2 正则化项的权重，均取 1.0。

2.3 模型评估

分类准确度是评估模型的最常使用的标准。混淆矩阵(Confusion Matrix)可以用作二元分类问题，混淆矩阵有四个元素：真正类(True Positives，TP)、真负类(True Negatives，TN)、假正类(False Positives，FP)和假负类(False Negatives，FN)，这四个元素表示观察到的结果和预测的结果是否一致，具体如表 2 所示。TP 和 TN 分别为事故是否发生的正确预测；FP 和 FN 检验结果分别为事故是否发生的错误预测。

混淆矩阵 表 2

混淆矩阵		实际情况	
		Negative(0)	Positive (1)
预测情况	Negative (0)	TN	FN
	Positive (1)	FP	TP

一般来说，预测准确度按公式(10)计算，公式(10)是文献[30]中最常见的指示预测模型验证的公式，其中 TP、TN、FN、FP 代表上述四种类别中每个类别的预测结果个数。

$$\text{Accurancy}=\frac{TP+TN}{TP+TN+FN+FP} \tag{10}$$

分类准确度方程提供了总体预测准确度测量。然而，准确度并不衡量每个目标类别(发生事故与未发生事故)的预测准确性。由于数据是不平衡数据，大多数观测值属于未发生事故的类别，整体预测准确度主要由模型未发生事故类别的性能来表示。模型在预测发生事故类别的准确度可能被模型在预测总体准确度方面的优异结果所掩盖。因此，引入了敏感度、特异度、精确度、NPV 和 F1 分数，以分析模型对不平衡数据更全面的表现。

敏感度定义为式(11)[30]，它通过描述模型在实际结果为正时模型预测也为正的效果。换句话说，它代表了模型预测正类(TP)与实际总正类(TP 和 FN)的百分比。

$$\text{Sensitivity}=\frac{TP}{TP+FN} \tag{11}$$

可以看出，敏感度忽略了假正类(FP)的描述。一个模型可以通过牺牲大量的假正类(FP)预测来增加它的敏感度。如等式(12)中所定义的，特异度(Specificity)评估当实际结果为负时，模型预测也为负类的结果是否良好。假正类的比率 FPR

(False Positive Rate)被称为反向真负类比率[30]，如等式(13)中所示。等式(13)总结了当实际结果为负时,预测结果为正的频率。敏感度、特异度和FPR都侧重于检测观测指标的覆盖范围,而不是着眼于模型预测性能。对于不平衡的事故数据,占优势的数据将不产生虚报率。因此,即使特异度和FPR考虑假警报,它们也不能单独作为性能评估的指标。

$$\text{Specificity}=\frac{\text{TN}}{\text{TN}+\text{FP}} \tag{12}$$

$$\text{FPR}=1-\text{Specificity}=\frac{\text{FP}}{\text{TN}+\text{FP}} \tag{13}$$

为了评估预测模型预测技能,引入了由等式(14)定义的精确度[30]，也被称为PPV(Positive Predictive Value)指标。精确度精确描述了一个模型在预测正类方面的准确程度。它评估TP预测相对于模型预测总正类(TP和FP)预测的百分比。该指标是对模型预测正类的性能评价。

$$\text{Precision}=\frac{\text{TP}}{\text{TP}+\text{FP}} \tag{14}$$

在样本中存在不平衡数据的情况下,检查精确度和特异度非常重要。大多数交通事故数据是不平衡的数据,其中有许多事件不发生(类别0)的情况,而事件发生(类别1)的情况很少,在本次研究中,类别0对应的是伤人事故,而类别1对应的是死亡事故,伤亡事故本身就是不平衡数据。如前所述,大量的不发生样本表明类别0的模型预测率高,导致大量的TN,因此特异度对FN不敏感,通常产生较高的值。精确度通过对少数类的正确预测来揭示一个模型的真正事件预测能力。

式(15)中描述的NPV(Negative Predictive Value)评估模型在预测事故为多数量类别0的真实表现[32]。它评估TN预测相对于模型预测总负类(TN和FN)预测的百分比。精确度和NPV是两个可以用来评估模型的真实预测性能的度量。因此,敏感度、特异度和FPR侧重于检测模型准确预测的覆盖范围,而精确度和NPV侧重于评估模型的实际预测性能。

$$\text{NPV}=\frac{\text{TN}}{\text{TN}+\text{FN}} \tag{15}$$

同时总结精确度和敏感度的综合分数也很重要。由等式(16)定义的F1分数计算精确度和敏感度的谐波平均值。它总结了模型的综合准确度,1表示完美的精确度和敏感度,0表示最坏的情况。此外,研究指出F1分数对数据不平衡也很敏感[33]。

$$\text{F1}=\left(\frac{\text{sesitivity}^{-1}+\text{precison}^{-1}}{2}\right)^{-1}=2\,\frac{\text{sesitivity}\times\text{precison}}{\text{sesitivity}+\text{precison}} \tag{16}$$

在本研究中,马修斯相关系数(Matthews Correlation Coefficient,MCC)被选择为二分类的预测性能的另一个综合衡量指标。MCC最早由BW Matthews引入,由于它对不平衡数据的检测结果更可靠、更客观,同时在一定程度上弥补F1分数的不足[34-35]，因此在生物医学中被大量使用。MCC可以看作是二元变量Pearson相关性的离散化[34]。MCC由等式(17)定义。它是一个介于-1和1之间的值,其中1表示完美预测,-1表示预测和观察完全不一致。

$$\text{MCC}=\frac{\text{TP}\cdot\text{TN}-\text{FP}\cdot\text{FN}}{\sqrt{(\text{TP}+\text{FP})\cdot(\text{TP}+\text{FN})\cdot(\text{TN}+\text{FP})\cdot(\text{TN}+\text{FN})}} \tag{17}$$

本研究提出了一个完整的预测能力评估,以避免过度乐观的验证和使用上述所有测量的误导性错觉,然而以往文献在敏感度、特异度、精确度、NPV和F1分数很少被同时应用评估,马修斯相关系数在交通事故预测领域的应用也极少。最后,引用以往文献中常用的ROC曲线与AUC指标进行补充对比。

2.4 模型解释

本研究使用Lundberg和Lee[18]提出的SHAP程序包对XGBoost模型进行解释。SHAP基于博弈论和局部解释来估计每个特征的贡献。假设一个XGBoost模型,其中一个组N(包含n个特征)用于预测输出,在SHAP中,各特征的贡献Φ_i是基于其边际贡献进行分配的[17]，详细可参考Lundberg和Lee的相关研究[18]。Shapely值通过以下公式(18)确定:

$$\Phi_i=\sum_{S\subseteq N\setminus\{i\}}\frac{|S|!(n-|S|-1)!}{n!}\left[v(S\cup\{i\})-v(S)\right] \tag{18}$$

式中:n——特征的总数;

S——任何特征N的子集;

$v(S)$——S的贡献值。

二元特征g的线性函数根据以下可加性特征属性方法定义[31]:

$$g(z')=\Phi_0+\sum_{i=1}^{M}\Phi_i z_i' \tag{19}$$

式中,$z' \in \{0,1\}^M$ 观察到特征时取值为1,否则为0,M 为输入特征的个数。

3　结果与分析

3.1　结果对比

RF 模型和 XGBoost 模型预测测试数据集的混淆矩阵如表3所示。表4显示了六个模型的各个指标比较结果。很明显,这两个模型的预测准确度均超过了85%,达到较好的预测分类结果,二者的特异度明显高于预测的敏感度,虽然模型能够表现出良好的预测准确度和特异度,但不意味着它们具有很强的预测能力。这种现象的根本原因是机动车交通事故数据是不平衡数据集。因此需要使用其他指标进行综合对比。

RF 模型和 XGBoost 模型的混淆矩阵　表3

RF 模型	实际伤人事故(0)	实际死亡事故(1)
预测伤人事故(0)	2172(TN)	225(FN)
预测死亡事故(1)	146(FP)	248(TP)
XGBoost 模型	实际伤人事故(0)	实际死亡事故(1)
预测伤人事故(0)	2208(TN)	168(FN)
预测死亡事故(1)	165(FP)	250(TP)

表4显示,RF 模型和 XGBoost 模型在大部分测量指标的表现优于其他数据挖掘模型。朴素贝叶斯模型虽然 NPV 指标是所有模型中最高的,然而,该模型显著牺牲了模型的精确度,仅为0.3717,比其他模型低了至少20%,也就是说,该模型假正类的数据很高,意味着模型会高估机动车事故严重程度,误导事故结果。决策树模型的精确度是所有模型中最高的,但该模型显著牺牲了模型的敏感度和 NPV 指标,即该模型假负类的数据很高,意味着模型会低估机动车事故严重程度,将严重误导事故结果。

RF 模型在特异度和精确度方面分别超过 XGBoost 模型约0.65%与2.70%。但是,XGBoost 模型在准确度、敏感度、NPV 指标这三个方面分别超过 RF 模型约1.36%、7.38%、2.32%。也就是说,XGBoost 模型在防止假负类(FN)错误方面具有更好的性能;RF 模型在防止假正类(FP)错误方面具有更好的性能,二者在数据预测能力上各有优势。RF 模型和 XGBoost 模型在准确度、敏感度、特异度和 FPR 均优于其他四个模型,在精确度和 NPV 指标上也具有很好的表现。

六个数据挖掘模型的指标对比　表4

项目	Logistic	Bayes	DT	SVM	RF	XGBoost
Accuracy	0.7621	0.8799	0.7420	0.7832	0.8671	0.8807
Sensitivity	0.3377	0.5816	0.3041	0.3825	0.5243	0.5981
Specificity	0.9238	0.9079	0.9280	0.9136	0.9370	0.9305
FPR	0.0762	0.0921	0.0720	0.0864	0.0630	0.0695
Precision	0.6280	0.3717	0.6421	0.5901	0.6294	0.6024
NPV	0.7854	0.9586	0.7584	0.8198	0.9061	0.9293
F1	0.4392	0.4535	0.4127	0.4641	0.5721	0.6002
MCC	0.3288	0.4021	0.3049	0.3483	0.4971	0.5313

为了确定模型对不平衡类别数据的真实预测能力,应同时考虑评估 F1 得分,因为 F1 分数对数据不平衡不仅敏感,而且同时考查了精确度和敏感度。与 RF 模型相比,XGBoost 模型具有更高的 F1 分数,提高了约2.81%,这表明 XGBoost 模型在综合预测能力方面具有更好的性能。此外,另一个综合衡量指标马修斯相关系数也应该得到重视。XGBoost 模型的 MCC 最高,最接近与1,说明 RF 模型和 XGBoost 模型在不平衡数据中具有了良好的预测能力。在其他模型中,Logistic 模型、决策树和支持向量机的 MCC 相近,说明它们对不平衡数据的预测能力相近;而朴素贝叶斯模型仅次于 RF 模型和 XGBoost 模型,说明该模型在不平衡数据中具有不错的预测能力。

综合来看,朴素贝叶斯的综合表现仅次于 RF 模型和 XGBoost 模型。Logistic 模型具有最高的特异度和较好的精确度;而支持向量机 SVM 在特异度方面也较高,在 F1 评分和 MCC 中与 Logistic 模型相近,这表明Logistic模型与支持向量机SVM在不平衡数据的总体预测能力是相似。值得注意的是,支持向量机SVM在F1分数中高于朴素贝叶斯模型,但是在MCC中却得到了相反的结果,这是因为在F1分数中没有反应真负类(TN),从而导致支持向量机SVM的F1分数产生了虚高的结果。

总之,敏感度、特异度、FPR指标、精确度、NPV指标和F1分数能够表现不同类别的预测性能。然而,他们倾向于高估不平衡数据集的预测能力。精确度能够表明模型对少数类别的真实预测能力,但在事故分析以及以往的文献中应用较少,同时,NPV指标和F1分数同样很少被同时应用评估。此外,准确度确实受到了敏感度、特异度、FPR、精确度和NPV指标的影响,但它容易高估不平衡数据的预测能力。F1评分可以作为谐波平衡指标,它对数据不平衡很敏感,但是也会产生具有误导性的虚高结果,为此,本研究引入考察了混淆矩阵所有元素综合性更强的马修斯相关系数指标,它在一定程度上弥补F1分数的不足。综上所述,XGBoost模型在不平衡数据的模型预测性能中表现稍微好于RF模型。

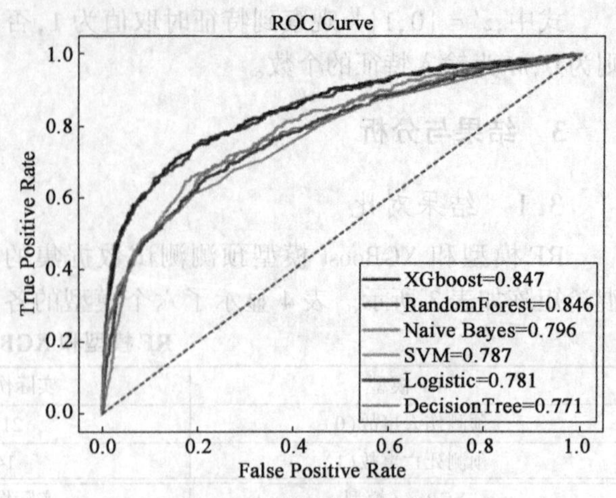

图1　ROC曲线与AUC指标

六种模型的ROC曲线如图2所示。图3中可以看出,决策树、朴素贝叶斯、Logistic回归、支持向量机、RF模型与XGBoost模型的AUC指标均保持在0.75~0.85之间。其中,RF模型和XGBoost模型的AUC值均接近0.85,分别为0.846和0.847,说明这两种模型均能达到较好的预测效果,且两者效果极其相近;XGBoost模型比RF模型的AUC值高0.001,说明XGBoost模型的表现稍微优于RF模型。

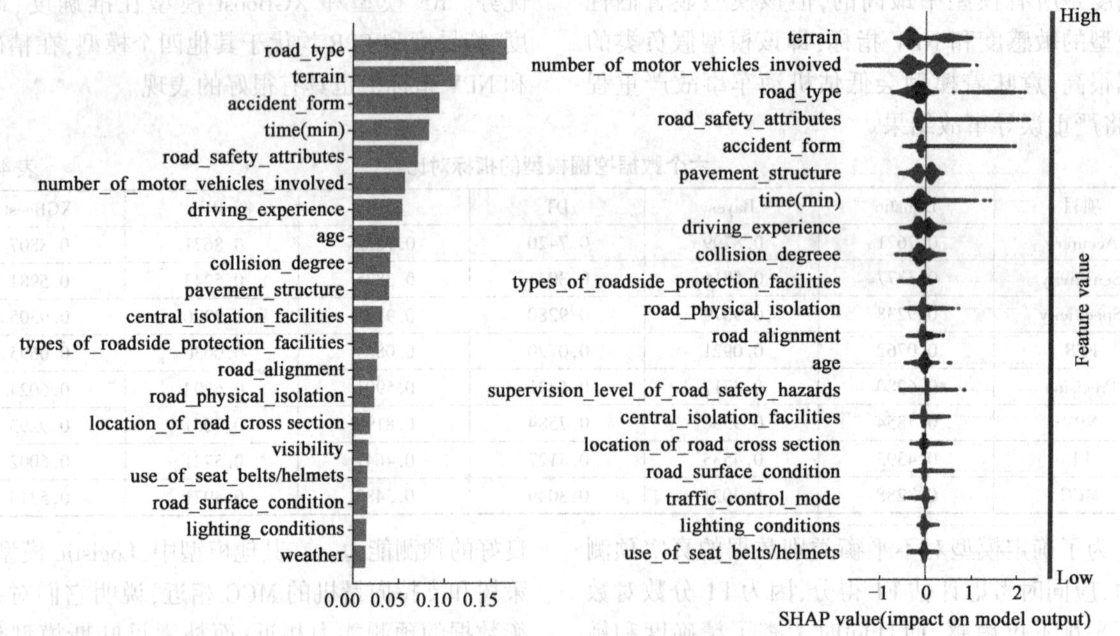

图2　RF和XGBoost模型的变量重要度排序

将变量重要性分别按照模型平均精度下降(Mean Decrease Accuracy)作排序,然后再提取导致严重的死亡事故影响因素做排序。图3左边为RF模型中各变量重要度的排序,图3右边为XGBoost模型利用SHAP解释器输出的各变量重要度的排序。结果表明RF与XGBoost的变量重要性排序结果类似,可以看出两种模型的结果相近,道路类型、道路所处地形、事故时间、涉事机动车数量和道路安全属性是最重要的影响变量,其次,年龄、驾龄、碰撞程度、能见度和佩戴头盔及系安全带对事故严重程度的影响较大。

3.2 特征依赖分析

在图3a)和图3b)中,在 x 轴绘制数据特征的值(主要选取了连续变量的特征),y 轴为该特征的 SHAP 值,由于篇幅有限,本研究选取具有代表性的两个特征图进行分析。

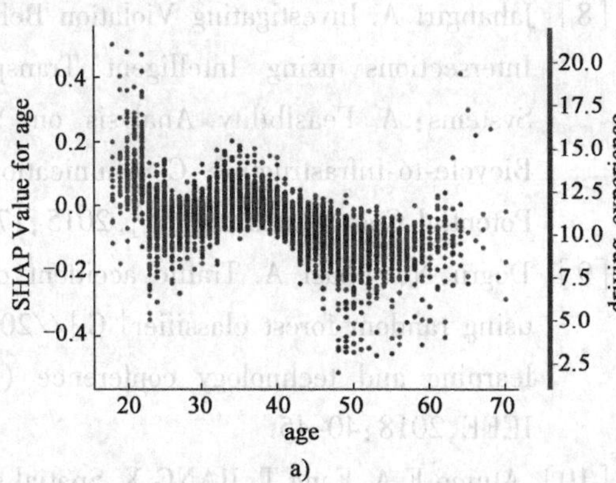

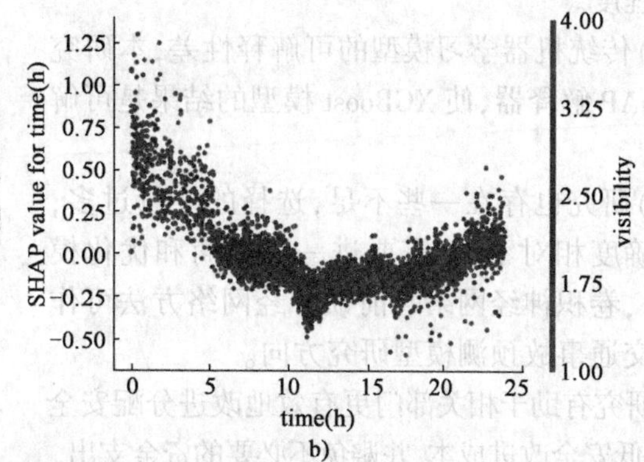

图3 SHAP 依赖分析

图3a)中显示了的驾驶人年龄与驾龄对机动车交通事故严重程度的影响。可以看出,驾驶人年龄在35岁以前,驾龄大部分集中在5年以内,年龄超过40岁以后,驾龄普遍较长。有趣的是,年龄在18~23周岁之间,SHAP值普遍较高(大于0),过了23周岁以后,出现了断崖式的下降(小于0),这意味着年轻且无驾驶经验的驾驶员易导致交通事故,这与以往的研究结果相似[36]。然而,年龄在35周岁附近时,SHAP值有所上升,这可能与驾驶人的社会压力有关。年龄在40周岁以上的驾驶人群体的SHAP值普遍低于0,在此区间的驾驶人驾龄普遍在10年以上,说明随着年龄的增加,具有丰富驾驶经验的驾驶人发生交通事故的概率较低,但也存在极少数高龄驾驶人发生严重交通事故的现象,这同样与以往的研究结果相似[37]。

在图3b)中,本文选择事故时间(单位:h)作为特征来确定能见度从高(200m以上取值为1)到低(50m以下取值为4)的影响。可以看出,大部分能见度较高的时间集中在早晨8点至下午6点之间,意味着在早上至下午的时候,一般能见度也较高,是比较符合当地的天气气候变化的。在这个时间段中,SHAP值均低于0,表明良好的能见度能显著降低机动车交通事故的严重程度。在18点至24点时,SHAP值有明显的提升趋势,超过21点后,SHAP值高于0,而且能见度显著降低,点的密度大幅增加,这说明晚上的机动车交通事故的严重程度较高。在凌晨0点至5点之间,虽然点的密度明显比其他时间段稀疏,但是SHAP值显著高于其他时间段,意味着此时间段的机动车交通事故发生次数虽然较少,但是事故一旦发生,事故死亡概率会很高。

结合事故影响因素排序图与特征依赖分析,对于交通部门来说,首先需要对各类型的驾驶员群体开展系统的安全教育培训,尤其针对年龄在20周岁左右的年轻驾驶员群体,规范全体驾驶员的安全意识,同时加强道路设施的完善。对于行政执法部门来说,需要加大执法力度,合理规范设置道路路段行驶速度,以减少因超速行驶或速度差过大导致的道路交通事故发生。对于广大机动车驾驶员来说,自觉并严格遵守交通规则,加强自身交通安全意识,并尽可能减少夜间不必要的机动车驾驶出行。

4 结语

本文提出了通过八个预测性能指标进行数据挖掘模型的评估,利用2015—2020年陕西省某市的机动车交通安全事故数据,建立了六种数据挖掘模型,以此得到混淆矩阵并计算出各预测性能指标。分析结果表明:

(1)准确度、敏感度、特异度、FPR指标、精确度和NPV指标能够显示出模型在不同类别的预测性能。RF模型和XGBoost模型在大部分测量指标的表现优于其他数据挖掘模型。随机森林模型和XGBoost模型显著地提高了预测准确度,而没有提供额外的错误的正向和反向预测。

(2)综合以上六个指标、F1评分、MCC指标和AUC指标,发现XGBoost模型在机动车交通事故不平衡数据的严重程度预测性能中表现稍微比

RF 模型更好。

(3)针对事故伤亡程度的重要度排序和特征依赖分析,提出相关建议以缓解机动车交通事故的严重程度。

(4)传统机器学习模型的可解释性差,本研究利用 SHAP 解释器,使 XGBoost 模型的结果是可解释的。

(5)研究也存在一些不足,选择的变量过多,模型准确度相对不高,需要进一步精简和优化模型;此外,卷积神经网络与前馈神经网络方法可作为新的交通事故预测模型研究方向。

本研究有助于相关部门更有效地改进分配安全预算,降低安全改进成本,并避免不必要的资金支出。

参考文献

[1] Chiou Y C. An artificial neural network-based expert system for the appraisal of two-car crash accidents[J]. Accident Analysis & Prevention, 2006,38(4):777-785.

[2] Zeng Q, Huang H L. A Stable and Optimized Neural Network Model for Crash Injury Severity Prediction [J]. Accident Analysis and Prevention 2014,73:35-81.

[3] Luca M D, Mauro R, Russo F, et al. Before-after Freeway Accident Analysis Using Clustering Algorithms[J]. Social and Behavioral Science 2011,20:723-731.

[4] Luca M D, Mauro R, Russo F, et al. Road Safety Management Using Bayesian and Clustering Analysis [J]. Social and Behavioral Science 2012,54:1260-1269.

[5] Ona J D, Lopezz Z, Mujalli r, et al. Analysis of Traffic Accident on Rural Highway Using Latent Class Clustering and Bayesian Networks[J]. Accident Analysis and Prevention 2013, 51: 1-10.

[6] Magazzu D, Comelli M, Marinoni A. Are Car Drivers Holding a Motorcycle License Less Responsible for Motorcycle-car Crash Occurrence? A Non-parametric Approach[J]. Accident Analysis and Prevention 2006, 38 (3):65-70.

[7] Kashani A T, Rabieyan R, Besharati M M. A Data Mining Approach to Investigate the Factors Influencing the Crash Severity of Motorcycle Pillion Passengers [J]. Journal of Safety Research 2014,51:93-101.

[8] Jahangiri A. Investigating Violation Behavior at Intersections using Intelligent Transportation Systems: A Feasibility Analysis on Vehicle/Bicycle-to-Infrastructure Communications as a Potential Countermeasure[M]. 2015,170.

[9] Dogru N, Subasi A. Traffic accident detection using random forest classifier[C]//2018 15th learning and technology conference (L&T). IEEE,2018:40-45.

[10] Atumo E A, Fang T, JIANG X. Spatial statistics and random forest approaches for traffic crash hot spot identification and prediction [J]. International journal of injury control and safety promotion,2021:1-10.

[11] Yassin SS. Road accident prediction and model interpretation using a hybrid K-means and random forest algorithm approach [J]. SN Applied Sciences,2020,2(9):1-13.

[12] Meng H L, Wang X H. Expressway crash prediction based on traffic big data. 2018 Int. Conf. Signal Process. Mach. Learn. 1-6.

[13] Mousa S R, Bakhit P R, ISHAK S. An extreme gradient boosting method for identifying the factors contributing to crash/near-crash events: a naturalistic driving study[J]. Canadian Journal of Civil Engineering,2019,46.

[14] Schlögl M, Stütz R, Laaha G, et al. A comparison of statistical learning methods for deriving determining factors of accident occurrence from an imbalanced high resolution dataset[J]. Accident Analysis & Prevention, 2019:134-149.

[15] Parsa A B, Movahedi A, Taghipour H, et al. Toward safer highways, application of XGBoost and SHAP for real-time accident detection and feature analysis [J]. Accident Analysis & Prevention,2020,136:105405.

[16] Mokoatle M, Marivate V, Esiefarienrhe M. Predicting Road Traffic Accident Severity using Decision Trees and Time-Series Calendar

Heatmaps [C]. 2019 IEEE Conference on Sustainable Utilization and Development in Engineering and Technologies (CSUDET). IEEE,2019:11-17.

[17] Shapley L S. 17. A value for n-person games [M]. Princeton University Press,2016.

[18] Lundberg S M,Lee S I. A unified approach to interpreting model predictions [C] // Proceedings of the 31st international conference on neural information processing systems, 2017, 4768-4777.

[19] Mihaita A S,Liu Z,Cai C,et al. Arterial incident duration prediction using a bi-level framework of extreme gradient-tree boosting [J]. arXiv preprint arXiv:1905.12254,2019.

[20] Kumar S. Severity analysis of powered two wheeler traffic accidents in Uttarakhand,India [J]. European Transport Research Review, 2017,9(2):1-10.

[21] Ona J. Analysis of traffic accidents on rural highways using latent class clustering and Bayesian networks[J]. Accident Analysis and Prevention,2013,51(2):1-10.

[22] 李英帅,张旭,王卫杰,等.基于随机森林的电动自行车骑行者事故伤害程度影响因素分析[J].交通运输系统工程与信息,2021,21(01):196-200.

[23] Da Cieslak, Chawla N V. Learning Decision Trees for Unbalanced Data [C]. Machine Learning and Knowledge Discovery in Databases,European Conference,ECML/PKDD 2008, Antwerp, Belgium, September 15-19, 2008, Proceedings,Part I. Springer-Verlag,2008.

[24] Chang LY, Chen W C. Data Mining of Tree-based Models to Analyze Freeway Accident Frequency [J]. Journal of Safety Research, 2005,36(3):65-75.

[25] Pande A,Aty Ma,Das A. A Classification Tree Based Modeling Approach for Segment Related Crashes on Multilane Highways[J]. Journal of Safety Research,2010,41:391-398.

[26] Chang L Y,CHIEN J T. Analysis of Driver Injury Severity in Truck-involved Accidents Using a Non-parametric Classification Tree Model[J]. Safety Science,2013,51:17-22.

[27] Han H, Wang W Y, Mao B H. Borderline-SMOTE:a new over-sampling method in imbalanced data sets learning [C]//International conference on intelligent computing. Springer, Berlin,Heidelberg,2005:878-887.

[28] Zhou X Y, Lu P, Zheng Z J, et al. Accident prediction accuracy assessment for highway-rail grade crossings using random forest algorithm compared with decision tree [J]. Reliability Engineering & System Safety, 2020, 200:106931.

[29] Prajwala T R. A Comparative Study on Decision Tree and Random Forest Using R Tool [J]. International Journal of Advanced Research in Computer and Communication Engineering January,2015.

[30] Rachman A,Chandima R M. Machine Learning Approach for Risk-Based Inspection Screening Assessment[J]. Reliability Engineering & System Safety,2019,185:518-532.

[31] Chen T Q,Guestrin C. Xgboost:a scalable tree boosting system [J]. International Journal of Intelligence Science,2016:785-794.

[32] Zhou X,Lu P,Zheng Z,et al. Accident prediction accuracy assessment for highway-rail grade crossings using random forest algorithm compared with decision tree[J]. Reliability Engineering & System Safety,2020,200:106931.

[33] Matthews B W,Matthews B. Comparison of the predicted and observed secondary structure of T4 phage lysozyme[J]. Biochimica et Biophysica Acta,1975,405(2):442-451.

[34] Boughorbel S, Jarray F, El-anbari M. Optimal classifier for imbalanced data using Matthews Correlation Coefficient metric [J]. PloS one, 2017,12(6):e0177678.

[35] Chicco D, Jurman G. The advantages of the Matthews correlation coefficient (MCC) over F1 score and accuracy in binary classification

evaluation[J]. BMC genomics, 2020, 21(1): 1-13.

[36] 贾云帆,张李斌,段亚妮,等.驾驶人员路怒情绪与驾驶风格及攻击行为相关分析[J]. 中国公共卫生,2016,32(10):1373-1377.

[37] 胡江碧,曹新涛.道路交通事故肇事驾驶员特征分析[J].中国公路学报,2009,22(06):106-110.

1980—2020 年中国交通事故空间分布特征研究

应江龙[1,2] 郭建群[1,2] 蒋仲廉*[1] 初晓[1,2] 余诚强[1,2,3]

(1.武汉理工大学国家水运安全工程技术研究中心;
2.武汉理工大学交通与物流工程学院;3.闽江学院海洋研究院)

摘 要 随着我国交通运输行业的蓬勃发展,交通安全问题得到了更多学者的关注。本文根据EM-DAT(Emergency Events Database)数据库,以发生在1980—2020年间的道路、水路、航空、轨道交通运输重大级以上事故数据为基础,采用重心分析和标准差椭圆统计方法分析交通事故空间特征,研究结果表明:道路交通事故数量占总事故数比例约49.7%,其人口损失空间分布由东南-西北向逐渐向西扩张,发展为东-西方向分布;水路交通事故人口损失由最初的东北-南分布逐渐逆时针旋转,逐步发展为南-北方向分布;航空交通人口损失保持东南-西北方向分布特征,但东西向分布范围逐渐收缩;轨道交通人口损失由东北-西南方向分布逐渐转变为东南-西北方向,且各方向上的分布范围都大幅收缩。本文研究结果可为交通事故防控及应急资源配置提供参考。

关键词 交通事故 空间分布特征 重心分析 标准差椭圆 EM-DAT 数据库

0 引言

交通运输是国民经济基础性、先导性、战略性产业和重要服务业,降低行业风险、避免发生重大事故一直是行业和学术界关注的重点问题之一。Li 等[1]针对城市内机动车碰撞事故提出了一种基于地理信息系统(Geographic Information System, GIS)的贝叶斯方法,并通过此方法对德克萨斯州哈里斯县五年内的汽车碰撞事故数据开展分析,识别了潜在高碰撞风险的路段。Acharya 等[2]研究了韩国近岸水域水上交通事故空间分布,通过GIS直观展示了安全事故的空间分布情况,确定了事故高发区和安全缺陷区。Huang 等[3]基于全球综合船舶信息系统(Global Integrated Shipping Information System, GISIS)中的海上伤亡和事故(Marine Casualties and Incidents, MCI)数据,分析了2002—2011年间的水路交通事故空间分布,利用GIS实现了结果可视化分析,研究结果表明:大约51.1%的水路交通事故发生在距离大陆25mile❶范围内,62.2%的事故发生在距离大陆50mile范围内。Nezval 等[4]使用核密度估计(Kernel Density Estimation, KDE)方法分析了捷克境内火车与野生动物碰撞数据,最终识别出了208个碰撞热点,并通过风险参数对上述热点进行了排序,为铁路部门完善、提升安全防护措施奠定了基础。作为免费开放的灾害数据库,EM-DAT数据库得到了国内外学者的广泛关注。Shen 等[5]利用EM-DAT数据库记录的技术灾难相关数据,建立了风险预测模型,开展了全球各国技术灾难人口损失、受伤害人数、经济损失等预测和验证,结果整体符合预期。目前,针对交通运输事故时空分布的相关研究,通常采用政府公报或者商业数据库中的数据,无法在保证基础数据的完整性和一致性,且获取难度较大;EM-DAT数据库在数据标准化及开

1. 基金项目:国家自然科学基金项目(52071250, 51709220),中央高校基本科研业务费专项资金(2018IVB078, 2019III096CG)资助。

❶1mile = 1609.344m。

放获取中具有显著优势，使得长时距、大范围、多种运输方式的交通事故空间分布及演化规律研究成为可能。本文基于 EM-DAT 数据库中记录的中国交通运输领域重大级以上事故相关数据，采用 ArcGIS 软件开展交通事故标准差椭圆分析，揭示交通事故时空分布特征，为不同类型交通事故防控及应急资源配置提供参照。

1 数据来源和处理

1.1 数据来源

EM-DAT 数据库是由世界卫生组织和灾后流行病研究中心于 1988 年共同创建，面向公众免费开放[6]。EM-DAT 数据库中的数据来源于联合国、各国政府、国际联合会、世界银行、保险公司等，数据库仅收录人口损失 10 人以上或受灾难影响人数 100 人以上或者使国家宣布紧急状态、呼吁国际援助的灾难事件；其记录的灾难类型包括自然灾难、技术性灾难、多种因素造成的复杂灾难等。其中，技术性灾难数据中包含了工业、运输和其他三类。运输类的灾难数据涵盖道路、水路、航空、轨道交通四类，共记录全球范围内共计 6040 条事故，最早的事故记录可以追溯到 1906 年，但是由于时间较早，1900—1980 年间的数据可信度不高[7]；对于 1980 年以后的数据，由于设置了较为严格的筛选标准，且国内对于重大级以上事故通常有可靠的官方新闻报道及大额保险理赔流程，使得这部分数据可信度较高且覆盖面相对完整。

1.2 数据处理

(1)重心分析

地理学常引入物理学中的“重心”概念，对区域中某种要素进行空间分析。通过计算不同的时间段的重心坐标，可刻画要素的空间聚集特征及移动轨迹；重心分析法在经济学、人口与粮食问题等领域的空间特征研究中有广泛的应用。对于某一大区域中包含若干重心坐标已知的小区域，大区域重心坐标计算方法定义如下[8]：

$$\begin{cases} \overline{x_i} = \dfrac{\sum_{j=1}^{n} x_j w_j}{\sum_{j=1}^{n} w_j} \\ \overline{y_i} = \dfrac{\sum_{j=1}^{n} y_j w_j}{\sum_{j=1}^{n} w_j} \end{cases} \tag{1}$$

式中：(x_i, y_i)——子区域重心坐标；

w_i——该子区域对应的要素值；

$(\overline{x_i}, \overline{y_i})$——大区域重心坐标。

(2)标准差椭圆

标准差椭圆是一种对数据的方向和分布进行分析的方法。椭圆中心表示所有要素的中心位置，长半轴表示要素分布方向，短半轴代表要素分布范围。长半轴与短半轴之间的差值越大，代表要素分布的方向性越明显，反之则越不明显[9]。另外，当短半轴的长度越大，说明要素分布范围广泛，离散程度高。标准差椭圆中心计算如下[10-11]：

$$\begin{cases} x = \sqrt{\dfrac{\sum_{i=1}^{n} (x_i - X)^2}{n}} \\ y = \sqrt{\dfrac{\sum_{i=1}^{n} (y_i - Y)^2}{n}} \end{cases} \tag{2}$$

式中：(x_i, y_i)——各要素的坐标；

(X, Y)——区域重心坐标。

椭圆的转角代表数据的分布方向，其计算如式(3)所示：

$$\tan\theta = \frac{\left(\sum_{i=1}^{n} x_i'^2 - \sum_{i=1}^{n} y_i'^2\right) + \sqrt{\left(\sum_{i=1}^{n} x_i'^2 - \sum_{i=1}^{n} y_i'^2\right)^2 + 4\left(\sum_{i=1}^{n} x_i' y_i'\right)^2}}{2\sum_{i=1}^{n} x_i' y_i'} \tag{3}$$

其中，$x_i' = x_i - X$，$y_i' = y_i - Y$。椭圆的长、短半轴计算表达式如下：

$$\delta_x = \sqrt{\frac{\sum_{i=1}^{n} (x_i' \cos\theta - y_i' \sin\theta)^2}{n}} \tag{4}$$

$$\delta_y = \sqrt{\frac{\sum_{i=1}^{n} (x_i' \sin\theta + y_i' \cos\theta)^2}{n}} \tag{5}$$

本文拟采用重心分析，刻画 1980—2020 年间中国交通事故的空间聚集特征以及移动轨迹，同时结合标准差椭圆开展事故分布方向、分布范围和离散程度研究，并利用 ArcGIS 10.2 软件实现研究结果的可视化分析，直观呈现 1980—2020 年间中国四类交通运输事故的空间分布特征。

2 交通事故空间分布特征

根据 EM-DAT 数据库，1980—2020 年期间在

中国境内共发生重大级以上交通事故292起,造成人口损失11796人,其中道路交通事故145起(占比约49.7%)、造成人口损失3638人,水路交通事故87起(占比约29.8%)、造成人口损失4226人,轨道交通事故28起(占比约9.6%)、造成人口损失1643人,航空交通事故32起(占比约10.9%)、造成人口损失2289人,各类交通事故的发生次数及人口损失空间分布如图1所示。由图可知:道路交通事故与水路交通事故覆盖的省级行政区基本一致,主要集中在经济发展迅速、交通运输网络较发达的华中、华东、华南地区。航空运输平均单次事故人口损失约71人,位居四类交通运输方式之首,其分布范围较分散,区别于其他三类。轨道交通是所有交通方式中重大级以上事故发生次数最少的,同时,其分布的省级行政区域数量也是最少的。

本文以10年为时间间隔,分别计算了不同交通事故类型的标准差椭圆及其重心,结合其时空变化特征,可揭示交通事故空间分布规律及演化特征。

2.1 道路交通事故空间演化趋势

道路交通事故人口损失的重心落在华中地区(27.990N~32.119N,108.582E~114.039E)。道路交通事故人口损失最初呈现东南-西北向分布格局,之后逆时针旋转发展为东北-西南向分布格局发展,后来又向顺时针方向旋转重新回到东南-西北向分布的格局,但较第一个十年(1980—1990年)而言,总体呈现逆时针旋转趋势。在最后一个十年(2010—2020年)内,椭圆依旧向逆时针方向旋转呈现接近东-西向分布的格局。根据标准差椭圆计算结果,道路交通事故数据离散程度先增大后减少,最后再增大;道路交通事故人口损失的分布格局在南-北向变化不大,但呈现逐渐向西发展的趋势。

2.2 水路交通事故空间演化趋势

与道路交通事故空间分布相似,水路交通事故人口损失的重心在华中地区,但其东西向跨度明显更小,重心更加集中(29.133N~31.618N,112.886E~116.058E)。在1980—1990年间,水路交通事故人口损失呈现出东北-西南向分布格局;1990—1999年间,空间分布格局呈逆时针旋转,南北向的分布格局得到加强;在2000—2010年间,顺时针转旋转角度增大,东西向分布格局重新得到加强;在2010—2020年间,水路交通事故人口损失呈现南-北向分布格局。根据标准差椭圆计算结果,水路交通事故数据离散程度总体呈现逐渐减小的趋势;水路交通事故人口损失分布格局在南北向有所收缩,同时也有向西逐渐扩张的趋势。

2.3 航空交通事故空间演化趋势

航空交通事故人口损失重心落在湖南、江西、浙江三省,与前两类交通方式相比,其南北向的跨度减小,但东西向的跨度有较大程度的增加,分布较为分散(27.536N~29.027N,113.466E~118.887E)。在1980—1990年间,重大级以上航空事故人口损失呈现出东南-西北向分布格局;在之后的1990—2000年间,标准差椭圆顺时针旋转,南-北向的分布格局得到加强;2000—2010年间,标准差椭圆进一步顺时针旋转,同时东西向分布格局大幅削弱,呈接近南-北向分布的格局;在2010—2021年间,标准差椭圆逆向旋转,回到东南-西北的格局,相较于1980—1990年,南北向有所扩张,东西向则大幅缩减。在1980—2020年间,航空交通事故人口损失标准差椭圆的长短轴之比一直呈现增大趋势,说明数据的离散程度不断减小,方向性特征愈发明显;航运交通事故人口损失在东西向的分布格局有所收缩,而南北向呈现扩张趋势。

2.4 轨道交通事故空间演化趋势

轨道交通重大级以上事故人口损失的重心分别落在湖南、安徽、江苏、浙江四省行政区境内,是四类交通运输事故中最为分散的(27.401N~34.301N,112.531E~119.930E)。轨道交通事故人口损失在最初1980—1999年间呈现东北-西南向分布格局;在1990—2000年间,分布格局逆时针旋转,南北向的分布格局得到加强而东西向减弱;在2000—2010和2010—2020年间,标准差椭圆依旧逆时针旋转,呈现接近南-北向的分布格局,但在东西向、南北向的分布范围大幅减小。根据标准差椭圆计算结果,轨道交通事故数据离散程度先增大后减少,随后再次增大;轨道交通事故空间分布范围呈现减小的趋势,其空间分布方向逐渐发展为南-北向(表1)。

1980—2020 年间交通事故重心及标准差椭圆参数　　表 1

交通方式	年　份	重心经度	重心纬度	重心移动距离（km）	长半轴长度（km）	短半轴长度（km）	椭圆转角（°）
道路	1980—1989	114.040	30.563	0	796.1872	573.2932	155.717
	1990—1999	111.759	27.990	276.94	739.235	712.2763	86.33053
	2000—2009	108.582	29.728	359.46	1053.563	826.9476	112.1763
	2010—2021	112.056	32.119	397.09	976.0816	855.8673	94.83596
水路	1980—1989	113.728	29.675	0	1405.616	725.8265	36.99611
	1990—1999	116.058	29.133	260.32	782.0408	660.0444	30.57388
	2000—2009	113.240	31.618	333.80	844.2719	763.8082	77.80432
	2010—2021	112.887	29.916	83.89	426.888	309.9276	5.459031
航空	1980—1989	113.467	27.710	0	961.0482	815.7234	104.8593
	1990—1999	114.116	27.536	72.59	902.6493	716.6398	130.2258
	2000—2009	118.888	29.027	535.72	1000.863	271.0326	160.9814
	2010—2021	116.142	28.160	308.56	1284.661	236.0273	131.9451
轨道	1980—1989	112.531	28.300	0	843.9791	424.684	57.67664
	1990—1999	115.981	32.265	424.03	1066.954	684.7255	37.58081
	2000—2009	118.604	34.302	309.57	685.2449	154.4732	167.8857
	2010—2021	119.930	27.402	402.79	365.0351	240.2901	162.2243

3　结语

安全可靠是发展现代化高质量国家综合立体交通网的重要特征。受环境因素、基础设施条件、人因等多重因素影响，不同交通方式的事故数据呈现出复杂的时空特征，受到学术界的广泛关注。本文基于 EM-DAT 数据库记录的 1980—2020 年重大级以上交通事故数据，采用 ArcGIS 10.2 开展事故数据标准差椭圆、重心分布计算和分析，研究结果总结如下：

1980—2020 年期间在中国境内共发生重大级以上交通事故 292 起，其中道路交通事故数量最多，占比约为 49.7%；轨道事故数量最少，占比约为 9.6%。道路交通事故人口损失空间分布由东南-西北向分布格局逐渐发展为东-西向格局，数据离散程度总体呈增大趋势；水路交通事故人口损失空间分布由东北-南分布格局逐渐逆时针旋转发展为南-北向分布格局，数据离散程度总体呈增大趋势；航空交通事故人口损失空间分布始终保持东南-西北向分布格局，但东西向分布范围逐渐收缩，数据离散程度呈减小趋势；轨道交通事故人口损失空间分布由东北-西南向分布格局逐渐转变为东南-西北向、东西向、南北向的分布范围大幅收缩，数据离散程度呈减小趋势。

通过对长时序交通事故数据空间分布特征研究，可进一步揭示不同交通方式事故数据演化趋势和局部变化，为交通事故防控和应急资源配置优化提供参考。

参考文献

[1] Li L, Zhe L, Sui D Z. A GIS-based Bayesian approach for analyzing spatial-temporal patterns of intra-city motor vehicle crashes [J]. Journal of Transport Geography, 2007, 15(4): 274-285.

[2] Acharya T D, Yoo K W, LEE D H. GIS-based Spatio-temporal Analysis of Marine Accidents Database in the Coastal Zone of Korea [J]. Journal of Coastal Research, 2017, 79 (S1): 114-118.

[3] Huang D Z, Hu H, Li Y Z. Spatial Analysis of Maritime Accidents Using the Geographic Information System [J]. Transportation Research Record, 2013, 232(6): 39-44.

[4] Nezval V, Bil M. Spatial analysis of wildlife-train collisions on the Czech rail network [J]. Applied Geography, 2020, 125: 102304-102311

[5] Shen G Q, Hwang S N. Revealing global hot spots of technological disasters: 1900-2013 [J]. Journal of Risk Research, 2018, 21 (3): 361-393.

[6] CRED 2022. History. https://emdat. be/

history. [Accessed 2022 Jan 8]

[7] 司瑞洁,温家洪,尹占娥,等. EM-DAT 灾难数据库概述及其应用研究 [J]. 科技导报,2007(06):60-67.

[8] 吴金汝,陈芳,陈晓玲. 1900～2018 年全球自然灾害时空演变特征与相关性研究 [J]. 长江流域资源与环境,2021,30(04):976-991.

[9] 曹芳东,黄震方,余凤龙,等. 国家级风景名胜区旅游效率空间格局动态演化及其驱动机制 [J]. 地理研究,2014,33(06):1151-1166.

[10] Zhang X, Zhang B, Yao Y, et al. Dynamics and climatic drivers of evergreen vegetation in theQinling-Daba Mountains of China [J]. Ecological Indicators, 2022, 136(108625).

[11] Yuill R S. The standard deviational ellipse; an updated tool for spatial description [J]. Geografiska Annaler: Series B, Human Geography, 1971, 53(1):28-39.

城市道路畸形交叉口安全性评价与优化设计

金海英*

(武汉理工大学交通与物流学院)

摘　要　畸形交叉口随着城市道路网的发展逐渐显示出运行效率低和通行安全性低的缺陷,为了城市道路网的进一步发展,对畸形交叉口的安全评价与优化设计有着重要的现实意义。本文提出了基于几何设计、车流运作和交通控制三个方面的十二个评价指标,并通过查阅规范对各项指标按照优秀、良好、及格、差依次划分为 A、B、C、D 四个等级,从而构建了交叉口新型的安全评价指标体系。以北川路—粮食路—保康路交叉口为例,运用评价体系对交叉口现状和改善方案进行评价。评价结果显示,采用优化设计方案后,该交叉口的实际物理区面积与理论物理区面积的比值更低,路口偏角也更小,交叉口看起来更加规整,路权明确清晰,更能让驾驶员行车规范,且行车舒适性好。

关键词　城市道路畸形交叉口　安全性评价　优化设计　多路交叉口

0　引言

在实际建设中,由于地形条件受限、规划设计不当以及历史和社会等因素的制约,我国城市道路系统中存在一些畸形交叉口,这些畸形交叉口形态各异,存在的问题各具特色。

Shebeeb 和 Ousama[1] 从安全性和效率的角度研究了左转专用车道的设置条件并选取了评价指标,证明了在一定条件下设置左转专用车道可以有效地管理进入交叉路口的左转交通。Al-Salman 和 SalteRJ[2] 根据平面交叉口中右转车流的交通特性,提出了右转车流的通行能力与延误模型,并根据不同的右转车道路面结构构建了交通安全和效率方面的评价指标体系。孙林[3] 基于交通冲突技术选取了交叉口危险度为评价指标来构建交叉口交通安全评价模型并提出评价方法,提出了可行的改善措施,并通过实例证明改善后措施能提高交叉口安全性。侯丽婷[4] 通过对平面交叉口进行虚拟视景实验,建立了交叉口安全评价模型。汪莹[5] 研究了平面交叉口的安全性评价,探讨并建立交叉口安全性评价指标体系和安全评价模型。

国内对于交叉口安全性评价与优化设计所采用的评价方法比较单一,缺乏全面客观的评价体系,特别是对于畸形交叉口。因此,如何针对畸形道路交叉口进行科学合理的优化设计并评估其安全性是一个亟需解决的问题。

1　城市畸形交叉口现状

1.1　畸形交叉口交通特性

1.1.1　行驶距离

交叉口相邻道路交角越小车辆行驶的距离则越长,车辆通行的时间也就越长,大大增加了该方向的车流与其他方向车流的交叉、冲突的几率,从而影响到驾驶员的行车安全。

1.1.2 行驶车流

畸形交叉口的占地面积比较大,存在没有有效利用的区域。如果交叉口内没有进行合理的渠化和流向引导,容易导致车辆在交叉口内随意行驶,车流混乱,降低了交叉口的通行效率和增加安全隐患。

1.1.3 视距

畸形交叉口相邻道路交角多为小于75°的锐角,由于交叉角度较小,导致交叉口内的视距不良,容易使驾驶员在行驶的时候产生视觉上的盲区。视距有限,反应时间变长,均有可能导致事故发生的概率变大。

1.1.4 流向选择

当交叉口相交道路过多,且相交道路的横断面类型比较相似,对于不熟悉路况和注意力不集中的驾驶员容易因为车流转向特征不明显或者流向指示设施不完善的情况下选择错误的出口道,使得车辆绕行成本增加。

1.1.5 车辆转弯

畸形交叉口内路缘石转角半径较大时,由于视线良好,右转车辆转弯时容易车速过高,安全风险较大;路缘石转角半径较小时,对于大型货车、公交车来说,因其车辆实际宽度和车辙宽度差距比较大,转弯的时候需要占用更多的道路空间,若是两个冲突方向的车辆同时转弯的话,容易导致交叉口出现"死锁"现象。

1.2 畸形交叉口安全影响因素分析

从交叉口规划设计来看,安全风险主要来源于几何设计、渠化设计、交通控制设计等。

(1)几何设计因素

部分畸形交叉口设计参数一般采用规范下限值,常存在车行道布置不合理、车道渐变段长度过短、车辆轨迹设计不合理、交叉口内纵坡度偏大、转弯半径比较小、视距视区不足等问题,这些问题对于交叉口行车安全有较大影响。

(2)渠化设计因素

部分畸形交叉口渠化不合理、不完善或没有进行渠化,或渠化设施破损而没有修复,或进出口车道数不匹配。

(3)交通控制设计因素

交通标线施划不足或不合理使机动车、非机动车、行人路权不明确造成运行混乱,信号相位设置不合理使车流发生冲突造成交通拥堵。

2 安全性评价指标

安全性评价是交叉口方案设计中的一个十分重要的环节,如何对交叉口安全进行全面、客观、有效的评价,并建立交叉口安全综合评价体系,对提高整个城市道路网的安全水平有重要意义。对交叉口安全风险有影响的因素比较多,本文将从几何设计、车流运作、交通控制三方面选取评价指标,通过构建的评价指标体系对设计方案进行评价,具体见表1。

交叉口安全评价指标评价等级标准 表1

评价指标	评价内容	评价等级			
		A	B	C	D
几何设计	物理区构型	A2/A1 1~1.2	A2/A1 1.2~1.5	A2/A1 1.5~2	A2/A1 >2
	交叉路口交角	>75°	60°~75°	45°~60°	<45°
	道路功能阶差	0	±1	=2	>2
	路口偏角	<3°	3°~5°	5°~10°	>10°
	路口偏移量	偏移小于1个车道	偏移1~2个车道	偏移2~3个车道	偏移大于三个车道
车流运作	相邻交叉口间距	主集散道路>300m 次集散道路>220m	主集散道路250~300m 次集散道路180~220m	主集散道路200~250m 次集散道路150~180m	主集散道路<200m 次集散道路<150m
	车道配置	各方向有专用车道	部分方向有专用车道	无专用车道	机非混行
	视距视区状况	视距三角形内无任何视线障碍物,通视条件优秀	有0.2~0.6m高障碍物,通视条件良好	有超过0.6m高的视线障碍物,通视条件一般	有超过1.2m的视线障碍物,通视条件差

续上表

评价指标	评价内容	评价等级			
		A	B	C	D
	标志标线(空间路权)	突起路标+双白线	突起路标+单白线	白线清晰	白线不清晰
交通控制	通行优先权	有信号控制,设置合理,行人等候时间短	有信号控制,设置不够合理,行人等候时间长	固定优先权:有停让标志或者全停标志	全无控制
	执法系统	白天有交警指挥,且设有电子执法	白天有交警指挥,无电子执法	有电子执法,无交警	既无交警指挥,也无电子执法
	导流设施(机动车左转、行人过街)	有左转导流线、路侧等候岛	有左转导流线、无等候岛	无左转导流线、有等候岛	都没有

注:A为优,B为良,C为及格,D为不及格;A1为交叉口理论物理区,A2为交叉口实际物理区。

2.1　物理区构型

如图1所示,A2表示交叉口的实际物理区(停止线围起来的阴影部分)面积,A1表示交叉口的理论物理区面积,根据A2/A1的比值可以来判断交叉口设计的合理性、安全隐患的大小,通常认为A2/A1的值在1.1~1.2之间是比较合理的。若A2/A1愈大,交叉口内的安全风险就愈高[6]。

2.2　交叉路口交角

一般而言,对于交叉角度,美国联邦公路管理局(FHWA)建议平面交叉的交角以直角(或接近直角)最好,斜交时其交角宜大于75°,不宜小于60°[6],国内《城市道路工程设计规范》(CJJ 37—2012)规定,不得出现交叉角度小于70°(特殊困难时为45°)的斜交交叉口。交叉角度过小会出现视野被遮挡等问题出现,阻碍车辆以及行人的通行。

2.3　相交道路功能位阶差

阶差是指两条相交的道路交通功能位阶的差值[6],道路按交通功能可划分成八大阶层,要形成合理的路网结构两条相交道路交通功能阶差应小于或等于2。

2.4　路口偏角

路口偏角是指交叉口道路中心线的偏移角度,如图2所示,路口偏角的合理范围应该是在3°~5°之间,如果偏角太大,视距、视区可能不够,会影响驾驶员对路口情况的判断,从而产生安全隐患。

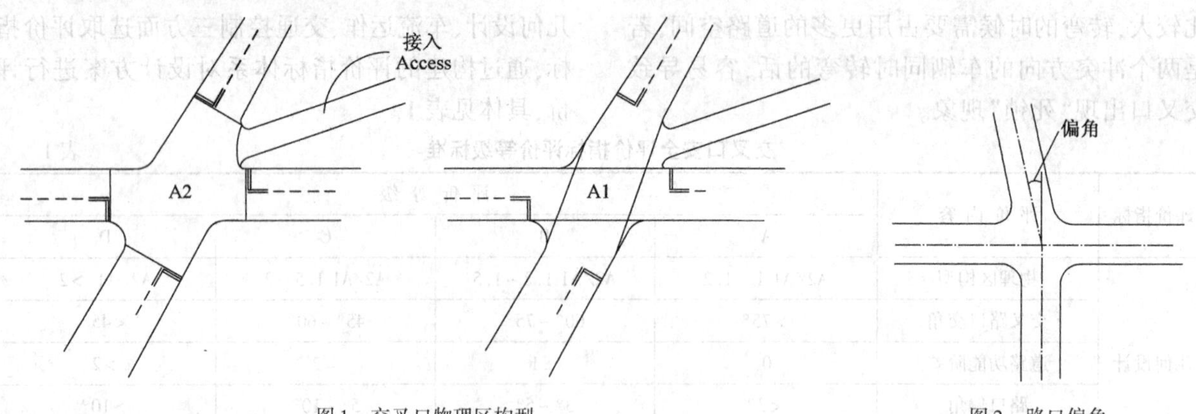

图1　交叉口物理区构型　　图2　路口偏角

2.5　路口偏移量

路口偏移量是指相对的两条道路的中心线的偏移距离,如图3所示,W表示路口的偏移量,当偏移量比较小时,驾驶员能清楚看到对面路口的情况,行车顺畅且比较安全;当偏移量比较大时,某一道路的进口道与对面道路的出口道偏移得很远,驾驶员看不清对面路口情况,行车轨迹也比较复杂,行车安全风险高。

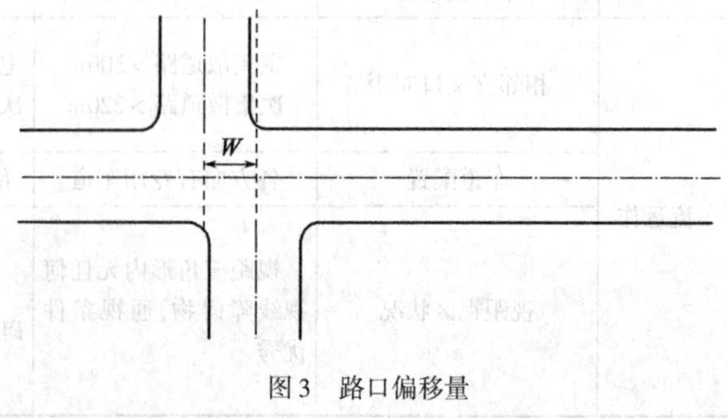

图3　路口偏移量

路口偏移量可根据车道的偏移个数来划分等级。

2.6 相邻交叉口间距

根据文献《公路交叉口合理间距研究》[7]和文献《交织区交通特性的微观仿真研究》[8]中的数据及分析结果，集散公路和地方公路信号交叉口的最小间距取值如表2所示。

集散公路和地方公路信号交叉口最小间距 表2

速度(km/h)	20	30	40	50	60	70	80	90	100
上游段长度(m)	73	95	121	152	187	226	269	317	369
下游段长度(m)	24	42	65	93	126	163	204	251	301
平稳段长度(m)	50	75	100	140	180	220	250	250	250
间距计算值(m)	147	212	286	385	493	609	723	818	920
间距采用值(m)	150	210	290	390	490	610	720	820	920

注：主集散道路速度取40km/h，次集散道路速度取30km/h，可根据本表划分等级。

2.7 其他指标

车道配置(专用路权/共享路权)根据路权分配合理程度划分等级；视距视区状况根据视距三角形内是否有障碍物、障碍物的高度和通视条件来划分等级；标志标线(空间路权)根据是否设有突起路标、白线设置情况来划分等级；通行优先权根据有无信号控制、配时方案设置是否合理来划分等级；执法系统根据有无交警指挥、是否配备电子执法系统划分等级；导流设施(机动车左转、行人过街)根据是否设置左转导流线、行人路侧等候岛来划分等级。

3 实例分析

位于武穴市的北川路—粮食路—保康路交叉口属于典型的六路畸形交叉口，通过畸形交叉口的道路几何条件、交通运行情况等数据，在对交叉口现状问题分析的基础上提出改善措施，并拟定改善方案，以期达到增加通行效率、降低交通事故发生概率、维护交通安全等目的。

3.1 现状分析

3.1.1 交叉口渠化分析

北川路—粮食路—保康路为六路畸形交叉口，现状图如图4所示，车道配置情况如表3所示。

3.1.2 交通流量调查

在本次调查中，对该交叉口早晚高峰的高峰小时流量进行了调查，具体数据如表4所示，从表中可以看出，该交叉口西进口早晚高峰流量最大，其次是南进口，东进口和北进口交通量相对较少。

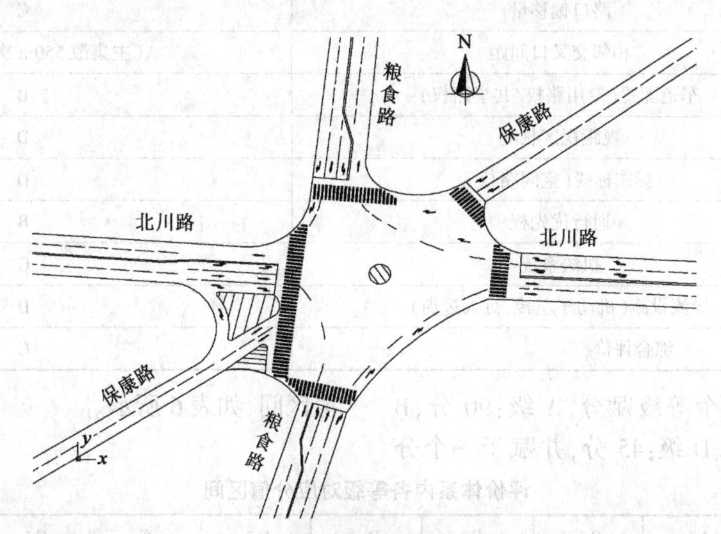

图4 交叉口现状图

北川路—粮食路—保康路交叉口车道配置情况　　表3

进口方向	东进口	南进口	西进口	北进口	东北进口	西南进口
道路名称	北川路	粮食路	北川路	粮食路	保康路	保康路
入口车道数	2机	3机	3机	3机	2机	0
出口车道数	2机	1机	1机	1机	0	2机
左转专用车道	0	1	1	1	0	0
直行左转车道	1	0	0	0	0	0
直行专用车道	0	1	1	2	0	0
直行右转车道	0	0	0	0	0	0
右转专用车道	1	1	1	1	2	0

北川路—粮食路—保康路交叉口早晚高峰高峰小时交通量　　表4

地　点	方　向	早高峰高峰小时流量(pcu/h)	晚高峰高峰小时流量(pcu/h)
北川路与粮食路、保康路交叉口(老人民医院)	东进口	136	200
	西进口	476	392
	南进口	382	292
	北进口	106	50

3.1.3　交叉口存在的主要问题分析

通过分析畸形交叉口现状,发现存在道路夹角过小、视距不足、进出口车道不匹配、出口道方向不明确和道路标线破损严重等几何条件问题以及行车轨迹混乱、单向交通路段存在逆行现象、交叉口清空时间不足、信号相位利用不充分等交通运行问题。

3.1.4　安全水平评价

依据第2章内容的各评价指标,得出该交叉口的安全性评价结果如表5所示。

北川路—粮食路—保康路现状安全性评价结果　　表5

评价指标	评价内容	现　状
几何设计	物理区构型	D(5.2)
	交叉路口交角	C(49°)
	道路功能阶差	B
	路口偏角	D(11°)
	路口偏移量	C
车流运作	相邻交叉口间距	A(主集散550m次集散270m)
	车道配置(专用路权/共享路权)	B
	视距视区状况	D
交通控制	标志标线(空间路权)	D
	通行优先权	B
	执法系统	C
	导流设施(机动车左转、行人过街)	D
综合评价		C

对A、B、C、D四个等级赋分,A级:90分、B级:75分、C级:60分、D级:45分,并赋予一个分值区间,如表6所示。

评价体系内各等级对应分值区间　　表6

划分等级	A	A⁻	B⁺	B	B⁻	C⁺	C	C⁻	D⁺	D
分值区间	90	90~85	85~80	80~75	75~70	70~65	65~60	60~55	55~50	50~45

计算该交叉路口总得分之后求平均值,得总分720,平均值为60,所以该路口等级为C。

3.2 优化方案

交叉口优化设计方案如图5所示。

具体改善措施:

(1)拓宽进口道,保持出口道两车道,除西向的北川路进口道右转车辆受信号灯控制,其余进口道右转车辆改为不受信号控制行驶,信号相位与原来相同。

(2)南北向粮食路与东向北川路进口道前移,并增画左转导流线,优化行车动线顺畅程度,并增加相应的路面指示箭头,引导驾驶员方向。

(3)增设7处行人安全岛,将右转车辆从空间上进行分离,规范右转车辆行驶轨迹,并增设减速让行标志标线,保护行人过街。

(4)基于东北向的保康路的车流量不大,由原来两车道行驶改为一车道行驶,另一车道设置路边停车,为了使进出口车道数匹配西南向的保康路直行进口道由两条改为一条,规范行车轨迹。

(5)在西向北川路安全岛前适当位置设置右转路口指示标志,避免需要右转进粮食路的车辆提前右转而进入了保康路。

(6)在东北口保康路进口道处增设抓拍摄像头,借此严禁机动车及非机动车逆向驶入单向行驶的保康路。

3.3 优化方案评价

对交叉口进行改善后,交叉口评价指标对比如表7所示。

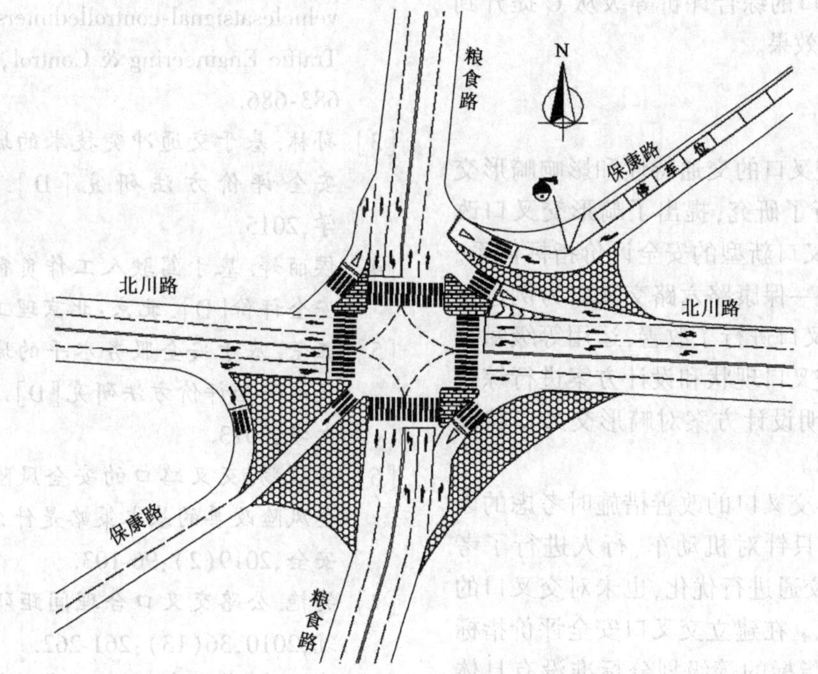

图5 交叉口改善图

北川路—粮食路—保康路现状与改善方案安全性评价结果 表7

评价指标	评价内容	现状	设计方案
几何设计	物理区构型	D(5.2)	A(1.1)
	交叉路口交角	C(49°)	C(49°)
	道路功能阶差	B	B
	路口偏角	D(11°)	A(1°)
	路口偏移量	C	A
车流运作	相邻交叉口间距	A(主集散550m 次集散270m)	A(主集散550m 次集散270m)
	车道配置(专用路权/共享路权)	B	A
	视距视区状况	D	B

续上表

评价指标	评价内容	现状	设计方案
交通控制	标志标线(空间路权)	D	C
	通行优先权	B	A
	执法系统	C	C
	导流设施(机动车左转、行人过街)	D	A
综合评价		C	B⁺

根据上文等级赋分求得设计方案总分为 960，平均值为 80，故等级为 B⁺。

设计方案相较于现状路口，交叉口的实际物理区面积与理论物理区面积的比值更低，路口偏角也更小，交叉口看起来更加规整，每条道路各方向的车流都设有专用车道，并设有左转导流线，路权明确清晰，更能让驾驶员行车规范，且行车舒适性好。最终，使路口的综合评价等级从 C 提升到 B⁺，有一定的改进效果。

4　结语

本文对畸形交叉口的交通特性和影响畸形交叉口安全因素进行了研究，提出了畸形交叉口改善方法，构建了交叉口新型的安全评价指标体系。以北川路—粮食路—保康路六路交叉口为例进行了实例分析，对交叉口进行了改善，运用等级赋分的方法对该六路交叉口现状和设计方案进行综合评价，评价结果表明设计方案对畸形交叉口状况有一定的改善作用。

但本文对畸形交叉口的改善措施时考虑的因素不够全面，重点只针对机动车、行人进行了考虑，未对非机动车交通进行优化，也未对交叉口的信号配时进行优化。在建立交叉口安全评价指标体系时，部分评价指标的等级划分标准没有具体的论文和规范作为理论支撑，且在构建评价指标体系时，未说明各评价指标的重要性程度，也没有对指标之间的关联度进行分析，希望能在今后的相关研究进一步深化。

参考文献

[1] Shebeeb, Ousama. Safety and efficiency for exclusive left-turn lanes at signalized intersections [J]. Institute of Transportation Engineers,1995,65(7):50-56.

[2] Al-Salman, Salter R J. Controlofright-turning-vehiclesatsignal-controlledintersections [J]. Traffic Engineering & Control,1974,115(15):683-686.

[3] 孙林. 基于交通冲突技术的城市交叉口交通安全评价方法研究[D]. 陕西:长安大学,2015.

[4] 侯丽婷. 基于驾驶人工作负荷的道路交叉口安全评价[D]. 北京:北京理工大学,2016.

[5] 汪莹. 基于安全服务水平的城市道路交叉口交通安全评价方法研究[D]. 南京:南京林业大学,2013.

[6] 徐耀赐. 交叉路口的安全风险因素有哪些安全风险改善的基本策略是什么?[J]. 汽车与安全,2019(2):96-103.

[7] 吴艳. 公路交叉口合理间距研究[J]. 山西建筑,2010,36(13):261-262.

[8] 陈小鸿,肖海峰. 交织区交通特性的微观仿真研究[J]. 中国公路学报,2001,14:88-91.

数据聚合方法对快速路事故预测影响分析

万 壮[1,2] 张 晖*[1,2] 侯宁昊[1,2] 郭雯慧[1,2] 刘嘉丽[1,2]
(1.武汉理工大学智能交通系统研究中心;2.国家水运安全工程技术研究中心)

摘 要 本文探讨了使用事故聚合数据与分解数据对城市快速路追尾事故频率进行预测时所产生的差异。所采用的事故预测模型基于历史事故数据与实时交通流数据,利用负二项回归模型对聚合数据与分解数据分别进行建模分析,最后比较了模型参数估计值、过分散参数和预测事故频率的差异性。结果表明,聚合数据和分解数据进行事故频率预测建模时参数估计值比较相似,但也存在逐年变化的变量,如交通量参数估计值不一致。同时,聚合数据与分解数据的过分散参数相差较大,这与聚合数据将事故特征平均化有关。本研究得出,在进行事故频率预测时,最佳的数据整合方式是使用时间跨度一致的数据进行模型建立和预测,对预测效果不好的模型则应使用时间跨度更长的数据集进行建模预测。

关键词 交通安全 事故预测 负二项回归 数据聚合 实时交通流 城市快速路

0 引言

对事故频率预测建模通常用统计计数回归模型,常用的模型包括线性回归模型、泊松回归模型、负二项回归模型、灰色模型等,其中负二项回归模型可解决数据离散问题,且对均值方差不作要求[1],因此被广泛应用。事故中交通流特性对发生频率和严重程度都有非常大的影响,也会显著影响追尾事故的发生可能性[2]。

研究表明事故预测模型显示出在时间上的不稳定性[3],即模型参数对事故严重程度和频率的影响可能会随时间发生变化。目前大多数事故预测模型是基于几年内发生的事故数据汇总,这种方法可以解决过多零碰撞事故的情况,但会丢失事故的纵向特征如逐年变化的交通流量特征[3]。使用聚合和分解数据集进行事故预测建模的差异在以往的研究中受到关注较少,特别是以交通流特性为研究对象时。Kweon Y J[4]等使用聚合和分解数据集比较了安全性能函数,将几个分解模型的过分散参数均值作为最佳模型选择标准。然而,这些研究没有研究聚合与分解模型中变量以及参数估计值的差异,以及不同时间跨度事故数据建模预测的影响。

本文对武汉市三环线追尾事故和相关交通流数据进行负二项回归建模分析,针对聚合模型和分解模型进行了对比,还比较了不同时间跨度模型进行预测的效果。研究结果可以指导事故预测模型选择合适的输入数据,从而更加精确的预测事故数,为道路安全预警提供有力的理论支撑。

1 交通事故及关联数据聚合方法

1.1 数据集基本信息

本文采用武汉市三环线快速路共约37km路段上2018年9—11月以及2019年3—5月共716条追尾事故数据。表1描述了本文三个数据集的构成。并通过沿线共27组平均间隔为1.37km的微波检测器得到事故点相邻上游检测器在事故发生前5~10min相关交通流数据,如表2所示。

数据集描述 表1

类型			时间区间	事故数
分解数据集	1	2018年	2018年9—11月	462条
	2	2019年	2019年3—5月	254条
聚合数据集	3	聚合数据	2018年9—11月与2019年3—5月	716条

1.资助项目:国家重点研发计划项目(编号:2019YFB1600800);国家自然科学基金(编号:52072289)。

事故对应流量数据集统计数据　　表 2

变量		聚合数据	2018 年	2019 年
平均速度(km/h)	平均值	51.6865	50.6898	53.4994
	标准差	15.1173	13.9094	16.9767
	最小值	3.4	8.3	3.4
	最大值	77.52	73.4	77.52
车道间速度差(km/h)	平均值	5.63842	5.26093	6.32504
	标准差	4.14846	4.09391	4.16695
	最小值	0.27	0.3	0.27
	最大值	39.69	39.5	39.69
车道内速度度差(km/h)	平均值	4.53128	4.62234	4.36567
	标准差	3.53164	3.66058	3.28473
	最小值	0.67	0.67	0.81
	最大值	51.4	51.4	26.39
交通量(pcu/lane)	平均值	225.398	249.753	181.098
	标准差	106.815	107.842	89.4415
	最小值	9	10	9
	最大值	523	523	429
大车比例(%)	平均值	0.067905	0.060498	0.081378
	标准差	0.060356	0.56897	0.06414
	最小值	0	0	0
	最大值	0.63	0.63	0.53

1.2　事故数据处理过程

本文采用基于交通流状态的统计方法,通过描述实际事故状态来分析对事故的影响[5]。表 3 描述了事故流量数据集的分位数情况。事故场景划分流程如图 1 所示,首先根据平均速度的累计分布以 25% 的步长划分为 4 等份,同样的,对交通量划分 4 等份,车道内速度差、车道间速度差、大车比例划分 3 等份,最终得到 432 种事故场景,包含了交通流参数的所有可能组合,将场景与事故匹配后,将分组到相同场景的事故数据进行统计形成分析数据集,例如在交通流场景 1 下有四条事故数据,则事故频率记为 4(次)。

为了便于场景间的事故概率比较,引入一个暴露变量。基于事故场景的数据集的偏移量,暴露变量被设为各场景下所花费的车辆行驶时间,即每公里平均行驶时间乘以交通量。利用各组内交通参数的中值表示与事故频次相对应的交通特性并作为自变量,同一场景的事故频次作为因变量。

事故对应流量数据集分位数表　　表 3

变量	百分位数	聚合数据	2018 年	2019 年
平均速度(km/h)	25%	48.795	48.21	50.36
	50%	56.075	54.21	59.19
	75%	61.335	59.51	63.31
车道间速度差(km/h)	25%	3.07	2.95	3.77
	50%	4.575	4.06	5.765
	75%	7.065	6.08	8.17
车道内速度差(km/h)	25%	2.795	2.93	2.48
	50%	3.64	3.635	3.72
	75%	5.08	5.09	4.99

续上表

变量	百分位数	聚合数据	2018 年	2019 年
交通量 (pcu/lane)	25%	147	177	114
	50%	233	260	190
	75%	302	330	241
大车比例 (%)	25%	0.03	0.03	0.04
	50%	0.06	0.05	0.08
	75%	0.09	0.09	0.1

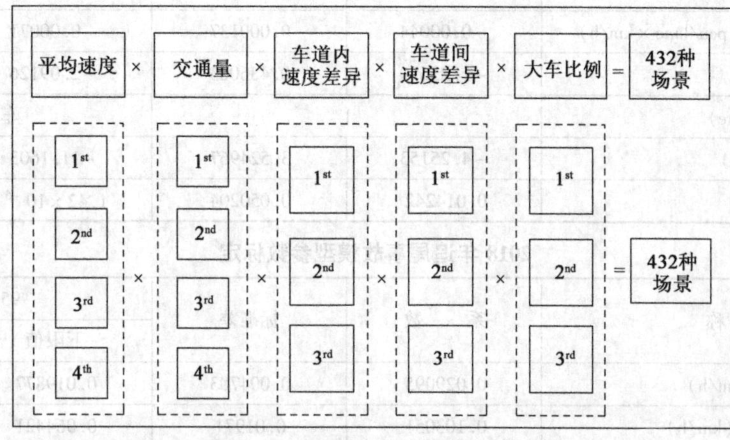

图 1　事故场景划分流程

2　不同聚合方法下的事故预测建模影响分析

2.1　负二项回归模型

交通事故的发生具有随机性、离散性和独立性等特点，可用泊松回归得到事故频次与事故影响因素之间的关系，但前提假设是事故数量的均值等于方差，然而事故频次通常有偏大离差，即其均值小于方差，这种现象被称为过分散[1]。负二项回归在泊松模型的基础上添加了一个服从Gamma分布的误差项来解决过分散问题，因此被广泛应用：

$$\lambda_{ik} = \exp\ (\beta_{ik} x_{ik} + \epsilon_{ik}) \tag{1}$$

式中：λ_{ik}——事故频次；

β_{ik}——参数系数；

x_{ik}——参数值；

ϵ_{ik}——假设泊松分布允许均值和方差不相等而产生的误差项。

$\exp\ (\epsilon_{ik})$服从均值为 1、方差为α^2的 Gamma 分布，使得事故频次分布的方差变为：

$$V_{ik} = E_{ik} \cdot (1 + \alpha \cdot E_{ik}) = \lambda_{ik} \cdot (1 + \alpha \cdot \lambda_{ik}) \tag{2}$$

式中：E_{ik}——事故频次期望；

α——过分散参数。

负二项模型在事故影响因素基础上增加了扰动项ϵ_{ik}，来体现事故次数均值的随机变化特性，同时允许方差大于均值，因此，本文使用负二项模型对事故数据进行预测建模。

2.2　模型参数标定及对比分析

本文以城市快速路 716 条追尾事故数据以及对应交通流数据为基础，分别将三个数据集的 66.7% 作为训练集，33.3% 作为测试集。对三个训练集采用负二项回归分别进行建模，采用模型精度检验指标对三个模型的精度进行检验。表 4 ~ 表 6 分别列出了三个训练集的参数估计结果。

聚合模型、2018 年模型和 2019 年模型的参数系数估计值如表 7 所示。三个模型的参数估计存在明显差异，例如车道内速度差和大车比例，系数显示出对事故频次的影响效果截然相反。检查变量分位值表却未发现较大差异，这说明在相似交通流场景下，事故的发生也是随机的，需要结合更多相关联的交通流参数以进行更精确的预测。聚合模型与分解模型同一系数的估计值最高差异为 64%，因为聚合模型倾向于忽略由于聚合期间的平均化处理而导致的变量短期变化。

总体追尾事故模型参数标定　表 4

变量名称	系数	标准差	95%置信区间	
			下限值	上限值
平均速度(km/h)	0.019443	0.006013	0.007658	0.031228
车道间速度差(km/h)	0.095295	0.02463	0.047022	0.143569
车道内速度差(km/h)	-0.07565	0.054533	-0.18253	0.031233
交通量(pcu/lane)	-0.00259	0.000956	-0.00446	-0.00072
大车比例(%)	1.568442	0.60264	0.38729	2.749593
平均速度×车道内速度差(km/h×km/h)	0.001451	0.001103	-0.00071	0.003612
交通量×车道间速度差(pcu/lane×km/h)	-0.00044	0.000137	-0.00071	-0.00017
截距	-1.23659	0.436063	-2.09126	-0.38193
ln(exposure)	1		车辆行驶时间	
ln(alpha)	-4.25153	3.524967	-11.1603	2.65728
alpha	0.014242	0.050204	1.42×10^{-5}	14.25746

2018 年追尾事故模型参数标定　表 5

变量名称	系数	标准差	95%置信区间	
			下限值	上限值
平均速度(km/h)	0.029095	0.004703	0.019877	0.038313
车道间速度差(km/h)	0.103051	0.01971	0.064421	0.141682
车道内速度差(km/h)	0.03317	0.041345	-0.04787	0.114205
交通量(pcu/lane)	-0.00093	0.000813	-0.00252	0.000665
大车比例(%)	-0.04514	1.159119	-2.31698	2.226687
平均速度×车道内速度差(km/h×km/h)	-0.00078	0.000892	-0.00253	0.000967
交通量×车道间速度差(pcu/lane×km/h)	-0.00053	0.00012	-0.00077	-0.0003
截距	-2.13744	0.290938	-2.70767	-1.56721
ln(exposure)	1		车辆行驶时间	
ln(alpha)	-16.00673	0.3985946	-16.788	-15.2255
alpha	1.12×10^{-7}	4.46×10^{-8}	5.12×10^{-8}	2.44×10^{-7}

2019 年追尾事故模型参数标定　表 6

变量名称	系数	标准差	95%置信区间	
			下限值	上限值
平均速度(km/h)	0.012083	0.007359	-0.00234	0.026505
车道间速度差(km/h)	0.041835	0.03137	-0.01965	0.10332
车道内速度差(km/h)	-0.07414	0.094343	-0.25905	0.110768
交通量(pcu/lane)	-0.00632	0.001161	-0.0086	-0.00405
大车比例(%)	2.902597	0.644374	1.639647	4.165548
平均速度×车道内速度差(km/h×km/h)	0.001332	0.00165	-0.0019	0.004567
交通量×车道间速度差(pcu/lane×km/h)	1.71×10^{-5}	0.000165	-0.00031	0.00034
截距	-0.63278	0.402562	-1.42178	0.156229
ln(exposure)	1		车辆行驶时间	
ln(alpha)	-18.3284	0.873093	-18.4995	-19.1573
alpha	1.10×10^{-8}	9.58×10^{-10}	9.24×10^{-9}	1.30×10^{-8}

聚合模型与分解模型参数系数估计值对比 表7

变量名称	聚合数据	2018年	2019年
平均速度(km/h)	0.019443	0.029095	0.012083
车道间速度差(km/h)	0.095295	0.103051	0.041835
车道内速度差(km/h)	−0.07565	0.03317	−0.07414
交通量(pcu/lane)	−0.00259	−0.00093	−0.00632
大车比例(%)	1.568442	−0.04514	2.902597
平均速度×车道内速度差(km/h×km/h)	0.001451	−0.00078	0.001332
交通量×车道间速度差(pcu/lane×km/h)	−0.00044	−0.00053	1.71×10^{-5}
截距	−1.23659	−2.13744	−0.63278
ln(alpha)	−4.25153	−16.00673	−18.3284
alpha	0.014242	1.12×10^{-7}	1.10×10^{-8}

聚合模型与分解模型更重要的差别在于过分散参数(alpha)。负二项回归解释了事故数据中通常存在的过度分散问题,而过分散参数表示方差大于碰撞频率分布均值的程度,通常是先验未知,通过模型计算得到。对于两个分解模型而言,均比聚合模型要小很多,且标准误差也明显更小,这是由于将每个场景的事故频率汇总时通常会减少场景中事故的变化特性。在单独的分解数据集中,高于平均水平的事故频率可能会受到其他年份低于平均水平事故频率的影响,这反过来又会减少由分解数据集汇总得到的聚合数据集中事故频率的变化特征,从而减少数据中存在的过度分散程度,见表8。

聚合模型与分解模型过分散参数对比 表8

过分散参数取对数/ln(alpha)		聚合数据	2018年	2019年
系数		−4.25153	−16.00673	−18.3284
标准差		3.524967	0.3985946	0.873093
95%置信区间	上限值	−11.1603	−16.788	−18.4995
	下限值	2.65728	−15.2255	−19.1573

对于模型而言,聚合模型的拟合优度 R^2 更高,这意味着聚合模型相比默认模型在解释数据时效果最好。而当使用模型的其他评价指标时,分解模型明显优于聚合模型,见表9。

模型评价指标对比 表9

评价指标	聚合数据	2018年	2019年
Rseudo R^2	0.1731	0.1542	0.1059
Wald检验	141.19	161.43	316.34
LL	−387.1959	−267.3764	−141.7385
AIC	792.3917	552.7528	299.4769
BIC	823.3735	581.4894	320.8595
MSE	3.94525	2.697733	2.396038

本文采用正态分布 $\mu\pm2\sigma$ 即95.5%的置信区间,来验证模型的拟合效果,绘制累积残差(Cumulative Residual, CURE)图。图2~图4为分别使用聚合、2018年和2019年事故预测模型分别对三个测试集进行拟合的CURE图。结果显示基于聚合和分解模型的预测CURE图存在很大差异。2019年事故预测模型对三个测试集的预测效果均较差,这与之前较低的模型评价指标值不谋而合。而2018年模型则表现优秀,对三个测试集均能较好地预测。聚合数据模型吸收了两年的事故特征,对2019年测试集也能进行较好的预测,这说明通过聚合时间跨度更长的事故数据,能够得到预测效果更好的模型。

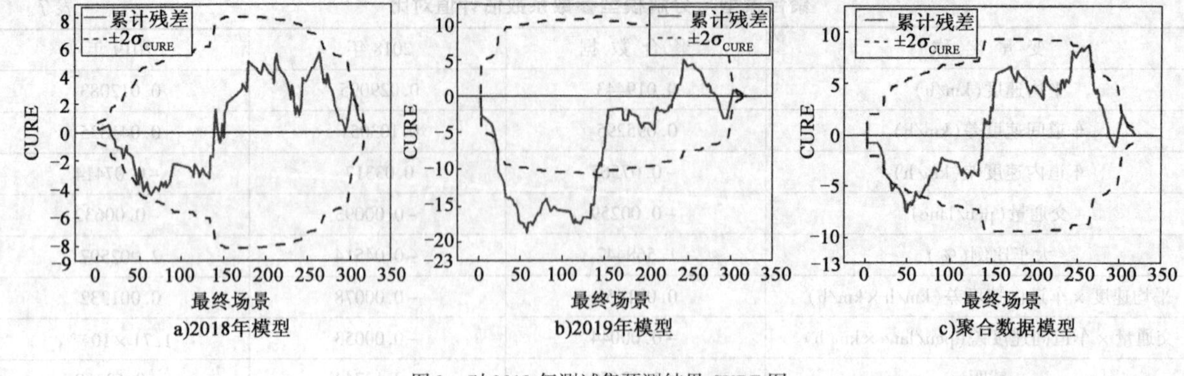

图2　对2018年测试集预测结果CURE图

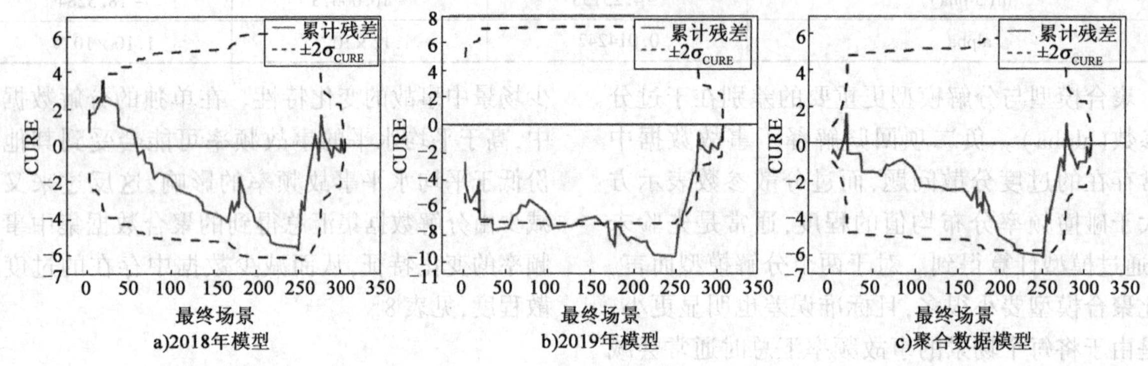

图3　对2019年测试集预测结果CURE图

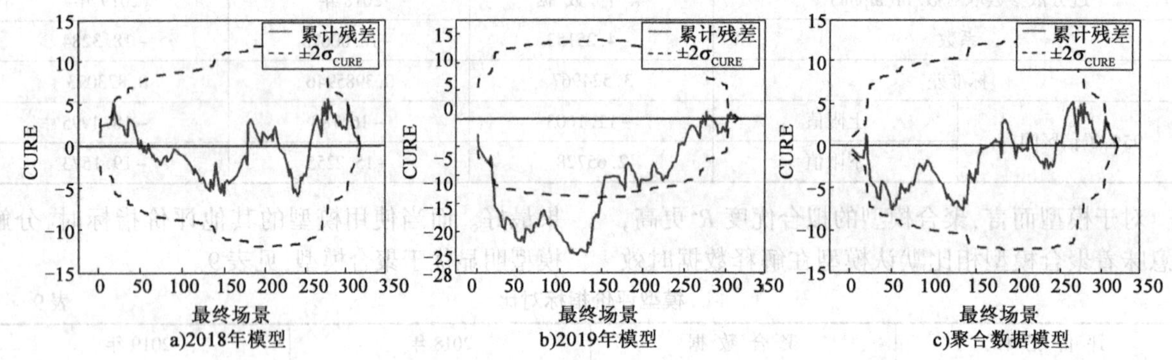

图4　对聚合数据测试集预测结果CURE图

3　结语

本文使用武汉市三环线快速路追尾事故研究了事故数据聚合与分解时对事故预测的影响。通过对事故预测模型更好的研究，能够让交管部门提前进行预警和管控。结果表明，聚合模型与分解模型有很大的差异性。首先，聚合模型与分解模型的参数系数基本相似，但在某些参数上也存在较大差异，特别是容易随时间变化的解释变量(如交通量)，这与每个数据集的事故特征相关，其中同一系数估计值的最大差异为64%，因为聚合数据可能会在数据汇总时平均化处理变量，忽略短期变化。同时，聚合模型更高的R^2也表明聚合模型对数据的解释效果更好。

聚合模型与分解模型更重要的差别在于过分散参数(alpha)。聚合模型与分解模型的过分散参数有明显的差异，这些差异也反映到对测试集的预测效果上，聚合模型不稳定的过分散参数(标准差过大)会导致无法捕捉短期事故的事故特征，进而导致预测不准确，但相比质量不佳的分解模型预测效果要好得多。同时，对聚合数据测试集预测时，聚合模型的预测效果又是最佳的。因此，在进行事故频率预测时，最佳的数据整合方式是使用时间跨度一致的数据进行模型建立和预测，当模型质量不佳时则应通过时间跨度更长的数据进行建模预测。

未来可以在划分分解数据集时,选择更加精细的时间维度进行分析。建模时使用更加复杂的建模方法,如随机参数模型,以更好地捕捉数据中未观察到的异质性。

参考文献

[1] 张迎. 考虑数据异质性的高速公路交通事故预测研究[D]. 西安:长安大学,2018.

[2] Dimitriou L, Stylianou K, ABDEL-ATY M A. Assessing rear-end crash potential in urban locations based on vehicle-by-vehicle interactions, geometric characteristics and operational conditions[J]. Accident Analysis & Prevention, 2018,118:221.

[3] Ab A, Fm B. Time-of-day variations and temporal instability of factors affecting injury severities in large-truck crashes - ScienceDirect[J]. Analytic Methods in Accident Research, 23 (C): 100102-100102.

[4] Kweon Y J, Lim I K. Appropriate Regression Model Types for Intersections inSafetyAnalyst[C] //Transportation Research Board Meeting. 2011.

[5] Imprialou M I M, Quddus M, Pitfield D, et al. Re-visiting Crash-speed Relationships: A New Perspective in Crash Modelling[J]. Accident Analysis and Prevention, 2016, 86:173-185.

基于货车侧翻模型的枢纽互通环形匝道交通安全改善研究

陈亚振[1] 高 阳*[2]

(1. 中交第二公路勘察设计研究院有限公司;2. 武汉中交交通工程有限责任公司)

摘 要 本文针对某高速公路营运阶段枢纽互通立交环形匝道,对其现有路况影响行车安全的因素进行分析。具体通过分析车辆在匝道行驶时的转弯半径、视距以及弯道超高等因素对车辆运行安全的影响,辨识其关键因素;通过实地调研勘测道路现状,通过雷达获取道路断面车辆速度数据,并对运行车速进行分析;结合交通事故的调查分析及 TruckSim 建模找出交通事故发生的主要原因及规律,并提出交通安全改善建议。

关键词 交通工程 交通安全改善 货车侧翻模型 环形匝道

0 引言

某高速公路枢纽互通匝道由于地形条件受限,先是上坡(1.8%)通过匝道桥上跨被交高速公路主线,然后是下坡急弯(-3.24%,R=65m)进入被交高速,通车后共发生9起交通事故,分别为拖挂车8起,小轿车1起。其中,2018年发生6起交通事故,经各方研讨采取了相应措施,取得了一定效果,但2019年4月中旬4天内又连续发生3起交通事故。这9起交通事故多为货车侧翻事故。

本次安全改善研究的目的为:

(1)针对高速公路营运阶段枢纽互通环形匝道,对其现有路况影响行车安全的因素进行分析。具体通过分析车辆在匝道行驶时的转弯半径、视距以及弯道超高等因素对车辆运行安全的影响,辨识其关键因素;通过实地调研勘测道路现状,通过雷达获取道路断面车辆速度数据,并对运行车速进行分析;结合交通事故的调查分析及 TruckSim 建模找出交通事故发生的主要原因及规律。

(2)在交通事故统计分析的基础上,根据车速观测结果、驾驶员行为特性以及车辆动力学仿真结果,提出针对枢纽互通环形匝道的交通安全改善意见。

1　概述

1.1　项目概况

本文研究对象为两条高速公路的枢纽互通立交 H 匝道。高速公路主线设计速度 120km/h,双向四车道,路基宽度 28m;被交高速公路设计速度 100km/h,双向四车道,路基宽度 26m。

枢纽环形匝道先是上坡(1.8%)通过匝道桥上跨被交高速公路主线,然后是下坡急弯(-3.24%,R=65m)进入被交高速公路,设计速度 40km/h,如图 1 所示。

从 2017 年 12 月底通车至 2019 年 4 月,枢纽互通 H 匝道共发生 9 起交通事故,分别为拖挂车 8 起,小轿车 1 起。其中,2018 年发生 6 起交通事故,经各方研讨采取了相应措施,取得了一定效果,但 2019 年 4 月中旬 4 天内又连续发生 3 起交通事故。这 9 起交通事故多为货车侧翻事故。

1.2　研究内容及技术路线

研究内容主要包含以下四部分:

(1)互通环形匝道交通事故统计分析。

(2)安全重点路段车速及行为特性研究。

(3)复杂线形组合的大车侧翻规律分析。

(4)安全重点路段综合评价及改善建议。

图 2 所示为项目总体研究框架和技术路线示意图。

图 1　枢纽互通 H 匝道现状

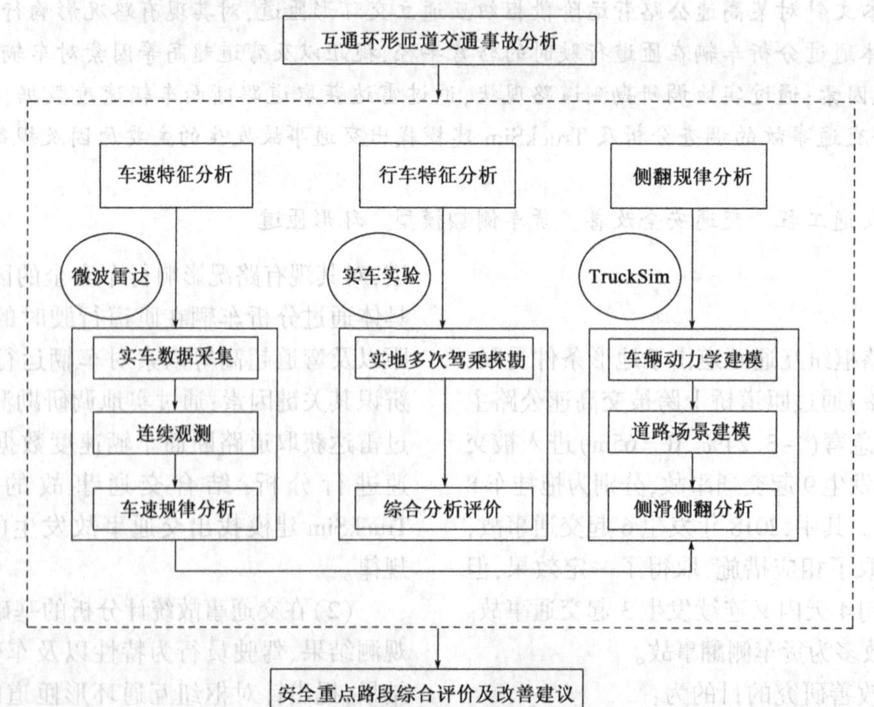

图 2　项目总体研究框架和技术路线

2　交通事故统计分析

道路交通事故分析工作作为预防道路交通事故的有效手段之一[1]，运用统计方法进行全面分析，找出交通事故发生的时间和空间规律性[2]，从而得出安全重点路段的事故原因等初步结论，为制定交通安全改善措施提供依据。

枢纽互通H匝道弯道处事故多发月份为3、4、5月份，近一半的事故发生在雨天，主要为大车侧翻事故（图3）。虽然该高速公路设计符合现行规范要求，但是在车速、车型的耦合影响下，极端条件易诱发交通事故，且重型货车在互通立交特性的匝道环境中易发生事故，主要原因为重型货车重心较高以及超载、超速等极端因素的影响。

图3　H匝道弯道处的货车侧翻事故现场

3　道路线形符合性检查

枢纽互通匝道为半定向+环形匝道枢纽互通，事故多发点为H匝道，起讫桩号为K759+010～K760+670（图4）。其主线线形：平面R为3500m的圆曲线，最大纵坡1.50%，最小纵坡1.040%，竖曲线最小半径为45000m（凸形）；互通范围全线处于2%超高段落上。匝道线形：最小平曲线半径为65m，最大纵坡为3.24%，凸形竖曲线最小半径为1300m，凹形竖曲线最小半径为1500m；最大超高横坡度为6%。

枢纽互通匝道道路设计线形符合设计规范，竖曲线、平曲线设计指标接近规范规定的极限值。但是匝道坡弯组合较为复杂，该处路线是上坡后紧接一个小半径的转弯，导致驾驶员的视野较差。

图4　枢纽互通H匝道现状图

4　车速分析

车辆运行速度是评价交通流稳定性的重要指标，对道路安全性的评价也有着极为重要的意义。运行速度是一个统计学指标，在驾驶行为、心理、视觉需求、汽车性能特征、几何线形设计等因素的综合影响下是连续变化的[3]，比设计速度更贴近实际行驶速度。

4.1　实车调查及数据分析

本次调查通过开展实车测试，提取了12段驾驶人驾驶实验车通过互通H匝道的车速数据,并将在此期间内捕捉到的周围车辆车速信息作为样本补充,通过统计方法计算出行驶速度的分位值,并以此为基础评价互通H匝道的交通运行状态。互通H匝道实车测试车速数据见表1。

实验结果表明,小汽车通过互通H匝道时的速度相比该路段限速要快很多,该路段的限速标志和交通设施并不能有效控制小汽车的车速。互通H匝道的事故形态多为大货车侧翻,但在互通车流量较大的情况下,小汽车的车速也会对大货车的车速产生影响。

4.2 定点雷达测速及数据分析

本研究在互通H匝道上选择2个定点,分别于第一天、第二天布置测速雷达,如图5、图6所示,每个测速雷达工作24小时。测试期间采集的大型车车速数据如表2所示,雷达观测点车速统计分析如图7、图8所示。

互通H匝道实车测试车速数据 表1

速度类型	v_{95}	v_{85}	路段限速
速度大小	59.50km/h	55.82km/h	40km/h
实验次数	12次		

图5 互通H匝道雷达布设位置

图6 雷达观测点布设实况

互通H匝道雷达测速统计 表2

测速位置	v_{85}	v_{95}	v_{99}	车辆数	匝道限速	超速比例
观测点1	39.87km/h	45.94km/h	49.57km/h	278km/h	40km/h	14.85%
观测点2	41.63km/h	46.46km/h	51.12km/h	309km/h		16.66%

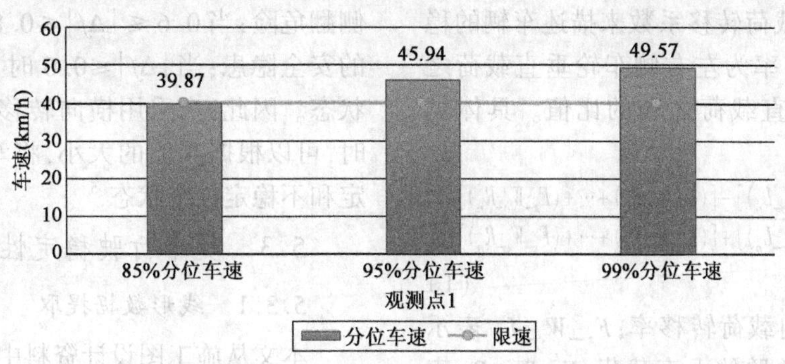

图7　互通 H 匝道雷达观测点 1 车速统计分析

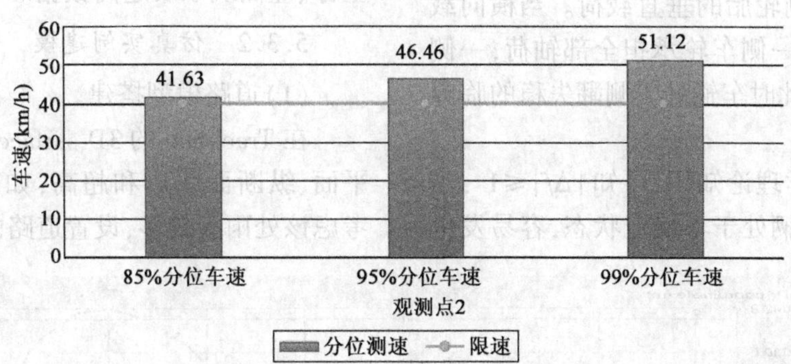

图8　互通 H 匝道雷达观测点 2 车速统计分析

从 H 匝道雷达测速获取的数据来看，虽然该匝道布置了很多道路交通设施并设置了明确的限速标准，但大型车行驶速度仍然较快，超速比例也比较高。

5　行车稳定性分析

本文利用 CarSim/TruckSim 和 Simulink 仿真软件构建危险匝道的真实道路环境模型、车辆动力学模型及数据求解模型，通过仿真模拟车辆在安全重点路段的运行情况，分析车辆的行驶稳定性[4]。

5.1　联合仿真设计思路

为了模拟车辆行驶时的侧翻危险性能，本文通过动力学仿真软件 CarSim/TruckSim 分别与 Simulink 构建联合仿真环境，进行大型车的行驶稳定性仿真。CarSim/TruckSim 与 Simulink 的联合仿真原理如图 9 所示。

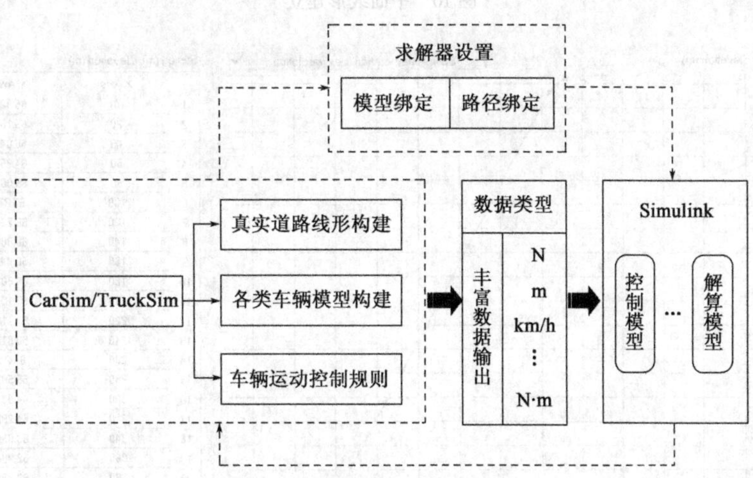

图9　CarSim/TruckSim 与 Simulink 的联合仿真原理

5.2　行车稳定性评价指标

汽车在弯道上行驶时，由于轮胎受力不均匀，可能导致受力小的一侧发生翻车。轮胎承受的垂直载荷力 F_Z 是衡量车辆发生侧翻的一个重要数值。通常采用横向载荷转移系数来描述车辆的稳定性,横向载荷转移率为左右侧车轮垂直载荷之差与左右侧车轮垂直载荷之和的比值。具体见下式:

$$\Delta f=\frac{[(F_{z}\_W_{c}\_L_{1})+\cdots+(F_{z}\_W_{c}\_L_{n})]-[(F_{z}\_W_{c}\_R_{1})+\cdots+(F_{z}\_W_{c}\_R_{n})]}{[(F_{z}\_W_{c}\_L_{1})+\cdots+(F_{z}\_W_{c}\_L_{n})]+[(F_{z}\_W_{c}\_R_{1})+\cdots+(F_{z}\_W_{c}\_R_{n})]} \tag{1}$$

式中:Δf 为横向载荷转移率;$F_z\_W_c\_L_n$ 表示车辆的第 n 轴左侧轮胎的垂直载荷;$F_z\_W_c\_R_n$ 表示车辆的第 n 轴右侧轮胎的垂直载荷。当横向载荷转移率达到 1 时,一侧车轮承担全部轴荷,一侧车轮垂直载荷为 0,此时车辆处于侧翻失稳的临界状态。

根据汽车动力学理论知识,可知 $|\Delta f|\leqslant 1$,当 $0.8\leqslant|\Delta f|\leqslant 1$ 时车辆处于不稳定状态,容易发生侧翻危险;当 $0.6\leqslant|\Delta f|\leqslant 0.8$ 时,车辆存在一定的安全隐患;当 $|\Delta f|\leqslant 0.6$ 时,车辆处于较安全的状态。因此,当采用横向转移系数作为评价指标时,可以根据其值的大小,将车辆分为稳定、亚稳定和不稳定三个状态[5]。

5.3　货车行驶稳定性仿真

5.3.1　线形数据提取

本文从施工图设计资料中提取 H 匝道的逐桩坐标、竖曲线以及超高数据。

5.3.2　仿真实例建模

(1)道路模型搭建。

在 TruckSim 的 3D surface 模块中建立匝道的平面、纵断面线形和超高,如图 10 ~ 图 12 所示。考虑该处雨天较多,设置道路的摩擦系数为 0.4。

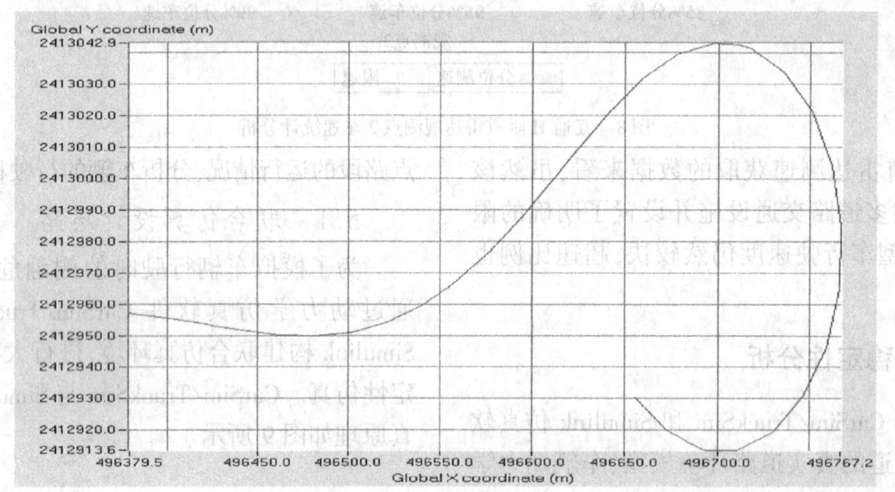

图 10　平面线形建立

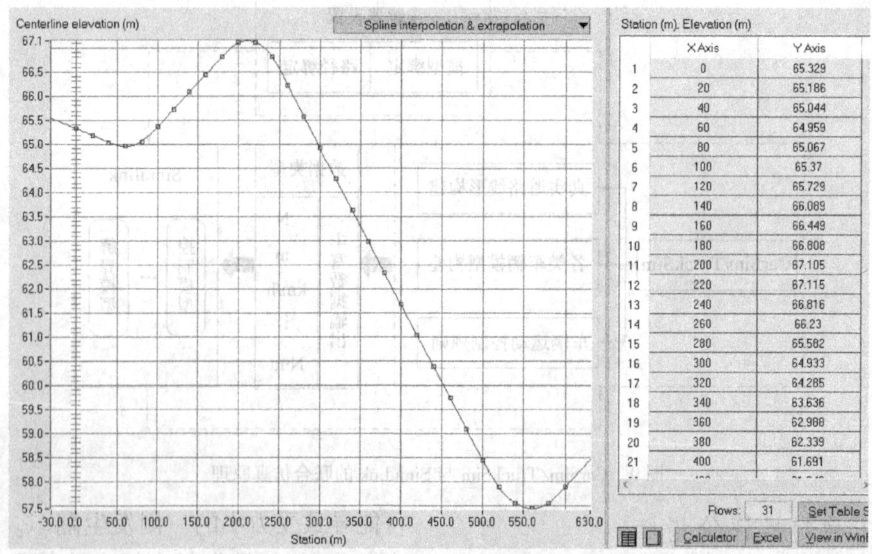

图 11　纵断面线形建立

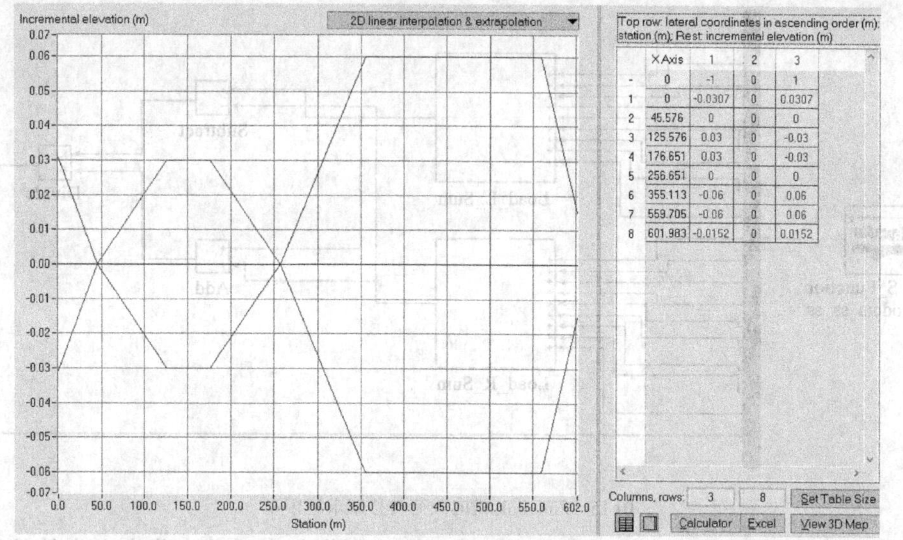

图 12　匝道超高设置

(2)车辆模型搭建。

在 TruckSim 车辆配置中构建 5 轴(3 轴牵引车 +2 轴挂车)重型货车模型,如图 13 所示,车辆以 50km/h 的初始速度运行。

图 13　仿真车辆模型构建

(3)仿真输出数据设置。

在 TruckSim 界面选择输出货车各个轮胎的实时垂直载荷以及车辆从匝道起始点开始的累计行驶里程,如图 14 所示。

(4)计算模型搭建。

在 TruckSim 与 Simulink 构建联合仿真环境后,将 TruckSim 中的模型加载至 Simulink 中即可模拟运行,并得到预期的数据。其中,构建的求解模型如图 15 所示。

上图中最右侧的 deltaf_S 模块为横向载荷转移率曲线图,即为评价货车行驶侧翻危险的指标信息。

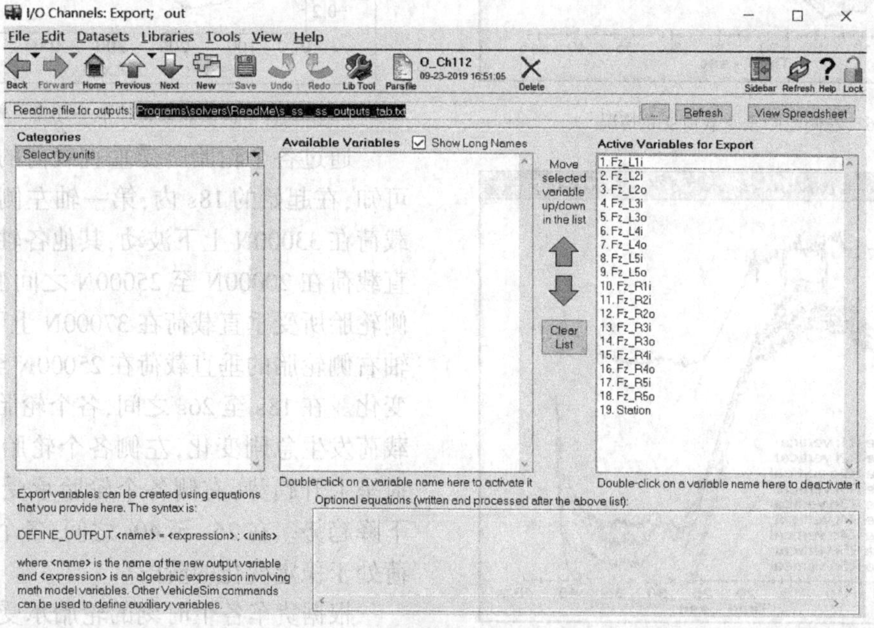

图 14　仿真输出数据类型控制

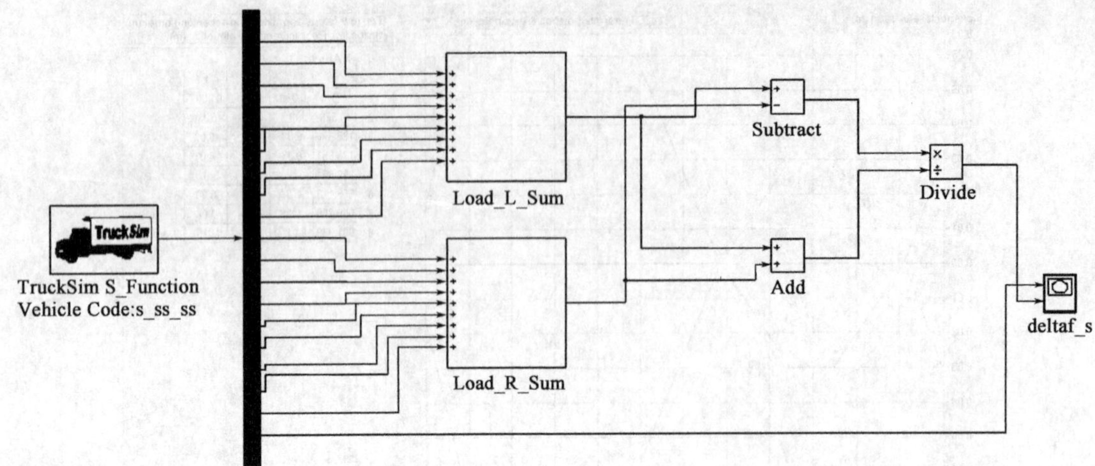

图15　Simulink横向载荷转移率求解模型

5.3.3　仿真结果及分析

通过运行模型,可以实时观测垂直载荷曲线。其中,货车左右两侧每个轮胎所承受的垂直载荷如图16、图17所示。

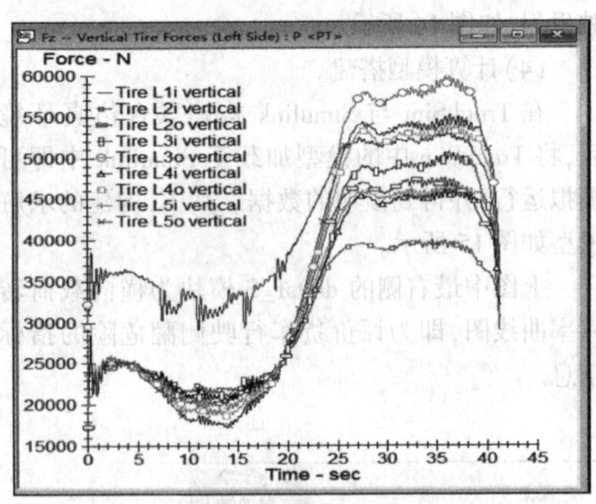

图16　左侧轮胎垂直载荷变化情况

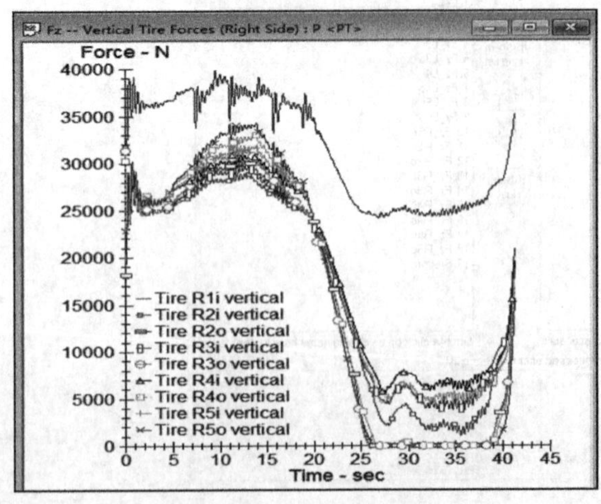

图17　右侧轮胎垂直载荷变化情况

根据行驶过程中货车左右侧轮胎所承受的实时垂直载荷数据,由Simulink模型可直接查看横向载荷转移率曲线,具体如图18所示。其中,横轴为货车从该处匝道起始点处开始的累计行驶里程,纵轴为实时横向载荷转移率。

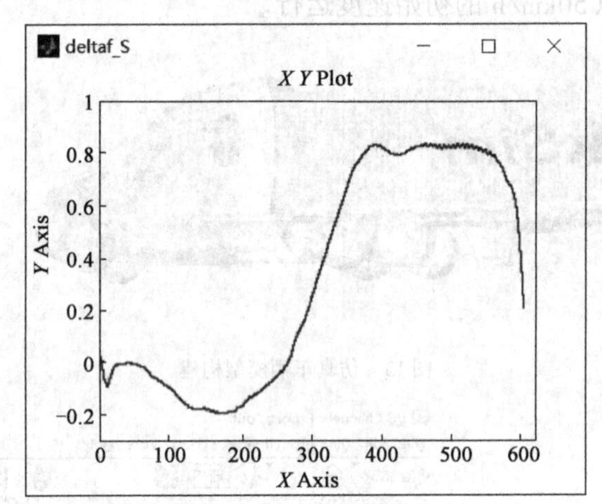

图18　横向载荷转移率—行驶距离曲线图

通过各个轮胎所受垂直载荷的实时变化曲线可知,在起始的18s内,第一轴左侧轮胎所受垂直载荷在33000N上下波动,其他各轴左侧轮胎的垂直载荷在20000N至25000N之间变化;第一轴右侧轮胎所受垂直载荷在37000N上下波动,其他各轴右侧轮胎的垂直载荷在25000N至30000N之间变化。在18s至26s之间,各个轮胎所承受的垂直载荷发生急剧变化,左侧各个轮胎承受的垂直载荷呈上升趋势,右侧各个轮胎承受的垂直载荷呈下降趋势。在26s至40s之间,各个轮胎的垂直载荷处于稳定变化的阶段。

根据货车各个时刻的轮胎承受的垂直载荷数据,并结合在Simulink模型中求解得到的横向载荷转移率曲线可知，当货车行驶在 HK0 + 157.698 ~ HK0 + 454.898 时，横向载荷转移率 Δf 为 -0.2 ~ 0.2，货车行驶的稳定性很好。当货车行驶在HK0 + 454.898 ~ HK0 + 501.566 时，横向载荷转移率 Δf 快速上升，最大值接近 0.6，货车行驶稳定性较好。当货车行驶在 HK0 + 501.566 ~ HK0 + 534.497 时，横向载荷转移率 Δf 接近 0.8，表明货车从较安全状态转变为存在一定安全隐患的状态。当货车行驶在 HK0 + 534.497 ~ HK0 + 714.628 时，横向载荷转移率 Δf 维持在 0.8 以上，此时车辆处于不稳定状态，容易发生侧翻危险。当货车在该处匝道的结束部分行驶在 HK0 + 714.628 ~ HK0 + 762.378 时，横向载荷转移率 Δf 逐渐下降，货车向安全稳定行驶状态转变。

6 研究结论及改善措施

(1)从事故统计来看，互通 H 匝道事故发生形态主要为碰撞和翻车，这两类事故分别占事故总数的 44% 和 45%，事故车型以大型货车为主。可见，上述原因和结论分析与事故形态一致。大型货车超载导致车辆重心提高、惯性增大，如果在极端天气摩擦系数较小的情况下超速行驶，很容易向匝道外侧发生碰撞或侧翻。

(2)互通 H 匝道的坡弯组合较为特殊。该处路线是上坡后紧接一个半径 65m 的小半径转弯。驾驶员由于受纵坡影响视距有限，可能无法观察和预计坡后的平曲线走向，导致车速与线形不匹配，进而引发事故。为解决尤其是在夜晚容易出现的视距问题，建议在护栏立柱上设置反光线形诱导标。

(3)根据 2 个测速点观测的数据，两处的 v_{85} 均超过 45km/h，最高达到 49.98km/h，v_{95} 均超过 50km/h，v_{99} 均超过 69km/h；两个测速点大型车 v_{99} 分别达到 49.57km/h 和 51.12km/h；虽然该匝道设置了明确的限速标准，但车辆行驶速度仍超出限速值。

考虑到该路段在匝道入口处设置了匝道急弯警示标志(图 19)，但未能对车辆运行速度起到良好的控制效果，建议在匝道急弯处等间隔设置多个标志，增强对驾驶员的提醒效果，控制车辆入弯速度。

图 19 匝道急弯警示标志

另外，建议增加车牌 + 车速反馈系统，将超速车辆的车牌连同车速一起显示(图 20)，对驾驶员起到警示作用。同时，建议对超速进行处罚，威慑违法行为。

图 20 车牌识别及车速显示系统

为进一步减少车辆超速(尤其是大货车超速)现象，将货车实际 v_{99} 车速控制在 40km/h 以下，建议从主线出口至 H 匝道连续设置横向减速振动标线。

(4)通过利用 TruckSim 与 Simulink 联合仿真构建重型货车、真实道路以及控制等模型，模拟重型货车在互通H匝道上的行驶状态,求得横向载荷转移率曲线。结果表明重型货车行驶在HK0+501.566~HK0+534.497时,横向载荷转移率Δf接近0.8,表明货车存在一定的安全隐患;行驶在HK0+534.497~HK0+714.628时,横向载荷转移率Δf维持在0.8以上,此时车辆处于不稳定状态,容易发生侧翻危险。因此,在目前的65m半径、6%超高、满载或超载环境及大车v_{99}为51km/h的组合下,不能保证超载大货车的行车稳定性,这种极端条件应加以限制。

为此,建议在HK0+420处增加一处横杆式或者路侧式测速装置(图21),对车速进行全程监控,避免驾驶员越过测速装置后立即提速,以解决H匝道尾段行车稳定性不强的问题。

图21　雷达测速系统

如上述措施仍不能有效改善,说明该道路在设计层面存在安全隐患,结合本文仿真建模的研究结果,建议通过工程手段改造H匝道的线形要素,该方案涉及原有互通线形设施的改建,需联合主体设计单位进行论证。

(1)针对车辆未能预知小半径平曲线可能导致在平曲线偏离车道的问题,建议对匝道HK0+534.497~HK0+714.628左侧(外侧)进行加宽处理[6],如图22所示,以提高车辆偏离车道的宽容性。

图22　匝道左侧拓宽

(2)为减小大型货车在H匝道侧翻的严重程度,建议改造H匝道护栏,加密护栏立柱并加大护栏的强度及埋深,如有必要可将护栏改为混凝土护栏,将左侧护栏增加到1.1m高,避免车辆出现翻越护栏的情况,减小侧翻后的损失。

(3)建议改造匝道最后一段的超高,将超高由1.5%增加到4%。由于涉及土建,该方案需联合主体设计单位进行论证。

(4)互通H匝道的坡弯组合较为特殊,是小半径竖曲线+R65m的平曲线半径,在该路段驾驶员不易预置竖曲线之后的小半径,在超速行驶或者操作不当的情况下易发生碰撞护栏或侧翻事故。建议在今后互通匝道的设计中避免小半径竖曲线+小半径平曲线的组合,在行车视距范围内保证小半径曲线的可视性。

7 结语

本文针对某高速营运阶段枢纽互通环形匝道,对其现有路况影响行车安全的因素进行分析,对现有公路运行速度协调性进行评价;结合实际道路条件提出必要的横坡优化策略及设置相应的交通安全设施,以保障高速公路交通运行安全,切实提升项目运营安全。

高速公路的事故是人、车、路、环境耦合作用下各因素失调的结果,本文从线形分析、事故形态分析、实地勘察测速、动力学仿真等多方面开展综合分析,找出了可能的原因,并提出了改善措施。高速公路的事故原因非常复杂,因此建议对改善措施进行跟踪评估,使其不断完善,以提高事故多发路段的安全水平。

参考文献

[1] 支野,王大珊,丛浩哲,等.道路交通事故数据深度挖掘技术与应用——以深圳市为例[J].城市交通,2018,16(3):28-32,61.

[2] 毛应萍,于丰泉,孙烨垚,等.道路交通事故数据挖掘分析技术及应用研究[J].交通与运输,2020,36(S2):106-111.

[3] 向辉.基于运行速度的公路设计方法[J].交通世界,2020(4):87-88.

[4] 杨炜,马浩越,郭祥靖.基于TruckSim与Simulink联合仿真的半挂汽车列车横向稳定性控制[J].中国科技论文,2018,13(4):390-398.

[5] 金智林,严正华.基于二次预测型横向载荷转移率的汽车侧翻预警研究[J].中国机械工程,2019,30(15):1790-1795.

[6] 骆中斌,靳媛媛,史恒,等.双车道公路及立交匝道的曲线段路面加宽研究[J].中外公路,2021,41(4):84-89.

基于ETC门架数据的高速公路交通事故风险动态辨识模型

焦利娟*[2] 汤厚骏[1] 杜逸[1] 彭畅[2] 罗曦[1] 徐铖铖[2]

(1.浙江省交通投资集团有限公司智慧交通研究分公司;2.东南大学交通学院)

摘 要 为了有效利用高精度交通流数据,主动调节交通流运行状态,达到快速降低交通事故风险、提升交通安全的目的,本文基于ETC门架数据建立高速公路交通事故风险动态辨识模型。首先,通过车牌匹配获得高精度交通流数据。然后,建立随机式数据样本,采用非配对病例-对照研究方法进行研究。最后,利用二元logit回归建立高速公路交通事故风险动态辨识模型,并对模型的预测精度和有效性进行验证。结果表明,模型的解释变量具有较强的显著性,解释变量的符号可以得到合理的解释;当概率分割值取0.0760时,模型对训练集的敏感度、特异度、预测正确率和AUC分别为66.02%、65.45%、65.50%和0.7306,对测试集的敏感度、特异度、预测正确率和AUC分别为71.11%、65.48、65.99%和0.7714。

关键词 交通工程 事故风险动态辨识模型 二元logit回归 高速公路

0 引言

传统交通安全管理由于缺乏高精度实时交通流数据,通常将交通事故数据在时间和空间上进行集计,建立交通事故频次与某一较长时间段内(通常为一年)交通流参数平均值、道路特征和环境条件等影响因素的关系[1-3]。由于模型中的交通流变量是较长时间段内的平均值,无法反映交通流的动态特征,此类模型难以揭示交通流动态特征对交通事故风险的影响。

1.基金项目:国家重点研发计划项目(2020YFB1600500),国家自然科学基金项目(52172343),江苏省自然科学基金项目(BK20211515)。

动态交通安全管理利用高精度实时交通流数据建立事故风险辨识模型,可主动地调节交通流运行状态,达到快速降低交通事故风险、主动提升交通安全的目的。根据建模思路和样本结构可以将现有的事故风险辨识模型分为三类:基于事故发生前实时交通流数据的模型、基于配对式数据样本的模型和基于随机式数据样本的模型[4]。

第一类模型基于事故发生前的实时交通流数据进行建模。Lee 等[5]基于事故发生前 5min 内的交通流动态特征,构建二项 Logistic 回归模型判别侧向碰撞与追尾两种事故形态,认为换道行为对事故形态有显著的影响。Golob 等[6]从事故发生前的交通流数据中提取了 36 个交通流参数,用于研究交通流动态特征对事故严重程度、碰撞类型、发生位置、涉及车辆数的影响,结果表明研究选取的部分交通流参数可以很好地解释不同交通流状态下的碰撞类型。此类模型虽利用了实时交通流数据,但仅考虑了事故发生前的交通流特征,只能描述可能发生事故的形态的概率,无法评估或预测事故风险。

第二类模型基于配对式数据样本,采用配对病例-对照研究方法进行建模。通过调查事故相关的交通状态和正常交通状态,确定事故前兆及其对事故风险的影响[7-10]。Abdel-Aty 等[11]采用条件 Logistic 回归建立高速公路实时事故风险模型。Hossain 等[12]采用随机多项 logit 回归模型确定最重要的影响事故的因素和最合适的安装检测器的位置,并基于贝叶斯网络建立事故实时预测模型。Xu 等[13]采用 K 均值聚类分析方法划分高速公路交通流状态,并采用条件 Logistic 回归建立不同交通流状态下的事故风险模型,确定了不同交通流状态下交通流动态特征对事故风险的影响。此类模型虽能在样本设计阶段有效控制混杂因素对研究结果的影响,但无法反映道路特征和天气信息对事故风险的影响。

第三类模型基于随机式数据样本,采用非配对病例-对照研究方法进行建模。Xu 等[14]采用此研究方法发现天气特征和道路特征是影响事故风险的重要因素。在之后的研究中发现,对于给定的敏感性水平,基于随机式数据样本建立的事故风险模型的可预测性总是优于使用配对式数据样本建立的模型[15]。

综上,本文基于随机式数据样本,采用非配对病例-对照研究方法进行建模,建立基于 ETC 门架数据的高速公路交通事故风险动态辨识模型。

1　数据获取

1.1　数据来源

为实现研究目标,本研究从中国某高速公路上获取交通、环境、事故等数据。其中,交通和环境数据来源于高速公路上的 ETC 门架,事故数据来源于交管中心的报告。

研究路段总长约 85km,共包含 44 台 ETC 门架,上行方向和下行方向各有 22 台,各 ETC 门架的相对位置如图 1 所示,图中数字代表 ETC 门架与研究路段起点的距离,单位为 km,箭头表示下行方向,反之为上行方向。下行方向的 ETC 门架平均间距为 4.03km,最小间距为 0.51km,最大间距为12.61km。上行方向 ETC 门架平均间距为 3.86km,最小间距为 0.32km,最大间距为 11.80km。ETC 门架数据包含门架 ID、车牌号和时间戳等信息,每一辆车通过 ETC 门架都会产生一条 ETC 门架数据。

交通事故数据来源于交管中心 2020 年 8 月至 2021 年 8 月的报告,包含事故发生位置、事故发生时间、事故结束时间和事故类型等信息。在研究时间段内,共获取交通事故数据 898 条。

1.2　高精度交通流数据提取

本研究基于 ETC 门架数据获取高精度交通流数据,利用 ETC 门架数据中的门架 ID、时间戳、车牌号等信息,将每台 ETC 门架在 1min 内采集的数据合并为一条高精度交通流数据,44 台 ETC 门架在同 1min 可形成 44 条高精度交通流数据。每一条高精度交通流数据所包含的信息如表 1 所示,包括几何特征(如 DriDir, Interval)、时间特征(如 Hour, Season)、流量特征(如 SecCou, PasNum)、密度特征(如 Density, $Density_s$)、速度特征(如 MeaSpe, $MeanSpe_u$)等五类,见表 1。

1.3　样本结构设计

本研究采用随机式抽样方法抽取非事故交通流数据,将随机式抽样方法获得的非事故交通流数据和事故交通流数据组合成非配对样本,用于非配对-病例对照研究。在随机式样本结构中,事故交通流数据和非事故交通流数据采用 1∶10 的比例。

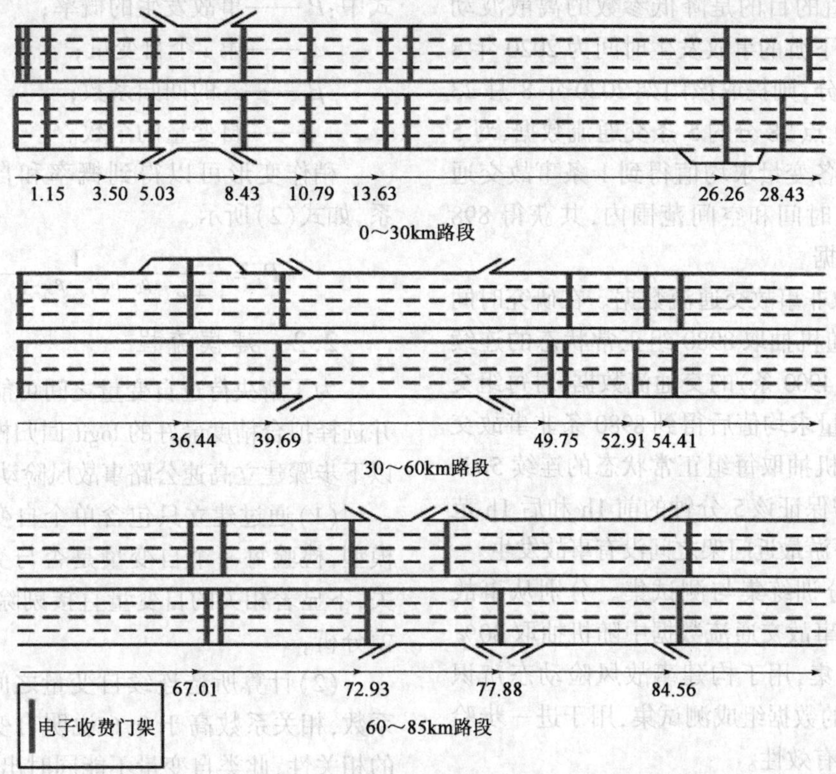

图1 ETC门架相对位置

变量名称及其描述 表1

变量名称	变量含义
GanOrd	门架编号顺序,每个方向从上游至下游依次增加
DriDri	车辆行驶方向,0代表下行方向,1代表上行方向
Interval	路段长度,当前门架与下游门架之间的距离,km
Hour	0代表白天(6:00—18:00),1代表晚上(18:00—6:00)
Season	季节(0代表春季,1代表夏季,2代表秋季,3代表冬季)
SecCou	1min内通过当前门架的车辆数,veh/min
PasNum	1min内通过当前门架且将会通过下游最近门架的车辆数,veh/min
LosNum	1min内当前门架与下游最近门架之间的分流交通量,veh/min
NewNum	1min内当前门架与下游最近门架之间的合流交通量,veh/min
CelFlo	路段总流量,veh/h/lane
InpGin	1min内车辆到达的Gini系数
Density	对应分钟路段平均密度,veh/km/lane
$Density_s$	对应分钟开始时刻的路段密度,veh/km/lane
$Density_e$	对应分钟结束时刻的路段密度,veh/km/lane
MeaSpe	1min内通过当前门架的车辆行驶速度的平均值,km/h
$MeaSpe_u$	1min内通过当前门架的上游最近门架的车辆行驶速度的平均值,km/h
$MeaSpe_d$	1min内通过当前门架的下游最近门架的车辆行驶速度的平均值,km/h
SpeDif	MeaSpe与$MeaSpe_u$之差的绝对值,km/h

第1步,抽取事故交通流数据。距离事故发生时间越近的交通流数据对事故风险的影响越大,提取事故发生前10～5min的交通流数据可以在事故发生前识别危险交通流特征[4]。通过位置信息将事故数据与事故发生位置上游最近的电子收费门架数据进行匹配,通过时间信息提取该门架在事故发生前10～5min的5条交通流数据,对5条交通流数据中各变量求均值得到1条事故交

通流数据,求均值的目的是降低参数的离散波动性。如某一门架下游的事故发生时间为 2020 年 8 月 23 日 9 点 34 分,则提取该门架 2020 年 8 月 23 日 9 点 24 分至 9 点 28 分的 5 条交通流数据,对 5 条交通流数据中各变量求均值得到 1 条事故交通流数据。在研究时间和空间范围内,共获得 898 条事故交通流数据。

第 2 步,抽取非事故交通流数据。在研究时间和空间范围内,随机抽取 8980 组正常状态的连续 5min(8980 ×5 =44900 条)的交通流数据,对每组交通流数据中各变量求均值后得到 8980 条非事故交通流数据。在随机抽取每组正常状态的连续 5min 交通流数据时,需保证该 5 分钟的前 1h 和后 1h 范围内,该门架与下游最近门架之间没有事故发生。

第 3 步,划分训练集与测试集。分别从事故交通流数据和非事故交通流数据中随机抽取 80% 的数据组成训练集,用于构建事故风险动态辨识模型,剩余 20% 的数据组成测试集,用于进一步验证模型的精度和有效性。

2　模型构建

2.1　二元 logit 模型

二元 logit 模型的被解释变量为二分类变量,模型常用于研究分类概率与解释变量之间的关系。是否发生交通事故作为被解释变量属于二分类变量,故本研究采用二元 logit 回归模型建立高速公路交通事故风险动态辨识模型。二项 logit 模型的基本形式如式(1)所示。

$$\mathrm{logit}(P_i) = \ln\frac{P_i}{1-P_i} = \beta_0 + \beta_1 x_{1,i} + \beta_2 x_{2,i} + \cdots + \beta_n x_{n,i} \tag{1}$$

式中:P_i——事故发生的概率;

x_i——第 i 个自变量;

β_i——x_i 的回归系数;

n——自变量的个数。

稍作变形可以得到概率和自变量之间的关系,如式(2)所示。

$$P_i = \frac{1}{1+e^{-(\beta_0+\beta_1 x_{1,i}+\beta_2 x_{2,i}+\cdots+\beta_n x_{n,i})}} \tag{2}$$

2.2　建模流程

为了解决待选自变量之间可能存在的相关性,并选择拟合精度最好的 logit 回归模型,本研究通过以下步骤建立高速公路事故风险动态辨识模型:

(1)通过建立只包含单个自变量的 logit 回归模型,检验每一个自变量是否与交通事故风险相关,不显著相关的自变量直接剔除,不参与后续建模分析;

(2)计算所选连续自变量之间的皮尔逊相关系数,相关系数高于 0.6 说明自变量间存在较强的相关性,此类自变量不能同时出现在模型中;

(3)将变量自由组合,进行 logit 回归模型建模,注意避免将相关性较强的变量同时添加到模型中,选择对数似然函数值最大的模型作为最终的高速公路事故风险动态辨识模型。

2.3　建模结果

根据上述步骤,本研究建立的高速公路事故风险动态辨识模型的参数估计如表 2 所示,模型包括 1 个分类变量、1 个几何特征变量和 4 个交通流连续变量。对 4 个交通流连续变量进行相关性检验,得到皮尔逊相关系数的取值范围为 -0.2907 ~ 0.3332,表明各个交通流连续变量之间的相关性较小,都可以加入到模型中。

模型的参数估计　　表 2

变　量	系　数	标　准　差	z	$p>\|z\|$	95% 置信区间	
MeaSpe	-0.0757518	0.0050701	-14.94	0.000	-0.0856889	-0.0658146
SpeDif	0.0424268	0.005694	7.45	0.000	0.0312669	0.0535868
SecCou	0.0274775	0.0030298	9.07	0.000	0.0215392	0.0334158
Interval	0.0333786	0.0103813	3.22	0.001	0.0130317	0.0537256
NewNum	0.0453309	0.0116654	3.89	0.000	0.0224671	0.0681947
DriDri	0.4999147	0.0906297	5.52	0.000	0.3222838	0.6775456
常数项	2.88177	0.4765486	6.05	0.000	1.947752	3.815789

从表 2 中可以看出,模型中各个解释变量的 p 值都小于 0.05,说明各个解释变量对交通事故风险的影响都很显著。系数为负,表明随着该变量值的增大,发生事故的风险越低;系数为负,表明随着该变量值的增大,发生事故的风险越高。MeaSpe 系数为负,表明平均速度越大,发生事故

的可能性越小,而 SpeDif 系数为正,表明上下游断面速度差的绝对值越大,发生事故的可能性越大,与事实相符。模型中其他自变量的符号也可以得到合理的解释。

3 模型评价

3.1 模型对训练集的预测精度

事故风险动态辨识模型在训练集上不同误报率下的预测精度如表3所示。

当概率分割值取0.0760时,事故风险动态辨识模型对训练集的分类预测结果如表4所示,模型对训练集的正确预测率为65.50%。

事故风险动态辨识模型对训练集的ROC曲线图如图2所示,纵坐标为敏感度,横坐标为1-特异度。图2中的AUC为0.7306,说明建立的模型对训练集具有一定的准确性。

3.2 模型对测试集的预测精度

事故风险动态辨识模型在测试集上不同误报率下的预测精度如表5所示。

模型在训练集上的预测精度 表3

误报率	阈值	敏感度	特异度	正确分类率
0.05	0.1651	35.52%	95.00%	89.59%
0.10	0.1275	43.04%	90.00%	85.73%
0.15	0.1097	49.03%	85.00%	81.73%
0.20	0.0970	54.18%	80.00%	77.65%
0.25	0.0878	59.47%	75.00%	73.59%
0.30	0.0808	63.37%	70.00%	69.40%
0.35	0.0754	66.43%	65.00%	65.13%
0.40	0.0704	70.19%	60.00%	60.93%
0.45	0.0661	74.37%	55.00%	56.76%
0.50	0.0621	76.88%	50.00%	52.44%

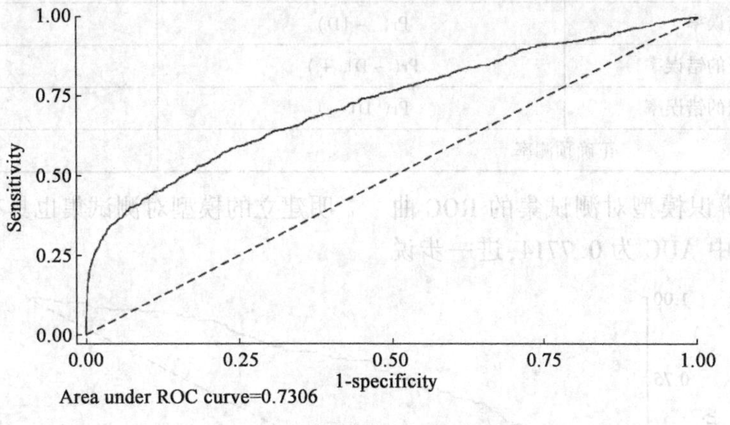

图2 模型对训练集的ROC曲线图

模型对训练集的分类预测结果 表4

类别	符号	概率
灵敏度	Pr(+ | D)	66.02%
特异度	Pr(+ | ~D)	65.45%
阳性预测值	Pr(D| +)	16.04%
阴性预测值	Pr(~D| −)	95.06%
事件未发生的错误率	Pr(+ | ~D)	34.55%
事件发生的错误率	Pr(− |D)	33.98%
概率值大于分割点的错误率	Pr(~D| +)	83.96%
概率值小于分割点的错误率	Pr(D| −)	4.94%
正确预测率		65.50%

模型在测试集上的预测精度 表5

误报率	阈值	敏感度	特异度	正确分类率
0.05	0.1705	42.78%	95.00%	90.28%
0.10	0.1293	47.78%	90.00%	86.18%
0.15	0.1086	56.67%	85.00%	82.44%
0.20	0.0969	54.18%	80.00%	77.65%
0.25	0.0878	65.56%	75.00%	74.14%
0.30	0.0814	68.33%	70.00%	69.89%
0.35	0.0755	71.11%	65.00%	65.59%
0.40	0.0698	75.56%	60.00%	61.44%
0.45	0.0643	80.00%	55.00%	57.29%
0.50	0.0608	80.56%	50.00%	52.78%

当概率分割值取0.0760时,事故风险动态辨识模型对测试集的分类预测结果如表6所示,模型对训练集的正确预测率为65.99%。

模型对测试集的分类预测结果 表6

类别	符号	概率
灵敏度	Pr(+|D)	71.11%
特异度	Pr(-|~D)	65.48%
阳性预测值	Pr(D| +)	17.11%
阴性预测值	Pr(~D| -)	95.77%
事件未发生的错误率	Pr(+|~D)	34.52%
事件发生的错误率	Pr(-|D)	28.89%
概率值大于分割点的错误率	Pr(~D| +)	82.89%
概率值小于分割点的错误率	Pr(D|-)	4.23%
正确预测率		65.99%

事故风险动态辨识模型对测试集的ROC曲线图如图3所示,图中AUC为0.7714,进一步说明建立的模型对测试集也具有一定的准确性。

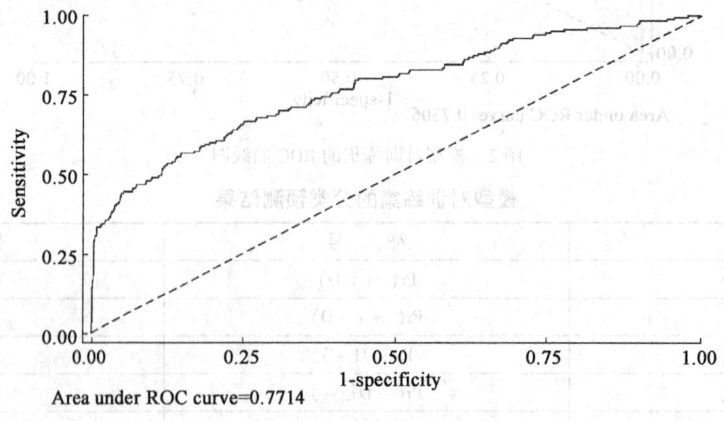

图3 模型对训练集的ROC曲线图

4 结语

本研究基于ETC门架数据获取高精度交通流数据,建立随机式数据样本,采用非配对病例-对照研究方法进行研究,基于二元logit回归模型建立高速公路交通事故风险动态辨识模型,得出以下结论：

(1)基于 ETC 门架数据,可以获取以分钟为单位的高精度交通流数据用于高速公路事故风险动态辨识模型建模,每一条高精度交通流数据包括几何特征、时间特征、流量特征、密度特征、速度特征等五种类型的变量。

(2)logit 回归分析结果表明,高速公路交通事故风险受平均速度、上下游断面速度差、交通量、路段长度、汇入流量和行车方向共同影响的。其中平均速度的系数为负,其余自变量的系数为正。

(3)随着概率分割值的增大,模型的敏感度降低,特异度升高。当概率分割值取 0.0760 时,模型对训练集的敏感度为 66.02%,特异度为 65.45%,预测正确率为 65.50%,AUC 为 0.7306;模型对测试集的敏感度为 71.11%,特异度为 65.48,预测正确率为 65.99%,AUC 为 0.7714。可以看出,模型对测试集表现出较好的预测性能。

(4)后续研究中,可以进一步考虑天气状况、事故发生地点是否位于分合流区域等因素对事故风险的影响。

参考文献

[1] Lord D, Mannering F. The statistical analysis of crash-frequency data: A review and assessment of methodological alternatives[J]. Transportation research part A: policy and practice, 2010, 44(5): 291-305.

[2] Malyshkina N V, Mannering F L, Tarko A P. Markov switching negative binomial models: an application to vehicle accident frequencies[J]. Accident Analysis & Prevention, 2009, 41(2): 217-226.

[3] Quddus M A. Time series count data models: an empirical application to traffic accidents[J]. Accident Analysis & Prevention, 2008, 40(5): 1732-1741.

[4] 徐铖铖. 高速公路交通流运行状态与交通安全关系研究[D]. 2014.

[5] Lee C, Abdel-Aty M, Hsia L. Potential real-time indicators of sideswipe crashes on freeways[J]. Transportation research record, 2006, 1953(1): 41-49.

[6] Golob T F, Recker W, Pavlis Y. Probabilistic models of freeway safety performance using traffic flow data as predictors[J]. Safety science, 2008, 46(9): 1306-1333.

[7] Kwak H C, Kho S. Predicting crash risk and identifying crash precursors on Korean expressways using loop detector data[J]. Accident Analysis & Prevention, 2016, 88: 9-19.

[8] 付存勇,王俊骅. 基于监控数据的高速公路实时事故风险模型[J]. 交通信息与安全, 2017, 35(5): 11-17.

[9] 游锦明,方守恩,张兰芳,等. 高速公路实时事故风险研判模型及可移植性[J]. 同济大学学报(自然科学版), 2019, 47(3): 347-352.

[10] 樊博. 基于实时交通流的高速公路事故风险预测与致因分析方法研究[D]. 2021.

[11] Abdel-Aty M A, Hassan H M, Ahmed M, et al. Real-time prediction of visibility related crashes[J]. Transportation research part C: emerging technologies, 2012, 24: 288-298.

[12] Hossain M, Muromachi Y. A Bayesian network based framework for real-time crash prediction on the basic freeway segments of urban expressways[J]. Accident Analysis & Prevention, 2012, 45: 373-381.

[13] Xu C, Liu P, Wang W, et al. Evaluation of the impacts of traffic states on crash risks on freeways[J]. Accident Analysis & Prevention, 2012, 47: 162-171.

[14] Xu C, Wang W, Liu P. Identifying crash-prone traffic conditions under different weather on freeways[J]. Journal of safety research, 2013, 46: 135-144.

[15] Xu C, Liu P, Wang W. Evaluation of the predictability of real-time crash risk models[J]. Accident Analysis & Prevention, 2016, 94: 207-215.

三对应原理之实施 13——三个真法理联进

黄剑飞*
(浙江杭州市公安局)

摘　要　本文继续论述、道路交通安全三对应原理的实施真法理,“提前识险”“三三归一”“注意维护”的联进(即联合进行);即三者继续联进提醒与消除事故原因鉴定、立法规、供路供车供驾驶、用路用车用驾驶、执法规中的不对应,以不断地维护对应而实现交通安全。

关键词　原理实施　三个真法理　不对应

0　引言

笔者已经提出了道安(道路交通安全的简称,下同)的三对应原理(以下均称原理),以及原理实施的真法理“提前识险”“三三归一”“注意维护”;也已对三个真法理的同行(也就是联进)进行了论述,即以全体用路人(用路用车用驾驶人的简称,下同)选举出来的“用路人代表大会”(以下均称“代表会”)、事故原因(含当事人责任)鉴定(以下均称原因鉴定)委员会”(以下均称“鉴定会”)、“道安立法规委员会”(以下均称“立法规会”)、“道安监督委员会”(以下均称“监督会”)等,联进进行“提前识险”“三三归一”“注意维护”;这些笔者不再重复了。由于道安系统中具体的不对应很多,因此笔者对三者的联进继续论述,以不断地消除不对应而维护对应。

1　原因鉴定中的联进

根据原理,如果道路上的绿化丛高就会遮挡驾驶人(用路人之一,下同)的视线,使驾驶人没有反应时间与措施距离而与他车相撞,因此及时割低绿化丛是供路人(供路供车供驾驶人之一,下同)中的养护人对应的注意义务(安全注意义务的简称,下同),原因鉴定必须以此为准绳,否则就是不对应。“代表会”在原因鉴定前就要识别这个不对应危险,并提醒鉴定人消除,否则将会产生这种不对应原因鉴定的危险。例 1:甲驾轿车由北向南行驶,与由东向西横过道路乙骑的二轮电动自行车相撞,造成车损人伤,事后甲、乙均称“道路中间的绿化丛太高而看不到对方,等看到时已经相撞”;由于道路交通安全法及其实施条例中对绿化丛只有“不得妨碍安全视距”的模糊要求,而没有精确要求,即没有“绿化丛高度”最大允许的“标准值”(即大于“标准值”就属于妨碍安全视距),法规中也没有“道路安全技术标准”(本来这里也可规定这个“标准值”);于是交警部门(中国的原因鉴定人)就作出“因绿化丛高度妨碍安全视距、没有法律依据,故甲未确保安全、乙未按规定让行是事故的两个原因,甲乙各负同等的当事人责任”的事故认定结论(中国的原因鉴定结论);甲、乙就不满而称“都看不到对方了”“还怎么确保安全”“还怎么让行”。此其一,其二,如果例 1 的不对应原因鉴定发生了,那就必须由“三三归一”进行重新鉴定予以消除。根据“三三归一”“鉴定会”鉴定如下:由于道路交通安全法及其实施条例对绿化丛的高度没有精确要求,即没有规定这个“标准值”(如道路内及路口周边两个路宽范围的绿化丛高度不得超过 30cm),而且我国的公路法及公路工程技术标准,也没有规定这个“标准值”;因此由于法规没有规定、造成养护人没有割低绿化丛,从而导致了事故的发生,所以事故原因的原因是中国的立法规人没有履行正确(即对应)的立法规注意义务,负全部的当事人责任。其三,由于“三三归一”是以原理(而不是以现有法规)为准绳进行鉴定的,因此“三三归一”的鉴定结论,能为立法规(包括修正法规,下同)提供依据。反之,如果原因鉴定的结论错误(即不对应),那就为立法规人提供错误(即不对应)的依据。

2　立法规与提供及用路中的联进

(1)“代表会”运用“提前识险”识别各种不对应危险后、就要提醒“立法规会”消除,而“立法规会”则运用“注意维护”具体消除立法规中的各种不对应。比如:“代表会”在提前识别(例1)中的不对应危险、提醒“鉴定会”消除后,还要继续提醒“立法规会”消除,而“立法规会”根据“代表会”的提醒、“鉴定会”重新鉴定的依据,运用“注意维护”修正法规、即在法规中补上这个“标准值”(以及“道路安全技术标准”),这样就消除了立法规中的不对应而维护对应;如果立法规人不肯消除不对应,那就必须由“监督会”“代表会”对立法规人实施弹劾予以消除。

(2)根据原理,如果原因鉴定人与立法规人已经消除了各自的不对应,但提供人(供路供车供驾驶人的简称,下同)没有消除提供中的不对应,那不对应仍然存在、事故仍会发生。比如如果前面2(1)中法规已补上了这个“标准值”(即已消除了立法规中的不对应),但提供人中的供路人没有履行(即没有做到)法规要求的注意义务(即没有消除提供中的不对应),那不对应仍会传播到用路中而发生例1这样的事故。因此,只有提供人也履行了法规要求的注意义务,才是达到了提供中的对应;如果提供人不肯履行(即不肯消除不对应),那就必须由道安监理的执法规人运用“注意维护”强制消除(包括对提供人进行处罚以阻止不对应的传播)。比如:根据原理,如果机动车左转弯时靠外侧大转弯(即未靠内侧小转弯),就会增大机动车与其他进口道上车辆空间上的冲突程度,从而增大发生事故的概率;因此这种行驶方式是不对应。“代表会”在提供前就要识别这个不对应危险,并提醒提供人中的供驾驶人消除,即供驾驶人在教授与许可时要求驾驶人做到“靠内侧小转弯”,否则不对应会传播到用路中而发生事故。

(3)根据原理,如果原因鉴定人、立法规人、提供人已经消除了各自的不对应,但用路人没有消除用路中的不对应,那不对应仍然存在、事故仍会发生。比如:如果前面2(2)中供驾驶人已经要求驾驶人“靠内侧小转弯”,但驾驶人没有做到,则仍是用路中的不对应;“代表会”在用路前就要识别这个不对应危险,并提醒用路人消除,否则将会产生这种不对应用路的危险。例2:乙骑二轮电动自行车、在四岔路口由西向北左转弯,因避让前方右偏的同类车,而被由东向南行驶、靠外侧左转弯的轿车剐倒、造成车损人伤,事后乙称“你(指轿车),左转弯为什么开在这里?”。如果例2的不对应用路发生了,那就必须由“注意维护”进行消除,即由道安监理的执法规人对轿车驾驶人进行处罚,以阻止类似事件的发生。因此,只有用路人也履行了法规、提供人要求的注意义务,才是达到了用路中的对应。

(4)前面1“其一”中的原因鉴定、也是常常被质疑的“中国式原因鉴定”的表现,其导致了立法规中的不对应、并传播到供路中与用路中;根据原理,只有消除了“中国式原因鉴定”这个不对应,才能消除立法规中的不对应及其传播。

3 执法规中的联进

(1)根据原理,如果原因鉴定人、立法规人已经消除了各自的不对应,但提供人、用路人不肯消除自己的不对应,那就必须由执法规人进行消除;但如果执法规人没有进行消除,那这个不对应就又成为了执法规中的不对应,如果执法规人进行了错误的消除,那执法规中就又产生了新的不对应;执法规中的不对应仍会导致事故的发生。比如:根据原理,如果例2的不对应用路是执法规人造成的,即由于当地交警部门(中国的道安监理执法规人,下同)将该路口的左转弯机动车道设置于(同进口道的)最右边,右转弯机动车道设置于(同进口道的)最左边,并规定“未按规定车道行驶的、一律处罚”,才造成轿车驾驶人靠外侧左转弯;那就是执法规中产生的新的不对应,必须由“监督会”运用“注意维护”撤消这个处罚。因此,只有执法规人也履行了法规要求的注意义务,才是达到了执法规中的对应。

(2)根据原理,当人行横道线上没有行人而机动车进行停车“让行”时,本来能够按时离开的机动车就被滞留,本来不会与行人相遇的机动车就因相遇,并(真)让行而再被滞留,再加上后面机动车的拥到,从而使机动车之间的时空冲突增大、反应时间与措施距离不够的驾驶人出现的概率增大,发生事故的概率也增大。而且,这种停车会使其他车辆产生误判,从而产生新的反应时间与措施距离不够的驾驶(骑车)人、新的事故也产生。再则,如果每条横道线都这么停车,就会影响驾驶人驾驶任务的完成,驾驶人就会有意无意地去减小其他通行时的反应时间与措施距离,从而增大事故发生的概率;如果每辆机动车都这么停车,则除了会使前面的情况叠加外,还会阻却交通流,从而又增大事故发生的概率(原因见笔者以前的文章)。由此可见,这种停车"让行"是无故停车、是错让行、是不对应,如果执法规人强制要求驾驶人这么做,那就是执法规中的不对应。"代表会"在执法规前就要识别这个不对应危险、并提醒执法规人消除,否则将会产生这种不对应执法规的危险。例 3:某地交警部门要求所有机动车遇到人行横道线时,不管横道线上有无行人都必须先停车、再观察、再起步行驶,否则,一律按未按规定让行处罚;于是机动车因停车而被滞留、被滞留机动车之间的事故多发了(尤其在车流量大的地方),后面的二轮电动自行车见机动车停车以为安全,左转被撞的事故发生了,机动车驾驶人为了挽回多次停车损失的时间、加速行驶而与别车相剐的事故增多了,每辆机动车都停车造成交通堵塞、而使堵塞开始与结束的地方事故多发了……。如果例 3 的不对应执法规发生了,那就必须由"注意维护"进行消除,即由"监督会"对执法规人实施监督、撤消这个处罚。

4　结束语

如果"三三归一"的鉴定结论是立法规人负全部的当事人责任,那事故的民事赔偿就必须进行国家赔偿。法规是公开的、透明的,未履行者是要对全社会负责而承担法律责任的,而部门的内部规定是不公开、不透明的,未做到者是不用承担法律责任的。比如例 1 的绿化丛高度,养护部门内部是可能有个"目标值",但由于其是不公开、不透明的,因此就算这个"目标值"是准确的,如果养护人自己没有做到是不用负责的。所以,对不对应(尤其是危害大的不对应)必须以法规(即列入法规之中)来阻止,这样才权责对应。从安全上说,立法规、执法规是对提供人、用路人行为的控制,因此他们的对应不对应决定了所有提供人、用路人的对应不对应;像例 1 法规没有规定"标准值"、提供人不对应也变成对应了,像例 3 与例 2(指由执法规造成的情况)由于执法规不对应、驾驶人就都被不对应了。因此必须对立法规有弹劾机制、对执法规有监督机制,才能权责对应。由于道安系统中具体的不对应很多,因此三个真法理必须在联进中不断地提醒与消除不对应,才能消除所有的不对应、而实现交通安全。

参考文献

[1] By Jianfei Huang. The Three Corresponding Principles of Road TrafficSafety and Their Supplements [C]. Proceeding of the 15th International Forum of Automotive Traffic Safety, 2018:41-46.

Real-time Crash Analysis for Expressways Considering Distances between Detectors

Chunjie Li[1,2]　Qikang Zheng[*2]　Chengcheng Xu[2]　Yiheng Lu[2]　Ling Deng[2]

(1. Hebei Provincial Communications Planning, Design and Research Institute Co., Ltd.;

2. School of Transportation, Southeast University)

Abstract　Many studies have been conducted to establish real-time crash prediction models. However, few of them have focused on the layout location of traffic detectors. This study aims at evaluating the effects of distance between detectors on the predictive performance of real-time crash models. Crash data and real-time traffic data in the year of 2017 were collected from the I-880 highway northbound in California. The study corridor was classified into 6 categories based on the distance between the upstream and downstream detectors. Stepwise Logistic Regression was used to identify significant variables and build real-time crash prediction models for each category. Predictive abilities of all models were compared. The results indicate that when the distance between detectors ranges from 0.45 to 0.6 miles, the models perform best. Prediction performance of models increases before detector distances rise to 0.45 miles, and decreases with detector distances beyond 0.6 miles. The study results could be used by transportation management departments when decide the layout location and spacing of detectors from the point of view of improving the prediction accuracy of crashes.

Keywords traffic safety crash prediction traffic detectors express way

0 Introduction

With the developemt of proactive safety intervention measurements such as Advanced Traffic Management (ATM) Systems, real-time crash prediction models are of vital significance (Lee et al., 2006). The models can serve as a tool for identifying crash precursors and exploring crash mechanisms for ATM systems (Hossain and Muromachi, 2011). The original intention for real-time crash models was to link real-time crash probability with dynamic traffic flow conditions prior to the occurrence of crashes (Oh et al., 2001; Xu et al., 2015). Traffic flow characteristics prior to crash occurrence could be identified and matched with the crashes.

Loop detector data was most frequently used data in previous real-time crash prediction. Most studies collected traffic data 5-10 minutes before crash occurrence (Hossain and Muromachi, 2013; Yu and Abdel-Aty, 2013; Wang et al., 2019; Haule et al., 2021). Jiang et al. (2020) proposed that traffic data of only one temporal resolution cannot fully represent traffic trend and dynamic transitions in different time intervals, and they predicted real-time crash risk in different time intervals.

Recently, detector data of more sources have been collected and used in real-time traffic crash, such as radar detectors and camera detectors. Ahmed and Abdel-Aty (2012) examined the identification of freeway locations with high crash potential using real-time speed data collected from automatic vehicle identification (AVI). Wu et al. (2020) extracted trajectory of road users from roadside LiDAR data to identify near-crash cases. Trajectories extracted from camera video data were also applied for real-time traffic safety evaluation (Guo et al., 2020; Zheng et al., 2020).

However, whether the research was based on loop detector data, or based on other datasets, the distance between detectors was assumed to be constant. In fact, the detectors utilized to obtain the data are not equally spaced, and the distance between detectors are of difference, which can affect the exposure rate of crashes on a single segment between the detector pair. A limitation of previous studies is that the section length variable was always omitted from models or even not be mentioned. Therefore, it is essential to establish real-time crash risk models considering the layout spacing of detectors.

To address the above limitations, themain goal of this study was proposed: to evaluate the effects of distance between detectors on the predictive performance of real-time crash models. Stepwise Logistic Regression was used in this study to predict the crash risk.

The remainder of this study is organized as follows. Following this section, the second section describes the data and conducts descriptive analysis of the collected variables. The third section presents the methodology. The fourth section shows the model results, and the fifth section summarizes the findings, conclusions and limitations of this study.

1 Data Description

The study chose a 28 miles long corridor of the I-880 highway northbound in California, US as the study subject. The study corridor is illustrated in Fig. 1. The study period was the whole year of 2017 from January to December. Two datasets were collected, including the crash data and the traffic data.

Crash data were obtained from the State-wide Integrated Traffic Records System (SWITRS) of the California Departmentof Transportation. SWITRS offers detailed information on state-wide collisions on all types of roads, excluding private roads. After screening, 695 crashes happening in the study period were collected.

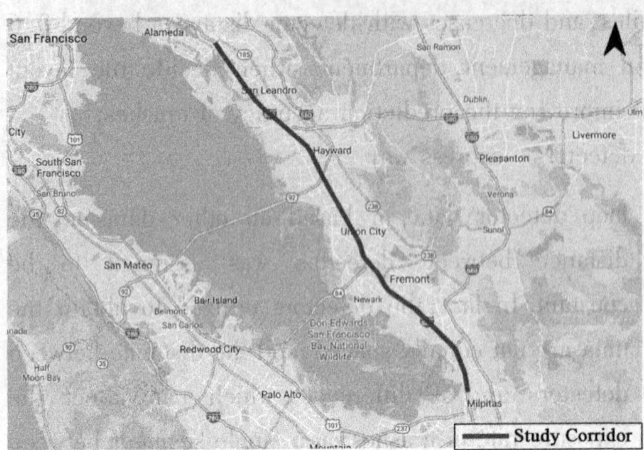

Fig. 1 Study Corridor

Traffic data were collected from the Highway Performance Measurement System (PeMS). PeMS provides real-time and historical traffic data obtained by loop detectors in a 30 second interval, including volume data, occupancy data and speed data. There are 53 detectors on the study corridor, combined into 52 target segments, the length of which ranges from 0.14 miles to 1.38 miles.

Traffic data 5-10 minutes prior to the crash time were selected to represent the disturbance condition that contributes to the occurrence of a crash. Case-control method was used in this study to collect non-crash dataset. The ratio of cases to controls equals to 1 : 4 as previous researchers did (Abdel-Aty et al., 2005; Zheng et al., 2021). Non-crash samples were collected from normal traffic conditions, which neither result in nor are impacted by any crashes. Hence, non-crash dataset consists of 2780 samples.

The raw 30s data from the two detectors nearest to the target segments (i.e., the nearest upstream detector and the nearest downstream detector) was obtained and converted into traffic variables at a 5-min interval, including the average (*avg*), standard deviation (*std*) of the upstream (*up*) and downstream (*down*) volume (*vol*), speed (*spd*) and occupancy (*occ*), along with the difference between the upstream and downstream traffic variables (*up_down*). In total, 15 traffic variables were obtained, comprising *avg_vol_up*, *avg_occ_up*, *avg_spd_up*, *avg_vol_down*, *avg_occ_down*, *avg_spd_down*, *std_vol_up*, *std_occ_up*, *std_spd_up*, *std_vol_down*, *std_occ_down*, *std_spd_down*, *vol_up_down*, *occ_up_down*, *spd_up_down*.

The 52 target segments were classified into 6 categories by the distance between the upstream and downstream detectors, i.e., section length. In order to avoid the impact of different sample sizes, the sample sizes of each category were tried to keep similar. The classification result and the distribution of data are shown in Tab. 1.

Distribution of Data Tab. 1

Section Length	Crash Cases	Non-crash Cases
<0.3	123	492
0.3-0.45	143	572
0.45-0.6	136	544
0.6-0.8	145	580
>0.8	148	592
Total	695	2780

2 Methodology

In crash risk modelling, relationship between traffic crashes and traffic flow variables need to be established. Stepwise Logistic Regression was used in this paper to filter variables and build real-time crash risk models at the 90% confidence interval. There are 15 traffic variables used for Stepwise Logistic Regression analysis. A forward stepwise procedure was used to select the independent variables that should have been included in the model to predict crashes. A variable was progressively entered into the model if the significance level of its statistical score was smaller than 0.1. The regression equation derived from each of the training subsets was applied to the just removed cross-validation subset to estimate the individual probability of having a malignant breast tumour. This probability (P) can be calculated as follows:

$$P = \frac{1}{1 + e^{-Z}} \tag{1}$$

where e is the base of natural logarithms and Z is the linear combination calculated as:

$$Z = \beta_0 + \sum_{k=1}^{n} \beta_k x_k \tag{2}$$

where β_0 is the constant term, and β_k is the

coefficient estimated from data, and x_k is the predictor variable included in the model.

By combining equation (1) and equation (2), the probability P can be calculated as:

$$P = \frac{1}{1 + e^{-(\beta_0 + \sum_{k=1}^{n} \beta_k x_k)}} = \frac{e^{\beta_0 + \sum_{k=1}^{n} \beta_k x_k}}{e^{\beta_0 + \sum_{k=1}^{n} \beta_k x_k} + 1} \quad (3)$$

The probability P estimated by Logistic Regression always ranges between 0 to 1, regardless of the value of Z (Chou et al., 2001). Once P is greater than the threshold, then the event will be classified as a crash event. When the estimated probability was less than threshold, the event will be classified as a non-crash event.

3 Results

3.1 Crash Precursor Identification by Logistic Model

The data contains 695 crash cases and 2780 non-crash cases. The ratio between the two is 1:4. The data was classified almost evenly into six categories by the length of sections. Stepwise Logistic Regression was used to test the significance of each independent variable and identify crash precursors for each category of data. Specifically, the independent variables were introduced step by step. In each step, the most significant independent variable was introduced into the model at the 90% confidence interval, while the existing variables were tested one by one, and the insignificant variables were eliminated. The performance of the models was evaluated by the area under the Receiver Operating Characteristic (ROC) curve (AUC). AUC is a commonly used indicator to measure the predictive ability of a model. The range of AUC is from 0.5 to 1.0, and a higher AUC value is preferred.

In total, six Logistic Regression models were established according to the section lengths. The models' results are shown in Tab.2. The t-test results indicate that of all the variables in the table are significant at the 90% confidence interval.

Logistic Regression Result Tab. 2

Section Length(miles)	Variable	Coef.	Std.	t-test result	AUC
<0.3	*avg_vol_up*	−0.133	0.042	−3.19	0.7303
	std_occ_down	0.151	0.036	4.26	
	vol_up_down	0.239	0.129	1.86	
	constant	−3.714	0.436	−8.51	
0.3 ~ 0.45	*avg_spd_up*	−0.033	0.015	−2.16	0.7491
	avg_spd_down	−0.036	0.014	−2.63	
	std_occ_up	0.032	0.012	2.62	
	std_vol_down	0.435	0.117	3.73	
	constant	1.581	0.604	2.62	
0.45 ~ 0.6	*avg_occ_up*	0.125	0.031	4.04	0.7840
	avg_occ_down	−0.061	0.036	−1.68	
	std_vol_up	0.237	0.114	2.07	
	std_spd_up	0.108	0.042	2.57	
	std_occ_down	0.223	0.055	4.04	
	constant	−0.223	0.055	−7.99	
0.6 ~ 0.8	*avg_occ_up*	0.156	0.055	2.82	0.7740
	avg_spd_up	−0.108	0.032	−3.46	
	avg_occ_down	−0.171	0.074	−2.31	

continued

Section Length(miles)	Variable	Coef.	Std.	*t*-test result	AUC
0.6 ~ 0.8	*avg_spd_down*	0.044	0.024	1.81	0.7740
	occ_up_down	0.1399	0.0668	2.09	
	spd_up_down	0.057	0.028	2.04	
	constant	2.784	1.53	1.82	
>0.8	*avg_spd_up*	−0.069	0.027	−2.51	0.7239
	avg_vol_down	0.103	0.041	2.49	
	avg_occ_down	−0.201	0.075	−2.69	
	avg_spd_down	−0.026	0.013	−1.91	
	std_occ_down	0.264	0.130	2.03	
	std_spd_down	−0.198	0.072	−2.75	
	occ_up_down	0.145	0.048	3.02	
	constant	5.14	2.079	2.47	

The result presented inTab. 2 aimed at selecting variables to prevent overfitting in modelling. If the coefficient of a variable is greater than zero, crash risk can be considered to increase with the rise of the variable. On the contrary, crash risk can be considered to decrease with the rise of the variable. Over all, crash risk increases with the decrease in velocity, the increase in traffic volume and occupation, and the increase in variables reflecting traffic oscillation, including the standard deviation of traffic flow variables and the difference between upstream and downstream traffic flow variables.

For sections shorter than 0.3miles, it can be seen there are three significant variables in the model, e.g., average value of upstream flow (*avg_vol_up*), standard deviation of downstream occupation (*std_occ_down*), and difference between upstream and downstream speed (*vol_up_down*). The parameter of *avg_vol_up* is less than zero, which means that the crash probability decreases with the increasement of upstream speed. It is rational for the reason that the high speed represents the non-obstruction of road. Parameters of *std_occ_down* and *vol_up_down* are positive, which reflects the rise of crash risk with fluctuations in traffic flow. For sections whose lengths are between 0.3 to 0.45 miles, parameters of average speed of upstream and downstream are both negative. Meanwhile, parameters of standard deviation of upstream occupation and downstream volume have positive values.

Acurious phenomenon can be found in sections range from 0.45 to 0.6 miles and sections range from 0.6 to 0.8 miles, that parameters of *avg_occ_up* are both positive, but parameters of *avg_occ_down* are both negative, which means that crashes tend to happen when upstream occupation is larger while the downstream occupation is relatively small. This phenomenon signifies that congestion is likely to happen, because more cars are entering than leaving the section. As a result, risk of crashes goes up.

And for sectionslonger than 0.8 miles, as expected, *avg_spd_up*, *avg_spd_down* and *avg_occ_down* have negative parameters, while *avg_vol_down*, *std_occ_down* and *occ_up_down* have positive parameters. However, the parameter of *std_spd_down* is less than zero, which means that the crash risk will decrease with the fluctuation in downstream speed. This seems unreasonable, but it can be interpreted that when the section length is too long, the downstream detector can be too far away from the risk spot, resulting in the failure of crash risk prediction.

The AUC value of the six models are also presented in the table. The model where section length ranges from 0.45 miles to 0.6 miles owns the largest AUC value, indicating that crashes can be predicted most accurately when the distance between the detectors used for crash prediction falls in this range.

3.2 Effects of Distances between Detectors

The results of theLogistic Regression models were also evaluated by AUC. And the AUC values of the six models were calculated to be 0.7303, 0.7491, 0.7840, 0.7740, and 0.7239 respectively. The results of Logistic Regression models are shown in Fig. 2.

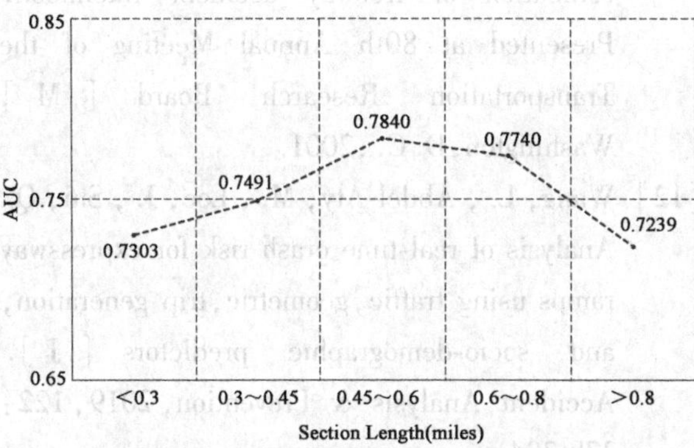

Fig. 2 Results of Logistic Regression

Fig. 2 clearly delineates the effects of distances between detectors to the predictive ability of real-time crash risk models. When the section length is in the range of 0.45 miles to 0.6 miles, the model has the largest AUC. When the section length is shorter than 0.45 miles, the predictive ability rises with increase of section length. And then, once the distance between detectors surpasses 0.6 miles, predictive ability decreases sharply.

The result is fairly apparent and reasonable. When the two detectors are too close, the section length will be too small to observe the inordinate traffic flow phenomenon before crashes. The reason may be explained as that too short a distance increases the randomness of the vehicles observed because of the relatively small sample. Whereas, when the distance between detectors is too large, the detectors will be too far away from the study object. As a result, with the propagation of traffic flow, the characteristics of traffic flow that should have been observed may be washed away.

Hence, the result indicates that the best rangeof distances between detectors on expressways is from 0.45 miles to 0.6 miles.

4 Conclusions

Numerous studies have been conducted topredict real-time crash risks. However, the detectors along freeways were not equally spaced, and few of previous studies have focused on the layout location of traffic detectors. This study aims to estimate the effects of distance between detectors on the predictive performance of real-time crash models.

A 28 miles long corridor of the I-880 highway northbound in California, US was selected as the testbed of this study. Case-control method was used to collect crash and real-time traffic data in the year of 2017. Thedataset was classified into six categories by the length of sections. Stepwise Logistic Regression was applied for variable sheltering and model establishing. AUC value was employed to evaluate the prediction performance of the models. By plotting the line charts of the results, it was found that the model performs best when the section length is in the range of 0.45 miles to 0.6 miles. If the section length is shorter than 0.45 miles, the predictive ability rises with the increase of section length. On the contrary, if the distance between detectors is greater than 0.6 miles, predictive ability decreases with the increase of section length.

There are still some limitations in this study. The section length could be classified in more detail, and a more precisely optimal distance range could be suggested.

5 Acknowledgements

This work was supported by the National Natural Science Foundation of China (No. 51925801 and 52172343), and the National Key Research and Development Program of China (No. 2020YFB1600500). The authors would like to thank the editor and the reviewers for their constructive comments and valuable suggestions to improve the quality of this article

References

[1] Abdel-Aty, M., Uddin, N., and Pande, A. Split models for predicting multivehicle crashes during high-speed and low-speed operating conditions on freeways [J]. Transportation Research Record: Journal of the Transportation Research Board 2005, 1908, 51-58.

[2] Ahmed, M., and Abdel-Aty, M. The viability of using automatic vehicle identification data for real-time crash prediction. IEEE Transactions on Intelligent Transportation Systems, 2012, 13 (2), 459-468.

[3] ChouY., Tiu C., Hung G., Wu S., Chang T., and Chiang H. Stepwise logistic regression analysis of tumor contour features for breast ultrasound diagnosis [J]. Ultrasound in Medicine & Biology, 2001, 27 (11), 1493-1498.

[4] Guo, Y., Sayed, T., and Essa, M. Real-time conflict-based bayesian tobit models for safety evaluation of signalized intersections [J]. Accident Analysis & Prevention, 2020, 144, 105660.

[5] Haule, H. J., Ali, M. S., Alluri, P., et al Evaluating the effect of ramp metering on freeway safety using real-time traffic data. Accident Analysis & Prevention 2021, 157, 106-181.

[6] Hossain, M., and Muromachi, Y. Understanding crash mechanisms and selecting interventions to mitigate real-time hazards on urban expressways. Transportation Research Record: Journal of the Transportation Research Board, 2011, 2213, 53-62.

[7] Hossain, M., Muromachi, Y. A real-time crash prediction model for the ramp vicinities of urban expressways [J]. IATSS Research, 2013, 37, 68-79.

[8] Jiang, F., Yuen, K., Lee, E. A long short-term memory-based framework for crash detection on freeways with traffic data of different temporal resolutions. Accident Analysis & Prevention, 2020 141, 105520.

[9] Kotsiantis, S. B. Supervised machine learning: A review of classification techniques [J]. Informatica, 2007, 31, 249-268.

[10] Lee, C., Abdel-Aty, M., Hsia, L. Potential real-time indicators of sideswipe crashes on freeways[J]. Transportation Research Record: Journal of the Transportation Research Board, 2006, 1953: 41-49.

[11] Oh, C., Oh, J., Ritchie, S. Real-time estimation of freeway accident likelihood. Presented at 80th Annual Meeting of the Transportation Research Board [M] Washington, D. C., 2001.

[12] Wang, L., Abdel-Aty, M., Lee, J., Shi, Q. Analysis of real-time crash risk for expressway ramps using traffic, geometric, trip generation, and socio-demographic predictors [J]. Accident Analysis & Prevention, 2019, 122: 378-394.

[13] Wu, J., Xu H., Zhang Y., et al. An improved vehicle-pedestrian near-crash identification method with a roadside lidar sensor [J]. Journal of Safety Research, 2020, 73, 211-224.

[14] Xu, C., Wang, W., Liu, P., et al, Calibration of crash risk models on freeways with limited real-time traffic data using Bayesian meta-analysis and Bayesian inference approach[J]. Accident Analysis & Prevention, 2015, 85, 207-218.

[15] Yu, R., Abdel-Aty, M. Multi-level Bayesian analyses for single-and multi-vehicle freeway crashes[J]. Accident Analysis & Prevention, 2013, 58, 97-105.

[16] Zheng, L., Sayed, T. A novel approach for real time crash prediction at signalized intersections. Transportation Research Part C: Emerging Technologies, 2020, 117, 102683.

[17] Zheng, Q., Xu, C., Liu, P., et al. Investigating the predictability of crashes on different freeway segments using the real-time crash risk models[J]. Accident Analysis & Prevention, 2021, 159, 106213.

Design and Evaluation of Overspeed Behavior Control Scheme based on Information and Behavior Fusion Strategy

Hao Zhao Jianjun Shi Yan Han* Linfeng Guo
Key Laboratory of Traffic Engineering, Beijing University of Technology;

Abstract The number of urban traffic accidents caused by overspeed remains high and various intervention measures have been put forward, but the containment effect of overspeed is limited. Considering the continuous development of on-board information technology and the advantages of timeliness and accuracy, this paper proposed to optimize and integrate on-board information system and design an overspeed behavior information control fusion scheme. The drivers' overspeed behaviorprocess and the release process of on-board information were discussed and a series of on-board information control schemes were integrated and designed. Through the synergism of various media in the vehicle, different contexts were built and an on-board information control system is established to effectively control drivers' overspeed behavior. A questionnaire survey on the control effect of overspeed behavior information control fusion scheme is designed and completed. Two aspects are selected to investigate: personal socio-economic attributes and drivers' overspeed control intention when releasing different on-board information in different scenarios. The results of the questionnaire show that drivers aged 31-40 and driving for 1-3 years are better controlled. Then a speed control model based on the ordered logit model is constructed. The results show that the significance of 31-40 years old, 1-3 years driving age, reminder context and warning context is $p < 0.05$, indicating that age and driving age have a significant impact on the control effect, and the control effect of the whole control system increases with the progression of context.

Keywords On-board information Information and behavior fusion strategy Overspeed behavior control scheme Speed control model

0 Introduction

In recent years, with the rapid development of the economy, the transportation industry has developed steadily and rapidly. Both vehicle population and traffic volume have significantly increased[1]. At the same time, traffic accidents caused by overspeed occur frequently and show an upward trend year by year. Overspeed will not only affect the safety performance of the vehicle, but also lead to the driver's inability to operate timely and accurately and making wrong decisions. Various overspeed intervention measures have been proposed around the world and can be dived into two types:

(1) Set up physical devices on the road to slow down the vehicle, or set up signs to warn the drivers[2]. (2) Regulate drivers' behavior by formulating laws and regulations and some more effective punishment mechanisms are excavated to make sure that the drivers can control their behavior to alleviate overspeed. But there exist some questions: the construction of road infrastructure requires a lot of capital investment, and faces the challenges of limited urban available space and a long construction cycle. The laws and regulations are mostly mandatory for driver's behavior and their promulgation needs to consider many factors with a long cycle.

Based on this, on-board information system such

as ISA (intelligent speed adaptation) and ISPA (intelligent speed in prediction system) are constantly emerging and applied to control driver overspeed behavior. The control method of on-board information has the advantages of timeliness and accuracy. The driver can receive certain information during driving. Based on on-board information system, the on-board information is released in time to remind the driver to perceive and control the speed. Although the on-board information control method is more effective than the traditional road facility construction and law promulgation, the driver's behavior process is not considered, the continuous tracking and feedback of on-board information release also be ignored[3]. Without a step-by-step control measure, its effect is still limited. Therefore, it is necessary to carry out the fusion scheme design combining the driver's behavior process with the on-board information release process and finally evaluate its effect.

The rest of the paper is organized as follows. Section 2 summarizes the relevant literature on overspeed control method. It also indicates the shortage of existing research. Section 3 analyzes the overspeed behavior process based onbehavioral science and designs the process of vehicle information release with different contexts based on the principle of information science, then integrates the overspeed behavior process with the on-board information release process to design the fusion scheme, and an ordered logit model is proposed. Section 4 introduces a questionnaire and survey results, and the estimation results of the Ordered Logit model are calculated to verify whether the different contextual intensities of the design are progressive and effective.

1 Literature Review

Domestic and foreign scholars have carried out some corresponding discussions on overspeed behavior control strategy and scheme. Soole et al.[4] analyzed the interval overspeed capture system through a systematic literature review, compared and analyzed the operation mode and intervention effect of different types of overspeed capture systems. Montella et al.[5] conducted an empirical Bayesian experiment to observe the effect of the speed enforcement system before and after, and concluded that the enforcement system has different intervention effects on different road types, different times, and vehicle types. Thornton et al.[6] analyzed the intervention effects of four kinds of anti-overspeed advertisements with different intimidation modes on overspeed drivers through a questionnaire survey and repeated measurement covariance. Elliott et al.[7] applied the intermediary effect analysis to discuss the intervention effect based on the theory of planned behavior and found that the intervention effect of print speculation advertising is more significant which contains some factors such as behavior concept and perceived behavior control. Houten et al.[8] analyzed the intervention effects of strict standards and loose standards on overspeed through experiments and concluded that loose standards are easier for drivers to accelerate. To sum up, the existing research mainly focuses on the behavior control of drivers using external facilities or publicity and law promulgation. There are only a few studies on on-board information release.

The effect of driver's driving behavior before and after ISA (intelligent speed adaptation) installation has long drawn the interest of researchers. Vlassenroot et al.[9] compared the changes of drivers before and after installing ISA (intelligent speed adaptation) through questionnaire survey and comparative experiment, mainly evaluated the changes in vehicle speed, traffic safety, driver attitude, and driver acceptance, and concluded that although ISA can reduce the overspeed ratio, the average vehicle speed will increase greatly. Warner et al.[10] tested 27 drivers equipped with prompt ISA and found that prompt ISA can control driver attitude, subjective norms and self-reported behavior, but had few effects on perceived behavior control. Based on the theoretical model of planned behavior, Chorlton et al.[11] tested the change of overspeed behavior caused by voluntary ISA through ABA design. The results showed that voluntary ISA significantly reduced the percentage of driving distance exceeding the speed limit. Mari et al.[12] analyzed and tested the ISA control effects under different speed limits, different types of ISA and different driving environments through comparative experiments. The results showed that all of the percentages of overspeed time decreased under speed limits of 40,70 and 80 km/h, but the percentage of overspeed events increased by 15.5% under speed limits of 60km/h. Wu[13] conducted a driving simulator experiment on 40 drivers to test the intervention effects of the four systems: no system, ISPS (intelligent speed prediction system), ISA, and the system combining ISA and ISPS. It is proved that both ISPS and the combined system have high intervention effects. Combined with the research of existing scholars, it is concluded that the overspeed intervention effect of mandatory ISA is better than that of the other two types of ISA. The effect of prompt ISA is better for experienced drivers, and the effect of prompt ISA with high prompt intensity is more significant. The intervention effect of voluntary ISA in the high-speed limit section is better than that in the low-speed limit section, and the overspeed intervention effect for experienced drivers is better. Although the intervention effect of ISPS is higher than that of prompt ISA, it is lower than that of the combination. However, the effects of these four control methods have some disadvantages. For example, in those four control methods, the number of information interactions between the platform and the drivers are only once and the driver's following behavior process is not considered after releasing the information, it is difficult to achieve the desired control effect.

To sum up, the paperanalyzed the overspeed behavior process and the on-board information release process based on behavioral science and information science. An overspeed behavior-information control fusion process was designed. A questionnaire survey on the driver's acceptance of the control scheme was carried out and the effect was evaluated.

2 Methodology

2.1 Overspeed behavior process based on Behavioral Science

Behavioral science theory is a new discipline to study human behavior, which was formed in the 1930s. It grasps the law of human behavior through the study of human psychological activities to find new methods to get along with others and improve labor efficiency.

Inbehavioral science theory, needs and motivation are considered as the starting point of human research and further extend the psychological law to the behavior field based on psychology. A set of consensuses reflecting the causality of human behavior were summarized. Behavioral science believes that humans are stimulated by their self-functions and external things, and then they generate various needs, motivation, and finally lead to their actual behavior. The overall process is shown in Fig. 1.

Traffic behavior is alsoa kind of social behavior, which is determined by traffic needs. Hence, the process of traffic behavior conforms to the general behavior process proposed by behavioral scientists. In the process of general behavior, it can be divided into conscious behavior, self-control behavior, passive behavior and rational behavior. When the drivers are in the state of conscious behavior, they will have correct cognition and take the initiative to do something right; In the state of self-control behavior, the behavior can be initiated or terminated according to the situation requirements; In the state of passive behavior, the behavior occurs due to the promotion of external force or the influence and restraint of others; In the state of rational behavior, the behavior motivation is consistent with the effect of behavior. From the perspective of behavioral science, the process and the influencing factors of drivers' overspeed behavior were analyzed. Only on the basis of understanding their needs and motivation, the strategy of driver speed could be formulated, which can produce a better control effect. The process of driver overspeed behavior is shown in Fig. 2.

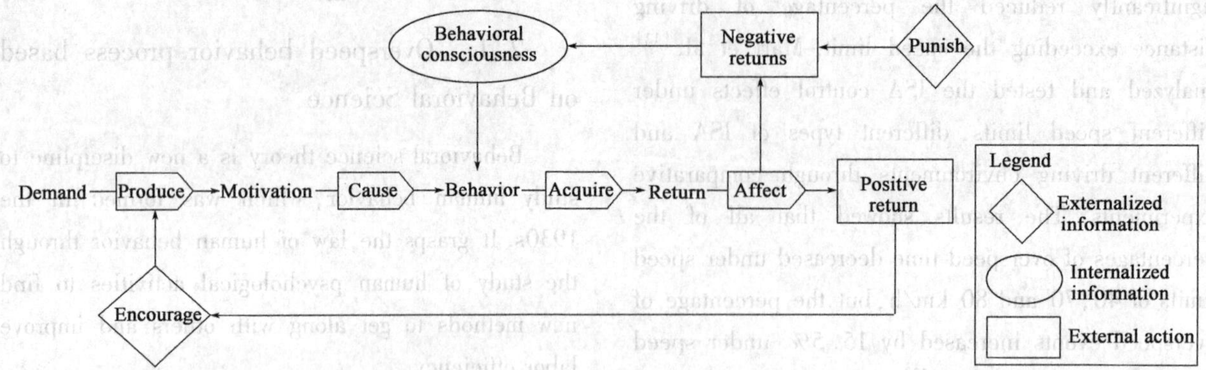

Fig. 1 General behavior process in behavioral science theory

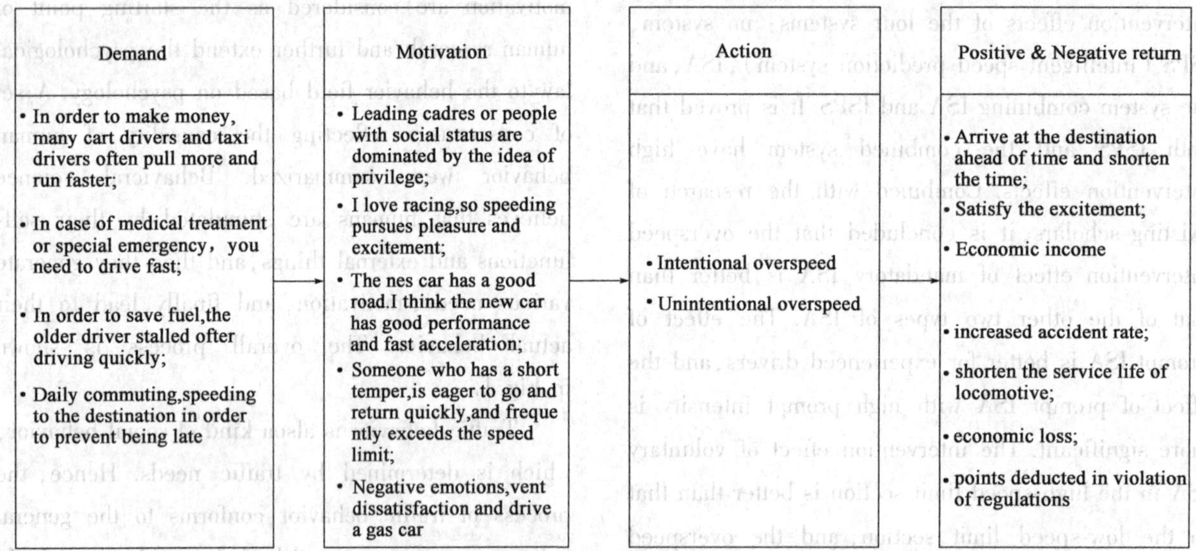

Fig. 2 Process analysis of driver overspeed behavior

Human behavior is determined by the joint restriction of subjective needs and objective things. According to the law revealed by behavioral science, needs can cause motivation, and motivation can drive human behavior. When the driver has a certain need, they will have psychological tension and become an internal driving force, that is, motivation. It drives the driver to choose goals and carry out activities that can be realized to satisfy their needs. After the needs are satisfied, new needs will be generated, which will lead to new behavior. The overspeed behavior is not always caused by needs, it may also be unintentional overspeed. When the driver unintentionally overspeed, the on-board information system only needs a voice prompt which can avoid the driver's continued overspeed behavior, while intentional overspeed needs to be corrected by layer-by-layer progressive control method. After overspeed, the driver will get a series of returns, including positive and negative returns. Positive returns are the economy and time saved, while negative returns are the economic or corporeal losses. When the driver obtains positive returns, it will have an incentive effect on the next behavior. When the driver has the needs to overspeed again, motivation for overspeed will be produced because of the positive returns obtained from the last overspeed. If negative benefits are obtained, the driver will be urged by behavior awareness at the next overspeed behavior.

2.2 Analysis of on-board information release process based on the principle of Information Science

The information control system discerns the

initial state and mode of human movement and realizes cognition by collecting, transmitting and processing information, and "regenerates" the control information accordingly. The function of control is to execute strategy information. With the generation of control behavior, the information system is guided to achieve the specified target state. Finally, complete the change of human behavior state by the control system as shown in Fig. 3.

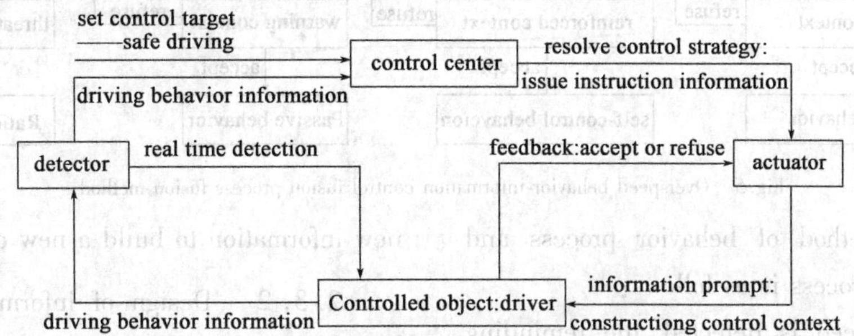

Fig. 3 On-board information transmission process

When the information systemreleases on-board information to control overspeed, the information control process is as cyclical as the behavioral process.

After the on-board information is released, the driver receives theoverspeed voice reminder, generates the intention of speed control and adopts control behavior. Whether the speed control is effective depends on the driver's behavior process. Therefore, it is necessary to carry out the information release process of multiple times speed detection- information control- driver speed control. The information release process of controlling vehicle speed is shown in Fig. 4.

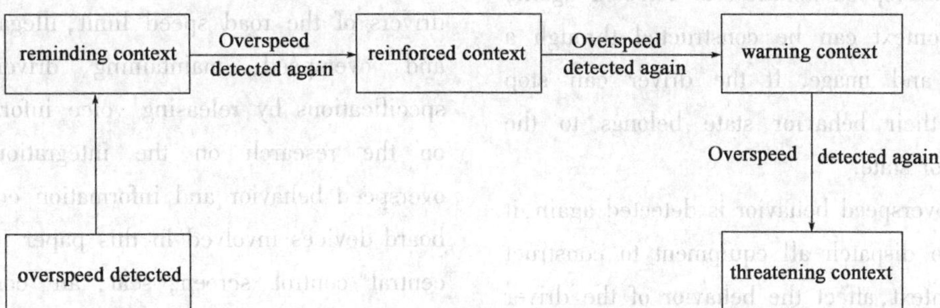

Fig. 4 Context and process of information release

The information control process is divided into four stages. Constructing different contexts in different stages: reminder, reinforcement, warning and threat. Firstly, construct the reminding context to remind the driver of the fact of overspeed. Then construct the reinforced context to further emphasize and remind the driver that he has exceeded the speed limit. Then construct warning context to warn drivers of the consequences of overspeed. Finally, the threatening context is used to force the driver to slow down. The above four contexts are progressive layer by layer and gradually carried out in the process of drivers' overspeed behavior. If drivers stop overspeed behavior in a certain context, the on-board information system does not need to continue to build a new context.

2.3 Scheme design of overspeed behavior-information control fusion process

2.3.1 Fusion method of driving behavior and information control

Byanalyzing the overspeed behavior process and information release process, it can be found that during the overspeed control process, the on-board information process is related to the driver's behavior process, the circulation of behavior process and the circulation of information release process related closely. This paper designs the overspeed behavior-information control fusion process, as shown in Fig. 5.

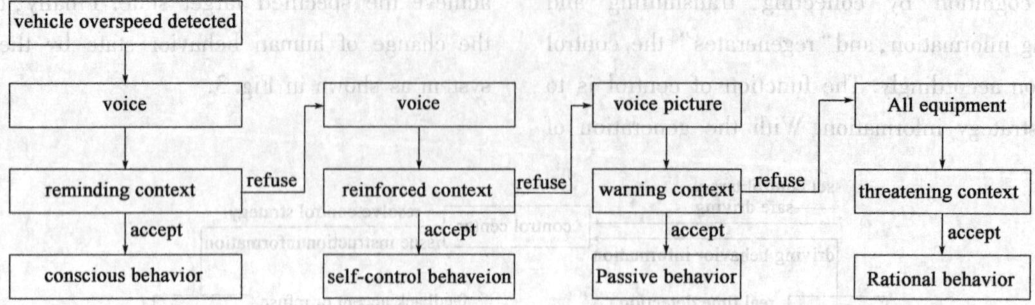

Fig. 5　Overspeed behavior-information control fusion process fusion method

The fusion method of behavior process and information release process is as follows:

①When overspeed is detected, the reminding context can be constructed through a voice prompt firstly. If the driver can stop overspeeding, their behavior states belong to the conscious behavior state.

②If the overspeed behavior is detected again, the reinforced context can be constructed through voice emphasis. If the driver can stop overspeeding, their behavior state belongs to the self-control behavior state.

③If the overspeed behavior is detected again, the warning context can be constructed through a stronger tone and image. If the driver can stop overspeeding, their behavior state belongs to the passive behavior state.

④If the overspeed behavior is detected again, it is necessary to dispatch all equipment to construct threatening context, affect the behavior of the driver and terminate overspeed. If overspeed behavior continues, it is determined that the behavior of the driver is not rational, and there is no need to release new information to build a new context.

2.3.2　Design of information release device based on fusion scheme

The existing on-board speed limiting devices such as the central control screen, can set the vehicle speed limit in advance. When the speed limit is exceeded, the central control screen will send an alarm to remind the speeding driver. Some high-end cars install vibration motors under the seats to remind the driver. Amap, Baidu Maps and other apps remind drivers of the road speed limit, illegal photography and overspeed, maintaining driver's driving specifications by releasing voice information. Based on the research on the integration process of overspeed behavior and information control, the on-board devices involved in this paper include audio, central control screen, seat, air conditioner and flashlight. The on-board devices and their information release contents in different contexts in the process of information control are designed, as shown in Tab. 1.

Design of on-board equipment and its information release function　　Tab. 1

On board equipment	Control context			
	Reminding context	Reinforced context	Warning context	Threatening context
Audia	Plav voice: "the current road speed limit is 60, you have exceeded the speed limit."	Play voice: "speeding will cause serious traffic accidents. Please slow down for the sake of yourself and others."	Play voice: "this is the photo of your last accident caused by speeding. Please slow down and pay attention to safety."	Play voice: "if you continue to overspeed, it will lead to irreparaole consequences."
Central control screen		Display photos of violation tickets, traffic accident videos and driver's family photos		

continued

On board equipment	Control context			
	Reminding context	Reinforced context	Warning context	Threatening context
Air conditioner			Release mentholum to stemmate the driver through smell	
Seat			Vibration effect of 40 ~ 804HZ vibration frequency	
Flashlight			The warning effect is alternation through light flashing and light color alternation	

Integrate all media scheduling into the design scheme. The specific integration scheme is shown in Fig. 6.

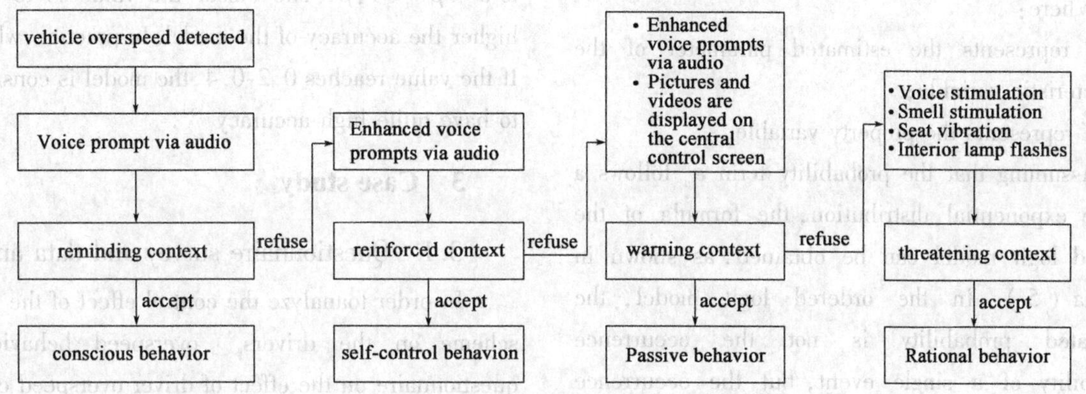

Fig. 6 Overspeed behavior-information control fusion scheme based on on-board equipment

2.4 Introduction of ordered logit model

To quantitativelyanalyze the driver's control behavior in different contexts, the degree of control effect by on-board information and the relationship and effect between various factors, a speed control model based on the ordered logit model is constructed.

In the discrete selection model, the selection of agents has sorting characteristics, which are represented by 1, 2, 3,... Respectively. The model that takes it as the explained variable is called the ordered selection model. It is observed that the option selected by the sample ($n = 1, 2, \ldots, N$) (the explained variable Y_n) is discrete data. In random utility theory, its utility is usually U_n is divided into random variation part (probability term) ε_n and non-random variation part (fixed term) V_n. And assume that they are linear.

$$U_n = V_n + \varepsilon_n \tag{1}$$

There are many kinds of relationships between V_n and explanatory variable X_{nk}, which are usually assumed to be linear.

$$V_n = \theta_0 + \sum_{K=1}^{K} \theta_k X_{nk} \tag{2}$$

Where: θ_0——the fixed coefficient;

k——the number of revealing (or influencing) variables;

θ_k——the parameter corresponding to the Kth variable;

X_{nk}——the Kth influencing variable of the nth sample (such as age, driving age, etc.).

Here, the utility U_n is the latent variable, which is continuous data. The corresponding relationship between the observed value Y_n and U_n is shown in eq. (3).

$$Y_n = \begin{cases} 1 & \text{If } U_n \leqslant \mu_1 \\ 2 & \text{If } \mu_1 \leqslant U_n \leqslant \mu_2 \\ \vdots \\ \vdots \\ J & If^{\mu_{j-1}} \leqslant U_n \end{cases} \quad (3)$$

In equation (3), $\mu_k (k = 1,2,3,\cdots,J-1)$ is the threshold, and U_n and the threshold in parameter estimation μ_k estimated together.

It is assumed that the likelihood ratio $odds(P_j)$ of the selection order of the dependent variable Y_n is shown in equation (4).

$$odds(P_j) = \frac{P(\leqslant j)}{P(>j)} = \frac{P(\leqslant j)}{1-P(\leqslant 1)} = \exp(\mu_j - \vec{\theta}\vec{X}) \quad (4)$$

Where:

$\vec{\theta}$ represents the estimated parameter of the characteristic variable;

$\vec{X}$ represents the property variable.

Assuming that the probability term ε_n follows a double exponential distribution, the formula of the ordered logit model can be obtained, as shown in formula (5). In the ordered logit model, the calculated probability is not the occurrence probability of a single event, but the occurrence probability of cumulative events. Therefore, the probability value of delay time can be obtained by processing the obtained cumulative probability value, and the formula is shown in formula (6).

$$P(Y_n \leqslant j \mid X,\theta,\mu) = \frac{\exp(\mu_j - \vec{\theta}\vec{X})}{1+\exp(\mu_j - \vec{\theta}\vec{X})} = F(\mu_j - V_n) \quad (5)$$

The probability of each dependent variable Y_n is shown in equation (6):

$$P(Y_n = 1 \mid X,\theta,\mu) = F(\mu_1 - V_n)$$

$$P(Y_n = 2 \mid X,\theta,\mu) = F(\mu_2 - V_n) - F(\mu_1 - V_n)$$

$$\cdots\cdots \quad (6)$$

$$P(Y_n = J \mid X,\theta,\mu) = 1 - F(\mu_{j-1} - V_n)$$

In eq. (6), F is the cumulative distribution function of ε, $V_n = \sum_{i=1}^{I}\theta_i X_{in}$。

After simplification, the probability of each dependent variable Y_n can be expressed by eq. (7):

$$P(Y_n = J) = \frac{1}{1+\exp(\sum_{i=1}^{I}\theta_i X_{in} - \mu_{j-1})} - \frac{1}{1+\exp(\sum_{i=1}^{I}\theta_i X_{in} - \mu_j)} \quad (7)$$

In the formula, $\mu_0 = +\infty$, $\mu_j = -\infty$。

After estimating the parameters of the model, the model can be tested by t-test and goodness ratio.

For t-test, at the significance level of 5%, when the absolute value of t is greater than 1.96, the original hypothesis $H_0:\theta_k = 0$ can be rejected; When the absolute value of T is less than 1.96, the original hypothesis of $\theta_k = 0$ cannot be rejected[14].

ρ^2 It is called goodness ratio, and its value range is $0 < \rho^2 < 1$, ρ^2 The closer the value is to 1, the higher the accuracy of the model. In practice, when ρ^2 If the value reaches 0.2-0.4, the model is considered to have quite high accuracy[15].

3 Case study

3.1 Questionnaire survey and data analysis

In order toanalyze the control effect of the fusion scheme on the drivers' overspeed behavior. A questionnaire on the effect of driver overspeed control is designed and carried out. The survey is divided into two parts, including personal socio-economic attributes (region (municipality directly under the central government, provincial city, prefecture-level city, county-level city), gender, age and driving age), and drivers' intention to overspeed control when releasing different on-board information in different scenarios. Scenario 1: reminding context of voice information only. Scenario 2: warning context controlled by voice information and image information. Scenario 3: mobilize all equipment to build a threatening context. The respondent will be asked "when driving on a road with a speed limit of 80km/h, if your current speed is 100km / h, what do you think your speed will change in different scenarios?" In the reminding context constructed in scenario 1, the audio player will play "the current road speed limit is 80km/h, you are currently overspeed, please drive normally and slow down.". In the warning context constructed in scenario 2, the audio player will play "this is your ticket for overspeed last time, deduct 2 points and a fine of 200 yuan", and show photos of tickets for previous violations on the central control screen. In the threat context constructed in scenario 3, the audio player will play "if you continue to overspeed, it will lead to irreparable consequences", the seat starts to vibrate slightly, and the interior lights flash red. The four control contexts of reminder, reinforcement, warning and threat are mentioned above. Considering the reinforcement context just repeats the content of reminding context with a enhancing intonation, the reminding context and reinforcement context are combined into Scenario 1 in the questionnaire.

Introduction to survey scenarios Tab. 2

Scenario	Description of the scenario	Behavior choice
Reminding context	a) Audio: "The current road speed limit is 80km/h. You are currently overspeed. Please drive normally and slow down."	When driving on a road with a speed limit of 80km/h, if your current speed is 100km / h, what do you think your speed will change in different scenarios? A. Reduce the vehicle speed below 80km / h B. Control the vehicle speed at 80-90km / h C. Control the vehicle speed at 90-95km / h D. Control the vehicle speed at 95-100km / h E. Maintain existing speed
Warning context	a) Audio: "This is your ticket for overspeed last time. Deduct 2 points and a fine of 200 yuan." b) Central control screen: photos of ticket violations before delivery	
Threatening context	a) Audio: "If you continue overspeed, it will lead to irreparable consequences." b) Seat: vibrate slightly c) Interior lamp: flashing red light	

The questionnaireswere issued through the www.wjx.cn. The survey was conducted from October 9 to October 17, 2021, and a total of 318 valid questionnaires were collected.

In the questionnaire survey results, the composition of respondents' socio-economic attributes is shown in Tab. 3.

Composition of respondents' socio-economic attributes Tab. 3

Variable		Quantity (percentage)	Variable		Quantity (percentage)
Gender	Male	159 (50%)	Region	Municipality	81 (25.5%)
	Female	159 (50%)		Provincial city	76 (23.9%)
Age	18-22	80 (25.2%)		Prefecture level city	76 (23.9%)
	23-30	86 (27%)		County-level city	85 (26.7%)
	31-40	93 (29.2%)	Driving age	Less than 1 year	87 (27.4%)
	Over 40	59 (18.6%)		1-3 years	100 (31.4%)
				3-5 years	74 (23.3%)
				More than 5 yeara	57(17.9%)

1) About age

It can be seen that in the reminding context and warning context, the proportion of drivers aged 31-40 who choose to slow down to 80km/h is significantly higher than that of drivers of other ages. The mean plots in Fig. 8 also shows that drivers aged 31-40 in the third age group receive higher control effects than drivers in other age groups. That is to say, such drivers reduce their speed the most and receive the best control effect in these two contexts. However, the control effect of 31-40 years old drivers in the threatening context is the worst. After consulting data and analysis, it is found that some adults may have the same rebellious behavior as adolescence in a certain period, which is called the "adult rebellious period". Tao Li[16] also analyzed the influence of age on improper driving behavior. Among them, drivers aged 31-35 are higher than drivers aged 25-30 and over 36 in "emotion" and "risk". Therefore, emotional changes or inspired risk-taking spirit under threatening context may prompt them to make different judgments from drivers of other ages.

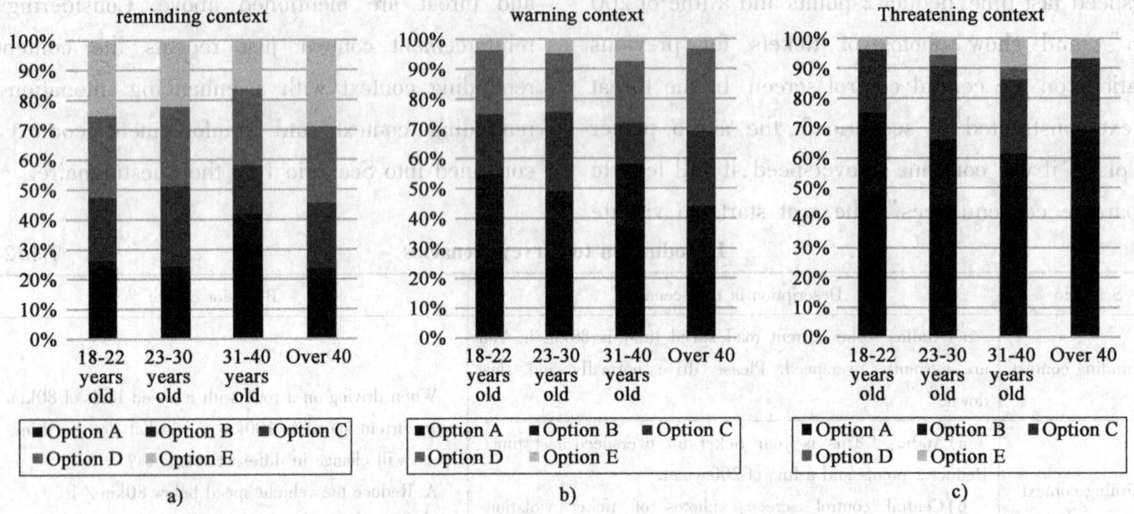

Fig. 7　Effect of fusion scheme on drivers of different ages

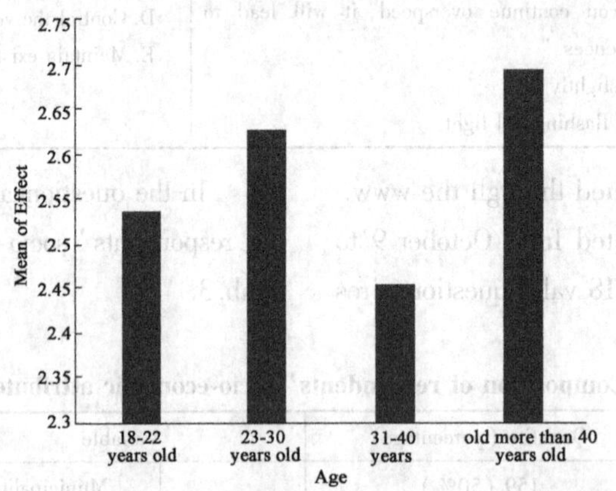

Fig. 8　Mean plots of the effect of fusion scheme on drivers of different ages

2) About driving age

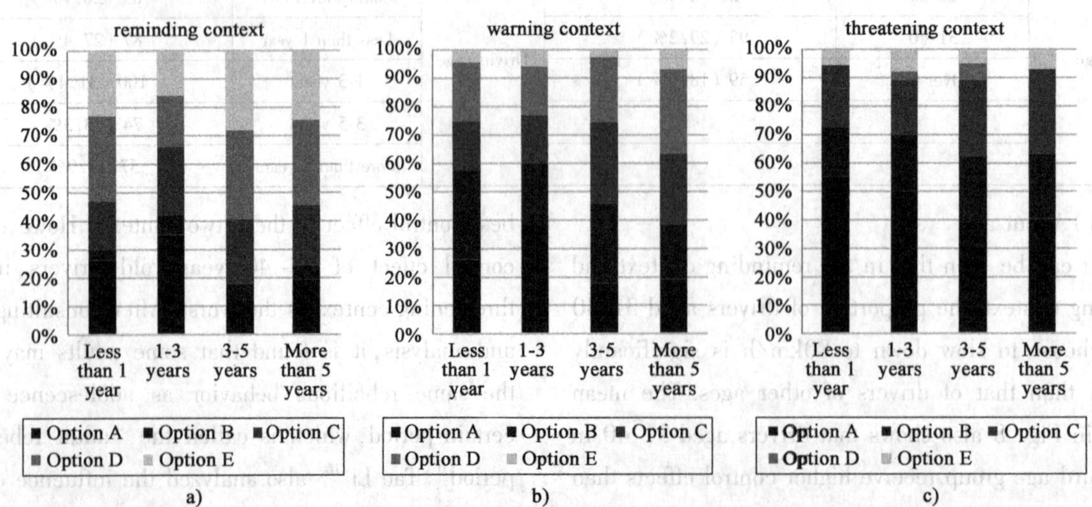

Fig. 9　Effect of fusion scheme on drivers of different driving ages

The deceleration degree of drivers with a driving age of 1-3 years under thereminding context and warning context is significantly higher than that of drivers with other driving ages, but in threatening context, drivers with less than 1 year of driving age and drivers with 1-3 years of driving age received almost the same control effect. The mean plots in Fig. 10 also shows that drivers of 1-3 years of driving age in the second group receive higher control effects than drivers of other driving ages. This may be caused that the drivers within 1 year are inexperienced and easier to make mistakes, so that their experience is not enough to support their judgment. Old drivers over 3 years are not careful enough because of their rich experience. Drivers with driving age of 1-3 years are neither inexperienced as novice drivers nor as careless as experienced old drivers. Therefore, such drivers receive the best information control effect. Guo Yanli[17] also drew a similar conclusion in her article, that is, drivers with a driving age of 1-3 years perform best in driving behavior.

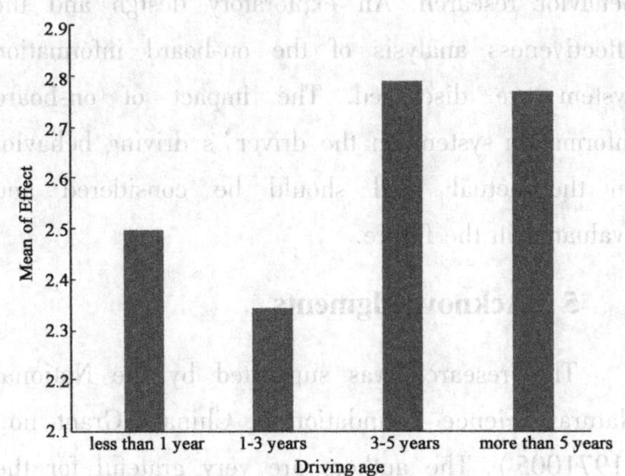

Fig. 10 Mean plots of the effect of fusion scheme on drivers of different driving ages

3) About region, gender

The survey of socio-economic attributes in the questionnaire also includes region and gender. Regions are divided into four levels: municipalities directly under the central government, provincial cities, prefecture-level cities and county-level cities. There is no great difference in the control effect of different regions and gender.

3.2 speed control model based on ordered logit model

The dummy variable settings of model variables are shown in Tab. 4。

Dummy variable settings in the model

Tab. 4

Variable name	Coefficient	Classify	Dummy variable		
Gender	X_1	Male	1	—	—
Age	X_2	18-22 years old	1	0	0
	X_3	23-30 years old	0	1	0
	X_4	31-40 years old	0	0	1
Zone	X_5	Municipality	1	0	0
	X_6	Provincial City	0	1	0
	X_7	Prefecture-level city	0	0	1
Driving age	X_8	Less than 1 year	1	0	0
	X_9	1-3 years	0	1	0
	X_{10}	3-5 years	0	0	1
circumstances	X_{11}	Reminding context	1	0	—
	X_{12}	Warning context	0	1	—

After cross contingency table analysis, the variables brought into the model include: age, gender, driving age, region, etc. the calibration results ofthe sorted logit model are shown in Tab. 5. The goodness ratio of data ρ^2 is 0.145, which is within the accuracy requirements.

In Tab. 5, it can be seen that the conspicuousness of drivers aged 31-40, drivers with driving experience of 1-3 years, reminding context only releasing voice information and warning context controlled by voice information and image informationare $p < 0.05$. It is concluded that drivers aged 31-40 have a stronger control effect than drivers of other ages, and drivers with driving age of 1-3 years have a stronger control effect than drivers of other driving ages. The control effect caused by the reminding context of only releasing voice control information and the warning context of cooperative control of voice information and image information is weaker than that of the threatening context constructed by mobilizing all equipment, and the intensity of the constructed context is positively correlated with the control effect, that is, the control intensity of the three contexts is progressive layer by layer.

calibration resultsof the model　　Tab. 5

		Estimeate	Std. Error	Wald	df	Sig.	95% Confidence Interval Lower Bound	Upper Bound
Threshold	θ_1	-0.499	0.240	4.335	1	0.037	-0.969	-0.029
	θ_2	0.296	0.240	1.528	1	0.216	-0.173	0.766
	θ_3	1.382	0.244	32.180	1	0.000	0.905	1.860
	θ_4	2.610	0.256	104.256	1	0.000	2.109	3.111
Location	X_1	0.152	0.119	1.631	1	0.202	-0.081	0.385
	X_2	-0.222	0.180	1.511	1	0.219	-0.575	0.132
	X_4	-0.358	0.176	4.163	1	0.41	-0.702	-0.14
	X_7	-0.292	0.167	3.064	1	0.080	-0.619	0.35
	X_8	-0.327	0.180	3.309	1	0.069	-0.680	0.025
	X_9	-0.574	0.178	10.369	1	0.001	-0.923	-0.225
	X_{11}	1.658	0.151	120.320	1	0.000	1.362	1.954
	X_{12}	0.773	0.146	27.877	1	0.000	0.486	1.060

4　Conclusions

Based on the behavior process inbehavioral science and the information release process in the principle of information science, this paper analyzes the driver ' s needs, motivation, behavior and return when overspeed, and summarizes the different behavioral states of drivers in overspeed behavior, from the conscious state to self-control state to passive state to rational state. Compared with the existing physical equipment or laws and regulations, this paper combines traffic engineering, behavioral science, psychology and information theory to finally complete the innovative design of the control system. The integration process of driver ' s overspeed behavior-information control in the process of overspeed is constructed, and the on-board devices and their information release contents in the context of reminding, enhanced, warning and threatening in the process of information control are designed. A speed control model based on the ordered logit model is constructed. The results show that drivers aged 31-40 and drivers with 1-3 years of driving experience have a more significant impact on the control effect, and the control effect of each context increases gradually, which proves that the on-board equipment control scheme designed in this paper is effective and efficient.

Considering the continuous development of on-board information technology and the advantages of timeliness and accuracy, the on-board information system will become the general trend of future driving behavior research. An exploratory design and the effectiveness analysis of the on-board information system are discussed. The impact of on-board information system on the driver ' s driving behavior on the actual road should be considered and evaluated in the future.

5　Acknowledgments

This research was supported by the National Natural Science Foundation of China (Grant no. 71971005). The authors are very grateful for the comments from the anonymous reviewers. The authors would like to thank one anonymous referee for his (her) helpful comments and suggestion, which improved the content and composition substantially.

References

[1] Wang Chang-jun, Huang Yan. Discussion on the Countermeasures of Speeding Driving [J]. Journal of Transportation Engineering and Information, 2005, 10-15, 28.

[2] Chi Cheng, Pan Xiao-dong. Setting of Speed

Limit Signs Based on the Speeding Behavior on Freeway [J]. Journal of Transportation Engineering and Information, 2010:110-116.

[3] Jiang Xin-guo, Liu hai-yue. Systematic Review on Anti-speeding Counter measure Research [J]. China Journal of Highway and Transport, 2020, 1-31.

[4] Soole D W, Watson B C, Fleiter J J. Effects of average speed enforcement on speed compliance and crashes: A review of the literature [J]. Accident Analysis & Prevention, 2013, 54 (may):46-56.

[5] Montella A, Imbriani L L, Marzano V, et al. Effects on speed and safety of point-to-point speed enforcement systems: Evaluation on the urban motorway A56 Tangenziale di Napoli[J]. Accident Analysis & Prevention, 2014, 75C (7):164-178.

[6] Thornton J, Rossiter J R. Advertisingwearout of shock-value anti-speeding ads[J]. 2001:5-7.

[7] Elliott M A, Armitage C J. Promoting drivers' compliance with speed limits: Testing an intervention based on the theory of planned behaviour[J]. British Journal of Psychology, 2008, 100(Pt 1):111-132.

[8] Houten R V, Nau P A. Feedback interventions and driving speed: A parametric and comparative analysis [J]. Journal of Applied Behavior Analysis, 1983, 16(3):253-281.

[9] Vlassenroot S, Broekx S, Mol J D, et al. Driving with intelligent speed adaptation: Final results of the Belgian ISA-trial [J]. Transportation Research Part A: Policy and Practice, 2007, 41 (3):267-279.

[10] Warner H W, Berg L. The long-term effects of an ISA speed-warning device on drivers' speeding behaviour [J]. Transportation Research PartF Psychology & Behaviour, 2008, 11(2):96-107.

[11] Chorlton K, Conner M. Can enforced behaviour change attitudes: exploring the influence of Intelligent Speed Adaptation [J]. Accident Analysis and Prevention, 2012, 48:49-56.

[12] Mari Päätalo, Peltola H, Kallio M. Intelligent speed adaptation - effects on driving behaviour [J]. Plant & Soil, 2001, 228(2):265-273.

[13] Zhao G, Wu C. Effectiveness and acceptance of the intelligent speeding prediction system (ISPS)[J]. Accident Analysis & Prevention, 2013, 52:19-28.

[14] Wang Xiao-yuan Yang Jing-lei. Key theories and methods of traffic flow data cleaning, state identification and optimal control[M]. 217.

[15] Galhardas H, Florescu D. An Extensible Framework for Data Cleaning [C]. In: Proceedings of the 16th IEEE International Conference on Data Engineering. San Diego, California, 2000: 312-314.

[16] Tao Li. Research on Drivers' Aberrant Driving Behavior Styles and Their Discriminant Indices [D]. 40-47.

[17] Guo Yan-li. Research on Aberrant Driving Behavior of Drivers in Baotou[D]. 35-58.

海员心理特性及改善研究

叶素素 万 征*

(上海海事大学交通运输学院)

摘 要 本文以海员的人际关系、工作满意度为切入点,结合 809 名中国海员的调查数据来考察海员的人际关系、工作满意度与心理健康之间的关系。研究发现,海员人际关系与工作满意度、心理健康呈

1. 基金项目:国家自然科学基金(52071202),海员心理压力与决策风险演化机制研究:理论模型与干预策略,在研。

显著的正相关,而海员工作满意度与心理健康也呈显著正相关;海员工作满意度在人际关系与心理健康之间起到中介作用。此外,最高学历、海龄、担任职务、每日平均睡眠时间、体育与娱乐时间以及娱乐方式会显著影响海员心理健康水平。因此,可以通过航运企业制定合理工作时间安排表以及相关航运协会组织减少不必要的检查程序来保障海员的睡眠休闲时间,提高船上体育运动休闲娱乐设施的设置丰富海员的精神生活以及提高身体素质,加大船舶通信技术的研究与投入以保障船员能及时与家人取得沟通联系来提高海员的工作满意度。加强对领导者的管理能力的培训来发挥领导的调节作用来调节船上海员之间的人际关系与沟通从而进一步提高海员的心理健康水平。

关键词 海员 心理健康 人际关系 工作满意度 中介效应

0 引言

截至2020年底,我国共有注册海员超过171.6万人。党的十八大提出要建设海洋强国这一战略目标,但是由于海员这一职业的特殊性,远离陆地常年漂泊在海上,因此海员需要承受更多的心理压力,从而对海员的心理健康提出更高的考验。海员的心理健康状况,不仅直接关系海员本人的身心健康,也关系到船舶的航行安全,还关系到企业、社会的和谐与稳定,也会影响到中国航运企业的市场竞争力,还会影响到中国海员的强国建设[1]。因此,关注海员心理健康,提升海员心理健康水平,有助于减少因心理因素引发的海难事故,有助于我国由海员大国向海员强国转变[2]。

影响海员心理健康状况的因素是多方面的,如生活事件、社会支持、婚姻质量、人格和行为特征等。这些因素与其他相关生物、理化因素交织在一起对海员产生影响[3]。Song等[4]研究发现,契约类型、家庭支持以及选择航海职业的动机对海员职业健康有显著的影响,孤立和孤独[5]、家庭分离[6]以及岸上休假减少和不同国籍海员的文化差异[7]等因素会对海员心理造成影响。CaRter等[8]研究发现,来自低收入和中等收入国家的海员所经历的不平等,会影响他们的心理健康。邬远和等[9]研究显示,现职海员(部分)的心理问题较正常人群严重,心理健康的水平低于中国正常成人。王慧玲等[10]研究发现,健康成人的年龄、学历、工作年限、婚姻状态是海员心理状况的主要影响因素。谢鸣等[11]研究显示,国籍与宗教类别对海员心理健康状况产生重要影响。李静[12]等研究显示,个人的身体健康是影响海员的心理健康的一个因素。胡学文等[13]研究显示,收入差距会影响海员心理健康。海员是以特殊职业为纽带形成独特的社会组织群体,与陆地人群的人际关系有着很大的差别。谢特秀等[14]研究发现,由于海员间可能存在生活习惯不同、文化差异,海员间的交往容易发生障碍,以及海员值班频繁、交际空间主要集中在餐厅和娱乐室,与他人心理沟通与情感交往机会较少,从而影响海员之间建立良好的人际关系。

众多研究结果显示,工作满意度可能是人际关系与心理健康的中介变量。首先,Friendlander通过因素分析抽出三个影响工作满意度的因素:社会及技术环境因素(包括上司、人际关系、工作条件等)、自我实现因素(个人能力得到发挥)、被人承认因素(工作挑战、责任、工资、晋升等),可见人际关系是影响工作满意度的一个重要的因素。其次,工作满意度是影响心理健康的一个因素,因为不满意的状态的本身即是一种不愉快的心理状态[15]。因此我们提出假设,工作满意度在人际关系与海员心理健康之间起到中介作用。

国内关于心理健康的探讨主要集中于教师、警察、医生等服务业行业也取得了一些进展,但关于海员的心理健康造成的后果及其关系的实证研究尚不多见。尽管已有研究结果显示,人际关系是影响海员心理健康的一个重要因素,但是并没有直接研究二者之间的因果联系。此外,在研究海员心理健康状况中鲜有涉及工作满意度问题。为此,本研究通过结合809名中国海员的调查数据来弥补这方面的缺陷。

1 数据与方法

在中国航海学会的大力支持下,我们通过随机发放在线问卷的方式收集数据。问卷发放对象为四家大型海员服务公司的所有员工。本次调查共回收有效样本809份,他们的人口学信息见表1。其中,7.3%的海员是18~25岁,19.3%的海员是26~30岁,46.7%的海员是31~40岁,26.7%的海员是41岁或以上;81.2%的海员已婚,78%的海员有孩子;工程部海员占30.5%,甲板部海员占

38.1%,而普通海员占 31.4%。本研究采用 SPSS25 版本进行数据整理和统计分析,主要统计方法有独立样本 t 检验、单因素方差分析、Pearson 相关分析、分层回归分析。本研究的问卷设计主要参考以前量表,结合海员生活实际情况,设计潜变量测试项。

人口学变量频率分析 表 1

变量	选项	频率	百分比(%)	平均值	标准偏差
年龄	18~25 岁	59	7.3	3.93	0.86
	26~30 岁	156	19.3		
	31~40 岁	378	46.7		
	41 岁及以上	216	26.7		
婚姻状况	单身	152	18.8	1.81	0.39
	已婚	657	81.2		
是否有孩子	没有	178	22	2.13	0.78
	1 个	368	45.5		
	2 个	243	30		
	2 个以上	20	2.5		
学历	高中及以下	248	30.7	1.84	0.65
	大专	446	55.1		
	大学本科及以上	115	14.2		
海龄	少于 1 年	38	4.7	4.08	1.16
	1~3 年	66	8.2		
	3~5 年	84	10.4		
	5~10 年	227	28.1		
	10 年以上	394	48.7		
担任职务	船长	68	8.4	5.73	2.89
	大副	99	12.2		
	二副	73	9		
	三副	69	8.5		
	轮机长	56	6.9		
	大管轮	66	8.2		
	二管轮	79	9.8		
	三管轮	45	5.6		
	其他	254	31.4		
服务船型	货船	553	68.4	1.59	1
	集装箱船	94	11.6		
	油船、液化气船	132	16.3		
	邮轮	2	0.2		
	其他	28	3.5		
服务航线	内河航线	12	1.5	2.96	0.89
	沿海航线	303	37.5		
	近洋航线	203	25.1		
	远洋航线	291	36		
年薪水平	20 万元以下	379	46.8	2.02	1.2

续上表

变　量	选　项	频　率	百分比(%)	平均值	标准偏差
年薪水平	10 万 ~15 万	197	24.4	2.02	1.2
	15 万 ~20 万	111	13.7		
	20 万 ~30 万	85	10.5		
	30 万元以上	37	4.6		
睡眠时间	0 ~3h	27	3.3	2.48	0.62
	4 ~6h	390	48.2		
	7 ~9h	365	45.1		
	9h 以上	27	3.3		
体育运动时间	0 ~30min	621	76.8	1.26	0.5
	30min ~1h	170	21		
	1 ~3h	16	2		
	3h 以上	2	0.2		
休闲娱乐时间	小于 30min	279	34.5	2.05	0.93
	30min ~1h	259	32		
	1 ~3h	223	27.6		
	3h 以上	48	5.9		
娱乐方式	打牌或打麻将	28	3.5	3.22	1.37
	玩手机或平板电脑	351	43.4		
	聊天	57	7		
	看书看电影或唱歌	206	25.5		
	无娱乐	123	15.2		
	其他	44	5.4		

2　研究结果

2.1　信效度分析

2.1.1　信度分析

信度分析主要指检测测量结果的可靠性。在信度方面,采用克隆巴赫系数进行检验。由表 2 可知,问卷总体 α 系数为 0.885,则表示总体信度非常理想。由表 3 可知,各潜变量的 α 系数均在 0.5 ~0.9之间,则表示各变量的信度是可以接受的。

总体信度检验　　表 2

克隆巴赫 Alpha	基于标准化项的克隆巴赫 Alpha	项数
0.884	0.887	14

各变量的信度检验　　表 3

变量	题数	α
人际关系	2	0.52
工作满意度	8	0.84
心理健康	4	0.81

2.1.2　内容效度分析

内容效度分析就是检测测量量表能否准确测量调查问卷中的构念,本文采用探索性因子分析实现检验过程。由表 4 可知,KMO 检验的系数为 0.906,且 Bartlett 检验结果显著,则表示问卷的效度非常理想。

KMO 和 Bartlett 检验　　表 4

KMO 取样适切性量数		0.906
巴特利特球形度检验	近似卡方	4348.494
	自由度	91
	显著性	0.000

2.2　变量的描述性统计分析

2.2.1　海员的人际关系

由表 5 可知,海员的人际关系变量均值为 3.71,则表明海员的人际关系较好。

海员人际关系描述性统计 表5

选项	N	最小值	最大值	均值	标准偏差	变量均值
与同事之间相处良好,同事之间氛围良好	809	1	5	4.01	0.96	3.71
与家人之间的关系亲密,联系紧密	809	1	5	3.41	1.32	

2.2.2 海员的心理健康

由表6可知,海员心理健康变量的均值为2.51,则表明海员心理健康水平低于一般水平。为深入探讨海员心理健康的基本特征,本研究以年龄、婚姻状况、孩子数量、最高学历、海龄、担任职务、服务船舶类型、服务的航线、年薪、每日平均睡眠时间、体育运动时间、娱乐时间、娱乐方式为自变量,心理健康为因变量,进行 t 检验、单因素方差分析等,结果发现:根据表7和表8得到年龄、婚姻状况、孩子数量、服务船型、服务航线、年薪六个变量的主效应不显著,根据表9可得其余七个变量的主效应显著,具体结果如下:

(1)高中及以下学历的海员心理健康水平分别大于大专学历和本科及以上学历的海员心理健康水平;

(2)海龄少于1年的海员心理健康水平分别海龄大于3~5年、5~10年、10年以上的海员心理健康水平,海龄1~3年的海员心理健康水平分别海龄大于3~5年和10年以上的海员心理健康水平;

(3)船长的心理健康水平分别大于轮机长与二管轮的心理健康水平,大副的心理健康水平小于三副的心理健康水平,二副的心理健康水平大于二管轮的心理健康水平,三副的心理健康水平分别大于轮机长和二管轮的心理健康水平;

(4)睡眠时间只有0~3h的海员心理健康水平分别小于4~6h、7~9h和9h以上的海员心理健康水平,而睡眠时间4~6h的海员心理健康水平分别小于7~9h和9h以上的海员心理健康水平;

(5)体育运动时间小于30min的海员心理健康水平分别小于0.5~1h和1~3h的海员心理健康水平;

(6)在娱乐方式上,有娱乐方式的海员心理健康水平大于没有娱乐方式的海员心理健康水平。

海员心理健康描述性统计 表6

选项	N	最小值	最大值	均值	标准偏差	变量均值
感到精力旺盛	809	1	5	2.52	1.05	2.51
有焦虑、过分担忧或心情低落等情绪	809	1	5	2.43	1	
有失眠的问题	809	1	5	2.43	1.02	
工作会使我情绪激动或者不安	809	1	5	2.66	1.03	

心理健康在婚姻上的差异分析 表7

维度	选项	个案数	平均值	标准偏差	t	sig
婚姻	单身	152	9.97	3.254	−0.315	0.753
	已婚	657	10.06	3.258		

心理健康在年龄、孩子数量、服务船型、服务航线和年薪上的差异分析 表8

维度	选项	个案数	平均值	标准偏差	F	sig	多重比较
年龄	18~25岁	59	10.36	3.50	2.30	0.08	—
	26~30岁	156	9.71	3.02			
	31~40岁	378	9.89	3.28			
	41岁及以上	216	10.47	3.28			
孩子数量	没有	178	9.67	3.23	1.19	0.31	—
	1个	368	10.13	3.16			
	2个	243	10.21	3.35			
	2个及以上	20	9.65	3.88			

续上表

维度	选项	个案数	平均值	标准偏差	F	sig	多重比较
服务船型	货船	553	10.14	3.37	0.43	0.78	—
	集装箱船	94	9.83	2.98			
	油船、液化气船	132	9.82	3.02			
	邮轮	2	9.00	4.24			
	其他	28	9.96	2.97			
服务航线	内河航线	12	10.92	3.06	0.80	0.49	—
	沿海航线	303	9.89	3.52			
	近洋航线	203	10.25	3.11			
	远洋航线	291	10.02	3.07			
年薪	10万元及以下	379	10.29	3.53	1.72	0.14	—
	10万~15万元	197	9.60	2.91			
	15万~20万元	111	9.92	3.05			
	20万~30万元	85	9.91	2.89			
	30万元及以上	37	10.51	3.34			

心理健康在七个其余变量上的差异分析　　表9

维度	选项	个案数	平均值	标准偏差	F	sig	多重比较
学历	高中及以上	248	10.71	3.46	7.72	0.00	1>2、1>3
	大专	446	9.77	3.13			
	大学本科及以上	115	9.64	3.09			
注:其中1代表为高中及以上、2代表为大专、3代表为大学本科及以上							
海龄	少于1年	38	11.58	3.37	3.67	0.01	1>3、1>4、1>5、2>3、2>5
	1~3年	66	10.77	3.18			
	3~5年	84	9.58	3.37			
	5~10年	227	10.03	3.15			
	10年以上	394	9.88	3.25			
注:其中1代表为少于1年、2代表为1~3年、3代表为3~5年、4代表为5~10年、5代表为10年以上							
职务	船长	68	10.19	2.95	5.08	0.00	1>5,1>7,2<4,2<9,3>7,4>5,4>7,5<9,6<9,7<9,8<9
	大副	99	9.25	2.96			
	二副	73	10.07	2.98			
	三副	69	10.59	2.88			
	轮机长	56	8.96	3.23			
	大管轮	66	9.83	3.09			
	二管轮	79	9.03	2.68			
	三管轮	45	9.51	3.39			
	其他	254	10.85	3.58			
注:其中1代表为船长、2代表为大副、3代表为二副、4代表为三副、5代表为轮机长、6代表为大管轮、7代表为二管轮、8代表为三管轮、9代表为其他							
睡眠时间	0~3h	27	8.26	3.10	11.82	0.00	1<2,1<3,1<4,2<3,
	4~6h	390	9.53	3.14			
	7~9h	365	10.62	3.27			

续上表

维度	选项	个案数	平均值	标准偏差	F	sig	多重比较
睡眠时间	9h 以上	27	11.44	2.89	11.82	0.00	2 <4
注:其中1代表为0~3小时,2代表为4~6小时,3代表为7~9小时,4代表为9小时以上							
体育运动时间	0~30min	621	9.68	3.07	11.31	0.00	1 <2,1 <3
	30min~1h	170	11.20	3.62			
	1h~3h	16	11.50	3.22			
	3h 及以上	2	11.50	0.71			
注:其中1代表为0~30min,2代表为30min~1h,3代表为1~3h,4代表为3h及以上							
娱乐时间	小于30min	279	9.35	3.27	6.67	0.00	1 <2,1 <3
	30min~1h	259	10.37	3.28			
	1~3h	223	10.48	3.11			
	3h 以上	48	10.27	3.11			
注:其中1代表为小于30min,2代表为30min~1h,3代表为1~3h,4代表为3h以上							
娱乐方式	打牌或打麻将	28	10.54	3.43	9.69	0.00	1 >5,2 >5,3 >5,4 >5,6 >5
	玩手机或平板电脑	351	10.12	3.06			
	聊天	57	10.30	2.76			
	看书看电影或唱歌	206	10.64	3.46			
	无娱乐	123	8.30	2.80			
	其他	44	10.84	3.85			
注:其中1代表为打牌或打麻将,2代表为玩手机或平板电脑,3代表为聊天,4代表为看书看电影或唱歌,5代表为无娱乐,6代表为其他							

2.2.3 海员的工作满意度

由表10可知,海员的工作满意度的平均水平为2.91,总体属于中等水平(表7)。

工作满意度的描述性统计 表10

项目	N	最小值	最大值	均值	标准偏差	变量均值
我的工作量分配均匀(不会在某一时间段工作量激增、集中工作)	809	1	5	2.47	1.29	2.91
我有足够的时间来完成工作任务(我无需加班)	809	1	5	2.55	1.32	
我能在工作中提高自己的能力或学习新知识	809	1	5	3.65	1.14	
我的工作很有意义,我很愿意继续从事航海的工作	809	1	5	2.39	1.28	
我认为我的工作很重要	809	1	5	3.47	1.37	
我的上司(如船长等)善于统筹安排工作,解决冲突等	809	1	5	3.18	1.19	
我的上司了解我的工作内容,经常与我沟通并支持我的工作	809	1	5	3.21	1.18	
我的上司能确保每一位员工都有升职加薪的机会	809	1	5	2.38	1.24	

2.3 人际关系、工作满意度、心理健康等变量之间的相关性分析

由表11可知,海员心理健康与人际关系的相关系数为0.495,则说明它们呈现显著的正相关;海员心理健康与工作满意度的相关系数为0.583,则说明它们相关性较大;海员的工作满意度与人际关系的相关系数为0.615,则说明它们呈现显著的正相关。由此可见,海员的人际关系、工作满意度与心理健康之间呈显著正相关。

相关性分析 表11

变量	相关性	人际关系	工作满意度	心理健康
人际关系	皮尔逊相关性	1		
工作满意度	皮尔逊相关性	0.615**	1	
心理健康	皮尔逊相关性	0.495**	0.583**	1

注:在0.01级别(双尾),相关性显著。

2.4 工作满意度的中介作用分析

本研究基于温忠麟等人的中介效应检验流程[16],在控制学历、海龄、担任职务、每日平均睡眠时间、体育运动时间、休闲娱乐时间、娱乐方式等变量的基础上,通过三步回归分析来检验工作满意度在人际关系和心理健康之间的中介效应。第一步,以人际关系 X 为自变量、心理健康为因变量进行回归分析;第二步,以人际关系为自变量、工作满意度 W(工作资源满意度 $W1$、领导资源满意度 $W2$)为因变量进行回归分析;第三步,同时以人际关系和工作满意度(工作资源满意度、领导资源满意度)为自变量、心理健康水平为因变量进行回归分析中介检验结果如表12所示。

中介效应检验 表12

项目	标准化回归方程	回归系数检验	
工作满意度 W			
第一步	$Y=0.781X+3.446$	SE=0.042	$t=14.746$
第二步	$W=2.064X+3.2$	SE=0.082	$t=20.855$
第三步	$Y=0.196W+0.378X+2.821$	SE=0.049	$t=11.091$
		SE=0.017	$t=6.159$
工作资源满意度 $W1$			
第一步	$Y=0.781X+3.446$	SE=0.042	$t=17.758$
第二步	$W1=1.311X+0.936$	SE=0.055	$t=19.476$
第三步	$Y=0.265W1+0.434X+3.198$	SE=0.048	$t=10.095$
		SE=0.025	$t=7.163$
领导资源满意度 $W2$			
第一步	$Y=0.781X+3.446$	SE=0.042	$t=17.758$
第二步	$W2=0.753X+2.263$	SE=0.041	$t=15.025$
第三步	$Y=0.285W2+0.567X+2.801$	SE=0.045	$t=9.803$
		SE=0.034	$t=7.912$

由表12可知,人际关系直接作用于海员的心理健康($\beta=0.523$, $P<0.001$),也通过工作满意度间接作用于海员的心理健康,中介效应占总效应的比例为$(2.064\times0.196)/0.781=0.518$,说明工作满意度中介效应影响较大。其中,工作资源满意度和领导资源满意度均具有显著性。工作资源满意度的中介效应占总效应的比例为$(1.311\times0.265)/0.781=0.726$,领导资源满意度的中介效应占总效应的比例为$(0.753\times0.285)/0.781=0.275$。

3 总结与展望

3.1 总结

本文主要研究海员人际关系、工作满意度和心理健康的关系。研究发现，海员人际关系与工作满意度、心理健康呈显著的正相关，而海员工作满意度与心理健康也呈显著正相关；海员工作满意度在人际关系与心理健康之间起到中介作用。

此外，最高学历、海龄、担任职务、每日平均睡眠时间、体育与娱乐时间以及娱乐方式会显著影响海员心理健康水平。

3.2 建议

基于研究结果，分别针对航运企业、海员自身和航运协会以及政府三方提出如下建议：

1）航运企业

（1）应对船员心理问题加以关注并且重视，比如改善船员的工作生活条件，提高船舶生活功能，增加生活、娱乐设施，提供免费的互联网访问条件等，将硬件设施尽可能的完善，让海员在船上的休闲娱乐的需求得到最大的满足，增加船员社会信息的接收和社会交往渠道，安排家属不定期到船探亲，让海员减少与陆地生活的差异感；

（2）建立船员电子化心理档案，这样便于留档保存以及调用，方便及时查看海员的心理健康状况。

（3）企业要多一些人文关怀，船上的生活总的来说是比陆地会更加的辛苦与危险，但近几年船上的海员收入与陆地的收入在逐渐的缩小，这会较大的影响海员的积极性，所以应以实际行动切实解决好船员最关心、最直接、最现实的利益问题，提高海员的福利待遇。

2）海员自身

（1）要掌握一定的心理健康知识，学会自我减压，控制情绪。加强人际关系理论的学习，转变观念让自己拥有一个良好的心理素质。

（2）注重人际交往技能的培养。首先将所学的人际交往的知识与行动结合起来，正确选择交际手段，克服人际交往障碍。

（3）船长在船上要充分发挥领导功能，促进海员之间的理解与对话，对于海员之间发生的矛盾要及时调节，避免矛盾升级恶化造成不可挽回的后果，也可以在闲暇时间组织相关活动比赛来提高海员之间的交往，促进海员之间的熟悉与认识。

3）航运协会以及政府相关部门

（1）政府和航运协会可以提升社会对船员职业的关注度，创造尊重船员，关爱船员的良好氛围，对于增加船员职业自豪感和自信心。政府可以引导媒体多关注海员的正面形象，宣传海员为社会经济发展所做的巨大贡献，宣扬海员的英雄模范事迹，树立典型，加大航海科学知识的普及，鼓励拍摄海员相关的影视作品，提高海员的社会影响力。

（2）航海院校可以将海员心理健康作为必修学科，让海员在校期间能尽可能多地提高自身的心理素质，以及对心理健康问题加以重视与初步的了解，这将为后面的船上生活打下基础，同时学校的课程教学与引导会比海员自学或者企业内的一些讲座更加的专业性。

（3）有关部门也可将心理健康纳入船员考试发证规则，现场检查时关注船员心理问题，这样可以在源头上做好预防工作。

（4）政府可以成立专门的船员心理疏导机构，像学校有心理咨询部门一样，社会也需要一个专门的海员可以诉诸心理压力的地方，为海员提供多种渠道的心理咨询与引导，帮助船员解决心理问题。

3.3 局限

本研究的人际关系主要从同事、家人两个层面探讨人际关系对心理健康的影响，未来可以进一步扩大人际关系的范围进行探讨。

参考文献

[1] 卢琳际. 海员心理健康问题与影响及对策[J]. 管理观察，2015(35)：9-12.

[2] 童颖，李雪松. 维护我国海员心理健康探析[J]. 中国海事，2018(04)：40-42.

[3] 谢鸣. 上海港出入境国际海员心理健康状况调查及其影响因素分析[D]. 上海：复旦大学，2012.

[4] Song L，Huang Z，Zhang H，et al. The urgency to address the occupational health ofchinese seafarers for sustainable development [J]. Marine Policy，2021，129(2)：104518.

[5] Mellbye A，Carter T. Seafarers' depression and suicide. [J]. International maritime health，2017，68(2)：108-114.

[6] Oldenburg M，Jensen H J，Wegner R. Burnout

syndrome in seafarers in the merchant marine service [J]. International Archives of Occupational & Environmental Health,2013,86(4):407-416.

[7] Maria, Borovnik. Occupational health and safety of merchant seafarers from Kiribati and Tuvalu [J]. Asia Pacific Viewpoint, 2011, 52(3): 333-346.

[8] CaRter T . Working at sea and psychosocial health problems Report of an International Maritime Health Association Workshop [J]. Travel Medicine & Infectious Disease, 2005, 3(2):61-65.

[9] 郇远和,张蓓.海员职业心理适应能力的培养[J].航海教育研究,2005(02):96-99.

[10] 王慧玲,杨烨,尹耀兴,等.远洋航行对健康海员心理卫生的影响[J].医学理论与实践,2005(10):1151-1152.

[11] 谢鸣,俞秋蓉,王征.上海外高桥口岸国际海员心理健康状况及其相关因素调查[J].中国国境卫生检疫杂志,2015(01):42-45.

[12] 李静.影响海员心理健康的因素及心理援助对策[C]// 2010 年全国航海心理学术交流会.

[13] 胡学文,钱轶梅.影响海员心理健康的因素及对策探析[J].交通医学,2010,24(5):495-495.

[14] 谢特秀.海员工作特点与常见心理问题的探讨[J].中国水运(下半月),2008(10):22-23.

[15] 曾明,秦璐.工作满意度研究综述[J].河南教育学院学报(哲学社会科学版),2003(01):101-104.

[16] 温忠麟,张雷,侯杰泰,等.中介效应检验程序及其应用[J].心理学报,2004,36(5):614-620.

基于网络时空核密度的不良驾驶行为多发点识别研究

王建伟[1]　付佳杨*[2]　付　鑫[2]

(1.交通基础设施数字化教育部工程中心;2.长安大学运输工程学院大数据管理与应用系)

摘　要　不良驾驶行为是导致交通事故的主要原因之一,为降低交通事故的发生率,应加强对不良驾驶行为的有效监管。本文采用网络时空核密度分析方法结合高斯函数,以昆明市部分地区为研究区域,该区域内两周产生的不良驾驶行为为研究对象。在研究区域内生成时空子路段,计算各时空子路段的网络时空核密度值。分析了不良驾驶行为的时空分布特征,最终采用累计频率法确定不良驾驶行为多发时空子路段的识别阈值,最终鉴别出 14880 条不良驾驶行为的多发时空子路段,并对这些子路段进行简要时空分析。

关键词　交通安全　多发点识别　时空网络核密度估计　不良驾驶行为

0　引言

作为道路交通运行的重要参与者,驾驶员在驾驶车辆过程中,不断接收、处理、判断交通运行信息,并根据自己的判断做出相应的驾驶行为,这就要求驾驶员在驾驶车辆过程中时刻保持精神高度集中,但多数驾驶员在日常的驾驶中会放松警惕性,出现打手机、抽烟、跟车过近、疲劳驾驶等一系列不良驾驶行为。不良驾驶行为存在多发点、多发路段以及多发时间段,此类地点、时间点我们称之为不良驾驶行为的“黑点”“黑段”,在这些地点、时间段中通过“提醒”“重点监管”等手段,提示驾驶员此地容易产生哪种不良驾驶行为,有效降低不良驾驶行为的发生频率,将对预防交通事故的发生有较大帮助[1]。

传统针对驾驶人行为的研究主要集中在试验性研究方面[2],研究人员大多从驾驶员个体的间接属性,即工作经验[3]、年龄[3-4]、性别[4]等条件出发。对于多发点的识别还存在一定的不足,但对于犯罪行为、交通事故等多发点研究已经较为成熟。

研究方法层面。核密度方法是空间分析方法中比较成熟的一种算法[5],但传统核密度估计无论在最优窗宽计算还是时间分析上都存在一定的不足,忽略不良驾驶行为的一个重要方面,即位置受限于道路网络[6]。Atsuyuki Okabe 等[7]开发了一种用于估计网络上点密度的核密度估计方法,这种方法可用于寻找交通事故、街头犯罪或油气管道泄漏的"热点"。Loo B 等[8]采用基于地理信息系统的网络约束核密度方法,分析道路交通事故的空间分布。禹文豪等[9]通过实际 POI 数据分析发现,考虑街道网络约束的热点范围可凸显设施功能沿交通网络布局的空间特征。Mohaymany A S 等[10]通过检查三年研究(2006—2008 年)期间得出的网络估计核密度,提出了一种高碰撞路段检测方法,并说明了危险路段的稳定性。但像不良驾驶行为和交通事故这种"点"数据除了就空间属性外,还包括时间属性,因此分析这类"点"数据的时间分布情况也非常必要。Benjamin Romano 等[6]提出时空网络核密度估计(STNKDE)方法,该方法解决了交通事故热点受限于道路网络的问题,并将事故热点的时间维度和时间动态结合到核密度分析中。

研究内容层面。对于"热点"、多发路段、高发区域、多发点、黑点研究在交通事故和盗窃犯罪等研究中频繁出现,随着 GIS 和 GPS 的普及,多发点的研究方法越来越丰富,研究范围也越来越广泛。常安德等[11]在定义道路交通事故多发点段和充分考虑交通事故空间定位信息的基础上,基于聚类分析技术研究了一种道路交通事故多发点段的识别方法,进而利用当量总事故率法将交通事故多发点段划分为 3 个风险等级。姜燕等[12]以核密度估计和计数数据模型为理论基础,提出了一种基于空间聚类分析技术的城市道路事故多发位置鉴别方法,实现分析结果的可视化。多发点研究在空间范围内已经非常普遍,但是拓展时空范围进行研究的并不多见。刘尧等[13]针对目前交通事故分析中时空维度分离的不足,以 H 市 2013—2015 年的交通事故数据为研究对象,基于时空网络核密度估计、热点分析法,分别从行政区划以及道路网络上进行交通事故的时空特征分析,从宏观和微观角度揭示交通事故的时空热点区域。

综上,时空网络核密度分析已成为时空集聚研究方面较为先进的综合性分析方法。多发点的鉴别在交通事故、犯罪等领域已相当成熟,但对于不良驾驶行为的多发点鉴别研究还很少见,本文将以昆明市部分城区为研究区域,以 2020 年 7 月 12-25 日该区域内部分货运车辆发生的不良驾驶行为为研究对象,以时空网络分析为方法,结合高斯函数和累计频率法,生成一套适用于不良驾驶行为多发点的识别方法。

1 数据来源及研究区域

本文研究区域为昆明市部分城区,数据分为两大主体,一部分是不良驾驶行为数据,另一部分是路网矢量数据。不良驾驶行为数据为该地 2020 年 7 月中两周内的货运车辆发生的不良驾驶行为产生记录,经管处理、筛选、去重后剩余 15698 条点数据。路网数据源于全国路网数据,根据需要裁剪出昆明市部分城区,经过人工补全和疏通后,共计 837 条路段。

不良驾驶行为数据字段包括车辆编号、发生地点经纬度、发生时间(年月日时分秒)、不良驾驶行为类型。该数据采集自车载 ADAS 系统,随时记录车辆在行驶过程中发生的不良驾驶行为。数据采集过程中存在一定的空值、误差、重复的"脏数据",数据清洗过程目的就在于去除这些"脏数据"。

由于原始的路网数据存在较多断点以及重复路线,因此需要将路网进行裁剪,经过预处理后的路网与不良驾驶行为数据匹配如图 1 所示。

图 1 路网与不良驾驶行为点匹配

2　分析方法

2.1　时空网络核密度估计

因自然路段存在长短不一的现象,因此需要将路段分割成子路段,使大部分的子路段长度一致,本文以最优窗宽的 1/10 为空间子路段的长度,依据高斯函数中积分均方差最小原则来求取最优窗宽,最终推导形成的最优窗宽计算公式为[5]:

$$h_{opt} = 1.06\sigma n^{-\frac{1}{5}} \tag{1}$$

式中:h_{opt}——最优窗宽;

σ——高斯核函数的标准差;

n——目标对象总量。

本文中,n 为不良驾驶行为数据的总量,σ 为不良驾驶行为数据的网络距离的标准差,通过计算得到的空间最优窗宽为 466m。空间子路段长度为 46m,按照子路段长度划分子路段,得到空间范围内 7624 条子路段,空间子路段序号定义为 0 ~7623。由于实际求得的时间最优窗宽极大地加剧了计算量,因此本文中直接设定时间窗宽为 3 时,时间子路段长为 1 时,最终得到时空子路段 7624 条 ×24 条。

本文应用基于路网距离的网络时空核密度估计方法进行货运不良驾驶行为多发点识别研究,估计公式如下所示:

$$\lambda = \frac{1}{h_{opt1} h_2}\sum_{i=1}^{n} \frac{1}{\sqrt{2\pi}} e^{\left[-\frac{1}{2}\left(\frac{d_i}{h_{opt1}}\right)^2\right]} \cdot \frac{1}{\sqrt{2\pi}} e^{\left[-\frac{1}{2}\left(\frac{t_i}{h_2}\right)^2\right]} \tag{2}$$

式中:λ——某一时空子路段的网络时空核密度估计值;

h_{opt1}——空间最优宽窗;

h_2——时间最优宽窗;

d_i——第 i 个不良驾驶行为到时空子路段的路网距离;

t_i——第 i 个不良驾驶行为到时空子路段的时间距离。通过计算,得到了 7624 条 ×24 条时空子路段的网络时空核密度估计值。

2.2　时空网络核密度估计值分析

以各个小时各子路段的时空网络核密度值为依据形成热力图,从图中可以看出每个小时的不良驾驶行为高发点的范围。随着时间推移,不同时间段的不良驾驶行为高发路段有所不同。以图中方框内的路网为例,在前 5h 时空网络核密度值比较低,从第 6h 起核密度值突增,并在接下来的 19h 内居高不下。方框以外的路网刚好相反,在前 8h 中网络核密度值较高,从第 9h 起,时空网络核密度值持续降低,如图 2 所示。

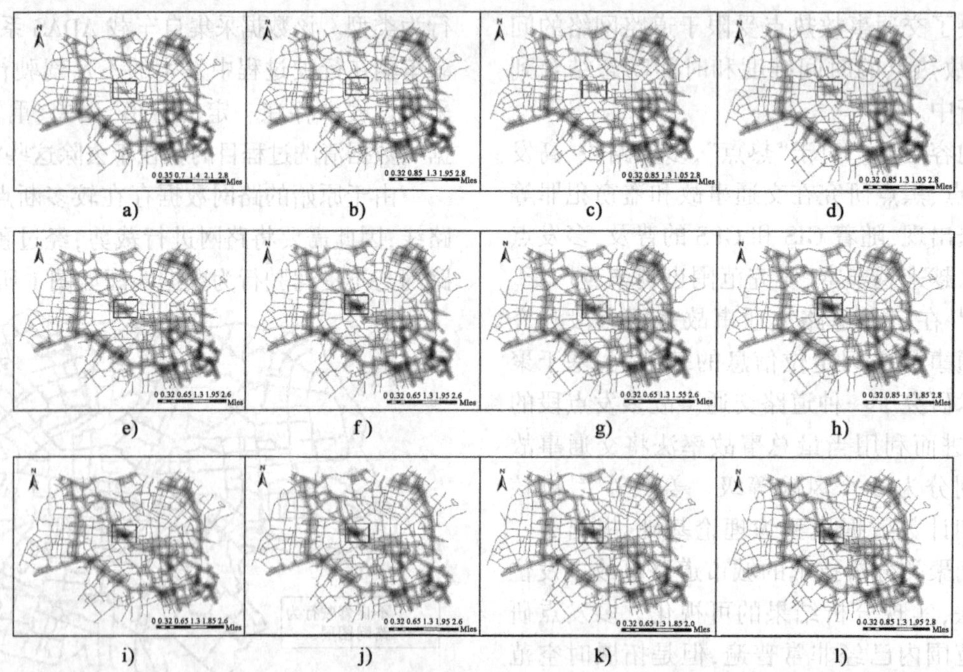

图　2

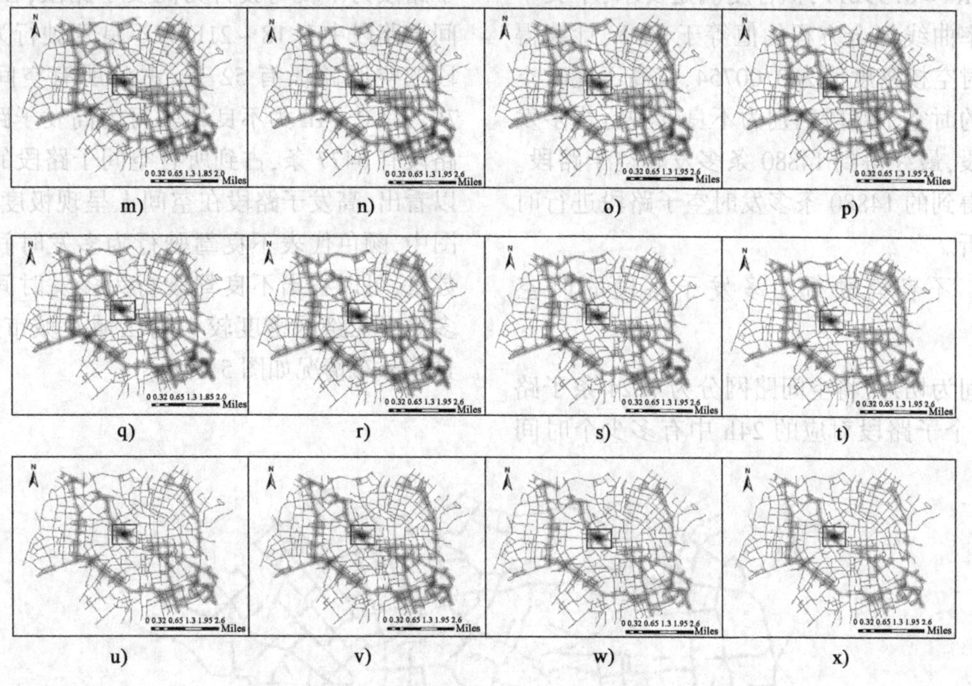

图2 24h 的时空核密度值热力图

3 不良驾驶行为多发路段的识别与特征分析

3.1 不良驾驶行为多发路段的识别

交通事故的多发点鉴别多采用累计频率法[14]，本文将得到的 7624 条 ×24 条子路段的网络时空核密度值按照大小顺序，对比不同的划分标准，最终确定均匀划分成 30 个区间，统计每个区间的时空子路段数量，并计算该区间的频率及累计频率，然后根据累计频率法来确定不良驾驶行为多发时空子路段的阈值。

大多数时空子路段的核密度值较低，从第 10 个区间，累计频率就已经高达 0.992%，由此可知大部分的不良驾驶行为发生在极少量的时空子路段上。根据累计频率法得到各时空核密度值区间的频率分布如图 3 所示。

依据统计结果，利用累计频率曲线法得到的时空核密度值的累计频率散点图如图 4 所示。

对一系列散点进行拟合，最终得到时空核密度值区间和累计频率的拟合结果，拟合出的方程为：

$$y = \frac{1.048x}{0.00124 + x} \tag{3}$$

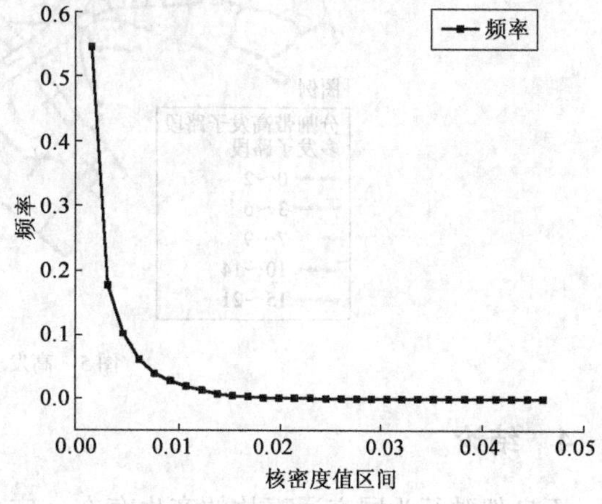

图3 各时空核密度值区间的频率分布图

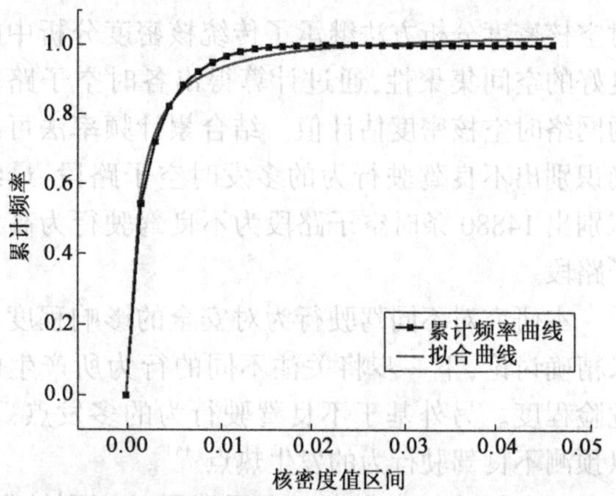

图4 各时空核密度值区间的累计频率散点图

其中,$R^2 = 0.99211$,拟合度满足要求,本文中令累计频率曲线拟合方程的值等于90%,计算得到相应的时空核密度值为0.00754,将高于此时空核密度值的时空子路段判别为不良驾驶行为多发时空子路段,最终得到14880条多发时空子路段。接下来对得到的14880条多发时空子路段进行时空特征分析。

3.2 不良驾驶行为多发子路段的时空特征分析

以空间为切片,将空间路网分为7624条子路段,观察每个子路段对应的24h中有多少个时间子路段为不良驾驶行为高发子路段,在7624条空间子路段中有18~21h为不良驾驶行为高发子路段的空间路段有52条,占到所有空间子路段的7%;有0~4h为不良驾驶行为高发子路段的空间路段有6477条,占到所有空间子路段的85%,可以看出,高发子路段在空间上呈现极度集中现象。图中,颜色代表不良驾驶行为多发时间子路段的数量,可以看出不良驾驶行为多发时间子路段大多集中在路网密度较大的区域及城市路网环线。具体分布情况如图5所示。

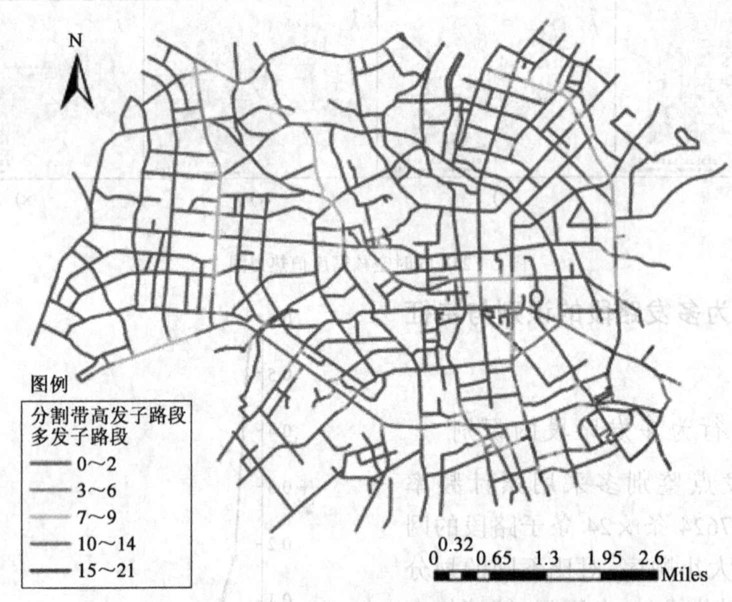

图5 高发子路段的时空分布特征

4 结论

不良驾驶行为同交通事故的产生存在一定关系,且在时间与空间上呈现一定的集聚性。网络时空核密度分析方法继承了传统核密度分析中的良好的空间集聚性,通过计算得出各时空子路段的网络时空核密度估计值。结合累计频率法可准确识别出不良驾驶行为的多发时空子路段,最终识别出14880条时空子路段为不良驾驶行为高发子路段。

本研究对不同驾驶行为对安全的影响程度尚未精确讨论,下一步将关注不同的行为所产生的危险程度。另外基于不良驾驶行为的多发点,可以预测不良驾驶行为的发生热点[15]。

不良驾驶行为多发时空子路段的识别结果,为监管部门为减少不良驾驶行为的产生所采取措施提供参考,可在多发时空子路段重点设置提示牌,提醒驾驶员此处易产生不良驾驶行为,也可在多发时间段内多出动监管人员,进行人为监管,以减少不良驾驶行为的产生,最终达到减少交通事故的目的。

参考文献

[1] Dula C S, Ballard M E. Development and Evaluation of a Measure of Dangerous, Aggressive, Negative Emotional, and Risky Driving [J]. Journal of Applied Social Psychology,2010,33(2):263-82.

[2] Yuan Y A, YI A, Qi W A. Adaptive forward vehicle collision warning based on driving behavior - ScienceDirect [J]. Neurocomputing, 2020,408:64-71.

[3] Tseng C M. Operating styles, working time and daily driving distance in relation to a taxi driver's speeding offenses in Taiwan [J]. Accid Anal Prev, 2013, 52: 1-8.

[4] Palk G, Freeman J, Kee A G, et al. The prevalence and characteristics of self-reported dangerous driving behaviours among a young cohort [J]. Transportation Research Part F Traffic Psychology & Behaviour, 2011, 14(2): 147-54.

[5] 陈金林. 基于网络核密度估计城市路网事故黑点鉴别研究[D]. 南京:东南大学,2015.

[6] Benjamin Romano, Zhe Jiang. Visualizing Traffic Accident Hotspots Based on Spatial-Temporal Network Kernel Density Estimation[P]. Advances in Geographic Information Systems, 2017.

[7] Atsuyuki Okabe, Toshiaki Satoh, Kokichi Sugihara. A kernel density estimation method for networks, its computational method and a GIS-based tool [J]. International Journal of Geographical Information Science, 2009, 23(1).

[8] Loo B, Yao S, Wu J. Spatial point analysis of road crashes in Shanghai: A GIS-based network kernel density method[C]// IEEE. IEEE, 2011.

[9] 禹文豪,艾廷华,刘鹏程,等. 设施 POI 分布热点分析的网络核密度估计方法[J]. 测绘学报,2015,44(12):1378-1383,1400.

[10] Mohaymany A S, Shahri M, Mirbagheri B. GIS-based method for detecting high-crash-risk road segments using network kernel density estimation[J]. 地球空间信息科学学报(英文版),2013,16(002):113-119.

[11] 常安德,张朝旭,陈松. 基于聚类分析的道路交通事故多发点段评价方法[J]. 中国人民公安大学学报(自然科学版),2020,26(02):47-52.

[12] 姜燕,刘利华. 城市道路交通事故多发位置鉴别[J]. 交通信息与安全,2014,32(03):32-35,52.

[13] 刘尧,王颖志,王立君,等. 交通事故的时空热点分析[J]. 浙江大学学报(理学版),2020,47(01):52-59.

[14] 孙平,黄建峰. 泉南高速公路柳南段事故黑点鉴别及组合因素影响分析[J]. 路基工程,2018(05):227-232.

[15] Aslam Al-Omari, Nawras Shatnawi, Taisir Khedaywi, Tasneem Miqdady. Prediction of traffic accidents hot spots using fuzzy logic and GIS[J]. Applied Geomatics, 2019.

风险驾驶行为对高速公路事故影响因素研究

马潇驰[1,2,3] 陆 建*[1,2,3]

(1. 东南大学江苏省城市智能交通重点实验室;

2. 东南大学现代城市交通技术江苏高校协同创新中心;3. 东南大学交通学院)

摘 要 为降低高速公路的交通事故,分析驾驶员行为对交通事故的影响因素,为交通管控和规避风险提供理论依据,以宁杭高速公路长兴—溧阳段的驾驶行为和事故数据集为基础,研究风险驾驶行为对高速公路事故的影响因素。使用高德车载 GPS 采集的车辆轨迹,筛选紧急左变道、紧急右变道、紧急加速和紧急制动四种风险驾驶行为。将宁杭高速公路长兴—溧阳段按互通匝道进出口和一般长直道路划分为123个子区间,使用 GIS 技术将事故和驾驶行为投影到各子区间内。利用泊松回归分析风险驾驶行为和事故间的相关关系。研究结果表明:(1)紧急左变道驾驶行为对事故的发生影响最大,其他三个行为的影响系数较小或不具有显著影响,每多1次紧急左变道行为,事故率较平均水平提高3.5%。(2)高速

1. 基金项目:国家自然科学基金(No. 52072071);道路交通安全公安部重点实验室开放基金(No. 2021ZDSYSKFKT12)。

公路互通匝道进出口是事故高发路段,且紧急左变道驾驶行为影响更剧烈,在互通上的1次左变道行为比长直路段发生事故的概率提高20.7%。最后,针对可能导致频繁急左变道的原因提出三点假设,并给出相应的建议以规避事故风险。

关键词　交通工程　事故影响因素　泊松回归　风险驾驶行为　高速公路　交通安全

0　引言

明确交通事故致因是预测事故和风险管控的首要前提,在明确了导致交通事故的因素后才能有的放矢,制定相应的管理政策,减小道路风险,降低交通事故。国内外学者对交通事故的风险致因已有长期的探索,取得了诸多成果。交通系统是一个人、车、路、环境等多要素共同作用的复杂系统,对交通事故的影响因素分析一般也从这四个方面入手。交通流在事故中的作用已得到了深入研究,有大量学者研究了实时交通流和事故之间的关系[1],并相应提出了利用实时交通流信息预测预警交通事故的方法,交通量[2]、平均车速[3]和拥堵指数[4]是导致交通事故的显著因素。道路线形和天气也会表现出高度的风险特征,由于线形设计不佳[5]或极端天气[6,7]导致的视距不良会大大增高事故的风险。

交通流、道路和环境对事故的影响因素研究已经有了长足的进展,驾驶员作为道路交通系统的另一个重要组成部分,其行为对交通事故的发生亦有不可估量的影响。一个驾龄长、经验丰富的驾驶员能更好地在复杂交通状态下从容驾驶[8],规避可能的事故风险,而青少年在驾驶过程中表现出更多的进攻性和鲁莽性。目前,针对驾驶行为的研究多使用驾驶行为问卷(Driver Behavior Questionnaire,DBQ)的形式,间接地从驾驶员渠道获得行为数据加以分析。Eboli(2017)等[9]通过问卷调查研究了不同驾驶员在事故多发路段的行为,并对驾驶员进行了风险评级,指出需要给予高风险的驾驶员更多关注。根据多位学者的研究和调查发现,分心驾驶[10]、疲劳[11]、酒驾[12]、驾驶时使用手机[13]极大地增大了事故发生的风险。然而问卷调查的行为和驾驶员实际的行为一定存在偏差,问卷的定性问题设计也会使数据失真。使用手机信令数据或GPS数据采集驾驶员行为成本高昂,因此对真实发生的驾驶员行为数据研究较为稀少。驾驶员真实行为和事故之间的关系研究可以探明导致事故的高风险行为,对进一步研究驾驶员为何做出风险行为以及制定管控措施规避风险提供理论依据。

本文利用高德GPS采集的高速公路行车急变道、急加速和急减速行为数据,以采样时间内各路段的不同风险驾驶行为数为自变量,事故总数为因变量,使用泊松回归分析了前述风险驾驶行为和事故之间的关系,填补相关领域内的空白,并对可能造成风险驾驶行为的危险因素提出假设,为后续排除风险提出政策意见。本文的各章节内容为:第一节介绍使用的统计分析方法,第二节介绍采集的高德GPS风险驾驶行为数据集,第三节展示回归结果,分析驾驶行为对交通事故的影响,并提出相应的建议规避风险,最后总结本文的创新点和未来的计划。

1　方法简述

在对因变量是离散型变量的问题进行回归分析时,可以使用线性回归模型,当因变量是计数变量时,由于计数变量都是大于等于0的整数,且可能存在较多因变量为0的情况,故常规的线性模型无法很好地完成计数变量回归任务。采用泊松回归的广义线性模型具有良好的回归效果,一般地,泊松回归要求统计量服从泊松分布:

$$P(y = k) = \frac{\lambda^k}{k!}e^{-\lambda} \tag{1}$$

其中,y为事件发生的频数,λ为泊松分布的特征参数,亦是泊松分布的均值和方差,满足式(2)的数学关系:

$$E(Y) = D(Y) = \lambda \tag{2}$$

由于期望λ是连续变量,因此可以建立解释变量和λ之间的广义线性回归模型:

$$\lambda = e^{x\beta} \tag{3}$$

其中,$\boldsymbol{x}$为样本的解释变量向量,$\boldsymbol{\beta}$为回归参数向量,亦可写成非矩阵形式:

$$\ln(\lambda) = \beta_0 + \beta_1 x_1 + \cdots + \beta_m x_m \tag{4}$$

对具有N个样本的数据集$\{X_i, i = 1:n\}$,每一个样本点对为$\{x_i, y_i\}$,根据式(1)假定的模型,该样本的概率为

$$P(y_i = k_i) = \frac{\lambda(x_i)^{k_i}}{k_i!}e^{-\lambda(x_i)} \tag{5}$$

则对数据集中的所有样本点对,列出关于 λ 的似然函数:

$$L(\Theta) = \prod_{i=1}^{N} \frac{\lambda(\mathbf{x}_i)^{k_i}}{k_i!} e^{-\lambda(x_i)} \tag{6}$$

其中,$\Theta = [\beta_0, \beta_1, \cdots, \beta_m]$ 为拟得到的一组参数向量,通过求式(6)的对数函数的极值获得参数估计值

$$\hat{\Theta} = [\hat{\beta}_0, \hat{\beta}_1, \cdots, \hat{\beta}_m] \tag{7}$$

在参数估计完成后,使用 T 检验评价模型参数的显著性水平。使用 SPSS 软件完成泊松回归参数估计和显著性检验。

2 数据准备

采集宁杭高速 2020 年 9 月 26 日到 10 月 2 日的风险驾驶行为和事故数据,时间段覆盖工作日和节假日,具有典型性。采样区域为杭州-南京方向在长兴、宜兴和溧阳辖区内的路段。

事故数据来源于宜兴市公安局,风险驾驶行为数据来源于高德软件有限公司,利用车载导航获取车辆的行驶轨迹,判断车辆是否有急变道、急加速、急刹车的风险驾驶行为,并记录风险驾驶行为的类型和经纬度信息。共采集 374 起事故和 13 万余条驾驶行为数据。按照一般长直道路和互通匝道进出口道路的种类将采样区域全段划分为 123 个子区间,通过 GIS 手段将驾驶行为数据和事故数据投影到子区间上,每个子区间为一条数据,因变量为在此区间内发生的事故次数,自变量为各风险驾驶行为的发生次数,数据结构及描述性统计结果见表 1。

数据结构及描述性统计结果 表 1

变量名	含义	变量类型	最小值	最大值	均值	标准差
Crash	事故数(起)	计数	0	40	2.85	5.16
Left	急左变道行为次数(次)	计数	0	90	8.02	13.97
Right	急右变道行为次数(次)	计数	0	1326	17.26	119.51
Accel	急加速行为次数(次)	计数	5	6510	511.63	911.40
Brake	急刹车行为次数(次)	计数	1	7162	549.28	1062.21
Position	位置(HT = 互通匝道进出口,NM = 一般长直路段)	名义	—	—	—	—

3 结果分析

3.1 参数解释

对第 2 节中采集的数据进行泊松回归,在最初的模型中纳入所有的变量和它们的二阶交互,以 95% 置信度为阈值,每次迭代删除显著性最差的变量,直到所有变量的显著性 p 值都在 0.05 以下。回归参数估计结果如表 2 所示。回归结果清晰地显示急左变道行为的参数权重最大,其他三个高显著的变量影响很小,几乎可以忽略不计。在经验认识中,急刹车应是一个高危因素,容易导致追尾和碰撞,但分析结果表示急刹车的影响很小。急左变道行为的参数的指数估计值为 1.035,其含义是在各子路段上每多一个急左变道行为,发生事故的概率变为 1.035 倍,根据表 2 中急左变道行为的取值范围,以平均值 2.85 为基准,最大值 40 出现的路段的事故发生概率会是普通路段的 3.59 倍。

将事故数为 0 的路段剔除,只留下至少发生 1 次的路段,并考虑发生事故的地点是互通还是一般长直路段,再次进行相同步骤的泊松回归,结果如表 3 所示。在已发生事故的路段上,急左变道行为的权重进一步加大,而互通包括它的分流、合流匝道和交织区都是事故多发的地段,相同的左转行为若发生在互通上,其事故概率比发生在一般长直道路上高 20.7%,这和人们普遍的经验认识相符。

驾驶行为与事故的泊松回归结果 表 2

变量	参数估计	标准误差	显著性	指数估计值
Left	0.034	0.008	0.000	1.035
Brake	0.001	0.000	0.000	1.001
Left * Accel	0.000	0.000	0.001	1.000
Left * Brake	0.000	0.000	0.000	1.000

考虑不同位置的驾驶行为对事故的影响　　表3

变量	参数估计	标准误差	显著性	指数估计值
Left	0.043	0.001	0	1.044
Right	0.000	0.000	0.000	1.000
HT * Left	0.188	0.076	0.013	1.207
HT * Right	-0.160	0.077	0.031	0.847

3.2 政策意见

在分析了宁杭高速长兴、宜兴和溧阳辖区内的风险驾驶行为对交通事故的影响因素后,仅明确事故的致因是不够的,需对症下药研究控制急左变道行为的政策,进而减少交通事故,如图1所示。实际导致急左变道的原因需要在多条高速公路现场进行调研、勘探才能确定,在此提出三条假设和对应整治的建议。

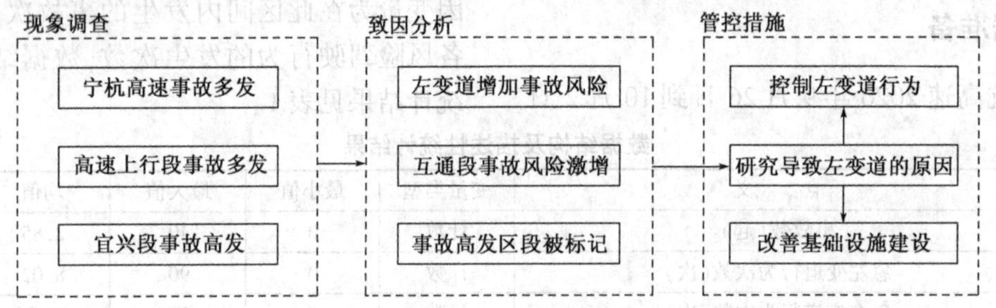

图1　调查分析与实践操作流程图

(1)区段交通流量较大,需提高区段道路通行能力

较高的交通量和较大的客货比会使交通状态复杂。在交通量较多时,小轿车会频繁左变道进入快车道超车,若此时前方有大型车辆遮挡视野,容易发生交通事故,在无法控制交通出行总量的情况下,需要拓宽瓶颈路段以提高道路交通能力;对大型车辆较多的路段,视道路线形条件还需要建设爬坡车道和紧急避险车道。

(2)交通设施设计问题,需排查不良标志标线设计

在分流匝道入口前的指示标志若设置不当,可能会造成欲前往匝道的车辆反复变道,最终在匝道入口处紧急变道,造成事故。

(3)入口交织存在风险,需建设现代智慧高速公路

在交织段合流与分流车辆行为复杂,容易发生交通事故,且此类事故难以通过标志标线引导解决,可以考虑引入交通事故预测系统,对路段内的交通流信息和事故风险进行实时预测,并在超过预警阈值时及时关闭匝道,降低交通流量,规避风险。

4　结语

本文使用真实驾驶行为数据研究了驾驶员行为和交通事故之间的关系,避免了DBQ问卷形式的主观性较大、信息失真的问题,利用GPS提取车辆轨迹获得的行为数据能真实地反应驾驶员行为。对每一区段的驾驶行为和事故数进行泊松回归,得到了风险驾驶行为和事故在空间分布上的重要结论:

(1)在驾驶行为对高速公路事故的影响因素中,急左变道行为是一个权重很大的因素,每增加一次急左变道行为,相应的事故发生率会比通常水平提高3.5%,而急加速、急减速的显著性水平和权重都不高。

(2)将事故地点按照一般长直道路和互通匝道进出道路进行分类,用统计分析方法验证了互通处为事故多发地点的经验认识,在互通处增加一次急左变道行为,会比在一般长直路段增加20.7%的事故概率。

本文研究了驾驶行为和事故在空间分布上的相关关系,具有创新性,但也存在一些限制。首先,缺少对时空异质性的处理,同时探索的结果也

不是精确的函数关系，下一步将从时间维度来研究发生事故前车辆的驾驶行为变化是否与事故的发生有因果关系。

参考文献

[1] YANG K, WANG X, YU R. A Bayesian dynamic updating approach for urban expressway real-time crash risk evaluation[J]. Transportation Research Part C: Emerging Technologies, 2018, 96: 192-207.

[2] ZHENG Q, XU C, LIU P, et al. Investigating the predictability of crashes on different freeway segments using the real-time crash risk models[J]. Accident Analysis & Prevention, 2021, 159: 106213.

[3] YU R, QUDDUS M, WANG X, et al. Impact of data aggregation approaches on the relationships between operating speed and traffic safety[J]. Accident Analysis & Prevention, 2018, 120: 304-310.

[4] SHI Q, ABDEL-ATY M. Big Data applications in real-time traffic operation and safety monitoring and improvement on urban expressways[J]. Transportation Research Part C: Emerging Technologies, 2015, 58: 380-394.

[5] MA Q, YANG H, WANG Z, et al. Modeling crash risk of horizontal curves using large-scale auto-extracted roadway geometry data[J]. Accident Analysis & Prevention, 2020, 144: 105669.

[6] M. A A, R. P. Calibrating a real-time traffic crash-prediction model using archived weather and ITS traffic data[J]. IEEE Transactions on Intelligent Transportation Systems, 2006, 7(2): 167-174.

[7] AYON B D, OFORI-AMOAH B, MENG L, et al. Modeling the effects of lake-effect snow related weather conditions on daily traffic crashes: A time series count data approach[J]. Accident Analysis & Prevention, 2020, 144: 105510.

[8] WEN H, XUE G. Injury severity analysis of familiar drivers and unfamiliar drivers in single-vehicle crashes on the mountainous highways[J]. Accident Analysis & Prevention, 2020, 144: 105667.

[9] EBOLI L, MAZZULLA G, PUNGILLO G. How to define the accident risk level of car drivers by combining objective and subjective measures of driving style[J]. Transportation Research Part F: Traffic Psychology and Behaviour, 2017, 49: 29-38.

[10] STAVRINOS D, MCMANUS B, BECK H. Demographic, driving experience, and psychosocial predictors of adolescent distracted driving beliefs[J]. Accident Analysis & Prevention, 2020, 144: 105678.

[11] CORI J M, DOWNEY L A, SLETTEN T L, et al. The impact of 7-hour and 11-hour rest breaks between shifts on heavy vehicle truck drivers' sleep, alertness and naturalistic driving performance[J]. Accident Analysis & Prevention, 2021, 159: 106224.

[12] FEI G, LI X, SUN Q, et al. Effectiveness of implementing the criminal administrative punishment law of drunk driving in China: An interrupted time series analysis, 2004-2017[J]. Accident Analysis & Prevention, 2020, 144: 105670.

[13] RISPLER C, LURIA G. Employee perseverance in a "no phone use while driving" organization-al road-safety intervention[J]. Accident Analysis & Prevention, 2020, 144: 105689.

Exploring the Relationships between Work Stress, Psychological Stress and Driver Stress-A Case Study of Chinese Drivers

Liu Yang [1] Zhangwei Chen [2] Wenyi Zhang [*2] Yuting Zhang [3] Ziyang Wang [1]
(1. School of transportation and logistics engineering, Wuhan University of Technology
2. School of transportation, Beijing Jiaotong University
3. College of Transportation Engineering, Chang'an University)

Abstract In order to study the impact mechanism of work stress on driver stress and the mediating effect of psychological stress, a questionnaire survey consisting of three subscales was conducted. Subscale 1 was about work stress; Subscale 2 was associated with psychological stress, while Subscale 3 focused on driver stress. A total of 596 valid questionnaires were collected. Descriptive statistical analysis, correlation analysis, and structural equation model were used to verify the hypothesis. The results showed that there was a significant positive correlation between driver's work stress, psychological stress and driver stress. The work stress and psychological stress of drivers were important sources of driver stress. Specifically, the organizational structure, co-worker relationships, intrinsic work factors of work stress and the sense of out of control and difficulty of psychological stress were the main sources of driver stress. Psychological stress played a significant and complete intermediary role in the process of work stress affecting driver stress, and its total effect on driver stress was greater than that of work stress.

Keywords Impact mechanism Structural equation model Work stress Psychological stress Driver stress

0 Introduction

Nowadays, with the constant refinement of the social division oflabor and the acceleration of the pace of people's life and work, the life stress, psychological stress and work stress become greater and greater. So for the drivers, when they encounter bad commuting and traffic congestion, drive stress will be induced easily, which will lead to driving errors, and hence aggravate the road risk. As shown by Yan et al. (2019), drivers' personal factors were one of the main causes of road traffic accidents, and about 90% of road traffic accidents were related to them.

Existing studies mainly focus on four factors in exploring the impact mechanism of driver stress, for example, drivers' personal characteristics, drivers' physical and mental status, road and traffic conditions, vehicle conditions and external environment.

Drivers' personal characteristics mainly consist of personality traits, gender, age, occupation and so on. According to Piotr et al. (2019), there was a significant positive correlation between personality traits and driver stress and work stress. Qu et al. (2016) confirmed the gender differences in driver stress with the help of Driver Stress Inventory (DSI) and revealed that female drivers scored higher in the dimension of dislike of driving and lower in the dimension of hazard monitoring. And Daghan et al. (2019) also noted that female drivers had significantly higher driver stress through driving simulation experiments. Besides, Age differences of driver stress were also corroborated. Zhao et al. (2020) suggested that the old drivers' driver stress was significantly lower than that of the younger drivers. And according to Ortoncelli et al. (2020), student drivers usually had greater driver stress.

Many researches were carried out to test drivers'

physical and mental status, including the psychological stress, work stress, self-control ability and so on. Shalini et al. (2021) proved that excessive psychological stress of drivers would affect driving and led to traffic accidents. In terms of work stress, Useche et al. (2017) showed that work stress was a relevant predictor of dangerous driving for bus rapid transport (BRT) drivers. In addition, the correlation between the driver's self-control ability and driver stress were also reported in Yeon et al. (2019).

The road and traffic conditions, which is composed of narrow sections, tunnel sections, congestion conditions, complex traffic conditions, etc. is another important factor leading to the explanation of the impact mechanism of drive stress. Schießl (2007) introduced that driving on narrow and curved roads would increase the driver's stress perception level. what's more, driver's stress level would increase significantly when driving at the tunnel entrance and in the tunnel section (Erika et al., 2015 and Marcel et al., 2014). The median of expressway would also affect the driver's stress. Ratthaphong et al. (2020) found that the setting of elevated curb median could significantly increase the driver's stress. In terms of traffic conditions, there was evidence for congestion being an indicator of increased crash risk (Stempfel et al., 2016). And Bitkina et al. (2019) reported that driving in cities was more stressful than driving on highways through real vehicle experimental research, and traffic congestion also significantly affected the driver's stress level. Madlen et al. (2019) verified through driving simulation experiments that driving on roads with complex traffic conditions, such as residential areas, auxiliary roads and speed limit areas would also increase the driver's stress.

Influences of the vehicle condition and external environment on drivers' stress level have also been examined. Magaña et al. (2020) testified in a driving simulation experiment that the environmental conditions in the vehicle, such as temperature, humidity and carbon dioxide level, would have a great impact on the driver's stress level. Serrano et al. (2019) found that the comfort of seats could be used to predict driver stress. By setting up autopilot vehicle without noise driving control group, Nicholas et al. (2012) suggested that the presence of noise inside the driver would significantly increase the stress level of the driver. Notably, John et al. (2006) revealed that the driving stress was closely related to the driver's driving environment. When driving in heavy rain and fog (low visibility), drivers had greater stress, and the worse the weather conditions, the greater the driver stress will be.

Apparently, most studies on the influence mechanism of driver stress examined the relationship between driver stress and driving behaviour, less has been done on the more basic issue of how driver stress itself forms (i. e. the relationship between driver stress and basic stress such as work stress and psychological stress). To fill the gap, this study explores the relationship between driver stress and more basic psychological stress and work stress and constructs the mechanism model among the three. Thus, the influence mechanism of work stress and psychological stress on driver stress is revealed, which can help prevent traffic accidents and improve the level of road traffic safety by reducing the source of driver stress.

1 Method

1.1 Participants and procedure

Based on the principle of simple random sampling, a combination of online and offline method is adopted to investigate drivers in China. Online questionnaires are mainly distributed on WeChat, QQ and other online platforms, while offline questionnaires are mainly distributed and collected at parking lots, communities, railway stations and business districts. The survey was conducted anonymously. A total of 1635 questionnaires were collected (Participants would be paid about 2 RMB). In order to ensure the quality of the answers, they were eliminated according to strict screening principles, such as time length control, reverse scoring control and logical relationship control. A total of 596 valid questionnaires were collected, with an effective rate of 36.5%. The questionnaire was processed by SPSS24.0 and AMOS22.0.

1.2 Instrument

There are 12 items in the Subscale 1, which referred to Cooper (1988). The objective of Subscale 1 is to investigate drivers' work stress, including the four dimensions of intrinsic work factors, career and achievement, organizational structure and co-worker relationships. Subscale 2 consists of 14 items with reference to Cohen (1983) and Yang (2003). Subscale 2 mainly measures the three dimensions of psychological stress received by the subjects through their perceptual feelings, containing tension, out of control and difficulty. Subscale 3 was derived from Matthews et al. (1999), the Institute of Psychology of the Chinese Academy of Sciences (2015), Daghan (2019) and the suggestions of front-line senior drivers with more than 10 years' driving age. And Subscale 3 comprises 24 items, with the four dimensions of thrill seeking, driving tension, hazard monitoring and dislike of driving. A five-point Likert scale (1 = Never, 5 = Always) was adopted to report the frequency of the depicted situations of the three subscales.

In addition to these three subscales, the study also collected participants' demographic information, including gender, age, driving age, professional driver or not, education level, profession, traffic violations or not during the last 3 years and traffic accidents or not during the last 3 years.

1.3 Research hypothesis

Peter et al. (2011) pointed out that the driver stress was related to the stress in other fields, including work and family life. Useche et al. (2017) noted that work stress was a relevant predictor of dangerous driving for bus rapid transport (BRT) drivers. Li et al. (2011) showed that work, family, society and other factors would make drivers have high stress in the process of driving. In addition, stress would affect the driver's overall health (Mohammad et al., 2018). Copsey et al. (2010) found that work stress would affect the driver's health level, which would lead to high psychological workload (Frasson et al., 2014), and also stimulated the driver's negative emotions (Henrik et al., 2015). Based on the research status and combined with the actual situation of drivers, the research assumptions are shown in Tab. 1.

Research Hypotheses Tab. 1

Number	Hypothetical Content	Number	Hypothetical Content
H1	The work stress of drivers is positively correlated with their driver stress	H3	The work stress of drivers is positively correlated with their psychological stress
H1a	Intrinsic work factors is positively correlated with driver stress	H3a	Intrinsic work factors is positively correlated with psychological stress
H1b	Career and achievement is positively correlated with driver stress	H3b	Career and achievement is positively correlated with psychological stress
H1c	Co-worker relationships is positively correlated with driver stress	H3c	Co-worker relationships is positively correlated with psychological stress
H1d	Organizational structure is positively correlated with driver stress	H3d	Organizational structure is positively correlated with psychological stress
H2	The psychological stress of drivers is positively correlated with their driver stress	H4	Work stress can directly affect driver stress
H2a	The sense of tension is positively correlated with driver stress	H5	Psychological stress can directly affect driver stress
H2b	The sense of out of control is positively correlated with driver stress	H6	Work stress can affect driver stress through psychological stress
H2c	The sense of difficulty is positively correlated with driver stress	—	—

2 Results

2.1 Demographic and descriptive variables

Among the 596 valid receipts, the ages of the participants (396 males, 200 females) ranged from 19 to 58 years (M = 30.85, SD = 8.84). Most participants were 26-30 years old (32.38%). The participants who were younger than 26 and older than 30 accounted for 29.36% and 38.26% of the total sample, respectively. The participants' average driving age was 5.56 years (SD = 5.18). And 43.29% participants were professional drivers. Most participants (40.27%) reported that their education level was bachelor degree, the next two were junior college degree (28.86%) and high school education (20.81%). Besides, the most common profession was professional technicians (28.36%), such as teachers, doctors, writers and so on. In addition, 55.20% of the participants indicated that they had no traffic violations over the last three years, while 73.66% reported they had no traffic accidents over that same period.

2.2 Questionnaire test

2.2.1 Normality test

Mardia (1983) proposed that the skewness and kurtosis of variables could reflect whether the questionnaire variables conform to the normal distribution. When the absolute values of both are less than 2, it can be considered that the normality of the questionnaire variables passes the test and obeys the normal distribution. The kurtosis and skewness values of 50 items in 596 answers were calculated by SPSS24.0, and the absolute values were less than 2, indicating that the whole obeyed the normal distribution.

2.2.2 Reliability and validity test

Cronbach's Alpha was used to measure the internal consistency of the questionnaire. It is found that the Cronbach's Alpha values of variables in each dimension and overall reliability were greater than 0.7. As shown in Tab. 2, the internal consistency and stability of the evaluation scale were good, and the questionnaire data were acceptable.

Reliability Values of Variables in Each Dimension Tab. 2

Variable Dimension	Cronbach's Alpha	Variable Dimension	Cronbach's Alpha
Intrinsic Work Factors	0.800	Sense of Difficulty	0.904
Career and Achievement	0.868	Psychological Stress	0.703
Co-worker Relationships	0.912	Thrill Seeking	0.880
Organizational Structure	0.903	Driving Tension	0.911
Work Stress	0.923	Hazard Monitoring	0.827
Sense of Tension	0.896	Dislike of Driving	0.713
Sense of Out of Control	0.871	Driver Stress	0.931

Factor analysis was used to test the validity of the questionnaire. The Kaiser-Meyer-Olkin (KMO) value of work stress scale was 0.914, and Bartlett spherical test was significant, which meant the scale was suitable for factor analysis. Four common factors with eigenvalues greater than 1 were extracted, and the cumulative variance contribution rate was 80.151%, which was more than 50%. The factor load values under the common factor were greater than 0.4, which met the requirements. It showed that the overall structure validity of the scale was good. Similarly, the validity of psychological stress scale and driver stress scale was also good. The results are shown in Tab. 3.

Validity Index Values of the Scale Tab. 3

Variable	KMO Value	Sig.	Common Factor Number	Cumulative Variance Contribution Rate	Factor Load Values
Work Stress	0.914	0.000	4	80.151%	>0.4
Psychological Stress	0.917	0.000	3	64.926%	>0.4
Driver Stress	0.953	0.000	4	64.092%	>0.4

2.3 Correlation analysis

Taking the Person correlation coefficient as the judgment standard, the person correlation coefficient between working stress and driver stress was 0.637, indicating that there was a significant positive correlation between work stress and driver stress at the level of 0.01, and the hypothesis H1 was proved. Similarly, it could be concluded that psychological stress and driver stress, work stress and psychological stress were significantly positively correlated at the level of 0.01. Hypothesis H2 and hypothesis H3 were proved. The results are shown in Tab. 4.

Correlation Analysis Matrix of Work Stress, Psychological Stress and Driver Stress Tab. 4

		Work Stress	Psychological Stress	Driver Stress
Work Stress	PearsonCorrelation	1	0.475 * *	0.637 * *
	Sig. (2-tailed)		0.000	0.000
Psychological Stress	Pearson Correlation	0.475 * *	1	0.310 * *
	Sig. (2-tailed)	0.000		0.000
Driver Stress	Pearson Correlation	0.637 * *	0.310 * *	1
	Sig. (2-tailed)	0.000	0.000	

* * Correlation is significant at the 0.01 level (2-tailed).

Additionally, the Person correlation coefficients of each dimension of working stress and driver stress were 0.510, 0.460, 0.559 and 0.565 respectively, and the significance was 0.000, indicating that each dimension of working stress showed a significant positive correlation with driver stress. It is assumed that hypothesis H1a, H1b, H1c and H1d were proved. Similarly, it could be seen that all dimensions of work stress were significantly positively correlated with psychological stress at the level of 0.01. Assuming that hypothesis H3a, H3b, H3c and h3d were proved, the results are shown in Tab. 5. According to Tab. 6, each dimension of psychological stress showed a significant positive correlation with driver stress. It is assumed that hypothesis H2a, H2b and H2c were proved.

Correlation Analysis Matrix of Each Dimension of Work Stress, Driver Stress and Psychological Stress Tab. 5

		Intrinsic Work Factors	Career and Achievement	Co-worker Relationships	Organization and Management Stress
Driver Stress	PearsonCorrelation	0.510 * *	0.460 * *	0.559 * *	0.565 * *
	Sig. (2-tailed)	0.000	0.000	0.000	0.000
Psychological Stress	PearsonCorrelation	0.325 * *	0.358 * *	0.415 * *	0.453 * *
	Sig. (2-tailed)	0.000	0.000	0.000	0.000

* * Correlation is significant at the 0.01 level (2-tailed).

Correlation Analysis Matrix between Psychological Stress and Driver Stress Tab. 6

		The Sense of Tension	The Sense of Out of Control	The Sense of Difficulty
Driver Stress	PearsonCorrelation	0.713 * *	0.914 * *	0.494 * *
	Sig. (2-tailed)	0.000	0.000	0.000

* * Correlation is significant at the 0.01 level (2-tailed).

2.4 Structural equation model analysis

Structural equation model was used to further explore the action path and effectiveness of work stress and psychological stress on driver stress. And three measurement models were constructed as follows: ①Taking work stress as potential variable, taking intrinsic work factors, career and achievement, co-worker relationships and organizational structure as observation variables. ② Taking psychological stress as potential variable, and the sense of tension, out of control and difficulty were the observation variables of psychological stress. ③Taking driver stress as potential variable, and thrill seeking, driving tension, hazard monitoring and dislike of driving were the observed variables. At the same time, a structural model was constructed: taking work stress and psychological stress as external derivative potential variables and driver stress as internal derivative potential variables to obtain the initial model.

AMOS 22.0 was used for model fitting, and the maximum likelihood method was used for estimation to obtain the standardized fitting results of the initial model. Since the fitness index of the initial model did not meet the standard, it is necessary to modify the initial model.

Results ofInitial Model Fitness Test. Tab. 7

Fitness Index	CMIN/DF	GFI	AGFI	CFI	IFI	RMSEA
Index Value	21.104	0.765	0.621	0.822	0.823	0.197
Adaptation Standard	<5	>0.9	>0.9	>0.9	>0.9	<0.08

Combined with the correction index and critical ratio output by AMOS22.0, relaxed the measurement parameters to correct the model, that is, added the covariance relationship between error variables, and change the relevant error term into free parameters. The correction model diagram was shown as Fig. 1. Firstly, the basic adaptation index was tested. The factor load between the potential variables and their observation variables was between 0.42 ~ 0.98, indicating that the 11 observation variables in this model could better explain their corresponding potential variables. All the error variations of the model reached a significant level (the critical ratio was greater than 1.96), indicating that the basic adaptation indexes of the modified model were well adapted. Continue to test the overall fitness index, as shown in Tab. 8. The overall fitness index of the modified model had been met, indicating that the modified model was more reasonable.

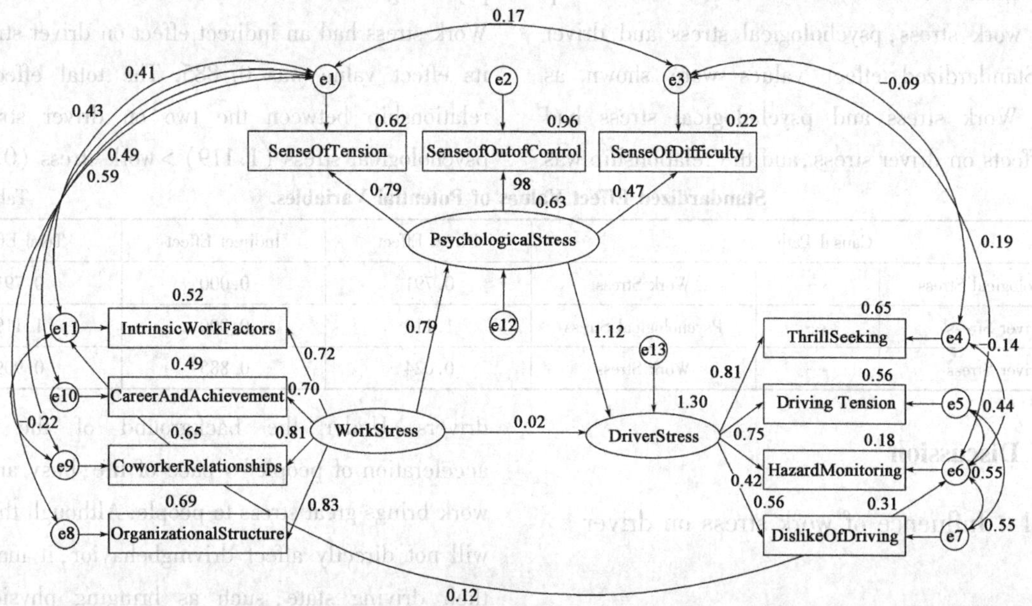

Fig. 1 Modified Model of Work Stress-Psychological Stress-Driver Stress Coupling Mechanism (Standardized)

Test Results of Modified Model Fitness Tab. 8

Fitness Index	CMIN/DF	GFI	AGFI	CFI	IFI	RMSEA
Index Value	3.853	0.969	0.926	0.985	0.985	0.069
Adaptation Standard	<5	>0.9	>0.9	>0.9	>0.9	<0.08

The path analysis was carried out for the modified model. The path coefficients and significance test results between potential variables were shown in Tab. 9. The path critical ratio of work stress to psychological stress C. R. = 18.662 > 1.96, $P < 0.001$, indicating that work stress could directly act on psychological stress, and its standardized path coefficient was 0.791, indicating that when other variables were constant, psychological stress would increase by 0.791 for every 1 unit increase in work stress. Similarly, it can be seen that psychological stress could directly act on driver stress, and when other variables were constant, driver stress would increase by 1.119 units for every increase of psychological stress, assuming that hypothesis H5 was proved. The critical path ratio of working stress to driver stress C. R. = 1.317 < 1.96, $P = 0.188 > 0.05$, indicating that working stress could not directly act on driver stress, and hypothesis H4 was not proved.

Because the paths of work stress→ psychological stress and psychological stress → driver stress were significant, it can be seen from the judgment standard of step-by-step method that psychological stress played an intermediary role in the path of work stress → driver stress. And the path from work stress to driver stress was not significant, it can be considered that psychological stress had a significant mediating effect between work stress and driver stress, and it was a complete mediating effect. It is assumed that hypothesis H6 was proved.

Path Coefficient and Significance Test among Variables Tab. 9

Causal Path			Unstandardized Coefficients	Standardized Coefficients	Std. Error of the Estimate	C. R.	P	Sig.
Psychological Stress	←	Work Stress	1.223	0.791	0.066	18.662	* * *	Remarkable
Driver Stress	←	Psychological Stress	1.205	1.119	0.049	24.525	* * *	Remarkable
Driver Stress	←	Work Stress	0.041	0.024	0.031	1.317	0.188	Unremarkable

* * * indicates $P < 0.001$, ← indicates causality.

Continue to analyse the effect relationship between work stress, psychological stress and driver stress. Standardized effect values were shown as Tab. 10. Work stress and psychological stress had direct effects on driver stress, and the relationship was psychological stress (1.119) > work stress (0.024). Work stress had an indirect effect on driver stress, and its effect value was 0.885. The total effect value relationship between the two on driver stress was psychological stress (1.119) > work stress (0.909).

Standardized Effect Values of Potential Variables. Tab. 10

Causal Path			Direct Effect	Indirect Effect	Total Effect
Psychological Stress	←	Work Stress	0.791	0.000	0.791
Driver Stress	←	Psychological Stress	1.119	0.000	1.119
Driver Stress	←	Work Stress	0.024	0.885	0.909

3 Discussion

3.1 Influence of work stress on driver stress

Work stress is the most common stress faced by drivers. Under the background of the gradual acceleration of people's pace of life, busy and tense work brings great stress to people. Although this stress will not directly affect drivingbehavior, it may affect their driving state, such as bringing physical and mental fatigue and reducing the driver's judgment ability,so as to make them have stress during driving. This situation is consistent with the result of this study that " work stress is positively correlated with driver stress" ,which verifies the validity of hypothesis H1a.

The positive correlation between co-worker relationships and driver stress shows that there is a certain stress for drivers to deal with interpersonal relationship well. If you are unhappy with your colleagues before driving, you will inevitably be distracted during driving. But driving requires attention, and the driver needs to monitor the road conditions at all times, which will lead to conflict and virtually lead to driver stress (verify that hypothesis H1c is proved).

There is also a positive correlation between organizational structure and driver stress, indicating that organizational structure is also one of the sources of driver stress. If there are problems in the organizational structure of the work unit, employees can't get a good experience at work, and this poor sense of experience will bring some discomfort to their psychology and keep it, When they encounter bad traffic conditions such as congestion during driving, it may lead to driver stress, which indirectly leads to the decline of driving experience. Therefore, organizational structure will also increase drivers' driver stress, which is consistent with the research result that " there is a positive correlation between organizational structure and driver stress". Hence, the validity of hypothesis H1d is proved.

In addition, according to the structural equation model analysis in section 3.4, the working stress→ driver stress path is not significant, indicating that the working stress can not directly act on the driver stress (the validation hypothesis H4 is not valid). Alonso et al. (2020) suggested that work stress affected driving decision-making, Useche et al. (2018) proposed that work stress affected mental health, and Wang et al. (2019) noted that work stress affected driving behavior. These researches show that work stress is likely to indirectly cause driver stress by affecting driving decision-making, psychology and behavior.

3.2 Influence of psychological stress on driver stress

According to the analysis in section 4.1, work stress does not directly affect driver stress, but through a variety of intermediaries. The results of this study indicate that psychological stress is one of the mediators. Useche et al. (2018) reported that the driver's work stress was related to his psychological factors. Psychological stress will not occur for no reason, but there must be external incentives, and the stress generated by work is the incentive. The stress brought by work itself, the stress brought by dealing with interpersonal relationships and the stress brought by the organization and management of the work unit will intervene in the drivers' psychology, bring them the feeling of out of control and difficulty, and form a psychological sense of out of control and difficulty (verify the establishment of hypothesis H3 and hypothesis H3a ~ H3d). This psychological sense of out of control and difficulty will directly become a source of stress during his driving, It promotes the increase of driver stress, which supports the judgment of Li et al. (2010) that " the increase of drivers' psychological load will bring driver stress" , which is also consistent with the result of the study that " psychological stress can directly act on driver stress, and psychological stress has a significant intermediary effect between work stress and driver stress".

3.3 Limitations

Some limitations encountered by the current study should be noted. Firstly, a sample size of 596 were still slightly insufficient, which may affect the validity of the conclusions. Besides, the sample was more young novice drivers and less senior drivers, so the applicability of conclusions to non-novice drivers needs to be discussed. In future research, more participants should be invited to expand present study, especially the sample proportion of non-novice drivers.

3.4 Implications

Combined with the actual situation of the driver group, the study obtained some strategies to alleviate the driver stress. In terms of interpersonal relationship, the working environment atmosphere and interpersonal relationship will directly affect people's work stress, and this stress will transfer to the driver's driver stress along with the driving process. For this, drivers need to deal with their interpersonal relationship and maintain a good working atmosphere. And for organization management, organizational structure in work stress is one of the important sources of driver stress. Therefore, enterprises should refine employee management, clarify employee job responsibilities and work scope, and give employees a good working environment. Moreover, psychological stress not only directly affects the driver's driver stress, but also affects the driver as an intermediary of work stress, so it is more and more necessary to pay attention to the driver's mental health. In this regard, drivers should actively participate in cultural and sports activities, reduce the bad state caused by stress and maintain mental health. All of these strategies can help traffic management departments or driver education and training institutions provide more targeted education and training, thus prevent traffic accidents from the source.

4 Conclusions

This study conducted a questionnaire survey to deeply explore the relationship between work stress, psychological stress and driver stress. It analysed the sources of driver stress from two aspects of work and psychology, and defined the main sources of driver stress. The study found that the psychological stress of drivers would increase with the increase of work stress, and the driver stress would increase significantly with the increase of work stress and psychological stress. The driver's work stress and psychological stress were the important sources of driver stress, especially the organizational structure, co-worker relationships, intrinsic work factors of work stress and the sense of out of control and difficulty of psychological stress. Additionally, driver's work stress could not directly affect driver stress, but would indirectly affect driver stress through psychological stress, and the impact of psychological stress on driver stress was higher than work stress. These findings can help to realize the driver's self-decompression, and can provide a theoretical basis for relevant departments to formulate strategies.

5 Acknowledgements

This work was supported by the National Natural Science Foundation of China (Nos. 72001163 and Nos. 71901036).

References

[1] Alonso, F., Esteban, C., Gonzalez, M. A., et al. Job stress and emotional exhaustion at work in Spanish workers: Does unhealthy work affect the decision to drive? [J]. PLOS ONE, 2020, 15(1), 227-328.

[2] Bitkina, O. V., Kim J., Park J., et al. Identifying Traffic Context Using Driving Stress: A Longitudinal Preliminary Case Study. Sensors (Basel, Switzerland), 2019, 19(9).

[3] Copsey, L., Drupsteen, J., Kampen, L., et al. A review of accidents and injuries to road transport drivers. European Agency for Safety and Health at Work.

[4] Daghan, D., Seta, B., Tankut, A.. Evaluation of driver stress level with survey, galvanic skin response sensor data, and force-sensing resistor data. Advances in Mechanical Engineering, 2019, 11(12).

[5] Erika, E. M., Linda N. B.. Driver Behavior in Road Tunnels: Association with Driver Stress and Performance [J]. Transportation Research Record, 2015, 2518(1).

[6] Frasson, C., Brosseau, P. O., Tran, THD. Virtual environment for monitoring emotional behaviour in driving [J]. In Intelligent Tutoring Systems. Springer, 2014, 8474: 75-83.

[7] Henrik, W., Emma, N., Per L., et al. Physiological responses related to moderate mental load during car driving in field conditions [J]. Biological Psychology, 2015, 108: 115-125.

[8] John, D. H., Boyle, L. N.. Driver stress as influenced by driving maneuvers and roadway conditions[J]. Transportation Research Part F: Psychology and Behaviour, 2006, 10(3): 177-186.

[9] Li, Y. Z., Jia, J., Xu, Y., et al. Reliability and validity of Chinese version of driver stress scale [J]. Chinese Journal of behavioral medicine and brain science, 2010, 19(5): 472-474.

[10] Li, Y. Z., Jia, J., Yin, L., et al. The characters of non-professional drivers' stress[J]. Chinese Journal of behavioral medicine and brain science, 2011(1): 62-64.

[11] Madlen, R., Mark, V.. Effect of complex traffic situations on route choice behaviour and driver stress in residential areas [J]. Transportation Research Part F: Psychology and Behaviour, 2019, 60.

[12] Magaña, V. C., Scherz, W. D., et al. The Effects of the Driver's Mental State and Passenger Compartment Conditions on Driving Performance and Driving Stress. Sensors (Basel, Switzerland), 20(18).

[13] Marcel, M., Andreas, R.. Evaluation of Driver Stress while Transiting Road Tunnels. Automotive User Interfaces and Interactive Vehicular Applications, 2014.

[14] Mardia, K. V., Foster, K. Omnibus tests of multinormality based on skewness and kurtosis [J]. Communication in Statistics-Theory and Methods, 1983, 12(2): 207-221.

[15] Mohammad, N. R., Bahareh, N., Andry, R., et al. A Critical Review of Proactive Detection of Driver Stress Levels Based on Multimodal Measurements [J]. ACM Computing Surveys (CSUR), 2018, 51(5).

[16] Nicholas, D. C., Benjamin, K. B.. The impact of artificial vehicle sounds for pedestrians on driver stress[J]. Ergonomics, 2012, 55(12).

[17] Ortoncelli, A. R., Silva, L., et al. Summarizing Driving Behavior to Support Driver Stress Analysis. 15th IEEE International Conference on Automatic Face and Gesture Recognition, 2020.

[18] Peter, R., Gerald, M., Barry, W., et al. The relative impact of work-related stress, life stress and driving environment stress on driving outcomes [J]. Accident Analysis and Prevention, 2011, 43(4).

[19] Piotr, M., Paulina, D., Lucia, M., et al. Level of occupational stress, personality and traffic incidents: Comparative study of public and freight transport drivers [J]. Transportation Research Procedia, 2019, 40.

[20] Ratthaphong, M., Kunnawee, K, Piyapong, J. Investigating the influence of highway median design on driver stress [J]. Transportation Research Interdisciplinary Perspectives, 2020, 4.

[21] Schießl, C. Stress and strain while driving. Proc[J]. European Conf. Transport Research Institutes, 2007: 1-11.

[22] Serrano, F., María, J., Boada, G. J., Robert, S. L., et. al. Predictive power of selected factors on driver stress at work [J]. International journal of occupational safety and ergonomics: JOSE, 2019.

[23] Shalini, B., Rakshana, M., et al. Driver's Stress Analysis and Automated Emergency Call Using IOT and Data Analytics [J]. Lecture Notes in Electrical Engineering, 2021, 709: 403-412.

[24] Stempfel, J., Guler, S. I., Menendez, M., Brucks, W. M.. Effects of urban congestion on safety of networks [J]. Journal of Transportation Safety & Security, 2016, 8(3): 214-229.

[25] Useche, S. A., Cendales, B., Montoro, L., et al. Work stress and health problems of professional drivers: a hazardous formula for their safety outcomes [J]. PeerJ, 2018, 6: 49-62.

[26] Useche, S. A., Ortiz, V. G., Cendales, B. E. Stress-related psychosocial factors at work, fatigue, and risky driving behavior in bus rapid transport (BRT) drivers [J]. Accident

Analysis and Prevention,2017,104:106-114.

[27] Wang, Y., Qin, H., You, Z., et al. The influence of driver's psychological factors on their risky driving behavior[J]. Automobile and safety,2019(3):83-88.

[28] Weina, Q., Qian, Z., Wenguo, Z., et al. Validation of the Driver Stress Inventory in China: Relationship with dangerous driving behaviors [J]. Accident Analysis and Prevention,2016,87.

[29] Yanning,Z.,Toshiyuki,Y.,Ryo,K.. Study of older male drivers' driving stress compared with that of young male drivers[J]. Journal of Traffic and Transportation Engineering (English Edition),2020,7(04):467-481.

[30] Yan,X.,Wu,B.,He,Y.,et al. Research on traffic safety concept and implementation strategy of "zero death vision" in China[J]. Traffic information and safety,2019,37(1):1-6.

[31] Yeon, H. D., Dong, K. H.. Research on Relationship between Drivers' Self-control, Driving Behavior and Driving Stress [J]. Journal of Korea Entertainment Industry Association,2019,13:229-238.

智能技术对山区商用车的交通安全影响研究

张佳涛*　韩天园　刘传攀

(长安大学汽车学院)

摘　要　我国山区公路商用车事故发生后损伤严重及重特大交通事故率高,智能技术的应用有助于提高山区公路商用车运行安全。运用人-车-路协同理论系统分析了山区公路特性、商用车固有属性和商用车驾驶员属性及各因素的耦合对道路交通事故的诱发机理,并研究智能车辆、智慧公路及智能交通对驾驶员-商用车-山区公路行车安全系统稳定性和鲁棒性的作用路径。研究表明,智能车辆、智慧公路及智能交通技术在感知、判断、决策和操作的驾驶过程中提高了危险条件和随机事件影响的系统内部协调性,促进驾驶员-商用车-山区公路协调运行安全,为山区公路商用车加强运行安全提供了新的解决方案。

关键词　山区公路　商用车　智能技术　运行安全

0　引言

急弯、长大下坡、道路线形不良组合及极端路侧环境是我国山区公路事故频发的客观因素之一,一方面车辆制动和操稳固有属性无法完美适配山区公路复杂的几何特征和道路环境,另一方面弯陡坡和临崖临水路段影响驾驶员视觉、心理和行为特性[1]。商用车普遍质量大、质心高,在转弯车速过高和频繁制动时易发生车辆横向失稳和制动热衰退[2]。据统计,我国山区公路上发生的约20%的重大交通事故与车辆状况有关[3]。93%以上的交通事故与驾驶员因素有关[4],道路、环境与设施的协调性限制下的山区公路和商用车固有属性、商用车运输特性下的驾驶员因素的耦合增大了山区公路商用车行车安全隐患,提高驾驶员-商用车-山区公路联合运行协调性对运行安全意义重大。

山区公路商用车行车事故生成路径多元,容易引发碰撞、翻车、坠车等连锁反应而导致事故后更高的损伤概率和严重程度[5],事故损伤严重及重特大交通事故率高是我国山区公路商用车交通安全形势的两个显著特征[6]。Li 对我国特大交通事故数据分析发现 49.64% 的单车事故的案例发生于云南、贵州、广西、四川、西藏和和重庆六个山区地域,77.5% 的多车事故是客车-货车碰撞和客

1. 基金项目:陕西省重点研发计划项目(2020ZDLGY16－08);教育部人文社会科学青年基金项目(18YJCZH110);中央高校基本科研业务费专项资金项目(300102220111,300102229668);省级大学生创新创业训练计划项目(S201910710064)。

车-客车碰撞[7]。袁泉研究表明车辆驶离道路是特大交通事故发生的第一事件,恶劣的地理环境和驾驶员因素是此类事故直接因素,其中坠车事故的比例与死亡率更高[8]。

目前,智能车辆、智慧公路和智能交通技术的快速发展为山区商用车行车主动安全提供了借鉴。基于传感器的道路环境感知、基于智能网联的信息交互以及基于机器学习的目标检测、定位和分类技术实现了智能车辆对道路环境和交通状况信息的感知和预知[9],通过车道线检测、交通标志识别、目标车辆跟踪等技术和车辆主动安全控制技术融合开发的高级辅助驾驶系统有效降低了事故发生率,如车道偏离警告(LDW)和自动紧急制动(AEB)等可防止驾驶员分心导致的交通事故[10]。具备感知、传输、管控决策能力的智慧公路,基于面向主动安全的道路控制技术智慧可以通过车路情境感知、危险警示与安全提醒、事故通知、道路盲区监测预警等有效预警通知实现与驾驶员的信息交流[11],通过道路设施与智能车辆通信掌控交通流和周围车辆运行状态,避免因路况信息缺乏及雾天或弯道行驶时驾驶视距不良导致的交通事故[12]。智能交通系统融汇人-车-路与交通管理数据信息,基于全局的交通分析研判技术和智能化交通控制设施设计、优化时间全域与空间全域的道路安全行车,避免因人-车-路与管理协调不良而增大交通事故隐患。本文聚焦于山区公路商用车运行交通安全,针对山区道路商用车安全运行隐患,论述智能技术在商用车驾驶感知、决策和控制执行的应用前景。

1 驾驶员-商用车-山区公路协调运行的安全隐患

由于道路交通事故是人、车、路和环境构成的交通系统协调不良的结果,因此道路交通安全的研究必须从交通系统各要素及其之间的安全性与协调性出发。

1.1 山区公路和道路环境的事故诱因

工程造价、地质地形、技术标准和社会效益等多重因素约束着山区低等级公路路线,使得我国山区公路蜿蜒曲折、地势险恶,环境复杂多变。如图1所示,山区公路各因素协调性差、公路诱导能力不良、容错能力差,增大了山区道路车辆交通事故发生的几率。

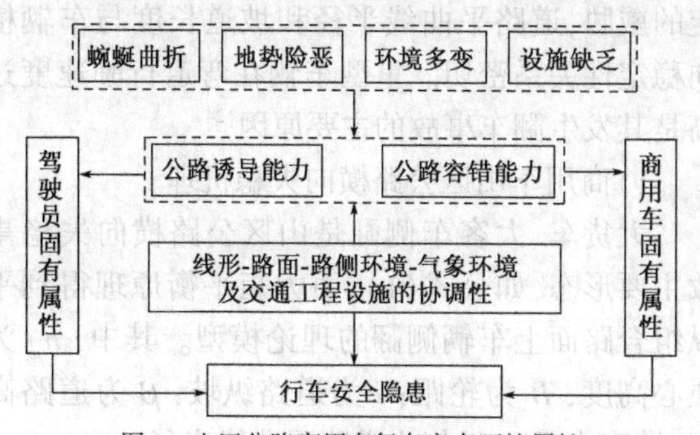

图1 山区公路商用车行车安全环境属性

1)山区公路复杂的几何特征

急弯与连续急弯、陡坡与连续下坡及弯坡危险组合是山区公路交通车辆追尾、碰撞和翻车的重要诱因[13]。商用车在陡坡与连续下坡及不同竖曲线组合路段由于频繁或持续制动造成制动器温度过高导致的制动热衰退而发生车辆失控的风险较高[14]。Yue L 基于车-路协同分析了平曲线半径过小对车辆侧向稳定性的不利影响[15]。王华荣研究发现山区公路纵坡长度车辆追尾事故有很强的正相关[16]。Shuming 研究了道路线形对安全行车速度和驾驶视距的不利影响。

2)山区公路极端的路侧特征

商用车(尤其客车)在山区公路危险边坡倾翻和临崖临水路段坠车,极易造成特重大交通事故[18]。据统计显示,约60%的特重大交通事故为坠车形态。西藏拉萨8·9重大道路交通事故中大客车转弯下坡路段碰撞对向来车而坠崖,丹巴7·18重大道路交通事故中大客车因雨天路面湿滑及驾驶员操作错误而坠河,充分说明道路线形、路面条件等因素综合作用会触发危险路侧交通事故[19]。

3)山区公路多变的天气环境

我国南方山林多雨雾,北方冬天及高原地区多降雪。由于雨、雪、雾天气驾驶视距不足和制动距离变大,增大了山区公路商用车驾驶难度和交通事故发生概率[20]。Aty 研究表明正面碰撞和追尾碰撞是雾天等视线不良环境的主要事故形式[21]。Yu 研究表明陡坡等曲线段道路交通事故与环境能见度和降雨量有很大的相关性[22]。胡立伟研究了雨、雪、雾和风等气象环境与其他公路交通风险因素耦合对交通安全的不利影响[23]。

1.2 商用车山区公路运行的横纵向失稳机理

商用车安全行车受到横向不稳定和纵向不稳

定的威胁，道路平曲线半径和坡道长度与车辆横向稳定性关系密切。重型车辆在弯道行驶速度过高是其发生翻车事故的主要原因[24]。

1）商用车山区公路横向失稳机理

大货车、大客车侧翻是山区公路横向失稳事故主要形态，如公式(1)，由力矩平衡原理得到平纵组合路面上车辆侧翻的理论模型。其中，h_g 为质心高度；B 为轮距；i 为道路纵坡；β 为道路高程；转弯半径 R 近似为道路平曲线半径。

$$V_{\max} < \sqrt{127R\left(\frac{B/h_g+\beta}{1-\frac{B}{h_g}\cdot\beta}\right)\cos i} \quad (1)$$

由上式可知，质心高度 h_g 和纵坡 β 越大、平曲线半径 R 越小，车辆越倾向于横向失稳。

此外，车辆在弯坡组合路段行驶时车辆转向性能因载荷分配变化而变化，如图2所示，下坡时出现过多不足转向倾向，上坡时出现过度转向倾向。

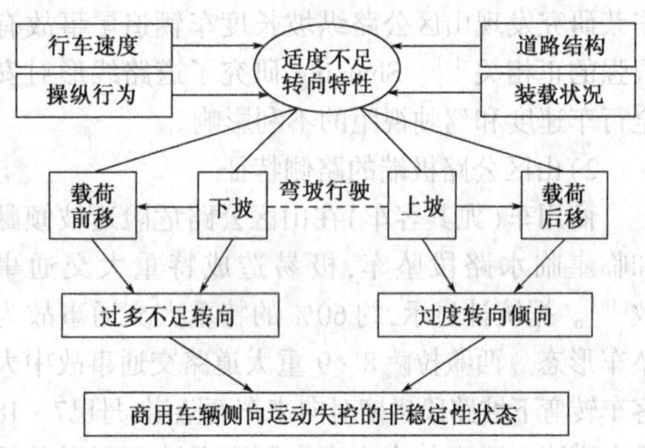

图2　商用车辆侧向非稳定性

2）商用车山区公路纵向制动失稳机理

一般重型商用车辆制动器以铸铁作制动鼓，石棉摩擦材料作摩擦片。如图3所示，由于车辆连续制动或高速制动，导致摩擦片温度急剧上升，此时有机物便会分解产生一些气相或液相化学物质并在两接触面间形成润滑作用的薄膜，降低制动器摩擦因数而影响制动效能。

由能量守恒定理可知，汽车制动时动能和势能转化为热能，因此制动器因摩擦产生的热量 Q 为：

$$Q = (1-s)\cdot\left(\frac{1}{2}mv_0^2 - \frac{1}{2}mv_t^2 + mg(\pm i - f)S\right) \quad (2)$$

式中：m ——商用车质量；

s ——滑移率；

v_0、v_t ——制动初始与 t 时刻的速度；

f ——道路滚动阻力系数；

S ——制动距离；

i ——坡度，下坡取正。

由上式分析可知，车辆超载加剧了山区公路陡坡与连续下坡路段行驶时车辆制动器热衰退而发生纵向失稳现象。

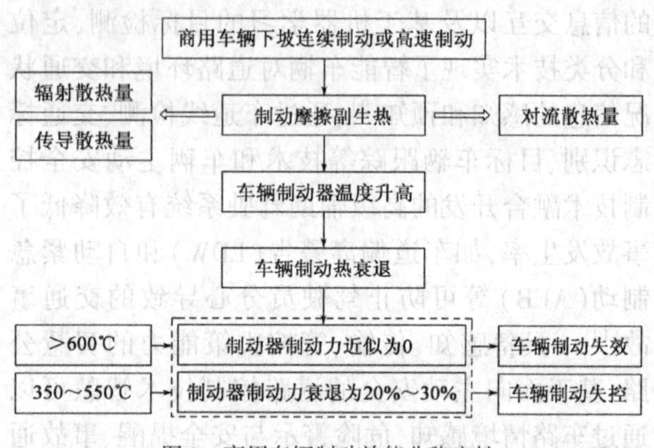

图3　商用车辆制动效能非稳定性

1.3　商用车驾驶员心理与行为的不稳定性

驾驶员的信息需求属性、驾驶行为属性、性格和素质多样式属性决定了驾驶员是道路交通系统中最活跃、最核心且最不稳定的要素这一客观事件，如图4所示。驾驶员与车辆和道路直接进行全方位实时地动态信息交流，通过感知、判断与决策等心理活动操作车辆和控制车速。山区公路道路环境情况复杂，交通状况信息密度大，驾驶员可能处于信息过载状况，存在有选择性地放弃一些自认为(潜意识)无关的目标信息，如果经验不足则可能发生信息错误，导致判断错误。

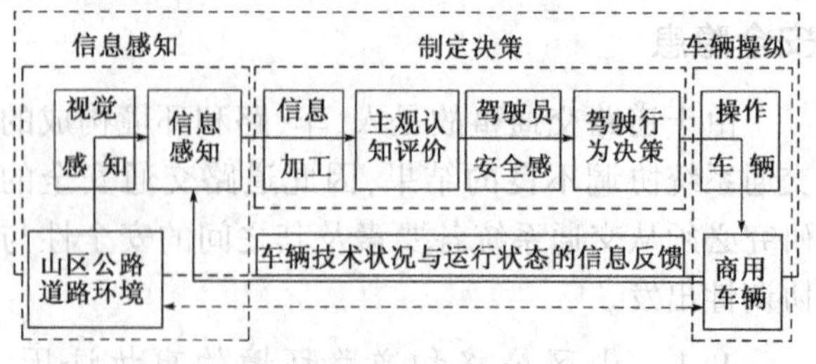

图4　驾驶员不确定与不稳定因素

商用车驾驶员因为驾驶任务、睡眠不足、长时间连续驾驶、工作时间不规律容易引起疲劳驾驶，据研究，全世界20%～50%的商用车事故是由于疲劳驾驶造成的[25]。车内环境差，振动、噪音、高温、阳光等和山区公路道路线形、天气能见度、路侧特征、驾驶速度等加大了驾驶员精神和身体负荷[26]。长时间的信息过载和任务过载驾驶使得驾驶员体力与精神负荷的激增,极易造成驾驶疲劳而增加发生交通事故的可能性。此外,驾驶次任务的执行导致驾驶分心、酒后驾驶导致反应迟缓等。此类驾驶状态影响了驾驶员心率、血压和对光与声音的反应时间,致使驾驶员驾驶能力的下降和驾驶行为出错[27],如图5所示。

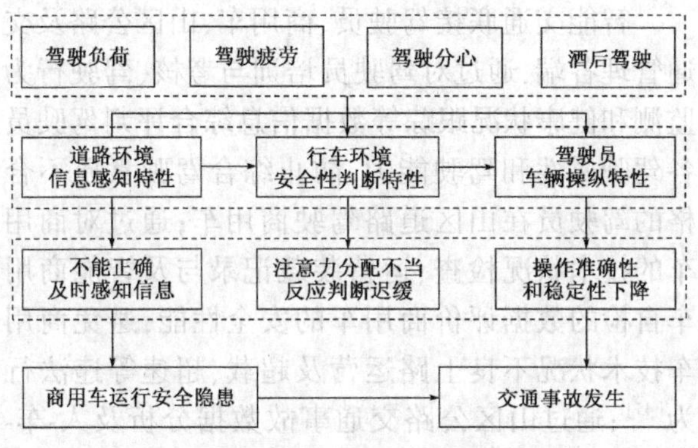

图5 驾驶员异常行为表现的事故诱因

2 智能技术的应用

目前,智能车辆、智慧公路和智能交通技术的快速发展为山区商用车行车主动安全提供了借鉴,其作用于传统的感知、判断、决策和操作的驾驶全过程与交通事故机理,消除或减轻驾驶员-商用车-山区公路行车安全系统不稳定因素,有利于从事故源头减少山区公路商用车交通安全隐患,如图6所示。

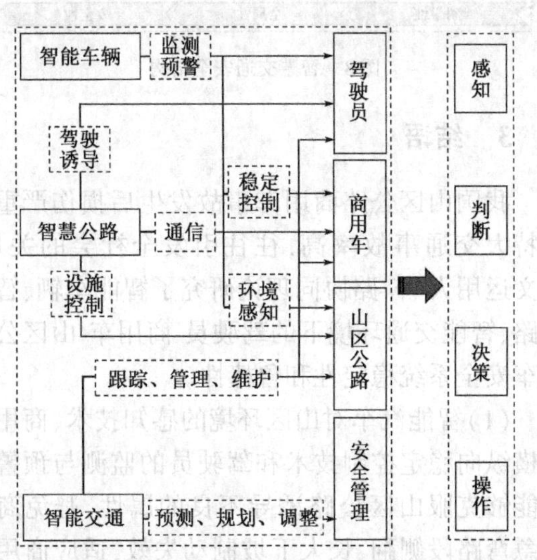

图6 智能技术对山区公路商用车交通安全作用路径

2.1 智能车辆技术对车辆运行的应用

1)山区公路复杂环境的感知技术

智能车辆感知技术是理解及辨析交通场景的重要途径,补充驾驶员视觉和认知极限,及时准确地响应与接收山区道路结构、交通环境综合诱导信息。

基于传感设备的感知技术主要应用于车辆驾驶辅助系统,辅助驾驶员实现对目标物的测距、跟踪与道路危险感知。然而雷达、摄像头等设备对道路交通环境的综合感知能力并不优于驾驶员,对此Han提出了一种基于高精度地图匹配的车辆定位技术,以提高车辆传感器失效或失灵时环境感知的鲁棒性[28]。基于高精度地图的环境感知技术被认为是车辆"超感知"技术发展的关键方向[29]。高精度地图具有厘米级的导航定位精度,既包含准确而全面的道路结构参数,如道路线形、道路结构参数等定量数据,又能反映特定路段的交通标线、交通流、天气状况等定性因素,为驾驶员或车辆提供实时的高精度的定位、车道级规划能力以及车道级驾驶引导。

2)商用车辆主动性安全控制与行车规划

近年来,车辆主动安全技术逐渐演变为集成化、智能化的高级辅助驾驶系统(ADAS),各技术结构体系主要分为道路环境感知、决策和控制以及车辆平台操纵三类[30]。高级驾驶辅助系统(ADAS)在山区公路场景中自适应干预商用车有效降低事故伤害风险[31]。Montani介绍了一种商用车稳定性控制系统,通过控制车辆制动与动力保证了在各种运动或操作极限及低附着道路的车辆动力性与安全性[32];Camde通过对自动紧急制动(AEB)、车道偏离警告(LDW)成本效益分析,认为此类技术对大型卡车有很好的安全和成本效益[33];Alejandra研究发现车道偏离警告(LDW)系统和侧倾稳定性控制(RSC)系统有利于商用车辆行车安全[34]。

根据地图和动态交通信息的先验知识,基于全局路径规划道路全线段或复杂路段的安全行驶策略,可以有效提高山区公路商用车主动安全。基于高精度地图精细化的山区公路信息获取辅助车辆实现高精度定位,并基于商用车的制动效力计算模型和横向稳定性评价模型,设计特定路段或危险路段的行车控制策略[35],如图7所示,防止商用车辆在山区公路急弯处发生侧翻横向失稳、长大下坡的制动失效,以及适应坡道载荷变化下的不足或过度转向变化。

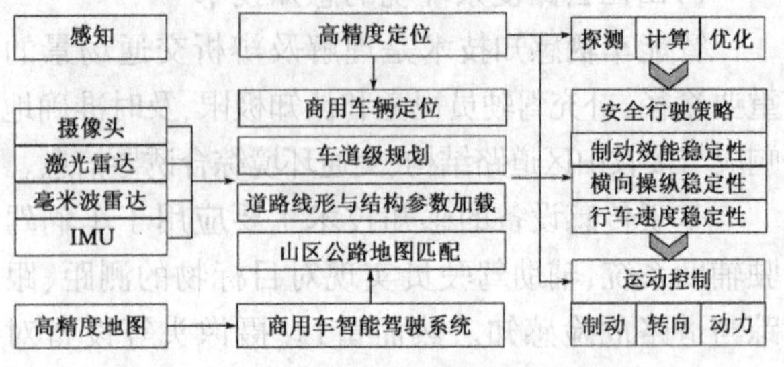

图7　全局路径与行驶策略规划过程

3)驾驶员行为监测与危险预警

以驾驶员为作用目标的商用车智能技术主要可分为两类,一类是基于对交通环境危险隐患的检测与驾驶员预警,如大雾智能预警系统有利于商用车驾驶员谨慎驾驶[36],追尾碰撞警告与车道偏离警告可有效防止大型卡车发生碰撞[33]。另一类是基于对驾驶员驾驶能动性的监测与预警,主要针对山区公路商用车驾驶员困倦、疲劳、酒后和分心驾驶[37]。车载安全监测系统(OSM)能主动收集、处理商用车驾驶员驾驶表现行为,并警示驾驶过程的不良行为、驾驶错误和安全隐患,包括驾驶员意识不到的错误[38]。驾驶员疲劳预警系统基于驾驶员面部表情变化、眼球运动、肢体动作和车辆特征来表征驾驶员疲劳状态,并通过视觉、听觉(警报和语音)、触觉和电刺激等方法警示商用车驾驶员在山区公路安全驾驶[39]。

2.2　智慧公路技术对公路运行的应用

智慧公路通过沿线布设的感知设备、监控设备、通信设施等基础设施和卫星的多网融合通信并基于云控平台实现人、车、路、基础设施、环境等综合要素协调运行[40]。Maram研究表明智慧公路可以改善山区公路安全运行条件,有效降低商用车辆事故发生率[41]。

山区智慧公路系统通过多种传感器采集道路全线内气象特征、交通状况及突发交通事件等多种信息,分析计算雨雾天气能见度、冰雪路面附着系数等道路通行能力,检测山区公路落石、塌陷和交通事故等突发事件,监测道路车辆运行速度[42]。并基于车路通信信息网络实现道路交通信息的实时有序传输,基于卫星通信信息网络为运行商用车提供高精度定位与高精度地图服务,为智能商用车与驾驶员预先、全面感知山区公路交通环境[43],提高山区公路的诱导能力。

2.3　智能交通对交通运行的应用

我国智能交通的发展主要包括智能化交通管理、智能化交通服务、智能化决策支持三方面,智能化交通管理和智能化决策支持对山区公路商用车运行安全意义重大。Hou研究表明智慧交通对驾驶员、商用车、山区公路和运输运营的智能化安全管理,可以更好地实现驾驶员-商用车-山区公路协调运行安全[44]。

智能交通联接驾驶员、商用车、山区公路及交通管理各端,通过对驾驶员培训与考核、驾驶行为监测和健康状况跟踪等数据信息综合评判驾驶员各驾驶属性和驾驶能力,防止综合驾驶素质不合格的驾驶员在山区道路驾驶商用车;通过对商用车的技术状况检查、运营装载记录与及智能商用车自检的数据评价商用车的安全性能,避免商用车技术状况不良上路运营及超载、超速等违法行为[45];通过山区公路交通事故数据分析及人-车-路协同仿真评价及改进山区公路运行安全性能和山区智慧公路系统的基础设施智能化控制,提高山区公路诱导能力、容错能力及道路与环境的协调性[46],如图8所示。

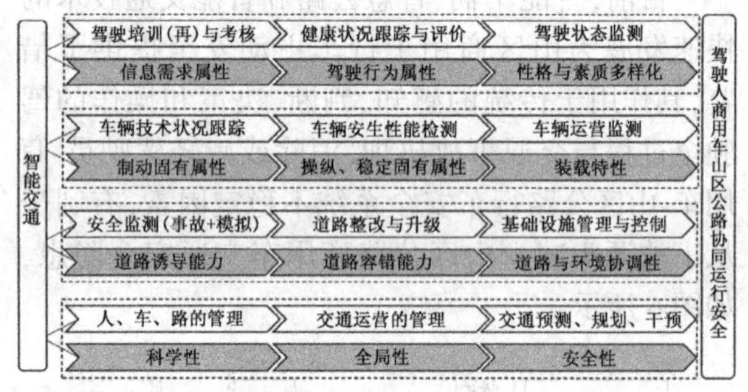

图8　智慧交通安全结构

3　结语

我国山区公路商用车事故发生后损伤严重及重特大交通事故率高,往往引发全社会的关切。本文运用人-车-路协同理论研究了智能车辆、智慧公路、智能交通环境下的驾驶员-商用车-山区公路行车安全系统稳定性和鲁棒性。

(1)智能汽车对山区环境的感知技术、商用车辆横纵向稳定控制技术和驾驶员的监测与预警技术能够克服山区公路诱导不良的属性,避免商用车急弯路段侧翻、长大下坡制动失效,适应商用车弯坡路段载荷变化引发的转向特性变化,减轻驾驶员不确定及不稳定因素对山区公路商用车行车安全的消极影响。

(2)智慧公路能通过道路交通信息采集与传输、交通诱导与危险预警等手段改善驾驶员及智能商用车对山区公路交通环境的感知,提高山区公路的诱导能力、容错能力和道路结构与环境的协调性。

(3)智能交通通过交通分析研判和智能化交通控制以确保合格的驾驶员、商用车、山区公路,以及规范的运输运营过程,更好地实现驾驶员-商用车-山区公路协调运行安全。

参考文献

[1] 赵丹,马社强,张雨萌,等.农村公路交叉口交通事故特征关联性与风险因素分析[J].中国安全科学学报,2020,30(7):146-151.

[2] Lsbib M F,Rifat A. S,Hossain M. M.,et al. Road Accident Analysis and Prediction of Accident Severity by Using Machine Learning in Bangladesh [C] // 7th International Conference on Smart Computing & Communications (ICSCC). Sarawak, 2019: 1-5.

[3] 王芳,郭艳,刘洪启,等.山区等级公路事故成因及对策分析[J].公路, 2011 (11): 126-129.

[4] 张旭欣,王雪松,马勇,等.驾驶行为与驾驶风险国际研究进展[J].中国公路学报,2020,33(06):1-17.

[5] Rusli R,Haque M,Saifuzzaman M,et al. Crash Severity Along Rural Mountainous Highways in Malaysia: An Application of A Combined Decision Tree and Logistic Regression Model [J]. Traffic Injury Prevention, 2018, 19 (7), 741-748.

[6] Yu B, Chen Y R, Bao S, et al. Quantifying Drivers' Visual Perception to Analyze Accident-Prone Locations on Two-Lane Mountain Highways[J]. Accident Analysis & Prevention, 2018,119: 122-130.

[7] Li F Y, Hu D W, Zhou C X, et al. Factor Analysis of Grievous Road Traffic Accidents in China[C] // 11th International Conference of Chinese Transportation Professionals (ICCTP). Nanjing,2011: 1966-1977.

[8] 袁泉,李一兵,陈康.引发重大交通事故的显著因素特点分析及安全对策[J].中国司法鉴定,2015(5): 34-40.

[9] Sirohi D, Kumar N, Rana P S. Convolutional Neural Networks for 5g-Enabled Intelligent TransportationSystem: A Systematic Review[J]. Computer Communications,2020,153: 459-498.

[10] Di Mare G, Vico F, Crisci F. An Innovative Real-Time Test Setup for Adas'S Based on Vehicle Cameras[J]. Transportation Research Part F: Traffic Psychology and Behaviour, 2019,61: 252-258.

[11] 徐志刚,李金龙,赵祥模,等.智能公路发展现状与关键技术[J].中国公路学报,2019,32(8): 1-24.

[12] Wu Y N,Abdel-aty M,Park J,et al. Effects of Crash Warning Systems on Rear-End Crash Avoidance Behavior Under Fog [J] Conditions, Transportation Research Part C: Emerging Technologies,2018,95: 481-492.

[13] Liu Z Y,He J,Zhang C. The Impact of Road Alignment Characteristics on Different Types of Traffic Accidents [J]. Journal of Transportation Safety & Security, 2020 12 (5): 697-726.

[14] Apronti D T, Saha P, Moomen M, et al. Truck Safety Evaluation on Wyoming Mountain Passes[J]. Accident Analysis & Prevention, 2019,122: 342-349.

[15] Yue L,Wang H,Xu Z C. Optimized Geometric Design of Mountain Highways based on A Vehicle-Road Coordination Model[C] // 5th International Conference on Transportation Information and Safety (ICTIS). Liverpool, 2019: 1251-1257.

[16] 王华荣,孙小端,贺玉龙,等.山区双车道公路尾随相撞事故与道路线形的关系[J].北京工业大学学报,2010,36(9): 1236-1241.

[17] Shi S M,Liu X D,Cao K Z,et al. Study on Cloud Model of Operating Speed Based on Road Alignment and Sight Distance [C] // Proceedings 2011 International Conference on Transportation, Mechanical, and Electrical Engineering (TMEE), Changchun, 2011:

648-651.

[18] Xu CC, Bao J, Wang C, et al. Association Rule Analysis of Factors Contributing to Extraordinarily Severe Traffic Crashes in China [J]. Journal of Safety Research, 2018, 67: 65-75.

[19] 赵俊玮,华珺,刘永涛,等.道路交通事故信息采集技术及应用[J].重庆理工大学学报(自然科学),2019,33(7):28-36.

[20] Pennelly C, Reuter G W, Tjandra S. Effects of Weather on Traffic Collisions in Edmonton, Canada [J]. Atmosphere-Ocean, 2018, 56 (5): 362-371.

[21] Abdel-aty M, Ekram A, Huang H L, et al, A Study on Crashes Related to Visibility Obstruction Due to Fog and Smoke [J]. Accident Analysis & Prevention, 2011, 43 (5): 1730-1737.

[22] Yu R J, Xiong Y G, Abdel-aty M, A Correlated Random Parameter Approach to InvestigateThe Effects of Weather Conditions on Crash Risk For A Mountainous Freeway [J]. Transportation Research Part C: Emerging Technologies, 2015 (50): 68-77.

[23] 胡立伟,薛刚,李林育,等.高原地质及气象环境下公路交通风险致因耦合分析[J].中国公路学报,2018,31(1):110-119.

[24] Chu D F, Li Z L, Wang J M, et al, Rollover Speed Prediction on Curves for Heavy Vehicles Using Mobile Smartphone [J]. Measurement, 2018(130): 404-411.

[25] Davidović J, Pešić D, Antić B. Professional Drivers' Fatigue as A Problem of The Modern Era [J]. Transportation Research Part F: Traffic Psychology andBehaviour, 2018(55): 199-209.

[26] Anund A, Fors C, Ihlström J, et al. An on-road study of sleepiness in split shifts among city busdrivers, Accident Analysis & Prevention, Volume 114, 2018: 71-76.

[27] Zhang X J, Zhao X H, Du H J, et al. A Study on the Effects of Fatigue Driving and Drunk Driving on Drivers' Physical Characteristics [J]. Traffic Injury Prevention, 2014, 15(8): 801-808.

[28] Han S, Kang J, Jo Y, et al. Robust Ego-motion Estimation and Map Matching Technique for Autonomous Vehicle Localization with High Definition Digital Map [C] // 2018 International Conference on Information and Communication Technology Convergence (ICTC). Jeju, 2018: 630-635.

[29] Hamieh I, Myers R, Rahman T. Construction of Autonomous Driving Maps employing LiDAR Odometry [C] // 2019 IEEE Canadian Conference of Electrical and Computer Engineering (CCECE). Edmonton, 2019: 1-4.

[30] Behere S, Törngren M. A Functional Reference Architecture for Autonomous Driving [J]. Information and Software Technology, 2016 (73): 136-150.

[31] Vangi D, Virga A, Gulino M. Combined Activation of BrakingAnd Steering for Automated Driving Systems: Adaptive Intervention by Injury Risk-Based Criteria [J]. Procedia Structural Integrity, 2019(24): 423-436.

[32] Montani M, Capitanl R, Annicchiarico C. Development of A Brake by Wire System Design for Car Stability Controls[J]. Procedia Structural Integrity, 2019(24): 137-154.

[33] Camden M C, Medina-flintsch A, Hickman J S, et al. Do the Benefits Outweigh the Costs? Societal Benefit-Cost Analysis of Three Large Truck Safety Technologies [J]. Accident Analysis & Prevention, 2018(121): 177-184.

[34] Medina-flintsch A, Hickman J S, GUO F et al. Benefit-Cost Analysis of Lane Departure Warning and Roll Stability Control in Commercial Vehicles [J]. Journal of Safety Research, 2017(62): 73-80.

[35] Moon S, Cho W, Yi K. Intelligent VehicleSafetycontrol Strategy in Various Driving Situations[J]. Vehicle System Dynamics, 2010 (48): 537-554.

[36] Chang X, Li H, Rong J, et al. Effects of Warning Systems on Longitudinal Driving Behavior and Safety under Fog Conditions[C]

// 2019 IEEE Intelligent Transportation Systems Conference (ITSC). Auckland, 2019:2154-2159.

[37] Rezaei M, Terauchi M. Vehicle Detection Based on Multi-feature Clues and Dempster-Shafer Fusion Theory[C]// 6th Pacific-Rim Symposium on Image and Video Technology (PSIVT). Image and Video Technology, 2014 (80): 60-72.

[38] Horrey W J, Lesch M F, Dainoff M J, et al. On-Board Safety Monitoring Systems for Driving: Review, Knowledge Gaps, and Framework [J]. Journal of Safety Research, 2012, 43 (1): 49-58.

[39] Meng F X, Li S L, Cao L Z, et al. Designing Fatigue Warning Systems: The Perspective of Professional Drivers[J]. Applied Ergonomics, 2016(53): 122-130.

[40] 岑晏青,宋向辉,王东柱,等.智慧高速公路技术体系构建[J].公路交通科技,2020,37 (7): 11-121.

[41] Younes M B, Boukerche A. Safety and Efficiency Control Protocol for Highways Using Intelligent Vehicular Networks[J]. Computer Networks, 2019(152): 1-11.

[42] Finogeev A, Finogeev A, FIONOVA L, et al. Intelligent Monitoring System for Smart Road Environment [J]. Journal of Industrial Information Integration, 2019(15): 15-20.

[43] Manivannan P V, Ramakanth P. Vision Based Intelligent Vehicle Steering Control Using Single Camera for Automated Highway System [J]. Procedia Computer Science, 2018 (133): 839-846.

[44] Hou Z X, Zhou Y C, Du R H. Special issue on intelligent transportation systems, big data and intelligent technology [J]. Transportation Planning and Technology, 2016, 39 (8): 747-750.

[45] Sandt A, Al-deek H. An Optimization Approach for Deployment of Intelligent Transportation Systems Wrong-Way Driving Countermeasures [J]. Journal of Intelligent Transportation Systems, 2020, 24(1): 40-53.

[46] Galkin A, Sysoyev A. Formalizing Criteria of Intelligent Transportation andLogistic Systems Functioning [J]. Transportation Research Procedia, 2020(45): 514-521.

车路协同技术在智慧高速中的应用

李佳晨* 雷 斌 张 鹏

(西安建筑科技大学土木工程学院)

摘　要　为了避免发生交通事故,保证行车安全,提高高速公路运行效率,在高速公路建设运营过程中,建议采用车路协同技术开展智慧交通管理。本文通过整理文献详细介绍了国内外智慧高速车路协同系统的发展情况,从系统感知、网络通信和平台应用等方面介绍其系统架构。研究结果显示,目前该系统主要应用于辅助安全驾驶,且处于试验阶段,应用等级不高,在政策、规范、网络、系统对接上均存在问题。通过智慧高速车路协同系统的实践应用发现,车路协同系统对自动驾驶的安全保证至关重要,应从辅助安全驾驶定位,不断增加场景应用,逐步完成高级自动驾驶。

关键词　交通工程　智慧高速公路　车路协同技术　关键技术　建议

0　引言

近年来,随着智能化交通系统的不断发展,高速公路系统被赋予了新的内涵。国家提出的《交通强国建设纲要》和《推进智慧交通发展行动计划》等文件中都提出关于“智慧高速”的建设要求。当下智慧高速建议的重点方向是依据车路协同技术开展自动驾驶示范工程建设,这不但需要满足高等级 V2X(Vehicle to everything)网联车辆的自动驾驶测试需求,而且需要提高高速公路管理水平和服务质量[1]。本文首先对智慧高速与车路协同技术的相关概念和发展现状进行梳理,其次提出面向智慧高速的车路协同系统架构并梳理其具体应用,最后提出了对我国智慧高速车路协同技术发展的建议和展望,以期及时发现新型智慧高速发展过程中的不足之处,从不同维度进行改进,为智慧高速系统的快速高质量发展提供一定的基础。

1　智慧高速与车路协同概述

1.1　智慧高速

20 世纪 40 年代国际上就已提出智慧高速公路[2]概念。智慧高速是智慧交通在高速公路系统的延伸,即运用网络技术和智能技术,科学配置各类资源,融合智能管理和智能服务的高速公路。高速公路的车道线和标志等静态信息功能清晰,交通环境相对简单。未来,它可能成为智能网联车辆(Intelligent and Connected Vehicle,ICV)技术的优先落实和应用场景之一[3]。

1.2　车路协同

车路协同系统[4-5](Intelligent Vehicle Infrastructure Cooperative Systems,IVICS)采用 5G、云计算、大数据、物联网、人工智能等先进信息技术手段,实现车路(Vehicle to Infrastructure,V2I)、车车(Vehicle to Vehicle,V2V)之间的实时动态信息交互,目标是通过协同人、车、路与环境,保障交通安全,提高交通效率,构建高效、环保、安全的道路交通体系[6]。车路协同技术是智慧高速系统的有机组成部分,是未来智慧高速的重要发展方向,二者的融合联系如图 1 所示。

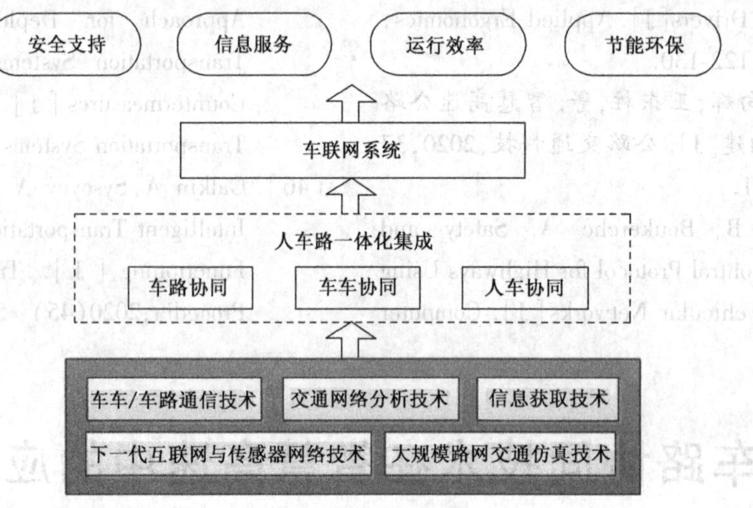

图 1　车路协同与智慧交通的融合联系

1.3　国内发展现状

根据智慧高速中车路协同技术提供的功能和性能等级,对具有不同功能的道路进行分级,见表 1。

智慧高速车路协同分级　　表 1

能力等级	道路条件	车路协同能力	车路通信能力
1 级车路通信能力	完备的道路交通标志和标线设施	1. 标志标线:仅静态标志标线,无电子标识 2. 信息发布:红绿灯、车道通行灯、情报板等常规标志 3. 路测设施:道路感知设备(气象传感器、雷达、摄像机)自成体系,未网联化	无数据信息交互,车辆识别道路标志
2 级数字化道路	安装路侧智能感知、通信、计算设备	1. 标志标线:可进行车道级标志标线信息推送 2. 信息发布:具备非视距信息推送功能,可将动态事件、气象、施工、信号灯、限速、车道线、预警等信息推送至车辆 3. 路侧设施:支持 C-V2X 和蜂窝车路直线通信,能提供动态事件感知、本地交通流计算、车联网 V2N(Vehicle to netword)业务、高精地图及定位辅助	具备交通信息推送能力,路侧设施网联化部署

续上表

能力等级	道路条件	车路协同能力	车路通信能力
3级多源融合感知道路	可以基于云控平台提供道路管控服务,支持全城交通信息采集、车路协同融合感知、交通信息处理	1.双向信息交互:具备RSU-OBU双向通信功能。 2.路侧设施:C-V2X支持单播、组播,可以为自动驾驶车辆提供高精地图及定位辅助信息。 3.交通控制:具备全域交通感知和交通流控制调节能力,可提供分合流预警、紧急情况预警等服务	车辆与道路数据信息实时交互
4级协同控制道路	支持自动驾驶在线调度和车队编队行驶	交通控制:支持自动驾驶车辆协同决策,具备快速交通决策和调度能力	车路一体化信息交互和协同控制

车路协同智能化等级可由下列公式获得:

$$S = f(V, I)$$

式中:S——车路协同系统智能等级;

V——车辆智能化等级;

I——道路智能化等级。

智慧高速和智能网联车辆是促进国家经济高速发展的重要战略。同时,高速公路也是智能网联车辆实际应用的重要场景和重要基础,二者的融合发展已成为当前交通和汽车领域探索的热点。近年来,我国各地积极响应政策要求,不断创新实验,取得了较好的成果。表2列出了我国高速公路车路协同应用案例。目前我国智慧高速车路协同项目的建设大多数还处于2级的水平,以实现辅助安全驾驶为主。随着5G技术的发展和基础设施的建设,最新项目已经可以实现3级车路协同要求,更高等级智慧高速的实现依赖车辆自身技术性能的提高,故4级车路协同要求的实现取决于智能网联汽车自动驾驶能力的提升[7]。

中国车路协同应用案例 表2

高速公路	项目概况	关键时间点	建设特色
大兴机场高速	大兴国际机场至北京南五环,全长27km	2020年7月全线开放	移动网联收费、综合监控系统、大数据智能分析、仿真推演、电子沙盘
吉林珲乌高速	连接乌兰浩特和珲春,全长885km	2019年建设完成	不停车移动支付、动态无线充电、低温条件下的气象预测及预防性养护、辅助驾驶
浙江杭绍甬高速	杭甬复线高速公路,全长约174km	2022年建成通车	高精度定位、5G通信、新能源无线充电、无人驾驶、自由流收费、智慧云控平台、自动驾驶及货车编队系统
杭绍台高速公路绍兴金华段	列为浙江省智慧高速示范项目的绍兴金华段约115.4km	于2016年正式动工,力争2020年建成通车	“客货运输网”“传感通信控制网”和“绿色能源网”三网合一、智慧隧道、智慧服务区、准全天候通行
山东滨莱高速	连接淄博和莱芜,全长72.8km	2019年7月开始进行封闭试运营	智能网联汽车高速公路场景、辅助驾驶、智能网联车队列行驶
机西高速	周口至西华郑州新郑国际机场,在已通车运营的机西高速一期工程(106km)和在建的二期工程(45km)	2019年11月招标	基础设施数字化感知体系、多维度的交通运行数字化感知体系、基于大数据决策的高速公路智慧管理系统、高速公路交通运行管控系统、陆空信息一站式服务区、1个云数据中心
长常北线长益段	长沙绕城高速西北段、西南段63km以及G5517长益北线	2020年8月31日全线开通	网联辅助驾驶、智慧高速运营监管、实现L3级自动驾驶,示范段满足L4级自动驾驶车辆测试需求
成宜高速	起于成都经济区环线高速公路,止于乐宜高速公路中峰,全长157km	2020年12月31日通车	满足L3.5级自动驾驶标准,全路段人工智能视频分析、预判、报警功能,全路段5G覆盖
京雄高速公路河北段、荣乌高速	京雄高速公路从北京到达雄安新区与荣乌高速公路连接	2021年5月建成通车	自动驾驶专用车道、智慧照明系统、智慧化货运系统车道级主动控制系统、车辆轨迹追踪

续上表

高速公路	项目概况	关键时间点	建设特色
五峰山未来高速公路	自京沪高速公路与沪陕高速公路交叉的正谊枢纽,止于泰镇高速公路与江宜高速公路交叉的大港枢纽,全长33km	2021年6月建成通车	单车自动驾驶、重载车队编队自动驾驶、车道级雾天行车诱导系统、消雪融冰系统、交通事件极速感知系统、基于4K+5G无人机的数据采集与分析研究系统
沙吴高速	南宁沙井至吴圩高速公路,全长28.5km	2021年9月建成通车	北斗高精度增强网工程、全生命周期高精度多模态空间数据工程、车路协同数据互联与云管控平台工程、基于5G的车路协同通信工程、交通控制工程以及数字化施工、智慧服务区示范

1.4　国外发展现状

在20世纪60年代,美国和日本已经开始进行车路通信的研究,但是车路协同的快速发展期应该是从美国联邦交通运输部于2015年启动的Connected Vehicles Pilot项目开始的。据报道,美国当前50%的州已经开始进行车路协同的示范建设,其中怀俄明州、纽约市和佛罗里达州Tampa市的三个示范最为典型[8]。

欧洲早在2009年就启动了CVIS(Cooperative Vehicle-Infrastructure System)项目,目前逐步发展到了Horizon 2020地平线计划。日本则以VICS(Vehicle Infrastructure Communication Systems)项目为基础,提出了SmartWay计划,发展成至今的ETC2.0项目,进行自动驾驶系统的研发,具体如图2所示。

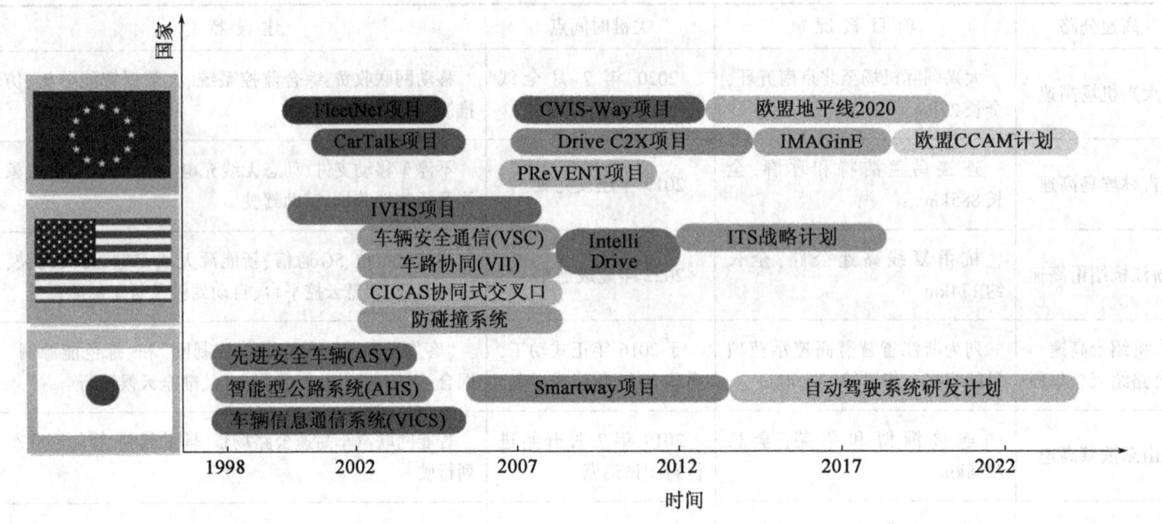

图2　国外车路协同技术发展历程

2　系统架构及存在的问题

车路协同系统以智能网联车辆的需求为导向,从感知设备、感知能力、网络信息交互方式、智能联控机制、信息可视化等方面考虑,多模式兼容的感知设备能够保证信息获取的稳定性,基于协同感知的环境感知能力能够保证获取信息的及时性,基于可信交互的信息交互模式可以保证信息的安全性,动态分层形式的控制机制可以保证控制行为的合理性,以边缘云端形式的计算实现可以提高计算效率。因此,随着系统功能的不断升级,车路协同系统会使大众出行更加安全、高效和舒适。车路协同系统涉及多方面、多领域、多层次的新技术的集成与应用,涉及5G、物联网、大数据、AI和云计算等多个领域,其技术架构可以分为系统感知层、网络通信层、平台层和应用层[9]。图3为车路协同技术架构分析。

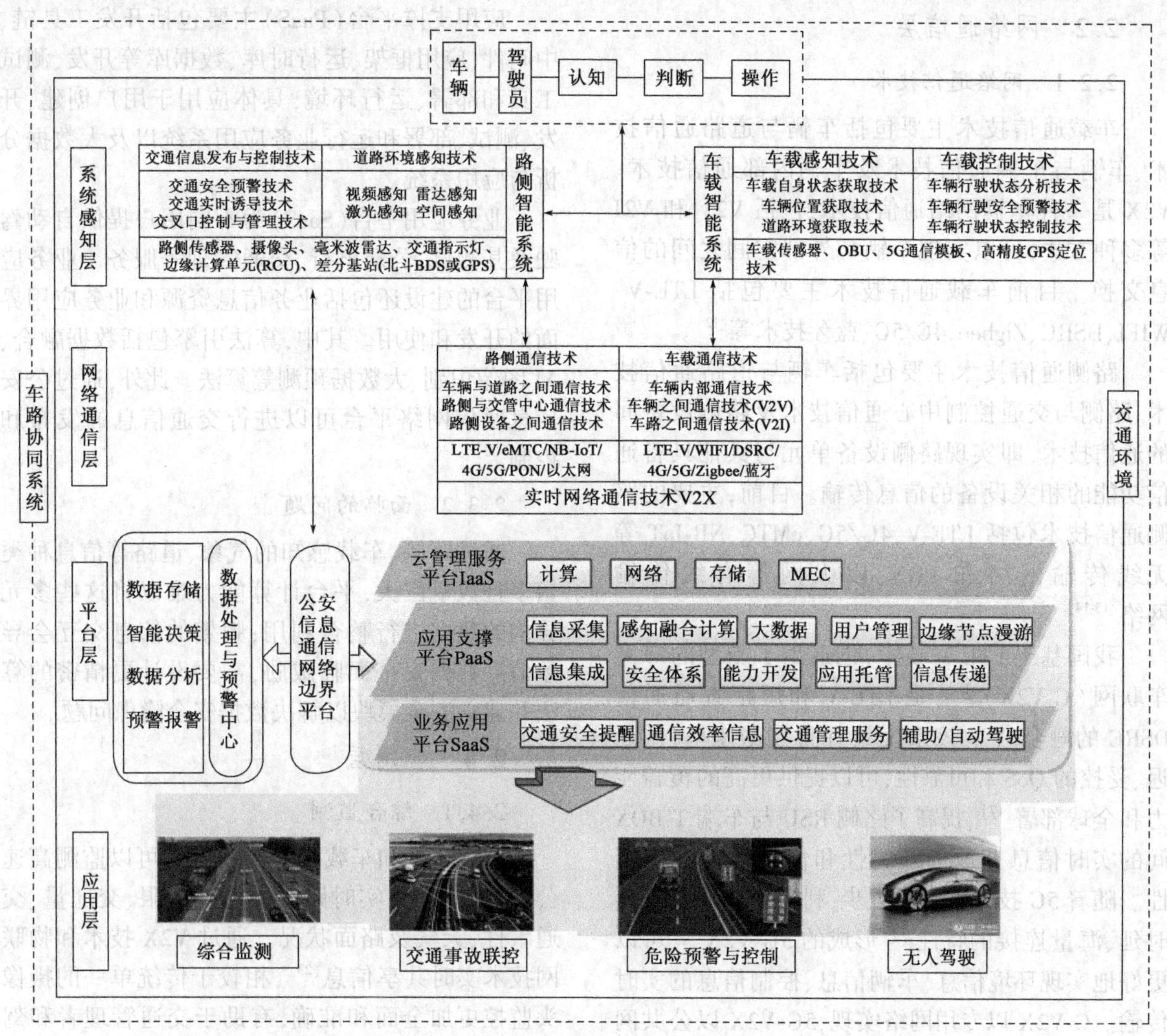

图3 车路协同技术架构

2.1 系统感知层

2.1.1 智能感知技术

车载智能感知技术主要包括车辆状态采集技术、车辆位置采集技术和道路环境采集技术。车载信息采集子系统(Vehicle Information Acquisition system)利用传感器、车载摄像头和其他终端设备(OBU)的感知能力和与视觉感知融合的高精度GPS定位技术,实现车辆行驶状态、车辆位置、道路环境状况等相关信息的采集。

道路环境感知技术使用路侧RSU设备和交通指示灯等来获取环境信息,主要用于监测道路气象环境、道路交通状态以及行人和非机动车的行为。目前,道路环境感知技术主要有视频监测、雷达感知、激光感知、空间定位、微波感应、超声波等。其中,高精度地图(HDM)是车方和路方的重要纽带和车路协同的重要载体[10],它包含着大量行车辅助信息:一类是道路数据,另一类是车道周边的固定对象信息[11]。高精度地图对路网精确的三维表征可以达到厘米级,在此基础上联合V2X技术和仿真技术,可以提前感知前方超视距范围内的动态信息,实现动态实时信息可视化,为驾驶人和交通管理者提供更准确的信息,使驾驶人更加安全地参与交通,使管理者更便捷地管理交通。

2.1.2 面临的问题

目前车载感知主要依赖摄像头感知技术,其在大雨、大雾等恶劣天气下感知能力严重受限;路侧激光雷达的使用寿命低,使用成本较高;车载感知设备和路侧感知设备由不同设备供应商提供,而不同供应商之间信任度有限,限制了测试场景的应用。

2.2 网络通信层

2.2.1 网络通信技术

车载通信技术主要包括车辆与道路通信技术、车辆与车辆通信技术及车辆内部通信技术。V2X是一种车辆网络通信技术,包括V2V和V2I等多种方式,可以实现车辆与外部空间之间的信息交换。目前车载通信技术主要包括LTE-V、WIFI、DSRC、Zigbee、4G/5G、蓝牙技术等[12]。

路侧通信技术主要包括车辆与道路通信技术、路侧与交通控制中心通信技术及路侧设备间的通信技术,即实现路侧设备单元与其他具备通信功能的相关设备的信息传输。目前,主要的路侧通信技术包括LTE-V、4G/5G、eMTC、NB-IoT等无线传输网络和PON、以太网等有线传输网络[13-14]。

我国基于LTE-V技术,创造出了新型的蜂窝车联网(C-V2X)[15],是LTE-V和短距直通通信DSRC的融合[16]。该系统具有高数据速率、低延迟、受控的QoS和可靠性,可以提供更高的覆盖能力和全球部署[17],提高了路侧RSU与车端T-BOX间的实时信息获取的及时性和信息传递的稳定性。随着5G技术的不断进步,利用5G高速率、低时延、海量连接的特性[18]形成的5G-V2X[19]可以更好地实现环境信息、车辆信息、控制信息的实时传输。C-V2X以专用网络实现,5G-V2X以公共网络实现,两者相辅相成,可以满足车路协同系统的通信要求。

2.2.2 面临的问题

C-V2X专网安全性好,传输稳定,但所需服务费较高,且不同品牌的设备不兼容,容易造成资源浪费;5G传输需要大量的基站部署,建设成本太高;车路协同系统的商业化运营困难[20]。

2.3 平台层

2.3.1 平台建设

云管理服务平台(IaaS)负责主机、存储、网络、安全等物理资源虚拟化管理,实现计算、存储、网络软件等物理资源的软件定义,为业务应用系统提供虚拟资源库及相关管理服务,实现自动分配、回收、监控和统一管理物理资源,降低能源消耗和使用IT基础设施的成本,提高IT基础设施的使用效率和灵活性[21]。

应用支撑平台(PaaS)主要包括开发工具链、中间件、应用框架、运行时库、数据库等开发、测试工具和部署、运行环境,具体应用于用户创建、开发、测试、部署和运行业务应用系统以及大数据分析与应用系统。

业务应用平台(SaaS)为不同用户提供自动驾驶及其测试、公众出行、交通管理等服务。业务应用平台的建设还包括业务信息资源和业务应用界面的开发和使用。其中,算法引擎包括数据融合、AI图像识别、大数据预测等算法。此外,通过公安信息通信网络平台可以进行交通信息的发布和控制[22]。

2.3.2 面临的问题

通过路侧、车载感知的气象、道路等信息种类繁多且数量巨大,平台计算能力难以将这些多元异构的数据进行整合利用;频繁的信息交互会导致信息数据安全面临威胁,需要设计更精密的算法并建立安全模块以解决数据安全隐患问题。

2.4 应用层

2.4.1 综合监测

利用路侧和车载智能传感技术可以监测高速公路基础设施、实时路况、路标、超限、交通量、交通事件、天气及路面状况。通过V2X技术和物联网技术实时共享信息[23],相较于传统单一的摄像头监控更加全面和准确,有助于交通管理者和驾驶员及时获取高速公路状况,掌握交通的变化态势,可以帮助管理人员作出交通管制决策,辅助驾驶员完成安全驾驶行为。在新建的宜昭高速和杭绍台高速中构建的准全天候通行系统包含精准交通气象系统和凝冰除雪监测,首次实现了高速公路主动交通管控和服务。

2.4.2 交通事故联控

对于事故发生区域,利用综合监测获取信息,数据通过RSU单元和5G基站传输网络快速准确地上传到后台数据中心,平台层整合、计算数据,判断事故发生的具体位置、严重程度等事故信息,为故障车辆就近提供维修及拖车等服务。同时,将智能优化决策算法用于联动控制外场装置设备,以发布预警信息,并向后续车辆发送事故指令,使其进行规避并为其提供可更换路线,避免道路拥堵或二次事故,提高事故处理效率[24]。京沪高速基于准全天候辅助设施,结合高精度地图和车载终端提供的车道级差异化服务中包含的危险车辆避让、救援车辆应急车道行驶诱导功能充分体现了交通事故联控的有效性。

2.4.3 危险预警与控制

当路侧和车载智能感知设备发现危险隐患时,通过V2V和V2I通信技术,将道路前方的道路病害、障碍物的位置、前进方向和限速等信息传递给驾驶员,达到提前预警的效果,预防危险物影响车辆行驶,防止车辆在换道过程中与其他车辆发生碰撞。此外,网络通信平台通过筛选算法和AI技术将此信息传递至道路管理部门进行危险排除[25]。在五峰山高速实现的车路协同应用中,道路遗撒、道路施工、匝道汇入、交通事故预警、大雾预警和隧道危险预警等技术将在高速公路的行车安全防控中发挥巨大的作用。

2.4.4 自动驾驶

自动驾驶技术是全世界都在研究的新技术,车路协同是实现完全自动驾驶的必经之路。随着V2X技术的不断扩充,车路协同技术不断更新,最终将满足高等级的完全自动驾驶。已建成的长常北线长益段和成宜高速已经可以实现3级以上的自动驾驶。随着高标准的新型基础建设不断完善,专用自动驾驶车道投入应用,自动驾驶车辆性能不断提高,高等级自动驾驶技术也会逐渐成熟。

3 智慧高速建设思考

随着以车路协同为重点的新型高速公路基础设施的快速发展,高速公路也被规划、设计为一个特定的应用场景,结合存在的问题,本文对我国智慧高速系统的发展提出以下建议。

3.1 统筹管理、积极协调

政府应起到自身的领导和管理作用,积极组织相关事宜,在车路协同项目开始阶段成立专项工作领导组,组织分级管理,建立一个学术和产业并重的专家团队,以论证项目的战略目标和整体规划;坚决维护自动驾驶市场秩序,规范企业市场行为。公路基建是车路协同项目的基础,要有效地统筹管理,按需建设,不断完善设计管控策略及设计主动安全技术和管理方法,实现交通安全运行防控一体化;可以增加相关方面的补贴,为建设高质量智慧高速系统保驾护航。

3.2 法规标准、鼓励创新

目前,车路协同的技术水平与相应规范标准不平衡,规范标准不能满足智能化的需要。对此,政府应学习相关知识,与时俱进,结合实践,制定与技术发展相匹配的法律法规,积极引入保险机制,明确系统运行过程中的责任划分。项目管理者应统一C-V2X技术标准,明确数据采集和信息传输技术标准,保证不同项目之间信息技术的互联互通,为未来全国性智慧高速网络工程的建设提供基础。此外,智慧高速最终要落实到现实使用中,所以应对民众进行车路协同自动驾驶技术的普及和宣传。

3.3 定位准确、充分利用

车路协同和智慧高速建设都要定位于解决实际运营问题,智慧高速可以充分利用现有系统,并在此基础上结合所需的新型技术设备进行建设。现在高速公路已经有通信、监控、收费、指挥调度、出行服务、道路养护等一系列系统,智慧高速要满足多样化功能场景需求,就要把现有系统互通融合起来,从信息感知维度统筹考虑业务目标,从信息处理维度全面推动AI应用,从用户服务触达维度充分利用现有系统,充分发挥每一个已经布设的设备的价值,发挥聚合效应。在实施过程中可以分阶段、分层次进行不同模块的搭建,为后期多功能融合提供基础,避免出现单一性的场景适应。

3.4 跨行融合、持续发展

车路协同技术涉及通信、道路基建、计算机等多个行业,应由政府主导,促进多行业之间的合作,通过产学研协作,推动跨行业的发展平台建设。基础建设应与"本土产业"深度融合,各个基础设备的设计和应用采用统一的标准,解决基础建设所需的大量资金投入;通信网络可以由网络运营商进行统一建设;平台的建设要避免低水平重复投资,不同企业间应紧密合作,推进项目可持续发展,激活车路协同发展的内生动力。

4 结语

高速公路运营期间发生的交通事故不同于城市道路事故,不仅会影响正常行车,造成道路拥堵,而且所造成的人身伤害及经济损失更加严重。为了保证安全行车,避免交通事故的发生,将车路协同技术应用到智慧高速的管理中可以大幅度提高高速公路运行效率。先进的技术是智慧高速公路不断发展的重要前提。随着大数据、物联网、信息通信、人工智能技术的飞速发展,人们的出行特征和出行方式发生了巨大变化。随着智慧网联车辆核心技术取得了较大的突破,智能高速公路建设不断加快。实践证明,利用车路协同技术建设智慧高速公路,可以显著提高道路交通系统的通行效率,保证车辆安全绿色出行,具有巨大的社会效益与经济效益。车路协同应用服务等级的提高依托车辆智能和路侧智能的同步发展,要让"智慧"的车行驶于"智慧"的路上,让二者相互促进。通过推进车路协同技术辅助自动驾驶,规范新技术的健康发展,可以促进自动驾驶车辆产业高速发展,减少交通拥堵、提高交通效率、确保行车安全。车路协同技术的实时感知周边环境并进行预警的能力是解决交通安全问题的重要一环,将成为自动驾驶技术的重要支撑点,使出行更高效、更安全。在此基础上,智慧交通系统将有望进一步实现高质量发展。

参考文献

[1] 李向峰,基于车路协同技术的智慧高速系统架构分析[J]. 中国高新科技,2020,78(18):36-38.

[2] 齐为.我国智慧高速公路建设标准化现状研究[J]. 标准科学,2015,497(10):47-49.

[3] 吴戡,宋晓峰,季玮,等. 智慧高速车路协同系统发展现状与趋势[C]. 中国智能交通协会. 第十五届中国智能交通年会科技论文集,中国智能交通协会,2020.

[4] 柴琳果. 智能车路协同交叉口间隙耦合运行控制方法[D]. 北京:北京交通大学,2018.

[5] 石勇. 基于无线信道衰落模型的智能车路协同系统通信性能分析[D]. 北京:清华大学,2015.

[6] 崔晓丹. 基于车路协同的区域化无信号交叉口控制方法研究[D]. 北京:北京交通大学,2017.

[7] 李大成. 车路协同在智慧高速领域的应用探索[J]. 互联网经济,2020(11):64-70.

[8] 沙锐,梁德建. 智慧公路发展现状、趋势分析及对策[J]. 科技中国,2020,279(12):7-9.

[9] 燕崇麒. 探索车路协同技术在智慧高速公路建设中的应用[J]. 智能城市,2021,7(9):1-2.

[10] 李智,张江,仲跻冲,等. 高精度地图在车路协同系统中的统一化应用探索[J]. 中国交通信息化,2021,252(1):94-97.

[11] 潘霞,张庆余,朱强. 高精度地图在自动驾驶领域的作用及意义解析[J]. 时代汽车,2019,307(4):51-52,55.

[12] 洪伟权,陈久雨. 车路协同业务产业细分和市场空间[J]. 通信企业管理,2021,410(6):61-63.

[13] 李凯旋. 智慧城市:车路协同技术对智能交通管理的贡献与影响[J]. 中华建设,2019(5):85-89.

[14] 程璐明. 基于5G万物互联的智慧交通探索[J]. 智能城市,2019,5(4):98-99.

[15] G. Araniti, C. Campolo, M. Condoluci, A. Iera, A. Molinaro, Lte for vehicular networking: a survey, IEEE Commun [C]. Mag. 51 (5) (2013):148-157.

[16] 刘爽,吴韶波. V2X车联网关键技术及应用[J]. 物联网技术,2018,8(10):39-40,43.

[17] T. Toukabri, A. M. Said, E. Abd-Elrahman, H. Afifi, Cellular vehicular networks (cvn): prose-based its in advanced 4g networks, in: Proc. of IEEE 11 th International Conference on Mobile Ad Hoc and Sensor Systems (MASS), IEEE, 2014:527-528.

[18] 缪立新,王发平. V2X车联网关键技术研究及应用综述[J]. 汽车工程学报,2020,10(1):1-12.

[19] C. Campolo, A. Molinaro, A. Iera, et al . 5G network slicing for vehicle-to-everything services[J] IEEE Wirel. Commun, 2017, 24(6):38-45.

[20] 于力,陶永峰. 智慧快速路车路协同系统应用及展望[J]. 中国交通信息化,2021,256(S1):158-159.

[21] 李艳艳,王小雄,邵永军. 智慧高速平台的设计与实现[J]. 科技创新与应用,2018(18):93-94.

[22] 孙敏,王妍颖,黄宇. 基于多场景下车路协同应用的研究[J]. 交通节能与环保,2020,16(5):59-61.

[23] 陈漩,蔡子华. 面向下一代车联网的V2X关

键技术研究[J].广东通信技术,2018,38(4):22-25.
[24] 孟永帅.高速公路车路协同技术应用探讨[J].交通世界,2021,571(13):7-8,12.
[25] 郭丽苹,张兴宇.车路协同技术应用与推广探讨[J].中国交通信息化,2021,256(S1):163-165.

Experimental Design of Test Platform for Operation Design Domain of Autonomous Driving: A Case Study in China

Jingliang Ming [1,3] Chuan Sun [*2,3] Sifa Zheng [3,4] Zhixiong Li [1] Guisheng Li [5,3] Yujun Yue [5,3] Haoran Li [3]

(1. College of Engineering, Ocean University of China;
2. Department of Civil and Environmental Engineering, The Hong Kong Polytechnic University;
3. Suzhou Automotive Research Institute, Tsinghua University;
4. School of Vehicle and Mobility, Tsinghua University;
5. Mechanical and Electrical Engineering College, Hainan University)

Abstract To ensurethe operational safety of autonomous driving and address the fuzziness of boundary conditions regarding their operation, an operational design domain (ODD) of intelligent connected vehicles (ICVs) was designed based on the actual transportation in China, and a test platform for the ODD was constructed. The test platform comprises road sections of circle island and tunnel, as well as ramps, straight and curved; on board units (OBUs) were deployed on the vehicle terminal and multi-module road side units (RSUs) on the roadside. A case study on the test platform shows that within the ODD, ICVs are able to drive along the path planning and complete a range of autonomous driving functions from starting, recognizing traffic signs, markings and obstacles, changing lanes to pass, simulating accident scenes, driving straight, recognizing and responding to traffic lights, passing tunnel and circle island, to fixed-point parking. The problem of blurred operational boundary conditions for autonomous driving is addressed, providing certain guidance for normalization and standardization of subsequent ODD for autonomous driving in China.

Keywords Traffic engineering Operation design domain Experimental design Autonomous driving Intelligent connected vehicles

0 Introduction

In recent years, many countries have tested and operated vehicles with different levels of autonomous driving. The Society of American Engineers (SAE) classifies autonomous driving into five levels. Specifically, L1-L2 cover driver assistance system. Despite the fact that automobile enterprises in many countries have commercially applied L1 and L2 technologies, many driver assistance functions have risks of inadequate response or failure in certain scenes (Galceran et al., 2017). L3-L5 represent autonomous driving systems. Presently, automobile manufacturers are still using different combinations of sensors (e.g., the global navigation satellite system (GNSS), inertial measurement unit (IMU), LIDAR, high-definition camera, millimeter-wave radar, ultrasonic radar), high-definition maps, computing processors, drive-by-wire systems and other assistance components to fulfill vehicle positioning, environmental perception, computational decision-making and control execution (Haghzare et al. ,2021, Yu et al. ,2016, Merriman et al. ,2021). However, due to the limitations of autonomous vehicles in terms of the capabilities of sensor perception, computation, planning and decision-making, it is difficult to ensure the operational safety of autonomous driving in all complicated working conditions (Malekzadeh et al., 2021). The reliability of autonomous driving and its capability to adapt to challenging traffic scenes still need to be improved. Therefore, autonomous vehicles can operate normally only in a limited range of conditions (Kaye et al., 2021, Winter et al. ,2021).

The operational design domain (ODD) of autonomous driving refers to the operational conditions set by theautonomous driving system, including environmental, geographic and timeslot limitations, traffic flow and road characteristics (P Joshué et al., 2011). Many factors can impose a limitation on ODD for autonomous driving. They include, for example, road conditions such as highway, uncontrolled intersections, urban and rural roads; environmental, weather (rain, snow and fog) and lighting conditions (day or night, backlighting, tunnel entrance/exit, night with or without road lamp lighting). Other factors include height limiting frame, vehicles involving failures or accidents, toll stations, puddles, low-hanging plants, road icing, snow accumulation, littered objects and human behaviors in violation of traffic rules (Stoll et al. ,2021).

The long-tail problem confronting vehicle perception is one of the main obstacles for the ODD ofautonomous vehicles. Subject to restrictions of sensor mounting locations on the vehicle, detectable distance, field of view, data throughput, calibration definition and time synchronization, vehicles still struggle to completely fulfill accurate perception and recognition and high-definition positioning when operated in conditions involving busy intersections, harsh weather, small objects, traffic signals and backlighting (Bian et al. ,2018). The restrictions of ODD are an important way to ensure vehicle safety, but they are not conducive to the large-scale commercialization of autonomous driving (Du et al., 2020). For example, the U. S. Congress hasn't passed any nationwide legislation about autonomous driving up to date; local governments like Arizona and Florida only require autonomous driving tests and pilot operations within prescribed areas to be implemented for autonomous vehicles (Siddiqui et al. ,2021).

Vehicle to Everything (V2X), a concept originating from the Internet of Things (IoT), allows the vehicle to communicate with traffic participants or infrastructural facilities nearby in forms of the communication between vehicles, vehicle and infrastructure, vehicle andpedestrians and vehicle and networks (Molina-Masegosa et al., 2017). With V2X, on the one hand, vehicles are able to use network communication as a means of perception to obtain information from other traffic participants or perceive a richer body of information by themselves, thus breaking the blind area of traditional vehicle-mounted sensors and promoting the study and development of the autonomous driving technology (Lu et al., 2021, Yu et al., 2021). On the other hand, by connecting traffic participants and elements like "pedestrians, vehicles, roads and clouds", the network infrastructure of a smart traffic system can be constructed, where the collaborative optimization technology can be used to fulfill the purposes of improving driving safety, traffic efficiency and passenger experience. V2X can essentially address the technological bottlenecks encountered by autonomous driving and improve autonomous driving capabilities, thereby ensuring safety and expanding the ODD of autonomous driving.

Drawing on methods and approaches adopted by developed countries in developing ODD of autonomous driving and in combination with the complexity and particularity of the actual transportation in China, an ODD test platform was designed and employed to test part of the functions of intelligent connected vehicles (ICVs), with a view of addressing the most pressing problems regarding autonomous driving test and safety of pilot operations.

1 Architecture design of Odd

Using built-in environmental models in combination with other vehicle-mounted sensors like the rain sensor, camera, high-definition map, wheel speed sensor, temperature sensor, LIDAR and millimeter-wave radar, information on known weather and road conditions, vehicle speed and traffic flow can be measured and matched with specific operational conditions of the autonomous driving system to ensure autonomous driving functions fall within an applicable safe environment (R Aufrère et al., 2003).

The conditions of ODD forautonomous driving are mainly comprised of road and driving conditions, traffic control facilities and roadside obstacles, environmental and V2X conditions. In this study, the specific restrictions for the ODD of ICVs are given and a test platform of the ODD for autonomous driving is constructed with a view of improving the safety of the tests and pilot operations of ICVs, thereby accelerating large-scale commercialization of advanced autonomous driving (Lerher et al., 2021, Rossi et al., 2021).

1.1 Road and Driving Conditions

Road condition requirements involve road types, road surface, road boundaries, road alignment and lane specifications. Road types mainly cover urban roads, crossings (intersections, circle island), tunnels and bridges; road surfaces are required to be paved with asphalt without cracks, potholes, slipperiness or accumulated water, snow and ice, but deceleration strips are allowed; for road boundaries, the presence of road shoulders, street lamps, roadside plants and lawns, guardrails and median strips is required, and roadside architecture like buildings are allowed; road alignments can be straight, curved, uphill/downhill roads; in terms of lane specifications, the minimum requirement is two-way four-lane roads which may be comprised of pedestrian crossings, sidewalks and non-motorized vehicle lanes, with clear and nonblurry lane markings.

For driving conditions, it is required that there must be limits on speed and traffic conditions. The traveling speed is limited to somewhere lower than 50 km/h; for traffic conditions, the traffic flow should be smooth with temporary minor traffic accidents, road closure, pedestrians and riders allowed.

1.2 Traffic Control Facilities and Roadside Obstacles

For traffic control facilities and roadside obstacles, traffic signs and movable/stationary obstacles are allowed. Specifically, the traffic signs are required to be signboards and LED display boards made in accordance with applicable specifications of China, which require the boards to be easily identifiable and traffic lights are not occluded by obstacles like trees and function normally so that the ICVs can easily recognize and read traffic semantic information; movable/stationary obstacles can be vehicles involving accidents and unknown littered objects on the ground, and other ICVs traveling in conformity with traffic rules are allowed.

1.3 Environmental and V2X Conditions

The environmental conditions mainly include weather and lighting conditions. Specifically, sunny and fog-free weather and daytime good lighting conditions are required.

The V2X compriseson board units (OBUs) and road side units (RSUs). Specifically, the OBUs involve vehicles with different connection and automation levels (Abboud et al., 2016); the RSUs encompass intelligent perception facilities (cameras, millimeter-wave radars, LIDARs); roadside communication facilities (direct wireless communication facilities, cellular mobile communication facilities); computational control facilities (edge computing nodes and cloud platforms); high-definition maps and assisted positioning facilities; and auxiliary facilities like electric utility facilities.

2 Driving Scenes Design of Odd

Thedriving scenes design in the test platform of ODD for autonomous driving include static driving scenes design and dynamic driving scenes design.

Specifically, the static driving scenes design refer to the planning and design of the test platform; while the dynamic driving scenes design involve the design of test routes and plans.

2.1 Static Driving Scenes

While considering road conditions, driving conditions, traffic control facilities, roadside obstacles, environmental conditions and V2X in the ODD forautonomous driving, the infrastructural facilities of the test platform include portable traffic signal lights, intersection video surveillance, bridges, rivers, trees, test buildings, street lamps, guardrails, concrete walls and vegetation. Road layout involves straight and curved road sections, entrances and exits and ramps. LED display boards that distinctly display test status reminders and warnings, as well as the simulated tunnel facilities capable of emulating different lighting and weather conditions, are deployed in the test field. To satisfy test requirements, lane specifications, traffic signal lights and signboards must be in conformity with applicable traffic standards.

The test platform established in this research is located in Tsinghua University Suzhou Automotive Research Institute. Fig. 1 is a real-scene photo of the completed test platform; Fig. 1a) shows the simulated tunnel entrance; Fig. 1b) shows the 4-lanestraight road area, which is also the main validation area for the test; Fig. 1c) depicts a fork road and ramps areas; Fig. 1d) shows the circle island and parking test areas.

a)tunnel

b)straight road

c)ramps

d)the circle island and parking

Fig. 1 The Test Platform Scenario

To meet the requirements ofICVs test, multi-module communication RSUs are deployed in addition to the OBUs deployed on vehicles to achieve not only V2X communication but also a roadside intelligent system encompassing roadside cameras, roadside tracking microwave radars that fulfill perception of pedestrians and vehicles, GNSS differential base stations aiming to enhance vehicle terminal perception and traffic lights supporting network connection - facilities that cover the whole test section (Xing et al., 2021). Network facilities and cloud control system servers are deployed at the cloud control center as the base cloud control platform. The distribution of facilities is shown in Fig. 2.

The diversified traffic conditions and network facilities of the test platform are able to satisfy the multi-scenario requirement of theICVs test. Fig. 3 is the real-scene image of hardware facilities; Fig. 3a) shows the cloud server and network facilities; Fig. 3b) shows the portable roadside intelligent system integrating network-connected traffic lights, RSUs and solar power supply facility; Fig. 3c) shows the roadside cameras and RSUs on vertical poles; Fig. 3d) shows the OBU and shark fin antenna.

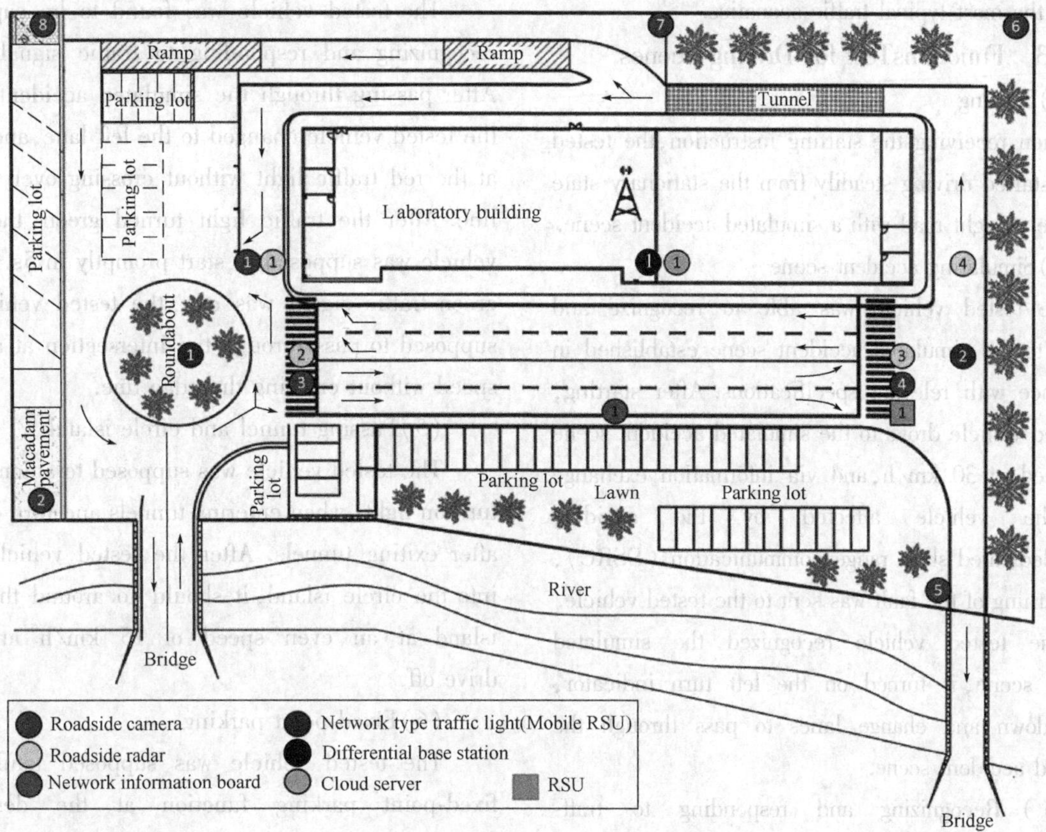

Fig. 2　The Distribution of Roadside Facilities

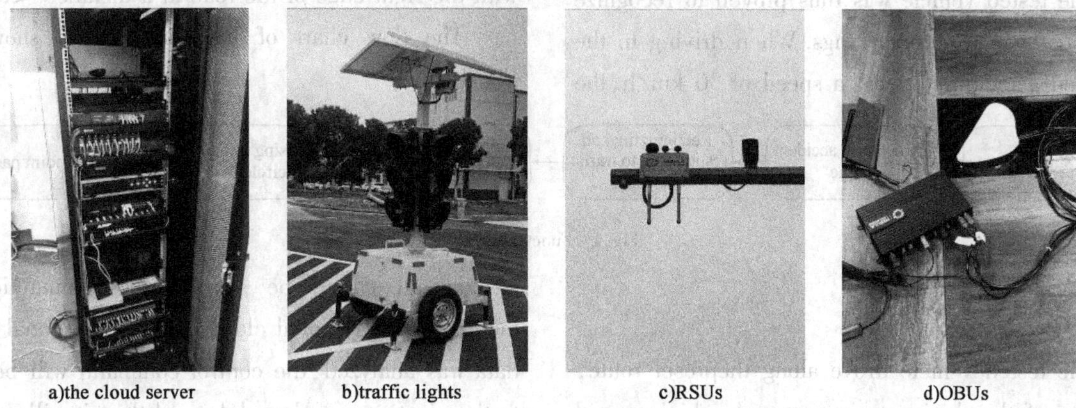

a)the cloud server　b)traffic lights　c)RSUs　d)OBUs

Fig. 3　Hardware Facilities

2.2　Dynamic Driving Scenes

The question of whether smartICVs were able to fulfill certain autonomous driving functions within the ODD was explored to validate the reasonability of ODD. The typical application scenarios of V2X included early warnings for collision and road hazards (Maimone et al., 2005, Sotelo et al., 2004). The ICV was able to recognize pedestrians, obstacles, motor vehicles, non-motor vehicles, traffic markings and lights, and complete autonomous driving within the ODD (including starting, vehicle following, lane changing and overtaking). In the meantime, the tested vehicle also fulfilled functions like driving through the circle island, obstacle avoidance, fixed-point parking, emergency braking and manual takeover. A test scheme of functions of the autonomous driving system was designed with a consideration of some of the most typical traffic scenarios.

2.3 FunctionsTest for Driving Scenes

(1)Starting

When receiving the starting instruction, the tested vehicle started driving steadily from the stationary state along the straight road with a simulated accident scene.

(2)Simulating accident scene

The tested vehicle was able to recognize and respond to the simulated accident scene established in accordance with relevant specifications. After starting, the tested vehicle drove to the simulated accident scene at a speed of 30 km/h, and via information exchange with the vehicle affected by the accident throughdedicated short range communication (DSRC), early warning of the fault was sent to the tested vehicle. After the tested vehicle recognized the simulated accident scene, it turned on the left turn indicator, slowed down and change lanes to pass through the simulated accident scene.

(3) Recognizing and responding to traffic markings

The tested vehicle was thus proven to recognize and respond to traffic markings. When driving to the simulated accident scene at a speed of 30 km/h, the tested vehicle was required to recognize the broken lane boundary lines and choose to cross over the crossable boundary line area to bypass the obstacle.

(4)Recognizing and responding to traffic lights

The tested vehicle was found to be capable of recognizing and responding to traffic signal lights. After passing through the simulated accident scene, the tested vehicle changed to the left lane, and waited at the red traffic light without crossing over the stop line. After the traffic light turned green, the tested vehicle was supposed to start promptly in 5s. When a green traffic signal was one, the tested vehicle was supposed to pass through the intersection at a steady speed without crossing the edge line.

(5)Passing tunnel and circle island

The tested vehicle was supposed to automatically turn on lights when entering tunnels and turn off them after exiting tunnels. After the tested vehicle drove into the circle island, it should go around the circle island at an even speed of 15 km/h and then drive off.

(6)Fixed-point parking

The tested vehicle was supposed tofulfill the fixed-point parking function at the designated location, with the vehicle body basically in parallel with the right edge of the road at a distance ≤50cm.

The flow chart of functions test is shown in Fig. 4.

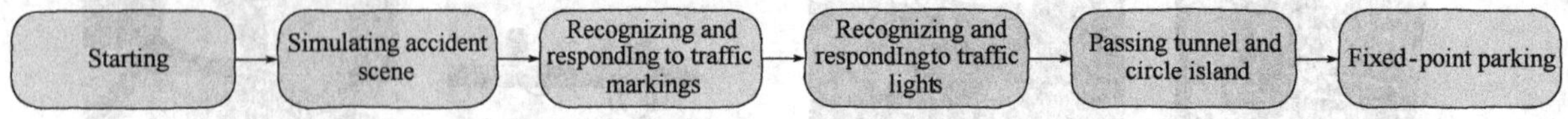

Fig. 4　Functions Test

3 A Case Study

The tested vehicle drove along thepreset route, and data of the driving trajectory and vehicle speed were transmitted by the OBUs via V2X to the cloud platform, RSUs received data packets from OBUs, and the edge cloud maintained the connection between cloud platform and RSUs device through the data communication module to receive and parse data packets (Nsp et al., 2019). If it is a request that needs to be sent to the regional cloud for application scheduling, it will be sent to the communication module of the regional cloud. After the regional cloud data was analyzed, the control command will be sent to the cluster control module, and then it will call the interface of Kubernetes for scheduling control of container applications on the edge cloud. This part of the task is completed by the cluster communication component of Kubernetes. Whether creating a new computing task container or migrating the original container, the deployment of the computing task module container will be completed on the target node according to the request (Zhang et al., 2019). After that, when the terminal sent the calculation task execution data, the communication module of the device directly forwarded the data to the Service discovery module, and then transferred the calculation data to the calculation task module. The data was sent back to OBUs through the RSUs to complete the calculation task execution process (Chen et al., 2017, Huang et al., 2020). And the connectivity test is conducted the principle of information interaction is shown in Fig. 5.

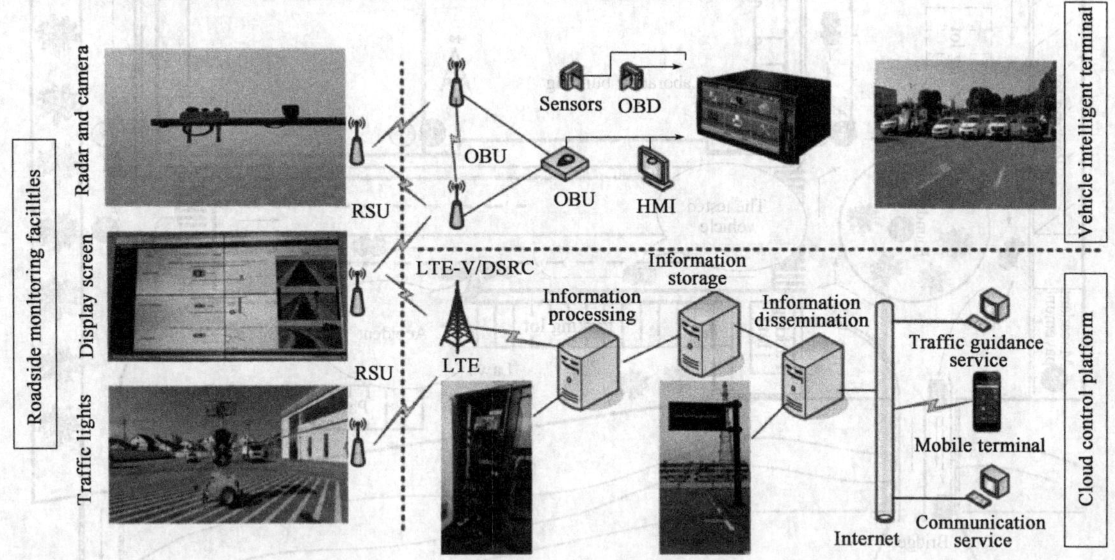

Fig. 5 Information Interaction Principle

3.1 Experimental Design

An intelligent connected vehicle was used as the tested vehicle, which consisted of the following parts: 1 32-wire LIDAR, 2 16-wire LIDARs, 1millimeter-wave radar, 3 front cameras, 1 rear camera, 4 side cameras, 1 GPS antenna, 1 inertia measurement unit, 1 industrial computer and OBUs. The OBUs of the tested vehicle were able to directly communicate with RSUs to fulfill information interaction and sharing between vehicle and road. The driving route is shown in Fig. 6. Functions tested included vehicle starting, recognition of traffic signs, markings and obstacles, passing through the simulated scene by changing lanes, driving straight, passing through tunnels, passing through circle islands and curb parking with a view of validating the performance of the intelligent connected vehicle system within the predesigned ODD.

3.2 Results

The speed-time data of the tested vehicle is shown in Fig. 7. As shown in the figure, the tested vehicle started at 0-2s, accelerated during 3-10s, reached a speed of 30km/h at the point of 11s, and drove at an even speed of 30 km/h during 11-19s. At this moment, the vehicle recognized the simulated accident scene 20m ahead. By recognizing that there were crossable lane lines, the tested vehicle made the decision to slow down and change lanes by turning on the left-turn indicator. The tested vehicle successfully changed lanes during 19-22s, retained the speed of 30km/h during 22-28s and traveled at the even speed of 30km/h during 28-36s. When detecting a red traffic signal ahead, the tested vehicle started to slow down and stop. The 46-64s interval was the time when the tested vehicle waited at the red light. During 65-68s, the green light was on, the tested vehicle started and passed through the intersection in a left turn. Around 76-81s, the tested vehicle entered the tunnel, where it turned on the lights and passed through the tunnel at an even speed of 30km/h. During 93-107s, the tested vehicle accelerated its speed after exiting from the tunnel, and then slowed down to turn left. Around 113-117s, it entered the circle island. During the 117-128s, the vehicle passed through the circle island at an even speed of 15 km/h. After the 129s, the vehicle exited the circle island and eventually pulled over at an appropriate place.

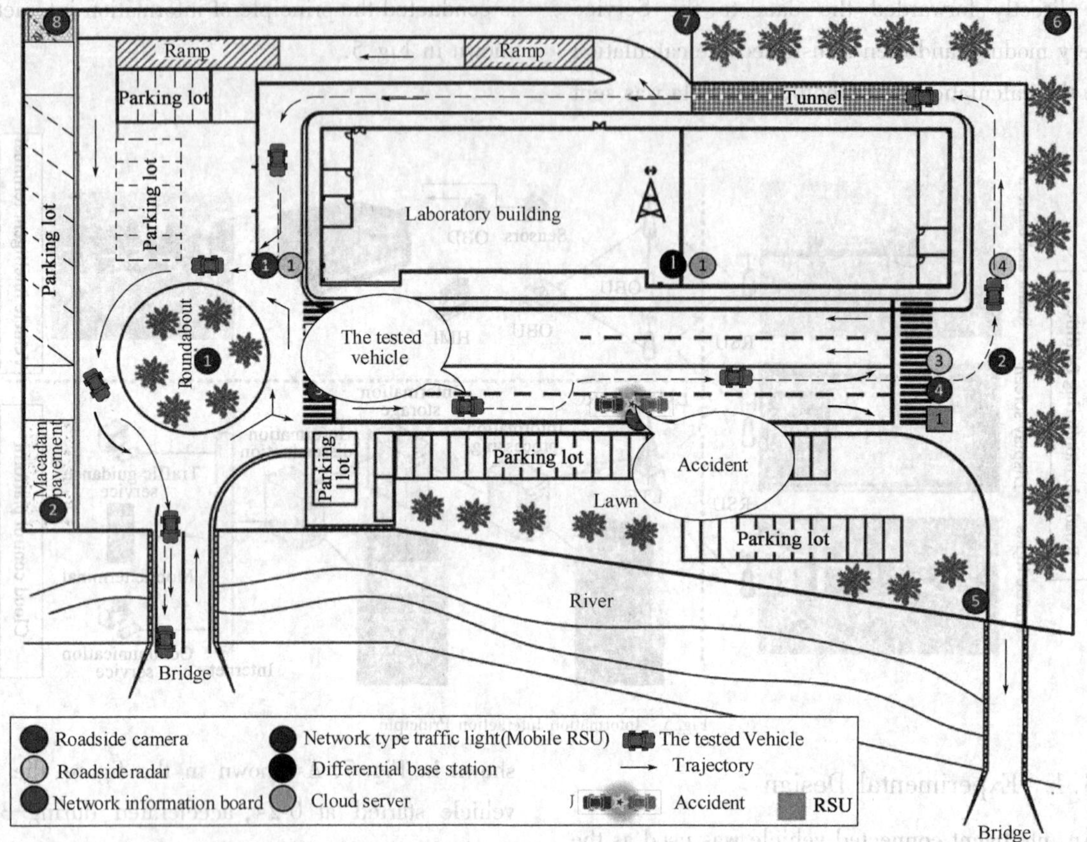

Fig. 6 The Driving Route

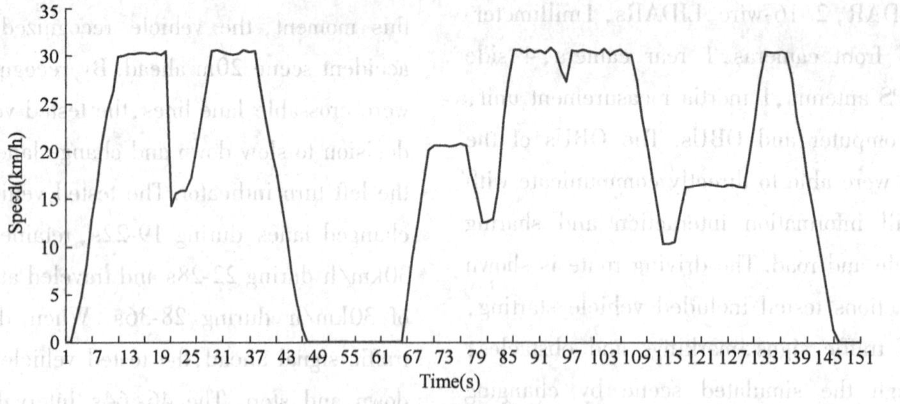

Fig. 7 Speed-Time Chart

4 Conclusions

Based on the present transportations and typical traffic scenarios in China, in combination with the specific conditions relating to ODD for autonomous driving, a test platform of ODD for autonomous driving was established. A real vehicle test validated that the platform fulfills the requirements of test and pilot operation of ICVs. The research represents an exploratory attempt to design the ODD for autonomous driving in China, lays a foundation for subsequent experiments and provides references for future studies.

The test of V2X technology plays a positive role

in promoting ICVs and intelligent roads in China. To fulfill the large-scale commercialization of autonomous driving, challenges and problems relating to safety, ODD restrictions and economic efficiency should be addressed. With present autonomous driving capabilities, there is still an inability to find a balance among these targets. Therefore, to achieve early large-scale commercialization of autonomous driving, it is imperative to conduct in-depth research and tests of the deep integration of vehicle and road and accelerate the deployment of advanced intelligent roads, thereby providing higher-dimensional data for smart traffic, trips and cities and bringing more smart applications while ensuring the safety and rapid commercialization of autonomous driving.

5 Acknowledgements

This work is supported by the National Natural Science Foundation of China (52002215); the Jiangsu Science and Technology Project (BE2021011-4); the Research Project of Hubei Provincial Department of Education (D20212901); the Hubei Science and Technology Project (2021BEC005, 2021BLB225) and the Hong Kong Scholars Program (XJ2021028). Special thanks go to the lion team of TSARI for providing field test data.

References

[1] Abboud, K., Omar, H., Zhuang, W. Interworking ofdsrc and cellular network technologies for v2x communications: a survey [J]. IEEE, Transactions on Vehicular Technology, 2016: 9457-9470.

[2] Bian, M., Li, K. Strategic analysis on establishing an automobile power in china based on intelligent connected vehicles [J]. Chinese Journal of Engineering Science, 2018, 20 (1): 52.

[3] Chen, S., Hu, J., Yan, S., et al. Vehicle-to-everything (v2x) services supported bylte-based systems and 5g [J]. IEEE Communications Standards Magazine, 2017, 1(2): 70-76.

[4] Du, X., Lv, D., Li, S., et al. Coordinated control algorithm at non-recurrent freeway bottlenecks for intelligent and connected vehicles [J]. IEEE Access, 2020.

[5] Galceran, E., Cunningham, A. G., Eustice, R. M., & Olson, E. Multipolicy decision-making for autonomous driving via changepoint-based behavior prediction: theory and experiment [J]. Autonomous Robots, 2017, 41(6): 1-16.

[6] Haghzare, S., Campos, J. L., Bak, K., et al. Older adults' acceptance of fully automated vehicles: effects of exposure, driving style, age, and driving conditions [J]. Accident Analysis & Prevention, 2021, 150(5), 105919.

[7] Huang, J., Fang, D., Qian, Y., et al. Recent advances and challenges in security and privacy for v2x communications [J]. IEEE Open Journal of Vehicular Technology, 2020, 1: 244-266.

[8] Kaye S. A., Demmel S., Oviedo-Trespalacios O., et al. Young drivers' takeover time in a conditional automated vehicle: the effects of hand-held mobile phone use and future intentions to use automated vehicles [J]. Transportation Research PartF Traffic Psychology and Behaviour, 2021, 78(2): 16.

[9] Lerher T., Ficko M., Pali, I. Throughput performance analysis of automated vehicle storage and retrieval systems with multiple-tier shuttle vehicles [J]. Applied Mathematical Modelling, 2021, 91: 1004-1022.

[10] Lu Q. L., Qurashi M., Varesanovic D., et al. Exploring the influence of automated driving styles on network efficiency [J]. Transportation Research Procedia, 2021, 52(9): 380-387.

[11] Maimone M., Biesiadecki J. J., Leger C. Tradeoffs between directed and autonomous driving on the mars exploration rovers [J]. The International Journal of Robotics Research, 2005, 26(1): 91-104.

[12] Malekzadeh M., Papamichail I., Papageorgiou M. Internal boundary control of lane-free automated vehicle traffic using a model-free adaptive controller -sciencedirect [J]. IFAC-PapersOnLine, 2021, 54(2): 99-106.

[13] Merriman S. E., Plant K. L., Revell K., et al.

Challenges for automated vehicle driver training: a thematic analysis from manual and automated driving[J]. Transportation Research Part F: Traffic Psychology andBehaviour, 2021,76:238-268.

[14] Molina-Masegosa R., Gozalvez J. Lte-v for sidelink 5g v2x vehicular communications: a new 5g technology for short-range vehicle-to-everything communications [J]. IEEE Vehicular Technology Magazine,2017,12(4):30-39.

[15] Nsp B., Hr A. Review of research on v2x technologies, strategies, and operations. Renewable and Sustainable Energy Reviews, 2019,105:61-70.

[16] P Joshué, Vicente, M., Tere D. P., et al. Autonomous driving manoeuvres in urban road traffic environment: a study on roundabouts. IFAC Proceedings Volumes, 2011, 44 (1): 13795-13800.

[17] R Aufrère Gowdy J., Mertz C., et al. Perception for collision avoidance and autonomous driving[J]. Mechatronics, 2003, 13(10):1149-1161.

[18] Rossi R., Gastaldi M., Orsini F., et al. A comparative simulator study of reaction times to yellow traffic light under manual and automated driving[J]. Transportation Research Procedia,2021,52:276-283.

[19] Siddiqui A. J., Boukerche A. A novel lightweight defense method against adversarial patches-based attacks on automated vehicle make and model recognition systems [J]. Journal of Network and Systems Management, 29(4):1-33.

[20] Sotelo M. N., F J Rodríguez, Magdalena L., et al. A color vision-based lane tracking system for autonomous driving on unmarked roads. Autonomous Robots,2004,16(1):95-116.

[21] Stoll T., K Mühl, Baumann M. Do drivers accept cooperative behavior of their automated vehicle on highways? -sciencedirect[J]. Transportation Research Part F: Traffic Psychology and Behaviour,2021,77:236-245.

[22] Winter K., Cats O., Martens K., et al. Parking space for shared automated vehicles: how less can be more[J]. Transportation Research Part A Policy and Practice, 2021, 143(143):61-77.

[23] Xing Y., Lv C., Cao D., et al. Toward human-vehicle collaboration: review and perspectives on human-centered collaborative automated driving [J]. Transportation Research Part C Emerging Technologies,2021,128(5),103199.

[24] Yu, Richard F. Connected vehicles for intelligent transportation systems [guest editorial][J]. IEEE Transactions on Vehicular Technology,2016,65(6):3843-3844.

[25] Yu B., Bao S., Zhang Y., et al. Measurement and prediction of driver trust in automated vehicle technologies: an application of hand position transition probability matrix [J]. Transportation Research Part C Emerging Technologies,2021,124(5),102957.

[26] Zhang D, Liu Y, Dai L, et al. Performance analysis of fd-noma-based decentralized v2x systems [J]. IEEE Transactions on Communications,1-1.

L3自动驾驶接管过程中的TTC分析

张子号 潘梦妞 刘 钦 李振龙*

(北京工业大学城市建设学部)

摘 要 为研究非驾驶相关任务(NDRT)和驾驶人属性对L3自动驾驶接管全过程中纵向安全性的

精细化影响。本文基于驾驶模拟器搭建了高速公路事故接管场景,招募42名驾驶人进行驾驶模拟实验,以碰撞预警时间(Time To Collision,TTC)为基础,从接管全过程中提炼出接管点TTC、避险点TTC、危险段TTC均值和标准差四个指标精准表征车辆的纵向安全性。运用统计分析方法分析NDRT、性别、年龄、驾龄对接管点TTC、避险点TTC、危险段TTC均值和标准差是否具有显著影响。结果表明,性别属性对避险点TTC、危险段TTC均值和标准差有显著影响;驾龄对危险段TTC的均值和标准差有显著影响;年龄对危险段TTC均值有显著影响。研究结论可用于L3自动驾驶车辆接管后纵向安全性预警设计。

关键词 L3自动驾驶 碰撞预警时间 统计分析 接管 驾驶人属性

0 引言

汽车自动驾驶技术近年来发展迅速。在谷歌、特斯拉等公司推出了自动驾驶系统之后,宝马、奔驰和奥迪等老牌汽车厂商也相继发布了功能相似的自动驾驶系统,并且在一定的技术范围内开展了道路测试[1]。美国、日本、英国等发达国家也制定了完全自动驾驶汽车的发展规划,明确指出了自动驾驶汽车在减少道路交通事故方面的重要作用[2]。

可以预见的是,随着自动驾驶技术的发展,自动驾驶汽车将在人们的出行中占有重要地位,为此国际汽车工程师协会将自动驾驶汽车划分为L0~L5共六个等级,因为技术和法律的限制,目前自动驾驶汽车研究的聚焦点主要集中在L3级自动驾驶。L3自动驾驶也称有条件自动驾驶(SAE,L3级),它是指系统自己执行全部的动态驾驶任务,驾驶人不必一直从事驾驶任务,而是可以从事其他非驾驶相关任务,例如,玩手机、听音乐、看视频等,但是当车辆面临的情况是自动驾驶系统无法处理的,系统就会发出接管请求,这时要求驾驶人能够及时安全的接管车辆的控制权[3]。早期道路安全仿真模型中常用的冲突度量方法是[4]碰撞预警时间(TTC),TTC的一般定义[5]为"当两辆车以当前车速沿同一路线行驶时发生碰撞的时间"。在国内外研究中,TTC常用于确定道路安全性,或用它来确定车辆能否安全通过前方事故[6]。在L3自动驾驶接管领域,TTC也作为接管绩效的一部分用于表征接管时的纵向安全性。Happee等[7]的研究发现,TTC和最小距离障碍物的间距在评价紧急接管避让操作时是非常好的指标。Gold等[8]建立了以接管时间、最小碰撞时间(最小TTC)、刹车应用和碰撞概率为接管绩效变量的预测模型,研究结果表明,接管时间、最小碰撞时间对碰撞概率模型具有较好的预测效果。林庆峰等[9]研究了城市道路环境高度自动驾驶下非驾驶相关任务和接管紧迫度对接管绩效的影响,结果表明在紧急接管情况下,接管紧迫度对合成加速度和最小TTC有影响,而对接管时间无影响,非驾驶相关任务对接管时间和最小TTC有影响。

以往的研究中不仅将TTC作为接管绩效的一部分来分析接管过程的好坏,也研究了非驾驶相关任务、接管紧迫度等因素对接管绩效中TTC的影响。然而,关于对接管后TTC精细化分析及其影响因素方面的研究相对较少,进而从接管过程中TTC分布上评估驾驶员接管车辆后的纵向安全性方面的研究有所缺失。为解决这一问题,本文利用高速公路上常见的事故场景来获取接管数据,分析驾驶员从接管时刻点到安全变换车道完成点之间TTC的分布情况,探究不同的非驾驶相关任务和驾驶人自身属性在接管过程中TTC的差异性,研究结论可以帮助我们了解接管后驾驶员驾驶车辆时的纵向安全情况,为后续自动驾驶车辆接管后的安全评估提供理论参考。

1 实验方法

1.1 实验被试

该实验共招募了42名被试(男性32名,女性10名),被试的平均年龄为42.53岁(标准差15.85岁),平均驾龄为17.06年(标准差12.17年),所有被试均具有有效的驾驶执照资格。驾驶员类型划分符合我国驾驶员群体个人特征分布[10]。实验前,每位受试者填写基本信息表和KSS疲劳量表,确定自己的身体健康状况、疲劳程度以及是否服用药物。被试需在实验前了解整个实验过程,然后如实填写知情同意书。

1. 基金项目:国家自然科学基金项目(10038002201801)。

1.2　驾驶模拟器

本研究依托于建有驾驶模拟器的自动驾驶接管测试平台(图1),实验平台所用设备为北京工业大学 Auto-Sim-AS 驾驶模拟系统、硬件包络驾驶模拟舱、6 台高性能电脑、HMI 平板电脑、Eye-Tracking-Core + 眼镜眼动仪等设备,驾驶模拟器内置软件为 SCANeR1.9 系统,系统通过外部接口连接,实现人、车、路的整体连接。在此基础上,本文以驾驶仿真实验为核心,开发了一套适用于自动驾驶接管测试的典型场景,自动驾驶接管测试通过合理的实验设计,可以获得驾驶人在自动驾驶接管过程中的车辆运动学数据,如车速、方向盘转角、横向和纵向加速度、车辆行驶里程等,可用于综合评估驾驶人接管行为。

图1　驾驶模拟实验平台

1.3　非驾驶相关任务的类型和接管时间预算

驾驶人在车辆自动驾驶过程中会做一些与驾驶无关的事情,称为非驾驶相关任务(Non-driving-related tasks,NDRT),与驾驶无关的任务造成的沉浸感会影响驾驶人将注意力转移到驾驶任务上的效率,本次实验选取了两种常见的非驾驶相关任务,即工作任务(发微信)和娱乐任务(看视频)。接管时间预算(Take over request time,TOR)是指从系统发送"接管请求消息"到驾驶员接管车辆的持续时间,且 Ito 等[11] 发现 5s 的接管时间预算恰好能够完成接管任务,所以本次实验我们预设的接管时间预算为 5s。

1.4　接管场景

接管场景是选取的事故接管场景,测试道路为双向四车道的高速公路,道路状况良好,事故点处正常车道无法通行,被试需要接管车辆后绕道从应急车道通过事故路段(图2),为了避免驾驶员在接管场景中受到交互效应的影响,两种接管场景被随机划分在不同的道路上,路段1:内蒙古高速公路—接管时间预算 5s—发微信;路段2:北京城郊高速公路—接管时间预算 5s—看视频。高速公路正常路段限速值 120km/h,自动驾驶时车速为 100km/h。前方出现预设的事故时,自动驾驶系统按照预先设定的接管时间预算向被试发出接管请求提示信息(声音 + HMI 界面闪烁提示)。接管提示声音为"前方 XX,请接管车辆!"事故路段被试接管车辆后需按照 HMI 限速提示在 60km/h 以下行驶,从手动驾驶切换成自动驾驶后,车速逐渐恢复到 100km/h。

1.5　实验流程

根据实验设计,本实验需进行两个场景的驾驶模拟测试,同时为保证实验数据的有效性,每位被试在实验场景里的起点随机,实验具体流程如下:

(1)被试实验前需要填写基本信息表,生理状态表(疲劳程度等)、知情同意书(告知参与本次实验的相关事项并征得本人同意)。

(2)对被试进行实验前的驾驶培训和练习。

(3)被试佩戴好测试设备后,按照实验指导员指令完成第一个实验场景测试。

(4)被试完成第一个实验场景测试后,休息 10 ~ 15min。

(5)休息结束后开始第二个实验场景测试。

(6)实验结束后。被试填写主观问卷并登记劳务信息。

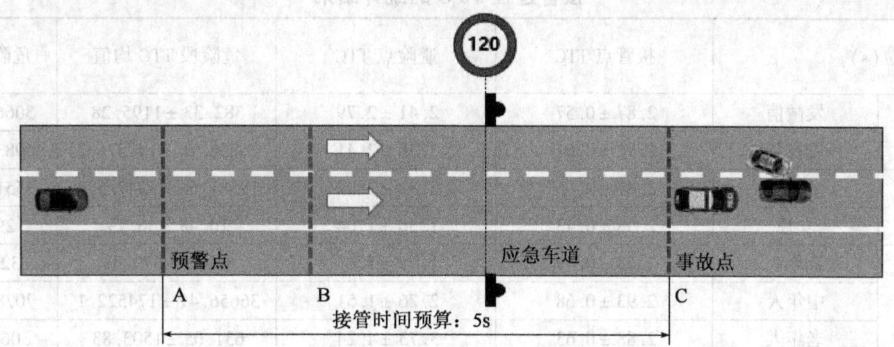

图 2 事故接管场景

1.6 数据预处理和和指标的选取

本次实验共获得事故场景下的 84 条接管数据，剔除掉 16 条无效数据后可获得 68 条有效数据，本文选取接管过程中的 TTC 作为评价指标，接管过程中的 TTC 按照接管过程可划分为接管点 TTC、避险点 TTC、危险段 TTC 均值、危险段 TTC 标准差。具体定义如下：

（1）碰撞预警时间（TTC）

碰撞预警时间是指自车与前方道路上事故点的碰撞时间（TTC）。碰撞预警时间的计算公式如式（1）所示：

$$\mathrm{TTC} = \frac{S}{V} \tag{1}$$

式中：TTC——自车的碰撞预警时间，s；

S——自车距离前方事故点的距离，m；

V——自车当前的速度，m/s。

（2）接管点 TTC

被试在收到系统发出的接管请求信息后，被试反应过来按下手动驾驶接管按钮那一刻的碰撞预警时间。

（3）避险点 TTC

被试接管车辆后，需要变换车道在应急车道上行驶才可以安全通过事故点，驾驶员在从正常车道向应急车道换道时的碰撞预警时间称为避险点 TTC。

（4）危险段 TTC 均值和标准差

危险段是指从被试接管车辆时的接管点至避险点之间的区段。该区段所有 TTC 的均值称为危险段 TTC 均值，用来衡量驾驶员在该区段内 TTC 的平均水平；该区段所有 TTC 的标准差称为危险段 TTC 的标准差，用来衡量区段内 TTC 的波动幅度。

使用 python 提取和计算事故场景下的接管点 TTC，避险点 TTC、危险段 TTC 均值、危险段 TTC 标准差，事故场景下接管过程中 TTC 的关键点位置如图 3 所示。

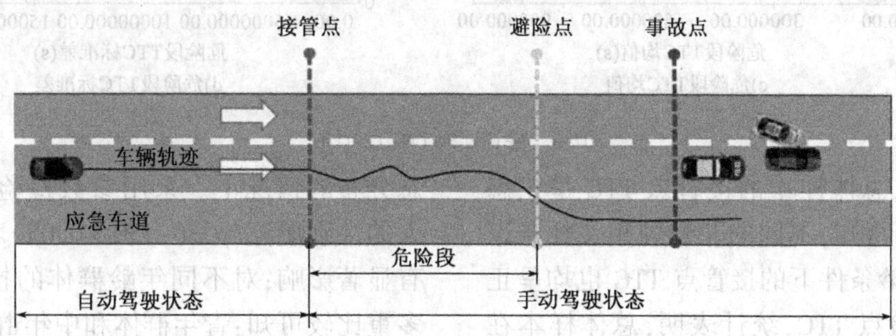

图 3 事故接管场景指标示意图

2 结果分析

2.1 统计分析

对获得的有效数据进行统计分析，分析数据时需要考虑的影响因素包括非驾驶相关任务（发微信、看视频）、性别（男性、女性）、年龄（青年人、中年人、老年人）、驾龄（低驾龄、中驾龄、高驾龄）等条件对 TTC 的影响，不同条件下接管过程 TTC 的统计结果如表 1 所示。图 4 为接管点 TTC、避险点 TTC、危险段 TTC 均值、危险段 TTC 标准差的统计直方图。

接管过程 TTC 的统计结果　　表 1

单位(s)		接管点 TTC	避险点 TTC	危险段 TTC 均值	危险段 TTC 标准差
非驾驶相关任务	发微信	2.87 ±0.57	2.41 ±2.79	382.33 ±1195.28	3066.62 ±12093.84
	看视频	2.92 ±0.64	2.38 ±2.41	25856.76 ±147578.7	498301.4 ±2857553
性别	男性	2.87 ±0.66	2.82 ±2.92	18581.66 ±124725.8	355123.4 ±2415337
	女性	2.98 ±0.43	1.36 ±1.04	10.48 ±36.79	29.63 ±126.51
年龄	青年人	2.88 ±0.49	1.75 ±1.69	81.38 ±379.33	323.29 ±1566.8
	中年人	2.93 ±0.68	2.26 ±1.51	36656.41 ±174522.1	707850.1 ±3379177
	老年人	2.88 ±0.63	3.73 ±4.24	631.05 ±1503.83	3066.18 ±7111.07
驾龄	低驾龄	2.89 ±0.47	1.71 ±1.59	71.83 ±355.73	283.44 ±1469.40
	中驾龄	2.76 ±0.71	2.74 ±1.89	44012.97 ±190328.3	849510.5 ±3685404
	高驾龄	3.07 ±0.64	3.34 ±4.17	598.20 ±1510.94	2952.05 ±7140.89

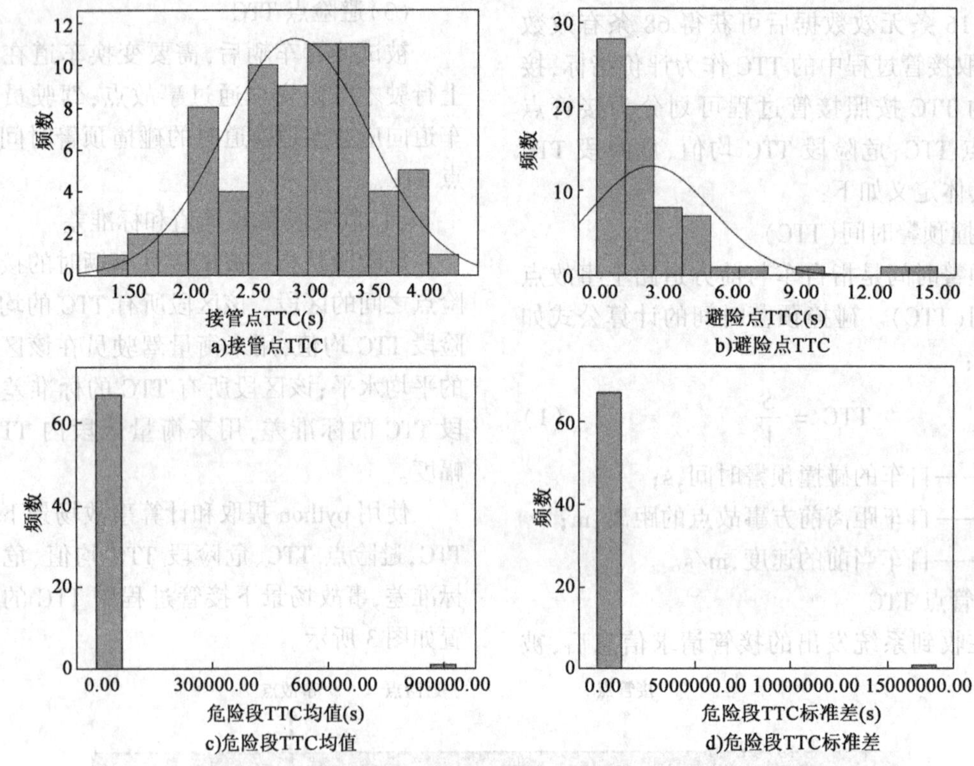

图 4　接管过程 TTC 直方图

如图 4 所示,总体样本的接管点 TTC 呈正态分布,进一步分析可知,不同的非驾驶相关任务以及性别、年龄、驾龄条件下的接管点 TTC 也均呈正态分布;对于避险点 TTC,统计表明,总体样本在不同非驾驶相关任务、性别、年龄、驾龄条件下均不呈正态分布;危险段 TTC 均值、危险段 TTC 标准差的样本数据均不呈正态分布。

2.2　非驾驶相关任务和驾驶人属性对接管过程中 TTC 的影响

从图 5a) 可以看出,在接管点 TTC 总体成正态分布的情况下。采用参数检验分析可知,驾驶人的性别属性($p=0.430>0.05$)对接管点 TTC 没有显著影响;对不同年龄群体的接管点 TTC 进行多重比较可知:青年群体和中年群体($p=0.771$),青年群体和老年群体($p=0.999$),中年群体和老年群体($p=0.801$)条件下的接管点 TTC 均无显著性差异;从表 4 能看出接管点 TTC 均值:高驾龄 > 低驾龄 > 中驾龄,但对驾龄群体的接管点 TTC 进行方差分析知,不同驾龄群体之间($p=0.305$)的接管点 TTC 没有显著性差异。

由图 4b) 可知,避险点 TTC 样本数据未成正态分布，因此对样本数据做非参数检验。如图5b)所示，男性群体的避险点TTC均值为2.82s，女性群体的避险点TTC均值为1.36s，男性群体的避险点TTC大于女性群体避险点TTC，表明性别属性($p=0.02<0.05$)在避险点TTC上有显著性差异，其原因可能是男性驾驶员能够在接管车辆后较早的操纵车辆完成变道避让事故车辆，进而导致男性驾驶员和女性驾驶员在避险点处的纵向安全性不同；不同年龄群体条件下($p=0.267$)的避险点TTC无显著性差异；驾龄群体的避险点TTC($p=0.167$)无显著性差异。

对于危险段TTC，由图5c)可知，危险段TTC均值在性别属性上：男性群体>女性群体，性别属性($p=0.02<0.05$)对危险段TTC均值有显著影响，出现这一结果的原因可能与大部分男性驾驶员在接管车辆后减速控制车辆的动作比女性驾驶员快有关。年龄属性($p=0.017<0.05$)和驾龄属性($p=0.036<0.05$)在危险段TTC均值上也有显著性差异，具体表现为青年人群体和中年人群体($p=0.044$)的危险段TTC均值存在显著性差异，中年人的危险段TTC均值高于青年人；说明中年人在遇到危险事件接管车辆后可能大多选择减速观望道路状况，在处理道路突发情况上比青年人持有更为谨慎的态度，进而导致中年人的危险段TTC均值高于青年人；低驾龄群体和高驾龄群体的危险段TTC均值有显著性差异，低驾龄群体的危险段TTC均值低于高驾龄。这可能与低驾龄群体驾驶员相较于高驾龄群体的驾驶经验更为匮乏，在突发情况下更多选择较低的速度通过突发事件现场的驾驶心理有关。

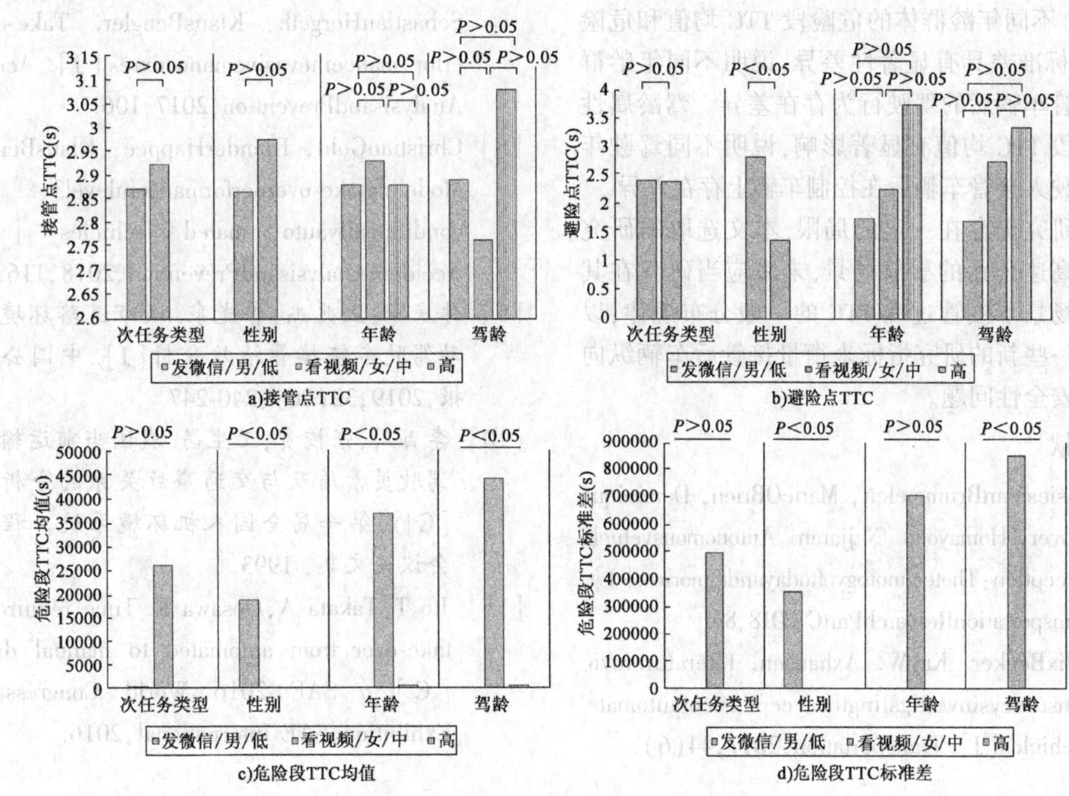

图5 非驾驶相关任务和驾驶人属性对TTC的影响

图5d)表明，危险段TTC标准差在性别属性($p=0.004<0.05$)上有显著性差异，男性驾驶员的危险段TTC波动幅度相较女性更大，表明男性驾驶员接管后的驾驶行为可能比女性驾驶员更为激进，出现急刹车、急加速的情况更多；年龄属性($p=0.056$)的危险段TTC标准差均无显著性差异；驾龄群体之间($p=0.032<0.05$)的危险段TTC标准差有显著性差异，具体表现为低驾龄群体和高驾龄群体之间的危险段TTC标准差有显著性差异，危险段TTC标准差：高驾龄>低驾龄，体现了高驾龄驾驶员相比低驾龄驾驶员在驾驶控制车辆上可能更为流畅、平稳地把握车辆行驶状态。

非驾驶相关任务对接管点TTC、避险点TTC、危险段TTC均值、危险段TTC标准差均不存在显著性影响。

3　结语

本研究基于驾驶仿真实验获得了高速公路上事故场景下的接管数据,分析了 L3 自动驾驶中非驾驶相关任务和驾驶人属性对接管过程中 TTC 的影响,具体的结论如下:

(1)非驾驶相关任务对接管过程中的 TTC 没有显著性影响,驾驶人的属性在接管点 TTC 上没有显著性差异,驾驶人的年龄、驾龄对避险点 TTC 均没有显著性影响。

(2)性别属性对避险点 TTC、危险段 TTC 均值、标准差均有显著影响,且呈现为男性驾驶人的避险点 TTC、危险段 TTC 均值、危险段 TTC 标准差均大于女性驾驶人,表明男性驾驶人和女性驾驶人在接管车辆后的驾驶行为上存在差异。

(3)不同年龄群体的危险段 TTC 均值和危险段 TTC 标准差具有显著性差异,说明不同年龄群体在接管车辆后的驾驶行为存在差异。驾龄属性对危险段 TTC 均值有显著影响,说明不同驾驶年限的驾驶人接管车辆后在控制车辆上存在差异。

本研究仍存在一定的局限,本文选取的研究场景是高速公路的事故场景,未来应当研究在其他道路场景下接管过程 TTC 的一般分布规律,以及提取一些新的研究指标来衡量接管后车辆纵向行驶的安全性问题。

参考文献

[1] JessicaVanBrummelen, MarieOBrien, Dominique Gruyer, Homayoun Najjaran. Autonomousvehicle perception: Thetechnologyoftodayandtomorrow[J]. TransportationResearchPartC,2018,89.

[2] FelixBecker, KayW. Axhausen. Literaturereviewonsurveysinvestigatingtheacceptanceofautomatedvehicles[J]. Transportation,2017,44(6).

[3] SayedT, BrownG, NavinF. Simulation oftrafficconflictsatunsignalizedinterse ctionswithTSC-Sim[J]. Accident Analysis& Prevention, 1994, 26(5):593-607.

[4] SayedTarek, BrownGerald, NavinFrancis. Simulationoftrafficconflictsatunsignalizedintersections withTSC-Sim [J]. AccidentAnalysis&Prevention,1994,26(5).

[5] HaywardJC. Nearmissdeterminationthroughuseof ascaleof danger[J]. HighwayResearch Record,1972.

[6] WilliamH. Levison. InteractiveHighwaySafety DesignModel: IssuesRelatedtoDriverModeling [J]. Transpor tation ResearchRecord, 1998, 1631(1).

[7] RienderHappee, ChristianGold, JonasRadlmayr, SebastianHergeth, KlausBengler. Take-overperfor manceinevasivemanoeuvres[J]. Accident AnalysisandPrevention,2017,106.

[8] ChristianGold, RienderHappee, KlausBengler. Modelingtake-overperformanceinlevel3 conditionallyauto mated vehicles [J]. AccidentAnalysisandPrevention,2018,116.

[9] 林庆峰,王兆杰,鲁光泉. 城市道路环境下自动驾驶车辆接管绩效分析[J]. 中国公路学报,2019,32(06):240-247.

[10] 李百川,张校贵,王生昌. 我国当前运输生产驾驶员素质及与交通事故关系的分析研究[C]//第一届全国人机环境系统工程学术会议论文集, 1993.

[11] Ito T, Takata A, Oosawa K. Time required for take-over from automated to manual driving [C] // SAE 2016 World Congress and Exhibition. SAE International,2016.

城市道路交通异常事件检测研究综述

陈　华　刘　伟*

(重庆交通大学交通运输学院)

摘　要　为确保城市交通整体运行更加安全、协调,实时检测城市运营中的交通异常事件具有重要实际价值。传统交通异常事件检测大都是在交通事件发生后采取补救措施,但这种事后检测的实际意义不大。为确保事件发生后损失最低,需要对交通事件进行事前的识别、检测、预警,以此保证良好的城市交通整体运行状态。在智慧交通的建设背景下,交通异常事件事前检测预警已成为一种大趋势。为了从宏观层面掌握交通异常事件检测的研究状况,本文主要从交通异常事件识别算法、视频监控检测及数据预测分析三个方面对交通异常事件的研究现状进行阐述,然后在此基础上根据自己的认识交通异常事件检测的未来做出展望。

关键词 城市交通 交通异常检测 交通异常事件 智慧交通

0 引言

城市作为大规模复杂系统,局部异常事件会影响整体系统正常运行。若能精确预警、识别异常事件,对城市建设服务具有实际应用价值意义[1]。交通作为城市基本功能之一,随着城市快速发展,也会产生不同交通异常事件。交通事件是指导致通行能力下降或交通需求不正常升高的偶发性事件,包括交通事故、车辆故障、货物散落等,总之任何打断路段上交通流正常运行的突发情况都可称为交通事件[2]。城市通行车辆的供需不平衡,导致交通异常事件频发,针对此类情况,在道路交通安全管理过程中,构建交通异常事件检测系统的应用价值逐渐凸显,城市道路交通异常检测在交通管理和道路安全方面的巨大潜力成为一项重要的任务[3]。为降低交通异常事件的负面影响,除采取必要措施外,关键在于及时发现、清除、缩短事件持续时间,进而减少对交通的影响。为检测偶发性交通异常事件,部分学者从交通异常事件识别算法、计算机视觉检测以及大数据分析等方面作一系列探索,进而对异常事件分析、识别、预警。

1 交通异常事件识别/算法

交通异常事件检测实质就是依据事件发生前后交通流参数的变化进而判断。如今已存在早期成熟交通异常事件主动检测算法,如加州算法、McMaster算法、低通滤波算法等。但这些异常事件检测算法不适应当今复杂的交通场景。随着交通流理论、人工智能等新技术的快速发展,相继提出新的交通异常事件自动检测模型[4-11],相关检测模型如表1所示。

道路交通事件自动检测算法 表1

作　者	初始变量集	数据处理	事件检测模型/算法
邴其春等[4]	交通事件检测初始变量集	随机森林	组合核函数相关向量机模型
李红伟等[5]	流量、速度、占有率	—	基于突变强度纵向时间序列算法
郭爽[6]	车速、流量、占有率等	机器学习	车辆碰撞机器学习检测模型
魏丹[7]	车道平均占有率、上下游数据差	小波变换	GA优化的BP神经网络检测算法
孙熙等[9]	流量、速度、占有率	Boosting	基于boosting模糊分类检测
万福才等[10]	加速度、方向、位置	视频提取	车辆碰撞检测算法
Aoki, et al[11]	公交车GPS轨迹数据	插值	BusBeat早期事件检测技术

1.1 交通拥堵识别

交通拥堵作为常见交通异常事件,分常发性拥堵和偶发性拥堵两种。常发性拥堵是居民上、下班通行的规律性事件,此类拥堵不能消除,只能缓解;而偶发性拥堵主要是由突发情况引起。针对后者,王芜等[12]以速度-占有率比、速度差两个指标判定交通拥堵的起始、结束时刻;Liu等[13]利用多目标跟踪技术进行车辆检测,实现对交通拥堵的实时感知、识别;张驰远等[14]对快速路交通密度进行估计,并将路段密度估计值与临界拥堵密度进行对比进而判别拥堵。

1.2 交通安全事件检测

城市道路除交通拥堵外,还会产生交通安全事件。在实际道路运行中也会产生各种交通安全事故,相关学者针对交通安全[15-20]事故预防早期检测方法也有相关研究,如表2所示。

交通安全事件检测　　表2

作　者	数　据　集	检　测　方　法	安　全　类　型
Athanesious, et al[15]	real time dataset	DBSCAN	违规掉头、行人横穿、错边驾驶和频繁换道
Hu, Work[16]	real time dataset	基于光纤离群值的鲁棒张量恢复方法	车祸、施工车道关闭
Lee, et al[17]	real time dataset	CNN	车辆交通事故
Wan, et al[18]	DAQUAR-ALL	视频检测	车辆交通事故
Zhang, et al[19]	SUMO stimulation	机器学习	鲁莽驾驶
Wang, et al[20]	real-world smartcard data	异常流量检测	公共安全

城市道路是场景复杂的开放性系统，不具有高速公路的封闭性，故城市道路频发行人、驾驶员等交通参与者安全性的交通事件。为有效检测城市道路交通异常行为事件，Athanesious等[15]基于机器学习检测车辆违规掉头、行人横穿道路、错边驾驶和频繁换道等异常事件，为后续救助伤员节约宝贵的救护时间并为划定事故责任提供证据。交通作为服务型行业，时刻产生大量数据，随着交通大数据技术迅猛发展，基于数据层面研究异常事件也引起学者广泛关注。Hu和Work[16]基于大型交通数据集，并估算常规条件下的缺失数据，以此识别车祸现场；Wan等[18]基于超帧分割的长视频事件检索算法，利用交通监控摄像头检测车辆交通事故。

2　计算机视觉检测

近些年人工智能快速发展，计算机视觉领域也成为了人工智能的热门研究方向，通过处理采集的图片或视频以获得相应场景的三维信息、特征信息。基于计算机视觉提取场景特征的方法，成熟应用于交通。

2.1　视频监控研究

为实时检测道路交通异常事件，基于视频监控研究成为近年热门研究方向。交通场景中异常事件检测非常具有挑战性，是视频监控中的一个重大问题[21-22]，自动监控异常事件同样也是城市管理中的一个重大未解决的问题[23]。基于视频监控的交通异常事件研究不断深入，部分学者基于视频监控及图像识别技术研究交通异常事件，借助高清摄像头对城市道路关键性节点进行实时监控，如高等[24]人通过视频监控、图像处理技术判断车辆是否在黄网格区域违章停车。但此类方法的高清摄像头位置固定，不能对节点上下游进行监测，针对此缺陷，李等[25]人在此基础提出“预置位时域控制+定位识别技术”的主动监控技术，能有效监测地点的上下游交通状况。如今信息化时代的到来，为交通的发展带来新的挑战和机遇，对传统视频监控的不足发起了冲击。

2.1.1　车辆检测

交通事件发生后，需要对车辆进行检测，传统处理方式是调研现场后再调取视频监控进行事后追踪。这类方法趋向于事后监测，具有时滞性，且城市交通场景复杂，特定场合下车辆的速度快，检测难度较大。因此，李浩等[26]基于快速候选区域及深度学习提出多角度车辆动态检测方法，但该方法并未涉及视频中车辆间、车辆与其阴影是否存在遮挡。针对此不足，为准确提取广域道路场景交通信息，彭博等[27]人以无人机进行高空视频拍摄并融合形态检测与深度卷积网络，提出高空视频车型识别方法；周君等[28]人在原ST-MRF方法上提出基于模式识别与ST-MRF相结合的检测方法。虽然这类方法能提升异常事件检测的准确率，但是没有明确鉴定监测稳定性如何。针对稳定性不能满足多变视频检测需求，高新文等[29]人提出多目标跟踪的交通异常事件自动检测方法。近些年人工智能及机器学习在交通领域的广泛应用，有效提升传统视频交通异常事件检测精度、稳定性。尽管机器学习目标检测算法提升视频检测的准确性、稳定性，但执行效率却还达不到相应要求。为提升检测效率，宋等[30]人针对实际交通场景下的车辆，应用深度学习目标分类算法对车辆检测识别。

2.1.2　轨迹异常检测

轨迹信息反应交通参与者动态过程，可以根据车辆历史行车轨迹进而判断车辆行驶情况正常与否。也有学者们基于轨迹进行异常事件检测研究，Roy和Bilodeau[31]建立深度自编码器模型和数据增强方法，来检测行人、自行车或车辆在道路交叉口的异常轨迹。此外,轨迹信息只有正常和异常两种情况,可将轨迹正常与否视为二分类问题。因此 Roy 和 Bilodeau 用新的对抗方法来构建无监督方式训练深度神经网络二分类器,可在不需设置人工检测阈值情况下区分基于轨迹的正常和异常事件[32]。现有轨迹信息都是通过无人机、交通监控摄像头对实际交通场景拍照录像后进行加工提取,Giannakeris 等[33]利用深度 CNN 提取车辆的轨迹特征以此检测视频场景的异常事件;Wang 等[34]基于多特征融合对交通视频中的行人进行检测并跟踪,进而确定异常行为事件。

3 大数据分析、预测

交通作为服务型行业,随着通信技术、传感技术的发展,随时在客户端产生海量多源异构数据,如车辆轨迹、社交平台数据、地理信息系统等。但如何分析这些海量数据并得到城市交通是否发生异常事件,也是值得研究的课题。主要有两种方法从数据方面对城市交通异常事件进行识别,一种是对现有历史数据、实时数据进行分析,从而预测道路交通流状态;另一种就是依据车辆轨迹数据进行识别。

异常事件发生后交通流状态的预测就是以过去城市路网的历史状况,预测未来路网状况,进而确定未来路网是否存在异常行为。数据预测一般有两种方法:数据预测及基于预测数据的异常判别。在数据预测方面,早期利用浮动车搜集数据进行交通异常事件预测研究;安实等[35]人以城市异常数据为基础,构建交通异常预测模型。在预测数据异常判别方面。常规方法基于历史数据训练出一个多变量模型,从而对异常交通事件发生后的交通流状态进行预测判别,若模型移植性较好,可以判断识别其他路段的异常状态。陈佳良等[36]人为更好对无交通流检测器路段进行交通流状态估计,研究了基于时空特征序列匹配的交通流状态估计模型。

3.1 轨迹数据研究

车辆轨迹数据由于更新快、频率高,可以得到居民出行和交通运行状态等重要信息,成为数字交通的建设基石[37]。轨迹数据在城市研究中是一种非常具有实际研究价值,可以用于研究众多城市问题。交通异常事件发生后,车辆行驶轨迹会有明显的突变。针对轨迹变化,传统轨迹分析方法主要考虑的是轨迹的空间特性,因而异常行为识别能力较弱,只能识别简单的异常行为[38]。为提高识别能力,王雪等[39]人以出租车异常行驶轨迹数据作为数据源提出交通异常事件识别算法。除此之外, Zhou 等[40]基于历史车辆 GPS 大数据研究挖掘,可以准确识别驾驶员异常驾驶行为,如绕行和异常停车

3.2 社交数据

交通作为大型的输入、输出开放性复杂系统,每天都有大量的实时交通数据,对于这些数据如何利用是学者们关注的重点。随着移动设备的普及和网络设施的发展,社交媒体作为一种新的灾害数据来源受到了广泛关注,社会感知已成为通过探索社交媒体上的"群体智慧"来观察物理世界的新感知范式。Yang 等[41]采用自然语言处理和深度学习等多种方法,提取社交媒体文本中包含的细粒度路况信息和公共情感信息,对暴雨灾害期间的交通影响区域进行综合检测和分析。Zhang 等[42]研究使用社交媒体感知对异常交通事件进行精确定位问题。刘昭等[43]人以微博信息作为数据源提出交通突发事件识别方法。

4 未来展望

随着智慧城市概念提出后,则需要对城市进行更加精细化管理。发展至今,交通经过多个阶段变化。从传统交通过渡到智能交通,再到如今智慧交通。传统交通则主要是对交通系统的组成:人、车、路、环境进行综合分析;智能交通则是重于解决交通道路上突发紧急事件的检测和处理决策,一定程度上促进了交通的发展、也有效解决了一系列城市交通难题。然而在如今智慧城市背景下的智慧交通则需要更加智能化、超前性的对交通问题进行识别。在当前智慧城市广泛建设的大背景下,需要对异常事件识别更加精准。

随着物联网技术的发展,针对现有的城市问题。我们可以采集城市中人、车、物、时间等多维度、跨时空数据,融合现有历史数据与信息做出综合推理与及时响应。可利用现有城市联网基础设施,实现感知更为细粒度,更精准人车物的属性,通过机器视觉、多模态机器学习、多传感融合、自监督学习等手段,从城市感知物联网与现有历史数据发现城市运行中的交通异常事件。这迫切需要融合多源空间数据进而提升城市管理水平[44]。

但传统单一数据在城市异常事件管理中存在一定的局限,此外利用多源时空数据是当今加强城市交通控制、异常事件检测等领域建设智慧交通的关键[45]。在智慧交通的背景下,为提升异常事件检测的准确性,有人以多时空数据为基础,提出区分目标类型的停车和掉落物体检测算法[46],也有人建立有效区分城市交通异常时间与正常的交通状态变化的无监督异常检测系统[47],不断为智慧交通的未来进行探索。

参考文献

[1] Kong X, Gao H, Alfarraj O, et al. HUAD: Hierarchical Urban Anomaly Detection Based on Spatio-Temporal Data [J]. IEEE ACCESS, 2020,8:26573-26582.

[2] Fang Yuan,Ruey Long Cheu. Incident detection using support vector machines [J]. TRANSPORTATION RESEARCH PART C-EMERGING TECHNOLOGIES,2003,11(3):309-328.

[3] Xu Y, Ouyang X, Cheng Y, et al. Dual-Mode Vehicle Motion Pattern Learning for High Performance Road Traffic Anomaly Detection [C]//IEEE Comp Soc. PROCEEDINGS 2018 IEEE/CVF CONFERENCE ON COMPUTER VISION AND PATTERN RECOGNITION WORKSHOPS (CVPRW),2018:145-152.

[4] 郇其春,龚勃文,林赐云,等.城市快速路交通事件自动检测算法[J].中南大学学报(自然科学版),2017,48(06):1682-1687.

[5] 李红伟,姜桂艳,李素兰,等.基于突变强度的交通事件自动检测算法[J].交通运输系统工程与信息,2019,19(05):59-65.

[6] 郭爽.基于流数据的交通异常事件检测方法研究[D].北京:中国石油大学,2018.

[7] 魏丹.基于机器学习的交通状态判别与预测方法[D].长春:吉林大学,2020.

[8] Gao J,Zheng D,Yang S. Sensing the disturbed rhythm of city mobility with chaotic measures: anomaly awareness from traffic flows [J]. JOURNAL OF AMBIENT INTELLIGENCE AND HUMANIZED COMPUTING, 2021, 12 (4):4347-4362.

[9] 孙熙,李夏苗.基于boosting算法的交通事件检测[J].交通运输系统工程与信息,2007(05):37-41.

[10] 万福才,尹承祥,韩晓微,等.城市道路交通异常事件自动检测方法[J].沈阳大学学报(自然科学版),2015,27(01):30-33,43.

[11] Aoki S,Sezaki K,Yuan N J,et al. BusBeat: Early Event Detection with Real-Time Bus GPS Trajectories [J]. IEEE TRANSACTIONS ON BIG DATA,2021,7(2):371-382.

[12] 王尧,邵长桥,刘洋.城市快速路交通拥堵判定方法研究[J].交通信息与安全,2014,32(02):23-27.

[13] Liu X,Gao W,Feng D,et al. Abnormal Traffic Congestion Recognition Based on Video Analysis[C]//IEEE IEEE Comp Soc Huawei Cloud Hisense Kuaishou Technol NEC. Third International Conference on Multimedia Information Processing and Retrieval (MIPR, 2020),2020:39-42.

[14] 张驰远,陈阳舟,郭宇奇.基于卡尔曼滤波的城市快速路交通密度估计与拥堵识别[J].交通信息与安全,2017,35(05):55-61,82.

[15] Athaneaious J J, Vasuhi S, Vaidehi V, et al. Adaptive density based data mining technique for detection of abnormalities in traffic video surveillance[J]. JOURNAL OF INTELLIGENT & FUZZY SYSTEMS, 2020, 39(3):3737-3747.

[16] Hu Y,Work D B. Robust Tensor Recovery with Fiber Outliers for Traffic Events [J]. ACM TRANSACTIONS ON KNOWLEDGE DISCOVERY FROM DATA,2021,15(1).

[17] Lee H,Kang M,Song J,et al. The Detection of Black Ice Accidents for Preventative Automated Vehicles Using Convolutional Neural Networks[J]. ELECTRONICS,2020,9(12).

[18] Wan S, Xu X, Wang T, et al. An Intelligent Video Analysis Method for Abnormal Event Detection in Intelligent Transportation Systems [J]. IEEE TRANSACTIONS ON INTELLIGENT TRANSPORTATION SYSTEMS, 2021, 22 (7):4487-4495.

[19] Zhang L, Yan L, Fang Y, et al. A Machine Learning-Based Defensive Alerting System Against Reckless Driving in Vehicular Networks [J]. IEEE TRANSACTIONS ON VEHICULAR TECHNOLOGY, 2019, 68(12): 12227-12238.

[20] Wang H, Li L, Pan P, et al. Early warning of burst passenger flow in public transportation system[J]. TRANSPORTATION RESEARCH PART C-EMERGING TECHNOLOGIES, 2019, 105: 580-598.

[21] Athanesious J, Srinivasan V, Vijayakumar V, et al. Detecting abnormal events in traffic video surveillance using superorientation optical flow feature[J]. IET IMAGE PROCESSING, 2020, 14(9): 1881-1891.

[22] Ramchandran A, Sangaiah A K. Unsupervised deep learning system for local anomaly event detection in crowded scenes [J]. MULTIMEDIA TOOLS AND APPLICATIONS, 2020, 79(47-48): 35275-35295.

[23] Gao X, Xu G, Li S, et al. Particle Filter-Based Prediction for Anomaly Detection in Automatic Surveillance [J]. IEEE ACCESS, 2019, 7: 107550-107559.

[24] 高韬,刘正光,张军,等.智能交通黄网格违章车辆监测[J].交通运输系统工程与信息,2008(03):34-39.

[25] 李国锋,方正鹏,龚柏岩.带云台摄像机异常交通事件视频识别技术研究[J].公路交通科技,2007(11):168-169,173.

[26] 李浩,张运胜,连捷,等.基于深度学习的多角度车辆动态检测方法[J].交通信息与安全,2017,35(05):37-44.

[27] 彭博,蔡晓禹,唐聚,等.基于形态检测与深度学习的高空视频车辆识别[J].交通运输系统工程与信息,2019,19(06):45-51.

[28] 周君,包旭,高焱,等.基于模式识别与ST-MRF相结合的车辆检测方法[J].交通信息与安全,2021,39(02):95-100,108.

[29] 高新闻,沈卓,许国耀,等.基于多目标跟踪的交通异常事件检测[J].计算机应用研究,2021,38(06):1879-1883.

[30] 宋焕生,张向清,郑宝峰,等.基于深度学习方法的复杂场景下车辆目标检测[J].计算机应用研究,2018,35(04):1270-1273.

[31] Roy P R, Bilodeau G-A. Road User Abnormal Trajectory Detection Using a Deep Autoencoder [C] // Bebis, G; Boyle, R; Parvin, B, et al. ADVANCES IN VISUAL COMPUTING, ISVC 2018, 2018: 748-757.

[32] Roy P R, Bilodeau G-A. Adversarially Learned Abnormal Trajectory Classifier [C] // IEEE Comp Soc Canadian Image Proc & Pattern RecognitiSoc. 2019 16TH CONFERENCE ON COMPUTER AND ROBOT VISION (CRV 2019), 2019: 65-72.

[33] Giannakeris P, Kaltsa V, Avgerinakis K, et al. Speed Estimation and Abnormality Detection from Surveillance Cameras [C] // IEEE Comp Soc. PROCEEDINGS 2018 IEEE/CVF CONFERENCE ON COMPUTER VISION AND PATTERN RECOGNITION WORKSHOPS (CVPRW), 2018: 93-99.

[34] Wang X, Song H, Cui H. Pedestrian abnormal event detection based on multi-feature fusion in traffic video[J]. OPTIK, 2018, 154: 22-32.

[35] 安实,王雷,周超.基于神经网络及关联性修正的交通异常预测研究[J].交通信息与安全,2019,37(02):10-17.

[36] 陈佳良,胡钊政,李飞.基于时空特征序列匹配的交通流状态估计方法[J].交通信息与安全,2021,39(03):68-76,120.

[37] 黄士琛,邵春福,李娟,等.基于深度学习的车辆轨迹重建与异常轨迹识别[J].交通运输系统工程与信息,2021,21(03):47-54.

[38] 李明之,马志强,单勇,等.基于轨迹分析的交通目标异常行为识别[J].电视技术,2012,36(01):106-112.

[39] 王雷,安实,杨海强,等.基于出租车轨迹数据的交通异常识别算法[J].科学技术与工程,2018,18(32):239-247.

[40] Zhou Tong, Shi Wenzhong, Liu Xintao, et al. A Novel Approach for Online Car-Hailing Monitoring Using Spatiotemporal Big Data[J]. IEEE ACCESS, 2019, 7: 128936-128947.

[41] Yang T, Xie J, Li G, et al. Traffic Impact Area Detection and Spatiotemporal Influence Assessment for Disaster Reduction Based on Social Media: A Case Study of the 2018 Beijing Rainstorm [J]. ISPRS INTERNATIONAL JOURNAL OF GEO-INFORMATION, 2020, 9 (2).

[42] Zhang Y, Dong X, Zhang D, et al. A Syntax-based Learning Approach to Geo-locating Abnormal Traffic Events using Social Sensing [C] // Spezzano, F; Chen, W; Xiao, X. PROCEEDINGS OF THE 2019 IEEE/ACM INTERNATIONAL CONFERENCE ON ADVANCES IN SOCIAL NETWORKS ANALYSIS AND MINING (ASONAM 2019), 2019: 663-670.

[43] 刘昭,何赏璐,刘英舜.基于社交网络数据的交通突发事件识别方法[J].交通信息与安全,2021,39(02):53-60.

[44] 左海龙,罗红霞.多源空间数据融合的城市精细化管理[J].测绘通报,2019(12):108-111,151.

[45] Zhou F, Li L, Zhang K, et al. Urban flow prediction with spatial-temporal neural ODEs [J]. TRANSPORTATION RESEARCH PART C-EMERGING TECHNOLOGIES,2021,124.

[46] Li G, Song H, Liao Z. An Effective Algorithm for Video-Based Parking and Drop Event Detection[J]. COMPLEXITY,2019.

[47] Zameni M, He M, Moahtaghi M, et al. Urban Sensing for Anomalous Event Detection: Distinguishing Between Legitimate Traffic Changes and Abnormal Traffic Variability[C] // Brefeld, U; Curry, E; Daly, E, et al. MACHINE LEARNING AND KNOWLEDGE DISCOVERY IN DATABASES, ECML PKDD 2018, PT III, 2019: 553-568.

城市交通事故黑点治理新模式研究

李泽炜 张敏捷* 张浩霖 黎健侃
(宁波工程学院建筑与交通工程学院)

摘 要 传统道路交通事故预防和治理体系存在着不足之处。为有效治理城市交通事故黑点,改善城市交通安全状况,提出全生命周期的交通事故黑点治理新模式,有机整合事故数据采集、交通黑点识别、黑点致因分析、方案效果评估。将该模式应用于2021年的宁波市道路交通安全治理提升工程,取得了良好的治理效果。以宁波市中兴南路和宋诏桥路交叉口黑点发现和治理为例,其事故量由每月56.6起降至每月19.6起,同比下降65.4%。该模式的应用为城市道路交通黑点的识别和治理提供了有效的工程样板。

关键词 交通安全 治理模式 全生命周期 事故黑点

0 引言

随着世界经济的高速发展,城市交通系统也有了巨大的飞跃,人们在出行时享受巨大便利的同时,也见证和经历着大量的事故的发生[1]。据世界卫生组织报告的数据显示,全球因道路交通碰撞而死的人数每年高达135万人[2-3],即平均每24s就有1人因道路交通事故而失去生命;道路交通事故已逐渐成为15~29岁人群死亡的主要原因[3]。因此如何减少交通事故量的发生是全世界都需要关注的重点。

1. 基金项目:浙江省公益计划项目(LGF20F030004),宁波市自然科学基金项目(2018A610119)。

事故黑点是单位路段内发生的事故数量超过某一限定值的路段或区域,即交通事故高发点位,许多重大伤亡事故往往就发生在这些黑点中。道路交通事故黑点的交通事故发生频率显著大于其他正常区域[4],每年在该类点位发生的交通事故严重影响了道路交通的安全性,是道路交通事故的主要原因。第16届国际道路会议报告指出,道路交通事故黑点仅占路网总长的0.25%,却发生了占事故总数的25%的事故量[5]。因此形成一套有效、便捷的道路交通事故黑点治理模式,对于有效地提高道路交通的安全性,降低事故的发生率、确保人民的出行具有重要的现实意义。

目前国内外在黑点治理模式的研究上,缺乏完善闭合的治理体系,以及缺乏与治理体系相匹配的有效治理方法。本文首先对目前的事故黑点治理模式进行了系统性综述,具体分析存在的弊端,在此基础上提出基于全生命周期的城市交通事故黑点治理新模式;然后以宁波为例,将该新模式应用至道路交通安全提升工程;最后,根据统计数据验证新模式的有效性。

1 城市交通事故黑点治理模式综述

1.1 现行治理模式

良好的交通事故黑点治理模式是有效解决事故黑点,全面改善交通状况的前提、基础和规范。目前国内外现行较成熟的交通事故黑点识别方法,主要包括事故率法[6-7],当量事故频数法[7],聚类算法[8]等,但对于交通事故黑点的治理模式的研究仍停留在事故黑点识别以及典型事故原因分析阶段,缺乏对事故数据的深入研究及挖掘,无法准确研判事故整体分布。

1.2 存在的缺陷

全面和准确地识别黑点,并实施有效治理,是交通事故治理的核心问题。目前国内城市道路交通事故高发,交通事故数据采集任务繁重,现行治理模式中缺乏有效应对采集手段,且在数据的全面性和准确性方面有所缺失,导致事故黑点全面和准确识别存在很大难度。其次现行治理模式缺乏方案的有效性和治理效果的后验评价,实用性和可靠性受到制约。因此对于事故数据应当不断地深入挖掘,研究治理后的事故数据量,通过数据来提供决策支持和研判证据,降低治理失误的可能性,在事故量没有明显降低的情况下进行二次研判分析,以保障事故黑点治理的有效性。

1.3 新治理模式方向

基于目前的交通事故状况的背景,以治理效果为依据,构成新治理模式的主要方向,其主要为全生命周期的闭环治理模式。该模式以准确、全面的事故数据采集为起点,合理有效的效果评判为终点,并以评判结果作为依据来确认是否进行二次整改,从而将原本各自为政的治理模式向闭环运作转变,建立统一完善的流程方法,突出精细化的治理水平,构建符合中国交通现状的治理模式,以零事故伤亡为愿景目标,真正做到减少事故量,改善道路交通状况,保障人民出行的出行安全。

2 全生命周期的黑点治理模式

2.1 新治理模式的框架

基于全生命周期的治理模式为交通事故黑点治理的闭环体系,可分为以下四个步骤实施:

(1)基础事故数据采集。

完善目前的黑点采集方式,从传统的黑点治理方法入手,分别对黑点识别、黑点治理、效果评估三方面的方法进行需求讨论,研发出适合于当地道路交通状况的数据采集平台,以对各事故黑点进行量化分析。在保障基础事故数据的采集丰度满足后续分析需求的同时,尽可能优化和简化操作步骤,在采集时间和数据丰度之间取得平衡,以提高采集效率。

(2)黑点识别。

通过各种算法效率优劣、算法适性对比,借鉴当量事故频数法和聚类均值算法的思想,开发新算法进行事故黑点识别,在吸纳各种算法的优点的同时,避免识别缺陷,并将新算法实际应用到适合的道路上,模拟识别黑点的实验,并与其他算法的结果进行对比,降低识别误差,为后期的治理阶段提供依据。

(3)黑点致因分析。

黑点致因分析需要结合数据采集和黑点识别所得到的数据进行分析治理,目前对于黑点的治理没有形成一个有效的体系,仅是针对性的进行点对点改造,工作量太大。有效的解决方案是建立一个标准化的黑点治理方案库,通过收集大量的事故治理方案并整理归纳到方案库中;并根据事故黑点的致因分析得到的结论,快速生成相应的解决方案。

(4)方案效果评估。

治理方案在一系列审核后将会上报进行实施,施工完成后将持续跟进方案整改效果并进行评估,若治理效果未达到预期,则将重复致因分析阶段,重新提出相关治理方案进行二次施工,直至事故数据降至定义的黑点标准之下。

这四步法初步构成了全生命周期的闭环治理模式的框架,其结构如图1所示。将为后续具体治理方式的代入提供基础,确保治理模式的先进性和科学性。

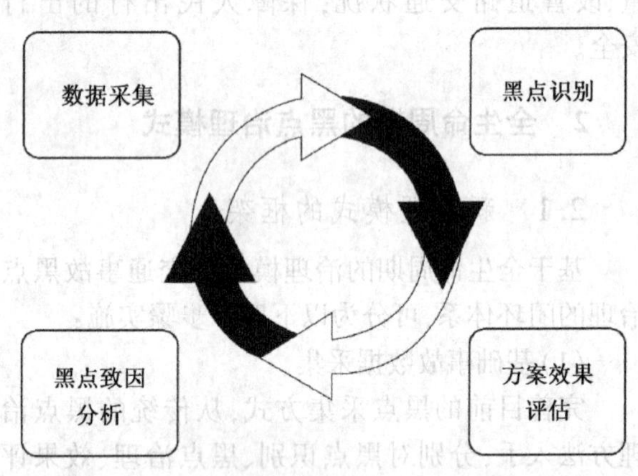

图1　全生命周期的黑点治理框架

2.2　事故数据采集方法

根据宁波市的交通状况,结合数据采集技术需求,并参照《道路交通管理信息采集规范第3部分:道路交通事故处理信息采集》(2011)[9,12],开发事故数据采集程序,为黑点识别及致因分析提供数据支持,事故信息采集字段如表1所示。

2.3　黑点识别算法设计

提出基于积分阈值的k-means聚类算法,即赋予不同严重程度的交通事故分值,将其代入黑点识别密度聚类算法。黑点识别的流程如图2所示。

基于德尔菲法将伤人事故的权重定义为0.75,物损事故的权重定义为0.25,再由每起事故乘以权重得出每起事故的分值。团队以任意事故发生点为圆心,100m(城市),150m(乡镇)为半径进行GIS扫描,将在一个统计周期(一般以季度为单位)内,城区、乡镇平均产生的道路交通事故事故积分累计达到6分(城市),4.5分(乡镇)以上即为交通事故高发点位;然后设定事故单位点为0.25分,伤人事故点位等效为3个事故单位点,由此对筛选出来的交通事故高发点位进行事故单位点代入,运用改进的k值算法对事故单位点进行点位处理,将处理后得出的质心作为黑点的圆心,100m(城市)或150m(乡镇)为半径,最终得出交通事故黑点。发生死亡事故的点位将直接设定为黑点,在后续进一步排查,确认事故是否非偶然。

该算法量化了事故严重程度和事故数量在事故黑点识别中影响因子,使事故黑点更加精准。最后运用ArcGIS技术将已识别的黑点标记在图中,绘制黑点热力图,将审核过的黑点记录整理,此阶段为后期的治理方案的制定提供依据。

事故信息采集程序所采集字段　　表1

序号	字段名称	字段类型	详细说明
1	事故所属中队	文本	根据民警所属中队自动分配
2	事故时间	日期/时间	根据录入时间自动生成
3	位置	数值	根据事故采集位置自动生成
4	事故类型	文本	选项:机动车-机动车冲突、机动车-非机动车冲突、机动车-行人冲突等
5	事故当事人	文本	选项:老年人、青年人、学生等
6	事故原因	文本	选项:21种快速处理情形[13]
7	事故严重程度	文本	选项:物损、受伤、死亡
8	事故点位置	文本	选项:路段、交叉口、高架等
9	天气因素	文本	选项:晴天、雨天、雪天等
10	事故发生环境	文本	选项:正常环境、夜间照明不良、绿化遮挡视线等
11	事故现场照片	图片	拍摄事故照片上传

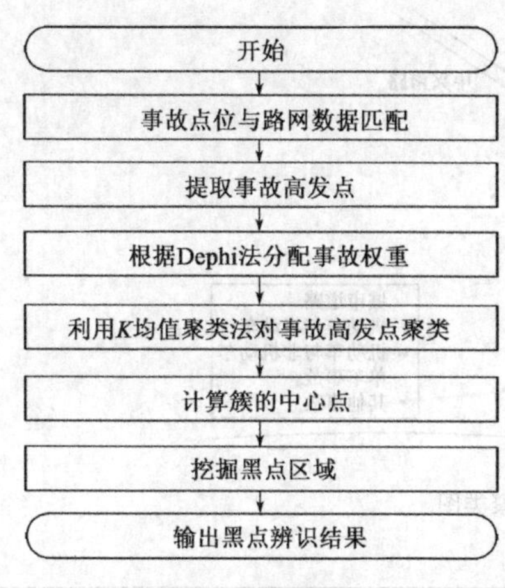

图2 算法结构

2.4 黑点治理方法设计

传统事故黑点治理方法为通过事故数据分析得出事故的主要致因，针对主要致因采取相对应的措施进行治理，一点一策的设计使工作量大。在事故基础数据和对应的方案集数据的基础上，构建标准方案库，并在全生命周期治理的过程中，持续针对方案库进行迭代更新和完善，如图3所示。事故黑点能够根据黑点致因的细分类型，其治理方案按照方案库的标准模板进行设计，实现治理方案设计的高效化和快速化。根据历史数据和专家经验，将事故黑点致因分为设施类、设计类、管控类等三类，再提取已绘制治理方案图进行参考，提升已分类的事故黑点的治理方案的设计速度和标准化。

根据对已识别事故黑点的事故数据进行统计分类，得出其特性的分布特征并绘制事故数据特性分布图。对已识别黑点通过实验室视频观测得出道路数据，并绘制道路基础设施及其附属设施图。依据上述分类数据和分析图，综合定性分析事故黑点的成因，并将其归类。

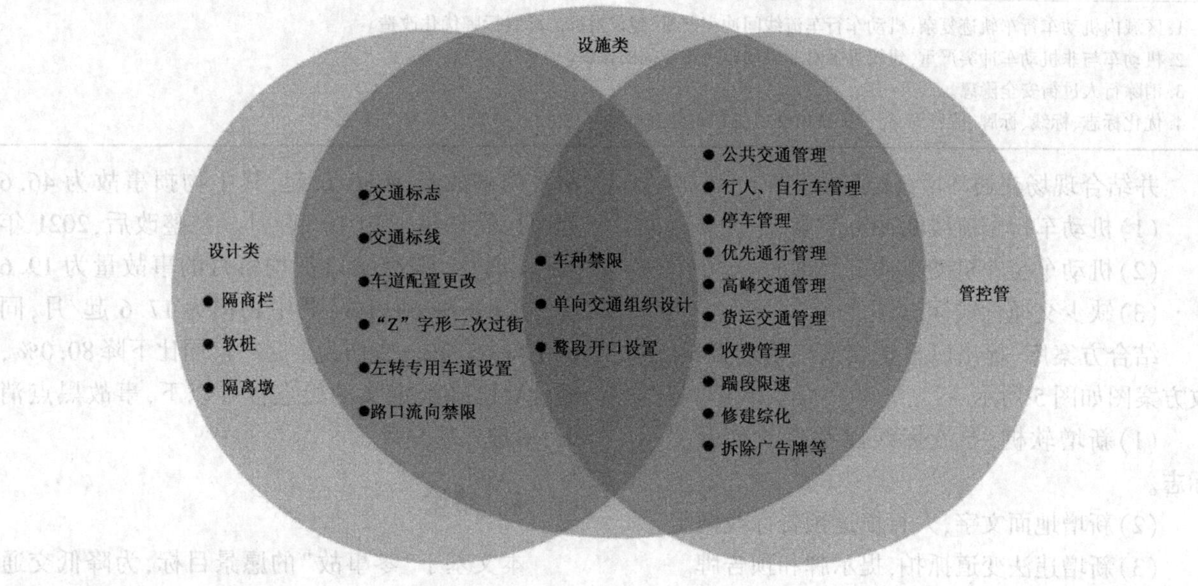

图3 事故黑点的事故数据分类

治理方案制定完成后将会上报给相关专家进行审核，在通过后最终交由施工部门进行施工整改，在改进的过程中将持续通过采集的事故数据跟进方案治理效果，通过分析事故数量及严重程度进行研判，判断黑点是否依旧存在，若黑点消失，则证明黑点治理效果优良，反之则需重新进行黑点的致因分析，提出新的治理方案，确保黑点问题得到真正解决。

3 实证分析

以宁波市中兴南路与宋诏桥路交叉口的治理为例，展示基于全生命周期的黑点治理模式的应用过程。

3.1 黑点的识别与确认

2021年1～5月在该区域采集的事故数据为283条，基于积分阈值的k-means聚类算法将其识别为事故黑点，事故点位的聚类结果如图4所示。

3.2 黑点的治理设计

事故数据的详细分析如表2所示。

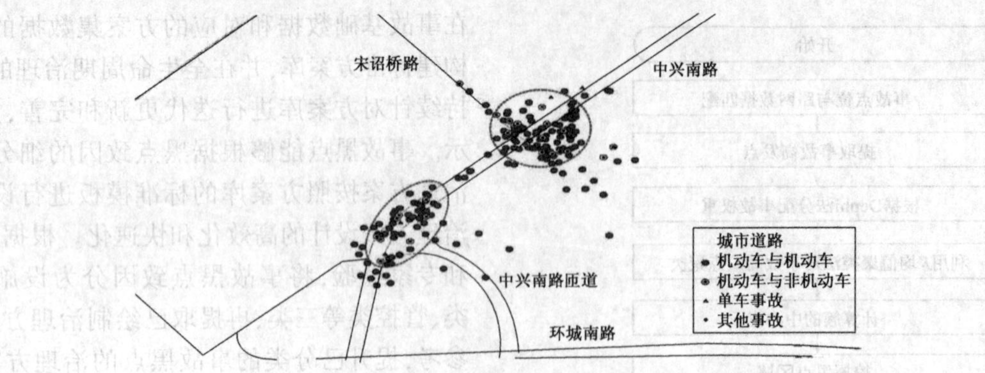

图4　宁波中兴南路区域事故点位聚类图

事故数据分析表　　表2

事故点位分布	事故类型分布
路段(227 起,80.2%)	机动车1与机动车2,88.0%
交叉口(51 起,18.0%)	机动车与非机动车,9.2%
高架(1 起,0.4%)	单车事故,2.5%
路外(4 起,1.4%)	其他事故,0.3%
排查整治重点方向	
1. 区域内机动车行车轨迹复杂,机动车行车流线间冲突严重,建议对标志标线标牌优化改造。 2. 机动车与非机动车冲突严重,建议加强对非机动车行驶空间的保障。 3. 消除行人过街安全隐患。 4. 优化标志、标线、标牌、信号等,完善区域内交通信息的提前告知	

并结合现场交通环境,认定问题如下:

(1)机动车行车流线间冲突严重。

(2)机动车与非机动车冲突严重。

(3)缺少交通标线标志。

结合方案库,提出以下该交叉口治理方案,整改方案图如图5 所示。

(1)新增软桩,导流标线以及事故预警提示标志。

(2)新增地面文字,人行横道预告标线两组。

(3)新增违法变道抓拍,提示牌和预告牌。

(4)中兴南路南进口新增机非隔离栏。

(5)新增纵向减速线,直右车道改为左右转车道。

(6)绿化降低,广告牌移除。

(7)人行横道标线补画。

(8)加油站实行单向交通组织。

(9)中兴南路宋诏桥路沿线开口新增减速让行标线。

(10)补画公交车站标线。

(11)新增软桩、隔离栏以及非机动车指示标志。

黑点整改方案经实施后进行效果评估。数据显示,未整改时,2021 年1 ~5 月中,该交叉口平均每月的事故量为 56.6 起,其中物损事故为 46.6 起/月,受伤事故为 10 起/月。经整改后,2021 年 7 ~11 月中,该交叉口平均每月的事故量为 19.6 起,同比下降 65.4%;其中物损为 17.6 起/月,同比下降62.2%;受伤为2 起/月,同比下降80.0%,经计算已降至定义的黑点标准以下,事故黑点消失,治理效果显著。

4　结论

本文基于“零事故”的愿景目标,为降低交通事故发生绝对数量、改善交通出行环境而提出的新型黑点治理模式,可总结为以下内容:

(1)在目前已有的事故黑点治理模式的基础上进行优化,采用全生命周期的闭环治理模式,实现对城市道路交通事故黑点治理的高效化并保证了治理的有效性,该模式取得了较好的社会效益,有望在全国其他城市进行模式和技术推广。

(2)基于黑点治理模式中需要的事故数据结合宁波市实际道路交通状况进行小程序的开发,合理制定小程序的功能及选项,有利于整个黑点治理模式的实行。

(3)在提出全新黑点治理模式的基础上改进

其中的算法流程,在黑点识别板块采用基于积分阈值的 k-means 聚类算法,并引入事故单位点的概念,弥补其他算法的不足,有效提高黑点识别的准确性。

(4)为达到治理黑点高效、准确的目的,提出方案库的思想,将事故黑点进行分类,使事故黑点治理标准化,模块化。

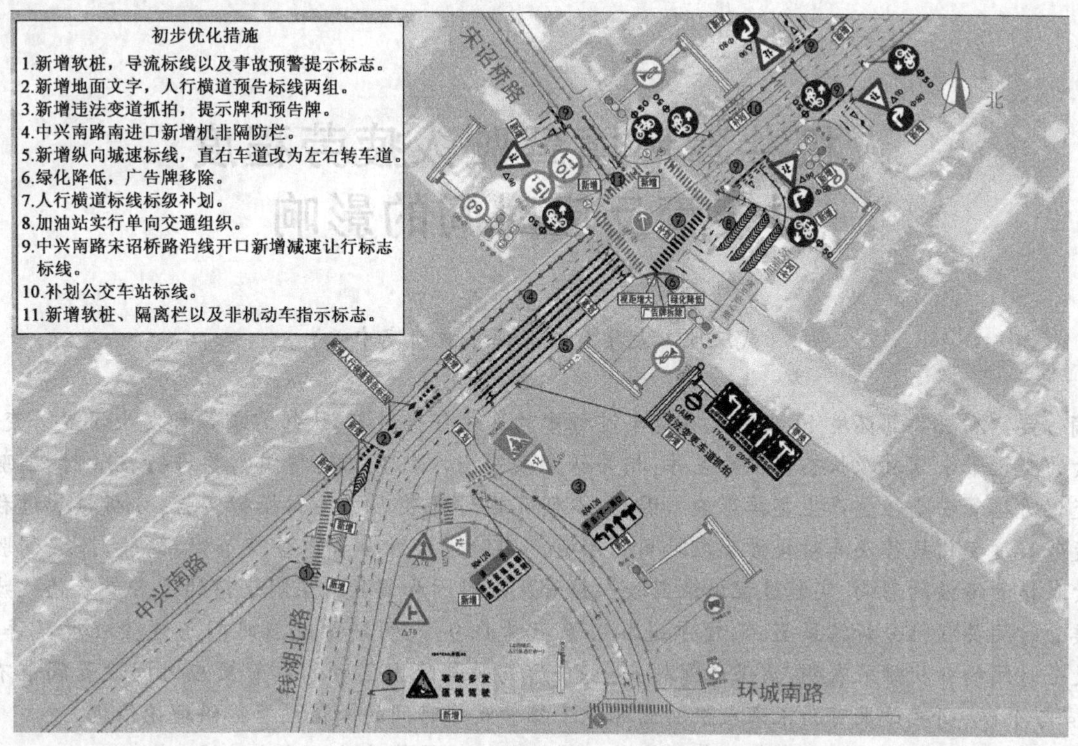

图 5　黑点整改方案图

参考文献

[1] 郝建勋. 道路交通事故分析方法应用研究[D]. 长春:吉林大学,2008.

[2] 王文博,周继彪,陈红,等. 基于 VISSIM 仿真的事故路段通行能力估算方法[J]. 公路交通科技,2015,32(12):120-127.

[3] World Health Organization. Global status report on road safety 2015[R]. Geneva:World Health Organization,2015.

[4] 周昱. 基于多源数据的地面道路交通事故黑点研究[J]. 中国公共安全,2020,(Z1):100-103.

[5] 张殿业,方守恩. 道路交通事故与黑点分析[M]. 北京:人民交通出版社,2005.

[6] 胡新民,刘涛,张天华,等. 道路黑点识别与改善[J]. 交通运输工程学报,2004(01):106-109.

[7] 肖慎,过秀成,宋俊敏. 公路交通事故黑点鉴别方法研究[J]. 公路交通技术,2003(02):70-73.

[8] 郭璘,周继彪,董升,等. 基于改进 K-means 算法的城市道路交通事故分析[J]. 中国公路学报,2018,31(04):270-279.

[9] Guo Y, Sayed T, Zaki M H, et al. Safety Evaluation of Unconventional Outside Left-Turn Lane Using Automated Traffic Conflict Techniques[J]. Canadian Journal of Civil Engineering,2016,43(7):631-642.

[10] Stewart B,Yankson I K,Afukaar F,et al. Road Traffic and Other Unintentional Injuries Among Travelers to Developing Countries[J]. The Medical clinics of North America,2016,100(2):331.

[11] Gregoriades A, Mouskos K C. Black Spots Identification Through a Bayesian Networks Quantification of Accident Risk Index[J]. Transportation Research part C: emerging technologies,2013,28:28-43.

[12] Erdogan S, Yilmaz I, Baybura T, et al. Geographical Information Systems Aided Traffic Accident Analysis System Case Study:

City of Afyonkarahisar[J]. Accident Analysis & Prevention,2008,40(1):174-181.

[13] 龙岩高速交警."互联网+手机",轻松解决道路交通事故快处快赔[EB/OL]. https://m. thepaper. cn/baijiahao_4819090, 2019-10-30.

人机共驾环境驾驶人疲劳程度对接管反应时间的影响

胡 宸 毛 喆 张 晖*

(武汉理工大学智能交通系统研究中心)

摘 要 人机共驾环境下,驾驶人在行车过程中的驾驶任务时长、认知需求等都发生了显著变化;以上要素的变化带来驾驶人状态特征的差异,相关研究表明当人机共驾过程中需要进行接管时,驾驶人状态的变化对接管安全性会产生直接影响。因此,本研究通过开展人机共驾模拟实验,分析接管过程中驾驶人疲劳程度变化规律及其对接管反应时间的影响。实验设计综合考虑昼夜节律、驾驶时长、驾驶疲劳等因素对接管绩效的影响,实验过程记录驾驶人接管反应时间和驾驶人主观反馈的疲劳量表值。疲劳程度和接管时间关联性分析结果显示:皮尔逊相关系数为0.9,表明接管反应时间与疲劳程度显著相关。接管反应时间的分析结果表明:为保证驾驶安全,午后驾驶与晚上驾驶的接管反应时间设置阈值不应超过4.4s与4.6s,研究结果可为未来人机共驾环境下接管反应时间的阈值设置提供理论依据。

关键词 交通安全 人机共驾 驾驶疲劳 模拟驾驶 接管绩效 反应时间

0 引言

人机共驾阶段的驾驶行为安全性是当前研究的热点,国内外研究学者针对人机共驾环境下的行为差异、行为变化、接管绩效等展开了研究。钮建伟等[1]收集了36名驾驶人在模拟驾驶的2种险情下切换驾驶方式过程中的驾驶行为数据,研究影响驾驶人驾驶方式切换过程的因素。严利鑫等[2]用驾驶人主观经验将驾驶模式划分为人工驾驶、警示辅助、自动驾驶3种状态,通过实车试验分析驾驶模式决策影响因子。人机交互驾驶环境下,驾驶人的驾驶疲劳变化,相比较于传统的手动驾驶,自动驾驶模式下的驾驶人更容易产生驾驶疲劳,进而影响驾驶行为和接管能力[3-5,7]。Strand等针对驾驶切换时所处的不同交通场景,研究了其对驾驶人接管能力的影响,发现系统失效方式、失效程度、与前方障碍物的距离等条件的不同会引起驾驶人接管能力的巨大差异[6]。GOLD等通过模拟驾驶实验,发现反应时间、交通密度和接管次数对接管绩效有较明显的影响[9]。在Dambock的研究中,也证明了接管反应时间可以用来评估接管绩效[10]。综上,目前国内外研究针对人机共驾环境下驾驶疲劳与接管绩效之间的交互作用研究还较少,表征接管绩效的指标也并不统一。本文将研究驾驶疲劳对接管绩效的影响,通过人机共驾模拟驾驶实验进行驾驶疲劳数据的采集,以接管反应时间作为接管绩效的最优指标,进而分析驾驶疲劳对接管绩效的影响机制,为人机共驾环境下接管绩效的阈值设定提供理论支持。

1 实验方法

本研究搭建了人机共驾模拟驾驶平台,筛选被试进行人机共驾模拟驾驶实验,对实验中采集的疲劳和接管绩效指标进行研究。

1.1 驾驶模拟器

人机共驾实验采用UC-winRoad软件来进行场景设计,驾驶舱由实车改造而来,两个小型液晶显示

1. 基金项目:国家重点研发计划项目(编号:2019YFE0104600);国家自然科学基金(编号:52072289)。

屏作为左右后视镜由 UC-winRoad 软件控制,五通道环幕用于人机交互驾驶环境的显示,如图1 所示。

图1 实验设备

1.2 被试人员

通过筛选,被试人员为 7 名男性和 2 名女性。年龄为 24.56 岁 ±0.88 岁(平均值 ± 标准差,下同),驾龄为 4.56 年 ±1.13 年,最近 5 年内无重大疾病且睡眠情况正常,并对模拟驾驶器有较好的适应性。在实验前的 24h 内,保证 7h 睡眠并且实验当天不能午睡。实验前不可饮用咖啡、功能饮料等饮品。

1.3 实验情景设计

驾驶场景为车道宽为 3.75m 的双向 6 车道高速公路。实验车辆行驶的中间车道上的交通流量为 900pcu/h,道路限速为 80 ~ 100km/h,实验路线全长为 49250m。设有中央分隔带、路侧护栏和相应的限速标志牌,模拟场景如图 2 所示。

图2 早上、午后、晚上三个时刻的驾驶场景示意图

研究表明,驾驶疲劳会受到昼夜节律的影响,因此,本研究在实验设计过程中,将实验分为早上组、午后组、晚上组三组进行。每位被试人员都需要完成 3 组实验,分别是:早上组(7:30—8:35)人机共驾实验、午后组(13:30—14:35)人机共驾实验、夜间组(19:00—20:05)人机共驾实验。考虑到驾驶员进行非驾驶任务的随机性,因此在自动驾驶期间,不对被试人员的行为进行限制,被试人员可以自行安排自己的活动(读书、处理公务、休息等)。

实验中每次驾驶任务包括三个阶段,第一阶段:车辆以 80km/h 的速度在自动驾驶模式下匀速行驶。第二阶段:自动驾驶模式下,在接管点,车辆向驾驶人发送接管请求信号,驾驶人接管后,驾驶权由车辆转移到驾驶人。第三阶段:驾驶人手动驾驶一段时间后(车速限制:80 ~ 100km/h),驾驶权重新分配给车辆,此时车辆和驾驶人共同完成了一个完整的人机共驾接管过程,如图 3 所示。其中,T0 为发出接管请求信号的时刻,T1 为驾驶人接管驾驶的时刻,T0 和 T1 时刻之间的时间差称为驾驶人的接管反应时间。

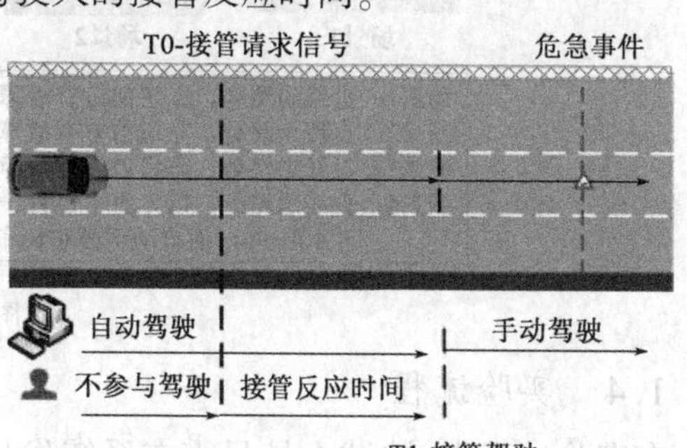

图3 接管过程

完成一次接管后,车辆再度以自动驾驶模式行驶至下一个接管点,整个实验中共设有 7 次接管过程,分别在实验中预设的位置出现,如图4 所示。但为了防止驾驶人对接管场景产生重复认知,设置 4 种接管触发的场景,如图 5min,每个被试在实验过程中的场景变换顺序均为 1—2—3—4—2—1—4—3。实验期间实验员需要每隔 5min 对被试的疲劳程度进行询问并记录,所用疲劳评定量表为卡罗林斯卡嗜睡量表(Karolinska Sleepiness Scale,KSS)。

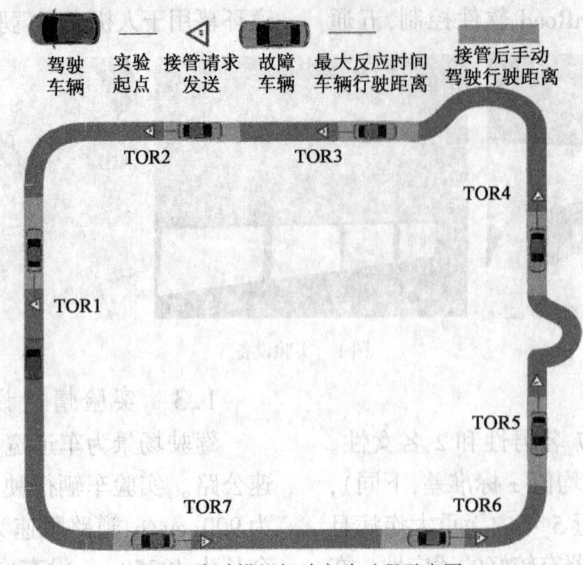

图4　自动模拟驾驶实验过程示意图

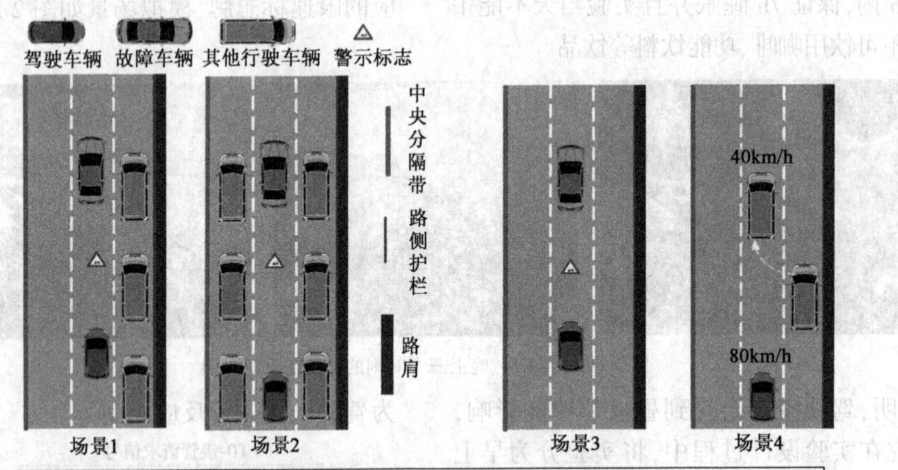

场景1：直线道路处，车道前方有故障车停滞，右车道有较密集的交通流。
场景2：直线道路处，车道前方有故障车停滞，左、右车道均有密度较大的交通流。
场景3：直线道路处，车道前方有故障车停滞，左、右车道均没有交通流。
场景4：直线道路处，前方右车道有一辆大型SUV以80km/h的速度向左换道，换道后急减速至40km/h，而自动驾驶车辆车速为80km/h。

图5　4种接管场景

1.4　实验流程

在实验过程中，被试人员只需在系统发出接管请求（驾驶操作由车辆切换给驾驶人）后操作车辆，系统会语音提示“请接管驾驶”。接管后要求被试驾驶车辆在中间车道行驶，手动驾驶一段距离，当看到道路右侧出现“stop”的标志时，将车停在与stop齐平的位置。之后系统会切换到下一次自动驾驶，总计手动驾驶时间为15min。

1.5　数据预处理

对于驾驶疲劳数据，为了能够表征三个不同时段实验组的整体疲劳变化规律，将各组内的被试人员KSS数据进行均值求解，得到能够反映各组整体疲劳变化规律的KSS数据。并使用三次样条插值法将离散分布的KSS数据拟合为连续数据。对于驾驶人操作行为数据，通过补全缺失数据、剔除异常值、数据截取、数据筛选等处理来完善实验数据。

2　疲劳与接管绩效分析

2.1　驾驶疲劳变化特征分析

通过T检验（Student’s test）分析各组单个被试疲劳数据和所有被试疲劳均值数据之间的差异性及其显著性，若分析结果未表现出显著性差异，则证明KSS均值能够表征整体的疲劳变化趋势。

为了能够表征三个不同时段实验组的整体疲劳变化规律,将各组内的被试人员 KSS 数据进行均值求解,得到能够反映各组整体疲劳变化规律的 KSS 数据。经验证数据均满足正态分布,即满足 T 检验的先决条件。

用单总体 t 检验对各被试人员数据样本和被试均值样本进行检验分析。其计算公式见式(1)。

$$t = \frac{\bar{X} - \mu}{\frac{\sigma_X}{\sqrt{n-1}}} \tag{1}$$

式中:$i = 1, \cdots, n$;

$\bar{X} = \frac{\sum_{i=1}^{n} x_i}{n}$——样本平均数;

$S = \sqrt{\frac{\sum_{i=1}^{n}(x_i - \bar{x})^2}{n-1}}$——样本标准偏差;

n——样本数。

验证可得,早上组、午后组、晚上组的 KSS 数据少数存在差异,但是差异值均大于 0.01 且小于 0.05,未表现出显著性差异,其他数据在统计上可以认为来自于同一分布的数据。附三组 KSS 数据 T 检验结果如表 1 所示。

各实验组 KSS 数据 t 检验结果 表 1

项目	早上组			午后组			夜间组		
参数	h	P	c	h	P	c	h	P	c
被试 1	0	0.076	[-1.17,0.06]	0	0.5039	[-0.47,0.93]	1	0.0091	[0.17,1.07]
被试 2	0	0.6765	[-0.90,1.36]	1	0.015	[0.76,1.56]	0	0.4564	[-0.45,0.98]
被试 3	0	0.0593	[-1.13,0.02]	0	0.8826	[-0.82,0.71]	0	0.9268	[-0.55,0.50]
被试 4	1	0.0176	[0.21,1.97]	0	0.0329	[0.03,0.71]	0	0.2226	[-0.17,0.69]
被试 5	1	0.0414	[-1.51,-0.31]	1	0.019	[-1.08,-0.17]	0	0.3635	[-0.41,1.07]
被试 6	0	0.1055	[-0.12,1.15]	0	0.0268	[-1.18,-0.08]	0	0.7103	[-0.53,0.77]
被试 7	0	0.7585	[-0.96,0.71]	0	0.0088	[-1.21,-0.19]	0	0.2334	[-0.83,0.21]
被试 8	0	0.3284	[-0.82,0.29]	1	0.0192	[0.16,1.02]	0	0.1213	[-1.36,0.17]
被试 9	0	0.0882	[-0.09,1.27]	0	0.182	[-0.85,0.17]	1	0.0418	[-1.31,-0.03]

参数说明:$h = 0$,则表明零假设在 5% 的置信度下不被接受,在统计上可看作来自同一分布的数据;$h = 1$,表明零假设被拒绝统计上认为是来自不同分布的数据。

P 表示设定的显著差异的标准,等于 0.05,一般 <0.05 认为差异,<0.01 认为差异极其显著。c 为真正均值的置信区间。

2.2 接管反应时间相关性分析

本研究选用皮尔逊相关系数(Pearson Correlation Coefficient)法进行指标与疲劳的相关性分析。同时对相关性分析结果的显著性意义这一项参数进行分析,用 P 值表示显著性,$P < 0.05$ 表示结果具有显著性意义。

KSS 数据为每隔 5min 采集的疲劳等级数值,为了提高相关性分析的精确度,首先利用三次样条插值(Cubic Spline Interpolation)也称为 Spline 插值,通过所有数据点的一条光滑曲线,并通过求解三弯矩方程组得出曲线函数组的过程,即可得到缺失数据段的数据,获取采样频率与驾驶人反应时间一致的数据集。得出接管反应时间与疲劳数据的皮尔逊相关系数 $\rho_{X,Y} = 0.9$,$P = 0.007 < 0.05$,结果证明接管反应时间与疲劳数据即 KSS 显著相关。

3 驾驶疲劳对接管绩效的影响分析

驾驶人疲劳量表值与接管反应时间的显著性分析结果表明驾驶人疲劳程度对接管绩效存在显著影响,为了描述驾驶人疲劳程度与接管绩效之间的关系,根据实验采集的三组数据,以驾驶人编号为 X 轴坐标、65min 实验驾驶时长为 Y 轴坐标、以疲劳度(KSS 值)和接管反应时间为 Z 轴坐标,不同驾驶人的疲劳程度随驾驶时间变化和驾驶人接管反应时间随驾驶时间变化如图 6 所示,其中图 6a)表示早上组,图 6b)表示午后组,图 6c)表示晚上组),驾驶人疲劳程度与接管绩效之间的影响关系分析结果如下:

(1)早上组被试的接管反应时间与驾驶疲劳以及驾驶时间整体呈正相关线性关系,如图 6a)所示,随驾驶疲劳程度以及驾驶时间的增加而递增。疲劳等级分布在[2,4],整体的疲劳程度尚未达到疲劳驾驶的标准。在驾驶疲劳等级为 3.5 左右时,接管反应时间的变化趋势发生了明显的变化,在早上(7:30—8:35)进行驾驶时,当驾驶疲劳增长至 3.5 ~4 级范围内,接管反应时间均值为 3.8s,

驾驶员的接管绩效有较明显的下降。

(2)午后组被试的接管反应时间随着驾驶疲劳以及驾驶时间的增长表现出增长的趋势,如图6b)所示。同时接管反应时间表现出了相应的时变规律,在驾驶时间0~30min内,接管反应时间随驾驶时间增加;在驾驶30~45min内,接管反应时间有所下降;在驾驶时间45~65min内,接管反应时间随驾驶时间增加。在午后(13:30—14:35)进行驾驶时,当疲劳等级增长至5~6级范围内,接管反应时间均值为4.53s,疲劳驾驶行为对接管绩效有着明显的降低作用。

(3)晚上组被试的接管反应时间随着驾驶疲劳以及驾驶时间的增长同样表现增长的趋势,如图6c)所示。在疲劳等级[4,5]范围内,接管反应时间和驾驶疲劳为正弦关系。在晚上(19:00—20:05)进行驾驶时,当疲劳处于5~6级范围内,接管反应时间均值为4.55s,疲劳驾驶行为对接管绩效有着明显的降低作用。

从整体分析,由于驾驶疲劳程度的不同,反映出接管反应时间的趋势,午后驾驶接管反应时间设置阈值不应超过4.5s,晚上驾驶接管反应时间阈值不应超过4.6s。当驾驶员的疲劳等级超过6时,不建议驾驶员执行接管任务。考虑早上组实验后,驾驶人对接管场景有一定的熟悉度,导致对后续实验组(午后组、晚上组)的准确性有一定影响。另外,不同驾驶人的操作习惯不同也会导致接管平稳度有所差异。

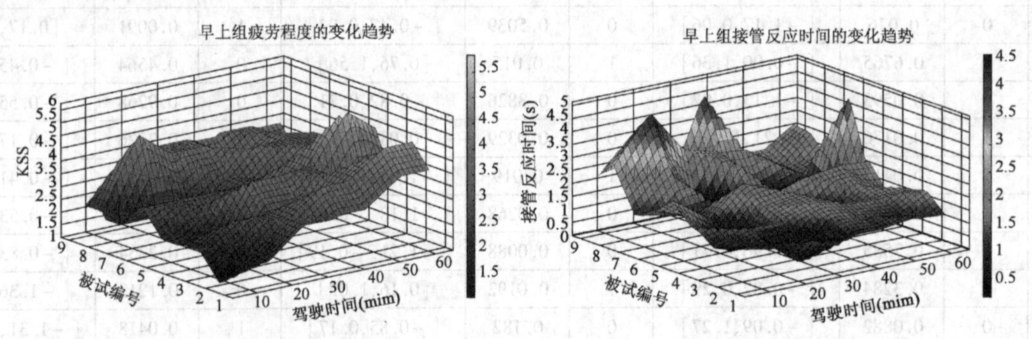

a)早上组实验接管绩效变化

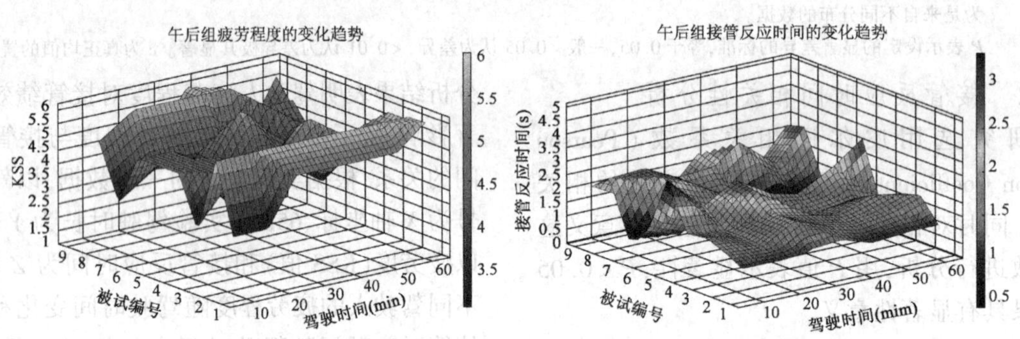

b)午后组实验接管绩效变化

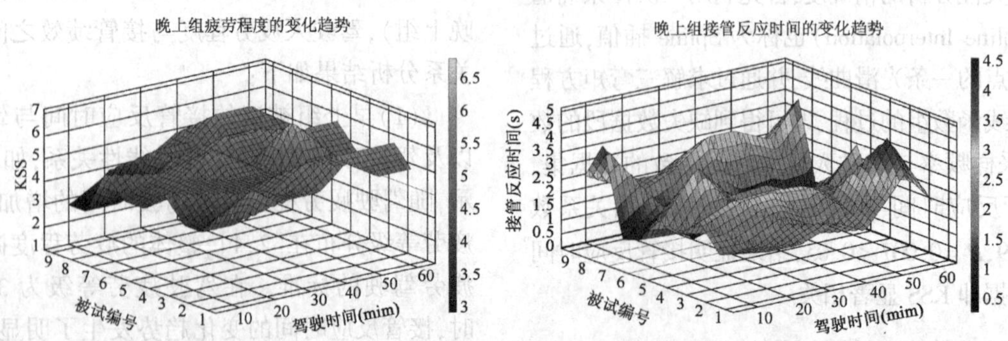

c)晚上组实验接管绩效变化

图6　接管绩效变化

4 结论与展望

本文通过开展人机共驾模拟实验,分析驾驶权限由自动驾驶切换至人工驾驶该模式下接管绩效的变化。根据人机共驾环境下接管反应时间的峰值和均值数据,可以根据驾驶时段的不同,午后驾驶接管反应时间设置阈值不应超过4.5s,晚上驾驶接管反应时间阈值不应超过4.6s。当驾驶人的疲劳等级超过6时,不建议驾驶人执行接管任务,为人机共驾环境下接管时间的阈值设定提供理论支持。但本研究还存在一些不足:

(1)疲劳数据采集方法采用的是主观评价法,在未来的研究中可以将主观评价法和客观设备评定法进行结合,期望能做出一个精度较高的统一疲劳评定方法。

(2)目前大部分学者进行自动驾驶与驾驶疲劳的相关研究都基于模拟器,本文的研究亦是,其数据分析结论对实车驾驶的契合程度还未可知。希望进一步完成实车环境下的人机共驾实验,届时考虑到驾驶环境的复杂性,将会对驾龄、年龄、性别、驾驶风格等因素进行综合考虑,从而增强人机交互环境中接管驾驶的安全稳定性。

参考文献

[1] 钮建伟,张雪梅,孙一品,等.险情中驾驶人接管自动驾驶车辆的驾驶行为研究[J].中国公路学报,2018,31(6):272-280.

[2] 严利鑫,吴超仲,贺宜,等.人机共驾智能车驾驶模式决策属性析取研究[J].中国公路学报,2018,31(1):120-127.

[3] 冯舒,段靓瑜,江朝晖,等.长时间单调模拟驾驶对疲劳的影响研究[J].中国安全科学学报,2007,17(2):66-71.

[4] Vogelpohl T,Kuehn M,Hummel T,et al. Asleep at The Automated Wheel—Sleepiness and Fatigue During Highly Automated Driving[J]. Accident Analysis & Prevention,2018,126:70-84.

[5] Körber M, Cingel A, Zimmermann M, et al. Vigilance Decrement and Passive Fatigue Caused by Monotony in Automated Driving[J]. Procedia Manufacturing,2015,3:2403-2409.

[6] Strand N, Nilsson J, Karlsson M A, et al. Semi-automated versus highly automated driving in critical situations caused by automation failures [J]. Transportation Research Part F Psychology & Behaviour,2014,27:218-228.

[7] Schmig N, Hargutt V, Neukum A, et al. The Interaction Between Highly Automated Driving and the Development of Drowsiness[C]// 6th International Conference on Applied Human Factors and Ergonomics (AHFE 2015) and the Affiliated Conferences, AHFE 2015. 2015.

[8] Caponecchia C, Williamson A. Drowsiness and Driving Performance on Commuter Trips[J]. Journal of Safety Research,2018,66:179-186.

[9] Gold C, Damböck D, Bengler K, et al. Partially Automated Driving as aFallback Level of High Automation [J]. Tagung Fahrerassistenzsysteme. Der Weg zum automatischen Fahren,2013,28(29.11):2013.

[10] Nilsson J, Strand N, Falcone P, et al. Driver Performance in the Presence of Adaptive Cruise Control Related Failures: Implications for Safety Analysis and Fault Tolerance[C]. New York: Dependable Systems and Networks Workshop (DSN-W), 2013 43rd Annual IEEE/IFIP Conference on. IEEE,2013: 1-10.

Environmental Impact on Connected and Automated Vehicle in Heterogeneous State Considering Different Penetration Rates

Yixin Zhang[1] Xumei Chen[*1,2] Xiaoyue Liu[3] Yu Zhang[1]

(1. Key Laboratory of Transport Industry of Big Data Application

Technologies for Comprehensive Transport, Beijing Jiaotong University;
2. School of Traffic and Transportation, Xuchang University;
3. Department of Civil & Environmental Engineering, University of Utah)

Abstract With the rapid development of Connected and Automated Vehicle (CAV) technology, vehiclesequipped with such technology have gradually entered the commercialization stage. For a long time to come, road traffic will be heterogeneous. In this environment, whether different mixes of human-driven vehicles (HVs) and CAVs can achieve the expected benefits and whether the overall benefits on the road will improve are important questions. The main goal of this paper is to quantify the impact of CAV technology on traffic efficiency and traffic environment in complex environments. First, the driving behavior of HV and CAV is characterized based on the Wiedemann model. Then, the measurement model of energy consumption and emission is established based on the kinetic principle. Finally, a simulation platform is developed based on VISSIM for a case study. The traffic efficiency and environmental benefit characteristics of vehicles on an expressway in Beijing are measured at different CAV penetration rates. The results show that with the increase of CAV penetration, the average operating time, average energy consumption, and average vehicle emissions are significantly reduced. This study will effectively support the formulation of relevant road traffic management policies.

Keywords Wiedemann model Connected and automated vehicle Energy consumption emission Vissim

0 Introduction

Economic and social development has led to a significant increase in urban vehicle ownership, which hasinduced a series of traffic-related issues, including reduced travel efficiency, increased energy consumption, and increased emissions (Ou et al., 2018). Many solutions have been proposed to address these problems, among which, improving vehicles' operational stability is considered to be one of the effective and economical solutions (Milanés et al., 2014).

In recent years, Connected and Automated Vehicle (CAV) technology has developed rapidly, which uses onboard detection devices, connected devices, etc., to obtain information such as acceleration and speed of the vehicle in front and achieve acceleration optimization control through theintelligent control system (Zhou et al., 2017). This technology can improve vehicle sensing, decision-making, and control capabilities across the board. Therefore, vehicles equipped with CAV devices are more stable and can provide an effective solution to traditional traffic problems (Rios-Torres et al., 2018).

Vehicles equipped with primary CAV systems are currently available on the market, mainly for premium vehicles but also some for mid-range vehicles (Shladover et al., 2018). Furthermore, with the gradual maturity of CAV technology, market acceptance, application reliability, and application cost of this technology will improve, and the number of vehicles operating on urban roads applying related technology will gradually increase. Therefore, the market penetration of CAV is likely to show a rapid growth trend in recent years.

The popularity of CAV technology makes the future traffic flow consist of a random mix of traditional human-driven vehicles (HV) and CAVs. Whether CAV technology can achieve the expected benefits insuch complex traffic environment is a research topic of outstanding research significance and application value. The purpose of this paper is to quantify the changing characteristics of traffic efficiency and traffic environment impact under different CAV market penetration rates. The driving behavior of HVs and CAVs is characterized based on the Wiedemann model considering operating characteristics and different vehicle types. A vehicle energy consumption measurement method is proposed based on kinematic and kinetic principles. Based on the principle of carbon conservation and considering the energy structure of urban power generation, CO_2 emissions from a vehicle are measured. Finally, a simulation platform for a section of an expressway in Beijing is built in VISSIM, and a case study is conducted to measure the average travel time, average energy consumption, and average CO_2 emissions of vehicles.

The rest of this paper is structured as follows. The literature review on related methods is presented in Section 2. The methodology on the establishment of the car-following model for HV and CAV, and the establishment of the energy consumption and emission model is in the third section. The Case study is in the fourth section. The results and discussion are in the fifth section. The conclusion is presented in the final section.

1 Literature Review

In this paper, Wiedemann model is used to characterize the drivingbehavior of HVs and CAVs, and complex traffic environments are simulated in VISSIM.

Wiedemann model is a classiccar-following model that takes into account the physiological-psychological characteristics of the driver. The model is widely used because it considers numerous factors and can achieve a more accurate portrayal of microscopic driving characteristics (Durrani et al., 2016; Mai et al., 2019; Song et al., 2015). In recent years, with the development of CAV technology, Wiedemann model has also been used to characterize the driving behavior of CAVs (Correia et al., 2019; Stanek et al., 2018). The benefit of this solution is the ability to characterize the driving behavior of a primary CAV with driver involvement. At the same time, the adjustments to the following distance and reaction time of the subject vehicle are in accordance with the essential properties of CAV from the traffic engineering perspective.

The IDM model and the PATH lab model are currently used to characterize the car-followingbehavior of CAV (Qin et al., 2017; Milanés and Shladover, 2014). However, these models are essentially a data fit with weak physical support. At the same time, the implementation cost on some traffic simulation software is relatively high and not suitable for rapid application. In a physical sense, the modification and modeling using the existing Wiedemann model is an automated retrofit and upgrade of existing HVs. At the same time, the learning and application costs are relatively lower for the researcher.

As one of the most commonly used microscopic traffic simulation platforms, Vissim has been widely recognized for its role in supporting the study of microscopic traffic simulation (Huang et al., 2018; Yang et al., 2019). Moreover, with the increasing popularity of CAV research, more and more scholars are analyzing strategies, impacts, and policies using Vissim platform (Hu et al., 2019; Virdi et al., 2019; Zhang et al., 2020). Vissim has powerful microscopic traffic simulation capabilities that enable researchers to set up their own needs for traffic infrastructure, traffic management measures, vehicle operating characteristics, etc. At the same time, Vissim is able to output important information, including vehicle trajectory data and operating time, which is essential for the efficiency of the study.

Therefore, in this paper, the research framework constructed based on the Wiedemann model-Vissim software can effectively analyze vehicle operation characteristics under different market penetration rates in complex traffic environments. Meanwhile, based on the trajectory data output from Vissim, combined with the energy consumption and emission model measurement method proposed in this paper, the environmental impact of CAV can be studied. The research method in this paper can effectively support the achievement of the research objectives and provide guidance for CAV research in related fields.

2 Methdology

2.1 Characterization of Driving Behavior

2.1.1 Wiedemann model

In this paper, Wiedemann model is used to characterize the car-following behavior of HV and

CAV. In Wiedemann model, the car-following behavior of the rear vehicle (target vehicle) is dictated by the speed difference (Δv) and distance difference (Δx) between the rear vehicle and the preceding vehicle. The perception thresholds of the rear driver result in four driving conditions and corresponding driving strategies are determined: (1) Approaching, (2) Following, (3) Braking, and (4) Free. In each condition, a different calculation method is used to calculate the acceleration required by the subject vehicle at the current time stamp. The driving process is shown in Fig. 1.

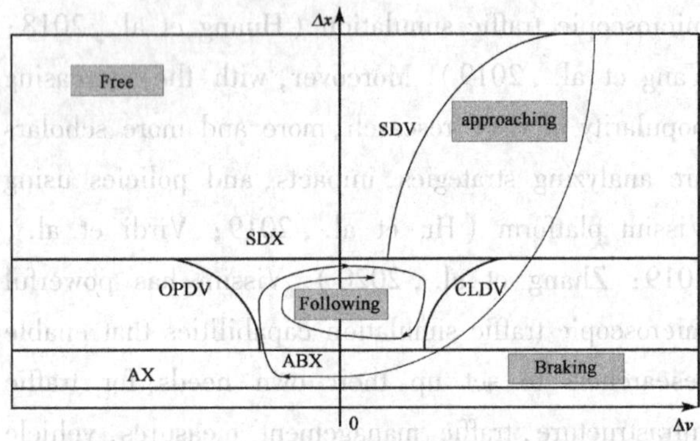

Fig. 1 Wiedemann Model

As shown inFig. 1, AX, OPDV, SDX, ABX, CLDV, and SDV are the thresholds for the rear vehicle response. A driving condition is defined by several thresholds. When the vehicle is in a certain condition, the vehicle apply the corresponding acceleration. The four thresholds SDV, SDX, OPDV, and ABX, altogether determine the "Following" condition, and when the vehicle enters this condition, $a_{\text{following}}$ is adopted as the acceleration of the subject vehicle. In the "Following" condition, since the driver cannot accurately judge the distance difference, speed is in a fluctuating state. That is, when the driver feels far away from the car in front, the driver accelerates, and when the vehicle is close in distance, the driver decelerates. The "Braking" condition is determined by the threshold values ABX and AX. When the vehicle is in "Braking" condition, the acceleration for the vehicle is $d_{braking}$. When the vehicle is above the threshold SDX and SDV, it is in a "Free" condition. At this moment, there are no vehicles or signals within a specific range directly in front of the target vehicle, and the goal of the driver or control system is to maximize travel speed, so the vehicle uses the maximum acceleration ($a_{\max}$) to reach the desired speed. When the vehicle is on the right side of SDV or CLDV, it enters the "Approaching" state, and the acceleration is $a_{\text{approaching}}$. The main thresholds and accelerations are calculated as shown in Eqs (1)-Eqs (7).

$$AX = L_{n-1} + AX_{\text{add}} + RND1_n \times AX_{\text{mult}} \quad (1)$$

$$ABX = AX + BX \quad (2)$$

$$BX = (BX_{\text{add}} + \text{BX}_{\text{mut}} \times RND1_n) \times \sqrt{v} \quad (3)$$

$$v = \min(v_n, v_{n-1}) \quad (4)$$

$$a_{\text{following}} = \text{following}_{\text{mult}} \times (RND4_n + NRND) \quad (5)$$

$$a_{\text{approaching}} = \frac{1}{2} \times \frac{(Av)^2}{ABX - (AX - L_{n-1})} + b_{n-1} \quad (6)$$

$$d_{\text{braking}} = \frac{1}{2} \times \frac{(Av)^2}{ABX - (AX - L_{n-1})} + b_{n-1} + b_{\min} \times \frac{ABX - (AX - L_{n-1})}{BX} \quad (7)$$

Where, L_{n-1} is the length of the front vehicle, *AXadd*, *AXmult*, *Bxadd*, and *BXmult* are constants, and *RND1n* is a normally distributed parameter. v_n, v_{n-1} are the speeds of the rear and preceding vehicles, respectively. $following_{mult}$ is a calibration parameter, and *RND4n* and *NRND* are normally distributed parameters. b_{n-1} is the deceleration of the preceding vehicle. b_{min} is the maximum deceleration of the subject vehicle.

Based on the above theories and models, two models, Wiedemann 74 and Wiedemann 99 were developed, the former mainly for urban roads and the latter mainly for highways or expressways. This paper is based on Wiedemann 99 according to the experimental research needs and calibrates the relevant parameters according to the actual situation in order to characterize the car-followingbehavior of HV or CAV.

2.1.2 HV

The default parameters of the Wiedemann model are not designed for thereal-world conditions in

China, so relevant parameters need to be calibrated to simulate the actual road conditions as much as possible. There are ten main parameters of the Wiedemann model, as shown in Tab. 1.

Description of the parameters Tab. 1

Parameters	Description
CC0	The average desired standstill distance between two vehicles
CC1	It restricts the distance difference (longitudinal oscillation) or how much more distance than the desired safety distance a driver allows before he intentionally moves closer to the car in front.
CC2	It restricts the distance difference (longitudinal oscillation) or how much more distance than the desired safety distance a driver allows before he intentionally moves closer to the car in front.
CC3	It controls the start of the deceleration process, i. e. the number of seconds before reaching the safety distance. At this stage the driver recognizes a preceding slower vehicle.
CC4	It defines negative speed difference during the following process.
CC5	It defines positive speed difference during the following process.
CC6	Influence of distance on speed oscillation while in following process.
CC7	Oscillation during acceleration
CC8	Desired acceleration when starting from standstill
CC9	Desired acceleration at 80 km/h

Firstly, some parameters are set directly based on relevant literature andexisting studies. Then, several road sections are selected for calibrating the parameters in VISSIM. The range of alternative parameter values is set on the basis of relevant studies, and the parameters are calibrated using the orthogonal experimental method. Finally, parameters such as "Lane Change" and "Lateral" are also set according to the actual situation.

2.1.3 CAV

There are two ways in VISSIM to characterize the driving behavior of CAV, internally and externally. The internal method refers to the adjustment of the parameters of the Wiedemann model to characterize the CAV behavior. On the other hand, the external method refers to the use of Component Object Model (COM) or External Driver Model (EDM) interfaces to take over the control logic of a specific vehicle to achieve the simulation of the CAV driving behavior. The internal method is more efficient than the COM or EDM method. Moreover, the learning cost and usage cost of this method make it easy to adopt. Therefore, the parameters of the Wiedemann model are modified to characterize the driving behavior of the CAV, as shown in Tab. 2.

Parameter setting for CAV. Tab. 2

Parameters	Automated Car (AC)	Automated Bus (AB)
CC0	1.50	3.00
CC1	1.40	1.80
CC2	0.00	0.00
CC3	-16.00	-20.00
CC4	0.00	0.00
CC5	0.00	0.00
CC6	0.00	0.00
CC7	0.00	0.00
CC8	2.50	2.00
CC9	1.50	1.50

By setting these parameters, the vehicle's speed oscillation and acceleration oscillation are essentially minimized, which is in line with the operating characteristics of the CAV being controlled by the system. The visual field of view of the vehicle is also expanded, which is in line with the increased capability of the CAV due to sensors, radar, and other equipment.

Compared with HV, CAV has significant advantages in speedstability, following distance, and sensitivity because they rely on sensors, radar, and onboard computers for perception, decision-making, and control. Therefore, the setting of the parameters related to the speed stability and the following spacing in Widemann model enables the characterization of the longitudinal behavior of CAV.

In order to verify the effectiveness of the CAV model proposed in this paper, a series of tests are conducted. The response of the rear vehicle is tested on a section of the urban expressway where the front vehicle is a human-driven car (HC) operating at a constant speed of 40km/h. Based on the above study, four models of HC, automated car (AC), human-driven bus (HB), and automated bus (AB), are designed and defined as the rear vehicle, respectively. Fig. 2 shows the test results.

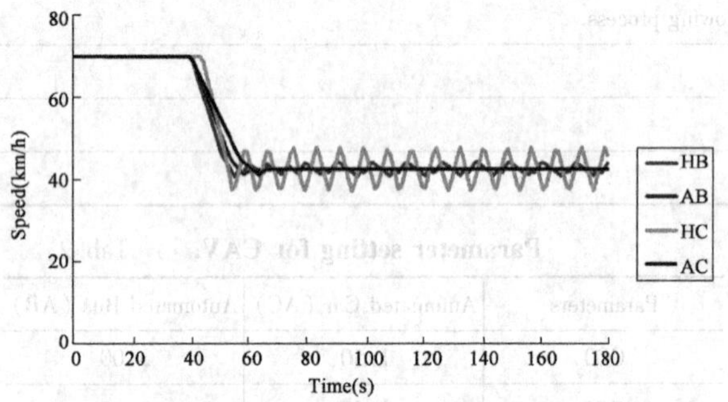

Fig. 2 Response of four vehicles

As shown in Figure 2, the AC and AB equipped with CAV technology react earlier andenter " Following" condition faster. Moreover, the operation of these two vehicle types in the " Following" condition is more stable. The results show that the CAV model proposed in this paper is effective.

2.2 Emission and Energy Consumption Model

The model set up above is configured on theVissim software, and the simulated road network is constructed according to the actual conditions. After a successful run, second-by-second trajectory data for each vehicle is generated. In each time step, the speed and acceleration of individual vehicles are used to calculate the energy consumption and emission for every vehicle. For the purpose of this paper, it is assumed that all vehicles are electric vehicles.

The energy consumption model in this study first obtains the instantaneous traction force required by the electricvehicle based on the basic theory of vehicle dynamics, and then integrates it to estimate the total energy consumption. The traction force is calculated by Eq. (8).

$$F(t) = F_r(t) + F_a(t) + F_s(t) + F_l(t) + F_g(t) \tag{8}$$

Where, $F_r(t)$ is the rolling resistance, $F_a(t)$ is the air resistance, $F_s(t)$ is the slope resistance, $F_l(t)$ is the linear acceleration force, and is the $F_g(t)$ rotational acceleration force. The detailed calculation is shown in Eqs. (9) - (13). According to existing studies, the rotational acceleration force is about 5% of the linear acceleration force.

$$F_r(t) = u_r mg \tag{9}$$

$$F_a(t) = 0.5\rho C_d A_f^2 v(t)^2 \tag{10}$$

$$F_s(t) = mg\sin\theta \tag{11}$$

$$F_l(t) = ma \tag{12}$$

$$F_g(t) = 0.05ma \tag{13}$$

Where, u_r is the coefficient of friction, m is the total vehicle mass, g is the acceleration of gravity, ρ is the air density, C_d is the air resistance coefficient, A_f is the windward area, $v(t)$ is the vehicle speed, θ is the slope, and a is the vehicle acceleration.

The parameters represented are known and constant, except for the acceleration and speed of the vehicle, so that the instantaneous power of the vehicle ($P(t)$) is shown in Eq (14).

$$P(t) = F(t)v(t) \tag{14}$$

The formula for calculating the total energy consumption of a vehicle (E_c) is Equation (15).

$$E_c = \int P(t)\,dt \tag{15}$$

CO_2 emissions from electric vehicles are mainly generated by power plants when they generate electricity. Typical types of power generation in Beijing (coal, hydrogen, hydroelectric, nuclear, wind power, etc.) are considered, and the CO_2 emissions of an electric vehicle (E_m) in this paper are shown in Eq (16).

$$E_m = E_c f \tag{16}$$

Where, f is the CO_2 emissions intensity per unit of energy consumption.

3 Case Study

The study is based onVissim software. The study area is a road section along Lianshi East Road in Beijing, as shown in Fig. 3.

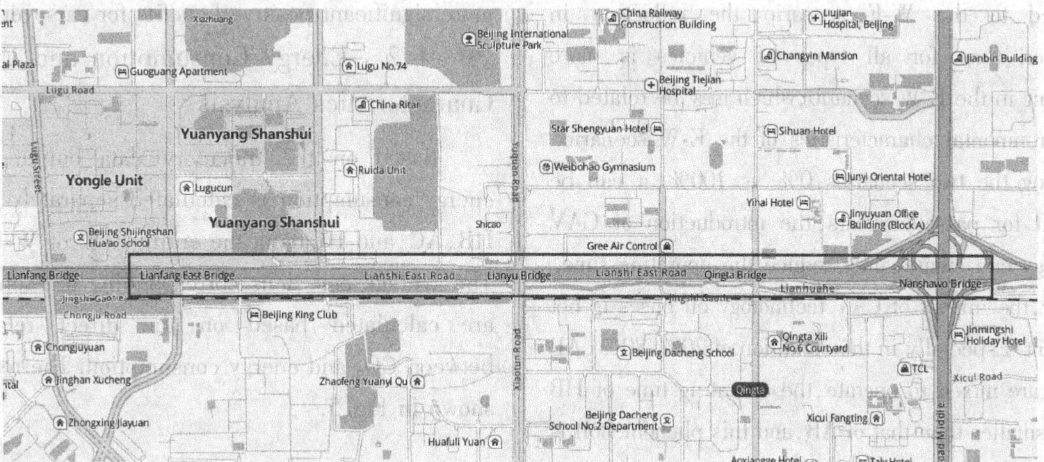

Fig. 3　Study area

Based on the datacollected, key parameters such as vehicle composition, vehicle routes, and desired speed distribution are set. The longitudinal and lateral models of Vissim are calibrated according to the traffic flow of critical sections and the actual situation in Beijing, and the simulation platform is finally established.

In order to facilitate the study, in this paper, the simulation platform is developed and analyzed mainly for two types of vehicles-buses, and passenger cars.

Six scenarios are set based on the CAV market penetration, including 0%, 20%, 40%, 60%, 80%, and 100%. 0% means that all vehicles are HVs while 100% is when all vehicles are equipped with CAV system.

4 Results and Discussion

The first 1200s are considered warm-up period to better simulate the actual situation, and the results from this period are not used in this study. Moreover, for comparison purposes, in this paper, only vehicles that completed the entire route (i. e., vehicles whose start and endpoints are located on the main road and whose start time is after the 1200s and end time is before 4800s) are analyzed.

4.1 Operation Characteristics Analysis

After the warm-up period, the average operating time of vehicles traveling the entire distance in the east-to-west (E-W) or west-to-east (W-E) direction isrecorded. The entire distance in both directions is 3900m. Under free flow, the desired speed of both HC and AC is 80km/h, and the desired speed of both HB and AB is 60km/h. The results of the average operating time are shown in Fig. 4.

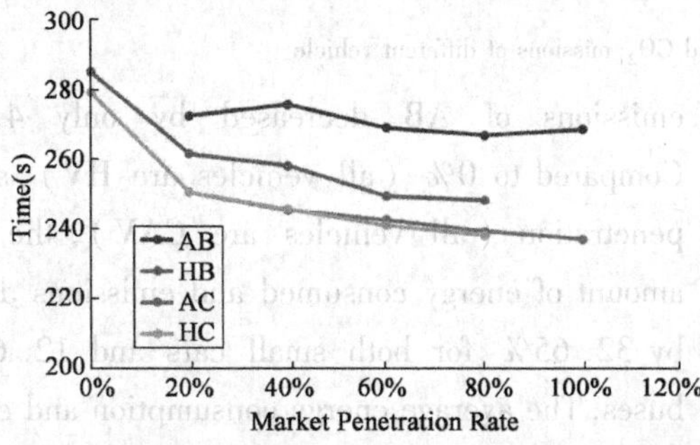

a)Average vehichle operating time from east to west

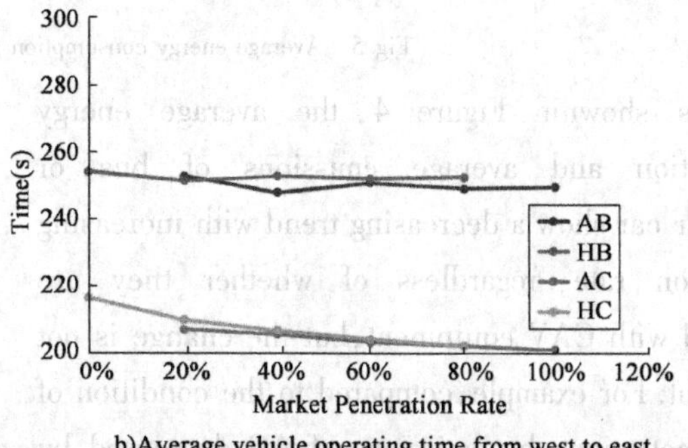

b)Average vehicle operating time from west to east

Fig. 4　Average vehicle operating time

According to Fig. 4, as market penetration rate increases, the average operating time to complete the entire journey decreases for both types of vehicles. Compared to the W-E scenario, the reduction in completion time for all types of vehicles is more significant in the E-W scenario, which may be related to the environmental characteristics of the E-W scenario. Combining the two scenarios, 0% vs. 100%, it can be seen that for passenger cars, the introduction of CAV technology can significantly reduce the operating time. However, the impact of CAV technology on buses is not significant. Especially in the condition of 20%-80%, AB and HB are mixed to operate, the operating time of HB may be smaller than that of AB, and this phenomenon is more obvious in the E-W scenario.

The results show that the introduction of CAV technology has a positive impact on traffic flow, with more significant positive benefits for carsover buses.

4.2 Energy Consumption and Emission Characteristics Analysis

Based on the trajectory data output, average energy consumption is calculated separately for AB, HB, AC, and HCalong the entire E-W or W-E route. The average emissions corresponding to each vehicle are calculated based on the direct relationship between CO_2 and energy consumption. The results are shown in Fig. 5.

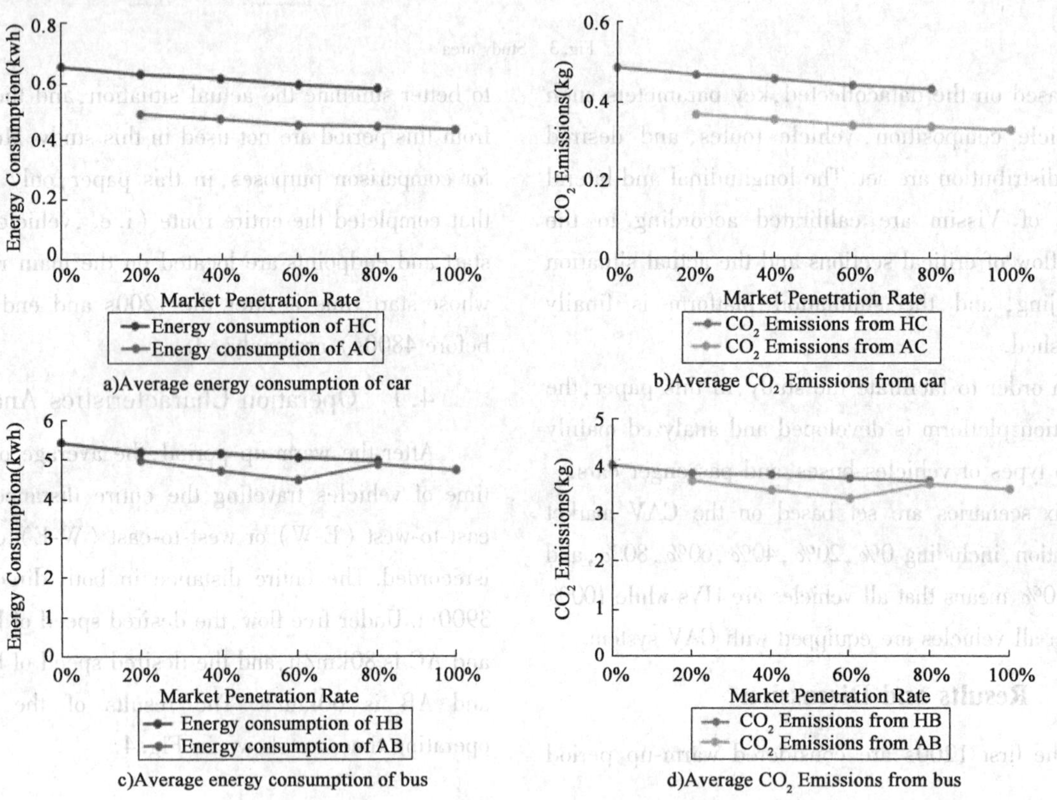

Fig. 5　Average energy consumption and CO_{2e}missions of different vehicle

As shownin Figure 4, the average energy consumption and average emissions of bus or passenger car show a decreasing trend with increasing penetration rate, regardless of whether they are equipped with CAV equipment, but the change is not significant. For example, compared to the condition of 20% penetration, the emissions of AC decreased by only 10.76% in the 100% condition, while the emissions of AB decreased by only 4.75%. Compared to 0% (all vehicles are HV), at 100% penetration (all vehicles are CAV), the average amount of energy consumed and emissions decreased by 32.65% for both small cars and 12.60% for buses. The average energy consumption and emissions of CAV vehicles are lower than those of HV for the same penetration rate. At a 60% penetration rate, the average energy consumption and emissions of AC decreased by 23.22% compared to HC, while the average energy consumption and emissions of AB decreased by 11.12% compared to HB.

Because of the direct relationship between CO_2 and energy consumption, and both buses and cars are electric, the trend in emissions is consistent with the trend in the amount of energy consumption, regardless of the vehicle types. The average energy consumption and emissions of CAV (AB or AC) are lower than those of HV (HB or HC) for any penetration rate. CAV technology has a more significant reduction in energy consumption and emissions for passenger cars than for buses. The energy consumption and emissions of buses, whether equipped with CAV equipment or not, are much higher than those of cars.

5 Conclusions

In this paper, the impact of CAV technology on traffic efficiency, energy consumption, and emissions areanalyzed and measured for the gradual introduction of CAV technology into road traffic. Wiedemann model is used to characterize the driving behavior of HVs and CAVs, respectively. Based on the physics fundamentals, calculation of the energy consumption and emissions of the vehicle is proposed. Finally, based on the actual expressway in Beijing, a simulation platform is built in VISSIM to analyze the changing characteristics of average vehicle travel time, average energy consumption, and average emission under different market penetration rates. The main findings are as follows.

(1) The introduction of CAV technology can reduce the average travel time of all vehicles on a road section and improve the efficiency of the road. The improvement is more significant in congested conditions.

(2) The average energy consumption and emissions of CAVs are lower than those of HVs due to the stability of vehicle operating as a result of the CAV technology, and the average energy consumption and emissions of vehicles show a decreasing trend as the penetration rate increases.

Although the study successfully demonstrated the advantages of CAV technology in the traffic and environment domain without considering the unique features of CAV, it has certain limitations in terms ofmodeling. In the future, the CAV model can be developed in greater depth rather than being modified using existing human-driving models. Meanwhile, environmental impact measurement models can be developed based on actual data. The applicability and reliability of the method proposed in this paper can be analyzed by comparing it with the existing methods based on the IDM model and PATH model. Furthermore, the sensitivity analysis of the results can be performed by considering factors such as speed and traffic flow.

6 Acknowledgements

The authors acknowledge that this paper is prepared based on the Fundamental Research Funds for the Central Universities # 2020YJS087 and the National Natural Science Foundation of China (NSFC) under grant #71871013. Thanks are also given to the anonymous reviewers for their helpful comments on this paper.

The authors confirm contribution to the paper as follows: study conception and design: Yixin Zhang, Xumei Chen; data collection: Yixin Zhang and Yu Zhang; analysis and interpretation of results: Yixin Zhang and Xumei Chen; draft manuscript preparation: Yixin Zhang, and Xumei Chen. All authors reviewed the results and approved the final version of the manuscript.

References

[1] Correia L. P., Rafael S., Lopes D., et al. Assessment of local air quality for different penetration levels of connected autonomous vehicles[J]. WIT Transactions on the Built Environment, 2019, 186, 153-162.

[2] Durrani U., Lee C., Maoh H. Calibrating the Wiedemann's vehicle-following model using mixed vehicle-pair interactions[J]. Transportation Research Part C: Emerging Technologies, 2016,

67,227-242.

[3] Eilbert A., L. Jackson., G. Noel, et al. A framework for evaluating energy and emissions impacts of CCAV traffic microsimulations. in "Transportation Research Board 92th Annual Meeting", Washington, D. C., Untied State, January 16-27,2018,915(5):1-19.

[4] Hu X., Sun J. Trajectory optimization of connected and autonomous vehicles at a multilane freeway merging area[J]. Transportation Research Part C: Emerging Technologies, 2019, 101 (January):111-125.

[5] Huang K., Yang X., Lu Y., et al. Ecological driving system for connected/automated vehicles using a two-stage control hierarchy[J]. IEEE Transactions on Intelligent Transportation Systems,2018,19(7):2373-2384.

[6] Mai M., Wang L., Prokop, G. Advancement of the car following model of Wiedemann on lower velocity ranges for urban traffic simulation[J]. Transportation Research Part F: Traffic Psychology and Behaviour,2019,61:30-37.

[7] Milané s V., Shladover S. E. Modeling cooperative and autonomous adaptive cruise control dynamic responses using experimental data [J]. Transportation Research Part C: Emerging Technologies,2014,48:285-300.

[8] Milané s V., Shladover S. E. Modeling cooperative and autonomous adaptive cruise control dynamic responses using experimental data [J]. Transportation Research Part C: Emerging Technologies,2014,48:285-300.

[9] Ou H., Tang, T. Q. An extended two-lane car-following model accounting for inter-vehicle communication. Physica A: Statistical Mechanics and Its Applications,2018,495:260-268.

[10] Qin Y. Y., Wang H., Wang W., et al. Fundamental Diagram Model of Heterogeneous Traffic Flow Mixed with Cooperative Adaptive Cruise Control Vehicles and Adaptive Cruise Control Vehicles [J]. Zhongguo Gonglu Xuebao/China Journal of Highway and Transport,2017,30(10):127-136.

[11] Rios-Torres J., Malikopoulos, A. A. Impact of partial penetrations of connected and automated vehicles on fuel consumption and traffic flow [J]. IEEE Transactions on Intelligent Vehicles,3(4):453-462.

[12] Shladover S. E. Connected and automated vehicle systems: Introduction and overview. Journal of Intelligent Transportation Systems: Technology, Planning, and Operations, 2018, 22(3):190-200.

[13] Song G., Yu L., Geng Z. Optimization of Wiedemann and Fritzsche car-following models for emission estimation [J]. Transportation Research Part D: Transport and Environment, 2015,34:318-329.

[14] Stanek D., Huang E., MilamR. T., et al. Measuring autonomous vehicle impacts on congested networks using simulation [C] // Transportation Research Board 92th Annual Meeting, Washington, D. C., Untied State, January 16-27,2018,18(04585):1-19.

[15] Virdi N., Grzybowska H., Waller S. T., et al. A safety assessment of mixed fleets with Connected and Autonomous Vehicles using the Surrogate Safety Assessment Module. Accident Analysis and Prevention, 2019, 131 (June): 95-111.

[16] Yang Z., Feng Y., Gong X., et al. Eco-trajectory planning with consideration of queue along congested corridor for hybrid electric vehicles[J]. Transportation Research Record.

[17] Zhang J., Wu K., Cheng M., et al. Safety evaluation for connected and autonomous vehicles' exclusive lanes considering penetrate ratios and impact of trucksusing surrogate safety measures. Journal of Advanced Transportation,2020.

[18] Zhou Y., Ahn S., Chitturi M., et al. Rolling horizon stochastic optimal control strategy for ACC and CACC under uncertainty [J]. Transportation Research Part C: Emerging Technologies,2017,83:61-76.

天气对公共自行车出行的影响研究

甘雷琼*

(华设设计集团股份有限公司)

摘　要　在各种出行方式中,自行车出行对天气的敏感性是最强的,本文通过对华盛顿 Capital Bike 原始数据进行分析,系统研究了天气因素对公共自行车出行量的影响。首先,运用 SPSS 方差分析模型讨论了降水、温度和风速影响下公共自行车出行量的变化,发现降水对自行车出行量的影响是最大的;其次,引入负二项回归模型,深入研究了天气因素不同等级下公共自行车出行量的变化,研究表明,降水量越大、温度越高、出行距离越长,自行车出行量减少越多。

关键词　天气　公共自行车出行量　方差分析模型　负二项模型

0　引言

自行车出行属于需要长期暴露于户外环境中的主动出行方式之一,任何时间交通环境中所出现的因素都会对出行者是否选择公共自行车出行产生相应的影响。而在现实中的交通环境中自行车出行者最能切身感受到的便是天气的变化。同时,在实际中每天的天气因素又会包含多种类型,如降水、温度、风速、能见度等,因此,各类型天气因素之间又可能存在某种交互作用,这都将会对自行车出行产生影响,都值得我们进行深入研究[1]。

现有文献中,Cantelmo 等[2]基于天气因素构建了共享单车的需求预测模型。Wessel 等[3]运用对数线性回归和负二项式回归的方法研究了温度、降水、风速等天气因素影响下自行车出行的需求,模型结果表明降雨对自行车出行产生的影响最大,而且还会带来滞后效应。黎鹏[4]选取气温和降雨量作为天气指标,采用 BP 神经网络定量预测的方法,就天气指标对区域单车骑行量进行了预测研究。总结发现,讨论天气因素交互作用对出行量影响的文献相对较少。在实际的户外环境中,骑行者所能感受到的天气条件并不是单一的,而是多种天气状况交织的一种混合天气。因此,本文在现有研究的基础上,基于 2017 年 9 月至 2018 年 10 月华盛顿 Capital Bike 的出行数据,就天气因素交互作用对自行车出行量产生的影响展开了相关研究。

1　多因素方差分析模型

1.1　模型概述

多因素方差分析主要用于研究两个或两个以上影响因子不同水平是否对因变量产生显著影响。通过多因素方差分析模型既能够得出各种影响因子独立对因变量产生影响的显著性,又能够得出两个或两个以上影响因子的交互作用对因变量产生影响的显著性。以三因素方差分析为例,本文将降水、温度、风速作为公共自行车出行量变化的主要影响因素,其中,降水有 r 个水平,记为 A_1、A_2、A_3、$\cdots$ A_r,温度有 s 个水平,记为B_1、B_2、B_3、$\cdots$ B_s,因素 C 有 t 个水平,记为C_1、C_2、C_3、$\cdots$、C_t,在(A_r,B_s,C_t)的水平组合下进行 m 次独立实验,实验结果记为x_{ijkn},其中 i、j、k 分别代表降水、温度、风速的相应水平,n 代表第 n 次独立实验,假定 x_{ijkn}服从正态分布,即$x_{ijkn} \sim N(\mu_{ijk},\sigma^2)$,其数学表达式为:

$$\begin{cases} x_{ijkn} \sim N(\mu_{ijk},\sigma^2) \\ x_{ijkn} = \mu + \alpha_i + \beta_j + \gamma_k + \eta_{ij} + \eta_{ik} + \eta_{jk} + \eta_{ijk} + \varepsilon_{ijkn} \end{cases} \tag{1}$$

式中:　$i=1,2,3,\cdots,r;j=1,2,3,\cdots,s;k=1,2,3,\cdots,t$;

x_{ijkn}——自行车出行量在降水第 i 个水平,温度第 j 个水平,风速第 k 个水平下第 n 次实验的均值;

μ——公共自行车的出行量均值;

α_i、β_j、γ_k——出行量在降水第 i 个水平、温度第 j 个

水平风速第 k 个水平下的总体均值;

η_{ij}、η_{ik}、η_{jk}——出行量在两种天气因素相交互作用下的总体均值;

η_{ijk}——自行车出行量在三种天气因素交互作用下的总体均值;

ε_{ijkn}——第 n 次实验的随机误差项。

以本文所用的三因素方差分析为例,在进行影响因素显著性分析时其零假设是各类型天气因素不同水平下公共自行车出行量的各总体的均值无显著差异,各类型天气因素及其交互作用的效应同时为0,记为 H_0: $a_1=a_2=\cdots=a_r=0$: $b_1=b_2=\cdots=b_s=0$: $c_1=c_2=\cdots=c_t=0$: $(ab)_{rs}=(ac)_{rt}=(bc)_{st}=0$: $(abc)_{rst}=0$。多因素方差分析模型中各种因素的显著性检验也是比较各种因素以及它们之间交互作用的概率 p 值与给出的显著性水平 α:

(1)若 p_{F_A}、p_{F_B}、p_{F_C} 小于 α,则拒绝零假设,认为公共自行车出行量在降水、温度、风速不同水平下的各总体均值具有显著差异,即降水、温度、风速不同水平对公共自行车出行量产生显著影响;否则,接受零假设。

(2)若 $p_{F_{AB}}$、$p_{F_{AC}}$、$p_{F_{BC}}$、$p_{F_{ABC}}$ 小于 α,则拒绝零假设,认为公共自行车出行量在天气因素交互作用下的各总体均值具有显著差异,即天气对公共自行车出行量具有交互影响;否则,接受零假设。

1.2　变量处理

本文将从气象站获得的原始天气数据,按照一定的分类标准对温度、降水、风速、能见度等天气因素进行了详细划分,即方差分析模型中所提到的天气因素不同水平。各种天气因素的划分标准和调查期间的发生频次及其分布情况如表1所示。

天气类型的定义、发生频次及所占比例分布　　表1

天气类型		分类标准	比例	参考文献
降水	无降水	日累积降水量为0mm	58.08%	Li 等[5];Yang 等[6]
	阵雨	日累积降水量在0~10mm范围内或有降水迹象,且气象站描述的天气状况为雨	24.66%	
	普通降雨	日累积降水量在10~25mm范围内,且气象站描述的天气状况为雨	6.85%	
	暴雨	日累积降水量超过25mm	6.85%	
	降雪	日累积降水量大于0mm且气象站描述的当天天气状况为雪	2.19%	
	雨夹雪	日累积降水量大于0mm,且气象站描述的当天天气状况雨/雪	1.37%	
	下雪后两天	发生降雪事件之后的两天	4.38%	
温度	较为舒适的温度	气温介于4℃和30℃之间,且相近两天温度差小于5℃	50.41%	Nankervis[7],Li 等[5],Chardon 等[8],An 等[9],Yang 等[6]
	极冷	气温低于4℃	20.27%	
	极热	气温高于30℃	13.97%	
	大温差	气温介于4℃和30℃之间,且相近两天温度差大于5℃	15.34%	
风速	无风	当日最高风速小于5.7m/s	39.73%	Nankervis[7],Corcoran 等[10],Yang 等[6]
	微风	当日最高风速介于5.7m/s和10.8m/s之间	57.26%	
	强风	当日最高风速大于10.8m/s	3.01%	
能见度	无雾	当日最低能见度大于1km且气象站描述的天气状况没有薄雾/霾	91.23%	Yang 等[6]
	有雾	当日最低能见度小于1km,或气象站描述的当天天气状况为薄雾/霾	8.77%	

1.3　模型结果

考虑天气因素交互方差分析模型的零假设为:各种天气不同水平的公共自行车出行量各总体均值无显著差异,各种天气因素无交互作用。表2为各种天气因素及其交互作用与出行量的方差分析结果。

各种天气因素及其交互作用与出行量的方差分析结果 表2

源	Ⅲ类平方和	自由度	均方	F	显著性
修正模型	12.178a	42	0.290	5.311	0.000
截距	1.804	1	1.804	33.047	0.000***
降水	3.671	6	0.612	11.204	0.000***
温度	0.489	3	0.163	2.985	0.031*
风速	0.533	2	0.267	4.882	0.008**
降水/温度	0.599	12	0.050	0.914	0.533
降水/风速	0.607	7	0.087	1.589	0.138
温度/风速	0.523	5	0.105	1.916	0.091
降水/温度/风速	0.313	6	0.052	0.954	0.456
误差	17.581	322	0.055	—	—
总计	29.781	365	—	—	—
修正后总计	29.759	364	—	—	—

注：*** p_value < 0.001，** 0.001 < p_value < 0.01，* 0.01 < p_value < 0.05。

根据方差分析结果，可以得出，当显著性水平取0.05时，对自行车出行量影响最显著的天气因素依次是降水（$F=11.204, p=0.000$）、风速（$F=4.882, p=0.008$）和温度（$F=2.985, p=0.031$）；当显著性水平取0.1时，温度和风速的交互项对出行量产生的影响比其他天气因素交互项对自行车出行量产生的影响明显。

2 负二项回归模型

2.1 模型概述

负二项分布可以看作是一个连续的混合poisson分布，负二项回归模型也是poisson回归模型的一个延伸发展。因此，本小节首先对poisson回归模型进行了简单概括。

本文将不同距离范围内公共自行车的实际出行量作为回归分析的因变量，在对计数模型进行回归分析时，通常采用的是poisson回归模型，该模型假设公共自行车实际出行量服从poisson分布，其概率分布函数为：

$$\begin{cases} P(y_i) = \dfrac{\lambda_i^{y_i}\exp(-\lambda)}{y_i!} \\ \lambda_i = E(y_i \mid x_i) = \mathrm{Var}(y_i \mid x_i) \end{cases} \tag{2}$$

式中：$P(y_i)$——第i类出行距离下公共自行车实际出行量为y的概率；

$E(y_i|x_i)$——第i类出行距离下公共自行车实际出行量的期望值；

$\mathrm{Var}(y_i|x_i)$——第i类出行距离下公共自行车实际出行量的方差。

当研究公共自行车实际出行量与各影响因素之间关系时，通常建立如下关系：

$$\lambda_i = E(y_i \mid x_i) = \exp(\beta_0 + \beta_1 x_1 + \beta_2 x_2 + \cdots + \beta_n x_n) \tag{3}$$

式中：x_i——公共自行车出行量的各类影响因素；

β_i——各影响因素的参数估计值$i=1,2,3,\cdots,n$。

Poisson回归模型的连结函数一般为对数函数，其回归方程表达式为：

$$\log(\lambda) = \beta_0 + \beta_1 x_1 + \beta_2 x_2 + \cdots + \beta_n x_n \tag{4}$$

在poisson回归中，隐含一个重要的前提假设：

$$E(y_i \mid x_i) = \mathrm{Var}(y_i \mid x_i) \tag{5}$$

即因变量的期望与方差相等。

但在实际中，不同出行距离范围内公共自行车出行量存在过度离散的情况，这种情况下poisson回归便不再适用，因此，需要引入负二项回归。负二项式回归是在poisson回归模型的基础上，添加了一个ε_i作为随机效应来表示未观察到的个体异质性，因此，负二项回归模型的函数表达式为：

$$\ln\lambda_i = \beta_0 + \beta_i X_i + \varepsilon_i \tag{6}$$

此时，λ_i满足：

$$\lambda_i = E(y_i \mid x_i) = \exp(\beta_0 + \beta_1 x_1 + \beta_2 x_2 + \cdots + \beta_n x_n)\exp(\varepsilon_i) \tag{7}$$

其中，$\exp(\varepsilon_i) \sim \Gamma(1,\alpha)$。

因此，负二项分布的概率密度函数表达式为：

$$P(y_i) = \frac{\Gamma(y_i + \alpha^{-1})}{\Gamma(y_i + 1)\Gamma(\alpha^{-1})}\left(\frac{\alpha^{-1}}{\alpha^{-1} + \lambda_i}\right)^{\alpha^{-1}}$$

$$\left(\frac{\lambda_i}{\alpha^{-1}+\lambda_i}\right)^{\alpha^{-1}} \tag{8}$$

概率分布函数表达式为:

$$P(y_i)=\frac{\Gamma(y_i+\alpha)}{y_i!\Gamma(\alpha)}\left(\frac{\alpha}{\lambda_i+\alpha}\right)^{\alpha}\left(\frac{\lambda_i}{\lambda_i+\alpha}\right)^{y_i} \tag{9}$$

式中:α——模型的离散系数;$\Gamma(\cdot)$表示伽马分布。

在负二项分布中,$E(y_i)=\lambda_i$,$Var(y_i)=\lambda_i+\alpha\lambda_i^{\ 2}$,当离散系数$\alpha$为0时,负二项模型便可以转化为poisson模型,因此,可以说poisson模型是负二项模型的一种特殊情况,负二项模型是由poisson模型发展而来的。

2.2　分类变量处理

(1)定义天气事件

回归模型中天气变量分为数值型变量和分类变量两种,其中,数值型变量为温度、降水、风速、能见度等普通天气的度量值;分类变量为包括冷天、热天、强风、暴雨、雾天、雪天等恶劣天气变量。对于各分类变量的定义如表3所示。

分类变量定义标准　表3

变量类型	变　量	分　类	占　比
恶劣天气变量	冷天(Coldday)	日最低气温≤-0.6℃(10%分位数)	10.68%
	热天(Hotday)	日最高气温≥31.7℃(90%分位数)	10.14%
	强风(Strongwind)	日最高风速≥10m/s	9.86%
	暴雨(Heavyrain)	日累计降水量≥15mm;0代表非暴雨,1代表暴雨	11.51%
	雾天(Heavyfog)	能见度≤1km;0代表无雾,1代表有雾	0.14%
	雪天(Snow)	发生降雪,且日累计降水量>0(降雪/雨夹雪);0代表无雪,1代表有雪	2.47%
时间周期变量	周末(Weekend)	0代表非周末;1代表周末	28.77%
	节假日(Holiday)	0代表非节假日;1代表节假日	3.56%

(2)定义出行距离

在进行回归分析时,将公共自行车的出行距离作为分类变量处理,设置两个虚拟变量,分别为出行距离在2~4km范围内、大于4km时取1,其他取0,以单次出行距离在2km以内的公共自行车出行为参考标准。

2.3　模型构建

按照出行距离的划分标准,将每天的公共自行车出行数据划分为三种类型,分别统计出每天三种出行距离范围内的实际公共自行车出行量作为模型的因变量;自变量分为两种类型:一种是数值型变量包括降水、温度、风速、能见度作为基础天气变量,另一种是分类变量包括暴雨、低温、高温、强风、雾天、雪天作为恶劣天气变量以及周末、节假日、季节作为时间周期变量。本节构建了考虑恶劣天气与出行距离之间交互作用的负二项回归模型,以恶劣天气下短距离出行为参考标准,研究了恶劣天气影响下不同出行距离自行车出行量差异的显著性。构建的考虑恶劣天气与出行距离交互作用的回归方程表达式为:

$$\log y_{it}=\beta_0+\beta_i(A_j+B_k+C_l+BC_{kl}+D_m) \tag{10}$$

式中:y_{it}——第t天第i种距离范围内的公共自行车出行量;

β_0、β_i——常数项和回归系数;

A_j——温度(Tem)、降水量(Pre)、风速(Win)和能见度(Vis)的普通天气度量值(数值型变量);

B_k——恶劣天气事件,包括极冷(Coldday)、极热(Hotday)、暴雨(Heavyrain)、强风(Strongwind)、大雾(Heavyfog)、降雪(Snow)均为分类变量;

C_l——出行距离为分类变量,包括中距离(middle_distance)、长距离(long_distance);

BC_{kl}——恶劣天气与出行距离的交互作用,例如极冷天气下中距离出行用Coldday * middle_distance表示;

D_m——时间周期,包括夏季(Summer)、秋季(Autumn)、冬季(Winter)、周末(Weenend)、节假日(Holiday)。

2.4　模型结果

将每天三种距离范围公共自行车出行量作为因变量,天气因素、出行距离、时间周期以及恶劣天气与出行距离的交互项作为自变量的负二项回归模型结果如表4所示。

考虑恶劣天气与出行距离交互的负二项回归结果　表4

自变量	系数	Exp(β_i)	标准误	z	$P>z$
常数项	8.0129	3019.6614	0.0664	120.72	0.00
Temperature	0.0335	1.0341	0.0016	20.85	0.00***
Precipitation	-0.0026	0.9974	0.0008	-3.21	0.00***
Wind_speed	-0.0209	0.9793	0.0060	-3.48	0.00***
Visibility	0.0236	1.0239	0.0024	9.77	0.00***
Cold_day	-0.0050	0.9950	0.0565	-0.09	0.93
Hot_day	-0.2166	0.8053	0.0538	-4.03	0.00***
Heavyrain	-0.1992	0.8194	0.0598	-3.33	0.00***
Strongwind	-0.0473	0.9538	0.0579	-0.82	0.41
Heavyfog	0.0162	1.0163	0.1322	0.12	0.90
Snow	-0.1108	0.8951	0.0855	-1.30	0.20
middle_distance	-0.6826	0.5053	0.0263	-25.96	0.00***
long_distance	-2.0720	0.1259	0.0264	-78.51	0.00***
Cold_day * middle_distance	-0.2042	0.8153	0.0723	-2.82	0.01**
Cold_day * long_distance	-0.3825	0.6822	0.0731	-5.23	0.00***
Hot_day * middle_distance	0.0095	1.0095	0.0705	0.13	0.89
Hot_day * long_distance	0.0368	1.0375	0.0707	0.52	0.60
Heavyrain * middle_distance	-0.0510	0.9503	0.0669	-0.76	0.45
Heavyrain * long_distance	-0.0593	0.9424	0.0673	-0.88	0.38
Strongwind * middle_distance	-0.0542	0.9472	0.0723	-0.75	0.45
Strongwind * long_distance	-0.0961	0.9084	0.0729	-1.32	0.19
Heavyfog * middle_diatance	-0.0800	0.9231	0.1819	-0.44	0.66
Heavyfog * long_distance	-0.1514	0.8595	0.1829	-0.83	0.41
Snow * middle_distance	-0.1028	0.9023	0.1178	-0.87	0.38
Snow * long_distance	-0.2370	0.7890	0.1194	-1.99	0.05*
Summer	-0.0889	0.9149	0.0311	-2.86	0.00***
Autumn	0.1971	1.2179	0.0262	7.53	0.00***
Winter	0.0440	1.0450	0.0361	1.22	0.22
Weekend	-0.2327	0.7924	0.0195	-11.96	0.00***
Holiday	-0.4077	0.6652	0.0478	-8.52	0.00***
/lnalpha	-2.5191	0.08	0.0432		
alpha	0.0805	1.08	0.0035		

注：*** p_value < 0.001，** 0.001 < p_value < 0.01，* 0.01 < p_value < 0.05。

如果显著性水平为0.05，根据模型结果可以得出：

(1)不同距离的自行车出行均受到温度、降水、风速、能见度等天气因素的影响,其中,温度和能见度水平与自行车出行量呈正相关,降水量和风速与自行车出行量呈负相关,这与方差分析的研究结论是一致的;

(2)在恶劣天气因素中,极热(Hotday)和暴雨(Heavyrain)下不同出行距离的差异是显著的,且均会导致自行车出行量的减少;

(3)出行距离越长出行量越少,其中,出行距离大于 4km 的出行量是 2km 范围内出行量的 12.59%;

(4)在恶劣天气与出行距离的交互作用中,与恶劣天气下短距离出行相比,极冷天气中、长距离出行量和降雪天气下长距离出行量变化较为明显。与极冷天气下短距离出行相比,中、长距离的公共自行车出行量分别减少 18.47%、31.78%;与降雪天气下短距离出行相比,雪天长距离公共自行车出行量比短距离减少 21.1%;

(5)不同时间段公共自行车出行距离也会有所变化。其中,与春季相比夏季和秋季不同出行距离的出行量变化是显著的;与工作日和非节假日相比,不同出行距离的自行车出行量在周末和节假日的变化也是显著的。

3 结语

本文基于 Capital-Bike 的出行数据和天气数据,构建了天气因素、出行距离与公共自行车出行量的多因素方差分析模型和负二项回归模型,由定性分析到定量分析,系统研究了天气因素影响下自行车出行量的变化。主要研究结论如下:

(1)工作日和夏季自行车出行量明显较多,而节假日和冬季其出行量会明显减少;相同天气类型下出行距离越长,出行量越少。

(2)降水是影响公共自行车出行量的主要因素,且出行距离越长,影响越显著;温度、风速和能见度对不同距离范围内出行量均产生显著影响,且不同距离范围自行车出行量会随温度和能见度的增加而增加,随风速和降水量的增加而减少。

(3)恶劣天气对不同距离自行车出行量影响的差异性是显著的,相同天气条件下,出行距离越长,出行量的减少就越多。

虽研究区域及样本非最新数据,但本文的研究方法以及所用的模型适用性较强,均可使用不同地区的公共自行车或共享单车出行数据研究天气因素对其出行量的影响,得出的相关结论也具有实际意义。

参考文献

[1] 王永强.天气因素对城市共享单车出行的影响研究[D].北京:北京交通大学,2019.

[2] Cantelmo G, Kucharski R, Antoniou C. Low-Dimensional Model for Bike-Sharing Demand Forecasting that Explicitly Accounts for Weather Data[J]. Transportation Research Record, 2020,2674(8):132-144.

[3] Wessel J. Using weather forecasts to forecast whether bikes are used[J]. Transportation Research Part A,2020(138):537-559.

[4] 黎鹏.基于天气因素的共享单车骑行量预测[D].北京:电子科技大学,2020.

[5] Li J L, Li X H, Chen D W, et al. Assessment of metro ridership fluctuation caused by weather conditions in Asian context: Using archived weather and ridership data in Nanjing[J]. Journal of transport geography, 2018(66):356-368.

[6] Yang X B, Yue X F, Sun H J, Gao Z Y, Wang W C. Impact of weather on freeway origin-destination volume in China[J]. Transportation Research Part A,2021(143):30-47.

[7] Nankervis M. The effect of weather and climate on bicycle commuting[J]. Transportation Research Part A,1999,33(6):417-431.

[8] Chardon D, Medard C, Caruso, et al. Bicycle sharing system 'success' determinants[J]. Transportation Research Part A, 2017(100):202-214.

[9] An R, Zahnow R, Pojani D, et al. Weather and cycling in New York: The case of Citibike[J]. Journal of Transport Geography, 2019(77):97-112.

[10] Corcoran J, Li T B, Rohde D, et al. Spatio-temporal patterns of a Public Bicycle Sharing Program: the effect of weather and calendar events[J]. Journal of Transport Geography, 2014(41):292-305.

航空运输篇

民航业务泛化数据仓库架构设计研究

杨伟伟　郑贵德　严　丹*
（南大通用数据技术股份有限公司）

摘　要　数据仓库已经广泛深入应用于各行各业的数据分析，对于民航业务，比如定价、安检、值机、运营、客服等机场决策，数据仓库提供了重要的支撑。随着数字化业务在民航业的快速发展，民航业务对数据仓库平台处理数据源的广度及分析响应的速度，都提出更高要求。本研究利用大数据先进技术对传统数据仓库进行改进与提升，为民航业务提供适应能力更强、响应效率更高的新型数据仓库。

关键词　泛化数据仓库　数据湖　大数据　民航业

0　引言

随着大数据技术的快速发展，民航业务管理决策对数据仓库提出了更高要求，不仅需要更广泛的数据来源支撑，还需要快速的分析响应。在数据源上，传统数据仓库通常是对结构化数据进行存储和处理，而类似客户的活动、轨迹、行为以及旅客投诉等非结构化数据也将成为应用分析的重要数据来源。在数据加工处理上，传统数据仓库通过层与层数据移动，加工周期长，无法满足许多新业务场景的实时性需要，而一些应用，比如安防、值机服务、延误反馈、航班提醒等多个场景对实时分析要求越来越高。

本设计提出的泛化数据仓库，是对传统数据仓库能力的扩展，除了具备经典数据仓库的基本特点外，还能够处理非结构化数据，具备了数据湖能够处理多类型数据的特点，泛化数据仓库需要对接入的数据预先进行组织、转换、处理。

泛化数据仓库可以有对应经典数据仓库的ODS（操作数据存储层）、DW（数据仓库明细层）、DM（数据集市层）三个大的层次结构考虑到实时响应的需要，泛化数据仓库各层的数据模型还可通过关系映射以快速反映数据变化。本设计引入了Lambda 架构技术，提升泛化数据仓库的实时响应能力。经过实际应用和测试，效果显著。

1　研究背景及需求分析

1.1　传统数据仓库架构

多年来，数据仓库已经广泛为众多企业提供管理分析服务。民航业典型的传统数据仓库架构示意如图1 所示。

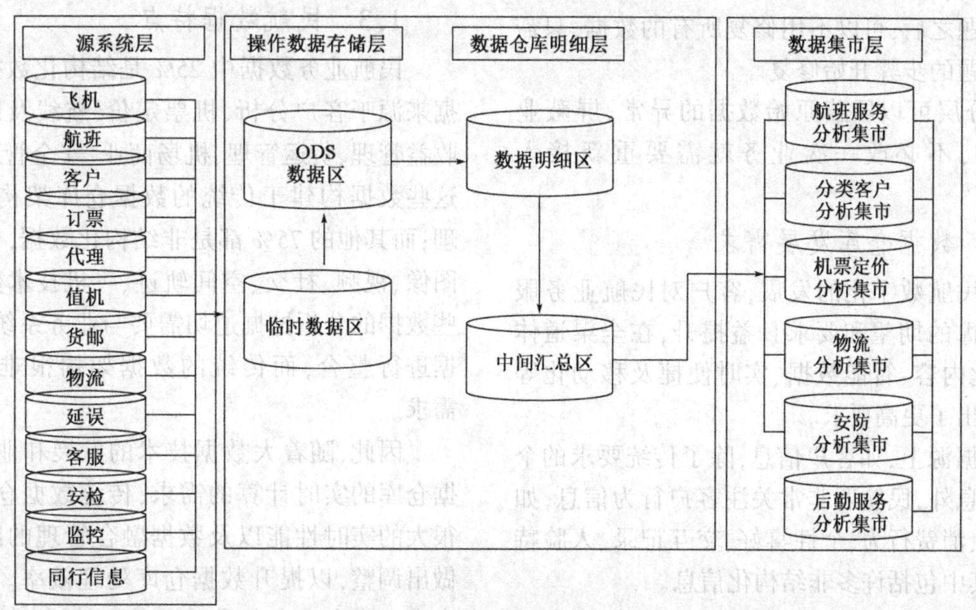

图1　民航业典型的传统数据仓库架构示意

总体上,民航传统数据仓库除了数据源外,通常包含操作数据存储层(ODS)、数据仓库明细层(DW)和数据集市层(DM):

ODS层,即操作数据存储层。数据仓库源头系统的数据表通常会原封不动地存储一份在这一层,也称为准备区。它们是后续数据仓库层数据加工的来源。

DW层,即数据仓库明细层,是数据仓库汇总层,DW层的表通常包括两类,一个用于存储当前需要加载的数据,一个用于存储处理完后的历史数据。

DM层,即数据集市层,是基于DW上的基础数据,整合汇总成分析某一个主题域的服务数据,一般是宽表,用于提供后续的业务查询、OLAP分析等。

传统数据仓库之所以分层,其主要原因如下:

(1)分层可以清晰数据结构,为不同数据分层定义的作用域,这样在使用数据的时候能更方便地定位和理解。

(2)分层可以追踪数据血缘,简单来说可以这样理解,由于数据来源有很多,当发现数据问题时,能够快速准确地定位到问题,并清楚它的危害范围。

(3)分层可以减少重复开发:规范数据分层,开发一些通用的中间层数据,能够减少重复计算。

(4)分层可以把复杂问题简单化。通过复杂的任务分解,每一层只处理单一的步骤,比较简单和容易理解。而且便于维护数据的准确性,当数据出现问题之后,可以不用修复所有的数据,只需要从有问题的步骤开始修复。

(5)分层可以屏蔽原始数据的异常,屏蔽业务的影响,不必改一次业务就需要重新接入数据。

1.2　数据仓库发展需求

随着民航数字化的发展,客户对民航业务服务能力支撑的期望和要求日益提升,在全渠道体验、定制化内容、智能数据、实时便捷及移动化等方面都提出了更高要求。

在数据源上,如客户信息,除了传统要求的个人基本信息外,民航还非常关注客户行为信息,如订票行为、消费行为、个性喜好、交互记录、人脸特征等,这其中包括许多非结构化信息。

在数据分析响应速度上,实时性分析要求越来越高,比如:对于风险管理,要求主动识别异常行为,采集分析异常行为数据;对于飞行延误,实时提示可能延误的时间,安排延误需要的准备服务,实时动态部署智能化监控,实现精准化高风险识别,及时有效保障飞行安全。

为了结合大数据技术发展与客户需求,传统数据仓库重点在以下方面进行改进发展:

(1)异构数据源融合

随着数字化的发展,业务分析应用更加依赖广泛的数据源,这些数据源很可能来自多种异构系统,数据类型不仅有结构化数据,还有非结构化数据及流数据等。而传统数据仓库是面向结构化数据,需要增强非结构化数据处理能力。

(2)实时处理

传统数据仓库面向OLAP应用,主要提供全量的批处理。随着业务需求的发展,许多业务场景的应用分析,如风险预警、问题响应等都有实时性分析的要求。为了满足这种需求,传统数据仓库需要在实时分析能力上进行提升。

(3)快速更新响应

传统数据仓库通常对数据源逐层进行加工,加工步骤多、中间过程长,这种层次加工在一定程度上有助于系统稳定性,但对数据源的变化反应慢,难以及时反映业务变化。同时,层与层之间数据需要移动,数据冗余大,加大了维护难度。故此,快速反应数据源变化,也是数据仓库的发展需求。

1.3　民航数据特点

民航业务数据中25%是结构化数据,这些数据来源于客户分析、机票定价、航线及网络规划、收益管理、货运管理、机场商业、安全管理等系统,这些数据构建于传统的数据仓库架构上进行处理;而其他的75%都是非结构化数据,包括文字、图像、视频、社交、空间轨迹、飞机技术数据等,这些数据的分析挖掘迫切需要与业务系统结构化数据进行整合,而传统的数据架构很难支撑这些需求。

因此,随着大数据技术的发展和业务上对数据仓库的实时计算的需求,传统数据仓库面临着很大的实时性能以及数据融合管理的问题,亟须做出调整,以提升数据仓库处理效率。泛化数据仓库正是在这个背景下提出的。

2 泛化数据仓库技术架构与实现

2.1 泛化数据仓库架构设计

泛化数据仓库将突破传统数据仓库的局限，扩展传统数据仓库的泛化和实时能力，融合结构化数据、文档数据、流数据、图数据等多类型数据。

泛化数据仓库系统总体结构如图2所示。

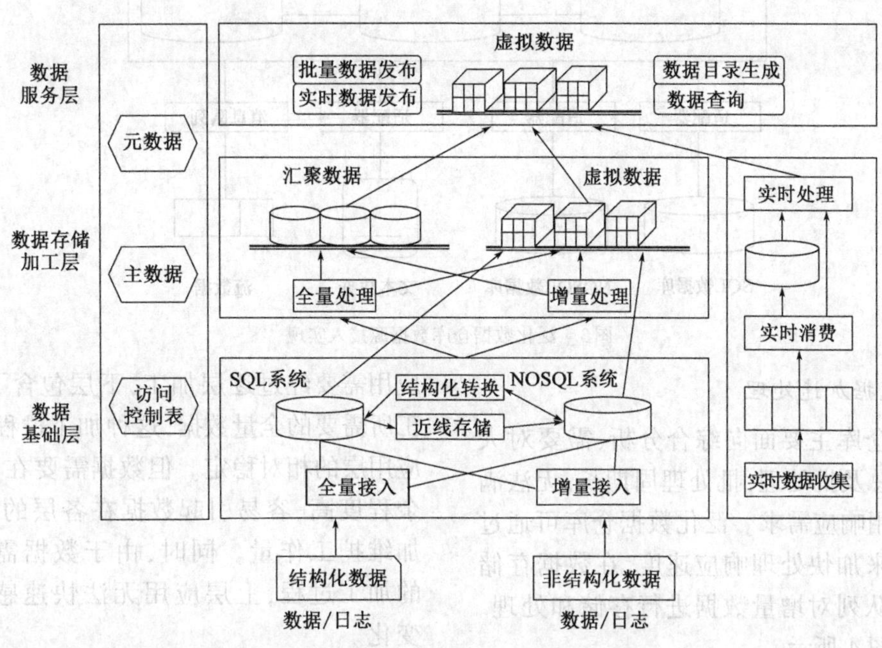

图2 泛化数据仓库系统总体结构示意图

泛化数据仓库总体上分为数据基础层、数据存储加工层、数据服务层三大层。

(1)数据基础层，通过ETL、CDC及流数据导入工具等接入各种数据源，该层的数据与源数据结构基本保持一致。数据接入还包括数据清洗、加载、转换、和数据质量处理，数据基础层需要支持结构化、非结构化数据及流数据。非结构化数据主要指Key-value stores键值数据、Table-oriented面向表列数据、Document-oriented面向文档数据、Graph-oriented面向图论的图数据及文本数据。

(2)数据存储加工层，是在数据基础层的基础上，对数据做轻度聚合操作、加工形成明细事实数据、维表数据并构建业务数据模型，生成公共指标汇总数据。为了能够加工处理异构数据和非结构化数据，数据存储加工层还支持异构数据查询，同时通过虚拟数据映射，快速反映数据源的更新变化。

(3)数据服务层，是依据业务主题，综合批量处理与实时处理，构建逻辑数据，形成面向主题的数据指标或数据视图，同时提供数据API服务，支撑BI、AI及应用开发等服务。数据服务层也可以通过虚拟数据技术，直接映射下层或跨层数据源，用于快速响应数据源更新变化。

其中，数据基础层和数据存储加工层通过实时操作可以在接入增量数据、流数据的基础上，在一定时间窗口内，通过实时计算处理，实现实时分析。泛化数据仓库综合了传统数据库与数据湖的特色，可以支撑更加复杂的大数据应用需求。

2.2 关键技术实现

泛化数据仓库实现的关键技术包括多源数据接入、数据加速处理、虚拟化数据、跨引擎的数据统一查询等。

2.2.1 多源数据接入

结构化数据接入技术已经成熟，而且效率很高，可以通过数据同步或日志同步根据预置的业务内容抽取；增量数据可以通过带有时间戳的CDC(Change Data Capture)工具实现增量抽取；文本文件数据可以通过FTP或基本操作脚本导入到分布式文件系统；NOSQL数据可以采用系统自带或第三方工具导入相应系统；流数据可以采用消息队列工具接入到分布式文件系统。增量数据和流数据都是实时数据的基础。

总的来说，数据接入综合采用ETL技术及

CDC工具来完成。接入功能同时还具备预置的公式、函数、数据汇总和计算能力,支持分区技术、数据清洗转换、元数据的集成。其接入实现方式如图3所示。

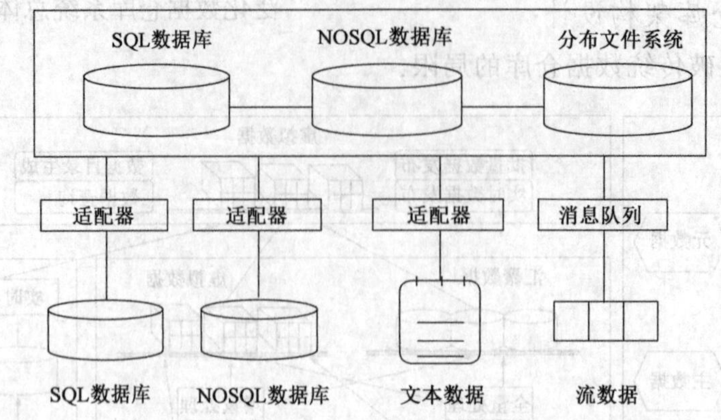

图3　泛化数据仓库数据源接入实现

2.2.2　数据加速处理

传统数据仓库主要面向综合分析,需要对大量数据进行汇总及批处理,批处理周期长,无法满足部分快速应用响应需求。泛化数据仓库可通过增量数据处理来加快处理响应速度,在数据存储层可通过消息队列对增量数据进行存储和处理。其实现机制如图4所示。

在此基础上,数据存储加工层将分别实现批处理和增量处理。批数据处理支持传统数据仓库的数据分析,增量数据处理支持实时数据分析。数据加速处理机制如图5所示。

2.2.3　虚拟化数据

传统数据仓库通常分为多层,数据从接入到应用需要经过逐层加工,下层包含了上层数据加工所需要的全量数据,这种加工过程,虽然保持了应用层的相对稳定。但数据需要在各层移动,冗余程度高,容易引起数据在各层的不一致性,增加维护工作量。同时,由于数据需要经过各层的加工过程,上层应用无法快速感知数据源的变化。

泛化数据仓库提供了虚拟化数据,通过虚拟化数据对象,构建与下层或跨层的数据源映射关系,从而使一些需要快速响应的应用数据不必经过数据的层层上移及聚合。虚拟化数据的数据源可直接来自下层或跨层的多源数据,其数据关系映射如图6所示。

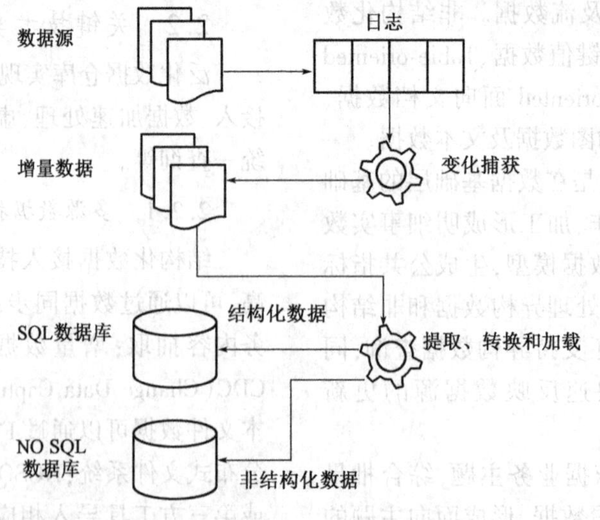

图4　泛化数据仓库增量数据处理实现

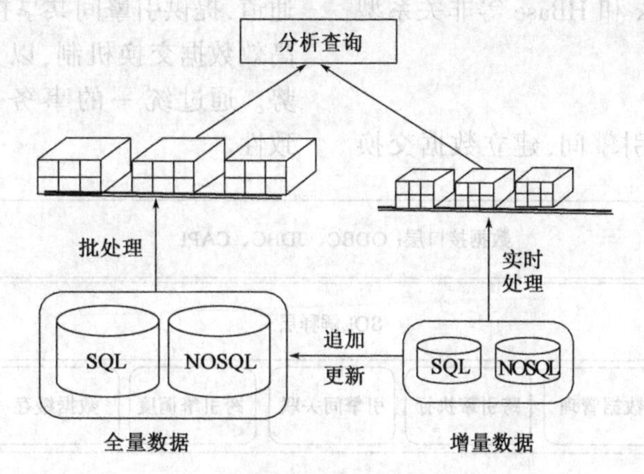

图5　泛化数据仓库数据加速处理

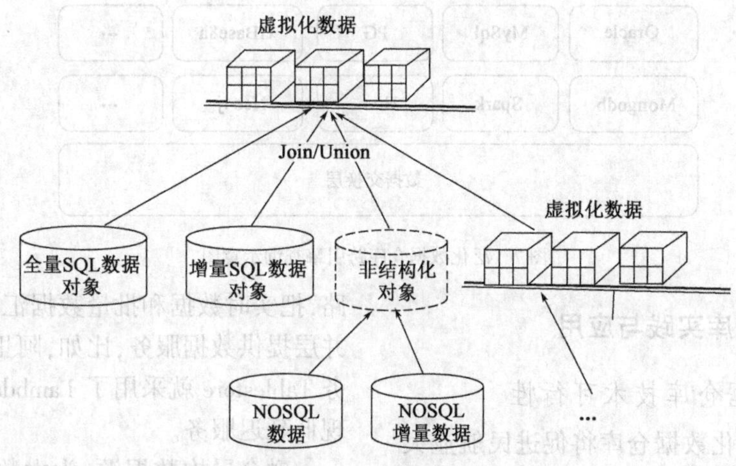

图6　泛化数据仓库虚拟化数据关系映射

虚拟化数据可以映射(含 Join、Union 及汇聚计算)到全量结构化数据的对象、增量数据对象、非结构化对象及其他的虚拟存储数据。全量或增量数据对象可以是各种数据表、事实表、维度表、视图等,非结构化对象可以转换加载非结构化数据,同时虚拟化数据还可以对接其他虚拟化数据,进一步增加虚拟化数据的灵活度。

2.2.4　*跨引擎的数据统一查询*

为了支持多源、多类型数据,泛化数据仓库需要具备异构数据查询能力,融合异构数据库查询引擎及非结构化数据查询引擎,提供高效的统一查询服务。

泛化数据仓库数据统一查询实现示意如图7所示。

其主要实现技术包括:

(1)解析标准 SQL

接收用户发来跨数据源的 SQL 指令,将接收到的接口指令转换为模块内各引擎支持的指令。在标准 SQL 的基础上,扩展部分 DDL 语句,DML 语句使用标准 SQL 语句,提供统一查询语言访问各引擎。

(2)跨引擎统一调度

提供对数据的统一调度能力,根据业务需要对多引擎上的数据进行调度,透明地实现跨引擎的数据关联。统一调度按照工作流程间的依赖关系有序、自动地调度执行,它将贯穿业务处理的全流程,从数据资源的整合、加工到后续的数据处理和结果输出。

(3)引擎间关联数据存储与运算

当 SQL 涉及有多个引擎需要进行数据关联时,负责数据的关联运算,根据执行计划将参与的数据进行本地化存储,从而减少运算过程中拉数据,确保运算性能。

(4)插件扩展服务

通过可动态扩展的插件体系架构,实现下层数据查询引擎的动态扩展。支持 Oracle、MySQL、国产数据库以及Hive、Spark和HBase等非关系型数据库等。

(5)数据交换

在不同的数据库处理引擎间,建立数据交换通道,提供引擎间共享接口,支持引擎间多对多的高效数据交换机制,以充分发挥跨多个引擎的优势。通过统一的事务机制保证迁移数据的一致性。

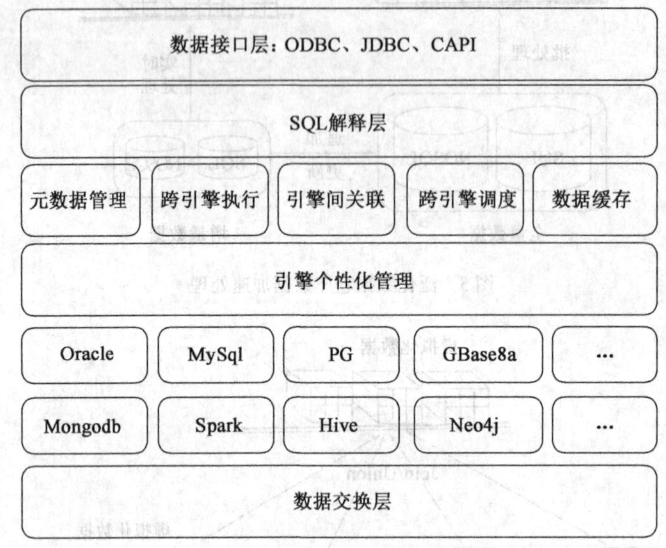

图7　泛化数据仓库跨引擎查询示意图

3　泛化数据仓库实践与应用

3.1　泛化数据仓库技术可行性

本研究提出的泛化数据仓库将促进民航业大数据分析应用的新突破。多源数据接入可以为分析应用提供广泛的、多视角的数据源,虚拟化数据可以及时响应数据源变化、方便大数据智能运维,增量数据加速可以更好应对实时处理,统一跨引擎查询为分析应用提供高效支持。

目前,支撑泛化数据仓库实现的理论和技术工具都很成熟。在数据接入上,有多种产品和工具可以支持,开源的kettle、GBase RTSync等ETL工具,都可以全量和实时接入结构化数据源;同时开源的Flume、Kafka、Flink、FTP工具可以接入非关系型数据源。

虚拟化数据概念并不陌生,在多年前Gartner就提出了逻辑数据仓库概念及其优势,国际著名的数据仓库供应商SAP,也大刀阔斧地对传统数据仓库技术进行改进,利用如今更高的数据库算力,压缩了传统数据仓库技术分层的层级,实现了数据仓库跨层直接映射的虚拟化数据层功能。

面对企业对大数据应用低延时的需求,国际业界专家提出了Lambda体系架构。逻辑上是在传统大数据批处理的基础上引入实时数据处理链路,把实时数据和批量数据汇总到一起,再通过合并层提供数据服务,比如,阿里云的大数据存储服务Tablestore就采用了Lambda架构加Spark来实现低延迟服务。

融合异构数据源、为大数据应用提供统一跨引擎查询技术也已成熟,南大通用的UP跨引擎统一查询工具,综合采用了索引技术、缓存技术、冗余策略、调度策略、SQL优化、预计算等技术,已经为国内多个大型金融数据仓库提供服务。

3.2　泛化数据仓库应用效果

本研究提出的泛化数据仓库关键技术已经在多个实际项目中取得成功应用。在能源行业的智能数据仓库平台,接入了多种类型数据,包括生产运行数据、报告、施工文档、施工报告、设备状态和GIS地理信息等。在电信、电力等行业,通过跨引擎查询技术,有力支撑了基于大数据的商业智能、机器学习等客户营销分析应用,提高了数据应用分析的效率。泛化数据仓库的虚拟化数据技术为多家大型金融企业构建了逻辑数据仓库集市,极大提高了数据业务建模效率,减少了数据冗余,保障了多源数据的一致性。同时,更好地实现了数据源的追溯与数据质量管控。

泛化数据仓库典型应用是金融行业的智能数据仓库平台应用,该平台提供了客户管理系统、贷记卡、银行卡、电子银行和财务系统等52个核心系统的分析应用支持,系统部署集群280个节点,实际入库数据量1PB,每日增量1.1TB。最大表超过1000亿行,每天运行60000个以上的数据加工作业和交互式数据查询任务。通过应用泛在数据仓库的架构优化,在每天提供 $T+1$ 的海量大数据批处理的同时也提供低延时的综合在线查询服务,个人集市的拉链运算从分钟级降低到秒级。

经过行业的实际应用,泛化数据仓在数据加载、数据转换、数据重复利用、性能提升、数据处理模式以及查询模式上比传统数据库都有很大的提升,如表1所示。

传统数据仓库与泛化数据仓库的对比 表1

比较项	传统数据仓库	泛化数据仓库
数据加载	支持全量、增量接入	支持全量、增量接入,同时支持非结构化、半结构化数据接入,可以达到10TB/h
数据转换能力	通过维护数据对照表,将源系统中的编码转换为合并系统编码	采用多种数据转换工具,实现数据自动转换
数据冗余程度	数据在源系统、合并系统、分析系统(多维模型)及数据转换过程中存在多个副本	通过数据源映射,数据在合并系统与分析使用同一份数据,减少数据副本,确保数据源唯一
数据重复利用	通过新增加数据副本实现数据重复利用,保证数据一致性,工作量大	使用逻辑建模技术实现虚拟模型,一份数据多处使用,无须层与层之间的数据同步
系统性能提升	数据更新过程复杂,链路长,数据冗余,计算脚本多,性能数小时甚至更长	数据更新链路短,基于配置规则运行标准合并程序,处理性能高,可以达到小时级或分钟级
数据处理模式	主要支持批处理,一般不支持实时处理	同时支持批处理和实时处理,实时处理性能可达到秒级响应
查询引擎	支持数据查询,一般不支持异构数据查询	融合常用查询引擎,提供统一查询引擎,并对异构查询统一优化
与Hadoop集成能力	一般不支持Hadoop集成	能够实现与Hadoop数据的互联互通和数据交换

4 泛化数据仓库民航应用研究展望

民航业务如客户分析、机票定价、航线及网络规划、收益管理、货运管理、机场商业、安全管理等都可以通过泛化数据仓库技术,进一步提升管理决策水平。目前,南大通用已经为民航局信息中心构建了数据仓库,该数据仓库采集并存储了大量关于机场、运输生产及通航生产等数据信息,实现对数据精细化提取、挖掘分析,并以Cognos、Arcgis、Echarts等工具对仓库数据进行可视化多维度多层次的实时展现。

在业务场景上,民航业务数据中的非结构化数据,将是南大通用下一步重点采集的数据范围为民航业务大数据分析提供更广的数据视角。同时通过泛化数据仓库技术,实现数据实时分析的综合应用,支持智慧安监及实时客户行为分析、异常事件响应。

在此基础上本研究下一步将继续优化泛化数据仓库性能,继续研究基于新型硬件FPGA、NVMe和RDMA等技术优化提升性能;通过智能化感知模块,提供泛化数据仓库计算能力;结合信息技术应用创新提出的新要求,进行国产化平台的适配和优化工作。与此同时,随着云上应用需求的增加,泛化数据仓库将进一步实现与云原生的融合。

参考文献

[1] 张远,熊静,王羽. 民航大数据资源治理机制研究[J]. 大经贸. 创业圈, 2019(1).

[2] 郑广,李建政,张义军. 应用数据仓库技术实现民航决策支持系统[J]. 计算机工程与应用,2002(5):249-252.

[3] 陈卫卫. 数据仓库与数据技术的研究与应用[J]. 信息与电脑(理论版),2014(24):23.

[4] 王锋. 维数据仓库及其在复杂数据建模中的应用研究[J]. 通讯世界,2015(03):198.

[5] 李澍. 关于采用云计算技术构建大型数据仓库平台的探究[J]. 计算机光盘软件与应用,2014,17(16):48,50.

[6] 陈诚,石莉,丁雪红,等.大数据处理框架现状分析[J].宜宾学院学报,2019,19(12):39-46.
[7]江佳原.实时大数据平台的设计与实现[J].金融科技时代,2020(02):75-78.
[8] 胡智慧,徐飒英.证券行业大数据平台建设及未来展望[C]//创新与发展:中国证券业2018年论文集(下册),2019:372-381.
[9] 滕长青.大数据平台建设关键技术研究[J].数字通信世界,2019(12):62.
[10] 刘志勇,何忠江,刘敬龙,等.统一数据湖技术研究和建设方案[J].电信科学,2021,37(01):121-128.
[11] 李卓蓉,薛羽.数据湖新一代大数据解决方案[N].中国城乡金融报,2021-11-12.
[12] 陆生强.时空数据湖的研究与应用[J].国土资源信息化,2021(03):28-33,53.
[13] 苏洁.金融企业数字化营销是机遇更是使命[N].中国银行保险报,2019.
[14] 任仲晟.基于数据仓库的数据挖掘技术[J].数字技术与应用,2021,39(09):59-61.
[15] 狄程,杨中国,韩燕波,等.面向流数据的实时处理及服务化系统[J].重庆大学学报,2020,43(07):75-83.
[16] 于自强.海量流数据挖掘相关问题研究[D].山东:山东大学,2015.
[17] 田森.分布式异构数据库同步中间件的设计与实现[D].西安:西安电子科技大学,2012.
[18] 刘辉,陈刚.基于Flink的工业大数据实时分析平台[J].电子技术与软件工程,2021(06):185-187.
[19] Bitencorte J, Rech T, Lunge V R, et al. Association of Interferon Iambda-4 rs12979860 Polymorphism with Hepatocellular Carcinoma in Patients with Chronic Hepatitis C Infection [J]. World Journal of Hepatology, 2021, 13(1):109-119.

基于迁移AdaBoost的航线节假日客流量预测

左海超*[1,2]　孙媛媛[1]　杨晓东[1]　徐　涛[1,2]
(1.中国民航大学计算机科学与技术学院;2.中国民航大学信息技术科研基地)

摘　要　节假日出行需求逐渐增大,航空公司有必要对客流量进行准确预测以便采取相应的措施提高客座率和增加收益。由于节假日周期普遍偏短,旅客出行数据积累相对匮乏,现有的航线客流量预测方法需依赖大量旅客出行历史数据,较难进行准确预测。针对此问题,提出一种基于迁移AdaBoost的航线节假日客流量预测模型,该模型通过定义二元关系网络表示航空公司的航线网络,并定义起飞机场和目的机场的正负出入度、公共邻居数及度中心性等构造航线属性,然后利用迁移学习方法将相似航线属性迁移到目标航线的属性中,再运用AdaBoost算法对航线节假日客流量进行预测。实验结果表明,本文提出的针对数据相对匮乏的节假日航线客流量预测模型在北京—三亚航线和广州—昆明航线的预测平均相对误差仅为3.25%和2.89%,具有更强的预测稳定性和更高的预测准确率。

关键词　航空运输　航线客流量　迁移AdaBoost　航线网络　节假日

0　引言

随着旅客出行需求的逐步增长,越来越多旅客选择飞机出行,而节假日期间更是旅客出行的高峰期。航线客流量的准确预测,不仅为航空公司的航线规划、动态定价和运营决策提供参考,而且有助于航空公司对有限资源进行优化配置以提供更好的服务。为此,如何准确预测节假日期间

1.基金项目:中央高校基本科研业务费中国民航大学专项(3122014D032)资助。

航线客流量是航空公司面临的一个重要问题。

国内外学者在客流量预测模型做了大量的研究，从早期的统计模型、计量经济模型到现阶段的神经网络、支持向量机等。Pitfield 验证了自回归积分滑动平均模型 ARIMA（Autoregressive Integrated Moving Average Model）在旅客流量预测问题上的有效性。Li 基于三亚机场 2008—2016 年的客流量数据，构建了 ARIMA 模型，以发掘客流的通用趋势和季节变化规律。由于航线客流量具有强非线性特征，ARIMA 模型需以大量历史客流量数据为基础，而且不能解决非线性预测问题。Wang 等提出利用神经网络模型对城际高速铁路客流量进行预测，提出了将现行政策与专用交通预测时间相结合的方法，建立了定量与定性相结合的城际高速铁路客流量预测新流程。求森以小波分析方法将原始客流数据进行分解去噪，使得客流数据信号光滑平整，再用时间序列方法对去噪后的主信号进行预测，最后用神经网络的方法对原始信号经小波分析后的噪声进行预测，由时间序列的预测值和神经网络的误差预测值一起得到真正的最终预测值。李伟等将 SARIMA 模型和 SVM 模型相融合建立一种短时客流量预测模型，采用北京市轨道交通具体站点客流量数据，对模型进行验证，并通过 RMSE、MAE、MAPE 多种指标对预测结果进行对比分析，结果表明，SARIMA-SVM 融合模型提高了车站客流量预测精度，降低了预测误差，预测数据和实测数据拟合良好，能更全面刻画车站客流量变化规律，适用于城市轨道交通日常客流预测。余涛使用 SVM 和 BP 神经网络对短时交通流进行了预测与实现，两种模型的结合虽然提升了预测的精度，但模型生成的复杂度也直线上升。

综上所述，当前航线客流量预测模型存在如下的不足：①依赖大量历史数据，针对数据匮乏的航线较难进行预测；②采用单一模型进行预测易受模型自身的限制降低预测精度，而组合模型虽可提升预测精度，但也大大增加了模型生成的复杂度。

针对上述问题，本文首先通过构建二元关系网络表示航线网络，定义航线属性，再利用迁移学习方法将相似航线和目标航线属性相融合扩充领域知识。采用 AdaBoost 算法将若干弱学习模型整合成高预测精度的强学习模型对航线节假日客流量进行预测，在简化模型生成复杂度的同时，提升模型的预测精度。

1　相关工作

针对节假日数据匮乏航线，利用迁移学习方法将源域数据集中数据之间的关系迁移应用于目标域的学习任务中扩充领域知识，通过定义二元关系网络表示航线网络，利用二元关系网络的正负出入度特性，更有助于相似航线的确定以及客流量的准确预测。

1.1　迁移学习

迁移学习作为机器学习领域的一个新的研究方向近年来受到越来越多的关注和研究。传统的机器学习方法要求源领域数据和目标领域数据同分布，而迁移学习放松了这一限制要求，能够把已经获得的知识应用到不同但相似的领域中，解决了目标领域中可用训练样本不足的学习问题。

迁移学习利用标记的源或辅助域来实现目标任务，可以大大降低收集足够训练标签的成本和精力，以在新目标分布中创建有效模型。最近，已经开发出异构转移学习方法，可以应用到如跨语言文本分类、文本到图像分类以及许多其他的实际任务中。

1.2　二元关系网络

定义有向带权图 $G=(V,E,W)$ 为二元关系网络如图 1 所示，其中 V 是节点的集合，E 是边的集合，W 是边上权值的集合，+/- 代表节点间的正负关系（边上的权值大于平均权值为正关系，反之为负关系）。

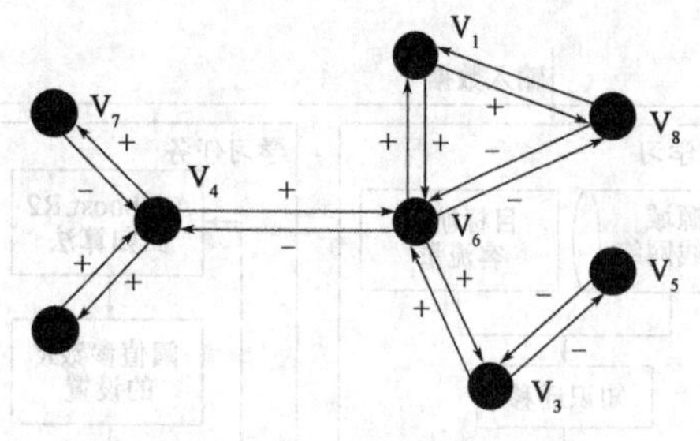

图1　二元关系网络结构图

对于有向图而言，一个节点的度包括了节点的出度与入度；而对于具有二元关系的网络而言，出度又分为正出度及负出度，入度分为正入度与负入度。几个有关二元关系网络的相关概念如下：

(1)节点度(Degree):与节点相关联的边的条数。

(2)节点入度(In-Degree):进入该节点的边的条数。

(3)节点出度(Out-Degree):从该节点出发的边的条数。

(4)节点正入度(In-Degree^+):进入该节点且边上关系为正的边的条数。

(5)节点负入度(In-Degree^-):进入该节点且边上关系为负的边的条数。

(6)节点正出度(Out-Degree^+):从该节点出发且边上关系为正的边的条数。

(7)节点负出度(Out-Degree^-):从该节点出发且边上关系为负的边的条数。

2　基于迁移 AdaBoost 的航线节假日客流量预测

2.1　预测模型框架

图2给出了从迁移学习的视角对节假日期间航线客流量进行预测的模型框架图,该模型由两部分组成:迁移学习和学习任务。迁移学习部分中,输入是航空公司整个航线网络的节假日客流量数据,并用二元关系网络表示航线网络 $G=(V,E,W)$ 构造航线属性。为预测节假日目标航线客流量,在源域中寻找相似航线进行知识迁移,并与目标航线的公共知识进行融合。学习任务部分中,采用 AdaBoost. R2 回归算法对航线网络中的航线属性及客流量进行训练,设置阈值参数 R 后,实现以相似航线和目标航线公共知识为输入的航线节假日客流量预测。

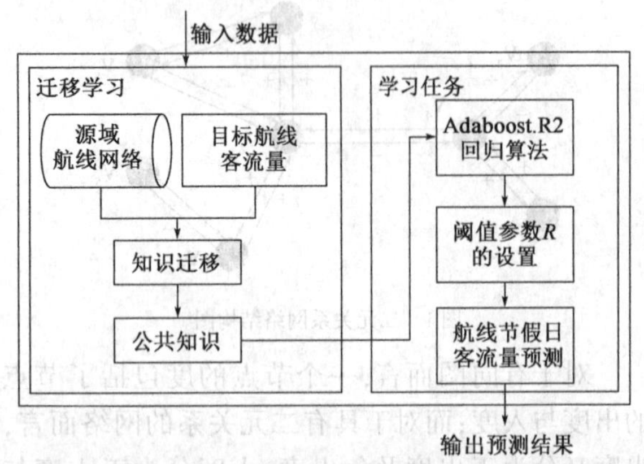

图2　基于迁移 AdaBoost 的航线节假日客流预测模型框架图

2.2　航空公司航线网络构建及航线属性构造

用二元关系网络表示航空公司航线网络,定义航线属性,通过航线属性及客流量确定相似航线并进行知识迁移,得到包含相似航线与目标航线公共知识的航线属性。

2.2.1　航空公司航线网络构建

航空公司航线网络 $G=(V,E,W)$,节点代表机场,有向边代表起飞机场到目的机场的航线,边上的权值代表航线上的客流量,航线客流量大于航线网络客流量均值表示节点间的正关系,反之为负关系。

对于航线网络 $G=(V,E,W)$,$n=|V|$ 为机场个数,$m=|E|$ 为航线网络中航线总条数,设具有反自反性的邻接矩阵为 $A=\{a_{ij}\}$,$\forall v_i,v_j\in V$,$\exists e_{ij}\in E$,则 $a_{ij}=1$,否则 $a_{ij}=0$。同时,对于 $\forall v_i,v_j\in V$,$w_{ij}\in W$,如果起飞机场 v_i 至目的机场 v_j 无直达航线即 $e_{ij}\notin E$,则记 $w_{ij}=0$,表示其客流量为0。

2.2.2　航线属性的定义及构造

采用机场正负出入度、公共邻居数、度中心性定义航线属性。定义如下:

(1) 起飞(目的)机场正出(入)度:起飞机场 $v_i\in V$ 的正出度定义为从 v_i 出发(目的机场为 $v_j\in V$)的所有航线 $e_{ij}\in E$ 上权值不小于航线网络中航线平均权值的航线数,计算公式为:

$$v^{+}_{i,out}=\sum_{j=1}^{n}I\left(w_{ij}\geqslant\frac{\sum\limits_{p=1}^{n}\sum\limits_{q=1}^{n}w_{pq}}{m}\right)\tag{1}$$

式中:w_{ij}——从起飞机场 v_i 至目的机场 v_j 的航线权值;

$\sum\limits_{p=1}^{n}\sum\limits_{q=1}^{n}w_{pq}$——航线网络中航线权值之和;

$\frac{\sum\limits_{p=1}^{n}\sum\limits_{q=1}^{n}w_{pq}}{m}$——航线权值的均值;

$I(B)$——指示函数,当条件 B 成立时取值为1,否则为0。

同理,目的机场 $v_j\in V$ 正入度 $v^{+}_{j,\text{in}}$ 类比 $v^{+}_{i,out}$ 定义。

(2) 起飞(目的)机场负出(入)度:起飞机场 $v_i\in V$ 的负出度定义为从 v_i 出发(目的机场为 $v_j\in V$)的所有航线 $e_{ij}\in E$ 上权值小于航线网络中航线平均权值的航线数,计算公式为:

$$v_{i,out}^{-}=\sum_{j=1}^{n}I\left(w_{ij}<\frac{\sum_{p=1}^{n}\sum_{q=1}^{n}w_{pq}}{m}\right) \quad (2)$$

同理，目的机场 $v_j\in V$ 负入度 $v_{j,\text{in}}^{-}$ 类比 $v_{i,\text{out}}^{-}$ 定义。

(3)公共邻居数：对于航线网络 $G=(V,E,W)$，邻接矩阵为 $A=\{a_{ij}\}$，记 $NB_{v_i}=\{v_j|v_j\in V,a_{ij}=1\}$ 表示起飞机场 v_i 的邻居集合，则对于任意相邻的起飞机场 v_i 和目的机场 v_j，其公共邻居数的计算为：

$$M_{v_iv_j}=|NB_{v_i}\cap NB_{v_j}| \quad (3)$$

(4) 起飞机场度中心性：对于航线网络 $G=(V,E,W)$，邻接矩阵为 $A=\{a_{ij}\}$，对于 $\forall v_i\in V$，起飞机场 v_i 与其余 $n-1$ 个机场有直接联系的机场个数，计算公式为：

$$C_D(v_i)=\sum_{j=1}^{n}a_{ij} \quad (4)$$

同理，目的机场 $v_j\in V$ 度中心性 $C_D(v_j)$ 类比 $C_D(v_i)$ 定义。

对于航线网络中的 m 条航线，令：

$$u_{e_{ij}}=(v_{i,\text{out}}^{+},v_{i,\text{out}}^{-},v_{j,\text{in}}^{+},v_{j,\text{in}}^{-},M_{v_iv_j},C_D(v_i),C_D(v_j)) \quad (5)$$

式中：$u_{e_{ij}}$——航线 e_{ij} 的属性；

$v_{i,\text{out}}^{+}$、$v_{i,\text{out}}^{-}$——分别为航线 e_{ij} 起飞机场 v_i 的正出度和负出度；

$v_{j,\text{in}}^{+}$、$v_{j,\text{in}}^{-}$——分别为航线 e_{ij} 目的机场 v_j 的正入度和负入度；

$M_{v_iv_j}$——度量航线 e_{ij} 起飞机场与目的机场相似性的公共邻居数；

$C_D(v_i)$、$C_D(v_j)$——分别为衡量航线 e_{ij} 起飞机场和目的机场在网络中重要程度的度中心性。

2.2.3 基于迁移学习的航线属性构造

为预测目标域中航线客流量，将源域中相似航线的属性迁移到目标航线属性中，并融合相似航线与航线自身的属性，得到包含公共知识的航线属性。

(1)相似航线选取。通常用距离度量航线属性之间的差异，距离越小属性差异越小，其相似度越高。欧氏距离是较常用的距离计算形式，依据式(5)定义的航线属性计算航线属性相似度。

相似航线同时取决于航线属性和客流量的相似度，运用夹逼准则计算航线间属性差异最小的参数以及客流量差异最小的值来确定相似航线。

(2)公共知识融合。为提高预测精度，将目标航线和相似航线的公共知识进行融合，计算目标航线和相似航线属性的均值，作为目标航线的属性。

2.3 面向航线属性的 AdaBoost. R2 回归算法

在多数情况下，由于预测模型的精确性受训练数据及其分布等因素的影响很大，直接构建出精确预测模型较难，然而获得预测精度相对较差的弱学习模型容易得多。预测模型精度提升(Boosting)的方法是将易获取的弱学习模型整合成高预测精度的强学习模型，从而简化模型生成的复杂度和提升模型的预测精度。

AdaBoost 算法能够应用于实际问题成为 Boosting 家族的代表算法，Drucker 最早将其改进为 AdaBoost. R2 应用到实际的回归问题中。面向航线属性的 AdaBoost. R2 回归算法的思想是在航线属性及客流量的训练集中用初始权重 $D_{t=1}(k)$ 训练出一个弱学习器 1，根据弱学习器的客流量误差率$\bar{L}_t$更新训练样本的权 $D_{t=2}(k)$，使之前在弱学习器 1 中客流量误差率高的样本的权重变高，客流量误差率低的样本的权重变低，再根据更新权重后的训练集训练得到弱学习器 2，重复执行若干次，直到获得的弱学习器数目达到事先设定的最大迭代次数 T，最后将这 T 个弱学习器进行整合，得到强学习器。面向航线属性的 AdaBoost. R2 回归算法步骤如下：

(1)输入

将 m 条航线属性 $u_{e_{ij}}$ 以及航线上的客流量 $w_{ij}\in W$ 作为训练集。

确定弱学习器。

确定最大迭代次数 T。

(2)初始化

迭代次数 $t=1$。

$$D_t(k)=\frac{1}{m},k=1,2,\cdots,m \quad (6)$$

(3)当 $t\leqslant T$ 时进行迭代

根据 $D_t(k)$ 训练弱学习器。

建立回归模型：$f_t(u_e)\rightarrow W$。

计算每个训练样本的相对误差

$$L_t(k)=\frac{|f_t(u_{e_{ij}})-w_{ij}|}{\max\limits_{k=1,\cdots,m}(|f_t(u_{e_{ij}})-w_{ij}|)} \tag{7}$$

计算样本误差率

$$\overline{L_t}=\sum_{k=1}^{m}L_t(k)D_t(k) \tag{8}$$

计算弱学习器系数

$$\beta_t=\frac{\overline{L_t}}{(1-\overline{L_t})} \tag{9}$$

更新 $D_{t+1}(k)$

$$D_{t+1}(k)=\frac{D_t(k)\beta_t^{1-Lt(k)}}{\sum\limits_{k=1}^{m}D_t(k)\beta_t^{1-Lt(k)}} \tag{10}$$

令 $t=t+1$。

(4)强学习器合成:将得到的 T 个弱学习器合成为强学习器

$$f(u_e)=\sum_{t=1}^{T}(\ln\frac{1}{\beta_t})F(u_e) \tag{11}$$

式中:$F(u_e)$——所有 $\beta_t f_t(u_e)$ 的中位数,$t=1,\cdots,T$。

2.4　基于迁移 AdaBoost 的航线节假日客流量预测模型

基于迁移 AdaBoost 的航线节假日客流量预测模型流程图如图 3 所示,具体步骤如下:

(1)输入属性的选取。由于航线属性和航线上的客流量能确定航线的基本信息,于是将起飞机场正负出度、目的机场正负入度、公共邻居数、度中心性以及航线客流量作为预测模型的输入属性。

(2)弱学习模型的选取。考虑到航线客流量的强非线性,BP 神经网络具有很强的非线性处理能力,所以采用 BP 神经网络作为弱学习器,随机初始化神经网络的权值和阈值。

(3)初始化训练样本权重分布。样本初始化权重取值如式(6)所示,这里选取 m 条航线属性与客流量的集合作为训练集,基于迁移学习的航线属性及目标航线的客流量作为测试集进行验证,因此初始权重 $D_{t=1}(k)=\frac{1}{m},k=1,\cdots,m$。

(4)弱学习模型训练及权重更新。训练弱学习器 BP 神经网络,并根据式(7)~式(10)计算弱学习器系数 β_t 及更新后的权重 $D_t(k)$。

(5)强学习器合成。设置 AdaBoost. R2 算法迭代次数 T,根据式(7)~式(9)可以得到 T 个预测序列弱学习器的系数 $\beta_t,t=1,2,\cdots,T$ 以及 $\beta_t f_t(u_e),t=1,\cdots,T$,并在此基础上根据式(11)合成最终的强学习器。

(6)阈值参数 R 的设置。求森鉴于对客流特征的分析得知,历年节假日变化规律相似且对客流的影响较大,所以通过设置阈值参数 R 将与目标航线节假日天数相同的相似节假日的客流量涨幅特征迁移到目标航线节假日客流量的预测中,最后实现航线节假日客流量的预测。

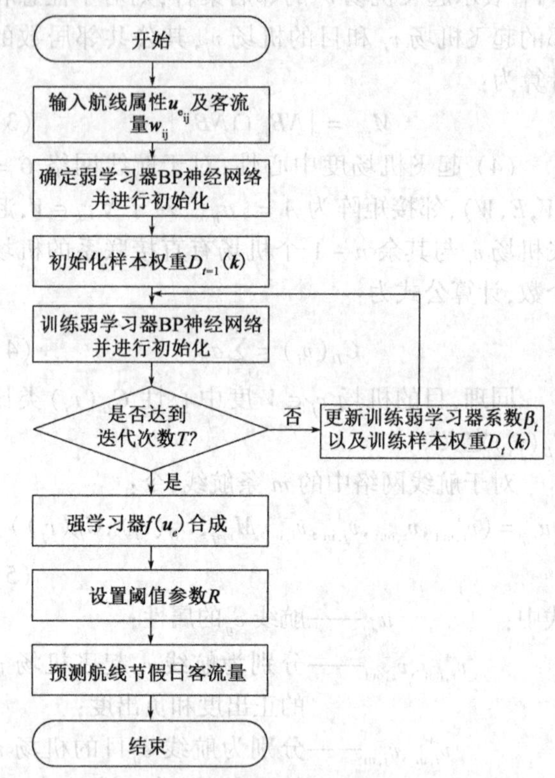

图 3　基于迁移 AdaBoost 的航线节假日客流量预测模型流程图

3　实验结果与分析

3.1　实验数据集

选取北京—三亚和广州—昆明航线进行国庆节假日期间的客流量预测,由于人们在节假日出行通常具有很强的计划性,且提前一天出发或者推迟一天返程的现象较多,所以把节假日前一天和后一天以及节假日统称为节假日期间。训练数据选用中国民航旅客订票(PNR)系统中 201×年 9 月 30 日—10 月 8 日(国庆期间),201×年 2 月 12 日—2 月 20 日(春节期间)以及次年 2 月 1 日—2 月 9 日(春节期间)脱敏后的真实订票数据作为源域,对国庆期间航线数据建立航线网络,构造航线属性,并确定相似航线进行知识迁移,实现对次年 9 月 30 日—10 月 8 日(国庆期间)目标航线的客流量预测。

3.2 数据预处理

从 PNR 数据中筛选出某航空公司所有航线的旅客订票数,滤除订票后退票即没有实际乘坐的订票数,对得到航线-客流量数据构建航线网络,提取并生成节假日期间不同时间北京—三亚和广州—昆明的航线属性,如表1 和表2 所示。

北京—三亚航线属性 表1

日期	航线属性
9月30日	[25.0,22.0,4.0, 12.0,0.0,12.777,1.053]
10月1日	[23.0,22.0,5.0,13.0, 5.0,11.871,5.874]
10月2日	[28.0,15.0,4.0,14.0, 9.0,10.814,2.521]
10月3日	[25.0, 19.0,4.0,13.0,0.0,12.986,1.489]
10月4日	[23.0,18.0,3.0,14.0,2.0, 10.216,6.744]
10月5日	[25.0,21.0,3.0,15.0,3.0, 13.318,2.462]
10月6日	[22.0,24.0,3.0,15.0, 4.0,12.716,6.157]
10月7日	[25.0,21.0,3.0,15.0,2.0,13.439,2.247]
10月8日	[21.0,23.0,3.0,13.0,4.0,12.663,3.591]

广州—昆明航线属性 表2

日期	航线属性
9月30日	[38.0,40.0,8.0,17.0,3.0,43.710,1.879]
10月1日	[38.0,42.0,9.0,15.0,2.0,44.132,1.386]
10月2日	[38.0,37.0,7.0,18.0,2.0,44.598,2.721]
10月3日	[35.0,44.0,8.0,16.0,0.0,49.154,1.923]
10月4日	[33.0,42.0,7.0,17.0,0.0,43.883,1.447]
10月5日	[35.0,43.0,7.0,17.0,2.0,45.815,1.934]
10月6日	[34.0,44.0,9.0,16.0,0.0,46.481,1.431]
10月7日	[35.0,42.0,6.0,20.0,1.0,46.114,2.831]
10月8日	[34.0,43.0,9.0,16.0,0.0,44.805,1.484]

3.3 实验评价指标

用预测客流量与真实客流量的相对误差对实验结果进行评价。其计算公式如下:

$$X_{RE} = \frac{|X' - X|}{X} \times 100\% \tag{12}$$

式中:X'——客流量预测值;

X——客流量真实值。

3.4 实验参数设置

阈值参数 R 的计算如下:

$$R = \frac{(r' - r)}{r} \times h + h \tag{13}$$

式中:r——201×年春节假期的客流量;

r'——次年春节假期的客流量;

h——201×年国庆假期的客流量。

根据阈值和时间限制,进行多次试验得出的经验,将 AdaBoost. R2 算法中迭代次数 T 设置为默认值50。

3.5 实验方法

传统机器学习方法需在大量历史客流量数据的基础上进行预测,针对无长期节假日客流量数据积累的航线,传统机器学习方法较难准确预测,所以基于迁移 AdaBoost 的航线节假日客流量预测模型(简记为"模型 C")与传统机器学习方法作对比意义不大,故对比实验选择基于客流量增长的航线节假日客流量预测模型(简记为"模型 A")与基于航线属性的航线节假日客流量预测模型(简记为"模型 B")进行。

(1)模型 A:通过统计方法将相邻两年春节期间航线客流的增长趋势以及前一年国庆期间客流量迁移到次年国庆假期客流量的预测中,实现对国庆假期航线客流量的预测。

(2)模型 B:建立航空公司航线网络,计算前一年国庆节假日期间航线属性,采用 AdaBoost. R2 回归算法对次年国庆假期客流量进行预测。

3.6 实验结果分析

图4、图5 给出了模型 A、模型 B、模型 C 的客流量预测相对误差 X_{RE}。

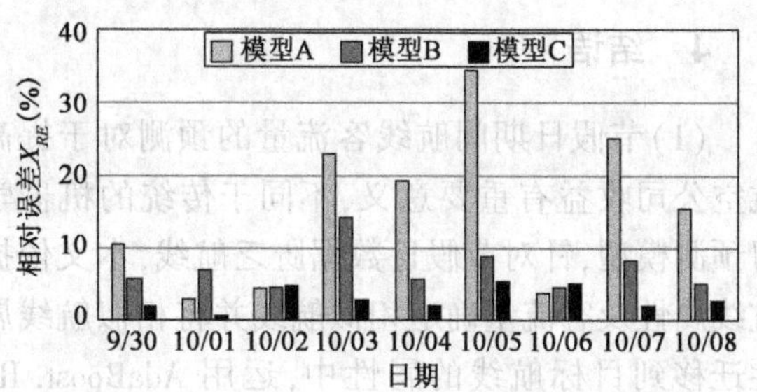

图4 北京—三亚国庆期间客流量预测相对误差对比图

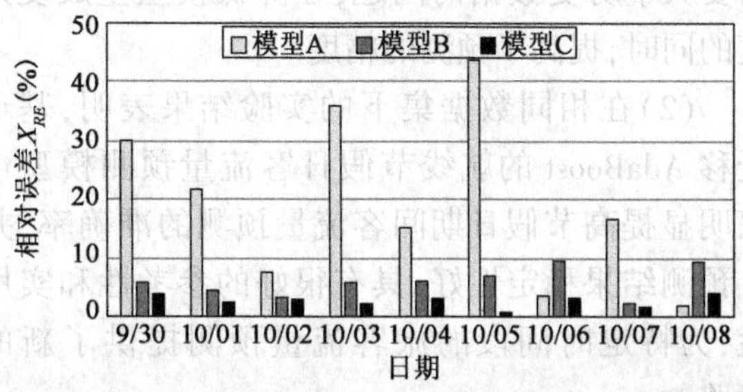

图5 广州—昆明国庆期间客流量预测相对误差对比图

模型A预测相对误差最大,其中北京—三亚航线10月5日预测相对误差高达34%,而10月1日预测结果比较准确,相对误差为3.11%。同样广州—昆明航线10月5日预测相对误差高达43%,而10月6日和10月8日预测结果相对准确,说明该模型的预测结果相当不稳定。

模型B明显比模型A预测结果准确,说明结合航线属性更有助于进行航线客流量预测,但是总体而言预测精度尚不够高。

模型C预测相对误差一般都比其他两种模型都低,除北京—三亚航线10月6日的预测结果例外,该模型对节假日客流量预测结果的稳定性也最好。针对平均相对误差,模型A预测误差较高,两条航线的平均相对误差分别在15.42%和19.72%左右(表3),模型B较模型A预测平均相对误差有大幅度的提升,而模型C的平均相对误差最低,两条航线的平均相对误差分别在3.25%和2.89%左右,说明模型C更适合节假日期间航线客流量的预测。

模型对比　　表3

模　型	平均相对误差	
	北京—三亚	广州—昆明
模型A	15.42%	19.72%
模型B	7.05%	6.05%
模型C	3.25%	2.89%

4　结语

(1)节假日期间航线客流量的预测对于提高航空公司收益有重要意义,不同于传统的机器学习预测模型,针对节假日数据匮乏航线,本文依据航线属性及客流量确定相似航线并将相似航线属性迁移到目标航线的属性中,运用AdaBoost.R2回归算法进行预测,克服了传统机器学习方法中需要大量历史数据的问题,在降低模型生成复杂度的同时,提高了预测的精度。

(2)在相同数据集下的实验结果表明,基于迁移AdaBoost的航线节假日客流量预测模型可以明显提高节假日期间客流量预测的准确率,并且预测结果稳定性好,具有很好的参考性和实用性,为特定时间段的旅客流量预测提供了新的思路。

(3)因航线客流量受诸多因素的影响,后续考虑对节假日客流量影响因素进行分析,进一步提高预测的准确率。

参考文献

[1] Wu X F, Xiang Y, Mao G, et al. Forecasting Air Passenger Traffic Flow Based on the Two-phase Learning Model [J]. The Journal of Supercomputing, 2021, 77: 4221-4243.

[2] 李易容. 结合OD矩阵的城市地铁客流量预测研究[D]. 南京:南京大学, 2020.

[3] 邢志伟,何川,罗谦,等. 基于双层K近邻算法航站楼短时客流量预测[J]. 北京航空航天大学学报, 2019, 45(01): 26-34.

[4] Carmen Bas M D, Ortiz J, Ballesteros L, et al. Evaluation of a Multiple Linear Regression Model and SARIMA Model in Forecasting 7 Be air Concentrations [J]. Chemosphere, 2017, 177(6): 326-333.

[5] Emami A, Sarvi M, Bagloee S A. Short-term Traffic Flow Prediction Based on Faded Memory Kalman Filter Fusing Data from Connected Vehicles and Bluetooth Sensors[J]. Simulation Modelling Practice and Theory, 2020, 102:102025.

[6] 李洁,彭其渊,杨宇翔. 基于SARIMA模型的广珠城际铁路客流量预测[J]. 西南交通大学学报, 2020, 55(01): 41-51.

[7] 马超群,李培坤,朱才华,等. 基于不同时间粒度的城市轨道交通短时客流预测[J]. 长安大学学报(自然科学版), 2020, 40(03): 75-83.

[8] 白丽. 城市轨道交通常态与非常态短期客流预测方法研究[J]. 交通运输系统工程与信息, 2017, 17(01): 127-135.

[9] 李若怡. 基于改进时空LSTM模型的城市轨道交通系统OD客流短时预测[D]. 北京:北京交通大学, 2019.

[10] Chen Q X, Song Y, Zhao J F. Short-term Traffic Flow Prediction Based on Improved Wavelet Neural Network [J]. Neural Computing and Applications, 2020, 33(14): 8181-8190.

[11] Gallo M, De Luca G, D'Acierno L, et al.

ArtificialNeuralNetworks for Forecasting Passenger Flows on Metro Lines [J]. Sensors (Basel), 2019, 19(15): 3424.

[12] 梁强升. 城市轨道交通大型活动客流预测方法研究[D]. 北京:北京交通大学, 2020.

[13] Liu S S, Yao E J. Holiday Passenger Flow Forecasting Based on the Modified Least-Square Support Vector Machine for the Metro System [J]. Journal of Transportation Engineering, 2017, 143(2): 04016005.

[14] 黄益绍,韩磊. 基于 RS-IPSOSVM 的公交客流量预测方法[J]. 重庆交通大学学报: 自然科学版, 2020, 39(11): 11-19.

[15] Wang X M, Zhang N, Zhang Y L, et al. Forecasting of Short-Term Metro Ridership with Support Vector Machine Online Model [J]. Journal of Advanced Transportation, 2018.

[16] CHENG A Y, Jiang X, Li Y F, et al. Multiple Sources and Multiple Measures Based Traffic Flow Prediction Using the Chaos Theory and Support Vector Regression Method [J]. Physica A: Statistical Mechanics and its Applications, 2017, 466: 422-434.

[17] Pitfiled D E. Predicting Air-Transport Demand [J]. Environment & Planning A, 1993, 25 (4): 459-466.

[18] Li Y H, Han H Y, Liu X, et al. Passenger Flow Forecast of Sanya Airport Based on ARIMA Model [C]. ICPCSEE 2018: Data Science, 2018, 902(12): 442-454.

[19] Wang Y, Cheng H, Li S. Passenger Flow Forecast Model for Intercity High Speed Railway-A Neural Network-Based Analysis [J]. Journal of Interdisciplinary Mathematics, 2018, 21(4): 897-906.

[20] 求森. 基于小波分析和神经网络的城市轨道交通客流时间序列预测[D]. 北京:北京交通大学, 2017.

[21] 李伟,董海荣,高士根,等. 基于 SARIMA-SVM 模型的城市轨道交通短时客流预测研究[C]//中国自动化学会过程控制专业委员会. 第 28 届中国过程控制会议(CPCC 2017)暨纪念中国过程控制会议 30 周年摘要集,中国自动化学会过程控制专业委员会, 2017.

[22] 余涛. 基于 SVM 和 BP 神经网络的短时交通流预测与实现[D]. 南京:南京邮电大学, 2018.

[23] Day O, Khoshgoftaar T M. A Survey on Heterogeneous Transfer Learning[J]. Journal of Big Data, 2017, 4(1): 1-42.

[24] Zhuang F Z, Qi Z Y, Duan K Y, et al. A Comprehensive Survey on Transfer Learning [J]. Proceedings of the IEEE, 2021, 109 (1): 43-76.

[25] 王玲娣. Adaptive Boosting 算法及组合分类器的构建研究[D]. 无锡:江南大学, 2018.

空域运行复杂度评估方法研究

梁卜予[1] 张 斌[2] 张矚熹*[3] 刘洪岩[4] 石婉君[4]

(1. 北京航空航天大学大型飞机高级人才培训班;2. 国能朔黄铁路发展有限责任公司科技发展部;3. 后勤保障部信息中心;4. 北京航空航天大学电子信息工程学院)

摘 要 我国航空业飞速发展,航班量居高不下,导致空域运行的复杂程度较高,对实现安全有序的空域管制带来了较大压力。因此,亟须对空域运行复杂度进行准确评估,从而准确定位运行风险分布,为空域结构规划、空域管制资源配置提供关键参考信息,提高空域运行效率。由于现有大多数空域运行复

1. 基金项目:国能朔黄铁路发展有限责任公司科技创新项目"朔黄铁路桥梁设施无人机巡检系统应用研究"(项目编号 CJNY-19-90)。

杂度评估模型只能基于空域运行数据集构建,导致空域结构调整后该类模型对于新出现空域的评估效果差。针对该问题,本文提出了一种对于新空域具有较强适应性的空域运行复杂度深度无监督评估方法。该方法基于25维描述运行动态复杂性的因子和18维描述静态空域结构的复杂性因子对空域运行复杂度等级进行评估,使用稀疏输出的自编码网络实现关键特征成分提取,并基于Gumble-Softmax引入了概率型的复样本等级聚类方法,通过自编码损失与聚类损失联合优化的方式对网络参数和聚类过程进行迭代,提升了模型在评估新空域时的性能。基于全国200多个扇区空域实际运行数据进行的实验表明,本文方法对于"新出现"扇区空域的运行复杂度具有较好的评估效果。

关键词　空域态势　空域运行复杂度　无监督学习　深度学习　自编码网络

0　引言

近年来,民航事业飞速发展,带来更多机遇的同时也给航空交通管制带来了更大的挑战。我国的空管部门将管制空域划分为小的管制扇区,各个扇区内的空中交通由空域管制员负责调控。拥挤的空域和复杂的民航运行态势,给管制员的工作带来了巨大的压力。当管制员工作能力无法负荷高复杂空域态势时,带来的就是航班延误以及不安全事件的发生。是否能准确评估空域运行复杂度,是空域管制工作能否高效开展的重要因素。

复杂的空域结构、逐年上升的航空流量、多变的空中交通态势等原因使得空域运行复杂度评估十分困难,是空中交通领域多年的重点研究内容。空域运行复杂度一般被描述为不断变化的空域配置和交通模式。由于这种概念的模糊性,尽管经过多年的研究,空域运行复杂度的概念仍然没有一个统一的定义。因此,研究人员们开始从影响空域运行复杂度的根本原因入手,探究空域的交通特性以及飞机运行期间的动态变化。大量与描述空域复杂状态相关的复杂度因子被研究出来作为复杂度评估的指标。早在1995年,研究人员们就已提出了40多种复杂度因子[1]。1998年,NASA提出了动态密度的复杂度评估方法[2],提取了十余项复杂度因子如飞机数量、飞机速度变化、飞机航向变化等,通过线性加权的方式得到复杂度值。Keumjin Lee等将复杂度定义为管制员管制额外进入扇区飞机的工作量。Zhang Chen等定义了接近因子来反应飞机对彼此空间的接近关系和风险[3];Maria Prandini等考虑了未来飞机位置的不确定性,设计了一种概率方法来计算空域可能的占用率[4]。

随着计算机科学的发展,许多学者将机器学习和深度学习引入了空中交通管制的研究中。这种方法能够建立多维复杂度因子与复杂度之间的非线性关系,为这种很难找到最优解路径的复杂度问题提供了新的解决思路,并成为主流的评估方法。David Gianazza等使用PCA主成分分析方法实现了复杂度数据的降维[5],并通过神经网络判断了指标组合的有效性,最终确定了包括飞机数量、飞机平均速度、未来15min进入空域的飞机数量在内的最佳指标体系[6]。Xiao等使用GA遗传算法[7],构建了高维和低维数据的非线性联系,结合神经网络实现了复杂度评估。Petar Andrai等也使用了遗传算法加神经网络的方式进行了复杂度评估,并通过与线性模型的比较验证了神经网络评估方法的有效性[8]。近期方法中,Zhang等针对复杂度标签中可能存在的噪声,使用mRMR置信学习进行了标签噪声的过滤,并基于XGboost进行了复杂度的评估[9]。

对于以上提出的各种方法,其中用单一指标进行评估的方法仅从某一个角度对空域运行复杂度给出了定义,考虑的角度比较片面。动态密度相关的方法由于使用线性加权的方式,没有考虑复杂度指标体系与复杂度等级之间的非线性联系。而尽管机器学习方法解决了这个问题,其在实际工作中也有一定的限制:一是复杂度等级标定样本的稀缺,二是空域结构时常调整造成的模型评估效果变差。

针对以上两点局限,本文提出一种对新出现扇区评估鲁棒性较好的空域运行复杂度无监督评估方法。在传统的影响复杂度评估的25维动态指标的基础上,增加了18维静态指标用于描述空域扇区的静态结构;使用稀疏自编码网络进行多维空域运行复杂度数据的降维;并基于Gumble-Softmax引入了概率型的聚类方法。使用全国范围扇区的无标签数据构建了动静态指标数据集进行训练,提升了模型在"新出现"空域结构扇区中的复杂度评估效果。并使用了几种经典的无监督模型作为基准进行了方法的对比和分析。结果表明,对于“新出现”的空域结构扇区进行评估时,本文提出的方法有较为不错的效果。

1 空域运行复杂度评估问题分析

1.1 问题描述与分析

在过去学者的研究以及空管的实际工作情况中,都是将空域运行复杂度分为高、中、低三个等级[10],由低到高,代表了空域运行的复杂程度逐渐递增,管制员进行空域管制的压力和空中交通运行的风险也随之递增。这种分类方法在实际工作中能够让空域管制员更直观地了解管辖区域内的复杂情况以进行相关的管制措施。在复杂度评估的学术研究中,各种研究人员使用的机器学习评估方法也是将复杂度指标数据集与这三个复杂度等级做数学模型上的映射。由此可知,基于机器学习的空域运行复杂度评估实际上是一个复杂度等级的三分类问题。

使用机器学习方法进行空域运行复杂度评估的方法流程一般为:①选择影响空域运行复杂度的多种复杂度因子作为构建训练数据集的体系结构;②选择一种分类的机器学习模型加以改进后,用空域运行复杂度指标训练数据进行模型训练,得到一个训练好的分类器;③基于复杂度指标体系,收集想要进行复杂度评估的目标扇区的复杂度指标数据,并应用在机器学习分类模型中,得到高、中、低的分类结果。最终完成空域运行复杂度评估。

针对复杂度等级标定样本的稀缺问题,本文通过设计深度无监督学习方法数据进行等级评定,这样可以避免由于标定样本的稀缺导致的数据规模较小的问题,在测试阶段以中国西南空域的 6 个扇区 CD01、CD02、CD04、GZ01、GZ02 以及 KM03 的真实复杂度数据作为测试数据来验证本文所提模型的有效性、准确性。针对空域结构时常调整造成的模型评估效果变差问题,本文在传统的影响复杂度评估的多维动态指标的基础上,增加了 18 维静态指标用于描述空域扇区的静态结构。通过全面描述空域扇区的动静态因素提升模型对于非训练集空域扇区的评估效果,保证模型在对“新出现”扇区进行复杂度等级评定时的泛化能力。

1.2 复杂度影响因子集构建

本节对本文使用的空域运行复杂度影响因子体系做描述。在传统的多维动态指标基础上,本文加入了 18 维静态指标,用来描述影响空域运行复杂度的动静态因素。过去的机器学习方法中仅着眼于某个目标扇区的复杂度评估,使用的训练数据也仅为该目标扇区某个时间段的动态指标体系数据。然而由于不同空域扇区在静态结构上大有不同(例如广州 01 扇区和成都 01 扇区在扇区大小和航路航线分布上有很大差异),因此在训练出来的模型在非目标扇区上评估效果往往不尽人意。针对以上问题,本文加入与空域结构相关的静态指标的目的是一定程度上消除空域结构对于模型评估的影响,使模型能在非目标扇区上也能有较好的评估效果。需要说明的是,本文所使用的的动态复杂度影响因子在过去的研究中已被研究人员证明对空域运行复杂度评估有效[11],静态因子见表 1。

空域运行复杂度静态影响指标 表 1

序号	名称	详细解释
1	扇区体积	管制扇区所占的空域体积,是决定飞机密度的重要因素。相同数量的飞机在不同体积的管制扇区内,对复杂度的影响可能相差很远
2	扇区交叉点个数	管制扇区内航路航线互相交叉的数量,一般来说,该值越大,飞机飞行路线上的重合就越多,飞机间的潜在冲突越多,复杂度越高
3	扇区交叉点密度	交叉点在单位管制扇区体积内的数量,代表了潜在冲突的密集程度,该值越大,潜在冲突的风险就越高,复杂度越高
4	交叉点到扇区边界的平均距离	除了交叉点以外,扇区边界也是管制员需要重点关注的空域结构。飞机在接近或跨越扇区边界的时候需要不同扇区的管制员投入额外的管制精力。因此这两个指标也被引入
5	交叉点到扇区边界的最小距离	

续上表

序 号	名 称	详细解释
6	交叉点通过航路到扇区边界的平均距离	与4、5不同的是,4、5更代表了飞机飞行中的不确定性,6、7代表的是按照飞行计划的航路飞行时,接近或跨越扇区边界所带来的潜在冲突,进而造成复杂度的提高
7	交叉点通过航路到扇区边界的最小距离	
8	航路扇区边界的交叉点个数	用来描述飞机按照飞行计划中的航路飞行时可能跨越扇区边界的数量。与6、7类似,这个数量越大,代表管制员投入的管制精力越大,复杂度越高
9	交叉点引出的航路数量平均值	交叉点引出的航路数量越多,代表了经过交叉点后飞机飞行的变化就越多,潜在冲突越多,管制员管制压力越大,复杂度就越高
10	交叉点引出和航路数量最大值	
11	扇区安全高度上限	飞机飞行的时候是有高度分层的,扇区从垂直角度上也分为高空扇区和低空扇区等,不同类型的扇区有不同的高度上下限
12	扇区安全高度下限	
13	扇区横截面面积	用来描述扇区面积、周长等静态特征
14	扇区横截面周长	
15	航路总里程	用来描述管制扇区内航路的里程数之和
16	无交叉点航路段平均距离	用来描述理论上潜在冲突风险较低的航路平均距离,飞机按照飞行计划平稳飞行,一般来说潜在冲突较少,管制资源投入的也较少
17	无交叉点航路段最大距离	
18	扇区容量	管制扇区内的飞机数量的阈值,代表了空管部门认为的管制扇区的管制员工作量上限,一般会根据扇区运行状况进行动态调整

2 基于深度无监督学习的复杂度评估方法设计

本节中,我们提出了一个深度无监督模型。在深度自编码网络的基础上,本文在原有的损失函数中加入了抑制神经元活跃度的部分,使得隐藏层的神经元稀疏输出,提高了隐藏层神经元的特征学习能力。模型结构如图1所示。

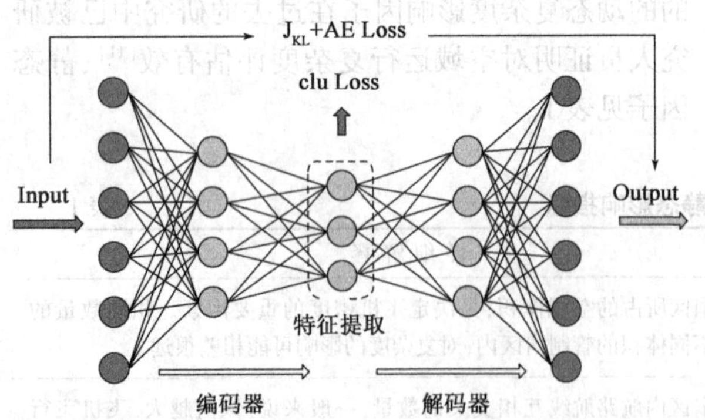

图1 深度无监督模型结构

2.1 基于稀疏自编码网络的复杂度因子关键特征提取

针对复杂度评估问题,对于自编码这种用输出重构输入的网络模型来说,有两点是衡量其效果的关键:①重构误差是否足够小。误差的大小直接决定了自编码网络的优劣,也是最基础的自编码网络衡量标准;②隐藏层的神经元是否能学习到更多的数据内在特征。由于我们使用自编码网络对空域运行复杂度数据进行降维,因此降维后的数据越具备复杂度数据特征,越有更好的分类效果。

对于第一点,我们通过用损失函数约束输入数据与输出数据的误差即可完成。一般来说,这部分的损失函数使用 MSE(Mean Square Error,均方误差)或者 KL 散度均可实现。本文选择 MSE 作为自编码网络的损失函数,其数学表达式为:

$$L_{AE}=\frac{1}{m}\sum_{i=1}^{m}\|x-g_{\tilde{\theta}}[f_{\theta}(x_i)]\|_2^2 \tag{1}$$

式中:m——数据点的个数;

x_i——输入的原始复杂度指标数据;

$f_{\theta}(x_i)$——由 Encoder 编码后在隐藏层中的表征数据;

$g_{\tilde{\theta}}(x)$——由 Decoder 解码后输出的数据。

上述公式衡量了原始数据与经过自编码变换的重构数据之间的差异。该值可以通过随机梯度下降算法与反向传播实现迭代优化。

针对第二点,我们希望自编码网络能够在隐

藏层中学习到更多复杂度数据的内在特征。因此本文引入稀疏模式的自编码网络实现空域运行复杂度数据的降维。出于上述目的,我们让隐藏层中的神经元数量小于输入层和输出层,这样隐藏层中的数据能够以更少的维度包含全部的数据信息。为了提升这种效果,同时保证自编码的损失函数在一定范围内,我们希望隐藏层的神经元能够尽可能学习到更多的数据特征,这就需要隐藏层进行稀疏输出。

隐藏层的稀疏性可以被解释为:当我们选择的网络模型激活函数为 sigmoid 函数(取值在 0 和 1 之间)时,神经元的输出接近 1 则认为它是“活”的,而当其输出接近 0 则认为它是“死”的。我们通过改变自编码的损失函数使得隐藏层的神经元大部分处于这种“死”的状态,即可认为隐藏层进行了稀疏输出。这样做的优势在于:在如此“恶劣”的条件下,活跃的神经元依然能够实现数据的重构,那么这些神经元所学习到的数据内在特征是更加“重要”的。除此之外,隐藏层稀疏输出的好处还在于,网络的稀疏性会降低参数之间的互相耦合联系,不但能降低网络模型的训练时间复杂度,还能有效改善模型的过拟合问题。

为了实现这种“稀疏性”,本文在编码网络的损失函数中加入了基于 KL 散度的限制项,保证大多数神经元的输出为 0。限制项的数学公式为:

$$L_S = KL(\rho \| \hat{\rho}_j) = \rho \log \frac{\rho}{\hat{\rho}_j} + (1-\rho) \log \frac{1-\rho}{1-\hat{\rho}_j} \quad (2)$$

式中:$\hat{\rho}_j$——隐藏层神经元的平均激活程度;

$$\hat{\rho}_j = \frac{1}{m} \sum_{i=1}^{m} [a_j^{(n)}(x_i)] \quad (3)$$

$a_j^{(n)}(x)$——在输入为 x 的情况下,第 n 层的神经元 j 的活跃度,由 sigmoid 函数的输入决定。

整个限制项由 KL 散度作为衡量公式。其中的 ρ 是人为引入的参数,称为稀疏性参数。一般来说,需要将其设置为一个很小的值,通过 KL 散度的衡量,当 ρ 与 $\hat{\rho}_j$ 很相近时,KL 散度很小;而当 $\hat{\rho}_j$ 趋于 0 或者 1 时,KL 散度趋于无穷。二者变化带来的 KL 散度值如图 2 所示(图中设置 ρ 为 0.2)。

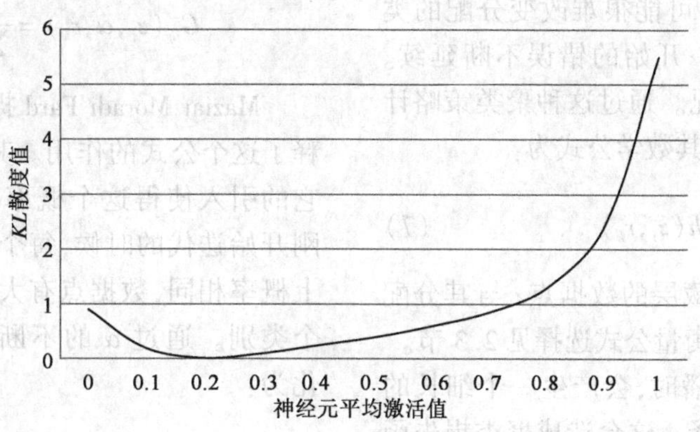

图 2　KL 散度变化图

基于这个特性,把衡量二者相似度的 KL 散度引入自编码网络的损失函数中,通过惩罚离 ρ 相差较大的 KL 散度值,来保证 $\hat{\rho}_j$ 随着迭代稳定在 ρ 这一数值附近。进而保证自编码隐藏层中活跃的神经元保持在这个比例,进而实现自编码网络的稀疏输出。整个自编码网络损失函数的数学公式为:

$$L = L_{AE} + \lambda L_S$$

$$L = \frac{1}{m} \sum_{i=1}^{m} \left\{ x_i - g_{\hat{\theta}}[f_\theta(x_i)] \right\}^2 + \lambda \sum_{j=1}^{n} \left\{ \rho \log \frac{\rho}{\hat{\rho}_j} + (1-\rho) \log \frac{1-\rho}{1-\hat{\rho}_j} \right\} \quad (4)$$

式中:n——神经网络的第 n 层。

与普通的自编码类似,稀疏自编码网络的参数同样以反向传播的方式更新,其迭代的偏导数公式为:

$$z_i^{(n)} = f(x_i^n)$$

$$\delta_i^{(n)} = \frac{\partial L}{\partial \theta_{ij}^{(S)}} = \left\{ \begin{array}{l} [\sum_{j=1}^{n} \theta_{ji}^{(n)} \delta_j^{(n+1)}] + \\ \lambda \left(-\frac{\rho}{\hat{\rho}_j} + \frac{1-\rho}{1-\hat{\rho}_j} \right) \end{array} \right\} f(z_i^{(n)}) \quad (5)$$

经过反向传播迭代更新后,最终自编码网络的损失函数为:

$$L_{SAE} = \min_{\theta,\tilde{\theta}} L_{AE} + \lambda L_S = \min_{\theta,\tilde{\theta}} \frac{1}{m}\sum_{i=1}^{m}\left(x_i - g_{\tilde{\theta}}\left[f_\theta(x_i)\right]\right)^2 + \lambda\sum_{j=1}^{n}\left[\rho\log\frac{\rho}{\hat{\rho}_j} + (1-\rho)\log\frac{1-\rho}{1-\hat{\rho}_j}\right] \quad (6)$$

2.2　基于 Gumbel-Softmax 的复杂度样本概率型聚类

通过自编码隐藏层神经元的稀疏输出,我们获得了更有特征代表性的低维数据,将每一个 mini-batch 里得到的每一条低维数据转换为一个一维向量,假定一个 mini-batch 有 m 条数据,每条 43 维数据经过自编码器后得到降维后的 n 维数据,则可得到 m 个一维向量,每个向量包含 n 个元素,将数据映射到对应的 n 维线性空间中,即是线性空间中的 m 个数据点,在此基础上直接进行聚类,其效果也会有一定程度的提升。

然而,空域运行复杂度数据在高、中、低三个类别之间的分类边界并不明显。由于 K-means 随机初始化簇中心的特性,如果在迭代前期就明确地将数据点分配给各个类别,那么在后面的迭代过程中可能沿着这个聚类方向不断前进。若一开始分类出错,在迭代后期可能很难改变分配的类别,聚类过程也会随着一开始的错误不断延续。这是我们不想看到的情况。通过这种聚类策略计算得到的聚类损失函数,其数学公式为:

$$L_{\text{clu}} = \sum_{i=1}^{m} h(z_i, r_k) \quad (7)$$

式中,$h(z_i, r_k)$衡量了隐藏层的数据点z_i与其分配的簇中心r_k的距离,距离衡量公式选择见 2.3 节。

在神经网络反向传播时,会产生一个细长的梯度反馈给随机梯度下降。这会造成聚类损失函数缓慢更新,最终整个网络的损失函数仅仅受L_{SAE}的影响。进而导致模型只考虑了数据重构的准确度,却忽略了聚类的效果。

为了解决这种问题,使得数据点的分配能够随着神经网络迭代而逐渐进行,本文在 Eric Jang 等研究的基础上,引入了一种基于 Gumbel-Softmax 的概率型聚类方法。这种方法将分类问题中无法计算梯度的难题通过 Gumbel-Softmax 函数转换为一个概率表示的向量,分类方向为最大或者最小的概率值。这样,离散的分类问题就可以通过反向传播计算梯度进行更新,并且通过调整参数,最终概率值会收敛为 0 和 1,最终完成类别的分配。

首先,我们提出,在模型迭代过程中,聚类的损失函数为:

$$L_{\text{clu}} = h(z_i, R) = \begin{cases} h(z_i, r_k), \text{如果} r_k = \operatorname{argmin} h(z_i, R) \\ 0, \text{其他情况} \end{cases} \quad (8)$$

上述公式的含义为:只有当r_k是离数据点最近的簇中心时,这个距离才被列入聚类损失函数的计算中。那么确定一个能够以概率代表数据点类别分布,且能随着网络模型迭代更新最终实现收敛的 $h(x)$ 是这个损失函数的关键。

为了避免迭代前期聚类方向错误导致后期难以调整的问题,我们在自编码的隐藏层中将每一个数据点与每一个簇中心的距离都考虑进去,用欧式距离作为数据点距离的衡量公式。数据点与簇中心的距离数学表达式为:

$$D_{ik} = \|z_i - r_k\|_2^2 \quad k \in 0,1,2 \quad (9)$$

基于 Gumbel-Softmax 方法,本文引入一个概率型的分配方式为:

$$G_{ik}(z_i, \alpha, r_k) = \frac{\exp(-\alpha D_{ik})}{\sum_K \exp(-\alpha D_{ik})} \quad (10)$$

Maziar Moradi Fard 提出的深度 K-means 中解释了这个公式的作用。其中 α 作为一个超参数,它的引入使得这个概率公式参数化。网络模型刚开始迭代的时候,每个数据点的聚类分配大致上概率相同,数据点有大致相同的机会分配给每个类别。通过 α 的不断迭代,这个公式发生变化为:

$$\lim_{\alpha\to\infty} G_{ik}(z_i, \alpha, R) = \begin{cases} 1, \text{如果} r_k = \operatorname{argmin} h(z_i, R) \\ 0, \text{其他情况} \end{cases} \quad (11)$$

也就是说,随着对 α 的调整,当 α 到一个较大值的时候,$G_{ik}(z_i, \alpha, r_k)$会趋近于 0 或者 1,这与我们对 $h(x)$ 的期望不谋而合。以这种方式迭代的模型,数据点会从一开始在每个类别分配上有大体相同的概率,逐渐趋向于某一个确定的类别,经过一次次的迭代,最终,模型完成聚类结果分配。

综上所述,聚类部分的损失函数数学公式为:

$$L_{\text{clu}} = \min_{\theta,\tilde{\theta},R} \|f_\theta(x_i) - GR^T\|_2^2 \quad (12)$$

结合上一小节提出的稀疏自编码损失函数，整个网络模型的损失函数为：

$$L = L_{AE} + \lambda L_S + L_{clu}$$

$$L = \min_{\theta,\tilde{\theta}} \frac{1}{m}\sum_{i=1}^{m}\left(x_i - g_{\tilde{\theta}}[f_\theta(x_i)]\right)^2 + \lambda\sum_{j=1}^{n}\left[\rho\log\frac{\beta}{\hat{\rho}_j} + (1-\rho)\log\frac{1-\rho}{1-\hat{\rho}_j}\right] + \|f_\theta(x_i) - GR^T\|_2^2 \tag{13}$$

2.3 模型迭代方法

与常规的神经网络模型相似，本文提出的方法使用反向传播和随机梯度下降的方式进行损失函数的优化和参数的迭代。在深度无监督模型中，有两点是模型迭代过程中的难题：一是自编码网络在预训练时期的参数初始化；二是聚类簇中心作为一个离散空间，簇中心的更新是无法对损失函数微分的，导致随机梯度下降不可用。基于过去研究人员在深度学习中的工作，本文使用常用的深度学习模型参数初始化的方法。同时引入一个改进后的可微聚类损失函数，使其能够随着模型迭代而更新。整个过程通过随机梯度下降和反向传播完成。

自编码预训练部分，我们使用逐层预训练的方式，将上一层的输出作为下一层网络的输入来训练。这部分的预训练过程与聚类无关，仅仅为了实现空域运行复杂度数据的重构，也就是稀疏自编码网络模型的部分。在梯度下降的步骤中，我们使用 mini-batch 的方法将数据集分为几个 batches，这样做的好处在于不用等到全部的数据集遍历后再更新模型参数，而是在每一个 mini-batch 训练后就进行更新。这种方式能够显著提升网络模型训练效率。整个过程使用随机梯度下降即可完成。通过这一预训练过程，我们得到网络模型的参数与隐藏层数据，其数学公式为：

$$(\theta,\tilde{\theta},z)\leftarrow(\theta,\tilde{\theta},z) - \beta\frac{1}{|\tilde{\chi}|}[\nabla_{(\theta,\tilde{\theta},z)}L_{AE} + \nabla_{(\theta,\tilde{\theta})}L_s(\theta,\tilde{\theta})] \tag{14}$$

式中：β——网络模型训练的学习率（learning rate），其大小影响了随机梯度下降时的参数更新幅度，以及模型的收敛速度；

$\tilde{\chi}$——复杂度数据集的一个随机 mini-batch。

二者均为模型超参数，通过调整设置影响模型效果。若β过大，则模型收敛过快，容易进入局部最优解，若过小，则收敛速度过慢，迭代之间看不到效果变化。$\tilde{\chi}$的大小根据数据量的大小和计算资源我们选择为 100。

经过了预训练的自编网络，我们得到一组网络参数以及隐藏层。接着我们将原始空域运行复杂度数据通过预训练后的 Encoder 层进行降维，得到了一组低维表示的数据。接着使用基本的 K-means 对隐藏层低维数据进行聚类，得到一组初始化的簇中心 $R=[r_1,r_2,r_3]$。至此完成了自编码网络以及隐藏层数据聚类的预训练。

参数微调部分，我们引入变量p_{ik}，用来衡量隐藏层中每一个数据点对于其大概率分配至的类别的影响，其数学公式为：

$$p_{ik} = \begin{cases} 1,\text{如果} r_k = \operatorname{argmin} h(z_i, r_k) \\ 0,\text{其他情况} \end{cases} \tag{15}$$

上述公式的意义在于，每次迭代时选择距离最近的簇中心作为聚类损失函数的加和项，乘以该点分配到这一类别的概率，即为这一迭代轮次的聚类损失。由此，整体的聚类损失函数为：

$$L_{clu} = \min_{\theta,\tilde{\theta},z,R}\sum_{k=1}^{K}p_k\|f_\theta(\chi) - GR_k^T\|_2^2 \tag{16}$$

结合自编码网络的损失函数，整个网络模型的参数均可以通过随机梯度下降进行联合更新，此过程由反向传播的方式进行迭代。其数学公式为：

$$(\theta,\tilde{\theta},z,R)\leftarrow(\theta,\tilde{\theta},z,R) - \beta\frac{1}{|\tilde{\chi}|}[\nabla_{(\theta,\tilde{\theta},z)}L_{AE} + \nabla_{(\theta,\tilde{\theta})}L_s(\theta,\tilde{\theta}) + \nabla_{(\theta,\tilde{\theta},z,R)}L_{clu}] \tag{17}$$

每轮迭代，在网络模型的参数更新后，需要重新确定簇中心，以这种方式逐渐确定最合适的聚类结果。传统的 K-means 聚类，在更新簇中心时，其逻辑流程为：从数据集中选择一个数据点，计算其与每一个簇中心的距离，选择距离最短的分配到该类别中，并选择“中间”的数据点作为新的簇中心。数学公式为：

$$R\leftarrow\frac{1}{|C_k|}\sum_{i}^{m}z_i \tag{18}$$

其中C_k代表了 k 类别的数据点数量。这种更新方式的弊端在于，迭代初期可能不是每个点都分配到了正确的类别，将这些分配错误的点加入计算过程导致了聚类方向有所偏差。因此,本文将 k 类别附近的所有数据点都考虑进来,根据它们的位置共同决定聚类的走向。由此,聚类簇中心的更新公式为:

$$R \leftarrow R - \frac{1}{|C_k|}[R - f_\theta(\chi)]p_{ik} \tag{19}$$

其中,$p_{ik} = \begin{cases} 1, 如果 r_k = \mathrm{argmin} h(z_i, r_k) \\ 0, 其他情况 \end{cases}$

3　实验结果与分析

3.1　数据集

为了得到适用于中国任意一个空域扇区的空域运行复杂度评估模型。我们选择 2018 年 10 月 1 日凌晨 2 点至夜晚 24 点时间段内,中国管辖空域的 200 个高空扇区的复杂度数据构成测试数据集。选择这个时间段的理由是通过对航班数量的统计,0 点至 2 点内的运行飞机数量较少。相对而言,这个时间内空中交通的复杂程度以及管制员的工作压力都是较小的。我们设定这一时间段内的复杂度均为"低",学习这一时间段的数据对于飞机数量较多的空域情况是意义较小的。

结合航迹数据与扇区结构数据,通过程序计算得到的空域运行复杂度数据,我们以每一分钟作为一条数据样本,每条样本包括 25 维动态指标和 18 维静态指标。基于此构成了共 264000 条数据的复杂度训练数据集。

由于复杂度等级标签的获取难度较大,我们仅选择中国西南空域的 6 个扇区 *CD*01、*CD*02、*CD*04、*GZ*01、*GZ*02 以及 *KM*03 的真实复杂度数据作为测试数据。基于相同的原因,我们选择 2 点至 16 点(数据仅涵盖到 16 点)时间段内每一分钟的数据,共 5040 条样本作为测试数据集。同样的,每条样本包含 25 维动态指标、18 维静态指标以及 1 个标定的复杂度等级。其中,复杂度等级由熟悉扇区的管制员人工标定。

为了模拟"新出现"的空域结构以验证模型对于调整后空域结构的复杂度评估效果,我们在训练数据集中去除了测试数据集内包含的 6 个扇区,使用余下的 194 个扇区作为训练数据集。用测试数据集的 6 个扇区代表新的空域结构。

综上,本文使用程序计算得到的中国 194 个扇区复杂度数据共 256080 条样本构成训练数据集;使用真实的西南地区 6 个标定的扇区复杂度数据共 5040 条样本构成测试数据集。

3.2　模型性能验证

本文选用无监督学习中的一些经典模型以及深度聚类的相关模型作为基准对本文提出的方法进行对比和评估。选择 Acc、NMI、ARI 作为评估模型效果的指标。其中 Acc 的计算由于聚类后的数据标签与真实标签并不一定是一一对应的关系,因此我们使用 Kuhn-Munkres 算法将聚类后的标签映射到真实的标签中。最终,本文提出模型与各个基准模型对测试数据的评估结果如表 2 所示。

实验结果与 Baseline 对比　　表 2

	本文方法	K-means	PCA_K-means	AE_K-means	DEC
Acc	71%	32.5%	46.5%	47.8%	57.7%
NMI	0.305	0.073	0.079	0.089	0.183
ARI	0.288	0.035	0.037	0.069	0.141

本文所提出的方法在各项指标中均比基准模型有着更好的表现。说明本文方法在进行"新出现"空域结构的复杂度评估问题中是有不错的效果的。进一步分析,对比 K-means、PCA_K-means 与 AE_K-means,我们可以看到,PCA_K-means 与 AE_K-means 有着明显的效果提升,这证明了降维方法确实可以有效挖掘空域运行复杂度特征。而对比 PCA_K-means 与 AE_K-means,后者的效果并没有显著提升,一方面可能是 AE 的性能受调参的影响并没有达到最优的结果;另一方面,这种先降维再聚类的方式,其分类效果更多的还是受到 K-means 的限制,这一点从 DEC 的评估结果中也能证明。由于 DEC 通过 KL 散度约束了聚类过程与自编码网络迭代,进而一同优化了网络参数和聚类分配,使得网络模型中的特征选择与聚类效果强相关,因此也有着更好的结果。这种无监督学习方式也是更适用于空域运行复杂度评估的方法。

4 结语

本文以中国整体空域为研究目标,针对现有基于机器学习的空域运行复杂度评估方法的两点局限性,旨在设计一种不依赖管制员人工标定复杂度样本的对新出现扇区鲁棒性较好的复杂度评估方法。主要工作如下。

(1)本文在传统的影响复杂度评估的多维动态指标的基础上,增加了18维静态指标用于描述空域扇区的静态结构。通过全面描述空域扇区的动静态因素提升了对于非训练集空域扇区的评估效果。

(2)使用稀疏自编码网络进行多维空域运行复杂度数据的降维。通过在自编码网络中加入稀疏项限制隐藏层神经元的输出,在保证自编码性能的同时提升了其特征学习能力,进而提升了模型的鲁棒性。提升了模型对于"新出现"空域结构下复杂度评估的性能。

(3)基于Gumble-Softmax引入了概率型的聚类方法。与传统的聚类方法相比,概率型的聚类方法通过迭代将数据点逐渐引导到概率最大的簇中心,避免了一开始聚类方向出错导致迭代后期难以调整的问题。提升了聚类效果。

基于以上工作,本文设计了一种深度无监督复杂度评估算法。使用全国范围扇区的无标签数据构建了动静态指标数据集进行训练,提升了模型在"新出现"空域结构扇区中的复杂度评估效果。并使用了几种经典的无监督模型作为基准进行了方法的对比和分析。结果表明,对于"新出现"的空域结构扇区进行评估时,本文提出的方法有较为不错的效果。然而,本文提出的方法仍然有一定的问题。和使用复杂度等级标定样本训练的有监督模型相比,无监督模型在准确率方法仍然存在一定的差距。同时,空管工作是与时俱进的。随着新一代空管系统的研制和开发,扇区将不再是划分空域的管制单位,基于航迹的管制方式将被广泛应用。在四维航迹的空中交通模式下,空管的模式将变得更加灵活多变,过去的复杂度指标可能不再有意义。因此,空域运行复杂度评估的方法也要随之更新优化。

参考文献

[1] Mogford R H , Guttman J A , Morrow S L , et al. The Complexity Construct in Air Traffic Control: A Review and Synthesis of the Literature[J]. Complexity Construct in Air Traffic Control a Review & Synthesis of the literature, 1995.

[2] Laudeman L V , Shelden S G , Branstrom R , et al. Dynamic Density: An Air Traffic Management Metric[J]. Density, 1998.

[3] Chen Z , Jin Z , Hu M . Air Traffic Complexity Based on Alliance Effects, IEEE, 2009.

[4] Prandini M, Putta V , Hu J . A Probabilistic Measure of Air Traffic Complexity in 3-D Airspace[M]. Springer Berlin Heidelberg,2017.

[5] Gianazza D , Guittet K . Évaluation of Air Traffic Complexity Metrics Using Neural Networks and Sector Status, 2006.

[6] Chatterji G , Sridhar B . Measures for Air Traffic Controller Workload Prediction[C]// 1st AIAA, Aircraft, Technology Integration, and Operations Forum, 2001.

[7] Xiao M, Zhang J , Cai K , et al. ATCEM: A Synthetic Model for Evaluating Air Traffic Complexity [J]. Journal of Advanced Transportation, 2016, 50(3):315-325.

[8] Andrai P, Radii T ,Novak D , et al. Subjective Air Traffic Complexity Estimation Using Artificial Neural Networks[J]. Promet-traffic & Transportation, 2019, 31(4):377-386.

[9] Zhang M, Xie H, Ge J, et al. Air Traffic Complexity Evaluation withNovel Complexity Features and mRMR-XGBoost [J]. IOP Conference Series: Earth and Environmental Science, 2021, 638(1):012036.

[10] 丛玮,胡明华,谢华,等.基于指标体系的扇区复杂性评估方法[J].交通运输系统工程与信息,2015,15(05):136-141.

[11] Gianazza D, Guittet K. Selection and Evaluation of Air Traffic Complexity Metrics [C]// Digital Avionics Systems Conference, IEEE, 2014.

气象影响下的机场动态容量预测方法研究

李　琛[1]　张瞩熹*[2]　石婉君[3]
(1.北京航空航天大学大型飞机高级人才培训班;2.后勤保障部信息中心;
3.北京航空航天大学电子信息工程学院)

摘　要　为有效实施机场航班起降调控,提升机场运行效率,减少航班延误现象的发生,本文以气象为切入点,开展机场动态容量预测方法研究。首先,相比于传统方法仅考虑风速、风向、云底高及能见度等一维气象特征,本文引入雷达回波图二维时空气象特征,获得机场周边对流天气的空间分布对机场容量的影响规律;其次,采用长短期记忆神经网络模型设计了一种基于注意力机制的时序预测方法捕捉机场动态容量的时序关联性;最后,以北京首都国际机场作为研究对象开展机场动态容量预测实证探究,与机器学习方法、统计回归等方法进行对比分析,验证了本文方法的有效性。

关键词　机场动态容量　容量预测　气象影响　长短期记忆模型　注意力机制

0　引言

随着我国经济的快速发展,民航旅客不断增长,全国各机场起降航班持续增多,机场起降流量时常超过机场动态容量限制,导致航班延误问题日益凸显。因此,准确预测评估机场动态容量,为航空管制员优化进离港航班计划,缓解航班延误现象显得尤为重要。

本文以《机场容量评估管理暂行管理办法》中四种主要方法作为研究对象,通过国内外文献的调研,将目前较为流行的机场动态容量预测评估方法概述为:以航空管制员为核心的基于管制员工作负荷的机场容量评估方法、以机场航班运行数据为基础的基于历史数据统计分析的机场容量评估方法、以机场空域为研究对象的基于计算机仿真的机场容量评估方法以及以数学建模为目标的基于数学模型的机场容量方法。

目前对于机场动态容量的评估方法很多,且已有非常成熟的成果,但是仍有部分不足:一是理论方法方面,目前对于气象因素的考虑,主要是风速、风向、能见度、云底高等较为简单的一维气象特征,对于气象的考究较为简单且不够全面,未考虑气象随时间推进而变化的趋势信息,导致对于机场动态容量的预测精度不够;二是实际业务开展方面,根据《机场容量评估管理暂行办法》规定,各民航地区管理局对于机场容量的评估工作只在每年的4月和10月开展,得到的评估结果为静态容量。但是机场容量并非是一成不变的,而是随着气象条件、跑道配置、空中交通管制等各类因素实时动态变化的,因此目前实际业务中开展的机场容量评估很难满足机场运行需要,亟须能够对机场动态容量进行在线评估预测的方法。

1　机场动态容量预测问题分析

机场动态容量被定义为在特定的条件下(例如跑道配置条件和天气条件),某一特定机场在一个确定的时间间隔内(例如15min或1h)可以起降航班的最大数量。在经济计量学中有专有名词——时序数据。时序数据是在同一统一指标下按时间顺序记录的数据列。在同一数据列中的各个数据必须是同口径的,要求具有可比性,可见,机场动态容量预测问题是典型的时序数据预测问题,通过对时间序列数据进行分析,进而找到样本时间序列的统计特性和发展规律,构建时间序列模型,进行样本外的预测。

同时机场动态容量受到气象条件、跑道配置条件、航班起降比率以及执飞航班机型等多方面因素的影响。其中气象是最主要的因素,大风和低能见度会拉长航班之间的最小安全间隔,使机场容量降低;对流天气会降低机场终端区空域的

1.基金项目:科技部国家重点研发计划项目2020YFC0832600。

开放程度,造成跑道关闭,直接影响机场容量,雷达回波图可以根据雷达反射的强度进行颜色标注,通过颜色的不同判断其降雨的强度,并根据其雷达回波的移动范围及方向预测未来该地区的降雨情况。同时目前雷达回波图的频率可以达到6min一次,能够快速地展现出气象变化的趋势和范围,对于研究气象如何影响机场日常航班运行具有非常重要的意义。因此,本文通过研究气象与机场动态容量之间的关联性,研究气象影响下的机场动态容量之间的时序关联性,预判机场未来承载航班的能力,为民航管制员优化进离港航班计划提供理论方法和系统支撑。

2 气象影响下的机场动态容量预测模型设计

2.1 模型构建思路与框架设计

气象影响下的机场动态容量预测问题是一个关于多因素特征因子时序预测问题,本文将影响机场动态容量的影响因子分为:气象因子、起降流量因子和其他因子。通过卷积神经网络对气象特征因子中的雷达回波图进行特征提取,以掌握气象变化的趋势和范围。其他特征因子通过Python语言进行解析、翻译和提取,其相关特征因子见表1。

18维基础训练数据 表1

变　量	变量描述
气象相关变量因子	
FEATURE_1~8	8维雷达回波图气象特征,无量纲
CROSS_WIND	侧风风速,单位:m/s
VISIBILITY	能见度,单位:m
CEILING	云底高,单位:ft
起降流量相关变量因子	
DEP_PLAN	小时计划起飞航班数量,单位:架次/h
ARR_PLAN	机场小时计划降落数量,单位:架次/h
RATIO_PLAN	机场跑道配置变量,无量纲
FLOW_AVERAGE	该时段的平均小时流量,单位:架次/h
FLOW	真实小时流量,单位:架次/h
其他相关变量因子	
IS_WEEKEND	该日是否为周六日,bool类型
IS_HOLIDAY	该日是否为节假日,bool类型

同时该问题作为时序数据预测问题,拟采用长短期记忆模型作为模型的主框架,以此掌握机场动态容量的时序关联性;在长短期记忆模型的基础上,采用缩放点积模型对长短期记忆模型的训练结果进行软注意力模型的训练,最终是一个输入序列为n,输出序列为1的神经网络模型。最终的模型框架如图1所示。

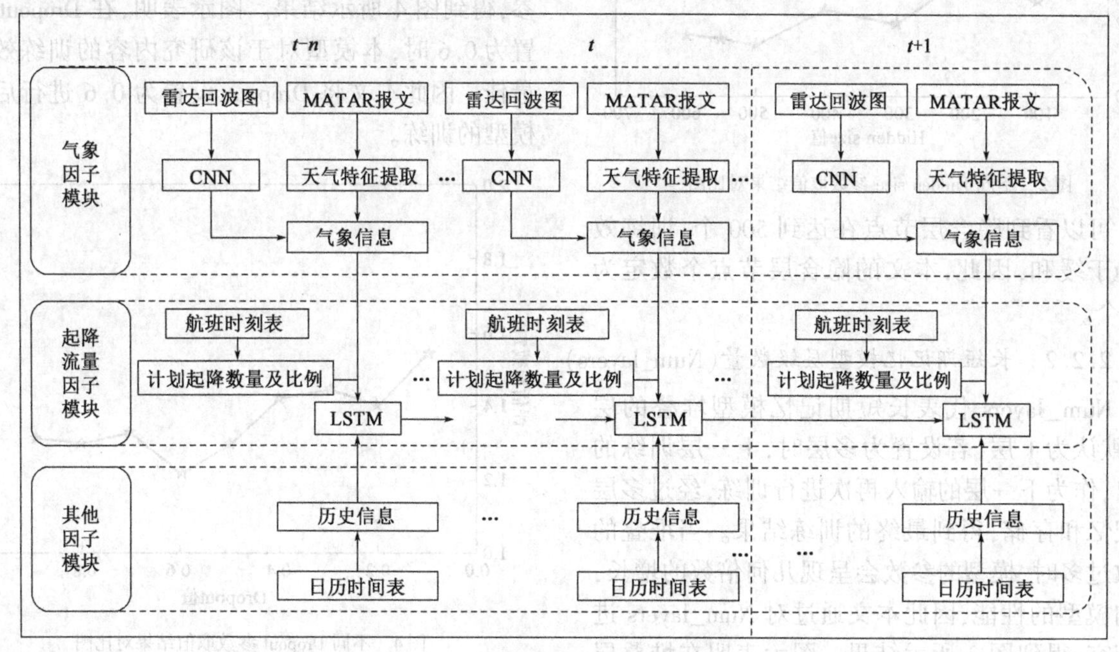

图1 机场动态容量预测模型框架

2.2　机场动态容量预测模型参数选择

根据上述模型构建思路搭建的机场动态容量时序预测模型，本小节对相关参数进行适应性改造的相关探究，采用 3.1 小节的方法评价指标作为评价标准，采用 Adam 优化算法和均方误差损失函数进行参数的更新和模型的优化。

2.2.1　隐藏层节点数量(Hidden size)

Hidden size 代表隐含层的节点个数，本文中输入层包括了气象因子等 18 维机场动态容量影响因子，通过隐含层用于记忆和存储过去的状态，从而实现时序数据的关联性。隐含层的维度大小对结果有着一定的影响，维度过小，记忆和存储能力过弱，容易导致其结果造成偏差；维度过大，造成模型运算过慢，硬件资源利用过高。因此本文通过对隐含层的节点个数进行探究，得到图 2 所示结果。

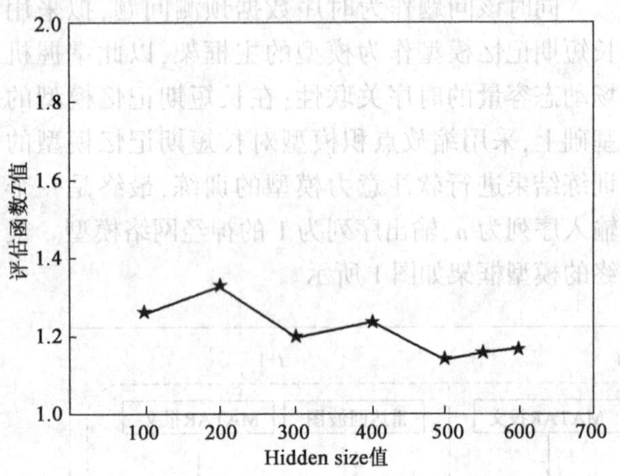

图 2　不同 Hidden size 参数取值结果对比图

可以看到隐含层节点在达到 500 个，训练效果趋于缓和，因此，本文的隐含层节点个数定为 500 个。

2.2.2　长短期记忆模型层级数量(Num_layers)

Num_layers 代表长短期记忆模型堆叠的层数，默认为 1 层，若设置为多层时，上一层训练的输出，作为下一层的输入再次进行训练，经过多层的记忆和存储，得到最终的训练结果。当堆叠的层数过多时，模型的参数会呈现几何倍数的增长，影响模型的性能，因此本文通过对 Num_layers 进行探究，得到图 3 所示结果。图示表明在堆叠层数为 2 层时，本模型对于该研究内容的训练效果最佳。

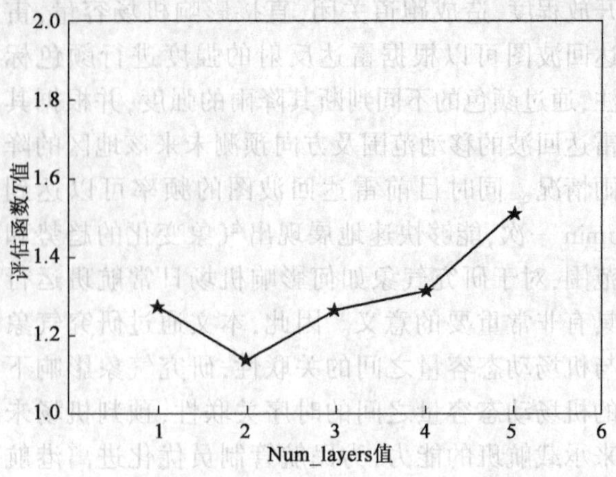

图 3　不同 Num_layers 参数取值结果对比图

2.2.3　长短期记忆网络单元丢弃概率参数(Dropout)

Dropout 是 Hinton 于 2012 年提出来用于提高训练结果的方法。在训练过程的前向传播中，让每个神经元以一定的概率 p 处于不激活的状态，以达到减少过拟合的效果，在测试阶段把 Dropout 进行关闭。同时将 Dropout 应用到输入张量上，使得每个输入张量以服从伯努利分布的概率值 p 进行随机变化为 0，以此来模拟现实生活中的某些数据缺失的情况，以期达到数据增强的目的。

本文中通过对 Dropout 从 0.1 ~ 0.9 进行调参，得到图 4 所示结果。图示表明，在 Dropout 设置为 0.6 时，本模型对于该研究内容的训练效果最佳。因此本文将 Dropout 设置为 0.6 进行后续模型的训练。

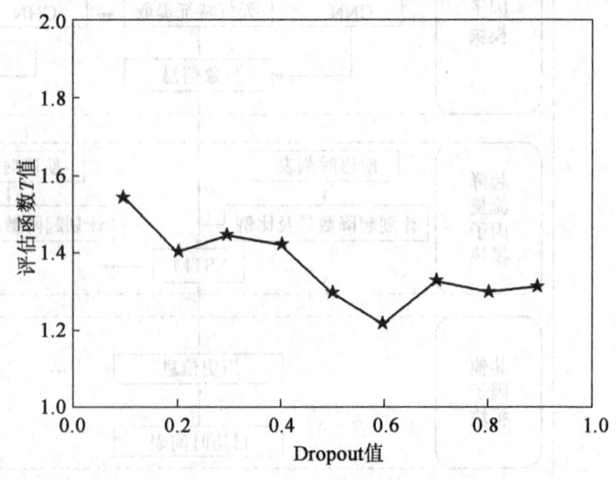

图 4　不同 Dropout 参数取值结果对比图

2.2.4　训练集训练次数(Epoch)

Epoch 代表训练时，所有训练数据集训练的次数。本文采用 Adam 优化算法和均差误差损失函数进行参数的更新和模型的优化。模型参数在每个 Epoch 内迭代,当 Epoch 偏小时,模型的学习不足,泛化能力不强,难以得到较好的训练结果,当训练结果达到一定程度时,再次增加迭代次数,往往会导致模型发生过拟合,验证集的效果不再有提升;本文从 Epoch 设置为 100 开始,并记录其迭代次数中均方误差损失函数(loss)的变化,得到图5不同 Epoch 参数取值损失函数对比图和图 6 不同 Epoch 参数取值结果对比图。

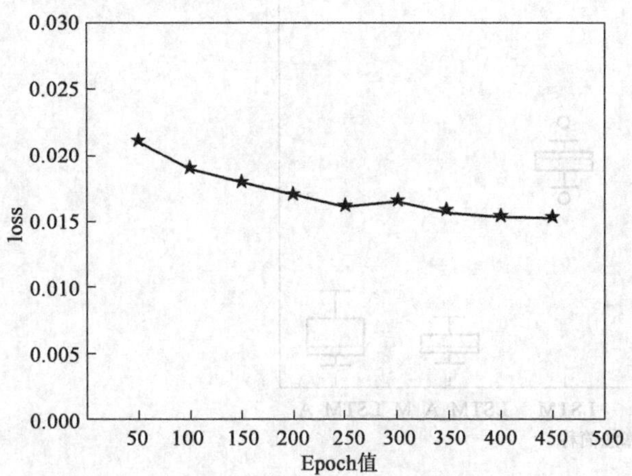

图5 不同 Epoch 参数取值损失函数对比图

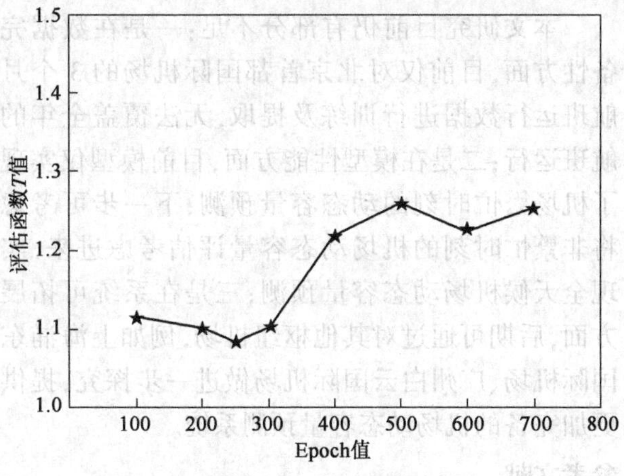

图6 不同 Epoch 参数取值结果对比图

由图 5、图 6 分析可知,当训练次数达到 250 左右时,验证集的预测效果趋于最佳,当再次增大训练次数时,均方误差损失函数虽然有略微下降,但是此时模型发生过度学习,验证集的预测效果反而下降。因此通过对 Epoch 训练数据集训练次数的探究,本文最终将迭代次数确定为 250 次。

2.2.5 长短期记忆模型序列长度(Seq_len)

Seq_len 表示序列的长度,在自然语言处理中代表句子的长度,在本文中 Seq_len 则代表了机场动态容量预测序列的长度,以 Seq_len 为 3 为例,代表根据前三个小时气象特征因子、起降流量特征因子以及其他特征因子来预测三个小时后的机场动态容量。因为本身训练集是有限的,当 Seq_len 变大时,相应的 batch_size 变小,训练样本减少。本文从 Seq_len 为 1 时进行探究,逐渐增加到 5,其相关结果见表 2。可知当 Seq_len 为 2 时,预测效果最优。故本文将 Seq_len 定为 2。

不同 Seq_len 参数取值结果对比 表 2

Seq_len	Batch_size	T	T/batch_size
1	268	2.41180	0.00900
2	134	1.10522	0.00825
3	89	0.909032	0.01021
4	67	0.712625	0.01064
5	53	0.53708	0.01013

3 实证及模型对比分析

3.1 方法性能评价指标简介

机场动态容量预测问题本质上是一个回归问题,在评价算法优劣时,本文借鉴了 Kicinger 在 2016 年发表的有关评估方法均方误差损失函数,其评估函数为:

$$T = \frac{\sum_{i=1}^{n}(P_i - A_i)^2}{\sum_{i=1}^{n}A_i^2}$$

式中:P_i——该时刻算法模型预测的机场动态容量;

A_i——该时刻实际的机场动态容量;

T——整个测试集的所有时刻动态容量预测偏差总和。

3.2 模型方法性能及气象特征因子效果验证及对比

本节基于北京首都国际机场的研究数据和构建的注意力机制下的长短期记忆模型进行实例验证,通过与当下机器学习、统计回归等方法进行对比,分析不同模型方法所预测的机场动态容量的异同,并通过加入该气象特征因子与不加气象特征因子的对比研究,探究该气象特征因子模块对于模型效果的影响。

本文以北京首都国际机场作为研究对象,以 2019 年 7 月 29 日—2019 年 10 月 21 日共 85 天的机场繁忙时刻(10:00—20:00)运行航班数据及气象数据为基础,开展探索与研究,共获得892组数据,将其分为70%的训练集及30%的测试集。为防止偶然性的发生,本文在同样数据与代码逻辑的基础上,进行了20次独立训练。

如图7所示,RF代表加入了气象特征因子的随机森林方法,Ba代表加入了气象特征因子的贝叶斯回归方法,Ga代表加入了气象特征因子的高斯过程回归方法,LSTM表示加入了气象特征因子的长短期记忆模型方法,LSTM_A_M代表加入了气象特征因子的注意力机制下的长短期记忆模型方法,LSTM_A代表未加入气象特征因子的注意力机制下的长短期记忆模型方法。

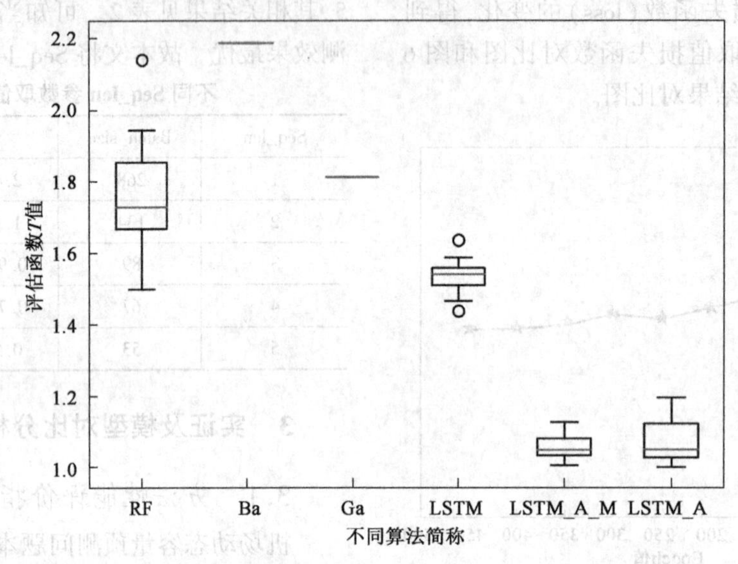

图7　不同算法模型及气象特征取值结果对比图

从气象特征因子的添加与否观察分析可知,添加气象特征因子使得机场动态容量的预测结果更加稳定,同时通过对20次独立训练的结果观察可知,添加气象特征因子的训练结果稍好于未添加气象特征因子的训练结果。

从模型方法性能方面对比可知,对于134组相同的测试数据,贝叶斯回归方法效果一般,高斯过程回归方法、随机森林方法两者效果相当,长短期记忆模型相较随机森林方法模型更加稳定,效果更好,本文提出的基于注意力机制的长短期记忆网络方法相比上述四种方法效果最佳,更能够准确地预测机场动态容量,为航空管制员提供更加有效的数据支撑。

4　结语

本文聚焦于气象因素的研究,探究气象因素与机场动态容量的变化关系。并以北京首都国际机场作为研究对象,采用基于注意力机制的长短期记忆模型对其进行训练,与目前较为流行的机器学习算法和统计回归算法进行实例验证及模型对比,对比结果显示,本文方法能够更好地对北京首都国际机场的动态容量进行有效的预测。

本文研究目前仍有部分不足:一是在数据完备性方面,目前仅对北京首都国际机场的3个月航班运行数据进行训练及提取,无法覆盖全年的航班运行;二是在模型性能方面,目前模型仅实现了机场繁忙时刻的动态容量预测,下一步可考虑将非繁忙时刻的机场动态容量评估考虑进来,实现全天候机场动态容量预测;三是在系统可拓展方面,后期可通过对其他枢纽机场,例如上海浦东国际机场、广州白云国际机场做进一步探究,提供更加完备的机场动态容量预测系统。

参考文献

[1] 马杨. 浅谈基于管制员工作负荷的容量评估方法[J]. 科技风,2015, 21:11.

[2] International Civil Aviation Organization: Air traffic service planning manual (DO-C9426) [M]. Montreal: International Civil Aviation Organization, 1984.

[3] TofukujiN. An Airspace Design and Evaluation of Enroute Sector by Air Traffic Control-simulation Experiments [J]. Eletronics and

Communications in Japan (Part I: Communications), 1996, 79(8): 35-38.

[4] 朱聃，徐晨，刘继新. 基于语音识别的管制员工作负荷评估[J]. 计算机应用研究, 2020, 37(S1): 24-26,33.

[5] 李建光. 某中小型机场管制员工作负荷及疲劳度分析[J]. 民航管理. 2020, 13(30): 201-241.

[6] Gilbo E P. Airport Capacity: Representation, Estimation, Optimization[J]. IEEE Transactions on Control System Technology, 1993, 1(3): 144-154.

[7] Newell G F. Airport Capacity and Delays[J]. Transporation Science, 1979, 13(30): 201-241.

[8] 刘建彬. 郑州新郑国际机场容量评估分析[J]. 河南科技,2015, 12: 92-95.

[9] 邹石. 试论机场航空容量评估的计算机仿真方法[J]. 计算机产品与流通, 2019(09): 143.

[10] 鱼海洋，胡华清，姚津津. 机场航空容量评估的计算机仿真办法[J]. 空中交通管理, 009, 2: 21-25.

[11] 王哲，李丘，杨子晴. 基于 AirTOP 的珠三角机场群航班增量仿真研究——以广州白云机场为例[J]. 科技和产业: 2018, 18(07): 53-56.

[12] 王强，左杰俊，钟琦，等. 基于 AnyLogic 仿真的中小机场容量评估分析[J]. 航空计算技术, 2020, 1(3): 21-24.

[13] 伊嘉男，胡明华，赵征. 多跑道机场地面容量评估模型[C]. 2010 年航空器适航与空中交通管理学术年会论文集,2010:5.

[14] Bowen E G, Pearcey T. Delays in the Flow of Air Traffic[J]. The Aeronautical Journal, 1948, 52(448): 251-258.

[15] 冯奎奎，翟文鹏，王玮卿. 基于排队模型的乌鲁木齐机场容量评估[J]. 数学的实践与认识, 2019, 49(21): 1-8.

[16] 董睿，王嫣. 基于蒙特卡洛方法的美兰机场平行跑道容量评估[J]. 现代商贸工业, 2018, 39(30): 191-193.

[17] Liu P B, Hansen M, Mukherjee A. Scenario-based Air Traffic Flow Management: From Theory to Practice[J]. Transportation Research Part B, 2008, 42(7): 685-702.

[18] Buxi G, Hansen M. Generating Day-of-operation Probabilistic Capacity Scenarios from Weather Forecasts [J]. Transportation Research Part C, 2013,33: 153-166.

[19] 翟文鹏，陈梵驿，金嗣博. 基于分位数回归的机场容量评估[J]. 飞行力学,2016, 34(04): 86-89.

[20] Provan C A, Cook L, Cunningham J. A Probabilistic Airport Capacity Model for Improved Ground Delay Program Planning[C]. IEEE/AIAA 30th Digital Avionics Systems Conference, 2011.

[21] Cox J, Kochenderfer M J. Probabilistic Airport Acceptance Rate Prediction[C]. AIAA Modeling and Simulation Technologies Conference, 2016.

[22] Murça M R, Hansman R J. Predicting and Planning Airport Acceptance Ratesin Metroplex Systems for Improved Traffic Flow Management Decision Support [J]. Transportation Research Part C, 2018, 97: 301-323.

[23] Liu Y, Hansen M. Predicting Aircraft Trajectories: A Deep Generative Convolutional Recurrent Neural Networks Approach[J]. arXiv preprint arXiv:1812.11670, 2018.

[24] Hochreiter S, Schmidhuber J. Long Short-term Memory[J]. Neural Computation,1997,9(8): 1735-1780.

[25] Hinton G E, SrivastavaN, Krizhevsky A, et al. Improving Neural Networks by Preventing Coadaptation of Feature Detectors[J]. arXiv preprint arXiv: 1207.0580, 2012.

[26] Kicinger R, Chen J T, Steiner M, et al. Airport Capacity Prediction with Explicit Consideration of Weather Forecast Uncertainty[J]. Journal of Air Transportation, 2016, 24(1): 18-28.

面向流式大数据的航迹模式在线挖掘方法研究

田　旺*[1]　冯俊池[2]　张　斌[3]　安宇航[1]　高亚玲[1]
(1. 北京航空航天大学电子信息工程学院
2. 军事科学院系统工程研究院后勤科学与技术研究所
3. 国能朔黄铁路发展有限责任公司科技发展部)

摘　要　基于某块空域近一段时期的海量航迹数据挖掘出该空域内的若干航迹模式,能够为航班异常行为预警、空域航路结构优化等空管业务提供关键参考信息。现有航迹模式挖掘方法仅能够处理离线的历史航迹数据,所得到的航迹模式是静态且易过时的;为满足实际空管业务对于航迹模式实时更新需求,亟待对动态航迹模式在线挖掘方法开展研究。然而,该问题面临着海量航迹数据难以实时快速计算处理的挑战。对此,本文提出了一种适用于分布式计算的动态航迹模式挖掘算法,并在 Spark 大数据计算框架中,重构了该算法的分布式执行过程,极大压缩了航迹模式在线挖掘时间。基于西安进近区 2020 年 9 月航迹数据和 5 节点分布式计算平台的实验结果表明,本文所提出方法能够在准确挖掘航迹模式的前提下,较传统单机版方法提速 2.5 倍至 32 倍,有效解决了面向流式大数据的航迹模式在线挖掘难题,具有一定的实际应用意义。

关键词　航迹模式　流式大数据　航迹聚类　分布式计算

0　引言

相关数据表明,截至 2019 年底,在册的民航全行业运输飞机共有 3818 架,比上年底增加 179 架;全国民航运输机场完成起降架次 1166.05 万架次,比上年增长 5.2%;共有定期航班航线 5521 条,按重复距离计算的航线里程达 1362.96 万 km[1]。愈加繁忙的空中交通,给空中交通管理系统带来了严峻的挑战。

航线规划是空管系统中重要的组成部分。航班受到天气、管制事件、不同调度规则的影响,呈现出灵活的飞行航迹,产生了海量蕴含丰富交通模式信息的轨迹数据,反映出航班飞行与空中交通管制决策交互作用的结果[2]。通过对航迹进行挖掘,能够得到相关运动特征,从而支持空管部门对航班进行调控、航空公司对航班进行科学合理的排班等等,进而有效保障飞行安全,提高空管自动化水平,提高空域运行效率。

现有航迹模式挖掘方法可大致地分为有监督学习和无监督学习。其中,无监督学习由于不需要人为地提前标定模式分类,更能够适应航迹数据量愈发庞大、模式愈发复杂的现状,得到了更多的关注和应用。基于聚类的航迹模式分析是流行的无监督学习方法,依据航迹数据进行分类,总结出飞行模式[3]。传统的方法通常使用以 K-Means 为代表的基于划分的聚类算法挖掘航迹模式[4-6]。该类方法可实现性强、算法复杂度低,但是需要提前确定聚类数量,且不能处理非凸的航迹类簇,难以满足现实需求。为处理非凸航迹类簇,现有研究普遍使用以 DBSCAN 为代表的基于密度的聚类算法[7-8]。该类算法能获得良好的聚类效果,有效区分出不同的航迹模式。不同于无监督学习,有监督学习人为标定模式类别,通过神经网络等有监督学习方法训练分类模型,达到挖掘航迹模式的目的[9-10]。然而,该类方法需要人工标定,难以适应复杂的航迹模式,导致实际应用受限。另一方面,当前研究大多仅能够基于离线的历史航迹数据进行计算,所得到的航迹模式是静态且易过时的,而无法反映航迹模式动态演化的过程。如何从航迹流式大数据中实时在线挖掘航迹动态模式,亟需进一步的研究。

针对航迹纷繁复杂,数据海量且实时多变的

1. 基金项目:国能朔黄铁路发展有限责任公司科技创新项目“朔黄铁路桥梁设施无人机巡检系统应用研究”(项目编号 GJNY-19-90)。

特点，本文旨在将基于数据流聚类的动态航迹模式挖掘方法和流式大数据计算框架相结合，采用分布式计算实现对海量流式航迹大数据航迹模式的高效处理。以 K-Means 为基础，结合航迹作为流式数据的特征，提出了动态航迹模式挖掘算法，算法计算时间复杂度低，能够在线实时地对航迹模式进行分析，且多个环节可以并行化处理，有利于其在大数据计算框架下实现。针对算法中涉及大量数据计算的环节，进一步调整数据的表达方式，优化处理流程，最大限度提升算法的可并行化程度。结合 Spark 计算框架，将航迹重采样、航迹间距离计算、最近类簇判断三个主要计算量较大的环节在 Spark 中进行实现，充分利用集群分布式计算的能力，提升整体的数据处理能力。实验结果表明，在分布式计算集群中的算法运行效率相较于传统单机版，在航迹模式挖掘的各环节中取得了 2.5 倍至 32 倍不等的提升，具有实际应用价值。

1　动态航迹模式挖掘算法

1.1　航迹模式挖掘问题分析

一架飞机的航迹点主要包含经纬度、高度和时间 4 个维度的信息。将航迹点抽象为一个二维平面上的轨迹点，将轨迹点按时间排列成一条二维平面上的轨迹。航迹模式挖掘问题可转化为多个轨迹间的聚类问题，航迹模式可使用一类轨迹中具有代表性的轨迹表示。如图 1 所示，蓝色轨迹本身即可代表一种航迹模式。绿色和橙色则生成了新的代表性轨迹，用来概括该类所有轨迹的形状特征。

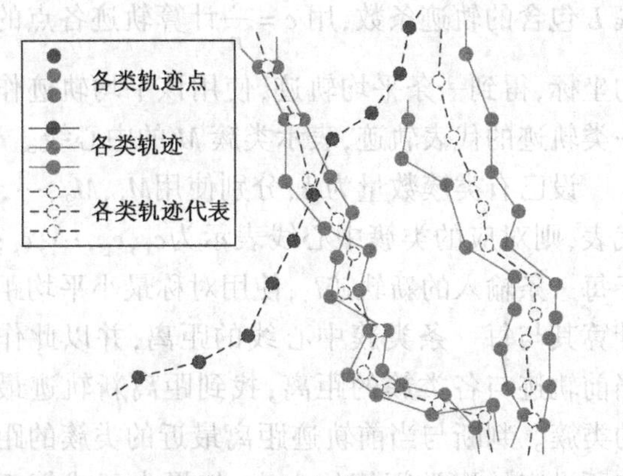

图 1　航迹模式示意

为方便准确描述算法，有关轨迹点、轨迹和轨迹类的数学表示定义如下。

使用一个 $\mathbb{R}^{1\times2}$ 的矩阵 $\boldsymbol{p}$ 表示轨迹点，$\boldsymbol{p}=[x \quad y]$，其中 x 为横坐标，其值为原航迹点的经度值，y 为纵坐标，其值为原航迹点的纬度值。一条轨迹中不同位置序号的轨迹点用 $p_1, p_2, \cdots, p_{num}$ 表示，其中，num 表示该条轨迹包含 num 个轨迹点。考虑到轨迹中的各个轨迹点具有时序性，一条轨迹使用一个 $\mathbb{R}^{num\times2}$ 的矩阵 $\boldsymbol{l}$ 表示，$\boldsymbol{l}=\begin{bmatrix} p_1 \\ p_2 \\ \vdots \\ p_{num} \end{bmatrix}$。对于一个包含有 n 条轨迹集合，使用 L 表示，$L=\{l_1, l_2, \cdots, l_n\}$。满足一定距离相似条件的轨迹的集合，定义为一个类簇，使用 M 表示。

1.2　动态航迹模式挖掘算法设计

本文主要使用了聚类的思想解决航迹模式挖掘问题。对于类似于航迹模式挖掘的轨迹数据，Garyfallidis E 等人[11]为对通过 CT 图像得到的神经纤维进行聚类分析，提出了一种适用于轨迹数据的聚类方法。该方法计算复杂度低，可以对复杂且密集的神经纤维进行分类展示。但是相较于神经纤维，航迹数据之间长度形状差异较大，且相较于处理一次静态扫描的 CT 图像数据，航迹本身处于不断的生成当中。结合流式航迹数据的特征，在 Garyfallidis E 等人[11]工作的基础上，本文提出的动态航迹模式聚类算法整体架构见图 2。

在航迹问题中，本文关注轨迹本身形状，使用对称最小平均距离计算方法计算轨迹间的相似性。对称最小平均距离计算方法要求参与计算的两条轨迹具有相同数量的点，本文先对原始轨迹进行重采样，重采样的规则为等距重采样。重采样时，保留原始轨迹端点的两个点，对其余中间的轨迹点等距离按照原始轨迹的斜率进行插值。重采样效果如图 3 所示。

完成到 N 个点的重采样后的轨迹 l，转变为一个 $\mathbb{R}^{N\times2}$ 的矩阵 $\boldsymbol{l}=\begin{bmatrix} p_1 \\ p_2 \\ \vdots \\ p_N \end{bmatrix}$。对所有轨迹进行重采样后，得到的轨迹便具有统一的轨迹点数量 N。

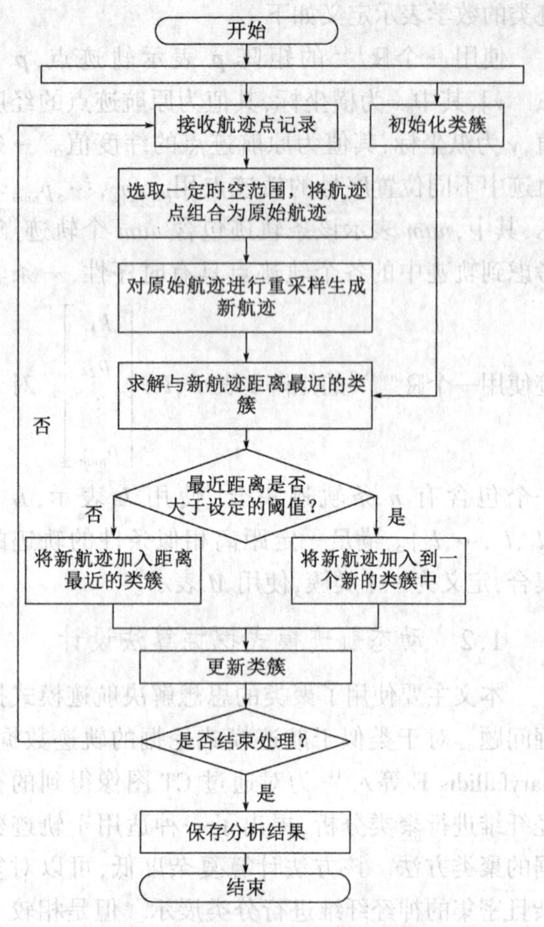

图2　动态航迹模式聚类算法整体流程

图3　轨迹等距重采样示例

对于轨迹矩阵 $l=[p_1\quad p_2\quad \cdots\quad p_N]^{\mathrm{T}}$，定义其对称轨迹矩阵为 $l^R=[p_N\quad p_{N-1}\quad \cdots\quad p_1]^{\mathrm{T}}$。$T$ 表示矩阵的转置运算。设有两条已经完成重采样的轨迹 $a=[p_{a1}\quad p_{a2}\quad \cdots\quad p_{aN}]^{\mathrm{T}}, b=[p_{b1}\quad p_{b2}\quad \cdots\quad p_{bN}]^{\mathrm{T}}$，其直接距离定义见式(1)，对称距离定义见式(2)，其对称最小平均距离 $D(a,b)$ 定义见式(3)：

$$d_d(a,b)=\frac{1}{N}\sum_{i=1}^{N}|p_{ai}-p_{bi}| \tag{1}$$

$$d_r(a,b)=d_d(a^R,b)=d_d(a,b^R) \tag{2}$$

$$D(a,b)=\min\ (d_d(a,b),d_r(a,b)) \tag{3}$$

对称最小平均距离 $D(a,b)$ 的计算过程如图4所示。$|p_{ai}-p_{bi}|$ 表示空间中两个点的欧式距离，$d_d(a,b)$ 为直接距离，代表两条轨迹各轨迹点间一一对应距离的平均值，$d_r(a,b)$ 为对称距离，表示将其中一条轨迹进行颠倒后，再一一计算对应轨迹点间的距离的平均值。最后，取 $d_d(a,b)$ 和 $d_r(a,b)$ 中的最小值作为对称最小平均距离 $D(a,b)$。

为了能够处理不断产生的流式航迹数据，在类簇的表示上，考虑保留过往航迹的信息，用于在新航迹到达时，增量式地更新类簇。为此，考虑将一类轨迹中，所有轨迹具有相同序号的点的横纵坐标分别求和，组成一条“和轨迹”，然后再取各点横纵坐标的平均值组成“平均轨迹”，由“平均轨迹”作为一类轨迹的代表。

设包含有同样 N 个点的两条轨迹 $l_a=[p_{a1}\quad p_{a2}\quad \cdots\quad p_{aN}]^{\mathrm{T}}$ 和 $l_b=[p_{b1}\quad p_{b2}\quad \cdots\quad p_{bN}]^{\mathrm{T}}$，其中 $p_{ai}=(x_i^a,y_i^a)$，$p_{bi}=(x_i^b,y_i^b)$。则其“和轨迹” l_S 可表示为式(4)：

$$l_S=l_a+l_b=\begin{bmatrix}(x_1^a+x_1^b,y_1^a+y_1^b) & (x_2^a+x_2^b,y_2^a+y_2^b)\\ \cdots & (x_N^a+x_N^b,y_N^a+y_N^b)\end{bmatrix}^{\mathrm{T}} \tag{4}$$

其“平均轨迹” l_A 可表示为式(5)：

$$l_A=\frac{l_a+l_b}{2}=\begin{bmatrix}\left(\frac{x_1^a+x_1^b}{2},\frac{y_1^a+y_1^b}{2}\right) & \left(\frac{x_2^a+x_2^b}{2},\frac{y_2^a+y_2^b}{2}\right)\\ \cdots & \left(\frac{x_N^a+x_N^b}{2},\frac{y_N^a+y_N^b}{2}\right)\end{bmatrix}^{\mathrm{T}} \tag{5}$$

使用 M 表示一个类簇，定义 $M=(L,s,n)$，其中，L 表示类簇 M 包含的轨迹序列 $\{l_1,l_2,\cdots,l_n\}$，s 为一个 $\mathbb{R}^{N\times 2}$ 矩阵，为 L 中所有表示轨迹的矩阵之和，即 $s=\sum_{i=1}^{n}l_i$，用于存储和轨迹信息，n 为当前类簇 L 包含的轨迹条数，用 $c=\frac{s}{n}$ 计算轨迹各点的平均坐标，得到一条平均轨迹，使用该平均轨迹作为一类轨迹的代表轨迹，表示类簇 M 的中心线。

设已有类簇数量为 k，分别使用 $M_1,M_2,\cdots,M_k$ 代表，则对应的类簇中心线表示为 $c_1,c_2,\cdots,c_k$；对于每一条输入的新轨迹 l_g，使用对称最小平均距离计算其与每一条类簇中心线的距离，并以此作为当前轨迹与各类簇的距离，找到距离新轨迹最近的类簇。判断与当前轨迹距离最近的类簇的距离和所设定的聚类阈值的大小，如果小于或等于聚类阈值，则将当前轨迹加入该距离最近的类簇，并更新类簇。如果大于聚类阈值，则将当前轨迹划分到新的类簇中。在将新轨迹加入到其最近类簇的时候,需要判断该最近距离是有直接距离取得还是对称距离取得。如果是直接距离取得,直接将轨迹加入该类簇即可,如果是对称距离取得,需要将轨迹对称翻转后的对称轨迹加入该类簇。

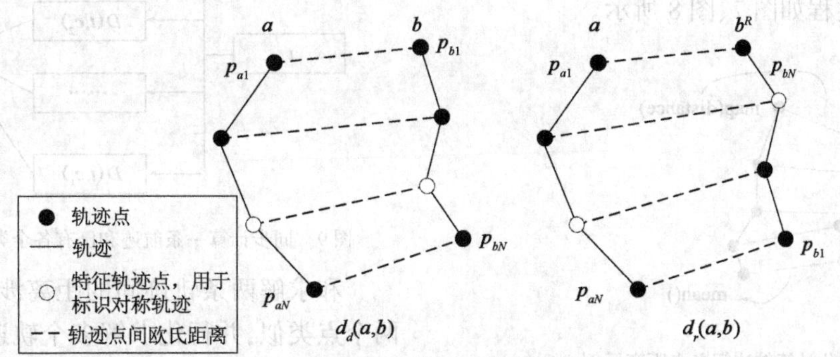

图4 对称最小平均距离求解过程示例

在这种方式下,已被归类的轨迹不会再重新计算其分类,类簇可以在新的轨迹加入时,增量式计算变化的部分,由此实现轨迹模式随着新轨迹的加入而不断更新。

2 基于Spark的航迹模式在线挖掘

将轨迹点,轨迹以及类簇进一步抽象为使用程序中的数组表示,则可以分别使用一维数组、二维数组和三维数组依次表示点、线以及线集合。具体地,一个点可以表示为$p=[x,y]$,一条包含有N个点的轨迹线可以表示为$l=[p_1,p_2,\cdots,p_N]$,一个包含了n条轨迹线的集合可以表示为$L=[l_1,l_2,\cdots,l_n]$。针对航迹重采样、航迹点距离计算、求解最近类簇三个运算量最大的环节,本文采用Spark框架,利用分布式集群的算力进行优化。

在航迹并行化重采样环节,将多条航迹组合成一个集合,将航迹重采样算法以函数resample(streamline, point_num)进行实现,其中,streamline为一个二维数组,表示一条轨迹线,point_num为一个整数,表示需要重采样到的点数量,函数返回一个二维数组,表示完成采样后的轨迹线。使用数组$L=[l_1,l_2,\cdots,l_n]$表示轨迹线的集合,则可以使用L. map(resample)的方式,对数组L中的各条航迹进行并行化重采样。图5给出了三条航迹组成的集合使用map的方式将重采样函数应用到每一条航迹上最后到采样到10个点示例。

在Spark中,参与运算的RDD相关操作构成的有向无环图如图6所示。其中parallelize操作将原始的轨迹数组转变为RDD存储在内存中,map操作对RDD进行了映射转换,最后collect操作将分布在集群内存中的转换后的新RDD进行了输出。

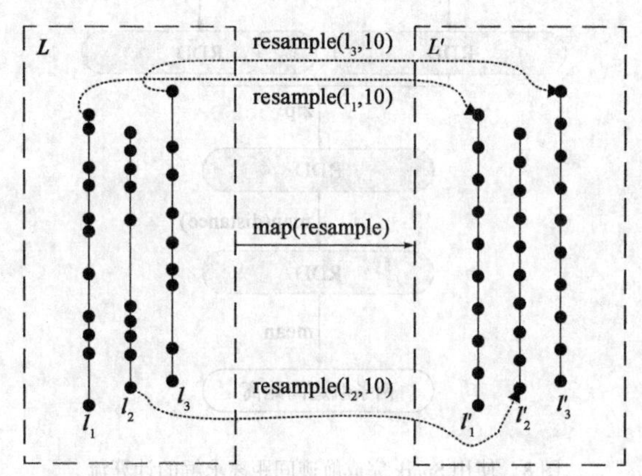

图5 多条航迹并行化重采样示例

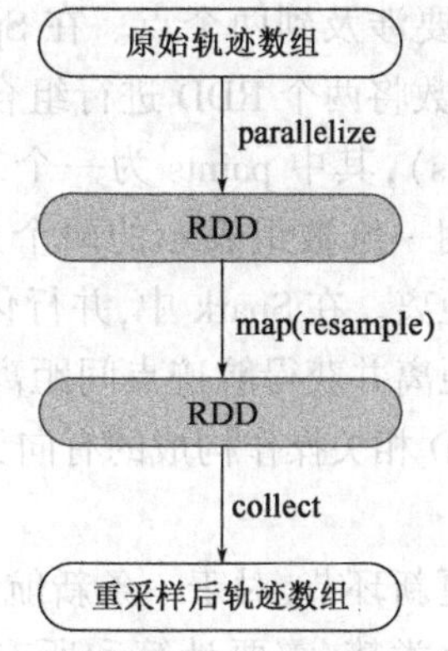

图6 使用Spark完成航迹重采样的计算流

航迹间距离的计算,涉及大量航迹点间欧式距离的计算。由于最后是以平均值为结果,因此各航迹点间的距离计算没有先后顺序,可以进行分布式地求和,最后汇总得到平均值。定义两点之间欧式距离的计算函数为 distance(point1, point2),其中,point1 和 point2 均为一个包含两个元素的一维数组,表示一个点,并行化求解多个航迹点间的距离其过程如图 7、图 8 所示。

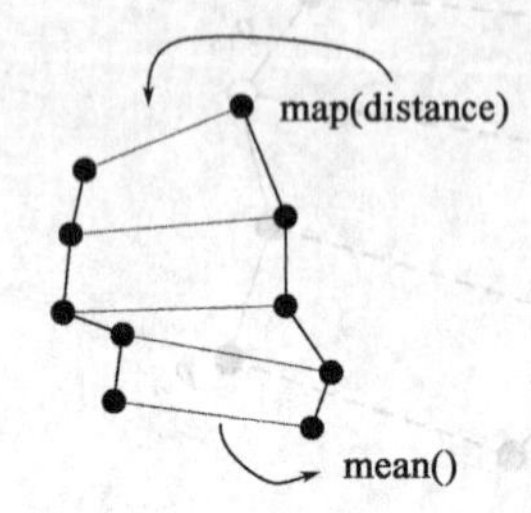

图 7　并行化计算航迹间各点距离示例

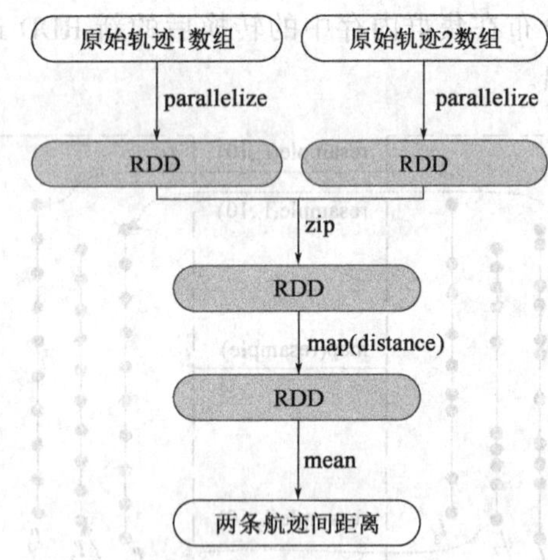

图 8　使用 Spark 完成航迹间距离求解的计算流

由于在使用 map(function)时,map 只能对集合中的一个元素映射相应的 function,而航迹点的距离,至少需要涉及到两个点。在 Spark 中,可以使用 zip()函数将两个 RDD 进行组合。定义函数 distance(points),其中 points 为一个二维数组,数组元素为使用一维数组表示的两个点,返回两点之间的欧式距离。在 Spark 中,并行化计算两条航迹各点之间距离并获得航迹点间距离平均值的过程涉及的 RDD 相关操作构成的有向无环图如图 8 所示。

在类簇更新环节,对于一条新航迹,为了判断其属于哪一个类簇,需要计算和所有已有类簇的距离,且该过程可以分别独立同步进行。如图 9 所示,对于一条新航迹 t,可以同时计算其和已有聚类中心线c_1至c_k的对称最小平均距离,最后取最小值 $D(t,c_j)$(此处假设距离最近的类簇中心线为c_j)。

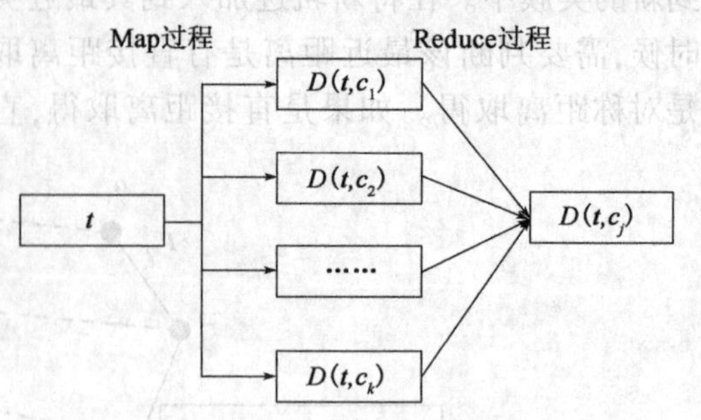

图 9　同步计算一条航迹和已有各个类簇之间距离示意

和求解两条轨迹间的距离涉及需要同时处理两个点类似,并行化求解多个轨迹间的距离,需要同时处理两条轨迹。考虑使用 Spark 中的广播变量。将新航迹 r 转变为 RDD 后,进行全局共享。定义函数 findNearestCentroid(centroid_line),函数只需要接收一条中心线作为变量,即可返回中心线和 r 的对称最小平均距离。对航迹中心线的集合进行 map(findNearestCentroid)操作,即可以实现对多个中心线同时求解和新航迹 r 的距离。使用 Spark 寻找一条新航迹距离最近的类簇的过程涉及的 RDD 计算关系形成的有向无环图如图 10 所示。

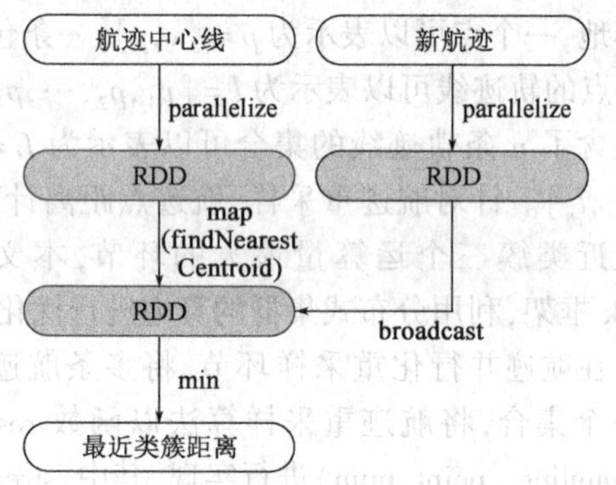

图 10　使用 Spark 寻找新航迹最近类簇的计算流

3　实验结果分析

3.1　实验环境及数据集介绍

在实验部分,共使用 5 台虚拟机进行,均配置了 16GB 内存,1TB 硬盘,8 核心 Intel Xeon Processor (Skylake) @2GHz 中央处理器,操作系统为 Ubuntu 18.04.6 LTS。目标集群按照 Hadoop Yarn 架构进行搭建。其中,虚拟机 yj-8631-1 作为集群主节点,承担 Yarn 架构中的 Resource Manager 角色,yj-8631-2 至 yj-8631-5 共 4 台虚拟机作为 Node Manager。同时,yj-8631-2 作为 Spark 运行在

Yarn 上的驱动节点,承担 Spark Driver 的角色。yj-8631-3 至 yj-8631-5 则是 Spark 应用程序的执行节点,承担 Spark Executor 的角色。

航迹数据由民航数据公司实时 ADS-B 报文提供。经过处理后的结构化数据包括基础的三维位置信息,飞行状态信息,时间信息,以及航班信息等。原始航迹数据范围为 2020 年 9 月以西安咸阳国际机场为起降机场的所有航班飞行记录。本研究筛选了以西安进近区为封闭区域内的航迹数据作为研究对象,便于航迹模式的可视化集中展现。

3.2 航迹模式挖掘实验结果分析

选取西安进近区 2020 年 9 月航班数量最多的一天 9 月 26 日的航迹数据进行分析,共包含进港航迹 439 条,出港航迹 464 条。其中,进港航迹平均包含 184 个航迹点,出港航迹平均包含 107 个航迹点。按照平均值对原始航迹进行重采样,设定聚类阈值为 0.2。

进港航迹的航迹模式分析结果详情见表 1。按照统计学方法,将包含航迹条数的数量在所有航迹模式包含的航迹条数上四分位数外的航迹模式设为小规模航迹模式,图 11 给出了主要航迹模式的可视化结果展现。

进港航迹模式详情 表 1

航迹模式序号	包含的航迹条数	航迹模式类别
1	167	主要航迹模式
2	134	主要航迹模式
3	87	主要航迹模式
4	15	主要航迹模式
5	12	主要航迹模式
6	6	小规模航迹模式
7	3	小规模航迹模式
8	2	小规模航迹模式
9	1	小规模航迹模式
10	1	小规模航迹模式
……	……	……

如果不考虑展现主要航迹模式,亦可以单独关注小规模的航迹模式。在这种情况下,可以更直观地发现一些比较特殊的航迹,进一步地,可以为研究异常航迹提供参考。

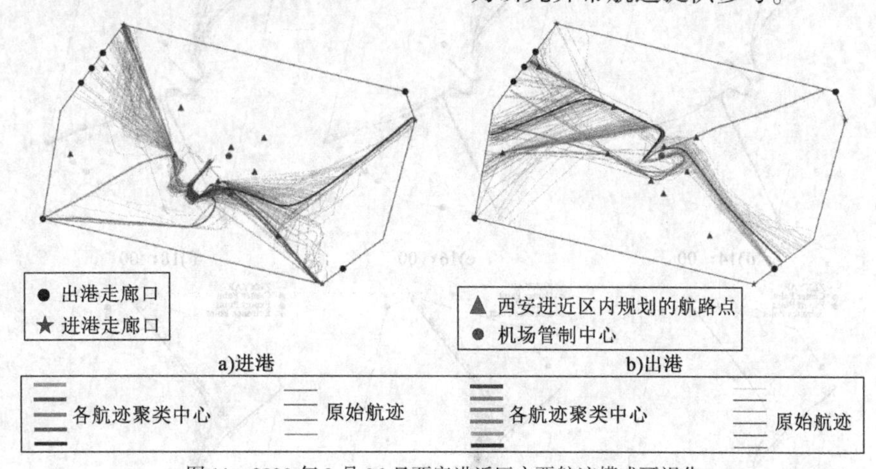

图 11 2020 年 9 月 26 日西安进近区主要航迹模式可视化

通过观察一天内进出港的航迹模式分析结果,可以看出,算法能准确地对不同形状的航迹进行分类,主要航迹模式类别可以得到较为明显的区分,聚类分析得到的航迹模式中心线能很好地反映某一类航迹的主要轨迹形状,具有代表性。对航迹模式进行可视化展示的结果验证了航迹模式聚类算法的有效性。

航迹模式并不是一成不变的,随着一天中航班轨迹数量的增加,为了验证流式聚类的效果,依旧选取 9 月 26 日的航迹进行分析,将存储的历史航迹输入算法中,模拟实时接收流式数据的情形,以每两个小时为时间切片,由于当日 0 点至早上 6 点没有进港航班,因此共抓取 9 张航迹模式分析结果展示如图 12 所示。其中,每一种航迹模式类簇的中心线均使用黑色粗实心线条表示,细虚线条代表原始航迹,且在同一张子图中,相同颜色的原始航迹表示属于同一种航迹模式。

图 13 关注的是主要航迹模式的变化,对比图 12a) ~ g) 各图可以看出,随着航迹数量的增加,航迹模式也会不断修正以吻合新出现的航迹,

相关航迹模式类簇中心线明显更加光滑且更具有代表性。对比图12g)、h)、i)可以看出,当出现了新的航迹和已有的航迹模式相差较大且有一定规模时,算法会随着新航迹的出现而增加相应的航迹模式。分析航迹模式的变化,可以对空域运行的指导规则进行优化。例如,图12h)相较于图12g)新出现的航迹模式,和现有的航迹模式从同一个进港走廊口抵达机场,但是飞行了更多的拐弯路程,降落在了另一边的跑道上。背后的原因可能是,原有跑道出现容量不足或者调度规则出现变化。有了航迹模式作为参照遵循,可以为后续的空域管制规则优化提供有力参考。

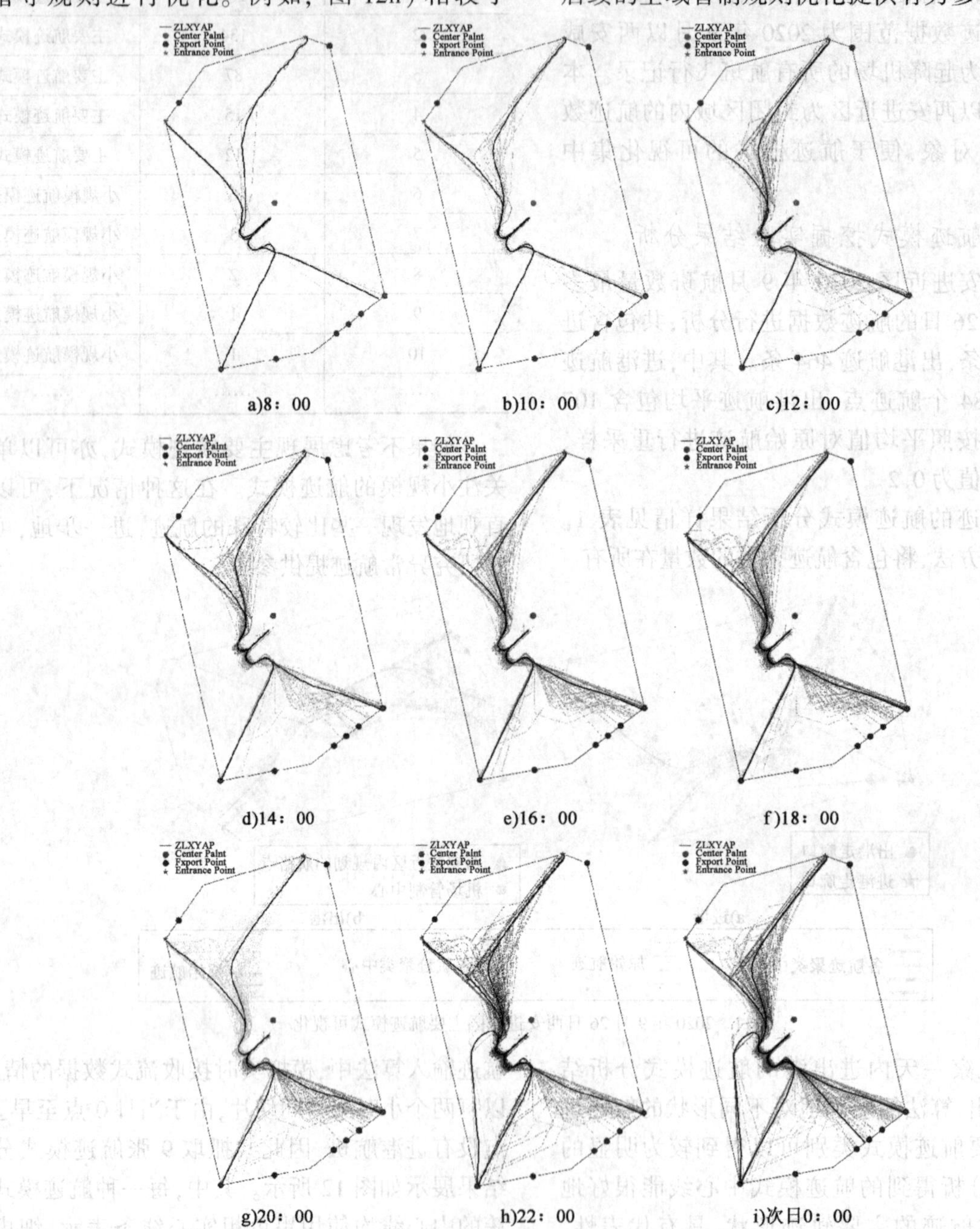

图12 每2h为时间切片的航迹模式分析结果

3.3 Spark集群分布式计算实验结果分析

前文2.1对原始算法的几个关键环节进行了并行化改造,而原始算法主要是对1.2中描述的方法和伪代码使用Python进行了实现。在yj-8631-2服务器上运行原始算法作为对照。下面将对3个关键环节的效率提升效果进行分析。

在航迹重采样环节,选取了西安进近区整个9月的航迹作为原始数据,总计包含26834条航迹,共有航迹点3981579个,平均每条航迹包含148个航迹点。设置Spark集群调用3个Executor,每个Executor启用6个vCPU,共包含18个vCPU,对26834条航迹全部执行重采样到148个航迹点的操作所需时间和原始算法的对比见图13。

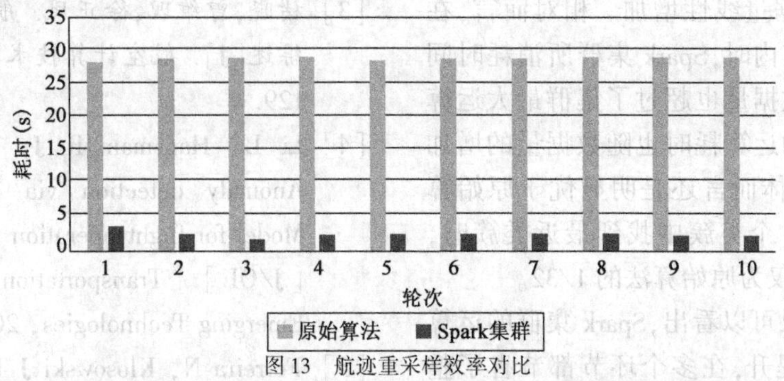

图13 航迹重采样效率对比

为了避免偶然环境因素的影响,一共进行了10次实验。平均下来,原始算法完成对26834条航迹的重采样需要33.0608s,而Spark集群平均仅需要3.2329s即可完成重采样的任务,效率提升了约10倍,有效应证了算法并行化改造后在Spark集群上运行效率的提升。

在计算航迹间距离环节,使用随机数生成点,并将不同数量的点组合成数组代表一条轨迹,用于模拟航迹。同样的,每次计算均进行10次,取平均耗时作为最后的结果。Spark集群配置为使用3个Executor,每个Executor使用6个vCPU,共18个vCPU。图14给出了相应的对比结果。

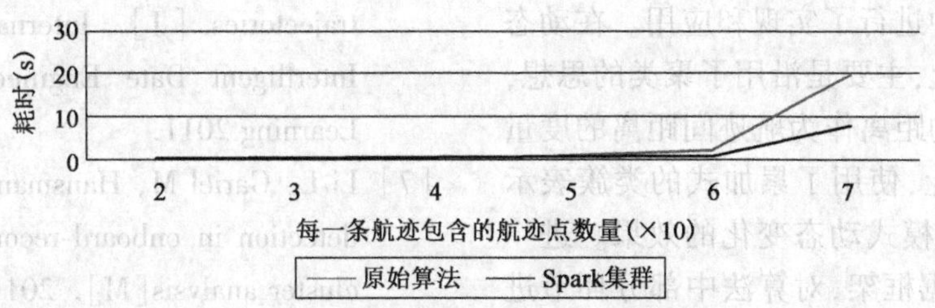

图14 航迹间距离计算效率对比

对比Spark集群的计算耗时可以看出,在数据量较低的情况下,Spark集群运算并没有优势,这主要是因为集群中各个工作节点之间涉及任务调度还有数据状态的传输消耗了较多的时间。但是随着数据量的增加,Spark集群运算的优势逐渐凸显。主要表现在,当每条轨迹包含的点在100000个以内时,Spark集群可以借助分布式的算力,维持基本不变的时间消耗,而不会像原始算法所需时间一样呈现线性增长。直到超过集群最大并行化能力,Spark集群所需耗时也会随数据量的增加呈现线性相关,但是整体而言,依然可以在每条轨迹包含10000000点时比原始算法有2.5倍的效率提升。

在求解最近类簇的环节,为了方便探测集群的运算能力,同样使用模拟数据进行实验。使用随机数生成点,设定每一条轨迹包含1000个点,随机生成不同数量的轨迹代表不同的航迹类簇中心线,使用原始算法和Spark集群计算距离一条新的轨迹距离最近的轨迹,同样的,每次计算均进行10次,取平均耗时作为最后的结果,Spark集群配置同上。对比结果见图15。

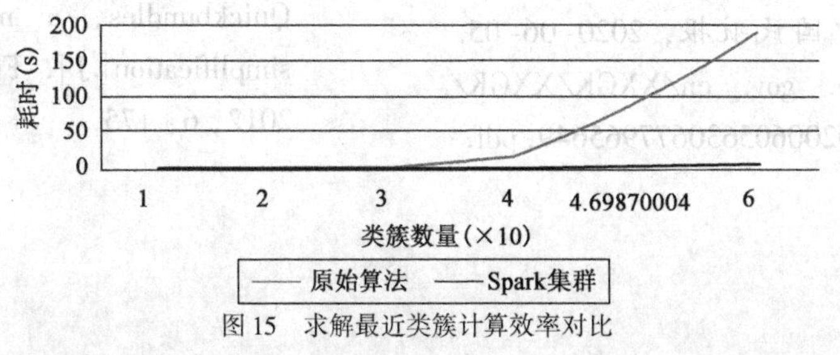

图15 求解最近类簇计算效率对比

从图 15 可以看出,和计算航迹间距离的结果类似,在类簇数量较少的情况下,Spark 集群的效率优势并不突出。但是随着数据量的增大,原始算法耗时明显随数据量线性增加。相对而言,在类簇数量在 10000 以内时,Spark 集群所消耗时间基本维持不变。当数据量也超过了集群最大运算能力时,Spark 集群的运算耗时也随数据量的增加而线性增长,但是整体而言还是明显优于原始算法,在需要在 100000 个类簇中找到最近类簇时,Spark 集群所需时间仅为原始算法的 1/32。

从上述实验结果可以看出,Spark 集群的运算带来了明显的性能提升,在多个环节都节省了整体的运行时间。

4　结语

本文旨在研究面向流式航迹大数据的动态航迹模式在线挖掘方法。主要的核心工作是提出了一种基于聚类的动态航迹模式挖掘算法,并将其在大数据计算集群中进行了实现和应用。在动态航迹模式挖掘算法上,主要是沿用了聚类的思想,使用了对称最小平均距离作为航迹间距离的度量方式。在类簇表示上,使用了累加式的类簇表示方法,达到跟踪航迹模式动态变化的效果。进一步,结合 Spark 大数据框架,对算法中部分环节进行了航迹数据结构设计和算法并行化改造。在实验环节,使用 5 台服务器搭建了基于 Yarn 架构的 Spark 集群,通过生成不同数量级的测试数据,对每一个计算环节进行多轮实验,结果显示,使用 Spark 集群后和原始算法相比计算耗时均加快了数倍至数十倍,具有实际应用价值。各式航迹的模式背后可能反映了航班的运行规律。挖掘航迹模式背后的成因和利用航迹模式进一步指导空域运行规则的顶层设计,推动空管系统的智能化管理水平是一个具有挑战性的研究方向。

参考文献

[1] 中国民用航空局. 2019 年民航行业发展统计公报[N/OL]. 中国民航报, 2020-06-05. http://www.caac.gov.cn/XXGK/XXGK/TJSJ/202006/P020200605630677965649.pdf.

[2] 王超, 郑旭芳, 卜宁. 基于小波聚类的终端区进场轨迹模式识别[J]. 计算机应用与软件, 2016, 33(11): 112-116.

[3] 褚晓,曾维理,徐正凤. 航空器轨迹聚类研究综述[J]. 航空计算技术, 2021, 51(5): 126-129.

[4] Li L, Hansman R J, Palacios R, et al. Anomaly detection via a Gaussian Mixture Model for flight operation and safety monitoring [J/OL]. Transportation Research Part C: Emerging Technologies, 2016, 64: 45-57.

[5] Ferreira N, Klosowski J T, Scheidegger C, et al. Vector Field k-Means: Clustering Trajectories by Fitting Multiple Vector Fields [J]. Computer Graphics Forum, 2013, 32 (3pt2): 201-210.

[6] Mace A, Sommariva R, Fleming Z, et al. Adaptive K-means for clustering air mass trajectories. [J]. International Conference on Interlligent Date Engineering and Automated Learning 2011.

[7] Li L, Gariel M, Hansman R J, et al. Anomaly detection in onboard-recorded flight data using cluster analysis[M]. 2011.

[8] Gariel M, Srivastava A N, Feron E. Trajectory Clustering and an Application to Airspace Monitoring [J]. IEEE Transactions on Intelligent Transportation Systems, 2011, 12 (4): 1511-1524.

[9] 谢廷尧, 姜伟, 吕宇宙, 等. 神经网络在航迹检测中的应用[J]. 无线电工程, 2020, 050 (01): 10-14.

[10] 谢春生, 赵龙, 柳跃朋. 基于自组织神经网络的终端区航迹识别研究[J]. 中国民航大学学报, 2021, 39(3): 6-9,33.

[11] Garyfallidis E, Brett M, Correia M M, et al. Quickbundles, a method for tractography simplification[J]. Frontiers in neuroscience, 2012, 6: 175.

飞行冲突网络建模方法研究

林福根* 温祥西 吴明功 衡宇铭
(空军工程大学空管领航学院)

摘 要 飞行冲突探测是空中交通研究的热点问题,针对目前大多数学者以微观分析为主,本文在传统飞行冲突网络的基础上,考虑了航空器的航速、航向、位置等信息,提出三维速度障碍法模型,并将其引入飞行冲突网络进行冲突判断。阐述了基于速度障碍法的椭球模型建模方法所具有的优越性。结论表明,椭球模型相比于位置、圆柱、球体模型的虚警率分别降低了40.05%、8.97%、59.3%;该建模方法能够有效感知潜在冲突,减少冲突网络的冗余连边,降低冲突的虚警概率;加入可视化元素后的冲突网络能够更加准确、直观地反映出空域的复杂情况,提高管制员的工作效率。

关键词 冲突探测 速度障碍法 保护区 飞行冲突网络

0 引言

航空业的高速发展,飞行量的激增加深了空域资源和空中交通流量之间的矛盾,为此,1994年美国联邦航空管理局(Federal Aviation Administration)提出“自由飞行”概念[1],在该飞行方式下,不用过分受制于管制员,飞行员能够自主、灵活地选择航路航线,有效地提高了空域利用率和容量。但是,自由飞行也会使得同一空域航空器密度增加,加之航向和航迹的不确定性,构成飞行冲突的可能性也极大提升。为了保证飞行的安全,对航空网络冲突进行高效、准确的预测是当下亟须解决的关键技术。

对于冲突的研究,首先要解决的是冲突探测问题。冲突探测被大量应用于机器人[2-3]和无人机[4-5]避障问题中,而在航空领域,飞行冲突探测是利用地面监视设备(ACAS等)探测航空器当前的位置与相关的运动信息,从而预测航空器的飞行趋势及轨迹,并基于此判断飞机之间是否会发生飞行冲突[6]。据现有学者的研究,检测冲突主要可以通过判断航空器位置、轨迹及所处空域保护区等方式,将以上检测冲突的办法归结为三种类型:

(1)确定型:在已编好的航路航线信息中,将航空器应运行的轨迹点视为一条确定的轨迹直线,通过判断航空器所处位置从而检测冲突[7-8]。

(2)概率型:通过判断航空器在各时刻所处的位置,将其拟合成一个时间序列的概率分布。越接近航空器现处位置的时间点预测精度越高,反之亦然[9-10]。

(3)建立保护区型:考虑航空器飞行信息参数(航向、位置、航速等)的基础上,以航空器为节点设置一个较大的保护区,若有航空器进去该保护区即视为存在冲突[11]。

复杂网络在航空领域有在航空领域中具有广泛的应用。王红勇等[12]考虑了航空器之间的内禀属性建立了内禀复杂度计算模型,并且基于复杂网络理论衡量了扇区交通的复杂性。曾小舟等[14]运用复杂网络理论,从度值、簇系数、介数等特征值进行实证分析,发现中国航空网络出现了以度值大的节点为中心的中心集群现象。在航空冲突网络的研究中,大多学者[15-17]由航空器和彼此之间位置关系作为航空器之间冲突连边的依据,并且利用复杂网络节点度、网络效率等分析指标对所构建的复杂网络特性进行分析。李昂等[18]利用航空器之间的相对速度和距离关系,建立了冲突网络,并以航空器距离等因素构建了航空器对的迫近效应,此判断方法仅在二维平面上进行飞行器冲突判断,缺乏航向和高度维的信息,具有一定的局限性。

从以上分析可知,在飞行冲突探测过程中,建立保护区型的冲突判断方法能够获取更多航空器综合信息。飞行状态网络的冲突关系往往由简单的航空器位置或在同一高度层考虑二维平面的速度关系决定,前者没有考虑航空器之间速度方向的关系,容易造成一定的冲突误警率,从而增加了管制员的负荷压力;加之没有对航空器在高度层之间演化作出冲突判断,在实际应用中缺乏了一定的可行性;为了解决上述问题,本文充分论证了椭球形保护区的优势,提出了一种基于三维速度障碍法的飞行态势冲突网络建模方法。建立"椭球形"保护区能够有效感知三维空间内的冲突关系,并且满足实际中的飞行安全边界条件,利用速度障碍法[19-20]能对航空器之间的位置和速度关系作出提前预测,既能降低管制员的负荷压力,又可减少冲突的误警率,为智能化空中交通管制提供一定的基础。

1　模型构建

1.1　保护区模型构建

在自由飞行条件下,航空器周围的空域从内至外被划分为保护区、避让区和预警区三个层次。依据飞行器保护区的定义,任意两架相同飞行高度的航空器水平距离不应小于 $R=5$ 海里(约10km)或垂直高度不应小于 $L=2000$ft(600m);Dowek 等人[21]以 R 为半径,$2L$ 为高提出了圆柱形保护区[图1a)],任意两航空器处于该保护区内即存在冲突,该保护区在飞行冲突探测问题的研究中应用极为广泛,但也存在一定问问题,Raghunathan[22]利用该保护区引入了一系列辅助量探测冲突,其目标函数随着辅助变量的增加出现了众多二次积分项,极大地增加了计算复杂度;再由圆柱的数学形状可知,其上下表面与柱面的连接处不可导,这又增加了后续的计算难度。因此,本文设置了更加符合实际且便于计算的冲突探测"椭球形"保护区[图1b)],其长轴焦距为 $d_v=10$km,短轴焦距 $d_l=600$m。

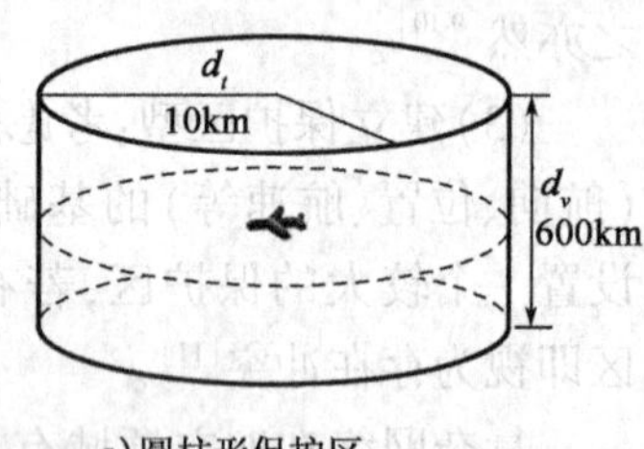

a)圆柱形保护区

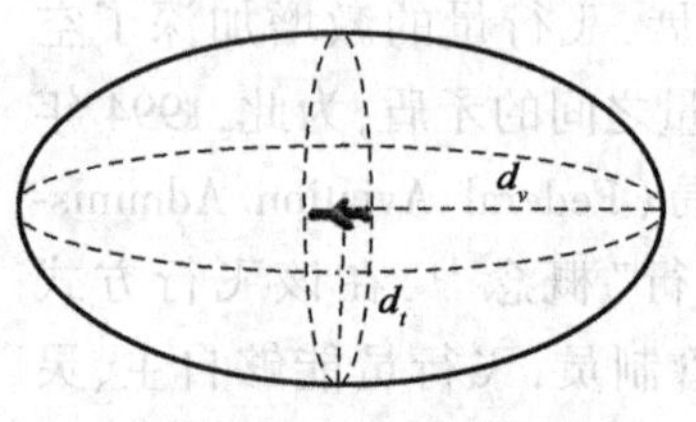

b)椭球形保护区

图1　保护区构建

当两航空器之间的保护区出现重叠时,即可认定其存在冲突,因此,对于飞行器冲突探测问题可以转化为判断保护区模型冲突域是否小于1的问题。依据保护区模型,构建冲突域判断式 C:

$$C=\left\{\frac{(x-x_c)^2}{d_v{}^2}+\frac{(y-y_c)^2}{d_v{}^2}+\frac{(z-z_c)^2}{d_l{}^2}\leqslant 1 \mid x,y,z\in R\right\} \tag{1}$$

式中:(x,y,z)——主机坐标;

(x_c,y_c,z_c)——潜在冲突机坐标。

1.2　冲突连边及权重确定

速度障碍法是通过获取两机位置和速度之间的关系,确定一个相对速度障碍区域,当两机相对速度落入该障碍区域时即认为有发生冲突的可能。该方法通常用于判断同一高度层航空器之间的冲突关系,而在自由飞行的条件下,航空器进行高度演化时会改变现有的冲突情况,仅考虑二维平面内的冲突显然是缺乏可行性的。因此,将速度障碍法应用到前文所构建的椭球保护区方可解决上述问题。

根据飞行探测区,采用速度障碍法确定彼此之间是否存在冲突建立连边,该方法只考虑某一时刻航空器的位置和速度状态。如图1所示,若已知两架航空器飞行方向 v_A、v_B,以 B 为参照点,A 做相对运动,相对速度为 $v_{AB}=v_A-v_B$,利用矢量三角形法则判断其合速度的方向 v_r、v_r 与 AB 连线的夹角为 γ,AB 连线与椭圆切线夹角为 $\alpha\alpha$,若 $\alpha>\gamma$ 时,则认为它们存在潜在冲突;$\alpha\leqslant\gamma$ 时就不存在冲突。

在数学上具体求解步骤如下:在速度任意的情况下,建立航空器速度、坐标与椭球之间的关系式:

$$\begin{cases}\dfrac{x^2}{d_v{}^2}+\dfrac{y^2}{d_v{}^2}+\dfrac{z^2}{d_l{}^2}=1\\[2ex]\dfrac{x-x_0}{v_1}=\dfrac{y-y_0}{v_2}=\dfrac{z-z_0}{v_3}=t\end{cases} \tag{2}$$

式中:v_1、v_2、v_3——x、y、z 方向上的速度分量。

利用上述关系解得：

$$(d_l^2v_1^2+d_l^2v_2^2+d_v^2v_3^2)t^2+2(d_l^2v_1x_0+d_l^2v_2y_0+d_v^2v_3z_0)t+(d_l^2x_0^2+d_l^2y_0^2+d_v^2z_0^2-d_l^2d_v^2)=0 \tag{3}$$

记冲突域 C 中交点个数为 n，根的判别式为 $\Delta=b^2-4ac$，其中 a、b、c 分别为多项式方程(3)中 t^2、t、1 的系数。$\Delta>0$ 时，判断其存在冲突边。

为了设定冲突连边的权重，我们假设：椭球体为 EPD，如图 2 所示，显然 $v_r\cap EPD\neq 0$ 时，合速度延长线交椭球与 I_1、I_2 两点，记交点坐标为 $|AI_1|$、$|AI_2|$，则有预计冲突时间 T：

$$T=\frac{\min\{|AI_1,AI_2|\}}{|v_r|} \tag{4}$$

基于椭球形速度障碍法冲突构建原则，航空器之间距离越小即 $|AI_1|$ 越小，边权越大；相对速度 $|v_r|$ 越小，冲突越紧迫，冲突时间 T 越长。依据上述关系，边权刚好与冲突时间 T 呈现反比关系，因此，引入负指数函数与冲突时间 T 建立联系。如式(5)，权重 ω_{ij} 会随着冲突时间 T 的减少而显著增大，较好地描述了冲突紧迫程度，并且权值在单位[0,1]范围内变化，起到单位化作用。

$$\omega_{ij}=(e-1)^{-T} \tag{5}$$

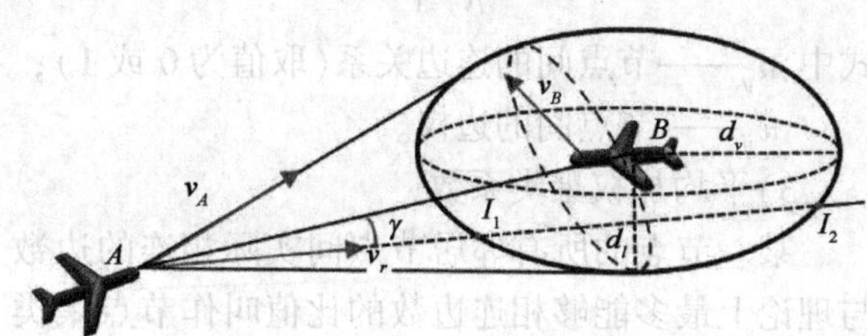

图 2 速度障碍冲突探测模型

1.3 冲突网络描述

在判断冲突连边时，文献[15]仅考虑航空器相对位置关系的冲突网络拓扑图如图 3a) 所示，红色箭头为飞行器航向，航空器小于距离阈值 $L=26$ 时则构成冲突连边，该网络有 6 条连边。因该冲突构成方式仅考虑了位置距离关系，称其所构成的网络为飞行状态网络；使用本文建模方法所构建网络时，如图 3b) 所示，该方法充分考虑了飞行器航向，取消了 3、4 及 5、6 之间的冲突连边，并且提前预测了 6、8 之间的冲突关系，构建的网络称为冲突网络。

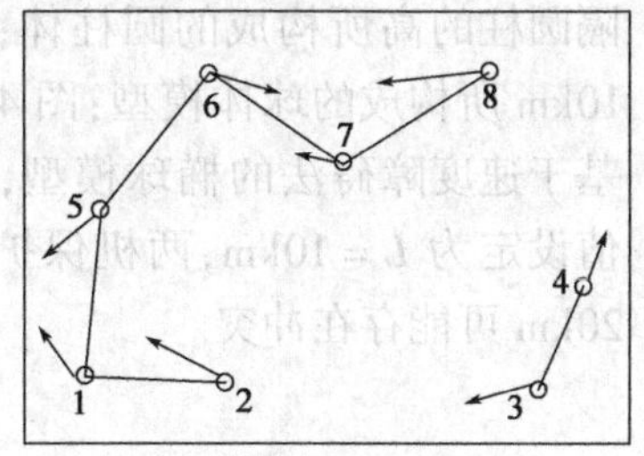

a)冲突状态网络拓扑图

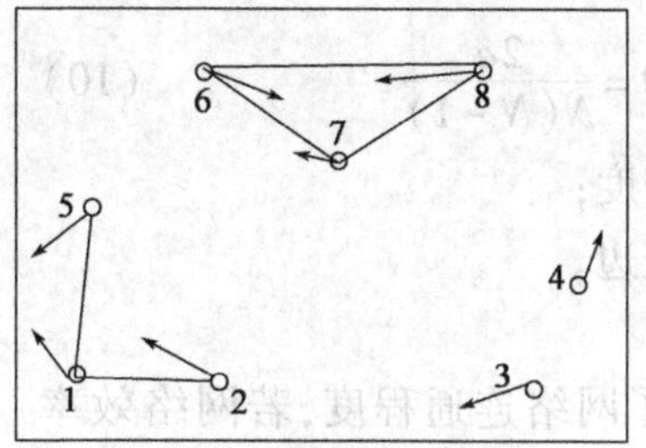

b)冲突态势网络拓扑图

图 3 飞行冲突拓扑图网络

由以上分析可知，飞行状态网络仅考虑了航空器之间的位置关系，同管制员主观判断相近，构成的连边可以较好反映冲突情况，但具有一定局限性；飞行冲突网络考虑了航空器的速度方向和位置之间的关系，对冲突有较好的预测性，减少了一定离散态势下的冲突连边，降低了误警率，并且能够从直观上获取冲突的紧急情况和急需调配的航空器。

2 指标选取

所构建的冲突网络有其特有的结构特性，通过定义相关网络特征参数，将复杂系统在网络层面进行表达，能够充分剖析该复杂网络的特性，参数设定如下所示：

1) 平均节点数

对于具有 N 个节点的飞行冲突网络，节点度可以表示某个节点所连接的冲突边数量，而平均节点度则是该网络所有节点度的平均值，能够反映网络航空器的总体冲突水平。用 $\bar{k}$ 表示：

$$\bar{k}=\frac{1}{N}\sum_{i=1}^{N}k_i \tag{6}$$

式中：N——总节点数；

k_i——单个节点度。

2) 平均点强

节点点强是某节点连边加入权值后的数值总和，而平均点强是网络中所有点强的平均值，能够反映某节点航空器冲突的紧急程度。用 $\bar{d}$ 表示：

$$\bar{d}=\frac{1}{N}\sum_{i=1}^{N}a_{ij}w_{ij} \tag{7}$$

式中：a_{ij}——节点间的连边关系(取值为0或1)；

w_{ij}——节点间的边权。

3)平均加权聚类系数

某一节点的所有邻居节点间实际相连的边数与理论上最多能够相连边数的比值叫作节点聚类系数。而加权聚类系数 $c(i)$ 还考虑了节点间的权重,两节点间距离越近,权重越大,对加权聚类系数的贡献越大。则平均加权聚类系数 $\bar{c}$ 则是所有节点加权聚类系数的平均值,其数值可以反映航空器冲突网络的复杂特征。用 $\bar{c}$ 表示：

$$\bar{c}=\frac{1}{N}\sum_{i=1}^{N}c(i) \tag{8}$$

式中：$c(i)$——聚集系数,计算方法如下：

$$c(i)=\frac{1}{(k_i-1)s_i}\sum_{m,n}\frac{\omega_{im}+\omega_{in}}{2}\cdot a_{im}a_{mn}a_{ni} \tag{9}$$

4)网络密度

网络密度是网络实际存在边数与网络最大边数的比值,该值能够反映该网络冲突的饱和程度,用于衡量网络冲突严重程度。

$$ND=\frac{2a}{N(N-1)} \tag{10}$$

式中：ND——网络密度；

a——实际连边。

5)网络效率

网络效率体现了网络连通程度,若网络效率越高,则网络中的节点联系越紧密,即可说明其网络越复杂。

$$NE=\frac{1}{N(N-1)}\sum_{i\neq j}^{N}\frac{1}{d_{ij}} \tag{11}$$

式中：d_{ij}——两节点 i 和 j 的最短路径长度。

若 i 与 j 之间没有连接时,$d_{ij}=\infty$,NE 的取值为0-1。

3　实验仿真

3.1　仿真场景设置

现有的航空器飞行高度层间隔是300m,因此,模拟200km×200km×300m的空域,在该空域中随机生成150架航空器(节点)。其中航空器的航速取700~800km/h,航向任意,任意选择 n 架航空器进行高度演化,航空器进行高度演化时的爬升/下降角度设置为0~30°。为了验证"椭球形"速度障碍保护区模型的可行性,现引入"圆柱形"速度障碍保护区、"球形"速度障碍保护区和仅考虑位置距离关系的模型与其进行对比。保护区模型如图4所示,图4a)的水平方向是以最小安全间隔10km为半径的圆,垂直方向是以300m为间隔圆柱的高所构成的圆柱体;图4b)是以半径为10km所构成的球体模型;图4c)是本文所构建的基于速度障碍法的椭球模型,因此统一将距离阈值设定为 $L=10\text{km}$,两机保护区有重叠时即 $d<20\text{km}$ 可能存在冲突。

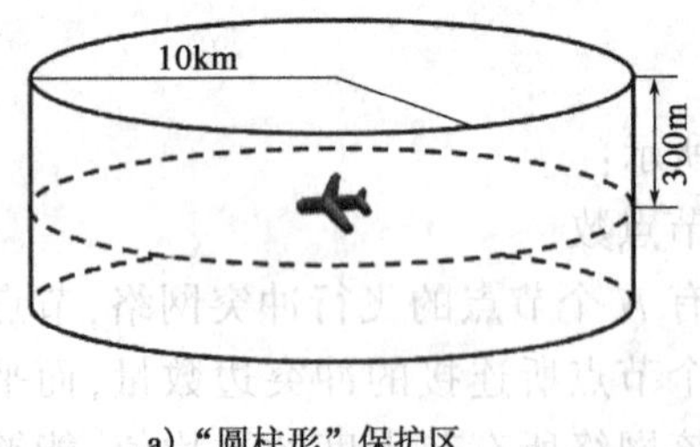

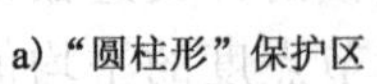
a)"圆柱形"保护区

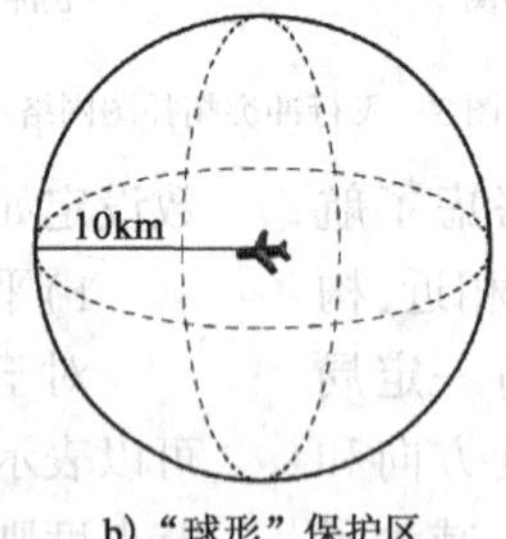

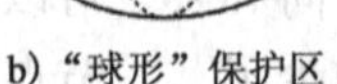
b)"球形"保护区

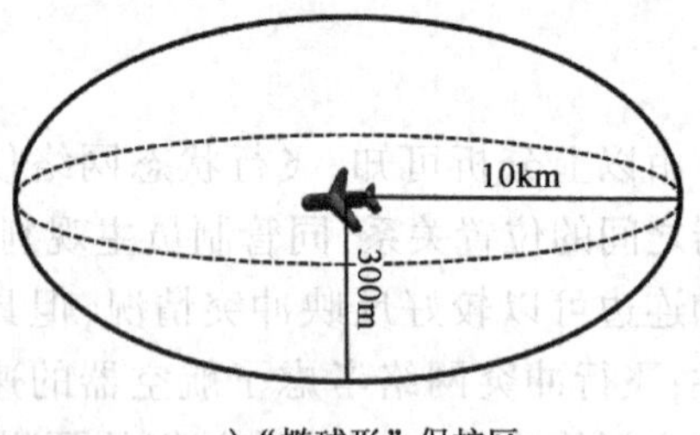

c)"椭球形"保护区

图4　各类保护区模型

3.2　仿真结果及分析

构建好仿真场景后,按照第1节所确定的冲突关系构建连边且确定边权,利用Matlab软件对所设置的场景进行仿真实验。本次实验数值是基于Intel Core i7-6700HQ四核处理器,NVIDIA GTX965M 2GGDDR5独立显卡,8GBDDR3L内存。三维空间图能够体现高度层之间的冲突连边关系,二维拓扑图能够研究复杂网络的拓扑特征,因此,为了更加准确地表示冲突关系,将三维空间图及其在二维的投影拓扑图一起展示(由于篇幅有限,此处只展示位置模型与椭球模型之间的对比仿真图,数据用表格表示)。

仿真结果如图5所示,图5a)、b)为依据"椭球形”速度障碍法并和冲突时间 T 确定边权所构建的飞行冲突网络,在冲突连边和航空器节点上增加了可视化元素如图 5b) 的节点 1 与节点 2,节点 2 的冲突程度较低,其节点红色填充相比于节点 1 较少,连边的宽度也较窄,表示该节点冲突程度轻。可视化方法使得冲突网络图更加直观,易于分辨;图 5c)、d) 为位置模型冲突网络图,仔细对比图 5b)、d) 的 3、4 节点,箭头表示飞机航向,因两机距离小于 20km 保护区有重叠,因此位置模型判断其存在冲突,但考虑飞机航向时实际则不存在冲突,本文所提的三维速度障碍法识别了这点,因此图 5b) 中 3、4 节点无连边。

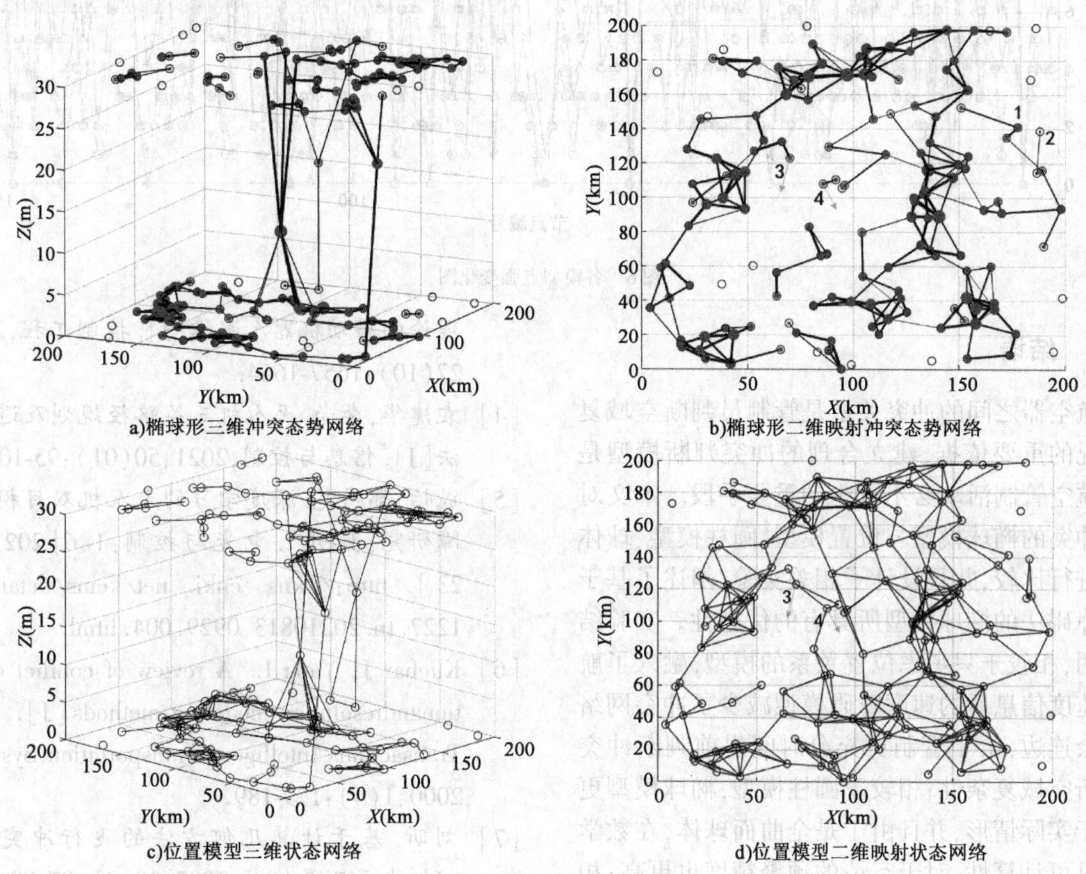

图 5 三维仿真及二维映射图

从二维图可知,图 5b) 与图 5d) 相比,图 5b) 的连边数量明显较少。表 1 给出了各种模型拓扑指标的对比。由表 1 可知,椭球模型 k 值最少即连边数量为 223,球体模型连边数量最多为 548,由此可以计算相比于其他三种模型,椭球模型虚警率依次减少了 40.05%、8.97%、59.30%;从网络的复杂程度 NE 和网络冲突严重程度 ND 的数值可知,椭球模型均优于其他模型;从其他拓扑指标来看,椭球模型的数值都是处于最低值,验证了该模型的检测效果准确性,因此可得到各模型预警有效程度为:球体 < 位置 < 圆柱 < 椭球。图 6 为各模型中节点的点强变化情况,可以看到椭球模型的变化幅度最小,进一步说明其冲突检测的准确性。

各模型特征指数

表 1

项 目	k	$\bar{k}$	$\bar{d}$	$\bar{c}$	ND	NE
椭球模型	223	1.486	10.981	0.283	0.087	0.208
位置模型	372	2.480	18.378	0.597	0.302	0.536
圆柱模型	245	1.633	12.683	0.309	0.112	0.296
球体模型	548	3.653	24.463	0.652	0.401	0.621

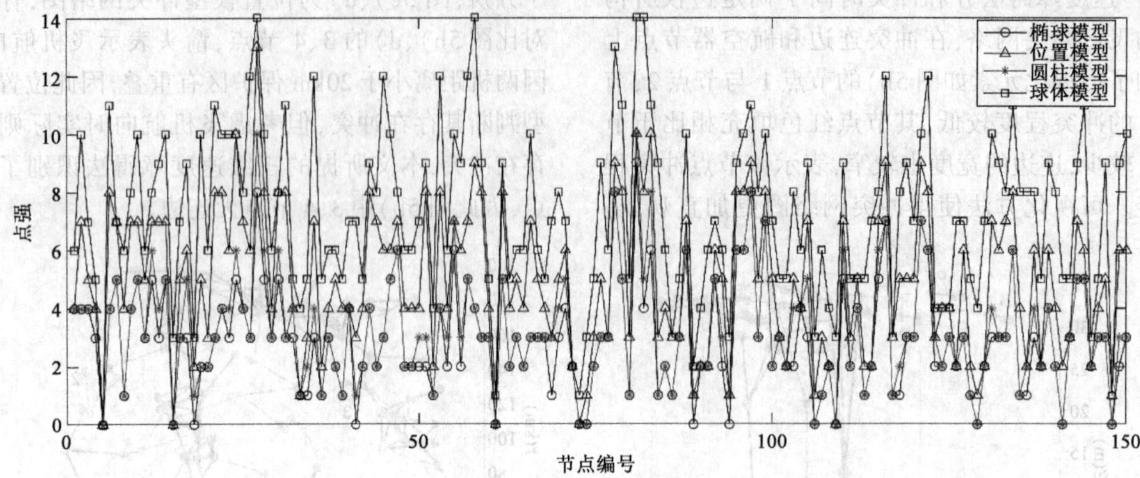

图6　各模型点强变化图

4　结语

航空器之间的冲突关系是管制员判断空域复杂情况的重要依据,建立合理的冲突判断模型是进行航空管制活动必不可少的重要手段。本文对判断冲突的椭球模型与位置模型、圆柱模型、球体模型进行比较,并且设计了相关实验,阐述了基于速度障碍法的椭球模型所具有的优越性。实验结果表明,相较于只考虑位置关系的模型,融入了航向和速度信息后的速度障碍模型减少了冲突网络的冗余连边,给予管制员充分时间提前判断冲突和分析空域复杂性;相较于圆柱模型,椭球模型更接近于实际情形,并且由于是全曲面球体,在数学上更具可计算性,对于空情的预警精度也更高;相较于球体模型,椭球模型规避了长短轴相同的壁垒,减少了高度层之间的冲突关系,提高了预警精度;加入了可视化元素,对冲突的判断更加直观、清晰,为进一步提高空管的效率和服务质量提供有力支撑。

参考文献

[1] Free flight (Air Traffic Control)-From Wikipedia, the free encyclopedia. Availablefrom: http://en.wikipedia.org/wiki/Free flight (air traffic control).

[2] 王梓强,胡晓光,李晓筱,等.移动机器人全局路径规划算法综述[J/OL].计算机科学:1-16[2021-08-23]. http://kns.cnki.net/kcms/detail/50.1075.TP.20210628.1829.043.html.

[3] 柴慧敏,陈奋增,方敏,等.贝叶斯网络与模糊理论的移动机器人避障[J].控制工程,2020,27(10):1657-1664.

[4] 袁建华,李尚.无人机三维路径规划及避障方法[J].信息与控制,2021,50(01):95-101.

[5] 成怡,郑腾龙.深度学习的无人机双目视觉避障研究[J/OL].电光与控制:1-6[2021-08-23]. http://kns.cnki.net/kcms/detail/41.1227.tn.20210813.0929.004.html.

[6] Kuchar J, Yang L. A review of conflict detectionandresolution modeling methods[J]. IEEE Transactions Intelligent Transportation Systems, 2000,1(4):179-189.

[7] 刘昕.基于计算几何方法的飞行冲突检测[J].电子测量技术,2007,30(4):87-89.

[8] Chakravarthy A, Ghose D. Obstacle avoidance in a dynamic environment: A collision cone approach[J]. IEEE Transactions on Systems Man & Cybernetics Part A Systems & Humans, 1998, 28(5): 562-574.

[9] Ford R, Powell D. A new threat detection criterion for airborne collision avoidance systems[J]. The Journal of Navigation, 1990, 43(3): 391-403.

[10] Ruiz S, Piera M, Pozo I. A medium-term conflict detection and resolution system for terminal maneuvering area based on spatial data structures and 4d trajectories[J]. Transportation Research Part C: Emerging Technologies, 2013, 26(1): 396-417.

[11] Paielli A, Erzherger H. Conflict probability estimation for free flight [J]. Journal of Guidance, Control, and Dynamics, 1997, 20 (3): 588-596

[12] 王红勇,赵嶷飞,温瑞英.基于复杂网络的空中交通复杂性度量方法[J].系统工程,2014,32(03):112-118.

[13] Wang H Y, Wen R Y, Zhao Y F. Analysis of topological characteristic in air traffic situation networks[J]. Proceedings of the Institution of Mechanical Engineers PartG: Journal of Aerospace Engineering, 2015, 229 (13): 2497-2505.

[14] 曾小舟,唐笑笑,江可申.基于复杂网络理论的中国航空网络结构实证研究[J].交通运输系统工程与信息,2011,11(06):175-181.

[15] 李昂,聂党民,温祥西,等.管制-飞行状态相依网络演化过程研究[J/OL].航空学报:1-14[2021-05-07]. http://kns.cnki.net/kcms/detail/11.1929.V.20201204.1016.004.html.

[16] 吴明功,王泽坤,甘旭升,等.基于复杂网络理论的关键飞行冲突点识别[J].西北工业大学学报,2020,38(02):279-287.

[17] 刘飞,余敏建,李佳威,等.基于复杂网络理论的飞行冲突关键点识别[J].空军工程大学学报(自然科学版),2019,20(04):19-25.

[18] 李昂,聂党民,温祥西,等.管制-飞行状态相依网络模型及特性分析[J].北京航空航天大学学报,2020,46(06):1204-1213.

[19] Nicolas Durand. Constant speed optimal reciprocal collision avoidance [J]. Transportation Research Part C, 2018, 96.

[20] Durand N, Barnier N. Does ATM need centralizedcoordination? Autonomous conflict resolution analysis in a constrained speed environment [J]. Air Traffic Control Quarterly, 2015, 23(4): 710-712.

[21] Dowek G., A. Geser. Tactical conflict detection and resolution in 3-D airspace[C]. 4th USA/Europe Air Traffic Management R&D Seminar, 2001, Santa Fe.

[22] Raghunathan A. U., V. Gopal, D. Subramanian, L. T. Biegler and T. Samad. Dynamic optimization strategies for 3D conflict resolution of multiple aircrafts [J]. AIAA Journal of Guidance, Control and Dynamics, 2004, 27 (4):586-594.

基于马尔科夫预测的管型航路网空间柔性化方法研究

倪　超　叶博嘉*　万莉莉　田　勇

(南京航空航天大学民航学院)

摘　要　管型航路是一种面向未来空中航行系统的新型空域概念,具有柔性高密度,占据空域少,动态激活/关闭等特性,但在目前的研究中,管型航路动态使用的研究较为缺乏。为了在实际运行中提供更高效、可靠的管型航路网络,基于马尔科夫链进行危险天气预测,提出了管型航路网络空间动态使用方法框架,基于马尔科夫链进行危险天气预测,以安全和经济为目标,构建了管型航路在水平和垂直方向的空间动态使用模型,以提升管型航路运行的可靠性。研究结果表明,该空间动态使用方法可在保证安全水平的前提下降低飞行成本。

关键词　空中交通管理　动态优化　多目标优化　管型航路　天气预测

1.基金项目:国家自然科学基金民航联合基金(U1933119)。

0　引言

随着航空运输业持续高速发展,民航空域紧张的局面已然呈现由点到面的发展趋势。各国都在积极探索空管系统升级和变革的新方法,欧美等航空发达国家率先提出了具备"大容量、自主间隔和柔性化"等崭新特点的管型航路运行概念。管型航路是可容纳多层、多股平行交通流的单向、管道型空域结构,具有高容量、高速度、高密度和柔性可变等特点,在提高空域容量、缓解延误方面具有较好的作用。

现阶段,诸多学者围绕管型航路运行概念展开了深入的研究,但在管型航路动态使用这一方面,大多数研究停留在战略层面对时间动态使用方法进行研究;在战术层面,管型航路空间动态使用方法的相关研究尚存在明显不足和空白,缺少时间与空间,战略与战术的结合,无法为管型航路提供真正具有说服力的运行方案。

由于管型航路空间动态使用方法的相关研究较少,本文将主要参考普通航路的结合气象预测的动态航迹进行研究。Arnab等将天气过程建模为一个平稳的马尔科夫链,使用动态规划算法来解决单飞机动态路由策略问题[1]。蒋昕构建天气运动预测模型,提出动态改航路径规划算法,并对空域动态容量进行评估[2]。Liu等在飞机和风动力学的不确定情况下,研究了飞机空中冲突解脱问题,利用马尔科夫链推导出最优控制方法[3]。杜实等采用灰色预测模型对危险天气边界点进行位置预测,对改航路径进行动态规划[4]。张兆宁等基于多重Morphin算法,研究了终端区航空器在危险天气下的改航方法[5]。Liu等提出了一种用于动态调整和优化飞行器轨迹的随机最优控制算法,采用马尔科夫链逼近方法进行求解[6]。毛利民等在对流天气变化条件下,建立了多目标整数规划模型生成战术阶段的改航路径[7]。王莉莉等将栅格环境和动态规划法相结合针对平行航路设计了一种新的单机改航路径规划方法[8]。赵元棣等构建了静态和动态的危险天气飞行限制区和改航路径快速规划模型,实现了在危险天气下改航路径的规划[9]。李海等提出了一种融合动态风险图和改进A^*算法的动态改航规划方法,构造算法的代价函数进行航迹规划[10]。根据以上研究可以发现,马尔科夫链比较适合气象变化随机性较强的特点,因此已被广泛地应用于气象预测的多个方面;而关于改航问题,相关的理论方法已经较为成熟,可以引入管型航路进行研究。

基于以上研究,本文提出了一个高效、可靠的管型航路网空间动态使用的框架,用动态的管型航路设计取代当前的静态设计。首先,基于马尔科夫链对管型航路附近空域的危险天气展开预测;其次,以降低管型航路内航空器的安全成本和飞行成本为目标,构建管型航路在水平方向和垂直方向的动态使用模型;最后,结合危险天气预测方法对动态使用模型进行求解,设计出战术层面的管型航路空间动态使用方法。

1　基于马尔科夫链的危险天气预测

在马尔科夫随机过程中,过去的历史状态对于预测未来的状态是无关的,$t+1$时刻的系统状态只与t时刻的状态有关,这一概念较好地契合了危险天气变化不确定性较强的特点。结合这一概念,本研究将危险天气预测模型视为以下三个部分:

1.1　栅格环境构建与危险天气识别计算

本研究采用侧向改航的方法规避危险天气,因此首先将管型航路的路径规划空间视为二维平面,采用栅格法划分为大小相同的$X \times Y$个方格,用i表示横坐标,j表示纵坐标。

随后,在RGB色彩空间内,对研究区域的基本反射率图像产品进行识别,将不同的颜色与不同的回波强度和对航空器的影响进行对应,如表1所示。

基本反射率对应关系表　　表1

颜　色	回波强度	描　述
无	[0,10)	无影响
蓝、青	[10,20)	几乎无影响
浅绿、深绿	[20,30)	轻度颠簸
黄、深黄	[30,40)	中度颠簸
橙、红	[40,50)	闪电、较大颠簸
镉红、砖红	[50,60)	积冰
深红、紫	[60,70)	严重积冰
湖紫	≥70	严重颠簸、结构受损

考虑到飞行成本和强对流天气快速变化带来的安全影响,航空器通常不会在危险天气范围内穿越或绕行,因此,可将危险天气范围视为凸多边形,采用凸包算法,对危险天气的范围边界进行计算。

1.2 危险天气几何中心的运动轨迹预测

Lee 等学者在研究对流单体时,将中心的移动分为水平和垂直两个方向分别进行预测和评估[11]。本文同样采用该思路,对危险天气几何中心的运动轨迹进行分解,并结合 Nilim 等学者提出的基于马尔科夫的天气预测模型进行预测[1]。

根据识别并划分的危险天气范围,可以计算获得该危险天气图形的重心作为中心点,并分别建立中心点垂直方向和水平方向的分速度模型,用矩阵$[v_1 v_2]$表示,并分别以北方向和东方向为正向。在垂直和水平方向速度变化绝对值的均值分别表示为$\bar{v}_1$和$\bar{v}_2$。

设$c_v(k) \in \{0,1\}$为k时段移动分速度的状态,分别表示k时段移动分速度为正向和负向,定义状态转移概率和一步状态转移矩阵为:

$$p = P\{c_v(k+1) = 0 \mid c_v(k) = 0\}$$
$$q = P\{c_v(k+1) = 1 \mid c_v(k) = 1\}$$
$$P = \begin{bmatrix} p & 1-p \\ 1-q & q \end{bmatrix}$$

根据 C-K 方程,计算得到k步状态转移矩阵为:

$$P(k) = P^k = (p_{a,b}(k))_{2\times 2}$$

式中:$p_{a,b}(k)$——移动分速度由初始状态a经过k个时段到达状态b的概率。

若当前处于 0 状态,经过k个时段的变化,中心点的移动分速度$v_1^k = \bar{v}_1 \cdot (p_{0,0}(k) - p_{0,1}(k))$;若当前处于 1 状态,经过$k$个时段的变化,中心点的移动分速度$v_1^k = \bar{v}_1 \cdot (p_{1,0}(k) - p_{1,1}(k))$。

通过以上根据马尔科夫链对速度的预测,可以计算危险天气中心点的移动路径,假设初始中心点位置为(X_0, Y_0),经过K个T时段的变化后,中心点的位置变为:

$$\begin{cases} X_K = X_0 + v_2^1 \cdot T + v_2^2 \cdot T + \cdots + v_2^K \cdot T \\ Y_K = Y_0 + v_1^1 \cdot T + v_1^2 \cdot T + \cdots + v_1^K \cdot T \end{cases}$$

1.3 危险天气几何结构的变化预测

对于危险天气几何结构,相关学者提出在划设不规则形状时,只需要找出能描述图形的关键点,形成描述危险天几何结构的不规则多边形[12]。随后,同样采用马尔科夫链对危险天气的几何结构进行预测。

根据以上思路,首先以危险天气几何结构中心点为极坐标原点,将所有顶点由笛卡儿坐标系转化至极坐标系,在该坐标系中求得ρ的两个极大值点以及与$\theta = 0°$、$\theta = 90°$、$\theta = 180°$和$\theta = 270°$相交的四个点,共计六个点,作为危险天气几何结构的特征边界点。用极坐标表示为$D_1(\rho_1, \theta_1)$,$D_2(\rho_2, \theta_2)$,$D_3(\rho_3, 0°)$,…,$D_6(\rho_6, 270°)$。

对于ρ,以增大为 0 状态,以减小为 1 状态,$\bar{\rho}$表示历史数据中长度变化绝对值的均值,定义状态转移概率为:

$$p = P\{c_\rho(k+1) = 0 \mid c_\rho(k) = 0\}$$
$$q = P\{c_\rho(k+1) = 1 \mid c_\rho(k) = 1\}$$

对于θ,以顺时针变化为 0 状态,以逆时针变化为 1 状态,$\bar{\theta}$表示历史数据中角度变化绝对值的均值,定义状态转移概率为:

$$p = P\{c_\theta(k+1) = 0 \mid c_\theta(k) = 0\}$$
$$q = P\{c_\theta(k+1) = 1 \mid c_\theta(k) = 1\}$$

ρ和θ的一步和k步状态转移矩阵及各时段的变化速度计算过程与 1.2 节相同。采用以上方法,可对ρ和θ(不包括固定值)进行预测。经过K个T时段的变化后,将危险天气多边形顶点转化为笛卡儿坐标系,可表示为:

$$D_1^K: \begin{cases} X_1 = X_K + \rho_1^K \cos\theta_1^K \\ Y_1 = Y_K + \rho_1^K \sin\theta_1^K \end{cases}$$

$$D_2^K: \begin{cases} X_2 = X_K + \rho_2^K \cos\theta_2^K \\ Y_2 = Y_K + \rho_2^K \sin\theta_2^K \end{cases}$$

$$D_n^K: \begin{cases} X_n = X_K + \rho_n^K \cos\theta_n^K \\ Y_n = Y_K + \rho_n^K \sin\theta_n^K \end{cases}$$

2 空间动态使用模型建立

本文在进行管型航路空间动态使用方法的研究时,主要考虑以安全成本和飞行成本作为优化目标,构建动态使用模型。管型航路在样本空间的动态使用主要分为水平方向内和垂直不同高度层内,两个层面的动态使用可同时进行。

为了保证管型航路在水平方向动态使用模型的科学性与合理性,做出如下假设如下:

(1)在管型航路内,航空器的运行仅考虑危险天气、风速风向的影响,不考虑其他气象因素的变化;

(2)我国探空资料发布时间间隔为12h,因此在各栅格内,除危险天气外的气象条件保持恒定;

(3)航空器在管型航路内可进行自主间隔管理而避免冲突;

(4)航空器在进行爬升或下降时,水平方向速度视为保持不变。

2.1　水平方向动态使用模型

在水平方向内,管型航路的搜索方向如图1所示,从由起点开始,可以向目标方向的正前/左/右/左前/右前方的栅格进行搜索。

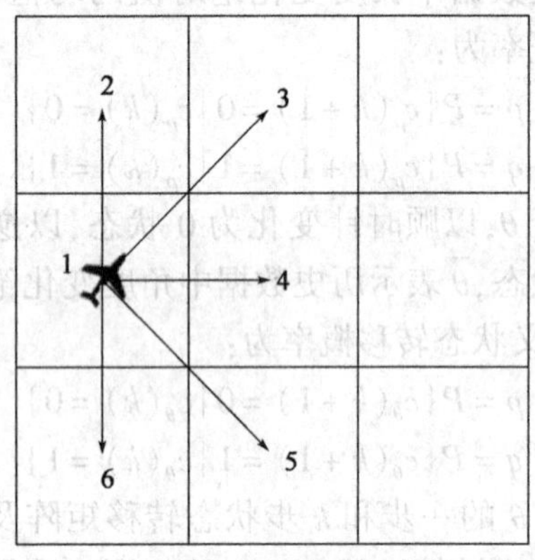

图1　路径搜索方向

本文结合气象条件,对管型航路进行水平方向动态使用方法建模,综合考虑了航空器的飞行安全和飞行成本(包括飞行时间和燃油消耗),以安全成本 $\mathrm{Cost_{safe}}$ 最小化和飞行成本 $\mathrm{Cost_{flight}}$ 最小化为目标构建多目标优化模型,表达式如下:

$$\mathrm{Min\ Cost_{safe}} = \mathrm{Min}\left(\sum_{ij \in \mathrm{Area}_{ij}} \mathrm{Cost}_{\mathrm{safe}}^{ij}\right)$$

$$\mathrm{Min\ Cost_{flight}} = \mathrm{Min}\left[\sum_{ij \in \mathrm{Area}_{ij}} \left(\mathrm{Cost}_{\mathrm{time}}^{ij} + \mathrm{Cost}_{\mathrm{fuel}}^{ij}\right)\right]$$

$$\mathrm{Cost}_{\mathrm{safe}}^{ij} = \sum_{k \in K} \eta_{ij} \cdot \varphi_{ij} \cdot n_k \cdot t_{k,ij}$$

$$\mathrm{Cost}_{\mathrm{time}}^{ij} = \sum_{ij \in \mathrm{Area}_{ij}} \eta_{ij} \cdot n_k \cdot t_{k,ij} \cdot C_t$$

$$\mathrm{Cost}_{\mathrm{fuel}}^{ij} = \sum_{ij \in \mathrm{Area}} \eta_{ij} \cdot n_k \cdot EG_k \cdot FF_k \cdot t_{k,ij} \cdot C_F$$

$$\eta_{ij} = \begin{cases} +\infty \text{网格 } ij \text{ 中存在恶劣天气} \\ 1 \text{ 否则} \end{cases}$$

$$\varphi_{ij} = \begin{cases} \alpha_1\ 30 < \gamma_{ij} \leqslant 40 \\ \alpha_2\ 20 < \gamma_{ij} \leqslant 30 \\ \alpha_3\ \gamma_{ij} \leqslant 20 \end{cases}$$

$$t_{k,ij} = L_{k,ij} / (V_{\mathrm{TAS}k} + WS_{ij} \cdot \cos WA_{ij})$$

决策变量:$\mathrm{Area}_z = \{z_{ij} \mid i \in [1,X], j \in [1,Y]\}$,表示管型航路经过的栅格集合,搜索样本区域记为 $Area$,$Area_z \in Area$。

模型中各参数的说明如下:

η_{ij}:网格 z_{ij} 中是否存在恶劣天气;

φ_{ij}:网格 z_{ij} 不存在恶劣天气时,不同基本反射率下的安全折减系数;

γ_{ij}:网格 z_{ij} 中基本反射率值;

n_k:机型 k 的数量;

$t_{k,z}$:机型 k 在网格 z_{ij} 中飞行的时间;

EG_k:机型 k 的发动机数量;

FF_k:机型 k 的燃油流率;

$L_{k,z}$:机型 k 在网格 z_{ij} 中的飞行距离;

$V_{\mathrm{TAS}k}$:机型 k 的真空速;

WS_{ij}:网格 z_{ij} 在目标高度层的平均风速;

WA_{ij}:网格 z_{ij} 在目标高度层的风角。

同时,模型要满足以下航路连续约束条件,即管型航路在栅格空间内进行搜索时,下一栅格需与上一栅格相邻:

$$i' \in \{i-1, i, i+1\}$$

$$j' \in \{j, j+1\}$$

式中:$i'j'$ 为管型航路路径搜索至 ij 的下一栅格。

2.2　垂直方向动态使用模型

在垂直方向上动态使用模型中,管型航路可在目标水平路径上的状态转换点进行多个高度层选择和转换,并保持该高度至下一状态转换点,以获得最有利的高空风,从而减少航空器的飞行成本,本研究设置的状态转换点为各栅格的中心位置。

由于在进行水平方向的动态使用规划时,已考虑了安全成本,对危险天气进行了规避,并且垂直方向的危险天气分布暂时无法准确获得,因此,在进行垂直方向动态使用模型构建时,仅考虑飞行成本。最终,以飞行成本 $\mathrm{Cost_{flight}}$ 最小化为目标,对管型航路进行垂直方向动态使用方法进行建模,表达式如下:

$$\mathrm{Min\ Cost_{flight}} = \mathrm{Min}\left[\sum_{z \in \mathrm{Area}_z} \left(\mathrm{Cost}_{\mathrm{time}}^{z} + \mathrm{Cost}_{\mathrm{fuel}}^{z}\right)\right]$$

$$\mathrm{Cost}_{\mathrm{time}}^{z} \approx \sum_{z \in \mathrm{Area}_z} n_k \cdot t_{k,z,FL} \cdot C_t$$

$$\mathrm{Cost}_{\mathrm{fuel}}^{z} = \sum_{z \in \mathrm{Area}_z} n_k \cdot \mathrm{EG}_k \cdot \mathrm{FF}_k \cdot t_{k,z,FL} \cdot C_F + \sum_{z \in \mathrm{Area}_z} \delta_z \cdot n_k \cdot \mathrm{EG}_k \cdot \mathrm{FF}_k^{CD} \cdot t'_{k,z,FL} \cdot C_F$$

$$t_{k,z,FL} = L_{k,z} / (V_{\mathrm{TAS}k} + \mathrm{WS}_z^{FL} \cdot \cos \mathrm{WA}_z^{FL})$$

决策变量：$FL=\{FL_z|z\in Area_z\}$，表示管型航路在各状态转换点的最优飞行高度层，可供选择的高度层记为 $FL_{all}=\{FL_1,FL_2,\cdots,FL_n\}$，$FL_z\in FL_{all}$。新增的参数说明如下：

δ_z：管型航路在状态转换点 z_{ij} 是否改变高度；

$t_{k,z,FL}$：机型 k 在网格 z_{ij} 中保持高度 FL 的飞行时间，不包括改变高度的时间；

$t'_{k,z,FL}$：机型 k 在网格 z_{ij} 中改变飞行高度的飞行时间；

FF_k^{CD}：机型 k 在进行相应爬升或下降时的燃油流率；

WS_{ij}^{FL}：网格 z_{ij} 在高度层 FL 的平均风速；

WA_{ij}^{FL}：网格 z_{ij} 在高度层 FL 的风角。

同时，模型要满足高度层搜索约束条件：

$$FL_z\in FL_{all}$$

式中：$FL_{all}=\{FL_1,FL_2,\cdots,FL_n\}$ 表示可供选择的高度层。

3 实例分析

本文的实例分析，将基于前期研究设计的管型航路网络展开研究，如图 2 所示。

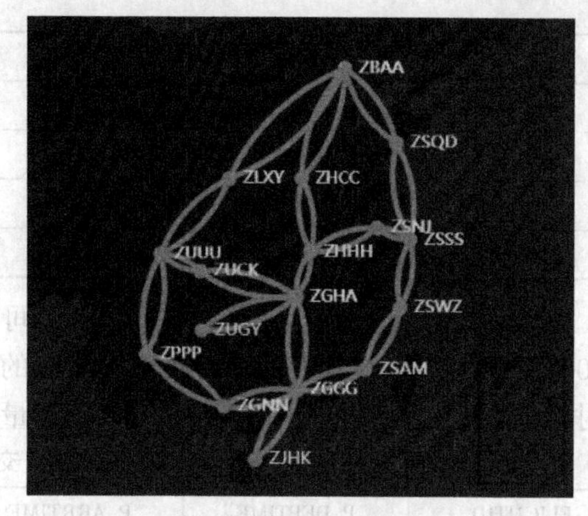

图 2 静态管型航路网络

3.1 数据处理

首先以 2021 年 3 月 11 日上海至青岛的大圆航迹管型航路为研究对象，进行管型航路空间动态使用方法的实例研究，并将该方法扩展至整个管型航路网络。

所用数据包括来自来自中国气象数据网的气象数据，来自民航局的航班运行数据，来自 BADA 数据库的航空器性能数据。

2021 年 3 月 11 日 15:00 华东雷达反射拼图，将其划分为 60 × 80 个大小相同的栅格，对危险天气进行识别，结果如图 3 所示。

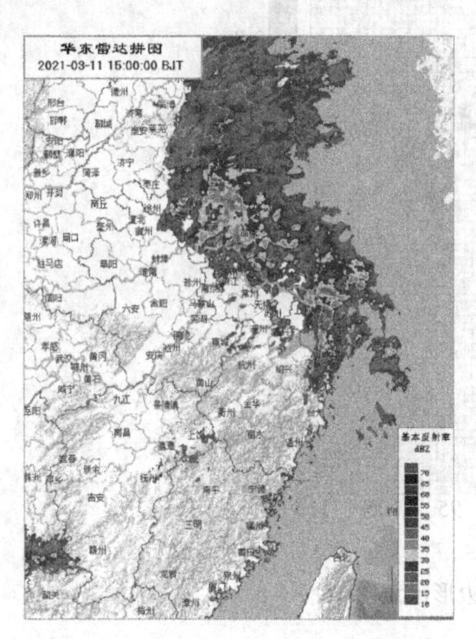

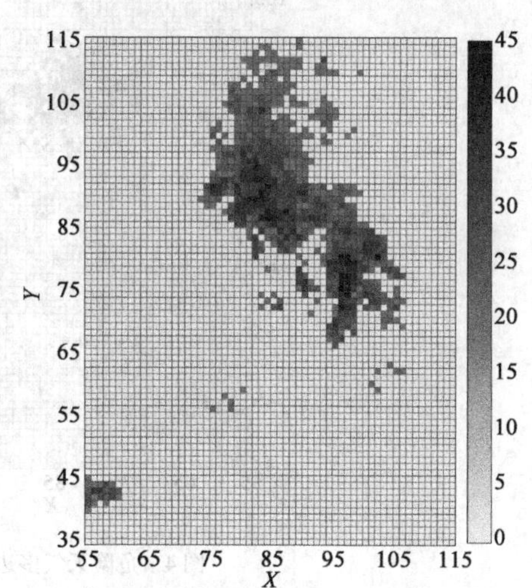

图 3 雷达拼图及其识别结果

获取上海区域青岛区域附近的 11 个探空站的高空气象数据，部分数据如表 2 所示。

高空气象数据示例 表 2

站点 ID	经度	纬度	高度(m)	风向(°)	风速(m/s)
54727	117.55	36.68	9563.0	253.0	47.3
54727	117.55	36.68	10829.0	256.0	48.2

续上表

站点 ID	经度	纬度	高度(m)	风向(°)	风速(m/s)
…	…	…	…	…	…
58424	116.97	30.62	9664.0	259.0	24.8
58424	116.97	30.62	12419.0	276.0	28.1
…	…	…	…	…	…

对于交通流，主要筛选预计起飞时间在15:00—16:00之间的航班，此外，由于在所选的研究时段前，附近空域出现强对流天气，导致大量航班延误积压，因此，还加入部分预计起飞时间在14:00—15:00的航班，如表3所示。

交通流数据　　表3

FLIGHTID	P_DEPTIME	P_ARRTIME	P_DEPAP	P_ARRAP	P_AIRCRAFTTYPE
CDG4670	201703111535	201703111644	ZSSS	ZSQD	B738
CES5574	201703111555	201703111707	ZSPD	ZSQD	A320
CES272	201703111510	201703111702	ZSPD	ZBAA	A321
…	…	…	…	…	…

根据上述航班流信息，从BADA数据库中获取以上各机型的性能数据，主要包括各高度层的最佳巡航速度、燃油流率和发动机个数等。

3.2　危险天气预测

本文设 T 为30min，分别对1h和2h后的危险天气范围进行预测。对影响管型航路运行的云团分别以30dBz、35dBz和40dBz为阈值(可根据实际需要选择)进行识别，采用凸包算法分别绘制危险天气多边形，结果如图4所示，计算得到中心点坐标为(28.6,54.2)，(28.8,54.1)，(28.5,54.1)。

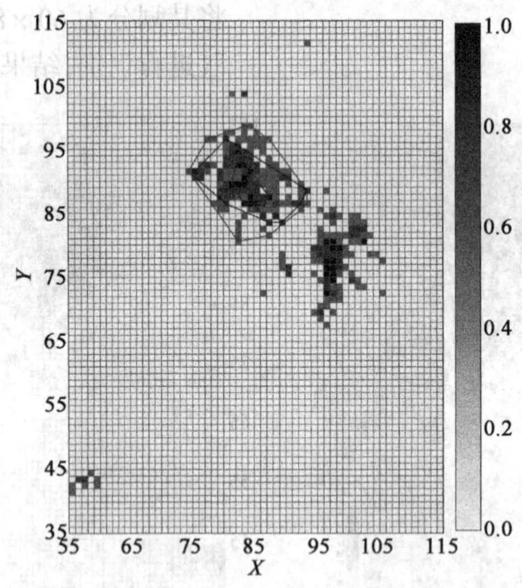

图4　危险天气多边形示意图

以基本反射率阈值为30dBz的多边形为例，中心点在 $\hat{x}_0$ 和 $\hat{y}_0$ 方向的初始速度分别为0.94和1.15，概率转移矩阵分别为：

$$P_1=\begin{bmatrix}0.90 & 0.10\\0.70 & 0.30\end{bmatrix}$$

$$P_2=\begin{bmatrix}0.95 & 0.05\\0.80 & 0.20\end{bmatrix}$$

根据1.2节中的方法，预测1h后，中心点 $\hat{x}_1$ 位置在30.1，中心点 $\hat{y}_1$ 位置在56.2，预测误差约为14.23km；预测2h后，中心点 $\hat{x}_2$ 位置在31.5，中心点 $\hat{y}_2$ 位置在57.8，预测误差约为17.5km。而对比该方面其他学者的研究，时效为1h的对流单体中心位置预测误差在19~26km之间[13-14]。

根据1.3节中的方法,求得各边界特征点相对于中心点的ρ与θ,并根据历史数据计算其概率转移矩阵,从而对各多边形边界相对中心的位置进行预测,结果如图5所示。

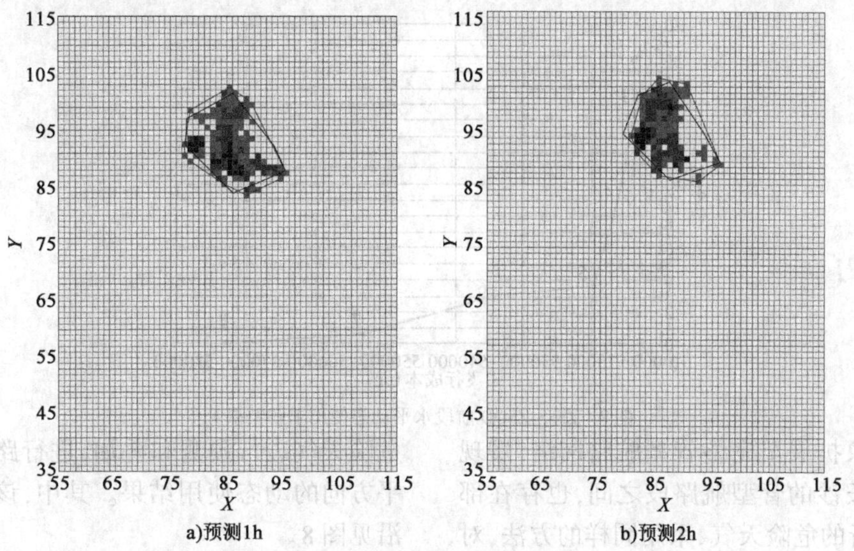

图5 预测1h/2h结果对比图(蓝色表示预测,红色表示实际)

接下来,以击中率POD、误警率FAR和临界成功指数CSI为指标,对结果进行评价,如表4所示。

危险天气范围预测结果评价表 表4

预测时段	POD	FAR	CSI
预测1h(阈值为40dBz)	88.6%	36.4%	58.8%
预测2h(阈值为40dBz)	72.7%	15.8%	64.0%
预测1h(阈值为35dBz)	91.5%	6.0%	86.4%
预测2h(阈值为35dBz)	88.4%	26.9%	66.7%
预测1h(阈值为30dBz)	81.3%	3.9%	78.7%
预测2h(阈值为30dBz)	78.6%	9.0%	72.9%

结果表明,采用此种方法,对危险天气的预测击中率较高,对变化趋势预测的效果较好,相比其他文献的结果[11],无论是击中率还是临界成功指数预测结果有明显提升。

3.3 管型航路网水平方向动态使用结果

管型航路的动态使用时间段设置为1h,为了保证在这一时段内所有航班在管型航路内的路径保持固定,需要将起始时间、预测1h、预测2h的气象进行叠加,如图6所示。

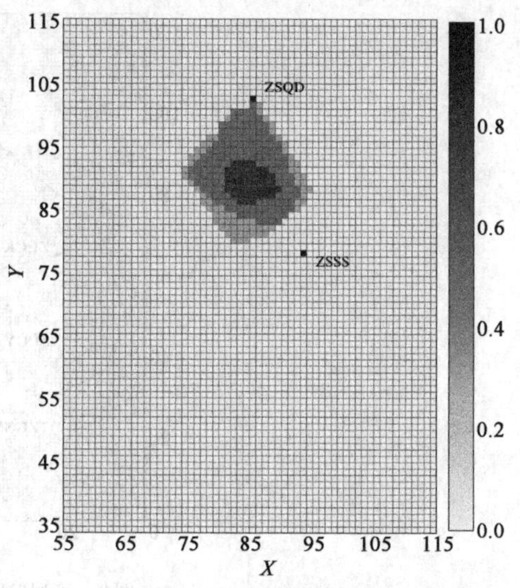

图6 15:00—17:00气象叠加结果图

设置基本反射率在30~35dBz栅格的安全成本为0.6,在35~40dBz栅格的安全成本为0.8,在40dBz以上栅格的安全成本为极大值。采用多目标进化算法NSGA-II(Non-dominated Sorting Genetic Algorithm-II,带精英策略的快速非支配排序遗传算法)对模型进行求解,通过迭代的方法选择收敛效果最佳的参数设置,具体如下:种群规模为 50,GA 终止代数为 500,交叉概率为 0.8,变异概率为 0.02,求解得到的帕累托前沿见图 7。

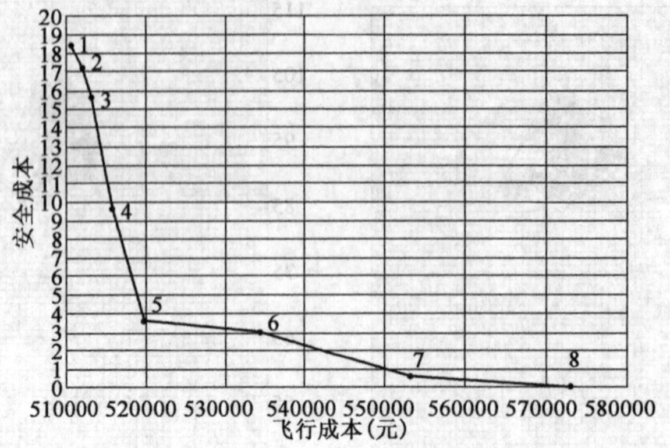

图 7　ZSSS-ZSQD 航段水平动态使用求解结果

将研究对象扩展至完整管型航路网络,发现在广州地区与长沙的管型航路段之间,也存在部分影响航路运行的危险天气,采用同样的方法,对危险天气进行预测和叠加,进行路径求解得到水平方向的动态使用结果。其中,该段的帕累托前沿见图 8。

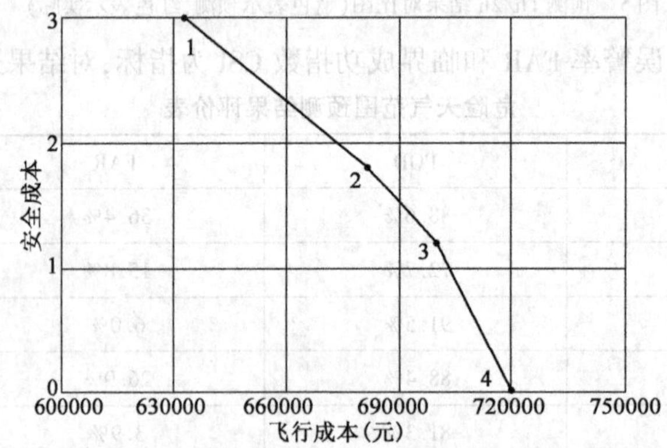

图 8　ZGGG-ZGHA 航段水平动态使用求解结果

各取其中 3 个方案,其余航段在水平方向上均按照大圆航迹进行构建,结果见图 9。

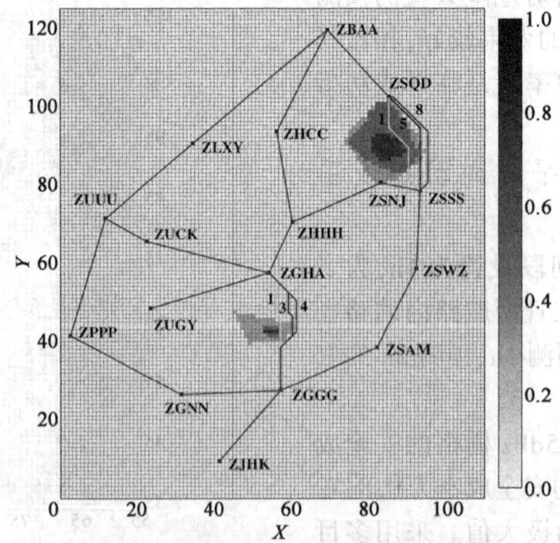

图 9　管型航路网动态使用路径可视化结果图

结果表明,基于马尔科夫链对危险范围的短时预测效果较好;以最小化安全成本和最小化飞行成本,构建水平方向的管型航路空间动态使用模型并求解,可以根据实际需求设置危险天气阈值,在保证安全性的前提下,有效降低飞行成本。

3.4 管型航路网垂直方向动态使用结果

由于可在每个状态转换点进行一次可选高度层的转换,故该问题可视为最短路径搜索问题,并采用 Dijkstra 算法进行求解。

对于上海地区至青岛航段,以方案 5 为例进行垂直方向动态使用模型的实例验证。默认情况下按照 FL350(10700m)飞行,分别设置一次和两次改变飞行高度,按照 2.2 节模型进行求解,结果如图 10、图 11 所示。

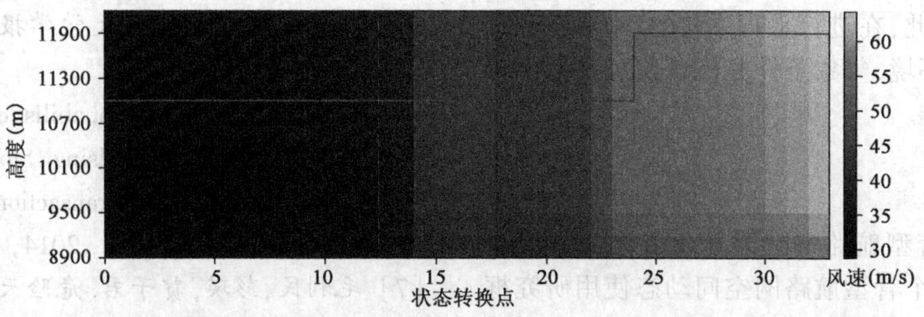

图 10 ZSSS-ZSOD 垂直方向动态使用方案(改变一次高度)

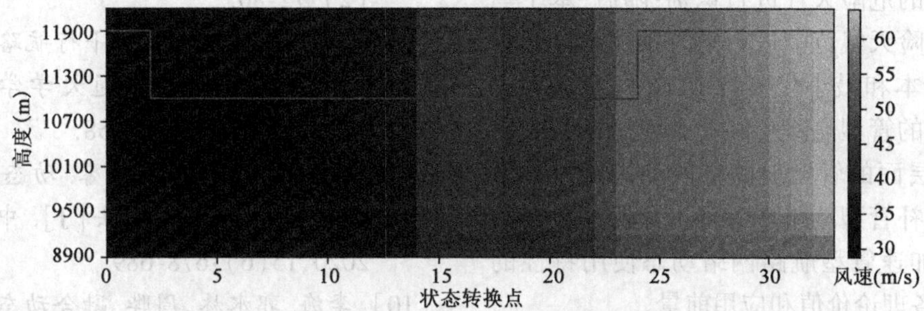

图 11 ZSSS-ZSQD 垂直方向动态使用方案(改变两次高度)

对以上方案的飞行成本进行计算,不改变高度层的飞行成本为 519858 元,改变一次高度层的飞行成本降低为 516814 元,成本降低了 0.6%;改变两次高度层的飞行成本升高为 516814 元,成本升高了 0.8%。

对于广州地区至长沙航段,采用同样方法进行求解,结果如图 12、图 13 所示。

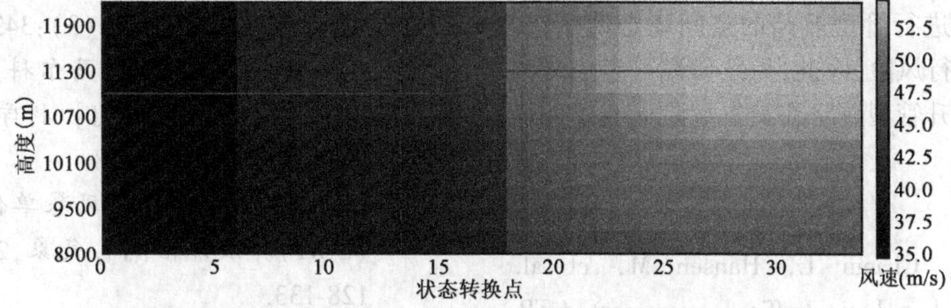

图 12 ZGGG-ZGHA 垂直方向动态使用方案(改变一次高度)

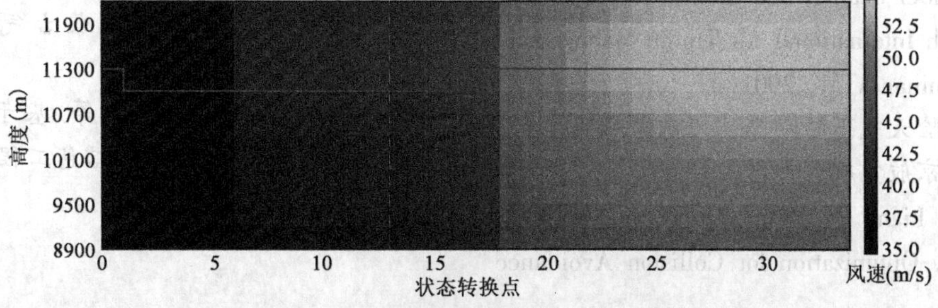

图 13 ZGGG-ZGHA 垂直方向动态使用方案(改变两次高度)

同样对飞行成本进行计算,不改变高度层的飞行成本为632857元,改变一次高度层的飞行成本降低为623592元,成本降低了1.5%;改变两次高度层的飞行成本降低为630634元,成本降低了0.4%。

由此可见,垂直方向的动态使用受空域环境差别的影响较大,改变飞行高度并不一定能降低飞行成本,因此,在进行垂直方向的动态使用时,应结合空域环境、气象条件和航班信息进行准确的计算和安排。

4 结语

本文以管型航路空间柔性化方法为研究对象,提出了一个管型航路网空间动态使用研究框架。首先构建管型航路附近的栅格化空域环境,并对不同等级的危险天气进行识别;随后,基于马尔科夫链对危险天气范围进行短时预测;最后,以最小化安全成本和最小化飞行成本,构建水平方向和垂直方向的管型航路空间动态使用模型并求解,实现战术层面的管型航路空间动态使用。该方法有助于填补管型航路现有理论和研究存在的不足和空白,加速管型航路网络动态使用特性的应用,同时具备理论价值和应用前景。

研究结果表明,水平方向动态使用方法可在保证安全性的前提下,有效较低管型航路内航空器的飞行成本;垂直方向动态使用方法最高可使飞行成本降1.5%。

由于实际强对流天气短时变化较快,依照危险天气的预测进行管型航路的空间动态使用,仍存在一定的运行风险,因此,后续研究可考虑提高预测精度或提升管型航路在突发危险天气下的应对能力。

参考文献

[1] Nilim A, Ghaoui L, Hansen M, et al. Trajectory-based air traffic management (TB-ATM) under weather uncertainty[C]//Proc. of the Fourth International Air Traffic Management R&D Seminar ATM, 2001.

[2] 蒋昕. 危险天气下的动态航班改航研究[D]. 南京:南京航空航天大学,2016.

[3] Liu W, Liang X, Ma Y, et al. Aircraft Trajectory Optimization for Collision Avoidance Using Stochastic Optimal Control[J]. Asian Journal of Control, 2019, 21(5): 2308-2320.

[4] 杜实,王俊凯,任景瑞. 基于改进多目标粒子群算法的航空器改航研究[J]. 安全与环境学报,2020,20(1):177-185.

[5] 张兆宁,魏中慧. 危险天气下基于多重Morphin算法的终端区三维实时改航方法[J]. 南京航空航天大学学报,2015,47(4):467-473.

[6] Liu W, Hwang I. Probabilistic Aircraft Midair Conflict Resolution Using Stochastic Optimal Control[J]. IEEE Transactions on Intelligent Transportation Systems, 2014, 15(1):37-46.

[7] 毛利民,彭瑛,贾子君. 危险天气下的战术改航方法[J]. 华东交通大学学报,2020,37(2):72-80.

[8] 王莉莉,刘子昂. 针对平行航路的改航路径规划研究[J]. 重庆交通大学学报(自然科学版),2020,39(8):45-58.

[9] 赵元棣,李瑞东,吴佳馨. 动态危险天气下改航路径快速规划方法[J]. 中国科技论文,2020,15(6):678-689.

[10] 李海,郭水林,周晔. 融合动态风险图和改进A^*算法的动态改航规划[J]. 航空科学技术,2021,32(5):61-71.

[11] Lee H, Kim J, Kim E, et al. A Novel Convective Storm Location Prediction Model Based on Machine Learning Methods[J]. Atmosphere. 2021, 12(3):343.

[12] 王清琦,张兆宁. 基于马尔科夫链的单体雷暴飞行受限区模型[J]. 科学技术与工程,2016,16(30):312-318.

[13] 王芬,李腹广,张辉. 风暴单体识别与跟踪(SCIT)算法评估[J]. 气象,2010,36(12):128-133.

[14] 张栋. 修正SCIT算法在冰雹识别、跟踪、预警中的应用[J]. 内蒙古气象,2020(1):40-44.

[15] 赖灿,王海江,李静,等. 基于ConvLSTM的雷达回波外推. 成都信息工程大学学报[J]. 2020,35(6):589-593.

基于尾流分类技术的机场跑道着落容量研究

吴　俊*
（湖南机场集团长沙机场分公司机场运行控制中心）

摘　要　随着航班量的增加，提高现有空域资源利用率显得尤为关键。本文分析了尾流形成机理及其对航空器运行的影响，梳理了国内外对尾流间隔进行划分的几种标准，包括现行标准及尾流重新分类标准，建立了跑道着落容量评估模型，研究了某机场着落航班机型构成情况，结合不同尾流间隔标准，应用容量评估模型，对其跑道着落容量进行了计算，确定了适应机场情况的最佳尾流分类标准，并进一步调整不同尾流类型航班数量，分析了各类型变化对跑道着落容量的影响程度。研究结果表明，现行尾流分类标准相对来说较为保守，通过采用尾流重新分类标准，跑道着落容量可以提升高达8.782%。

关键词　交通运输　跑道容量　尾流重新分类　平均尾流间隔　尾流影响

0　引言

随着航空业的发展，空域资源紧张问题越来越凸显，而尾流作为影响航空器运行安全的关键因素，直接制约间隔优化和跑道容量的提升，因此在保障运行安全的前提下，优化尾流分类标准缩小尾流间隔，从而有效提升空域和跑道容量，具有重要意义[1]。

国际民航组织（ICAO）根据最大允许起飞重量（MTOW）对航空器进行尾流分类，并制定相应尾流标准[2]。随着航空器抗尾流性能的提升，以及通信导航监视技术的进一步成熟，该标准较为保守，很大程度限制了空域资源的有效利用[3-4]。于是，在2007年，欧控（Euro Control）率先探索尾流标准重新分类技术（RECAT），以期待缩减尾流间隔，以实现提高空域利用率，提升容量。美国联邦航空局（FAA）也在不断探索尾流缩减新标准，改善既有空域利用情况，开始于2009年和欧控开展合作，讨论RECAT标准实施的可行性。日本于2010年也开展空管系统革新协同行动（CARATS），计划在2018年实现对RECAT技术的跟踪和吸收[5]。FAA于2012年开始将RECAT技术运用于孟菲斯机场[6]，并向美国主要机场推行，并于2014年进一步提出RECAT1.5尾流间隔标准[7-9]。欧控也于2013年开展RECAT-EU标准研究，考虑MTOW和翼展（WS）等，进一步细化尾流分类标准[10-11]。目前，国内主要采用的尾流间隔标准为ICAO标准，跟踪消化国外RECAT标准后[12-13]，尝试提出适合我国航空器分布情况的缩减标准（RECAT-CN），并于2018年下半年开始在广州和深圳机场进行试验运行[14]。

国内外研究对尾流重新分类标准的研究没有做区分考虑，没有考虑不同尾流标准在跑道着落容量提升上对机场机型分布情况的适用性。本文旨在研究不同分类标准对机场跑道着落容量提升上产生的效果，并进一步分析不同尾流类型航班数量变化对容量变化的影响程度。

1　航空器尾流影响

航空器运行过程中由于机翼上下表面存在压力差，机翼翼尖将伴随产生尾流，尾流向后、向下扩散从而对后随航空器造成重大安全影响[15]，图1是航空器尾流产生及扩散示意图。后随航空器一旦遭遇尾流，会发生机身抖动、下沉、发动机停车、改变飞行状态等危险，当超出航空器滚转力矩承受范围，甚至有可能会出现翻转情况。后随运行的航空器需要有效规避前机产生尾流影响，因此需要控制前后航空器间隔，不能使后随航空器与前机距离太近而遭遇尾流，造成运行安全事故[16-17]。为了运行安全，两航空器之间需要配备足够的尾流安全间隔，从而规避尾流影响，而过大的尾流间隔无疑会浪费空域资源，造成空域容量及跑道容量受限。

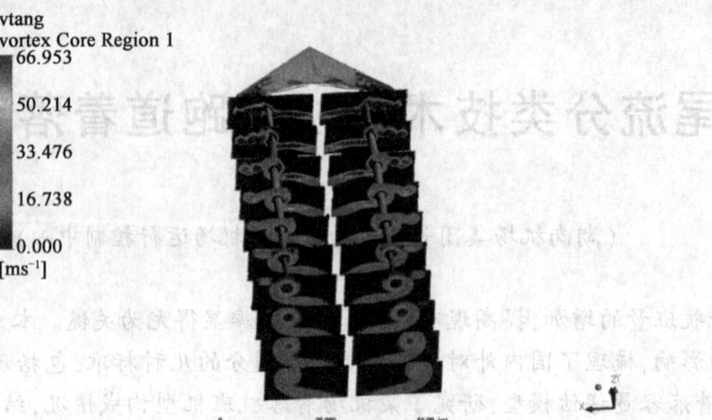

图 1　尾流生成及扩散示意图

2　航空器尾流分类及间隔标准

尾流的强弱大小与机型和翼展等有关,不同机型航空器将产生不同强度尾流,因此有必要对不同跟随组合航空器进行区分,以控制合理的跟随距离,既有效规避尾流影响,又能使得航空器运行效率有所提升,提高空域利用率,从而改善机场跑道运行容量情况。

2.1　ICAO 尾流分类及尾流间隔标准

国际民航组织(ICAO)基于航空器最大允许起飞重量(MTOW)将航空器分为三类,分别为重型(H)、中型(M)、轻型(L),如表 1 所示。从表中可以知道,此分类标准相对较为粗略,仅考虑了航空器重量,而重量是影响航空器所产生尾流强弱的因素之一。

ICAO 尾流分类标准　　表 1

尾流类型	分类依据
重型(H)	MTOW≥136000kg
中型(M)	7000kg < MTOW < 136000kg
轻型(L)	MTOW≤7000kg

经国外研究者分析和验证,得到 ICAO 标准下不同类型航空器组合间隔标准,如表 2 所示。

ICAO 尾流间隔标准　　表 2

前机	后机		
	重型(H)	中型(M)	轻型(L)
重型(H)	8km	10km	12km
中型(M)	MRS	MRS	10km
轻型(L)	MRS	MRS	MRS

注:MRS 表示前后航空器满足最小雷达间隔,为 5km。

从表 2 中可以知道,该分类标准下,不同航空器组合下间隔较大,重型和重型之间间隔至少为 8km,间隔过于保守,空域利用率较低,跑道起降容量受限,因此有进一步细化的空间。

2.2　欧控尾流分类及尾流间隔标准

从 2007 年发展至现阶段,欧控在考虑最大允许起飞重量(MTOW)的基础上,进一步结合其他影响尾流的因素,主要为航空器翼展(WS),提出来了相应的航空器尾流标准 RECAT-EU。该标准中将航空器分为 A ~ F 六类,如表 3 所示,该分类标准相较于国际民航组织标准更加细化。

RECAT-EU 尾流分类标准　　表 3

尾流类型	分类依据	
A	MTOW > 100t	72m < WS < 80m
B		60m < WS < 72m
*		WS > 52m
C		WS < 52m
D	MTOW < 100t	WS > 32m
E		WS < 32m
F	MTOW < 15t	—

注:* 表示对相应 MTOW、WS 范围内的机型进行分析,再将其划分至 B 类或者 C 类。

在 RECAT-EU 分类标准下,前后航空器之前的尾流间隔标准有所变化,具体满足表 4 要求。

RECAT-EU 尾流间隔标准　　表 4

前机	后机					
	A	B	C	D	E	F
A	3nm	4nm	5nm	5nm	6nm	8nm
B	MRS	3nm	4nm	4nm	5nm	7nm
C	MRS	MRS	3nm	3nm	4nm	6nm
D	MRS	MRS	MRS	MRS	MRS	5nm
E	MRS	MRS	MRS	MRS	MRS	4nm
F	MRS	MRS	MRS	MRS	MRS	3nm

注:MRS 表示前后航空器满足最小雷达间隔,为 2.5nm。

从表3可知,该尾流间隔标准下,由于航空器分类过程中考虑到了航空器机身翼展,不同航空器机型作了更加详细的区分,从表4中可以知道,对应地,不同航空器组合下间距也作了更加细致的分类。可利用的间隔从只有8km、10km、12km三种,优化到了3nm、4nm、5nm、6nm、7nm、8nm六种,当前后航空器均为A类时,由ICAO标准下的8km缩减到了3nm。而当前方航空器为A类,后随航空器为B类、C类、D类时,其尾流间隔均小于ICAO标准下前方航空器为重型,后随航空器为中型情形下的间隔。可见,RECAT-EU分类标准在很大程度上优化了尾流间隔。

2.3 FAA尾流分类及尾流间隔标准

FAA对不同机型进行分类时,考虑的因素基本与欧控一致,主要依据航空器的最大允许起飞重量及航空器翼展尺寸,有所区别的是,在分类中欧控采用的是公制单位,而FAA采用的则是英制单位。在发展探索过程中,先后提出了RECAT1和RECAT1.5,RECAT1.5在RECAT1的基本框架下做了一定的调整。类似地,RECAT1.5中将航空器分为A~F六类,见表5。

RECAT1.5尾流分类标准 表5

尾流类型		分类依据
A	MTOW≥300klb	WS>245ft
B		175ft<WS≤245ft
C	MTOW<300klb	125ft<WS≤175ft
D		90ft<WS≤125ft
E	MTOW>41klb	60ft<WS≤90ft
F	MTOW≤41klb	WS≤125ft
	MTOW<15.5klb	—

相应地,在RECAT1.5分类标准下,前后航空器尾流间隔标准如表6所示。

RECAT1.5尾流间隔标准 表6

前机	后机					
	A	B	C	D	E	F
A	MRS	5nm	6nm	7nm	7nm	8nm
B	MRS	3nm	4nm	5nm	5nm	7nm
C	MRS	MRS	MRS	3.5nm	3.5nm	6nm
D	MRS	MRS	MRS	MRS	MRS	4nm
E	MRS	MRS	MRS	MRS	MRS	MRS
F	MRS	MRS	MRS	MRS	MRS	MRS

注:MRS表示前后航空器满足最小雷达间隔,为2.5nm。斜体数字表示同一组合下尾流间隔较RECAT-EU标准更大。加粗部分表示同一组合下尾流间隔较RECAT-EU标准更小。

由表5和表6可知,同样地,RECAT1.5标准较ICAO标准在分类上更加细化,能更有效利用空域,改善容量。RECAT1.5标准可利用的间隔有3nm、3.5nm、4nm、5nm、6nm、7nm、8nm七种,而RECAT-EU标准只有六种,因此在间隔管理上更加严格,在表中对角线附近,RECAT1.5较RECAT-EU标准数值更小,可见RECAT1.5标准对于同一类型的前后航空器更为适用,在RECAT1.5标准下两航空器之间的间隔更小,间隔利用上更加优化。对于不同类型的前后航空器组合,RECAT1.5尾流间隔大于RECAT-EU标准。因此,两种RECAT标准各有其适用范围,而这取决于空域内运行航空器类型情况。

2.4 RECAT-CN尾流分类及尾流间隔标准

2019年开始,国内研究者结合我国机型分布及公英制运用实际,在主要考虑航空器最大允许起飞重量(MTOW)和翼展(WS)等因素下,提出了RECAT-CN标准[19],如表7所示,RECAT-CN对比原ICAO标准,分类更加细化,该标准中将航空器分为五类,分别为超级重型(J)、重型(B)、一般重型(C)、中型(M)、轻型(L),该尾流分类标准目前处于试运行阶段,在广州白云机场、深圳宝安机场等取得了很好的效果,有效提升机场起落容量。

RECAT-CN尾流分类标准 表7

尾流类型	分类依据	
超重型(J)	MTOW≥136000kg	WS≥75m
重型(B)		54m<WS<75m
一般重型(C)		WS≤54m
中型(M)	7000kg<MTOW<136000kg	WS≤54m
轻型(L)	MTOW≤7000kg	

在RECAT-CN试运行标准下,前后航空器尾流间隔标准如表8所示。

RECAT-CN尾流间隔标准 表8

前机	后机				
	J	B	C	M	L
J	5.6km	9.3km	11.1km	13.0km	14.8km
B	MRS	5.6km	7.4km	9.3km	13.0km
C	MRS	MRS	5.6km	6.5km	11.1km
M	MRS	MRS	MRS	MRS	9.3km
L	MRS	MRS	MRS	MRS	5.6km

注:MRS表示前后航空器满足最小雷达间隔,为5km。

从表7和表8中可知,通过吸收了FAA和欧控尾流重新分类标准考量因素,RECAT-CN试运行标准较我国目前主要采用的ICAO分类标准,分类更加科学严格,将尾流间隔进一步细化为5.6km、6.5km、7.4km、9.3km、11.1km、13.0km、14.8km七类。当前机为J类,除了后机组合为M类或L类,两机之间的间隔将大于ICAO分类标准下的间隔,其他与前机J类组合都有一定的优化,分别优化了6.66%(J-J组合)、7%(J-B组合)、7.5%(J-C组合),其他前后机组合类似。

3 尾流间隔模型的建立

在运行过程中,前后航空器既要克服尾流影响,又要满足相应间隔标准要求。不同前后航空器组合存在某一概率,该概率大小取决于某机场运行航空器机型分布情况。同时,当两航空器以一定的组合进场着落时,不同的尾流间隔标准下航空器会有对应的分类类型,从而获得各自尾流间隔标准值。通过计算,进一步可以得到不同航空器组合下平均尾流间隔 S_{mn},其计算方式见下:

$$S_{mn} = \sum_{m}^{h}\sum_{n}^{h}\sigma_{mn}p_{mn}$$

克服尾流影响的安全间隔距离 x 为:

$$x = \frac{\gamma}{24}\frac{W_m E_n E_n l_n}{W_n E_m E_a l_a}\frac{l_n c_{rm} U_n}{K}$$

而克服尾流影响的平均尾流间隔 S 应为:

$$S = \max[S_{mn} \quad x]$$

平均尾流间隔大小反映机场跑道起降容量 λ 为:

$$\lambda = \frac{1}{S}$$

式中:σ_{mn}——在尾流分类标准前机为 m;

后机为 n 组合下航空器尾流间隔值;

p_{mn}——前机为 m,后机为 n 组合下的概率;

h——尾流分类标准下航空器种类;

γ——机翼外形无量纲系数;

W——航空器重量;

E_m——前机机翼面积;

E_a——后机副翼面积;

l_a——后机副翼力臂;

l——翼展;

c_r——翼根弦长;

U——真空速;

K——飞行安全阈值。

由上式可知,当 S 取值较小时,表示所有航空器运行组合下平均尾流间隔较小,机场可利用起落时隙较多,可容纳航空器起降数量更多,机场采用该类尾流间隔标准更为合适。

4 机场跑道容量分析计算

现对某机场连续10天内着落航空器机型分布情况进行统计分析,见表9,得出不同尾流分类标准下各机型种类数量情况。

某机场连续10天着落航空器机型分布情况 表9

机 型	ICAO	RECAT-EU	RECAT1.5	RECAT-CN	着落航班量
A319	M	D	D	M	93
A320	M	D	D	M	967
A320NEO	M	D	D	M	123
A321	M	D	D	M	388
A321NEO	M	D	D	M	12
A325	M	D	D	M	2
A332	H	B	B	B	35
A333	H	B	B	B	60
A343	H	B	B	B	3
ARJ21-700	M	E	E	M	9
B733	M	E	D	M	11
B734	M	E	D	M	6
B737	M	D	D	M	66
B738	M	D	D	M	1336

续上表

机　型	ICAO	RECAT-EU	RECAT1.5	RECAT-CN	着落航班量
B739	M	D	D	M	44
B744	H	B	B	B	4
B747	H	B	B	B	7
B752	M	C	D	M	18
B773	H	B	B	B	14
B773ER	H	B	B	B	2
B787	H	B	B	B	5
B788	H	B	B	B	13
B789	H	B	B	B	13
C525	L	F	F	L	3
C560	L	F	F	L	2
CL604	M	E	E	M	3
CRJ9	M	E	E	M	7
E190	M	E	D	M	86
E195	M	D	D	M	8
EMB505D	M	F	F	M	2
FA7X	M	E	E	M	2
G450	M	E	E	M	1
G550	M	E	E	M	2
G650	M	E	E	M	1
G650ER	M	E	E	M	5
GL5T	M	E	E	M	2
GLF4	M	E	E	M	1
MA60	M	E	E	M	31
TU204	M	C	D	M	2
Y12	L	F	F	L	2

根据机型数量占比情况进行不同航空器之间配对组合得到相应概率密度分布，即 p_{mn} 值，不同尾流分类标准下，各尾流类型占比及其概率密度分布如表10～表13所示。

ICAO 标准下尾流类型占比及概率密度分布情况 表10

前　机	后　机			
	重型(H)	中型(M)	轻型(L)	机型占比
重型(H)	0.00212	0.04379	9.49658E-05	4.6%
中型(M)	0.04379	0.90617	0.00197	95.193%
轻型(L)	9.49658E-05	0.00197	4.26128E-06	0.207%

RECAT-EU 标准下尾流类型占比及概率密度分布情况 表11

前　机	后　机					
	B	C	D	E	F	机型占比
B	0.00212	0.00027	0.04123	0.00227	0.00012	4.6%
C	0.00027	0.00003	0.00529	0.00029	0.00002	0.59%

续上表

前　机	后　机					
	B	C	D	E	F	机型占比
D	0.04123	0.00529	0.80317	0.04414	0.00237	89.62%
E	0.00227	0.00029	0.04414	0.00243	0.00013	4.925%
F	0.00012	0.00002	0.00237	0.00013	7.0225E-06	0.265%

RECAT1.5 标准下尾流类型占比及概率密度分布情况　表12

前　机	后　机				
	B	D	E	F	机型占比
B	0.00212	0.04289	0.00087	0.00012	4.6%
D	0.04289	0.86950	0.01760	0.00248	93.247%
E	0.00087	0.01760	0.00036	5.01942×10^{-5}	1.887%
F	0.00012	0.00248	5.01942×10^{-5}	7.0756×10^{-6}	0.266%

RECAT-CN 标准下尾流类型占比及概率密度分布情况　表13

前　机	后　机			
	B	M	L	机型占比
B	0.00212	0.04379	0.00010	4.6%
M	0.04379	0.90617	0.00197	95.193%
L	0.00010	0.00197	4.2849×10^{-6}	0.207%

进一步结合对应标准下尾流间隔标准,计算航空器平均尾流间隔 S,通过对比现有 ICAO 标准,从而得到其他尾流标准下跑道着落容量变化情况,如表14所示。

不同尾流标准下平均尾流间隔及跑道着落容量变化情况　表14

尾流分类标准	ICAO	RECAT-EU	RECAT 1.5	RECAT-CN
平均尾流间隔 S(m)	5235.80	4775.97	4842.49	5198.80
容量提升情况	0	+8.782%	+7.512%	+0.707%

从表14可知,对于某机场现有机型分布,在实施现有ICAO尾流标准充分利用和发挥好间隔资源的前提下,能将平均尾流间隔 S 有效缩减至5235.80 m。而我国结合全国实际最新提出并试行的RECAT-CN标准,对于某机场的容量虽然也有一定提升作用,但效果并不是很明显,仅在现有标准上提升0.707%。而对于某机场来说,对容量提升效果最佳的是RECAT-EU尾流标准,对比现有标准,RECAT-EU尾流标准将提升容量8.782%。

由于采用RECAT-EU尾流标准对某机场容量提升最明显,因此在使用RECAT-EU尾流标准下,进一步改变机场机型分布情况,通过增加不同尾流类型航班数量,分析研究改变某一尾流类型航班数量对跑道着落容量提升的作用,结果如图2、图3所示。

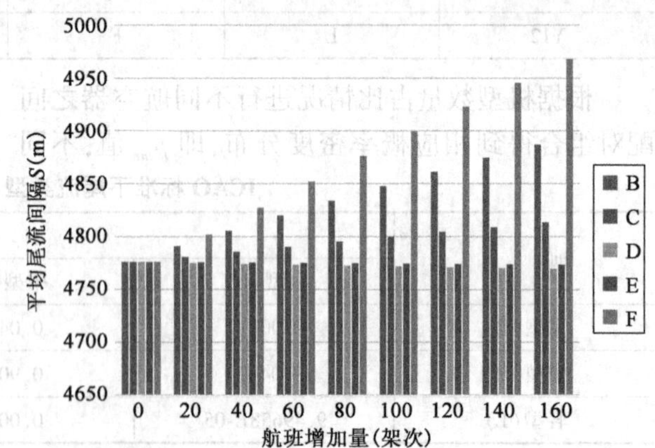

图2　改变航班数量对平均尾流间隔影响情况

由图2、图3可知,当增加不同尾流类型航班数量对容量提升的效果不同。在RECAT-EU标准下,当增加B类、C类、F类航班数量时,虽较现有ICAO标准下,平均尾流间隔 S 有明显减少,跑道着落容量有较大幅度提升,但是随着航班数量的增多,平均尾流间隔 S 不断增大,容量提升率不断减小,其中F类航空器平均尾流间隔增长最明显,容量提升率减小幅度最大,为对容量影响最敏感机型,其次是B类尾流航空器,再次是C类。当增加D类、E类航班数量时,平均尾流间隔 S 变化不明显,略有减小,跑道着落容量随着航班数量的增多,容量提升率还将增大,但增幅较小。因此,对于某机场来说可以适当增加D类、E类航空器数量占比,进一步较大幅度提升跑道着落容量。

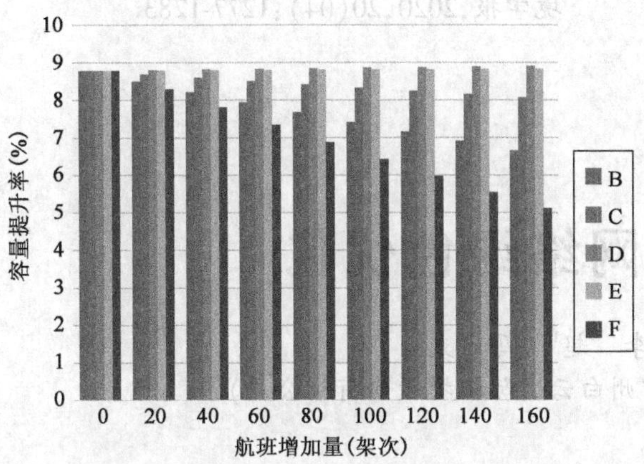

图3 改变航班数量对跑道着落容量影响情况

5 小结

分析了尾流对前后航空器运行安全影响以及空间资源利用影响,总结了目前几种主要尾流分类标准,建立了跑道容量模型,通过分析某机场机型分布情况及不同尾流标准对其跑道着落容量的影响情况,得出了以下结论:

(1)现行尾流分类标准相对来说较为保守,更多的是考虑了运行的安全,相对其他尾流重新分类标准,在效率提升上有很大优化空间,能进一步改善跑道着落容量。

(2)不同尾流分类标准适用于机场不同航班机型构成,对着落容量的影响不同,因此,采用适宜的标准既能有效保障运行安全,又能充分利用间隔资源,实现提升容量最佳效果。

(3)调整不同尾流类型航空器相同数量,对平均尾流间隔以及整体容量所起的效果不同,因此,可以通过调整敏感尾流类型航空器来实现空域容量或机场跑道着落容量的优化。

新的尾流分类标准的实施和推广应用对整个空管系统来说无疑是个巨大挑战,包括需要对一些系统进行配套升级以及对一些人员进行资质培训,更需要民航局、空管部门、机场、航空公司等有关单位协同合作,下一步将持续关注试运行效果,并分析研究相关技术问题,助推新技术安全高效运用。

参考文献

[1] 徐肖豪,赵鸿盛,王振宇. 尾流间隔缩减技术综述[J]. 航空学报,2010 ,31(4):655-662.

[2] 胡军. 空中交通中的尾流安全间隔研究[D]. 南京:南京航空航天大学,2001.

[3] ICAO. Working Document For The Aviation System Block Upgrades[Z]. 28 March 2013.

[4] ADAMSON P, PHYTHIAN D. European Wake Tur-bulence Categorisation and Separation Minima on Approach and Departure [Z]. RUROCONTROL,2015.

[5] MATAYOSHI N. Reduced Wake Vortex Separation Using Weather Information [M]. Matayoshi N. eds. Lecture Notes in Electrical Engineering, Air Traffic. Management and Systems. Tokyo: Springer Japan,2014: 49-68.

[6] HENRY J, VEIGH M. Recategorization (RECAT) of FAA Wake Turbulence Separation Categories at Memphis International Airports (MEM) [R]. W ashington DC: Federal Aviation Administration, 2013.

[7] SORIA L, PEETERS B, ANTHONISJ, et al. Operational Modal Analysis and the Performance Assessment of Vehicle Suspension Systems[J]. Shock &. Vibration, 2015, 19 (5): 1099-1113.

[8] LISA W, CLARK R L, JEFFREY A, et al. Development of Approach and Departure Aircraft Speed Profiles[J]. Journal of Aircraft, 2016, 54(1): 1-10.

[9] HEIMLICH J. Joint Analysis Team: Wake ReCat in IND/PHL &. Fuel Analysis in North Texas [Z]. Next Gen Advisory Committee, 2017.

[10] LANG S, LUNSFORD C. RECAT I: Lessons Learned from MEM[Z]. FAA,2013.

[11] BORENER S S, GUZHVA V S, CROOK I, et al. Safety Assessment of Implemented Next

Gen Operational Improvements [J]. Transportation Research Procedia, 2016, 14: 3731-3740.

[12] 聂润兔,李冰冰. 尾流分类新标准(RECAT)对跑道容量影响分析[J]. 航空计算技术, 2015,45(4):4-7.

[13] 魏志强,牟明江,李志远. RECAT 间隔标准的差异性对比与计算分析[J]. 航空计算技术,2017,47(4):6-9.

[14] 李芳芳. 民航空管推动 RECAT 等新技术应用[N]. 中国民航报,2018-06-07 (001).

[15] 谷润平,吴俊,卢飞. 近距平行跑道配对进近程序及其碰撞风险研究[J]. 河南科技大学学报(自然科学版),2019,40(01):37-41.

[16] 魏志强,李志远,刘薇. 侧风影响下的飞机尾流强度消散与涡核运动[J]. 空军工程大学学报:自然科学版,2017,18(6):27-33.

[17] 何昕,侯宇杰,陈亚青,等. 基于侧风影响的 CSPRs 起飞尾流间隔优化[J]. 安全与环境学报,2019,19(02):411-418.

[18] 赵宁宁,陈越,李晓晨,等. 航空器尾流重新分类标准的安全性评估方法[J]. 安全与环境学报,2020,20(04):1277-1283.

非严格枢纽航线网络绿色优化

刘　璐[1]　田　勇[*1]　李　超[1]　马　克[2]

(1. 南京航空航天大学民航学院;2. 广州白云国际机场股份有限公司)

摘　要　枢纽航线网络的设计主要关注经济性和环保性,为了减少运营成本,减轻航空排放的环境影响,提出了一种多目标枢纽航线网络绿色优化模型。该模型基于非严格枢纽航线网络结构,以二氧化碳排放量、有害气体排放量和运输成本最小为目标,采用二维实数编码方式,设计了带精英策略的非支配排序遗传算法(NSGA-Ⅱ)。实验结果表明,通过调整运输成本的宽容值,可以达到在提高 3.9% 的枢纽航线网络运输成本的情况下,降低 17.6% 的 CO_2 排放量,同时降低 18.2% 的有害气体排放量的优化结果,实现经济成本与环境成本较好的平衡。

关键词　航空运输　非严格枢纽网络设计　多目标绿色优化　污染物排放

0　引言

在公众绿色环保意识日益增强的今天,航空排放问题已经引起了人们的观注,成为重大的国际民航问题。目前对于航线网络的研究多集中在提高航线网络的经济效益方面,缺少对环境效益的考虑,因此考虑降低环境影响的航线网络优化研究,是当下研究的新方向。

国内外在该方向上已经有了一定的研究基础。文献[1]构建了多目标枢纽选址模型,其中第一个目标是最小化总运输成本,而第二个目标是最小化两站路线的总运输成本,同时提出了一个双目标变量邻域搜索启发式算法,并验证了模型和算法的有效性。文献[2]在优化客流总成本的同时,建立枢纽和环境目标,结果表明,与经典的枢纽选址问题模型相比,新措施可以有效地降低原预计累计二氧化碳排放量的 8% ~10%。文献[3]研究市场补贴对航空公司枢纽选址和航线选择的影响,建立了双层联合规划模型,最后通过实例分析详细的介绍了市场补贴对 HS 航线网络设计的影响。文献[4]针对枢纽拥堵问题的非严格枢纽航线网络模型,在枢纽机场拥堵成本过高时选择直航来缓解拥堵、降低运行成本,最后利用同时具有突跳性和快速寻优特点的模拟退火粒子群算法进行了求解。在模型求解方面,现有求解方法多数是基于严格的枢纽航线网络而改进启发式方法[5-8]。不能解决非严格的枢纽航线网络结构带来的变量结构复杂和解空间规模大的问题。

上述研究中,国内外学者在枢纽航线网络的优化过程中有着较为全面的研究,缺少对枢纽航线网络的航空排放研究；在枢纽航线网络结构优化方面，相关研究主要基于严格的枢纽航线网络结构进行建模优化，没有考虑直航情况。

本研究在“绿色航空”以及枢纽航线网络的概念基础上，提出航线网络的污染物排放量计算模型，结合已有的枢纽航线网络模型，以降低航线网络运输成本和二氧化碳、有害气体排放量为目标，构建非严格枢纽航线网络绿色优化模型，并利用NSGA-Ⅱ算法进行求解。以我国15个城市为例，对比三种不同结构的航线网络在成本和污染物排放方面的表现差异，并得到非严格枢纽航线网络绿色优化方案。

1 问题描述

全连通航线网络是指每个城市对之间全都采用直接相连接的方式，形成全部互连的航线网络；枢纽航线网络是指城市对之间可以通过枢纽城市转运而形成互连，按照是否允许直航，枢纽航线网络的结构可以分为严格和非严格。

严格枢纽航线网络指的是非枢纽城市间只能通过枢纽转运的方式形成连接，不允许直航；非严格枢纽航线网络则指的是允许非枢纽城市间枢纽转运和直航两种连接方式共存。图1分别给出了严格和非严格枢纽航线网络的示意图。

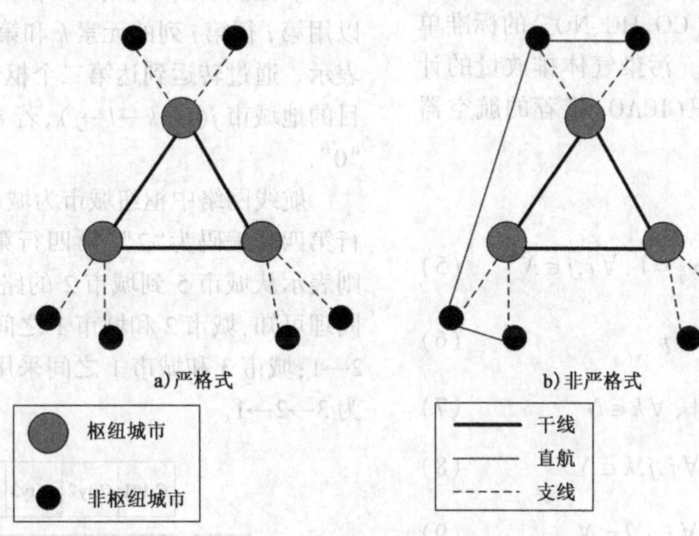

图1 严格和非严格枢纽航线网络

本文采用非严格枢纽航线网络，假设枢纽城市之间完全相互连接，非枢纽城市之间可以经过枢纽城市进行转运，也可以直接连接；一个非枢纽城市可以和多个枢纽城市相连接；城市对之间客流需求稳定；机场和航线没有容量的限制；旅客中转次数不能大于2次。

2 模型构建

2.1 优化模型

非严格枢纽航线网络绿色优化模型以航线网络的总成本 TotalCost，二氧化碳的排放量 $\mathrm{TotalCO_2}$，有害气体排放量 TotalHarmfulGas 最低为目标函数。

$$\mathrm{Min}\quad\{\mathrm{TotalCost},\mathrm{TotalCO_2},\mathrm{TotalHarmfulGas}\}\tag{1}$$

$$\mathrm{TotalCost}=\sum_{i\in N}\sum_{j\in N}\sum_{k\in N}\sum_{l\in N}w_{ij}C_{ijkl}x_{ijkl}+\sum_{i\in N}\sum_{j\in N}\sum_{k\in N}w_{ij}C_{ijk}x_{ijk}+\sum_{i\in N}\sum_{j\in N}w_{ij}c_{ij}x_{ij}\tag{2}$$

$$\begin{aligned}\mathrm{TotalCO_2}=&\sum_{i\in N}\sum_{j\in N}\sum_{k\in N}\sum_{l\in N}w_{ij}(c_{ik}^{co_2}+c_{kl}^{co_2}+c_{lj}^{co_2})x_{ijkl}+\sum_{i\in N}\sum_{j\in N}\sum_{k\in N}w_{ij}(c_{ik}^{co_2}+c_{kj}^{co_2})x_{ijk}\\&+\sum_{i\in N}\sum_{j\in N}w_{ij}c_{ij}^{co}x_{ij}\end{aligned}\tag{3}$$

$$\begin{aligned}\mathrm{TotalHarmfulGas}=&\sum_{i\in N}\sum_{j\in N}\sum_{k\in N}\sum_{l\in N}w_{ij}(c_{ik}^{hg}+c_{kl}^{hg}+c_{lj}^{hg})x_{ijkl}\\&+\sum_{i\in N}\sum_{j\in N}\sum_{k\in N}w_{ij}(c_{ik}^{hg}+c_{kj}^{hg})x_{ijk}+\sum_{i\in N}\sum_{j\in N}w_{ij}c_{ij}^{hg}x_{ij}\end{aligned}\tag{4}$$

式(2)为枢纽航线网络的总成本，等式右边第一项和第二项为枢纽转运航线运营成本，w_{ij}表示

从城市 i 到达城市 j 之间的客流量；C_{ijkl} 表示从城市 i 出发经过枢纽城市 k 和 l 转运到达城市 j 的单位运输成本；x_{ijkl} 表示从城市 i 出发经过枢纽城市 k 和 l 转运到达城市 j 的客流占 w_{ij} 的比例；C_{ijk} 表示从城市 i 出发经过枢纽城市 k 转运到达城市 j 的单位运输成本；x_{ijk} 表示从城市 i 出发经过枢纽城市 k 转运到达城市 j 的客流占 w_{ij} 的比例；第三项为直航航线运营成本，c_{ij} 表示从城市 i 到达城市 j 的标准单位运输成本；x_{ij} 表示从城市 i 到达城市 j 的直航客流占 w_{ij} 的比例。

c_{ij}^{co2} 表示从城市 i 到达城市 j 过程中 CO_2 的标准单位排放量，其他符号同理。c_{ij}^{hg} 表示从城市 i 到达城市 j 过程中有害气体（CO、HC、NO_x）的标准单位排放量，其他符号同理。污染气体排放量的计算方法参照国际民航组织（ICAO）推荐的航空器污染物排放计算模型[9]。

2.2 约束条件

$$\sum_{k\in N}\sum_{l\in N}x_{ijkl}+x_{ijk}+x_{ij}=1,\ \forall i,j\in N \tag{5}$$

$$\sum_{k\in N}H_k=p \tag{6}$$

$$H_k\in(\{0,1\},\ \forall k\in N \tag{7}$$

$$\sum_{l\in N}x_{ijkl}\leqslant H_k,\ \forall i,j,k\in N \tag{8}$$

$$\sum_{k\in N}x_{ijkl}\leqslant H_l,\ \forall i,j,l\in N \tag{9}$$

$$x_{ijkl}\geqslant 0,\ \forall i,j,k,l\in N \tag{10}$$

$$x_{ijk}\geqslant 0,\ \forall i,j,k\in N \tag{11}$$

$$x_{ij}\geqslant 0,\ \forall i,j\in N \tag{12}$$

式(5)表示任意两个城市之间经过两次枢纽城市转运和一次枢纽城市转运的客流占比和直航的客流占比之和为1；H_k 为逻辑变量，若 k 为枢纽城市，则 $H_k=1$，反之 $H_k=0$；式(8)表示转运城市 k 必须为枢纽城市，否则转运客流量为0。式(9)表示转运城市 l 必须为枢纽城市，否则转运客流量为0；式(10)、式(11)、式(12)为客流比例的非负约束。

3 算法设计

面对大型枢纽航线网络存在解空间规模较大，且容易陷入局部最优解的问题，模型中有三个目标函数，采用 NSGA-Ⅱ算法作为多目标算法框架，为帕累托解集的求取提供可能，且算法可降低时间复杂度，实现同一级个体间的快速排序。将算法根据功能的不同分为多个模块，分别进行具体的设计工作，最后，利用模块化的算子具体演示整个算法的实现过程。

3.1 编码方式

将城市编号，形成城市集 $N=\{1,2,3,\cdots,n\}$，用二维数组的形式同时表示枢纽城市和分配方式。每个城市对之间都有两个编码位置，对应两个转运枢纽城市，若采用单枢纽城市转运，则两个位置编码相同，若采用直航，则两个位置都编码为“-1”。如图2所示，城市 i 和城市 j 之间的路线可以用第 i 行第 j 列的元素 k 和第 j 行第 i 列的元素 l 表示。通过转运到达第二个枢纽城市 l，最后到达目的地城市 $j(i\to k\to l\to j)$，若 $i=j$，则对应编码为“0”。

航线网络中枢纽城市为城市2和城市3；第五行第四列编码为“2”，第四行第五列编码为“3”，则表示从城市5到城市2的路线为5→2→3→4；同理可知，城市2和城市1之间采用直航，路线为2→1；城市3和城市1之间采用单枢纽转运，路线为3→2→1。

	City1	City2	City3	City4	City5
City1	0	-1	2	3	-1
City2	-1	0	-1	-1	-1
City3	2	-1	0	-1	-1
City4	2	-1	-1	0	3
City5	-1	-1	-1	2	0

图2 航线方案的编码示意图

3.2 航线方案初始化

初始化算法如下：

Step 1：输入待选枢纽城市集 HUB，种群数 N，枢纽数目 p，个体编号 $d=1$。

Step 2：选取 p 个枢纽城市组成集合 hub，对第 d 个个体 I_d 进行初始化。

Step 3：从个体 I_d 中选取城市对 i 和 j。

Step 4：从 hub 中选取分别距离城市对 i 和 j 最近的枢纽城市 k 和 l。

Step 5:比较运输成本,选取转运($i \to k \to l \to j$)和直航($i \to j$)方案中成本低者。

Step 6:重复 Step 3 ~ Step 5,直到 I_d 中所有城市对之间均有运输方案,$d++$。

Step 7:重复 Step 3 ~ Step 5,直到 $d > N$。

3.3 算法整体实现过程

对初始化的航线方案依次进行基因重组、基因突变、非支配快速排序和精英策略选择,实现整体的多目标遗传算法,算法流程示图3。

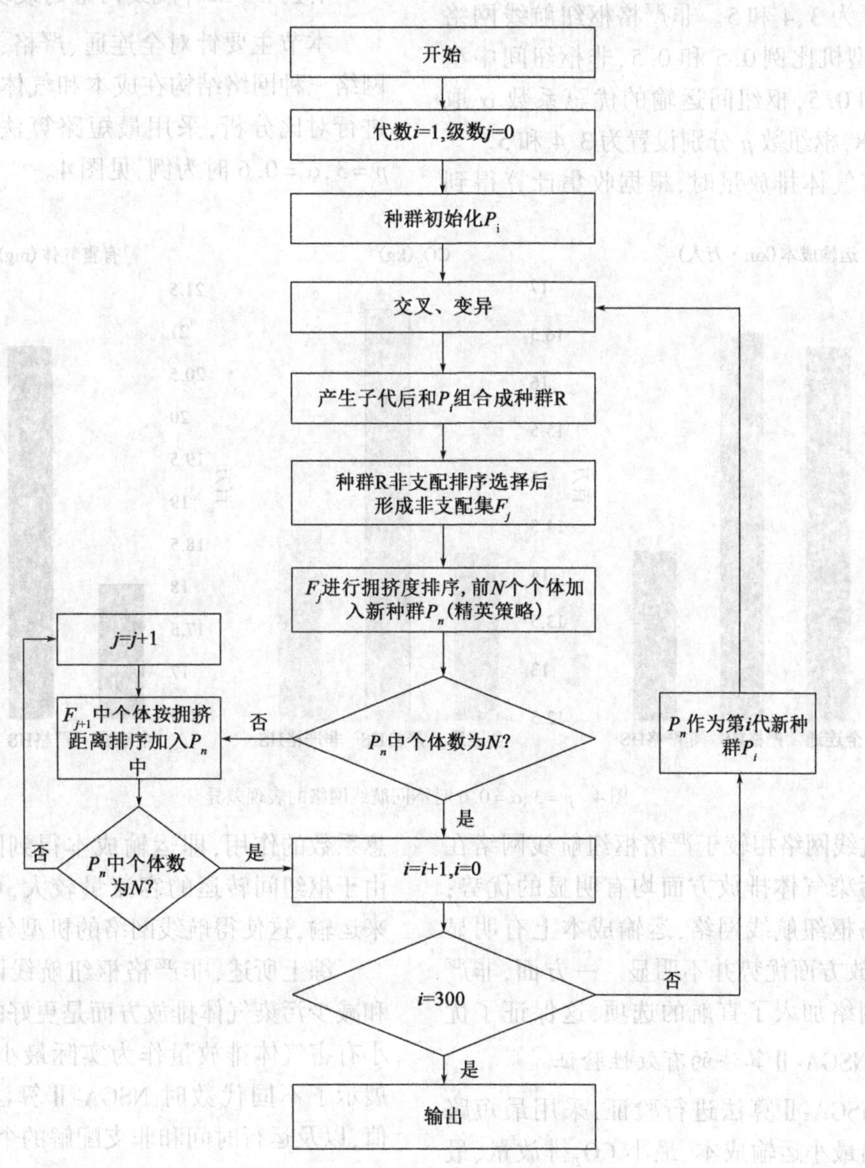

图3 NSGA-Ⅱ算法流程图

4 实验结果与分析

4.1 实验数据和参数设置

本文选取北京、广州、成都、昆明、西安、上海、郑州、青岛、乌鲁木齐、沈阳、武汉、杭州、长沙、兰州、哈尔滨等 15 个城市构建航线网络,按顺序编号为 1 ~ 15。利用城市距离与客运总量的乘积表征运输成本。通过 Flightaware 查询这 15 个城市间的航班信息和飞行剖面,每个城市对分别取 A300、A320、A330 和 B737 四种机型各一次航班飞行任务数据。从 BADA 数据库中获得各机型燃油流率随高度变化的相应数值,计算燃油消耗和污染物排放量。算法由 Python 编写,运行硬件环境为 Intel(R) Core(TM) i5-8250U、1.60GHz主频、8GB 内存的计算机。

计算整个航线网络污染物排放量时,全连通

航线网络的重型机(A300 和 A330)比例为 0.25 和 0.25;中型机(A320 和 B737)比例为 0.25 和 0.25。严格枢纽航线网络中,枢纽间重型机比例为 0.5 和 0.5;非枢纽间中型机比例为 0.5 和 0.5。枢纽间运输的优惠系数 α 取 0.4、0.6 和 0.8,枢纽数 p 分别设置为 3、4 和 5。非严格枢纽航线网络中,枢纽间重型机比例 0.5 和 0.5,非枢纽间中型机比例 0.5 和 0.5,枢纽间运输的优惠系数 α 取 0.4、0.6 和 0.8,枢纽数 p 分别设置为 3、4 和 5。

计算有害气体排放量时,根据收集计算得到的排放数据,为统一三者的数量级,将 NO_x 的权重系数取 0.2,CO 的权重系数取为 0.7、HC 的权重系数取为 0.1。

4.2　实验结果分析

4.2.1　三种航线网络的表现差异

本节主要针对全连通、严格、非严格枢纽航线网络三种网络结构在成本和气体排放方面的表现进行对比分析,采用最短路算法,以参数设置为 $p=3,\alpha=0.6$ 时为例,见图 4。

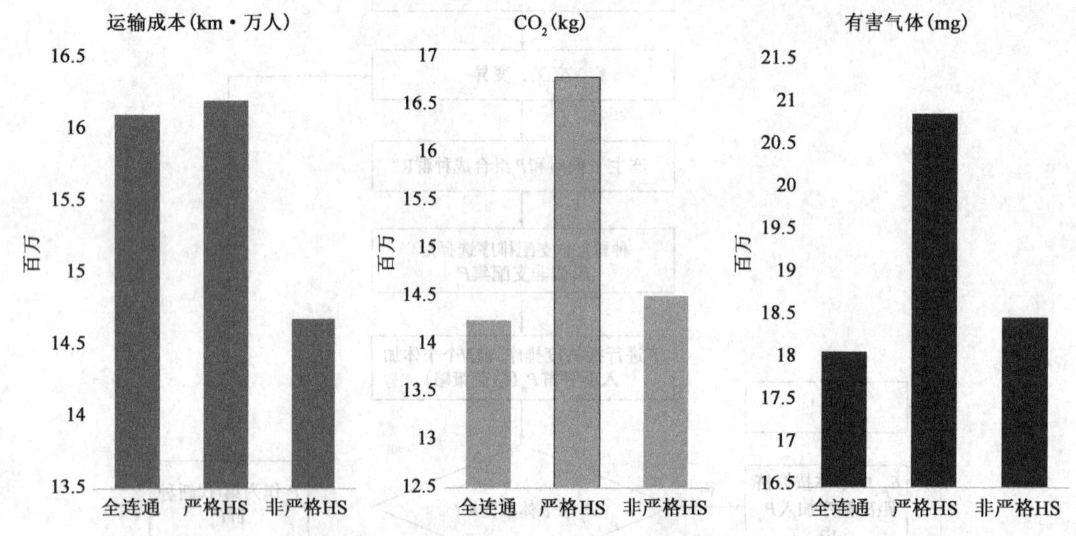

图 4　$p=3$、$\alpha=0.6$ 时不同航线网络的表现差异

全连通航线网络相较于严格枢纽航线网络在运输成本和污染气体排放方面均有明显的优势;相较于非严格枢纽航线网络,运输成本上有明显劣势,气体排放方面优势并不明显。一方面,非严格枢纽航线网络加入了直航的选项,这保证了优惠系数的作用,即运输成本得到降低,另一方面,由于枢纽间转运的客流量较大,可以采用重型机来运输,这使得航线网络的机型分配更加合理。

综上所述,非严格枢纽航线网络在降低成本和减少污染气体排放方面是更好的选择。

4.2.2　NSGA-Ⅱ算法的有效性验证

为了对 NSGA-Ⅱ算法进行验证,采用最短路算法分别求出最小运输成本、最小 CO_2 排放量、最小有害气体排放量作为实际最小值参考,表 1 中展示了不同代数时 NSGA-Ⅱ算法求解出的最小值,以及运行时间和非支配解的个数。

NSGA-Ⅱ算法运行结果　　表 1

项　目	实际最小值	100 代	200 代	300 代	400 代	500 代
最小 Cost(km·万人)	14673857	15056033	15057772	15052532	15096345	15129863
最小 CO_2 排放量(kg)	1155944	1180422	1182100	1194154	1182380	1180174
最小有害气体排放量(mg)	1485060	1490878	1499780	1513364	1500584	1497618
运行时间(s)	无	120	232	341	442	569
非支配解数	无	895	1130	1602	1829	2204

由图6可知，NSGA-Ⅱ算法在求解运输成本、CO_2、有害气体排放量的最小值方面可以将误差控制在4%以内，即其得到的非支配解足够靠近帕累托边界；随着迭代次数的增加得到的非支配解个数也在逐渐增加，运行时间均匀增加并在合理的范围之内。将支配解剔除后可以得到帕累托前沿图。

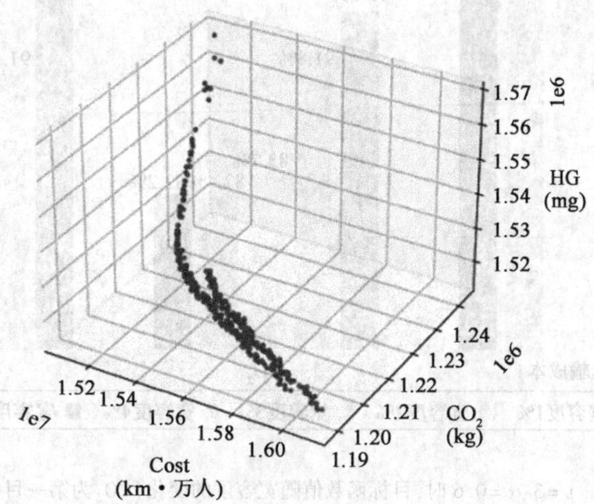

图5 帕累托前沿示意图

4.2.3 非严格枢纽航线网络绿色优化方案

按照4.2.1中的方法可以得到帕累托解集，现从该解集中搜索绿色优化方案。以 $p=3$、$\alpha=0.6$ 为例，从表1中可知，最低运输成本：14673857km · 万人；CO_2 排放量：1448219kg；有害气体排放量：1846698mg；以此为基准量，现在将最低运输成本分别放宽1%、2%、3%、4%、5%，在帕累托解集中寻找最低 CO_2 排放的解，并求出此时运输成本、CO_2 排放量、有害气体排放量占基准量的百分比。

由图5可以看出，在增加0.74%成本的前提下，可以降低3.43%的 CO_2 排放量以及降低2.07%的有害气体排放量。随着宽容度的继续增加，目标函数值的变化跨度由于边际效应而减小。在从4%增加到5%过程中变化非常小，已经接近边际。

由图6可以看出，同样地，在增加0.74%成本的前提下，可以降低3.43%的 CO_2 排放量以及降低2.07%的有害气体排放量。随着宽容度的继续增加，目标函数值的变化跨度由于边际效应而减小。在宽容度增加到5%时两图略有不同。

综上所述，以CO或有害气体为第一目标得到的结果几乎相同，因此从决策者的角度出发，以图6和图7为参考，可以通过增加3.9%的成本来获得17.6%的 CO_2 排放量降低、18.2%的有害气体排放量降低。此时，枢纽城市从原本的{1,2,3}，变为{1,3,7}，城市对之间具体的运输路线见表2。

绿色优化航线方案 表2

优化前	优化后	优化前	优化后	优化前	优化后
1→2	1→7→2	3→6	3→7→6	4→3→1→15	4→3→7→15
1→3	1→7→3	3→1→8	3→7→8	5→8	5→7→8
1→3→4	1→7→3→4	3→1→10	3→7→10	6→9	6→7→9
1→5	1→7→5	3→1→15	3→15	8→9	8→7→9
1→11	1→7→11	4→5	4→3→5	8→13	8→7→13

注：城市编号见4.1节。

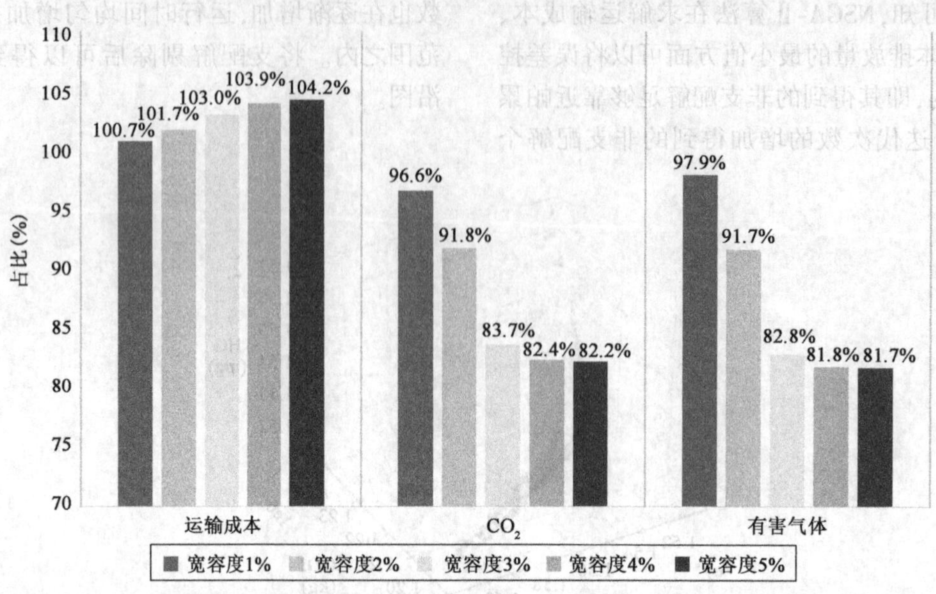

图 6　$p=3$、$\alpha=0.6$ 时,目标函数值随宽容度的变化(CO_2为第一目标)

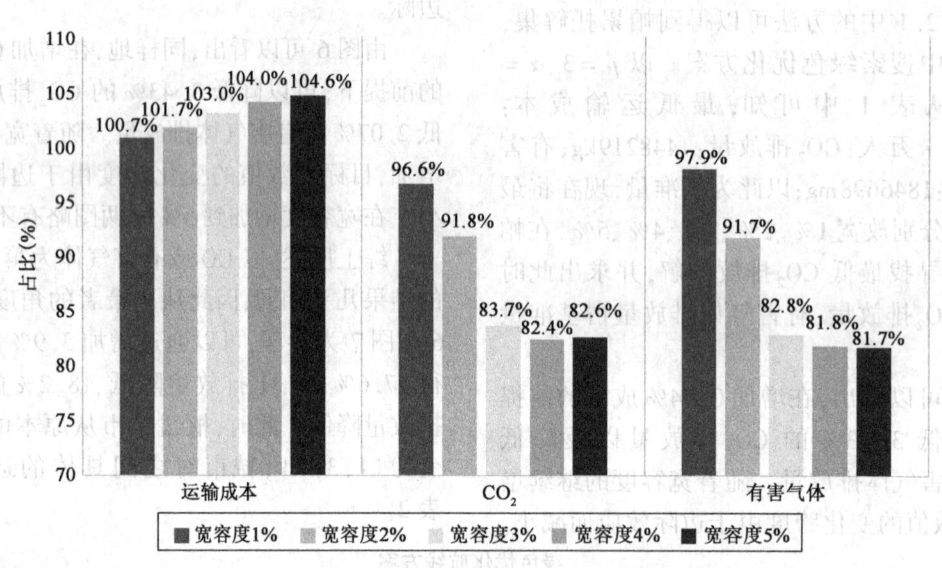

图 7　$p=3$、$\alpha=0.6$ 时,目标函数值随宽容度的变化(有害气体为第一目标)

5　结语

本文基于非严格枢纽航线网络,考虑直航和枢纽转运同时存在的情况,设计枢纽航线网络的绿色优化模型,实现经济成本与环境成本的较好平衡。在模型求解方面,设计了二维实数编码的NSGA-Ⅱ算法并验证了算法的有效性。实验结果表明,相较于全连通和严格枢纽航线网络,非严格枢纽航线网络在降低成本和减少污染气体方面具有优势;以枢纽数 p 为 3,枢纽间运输的优惠系数 α 设置为 0.6 为例,通过调整运输成本的宽容值,可以达到枢纽航线网络运输成本提高 3.9%,降低 17.6% 的 CO_2 排放量、降低 18.2% 有害气体排放量的绿色优化方案。

后续可在枢纽和航线间考虑容量限制,考虑实际中客流量在全年分布的差异,还可加入旅客满意度等优化目标。

参考文献

[1] Parsa M, Nookabadi A S, Flapper S D, et al. Green hub-and-spoke network design for aviation industry [J]. Journal of cleaner production, 2019, 229: 1377-1396.

[2] Soylu B, Katip H. A multiobjective hub-airport location problem for an airline network design [J]. European Journal of Operational Research, 2019, 277(2): 412-425.

[3] 王谦. 市场补贴提供者参与下的枢纽航线网络设计研究[D]. 德阳: 中国民用航空飞行学院, 2020.

[4] 徐涛, 吴志帅, 卢敏, 等. 面向拥堵问题的枢纽航线网络优化模型[J]. 系统工程与电子技术, 2020, 42(11): 2553-2559.

[5] Wu W W, Zhang H Y, Wei W B. Optimal design of hub-and-spoke networks with access to regional hub airports: a case for the Chinese regional airport system [J]. Transportmetrica A: Transport Science, 2018, 14 (4): 330-345.

[6] Huang X L, Chen Y Y. An optimization model for multimodal transportation decisions based on congestion information[C]// Proc. Of the 11th World Congress on Intelligent Control and Automation, 2014: 610-615.

[7] Hamid M, Mohan K, Andreas T, et al. A modified benders method for the single and multiple allocation P-hub median problem[J]. Operations Research Proceedings, 2018, 1(1): 135-141.

[8] Niraj R D, Krishnamoorthy M, Ernst A T. Efficient models, formulations and algorithms for some variants of fixed interval scheduling problems[J]. Data and Design Sciences in Action, 2018, 8(4): 43-69.

[9] ICAO. Airport Air Quality Manual: Doc 9889. Montreal: International Civil Aviation Organization, 2011.

网格体系下基于 K-Means 空域聚类的冲突检测方法

蔡明　万路军*　高志周　徐鑫宇

（空军工程大学空管领航学院）

摘　要　针对传统的空域冲突检测方法运算量大，无效检测过多，实际应用中适用性不强的问题，提出了在网格体系下基于 K-Means 空域聚类的冲突检测方法。首先，梳理总结了 K-Means 聚类方法和 GeoSOT 剖分网格的应用基础；其次，利用 K-Means 聚类方法将空域进行聚类，规划设计了空域簇的划分流程，为聚类后的空域冲突检测打下基础。最后，利用实验仿真验证了基于 K-Means 空域聚类的冲突检测方法的高效性和准确性。

关键词　空中交通管制　空域冲突检测　聚类算法　K 均值聚类　GeoSOT 网格

0　引言

随着全球经济一体化的推进，世界航空运输蓬勃发展，中国民用航空运输产业增长尤为迅猛。加之国际形势日趋紧张，我国军事用空计划愈加频繁，军民航冲突和军种间冲突矛盾不断升级，给空中交通管理系统带来了严峻的挑战。在众多类型的空域中，低空空域是国家通用航空和军航

1. 基金项目：空军工程大学研究生创新实践基金（CXJ2021087）。

日常航行的活动领域,随着低空空域的持续开放和发展,空域内各类飞行器密集度也随之上升,不同飞行器之间需要协同规划和调度以保证飞行的安全性以及空域资源的利用效率,这使得低空空域管理的压力越来越大。如何快速准确地判别空域使用计划的冲突空域并实时给出解脱方案,是未来大规模空域协同划设的一个关键问题[1]。

当前民用航空方面空管系统将空域划分为若干扇区,每个扇区的交通管制工作由对应管制员负责。可以说各个扇区的平稳高效运行是保障航空交通安全运行的前提与基础。因此,如何科学合理地规划扇区结构,均衡扇区内管制员的工作负荷,充分挖掘空域扇区的潜在容量,成为中国民航业发展研究的主要方向。国内外专家学者在扇区规划方面取得了丰富成果。主要包括基于管制员负荷的扇区划分、基于交通流的扇区划分、基于空域结构的扇区划分以及目前比较流行的基于空域扇区复杂度的扇区划分方法[2-5]。这其中,空域规划专家 Yousefi A 等人提出了正六边形分割理论等多个空域扇区切割算法,大大推动了全球扇区划分创新研究进程[6]。

而在军用航空方面,由于空中任务行动的载体往往是单个独立的空域,因此管制员不仅要关注整个扇区内的空域使用情况,而且要更加关注任务空域之间是否存在使用冲突,也是空中交通管制的重要环节——空域冲突探测与消解[7-8]。在目前的空域冲突探测工作中,管制员主要是依靠上报的计划划设空域的中心位置、形状、大小和安全距离,在经纬度坐标体系下,采用几何解析的方法进行粗略判断,进行冲突空域调配消解则是根据基本的管制规则和个人经验进行调配,使得管制人员需要花费大量精力在空域冲突识别与消解方面来保证用空安全。

同时,在空域冲突检测与消解的算法中,采用的是通过遍历计算,逐一对比、逐对检测的方法。利用这种方法,无论是检测还是消解都将面临极大的解空间,检测算法复杂度至少是 $o(n^2)$,计算量巨大的同时还会进行大量距离较远或用途类型本不冲突的无用空域对冲突检测。同时,按照目前的技术支持,各用空分域在做空域使用计划时,很难获取所有空域的实时数据,提报的空域需求就很难避免与其他用空单位的空域需求产生冲突。

受到民用航空划分空域扇区的启发,本文通过先在时间和空间维对空域进行检测,建立核心冲突网,再利用 K-Means 聚类将核心关联网之外的空域聚类,从而达到先划分空域簇再检测的目的,精简解空间提高了求解效率。

1　理论基础

1.1　K-Means 聚类方法

机器学习是一门多学科交叉专业,涵盖概率论知识、统计学知识、近似理论知识和复杂算法知识,使用计算机作为工具并致力于真实实时的模拟人类学习方式,并将现有内容进行知识结构划分来有效提高学习效率。主要分为有监督学习、半监督学习、无监督学习和强化学习。有监督学习知道从对象(数据)中学习什么,而无监督学习不需知道所要搜寻的目标,它是根据算法得到数据的共同特征。聚类是指将数据集划分为若干类,使得类内之间的数据最为相似,各类之间的数据相似度差别尽可能大。聚类分析就是以相似性为基础,对数据集进行聚类划分,属于无监督学习。

K-Means 算法是一种简单的迭代型聚类算法,采用距离作为相似性指标,根据给定数据集中的类数量 k,且每个类的中心是根据类中所有值的均值得到,每个类用聚类中心的位置来描述[9-11]。对于给定的一个包含 n 个 d 维数据点的数据集 X,选取欧式距离作为相似度指标,聚类目标是使得各类的聚类平方和最小:

$$S = \sum_{j=1}^{k} \sum_{i=1}^{n} \| x_i - u_k \|^2 \quad (1)$$

式中:k——要划定的目标类的数量;

n——第 j 个类内的样本数量;

u_k——对应质心(位置中心)[12]。算法具体迭代步骤如下:

(1)选取数据空间中的 k 个对象作为初始中心,每个对象代表一个聚类中心;

(2)对于样本中的数据对象,根据它们与这些聚类中心的欧氏距离,按距离最近的准则将它们分到距离它们最近的聚类中心所对应的类;

(3)更新聚类中心:将每个类别中所有对象所对应的均值作为该类别的聚类中心,同时计算目标函数的值;

(4)判断聚类中心和目标函数的值是否发生改变,若不变,则输出结果,若改变,则返回至步骤(2)。

1.2 GeoSOT 剖分网格坐标体系

传统的地理参考系统或测绘参考系统,根据地球的椭球特点,建立的经纬度的地理标识,经纬度以"度-分-秒"的形式,描述地球上某一"点"的位置,其他形状或区域则用"点"集合进行标定即由"点"描述"线",再由线描述"面",如果增加高度参数则可以构建空间"体"的描述。在进行涉及空间位置关系的探测判断时,用低维度的"点",描述其他维度更高的空间位置,难度较大且效率较低。针对经纬度点坐标体系存在的不足与缺点,国内外自20世纪90年代以来不断探索空间网格系统,采用网格描述方法,对地理空间进行建模。美军发展并推广使用了全球区域参考系统(Global Area Reference System,GARS)和军事网格参考系统(Military Grid Reference System,MGRS),我国北京大学程承旗教授提出的全球空间网格参考系统(Global Spatial Grid Reference System,GSGRS)在当今地理测绘以及空间位置关系判断上得到了极大应用[13-15]。

本文列出并利用我国国家军用标准、由北京大学程承旗教授团队提出的 2^n 一维整型数组全球经纬剖分网格(Geographic Coordinate Subdividing Grid with One Dimension Integral Coding on 2^n-Tree,GeoSOT),这是一种经纬度的四叉树剖分网格体系,较完备地实现了大到整个地球、小到厘米级面片的全球四叉树格网结构。将地球表面进行了三次扩展,格网上下级别之间的父子面片,面积之比大致都为4:1,并且与我国及世界各国主要的规格地理格网之间都具有一致性聚合特性。GeoSOT各层级面片与尺度对应关系见表1。

GeoSOT 各层级及对应属性参数 表1

层 级	网格大小	赤道附近大致尺度	层 级	网格大小	赤道附近大致尺度
G	512°		17	16″	512m
1	256°		18	8″	256m
2	128°		19	4″	128m
3	64°		20	2″	64m
4	32°		21	1″	32m
5	16°		22	1/2″	16m
6	8°	1024km	23	1/4″	8m
7	4°	512km	24	1/8″	4m
8	2°	216km	25	1/16″	2m
9	1°	128km	26	1/32″	1m
10	32′	64km	27	1/64″	0.5m
11	16′	32km	28	1/128″	25cm
12	8′	16km	29	1/256″	12.5cm
13	4′	8km	30	1/512″	6.2cm
14	2′	4km	31	1/1024″	3.1cm
15	1′	2km	32	1/2048″	1.5cm
16	32″	1km			

2　空域簇划分流程

在利用 K-Means 聚类算法划分空域簇之前需要提前知道待划分样本数据有多少类即 K 的数值。为了达到较好的聚类效果,需要提前对分类数进行设定。目前比较常用的方法是根据误差平方和(Sum of Squared Error,SSE)来判断,SSE 越小表示数据点越接近它们的质心,聚类的效果相对来说也就最好。或者是人工考虑"肘部法则"来选择,即画出不同 K 值下的代价函数图,图形很像一个人的肘部,观察判断可知,当达到一个点时 SSE 下降的非常快,之后会很慢,由此来选择 K。

本文旨在通过划分空域簇后以各空域簇为单位进行空域的冲突检测与消解。空域簇的划分实现了在同一空域簇内可能存在一对或多对冲突空域;不同空域簇(及其包含的空域)之间不存在空域使用冲突。这样达到了在进行空域冲突检测时不需要逐一检测,只需要在簇内检测,大大降低了求解效率,同时也提高了检测精度[16]。具体方法流程如下:

(1)基于空域簇进行冲突检测方法核心是构建起核心冲突空域群,就是利用传统的空域冲突与检测方法找出存在使用冲突的空域对,将这些空域进行初聚类并作为各个簇的初始点;

(2)将初聚类簇以外的空域点利用 K-Means 聚类算法进行聚类;

(3)检查所有空域是否有遗漏;

(4)输出聚类结果,格式如下:

$$C_1 = \{x_1, x_2, x_3, x_7, x_8, x_9\}$$

$$C_2 = \{x_4, x_6\}$$

$$C_3 = \{x_5, x_{10}\}$$

K-means 聚类算法是一个反复迭代的过程,利用 K-means 聚类算法进行空域簇划方法流程图见图 1。

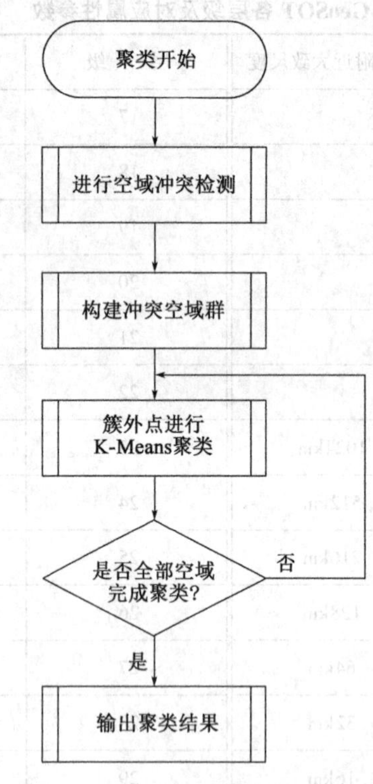

图 1　空域簇划分方法流程图

3　冲突检测实验仿真

3.1　空域参数设定

实验仿真前首先要对空域参数进行设定,空域的主要参数包括使用时间、空间位置、空域形状、大小范围和注意事项等。为了方便确定空域位置和实验仿真,下文通过将空域投影至地面二维平面确定位置坐标,将空域的经纬度值转化成一维四进制网格坐标(网格尺度为 1km),并结合传统空域划设的方法将 20 个空域参数定义如表 2 所示。

表2

空域参数属性

空域编号	网格坐标	空域形状	长宽/半径(km)	使用时间
1	G000223011-102131	圆形	5	6:00—7:00
2	G000223011-302100	正方形	10	7:00—8:00
3	G000223011-100211	正方形	12	8:00—9:00
4	G000223011-120031	圆形	5	9:00—10:00
5	G000223110-301023	正方形	10	10:00—11:00
6	G000223011-102231	圆形	12	11:00—12:00
7	G000223011-1221330	正方形	10	12:00—13:00
8	G000223011-102033	长方形	20×10	13:00—14:00
9	G000223011-121030	圆形	10	14:00—15:00
10	G000221232-302230	正方形	15	15:00—16:00
11	G000223011-302312	圆形	5	16:00—17:00
12	G000223011-123023	长方形	8×15	17:00—18:00
13	G000223011-230132	长方形	8×20	18:00—19:00
14	G000223011-321001	圆形	8	19:00—20:00
15	G000223011-121033	圆形	15	21:00—22:00
16	G000223011-321011	正方形	10	23:00—24:00
17	G000223011-333010	长方形	12×20	9:00—10:00
18	G000223011-301011	圆形	10	8:00—10:00
19	G000223011-302311	圆形	10	10:00—12:00
20	G000223011-323011	正方形	16	14:00—16:00

3.2 构建空域冲突群

将各个空域的中心位置定为该空域的位置参数,利用 Matlab 软件仿真将设定的空域表示出来如图2所示,并通过算法检测找到存在冲突的空域群。

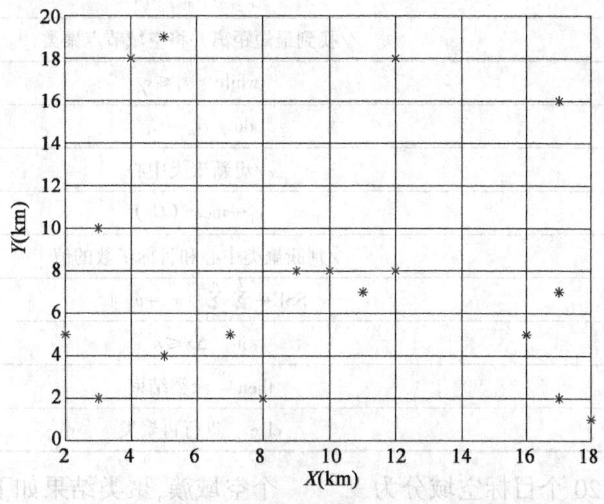

图2 空域位置标示图

在进行空域冲突检测时,结合空域位置标示图先对任务空域的时间使用情况进行检测,发现以下空域之间可能存在冲突,如表3所示。

存在潜在冲突空域列表　表3

空域编号	冲突时间(h)	空域编号	冲突时间(h)
4-17	9:00—10:00	6-19	11:00—12:00
3-18	8:00—9:00	9-20	14:00—15:00
4-18	9:00—10:00	10-20	15:00—16:00
5-19	10:00—11:00		

通过时间维度的检测筛选出了可能存在冲突的7对空域,对这7对空域再进行空间维度的冲突检测,在这里设置空域之间存在安全缓冲距离 $d=10\text{km}$,空间维度的检测算法伪代码如表4所示。

空间维度检测算法　表4

//将待检测空域位置参数信息进行赋值

$x \leftarrow X$

$y \leftarrow Y$

//计算待检测空域之间的距离

$D \leftarrow \mathrm{sqrt}(\Delta x^2+\Delta y^2)$

//冲突检测判断

if　$D \leq d_1+d_2+d$

then　存在冲突

else　不存在冲突

通过算法计算得到存在冲突的空域对分别为4号空域和17号空域、3号空域和18号空域以及10号空域和20号空域。

3.3　空域节点聚类构建空域簇

由此可以确定三个初始聚类簇,以初始簇的中心位置坐标作为聚类初始中心 c_1、c_2 和 c_3,将初始簇以外的空域点利用K-Means聚类算法进行聚类,聚类算法伪代码如表5所示。

空域聚类算法　表5

//计算初始簇外空域节点距离各簇的距离 s

$s_{ui} \leftarrow |A_u - C_i|$

//找到最短距离并将空域节点聚类

while　$s_i \leq s_j$

do　$A_u \rightarrow C_i$

//更新聚类中心

$c_i \leftarrow \mathrm{mean}(C_i)$

//判断聚类中心和目标函数的值

$\mathrm{SSE} \leftarrow \sum_{j=1}^{k}\sum_{i=1}^{n}\| x_i - u_k \|^2$

if　$\Delta S \leq \varepsilon$

then　聚类结束

else　进行再聚类

经过多轮聚类运算,将20个目标空域分为三个空域簇,聚类结果如下:

$C_1 = \{A_4, A_6, A_9, A_{11}, A_{12}, A_{15}, A_{17}\}$

$C_2 = \{A_3, A_7, A_8, A_{18}, A_{19}\}$

$C_3 = \{A_1, A_2, A_5, A_{10}, A_{13}, A_{14}, A_{16}, A_{20}\}$

3.4 对比仿真分析

算法的效率指的是算法运行的时间,算法运行所占据电脑运行空间的大小,一个算法的优劣往往可以用空间复杂度和时间复杂度来衡量。由于在运行空域冲突检测算法时,大部分电脑机器运行空间都能满足算法需求,因此,本文主要通过 O 运算表示法讨论算法的时间复杂度。传统空域冲突检测方法是通过逐一对比,遍历比较,空域冲突检测算法时间复杂度至少是 $o(N^2)$;在先进行空域聚类、后进行空域冲突检测的方法中,算法时间复杂度为 $o(N_1{}^2 + N_2{}^2 + N_3{}^2)$。由于 $N = N_1 + N_2 + N_3$,不难得到 $N^2 \geqslant N_1{}^2 + N_2{}^2 + N_3{}^2$,因此理论分析不难得到先聚类后检测的空域冲突检测方法效率更高。

为了检验理论分析的结果,通过改变空域数量 N,将两种检测方法的运行时间进行比较。将空域数量分别设定为 300、600、800 和 1000,通过四次仿真对比运行时间,仿真结果如图 3 所示。

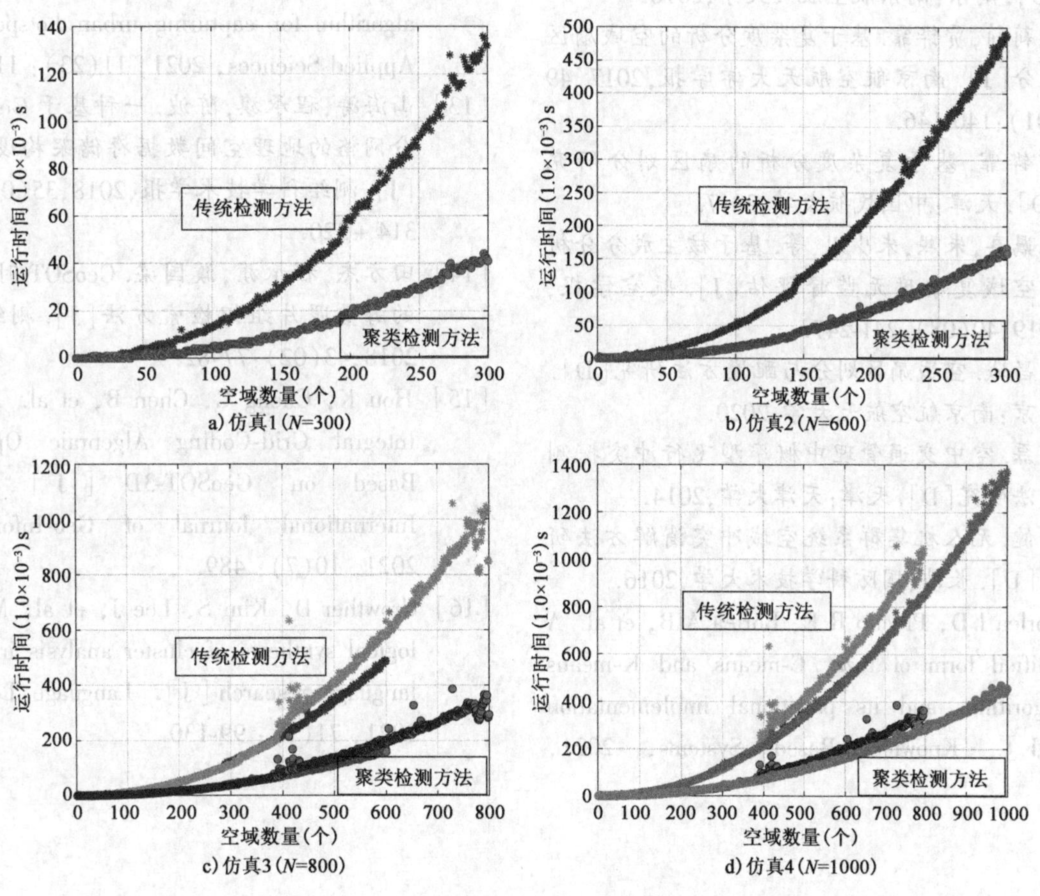

图 3 实验对比仿真图

从上述四个对比实验仿真发现,随着空域数量的增多,传统空域冲突检测方法的时间复杂度呈现出几何爆发式增长,聚类检测方法的时间复杂度则始终保持在 $o(N^2)$。同时,随着空域数量的增加,聚类检测方法效率优势和计算简便性越明显,体现在两个方法用时差距越来越大。通过仿真实验,验证了聚类检测方法在稳定性与高效性方面的优势,在满足空域冲突检测任务需求的同时,还提高了冲突探测的稳定性与高效性。

4 结语

本文提出了一种网格体系下基于 K-Means 聚类的空域簇划分方法,并在空域分类成簇的基础之上进行冲突检测。传统的空域冲突检测主要按照逐一检测,遍历计算的思路进行运算,导致了解空间巨大,运算速度较慢。基于空域聚类的冲突检测方法,在检测之前先将空域分类成簇,避免了大量非必要的检测运算,精简了待解空间,弥补了传统空域冲突检测方法运算冗余,无效检测过多和效率低下的不足。通过仿真实验,验证了基于空域聚类的冲突检测方法在高效性与准确性方面的优势,能够满足目前日趋紧张、计划频繁的用空需求。

参考文献

[1] 徐鑫宇,万路军,陈平,等.基于 GeoSOT 网格的空域栅格化表征方法[J].空军工程大学学报(自然科学版),2021,22(02):15-22.

[2] 亢继方.空域复杂性因素下的扇区划分研究[D].南京:南京航空航天大学,2016.

[3] 王莉莉,贾铧霏.基于复杂度分析的空域扇区划分[J].南京航空航天大学学报,2017,49(01):140-146.

[4] 贾铧霏.基于复杂度分析的扇区划分研究[D].天津:中国民航大学,2017.

[5] 张瞩熹,朱熙,朱少川,等.基于核主成分分析的空域复杂度无监督评估[J].航空学报,2019,40(08):241-247.

[6] 李昌城.空域扇区划分与配置方法研究[D].南京:南京航空航天大学,2020.

[7] 石磊.空中交通管理中概率型飞行冲突探测算法研究[D].天津:天津大学,2014.

[8] 杨健.无人机集群系统空域冲突消解方法研究[D].长沙:国防科学技术大学,2016.

[9] Borlea I D, Precup R E, Borlea A B, et al. A unified form of fuzzy C-means and K-means algorithms and its partitional implementation[J]. Knowledge-Based Systems, 2021, 214: 106731.

[10] Estupiñán Ricardo J, Domínguez Menéndez J J, Barcos Arias I F, et al. Neutrosophic K-means for the analysis of earthquake data in Ecuador[J]. Neutrosophic Sets and Systems, 2021, 44(1): 29.

[11] 邬春明,齐森南.改进 K-means 聚类的自适应加权 K 近邻指纹定位算法[J].重庆邮电大学学报(自然科学版),2021,33(06):946-954.

[12] Ran X, Zhou X, Lei M, et al. A novel k-means clustering algorithm with a noise algorithm for capturing urban hotspots[J]. Applied Sciences, 2021, 11(23): 11202.

[13] 山海涛,程承旗,陈波.一种基于 GeoSOT 剖分网格的地理空间数据存储架构设计方法[J].测绘科学技术学报,2018,35(03):311-314+320.

[14] 田方杰,程承旗,濮国梁.GeoSOT 时空编码的海量照片组织检索方法[J].测绘科学,2018,43(02):77-82.

[15] Hou K, Cheng C, Chen B, et al. A Set of Integral Grid-Coding Algebraic Operations Based on GeoSOT-3D[J]. ISPRS International Journal of Geo-Information, 2021, 10(7): 489.

[16] Crowther D, Kim S, Lee J, et al. Methodological synthesis of cluster analysis in second language research[J]. Language Learning, 2021, 71(1): 99-130.

基于功能性的终端区三维管制扇区划设方法研究

徐　灿[1]　田　勇[*1]　李传家[1]　巩文健[2]

(1.南京航空航天大学民航学院;2.中国民用航空华东地区空中交通管理局)

摘　要　为缓解终端区日益增长的交通需求与有限的空域容量之间矛盾,避免现有的管制扇区主观

1.基金项目:国家自然科学基金民航联合基金项目(U1933119);南京航空航天大学创新计划项目(xcxjh20210703)。

划设导致空域资源的不合理配置，本文提出了一种基于空域功能的三维管制扇区划设方法，以生成与空中交通流功能属性一致的扇区。首先，采用航迹聚类方法对空中交通流的功能属性进行分类。在此基础上，提出了功能性扇区划设框架，首次提出了管制扇区与空中交通流之间的功能一致性优化目标。接着，设计相应的高效算法，生成范围准确的功能扇区，能够很好地分离不同功能的交通流。最后，利用上海终端区实际运行数据对所提出的框架和算法进行实例验证。结果表明，该方法能够根据复杂终端区内的交通流生成具有特定功能的三维扇区，有利于提高空域的安全水平，增大空域容量。具体地，降低了潜在的冲突风险，增加了平均扇区飞行时间，优化了管制负荷。

关键词 航空运输 空域扇区划设 功能性扇区 终端区 航迹聚类

0 引言

随着民用航空的稳步发展[1]，现有空域容量无法满足快速增长的交通需求。终端区作为航空器运行的重要区域，空域容量时常逼近阈值。目前终端区扇区大多参照国际民航组织的原则，结合主观经验设计，显然不能满足持续增长的交通需求，容易出现管制负荷不均匀的问题，最终成为限制空域容量的短板[2]。

国内外一直积极探索科学的扇区划设方法。Delahaye 等最早提出了基于 Voronoi 图的扇区划设方法[3-4]。韩松臣等进一步提出了蜕变的空域 Voronoi 图[5-7]。2005 年，Yousefi、Klein 等使用混合整数规划（Mixed Integer Programming，MIP）划设扇区[8-9]。2008 年，Brinton 等基于航迹聚类生成扇区[10]。2016 年，Zenlinski 总结了 Voronoi 图、MIP 和航迹聚类三种方法的优缺点[11]。

近年来，学者们开始考虑三维扇区划设。2008 年，Delahaye 等在水平分割的基础上对高度进行划分，并引入直棱柱约束[12]。2009 年，Kicinger 等基于智能体模型（Agent Based Model，ABM）生成扇区[13]。2011 年，Tang 等改进了 ABM 模型，较好地满足了相关约束[14]。2012 年，Min 提出了优化管制扇区数量的方法[15]。2015 年，王超等使用二叉空间分割法划设扇区[16]。2019 年，Wong 等提出了考虑下一小时流量的动态扇区配置方法[17]。2021 年，Wong 等提出了一种滚动优化方法，根据流量的不同实现扇区的渐变[18]。

相比于高空区域，终端区扇区划设的研究较少。2014 年，Wei 等先在垂直方向上进行分割，而后对分割的高度层分别采用 MIP 划设扇区[19]。2017 年，Granberg 等提出新的扇区划分方法以解决未来终端区航班拥挤问题[20]。2019 年，Granberg 等以斯德哥尔摩阿兰达机场为实例，为高度灵活的终端区扇区划设提供了概念验证[21]。

总的来说，现有研究主要采用几何计算、航迹聚类、整数规划等方法，以管制负荷为主要优化目标划设扇区，取得了较为丰硕的成果。但生成的扇区覆盖多种类别的交通流，不具备特定的功能性。此外，对于垂直高度往往进行简单分层，导致生成扇区垂直范围较为粗糙，仍有进一步优化的空间。最后，现有针对终端区的扇区划设的研究，很少考虑多机场终端区与飞越的交通流。对此，本文率先从空域及扇区功能性的角度出发，研究终端区内三维扇区划设问题，主要贡献如下：

(1)本文首次明确了空中交通流和空域扇区的功能属性，提供了一个使不同扇区具有不同功能的扇区划设框架，具体提出了空中交通流和空域扇区之间的功能一致性目标。

(2)首次结合初始生成规则、判断调整规则、间隙填充规则和优化过程，设计出高效的功能性扇区划设算法，生成水平和垂直范围准确的功能性扇区。

(3)以典型的繁忙终端区的实际运行数据集，对功能性扇区的划设框架和算法进行了实例验证。为了对现有扇区和功能性部门进行比较，选择了性能指标进行对比。

本文主要内容安排如下：第 1 节通过航迹聚类对交通流的功能进行了分类；第 2 节提出功能性扇区划设框架；第 3 节设计相应的规则与算法；第 4 节以上海终端区为实例验证；第 5 节得出结论。

1 空中交通流功能分类

1.1 航迹描述

本研究基于二次雷达航迹数据，更新率为 4 ~ 10s，每次更新记录一个离散的坐标点。图 1 展示了终端区内高峰小时航迹。

图1　终端区内高峰小时航迹

设在某一时间段内终端区内航空器架次为 m 架,航迹数据的集合 T 表示为:

$$T = \{P_1, P_2, \cdots, P_m\} \tag{1}$$

式中:P_i——第 i 条航迹数据,每条航迹数据为如下集合:

$$P_i = \{p_{i,1}, p_{i,2}, \cdots, p_{i,n_i}\} \tag{2}$$

式中:$p_{i,j}$——第 i 条航迹的第 j 个航迹点,该航迹共有航迹点 n_i 个,$j \in \{1, n_i\}$ 为航迹点的编号,按时间顺序排列。每个航迹点为一个六维向量:

$$p_{i,j} = \{x, y, h, d, v, t\} \tag{3}$$

式中:x——经度;

y——纬度;

h——高度;

d——航向;

v——速度;

t——获取雷达数据的时间。

聚类分析需要通过航迹间的相似性,将航迹集合 T 分解为若干个不相交的子集 C,共形成 K 个聚簇,使得每一类聚簇都包含一个聚类中心,各聚簇内部与聚簇中心间的距离和最小。

$$C = \{c_1, c_2, \cdots, c_K\} \tag{4}$$

式中,c_i 由 m_i 条航迹组成,表示第 i 个聚簇:

$$c_i = \{P_1, P_2, \cdots, P_{m_i}\} \tag{5}$$

聚簇之间互不相交,每个航迹只属于一类聚簇:

$$c_1 \cup c_2 \cdots \cup c_K = C = T \tag{6}$$

$$c_i \cap c_j = \varnothing \quad (1 \leqslant i, j \leqslant K, i \neq j) \tag{7}$$

将航迹间的距离定义为 $d_{P_i,P_j}(1 \leqslant i, j \leqslant m)$,所有聚簇的距离和为:

$$D(c, u) = \sum_{i=1}^{m} d(P_i, u_{c_i}) \tag{8}$$

式中:P_i——第 i 条航迹;

c_i——第 i 条航迹所属聚簇;

u_{c_i}——聚簇对应的中心点。

需求解聚簇划分方案 C 使得总距离和 $D(c, u)$ 最小。

1.2　航迹聚类

1.2.1　相似性度量

航迹聚类的首要步骤就是选择合适的相似度系数,以准确表示航空器航迹间的相似性。空中交通航迹数据具有离散、航迹数不相等、具有不同的起止点等特性,使得航迹数据的相似度系数变得更加复杂,常用的无监督学习的相似度量方法变得不再适用。本文采用相邻航迹点欧式距离作为度量,建立基于欧式距离的相似度系数计算方法,如图2所示。

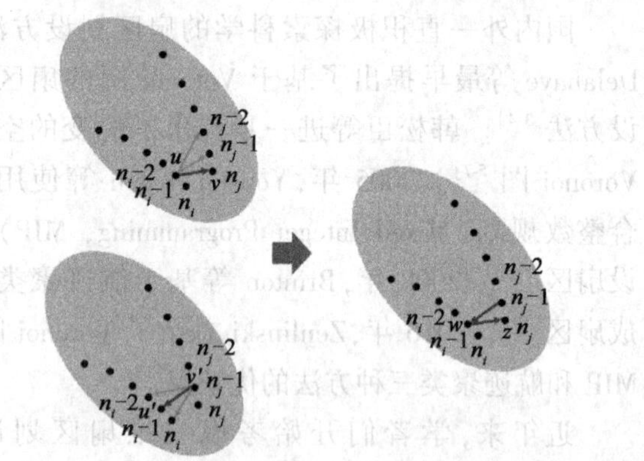

图2　两航迹间距离计算过程

Step1:输入两条航迹 P_i 与 P_j,以每个航迹倒数第二个点 (p_{n_i-1}, p_{n_j-1}) 作为初始航迹点对 (g, h) 开始遍历。

Step2:分别计算航迹 i 中对应点 $p_{i,g}$ 与 j 中对应点 $p_{j,h}$ 及其相邻两点 $p_{j,h-1}, p_{j,h+1}$ 间的距离,其中距离最小的点对作为 (u, v)。分别计算航迹 j 中对应点与 i 中对应点及其相邻两点间的距离,其中距离最小的点对作为 (u', v'),有

$$d(u, v) = \min\{d(p_{i,g}, p_{j,h-1}), d(p_{i,g}, p_{j,h}), d(p_{i,g}, p_{j,h+1})\} \tag{9}$$

$$d(u', v') = \min\{d(p_{i,h}, p_{j,g-1}), d(p_{i,h}, p_{j,g}), d(p_{i,h}, p_{j,g+1})\} \tag{10}$$

Step3:比较点对 (u, v) 的距离与 (u', v') 的距

离,选取距离较小的点作为(w,z),将点对(w,z)间的距离加入总距离和$d(P_i,P_j)$。

$$d(w,z)=\min\{d(p_{i,u},p_{j,v}),d(p_{i,u'},p_{j,v'})\} \tag{11}$$

Step4:令$(w-1,z-1)$为新的初始点对(g,h),判断是否满足终止条件$g==0 \vee h==0$。若不满足,返回步骤(2)。对m条航迹两两计算相似度系数,相似度矩阵S如下:

$$S=\begin{pmatrix} s_{1,1} & s_{1,2} & \cdots & s_{1,m} \\ s_{2,1} & s_{2,2} & \cdots & s_{2,m} \\ \cdots & \cdots & \ddots & \cdots \\ s_{m,1} & s_{m,2} & \cdots & s_{m,m} \end{pmatrix} \tag{12}$$

式中:$s_{i,j}(i\neq j,1\leqslant i,j\leqslant m)$——两条不同航迹间的相似度系数,相同航迹的相似度系数$s_{i,i}=0$。

1.2.2　DBSCAN 算法

目前,经典的聚类算法按照方式分类主要包括:基于层次的聚类树、基于划分的 K-Means 和基于密度的 DBSCAN 等,其中基于密度的 DBSCAN 聚类算法是根据聚集的密集程度进行聚类,相比于传统的基于距离的 K-Means 容易导致球状的聚类结果,DBSCAN 具有能够发现任意形状的聚类、不需要先验地设置簇的个数等优点,并且能够分离核心点、噪声。而根据上文的分析,空中交通航迹数据具有分布不规则、非常规数据多、按照运行模式聚集等特点,因此非常适合采用 DBSCAN 算法进行聚类分析。

算法首先任意选取初始点,然后根据设定的关键参数 eps 对附近的航迹点进行遍历,标记核心样本和噪声,其中噪声即为附近点数少于阈值的点,大于阈值即为核心样本,其余为边界点,遍历直到 eps 距离内没有核心样本,便得到一个聚簇,再选取一个未被访问过的点重复上述过程。如图3所示,核心点用红色标记,边界点用黄色标记,噪声用蓝色标记。

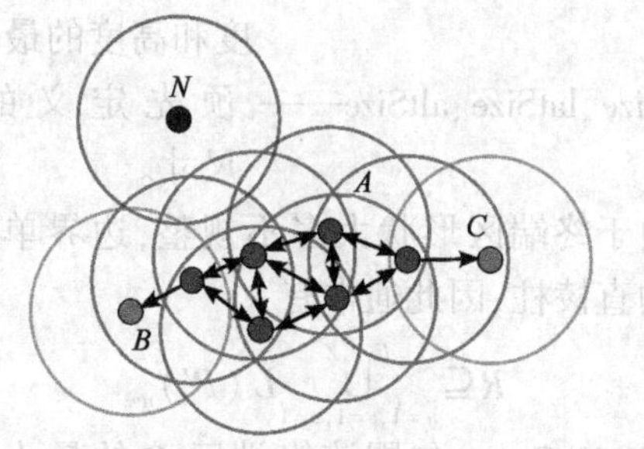

图3　DBSCAN 算法示意图

DBSCAN 算法中,参数 eps 和 min_samples 的选择非常重要,设置过小易导致噪声过多,设置过大则使得簇的个数较少,图4显示了不同参数设置对分类结果的影响,其中实点为属于簇的点,核心样本点显示为较大标记,空点为噪声。

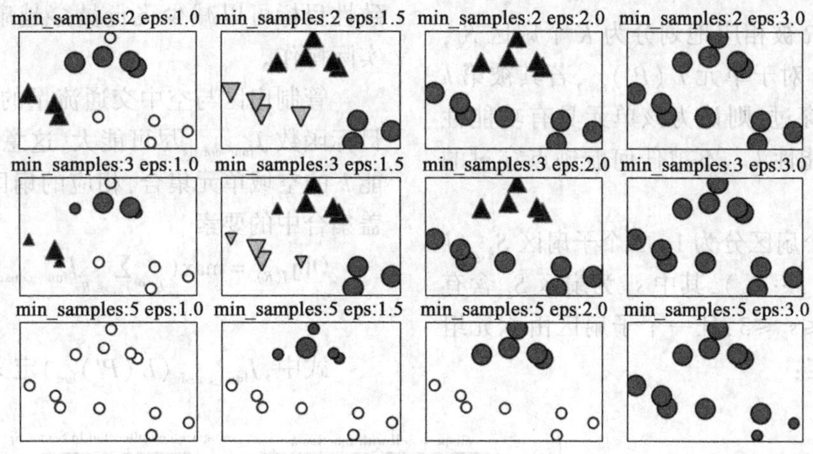

图4　不同参数设置得到的分类结果

2　功能性扇区划设框架建立

2.1　空域离散化

本文采用离散化的方法,对空域进行栅格化,分割为一个个小的直棱柱单元格,再根据航迹聚类的结果对栅格的功能性进行设置。模型的输入包括空域范围和航迹数据两部分,终端区空域可表示为:

$$R=\bigcup_{u,v,z} L(P')_{uvz} \tag{13}$$

式中:$L(P')_{uvz}$——三维空域单元。

该单元中包含的航迹点的集合 $P'=\{p_{i_1,j_1},p_{i_2,j_2},\cdots,p_{i_n,j_n}\}(1\leqslant i_t\leqslant m,1\leqslant j_t\leqslant n_{i_t})$。$u$、$v$ 和 z 分别表示单元 $L(P')_{uvz}$ 的经度、纬度和高度索引：

$$\begin{cases}u=\dfrac{\text{lng}-\text{minLng}}{\text{lngSize}}+1\\ v=\dfrac{\text{lat}-\text{minLat}}{\text{latSize}}+1\\ z=\dfrac{\text{alt}-\text{minAlt}}{\text{altSize}}+1\end{cases}\tag{14}$$

式中：lng、lat、alt——该单元底面中心点的经度、纬度、高度；

minLng、minLat、minAlt——所有单元中经度、纬度和高度的最小值；

lngSize、latSize、altSize——预先定义的单元尺寸。

由于终端区形状大多不规整，边界单元不是标准的直棱柱，因此通常有

$$R\subseteq\bigcup_{u=1,v=1,z=1}^{U,V,Z}L(P')_{uvz}\tag{15}$$

式中：U、V、Z——包围该终端区 R 的最小直棱柱的各单元中经度、纬度和高度最大值的索引。

聚类集合 $C=\{c_1,c_2,\cdots,c_K\}$，$c_i=\{P_1,P_2,\cdots,P_{m_i}\}$，相应空域单元功能定义如下：

$$F(L(P')_{uvz},k)=\begin{cases}1,\ \text{when}\ \exists p_{i_t j_t}\in P',P_{i_t}\in c_k\\ 0,\ \text{when}\ \forall p_{i_t j_t}\in P',P_{i_t}\notin c_k\end{cases}\tag{16}$$

终端区空域 R 被相应地划分为 K 个扇区 S_k，$(k=1,2,\cdots,K)$。对于单元 $L(P')_{uvz}$，若其被第 k 类聚簇的航迹点穿过，则认为该单元具有功能性 k，否则不具有功能性 k。不被任何航迹点穿过的单元为空白。

进一步将每个扇区分为 1~3 个子扇区 $S_{k,g}(k=1,2,\cdots,K;g=1,\cdots,s_k)$，其中 s_k 为扇区 S_k 含有的子扇区数目，$1\leqslant s_k\leqslant 3$，任一个子扇区由六元组 $\text{Six}(S_{k,g})$ 唯一确定：

$$\text{Six}(S_{k,g})=\{u_{\text{left}},u_{\text{right}},v_{\text{back}},v_{\text{front}},z_{\text{bottom}},z_{\text{top}}\}\tag{17}$$

$$\begin{cases}1\leqslant u_{\text{left}},u_{\text{right}}\leqslant u_{\max}\\ v_{\min}(u_{\text{left}},u_{\text{right}})\leqslant v_{\text{back}},v_{\text{front}}\leqslant v_{\max}(u_{\text{left}},u_{\text{right}})\\ 1\leqslant z_{\text{bottom}},z_{\text{top}}\leqslant z_{\max}\end{cases}\tag{18}$$

式中，$u_{\max}$ 为终端区 R 的经度索引的最大值；$v_{\min}(u_{\text{left}},u_{\text{right}})$，$v_{\max}(u_{\text{left}},u_{\text{right}})$——在 u_{left}、u_{right} 范围内纬度最窄的范围的上下限，$z_{\max}$ 为高度索引的最大值。

$$S_{k,g}=\bigcup_{u=u_{\text{left}},v=v_{\text{back}},z=z_{\text{bottom}}}^{u_{\text{right}},v_{\text{front}},z_{\text{top}}}L(P')_{uvz}\tag{19}$$

因此功能性扇区划分的问题便转化为求 $\sum_{k=1}^{K}s_k$ 个六元组的问题。

2.2　目标函数

目标函数的区别是功能性扇区与传统扇区划设的最根本的区别。传统的扇区划设以优化管制员的工作负荷为目标，主要包括两部分：平衡不同扇区之间的监视负荷，最小化扇区间的协调负荷之和。许多研究表明，这两个目标函数存在着内在的冲突[6,12,14]。而使得生成的扇区与交通流之间的功能具有一致性是本文提出的一种新的优化目标。从空中交通管制的角度来看，功能一致性目标有利于管制员更好地建立情景意识，并提高扇区内安全水平。从飞行员的角度来看，功能一致性目标可以减少飞行员穿越扇区数量，简化了实际操作。

管制扇区与空中交通流量的功能一致性要求目标函数 $J_{\text{func-consis}}$ 尽可能大，这意味着对于具有功能 k 的空域单元集合，相应的扇区 S_k 应尽可能覆盖集合中的要素。

$$\text{Obj}_{J(R)}=\max\Big(\sum_{L(P')_{uvz}\in R}J_{\text{func\_consis}}(L(P')_{uvz})\Big)\tag{20}$$

式中，$J_{\text{func\_consis}}(L(P')_{uvz})$ 定义如下：

$$J_{\text{func-consis}}(L(P')_{uvz})=\begin{cases}1,\text{if}\ \overbrace{F(L(P')_{uvz},k)==1}^{\text{airspace cell with function }k}\wedge\overbrace{L(P')_{uvz}\in S_k}^{\text{airspace cell allocated to Sector }S_k}\\ 0,\begin{matrix}\text{if}F(L(P')_{uvz},k)==1\wedge L(P')_{uvz}\notin S_k\\ \vee F(L(P')_{uvz},k)==0\wedge L(P')_{uvz}\in S_k\end{matrix}\end{cases}\tag{21}$$

由式(15)可知，空域单元的功能由通过该单元的航迹的功能决定。因此，式(21)描述了目标函数的值取决于是否将具有功能性的空域单元分配给相应的扇区，这本质上反映了生成的扇区与交通流的功能的一致性。生成的扇区功能与交通流功能越一致，目标函数越大。

2.3 约束条件

(1)直棱柱约束

管制屏幕上只能显示3D扇区的平面投影,因此需将扇区设计为直棱柱的形状,如图5所示。本文通过六元组表示扇区,因此一定满足直棱柱约束。

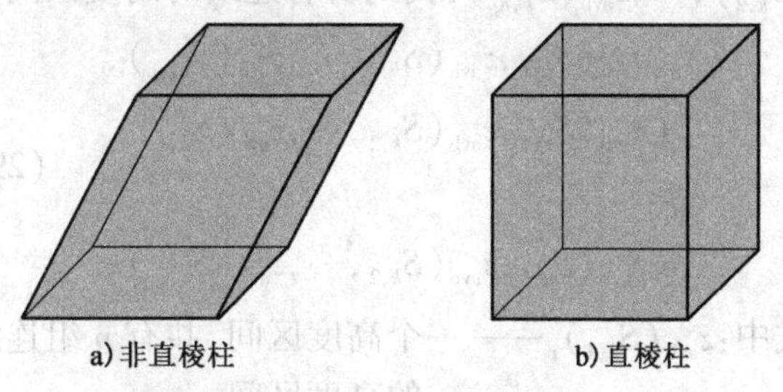

a)非直棱柱　　b)直棱柱

图5　直棱柱约束

(2)唯一性约束

考虑到管制责任的唯一性,每一个空域单元只能分配给一个扇区:

$$L(P')_{uvz} \in S_{k,g} \Rightarrow L(P')_{uvz} \notin (R/S_{k,g}) \quad (22)$$

以六元组的方式表示为:

$$\begin{aligned}&((u_{\text{left}},u_{\text{right}})_{S_{k,g}} \cap (u_{\text{left}},u_{\text{right}})_{S_{i,j}} = \varnothing) \vee \\ &((v_{\text{back}},v_{\text{front}})_{S_{k,g}} \cap (v_{\text{back}},v_{\text{front}})_{S_{i,j}} = \varnothing) \vee \\ &((z_{\text{bottom}},z_{\text{top}})_{S_{k,g}} \cap (z_{\text{bottom}},z_{\text{top}})_{S_{i,j}} = \varnothing), \\ &(i \neq k \vee j \neq g)\end{aligned} \quad (23)$$

(3)连通性约束

扇区应当为一个封闭的空间,任一子扇区由一个六元组确定,内部连通,同时各子扇区也应连通:

$$u_{\text{left}}(S_{k,g+1}) = u_{\text{right}}(S_{k,g}) + 1 \quad (24)$$

$$\begin{aligned}&((v_{\text{back}},v_{\text{front}})_{S_{k,g}} \cap (v_{\text{back}},v_{\text{front}})_{S_{i,g+1}} = \varnothing) \vee \\ &((z_{\text{bottom}},z_{\text{top}})_{S_{k,g}} \cap (z_{\text{bottom}},z_{\text{top}})_{S_{i,g+1}} = \varnothing)\end{aligned} \quad (25)$$

(4)反复移交约束

国内外研究文献中常设置扇区凸性约束,以避免同一架航空器被反复移交,如图6所示。但功能性扇区包围主流航迹,自然满足反复移交约束。

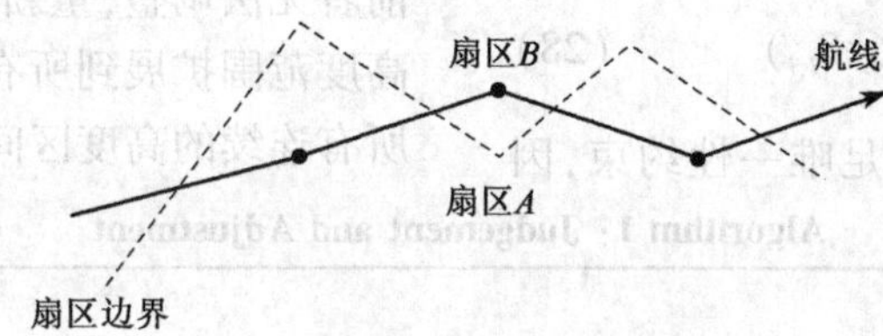

图6　反复移交约束

(5)完整性约束

所有扇区应组成完整的终端区空域,因此算法设计时需考虑如何对空白单元进行分配,并保证分配后仍满足上述4种约束。

3 功能性扇区划设算法设计

3.1 初始生成规则

初始生成规则通过产生 $\sum_{k=1}^{K} s_k$ 个六元组,确定各功能性扇区的初始范围。

步骤1:获取第 k 类航迹穿过的单元区域的水平左、右边界,作为第 k 类功能性扇区的 S_k 的左右范围 u_{left} 和 u_{right},并在该范围内随机产生数字 $u1$ 和 $u2$,将扇区 S_k 分为三个连续的子扇区 $S_{k,1}$、$S_{k,2}$、$S_{k,3}$,分别得到三类子扇区的左右边界($u_{\text{left}}, u1$)、($u1+1, u2$)、($u2+1, u_{\text{right}}$)。

步骤2:在各子扇区左右边界范围内,获取被该类航迹单元穿越区域的水平前、后边界,作为各子扇区的前后边界($v_{\text{down}}, v_{\text{up}}$),以及最低和最高边界,作为垂直范围($z_{\text{bottom}}, z_{\text{top}}$)。

步骤3:获得第 k 类功能性扇区初始解的六元组如下:

$$\begin{cases} S_{k,1} = \{u_{\text{left}}, u1, v_{\text{down}}, v_{\text{up}}, z_{\text{bottom}}, z_{\text{top}}\} \\ S_{k,2} = \{u1+1, u2, v_{\text{down}}, v_{\text{up}}, z_{\text{bottom}}, z_{\text{top}}\} \\ S_{k,3} = \{u2+1, u_{\text{right}}, v_{\text{down}}, v_{\text{up}}, z_{\text{bottom}}, z_{\text{top}}\} \end{cases} \quad (26)$$

重复以上步骤 K 次,分别为每类功能性扇区产生初始解。图7为航迹对应的功能性扇区初始解范围。

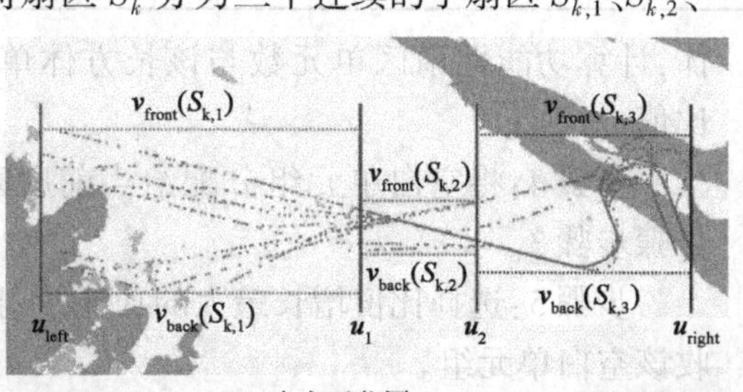

a)水平范围

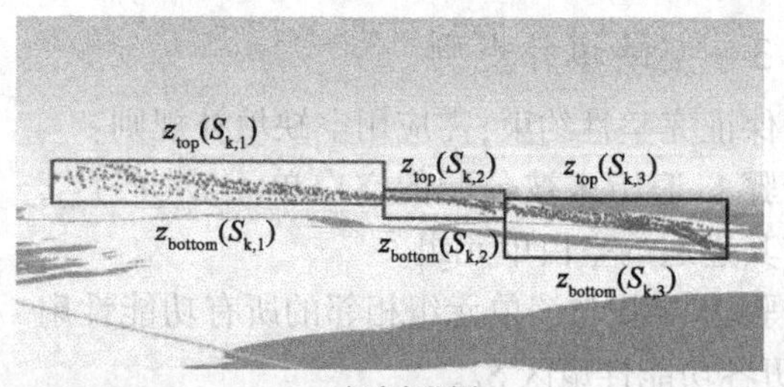

b)垂直范围

图7　功能性扇区初始解范围

3.2　判断调整规则

基于初始解产生规则,算法生成了各类功能性扇区的满足连通性约束的初始解,然而这些扇区的范围可能有所交叉,未必满足唯一性约束,因此需要对每类航迹之间进行交叉判定和调整。设扇区划设顺序 $\text{OrderS}=\{S_{i_1},S_{i_2},\cdots,S_{i_K}\}$,前一类扇区为 S_k,后一类扇区为 S_i。

判断两个扇区是否交叉,即等价于判断两个扇区的各子扇区是否交叉,用符号⊗表示交叉,判断子扇区交叉的方式可用六元组表示为:

$$S_{k,g}\otimes S_{i,g}=\begin{matrix}((u_{\text{left}},u_{\text{right}})_{S_{k,g}}\cap(u_{\text{left}},u_{\text{right}})_{S_{i,j}}\neq\varnothing)\ \wedge\\((v_{\text{down}},v_{\text{up}})_{S_{k,g}}\cap(v_{\text{down}},v_{\text{up}})_{S_{i,j}}\neq\varnothing)\ \wedge\\((z_{\text{bottom}},z_{\text{top}})_{S_{k,g}}\cap(z_{\text{bottom}},z_{\text{top}})_{S_{i,j}}\neq\varnothing)\end{matrix}\tag{27}$$

则两扇区是否交叉可表示为:

$$S_k\otimes S_i=\bigcup_{g=1,j=1}^{n_k,n_i}(S_{k,g}\otimes S_{i,j})\tag{28}$$

生成的初始扇区可能不满足唯一性约束,因此需要应用调整规则。设扇区划设顺序 $\text{OrderS}=\{S_{i_1},S_{i_2},\cdots,S_{i_K}\}$,前一类扇区为 S_k,后一类扇区为 S_i。

步骤1:遍历可用的高度范围 $z_{\text{avb}}(S_{k,1})$,$z_{\text{avb}}(S_{k,2})$,…,$z_{\text{avb}}(S_{k,n_k})$,找到所有连续的高度区间:

$$\begin{matrix}(z_{\text{avb}}(S_{k,1},z_{\text{avb}}(S_{k,2},\cdots,z_{\text{avb}}(S_{k,s_k}),\\(z_{\text{avb}}(S_{k,1},z_{\text{avb}}(S_{k,2},\cdots,z_{\text{avb}}(S_{k,s_k}),\\\cdots\\(z_{\text{avb}}(S_{k,1},z_{\text{avb}}(S_{k,2},\cdots,z_{\text{avb}}(S_{k,s_k})\end{matrix}\tag{29}$$

式中:$z_{\text{avb}}(S_{k,1})_p$——一个高度区间,共有 p 组连续的高度区间。

步骤2:若找到连续的高度区间,则计算 p 组高度区间的范围,将区间范围最大的一组作为新的高度范围。

步骤3:若无法找到一组连续的高度区间,则前者无法调整,重新对后者 S_i 进行调整。将可用高度范围扩展到所有高度范围$(1,z_{\max})$,重新寻找所有连续的高度区间。

Algorithm 1: Judgement and Adjustment

```
Input: All Functional Sectors and OrderS
Output: Adjusted Sectors

for i in OrderS do
    S_k ⇐ All Sectors(i)
    for j in 1,2,…,i-1 do
        S_j ⇐ All Sectors(j)
        if S_k intersect with S_j then
            z_ava(S_k,g) ⇐ (z_bottom,z_top)_{S_k,g} - (z_bottom,z_top)_{S_i,j}
        end if
    find all consecutive height intervals z_ava
    if z_ava exists then
        find the height interval z_ava(S_k,1)_p with longest interval length
        (z_bottom,z_top)_{S_k} ⇐ z_ava(S_k,1)_p
    else
        extend available vertical range to (1, z_max)
        go to  find all consecutive height intervals z_ava
end if
```

3.3　空缺填补规则

为保证完整性约束,需应用空缺填补规则:

步骤1:遍历未被分配的空白单元 $L(P')_{uvz}$,找到与其连通的空白单元组。

步骤2:寻找与该单元组相邻的所有功能性扇区,遍历各功能性扇区 S_k。

步骤3:计算包围当前功能性扇区的最小长方体,计算功能性扇区单元数与该长方体单元数的比值。

步骤4:将空白单元组分配给当前扇区,重复步骤步骤3。

步骤5:选择比值增长最大的功能性扇区来接收该空白单元组。

步骤6:重复上述步骤,直至所有空白单元都已分配。

3.4 基于模拟退火算法的优化求解

本文利用模拟退火算法,对六元组的各要素进行优化求解。

(1)解的表示

扇区划设的结果受到水平、垂直范围和扇区划设顺序的影响,因此选择上述因素作为变量。生成的所有扇区的解表示为:

$$\mathrm{Sol}(R)=\begin{bmatrix}\mathrm{Sol}_1\\ \cdots\\ \mathrm{Sol}_K\\ \mathrm{OrderS}\end{bmatrix} \tag{30}$$

式中:OrderS——1,2,…,K 的一个排列;

Sol(R)——终端区 R 功能性扇区划设的解。

(2)解的转移

模拟退火算法在温度变化时,转移幅度太大无法收敛,而幅度太小则跳跃能力变差,容易陷入局部最优。本文中解的转移步骤如下:

步骤1:对水平划分位置进行转移,产生随机转移幅度 $\delta 1,\delta 2\in\{-3,0,3\}$,令 $u1,u2$ 进行转移。

步骤2:判断转移后的水平划分位置是否合法:$u_{\text{left}}\leqslant u1\leqslant u2\leqslant u_{\text{right}}$,若不合法,则回退。

步骤3:根据当前 $u1$ 和 $u2$ 的值,获取各子扇区水平范围内的最前最后范围和最低最高范围作为新的前后范围($v_{\text{down}},v_{\text{up}}$)和高度范围($z_{\text{bottom}},z_{\text{top}}$)。

步骤4:产生新的转移幅度 $\delta 1',\delta 2'\in\{-1,0,1\}$,对前后范围和高度范围进行转移。

步骤5:判断新的前后范围和高度范围是否合法:$v_{\text{down}}\leqslant v_{\text{up}},z_{\text{bottom}}\leqslant z_{\text{top}}$,若不合法,则回退。

模拟退火具体优化过程如下所示。

Algorithm 2: Simulated Annealing

```
Input: Energy ObjectiveJ( )
Output: the optimal solution s_optimal
Set initial temperature T_0←T_min
generate initial solutions_0←Initial generation rule( )
initiate control parameters iterMax, T_max, coolrate
T←T_max
calculate initial objectiveJ(s_0), set J(s_optimal)←J(s_0)
* the stopping criterion
while T > T_min do
    s_new←transform(s)
* neighbor selecting
        calculate E(s_new)
        calculate the acceptance probabilityP(E(s), E(s_new), T)
    if P(E(s), E(s_new), T) ≥ random(0,1) then
            move to the new solution: s←s_new
end if
if E(s_new) < E(s_optimal) then
            s_optimal←s_new
end if
T←T * coolrate

Transform Function( ):
    input: solution s
    output: new neighbor solution s_new

for each sector in s do
        randomly adjust vertical range and horizontal range within (-3,3)
    check legality of new solution s_new
if legal then
        return s_new
else
        apply adjust rule to s_new
```

4　实例分析

4.1　数据准备

上海终端区为全国最繁忙的终端区，主要负责向上海虹桥、浦东国际机场进离场航班，和辖区内其他机场以及周边机场的飞越航班提供空中交通管制服务。目前上海终端区内划分为图 8 所示的 11 个扇区。

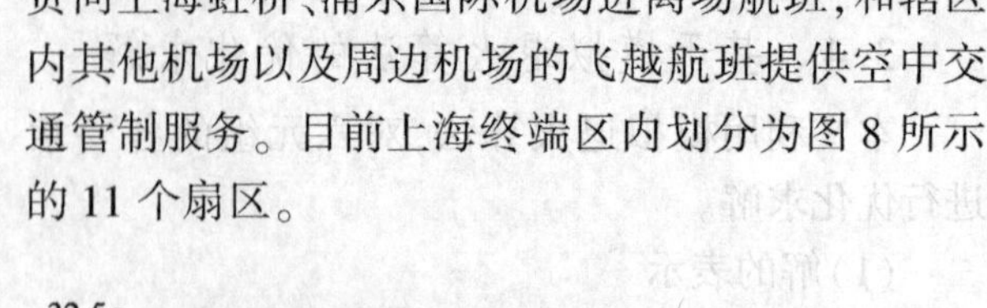

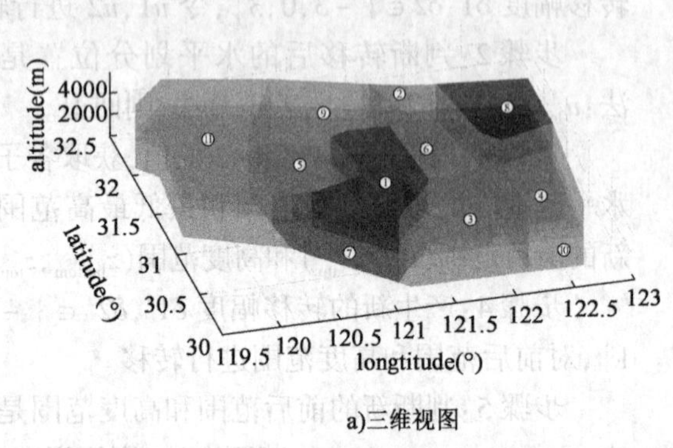

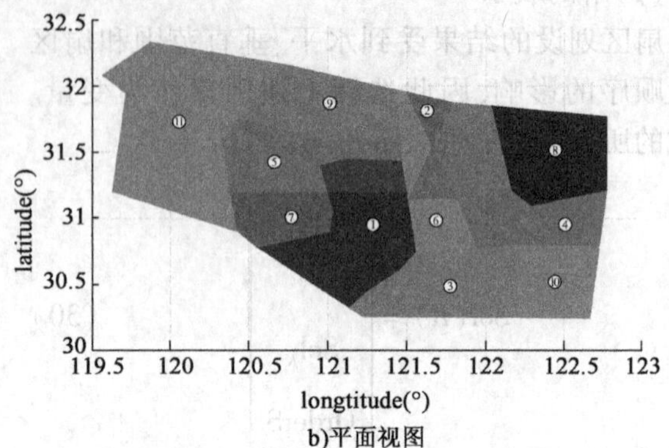

图 8　上海终端区现行扇区

选取 2021 年 6 月 15 日 9:00 至 11:00 上海终端区内的 167 条雷达航迹数据，对原始航迹数据进行预处理，包括异常航迹的清洗与等时间间隔的雷达航迹重采样。重采样时间间隔为 5s。

4.2　功能性扇区生成过程

建立基于逐点对比的相似性矩阵，部分结果如图 9 所示。

	ABW119	ANA8433	AZG040	CAL501	CBJ5377	CCA139	CCA1590	CCA1854	CCA1907	CCA1943
ABW119	0	7.303e+04	7.983e+04	998.7	5.043e+04	5.933e+04	8.554e+04	5.911e+04	8.469e+04	8.948e+04
ANA8433	7.303e+04	0	1.195e+05	6.661e+04	9.313e+04	7.848e+04	1.4e+05	1.365e+05	1.329e+05	1.114e+05
AZG040	7.983e+04	1.195e+05	0	4.601e+04	6.903e+04	7.717e+04	7200	6.013e+04	8.371e+04	5457
GAL501	998.7	6.661e+04	4.601e+04	0	4.917e+04	5.295e+04	8.516e+04	6.312e+04	8.13e+04	5.629e+04
CBJ5377	5.043e+04	9.313e+04	6.903e+04	4.917e+04	0	6172	7.674e+04	2.177e+04	1.478e+04	6.225e+04
CCA139	5.933e+04	7.848e+04	7.717e+04	5.295e+04	6172	0	8.417e+04	1.867e+04	1.411e+04	7.234e+04
CCA1590	8.554e+04	1.4e+05	7200	8.516e+04	7.674e+04	8.417e+04	0	5.892e+04	8.947e+04	2.039e+04
CCA1854	5.911e+04	1.365e+05	6.013e+04	6.312e+04	2.177e+04	1.867e+04	5.892e+04	0	1.559e+04	4.848e+04
CCA1907	8.469e+04	1.329e+05	8.371e+04	8.13e+04	1.478e+04	1.411e+04	8.947e+04	1.559e+04	0	7.767e+04
CCA1943	8.948e+04	1.114e+05	5457	5.629e+04	6.225e+04	7.234e+04	2.039e+04	4.848e+04	7.767e+04	0

$\times 10^4$　12　10　8　6　4　2　0

图 9　部分航迹相似性矩阵

由图 9 可见，较远航迹与较近航迹相似性距离相差较大，说明本文提出的相似性举例能够较好地衡量航迹间的相似性，将较近与较远的航迹分开。使用 DBSCAN 算法基于该距离矩阵进行聚类，并改变 DBSCAN 算法的两个主要参数。图 10 给出了不同参数值下航迹的聚类结果。

灰色航迹点为噪声，其余不同颜色的航迹点表示不同的航迹簇。对比以上结果，我们可以发现不同的参数设置对航迹的聚类结果有很大的影响。在图 10a）中航迹簇共有 11 个，而在图 10b）、c）中航迹簇共有 6 个，说明 eps 越大，航迹越容易聚成一簇，聚类簇数越少。此外，随着 min_samples 的增加，部分飞越航迹被误分类为噪声点。由于飞越航迹与其他航迹的距离较远，所以当飞越航迹较大时，附近没有足够的航迹来满足要求。

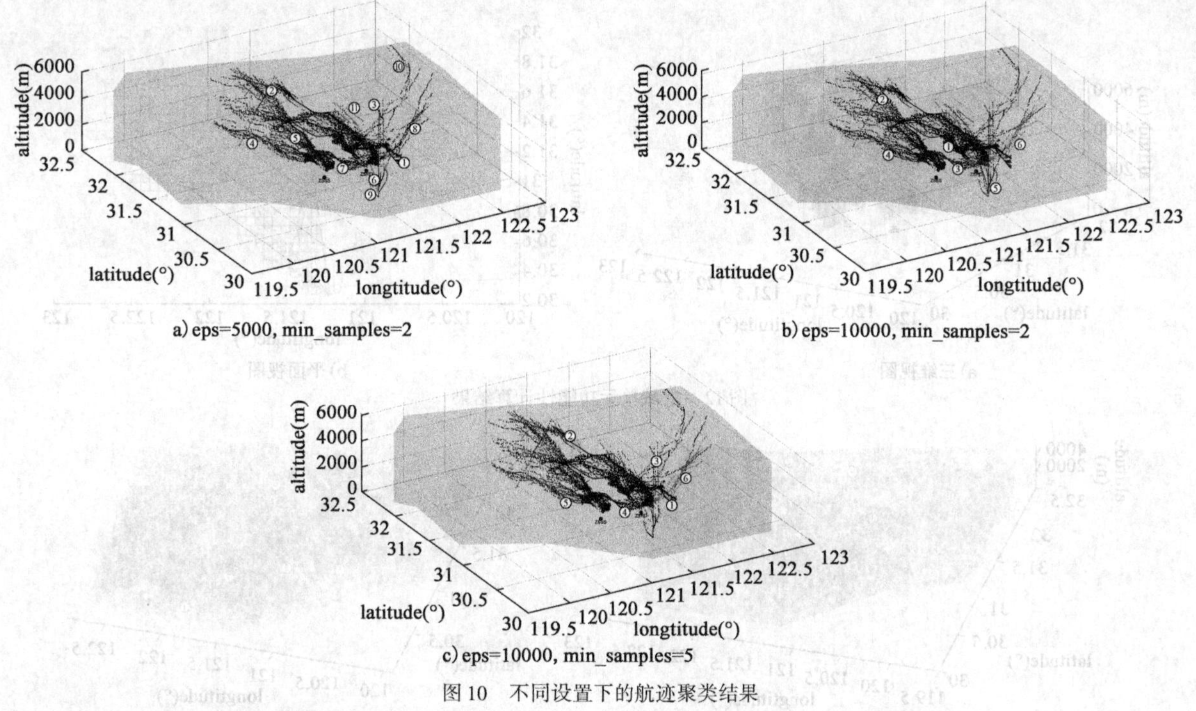

a) eps=5000, min_samples=2　　b) eps=10000, min_samples=2

c) eps=10000, min_samples=5

图10　不同设置下的航迹聚类结果

通过多次调整参数，确定参数 eps = 10000，min_samples = 2。然后结合飞行程序，最终得到 11 个航迹簇，如图 11 所示。

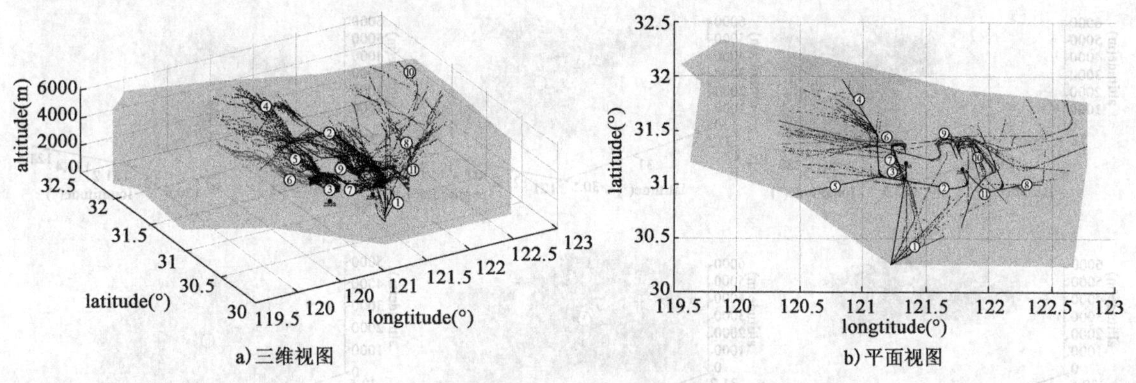

a) 三维视图　　b) 平面视图

图11　最终 11 类航迹聚类结果

在图 11 中，不同的功能的航迹被很好地分离。第 1 簇航迹为飞越航迹，第 2 簇航迹为浦东西北方向离场的初始航迹，第 3 簇航迹为虹桥西北方向离场的航迹，第 4 簇航迹为浦东和虹桥西北方向离场的共同航迹，第 5 簇航迹为浦东向西离场的航迹，第 6 簇航迹为虹桥西向进场的航迹，第 7 簇航迹为虹桥南向进场的航迹，第 8 簇航迹为浦东向东离场的航迹，第 9 簇航迹为浦东西向进场的航迹，第 10 簇航迹为浦东东向进场的航迹，第 11 簇航迹为浦东向东离场的初始航迹。

空域栅格采用正方体，边长 3.82km，高 300m，以虹桥机场跑道基准点为中心，起始角度 0°。接着计算各单元功能，若一个单元中包含多种航迹点，则具有多种功能，最终空域栅格化及各单元功能确定结果如图 12 所示。

空域栅格化后共有 1612 个空域单元被航迹穿越。经多次实验，设置模拟退火算法参数为：初始温度 $T_{max} = 1000$，冷却率 delta = 0.95，每一个温度内迭代次数 iterNum = 100，最低终止温度 $T_{min} = 1.0$。优化后目标函数为 1503，相应功能性扇区如图 13 所示，该划设方案能将 93.24% 被航迹穿越的单元分配至相应的扇区。由于约束条件，特别是右棱柱约束，剩余的 6.76% 功能单元无法分配到相应的扇区。

图 14 进一步展示了功能性扇区划设方案中每一个功能性扇区及其覆盖的航迹情况。

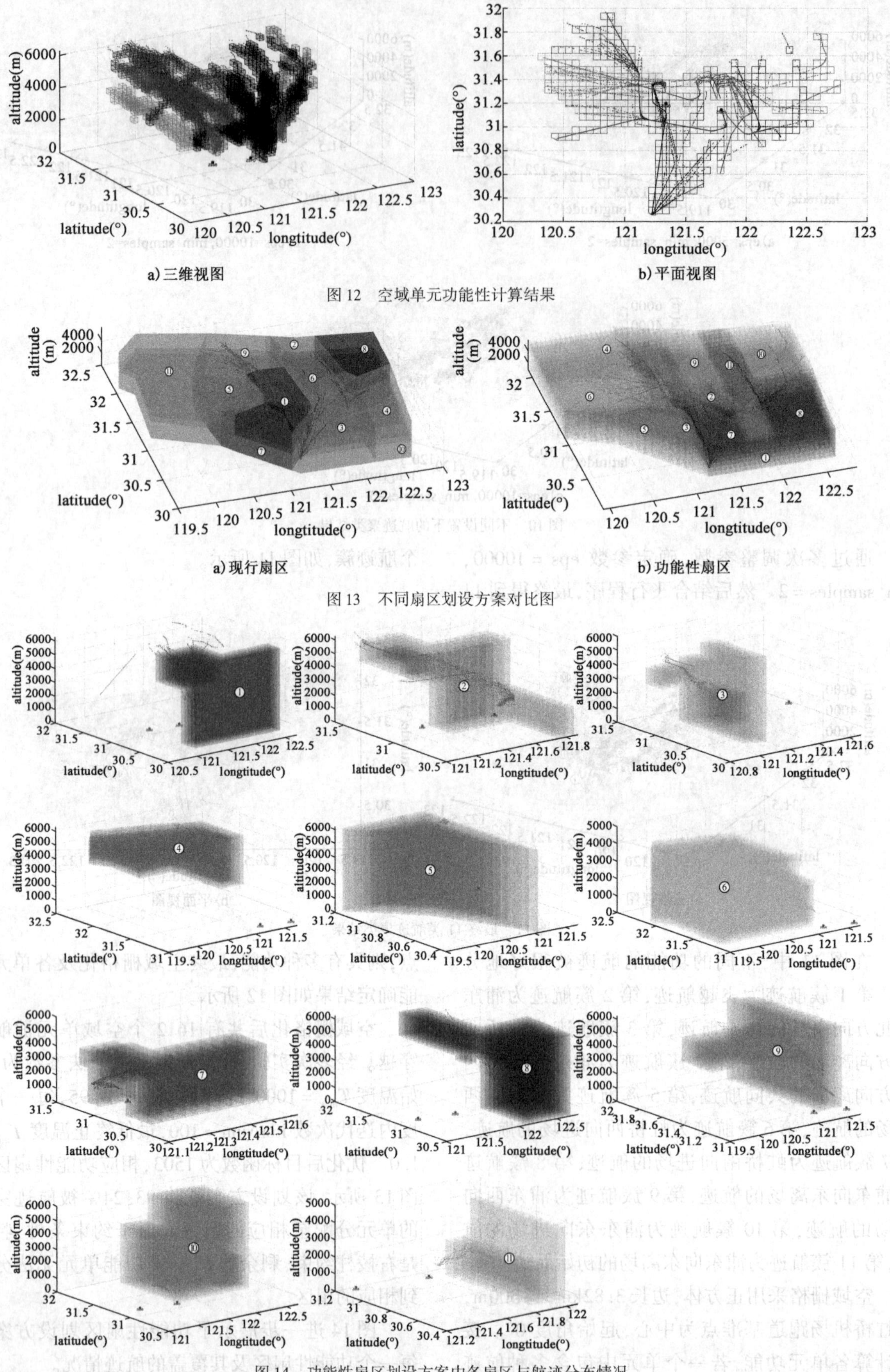

图12 空域单元功能性计算结果

图13 不同扇区划设方案对比图

图14 功能性扇区划设方案中各扇区与航迹分布情况

可以看出,相对于现行同一扇区同时存在不同的航迹簇,不同的航迹簇在不同扇区中得到了很好的区分和识别,即每个功能扇区准确覆盖一簇相应功能的航迹,验证了算法的有效性。

4.3 结果分析

虽然当前对空域系统性能评价的研究已经相当多,但对扇区划分特别是终端区中的扇区划分的研究还很少。为了进一步评价扇区划设方案的优劣,本研究从安全与效率两个方面选取了以下四个指标。

(1)扇区内潜在冲突次数:文献[14]中称这些潜在冲突为交叉点,用以衡量扇区的安全水平。但文献[14]中将时间间隔定义为300s,与当前的操作现实不符。经过多次实验,结合管制员的经验,本文对文献[14]的定义进行了如下改进:

$$d(p_m(\text{lng}_{p_m},\text{lat}_{p_m}),q_n(\text{lng}_{q_n},\text{lat}_{q_n}))\leqslant 10km \vee$$
$$|p_m(\text{alt}_{p_m})-q_n(\text{alt}_{q_n})|\leqslant 300m \vee$$
$$|\text{time}_{p_m}-\text{time}_{q_n}|\leqslant 60s \tag{31}$$

式中:p_m、q_n——两架航空器 p、q 在时间 time_{p_m}、time_{q_n} 的位置。

(2)平均扇区飞行时间:平均扇区飞行时间为各扇区航班的平均飞行时间。扇区飞行时间长意味着扇区与交通流的对齐,扇区内交通量削减量小[14]。研究表明,各扇区的容量与平均扇区的容量直接相关,平均飞行时间越长扇区的容量越大[11]。

(3)交通密度方差:交通密度方差是给定时间段内各扇区航班数的方差。交通密度是衡量管制员监控负荷的指标之一,交通密度高的扇区监控负荷大。因此,交通密度方差反映了不同扇区空中交通管制监控工作量的公平性,这是传统扇区划分的主要优化目标[4-7]。

(4)平均穿越扇区数量:平均穿越扇区数量可衡量管制协调负荷,较小的平均穿越扇区数量意味着较少的协调交接次数以及更高的管制效率,这也是传统扇区划分的主要优化目标[4-7]。

总体而言,扇区内潜在冲突次数表示扇区划分的安全水平,扇区平均飞行时间表示扇区容量,交通密度方差和平均穿越扇区数量表示管制员工作负荷。图15显示了当前扇区和功能性扇区划分方案中各扇区的潜在冲突数量、飞行时间和交通密度。

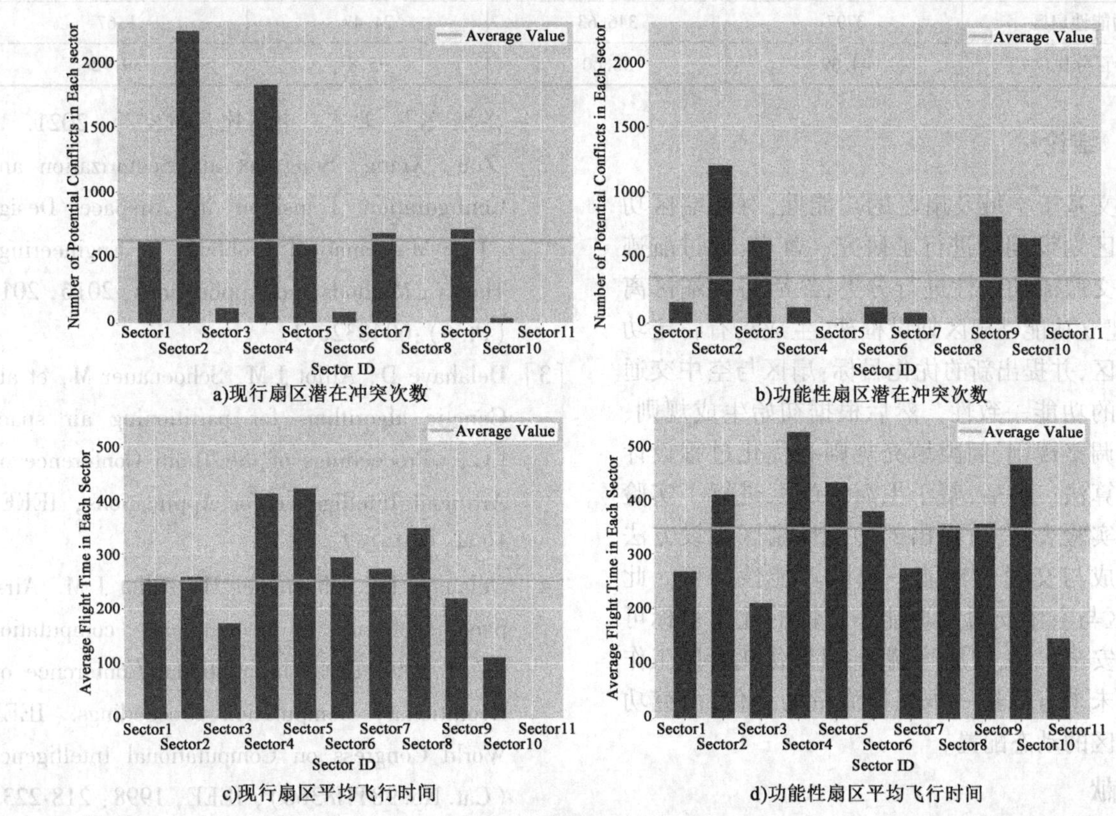

a)现行扇区潜在冲突次数 b)功能性扇区潜在冲突次数

c)现行扇区平均飞行时间 d)功能性扇区平均飞行时间

图 15

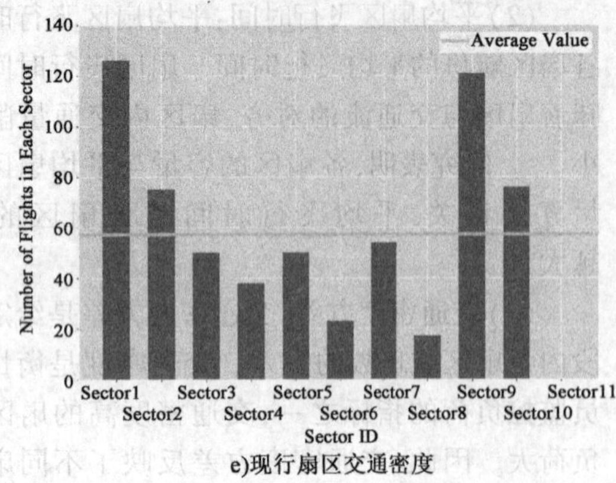

e)现行扇区交通密度

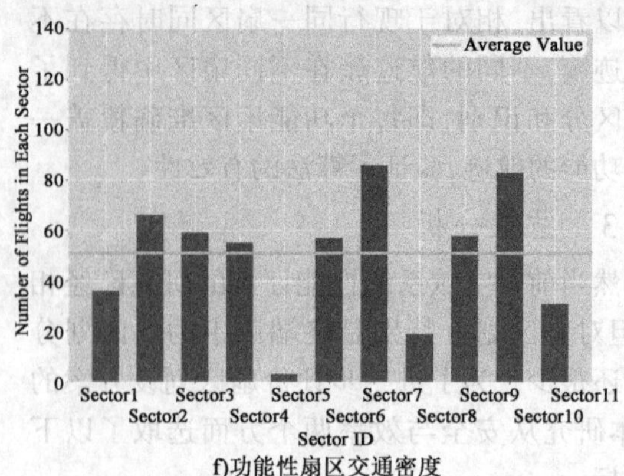

f)功能性扇区交通密度

图 15 现行扇区与功能性扇区不同指标对比情况

从图 15 可以看出,几乎每个扇区在这三个指标上都有所改善。这是因为功能性扇区可以覆盖主流交通流,所以大多数航班只需要通过一个扇区,平均穿越扇区数量减少,每个扇区中的飞行时间增加,从而减少管制员的协调负荷。而管制员监视负荷的平衡主要依靠于终端区内不同功能交通流分布的均匀性。此外,不同功能的交通流往往存在交叉冲突的风险,这就需要管制员的人为干预,以便及时解决冲突。职能部门可以将不同职能的交通流分开,减少部门内飞机的潜在冲突,从而保证空域资源的合理分配

表 1 为现行扇区与功能性扇区的总体比较。与当前扇区相比,功能性扇区的 4 项指标均有所改善,其中扇区内潜在冲突减少了 44.89%,平均扇区飞行时间增加了 38.60%,交通密度方差减少了 35.8%,平均穿越扇区数量减少了 39.92%。

现行扇区与功能性扇区总体比较 表 1

项 目	扇区内潜在冲突数量	平均扇区飞行时间(s)	交通密度方差	平均穿越扇区数量
现行扇区	6890	250.10	38.16	2.78
功能性扇区	3797	346.63	24.47	1.67
改善百分比(%)	44.89	38.60	35.8	39.92

5 结论

本文基于空域及扇区的功能性,对终端区功能性扇区划设问题进行了研究。首先,通过航迹聚类对交通流功能性进行分类;然后将终端区离散化,建立功能性扇区划设框架,生成具有特定功能的扇区,并提出新的优化目标:扇区与空中交通流之间的功能一致性。然后根据初始生成规则、判断与调整规则、间隙填充规则和优化过程设计相应的算法。最后,基于上海终端区进行了实验评价。实验表明,所提出的功能性扇区划设方法能够生成与交通流功能一致的功能性扇区。此外,扇区与空中交通流功能一致性的优化目标可以提高安全水平,增加终端区容量,优化管制工作负荷。未来可以进一步根据流量的变化,研究功能性扇区的动态配置。

参考文献

[1] 中国民用航空局. 2020 年民航行业发展统计公报[R]. 北京:中国民用航空局, 2021.

[2] Zou, Xiang, Song, et al. Sectorization and Configuration Transition in Airspace Design [J]. Mathematical Problems in Engineering: Theory, Methods and Applications, 2016, 2016 (Pt.6):6048326.1.

[3] Delahaye D, Alliot J M, Schoenauer M, et al. Genetic algorithms for partitioning air space [C]. Proceedings of the Tenth Conference on Artificial Intelligence for Applications, IEEE, 1994: 291-297.

[4] Delahaye D, Schoenauer M, Alliot J M. Airspace sectoring by evolutionary computation [C]. 1998 IEEE International Conference on Evolutionary Computation Proceedings. IEEE World Congress on Computational Intelligence (Cat. No. 98TH8360), IEEE, 1998: 218-223.

[5] 韩松臣, 张明, 黄卫芳. 管制扇区优化划分

的方法及计算机实现技术[J]. 交通运输工程学报, 2003(01):101-104.

[6] Songchen H, Ming Z. The Optimization Method of the Sector Partition Based on Metamorphic Voronoi Polygon [J]. Chinese Journal of Aeronautics, 2004, (01): 7-12.

[7] 张明, 韩松臣. 基于变精度粗集的动态扇区数规划[J]. 西南交通大学学报, 2009,44(03):410-414.

[8] Yousefi A, Donohue G. Temporal and Spatial Distribution of Airspace Complexity for Air Traffic Controller Workload-Based Sectorization [C]// Aiaa Aviation Technology, Integration & Operations,2004.

[9] Klein A. An efficient method for airspace analysis and partitioning based on equalized traffic mass[C]. Proceedings of the 6th USA/Europe Air Traffic Management R & D Seminar,2005.

[10] Brinton C, Hinkey J, Leiden K. Airspace sectorization by dynamic density [C]. 9th AIAA Aviation Technology, Integration, and Operations Conference (ATIO) and Aircraft Noise and Emissions Reduction Symposium (ANERS),2009: 7102.

[11] Zelinski S. A Comparison of Algorithm Generated Sectorizations [J]. Air Traffic Control Quarterly, 2016, 18(26):279-301.

[12] Delahaye D, Puechmorel S. 3D airspace sectoring by evolutionary computation: Real-world applications[C]. Proceedings of the 8th annual conference on genetic and evolutionary computation. 2006: 1637-1644.

[13] Kicinger R, Yousefi A. Heuristic Method for 3D Airspace Partitioning: Genetic Algorithm and Agent-Based Approach [C]// Aiaa Aviation Technology, Integration, & Operations Conference,2009.

[14] Tang J, Alam S, Lokan C, et al. A multi-objective evolutionary method for dynamic airspace re-sectorization using sectors clipping and similarities[C]. 2012 IEEE Congress on Evolutionary Computation. IEEE, 2012: 1-8.

[15] 王超, 陈昱. 基于BSP和动态规划的大规模空域扇区划分[J]. 计算机应用研究, 2015,32(11):3259-3263.

[16] Min X. Three Dimensional Sector Design with Optimal Number of Sectors [C]// Aiaa Guidance, Navigation, & Control Conference. American Institute of Aeronautics and Astronautics (AIAA), 2012: 609-618.

[17] Wong C S Y, Sundaram S, Sundararajan N. CDAS: A Cognitive Decision-Making Architecture for Dynamic Airspace Sectorization for Efficient Operations [J]. IEEE Transactions on Intelligent Transportation Systems, 2018, 20(5): 1659-1668.

[18] Wong C S Y, Suresh S, Sundararajan N. A rolling horizon optimization approach for dynamic airspace sectorization [J]. IFAC Journal of Systems and Control, 2020, 11: 100076.

[19] Wei J, Sciandra V, Hwang I, et al. Design and Evaluation of a Dynamic Sectorization Algorithm for Terminal Airspace[J]. Journal of Guidance, Control, and Dynamics, 2014, 37(5): 1539-1555.

[20] Granberg T A, Polishchuk T, Polishchuk V, et al. Convex sectorization-a novel integer programming approach[C]. 2017 Integrated Communications Navigation and Surveillance (ICNS) Conference,2017.

[21] Granberg T A, Polishchuk T, Polishchuk V, et al. Integer Programming-Based Airspace Sectorization for Terminal Maneuvering Areas with Convex Sectors [J]. Journal of Air Transportation, 2019, 27(4): 169-180.

基于VMD-LSTM的民航运输量预测

王 飞* 韩翔宇
(中国民航大学空管学院)

摘 要 为准确预测受疫情影响后我国民航运输量,本文提出了基于分解-集成模型的民航运输量预测方法。首先,收集了2005年1月至2021年10月的运输总周转量、旅客运输量和货邮运输量统计数据,构建了相应时间序列。其次,考虑到所用时间序列的分布总体呈上升趋势但部分数据突变较大的特点,采用变分模态分解方法分解相应时间序列,并运用中心频率的方法确定分解模态数量。再次,使用长短期记忆网络对分解后的模态分量进行多次一步预测。最后进行实例计算和分析。结果表明,应用VMD-LSTM模型,运输总周转量、旅客运输量和货邮运输量预测准确度分别为94.22%、94.64%和97.57%;与使用单一LSTM模型相比,3种运输量预测准确性分别提高7.1%、9.62%和2.69%;与使用VMD-XGboost模型相比,3种运输量预测准确性分别提高4.73%、9.15%和2.5%。说明应用VMD-LSTM模型对民航运输量进行预测是可行的和准确的。

关键词 民航运输 民航运输量预测 分解集成模型 时间序列

0 引言

航空运输业是国家战略性产业,在整个国民经济发展中发挥重要的支撑作用。民航运输量的科学预测是准确把握民航业发展趋势、制定发展规划目标的重要基础。运输总周转量、旅客运输量和货邮运输量是民航运输量的三个核心指标,这三个指标能从整体上反映民航运输量的发展趋势。围绕这三个指标,诸多学者展开了各种方法的预测研究,大体上可分为4类。第一类是建立一元或多元回归模型,该方法综合考虑多种影响因素,如国内生产总值,国际国内局势,进出口贸易额、人均消费水平、人口数量等,再通过预测相关因素的数值来计算民航运输量[1-2],这种方法本质上需要对多个因素进行预测,存在误差累积的弊端。第二类是时间序列方法,应用灰色模型(Grey Model, GM)[3-4]、自回归移动平均模型(Autoregressive Integrated Moving Average model, ARIMA)[5-6]、XGboost、指数平滑模型[7-8]等进行预测,这一类方法对时间序列自身特性要求较高,且普适性较差。第三类是人工智能方法,应用支持向量机[9]、神经网络[10]等模型实现预测,这一类方法需要大量样本进行训练,耗时长,且科学合理确定模型参数难度较大。第四类是上述三类方法的组合预测方法[11-14],这类方法能改善预测精度,但需要计算多个模型预测值,且各模型的权重值仍以经验为主,主观性较大。上述方法都利用数学模型对历史数据进行拟合,进而进行预测,无法客观、全面反映数据的内在结构和特性,同时预测精度有待提高。

近年来,快速发展的分解-集成模型为解决自然科学和社会科学领域中诸多问题提供了一种新的思路,在原油价格[15]、水库的月径流[16]、风电功率[17]、医学治疗[18]等预测方面取得了一些成果,且可以有效解决上述方法存在的弊端,特别是在地面交通流预测[19]领域的研究成果为分解-集成模型在民航运输领域应用提供了有益借鉴。

本文根据"先分解、后集成"的整体框架,首先应用变分模态分解(Vibrational Mode Decomposition, VMD)将原始时间序列分解为若干个模态时序,其中VMD分解方法较其他方法有着可以选择模态分解个数的特点,故在时序分解结果方面有着更好的可控性。接着采用长短期记忆(Long Short-Term Memory, LSTM)方法对模态进行

1. 基金项目:国家科学自然基金(U1833103);中央高校基本科研业务费项目中国民航大学专项(3122019129)。

预测,然后将模态预测结果采用加和方式实现集成预测,最后进行实例分析。

1 基于 VMD 的时间序列分解

VMD 是一种自适应的分解方法,可以有效降低非线性时间序列的复杂度。VMD 的核心思想是构建和求解变分问题,其中变分模态分解原理如式(1)所示:

$$\begin{cases} \min\limits_{\{u_k\},\{\omega_k\}} \sum\limits_k \left\| \partial_t \left[\left(\delta(t) + \frac{j}{\pi t} \right) * u_k(t) \right] e^{-j\omega_k t} \right\|^2 \\ \text{s.t.} \sum\limits_k u_k(t) = f(t) \end{cases} \tag{1}$$

式中:k——需要分解的模态个数;

t——自变量;

j——虚部;

$u_k(t)$——模态分量;

$\{\omega_k\}$——各模态分量的频率中心;

$\delta(t)$——狄拉克函数;

$*$——卷积运算符;

$\|\cdot\|$——二范数;

$f(t)$——原始时间按序列。

为求解式(1),将上式转变为无约束变分问题,如式(2)所示:

$$L(\{u_k\},\{\omega_k\},\lambda) = \alpha \sum_k \| \partial_t [(\delta(t) + \mathrm{j}/\pi t) * u_k(t)] e^{-\mathrm{j}\omega_k t} \|_2^2 + \| f(t) - \sum_k u_k(t) \|_2^2 + \langle \lambda(t), f(t) - \sum_k u_k(t) \rangle \tag{2}$$

式中:λ——Lagrange 算子;

$\langle \cdot \rangle$——求内积;

α——二次惩罚因子,用以降低高斯噪声的干扰。

利用交替方向乘子(Alternating Direction Method of Multipliers, ADMM)迭代算法结合 Parseva / Plancherel、傅里叶等距变换,优化得到的各模态分量和中心频率,并搜寻增广 Lagrange 算子的鞍点,计算得到 u_k、ω_k 和 λ,如式(3)~式(5)所示:

$$\hat{u}_k^{n+1}(\omega) \leftarrow \frac{\hat{f}(\omega) - \sum_{i \neq k} \hat{u}_i(\omega) + \hat{\lambda}(\omega)/2}{1 + 2\alpha(\omega - \omega_k)^2} \tag{3}$$

$$\omega_k^{n+1}(\omega) \leftarrow \frac{\int_0^\infty \omega \left| \hat{u}_k^{n+1}(\omega) \right|^2 d\omega}{\int_0^\infty \left| \hat{u}_k^{n+1}(\omega) \right|^2 d\omega} \tag{4}$$

$$\hat{\lambda}^{n+1}(\omega) \leftarrow \hat{\lambda}^n(\omega) + \gamma \left(\hat{f}(\omega) - \sum_k \hat{u}_k^{n+1}(\omega) \right) \tag{5}$$

式中:$\hat{}$——估计值;

ω——自变量;

$d\omega$——对 ω 求导;

γ——噪声容限;

$u_k(\omega)$——分解后的单分量调幅调频信号;

ω_k——每个单分量调幅调频信号的中频率;

n——迭代发生次数。

VMD 分解的具体方法表示见图 1。

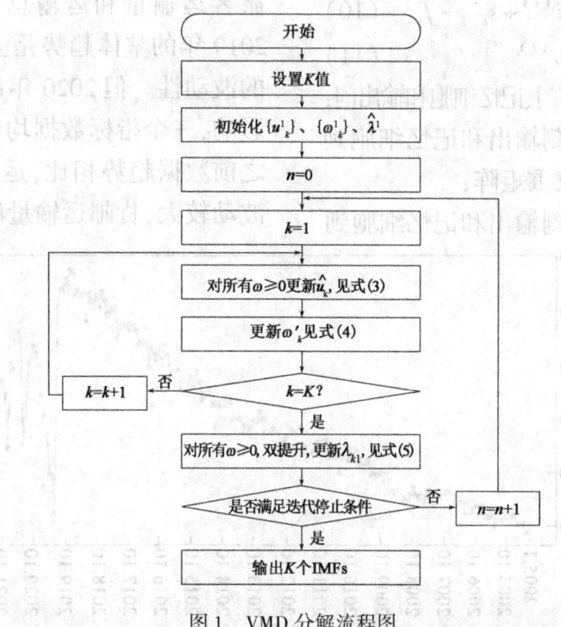

图 1 VMD 分解流程图

(1)通过中心频率确定 K 取值；

(2)初始化 $\{u_k\}$、$\{\omega_k\}$、λ_k 和 $k=0$, $n=0$；

(3)$n=n+1$,迭代；

(4)依据式(3)、式(4)更新 u_k 和 ω_k,直至分解个数达到 K 时停止内迭代；

(5)依据式(5)迭代 λ；

(6)给定精度 ε,若满足式(6)的停止条件则停止,否则进入步骤(3)继续迭代。

$$\sum_k \| u_k^{n+1} - u_k^n \|_2^2 / \| u_k^n \|_2^2 < \varepsilon \tag{6}$$

2　长短期记忆网络预测模型

LSTM是一种特殊的RNN(Recurrent Neural Network)模型,解决了RNN模型在处理长期数据依赖时的梯度消失问题,具有学习长期的规律效率较高的特点。LSTM由3个控制门、遗忘门、输入门、输出门和记忆细胞组成。其中输入门控制输入信息输入记忆细胞,输出门筛选并确定输出进入下一次迭代的信息,遗忘门选择输入信息中需要被遗弃的信息,记忆细胞用于储存每个时刻的状态信息。记忆细胞的输入、输出和遗忘通过矩阵乘法实现。

LSTM模型的主要思想是将RNN中的每个隐藏单元换成了具有记忆功能的细胞。每个记忆细胞组成如图2所示。根据文献[20],LSTM输出 h 计算如式(7)~式(11)所示：

$$i_t = \sigma(\boldsymbol{W}_{ix}x_t + \boldsymbol{W}_{ih}h_{t-1} + \boldsymbol{W}_{is}s_{t-1} + b_i) \tag{7}$$

$$f_t = \sigma(\boldsymbol{W}_{fx}x_t + \boldsymbol{W}_{fh}h_{t-1} + \boldsymbol{W}_{fs}s_{t-1} + b_f) \tag{8}$$

$$o_t = \sigma(\boldsymbol{W}_{ox}x_t + \boldsymbol{W}_{oh}h_{t-1} + \boldsymbol{W}_{os}s_t + b_o) \tag{9}$$

$$s_t = \varphi(\boldsymbol{W}_{sx}x_t + \boldsymbol{W}_{sh}h_{t-1} + b_c) \cdot i^{(i)} + s_{t-1} \cdot f_t \tag{10}$$

$$h^{(t)} = s^{(t)} \cdot o^{(t)} \tag{11}$$

式中：i、f、s、o——输入门、遗忘门、记忆细胞和输出门；

$\boldsymbol{W}_{ix}$、$\boldsymbol{W}_{ih}$、$\boldsymbol{W}_{os}$——输入、上时刻输出和记忆细胞到输入门的权重矩阵；

$\boldsymbol{W}_{fx}$、$\boldsymbol{W}_{fh}$、$\boldsymbol{W}_{fs}$——输入、上时刻输出和记忆细胞到遗忘门的权重矩阵；

$\boldsymbol{W}_{ox}$、$\boldsymbol{W}_{oh}$、$\boldsymbol{W}_{os}$——输入、上时刻输出和记忆细胞到输出门的权重矩阵；

$\boldsymbol{W}_{sx}$、$\boldsymbol{W}_{sh}$——输入,上时刻输出到记忆细胞的权重矩阵；

b_i、b_f、b_o、b_s——输入门、输出门、遗忘门和记忆细胞的偏置量；

$\cdot$——点乘。

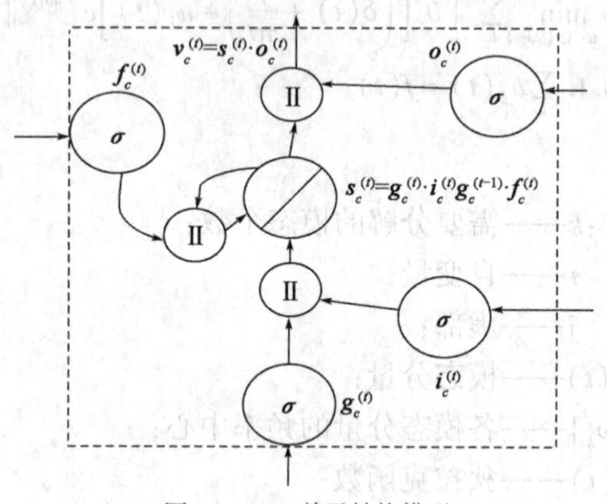

图2　LSTM单元结构模型

3　实例分析

3.1　数据描述

本部分以旅客运输量、货邮运输量和运输总周转量3个关键的民航运输量指标为例来进行实例分析。从国家统计局、民航局官网上收集到2005年1月至2021年10月的数据,构建相应的时间序列,其变化趋势见图3~图5。可以看出,旅客运输量和运输总周转量时间序列在2005—2019年的整体趋势是上升的,相邻数据没有明显的波动性。但2020年以来,受疫情及出行管控的影响,三个指标数据均出现明显波动。与2020年之前数据趋势相比,运输总周转量和旅客运输量波动较大,货邮运输量波动相对较小。

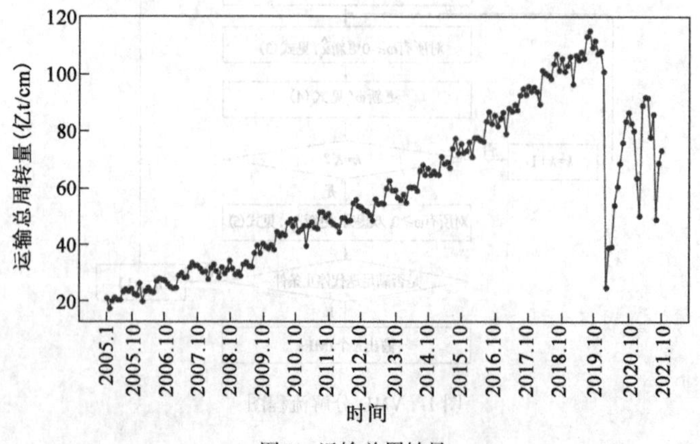

图3　运输总周转量

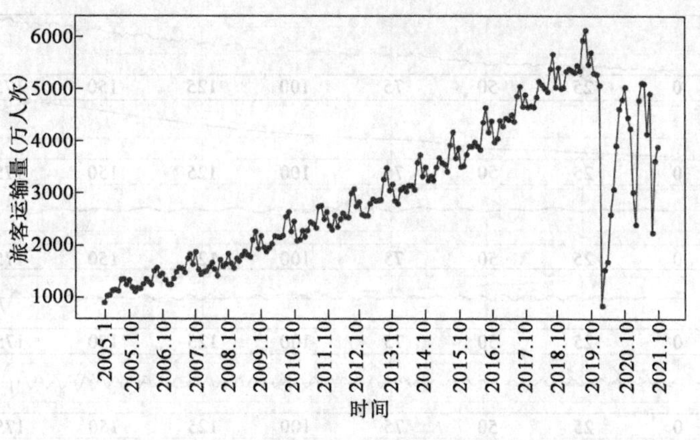

图4 旅客运输量

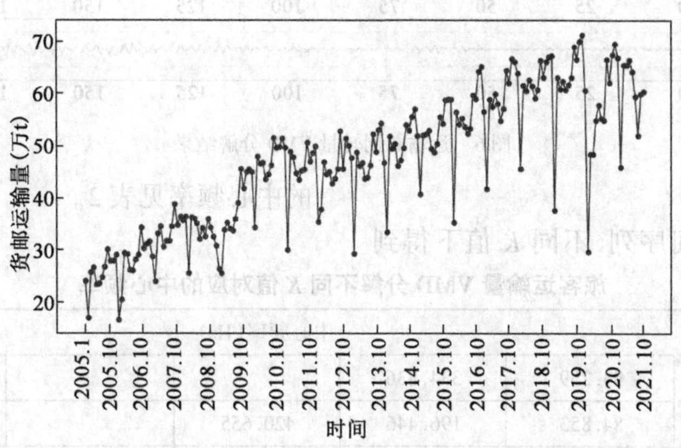

图5 货邮运输量

3.2 VMD分解

VMD分解需要首先确定分解模态数 K。如果模态数过多容易导致两个相邻模态过于接近,从而产生模态的混叠[21-22];如果模态个数过少将导致分解不充分,出现部分序列丢失现象。各模态主要区别体现在其中心频率上,故本文通过设置不同的 K,观察不同 K 对应的中心频率分布,从而确定最终的 K 值。

(1)运输总周转量分解

针对运输总周转量时间序列,不同 K 值下得到的中心频率见表1。

运输总周转量 VMD 分解不同 K 值对应的中心频率 表1

模态数 K	中心频率(Hz)						
3	0.300	84.082	270.794				
4	0.291	77.018	195.456	417.953			
5	0.285	71.904	173.034	282.212	429.949		
6	0.283	70.199	169.160	260.171	343.154	437.521	
7	0.282	69.445	168.233	258.172	338.705	422.206	482.440

当 K 值取7时,422.206Hz与482.440Hz之间差较小,可能存在有模态的混叠现象,故模态数 K 的取值应为6。VMD分解的6个模态(Intrinsic Mode Function,IMF)结果如图6所示。

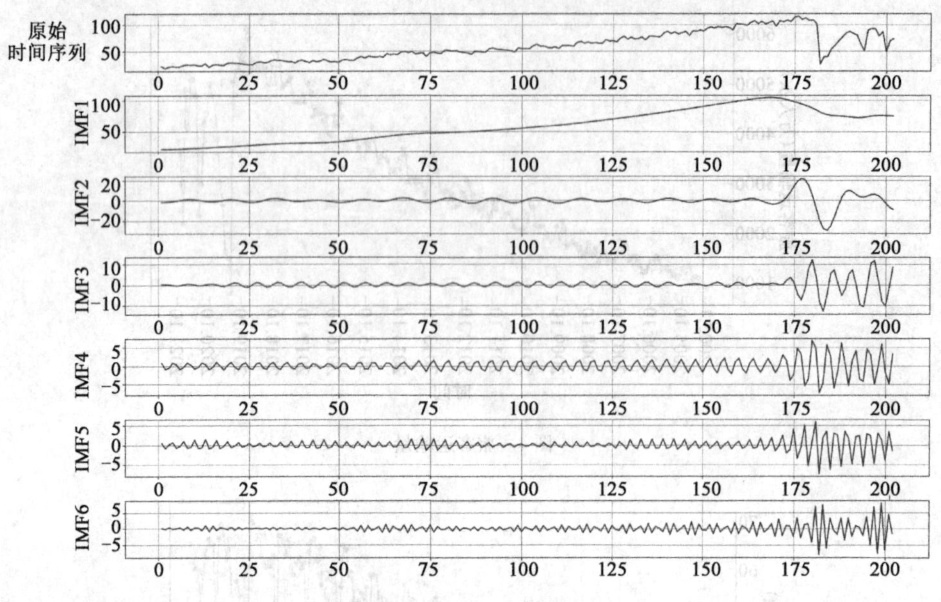

图 6　运输总周转量 VMD 分解结果

(2)旅客运输量分解

针对旅客运输量时间序列,不同 K 值下得到的中心频率见表 2。

旅客运输量 VMD 分解不同 K 值对应的中心频率　　表 2

模态数 K	中心频率(Hz)						
3	0.291	93.259	334.836				
4	0.279	84.853	196.446	420.655			
5	0.274	81.263	173.917	290.150	432.296		
6	0.272	80.216	171.412	269.010	344.450	438.014	
7	0.272	79.428	170.675	267.908	341.065	425.834	471.976

当 K 值取 7 时,425.834Hz 与 471.976Hz 之间差较小,可能存在有模态的混叠现象,故模态数 K 的取值应为 6。VMD 分解的 6 个 IMF 结果如图 7 所示。

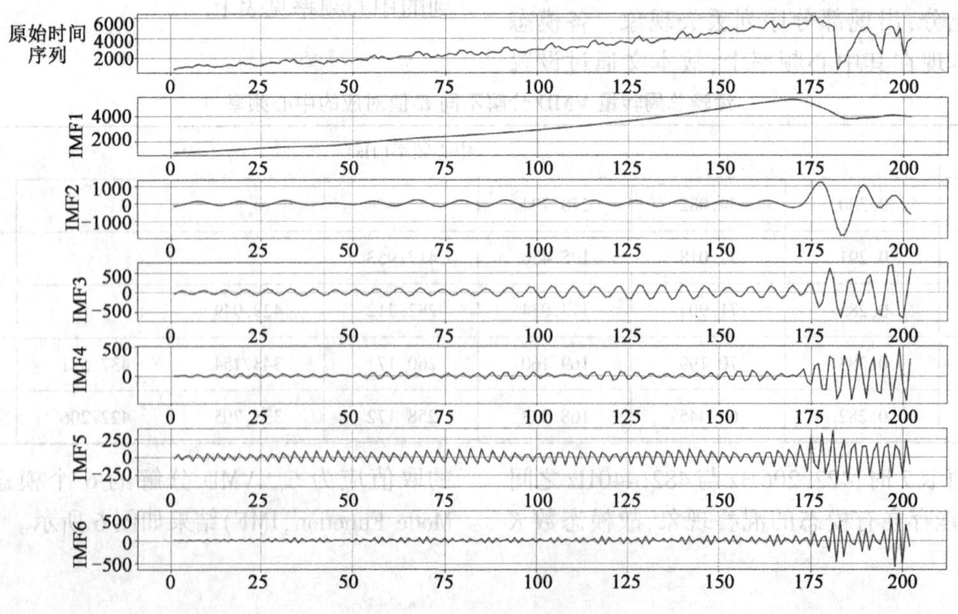

图 7　旅客运输量 VMD 分解结果

(3)货邮运输量分解

针对货邮运输量时间序列,不同 K 值下得到的中心频率见表3。

货邮运输量 VMD 分解不同 K 值对应的中心频率 表3

模态数 K	中心频率(Hz)							
3	0.107	165.413	334.889					
4	0.107	158.073	261.836	454.076				
5	0.092	87.174	233.351	334.993	482.324			
6	0.090	80.808	166.704	253.214	337.555	481.042		
7	0.089	80.064	166.743	249.998	332.858	415.943	490.500	
4938968	0.089	7.2068	166.435	249.395	333.399	336.033	419.204	

当 K 值取8时,333.399Hz 与 336.033Hz 之间差较小,可能存在有模态的混叠现象,故模态数 K 的取值应为7。VMD 分解的7个 IMF 结果如图8所示。

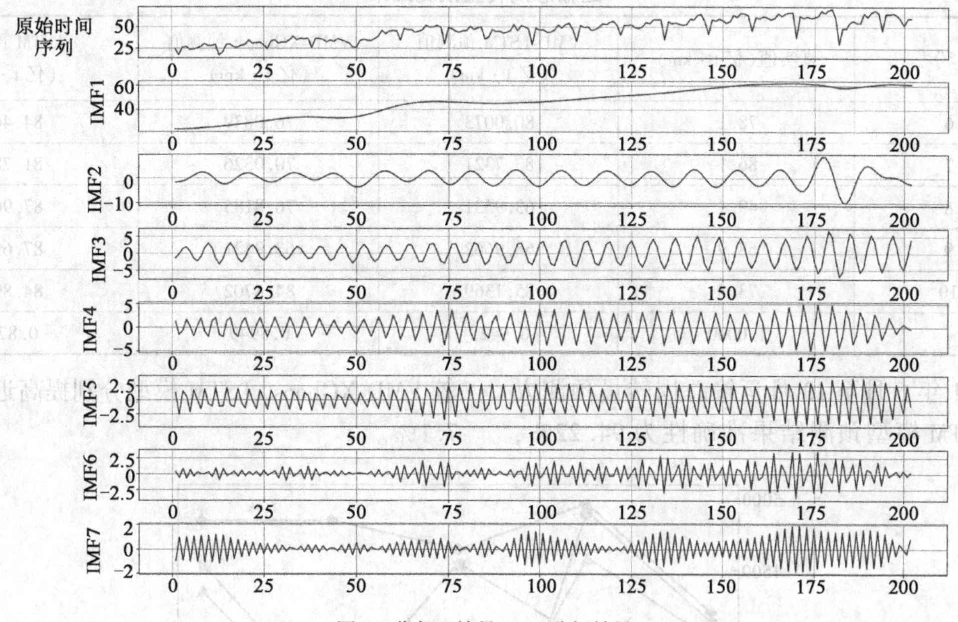

图8 货邮运输量 VMD 分解结果

3.3 LSTM 预测

应用 VMD 方法分别将原始时序分解为若干个 IMF,针对每个 IMF 应用 LSTM 进行预测,然后将个 IMF 预测结果累加求和,即为最终的预测结果。以 2005 年 1 月至 2021 年 5 月数据作用以训练模型,采用滑动窗方式,每组连续 6 个数值预测下一个数值。用 2021 年 6 月至 2021 年 10 月数据作为测试集,共 5 组数据。鉴于 LSTM 具有快速适应趋势中急剧变化的固有能力,因此最终预测结果常有波动,故本文将多次预测结果取平均值作为最终预测结果。采用均等系数 R_{EC} 指标来衡量 5 组数据预测准确性,其计算公式如式(12)所示。R_{EC} 值越接近 1,说明预测精度更高。

$$R_{EC} = 1 - \frac{\sqrt{\sum_{t=1}^{N}(\hat{y}_t - y_t)^2}}{\sqrt{\sum_{t=1}^{N}(\hat{y}_t)^2} + \sqrt{\sum_{t=1}^{N}(y_t)^2}} \tag{12}$$

式中:y_t——真实值;

$\hat{y}_t$——预测值。

为了进一步评价本文模型预测性能,将本文模型与 VMD-XGboost 模型及 LSTM 单一模型进行对比,其中 XGboost 模型是一个开源的机器学习项目,是 GBDT(Gradient Boosting Decision Tree)模型在算法上和工程上的改进,在非线性时间序列的预测上展现出较大优势,同时在诸多机器学习竞赛中取得过不错的成绩。最终预测结果如图 9 ~ 图 11 及表 4 ~ 表 6 所示。

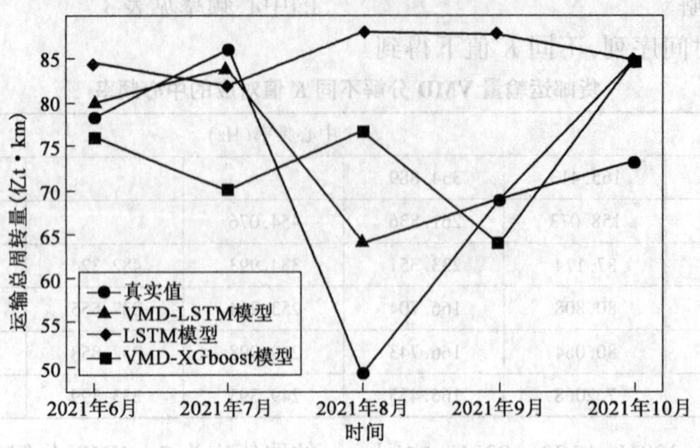

图9　运输总周转量各方法预测结果对比

运输总周转量预测结果　　表4

年　份	真实值(亿 t·km)	VMD-LSTM 预测值(亿 t·km)	VMD-XGboost 预测值(亿 t·km)	LSTM 预测值(亿 t·km)
2021.6	78.1	80.0073	76.0839	84.4687
2021.7	86.1	83.7321	70.0326	81.7805
2021.8	49.1	63.9531	76.8185	87.9627
2021.9	68.9	68.9662	63.9421	87.6964
2021.10	73.3	85.1369	84.8702	84.8994
R_{EC}	1.0000	0.9422	0.8949	0.8712

在2021年6月至10月运输总周转量预测方面VMD-LSTM模型预测结果准确性为94.22%，较VMD-XGboost、LSTM模型分别提高近4.73%和7.1%。

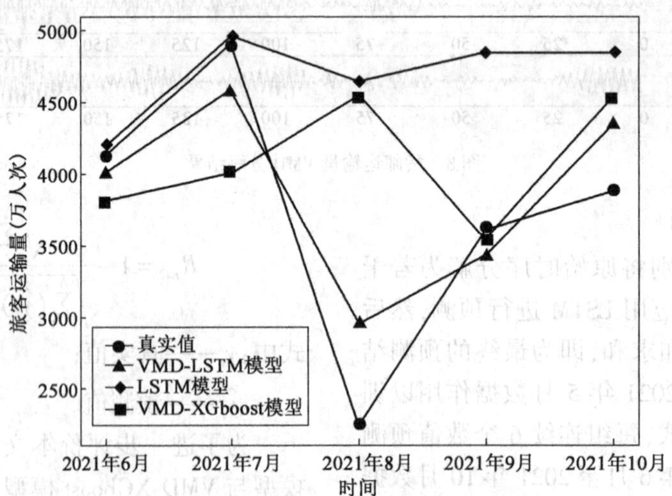

图10　旅客运输量各方法预测结果对比

旅客运输量预测结果　　表5

年　份	真实值(万人次)	VMD-LSTM 预测值(万人次)	VMD-XGboost 预测值(万人次)	LSTM/预测值(万人次)
2021.6	4127.7	4014.16	3803.6	4184.35
2021.7	4911.7	4583.32	4009.68	4963.67

续上表

年 份	真实值(万人次)	VMD-LSTM 预测值(万人次)	VMD-XGboost 预测值(万人次)	LSTM/预测值(万人次)
2021.8	2240.7	2947.95	4548.91	4641.9
2021.9	3611.7	3435.09	3539.23	4846.18
2021.10	3886.1	4348.05	4532.4	4845.61
R_{EC}	1.0000	0.9464	0.8549	0.8502

在2021年6月至10月旅客运输量预测方面VMD-LSTM模型预测准确性为94.64%，较VMD-XGboost、LSTM模型分别提高近9.15%和9.62%。

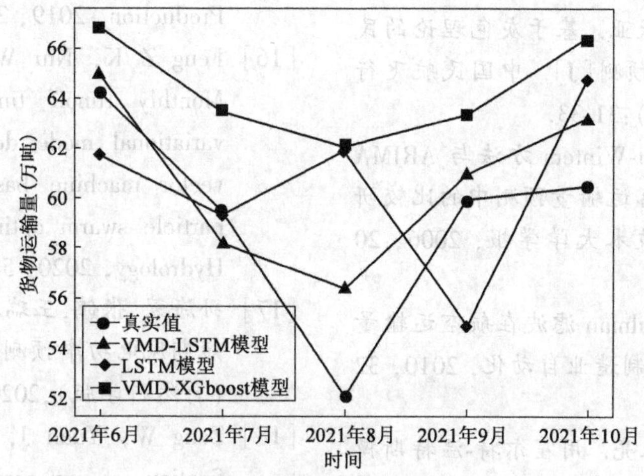

图11 货邮运输量各方法预测结果对比

货邮运输量预测结果 表6

年 份	真实值(万 t)	VMD-LSTM 预测值(万 t)	VMD-XGboost 预测值(万 t)	LSTM 预测值(万 t)
2021.6	64.2	65.0127	61.7304	66.8325
2021.7	59.4	58.1822	59.3528	63.4347
2021.8	52.0	56.3621	61.9015	62.04
2021.9	59.9	60.9532	54.8633	63.2959
2021.10	60.4	63.2197	64.7488	66.4048
R_{EC}	1	0.9795	0.9545	0.9526

在2021年6月至10月货邮运输量预测方面VMD-LSTM模型预测准确性为97.95%，较VMD-XGboost、LSTM模型分别提高近2.5%和2.69%。

可以看出，针对运输总周转量、旅客运输量和货邮运输量，使用VMD-LSTM混合模型均具有较好的预测效果。VMD-LSTM和VMD-XGboost模型预测效果，优于LSTM单一模型预测效果。

4 结论

本文应用分解-集成模型对受新型冠状病毒影响下的国内旅客运输量、货邮运输量和运输总周转量进行分析和预测，得出如下结论：

(1) VMD-LSTM混合模型预测准确度较高，特别是受疫情影响造成数据波动性较大情况下，分解集成预测方法依然是可行有效的。

(2)通过不同模型对比分析，分解集成预测模型预测效果要优于使用单一模型直接预测的预测效果。

(3)因LSTM模型具有预测结果不固定的特征，因此后续研究可针对VMD分解时间序列中数据尺度较大的分量采用其他的预测方法进行预测，分析不同模态不同预测预测方法的预测效果。

参考文献

[1] 何军辉. 中国民航货运总量的两种预测方法[J]. 番禺职业技术学院学报,2002, 1(1): 64-67.

[2] 蔡文婷, 彭怡, 陈秋吉. 基于多元回归模型的航空运输客运量预测[J]. 航空计算技术, 2019(4):50-53,58.

[3] 田俊改, 许红军. 基于灰色马尔可夫链的航空货邮预测[J]. 中国民航大学学报, 2009, 27(1):35-38.

[4] 李明捷, 周阳, 史跃亚. 基于灰色理论的民航旅客运输周转量预测[J]. 中国民航飞行学院学报, 2011(05):31-33.

[5] 张丽, 闫世锋. Holt-Winters 方法与 ARIMA 模型在中国航空旅客运输量预测中的比较研究[J]. 上海工程技术大学学报, 2006, 20(3):280-283.

[6] 雷开洪, 游庆山. Kalman 滤波在航空运输量预测中的应用[J]. 制造业自动化, 2010, 32(5):193-196.

[7] 赵巍飞, 王红勇, 张亮. 用霍尔特-温特斯模型预测航空运输总周转量[J]. 中国民航大学学报, 2007, 25(2):1-3,11.

[8] 李明捷. 基于三次指数平滑法的航空旅客运输量预测[J]. 中国民航飞行学院学报, 2009, 20(1):43-44,47.

[9] 黄文强. 支持向量机在航空运输量预测中的应用[J]. 计算机工程,2005, 31(增刊): 253-255.

[10] 吴璇. 基于BP神经网络的航空运输量短期预测模型[J]. 西安电子科技大学学报:社会科学版, 2007, 17(3):67-70.

[11] 尧姚, 陶静, 李毅. 基于 ARIMA-BP 组合模型的民航旅客运输量预测[J]. 计算机技术与发展, 2015, 25(12):147-151.

[12] 王振华. 组合预测模型在航空客运量预测中的应用[D]. 福州:福州大学,2017.

[13] 杨新湦, 王翩然. 基于组合预测的民航运输量分析——以珠三角地区为例[J]. 数学的实践与认识, 2019(8):301-310.

[14] Sulistyowati R, Suhartono, Kuswanto H, et al. Hybrid forecasting model to predict air passenger and cargo in Indonesia[C]// 2018 International Conference on Information and Communications Technology(ICOIACT). 2018.

[15] Chai J, Wang Y R, Wang S Y, et al. A decomposition-integration model with dynamic fuzzy reconstruction for crude oil price prediction and the implications for sustainable development [J]. Journal Of Cleaner Production, 2019, 229: 775-786.

[16] Feng Z K, Niu W J, Tang Z Y, et al. Monthly runoff time series prediction by variational mode decomposition and support vector machine based on quantum-behaved particle swarm optimization[J]. Journal Of Hydrology, 2020, 583.

[17] 孙海蓉,张鸽,王瑞珈. 基于组合优化算法的短期风电功率预测[J]. 华北电力大学学报(自然科学版),2020,47(01):33-41.

[18] Zeng W, Yuan J, Yuan C, et al. Classification of myocardial infarction based on hybrid feature extraction and artificial intelligence tools by adopting tunable-Q wavelet transform (TQWT), variational mode decomposition (VMD) and neural networks [J]. Artif Intell Med, 2020, 106: 101848.

[19] 朱永强,王小凡. 基于互补型集成经验模态分解和遗传最小二乘支持向量机的交通流量预测模型[J]. 科学技术与工程,2020,20(17):7088-7092.

[20] S Hochreiter, J Schmidhuber. Long Short-Term Memory [J]. Neural Computation. 1997,9(8): 1735-1780.

[21] 陈东宁,张运东,姚成玉,等. 基于变分模态分解和多尺度排列熵的故障诊断[J]. 计算机集成制造系统,2017,23(12):2604-2612.

[22] 郑小霞,周国旺,任浩翰,等. 基于变分模态分解和排列熵的滚动轴承故障诊断[J]. 振动与冲击,2017,36(22):22-28.

附:参数解释表

参数	含义解释
k	需要分解的模态个数
t	自变量
j	指代虚部
$u_k(t)$	模态分量
$\{\omega_k\}$	模态中心频率
$\delta(t)$	狄拉克函数
$*$	卷积运算符
$\\|\bullet\\|$	二范数
$f(t)$	原始时间序列
λ	Lagrange 算子
$\langle\bullet\rangle$	求内积
α	二次惩罚因子函数
$\hat{}$	估计值
ω	自变量
γ	噪声容限
$u_k(\omega)$	分解后的单分量调幅调频信号
ω_k	每个单分量调幅调频信号的中频率
n	迭代次数
i,f,s,o	输入门、遗忘门、记忆细胞和输出门
W_{ix}、W_{ih}、W_{os}	输入、上时刻输出和记忆细胞到输入门的权重矩阵
W_{fx}、W_{fh}、W_{fs}	输入、上时刻输出和记忆细胞到遗忘门的权重矩阵
W_{ox}、W_{oh}、W_{os}	输入、上时刻输出和记忆细胞到输出门的权重矩阵
W_{sx}、W_{sh}	输入,上时刻输出到记忆细胞的权重矩阵
b_i、b_f、b_o、b_s	输入门、输出门、遗忘门和记忆细胞的偏置量
y_t	真实值
$\hat{y}_t$	预测值
R_{EC}	均等系数

基于最小成本的飞机下降性能参数计算方法

陆松麟[1]　韩孝兰[1,2]　魏志强*[2]

(1. 中国东方航空股份有限公司运行控制中心;2. 中国民航大学空管学院)

摘　要　为计算下降阶段的性能参数,本文首先建立下降阶段的飞行动力学模型和飞行成本计算模型;然后根据基础性能数据编写下降性能参数计算软件;之后以我国某型处于设计阶段的宽体飞机为例,对下降性能计算结果进行分析;最后基于最小成本的优化目标对性能参数进行优化,并分析优化参数的影响因素。结果表明,优化后的下降策略相对最省油和最省时的下降策略能分别降低 1.05% 和 3.16% 的飞行成本。

关键词　下降性能　飞行成本　成本指数　性能优化

0 引言

下降是飞行任务的重要组成部分,通常采用固定马赫数/表速、慢车推力的方法,降低飞机的油耗。一些学者针对传统的梯级爬升、固定高度巡航和梯级下降做了性能优化,并尝试了不同的优化算法。Turgut 等通过优化下降角来减少下降阶段的油耗[1];Jensen 等对巡航速度的效率进行了系统分析,并量化了速度优化的影响[2];Takeichi 等运用四维下降航迹优化方法降低油耗、时间和运行成本[3];Alejandro 等利用 Dijkstra 算法和蚁群算法优化飞行的垂直和水平剖面,有效减少了燃料和飞行成本[4-5]。另外,随着飞机持续爬升运行(Continuous Climb Operation,CCO)和持续下降运行(Continuous Descent Operation,CDO)的提出和实施,一些学者研究了基于飞机 CCO 和 CDO 运行的性能优化问题。Jin 等研究了连续下降进近(Continuous Descent Approach,CDA)过程中的节油问题[6];Park 等研究了在 CDA 的飞行时间和油耗指标下的性能边界问题[7]。

在国内,吕开妮等利用自适应遗传算法针对时间和油耗对飞机爬升段垂直轨迹进行了优化[8];李文娟等以巡航阶段为例,研究了 Fibonacci 搜索技术在垂直剖面优化方面的应用[9];许跃凤等基于 BADA(Base of Aircraft Data,BADA)的航空器性能模型研究了飞机持续爬升运行对噪声的影响[10];魏志强等针对终端区多机协同进场问题对下降性能参数进行了优化,之后研究了考虑排放因素的下降性能优化方法[11-12]。

本文以我国某型处于设计阶段的宽体飞机为例,研究建立了下降阶段动力学计算模型,对下降成本进行计算;然后从成本角度出发,对下降性能参数进行优化,并对有关影响因素进行分析。研究成果有助于民机设计单位更好地开展概念设计阶段的飞行任务性能评估与迭代优化。

1 下降性能参数计算模型与实现

对下降性能进行分析时,总飞行距离取固定值,起始点为巡航公共点,结束点为下降结束点。其中,巡航段为巡航公共点至下降顶点(Top of Descent,TOD),下降段为 TOD 点至下降结束点。下降阶段采用等表速-等马赫数(V_c,M)组合的方式下降。本文利用质点性能模型将飞行中的飞机视为一个质点,将不同飞行阶段分割为许多小段。下降段示意图如图1所示。

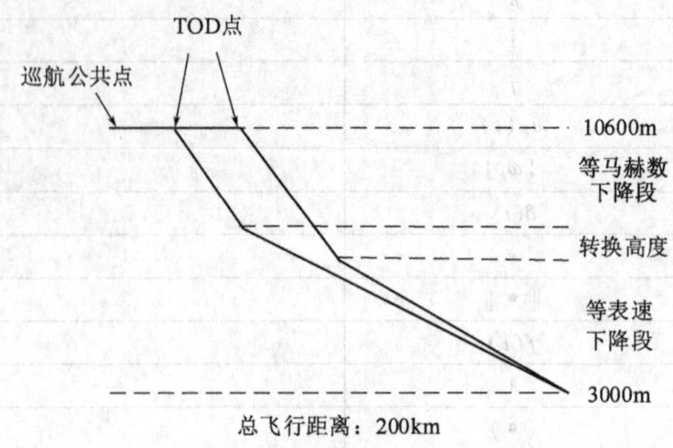

图1 下降阶段示意图

1.1 下降阶段飞行动力学模型

飞机下降时的飞行动力学模型可以表示为:

$$L + T\sin\alpha - W\cos\theta = \frac{W}{g}\frac{d\theta}{dt}V_T \tag{1}$$

$$T\cos\alpha - D + W\sin\theta = \frac{W}{g}\frac{dV_T}{dt} \tag{2}$$

式中:L——升力,N;

T——推力,N;

W——航空器重量,N;

α——迎角;

θ——航迹角;

D——阻力,N;

V_T——真空速;t 为时间。

考虑到下降段的飞机迎角较小,$\sin\alpha\approx 0$,$\cos\alpha\approx 1$,飞行动力学方程可以表示为:

$$L - W\cos\theta = \frac{W}{g}\frac{d\theta}{dt}V_T \tag{3}$$

$$T - D + W\sin\theta = \frac{W}{g}\frac{dV_T}{dt} \tag{4}$$

下降率:

$$\gamma = -\frac{dh}{dt} = V_T\sin\theta \tag{5}$$

将式(4)代入式(5)得:

$$\gamma = \frac{\frac{T-D}{W}\cdot V_T}{1+\frac{V_T}{g}\frac{dV_T}{dh}} \tag{6}$$

第 i 段下降高度间隔下的下降率 γ_i:

$$\gamma_i = M_i a\frac{D_i - T_i}{gm_{de,i}}\cdot f\{M_i\},(i=1,\cdots,j) \tag{7}$$

式中,$m_{de,i}$ 为第 i 段高度下的飞机质量,kg;

j 为下降结束高度对应的高度层数。

第 i 个下降段由高度 h_{i-1} 到 h_i 的时间 t_i、油耗 $F_{\mathrm{de},i}$ 和飞行距离 $X_{\mathrm{de},i}$ 分别为：

$$\begin{cases} t_i = \int_{h_{i-1}}^{h_i} \dfrac{\mathrm{d}h}{\gamma_i} \\ F_{\mathrm{de},i} = \int_{h_{i-1}}^{h_i} \dfrac{W_{\mathrm{fde},i}}{\gamma_i}\mathrm{d}h, (i=1,\cdots,j) \\ X_{\mathrm{de},i} = t_i \cdot M_i \cdot a \end{cases} \tag{8}$$

式中，$W_{\mathrm{fde},i}$ 为第 i 个下降段的燃油流量，kg/h。

整个飞行过程的总油耗 F、总时间 t 和总水平距离 R 定义为：

$$\begin{cases} F = F_{\mathrm{cr}} + F_{\mathrm{de}} \\ t = t_{\mathrm{cr}} + t_{\mathrm{de}} \\ R = R_{\mathrm{cr}} + R_{\mathrm{de}} \end{cases} \tag{9}$$

式中，F_{de}、t_{de}、R_{de} 分别为下降阶段的总油耗、总时间和总水平距离，F_{cr}、t_{cr}、R_{cr} 分别为巡航段的总油耗、总时间和总水平距离。

1.2 飞行成本计算模型

选择不同的飞行方式可以节省燃油或时间，而经济性是飞行中需要考虑的重要因素。航空公司与飞行有关的航班成本包括时间成本和燃油成本，即

$$C = C_f \cdot F + C_t \cdot t \tag{10}$$

式中，C 为飞行成本，元；C_f 为燃油成本，元/kg；C_t 为时间成本，元/min。

飞行成本指数 CI 取值 0-999，定义如下：

$$CI = \frac{C_t}{C_f \cdot 100} \tag{11}$$

1.3 飞行动力学模型的软件实现

飞行动力学模型的实现流程如图 2 所示，相应的计算软件界面如图 3 所示。根据飞机基础性能数据和软件界面输入的发动机参数、下降策略、飞机质量、温度偏差、下降限制条件及高度相关数据，可详细计算出整个下降阶段的性能参数。

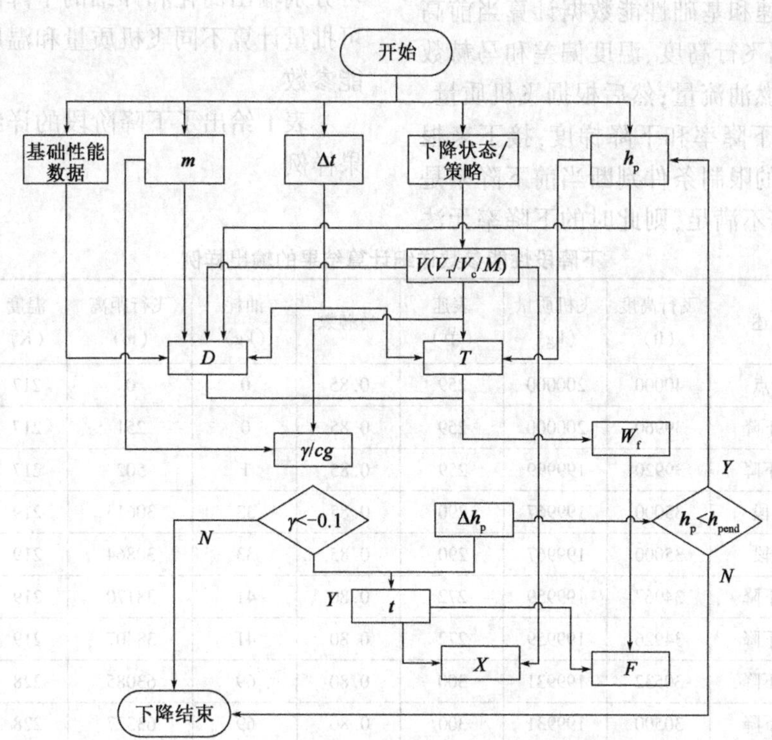

图 2 下降阶段飞行动力学模型的实现流程图

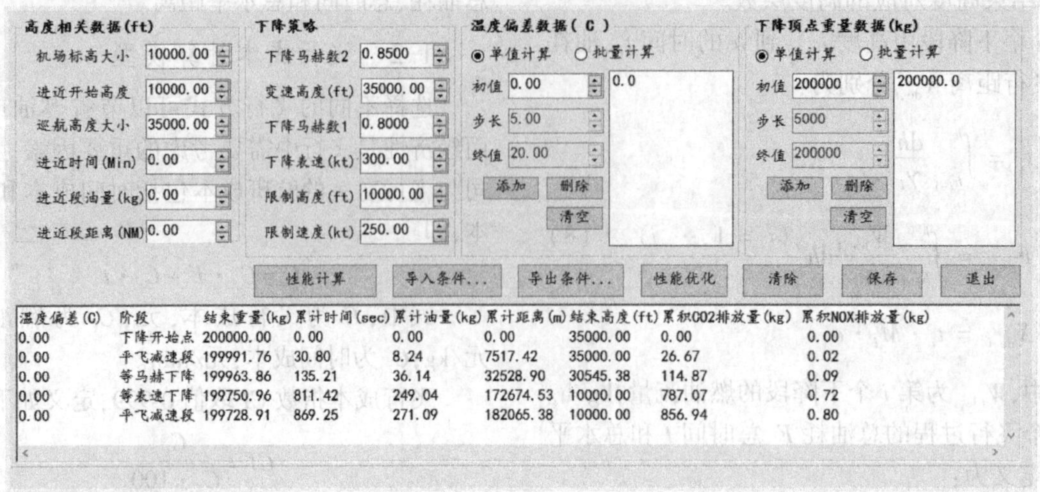

图3 下降阶段性能参数计算软件界面

2 下降性能计算分析

2.1 计算结果分析

给定飞机质量、温度偏差、飞行高度后,本文根据当前的下降状态(等表速-等马赫数下降)确定下降的速度类型和速度大小,进而计算当前高度的真空速和马赫数;再通过飞机质量、温度偏差、飞行高度、真空速和基础性能数据计算当前高度的阻力;之后根据飞行高度、温度偏差和马赫数计算出慢车推力和燃油流量;然后根据飞机质量、阻力和推力计算出下降率和下降梯度;接下来根据设定的下降升限的限制条件判断当前下降率是否满足下降条件,若不满足,则此时的下降率无法满足继续下降的要求,停止下降。若满足,则说明可继续下降;之后由固定小段高度和下降率计算出小段时间,由小段时间和真空速计算飞行距离,由小段时间和燃油流量计算小段油耗;最后进一步计算累积飞行高度、飞行时间、飞行距离、油耗以及下一阶段飞机质量,直到达到下降结束高度或设定的下降率,下降结束。参数计算软件界面可分别输出简化和详细的下降阶段性能参数。还可批量计算不同飞机质量和温度偏差下的下降性能参数。

表1给出了下降阶段的详细性能参数计算结果样例。

下降段性能参数详细计算结果的输出样例 表1

时间(s)	阶段描述	飞行高度(ft)	飞机质量(kg)	表速(节)	马赫数	油耗(kg)	飞行距离(m)	温度(K)	下降率(m/s)	燃油流量(kg/min)
0	下降开始点	40000	200000	259	0.85	0	0	217	0	0
1	等马赫数下降	39960	200000	259	0.85	0	251	217	-12	8
2	等马赫数下降	39920	199999	259	0.85	1	502	217	-12	8
122	平飞减速段	35000	199967	290	0.85	33	30613	219	0	8
123	平飞减速段	35000	199967	290	0.85	33	30864	219	0	8
153	等马赫数下降	34967	199959	272	0.80	41	38170	219	-12	8
154	等马赫数下降	34926	199959	272	0.80	41	38407	219	-12	8
257	等表速数下降	30532	199931	300	0.80	69	63085	228	-10	8
258	等表速数下降	30500	199931	300	0.80	69	63327	228	-10	8
933	平飞减速段	10000	199718	300	0.54	282	203166	268	0	12
934	平飞减速段	10000	199718	299	0.54	282	203343	268	0	12
991	等表速下降	9991	199696	250	0.45	304	212574	268	-6	11

续上表

时间(s)	阶段描述	飞行高度(ft)	飞机质量(kg)	表速(节)	马赫数	油耗(kg)	飞行距离(m)	温度(K)	下降率(m/s)	燃油流量(kg/min)
992	等表速下降	9970	199696	250	0.45	304	212723	268	-6	11
1533	下降结束点	50	199484	0	0.00	516	271538	288	0	0

在指定的飞行时刻,可以显示出当前飞行阶段(等马赫数下降M0.85、M0.8,平飞减速,等表速下降300kt、250kt)、当前飞行高度、当前飞机质量、飞行表速、马赫数、油耗、飞行距离、当前高度外界温度、爬升率、燃油流量等性能参数。

2.2 基于飞行成本的下降性能优化结果分析

本文基于1.2节建立的飞行成本计算模型,计算下降飞行成本最小对应的(V_c,M)组合。计算条件如下:温度偏差为ISA-5℃,巡航公共点处飞机质量200000kg,燃油价格6000¥/t,成本指数25,飞行距离为200km,V_c的变化范围为[250,300],M的变化范围为[0.7,0.8]。根据计算结果分别得到飞行成本、油耗和飞行时间最小对应的(V_c,M)组合,结果如表2所示。

基于飞行成本的下降阶段优化结果对比　表2

优化目标	优化结果	飞行成本/¥	油耗/kg	飞行时间/s
飞行成本	(266,0.74)	4086.94	352.27	1044.11
油耗	(250,0.71)	4130.44	341.7	1100.67
飞行时间	(300,0.8)	4220.29	405.04	947.15

由表2可以看出,整体上,油耗最低对应的飞行速度最小,而飞行时间最少对应的飞行速度最大。基于飞行成本优化后的组合优化值相对最省油的组合降低1.05%,相对最省时的组合降低3.16%。通过引入飞行成本能够平衡飞行中油耗和时间的关系。

对于某一特定机型和飞行距离,飞行成本的大小取决于成本指数、飞机质量和温度偏差等。保持初始计算条件不变,计算不同成本指数下飞行成本最小对应的(V_c,M)组合。结果如表3所示。

不同飞行成本下的优化参数对比　表3

CI值	0	10	20	30	40	50	60	70	80	90	100
V_c/kt	250	254	262	270	282	292	300	300	300	300	300
M	0.71	0.71	0.73	0.74	0.74	0.75	0.76	0.78	0.79	0.8	0.8
飞行成本/¥	2050	2879	3690	4478	5244	5990	6719	7440	8158	8875	9591

由表3可以看出,随着成本指数的增加,飞行成本最小对应的飞行速度整体呈上升趋势。当CI=0时,对应最省油的(V_c,M)组合,当CI大于70时,速度组合与最省时的(V_c,M)组合相同,即随着成本指数的增加,时间成本占飞行成本的比例增加,此时需要通过提高飞行速度来降低整体飞行成本。

保持初始计算条件不变,计算不同飞机质量下飞行成本最小对应的(V_c,M)组合,结果如表4所示。

不同飞机质量下的优化参数对比　表4

W/kg	190000	195000	200000	205000	210000
(V_c,M)	(264,0.71)	(266,0.72)	(266,0.74)	(270,0.74)	(270,0.76)
飞行成本/¥	4126	4106	4087	4070	4054

由表4可以看出,随着飞机质量的增加,飞行表速和马赫数均呈现增加趋势,但下降阶段的飞行成本整体呈减少趋势。当飞机质量增加时,针对某一段固定下降高度,同一飞行速度下油耗和飞行时间均增加。此时需要通过提高飞行速度来减少油耗和飞行时间,从而降低飞行成本。

保持初始计算条件不变,计算不同温度偏差下飞行成本最小对应的(V_c,M)组合,结果如表5

所示。

不同温度偏差下的优化参数对比 表5

t/℃	-10	0	10	20
(V_c,M)	(268,0.71)	(266,0.76)	(284,0.8)	(300,0.8)
飞行成本/¥	4232	3935	3665	3532

由表5可以看出,随着外界温度偏差的增加,飞行表速和马赫数整体上均呈增加趋势,飞行成本呈下降趋势,当温度增加至20℃时,表速和马赫数均达到最大值。当温度增加时,相同飞行条件下燃油流量增加,油耗随之增加。通过适当提高飞行速度,能有效降低飞行成本。

3 结语

本文基于下降阶段的性能参数计算模型,建立了下降阶段性能参数计算软件,详细计算出每个下降时刻的下降速度、下降率、高度、飞行距离、燃油流量、油耗、飞机质量、飞行成本等性能参数,并基于飞行成本对下降性能参数进行优化。结论表明,基于飞行成本最小的下降策略相对最省油和最省时的下降策略能够分别降低1.05%和3.16%的飞行成本。

参考文献

[1] Turgut E T, Usanmaz O, Cavcar M, et al. Effects of descent flight-path angle on fuel consumption of commercial aircraft [J]. Journal of Aircraft, 2019, 56(1): 313-323.

[2] Jensen L L, Hansman R J, Venuti J, et al. Commercial Airline Speed Optimization Strategies for Reduced Cruise Fuel Consumption[C]. 2013 Aviation Technology, Integration, and Operations Conference, Reston, Virginia: American Institude of Aeronautics and Astronautics, 2013:1-13.

[3] Takeichi N, Ishihara J, Abumi Y. Validation Study On Descent Trajectory Optimization and Scheduling Improvement Using Actual Operation Data [C]//American Institute of Aeronautics and Astronautics. AIAA Modeling & Simulation Technologies Conference. San Diego, California, USA; American Institute of Aeronautics and Astronautics, 2015: 1-9.

[4] Alejandro M M, Paul M, Ruxandra M. Vertical and Horizontal Flight Reference Trajectory Optimization for A Commercial Aircraft[C]// AIAA Guidance, Navigation, and Control Conference, Grapevine, Texas: January 9-13, 2017.

[5] Alejandro M M, Antoine H, Ruxandra M B. Lateral Reference Trajectory Algorithm Using Ant Colony Optimization [C]//16th AIAA Aviation Technology, Integration, and Operations Conference, Washington, D. C.: June 13-17, 2016.

[6] Jin L, Cao Y, Sun D. Investigation of potential fuel savings due to Continuous-Descent Approach[J]. Journal of Aircraft, 2013, 50 (3): 807-816.

[7] Park S G, Clarke J P. Optimal control based vertical trajectory determination for continuous descent arrival procedures [J]. Journal of aircraft, 2015, 52(5):1469-1480.

[8] 吕开妮,南英. 基于自适应遗传算法的客机爬升段轨迹优化[J]. 计算机仿真,2017,34(1):66-69.

[9] 李文娟,贺尔铭,马存宝,等. 垂直剖面轨迹寻优算法的研究与仿真[J]. 计算机仿真,2013,30(10):133-137.

[10] 许跃凤,胡荣,张军峰,等. 基于BADA模型的飞机持续爬升运行减噪效果研究[J]. 交通运输系统工程与信息,2017,17(4):201-206.

[11] 魏志强,曹格. 终端区多机协同进场下的飞机性能参数优化方法[J]. 飞行力学,2020,38(2):5-11.

[12] 魏志强,韩孝兰. 考虑排放因素的飞机下降性能优化方法[J]. 安全与环境学报,2020,20(3):1126-1131.

基于陆空通话反应时的管制员疲劳风险研究

潘卫军 张钰沁* 姜沿强
（中国民用航空飞行学院 空中交通管理学院）

摘 要 统计表明，超过70%的航空事故可归因于人为因素。人为因素被认为是管理和改善飞行安全的决定因素之一，其中管制员疲劳这一危险因素造成的不安全事件高达52000起。深入分析造成管制员疲劳的风险因素，评估风险的严重程度有利于改进安全防护措施，降低民用航空器的事故率。本研究的主要目标为分析造成管制员疲劳的因素、疲劳对管制员工作的影响，着重以管制员的陆空通话反应时为参考指标，对管制员的疲劳风险程度进行定量评估。结果表明，在置信度为99%的情况下，运用疲劳风险评估模型测量出的疲劳值与管制员的NASA-TLX量表数值呈正相关，相关系数为0.954，表明利用正态分布建立的疲劳风险评估模型对疲劳的评估具有一定的参考价值。

关键词 航空运输 疲劳风险评估模型 风险可接受性二维矩阵 陆空通话反应时

0 引言

随着我国民用航空业的飞速发展，航班量日益庞大，飞行安全成为民航事业继续蓬勃发展的重要前提。在航空器运行事故中，由空中交通管制员疲劳因素所导致的运行差错的比例为13%。疲劳会使管制员产生一系列负面状态，包括但不限于反应时间变长、决策能力降低、注意力涣散、睡岗等情况[1]。管制员不良的身体或精神状况可能会导致严重的飞行事故。本文结合相关疲劳风险研究的成果，以管制员的陆空通话反应时间为测量指标，建立管制员疲劳风险评估模型，对管制员的疲劳状态进行定量研究。

1 管制员疲劳风险管理方法

1.1 国内外研究综述

国际民航组织针对飞行安全中的疲劳问题，制定了《疲劳风险管理系统手册》和《运营人疲劳风险管理制度(FRMS)实施指南》。2007年以来，各国逐渐开始实施疲劳风险管理体系(Fatigue Risk Management System，FRMS)的建设工作。美国、加拿大、澳大利亚于2010年左右相继颁布了疲劳风险管理的相关建设与实施方案，但至今我国仍缺少对管制员疲劳风险系统性管理的研究[2]。我国的疲劳风险测定目前尚处在研究阶段，已经取得了初步的成果：孙瑞山等通过建立关于警觉性的心理疲劳风险模型[3]，将警觉度作为量化指标，在一定程度上反映心理疲劳，为管制员心理疲劳防控提供一种解决思路；王莉莉等基于脑电数据的管制架次对管制员疲劳影响的研究；运用眼动指标的管制员疲劳检测技术、面部特征识别技术等。

研究现状总结与分析调查表明，目前针对管制员疲劳风险定量评估的研究较少，管制员的自愿报告系统也不够完善。为了保障飞行安全，管制员疲劳风险管理除了要建立稳定的疲劳检测与疲劳预防体系，还要对管制员疲劳风险进行定量评估。

1.2 疲劳风险评估的方法及思路

孙瑞山等的研究发现，管制员与飞行员陆空通话反应时的长短，在一定程度上能体现管制员在工作中的警觉性——管制员处于非疲劳状态时，其反应时间会在其平均反应时间的一定范围内小幅度波动，总体上会呈现出正态分布的特征；管制员处于疲劳状态时，其反应时会随着疲劳程度的提高而变长，逐渐远离平均反应时，并且反应时间的稳定性也会降低，故反应时呈现出的正态分布特征会变得不显著，或者不再呈现出正态分布特征。综上所述，可通过测量飞行员呼叫管制员，管制员首次应答的通话反应时间，作为测量指标来测定管制员的疲劳程度。本文将利用这一指标对疲劳的测定方法进行一系列假设检验，并通过建立相应的模型对管制员的疲劳风险进行定量评估。

1.3 风险可接受性二维矩阵

风险可接受性二维矩阵是判定单一风险的定量评估法,对于疲劳这一单一的风险评估具有一定的适用性。风险可接受性的公式为:

可接受性=严重性×可能性

某一风险的严重性和可能性的乘积可表示该风险的可接受程度,其结果的取值范围为1~25。可接受性数值越大表明风险越大,可接受性越差。风险可接受性二维矩阵见表1。

风险可接受性二维矩阵 表1

风险等级	可能性	1	2	3	4	5
严重性	5	5 可接受的	10 可容忍的	15 不可接受的	20 不可接受的	25 不可接受的
	4	4 可接受的	8 可容忍的	12 可容忍的	16 不可接受的	20 不可接受的
	3	3 可接受的	6 可接受的	9 可容忍的	12 可容忍的	15 不可接受的
	2	2 可接受的	4 可接受的	6 可接受的	8 可容忍的	10 可容忍的
	1	1 可接受的	2 可接受的	3 可接受的	4 可接受的	5 可接受的

上述风险评价矩阵将风险划分为可接受的、可容忍的和不可接受的三个等级,不同风险等级采取不同的控制措施。“可接受的”表示低风险状况,只需对此风险进行监控,保持正常的运行即可;“可容忍的”表示中风险状况,需要对其采取一定的控制措施,也可以正常运行;“不可接受”的为高风险状况,应立即采取相应的控制措施,并立即停止运行,直到风险降低到可接受水平。

2 疲劳风险评估模型的建立

2.1 建立对照组

该实验选取的测量疲劳程度的指标为管制员的陆空通话反应时间。陆空通话反应时间是指塔、进、区管制人员接收到机组呼叫后回复机组的反应时间。孙文洲等在《民航管制员疲劳风险评估模型研究》中对管制员某一周期内非疲劳状态下的大量语音数据进行数理统计与分析[4],将其得出的反应时间进行频数统计后,发现结果近似呈现正态分布。本文根据这一结论建立正态分布函数算法,利用概率密度函数对疲劳进行定量测定。

本研究采集若干组陆空通话的语音记录数据进行处理,通过SPSS对采集到的所有有效语音数据进行频数统计,得出其分布图像,然后选取其中出现频率较高的通话反应时间范围,定为非疲劳状态下通话反应时间的总体均值。

2.2 建立实验组

随机选取管制员除对照组之外的任意一组通话数据进行处理,该组数据的均值记为$\overline{X_t}$、统计量方差记为s_t^2,公式如下:

$$\overline{X}=\frac{1}{n}\sum_{i=1}^{n}X_i, i\in[1,n] \tag{1}$$

$$s_t^2=\sum_{i=1}^{n}(X_i-\overline{X})^2, i\in[1,n] \tag{2}$$

2.3 建立模型

设P为疲劳事件发生的可能性,C为疲劳事件的严重程度,R为疲劳事件的风险值,可得出公式:

$$R=P\times C \tag{3}$$

在正态分布的密度函数中,令分布函数中对照组的期望值μ为对称轴,则$x\in[2\mu-\mu_t,\mu_t]$,如公式(4),与概率密度曲线围成的面积可表示为事件发生的概率,即疲劳事件发生的可能性P,如公式(5):

$$\begin{cases}2\mu-\mu=\mu-(\mu_t-\mu)\\ \mu_t=\mu_t\end{cases} \tag{4}$$

$$\begin{cases} P = \left(\frac{2}{\sqrt{2\pi\sigma}}\int_{-\infty}^{\mu_t} e^{\frac{(x-\mu)^2}{2\sigma^2}}dx\right) - 1, \mu_t > \mu & ,0 < P < 1 \\ P = 0, \mu \leqslant \mu_t \end{cases} \quad (5)$$

疲劳事件的严重程度 C，可用 μ_t 与总期望值 μ 之间的偏离程度来表示，如公式(6)，μ 与 μ_t 的距离越远，则疲劳事件的严重程度越高。

$$\begin{cases} C = \frac{\mu_t - \mu}{\sigma}, \mu_t > \mu \\ C = 0, \mu_t \leqslant \mu \end{cases} \quad (6)$$

2.4 风险值修正

在正态分布模型中，概率密度曲线是由 μ_t 与 σ_t^2 共同决定的，在期望 μ_t 一定的情况下，曲线的区间能够确定，但对于不同的 σ_t^2，函数的概率分布也不同。当方差越小，即 σ^2 的数值越小，代表数据越向均值收敛，表示反应时间越集中且稳定性越高，产生疲劳的可能性越低；反之则疲劳的可能性越高。为了完善疲劳风险评估模型的有效性和实用性，可引入统计学中的变异系数 C_v 对其离散程度进行比较。变异系数是原始数据标准差与平均数的比，且没有量纲，可消除量纲的影响。$R_{修正}$ 表示修正后的疲劳风险值，C_v 表示对照组的变异数据，$C_{v(t)}$ 表示实验组的变异数据，公式如下：

$$C_v = \frac{\sigma}{\mu} \times 100\% \quad (7)$$

$$C_{v(t)} = \frac{\sigma_t}{\mu_t} \times 100\% \quad (8)$$

所以，疲劳值的修正公式为：

$$\begin{cases} R_{修正} = R_t, C_{v(t)} \leqslant C_v \\ R_{修正} = R_t \times \frac{C_{v(t)}}{C_v}, C_{v(t)} > C_v \end{cases} \quad (9)$$

2.5 疲劳风险值等级划分

根据上述正态分布模型可知，疲劳的可能性 P 与严重程度 C 呈现出相关性，即疲劳的风险值与发生的可能性存在对应关系。根据正态分布的性质，正态分布的概率密度图形与 x 坐标轴围成区域的面积表示发生的概率为 1，那么疲劳事件发生的可能性 P 可用 3σ 原则进行划分，公式如下：

$$\begin{cases} P(\mu - \sigma < \mu_t < \mu + \sigma) = 68.3\% \\ P(\mu - 2\sigma < \mu_t < \mu + 2\sigma) = 95.4\% \\ P(\mu - 3\sigma < \mu_t < \mu + 3\sigma) = 99.7\% \\ P(\mu_t > 3\sigma) = 99.9\% \end{cases} \quad (10)$$

同理，疲劳事件的严重程度 C 也可利用 3σ 原则进行划分。综上所述，当已知一组数据的 μ_t 与 σ_t 时，可将其与对照组 μ 代入正态分布模型进行计算，从而对疲劳风险值进行定量评估。以 σ、2σ、3σ 为划分界限，根据风险可接受性二维矩阵原理可对疲劳风险值定量评估，如表 2 所示。

风险等级划分表 表2

严重程度	可能性	风险值	风险等级
0~1	0~0.68	0~0.68	1
1~2	0.68~0.95	0.68~1.98	2
2~3	0.95~0.99	1.98~2.97	3
>3	0.99~0.999	2.97~3	4
>3	>0.999	>3	5

3 疲劳风险评估模型的验证

3.1 数据采集处理

本文将华北空管局在岗管制员通话数据作为实验数据，对该管制员一个月内的陆空通话录音进行提取处理。具体处理方案为：将收集到的全部音频导入音频处理软件，筛选截取其中飞行员呼叫管制员，管制员应答飞行员过程中间隔的时间，并进行记录。为了便于数据收集与处理，提取通话录音的具体标准为：从飞行员呼叫管制员的时间点开始，直到管制员收到飞行员呼叫后，经过一定的反应时间做出回应为止。这一短暂的时间段即可作为管制员陆空通话反应时间的一个样本。

经过数据处理，本研究得出八组实验数据，如表3 所示。

均值方差表　　表3

组　别	μ_t 均值/(ms)	σ_t^2 方差
1	453	101^2
2	455	101^2
3	488	104^2
4	571	150^2
5	526	109^2
6	551	124^2
7	570	153^2
8	504	115^2

3.2　数据计算及验证

将数据编入计算模型中,所得结果如表4所示。

疲劳值计算结果　　表4

组　别	P_t	C_t	R_t	$R_{t修正}$	疲劳风险等级	NASA-TLX 量表得分值
1	0	0	0	0	1	28
2	0	0	0	0	1	34
3	0	0	0	0	1	38
4	0.3203	0.3	0.0961	0.1218	1	47
5	0	0	0	0	1	42
6	0.1814	0.2016	0.0366	0.0397	1	4
7	0.3135	0.2876	0.0901	0.1168	1	49
8	0	0	0	0	1	44

为了验证上述计算结果的有效性,本研究将计算结果与该名管制员对自身疲劳程度的自评表进行对比分析。结果表明,$R_{t修正}$ 和 NASA-TLX 值之间的相关系数值为0.954,并且呈现出0.01水平的显著性,说明 $R_{t修正}$ 和 NASA 表得分值之间有着显著的正相关关系。

3.3　实验结论

经过模型计算,由该管制员的实验数据得出的疲劳风险等级与其自评表数据结果呈现出相关性,表明该实验数据具有可靠性。上述风险评估模型得出的疲劳值的有效性,表明该模型可以为管制员疲劳风险评估的研究提供新的方向,也可为管制员实时疲劳风险评估提供方案。

4　结语

本文通过使用陆空通话反应时来评估管制员的疲劳程度,对管制员疲劳风险设计了一种评估模型和检测方法,为建立健全管制员疲劳风险评估提供了思路。但本研究尚处于理论实验阶段,希望为今后有关管制员疲劳风险的测定与评估方面的研究提供一些参考的思路。

参考文献

[1] 杨昌其,马梦尧.管制员疲劳致因及防控措施[J].科技创新与应用,2018(35):139-141.

[2] 潘卫军,吴量,陈华群,等.空中交通无线电陆空通话错误分析[J].中国西部科技,2008(30):1-3.

[3] 孙瑞山,马广福,袁乐平.语音反应时特性的管制员疲劳风险分析[J].中国安全科学学报,2016,26(12):7-12.

[4] 孙文舟,王慧,柳震.民航管制员疲劳风险评估模型研究[J].滨州学院学报,2020,36(6):31-37.

美国航空应急救援空域管理制度及其启示

陈忠莹*[1]　刘俊丽[1]　张　弢[2]　周俊杰[3]
(1. 空军航空大学;2. 空军石家庄飞行学院
3. 95926 部队)

摘　要　美国航空应急救援空域管理制度在西方国家具有代表性,其航空应急救援任务由美国联邦航空管理局和各级相关机构共同承担,主要负责发布预警特别通知、标定空域协调区和设置临时飞行限制等。研究美国航空应急救援空域管理制度的有益经验,在此基础上充分发挥我国制度优势,建立权责清晰组织网络、构建应急救援空域管理机制,促进救灾空域管理安全高效。

关键词　航空应急救援　空域管理　救灾空域

0　引言

我国是世界上自然灾害最为严重的国家之一,同时,各类事故隐患和安全风险交织叠加、易发多发,影响公共安全的因素日益增多。航空应急救援是国家应急管理体系的重要组成部分,完善应急救援空域管理制度是实现航空应急救援管理体系和能力现代化的必然要求。当前,域外很多国家就航空应急救援空域管理形成了一系列有益经验,美国就是其中的典型代表。鉴此,本文试图对美国航空应急救援空域管理制度及其启示进行探讨,希冀裨益于我国航空应急救援空域的开放和管理,确保救援飞机安全高效运行。

1　美国航空应急救援空域管理的确立动因

航空应急救援是基于无人机、直升机、固定翼等航空器,对各类自然灾害和事故实施应急救援的一种救援方式,通常具有区域覆盖广、应急响应快、救援能力强、受地形限制少等优势,主要担负空中侦察勘测、调度指挥、消防灭火、紧急输送、搜寻救助、特殊吊载、应急通信等救援任务。由于每个灾难出现的状况都是独一无二的,航空应急救援机构安全有效地进行应急救援行动的能力一直面临着许多空域管理方面的矛盾,这些矛盾也成为推动航空应急救援空域管理不断发展的源泉和动力。与空域常态化管理使用相比,救灾空域管理主要面临以下矛盾问题:一是保障飞行的空地资源紧张。灾难发生后,由美国联邦航空管理局提供的空中交通管理和其他空中导航服务,如通信、导航辅助和监控(如雷达)通常会被破坏或降级;除了缺乏空中导航服务外,通常还伴随着机场服务不可用或降级(包括加油、乘客/货物装卸、守卫等地面支援服务),导致应急救援和灾后恢复所需要的机场和航空用地限制救援能力和最大停机数量。二是管理低空空域的难度增大。由于需要执行大量的低空任务比如搜索和救援,所以飞机需要在目视飞行规则和目视气象条件下执行任务,并且各种式样的无人机、直升机和固定翼飞机常常同时出现在低空空域参与航空应急救援行动。三是参与救灾空域交通的主体复杂。应急救援行动通常由来自不同机构的多种执行人员组成,飞行员大多不熟悉灾区并且不习惯配合进行应急飞行操作;某些类型的救灾临时飞行限制区允许许多不参与救灾工作的飞机进入,包括机上媒体转播、居民乘坐私人飞机撤离、通用航空和商业航空公司飞机的运营等,这些活动均涉及与应急救援飞机的避撞问题,由此增加了灾区空中交通的复杂性;部分救灾行动由私人或非政府组织(如美国红十字会)执行,与应急救援指挥中心使用的航空行动管理机制之间存在不清晰的协调链,甚至没有被纳入应急救援行动的统一指挥体系。灾难中,上述矛盾问题经常组合出现,成为同空域内救灾飞机需要重视并妥善解决的关键所在。

2　美国航空应急救援空域的相关管理机构

美国联邦航空管理局和各级相关机构(通常还

包括私人部门利益相关者)共同承担航空管理应急规划、救灾和灾后恢复等航空应急救援空域管理职责。

其中,美国联邦航空管理局是美国运输部下属负责民用航空管理的机构,分总部、地区机构和地方机构三级。它运行着一套复杂性高、使用非常频繁的航空系统,对美国国家领空拥有全权管理权,通过运用一套复杂、高效、冗余的弹性网络实现空中交通管理、通信、导航服务和基础设施监控,保障其国家空域系统正常运行。美国联邦航空管理局作为美国国家级空域控制机构和主要空中导航服务提供者,其下设的航管应急响应管理中心、系统运营支持中心、空域访问响应小组等机构主要负责美国航空应急救援空域管理,履行救灾空域飞机访问限制、访问审查、参与机识别、参与机交通流量管理和时段调度以及无人机参与应急救援的授权等职责,并在最大可行范围内为灾区提供空中交通管理和其他航空导航服务。

除了美国联邦航空管理局之外,其他各级相关机构主要有国土安全部、国防部、内政部、商业部、州应急管理局、州国民警卫队、私人空中行动方*、民航行动小组(空中交通协会和飞机所有者与飞行员协会),以及其他州和地方的执法部门、应急医疗部门和环境管理部门等。

3 美国航空应急救援空域管理的运行模式

航空应急救援空域管理的高效安全运行不仅可以减轻灾难本身和航空应急救援工作对国家空域系统安全性和效率的影响,约束、审查和管理灾区空域或进入救灾指定机场和机场用地的航班流量,还可以通过帮助捕获、跟踪、消除冲突和协调救灾行动,协助统一指挥部或事故指挥官有效管理稀缺的空中资源。下面概述的核心措施构成了美国联邦航空管理局实施航空应急救援空域管理的基本运行模式,主要包括发布预警特别通知、标定空域协调区和设置临时飞行限制等。

3.1 发布预警特别通知

联邦航空管理局可以发布《预警特别通知》,警告灾区上空或附近的飞行员具体的危险(例如石油火焰烟羽)或随着参与机行动出现安全风险增加,尤其是低空,目视飞行规则活动,如作业中的搜救机。

3.2 标定空域协调区

通过前文提到的《预警特别通知》,联邦航空管理局可以建立一个空域协调区,指出灾区上空参与飞机活动的空域范围,以引起所有经常在附近活动的飞行员的警惕。这个空域协调区通常范围很大,包含一个或多个临时飞行限制区。空域协调区通常在《预警特别通知》中定义,警告在目标空域参与航空作业的飞行员,风险已经升级,这些特别通知也会对预期低空目视飞行规则救灾航空作业航线提供预警性细节。根据需要,会要求美国北方空军,将北方司令部给民政部门国防支持的联合行动区和空域协调区整合,一起推动航空应急救援任务的执行。

3.3 设置临时飞行限制

美国联邦航空管理局根据联邦法规,区分不同情况,设置相应的临时飞行限制,在临时飞行限制区内通常仅允许执行搜救、空中救护、事故评估、执法、关键物资供应,空中疏散和其他重要任务的政府或私人飞机通行。在临时飞行限制区内主要采用以下具体做法:

(1)任务类型高度层分离

如果需要相对高密度、低高度目视飞行规则救灾行动(例如,搜救和吊索负载),联邦航空管理局可采用临时飞行限制区内的高度层按任务类型分离选择运行(图1)。这些基于任务类型的高度分层旨在用于目视飞行规则的行动(即"目视避撞"的飞行)。在指定高度层内工作的飞机必须遵守目视飞行规则并保持在目视气象条件内。如果飞行员预判将要遇到或已经遇到仪表气象条件,无法够遵守目视飞行规则,那么飞机必须通过安全性最高的航路离开划定的临时飞行限制高度层。

(2)着陆区进入/退出方向

除了空中机动飞行和高空行动,空域管制区和临时飞行限制区内的大多数应急救援行动将采用目视飞行规则进行。由于无法提供航管和其他空中导航服务(例如导航辅助设备),旋翼机搜救行动将经常使用"荷叶"或着陆区,例如学校运动场、停车场、牧场、农田等。为提高这些行动的安全

---

*指在航空应急救援工作中与各级合作机构签订合同的参与者,还有为保护私人重要基础设施(比如炼油厂和管道)或其他资产而自发进行救灾开展空中行动的人。

性,联邦航空管理局为使用不受控机场用地或“荷叶”/着陆区的目视飞行规则救灾飞机建立进入/退出方向和/或报告点(和频率)。一般规则是,这些进入/退出方向和点将按照图2中的描述进行配置,在第四边最后转向着陆和起飞时的盛行风向。

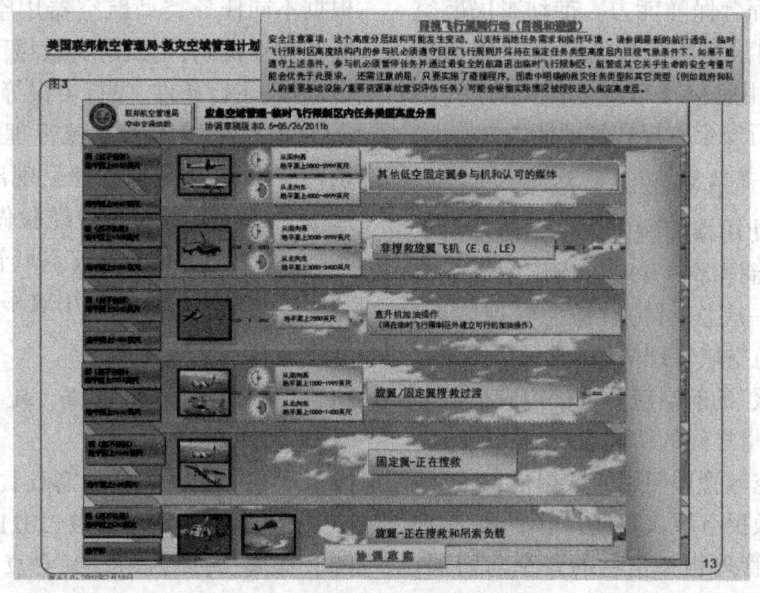

图1　基于任务类型的高度分层

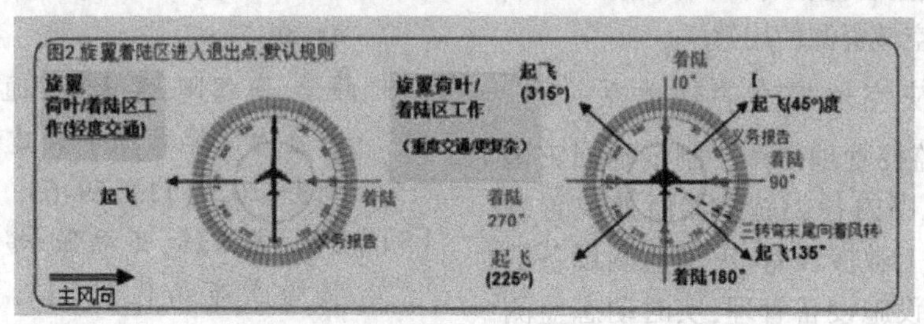

图2　旋翼机进入/退出点规则

(3)临时飞行限制区进入/退出点和航路

联邦航空管理局为目视飞行规则参与机进入或退出救灾空域管制区或临时飞行限制区建立进入/退出点(纬度/经度和高度)。该机构还可以扩大这些初始进入/退出点的使用,以建立多段、辐射任务特定航线,旨在消除向台和背台空中交通(有时称为“蜘蛛航线”)的冲突,由连接空域管制区和/或临时飞行限制区边界到指定航空装载/卸载港、荷叶/着陆区或灾区内其他指定位置的协调点确定。沿蜘蛛航线飞行时,飞行员应向右偏置1/2n mile。所有救灾飞机都应该预料到蜘蛛航线附近和沿线的目视飞行规则空中交通量会增加,并保持向外观察的警惕。

上述运行措施通常会得到联邦航空管理局采取的其他运行措施的补充,以减轻对国家空域系统运行的影响,并帮助维持其正常运行。其他运行措施包括实施交通管理新方案(例如地面延误计划),实施行动应急方案(例如设计应急路线),部署移动空中导航服务资产(例如移动空中交通管制塔),以及空域的剥夺等。

4　美国航空应急救援空域管理的启示意义

航空应急救援空域管理是空域管理的重要组成部分,在全面加强空域管理效率、有效应对重特大自然灾害和事故灾难中具有非常重要的作用。学习和借鉴美国航空应急救援空域管理制度的有益经验,对于构建我国航空应急救援空域管理制度,形成安全高效、结构合理、规模适度、各方参与的救灾空域管理体系意义重大。

4.1　完善救灾空域管理机制

要建立统一的航空应急救援救灾空域管理机制。在全国空域管理体系下,加强军航、民用运输航空、通用航空等与各级应急救援管理部门的协同配合,形成全国统一的救灾空域管理机制。加快应急救援飞行计划申请“绿色通道”建设,增强航空应急救援空域综合保障能力。推动军民航空管部门主导、社会力量参与的救灾空域使用保障机制。加快完善通用航空飞行服务保障体系,不断增强低空空域飞行安全监控和管理能力。

4.2　建立权责清晰组织网络

构建救灾空域使用指挥响应体系。结合由上至下的“国家应急指挥部—省应急指挥中心—市级基地—区域基地—应急起降点”应急管理体系,建立各级各类军民航空域管理协调机制预案,建立“统一指挥、逐级上报”的航空应急救援响应空域使用流程,实现不同力量之间的协同运行、互联互通。整合航空应急救援空域管理使用的数据信息,搭建跨部门的航空应急救援空域大数据共享平台,实现航空应急救援空域管理相关信息的共享与协同。实现与军航信息对接,与民航、警航等航空力量在区域布局、指挥调度、空管监控等方面的相互开放、相互保障,提高救灾空域资源使用效率。

4.3　构建救灾空域安全管理体系

搭建救灾空域监控管理体系。制定不同灾害类型中,救灾空域范围内各类航空器所处位置及任务类型,救援飞机上救援设备、灾情监测设备的参数,加强航空救援设施设备管理,实时动态监测各类航空器空中位置数据。建立三维展示系统,搭建航空应急救援指挥空域管理可视化系统,辅助灾害空域救援决策。强化救灾空域范围内飞行安全,健全完善应急救援飞行空域安全管理制度,根据不同任务类型航空器用空需求,建立相应的协调管控机制,全面落实救援飞机执飞航空器、机组成员、飞行条件、飞行申报等标准规范。

总之,随着国家空域管理体系和应急救援体系的发展,救灾空域管理呈现出新的需求和特点,借鉴美国等国家成熟的经验做法,立足我国发展实际,推动完善我国救灾空域管理机制,有助于增强应急条件下的空域使用效率和安全性。

参考文献

[1]　美国航空管理局.救灾空域管理计划[Z].2012.

[2]　钟实,王刚.航空应急救援现状及发展建议的思考[J].内江科技,2021,42(08):1-2.

[3]　闫鹏,杨帅,张强.航空应急救援专业化力量建设的战略性思考(上)——航空应急救援概述及发展现状[J].中国减灾,2019(01):44-49.

[4]　薛峰,商朝阳,李天宇.通用航空应急救援服务资源保障数据平台建设及前瞻[J].空运商务,2021(11):59-63.

[5]　皮骏,吉亚铭,齐福强.超大城市航空应急救援场点布局优化[J].安全与环境工程,2020,27(06):140-146.

无人机城区栅格环境下的能耗问题研究

刘明欢　李亚飞*

(中国民航大学空中交通管理学院)

摘　要　为了提高无人机在城市低空空域中的生存能力,运用蚁群算法求解无人机在栅格环境中不同飞行高度下的安全路径,并考虑了无人机避障路径规划中电池能耗问题。本研究考虑空气密度的影响,建立无人机水平飞行和垂直飞行精细化能量消耗模型。运用能量消耗模型求解在不同飞行高度下无人机水平飞行阶段和垂直飞行阶段的能耗,得到无人机能耗最小的飞行剖面。研究表明无人机在较低高度飞行能耗较小,随着飞行高度的增加,能耗增大。本研究可为无人机选择最优飞行能耗提供理论支持。

关键词　航空运输　最小能耗　蚁群算法　无人机(UAV)　路径规划

1.基金项目:教育部人文社会科学研究青年基金项目(21YJCZH075)。

0 引言

近年来,无人机(Unmanned Aerial Vehicle,UAV)的研究和应用呈现出迅猛发展的势头[1]。民航局发展统计公报指出,截至2020年底,全行业无人机拥有者注册用户约55.8万个,其中,个人用户约49.8万个,企业、事业、机关法人单位用户约6万个。全行业注册无人机共51.7万架,无人机有效驾驶员执照达到88994本。无人机因其使用灵活、节省人力、使用成本低、可大规模生产、能精准完成点对点任务等特点,被广泛用于物流配送、影像拍摄、电力巡检、抢险救灾、作物喷洒等领域。

随着无人机数量的增加,无人机空中交通管理成为国内外学者广泛关注的问题。无人机空中交通管理目的是让无人机飞行更加安全、高效、有序,规划无人机路径成为无人机核心问题之一。无人机路径规划是综合考虑各种因素,规划一条从起点到终点的最优路径。无人机避开障碍物安全飞行又是路径规划首要考虑的问题,国内外学者做了大量该问题的研究。文献[2]将Theta*算法在三维路径规划运用于地形障碍和城市环境中,以评估不同类型障碍的解决方案;文献[3]设计了一种新的多阶段动态路径规划算法,将人工势场法和调和函数、卡尔曼滤波和马尔可夫决策过程相结合,主要针对城市空中交通领域的应用;文献[4]提出了一种关键障碍和周围点集的路径规划方法,可在三维环境中快速生成路径;文献[5]研究了无人机机群的协同路径规划问题,通过对无人机损失概率建模,优化路径以考虑环境中的不确定性,使用直线路径估计每个任务的飞行时间和风险;文献[6]构建了无人机空中风险指数和地面风险指数,建立了指标筛选模型和无人机飞行风险评估模型,提出了基于k-均值聚类的无人机飞行风险评估模型;文献[7]在考虑无人机航路安全成本的基础上,提出了基于地面风险评估的最优航路规划模型,以每飞行小时地面上的死亡概率为定量指标,定义每个栅格的安全系数;文献[8]考虑不同任务场景的地面人口密度和遮蔽物保护能力,并引入环境影响因子,用以分析不同环境场景的气象、地理和通信等要素;文献[9]考虑地面人员伤亡率和人口数量等因素构建栅格风险因子,建立航路安全代价评估模型,探究距离和安全双重约束条件下的航路规划方法。

这些文献主要考虑了无人机飞行时的路径风险值,规划路径避开障碍物,使无人机飞行时风险最小,但较少考虑无人机电池消耗问题。无人机电池消耗过多是引起无人机坠落的一个主要原因,本研究将考虑无人机在路径规划中电池能耗的问题。以小型电动垂直起降无人机为研究对象,分析无人机在垂直飞行阶段和水平飞行阶段的能耗问题。在满足安全飞行的前提下,以最小能耗为目标优化飞行剖面,选择无人机最优飞行高度。

1 无人机电池消耗模型

1.1 电池输出功率

从飞行剖面角度看,小型电动垂直起降无人机在整个飞行过程中可分水平飞行阶段和垂直飞行阶段。

在水平飞行阶段,无人机电动推力主要克服飞行时受到的飞行阻力,电池的输出功率可以表示为[10]:

$$P_1=\frac{1}{\eta_P\eta_M\eta_{ESC}}\left(\frac{1}{2}\rho V_C{}^3SC_{D0}+\frac{2kM^2g^2}{\rho SV_C}\right) \tag{1}$$

式中: S——无人机水平迎风面积,m^2;

C_{D0}——零升力阻力系数;

ρ——空气密度,kg/m^3;

V_C——水平飞行速度,m/s;

k——诱导阻力因子;

M——无人机起飞质量,kg;

g——重力加速度,取9.8m/s^2;

η_P,η_M,η_{ESC}——螺旋桨、无刷电机和无刷电调的工作效率,一般均取值为0.8[11]。

在垂直飞行阶段,无人机缓慢匀速运行,电动推力主要克服无人机重量,电池的输出功率可以表示为[11]:

$$P_2=\frac{1}{\eta_P\eta_M\eta_{ESC}}\sqrt{\frac{(Mg)^3}{2\rho A\kappa}} \tag{2}$$

式中:A——无人机桨盘面积(m^2);

κ——桨盘修正因子,一般取0.9~0.94[11]。

1.2 能量消耗

本研究考虑到在标准状态下空气密度与距离海平面的高度有关,无人机在不同飞行高度下电池输出功率有一定程度的变化。根据公式(1)和公式(2),小型电动垂直起降无人机在水平飞行阶段和垂直飞行阶段的电池输出功率与空气密度有关。考虑飞行高度对电池输出功率的影响,能更加精确求解电池消耗的能量。

依据BADA手册,标准大气海平面高度的空气密度 $\rho_0 = 1.225\text{kg/m}^3$,温度 $T_0 = 288.15\text{K}$。

在海平面高度以上 $H(H<11000\text{m})$ m时,温度 T 和空气密度 ρ 随着高度的增大而减小,其变化规律为:

$$T = T_0 - 0.0065H \tag{3}$$

$$\rho = \rho_0 \left(\frac{T}{T_0}\right)^{\frac{-g}{K_T R}-1} \tag{4}$$

式中:R——空气的气体常数,其值为 $287.05287\text{m}^2/\text{Ks}^2$;

K_T——低于对流层顶的温度梯度,其值为 $-0.0065°\text{K/m}$。

结合式(1)、式(3)、式(4),无人机飞行高度为 H 时,水平飞行距离为 L 时,水平飞行阶段电池消耗的能量 Q_1 可表示为:

$$Q_1 = \frac{L}{V_C \eta_P \eta_M \eta_{ESC}} \left(\frac{1}{2}\rho V_C{}^3 S C_{D0} + \frac{2kM^2 g^2}{\rho_0 \left(\frac{T_0 - 0.0065H}{T_0}\right)^{\frac{-g}{K_T R}-1} S V_C} \right) \tag{5}$$

结合式(2)、式(3)、式(4),无人机在垂直飞行阶段速度为 V_T、飞行高度为 H 时,无人机垂直起飞和垂直降落的电池消耗能量 Q_2 可以表示为:

$$Q_2 = \int_0^{\frac{H}{V_T}} \frac{1}{\eta_P \eta_M \eta_{ESC}} \sqrt{\frac{(Mg)^3}{2\rho_0 \left(\frac{T_0 - 0.0065 V_T t}{T_0}\right)^{\frac{-g}{K_T R}-1} A\kappa}}\, dt \tag{6}$$

无人机整个飞行过程中电池消耗的能量 Q 可以表示为:

$$Q = Q_1 + 2Q_2 \tag{7}$$

结合式(5)和式(6),无人机电池消耗的能量与无人机飞行高度和水平飞行阶段的路径长度有关。无人机垂直飞行阶段电池耗能随飞行高度增大而增大。在城市环境中,由于建筑物高度不同,无人机在不同飞行高度下要避开的建筑物数量和位置不同,飞行路径长度不同,水平飞行阶段电池消耗也不同。研究无人机路径规划中的电池耗能问题,探究无人机垂直飞行阶段和水平飞行阶段的电池耗能,可为无人机选择最小能耗的飞行路径提供决策。

2　基于蚁群算法的无人机栅格路径规划

2.1　栅格路径

城市区域是人员高度集中,建筑物密集的区域。无人机在城市区域飞行首要考虑的障碍物是城市建筑物。由于城市建筑物大多数都是垂直于地面,在不同的高度上横截面基本一致,从俯视的角度看为矩形,可以把城市建筑物简化成长方体。无人机城区飞行示意图如图1所示,黑色的长方体为简化后的建筑物。

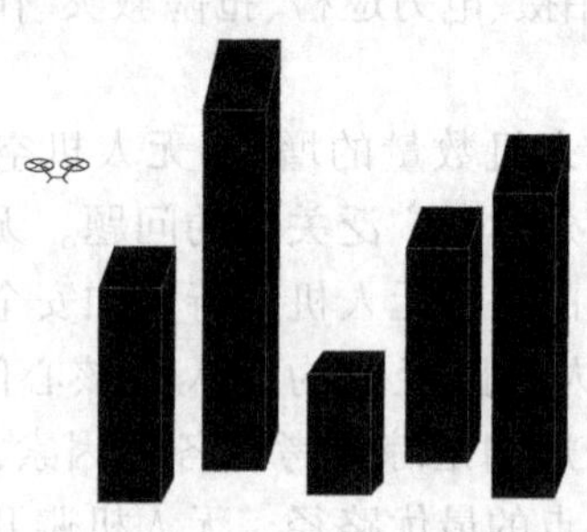

图1　无人机城区飞行

无人机在城区飞行时,高于无人机飞行高度的建筑物会影响无人机飞行,为保证无人机安全飞行,需要规划无人机路径绕过建筑物。对于高度低于飞行高度的建筑物,无人机可以直接飞越,不影响无人机飞行。由于城市建筑物高度不一致,无人机在不同飞行高度下需要绕飞的建筑物数量、位置不同,无人机飞行路径也不同。

栅格法是将一定范围的空间分成若干个大小相同的小正方体,其中黑色的小正方体表示该区域内存在障碍物,无人机不能进入该区域,白色的小正方体则表示该区域无障碍物,无人机可以安全飞行。

将城市区域栅格化,在某一高度下,建筑物占据的空间可表示为黑色区域。无人机可飞的区域为白色,该模式如图2所示。

图2　栅格化城市区域

在不同飞行高度下,无人机水平飞行阶段需要绕开建筑物的数量、位置不同,栅格化图形中黑色区域也不相同。

2.2 蚁群算法求解栅格路径

蚁群算法是无人机路径规划中一种常用的智能算法。蚁群算法是一种基于正反馈机制的启发式寻优方法,具体依赖于启发信息和信息素,通过个体努力与群体协作在位置领域进行搜索,基于正反馈增大较优路径上的信息素,选出最优路径[12]。蚁群算法可以解决无人机在栅格图形中路径规划的问题,找出一条从起点到终点避开障碍物的最优路径。无人机在栅格图形中最优路径如图3所示。

图3 无人机路径

在不同高度下,无人机水平飞行路径长度不同。高度越大,无人机需要绕开的建筑物越少,路径长度越小。运用蚁群算法可求解无人机在某个已知飞行高度时的水平飞行路径长度与飞行轨迹,可进一步求解无人机整个飞行剖面的电池能耗。

3 算例仿真

选取无人机飞行场景为200m×200m的空间范围,无人机起点坐标为(0,200),无人机终点坐标为(200,0),无人机有关参数参考文献[13]中的数据,相关参数见表1。

无人机及其他参数 表1

V_C $(m \cdot s^{-1})$	15	V_T $(m \cdot s^{-1})$	2.5	M (kg)	6.2	k	0.13
$S(m^2)$	1.313	$A(m^2)$	1.313	C_{D0}	0.015	k	0.94

设置蚁群算法中种群规模为80,迭代次数为200次,信息素蒸发系数为0.3,信息素重要程度参数为1,启发式因子重要程度参数为7,信息素增加强度系数为1。运用蚁群算法,分别求解栅格化图形中无人机在20m、30m、40m、50m和60m飞行高度时的最优路径。

无人机在不同高度的飞行轨迹如图4所示。

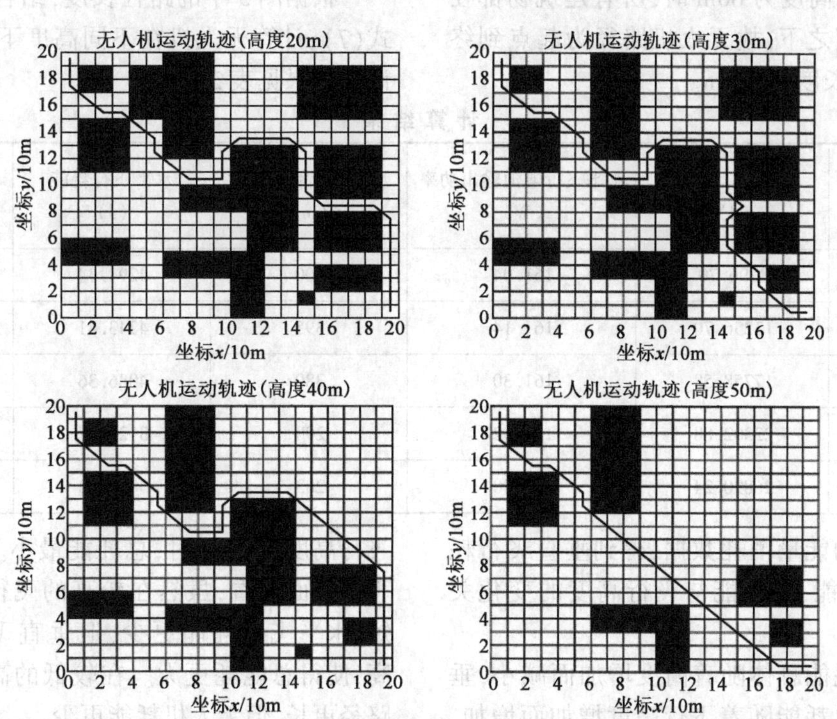

图4 无人机飞行轨迹

无人机水平飞行路径长度如图5所示。

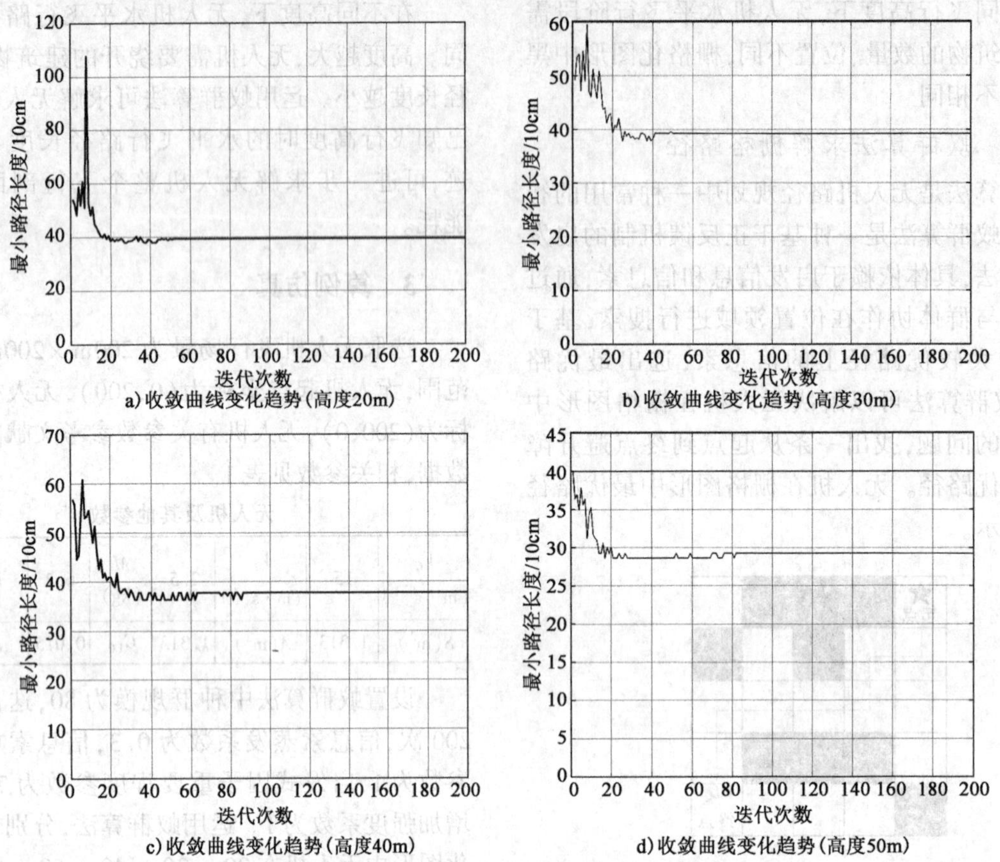

图5　无人机水平飞行路径长度

无人机飞行高度为60m时,所有建筑物都在无人机飞行高度之下,故无人机路径为起点到终点的直线,路径长度为283m。

根据图5中的路径长度,结合式(5)、式(6)、式(7),计算无人机在不同高度下的电池消耗量,计算结果见表2。

计算结果　　表2

飞行高度(m)	垂直飞行耗能(J)	水平飞行电池输出功率(W)	水平飞行路径长度(m)	水平飞行耗能(J)	总耗能(J)
20	8796.70	161.04	400	4294.34	13091.04
30	13256.70	161.14	395	4243.41	17500.11
40	17758.58	161.30	380	4086.36	21844.94
50	22302.88	161.52	290	3122.77	25425.65
60	26890.24	161.80	283	3052.63	29942.87

由表2中的能量消耗数据,得到垂直飞行耗能、水平飞行耗能、总耗能与飞行高度的变化关系,如图6所示。

水平飞行耗能总体随着高度增加而减小,垂直飞行耗能与总耗能随着飞行高度增加而增加。飞行高度为20m时,总耗能最小。从无人机整个飞行剖面来看,虽然在较高的飞行高度上路径更短,水平飞行耗能更少,但垂直飞行阶段耗能较高,使得总能耗更大。在较低的高度飞行时虽然路径更长,但无人机耗能更少。

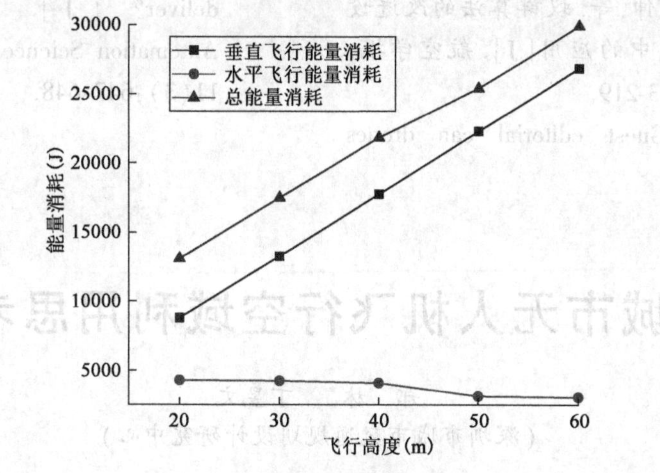

图6　能量消耗变化

4　结语

本文在小型电动垂直起降无人机水平与垂直飞行的电池输出功率研究的基础上,引入空气密度随高度变化的表达式,使得能耗计算更加精确。同时将城市区域栅格化,考虑到城市建筑物高度不一,运用蚁群算法求解在不同飞行高度下无人机飞行路径的轨迹长度。结合无人机电池消耗和飞行路径建立无人机路径的能耗模型。在算例仿真中,运用蚁群算法计算无人机路径长度,并从无人机垂直和水平飞行剖面角度,研究无人机垂直与水平飞行阶段的电池能耗。分析电池能量消耗与飞行高度和路径长度的变化关系,在比较分析后,发现在所测试的高度中,无人机飞行高度为20m时虽然路径长度最长,但其总能耗最小。本文中建立的模型可为无人机选择最小能耗的安全飞行路径提供决策依据,后续可进一步研究在城市风场影响下的无人机电池能量消耗。

参考文献

[1] Tan Y H, Lai S, Wang K, et al. Cooperative Ccontrol of Multiple Unmanned Aerial Systems for Heavy Duty Carrying[J]. Annual Reviews in Control, 2018, 46:44-57.

[2] Filippis L D, Guglieri G, Quagliotti F. Path Planning Strategies for UAVS in 3D Environments[J]. Journal of Intelligent and Robotic Systems, 2012, 65(1-4):247-264.

[3] He T, Mantegh I, Chen L, et al. UAS Flight Path Planning for Dynamic, Multi-Vehicle Environment[C]. 2020 International Conference on Unmanned Aircraft Systems (ICUAS), 2020:211-219.

[4] Han J. An Efficient Approach to 3D Path Planning[J]. Information Sciences, 2018, 478.

[5] Bellingham J S, Tillerson M, Alighanbari M, et al. Cooperative Path Planning for Multiple UAVs in Dynamic and Uncertain Environments[J]. Proceedings of the IEEE Conference on Decision & Control, 2002.

[6] 卜建,张洪海,胡明华,等.基于K-means聚类的无人机飞行风险评估(英文)[J]. Transactions of Nanjing University of Aeronautics and Astronautics,2020,37(02):263-273.

[7] 韩鹏,赵巍飞.基于地面安全约束的无人机航路规划研究(英文)[J]. Transactions of Nanjing University of Aeronautics and Astronautics,2021,38(02):298-305.

[8] 韩鹏,赵巍飞.基于飞行环境建模的UAV地面撞击风险研究[J].中国安全科学学报,2020,30(01):142-147.

[9] 韩鹏,张冰玉.基于改进蚁群算法的无人机安全航路规划研究[J].中国安全科学学报,2021,31(01):24-29.

[10] 赵巍飞,郑雨欣.城市物流无人机飞行任务剖面构建与优化[J].飞行力学,2021,39(03):54-59,67.

[11] 唐伟,宋笔锋,曹煜,等.微小型电动垂直起降无人机总体设计方法及特殊参数影响[J].航空学报,2017,38(10):22097.

[12] 李宪强,马戎,张伸,等.蚁群算法的改进设计及在航迹规划中的应用[J].航空学报,2020,41(S2):213-219.

[13] D'Andrea R. Guest editorial can drones deliver? [J]. IEEE Transactions on Automation Science and Engineering, 2014, 11(3):647-648.

城市无人机飞行空域利用思考

郑　林*　丁昱文

(深圳市城市交通规划设计研究中心)

摘　要　无人机种类众多且性能差异较大,与有人驾驶航空器有较大差别,对空域管理提出了新的挑战。各国空域管理机构基于对无人机稳定性、安全性等方面的顾虑,对无人机飞行采用以隔离运行为主的管理方法,一定程度上限制了无人机的飞行以及行业的发展。本文深入分析了无人机在飞行空域利用中遇到的体制机制、规则体系、服务保障等方面的限制及其背后的原因,并提出了在现有空域管理体制下缓解空域限制的办法,包括建立场景试验、试运行机制,引入可接受安全水平理念,基于无人机的智慧化属性建立智能管理平台以提升空域利用效率。特别是创新性地提出了特殊隔离飞行空域形式,以解决当前规则制定遇到的难题,为无人机空域的高效利用提供指引。

关键词　空域　无人机通道　无人机运行　空域形式　空域使用效率

0　引言

城市无人机飞行是利用无人机面向城市开展物流运输、执法监察、消防救援、环境保护、应急减灾等应用的飞行活动。随着无人机技术的进一步发展,其在城市管理以及交通运输等领域发挥着越来越重要的作用。因此,各国政府对城市无人机应用越发重视,出台了一系列规章引导无人机的空域利用。美国联邦航空管理局(FAA)推出了非管制的、面向服务的无人机交通管理系统(UTM)及相关操作指引,欧洲航空安全局(EASA)为无人机安全、高效融入各国空域推出了无人机飞行管理体系(U-Space)[1]。但无人机属于新兴产业,在飞行空域利用,特别是城市地区空域利用上,可参照的先例较少,无人机飞行空域划设与管理尚处于探索阶段[2-4]。同时,无人机强制认证或适航审定等工作尚未全面开展,监管机构因性能疑虑而大多要求无人机隔离运行[5]。但是,各国均未对隔离空域的划设做出具体规定,且隔离空域内的运行规则也尚不明确,导致无人机在实际的空域利用中困难重重。另一方面,无人机飞行空域限制也制约了应用数据累积,导致空域规则制定难以获得实际数据支撑,规则制定进展缓慢,无人机空域利用限制难以缓解。

1　城市无人机飞行及其空域特点

1.1　无人机种类众多,性能特点差异较大

按照国家空中交通管制委员会办公室组织起草的《无人驾驶航空器飞行管理暂行条例(征求意见稿)》,无人机是指机上没有驾驶员进行操控的航空器,主要包括遥控航空器和自主航空器。从无人机的概念我们可以看出,无人机包括的航空器范围较大[6],从消费级的无人机到接受远程驾驶操控的运-5型货机都可列入无人机的范畴。不同机型的动力系统、通信系统、导航系统各不相同,性能参数也有差异,导致不同机型的空域保持能力以及通信导航能力差别较大。各国的监管机构也尝试通过分类对无人机实施分类管理,如欧盟航空管理局根据风险等级将无人机划分为开放类、限制类以及适航审定类[7-9],日本政府在其航空法中增加了无人机安全运行法规[10],而我国《无人驾驶航空器飞行管理暂行条例(征求意见稿)》根据重量以及速度将无人机分为微型、轻型、

小型、中型和大型无人机,但目前这些规定尚未对无人机的空域保持能力以及通信导航性能做出细致划分,难以根据现有分类对无人机的飞行空域实施管理。

在实际的空域使用过程中,不同类型无人机对空域的需求差别较大,使用无差别的飞行规则难以适应不同种类无人机的需求。按照《无人驾驶航空器飞行管理暂行条例(征求意见稿)》的有关规定,微型无人机的飞行高度不超过真高50m,而大型无人机由于重量需按照适航类飞行器进行管理,飞行高度在平原地区应不小于真高100m[11]。因此,难以对不同类型的无人机实施无差别的飞行管理。同时,无人机作为新兴行业,在起始发展阶段难以要求管理机构对每一种无人机机型的空域保持以及通信导航等参数做出认证,也缺乏相关标准对需要进行适航认证的机型进行审定。因此,现阶段的无人机空域管理难以通过严格的空域保持能力以及风险分类认定进行。

1.2 飞行空域高度较低,与有人驾驶飞行重叠度高

相比城市外的无人机飞行,城市无人机应用集中在真高120m以下的适飞空域以及作业上方一定高度范围。正在快速发展的城市无人机物流以及无人机载人运输,由于飞行性能以及能耗等原因,飞行高度也主要集中在600m以下。美团主要使用轻微型无人机在120m以下进行终端配送,迅蚁、顺丰无人机在城市内的飞行高度也在真高600m以下。虽然城市内的物流无人机由于以小件货物的运输为主,载重以及机型较小,但为满足运输的需要飞行区域并不固定,需要根据运输需求进行大范围机动,空中运行范围相对较大[12]。同时,无人机物流以及载人飞行需要根据物流和出行需求选择运行起降点和路线,因此主要集中在城市内商务需求较大的地区,与从事商务接驳的传统有人驾驶飞行的使用空域存在较大的重叠。

1.3 无人机飞行对通信导航等基础保障要求更高

无人机由于没有驾驶员进行操纵,导航控制都依赖信号传输,对导航通信等保障要求较高[13]。无人机视距内飞行依靠地面操纵员对无人机状态进行感知,但仍需通过稳定高效的通信保证操纵员的飞行意图传输到无人机。而超视距飞行由于感知与操纵都依赖无人机信号,对通信保障要求更高。特别是物流无人机,其地形摄影探测多为超视距飞行,长距离通信对无线电通信资源提出了一定的要求。此外,由于超视距无人机需要时通过通信频率保持对无人机的控制,基于通信安全的需要有时需占用专有公共频率。目前,无人机通信主要使用两个公共频率,但由于公共频率容易被第三方干扰,无人机产业正在研究使用5G等新型通信方式实现加密通信,保障超视距飞行的通信安全。

1.4 无人机飞行自动化、信息化程度高

无人机采用自动化的飞行系统以及信息传输系统,可以支撑以信息共享为基础的空中交通调配机制,并基于信息共享的及时性和准确性提升空域利用效率,这对空中交通调配的自动化以及效率提升提出新的要求。而传统有人驾驶飞行规则基于飞行员的目视自主观察或管制员的统一调配,难以适应无人机无人化、自动化的运行需求。另一方面,无人机的运行需要考虑通信延迟以及通信失效情况下需要预留的间隔余度以及反应时间,因此无人机急需一套适应其飞行特点的规则体系,以充分发挥无人机的信息化优势,提升飞行空域利用效率。

2 城市无人机飞行空域利用遇到的问题

2.1 飞行空域利用限制严格

由于无人机飞行性能相差较大且认证体系尚不完善,目前监管部门大多采用隔离飞行的方法保证无人机与有人驾驶航空器的飞行安全。美国NASA提出无人机走廊的方式实现无人机与有人驾驶飞行的隔离运行[14],而我国按照《无人驾驶航空器飞行管理暂行条例(征求意见稿)》的要求,无人机飞行以隔离飞行为主,兼顾融合飞行需求。但是,各国监管机构并未出台相应的隔离飞行空域划设规则,不同隔离空域需要的间隔尚不明确,导致不同空域管理者对隔离飞行空域的划设标准各不相同,且极易出于安全考虑加大相应间隔余度,使空域利用效率难以保证。

另一方面,各国目前普遍采用“无人飞行避让有人飞行”的调配管理原则。例如,FAA在特殊运行许可中明确无人机飞行不得干扰现有的运输航

空飞行[15],《无人驾驶航空器飞行管理暂行条例(征求意见稿)》规定无人飞行避让有人飞行。因此,在实际运行管理中,无人机飞行需要避让其他有人驾驶飞行。而在城市低空空域资源有限且空域划设规则不明确的情况下,无人机飞行往往需要等待有人驾驶航空器确认离开相关空域后才能开展。此外,根据《民用无人驾驶航空器系统空中交通管理办法》的相关规定,无人机在隔离空域飞行与其他有人驾驶飞行需要保持600m 的垂直间隔[16],但在有限的城市空域内基本难以配备此类间隔。无人机空域利用面临较大困难。

2.2　规则尚未明确阻碍高效运行

无人机产业属于新兴产业,其管理体系以及规则体系尚未明确。空域管理机构沿用传统有人驾驶航空器的飞行规则对其进行管理,无人机飞行效率受到较大制约。在飞行过程中,无人机由于缺乏机上驾驶员,不能按照目视飞行规则进行飞行,只能按照仪表飞行规则,并保持较大的间隔。但无人机飞行的速度、高度与有人驾驶仪表飞行相差较大,且其可以通过高效的信息共享实现统一管理调度,按照仪表飞行间隔调配飞行的必要性较小。另一方面,无人机具备通过协同算法调配集群内飞行的能力,按照现有的仪表飞行规则调配不同集群,甚至集群内飞行难以满足无人机高效运行的需求[17]。

2.3　飞行服务保障缺失,安全难以保障

目前,无人机通信导航等配套设施严重缺乏,飞行应用范围受限[18]。无人机基于飞行器与地面站或控制者的信号通信实现安全飞行,因此无人机与地面基站之间的通信成为控制或者介入无人机运行的重要保障。但当前物流等领域应用的无人机由于频率资源有限,大部分还使用公共频率与地面基站进行通信,难以保障无人机接收到正确的地面指令,甚至可能导致无人机接收到违法者发出的欺骗指令而做出错误的动作。同时,无人机目前依靠的通信链路仍然采用视距传播,即必须在信号传输路线上没有障碍物遮挡,否则无人机与地面基站之间的通信就会受到干扰。特别是超视距飞行需求强烈的物流无人机,其在城市范围内的飞行难免会受到山体或高层建筑物的遮挡,通信质量难以保障。为了防止无人机在运行过程中难以收到正确的指令,当前大部分无人机运行者采用在城市高层建筑零星布设中继站的方式解决通信问题,但飞行线路以及飞行范围大大受限。

通信设施等飞行保障的缺失也阻碍了无人机通过实时的信息共享实现安全飞行。无人机可以通过在调度系统上及时共享位置、高度、速度等信息,实现不同无人机的动态调度,在提升空域利用效率的同时保障运行安全。气象信息、动态空域地图以及空中情报等飞行保障也需要通过通信与空域无人机及时共享。但目前无人机的气象信息、空中情报等服务缺失,实现信息共享的通信保障网络也亟须构建。

2.4　缺乏实际运行数据支撑规则制定

管理机构已经意识到制定无人机飞行规则的重要性,国家空中交通管制委员会办公室组织起草了《无人驾驶航空器飞行管理暂行条例(征求意见稿)》并有望于2022 年发布生效。但是,地方政府以及民航管理机构在《无人驾驶航空器飞行管理暂行条例(征求意见稿)》等上位法的基础上制定无人机管理细则时,往往遇到缺乏实际运行数据支撑的难题。而实际运行数据需要无人机在特定场景下经历一定周期的常态化运行才可得到,但无人机,特别是城市无人机的常态化运行,因与其他用户空域重叠情况严重,难以在规则缺失的情况下开展,一定程度上延迟了有关规则的制定实施。

3　创新空域利用形式与理念,缓解空域限制

3.1　推行场景试验机制,为应用推广提速

作为一种新兴业态,无人机产业的规则体系构建是一个长期渐进的过程。但由于无人机产业发展迅猛,无人机物流等部分应用场景已经具备投入商用的条件,传统的从实验室获得性能数据,到实际场景试飞,再到制定相应规则以及验证试飞循序渐进的流程难以满足无人机快速发展的需要,也难以在短时期内支撑种类众多的无人机标准的制定。因此,建议采用基于设计参数的实际场景试验机制,在保障安全的基础上加快规则体系建设。行业管理部门可以联合地方政府打造相关的无人机试验区或实验项目,基于当地的空域条件,对指定的无人机机型颁发试运行许可或试验许可。在相关机型经过设计论证及必要的试验

验证后，允许无人机运营人在实验室试验的同时，提前按照相关经审核的运行方案进行试验运行，并基于运行实践和数据制定相关的试行规则和标准。获得的实际场景运行数据以及规则草案可以与同步进行的实验室试验获得的数据融合并相互验证，为规则完善提供支撑，缩短规则验证流程。

FAA已经为运行方案获得认可的运行人颁发了特殊运行许可[19-20]；中国民航局也已经为多个无人机运营人颁发了试运行许可[21]，并出台《民用无人驾驶航空试验基地(试验区)建设工作指引》[22]，推进无人机试验区的建设。但在实际运行过程中，运行人或试验区管理方依然遇到由规则未健全导致的空域利用难题。因此，各方需要在试验过程中抓住空域利用的主要矛盾，更新安全管理理念，在保证安全的前提下创新空域利用形式以推动无人机产业的应用。

3.2 引入可接受安全水平理念，逐步构建运行规则体系

空域管理的目标是保障飞行安全与效率。由于当前各方尚未就安全管理的目标和方法达成一致，往往出现以牺牲效率换取安全的情况，阻碍了无人机等与空域关系密切的行业的发展。因此，相关行业亟须更新安全管理的理念和方法，明确安全管理的目标，在保障安全的情况下为行业发展松绑。空域参与方应引入"可接受安全水平"[23]的理念，制定可达到且可接受的安全水平目标，在可接受安全水平下构建规则体系，保障空域的安全科学利用。

按照国际民用航空组织(ICAO)发布的安全管理系统指引文件(ICAO8084)，安全目标水平(Target Level of Saftey，TLS)是风险评估的最终目标。ICAO的相关评估专家把安全目标定义为可以接受的风险水平。例如，对于航空器的碰撞风险，其规定的标准为8105.1(次事故/飞行小时)，而且规定一次碰撞相当于两次事故；对于民航整体的风险水平，标准为710(次事故/飞行小时)[24-25]。可接受安全水平，即安全水平已经得到各方的认可，且可以以安全运行的时间或发生可控制事故的概率进行衡量。通过制定可接受安全水平，各方明确其应达到的安全目标，并通过不断的行为修正保证其安全水平在目标之上。而在此安全水平之上，结果可控的事件具备发生的概率，但其将作为安全管理学习的触发事件，从而促进安全水平的提升。作为一种新兴行业，无人机应用在缺乏完善规则体系的情况下必然发生超出预期的各种小型事件，这也是行业进行试验运行或试运行的原因。无人机应用各参与方可借助可接受安全水平的理念，由管理方发布安全水平目标和指引，运行方通过制定操作规范以及风险缓解措施、事件应对措施保证安全风险可控，从而在保障安全的情况下进行规则试验验证，为规则制定提供数据支撑，逐步构建运行规则体系。

3.3 创新空域利用形式，减少隔离飞行限制

在无人机飞行空域划设等有关规定尚不明确的情况下，各方应充分利用试验区、试运行等试验机制尝试新型空域形式，在不同空域内探索实行不同规则，缓解空域限制[26]。物流、载人等以实现位移为目标的无人机应用可以探索利用无人机通道、走廊等空域形式[27-28]，并利用智慧化空域管理平台实现实时动态管理，改变以往片状固定空域与其他低空用户协调难度大的情况。对于重量小、飞行高度低的无人机，可以考虑根据对地风险以及对空影响的评估结果进行分类管理，沿用我国已经在部分地区试行的适飞空域。通过科学分类评估可进入适飞空域的机型并控制适飞空域高度，在适飞空域内实行操纵者自主避让的管理原则。

针对物流无人机重量、航程以及空域保持能力将不断地接近甚至超过现有的有人驾驶航空器的情况，无人机通道可以充分借鉴可接受安全水平的理念，评估保证无人机在通道内运行的通道尺寸以及保护空间。同时，针对城市地区空域资源紧张的情况，可在确保无人机保持在指定空域范围内的前提下，基于其他航空器的空域保持能力配备不同隔离飞行空域的间隔。而针对集群飞行需求巨大的无人机用户，可以践行民航局提出的"放管服"思维，在无人机空域内探索属于同一用户的无人机飞行间隔，由无人机操纵者统一调配，并对安全负责，而不同用户的无人机则必须满足规定的空域间隔，以利于发挥无人机集群统一调度的算法优势，提升空域利用效率。

3.4 建立服务保障体系，提升安全监控水平

(1)低空空域融入智慧城市管理，无人机低空

调度智慧化。随着大量无人机投入实际应用,无人机的空中交通管理数量和密度将较大地超过现有的空管模式,以人工方式为主的空中调度管理将难以适应无人机的调度续期。加上物流无人机的智能化属性以及大量自动化技术在无人机上的应用,智能化的空中交通管理平台将成为未来城市低空调度的主流模式。而在调配的过程中,无人机调度系统还需考虑城市的自然山体以及高层建筑对无人机运行路线的影响。因此,城市应将低空空域空间作为城市国土空间资源之一列入城市国土空间规划,通过智慧城市平台统一管理高层建筑、低空空域空间规划以及生态敏感保护区域,并同步将城市无人机空中调度管理系统纳入智慧城市体系,利用智慧城市体系对低空无人机进行统一调度管理,实现无人机空中管理调度智慧化。

(2)建设智慧监视体系,支撑空域动态管理。城市应在智慧城市的平台建设低空空域监视体系,利用5G等专用网络为低空用户提供更为精确稳定的定位导航服务,并利用专用高速网络将空域中的运行信息实时传送至军民航监管机构,支撑空域动态划设。在现有空域管理体制下,充分利用城市中军民航各方使用较少的空域,建立协同动态管理空域。在协同管理空域无特殊飞行需求的情况下,允许物流无人机等低空用户在空域中自主组织飞行,并对飞行的安全负责,同时通过智慧城市平台与空域用户保持通信联系。在军方或其他空域用户对空域有使用需求时,军方单位可通过监视手段掌握空域内的航空器动态,并通过专用频率或其他通信方式及时组织各方退出空域,保障在特殊情况下空域的可回收性。

城市应在智慧城市平台融入低空飞行保障服务,搜集储存城市地形等航空情报信息,并实时更新相关气象信息,为包括物流无人机在内的低空用户提供实时飞行服务。地方政府应联合民航部门以及无人机企业,统筹规划,利用城市5G网络等智慧化设施,建设无人机发展所需的通信导航体系,解决当前无人机在运行过程中遇到的通信导航难题。建议为包括物流无人机在内的应用级无人机分配专有的频率,并统筹在铁塔或者现有导航设施上加装中继设备,满足应用级无人机的超视距运行需求。同时,为了提高通信导航设施的效率,建议将加建的无人机通信导航设施与传统通航飞行器服务设施融合使用,并融入统一的飞行服务保障平台,实现相关信息的互联共享。

4 结语

随着无人机应用在城市中的深入,低空空域,特别是城市低空空域必将迎来更大的需求。通过空域利用方式创新等方法可以在以隔离飞行为主的管理架构下提升空域的利用效率,但难以达到融合飞行空域的空域利用率。因此,要满足无人机应用不断扩展带来的空域需求,管理机构需要探索融合飞行框架下的管理规则。特别是从场景试验机制下获取的实际运行数据,可以用于进一步评估无人机的空域保持能力等性能,并基于不断完善的无人机飞行服务保障体系,在满足可接受安全水平的基础上探索融合飞行,以提升空域利用效率,满足无人机产业进一步发展的需求。

参考文献

[1] Prevot T, Rios J, Kopardekar P, et al. UAS traffic management (UTM) concept of operations to safely enablelow altitude flight operations [C]// 16th AIAA aviation technology, integration, and operations conference. AIAA 2016-3292. Washington D C, USA: AIAA, 2016.

[2] O. Schneider, S. Kern, F. Knabe, et al. Metropolis-urban airspace design. Delft University of Technology, Delft, 2014.

[3] E. Sunil, J. Hoekstra, J. Ellerbroek, et al. Metropolis: Relating airspace structure and capacity for extreme traffic densities. ATM seminar 2015, 11th USA/EUROPE Air Traffic Management R&D Seminar, Lisbon, Portugal, 2015.

[4] Amazon. Revising the Airspace Model for the Safe Integration of Small Unmanned Aircraft Systems. July 2015. [Online]. Available: https://utm. arc. nasa. gov/docs/Amazon_Revising% 20the% 20Airspace% 20Model% 20for% 20the% 20Safe% 20Integration% 20of% 20sUAS[6]. pdf. [Accessed 2016 October 12].

[5] 王杰,田红安. 无人机融入非隔离空域感知与规避技术研究[C]. 中国航空学会. 第七届中国航空学会航空通信导航监视及空管学术会议暨航电与空管分会 2016 年学术年(CCATM2016)论文集,2016:260-263.

[6] 张旭,焦庆宇. 无人机空中交通管理体系架构研究[J]. 武汉理工大学学报, 2020, 42(9):29-37 +58.

[7] European Union Aviation Safety Agency. Regulation(EU) 2018/1139 of the European Parliament and of the Council [EB/OL]. (2018-08-22) [2019-12-30]. https://eur-lex. europa. eu /legal-content/EN/TXT/? uri = CELEX:32018R1139.

[8] European Union Aviation Safety Agency. Commission delegated regulation (EU) 2019/945[EB/OL]. (2019-06-11)[2019-12-30]. https://www. easa. europa. eu/documentlibrary/regulations/commission-delegated-regulation-eu-2019945.

[9] European Union Aviation Safety Agency. Standard scenarios foruas operations in the "specific" category [EB/OL]. (2019-11-07) [2020-01-11]. https://www. easa. euro-pa. eu/document-library/opinions/opinion-052019.

[10] Ministry of Land, Infrastructure, Transport and Tourism. Flight rules for UAVs (Drones, radio- controlled air vehicles, etc.) [EB/OL]. 2015-10-17 [2020-10-01]. http://www. mlit. go. jp/koku/koku_tk10_000003. html.

[11] http: //www. caac. gov. cn/XXGK/XXGK/MHGZ/201511/P020151103349925173206. pdf.

[12] Anders L, Schiøler H. Probability of low-altitude midair collision between general aviation and unmanned aircraft [J]. Risk Analysis, Johu Wileg & Sons, 2019, 39(11): 2499-2513.

[13] LakshmiPathiyil, K. H. Low, Boon Hai Soon, Shixin Mao Enabling Safe Operations of Unmanned Aircraft Systems in an Urban Environment: A Preliminary Study.

[14] B. Lascara, A. Lacher, M. DeGarmo, D. Maroney, R. Niles, L. Vempati, Urban Air Mobility Airspace Integration Concepts, 2019.

[15] One hundred fifteenth congress of the United States of America. FAA reauthorization act of 2018 [EB/OL]. (2018-04-25) [2020-01-14]. https://www. congress. gov/ 115/bills/hr302/BILLS-115hr302enr. pdf.

[16] http://www. caac. gov. cn/XXGK/XXGK/GFXWJ/201610/P020161008345668760913. pdf.

[17] 武喜萍,杨红雨,韩松臣. 基于复杂网络的空中交通特征与延误传播分析[J]. 航空学报, 2017,38(S1):113-119.

[18] 全权,李刚,柏艺琴,等. 低空无人机交通管理概览与建议[J]. 航空学报,2020,41(1):6-34.

[19] Federal Aviation Administration. Small Unman-ned Aircraft Systems (SUAS)[EB/OL]. (2016-06-21)[2020-01-14]. https://www. faa. gov/documentLibrary/media/Advisory_Circular/AC_107-2. pdf.

[20] Federal Aviation Administration. Part 107-small un-manned aircraft system [EB/OL]. (2016-06-28) [2020-01-14]. https://www. ecfr. gov/cgi-bin/text-idx? SID = 134a6a84e849d78e5722100ee018a452&mc = true&node = pt14. 2. 107&rgn = div5.

[21] http://www. caac. gov. cn/XWZX/MHYW/201910/t20191021_199030. html.

[22] http://www. gov. cn/zhengce/zhengceku/202005/27/5515320/files/1d03b8f9cb98488-baeb34562e1abc9b5. pdf.

[23] Doc 9859. Safety Management Manual Safety Management Manual Fourth Edition (advance unedited) [S]. ICAO, 2018.

[24] Eurocontrol. A method for states to determine national ATM safety minina [R]. European Organisation for the Safety of Air Navigation, Safety Regulation Commission, 2004.

[25] Doc 7300. Convention oninternational civil aviation[S]. ICAO, 2006.

[26] 石潇竹. 我国低空空域结构调整与划设探讨[J]. 指挥信息系统与技术,2010,1(3):

23-26.
[27] 张宏宏,甘旭升,李双峰,等.复杂低空环境下考虑区域风险评估的无人机航路规划[J].仪器仪表学报,2021,42(1):257-266.
[28] Sunil E, Hoekstra J, Ellerbreok J, et al. Metropolis: relating airspace structure and capacity for extreme traffic densities [C]. Proceedings of the 11th USA/Europe Air Traffic Management Research and Development Seminar. Lisbon: FAA/EUROCONTROL, 2015: 01168662.

我国机场 BIM 技术应用现状及运维阶段信息传递方法初探

戴 轩 王瀚雪 蔡 靖* 李 岳 刘 昱
(中国民航大学交通科学与工程学院)

摘 要 机场工程具有参与专业多、造价高、周期长、信息大的特点。传统机场工程建设与运维过程中的信息传递和协同效率较低,工程信息从建设阶段至运维阶段丢失严重。针对上述问题,通过数据调查方法对机场 BIM 技术的使用现状进行调研分析;并在此基础上提出了基于 IFC 标准的机场工程信息传递流程。研究表明:目前国内机场较多在设计与施工阶段应用 BIM 技术,而 BIM 数据较少传递至运维阶段并加以应用;对于旅客年吞吐量超过 300 万的机场,可按需开展不同程度 BIM 技术应用;在机场现有的信息系统中,应加强融入结构化、关联性的建设阶段 BIM 数据;所提出的基于 IFC 标准的数据传递流程可在机场运维阶段发挥作用,通过实际案例证明其具有一定可行性。本文研究成果可为机场场道结构基于 BIM 技术的智慧化管理提供参考。

关键词 机场工程 建筑信息模型 数据交互 工业基础类(IFC) 运行维护

0 引言

BIM(Building Information Modeling)即建筑信息模型,是指将建筑信息数据组织成完整个体并为建筑全生命周期过程中的决策提供支持的一项技术[1-3]。BIM 的概念最先由 Chuck Eastman 教授在 1975 年提出,此后在国外经历了数十年的发展,美国、欧洲均针对 BIM 核心技术问题开展了相关研究工作。我国 BIM 技术起步相对较晚,近年来相关部门出台了一系列文件促进 BIM 技术在不同行业的应用,2011 年 5 月住建部发布《2011—2015 年建筑业信息化发展纲要》,在总体目标和专项信息技术应用中 9 次提到 BIM;2015 年住建部发布《关于推进建筑信息模型应用的指导意见》,指出在工程项目全生命周期普及深化 BIM 应用的同时需要聚焦经济、社会和环境效益;2020 年包括中国民航局在内的十三部委联合发布《住房和城乡建设部等部门关于推动智能建造与建筑工业化协同发展的指导意见》,指出在建造全过程加大 BIM 等技术的创新与应用。目前,关于 BIM 技术的研究主要集中在数据传递标准[4]、可视化编程[5]、MVD[6]、信息管理[7]、BIM 技术与数值计算的结合[8]等方面,其中 IFC 传递标准是目前 BIM 技术研究的热点问题。

1. 基金项目:中央高校基本科研业务费中国民航大学专项(3122022043)。

IFC(Industry Foundation Classes)源于 buildingSMART 提出的 OpenBIM 的理念,其作为 BIM 信息交换的一种较为主流的格式,提供一个信息传递且不依赖任何系统的载体,不仅可以描述整个项目全生命周期内的数据与信息,还可以实现不同信息间的传递与共享[4]。国内外针对其进行了大量研究,如陈国良等[9]基于 IFC 标准,扩展了三维地质模型的标准化表达;赖华辉等[4]研究了基于 IFC 标准的结构模型数据转换与 BIM 数据集成的关键技术;徐照等[10]提出了一种结合 WebGL 和 IFC 标准的模型可视化分析方法,实现了矢量数据和模型信息的完整匹配;钟宇[11]根据 IFC 标准的扩展机制,从不同方面实现了针对盾构隧道、矿山法隧道的空间和物理结构的扩展;Filip Biljecki 等[12]研究出一种多用途应用程序域扩展(ADE)来支持保留 IFC 的相关信息,并生成丰富的数据集。可以看出,为实现 BIM 数据交换的目的,针对 IFC 标准各个领域均开展了实体扩展工作,而在机场工程领域尚未见系统报道。

BIM 在解决大型复杂建筑建设方面有着不可替代的作用。在机场建设过程中,大型枢纽机场航站楼往往体型庞大、结构复杂、涉及专业多,因此亟须将 BIM 相关数据格式标准进行扩展,并考虑其基础设施特点进行相关基础性研究。《民用运输机场建筑信息模型应用统一标准》[13]于 2020 年颁布实施,对行业 BIM 技术发展有一定促进作用,然而基于该标准的具体 BIM 技术尚待深入研究。目前,大型民用运输机场均采用了 BIM 技术辅助进行项目的设计、施工,如浦东国际机场[13]、南京禄口机场[15]、博鳌机场[16]、马尔代夫机场[17]、阿布扎比国际机场[18]。然而现有报道大多为采用相关软件的建模与应用,针对关键技术问题的深入研究还较为缺乏。本文首先基于大量数据调查对目前我国机场 BIM 应用现状进行分析,在此基础上探索了机场领域 IFC 标准的应用路径。

1 我国民用运输机场 BIM 技术发展现状

早在 2004 年,北京首都国际机场 T3 航站楼的建设就基于 BIM 技术开展了设计管理与协同方面的应用[19]。此后,2011 年南京禄口机场在建设二期航站楼过程中应用了 BIM 技术,在设计、施工、协同三方面开展了相关应用[15]。

上海浦东国际机场 2012 年在 T1 航站楼的运营维护过程中,设计与开发了基于 BIM 的运维管理系统,虽未使用数据标准进行数据模型的传递,但为其高效运维和管理提供了基础[14]。

2015 年,广州白云国际机场在扩建工程中利用 BIM 技术在桩基检测验收进度管理、同屏进度对比分析和交叉施工作业模拟优化三大方面取得了良好的效果。同时响应国家提出的相关政策,实现了绿色机场的建设,自主开发了 Revit 插件,实现了多类别模型的技术整合[20]。

在 2016 年北京大兴机场建设的过程中,在首都国际机场建设技术条件的基础上得到了进步,如在三维模型中加入时间信息进行了 4D 模拟施工,增加造价信息后实现了 5D 模拟;机械化、自动化、工程装配化程度得到不同程度的提升,施工现场利用软件翻样技术降低劳动强度的同时提高了效率[21]。

2017 年成都天府国际机场通过将 BIM 思维模式与行业工作模式相互融合,提出了将 BIM 技术融入施工过程的流程。此后湖北鄂州花湖机场建立了构件级甚至零件级的 BIM 模型,并对模型进行精细化编码,利用 BIM 技术开展正向设计、施工等过程,针对 BIM 技术在机场的精细化应用进行了探索。

总结上述国内机场 BIM 应用情况可以发现,民用运输机场建设阶段产生的大量 BIM 数据鲜有传递至运维阶段并加以应用之案例,缺乏较为基础的数据格式、信息传递方法等底层技术研发。

本文通过数据调查法对国内机场的相关从业人员开展了数据调查,并对结果进行统计与分析,共收回 117 份有效数据,其中参与的从业部门分别为机场设计单位、机场施工单位、机场集团管理部门、机场建设咨询单位、机场扩建指挥部门、机场运行指挥部门、从事机场相关其他单位和从事机场相关以外的企业。图 1 为各利益相关方在实际工程中对 BIM 技术使用情况及水平调查结果,总体上应用过 BIM 技术的占总数的 83.76%,占比虽较大,但还有未使用 BIM 技术的相关从业部门,仍需大力推广并制定相关政策;不同主体使用 BIM 技术的水平参差不齐,如机场设计单位和机场施工单位应用 BIM 技术的水平集中于初、中级阶段,占比超 50% 以上,这体现了机场设计、施工单位目前 BIM 技术应用尚存在较大发展空间,BIM 应用水平的参差不齐将导致工程设计和施工阶段的大量数据资源无法发挥其价值。

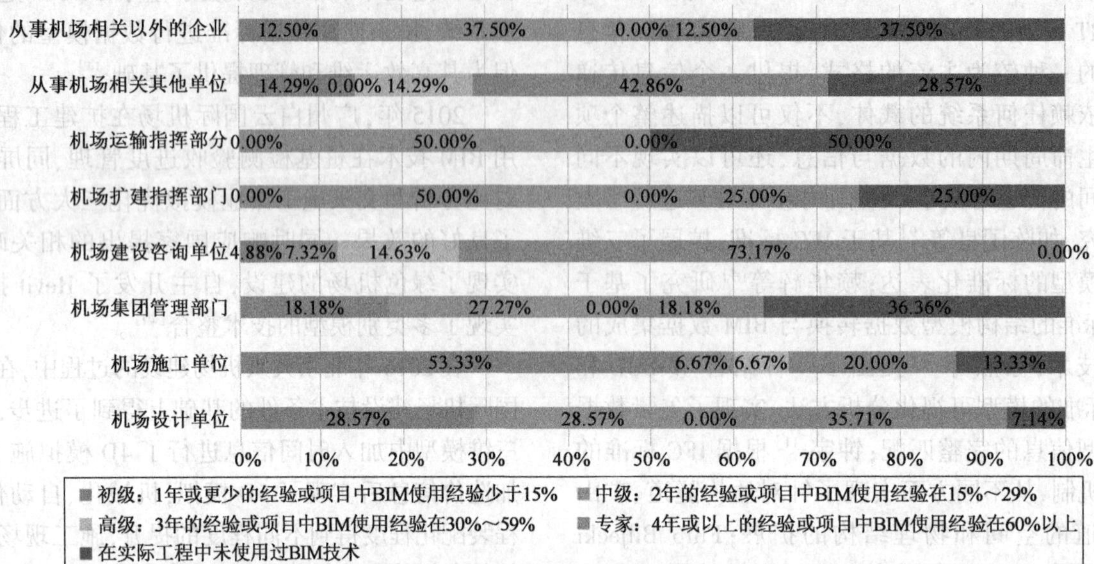

图1　各相关方 BIM 技术使用程度

何种规模的机场建议在运维阶段应用 BIM 技术的结果如图2所示。可以看出，有25%的被调查者认为当机场旅客年吞吐量达50万～300万人次时需应用 BIM 技术，而仅有2%的被调查者认为旅客年吞吐量达5000万人次才需使用 BIM 技术。总体上讲，认为机场年吞吐量大于300万人次以上可以在运维阶段开展 BIM 应用的占总调查者的56%，因此可建议对于年吞吐量超过300万人次的机场在运维阶段开展不同程度的 BIM 技术应用。

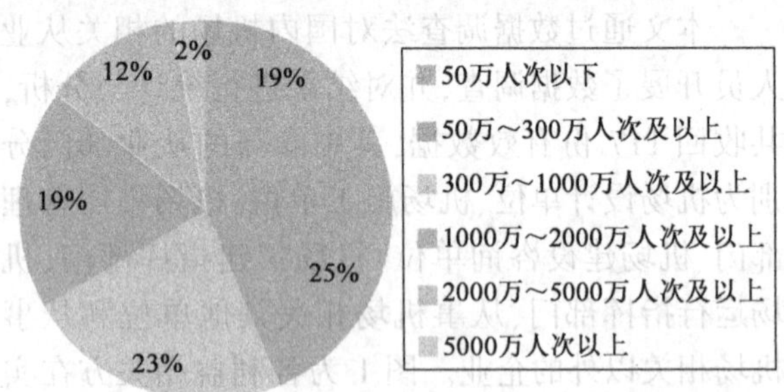

图2　建议应用 BIM 技术开展运维的机场规模

针对 BIM 技术的数据交换标准，调查了当前机场工程相关从业单位对数据交换标准的应用情况，如图3所示。可以看出 IFC 作为数据交换的常用标准使用率较高，COBie 和 Omniclass 两种交换方式在国内机场领域应用较少。此外，仍存在未使用过相关数据标准的情况，在机场扩建部门中未应用过 BIM 数据标准的比例高达68%，在调查的机场集团管理部门中该比例为44%，可以看出目前机场管理方在 BIM 数据标准方面了解及应用较少，这是制约 BIM 技术在机场领域发展的重要因素之一。

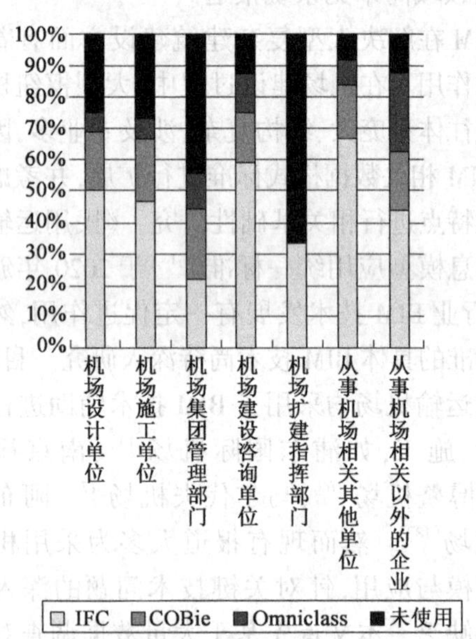

图3　不同企业进行 BIM 数据交换的方式

2　民用运输机场运维阶段信息传递方法

数据传递是 BIM 实现的关键技术，开放的数据标准突破了平台与软件供应商的制约，是 BIM 技术发展最为重要的技术手段，较为常用的 BIM 数据传递标准有 IFC、COBie 和 OmniClass 等，从上述调研分析可知，IFC 为目前较为主要的 BIM 数据交换格式，而现有 IFC 体系主要针对房屋建筑领域，在各自行业中缺乏相应的数据交换标准与交换方法。针对此问题,IFC 标准在铁路[22]、公路[23]、隧道[11]等领域进行了大量研究与实体扩展,在机场领域还未形成较为成熟的 IFC 标准,IFC 标准中尚缺乏机场相关实体,例如助航灯光、登机桥、机场道面、行李系统等,导致数据在不同模型间的传递较为困难。IFC 标准的数据模型根据其功能的不同划分为资源层、核心层、共享层、邻域层[24]。每层都包含相关一系列信息描述模块,并且结构层遵循阶梯原则,每一个层级的类别可参照同一层级或者较低层级的其他类别,但不能参照较高层级的类别。

经过大量的建模研究,以机场跑道建模为例,提出的基于 IFC 的机场跑道模型关联数据传递流程如图 4 所示。首先,基于某机场的实例跑道,通过建立满足初始跑道设计要求的道面板族,并将所建族模型的格式导出成可修改编辑的 IFC 中性文件;其次根据需求整理机场道面属性,利用检测、监测、数值分析等方法获取道面力学信息和状态信息;在此基础上扩展属于跑道的新实体,利用属性信息存储的方法进行新属性的添加,并寻找相关数据信息和新实体的映射关系,将所需属性信息赋予到扩展的实体中,形成跑道信息模型的通用数据环境(Common Data Environment);此后,当需要利用网络端对 BIM 数据管理时,将 IFC 中性文件转换为网页外部调用文件 OBJ 格式[10],进行模型的轻量化处理进行信息的融合,最终呈现出可通过浏览器或客户端 App 对机场 BIM 数据进行运维阶段管理。

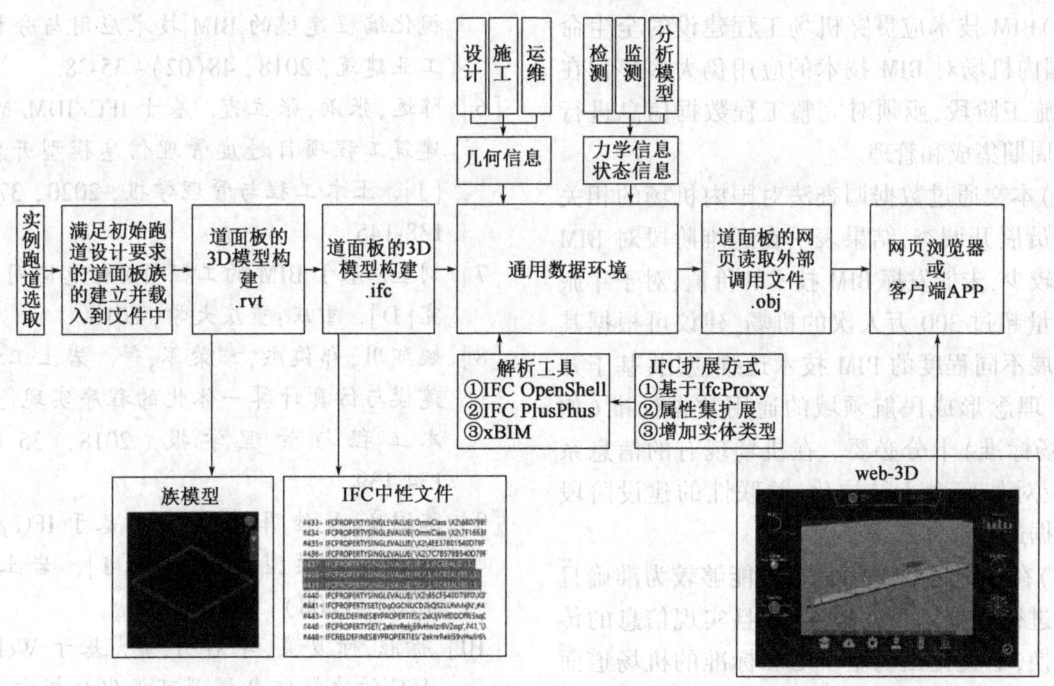

图 4 基于 IFC 的跑道运维信息传递路径

利用上述跑道运维信息路径建立适用于跑道运维阶段病害管理的道面单元如图 5a)所示,基于 IFC 标准对机场道面板族关键属性进行了扩展,添加的属性分别为国际平整度指标(IRI)、道面状况指数(PCI)、道面结构状况指数(SCI),这些属性信息可随着道面的运行不断添加,从而实现跑道基础设施运维的目的。如图 4 中的道面板模型 IFC 中性文件,可以在 IFC 中性文件中读取出道面板族中的新属性 IRI、PCI、SCI。图 5b)为可视化解析软件对添加属性信息后的 IFC 文件的可视化展示,验证了 IFC 的数据互操作性和中性文件的可读性,后续使用扩展的道面单元进行跑道模型的建立,这样可对整条跑道的不平整度、病害等指标进行动态管理与维护,并与机场整体的 BIM 数据融合。

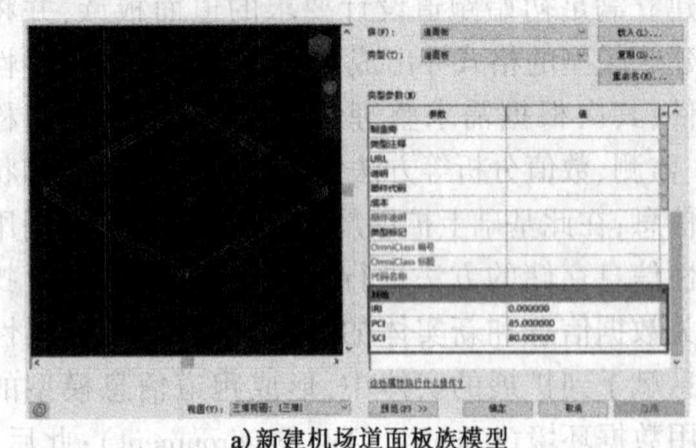
a)新建机场道面板族模型

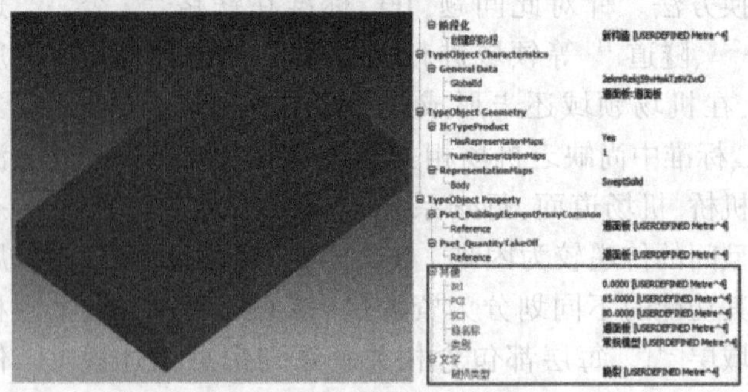
b)对新建机场道面板IFC文件的读取

图5 道面板族 IFC 新属性集的扩展

3 结论

本文针对 BIM 技术在机场工程中的应用开展了相关研究,主要研究成果和结论如下:

(1)BIM 技术应贯穿机场工程建设的全生命周期,国内机场对 BIM 技术的应用仍大多停留在设计和施工阶段,亟须对完整工程数据信息进行全生命周期集成和管理。

(2)本文通过数据调查法对国内机场的相关从业人员展开调查,结果表明在运维阶段对 BIM 的使用较少,未能发挥 BIM 技术的价值;对于年旅客吞吐量超过 300 万人次的机场,建议可根据其需求开展不同程度的 BIM 技术运维应用;基于开放 BIM 理念形成民航领域的通用数据标准(如 IFC 机场标准)十分必要。在机场现有的信息系统中,应对如何融入结构化、关联性的建设阶段 BIM 数据进行总体部署。

(3)在一定程度内,IFC 标准能够较为准确且高效地进行数据信息的描述,并且实现信息的传递与交换,本文提出的基于 IFC 标准的机场道面运维应用路径可应用于机场自定义族扩展、运维阶段道面结构属性添加、利用 Web 端对运维数据进行综合管理,具有一定可行性。

参考文献

[1] 清华大学软件学院 BIM 课题组. 中国建筑信息模型标准框架研究[J]. 土木建筑工程信息技术, 2010, 2(02): 1-5.

[2] 何清华, 钱丽丽, 段运峰, 等. BIM 在国内外应用的现状及障碍研究[J]. 工程管理学报, 2012, 26(01): 12-16.

[3] 成丽媛. BIM 在全球的应用现状[J]. 中国高新区, 2017(11): 27.

[4] 赖华辉, 邓雪原, 刘西拉. 基于 IFC 标准的 BIM 数据共享与交换[J]. 土木工程学报, 2018, 51(04): 121-128.

[5] 吴生海, 刘陕南, 刘永晓, 等. 基于 Dynamo 可视化编程建模的 BIM 技术应用与分析[J]. 工业建筑, 2018, 48(02): 35-38.

[6] 陈远, 张雨, 张立霞. 基于 IFC/IDM/MVD 的建筑工程项目进度管理信息模型开发方法[J]. 土木工程与管理学报, 2020, 37(04): 138-145.

[7] 刘星. 基于 BIM 的工程项目信息协同管理研究[D]. 重庆: 重庆大学, 2016.

[8] 姚翔川, 郑俊杰, 章荣军, 等. 岩土工程 BIM 建模与仿真计算一体化的程序实现[J]. 土木工程与管理学报, 2018, 35(05): 134-139.

[9] 陈国良, 吴佳明, 钟宇, 等. 基于 IFC 标准的三维地质模型扩展研究[J]. 岩土力学, 2020, 41(08): 2821-2828.

[10] 徐照, 徐夏炎, 李启明, 等. 基于 WebGL 与 IFC 的建筑信息模型可视化分析方法[J]. 东南大学学报(自然科学版), 2016, 46(02): 444-449.

[11] 钟宇, 陈健, 陈国良, 等. 基于建筑信息模型技术的盾构隧道结构信息模型建模方法[J]. 岩土力学, 2018, 39(05): 1867-1876.

[12] Biljecki F, Lim J, Crawford J, et al. Extending CityGML for IFC-sourced 3D city models [J]. Automation in Construction, 2021, 121.

[13] 中国民用航空局. 民用运输机场建筑信息模型应用统一标准: MH/T 5042—2020[S]. 北京: 中国民航出版社, 2020.

[14] 董政民. BIM 技术在航站楼运维管理中的应用——以浦东国际机场 T1 航站楼为例[J]. 建筑经济, 2013(09): 91-93.

[15] 赵健,房健康,宋扬,等. BIM 技术在南京禄口国际机场运维阶段的深入应用[J]. 土木建筑工程信息技术, 2015, 7(02): 50-55.

[16] 肖婧,曹乐,莫玳,等. BIM 开启民航建造新未来——博鳌机场 BIM 实践[J]. 土木建筑工程信息技术, 2016, 8(05): 1-9.

[17] 张凤林,关书安. 马尔代夫维拉纳国际机场改扩建项目——基于 BIM 技术的飞行区全过程数字化施工[J]. 土木建筑工程信息技术, 2019, 11(05): 90-96.

[18] BIM技术在阿布扎比国际机场项目中的成功应用[J]. 土木建筑工程信息技术, 2016, 8(06): 67.

[19] 邵韦平. T3——面向未来的首都机场新航站楼[J]. 建筑设计管理, 2012, 29(02): 22-25.

[20] 肖金水,黄健. BIM 技术在大型复杂公共建筑进度管理中的研究应用——以广州白云国际机场 T2 航站楼为例[J]. 建筑施工, 2019, 41(06): 1179-1181.

[21] 张晋勋,李建华,段先军,等. 从首都机场到北京大兴国际机场看工程建造施工技术发展[J]. 施工技术(中英文), 2021, 50(13): 27-33.

[22] 艾山丁,毛宁,贺欣. 基于 IFC4 扩展的轨道 BIM 数据存储标准研究[J]. 铁路技术创新, 2017(04): 48-54.

[23] Tang F, Ma T, Zhang J, et al. Integrating three-dimensional road design and pavement structure analysis based on BIM[J]. Automation in construction, 2020, 113: 103152.

[24] 邱奎宁,张汉义,王静,等. IFC 技术标准系列文章之一:IFC 标准及实例介绍[J]. 土木建筑工程信息技术, 2010, 2(01): 68-72.

四型机场的协同优化与生态建构

张 洪*

(中国民航局第二研究所)

摘 要 为推进"十四五"期间我国四型机场建设,根据民航四型机场建设的理念认知,基于政策导向、创新实践与建设成果,针对我国目前四型机场建设的推进现状与不足之处,应用系统性思维提出了四型机场生态的基本概念及重要属性,探析了数字化创新优化路径、智慧化协同演进路线,并探讨了科技创新赋能四型机场生态的对策建议。

关键词 航空运输 四型机场 协同优化 生态建构 科技创新

0 引言

民用机场作为民航行业及综合交通的重要基础设施,是区域对外开放的重要空中通道与国民经济发展的重要动力源。当前,我国机场发展已经进入规划建设高峰期、运行安全高压期、转型发展关键期和国际引领机遇期。四型机场作为中国机场未来的发展理念与战略方向,既是民航基础设施建设与航空运输业务发展之间的解决方案,也是促进我国机场从量优式发展转变为质优式发展的实施对策,更是筑牢民航安全底线、夯实智慧民航建设基石的重要载体。

1 四型机场建设的推进成果

2019 年 9 月 25 日,习近平总书记出席北京大兴国际机场投运仪式时作出重要指示,要把大兴国际机场打造成为国际一流的平安机场、绿色机场、智慧机场、人文机场,打造世界级航空枢纽❶。

❶习近平出席投运仪式并宣布北京大兴国际机场正式投入运营[N]. 人民日报, 2019-09-26(01)。

近年来,民航局加强政策引导与顶层设计,不断深化四型机场的内涵与外延,相继出台了《中国民航四型机场建设行动纲要(2020—2035年)》《四型机场建设导则》、民航新基建、蓝天保卫战、行业智能建造等相关政策与指导文件。相关参与各方在机场的基础设施改造、业务流程优化、运行模式创新、服务品质提升等方面探索实践,我国各地机场基础设施建设取得了显著的成果,一系列新技术、新产品、新装备广泛应用推广,若干技术产品打破国外垄断,涌现了以北京大兴国际机场、成都天府国际机场、深圳宝安国际机场等为代表的一大批各具特色、成效突显的四型机场示范项目,有力促进了我国机场的安全运营、服务保障与绿色发展,初步构建了政策链、创新链、产业链、供应链"四链"融合发展的格局。

2　四型机场建设的协同不足

四型机场的四大要素相辅相成、不可分割,四者之间是多维互嵌、耦合共容、高效联动、互促共生的关系。综观我国四型机场的探索与实践情况,坚持问题导向,通过调研,在协同推进实施方面还存在以下不足。

(1)四大要素协同不足,一体化推进不协调。

片面地把四型机场简单理解为新技术应用,将现代化机场的四大要素割裂开来,没有把四者充分有机融合、一体规划与协同共建,同时行业单位之间的运行衔接有待加强,与城市公共交通数据互联互通还不顺畅,与智慧交通、智慧城市、全域旅游与现代物流的协调发展还不够。

(2)软硬件协同不足,内涵落地还不到位。

片面追求"高、大、上",突出地区特色,因地制宜建设运营机场做得不够,个性不突出,同质化趋势日益加剧。只在机场硬件建设上不断加大投入,在业务流程改进、旅客服务品质提升、从业员工培训等软件方面还存在短板,对旅客及员工的人文关怀还不够。

(3)创新力量协同不足,产研融合还不充分。

四型机场关键核心技术掌握不多,自主创新产品应用推广难,行业内外创新力量的汇集与凝聚不够,相互之间竞争大于协作,缺乏统筹合作与优势互补,还没有形成完善的产学研用协同创新机制。

(4)制度实践协同不足,规范标准体系还不完善。

由于新兴技术的迭代周期很短,但是现有技术设备有关规定修订较慢,四型机场建设中的有些新技术、新系统没有对应的具体规范标准用于指导实践,或者应用新技术的业务流程变更不符合现行规范制度。

3　以系统观念创建四型机场生态

四型机场建设中,智慧机场建设是基础工程,因为平安、绿色、人文更多体现的是四型机场建设的结果和状态,都需要利用智慧化的措施、手段来实现。四型机场的四大要素相辅相成、不可分割,四者之间是多维互嵌、耦合共容、高效联动、互促共生的关系。为此,要以系统观念促进四型机场全方位协同优化,全面塑造高品质的四型机场生态体系。

3.1　四型机场生态的丰富内涵

四型机场生态是一个拥有"强壮躯体、智慧大脑、健康体质、文明灵魂"的多维立体有机生命体,是一个植入科技基因与创新元素的多元业态复合、协同共建共享的可持续发展体系,其总体框架包含目标层、特征层、路径层和实践层四个层面(图1)。建构四型机场生态,就是以新技术、新理念为驱动力,以品质工程为指引,融合智能机场、海绵机场、韧性机场、生态机场、文明机场等内涵,使"平安、绿色、智慧、人文"四方面特质不断显现与增强,从机场规划设计到实际运行全生命周期的动态优化、协同革新的演化升级过程,以推动形成自治运行、自我进化、智慧发展的四型机场生态价值链,最终体现为机场的安全运行保障有力、生产管理精细智能、旅客出行便捷高效、环境生态绿色和谐,全面促进民航行业的格局重塑、流程再造和体系重构,建设经得起人民检验、历史考验的新时代中国特色机场新文明。

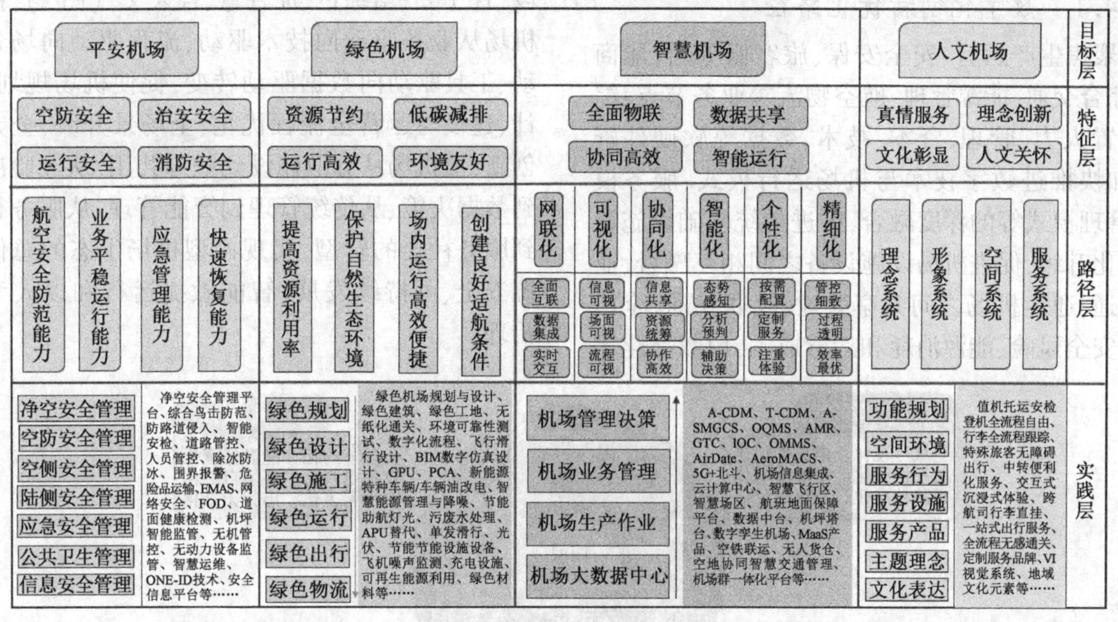

图1 四型机场生态的总体框架

3.2 四型机场生态的属性特征

3.2.1 以多元融合为特点的综合系统性

四型机场生态是由众多复杂系统组成,多进程时间协同、多元主体运行空间协同,综合配置人力、管理、资本、技术等软硬件资源,将新技术与机场建设运行流程相结合,持续改进提升工程品质以及建设运营的系统集成,实现全场景无缝耦合、全链条全面融合、全领域时空一体,创造高附加值的机场体验、高效率的生产运行和高颜值的互动体验,呈现机场生产运行各类资源要素有机融合的生态圈。

3.2.2 以全面协作为特点的开放包容性

四型机场生态是打破组织壁垒与业务边界,应用新兴技术提升服务体验、优化业务流程、赋能商业创新,拓展产业技术价值空间,通过空地协同、多机场协同、综合交通协同,加强与四强空管、智慧航司、智慧物流、智慧口岸等的泛在互联、协同交互,提高行业主体间的协同运行水平和服务保障能力,实现机场与智慧城市在安防、交通、物流、服务、旅游等多方信息共享,将传统的"机场到机场"运输升级为高品质的"门到门"服务,促进机场群与现代化都市圈、区域城市群的系统联动、协同运作。

3.2.3 以持续变革为特点的服务驱动性

四型机场生态是通过理念创新、技术创新、制度创新与模式创新,不断创造新产品新业态、应用新技术新模式,从点的突破迈向系统能力提升,全面提高行业基础设施的智能化、自主化和绿色化水平,实现四型机场的政策标准、制度机制、设施设备、治理方式、人员队伍的新陈代谢、进化迭代,全链路促进人流、物流、资金流、信息流、数据流在机场及其周边临空经济区集聚与交融,突显机场的交通功能性、产业引致性和经济带动性,使机场成为驱动多领域民航强国、新时代交通强国的强大引擎。

3.2.4 以转型蜕变为特点的创新生长性

四型机场生态是对标"四个智慧"和"五个一"要求,聚焦未来机场场景化需求,采用新技术、新能源、新材料,使机场从分散建设到统筹共用、从经验决策到数据决策、从传统管理到智能管理、从服务行业到服务社会的转变,向技术贡献度更高、服务体验更佳、资源利用更集约、生态环境更友好的方向升级,推动机场发展质量全方位提高、治理体系全方位提升、发展方式全方位变革,加快构建更高层次、更高品质的国家现代化机场体系。

4 四型机场生态的协同优化范式

针对四型机场的协同方面现存的四点不足,结合四型机场生态的四项属性,通过深度融合应用新技术、新材料、新能源等,面向未来提出四型机场的数字化优化路径与智慧化演进路线。

4.1　数字化创新优化路径

聚焦生产运行、安全安保、旅客服务、智能商业、综合交通、能源管理、航空物流等业务节点,综合配置人力、管理、资本、技术、数据等软硬件资源,加快推进数字技术与机场运行模式、服务模式、管理模式等的深度融合,推进传统基础设施设备优化升级,促进机场设施设备之间相互融合、业务互通,通达机场之间共享共建、互联互通,全面降低安全风险、能源消耗和运营成本,用数字化手段“保平安、增绿色、促智慧、合人文”(图2),推进机场从业务驱动向技术驱动、流程驱动向场景驱动、工具驱动向数据驱动转变,促使机场规划、设计、建设与运营全流程优化、全场景升级、全方位创新,使机场从分散建设到统筹共用、从经验决策到数据决策、从传统管理到智能管理、从服务行业到服务社会的转型,实现四型机场生态的总体系统安全、可持续发展、智能敏捷运行和以人为本治理。

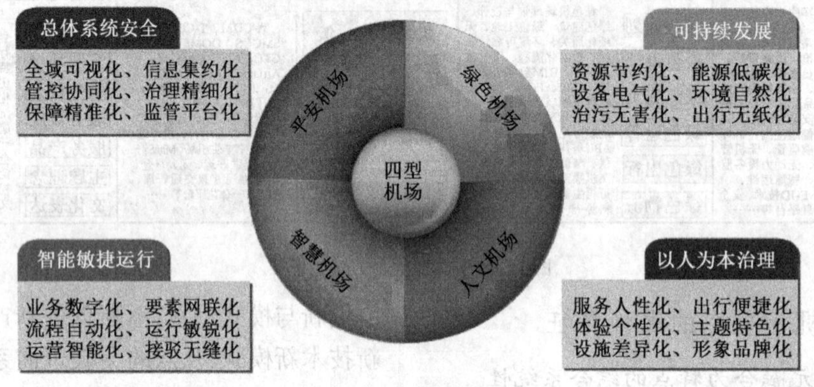

图2　四型机场生态的数字化创新优化

4.2　智慧化协同演进路线

四型机场生态的发展分为培育、成长、成熟三个阶段,遵循“政策指导—重点突破—典型示范—标准规范—全程协同—动态优化—治理升级—全域更新—总体迭代”的演进路线(图3),通过智慧化手段推进四型机场资源协同化、技术协同化、流程协同化、业务协同化,加快四型机场建设的全过程、全要素、全方位智慧化协同升级,全生命周期提升平安机场可靠度、绿色机场友好度、智慧机场敏捷度和人文机场满意度,成为民航新基建先进范式、智慧城市标杆工程与综合立体交通核心枢纽,在全球机场建设运营领域建树引领标杆。

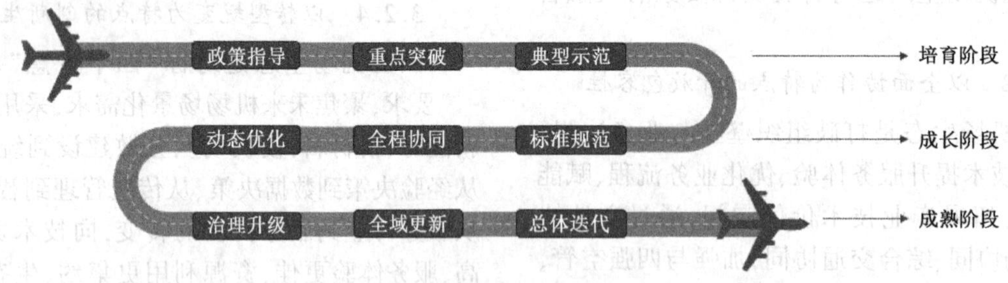

图3　四型机场生态的智慧化演进路线

5　科技创新建构四型机场生态的对策建议

在“十四五”智慧民航建设背景下,要将智慧技术融入四型机场全领域、全流程和全周期,促进“平安、绿色、智慧、人文”一体化融合发展,实现从规模扩张向品质提升转变、从封闭运行向开放发展转变,从粗放管理向精益治理转变,真正达到“人享其行、货畅其流”,打造精益成长、价值增长的中国特色、世界一流的现代化机场生态体系。

5.1　聚集资源交融裂变,创建四型机场新动力源

5.1.1　应用智慧技术,集智攻关提升科技供给质量

强化数据驱动、集成创新、智慧管控、流程再造

等理念，综合运用“云大物智移链”等新兴技术，聚焦重点环节和薄弱环节，精准把握“卡脖子”问题，施力于机场智能感知、互联互通、数字孪生和智慧协同的关键核心技术研发，不断突破国外的技术垄断，应用新兴技术提升服务体验、优化业务流程、使能商业创新，通过对飞机流、旅客流、货物流、行李流、交通流作数字化处理，智能化响应和智慧化支撑，实现四型机场规划建设、安全运行、服务保障等环节的全区域覆盖、全流程管控、全场景赋能。

5.1.2 强化协同创新，构建政产学研用科技共同体

按照“开放、合作、共享”的原则，促进航空巨头、国内外知名高校、研究机构、科技企业和机场集团的合作力度与深度，建立优势互补、项目共建、资源共享、利益共赢的战略伙伴关系，搭建多学科融合、多团队协同、多技术集成的协同创新平台，并加强行业各主体间、各交通方式、产业链上下游间的协同合作，构建“开放协同、合作共赢”的联合创新模式，健全从技术攻关、测试验证、行业应用的四型机场创新网络体系。

5.1.3 服务全生命周期，健全四型机场技术产品谱系

按照“全面感知、泛在互联、人机协同、全球共享”的理念，从规划咨询、建设实施、安全运行、服务保障等多个维度，以“补链、强链、延链”为重点，抓好系统布局、系统组织、跨界集成，在智能感知、时空协同、泛在互联、数据活化、安全可信、服务优质等方面实现技术创新性应用，打造兼容安全、智能、集约、低碳的全生命周期服务总体解决方案，为旅客、货主及员工提供卓越高效服务与极致化品质体验。

5.2 聚焦民航可持续发展，创建四型机场新策源地

5.2.1 对标国际航空前沿，掌握智慧发展主动权

把握国际机场建设发展的新趋势、新理念和新技术，以民航科创园区、工程技术中心、重点实验室等创新平台为载体建立国际民航科技合作平台，推动项目、基地、人才、资金一体化配置，面向未来机场做好技术沉淀储备、方案试验验证、产品迭代升级，发展四型机场战略咨询、技术总体、平台产品、运营服务、技术创新等业务，打造全域智慧、数字治理、智能变革、精致发展的四型机场生态典范。

5.2.2 顺应绿色低碳趋势，增强可持续发展力

融会贯通“碳达峰碳中和”理念，在规划、设计与建设中注重经济、实用、适用，推动新能源、新材料和绿色技术的应用推广，持续推进机场能效提升、节能管理、污染防治、新能源特种车辆、绿色建筑、资源集约节约等工作，更新换代机场节能环保设备设施，着力提高航班正常率，全面提高机场全要素生产率，广泛应用先进技术催生以集约共享为核心的四型机场发展模式。

5.2.3 融入综合立体交通，服务双循环新格局

运用5G、北斗、星链、区块链等新技术深度融合交通联运资源，运用信息技术深度融合行业生产资源，促进机场与航司、空管、保障部门的融合运行，打造机场全时空一体化数智化管理平台，助力机场网与航线网、运行信息监控网的高效协同，推动空地交通信息的互联互通与多式联运的无缝衔接，促使机场成为“双循环”发展格局下的综合立体交通枢纽。

5.3 聚力自主创新航向，创建四型机场新增长极

5.3.1 加快首台套应用推广，加速机场重大装备国产化

加快智慧场面、智慧监测、智慧机坪、智慧跑道、智慧安检、净空管理等四型机场相关领域先进技术和成果加快落地，不断增强创新成果转化能力与新兴技术综合集成能力，促进首台套重大技术装备示范应用，大幅提升机场设备国产化率，有效防范化解机场的运营安全、网络安全、数据安全等各类风险，进一步健全从研发智造、转化应用到产业推广的自主创新链条，确保四型机场生态体系的安全可靠、自主可控。

5.3.2 矢志追求精益求精，匠心智造卓越品质工程

对标“四个工程”要求，以“品质工程”理念为主导，树牢“三个敬畏”作风，夯实“三基”建设，全面推行现代工程管理，积极践行工匠精神，实施精品智造、智能建造与精细化管理，创建基于民航生产运行全场景的智慧仿真模型，提升四型机场基础工程技术、关键技术研究及测试验证的总体集成水平，推动四型机场的高水平规划设计、高标准建设与高品质运营，致力于将四型机场打造成全国新基建样板。

5.3.3　依托“一带一路”建设，助推中国方案“走出去”

依托民航“一带一路”建设合作平台，促进机场国产先进装备与自主创新技术的全球推广，优化布局与协同架构“空中丝绸之路”全球航空运输网络体系，以产品输出、技术输出带动标准输出、服务输出、管理输出，推动民航优势技术与标准国际化，以民航新基建构建新的国际竞争优势，不断增强我国在全球航空业界的影响力和话语权，全力提升我国引领国际民航业发展的创新能力。

6　结语

本文结合民航局打造民用机场品质工程建设要求，较全面总结了四型机场的建设现状与协同不足，基于系统思维提出了四型机场生态的基本概念、重要属性与优化协同范式，并深入研讨了科技创新建构四型机场生态的对策建议，将有益于“十四五”期间建树国际民航基建标杆，引领世界机场发展，增强我国民航的国际竞争优势与影响力。

参考文献

[1] 民航局发布《四型机场建设导则》[J]. 民航管理，2020(11)：66.

[2] 冯正霖. 推动民航高质量发展开启新时代民航强国建设新征程[J]. 人民论坛，2018(5)：6-8.

[3] 屈建华. “四型机场”协同一体化建设浅见[J]. 民航管理，2021(04)：87-88.

[4] 冯广东，李彤阳，吴程程. 智慧机场建设的探索与思考[J]. 中国民用航空，2021(7)：29-32.

[5] 李哲. 民用航空区域多机场系统发展趋势分析[J]. 中国民用航空，2020(12)：50-52.

土质道面上飞机起飞滑跑距离的改进计算方法

白鹏坤　种小雷*　张万衡　张继超
(空军工程大学航空工程学院)

摘　要　针对目前土质跑道长度计算中采用定值摩擦系数来简化因地面摩擦和轮辙引起的阻力的现状，通过分析机轮与土的相互作用机理，结合飞机起飞过程中三点滑跑和两点滑跑两阶段的特征，综合考虑地面摩擦和轮辙影响，提出了基于起飞滑跑两阶段特征的综合摩擦阻力计算方法，改进了传统土质跑道长度估算方法中定值摩擦系数的不足，并以某型飞机为例说明了该方法的应用过程，为土质跑道长度计算提供了一种新的思路和方法。

关键词　机场基础设施　土质道面　摩擦系数　起飞滑跑距离

0　引言

由于承载力的不同，飞机在土质跑道上运行时除了会受到摩擦力之外，还会受到因土质道面沉陷而产生的阻力。并且随着飞机升力逐渐增大，产生的轮辙深度发生变化，其阻力也随之改变。传统的土质跑道长度计算中，采用定值摩擦系数来简化计算飞机起飞过程中的摩擦阻力，对长度计算结果造成一定的误差。

目前关于土质跑道的研究主要集中在飞机轮胎与土质道面的相互作用机理上，黄炜等[1]提出了机轮尺寸、驱动力、驱动效率、越障要求等影响飞机在土质道面上通行性能的关键设计参数选择依据。张铎耀等[2]提出了基于车辙深度和累积疲劳的机场土质路面设计方法。谭滔等[3]实现了土质跑道在不同基层材料强度和覆盖作用次数下的道面强度与厚度设计。刘军忠等[4-5]研究了土质道面结构的累积塑性变形、回弹弯沉和弯沉盆曲线随飞机荷载、施加荷载频率和荷载作用次数的变化情况及其平面分布规律。E Heymsfield[6]提出了一种稳定土在重复荷载作用下的数值模拟方法。尚未见到关于土质跑道长度计算方面的系统研究，土质道面长度估算是在混凝土跑道长度计算模型的基础上修正摩擦系数来完成的。

本文分析了飞机在土质跑道上起飞滑跑过程，以机轮与土质道面相互作用模型为基础，将飞机起飞滑跑分为两个阶段，综合考虑飞机在土质道面上因轮辙产生的滚动阻力和道面本身的摩擦阻力，提出一种基于三点滑跑和两点滑跑两个阶段来计算飞机在土质道面上起飞所需距离的方法，为运输机在土质跑道上运行时的跑道长度设计提供参考。

1 土质道面上飞机起飞滑跑距离的估算方法

1.1 飞机在土质跑道上的起飞过程

飞机起飞是指飞机从停机坪滑出，通过滑行道、端联络道进入跑道，对准跑道中线后刹车停住，然后加大油门，提高发动机转速，待发动机转速达到起飞转速后就松开刹车，以停机迎角进行三点滑跑。待加速到抬前轮速度 V_R 时，飞行员拉杆开始抬起前轮，飞机迎角很快增加至预定迎角，此后飞机进入两点滑跑状态，当飞机速度达到离地速度 V_{lof}时，飞机开始离开地面，作加速上升飞行，上升到10.7m（或15.2m）高度时，起飞过程结束。飞机从起飞线开始滑跑加速上升到起飞安全高度的整个运动过程，称为起飞。

1.2 飞机起飞过程中的受力分析

飞机在跑道上滑跑时，会同时受到多个力的作用，受力情况如图1所示。

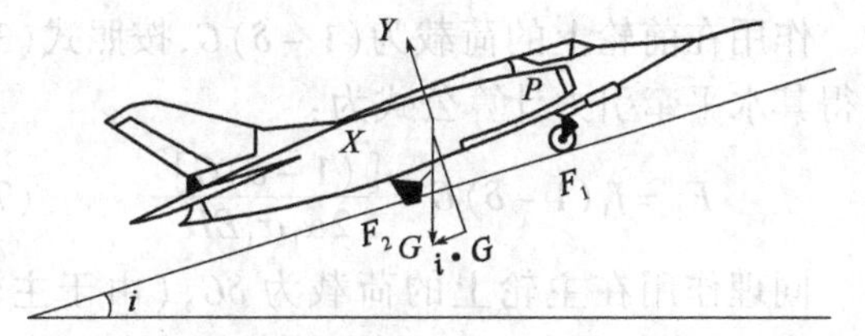

图1 飞机地面滑跑受力示意图

根据牛顿运动定律，该动力学方程为如公式(1)所示：

$$a=\frac{H}{m}=[J\cos(\beta+\alpha_p)-Q\pm Q_i]\frac{1}{m} \tag{1}$$

式中：m——飞机质量；

H——作用在飞机上沿滑跑方向的合力；

J——发动机推力；

β——飞机滑跑迎角；

α_p——推力线和机身轴线的夹角（发动机安装角）；

Q——综合阻力；

Q_i——飞机重力在跑道纵向坡度上的分力。

1.3 飞机起飞滑跑距离计算公式

在上述力学模型的基础上，蔡良才[7]将飞机起飞滑跑距离计算公式简化为公式(2)：

$$S=\int_0^{V_{lof}}\frac{1}{\frac{J}{G}\cos(\beta+\alpha_p)-f\left\{1+\left[(C_x+C_{xs})\frac{1}{f}-C_y\right]\frac{\rho S_y V^2}{2G}\right\}+i}\cdot\frac{V\mathrm{d}V}{g} \tag{2}$$

式中：S——地面滑跑距离；

G——飞机重力；

f——机轮与地面的摩擦系数；

C_x——空气阻力系数；

ρ——机场实际空气密度；

S_y——机翼面积；

C_{xs}——以机翼面积；

S_y——参考面积的减速伞阻力系数（起飞时为0）；

C_y——升力系数；

i——跑道坡度。

上述参数可分三类，即环境参数（空气密度）、跑道参数（坡度、摩擦系数）、飞机参数（空气阻力系数、飞机重量、发动机推力、滑跑迎角、机翼面积、升力系数、阻力系数、减速伞阻力系数、离地速度）。由此可见，在道面满足承载力要求的前提下，计算起飞滑跑长度中与道面相关的参数为坡度与摩擦系数。飞机在土质跑道上运行时，同样可采用该模型估算其起飞长度，与混凝土道面跑道长度计算不同的是摩擦系数取值为0.15～0.30[8]，为混凝土道面的15倍。

2 土质跑道上机轮与道面相互作用机理分析

在实际土质道面起飞过程中，机轮不仅有道面的摩擦阻力还有轮辙带来的滚动阻力，而且这种阻力随飞机姿态的变化而变化，采用定值摩擦系数来简化计算飞机起飞过程中受到摩擦阻力，会给跑道长度计算带来误差。为此有必要在分析机轮与土质道面相互作用机理的基础上确定阻力计算方法，从而建立更加准确的土质跑道长度计算模型。

2.1 机轮与土质跑道力学作用模型

当飞机在土质跑道上滑行时，会产生较深的轮辙,使土体受到挤压产生径向反力,从而飞机会受到较大的滚动阻力。为了研究飞机在土质跑道上的受力情况,就必须研究机轮与土的接触受力模型。

当不变的刚性轮在土质道面表面运动时,刚性轮与土质道面的受力情况如图 2 所示。

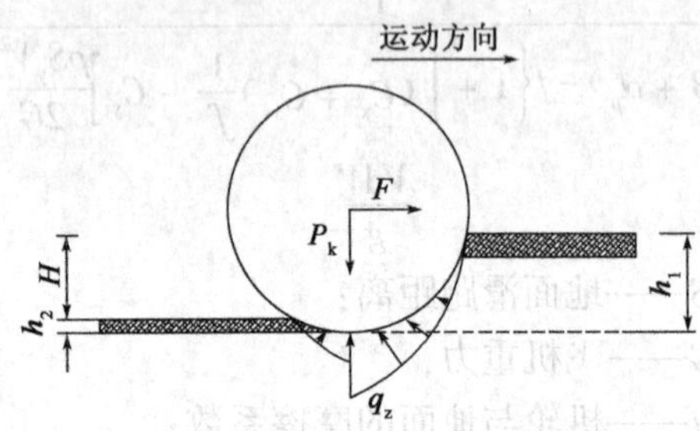

图 2　刚性轮轮辙计算图

图中 P_K 为机轮荷载,F 为水平牵引力。刚性轮宽度为 B,直径为 D,设机轮压入土中深度为 h_1。由于土体具有弹性,因而一部分变形是可以恢复的,设为 h_2,可得轮辙深度 $H=h_1-h_2$。机轮压入土中以后,土即在轮缘面积上的径向反力 q_z。

2.2　飞机在土质跑道上运行时摩擦系数的计算

为分析土质道面上摩擦阻力计算方法,本文引用翁兴中[8]教授针对常见飞机起落架构型建立的土质道面摩擦阻力系数计算公式,具体如下。

2.2.1　双轮起落架

$$f=\frac{P}{2\alpha\sigma BD} \tag{3}$$

式中:P——作用在一个起落架上的总荷载;

σ——机轮滚动时土的承载力系数;

α——轮胎的变形系数。

2.2.2　四轮起落架

$$f=\frac{P}{2\alpha_1\sigma_1 BD}\times\frac{K^2+C}{(K+1)^2} \tag{4}$$

$$C=\frac{\alpha_1\sigma_1}{\alpha_2\sigma_2} \tag{5}$$

式中:σ_1、σ_2——前后轮滚动时土的承载力系数;

α_1、α_2——前后轮轮胎的变形系数;

K——作用在前后轮上的荷载比值。

2.2.3　六轮起落架

$$f=\frac{P}{2\alpha\sigma BD(K_1+K_2+1)^2}\times\left(\frac{{K_1}^2}{2\alpha_1\sigma_1}+\frac{{K_2}^2}{2\alpha_2\sigma_2}+\frac{1}{2\alpha_3\sigma_3}\right) \tag{6}$$

式中:σ_1、σ_2、σ_3——前轮、中间轮、后轮滚动时土的承载力系数;

α_1、α_2、α_3——前轮、中间轮、后轮轮胎的变形系数;

K_1——作用在前轮与后轮上的荷载比值;

K_2——作用在中间轮与后轮上的荷载比值。

2.3　土质跑道上飞机起飞中摩擦系数的确定方法

2.3.1　土质跑道上摩擦阻力系数的变化特征

当飞机在土质跑道上起飞滑跑时,其速度从零开始逐渐增加,先增加至抬前轮速度后增至飞机离陆速度脱离跑道。随着飞机速度的逐渐增大,飞机的升力逐渐增加,在土质跑道上产生的轮辙深度逐渐逐渐减小,同时轮辙产生的阻力也会减小。在这个过程中,飞机抬起前轮的时刻,飞机的荷载作用形式会发生改变,由前轮和主轮共同承受荷载变为主轮承受荷载,会使主轮产生的轮辙深度发生突变,阻力也会发生变化,因而需要对抬前轮前后两个阶段分别进行计算。

2.3.2　两阶段摩擦阻力系数计算方法

设机型前轮为单轴双轮,主轮为双轴四轮,设其荷载分布比例为 δ,即在主轮上为所占总荷载比例为 δ,前轮上为 $1-\delta$,设飞机的总荷载为 G。

作用在前轮上的荷载为 $(1-\delta)G$,按照式(3)可得其水平牵引力计算公式为:

$$F_1=f_1(1-\delta)G=\frac{[(1-\delta)G]^2}{2\alpha_1\sigma_1 BD} \tag{7}$$

同理作用在主轮上的荷载为 δG,(由于主轮有两个,对称分布在飞机两侧,则作用在每个主轮上的荷载为 $0.5\delta G$)按照式(4)可得其水平牵引力计算公式为:

$$F_2=f_2\delta G=\frac{(\delta G)^2}{4\alpha_1\sigma_1 BD}\times\frac{K^2+C}{(K+1)^2} \tag{8}$$

则飞机所受的水平牵引力为:

$$F=F_1+F_2 \tag{9}$$

由摩擦系数的定义可得飞机在三轮滑跑时的摩擦系数计算公式为:

$$\begin{aligned}f&=\frac{F_1+F_2}{G}=\delta f_2+(1-\delta)f_1\\&=\frac{\delta^2 G}{4\alpha_{11}\sigma_{11}BD}\times\frac{K^2+C}{(K+1)^2}+\frac{(1-\delta)^2 G}{2\alpha_{12}\sigma_{12}BD}\end{aligned} \tag{10}$$

在两轮滑跑时前轮抬起，荷载全部作用在主轮时($\delta=1$时)摩擦系数计算公式为：

$$f=f_2 \tag{11}$$

式中：α_{11}——主轮中前轮轮胎的变形系数；

σ_{11}——主轮中前轮滚动时的土的承载力系数；

α_{12}——前轮轮胎的变形系数；

σ_{12}——前轮滚动时的土的承载力系数。

2.3.3 基于分段摩擦系数的起飞滑跑距离计算方法

对飞机滑跑起飞进行分段计算，从飞机开始滑跑到抬起前轮，即三轮滑跑过程中，滑跑距离计算如式(12)所示：

$$S_1=\int_0^{V_R}\frac{VdV}{g\left\{\frac{J}{G}\cos(\beta+\alpha_p)-\left[\delta f_2+(1-\delta)f_1\right]\left(1+\left[(C_X+C_{XS})\frac{1}{\delta f_2+(1-\delta)f_1}-C_y\right]\frac{\rho S_y V^2}{2G}\right)+i\right\}} \tag{12}$$

当前轮抬起后，即二轮滑跑过程中，滑跑距离为计算如式(13)所示：

$$S_2=\int_{V_R}^{V_{lof}}\frac{VdV}{g\left[\frac{J}{G}\cos(\beta+\alpha_p)-f_2\left\{1+\left[(C_X+C_{XS})\frac{1}{f_2}-C_y\right]\frac{\rho S_y V^2}{2G}\right\}+i\right]} \tag{13}$$

3 算例

3.1 计算参数

飞机起落架参数：

飞机参数：起落架：前轮为四轮，主轮为八轮，前轮 $B=0.33\text{m}$，$D=1.1\text{m}$；主轮 $B=0.48\text{m}$，$D=1.3\text{m}$；起飞时襟翼角为43°，缝翼角为25°，发动机安装角为0°，机翼面积为300m²；在土质跑道上起飞质量为152t；发动机为四台，单台推力为117.6kN；在土质跑道上运行时抬前轮速度为57m/s，离地速度=61m/s，土质道面承载力系数为0.6MPa，$\alpha=1.1$。其余参数见表1。

飞机部分参数 表1

起飞阶段	滑跑迎角	升力系数	阻力系数	前轮荷载	主轮荷载
三轮滑跑	3°	1.4	0.17	119.17kN	685.22kN
两轮滑跑	8°	2.1	0.25	0	744.8kN

在飞机起飞滑跑时迎角时逐渐变化的，为简化运算，根据飞行手册，将滑跑迎角在三轮滑跑时取为3°，两轮滑跑时取为8°。

环境参数：气温0℃，标准大气压，无风，空气密度取1.293kg/m³。

道面参数：土质跑道坡度为0。

3.2 起飞滑跑距离计算

按照等效面积对本机模型进行简化，将前轮简化为双轮，主轮简化为四轮，简化模型的轮胎为真实轮胎面积的两倍。由荷载分配知，前轮每个轮胎承受荷载基本相同，即可认为前轮的四个轮胎变形系数相同，荷载比值为1，主轮亦是。

首先计算三轮滑跑距离，按照式(3)、式(4)、式(10)可得 $f=0.2$，按照式(12)可得三轮滑跑阶段的距离 $S_1=1210.4\text{m}$。

其次计算两轮滑跑距离，按照式(4)、式(11)可得 $f=0.226$，按照式(13)可得三轮滑跑阶段的距离 $S_2=127.1\text{m}$。

起飞滑跑距离为 $S=S_1+S_2=1337.5\text{m}$，取整为1340m。

若是采用传统计算方法，取摩擦系数为0.15，则根据式(2)可得起飞滑跑距离为1030m。

通过两种计算的结果可知，采用分段摩擦系数计算的跑道长度比采用定值摩擦系数计算的结果大310m。通过与飞行手册提供的数据进行对比，采用分段摩擦系数计算的土质跑道长度与手册上的数据更接近，与实际情况更相符，进一步说明了两阶段计算方法比定值计算方法更加合理。

4 结语

本文在分析机轮与土质道面相互作用机理的基础上，结合飞机起飞滑跑的过程特征，提出了考虑两阶段摩擦系数的飞机在土质道面上起飞滑跑距离的计算方法，并给出了算例，为土质道面上飞机起飞滑跑距离的计算提供了一种新的思路与方法。后期可以考虑按照飞机升力或轮辙深度的变化来更加精确地计算由摩擦而引起的阻力,进一步完善土质跑道长度设计理论。

参考文献

[1] 黄炜, 许巍, 刘从军. 简易机场加固土道面飞机通行性能理论分析[J]. 机场工程, 2014(2):6.

[2] Zhang D, Cai L, Zhou S. An Airfield Soil Pavement Design Method Based on Rut Depth and Cumulative Fatigue [J]. Journal of Advanced Transportation, 2019, 2019:1-11.

[3] 谭滔, 蔡良才, 刘晓军, 等. 简易机场土质跑道设计方法[J]. 空军工程大学学报: 自然科学版, 2012, 13(6):4.

[4] 刘军忠, 翁兴中, 张俊, 等. 应急机场土质道面疲劳变形特性模型试验[J]. 西南交通大学学报, 2014, 49(3):7.

[5] 刘军忠, 翁兴中, 张俊, 等. 简易机场纤维格栅-水泥土基层使用性能研究[J]. 建筑材料学报, 2014, 017(06):1043-1048.

[6] Heymsfield E, Wahl R E, Hodo W. Developments of a Damage Model for Stabilized Soil Layers Subjected to Repetitive Aircraft Loadings [C]. Airfield & Highway Pavements the Airfield & Highway Pavement Specialty Conference, 2006.

[7] 蔡良才, 邵斌, 王观虎. 机场规划设计[M]. 北京:国防工业出版社, 2018.

[8] 翁兴中, 蔡良才. 机场道面设计[M]. 北京:人民交通出版社股份有限公司, 2016.

Optimal Design of the Asphalt Overlay on Rigid Pavement of Runways

Fenglei Zhang [1]　Wei Huang[1]　Chao Shi[2]　Pengfei Yao[1]　Lei Zhang [*1]

(1. Intelligent Transportation System Research Center, Southeast University;

2. China Airport Construction Group Corporation of CAAC)

Abstract　In China, Portland concrete is major pavement type in runways, whereas in U.S. and European countries HMA is prevalent in the airfield. Since the structure of HMA overlay on the origin Portland cement concrete pavement is more complex, the mechanic behavior of this composite is studied to make advices for pavement overlay design. The full depth composite model of runway pavements was established based on Finite Element Method, including joints and tie/dowel bars between concrete slabs. The model was verified using test data of the specific airfield pavement experimental section provided by the National Airport Pavement Test Equipment (NAPTF). The response of the overlay on rigid pavement to New Generation Large Aircrafts (NGLA) was then analyzed based on this composite model. The stress distribution and high stress area were obtained from the simulation. In addition, Parameter sensitivity analysis was carried out to show effects of overlay thickness and modulus. Furthermore influences of these two parameters on the runway rutting were also studied using the vertical compressive strain variation trends along the depth. Suggestions composed of both the structural and material considerations were proposed for runway pavement design. Finally, the appropriate design parameters of overlay thickness and modulus were optimized by balancing both critical tensile stress and high temperature performance.

Keywords　Runway　Overlay　Pavement　Concrete　New Generation Large Aircraft

0 Introduction

The runway is main part of the airport, which catches much attention of both the designers and researchers (Chen et al., 2021, Zhang et al., 2013). However, the distresses of airfield pavement often occurred in the metropolitan airports. Investigations by Kelvin C. P. Wang (2002), Jim Hall (2014) and Abu Siddique (2008) showed that crack is major types of the deterioration. Surveys conducted by Xianyi Wang (2005) and M. Wensel (2002) denoted that rutting is the large portion of the airport pavement distresses. Furthermore, as New Generation Large Aircraft (NGLA) became a member of airlines in China, both crack and rutting problems could be more serious (Ling et al., 2021), due to the heavy load and high contact pressure introduced by the new gear. This indicated that the consideration for such new load patterns is of much importance during runway design period.

In China, Portland Cement Concrete (PCC) was major pavement type in runways with percentage of more than 70%, whereas in U. S. and European countries Hot Mix Asphalt (HMA) was prevalent in the airfield (Su et al., 2009, Rushing and Little, 2014). And near fifty airport runways in China had overlaid with HMA. Furthermore, according to The 14th Five-Year Plan of China (Wei et al., 2020), there will be 400 civil airports by 2035, i. e. about 150 new airports will be built. Therefore, much attention should be paid to this issue in China to prevent severe pavement distresses. The goal of this research is to obtain stress distribution characteristics of runway overlay pavement due to the HMA + PCC composite structure under passes of New Generation Large Aircraft (NGLA) and to provide suggestions for reducing crack and rutting.

Although much studies has been done on the overlay of PCC roads, the results can hardly be applied to runways directly, as there are four major differences between the two types of overlays. Firstly, the traffic conditions are different that in most countries, road traffic loading is converted to the legal axle load or standard axle load such as the equivalent 80kN axle load i. e. 40kN per dual wheel loading and typically a 0.7MPa contact pressure. Whereas, a typical design aircraft for runways such as the Airbus 380 has a wheel load of approximately 267kN per wheel on their main gear and a tire pressure of 1.40MPa per wheel

Secondly, the wandering of wheels on runways are much wider than on roads and the repetitions of loading are far less than that on roads. The busiest parts of the busiest airfields in the USA can experience up to 20 times less traffic loading than a busy highway, as reported by Cooley (2007). The situation in China is more significant, about 750 flights with comparison to 8000 vehicles passes.

Thirdly, there is less sunlight shields such as trees and vehicle shade on runways than on roads, which will lead to more severe pavement aging on the runways.

However, as pointed out by Horak (2011), it is often found though that the more dominant market leader in flexible pavements is the roads field and designs tend to be transferred blindly from this field to that of airfields with little consideration for the actual operating and performance differences.

In the following sessions, flexible overlay i. e. asphalt pavement surfacing was discussed, taking one newly-overlaid airport as example. Firstly, by employing the multilayered elastic theory, the FE model was built. The model was also refined to include structural details such as joints, dowel bars and tie bars, according to the origin PCC pavement design. Secondly the critical stresses under New Generation Large Aircraft (NGLA) Airbus 380 were calculated and then the critical load case was determined. Thirdly, the stress distribution due to HMA overlay thickness and modulus variations, were analyzed respectively. Finally, design suggestions compose of both the structural and material considerations were proposed to reduce the potential cracking and rutting of the overlay on the existing runway rigid pavement.

1 Modeling

One civil airport was selected as study case, of which the runway had been overlaid recently. As showed in Fig. 1, the mid-section of flexible pavement of the runway in this airport includes four layers which are 12cm-Hot Mixed Asphalt (HMA), 24cm Portland Cement Concrete (PCC), 60cm base and subgrade downward. The input parameters for each layer were listed in Table 1 and the dimensions of reinforced bars for original concrete joints were showed in Tab. 2.

The FE model is 15m in length and 15m in width, containing 9 (3 × 3) concrete slabs jointed with dowel bars and tie bars, as shown in Fig. 1.

Fig. 1 Overall dimension diagram of pavement structure model

Different structural layers of the model are set according to the thickness parameters. Different structural layers are assigned specific material properties due to different materials. And the multilayer pavement structure is assumed to be continuous. Based on material parameters in literature research and the data provided by the maintenance and reconstruction project of the capital airport, the material and structural parameters applied in the finite element model are determined as shown in Tab. 1.

Material parameters for each layer Tab. 1

Structural layer	Material selection	Thickness(cm)	Reference value of elastic modulus in literature(MPa)	Material parameters used in the model(MPa)	Poisson's ratio
Overlay	HMA	12 (7~20)	1200~1600	1200 (400~2000)	0.30
Original pavement	Old cement concrete	40	27580	30000	0.15
			28500		
			30000		
			37000		
			27600		
Base course	Cement stabilized macadam	60	—	3000	0.25
Soil base course	Soil	—	—	60	0.40

According to the difference between the longitudinal or transverse joints of the cementslabs, tie bars and dowel bars are placed in the vertical and horizontal directions respectively. The parameters are shown in Tab. 2.

Parameters of reinforced bars for joints Tab. 2

Joint connecting rod	Elastic modulus(MPa)	Poisson's ratio	Diameter(mm)	Length(mm)	Spacing(mm)
Dowel bar	2.0×10^5	0.35	25	510	400
Tie bar	2.0×10^5	0.35	16	710	500

2 Validation of Finite Element Modeling Method for Airport Pavement

In order to verify the rationality of the above airport pavement finite element modeling method, this section uses the same method to model its specific test section with the help of the data provided by the National Airport Pavement Test Equipment (NAPTF). It compares the calculation results of ANSYS finite element simulation with the test measured data, to consider the mechanical properties of materials Under the comprehensive action of load distribution and other influencing factors of multi-wheel group, analyze the error between finite element modeling and actual loading condition, and correct the finite element model. It should be noted here that the actual test pavement corresponding to the model calculation is the No. 1 construction cycle section (CC1) of NAPTF. The loading equipment used in the test section is shown in Fig. 2, and two groups of loading modes can be overlapped accordingly: one is set as 6-wheel group, the other is set as 4-wheel group, and the wheel position arrangement is shown in Fig. 3 a); A typical medium strength flexible pavement section (MFC) is selected as the control structure to compare the finite element simulation with the test results. The pavement section is shown in Fig. 3 b).

Fig. 2 Wheelset loading device in large-scale loading test

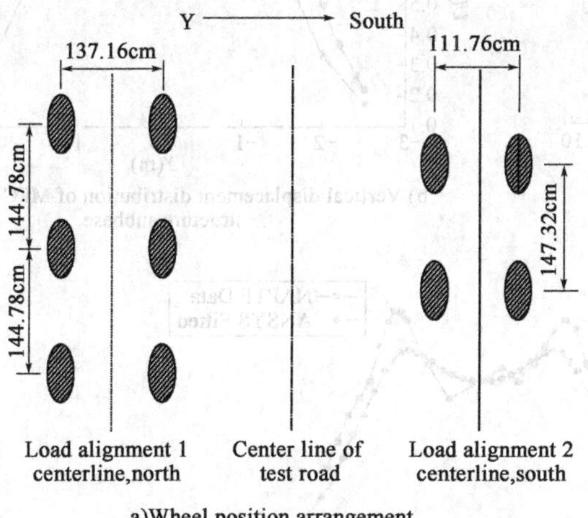

a)Wheel position arrangement

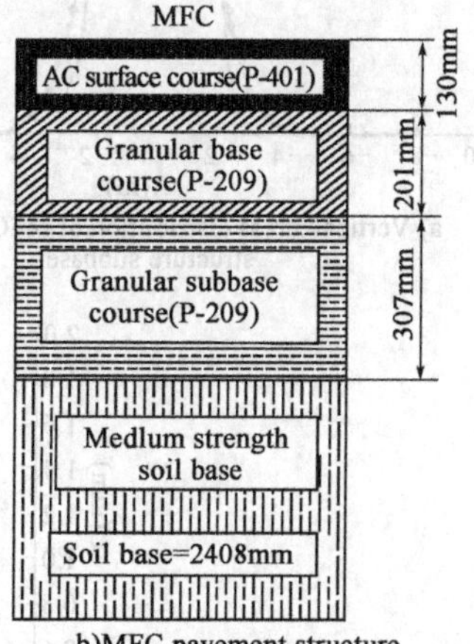

b)MFC pavement structure

Fig. 3 Schematic diagram of wheel group form and pavement structure in large-scale loading test

As shown in Fig. 4 a), the triaxial double wheel group (i. e. six wheel group) is selected for analysis. To simulate the test section more accurately, the circular zones of were loaded with tire pressure which coincide with tire contact areas. As shown in Fig. 4 b), the structure of MFC part is modeled by ANSYS finite element simulation software. In view of the symmetry of wheel load arrangement, the modeling adopts a quarter of the overall area for model simplification to have a finer grid near the loading position to save the overall operation time under the condition of ensuring the accuracy of calculation.

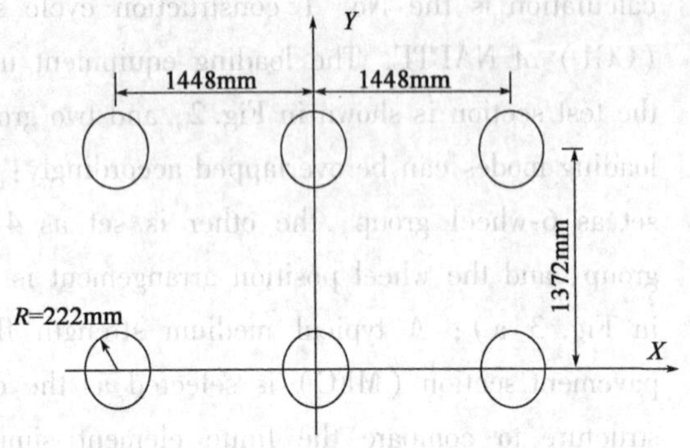

a)Triaxial double wheel group load distribution

b)Mesh generation of finite element model

Fig. 4 ANSYS finite element modeling based on naput measured data

Fig. 5 shows the comparison between the calculation results of the finite element model and the data using NAPTF. The calculation results in the post-processing are extracted by the calculation module of ANSYS finite element model. For the stress and displacement indexes in the vertical direction, the numerical value and change trend are generally consistent with the situation reflected by the measured data, and the maximum error is 13.5%.. The existence of partial deviation can be attributed to the difference in boundary constraints and dynamic characteristics under a wheel load. Therefore, within the allowable range of error, the above modeling method can be used to calculate airport pavement composite structure simulation calculation.

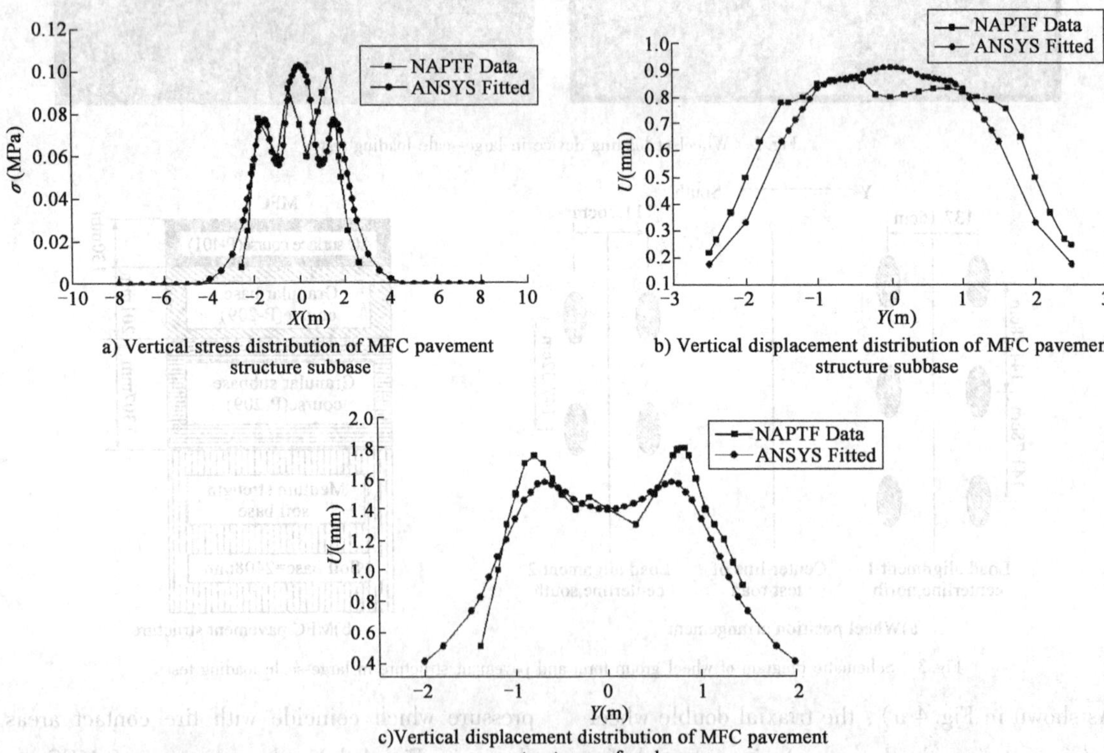

Fig. 5 Analysis and comparison of finite element calculated value and measured value

3 Stress Analysis

3.1 Load Pattern

Airbus A380-800, the largest passenger airplane was selected to represent New Generation Large Aircrafts (NGLA). Since the load on the front gear was far less than the rear gear (normally called main gear), the latter was chosen for pavement structural study as showed in Fig. 6.

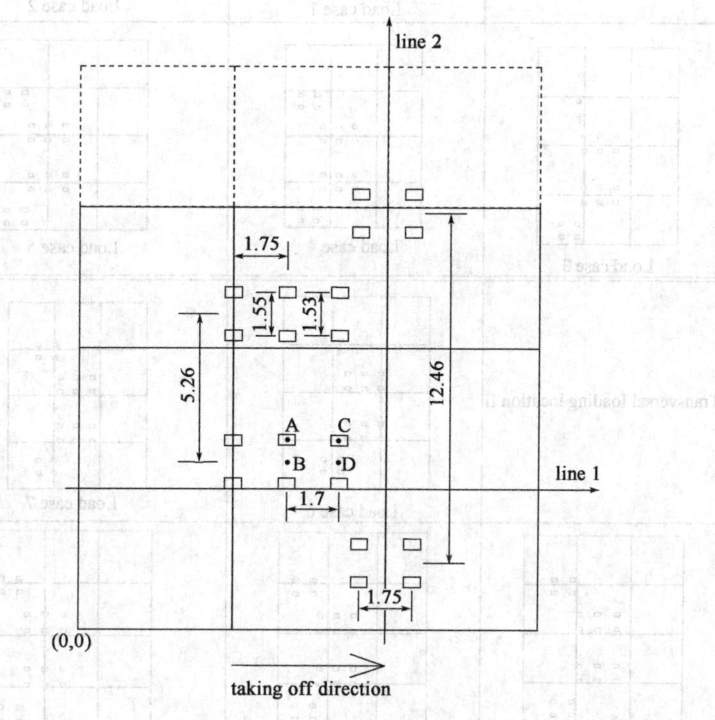

Fig. 6 Layouts of the typical airbus airplane A380-800 main gears (m)

As mentioned above, the reflective cracks on the overlay often occurred near the joints of PCC pavement, the different load cases were studied according to the layout ofthe PCC joints. Base on the arrangement of the main gear of A380-800, two transversal loading locations and five longitudinal locations were taken into account respectively, which makes ten load cases totally. Where the center line of the right-side dual tires of the rear tridem axles was aligned with the longitudinal joints, was transversal loading location I; whereas the external edge (right-side) of these dual tires aligned with the longitudinal joints, was transversal loading location II. When the main gear moved forward, the five longitudinal loading locations were made such as the transversal center line of tires and the center line between tires aligned with the transversal joint respectively, as illustrated in Fig. 7. It should be noted here longitudinal direction means taking off direction. Due to the rectangular mapping mesh grid was used in modelling, the contact area for each wheel in the main gear was simplified as a rectangle, as showed in Fig. 7 in turn.

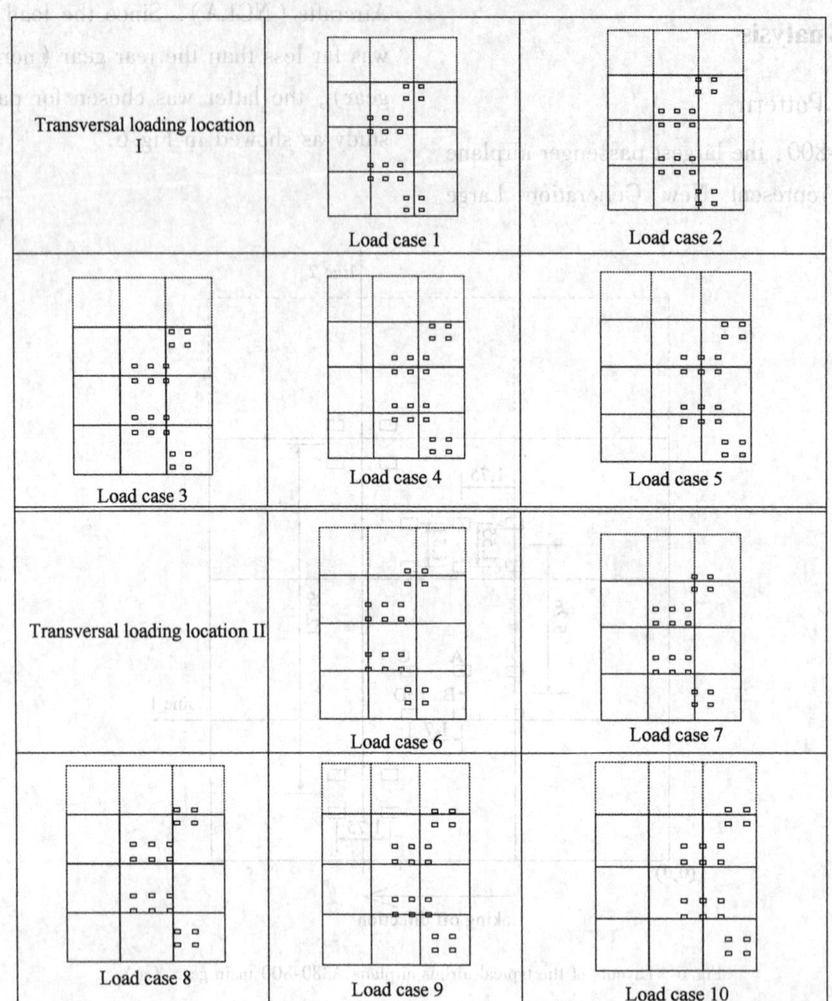

Fig. 7 Schematic of each load case

3.2 Stress Distribution

The response of the pavement under main gear was calculated by the FE program. the results showed that both the longitudinal and the transversal stresses in the overlay increased with the depth until the interface between PCC layer and HMA layer was reached, i. e. the critical stresses of overlay appeared at its bottom. Therefore only stress contours at the bottom of the overlay were plotted, as showed in Fig. 8. Notation SX represents longitudinal stress (along taking off direction) while SY represents transversal stress, and the load case numbering from 1 through 10 is consistent with that in Fig. 8. It could be seen both the maximum longitudinal stress and maximum transversal stress occurred under load case 6, and the former is larger than the latter with the value 0. 512MPa and 0. 438MPa respectively. Furthermore, load case 6, 7, 8, 9, 10 which belong to the transversal loading location II leads to larger tensile stress than corresponding load case 1, 2, 3, 4, 5 which belong to the transversal loading location I, respectively. In addition, wherever the longitudinal loading location is, the maximum transversal stress under transversal loading location I appeared at nearly the same position along the longitudinal joint, and when it is under transversal loading location II, the situation is similar except the maximum transversal stress position change to be along another longitudinal joint. It is also indicated when the main gear is moving, maximum transversal stress could be larger than maximum longitudinal stress. This means transversal loading location determined the maximum transversal stress position while longitudinal loading location influence its value. For the maximum longitudinal stress, the scenario is vice versa, i. e. longitudinal loading location determined the maximum longitudinal stress position while transversal loading location has more influence on its value. Trends of maximum tensile stresses with respect to load case number was also summarized in Fig. 9.

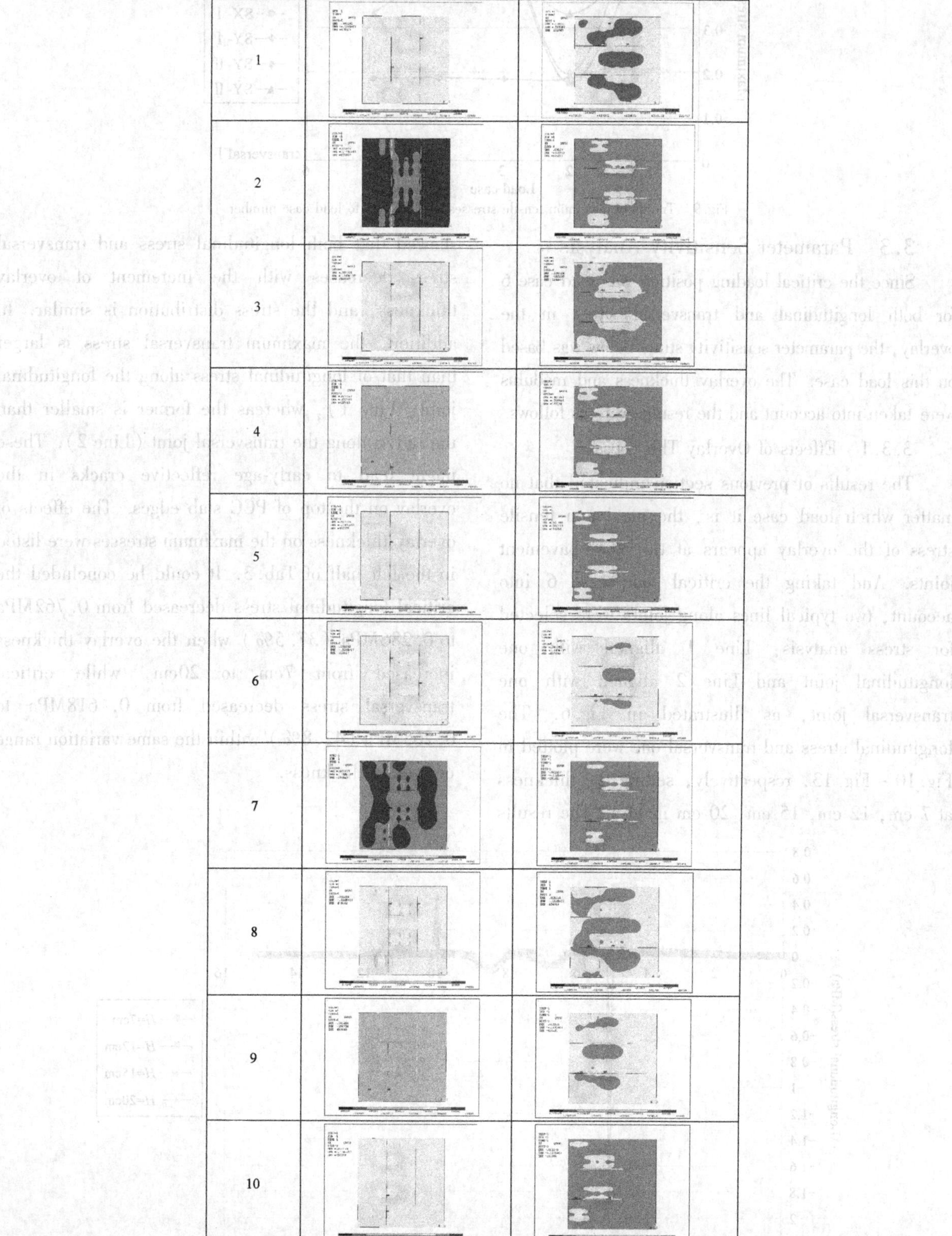

Fig. 8 Overlay tensile stress results of each load case

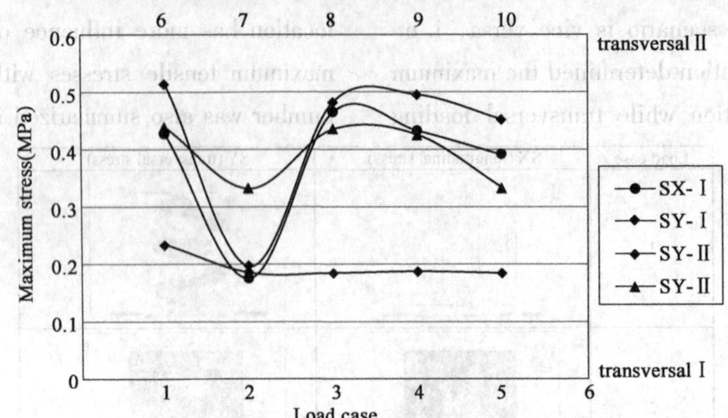

Fig. 9 Trends of maximum tensile stresses with respect to load case number

3.3 Parameter Sensitivity Analysis

Since the critical loading position was load case 6 for both longitudinal and transversal stress in the overlay, the parameter sensitivity study below was based on this load case. The overlay thickness and modulus were taken into account and the results were as follows.

3.3.1 Effects of Overlay Thickness

The results of previous section indicated that no matter which load case it is, the maximum tensile stress of the overlay appears at the PCC pavement joints. And taking the critical load case 6 into account, two typical lines along joints were selected for stress analysis: Line 1 aligned with one longitudinal joint and Line 2 aligned with one transversal joint, as illustrated in Fig. 6. The longitudinal stress and transversal one were plotted in Fig. 10 ~ Fig. 13, respectively, setting the thickness at 7 cm, 12 cm, 15 cm, 20 cm in turn. The results showed that both longitudinal stress and transversal stress decreases with the increment of overlay thickness, and the stress distribution is similar. In addition, the maximum transversal stress is larger than that of longitudinal stress along the longitudinal joint (Line 1), whereas the former is smaller than the latter along the transversal joint (Line 2). These might lead to early-age reflective cracks in the overlay on the top of PCC slab edges. The effects of overlay thickness on the maximum stresses were listed in the left half of Tab. 3. It could be concluded the critical longitudinal stress decreased from 0.762MPa to 0.286MPa (37.5%) when the overlay thickness increased from 7cm to 20cm, while critical transversal stress decreased from 0.618MPa to 0.265MPa (42.8%) within the same variation range of overlay thickness.

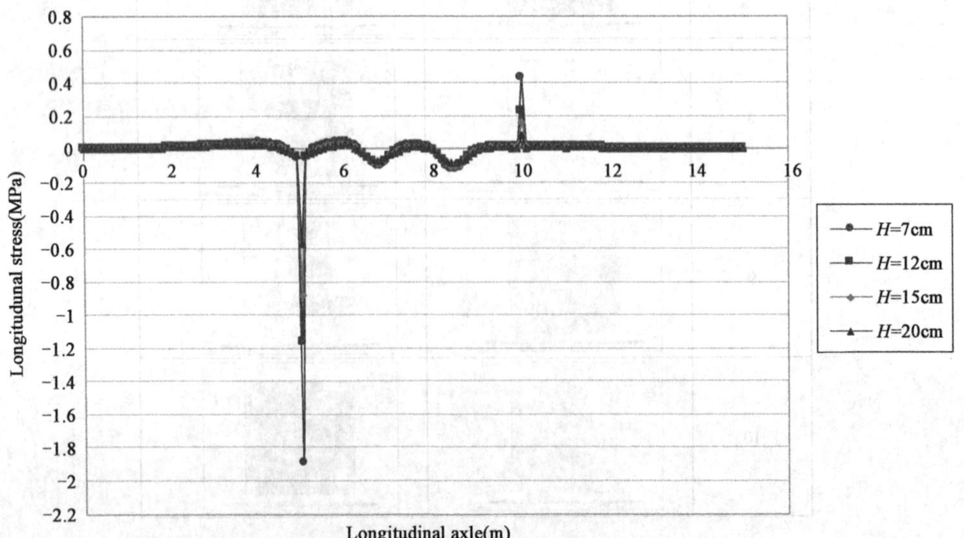

Fig. 10 Pavement longitudinal stress distribution due to overlay thickness (Line 1)

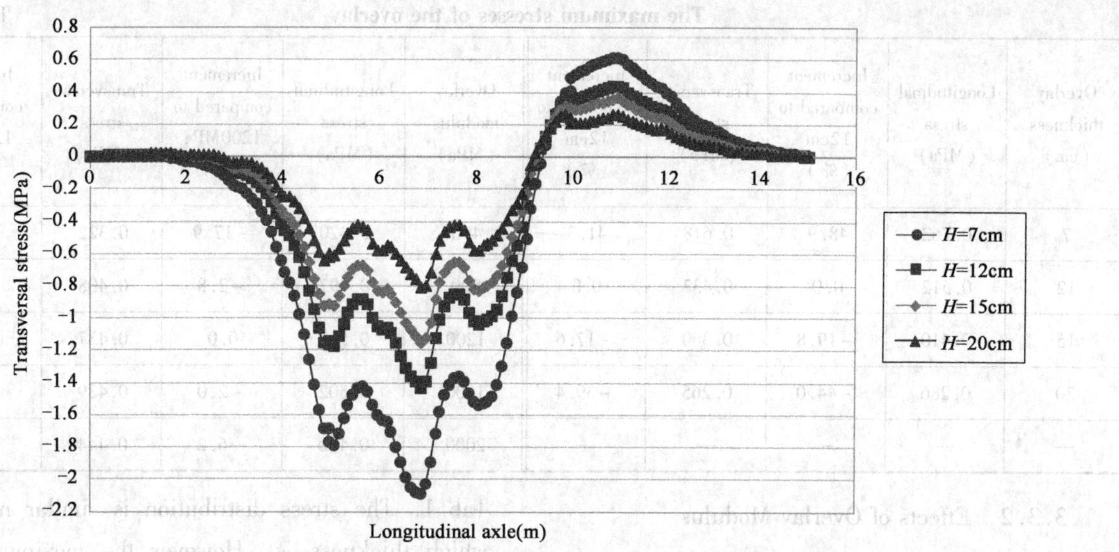

Fig. 11 Pavement transversal stress distribution due to overlay thickness (Line 1)

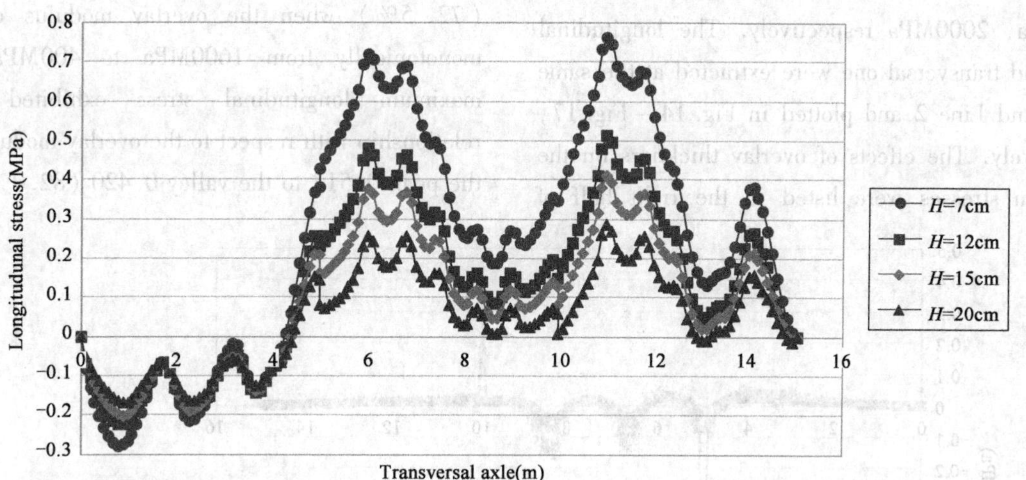

Fig. 12 Pavement longitudinal stress distribution due to overlay thickness (Line 2)

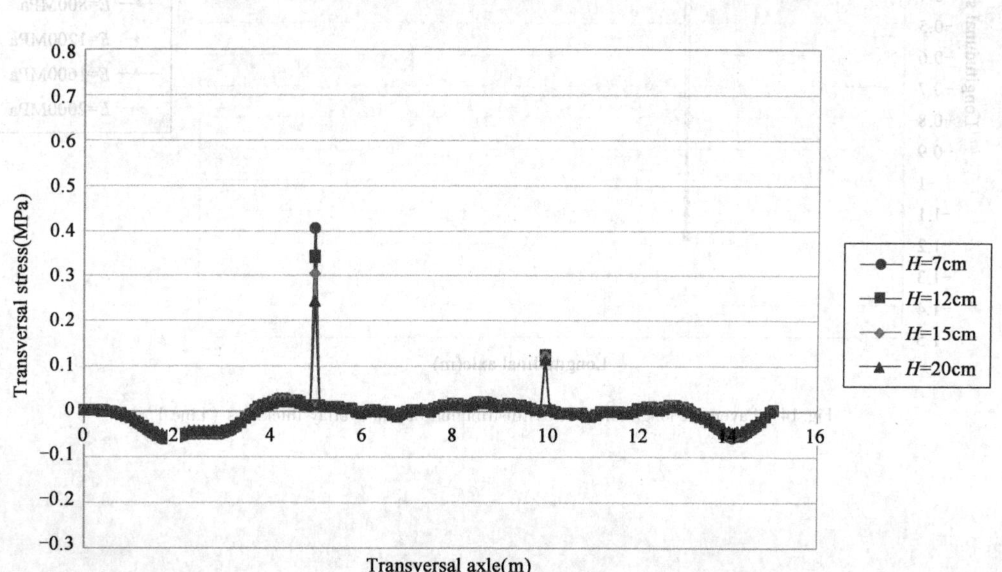

Fig. 13 Pavement transversal stress distribution due to overlay thickness (Line 2)

The maximum stresses of the overlay Tab. 3

Overlay thickness (cm)	Longitudinal stress (MPa)	Increment compared to 12cm (%)	Transversal stress (MPa)	Increment compared to 12cm (%)	Overlay modulus (MPa)	Longitudinal stress (MPa)	Increment compared to 1200MPa (%)	Transversal stress (MPa)	Increment compared to 1200MPa (%)
7	0.762	48.9	0.618	41.3	400	0.420	-17.9	0.322	-26.3
12	0.512	0.0	0.437	0.0	800	0.497	-2.8	0.408	-6.6
15	0.410	-19.8	0.360	-17.6	1200	0.512	0.0	0.437	0.0
20	0.286	-44.0	0.265	-39.4	1600	0.502	-2.0	0.439	0.5
—	—	—	—	—	2000	0.480	-6.2	0.444	1.6

3.3.2 Effects of Overlay Modulus

Simulations were carried out with the overlay modulus set to 400MPa, 800MPa, 1200MPa, 1600MPa, 2000MPa respectively. The longitudinal stress and transversal one were extracted at the same Line 1 and Line 2 and plotted in Fig. 14 ~ Fig. 17, respectively. The effects of overlay thickness on the maximum stresses were listed in the right half of Tab. 1. The stress distribution is similar no matter which thickness is. However the maximum transversal stress decreased from 0.444MPa to 0.322MPa (72.5%) when the overlay modulus decreased monotonically from 1600MPa to 400MPa, while maximum longitudinal stress exhibited quadric relationship with respect to the overlay modulus, from the peak 0.512 to the valley 0.420 (82.0%).

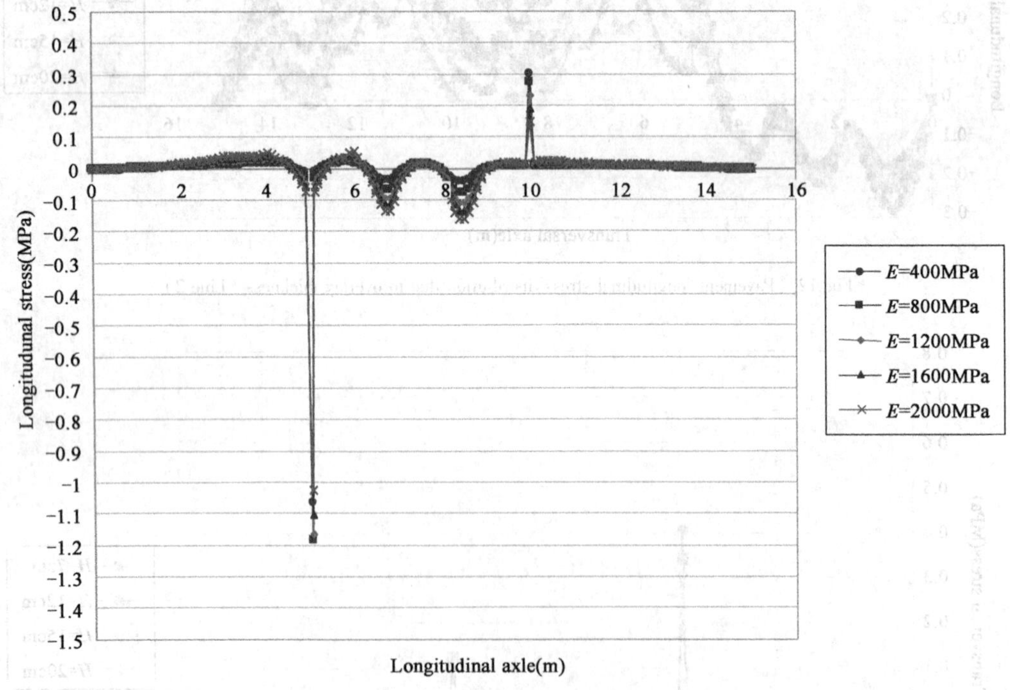

Fig. 14 Pavement longitudinal stress distribution due to overlay thickness (Line 1)

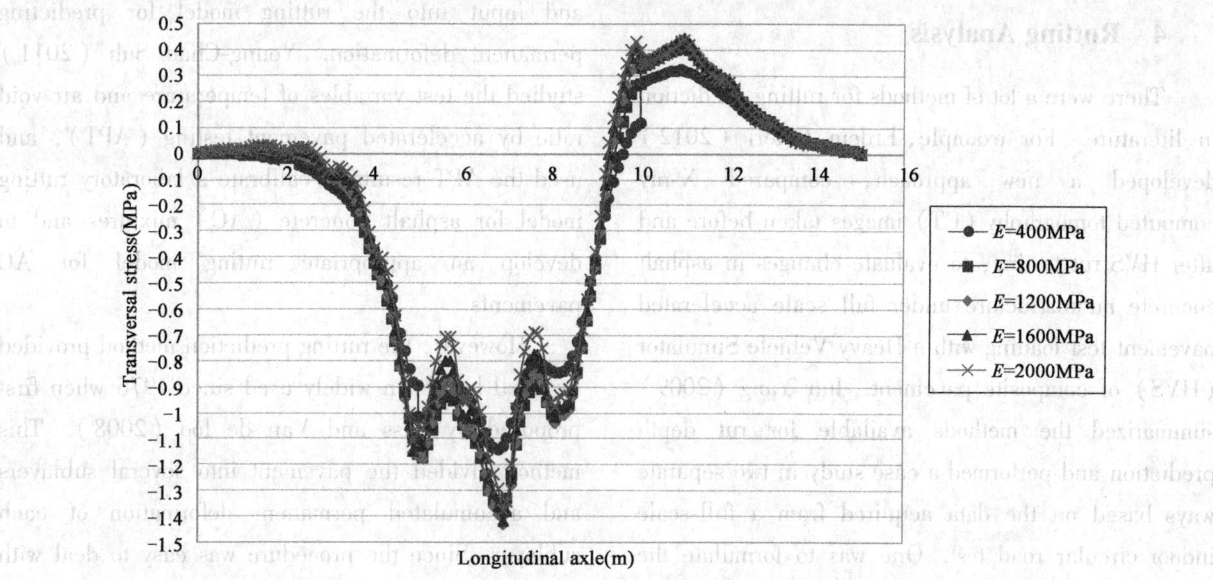

Fig. 15 Pavement transversal stress distribution due to overlay thickness (Line 1)

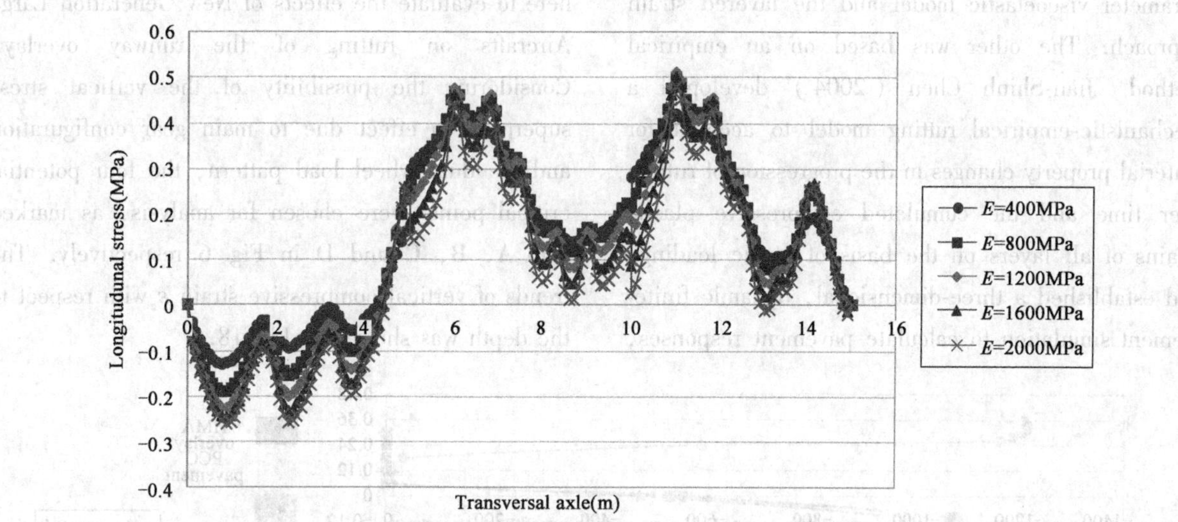

Fig. 16 Pavement longitudinal stress distribution due to overlay thickness (Line 2)

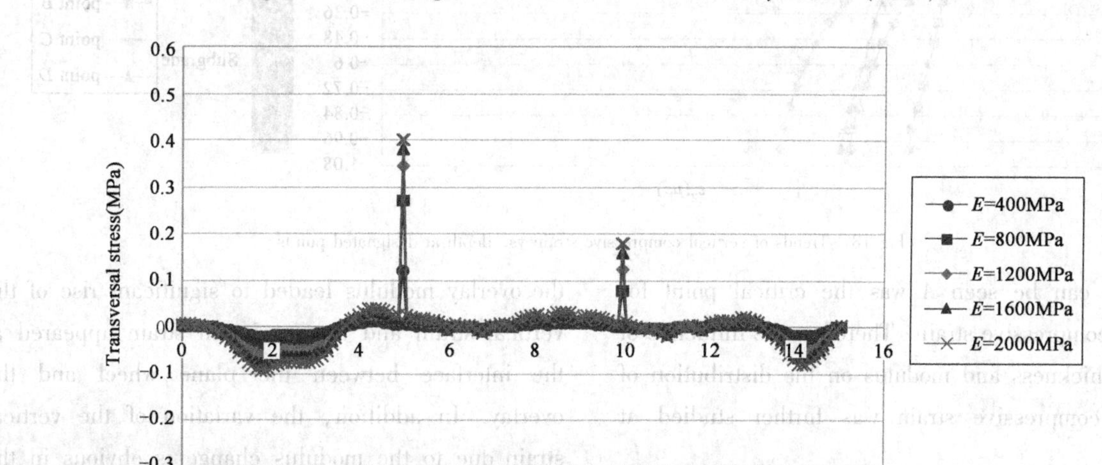

Fig. 17 Pavement transversal stress distribution due to overlay thickness (Line 2)

4 Rutting Analysis

There were a lot of methods for rutting prediction in literature. For example, Erdem Coleri (2012) developed a new approach, compared X-ray computed tomography (CT) images taken before and after HVS rut testing, to evaluate changes in asphalt concrete microstructure under full scale accelerated pavement test loading with a Heavy Vehicle Simulator (HVS) of composite pavement. Jun Yang (2009) summarized the methods available for rut depth prediction and performed a case study in two separate ways based on the data acquired from a full-scale indoor circular road test. One was to formulate the possible rut depth by integrating a four element five parameter viscoelastic model and the layered strain approach. The other was based on an empirical method. Jian-Shiuh Chen (2004) developed a mechanistic-empirical rutting model to account for material property changes in the progression of rutting over time and the cumulated compressive plastic strains of all layers on the basis of traffic loading, and established a three-dimensional, dynamic finite-element simulation to calculate pavement responses, and input into the rutting model for predicting permanent deformation. Young-Chan Suh (2011) studied the test variables of temperature and air void ratio by accelerated pavement testing (APT), and used the APT results to calibrate a laboratory rutting model for asphalt concrete (AC) mixtures and to develop an appropriate rutting model for AC pavements.

However, the rutting prediction method provided by Shell had been widely used since 1976 when first proposed by Hiss and Van de loo (2008). This method divided the pavement into several sublayers and accumulated permanent deformation of each sublayer. Since the procedure was easy to deal with based on simulation strain results, it was adopted here to evaluate the effects of New Generation Large Aircrafts on rutting of the runway overlay. Considering the possibility of the vertical stress superposition effect due to main gear configuration and the dual wheel load pattern, the four potential critical points were chosen for analysis, as marked with A, B, C and D in Fig. 6 respectively. The trends of vertical compressive strain ε_z with respect to the depth was showed in Fig. 18.

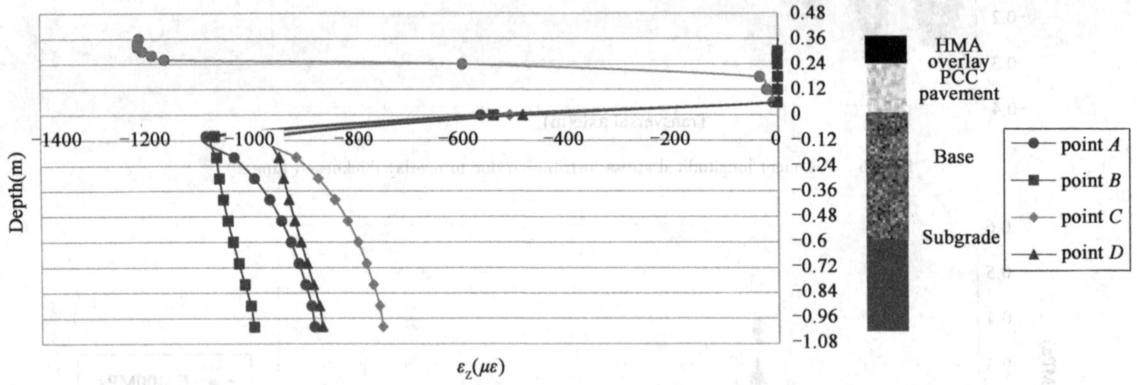

Fig. 18 Trends of vertical compressive strain vs. depth at designated points

As can be seen *A* was the critical point for vertical compressive strain. Therefore the influence of overlay thickness and modulus on the distribution of vertical compressive strain was further studied at point *A*.

The variation of each parameter was the same as above section. As showed in Fig. 19, the decrease of the overlay modulus leaded to significant rise of the vertical strain and the maximum strain appeared at the interface between the plane wheel and the overlay. In addition, the variation of the vertical strain due to the modulus change is obvious in the overlay, but it is much less in the PCC pavement and downward. The maximum strain appeared at the surface changed from 3600×10^{-6} to 730×10^{-6} (20.3%), corresponding to increase of modulus from 400MPa to 2000MPa. It can also be seen from Fig. 19 that the high temperature performance is more sensitive from 400MPa to 1200MPa than that from 1600MPa to 2000MPa.

Results also indicated that under A380, vertical compressive strain in the overlay decreased with the depth, as showed in Fig. 20. However it change very slowly near the surface. Extremely, when the thickness is small, for example 7cm, the vertical compressive strain in the overlay is nearly the same. This means less thickness could lead to higher compressive strain. Since the accumulated deformation depends on the product of the thickness and compressive strain, there could be an optimal overlay thickness when considering the rutting effect, and in this case it is between 7cm and 12cm.

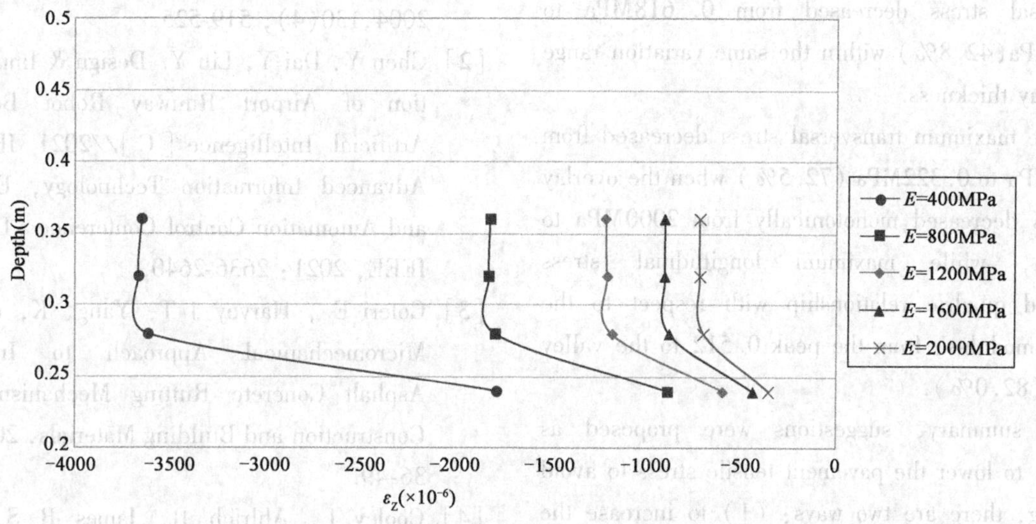

Fig. 19 The trend of vertical compressive strain vs. depth for different overlay modulus

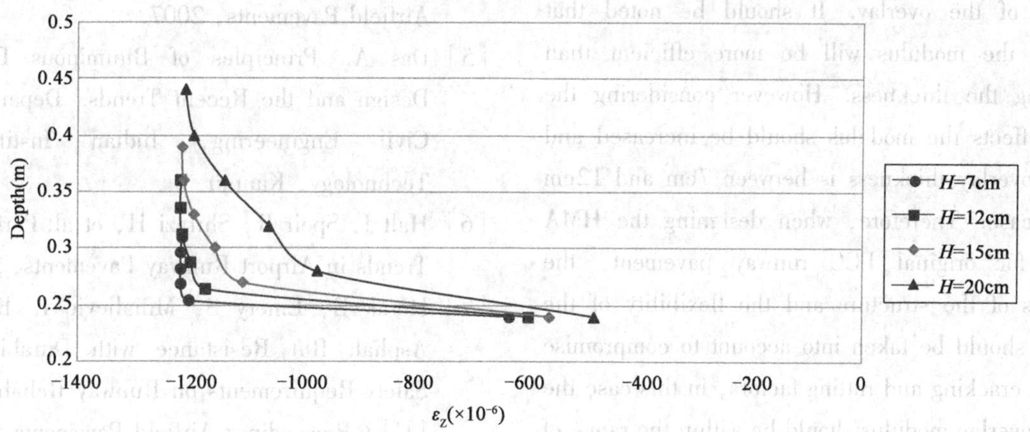

Fig. 20 The trend of vertical compressive strain vs. depth for different overlay thickness

5 Conclusions

The comparison between the simulation results and the test data from the National Airport Pavement Test Equipment (NAPTF) showed well consistence, which verified the modeling of the composite runway pavement structure. Model analysis indicated the critical loading position for New Generation Large Aircrafts (NGLA) was load case 6 for both longitudinal and transversal stress in the overlay, which were 0.512MPa and 0.438MPa respectively. Furthermore, the transversal loading location II leads to larger tensile stress than the transversal loading location I. In addition, no matter where the longitudinal loading location is, the maximum transversal stress under transversal loading location I appeared at nearly the same position along the longitudinal joint, whereas it is under transversal loading location II, the situation is similar.

Both the longitudinal stress and transversal stress decreases with the increment of overlay thickness, and the stress distribution is similar. the critical longitudinal stress decreased from 0.762MPa to 0.286MPa (37.5%) when the overlay thickness increased from 7cm to 20cm, while critical transversal stress decreased from 0.618MPa to 0.265MPa(42.8%) within the same variation range of overlay thickness.

The maximum transversal stress decreased from 0.444MPa to 0.322MPa (72.5%) when the overlay modulus decreased monotonically from 2000MPa to 400MPa, while maximum longitudinal stress exhibited quadric relationship with respect to the overlay modulus, from the peak 0.512 to the valley 0.420 (82.0%).

In summary, suggestions were proposed as follows: to lower the pavement tensile stress to avoid cracking, there are two ways: (1) to increase the thickness of the overlay; (2) to decrease the modulus of the overlay. It should be noted that reducing the modulus will be more efficient than increasing the thickness. However considering the rutting effects the modulus should be increased and optimal overlay thickness is between 7cm and 12cm in this case. Therefore, when designing the HMA overlay for original PCC runway pavement, the thickness of the structure and the flexibility of the material should be taken into account to compromise both the cracking and rutting factors, in this case the optimal overlay modulus should be within the range of 1600~2000MPa.

Furthermore, different kind of asphalt concrete has different ant-fatigue properties, thus the fatigue life should be further studied to validate the overlay design parameters more accurately.

6 Acknowledgements

This work was financially supported by the China Civil Aviation Science and Technology Innovation Fund (MHRD20140215), China Natural Science Foundation (51778142) and the Scientific Research Foundation of Graduate School of Southeast University (YBPY2044)

References

[1] Chen J S, Lin C H, Stein E, et al. Development of a Mechanistic-empirical Model to Characterize Rutting in Flexible Pavements [J]. Journal of transportation engineering, 2004,130(4), 519-525.

[2] Chen Y, Dai Y, Liu Y. Design & Implementation of Airport Runway Robot Based on Artificial Intelligence [C]//2021 IEEE 5th Advanced Information Technology, Electronic and Automation Control Conference (IAEAC), IEEE, 2021: 2636-2640.

[3] Coleri E., Harvey J T, Yang, K, et al. A Micromechanical Approach to Investigate Asphalt Concrete Rutting Mechanisms [J]. Construction and Building Materials, 2012, 30, 36-49.

[4] Cooley L, Ahlrich R, James R S, et al. Implementation of Superpave Mix Design for Airfield Pavements, 2007.

[5] Das A. Principles of Bituminous Pavement Design and the Recent Trends. Department of Civil Engineering, Indian Institute of Technology, Kanpur.

[6] Hall J, Speir R, Shirazi H, et al. Performance Trends in Airport Runway Pavements, 2014.

[7] Horak E, Emery S, Mihaljevic I. Balancing Asphalt Rut Resistance with Durability and Safety Requirements on Runway Rehabilitations [C]//Proceedings Airfield Pavements Seminar, XXIVth World Road Congress, Mexico City, Mexico, 2011: 28-29.

[8] Ling J, Ren L, Tian Y, et al. Analysis of Airfield Composite Pavement Rutting Using Full-scale Accelerated Pavement Testing and Finite Element Method [J]. Construction and Building Materials, 2021.

[9] Siddique A, Hoque A M. Crack Survey, Crack Repair Methodology and Overlay Design for

Rehabilitation of a Runway Pavement [J]. Journal of the Eastern Asia Society for Transportation Studies, 2008, 6:39-54.

[10] Suh Y C, Cho N H, Mun S. Development of Mechanistic-empirical Design Method for an Asphalt Pavement Rutting Model Using APT [J]. Construction & Building Materials, 2011, 25(4):1685-1690.

[11] Wang K C, Tee W Y, Watkins Q, et al. Digital Distress Survey of Airport Pavement Surface[C]. Federal Aviation Administration Airport Technology Transfer Conference, 2002: 69-82.

[12] Wang X Y, Liu Y H, Yuan J. Pavement Damage Evaluation and Analysis for Runway of Xiamen Gaoqi International Airport [J]. Journal of Civil Aviation University of China, 2005.

[13] Wei H, Meng N, Le L I. China's Strategies and Policies for Regional Development During the Period of the 14th Five-Year Plan[J]. Chinese Journal of Urban and Environmental Studies, 2020:2050008.

[14] Wensel M, Shalaby A, Thiessen M, et al. Investigation of Asphalt Pavement Rutting at Two Canadian Airfields [C]. 4th Transportation Specialty Conference of the Canadian Society for Civil Engineering, Montreal, Canada, 2002.

[15] Yang J, Lu H, Zhu H. Approaches to Rut Depth Prediction in Semirigid Asphalt Pavements [J]. Journal of Engineering Mechanics, 2009, 135(6): 510-516.

[16] Su K, Maekawa R, Hachiya Y. Laboratory Evaluation of WMA Mixture for Use in Airport Pavement Rehabilitation[J]. Construction and Building Materials, 2009, 23(7):2709-2714.

[17] Rushing J F, Little D N. Static Creep and Repeated Load as Rutting Performance Tests for Airport HMA Mix Design[J]. Journal of Materials in Civil Engineering, 2014, 26(9): 04014055.

[18] Zhang L A, Zhang L, Shi C, et al. Stress Distribution Characteristics of Runway Pavement under New Generation Large Aircrafts[J]. Advanced Materials Research, 2013, 811:218-222.

飞机轮胎与湿滑刻槽道面相互作用研究

蔡 靖*[1] 李 岳[1] 张 恒[2] 戴 轩[1]

(1. 中国民航大学机场学院;2. 上海民航职业技术学院)

摘 要 本文以A320的轮胎为研究对象,采用ABAQUS有限元软件,建立基于CEL算法的流固耦合飞机轮胎-刻槽纹理湿滑道面相互作用三维模型,基于上述模型从轮胎接地面积及与积水道面的接触面积、动水压强、轮胎所受道面支撑力等方面开展对比分析,研究结果表明:相同速度下刻槽道面上轮胎接地面积和接触面积均小于光滑道面上的值,二者差值分别为19.8%和6.2%;刻槽和光滑道面条件下着陆过程轮胎接触面积较起飞过程小12.5%和13.7%,且轮胎作用区域动水压强较起飞时高74.5%和40.25%;同一速度下刻槽道面对轮胎的支撑力比光滑道面高出约20kN,且刻槽道面临界滑水速度高出光滑道面约20km/h,因此基于上述结果得出飞机起飞、着陆存在上、下限两个临界滑水速度。

关键词 飞机轮胎 湿滑刻槽道面 临界滑水速度 接触面积 动水压强

1. 基金项目:国家自然科学基金项目(51508559)。

0 引言

民航作为重要运输业,安全运行至关重要,据统计,由轮胎滑水引起的飞机冲出跑道事故占全世界飞机安全事故总量的30%[1]。因此飞机轮胎与湿滑道面相互作用成为航空领域的热点研究问题之一。

早在1963年Horne[2]就基于光滑道面低轴载低胎压飞机轮胎试验提出轮胎临界滑水速度公式简称NASA公式。C W Oh[3](2007年)利用自编的轮胎花纹生成程序,生成了含复杂花纹的汽车轮胎有限元模型,分析研究汽车轮胎在光滑道面雨天行驶行为。Y S Wang[4](2009年)借助TYABAS软件从轮胎接地形状、轮胎胎压方面定性分析了光滑道面上飞机轮胎滑水行为,得到轮胎胎压是影响滑水主要因素的结论。H R Pasindu[5](2011年)基于有限元软件ADINA建立飞机-光滑道面有限元模型,分析积水厚度对飞机制动性能及运动特性的影响。

以上研究均针对光滑道面或低胎压、低轴载的飞机或汽车轮胎。带纹理道面与轮胎相互作用的研究方面,Wies[6](2009年)分析了道面沟槽方向、位置和面积对汽车发生滑水时轮胎受力状况的影响。S. K. Srirangam[7](2014年)采用激光扫描的方式,将真实沥青路面导入有限元软件中,考虑积水、复杂胎纹以及路面结构材料的影响,对汽车轮胎滑水进行了研究。杨军等[8](2016年)利用IFS插值方法在MATLAB中生成三维沥青路面,并建立轮胎-路面接触模型利用流体力学软件FLUNT计算得到水膜对轮胎作用力。上述对于纹理道面与轮胎相互作用的研究均针对沥青道面和汽车轮胎,而我国现有90%以上的机场道面均为水泥混凝土道面,为达到摩擦力的要求,道面均做刻槽处理,且高胎压、高轴载的大飞机已成为民航主流机型,以往基于低胎压,低轴载飞机轮胎或汽车轮胎与光滑道面相互作用的研究已不能适用于当前飞机轮胎滑水问题。

为此,本文以A320的轮胎为研究对象,采用ABAQUS有限元软件,建立基于CEL算法的流固耦合飞机轮胎-纹理(光滑)道面相互作用三维分析模型并验证,基于上述模型进行轮胎-光滑道面、轮胎-刻槽道面相互作用分析,通过其相互作用机理得到临界滑水速度上下限解的存在,进一步分析纹理湿滑道面条件下,不同飞机机型、不同道面积水状况对临界滑水速度的影响,从而提出NASA公式修正系数。

1 轮胎-湿滑道面相互作用三维模型

轮胎-湿滑道面相互作用中轮胎、道面为固体,道面上的水膜为液体,因此选择CEL(Coupled Eulerian-Lagrangian)流固耦合算法,并依照Horne试验的道面积水厚度7.66mm,建立轮胎-道面相互作用三维模型,模型由实体轮胎和积水道面两部分组成。

1.1 轮胎模型建立

以A320主起落架轮胎为研究对象,其型号为46×17R20。模型网格划分:轮胎环向网格由内壁向外壁均匀划分,轮胎径向网格绕转动中心 O 以均分角度划分,断面网格为均匀划分(图1),模型总节点数为53576,总单元数为40996。将轮胎内部帘线与胎面等效为具有统一弹性模量的超弹性均质橡胶材料[9-10],主要参数见表1。

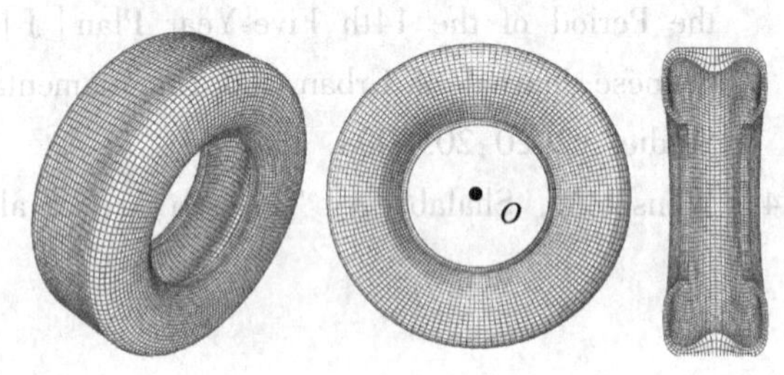

图1 A320轮胎模型

A320飞机主起落架轮胎参数 表1

参　数	数值
轮胎直径 D(cm)	115
轮胎宽度 B(cm)	43
轮胎胎压 P(kPa)	1140
橡胶正定常数C10	9.9×106
橡胶正定常数C01	8.8×106
橡胶不可压缩常数D1	10-7
单轮轴载 w(kN)	152

1.2 积水道面模型

为对比分析,本文分别建立了光滑积水道面

和方形刻槽积水道面(图2)。刻槽宽、深均为6mm,纵向间距为32mm。

根据Horne试验条件取水膜厚度为7.66mm,为表征液体流动界面,在水膜上层设置厚度为292mm的空气层,因此流体总厚度为300mm。参考文献[11]并考虑计算模型的优化性,将道面平面尺寸取为1.4 m×1.4 m,流域平面尺寸取为1m×1m。同时在流域前缘设置水流入口,后缘设置水流出口,流域两侧及底部设置为刚性不透水边界,如图2所示。模型网格划分:流域在厚度方向的网格由上至下逐渐加密,在平面方向的网格均匀划分,道面在厚度方向的网格由下至上逐渐加密,在平面方向均匀划分(图2)。流域单元数为75900,光滑道面单元数为361,刻槽道面单元数为3402。积水层模型参数如表2所示。其中:ρ_w^0为水的初始密度,c_0为声波在流体中的传播速度,n_w为水的动力黏度,表征流体内摩擦系数,s,Γ_0为无量纲材料常数,取值见表2。

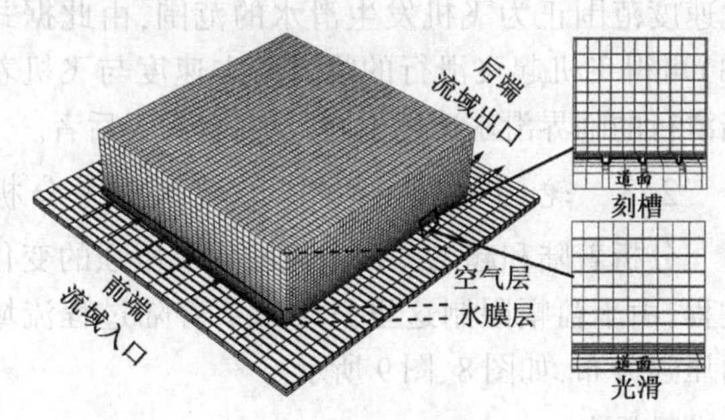

图2 积水道面模型

表2 积水层参数[12]

ρ_w^0 (kg/m³)	Mie-Grüneisen Parameters			n_w (Ns/m²)
	C_0 (m/s)	s (无量纲)	Γ_0 (无量纲)	
1000	1480	1.979	0.11	1.0×10^3

1.3 轮胎-湿滑道面相互作用三维模型

为了表征轮胎的力学和运动特征,对轮胎内壁施加均匀胎压P和单轮轴载F,同时绕转动中心O施加转动角速度ω,并以流域的运动代替轮胎的前进运动。为保证流域区的水流运动,在流域前缘设置初速度为v,加速度为a的水泵区使水流加速漫过流域,待水流覆盖整个流域后维持恒定速度使初始流域稳定。将转动轮胎与积水道面组合,就形成图3所示的轮胎-湿滑道面相互作用三维模型。

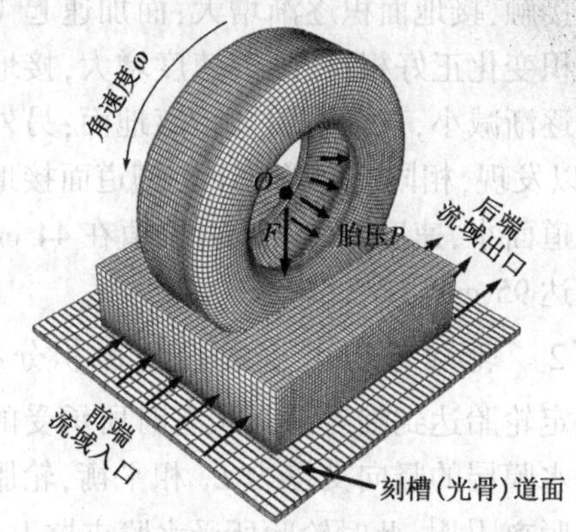

图3 轮胎-湿滑道面相互作用三维模型

2 刻槽湿滑道面与轮胎相互作用

2.1 轮胎接地面积分析

利用上述飞机轮胎-湿滑道面相互作用模型[14-16],对水流施加减速度和加速度,来模拟飞机着陆减速滑行和起飞加速滑行中轮胎-道面相互作用过程,得到轮胎接地面积变化云图和变化规律(图4、图5)。

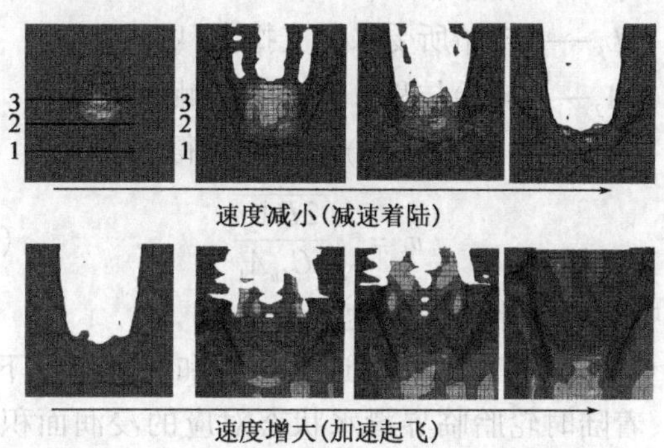

图4 轮胎接地面积云图

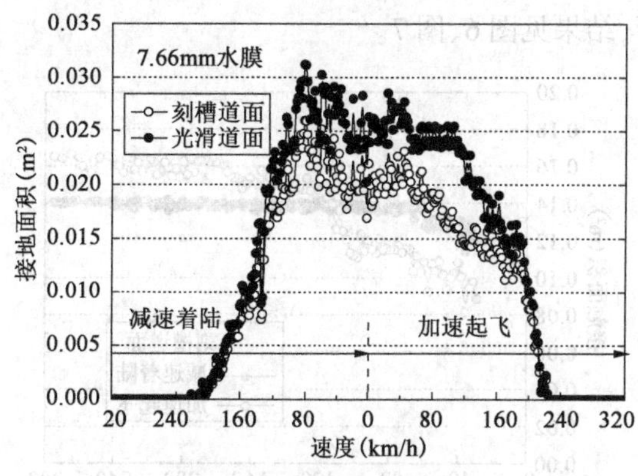

图5 轮胎接地面积变化曲线

由图4可以看出,减速着陆过程中,轮胎与道面分离,接地面积为零,随着速度降低,轮胎与地面开始接触,接地面积逐渐增大;而加速起飞过程接地面积变化正好相反,随着速度增大,接地面积由最大逐渐减小,直至轮胎被抬离地面;另外由图5还可以发现,相同速度条件下刻槽道面接地面积比光滑道面小,速度为0时二者差值在44 cm²,最大差值达95 cm²。

2.2 轮胎与积水道面接触面积分析

假定轮胎达到临界滑水状态时所承受的竖向载荷与水膜层的竖向支撑力 L_F 相平衡,轮胎与地面完全脱离[17-18],此时轮胎所受水膜支撑力为:

$$L_F = C_{Lh}T_F = \frac{1}{2}C_{Lh}\rho v^2 A_1 \tag{1}$$

式中:ρ——水膜密度,取1000 kg/m³;

C_{Lh}——动水压力分解系数,取0.7;

A_1——流体与轮胎的接触面积(m²),即浸润面积。

当 L_F 等于飞机单轮轴载时满足:

$$P = \frac{L_F}{A_2} \tag{2}$$

式中:P——轮胎胎压(kPa);

L_F——轮胎所受水膜支撑力(kN);

A_2——轮胎与积水道面的接触面积(m²)。

将式(2)带入式(1)中简化后得到:

$$v_h = \sqrt{\frac{2PA_2}{\rho C_{Lh}A_1}} \tag{3}$$

式中:v_h——临界滑水速度(km/h)。

公式(3)中在相同道面条件和水膜厚度下起飞、着陆时轮胎临界滑水状态对应的浸润面积 A_1 是相同的。利用上述模型对起飞和降落过程中轮胎与7.66mm水膜积水道面接触面积 A_2 进行分析,结果见图6、图7。

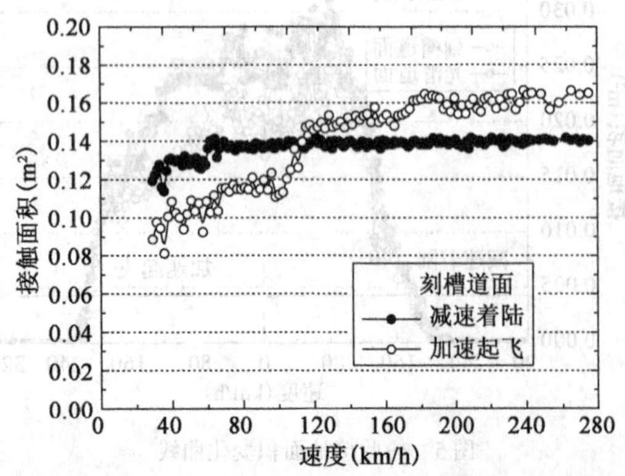

图6 轮胎与刻槽积水道面接触面积

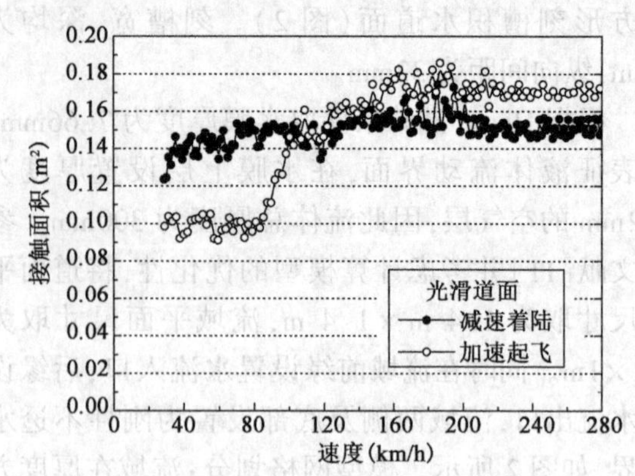

图7 轮胎与光滑积水道面接触面积

由图6、图7可以看出,在相同速度条件下,刻槽道面上轮胎与道面接触面积比光滑道面小,二者相差7.2%。光滑道面及刻槽道面上轮胎与积水道面接触面积 A_2 均随着滑行速度变化,且降落与起飞过程中 A_2 不同,在飞机滑行速度小于120 km/h时,降落时接触面积大于起飞;而滑行速度大于120 km/h时,起飞过程中 A_2 大于降落过程,此速度范围正为飞机发生滑水的范围,由此据式(3)可得飞机起飞滑行的临界滑水速度与飞机着陆滑行的临界滑水速度不同,且前者高于后者。

2.3 轮胎-水膜相互作用动水压强分析

分析着陆和起飞过程中流域动水压强的变化过程,由于篇幅限制这里只给出了着陆过程流域内压强分布,如图8、图9所示。

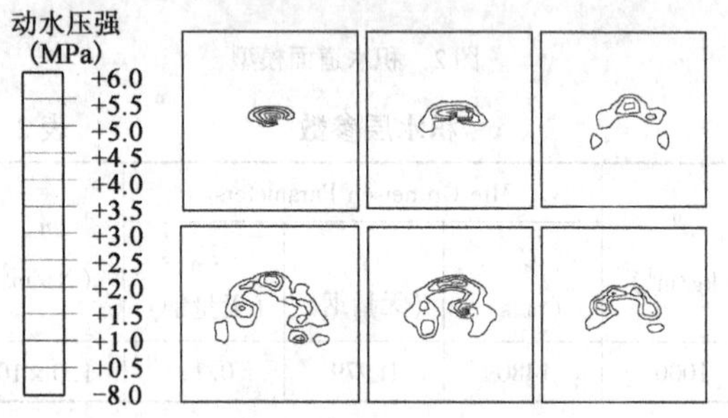

图8 刻槽道面着陆动水压强云图

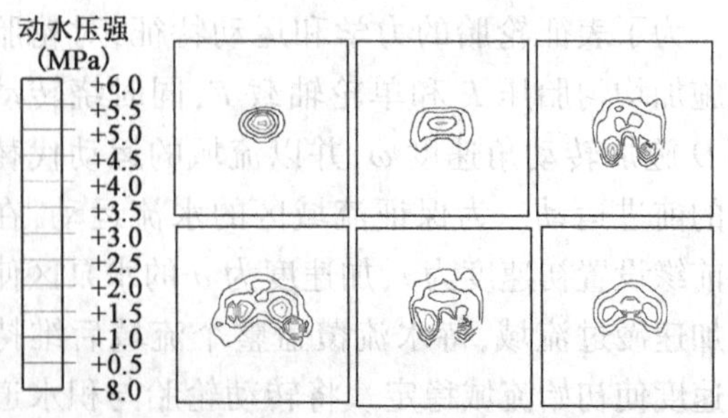

图9 光滑道面着陆动水压强云图

从图8、图9可以看出，着陆瞬时，接触面积内水膜压强较高，轮胎经减速后，水膜所受挤压作用减弱，流域内压强逐渐减小，但轮胎前缘压强仍较高；相比较而言，光滑道面上轮胎着陆所受水膜压强较刻槽道面高，且影响范围较大。

2.4 道面对轮胎支撑力及轮胎所受抬升合力分析

在模型中提取光滑、刻槽道面对轮胎支撑力，分析轮胎所受道面支撑力随滑行速度的变化规律，得到道面对轮胎支撑力趋近于零的点[19-21]，此时对应的滑行速度即为该工况下的临界滑水速度。结果如图10所示。

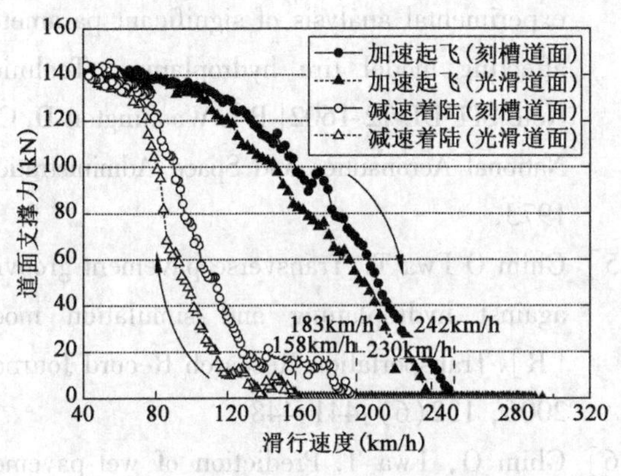

图10 道面支撑力(7.66mm水膜)

从图10可以看出，同一速度下刻槽道面对轮胎的支撑力均大于光滑道面，差值约为20 kN，且刻槽道面临界滑水速度大于光滑道面，差值约为20 km/h，光滑和刻槽道面上均有减速着陆临界滑水速度小于加速起飞临界滑水速度的规律，具体值见表3。

不同道面临界滑水速度对比(7.66mm水膜)

表3

项目	光滑道面 A(km/h)	刻槽道面 B(km/h)	提升率% (B-A)/A
减速着陆	158	183	15.8
加速起飞	230	242	5.2
差值 km/h	72	59	—

由图10和表3可以看出，在7.66mm积水道面条件下，光滑道面及刻槽道面均存在上下限临界滑水速度，加速起飞的临界滑水速度要比减速着陆的临界滑水速度高约60 km/h；同时刻槽道面的临界滑水速度均高于光滑道面，着陆和起飞时分别高出15.8%和5.2%。因此考虑道面刻槽对临界滑水速度的影响十分必要。

为进一步佐证以上滑水现象的发生，提取轮胎所受道面及水膜的作用合力进行分析，如表4所示。

轮胎所受合力(临界滑水时刻) 表4

道面状况	光滑道面		刻槽道面	
滑行状态	着陆	起飞	着陆	起飞
轮胎合力/kN	155.4	153.6	156.8	154.3

由表4可以看出，临界滑水速度时刻对应的轮胎合力均大于轴载(153 kN)，此时道面对轮胎支撑力为0，轮胎合力大于轴载，道面与轮胎分离，滑水发生。

2.5 临界滑水速度上下限的提出

基于上述轮胎-湿滑道面相互作用中轮胎与积水道面接触面积分析结果、动水压强分析结果、道面支撑力分析结果提出临界滑水速度具有上限和下限，上限即为起飞滑行的临界滑水速度，下限即为着陆滑行的临界滑水速度。

通过对大量试验数据回归分析，Horne[3]建议C_{Lh}等于0.7，带入式(3)，得到NASA临界滑水速度计算公式：

$$v_h = 6.36\sqrt{P} \tag{4}$$

根据NASA公式及本文研究成果提出以下临界滑水速度上下限公式：

上限临界滑水速度：

$$v_{\rm up} = 6.36\alpha\sqrt{P} \tag{5}$$

下限临界滑水速度：

$$v_{\rm low} = 6.36\beta\sqrt{P} \tag{6}$$

式中：α、β——与积水厚度、机型等相关的综合修正系数，考虑各个影响因素α、β为：

$$\alpha = \prod_{i=1}^{n}\alpha_i \tag{7}$$

$$\beta = \prod_{i=1}^{n}\beta_i \tag{8}$$

3 结论

(1)飞机在刻槽积水道面的起降与光滑积水道面相比，接地面积在减速着陆过程均是由小变大，加速起飞过程中，由于轮胎被水膜抬升接地面积逐渐减小为0，但其接地面积数值低于光滑道面19.4%，其上轮胎与道面接触面积较光滑道面低约7.2%；轮胎前缘动水压强影响范围低于光滑道面，动水压强数值也较光滑道面低37.2%。

(2)飞机发生滑水的速度范围内加速起飞接

触面积均高于减速着陆;飞机加速起飞产生的动水压强低于减速着陆,故而两个滑行状态下存在上、下限临界滑水速度,且两者差值约为 60 km/h。

参考文献

[1] 赵安家,孙丽莹,孟哲理.飞机轮胎滑水与预防措施研究综述[J].飞机设计,2015,35(5):46-51.

[2] Hoene W B, Dreher R C. Phenomena of pneumatic tire hydroplaning: NASA TN D-2056[R]. Washington, D. C.: NASA, 1963.

[3] Oh C W, Kim T W , Jeong H Y, et al. Hydroplaning simulation for a straight-grooved tire by using FDM, FEM and an asymptotic method[J]. Journal of Mechanical Science and Technology, 2008(22):34-40.

[4] Wang Y S, Wu J, Su B L. Analysis on the Hydroplaning of Aircraft Tire[J]. Advanced Materials Reseach., 2009(87-88 14):1-6.

[5] Pasindu H , Fwa T, Ghim O. Computation of Aircraft Braking Distances[J]. Journal of Transportation Research Board, 2011:126-135.

[6] Wies B, Rorger B, Mundl R. Influence of pattern void on hydroplaning and related target conflicts[J]. Tire Science and Technology, TSTCA, 2009, 37(3): 187-206.

[7] Srirangam S K, Anupam K, Scarpas A, et al. Safety Aspects of Wet Asphalt Pavement Surfaces Through Field and Numerical Modeling Investigations[J]. Transportation Research Record: Journal of the Transportation Research Board. 2014(2446), 37-51.

[8] 杨军,王昊鹏,吴琦.潮湿沥青路面抗滑性能数值模拟[J].长安大学学报,2016(5),36(3):25-32.

[9] 臧孟炎,陈高军,林银辉.湿滑路面轮胎制动距离有限元仿真分析[J].中国机械工程,2012(5),23(10):1246-1251.

[10] FwaT, Anupam K, Ghim O Relative Effectiveness of Grooves in Tire and Pavement in Reducing Vehicle Hydroplaning Risk[J]. Transportation Research Record: Journal of the Transportation Research Board, 2010, 2155(1):73-81.

[11] 王长键.复杂花纹下子午线轮胎滑水仿真分析与研究[D].广州:华南理工大学,2012.

[12] 庄继德.汽车轮胎学[M].北京:北京理工大学出版社,1999.

[13] Komandi G. Determination of adhesive parameters characterizing the interaction of pneumatic tires and concrete pavement from pull-slip curves[J]. Journal of Terramechanics, 1975, 12:109 - 117.

[14] Gilbert A W, Robert E I. A systematic experimental analysis of significant parameters affecting model tire hydroplaning: Technical Note SIT-DL-72-1602[R]. Washington D. C.: National Aeronautics and Space Administration, 1973.

[15] Ghim O Fwa T. Transverse pavement grooving against hydroplaning and simulation model[R]. Transportation Research Record Journal, 2006, 132(6):441-448.

[16] Ghim O, Fwa T. Prediction of wet-pavement skid resistance and hydroplaning potential[J]. Surface Properties-Vehicle Interaction, 2007:160-171.

[17] Horne W B. Wet Runways: NASA TM X-72650[R]. Washington D. C.: National Aeron-autics and Space Administration, 1965.

[18] Horne W B. Status of runway slipperiness[R]. Washington D. C.: NASA SP-416, 1976.

[19] 韩秀枝.子午线轮胎稳态滚动阻力及水滑特性的研究[D].北京:北京化工大学,2009.

[20] 赵坤.水漂动力学建模与仿真[D].哈尔滨:哈尔滨工业大学,2014.

[21] 陈高军.湿滑路面子午线轮胎制动性能有限元仿真研究[D].广州:华南理工大学,2012.

基于粒子群算法优化的 OGM 模型在航空业务量预测中的应用

张万衡[1] 邵 斌*[1] 白鹏坤[1] 张继超[1] 毕 征[2]
(1. 空军工程大学航空工程学院;2. 空军研究院工程设计研究所成都工程设计室)

摘 要 随着航空运输业的快速发展,机场建设工程规模越来越大,其规划建设需要更加科学合理的依据。航空业务量预测是机场选址、机场建设规模的重要考虑因素。本文通过建立粒子群算法优化的OGM(1,N)预测模型,选择经济因素、人口因素、贸易因素和旅游因素作为影响因素,航空旅客量作为预测目标,利用斜率关联度分析各因素对预测目标的影响程度,通过残差和平均相对误差绝对值(MAPE)评估预测模型的精度,得出该模型可用于航空业务量预测。

关键词 灰色预测 粒子群算法 OGM(1,N)模型 航空业务量

0 引言

近年来,我国民航运输业快速发展,机场吞吐量持续增长,机场规模也随之不断扩大。合理的机场建设规划对民用航空事业的发展意义重大,航空业务量预测结果对机场规模具有重要的影响,进而影响机场选址。

航空业务量预测通常采用专家判断法、类比法、趋势外推法、计量经济法和市场分析法 5 种[1],上述几种预测方法没有全面考虑影响航空业务量因素多样的实际情况,预测结果不够精确;陈太林等[2]基于 GM(1,1)模型的航空业务量预测模型,从理论上对传统预测模型进行了一定改进,具备较为精确的预测能力,但忽略了影响航空业务量多个因素间相互关联、共同制约的情况;葛折贵等[3]提出基于遗传算法和神经网络理论的航空业务量预测方法,考虑了多个影响因素的共同作用,但该模型需要大量数据学习,效率较低。

针对当前航空业务量预测模型未考虑多种因素共同影响以及需要大量学习样本的缺点,提出基于粒子群算法改进的 OGM(1,N)模型建立适用于特定机场特定条件下的航空业务量预测模型。该模型根据特定机场特定条件下的航空业务历史数据进行学习拟合,可以有效减少参数输入量,提高预测的精度和效率。

1 基于粒子群优化的 OGM(1,N)模型

1.1 模型提出背景

传统 GM(1,1)模型(含一个变量一阶方程的灰色预测模型),其建模主要依据仅为单一的时序数据,在建模时忽略了众多相关因素对整体发展趋势的共同影响。航空业务量预测的影响因素较多,因而 GM(1,1)模型不能反映外部环境变化对机场航空业务量预测变化趋势的影响。针对本文中机场建设的实际情况,采用多变量灰色预测模型进行航空业务量预测。

以 GM(1,N)为代表的经典传统多变量灰色预测模型虽能考虑相关因素的共同影响,但因其建模机理、参数估计和模型结构存在明显缺陷[4],导致该传统模型预测精度不够。因此,根据传统多变量灰色预测模型的缺陷,提出优化的模型结构 OGM(1,N)模型(Optimizing Grey Model)。

1.2 关联度分析

复杂系统的未来发展受到多种影响因素的制约,各种影响因素对结果发展的作用大小可以采用灰色关联度分析来计算。关联度用影响因素序列与输出序列的拟合程度来表征,拟合越好则关联度越高,该因素对结果的影响就越显著。关联度分析法有很多,本文采用斜率关联度分析法,其步骤为:

设母函数为 $X(t)$,子函数为 $Y_i(t)$ $(i=1,2,\cdots,n)$,取 $t_1,t_2,\cdots,t_n$ 个时刻的采样点,则 $X(t)$ 与

$Y_i(t)$在t时刻的灰色斜率应为：

$$\xi_i(t)=\frac{1+\left|\frac{1}{\bar{x}}\cdot\frac{\Delta x(t)}{\bar{x}}\right|}{1+\left|\frac{1}{\bar{x}}\cdot\frac{\Delta x(t)}{\Delta t}\right|+\left|\frac{1}{\bar{x}}\cdot\frac{\Delta x(t)}{\Delta t}-\frac{1}{\bar{y}_i}\cdot\frac{\Delta y_i(t)}{\Delta t}\right|} \tag{1}$$

式中：$\bar{x}$——母函数$X(t)$序列的平均值；

$\bar{y_i}$——子函数$Y_i(t)$序列的平均值；

$\frac{\Delta x(t)}{\Delta t}$——母函数$X(t)$序列在$t$到$t+\Delta t$时刻的斜率；

$\frac{\Delta y_i(t)}{\Delta t}$——子函数$Y_i(t)$序列在$t$到$t+\Delta t$时刻的斜率。

当$X(t)$，$Y_i(t)(i=1,2,\cdots,n)$为时间间隔为1的离散序列时，灰色斜率关系为：

$$\xi_i(t)=\frac{1+\left|\frac{\Delta x(t)}{\bar{x}}\right|}{1+\left|\frac{\Delta x(t)}{\bar{x}}\right|+\left|\frac{\Delta x(t)}{\bar{x}}-\frac{\Delta y_i(t)}{\bar{y_i}}\right|} \tag{2}$$

灰色斜率关联度：

$$\varepsilon_i=\frac{1}{n-1}\sum_{t=1}^{n-1}\xi_i(t) \tag{3}$$

1.3　建模方法

设$X_1^{(0)}$为系统特征数据序列(或称因变量序列)[5]：

$$X_1^{(0)}=(x_1^{(0)}(1),x_1^{(0)}(2),\cdots,x_1^{(0)}(m)) \tag{4}$$

序列$X_i^{(0)}=(i=2,3\cdots,N)$称为与序列$X_1^{(0)}$相关性解释变量序列(或称自变量序列)：

$$X_i^{(0)}=(x_i^{(0)}(1),x_i^{(0)}(2),\cdots,x_i^{(0)}(m)) \tag{5}$$

$X_i^{(1)}$为$X_i^{(0)}$进行一次累加后的1-AGO序列$(i=1,2,\cdots,N)$：

$$X_i^{(1)}=(x_i^{(1)}(1),x_i^{(1)}(2),\cdots,x_i^{(1)}(m)) \tag{6}$$

其中$x_j^{(1)}(k)=\sum_{g=1}^{k}x_j^{(0)}(g)$，$k=1,2,\cdots,m$。

$Z_1^{(1)}$为$X_1^{(1)}$的紧邻均值生成序列：

$$Z_1^{(1)}=(z_1^{(1)}(1),z_1^{(1)}(2),\cdots,z_1^{(1)}(m)) \tag{7}$$

其中$z_1^{(1)}(k)=\alpha x_1^{(1)}(k)+(1-\alpha)x_1^{(1)}(k-1)$，$k=2,3,\cdots,m$，则称为GM$(1,N)$的优化模型，即OGM$(1,N)$模型。

$$x_1^{(0)}(k)+az_1^{(1)}(k)=\sum_{i=2}^{N}b_ix_i^{(1)}(k)+h_1(k-1)+h_2 \tag{8}$$

式中：$h_1(k-1)$、h_2——OGM(1,N)模型的线性修正项和灰色作用量。

$X_1^{(0)}$，$Z_1^{(1)}$以及$X_i^{(1)}(i=1,2,\cdots,N)$如上文所述，分别代表系统特征数据序列(或称因变量序列)，相关性解释变量序列(或称自变量序列)以及$X_i^{(0)}$的1-AGO序列，则用最小二乘法估计OGM(1,N)模型参数列$\hat{p}=[b_1,b_2,\cdots,b_N,a,h_1,h_2]^{\mathrm{T}}$应满足：

$$\hat{p}=(B^TB)-1B^TY \tag{9}$$

其中，

$$B=\begin{bmatrix} x_2^{(1)}(2) & x_3^{(1)}(2) & \cdots & x_N^{(1)}(2) & -z_1^{(1)}(2) & 1 & 1\\ x_2^{(1)}(3) & x_3^{(1)}(3) & \cdots & x_N^{(1)}(3) & -z_1^{(1)}(3) & 2 & 1\\ \cdots & \cdots & & \cdots & \cdots & \cdots & \cdots\\ x_2^{(1)}(m) & x_3^{(1)}(m) & \cdots & x_N^{(1)}(m) & -z_1^{(1)}(m) & m-1 & 1 \end{bmatrix} \tag{10}$$

矩阵$\boldsymbol{Y}$为：

$$\boldsymbol{Y}=[x_1^{(0)}(2)\quad x_1^{(0)}(3)\quad\cdots\quad x_1^{(0)}(m)]^{\mathrm{T}} \tag{11}$$

OGM(1,N)模型的时间响应表达式为：

$$\hat{x}_1^{(1)}(k)=\sum_{t=1}^{k-1}[\mu_1\sum_{i=2}^{N}\mu_2^{t-1}b_ix_i^{(1)}(k-t+1)]+\mu_2^{k-1}\hat{x}_1^{(1)}(1)+\sum_{j=2}^{k-2}\mu_2^j[(k-j)\mu_3+\mu_4]\quad k=2,3,\cdots \tag{12}$$

其中，

$$\mu_1=\frac{1}{1+0.5a},\mu_2=\frac{1-0.5a}{1+0.5a},\mu_3=\frac{h_1}{1+0.5a},\mu_4=\frac{h_2-h_1}{1+0.5a}$$

同时，对式(9)累减还原可以计算出$\hat{x}_1^{(0)}(k)$，其累减还原表达式为：

$$\hat{x}_1^{(0)}(k)=\hat{x}_1^{(1)}(k)-\hat{x}_1^{(1)}(k-1) \tag{13}$$

可以看出，OGM$(1,N)$模型增加了线性修正项以及灰色作用量，使模型结构更加趋向合理，有效提高预测的精确度。

1.4 模型优化

对多变量灰色预测模型的优化主要是对模型背景值系数的优化。灰色预测模型的背景值 $z_1^{(1)}(k)=\alpha x_1^{(1)}(k)+(1-\alpha)x_1^{(1)}(k-1)$ 实际上是一个平滑公式,可以看作用微分近似计算曲线面积,为了提高精度,时间间距应尽量小且变化趋势越平缓,则准确度将越高[4]。在灰色理论系统中,背景值系数 α 是影响模型预测性能的关键参数。然而在实际操作中,往往为了简化运算过程,将背景值系数 α 取常数 0.5,这在很大程度上降低了模型的预测精度。

由 Eberhart 和 Kennedy[6] 在 1995 年提出的粒子群算法(Particle Swarm Optimization, PSO)被广泛应用于数据学习网络的优化[7]。针对本文所研究问题,采用粒子群算法优化 OGM(1,N)模型背景系数。利用最小平均相对误差作为求解灰色模型的最优阶数来解决模型优化问题:

$$\min f(\alpha)=\frac{1}{m-1}\sum_{k=2}^{n}\frac{\left|\hat{x}_1^{(0)}(k)-x_1^{(0)}k\right|}{x_1^{(0)}k} \tag{14}$$

式中:$\alpha\in R^{+}$;

n——训练数据个数;

$\hat{x}_1^{(0)}(k)$、$x_1^{(0)}(k)$——预测输出和期望输出。

粒子群优化流程如图 1 所示。

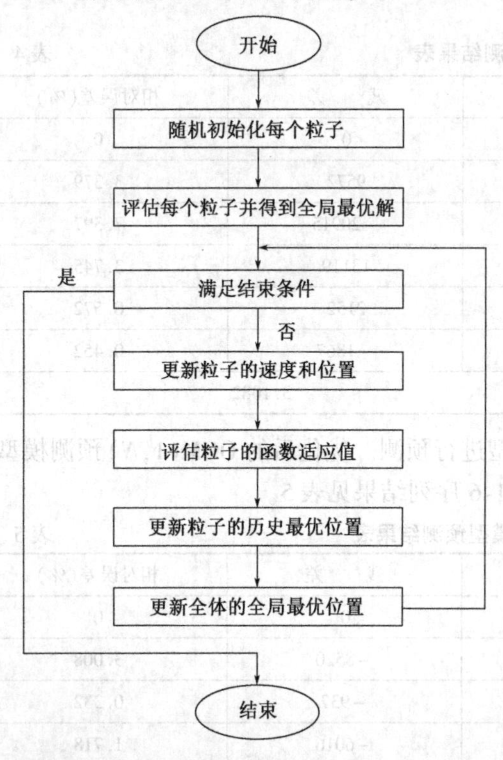

图 1 粒子群优化流程图

1.5 精度检验

模型通过残差和平均相对误差绝对值(MAPE)评估预测模型的精度[8]。

$$\mathrm{MAPE}=\frac{1}{n}\sum_{k=1}^{n}\frac{\left|\hat{x}^{(0)}(k)-x^{(0)}(k)\right|}{x^{(0)}(i)}\times 100\% \tag{15}$$

MAPE 精度检验表见表 1。

MAPE 精度标准检验表 表 1

MAPE 值	精度评价
小于 10%	高
10% ~20%	较高
20% ~50%	一般
大于 50%	差

2 实例分析

航空业务量的影响因素有很多[9],主要包括经济因素、人口因素、贸易因素和旅游因素。经济因素主要是指本地区的生产总值和人均生产总值,其分别代表着该地区的经济总体发展水平和地区居民的基本消费能力;人口因素主要为该地区的人口总数,反映了该地区人员可能产生流动的基数;贸易因素主要指外地企业(本地区行政市以外)在本地区的投资金额,商业往来也是产生人口流动的重要因素;旅游因素指的是本地区的旅游人数。

本文选择地区人口数、地区生产总值、人均生产总值、外地企业对地区投资总额、旅游人数 5 个指标作为预测参数,以航空旅客量作为预测指标,通过实例来验证和分析本文模型对航空业务量预测的有效性。

以实际运行中的 A 市某机场为例分析[10],本文通过文献[10]中公开的调查数据验证模型预测能力,数据在地方国民经济和社会发展统计公报中可查询。数据集见表 2。

A市航空旅客量及影响参数数据集　表2

运行年份(序列号k)	航空旅客量 $x_1^{(0)}$(人)	地区人口 $x_2^{(0)}$(万人)	地区生产总值 $x_3^{(0)}$(亿元)	人均生产总值 $x_4^{(0)}$(元)	外资企业对地区投资总额 $x_5^{(0)}$(亿元)	旅游人数 $x_6^{(0)}$(万人)
1	308559	621.4	1811.2	29147.1	251.0	1700.0
2	283296	614.8	2038.5	33157.1	336.4	2150.0
3	282885	607.2	2264.9	37300.7	478.4	2456.2
4	350301	608.7	2514.2	41304.4	556.4	2979.5
5	376384	609.2	2709.0	44468.2	646.0	3641.9
6	413484	611.0	2955.5	48371.5	696.2	4048.9

2.1　关联度分析

将航空旅客量作为母函数序列 $x_1^{(0)}$、地区人口 $x_2^{(0)}$、地区生产总值 $x_3^{(0)}$、人均生产总值 $x_4^{(0)}$、外资企业对地区投资总额 $x_5^{(0)}$、旅游人数 $x_6^{(0)}$ 代入式(2)、式(3)可以计算各影响因素与预测指标的关联度,数据见表3。

影响因素与预测指标关联度表　表3

参考序列	关联度 ε_{11}	关联度 ε_{12}	关联度 ε_{13}	关联度 ε_{14}	关联度 ε_{15}	关联度 ε_{16}
数据集	1.000	0.886	0.889	0.887	0.886	0.895

由结果可知 $\varepsilon_{16}>\varepsilon_{13}>\varepsilon_{14}>\varepsilon_{12}=\varepsilon_{15}$,旅游人数对该地区航空旅客量的影响最为显著。同时,地区人口数、地区生产总值、人均生产总值、外地企业对地区投资总额的关联度较高,结果表明这几种因素对航空业务量的预测也有重要的作用。根据关联度分析结果,可以看出航空旅客量受到多种因素共同影响,且作用明显,因此有必要建立多参数的预测模型进行预测。

2.2　模型预测

为了验证优化后的OGM(1,N)模型在航空业务量预测中的有效性,本文基于Matlab分别实现GM(1,1)预测模型和基于粒子群优化的OGM(1,N)预测模型的建立来进行比较。同时,采用残差和平均相对误差来检验模型精度。

GM(1,1)预测模型预测1-6序列结果见表4。

GM(1,1)预测模型预测结果表　表4

序　号	原始序列	预测值	残　差	相对误差(%)
1	308559	308559	0	0
2	283296	273724	9572	3.379
3	282885	303800	−20915	7.397
4	350301	337181	13119	3.745
5	376384	374231	2152	0.572
6	413484	415351	−1867	0.452
平均相对误差(%)		3.1082		

选取人均生产总值($x_4^{(0)}$)、外资企业对地区投资总额($x_5^{(0)}$)、旅游人数($x_6^{(0)}$)作为输入参数优化模型进行预测。优化后的OGM(1,N)预测模型预测1-6序列结果见表5。

优化后的OGM(1,N)预测模型预测结果表　表5

序　号	原始序列	预测值	残　差	相对误差(%)
1	308559	308559	0	0
2	283296	274776	−8520	3.008
3	282885	281947	−937	0.332
4	350301	344284	−6016	1.718

续上表

序　号	原始序列	预　测　值	残　差	相对误差(%)
5	376384	374206	-2178	0.579
6	413484	408816	-4668	1.129
平均相对误差(%)		1.3528		

图 2 为更直观分析训练模型预测效果,我们将 OGM(1,N)预测模型预测结果、优化后的 OGM(1,N)预测模型预测结果与原数据绘制折线图;图 3 为相对百分比误差条形图。

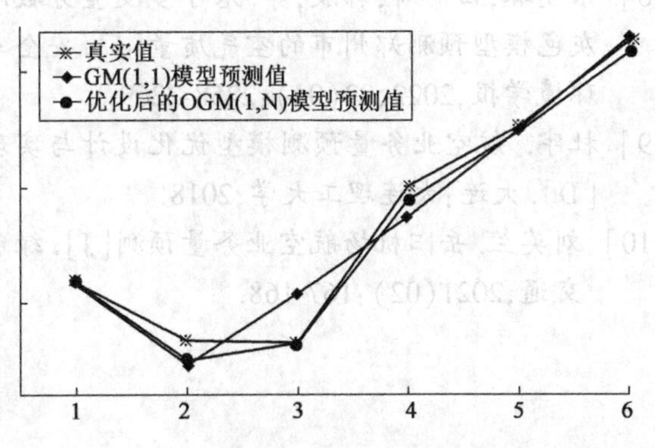

图 2　模型预测值

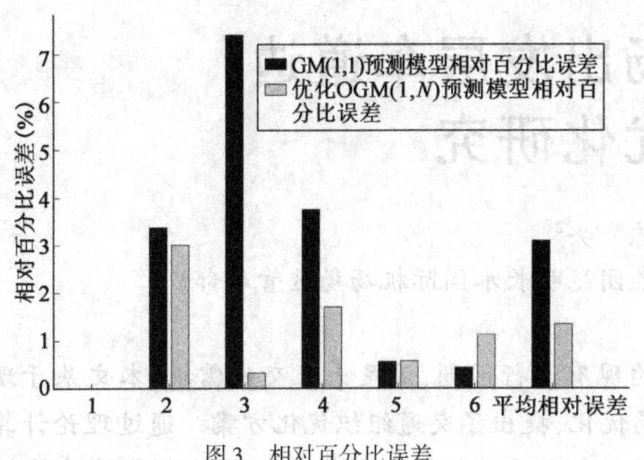

图 3　相对百分比误差

2.3　预测结果分析

从对数据集 1-6 序列学习模拟情况看,训练 GM(1,1)预测模型的相对百分比误差为 3.1082%,训练优化的 OGM(1,N)模型的相对百分比误差为 1.3528%。

根据 MAPE 精度标准,可认为其精度高,比 GM(1,1)预测模型提高了 1.7554%,由图 3、图 4 也能明显看出优化后的模型拟合程度更好。这表明,经过优化后,新的预测模型精度有了更好的保证,可以用于实现对航空业务量的预测功能。

国内机场建设相对比较缓慢,其航空业务量不仅受到人口数量、经济发展等的影响。同时,人们对于航空出行方式的认知并不成熟,随着时间推进,在经济和人口发展的同时,无论是受教育的水平或者是新事物对人的冲击,都会对主观心态造成很大的影响,出行方式越发多样并难以预测,采用航空出行的方式快速增多容易出现突破式的增长态势,样本数据往往会有较大的波动,而灰色预测中数据的波动是影响预测精度的重要原因,因此在选取样本时,应尽量选择发展平稳的样本,可以有效提高预测的准确性。另外,在影响因素选择时,会存在两个问题:一是选取影响因子过少,则可能会存在忽略关键因子的可能性,导致预测结果偏离实际或者精度不高;另一方面选取影响因子过多,则可能会导致主次不清、预测效率低的问题,同样会影响精度。因此,首先通过关联度分析,将各因子对预测目标的相关程度进行主次排序,并剔除影响较小的因素,实现对模型的简化和优化。

3　结论

(1)针对航空业务量预测提出基于粒子群算法优化的 OGM(1,N)预测模型,通过精度检验以及与已有的预测模型相比较,其精确度有了一定的提高,预测精度为高。在航空业务量预测中可以实现更好的预测功能。

(2)模型仍存在两点不足:一是在参数选择时,随意性较大,且选取的影响因素往往存在过多或者过少的问题,进而影响到预测结果的精确度;二是原始数据资料收集可靠性不足,在实际预测中,原始数据资料不齐全、样本量少、数据来源不可靠等问题也影响着预测结果的精确度。

(3)航空业务量也受到主观因素的影响,如机场的服务水平、居民的消费心理、交通是否便捷等,此类因素在本文中并未考虑,主要是其难以用数据形式进行量化表示;且通过调查打分形式,则工作量将大大增加,调查范围过大将不宜开展,调查范围过小则将不具有代表性。因此在数据样本选择时,建议选取情况相近的经济发展稳定的城市做类比,以此为新建机场提供更科学的建议。

预测是进行决策的基础工作,更加科学的预测模型将会使机场建设工程的决策更正确合理。本文主要通过建立优化模型并检验其可行性,提出一种可供航空业务量预测的新的思路。

参考文献

[1] 钱炳华,张玉芬. 机场规划设计与环境保护[M]. 北京:中国建筑工业出版社,2000.

[2] 陈太林,张伟,谢永亮,等. 预测机场航空业务量的灰色模型方法[J]. 工程力学,2001,525-529.

[3] 葛折贵,葛折圣. 基于遗传算法和神经网络理论的机场航空业务量的预测模型[J]. 现代交通技术,2005(04):65-67.

[4] 王锋刚,王勇传. 民用机场航空业务量预测[J]. 中国民用航空,2013(06):50-51.

[5] 曾波,尹小勇,孟伟. 实用灰色预测建模方法及其MATLAB程序实现[M]. 北京:科学出版社,2018.

[6] 唐超,陈妍颖,李庶林,等. 基于自适应变异粒子群算法改进OGM(1 ,N)及其在排土场变形预测中的应用[J]. 岩石力学与工程学报,2020,39(1):3197-3205.

[7] 田东平,赵天绪. 基于群体适应度方差的自适应粒子群优化算法[J]. 计算机工程与应用,2010,46(18):24-26.

[8] 张爱琳,白丽娜,韩液,等. 基于多变量分数阶灰色模型预测郑州市的空气质量[J]. 安全与环境学报,2022,22(04):2258-2269.

[9] 杜宇. 航空业务量预测模型优化设计与实现[D]. 大连:大连理工大学,2018.

[10] 刘英兰. 岳阳机场航空业务量预测[J]. 绿色交通,2021(02):167-168.

昆明长水国际机场出发层车道边交通组织优化研究

胡爱辉[*1] 陈 兴[2]

(1. 长安大学运输工程学院;2. 云南机场集团昆明长水国际机场场区管理部)

摘 要 为解决昆明长水国际机场出发层车道边的现有运行问题,满足未来交通需求,本文基于现状分析,考虑减少行人干扰、车道边空间分配调整与布局优化,提出了交通组织优化方案。通过理论计算与微观仿真分析,从通行能力、服务水平和平均车辆延误三个方面对各优化方案进行评估,并做未来交通压力测试。结果表明,提出的交通组织优化方案能较好地处理现有问题,保证该车道边在持续增长的未来交通压力下的良好性能。研究结果能够为其他机场出发层车道边的交通组织优化分析提供一定的参考。

关键词 出发层车道边 组织调整 交通评估 昆明长水国际机场

0 引言

随着社会经济的快速发展,航空需求不断增加。作为机场路侧交通系统的关键节点,航站楼出发层车道边的交通压力也随之增大。在此背景下,原有的出发层车道边交通组织方案开始逐渐显示出局部交通拥堵等问题,并且难以满足不断增加的未来交通需求。因此,对航站楼出发层车道边的交通组织进行优化极为重要,能够为车道边在未来交通压力下的持续良好工作提供一定的保障。

多年来,已有众多研究围绕机场航站楼车道边的容量评估和布局模式等方面展开探索。在容量评估方面,柳伍生等[1]基于有容量限制的排队理论,建立了机场出发层车道边的需求规模。欧阳杰等[2]利用可接受间隙理论对机场出发层车道边的容量进行了评估。王茹[3]基于时空消耗理论建立了多航站楼的车道边容量模型。在布局模式方面,宿百岩等[4]从车道边建设的角度对国内外机场航站楼车道边的布局特征进行归纳梳理。杨杰[5]基于机场车道边运行特征的分析,根据车辆停靠方式提出了不同类型的车道边布局模式。郑文昌[6]结合规划设计经验,对机场出发层车道边的布局模式选取与规模测算进行了研究。然而,目前针对车道边进行交通组织优化的研究还较少。

为此,本文以昆明长水国际机场为例,对出发层车道边的现有交通组织方案进行优化。通过理论分析和交通微观仿真,从多个方面对不同的交通组织优化方案进行评估,并考察各方案在未来交通压力下的可用性。

1 出发层车道边交通现状分析

昆明长水国际机场航站楼的出发层车道边设有3幅车道边,共9条车道(图1)。其中,中间车道边有2条行车道,而内侧和外侧车道边有1条行车道,并且内侧车道边有2条应急车道。整个车道边总长为300m,含有4条人行横道,宽度均为4m。

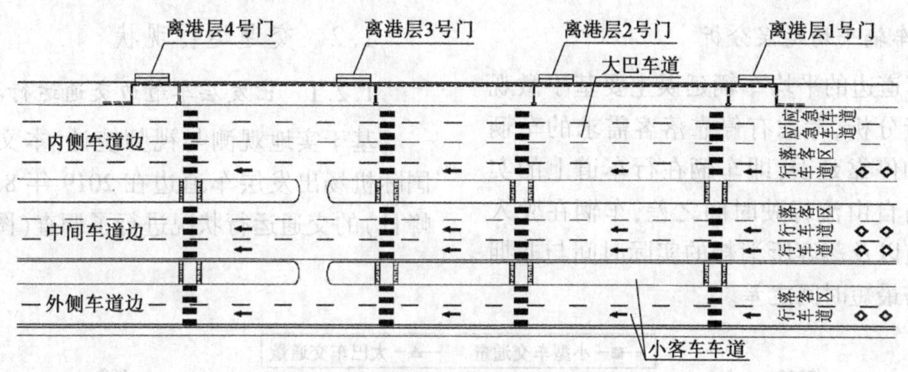

图1 昆明长水国际机场出发层车道边布局

1.1 分析方法

结合理论计算[7]与微观仿真,本文主要从通行能力、服务水平和平均车辆延误三个方面来分析出发层车道边的使用性能。其中,微观仿真模型主要基于VISSIM软件建立。

1.1.1 通行能力分析

由于机场车道边的落客车道上停靠的车辆数量与行车道的车流量相互影响,因而整体的车道边通行能力取两类车道通行能力的最小值,具体分析结合理论计算和微观仿真展开。

其中,在计算落客车道的通行能力时,通常仅考虑实际使用的车道边区域所能容纳的停靠车辆数量。单一车型下落客车道的通行能力可以表示为:

$$C_u = \frac{L_e}{\left(\frac{D_i}{60}\right) \cdot L_i} \tag{1}$$

式中:C_u——落客车道的通行能力(pcu/h);

L_e——有效车道边长度(m);

D_i——落客车道上车辆的平均停靠时间(min);

L_i——落客车道上车辆的平均占用长度(m)。

而出发层车道边的落客车道与行车道为并行设置,从行车道驶入落客车道的车流量与从落客车道驶入行车道的车流量相互交织。因此,可以基于交织区通行能力的计算方法[8]来分析行车道的通行能力,即密度法和交织需求量法结果的最小值,分别见式(2)、式(3)。

$$C_W = C_{IWL} \cdot N \cdot f_{HV} \cdot f_P \tag{2}$$

$$C_W = C_{IW} \cdot f_{HV} \cdot f_P \tag{3}$$

式中:C_W——交织路段的通行能力(pcu/h);

C_{IWL}——等效理想条件下交织路段的通行能力(pcu/h);

C_{IW}——等效理想条件下交织路段的总通行能力(pcu/h);

N——交织路段内的车道数;

f_{HV}——重型车修正系数;

f_P——驾驶员熟悉程度修正系数。

1.1.2　服务水平分析

同样地,车道边的整体服务水平取落客车道与行车道服务水平的最低值。

其中,落客车道的服务水平主要通过车道边利用率来评价,如式(4)所示:

$$CUF = \frac{L_d}{L_e} \tag{4}$$

式中:CUF——车道边利用率;

L_d——落客车道的设计需求长度(m)。

而行车道的服务水平则主要通过最大行车交通量与通行能力之比来体现,即 V/C。

结合表1和计算得到的 CUF 和 V/C,可以得出落客车道和行车道所对应的服务水平。其中,等级D是对现有车道边服务水平的基本要求。

车道边服务水平对照表　　表1

评价指标	车道边服务水平					
	A	B	C	D	E	F
CUF	0.70	0.85	1.00	1.20	1.35	>1.35
V/C	0.25	0.40	0.60	0.80	1.00	1.00

1.1.3　车辆平均延误分析

出发层车道边的平均车辆延误主要基于微观仿真模型进行分析,考虑有停靠落客需求的车辆的行驶延误和停靠延误,即车辆在行车道上的实际行驶时间与自由流行驶时间之差,车辆在驶入驶出落客车道以及落客所消耗的实际时间与非拥挤时段的所需最短时间之差。

1.2　交通运行现状

1.2.1　出发层车道边交通运行状况调查

基于实地观测与视频统计,本文对昆明长水国际机场出发层车道边在2019年8月30日(高峰日)的交通运行状况进行了调查(图2)。

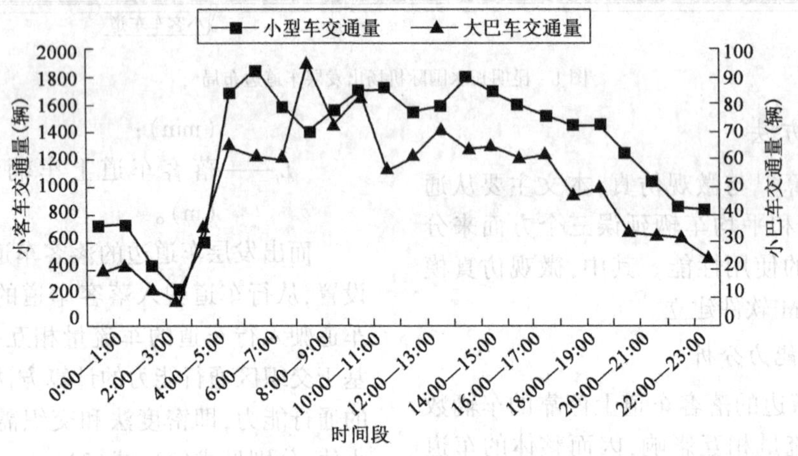

图2　出发层车道边高峰日交通量状况

如图2所示,鉴于小客车与大巴车的交通量悬殊,本文以小客车高峰小时(6:00—7:00)作为主要分析时段,相关调查数据见表2。并且,航站楼出发层车道边的平均自由流速度为20km/h,大巴车和小客车的平均停靠时间分别为1.82min和1.05min,平均占用长度分别为15m和8m。

出发层车道边早高峰流量数据　　表2

时　段	内侧车道边		中间车道边			外侧车道边		
	大巴(辆)	标准交通量	私家车(辆)	出租车(辆)	标准交通量	私家车(辆)	出租车(辆)	标准交通量
折算系数	2	—	1	1	—	1	1	—
6:00—6:15	35	70	201	29	230	189	18	207
6:15—6:30	29	58	233	38	271	187	16	203
6:30—6:45	25	50	233	17	250	193	32	225

续上表

时段	内侧车道边		中间车道边			外侧车道边		
	大巴(辆)	标准交通量	私家车(辆)	出租车(辆)	标准交通量	私家车(辆)	出租车(辆)	标准交通量
6:45—7:00	15	30	225	22	247	125	11	136
合计	104	208	892	106	998	694	77	771

通过实地调研发现,出发层车道边现状主要存在高峰时段局部路段拥堵、部分行人横穿道路、内侧车道边利用率低等问题。现状微观仿真效果如图3所示。

图3 现状微观仿真效果图

1.2.2 交通运行现状评价

结合前述分析方法,出发层车道边的交通运行现状评价结果见表3。

交通运行现状评价结果 表3

车道边		通行能力(pcu/h) 理论计算	仿真结果	对比	服务水平	平均车辆延误(s)
内侧车道边	落客车道	1240	672	93.3%	A	20.33
	行车道	720			B	
	结果	720			B	
中间车道边	落客车道	2020	1588	97.4%	B	39.28
	行车道	1630			D	
	结果	1630			D	
外侧车道边	落客车道	2020	1039	96.2%	A	24.15
	行车道	1080			D	
	结果	1080			D	
总体结果		3430	3299	96.2%	—	31.97

可以看到,在通行能力方面,因车道数优势,中间车道边的通行能力最大。但在相同车道数条件下,内侧车道边因服务车辆类型不同,通行能力小于外侧车道边。从服务水平来看,中间和外侧车道边的服务水平较内侧车道边低,已达D级,考虑未来需求增长,需加以改善,且各幅车道边的落客车道服务水平均低于行车道。就平均车辆延误而言,因车流量较大,中间和外侧车道边的平均车辆延误较内侧车道边长,且中间车道边受行人穿行影响,车辆延误更严重。而内侧车道边尽管车流量小,但易受行人穿行干扰。

2 交通组织优化方案

为解决出发层车道边现有问题,满足未来交通增长的需求,本文从以下几个方面来优化现有的交通组织:

(1)减少行人干扰。考虑在站台分隔带上设置行人栏杆,规范行人行为,尽量减少行人穿行的影响。

(2)调整车道边空间分配。虽然社会车辆与出租汽车均为小客车,但因落客目的不同,前者停靠时间长于后者。而现状方案中,社会车辆和出租汽车处于混行状态,给车辆运行带来了一定的负面影响。因此,考虑允许出租汽车同大巴车一起使用内侧车道边,在公共交通与私人交通层面对车辆行驶进行分离。同时,利用出租汽车停靠时间短、占用空间小的灵活性,弥补内侧车道边的时空利用不足问题。

(3)优化车道边布局。根据使用目的不同,出发层车道边的车道可以分为落客、过渡和直行车道[7],分别供车辆停靠落客、减速驶入或加速驶出落客车道和直行离开,三者需合理配置才得以发挥良好效用。而现状方案中,内侧和外侧车道边均依赖两条车道用于车辆停靠、过渡和直行,限制了车道的功能使用。因此,本文通过设置智能可变应急车道为内侧车道边增加1条过渡车道供日常所用;并通过调整车道宽度、利用站台和观光台等空间为外侧车道边增加1条过渡车道。

基于上述各类优化措施,本文提出两种交通组织优化方案,见表4。

交通组织优化方案　　表4

方　案	具体优化措施	VISSIM 仿真效果
A	• 添加行人栏杆; • 出租汽车使用内侧车道边; • 内侧车道边增加1条过渡车道	
B	• 添加行人栏杆; • 出租汽车使用内侧车道边; • 内侧车道边增加1条过渡车道; • 外侧车道边增加1条过渡车道	

3　交通组织优化方案评价

结合前文的分析方法,各交通组织优化方案的评价结果见表5。

交通组织优化方案评价结果　　表5

车 道 边	评价指标		现有方案	方案A	方案B
内侧车道边	通行能力(pcu/h)	公式计算	720	1370	1370
		仿真结果	672	1279	1279
		对比	93.3%	93.4%	93.4%
	服务水平	落客车道	A	B	B
		行车道	B	B	B
		结果	B	B	B
	平均车辆延误(s)		20.33	22.15	22.92

续上表

车道边	评价指标		现有方案	方案A	方案B
中间车道边	通行能力(pcu/h)	公式计算	1630	1630	1630
		仿真结果	1588	1588	1588
		对比	97.4%	97.4%	97.4%
	服务水平	落客车道	B	B	B
		行车道	D	C	C
		结果	D	C	C
	平均车辆延误(s)		39.28	37.3	32.8
外侧车道边	通行能力(pcu/h)	公式计算	1080	1080	1630
		仿真结果	1039	1039	1588
		对比	96.2%	96.2%	97.4%
	服务水平	落客车道	A	A	A
		行车道	D	D	C
		结果	D	D	C
	平均车辆延误(s)		24.15	10.31	6.86
综合评价	通行能力(pcu/h)	公式计算	3430	4080	4630
		仿真结果	3299	3906	4455
		对比	96.2%	95.7%	96.2%
	平均车辆延误(s)		31.97	25.4	20.19

可以看到,方案A和方案B的通行能力均较现状有所提升,其中,方案B在外侧车道边通行能力有进一步提高。并且,由于交通压力减小,两种方案在中间和外侧车道边的服务水平较现状更高,而内侧车道边的服务水平则相应更低,但仍处良好水平。同时,因通行能力提高,方案B在外侧车道边的服务水平比方案A更高。此外,方案A和方案B在整个车道边的平均车辆延误较现状有所缓解,主要体现在中间和外侧车道边。而内侧车道边的平均车辆延误则随交通压力增加略有增加。

基于出发层车道边现有的高峰小时交通量,结合统计预测的旅客年均增长率6%,本文可采用增长系数法计算出2020年至2030年的高峰小时交通量。在未来交通压力下,各方案的服务水平见表6。为保证车道边服务水平的要求,方案A和方案B可分别满足2023年、2025年的交通需求。

交通组织优化方案未来服务水平 表6

年份	车道边	现有方案	方案A	方案B
2020年	内侧车道边	B	C	C
	中间车道边	D	D	C
	外侧车道边	D	D	C
2023年	内侧车道边	B	C	D
	中间车道边	E	D	D
	外侧车道边	E	D	D
2025年	内侧车道边	C	D	D
	中间车道边	E	E	D
	外侧车道边	F	E	D

此外,方案A的实施涉及站台分隔带的行人栏杆和内侧车道边智能可变应急车道的设置,以

及出租汽车管理政策的调整,无须大规模的物理设施上的改变,因此施工难度较小,所需花费的资金也较少。而方案 B 的实施则在方案 A 的基础上还涉及外侧车道边的站台分隔带和车道的调整,较方案 A 而言,施工难度更大,资金要求也相应有所增加。

通过上述分析,方案 A 和方案 B 可分别用作近期和中期优化方案。

4　结语

以昆明长水国际机场的出发层车道边为研究对象,本文对现有运行状况进行了分析,针对存在的问题提出了交通组织优化方案。通过进行理论计算与交通微观仿真分析,对各组织方案进行评估,得到结论如下:

(1)通过调整出发层车道边的空间分配,可以在保证一定服务水平的前提下,均衡各幅车道边的交通压力,同时提高车道边的时空利用率。并且,从长远来看,为出租汽车、大巴车提供更便利的车道边空间可以鼓励公共交通的使用。

(2)通过优化车道边的布局,能够提供更合理的车道功能使用,在增加车道边通行能力的同时,提升车道边的服务水平。

(3)通过规范行人行为,可以避免行人对车辆运行的额外影响,一定程度上减少平均车辆延误时间。

参考文献

[1] 柳伍生, 周和平. 机场陆侧出发层车道边通行能力分析[J]. 交通科学与工程, 2010, 26(02): 98-102.

[2] 欧阳杰, 王茹. 基于可接受间隙理论的机场出发层车道边容量评估[J]. 科学技术与工程, 2015, 15(29): 193-198.

[3] 王茹. 基于时空消耗理论的多航站楼机场车道边容量评估[J]. 交通运输研究, 2016, 2(02): 53-58.

[4] 宿百岩, 刘海迅. 机场航站楼前车道边建设管理研究[J]. 中国民用航空, 2010(09): 40-43.

[5] 杨杰. 机场车道边设计要点及运行特性分析[J]. 中外建筑, 2015(07): 129-132.

[6] 郑文昌. 机场出发车道边布局模式及规模分析[J]. 交通与运输, 2021, 37(03): 12-16.

[7] Transportation Research Board. ACRP 40: Airport Curbside and Terminal Area Roadway Operations [R]. Washington D. C.: Transportation Research Board, 2010.

[8] Transportation Research Board. Highway Capacity Manual [M]. Washington D. C.: Transportation Research Board, National Research Council, 2010.

机场韧性内涵与提升措施

齐　麟*　怀永成　黄　信

(中国民航大学交通科学与工程学院)

摘　要　因自然灾害或突发事件引起机场运行能力下降或中断的情况时有发生,显示出机场韧性水平仍有待提高。在国家推进韧性交通的背景下,全面考虑机场系统构成各维度,以机场的高效运行为目标,从技术韧性和管理韧性两方面提出机场韧性的内涵。本文分析了我国机场韧性现状,从事故前、事故中、事故后三个阶段提出机场韧性提升措施,为韧性机场建设提供参考。

关键词　机场　韧性内涵　技术韧性　管理韧性　提升措施

1. 基金项目:国家重点研发计划项目“交通基础设施韧性评估与风险防控基础理论及方法”(项目编号:2021YFB2600500)。

0　引言

民航机场在运行时会面临不利环境条件与突发事件等各方面的风险,使机场的运行能力下降或中断。既有的机场风险防控研究聚焦于减弱扰动的影响,未反映机场对扰动的适应能力及恢复能力,因此需要新的指标对突发事件与自然灾害下的机场运行能力全过程进行评价,进而提出应对措施。

能够适应环境变化,具有较强的抵抗力和必要的冗余性,能承受突发事件并实现功能恢复的性能即为韧性。韧性的概念最早由机械、心理学科的学者提出,后延伸到生态学领域[1]。随着研究的深入,韧性的理念已经在建筑[2]、材料[3]、工业经济[4]、资源环境[5]等多领域得到应用。韧性的相关研究可以明确系统的运行状况,定位系统中韧性薄弱部分,有针对性地提出韧性提升措施,从而提高系统的运行能力。《中华人民共和国国民经济和社会发展第十四个五年规划和2035年远景目标纲要》中提出了建设韧性城市;《国家综合立体交通网规划纲要》将交通网络韧性作为系统指标之一;《交通强国建设纲要》中提出"实现立体互联,增强系统弹性"。

近年来,越来越多的学者对民航领域的韧性展开研究:Clark[6]采用复杂网络理论对航线网络韧性特征如恢复性、适应能力、脆弱性、鲁棒性、抗毁性等进行研究。其研究对象为航线网络,未涉及机场。Levenberg等人[7]研究了机场跑滑系统恢复力的计算方法,但未反映整个机场的韧性情况。Zhou[8]通过回归分析研究了机场恢复力的影响因素,但未考虑机场韧性的整个过程。Comes[9]采用仿真模拟评估了机场基础设施的抗灾能力。Huang等人[10]采用问卷调查或专家打分法对机场的抗灾能力和复原力进行计算,但未提出系统的理论方法。由此可见,目前对机场韧性的研究仍缺乏系统性,仍需开展深入研究。本文讨论了机场韧性的内涵,分析了我国民航机场韧性现状,并从事故前、事故中、事故后三个阶段提出了机场韧性提升措施。

1　机场韧性内涵

机场是一个体量庞大、组成复杂的系统,其构成如图1所示。

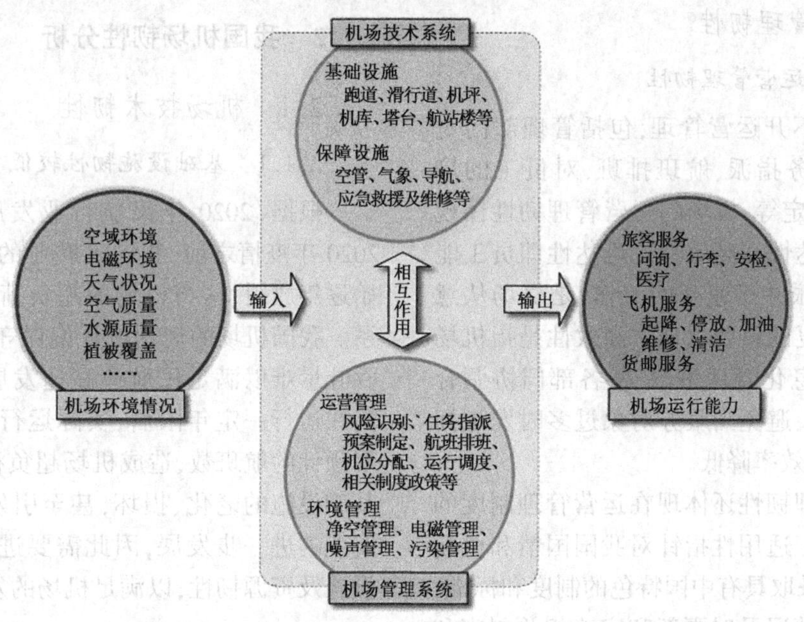

图1　机场系统构成

机场环境情况对灾害的发生、设备的故障概率有显著影响;机场技术系统是保证机场运行的基本手段;机场管理系统是机场运行的基本保障。机场技术系统与管理系统在机场环境条件下相互作用,实现机场的运行能力。

根据以上分析,本文从机场技术系统和管理系统两方面提出机场韧性的内涵。

1.1　机场技术韧性

1.1.1　机场基础设施韧性

机场基础设施韧性体现为基础设施的冗余性、可靠性和先进性。冗余性是指当意外发生后，机场可通过备用的基础设施来保证其正常运行。可靠性是指设置合理的日常检修和维护策略，以保证机场基础设施的正常使用，以及当出现故障后能够迅速维修以恢复其功能。先进性指保证机场基础设施的信息化程度，包括使用物联网、云计算等技术手段，将机场基础设施的使用状态和运行情况有效地同步到机场的相关部门，便于相关人员调用处理。

1.1.2　机场保障技术韧性

机场保障技术韧性指保障技术的可靠性、及时性和高效性。可靠性是指保障设施始终维持高性能状态，以充分应对机场可能发生的意外事件。及时性是指当机场基础设施故障或人为操作失误后，机场的正常运行受到扰动，各类保障技术及时发挥作用，可及时对各种扰动进行处理。高效性是指应用保障技术对扰动进行有效干涉，保证其处理质量与处理速度，使机场运行能力尽快恢复。

1.2　机场管理韧性

1.2.1　机场运营管理韧性

机场运行离不开运营管理，包括管理部门对各部门员工的任务指派、航班排班、对员工的培训、应急预案的制定等，机场的运营管理韧性体现在管理方案的可达性和高效性。可达性即员工能及时收到任务指派并迅速开始工作，是机场从意外事件中快速恢复的重要保证。高效性是指机场运营部门采取信息化管理手段，使各部门协调合作，提高工作效率，避免当服务对象过多时发生拥堵，使机场的运行效率降低。

机场运营管理韧性还体现在运营管理制度的适用性和灵活性。适用性指针对我国国情和机场的实际运营情况采取具有中国特色的制度和标准，按我国机场实际情况及时更新和完善相关制度和政策。灵活性指当重大事件发生后，相关部门能够迅速做出有效措施以快速恢复机场的运行能力。

1.2.2　机场环境管理韧性

机场环境管理包括对净空环境、电磁环境的管理，使机场的基础设施和保障设施能正常使用，保证飞机正常起飞，以维持机场的正常运行；还包括噪声、污染等方面的管理，保证机场对周边环境的干扰维持在标准范围内，降低对生态环境和周边居民生活的影响。

机场环境管理韧性体现为管理的落实性、有效性和先进性。落实性是指通过机场环境管理常态化，有专门的管理部门定期对机场的环境进行检查，保证机场环境维持正常状态。有效性是指，通过机场的环境管理，使机场环境满足飞机适航条件，对周边环境的影响处于较低水平。先进性指机场环境管理中先进手段的应用，例如智慧化噪声监控系统、智慧电磁监测与警告系统等。

综上，机场韧性是机场技术韧性和管理韧性的总和。技术韧性是管理韧性的基础，其中基础设施韧性保证了机场各类基础设施的高效安全运行，是机场各种服务得以开展的前提；保障技术韧性保证了机场面对突发事件的适应性。技术韧性提升了管理韧性，管理韧性推动了技术韧性。机场设施与技术韧性为管理韧性提升提供了载体与手段；管理韧性为推动机场设施和技术韧性的提升提供了规范与措施。两类韧性密切联系、相辅相成，共同构成了机场韧性。

2　我国机场韧性分析

2.1　机场技术韧性

2.1.1　基础设施韧性较低

根据《2020年民航行业发展统计公报》，在2020年疫情之前，我国民航业的吞吐量增速就开始逐年放缓，这与机场的超负荷运行有着密切关系。我国机场的规划设计偏保守，机场规模、设计吞吐量难以满足民航业高速发展的需要，造成机场在运行一定年限后，实际运行航班数远高于规划预计的航班数，造成机场超负荷使用，进而加速基础设施的老化、损坏，甚至引发事故，限制了民航业的进一步发展，因此需要进一步提高机场的设施及资源韧性，以满足机场的发展需要。

2.1.2　保障技术韧性不足

保障设施配备不足，保障技术水平不高，导致各部门处理流程连贯性和紧凑性较低。新型信息技术手段在大多数机场尚未广泛应用，大数据算力主要来源于采购设备的集成，算法相对局限，易出现精度不高、运行低效，甚至发生错误的现象。

2.2 机场管理韧性

2.2.1 机场运营管理韧性需要进一步提高

我国机场运营管理主要还是采用人工管理模式,不仅增加了运行成本,还使机场各管理部门的运行协调性降低,应对意外扰动事件缺乏有效的抵抗和应对能力。管理机构定位不清晰,导致无法充分发挥区域主体责任,与空管、政府部门的管辖区域存在部分重叠。

2.2.2 环境管理韧性较低

有关航空噪声方面的立法滞后,对飞机噪声控制管理方法研究甚少;净空管理工作缺乏统一标准,机场使用手册附图咨询通告不具有强制力;通信频率资源非常拥堵,机场电磁环境日趋复杂。

3 机场韧性提升措施

针对我国机场现状,重点考虑机场的高效运行,结合机场技术韧性和管理韧性,从事故前、事故中、事故后三个阶段提出以下机场韧性提升措施。

3.1 事故前措施

3.1.1 基础设施性能提升

考虑机场应对灾害或事故扰动的备用基础设施设计,适当提高其等级和数量,配置充足完善的维护、救援设备设施,提升其冗余性。研究长寿命设计理论,提高基础设施的耐久性与灾害抵抗性。对各类基础设施的运行、维护、维修、保养全过程进行智慧化升级,提升基础设施的适应性与可靠性。

3.1.2 常态化风险识别与预警

在新机场的规划设计阶段突出韧性机场的设计理念,充分考虑机场风险识别设计、风险防控设计、灾害处理流程设计、灾害后维护维修流程设计,提高机场的保障技术韧性。基于智慧化手段,对数据收集、数据处理分析、分析结果通知等全程进行信息化处理。分析机场各个服务设施的运行状态,预估可能发生的风险的类型和程度。加强智慧化技术的应用,包括自动识别环境问题和风险、无人操作技术产品的应用,全面提高机场的保障韧性。

3.1.3 人工智能与大数据应用

将先进的人员管理理念、任务分配理念应用到机场的实际运行中。采用协同运行管理模式,对机场的运营管理进行优化,在云计算、大数据技术的基础上不仅可以对机场的运行数据进行分析,与多个机场进行数据分享,从而共同面对大范围灾害或事故,保证机场网络的正常性能,形成更加完善的指挥运行服务体系,减少机场扰动后的恢复时间,以提高机场的运营管理韧性。加强环境管理中信息化技术的应用,使环境管理信息化、技术化,全面掌握对环境识别和处理过程的进度,从而全面提高机场环境管理韧性。

3.1.4 优化管理流程

明确统一的机场运行管理办法,保障机场的运行环境处于良好状态。采用协同运行管理模式对机场的运营管理进行优化,与多个机场进行数据分享,形成更加完善的指挥运行服务体系。政府有关部门采用以信息技术为基础的管治系统,针对机场的实际运行情况出台有效政策和措施,并保证政策和措施的有效性和及时性,实现扁平化组织架构。

3.2 事故中措施

3.2.1 提高部门协调运行能力

当灾害发生时,机场运行能力处于降低状态,要确保各部门信息互通、联系密切,部署工作迅速灵活。完善机场与地方政府、民航系统之间的应急响应、组织协调、协同保障等机制,加强应急防疫物资储备管理。依托信息化智能管理平台,推进应急管理信息化、智能化,提升机场应急救援能力。

3.2.2 信息化智能管理系统

通过智慧化的信息分析,以机场系统运行性能最高为目标,考虑各部门的关键指标,通过机器学习算法,自动进行求解,生成各部门的任务指派;采用多系统融合大屏控制技术,实时显示机场运行总体态势,并对救援或维护工作进行实施监控,为机场信息化智慧运行提供辅助决策。

3.2.3 发挥机场网络作用

发挥机场网络作用,基于机场群的航空运输冗余性,将航班适当分散于多层次式机场网络中,减轻事故中机场运行压力,提高机场网络资源利用率,保证航空运输系统的运行。

3.3 事故后措施

3.3.1 智慧决策技术

发展机场智慧化应急决策技术,利用大数据与人工智能算法自动筛选最优策略,使救援和维护工作迅速开展。形成由灾害发生前的预测、灾害发生时的应对到灾害后的处理整个过程的记录,分析每部分操作的合理性,将优良的处理策略和每阶段存在的不足之处纳入机器学习模型中,优化算法,提升应急决策的智慧化水平。

3.3.2 构建三方良性互动

在事故应急救援和应急处置中,政府应充分发挥主导作用,民航行政机关和机场管理机构三方应积极参与配合政府领导和组织的应急救援和应急处置,提供必要的专业技术支持,保持相关应急信息的互联互通,不断提升与地方应急力量的协同配合能力。

3.3.3 机场功能恢复

针对突发事件与自然灾害,分析对其预警、识别、处理的全过程,定位机场韧性的薄弱部位,完善机场应急保障决策系统,完善机场功能恢复策略,恢复或提升机场运行能力,进而全面提高机场韧性。

4 结语

本文分析机场系统的组成维度,从机场基础设施韧性与机场保障技术韧性等技术角度,以及机场运营管理韧性与环境管理韧性等管理角度提出机场韧性的内涵。本文分析了我国机场的韧性状态,以实现机场高效运行为目标,从基础设施性能提升、常态化风险识别与预警、人工智能与大数据应用、优化管理流程、提高部门协调运行能力、信息化智能管理系统、发挥机场网络作用、智慧决策技术、构建三方良性互动、机场功能恢复等各方面提出了机场韧性提升措施。

参考文献

[1] Holling S C. Resilience and Stability of Ecological Systems [J]. Annual Review of Ecology and Systematics, 1973, 4(1):1-23.

[2] 康现栋,付皓然,赵光,等.单体建筑抗震韧性评估方法研究与应用[J].土木工程学报,2021,54(08):37-42.

[3] 吴平,周飞,李庆华,等.超高韧性水泥基复合材料—纤维混凝土组合靶体抗两次打击试验研究[J].爆炸与冲击,2022,42(03):53-65.

[4] 李连刚,张平宇,王成新,等.区域经济韧性视角下老工业基地经济转型过程——以辽宁省为例[J].地理科学,2021,41(10):1742-1750.

[5] 吴浩,江志猛,林安琪,等.基于隐性—韧性—显性的武汉城市资源环境承载力空间特征[J].地理学报,2021,76(10):2439-2457.

[6] Clark K L. Mitigating Infrastructure Risk: Reducing Uncertainty in Resilience Modeling [D]. Boston: Northeastern University, 2018.

[7] Miller-Hooks, Elise, Levenberg, et al. Resilience ofNetworked Infrastructure with Evolving Component Conditions: PavementNetwork Application [J]. Journal of computing in civil engineering, 2017, 31(3):1-9.

[8] Zhou L, Chen Z. Measuring the Performance of Airport Resilience to Severe Weather Events [J]. Transportation Research Part D: Transport and Environment, 2020, 83: 102362.

[9] Comes T, Warnier M, Feil W, et al. Critical Airport Infrastructure Disaster Resilience: A Framework and Simulation Model for Rapid Adaptation [J]. Journal of Management in Engineering, 2020, 36(5): 04020059.

[10] Huang C N, Liou J, Lo H W, et al. Building an assessment model for measuring airport resilience[J]. Journal of Air Transport Management, 2021, 95(10):102101.

大型货运无人机与有人机同场滑行研究

刘俊丽[*] 陈忠莹 史彦斌 胡传生
(空军航空大学)

摘 要 物流公司已逐步将无人机推广应用到航空运输领域,大型货运无人机潜力巨大,与有人机合用现有机场成为必然趋势。由于大型货运无人机在性能上与有人机相比仍有差距且参差不齐,实现安全、有序、高效的有/无人机同场滑行面临着诸多现实挑战。通过对有/无人机滑行运动进行理论分析,在建立跑道、滑行道和停机坪系统场面网络图的基础上,将滑行运动抽象为描述横向运动的路线、纵向运动的滑行速度和滑行时间限制的滑行开始时刻三个参数,从而构建起三个滑行参数与自主控制、预先控制、外部控制三种滑行调度运行措施之间的矩阵图。通过分析矩阵,本着沿用现有机场交通规则、减少基础设施和机上设备改造、普遍适用于各型机场的原则,探索提出了解决大型货运无人机与有人机同场滑行困难的分段标准滑行方案。方案按照开飞前预先公布供机场所有用户使用的标准滑行路线,在标准滑行路线上划设强制停车点,滑行中由管制员触发通行指令这三大要点设计,具有安全性和可用性。

关键词 机场运行管理 分段标准滑行方案 矩阵图法 大型货运无人机 有人机 同场滑行

0 引言

早在2013年,顺丰就进行小型无人机或称旋翼无人机末端配送的首航,紧接着载重百公斤以上的中型无人机不断涌现,如上海优维斯水陆两栖的U650、STAR-650和新加坡F-drones公司无人机等。随着无人机技术的不断发展,商载在1000公斤以上的大型无人机应运而生,例如顺丰的FH-98、中通的鸿雁(HY100)、京东JDY-800“京鸿”、朗星AT200、美国Reliable Robotics公司的塞斯纳208等大型无人机。其具有载重大、航时长、航程远等优势,适于承担城市间中长距离的支干线货运任务,有力支撑了“大型有人运输机+支线大型无人机+末端小型无人机”三级航空货运体系的构建。

目前国内支线航空物流尚处于空白阶段,高效快速经济的航空物流需求迫切,而由于航空飞机较高的运营成本、飞行员短缺等市场痛点,以及大型无人机在提升流转效率、打破道路限制、助推产业转型方面的显著优势,使得其在物流网络的支干线上有非常大的用武之地。因而在当前无人航空货运需求急剧增长而无人机机场无法立即增加的情况下,实现大型货运无人机与有人机同场滑行控制,有助于扩大地面交通容量、均匀分布滑行道载荷,实现无冲突的连续滑行,提高场面运行效率,进而增加机场吞吐能力并相应减少航班延误。

1 现实困境:同场滑行面临的困境

目前,大型货运无人机与有人机通常使用机场不同区域实施滑行,虽然这在实践中是可行的,但只适合交通流量小(起飞架次较少、执行任务量少)的机场,无法满足航空货运物流量不断增加的需求。在当前技术阶段,基于“人在回路”控制的无人机系统,大型货运无人机与有人机同场滑行主要面临以下困境:

一是检测/感知与规避。滑行过程中,飞行员主要根据机坪管制员(以下简称“管制员”)发布的指令避撞。但是,在此过程中,飞行员必须能够看到其他交通工具(其他滑行或牵引车拖拽的飞机、地面车辆)或障碍物,才能与之保持安全距离,避免碰撞。除此之外,可能还存在管制员难以发现但飞行员易于发现的情况,如滑行道异物、损坏等。因此,飞行员在滑行阶段目视观察外部情况的能力对于确保滑行安全至关重要。目前,大型货运无人机尚无法模拟飞行员目视观察的能力。

二是标志/信号灯识别。机场设置了系统的标志标识和信号灯,例如跑道标志、滑行道标志、禁止进入标记牌、滑行引导标记牌、红色停车灯、塔台灯枪信号等。飞行员能够识别并判断这些标志/标识和信号,但是,截至目前,部分大型货运无人机却无法实现。

三是地面导航设施保障。飞行员驾驶飞机滑行过程中,主要以地面黄色标记,例如滑行边线、滑行道中线、跑道等待位置等标志,以及信号灯作为导航参照。目前,大型货运无人机采用链路导航、卫通导航等其他导航方法,这就需要专门为无人机配备与其导航性能匹配的滑行道和支持其滑行的特定设施,以保证其正常滑行。

四是应急情况处置。在操控大型货运无人机飞行过程中,地面站和无人机之间指挥控制链路的中断时有发生,一旦中断,飞行操控员无法操纵或监视无人机状态,无人机将由已安装的机载系统接管,转入自主滑行模式。在这种模式下,对于管制员、其他飞行员和机场人员来说,无人机滑行将处于不可预测和不可控制的状态,对机场交通其他参与者来说存在巨大的安全风险。

2　理论分析:滑行路径与调度措施分析

滑行是以机场滑行道系统为基础进行的场面运行活动,大型货运无人机与有人机滑行的有序整合对整个场面运行效率的提高起着至关重要的作用。因此,对大型货运无人机与有人机同场滑行的研究需要首先对机场场面运行进行分析,然后基于场面运行着重分析滑行过程。

2.1　机场场面运行

机场场面是指航空器在地面上运行的区域,主要包括场面资源中的跑道、滑行道和停机坪系统。使用网络建模分析能够将实际问题抽象,易于对复杂问题的处理分析,有必要将跑道、滑行道和停机坪系统抽象为场面网络图(图 1),由链路(E)和节点(V)组成,这是进行同场滑行研究的基础[1]。该网络图由任何一个跑道端、滑行道端与停机坪之间连接而成的所有路径组成,它是进行滑行控制研究的基础。机场场面的运行涉及着陆、脱离、滑行、推出、等待、起飞等一系列事件在跑道、滑行道和停机坪三个系统中的运作。

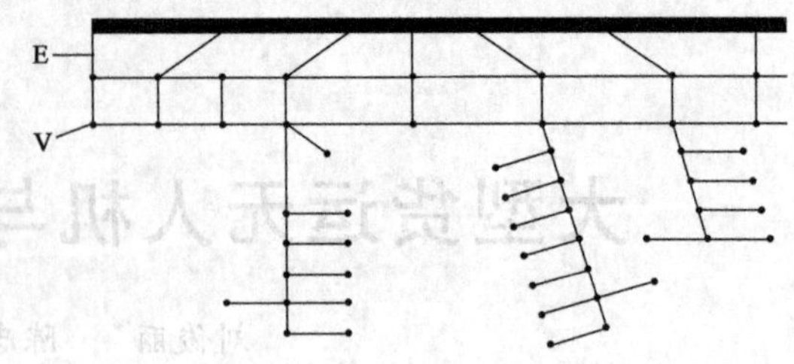

图 1　机场地面网络图

2.2　滑行调度运行

为了便于在上述机场场面网络中进行滑行调度分析,将大型货运无人机与有人机的滑行运动分解为以下三个参数:一是从起始位置滑行至目标位置的路线,描述横向运动;二是滑行速度,描述纵向运动;三是滑行开始的时刻,描述滑行时间限制。以上三个参数能够描述所有航空器在机场场面上的滑行路径。

在实际滑行控制过程中,地面管制席位通过所发布的停机位分配方案、跑道分配计划、离场航空器的最早推出时间、预计离场时间、跑道穿越时间等信息来控制航空器发动机启动时间、航空器进入滑行道系统时间、航空器的滑行路径和航空器通过主要控制点时间,确保不同的航班在满足间隔要求的前提下,在空间和时间上不发生冲突[2]。通常采用以下三种措施控制有/无人机滑行:一是外部控制,指外部决策者(例如管制员,不包括无人机飞行操控员)通过语音通信或者数据链、机场标志标识、信号灯、牵引车引导的方式控制航空器滑行;二是预先控制,指航空器根据已经公布的程序、规则或公告实施滑行;三是自主控制,是指无人机飞行操控员或飞行员、有/无人机的自主程序根据情况自行决定如何滑行。这些控制措施不仅可以单独使用,还可以组合使用。

下一步是建立一个矩阵,该矩阵同时面对不同的滑行参数和控制措施。

3　路径选择:分段标准滑行方案的提出

3.1　分段标准滑行方案的推导

如表 1 所示,该矩阵是所有理论上成立的滑行控制的一般框架,适用于大型货运无人机和有人机。

有/无人机滑行参数矩阵 表1

措施		横向运动(滑行路线)	纵向运动(滑行速度)	时间限制
自主控制	内容	无人机飞行操控员或者飞行员、有/无人机自主程序自行决定地面滑行路线	无人机飞行操控员或者飞行员、有/无人机自主程序自行决定速度	无人机飞行操控员或者飞行员、有/无人机自主程序自行决定滑行开始的时刻(无任何触发)
	现状	不适用于管制机场	根据其他有/无人机状态,采取停车/刹车操作,无人机需具备检测/感知和规避性能	不适用于管制机场
预先控制	内容	路线由已公布的程序、规则、公告规定	速度由已公布的程序、规则、公告规定	滑行开始时刻,由已公布的程序、规则、公告规定
	现状	标准滑行路线,如安塔利亚机场	尚未使用	尚未使用
外部控制(语音通信)	内容	路线由外部决策者通过语音发布	速度由外部决策者通过语音发布	滑行开始时刻由外部决策者通过语音发布
	现状	根据管制员发布的滑行许可路线	根据管制员的指示等待/继续滑行	管制员发布滑行许可(假定滑行在滑行许可发布后很快开始)

基于上述矩阵,分析发现:预先控制已经在有人机地面滑行路线确定方面得以使用,如安塔利亚机场标准滑行路线的建立。由于该滑行控制方法弱化了飞行员在飞机地面滑行过程中所起的作用,有助于将大型货运无人机在检测/感知和规避障碍物、地面导航、标志/标识和信号灯识别、管制员指令接收和执行方面与有人机之间的差异化降至最低。因此,拟将预先控制的方法用于大型货运无人机与有人机同场滑行控制中,本文提出了分段标准滑行方案这一新思路。

3.2 分段标准滑行方案的内容

分段标准滑行方案的设计要点如下:

首先,大型货运无人机从停机坪到跑道的滑行路线都是标准化的,这一路线被定义为标准滑行路线(见图2中的虚线),该路线是公开发布供机场所有用户使用的,并非通过管制员与飞行操控员通信后实时分配形成的。

其次,在大型货运无人机标准滑行路线上划定强制停车点(见图2中的编号圆圈),旨在将标准滑行路线分割为不同的路段。

最后,由外部决策者(通常为管制员)对每个路段发布一个简单触发的"通行"指令。此"通行"指令仅在大型货运无人机到达下一个强制停止点之前发出。管制员必须确保在发布"通行"指令时,已放行的路段没有其他机场交通工具和障碍物,每个路段有且只有一架大型货运无人机。对于本文讨论的主题,哪个通信信道将用于管制员向飞行员或者无人机飞行操控员发布"通行"指令并不重要,因为这对整个方案来说是次要的。

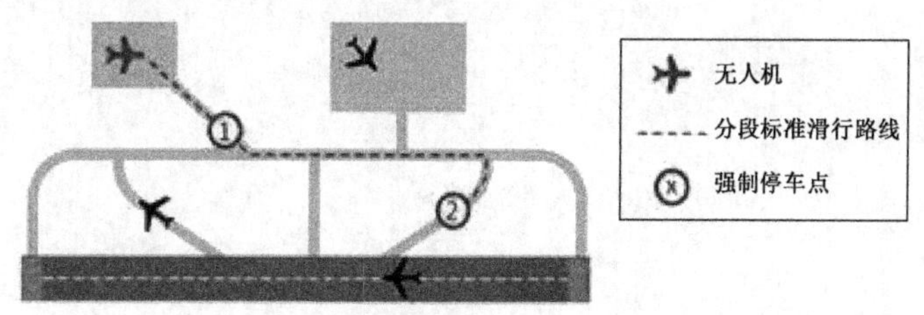

图2 分段标准滑行方案示意图

同时,为了保障分段标准滑行路线安全实施,还需注意以下事项:分段标准滑行路线的设计应尽可能遵循单向原则;滑行道可用性应与大型货运无人机的导航性能相关联;机场运营商应定期评估分段标准滑行路线的可用性;所有大型货运无人机都应具有特殊的颜色涂装或标记,并装配闪光灯,闪光灯应在应急情况(包括飞行操控员对大型货运无人机的操控被完全切断的情形)下闪烁,以使其他飞行员、塔台管制员和地面人员能够在第一时间做出判断,进而采取有效应对措施。

3.3　分段标准滑行方案的安全性

分段标准滑行方案是一个程序性构想,具有较高的安全性。因为其程序非常简单且明确,管制员与大型货运无人机之间的通信需求被简化为简单的触发指令,任何能够寻址和提交这种简单信号的通信手段均可完成,任何影响通信质量的风险都被降至最低,使得大型货运无人机在与有人机同场滑行中造成错误和误解的风险以及故障造成严重后果的风险被降至最低。同时,对管制员和所有其他机场交通参与者来说,由于提前发布了滑行路线,大型货运无人机的滑行具有稳定的可预测性和较高透明度。即使在通信中断或指挥控制链路中断的情况下,不管处于何种状态,无人机都将停在下一个强制停车点,可以确保机场所有交通参与者的安全。如果无人机不具备在强制停车点自动停车的能力,则可为所有滑行无人机设置一个"紧急停车"按钮。

4　结语

与当前大型货运无人机与有人机同场滑行的控制现状相比,在当前航空规则下,分段标准滑行方案真正实现了大型货运无人机融入机场地面交通的目标,实现了机场交通资源的最大化利用。并且,这一方案的概念与大型货运无人机系统的全自动滑行基本兼容,这是面向未来的优势。当然,分段标准滑行方案也存在一些缺点,如需要管制员给予较以往更高等级的关注,因为与大型货运无人机冲突的交通流量消除主要依靠管制员完成。并且,与单纯有人机参与的机场交通相比,灵活性和机场容量会有一定损失,因为引导大型货运无人机滑行的路线选择有限。这为以后不断优化大型货运无人机与有人机同场滑行方案留下了更多思考的空间。

参考文献

[1] 冯程. 机场场面运行优化及容量评估技术研究[D]. 南京:南京航空航天大学,2013.

[2] 陈浩. 机场航空器滑行路径优化技术研究[D]. 南京:南京航空航天大学,2015.